CHILTON®

FORD
SERVICE MANUAL
2010 EDITION
VOLUME I

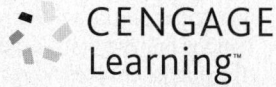
CENGAGE
Learning™

Australia • Brazil • Japan • Korea • Mexico • Singapore • Spain • United Kingdom • United States

CENGAGE
Learning™

CHILTON®
Ford Service Manual
2010 Edition
Volume I

Vice President,
Technology Professional
Business Unit:
  Gregory L. Clayton

Publisher,
Technology Professional
Business Unit:
  David Koontz

Director of Marketing:
  Beth A. Lutz

Production Director:
  Carolyn Miller

Production Manager:
  Andrew Crouth

Marketing Manager:
  Jennifer Barbic

Marketing Coordinator:
  Rachael Conover

Editorial Assistant:
  Tracey Gates

Chilton Content Specialist:
  Paula Baillie

Graphical Designer:
  Melinda Possinger

Art Director:
  Benj Gleeksman

Sr. Content Project Manager:
  Elizabeth C. Hough

Managing Editor:
  Terry L. Blomquist

Senior Editor:
  Christine L. Sheeky

Editors:
  Ken Burdette
  Eugene F. Hannon, Jr., A.S.E.
  Kyla Nyjordet
  Jonathan Wallace
  Lance Williams

For product information and technology assistance, contact us at **Professional & Career Group customer Support, 1-800-648-7450.** For permission to use material from this text or product, submit all requests online at **www.cengage.com/permissions.** Further permissions questions can be e-mailed to **permissionrequest@cengage.com.**

ISBN-13: 978-1-1110-3655-3
ISBN-10: 1-1110-3655-1
ISSN: 1939-621X

Delmar
5 Maxwell Drive
Clifton Park, NY 12065-2919
USA

Cengage Learning is a leading provider of customized learning solutions with office locations around the globe, including Singapore, the United Kingdom, Australia, Mexico, Brazil, and Japan. Locate your local office at: **international.cengage.com/region**

Cengage Learning products are represented in Canada by Nelson Education, Ltd.

NOTICE TO THE READER

Publisher does not warrant or guarantee any of the products described herein or perform any independent analysis in connection with any of the product information contained herein. Publisher does not assume, and expressly disclaims, any obligation to obtain and include information other than that provided to it by the manufacturer.

The reader is expressly warned to consider and adopt all safety precautions that might be indicated by the activities described herein and to avoid all potential hazards. By following the instructions contained herein, the reader willingly assumes all risks in connection with such instructions.

The publisher makes no representations or warranties of any kind, including but not limited to, the warranties of fitness for particular purpose or merchantability, nor are any such representations implied with respect to the material set forth herein, and the publisher takes no responsibility with respect to such material. The publisher shall not be liable for any special, consequential, or exemplary damages resulting, in whole or part, from the readers' use of, or reliance upon, this material.

Printed in the United States of America
1 2 3 4 5 6 7 13 12 11 10 09

Table of Contents

Sections

Model Index

USING THIS INFORMATION

Organization

To find where a particular model section or procedure is located, look in the Table of Contents. Main topics are listed with the page number on which they may be found. Following the main topics is an alphabetical listing of all of the procedures within the section and their page numbers.

Manufacturer and Model Coverage

This product covers 2008–2010 Ford Motor Company models that are produced in sufficient quantities to warrant coverage, and which have technical content available from the vehicle manufacturers before our publication date. Although this information is as complete as possible at the time of publication, some manufacturers may make changes which cannot be included here. While striving for total accuracy, the publisher cannot assume responsibility for any errors, changes, or omissions that may occur in the compilation of this data.

Part Numbers and Special Tools

Part numbers and special tools are recommended by the publisher and vehicle manufacturer to perform specific jobs. Before substituting any part or tool for the one recommended, you must be completely satisfied that neither your personal safety, nor the performance of the vehicle will be endangered.

ACKNOWLEDGEMENT

This product contains material that is reproduced and distributed under license from Ford Motor Company. No further reproduction or distribution of the Ford Motor Company material is allowed without express written permission from Ford Motor Company.

PRECAUTIONS

Before servicing any vehicle, please be sure to read all of the following precautions, which deal with personal safety, prevention of component damage, and important points to take into consideration when servicing a motor vehicle:

• Always wear safety glasses or goggles when drilling, cutting, grinding or prying.

• Steel-toed work shoes should be worn when working with heavy parts. Pockets should not be used for carrying tools. A slip or fall can drive a screwdriver into your body.

• Work surfaces, including tools and the floor should be kept clean of grease, oil or other slippery material.

• When working around moving parts, don't wear loose clothing. Long hair should be tied back under a hat or cap, or in a hair net.

• Always use tools only for the purpose for which they were designed. Never pry with a screwdriver.

• Keep a fire extinguisher and first aid kit handy.

• Always properly support the vehicle with approved stands or lift.

• Always have adequate ventilation when working with chemicals or hazardous material.

• Carbon monoxide is colorless, odorless and dangerous. If it is necessary to operate the engine with vehicle in a closed area such as a garage, always use an exhaust collector to vent the exhaust gases outside the closed area.

• When draining coolant, keep in mind that small children and some pets are attracted by ethylene glycol antifreeze, and are quite likely to drink any left in an open container, or in puddles on the ground. This will prove fatal in sufficient quantity. Always drain the coolant into a sealable container.

• To avoid personal injury, do not remove the coolant pressure relief cap while the engine is operating or hot. The cooling system is under pressure; steam and hot liquid can come out forcefully when the cap is loosened slightly. Failure to follow these instructions may result in personal injury. The coolant must be recovered in a suitable, clean container for reuse. If the coolant is contaminated it must be recycled or disposed of correctly.

• When carrying out maintenance on the starting system be aware that heavy gauge leads are connected directly to the battery. Make sure the protective caps are in place when maintenance is completed. Failure to follow these instructions may result in personal injury.

• Do not remove any part of the engine emission control system. Operating the engine without the engine emission control system will reduce fuel economy and engine ventilation. This will weaken engine performance and shorten engine life. It is also a violation of Federal law.

• Due to environmental concerns, when the air conditioning system is drained, the refrigerant must be collected using refrigerant recovery/recycling equipment. Federal law requires that refrigerant be recovered into appropriate recovery equipment and the process be conducted by qualified technicians who have been certified by an approved organization, such as MACS, ASI, etc. Use of a recovery machine dedicated to the appropriate refrigerant is necessary to reduce the possibility of oil and refrigerant incompatibility concerns. Refer to the instructions provided by the equipment manufacturer when removing refrigerant from or charging the air conditioning system.

• Always disconnect the battery ground when working on or around the electrical system.

• Batteries contain sulfuric acid. Avoid contact with skin, eyes, or clothing. Also, shield your eyes when working near batteries to protect against possible splashing of the acid solution. In case of acid contact with skin or eyes, flush immediately with water for a minimum of 15 minutes and get prompt medical attention. If acid is swallowed, call a physician immediately. Failure to follow these instructions may result in personal injury.

• Batteries normally produce explosive gases. Therefore, do not allow flames, sparks or lighted substances to come near the battery. When charging or working near a battery, always shield your face and protect your eyes. Always provide ventilation. Failure to follow these instructions may result in personal injury.

• When lifting a battery, excessive pressure on the end walls could cause acid to spew through the vent caps, resulting in personal injury, damage to the vehicle or battery. Lift with a battery carrier or with your hands on opposite corners. Failure to follow these instructions may result in personal injury.

• Observe all applicable safety precautions when working around fuel. Whenever servicing the fuel system, always work in a well-ventilated area. Do not allow fuel spray or vapors to come in contact with a spark, open flame, or excessive heat (a hot drop light, for example). Keep a dry chemical fire extinguisher near the work area. Always keep fuel in a container specifically designed for fuel storage; also, always properly seal fuel containers to avoid the possibility of fire or explosion. Do not smoke or carry lighted tobacco or open flame of any type when working on or near any fuel-related components.

• Fuel injection systems often remain pressurized, even after the engine has been turned OFF. The fuel system pressure must be relieved before disconnecting any fuel lines. Failure to do so may result in fire and/or personal injury.

• The evaporative emissions system contains fuel vapor and condensed fuel vapor. Although not present in large quantities, it still presents the danger of explosion or fire. Disconnect the battery ground cable from the battery to minimize the possibility of an electrical spark occurring, possibly causing a fire or explosion if fuel vapor or liquid fuel is present in the area. Failure to follow these instructions can result in personal injury.

• The EPA warns that prolonged contact with used engine oil may cause a number of skin disorders, including cancer! You should make every effort to minimize your exposure to used engine oil. Protective gloves should be worn when changing oil. Wash your hands and any other exposed skin areas as soon as possible after exposure to used engine oil. Soap and water, or waterless hand cleaner should be used.

• Some vehicles are equipped with an air bag system, often referred to as a Supplemental Restraint System (SRS) or Supplemental Inflatable Restraint (SIR) system. The system must be disabled before performing service on or around system components, steering column, instrument panel components, wiring and sensors. Failure to follow safety and disabling procedures could result in accidental air bag deployment, possible personal injury and unnecessary system repairs.

• Always wear safety goggles when working with, or around, the air bag system. When carrying a non-deployed air bag, be sure the bag and trim cover are pointed away from your body. When placing a non-deployed air bag on a work surface, always face the bag and trim cover upward, away from the surface. This will reduce the motion of the module if it is accidentally deployed.

• Electronic modules are sensitive to electrical charges. The ABS module can be damaged if exposed to these charges.

• Brake pads and shoes may contain asbestos, which has been determined to be a cancer-causing agent. Never clean brake surfaces with compressed air. Avoid inhaling brake dust. Clean all brake surfaces with a commercially available brake cleaning fluid.

• When replacing brake pads, shoes, discs or drums, replace them as complete axle sets.

• When servicing drum brakes, disassemble and assemble one side at a time, leaving the remaining side intact for reference.

• Brake fluid often contains polyglycol ethers and polyglycols. Avoid contact with the eyes and wash your hands thoroughly after handling brake fluid. If you do get brake fluid in your eyes, flush your eyes with clean, running water for 15 minutes. If eye irritation persists, or if you have taken brake fluid internally, immediately seek medical assistance.

• Clean, high quality brake fluid from a sealed container is essential to the safe and proper operation of the brake system. You should always buy the correct type of brake fluid for your vehicle. If the brake fluid becomes contaminated, completely flush the system with new fluid. Never reuse any brake fluid. Any brake fluid that is removed from the system should be discarded. Also, do not allow any brake fluid to come in contact with a painted or plastic surface; it will damage the paint.

• Never operate the engine without the proper amount and type of engine oil; doing so will result in severe engine damage.

• Timing belt maintenance is extremely important! Many models utilize an interference-type, non-freewheeling engine. If the timing belt breaks, the valves in the cylinder head may strike the pistons, causing potentially serious (also time-consuming and expensive) engine damage.

• Disconnecting the negative battery cable on some vehicles may interfere with the functions of the on-board computer system (s) and may require the computer to undergo a relearning process once the negative battery cable is reconnected.

• Steering and suspension fasteners are critical parts because they affect performance of vital components and systems and their failure can result in major service expense. They must be replaced with the same grade or part number or an equivalent part if replacement is necessary. Do not use a replacement part of lesser quality or substitute design. Torque values must be used as specified during reassembly.

FORD, LINCOLN AND MERCURY

Crown Victoria • Grand Marquis • Town Car

SPECIFICATIONS AND MAINTENANCE CHARTS

ENGINE AND VEHICLE IDENTIFICATION

	Engine						Model Year	
Code ①	Liters (cc)	Cu. In.	Cyl.	Fuel Sys.	Type	Eng. Mfg.	Code ②	Year
W	4.6 (4593)	281	8	SFI	SOHC	Ford	8	2008
V	4.6 (4593)	281	8	SFI	SOHC	Ford	9	2009

SOHC: Single Overhead Camshaft

V: Flex Fuel/E-85 Compliant

① 8th digit of the Vehicle Identification Number (VIN)

② 10th digit of the Vehicle Identification Number (VIN)

36578_CVIC_C0001

GENERAL ENGINE SPECIFICATIONS

Year	Model	Engine Displacement Liters	Engine ID/VIN	Net Horsepower @ rpm	Net Torque @ rpm (ft. lbs.)	Bore x Stroke (in.)	Compression Ratio	Oil Pressure @ rpm
2008	Crown Victoria	4.6	W,V ④	①	②	3.60x3.60	③	40-70@2500
	Grand Marquis	4.6	W,V ④	①	②	3.60x3.60	9.4:1	20-45@1500
	Town Car	4.6	W,V ④	①	②	3.60x3.60	9.4:1	20-45@1500
2009	Crown Victoria	4.6	W,V ④	①	②	3.60x3.60	③	20-45@1500
	Grand Marquis	4.6	W,V ④	①	②	3.60x3.60	9.4:1	20-45@1500
	Town Car	4.6	W,V ④	①	②	3.60x3.60	9.4:1	20-45@1500

① Single exhaust: 220@4750

Dual exhaust: 235@4000

Crown Victoria with natural gas: 178@4500

② Single exhaust: 265@4000

Dual exhaust: 275@4000

Crown Victoria with natural gas: 237@3500

③ Gasoline engine: 9.4:1

Natural gas engine: 10.0:1

④ VIN V not available on taxi and police models

36578_CVIC_C0002

ENGINE TUNE-UP SPECIFICATIONS

Year	Engine Displacement Liters	Engine ID/VIN	Spark Plug Gap (in.)	Ignition Timing (deg.)	Fuel Pump (psi) ①	Idle Speed (rpm)	Valve Clearance Intake	Valve Clearance Exhaust
2008	4.6	W	0.054	10BTDC	25-40	②	HYD	HYD
	4.6	V	0.054	10BTDC	25-40	②	HYD	HYD
2009	4.6	W	0.054	10BTDC	25-40	②	HYD	HYD
	4.6	V	0.054	10BTDC	25-40	②	HYD	HYD

NOTE: The Vehicle Emission Control Information label may reflect specification changes made during production. The label specifications differ from those in this chart.

BTDC: Before Top Dead Center

HYD: Hydraulic

① Fuel pressure with engine running, pressure regulator vacuum hose connected

② Refer to Vehicle Emission Control Information label

36578_CVIC_C0003

CAPACITIES

Year	Model	Engine Displacement Liters	Engine ID/VIN	Engine Oil with Filter (qts.)	Automatic Transmission (pts.) ①	Rear Drive Axle (pts.)	Fuel Tank (gal.)	Cooling System (qts.)
2008	Crown Victoria	4.6	W,V	6.0	②	5.0	19.0	19.0
	Grand Marquis	4.6	W	6.0	②	5.0	19.0	19.0
	Town Car	4.6	W	6.0	②	5.0	19.0	19.0
2009	Crown Victoria	4.6	W,V	6.0	②	5.0	19.0	19.0
	Grand Marquis	4.6	W	6.0	②	5.0	19.0	19.0
	Town Car	4.6	W	6.0	②	5.0	19.0	19.0

NOTE: All capacities are approximate. Add fluid gradually and ensure a proper fluid level is obtained.

① Includes torque converter

② Police package: 12.8 qts.

Non-Police package: 14 qts.

36578_CVIC_C0004

FLUID SPECIFICATIONS

Year	Model	Engine Displacement Liters	Engine ID/VIN	Engine Oil	Auto. Trans. ①	Drive Axle	Power Steering Fluid	Brake Master Cylinder
2008	Crown Victoria	4.6	W,V ②	5W-20	Mercon V	80W-90	Mercon MP ATF	DOT 3
	Grand Marquis	4.6	W	5W-20	Mercon V	80W-90	Mercon MP ATF	DOT 3
	Town Car	4.6	W	5W-20	Mercon V	80W-90	Mercon MP ATF	DOT 3
2009	Crown Victoria	4.6	W,V ②	5W-20	Mercon V	80W-90	Mercon MP ATF	DOT 3
	Grand Marquis	4.6	W	5W-20	Mercon V	80W-90	Mercon MP ATF	DOT 3
	Town Car	4.6	W	5W-20	Mercon V	80W-90	Mercon MP ATF	DOT 3

① MERCON V = XT-5-QM or XT-5-QMC (US); CXT-5-LM12 (Canada)

② VIN V Not available on taxi and police models

36578_CVIC_C0005

VALVE SPECIFICATIONS

All measurements are given in inches.

Year	Engine Displacement Liters	Engine ID/VIN	Seat Angle (deg.)	Face Angle (deg.)	Spring Test Pressure (lbs. @ in.)	Spring Installed Height (in.)	Stem-to-Guide Clearance (in.) Intake	Stem-to-Guide Clearance (in.) Exhaust	Stem Diameter (in.) Intake	Stem Diameter (in.) Exhaust
2008	4.6	W	45	45.5	132@1.10	1.598-1.717	0.0008-0.0027	0.0018-0.0037	0.2746-0.2754	0.2736-0.2744
	4.6	V	45	45.5	160@1.03	1.598-1.717	0.0008-0.0027	0.0018-0.0037	0.2746-0.275	0.2736-0.2744
2009	4.6	W	45	45.5	132@1.10	1.598-1.717	0.0008-0.0027	0.0018-0.0037	0.2746-0.2754	0.2736-0.2744
	4.6	V	45	45.5	160@1.03	1.598-1.717	0.0008-0.0027	0.0018-0.0037	0.2746-0.275	0.2736-0.2744

36578_CVIC_C0006

CAMSHAFT AND BEARING SPECIFICATIONS CHART

All measurements are given in inches.

Year	Engine Displ. Liters	Engine ID/VIN	Journal Dia.	Brg. Oil Clearance	Shaft End-play	Runout	Journal Bore	Lobe Height Intake	Lobe Height Exhaust
2008	4.6	W,V	1.0605-1.0615	0.0010-0.0030	0.0011-0.0075	0.0035	1.0625 1.0635	0.2799	0.2952
2009	4.6	W,V	1.0605-1.0615	0.0010-0.0030	0.0011-0.0075	0.0035	1.0625 1.0635	0.2799	0.2952

36578_CVIC_C0007

CRANKSHAFT AND CONNECTING ROD SPECIFICATIONS

All measurements are given in inches.

Year	Engine Displacement Liters	Engine ID/VIN	Crankshaft Main Brg. Journal Dia.	Crankshaft Main Brg. Oil Clearance	Crankshaft Shaft End-play	Crankshaft Thrust on No.	Connecting Rod Journal Diameter	Connecting Rod Oil Clearance	Connecting Rod Side Clearance
2008	4.6	W	2.6500-2.6570	0.0009-0.0026	0.0051-0.0119	5	2.0870-2.8670	0.0009-0.0026	0.0006-0.0177
	4.6	V	2.6567-2.6577	0.0001-0.0018	0.0051-0.0119	5	2.0859-2.0867	0.0011-0.0027	0.0006-0.0177
2009	4.6	W	2.6500-2.6570	0.0009-0.0026	0.0051-0.0119	5	2.0870-2.8670	0.0009-0.0026	0.0006-0.0177
	4.6	V	2.6567-2.6577	0.0001-0.0018	0.0051-0.0119	5	2.0859-2.0867	0.0011-0.0027	0.0006-0.0177

36578_CVIC_C0009

PISTON AND RING SPECIFICATIONS

All measurements are given in inches.

Year	Engine Displacement Liters	Engine ID/VIN	Piston Clearance ①	Ring Gap Top Compression	Ring Gap Bottom Compression	Ring Gap Oil Control	Ring Side Clearance Top Compression	Ring Side Clearance Bottom Compression	Ring Side Clearance Oil Control
2008	4.6	W	0.0002-0.0010	0.005-0.012	0.012-0.022	0.006-0.026	②	0.008-0.0024	0.0010-0.0077
	4.6	V	0.0002-0.0010	0.005-0.012	0.012-0.022	0.006-0.026	②	0.008-0.0024	0.0010-0.0077
2009	4.6	W	0.0002-0.0010	0.005-0.012	0.012-0.022	0.006-0.026	②	0.008-0.0024	0.0010-0.0077
	4.6	V	0.0002-0.0010	0.005-0.012	0.012-0.022	0.006-0.026	②	0.008-0.0024	0.0010-0.0077

① Measured 1.96 in. (43mm) from the top
② On 10:1 engines: 0.0012-0.0028 in.
  On 9:1 engines: 0.0008-0.0024 in.

36578_CVIC_C0008

TORQUE SPECIFICATIONS
All readings in ft. lbs.

Year	Engine Displacement Liters	Engine ID/VIN	Cylinder Head Bolts	Main Bearing Bolts	Rod Bearing Bolts	Crankshaft Damper Bolts	Flywheel Bolts	Manifold Intake	Manifold Exhaust	Spark Plugs	Oil Pan Drain Plug
2008	4.6	W	①	②	③	118	59	18	18	11	10
	4.6	V	①	②	③	118	59	18	18	11	10
2009	4.6	W	①	②	③	118	59	18	18	11	10
	4.6	V	①	②	③	118	59	18	18	11	10

NOTE: Stretch bolts are used in all procedures that require rotating the fastener a certain number of degrees. The bolts stretch and cannot be reused. For reassembly, replace with new fasteners.

① Step 1: 30 ft. lbs.
   Step 2: Rotate 90 degrees
   Step 3: Loosen 360 degrees
   Step 4: 30 ft. lbs.
   Step 5: Rotate 90 degrees
   Step 5: Rotate an additional 90 degrees

② Step 1: Main bearing cap bolts: 30 ft. lbs.
   Step 2: Rotate each bolt 90 degrees
   Step 3: Main bearing cap adjusting screws: 44 in. lbs. then 89 in. lbs.
   Step 4: Main bearing cap side bolts: 89 in. lbs. then 15 ft. lbs.

③ Step 1: 32 ft. lbs.
   Step 2: 12 ft. lbs.
   Step 2: Rotate 90-120 degrees

36578_CVIC_C0010

WHEEL ALIGNMENT

Year	Model		Caster Range (+/-Deg.)	Caster Preferred Setting (Deg.)	Camber Range (+/-Deg.)	Camber Preferred Setting (Deg.)	Toe-in (in.)
2008	Crown Victoria	F	0.75	+0.50	0.75	0	-0.25 +/- 0.25
		R	—	—	—	—	—
	Town Car	F	0.75	0	0.75	0	-0.12 +/- 0.25
		R	—	—	—	—	—
	Grand Marquis	F	0.75	+0.50	0.75	0	-0.13 +/- 0.25
		R	—	—	—	—	—
2009	Crown Victoria	F	0.75	+0.50	0.75	0	-0.25 +/- 0.25
		R	—	—	—	—	—
	Town Car	F	0.75	0	0.75	0	-0.12 +/- 0.25
		R	—	—	—	—	—
	Grand Marquis	F	0.75	+0.50	0.75	0	-0.13 +/- 0.25
		R	—	—	—	—	—

Note: Specifications apply to all models, including taxi, police, and vehicles equipped with air suspension

36578_CVIC_C0011

TIRE, WHEEL AND BALL JOINT SPECIFICATIONS

Year	Model	OEM Tires Standard	OEM Tires Optional	Tire Pressure Front	Tire Pressure Rear	Wheel Size	Ball Joint Inspection	Lug Nut (ft. lbs.)
2008	Crown Victoria	P225/60SR16	P225/60TR16	32	32	7J	U ①	100
			P235/55HR17	35	35		L ①②	
	Crown Victoria Police Special	P225/60SR16	P225/60VR16	35	35	7J	U ① L ①②	100
	Grand Marquis	P225/60SR16	NA	32	32	6-JJ	U ① L ①②	100
	Grand Marquis w/Handling package	P225/60TR16	P225/60VR16	35	35	6-JJ	U ① L ①②	100
	Town Car	P225/60R17	NA	32	32	Std: 7-JJ	U ① L ①②	100
2009	Crown Victoria	P225/60SR16	P225/60TR16	32	32	7J	U ①	100
			P235/55HR17	35	35		L ①②	
	Crown Victoria Police Special	P225/60SR16	P225/60VR16	35	35	7J	U ① L ①②	100
	Grand Marquis	P225/60SR16	NA	32	32	6-JJ	U ① L ①②	100
	Grand Marquis w/Handling package	P225/60TR16	P225/60VR16	35	35	6-JJ	U ① L ①②	100
	Town Car	P225/60R17	NA	32	32	Std: 7-JJ	U ① L ①②	100

NA: Not Available

OEM: Original Equipment Manufacturer

PSI: Pounds Per Square Inch

U: Upper

L: Lower

① Replace if any measurable movement is found.

② Do not lift car. Inspect the boss into which the grease fitting is threaded. Replace if the boss is flush or receded below the surface of the ball joint.

36578_CVIC_C0012

BRAKE SPECIFICATIONS
All measurements in inches unless noted

Year	Model	Front Brake Disc Original Thickness	Front Brake Disc Minimum Thickness	Front Brake Disc Maximum Run-out	Rear Brake Disc Original Thickness	Rear Brake Disc Minimum Thickness	Rear Brake Disc Maximum Run-out	Minimum Lining Thickness	Brake Caliper Bracket Bolts (ft. lbs.)	Mounting Bolts (ft. lbs.)
2008	Crown Victoria	1.063	1.037	0.002	NA	0.790	0.003	0.039	118	27
	Grand Marquis	1.063	1.037	0.002	NA	0.790	0.003	0.039	118	27
	Town Car	1.063	1.037	0.002	NA	0.790	0.003	0.039	118	27
2009	Crown Victoria	1.063	1.037	0.002	NA	0.790	0.003	0.039	118	27
	Grand Marquis	1.063	1.037	0.002	NA	0.790	0.003	0.039	118	27
	Town Car	1.063	1.037	0.002	NA	0.790	0.003	0.039	118	27

NOTE: Follow specifications stamped on rotor or drum if figures differ from those in this chart.

NA: Not Available

36578_CVIC_C0013

SCHEDULED MAINTENANCE INTERVALS
Ford—Crown Victoria, Mercury—Grand Marquis & Lincoln—Town Car

TO BE SERVICED	TYPE OF SERVICE	VEHICLE MILEAGE INTERVAL (x1000)												
		5	10	15	20	25	30	35	40	45	50	55	60	65
Engine oil & filter	R	✓	✓	✓	✓	✓	✓	✓	✓	✓	✓	✓	✓	✓
Rotate tires	S/I	✓		✓		✓		✓		✓		✓		✓
Cooling system, hoses, clamps & coolant strength	S/I			✓			✓			✓			✓	
Lubricate steering linkage	S/I			✓			✓			✓			✓	
Air cleaner element	R						✓						✓	
Automatic transaxle fluid & filter	R						✓						✓	
Spark plugs ①	R													
Exhaust heat shields	S/I						✓						✓	
Fuel filter (NGV Crown Victoria) ②	R					✓					✓			
Front & rear brakes	S/I						✓						✓	
Lubricate suspension (Town Car)	S/I						✓						✓	
Engine coolant ③	R										✓			
PCV valve	R												✓	
Accessory drive belt	S/I												✓	

R: Replace   S/I: Service or Inspect

① Replace every 100,000 miles.

② Also drain coalescer assembly. Perform every 24,000 miles for severe service.

③ Change initially at 5 years/100,000 miles, and every 50,000 miles thereafter.

FREQUENT OPERATION MAINTENANCE (SEVERE SERVICE)

If a vehicle is operated under any of the following conditions it is considered severe service:

- Extremely dusty areas.

- 50% or more of the vehicle operation is in 32°C (90°F) or higher temperatures, or constant operation in temperatures below 0°C (32°F).

- Prolonged idling (vehicle operation in stop and go traffic).

- Frequent short running periods (engine does not warm to normal operating temperatures).

- Police, taxi, delivery usage or trailer towing usage.

Oil & filter change: change every 3000 miles.

Rotate tires at 6000 miles & every 9000 miles thereafter.

Automatic transmission fluid & filter: change every 21,000 miles.

36578_CVIC_C0014

PRECAUTIONS

Before servicing any vehicle, please be sure to read all of the following precautions, which deal with personal safety, prevention of component damage, and important points to take into consideration when servicing a motor vehicle:

• Never open, service or drain the radiator or cooling system when the engine is hot; serious burns can occur from the steam and hot coolant.

• Observe all applicable safety precautions when working around fuel. Whenever servicing the fuel system, always work in a well-ventilated area. Do not allow fuel spray or vapors to come in contact with a spark, open flame, or excessive heat (a hot drop light, for example). Keep a dry chemical fire extinguisher near the work area. Always keep fuel in a container specifically designed for fuel storage; also, always properly seal fuel containers to avoid the possibility of fire or explosion. Refer to the additional fuel system precautions later in this section.

• Fuel injection systems often remain pressurized, even after the engine has been turned **OFF**. The fuel system pressure must be relieved before disconnecting any fuel lines. Failure to do so may result in fire and/or personal injury.

• Brake fluid often contains polyglycol ethers and polyglycols. Avoid contact with the eyes and wash your hands thoroughly after handling brake fluid. If you do get brake fluid in your eyes, flush your eyes with clean, running water for 15 minutes. If eye irritation persists, or if you have taken brake fluid internally, IMMEDIATELY seek medical assistance.

• The EPA warns that prolonged contact with used engine oil may cause a number of skin disorders, including cancer. You should make every effort to minimize your exposure to used engine oil. Protective gloves should be worn when changing oil. Wash your hands and any other exposed skin areas as soon as possible after exposure to used engine oil. Soap and water, or waterless hand cleaner should be used.

• All new vehicles are now equipped with an air bag system, often referred to as a Supplemental Restraint System (SRS) or Supplemental Inflatable Restraint (SIR) system. The system must be disabled before performing service on or around system components, steering column, instrument panel components, wiring and sensors. Failure to follow safety and disabling procedures could result in accidental air bag deployment, possible personal injury and unnecessary system repairs.

• Always wear safety goggles when working with, or around, the air bag system. When carrying a non-deployed air bag, be sure the bag and trim cover are pointed away from your body. When placing a non-deployed air bag on a work surface, always face the bag and trim cover upward, away from the surface. This will reduce the motion of the module if it is accidentally deployed. Refer to the additional air bag system precautions later in this section.

• Clean, high quality brake fluid from a sealed container is essential to the safe and proper operation of the brake system. You should always buy the correct type of brake fluid for your vehicle. If the brake fluid becomes contaminated, completely flush the system with new fluid. Never reuse any brake fluid. Any brake fluid that is removed from the system should be discarded. Also, do not allow any brake fluid to come in contact with a painted surface; it will damage the paint.

• Never operate the engine without the proper amount and type of engine oil; doing so WILL result in severe engine damage.

• Timing belt maintenance is extremely important. Many models utilize an interference-type, non-freewheeling engine. If the timing belt breaks, the valves in the cylinder head may strike the pistons, causing potentially serious (also time-consuming and expensive) engine damage. Refer to the maintenance interval charts for the recommended replacement interval for the timing belt, and to the timing belt section for belt replacement and inspection.

• Disconnecting the negative battery cable on some vehicles may interfere with the functions of the on-board computer system(s) and may require the computer to undergo a relearning process once the negative battery cable is reconnected.

• When servicing drum brakes, only disassemble and assemble one side at a time, leaving the remaining side intact for reference.

• Only an MVAC-trained, EPA-certified automotive technician should service the air conditioning system or its components.

BRAKES

GENERAL INFORMATION

PRECAUTIONS

• Certain components within the ABS system are not intended to be serviced or repaired individually.

• Do not use rubber hoses or other parts not specifically specified for and ABS system. When using repair kits, replace all parts included in the kit. Partial or incorrect repair may lead to functional problems and require the replacement of components.

• Lubricate rubber parts with clean, fresh brake fluid to ease assembly. Do not use shop air to clean parts; damage to rubber components may result.

• Use only DOT 3 brake fluid from an unopened container.

• If any hydraulic component or line is removed or replaced, it may be necessary to bleed the entire system.

• A clean repair area is essential. Always clean the reservoir and cap thoroughly before removing the cap. The slightest amount of dirt in the fluid may plug an orifice and impair the system function. Perform repairs after components have been thoroughly cleaned; use only denatured alcohol to clean components. Do not allow ABS components to come into contact with any substance containing mineral oil; this includes used shop rags.

ANTI-LOCK BRAKE SYSTEM (ABS)

• The Anti-Lock control unit is a microprocessor similar to other computer units in the vehicle. Ensure that the ignition switch is **OFF** before removing or installing controller harnesses. Avoid static electricity discharge at or near the controller.

• If any arc welding is to be done on the vehicle, the control unit should be unplugged before welding operations begin.

WHEEL SPEED SENSORS

REMOVAL & INSTALLATION

Refer to Wheel Bearing and Hub under Suspension.

BRAKES **BLEEDING THE BRAKE SYSTEM**

BLEEDING PROCEDURE

Manual Bleeding

✻✻ WARNING

Use of any brake fluid other than approved DOT 3 will cause permanent damage to brake components and will render the brakes inoperative. Failure to follow these instructions may result in personal injury.

✻✻ CAUTION

Brake fluid contains polyglycol ethers and polyglycols. Avoid contact with eyes. Wash hands thoroughly after handling. If brake fluid contacts eyes, flush eyes with running water for 15 minutes. Get medical attention if irritation persists. If taken internally, drink water and induce vomiting. Get medical attention immediately. Failure to follow these instructions may result in personal injury.

✻✻ WARNING

Do not allow the brake master cylinder reservoir to run dry during the bleeding operation. Keep the brake master cylinder reservolr fllled with the specified brake fluid. Never reuse the brake fluid that has been drained from the hydraulic system.

✻✻ WARNING

Brake fluid is harmful to painted and plastic surfaces. If spilled, wipe up immediately before damage to the painted or plastic surfaces occurs.

➡When any part of the hydraulic system has been disconnected for repair or installation of new components, air can get into the system and cause spongy brake pedal action. This requires bleeding of the hydraulic system after it has been correctly connected.

➡If the hydraulic control unit (HCU) or any component upstream of the HCU are installed new, carry out the brake system bleed procedure first without the diagnostic tool, followed by the brake system bleed procedure using the diagnostic tool. This reduces the risk of trapping air in the HCU.

1. Before servicing the vehicle, refer to the precautions in the beginning of this section.
2. Connect the diagnostic tool DCL cable adapter into the vehicle data link connector (DLC) under the dash and follow the diagnostic tool instructions.
3. Clean all dirt from and remove the brake master cylinder filler cap and fill the brake master cylinder reservoir with clean motor vehicle brake fluid.
4. For ABS vehicles only, open the master cylinder bleed screw until clear, bubble-free fluid flows from the tube into the cup.
5. Bleed the brake system in the order displayed on the diagnostic tool or bleed from the longest to the shortest brake line. Place a box end wrench on the bleeder screw. Attach a rubber drain tube to the bleeder screw and submerge the free end of the tube in a container partially filled with clean brake fluid.
6. Have an assistant hold firm pressure on the brake pedal.
7. Loosen the bleeder screw until a stream of brake fluid comes out. While the assistant maintains pressure on the brake pedal, tighten the bleeder scrcw.

- Repeat 3 times until clear, bubble-free fluid comes out.
- Refill the brake master cylinder reservoir with clean motor vehicle brake fluid as necessary.

8. Tighten the bleeder screw.
9. Repeat the for the remaining bleeder screws in the system.

Pressure Bleeding

1. Before servicing the vehicle, refer to the precautions in the beginning of this section.

2. Clean all dirt from and remove the brake master cylinder filler cap and fill the brake master cylinder reservoir with clean motor vehicle brake fluid.
3. Master cylinder pressure bleeder adapter tools are available from various manufacturers of pressure bleeding equipment. Follow the instructions of the manufacturer when installing the adapter.
4. Install the bleeder adapter to the brake master cylinder reservoir, and attach the bleeder tank hose to the fitting on the adapter.

- Refill the brake master cylinder reservoir with clean motor vehicle brake fluid as necessary.

5. Bleed from the longest to the shortest brake line. Make sure the bleeder tank contains enough clean motor vehicle brake fluid to complete the bleeding operation.
6. Place a box end wrench on the bleeder screw. Attach a rubber drain tube to the bleeder screw, and submerge the free end of the tube in a container partially filled with clean brake fluid.
7. Open the valve on the bleeder tank.
8. Loosen the bleeder screw. Leave open until clear, bubble-free brake fluid flows. Have an assistant pump the brake pedal once every 2 seconds after the diagnostic tool runs the HCU pump Wait 15 seconds after clear, bubble-free fluid flows through the rubber hose. Then, tighten the bleeder screw and remove the rubber hose.
9. Continue bleeding the rear of the system repeating Stcp 4 and 5.
10. Close the bleeder tank valve. Remove the tank hose from the adapter, and remove the adapter.
11. Fill the master cylinder reservoir with clean motor vchicle brake fluid
12. Install a new reservoir cap.

BLEEDING THE ABS SYSTEM

The ABS system is bled in the same manner as non-ABS brakes on this vehicle. Please refer to the Bleeding Procedures located earlier in this section.

BRAKES   FRONT DISC BRAKES

BRAKE CALIPER

REMOVAL & INSTALLATION

See Figure 1.

> ❋❋ **CAUTION**
>
> If the vehicle is equipped with air suspension, the electrical power to the air suspension system must be shut off prior to hoisting, jacking or towing an air suspension vehicle. This can be accomplished by turning off the air suspension switch located in the luggage compartment. Failure to do so can result in unexpected inflation or deflation of the air springs, which can result in shifting of the vehicle during these operations. Failure to follow these instructions may result in personal injury.

> ❋❋ **CAUTION**
>
> Dust and dirt accumulating on brake parts during normal use may contain asbestos fibers from production or aftermarket brake linings. Breathing excessive concentrations of asbestos fibers can cause serious bodily harm. Exercise care when servicing brake parts. Do not sand or grind brake lining unless equipment used is designed to contain the dust residue. Do not clean brake parts with compressed air or by dry brushing. Cleaning should be done by dampening the brake components with a fine mist of water, then wiping the brake components clean with a dampened cloth. Dispose of cloth and all residue containing asbestos fibers in an impermeable container with the appropriate label. Follow practices prescribed by the Occupational Safety and Health Administration (OSHA) and the Environmental Protection Agency (EPA) for the handling, processing, and disposing of dust or debris that may contain asbestos fibers.

➥ Before continuing with this procedure, make sure to have available, 2 new disc brake caliper guide pin bolts and 2 banjo bolt sealing washers, per caliper. Once removed, these parts lose their torque holding ability or retention capability and must not be reused.

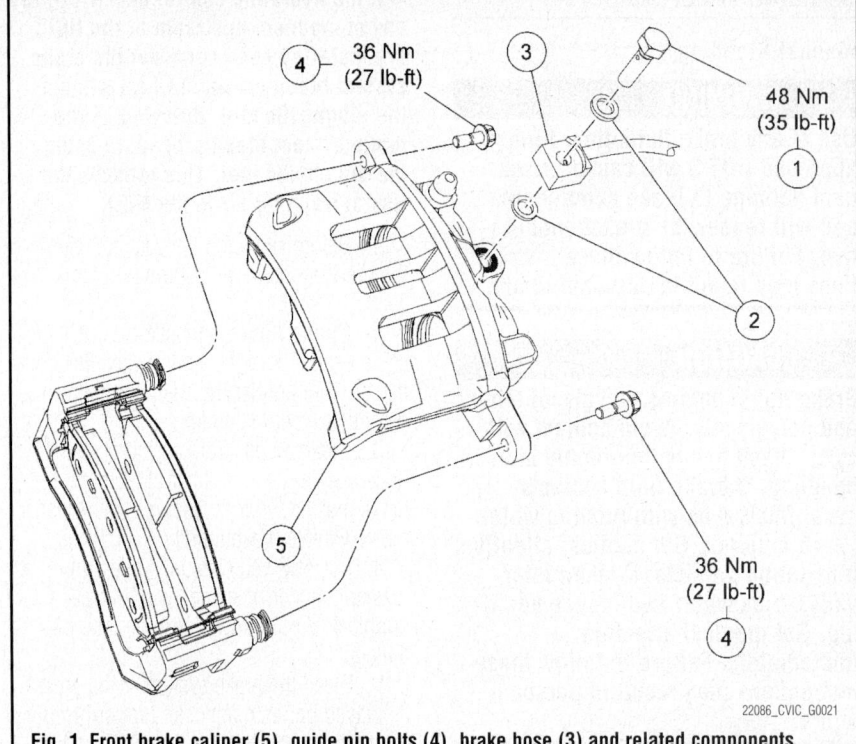

Fig. 1 Front brake caliper (5), guide pin bolts (4), brake hose (3) and related components

22086_CVIC_G0021

Front brake caliper components (see figure):

1. Brake caliper flow bolt
2. Copper washers (2 required)
3. Brake hose
4. Brake caliper bolts (2 required)
5. Brake caliper
6. If equipped with air suspension, the air suspension switch, located on the right-hand side of the luggage compartment, must be turned to the **OFF** position before raising the vehicle.
7. Remove or disconnect the following:
   - Front wheel and tire assembly
   - Banjo bolt securing the brake hose from the disc brake caliper. Plug the brake hose. Discard the sealing washers.
   - 2 disc brake caliper guide pin bolts and discard. If removing both calipers, mark the right and left sides so they may be reinstalled correctly.
   - Disc brake caliper off of the anchor plate

To install:

8. Retract the disc brake caliper piston fully in the piston bore, using an old brake pad or block of wood and a C-clamp.
9. Install or connect the following:
   - Disc brake pads to the caliper. Make sure that the brake pad insulators are correctly attached to the brake pad plate.
   - Disc brake caliper onto the anchor plate. Make sure the inner and outer pads are properly positioned and the anti-rattle spring is properly positioned. The caliper bleed screw should be positioned on top of the caliper when assembled on the vehicle.
   - 2 new caliper guide pin bolts and torque to 27 ft. lbs. (36 Nm)
   - Brake hose, after unplugging it, to the disc brake caliper using 2 new copper sealing washers on the banjo bolt. Torque the bolt to 35 ft. lbs. (48 Nm).
10. Bleed the brake system, filling the master cylinder as required. Only use clean DOT 3 brake fluid from a sealed container.
11. Install the wheel and tire assembly. Torque the lug nuts in a star pattern to 100 ft. lbs. (136 Nm).
12. If equipped with air suspension, turn the air suspension switch to the **ON** position.
13. Pump the brake pedal several times to position the brake pads prior to moving the vehicle.
14. Road test the vehicle and check for proper brake system operation.

DISC BRAKE PADS

REMOVAL & INSTALLATION

See Figure 2.

> ### ✳✳ CAUTION
>
> **If the vehicle is equipped with air suspension, the electrical power to the air suspension system must be shut off prior to hoisting, jacking or towing an air suspension vehicle. This can be accomplished by turning off the air suspension switch located in the luggage compartment. Failure to do so can result in unexpected inflation or deflation of the air springs, which can result in shifting of the vehicle during these operations. Failure to follow these instructions may result in personal injury.**

> ### ✳✳ CAUTION
>
> **Dust and dirt accumulating on brake parts during normal use may contain asbestos fibers from production or aftermarket brake linings. Breathing excessive concentrations of asbestos fibers can cause serious bodily harm. Exercise care when servicing brake parts. Do not sand or grind brake lining unless equipment used is designed to contain the dust residue. Do not clean brake parts with compressed air or by dry brushing. Cleaning should be done by dampening the brake components with a fine mist of water, then wiping the brake components clean with a dampened cloth. Dispose of cloth and all residue containing asbestos fibers in an impermeable container with the appropriate label. Follow practices prescribed by the Occupational Safety and Health Administration (OSHA) and the Environmental Protection Agency (EPA) for the handling, processing, and disposing of dust or debris that may contain asbestos fibers.**

➡ Before continuing with this procedure, make sure to have available, 2 new disc brake caliper anchor bracket mounting bolts, per caliper. Once removed, these parts lose their torque holding ability or retention capability and must not be reused.

Front disc brake components:
1. Brake caliper bolts (2 required)
2. Brake caliper

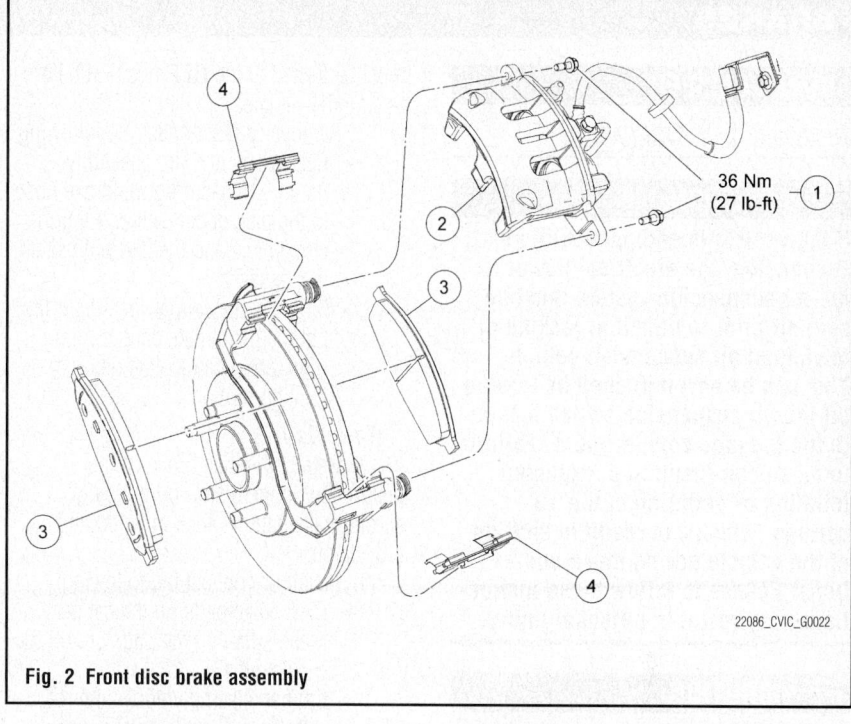

Fig. 2 Front disc brake assembly

22086_CVIC_G0022

3. Brake pads (2 required per side)
4. Stainless steel slides (2 required per side)
5. If equipped with air suspension, the air suspension switch, located on the right-hand side of the luggage compartment, must be turned to the **OFF** position before raising the vehicle.
6. Remove or disconnect the following:
   - ½ of the brake fluid from the brake master cylinder reservoir. Properly dispose of the used brake fluid.
   - Front wheel and tire assembly
   - 2 disc brake caliper anchor bracket mounting bolts and discard. Lift the caliper assembly from the disc brake rotor using a rotating motion. Suspend the caliper inside the fender housing with wire. Do not allow the caliper to hang from the brake hose.
   - Inner and outer disc brake pads. Inspect the rotor braking surfaces for scoring and machine as necessary. Refer to the minimum rotor thickness specification when machining. If machining is not necessary, hand-sand the glaze from the braking surfaces with medium grit sandpaper. Make sure to wear an approved respirator.

To install:
7. Use a C-clamp and an old brake pad, wood block to seat the caliper piston in its bore. Do not allow metal or sharp objects to come into direct contact with the plastic caliper piston surface or damage will result.
8. Remove all rust buildup from the inside of the caliper legs.
9. Make sure the anti-rattle spring is seated in the caliper lining inspection opening and that it is installed from the lining side.

To install:
10. Install or connect the following:
    - Inner disc brake pad to the caliper piston. Do not bend the pad clips during installation in the piston or distortion and rattles can occur. Install the outer disc brake pad. Make sure the clips are properly seated.
    - Caliper over the rotor and install 2 new anchor bracket mounting bolts. Torque the bolts to 118 ft. lbs. (160 Nm).
    - Wheel and tire assembly. Torque the lug nuts in a star pattern to 100 ft. lbs. (136 Nm).
11. If equipped with air suspension, turn the air suspension switch to the **ON** position.
12. Pump the brake pedal prior to moving the vehicle to seat the brake pads.
13. Fill the master cylinder reservoir with clean DOT 3 brake fluid from a closed container.
14. If the disc brake calipers were replaced or repaired be sure to bleed the system.
15. Road test the vehicle and check for proper brake system operation.

BRAKES

REAR DISC BRAKES

BRAKE CALIPER

REMOVAL & INSTALLATION

> **⁑ CAUTION**
>
> If the vehicle is equipped with air suspension, the electrical power to the air suspension system must be shut off prior to hoisting, jacking or towing an air suspension vehicle. This can be accomplished by turning off the air suspension switch located in the luggage compartment. Failure to do so can result in unexpected inflation or deflation of the air springs, which can result in shifting of the vehicle during these operations. Failure to follow these instructions may result in personal injury.

> **⁑ CAUTION**
>
> Dust and dirt accumulating on brake parts during normal use may contain asbestos fibers from production or aftermarket brake linings. Breathing excessive concentrations of asbestos fibers can cause serious bodily harm. Exercise care when servicing brake parts. Do not sand or grind brake lining unless equipment used is designed to contain the dust residue. Do not clean brake parts with compressed air or by dry brushing. Cleaning should be done by dampening the brake components with a fine mist of water, then wiping the brake components clean with a dampened cloth. Dispose of cloth and all residue containing asbestos fibers in an impermeable container with the appropriate label. Follow practices prescribed by the Occupational Safety and Health Administration (OSHA) and the Environmental Protection Agency (EPA) for the handling, processing, and disposing of dust or debris that may contain asbestos fibers.

➡Before continuing with this procedure, make sure to have available, 2 banjo bolt sealing washers, per caliper. Once removed, these parts lose their torque holding ability or retention capability and must not be reused.

1. If equipped with air suspension, the air suspension switch, located on the right-hand side of the luggage compartment,

must be turned to the **OFF** position before raising the vehicle.

2. Remove or disconnect the following:
   - Rear wheel and tire assembly
   - Banjo bolt securing the brake hose to the disc brake caliper. Plug the brake hose and discard both sealing washers.
   - 2 disc brake caliper locating bolts. Lift the disc brake caliper off the rotor and anchor plate using a rotating motion.

To install:

3. Retract the disc brake caliper piston fully in the piston bore, using an old brake pad or block of wood and a C-clamp.

4. Install or connect the following:
   - Disc brake pads on the caliper. Make sure that the pads are on the correct side.
   - Caliper assembly above the rotor with the anti-rattle spring located on the lower adapter support arm. Install the caliper over the rotor with a rotating motion.

5. Clean the inner surface of the caliper bushings and locating bolts. Lubricate the caliper locating bolts with a suitable silicone dielectric compound. Install and start the locating bolts by hand only. Torque both bolts to 27 ft. lbs. (36 Nm).
   - Brake hose, after unplugging it, to the disc brake caliper using 2 new copper sealing washers on the banjo bolt. Torque the bolt to 35 ft. lbs. (48 Nm).

6. Bleed the brake system, filling the master cylinder as required. Only use clean DOT 3 brake fluid from a sealed container.

7. Replace the rubber rear disc brake bleeder screw cap.

8. Install the wheel and tire assembly. Torque the lug nuts in a star pattern to 100 ft. lbs. (136 Nm).

9. If equipped with air suspension, turn the air suspension switch to the **ON** position.

10. Pump the brake pedal several times to position the brake pads prior to moving the vehicle.

11. Road test the vehicle and check for proper brake system operation.

DISC BRAKE PADS

REMOVAL & INSTALLATION

See Figures 3 and 4.

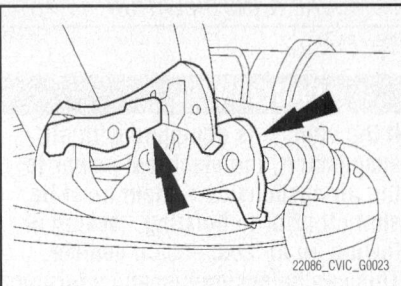
Fig. 3 Removal of rear disc brake pads from caliper

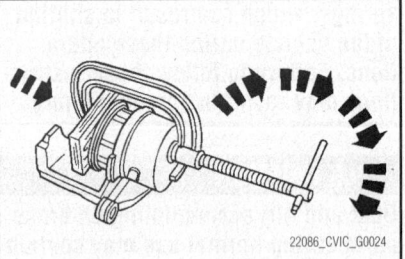
Fig. 4 Compress brake caliper piston as shown

> **⁑ CAUTION**
>
> If the vehicle is equipped with air suspension, the electrical power to the air suspension system must be shut off prior to hoisting, jacking or towing an air suspension vehicle. This can be accomplished by turning off the air suspension switch located in the luggage compartment. Failure to do so can result in unexpected inflation or deflation of the air springs, which can result in shifting of the vehicle during these operations. Failure to follow these instructions may result in personal injury.

> **⁑ CAUTION**
>
> Dust and dirt accumulating on brake parts during normal use may contain asbestos fibers from production or aftermarket brake linings. Breathing excessive concentrations of asbestos fibers can cause serious bodily harm. Exercise care when servicing brake parts. Do not sand or grind brake lining unless equipment used is designed to contain the dust residue. Do not clean brake parts with compressed air or by dry brushing. Cleaning should be done by dampen-

ing the brake components with a fine mist of water, then wiping the brake components clean with a dampened cloth. Dispose of cloth and all residue containing asbestos fibers in an impermeable container with the appropriate label. Follow practices prescribed by the Occupational Safety and Health Administration (OSHA) and the Environmental Protection Agency (EPA) for the handling, processing, and disposing of dust or debris that may contain asbestos fibers.

➡Before continuing with this procedure, make sure to have available, 2 new disc brake caliper anchor bracket mounting bolts, per caliper. Once removed, these parts lose their torque holding ability or retention capability and must not be reused.

1. If equipped with air suspension, the air suspension switch, located on the right-hand side of the luggage compartment, must be turned to the **OFF** position before raising the vehicle.
2. Remove or disconnect the following:
   • ½ of the brake fluid from the brake master cylinder reservoir. Properly dispose of the used brake fluid.

• Front wheel and tire assembly
• 2 disc brake caliper anchor bracket mounting bolts and discard. Lift the caliper assembly from the disc brake rotor using a rotating motion. Suspend the caliper inside the fender housing with wire. Do not allow the caliper to hang from the brake hose.
• Inner and outer disc brake pads. Inspect the rotor braking surfaces for scoring and machine as necessary. Refer to the minimum rotor thickness specification when machining. If machining is not necessary, hand-sand the glaze from the braking surfaces with medium grit sandpaper. Make sure to wear an approved respirator.

To install:

3. If installing new brake pads, use a C-clamp, and an old brake pad or a wood block to seat the caliper piston in its bore. Do not allow metal or sharp objects to come into direct contact with the plastic caliper piston surface or damage will result.
4. Remove all rust buildup from the inside of the caliper legs.
5. Make sure the anti-rattle spring is seated in the caliper lining inspection

opening and that it is installed from the lining side.
6. Install or connect the following:
   • Inner disc brake pad to the caliper piston. Do not bend the pad clips during installation in the piston or distortion and rattles can occur. Install the outer disc brake pad. Make sure the clips are properly seated.
   • Caliper over the rotor and install 2 new anchor bracket mounting bolts. Torque the bolts to 118 ft. lbs. (160 Nm).
   • Wheel and tire assembly. Torque the lug nuts in a star pattern to 100 ft. lbs. (136 Nm).
7. If equipped with air suspension, turn the air suspension switch to the **ON** position.
8. Pump the brake pedal prior to moving the vehicle to seat the brake pads.
9. Fill the master cylinder reservoir with clean DOT 3 brake fluid from a closed container.
10. If the disc brake calipers were replaced or repaired be sure to bleed the system.
11. Road test the vehicle and check for proper brake system operation.

BRAKES
PARKING BRAKE

PARKING BRAKE CABLES

ADJUSTMENT
See Figure 5.

⁂ **CAUTION**

The electrical power to the air suspension system must be shut off prior to hoisting, jacking or towing an air suspension vehicle. This can be accomplished by turning off the air suspension switch located in the luggage compartment. Failure to do so can result in unexpected inflation or deflation of the air springs, which can result in shifting of the vehicle during these operations. Failure to follow these instructions may result in personal injury.

1. Before servicing the vehicle, refer to the precautions in the beginning of this section.
2. Release the parking brake control using the parking brake release handle.
3. Raise and support the vehicle.

4. Pull the parking brake cable adjuster clip downward. The tensioner spring will take up the cable slack and preload the cables.
5. Push up on the bottom of the clip to lock the adjustment. If the clip does not slide up, move the assembly slightly to align the closest groove on the parking brake cable adjuster rod with the clip.

➡If new cables are installed, allow 20 minutes prior to releasing the parking brake control.

6. Apply the parking brake control fully and release using the parking brake release handle.

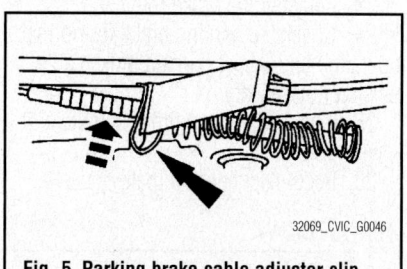

32069_CVIC_G0046
Fig. 5 Parking brake cable adjuster clip

7. Repeat Step 3 and Step 4 to complete the adjustment procedure.

PARKING BRAKE SHOES

REMOVAL & INSTALLATION
See Figure 6.

⁂ **CAUTION**

The electrical power to the air suspension system must be shut off prior to hoisting, jacking or towing an air suspension vehicle. This can be accomplished by turning off the air suspension switch located in the luggage compartment. Failure to do so can result in unexpected inflation or deflation of the air springs which can result in shifting of the vehicle during these operations. Failure to follow these instructions may result in personal injury.

Parking brake components
1. Parking brake shoe hold-down spring (2 required)

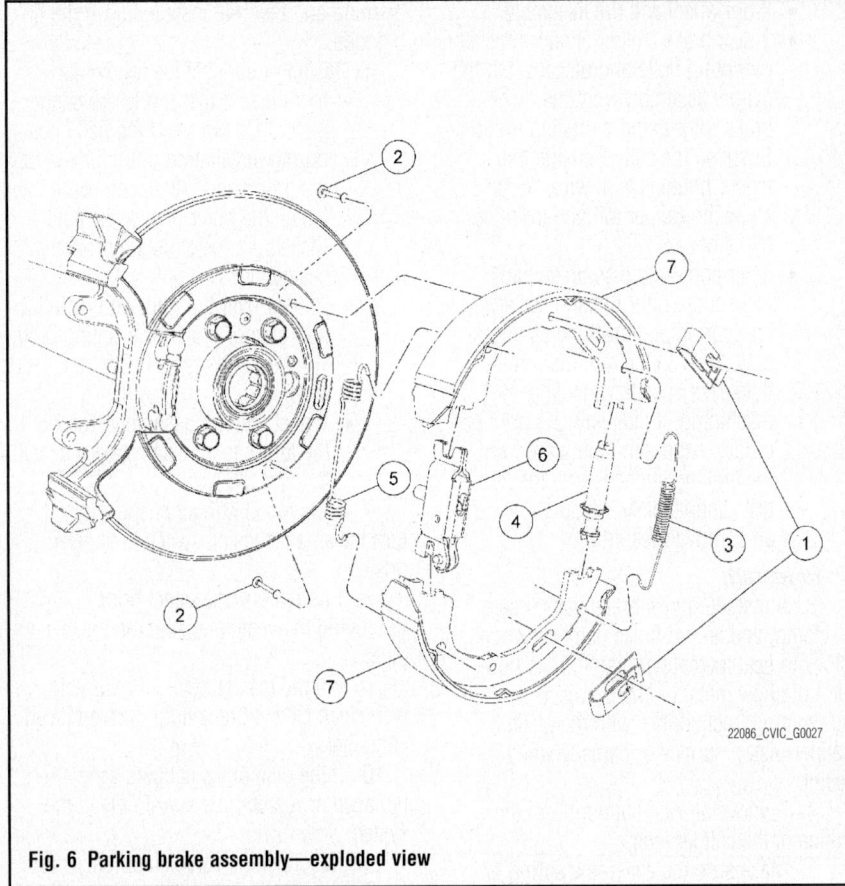

Fig. 6 Parking brake assembly—exploded view

2. Parking brake shoes hold–down spring anchor (2 required)

3. Parking brake shoe adjusting spring

4. Parking brake adjuster

5. Parking brake shoe return spring

6. Parking brake actuator

7. Parking brake shoes (2 required)

8. Before servicing the vehicle, refer to the precautions in the beginning of this section.

9. Disconnect battery negative cable from battery and properly isolate to prevent accidental reconnection.

10. Remove the rear brake disc.

11. Remove the adjuster by removing the brake shoe return spring and the adjusting spring.

➡A sharp-pointed tool such as a scratch awl is useful in removing and installing the springs.

12. Remove the parking brake actuator.

13. Push the parking brake shoes toward each other, then pull the parking brake actuator out. Unhook the parking brake cable end.

14. Remove the brake shoe hold-down springs.

15. Remove the parking brake shoe and linings.

To install:

16. Inspect the components for excessive wear or damage, and install new components as required.

17. Using anti-seize lubricant, lubricate the brake shoe contact point before installation of the rear brake shoes.

18. Lubricate the adjusting screw threads with anti-seize lubricant.

19. Install the parking brake shoe and linings.

20. Install the parking brake shoe hold-down springs.

21. Connect the parking brake cable and actuator.

22. Using a suitable brake adjusting gauge, set the rear brake shoe and lining diameter to 0.020 inch (0.5 mm) less than the inside diameter of the drum portion of the brake disc.

23. Reinstall the brake rotor.

24. Check the parking brake for normal operation and adjust parking brake cable tension if necessary.

25. Install wheel and tire assemble and lower vehicle.

26. Reconnect negative battery cable.

ADJUSTMENT

See Figure 7.

The electrical power to the air suspension system must be shut off prior to hoisting, jacking or towing an air suspension vehicle. This can be accomplished by turning off the air suspension switch located in the luggage compartment. Failure to do so can result in unexpected inflation or deflation of the air springs, which can result in shifting of the vehicle during these operations. Failure to follow these instructions may result in personal injury.

1. Before servicing the vehicle, refer to the precautions in the beginning of this section.

2. Disconnect battery negative cable from battery and properly isolate to prevent accidental reconnection.

3. Using the release handle, release the parking brake control.

➡Make sure the parking brake is fully released.

4. Remove the rear brake disc.

5. Inspect the parking brake shoes and drum for wear, damage or oil contamination. Install new components as necessary.

6. If the linings are oil contaminated, install a new rear axle oil seal.

7. Using a suitable brake adjusting gauge, measure the inside diameter of the drum portion of the rear brake disc. Record the measurement.

8. Using a suitable brake adjusting gauge, set the rear brake shoe and lining diameter to 0.020 inch (0.5 mm) less than the inside diameter of the drum portion of the rear brake disc.

9. Install the rear brake disc.

10. Test the parking brake for normal operation.

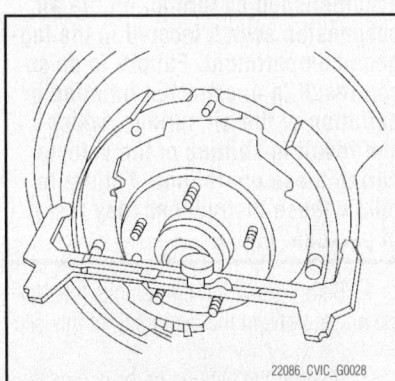

Fig. 7 Measure the shoe-to-brake clearance in this area.

CHASSIS ELECTRICAL | **AIR BAG (SUPPLEMENTAL RESTRAINT SYSTEM)**

GENERAL INFORMATION

✳✳ CAUTION

These vehicles are equipped with an air bag system. The system must be disarmed before performing service on, or around, system components, the steering column, instrument panel components, wiring and sensors. Failure to follow the safety precautions and the disarming procedure could result in accidental air bag deployment, possible injury and unnecessary system repairs.

SERVICE PRECAUTIONS

Disconnect and isolate the battery negative cable before beginning any airbag system component diagnosis, testing, removal, or installation procedures. Allow system capacitor to discharge for two minutes before beginning any component service. This will disable the airbag system. Failure to disable the airbag system may result in accidental airbag deployment, personal injury, or death.

Do not place an intact undeployed airbag face down on a solid surface. The airbag will propel into the air if accidentally deployed and may result in personal injury or death.

When carrying or handling an undeployed airbag, the trim side (face) of the airbag should be pointing towards the body to minimize possibility of injury if accidental deployment occurs. Failure to do this may result in personal injury or death.

Replace airbag system components with OEM replacement parts. Substitute parts may appear interchangeable, but internal differences may result in inferior occupant protection. Failure to do so may result in occupant personal injury or death.

Wear safety glasses, rubber gloves, and long sleeved clothing when cleaning powder residue from vehicle after an airbag deployment. Powder residue emitted from a deployed airbag can cause skin irritation. Flush affected area with cool water if irritation is experienced. If nasal or throat irritation is experienced, exit the vehicle for fresh air until the irritation ceases. If irritation continues, see a physician.

Do not use a replacement airbag that is not in the original packaging. This may result in improper deployment, personal injury, or death.

The factory installed fasteners, screws and bolts used to fasten airbag components have a special coating and are specifically designed for the airbag system. Do not use substitute fasteners. Use only original equipment fasteners listed in the parts catalog when fastener replacement is required.

During, and following, any child restraint anchor service, due to impact event or vehicle repair, carefully inspect all mounting hardware, tether straps, and anchors for proper installation, operation, or damage. If a child restraint anchor is found damaged in any way, the anchor must be replaced. Failure to do this may result in personal injury or death.

Deployed and non-deployed airbags may or may not have live pyrotechnic material within the airbag inflator.

Do not dispose of driver/passenger/curtain airbags or seat belt tensioners unless you are sure of complete deployment. Refer to the Hazardous Substance Control System for proper disposal.

Dispose of deployed airbags and tensioners consistent with state, provincial, local, and federal regulations.

After any airbag component testing or service, do not connect the battery negative cable. Personal injury or death may result if the system test is not performed first.

If the vehicle is equipped with the Occupant Classification System (OCS), do not connect the battery negative cable before performing the OCS Verification Test using the scan tool and the appropriate diagnostic information. Personal injury or death may result if the system test is not performed properly.

Never replace both the Occupant Restraint Controller (ORC) and the Occupant Classification Module (OCM) at the same time. If both require replacement, replace one, then perform the Airbag System test before replacing the other.

Both the ORC and the OCM store Occupant Classification System (OCS) calibration data, which they transfer to one another when one of them is replaced. If both are replaced at the same time, an irreversible fault will be set in both modules and the OCS may malfunction and cause personal injury or death.

If equipped with OCS, the Seat Weight Sensor is a sensitive, calibrated unit and must be handled carefully. Do not drop or handle roughly. If dropped or damaged, replace with another sensor. Failure to do so may result in occupant injury or death.

If equipped with OCS, the front passenger seat must be handled carefully as well. When removing the seat, be careful when setting on floor not to drop. If dropped, the sensor may be inoperative, could result in occupant injury, or possibly death.

If equipped with OCS, when the passenger front seat is on the floor, no one should sit in the front passenger seat. This uneven force may damage the sensing ability of the seat weight sensors. If sat on and damaged, the sensor may be inoperative, could result in occupant injury, or possibly death.

DISARMING THE SYSTEM

✳✳ CAUTION

Always wear safety glasses when repairing an air bag Supplemental Restraint System (SRS) vehicle and when handling an air bag module. This will reduce the risk of injury in the event of an accidental deployment.

✳✳ CAUTION

Never probe the connectors on the air bag module. Doing so can result in air bag deployment, which can result in personal injury.

✳✳ CAUTION

To reduce the risk of personal injury, do not use any memory saver devices.

➡ If a seat equipped with a seat mounted side air bag and/or a safety belt pretensioner (if equipped) system is being serviced, the Supplemental Restraint System (SRS) must be disarmed.

➡ The air bag warning lamp illuminates when the RCM fuse is removed and the ignition switch is ON. This is normal operation and does not indicate a Supplemental Restraint System (SRS) fault.

1. Turn all vehicle accessories OFF.
2. Turn the ignition switch to **OFF**.
3. At the central junction box (CJB), located on the LH end of the instrument panel, open the kick panel cover and remove the restraints control module (RCM) fuse F2.4 (10A).
4. Turn the ignition ON and visually monitor the air bag indicator for at least 30 seconds. The air bag indicator will remain

lit continuously (no flashing) if the correct RCM fuse has been removed. If the air bag indicator does not remain lit continuously, remove the correct RCM fuse before proceeding.

5. Turn the ignition **OFF**.

6. To avoid accidental deployment and possible personal injury, the backup power supply must be depleted before repairing or replacing any front or side air bag Supplemental Restraint System (SRS) components and before servicing, replacing, adjusting or striking components near the front or side air bag sensors or RCM, such as doors, instrument panel, console, door latches, strikers, seats and hood latches. The side impact sensors (if equipped) are located at or near the base of the B-pillars and C-pillars.

7. To deplete the backup power supply energy, disconnect the battery ground cable and wait at least one minute. Be sure to disconnect auxiliary batteries and power supplies (if equipped).

8. Disconnect the battery ground cable (14301) and wait at least one minute.

ARMING THE SYSTEM

✳✳ CAUTION

The restraint system diagnostic tool is for restraint system service only. Remove from vehicle prior to road use. Failure to remove could result in injury and possible violation of vehicle safety standards. Make sure all restraint system diagnostic tool(s) that may have been installed during the repair have been removed from the vehicle and all SRS components are connected.

1. Turn the ignition switch from **OFF** to **ON**.

2. Install the RCM fuse F2.4 (10A) to the CJB and close the cover.

✳✳ CAUTION

Be sure that nobody is in the vehicle and that there is nothing blocking or set in front of any air bag module when the battery ground cable is connected.

3. Connect the battery ground cable.

4. Prove out the Supplemental Restraint System (SRS) as follows:

• Turn the ignition key from **ON** to **OFF**.

• Wait 10 seconds, then turn the key back to **ON**.

• Visually monitor the air bag indicator with the air bag modules installed.

• The air bag indicator will light continuously for approximately six seconds and then turn off.

• If an air bag Supplemental Restraint System (SRS) fault is present, the air bag indicator will either fail to light, remain lit continuously or flash.

• The flashing might not occur until approximately 30 seconds after the ignition switch has been turned from the **OFF** to the **ON** position. This is the time required for the restraints control module (RCM) to complete the testing of the SRS. If the air bag indicator is inoperative and a SRS fault exists, a chime will sound in a pattern of five sets of five.

CLOCKSPRING CENTERING

➡ **A new clockspring is supplied in a centralized position and held there with a key. Remove the key from the clockspring, holding the rotor in its centralized position. Do not allow the clockspring rotor to turn.**

Vehicles needing clockspring recentering:

✳✳ WARNING

Incorrect centralization may result in premature component failure. If in doubt when centralizing the clockspring, repeat the centralizing procedure. Failure to follow this instruction may result in personal injury.

Make sure the road wheels are in the straight ahead position. If a clockspring has rotated out of center, follow through with this step.

1. Hold the clockspring outer housing stationary. Overturning will destroy the clockspring. The internal ribbon wire acts as the stop and can be broken from its internal connection. While turning the rotor counterclockwise, carefully feel for the ribbon wire to run out of length. Stop turning when a slight resistance is felt.

2. Turn the clockspring clockwise approximately three turns. This is the center point of the clockspring.

3. Do not allow the rotor to turn from this position.

DEPOWERING THE SRS SYSTEM

✳✳ WARNING

Always wear eye protection when servicing a vehicle. Failure to follow this instruction may result in serious personal injury.

✳✳ WARNING

Never probe the electrical connectors on air bag, Safety Canopy® or side air curtain modules. Failure to follow this instruction may result in the accidental deployment of these modules, which increases the risk of serious personal injury or death.

✳✳ WARNING

To reduce the risk of accidental deployment, do not use any memory saver devices. Failure to follow this instruction may result in serious personal injury or death.

➡ **The air bag warning indicator illuminates when the correct Restraints Control Module (RCM) fuse is removed and the ignition is ON.**

➡ **The Supplemental Restraint System (SRS) must be fully operational and free of faults before releasing the vehicle to the customer.**

1. Turn all vehicle accessories OFF.

2. Turn the ignition to OFF.

At the Central Junction Box (CJB), located on the LH end of the instrument panel, open the kick panel cover and remove the RCM fuse 22 (10A) from the CJB.

3. Turn the ignition ON and monitor the air bag warning indicator for at least 30 seconds. The air bag warning indicator will remain lit continuously (no flashing) if the correct RCM fuse has been removed. If the air bag warning indicator does not remain lit continuously, remove the correct RCM fuse before proceeding.

4. Turn the ignition OFF.

✳✳ WARNING

Always deplete the backup power supply before repairing or installing any new front or side air bag supplemental restraint system (SRS) component and before servicing, removing, installing, adjusting or striking components near the front or side impact sensors or the restraints

control module (RCM). Nearby components include doors, instrument panel, console, door latches, strikers, seats and hood latches.

5. To deplete the backup power supply energy, disconnect the battery ground cable and wait at least 1 minute. Be sure to disconnect auxiliary batteries and power supplies (if equipped).

➡**Failure to follow these instructions may result in serious personal injury or death in the event of an accidental deployment.**

6. Disconnect the battery ground cable and wait at least one minute.

REPOWERING THE SRS SYSTEM

✴✴ WARNING

Remove restraint system diagnostic tools from the vehicle prior to road testing. If tools are not removed, the supplemental restraint system (SRS) device may not deploy in a crash.

Failure to follow this instruction may result in serious personal injury or death in a crash and possibly violate vehicle safety standards.

1. Make sure all restraint system diagnostic tool(s) that may have been installed during the repair have been removed from the vehicle and all SRS components are connected.
2. Turn the ignition from OFF to ON.
3. Install the RCM fuse 22 (10A) to the CJB and close the cover.

✴✴ WARNING

Make sure no one is in the vehicle and there is nothing blocking or placed in front of any air bag module when the battery is connected. Failure to follow these instructions may result in serious personal injury in the event of an accidental deployment.

4. Connect the battery ground cable.
5. Prove out the SRS as follows:

a. Turn the ignition from ON to OFF. Wait 10 seconds, then turn the ignition back to ON and monitor the air bag warning indicator with the air bag modules installed. The air bag warning indicator will light continuously for approximately 6 seconds and then turn off. If an air bag SRS fault is present, the air bag warning indicator will:
- Fail to light
- Remain lit continuously
- Flash.

6. The flashing might not occur until approximately 30 seconds after the ignition has been turned from the OFF to the ON position. This is the time required for the RCM to complete the testing of the SRS .

a. If the air bag warning indicator is inoperative and a SRS fault exists, a chime will sound in a pattern of 5 sets of 5 beeps.

b. If this occurs, the air bag warning indicator and any SRS fault discovered must be diagnosed and repaired.

7. Clear all continuous DTCs from the RCM using a scan tool.

DRIVE TRAIN

AUTOMATIC TRANSMISSION ASSEMBLY

REMOVAL & INSTALLATION
See Figures 8 through 11.

✴✴ CAUTION

If the vehicle is equipped with air suspension, the electrical power to the air suspension system must be shut off prior to hoisting, jacking or towing an air suspension vehicle. This can be accomplished by turning off the air suspension switch located in the luggage compartment. Failure to do so can result in unexpected inflation or deflation of the air springs, which can result in shifting of the vehicle during these operations. Failure to follow these instructions may result in personal injury.

➡**Whenever a transmission has been disassembled to install new parts, the transmission fluid cooler tubes must be cleaned and backflushed using a suitable torque converter/fluid cooler cleaner. A new Oil-To-Air (OTA) transmission fluid cooler must also be installed.**

➡**When internal wear or damage has occurred in the transmission, metal particles, clutch plate material or band material may have been carried into the torque converter and fluid cooler. These contaminants are a major cause of recurring transmission concerns and must be removed from the system before the transmission is put back into service.**

➡**After the transmission is removed for a major overhaul, it is important to completely clean all transmission components, including torque converter, cooler inlet tube, main control valve body, clutches and all coasting booster valve shuttle balls after any transmission service that generates contamination. These contaminants are a major cause for recurring transmission concerns and must be removed from the system before the transmission is returned to service.**

✴✴ WARNING

Before servicing a vehicle equipped with a fire suppression system, depower the system.

1. Drain the transmission.
2. If equipped with air suspension, the air suspension switch, located on the right-

hand side of the luggage compartment, must be turned to the **OFF** position before raising the vehicle.

3. Disconnect the negative battery cable.

4. Install the transmission fluid pan and the old transmission fluid pan gasket. Position the transmission fluid pan gasket. Position the transmission fluid pan.

➡**To maintain the initial driveshaft balance, mark the rear driveshaft yoke and the axle pinion flange so they can be installed in their original positions.**

5. Mark the rear driveshaft yoke and the axle pinion flange and remove the 4 bolts.

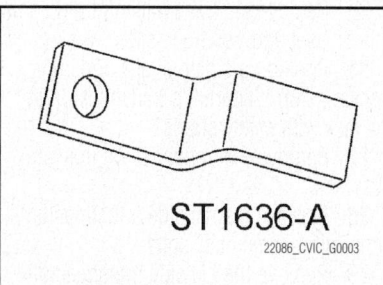

ST1636-A

22086_CVIC_G0003

Fig. 8 Special Tool no. 307-346 - Torque Converter Retainer

6. Index-mark the driveshaft and extension housing. Separate the driveshaft from the transmission.

7. Remove the torque converter access cover plug at the left rear engine block.

8. Remove the transmission inspection cover.

    a. Remove the 2 bolts.

    b. Remove the inspection cover .

    c. Remove the bolt for the separator plate.

➡**Make an identifying mark on the torque converter stud and the flexplate for correct alignment during assembly.**

9. Remove and discard the 4 torque converter-to-flexplate nuts.

10. Disconnect the RH Heated Oxygen Sensor (HO2S) connector.

11. Disconnect the RH catalyst monitor connector.

12. Remove the nuts from the RH exhaust flange.

13. Remove the RH catalytic converter-to-exhaust bolts.

14. Disconnect the LH HO2S connector.

15. Disconnect the LH catalyst monitor connector.

16. Remove the nuts from the LH exhaust flange.

17. Remove the LH catalytic converter-to-exhaust bolts.

➡**Make a reference mark on the selector lever cable to the transmission.**

18. Disconnect the selector lever cable.

19. Remove the selector lever cable bracket and position aside.

20. Remove the ground wire.

21. Remove the starter electrical connector cap.

22. Disconnect the electrical connectors.

23. Remove the 3 starter bolts and the starter.

➡**The case connectors must be held in place to prevent them from moving.**

24. Disconnect the transmission fluid cooler tubes.

25. Remove the transmission fluid cooler line bracket and position aside.

26. Position a suitable jack under the transmission. Secure the transmission to the jack with safety straps.

27. Remove the transmission insulator nuts.

28. Remove the RH side transmission support crossmember bolts.

29. Remove the LH side transmission support crossmember bolt.

30. Remove the bolts and remove the park cable bracket and position aside.

➡**The transmission support crossmember is a press fit in the transmission support crossmember pocket, it may be necessary to pry the transmission support crossmember out of the transmission support crossmember pocket. Be careful not to damage the transmission support crossmember.**

31. Lower the RH side of the transmission support crossmember.

➡**The transmission support crossmember is a press fit in the transmission support crossmember pocket, it may be necessary to pry the transmission support crossmember out of the transmission support crossmember pocket. Be careful not to damage the transmission support crossmember.**

32. Lower the LH side of the transmission support crossmember and remove the transmission support crossmember.

33. Remove the transmission insulator.

➡**It is not necessary to disconnect the transmission harness from all the transmission sensors at this time, the harness will come out with the transmission.**

34. Disconnect the wire harness connectors and remove them from the transmission fluid filler tube.

35. Remove the bolt.

36. Position the transmission fluid filler tube aside.

37. Remove the transmission retaining bolts.

38. Separate the transmission from the engine and lower. Partially lower the transmission from under the vehicle.

39. Disconnect the electrical connectors.

    a. Remove the catalyst monitor connector retainer from the stud.

    b. Disconnect the transmission vehicle harness connector.

40. Disconnect the electrical connectors and remove the wire harness from the transmission.

    a. Disconnect the Transmission Range (TR) sensor electrical connector.

    b. Disconnect the Output Shaft Speed (OSS) sensor electrical connector.

    c. Disconnect the Turbine Shaft Speed (TSS) sensor electrical connector.

    • Remove the catalyst monitor connector retainer from the stud.

    • Disconnect the wire harness retainers and remove the harness.

✳✳ WARNING

Secure the torque converter in the transmission during removal or installation. The torque converter is heavy and may result in injury if it falls out of the transmission. Failure to follow this instruction may result in serious personal injury.

41. Leaving the transmission in a horizontal position, slide it back far enough to install the Torque Converter Retainer. Install the Torque Converter Retainer.

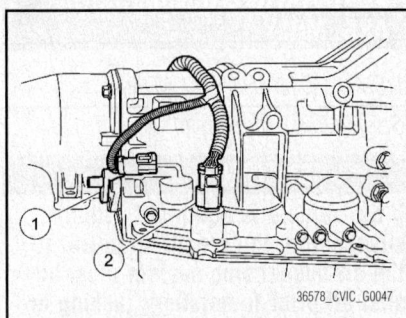

Fig. 10 Removing the catalyst monitor (1) and transmission vehicle harness connector (2)

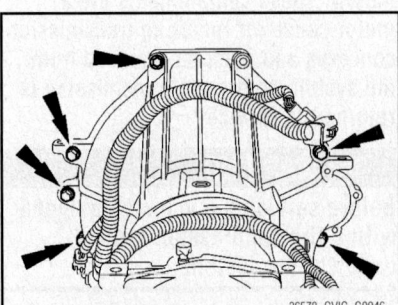

Fig. 9 Removing the transmission retaining bolts

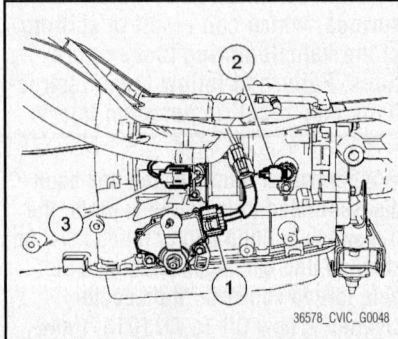

Fig. 11 Disconnecting the TR sensor (1), OSS sensor (2) and TSS sensor (3)

To install:

42. Reverse the removal procedure.

43. Tighten the following to specification:

  a. Transmission retaining bolts: 35 ft. lbs. (48 NM).

  b. The four NEW converter nuts: 27 ft. lbs. (36 Nm).

  c. Transmission inspection cover bolts: 26 ft. lbs. (35 Nm).

  d. Transmission separator plate bolt: 26 ft. lbs. (35 Nm).

  e. Transmission filler tube bolt: 35 ft. lbs. (48 Nm).

  f. Transmission insulator: 66 ft. lbs. (90 Nm).

  g. LH and RH transmission support cross member bolts: 52 ft. lbs. (70 Nm).

  h. Park cable bracket: 41 ft. lbs. (55 Nm).

  i. Transmission insulator nuts: 22 ft. lbs. (30 Nm).

  j. Transmission fluid cooler tubes: 177 inch lbs. (20 Nm).

  k. Transmission fluid cooler tube bracket: 133 inch lbs. (15 Nm).

  l. Ground wire: 17 ft. lbs. (23 Nm).

  m. Starter and bolts: 18 ft. lbs. (25 Nm).

  n. RH and LH exhaust flange nuts: 35 ft. lbs. (48 Nm).

  o. RH and LH catalytic converter-to-exhaust bolts: 30 ft. lbs. (40 Nm).

  p. Selector lever cable at the manual control lever: 22 ft. lbs. (30 Nm).

  q. Rear driveshaft: 76 ft. lbs. (103 Nm).

✳✳ WARNING

If the vehicle is equipped with a fire suppression system, repower the system.

44. Lower the vehicle.

45. Connect the battery ground cable.

46. Fill the transmission with automatic transmission fluid and inspect for correct operation.

REAR AXLE HOUSING

REMOVAL & INSTALLATION

See Figures 12 through 14.

✳✳ WARNING

The electrical power to the air suspension system must be shut off prior to hoisting, jacking or towing an air suspension vehicle. This can be accomplished by turning off the air suspension switch located in the LH side of the luggage compartment.

Failure to do so can result in unexpected inflation or deflation of the air springs, which can result in shifting of the vehicle during these operations.

1. Before servicing the vehicle, refer to the precautions in the beginning of this section.

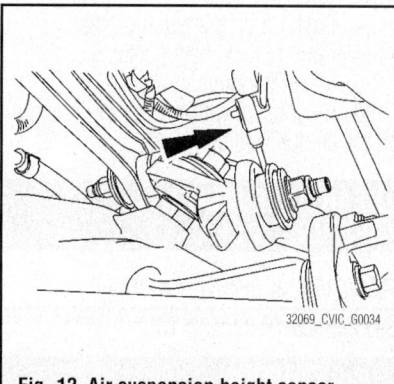

Fig. 12 Air suspension height sensor

2. Disconnect battery negative cable from battery and properly isolate to prevent accidental reconnection.

3. Remove or disconnect the following:

  • Drive pinion
  • Parking brake adjuster clip

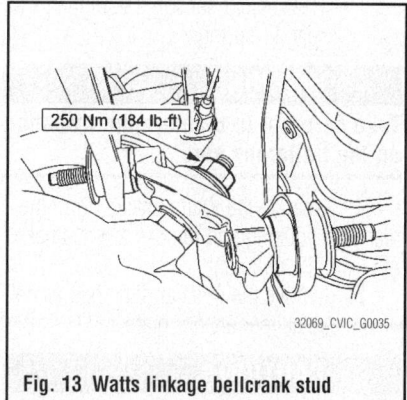

Fig. 13 Watts linkage bellcrank stud

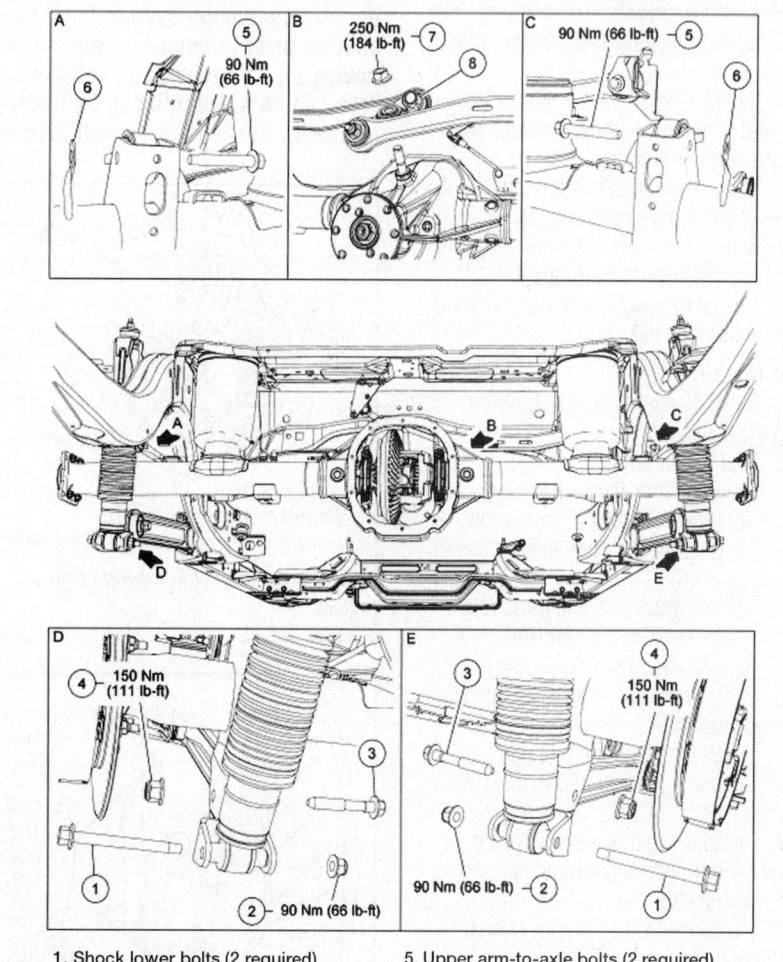

1. Shock lower bolts (2 required)
2. Shock lower nuts (2 required)
3. Lower arm-to-axle bolts (2 required)
4. Lower arm-to-axle flagnuts (2 required)
5. Upper arm-to-axle bolts (2 required)
6. Upper arm-to-axle flagnuts (2 required)
7. Watts link pivot nut
8. Watts link pivot

Fig. 14 Rear axle assembly

➡**Pull down on the parking brake cable at the control end. Push up on the parking brake adjuster clip to lock the adjuster.**

- Parking brake rear cables and conduit retainer bolts
- Two ABS sensor wire harness clips
- Rear stabilizer bar
- Rear height sensor, if equipped with rear air springs

✳✳ WARNING
Take care not to damage the threads on the bellcrank stud.

4. Separate the Watts linkage from the rear axle housing and remove the retainer nut from the bellcrank.
5. Remove the bolts and the rear wheel disc brake caliper anchor plate.

✳✳ CAUTION
Use additional support straps to secure the rear axle to the jack.

6. Support the rear axle housing with a suitable jack.
7. Remove the shock absorber lower nuts, and then remove the shock absorbers from the retainer brackets.
8. Remove the nuts and bolts retaining the LH and RH lower control arms.
9. Remove the nuts and bolts retaining the LH and RH upper control arms.
10. Unseat the air springs and lower the rear axle from the vehicle.

To install:
11. Raise the rear axle into position using a suitable jack.
12. Seat the air springs.
13. Install or connect the following:
- LH and RH upper control arms and torque the bolts to 69 ft. lbs. (93 Nm)
- Shock absorbers and torque the bolts to 66 ft. lbs. (90 Nm)
14. Remove the axle jack.
15. Install the Watts linkage on the rear axle housing.
16. Install the retainer nut on the bellcrank stud and tighten to 185 ft. lbs. (250 Nm)
17. Install the rear wheel disc brake caliper anchor plate and torque the bolts to 50 ft. lbs. (68 Nm)
18. If equipped with rear air springs, install the height sensor.
19. Install the rear stabilizer bar retainer bolts and tighten to 18 ft. lbs. (25 Nm)
20. Connect the ABS sensor harness routing clips.

21. Install the parking brake rear cables and conduit retainer bolts.
22. Connect the parking brake rear cables and conduit to the parking brake cable connector.
23. Pull down on parking brake cable at the control end, then pull the parking brake adjuster clip downward and release the cable.
24. Push up on the parking brake adjuster clip to lock the adjuster.
25. Install the drive pinion.
26. If equipped with rear air springs, turn on the air suspension switch.

REAR AXLE SHAFT, BEARING & SEAL

REMOVAL & INSTALLATION
See Figures 15 through 18.

✳✳ CAUTION
If the vehicle is equipped with air suspension, the electrical power to the air suspension system must be shut off prior to hoisting, jacking or towing an air suspension vehicle. This can be accomplished by turning off the air suspension switch located

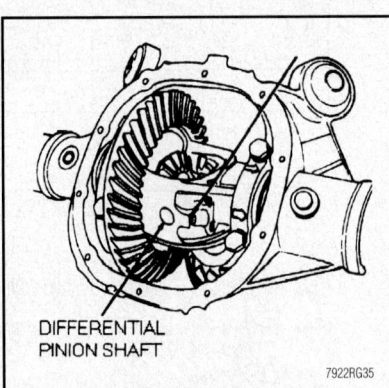
Fig. 15 Removal of differential pinion shaft

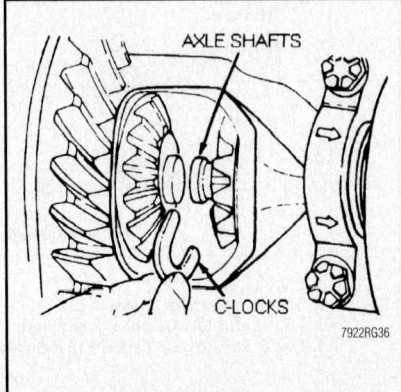
Fig. 16 Removing axle shaft C-lock clips

in the luggage compartment. Failure to do so can result in unexpected inflation or deflation of the air springs, which can result in shifting of the vehicle during these operations. Failure to follow these instructions may result in personal injury.

1. If equipped, turn the air suspension service switch to the **OFF** position before raising the vehicle.
2. Remove or disconnect the following
- Wheel
- Brake caliper and rotor
- Anti-lock brake speed sensor, if equipped
3. Clean all dirt from the area of the axle housing cover.
4. Place a drain pan under the axle housing.
5. Remove or disconnect the following:
- Axle housing cover retaining bolts and the cover, draining the axle lubricant from the housing
- Differential pinion shaft lock bolt and the differential pinion shaft
6. Push the flanged end of the axle shaft being removed toward the center of the vehicle
7. Remove or disconnect the following:
- C-lock from the button end of the axle shaft
- Axle shaft from the housing, being careful not to damage the oil seal and anti-lock brake sensor ring, if equipped.
8. Insert an axle bearing remover in the axle housing bore and position it behind the wheel bearing so the tangs on the tool engage the bearing outer race.
9. Remove the wheel bearing and seal as an assembly using an impact slide hammer attached to the bearing remover tool

To install:
10. Lubricate the new wheel bearing with rear axle lubricant.
11. Install the wheel bearing into the axle housing bore using a bearing installer.
12. Lubricate the lips of a new wheel bearing oil seal with wheel bearing grease.
13. Install or connect the following:
- New wheel bearing seal using a seal installer
- Axle shaft into the axle housing without damaging the bearing/seal assembly or anti-lock brake sensor ring, if equipped. Start the splines into the side gear and push firmly until the button end of the axle shaft can be seen in the differential case.

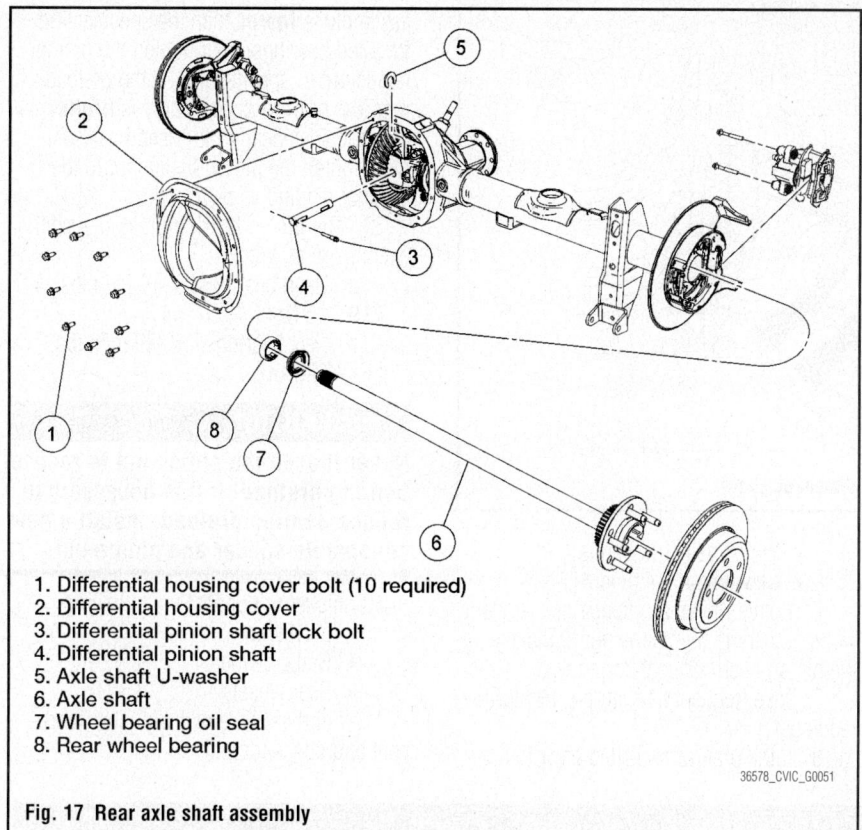

1. Differential housing cover bolt (10 required)
2. Differential housing cover
3. Differential pinion shaft lock bolt
4. Differential pinion shaft
5. Axle shaft U-washer
6. Axle shaft
7. Wheel bearing oil seal
8. Rear wheel bearing

36578_CVIC_G0051

Fig. 17 Rear axle shaft assembly

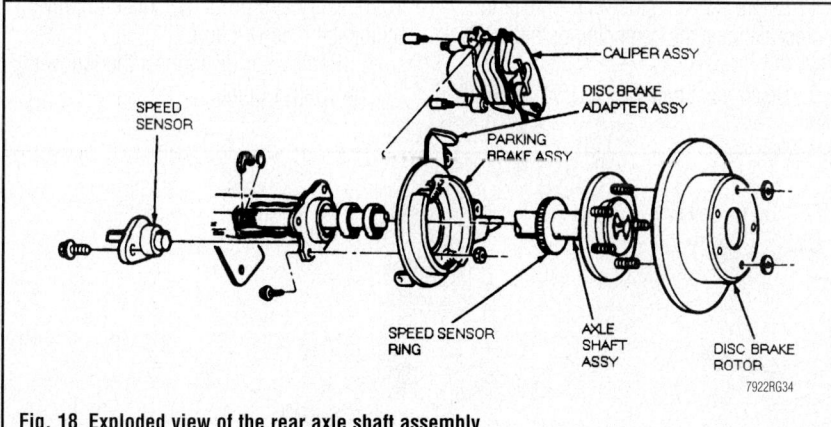

7922RG34

Fig. 18 Exploded view of the rear axle shaft assembly

- C-lock on the button end of the axle shaft splines, then push the shaft outboard until the shaft splines engage and the C-lock seats in the counterbore of the differential side gear.
- Differential pinion shaft through the case and pinion gears, aligning the hole in the shaft with the lock bolt hole
- Apply a thread locking compound to the lock bolt threads and place in the case and pinion shaft. Tighten to 22 ft. lbs. (30 Nm).

14. Cover the inside of the differential case with a shop rag and clean the sealing surface of the axle housing and the axle housing cover. Remove the shop rag.

15. Apply a 1/8–3/16 inch (3.18–4.76mm) wide bead of silicone sealer to the cover.

16. Install the axle housing and bolts and tighten in a star pattern. Final torque the cover retaining bolts to 33 ft. lbs. (45 Nm).

17. Add the appropriate rear axle lubricant to the axle housing to a level 1/4–9/16 inch (6–14mm) below the bottom of the fill hole. If equipped with a limited slip differential, add 4 oz. (118.3 ml) of the appropriate friction modifier.

18. Install or connect the following:
- Axle housing fill plug and tighten to 12 ft. lbs. (16 Nm)

- Anti-lock brake speed sensor, if equipped. Tighten the retaining bolt to 53 inch lbs. (6 Nm).
- Brake calipers and rotors
- Wheel

19. If equipped with air suspension, turn the air suspension switch to the **ON** position.

20. Road test the vehicle and check for proper operation.

REAR PINION SEAL

REMOVAL & INSTALLATION

See Figures 19 and 20.

✳✳ CAUTION

If the vehicle is equipped with air suspension, the electrical power to the air suspension system must be shut off prior to hoisting, jacking or towing an air suspension vehicle. This can be accomplished by turning off the air suspension switch located in the luggage compartment. Failure to do so can result in unexpected inflation or deflation of the air springs, which can result in shifting of the vehicle during these operations. Failure to follow these instructions may result in personal injury.

1. Remove or disconnect the following:
- Driveshaft
- Rear wheels
- Rear brake calipers

➡The rear brake calipers must be removed so that there is no additional drag when measuring pinion bearing preload.

2. Use an inch lb. torque wrench and measure the amount of torque required to maintain pinion rotation through several revolutions.

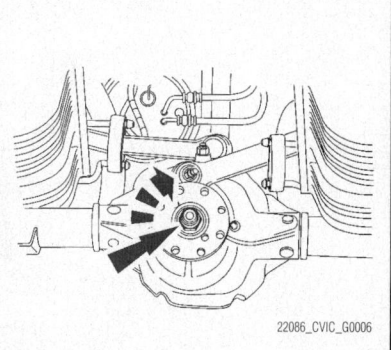

22086_CVIC_G0006

Fig. 19 Be sure to measure and record pinion bearing preload before removing the pinion nut

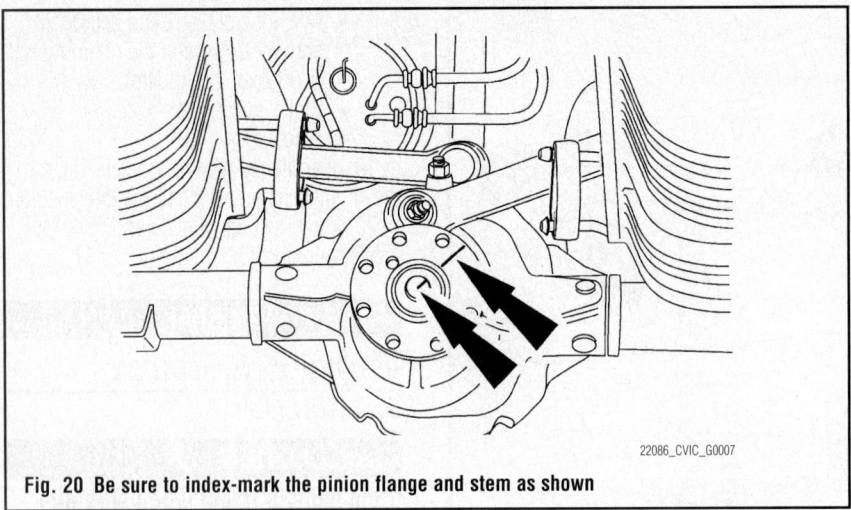

Fig. 20 Be sure to index-mark the pinion flange and stem as shown

22086_CVIC_G0007

3. Index mark the pinion flange and the drive pinion stem for correct alignment during installation

4. Remove the pinion flange and remove the seal.

To install:

5. Install or connect the following:

- Pinion seal and flange
- New pinion flange nut

6. Rotate the pinion flange occasionally while tightening the flange nut to make sure the pinion bearings seat correctly.

7. Take frequent bearing preload torque readings.

8. If the preload recorded prior to dis-

assembly is **lower** than the specification for used bearings, then tighten the pinion flange nut to specification. If the preload recorder prior to disassembly is **higher** than the specification for used bearings, then tighten the pinion flange nut to the original reading as recorded.

9. The pinion bearing preload specifications are as follows:
   a. Used bearings: 8–14 inch lbs. (0.9–1.6 Nm).
   b. New bearings: 16–29 inch lbs. (1.8–3.2 Nm).

⁕⁕ CAUTION

Never loosen the pinion nut to reduce bearing preload. If it is necessary to reduce bearing preload, install a new collapsible spacer and pinion nut.

10. Install or connect the following:
- Driveshaft
- Brake calipers
- Rear wheels

11. Fill the differential with gear lubricant and check for leaks.

ENGINE COOLING

ENGINE FAN

REMOVAL & INSTALLATION

See Figures 21 and 22.

1. Before servicing the vehicle, refer to the precautions in the beginning of this section.

2. Disconnect battery negative cable

from battery and properly isolate to prevent accidental reconnection.

3. Remove or disconnect the following:
- Degas bottle

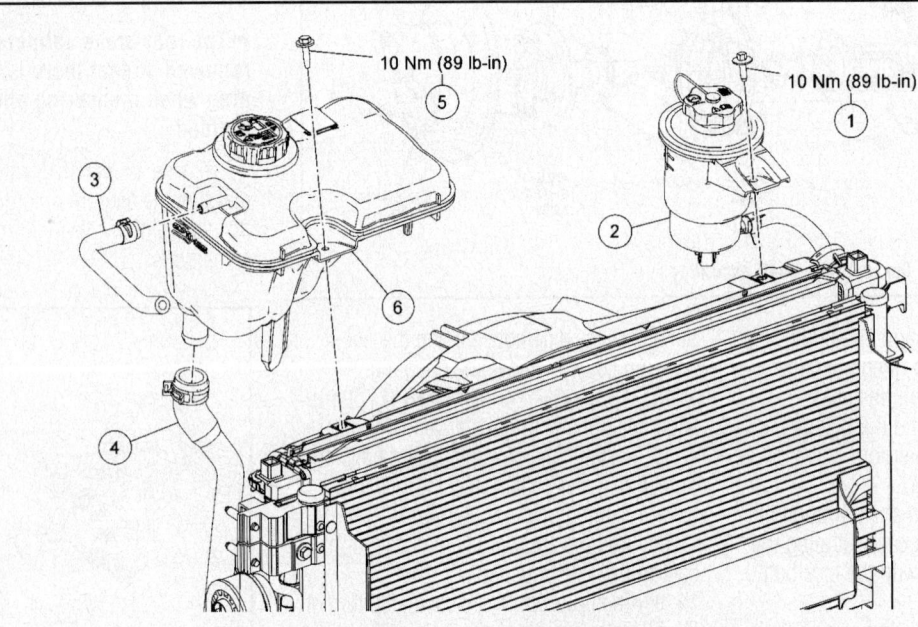

1. Power steering reservoir bolt
2. Power steering reservoir
3. Degas bottle overflow hose
4. Degas bottle supply hose
5. Degas bottle bolt
6. Degas bottle

10 Nm (89 lb-in)

36578_CVIC_G0056

Fig. 21 Degas bottle and power steering reservoir

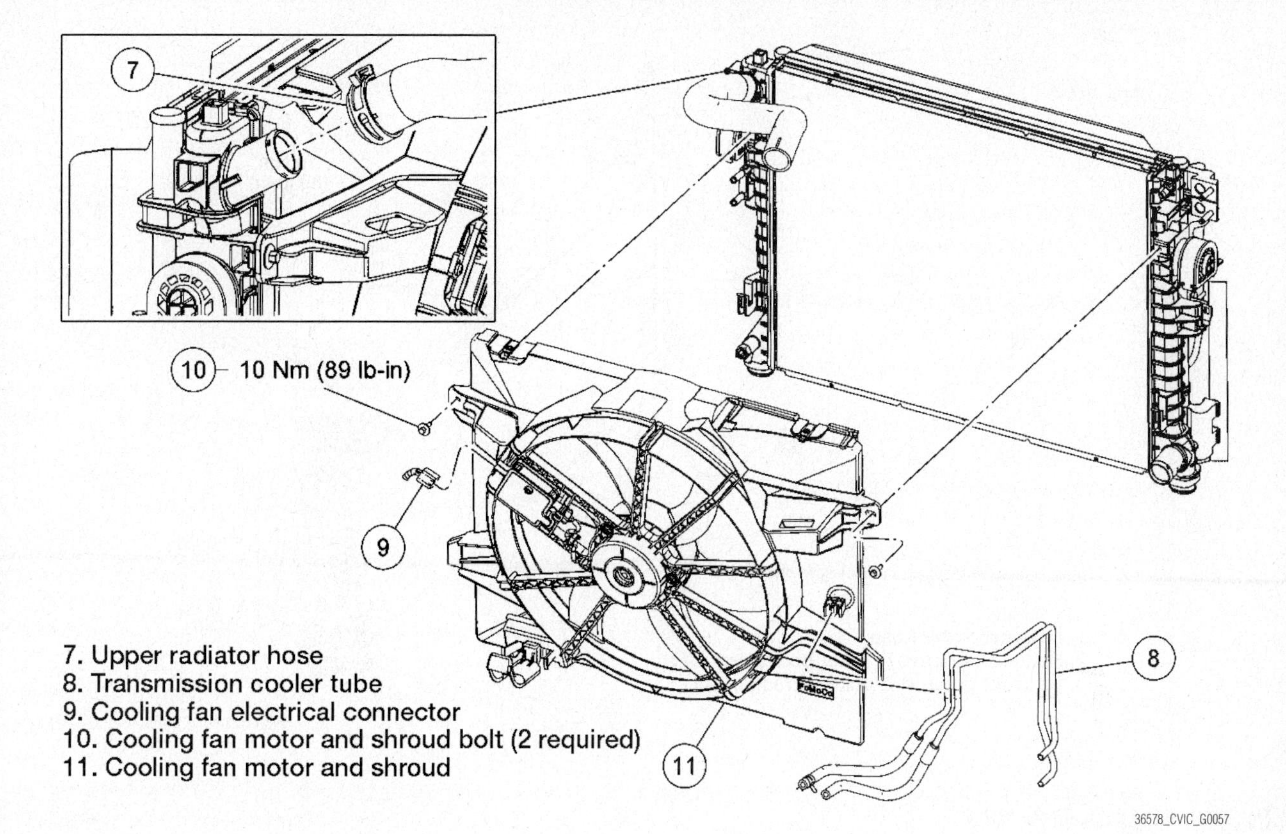

10 — 10 Nm (89 lb-in)

7. Upper radiator hose
8. Transmission cooler tube
9. Cooling fan electrical connector
10. Cooling fan motor and shroud bolt (2 required)
11. Cooling fan motor and shroud

36578_CVIC_G0057

Fig. 22 Cooling Fan Motor and Shroud

- Power steering reservoir and set aside
- Fan motor electrical connector
- Fan blade, motor and shroud assembly

To install:

4. Install or connect the following:
- Fan blade, motor and shroud assembly and tighten the bolts to 89 inch lbs. (10 Nm)
- Fan motor electrical connector
- Power steering reservoir and tighten the bolt to 9 ft. lbs. (12 Nm)
- Degas bottle and tighten the screws to 89 inch lbs. (10 Nm)

RADIATOR

REMOVAL & INSTALLATION

See Figures 23 through 26.

1. Before servicing the vehicle, refer to the precautions in the beginning of this section.

2. Disconnect battery negative cable from battery and properly isolate to prevent accidental reconnection.

3. Drain the engine cooling system.

4. Remove or disconnect the following:

- Fan blade, fan motor and fan shroud assembly
- Pin-type retainers and radiator sight shield
- Upper radiator hose
- Lower radiator hose
- Bolts and both radiator support brackets

5. Remove the top 2 LH and 2 RH pin-type retainers from the A/C condenser air deflectors.

6. Remove the A/C condenser and transmission cooler bolts and position them away from the radiator.

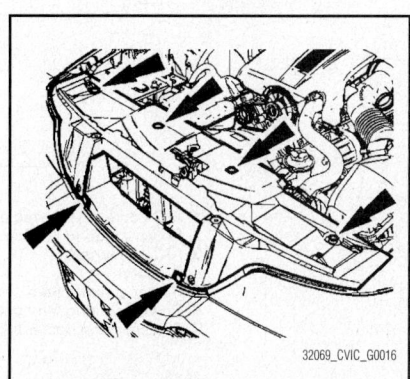

32069_CVIC_G0016

Fig. 23 Radiator sight shield screw locations

7. Remove the pin-type retainer from radiator-to-power steering fluid cooler.

8. Remove the bolt from the A/C condenser.

9. Release the 2 retainer clips and separate the power steering fluid cooler from the radiator.

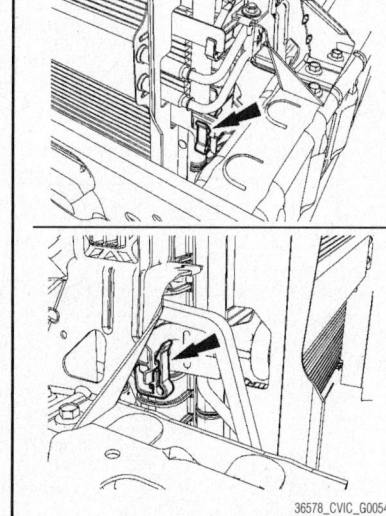

36578_CVIC_G0054

Fig. 24 Locating the retaining clips

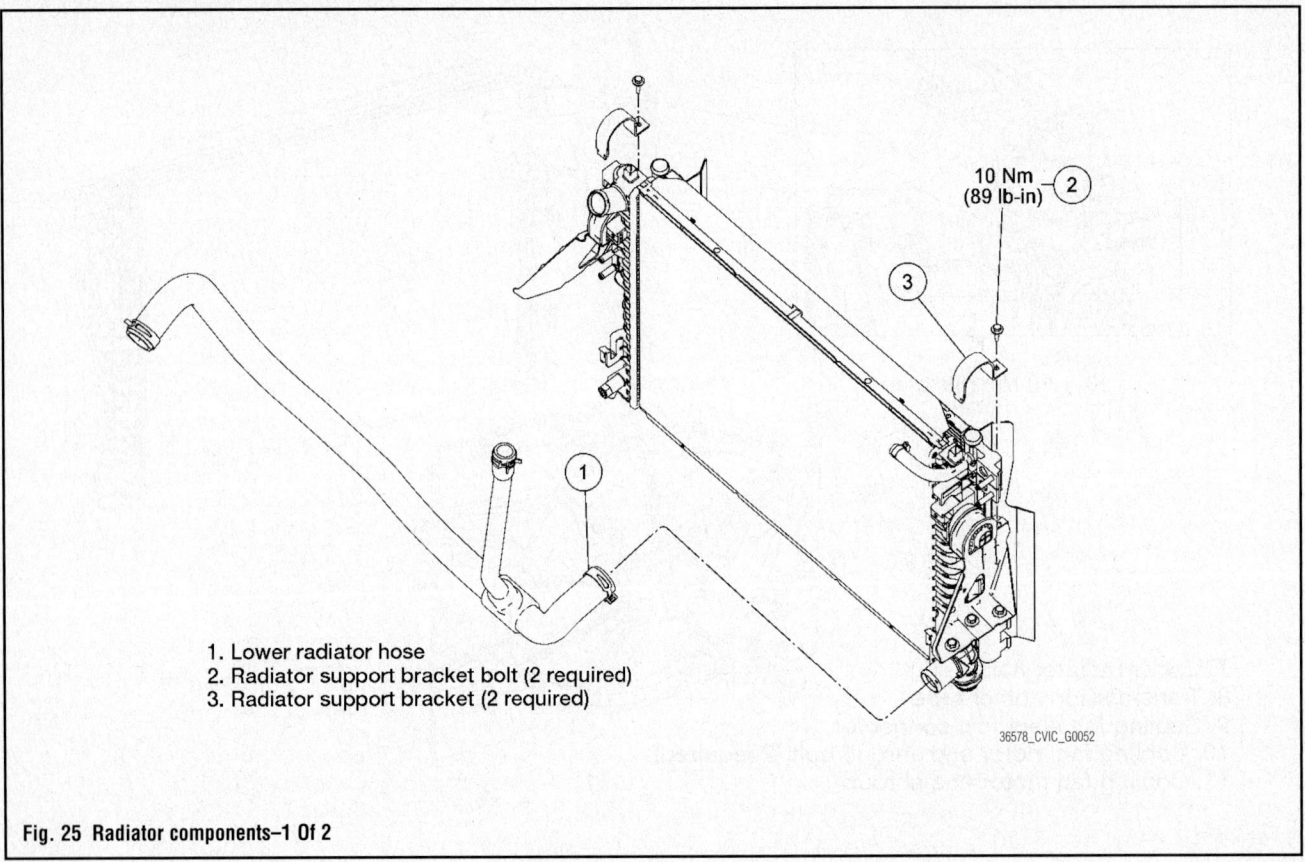

10 Nm
(89 lb-in) ─②

③

①

1. Lower radiator hose
2. Radiator support bracket bolt (2 required)
3. Radiator support bracket (2 required)

36578_CVIC_G0052

Fig. 25 Radiator components—1 Of 2

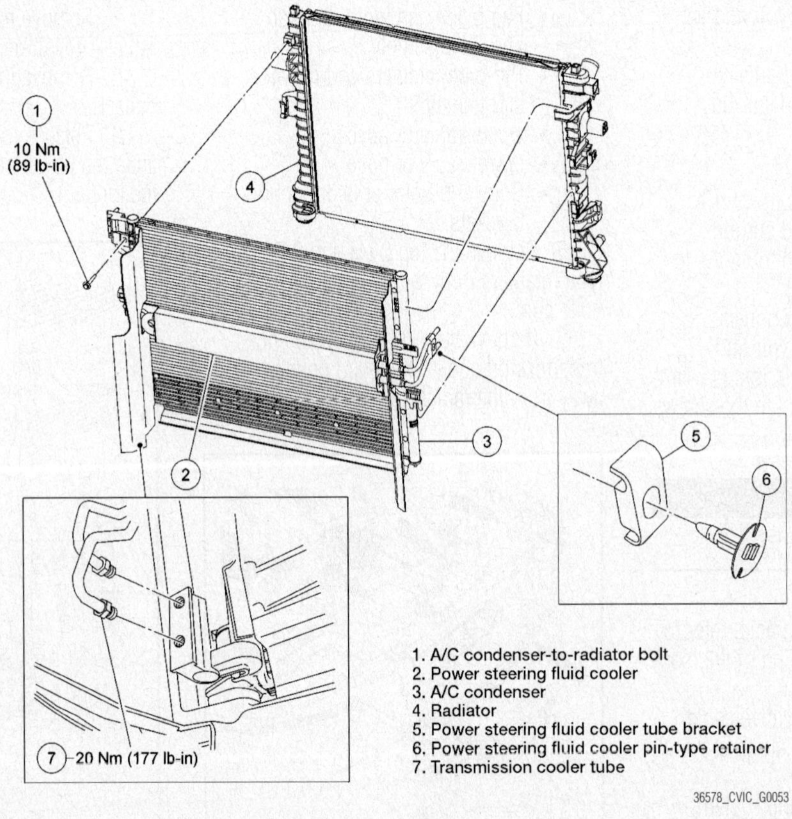

①
10 Nm
(89 lb-in)

④

③

⑤

⑥

②

⑦─20 Nm (177 lb-in)

1. A/C condenser-to-radiator bolt
2. Power steering fluid cooler
3. A/C condenser
4. Radiator
5. Power steering fluid cooler tube bracket
6. Power steering fluid cooler pin-type retainer
7. Transmission cooler tube

36578_CVIC_G0053

Fig. 26 Radiator components—2 Of 2

10. Separate the A/C condenser from the radiator by sliding from right to left.

11. Remove the radiator.

To install:

➡**Do not reuse hose clamps. Instead, use appropriately sized worm-style clamps in place of the constant tension clamps.**

12. To install, reverse removal procedure.

13. Bleed the cooling system.

14. Fill the transmission to the correct fluid level.

15. Reconnect the negative battery cable,

16. Check for leaks and repair if necessary.

THERMOSTAT

REMOVAL & INSTALLATION

See Figures 27 through 29.

1. Before servicing the vehicle, refer to the precautions in the beginning of this section.

2. Disconnect battery negative cable from battery and properly isolate to prevent accidental reconnection.

3. Drain the coolant below the water thermostat.

4. Remove or disconnect the following:
   - Engine cover
   - Two bolts and water outlet adapter and position aside
   - Water thermostat and the O-ring seal from the intake manifold

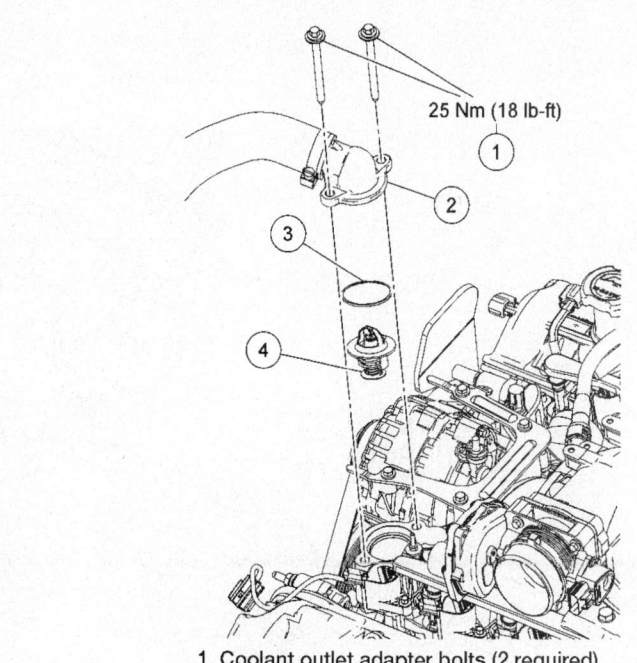

1. Coolant outlet adapter bolts (2 required)
2. Coolant outlet adapter
3. O-ring seal
4. Thermostat

36578_CVIC_G0055

Fig. 28 Thermostat components

To install:

5. Inspect the O-ring seal install a new seal if necessary.

6. Install or connect the following:
   - Thermostat into the intake manifold
   - Water outlet adapter and torque the bolts to 18 ft. lbs. (25 Nm)

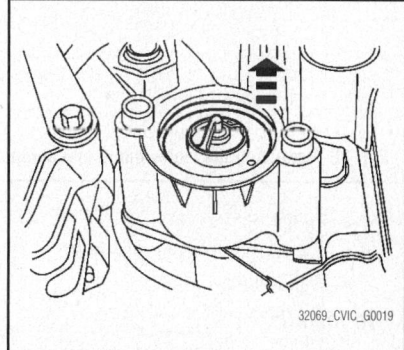

32069_CVIC_G0019

Fig. 29 Orientation of thermostat when installing

   - Engine cover
   - Refill the cooling system, check for leaks and repair if necessary

WATER PUMP

REMOVAL & INSTALLATION

See Figure 30.

1. Drain the cooling system.
2. Remove or disconnect the following:
   - Negative battery cable
   - Cooling fan and shroud
   - Accessory drive belt
   - 4 water pump pulley-to-water pump bolts

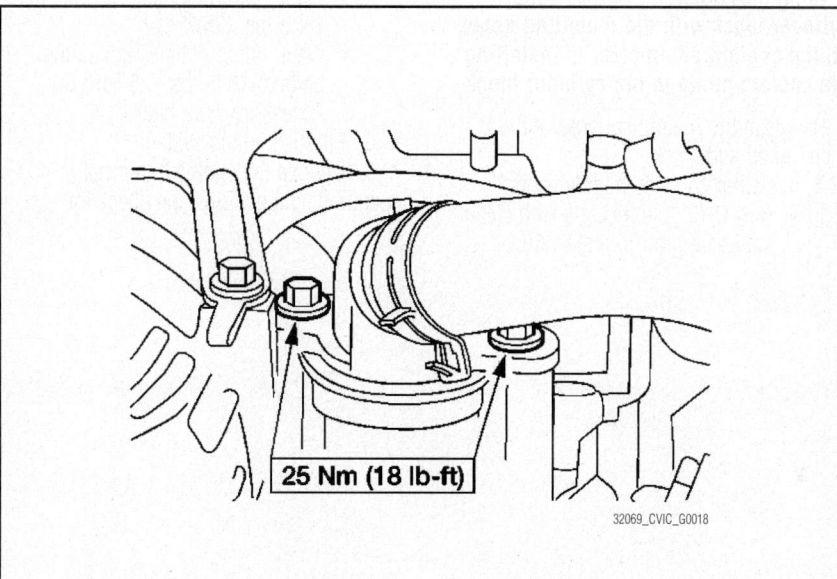

25 Nm (18 lb-ft)

32069_CVIC_G0018

Fig. 27 Position of thermostat housing

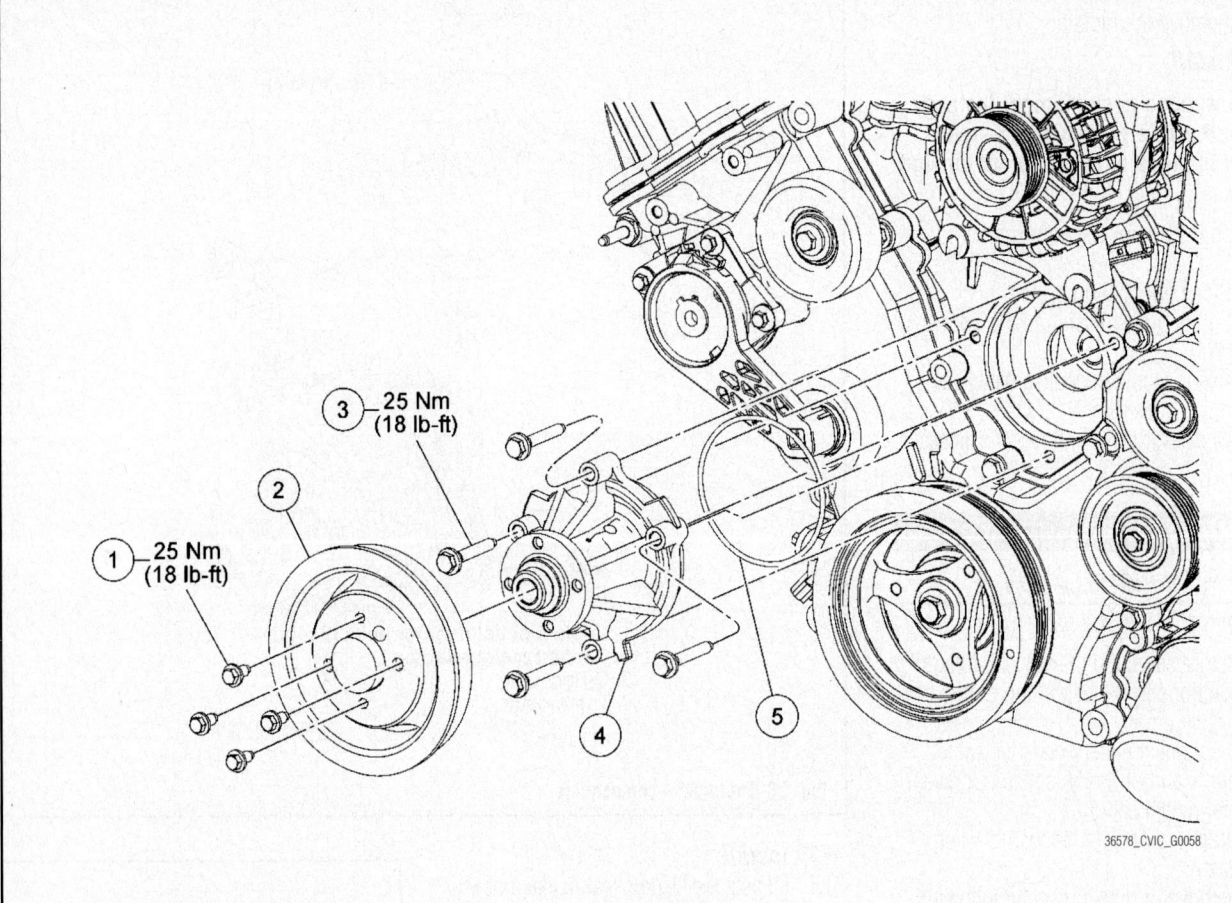

Fig. 30 Removing the water pump and components

- Pulley
- 4 water pump-to-engine bolts
- Water pump

To install:

➡**Do not rotate the coolant pump housing once installed in the engine. Damage to the O-ring seal can occur, causing the coolant pump to leak.**

➡**Align the mounting holes in the cylinder block with the mounting holes on the coolant pump prior to installing the coolant pump in the cylinder block.**

3. Clean the sealing surfaces of the water pump and block.
4. Install or connect the following:
    - New O-ring, lubricate it with clean antifreeze prior to installation

- Water pump. Tighten the bolts to 18 ft. lbs. (25 Nm).
- Water pump pulley. Tighten the bolts to 18 ft. lbs. (25 Nm).
- Accessory drive belt

5. Fill the cooling system.
6. Operate the engine to normal operating temperatures and check for leaks.

ENGINE ELECTRICAL   **CHARGING SYSTEM**

ALTERNATOR

REMOVAL & INSTALLATION

See Figures 31 and 32.

1. Before servicing the vehicle, refer to the precautions in the beginning of this section.

2. Remove or disconnect the following:
- Negative battery cable and properly isolate to prevent accidental reconnection.
- Engine cover
- Accessory drive belt

- Nut and electrical connector
- Battery cable harness pushpin from the generator bracket
- Mounting bolts
- Four bolts and alternator bracket
- Alternator

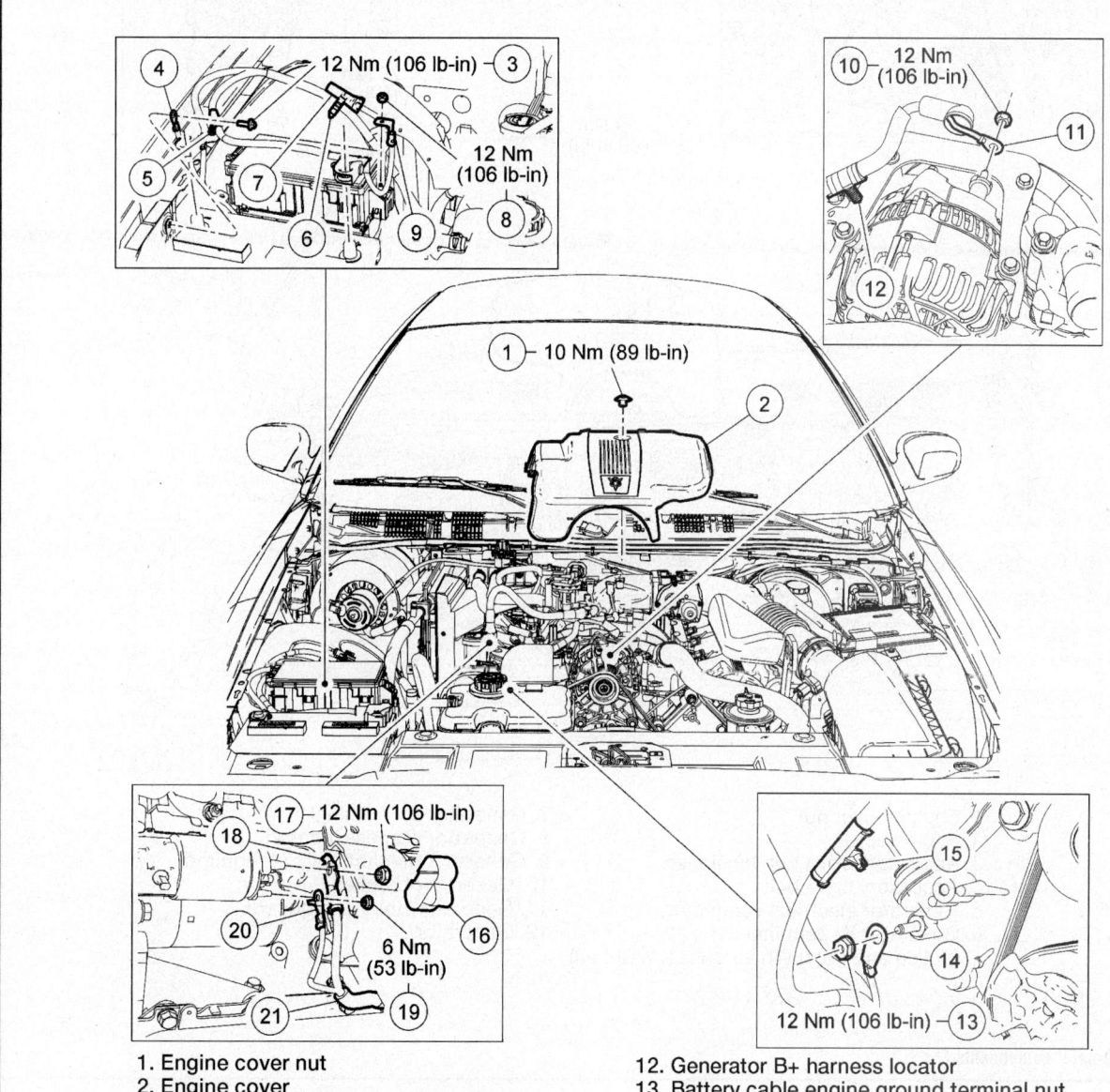

1. Engine cover nut
2. Engine cover
3. Battery cable body ground terminal bolt
4. Battery cable body ground terminal
5. Battery cable harness locator
6. Battery cable harness locator
7. Battery cable connector to 14290 harness
8. Battery Junction Box (BJB) cable terminal nut
9. BJB cable terminal
10. Generator B+ terminal nut
11. Generator B+ terminal
12. Generator B+ harness locator
13. Battery cable engine ground terminal nut
14. Battery cable engine ground terminal
15. Battery cable harness locator
16. Starter terminal cover
17. Starter solenoid positive terminal nut
18. Starter solenoid positive terminal
19. Starter solenoid wire terminal nut
20. Starter solenoid wire terminal
21. Battery cable harness

Fig. 31 Battery, alternator and starter components

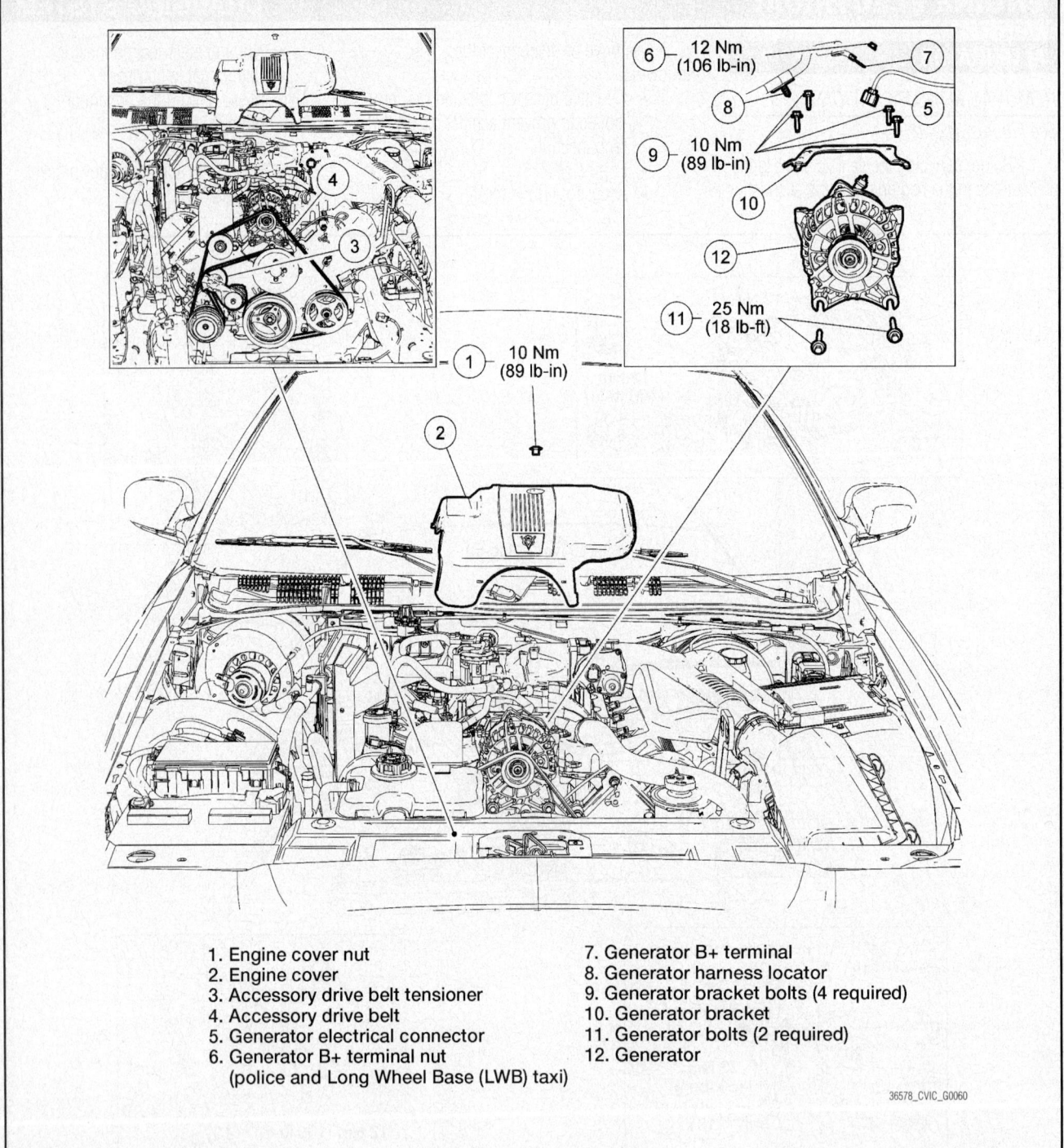

1. Engine cover nut
2. Engine cover
3. Accessory drive belt tensioner
4. Accessory drive belt
5. Generator electrical connector
6. Generator B+ terminal nut
   (police and Long Wheel Base (LWB) taxi)
7. Generator B+ terminal
8. Generator harness locator
9. Generator bracket bolts (4 required)
10. Generator bracket
11. Generator bolts (2 required)
12. Generator

36578_CVIC_G0060

Fig. 32 Alternator components

To install:

➡Two alternators are available; 130-amp and 200-amp. Their electrical connector torque value is different.

Install or connect the following:

- Alternator and tighten the mounting bolts to 18 ft. lbs. (25 Nm)
- Alternator bracket and tighten the bolts to 89 inch lbs. (10 Nm)
- Accessory drive belt
- Wire harness and torque the nut to 71 inch lbs. (8 Nm) for

vehicles equipped with 130-amp alternator
- Wire harness and torque the nut to 89 inch lbs. (10 Nm) for vehicles equipped with 200-amp alternator
- Engine cover
- Negative battery cable

ENGINE ELECTRICAL

IGNITION SYSTEM

FIRING ORDER

See Figure 33.

- Connector from the ignition coils
- Bolt from the ignition coil
- Ignition coil from spark plug

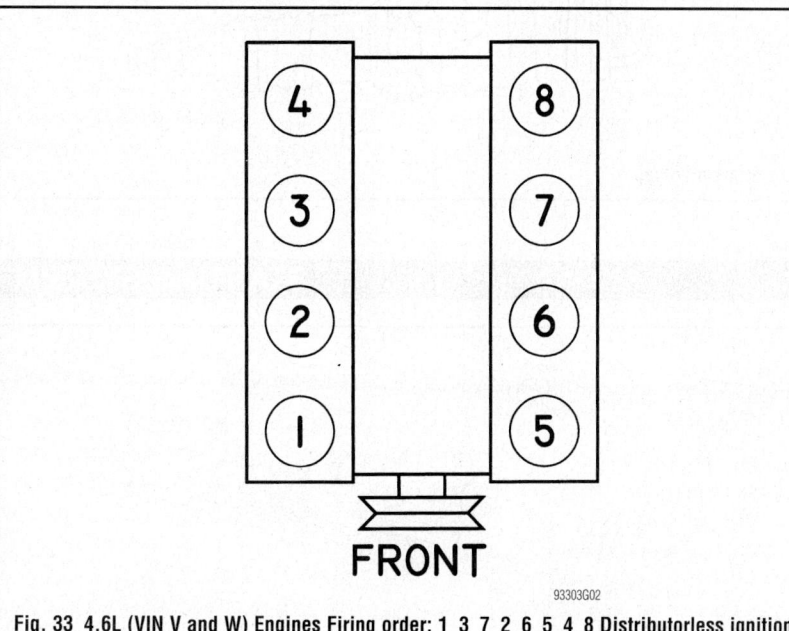

Fig. 33 4.6L (VIN V and W) Engines Firing order: 1 3 7 2 6 5 4 8 Distributorless ignition system—One coil per cyclinder

IGNITION COIL

REMOVAL & INSTALLATION

See Figures 34 and 35.

1. Before servicing the vehicle, refer to the precautions in the beginning of this section.
2. Disconnect battery negative cable from battery and properly isolate to prevent accidental reconnection.
3. Remove or disconnect the following:
   - Air cleaner outlet pipe

To install:

4. Install or connect the following:
   - Ignition coil to spark plug
   - Bolt and torque to 89 inch lbs. (10 Nm)

- Electrical connector
- Air cleaner outlet pipe

IGNITION TIMING

ADJUSTMENT

The ignition timing is controlled by the Powertrain Control Module (PCM). No adjustment is necessary or possible.

SPARK PLUGS

REMOVAL & INSTALLATION

See Figures 36 and 37.

1. Before servicing the vehicle, refer to the precautions in the beginning of this section.
2. Disconnect battery negative cable from battery and properly isolate to prevent accidental reconnection.
3. Remove the ignition coil on plug.

➡Use compressed air to remove any debris from the spark plug well before removing the spark plugs.

4. Inspect the spark plugs.

To install:

5. Adjust the spark plug gap to 0.052–0.056 inch (1.32–1.42 mm) as required and torque to 11 ft. lbs. (15 Nm)

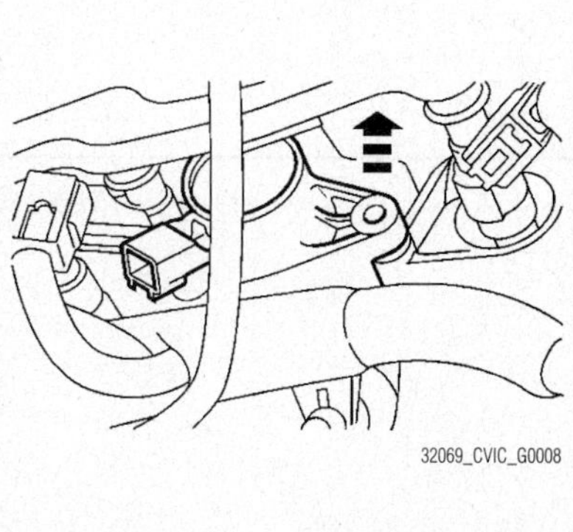

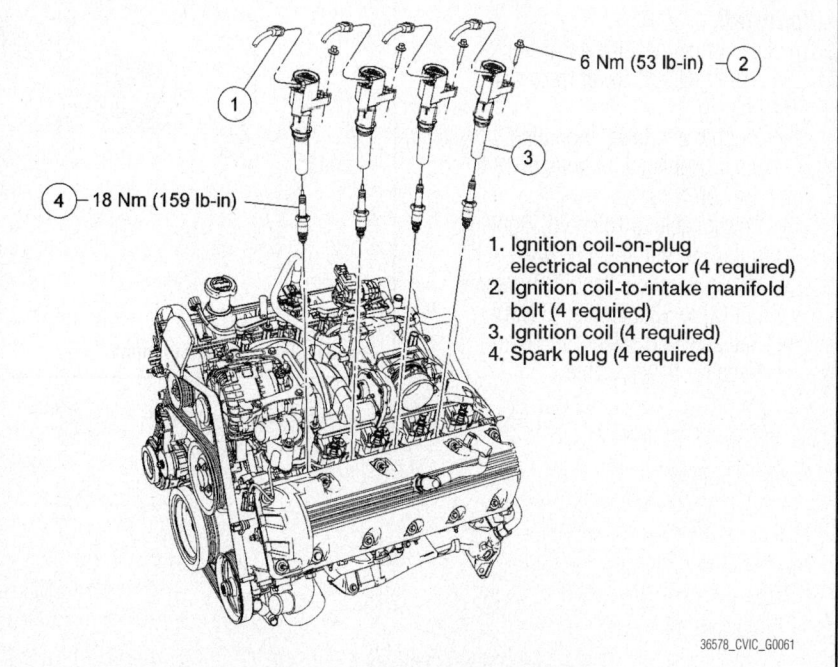

1. Ignition coil-on-plug electrical connector (4 required)
2. Ignition coil-to-intake manifold bolt (4 required)
3. Ignition coil (4 required)
4. Spark plug (4 required)

Fig. 35 Engine ignition components–Left side shown, right is similar

Fig. 34 Ignition coil, plug and bolt location

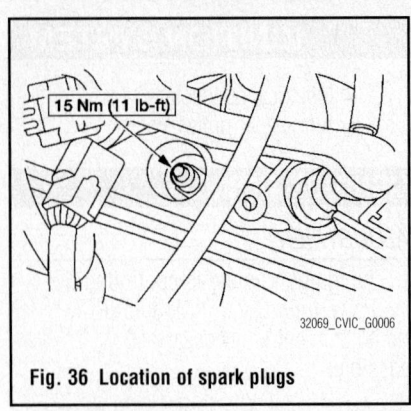

Fig. 36 Location of spark plugs

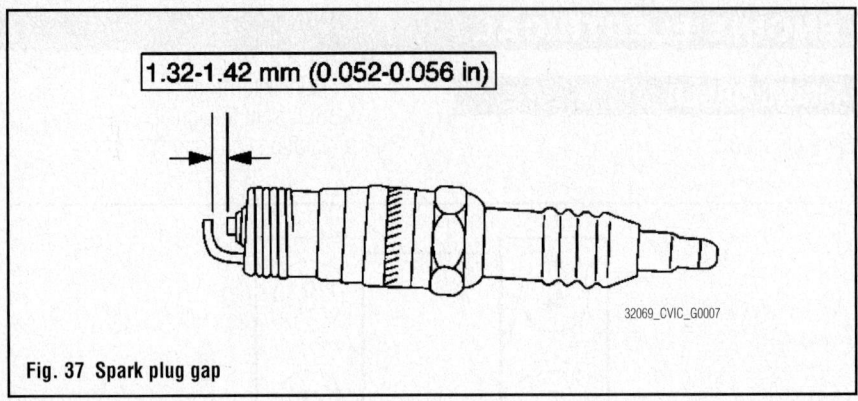

Fig. 37 Spark plug gap

ENGINE ELECTRICAL   STARTING SYSTEM

STARTER

TESTING

Carry out a Powertrain Control Module (PCM) self-test using an OBD-II scan tool.

REMOVAL & INSTALLATION

See Figure 38.

1. Remove or disconnect the following:
   - Negative battery cable and properly isolate to prevent accidental reconnection
   - Red solenoid safety cap
   - B-terminal nut and disconnect the wire
   - S-terminal nut and disconnect the wire
   - 2 upper bolts
   - 1 lower bolt and starter

To install:

2. Install or connect the following:
   - Starter (5) and lower mounting bolt (4)
   - 2 upper and lower mounting bolts. Tighten all 3 bolts to 18 ft. lbs. (25 Nm)
   - Power cable to solenoid. Tighten nut (3) to 9 ft. lbs. (12 Nm)
   - Exciter wire to solenoid. Tighten nut (2) to 53 inch lbs. (6 Nm)
   - Red solenoid safety cap (1)
   - Negative battery cable

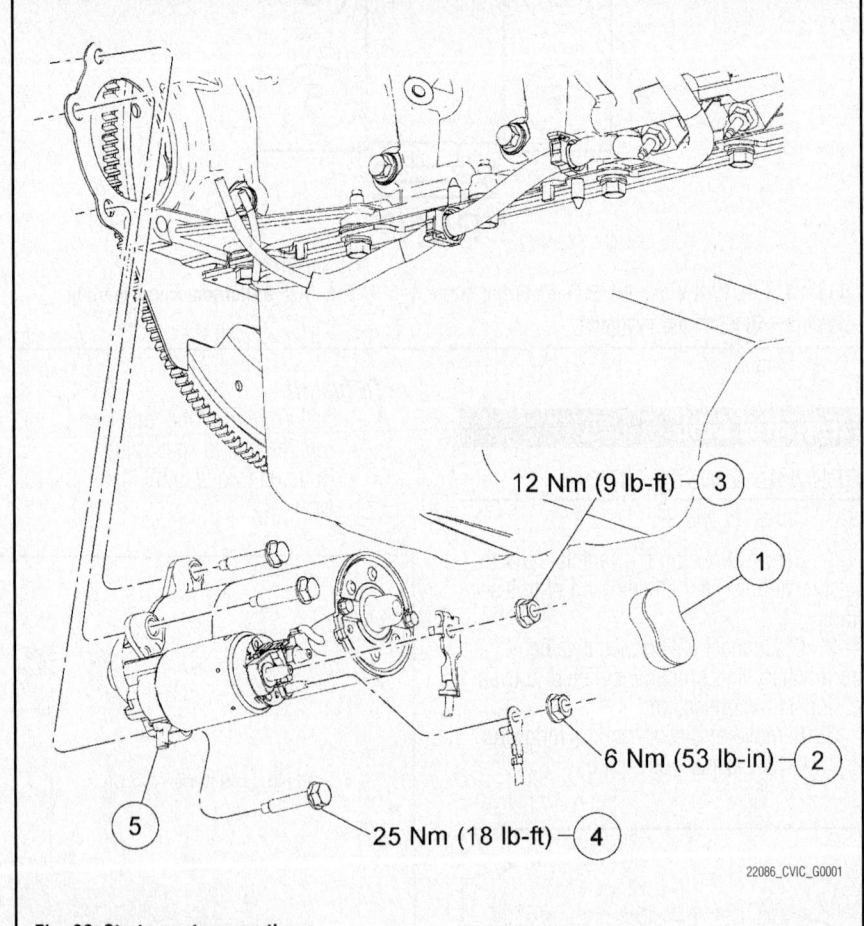

Fig. 38 Starter motor mounting

ENGINE MECHANICAL

ACCESSORY DRIVE BELTS

ACCESSORY BELT ROUTING

See Figure 39.

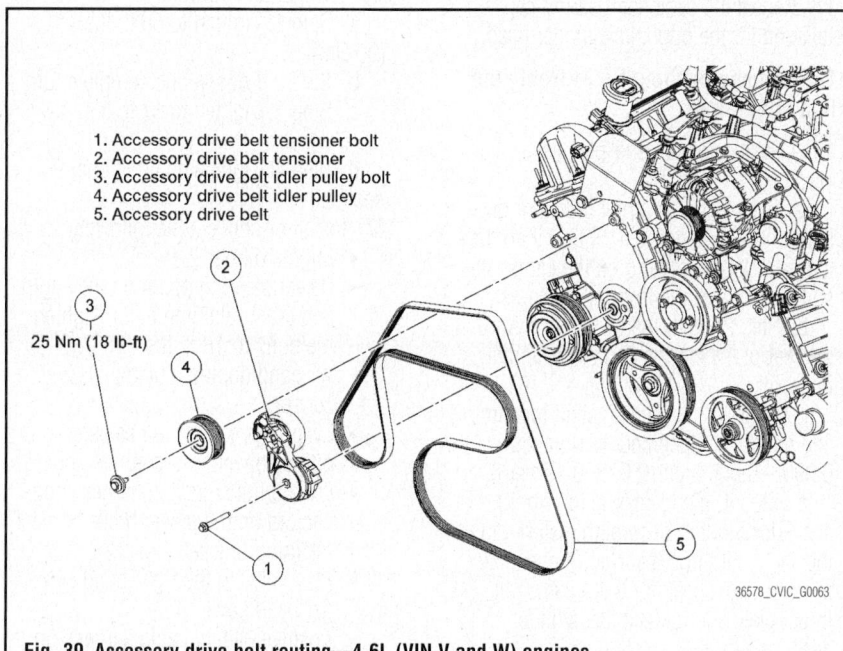

1. Accessory drive belt tensioner bolt
2. Accessory drive belt tensioner
3. Accessory drive belt idler pulley bolt
4. Accessory drive belt idler pulley
5. Accessory drive belt

25 Nm (18 lb-ft)

36578_CVIC_G0063

Fig. 39 Accessory drive belt routing—4.6L (VIN V and W) engines

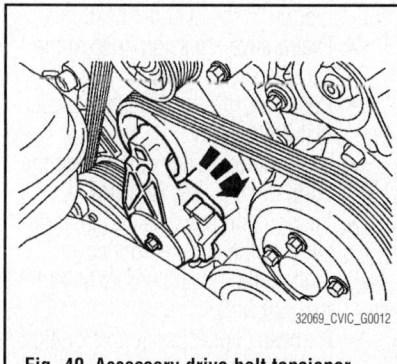

32069_CVIC_G0012

Fig. 40 Accessory drive belt tensioner

INSPECTION

Inspect the drive belt for signs of glazing or cracking. A glazed belt will be perfectly smooth from slippage, while a good belt will have a slight texture of fabric visible. Cracks will usually start at the inner edge of the belt and run outward. All worn or damaged drive belts should be replaced immediately.

ADJUSTMENT

The accessory drive belt tension is automatically adjusted with a spring-loaded tensioner.

REMOVAL & INSTALLATION

See Figures 39 through 40.

1. Before servicing the vehicle, refer to the precautions in the beginning of this section.

2. Disconnect battery negative cable from battery and properly isolate to prevent accidental reconnection.
3. Rotate the tensioner clockwise and remove the drive belt.

To install:
4. Rotate the tensioner clockwise.
5. Route the belt around the pulleys.
6. Slowly release the tensioner.

CAMSHAFT AND VALVE LIFTERS

REMOVAL & INSTALLATION

See Figure 41.

1. If equipped with air suspension, the air suspension switch, must be turned to the **OFF** position before raising the vehicle.
2. Properly relieve the fuel system pressure.
3. Drain the engine oil
4. Remove or disconnect the following:
   - Negative battery cable
   - Fan blade and fan shroud assembly
   - Fuel supply and return lines from the fuel injection supply manifold
   - Windshield wiper governor (module) assembly from the vehicle

- Engine air cleaner outlet tube
- Accessory drive belt
- Ignition wires from the spark plugs
- Ignition wire brackets from the cylinder head cover studs
- 2 bolts retaining the ignition wire separator to the ignition coil brackets and the bolt retaining the air conditioning pressure line to the right-hand ignition coil bracket.
- Connectors from both ignition coils and the Crankshaft Position (CMP) sensor
- Ignition coils with brackets attached
- Electrical connector from the alternator and at the power distribution box
- Water pump pulley
- Positive battery cable at the power distribution box
- Bolt from the positive battery cable bracket located on the right-hand cylinder head
- Fuel vapor hose from the EVAP canister purge valve and position the positive battery cable aside
- Positive Crankcase Ventilation (PCV) valve from the cylinder head cover and position aside
- Engine/transmission harness connector from the bracket on the power brake booster
- Crankshaft Position (CKP) sensor and air conditioning clutch harness connectors
- Bolts retaining the power steering pump to the cylinder block and wire the pump aside

➡**The front lower bolt on the power steering pump will not come all the way out.**

- Oil pan
- Crankshaft pulley bolt and washer and crankshaft pulley
- Engine oil filter
- Power steering control valve actuator and oil pressure sensor
- Oil filter adapter
- Cylinder head covers
- Engine front cover
- Timing chains

5. Rotate the crankshaft counterclockwise no more than 45 degrees from Top Dead Center (TDC) to ensure that all pistons are below the top of the engine block deck face.
6. Install a valve spring compressor under the camshaft and on top of one of the valve spring retainers.

7. Install Valve Spring Spacer T91P-6565-AH between the valve spring coils. Be sure that the valve being compressed is on its base circle. Compress the valve spring and remove the rocker arm. Repeat the procedure until all rocker arms are removed.

8. If required, pull the lash adjusters out of their bores in the cylinder head. Note their locations; they must be installed in the same bore they were removed from.

➡ **Do not mix the camshaft bearing caps. Note the camshaft bearing cap locations for installation.**

9. To remove each camshaft, unfasten the 14 bolts retaining the camshaft bearing caps (cluster assemblies) to the cylinder head. Tap upward on the camshaft bearing caps at points near the upper bearing halves and gradually lift the camshaft bearing cap clusters from the cylinder head.

10. Repeat the removal procedure for the opposite cylinder head.

11. Remove the camshaft straight upward to avoid bearing damage.

12. Clean and inspect the camshafts and related components for unusual wear or damage.

To install:

13. Clean and inspect the cylinder head covers, engine front cover and cylinder head sealing surfaces.

14. Apply clean engine oil to the camshaft journals and lobes. Position the camshafts on the cylinder heads.

15. Install and seat the camshaft bearing cap cluster assemblies. Install and hand start the retaining bolts. Tighten the camshaft cluster retaining bolts in sequence to 89 inch lbs. (10 Nm). Be sure to tighten each camshaft bearing cap cluster individually.

➡ **Each camshaft bearing cap cluster assembly is tightened individually.**

16. Loosen the camshaft bearing cap cluster retaining bolts approximately 2 turns or until the heads of the bolts are free. Tighten all bolts, again in sequence, to 89 inch lbs. (10 Nm).

17. Repeat the camshaft bearing cap installation for the opposite cylinder head.

➡ **The camshafts should turn freely but with a slight drag.**

18. Check camshaft end-play as follows:
   a. Step 1: Install a dial indicator on the front of the engine. Position it so the indicator foot is resting on the camshaft sprocket bolt or the front of the camshaft.
   b. Step 2: Push the camshaft toward the rear of the engine and zero the dial indicator.
   c. Step 3: Pull the camshaft forward and release it. Specified end-play is 0.0901–0.006 inch (0.025–0.190mm).
   d. Step 4: If end-play is too tight, check for binding or foreign material in the camshaft thrust bearing. If end-play is excessive, check for worn camshaft thrust plate and replace the cylinder head, as required.
   e. Step 5: Remove the dial indicator.

19. If removed, install the lash adjusters in their original positions.

20. If necessary, install Camshaft Positioning Tools T92P-6256-A on the flats of the camshafts and install the spacers and camshaft sprockets. Install the bolts and washers and tighten to 30 ft. lbs. (40 Nm), then tighten an additional 90 degrees.

21. Install a valve spring compressor under the camshaft and on top of the valve spring retainer.

22. Install Valve Spring Spacer T91P-6565-AH between the valve spring coils. Be sure that the valve being compressed is on its base circle. Compress the valve spring and install the rocker arm. Repeat the procedure until all rocker arms are installed.

23. Rotate the crankshaft clockwise 45 degrees to position the crankshaft at Top Dead Center (TDC).

➡ **The crankshaft must only be rotated in the clockwise direction and only as far as TDC.**

24. Install or connect the following:
   • Timing chains
   • Engine front cover
   • Cylinder head covers. Tighten the cylinder head cover bolts to 89 inch lbs. (10 Nm).

   • Power steering control valve actuator connector
   • Oil pressure sensor harness connector

25. Apply silicone sealer to the crankshaft keyway

26. Install the crankshaft pulley and tighten the bolt as follows:
   a. Step 1: Tighten to 66 ft. lbs. (90 Nm).
   b. Step 2: Loosen one complete turn.
   c. Step 3: Tighten to 37 ft. lbs. (50 Nm).
   d. Step 4: Tighten an additional 90 degrees.

27. Install or connect the following:
   • Engine oil pan
   • Power steering pump on the engine and the 4 retaining bolts. Tighten the bolts to 18 ft. lbs. (25 Nm).
   • Air conditioning clutch and CKP sensor
   • Evaporative emission canister purge valve harness connector
   • Engine/transmission harness connectors on the power brake booster retaining bracket
   • PCV valve to the right-hand cylinder head cover
   • Positive battery cable harness on the right-hand cylinder head
   • Bolt retaining the battery cable bracket to the cylinder head
   • Evaporative emission hose to the canister purge valve
   • Positive battery cable at the power distribution box
   • Water pump pulley and tighten the bolts to 18 ft. lbs. (25 Nm)
   • Ignition coil brackets and ignition wires to the engine front cover. Tighten the retaining nuts to 18 ft. lbs. (25 Nm).
   • Harness connectors to the ignition coils and the CMP sensor
   • Air conditioning pressure line on the right-hand ignition coil bracket and the retaining bolt
   • Ignition wires to the spark plugs and the brackets onto the cylinder head cover studs
   • Accessory drive belt
   • Windshield wiper governor
   • Fuel supply and return lines
   • Fan and shroud assembly
   • Negative battery cable

28. Fill the engine cooling system.

29. Fill the crankcase.

30. If equipped with air suspension, turn the air suspension switch to the **ON** position.

31. Start the engine and check for leaks.

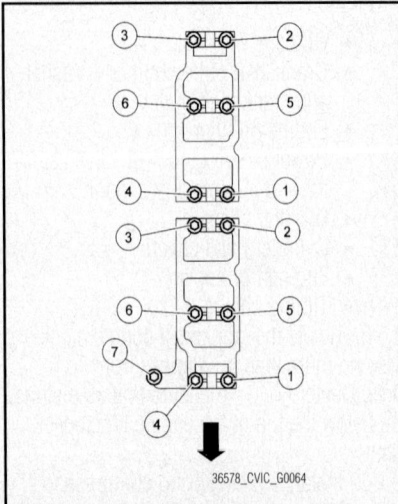

36578_CVIC_G0064

Fig. 41 Camshaft bearing cap torque sequence

32. Road test the vehicle and check for proper engine operation.

CATALYTIC CONVERTER

REMOVAL & INSTALLATION

✳✳ WARNING

Shut off the electrical power to the air suspension system prior to hoisting or jacking an air suspension equipped vehicle. Failure to do so may result in unexpected inflation or deflation of the air springs, which may result in shifting of the vehicle during these operations. Failure to follow this instruction may result in serious personal injury.

1. If equipped with a fire suppression system, depower the system
2. Raise and support the vehicle.
3. If equipped, turn the air suspension switch OFF.
4. For RH catalytic converter removal, disconnect the Heated Oxygen Sensor (HO2S) electrical connector.
5. Disconnect the Catalyst Monitor Sensor (CMS) electrical connector.
6. Remove and discard the 2 catalytic converter-to-exhaust manifold nuts. To install, alternately tighten the new nuts to 30 ft. lbs. (40 Nm).

➡Alternate tightening the catalytic converter-to-exhaust inlet pipe bolts to specifications to draw the flanges together evenly.

7. Remove the 2 catalytic converter-to-inlet pipe bolts, the 2 flagnuts, the damper (if equipped) and the catalytic converter. Discard the bolts, the flagnuts and the gaskets. To install, alternately tighten the new bolts to 30 ft. lbs. (40 Nm).

➡Clean the mating surfaces of the exhaust manifold, the outlet pipe and the catalytic converter.

➡Always install new exhaust system fasteners and gaskets. Do not tighten the fasteners until all components are assembled. Make sure to tighten all fasteners beginning at the front of the vehicle.

➡To correctly seat the converter, alternately tighten the catalytic converter-to-exhaust manifold nuts to specification.

8. To install, reverse the removal procedure.

9. If equipped with a fire suppression system, repower the system.

CRANKSHAFT DAMPER

REMOVAL & INSTALLATION
See Figure 42.

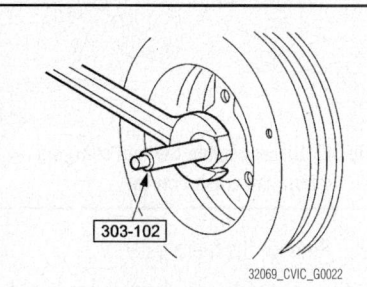

Fig. 42 Use special tool 303-102 (T74P-6316-B) or a suitable long bolt to install the crankshaft pulley

1. Before servicing the vehicle, refer to the precautions in the beginning of this section.
2. Disconnect battery negative cable from battery and properly isolate to prevent accidental reconnection.
3. Remove or disconnect the following:
   - Engine cooling fan and fan shroud
   - Accessory drive belt
   - Crankshaft pulley bolt
4. Remove the crankshaft pulley with special tool 303-009 (T58P-6316-D) or a suitable puller.

To install:

5. Apply sealant to the woodruff key slot on the crankshaft pulley and install within four minutes.
6. Use special tool 303-102 (T74P-6316-B) or a suitable installer to install the crankshaft pulley.
7. Install the bolt and washer. Tighten the bolt in four steps:
   - Tighten to 66 ft. lbs. (90 Nm)
   - Loosen the bolt
   - Tighten to 37 ft. lbs. (50 Nm)
   - Tighten an additional 90 degrees
8. Install the drive belt.
9. Install the engine cooling fan and the fan shroud.

CRANKSHAFT FRONT SEAL

REMOVAL & INSTALLATION
See Figure 43.

1. Before servicing the vehicle, refer to the precautions in the beginning of this section.
2. Disconnect battery negative cable

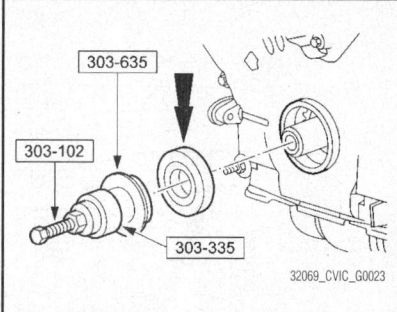

Fig. 43 Front engine cover, seal, and installation tool

from battery and properly isolate to prevent accidental reconnection.
3. Remove the crankshaft pulley.
4. Use special tool 303-107 (T74P-6700-A) or a suitable seal remover to remove the front cover seal.

To install:

5. Lubricate the engine front cover and the front oil seal inner lip with clean engine oil.
6. Use special tool 303-635 or a suitable seal installer to install the crankshaft front seal into the engine front cover.
7. Install the crankshaft pulley.
8. Reconnect negative battery cable, check for leaks and repair if necessary.

CYLINDER HEAD

REMOVAL & INSTALLATION
See Figures 44 through 50.

➡The cylinder head bolts are a torque-to-yield design and cannot be reused. Always use new cylinder head bolts for assembly.

1. If equipped with air suspension, the air suspension switch, located on the right-hand side of the luggage compartment, must be turned to the **OFF** position before raising the vehicle.
2. Drain the engine cooling system.
3. Properly relieve the fuel system pressure.
4. Remove the engine.
5. Remove the bolts and the flexplate.
6. Remove the engine/transmission spacer plate.
7. Using the Engine Lifting Bracket Set, mount the engine on a suitable engine stand.
8. If equipped with cylinder block drain plugs, remove the bolts and the RH engine mount.
9. If equipped, remove the drain plugs from the engine block. Allow the coolant to completely drain. Install the drain plugs when finished. Tighten to 177 inch lbs. (20 Nm).

Fig. 44 Disconnecting the radio ignition interference capacitor

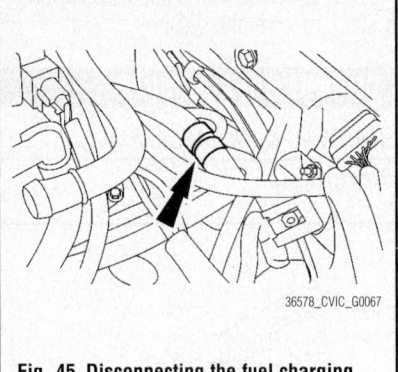

Fig. 45 Disconnecting the fuel charging wiring from the crash bracket

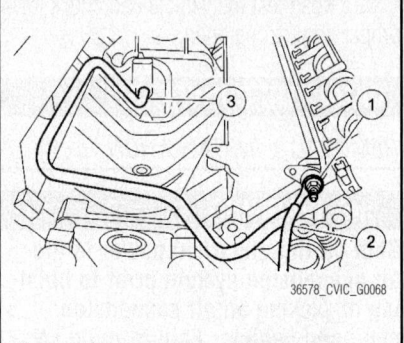

Fig. 46 Removing the retaining nut (1), the ground strap (2) and coolant bypass tube (3)

10. Remove the bolt and the battery cables from the engine.

11. Disconnect the EGR tube from the exhaust manifold.

12. Disconnect the 8 ignition coil electrical connectors.

13. Disconnect the 8 fuel injector electrical connectors.

14. Remove the 2 bolts and the intake manifold shield.

15. Remove the PCV tube and if equipped, disconnect the heated PCV valve electrical connector.

16. Disconnect the generator electrical connector and detach the wire harness retainer.

17. Remove the generator mounting bracket and 4 bolts.

18. Disconnect the throttle control and the Throttle Position (TP) sensor electrical connectors.

19. Disconnect the Cylinder Head Temperature (CHT) sensor electrical connector.

20. Disconnect the Camshaft Position (CMP) sensor electrical connector.

21. Disconnect the radio ignition interference capacitor and remove the engine control sensor wiring.

22. Disconnect the fuel charging wiring from the crash bracket and the wiring support bracket and remove the harness from the engine.

23. Disconnect the EGR tube nut from the EGR system module.

24. Remove the two bolts and the generator.

25. Remove the intake manifold crash bracket bolt and prevent the bolt from contacting the cylinder head with a rubber band or tie strap.

26. Remove the intake manifold crash bracket stud bolt.

27. Remove the 8 bolts and the 8 ignition coils (4 shown).

28. Remove the 2 bolts and the coolant outlet adapter.

29. Remove the thermostat.

➡️If the engine is repaired or replaced because of upper engine failure, typically including valve or piston damage, check the intake manifold for metal debris. If metal debris is found, install a new intake manifold. Failure to follow these instructions can result in engine damage.

30. Remove the 8 bolts and the intake manifold. Discard the intake manifold gaskets.

➡️Do not use metal scrapers, wire brushes, power abrasive discs or other abrasive means to clean the sealing surfaces. These tools cause scratches and gouges which make leak paths.

31. Clean the sealing surfaces.

32. Remove the coolant bypass tube.
   a. Remove the retaining nut.
   b. Remove the ground strap.
   c. Remove the coolant bypass tube.

33. Loosen the studs and bolts and remove the LH valve cover. Clean the mating surface and discard gasket.

34. Loosen the studs and bolts and remove the RH valve cover. Discard the gasket.

➡️Only use hand tools when removing or installing the spark plugs, damage may occur to the cylinder head or spark plug.

➡️Use compressed air to remove any foreign material from the spark plug well before removing the spark plugs.

35. Remove the spark plugs.

36. Position the lobe of the camshaft upward.

37. Install the Valve Spring Compressor Spacer between the valve spring coils to prevent valve stem seal damage.

➡️If the components are to be reinstalled, they must be installed in the

same positions. Mark the components for installation into their original locations. Failure to follow these instructions may result in engine damage.

38. Using the Valve Spring Compressor, compress the valve springs and remove the camshaft roller followers.

➡️If the components are to be reinstalled, they must be installed in the same positions. Mark the components for installation into their original locations. Failure to follow these instructions may result in engine damage.

39. Remove the 16 hydraulic lash adjusters.

40. Remove the bolt and the belt idler pulley.

41. Remove the A/C compressor pump pulley.

42. Remove the crankshaft pulley bolt.

43. Using the Crankshaft Vibration Damper Remover, remove the crankshaft pulley.

44. Using the Crankshaft Front Oil Seal Remover, remove the crankshaft front oil seal.

45. Remove the front 4 oil pan bolts.

➡️Correct fastener location is essential for the installation. Record fastener location.

46. Remove the engine front cover in sequence from the cylinder block. Discard the gaskets.

47. Remove the crankshaft sensor ring.

48. Position the crankshaft with the keyway at the 12 o'clock position.

49. Remove the timing chain tensioning system from both timing chains.
   a. Remove the bolts.
   b. Remove the timing chain tensioners.

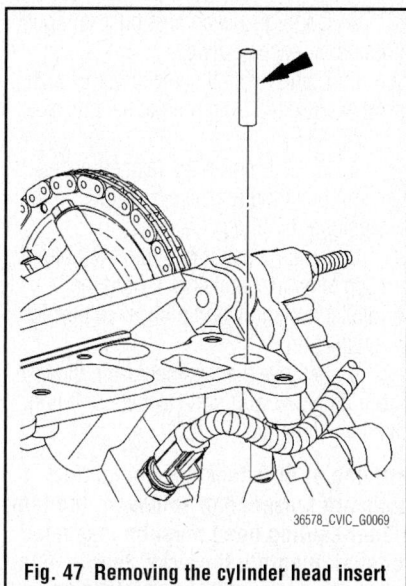

Fig. 47 Removing the cylinder head insert from the LH cylinder head

c. Remove the timing chain tensioner arms.

50. Remove the LH and RH timing chains and the crankshaft sprocket.

a. Remove the RH timing chain from the camshaft sprocket.

b. Remove the RH timing chain from the crankshaft sprocket.

c. Repeat for the LH timing chain and crankshaft sprocket.

51. Remove both timing chain guides.

a. Remove the bolts.

b. Remove the LH timing chain guide.

c. Remove the bolts.

d. Remove the RH timing chain guide.

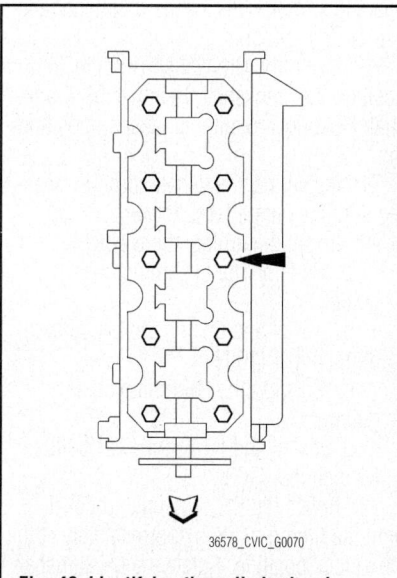

Fig. 48 Identifying the cylinder head bolts—RH side shown, LH similar

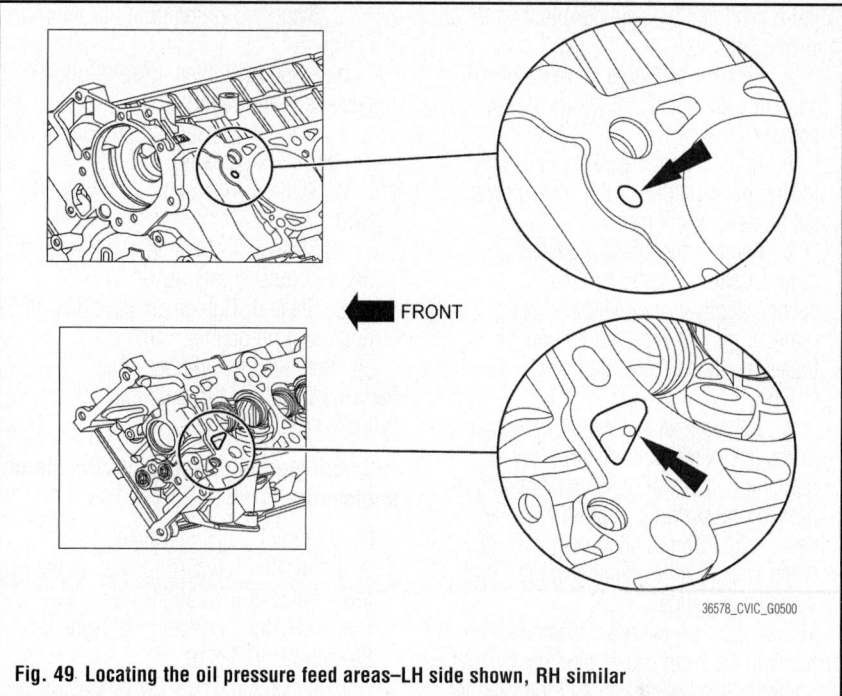

Fig. 49 Locating the oil pressure feed areas—LH side shown, RH similar

52. Remove the RH exhaust manifold.

a. Remove the nuts and discard.

b. Remove the RH exhaust manifold.

c. Remove and discard the RH exhaust manifold gasket.

d. Remove and discard the 8 RH exhaust manifold studs.

53. Remove the LH exhaust manifold.

a. Remove the nuts and discard.

b. Remove the LH exhaust manifold.

c. Remove and discard the LH exhaust manifold gaskets.

54. Remove and discard the 8 LH exhaust manifold studs.

55. Remove the bolt and the oil level indicator tube.

56. Remove the cylinder head insert from the LH cylinder head.

57. Clean and inspect the exhaust manifolds.

58. Install the Cylinder Head Remover/Installer on both ends of the cylinder head.

➡ The cylinder head must be cool before removing it from the engine. Cylinder head warpage may result if a warm or hot cylinder head is removed.

➡ Aluminum surfaces are soft and can be scratched easily. Never place the cylinder head gasket surface, unprotected, on a bench surface. The scratches may cause leak paths.

➡ Do not use metal scrapers, wire brushes, power abrasive discs or other abrasive means to clean the sealing surfaces. These tools cause scratches and gouges that make leak paths. Use a plastic scraping tool to remove all traces of the head gasket.

➡ Place clean shop towels over exposed engine cavities. Carefully remove the towels so foreign material is not dropped into the engine.

➡ The cylinder head bolts must be discarded and new bolts installed. They are a tighten-to-yield design and cannot be reused.

59. Remove the bolts and the LH cylinder head. Discard the cylinder head gasket. Discard the cylinder head bolts.

➡ Do not use metal scrapers, wire brushes, power abrasive discs or other abrasive means to clean the sealing surfaces. These tools cause scratches and gouges that make leak paths. Use a plastic scraping tool to remove all traces of the head gasket.

➡ Observe all warnings or cautions and follow all application directions contained on the packaging of the silicone gasket remover and the metal surface prep.

➡ If there is no residual gasket material present, metal surface prep can be used to clean and prepare the surfaces.

60. Clean the cylinder head-to-cylinder block mating surfaces of both the

cylinder head and the cylinder block in the following sequence.

a. Remove any large deposits of silicone or gasket material with a plastic scraper.

b. Apply silicone gasket remover, following package directions, and allow to set for several minutes.

c. Remove the silicone gasket remover with a plastic scraper. A second application of silicone gasket remover may be required if residual traces of silicone or gasket material remain.

d. Apply metal surface prep, following package directions, to remove any remaining traces of oil or coolant, and to prepare the surfaces to bond with the new gasket. Do not attempt to make the metal shiny. Some staining of the metal surfaces is normal.

61. Support the cylinder heads on a bench with the head gasket side up. Check the cylinder head distortion and the cylinder block distortion, paying particular attention to the oil pressure feed area.

To install:

➡ **The gasket sealing surfaces on the cylinder head and cylinder block must be clean.**

➡ **The use of sealing aids (aviation cement, copper spray and glue) is not permitted. The gasket must be installed dry.**

➡ **The new gasket has a film coating which is crucial to the gasket's ability to seal correctly. Do not scratch the gasket.**

➡ **Cylinder head machining or milling is not authorized by the Ford Motor Company. Cylinder head flatness must be within 0.0254 mm (0.001 in) across a 38.1 mm (1.5 in) square area.**

➡ **The gasket sealing surfaces on the cylinder head and cylinder block must be clean.**

➡ **The use of sealing aids (aviation cement, copper spray and glue) is not permitted. The gasket must be installed dry.**

➡ **Do not allow the dowels to scratch the sealing surface of the cylinder head during cylinder head installation.**

62. Install the cylinder head on the dowels and the head gasket. Loosely install new bolts.

63. Tighten the cylinder head bolts in 6 stages, in the sequence shown.

a. Stage 1: Tighten to 30 ft. lbs. (40 Nm).

b. Stage 2: Tighten an additional 90 degrees (one-quarter turn).

c. Stage 3: Loosen a minimum of one full turn (360 degrees).

d. Stage 4: Tighten to 30 ft. lbs. (40 Nm).

e. Stage 5: Tighten an additional 90 degrees (one-quarter turn).

f. Stage 6: Tighten an additional 90 degrees (one-quarter turn).

64. Remove the Cylinder Head Remover/Installer from both ends of the cylinder head.

➡ **Lubricate the O-ring seal with clean engine oil.**

65. For the LH cylinder head:

a. Install a new O-ring seal on the oil level indicator tube and install the oil level indicator tube and bolt. Tighten to 89 inch lbs. (10 Nm).

b. Install the 8 new LH exhaust manifold studs. Tighten to 106 inch lbs. (12 Nm).

c. Install a new LH exhaust manifold gasket the LH exhaust manifold and 8 new nuts. Tighten to 177 inch lbs. (20 Nm) in sequence.

66. For RH cylinder head :

a. Install the 8 new RH exhaust manifold studs. Tighten to 106 inch lbs. (12 Nm).

b. Install a new RH exhaust manifold gasket the RH exhaust manifold and 8 new nuts. Tighten to 177 inch lbs. (20 Nm).

67. Engines with ratcheting timing chain tensioners

➡ **Timing chain procedures must be followed exactly or damage to valves and pistons will result.**

➡ **Do not compress the ratchet assembly. This will damage the ratchet assembly.**

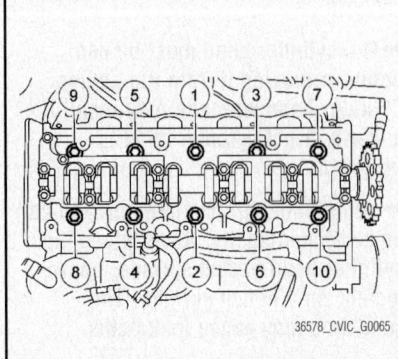

Fig. 50 Cylinder head torque sequence

36578_CVIC_G0065

a. Compress each tensioner plunger, using an edge of a vise.

b. Using a small screwdriver or pick, push back and hold the ratchet mechanism.

c. While holding the ratchet mechanism, push the ratchet arm back into the tensioner housing.

d. Install a paper clip into the hole of each tensioner housing to hold the ratchet assembly and plunger in during installation.

e. Remove the tensioner from the vise.

68. Engines with non-ratcheting timing chain tensioners.

➡**If one or both tensioner mounting bolts are loosened or removed, the tensioner-sealing bead must be inspected for seal integrity. If cracks, tears, separation from the tensioner body or permanent compression of the seal bead is observed, install a new tensioner or engine damage may occur.**

a. Inspect the RH and LH timing chain tensioners. Install new tensioners as necessary.

✳✳ CAUTION

Timing chain procedures must be followed exactly or damage to valves and pistons will result.

b. Compress each tensioner plunger, using an edge of a vise.

c. Install a Hydraulic Chain Tensioner Retaining Clip on the tensioner to hold the plunger in during installation.

69. For both cylinder heads: If the colored links are not visible, mark one link on one end and one link on the other end, and use as timing marks.

70. Using the Crankshaft Holding Tool, position the crankshaft. Remove the Crankshaft Holding Tool after crankshaft positioning.

71. Install the crankshaft sprocket, making sure the flange faces forward.

72. Install the timing chain guides.

a. Position the LH timing chain guide.

b. Install and tighten the LH bolts to 89 inch lbs. (10 Nm).

c. Position the RH timing chain guide.

d. Install and tighten the RH bolts to 89 inch lbs. (10 Nm).

73. Rotate the RH camshaft sprocket until the timing mark is approximately at the 11 o'clock position. Rotate the LH camshaft sprocket until the timing mark is approximately at the 1 o'clock position.

74. Position the LH (inner) timing chain on the crankshaft sprocket, aligning the colored (marked) link with the timing mark on the sprocket.

75. Install the LH timing chain on the camshaft sprocket, aligning the colored (marked) link with the timing marks on the sprocket.

➡ **The LH timing chain tensioner arm has a bump near the dowel hole for identification.**

76. Position the LH timing chain tensioner on the dowel pin and install the LH timing chain tensioner. Tighten to 18 ft. lbs. (25 Nm).

77. Remove the Hydraulic Chain Tensioner Retaining Clip from the LH timing chain tensioner.

78. Position the RH (outer) timing chain on the crankshaft sprocket, aligning the colored (marked) link with the timing mark on the sprocket.

79. Install the RH timing chain on the camshaft sprocket, aligning the colored (marked) link with the timing marks on the sprocket

80. Position the RH timing chain tensioner arm on the dowel pin and install the RH timing chain tensioner. Tighten to 18 ft. lbs. (25 Nm).

81. Remove the Hydraulic Chain Tensioner Retaining Clip from the RH timing chain tensioner.

82. Make sure that the colored (marked) chain links are lined up with the dots on the crankshaft sprockets and the camshaft sprocket.

83. Rotate the camshaft until the lobe is in the upward position.

84. Install the Valve Spring Compressor Spacer between the valve spring coils to prevent valve stem seal damage.

➡ **Lubricate the hydraulic lash adjusters with clean engine oil.**

85. Install the 16 hydraulic lash adjusters in their original locations (4 shown).

➡ **Lubricate the camshaft roller followers using clean engine oil. Position the cam lobe away from the camshaft roller follower location prior to installing each camshaft roller follower.**

86. Install the camshaft roller follower.
   a. Install the Valve Spring Compressor.
   b. Compress the valve spring.
   c. Install the camshaft roller followers in their original locations.

87. Remove the Valve Spring Compressor Spacer.

➡ **Only use hand tools when removing or installing the spark plugs, damage may occur to the cylinder head or spark plug.**

88. Install all 8 spark plugs.

89. Install the crankshaft sensor ring.

➡ **If not secured within 4 minutes, the sealant must be removed and the sealing area cleaned. To clean the sealing area, use silicone gasket remover and metal surface prep. Follow the directions on the packaging. Failure to follow this procedure can cause future oil leakage.**

90. Apply a bead of sealant along the head-to-block surface and the oil pan-to-block surface as specified.

91. Install a new engine front cover gasket on the engine front cover. Position the engine front cover onto the dowels. Install the fasteners finger-tight.

92. Tighten the front cover fasteners in sequence to 18 ft. lbs. (25 Nm).

93. Loosely install the 4 bolts, then tighten in 2 stages in sequence.
   a. Stage 1: Tighten to 15 ft. lbs. (20 Nm).
   b. Stage 2: Tighten an additional 60 degrees.

94. Install the RH and LH engine mounts and the bolts. Tighten to 52 ft. lbs. (70 Nm).

95. Lubricate the engine front cover and the front oil seal inner lip with clean engine oil.

96. Using the Crankshaft Front Oil Seal Installer, Front Cover Oil Seal Installer and Crankshaft Vibration Damper Installer, install the front oil seal.

➡ **If not secured within 4 minutes, the sealant must be removed and the sealing area cleaned. To clean the sealing area, use silicone gasket remover and metal surface prep. Follow the directions on the packaging. Failure to follow this procedure can cause future oil leakage.**

97. Apply sealant to the Woodruff key slot on the crankshaft pulley.

98. Using the Crankshaft Vibration Damper Installer, install the crankshaft pulley.

➡ **Use a Strap Wrench to hold the pulley.**

99. Tighten the crankshaft pulley bolt in 4 stages.
   a. Stage 1: Tighten to 89 ft. lbs. (120 Nm).

   b. Stage 2: Loosen 360 degrees.
   c. Stage 3: Tighten to 37 ft. lbs. (50 Nm).
   d. Stage 4: Rotate an additional 90 degrees (one-quarter turn).
   e. Position the coolant pump pulley on the coolant pump and install the bolts. Tighten to 18 ft. lbs. (25 Nm).

100. Install the accessory drive belt idler pulley and bolt. Tighten to 18 ft. lbs. (25 Nm).

➡ **If not secured within 4 minutes, the sealant must be removed and the sealing area cleaned. To clean the sealing area, use silicone gasket remover and metal surface prep. Follow the directions on the packaging. Failure to follow this procedure can cause future oil leakage.**

101. Apply sealant in 2 places where the engine front cover meets the cylinder head.

102. Install the new valve cover gasket into the valve cover and position on the cylinder head. Tighten the bolts in sequence. Tighten to 89 inch lbs. (10 Nm).

➡ **If not secured within 4 minutes, the sealant must be removed and the sealing area cleaned. To clean the sealing area, use silicone gasket remover and metal surface prep. Follow the directions on the packaging. Failure to follow this procedure can cause future oil leakage.**

103. Apply sealant in 2 places where the engine front cover meets the cylinder head.

104. Install the gasket into the valve cover and position on the cylinder head. Tighten the bolts in sequence. Tighten to 89 inch lbs. (10 Nm).

105. Inspect the O-ring seals. Install new seals if necessary.

106. Install the coolant bypass tube.

107. Install the ground strap on the rear of the RH cylinder head.
   a. Install the stud bolt and tighten to 18 ft. lbs. (25 Nm).
   b. Install the ground strap.
   c. Install the retaining nut and tighten to 89 inch lbs (10 Nm).

108. Install the insert into the LH cylinder head.

➡ **If the engine is repaired or replaced because of upper engine failure, typically including valve or piston damage, check the intake manifold for metal debris. If metal debris is found, install a new intake manifold. Failure to follow these instructions can result in engine damage.**

➡ **Align the gasket locator tabs to slots in cylinder head.**

109. Install the new intake manifold gaskets, intake manifold and hand-tighten the bolts.

110. Install the 8 ignition coils and tighten the 8 bolts (4 shown). Tighten to 53 inch lbs. (6 Nm).

111. Install the intake manifold bracket and loosely install the bolt and the stud bolt.

112. Install the thermostat.

113. Install the coolant outlet adapter and loosely install the 2 bolts. Tighten the bolts in sequence. Tighten to 18 ft. lbs. (25 Nm).

114. Tighten the stud bolt to 18 ft. lbs. (25 Nm).

115. Tighten the bolts to 18 ft. lbs. (25 Nm).

116. Connect the EGR tube to the EGR valve. Tighten to 32 ft. lbs. (43 Nm).

117. Connect the EGR tube-to-exhaust manifold connector. Tighten to 32 ft. lbs. (43 Nm).

118. Position the fuel charging wiring at 2 locations at the back of the intake manifold.

119. Install the generator and the 2 bolts. Tighten to 18 ft. lbs. (25 Nm).

120. Connect the throttle control and the Throttle Position (TP) sensor electrical connector.

121. Install the generator mounting bracket and the 4 bolts. Tighten to 89 inch lbs (10 Nm).

122. Attach the wire harness retainer and connect the generator electrical connector.

123. Connect the electrical connector to the EGR vacuum regulator solenoid.

124. Connect the crankcase ventilation tube and if equipped, the heated PCV valve electrical connector.

125. Install the intake manifold shield and the 2 bolts. Tighten to 89 inch lbs (10 Nm).

126. Connect the 8 fuel injector electrical connectors.

127. Connect the 8 ignition coil electrical connectors.

128. Connect the Camshaft Position (CMP) sensor electrical connector.

129. Connect the radio interference capacitor electrical connector.

130. Connect the Cylinder Head Temperature (CHT) sensor electrical connector.

131. Install the battery cables and the bolt.

132. Install the Engine Lifting Bracket to the RH cylinder head.

133. Install the Engine Lifting Bracket to the LH cylinder head.

134. Using the Engine Lifting Bracket Set, remove the engine from the engine stand.

135. Install the engine/transmission spacer plate.

136. Position the flexplate and install the bolts in the sequence shown. Tighten to 59 ft. lbs. (80 Nm).

137. Install the engine.

138. Connect the negative battery cable.

139. Fill the cooling system.

140. If equipped with air suspension, turn the air suspension switch to the **ON** position.

141. Refill the engine with the correct amount of oil and replace the filter.

142. Start the engine and bring to normal operating temperature while checking for leaks.

143. Road test the vehicle and check for proper engine operation.

ENGINE ASSEMBLY

REMOVAL & INSTALLATION
See Figures 51 and 52.

✳ CAUTION

If the vehicle is equipped with air suspension, the electrical power to the air suspension system must be shut off prior to hoisting, jacking or towing an air suspension vehicle. This can be accomplished by turning off the air suspension switch located in the luggage compartment. Failure to do so can result in unexpected inflation or deflation of the air springs, which can result in shifting of the vehicle during these operations. Failure to follow these instructions may result in personal injury.

1. Before servicing the vehicle, refer to the precautions in the beginning of this section.

2. Disconnect battery negative cable from battery and properly isolate to prevent accidental reconnection.

3. Drain the engine cooling system.

4. Recover the refrigerant from the air conditioning system.

5. Relieve the fuel system pressure.

6. Drain the engine oil.

7. Remove or disconnect the following:
   - Battery
   - Hood
   - Engine cooling fan, shroud and radiator
   - Windshield wiper governor and support bracket
   - Engine air cleaner outlet tube
   - Engine/transmission harness connector from the retaining bracket
   - Accelerator and cruise control cables at the throttle body
   - Electrical connector and vacuum hose from the evaporative emission canister purge valve
   - Positive battery cable from the power distribution box and harness
   - Vacuum supply hose from the throttle body adapter vacuum port
   - Both heater hoses
   - Alternator harness from the front fender apron and the power distribution box
   - Air conditioning hoses from the air conditioning compressor
   - Power steering control valve harness connector
   - Body ground strap from the dash panel
   - Exhaust system from the exhaust manifolds and support with wire hung from the crossmember
   - Retaining nut from the transmission line bracket
   - 3 bolts and 1 stud retaining the engine to the transmission knee braces
   - Starter motor
   - 4 bolts retaining the power steering pump to the cylinder block and position aside

8. Transmission housing cover from the cylinder block to access the torque converter nuts. Rotate the crankshaft until each of the 4 nuts is accessible and remove the nuts

9. Remove or disconnect the following:
   - 6 transmission-to-engine retaining bolts
   - Engine support insulator (mount) through-bolts

10. Support the transmission with a floor jack and a block of wood.
   - Bolt retaining the right-hand front engine support insulator to the front engine mount insulator support bracket

11. Install engine lifting bracket to the front of the left-hand cylinder head and to the rear of the right-hand cylinder head. Connect engine lifting equipment to the lifting brackets

12. Raise the engine slightly using a floor crane and carefully separate the engine from the transmission. Do not let the torque converter fall out of the transmission.

13. Carefully lift the engine out of the engine compartment and position on a workstand. Remove the engine lifting equipment.

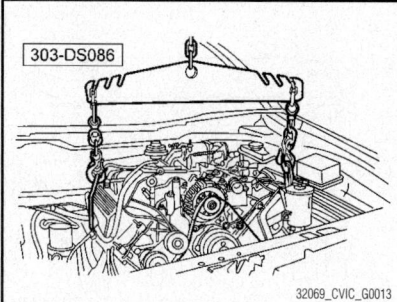

Fig. 51 Slightly lift the engine to access to two top bolts joining the transmission to the engine

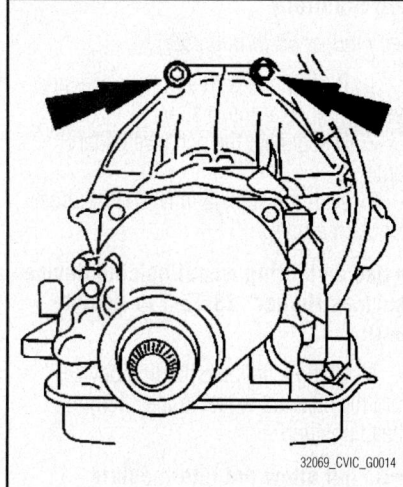

Fig. 52 Top two bolts joining engine to transmission

To install:

14. Engine lifting brackets. Support the engine using a floor crane installed to the lifting equipment and remove the engine from the workstand

15. Lower the engine into the engine compartment. Start the converter pilot into the flywheel and align the paint marks on the flywheel and torque converter. Be sure the studs on the torque converter align with the holes in the flywheel.

16. Fully engage the engine to the transmission and lower onto front engine support insulators.

17. Install or connect the following:

- Engine lifting equipment and brackets
- Bolt retaining the right-hand front engine support insulator to the front engine mount insulator support bracket
- 6 engine-to-transmission (bell housing) bolts and tighten to 35 ft. lbs. (48 Nm)

- Front engine support insulator through-bolts and tighten to 18 ft. lbs. (24 Nm)
- 4 torque converter retaining nuts and tighten to 25 ft. lbs. (34 Nm)
- Transmission housing cover to the cylinder block
- Power steering pump on the cylinder block and the 4 retaining nuts. Tighten to 18 ft. lbs. (24 Nm).
- Starter motor
- Engine-to-transmission brace and the 3 bolts and 1 stud. Tighten the bolts and stud to 22 ft. lbs. (30 Nm).
- Transmission line bracket to the brace stud and 1 retaining nut. Tighten to 18 ft. lbs. (24 Nm).
- Exhaust system to the exhaust manifolds. Tighten the 4 nuts to 18 ft. lbs. (25 Nm). Be sure the exhaust system clears the No. 3 crossmember. Adjust as necessary.
- Power steering valve harness connector
- Ground strap to the dash panel
- Air conditioning lines to the air conditioning compressor
- Alternator harness at the front fender apron and the power distribution box
- Both heater hoses
- Vacuum supply hose to the throttle body adapter vacuum port
- Positive battery cable to the power distribution box and harness
- Electrical connector and vacuum hose to the evaporative emission canister purge valve
- Accelerator and cruise control cables at the throttle body
- Engine/transmission harness connector to the retaining bracket on the power brake booster
- Windshield wiper governor and support bracket
- Fuel supply and return lines
- Radiator, cooling fan and shroud
- Engine air cleaner outlet tube
- Hood
- Battery

18. Fill the crankcase to the correct level.
19. Fill the cooling system.
20. Start the engine and allow it to reach normal operating temperature.
21. Check for leaks and proper fluid levels.
22. Evacuate and recharge the air conditioning system.
23. Road test the vehicle and check the engine and transmission for proper operation.

EXHAUST MANIFOLD

REMOVAL & INSTALLATION

Right Manifold

See Figures 53 through 55.

1. If equipped with a fire suppression system, depower the system.
2. Drain the engine cooling system.
3. Disconnect the negative battery cable.
4. Rotate the drive belt tensioner clockwise and remove the drive belt.
5. Disconnect the Crankshaft Position (CKP) sensor electrical connector.
6. Disconnect the A/C compressor electrical connector.
7. Remove the bolt from the transmission cooler tube bracket.
8. Remove the nut and position aside the transmission cooler tube assembly.
9. Remove the 3 bolts and position aside the A/C compressor.
10. Remove the catalytic converter-to-exhaust manifold nuts and position aside the catalytic converter flange. Discard the nuts.
11. Remove the 8 nuts, the exhaust manifold and the gasket. Discard the nuts and gasket.
12. Remove and discard the 8 exhaust manifold studs.
13. Clean and inspect the exhaust manifold for flatness.

To install:

14. Install the 8 new exhaust manifold studs. Tighten to 106 inch lbs. (12 Nm).
15. Install a new exhaust manifold gasket, the exhaust manifold and 8 new nuts. Tighten in sequence shown to 15 ft. lbs. (20 Nm).
16. Position the catalytic converter flange and install the new catalytic converter-to-exhaust manifold nuts. Tighten to 35 ft. lbs. (48 Nm).
17. Position the A/C compressor and install the 3 bolts. Tighten to 18 ft. lbs. (25 Nm).
18. Position the transmission cooler tube assembly and install the nut. To install, tighten to 80 inch lbs. (9 Nm).
19. Install the transmission cooler tube bracket bolt. To install, tighten to 11 ft. lbs. (15 Nm).
20. Connect the A/C compressor electrical connector.
21. Connect the CKP sensor electrical connector.
22. Rotate the drive belt tensioner clockwise and install the drive belt.
23. Connect the battery ground cable.
24. If equipped with a fire suppression system, repower the system.

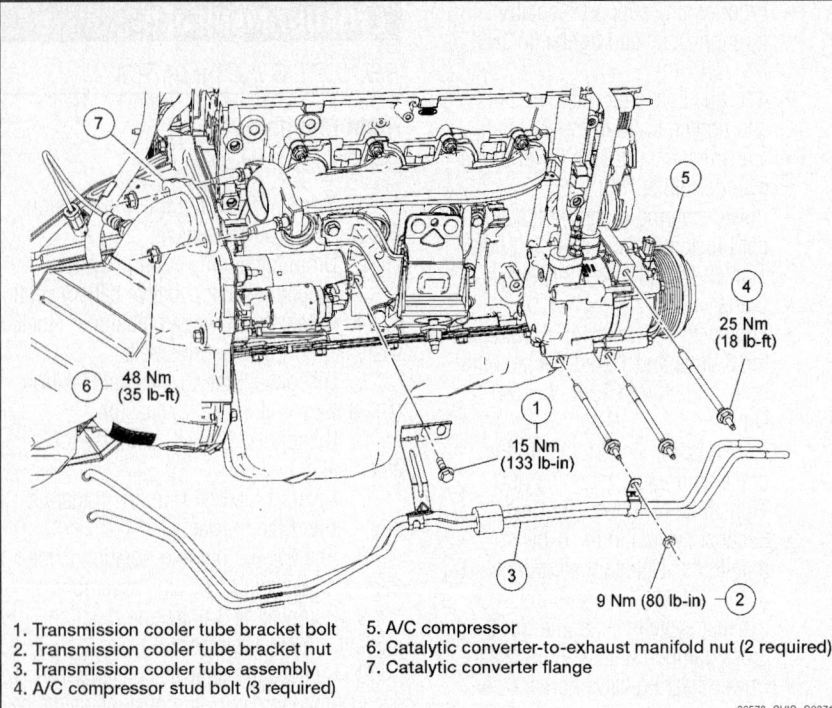

1. Transmission cooler tube bracket bolt
2. Transmission cooler tube bracket nut
3. Transmission cooler tube assembly
4. A/C compressor stud bolt (3 required)
5. A/C compressor
6. Catalytic converter-to-exhaust manifold nut (2 required)
7. Catalytic converter flange

36578_CVIC_G0071

Fig. 53 Components to be removed for right exhaust manifold (1 Of 2)

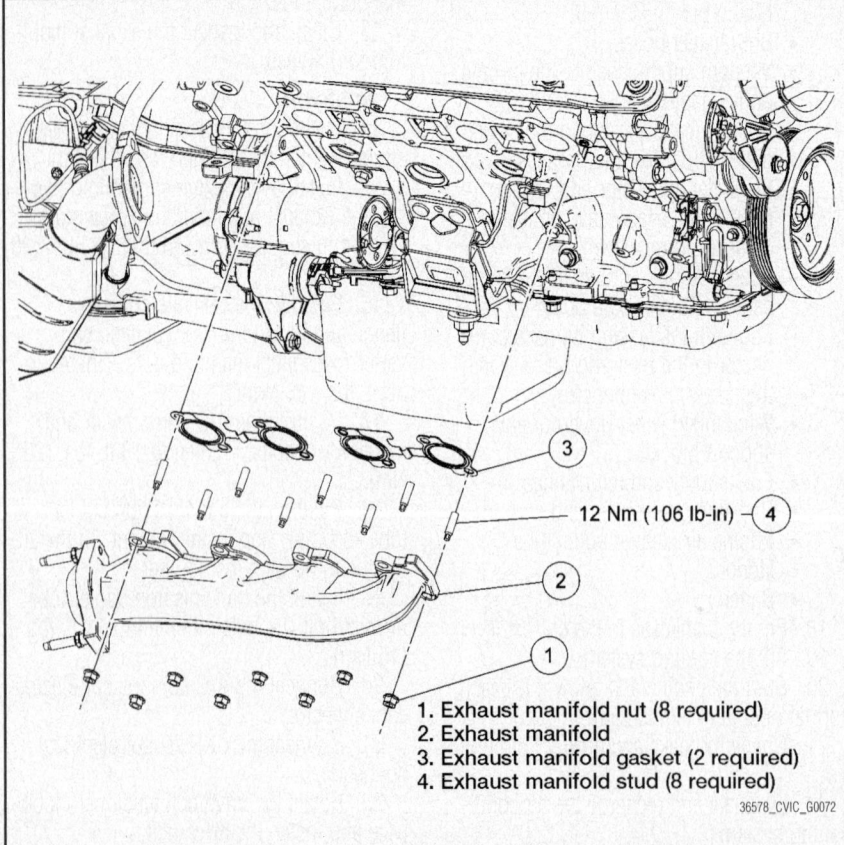

1. Exhaust manifold nut (8 required)
2. Exhaust manifold
3. Exhaust manifold gasket (2 required)
4. Exhaust manifold stud (8 required)

36578_CVIC_G0072

Fig. 54 View of the right exhaust manifold (2 Of 2)

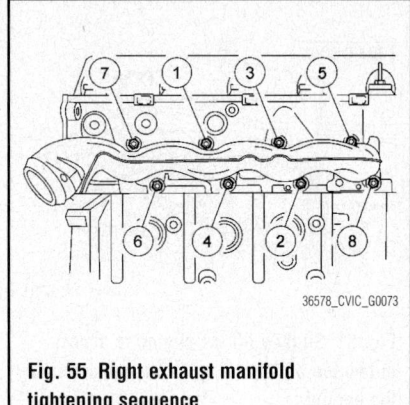

36578_CVIC_G0073

Fig. 55 Right exhaust manifold tightening sequence

Left Manifold

See Figures 56 through 58.

1. If equipped with a fire suppression system, depower the system.

2. Disconnect the negative battery cable.

3. With the vehicle in NEUTRAL, position it on a hoist.

➡**Use a steering wheel holding device (such as Hunter® 28-75-1 or equivalent).**

4. Using a suitable holding device, hold the steering wheel in the straight-ahead position

➡**Do not allow the intermediate shaft to rotate while it is disconnected from the steering gear or damage to the clockspring may result. If there is evidence that the intermediate shaft has rotated, the clockspring must be removed and recentered.**

5. Remove the intermediated shaft pinch bolt and detach the intermediate shaft from the steering gear and position aside.

6. Remove the 2 exhaust manifold heat shield bolts and the shield.

7. Remove the 2 catalytic converter-to-exhaust manifold nuts and position aside the catalytic converter flange. Discard the nuts.

8. Disconnect the EGR system module tube from the exhaust manifold.

9. Remove the LH Heated Oxygen Sensor (HO2S).

10. Remove the 8 nuts, the exhaust manifold and the gasket. Discard the nuts and gasket.

11. Remove and discard the 8 exhaust manifold studs.

12. Clean and inspect the exhaust manifold for flatness.

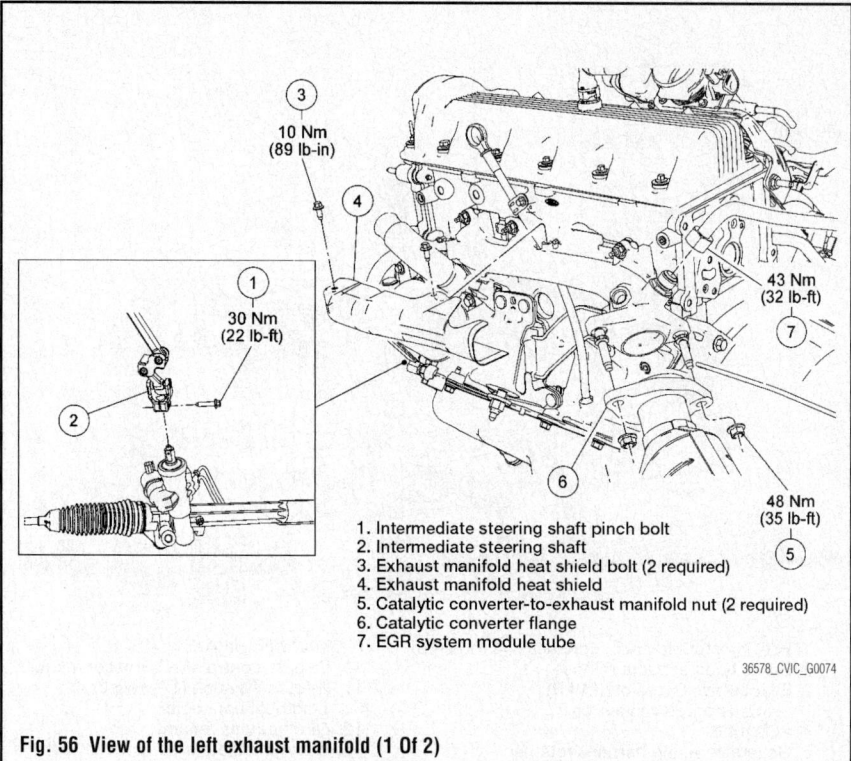

1. Intermediate steering shaft pinch bolt
2. Intermediate steering shaft
3. Exhaust manifold heat shield bolt (2 required)
4. Exhaust manifold heat shield
5. Catalytic converter-to-exhaust manifold nut (2 required)
6. Catalytic converter flange
7. EGR system module tube

36578_CVIC_G0074

Fig. 56 View of the left exhaust manifold (1 Of 2)

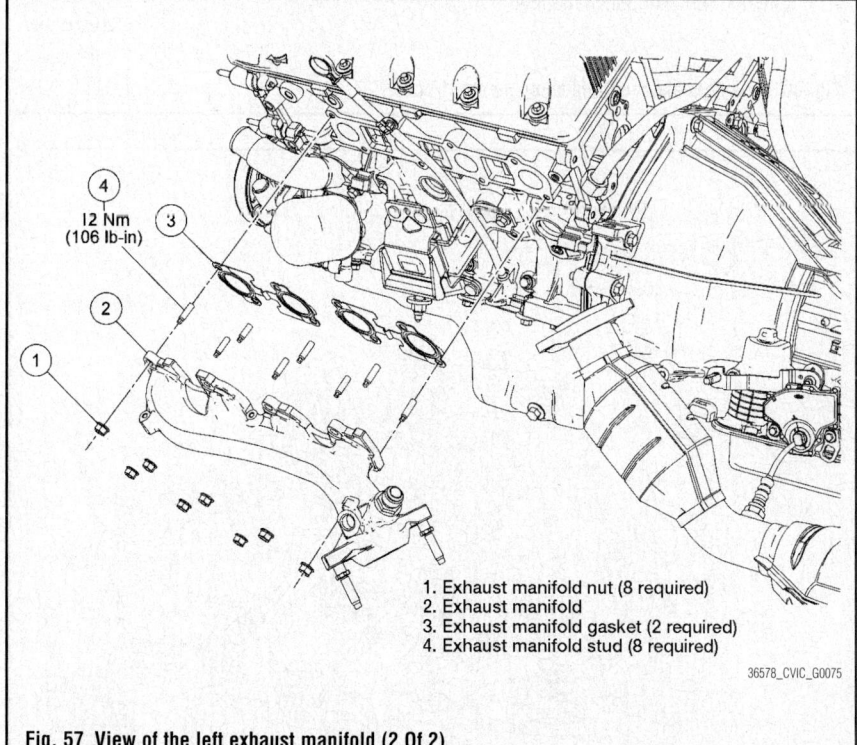

1. Exhaust manifold nut (8 required)
2. Exhaust manifold
3. Exhaust manifold gasket (2 required)
4. Exhaust manifold stud (8 required)

36578_CVIC_G0075

Fig. 57 View of the left exhaust manifold (2 Of 2)

To install:

13. Install the 8 new exhaust manifold studs. Tighten to 106 inch lbs. (12 Nm).

14. Install a new exhaust manifold gasket, the exhaust manifold and 8 new nuts. Tighten in sequence shown to 15 ft. lbs. (20 Nm).

15. Install the LH HO2S .

16. Connect the EGR system module tube to the exhaust manifold. Tighten to 32 ft. lbs. (43 Nm).

17. Position the catalytic converter flange and install the new catalytic converter-to-exhaust manifold nuts. Tighten to 35 ft. lbs. (48 Nm).

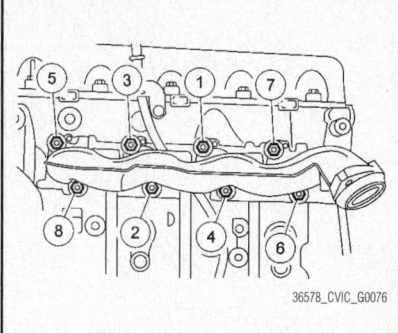

36578_CVIC_G0076

Fig. 58 Left exhaust manifold tightening sequence

18. Install the exhaust manifold heat shield and the 2 bolts. Tighten to 89 inch lbs. (10 Nm).

19. Position the intermediate shaft on the steering gear and install the pinch bolt. Tighten to 22 ft. lbs. (30 Nm).

20. Connect the battery ground cable.

21. If equipped with a fire suppression system, repower the system.

FLEXPLATE

REMOVAL & INSTALLATION

See Figure 59.

✳✳ CAUTION

If the vehicle is equipped with air suspension, the electrical power to the air suspension system must be shut off prior to hoisting, jacking or towing an air suspension vehicle. This can be accomplished by turning off the air suspension switch located in the luggage compartment. Failure to do so can result in unexpected inflation or deflation of the air springs, which can result in shifting of the vehicle during these operations. Failure to follow these instructions may result in personal injury.

1. Before servicing the vehicle, refer to the precautions in the beginning of this section.

2. Disconnect battery negative cable from battery and properly isolate to prevent accidental reconnection.

3. Remove the transmission.

4. Remove the bolts and the flexplate.

To install:

5. Position the flexplate and loosely install the bolts.

6. Tighten the bolts to 59 ft. lbs. (80 Nm) in the sequence shown.

7. Install the transmission.

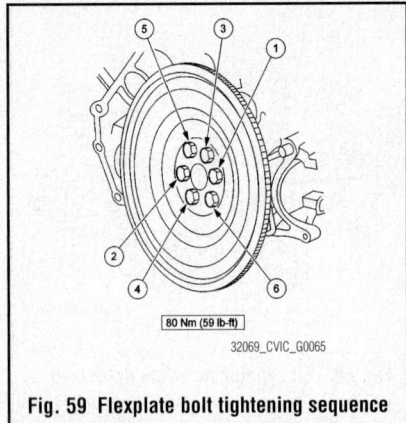

Fig. 59 Flexplate bolt tightening sequence

80 Nm (59 lb-ft)

32069_CVIC_G0065

INTAKE MANIFOLD

REMOVAL & INSTALLATION

See Figures 60 through 63.

1. If equipped with air suspension, the air suspension switch, located on the right-hand side of the luggage compartment, must be turned to the **OFF** position before raising the vehicle.

2. Disconnect negative battery cable.

3. Drain the engine cooling system.

4. Properly relieve the fuel system pressure.

5. With the vehicle in NEUTRAL, position it on a hoist.

6. Disconnect the fuel tube spring lock coupling.

7. Remove the air cleaner and outlet pipe.

8. Remove the wiper mounting arm and pivot shaft.

9. Disconnect the 8 fuel injector electrical connectors.

10. Remove the 8 ignition coil-on-plugs.

11. Remove the 2 bolts and the intake manifold shield.

12. Disconnect the brake booster vacuum hose from the intake manifold.

13. Disconnect the quick connect coupling Evaporative Emission (EVAP) canister purge valve hoses from the Throttle Body (TB) spacer and from the EVAP canister purge valve.

14. Disconnect the quick connect coupling PCV tube from the TB spacer.

15. Disconnect the EGR system module vacuum and electrical connectors.

16. Disconnect the intake manifold-to-TB spacer vacuum hose.

17. Disconnect the generator electrical connector.

18. Detach the 2 generator wiring harness retainers from the generator bracket.

19. Remove the 4 generator bracket bolts and the bracket.

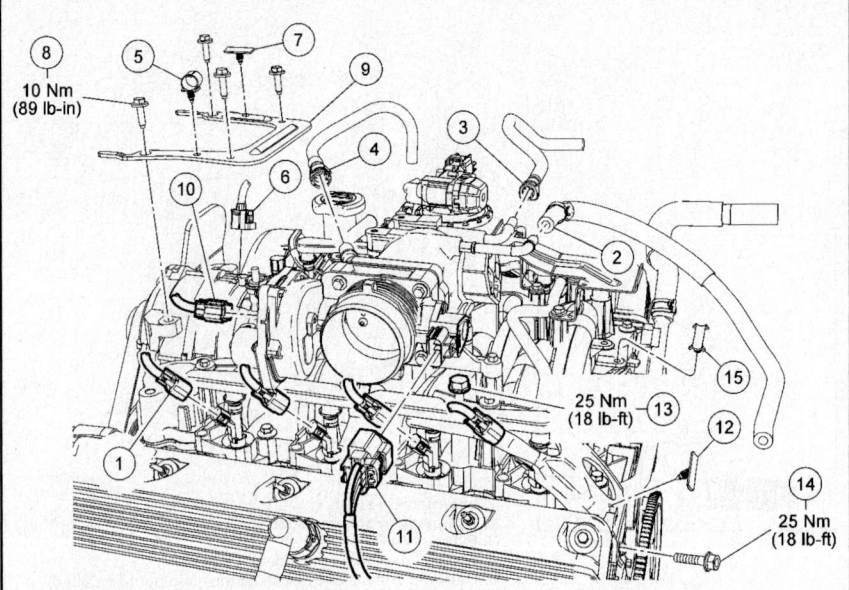

1. Fuel injector electrical connector (4 required)
2. Brake booster vacuum hose
3. Evaporative Emission (EVAP) canister purge valve tube
4. PCV tube
5. Generator wiring harness retainer
6. Generator electrical connector
7. Generator B+ wiring harness retainer
8. Generator bracket bolt (4 required)
9. Generator bracket
10. Throttle control electrical connector
11. Throttle Position (TP) sensor electrical connector
12. Wire harness retainer
13. Intake manifold crash bracket bolt
14. Intake manifold crash bracket bolt
15. Wire harness retainer

10 Nm (89 lb-in)

25 Nm (18 lb-ft)

25 Nm (18 lb-ft)

36578_CVIC_G0077

Fig. 60 View of intake manifold components (1 of 3)

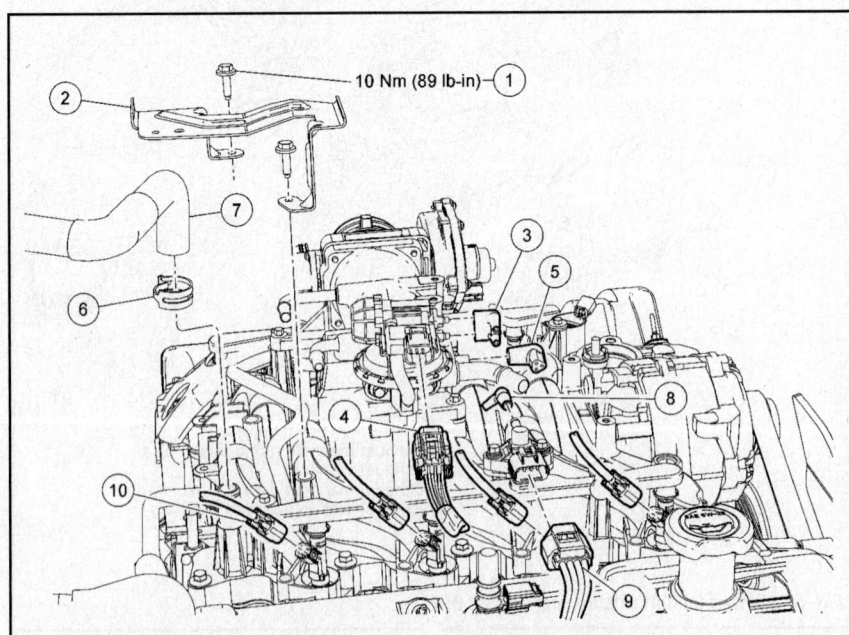

10 Nm (89 lb-in)

1. Intake manifold shield bolt (2 required)
2. Intake manifold shield
3. EGR system module vacuum connector
4. EGR system module electrical connector
5. Intake manifold vacuum hose connector
6. Heater hose spring clamp
7. Heater hose
8. Fuel rail pressure and temperature sensor vacuum connector
9. Fuel rail pressure and temperature sensor electrical connector
10. Fuel injector electrical connector (4 required)

36578_CVIC_G0078

Fig. 61 View of intake manifold components (2 of 3)

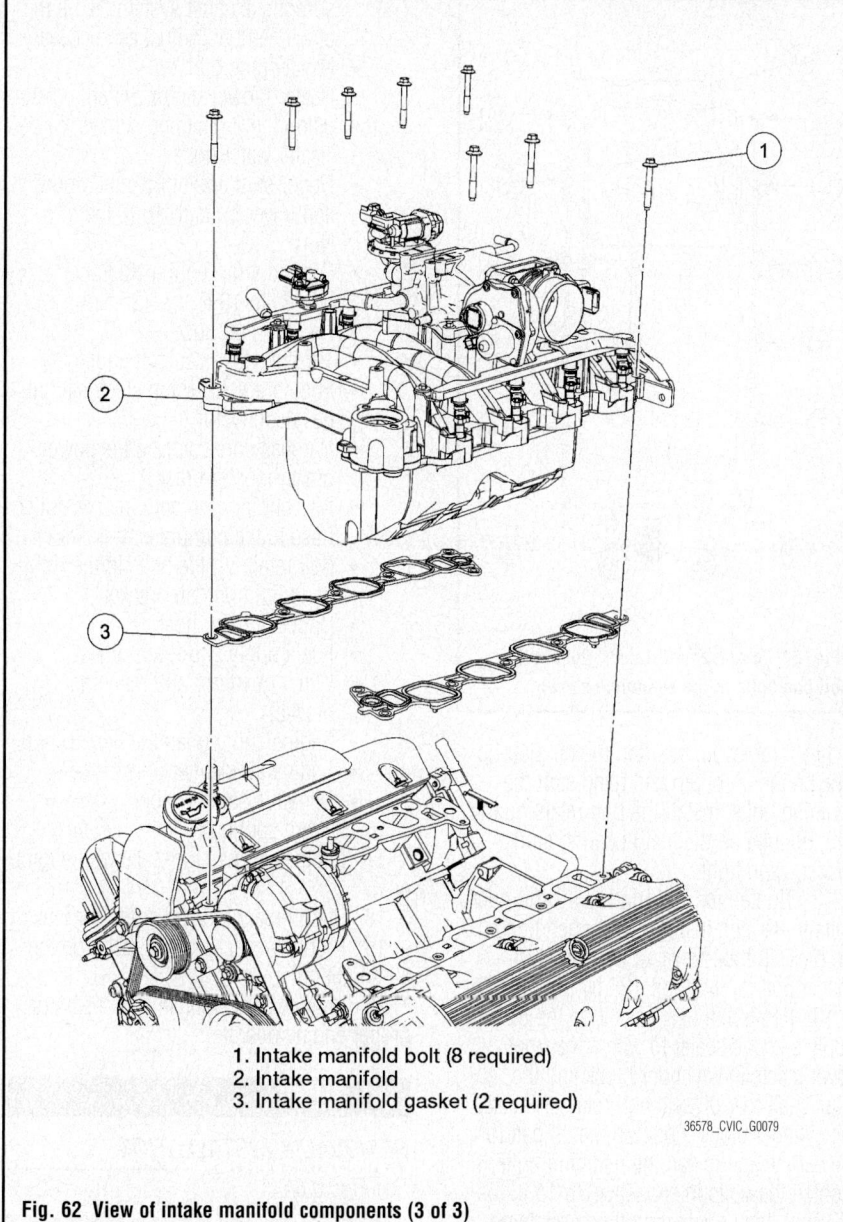

1. Intake manifold bolt (8 required)
2. Intake manifold
3. Intake manifold gasket (2 required)

36578_CVIC_G0079

Fig. 62 View of intake manifold components (3 of 3)

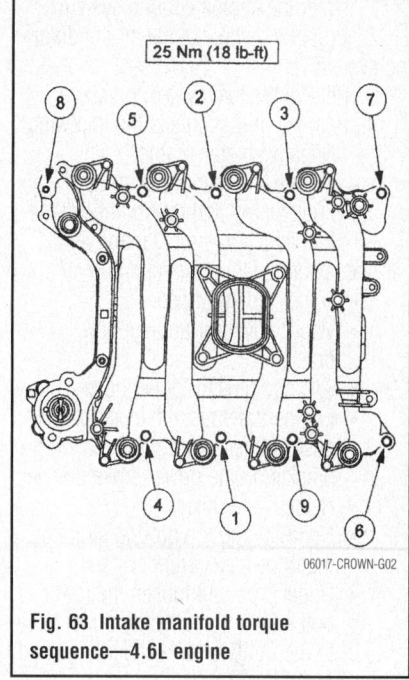

Fig. 63 Intake manifold torque sequence—4.6L engine

06017-CROWN-G02

before final tightening, then tighten the bolts, in sequence, to 18 ft. lbs. (25 Nm).

34. Inspect and if necessary, replace the O-ring seal on the thermostat housing. Position the housing and upper hose and install the 2 retaining bolts. Tighten to 18 ft. lbs. (25 Nm).

35. To complete installation, reverse remaining removal procedure.

36. Fill the engine cooling system.

37. If equipped with air suspension, turn the air suspension switch to the **ON** position.

38. Start the engine and check for leaks.

39. Road test the vehicle and check for proper operation.

OIL PAN

REMOVAL & INSTALLATION

See Figure 64.

✷✷ CAUTION

If the vehicle is equipped with air suspension, the electrical power to the air suspension system must be shut off prior to hoisting, jacking or towing an air suspension vehicle. This can be accomplished by turning off the air suspension switch located in the luggage compartment. Failure to do so can result in unexpected inflation or deflation of the air springs, which can result in shifting of the vehicle during these operations. Failure to follow these instructions may result in personal injury.

20. Remove the coolant thermostat.

21. Disconnect the throttle control and the Throttle Position (TP) sensor electrical connectors.

22. Release the heater hose spring clamp and disconnect the heater hose.

23. Remove the EGR system module tube.

24. If equipped, detach the wire harness retainer from the intake manifold crash bracket.

25. Remove the intake manifold crash bracket bolt and prevent the bolt from contacting the cylinder head with a rubber band or tie strap.

26. Remove the intake manifold crash bracket bolt.

27. Disconnect the fuel rail pressure and temperature sensor vacuum and electrical connectors.

28. Remove the wire harness retainer from the rear of the intake manifold.

29. Remove the 8 bolts and the intake manifold. Remove and discard the intake manifold gaskets.

30. Clean the sealing surfaces.

To install:

31. Clean all gaskets mating surfaces.

32. Position new intake manifold gaskets on the cylinder heads. Be sure the alignment tabs on the gaskets are aligned with the holes in the cylinder heads.

33. Install the intake manifold and the 9 retaining bolts. Hand-tighten the right-rear bolt (viewed from the front of the engine)

1. Drain the engine cooling system
2. Properly discharge the air conditioning system.
3. Relieve the fuel system pressure.
4. Remove or disconnect the following:
   - Negative battery cable
   - Engine air cleaner outlet tube
   - Fuel supply and return lines at the fuel injection supply manifold
   - Cooling fan and fan shroud
   - Upper radiator hose
   - Wiper governor and support bracket
   - A/C compressor outlet hose
   - Engine/transmission electrical harness connector from the retaining bracket on the power brake booster
   - Heater water hose
   - Nut retaining the ground strap to the right-hand cylinder head
   - Upper stud and loosen the lower bolt retaining the heater outlet hose to the right-hand cylinder head and position aside
   - Heater blower motor switch resistor
5. Drain the engine oil and reinstall the oil pan drain plug with a new gasket. Tighten the plug to 10 ft. lbs. (13 Nm).
6. Remove or disconnect the following:
   - Bolt retaining the right-hand engine support insulator to the lower front sub-frame
   - Bolts retaining the left-hand and right-hand front engine support insulators to the engine mount supports
   - Catalytic converter pipes from both exhaust manifolds. Lower the exhaust system and support it with wire from the transmission crossmember.
7. Position a jack and a block of wood under the oil pan, rearward of the oil drain hole. Raise the engine approximately 4 inches (100mm) and insert 2 wood blocks approximately 2½–2¾ inch (60–70mm) thick under each front engine support insulator. Lower the engine onto the wood blocks and remove the jack.
8. Remove the oil pan.
9. If necessary, remove the 2 bolts retaining the oil pick-up tube to the oil pump and remove the bolt retaining the pick-up tube to the main bearing stud spacer. Remove the pick-up tube.

To install:

10. Clean the engine oil pan and inspect for damage. Clean the sealing surfaces of the front cover and cylinder block. Clean and inspect the oil pick-up tube and replace the O-ring.

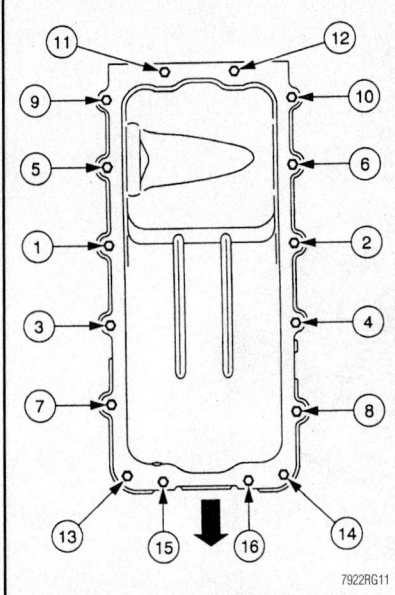

Fig. 64 To prevent oil leaks, tighten the oil pan bolts in the sequence shown

7922RG11

11. If removed, position the oil pick-up tube on the oil pump and hand start the 2 retaining bolts. Install the bolt retaining the pick-up tube on the main bearing stud spacer, hand tight.
12. Tighten the pick-up tube-to-oil pump bolts to 89 inch lbs. (10 Nm), then tighten the pick-up tube-to-main bearing stud spacer bolt to 18 ft. lbs. (25 Nm).
13. Position a new gasket on the oil pan. Apply silicone sealer to where the front cover meets the cylinder block and the crankshaft rear oil seal and retainer meets the cylinder block. Position the oil pan to the engine and install the retaining bolts. Tighten the bolts in sequence, to 14 ft. lbs. (20 Nm), then rotate the oil pan retaining bolts, in sequence an additional 60 degrees within 4 minutes of applying the silicone sealer.
14. Position the jack and wood block under the engine oil pan, rearward of the oil drain hole, and raise the engine enough to remove the wood blocks. Lower the engine and remove the jack.
15. Install or connect the following:
   - Left-hand and right-hand engine support insulator through-bolts and tighten to 18 ft. lbs. (25 Nm)
   - Bolt retaining the right-hand engine support insulator to the lower front sub-frame. Tighten the bolt to 18 ft. lbs. (25 Nm).
   - Exhaust system to the exhaust manifolds and tighten the 4 retaining nuts to 25 ft. lbs. (34Nm). Be

sure the exhaust system clears the crossmember. Adjust as necessary.
   - New engine oil filter
   - Heater blower motor switch resistor using the 2 retaining screws
   - Heater water hose
   - Upper stud and tighten the upper and lower bolts to 18 ft. lbs. (25 Nm)
   - Ground strap on the stud and tighten to 18 ft. lbs. (25 Nm)
   - Heater water hose
   - Throttle valve cable, if equipped
   - Engine/transmission electrical harness connector
   - Harness connector on the power brake booster bracket
   - Air conditioning compressor outlet hose to the compressor
   - Bolt retaining the hose to the right-hand ignition coil bracket
   - Upper radiator hose
   - Fuel supply and return lines
   - Wiper governor and retaining bracket
   - Engine cooling fan and fan shroud
   - Engine air cleaner outlet tube
   - Negative battery cable
16. Fill the cooling system.
17. Fill the engine crankcase with engine oil.
18. Start the engine and check for leaks.
19. Properly evacuate and recharge the air conditioning system.
20. Road test the vehicle and check for proper engine operation.

OIL PUMP

REMOVAL & INSTALLATION

See Figure 65.

1. Remove or disconnect the following:
   - Negative battery cable
   - Cylinder head covers
   - Engine front cover
   - Engine oil pan
   - Timing chains
   - 2 bolts retaining the oil pick-up tube to the oil pump and the bolt attaching the oil pick-up tube to the main bearing stud spacer
   - Pick-up tube
   - 4 bolts retaining the oil pump to the cylinder block
   - Oil pump

To install:

2. Rotate the inner rotor of the oil pump to align with the flats on the crankshaft and install the oil pump flush with the cylinder block. Install the 4 retaining bolts and tighten to 89 inch lbs. (10 Nm).

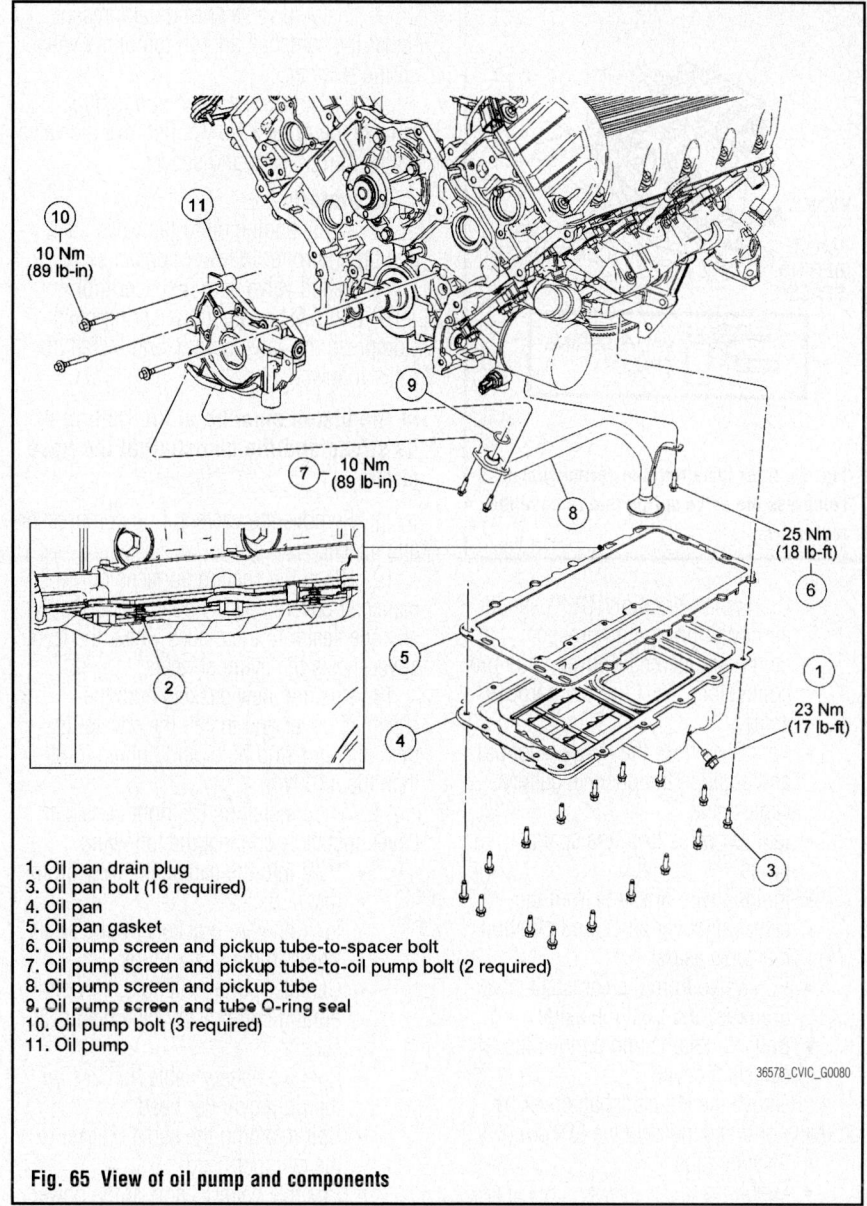

1. Oil pan drain plug
3. Oil pan bolt (16 required)
4. Oil pan
5. Oil pan gasket
6. Oil pump screen and pickup tube-to-spacer bolt
7. Oil pump screen and pickup tube-to-oil pump bolt (2 required)
8. Oil pump screen and pickup tube
9. Oil pump screen and tube O-ring seal
10. Oil pump bolt (3 required)
11. Oil pump

36578_CVIC_G0080

Fig. 65 View of oil pump and components

3. Clean the oil pick-up tube and replace the O-ring.

4. Place the pick-up tube on the oil pump and hand start the 2 retaining bolts. Install the bolt retaining the pick-up tube to the main bearing stud spacer hand tight. Tighten the pick-up tube-to-oil pump bolts to 89 inch lbs. (10 Nm). Tighten the pick-up tube to main bearing stud spacer bolt to 18 ft. lbs. (25 Nm).

5. Install or connect the following:
- New engine oil filter
- Timing chains
- Engine oil pan
- Engine front cover
- Cylinder head covers
- Negative battery cable

6. Fill the crankcase.

7. Start the engine and check for leaks and proper engine oil pressure.

8. Road test the vehicle and check for proper engine operation.

PISTON AND RING

POSITIONING

See Figures 66 and 67.

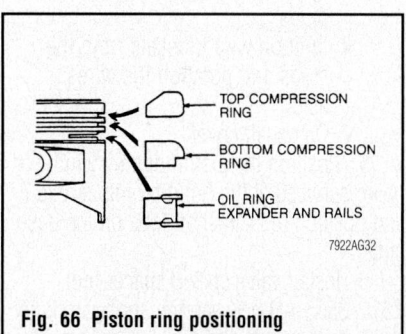

7922AG32

Fig. 66 Piston ring positioning

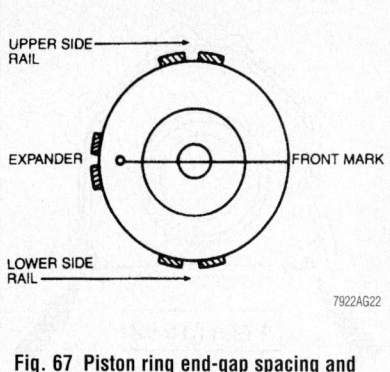

7922AG22

Fig. 67 Piston ring end-gap spacing and piston positioning

REAR MAIN SEAL

REMOVAL & INSTALLATION

See Figures 68 and 69.

✷✷ CAUTION

If the vehicle is equipped with air suspension, the electrical power to the air suspension system must be shut off prior to hoisting, jacking or towing an air suspension vehicle. This can be accomplished by turning off the air suspension switch located in the luggage compartment. Failure to do so can result in unexpected inflation or deflation of the air springs, which can result in shifting of the vehicle during these operations. Failure to follow these instructions may result in personal injury.

1. Remove or disconnect the following:
- Transmission
- Flexplate or flywheel

2. With a sharp awl, carefully punch a small hole in the metal portion of the seal.

3. Remove the seal using a slide hammer with a sheet metal screw attached.

➡If the oil leak is coming from around the seal retainer, the retainer must also be removed and resealed.

To install:

4. If the seal retainer was removed, carefully clean the sealant from the retainer and engine block using a plastic scraper. Remove any oil or grease residue from the sealing surfaces with a solvent.

5. Apply silicone sealant to the back of the retainer and immediately install it on the engine block. Tighten the bolts in sequence to 89 inch lbs. (10 Nm).

6. Lubricate the seal and the crankshaft with clean engine oil.

7. Install the seal with the spring side toward the engine.

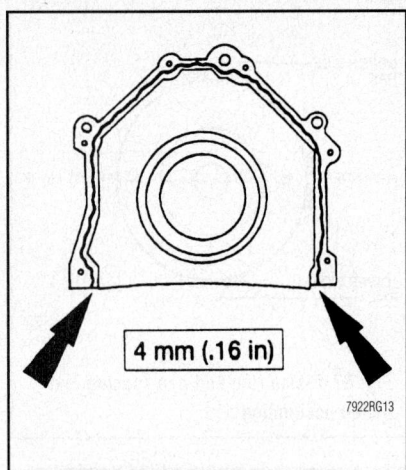

Fig. 68 Apply a continuous bead of silicone sealant to the back of the seal retainer before installing it on the engine

4 mm (.16 in)

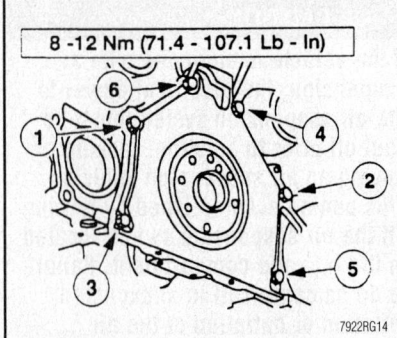

8 -12 Nm (71.4 - 107.1 Lb - In)

Fig. 69 To avoid leakage, be sure to tighten the crankshaft rear oil seal retainer bolts in the correct sequence

8. Remove the installation tool.
9. Install or connect the following:
   - Flexplate or flywheel. Tighten the bolts, in a star pattern, to 59 ft. lbs. (80 Nm).
   - Transmission
   - Negative battery cable
10. Check the engine oil level.
11. Start the engine and check for leaks.

ROCKER ARMS/SHAFTS

REMOVAL & INSTALLATION

See Figure 70.

1. Relieve the fuel system pressure.
2. Disconnect the negative battery cable.
3. Remove the right camshaft cover by removing or disconnecting the following:
   - Positive battery cable at the battery and at the power distribution box
   - Retaining bolt from the positive battery cable bracket located on the side of the right cylinder head

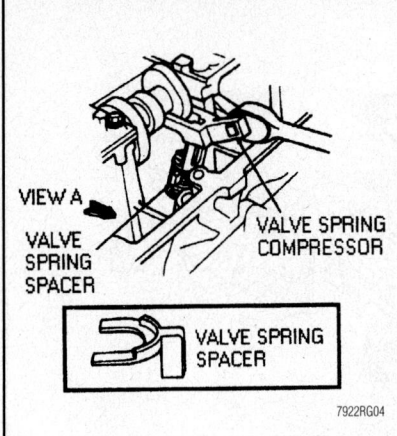

VIEW A
VALVE SPRING SPACER
VALVE SPRING COMPRESSOR
VALVE SPRING SPACER

Fig. 70 After installing the spring spacer, compress the valve spring and remove the rocker arm

   - Crankshaft Position (CKP) sensor, air conditioning compressor clutch and canister purge solenoid connectors. Position the harness aside.
   - Vent hose from the purge solenoid and position the positive battery cable aside
   - Ignition wires from the spark plugs
   - Ignition wire brackets from the camshaft cover studs and position the wires aside
   - PCV valve from the camshaft cover grommet and position aside
   - Bolts and studs and remove the camshaft cover.
4. Remove the left camshaft cover by removing or disconnecting the following:
   - Air inlet tube
   - Fuel lines
   - PSP switch and oil pressure sending unit and position the harness aside
   - 42-pin engine harness connector from the retaining bracket on the brake vacuum booster and position aside
   - Windshield wiper module
   - Ignition wires from the spark plugs
   - Ignition wire brackets from the studs and position the wires aside
   - Camshaft cover
5. Position the piston of the cylinder being serviced at the bottom of its stroke and position the camshaft lobe on the base circle.
6. Install valve spring spacer tool T91P-6565-AH between the spring coils to prevent valve seal damage.

7. Install a valve spring compressor under the camshaft and on top of the valve spring retainer.
8. Compress the valve spring and remove the roller follower. Remove the valve spring compressor and spacer.

To install:

9. Apply engine oil to the valve stem and tip and roller follower contact surfaces.
10. Install valve spring spacer tool T91P-6565-AH between the spring coils. Compress the valve spring, and install the roller follower.

➡**The piston must be at the bottom of its stroke and the camshaft at the base circle.**

11. Remove the valve spring compressor and spacer.
12. Clean the sealing surfaces of the camshaft covers and cylinder heads. Apply silicone sealer to the places where the front cover meets the cylinder head.
13. Position new gaskets onto the camshaft cover and install the covers. Install the bolts and stud bolts and tighten to 89 inch lbs. (10 Nm).
14. When installing the right camshaft cover, install or connect the following:
   - PCV into the camshaft cover grommet
   - Ignition wire brackets on the studs
   - Wires to the spark plugs
   - Canister purge solenoid, air conditioning compressor clutch and CKP sensor
   - Positive battery cable harness on the right cylinder head
   - Bolt retaining the cable bracket to the cylinder head
   - Positive battery cable at the power distribution box and the battery
15. When installing the left camshaft cover, install or connect the following:
   - Ignition wire brackets on the studs
   - Wires to the spark plugs
   - Windshield wiper module
   - 42-pin and transmission harness connectors
   - Retaining bracket
   - PSP switch and oil pressure sending unit harness.
   - Fuel lines
   - Negative battery cable
16. Start the engine and check for leaks.

TIMING CHAIN COVER AND SEAL

REMOVAL & INSTALLATION

See Figures 71 through 73.

1. Before servicing the vehicle, refer to the precautions in the beginning of this section.

2. Disconnect battery negative cable from battery and properly isolate to prevent accidental reconnection.

3. Raise and support the vehicle.

4. Remove both valve covers.

5. Remove the A/C compressor.

6. Remove the crankshaft front seal.

7. Remove the 3 bolts and position the power steering pump aside.

8. Drain the engine oil and install the drain plug when finished.

9. Remove the 4 front oil pan-to-engine front cover bolts.

10. Remove the bolt and the shield.

11. Remove the bolts and the stud bolts in the sequence shown.

12. Remove the engine front cover from the front cover-to-cylinder block dowel.

To install:

➡ **If not secured within 4 minutes, the sealant must be removed and the sealing area cleaned. To clean the sealing area, use silicone gasket remover and metal surface prep. Follow the directions on the packaging. Failure to follow this procedure can cause future oil leakage.**

13. Apply silicone gasket and sealant along the cylinder head-to-block surface and the oil pan-to-cylinder block surface.

14. Position the new engine front cover gaskets.

15. Install the engine front cover on the front cover-to-cylinder block dowel and loosely install the bolts.

16. Tighten the front cover fasteners in the sequence shown to 18 ft. lbs. (25 Nm).

17. Install the accessory drive idler pulley and the bolt. Tighten to 18 ft. lbs. (25 Nm).

18. Install the shield and the bolts Tighten to 18 ft. lbs. (25 Nm).

19. Loosely install the 4 front oil pan bolts.

➡ **Make sure to tighten the bolts in 2 stages.**

20. Tighten the 4 front oil pan bolts in 2 stages.

   a. Stage 1: Tighten to 177 inch lbs. (20 Nm).

   b. Stage 2: Tighten an additional 60 degrees.

➡ **The front lower hole in the power steering pump is not used.**

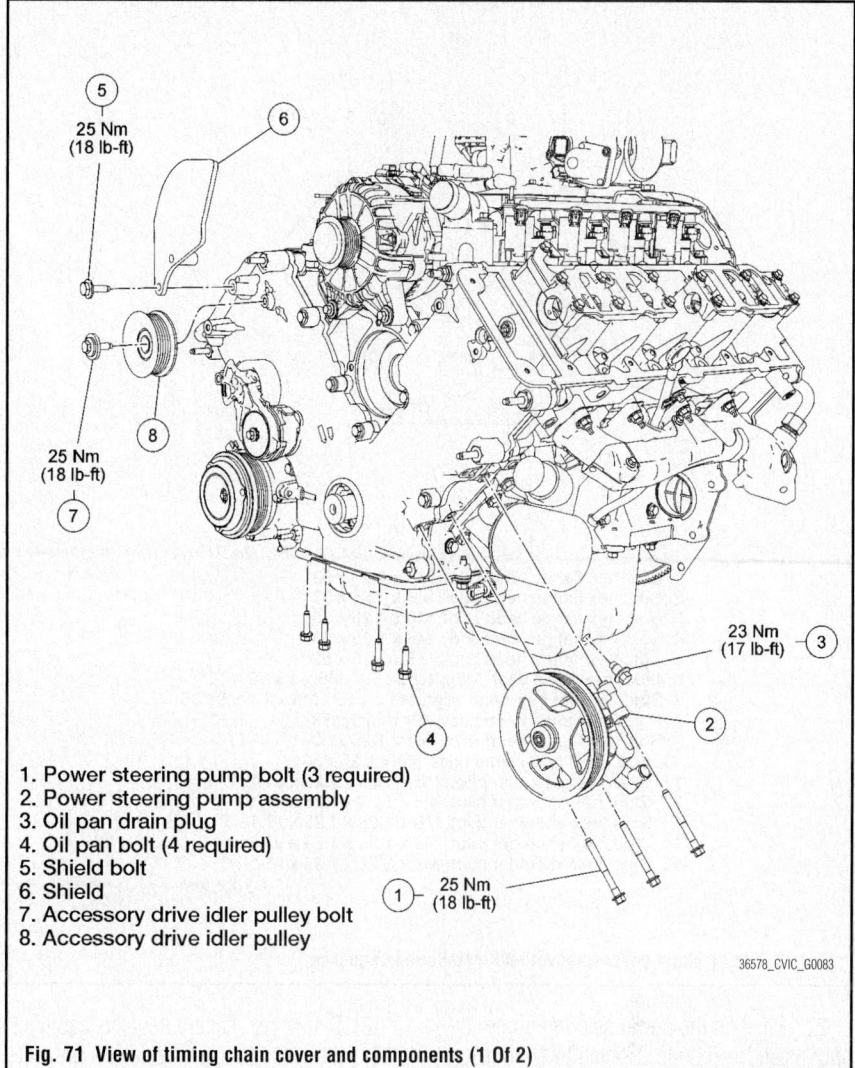

1. Power steering pump bolt (3 required)
2. Power steering pump assembly
3. Oil pan drain plug
4. Oil pan bolt (4 required)
5. Shield bolt
6. Shield
7. Accessory drive idler pulley bolt
8. Accessory drive idler pulley

36578_CVIC_G0083

Fig. 71 View of timing chain cover and components (1 Of 2)

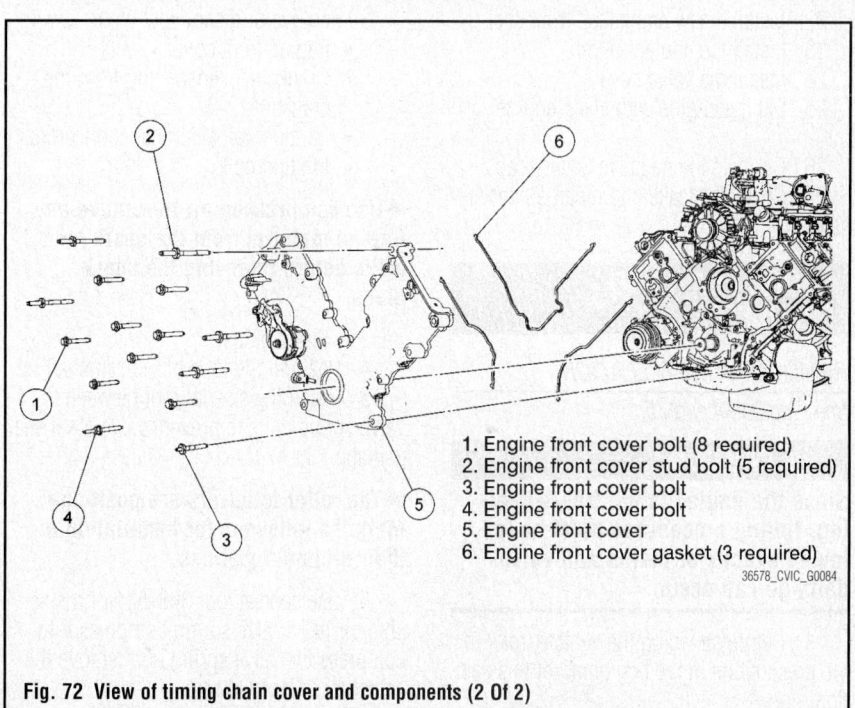

1. Engine front cover bolt (8 required)
2. Engine front cover stud bolt (5 required)
3. Engine front cover bolt
4. Engine front cover bolt
5. Engine front cover
6. Engine front cover gasket (3 required)

36578_CVIC_G0084

Fig. 72 View of timing chain cover and components (2 Of 2)

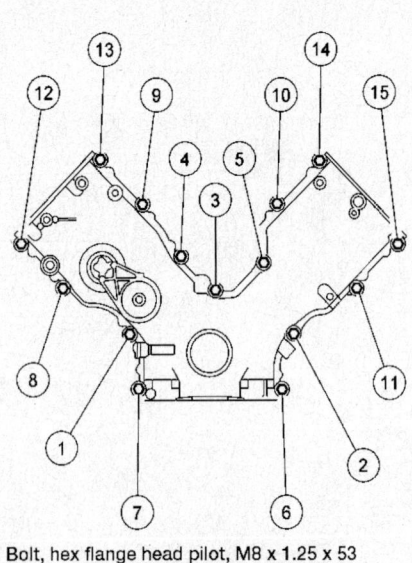

1. Bolt, hex flange head pilot, M8 x 1.25 x 53
2. Bolt, hex flange head pilot, M8 x 1.25 x 53
3. Bolt, hex flange head pilot, M8 x 1.25 x 53
4. Bolt, hex flange head pilot, M8 x 1.25 x 53
5. Bolt, hex flange head pilot, M8 x 1.25 x 53
6. Stud, hex-head pilot, M8 x 1.25 x 50 - M6 x 1 x 10
7. Stud, washer hex-head pilot, M8 x 1.25 - M6 x 1.0 x 86.35
8. Bolt, hex flange head pilot, M8 x 1.25 x 53
9. Bolt, hex flange head pilot, M8 x 1.25 x 53
10. Bolt, hex flange head pilot, M8 x 1.25 x 53
11. Stud, hex-shoulder pilot, M8 x 1.25 x 1.25 x 91.1
12. Stud, hex-shoulder pilot, M8 x 1.25 x 1.25 x 91.1
13. Stud, hex-shoulder pilot, M8 x 1.25 x 1.25 x 91.1
14. Stud, hex-shoulder pilot, M8 x 1.25 x 1.25 x 91.1
15. Stud, hex-shoulder pilot, M8 x 1.25 x 1.25 x 91.1

36578_CVIC_G0082

Fig. 73 Timing chain cover removal and installation sequence

21. Position the power steering pump and install the 3 bolts. Tighten to 18 ft. lbs. (25 Nm).
22. Install a new crankshaft front seal.
23. Install the coolant pump.
24. Install the valve covers.
25. Fill the engine with clean engine oil.
26. Connect the negative battery cable.
27. Check for leaks and repair as necessary.

TIMING CHAIN AND SPROCKETS

REMOVAL & INSTALLATION

See Figures 74 and 75.

❋❋ CAUTION

Since the engine is not free-wheeling, timing procedures must be followed exactly or piston and valve damage can occur.

1. Before servicing the vehicle, refer to the precautions in the beginning of this section.

2. Disconnect battery negative cable from battery and properly isolate to prevent accidental reconnection.
3. Remove or disconnect the following:
   - Engine front cover
   - Crankshaft sensor ring from the crankshaft
   - Ignition coil electrical connectors
   - Ignition coils

➡**Use compressed air to remove any foreign material from the spark plug wells before removing the spark plugs.**

   - Spark plugs
4. Position the lobe of the camshaft up.
5. Install the special tool between the valve spring coils to prevent valve stem seal damage.

➡**The roller followers are positional. Mark the followers for installation in their original locations.**

6. Use special tool 303-581 or a suitable on-head valve spring compressor to compress the valve spring and remove the camshaft roller followers.

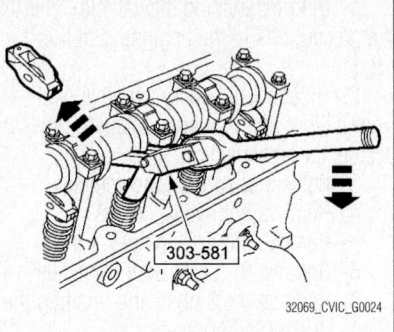

Fig. 74 Compressing valve spring to remove roller follower

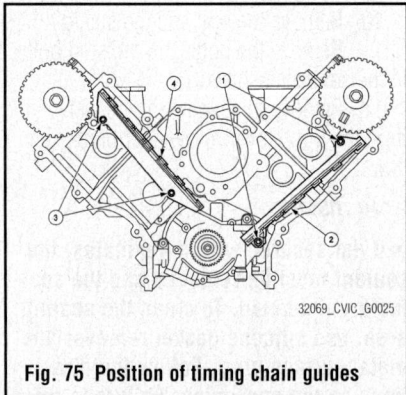

Fig. 75 Position of timing chain guides

7. Position the crankshaft with the keyway at the 12 o'clock position.
8. Remove the timing chain tensioning system from both timing chains.
   a. Remove the bolts.
   b. Remove the timing chain tensioners.
   c. Remove the timing chain tensioner arms.
9. Remove the LH and RH timing chains and the crankshaft sprocket as follows:
   - Remove the RH timing chain from the camshaft sprocket.
   - Remove the RH timing chain from the crankshaft sprocket.
   - Repeat for the LH timing chain and crankshaft sprocket.
10. Remove the timing chain guides as follows:
   - Remove the bolts.
   - Remove the LH timing chain guide.
   - Remove the bolts.
   - Remove the RH timing chain guide.

To install:

Engines With Ratcheting Timing Chain Tensioners

See Figures 76 through 79.

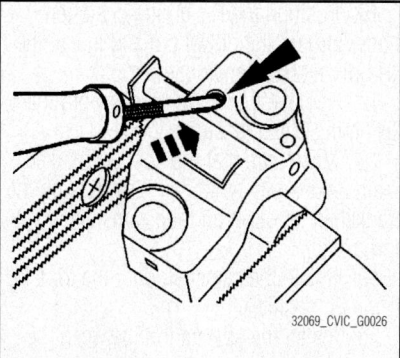

Fig. 76 Releasing the ratcheting timing chain mechanism

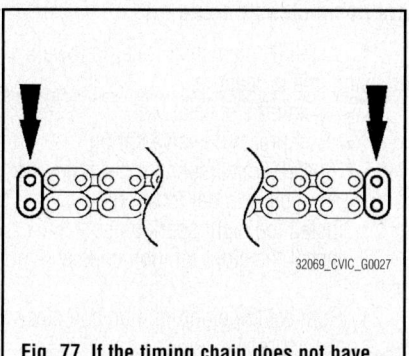

Fig. 77 If the timing chain does not have two copper index links, mark two links as shown

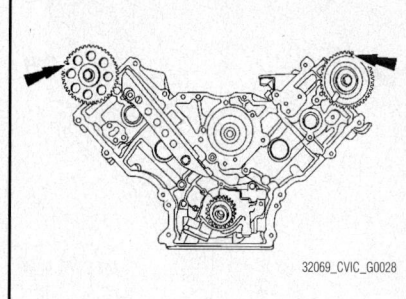

Fig. 78 Position the camshaft sprockets as shown when reinstalling timing chain

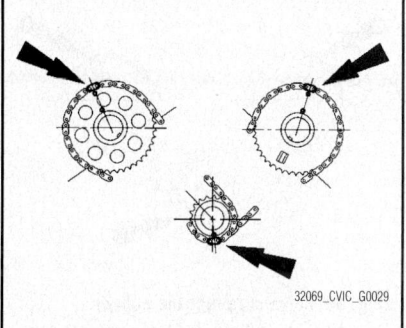

Fig. 79 Position of copper chain links to crank and cam sprockets

✳✳ WARNING

Timing chain procedure must be followed exactly or damage to valves and pistons will result.

✳✳ WARNING

Do not compress the ratchet assembly. This will damage the ratchet assembly.

1. Compress each tensioner plunger using an edge of a vise.
2. Using a small screwdriver or pick, push back and hold the ratchet mechanism.
3. While holding the ratchet mechanism, push the ratchet arm back into the tensioner housing.
4. Install a paper clip into the hole of each tensioner housing to hold the ratchet assembly and plunger in during installation.
5. Remove the tensioner from the vise.
6. If the copper links on the timing chain are not visible, mark one link on one end and one link on the other end and use as timing marks.
7. Install the camshaft sprockets and new bolts and tighten in two stages:

- Stage 1: Tighten the bolt to 30 ft. lbs. (40 Nm).
- Stage 2: Tighten the bolt an additional 90 degrees (1/4 turn).

8. Using the special tool, position the crankshaft so the number one cylinder is at top dead center (TDC).
9. Install the crankshaft sprocket, making sure the flange faces forward.
10. Install the timing chain guide as follows:

- Position the LH timing chain guide.
- Install and tighten the LH bolts.
- Position the RH timing chain guide.
- Install and tighten the RH bolts.

11. Rotate the RH camshaft sprocket until the timing mark is approximately at the 11 o'clock position.
12. Rotate the LH camshaft sprocket until the timing mark is approximately at the 12 o'clock position.
13. Position the LH (inner) timing chain on the crankshaft sprocket, aligning the copper (marked) link with the timing mark on the sprocket.
14. Install the LH timing chain on the sprocket, aligning the copper (marked) link with the timing marks on the sprocket.

➡The LH timing chain tensioner arm has a bump near the dowel hole for identification. Position the LH timing chain tensioner arm on the dowel pin and install the LH timing chain tensioner.

15. Remove the retaining clip from the LH timing chain tensioner.
16. Position the RH (outer) timing chain on the crankshaft sprocket, aligning the copper (marked) link with the timing mark on the sprocket.
17. Install the RH timing chain on the camshaft sprocket, aligning the copper (marked) link with the timing marks on the sprocket.
18. Position the RH timing chain tensioner arm on the dowel pin and install the RH timing chain tensioner.
19. Remove the retaining clip from the RH timing chain tensioner.

➡Lubricate the camshaft roller followers using clean engine oil.

20. Install the camshaft roller followers as using this procedure:

- Install the special tool.
- Compress the valve spring.
- Install the camshaft roller followers in their original locations.

21. Install the eight spark plugs.
22. Install the eight ignition coils and bolts.
23. Connect the eight ignition coil electrical connectors.
24. Install the crankshaft sensor ring on the crankshaft.
25. Install the engine front cover.
26. Reconnect negative battery cable, run engine to check for leaks and repair as necessary.

Engines With Non-Ratcheting Timing Chain Tensioners

See Figures 80 through 83.

✳✳ WARNING

If one or both tensioner mounting bolts are loosened or removed, the tensioner-sealing bead must be inspected for seal integrity. Any cracks, tears, cuts or separation from the tensioner body or permanent compression of the seal bead, will require replacement of the tensioner.

✳✳ WARNING

The timing chain procedure must be followed exactly or damage to valves and pistons will result.

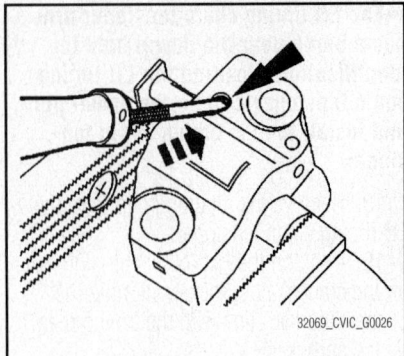

Fig. 80 Releasing the ratcheting timing chain mechanism

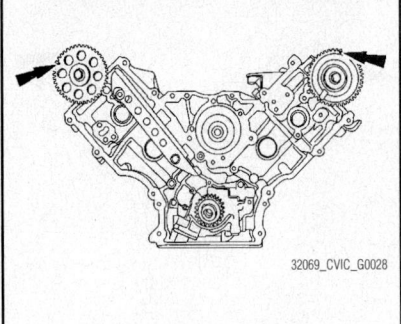

Fig. 82 Position the camshaft sprockets as shown when reinstalling timing chain

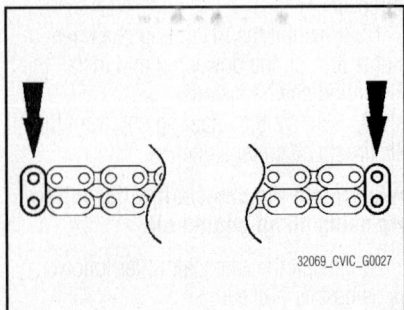

Fig. 81 If the timing chain does not have two copper index links, mark two links as shown

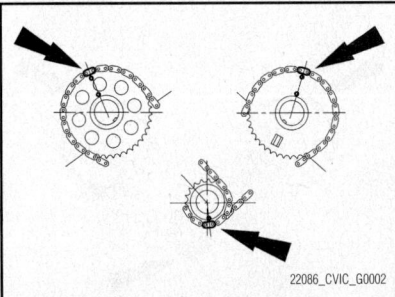

Fig. 83 Make sure that the copper (marked) chain links are lined up with the dots on the crankshaft and camshaft sprockets.`

1. Inspect the RH and LH timing chain tensioners and replace as necessary.

2. Compress each tensioner plunger, using a vise.

3. Install a retaining clip on each tensioner to hold the plunger in during installation.

4. If the copper links on the timing chain are not visible, mark one link on one end and one link on the other end and use as timing marks.

5. Install the camshaft sprockets and new bolts and tighten in two stages:
- Stage 1: Tighten the bolt to 30 ft. lbs. (40 Nm).
- Stage 2: Tighten the bolt an additional 90 degrees (1/4 turn).

6. Using the special tool, position the crankshaft so the number one cylinder is at top dead center (TDC).

7. Install the crankshaft sprocket, making sure the flange faces forward.

8. Install the timing chain guide as follows:
- Position the LH timing chain guide.
- Install and tighten the LH bolts.
- Position the RH timing chain guide.
- Install and tighten the RH bolts.

9. Rotate the RH camshaft sprocket until the timing mark is approximately at the 11 o'clock position.

10. Rotate the LH camshaft sprocket until the timing mark is approximately at the 12 o'clock position.

11. Position the LH (inner) timing chain on the crankshaft sprocket, aligning the copper (marked) link with the timing mark on the sprocket.

12. Install the LH timing chain on the sprocket, aligning the copper (marked) link with the timing marks on the sprocket.

➡ **The LH timing chain tensioner arm has a bump near the dowel hole for identification. Position the LH timing chain tensioner arm on the dowel pin and install the LH timing chain tensioner.**

13. Remove the retaining clip from the LH timing chain tensioner.

14. Position the RH (outer) timing chain on the crankshaft sprocket, aligning the copper (marked) link with the timing mark on the sprocket.

15. Install the RH timing chain on the camshaft sprocket, aligning the copper (marked) link with the timing marks on the sprocket.

16. Position the RH timing chain tensioner arm on the dowel pin and install the RH timing chain tensioner.

17. Remove the retaining clip from the RH timing chain tensioner.

18. Make sure that the copper (marked) chain links are lined up with the dots on the crankshaft sprocket and the camshaft sprockets.

19. Rotate the camshaft until the lobe is in the up position.

20. Install the special tool between the valve spring coils to prevent valve stem seal damage.

➡ **Lubricate the camshaft roller followers using clean engine oil.**

21. Install the camshaft roller followers as using this procedure:
- Install the special tool.
- Compress the valve spring.
- Install the camshaft roller followers in their original locations.

22. Install the eight spark plugs.

23. Install the eight ignition coils and bolts.

24. Connect the eight ignition coil electrical connectors.

25. Install the crankshaft sensor ring on the crankshaft.

26. Install the engine front cover.

27. Reconnect negative battery cable, run engine to check for leaks and repair as necessary.

VALVE COVERS

REMOVAL & INSTALLATION

Right Side

See Figures 84 through 87.

1. Before servicing the vehicle, refer to the precautions in the beginning of this section.

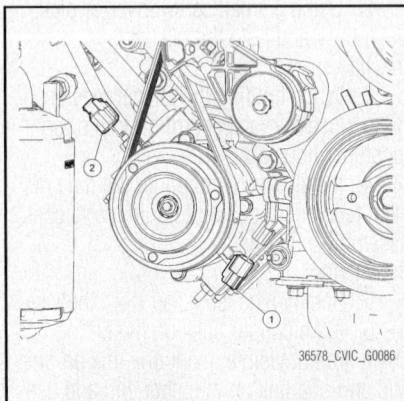

Fig. 84 Removing the CKP sensor (1) and A/C compressor electrical connectors (2)

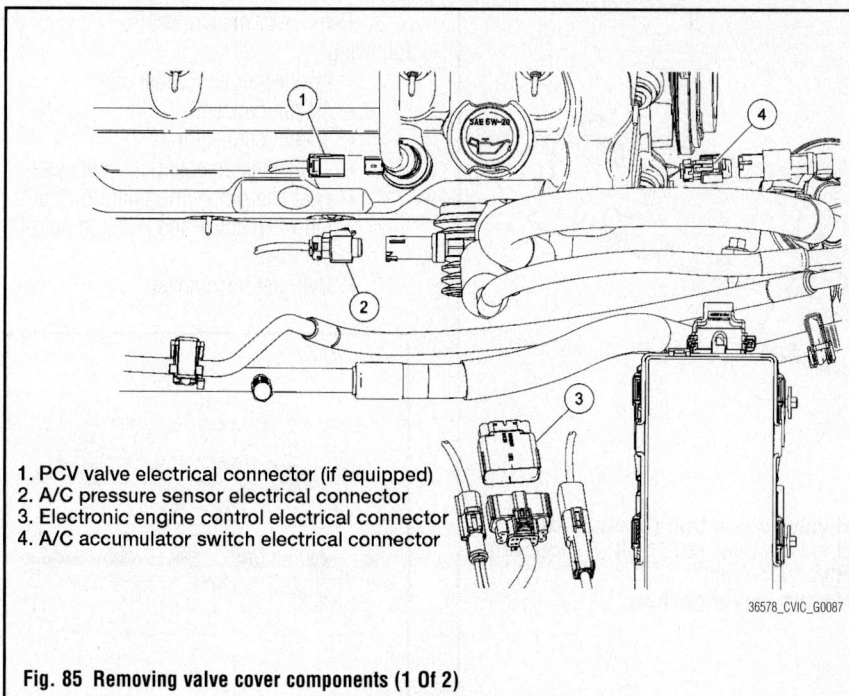

1. PCV valve electrical connector (if equipped)
2. A/C pressure sensor electrical connector
3. Electronic engine control electrical connector
4. A/C accumulator switch electrical connector

36578_CVIC_G0087

Fig. 85 Removing valve cover components (1 Of 2)

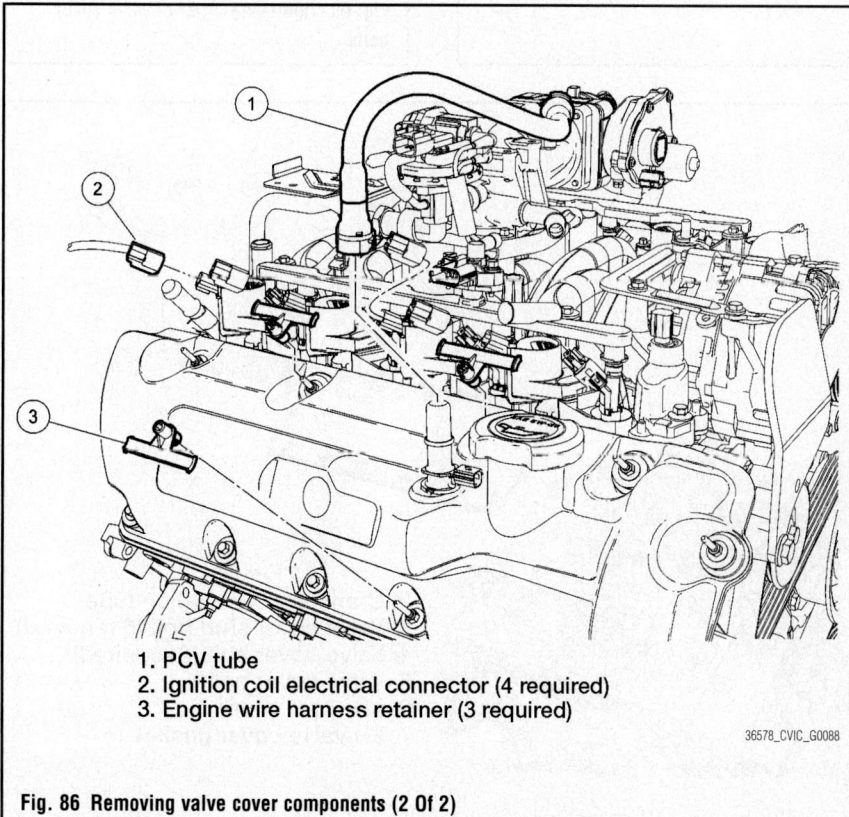

1. PCV tube
2. Ignition coil electrical connector (4 required)
3. Engine wire harness retainer (3 required)

36578_CVIC_G0088

Fig. 86 Removing valve cover components (2 Of 2)

2. Disconnect battery negative cable from battery and properly isolate to prevent accidental reconnection.
3. Remove or disconnect the following:
- Fuel line spring lock coupling
- LH engine mount
- Crankshaft Position (CKP) sensor electrical connector
- Power steering pressure (PSP) switch electrical connector
- A/C compressor electrical connector
- Engine wiring harness retainers
4. Lower the vehicle.
5. Continue removing:
- Power distribution center electrical connection cover
- Power distribution center electrical connection
- Ground wire
- Electrical connectors
- A/C high pressure switch electrical connector
- Evaporative emission (EVAP) canister purge valve hoses and the electrical connector
- Vacuum hose
- Nuts and EVAP canister purge valve
- Wiring harness and position aside
- Positive crankcase ventilation (PCV) hose
- Ignition coil electrical connectors

➡The valve cover harness retaining studs in retain the fuel charging wiring.

- Harness from valve cover and position out of the way
6. Lower the engine.

✳✳ WARNING

Do not use metal scrapers, wire brushes, power abrasive discs or other abrasive means to clean the sealing surface. These tools cause scratches and gouges that make leak paths. Use a plastic scraping tool to remove all traces of the gasket material. Remove the studs, the bolts and the valve cover.

- Clean the gasket surfaces with a plastic scraping tool and metal surface cleaner. If not secured within four minutes, the sealant must be removed and the sealing area cleaned with metal surface cleaner. Allow to dry until there is no sign of wetness, or four minutes, whichever is longer. Failure to follow this procedure can cause future oil leakage.

To install:
7. Apply sealant at the seam between the cylinder head and timing chain cover.
8. Install head cover and tighten bolts to 89 inch lbs. (10 Nm) in sequence shown.
9. Raise engine
10. Install or connect the following:
- Harness and studs to valve cover
- Ignition coil electrical connectors
- Positive crankcase ventilation (PCV) hose
- Wiring harness
- Nuts and EVAP canister purge valve
- Vacuum hose
- Evaporative emission (EVAP) canister purge valve hoses and the electrical connector

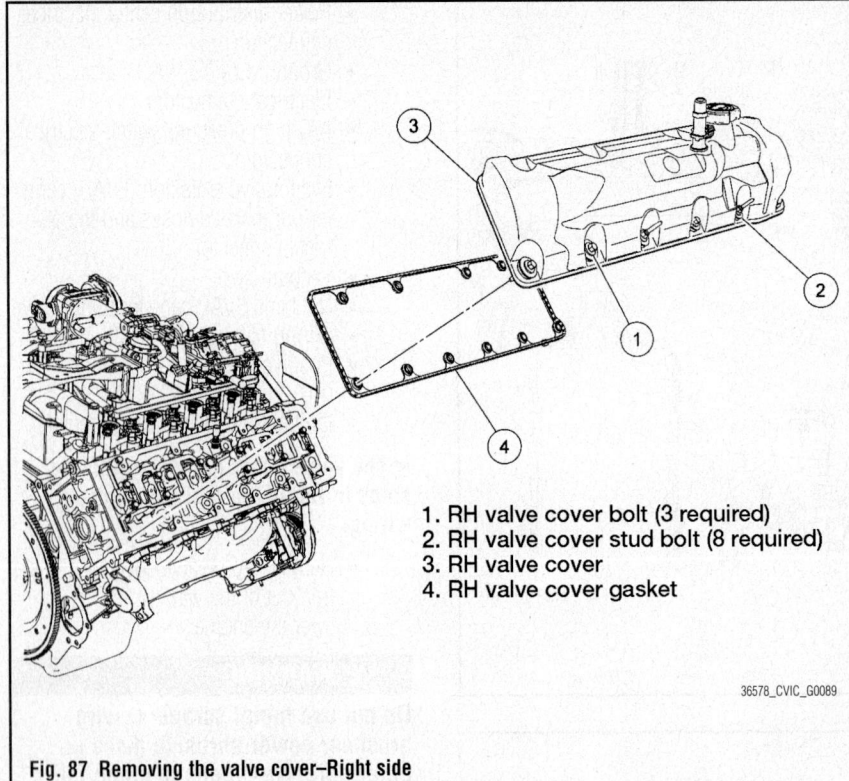

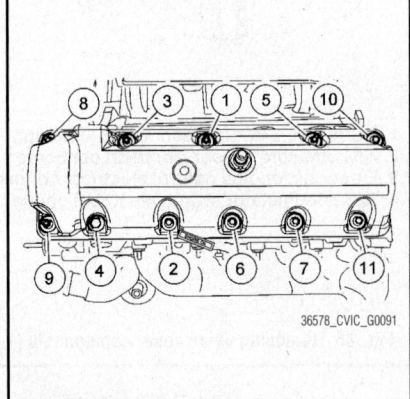

1. RH valve cover bolt (3 required)
2. RH valve cover stud bolt (8 required)
3. RH valve cover
4. RH valve cover gasket

36578_CVIC_G0089

Fig. 87 Removing the valve cover–Right side

Fig. 90 **Tightening order of valve cover bolts**

36578_CVIC_G0091

3. Remove or disconnect the following:
- Air cleaner and outlet pipe
- 42-pin connector
- 16-pin connector
- Transmission electrical connector
- Fuel charging wiring harness from the valve cover and position out of the way
- Cylinder head cover

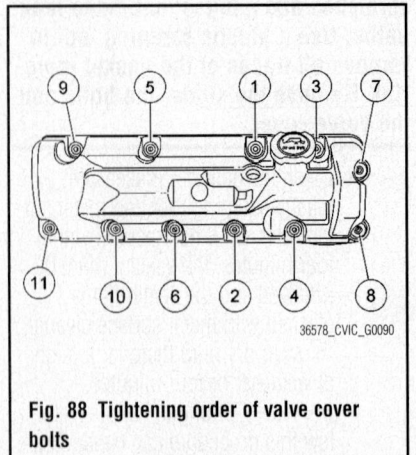

36578_CVIC_G0090

Fig. 88 Tightening order of valve cover bolts

- A/C high pressure switch electrical connector
- Ground wire
- Power distribution center electrical connection
11. Raise the vehicle and continue installing or connecting:
- Engine wiring harness retainers
- A/C compressor electrical connector
- LH engine mount
- Fuel line spring lock coupling
12. Lower vehicle and reconnect negative battery cable.

Left Side

See Figures 89 and 90.

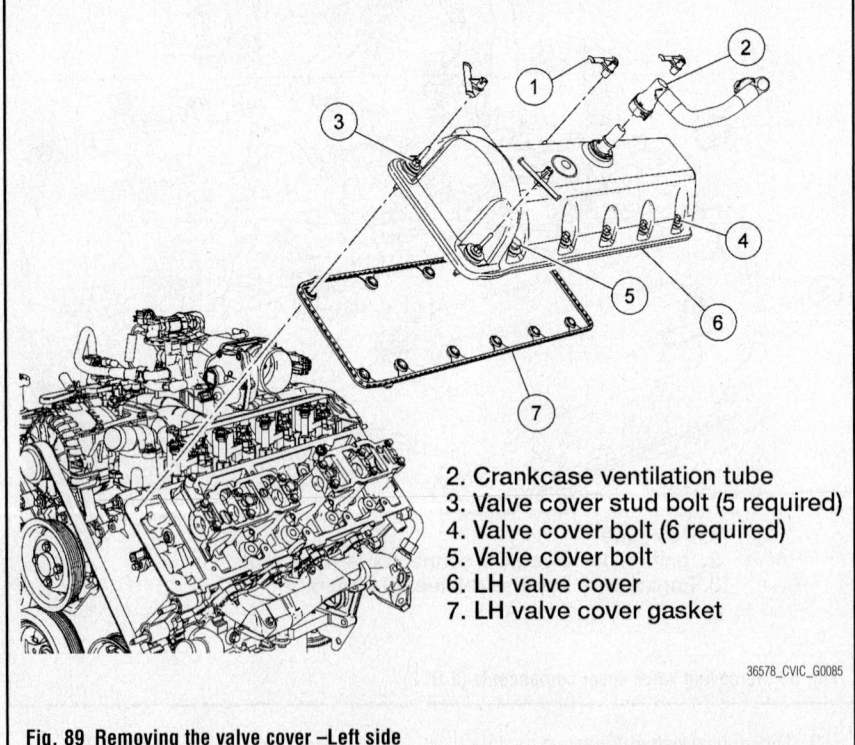

2. Crankcase ventilation tube
3. Valve cover stud bolt (5 required)
4. Valve cover bolt (6 required)
5. Valve cover bolt
6. LH valve cover
7. LH valve cover gasket

36578_CVIC_G0085

Fig. 89 Removing the valve cover –Left side

1. Before servicing the vehicle, refer to the precautions in the beginning of this section.

2. Disconnect battery negative cable from battery and properly isolate to prevent accidental reconnection.

✳✳ WARNING

Do not use metal scrapers, wire brushes, power abrasive discs or other abrasive means to clean the sealing surface. These tools cause

scratches and gouges that make leak paths. Use a plastic scraping tool to remove all traces of the gasket material. Remove the studs, the bolts and the valve cover.

- Clean the gasket surfaces with a plastic scraping tool and metal surface cleaner. If not secured within four minutes, the sealant must be removed and the sealing area cleaned with metal surface cleaner. Allow to dry until there is no sign

of wetness, or four minutes, whichever is longer. Failure to follow this procedure can cause future oil leakage.

To install:

4. Apply sealant at the seam between the cylinder head and timing chain cover.
5. Install or connect the following:
   - Cylinder head cover and tighten bolts to 89 inch lbs. (10 Nm) in sequence shown
   - Fuel charging wiring harness

- Transmission electrical connector
- 16-pin connector
- 42-pin connector
- Air cleaner and outlet pipe
- Negative battery cable

VALVE LASH

ADJUSTMENT

The 4.6L (VIN W and V) engines are equipped with hydraulic lash adjusters. Valve clearance is not adjustable.

ENGINE PERFORMANCE & EMISSION CONTROLS

ACCELERATOR PEDAL POSITION (APP) SENSOR

LOCATION
See Figure 91.

The Accelerator Pedal Position Sensor is located on top of the accelerator pedal assembly.

REMOVAL & INSTALLATION
See Figure 91.

1. Disconnect the battery ground cable.
2. Disconnect the accelerator pedal motor electrical connector.
3. Remove the two bolts and the accelerator pedal assembly.
4. To install, reverse the removal procedure.

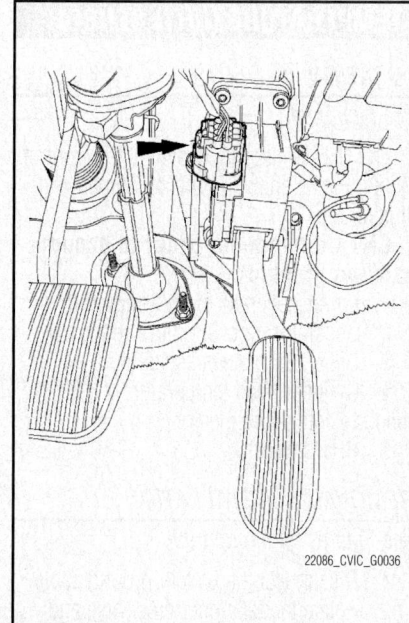

Fig. 91 Accelerator Pedal Position Sensor

CAMSHAFT POSITION (CMP) SENSOR

LOCATION
See Figure 92.

The Camshaft Position Sensors are located on the timing cover, just below each valve cover.

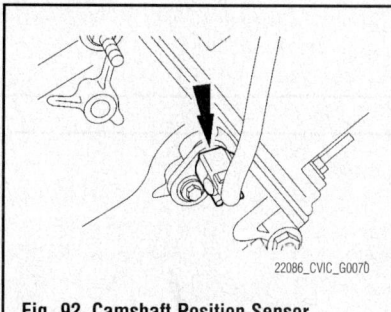

22086_CVIC_G0070

Fig. 92 Camshaft Position Sensor

REMOVAL & INSTALLATION
See Figure 93.

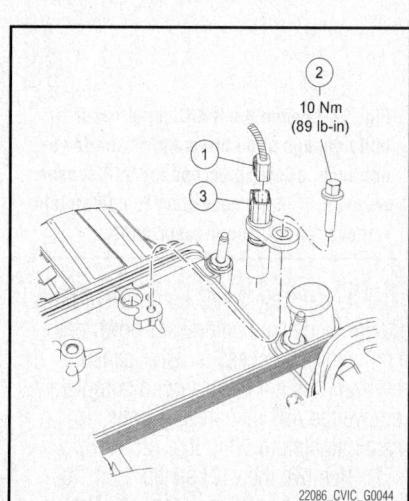

22086_CVIC_G0044

Fig. 93 Camshaft Position Sensor connector (1), bolt (2) and sensor (3)

1. Disconnect the battery ground cable.
2. Disconnect the camshaft position (CMP) sensor electrical connector.
3. Remove the CMP bolt.
4. Remove the CMP sensor.
5. To install, reverse the removal procedure, and tighten CMP bolt to 89 inch lbs. (10 Nm).

CRANKSHAFT POSITION (CKP) SENSOR

LOCATION
See Figure 94.

CKP sensor components (refer to accompanying illustration):
1. A/C compressor field coil electrical connector
2. A/C compressor bolt (3 required)
3. A/C compressor
4. Crankshaft position (CKP) sensor electrical connector
5. CKP sensor bolt
6. CKP sensor

REMOVAL & INSTALLATION
See Figures 95 through 97.

✸✸ WARNING

If equipped with fire suppression system, disable the system before performing repairs.

1. Disconnect the battery ground cable.
2. Rotate the drive belt tensioner clockwise, and remove the drive belt from the A/C compressor pulley.
3. Disconnect the A/C compressor field coil electrical connector.
4. Disconnect the crankshaft position sensor (CKP) sensor electrical connector.
5. Remove the nut and detach the wiring harness clips. To install, tighten to 80 inch lbs. (9 Nm)

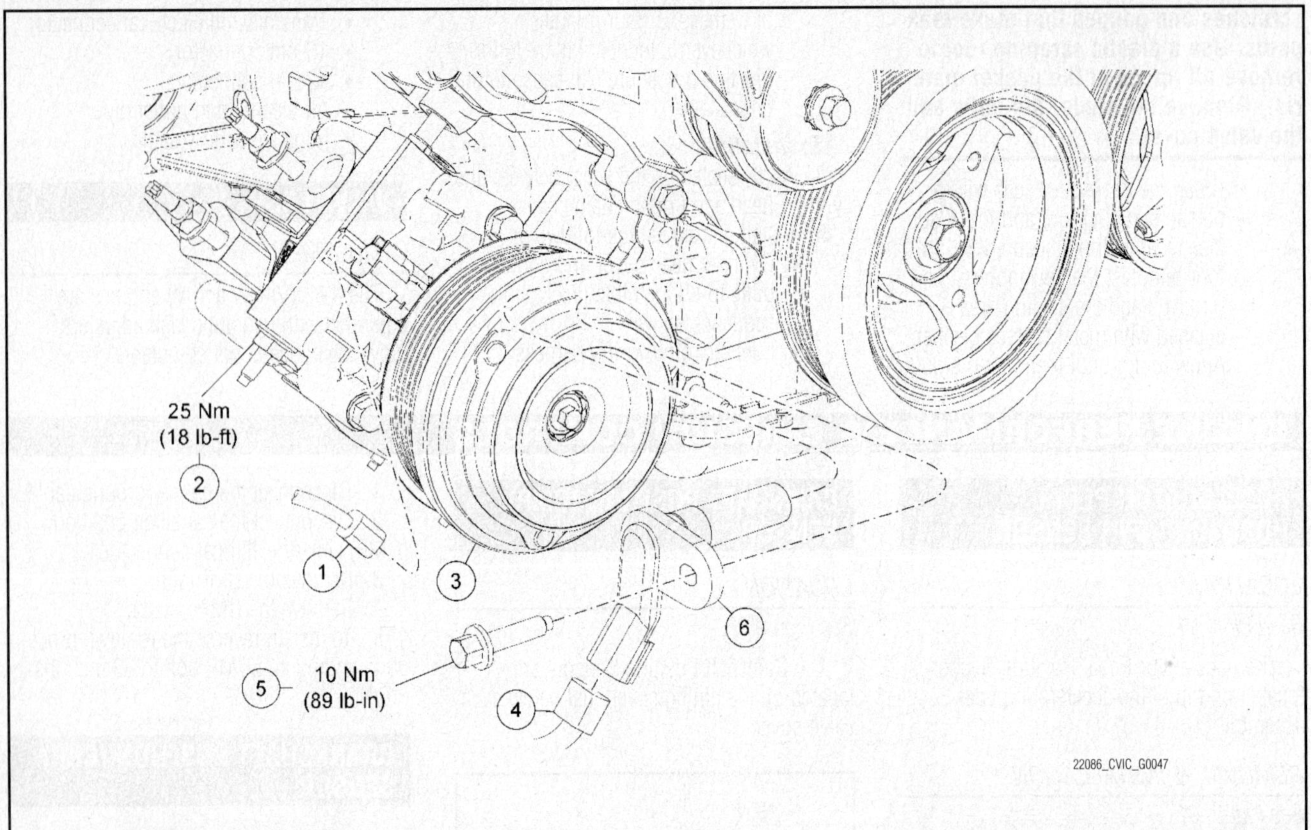

Fig. 94 Crankshaft Position (CKP) Sensor

2 25 Nm
(18 lb-ft)

1

3

6

5 10 Nm
(89 lb-in)

4

22086_CVIC_G0047

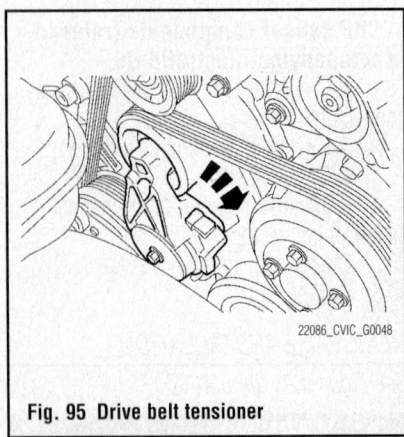

22086_CVIC_G0048

Fig. 95 Drive belt tensioner

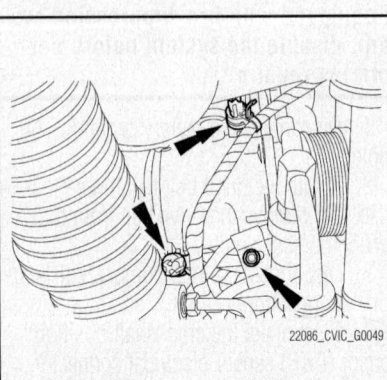

22086_CVIC_G0049

Fig. 96 Remove the nut and detach the wiring harness clips

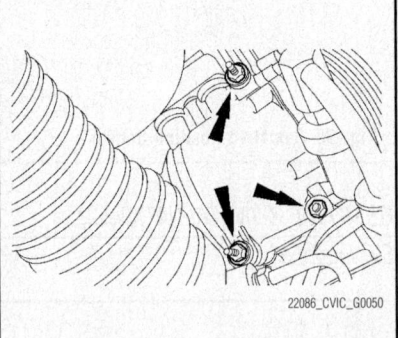

22086_CVIC_G0050

Fig. 97 Loosen the 3 A/C compressor bolts enough slide the compressor down one inch, allowing access for CKP sensor removal. It is not necessary to completely remove the A/C compressor bolts

6. Loosen the 3 A/C compressor bolts enough slide the compressor down one inch, allowing access for CKP sensor removal. It is not necessary to completely remove the A/C compressor bolts. To install, tighten to 18 ft. lbs. (25 Nm).

7. Remove the CKP sensor bolt. To install, tighten to 89 inch lbs. (10 Nm).

8. Remove the CKP sensor.

9. To install, reverse the removal procedure.

✳✳ WARNING

If equipped with fire suppression system, enable the system following assembly.

CYLINDER HEAD TEMPERATURE (CHT) SENSOR

LOCATION

See Figure 98.

The CHT Sensor is located at the front of the engine as shown in the accompanying illustration.

CHT Components (refer to accompanying graphic)

1. Lower generator bolt (2 required)
2. Generator bracket bolt (2 required)
3. Generator bracket assembly
4. Cylinder head temperature (CHT) sensor electrical connector
5. CHT sensor

REMOVAL & INSTALLATION

See Figures 98 through 99.

1. Disconnect the battery ground cable.

2. Rotate the tensioner clockwise and position the accessory belt aside.

3. Loosen the 2 lower generator bolts. To install, tighten to 18 ft. lbs. (25 Nm).

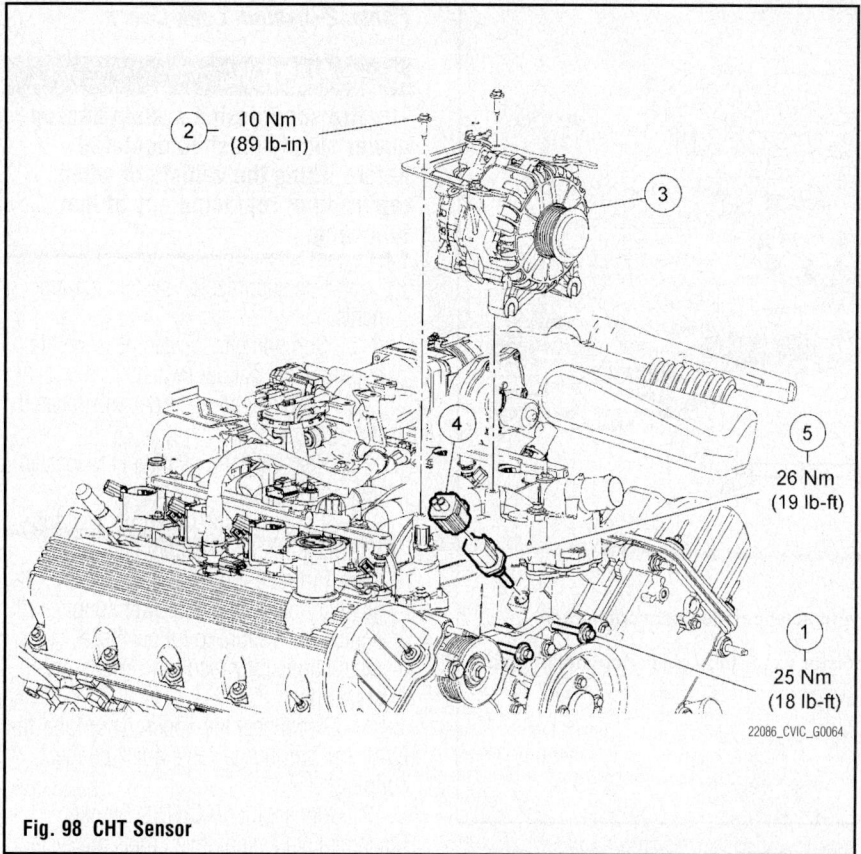

Fig. 98 CHT Sensor

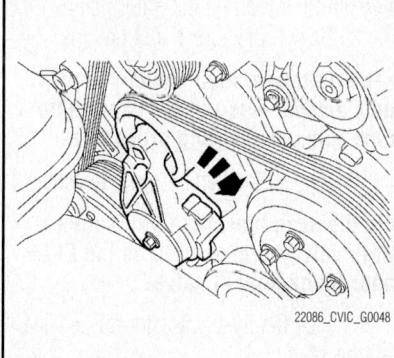

Fig. 99 Rotate the tensioner clockwise and position the accessory belt aside

4. Remove the 2 generator bracket bolts and position the generator and bracket aside. To install, tighten to 89 inch lbs. (10 Nm).

5. Disconnect the cylinder head temperature (CHT) sensor electrical connector.

6. Using a 19 mm (0.74 in) 12 point crows foot, remove and discard the CHT sensor. To install, tighten to19 ft. lbs. (26 Nm).

➡**The CHT sensor is not to be reused. Always install a new sensor.**

To install a new sensor, reverse the removal procedure.

ENGINE COOLANT TEMPERATURE (ECT) SENSOR

LOCATION
See Figure 100.

The ECT Sensor is located on top of the intake manifold, just below the throttle body.

REMOVAL & INSTALLATION
See Figure 100.

Remove the ECT Sensor as shown in illustration.

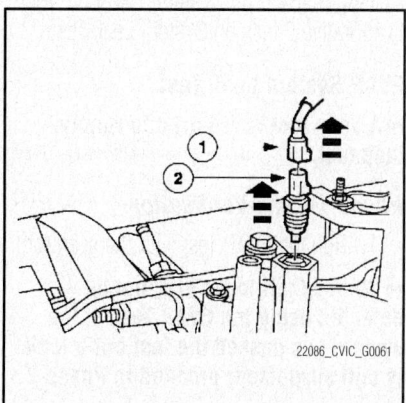

Fig. 100 ECT Sensor (2) and connector (1)

Components
1. Engine coolant temperature sensor electrical connector
2. ECT sensor

ENGINE OIL TEMPERATURE (EOT) SENSOR

LOCATION
See Figure 101.

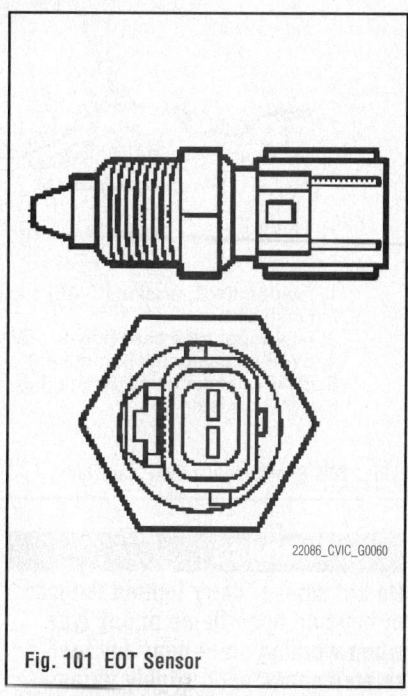

Fig. 101 EOT Sensor

EVAPORATIVE EMISSIONS (EVAP) CANISTER

LOCATION

The EVAP canister is located under the vehicle near the rear. Refer to the illustration under REMOVAL & INSTALLATION.

REMOVAL & INSTALLATION
See Figure 102.

❋❋ CAUTION

Observe all applicable safety precautions when working around fuel. Whenever servicing the fuel system, always work in a well ventilated area. Do not allow fuel spray or vapors to come in contact with a spark or open flame. Keep a dry chemical fire extinguisher near the work area. Always keep fuel in a container specifically designed for fuel storage; also, always properly seal fuel containers to avoid the possibility of fire or explosion.

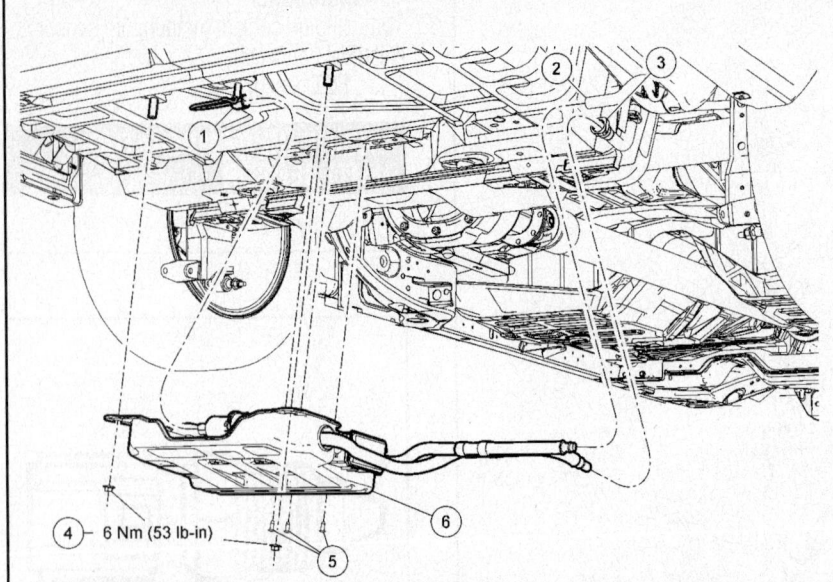

4 — 6 Nm (53 lb-in)

1. Evaporative Emission (EVAP) canister vent solenoid electrical connector
2. Fresh air hose
3. Fuel vapor tube assembly-to- EVAP canister vapor tube quick connect coupling
4. EVAP canister nuts (2 required)
5. EVAP canister rivets (3 required)
6. EVAP canister

36578_CVIC_G0092

Fig. 102 Removing the EVAP canister

✳✳ WARNING

Do not smoke, carry lighted tobacco or have an open flame of any type when working on or near any fuel-related component. Highly flammable mixtures are always present and may be ignited. Failure to follow these instructions may result in serious personal injury.

✳✳ WARNING

Do not carry personal electronic devices such as cell phones, pagers or audio equipment of any type when working on or near any fuel-related component. Highly flammable mixtures are always present and may be ignited. Failure to follow these instructions may result in serious personal injury.

✳✳ WARNING

Always disconnect the battery ground cable at the battery when working on an evaporative emission (EVAP) system or fuel-related component. Highly flammable mixtures are always present and may be ignited. Failure to follow these instructions may result in serious personal injury.

1. Disconnect the battery ground cable.
2. Disconnect the Evaporative Emission (EVAP) canister vent solenoid electrical connector.
3. Remove the 3 EVAP canister rivets. Drill out the center of the original rivets to remove and install new rivets upon installation.
4. Disconnect the fresh air hose from the dust separator.
5. Disconnect the fuel vapor tube assembly-to-EVAP canister vapor tube quick connect coupling.
6. Remove the 2 nuts and the EVAP canister.
7. To install, reverse the removal procedure. If equipped with a fire suppression system, repower the system. Carry out the Evaporative Emission System Leak Test.

EVAP System Leak Test

➡A scan tool is required to run the leak test.

Phase 1–Leak Verification

1. Run the EVAP Test with the scan tool.

➡Some small leaks may not be detected using the EVAP Test. If the system has passed the test but a leak is still suspected, proceed to Phase 2.

2. If the Evaporative Emission (EVAP) system failed the EVAP Test, proceed to Phase 2.

Phase 2–System Leak Check

✳✳ WARNING

The fire suppression system backup power supply must be depleted before lifting the vehicle or when repairing or replacing any of the following:

a. Fire suppression system components.
b. Components located near the fire suppression manual switch.
c. Fuel tank and components located near the fuel tank.
d. Rear axle and components located near the rear axle
e. To deplete the backup power supply, disconnect the battery and wait at least 1 minute. Be sure to disconnect all auxiliary batteries and power supplies (if equipped). Failure to follow these instructions may result in serious personal injury.

1. Disconnect the upper vapor tube-to-EVAP canister purge valve quick connect coupling.
2. Connect the VACUTEC Smoke Machine Fuel Evaporative Emission System Tester to the upper EVAP canister purge valve fitting. For additional information, refer to the manufacturer's instructions.

➡The battery ground cable was previously disconnected in the vapor tube quick connect coupling procedure.

3. Connect the battery ground cable.

➡In the scan tool, the EVAP canister purge valve is referred to as the EVAP vapor management valve.

4. Open the EVAP canister purge valve with the scan tool.
5. Close the canister vent solenoid with the scan tool.
6. Carefully turn the fuel tank filler cap counterclockwise until the thread disengages and position aside.

➡If smoke does not exit the fuel tank filler pipe neck area after the system is pressurized, open the canister vent solenoid with the scan tool to allow the air to purge. Once smoke is seen at the canister vent solenoid, close the canister vent solenoid with the scan tool.

7. Introduce smoke from the VACUTEC Smoke Machine Fuel Evaporative Emission System Tester into the EVAP system and verify that smoke is exiting the fuel tank filler pipe neck area.
8. Install the fuel tank filler cap once

smoke is observed exiting the fuel tank filler pipe neck area.

9. Continue to enter smoke into the system for 60 seconds to obtain pressure.

10. Press and release the remote start button in intervals of 15 seconds ON and 15 seconds OFF while checking for exiting smoke.

11. Use the halogen light provided with the VACUTEC Smoke Machine Fuel Evaporative Emission System Tester to follow the EVAP system path and look for smoke exiting at the source of the leak(s).

12. Repair any leaks as necessary.

⁕⁕ WARNING

If the vehicle is equipped with a fire suppression system, repower the system. Failure to follow these instructions may result in serious personal injury.

13. Repeat the leak test until the system passes. If equipped with a fire suppression system, repower the system.

EXHAUST GAS RECIRCULATION (EGR) VALVE

LOCATION

See Figure 103.

Components (refer to accompanying illustration):

1. Intake manifold shield retaining bolt (2 required)
2. Intake manifold shield
3. Exhaust gas recirculation system module electrical connector
4. EGR system module
5. EGR system module gasket
6. EGR vacuum connector
7. EGR system module retaining bolt (2 required)
8. EGR tube fitting
9. EGR tube

REMOVAL & INSTALLATION

See Figures 103 through 104.

1. Disconnect the exhaust gas recirculation (EGR) system module electrical connector and vacuum connector.

2. Remove the 2 bolts and the intake manifold shield. To install, tighten to 9 ft. lbs. (12 Nm).

3. Disconnect the EGR tube fitting from the EGR system module. To install, tighten to 30 ft. lbs. (40 Nm).

4. Remove the 2 bolts and the EGR system module.

5. To install, tighten to 18 ft. lbs. (25 Nm).

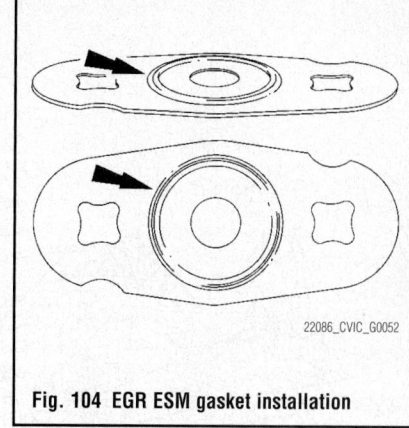

Fig. 104 EGR ESM gasket installation

6. Remove the EGR system module gasket and discard.

⁕⁕ CAUTION

Do not use metal scrapers, wire brushes, power abrasive discs or other abrasive means to clean the sealing surfaces. These tools cause scratches and gouges that make leak paths. Use a plastic scraping tool to remove all traces of the EGR system module gasket. If there is no residual gasket material present, metal surface cleaner may be used to clean and prepare the surfaces for assembly.

7. Clean the mating surfaces of any residual gasket material.

8. To install, reverse the removal procedure.

9. Install a new EGR system module gasket with the side that has the raised circle facing the intake manifold.

FUEL RAIL PRESSURE AND TEMPERATURE (FRPT) SENSOR

LOCATION

See Figures 105 and 106.

The FRPT Sensor is located on the fuel rail, on the passenger's side of the engine.

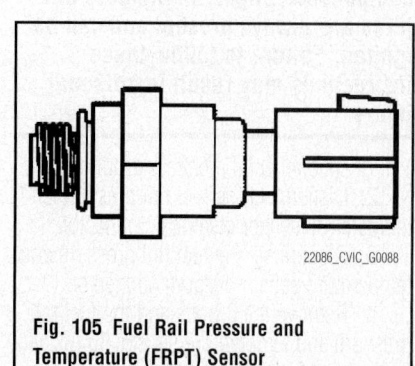

Fig. 105 Fuel Rail Pressure and Temperature (FRPT) Sensor

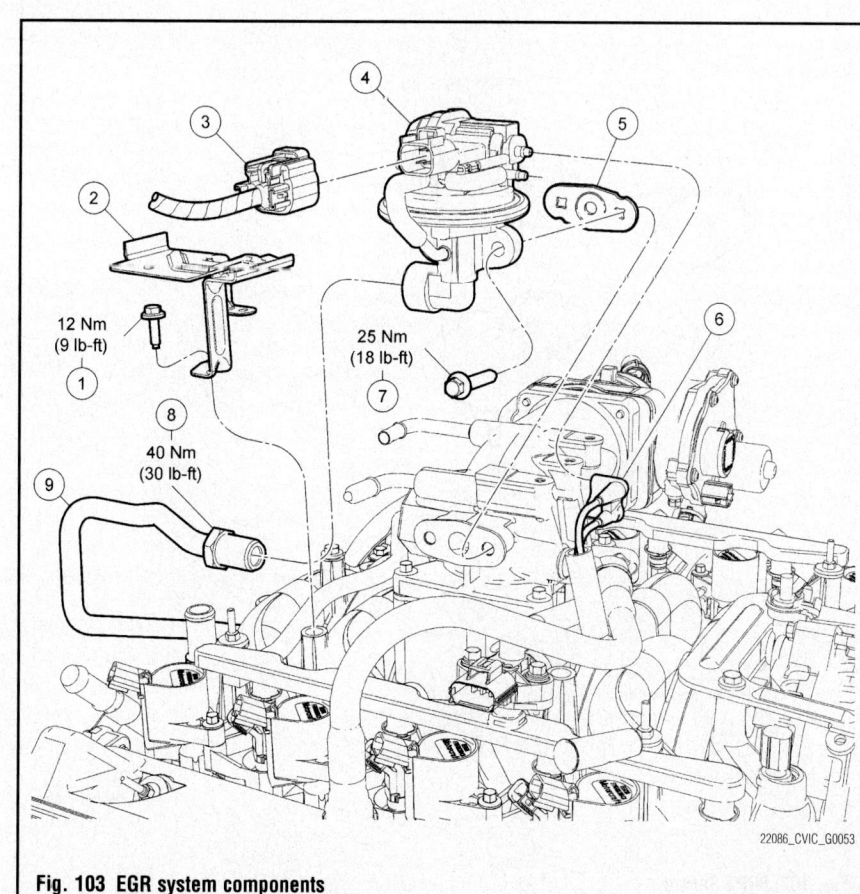

Fig. 103 EGR system components

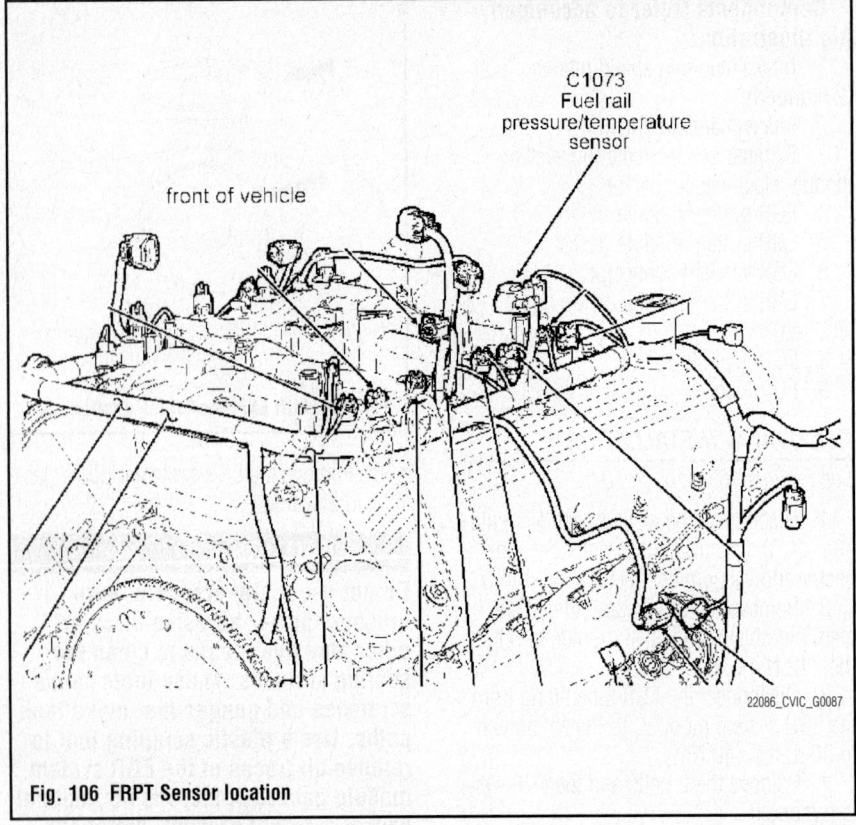

Fig. 106 FRPT Sensor location

REMOVAL & INSTALLATION

See Figure 107.

✳✳ WARNING

Do not smoke or carry lighted tobacco or open flame of any type when working on or near any fuel-related components. Highly flammable mixtures are always present and can be ignited. Failure to follow these instructions may result in personal injury.

✳✳ WARNING

Do not carry personal electronic devices such as cell phones, pagers, or audio equipment of any type when working on or near any fuel-related components. Highly flammable mixtures are always present and can be ignited. Failure to follow these instructions may result in personal injury.

1. Disconnect the battery ground cable.
2. Disconnect the fuel rail pressure and temperature sensor electrical connector.
3. Disconnect the fuel rail pressure and temperature sensor vacuum connector.
4. Remove the 2 bolts and the fuel rail pressure and temperature sensor. To install, tighten to 44 inch lbs. (5 Nm).

5. Remove and discard the O-ring seal. Install a new O-ring seal and lubricate it with clean engine oil.
6. To install, reverse the removal procedure.

Components (refer to accompanying illustration):
1. Fuel rail pressure and temperature sensor electrical connector
2. Fuel rail pressure and temperature sensor vacuum connector
3. Fuel rail pressure and temperature sensor bolts (2 required)
4. Fuel rail pressure and temperature sensor
5. Fuel rail pressure and temperature sensor O-ring

HEATED OXYGEN (HO2S) SENSOR

LOCATION

See Figure 108.

Components (refer to accompanying illustration):
1. L/H heated oxygen sensor connector
2. L/H HO2S

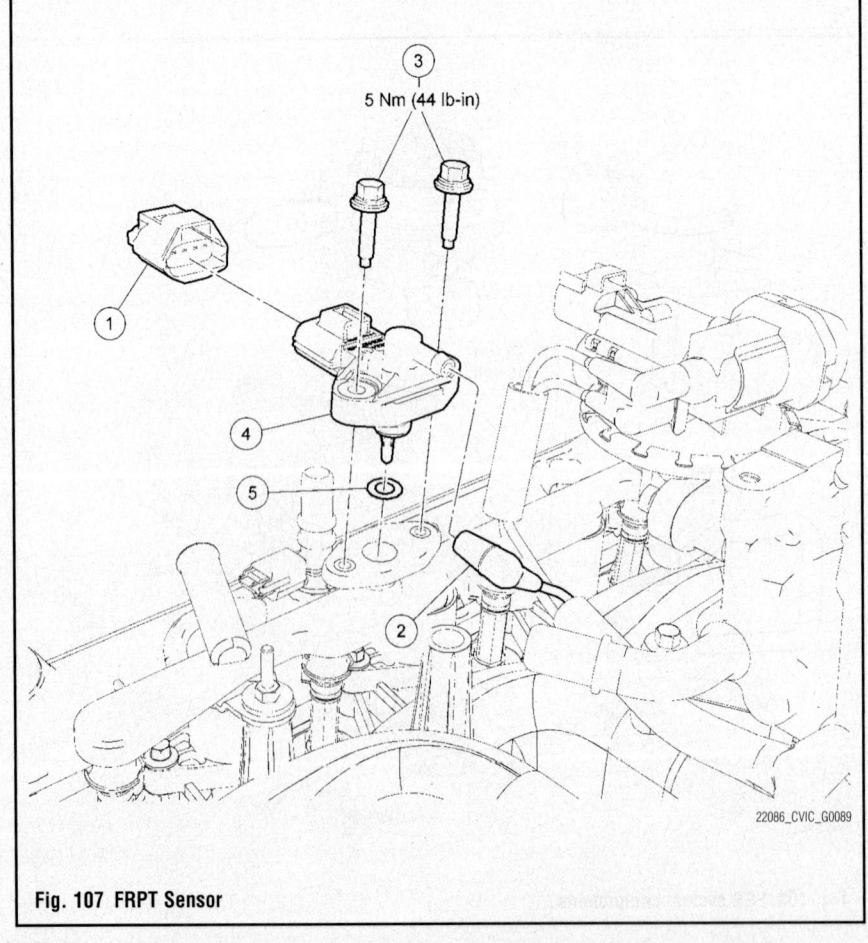

Fig. 107 FRPT Sensor

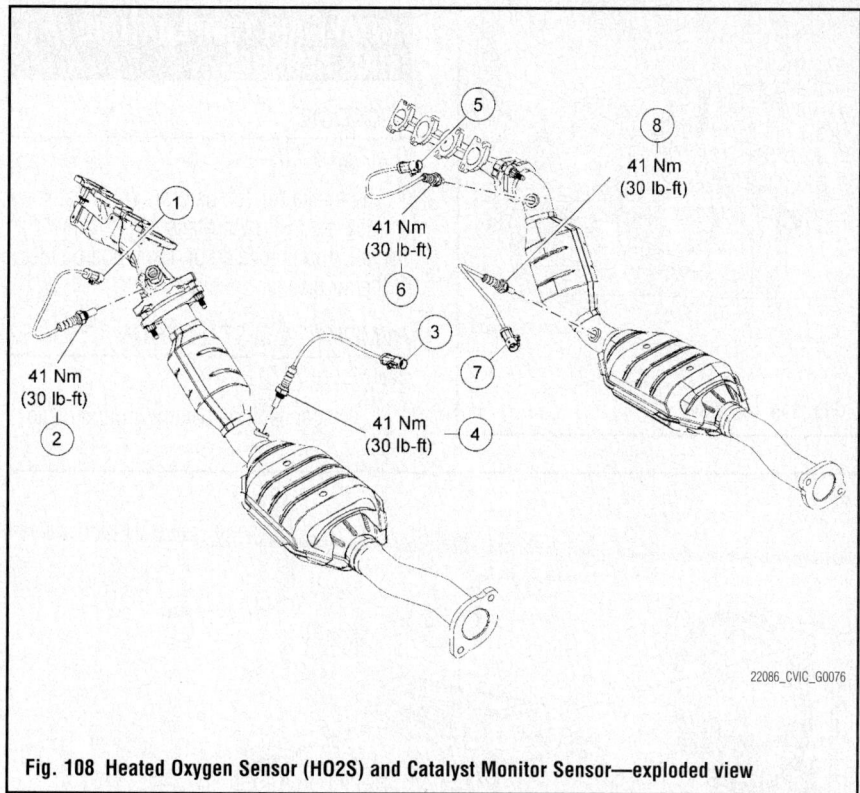

Fig. 108 Heated Oxygen Sensor (HO2S) and Catalyst Monitor Sensor—exploded view

3. L/H catalyst monitor sensor electrical connector
4. L/H catalyst monitor sensor
5. R/H heated oxygen sensor connector
6. R/H HO2S
7. R/H catalyst monitor sensor electrical connector
8. R/H catalyst monitor sensor

REMOVAL & INSTALLATION

See Figures 108, 109 through 113.

✻✻ WARNING

If equipped with fire suppression system, disable the system before performing repairs.

Heated Oxygen Sensor

1. Disconnect the battery ground cable.
2. Disconnect the right side heated oxygen sensor (HO2S) electrical connector.
3. Disconnect the left side HO2S electrical connector.
4. Remove the RH or LH HO2S as necessary. To install, tighten to 30 ft. lbs. (41 Nm).
5. To install, reverse the removal procedure. Apply a light coat of ant-seize lubricant to the threads of the HO2S.

✻✻ WARNING

If equipped with fire suppression system, enable the system following assembly.

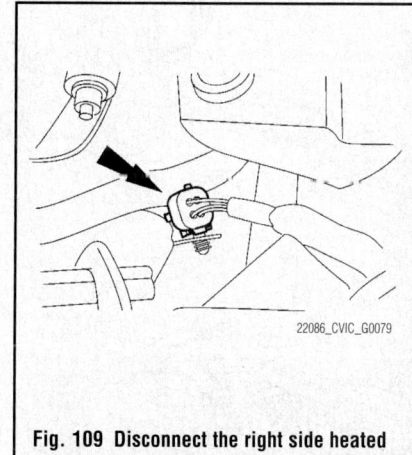

Fig. 109 Disconnect the right side heated oxygen sensor (HO2S) electrical connector

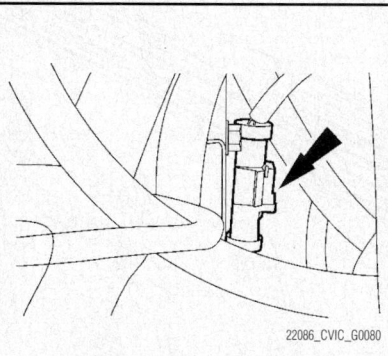

Fig. 110 Disconnect the left side HO2S electrical connector

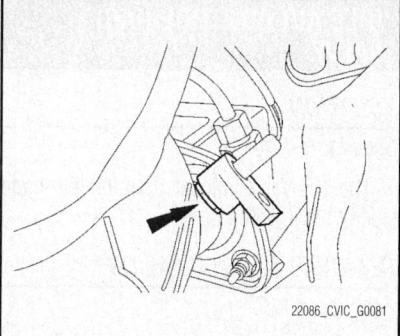

Fig. 111 Remove the RH or LH HO2S as necessary

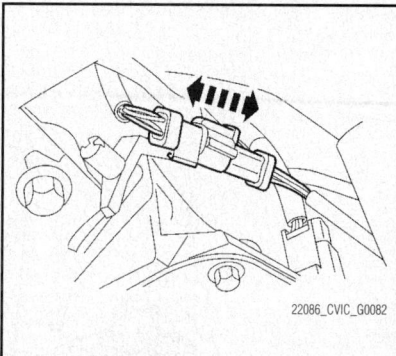

Fig. 112 Disconnect the catalyst monitor electrical connector

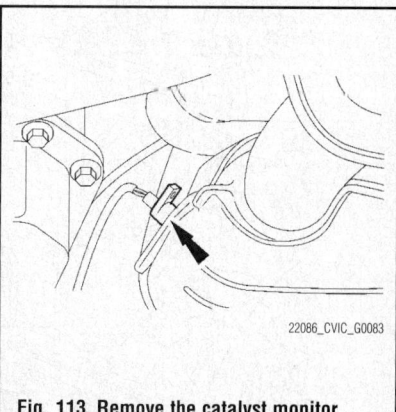

Fig. 113 Remove the catalyst monitor

Heated Oxygen Sensor

6. Disconnect the battery ground cable.
7. Disconnect the catalyst monitor electrical connector.
8. Remove the catalyst monitor. To install, tighten to 30 ft. lbs. (41 Nm).
9. To install, reverse the removal procedure. Apply a light coat of ant-seize lubricant to the threads of the HO2S.

✻✻ WARNING

If equipped with fire suppression system, enable the system following assembly.

IDLE AIR CONTROL (IAC) VALVE

LOCATION

See Figure 114.

The IAC Valve is located on the left–hand side of the Throttle Body.

REMOVAL & INSTALLATION

See Figure 115.

The IAC Valve is part of the Throttle Body, and the entire assembly must be removed for access.

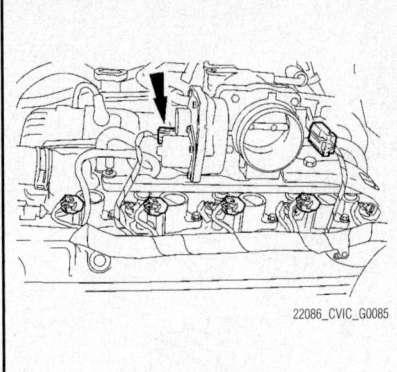

22086_CVIC_G0085

Fig. 114 IAC Valve

INTAKE AIR TEMPERATURE (IAT) SENSOR

LOCATION

See Figure 116.

The Intake Air Temperature (IAT) Sensor is integrated with the Mass Air Flow (MAF) Sensor, and is located on the inboard side of the air cleaner housing.

REMOVAL & INSTALLATION

See Figure 117.

1. Disconnect the battery ground cable.

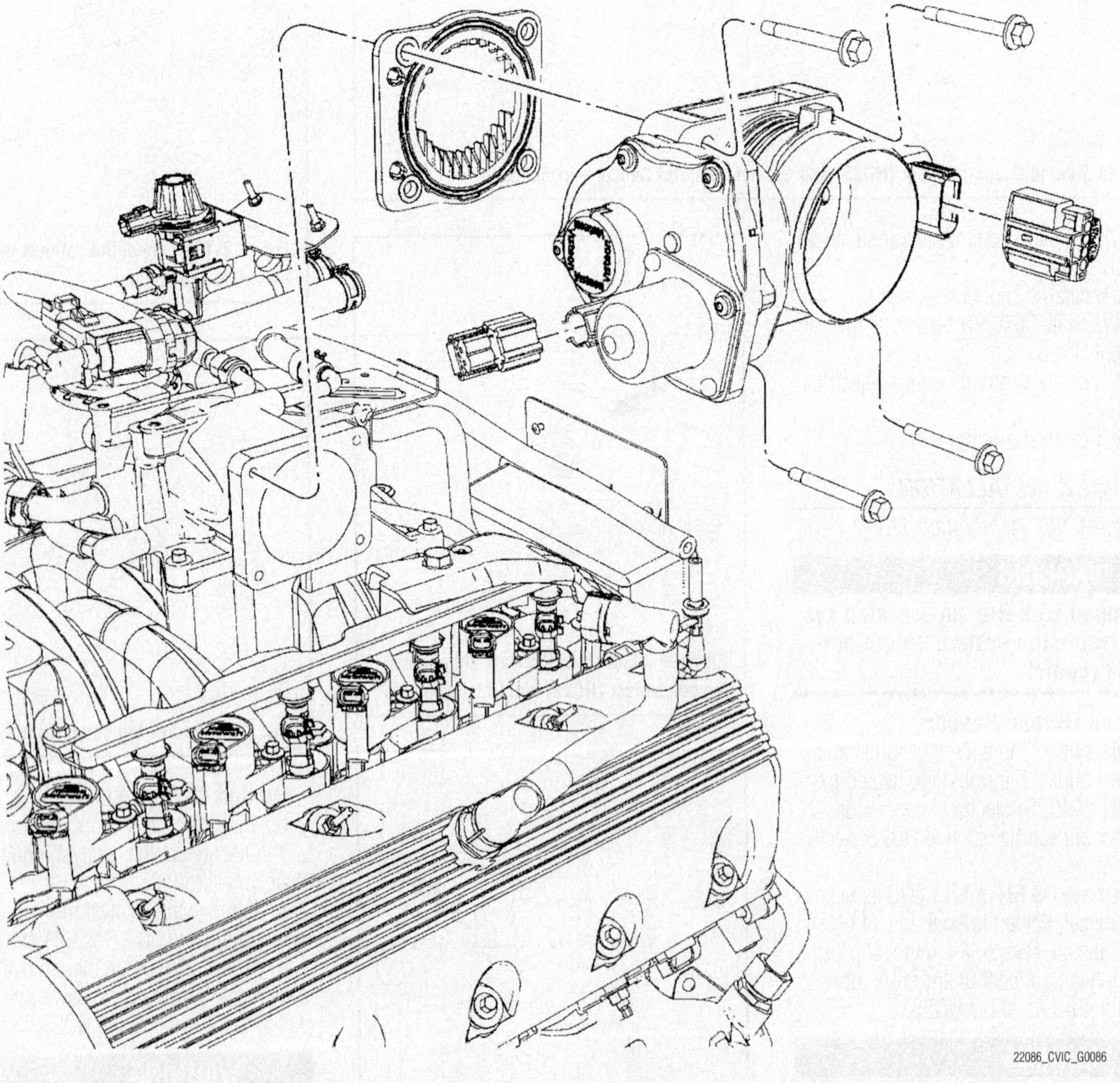

Fig. 115 Exploded view of the throttle body

22086_CVIC_G0086

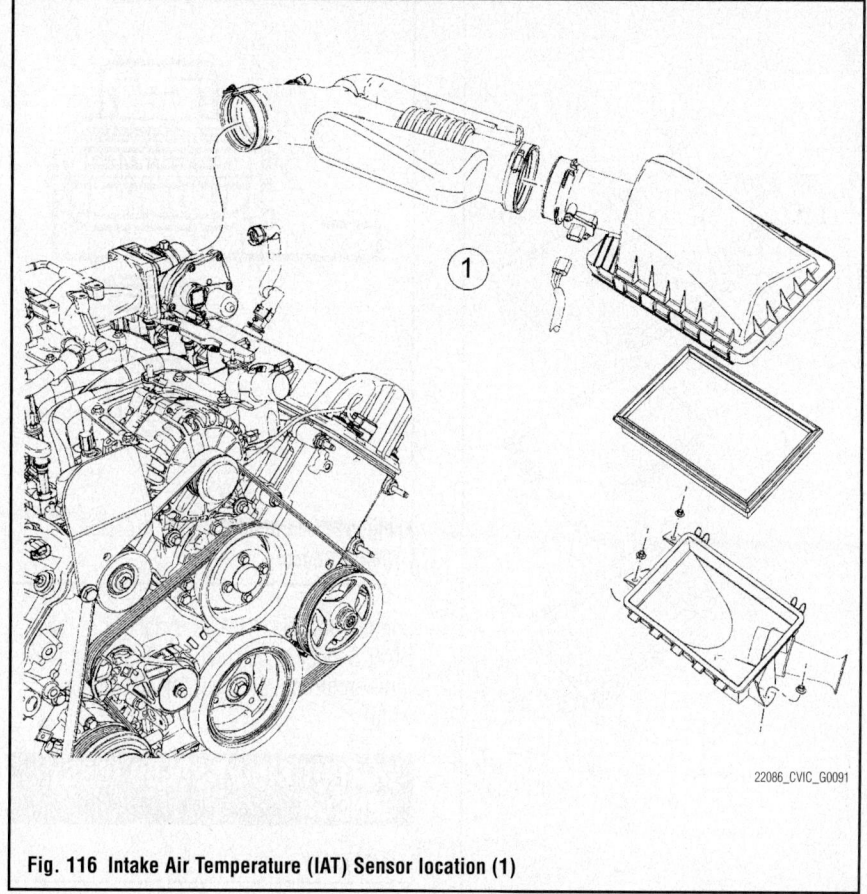

Fig. 116 Intake Air Temperature (IAT) Sensor location (1)

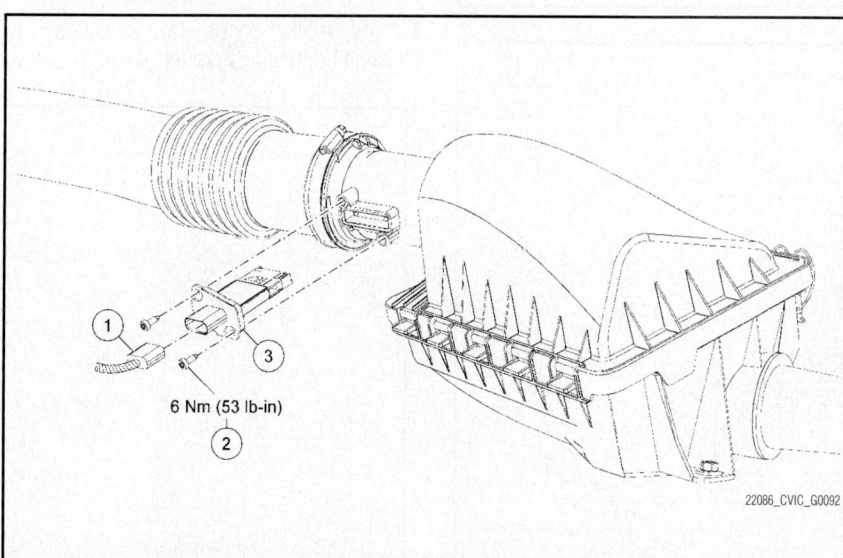

6 Nm (53 lb-in)

Fig. 117 View of the IAT/MAF connector (1), retaining screws (2) and sensor (3)

2. Disconnect the intake air temperature/mass air flow (IAT/MAF) sensor electrical connector.

3. Remove the IAT/MAF sensor retaining screws. To install, tighten to 53 inch lbs. (6 Nm).

4. Remove the IAT/MAF sensor.

5. To install, reverse the removal procedure.

KNOCK SENSOR (KS)

LOCATION

See Figure 118.

The Knock Sensors are located in the top of the engine block, under the intake manifold.

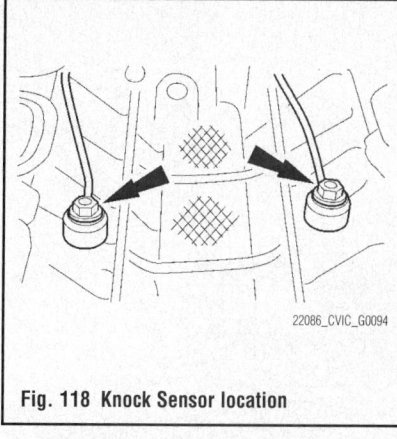

Fig. 118 Knock Sensor location

REMOVAL & INSTALLATION

See Figure 118.

❋❋ WARNING

Vehicle fuel systems are pressurized even when the engine is not running. To avoid fire or personal injury, disable the fuel delivery system and relieve fuel system pressure before removing any fuel system component. Refer to the fuel system information at the beginning of pinpoint HC. Failure to follow these instructions may result in personal injury.

For access to the Knock Sensors, refer to Engine Mechanical Components–Intake Manifold–Removal and Installation.

1. Remove the 2 Knock Sensor bolts, and remove the Knock Sensors.

2. To install, tighten the Knock Sensor bolts to 18 ft. lbs. (25 Nm).

MASS AIR FLOW (MAF) SENSOR

LOCATION

See Figure 119.

The Mass Air Flow (MAF) Sensor, and is located on the inboard side of the air cleaner housing.

REMOVAL & INSTALLATION

See Figure 120.

1. Disconnect the battery ground cable.

2. Disconnect the mass air flow (MAF) sensor electrical connector.

3. Remove the MAF sensor retaining screws. To install, tighten to 53 inch lbs. (6 Nm).

4. Remove the MAF sensor.

5. To install, reverse the removal procedure.

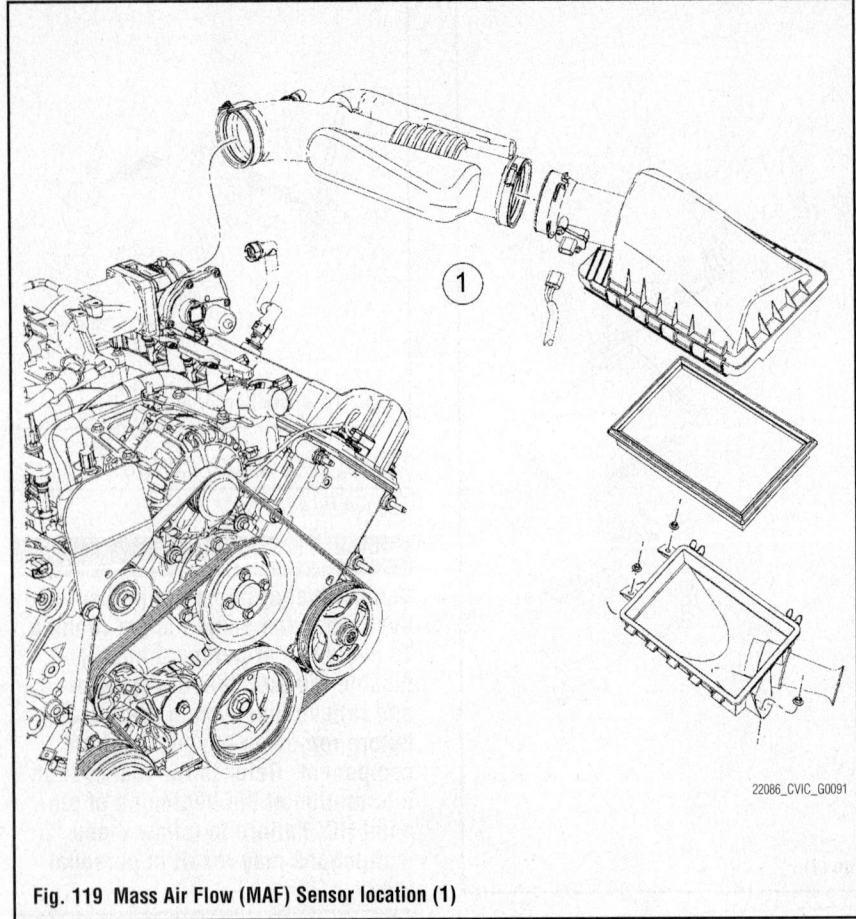

Fig. 119 Mass Air Flow (MAF) Sensor location (1)

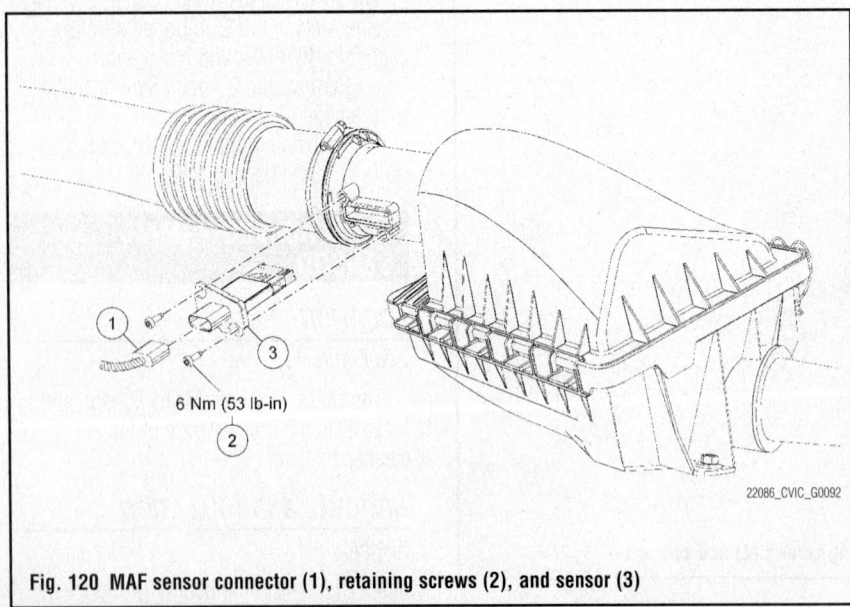

6 Nm (53 lb-in)

Fig. 120 MAF sensor connector (1), retaining screws (2), and sensor (3)

MANIFOLD ABSOLUTE PRESSURE (MAP) SENSOR

OPERATION

See Figure 121.

The Manifold Absolute Pressure (MAP) Sensor is a piezoelectric (pressure–sensitive) electronic device that monitors the intake manifold vacuum and atmospheric pressure. The MAP Sensor operates within a 5 volt DC reference range, and provides a linear input signal to the Powertrain Control Module (PCM) that is based upon a comparison of air density and intake manifold vacuum under measured operating

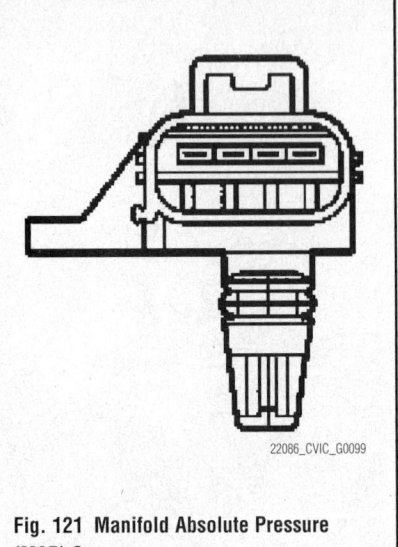

Fig. 121 Manifold Absolute Pressure (MAP) Sensor

conditions. The PCM uses data from the MAP Sensor to calculate air-fuel mixture, ignition timing, and fuel injector pulse width.

OUTPUT SHAFT SPEED (OSS) SENSOR

LOCATION

See Figure 122.

Output Shaft Speed (OSS) Sensor is located on the transmission.

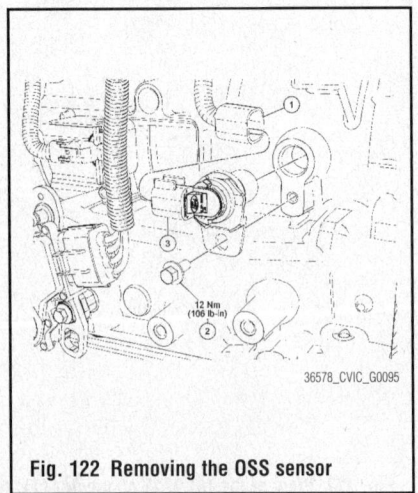

Fig. 122 Removing the OSS sensor

REMOVAL & INSTALLATION

See Figure 122.

1. Raise and support the vehicle.
2. Disconnect the OSS sensor connector.
3. Remove the OSS sensor bolt and connector.
4. To install, reverse removal procedure.

POSITIVE CRANKCASE VENTILATION (PCV) VALVE

LOCATION

The PCV valve is located on the right valve cover.

OPERATION

The PCV system consists of the breather tube and the PCV valve. The breather tube connects the crankcase to a contained fresh air source such as the air cleaner. Air passes into this tube and into the engine after being filtered through a spark arrestor screen in order to prevent a the possibility of an explosion within the engine in the case of a backfire.

REMOVAL & INSTALLATION

The PCV valve is integrated with the valve cover.

POWERTRAIN CONTROL MODULE (PCM)

LOCATION

See Figure 123.

The Powertrain Control Module (PCM) is located in the engine compartment, driver side, and is fender- mounted.

REMOVAL & INSTALLATION

See Figures 124 and 125.

➡ **Any Powertrain Control module (PCM) replacement will require that ALL customer**

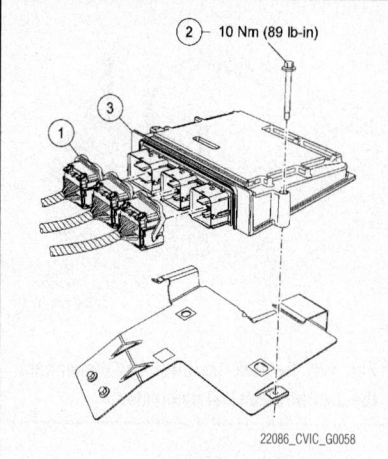

22086_CVIC_G0058

Fig. 124 Powertrain Control Module (PCM) connectors (1), retaining bolt (2) and PCM (3)

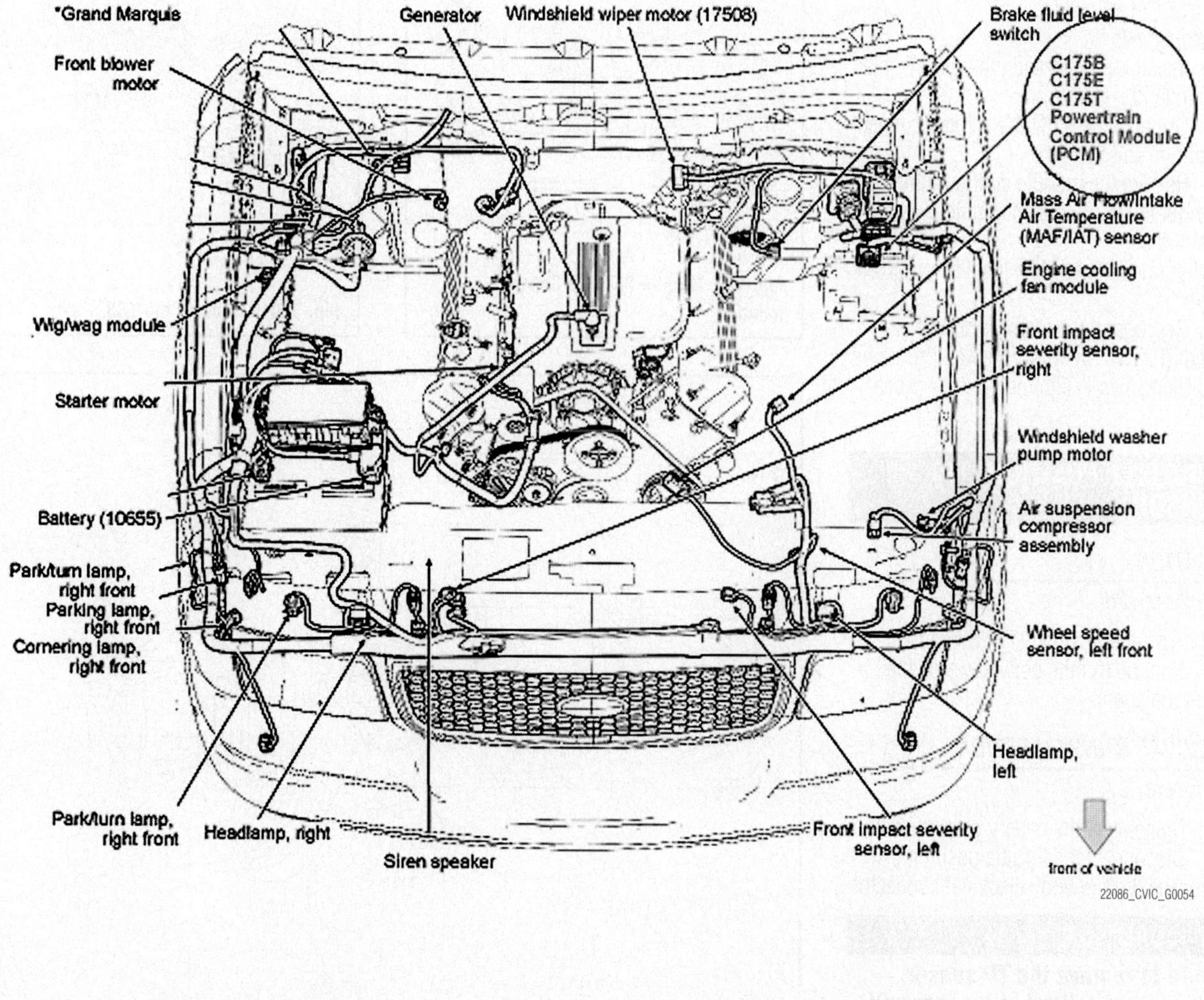

*Grand Marquis

Front blower motor

Generator

Windshield wiper motor (17508)

Brake fluid level switch

C175B
C175E
C175T
Powertrain
Control Module
(PCM)

Mass Air Flow/Intake Air Temperature (MAF/IAT) sensor

Engine cooling fan module

Wig/wag module

Front impact severity sensor, right

Starter motor

Windshield washer pump motor

Battery (10655)

Air suspension compressor assembly

Park/turn lamp, right front
Parking lamp, right front
Cornering lamp, right front

Wheel speed sensor, left front

Headlamp, left

Park/turn lamp, right front

Headlamp, right

Front impact severity sensor, left

Siren speaker

front of vehicle

22086_CVIC_G0054

Fig. 123 Powertrain Control Module location

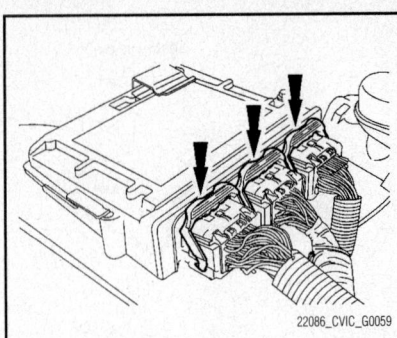

Fig. 125 Release the clips and disconnect the 3 PCM electrical connectors

keys are available to be programmed at the time of installation. PCM replacement DOES NOT require new keys. Retrieve the module configuration. Carry out the module configuration retrieval steps of the Programmable Module Installation procedure.

1. Release the clips and disconnect the 3 PCM electrical connectors.

To install:

2. Install the PCM and the bolts. Tighten to 89 inch lbs. (10 Nm).
3. Connect the 3 PCM electrical connectors and install the clips.
4. Restore the module configuration. Carry out the module configuration restore steps of the Programmable Module Installation procedure.
5. Reprogram the Passive Anti-Theft System (PATS). Carry out the Key Programming Using Two Programmed Keys procedure.

THROTTLE POSITION (TP) SENSOR

LOCATION

See Figure 126.

The Throttle Position (TP) Sensor is located on the throttle body, towards the rear of the engine.

REMOVAL & INSTALLATION

See Figure 127.

1. Disconnect the battery ground cable.
2. Disconnect the throttle position (TP) sensor the throttle body electrical connector.

✱✱ CAUTION

Failure to remove the TP sensor screws in the following manner will result in damage to the screws.

3. First loosen the screws 1-2 full turns using a hand tool, and then use a suitable high-speed driver to complete the removal.
4. Remove and discard the 2 screws and the TP sensor.

✱✱ CAUTION

Do not reuse the TP sensor and screws. A new TP sensor and screws must be installed.

To install:

✱✱ CAUTION

Do not use a high-speed driver to install the new screws or damage to the TP sensor can occur.

➡When installing the new TP sensor, make sure that the radial locator tab on the TP sensor is aligned with the radial locator hole on the throttle body.

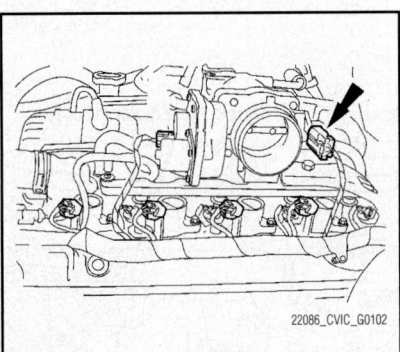

Fig. 126 Throttle Position Sensor location

5. Position the new TP sensor and install the 2 new screws. Tighten to 27 inch lbs. (3 Nm).
6. Connect the TP sensor electrical connector.

TURBINE SPEED SENSOR (TSS)

LOCATION

Turbine Speed Sensor (TSS) is located on the transmission. Refer to the illustration under REMOVAL & INSTALLATION.

REMOVAL & INSTALLATION

See Figure 128.

1. Raise and support the vehicle.
2. Disconnect the TSS sensor connector.
3. Remove the TSS sensor bolt and the sensor.
4. To install, reverse the removal procedure.

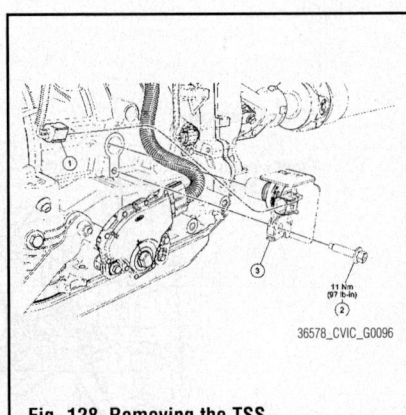

Fig. 128 Removing the TSS

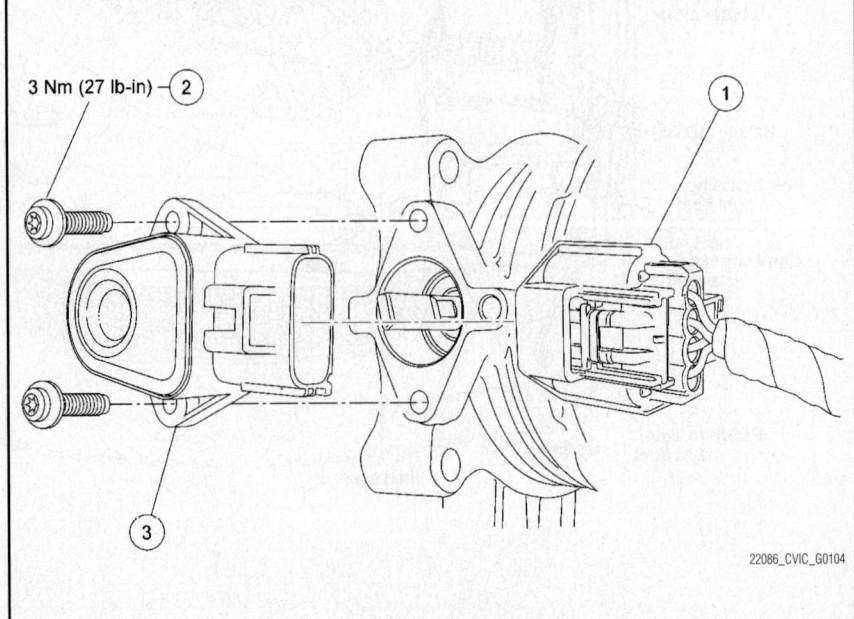

Fig. 127 Throttle Position (TP) sensor connector (1), retaining screws (2) and TP sensor (3)

VEHICLE SPEED SENSOR (VSS)

LOCATION

See Figures 129

REMOVAL & INSTALLATION

See Figures 130 and 131.

1. Position the vehicle on a hoist, and place the automatic transmission selector into the NEUTRAL position.
2. Disconnect the vehicle speed (VSS) sensor electrical connector.
3. Remove the VSS sensor bolt and the sensor. To install, tighten to 9 ft. lbs (12 Nm).
4. To install, reverse the removal procedure.

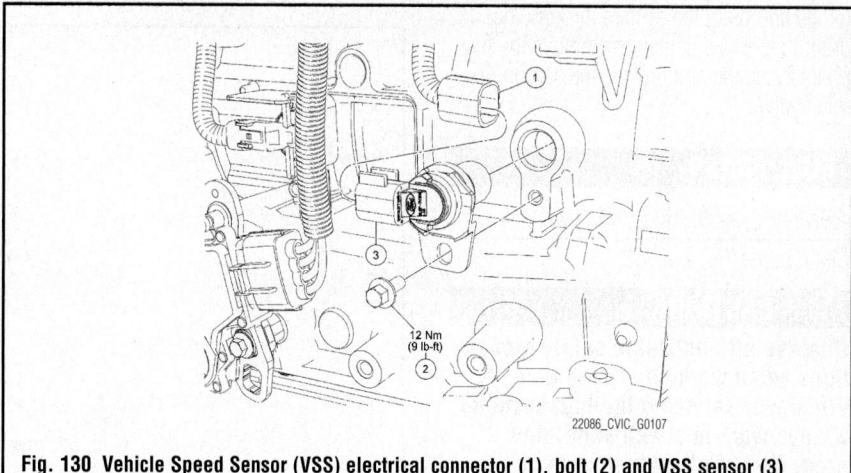

Fig. 130 Vehicle Speed Sensor (VSS) electrical connector (1), bolt (2) and VSS sensor (3)

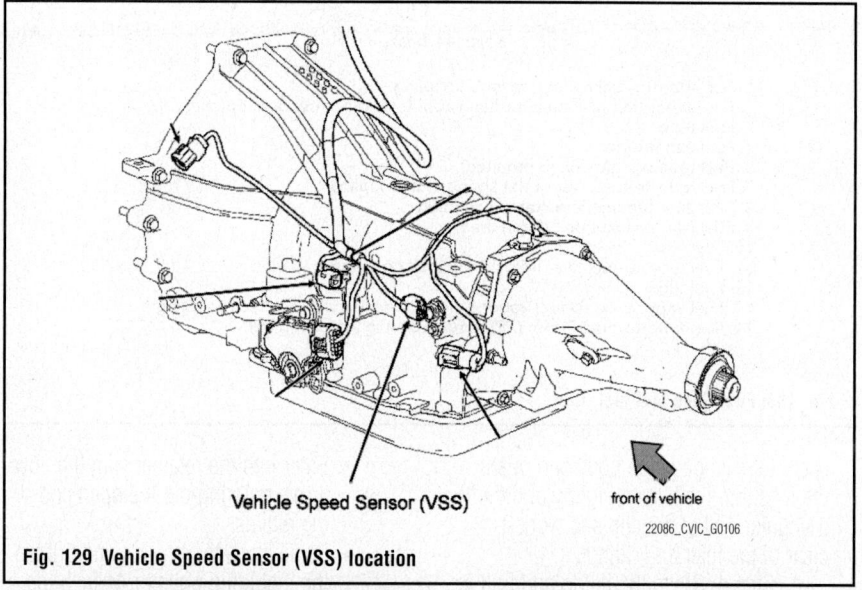

Vehicle Speed Sensor (VSS)

front of vehicle

22086_CVIC_G0106

Fig. 129 Vehicle Speed Sensor (VSS) location

22086_CVIC_G0108

Fig. 131 Remove the VSS sensor bolt and the sensor

FUEL

GASOLINE FUEL INJECTION SYSTEM

FUEL SYSTEM SERVICE PRECAUTIONS

Safety is the most important factor when performing not only fuel system maintenance but any type of maintenance. Failure to conduct maintenance and repairs in a safe manner may result in serious personal injury or death. Maintenance and testing of the vehicle's fuel system components can be accomplished safely and effectively by adhering to the following rules and guidelines.

• To avoid the possibility of fire and personal injury, always disconnect the negative battery cable unless the repair or test procedure requires that battery voltage be applied.

• Always relieve the fuel system pressure prior to disconnecting any fuel system component (injector, fuel rail, pressure regulator, etc.), fitting or fuel line connection. Exercise

extreme caution whenever relieving fuel system pressure to avoid exposing skin, face and eyes to fuel spray. Please be advised that fuel under pressure may penetrate the skin or any part of the body that it contacts.

• Always place a shop towel or cloth around the fitting or connection prior to loosening to absorb any excess fuel due to spillage. Ensure that all fuel spillage (should it occur) is quickly removed from engine surfaces. Ensure that all fuel soaked cloths or towels are deposited into a suitable waste container.

• Always keep a dry chemical (Class B) fire extinguisher near the work area.

• Do not allow fuel spray or fuel vapors to come into contact with a spark or open flame.

• Always use a back-up wrench when loosening and tightening fuel line connection fittings. This will prevent unnecessary stress and torsion to fuel line piping.

• Always replace worn fuel fitting O-rings with new. Do not substitute fuel hose or equivalent where fuel pipe is installed.

Before servicing the vehicle, make sure to also refer to the precautions in the beginning of this section as well.

RELIEVING FUEL SYSTEM PRESSURE

Fuel supply lines on all fuel injected engines will remain pressurized for some period of time after the engine is shut **OFF**. This pressure must be relieved before servicing the fuel system. Pressure is relieved through the fuel pressure relief valve, located on the fuel rail.

To relieve the fuel system pressure, first remove the fuel tank cap to relieve pressure in the tank, then remove the cap on the fuel pressure relief valve. Attach a fuel pressure gauge and drain the system through the drain tube into a container. Remove the fuel pressure gauge and replace the cap on the relief valve.

FUEL FILTER

REMOVAL & INSTALLATION

See Figures 132 and 133.

❄ CAUTION

Observe all applicable safety precautions when working around fuel. Whenever servicing the fuel system, always work in a well ventilated area. Do not allow fuel spray or vapors to come in contact with a spark or open flame. Keep a dry chemical fire extinguisher near the work area. Always keep fuel in a container specifically designed for fuel storage; also, always properly seal fuel containers to avoid the possibility of fire or explosion.

1. Disconnect the negative battery cable.
2. Relieve the fuel system pressure.
3. If equipped with air suspension, turn the air suspension switch to the **OFF** position.
4. Remove the hairpin clip push connect fittings from both ends of the fuel filter as follows:

   a. Step 1: Inspect the visible internal portion of the fitting for dirt accumulation. If more than a light coating of dust is present, clean the fitting before disassembly.

   b. Step 2: Some adhesion between the seals in the fitting and the filter will occur with time. To separate, twist the fitting on the filter, then push and pull the fitting until it moves freely on the filter.

   c. Step 3: Remove the hairpin clip from the fitting by first bending and breaking the shipping tab. Next, spread the 2 clip legs by hand about⅛inch

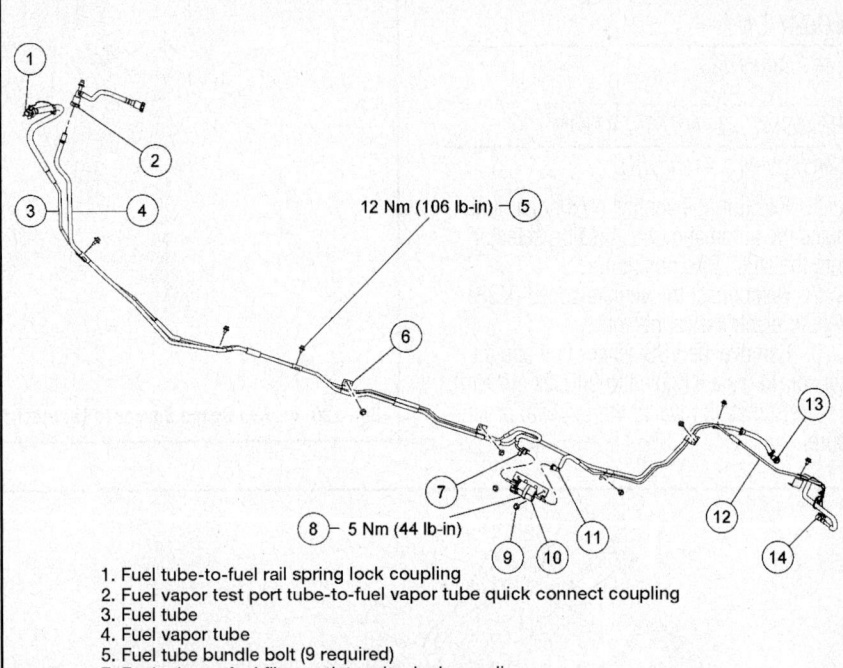

12 Nm (106 lb-in) — 5

6 — 5 Nm (44 lb-in)

1. Fuel tube-to-fuel rail spring lock coupling
2. Fuel vapor test port tube-to-fuel vapor tube quick connect coupling
3. Fuel tube
4. Fuel vapor tube
5. Fuel tube bundle bolt (9 required)
7. Fuel tube-to-fuel filter outlet spring lock coupling
8. Fuel filter bracket and clamp assembly
9. Fuel filter bracket bolt (2 required)
10. Fuel filter
11. Fuel tube-to-fuel filter inlet spring lock coupling
12. Fuel tube
13. Fuel vapor tube-to-fuel vapor tube assembly quick connect coupling
14. Fuel tube-to-Fuel Pump (FP) module spring lock coupling

36578_CVIC_G0099

Fig. 133 Fuel lines and fuel filter

each, to disengage the body and push the legs into the fitting. Lightly pull the triangular end of the clip and work it clear of the filter and fitting.

   d. Step 4: Grasp the fitting and pull in an axial direction to remove the fitting from the filter. Be careful on 90 degree elbow connectors, as excessive side loading could break the connector body.

   e. Step 5: After disassembly, inspect the inside of the fitting for any internal parts such as O-rings and spacers that may have been dislodged from the fitting. Replace any damaged connector.

5. Remove the filter retaining clamp and remove the fuel filter. Note the direction of the flow arrow on the filter, so the replacement filter can be reinstalled in the same position.

To install:

6. Install or connect the following:
   • Fuel filter with the flow arrow facing the proper direction and tighten the filter retaining clamp
   • Rubber insulator rings on the new filter. Replace the insulator rings if the filter moves freely after the retainer is installed.

   • Filter into the retainer with the flow arrow pointing out the open end of the retainer
   • Retainer on the bracket and tighten the mounting bolts to 44 inch lbs. (5 Nm)

7. Install the hairpin clip push connect fittings at both ends of the fuel filter as follows:

   a. Step 1: Install a new connector if damage was found. Insert a new clip into any 2 adjacent openings with the triangular portion pointing away from the fitting opening. Install the clip until the legs of the clip are locked on the outside of the body. Piloting with an index finger is necessary.

   b. Step 2: Before installing the fitting on the filter, wipe the filter end with a clean cloth. Inspect the inside of the fitting to be sure it is free of dirt and/or obstructions.

   c. Step 3: Apply a light coating of engine oil to the filter end. Align the fitting and filter axially and push the fitting onto the filter end. When the fitting is engaged, a definite click will be heard. Pull on the fitting to be sure it is fully engaged.

8. If equipped with air suspension, turn the air suspension switch to the **ON** position.

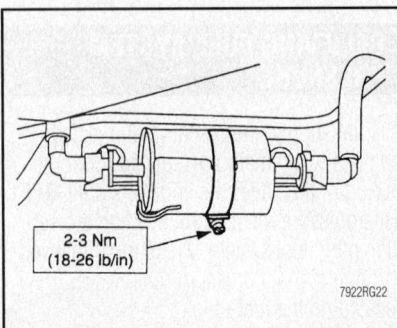

2-3 Nm
(18-26 lb/in)

7922RG22

Fig. 132 The fuel filter is located near the center of the vehicle on the frame rail

9. Reconnect the negative battery cable.

10. Start the engine and check for fuel leaks and proper operation.

FUEL LEVEL SENDING UNIT

REMOVAL & INSTALLATION

See Figure 134.

✳✳ CAUTION

Observe all applicable safety precautions when working around fuel. Whenever servicing the fuel system, always work in a well ventilated area. Do not allow fuel spray or vapors to come in contact with a spark or open flame. Keep a dry chemical fire extinguisher near the work area. Always keep fuel in a container specifically designed for fuel storage; also, always properly seal fuel containers to avoid the possibility of fire or explosion.

✳✳ CAUTION

If the vehicle is equipped with air suspension, the electrical power to the air suspension system must be shut off prior to hoisting, jacking or towing an air suspension vehicle. This can be accomplished by turning off the air suspension switch located in the luggage compartment. Failure to do so can result in unexpected inflation or deflation of the air springs, which can result in shifting of the vehicle during these operations. Failure to follow these instructions may result in personal injury.

1. Disconnect battery negative cable from battery and properly isolate to prevent accidental reconnection.

2. Relieve the fuel system pressure.

3. Remove the fuel pump module.

4. Remove the heat shrink tubing covering the fuel level sender electrical connector.

5. Disconnect the fuel level sender electrical connector.

6. Remove the screws, the ground wire eyelet and remove the fuel level sender from the fuel pump module.

7. To install, reverse the removal procedure.

FUEL PUMP MODULE

REMOVAL & INSTALLATION

See Figure 135.

✳✳ CAUTION

Observe all applicable safety precautions when working around fuel. whenever servicing the fuel system, always work in a well ventilated area. do not allow fuel spray or vapors to come in contact with a spark or open flame. keep a dry chemical fire extinguisher near the work area. always keep fuel in a container specifically designed for fuel storage; also, always properly seal

fuel containers to avoid the possibility of fire or explosion.

1. Disconnect the negative battery cable.

2. Relieve the fuel system pressure.

3. Remove any dirt that has accumulated around the fuel pump and fuel lines to prevent the entry of contaminants into the tank during fuel pump removal and installation.

4. Remove the fuel tank.

5. Disconnect the Fuel Pump (FP) module harness-to-Fuel Tank Pressure (FTP) sensor electrical connector.

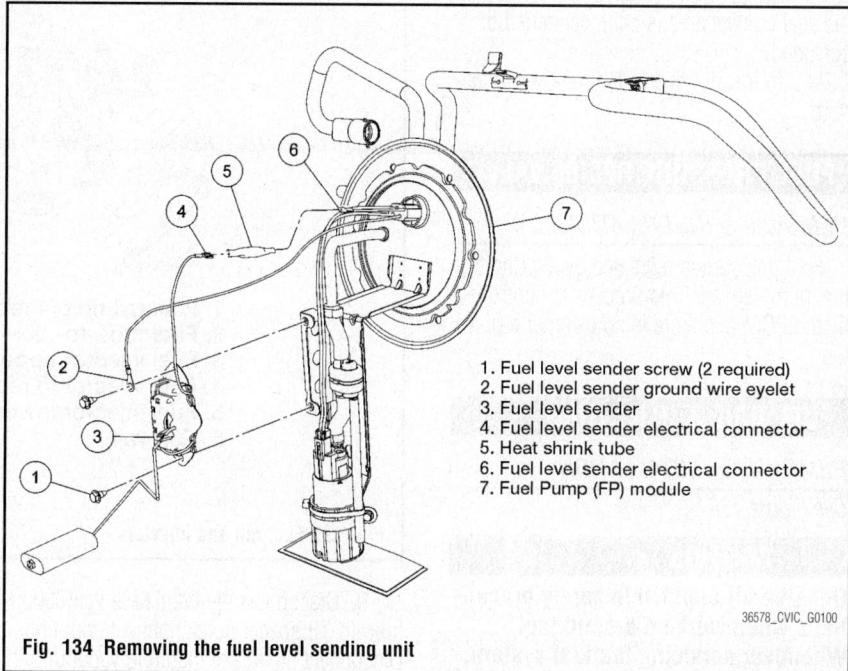

1. Fuel level sender screw (2 required)
2. Fuel level sender ground wire eyelet
3. Fuel level sender
4. Fuel level sender electrical connector
5. Heat shrink tube
6. Fuel level sender electrical connector
7. Fuel Pump (FP) module

36578_CVIC_G0100

Fig. 134 Removing the fuel level sending unit

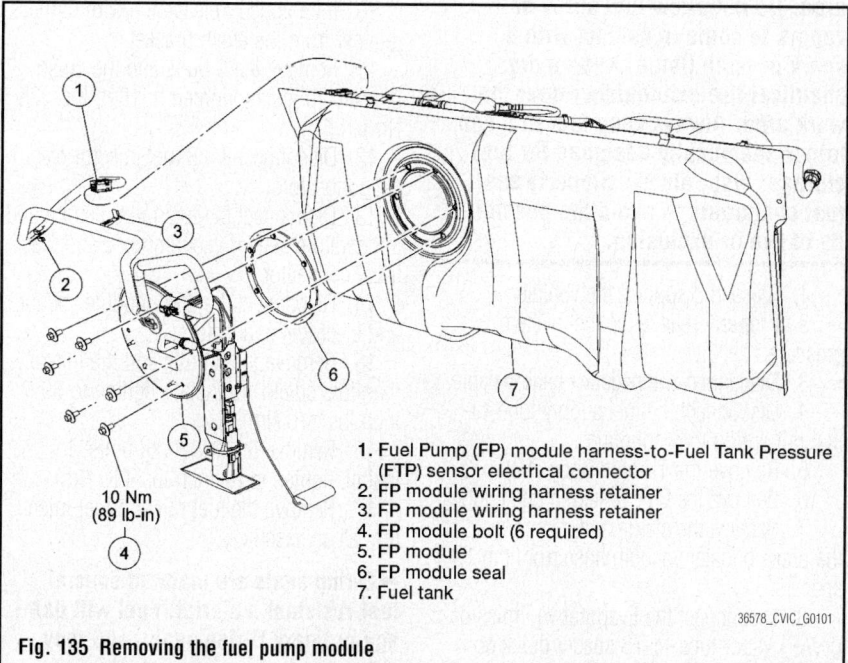

10 Nm (89 lb-in)

1. Fuel Pump (FP) module harness-to-Fuel Tank Pressure (FTP) sensor electrical connector
2. FP module wiring harness retainer
3. FP module wiring harness retainer
4. FP module bolt (6 required)
5. FP module
6. FP module seal
7. Fuel tank

36578_CVIC_G0101

Fig. 135 Removing the fuel pump module

6. Release the 2 fuel pump module wiring harness retainers.

7. Clean the FP module mounting flange and immediate surrounding area of any dirt or foreign material.

8. Remove the 6 bolts and the fuel pump module.

9. Remove and discard the fuel pump seal. Install a new FP module seal

10. Inspect the surfaces of the FP module flange and fuel tank seal contact surfaces. Do not polish or adjust the seal contact area of the FP module flange or fuel tank. Install a new FP module or fuel tank if the seal contact area is bent, scratched or corroded.

11. To install, reverse the removal procedure.

FUEL PRESSURE RELIEF VALVE

REMOVAL & INSTALLATION

Fuel pressure is regulated by altering the fuel pump speed. This process is controlled by the PCM and there is no external regulator.

FUEL RAIL & INJECTORS

REMOVAL & INSTALLATION

See Figure 136.

❊❊ CAUTION

Observe all applicable safety precautions when working around fuel. Whenever servicing the fuel system, always work in a well ventilated area. Do not allow fuel spray or vapors to come in contact with a spark or open flame. Keep a dry chemical fire extinguisher near the work area. Always keep fuel in a container specifically designed for fuel storage; also, always properly seal fuel containers to avoid the possibility of fire or explosion.

1. Raise and support the vehicle.
2. Properly relieve the fuel system pressure.
3. Disconnect the negative battery cable.
4. Disconnect the fuel supply tube-to-fuel rail spring lock coupling.
5. Remove the Throttle Body (TB).
6. Remove the EGR system module tube.
7. Release the clamp and disconnect the brake booster vacuum hose from the TB spacer.
8. Disconnect the Evaporative Emission (EVAP) vapor tube-to-TB spacer quick connect coupling.

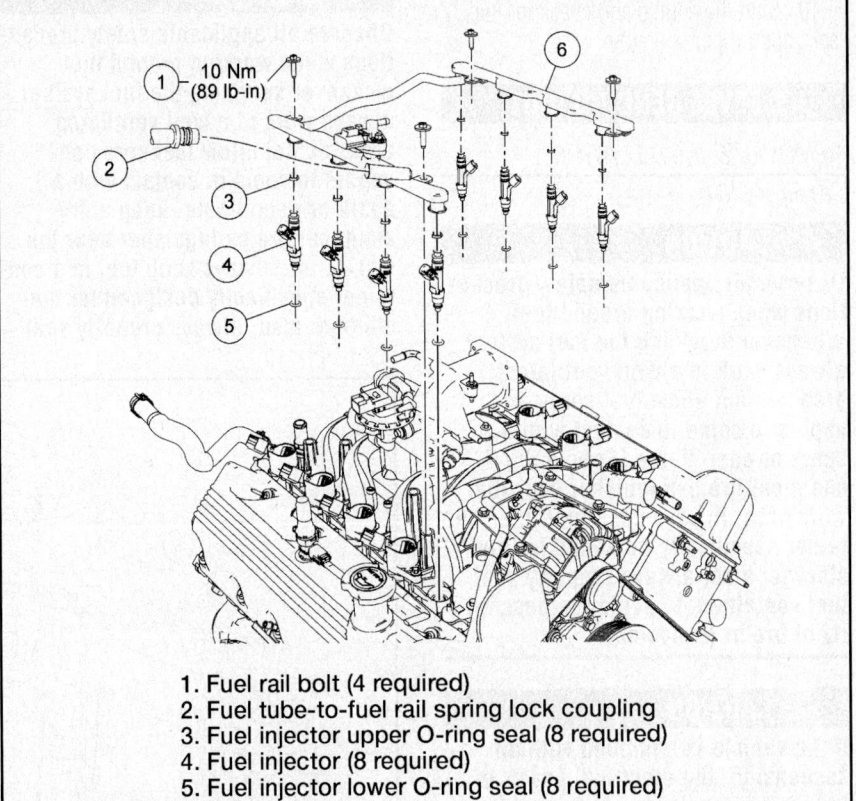

1. Fuel rail bolt (4 required)
2. Fuel tube-to-fuel rail spring lock coupling
3. Fuel injector upper O-ring seal (8 required)
4. Fuel injector (8 required)
5. Fuel injector lower O-ring seal (8 required)
6. Fuel rail

36578_CVIC_G0102

Fig. 136 Fuel rail and injectors

9. Disconnect the crankcase ventilation tube-to-TB spacer quick connect coupling. Disconnect the intake manifold vacuum hose from the TB spacer.

10. If equipped, release the wire harness retainer from the crash bracket.

11. Remove the 2 bolts and the crash bracket. To install, tighten to 18 ft. lbs. (25 Nm).

12. Disconnect the 8 fuel injector electrical connectors.

13. Disconnect the fuel rail pressure and temperature sensor vacuum hose and electrical connector.

14. Disconnect the EGR module vacuum and electrical connectors.

15. Remove the 2 bolts and the intake manifold shield. To install, tighten to 89 inch lbs. (10 Nm).

16. Remove the 4 fuel rail bolts. To install, tighten to 89 inch lbs. (10 Nm).

17. Remove the fuel rail and fuel injectors as an assembly.

➡O-ring seals are made of special fuel-resistant material. Fuel will damage ordinary O-ring seals, and may cause the fuel system to leak.

➡Do not reuse O-ring seals. The removal and installation process may damage the used O-ring seals, and may cause the fuel system to leak.

18. Remove the fuel injectors and O-ring seals. Discard the O-ring seals.

19. To install, reverse the removal procedure. If equipped with a fire suppression system, repower the system.

20. Install new upper and lower fuel injector O-ring seals and lubricate with clean engine oil prior to installation.

FUEL TANK

REMOVAL & INSTALLATION

See Figure 137.

❊❊ CAUTION

Observe all applicable safety precautions when working around fuel. Whenever servicing the fuel system, always work in a well ventilated area. Do not allow fuel spray or vapors to come in contact with a spark or open flame. Keep a dry

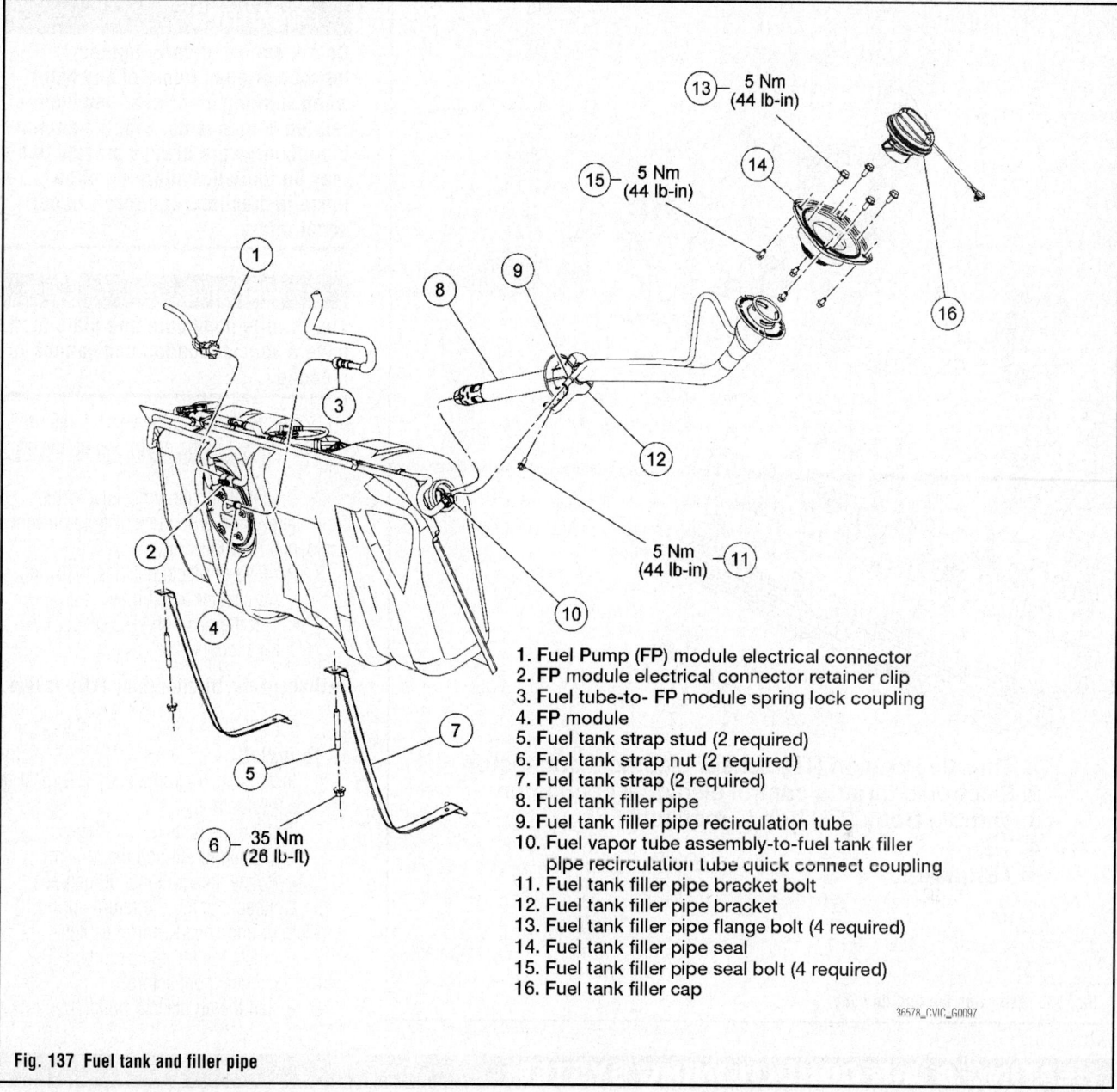

1. Fuel Pump (FP) module electrical connector
2. FP module electrical connector retainer clip
3. Fuel tube-to- FP module spring lock coupling
4. FP module
5. Fuel tank strap stud (2 required)
6. Fuel tank strap nut (2 required)
7. Fuel tank strap (2 required)
8. Fuel tank filler pipe
9. Fuel tank filler pipe recirculation tube
10. Fuel vapor tube assembly-to-fuel tank filler
    pipe recirculation tube quick connect coupling
11. Fuel tank filler pipe bracket bolt
12. Fuel tank filler pipe bracket
13. Fuel tank filler pipe flange bolt (4 required)
14. Fuel tank filler pipe seal
15. Fuel tank filler pipe seal bolt (4 required)
16. Fuel tank filler cap

36578_CVIC_G0097

Fig. 137 Fuel tank and filler pipe

chemical fire extinguisher near the work area. **Always keep fuel in a container specifically designed for fuel storage; also, always properly seal fuel containers to avoid the possibility of fire or explosion.**

1. Properly relieve the fuel system pressure.
2. Disconnect the negative battery cable.
3. Drain the fuel tank.
4. Disconnect the Fuel Pump (FP) module electrical connector and release the retainer clip.
5. Disconnect the fuel tube-to-FP module spring lock coupling.

6. Disconnect the fuel vapor tube assembly-to-fuel vapor tube quick connect coupling.
7. Disconnect the fuel vapor tube-to-fuel vapor tube assembly quick connect coupling.
8. Completely lower and remove the fuel tank.

➡**The fuel tank strap studs are manufactured as a break-off style. After installing the new fuel tank strap studs and fuel tank installation is completed, break-off the excess length at the recess in the studs.**

9. Remove and discard the fuel tank strap studs.
10. To install, reverse the removal proce-

dure. If equipped with a fire suppression system, repower the system.
11. Carry out the Evaporative Emission System Leak Test.

IDLE SPEED

ADJUSTMENT

Idle speed is maintained by the Powertrain Control Module (PCM). No adjustment is necessary or possible.

THROTTLE BODY

REMOVAL & INSTALLATION
See Figure 138.

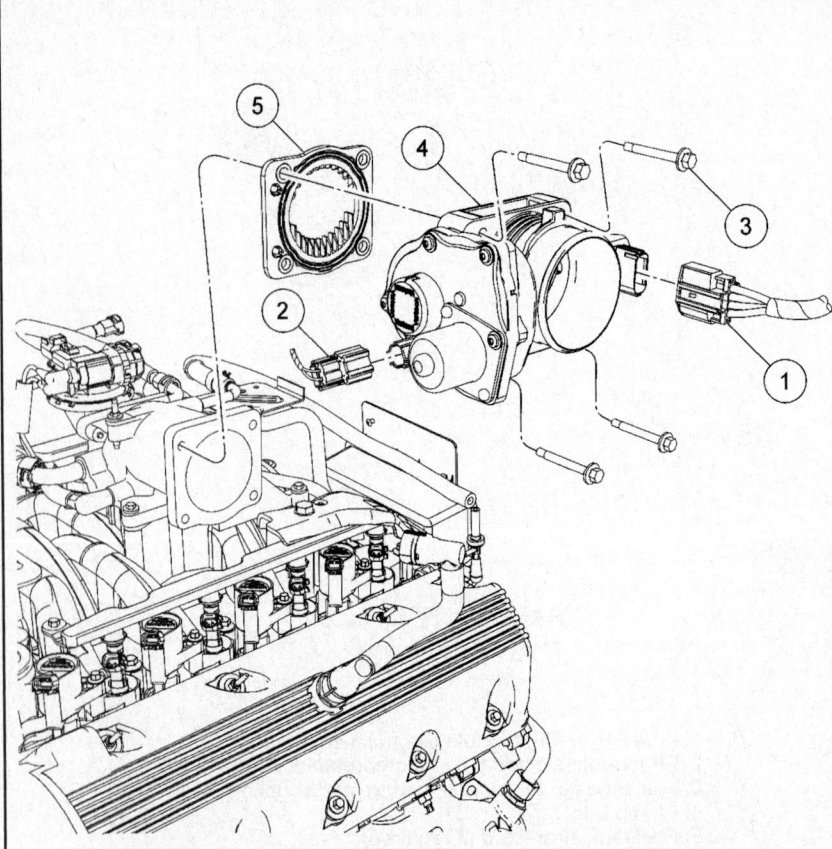

1. Throttle Position (TP) sensor electrical connector
2. Electronic throttle control electrical connector
3. Throttle Body (TB) bolt (4 required)
4. TB
5. TB gasket

36578_CVIC_G0103

Fig. 138 Removing the throttle body

✸✸ CAUTION

Do not smoke or carry lighted tobacco or open flame of any type when working on or near any fuel-related components. Highly flammable mixtures are always present and may be ignited. Failure to follow these instructions can result in personal injury.

✸✸ WARNING

The throttle body bore and plate area have a special coating and cannot be cleaned.

1. Before servicing the vehicle, refer to the precautions in the beginning of this section.
2. Disconnect battery negative cable from battery and properly isolate to prevent accidental reconnection.
3. Remove or disconnect the following:
   - Air cleaner outlet tube
   - Throttle position (TP) sensor electrical connector

➡ Discard the throttle body (TB) gasket.

   - Four bolts and the throttle body

To install:

4. Install a new throttle body (TB) gasket and the throttle body.
5. Tighten the bolts in two stages:
   - Tighten to 80 inch lbs. (9 Nm)
   - Rotate an additional 90 degrees.
6. Connect the throttle return spring, accelerator and speed control cables.
7. Connect the throttle position (TP) sensor electrical connectors.
8. Install the air cleaner outlet tube.

HEATING & AIR CONDITIONING SYSTEM

BLOWER MOTOR

REMOVAL & INSTALLATION

See Figures 139 through 141.

1. Before servicing the vehicle, refer to the precautions in the beginning of this section.
2. Disconnect battery negative cable from battery and properly isolate to prevent accidental reconnection.
3. Disengage the wire harness connectors from the retainer.
4. Disconnect the blower motor electrical connector.
5. Remove the motor cooling hose.
6. Remove the screws and remove the blower motor.

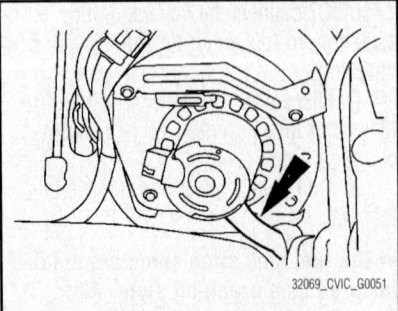

32069_CVIC_G0051

Fig. 139 Blower motor cooling hose

➡ Prior to removing a wheel that is to be reused, clean any corrosion from the blower motor shaft to prevent damage to the wheel mounting shaft.

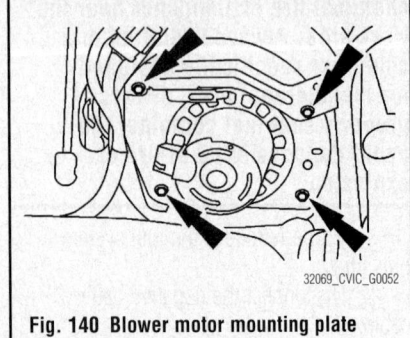

32069_CVIC_G0052

Fig. 140 Blower motor mounting plate

7. Remove the wheel from the blower motor as follows:
   - Remove the push clip.
   - Remove the wheel from the blower motor.

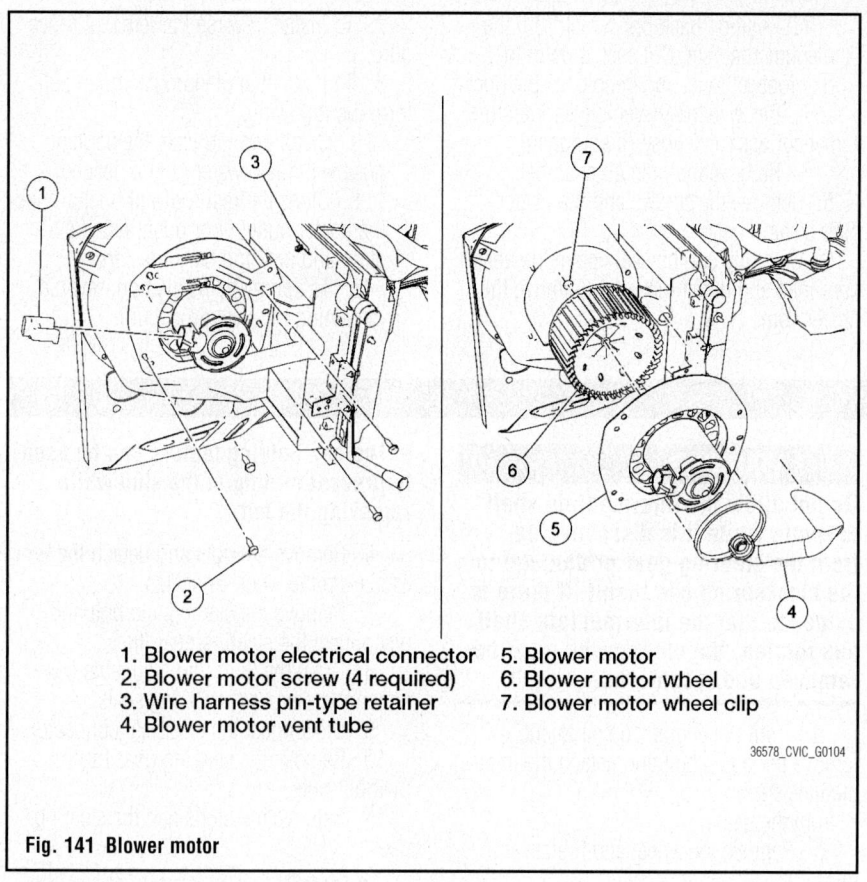

1. Blower motor electrical connector
2. Blower motor screw (4 required)
3. Wire harness pin-type retainer
4. Blower motor vent tube
5. Blower motor
6. Blower motor wheel
7. Blower motor wheel clip

36578_CVIC_G0104

Fig. 141 Blower motor

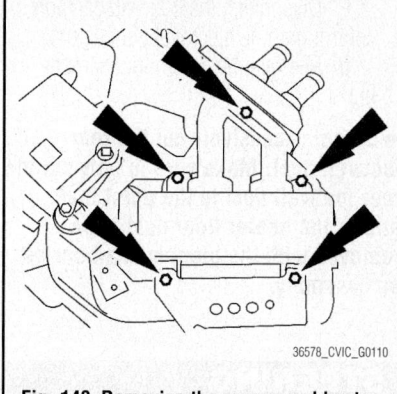

36578_CVIC_G0110

Fig. 143 Removing the screws and heater cover

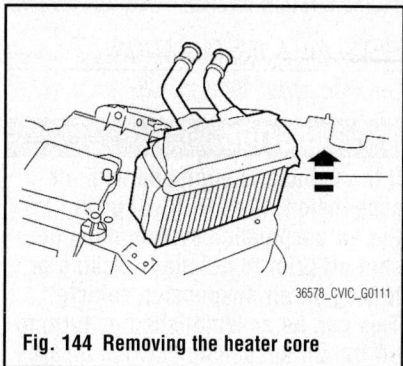

36578_CVIC_G0111

Fig. 144 Removing the heater core

To install:

8. Install or connect the following:
   - Wheel to the blower motor, if removed.
   - Blower motor and securely tighten the screws.
   - Motor cooling hose
   - Blower motor electrical connector
   - Wire harness retainers

HEATER CORE

REMOVAL & INSTALLATION

See Figures 142 through 144.

1. If equipped, turn the air suspension service switch to the **OFF** position before raising the vehicle.
2. Drain the cooling system.
3. Disconnect the negative battery cable.
4. Remove the plenum chamber by performing the following:

   a. Remove the instrument panel.

   b. Drain the engine coolant.

   c. Release the 2 heater hose clamps and disconnect the heater hoses at the heater core.

   d. Detach the plenum chamber vacuum harness from the plenum chamber.

   e. Disconnect the temperature blend door actuator electrical connector.

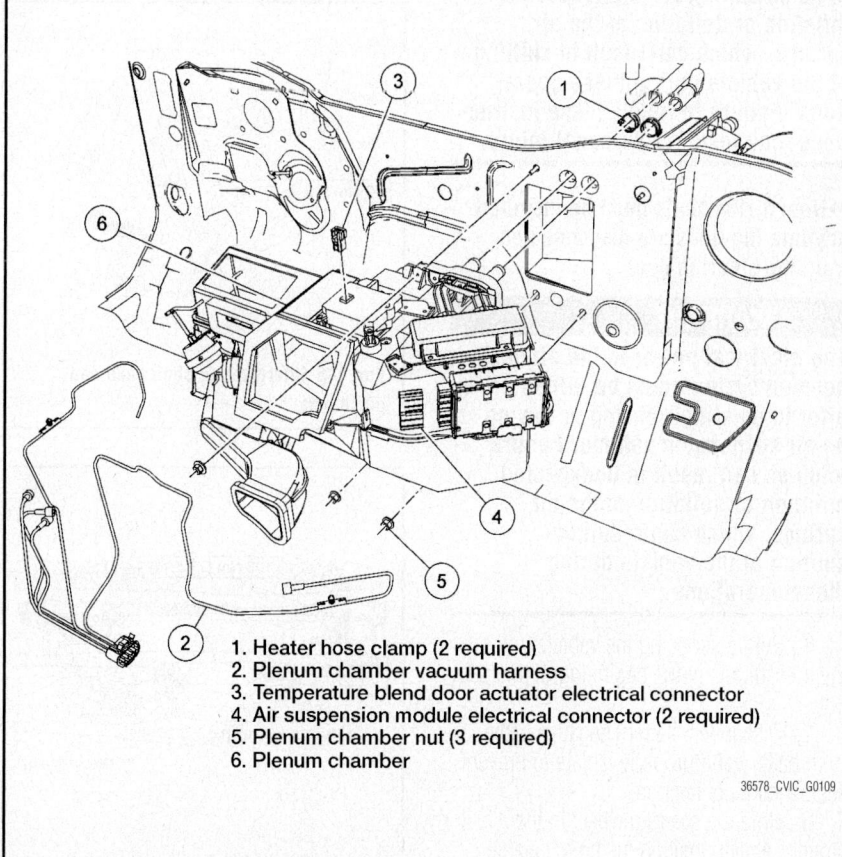

1. Heater hose clamp (2 required)
2. Plenum chamber vacuum harness
3. Temperature blend door actuator electrical connector
4. Air suspension module electrical connector (2 required)
5. Plenum chamber nut (3 required)
6. Plenum chamber

36578_CVIC_G0109

Fig. 142 Removing the plenum chamber

f. Disconnect the 2 air suspension control module electrical connectors.

g. Remove the 3 plenum chamber nuts.

➡Do not excessively cut the rear footwell duct. Make sure to only cut the rear footwell duct to the point that allows the heater floor duct to be removed with the plenum chamber as an assembly.

h. Position back the carpet from the plenum chamber. Cut each side of the rear footwell duct and bend back the duct.

i. Remove the in-vehicle temperature sensor aspirator hose (if equipped).

j. Remove the plenum chamber.

5. Remove the screws and the heater core cover.

6. Carefully cut the seal above the heater core inlet and outlet tubes and remove the heater core.

7. To install, reverse the removal procedure.

8. To install the plenum chamber, perform the following:

a. Clean and lubricate the coolant hose with plain water only if needed.

b. Close the rear footwell duct around the heater outlet floor duct, install a tie strap and position back the carpet.

c. To complete installation, reverse remaining removal procedure.

STEERING

POWER RACK & PINION STEERING GEAR

REMOVAL & INSTALLATION

See Figures 145 through 148.

❋❋ CAUTION

If the vehicle is equipped with air suspension, the electrical power to the air suspension system must be shut off prior to hoisting, jacking or towing an air suspension vehicle. This can be accomplished by turning off the air suspension switch located in the luggage compartment. Failure to do so can result in unexpected inflation or deflation of the air springs, which can result in shifting of the vehicle during these operations. Failure to follow these instructions may result in personal injury.

➡New O-ring seals must be installed anytime the lines are disconnected from the steering gear.

❋❋ WARNING

The electrical power to the air suspension system must be turned off prior to hoisting, jacking or towing an air suspension vehicle. Failure to do so can result in unexpected inflation or deflation of the air springs, which can result in shifting of the vehicle during these operations.

1. Before servicing the vehicle, refer to the precautions in the beginning of this section.

2. Disconnect battery negative cable from battery and properly isolate to prevent accidental reconnection.

3. Hold the steering wheel in the straight-ahead position, using a suitable holding device.

❋❋ WARNING

Do not allow the intermediate shaft to rotate while it is disconnected from the steering gear or damage to the clockspring can result. If there is evidence that the intermediate shaft has rotated, the clockspring must be removed and recentered.

4. From the engine compartment, remove the pinch bolt and detach the intermediate shaft from the gear.

5. Remove the wheel and tire assemblies.

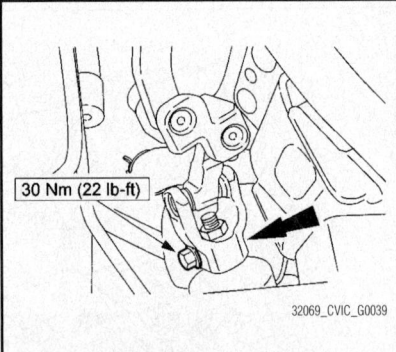

30 Nm (22 lb-ft)

32069_CVIC_G0039

Fig. 145 Intermediate shaft yoke and pinch bolt

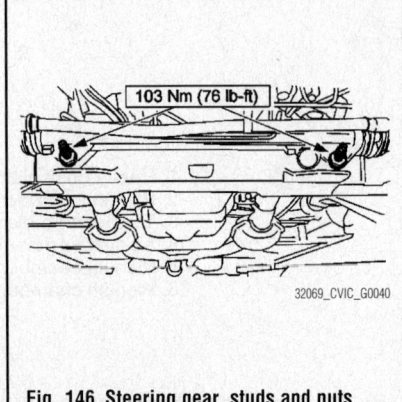

103 Nm (76 lb-ft)

32069_CVIC_G0040

Fig. 146 Steering gear, studs and nuts

➡The hex holding feature can be used to prevent turning of the stud while removing the nut.

6. Remove the nuts and detach the tie-rods from the wheel knuckles.

7. Remove the clamp plate bolt and disconnect the steering gear lines.

8. Drain the fluid into a suitable container and discard the O-ring seals.

9. Disconnect the electrical connector.

10. Remove the steering gear-to-crossmember nuts.

11. Remove the studs and the steering gear.

To install:

12. Install or connect the following:
- Steering gear studs and torque to 15 ft. lbs. (20 Nm)
- Steering gear and torque the nuts to 76 ft. lbs. (103 Nm)
- Electrical connector
- Power steering hydraulic lines with new O-rings on both the high pressure hose and return hose
- Clamp plate and torque the nuts to 13 ft. lbs. (18 Nm)
- Tie rods and torque the nuts to 59 ft. lbs. (80 Nm)
- Tire and wheel assemblies

13. Lower the vehicle.

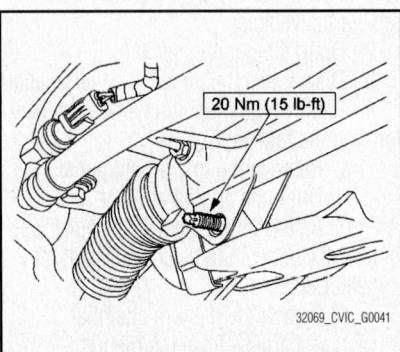

20 Nm (15 lb-ft)

32069_CVIC_G0041

Fig. 147 Installation of steering gear studs

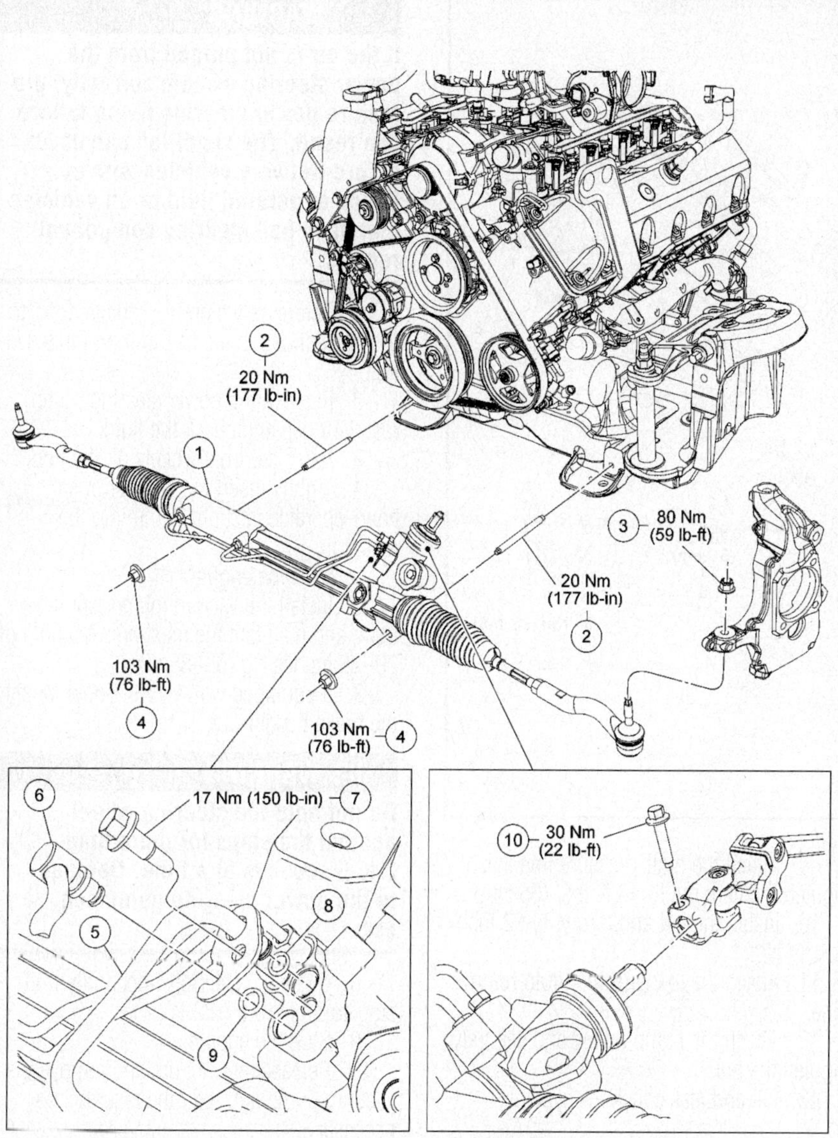

2
20 Nm
(177 lb-in)

1

3   80 Nm
(59 lb-ft)

20 Nm
(177 lb-in)
2

103 Nm
(76 lb-ft)
4

103 Nm
(76 lb-ft)
4

6   17 Nm (150 lb-in)   7

8

5

9

10   30 Nm
(22 lb-ft)

1. Steering gear
2. Steering gear studs (2 required)
3. Outer tie-rod end nut
4. Steering gear nuts (2 required)
5. Pressure line
6. Return line
7. Steering line clamp plate bolt
8. High-pressure O-ring seal
9. Low-pressure O-ring seal
10. Steering column shaft-to-steering gear coupling bolt

36578_CVIC_G0112

Fig. 148 Power rack and pinion steering gear

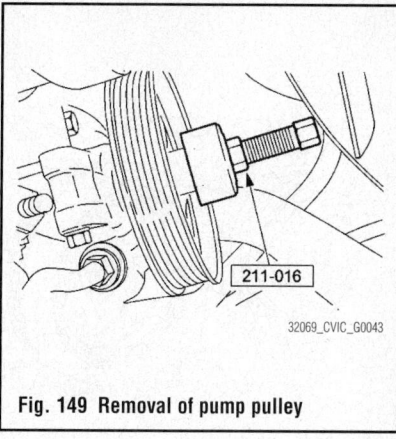

211-016

32069_CVIC_G0043

Fig. 149 Removal of pump pulley

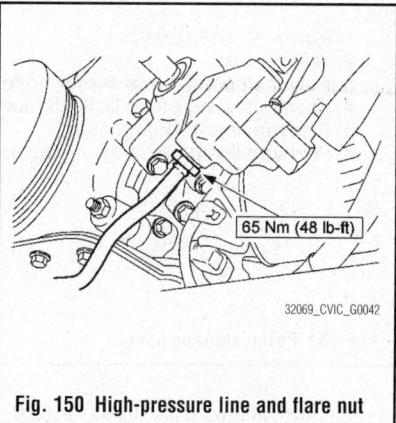

65 Nm (48 lb-ft)

32069_CVIC_G0042

Fig. 150 High-pressure line and flare nut

14. Install the steering wheel intermediate shaft and torque the pinch bolt to 22 ft. lbs. (30 Nm)

15. Ensure that the wheels and steering wheel are lined up.

16. Refill the power steering system, bleed, check for leaks and repair if necessary.

POWER STEERING PUMP

REMOVAL & INSTALLATION

See Figures 149 through 151.

❋❋ WARNING

While repairing the power steering system, care should be taken to prevent the entry of contaminants or premature failure of the power steering components can result.

❋❋ WARNING

The electrical power to the air suspension system must be turned off

prior to hoisting, jacking or towing an air suspension vehicle. Failure to do so can result in unexpected inflation or deflation of the air springs, which can result in shifting of the vehicle during these operations.

1. Before servicing the vehicle, refer to the precautions in the beginning of this section.

2. Remove the power steering pump pulley.

❋❋ WARNING

Installation of a new power steering pump pulley is necessary after being removed and installed two times.

  a. Remove the drive belt.
  b. Raise the vehicle.

❋❋ WARNING

Do not apply pressure on the power steering pump rotor shaft. Pressure will damage internal thrust areas of the power steering pump.

  c. Remove the pulley with a suitable puller.
  • Inspect the pulley for paint marks in the web area near the hub. If

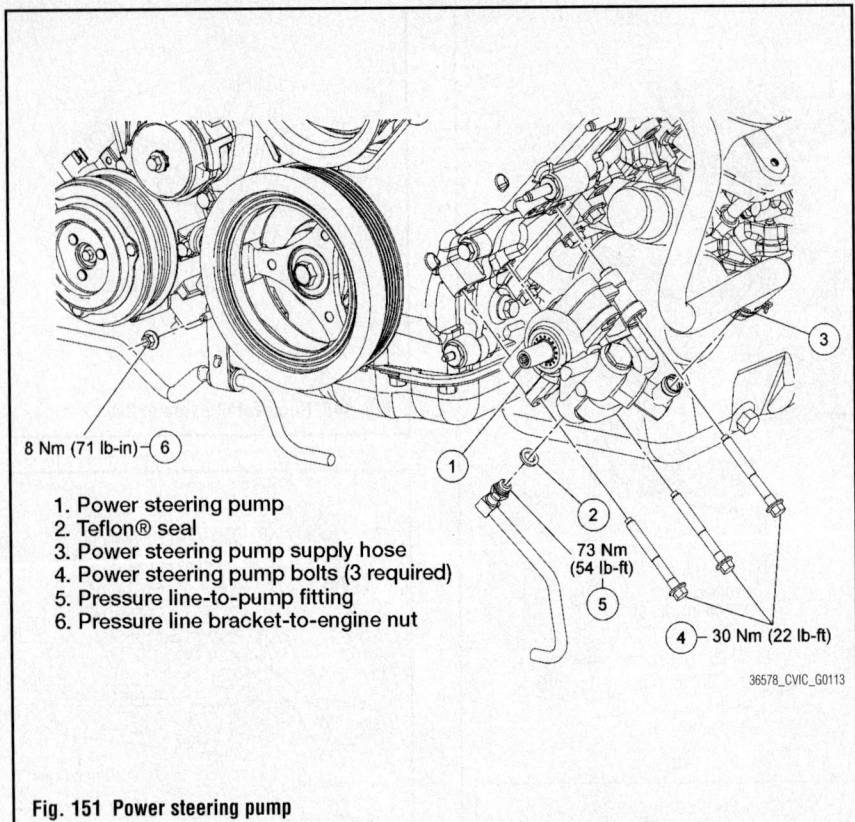

8 Nm (71 lb-in)—6

1. Power steering pump
2. Teflon® seal
3. Power steering pump supply hose
4. Power steering pump bolts (3 required)
5. Pressure line-to-pump fitting
6. Pressure line bracket-to-engine nut

73 Nm (54 lb-ft)

4—30 Nm (22 lb-ft)

36578_CVIC_G0113

Fig. 151 Power steering pump

there are two paint marks, discard the pulley. If there is no paint or one paint mark, use a paint pencil to mark the web area of the pulley near the hub.

3. Loosen the clamp and disconnect the hose and drain the fluid into a suitable container.

4. Remove the nut.

5. Disconnect the high-pressure line.

6. Remove the bolts and the power steering pump.

To install:

7. Install the power steering pump and torque the bolts to 18 ft. lbs. (25 Nm)

8. Install a new Teflon seal on the high-pressure line fitting.

9. Attach the high-pressure line and tighten the flare nut to 48 ft. lbs. (65 Nm)

10. Install the nut and torque to 62 inch lbs. (7 Nm)

11. Attach the low pressure fluid return line.

12. Attach the pump pulley and securely tighten the nut.

13. Fill and leak check the system..

BLEEDING

A whine heard from the power steering pump can be caused by air in the system. The power steering purge procedure must be carried out prior to any component repair for which power steering noise complaints are accompanied by evidence of aerated fluid.

✳✳ WARNING

If the air is not purged from the power steering system correctly, premature power steering pump failure can result. The condition can occur on pre-delivery vehicles with evidence of aerated fluid or on vehicles that have had steering component repairs.

1. Before servicing the vehicle, refer to the precautions in the beginning of this section.

2. Remove the power steering pump reservoir cap and check the fluid.

3. Raise the front wheels off the floor.

4. Tightly insert the stopper of a hand-operated vacuum pump into the reservoir.

5. Start the engine.

6. Install the vacuum pump, apply vacuum, and maintain the maximum vacuum of 20–25 inches Hg (68–85 kPa).

7. If equipped with Hydro-Boost, apply the brake pedal twice.

✳✳ WARNING

Do not hold the steering wheel against the stops for more than 3 to 5 seconds at a time. Damage to the power steering pump can occur.

8. Cycle the steering wheel fully from stop-to-stop 10 times.

9. Stop the engine.

10. Release the vacuum and remove the vacuum pump and refill the reservoir as necessary.

11. Start the engine and repeat the procedure.

12. Visually inspect the power steering system for leaks.

13. Fill the reservoir as needed and visually inspect the power steering system for leaks.

14. Install the reservoir cap.

SUSPENSION   **FRONT SUSPENSION**

COIL SPRING

REMOVAL & INSTALLATION

Refer to Strut to remove the coil spring.

STABILIZER LINKS

REMOVAL & INSTALLATION

See Figure 152.

➡Suspension fasteners are critical parts because they affect performance of vital components and systems and their failure may result in major service expense. New parts must be installed with the same part numbers or equivalent part, if replacement is necessary. Do not use a replacement part of lesser quality or substitute design. Torque values must be used as specified during reassembly to make sure correct retention of these parts.

1. Raise and support the vehicle.
2. Remove the wheel and tire.

➡Do not allow the caliper and anchor plate assembly to hang from the brake hose or damage to the hose may occur.

3. Remove the bolts and position the caliper, pads and anchor plate assembly aside. Support the caliper and anchor plate assembly using mechanic's wire.
4. Remove the brake disc.
5. Remove the stabilizer link upper nut and discard the nut. Use the hex-holding feature to prevent the stud from turning while removing the nut.
6. To install, reverse the removal procedure. For torque specifications, refer to the accompanying illustration.

LOWER BALL JOINT

REMOVAL & INSTALLATION

See Figures 153 through 155.

✷✷ CAUTION

If the vehicle is equipped with air suspension, the electrical power to the air suspension system must be shut off prior to hoisting, jacking or towing an air suspension vehicle. This can be accomplished by turning off the air suspension switch located in the luggage compartment. Failure to do so can result in unexpected inflation or deflation of the air springs, which can result in shifting of the vehicle during these operations. Failure to follow these instructions may result in personal injury.

1. If equipped with air suspension, the air suspension service switch to the **OFF** position before raising the vehicle.
2. Remove the steering knuckle.
3. Remove and discard the lower ball joint snap ring.
4. Using the C-Frame and Screw Installer/Remover and Ball Joint Installer/Remover, remove the lower ball joint.

To install:

➡Do not damage the lower ball joint boot when installing the ball joint or premature failure of the ball joint may occur.

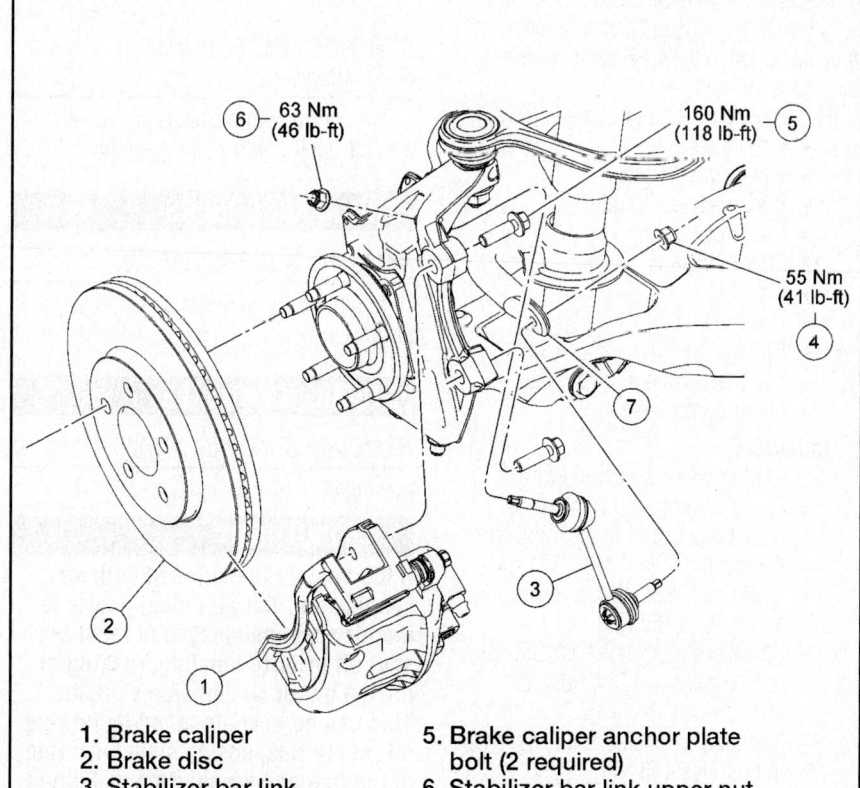

1. Brake caliper
2. Brake disc
3. Stabilizer bar link
4. Stabilizer bar link lower nut
5. Brake caliper anchor plate bolt (2 required)
6. Stabilizer bar link upper nut
7. Stabilizer bar

36578_CVIC_G0115

Fig. 152 Stabilizer link components

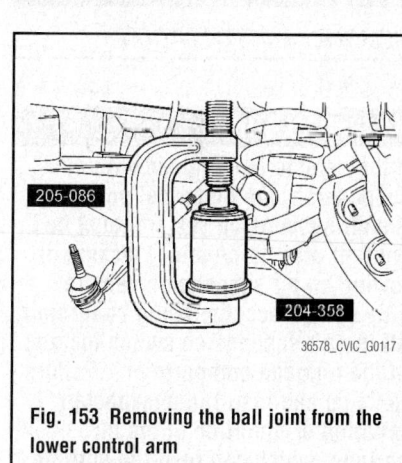

36578_CVIC_G0117

Fig. 153 Removing the ball joint from the lower control arm

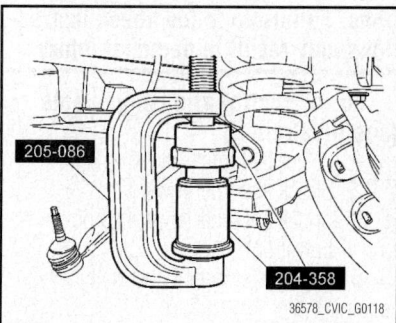

36578_CVIC_G0118

Fig. 154 Use a ball joint press to install the new ball joint into the lower control arm

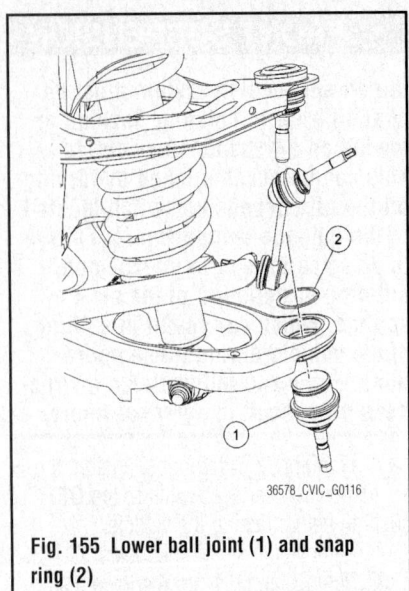

Fig. 155 Lower ball joint (1) and snap ring (2)

➡ **Make sure the ball joint snap ring is fully seated.**

5. Using the C-Frame and Screw Installer/Remover and Ball Joint Installer/Remover, install the lower ball joint.
6. Install the steering knuckle.

LOWER CONTROL ARM

REMOVAL & INSTALLATION

See Figure 156.

✳✳ CAUTION

If the vehicle is equipped with air suspension, the electrical power to the air suspension system must be shut off prior to hoisting, jacking or towing an air suspension vehicle. This can be accomplished by turning off the air suspension switch located in the luggage compartment. Failure to do so can result in unexpected inflation or deflation of the air springs, which can result in shifting of the vehicle during these operations. Failure to follow these instructions may result in personal injury.

Lower control arm components (see illustration):
1. Lower ball joint nut
2. Shock absorber lower nut
3. Shock absorber lower flag bolt
4. Lower arm
5. Lower bushing bracket bolt (3 required)
6. Lower arm cam nut
7. Lower arm cam bolt
8. Steering gear nut (2 required)
9. Steering gear

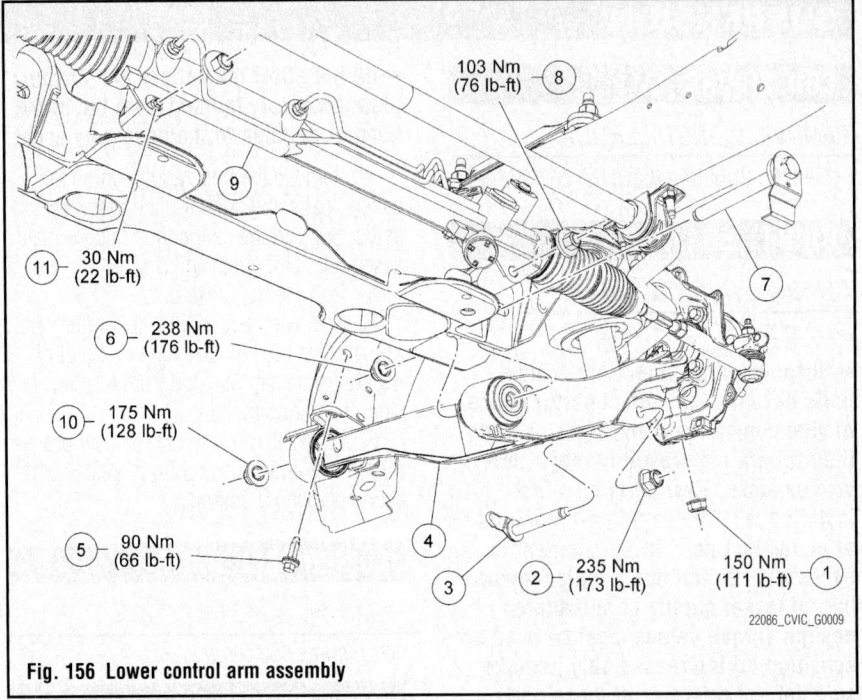

Fig. 156 Lower control arm assembly

10. Lower arm bushing nut
11. Steering gear studs (2 required)
12. If equipped with air suspension, the air suspension switch, located on the right-hand side of the luggage compartment, must be turned to the **OFF** position before raising the vehicle.
13. Remove or disconnect the following:
   - Front wheel
   - Wheel speed sensor
   - Brake caliper and rotor
   - Sway bar link
   - Shock absorber
   - Drag link
   - Lower ball joint
   - Coil spring
   - Lower control arm pivot bolts
   - Lower control arm

To install:
14. Install or connect the following:
   - Lower control arm. Tighten the pivot bolts to 111 ft. lbs. (150 Nm).
   - Coil spring
   - Lower ball joint. Tighten the nut to 111 ft. lbs. (150 Nm).
   - Shock absorber lower nut and flag bolt. Tighten to 176 ft. lbs. (238 Nm).
   - 3 lower arm bracket bolts. Tighten to 66 ft. lbs. (90 Nm).
   - 2 steering gear nuts. Tighten to 76 ft. lbs. (103 Nm).
   - Power steering rack studs. Tighten to 22 ft. lbs. (30 Nm).
   - Brake caliper and rotor
   - Wheel speed sensor
   - Front wheel

15. If equipped with air suspension, turn the air suspension service switch to the **ON** position.
16. Align the vehicle.

CONTROL ARM BUSHING REPLACEMENT

The control arm bushings are serviced with the control arm as an assembly.

SHOCK ABSORBERS

REMOVAL & INSTALLATION

To remove the shock absorber, refer to Strut.

STEERING KNUCKLE

REMOVAL & INSTALLATION

See Figure 157.

✳✳ CAUTION

If the vehicle is equipped with air suspension, the electrical power to the air suspension system must be shut off prior to hoisting, jacking or towing an air suspension vehicle. This can be accomplished by turning off the air suspension switch located in the luggage compartment. Failure to do so can result in unexpected inflation or deflation of the air springs, which can result in shifting of the vehicle during these operations. Failure to follow these instructions may result in personal injury.

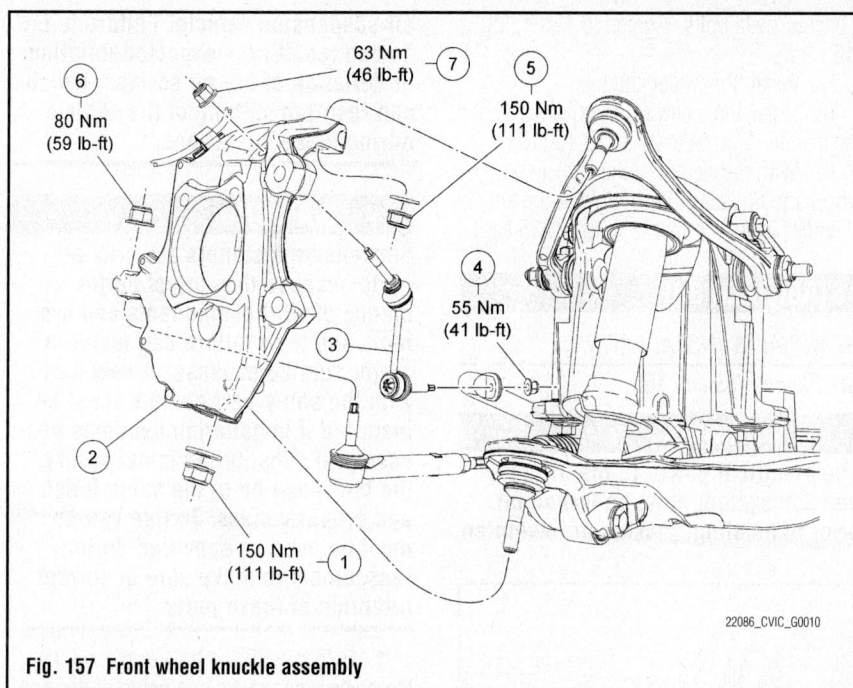

Fig. 157 Front wheel knuckle assembly

Front wheel knuckle components (see illustration):

1. Lower ball joint nut
2. Wheel knuckle
3. Stabilizer bar link
4. Lower stabilizer bar link nut
5. Upper ball joint nut
6. Outer tie rod end nut
7. Upper stabilizer bar link nut

8. If equipped with air suspension, the air suspension switch, located on the right-hand side of the luggage compartment, must be turned to the **OFF** position before raising the vehicle.

9. Remove or disconnect the following:
   • Wheel bearing and hub
   • Tie rod from knuckle

10. Raise the suspension arms and place a jack under them to release pressure from the stabilizer bar links.

11. Remove the upper control arm center nut.

12. Remove the stabilizer bar link nut and discard.

13. Disconnect the brake line retainer.

14. Remove the steering knuckle nuts and remove the steering knuckle.

To install:

15. Install or connect the following:
   • Steering knuckle and tighten the nuts to 111 ft. lbs. (150 Nm).
   • Brake line retainer.
   • Outer stabilizer bar link using a new nut and tighten to 46 ft. lbs. (63 Nm).
   • Inner stabilizer bar link using a new nut and tighten to 41 ft. lbs. (55 Nm).

   • Upper control arm center nut and tighten to 46 ft. lbs. (63 Nm).
   • Tie rod to knuckle and tighten to 59 ft. lbs. (80 Nm).
   • Wheel bearing and hub

16. If equipped with air suspension, turn the air suspension switch to the **ON** position.

STRUT

REMOVAL & INSTALLATION

See Figure 158.

➡Suspension fasteners are critical parts because they affect performance of vital components and systems and their failure may result in major service expense. New parts must be installed with the same part numbers or equivalent part, if replacement is necessary. Do not use a replacement part of lesser quality or substitute

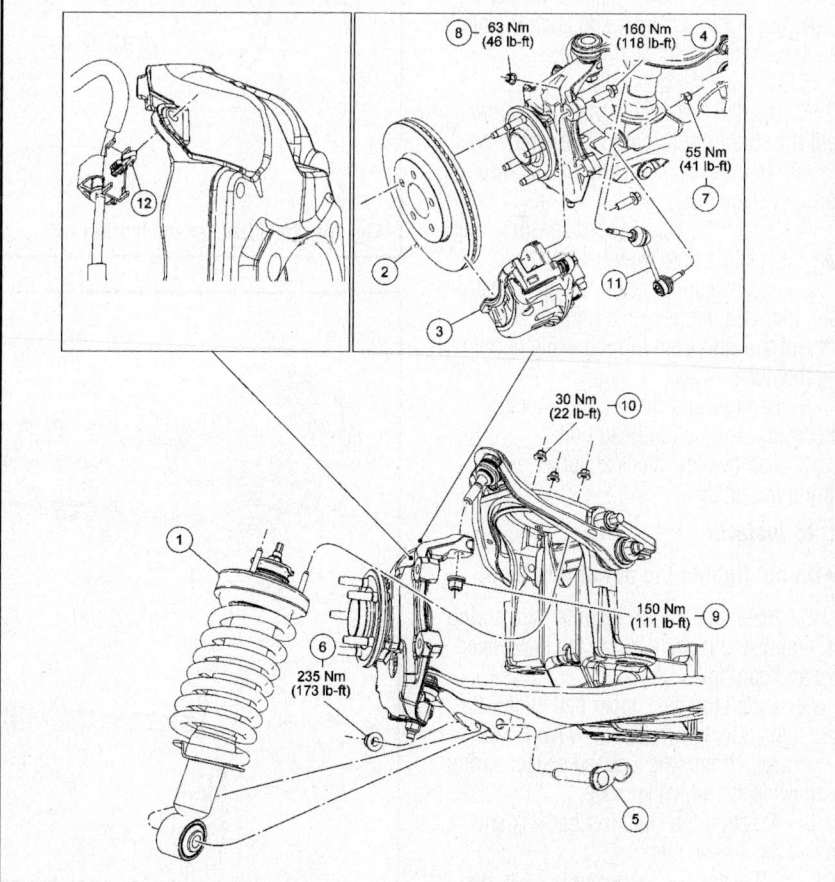

1. Shock absorber/coil spring assembly
2. Brake disc
3. Brake caliper and anchor plate
4. Brake caliper anchor plate bolt (2 required)
5. Shock absorber lower flag bolt
6. Shock absorber lower nut
7. Lower stabilizer bar link nut
8. Upper stabilizer bar link nut
9. Upper ball joint nut
10. Shock absorber mounting bracket nut (3 required)
11. Stabilizer bar link
12. Wheel speed sensor wiring harness retainer

Fig. 158 Shock absorber and spring assembly

design. Torque values must be used as specified during reassembly to make sure correct retention of these parts.

> ※ **WARNING**
>
> Before servicing a vehicle equipped with a fire suppression system, depower the system.

1. Raise and support the vehicle.
2. Remove the wheel and tire.

> ※ **WARNING**
>
> Do not remove the shock absorber center nut. Removal of this nut releases the spring tension and may result in serious personal injury.

3. Remove and discard the 3 shock absorber upper mount nuts.

➡ Do not allow the caliper and anchor plate assembly to hang from the brake hose or damage to the hose may occur.

4. Remove the 2 bolts and position the caliper, pads and anchor plate assembly aside. Support the caliper and anchor plate assembly using mechanic's wire.
5. Remove the brake disc.
6. Use the hex-holding feature to prevent the stud from turning while removing the nut. Remove and discard the stabilizer bar upper link nut.
7. Detach the wheel speed sensor wiring harness retainer from the wheel knuckle.
8. Remove and discard the upper ball joint nut. Use the hex-holding feature to prevent the stud from turning while removing the nut.
9. Remove and discard the shock absorber lower nut and flag bolt.
10. Remove the shock absorber and spring assembly.

To install:

➡ Do not tighten the nut at this time.

11. Install the shock absorber and spring assembly and loosely install the new lower nut and flag bolt.
12. Install the new upper ball joint nut and tighten to 111 ft. lbs. (150 Nm).
13. Attach the wheel speed sensor wiring harness to the wheel knuckle.
14. Position the stabilizer bar link and install the 2 new nuts.
   a. Tighten the lower nut to 41 ft. lbs. (55 Nm).
   b. Tighten the upper nut to 46 ft. lbs. (63 Nm).
15. Install the brake disc.
16. Position the brake caliper and anchor plate assembly and install the

2 anchor plate bolts. Tighten to 118 ft. lbs. (160 Nm).
17. Install the wheel and tire.
18. Install the 3 new shock absorber upper mount nuts. Tighten to 22 ft. lbs. (30 Nm).
19. With the weight of the vehicle on the wheel and tire assemblies, tighten the shock absorber lower nut to 173 ft. lbs. (235 Nm).

STABILIZER BAR

REMOVAL & INSTALLATION
See Figures 159 and 160.

> ※ **WARNING**
>
> The electrical power to the air suspension system must be turned off prior to hoisting, jacking or towing an

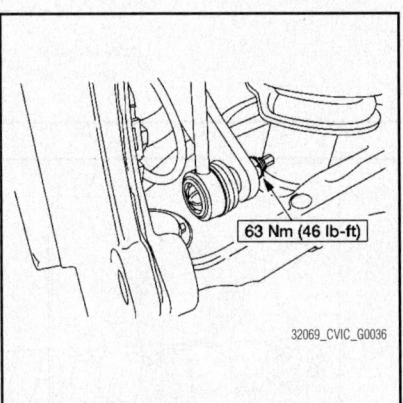

63 Nm (46 lb-ft)

32069_CVIC_G0036

Fig. 159 Stabilizer bar end link hex nut

air suspension vehicle. Failure to do so can result in unexpected inflation or deflation of the air springs, which can result in shifting of the vehicle during these operations.

> ※ **WARNING**
>
> Suspension fasteners are critical parts because they affect performance of vital components and systems and their failure can result in major service expense. A new part with the same part number must be installed if installation becomes necessary. If substitution is necessary, the part must be of the same finish and property class. Torque values must be used as specified during reassembly to make sure of correct retention of these parts.

1. Before servicing the vehicle, refer to the precautions in the beginning of this section.
2. Disconnect battery negative cable from battery and properly isolate to prevent accidental reconnection.
3. Turn the air suspension service switch off.
4. Raise the vehicle on a hoist.

➡ Use the hex holding feature to prevent the stud from turning while removing the nut.

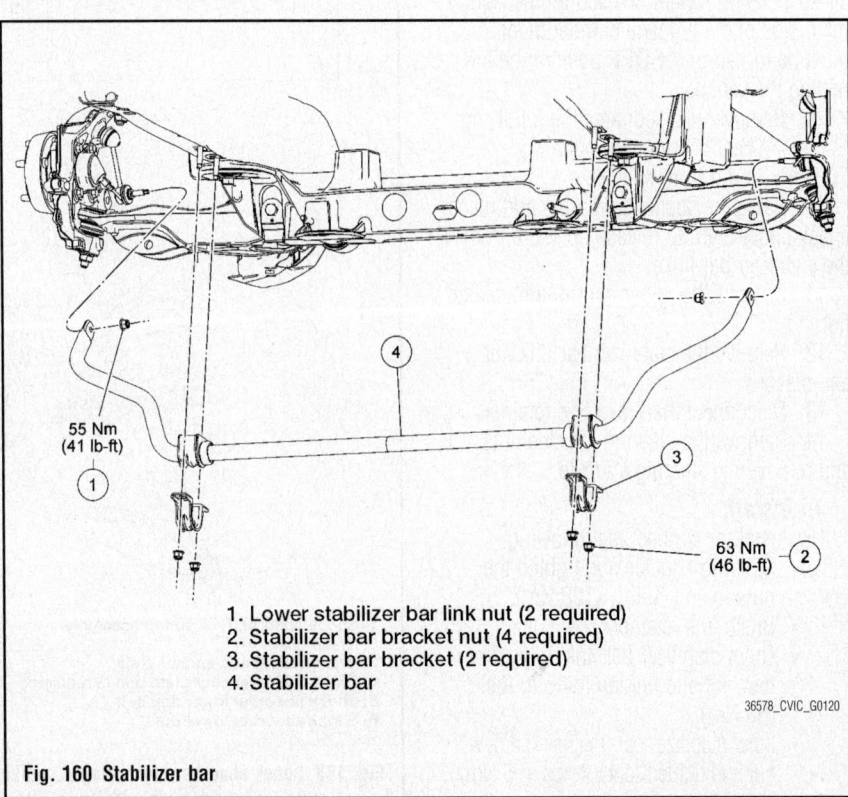

55 Nm (41 lb-ft) ①

63 Nm (46 lb-ft) ②

1. Lower stabilizer bar link nut (2 required)
2. Stabilizer bar bracket nut (4 required)
3. Stabilizer bar bracket (2 required)
4. Stabilizer bar

36578_CVIC_G0120

Fig. 160 Stabilizer bar

5. Remove or disconnect the following:
- Two nuts holding the stabilizer bar end links and discard.
- Stabilizer bar end links
- Four nuts holding the stabilizer bar brackets and discard.
- Stabilizer bar brackets
- Stabilizer bar

To install:

6. Install or connect the following:
- Stabilizer bar
- Stabilizer bar brackets with new nuts and torque to 46 ft. lbs. (63 Nm)
- Stabilizer bar end links with new nuts and torque to 46 ft. lbs. (63 Nm)

7. Turn air suspension switch on.

UPPER CONTROL ARM

REMOVAL & INSTALLATION

See Figure 161.

✳✳ CAUTION

If the vehicle is equipped with air suspension, the electrical power to the air suspension system must be shut off prior to hoisting, jacking or towing an air suspension vehicle. This can be accomplished by turning off the air suspension switch located in the luggage compartment. Failure to do so can result in unexpected inflation or deflation of the air springs, which can result in shifting of the vehicle during these operations. Failure to follow these instructions may result in personal injury.

1. If equipped with air suspension, the air suspension switch, located on the right-hand side of the luggage compartment, must be turned to the **OFF** position before raising the vehicle.

2. Remove or disconnect the following:

- Front wheel
- Upper ball joint. Support the lower control arm.
- Upper control arm pivot bolts
- Upper control arm

To install:

3. Install or connect the following:
- Upper control arm. Tighten the pivot bolts (1) to 111 ft. lbs. (150 Nm).
- Upper ball joint. Tighten the pinch bolt to 59 ft. lbs. (80 Nm).
- Front wheel

4. If equipped with air suspension, turn the air suspension service switch to the **ON** position.

5. Align the vehicle.

WHEEL HUB & BEARING

REMOVAL & INSTALLATION

See Figures 162 and 163.

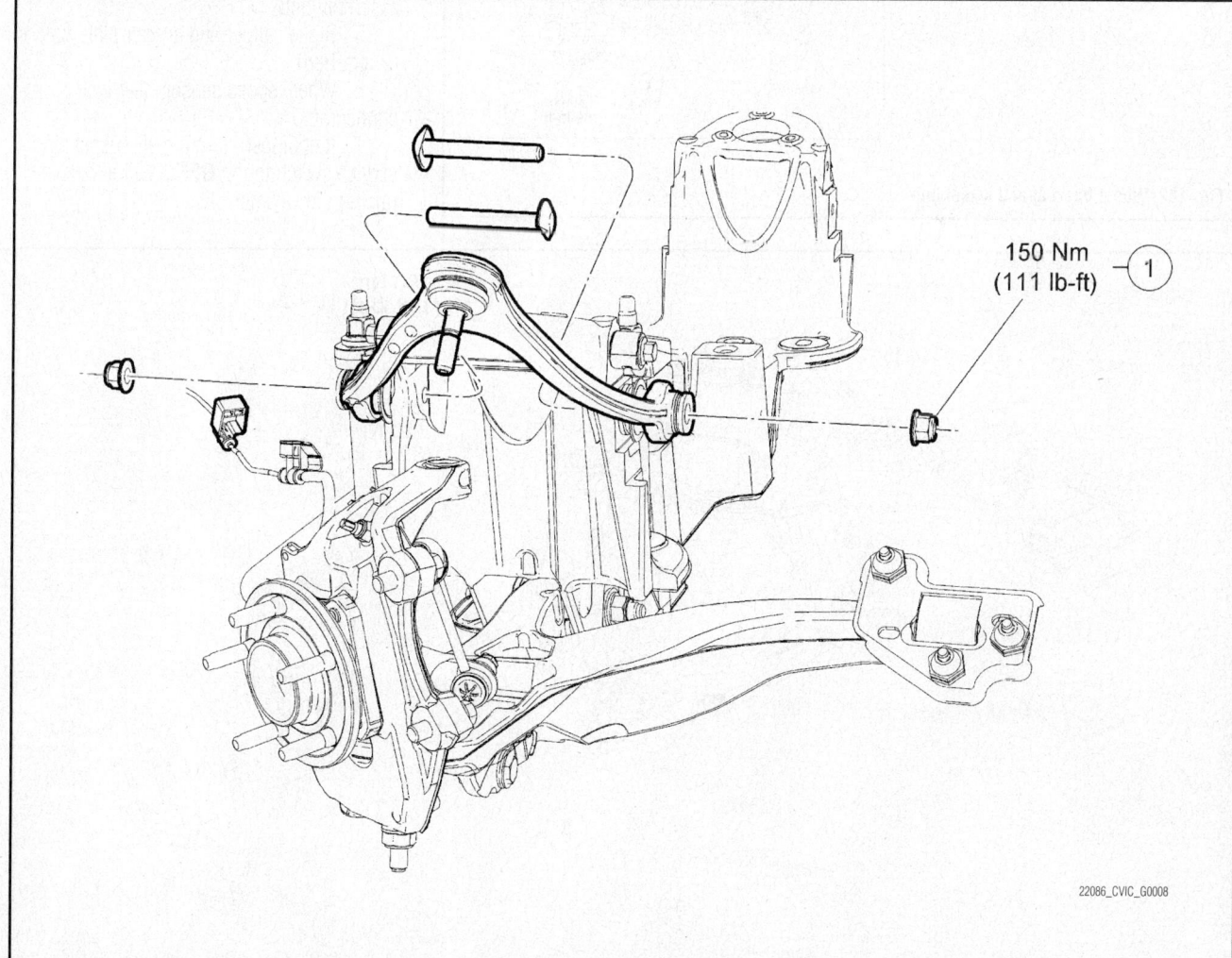

150 Nm (111 lb-ft) ①

22086_CVIC_G0008

Fig. 161 Upper control arm assembly

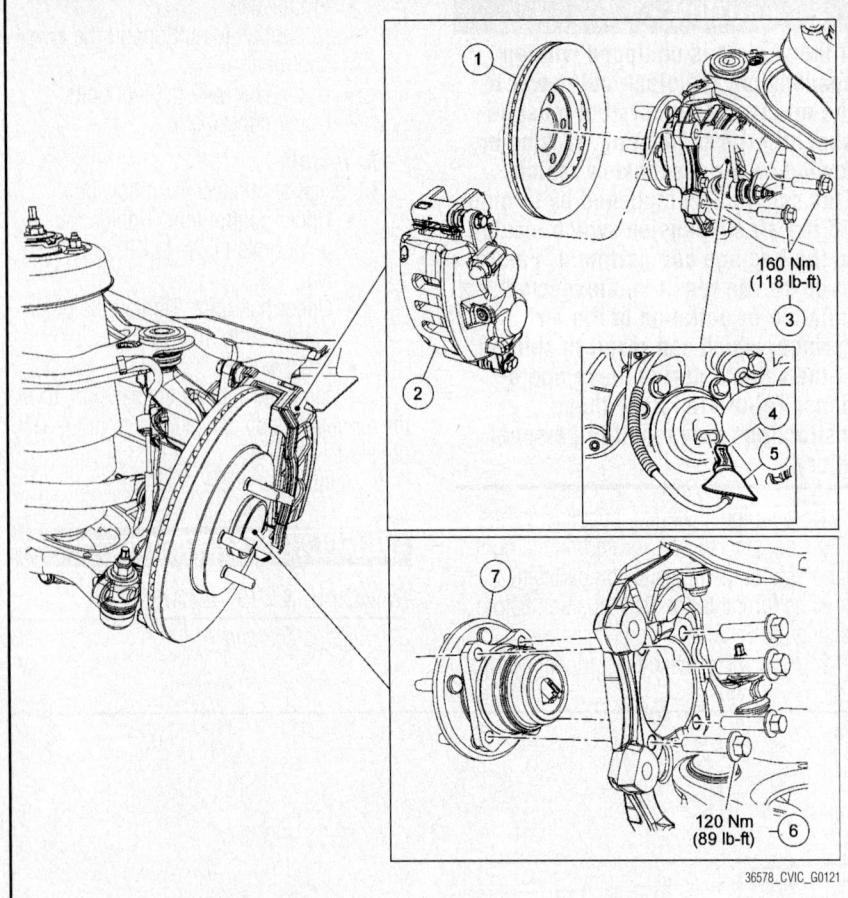

Fig. 162 Wheel bearing and wheel hub

✳✳ CAUTION

If the vehicle is equipped with air suspension, the electrical power to the air suspension system must be shut off prior to hoisting, jacking or towing an air suspension vehicle. This can be accomplished by turning off the air suspension switch located in the luggage compartment. Failure to do so can result in unexpected inflation or deflation of the air springs, which can result in shifting of the vehicle during these operations. Failure to follow these instructions may result in personal injury.

Wheel bearing and wheel hub components (see illustration):

1. Brake disc
2. Brake caliper
3. Wheel bearing and wheel hub assembly
4. Wheel bearing and wheel hub assembly bolt
5. Brake caliper and anchor plate bolt (2 required)
6. Wheel speed sensor electrical connector
7. If equipped, turn the air suspension service switch to the **OFF** position before raising the vehicle.

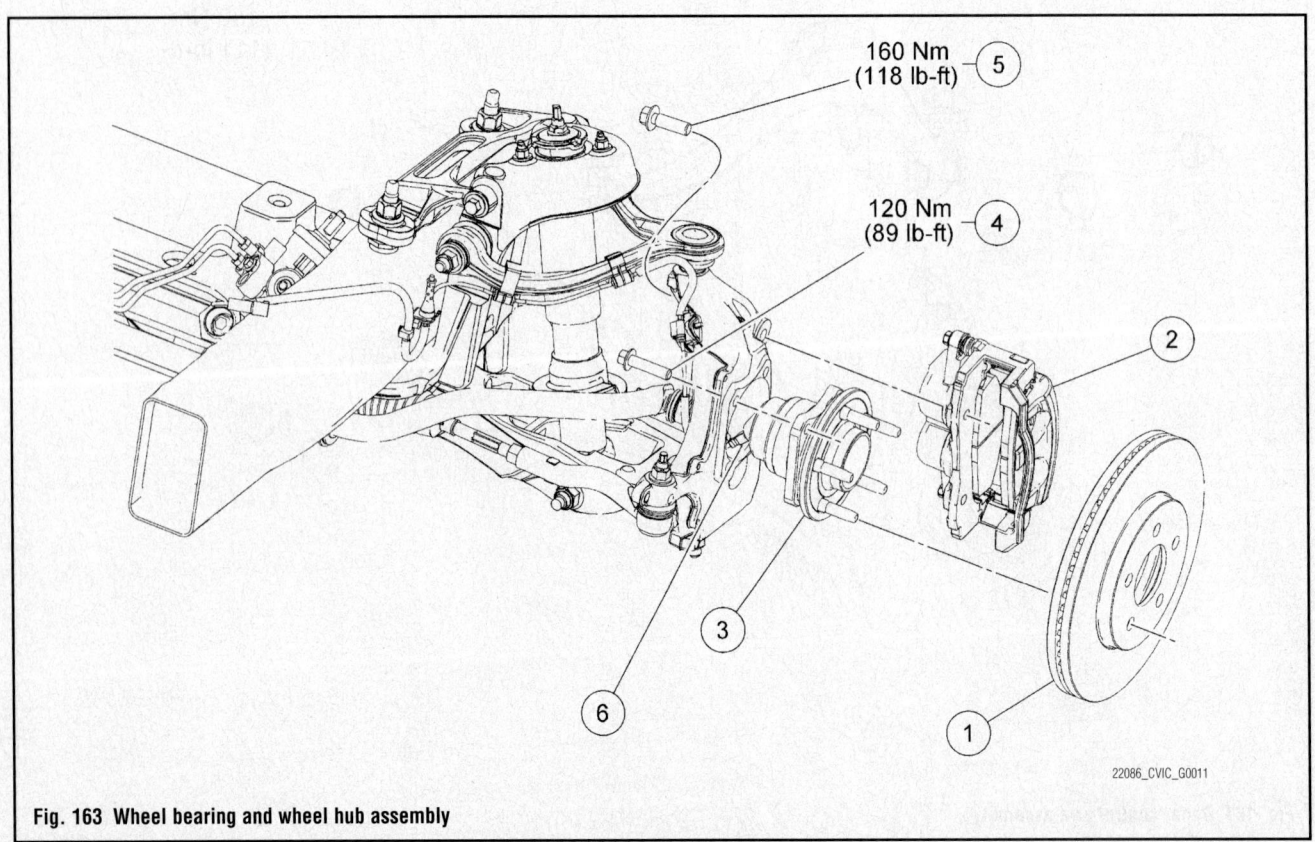

Fig. 163 Wheel bearing and wheel hub assembly

8. Remove or disconnect the following
- Front wheel
- Grease cap from the hub
- Disc brake caliper. Suspend the caliper with a length of wire. Do not let it hang from the brake hose. Discard the disc brake caliper mounting bolts.
- Disc brake rotor. If the factory installed push on nuts are installed, remove them first.
- Wheel hub retainer nut and discard
- Hub and bearing assembly

To install:

9. Install or connect the following:
- Hub and bearing assembly
- New wheel hub retainer nut and tighten to 118 ft. lbs. (160 Nm)
- Disc brake rotor and push on nuts, if equipped
- New grease cap seal
- Disc brake caliper using the 2 new disc brake caliper mounting bolts. Tighten the bolts to 89 ft. lbs. (120 Nm).
- Wheel. Tighten the lug nuts in a star pattern to 100 ft. lbs. (136 Nm).

10. If equipped with air suspension, turn the air suspension switch to the **ON** position.

11. Pump the brake pedal several times to position the brake pads prior to moving the vehicle.

12. Check the front end alignment.

ADJUSTMENT

The front wheel bearings are of a hub unit design and are pre-greased, sealed and require no maintenance. The bearings are preset and cannot be adjusted.

SUSPENSION

COIL SPRING

REMOVAL & INSTALLATION

See Figure 164.

✳✳ CAUTION

If the vehicle is equipped with air suspension, the electrical power to the air suspension system must be shut off prior to hoisting, jacking or towing an air suspension vehicle. This can be accomplished by turning off the air suspension switch located in the luggage compartment. Failure to do so can result in unexpected inflation or deflation of the air springs, which can result in shifting of the vehicle during these operations. Failure to follow these instructions may result in personal injury.

REAR SUSPENSION

Rear coil spring components (refer to graphic):
1. Lower shock bolt
2. Lower shock nut
3. Stabilizer bar link nut
4. Stabilizer bar link bushing
5. Rear spring
6. Rear spring insulator
7. Lateral arm bolt (2 required)
8. Lateral arm nut (2 required)
9. Lateral arm (2 required)

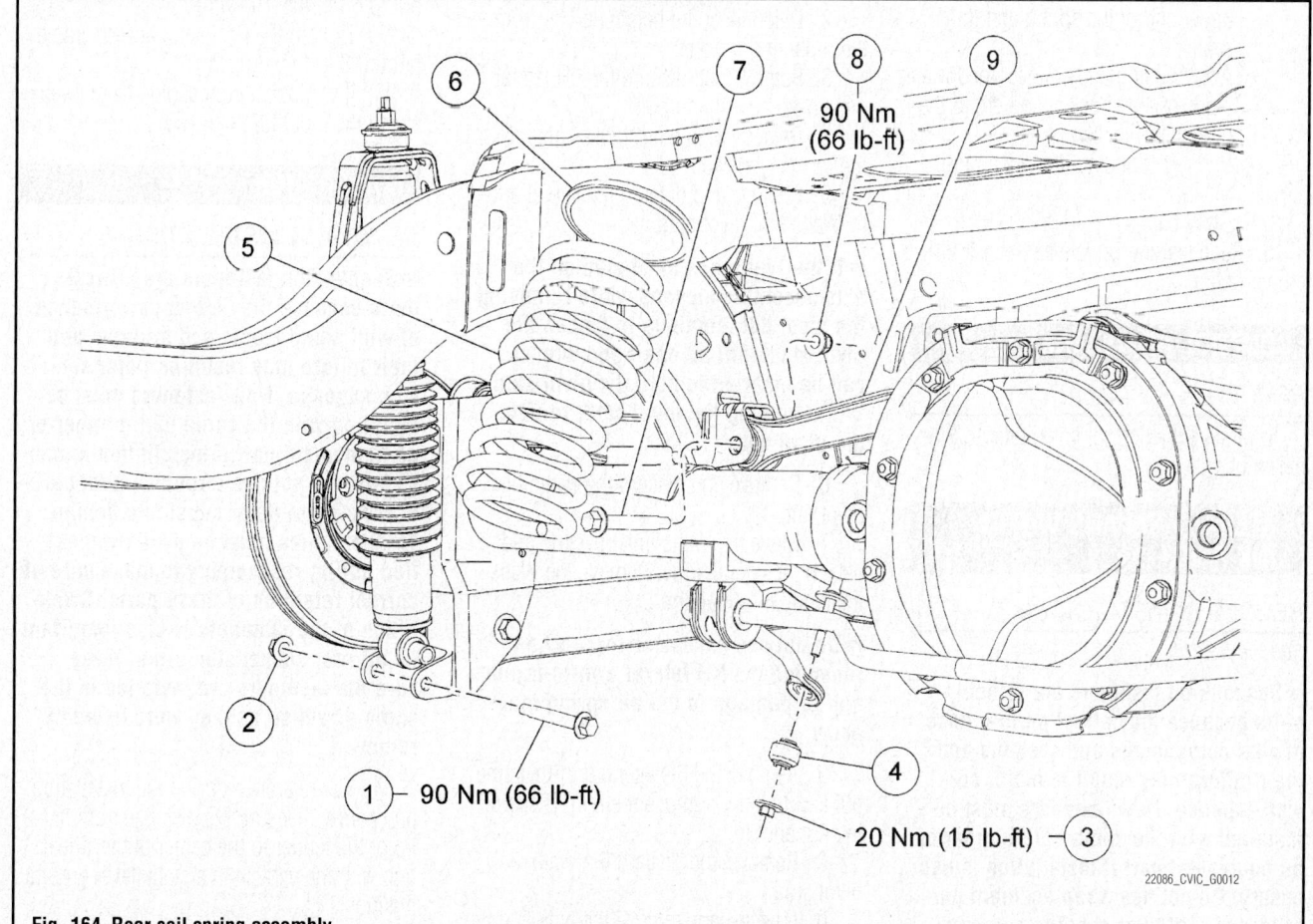

90 Nm (66 lb-ft)

90 Nm (66 lb-ft)

20 Nm (15 lb-ft)

22086_CVIC_G0012

Fig. 164 Rear coil spring assembly

10. Place a hoist under the rear axle housing and raise and safely support the vehicle.

11. Support the frame side rails with 2 jack stands.

12. Remove or disconnect the following:

- Rear stabilizer bar
- Lower studs of both rear shock absorbers from the mounting brackets on the axle tube
- Parking brake cable from the upper arm retainer before lowering the axle housing

13. Lower the axle housing until the coil springs are released. If the axle housing is supported by the hoist, lower the hoist allowing the rear of the vehicle to rest on the jack stands. If the vehicle's axle housing is supported by the jack stands, leave the hoist stationary and lower the jack stands or raise the hoist to release the tension on the coil springs.

14. Remove the coil springs and insulators.

To install:

15. Install or connect the following:

- Coil spring in the upper and lower seats with an insulator between the upper end of the spring and frame seat
- Axle housing and connect the lower studs of the shock absorbers to the mounting brackets
- Parking cable into the upper arm retainer
- Sway bar

16. Road test the vehicle and check for proper operation.

CONTROL ARMS/LINKS

REMOVAL & INSTALLATION

To remove the control links, refer to Stabilizer bar.

LATERAL ARM AND WATTS LINK PIVOT

REMOVAL & INSTALLATION

See Figure 165.

➡Suspension fasteners are critical parts because they affect performance of vital components and systems and their failure may result in major service expense. New fasteners must be installed with the same part number or an equivalent part if installation is necessary. Do not use a replacement part of lesser quality or substitute design. Torque values must be used as speci-

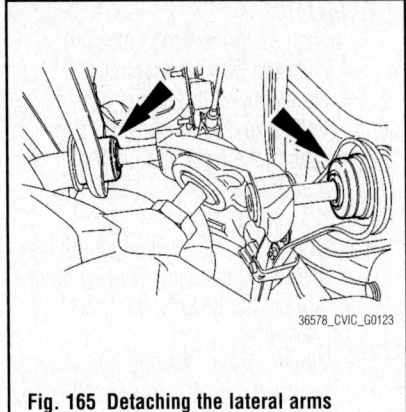

Fig. 165 Detaching the lateral arms

fied during reassembly to make sure of correct retention of these parts. Orientation of the fasteners is also important on all rear suspension arms. Make sure the fasteners are installed in the same direction as they were in when removed.

➡For reference during the installation procedure, measure the distance from the lip of the fender to the center of the wheel hub with the vehicle in a static level ground position.

1. Raise and support the vehicle.
2. Disconnect the height sensor from the mounting bracket.
3. Remove and discard the LH lateral arm-to-frame nut and bolt.
4. Detach the parking brake cable from the retainer bracket.
5. Remove and discard the lateral arm-to-Watts link pivot nuts.

➡If the Watts link pivot stud on the axle assembly loosens while removing the pivot nut, continue to loosen the pivot stud until an open-end wrench can be inserted to hold the pivot stud. While holding the pivot stud, remove the pivot nut.

6. Remove and discard the Watts link pivot nut.
7. Move the Watts link upwards and detach the lateral arms. Remove the Watts link and LH lateral arm.

➡Do not use excessive force when removing the RH lateral arm-to-frame bolt or damage to the air spring may occur.

8. Remove the RH lateral arm-to-frame nut and bolt and remove the arm. Discard the nut and bolt.
9. Remove and discard the Watts link pivot stud.
10. If necessary, remove the nuts and the height sensor bracket.

To install:

11. Position the LH lateral arm and loosely install the new LH lateral arm-to-frame nut and bolt.
12. If necessary, install the height sensor bracket.
13. Install the new Watts link pivot stud and tighten to 199 ft. lbs. (270 Nm).
14. Position the RH lateral arm and loosely install the new RH lateral arm-to-frame nut and bolt.
15. Position the Watts link pivot and loosely install the new lateral arm-to-Watts link pivot nuts.
16. Loosely install the new Watts link pivot nut.
17. Check and if necessary, align the front end.
18. Before tightening the fasteners, use a suitable jack to raise the suspension until the distance between the lip of the fender and the center of the wheel hub is equal to the measurement taken in the removal procedure.
19. Tighten the Watts link pivot nut to 184 ft. lbs. (250 Nm).
20. Tighten the lateral arm-to-Watts link pivot nuts to 66 ft. lbs. (90 Nm).
21. Tighten the LH lateral arm-to-frame nut to 66 ft. lbs. (90 Nm).
22. Tighten the RH lateral arm-to-frame nut to 66 ft. lbs. (90 Nm).
23. If equipped, connect the height sensor to the mounting bracket.

LOWER ARM

REMOVAL & INSTALLATION

➡Suspension fasteners are critical parts because they affect performance of vital components and systems and their failure may result in major service expense. New fasteners must be installed with the same part number or an equivalent part if installation is necessary. Do not use a replacement part of lesser quality or substitute design. Torque values must be used as specified during reassembly to make sure of correct retention of these parts. Orientation of the fasteners is also important on all rear suspension arms. Make sure the fasteners are installed in the same direction as they were in when removed.

1. For reference during the installation procedure, measure the distance from the lip of the fender to the center of the wheel hub with the vehicle in a static level ground position.
2. Raise and support the vehicle.

3. Remove the wheel and tire.

4. Remove and discard the lower arm-to-axle nut and bolt.

5. Remove the lower arm-to-frame bolt, flagnut and the lower arm.

6. Discard the flagnut and bolt.

To install:

→**The rear suspension lower arms are interchangeable from side-to-side, with OUTBOARD stamped on one side of the arms for positioning during installation.**

7. Position the lower arm and loosely install the new lower arm-to-frame bolt and flagnut.

8. Loosely install the new lower arm-to-axle nut and bolt.

9. Before tightening the fasteners, use a suitable jack to raise the suspension until the distance between the lip of the fender and the center of the wheel hub is equal to the measurement taken in the removal procedure.

10. Tighten the lower arm-to-frame nut to 111 ft. lbs. (150 Nm).

11. Tighten the lower arm-to-axle nut to 111 ft. lbs. (150 Nm).

12. Install the wheel and tire

SHOCK ABSORBER

REMOVAL & INSTALLATION

See Figure 166.

❋❋ CAUTION

If the vehicle is equipped with air suspension, the electrical power to the air suspension system must be shut off prior to hoisting, jacking or towing an air suspension vehicle. This can be accomplished by turning off the air suspension switch located in the luggage compartment. Failure to do so can result in unexpected inflation or deflation of the air springs, which can result in shifting of the vehicle during these operations. Failure to follow these instructions may result in personal injury.

Rear shock absorber components (refer to graphic):

1. Lower shock bolt
2. Lower shock nut
3. Shock absorber assembly
4. Shock washer and insulator
5. Upper shock nut
6. If equipped with air suspension, turn the air suspension service switch **OFF**.
7. Be sure the ignition switch is in the **OFF** position.
8. Support the rear axle assembly with a jack.
9. Remove or disconnect the following:

   • Top retaining nut, washer and bushing
   • Bottom retaining nut and washer
   • Shock absorber

To install:

10. Install or connect the following:

    • Shock absorber so the upper stud enters the hole in the frame

• Top bushing, washer and retaining nut. Tighten to 30 ft. lbs. (40 Nm).

11. Extend the shock absorber and place the lower stud through the hole in the bracket

12. Bottom retaining washer and nut. Tighten to 66 ft. lbs. (90 Nm).

13. Remove the jack from the axle assembly.

14. Turn the air suspension service switch to the **ON** position.

STABILIZER BAR & CONTROL ARMS/LINKS

REMOVAL & INSTALLATION

→**Suspension fasteners are critical parts because they affect performance of vital components and systems and their failure may result in major service expense. New fasteners with the same part number or an equivalent part must be installed if installation is necessary. Do not use a replacement part of lesser quality or substitute design. Torque values must be used as specified during reassembly to make sure of correct retention of these parts. Orientation of the fasteners is also important on all rear suspension arms. Make sure the fasteners are installed in the same direction as they were in when removed.**

1. Raise and support the vehicle.
2. Remove the 2 lower stabilizer bar link

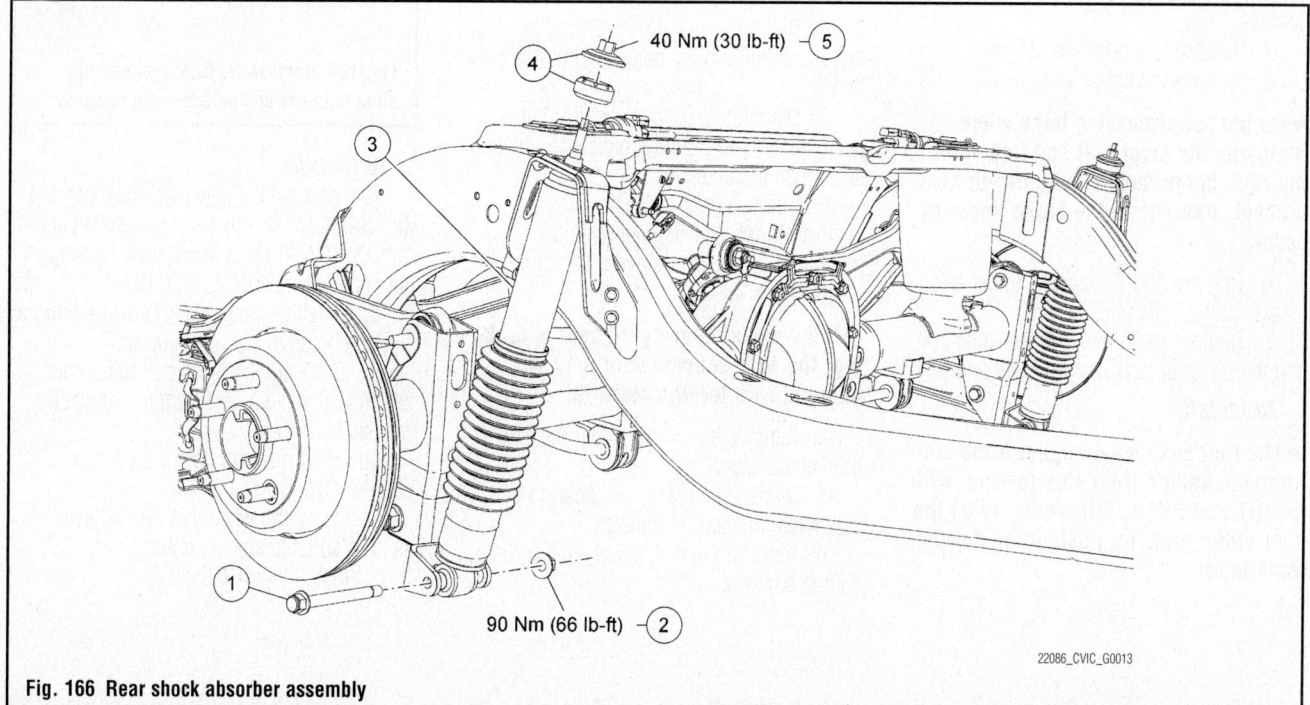

Fig. 166 Rear shock absorber assembly

22086_CVIC_G0013

nuts, washers and bushings. Discard the nuts.

3. Remove the 2 upper stabilizer bar link nuts, the washers and bushings, and the stabilizer bar links. Discard the nuts.

4. Remove the 2 stabilizer bar bracket bolts, 2 brackets and the stabilizer bar. Discard the 2 bracket bolts.

5. To install, reverse the removal procedure. For torque specifications, refer to the appropriate illustration under Component Locations.

UPPER ARM

REMOVAL & INSTALLATION

➡Suspension fasteners are critical parts because they affect performance of vital components and systems and their failure may result in major service expense. New fasteners must be installed with the same part number or an equivalent part if installation is necessary. Do not use a replacement part of lesser quality or substitute design. Torque values must be used as specified during reassembly to make sure of correct retention of these parts. Orientation of the fasteners is also important on all rear suspension arms. Make sure the fasteners are installed in the same direction as they were in when removed.

1. For reference during the installation procedure, measure the distance from the lip of the fender to the center of the wheel hub with the vehicle in a static level ground position.

2. Raise and support the vehicle.

3. Remove the wheel and tire.

➡Do not use excessive force when removing the pivot bolt and flagnut on the right upper suspension arm-to-axle bracket. Damage to the brake line may occur.

4. Remove and discard the upper arm-to-axle bolt and flagnut.

5. Remove the upper arm-to-frame bolt and the upper arm. Discard the nut and bolt.

To install:

➡The rear suspension upper arms are interchangeable from side-to-side, with FRONT and OUTBOARD stamped on the side of the arms for positioning during installation.

6. Position the upper arm and loosely install the new upper arm-to-frame bolt.

7. Loosely install the new upper arm-to-axle bolt and flagnut.

8. Before tightening the fasteners, use a suitable jack to raise the suspension until the distance between the lip of the fender and the center of the wheel hub is equal to the measurement taken in the removal procedure.

9. Tighten the upper arm-to-frame bolt to 111 ft. lbs. (150 Nm).

10. Tighten the upper arm-to-axle bolt to 66 ft. lbs. (90 Nm).

11. Install the wheel and tire.

WHEEL BEARINGS

REMOVAL & INSTALLATION

See Figures 167 through 169.

✳✳ CAUTION

If the vehicle is equipped with air suspension, the electrical power to the air suspension system must be shut off prior to hoisting, jacking or towing an air suspension vehicle. This can be accomplished by turning off the air suspension switch located in the luggage compartment. Failure to do so can result in unexpected inflation or deflation of the air springs, which can result in shifting of the vehicle during these operations. Failure to follow these instructions may result in personal injury.

1. Before servicing the vehicle, refer to the precautions in the beginning of this section.

2. Disconnect battery negative cable from battery and properly isolate to prevent accidental reconnection.

3. Remove the axle shaft.

a. If only the seal needs to be replaced, use care to avoid damaging the seal bore.

➡If the wheel bearing oil seal is leaking, the axle housing vent may be plugged with foreign material.

4. Remove the oil seal from the axle tube and discard.

5. Inspect the rear wheel bearing and axle shaft for wear or damage.

6. Remove the rear wheel bearing using a slide hammer.

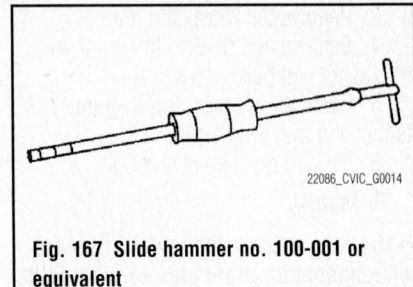

Fig. 167 Slide hammer no. 100-001 or equivalent

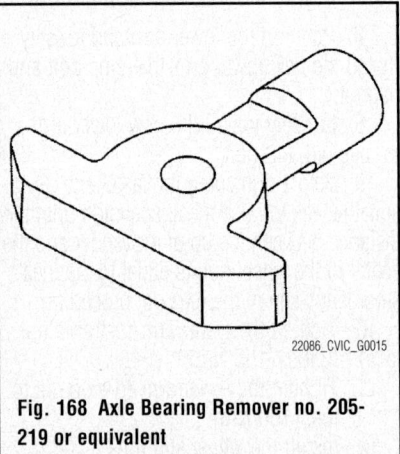

Fig. 168 Axle Bearing Remover no. 205-219 or equivalent

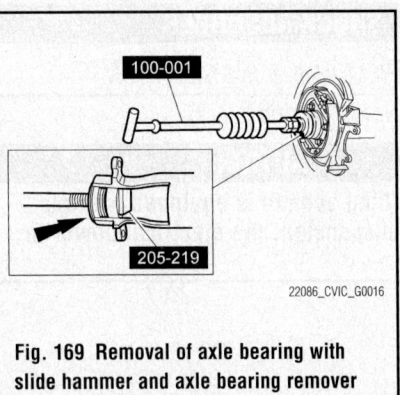

Fig. 169 Removal of axle bearing with slide hammer and axle bearing remover

To install:

7. Lubricate the new rear wheel bearing with SAE 80W-90 Premium Rear Axle Lubricant XY-80W90-QL or equivalent meeting Ford specification WSP-M2C197-A.

8. Install the rear wheel bearing using a suitable press or hammer and drift.

9. Lubricate the lip of the new wheel bearing oil seal using Premium Long-Life Grease XG-1-C or
equivalent meeting Ford specification ESA-M1C75-B.

10. Install the wheel bearing oil seal using a suitable seal installer.

11. Install the axle shaft.

FORD AND LINCOLN

Edge • MKX

SPECIFICATIONS AND MAINTENANCE CHARTS

ENGINE AND VEHICLE IDENTIFICATION CHART

Engine Code							Model Year	
Code	Liters (cc)	Cu. In.	Cyl.	Fuel Sys.	Engine Type	Eng. Mfg.	Code ①	Year
C	3.5 (3500)	214	6	SMFI	DOHC	Ford Motor Co.	8	2008
							9	2009

DOHC: Double Overhead Cam

SMFI: Sequential Multi-port Fuel Injection

① 10th position of VIN

36578_EDGE_C0001

GENERAL ENGINE SPECIFICATIONS

Year	Model	Engine Displacement Liters (VIN)	Net Horsepower @ rpm	Net Torque @ rpm (ft. lbs.)	Bore x Stroke (in.)	Compression Ratio	Oil Pressure @ rpm
2008	Edge	3.5 (C)	265@6250	250@4500	3.64x3.41	10.3:1	①
	MKX	3.5 (C)	265@6250	250@4500	3.64x3.41	10.3:1	①
2009	Edge	3.5 (C)	265@6250	250@4500	3.64x3.41	10.3:1	①
	MKX	3.5 (C)	265@6250	250@4500	3.64x3.41	10.3:1	①

① Minimum 30 psi @ 1500 rpm with engine at normal operating temperature

36578_EDGE_C0002

ENGINE TUNE-UP SPECIFICATIONS

Year	Engine Displacement Liters (VIN)	Spark Plug Gap (in.)	Ignition Timing (deg.) MT	AT	Fuel Pump (psi)	Idle Speed (rpm) MT	AT	Valve Clearance (in.) Intake	Exhaust
2008	3.5 (C)	0.051-0.057	—	NA	65	—	NA	0.006-0.010	0.012-0.016
2009	3.5 (C)	0.051-0.057	—	NA	65	—	NA	0.006-0.010	0.012-0.016

NOTE: The Vehicle Emission Control Information label often reflects changes made during production and must be used if they differ from this chart.

NOTE: The fuel pressure readings are with the engine running

NA: Not Available

36578_EDGE_C0003

CAPACITIES

Year	Model	Engine Displacement Liters (VIN)	Engine Oil with Filter (qts.)	Transmission (pts.) 5-Spd	Transmission (pts.) Auto.	Transfer Case (pts.)	Drive Axle Front (pts.)	Drive Axle Rear (pts.)	Fuel Tank (gal.)	Cooling System (qts.)
2008	Edge	3.5 (C)	5.5	—	20.0	①	—	2.43	②	11.7
	MKX	3.5 (C)	5.5	—	20.0	①	—	2.43	②	11.7
2009	Edge	3.5 (C)	5.5	—	20.0	①	—	2.43	②	11.7
	MKX	3.5 (C)	5.5	—	20.0	①	—	2.43	②	11.7

NOTE: All capacities are approximate. Add fluid gradually and check to be sure a proper fluid level is obtained.

① 18 ounces

② Front Wheel Drive (FWD): 19 gallons

All Wheel Drive (AWD): 20 gallons

36578_EDGE_C0004

FLUID SPECIFICATIONS

Year	Model	Engine Displacement Liters (VIN)	Engine Oil	Auto. Trans.	Drive Axle	Power Steering Fluid	Brake Master Cylinder
2008	Edge	3.5 (C)	①	Mercon® ATF Fluid	80W-90	Mercon® ATF Fluid	DOT 3
	MKX	3.5 (C)	①	Mercon® ATF Fluid	80W-90	Mercon® ATF Fluid	DOT 3
2009	Edge	3.5 (C)	①	Mercon® ATF Fluid	80W-90	Mercon® ATF Fluid	DOT 3
	MKX	3.5 (C)	①	Mercon® ATF Fluid	80W-90	Mercon® ATF Fluid	DOT 3

DOT: Department Of Transpotation

① 5W-20 Premium Synthetic Blend Motor Oil (US) or 5W-20 Super Premium Motor Oil (Canada)

36578_EDGE_C0005

VALVE SPECIFICATIONS

Year	Engine Displacement Liters (VIN)	Seat Angle (deg.)	Face Angle (deg.)	Spring Test Pressure (lbs. @ in.)	Spring Installed Height (in.)	Stem-to-Guide Clearance (in.) Intake	Stem-to-Guide Clearance (in.) Exhaust	Stem Diameter (in.) Intake	Stem Diameter (in.) Exhaust
2008	3.5 (C)	44.5-45.5	44.5-45.5	115 @ 1.08	1.4500	0.0008-0.0027	0.0013-0.0320	0.2157-0.2164	0.2151-0.2159
2009	3.5 (C)	44.5-45.5	44.5-45.5	115 @ 1.08	1.4500	0.0008-0.0027	0.0013-0.0320	0.2157-0.2164	0.2151-0.2159

NA: Not Available

36578_EDGE_C0006

CAMSHAFT SPECIFICATIONS
All measurements are given in inches

Year	Engine Displacement Liters (VIN)	Journal Diameter	Bearing Oil Clearance	Shaft End-play	Runout	Lobe Height Intake	Lobe Height Exhaust
2008	3.5 (C)	①	②	0.0012-0.0066	0.0015	0.3800	0.3800
2009	3.5 (C)	①	②	0.0012-0.0066	0.0015	0.3800	0.3800

① 1st journal: 1.2202-1.2209 in.

  Intermediate journals: 1.021-1.022 in.

② 1st journal: 0.0027 MAX

  Intermediate journals: 0.0029 MAX

36578_EDGE_C0007

CRANKSHAFT AND CONNECTING ROD SPECIFICATIONS
All measurements are given in inches

Year	Engine Displacement Liters (VIN)	Crankshaft Main Brg. Journal Dia.	Crankshaft Main Brg. Oil Clearance	Crankshaft Shaft End-play	Crankshaft Thrust on No.	Connecting Rod Journal Diameter	Connecting Rod Oil Clearance	Connecting Rod Side Clearance
2008	3.5 (C)	2.657	NA	0.0039-0.0114	NA	2.204-2.205	NA	NA
2009	3.5 (C)	2.657	NA	0.0039-0.0114	NA	2.204-2.205	NA	NA

NA - Not Available

36578_EDGE_C0008

PISTON AND RING SPECIFICATIONS
All measurements are given in inches

Year	Engine Displacement Liters (VIN)	Piston Clearance	Ring Gap Top Compression	Ring Gap Bottom Compression	Ring Gap Oil Control	Ring Side Clearance Top Compression	Ring Side Clearance Bottom Compression	Ring Side Clearance Oil Control
2008	3.5 (C)	0.0003-0.0017	0.0059-0.0098	0.0118-0.0216	0.0059-0.0177	NA	NA	NA
2009	3.5 (C)	0.0003-0.0017	0.0059-0.0098	0.0118-0.0216	0.0059-0.0177	NA	NA	NA

NA: Not Available

36578_EDGE_C0009

TORQUE SPECIFICATIONS
All readings in ft. lbs.

Year	Engine Displacement Liters (VIN)	Cylinder Head Bolts	Main Bearing Bolts	Rod Bearing Bolts	Crankshaft Damper Bolts	Flywheel Bolts	Manifold Intake	Manifold Exhaust	Spark Plugs	Oil Pan Drain Plug
2008	3.5 (C)	①	NA	NA	②	59	③	④	11	20
2009	3.5 (C)	①	NA	NA	②	59	③	④	11	20

① Step 1: 15 ft. lbs.
   Step 2: 26 ft. lbs.
   Step 3: +90 degrees
   Step 4: +90 degrees
   Step 4: +90 degrees

② Step 1: 89 ft. lbs.
   Step 2: Loosen one full turn
   Step 3: 37 ft. lbs.
   Step 4: +90 degrees

③ Upper intake manifold: 89 inch lbs.
   Lower intake manfold: 89 inch lbs.

④ Studs: 9 ft. lbs.
   Nuts: 15 ft. lbs.

36578_EDGE_C0010

WHEEL ALIGNMENT

Year	Model			Caster Range (+/-Deg.)	Caster Preferred Setting (Deg.)	Camber Range (+/-Deg.)	Camber Preferred Setting (Deg.)	Toe-in (in.)
2008	Edge	F	Left	4.4 +/- 0.75	NA	-0.50 +/- -0.75	NA	
			Right	4.4 +/- 0.75	NA	-0.50 +/- -0.75	NA	
		R		NA	NA	-0.40 +/- 0.75	NA	0.05 +/- -0.20
	MKX	F	Left	4.4 +/- 0.75	NA	-0.50 +/- -0.75	NA	
			Right	4.4 +/- 0.75	NA	-0.50 +/- -0.75	NA	
		R		NA	NA	-0.40 +/- 0.75	NA	0.05 +/- -0.20
2009	Edge	F	Left	4.3+/-0.75	NA	-0.1+/- -0.75	NA	NA
			Right	4.5+/-0.75	NA	-0.6 +/- -.075	NA	NA
		R		NA	NA	-0.45 +/- 0.75	NA	0.05 +/- -0.20
	MKX	F	Left	4.3+/-0.75	NA	-0.1+/- -0.75	NA	NA
			Right	4.5+/-0.75	NA	-0.6 +/- -.075	NA	NA
		R		NA	NA	-0.45 +/- 0.75	NA	0.05 +/- -0.20

36578_EDGE_C0014

TIRE, WHEEL AND BALL JOINT SPECIFICATIONS

Year	Model	OEM Tires Standard	OEM Tires Optional	Tire Pressures (psi) Front	Tire Pressures (psi) Rear	Wheel Size	Ball Joint Inspection	Lug Nut (ft. lbs.)
2008	Edge	P235/65R17	P245/60R18	①	①	NS	NS	100
	MKX	P235/65R17	P245/60R18	①	①	NS	NS	100
2009	Edge	P235/65R17	P245/60R18	①	①	NS	NS	100
	MKX	P235/65R17	P245/60R18	①	①	NS	NS	100

OEM: Original Equipment Manufacturer

PSI: Pounds Per Square Inch

NS: Not specified by manufacturer

① See the safety certification label on the driver side door jamb for tire pressures.

36578_EDGE_C0011

BRAKE SPECIFICATIONS

All measurements in inches unless noted

Year	Model		Brake Disc Original Thickness	Brake Disc Minimum Thickness	Maximum Runout	Brake Drum Diameter Original Inside Diameter	Brake Drum Diameter Max. Wear Limit	Brake Drum Diameter Maximum Machine Diameter	Minimum Lining Thickness Front	Minimum Lining Thickness Rear	Brake Caliper Bracket Bolts (ft. lbs.)	Brake Caliper Mounting Bolts (ft. lbs.)
2008	Edge	F	1.102	1.023	NA	—	—	—	0.118	—	98	65
		R	0.708	0.629	NA	—	—	—	—	0.118	66	19
	MKX	F	1.102	1.023	NA	—	—	—	0.118	—	98	65
		R	0.708	0.629	NA	—	—	—	—	0.118	66	19
2009	Edge	F	1.102	1.023	NA	—	—	—	0.118	—	98	65
		R	0.708	0.629	NA	—	—	—	—	0.118	66	19
	MKX	F	1.102	1.023	NA	—	—	—	0.118	—	98	65
		R	0.708	0.629	NA	—	—	—	—	0.118	66	19

F: Front

R: Rear

36578_EDGE_C0012

SCHEDULED MAINTENANCE INTERVALS

FORD EDGE, LINCOLN MKX

TO BE SERVICED	OF SERVIC	VEHICLE MILEAGE INTERVAL (x1000)															
		7.5	15	22.5	30	37.5	45	52.5	60	68	75	82.5	90	97.5	105	112.5	120
Accessory drive belts	I & A												✓				
Air cleaner element	R				✓				✓				✓				✓
Air conditioning filter	R																
Brake fluid	R																
Brake hoses & lines (including ABS)	I		✓		✓		✓		✓		✓		✓		✓		✓
Cooling system hoses & connections	I		✓		✓		✓		✓		✓		✓		✓		✓
Engine coolant	R								✓								
Engine oil	R	✓	✓	✓	✓	✓	✓	✓	✓	✓	✓	✓	✓	✓	✓	✓	✓
Engine oil and coolant levels	I	Inspect at each fuel stop															
Engine oil filter	R	✓	✓	✓	✓	✓	✓	✓	✓	✓	✓	✓	✓	✓	✓	✓	✓
Exhaust system	I		✓		✓		✓		✓		✓		✓		✓		✓
Fluid levels and condition	I		✓						✓		✓		✓		✓		✓
Front and rear brakes	I		✓		✓		✓		✓		✓		✓		✓		✓
Fuel lines & connection	I		✓												✓		
Halfshaft boots	I		✓						✓		✓		✓		✓		✓
Idle speed	I & A																
Parking brake system	I & A		✓						✓		✓		✓		✓		
Rear differential fluid	R														✓		
Rotate and inspect tires	I	✓	✓	✓	✓	✓	✓	✓	✓	✓	✓	✓	✓	✓	✓	✓	✓
Spark plugs	R												✓				
Suspension components	I		✓		✓		✓		✓		✓		✓		✓		✓
Tie rod ends, steering gear box & boots	I		✓		✓		✓		✓		✓		✓		✓		✓
Transmission fluid	R				✓				✓								✓
Valve clearance	I															✓	

R: Replace   I: Inspect   A: Adjust

FREQUENT OPERATION MAINTENANCE (SEVERE SERVICE)

If a vehicle is operated under any of the following conditions it is considered severe service:

- Towing a trailer or using a camper or car-top carrier.
- Repeated short trips of less than 5 miles in temperatures below freezing, or trips of less than 10 miles in any temperature.
- Extensive idling or low-speed driving for long distances as in heavy commercial use, such as delivery, taxi or police cars.
- Operating on rough, muddy or salt-covered roads.
- Operating on unpaved or dusty roads.
- Driving in extremely hot (over 90°) conditions.

Air cleaner element: replace every 15,000 miles

Engine oil and filter: replace every 3750 miles or 6 months, whichever occurs first.

Timing belt: replace every 60,000 miles if the vehicle is regularly driven in temperatures above 110°F or below -20°F.

Transmission fluid: replace every 30,000 miles.

Rear differential fluid: replace every 60,000 miles.

Front and rear brakes: inspect every 7500 miles or 6 months, whichever occurs first.

Locks and hinges: lubricate every 15,000 miles.

Tie rods, steering gear box, boots: inspect every 7500 miles or 6 months, whichever occurs first.

Suspension components: inspect every 7500 miles or 6 months, whichever occurs first.

Halfshaft boots: inspect every 7500 miles or 6 months, whichever occurs first.

PRECAUTIONS

Before servicing any vehicle, please be sure to read all of the following precautions, which deal with personal safety, prevention of component damage, and important points to take into consideration when servicing a motor vehicle:

• Never open, service or drain the radiator or cooling system when the engine is hot; serious burns can occur from the steam and hot coolant.

• Observe all applicable safety precautions when working around fuel. Whenever servicing the fuel system, always work in a well-ventilated area. Do not allow fuel spray or vapors to come in contact with a spark, open flame, or excessive heat (a hot drop light, for example). Keep a dry chemical fire extinguisher near the work area. Always keep fuel in a container specifically designed for fuel storage; also, always properly seal fuel containers to avoid the possibility of fire or explosion. Refer to the additional fuel system precautions later in this section.

• Fuel injection systems often remain pressurized, even after the engine has been turned**OFF**. The fuel system pressure must be relieved before disconnecting any fuel lines. Failure to do so may result in fire and/or personal injury.

• Brake fluid often contains polyglycol ethers and polyglycols. Avoid contact with the eyes and wash your hands thoroughly after handling brake fluid. If you do get brake fluid in your eyes, flush your eyes with clean, running water for 15 minutes. If eye irritation persists, or if you have taken brake fluid internally, IMMEDIATELY seek medical assistance.

• The EPA warns that prolonged contact with used engine oil may cause a number of skin disorders, including cancer. You should make every effort to minimize your exposure to used engine oil. Protective gloves should be worn when changing oil. Wash your hands and any other exposed skin areas as soon as possible after exposure to used engine oil. Soap and water, or waterless hand cleaner should be used.

• All new vehicles are now equipped with an air bag system, often referred to as a Supplemental Restraint System (SRS) or Supplemental Inflatable Restraint (SIR) system. The system must be disabled before performing service on or around system components, steering column, instrument panel components, wiring and sensors. Failure to follow safety and disabling procedures could result in accidental air bag deployment, possible personal injury and unnecessary system repairs.

• Always wear safety goggles when working with, or around, the air bag system. When carrying a non-deployed air bag, be sure the bag and trim cover are pointed away from your body. When placing a non-deployed air bag on a work surface, always face the bag and trim cover upward, away from the surface. This will reduce the motion of the module if it is accidentally deployed. Refer to the additional air bag system precautions later in this section.

• Clean, high quality brake fluid from a sealed container is essential to the safe and proper operation of the brake system. You should always buy the correct type of brake fluid for your vehicle. If the brake fluid becomes contaminated, completely flush the system with new fluid. Never reuse any brake fluid. Any brake fluid that is removed from the system should be discarded. Also, do not allow any brake fluid to come in contact with a painted surface; it will damage the paint.

• Never operate the engine without the proper amount and type of engine oil; doing so WILL result in severe engine damage.

• Timing belt maintenance is extremely important. Many models utilize an interference-type, non-freewheeling engine. If the timing belt breaks, the valves in the cylinder head may strike the pistons, causing potentially serious (also time-consuming and expensive) engine damage. Refer to the maintenance interval charts for the recommended replacement interval for the timing belt, and to the timing belt section for belt replacement and inspection.

• Disconnecting the negative battery cable on some vehicles may interfere with the functions of the on-board computer system(s) and may require the computer to undergo a relearning process once the negative battery cable is reconnected.

• When servicing drum brakes, only disassemble and assemble one side at a time, leaving the remaining side intact for reference.

• Only an MVAC-trained, EPA-certified automotive technician should service the air conditioning system or its components.

BRAKES

GENERAL INFORMATION

PRECAUTIONS

• Certain components within the ABS system are not intended to be serviced or repaired individually.

• Do not use rubber hoses or other parts not specifically specified for and ABS system. When using repair kits, replace all parts included in the kit. Partial or incorrect repair may lead to functional problems and require the replacement of components.

• Lubricate rubber parts with clean, fresh brake fluid to ease assembly. Do not use shop air to clean parts; damage to rubber components may result.

• Use only DOT 3 brake fluid from an unopened container.

• If any hydraulic component or line is removed or replaced, it may be necessary to bleed the entire system.

• A clean repair area is essential. Always clean the reservoir and cap thoroughly before removing the cap. The slightest amount of dirt in the fluid may plug an orifice and impair the system function. Perform repairs after components have been thoroughly cleaned; use only denatured alcohol to clean components. Do not allow ABS components to come into contact with any substance containing mineral oil; this includes used shop rags.

• The Anti-Lock control unit is a microprocessor similar to other computer units in the vehicle. Ensure that the ignition switch

ANTI-LOCK BRAKE SYSTEM (ABS)

is **OFF** before removing or installing controller harnesses. Avoid static electricity discharge at or near the controller.

• If any arc welding is to be done on the vehicle, the control unit should be unplugged before welding operations begin.

WHEEL SPEED SENSORS

REMOVAL & INSTALLATION

Front

See Figures 1 and 2.

1. Disconnect the negative battery cable.
2. Raise and safely support the vehicle.
3. Remove the wheel and tire assembly.

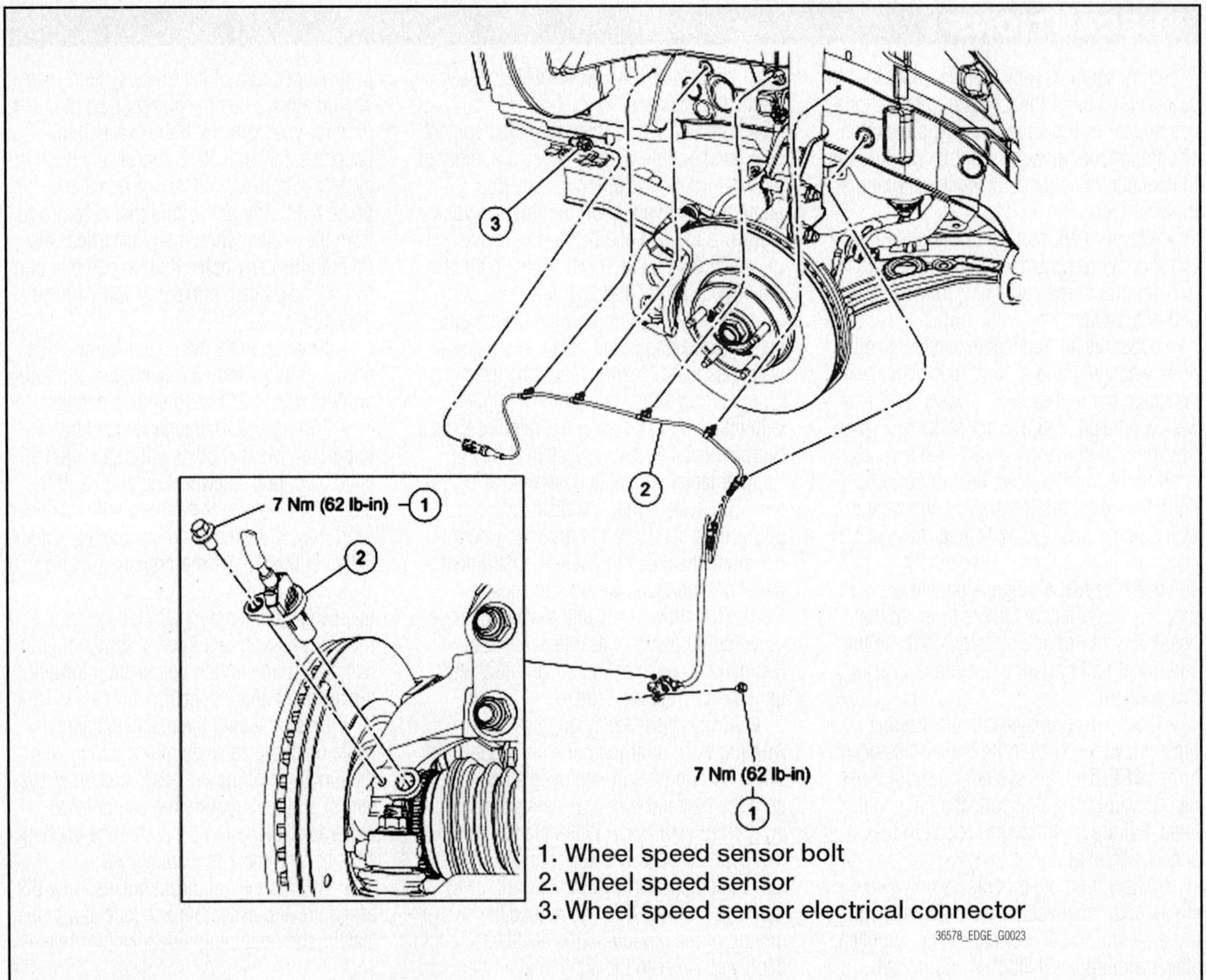

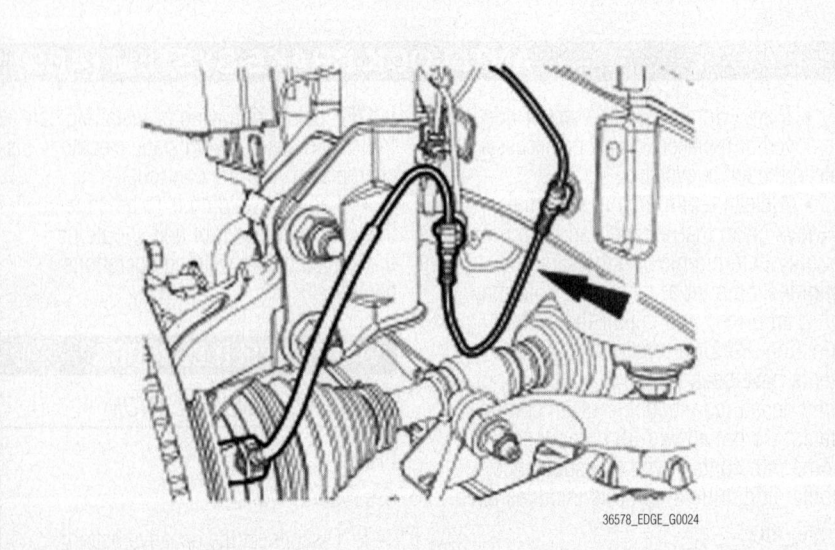

7 Nm (62 lb-in) — 1

2

7 Nm (62 lb-in)
1

1. Wheel speed sensor bolt
2. Wheel speed sensor
3. Wheel speed sensor electrical connector

36578_EDGE_G0023

Fig. 1 Exploded view of the front wheel speed sensor

36578_EDGE_G0024

Fig. 2 The wheel speed sensor harness must be properly routed, as shown, or damage to the harness during vehicle jounce and rebound can occur

4. Remove the retainers and position the fender splash shield aside.

5. Disconnect the wheel speed sensor electrical connector.

6. Disconnect the 6 pushpin fasteners.

7. Remove the front wheel speed sensor bolt and the wheel speed sensor.

✳✳ WARNING

The wheel speed sensor harness must be routed as shown in the accompanying illustration, or damage to the harness during vehicle jounce and rebound can occur.

8. Installation is the reverse of the removal procedure. Tighten the speed sensor bolt to 62 inch lbs. (7 Nm).

Rear

See Figures 3 and 4.

1. Disconnect the negative battery cable.

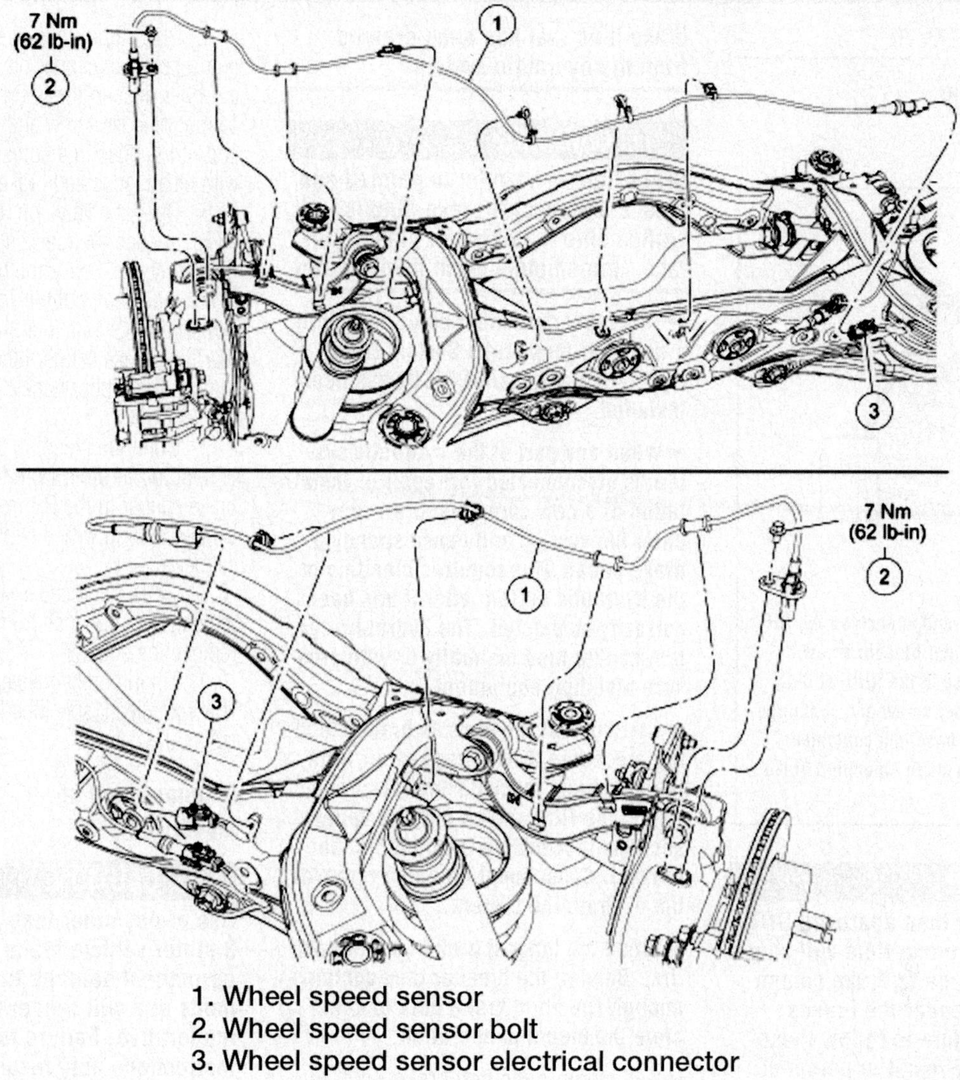

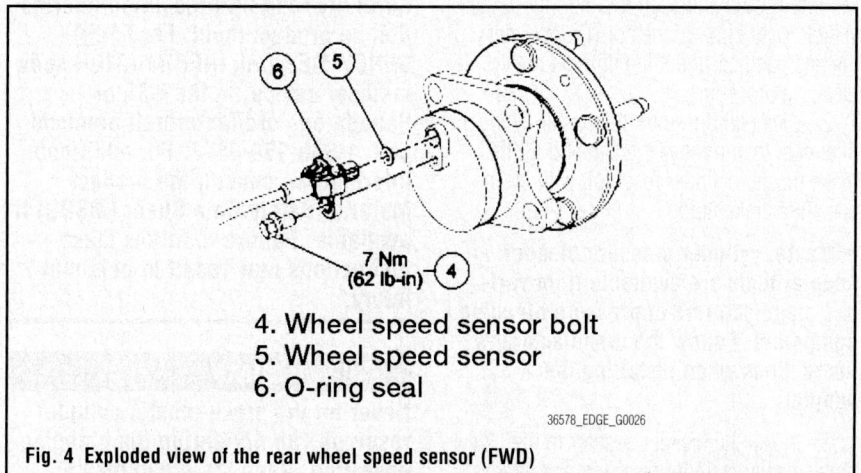

7 Nm
(62 lb-in)
②

①

③

7 Nm
(62 lb-in)
②

①

③

1. Wheel speed sensor
2. Wheel speed sensor bolt
3. Wheel speed sensor electrical connector

36578_EDGE_G0025

Fig. 3 Exploded view of the rear wheel speed sensor (AWD)

⑥ ⑤

⑥

7 Nm
(62 lb-in) ④

4. Wheel speed sensor bolt
5. Wheel speed sensor
6. O-ring seal

36578_EDGE_G0026

Fig. 4 Exploded view of the rear wheel speed sensor (FWD)

2. Raise and safely support the vehicle.

3. Remove the wheel and tire assembly.

4. Disconnect the wheel speed sensor electrical connector.

➡**It is not necessary to remove the harness routing brackets.**

5. Disconnect the wheel speed sensor harness from the brackets

6. Disconnect the pushpin fasteners.

7. Remove the wheel speed sensor bolt and the wheel speed sensor.

8. Installation is the reverse of the removal procedure Tighten the speed sensor bolt to 62 inch lbs. (7 Nm).

BLEEDING PROCEDURE

Pressure Bleeding
See Figure 5.

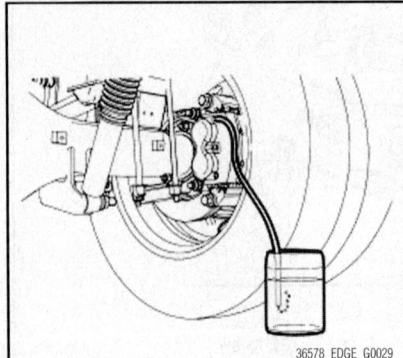

36578_EDGE_G0029

Fig. 5 Place a box-end wrench on the RH rear disc brake caliper bleeder screw. Attach a rubber hose to the RH rear disc brake caliper bleeder screw and submerge the free end of the hose in a container partially filled with clean, specified brake fluid

> ✳✳ **CAUTION**
>
> Use of any other than approved DOT 3 motor vehicle brake fluid will cause permanent damage to brake components and will render the brakes inoperative. Failure to follow these instructions may result in personal injury.

> ✳✳ **CAUTION**
>
> Carefully read all precaution information on product label. For EMERGENCY MEDICAL INFORMATION seek medical advice. In the USA or Canada on Ford/Motorcraft products call: 1-800-959-3673. For additional information, consult the product Material Safety Data Sheet (MSDS) if available. Failure to follow these instructions may result in personal injury.

> ✳✳ **WARNING**
>
> Never let the brake master cylinder reservoir run dry during the bleeding operation. Keep the brake master cylinder reservoir filled with clean, specified brake fluid. Never reuse the brake fluid that has been drained from the hydraulic system.

> ✳✳ **WARNING**
>
> Brake fluid is harmful to painted and plastic surfaces. If brake fluid is spilled onto a painted or plastic surface, immediately wash it with water.

➡ This procedure must be performed if a new Anti-lock Brake System (ABS) Hydraulic Control Unit (HCU) has been installed.

➡ When any part of the hydraulic system is disconnected for repair or installation of a new component, air may enter the system and cause spongy a brake pedal. This requires bleeding of the hydraulic system after it has been correctly connected. The hydraulic system can be bled manually or with pressure bleeding equipment.

➡ Carrying out the chassis brake bleeding procedure drives trapped air from the otherwise inaccessible lower section of the HCU valves into the upper sections (accessible by bleeding the brakes). Subsequent bleeding removes the air from the system.

➡ Bleed the longest brake tube or hose first. Be sure the bleeder tank contains enough specified brake fluid to complete the bleeding operation.

➡ Add clean, specified brake fluid as necessary throughout the procedure.

1. If the vehicle is equipped with an ABS, connect the Vehicle Communication Module (VCM) and scan tool into the vehicle Data Link Connector (DLC) under the dash and carry out the chassis brake bleeding procedure.

2. Clean all dirt from the master cylinder filler cap, then remove the cap and fill the brake master cylinder reservoir with clean, specified brake fluid.

➡ Master cylinder pressure bleeder adapter tools are available from various manufacturers of pressure bleeding equipment. Follow the manufacturer's instructions when installing the adapter.

3. Install the bleeder adapter to the brake master cylinder reservoir and attach the bleeder tank hose to the fitting on the adapter.

4. Place a box-end wrench on the RH rear disc brake caliper bleeder screw. Attach a rubber hose to the RH rear disc brake caliper bleeder screw and submerge the free end of the hose in a container partially filled with clean, specified brake fluid.

5. Open the valve on the bleeder tank.

6. Loosen the rear disc brake caliper bleeder screw. Leave the bleeder screw open until clear, bubble-free brake fluid flows into the container, then tighten the rear disc brake caliper bleeder screw and remove the rubber hose. Tighten to 71 inch lbs. (8 Nm).

7. Continue bleeding the rest of the system, going in order from the LH rear disc brake caliper to the RH front disc brake caliper, ending with the LH front disc brake caliper.

8. Close the bleeder tank valve and remove the tank hose from the adapter and remove the adapter.

9. Fill the brake master cylinder reservoir with clean, specified brake fluid and install the cap.

Manual Bleeding
See Figure 5.

> ✳✳ **CAUTION**
>
> Use of any other than approved DOT 3 motor vehicle brake fluid will cause permanent damage to brake components and will render the brakes inoperative. Failure to follow these instructions may result in personal injury.

> ✳✳ **CAUTION**
>
> Carefully read all precaution information on product label. For EMERGENCY MEDICAL INFORMATION seek medical advice. In the USA or Canada on Ford/Motorcraft products call: 1-800-959-3673. For additional information, consult the product Material Safety Data Sheet (MSDS) if available. Failure to follow these instructions may result in personal injury.

> ✳✳ **WARNING**
>
> Never let the brake master cylinder reservoir run dry during the bleeding operation. Keep the brake master cylinder reservoir filled with clean, specified brake fluid. Never reuse the

brake fluid that has been drained from the hydraulic system.

Brake fluid is harmful to painted and plastic surfaces. If brake fluid is spilled onto a painted or plastic surface, immediately wash it with water.

➡ This procedure must be performed if a new Anti-lock Brake System (ABS) Hydraulic Control Unit (HCU) has been installed.

➡ When any part of the hydraulic system is disconnected for repair or installation of a new component, air may enter the system and cause spongy a brake pedal. This requires bleeding of the hydraulic system after it has been correctly connected. The hydraulic system can be bled manually or with pressure bleeding equipment.

➡ Carrying out the chassis brake bleeding procedure drives trapped air from the otherwise inaccessible lower section of the HCU valves into the upper sections (accessible by bleeding the brakes). Subsequent bleeding removes the air from the system.

➡ Bleed the longest brake tube or hose first. Be sure the bleeder tank contains enough specified brake fluid to complete the bleeding operation.

➡ Add clean, specified brake fluid as necessary throughout the procedure.

1. Clean all dirt from the master cylinder filler cap, then remove the cap and fill the brake master cylinder reservoir with clean, specified brake fluid. Install the master cylinder filler cap.

2. If the vehicle is equipped with an ABS, connect the Vehicle Communication Module (VCM) and scan tool into the vehicle Data Link Connector (DLC) under the dash and carry out the chassis brake bleeding procedure.

3. Place a box-end wrench on the RH rear disc brake caliper bleeder screw. Attach a rubber hose to the RH rear disc brake caliper bleeder screw and submerge the free end of the hose in a container partially filled with clean, specified brake fluid.

4. Have an assistant pump the brake pedal and then hold firm pressure on the brake pedal.

5. Loosen the RH rear disc brake caliper bleeder screw until a stream of brake

fluid comes out. Have an assistant maintain pressure on the brake pedal while tightening the RH rear disc brake caliper bleeder screw:

   a. Repeat until clear, bubble-free fluid comes out.

   b. Refill the brake master cylinder reservoir as necessary.

6. Tighten the RH rear disc brake caliper bleeder screw. Tighten to 8 Nm (71 inch lbs.).

7. Repeat Steps 2 through 5 for the LH rear disc brake caliper.

8. Place a box-end wrench on the RH front disc brake caliper bleeder screw. Attach a rubber hose to the RH front disc brake caliper bleeder screw and submerge the free end of the hose in a container partially filled with clean, specified brake fluid.

9. Have an assistant pump the brake pedal and then hold firm pressure on the brake pedal.

10. Loosen the RH front disc brake caliper bleeder screw until a stream of brake fluid comes out. Have an assistant maintain pressure on the brake pedal while tightening the RH front disc brake caliper bleeder screw:

   a. Repeat until clear, bubble-free fluid comes out.

   b. Refill the brake master cylinder reservoir as necessary.

11. Tighten the RH front disc brake caliper bleeder screw to 71 inch lbs. (8 Nm).

12. Repeat Steps 7 through 10 for the LH front disc brake caliper.

Bleeding the Master Cylinder
See Figure 6.

Use of any other than approved DOT 3 motor vehicle brake fluid will cause permanent damage to brake compo-

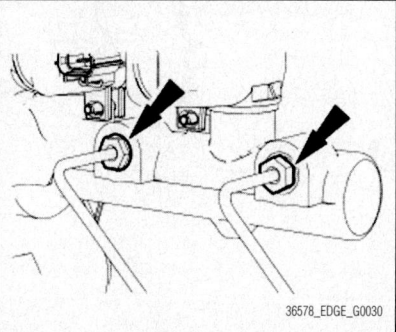

36578_EDGE_G0030

Fig. 6 Disconnect the brake master cylinder outlet tubes

nents and will render the brakes inoperative. Failure to follow these instructions may result in personal injury.

Carefully read all precaution information on product label. For EMERGENCY MEDICAL INFORMATION seek medical advice. In the USA or Canada on Ford/Motorcraft products call: 1-800-959-3673. For additional information, consult the product Material Safety Data Sheet (MSDS) if available. Failure to follow these instructions may result in personal injury.

Never let the brake master cylinder reservoir run dry during the bleeding operation. Keep the brake master cylinder reservoir filled with clean, specified brake fluid. Never reuse the brake fluid that has been drained from the hydraulic system.

Brake fluid is harmful to painted and plastic surfaces. If brake fluid is spilled onto a painted or plastic surface, immediately wash it with water.

➡ When any part of the hydraulic system is disconnected for repair or installation of a new component, air may enter the system and cause spongy a brake pedal. This requires bleeding of the hydraulic system after it has been correctly connected. The hydraulic system can be bled manually or with pressure bleeding equipment.

➡ Performing the chassis brake bleeding procedure drives trapped air from the otherwise inaccessible lower section of the HCU valves into the upper sections (accessible by bleeding the brakes). Subsequent bleeding removes the air from the system.

➡ Add clean, specified brake fluid as necessary throughout the procedure.

➡ When a new brake master cylinder has been installed or the system has been emptied, or partially emptied, it should be primed to prevent air from getting into the system.

1. Disconnect the brake master cylinder outlet tubes.

2. Install short brake tubes with ends submerged in the brake master cylinder reservoir and fill the brake master cylinder reservoir with clean, specified brake fluid.

3. Have an assistant pump the brake pedal until clear fluid flows from both brake tubes without air bubbles.

4. Remove the short brake tubes and install the brake outlet tubes.

5. Bleed each brake tube at the brake master cylinder as follows:

   a. Have an assistant pump the brake pedal and then hold firm pressure on the brake pedal.

   b. Loosen the rearmost brake tube fittings until a stream of brake fluid comes out. Have an assistant maintain pressure on the brake pedal while tightening the brake tube fitting.

   c. Repeat this operation until clear, bubble-free fluid comes out.

   d. Refill the brake master cylinder reservoir as necessary. Repeat the bleeding operation at the front brake tube.

   e. While the assistant maintains pressure on the brake pedal, tighten the brake tubes to 21 ft. lbs. (28 Nm).

BLEEDING THE ABS SYSTEM

Refer to the Bleeding Procedures located earlier in this section

BRAKES

✳✳ CAUTION

Dust and dirt accumulating on brake parts during normal use may contain asbestos fibers from production or aftermarket brake linings. Breathing excessive concentrations of asbestos fibers can cause serious bodily harm. Exercise care when servicing brake parts. Do not sand or grind brake lining unless equipment used is designed to contain the dust residue. Do not clean brake parts with compressed air or by dry brushing. Cleaning should be done by dampen-ing the brake components with a fine mist of water, then wiping the brake components clean with a dampened cloth. Dispose of cloth and all residue containing asbestos fibers in an impermeable container with the appropriate label. Follow practices prescribed by the Occupational Safety and Health Administration (OSHA) and the Environmental Pro-tection Agency (EPA) for the han-dling, processing, and disposing of dust or debris that may contain asbestos fibers.

FRONT DISC BRAKES

BRAKE CALIPER

REMOVAL & INSTALLATION
See Figure 7.

✳✳ CAUTION

Use of any other than approved DOT 3 motor vehicle brake fluid will cause permanent damage to brake compo-nents and will render the brakes inoperative. Failure to follow these instructions may result in personal injury.

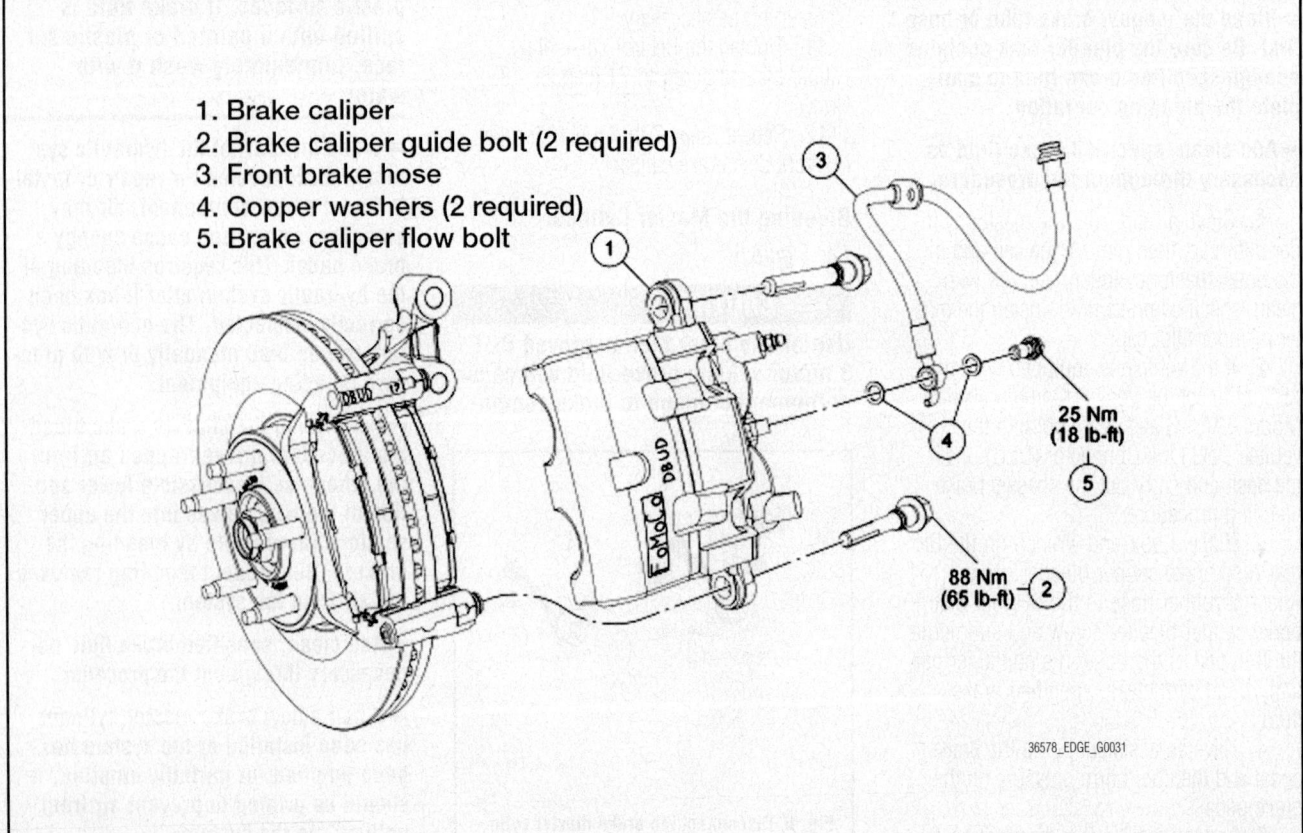

1. Brake caliper
2. Brake caliper guide bolt (2 required)
3. Front brake hose
4. Copper washers (2 required)
5. Brake caliper flow bolt

25 Nm (18 lb-ft)

88 Nm (65 lb-ft)

36578_EDGE_G0031

Fig. 7 Exploded view of the front brake caliper

❊❊ CAUTION

Carefully read all precaution information on product label. For EMERGENCY MEDICAL INFORMATION seek medical advice. In the USA or Canada on Ford/Motorcraft products call: 1-800-959-3673. For additional information, consult the product Material Safety Data Sheet (MSDS) if available. Failure to follow these instructions may result in personal injury.

❊❊ WARNING

Brake fluid is harmful to painted and plastic surfaces. If brake fluid is spilled onto a painted or plastic surface, immediately wash it with water.

1. Raise and safely support the vehicle.
2. Remove the wheel and tire assembly.
3. Remove the brake caliper flow bolt and position the hose aside. Discard the 2 copper washers.

➡ **The guide pin bolts are different sizes. The longer/bigger bolt is the upper guide pin bolt.**

4. Remove the 2 brake caliper guide pin bolts.
5. Remove the brake caliper.

To install:

6. Installation is the reverse of the removal procedure, noting the following:
   a. During installation, make sure that the brake caliper hose is not twisted.
   b. Tighten the caliper guide pin bolts to 65 ft. lbs. (88 Nm). Make sure to install the longer/bigger bolt in the upper position.
   c. Use new copper washers, then tighten the brake caliper flow bolts to 18 ft. lbs. (25 Nm).
   d. Bleed the brake system, as outlined in the beginning of the Brake Section.

DISC BRAKE PADS

REMOVAL & INSTALLATION

See Figure 8.

1. Check the brake fluid level in the brake master cylinder reservoir.
2. If necessary, remove the fluid until the brake master cylinder reservoir is ½ full.

3. Raise and safely support the vehicle.
4. Remove the wheel and tire assembly.

❊❊ WARNING

Do not pry in the caliper sight hole to retract the pistons as this can damage the pistons and boots.

❊❊ WARNING

NEVER let the brake caliper hang from the brake hose or damage to the hose can occur.

5. Remove the 2 brake caliper guide pin bolts and position the caliper aside. Support the caliper using a piece of wire.
6. Remove the brake pads, brake pad shims and stainless steel shims.
7. Inspect the brake pads and shims for wear or contamination.
8. Remove the brake pad slides.

To install:

❊❊ WARNING

Protect the caliper piston and boots when pushing the caliper piston into the bores.

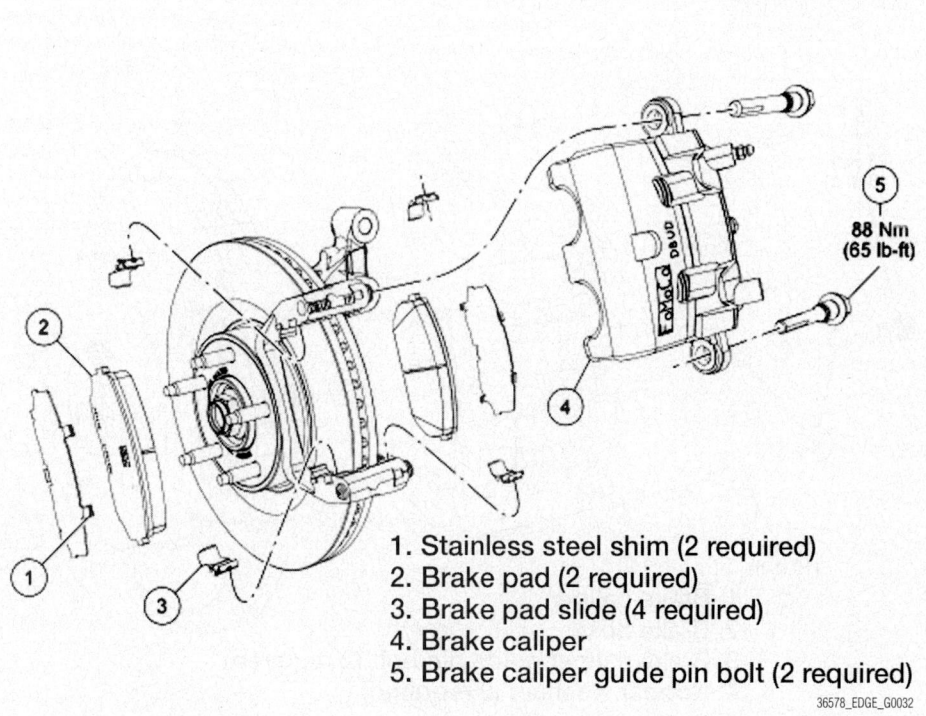

1. Stainless steel shim (2 required)
2. Brake pad (2 required)
3. Brake pad slide (4 required)
4. Brake caliper
5. Brake caliper guide pin bolt (2 required)

5
88 Nm
(65 lb-ft)

36578_EDGE_G0032

Fig. 8 Exploded view of the front brake pads and related components

✳✳ WARNING

Make sure that the caliper guide pin boots are fully seated or damage to the caliper guide pin boots can occur.

9. If installing new brake pads, using a C-clamp or equivalent suitable tool and a worn brake, compress the disc brake caliper pistons into the caliper.

10. Install the brake pad slides.

11. Apply a thin coating of the supplied grease to the shims and the shim contact area of the brake pads.

12. Install the stainless steel shims to the brake pads.

➡ The guide pin bolts are different sizes. The longer/bigger bolt is the upper guide pin bolt.

13. Position the brake caliper and install the 2 guide pin bolts. Tighten to 65 ft. lbs. (88 Nm).

14. Install the wheel and tire assembly.

15. Fill the brake master cylinder reservoir with clean, specified brake fluid.

16. Test the brakes for normal operation.

BRAKES

✳✳ CAUTION

Dust and dirt accumulating on brake parts during normal use may contain asbestos fibers from production or aftermarket brake linings. Breathing excessive concentrations of asbestos fibers can cause serious bodily harm. Exercise care when servicing brake parts. Do not sand or grind brake lining unless equipment used is designed to contain the dust residue. Do not clean brake parts with compressed air or by dry brushing. Cleaning should be done by dampening the brake components with a fine mist of water, then wiping the brake components clean with a dampened cloth. Dispose of cloth and all residue containing asbestos fibers in an impermeable container with the appropriate label. Follow practices prescribed by the Occupational Safety and Health Administration (OSHA) and the Environmental Protection Agency (EPA) for the handling, processing, and disposing of dust or debris that may contain asbestos fibers.

BRAKE CALIPER

REMOVAL & INSTALLATION

See Figure 9.

REAR DISC BRAKES

✳✳ CAUTION

Use of any other than approved DOT 3 motor vehicle brake fluid will cause permanent damage to brake components and will render the brakes inoperative. Failure to follow these instructions may result in personal injury.

✳✳ CAUTION

Carefully read all precaution information on product label. For EMERGENCY MEDICAL INFORMATION seek medical advice. In the USA or Canada on Ford/Motorcraft products call: 1-800-959-3673. For additional

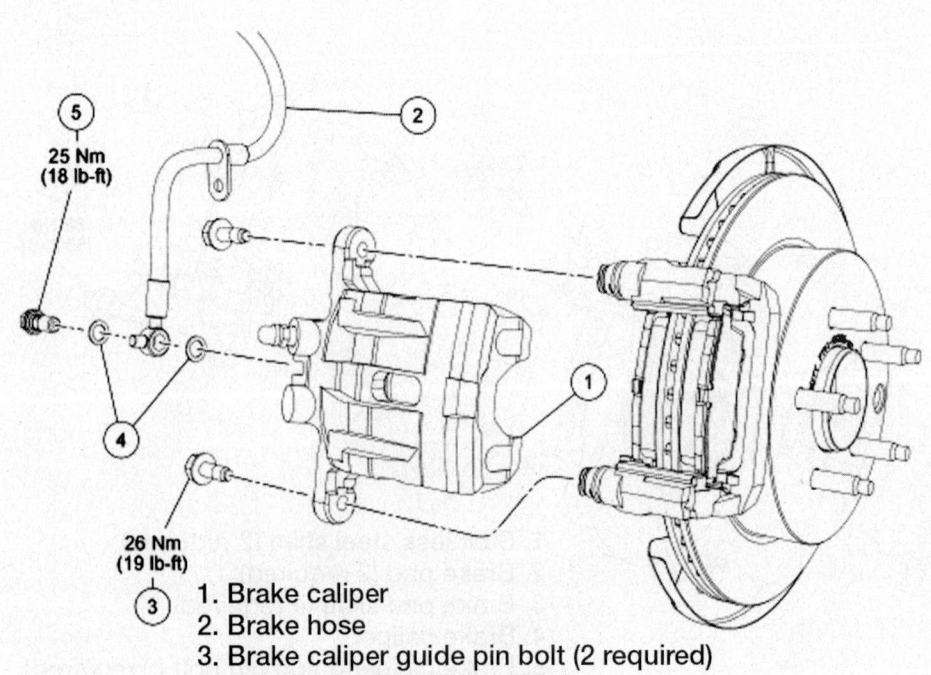

5. 25 Nm (18 lb-ft)

26 Nm (19 lb-ft)

1. Brake caliper
2. Brake hose
3. Brake caliper guide pin bolt (2 required)
4. Copper washers (2 required)
5. Brake caliper flow bolt

36578_EDGE_G0034

Fig. 9 Exploded view of the rear brake caliper

information, consult the product Material Safety Data Sheet (MSDS) if available. Failure to follow these instructions may result in personal injury.

✳✳ WARNING

Brake fluid is harmful to painted and plastic surfaces. If brake fluid is spilled onto a painted or plastic surface, immediately wash it with water.

1. Raise and safely support the vehicle.
2. Remove the wheel and tire assembly.
3. Remove the brake caliper flow bolt and position the brake hose aside. Discard the 2 copper washers.
4. Remove the 2 brake caliper guide bolts and the brake caliper.
5. If a leaking or damaged caliper piston boot is found, install a new disc brake caliper.

To install:

✳✳ WARNING

Make sure that the caliper guide pin boots are fully seated or damage to

the caliper guide pin boots can occur.

➡ **Make sure that the brake caliper hose is not twisted during caliper installation.**

6. Position the brake caliper onto the anchor plate and brake pads.
7. Install the 2 brake caliper guide pin bolts and tighten to 19 ft. lbs. (26 Nm).
8. Using 2 new copper washers, position the brake hose and install the brake caliper flow bolt. Tighten to 18 ft. lbs. (25 Nm).
9. Install the wheel and tire assembly.
10. Bleed the brake system, as outlined at the beginning of the Brake Section.
11. Test the brakes for normal operation

DISC BRAKE PADS

REMOVAL & INSTALLATION

See Figure 10.

✳✳ CAUTION

Use of any other than approved DOT 3 motor vehicle brake fluid will cause permanent damage to brake components and will render the brakes inoperative. Failure to follow these

instructions may result in personal injury.

✳✳ CAUTION

Carefully read all precaution information on product label. For EMERGENCY MEDICAL INFORMATION seek medical advice. In the USA or Canada on Ford/Motorcraft products call: 1-800-959-3673. For additional information, consult the product Material Safety Data Sheet (MSDS) if available. Failure to follow these instructions may result in personal injury.

✳✳ WARNING

Brake fluid is harmful to painted and plastic surfaces. If brake fluid is spilled onto a painted or plastic surface, immediately wash it with water.

1. Check the brake fluid level in the brake master cylinder reservoir.
2. If necessary, remove the fluid until the brake master cylinder reservoir is ½ full.
3. Remove the wheel and tire assembly.

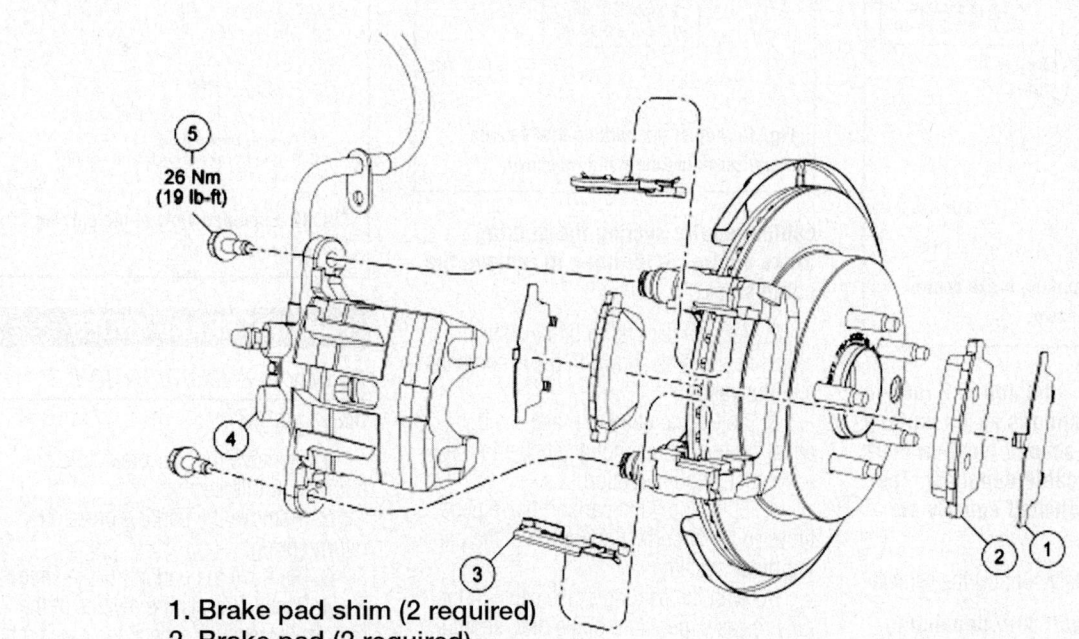

1. Brake pad shim (2 required)
2. Brake pad (2 required)
3. Brake pad slide clip (2 required)
4. Brake caliper
5. Brake caliper guide pin bolt (2 required)

36578_EDGE_G0035

Fig. 10 Exploded view of the rear brake pads and related components

※※ **WARNING**

Do not pry in the caliper sight hole to retract the pistons, as this can damage the pistons and boots.

※※ **WARNING**

Do not allow the brake caliper to hang from the brake hose or damage to the hose can occur.

4. Remove the 2 brake caliper guide pin bolts and position the caliper aside. Support the caliper using mechanic's wire.

※※ **WARNING**

Install new brake pads if they are worn past the specified thickness above the metal backing plates.

Install new brake pads in complete axle sets.

5. Remove the 2 brake pads, shims and slide clips. Inspect the brake pads and shims for wear, damage or contamination. Discard the slide clips.

To install:

※※ **WARNING**

Protect the caliper piston and boots when pushing the caliper piston into the bores.

➡Make sure the caliper piston boot is clean and free of foreign material.

6. If installing new brake pads, using a suitable tool and a worn brake pad, compress the disc brake caliper pistons into the caliper using a C-clamp..

7. Install the 2 brake pads, shims and new slide clips to the brake caliper anchor plate.

※※ **WARNING**

Make sure that the caliper guide pin boots are fully seated or damage to the caliper guide pin boots can occur.

➡Make sure that the brake caliper hose is not twisted during caliper installation.

8. Position the brake caliper on the anchor plate and install the 2 guide pin bolts. Tighten to 19 ft. lbs. (26 Nm).
9. Install the wheel and tire assembly.
10. Fill the brake master cylinder reservoir with clean, specified brake fluid.
11. Test the brakes for normal operation.

BRAKES | PARKING BRAKE

PARKING BRAKE CABLES

ADJUSTMENT

See Figures 11 and 12.

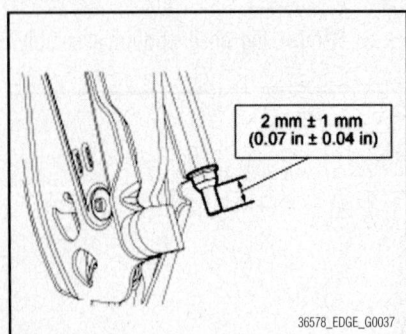

2 mm ± 1 mm
(0.07 in ± 0.04 in)

36578_EDGE_G0037

Fig. 11 Adjust the parking brake control adjustment nut as shown.

➡Cable tension is adjusted in 2 locations, the first location is at the parking brake control, the second location is at the parking brake cable equalizer. The tension must be adjusted equally at both locations.

1. Raise and safely support the vehicle.

➡The dimension will vary depending on the amount of cable stretch. New

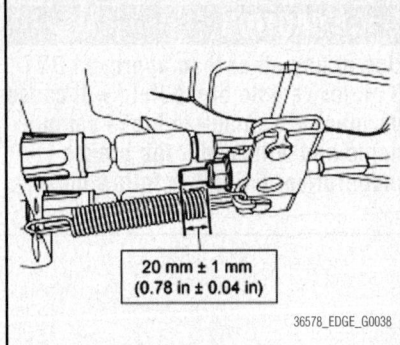

20 mm ± 1 mm
(0.78 in ± 0.04 in)

36578_EDGE_G0038

Fig. 12 Adjust the parking brake cable equalizer adjustment nut as shown

cables require cycling the parking brake control 5-10 times to remove the cable slack.

2. Adjust the parking brake control adjustment nut as shown in the accompanying illustration.
3. Adjust the parking brake cable equalizer adjustment nut as shown in the accompanying illustration.
4. Fully apply the parking brake pedal 3 times to verify correct operation of the parking brake system.
5. With the parking brake cable in the fully released position, brake drag should not be present

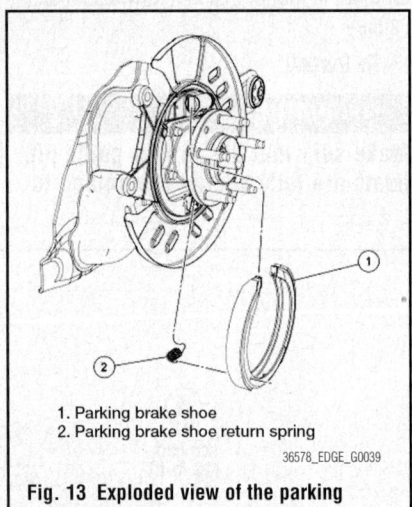

1. Parking brake shoe
2. Parking brake shoe return spring

36578_EDGE_G0039

Fig. 13 Exploded view of the parking brake shoes

PARKING BRAKE SHOES

REMOVAL & INSTALLATION

See Figure 13.

1. Remove the rear brake rotor, as outlined in this section.
2. Remove the parking brake shoe return spring.
3. Remove the parking brake shoe.
4. Installation is the reverse of the removal procedure. Check the parking brake for normal operation.

CHASSIS ELECTRICAL   AIR BAG (SUPPLEMENTAL RESTRAINT SYSTEM)

GENERAL INFORMATION

✳✳ CAUTION

Some vehicles are equipped with an air bag system. The system must be disarmed before performing service on, or around, system components, the steering column, instrument panel components, wiring and sensors. Failure to follow the safety precautions and the disarming procedure could result in accidental air bag deployment, possible injury and unnecessary system repairs.

SERVICE PRECAUTIONS

Disconnect and isolate the battery negative cable before beginning any airbag system component diagnosis, testing, removal, or installation procedures. Allow system capacitor to discharge for two minutes before beginning any component service. This will disable the airbag system. Failure to disable the airbag system may result in accidental airbag deployment, personal injury, or death.

Do not place an intact undeployed airbag face down on a solid surface. The airbag will propel into the air if accidentally deployed and may result in personal injury or death.

When carrying or handling an undeployed airbag, the trim side (face) of the airbag should be pointing towards the body to minimize possibility of injury if accidental deployment occurs. Failure to do this may result in personal injury or death.

Replace airbag system components with OEM replacement parts. Substitute parts may appear interchangeable, but internal differences may result in inferior occupant protection. Failure to do so may result in occupant personal injury or death.

Wear safety glasses, rubber gloves, and long sleeved clothing when cleaning powder residue from vehicle after an airbag deployment. Powder residue emitted from a deployed airbag can cause skin irritation. Flush affected area with cool water if irritation is experienced. If nasal or throat irritation is experienced, exit the vehicle for fresh air until the irritation ceases. If irritation continues, see a physician.

Do not use a replacement airbag that is not in the original packaging. This may result in improper deployment, personal injury, or death.

The factory installed fasteners, screws and bolts used to fasten airbag components have a special coating and are specifically designed for the airbag system. Do not use substitute fasteners. Use only original equipment fasteners listed in the parts catalog when fastener replacement is required.

During, and following, any child restraint anchor service, due to impact event or vehicle repair, carefully inspect all mounting hardware, tether straps, and anchors for proper installation, operation, or damage. If a child restraint anchor is found damaged in any way, the anchor must be replaced. Failure to do this may result in personal injury or death.

Deployed and non-deployed airbags may or may not have live pyrotechnic material within the airbag inflator.

Do not dispose of driver/passenger/curtain airbags or seat belt tensioners unless you are sure of complete deployment. Refer to the Hazardous Substance Control System for proper disposal.

Dispose of deployed airbags and tensioners consistent with state, provincial, local, and federal regulations.

After any airbag component testing or service, do not connect the battery negative cable. Personal injury or death may result if the system test is not performed first.

If the vehicle is equipped with the Occupant Classification System (OCS), do not connect the battery negative cable before performing the OCS Verification Test using the scan tool and the appropriate diagnostic information. Personal injury or death may result if the system test is not performed properly.

Never replace both the Occupant Restraint Controller (ORC) and the Occupant Classification Module (OCM) at the same time. If both require replacement, replace one, then perform the Airbag System test before replacing the other.

Both the ORC and the OCM store Occupant Classification System (OCS) calibration data, which they transfer to one another when one of them is replaced. If both are replaced at the same time, an irreversible fault will be set in both modules and the OCS may malfunction and cause personal injury or death.

If equipped with OCS, the Seat Weight Sensor is a sensitive, calibrated unit and must be handled carefully. Do not drop or handle roughly. If dropped or damaged, replace with another sensor. Failure to do so may result in occupant injury or death.

If equipped with OCS, the front passenger seat must be handled carefully as well. When removing the seat, be careful when setting on floor not to drop. If dropped, the sensor may be inoperative, could result in occupant injury, or possibly death.

If equipped with OCS, when the passenger front seat is on the floor, no one should sit in the front passenger seat. This uneven force may damage the sensing ability of the seat weight sensors. If sat on and damaged, the sensor may be inoperative, could result in occupant injury, or possibly death.

DISARMING THE SYSTEM

✳✳ CAUTION

Never probe the electrical connectors on air bag, safety canopy or side air curtain modules. Failure to follow this instruction may result in the accidental deployment of these modules, which increases the risk of serious personal injury or death.

✳✳ CAUTION

To reduce the risk of accidental deployment, do not use any memory saver devices. Failure to follow this instruction may result in serious personal injury or death.

➡ The air bag warning indicator illuminates when the Restraints Control Module (RCM) fuse is removed and the ignition switch is ON. This is normal operation and does not indicate a Supplemental Restraints System (SRS) fault.

1. Turn all vehicle accessories OFF.
2. Turn the ignition switch to the **OFF** position.
3. At the smart power distribution junction box (SPDJB), located in the LH lower kick panel, remove the lower kick panel fuse cover and the restraints control module (RCM) fuse 46 (7.5A) from the (SPDJB).
4. Turn the ignition **ON** and make sure that the air bag warning indicator lights up for at least 30 seconds. The air bag warning indicator will remain lit continuously (no flashing) if the correct RCM fuse has been removed. If the air bag warning indicator does not remain lit continuously, remove the correct RCM fuse before proceeding.
5. Turn the ignition switch to the **OFF** position.

✸✸ WARNING

To avoid accidental deployment and possible personal injury, the backup power supply MUST be depleted before repairing or installing any new front or side air bag SRS components and before servicing, installing, adjusting or striking components near the front or side air bag sensors, such as doors, instrument panel, console, door latches, strikers, seats and hood latches. Failure to follow this instruction may result in serious personal injury. The front impact severity sensors are located on the radiator support under the front bumper cover. The first row side impact sensors are located at or near the base of the B-pillars. The second row side impact sensors are located on the C-pillars.

6. To deplete the backup power supply energy, disconnect the negative battery cable and wait at least one minute. Be sure to disconnect auxiliary batteries and power supplies (if equipped).

7. Disconnect the negative battery cable and wait at least one minute.

ARMING THE SYSTEM

1. Turn the ignition switch from the **OFF** position to the **ON** position.

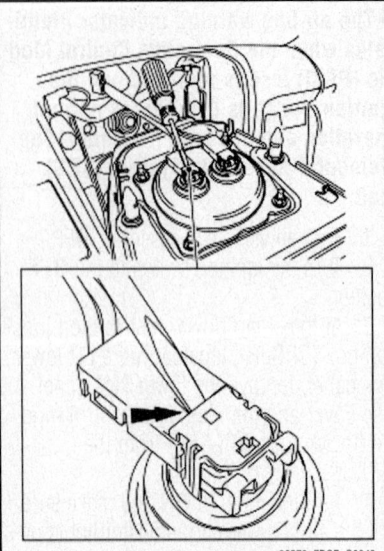

36578_EDGE_G0040

Fig. 14 Using a small screwdriver as shown, lift up and release the locking buttons on the driver air bag module electrical connectors. With the locking buttons released, remove the electrical connectors and the driver air bag module

2. Install RCM fuse 46 (7.5A) to the SPDJB and install the lower kick panel fuse cover.

✸✸ CAUTION

Make sure that nobody is in the vehicle and that there is nothing blocking or set in front of any air bag module when the negative battery cable is connected. Failure to follow this instruction may result in serious personal injury.

3. Connect the negative battery cable.

4. Prove out the SRS as follows:

a. Turn the ignition switch from ON to OFF. Wait 10 seconds, then turn the ignition switch back to ON and visually monitor the air bag warning indicator with the air bag modules installed. The air bag warning indicator will light continuously for approximately 6 seconds and then turn OFF. If an air bag SRS fault is present, the air bag warning indicator will:

- Fail to light.
- Remain lit continuously.
- Flash at a 5 Hz rate (RCM not configured).

5. The air bag warning indicator might not light until approximately 30 seconds after the ignition switch has been turned from the OFF to the ON position. This is the time required for the RCM to complete the testing of the SRS. If the air bag warning indicator is inoperative and a SRS fault exists, a chime will sound in a pattern of 5 sets of 5 beeps. If this occurs, the air bag warning indicator and any SRS fault discovered must be diagnosed and repaired.

6. Clear all continuous Diagnostic Trouble Codes (DTCs) from the RCM and Occupant Classification Sensor (OCS) module using a scan tool.

CLOCKSPRING CENTERING

See Figures 14 through 16.

➡ **This procedure covers removal and installation, and centering of the clockspring.**

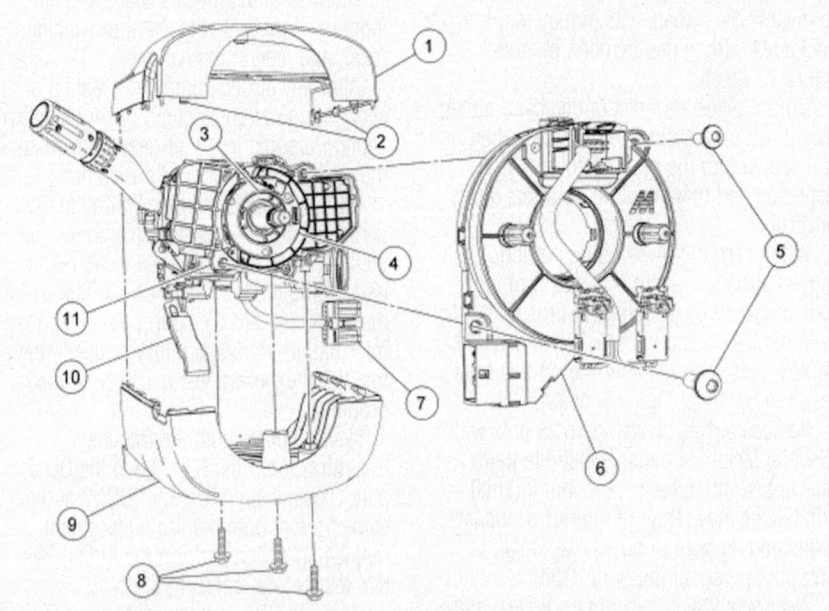

1. Upper steering column shroud
2. Upper steering column shroud tabs (2 required)
3. Steering angle sensor (if equipped)
4. Steering angle sensor ring (if equipped)
5. Clockspring screws (2 required)
6. Clockspring
7. Clockspring electrical connector
8. Lower steering column shroud screws (3 required)
9. Lower steering column shroud
10. Steering column tilt lock/unlock handle
11. Multifunction switch housing

36578_EDGE_G0041

Fig. 15 Exploded view of the SRS clockspring and related components

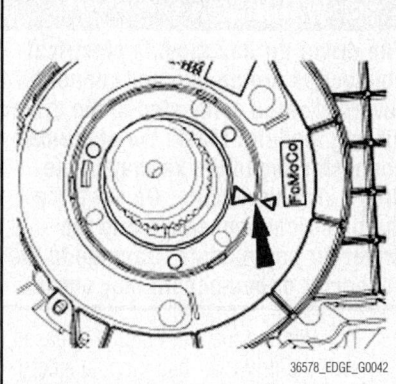

Fig. 16 Make sure the sensor ring arrow is lined up with the absolute steering angle sensor housing arrow as shown

✳✳ CAUTION

To reduce the risk of accidental deployment, do not use any memory saver devices. Failure to follow this instruction may result in serious personal injury or death.

➡The air bag warning indicator illuminates when the Restraints Control Module (RCM) fuse is removed and the ignition switch is ON. This is normal operation and does not indicate a Supplemental Restraint System (SRS) fault.

➡Repair is made by installing a new part only. If the new part does not correct the condition, install the original part and carry out the diagnostic procedure again.

1. Disarm the SRS, as outlined in this section.
2. Tilt the steering wheel in the downward position and lock the tilt handle.
3. Remove the driver air bag module, as follows:
   a. Using a 3-mm Allen wrench or a suitable tool through the access hole on the backside of the steering wheel, position the tool against the spring clip and push in, disengaging the clip from the locking pin. With the spring clip disengaged from the locking pin, gently pull back on that side of the driver air bag module to release it from the steering wheel. Repeat for the other locking pin.

✳✳ WARNING

NEVER pull the driver air bag module electrical connectors out by the locking buttons. Damage to the locking buttons can occur.

b. Using a small screwdriver as shown, lift up and release the locking buttons on the driver air bag module electrical connectors. With the locking buttons released, remove the electrical connectors and the driver air bag module.

✳✳ WARNING

Vehicles with absolute steering angle sensor and/or adaptive headlamps, do not allow the clockspring rotor to turn from the straight-ahead position after the steering wheel is removed. Failure to follow this instruction may result in component damage and/or system failure.

➡Make sure the vehicle's wheels are in the straight-ahead position.

4. Remove the steering wheel, as outlined in the Steering Section.
5. Tape the clockspring rotor to the steering column shaft to prevent the clockspring rotor from moving out of center.
6. Release the 2 tabs and position the upper steering column shroud upward.
7. Remove the 3 screws and the lower steering column shroud.
8. Disconnect the clockspring electrical connector.
9. Remove the tape from the clockspring rotor to the steering column shaft. Do not allow the clockspring rotor to move from center after tape is removed.

✳✳ WARNING

Vchicles with absolute steering angle sensor and/or adaptive headlamps, do not allow the clockspring rotor to turn from the straight-ahead position after the steering wheel is removed. Failure to follow this instruction may result in component damage and/or system failure.

➡Vehicles with absolute steering angle sensor and/or adaptive headlamps, after the clockspring has been removed make sure the arrow on the absolute steering angle sensor ring is lined up with the arrow on the absolute steering angle sensor housing as shown.

10. Remove the 2 clockspring screws and remove the clockspring.

To install:
Vehicle repairs re-using the same clockspring:

✳✳ CAUTION

If the clockspring is not correctly centralized, it may fail prematurely. If in doubt, repeat the centralizing procedure. Failure to follow these instructions may increase the risk of serious personal injury or death in a crash.

✳✳ WARNING

Make sure the vehicle's wheels are still in the straight-ahead position. Failure to follow this instruction may result in component damage and/or system failure.

11. If the vehicle's clockspring has rotated out of center, follow these steps to center the clockspring.
   a. Hold the clockspring outer housing stationary.

✳✳ WARNING

Overturning will destroy the clockspring. The internal ribbon wire acts as the stop and can be broken from its internal connection.

   b. While turning the rotor counterclockwise, carefully feel for the ribbon wire to run out of length and for a slight resistance. Stop turning at this point.
   c. Turn the clockspring clockwise (approximately 2.25 turns) until the clockspring rotor wiring and connector are in the 12 o'clock position. Clockspring is now centered.
   d. Do not allow the rotor to turn from this position.

➡Slight rotation of the absolute steering angle sensor ring is allowed to align the 2 arrows.

12. Make sure the sensor ring arrow is lined up with the absolute steering angle sensor housing arrow as shown.

✳✳ WARNING

If the clockspring is left unattended between centralizing the clockspring and installing it to the multi-function switch housing, the centralizing procedure must be repeated. Failure to follow this instruction may result in component damage and/or system failure.

➡On vehicles with absolute steering angle sensor and/or adaptive headlamps, slight rotation of the clockspring rotor might be needed to seat the clockspring 3 locator pins into the absolute steering angle sensor and or adaptive headlamps sensor ring. Very slight rotation is possible on a new clockspring with the sealing key installed.

➡Make sure the clockspring is fully seated into the multi-function switch housing before installing the clockspring screws.

13. Install the clockspring and the 2 screws.
14. Connect the clockspring electrical connector.
15. Install the lower steering column shroud and the 3 screws.
16. Attach the upper steering column shroud to the lower steering column shroud.

✳✳ WARNING

If not installing a new clockspring, and the vehicle is left unattended between the installation of the clockspring to the multi-function switch housing and installing the steering

wheel, the centralizing procedure can be repeated at this time with the clockspring being installed in the multi-function switch housing. Failure to follow this instruction may result in component damage and/or system failure.

17. Install the steering wheel, as outlined in the Steering Section.
18. If a new clockspring is being installed, and after the steering wheel installation, remove the clockspring sealing key.
19. Install the driver air bag module, as follows:

✳✳ WARNING

Do not install the driver air bag module electrical connectors by the locking buttons. Damage to the locking buttons can occur.

✳✳ WARNING

The driver air bag module electrical connector locking buttons must be in the released position when the connector is being installed or connector damage may occur.

✳✳ WARNING

The driver air bag module electrical connectors are unique and cannot be reversed when connected to the driver air bag module. Match the electrical connector key to the keyway in the driver air bag module. Do not force the electrical connectors into the driver air bag module. Damage to the connector or component may occur.

a. With the locking buttons released, install the driver air bag module electrical connectors fully into the driver air bag module and seat the locking buttons.

➡Audible clicks will be heard when both wire clips are seated in the driver air bag module. Align the driver air bag module locking pins to the steering wheel and, while pushing inward, seat the 2 driver air bag module locking pins to the steering wheel wire clips.

b. When the 2 locking pins are seated in place, there should be an even gap between the driver air bag module trim cover and the steering wheel
20. Rearm the SRS, as outlined in this section.

DRIVE TRAIN

AUTOMATIC TRANSAXLE ASSEMBLY

REMOVAL & INSTALLATION

See Figures 17 through 26.

1. Raise and safely support the vehicle.
2. Disconnect the Mass Air Flow (MAF) sensor electrical connector and the wiring harness fastener from the air cleaner assembly.
3. Disconnect the brake booster vacuum hose from the air cleaner outlet pipe.
4. Disconnect the engine breather from the air cleaner assembly.
5. Remove the air cleaner assembly bracket bolt.
6. Loosen the air cleaner outlet pipe clamp at the throttle body and remove the air cleaner and air cleaner outlet pipe assembly.
7. Disconnect the selector lever cable end from the manual control lever.

➡The coolant hoses do not need to be removed from the engine.

8. Remove the coolant hoses from the transmission fluid filler tube and position aside.

➡The coolant hoses have been removed for clarity.

9. Remove the transmission fluid level indicator.

➡The coolant hoses have been removed for clarity.

10. Remove the nut, rotate the transmission fluid filler tube counterclockwise 90 degrees and remove the transmission fluid filler tube.
11. Remove the 3 selector lever cable bracket bolts and position aside the selector lever cable.
12. Remove the starter motor electrical terminal cover.
13. Position the starter cable boot back

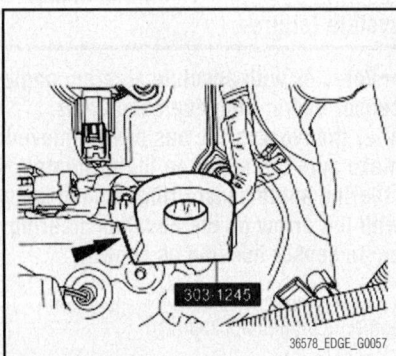

36578_EDGE_G0057

Fig. 17 Installing the engine lifting bracket on the LH cylinder head

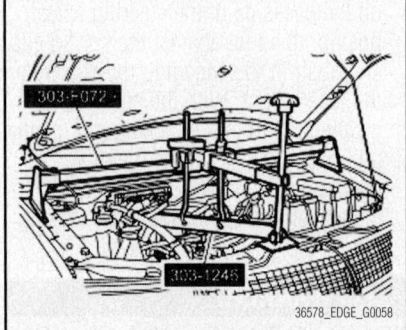

36578_EDGE_G0058

Fig. 18 Installing the engine support bar and engine spreader bar to support the engine

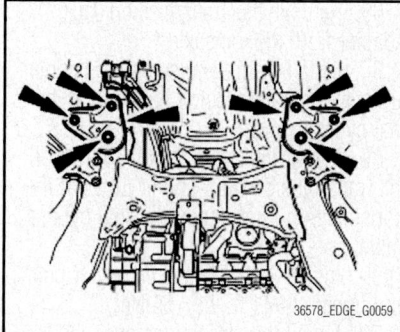

Fig. 19 Removing the subframe support brackets

and remove the starter terminals from the starter.

14. Disconnect the wiring harness fastener from the starter motor studbolt.

15. Remove the 2 bolts and the starter.

16. Disconnect the fuel hose routing clip from the transaxle stud and position the fuel hose aside.

17. Disconnect the transaxle electrical connector.

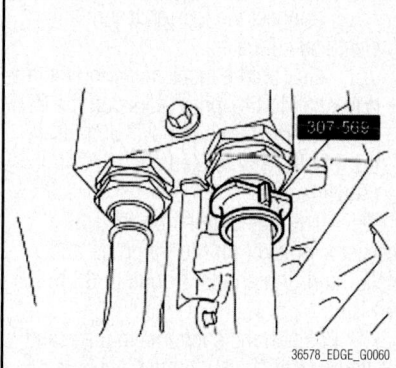

Fig. 20 Using the special tool, disconnect the transmission fluid cooler tubes from the transmission fluid cooler thermal bypass valve

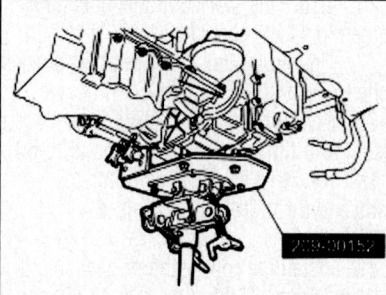

Fig. 21 Using the special tool and a suitable transmission jack, support the transaxle

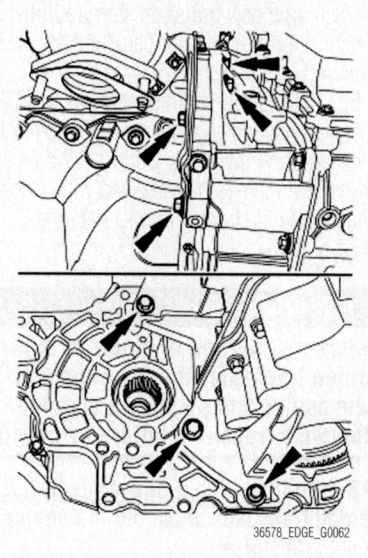

Fig. 22 Remove the 7 torque converter housing bolts and remove the transaxle from the vehicle

18. Remove the top 4 torque converter housing bolts.

19. Install the Engine Lifting Bracket on the LH cylinder head.

20. Remove the upper intake manifold.

21. Install the Engine Support Bar and Engine Spreader Bar to support the engine.

22. Remove the transaxle support insulator through bolt.

23. Remove the 3 nuts, the bolt and the transaxle support insulator bracket.

24. Remove the RH splash shield.

25. Remove the 3 pushpin fasteners, the 8 screws and the front splash shield.

26. Remove the 3 RH subframe to lower bumper nuts

27. Remove the 3 LH subframe to lower bumper nuts and separate the front support from the subframe.

28. Remove the 3 power steering tube bracket bolts from the subframe and position the power steering tube aside.

29. Remove the transmission fluid drain plug and allow the transmission fluid to drain.

30. Install the transmission fluid drain plug and tighten to 80 inch lbs. (9 Nm).

31. Remove the LH and RH front halfshafts.

32. Inspect the halfshaft hubs for wear or damage and replace the halfshafts if necessary.

    a. Inspect the differential seal surface.

    b. Inspect the halfshaft bushing surface. If this surface is damaged, inspect the halfshaft bushing for damage.

    c. Inspect the differential side gear splines.

33. Remove the bolts and the power steering rack heat shield.

34. Loosen the Y-pipe clamp and disconnect the 2 exhaust hangers.

35. Remove the 4 nuts and the Y-pipe assembly.

36. Remove the 4 bolts and position the steering gear aside, using a suitable length of mechanic's wire.

37. Remove the 4 bolts and position the sway bar aside, using a suitable length of mechanic's wire.

38. Remove the 2 nuts and the roll restrictor heat shield.

39. Remove the roll restrictor.

    a. Remove the roll restrictor-to-transaxle through bolt.

    b. Remove the 2 roll restrictor bracket bolts.

40. Support the subframe using the Powertrain Lift.

41. Remove the 2 nuts, 4 bolts and the subframe support brackets.

42. Remove the 2 front subframe nuts.

43. Remove the 2 middle subframe nuts and remove the subframe.

44. Remove the 3 bolts and the roll restrictor bracket.

45. All wheel drive (AWD) vehicles perform the following:

    a. Index-mark the driveshaft, remove the 4 bolts and position the driveshaft aside.

    b. Disconnect the RH catalyst monitor electrical connector.

    c. Remove the 2 catalytic converter support bracket bolts.

    d. Remove the 4 RH catalytic converter nuts and the RH catalytic converter.

    e. Remove the 5 bolts and the Power Transfer Unit (PTU) support bracket.

    f. Remove the 5 bolts and the PTU.

46. All vehicles, remove the 2 fasteners and the inspection cover.

47. Remove and discard the 3 torque converter bolts.

48. Remove the 2 secondary latches from the transmission fluid cooler tubes at the transmission fluid cooler thermal bypass valve.

49. Using the transmission cooler line disconnect tool, disconnect the transmission fluid cooler tubes from the transmission fluid cooler thermal bypass valve.

50. Using the special tool and a suitable transmission jack, support the transaxle.

51. Remove the 7 torque converter housing bolts and remove the transaxle from the vehicle.

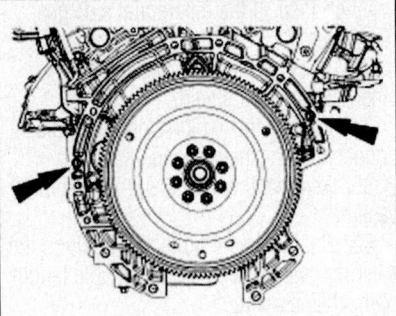

36578_EDGE_G0063

Fig. 23 Check the torque converter housing mating surface to make sure that the dowel pins did not come out of the engine block when the transaxle was removed. If the dowel pin is stuck in the torque converter housing, remove the dowel pin from the torque converter housing

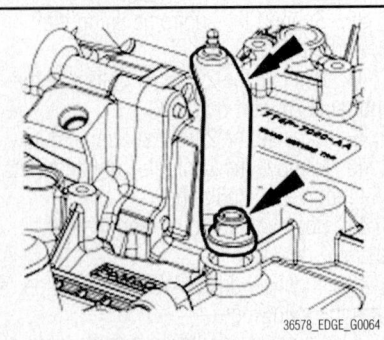

36578_EDGE_G0064

Fig. 24 Removing the manual control lever

52. Check the torque converter housing mating surface to make sure that the dowel pins did not come out of the engine block when the transaxle was removed. If the dowel pin is stuck in the torque converter housing, remove the dowel pin from the torque converter housing.

53. Remove the nut and the manual control lever.

54. Remove and discard the transmission fluid cooler tube bolts.

55. Remove the 2 transmission fluid cooler thermal bypass valve bracket nuts, pull the transmission fluid cooler thermal bypass valve and the transmission fluid cooler tubes straight up and remove the assembly from the transaxle.

56. Inspect the transaxle case to make sure that the transmission fluid cooler tube seals and backing rings were removed with the transmission fluid cooler tubes and are not stuck in the transaxle case. If the transmission fluid cooler tube seals or backing rings are stuck in the transaxle case, remove the seals and backing rings.

57. If the transaxle is to be overhauled or if installing a new transaxle, carry out the transmission fluid cooler backflushing and cleaning.

58. If a replacement transaxle assembly is being installed or a new solenoid body is installed, the Powertrain Control Module (PCM) will have to be reflashed with a new solenoid body strategy and ID data file.

To install:

✳✳ WARNING

Before installation of a new or overhauled transaxle, the transmission fluid cooler tubes must be cleaned. otherwise transaxle failure can occur.

➡**Before installing a new or overhauled transaxle, flush out the cooler and cooler lines.**

59. Inspect the transmission fluid cooler tube backing rings and seals for damage and install a new backing rings or seals if necessary. Lubricate the transmission fluid cooler tube seals with clean automatic transmission fluid and install the backing rings and seals on the transmission fluid cooler tube.

60. Position the transmission fluid cooler thermal bypass valve and transmission fluid cooler tube assembly in place and install the 2 nuts. Tighten to 80 inch lbs. (9 Nm).

61. Install new transmission fluid cooler tube bolts and tighten to 80 inch lbs. (9 Nm).

62. Lubricate the torque converter pilot hub with grease and install the torque converter into the transaxle.

➡**Make sure that when installing the manual control lever it is fully seated onto the manual control lever shaft or damage to the manual control lever shaft will occur and the lever will come loose.**

➡**Make sure to hold the manual control lever while tightening the manual control lever nut or damage to the manual control lever and park components will occur.**

63. Install the manual control lever and nut and tighten to 159 inch lbs. (18 Nm).

➡**If the transaxle is not positioned on the dowel pins, damage to the transaxle can occur.**

64. If the dowel pins were pulled out of the engine block during removal, install new dowel pins in the engine block.

65. Position the transaxle in place and install the 7 torque converter housing bolts. Tighten to bolts to 35 ft. lbs. (48 Nm).

66. Remove the Transmission Jack Adapter from the transaxle.

67. Install the transmission fluid cooler tubes in the transmission fluid cooler thermal bypass valve.

68. Install the 2 secondary latches on the transmission fluid cooler tubes at the transmission fluid cooler thermal bypass valve.

69. Install 3 new torque converter bolts and tighten to 41 ft. lbs. (55 Nm).

70. Install the inspection cover and the 2 fasteners.

71. All AWD vehicles perform the following:

   a. Position the PTU in place and install the 5 PTU-to-transaxle bolts. Tighten the bolts to 66 ft. lbs. (90 Nm).

   b. Position the PTU support bracket in place and install and tighten to 5 bolts to 52 ft. lbs. (70 Nm).

   c. Position the RH catalytic converter in place and install and tighten to 4 nuts to 30 ft. lbs. (40 Nm).

   d. Install the 2 RH catalytic converter support bracket bolts and tighten to 15 ft. lbs. (20 Nm).

   e. Connect the RH catalyst monitor electrical connector.

   f. Line up the index marks on the rear driveshaft to the index marks on the PTU flange made during removal and install the 4 bolts. Tighten to bolts to 52 ft. lbs. (70 Nm).

72. All vehicles, position the roll restrictor bracket on the transaxle and install and tighten the 3 bolts to 66 ft. lbs. (90 Nm).

73. Position the subframe in place and install and tighten the 2 middle nuts to 111 ft. lbs. (150 Nm).

74. Install and tighten the 2 front subframe nuts to 111 ft. lbs. (150 Nm).

75. Position the subframe support brackets in place and loosely install the bolts.

76. Install the rear subframe nuts and tighten to 111 ft. lbs. (150 Nm).

77. Tighten the subframe support bracket bolts to 76 ft. lbs. (103 Nm).

78. Position the roll restrictor in place, install and tighten the bracket bolts to 66 ft. lbs. (90 Nm) and the restrictor-to-transaxle through bolt to 85 ft. lbs. (115 Nm).

79. Install the roll restrictor heat shield and the 2 nuts. Tighten the nuts to 80 inch lbs. (9 Nm).

80. Position the stabilizer bar in place and install and tighten the 4 stabilizer bar bracket bolts to 35 ft. lbs. (48 Nm).

Fig. 25 Remove the 2 nuts, pull the transmission fluid cooler thermal bypass valve and the transmission fluid cooler tubes straight up and remove the assembly from the transaxle

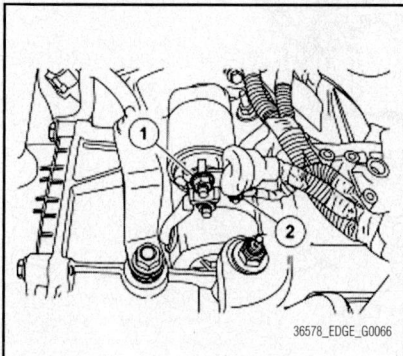

Fig. 26 Connecting the starter motor terminals

81. Position the power steering rack in place and install and tighten the 4 power steering rack bolts to 79 ft. lbs. (107 Nm).

82. Install the power steering rack heat shield and 2 bolts. Tighten the bolts to 53 inch lbs. (6 Nm).

83. Position the exhaust Y-pipe assembly in place and install and tighten to 4 exhaust Y-pipe nuts to 30 ft. lbs. (40 Nm).

84. Install the 2 exhaust hangers and tighten the exhaust clamp to 30 ft. lbs. (40 Nm).

85. FWD vehicles only, perform the following:

a. Position the RH halfshaft and intermediate shaft support bracket in the transaxle and in the steering knuckle. Install 1 stud bolt and 1 bolt. Tighten the bolts to 41 ft. lbs. (55 Nm).

b. Position the catalytic converter support bracket in place and install the bolt and the nut. Tighten the nut to 30 ft. lbs. (40 Nm). Tighten the bolt to 41 ft. lbs. (55 Nm).

c. Install the 2 RH catalytic converter

support bracket bolts and tighten to 15 ft. lbs. (20 Nm).

86. All vehicles, Install the LH and RH halfshafts.

87. Position the lower bumper on the subframe and install the 3 LH lower bumper to subframe nuts and tighten to 89 inch lbs. (10 Nm).

88. Install the 3 RH lower bumper to subframe nuts and tighten to 89 inch lbs. (10 Nm).

89. Install the front splash shield and install the 7 screws and the 3 pushpin fasteners.

90. Install the RH splash shield.

91. Install the transaxle support insulator bracket, bolt and the 3 nuts. Tighten the transaxle support insulator bracket nuts to 46 ft. lbs. (63 Nm). Tighten the transaxle support insulator bracket bolt to 59 ft. lbs. (80 Nm).

92. Install the transaxle support insulator through bolt and flagnut and tighten to 129 ft. lbs. (175 Nm).

93. Remove the engine support bar and engine spreader bar.

94. Remove the engine lift eye from the LH cylinder head.

95. If a new solenoid body was installed, wipe the surface of the existing solenoid body strategy tag on top of the transaxle case clean and install the new solenoid body strategy tag (supplied with the solenoid body service kit) over it.

96. Install the transmission fluid filler tube and nut and tighten to 97 inch lbs. (11 Nm).

97. Install the transmission fluid level indicator.

98. Route the coolant hoses in the transmission fluid filler tube.

99. Install the top 4 torque converter housing bolts and tighten to 35 ft. lbs. (48 Nm).

100. Connect the transaxle electrical connector.

101. Position the fuel hose routing clip on the transaxle stud.

102. Install the starter, bolt and studbolt and tighten to 19 ft. lbs. (26 Nm).

103. Install the wiring harness fastener on the starter motor studbolt.

104. Connect the starter motor terminals and position the starter terminal boot over the battery cable terminal. Tighten (1) to 106 inch lbs. (12 Nm). Tighten (2) to 53 inch lbs. (6 Nm).

105. Install the starter motor electrical terminal cover.

106. Position the selector lever cable and bracket in place and install the 3 bolts. Tighten the bolts to 106 inch lbs. (12 Nm).

107. Place the selector lever in **DRIVE**.

108. Place the manual control lever in **DRIVE**. Rotate the manual control lever clockwise until it stops. Rotate the manual control lever counterclockwise one detent until it stops.

109. Unlock the selector lever cable adjuster. Pry the latch up. Push the lock tab to slide it over.

110. Slide the cable end forward or backward to align it with the manual control cover. With the adjuster locking tab release, connect the selector lever cable end to the manual control lever. Slide the release tab back to lock the adjuster.

111. Install the upper intake manifold.

112. Install the battery tray and tighten the bolts to 89 inch lbs. (10 Nm). Connect the wiring harness fasteners to the battery tray.

113. Install the battery.

114. Position the ACL assembly in place and install and tighten to bolt to 97 inch lbs. (11 Nm).

115. Tighten the ACL outlet pipe clamp at the throttle body and tighten to 44 inch lbs. (5 Nm).

116. Connect the engine breather to the ACL assembly.

117. Connect the brake booster vacuum hose to the ACL assembly.

118. Connect the MAF sensor electrical connector and connect the electrical harness fastener.

119. Fill with clean transmission fluid to the correct level.

120. If a new solenoid body is installed, the solenoid body strategy and the solenoid body identification will need to by updated.

121. If a replacement transaxle assembly is being installed or a new solenoid body is installed, the PCM will have to be reflashed with a new solenoid body strategy and identification data file.

TRANSFER CASE ASSEMBLY

REMOVAL & INSTALLATION

See Figure 27.

➡**This procedure covers Removal and Installation of the Power Transfer Unit (PTU).**

➡**A new intermediate shaft seal and deflector must be installed whenever the intermediate shaft or**

1. Power Transfer Unit (PTU) is removed from the vehicle.

2. With the vehicle in NEUTRAL, position it on a hoist.

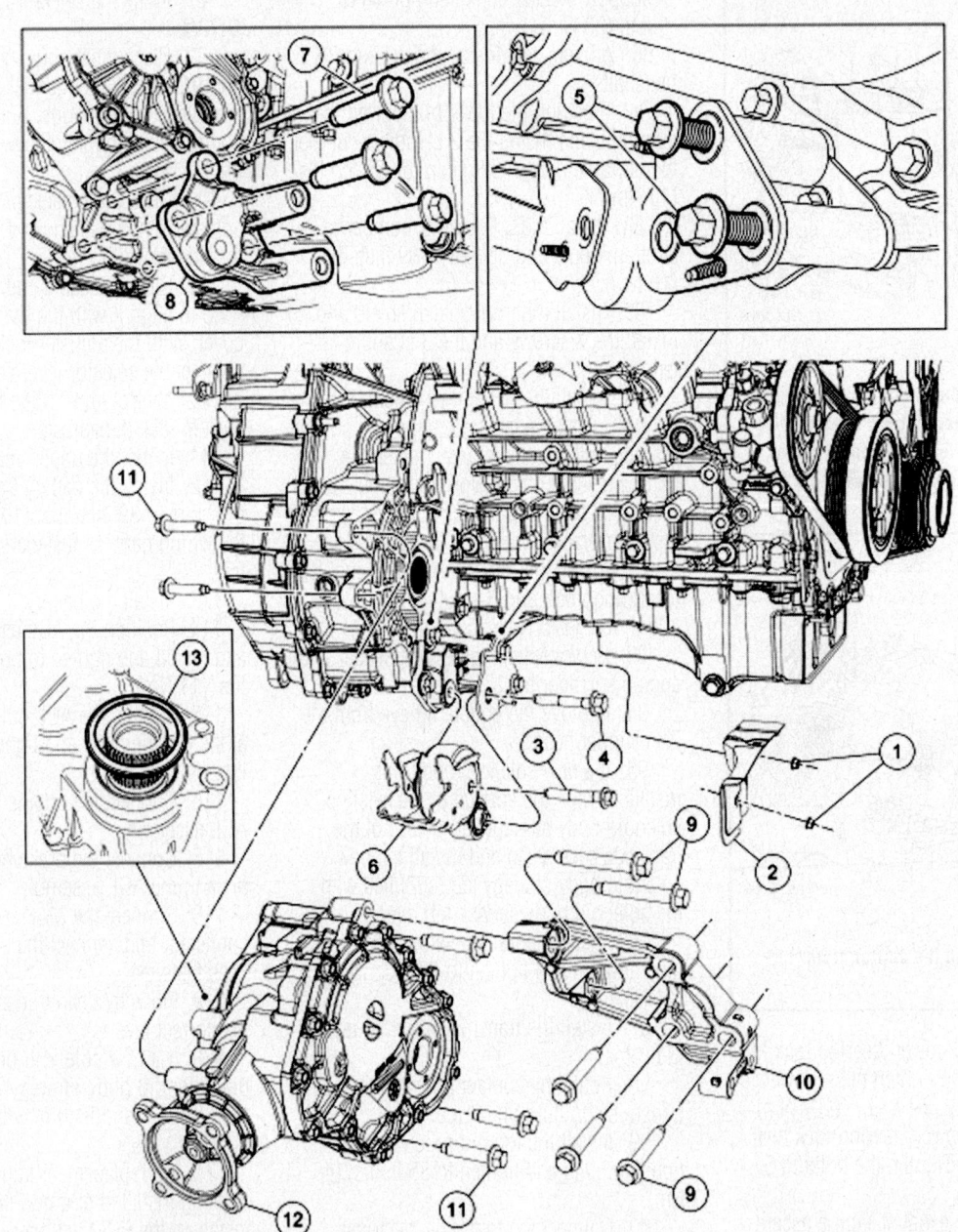

1. Roll restrictor shield nuts
2. Roll restrictor shield
3. Roll restrictor through bolt
4. Roll restrictor through bolt
5. Roll restrictor through bolts
6. Roll restrictor assembly
7. Roll restrictor bracket-to-transaxle bolt (3 required)
8. Roll restrictor bracket-to-transaxle
9. Power Transfer Unit (PTU)-to-support bracket bolts (5 required)
10. PTU support bracket
11. PTU-to-transaxle bolts (5 required)
12. PTU
13. Compression seal

36578_EDGE_G0080

Fig. 27 Exploded view of the Power Transfer Unit (PTU)

3. Remove the LH and RH wheel and tire.

4. Remove the intermediate shaft.

➡**Index-mark the driveshaft for installation.**

5. Remove the 4 bolts and support the driveshaft with a length of mechanic's wire.

6. Remove the exhaust flexible pipe and the RH catalytic converter.

7. Remove the 2 roll restrictor nuts and the roll restrictor shield

8. Remove the roll restrictor through bolt.

9. Remove the roll restrictor through bolt, 2 roll restrictor bracket bolts and the roll restrictor assembly.

10. Remove the 3 roll restrictor bracket-to-transaxle bolts and the roll restrictor-to-transaxle bracket.

11. Remove the 5 PTU support bracket bolts and the PTU support bracket.

12. Using a long extension, loosen but do not remove the 2 LH side PTU-to-transaxle bolts.

13. Remove the 3 RH side PTU-to-transaxle bolts and the 2 LH side PTU-to-transaxle bolts previously loosened.

14. Separate the PTU from the transaxle and remove it from the vehicle.

➡**A new compression seal must be installed whenever the PTU is removed from the vehicle.**

15. Using a suitable tool, remove the compression seal and discard.

To install:

➡**A new compression seal must be installed whenever the Power Transfer Unit (PTU) is removed from the vehicle.**

16. Using a suitable tool, install the new compression seal.

➡**A new PTU intermediate shaft seal must be installed whenever the intermediate shaft or PTU is removed from the vehicle.**

17. Using a suitable pry bar, move the engine forward. Install a block of wood to hold the engine in the forward position. Install the PTU with the output flange facing the passenger side, filler plug facing upward. Rotate the PTU to the transaxle. Install the 5 PTU-to-transaxle bolts. Tighten to 66 ft. lbs. (90 Nm).

18. Position the PTU support bracket into place and hand tighten the 5 PTU support bracket bolts. Tighten the bolts to the transaxle and to the engine to 52 ft. lbs. (70 Nm).

19. Install the roll restrictor-to-transmission bracket and the 3 roll restrictor bracket-to-transmission bolts and tighten to 66 ft. lbs. (90 Nm).

20. Install the roll restrictor through bolt and the 2 roll restrictor bracket bolts and tighten to 66 ft. lbs. (90 Nm).

21. Install the roll restrictor through bolt and tighten to 76 ft. lbs. (103 Nm).

22. Install the roll restrictor shield and the 2 roll restrictor nuts and tighten to 97 inch lbs. (11 Nm).

23. Install the exhaust flexible pipe and the RH catalytic converter.

24. Install the intermediate shaft.

25. Line up the index marks on the driveshaft to the index marks on the PTU flange made during removal and install the 4 bolts. Tighten the bolts to 52 ft. lbs. (70 Nm).

26. Fill the PTU, if necessary.

27. Install the LH and RH wheel and tire.

FRONT HALFSHAFTS

REMOVAL & INSTALLATION

Left Side

See Figures 28 through 30.

1. Raise and safely support the vehicle.

2. Remove the front tire and wheel.

➡**Depress the brake pedal to keep the halfshaft from rotating.**

3. Remove and discard the front wheel hub nut.

4. Remove and discard the ball joint pinch bolt from the knuckle and separate the lower control arm.

➡**Suspension fasteners are critical parts because they affect performance of vital components and systems and their failure may result in major service expense. New parts must be installed with the same part numbers or equivalent part, if replacement is necessary. Do not use a replacement part of lesser quality or substitute design. Torque values must be used as specified during reassembly to make sure of correct retention of these parts.**

5. Remove and discard the stabilizer bar link nuts and position the link aside.

6. Using the special tool, as shown in the accompanying illustration, separate the halfshaft from the wheel hub.

➡**Support the knuckle with a suitable jackstand.**

7. Pull the knuckle outboard and rotate it toward the rear of the vehicle.

※※ CAUTION

The sharp edges on the stub shaft splines can slice or puncture the oil seal. Use care when inserting the stub shaft into the transmission.

8. Using the special tools, as shown in the accompanying illustration, remove the halfshaft from the transmission.

9. Remove and discard the circlip from the stub shaft.

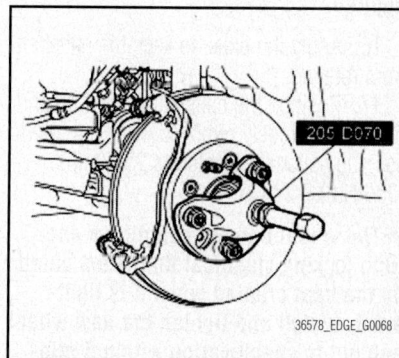

Fig. 29 Using the special tool, separate the halfshaft from the wheel hub

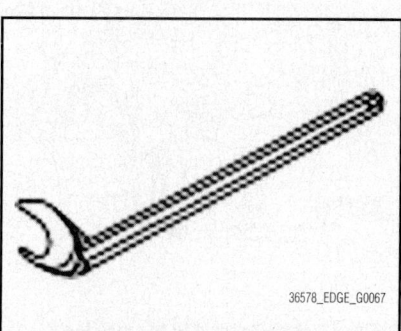

Fig. 28 A variety of special tools are required for left halfshaft removal and installation

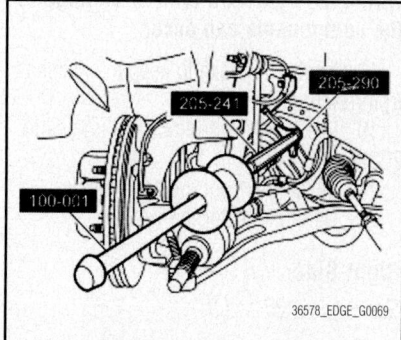

Fig. 30 Using the special tools, remove the halfshaft from the transmission

To install:

10. Install a new stub shaft circlip.

11. Insert the halfshaft into the wheel hub.

➡ **The sharp edges on the stub shaft splines can slice or puncture the oil seal. Use care when inserting the stub shaft into the transmission to avoid oil seal damage.**

➡ **After insertion, pull the halfshaft inner end to make sure the circlip is locked.**

12. Push the stub shaft into the transmission so the circlip locks into the differential side gear.

13. Rotate the knuckle into position.

14. Install the ball joint in the knuckle and install the pinch bolt. Tighten to 41 ft. lbs. (55 Nm).

15. Position the stabilizer bar links and install the link nuts. Tighten to 66 ft. lbs. (90 Nm).

➡ **Do not tighten the front wheel hub nut with the vehicle on the ground. The nut must be tightened to specification before the vehicle is lowered onto the wheels. Wheel bearing damage will occur if the wheel bearing is loaded with the weight of the vehicle applied.**

16. Apply the brake to keep the halfshaft from rotating.

17. Position the halfshaft in the hub and use the previously removed inner hub nut to seat the halfshaft. Tighten to 258 ft. lbs. (350 Nm).

➡ **The wheel hub nut contains a one-time locking chemical that is activated by the heat created when it is tightened. Install and tighten the new wheel hub nut to specification within 5 minutes of starting it on the threads. Always install a new wheel hub nut after loosening or when not tightened within the specified time or damage to the components can occur.**

18. Apply the brake to keep the halfshaft from rotating.

19. Install a new hub nut and tighten to 258 ft. lbs. (350 Nm).

20. Install the front tire and wheel.

21. Carefully lower the vehicle.

Right Side

See Figures 29 and 31.

1. Raise and safely support the vehicle.

2. Remove the front tire and wheel.

➡ **Depress the brake pedal to keep the halfshaft from rotating.**

3. Remove and discard the front wheel hub nut.

4. Remove the brake hose bracket bolt and disconnect the hose from the shock absorber.

5. Disconnect the wheel speed sensor harness from the shock absorber bracket.

6. Remove the RH brake disc.

➡ **Suspension fasteners are critical parts because they affect performance of vital components and systems and their failure may result in major service expense. New parts must be installed with the same part numbers or equivalent part, if replacement is necessary. Do not use a replacement part of lesser quality or substitute design. Torque values must be used as specified during reassembly to make sure of correct retention of these parts.**

7. Remove and discard the upper stabilizer bar link nut and position the link aside.

8. Remove and discard the ball joint bolt and nut. Separate the lower arm.

9. Using the special tool, separate the halfshaft from the wheel hub.

➡ **Support the knuckle with a suitable jackstand.**

10. Pull the knuckle outboard and rotate it toward the rear of the vehicle. Secure the knuckle assembly.

11. Use a brass drift to strike the right side halfshaft in the indicated area and separate the RH halfshaft from the intermediate shaft.

12. Remove and discard the circlip from the intermediate shaft.

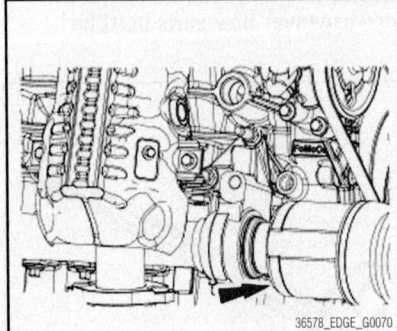

36578_EDGE_G0070

Fig. 31 Use a brass drift to strike the right side halfshaft where shown (arrow), and separate the RH halfshaft from the intermediate shaft

To install:

13. Install a new 1.181 inch (30 mm) intermediate shaft circlip.

➡ **Pull the right side inboard joint outward to make sure the circlip is locked.**

14. Align the splines on the right side shaft with the intermediate shaft and push the stub shaft in until the circlip locks the shafts together.

15. Insert the halfshaft into the wheel hub.

16. Rotate the knuckle into position.

17. Position the halfshaft and ball joint in the wheel knuckle. Install the new bolt and nut and tighten to 41 ft. lbs. (55 Nm).

18. Position the upper stabilizer bar link and install a new nut and tighten the 66 ft. lbs. (90 Nm).

19. Install the RH brake disc.

20. Position the brake hose bracket to the shock absorber and install the bolt. Tighten the bolt to 15 ft. lbs. (20 Nm).

21. Connect the wheel speed sensor harness to the shock absorber bracket.

⁕⁕ WARNING

Do not tighten the front wheel hub nut with the vehicle on the ground. The nut must be tightened to specification before the vehicle is lowered onto the wheels. Wheel bearing damage will occur if the wheel bearing is loaded with the weight of the vehicle applied.

➡ **Depress the brake pedal to keep the halfshaft from rotating.**

22. Install a the previously removed wheel hub nut to seat the halfshaft. Tighten to 258 ft. lbs. (350 Nm). Remove and discard the wheel hub nut.

➡ **The wheel hub nut contains a one-time locking chemical that is activated by the heat created when it is tightened. Install and tighten the new wheel hub nut to specification within 5 minutes of starting it on the threads. Always install a new wheel hub nut after loosening or when not tightened within the specified time or damage to the components can occur.**

➡ **Depress the brake pedal to keep the halfshaft from rotating.**

23. Install a new wheel hub nut and tighten to 258 ft. lbs. (350 Nm).

24. Install the front tire and wheel.

CV-JOINT OVERHAUL

See Figures 32 through 35.

1. Remove the halfshaft assembly, as outlined in this section.
2. For the inboard CV joint, remove and discard the boot clamps.
3. Remove the inboard CV joint retaining ring.

※※ WARNING

Do not let the roller bearings fall or damage to the component may occur.

4. For the inboard CV joint, carry out the following:
    a. Remove and discard the retainer circlip.
    b. Slide the boot away from the CV joint.
5. Using a suitable 3-jaw puller, remove the CV joint.
6. Remove and discard the inner CV boot.

➡ **The outboard CV joint is not removable from the halfshaft. The boot must be removed or installed from the inboard CV joint side of the shaft.**

7. For the outboard CV joint, carry out the following:

    a. Remove and discard the boot clamps.
    b. Remove and discard the boot.

To assemble:

➡ **Do not mix the boot clamps.**

8. Lubricate the outboard CV joint:
    a. Pack the outboard CV joint with grease from the kit. One-third of the grease must be installed in the joint with the remainder placed in the boot.
    b. Spread the remaining grease evenly inside the boot.
9. Position the boot so the rib on the boot is located in the groove of the shaft.
10. Position the outboard halfshaft boot and the outboard boot clamps.
11. Install the outboard CV boot clamps, using the special tool as shown.
12. Position the inboard clamp and boot.
13. Install the CV joint and snap ring on the halfshaft.
14. Fill the inboard CV joint housing with grease from the kit. One-half of the grease must be installed in the joint and the remainder placed in the boot.

※※ WARNING

Do not let the roller bearings fall.

15. Position the CV housing on the CV joint.
16. Install the retaining ring.
17. Position the inboard halfshaft boot and clamps:
    a. Position the boot in the housing groove.
    b. Position the boot clamps.
18. Set the halfshaft assembled length to specifications. Refer to the accompanying illustrations, and the following steps:

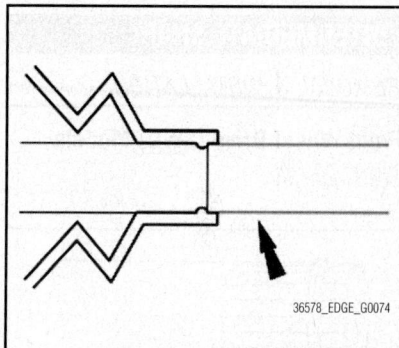

36578_EDGE_G0074

Fig. 33 Position the boot so the rib on the boot is located in the groove of the shaft

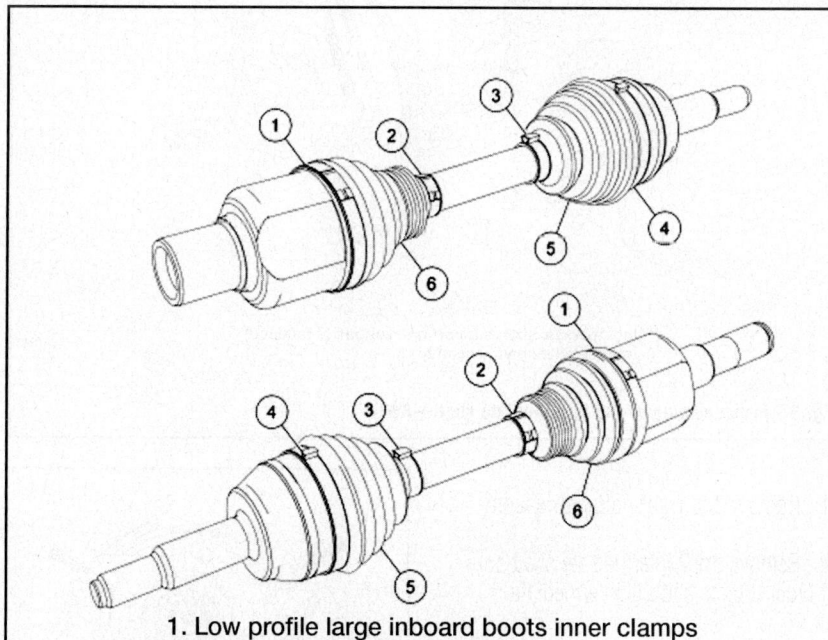

1. Low profile large inboard boots inner clamps
2. Low profile small inboard boots
3. Intermediate shaft boot clamps
4. Outboard boot outer clamps
5. Outboard CV joint boots
6. Inboard CV joint boots

36578_EDGE_G0073

Fig. 32 View of the halfshaft and CV-joint boots

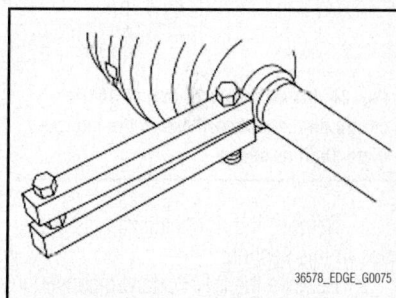

36578_EDGE_G0075

Fig. 34 Install the outboard CV boot clamps, using a suitable CV-Joint Boot Installation tool

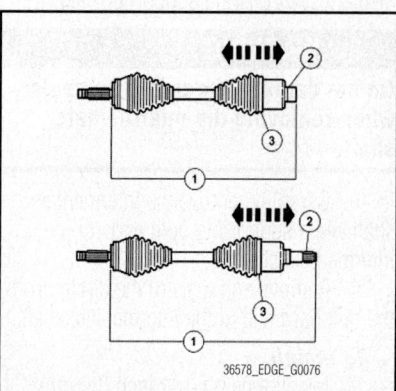

36578_EDGE_G0076

Fig. 35 Halfshaft assembled length specifications

a. Measure the entire assembly length (item 1 in illustration).

b. Push in or pull out on the inner joint as necessary to adjust the halfshaft assembled length (item 2 in illustration).

c. Hold the inner joint to prevent the assembled length from changing, and insert a small flat-blade screwdriver between the boot and the joint to equalize the pressure (item 3 in illustration).

19. Install the boot clamps.

20. Lever arm to the closed position and use a soft-faced hammer to close the tabs.

21. Install the halfshaft, as outlined in this section.

INTERMEDIATE SHAFT

REMOVAL & INSTALLATION

Front Wheel Drive (FWD) Models

See Figure 36.

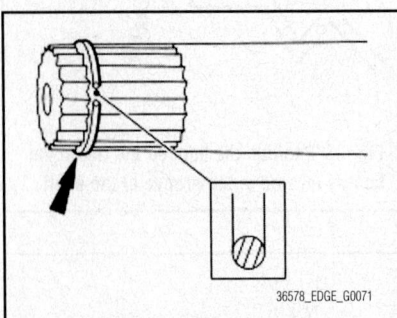

36578_EDGE_G0071

Fig. 36 Install a new 30 mm (1.181 in) circlip on the outboard end of the intermediate shaft as shown

1. Remove the right halfshaft, as outlined in this section.

2. Remove the 2 RH catalytic converter support bracket bolts.

3. Remove the bolt, nut and the RH catalytic converter support bracket.

4. Remove the 2 bolts from the intermediate shaft bearing support bracket.

✳✳ WARNING

Do not damage the transaxle seals when removing the intermediate shaft.

5. Carefully remove the intermediate shaft while supporting both ends of the intermediate shaft.

6. Remove and discard the circlip from the outboard end of the intermediate shaft.

To install:

7. Install a new 1.181 inch (30 mm) circlip on the outboard end of the intermediate shaft.

8. Position the intermediate shaft in the transaxle and engage the intermediate shaft splines with the transaxle side gears. Make sure the circlip is locked in the gear.

9. Install the 2 intermediate shaft support bracket stud bolts. Tighten to 30 ft. lbs. (40 Nm).

10. Install the RH catalytic converter support bracket, nut and bolt. Tighten to 30 ft. lbs. (40 Nm).

11. Install the 2 RH catalytic converter support bracket bolts. Tighten to 15 ft. lbs. (20 Nm).

12. Install the right halfshaft.

All Wheel Drive (AWD) Models

See Figure 37.

✳✳ WARNING

The intermediate shaft seal in the Power Transfer Unit (PTU) must be replaced whenever the intermediate shaft is removed. Refer to the Power Transfer Unit Seal Replacement procedure under the Transfer Case Section.

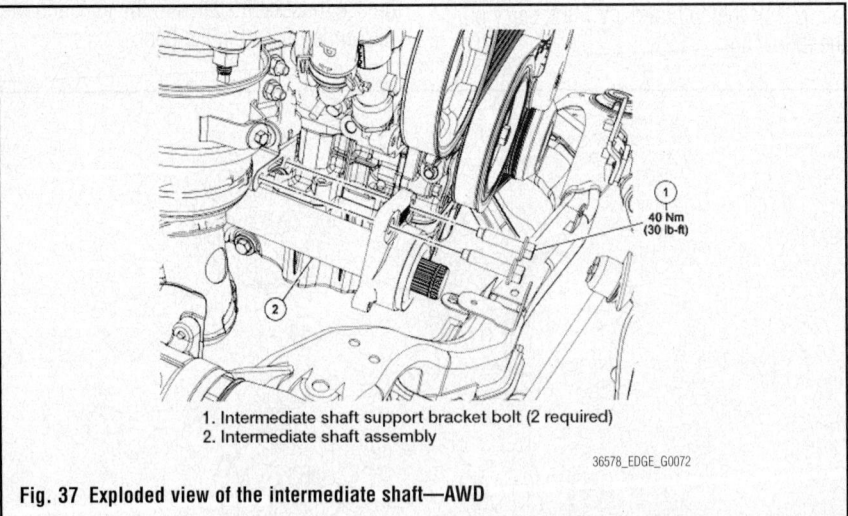

1. Intermediate shaft support bracket bolt (2 required)
2. Intermediate shaft assembly

36578_EDGE_G0072

Fig. 37 Exploded view of the intermediate shaft—AWD

1. Remove the right halfshaft assembly.

2. Remove the 2 intermediate shaft support bracket bolts and the intermediate shaft.

3. Remove and discard the circlip from the outboard end of the intermediate shaft.

To install:

4. Install a new 1.181 in (30 mm) circlip on the outboard end of the intermediate shaft.

5. Install a new intermediate seal in the PTU, as outlined in the Power Transfer Unit Seal procedure.

6. Position the intermediate shaft in the PTU and engage the intermediate shaft splines with the PTU gears.

7. Install the 2 intermediate shaft support bracket bolts. Tighten to 30 ft. lbs. (40 Nm).

8. Install the right halfshaft.

REAR AXLE SHAFT, BEARING & SEAL

REMOVAL & INSTALLATION

See Figure 38.

➡**This procedure covers replacement of the Stub Shaft, Bearing and Seal.**

1. Remove the driveshaft assembly.

2. Remove the rear halfshafts.

3. Remove the rear stabilizer bar and link.

4. Position a suitable transmission hydraulic jack to the axle housing. Securely strap the jack to the housing.

5. Disconnect the active torque coupling electrical connector at the front of the crossmember.

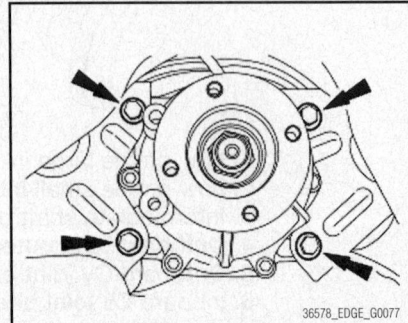

36578_EDGE_G0077

Fig. 38 Removing the differential housing to front insulator bracket bolts

6. Remove the 4 differential housing to front insulator bracket bolts. (To install tighten to 66 ft. lbs. (90 Nm)

7. Loosen the LH front insulator bracket to subframe bolt, and rotate the bracket aside. To install tighten to 66 ft. lbs. (90 Nm).

8. Loosen the RH front insulator bracket to subframe bolt and the bracket, and rotate the bracket aside. To install tighten to 66 ft. lbs. (90 Nm).

9. Remove the 2 RH side insulator bracket to rear axle differential bolts and the axle assembly. To install, tighten to 66 ft. lbs. (90 Nm).

10. Remove the 3 LH side insulator or bracket to rear axle differential bolts. To install, tighten to 66 ft. lbs. (90 Nm).

11. Lower the rear axle assembly.

12. To install, reverse the removal procedure.

REAR HALFSHAFTS

REMOVAL & INSTALLATION

See Figures 39 and 40.

1. With the vehicle in NEUTRAL, position it on a hoist.

2. Remove the rear wheel speed sensor.

3. Remove the inner and outer rear wheel hub nuts. Do not discard at this time.

4. Remove the brake caliper hose bracket bolt.

5. Remove the rear brake disc.

➡**Suspension fasteners are critical parts because they affect performance of vital components and systems and their failure may result in major service expense. New parts must be installed with the same part numbers or equivalent part, if replacement is necessary. Do not use a replacement part of lesser quality or substitute design. Torque values must be used a specified during reassembly to make sure of correct retention of these parts.**

6. Remove and discard the upper arm outboard bolt.

7. Lift the upper arm from the knuckle.

8. Support the lower arm and remove the lower shock nut and bolt.

9. Remove and discard the stabilizer link upper nut.

10. Remove and discard the outer toe link nut and bolt.

11. Support the wheel knuckle and remove the lower arm nut and bolt and discard the nut and bolt.

12. Using the front hub remover, separate the halfshaft from the rear axle hub assembly.

➡**DO NOT damage the oil seal when removing the axle halfshaft from the differential.**

13. Using a suitable pry bar, remove the halfshaft.

14. Position the halfshaft up through the wheel knuckle opening and remove the halfshaft.

15. Remove and discard the circlip from the stub shaft

To install:

16. Install a new 1.102 inch (28 mm) circlip on the stub shaft.

➡**Make sure the oil seal protector is correctly aligned with the differential oil seal during installation.**

17. Using the Axle Seal Protector, install the halfshaft in the differential.

18. Install the stub shaft in the rear drive unit. Make sure the circlip locks in the side gear.

19. Slide the outboard CV joint down through the knuckle.

20. Position the halfshaft outer CV joint through the hub bearing.

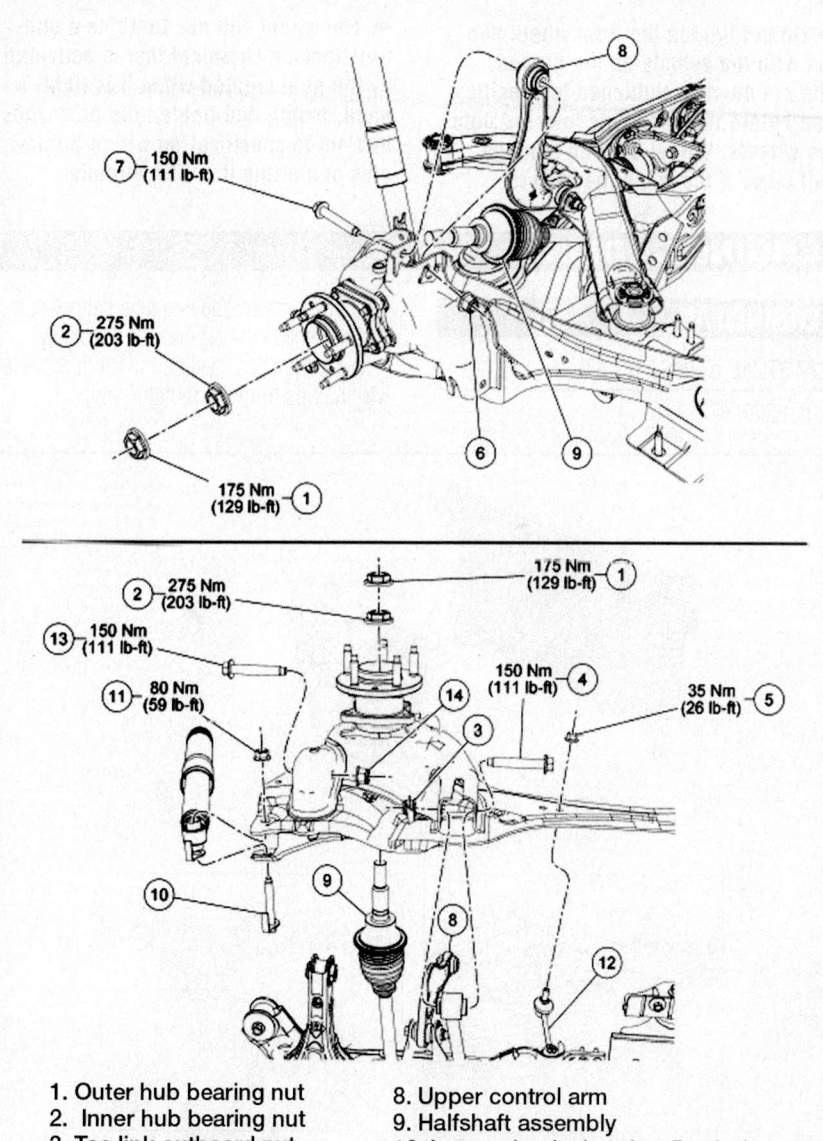

1. Outer hub bearing nut
2. Inner hub bearing nut
3. Toe link outboard nut
4. Toe link outboard bolt
5. Stabilizer bar link nut
6. Upper arm outboard nut
7. Upper arm outboard bolt
8. Upper control arm
9. Halfshaft assembly
10. Lower shock absorber flag bolt
11. Lower shock absorber nut
12. Stabilizer bar link
13. Lower arm outboard bolt
14. Lower arm outboard nut

36578_EDGE_G0078

Fig. 39 Exploded view of the rear halfshaft

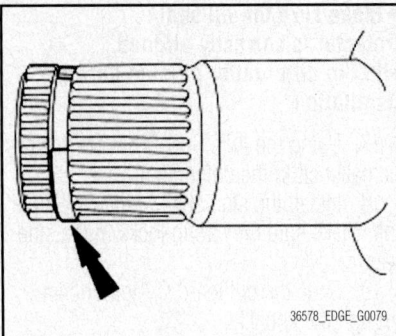

Fig. 40 Removing the circlip from the stub shaft

➡ **Do not tighten the front wheel hub nut with the vehicle on the ground. The nut must be tightened to specification before the vehicle is lowered onto the wheels. Wheel bearing damage will occur if the wheel bearing is** loaded with the weight of the vehicle applied.

➡ **Apply the brake to keep the halfshaft from rotating.**

21. Position the halfshaft in the hub and use the previously removed inner hub nut to seat the halfshaft. Tighten to 203 ft. lbs. (275 Nm). Remove and discard the hub nut.
22. Position the upper arm outboard end and install a new bolt. Tighten the bolt to 111 ft. lbs. (150 Nm).
23. Position the lower arm and install a new lower arm bolt and nut. Tighten to 111 ft. lbs. (150 Nm).

➡ **The wheel hub nut contains a one-time locking chemical that is activated by the heat created when it is tightened. Install and tighten the new wheel hub nut to specification within 5 minutes of starting it on the threads.**

Always install a new wheel hub nut after loosening or when not tightened within the specified time or damage to the components can occur.

➡ **Apply the brake to keep the halfshaft from rotating.**

24. Install the 2 new rear wheel hub nuts. Tighten the inner hub nut to 203 ft. lbs. (275 Nm). Tighten the outer hub nut to 129 ft. lbs. (175 Nm).
25. Install a new rear toe link bolt and tighten to 148 ft. lbs. (200 Nm).
26. Install a new stabilizer link upper nut and tighten to 26 ft. lbs. (35 Nm).
27. Install a new lower shock absorber bolt and tighten to 85 ft. lbs. (115 Nm).
28. Install the rear wheel speed sensor.
29. Install the rear brake disc.
30. Install the brake caliper hose bracket bolt and tighten to 133 inch lbs. (15 Nm).
31. Install the tire and wheel.

ENGINE COOLING

ENGINE FAN

REMOVAL & INSTALLATION

See Figure 41.

1. Disconnect the negative battery cable.
2. Remove the air cleaner assembly.
3. If equipped, detach the 2 block heater wiring clips from the radiator support.
4. Detach the 5 wiring harness retainers and position the harness aside.
5. Position aside the upper radiator hose from the cooling fan motor and shroud.
6. Disconnect the cooling fan motor and shroud electrical connector.
7. If equipped, remove the bolt and position aside the oil cooler bracket.
8. Remove the 2 bolts and the cooling fan motor and shroud.

To install:

9. Installation is the reverse of the removal procedure, noting the following tightening specifications:
    a. Tighten the oil cooler bracket bolt to 53 inch lbs. (6 Nm).
    b. Tighten the cooling fan motor and shroud bolts to 53 inch lbs. (6 Nm).

RADIATOR

REMOVAL & INSTALLATION

See Figures 42 and 43.

1. Drain the cooling system.
2. Remove the cooling fan motor and shroud.
3. Remove the front bumper cover.
4. Disconnect the upper radiator hose and lower degas bottle hose from the radiator.
5. Disconnect the lower radiator hose from the radiator.
6. Remove the compressor-to-condenser discharge line bracket bolt. To install, tighten to 62 inch lbs. (7 Nm).

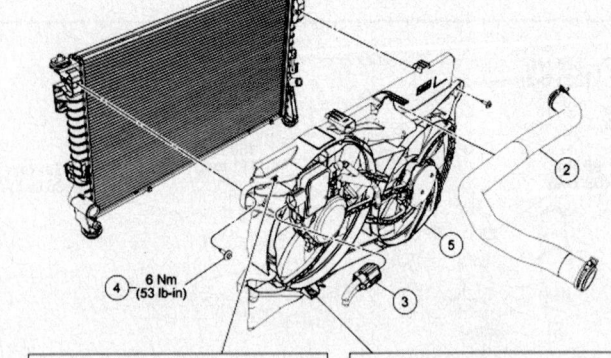
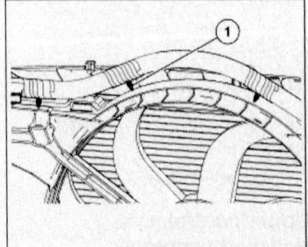

1. Wiring harness retainer
2. Upper radiator hose
3. Cooling fan motor and shroud electrical connector
4. Cooling fan motor and shroud bolt (2 required)
5. Cooling fan motor and shroud
6. Oil cooler bracket bolt (if equipped)
7. Oil cooler bracket (if equipped)

Fig. 41 Exploded view of the engine cooling fan and shroud and related components

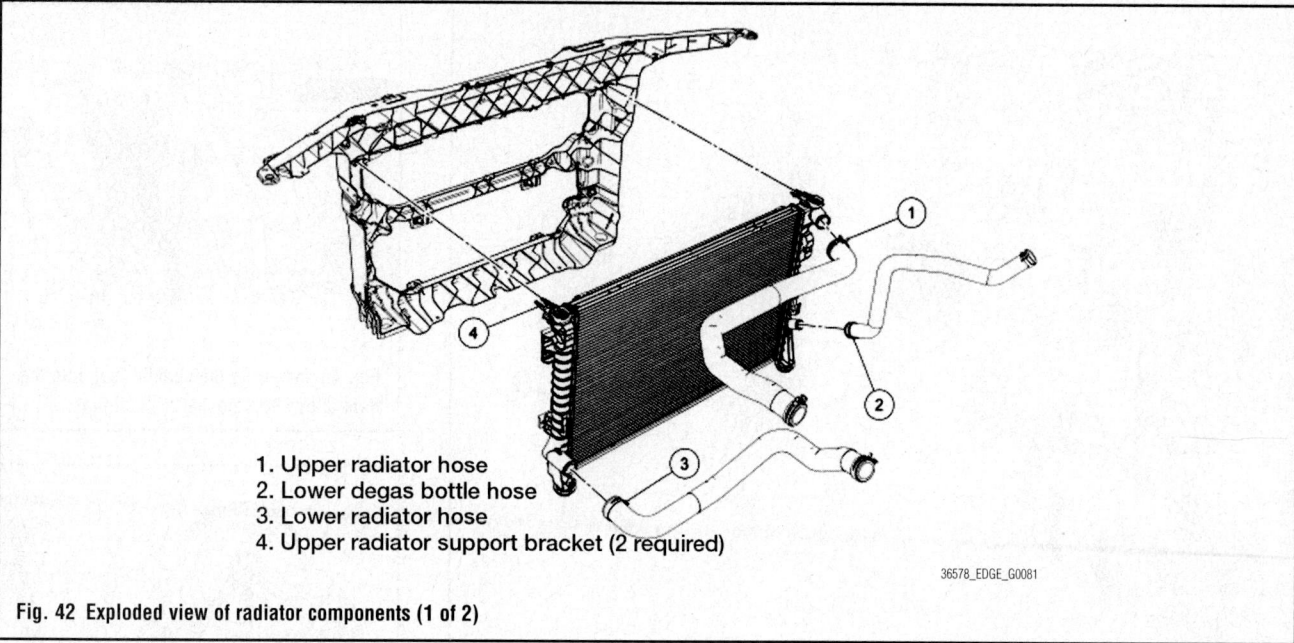

1. Upper radiator hose
2. Lower degas bottle hose
3. Lower radiator hose
4. Upper radiator support bracket (2 required)

36578_EDGE_G0081

Fig. 42 Exploded view of radiator components (1 of 2)

7. Lift and remove the tabs from the radiator support and position the radiator towards the engine.

8. Detach the 2 pin-type retainers from the radiator.

9. Remove the 2 A/C condenser bolts from the radiator and separate the condenser from the radiator. To install, tighten to 89 inch lbs. (10 Nm).

10. Remove the radiator.

11. To install, reverse the removal procedure.

12. Fill and bleed the cooling system.

THERMOSTAT

REMOVAL & INSTALLATION

See Figure 44.

1. Drain the cooling system.

2. Remove the air cleaner assembly and outlet pipc.

3. Remove the 2 bolts and position aside the thermostat housing cover.

4. Remove the O-ring seal and thermostat.

5. Clean and inspect the O-ring seal. Install a new scal if necessary.

To install:

➡Early build vehicle (built before January 19, 2009) cooling systems are filled with Motorcraft® Premium Gold Engine Coolant. Late build vehicle (built on or after January 19, 2009) cooling systems are filled with Motorcraft® Specialty Green Engine Coolant. Mixing coolant types degrades the corrosion protection of the coolant. Do not mix coolant types. Failure to follow these instructions may result in engine or cooling system damage.

6. Installation is the reverse of the removal procedure, noting the following:

a. Lubricate the thermostat O-ring seal with clean engine coolant.

b. Tighten the thermostat housing cover to 89 inch lbs. (10 Nm).

c. Fill and bleed the cooling system.

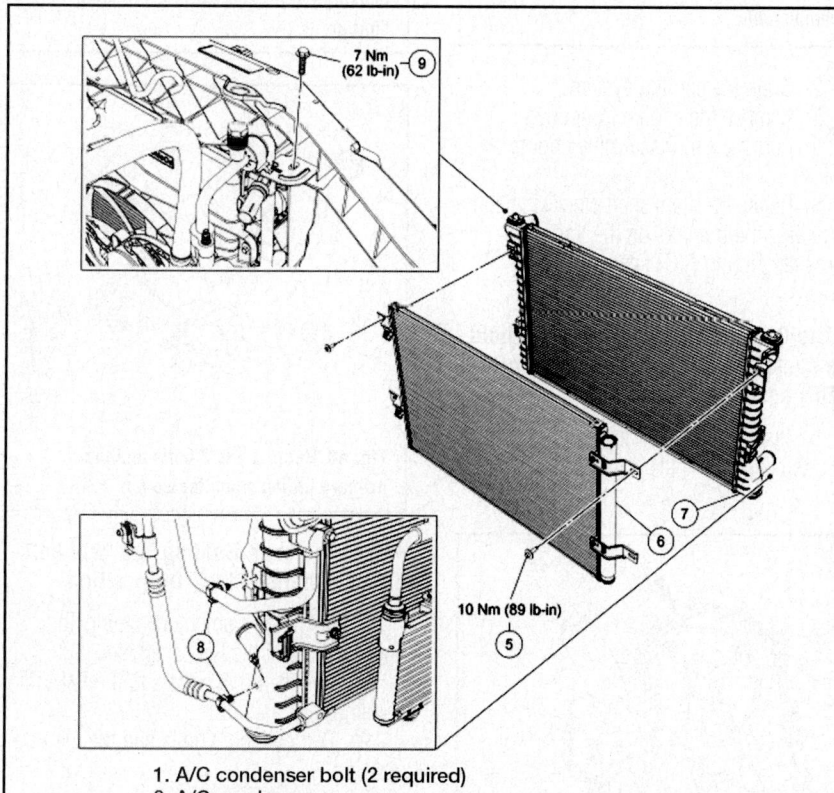

1. A/C condenser bolt (2 required)
2. A/C condenser
3. Radiator
4. Pin-type retainers (2 required)
5. Compressor-to-condenser discharge line bracket bolt

36578_EDGE_G0082

Fig. 43 Exploded view of radiator components (2 of 2)

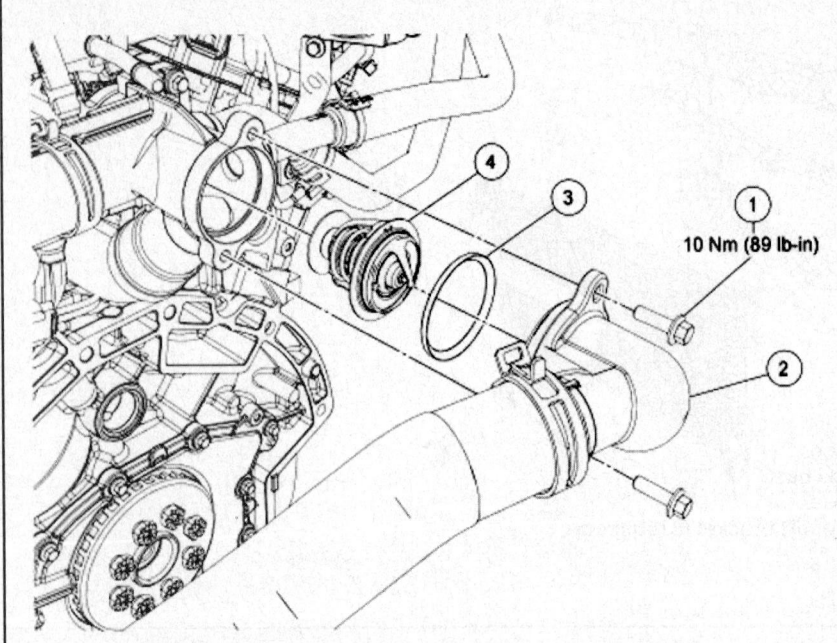

1. Thermostat housing cover bolt (2 required)
2. Thermostat housing cover
3. O-ring seal
4. Thermostat

36578_EDGE_G0084

Fig. 44 Exploded view of the thermostat and related components

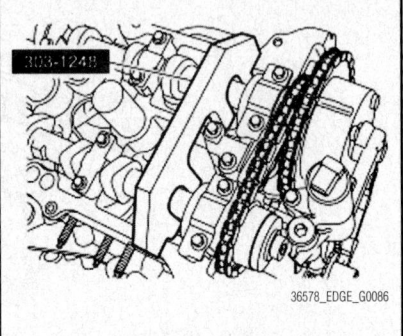

36578_EDGE_G0086

Fig. 46 Installing the special tool onto the flats of the RH camshaft (LH similar)

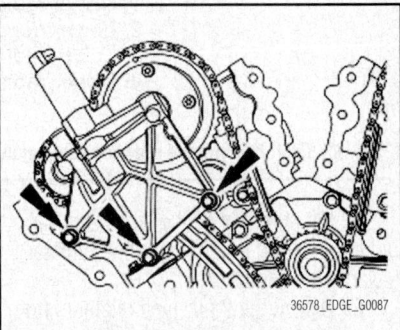

36578_EDGE_G0087

Fig. 47 Remove the 3 bolts and the VCT housing—right side shown, left side similar

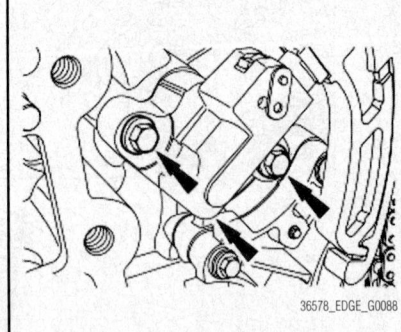

36578_EDGE_G0088

Fig. 48 Remove the 2 bolts and the primary timing chain tensioner

WATER PUMP

REMOVAL & INSTALLATION

See Figures 45 through 51.

➡**During engine repair procedures, cleanliness is extremely important. Any foreign material, including any material created while cleaning gasket surfaces, that enters the oil passages, coolant passages or the oil pan can cause engine failure.**

1. With the vehicle in NEUTRAL, position it on a hoist.

2. Drain the cooling system.
3. Remove the engine front cover.
4. Remove and discard the engine oil filter.
5. Rotate the crankshaft clockwise and align the timing marks on the Variable Camshaft Timing (VCT) assemblies as shown.

➡**The Camshaft Holding Tool will hold the camshafts in the Top Dead Center (TDC) position.**

6. Install the Camshaft Holding Tool onto the flats of the LH camshafts.

➡**The Camshaft Holding Tool will hold the camshafts in the TDC position.**

7. Install the Camshaft Holding Tool onto the flats of the RH camshafts.
8. Remove the 3 bolts and the RH VCT housing.
9. Remove the 3 bolts and the LH VCT housing.
10. Remove and discard the VCT housing seals.
11. Remove the 2 bolts and the primary timing chain tensioner.
12. Remove the primary timing chain tensioner arm.

36578_EDGE_G0085

Fig. 45 Aligning timing marks on the VCT assemblies

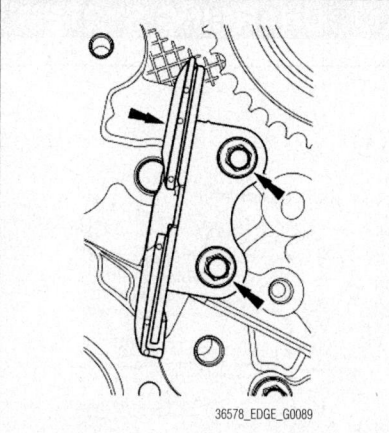

Fig. 49 Remove the 2 bolts and the upper LH primary timing chain guide

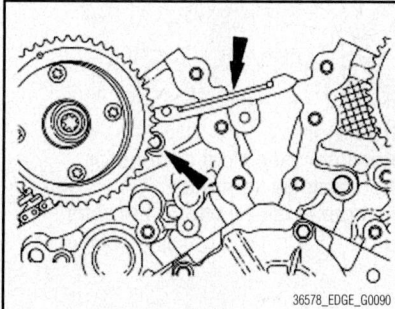

Fig. 50 Loosen the RH primary timing chain guide upper bolt. Rotate the guide and tighten the bolt

13. Remove the 2 bolts and the lower LH primary timing chain guide.

14. Remove the primary timing chain.

15. Remove the 2 bolts and the upper LH primary timing chain guide.

16. Remove the RH primary timing chain guide lower bolt.

➡ **The RH primary timing chain guide must be repositioned to allow the coolant pump to be removed.**

17. Loosen the RH primary timing chain guide upper bolt. Rotate the guide and tighten the bolt.

18. Place clean lint-free shop towels in the oil pan opening to prevent coolant from entering the oil pan during coolant pump removal.

19. Remove the 8 bolts and the coolant pump.

To install:

➡ **Clean and inspect all sealing surfaces.**

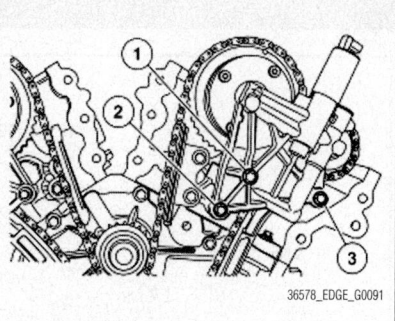

Fig. 51 Identifying the LH VCT housing bolt tightening sequence

20. Install the coolant pump and the 8 bolts. Tighten in the sequence shown to 89 inch lbs. (10 Nm).

21. Remove all of the shop towels from the oil pan opening.

➡ **Any coolant that has accumulated in the oil pan must be drained from the pan and any residual coolant cleaned from the front of the engine and oil pan. Failure to remove all traces of the coolant can result in oil contamination and severe engine damage.**

22. Remove the oil pan drain plug and allow any accumulated coolant to drain.

   a. Remove any residual coolant from the front of the engine and the oil pan using regulated compressed air and clean lint-free shop towels.

   b. Install the oil pan drain plug and tighten to 20 ft. lbs. (27 Nm).

23. Loosen the RH primary timing chain guide upper bolt.

   a. Position the RH primary timing chain guide and install the lower bolt. Tighten the 2 bolts to 89 inch lbs. (10 Nm).

24. Install the primary timing chain with the colored links aligned with the timing marks on the VCT assemblies and the crankshaft sprocket.

25. Install the upper LH primary timing chain guide and the 2 bolts. Tighten the bolts to 89 inch lbs. (10 Nm).

26. Install the lower LH primary timing chain guide and the 2 bolts and tighten to 89 inch lbs. (10 Nm).

27. Install the primary timing chain tensioner arm.

28. Reset the primary timing chain tensioner.

   a. Rotate the lever counterclockwise.

   b. Using a soft-jawed vise, compress the plunger.

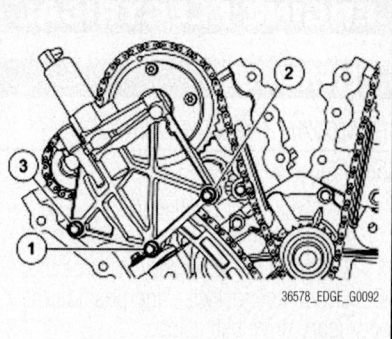

Fig. 52 Identifying the RH VCT housing bolt tightening sequence

   c. Align the hole in the lever with the hole in the tensioner housing.

   d. Install a suitable lock pin.

➡ **It may be necessary to rotate the crankshaft slightly to remove slack from the timing chain and install the tensioner.**

29. Install the primary tensioner and the 2 bolts. Tighten to 89 inch lbs. (10 Nm). Remove the lock pin.

30. As a post check, verify correct alignment of all timing marks.

31. Install new VCT housing seals.

➡ **Make sure the dowels on the Variable Camshaft Timing (VCT) housing are fully engaged in the cylinder head prior to tightening the bolts. Failure to follow this process will result in severe engine damage.**

32. Install the LH VCT housing and the 3 bolts. Tighten in the sequence shown to 89 inch lbs. (10 Nm).

➡ **Make sure the dowels on the Variable Camshaft Timing (VCT) housing are fully engaged in the cylinder head prior to tightening the bolts. Failure to follow this process will result in severe engine damage.**

33. Install the RH VCT housing and the 3 bolts. Tighten in the sequence shown to 89 inch lbs. (10 Nm).

➡ **Lubricate the engine oil filter gasket with clean engine oil prior to installing the oil filter.**

34. Install a new engine oil filter. Tighten to 44 inch lbs. (5 Nm) and then rotate an additional 180°.

35. Install the engine front cover.

36. Fill and bleed the cooling system.

ENGINE ELECTRICAL | CHARGING SYSTEM

ALTERNATOR

REMOVAL & INSTALLATION

See Figure 53.

1. Disconnect the battery.
2. Remove the cooling fan.
3. Rotate the accessory drive belt tensioner counterclockwise and position the accessory drive belt aside.
4. Position the generator B+ terminal protective cover aside, remove the nut and position the generator B+ terminal aside. To install, tighten to 106 inch lbs. (12 Nm).
5. Disconnect the alternator electrical connector. Detach the pin-type retainer and wiring harness.
6. Remove the alternator stud nut. To install, tighten to 35 ft. lbs. (47 Nm).
7. Remove the alternator stud. To install, tighten to 71 inch lbs. (8 Nm).
8. Remove the RH fender splash shield.
9. Loosen the alternator bolt and remove the generator. To install, tighten to 35 ft. lbs. (47 Nm).
10. To install, reverse the removal procedure.

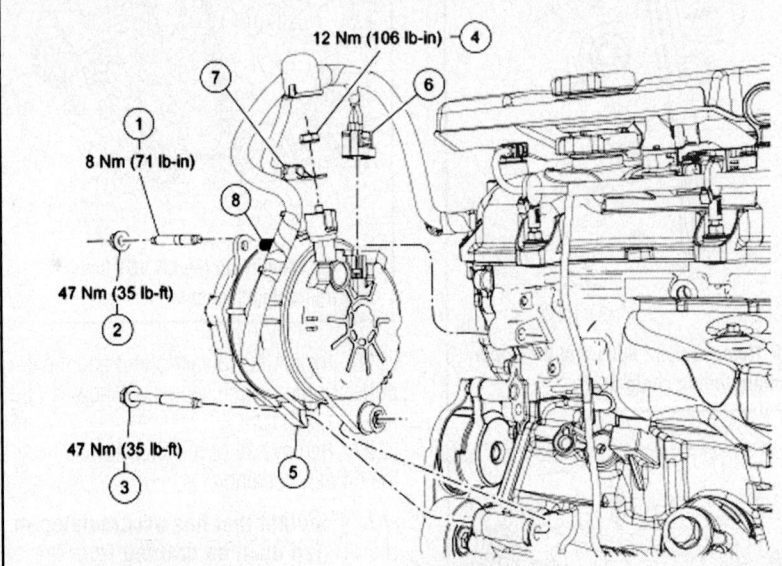

1. Alternator stud
2. Alternator nut
3. Alternator bolt
4. Alternator B+ terminal nut
5. Alternator
6. Alternator electrical connector
7. Alternator B+ terminal
8. Pin-type retainer, wiring harness

36578_EDGE_G0094

Fig. 53 Exploded view of the alternator

ENGINE ELECTRICAL | IGNITION SYSTEM

FIRING ORDER

The firing order goes as follows 1-4-2-5-3-6.

IGNITION COIL

REMOVAL & INSTALLATION

See Figures 54 and 55.

1. Disconnect the negative battery cable.
2. If removing the left side ignition coils, disconnect the crankcase vent tube quick connect coupling from the valve cover fitting and position it aside.
3. If removing the right side ignition coils, remove the upper intake manifold, as outlined in the Engine Mechanical Section.

➡ **The upper intake manifold must be removed to access the right side ignition coils only.**

4. Detach the 6 ignition coil-on-plug electrical connectors and unfasten the mounting bolts, then remove the ignition coils from the vehicle.

➡ **When removing the ignition coil-on-plugs, use a slight twisting motion to help break the seal and make removal easier.**

To install:

5. Install the 6 ignition coil-on-plugs and the 6 bolts, then tighten to 62 inch lbs. (7 Nm).
6. Attach the 6 ignition coil-on-plug electrical connectors.
7. If removed, install the upper intake manifold, as outlined in the Engine Mechanical Section.

IGNITION TIMING

ADJUSTMENT

The ignition timing is controlled by the Powertrain Control Module (PCM). No adjustment is necessary or possible.

SPARK PLUGS

REMOVAL & INSTALLATION

See Figures 54 through 56.

1. Disconnect the negative battery cable.
2. If removing the left side spark plugs, disconnect the crankcase vent tube quick connect coupling from the valve cover fitting and position it aside.
3. If removing the right side spark plugs, remove the upper intake manifold, as outlined in the Engine Mechanical Section.

➡ The upper intake manifold must be removed to access the right side spark plugs only.

4. Detach the 6 ignition coil-on-plug electrical connectors and unfasten the mounting bolts, then remove the ignition coils from the vehicle.

➡ **When removing the ignition coil-on-plugs, a slight twisting motion will help break the seal and make removal easier.**

✳✳ CAUTION

Only use hand tools when removing or installing the spark plugs, or you can damage the spark plug and/or cylinder head. Never use power tools.

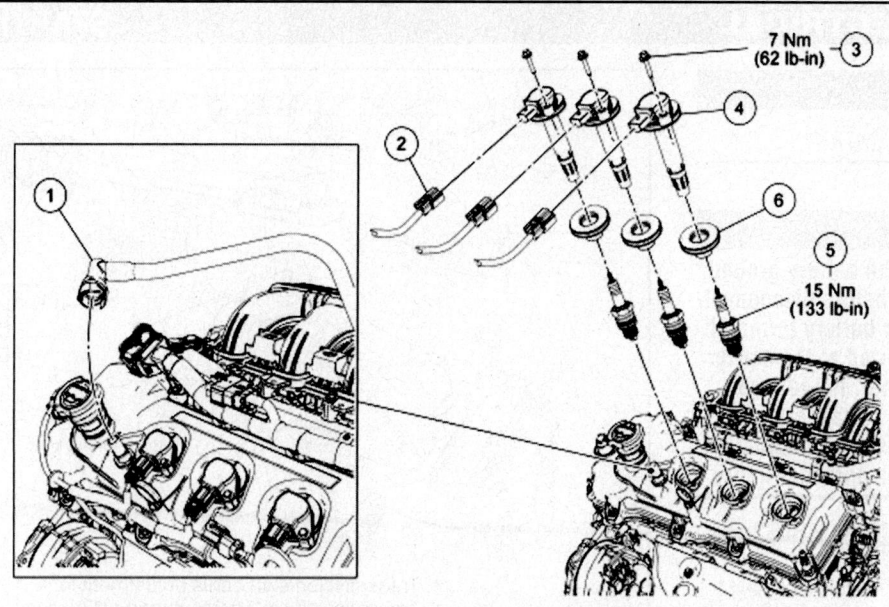

1. Crankcase vent tube-to-valve cover fitting quick connect coupling
2. Ignition coil-on plug electrical connector (3 required)
3. Ignition coil-on plug bolt (3 required)
4. Ignition coil-on plug (3 required)
5. Spark plug (3 required)

36578_EDGE_G0095

Fig. 54 Exploded view of the ignition system components—left side

➡**Use compressed air to remove any foreign material in the spark plug well before removing the spark plugs.**

5. Remove the 6 spark plugs.

To install:

6. Adjust the spark plug gap as necessary. The proper spark plug gap is 0.0051 0.0057 in. (1.29–1.45mm).

7. Install the spark plugs and tighten to 11 ft. lbs. (15 Nm).

8. Apply a little dielectric grease to the inside of the ignition coil-on-plug boots before attaching to the spark plugs.

9. Install the 6 ignition coil-on-plugs and the 6 bolts, then tighten to 62 inch lbs. (7 Nm).

10. Attach the 6 ignition coil-on-plug electrical connectors.

11. If removed, install the upper intake manifold, as outlined in the Engine Mechanical Section.

12. If disconnected, position and connect the crankcase vent tube quick connect coupling to the valve cover

13. Connect the negative battery cable.

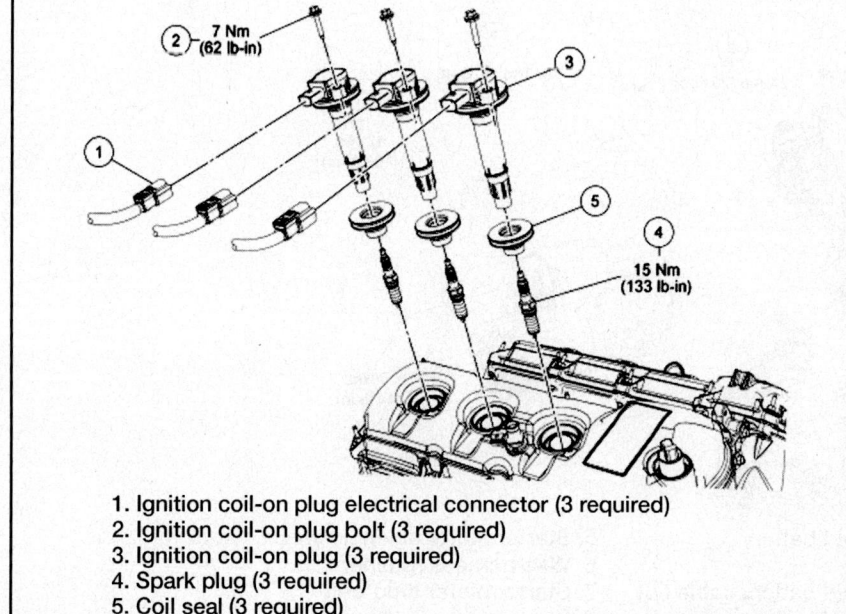

1. Ignition coil-on plug electrical connector (3 required)
2. Ignition coil-on plug bolt (3 required)
3. Ignition coil-on plug (3 required)
4. Spark plug (3 required)
5. Coil seal (3 required)

36578_EDGE_G0096

Fig. 55 Exploded view of the ignition system components—right side

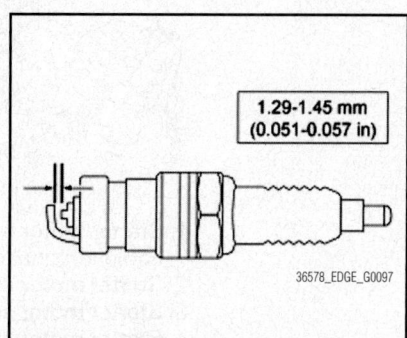

1.29-1.45 mm
(0.051-0.057 in)

36578_EDGE_G0097

Fig. 56 The proper spark plug gap is 0.0051–0.0057 in. (1.29–1.45mm)

ENGINE ELECTRICAL   **STARTING SYSTEM**

STARTER

REMOVAL & INSTALLATION

See Figures 57 and 58.

✳✳ WARNING

Always disconnect the battery ground cable at the battery before disconnecting the starter motor battery terminal lead. If a tool is shorted at the starter motor battery terminal, the tool can quickly heat enough to cause a skin burn. Failure to follow this instruction may result in serious personal injury.

1. Disconnect the negative battery cable.
2. Remove the air cleaner.
3. Disconnect the transmission shift cable and adjustment lock from the transmission manual control lever.
4. Disconnect the transmission shift cable rotating slide snap and position aside the transmission cable.
5. Remove the nut and the transmission manual control lever.
6. Remove the starter motor terminal cover.
7. Remove the starter motor solenoid battery cable nut.
8. Remove the starter motor solenoid wire nut.
9. Disconnect the wiring harness

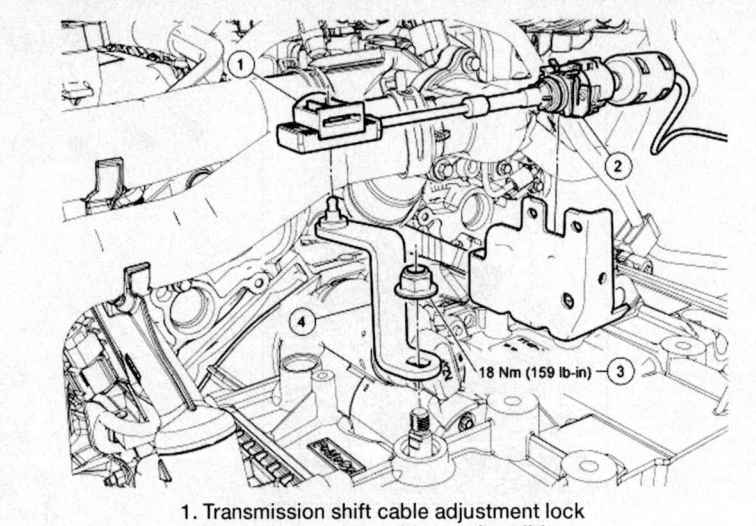

1. Transmission shift cable adjustment lock
2. Transmission shift cable rotating slide snap
3. Transmission manual control lever nut
4. Transmission manual control lever

36578_EDGE_G0101

Fig. 57 Exploded view of the transmission shift cable, control lever and related components

retainer from the starter motor stud bolt and position the wiring harness aside.

10. Unfasten the starter motor stud bolt, then remove the bolt and the starter

To install:

11. Installation is the reverse of the removal procedure, noting the following tightening specifications:

a. Starter mounting bolt(s) and stud bolt: 20 ft. lbs. (27 Nm)

b. Starter motor solenoid wire nut: 44 inch lbs. (5 Nm)

c. Starter motor solenoid battery cable nut: 9 ft. lbs. (12 Nm)

d. Transmission manual control lever nut: 13 ft. lbs. (18 Nm)

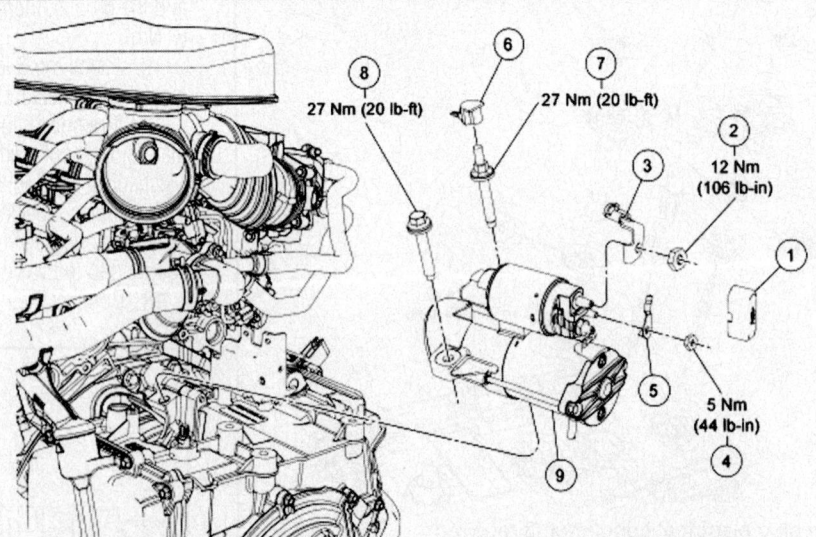

1. Starter motor solenoid battery cable terminal cover
2. Starter motor solenoid battery cable nut
3. Starter motor solenoid battery cable
4. Starter motor solenoid wire nut
5. Starter motor solenoid wire
6. Wire harness retainer
7. Starter motor stud bolt
8. Starter motor bolt
9. Starter motor

36578_EDGE_G0102

Fig. 58 Exploded view of the starter motor and components

ENGINE MECHANICAL

ACCESSORY DRIVE BELTS

ACCESSORY BELT ROUTING

See Figures 59 and 60.

INSPECTION

Inspect the drive belt for signs of glazing or cracking. A glazed belt will be perfectly smooth from slippage, while a good belt will have a slight texture of fabric visible. Cracks will usually start at the inner edge of the belt and run outward. All worn or damaged drive belts should be replaced immediately.

ADJUSTMENT

Belt tension is maintained by an automatic belt tensioner. No adjustments are necessary.

REMOVAL & INSTALLATION

See Figures 59 through 61.

❊❊ WARNING

NEVER lubricate the accessory drive belt, tensioner or pulleys as this will cause potential damage to the belt material and tensioner damping mechanism. Do not apply any fluids or any type of belt dressing to the accessory drive belt or pulleys.

1. Raise and safely support the vehicle.
2. Working from the top of the vehicle, use a suitable belt tensioner release tool to rotate the accessory drive belt tensioner clockwise and remove the accessory drive belt from the alternator pulley.
3. Remove the RH inner fender splash shield..
4. Working from underneath the vehicle, remove the accessory drive belt.

To install:

5. Working from underneath the vehicle, install the accessory drive belt on all pulleys, except the alternator pulley.

❊❊ WARNING

Make sure the belt is properly routed and correctly seated on all pulleys.

6. Working from the top of the vehicle, position the accessory drive belt on the alternator pulley, then use a suitable belt tensioner release tool to rotate the accessory drive belt tensioner clockwise and install the accessory drive belt on the alternator pulley.

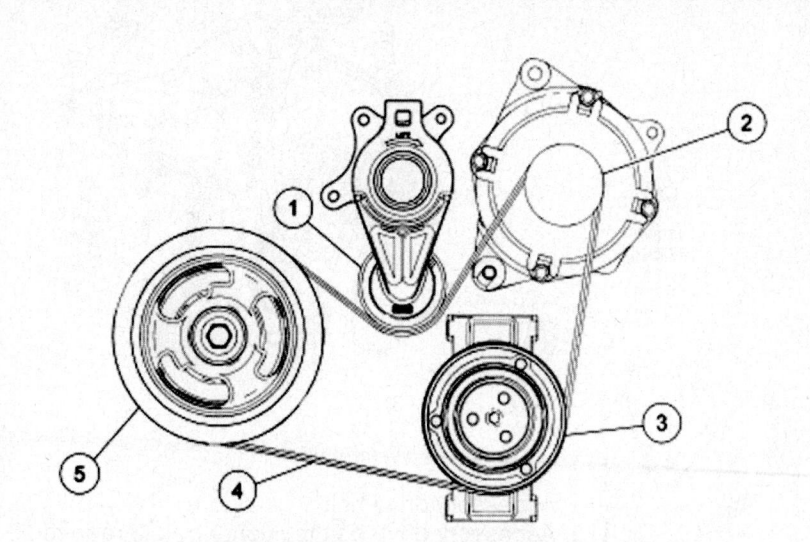

1. Accessory drive belt tensioner pulley
2. Generator pulley
3. A/C clutch pulley
4. Accessory drive belt
5. Crankshaft pulley

36578_EDGE_G0103

Fig. 59 Accessory drive belt routing

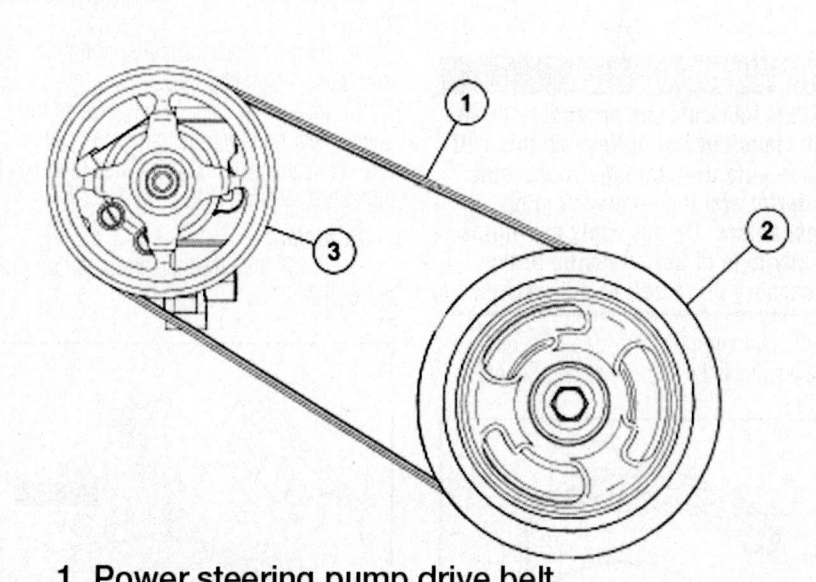

1. Power steering pump drive belt
2. Crankshaft pulley
3. Power steering pump pulley

36578_EDGE_G0104

Fig. 60 Power steering belt routing

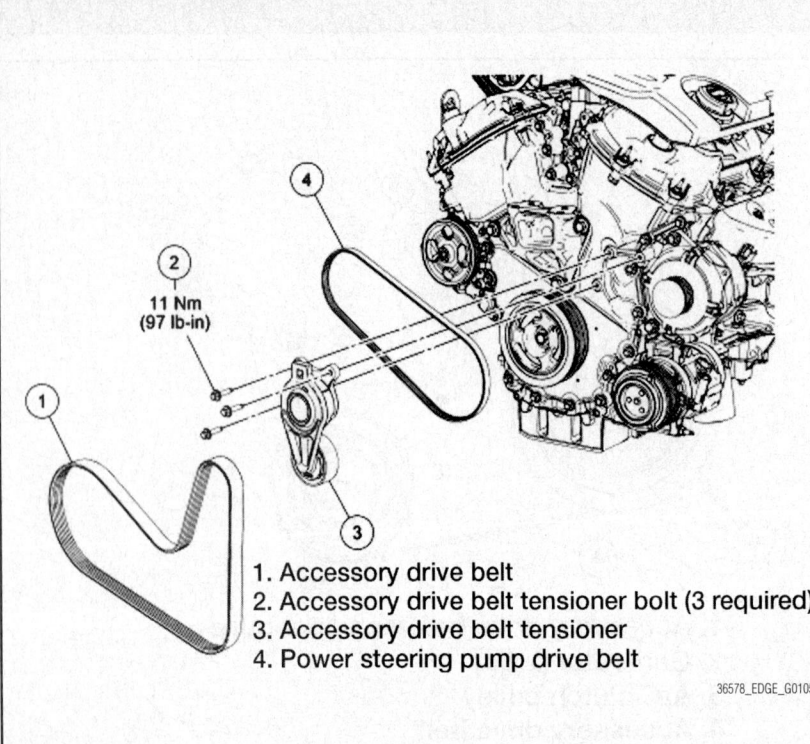

1. Accessory drive belt
2. Accessory drive belt tensioner bolt (3 required)
3. Accessory drive belt tensioner
4. Power steering pump drive belt

36578_EDGE_G0105

Fig. 61 Exploded view of the accessory drive belts

7. Install the RH inner fender splash shield.

8. Carefully lower the vehicle.

Power Steering Pump Belt

See Figures 62 through 64.

✸✸ WARNING

NEVER lubricate the accessory drive belt, tensioner or pulleys as this will cause potential damage to the belt material and tensioner damping mechanism. Do not apply any fluids or any type of belt dressing to the accessory drive belt or pulleys.

1. Working from the top of the vehicle, use a suitable belt tensioner release tool to

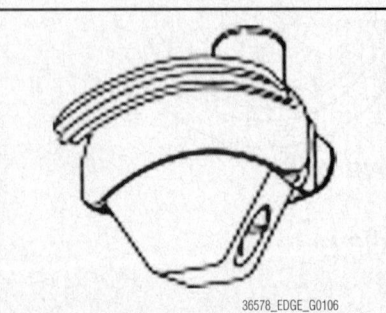

36578_EDGE_G0106

Fig. 62 You need these special tools, or their equivalents, to remove the power steering pump belt

rotate the accessory drive belt tensioner clockwise and remove the accessory drive belt from the alternator pulley.

2. Raise and safely support the vehicle.

3. Remove the RH inner fender splash shield..

4. Remove the accessory drive belt from the crankshaft pulley.

5. Install the special tool between the power steering pump belt and pulley, then turn the crankshaft bolt clockwise to remove the power steering belt.

To install:

6. Install the power steering belt on the crankshaft pulley.

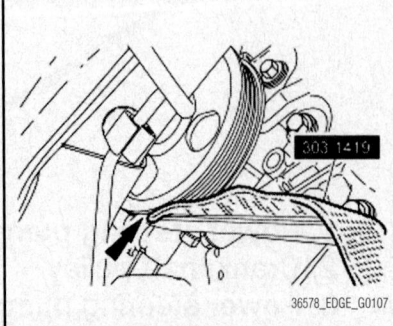

36578_EDGE_G0107

Fig. 63 Install the special tool between the power steering pump belt and pulley, then turn the crankshaft bolt clockwise to remove the power steering belt

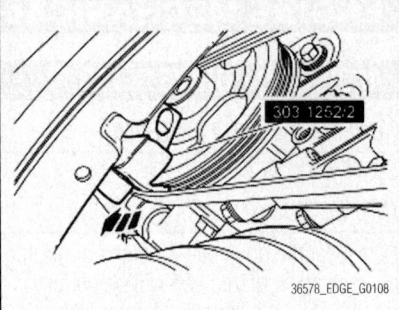

36578_EDGE_G0108

Fig. 64 Position the power steering belt around the special tool and the power steering pulley. Make sure that the belt is engaged with the power steering pulley and rotate the crankshaft clockwise to install the power steering belt

✸✸ WARNING

Make sure the belt is correctly seated on the crankshaft and power steering pulleys.

7. Position the power steering belt around the special tool and the power steering pulley. Make sure that the belt is engaged with the power steering pulley and rotate the crankshaft clockwise to install the power steering belt.

8. Install the accessory drive belt on the crankshaft pulley.

✸✸ WARNING

Make sure the belt is properly routed and correctly seated on all pulleys.

9. Working from the top of the vehicle, place the accessory drive belt on the alternator pulley. Using a suitable belt tensioner release tool, rotate the accessory drive belt tensioner clockwise and install the accessory drive belt on the generator pulley.

10. Install the RH inner fender splash shield.

CAMSHAFT AND VALVE LIFTERS

REMOVAL & INSTALLATION

See Figures 65 through 92.

✸✸ WARNING

Do not smoke, carry lighted tobacco or have an open flame of any type when working on or near any fuel-related component. Highly flammable mixtures are always present and may be ignited. Failure to follow these instructions may result in serious personal injury.

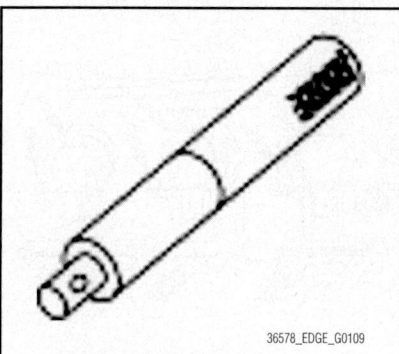

Fig. 65 Special tools needed for this procedure

➡**During engine repair procedures, cleanliness is extremely important. Any foreign material, including any material created while cleaning gasket surfaces that enters the oil passages, coolant passages or the oil pan, can cause engine failure.**

1. With the vehicle in NEUTRAL, position it on a hoist.
2. Recover the A/C system.
3. Release the fuel system pressure.
4. Drain the engine cooling system.
5. Remove the accessory drive belt and the power steering belt.
6. Remove the LH halfshaft and intermediate shaft.
7. Disconnect the power steering cooler hose and drain the power steering fluid into a suitable drain pan.
8. Remove the degas bottle.
9. Remove the engine Air Cleaner (ACL) and ACL outlet pipe.
10. Remove the battery tray.
11. Disconnect the battery harness electrical connector.
12. Remove the nut and disconnect the power feed from the battery terminal.
13. Remove the bolt and the ground wire. Detach the 2 wiring harness retainers from the cowl.

14. Disconnect the vacuum hose from the upper intake manifold.
15. Disconnect the Evaporative Emission (EVAP) tube quick connect coupling from the purge valve.
16. Disconnect the upper radiator hose, lower radiator hose and 2 heater hoses from the thermostat housing.
17. Detach the wiring harness retainer from the transaxle control cable bracket.
18. Disconnect the transaxle control cable from the control lever. Detach the control cable from the bracket.
19. Disconnect the transaxle control electrical connector.
20. If equipped, detach the engine block heater harness retainers from the radiator support and the A/C suction tube.
21. Remove the nut and disconnect the A/C pressure tube fitting. Discard the O-ring seal.
22. Remove the safety clip from the A/C fitting. Disconnect the A/C suction tube fitting.
23. Disconnect the hose from the power steering reservoir.
24. Disconnect the fuel supply tube.
25. Disconnect the fuel hose routing clip from the transaxle stud and position the fuel hose aside.
26. Disconnect the 2 engine wiring harness electrical connectors. Detach the electrical connector from the LH valve cover.
27. Remove the oil level indicator.
28. Detach the wiring harness retainer from the RH valve cover stud bolt.
29. Remove the bolt and the ground wire from the engine front cover.
30. Remove the nut, the ground wire and the radio interference capacitor wire from the engine front cover stud.
31. Loosen the exhaust flexible pipe clamp and disconnect the 2 exhaust hangers.
32. Remove the 4 nuts and the exhaust flexible pipe and Y-pipe as an assembly. Discard the nuts and the gasket.

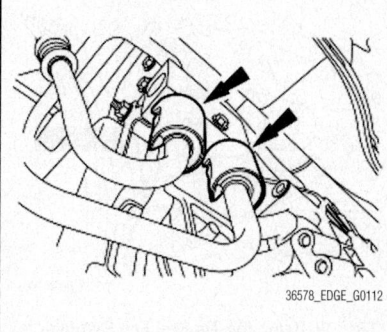

Fig. 68 Removing the 2 secondary latches from the transmission fluid cooler tubes

33. Remove the 3 pin-type retainers, the 7 screws and the radiator splash shield.
34. Remove the LH inner splash shield.
35. Remove the 2 secondary latches from the transmission fluid cooler tubes.
36. Using the Transmission Cooler Line Disconnect Tool, disconnect the transmission cooling tubes.
37. Remove the drain plug and drain the engine oil. Install the drain plug and tighten to 20 ft. lbs. (27 Nm).
38. Remove and discard the engine oil filter.
39. Remove the power steering cooler bracket bolt from the RH side of the subframe.

➡**Index-mark the driveshaft for installation.**

40. AWD vehicles, remove the 4 bolts and support the driveshaft with a length of mechanic's wire.

➡**Use a steering wheel holding device (such as Hunter 28-75-1 or equivalent).**

41. Using a suitable holding device, hold the steering wheel in the straight-ahead position.
42. Remove the 2 nuts and the roll restrictor heat shield.

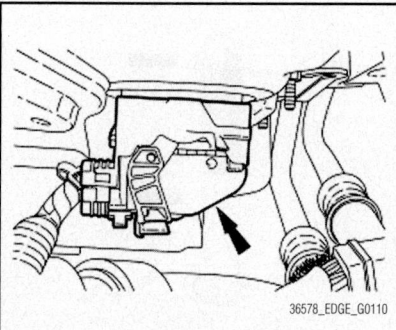

Fig. 66 Disconnecting the transaxle control electrical connector

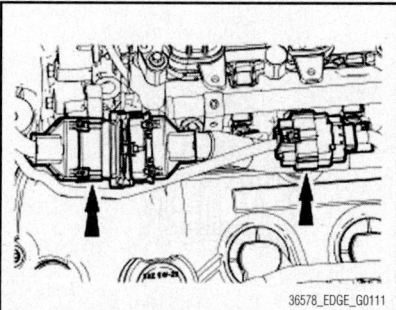

Fig. 67 Disconnecting the 2 engine wiring harness electrical connectors from the LH valve cover

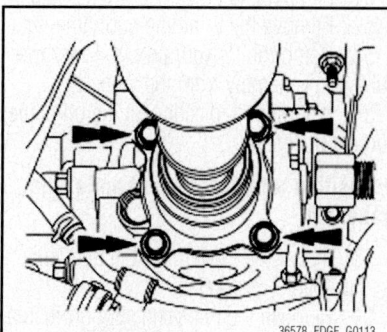

Fig. 69 Removing the 4 bolts and supporting the driveshaft

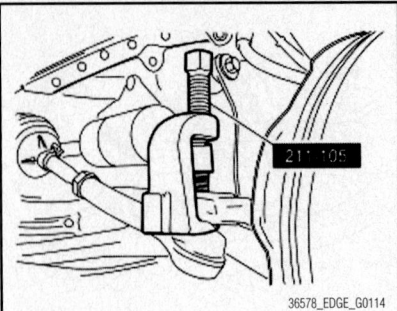

Fig. 70 Using the Tie Rod End Remover to separate the tie rod ends from the wheel knuckles

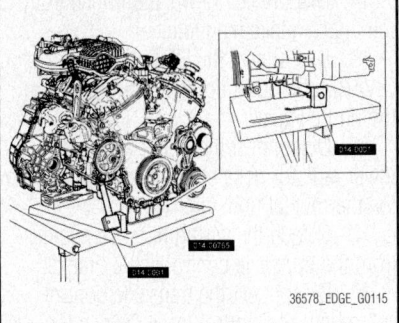

Fig. 71 Installing the Powertrain Lift and Universal Adapter Brackets

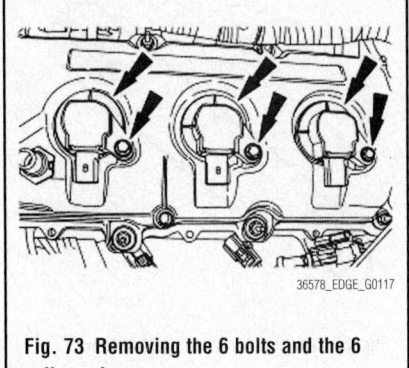

Fig. 73 Removing the 6 bolts and the 6 coil-on plugs

43. Remove the engine roll restrictor-to-subframe through bolt.

44. Remove and discard the Power Steering Pressure (PSP) tube-to-pump banjo bolt and the 2 seals.

➡ **Do not allow the intermediate shaft to rotate while it is disconnected from the gear or damage to the clockspring can occur. If there is evidence that the intermediate shaft has rotated, the clockspring must be removed and recentered.**

45. Remove and discard the steering intermediate shaft bolt. Separate the steering intermediate shaft from the steering gear.

➡ **RH shown, LH similar.**

46. Remove and discard the cotter pins and tie-rod end nuts. Using the Tie-Rod End Remover, separate the tie-rod ends from the wheel knuckles.

47. Remove the 3 RH subframe-to-lower bumper nuts.

48. Remove the 3 LH subframe-to-lower bumper nuts and separate the lower bumper from the subframe.

49. Position the Powertrain Lift under the subframe assembly.

50. Remove the 2 nuts, 4 bolts and the subframe support brackets.

51. Remove the 2 front subframe nuts.

52. Remove the 2 middle subframe nuts.

53. Using the Powertrain Lift, lower the subframe assembly from the vehicle.

54. If equipped, disconnect the oil cooler coolant hoses.

➡ **Position a block of wood under the transaxle.**

55. Install the Powertrain Lift and Universal Adapter Brackets.

56. Remove the transaxle support insulator through bolt and nut.

57. Remove the 3 nuts, the bolt and the transaxle support insulator bracket.

58. Remove the nut, bolt and engine mount brace.

59. Remove the 4 engine mount nuts.

60. Remove the 3 bolts and the engine mount.

61. Lower the engine and transaxle assembly from the vehicle.

62. If equipped, detach the engine block heater wiring harness retainers and position the harness aside.

63. Disconnect the PCV hose from the PCV valve.

64. Disconnect the Throttle Body (TB) electrical connector.

65. Detach the wiring harness retainers from the upper intake manifold.

66. Remove the upper intake manifold support bracket bolt.

67. Remove the 6 bolts and the upper intake manifold in the following sequence. Discard the gaskets.

68. Disconnect the RH Catalyst Monitor Sensor (CMS) electrical connector.

69. Disconnect the PSP switch electrical connector.

70. Disconnect the RH Variable Camshaft Timing (VCT) solenoid electrical connector.

71. Disconnect the 3 RH coil-on-plug electrical connectors.

72. Detach all of the wiring harness retainers from the RH valve cover and stud bolts.

73. Disconnect the LH VCT solenoid electrical connector.

74. Disconnect the 3 LH coil-on-plug electrical connectors.

75. Detach all of the wiring harness retainers from the LH valve cover and stud bolts.

➡ **LH shown, RH similar.**

76. Remove the 6 bolts and the 6 coil-on-plugs.

77. Loosen the 11 stud bolts and remove the LH valve cover. Discard the gasket.

78. Loosen the bolt, the 10 stud bolts and remove the RH valve cover. Discard the gasket.

➡ **VCT solenoid seal removal shown, spark plug tube seal removal similar.**

79. Inspect the VCT solenoid seals and the spark plug tube seals. Install new seals if damaged. Using the VCT Spark Plug Tube Seal Remover and Handle, remove the seals.

80. Remove the 3 bolts and the power steering pump.

81. Remove the 3 bolts and the accessory drive belt tensioner.

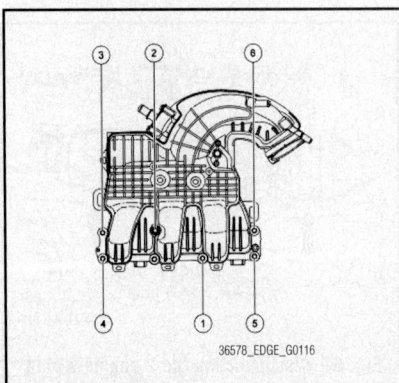

Fig. 72 Identifying the 6 bolts and upper intake manifold removal sequence

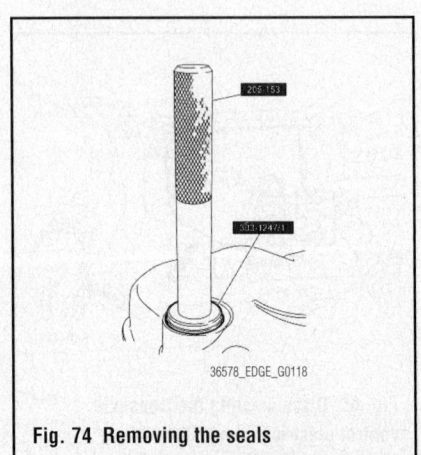

Fig. 74 Removing the seals

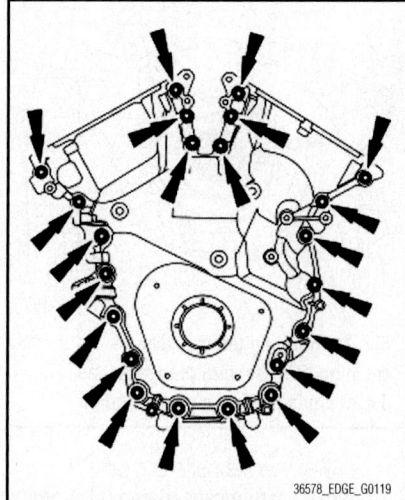

Fig. 75 Removing the 22 engine front cover bolts

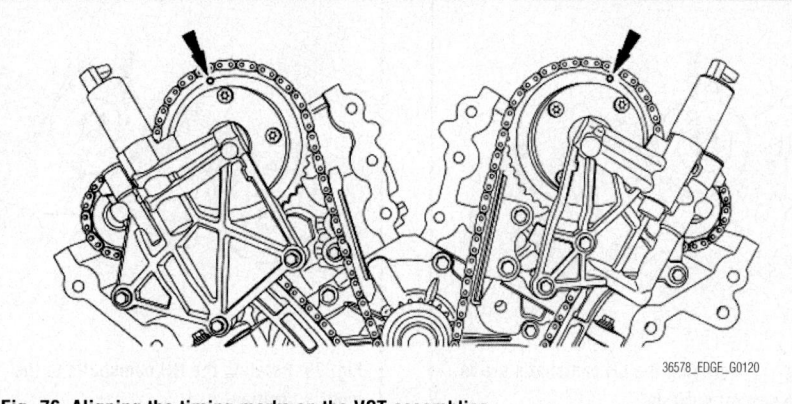

Fig. 76 Aligning the timing marks on the VCT assemblies

82. Using the Strap Wrench, remove the crankshaft bolt and washer. Discard the bolt.

83. Using the 3-Jaw Puller, remove the crankshaft pulley.

84. Using the Oil Seal Remover, remove and discard the crankshaft front seal.

85. Remove the 2 bolts and the engine mount bracket.

➡ **Only use hand tools to remove the studs.**

86. Remove the 2 engine mount studs.

87. Remove the 3 bolts and the engine mount bracket.

88. Remove the 22 engine front cover bolts.

89. Install 6 of the engine front cover bolts (finger tight) into the 6 threaded holes in the engine front cover. Tighten the bolts one turn at a time in a criss-cross pattern until the engine front cover-to-cylinder block seal is released. Remove the engine front cover.

➡ **Only use a 3M Roloc® Bristle Disk (2-in white, part number 07528) to clean the engine front cover. Do not use metal scrapers, wire brushes or any other power abrasive disk to clean the engine front cover. These tools cause scratches and gouges that make leak paths.**

90. Clean the engine front cover using a 3M Roloc® Bristle Disk (2-in white, part number 07528) in a suitable tool turning at the recommended speed of 15,000 rpm. Thoroughly wash the engine front cover to remove any foreign material, including any abrasive particles created during the cleaning process.

➡ **Place clean, lint-free shop towels over exposed engine cavities. Carefully remove the towels so foreign material is not dropped into the engine. Any foreign material (including any material created while cleaning gasket surfaces) that enters the oil passages or the oil pan, may cause engine failure.**

➡ **Do not use wire brushes, power abrasive discs or 3M Roloc® Bristle Disk (2-in white part number 07528) to clean the sealing surfaces. These tools cause scratches and gouges that make leak paths. They also cause contamination that will cause premature engine failure. Remove all traces of the gasket.**

91. Clean the sealing surfaces of the cylinder block in the following sequence.

a. Remove any large deposits of silicone or gasket material.

b. Apply silicone gasket remover and allow to set for several minutes.

c. Remove the silicone gasket remover. A second application of silicone gasket remover may be required if residual traces of silicone or gasket material remain.

d. Apply metal surface prep to remove any remaining traces of oil or coolant and to prepare the surfaces to bond. Do not attempt to make the metal shiny. Some staining of the metal surfaces is normal.

e. Make sure the 2 locating dowel pins are seated correctly in the cylinder block.

92. Rotate the crankshaft clockwise and align the timing marks on the Variable Camshaft Timing (VCT) assemblies as shown.

➡ **The Camshaft Holding Tool will hold the camshafts in the Top Dead Center (TDC) position.**

93. Install the Camshaft Holding Tool onto the flats of the LH camshafts.

➡ **The Camshaft Holding Tool will hold the camshafts in the TDC position.**

94. Install the Camshaft Holding Tool onto the flats of the RH camshafts.

95. Remove the 3 bolts and the RH VCT housing.

96. Remove the 3 bolts and the LH VCT housing.

97. Remove and discard the VCT housing seals.

98. Remove the 2 bolts and the primary timing chain tensioner.

99. Remove the primary timing chain tensioner arm.

100. Remove the 2 bolts and the lower LH primary timing chain guide.

101. Remove the primary timing chain.

102. LH camshafts perform the following:

a. Compress the LH secondary timing chain tensioner and install a suitable lockpin to retain the tensioner in the collapsed position.

➡ **The VCT bolt and the exhaust camshaft bolt must be discarded and new ones installed. However, the exhaust camshaft washer is reusable.**

b. Remove and discard the LH VCT assembly bolt and the LH exhaust camshaft sprocket bolt. Remove the LH VCT assembly, secondary timing chain and the LH exhaust camshaft sprocket as an assembly.

➡ **When the Camshaft Holding Tool is removed, valve spring pressure will rotate the LH camshafts approximately 3 degrees to a neutral position.**

c. Remove the Camshaft Holding Tool from the LH camshafts.

36578_EDGE_G0121

Fig. 77 Verifying the LH camshafts are in the neutral position

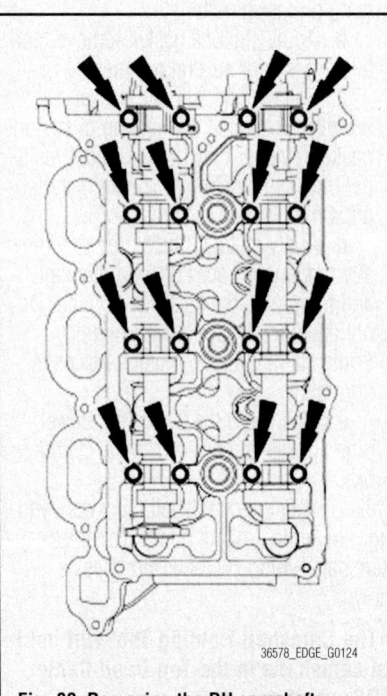

36578_EDGE_G0123

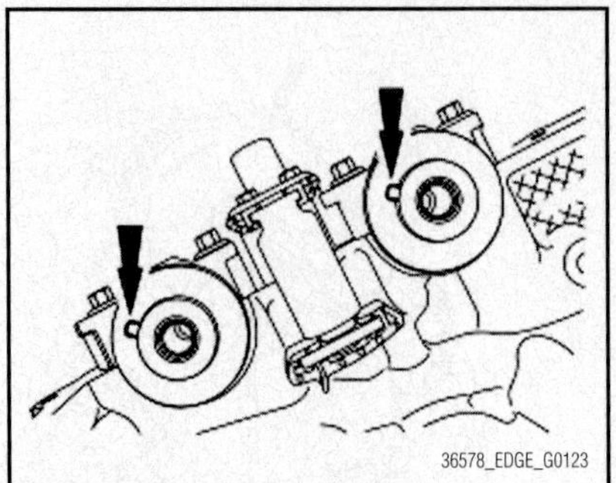

Fig. 79 Rotating the RH camshafts to the neutral position

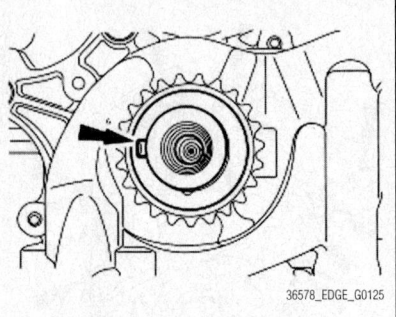

36578_EDGE_G0125

Fig. 81 Rotating the crankshaft counterclockwise until the crankshaft dowel pin is in the 9 o'clock position

➡The camshafts must remain in the neutral position during removal or engine damage may occur.

   d. Verify the LH camshafts are in the neutral position.

➡Cylinder head camshaft bearing caps are numbered to verify that they are assembled in their original positions.

   e. Remove the bolts and the LH camshaft bearing caps. Remove the LH camshafts.
103.RH camshafts perform the following:
   a. Compress the RH secondary timing chain tensioner and install a suitable lockpin to retain the tensioner in the collapsed position.

➡The VCT bolt and the exhaust camshaft bolt must be discarded and

new ones installed. However, the exhaust camshaft washer is reusable.

   b. Remove and discard the RH VCT assembly bolt and the RH exhaust camshaft sprocket bolt. Remove the RH VCT assembly, secondary timing chain and the RH exhaust camshaft sprocket as an assembly.
   c. Remove the Camshaft Holding Tool from the RH camshafts.

➡The camshafts must remain in the neutral position during removal or engine damage may occur.

   d. Rotate the RH camshafts counterclockwise to the neutral position.

➡Cylinder head camshaft bearing caps are numbered to verify that they are assembled in their original positions.

   e. Remove the bolts and the RH camshaft bearing caps. Remove the RH camshafts.

To install:

➡The crankshaft must remain in the freewheeling position (crankshaft dowel pin at 9 o'clock) until after the camshafts are installed and the valve clearance is checked/adjusted. Do not turn the crankshaft until instructed to do so. Failure to follow this process will result in severe engine damage.

   104. Rotate the crankshaft counterclockwise until the crankshaft dowel pin is in the 9 o'clock position.
   105. LH camshafts perform the following:

➡The camshafts must remain in the neutral position during installation or engine damage may occur.

➡Coat the camshafts with clean engine oil prior to installation.

   a. Position the camshafts onto the LH cylinder head in the neutral position.

➡Cylinder head camshaft bearing caps are numbered to verify that they are assembled in their original positions. If not reassembled in their original positions, severe engine damage may occur.

   b. Install the 8 camshaft caps and the 16 bolts. Tighten in the sequence shown to 89 inch lbs. (10 Nm).
   106. RH camshafts perform the following:
   107. RH camshafts perform the following:

➡The camshafts must remain in the neutral position during installation or engine damage may occur.

➡Coat the camshafts with clean engine oil prior to installation.

   a. Position the camshafts onto the RH cylinder head in the neutral position.

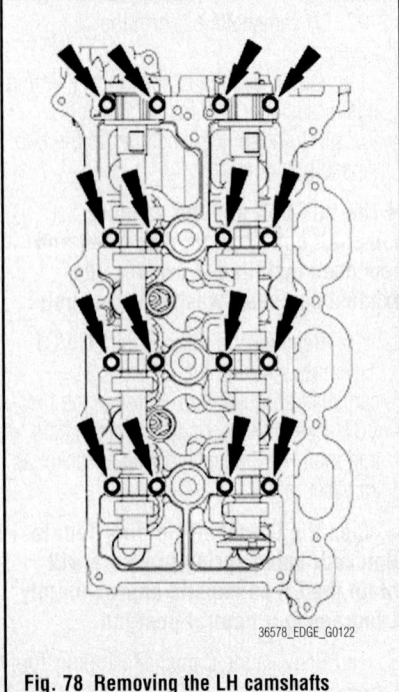

36578_EDGE_G0122

Fig. 78 Removing the LH camshafts

36578_EDGE_G0124

Fig. 80 Removing the RH camshafts

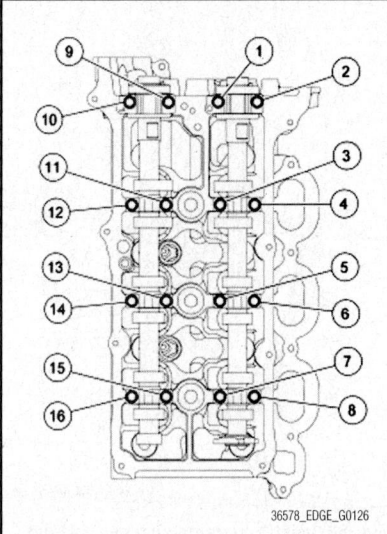

Fig. 82 **Installing the LH camshaft caps and bolts**

➡**Cylinder head camshaft bearing caps are numbered to verify that they are assembled in their original positions. If not reassembled in their original positions, severe engine damage may occur.**

   b. Install the 8 camshaft caps and the 16 bolts. Tighten in the sequence shown to 89 inch lbs. (10 Nm).

➡**If any components are installed new, the engine valve clearance must be checked/adjusted or engine damage may occur.**

➡**Use a camshaft sprocket bolt to turn the camshafts.**

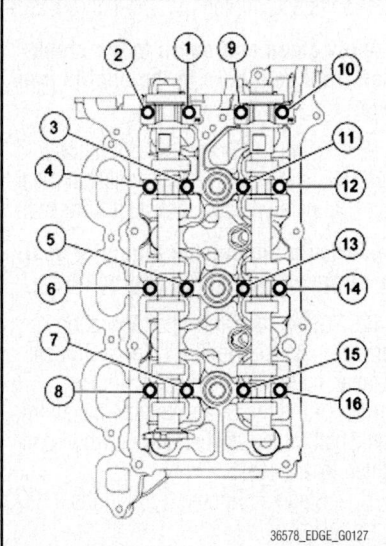

Fig. 83 **Installing the RH camshaft caps and bolts**

108. Using a feeler gauge, confirm that the valve tappet clearances are within specification. If valve tappet clearances are not within specification, the clearance must be adjusted by installing new valve tappet(s) of the correct size.

109. LH camshafts perform the following:

➡**Use a camshaft sprocket bolt to turn the camshafts.**

   a. Rotate the LH camshafts to the Top Dead Center (TDC) position and install the Camshaft Holding Tool on the flats of the camshafts.

   b. Assemble the LH Variable Camshaft Timing (VCT) assembly, the LH exhaust camshaft sprocket and the LH secondary timing chain. Align the colored links with the timing marks.

   c. Position the LH secondary timing assembly onto the camshafts.

   d. Install 2 new bolts and the original washer. Tighten in 4 stages.
- Stage 1: Tighten to 30 ft. lbs. (40 Nm)
- Stage 2: Loosen one full turn
- Stage 3: Tighten to 89 inch lbs. (10 Nm)
- Stage 4: Tighten 90°

   e. Remove the lockpin from the LH secondary timing chain tensioner.

110. RH camshafts perform the following:

➡**Use a camshaft sprocket bolt to turn the camshafts.**

   a. Rotate the RH camshafts to the TDC position and install the Camshaft Holding Tool on the flats of the camshafts.

   b. Assemble the RH VCT assembly, the RH exhaust camshaft sprocket and the RH secondary timing chain. Align the colored links with the timing marks.

   c. Position the RH secondary timing assembly onto the camshafts.

   d. Install 2 new bolts and the original washer. Tighten in 4 stages.
- Stage 1: Tighten to 30 ft. lbs. (40 Nm)
- Stage 2: Loosen one full turn
- Stage 3: Tighten to 89 inch lbs. (10 Nm)
- Stage 4: Tighten 90°

   e. Remove the lockpin from the RH secondary timing chain tensioner.

111. Rotate the crankshaft clockwise 60 degrees to the TDC position (crankshaft dowel pin at 11 o'clock).

112. Install the primary timing chain with the colored links aligned with the timing

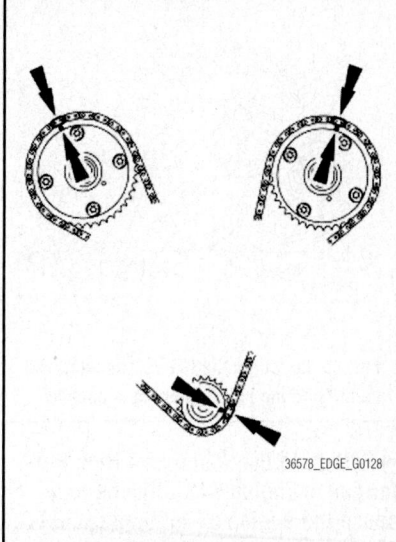

Fig. 84 **Installing the primary timing chain with the colored links aligned with the timing marks on the VCT assemblies and the crankshaft sprocket**

marks on the VCT assemblies and the crankshaft sprocket.

113. Install the lower LH primary timing chain guide and the 2 bolts and tighten to 89 inch lbs. (10 Nm).

114. Install the primary timing chain tensioner arm.

115. Reset the primary timing chain tensioner.

   a. Rotate the lever counterclockwise.

   b. Using a soft-jawed vise, compress the plunger.

   c. Align the hole in the lever with the hole in the tensioner housing.

   d. Install a suitable lockpin.

➡**It may be necessary to rotate the crankshaft slightly to remove slack from the timing chain and install the tensioner.**

116. Install the primary tensioner and the 2 bolts. Tighten to 89 inch lbs. (10 Nm). Remove the lockpin.

117. As a post-check, verify correct alignment of all timing marks.

118. Install new VCT housing seals.

➡**Make sure the dowels on the Variable Camshaft Timing (VCT) housing are fully engaged in the cylinder head prior to tightening the bolts. Failure to follow this process will result in severe engine damage.**

119. Install the RH VCT housing and the 3 bolts. Tighten the bolts in sequence shown to 89 inch lbs. (10 Nm).

120. Install the Alignment Pins.

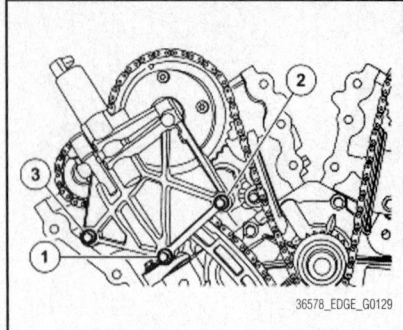

Fig. 85 Installing the RH VCT housing and identifying the bolt tightening sequence

➡ **Failure to use Motorcraft High Performance Engine RTV Silicone may cause the engine oil to foam excessively and result in serious engine damage.**

➡ **The engine front cover and bolts 17, 18, 19 and 20 must be installed within 4 minutes of the initial sealant application. The remainder of the engine front cover bolts and the engine mount bracket bolts must be installed and tightened within 35 minutes of the initial sealant application. If the time limits are exceeded, the sealant must be removed, the sealing area cleaned and sealant reapplied. To clean the sealing area, use silicone gasket remover and metal surface prep. Follow the directions on the packaging. Failure to follow this procedure can cause future oil leakage.**

121. Apply a 3.0 mm (0.11 in) bead of Motorcraft High Performance Engine RTV Silicone to the engine front cover sealing surfaces including the 3 engine mount bracket bosses. Apply a 5.5 mm (0.21 in) bead of Motorcraft High Performance Engine RTV Silicone to the oil pan-to-cylinder block joint and the cylinder head-to-cylinder block joint areas of the engine front cover in 5 places as indicated.

➡ **Make sure the 2 locating dowel pins are seated correctly in the cylinder block.**

122. Install the engine front cover and bolts 17, 18, 19 and 20. Tighten in sequence to 27 inch lbs. (3 Nm).

123. Remove the Alignment Pins.

➡ **DO NOT tighten the bolts at this time.**

124. Install the engine mount bracket and the 3 bolts.

➡ **Do not expose the Motorcraft High Performance Engine RTV Silicone to**

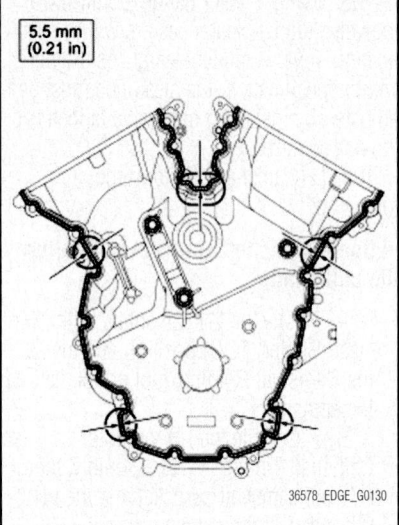

Fig. 86 Applying sealant to the engine front cover

engine oil for at least 90 minutes after installing the engine front cover. Failure to follow this instruction may cause oil leakage.

125. Install the remaining engine front cover bolts. Tighten all of the engine front cover bolts and engine mount bracket bolts in the sequence shown in 2 stages:
- Stage 1: Tighten bolts 1 thru 22 to 89 inch lbs. (10 Nm) and 23, 24 and 25 to 133 inch lbs. (15 Nm)
- Stage 2: Tighten bolts 1 thru 22 to 18 ft. lbs. (24 Nm) and 23, 24 and 25 to 55 ft. lbs. (75 Nm)

➡ **The thread sealer on the engine mount studs (including new engine mount studs if applicable) must be cleaned off with a wire brush and new**

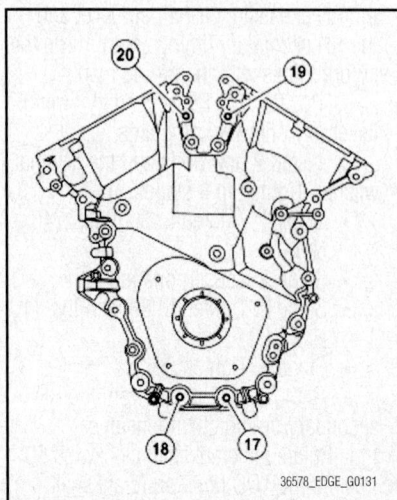

Fig. 87 Installing the engine front cover and bolts

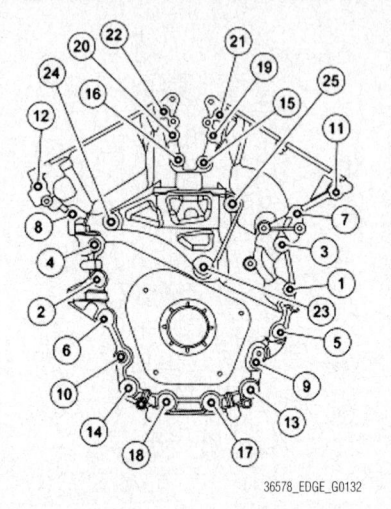

Fig. 88 Identifying remaining engine front cover bolt tightening sequence and torque specifications

thread sealer applied prior to installing the engine mount studs. Failure to follow this procedure may result in damage to the engine mount studs or engine.

126. Install the engine mount studs in the following sequence:
  a. Clean the front cover engine mount stud holes with pressurized air to remove any foreign material.
  b. Clean all the thread sealer from the engine mount studs (old and new studs).
  c. Apply new thread sealer to the engine mount stud threads.
  d. Install the 2 engine mount studs and tighten to 15 ft. lbs. (20 Nm).

127. Install the engine mount bracket and the 2 bolts and tighten to 22 ft. lbs (30 Nm).

➡ **Apply clean engine oil to the crankshaft front seal bore in the engine front cover.**

128. Using the Crankshaft Vibration Damper Installer and Front Crankshaft Seal Installer, install a new crankshaft front seal.

➡ **Lubricate the outside diameter sealing surfaces with clean engine oil.**

129. Using the Crankshaft Vibration Damper Installer and Front Cover Oil Seal Installer, install the crankshaft pulley.

130. Using the Strap Wrench, install the crankshaft pulley washer and new bolt and tighten in 4 stages.
- Stage 1: Tighten to 89 ft. lbs. (120 Nm)
- Stage 2: Loosen one full turn
- Stage 3: Tighten to 37 ft. lbs. (50 Nm)

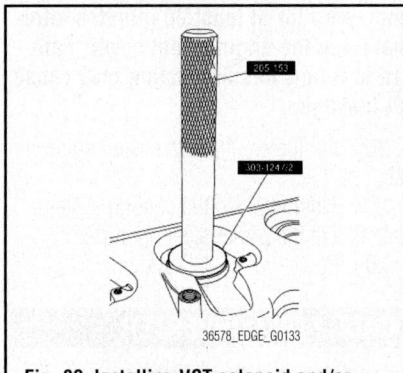

Fig. 89 Installing VCT solenoid and/or spark plug tube seals

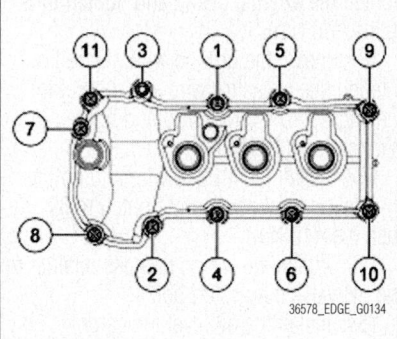

Fig. 90 Identifying the RH valve cover bolt and stud tightening sequence

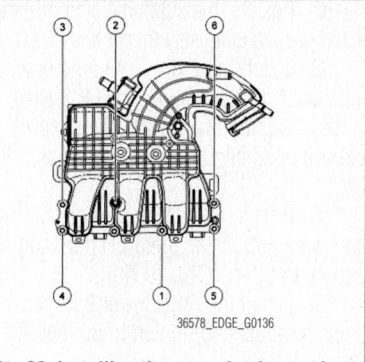

Fig. 92 Installing the upper intake manifold

• Stage 4 Tighten an additional 90°

131. Install the accessory drive belt tensioner and the 3 bolts and tighten to 97 inch lbs. (11 Nm).

132. Install the power steering pump and the 3 bolts. Tighten to 18 ft. lbs. (24 Nm).

➡Installation of new seals is only required if damaged seals were removed during disassembly of the engine.

➡Spark plug tube seal installation is shown, VCT seal installation is similar.

133. Using the VCT Spark Plug Tube Seal Installer and Handle, install a new VCT solenoid and/or plug tube seals.

➡Failure to use Motorcraft High Performance Engine RTV Silicone may cause the engine oil to foam excessively and result in serious engine damage.

➡If the valve cover is not installed and the fasteners tightened within 4 minutes, the sealant must be removed and the sealing area cleaned. To clean the sealing area, use silicone gasket remover and metal surface prep. Follow the directions on the packaging. Failure to follow this procedure can cause future oil leakage.

134. Apply a 0.31 inch (8 mm) bead of Motorcraft High Performance Engine RTV Silicone to the engine front cover-to-RH cylinder head joints.

135. Using a new gasket, install the RH valve cover, bolt and the 10 stud bolts. Tighten in the sequence shown to 89 inch lbs. (10 Nm).

➡Failure to use Motorcraft High Performance Engine RTV Silicone may cause the engine oil to foam excessively and result in serious engine damage.

➡If the valve cover is not installed and the fasteners tightened within 4 minutes, the sealant must be removed and the sealing area cleaned. To clean the sealing area, use silicone gasket remover and metal surface prep. Follow the directions on the packaging. Failure to follow this procedure can cause future oil leakage.

136. Apply a 8 mm (0.31 in) bead of Motorcraft High Performance Engine RTV Silicone to the engine front cover-to-LH cylinder head joints.

137. Using a new gasket, install the LH valve cover and 11 stud bolts. Tighten in the sequence shown to 89 inch lbs. (10 Nm).

138. Install the 6 coil-on-plug assemblies and the 6 bolts. Tighten to 62 inch lbs. (7 Nm).

Attach all of the wiring harness retainers to the LH valve cover and stud bolts.

139. Connect the 3 LH coil-on-plug electrical connectors.

140. Connect the LH camshaft VCT solenoid electrical connector.

141. Attach all of the wiring harness retainers to the RH valve cover and stud bolts.

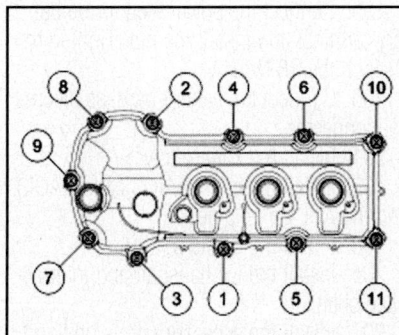

Fig. 91 Identifying the LH valve cover bolt tightening sequence

142. Connect the 3 RH coil-on-plug electrical connectors.

143. Connect the RH VCT solenoid electrical connector.

144. Connect the Power Steering Pressure (PSP) switch electrical connector.

145. Connect the RH Catalyst Monitor Sensor (CMS) sensor electrical connector.

146. Using new gaskets, install the upper intake manifold and the 6 bolts. Tighten in the sequence shown to 89 inch lbs. (10 Nm).

147. Install the upper intake manifold support bracket bolt and tighten to 89 inch lbs. (10 Nm).

148. Attach the wiring harness retainers to the upper intake manifold.

149. Connect the Throttle Body (TB) electrical connector.

150. Connect the PCV hose to the PCV valve.

151. If equipped, attach the engine block heater wiring harness retainers.

152. Raise the engine and transaxle assembly into the vehicle.

153. Install the engine mount and the 3 bolts. Tighten to 66 ft. lbs. (90 Nm).

154. Install the 4 engine mount nuts and tighten to 46 ft. lbs. (63 Nm).

155. Install the engine mount brace, the nut and the bolt and tighten to 15 ft. lbs. (20 Nm).

156. Install the transaxle support insulator bracket, the 3 nuts and the bolt. Tighten the 3 nuts to 46 ft. lbs. (63 Nm). Tighten the bolt to 59 ft. lbs. (80 Nm).

157. Install the transaxle support insulator through bolt and nut and tighten to 129 ft. lbs. (175 Nm).

158. If equipped, connect the oil cooler coolant hoses.

159. Using the Powertrain Lift, raise the subframe into the installed position.

160. Install the 2 middle subframe nuts and tighten to 98 ft. lbs. (133 Nm).

161. Install the 2 front subframe nuts and tighten to 98 ft. lbs. (133 Nm).

162. Position the subframe support brackets in place and loosely install the 4 bolts.

163. Install the 2 rear subframe bracket nuts and tighten to 98 ft. lbs. (133 Nm).

164. Tighten the 4 subframe support bracket bolts and tighten to 66 ft. lbs. (90 Nm).

165. Position the lower bumper on the subframe and install the 3 LH nuts and tighten to 80 inch lbs. (9 Nm).

166. Install the 3 RH lower bumper-to-subframe nuts and tighten to 80 inch lbs. (9 Nm).

167. Install the tie-rod ends and nuts. Tighten to 48 Nm (35 lb-ft). Install new cotter pins.

➡ **Do not allow the intermediate shaft to rotate while it is disconnected from the gear or damage to the clockspring can occur. If there is evidence that the intermediate shaft has rotated, the clockspring must be removed and recentered.**

168. Install the intermediate shaft onto the steering gear and install a new bolt and tighten to 35 ft. lbs. (48 Nm).

169. Install the engine roll restrictor-to-subframe through bolt and tighten to 76 ft. lbs. (103 Nm).

170. Install the roll restrictor heat shield and the 2 nuts and tighten to 80 inch lbs. (9 Nm).

171. AWD vehicles, line up the index marks on the rear driveshaft to the index marks on the PTU flange made during removal and install the 4 bolts. Tighten the bolts to 52 ft. lbs. (70 Nm).

172. Install the power steering cooler bracket bolt to the RH side of the subframe. Tighten to 80 inch lbs. (9 Nm).

173. Connect the power steering cooler hose.

➡ **Lubricate the engine oil filter gasket with clean engine oil prior to installing the oil filter.**

174. Install a new engine oil filter. Tighten to 44 inch lbs. (5 Nm) and then rotate and additional 180°.

175. Connect the 2 transmission fluid cooler tubes.

176. Install the 2 secondary latches onto the transmission fluid cooler tubes.

177. Install the LH inner splash shield.

178. Install the radiator splash shield, the 3 pin-type retainers and the 7 screws.

179. Using a new gasket, install the Y-pipe and exhaust flexible pipe assembly and 4 new nuts and tighten to 30 ft. lbs. (40 Nm).

180. Install the 2 exhaust hangers and tighten the exhaust clamp and tighten to 30 ft. lbs. (40 Nm).

181. Install the ground wire, the radio interference capacitor wire and the nut to the engine front cover stud and tighten to 89 inch lbs. (10 Nm).

182. Install the ground wire and bolt to the engine front cover and tighten to 89 inch lbs. (10 Nm).

183. Attach the wiring harness retainer to the RH valve cover stud bolt.

184. Install the oil level indicator.

185. Connect the 2 engine wiring harness electrical connectors. Attach the electrical connector to the LH valve cover.

186. Connect the fuel hose routing clip to the transaxle stud.

187. Connect the fuel supply tube.

188. Connect the hose to the power steering reservoir.

189. Connect the A/C suction tube fitting. Install the safety clip onto the A/C fitting.

190. Using a new O-ring seal, connect the A/C pressure tube fitting and install the nut and tighten to 71 inch lbs. (8 Nm).

191. If equipped, attach the engine block heater harness retainers from to the radiator support and the A/C suction tube.

192. Connect the transaxle control electrical connector.

193. Attach the control cable to the bracket. Connect the transaxle control cable to the control lever.

194. Attach the wiring harness retainer to the transaxle control cable bracket.

195. Connect the upper radiator hose, lower radiator hose and 2 heater hoses to the thermostat housing.

196. Connect the upper Evaporative Emission (EVAP) tube quick connect coupling to the purge valve.

197. Connect the vacuum hose to the upper intake manifold.

198. Install the ground wire and the bolt. Tighten to 89 inch lbs. (10 Nm). Attach the 2 wiring harness retainers to the cowl.

199. Connect the power feed to the battery terminal and install the nut. Tighten to 71 inch lbs. (8 Nm).

200. Connect the battery harness electrical connector.

201. Install the battery tray.

202. Install the engine Air Cleaner (ACL) and the ACL outlet pipe.

203. Install the degas bottle.

204. Install the LH halfshaft and intermediate shaft.

205. Install the accessory drive belt and the power steering belt.

➡ **Do not expose the Motorcraft High Performance Engine RTV Silicone to**

engine oil for at least 90 minutes after installing the engine front cover. Failure to follow this instruction may cause oil leakage.

206. Fill the engine with clean engine oil.

207. Fill and bleed the cooling system.

208. Fill the power steering system.

209. Recharge the A/C system.

CATALYTIC CONVERTER

REMOVAL & INSTALLATION

Left Side

See Figure 93.

➡ **Always install new fasteners and gaskets. Clean flange faces prior to new gasket installation to make sure of correct sealing.**

1. With the vehicle in NEUTRAL, position it on a hoist.

2. Disconnect the Catalyst Monitor Sensor (CMS) electrical connector.

3. Remove the exhaust Y-pipe.

4. Remove the 2 catalytic converter support bracket-to-transmission bolts. To install, tighten to 35 ft. lbs. (48 Nm).

5. Remove the 4 nuts and the LH catalytic converter. Discard the nuts and gasket. To install, tighten to 30 ft. lbs. (40 Nm).

6. Inspect the exhaust manifold studs for damage. If damaged, replace stud(s), or if stud comes out when removing nut(s), replace the stud(s). To install, tighten to 18 ft. lbs. (25 Nm).

7. To install, reverse the removal procedure. Install a new gasket and nuts.

Right Side

See Figure 94 and 95.

➡ **If necessary, the catalytic converter heat shield can be serviced separately.**

➡ **Always install new fasteners and gaskets. Clean flange faces prior to new gasket installation to make sure of correct sealing.**

1. With the vehicle in NEUTRAL, position it on a hoist.

2. Remove the catalyst monitor sensor.

3. Remove the exhaust Y-pipe.

4. AWD vehicles perform the following:

➡ **Index-mark the driveshaft for installation.**

a. Remove and discard the 4 u-joint flange bolts and separate the front driveshaft and secure it with a length of

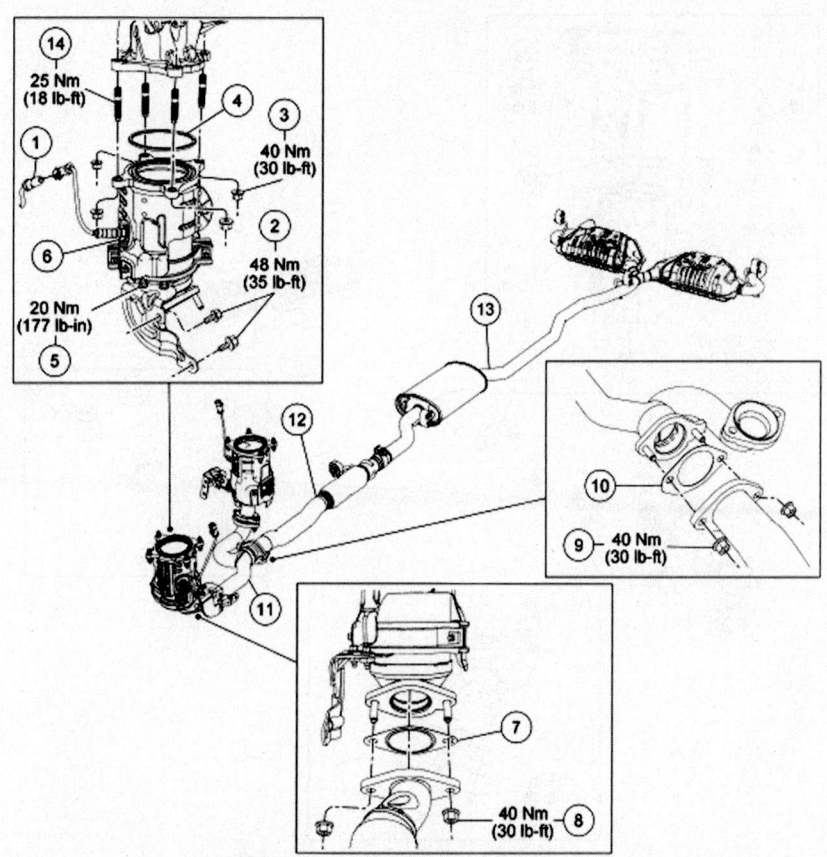

1. LH catalyst monitor sensor electrical connector
2. LH catalytic converter support bracket-to-transmission bolts (2 required)
3. LH catalytic converter-to-exhaust manifold nut (4 required)
4. Gasket
5. Bracket-to-LH catalytic converter bolt (2 required)
6. LH catalytic converter
7. Gasket
8. Exhaust Y-pipe-to-LH catalytic converter nut
9. Exhaust flexible pipe-to-exhaust Y-pipe nut (2 required)
10. Gasket
11. Exhaust Y-pipe
12. Muffler and tailpipe
13. LH catalytic converter-to-exhaust manifold (4 required)

36578_EDGE_G0137

Fig. 93 Exploded view of the LH catalytic converter and the Y-pipe

mechanic's wire. To install tighten to 52 ft. lbs. (70 Nm).

  b. Remove the intermediate shaft.

  c. Remove the 2 catalytic converter support bracket-to-engine block bolts. To install, tighten to 30 ft. lbs. (40 Nm).

5. All vehicles, remove the 2 bolts and the power steering gear heat shield. To install, tighten to 133 inch lbs. (15 Nm).

6. FWD vehicles, remove the catalytic converter support bracket-to-engine block bolt and nut. To install, tighten to 30 ft. lbs. (40 Nm).

7. All vehicles, remove the 2 nuts and

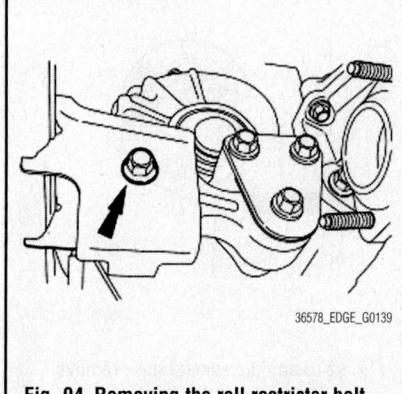

36578_EDGE_G0139

Fig. 94 Removing the roll restrictor bolt

the roll restrictor shield. To install, tighten to 97 inch lbs. (11 Nm).

8. Remove the roll restrictor bolt and rotate the engine forward. To install, tighten to 66 ft. lbs. (90 Nm).

9. Remove the 2 bracket-to-RH catalytic converter bolts. To install, tighten to 15 ft. lbs. (20 Nm).

10. Remove the 4 nuts and the RH catalytic converter. Discard the 4 RH catalytic converter nuts and gasket. To install, tighten to 30 ft. lbs. (40 Nm).

11. To install, reverse the removal procedure. Install a new gasket, nuts and studs.

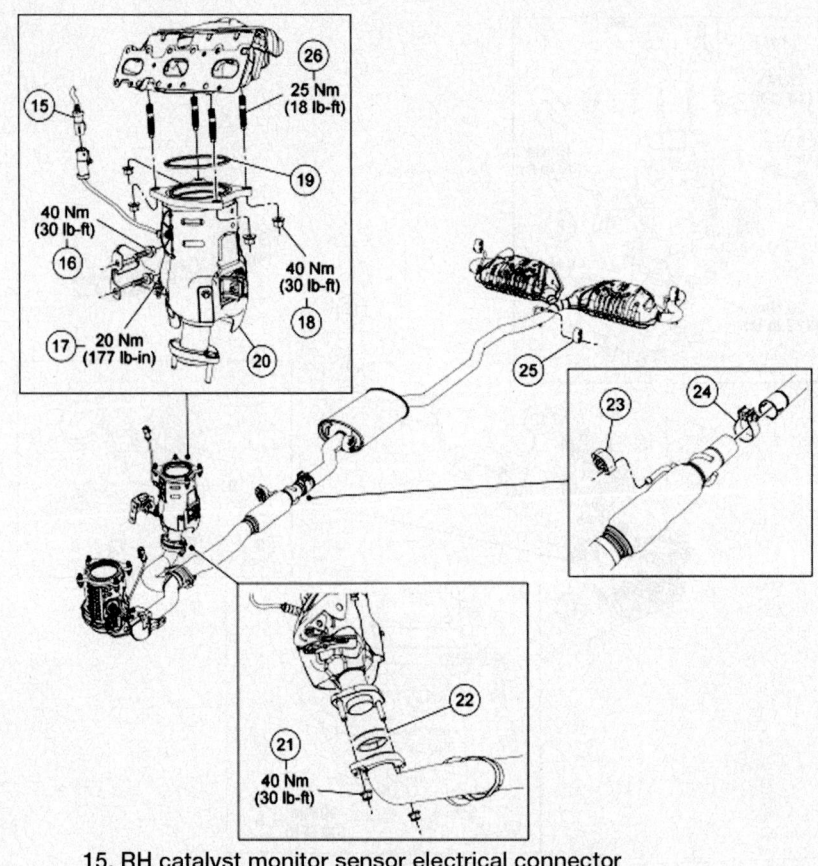

15. RH catalyst monitor sensor electrical connector
16. RH catalytic converter support bracket to engine
    block bolt (2 required) (FWD nut)
17. Bracket to RH catalytic converter bolt (2 required)
18. RH catalytic converter to exhaust manifold nut (4 required)
19. Gasket
20. RH catalytic converter
21. Exhaust Y pipe to RH catalytic converter nut (2 required)
22. Gasket
23. Exhaust flexible pipe isolator
24. Torca® clamp
25. Muffler and tailpipe isolator (4 required)
26. RH catalytic converter to exhaust manifold stud (4 required)

36578_EDGE_G0138

Fig. 95 Exploded view of the RH catalytic converter and the exhaust flexible pipe

CRANKSHAFT FRONT SEAL

REMOVAL & INSTALLATION

See Figures 96 and 97.

➡**This procedure requires the use of the following special tools or their equivalents:**

- Crankshaft Front Seal Installer 303-1251
- Oil Seal Remover 303-409 (T92C-6700CH)
- Crankshaft Damper Replacer 303-102 (T74P-6316-B)

1. Raise and safely support the vehicle.

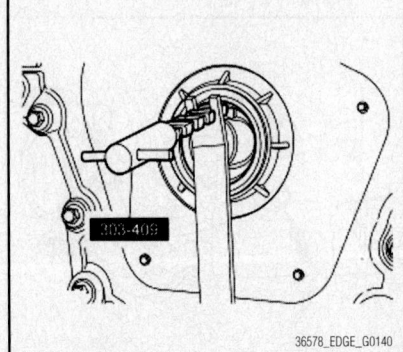

36578_EDGE_G0140

Fig. 96 Using the special tool, remove and discard the crankshaft front seal

2. Remove the crankshaft pulley, as outlined in this section.

3. Using the special tool shown, remove and discard the crankshaft front seal.

4. Thoroughly clean all sealing surfaces with a suitable metal surface cleaner.

To install:

➡**Apply clean engine oil to the crankshaft front seal bore in the engine front cover.**

5. Using the special tools, install a new crankshaft front seal.

6. Install the crankshaft pulley, as outlined in this section.

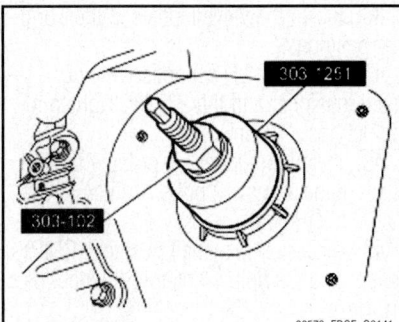

Fig. 97 Using the special tools, install a new crankshaft front seal

CYLINDER HEAD

REMOVAL & INSTALLATION

Left Side

See Figures 98 through 102.

> ❊❊ **WARNING**
>
> **During engine repair procedures, cleanliness is extremely important. Any foreign material, including any material created while cleaning gasket surfaces that enters the oil passages, coolant passages or the oil pan, can cause engine failure.**

1. Remove the LH camshafts, as outlined in this section.
2. If equipped, remove the heat shield and disconnect the block heater electrical connector.
3. Remove the block heater wiring harness from the engine.
4. Tag and detach the 6 fuel injector electrical connectors.
5. Disconnect the Cylinder Head Temperature (CHT) sensor electrical connector.
6. Disconnect the LH CMP sensor electrical connector.
7. Disconnect the LH Heated Oxygen Sensor (HO2S) electrical connector.
8. Disconnect the LH catalyst monitor sensor electrical connector.
9. Remove the wiring harness retainer bolt from the rear of the LH cylinder head.
10. Disconnect the A/C compressor electrical connector.
11. Remove the nut and disconnect the generator B+ cable.
12. Disconnect the generator electrical connector.
13. Detach the wiring harness retainer from the generator.
14. Disconnect the Engine Oil Pressure

(EOP) switch electrical connector and the wiring harness pin-type retainer.

15. Remove the nut, 2 bolts and the A/C compressor. Position the compressor aside, but DO NOT disconnect the refrigerant lines.
16. Remove the nut, bolt and the generator.
17. Remove the 2 LH catalytic converter bracket bolts.
18. Remove the 4 nuts and the LH catalytic converter. Discard the nuts and the gasket.
19. Remove the 3 bolts and the LH exhaust manifold heat shield.
20. Remove the 6 nuts and the LH exhaust manifold.
21. Discard the nuts and the exhaust manifold gasket.
22. Clean and inspect the LH exhaust manifold, as outlined under the Exhaust Manifold procedure in this section. Remove and discard the 6 LH exhaust manifold studs.
23. Remove the LH cylinder block drain plug. Allow the coolant to drain from

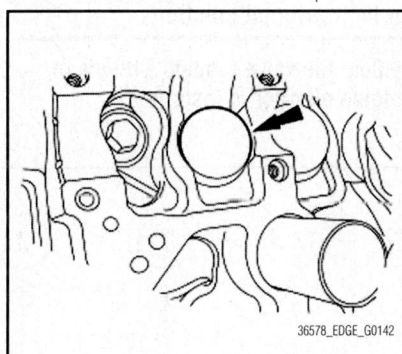

Fig. 98 Remove the valve tappets from the cylinder head

the cylinder block into a suitable container.

24. AWD vehicles remove the 2 RH catalytic converter bracket bolts.
25. Remove the 4 nuts and the RH catalytic converter. Discard the nuts and the gasket.
26. Remove the RH cylinder block drain plug or, if equipped, the block heater. Allow the coolant to drain from the cylinder block into a suitable container.
27. Remove the 4 bolts and the fuel rail and injectors as an assembly.
28. Remove the 3 thermostat housing-to-lower intake manifold bolts.
29. Remove the thermostat housing and discard the gasket and O-ring seal.
30. Remove the 10 bolts and the lower intake manifold. Discard the gaskets.
31. Remove the bolt and the LH CMP sensor.
32. Remove the 2 bolts and the upper LH primary timing chain guide.
33. Remove the 2 bolts and the LH secondary timing chain tensioner.

> ❊❊ **WARNING**
>
> **If the components are being reinstalled, they must be installed in the same positions. Mark the components for installation into their original positions.**

34. Remove the valve tappets from the cylinder head.
35. Remove and discard the M6 bolt.

> ❊❊ **WARNING**
>
> **Place clean rags over any exposed engine cavities. Also, carefully remove the towels so foreign materials do not drop into the engine.**

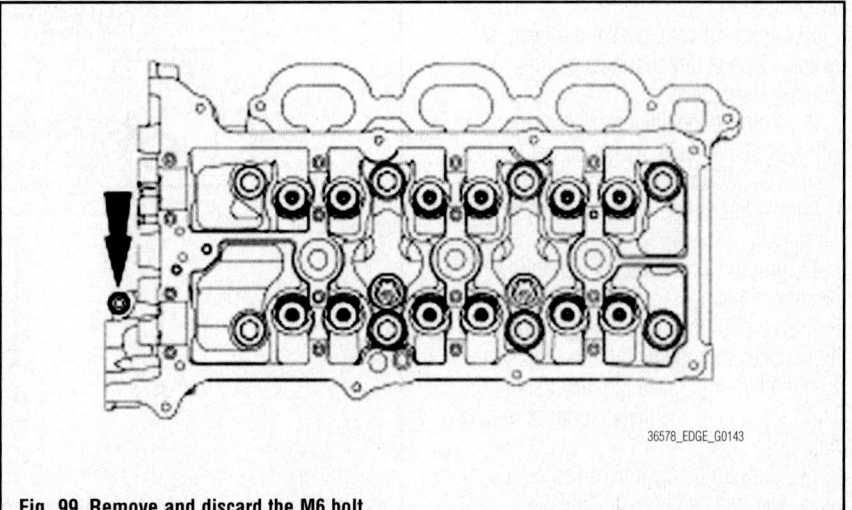

Fig. 99 Remove and discard the M6 bolt

※※ **WARNING**

The cylinder head bolts must be discarded and new bolts must be installed. They are tighten-to-yield designed and cannot be reused.

※※ **WARNING**

Aluminum surfaces are soft and can be easily scratched. Do NOT place the cylinder head gasket surface, unprotected, on a workbench surface.

36. Remove and discard the 8 bolts from the cylinder head.
37. Remove the cylinder head. Discard the cylinder head gasket.

※※ **WARNING**

NEVER use metal scrapers, wire brushes, power abrasive discs or other abrasive means to clean the sealing surfaces. These tools cause scratches and gouges that make leak paths. Use a plastic scraping tool to remove all traces of the head gasket.

➡Observe all warnings or cautions and follow all application directions contained on the packaging of the silicone gasket remover and the metal surface prep.

➡If there is no residual gasket material present, metal surface prep can be used to clean and prepare the surfaces.

38. Clean the cylinder head-to-cylinder block mating surfaces of both the cylinder heads and the cylinder block.
39. Remove any large deposits of silicone or gasket material with a plastic scraper.
40. Apply silicone gasket remover, following package directions, and allow to set for several minutes.
41. Remove the silicone gasket remover with a plastic scraper. A second application of silicone gasket remover may be required if residual traces of silicone or gasket material remain.
42. Apply metal surface prep, following package directions, to remove any remaining traces of oil or coolant and to prepare the surfaces to bond with the new gasket. Do not attempt to make the metal shiny. Some staining of the metal surfaces is normal.
43. Support the cylinder head on a bench with the head gasket side up.

➡The straightedge used must be flat within 0.0051 mm (0.0002 in) per foot of tool length. Inspect all areas of the deck face with a straightedge and feeler gauge. The cylinder head must not have depressions deeper than 0.0254 mm (0.001 in) across a 38.1 mm (1.5 in) square area, or scratches more than 0.0254 mm (0.001 in).

To install:

44. Install a new gasket, the LH cylinder head and 8 new bolts. Tighten in the sequence shown in 5 steps:
    a. Step 1: Tighten to 15 ft. lbs. (20 Nm).
    b. Step 2: Tighten to 26 ft. lbs. (35 Nm).
    c. Step 3: Tighten 90 degrees.
    d. Step 4: Tighten 90 degrees.
    e. Step 5: Tighten 90 degrees.
45. Install the M6 bolt and tighten to 89 inch lbs. (10 Nm).

※※ **WARNING**

The valve tappets must be installed in their original positions.

➡Coat the valve tappets with clean engine oil prior to installation.

46. Install the valve tappets in their original positions.
47. Install the LH secondary timing chain tensioner and the 2 bolts. Tighten to 89 inch lbs. (10 Nm).
48. Install the upper LH primary timing chain guide and the 2 bolts. Tighten to 89 inch lbs. (10 Nm).
49. Install LH camshaft position (CMP) sensor and the bolt. Tighten to 89 inch lbs. (10 Nm).
50. Using new gaskets, install the lower intake manifold and the 10 bolts. Tighten in the sequence shown to 10 Nm (89 inch lbs.).
51. Using a new gasket and O-ring seal, install the thermostat housing and the 3 bolts. Tighten to 10 Nm (89 inch lbs.).

※※ **WARNING**

Make sure to use O-ring seals that are made of special fuel-resistant material. Using regular O-rings can cause the fuel system to leak. Never reuse the O-ring seals.

※※ **WARNING**

The upper and lower O-ring seals are not interchangeable.

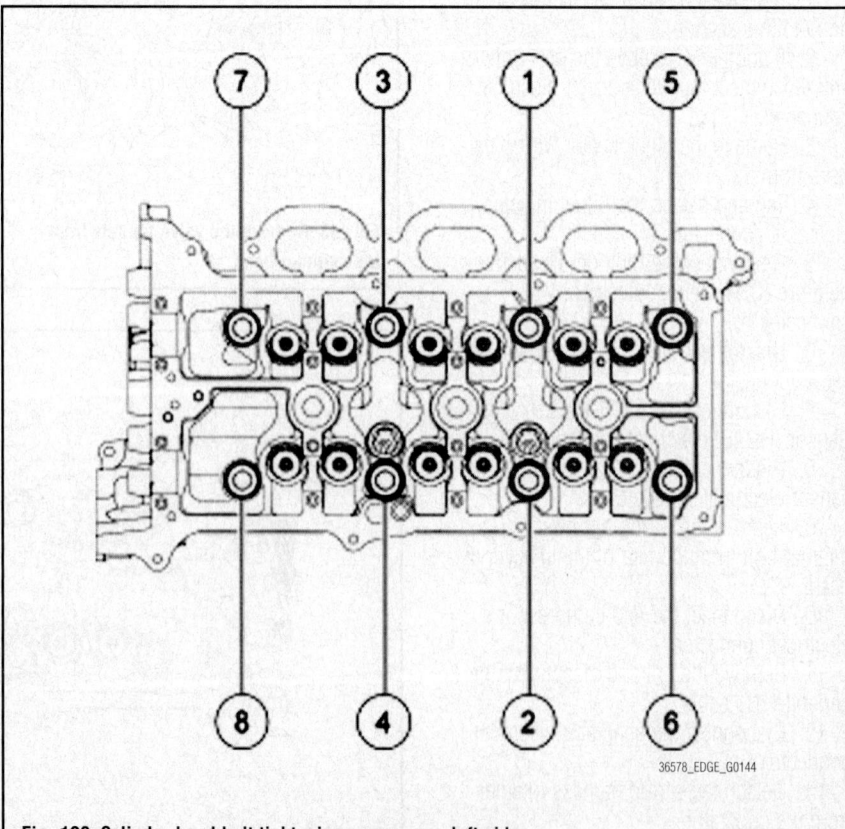

Fig. 100 Cylinder head bolt tightening sequence—left side

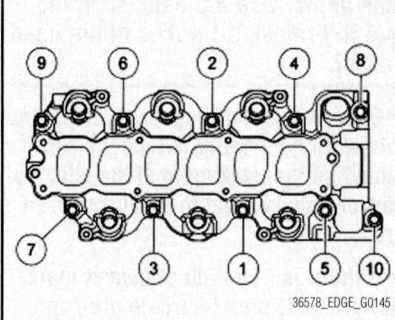

Fig. 101 Lower intake manifold bolt tightening sequence

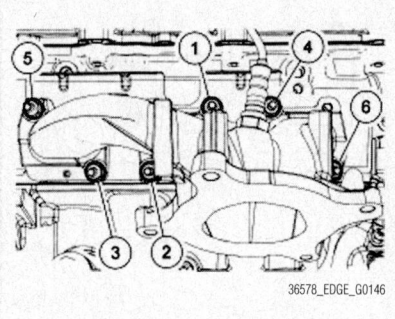

Fig. 102 Exhaust manifold tightening sequence—left side

52. Install new fuel injector O-ring seals, as follows:

    a. Remove the retaining clips and separate the fuel injectors from the fuel rail.

    b. Remove and discard the O-ring seals.

    c. Install new O-ring seals and lubricate with clean engine oil.

    d. Install the fuel injectors and the retaining clips onto the fuel rail.

53. Install the fuel rail and injectors as an assembly and install the 4 bolts. Tighten to 89 inch lbs. (10 Nm).

54. Install the RH cylinder block drain plug or, if equipped, the block heater. Tighten to 30 ft. lbs. (40 Nm).

55. AWD vehicles, install the 2 RH catalytic converter bracket bolts. Tighten the 4 catalytic converter nuts to 30 ft. lbs. (40 Nm). Tighten the 2 catalytic converter brackets to 15 ft. lbs. (20 Nm).

56. Using a new gasket, install the RH catalytic converter and 4 new nuts. Tighten to 30 ft. lbs. (40 Nm).

57. Install the LH cylinder block drain plug. Tighten to 20 Nm (15 ft. lbs.) plus an additional 180 degrees.

58. Install 6 new LH exhaust manifold studs. Tighten to 9 ft. lbs. (12 Nm).

➡**Failure to tighten the exhaust manifold nuts to specification a second time will cause the exhaust manifold to develop and exhaust leak.**

59. Using a new gasket, install the LH exhaust manifold and 6 new nuts. Tighten in the sequence shown.

    a. Stage 1: tighten to 15 ft. lbs. (20 Nm)

    b. Stage 2: tighten to 18 ft. lbs. (25 Nm)

60. Install the LH exhaust manifold heat shield and the 3 bolts. Tighten to 89 inch lbs. (10 Nm).

61. Using a new gasket, install the LH catalytic converter and 4 new nuts. Tighten to 30 ft. lbs. (40 Nm).

62. Install the 2 LH catalytic converter bracket bolts. Tighten to 15 ft. lbs. (20 Nm).

63. Install the generator, the bolt and the nut. Tighten to 35 ft. lbs. (47 Nm).

64. Install the A/C compressor, the nut and the 2 bolts. Tighten to 18 ft. lbs. (25 Nm).

65. Connect the EOP switch electrical connector and the wiring harness pin-type retainer.

66. Attach the wiring harness retainer to the generator.

67. Connect the generator electrical connector.

68. Connect the generator B+ cable and install the nut. Tighten to 53 inch lbs. (6 Nm).

69. Connect the A/C compressor electrical connector.

70. Install the wiring harness retainer bolt on the rear of the LH cylinder head. Tighten to 89 inch lbs. (10 Nm).

71. Connect the LH catalyst monitor sensor electrical connector.

72. Connect the LH HO2S electrical connector.

73. Connect the LH CMP sensor electrical connector.

74. Connect the CHT sensor electrical connector.

75. Connect the 6 fuel injector electrical connectors.

76. If equipped, install the block heater wiring harness onto the engine. Connect the block heater electrical connector and install the heat shield.

77. Install the LH camshafts, as outlined in this section.

Right Side

See Figures 103 through 109.

✳✳ WARNING

During engine repair procedures, cleanliness is extremely important. Any foreign material, including any material created while cleaning gas-

ket surfaces that enters the oil passages, coolant passages or the oil pan, can cause engine failure.

1. Remove the RH camshafts, as outlined in this section.

2. If equipped, remove the heat shield and disconnect the block heater electrical connector.

3. Remove the block heater wiring harness from the engine.

4. Disconnect the RH Heated Oxygen Sensor (HO2S) electrical connector.

5. Remove the bolt and position aside the RH radio interference capacitor.

6. Disconnect the RH Camshaft Position (CMP) sensor electrical connector.

7. Remove the bolt and the ground cable from the RH cylinder.

8. Tag and detach the 6 fuel injector electrical connectors.

9. Disconnect the Cylinder Head Temperature (CHT) sensor electrical connector.

10. Disconnect the LH Catalyst Monitor Sensor (CMS) electrical connector.

11. Remove the 2 LH catalytic converter bracket bolts.

12. Remove the 4 nuts and the LH catalytic converter. Discard the nuts and the gasket.

13. Remove the LH cylinder block drain plug. Allow the coolant to drain from the cylinder block into a suitable container.

14. AWD vehicles, remove the 2 RH catalytic converter bracket bolts.

15. Remove the 4 nuts and the RH catalytic converter. Discard the nuts and the gasket.

16. Remove the RH cylinder block drain plug or, if equipped, the block heater. Allow the coolant to drain from the cylinder block into a suitable container.

17. Remove the 3 bolts and the RH exhaust manifold heat shield.

18. Remove the 6 nuts and the RH exhaust manifold. Discard the nuts and exhaust manifold gaskets.

19. Clean and inspect the RH exhaust manifold. Refer to the Exhaust Manifold procedure in this section.

20. Remove and discard the 6 RH exhaust manifold studs.

21. Remove the 2 bolts and the RH primary timing chain guide.

22. Remove the 2 bolts and the RH secondary timing chain tensioner.

23. Remove the 2 bolts and the engine lifting eye.

➡**Matchmark the installed position of the bracket on the cylinder head for installation.**

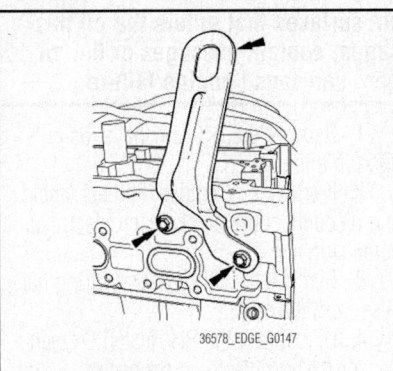

Fig. 103 Remove the 2 bolts and the engine lifting eye

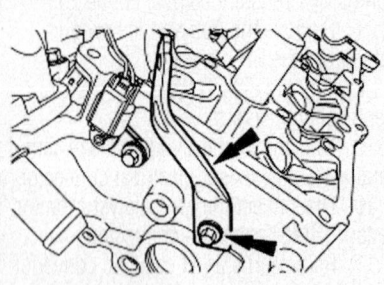

Fig. 104 Matchmark the installed position of the bracket on the cylinder head for installation, then remove the bolt and the upper intake manifold bracket

24. Remove the bolt and the upper intake manifold bracket.
25. Remove the bolt and the RH CMP sensor.
26. Remove the 4 bolts and the fuel rail and injectors as an assembly.
27. Remove the 3 thermostat housing-to-lower intake manifold bolts. Remove the thermostat housing and discard the gasket and O-ring seal.
28. Remove the 10 bolts and the lower intake manifold. Discard the gaskets.
29. Disconnect and remove the CHT sensor jumper harness.

✳✳ WARNING
If the components are being reinstalled, they must be installed in the same positions. Mark the components for installation into their original positions.

30. Remove the valve tappets from the cylinder head.
31. Remove and discard the M6 bolt.

✳✳ WARNING
Place clean rags over any exposed engine cavities. Also, carefully

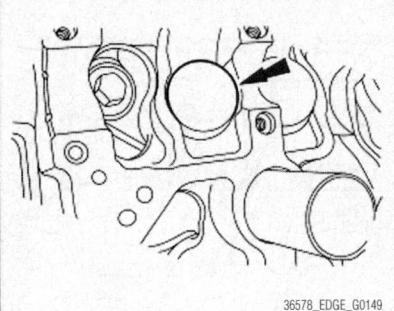

Fig. 105 Remove the valve tappets from the cylinder head

remove the towels so foreign materials do not drop into the engine.

✳✳ WARNING
The cylinder head bolts must be discarded and new bolts must be installed. They are tighten-to-yield designed and cannot be reused.

✳✳ WARNING
Aluminum surfaces are soft and can be easily scratched. Do NOT place the cylinder head gasket surface, unprotected, on a workbench surface.

32. Remove and discard the 8 bolts from the cylinder head. Remove the cylinder head. Discard the cylinder head gasket.

✳✳ WARNING
NEVER use metal scrapers, wire brushes, power abrasive discs or other abrasive means to clean the sealing surfaces. These tools cause scratches and gouges that make

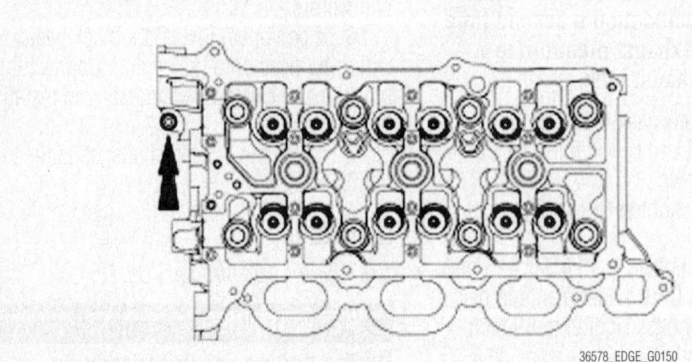

Fig. 106 Remove and discard the M6 bolt

leak paths. Use a plastic scraping tool to remove all traces of the head gasket.

➡ Observe all warnings or cautions and follow all application directions contained on the packaging of the silicone gasket remover and the metal surface prep.

➡ If there is no residual gasket material present, metal surface prep can be used to clean and prepare the surfaces.

33. Clean the cylinder head-to-cylinder block mating surfaces of both the cylinder heads and the cylinder block.
34. Remove any large deposits of silicone or gasket material with a plastic scraper.
35. Apply silicone gasket remover, following package directions, and allow to set for several minutes.
36. Remove the silicone gasket remover with a plastic scraper. A second application of silicone gasket remover may be required if residual traces of silicone or gasket material remain.
37. Apply metal surface prep, following package directions, to remove any remaining traces of oil or coolant and to prepare the surfaces to bond with the new gasket. Do not attempt to make the metal shiny. Some staining of the metal surfaces is normal.
38. Support the cylinder head on a bench with the head gasket side up.

➡ The straightedge used must be flat within 0.0051 mm (0.0002 in) per foot of tool length. Inspect all areas of the deck face with a straightedge and feeler gauge. The cylinder head must not have depressions deeper than 0.0254 mm (0.001 in) across a 38.1 mm (1.5 in) square area, or scratches more than 0.0254 mm (0.001 in).

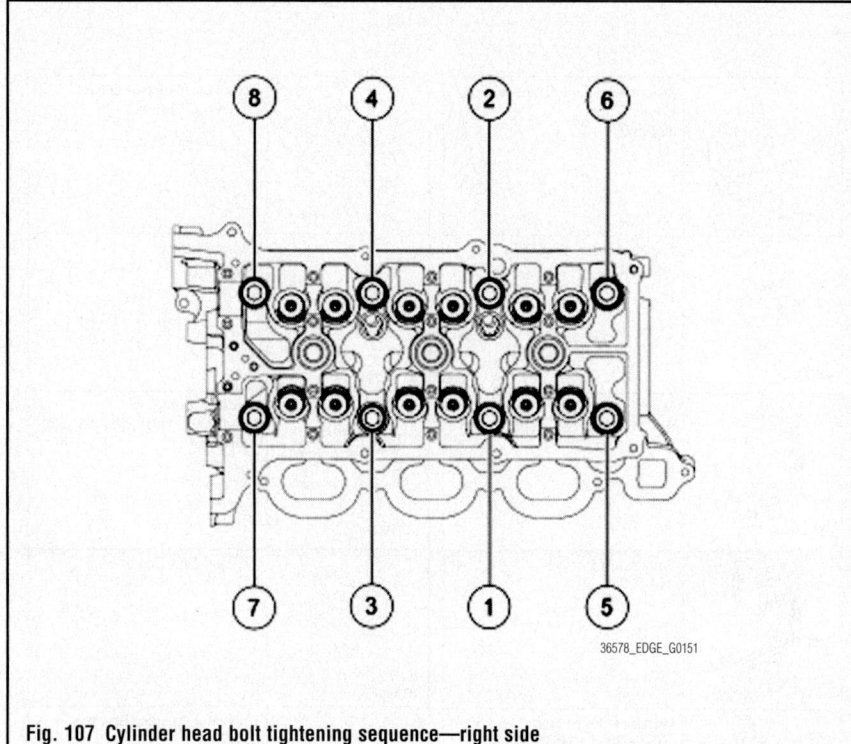

Fig. 107 Cylinder head bolt tightening sequence—right side

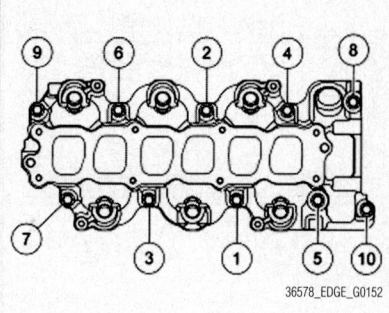

Fig. 108 Lower intake manifold bolt tightening sequence

To install:

39. Install a new gasket, the RH cylinder head and 8 new bolts. Tighten in the sequence shown in 5 steps:
   a. Step 1: Tighten to 20 Nm (15 ft. lbs.).
   b. Step 2: Tighten to 35 Nm (26 ft. lbs.).
   c. Step 3: Tighten 90 degrees.
   d. Step 4: Tighten 90 degrees.
   e. Step 5: Tighten 90 degrees.
40. Install the M6 bolt and tighten to 89 inch lbs. (10 Nm).

✷✷ WARNING

The valve tappets must be installed in their original positions.

➥**Coat the valve tappets with clean engine oil prior to installation.**

41. Install the valve tappets in their original, installed positions.
42. Install and connect the CHT sensor jumper harness.
43. Using new gaskets, install the lower intake manifold and the 10 bolts. Tighten in the sequence shown to 89 inch lbs. (10 Nm).
44. Using a new gasket and O-ring seal, install the thermostat housing and the 3 bolts. Tighten to 89 inch lbs. (10 Nm).

✷✷ WARNING

Only use O-ring seals that are made of special fuel-resistant material. Using regular O-rings can cause the fuel system to leak. Never reuse the O-ring seals.

✷✷ WARNING

The upper and lower O-ring seals are not interchangeable.

45. Install new fuel injector O-ring seals, as follows:
   a. Remove the retaining clips and separate the fuel injectors from the fuel rail.
   b. Remove and discard the O-ring seals.
   c. Install new O-ring seals and lubricate with clean engine oil.
   d. Install the fuel injectors and the retaining clips onto the fuel rail.
46. Install the fuel rail and injectors as an assembly and install the 4 bolts. Tighten to 89 inch lbs. (10 Nm).
47. Install the RH CMP sensor and the bolt. Tighten to 89 inch lbs. (10 Nm).

➥**Align the bracket with the index mark made during removal.**

48. Install the upper intake manifold bracket and the bolt. Tighten to 89 inch lbs. (10 Nm).

➥**Align the bracket with the index mark made during removal.**

49. Install the upper intake manifold bracket and the bolt. Tighten to 89 inch lbs. (10 Nm).

50. Install the engine lifting eye and the 2 bolts. Tighten to 18 ft. lbs. (24 Nm).
51. Install the RH secondary timing chain tensioner and the 2 bolts. Tighten to 10 Nm (89 inch lbs.).
52. Install the RH primary timing chain guide and the 2 bolts. Tighten to 10 Nm (89 inch lbs.).
53. Install 6 new RH exhaust manifold studs. Tighten to 9 ft. lbs. (12 Nm).
54. Using a new gasket, install the RH exhaust manifold and 6 new nuts. Tighten in the sequence shown.
   a. Stage 1: tighten to 15 ft. lbs. (20 Nm).
   b. Stage 2: tighten to 18 ft. lbs. (25 Nm).
55. Install the RH exhaust manifold heat shield and the 3 bolts. Tighten to 89 inch lbs. (10 Nm).
56. Install the RH cylinder block drain plug or, if equipped, the block heater. Tighten to 30 ft. lbs. (40 Nm).

➥**Do not tighten the 4 catalytic converter nuts at this time.**

57. Using a new gasket, install the RH catalytic converter and 4 new nuts.
58. AWD vehicles, install the 2 RH catalytic converter bracket bolts. Tighten the 4 catalytic converter nuts to 30 ft. lbs. (40 Nm). Tighten the 2 catalytic converter brackets to 15 ft. lbs. (20 Nm).
59. Install the LH cylinder block drain plug. Tighten to 15 ft. lbs. (20 Nm) plus an additional 180 degrees.
60. Using a new gasket, install the LH catalytic converter and 4 new nuts. Tighten to 30 ft. lbs. (40 Nm).
61. Install the 2 LH catalytic converter bracket bolts. Tighten to 15 ft. lbs. (20 Nm).
62. Connect the LH catalyst monitor sensor electrical connector.
63. Connect the CHT sensor electrical connector.

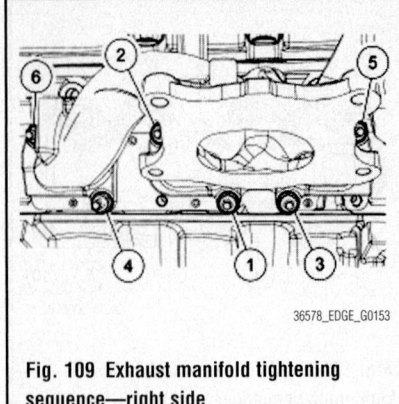

36578_EDGE_G0153

Fig. 109 Exhaust manifold tightening sequence—right side

64. Connect the 6 fuel injector electrical connectors.

65. Install the ground cable and the bolt. Tighten to 89 inch lbs. (10 Nm).

66. Connect the RH CMP sensor electrical connector.

67. Connect the RH HO2S electrical connector.

68. If equipped, install the block heater wiring harness onto the engine. Connect the block heater electrical connector and install the heat shield.

69. Install the RH camshafts, as outlined in this section.

ENGINE ASSEMBLY

REMOVAL & INSTALLATION

See Figures 110 through 118.

➡Engine removal and installation requires a number of specialized tools and equipment. Make sure to read the procedure and be sure you have all of the necessary tools and equipment before beginning the procedure.

✵ CAUTION

NEVER smoke or carry lighted tobacco or open flame of any type when working on or near any fuel-related components. Highly flammable mixtures are always present and may be ignited. Failure to follow these instructions may result in personal injury or death.

1. Raise and safely support the vehicle.

2. Recover the air conditioning system.

3. Release the fuel system pressure, as outlined in the Fuel System Section.

4. Disconnect the negative, then the positive battery cables.

5. Drain the engine cooling system.

6. Remove the accessory drive belt and

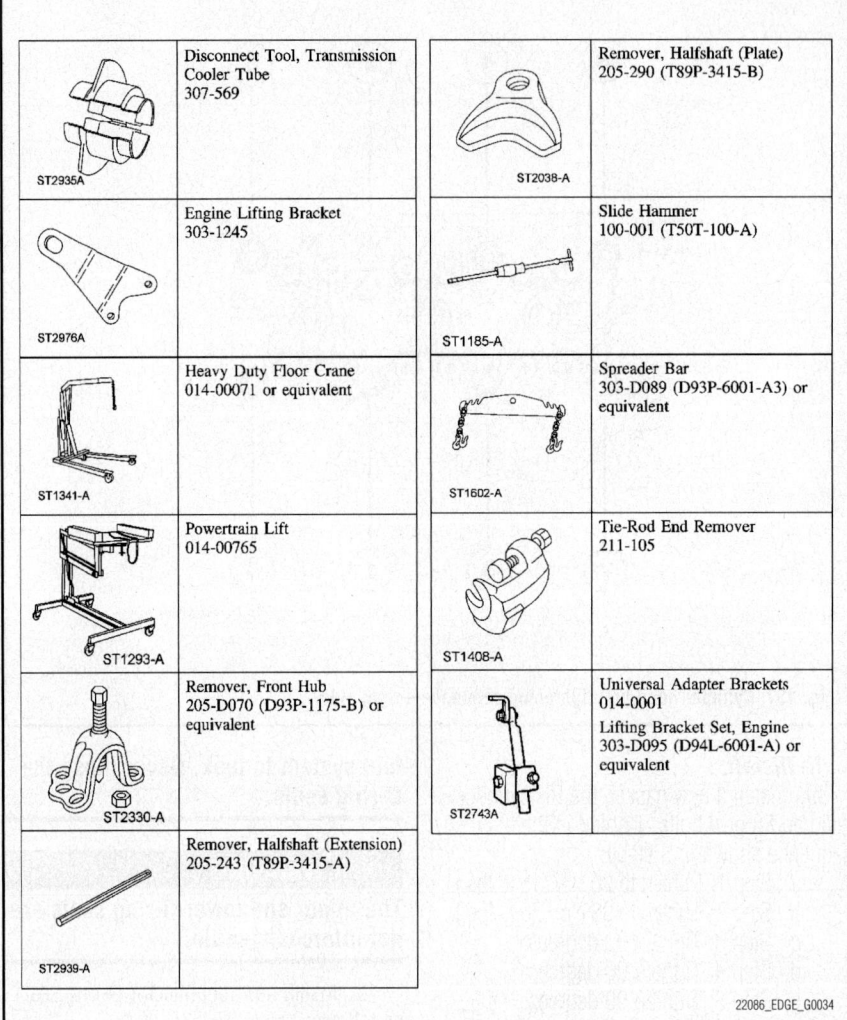

Disconnect Tool, Transmission Cooler Tube 307-569 ST2935A	Remover, Halfshaft (Plate) 205-290 (T89P-3415-B) ST2038-A
Engine Lifting Bracket 303-1245 ST2976A	Slide Hammer 100-001 (T50T-100-A) ST1185-A
Heavy Duty Floor Crane 014-00071 or equivalent ST1341-A	Spreader Bar 303-D089 (D93P-6001-A3) or equivalent ST1602-A
Powertrain Lift 014-00765 ST1293-A	Tie-Rod End Remover 211-105 ST1408-A
Remover, Front Hub 205-D070 (D93P-1175-B) or equivalent ST2330-A	Universal Adapter Brackets 014-0001 Lifting Bracket Set, Engine 303-D095 (D94L-6001-A) or equivalent ST2743A
Remover, Halfshaft (Extension) 205-243 (T89P-3415-A) ST2939-A	

22086_EDGE_G0034

Fig. 110 Special tools needed for engine removal and installation

the power steering belt, as outlined in this section.

7. Disconnect the power steering cooler hose and drain the power steering fluid into a suitable drain pan.

8. Remove the degas bottle.

9. Remove the engine air cleaner and air cleaner outlet pipe.

10. Remove the battery and the battery tray.

11. Disconnect the battery harness electrical connector.

12. Remove the nut and disconnect the power feed from the battery terminal.

13. Remove the bolt and the ground wire.

14. Detach the 2 wiring harness retainers from the cowl.

15. Disconnect the vacuum hose from the upper intake manifold.

16. Disconnect the upper Evaporative Emissions (EVAP) tube quick connect coupling from the purge valve.

17. Disconnect the upper radiator hose, lower radiator hose and 2 heater hoses from the thermostat housing.

18. Detach the wiring harness retainer from the transaxle control cable bracket.

19. Disconnect the transaxle control cable from the control lever.

20. Detach the control cable from the bracket.

21. Disconnect the transaxle control electrical connector.

22. If equipped, detach the engine block heater harness retainers from the radiator support and the A/C suction tube.

23. Remove the nut and disconnect the A/C pressure tube fitting.

24. Discard the O-ring seal.

25. Remove the safety clip from the A/C fitting.

26. Disconnect the A/C suction tube fitting.

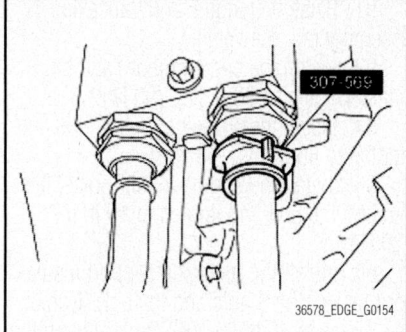

Fig. 111 Using the special tool shown, disconnect the transaxle cooling tubes

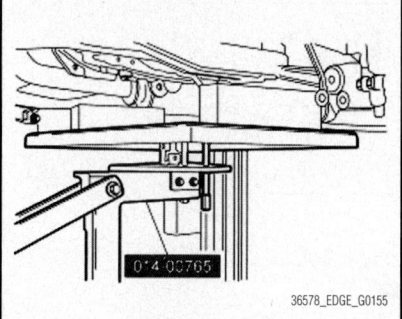

Fig. 112 Position the special tool under the subframe assembly

Fig. 113 Remove the 2 nuts, 4 bolts and the subframe support brackets

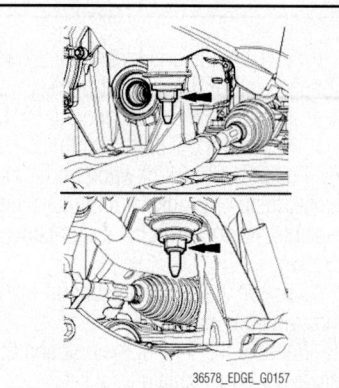

Fig. 114 Remove the 2 middle subframe nuts

27. Disconnect the hose from the power steering reservoir.

28. Disconnect the fuel supply tube.

29. Disconnect the fuel hose routing clip from the transaxle stud and position the fuel hose aside.

30. Disconnect the 2 engine wiring harness electrical connectors.

31. Detach the electrical connector from the LH valve cover.

32. Remove the oil level indicator dipstick.

33. Detach the wiring harness retainer from the RH valve cover stud bolt.

34. Remove the bolt and the ground wire from the engine front cover.

35. Remove the nut, the ground wire and the radio interference capacitor wire from the engine front cover stud.

36. Loosen the exhaust flexible pipe clamp and disconnect the 2 exhaust hangers.

37. Remove the 4 nuts and the exhaust flexible pipe and Y-pipe as an assembly.

38. Discard the nuts and the gasket.

39. Remove the 3 pin-type retainers, the 7 screws and the radiator splash shield.

40. Remove the LH inner splash shield.

41. Remove the 2 secondary latches from the transmission fluid cooler tubes.

42. Using the special tool shown in the accompanying illustration, disconnect the transaxle cooling tubes.

43. Remove the 4 oil pan-to-transaxle bolts.

44. Remove the 2 fasteners and the inspection cover.

45. Remove and discard the 3 torque converter bolts.

46. Remove the drain plug and drain the engine oil. Install the drain plug and tighten to 20 ft. lbs. (27 Nm).

47. Remove and discard the engine oil filter.

48. Remove the power steering cooler bracket bolt from the RH side of the subframe.

49. For All Wheel Drive (AWD) vehicles, match mark the driveshaft for installation, then remove the 4 bolts and support the driveshaft with a piece of wire.

50. Using a suitable holding device, hold the steering wheel in the straight-ahead position.

51. Remove the 2 nuts and the roll restrictor heat shield.

52. Remove the engine roll restrictor-to-subframe through bolt.

53. Remove and discard the power steering pressure (PSP) tube-to-pump banjo bolt and the 2 seals.

✷✷ WARNING

Do not let the intermediate shaft rotate while it is disconnected from the gear or damage to the clockspring can occur. If there is evidence that the intermediate shaft has rotated, the clockspring must be removed and recentered.

54. Remove and discard the steering intermediate shaft bolt.

55. Separate the steering intermediate shaft from the steering gear.

56. Remove and discard the cotter pins and tie-rod end nuts.

57. Remove the 3 RH subframe-to-lower bumper nuts.

58. Remove the 3 LH subframe-to-lower bumper nuts and separate the lower bumper from the subframe.

59. Position the special tool under the subframe assembly.

60. Remove the 2 nuts, 4 bolts and the subframe support brackets.

61. Remove the 2 front subframe nuts.

62. Remove the 2 middle subframe nuts.

63. Using the special tool, lower the subframe assembly from the vehicle.

64. If equipped, disconnect the oil cooler coolant hoses.

65. AWD vehicles perform the following:

a. Remove the RH Catalyst Monitor Sensor (CMS) electrical connector.

b. Remove the 2 RH catalytic converter support bracket bolts.

c. Remove the 4 nuts and the RH catalytic converter. Discard the gasket and the nuts.

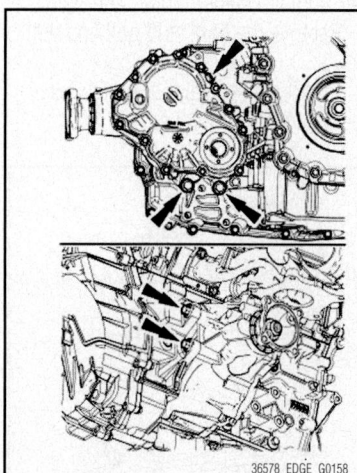

Fig. 115 Remove the 5 bolts and the Power Transfer Unit (PTU) support bracket—AWD models

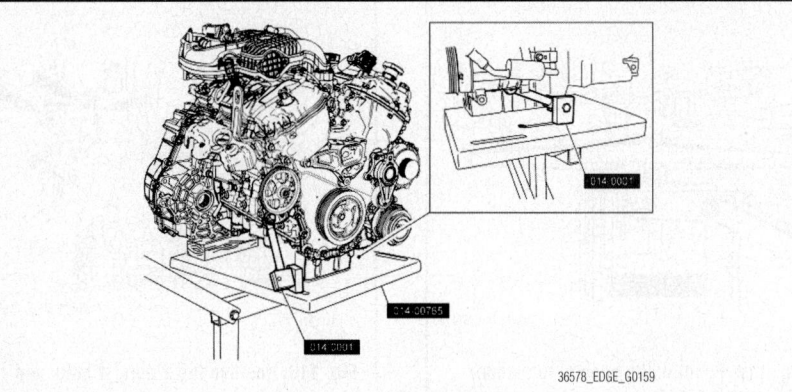

Fig. 116 Position a block of wood under the transaxle. Install the special tools, or their equivalents, as shown

d. Remove the 5 bolts and the Power Transfer Unit (PTU) support bracket.

e. Remove the 5 bolts and the PTU.

f. Remove the 5 bolts and the PTU.

66. Position a block of wood under the transaxle. Install the special tools, or their equivalents, as shown in the accompanying illustration.

67. Remove the transaxle support insulator through bolt and nut.

68. Remove the 3 nuts, the bolt and the transaxle support insulator bracket.

69. Remove the nut, bolt and engine mount brace.

70. Remove the 4 engine mount nuts.

71. Remove the 3 bolts and the engine mount.

72. Lower the engine and transaxle assembly from the vehicle.

73. Position the starter cable boot back and remove the 2 nuts.

74. Detach the 2 wire terminals from the starter.

75. Disconnect the wiring harness retainer from the starter motor stud bolt.

76. Remove the bolt, stud bolt and the starter.

77. Install the special tool on the LH cylinder head.

78. Using the special tools and a suitable engine crane, remove the engine and transaxle from the lift table.

79. Remove the 2 engine-to-transaxle bolts.

80. Remove the 5 transaxle-to-engine bolts.

81. Separate the transaxle from the engine.

To install:

82. Align the transaxle to the engine.

83. Install the 5 transaxle-to-engine bolts and tighten to 35 ft. lbs. (48 Nm).

84. Install the 2 engine-to-transaxle bolts and tighten to 35 ft. lbs. (48 Nm).

85. Using the special tools, position the engine and transaxle onto the lift table.

86. Position a block of wood under the transaxle. Install the special tools, as shown.

87. Install the starter, the bolt and the stud bolt. Tighten to 20 ft. lbs. (27 Nm).

88. Connect the wiring harness retainer to the starter stud bolt.

89. Attach the starter motor wire terminals and install the 2 nuts. Tighten as follows:

a. Tighten to 9 ft. lbs. (12 Nm).

b. Tighten to 44 inch lbs. (5 Nm).

90. Position the starter terminal boot over the starter terminal.

91. Raise the engine and transaxle assembly into the vehicle.

92. Install the engine mount and the 3 bolts. Tighten to 66 ft. lbs. (90 Nm).

93. Install the 4 engine mount nuts and tighten to 46 ft. lbs. (63 Nm).

94. Install the engine mount brace, the nut and the bolt and tighten to 15 ft. lbs. (20 Nm).

95. Install the transaxle support insulator bracket, the 3 nuts and the bolt. Tighten the 3 nuts to 46 ft. lbs. (63 Nm). Tighten the bolt to 59 ft. lbs. (80 Nm).

96. Install the transaxle support insulator through bolt and nut and tighten to 129 ft. lbs. (175 Nm).

97. For AWD vehicles, perform the following:

a. Position the Power Transfer Unit (PTU) in place and install the 5 bolts. Tighten to 66 ft. lbs. (90 Nm).

b. Position the PTU support bracket in place and install the 5 bolts. Tighten to 52 ft. lbs. (70 Nm).

➡ **Do not tighten the 4 catalytic converter nuts at this time.**

c. Using a new gasket, install the RH catalytic converter and 4 new nuts.

d. Install the 2 catalytic converter-to-bracket bolts.

e. Tighten the 4 catalytic converter nuts to 30 ft. lbs. (40 Nm).

f. Tighten the 2 catalytic converter-to-bracket bolts to 15 ft. lbs. (20 Nm).

g. Connect the RH catalyst monitor electrical connector.

98. If equipped, connect the oil cooler coolant hoses.

99. Using the special tool, raise the subframe into the installed position.

100. Install the 2 middle subframe nuts and tighten to 98 ft. lbs. (133 Nm).

101. Install the 2 front subframe nuts and tighten to 98 ft. lbs. (133 Nm).

102. Position the subframe support brackets in place and loosely install the 4 bolts.

103. Install the 2 rear subframe bracket nuts and tighten to 98 ft. lbs. (133 Nm).

104. Tighten the 4 subframe support bracket bolts to 66 ft. lbs. (90 Nm).

105. Position the lower bumper on the subframe and install the 3 LH nuts. Tighten to 80 inch lbs. (9 Nm).

106. Install the 3 RH lower bumper-to-subframe nuts. Tighten to 80 inch lbs. (9 Nm).

107. Install the tie-rod ends and nuts and tighten to 35 ft. lbs. (48 Nm). Install new cotter pins.

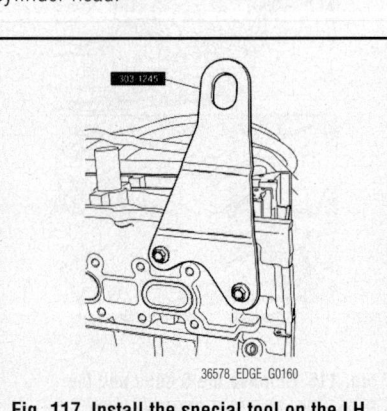

Fig. 117 Install the special tool on the LH cylinder head

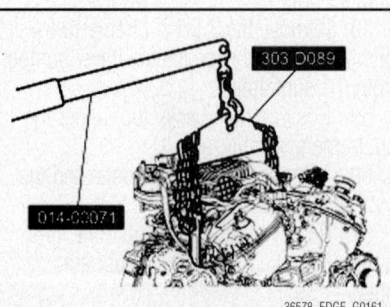

Fig. 118 Using the special tools and a suitable engine crane, remove the engine and transaxle from the lift table

⁂ WARNING

Do not let the intermediate shaft to rotate while it is disconnected from the gear or damage to the clockspring can occur. If there is evidence that the intermediate shaft has rotated, the clockspring must be removed and recentered, as outlined in the Chassis Electrical Section.

108. Install the intermediate shaft onto the steering gear and install a new bolt. Tighten to 17 ft. lbs. (23 Nm).

109. Using a new banjo bolt and 2 new seals, install the PSP tube. Tighten to 35 ft. lbs. (48 Nm).

110. Install the engine roll restrictor-to-subframe through bolt and tighten to 76 ft. lbs. (103 Nm).

111. Install the roll restrictor heat shield and the 2 nuts and tighten to 80 inch lbs. (9 Nm).

112. For AWD vehicles, align the match-marks on the rear driveshaft to the index marks on the PTU flange made during removal and install the 4 bolts. Tighten the bolts to 52 ft. lbs. (70 Nm).

113. Install the power steering cooler bracket bolt to the RH side of the subframe. Tighten to 80 inch lbs. (9 Nm).

114. Connect the power steering cooler hose.

➡ Lubricate the engine oil filter gasket with clean engine oil before installing the oil filter.

115. Install a new engine oil filter. Tighten to 44 inch lbs. (5 Nm) and then rotate an additional 180 degrees.

116. Install the 3 new torque converter bolts and tighten to 41 ft. lbs. (55 Nm).

117. Install the inspection cover and the 2 fasteners.

118. Install the 4 oil pan-to-transaxle bolts and tighten to 35 ft. lbs. (48 Nm).

119. Connect the 2 transmission fluid cooler tubes.

120. Install the 2 secondary latches onto the transmission fluid cooler tubes.

121. Install the LH inner splash shield.

122. Install the radiator splash shield, the 3 pin-type retainers and the 7 screws.

123. Using a new gasket, install the Y-pipe and exhaust flexible pipe assembly and 4 new nuts. Tighten to 30 ft. lbs. (40 Nm).

124. Install the 2 exhaust hangers and tighten the exhaust clamp. Tighten to 30 ft. lbs. (40 Nm).

125. Install the ground wire, the radio interference capacitor wire and the nut to the engine front cover stud. Tighten to 89 inch lbs. (10 Nm).

126. Install the ground wire and bolt to the engine front cover. Tighten to 89 inch lbs. (10 Nm).

127. Attach the wiring harness retainer to the RH valve cover stud bolt.

128. Install the oil level indicator.

129. Connect the 2 engine wiring harness electrical connectors.

130. Attach the electrical connector to the LH valve cover.

131. Connect the fuel hose routing clip to the transaxle stud.

132. Connect the fuel supply tube.

133. Connect the hose to the power steering reservoir.

134. Connect the A/C suction tube fitting. Install the safety clip onto the A/C fitting.

135. Using a new O-ring seal, connect the A/C tube fitting and install the nut. Tighten to 71 inch lbs. (8 Nm).

If equipped, attach the engine block heater harness retainers to the radiator support and the A/C suction tube.

136. Connect the transaxle control electrical connector.

137. Attach the control cable to the bracket.

138. Connect the transaxle control cable to the control lever.

139. Attach the wiring harness retainer to the transaxle control cable bracket.

140. Connect the upper radiator hose, lower radiator hose and 2 heater hoses to the thermostat housing.

141. Connect the upper EVAP tube quick connect coupling to the purge valve.

142. Connect the vacuum hose to the upper intake manifold.

143. Install the ground wire and the bolt and tighten to 89 inch lbs. (10 Nm).

144. Attach the 2 wiring harness retainers to the cowl.

145. Connect the power feed to the battery terminal and install the nut. Tighten to 71 inch lbs. (8 Nm).

146. Connect the battery harness electrical connector.

147. Install the battery tray and the battery.

148. Install the engine air cleaner and the air cleaner outlet pipe.

149. Install the degas bottle.

150. Install the accessory drive belt and the power steering belt, as outlined in this section.

151. Connect the positive, then the negative battery cables.

152. Fill the engine with clean engine oil.

153. Fill and bleed the cooling system.

154. Fill the power steering system.

155. Recharge the air conditioning system.

EXHAUST MANIFOLD

REMOVAL & INSTALLATION

Left Side

See Figures 119 and 120.

1. Remove the LH catalytic converter, as follows:

    a. Raise and safely support the vehicle.

    b. Disconnect the catalyst monitor sensor electrical connector.

    c. Remove the exhaust Y-pipe.

    d. Remove the 2 catalytic converter support bracket-to-transmission bolts.

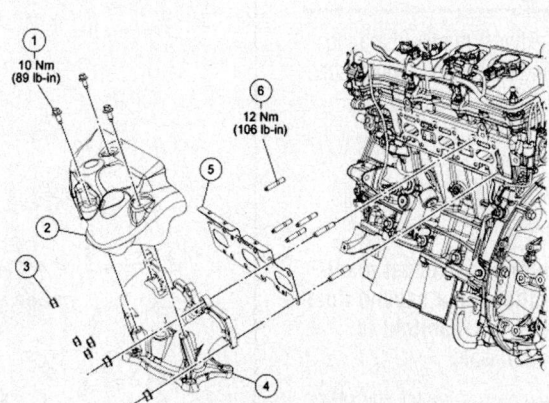

1. LH exhaust manifold heat shield bolt (3 required)
2. LH exhaust manifold heat shield
3. LH exhaust manifold nut (6 required)
4. LH exhaust manifold
5. LH exhaust manifold gasket
6. LH exhaust manifold stud (6 required)

36578_EDGE_G0162

Fig. 119 Exploded view of the left side exhaust manifold and related components

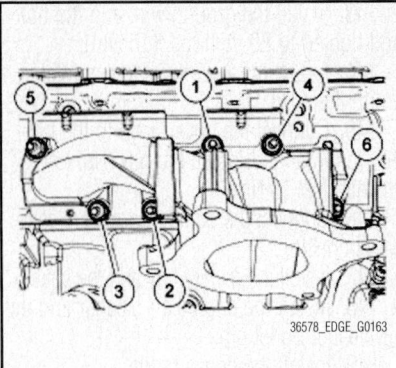

Fig. 120 Exhaust manifold tightening sequence—left side

e. Remove the 4 nuts and the LH catalytic converter.

f. Discard the 4 LH catalytic converter nuts and gasket.

2. Remove the LH Heated Oxygen Sensor (HO2S).

3. Remove the 3 bolts and the LH exhaust manifold heat shield.

4. Remove the 6 nuts and the LH exhaust manifold. Discard the nuts and gasket.

5. Clean and inspect the LH exhaust manifold.

6. Remove and discard the 6 LH exhaust manifold studs.

✳✳ WARNING

Do not use metal scrapers, wire brushes, power abrasive discs or other abrasive means to clean the sealing surfaces. These may cause scratches and gouges resulting in leak paths. Use a plastic scraper to clean the sealing surfaces.

7. Clean the exhaust manifold mating surface of the cylinder head with metal surface prep. Follow the directions on the packaging.

To install:

8. Install 6 new LH exhaust manifold studs and tighten to 9 ft. lbs. (12 Nm).

➡**Failure to tighten the exhaust manifold nuts to specification a second time will cause the exhaust manifold to develop an exhaust leak.**

9. Using a new gasket, install the LH exhaust manifold and 6 new nuts. Tighten in the sequence shown to 15 ft. lbs. (20 Nm). Then tighten to 18 ft. lbs. (25 Nm).

10. Install the LH exhaust manifold heat shield and the 3 bolts and tighten to 89 inch lbs. (10 Nm).

11. Install the LH HO2S.

➡**When installing the catalytic converter, always install new fasteners and gaskets. Clean the flange faces prior to new gasket installation to ensure proper sealing.**

12. Install the LH catalytic converter, with new gaskets and nuts, in the reverse of the removal procedure. Tighten the retainers as follows:

a. Catalytic converter nuts: 30 ft. lbs. (40 Nm).

b. Catalytic converter support bracket-to-transmission bolts: 35 ft. lbs. (48 Nm).

Right Side

See Figures 121 and 122.

1. Remove the right side catalytic converter, as follows:

a. Raise and safely support the vehicle.

b. Remove the catalyst monitor sensor.

c. Remove the exhaust Y-pipe.

d. For All Wheel Drive (AWD) models, Remove and discard the 4 universal joint (U-joint) flange bolts and separate the front driveshaft and secure it with a piece of wire.

e. For AWD models, remove the RH halfshaft assembly. Remove the 2 catalytic converter support bracket-to-engine block bolts.

f. For Front Wheel Drive (FWD) models, remove the 2 bolts and the power steering rack shield.

g. For FWD models, remove the catalytic converter support bracket-to-engine block bolt and nut.

h. Remove the 2 nuts and the roll restrictor shield.

i. Remove the roll restrictor bolt and rotate the engine forward.

j. Remove the 2 bracket-to-RH catalytic converter bolts.

k. Remove the 4 nuts and the RH catalytic converter.

l. Discard the 4 RH catalytic converter nuts and gasket.

2. Disconnect the RH Heated Oxygen Sensor (HO2S) electrical connector.

3. Remove the 6 nuts and the RH exhaust manifold. Discard the nuts and gasket.

4. Clean and inspect the RH exhaust manifold.

5. Remove and discard the 6 RH exhaust manifold studs.

✳✳ WARNING

NEVER use metal scrapers, wire brushes, power abrasive discs or other abrasive means to clean the sealing surfaces. These may cause scratches and gouges resulting in leak paths. Use a plastic scraper to clean the sealing surfaces.

6. Clean the exhaust manifold mating surface of the cylinder head with metal surface prep. Follow the directions on the packaging.

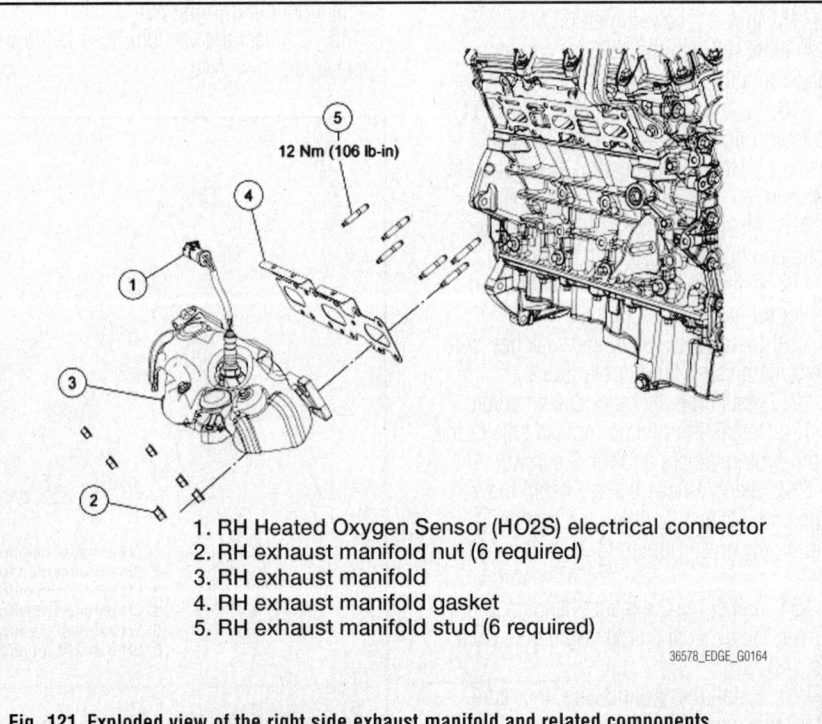

12 Nm (106 lb-in)

1. RH Heated Oxygen Sensor (HO2S) electrical connector
2. RH exhaust manifold nut (6 required)
3. RH exhaust manifold
4. RH exhaust manifold gasket
5. RH exhaust manifold stud (6 required)

Fig. 121 Exploded view of the right side exhaust manifold and related components

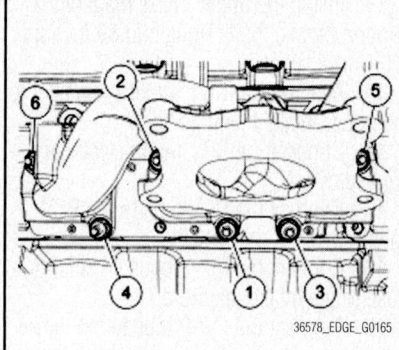

Fig. 122 Exhaust manifold tightening sequence—right side

To install:

7. Install 6 new RH exhaust manifold studs and tighten to 9 ft. lbs. (12 Nm).

➡**Failure to tighten the exhaust manifold nuts to specification a second time will cause the exhaust manifold to develop an exhaust leak.**

8. Using a new gasket, install the RH exhaust manifold and 6 new nuts. Tighten in the sequence shown to 15 ft. lbs. (20 Nm). Then tighten to 18 ft. lbs. (25 Nm).

9. Connect the RH HO2S electrical connector.

➡**When installing the catalytic converter, always install new fasteners and gaskets. Clean the flange faces prior to new gasket installation to ensure proper sealing.**

10. Install the right side catalytic converter, with new gaskets and nuts, in the reverse of the removal procedure. Tighten the retainers as follows:

a. Catalytic converter nuts: 30 ft. lbs. (40 Nm)

b. Bracket-to-RH catalytic converter bolts: 15 ft. lbs. (20 Nm)

c. Roll restrictor bolt: 66 ft. lbs. (90 Nm)

d. Roll restrictor shield: 8 ft. lbs. (11 Nm)

e. Catalytic converter support bracket-to-engine block bolt and nut (FWD models): 30 ft. lbs. (40 Nm)

f. Power steering rack shield (FWD models): 11 ft. lbs. (15 Nm)

g. Catalytic converter support bracket-to-engine block bolts (AWD models): 30 ft. lbs. (40 Nm)

h. U-joint flange bolts (AWD models): 52 ft. lbs. (70 Nm)

FLEXPLATE

REMOVAL & INSTALLATION

1. Raise and safely support the vehicle.
2. Remove the transaxle, as outlined in the Drive Train Section.
3. Remove the bolts and the flexplate.

➡**One of the 8 flexplate holes are offset so the flexplate can only be installed in one position.**

4. Installation is the reverse of the removal procedure. Tighten the flexplate bolts to 80 Nm (59 ft. lbs.).

INTAKE MANIFOLD

REMOVAL & INSTALLATION

Upper Intake Manifold

See Figures 123 through 125.

1. Disconnect the negative battery cable.
2. Remove the air cleaner outlet pipe.
3. Disconnect the throttle body electrical connector.
4. Disconnect the Evaporative Emissions (EVAP) tube from the intake manifold.
5. Disconnect the brake booster vacuum hose from the intake manifold.
6. Disconnect the Positive Crankcase Ventilation (PCV) tube from the PCV valve.
7. Disconnect the PCV fitting electrical connector.
8. Detach the wiring harness retainers from the upper intake manifold.
9. Remove the upper intake manifold support bracket bolt.
10. Remove the 6 bolts and remove the upper intake manifold.
11. Remove and discard the gaskets.

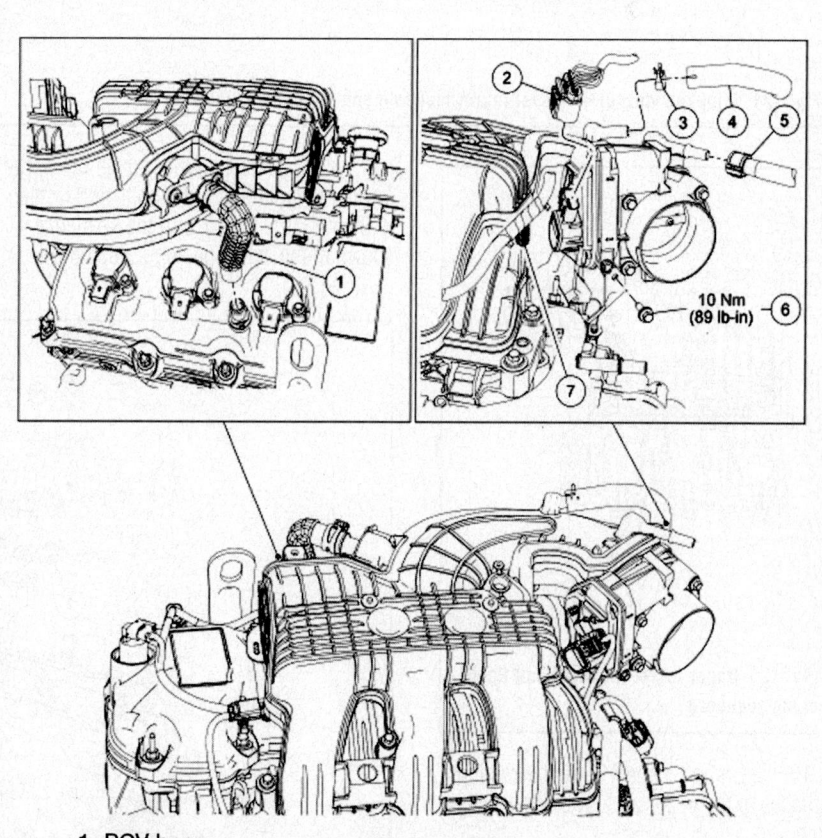

1. PCV hose
2. Throttle Body (TB) electrical connector
3. Brake booster-to-intake manifold vacuum hose clamp
4. Brake booster-to-intake manifold vacuum hose
5. Evaporative Emission (EVAP)-to-intake manifold tube
6. Upper intake manifold support bracket bolt
7. Engine control wiring harness retainer

Fig. 123 Installed view of the upper intake manifold and related components

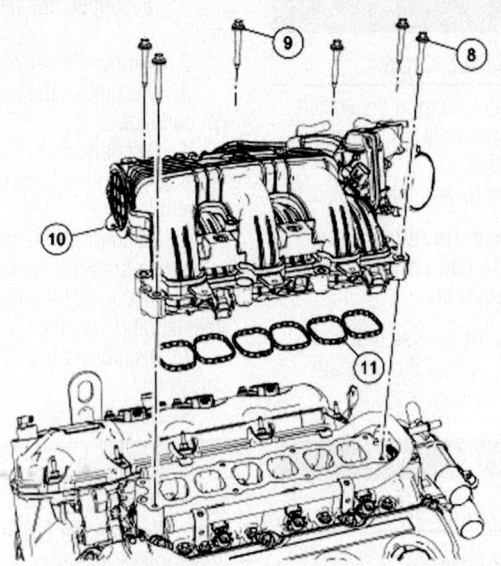

1. Upper intake manifold bolts (5 required)
2. Upper intake manifold bolt
3. Upper intake manifold
4. Upper intake manifold gasket (3 required)

36578_EDGE_G0167

Fig. 124 Exploded view of the upper intake manifold and related components

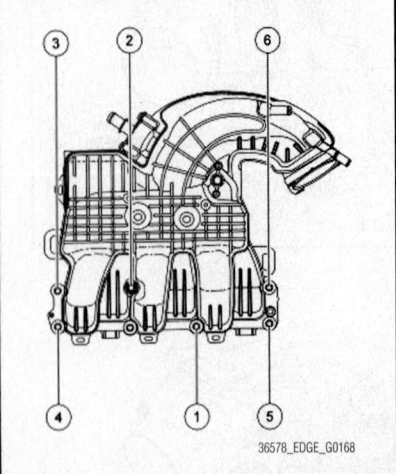

36578_EDGE_G0168

Fig. 125 Upper intake manifold bolt tightening sequence

12. Clean and inspect all of the sealing surfaces of the upper and lower intake manifold.

To install:

➡If the engine is repaired or replaced because of upper engine failure, typically including valve or piston damage, check the intake manifold for metal debris. If metal debris is found, install a new intake manifold. Failure to follow these instructions can result in engine damage.

13. Using new gaskets, install the upper intake manifold and the 6 bolts and tighten to 89 inch lbs. (10 Nm) in the sequence shown in the accompanying illustration.

14. Install the upper intake manifold support bracket bolt. Tighten to 89 inch lbs. (10 Nm).

15. Attach the wiring harness retainers to the upper intake manifold.

16. Connect the PCV fitting electrical connector.

17. Connect the PCV tube to the PCV valve.

18. Connect the brake booster vacuum hose to the intake manifold.

19. Connect the EVAP tube to the intake manifold.

20. Connect the throttle body electrical connector.

21. Install the air cleaner outlet pipe.

22. Connect the negative battery cable.

Lower Intake Manifold

See Figures 126 and 127.

✳✳ WARNING

During engine repair procedures, cleanliness is extremely important. Any foreign material, including any material created while cleaning gasket surfaces that enters the oil passages, coolant passages or the oil pan, can cause engine failure.

1. Raise and safely support the vehicle.

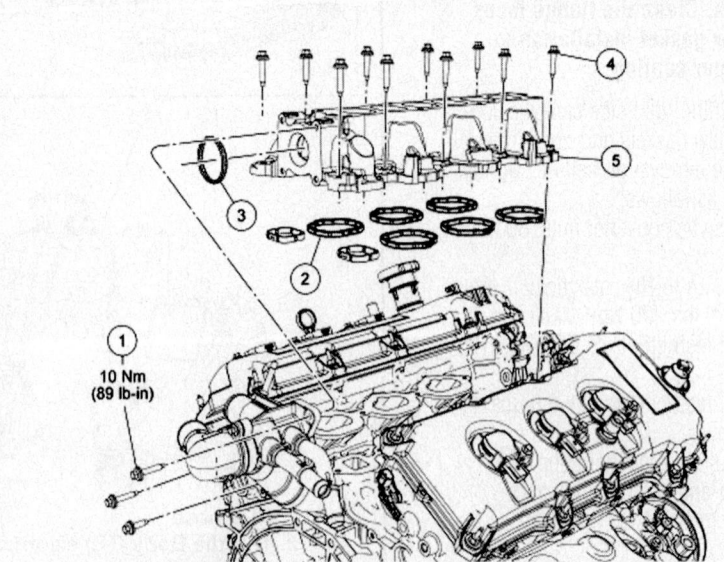

1. Thermostat housing-to-lower intake manifold bolt (3 required)
2. Lower intake manifold gasket (8 required)
3. Thermostat housing gasket
4. Lower intake manifold bolt (10 required)
5. Lower intake manifold

36578_EDGE_G0169

Fig. 126 Exploded view of the lower intake manifold and related components

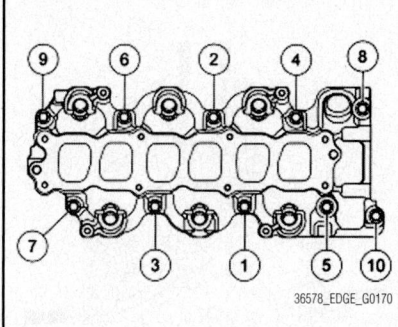

Fig. 127 Lower intake manifold bolt tightening sequence

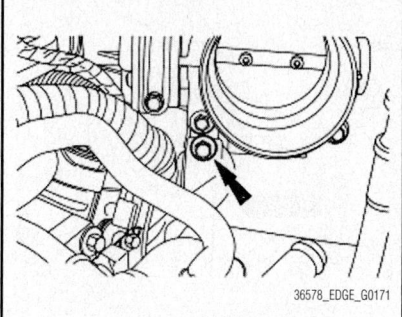

Fig. 128 Remove the upper intake manifold support bracket bolt

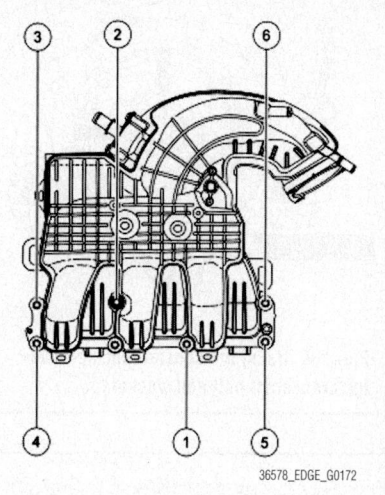

Fig. 129 Removing the 6 bolts and the upper intake manifold in sequence

2. Drain the cooling system.

3. Remove the fuel rail, as outlined in the Fuel System Section.

4. Remove the air cleaner assembly.

5. Remove the 3 thermostat housing-to-lower intake manifold bolts.

6. Unfasten the 10 bolts, then remove the lower intake manifold.

7. Remove and discard the intake manifold and thermostat housing gaskets.

8. Thoroughly clean and inspect all sealing surfaces.

To install:

➡ **If the engine is repaired or replaced because of upper engine failure, typically including valve or piston damage, check the intake manifold for metal debris. If metal debris is found, install a new intake manifold. Failure to follow these instructions can result in engine damage.**

9. Using new intake manifold and thermostat housing gaskets, install the lower intake manifold and the 10 bolts. Tighten to 89 inch lbs. (10 Nm) in the sequence shown in the accompanying illustration.

10. Install the 3 thermostat housing-to-lower intake manifold bolts. Tighten to 89 inch lbs. (10 Nm).

11. Install the air cleaner assembly.

12. Install the fuel rail.

13. Fill and bleed the cooling system.

OIL PAN

REMOVAL & INSTALLATION

See Figures 128 through 150.

➡ **This procedure requires engine removal, as well as a variety of specialized tools and equipment.**

➡ **During engine repair procedures, cleanliness is extremely important. Any foreign material, including any material created while cleaning gasket surfaces that enters the oil passages, coolant passages or the oil pan, can cause engine failure.**

1. Remove the engine from the vehicle, as outlined in this section.

2. Remove the 8 bolts and the flexplate.

3. Remove the crankshaft sensor ring.

⁂ **WARNING**

Install the engine stand bolts into the cylinder block only. Do not install the bolts into the oil pan.

4. Mount the engine on a suitable engine stand.

5. If equipped, remove the heat shield and disconnect the block heater electrical connector.

6. Detach all of the engine block heater harness retainers and remove the harness.

7. Disconnect the Positive Crankcase Ventilation (PCV) fitting electrical connector.

8. Disconnect the PCV hose from the PCV valve.

9. Disconnect the throttle body electrical connector.

10. Detach the wiring harness retainers from the upper intake manifold.

11. Remove the upper intake manifold support bracket bolt.

12. Remove the 6 bolts and the upper intake manifold in the sequence shown. Discard the gaskets.

13. Disconnect the Power Steering Pressure (PSP) switch electrical connector.

14. On Front Wheel Drive (FWD) vehicles, disconnect the RH catalyst monitor sensor electrical connector.

15. Disconnect the RH Variable Camshaft Timing (VCT) solenoid electrical connector.

16. Disconnect the 3 RH coil-on-plug electrical connectors.

17. Disconnect the heated PCV valve electrical connector.

18. Detach all of the wiring harness retainers from the RH valve cover and stud bolts.

19. Disconnect the LH catalyst monitor sensor electrical connector.

20. Disconnect the LH VCT solenoid electrical connector.

21. Disconnect the 3 LH coil-on-plug electrical connectors.

22. Detach all of the wiring harness retainers from the LH valve cover and stud bolts.

➡ **The A/C compressor must remain bolted to the engine block before installing the oil pan.**

23. Remove the A/C compressor nut and stud.

24. Remove the 3 bolts and the power steering pump.

25. Remove the 3 bolts and the accessory drive belt tensioner.

26. Remove the 4 nuts and the LH catalytic converter. Discard the nuts and the gasket.

27. On FWD vehicles, remove the 4 nuts and the RH catalytic converter. Discard the nuts and the gasket.

28. Remove the RH cylinder block drain plug or, if equipped, the block heater. Allow coolant to drain from the cylinder block into a suitable container.

29. Remove the LH cylinder block drain plug. Allow coolant to drain from the cylinder block into a suitable container.

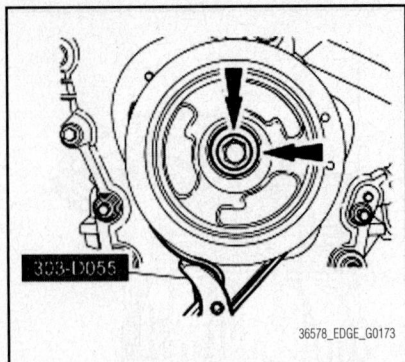

Fig. 130 Using the special tool, remove the crankshaft bolt and washer

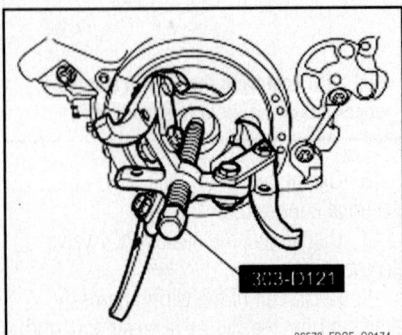

Fig. 131 Using the special tool, remove the crankshaft pulley

30. Remove the 6 bolts and the 6 coil-on-plugs.

31. Remove the 11 stud bolts and the LH valve cover. Discard the gasket.

32. Remove the bolt, the 10 stud bolts and the RH valve cover. Discard the gasket.

➡ **VCT solenoid seal removal shown, spark plug tube seal removal similar.**

33. Inspect the VCT solenoid seals and the spark plug tube seals. Remove any damaged seals.

   a. Using the special tools, remove the seal(s).

34. Using the special tool, remove the crankshaft bolt and washer. Discard the bolt.

35. Using the special tool, remove the crankshaft pulley.

36. Using the special tool, remove and discard the crankshaft front seal.

37. Remove the 2 bolts and the engine mount bracket.

➡ **Use only hand tools to remove the studs.**

38. Remove the 2 engine mount studs.

39. Remove the 3 bolts and the engine mount bracket.

40. Remove the 22 engine front cover bolts.

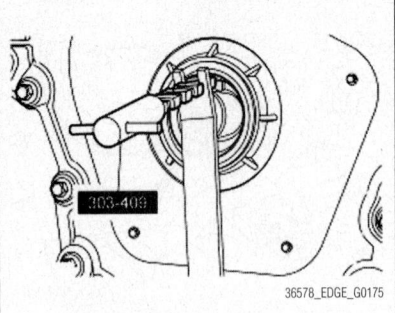

Fig. 132 Using the special tool, remove and discard the crankshaft front seal

41. Install 6 of the engine front cover bolts (finger tight) into the 6 threaded holes in the engine front cover. Tighten the bolts one turn at a time in a criss-cross pattern until the engine front cover-to-cylinder block seal is released.

42. Remove the engine front cover.

43. Remove the 16 oil pan bolts.

44. Install 2 of the oil pan bolts (finger tight) into the 2 threaded holes in the oil pan. Alternately tighten the 2 bolts one turn at a time until the oil pan-to-cylinder block seal is released. Remove the oil pan.

✳✳ WARNING

Only use a 3M Roloc® Bristle Disk, (2 inch, white, part number 07528) to clean the engine front cover and oil pan. Do not use metal scrapers, wire brushes or any other power abrasive disk to clean the crankshaft rear seal retainer plate. These tools cause scratches and gouges that make leak paths.

45. Clean the engine front cover and oil pan using a 3M Roloc® Bristle Disk, (2 inch, white, part number 07528) in a suit-

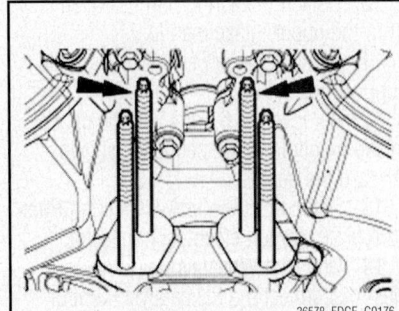

Fig. 133 Remove the 2 engine mount studs (arrows)

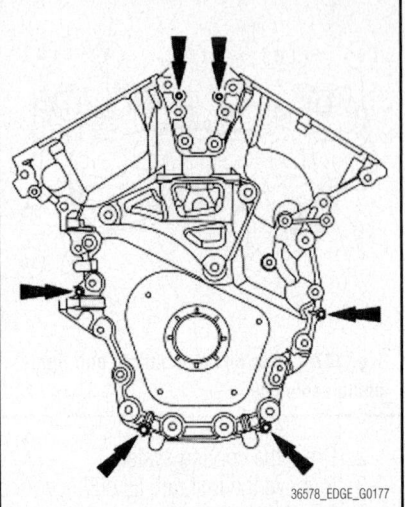

Fig. 134 Install 6 of the engine front cover bolts (finger tight) into the 6 threaded holes in the engine front cover. Tighten the bolts one turn at a time in a criss-cross pattern until the engine front cover-to-cylinder block seal is released

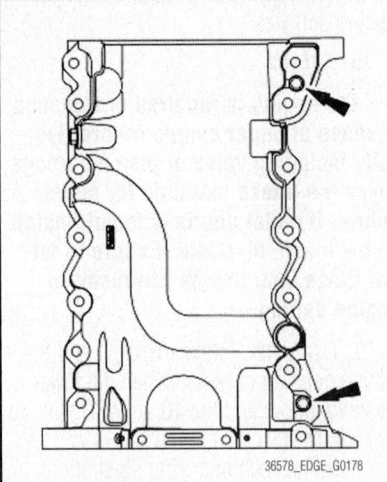

Fig. 135 Installing 2 of the oil pan bolts (finger tight)

able tool turning at the recommended speed of 15,000 rpm.

46. Thoroughly wash the engine front cover and oil pan to remove any foreign material, including any abrasive particles created during the cleaning process.

✳✳ WARNING

Place clean, lint free shop towels over all exposed engine cavities. Carefully remove the towels so foreign material is not dropped into the

engine. Any foreign material (including any material created while cleaning gasket surfaces) that enters the oil passages or the oil pan, can cause engine failure.

✳✳ WARNING

Do not use metal scrapers, wire brushes, power abrasive discs or other abrasive means to clean the sealing surfaces. These tools cause scratches and gouges that make leak paths. Use a plastic scraping tool to remove all traces of sealant.

✳✳ WARNING

Observe all warnings or cautions and follow all application directions contained on the packaging of the silicone gasket remover and the metal surface prep.

47. Clean the sealing surfaces of the cylinder block.

48. Remove any large deposits of silicone or gasket material with a plastic scraper.

49. Apply silicone gasket remover, following package directions, and allow to set for several minutes. Remove the silicone gasket remover with a plastic scraper. A second application of silicone gasket remover may be required if residual traces of silicone or gasket material remain.

50. Apply metal surface prep, following package directions, to remove any remaining traces of oil or coolant and to prepare the surfaces to bond. Do not attempt to make the metal shiny. Some staining of the metal surfaces is normal.

51. Make sure the 2 locating dowel pins are seated correctly in the cylinder block.

To install:

✳✳ WARNING

Failure to use the correct RTV Silicone Sealant (TA-357) may cause the engine oil to foam excessively and result in serious engine damage.

➡The oil pan and the 4 specified bolts must be installed and the oil pan aligned to the cylinder block and A/C compressor within 4 minutes of sealant application. Final tightening of the oil pan bolts must be carried out within 60 minutes of sealant application.

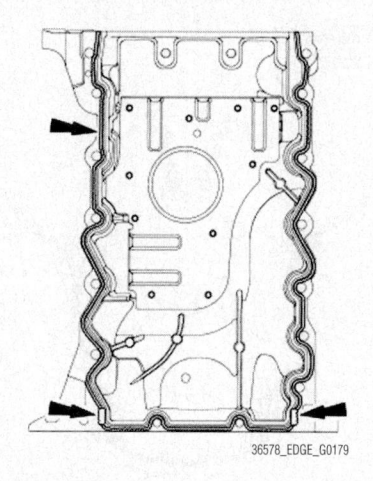

Fig. 136 Silicone sealant locations on the oil pan

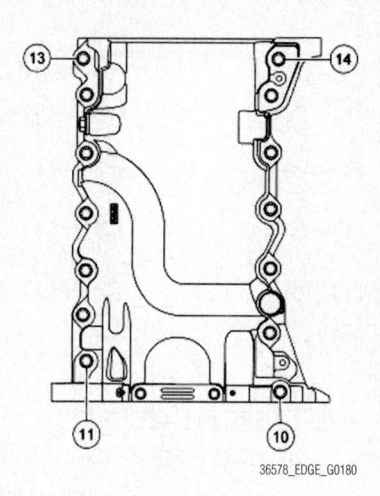

Fig. 137 Location of oil pan bolts 10, 11, 13 and 14

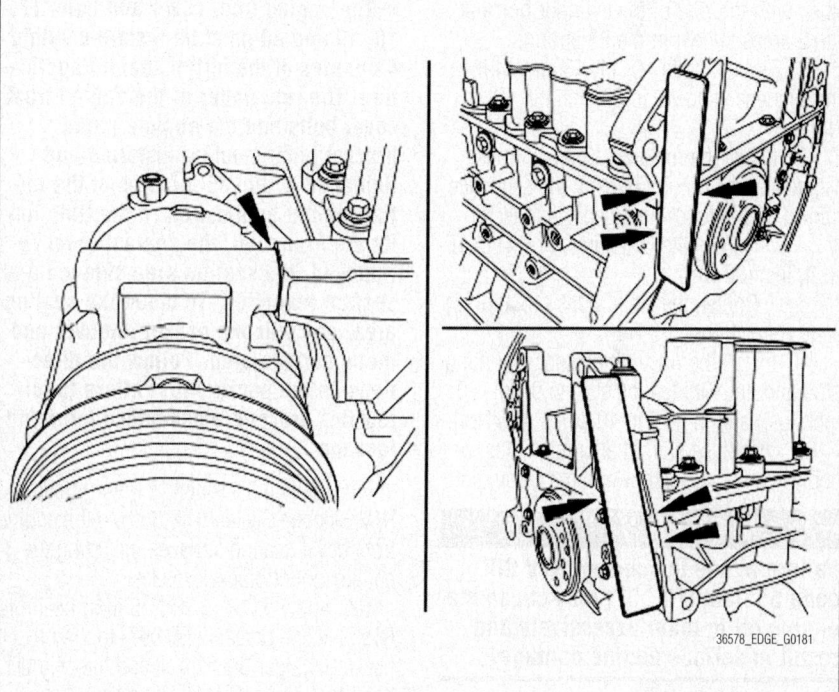

Fig. 138 Position the oil pan so the mounting boss is against the A/C compressor and using a straightedge, align the oil pan flush with the rear of the cylinder block at the 2 areas shown

52. Apply a 0.11 inch (3 mm) bead of RTV Silicone Sealant (TA-357) to the sealing surface of the oil pan.

53. Apply a 0.21 in (5.5 mm) bead of RTV Silicone Sealant (TA-357) to the 2 crankshaft seal retainer plate-to-cylinder block joint areas on the sealing surface of the oil pan.

➡The oil pan and the 4 specified bolts must be installed within 4 minutes of the start of sealant application.

54. Install the oil pan and bolts 10, 11, 13 and 14, as shown in the accompanying illustration. Tighten the bolts in the sequence shown to 27 inch lbs. (3 Nm) Loosen the bolts 180 degrees.

55. Align the oil pan to the cylinder block and the A/C compressor.

56. Position the oil pan so the mounting boss is against the A/C compressor and using a straightedge, align the oil pan

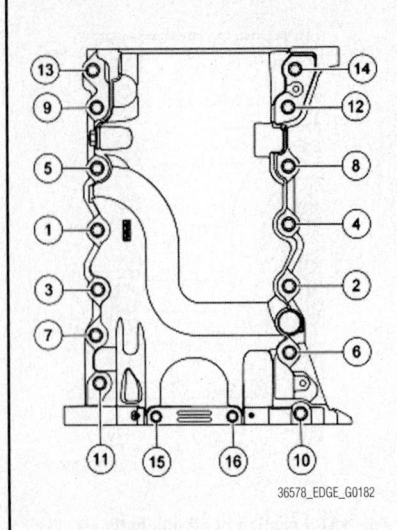

Fig. 139 Oil pan bolt locations and tightening sequence

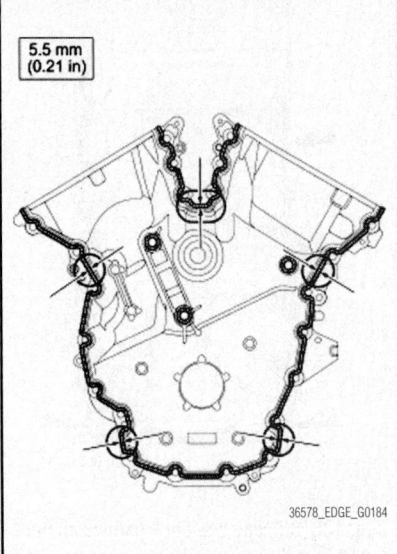

Fig. 141 Front cover sealant application locations

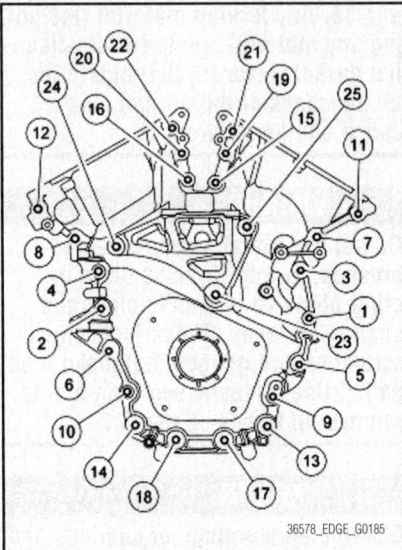

Fig. 142 Front cover bolt locations and tightening sequence

flush with the rear of the cylinder block at the 2 areas shown in the illustration.

57. Tighten bolts 10, 11, 13 and 14 in the sequence shown, to 27 inch lbs. (3 Nm).

58. Install the remaining oil pan bolts. Tighten all the oil pan bolts in the sequence shown, to the following specifications:

    a. Tighten the large bolts (1-14) to 15 ft. lbs. (20 Nm).

    b. Tighten the small bolts (15 and 16) to 89 inch lbs. (10 Nm).

59. Install the A/C compressor mounting stud and nut. Tighten the stud to 9 Nm (80 inch lbs.) and the nut to 18 ft. lbs. (25 Nm).

60. Install the special alignment pins, or equivalent tools, as shown in the illustration.

✸✸ WARNING

Failure to use the correct RTV Silicone Sealant (TA-357) may cause the engine oil to foam excessively and result in serious engine damage.

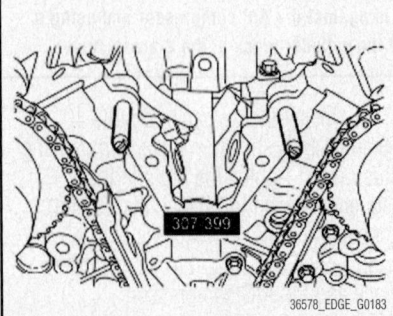

Fig. 140 Install the alignment pins, or equivalent special tools as shown

➡️**The engine front cover and bolts 17, 18, 19 and 20 must be installed within 4 minutes of the initial sealant application. The remainder of the engine front cover bolts and the engine mount bracket bolts must be installed and tightened within 35 minutes of the initial sealant application. If the time limits are exceeded, the sealant must be removed, the sealing area cleaned and sealant reapplied. To clean the sealing area, use silicone gasket remover and metal surface prep. Follow the directions on the packaging. Failure to follow this procedure can cause future oil leakage.**

61. Apply a 0.11 inch (3.0 mm) bead of RTV Silicone Sealant (TA-357) to the engine front cover sealing surfaces including the 3 engine mount bracket bosses.

62. Apply a 0.21 inch (5.5 mm) bead of RTV Silicone Sealant (TA-357) to the oil pan-to-cylinder block joint and the cylinder head-to-cylinder block joint areas of the engine front cover in 5 places as indicated.

➡️**Make sure the 2 locating dowel pins are seated correctly in the cylinder block.**

63. Install the engine front cover and bolts 17, 18, 19 and 20. Tighten in sequence to 27 inch lbs. (3 Nm).

64. Remove the special tools (alignment pins).

➡️**Do not tighten the bolt at this time.**

65. Install the engine mount bracket and the 3 bolts.

✸✸ WARNING

Do not expose the RTV Silicone Sealant (TA-357) to engine oil for at least 90 minutes after installing the engine front cover. Failure to follow this instruction may cause oil leakage.

66. Install the remaining engine front cover bolts. Tighten all of the engine front cover bolts and engine mount bracket bolts in the sequence shown in 2 steps:

    a. Step 1: Tighten bolts 1 thru 22 to 89 inch lbs. (10 Nm) and bolts 23, 24 and 25 to 11 ft. lbs. (15 Nm).

    b. Step 2: Tighten bolts 1 thru 22 to 18 ft. lbs. (24 Nm) and bolts 23, 24 and 25 to 55 ft. lbs. (75 Nm).

➡️**The thread sealer on the engine mount studs (including new engine mount studs if applicable) must be cleaned off with a wire brush and new thread sealer applied prior to installing the engine mount studs. Failure to follow this procedure may result in damage to the engine mount studs or engine.**

67. Install the engine mount studs in the following sequence:

    a. Clean the front cover engine mount stud holes with pressurized air to remove any foreign material.

    b. Clean all the threaded sealer from the engine mount studs (old and new studs).

    c. Apply new thread sealer to the engine mount stud threads.

    d. Install the 2 engine mount studs and tighten to 15 ft. lbs. (20 Nm).

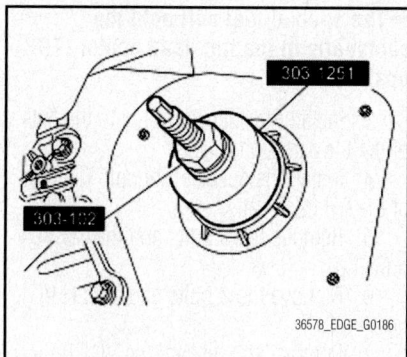

Fig. 143 Using the special tools, install a new crankshaft front seal

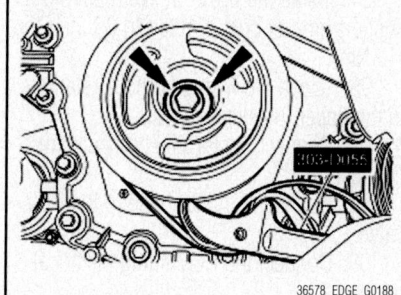

Fig. 145 Using the special tool, install the crankshaft pulley washer and new bolt and tighten in 4 steps

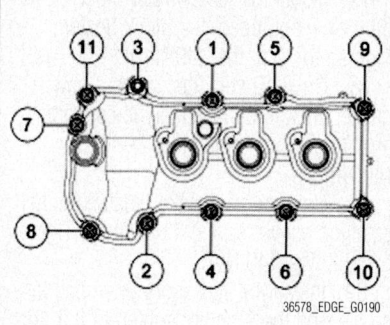

Fig. 147 Right side valve cover bolt tightening sequence

68. Install the engine mount bracket and the 2 bolts. Tighten to 22 ft. lbs. (30 Nm).

➡**Apply clean engine oil to the crankshaft front seal bore in the engine front cover.**

69. Using the special tools, install a new crankshaft front seal.

➡**Lubricate the outside diameter sealing surfaces with clean engine oil.**

70. Using the special tools, install the crankshaft pulley.

71. Using the special tool, install the crankshaft pulley washer and new bolt and tighten in 4 steps.

    a. Step 1: Tighten to 89 ft. lbs. (120 Nm).

    b. Step 2: Loosen one full turn.

    c. Step 3: Tighten to 37 ft. lbs. (50 Nm).

    d. Step 4: Tighten an additional 90 degrees.

➡**Installation of new seals is only required if damaged seals were removed during disassembly of the engine.**

72. Using the special tools, install new VCT solenoid and/or spark plug tube seals.

✳✳ WARNING

Failure to use the correct RTV Silicone Sealant (TA-357) may cause the engine oil to foam excessively and result in serious engine damage.

➡**If the valve cover is not installed and the fasteners tightened within 4 minutes, the sealant must be removed and the sealing area cleaned. To clean the sealing area, use silicone gasket remover and metal surface prep. Follow the directions on the packaging. Failure to follow this procedure can cause future oil leakage.**

73. Apply a 0.31 inch (8 mm) bead of RTV Silicone Sealant (TA-357) to the engine front cover-to-RH cylinder head joints.

74. Using a new gasket, install the RH valve cover, bolt and the 10 stud bolts. Tighten in the sequence shown to 89 inch lbs. (10 Nm).

75. Apply a 8 mm (0.31 in) bead of RTV Silicone Sealant (TA-357) to the engine front cover-to-LH cylinder head joints.

76. Using a new gasket, install the LH valve cover and 11 stud bolts. Tighten in the sequence shown to 10 Nm (89 inch lbs.).

77. Install the 6 coil-on-plug assemblies and the 6 bolts. Tighten to 62 inch lbs. (7 Nm).

78. Install the LH cylinder block drain plug. Tighten to 15 ft. lbs. (20 Nm) plus an additional 180 degrees.

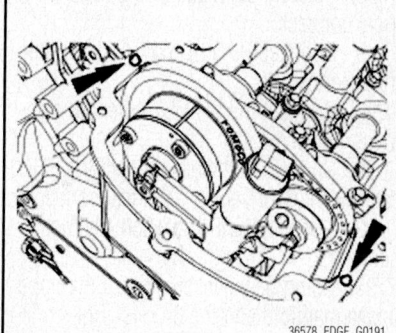

Fig. 148 Apply a 0.31 inch (8mm) bead of RTV Silicone Sealant (TA-357, or equivalent) to the engine front cover-to-LH cylinder head joints

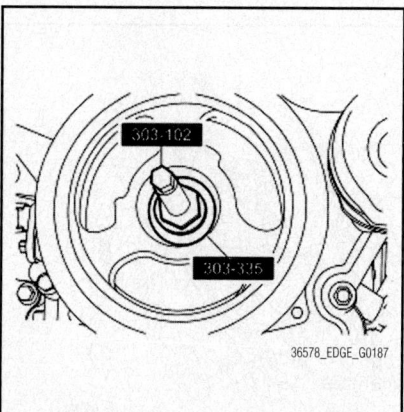

Fig. 144 Using the special tools, install the crankshaft pulley

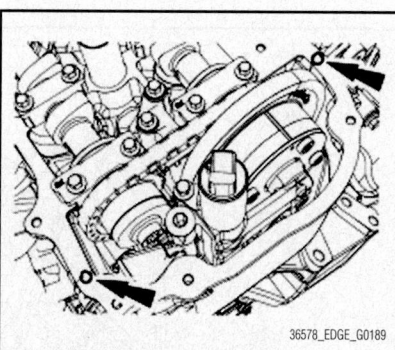

Fig. 146 Apply an 0.31 inch (8mm) bead of RTV Silicone Sealant (TA-357) to the engine front cover-to-RH cylinder head joints

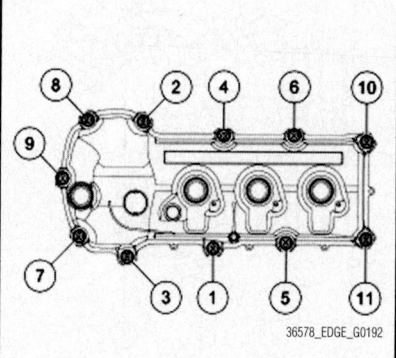

Fig. 149 Left side valve cover bolt tightening sequence

79. Install the RH cylinder block drain plug or, if equipped, the block heater. Tighten to 30 ft. lbs. (40 Nm).

80. On FWD vehicles, using a new gasket, install the RH catalytic converter and 4 new nuts. Tighten to 30 ft. lbs. (40 Nm).

81. Using a new gasket, install the LH catalytic converter and 4 new nuts. Tighten to 30 ft. lbs. (40 Nm).

82. Install the accessory drive belt tensioner and the 3 bolts. Tighten to 8 ft. lbs. (11 Nm).

83. Install the power steering pump and the 3 bolts. Tighten to 18 ft. lbs. (24 Nm).

84. Attach all of the wiring harness retainers to the LH valve cover and stud bolts. Connect the 3 LH coil-on-plug electrical connectors.

85. Connect the LH camshaft VCT solenoid electrical connector.

86. Connect the LH catalyst monitor sensor electrical connector.

87. Attach all of the wiring harness retainers to the RH valve cover and stud bolts.

88. Connect the heated PCV valve electrical connector.

89. Connect the 3 RH coil-on-plug electrical connectors.

90. Connect the RH VCT solenoid electrical connector.

91. On FWD vehicles, connect the RH catalyst monitor sensor electrical connector.

92. Connect the PSP switch electrical connector.

93. Using new gaskets, install the upper intake manifold and the 6 bolts. Tighten in the sequence shown to 89 inch lbs. (10 Nm).

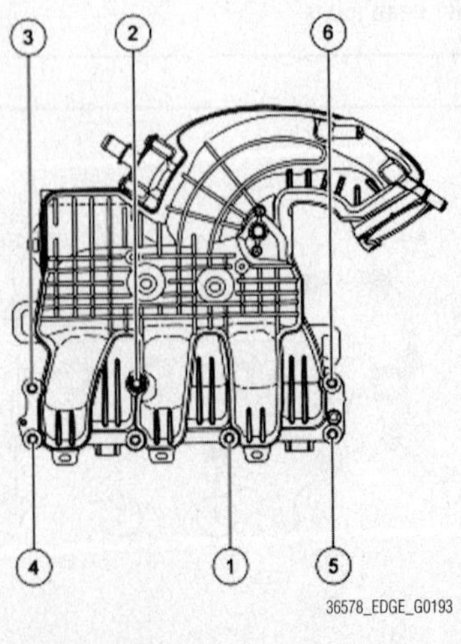

94. Install the upper intake manifold support bracket bolt. Tighten to 89 inch lbs. (10 Nm).

95. Attach the wiring harness retainers to the upper intake manifold.

96. Connect the throttle body electrical connector.

97. Connect the PCV hose to the PCV valve.

98. Connect the PCV fitting electrical connector.

99. If equipped, position the engine block heater harness on the engine and attach all of the harness retainers.

100. Connect the engine block heater electrical connector and install the heat shield.

101. Remove the engine from the stand.

102. Install the crankshaft sensor ring.

103. Install the flexplate and the 8 bolts. Tighten to 59 ft. lbs. (80 Nm).

104. Install the engine in the vehicle, as outlined in this section.

OIL PUMP

REMOVAL & INSTALLATION
See Figures 151 through 153.

✳✳ WARNING

During engine repair procedures, cleanliness is extremely important. Any foreign material, including any material created while cleaning gasket surfaces, that enters the oil passages, coolant passages or the oil pan may cause engine failure.

1. Remove the engine front cover, as outlined in this section.

2. Rotate the crankshaft clockwise and align the timing marks on the Variable Camshaft Timing (VCT) assemblies as shown.

➡**The special tool will hold the camshafts in the top dead center (TDC) position.**

3. Install the special tool onto the flats of the LH camshafts.

4. Install the special tool onto the flats of the RH camshafts.

5. Remove the 3 bolts and the RH VCT housing.

6. Remove the 3 bolts and the LH VCT housing.

7. Remove and discard the VCT housing seals.

8. Remove the 2 bolts and the primary timing chain tensioner.

9. Remove the primary timing chain tensioner arm.

10. Remove the 2 bolts and the lower LH primary timing chain guide.

11. Remove the primary timing chain. For more information, refer to the Timing Chain procedure in this section.

12. Remove the crankshaft timing chain sprocket.

13. Remove the 2 oil pump screen and pickup tube bolts.

14. Remove the 3 oil pump bolts. Rotate the oil pump clockwise and separate the oil pump from the oil pump screen and pickup tube. Remove the oil pump. Discard the oil pump screen and pickup tube O-ring seal.

To install:

➡**Install a new oil pump screen and pickup tube O-ring seal before installing the oil pump.**

15. Position the oil pump onto the crankshaft and rotate counterclockwise to position the pump onto the oil pump screen and pickup tube. Install the 3 bolts and tighten to 89 inch lbs. (10 Nm)

16. Install the 2 oil pump screen and pickup tube bolts. Tighten to 89 inch lbs. (10 Nm)

36578_EDGE_G0193

Fig. 150 Upper intake manifold bolt tightening sequence

36578_EDGE_G0085

Fig. 151 Aligning timing marks on the VCT assemblies

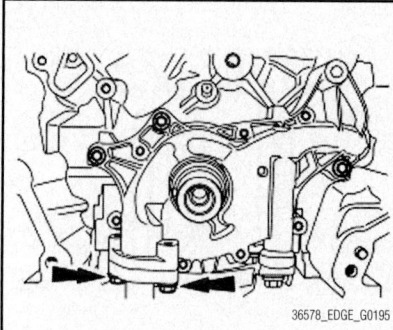

Fig. 152 Remove the 2 oil pump screen and pickup tube bolts

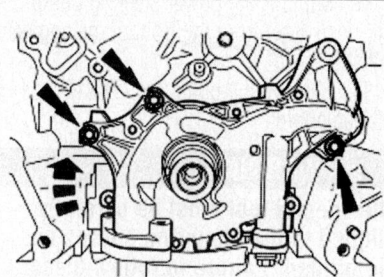

Fig. 153 Remove the 3 oil pump bolts. Rotate the oil pump clockwise and separate the oil pump from the oil pump screen and pickup tube. Remove the oil pump. Discard the oil pump screen and pickup tube O-ring seal

17. Install the crankshaft timing chain sprocket.

18. Install the primary timing chain with the colored links aligned with the timing marks on the VCT assemblies and the crankshaft sprocket.

19. Install the LH primary timing chain guide and the 2 bolts. Tighten to 89 inch lbs. (10 Nm)

20. Install the primary timing chain tensioner arm.

21. Reset the primary timing chain tensioner, as follows:

    a. Rotate the lever counterclockwise.

    b. Using a soft-jawed vise, compress the plunger.

    c. Align the hole in the lever with the hole in the tensioner housing.

    d. Install a suitable lockpin.

➡It may be necessary to rotate the crankshaft slightly to remove slack from the timing chain and install the tensioner.

    e. Install the primary tensioner and the 2 bolts. Tighten to 10 Nm (89 inch lbs.).

    f. Remove the lock pin.

22. As a post-check, verify correct alignment of all timing marks.

23. Install new VCT housing seals.

※ WARNING

Make sure the dowels on the variable camshaft timing (VCT) housing are fully engaged in the cylinder head prior to tightening the bolts. Failure to follow this process will result in severe engine damage.

24. Install the LH VCT housing and the 3 bolts. Tighten in the sequence shown to 10 Nm (89 inch lbs.).

※ WARNING

Make sure the dowels on the VCT housing are fully engaged in the cylinder head prior to tightening the bolts.

25. Install the RH VCT housing and the 3 bolts. Tighten in the sequence shown to 89 inch lbs. (10 Nm)

26. Install the engine front cover, as outlined in this section.

REAR MAIN SEAL

REMOVAL & INSTALLATION

See Figures 154 through 156.

➡This procedure requires the use of the following special tools, or their equivalents:

- Handle 205-153 (T80T-4000-W)
- Crankshaft Rear Seal Installer 303-1250
- Crankshaft Rear Seal Remover 303-519 (T95P-6701-EH)
- Slide Hammer 307-005 (T59L-100-B)

1. Raise and safely support the vehicle.
2. Remove the flexplate, as outlined in this section.

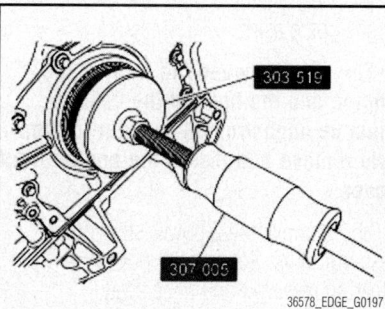

Fig. 154 Using the special tools shown in the illustration, remove and discard the crankshaft rear seal

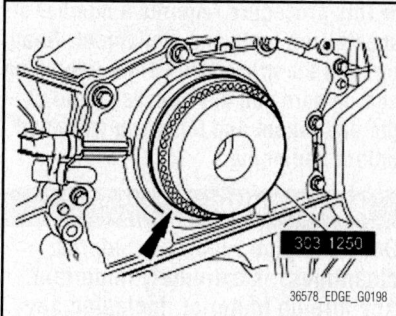

Fig. 155 Position the special tool onto the end of the crankshaft and slide a new crankshaft rear seal onto the tool

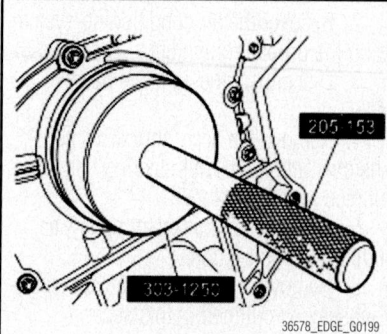

Fig. 156 Using the special tools, install the new crankshaft rear seal

3. Remove the crankshaft sensor ring.

4. Using the special tools shown in the illustration, remove and discard the crankshaft rear seal.

5. Clean all sealing surfaces with metal surface cleaner.

To install:

➡Lubricate the seal lips and bore with clean engine oil prior to installation.

6. Position the special tool onto the end of the crankshaft and slide a new crankshaft rear seal onto the tool.

7. Using the special tools, install the new crankshaft rear seal.

8. Install the crankshaft sensor ring.

9. Install the flexplate, as outlined in this section.

TIMING CHAIN COVER AND SEAL

REMOVAL & INSTALLATION

See Figures 157 through 162.

➡The Timing Chain Cover is also often referred to as the Engine Front Cover.

➡This procedure requires a number of specialized tools and equipment. Read through the procedure before beginning and be sure you have access to all of the equipment and tools you will need before beginning.

✳✳ WARNING

During engine repair procedures, cleanliness is extremely important. Any foreign material, including any material created while cleaning gasket surfaces that enters the oil passages, coolant passages or the oil pan, may cause engine failure.

1. Raise and safely support the vehicle.
2. Recover the air conditioning system, using the proper equipment.
3. Disconnect the negative battery cable.
4. Remove the accessory drive belt, tensioner and the power steering belt, as outlined in this section.
5. Remove the crankshaft pulley, as outlined in this section.
6. Remove and discard the crankshaft front seal, as outlined in this section.
7. Loosen the exhaust flexible pipe clamp and disconnect the 2 exhaust hangers.
8. Remove the 4 nuts, the exhaust flexible pipe and the Y-pipe as an assembly. Discard the nuts and the gasket.
9. Remove the 2 nuts and the roll restrictor heat shield.
10. Remove the roll restrictor through bolt and the 2 roll restrictor-to-transaxle bracket plate bolts.
11. Loosen the roll restrictor-to-subframe through bolt.
12. Position the roll restrictor and transaxle bracket plate aside.
13. Remove the 3 bolts and the transaxle bracket.
14. Remove and discard the RH front halfshaft nut.
15. Remove the RH stabilizer link-to-lower control arm nut.
16. Remove the RH lower control arm-to-knuckle pinch bolt.
17. Separate the lower control arm from the knuckle.
18. Using a suitable front hub removal tool, separate the RH halfshaft from the hub.
19. Using the special tools, separate the RH halfshaft from the intermediate shaft. Remove the RH halfshaft.
20. Remove the drain plug and drain the engine oil. Install the drain plug and tighten to 20 ft. lbs. (27 Nm)
21. If equipped, detach the engine block heater harness from the radiator support,

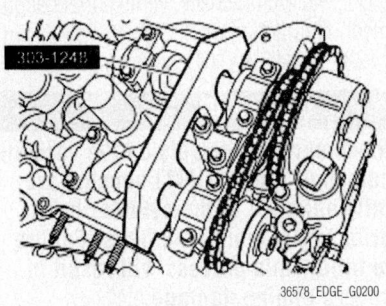

Fig. 157 Using the special tools, separate the RH halfshaft from the intermediate shaft. Remove the RH halfshaft

the A/C suction tube and the engine wiring harness.
22. Remove the engine air cleaner and air cleaner outlet pipe.
23. Remove the LH and RH valve covers, as outlined in this section.
24. Remove the safety clip from the A/C suction tube fitting.
25. Disconnect the A/C suction tube fitting and position the tube aside.
26. Remove the A/C pressure tube bracket bolt.
27. Remove the nut and disconnect the A/C pressure tube fitting. Discard the O-ring seal. Position the A/C pressure tube aside.
28. Disconnect the 2 engine wiring harness connectors.
29. Remove the bolt and the ground wire from the engine front cover.
30. Remove the nut, the ground wire and the radio interference capacitor wire from the engine front cover stud.
31. Remove the nut, the ground wire and the radio interference capacitor from the cowl stud.
32. Disconnect the purge valve electrical connector.
33. Disconnect the 3 Powertrain Control Module (PCM) electrical connectors and position the wiring harness aside.
34. Remove the 3 bolts and position the degas bottle aside.

➡The area between the front of the engine and the body of the vehicle must be unobstructed in order to properly remove and install the engine front cover.

35. Remove the 2 power steering reservoir nuts. Support the power steering reservoir and hose away from the front of the engine with a piece of wire.
36. Remove the 3 power steering pump bolts.

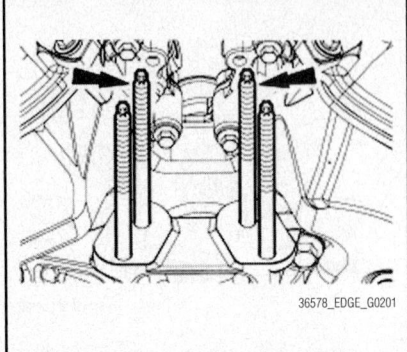

Fig. 158 Remove the 2 engine mount studs (arrows)

37. Support the power steering pump and hose away from the front of the engine with a piece of wire.
38. Remove the bolts, the LH and the RH VCT solenoids.

✳✳ WARNING

The special tool must be carefully aligned to the mounting bosses on the oil pan. Failure to follow these instructions may result in damage to the oil pan.

➡The special tool and floor jack are used to raise and lower the engine to access the engine front cover and engine mount bracket fasteners.

39. Position a floor jack and the special tool under the oil pan.

✳✳ WARNING

The transaxle through bolt must be loosened prior to removing the engine mount and lowering the front of the engine. Failure to follow these instructions may cause internal damage to the hydraulic transaxle mount and possible fluid leakage.

40. Loosen the transaxle mount through bolt.
41. Remove the nut, bolt and engine mount brace.
42. Remove the 4 engine mount nuts.
43. Remove the 3 bolts and the engine mount.
44. Remove the 2 bolts and the engine mount bracket.
45. Remove the 2 engine mount studs.
46. Remove the 2 upper engine mount bracket bolts.
47. Lower the engine to access the lower engine mount bracket bolt.
48. Loosen the lower engine mount bracket bolt and remove the engine mount bracket and bolt as an assembly.

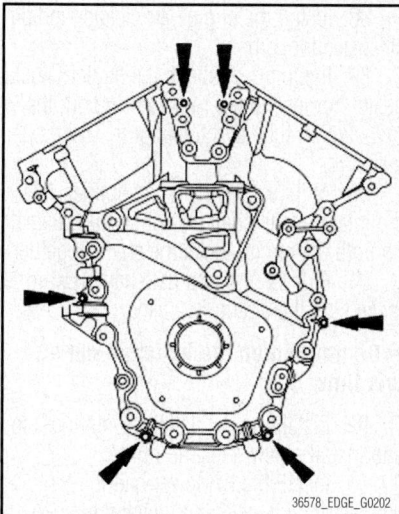

Fig. 159 Install 6 of the engine front cover bolts (finger tight) into the 6 threaded holes in the engine front cover. Tighten the bolts one turn at a time in a criss-cross pattern until the engine front cover-to-cylinder block seal is released

49. Remove the 22 engine front cover bolts.

50. Install 6 of the engine front cover bolts (finger tight) into the 6 threaded holes in the engine front cover. Tighten the bolts one turn at a time in a criss-cross pattern until the engine front cover-to-cylinder block seal is released. Remove the engine front cover.

To install:

51. Raise the engine to the installed position.

> ⁕⁕ **WARNING**
>
> **Only use a 3M Roloc® Bristle Disk, (2 inch, white, part number 07528) to clean the engine front cover. Do not use metal scrapers, wire brushes or any other power abrasive disk to clean the engine front cover. These tools cause scratches and gouges that make leak paths.**

52. Clean the engine front cover using a 3M Roloc® Bristle Disk, (2 inch, white, part number 07528) in a suitable tool turning at the recommended speed of 15,000 rpm.

53. Thoroughly wash the engine front cover to remove any foreign material, including any abrasive particles created during the cleaning process.

> ⁕⁕ **WARNING**
>
> **Place clean, lint-free shop towels over exposed engine cavities. Care-**

fully remove the towels so foreign material is not dropped into the engine. Any foreign material (including any material created while cleaning gasket surfaces) that enters the oil passages or the oil pan, can cause engine failure.

> ⁕⁕ **WARNING**
>
> **NEVER use metal scrapers, wire brushes, power abrasive discs or other abrasive means to clean the sealing surfaces. These tools cause scratches and gouges that make leak paths. Use a plastic scraping tool to remove all traces of sealant, including any sealant from the inner surface of the cylinder block and cylinder head.**

➡ Observe all warnings or cautions and follow all application directions contained on the packaging of the silicone gasket remover and the metal surface prep.

54. Clean the sealing surfaces of the cylinder heads, the cylinder block and the oil pan. Remove any large deposits of silicone or gasket material with a plastic scraper.

55. Apply silicone gasket remover, following package directions and allow to set for several minutes. Remove the silicone gasket remover with a plastic scraper. A second application of silicone gasket remover may be required if residual traces of silicone or gasket material remain.

56. Apply metal surface prep, following package directions, to remove any remaining traces of oil or coolant and to prepare the surfaces to bond. Do not attempt to make the metal shiny. Some staining of the metal surfaces is normal.

57. Make sure the 2 locating dowel pins are seated correctly in the cylinder block.

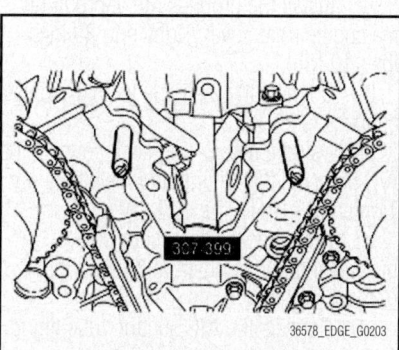

Fig. 160 Install the alignment pins, or equivalent special tools as shown

58. Install the special alignment pins, or equivalent tools, as shown in the illustration.

> ⁕⁕ **WARNING**
>
> **Failure to use the correct RTV Silicone Sealant (TA-357) may cause the engine oil to foam excessively and result in serious engine damage.**

➡ The engine front cover and bolts 17, 18, 19 and 20 must be installed within 4 minutes of the initial sealant application. The remainder of the engine front cover bolts and the engine mount bracket bolts must be installed and tightened within 35 minutes of the initial sealant application. If the time limits are exceeded, the sealant must be removed, the sealing area cleaned and sealant reapplied. To clean the sealing area, use silicone gasket remover and metal surface prep. Follow the directions on the packaging. Failure to follow this procedure can cause future oil leakage.

59. Apply a 0.11 inch (3.0 mm) bead of RTV Silicone Sealant (TA-357) to the engine front cover sealing surfaces including the 3 engine mount bracket bosses.

60. Apply a 0.21 inch (5.5 mm) bead of RTV Silicone Sealant (TA-357) to the oil pan-to-cylinder block joint and the cylinder head-to-cylinder block joint areas of the engine front cover in 5 places as indicated.

➡ Make sure the 2 locating dowel pins are seated correctly in the cylinder block.

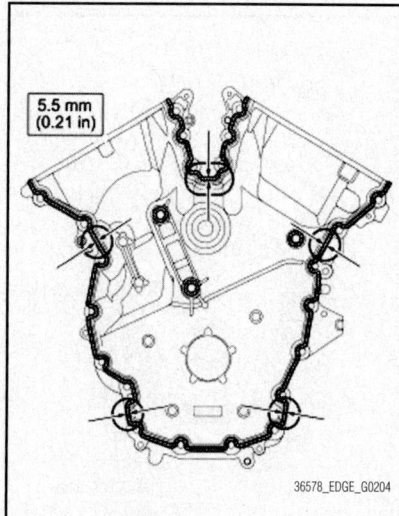

Fig. 161 Front cover sealant application locations

61. Install the engine front cover and bolts 17, 18, 19 and 20. Tighten in sequence to 27 inch lbs. (3 Nm).

62. Remove the special tools (alignment pins).

➡**Do not tighten the bolt at this time.**

63. Lower the engine to allow installation of the engine mount bracket and lower bolt.

64. Install the engine mount bracket and lower bolt as an assembly.

➡**Do not tighten the bolts at this time.**

65. Raise the engine to the installed position.

66. Install the 2 upper engine mount bracket bolts.

✲✲ WARNING

Do not expose the RTV Silicone Sealant (TA-357) to engine oil for at least 90 minutes after installing the engine front cover. Failure to follow this instruction may cause oil leakage.

67. Install the remaining engine front cover bolts. Tighten all of the engine front cover bolts and engine mount bracket bolts in the sequence shown in 2 steps:

    a. Step 1: Tighten bolts 1 thru 22 to 89 inch lbs. (10 Nm) and bolts 23, 24 and 25 to 11 ft. lbs. (15 Nm).

    b. Step 2: Tighten bolts 1 thru 22 to 18 ft. lbs. (24 Nm) and bolts 23, 24 and 25 to 55 ft. lbs. (75 Nm).

➡**The thread sealer on the engine mount studs (including new engine mount studs if applicable) must be cleaned off with a**

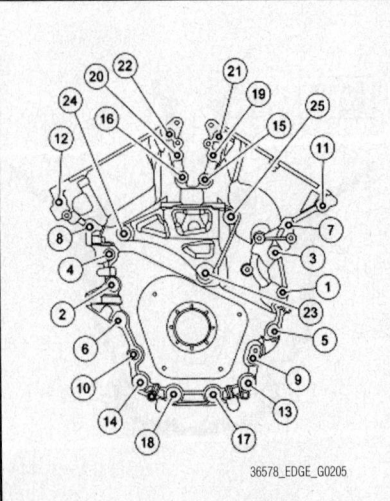

Fig. 162 Front cover bolt locations and tightening sequence

36578_EDGE_G0205

wire brush and new thread sealer applied prior to installing the engine mount studs. Failure to follow this procedure may result in damage to the engine mount studs or engine.

68. Install the 2 engine mount studs in the following sequence:

    a. Clean the front cover engine mount stud holes with pressurized air to remove any foreign material.

    b. Clean all the thread sealer from the engine mount studs (old and new studs).

    c. Apply new thread sealer to the engine mount stud threads.

    d. Install the 2 engine mount studs and tighten to 15 ft. lbs. (20 Nm).

69. Install the engine mount bracket and the 2 bolts. Tighten to 22 ft. lbs. (30 Nm).

70. Install the engine mount and the 3 bolts. Tighten to 66 ft. lbs. (90 Nm).

71. Install the 4 engine mount nuts. Tighten to 46 ft. lbs. (63 Nm).

72. Install the engine mount brace, nut and bolt. Tighten to 15 ft. lbs. (20 Nm).

73. Tighten the transaxle mount through bolt to 129 ft. lbs. (175 Nm).

74. Install the LH and RH VCT solenoids and bolts. Tighten to 10 Nm (89 inch lbs.).

75. Install the power steering pump and the 3 bolts. Tighten to 24 Nm (18 ft. lbs.).

76. Install the power steering reservoir and the 2 nuts. Tighten to 8 Nm (71 inch lbs.).

77. Install the degas bottle and the 3 bolts. Tighten to 80 inch lbs. (9 Nm).

78. Connect the 3 PCM electrical connectors.

79. Connect the purge valve electrical connector.

80. Install the radio interference capacitor, the ground wire and the nut to the cowl stud. Tighten to 89 inch lbs. (10 Nm).

81. Install the radio interference capacitor wire, the ground wire and the nut to the engine front cover stud. Tighten to 89 inch lbs. (10 Nm).

82. Install the ground wire and bolt on the engine front cover. Tighten to 89 inch lbs. (10 Nm).

83. Connect the 2 engine wiring harness connectors.

84. Using a new O-ring seal, connect the A/C pressure tube fitting and install the nut. Tighten to 71 inch lbs. (8 Nm).

85. Install the A/C pressure tube bracket and bolt. Tighten to 71 inch lbs. (8 Nm).

86. Connect the A/C suction tube fitting. Install the safety clip onto the fitting.

87. Install the LH and RH valve covers, as outlined in this section.

88. Install the engine air cleaner and air cleaner outlet pipe.

89. If equipped, attach the engine block heater harness to the radiator support, the A/C suction tube and the engine wiring harness.

90. Align the RH halfshaft splines with the intermediate shaft and push the halfshaft on until the circlip locks the shafts together.

91. Pull the inboard halfshaft outward to make sure the circlip is locked.

➡**Do not tighten the halfshaft nut at this time.**

92. Install the RH halfshaft into the hub and install a new halfshaft nut.

93. Install the RH lower ball joint into the steering knuckle and install the pinch bolt. Tighten to 41 ft. lbs. (55 Nm).

94. Install the RH stabilizer bar link into the lower control arm and install the nut. Tighten to 66 ft. lbs. (90 Nm).

95. Apply the brake to keep the halfshaft from rotating, then tighten the RH halfshaft nut to 258 ft. lbs. (350 Nm).

96. Install and the transaxle bracket and the 3 bolts. Tighten to 66 ft. lbs. (90 Nm).

97. Position the roll restrictor and transaxle bracket plate and install the 3 bolts. Tighten to 66 ft. lbs. (90 Nm).

98. Tighten the engine roll restrictor-to-subframe through bolt to 76 ft. lbs. (103 Nm).

99. Install the roll restrictor heat shield and the 2 nuts. Tighten to 80 inch lbs. (9 Nm).

100. Position the Y-pipe assembly in place and install the 4 nuts. Tighten to 30 ft. lbs. (40 Nm).

101. Install the 2 exhaust hangers and tighten the exhaust clamp. Tighten to 30 ft. lbs. (40 Nm).

➡**Apply clean engine oil to the crankshaft front seal bore in the engine front cover.**

102. Install a new crankshaft front seal, as outlined in this section.

➡**Lubricate the outside diameter sealing surfaces with clean engine oil.**

103. Install the crankshaft pulley, as outlined in this section.

104. Install the accessory drive belt, tensioner and the power steering belt, as outlined in this section.

105. Fill the engine with clean engine oil.

106. Connect the negative battery cable.

107. Evacuate and recharge the air conditioning system.

TIMING CHAIN AND SPROCKETS

REMOVAL & INSTALLATION

See Figures 163 through 168.

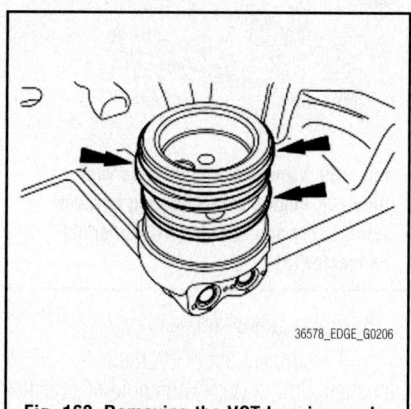

Fig. 163 Removing the VCT housing seals

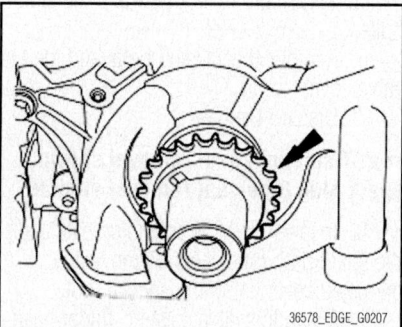

Fig. 164 Removing the crankshaft timing chain sprocket

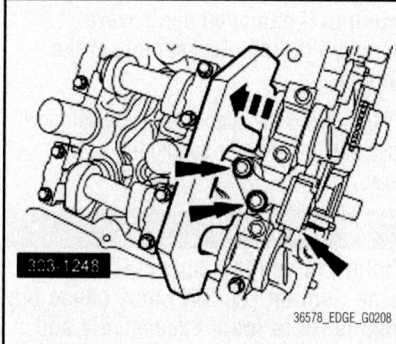

Fig. 165 Removing the 2 bolts and the RH secondary timing chain tensioner

➡During engine repair procedures, cleanliness is extremely important. Any foreign material, including any material created while cleaning gasket surfaces, that enters the oil passages, coolant passages or the oil pan may cause engine failure.

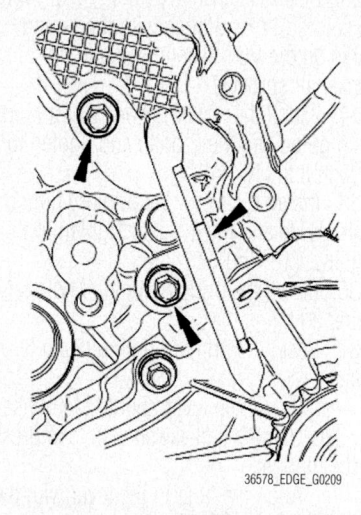

Fig. 166 Removing the 2 bolts and the RH primary timing chain guide

1. Remove the engine front cover.
2. Rotate the crankshaft clockwise and align the timing marks on the Variable Camshaft Timing (VCT) assemblies.

➡The special tool will hold the camshafts in the Top Dead Center (TDC) position.

3. Install the Camshaft Holding Tool onto the flats of the LH camshafts.
4. Install the Camshaft Holding Tool onto the flats of the RH camshafts.
5. Remove the 3 bolts and the RH VCT housing.
6. Remove the 3 bolts and the LH VCT housing.
7. Remove and discard the VCT housing seals.
8. Remove the 2 bolts and the primary timing chain tensioner.
9. Remove the primary timing chain tensioner arm.
10. Remove the 2 bolts and the lower LH primary timing chain guide.
11. Remove the primary timing chain.
12. Remove the crankshaft timing chain sprocket.
13. Remove the 2 bolts and the upper LH primary timing chain guide.
14. Compress the LH secondary timing chain tensioner and install a suitable lock-pin to retain the tensioner in the collapsed position.

➡The VCT bolt and the exhaust camshaft bolt must be discarded and new ones installed. However, the exhaust camshaft washer is reusable.

15. Remove and discard the LH VCT assembly bolt and the LH exhaust camshaft

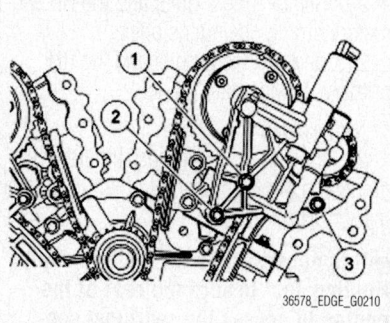

Fig. 167 Identifying the LH VCT housing tightening sequence

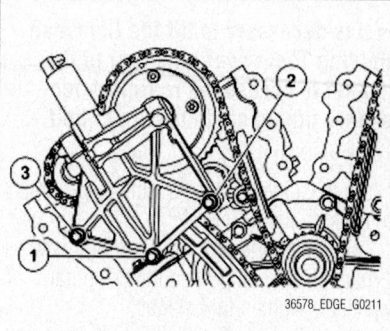

Fig. 168 Identifying the RH VCT housing tightening sequence

sprocket bolt. Remove the LH VCT assembly, secondary timing chain and the LH exhaust camshaft sprocket as an assembly.

➡It is necessary to tilt the camshaft holding tool toward the rear of the engine to access the rearmost secondary timing chain tensioner bolt.

16. Remove the 2 bolts and the LH secondary timing chain tensioner.
17. Compress the RH secondary timing chain tensioner and install a suitable lockpin to retain the tensioner in the collapsed position.

➡The VCT bolt and the exhaust camshaft bolt must be discarded and new ones installed. However, the exhaust camshaft washer is reusable.

18. Remove and discard the RH VCT assembly bolt and the RH exhaust camshaft sprocket bolt.
19. Remove the RH VCT assembly, secondary timing chain and the RH exhaust camshaft sprocket as an assembly.

➡It is necessary to tilt the Camshaft Holding Tool toward the rear of the engine to access the rearmost secondary timing chain tensioner bolt.

20. Remove the 2 bolts and the RH secondary timing chain tensioner.

21. Remove the 2 bolts and the RH primary timing chain guide.

To install:

22. Install the RH primary timing chain guide and the 2 bolts and tighten to 89 inch lbs. (10 Nm).

➡ **It is necessary to tilt the Camshaft Holding Tool toward the rear of the engine to access the rearmost secondary timing chain tensioner bolt.**

23. Install the RH secondary timing chain tensioner and the 2 bolts and tighten to 89 inch lbs. (10 Nm).

➡ **It is necessary to tilt the Camshaft Holding Tool toward the rear of the engine to access the rearmost secondary timing chain tensioner bolt.**

24. Install the RH secondary timing chain tensioner and the 2 bolts and tighten to 89 inch lbs. (10 Nm).

25. Install the new VCT bolt and new exhaust camshaft bolt and the original washers. Tighten in 4 stages:
   a. Stage 1: Tighten to 30 ft. lbs. (40 Nm).
   b. Stage 2: Loosen one full turn.
   c. Stage 3: Tighten to 89 inch lbs. (10 Nm).
   d. Stage 4: Tighten 90°

26. Remove the lockpin from the RH secondary timing chain tensioner.

➡ **It is necessary to tilt the Camshaft Holding Tool toward the rear of the engine to access the rearmost secondary timing chain tensioner bolt.**

27. Install the LH secondary timing chain tensioner and the 2 bolts and tighten to 89 inch lbs. (10 Nm).

28. Assemble the LH VCT assembly, the LH exhaust camshaft sprocket and the LH secondary timing chain. Align the colored links with the timing marks.

29. Position the LH secondary timing assembly onto the camshafts.

30. Install the new VCT and the new exhaust camshaft bolt and the original washers. Tighten in 4 stages.
   a. Stage 1: Tighten to 30 ft. lbs. (40 Nm).
   b. Stage 2: Loosen one full turn.
   c. Stage 3: Tighten to 89 inch lbs. (10 Nm).
   d. Stage 4: Tighten 90°

31. Remove the lockpin from the LH secondary timing chain tensioner.

32. Install the crankshaft timing chain sprocket.

33. Install the primary timing chain with the colored links aligned with the timing marks on the VCT assemblies and the crankshaft sprocket.

34. Install the upper LH primary timing chain guide and the 2 bolts and tighten to 89 inch lbs. (10 Nm).

35. Install the lower LH primary timing chain guide and the 2 bolts. Tighten to 89 inch lbs. (10 Nm).

36. Install the primary timing chain tensioner arm.

37. Reset the primary timing chain tensioner.
   a. Rotate the lever counterclockwise.
   b. Using a soft-jawed vise, compress the plunger.
   c. Align the hole in the lever with the hole in the tensioner housing.
   d. Install a suitable lockpin.

➡ **It may be necessary to rotate the crankshaft slightly to remove slack from the timing chain and install the tensioner.**

38. Install the primary tensioner and the 2 bolts. Tighten to 89 inch lbs. (10 Nm). Remove the lockpin.

39. As a post-check, verify correct alignment of all timing marks.

40. Install new VCT housing seals.

➡ **Make sure the dowels on the Variable Camshaft Timing (VCT) housing are fully engaged in the cylinder head prior to tightening the bolts. Failure to follow this process will result in severe engine damage.**

41. Install the VCT housing and the 3 bolts. Tighten in the sequence shown to 89 inch lbs. (10 Nm).

42. Install the engine front cover.

VALVE COVERS

REMOVAL & INSTALLATION

Left Side
See Figures 169 through 173.

❊❊ WARNING

During engine repair procedures, cleanliness is extremely important. Any foreign material, including any material created while cleaning gasket surfaces that enters the oil passages, coolant passages or the oil pan, can cause engine failure.

1. Remove the crankcase vent tube.
2. Remove the LH ignition coils, as outlined in the Engine Electrical Section.

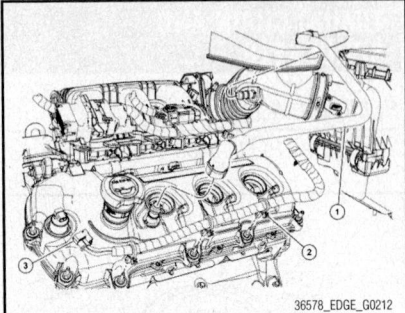

36578_EDGE_G0212

Fig. 169 View of the crankcase vent tube (1), engine control wiring harness retainer (2) and left side VCT solenoid connector (3)

3. Remove the oil level indicator.
4. Disconnect the LH Variable Camshaft Timing (VCT) solenoid electrical connector.
5. Detach all of the wiring harness retainers from the valve cover and the stud bolts.
6. Remove the 11 stud bolts and the LH valve cover.
7. Discard the gasket.

➡ **VCT solenoid seal removal shown, spark plug tube seal removal similar.**

8. Inspect the VCT solenoid seals and the spark plug tube seals. Remove any damaged seals using the special tool.

9. Clean the valve cover, cylinder head and engine front cover sealing surfaces with metal surface cleaner.

To install:

➡ **Installation of new seals is only required if damaged seals were removed during disassembly of the engine.**

10. Using the special tools, install new VCT solenoid and/or spark plug tube seals.

❊❊ WARNING

Failure to use the correct RTV Silicone Sealant (TA-357) may cause the engine oil to foam excessively and result in serious engine damage.

➡ **If the valve cover is not installed and the fasteners tightened within 4 minutes, the sealant must be removed and the sealing area cleaned. To clean the sealing area, use silicone gasket remover and metal surface prep. Follow the directions on the packaging. Failure to follow this procedure can cause future oil leakage.**

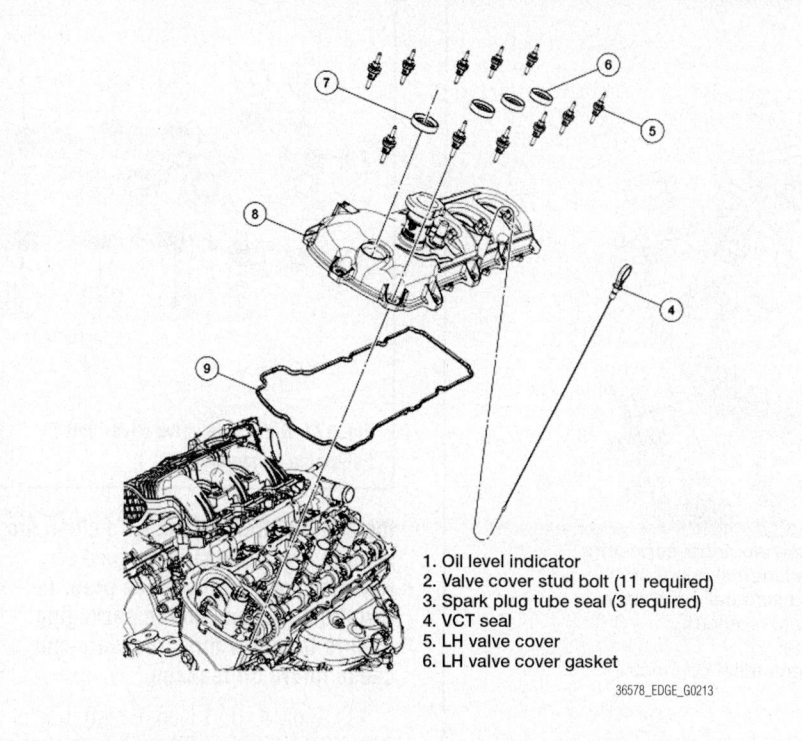

1. Oil level indicator
2. Valve cover stud bolt (11 required)
3. Spark plug tube seal (3 required)
4. VCT seal
5. LH valve cover
6. LH valve cover gasket

36578_EDGE_G0213

Fig. 170 Exploded view of the left side valve cover and related components

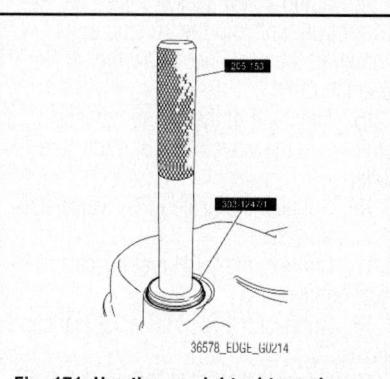

36578_EDGE_G0214

Fig. 171 Use the special tool to replace any damaged seals

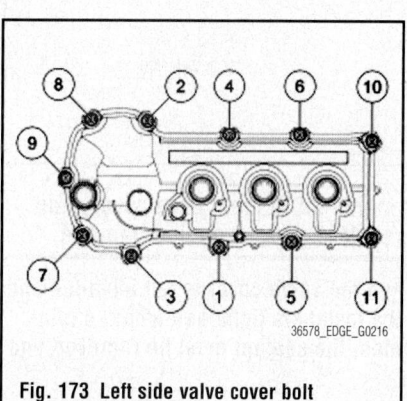

36578_EDGE_G0216

Fig. 173 Left side valve cover bolt tightening sequence

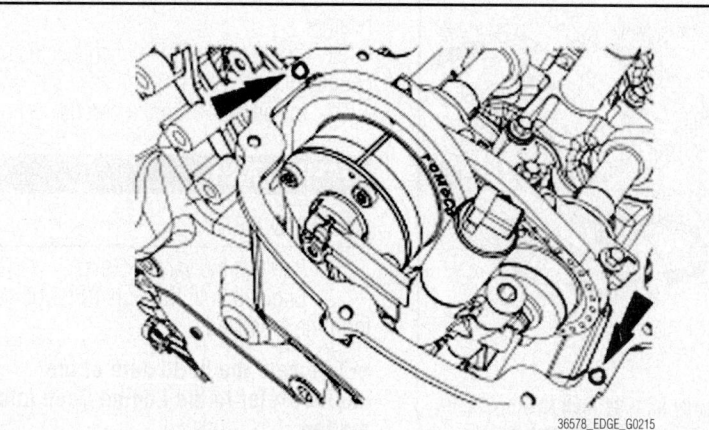

36578_EDGE_G0215

Fig. 172 Apply a 0.31 inch (8mm) bead of RTV Silicone Sealant (TA-357, or equivalent) to the engine front cover-to-LH cylinder head joints

11. Apply a 0.31 inch (8mm) bead of RTV Silicone Sealant (TA-357, or equivalent) to the engine front cover-to-LH cylinder head joints.

12. Using a new gasket, install the LH valve cover and 11 stud bolts. Tighten in the sequence shown to 89 inch lbs. (10 Nm).

13. Attach all of the wiring harness retainers to the valve cover and the stud bolts.

14. Attach the LH VCT solenoid electrical connector.

15. Install the oil level indicator.

16. Install the LH ignition coils.

17. Install the crankcase vent tube.

Right Side

See Figures 174 through 177.

> ✸✸ **WARNING**
>
> **During engine repair procedures, cleanliness is extremely important. Any foreign material, including any material created while cleaning gasket surfaces that enters the oil passages, coolant passages or the oil pan, can cause engine failure.**

1. Remove the RH ignition coils, as outlined in the Engine Electrical Section.

2. Disconnect the Power Steering Pressure (PSP) switch electrical connector.

3. Disconnect the RH catalyst monitor sensor electrical connector and pin-type retainer.

4. Disconnect the RH Heated Oxygen Sensor (HO2S) electrical connector.

5. Disconnect the RH Variable Camshaft Timing (VCT) electrical connector.

6. Disconnect the 3 RH fuel injector electrical connectors.

7. Detach all of the wiring harness retainers from the RH valve cover and the stud bolts.

8. Remove the bolt, the 10 stud bolts and the RH valve cover.

9. Discard the gasket.

➡**VCT solenoid seal removal shown, spark plug tube seal removal similar.**

10. Inspect the VCT solenoid seals and the spark plug tube seals. Remove any damaged seals using the special tool.

11. Clean the valve cover, cylinder head and engine front cover sealing surfaces with metal surface cleaner.

To install:

➡**Installation of new seals is only required if damaged seals were removed during disassembly of the engine.**

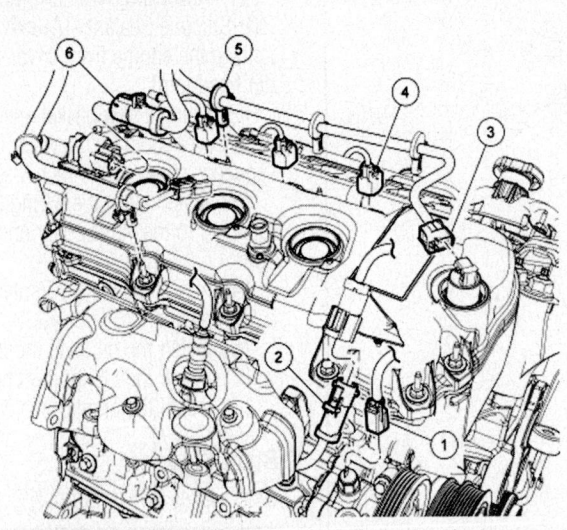

1. Power Steering Pressure (PSP) switch electrical connector
2. RH Catalyst Monitor Sensor (CMS) electrical connector
3. RH Variable Comshaft Timing (VCT) electrical connector
4. RH fuel injector electrical connector (3 required)
5. Engine control wiring harness retainer
6. RH Heated Oxygen Sensor (HO2S) electrical connector
12345_edge_g0218
7. Valve cover stud bolt (10 required)
8. Valve cover bolt
9. VCT seal
10. Spark plug tube seal (3 required)
11. RH valve cover
12. RH valve cover gasket

36578_EDGE_G0217

Fig. 174 Valve cover RH

12. Using the special tools, install new VCT solenoid and/or spark plug tube seals.

Failure to use the correct RTV Silicone Sealant (TA-357) may cause the engine oil to foam excessively and result in serious engine damage.

➡ If the valve cover is not installed and the fasteners tightened within 4 minutes, the sealant must be removed and

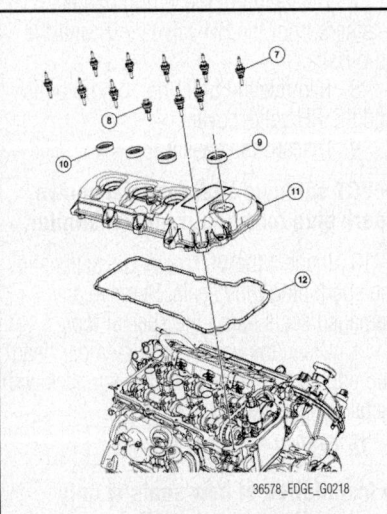

36578_EDGE_G0218

Fig. 175 Exploded view of the right side valve cover and related components

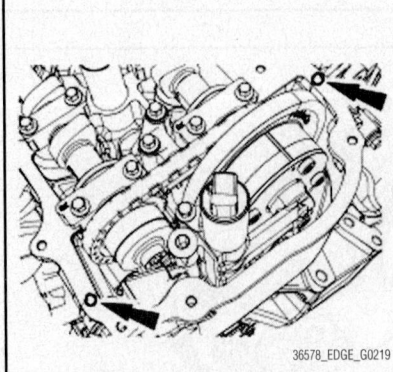

36578_EDGE_G0219

Fig. 176 Apply an 0.31 inch (8 mm) bead of RTV Silicone Sealant (TA-357) to the engine front cover-to-RH cylinder head joints

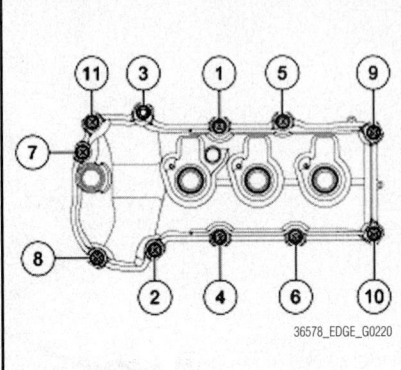

36578_EDGE_G0220

Fig. 177 Right side valve cover bolt tightening sequence

the sealing area cleaned. To clean the sealing area, use silicone gasket remover and metal surface prep. Follow the directions on the packaging. Failure to follow this procedure can cause future oil leakage.

13. Apply an 0.31 inch (8 mm) bead of RTV Silicone Sealant (TA-357) to the engine front cover-to-RH cylinder head joints.

14. Using a new gasket, install the RH valve cover, bolt and the 10 stud bolts. Tighten in the sequence shown to 10 Nm (89 inch lbs.).

15. Attach all of the wiring harness retainers to the valve cover and the stud bolts.

16. Connect the heated PCV valve electrical connector.

17. Connect the 3 RH fuel injector electrical connectors.

18. Connect the RH VCT electrical connector.

19. Connect the RH HO2S electrical connector.

20. Connect the RH catalyst monitor sensor electrical connector and pin-type retainer.

21. Connect the PSP switch electrical connector.

22. Install the RH ignition coils.

VALVE LASH

ADJUSTMENT

1. Remove the valve covers.
2. Engines built through 10/09/08 perform the following:

➡ To locate the build date of the engine, refer to the Engine Code Information.

➡ The valve clearance must be measured at room temperature.

➡The valve clearance must be measured with the camshaft at base circuit. The engine will have to be rotated with the crankshaft pulley bolt to bring each valve to base circle.

a. Use a feeler gauge to measure the clearance of each valve and record its location. A midrange clearance is the most desirable:
- Intake: 0.006-0.01 inch (0.15-0.25 mm)
- Exhaust: 0.0118-0.0157 inch (0.300-0.400 mm)

3. Engines built 10/10/08 and after perform the following:

➡To locate the build date of the engine, refer to Engine Code Information Label.

➡The valve clearance must be measured with the camshaft at base circle. The engine will have to be rotated with the crankshaft pulley bolt to bring each valve to base circle.

a. Use a feeler gauge to measure the clearance of each valve and record its location. A midrange clearance is the most desirable:
- Intake: 0.006-0.01 inch (0.15-0.25 mm)
- Exhaust: 0.0142-0.0181 inch (0.360-0.460 mm)

➡All engines perform the following:

➡The number on the valve tappet reflects the thickness of the valve tappet. For example, a tappet with the number 3.310 has the thickness of 0.13 inch (3.31 mm).

4. If any of the valve clearances are out of specification, select new tappets using this formula: tappet thickness = measured clearance + the base tappet thickness - most desirable thickness. Select the tappets and mark the installation location.

5. If required, install the new selected valve tappets in the marked locations.

ENGINE PERFORMANCE & EMISSION CONTROLS

ACCELERATOR PEDAL POSITION (APP) SENSOR

REMOVAL & INSTALLATION

See Figure 178.

➡ Release the safety lock tab mechanism on the accelerator pedal sensor electrical connector prior to disconnecting.

1. Disconnect the accelerator pedal sensor electrical connector.

2. Remove the 3 nuts and the accelerator pedal and sensor assembly. To install, tighten to 62 inch lbs. (7 Nm).

3. To install, reverse the removal procedure.

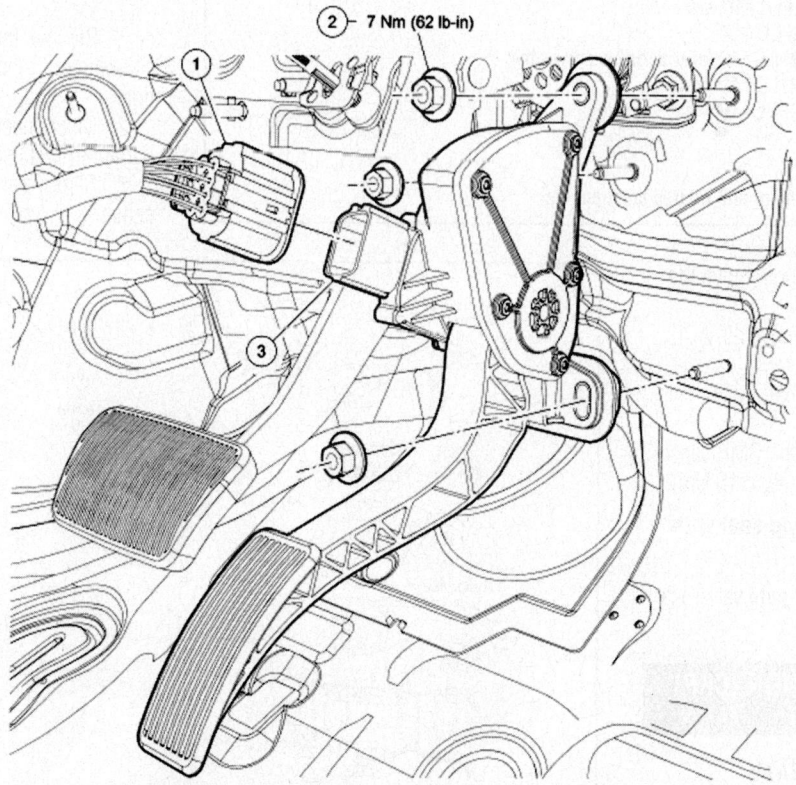

(2) 7 Nm (62 lb-in)

1. Accelerator Pedal Sensor electrical connector
2. Accelerator pedal nut (3 required)
3. Accelerator pedal and sensor assembly

36578_EDGE_G0221

Fig. 178 Removing and installing the Accelerator Pedal Position (APP) sensor

CAMSHAFT POSITION (CMP) SENSOR

REMOVAL & INSTALLATION

See Figure 179.

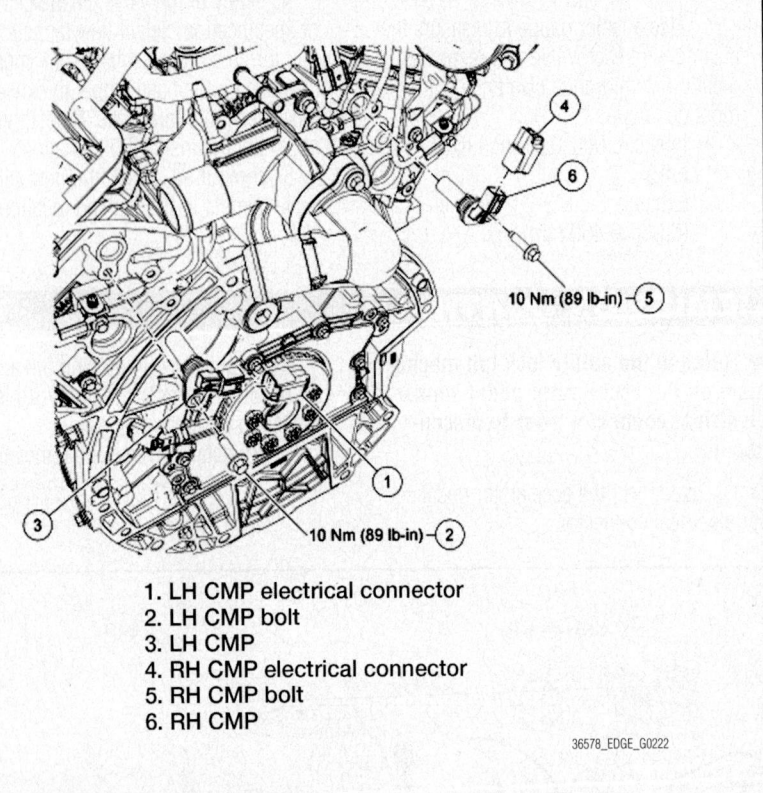

1. LH CMP electrical connector
2. LH CMP bolt
3. LH CMP
4. RH CMP electrical connector
5. RH CMP bolt
6. RH CMP

36578_EDGE_G0222

Fig. 179 Identifying CMP sensor and related components

1. For the right RH sensor, remove the Air Cleaner (ACL) outlet pipe.
2. For the LH sensor, remove the ACL assembly.
3. Disconnect the Camshaft Position (CMP) electrical connector.
4. Remove the bolt and the CMP sensor. To install, tighten to 89 inch lbs. (10 Nm).

➡ **Lubricate the CMP o-ring seal with clean engine oil.**

5. To install, reverse the removal procedure.

CRANKSHAFT POSITION (CKP) SENSOR

REMOVAL & INSTALLATION

See Figure 180.

1. With the vehicle in NEUTRAL, position it on a hoist.
2. Remove the LH catalytic converter.
3. Remove the bolt, nut and the heat shield. To install tighten to 89 inch lbs. (10 Nm).

4. Remove the rubber grommet cover.
5. Disconnect the Crankshaft Position (CKP) sensor electrical connector.
6. Remove the bolt and the CKP sensor. To install, tighten to 89 inch lbs. (10 Nm).
7. To install, reverse the removal process.

CYLINDER HEAD TEMPERATURE (CHT) SENSOR

REMOVAL & INSTALLATION

See Figure 181.

36578_EDGE_G0224

Fig. 181 Cylinder Head Temperature (CHT) sensor electrical connector (1) and sensor (2)

1. Remove the lower intake manifold, as outlined in the Engine Mechanical Section.
2. Disconnect the Cylinder Head Temperature (CHT) sensor electrical connector.
3. Remove and discard the CHT sensor.

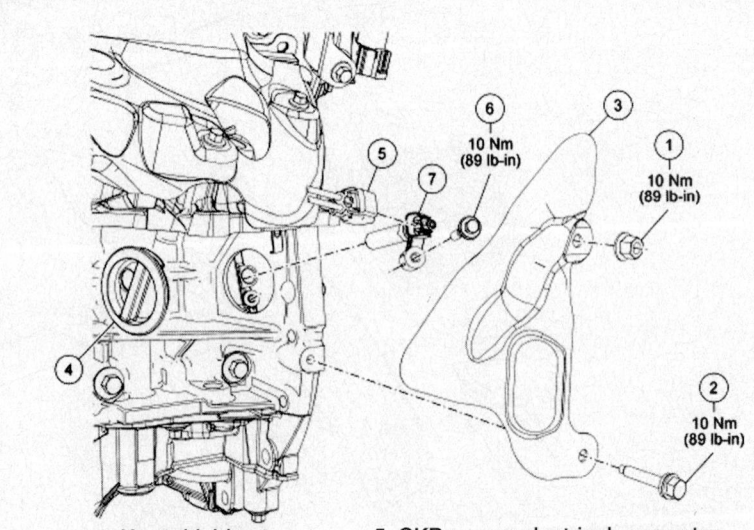

1. Heat shield nut
2. Heat shield bolt
3. Heat shield
4. Rubber grommet cover
5. CKP sensor electrical connector
6. CKP sensor bolt
7. CKP sensor

36578_EDGE_G0223

Fig. 180 Identifying the CKP sensor and related components

To install:

4. Install a new CHT sensor and tighten to 89 inch lbs. (10 Nm).

5. Attach the CHT sensor electrical connector.

6. Connect the negative battery cable.

EVAPORATIVE EMISSIONS (EVAP) CANISTER

REMOVAL & INSTALLATION

See Figure 182.

> ❋❋ **WARNING**
>
> Do not smoke, carry lighted tobacco or have an open flame of any type when working on or near any fuel-related component. Highly flammable mixtures are always present and may be ignited. Failure to follow these instructions may result in serious personal injury.

> ❋❋ **WARNING**
>
> Do not carry personal electronic devices such as cell phones, pagers or audio equipment of any type when working on or near any fuel-related component. Highly flammable mixtures are always present and may be ignited. Failure to follow these instructions may result in serious personal injury.

> ❋❋ **WARNING**
>
> Always disconnect the battery ground cable at the battery when working on an Evaporative Emission (EVAP) system or fuel-related component. Highly flammable mixtures are always present and may be ignited. Failure to follow these instructions may result in serious personal injury.

➡ Correct placement of the hoist arm to the frame lifting point is essential for the removal and installation of the Evaporative Emission (EVAP) canister.

1. With the vehicle in NEUTRAL, position it on a hoist.

2. Disconnect the battery ground cable.

3. Remove the 3 bolts, pin-type retainer and the EVAP shield. To install, tighten to 80 inch lbs. (9 Nm).

4. Disconnect the EVAP canister vent solenoid electrical connector.

5. Disconnect the fuel vapor tube-to-EVAP canister quick connect coupling.

6. Disconnect the vapor tube assembly-to-EVAP canister quick connect coupling.

7. Disconnect the fuel vapor tube to the dust separator.

8. Remove the 3 EVAP canister bolts. To install, tighten to 80 inch lbs. (9 Nm).

9. Release the pin-type retainer and remove the EVAP canister.

➡ When installing the EVAP canister, insert the alignment tab into the body first, then install the pin-type retainer and 3 bolts.

10. To install, reverse the removal procedure.

11. Carry out the FVAP system leak test.

HEATED OXYGEN SENSOR (HO2S)

REMOVAL & INSTALLATION

See Figure 183.

1. For the RH sensor, with the vehicle in NEUTRAL, position it on a hoist.

2. Disconnect the Heated Oxygen Sensor (HO2S) electrical connector.

➡ If necessary, lubricate the sensor threads with penetrating and lock lubricant to assist in removal.

3. Using the Exhaust Gas Oxygen Sensor Socket, remove the HO2S.

   a. Using the chart provided, calculate the correct torque wrench setting for the following torque.

   b. To install, tighten to 35 ft. lbs. (48 Nm).

➡ Apply a light coat of anti-seize lubricant to the threads of the HO2S.

4. To install, reverse the removal procedure.

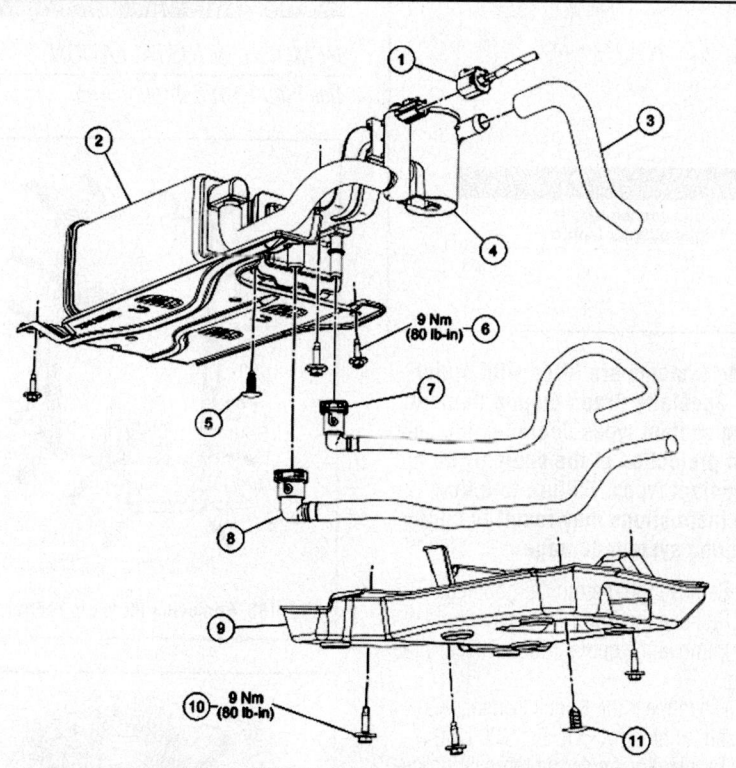

1. Evaporative Emission (EVAP) canister vent solenoid electrical connector
2. EVAP canister
3. Fuel vapor tube
4. EVAP canister vent solenoid/dust separator
5. EVAP canister pin-type retainer
6. EVAP canister bolt (3 required)
7. Fuel vapor tube-to-EVAP canister quick connect coupling
8. Fuel vapor tube assembly-to-EVAP canister quick connect coupling
9. EVAP shield EVAP shield bolt (3 required)
10. EVAP shield pin-type retainer

36578_EDGE_G0225

Fig. 182 Removing and installing the EVAP canister

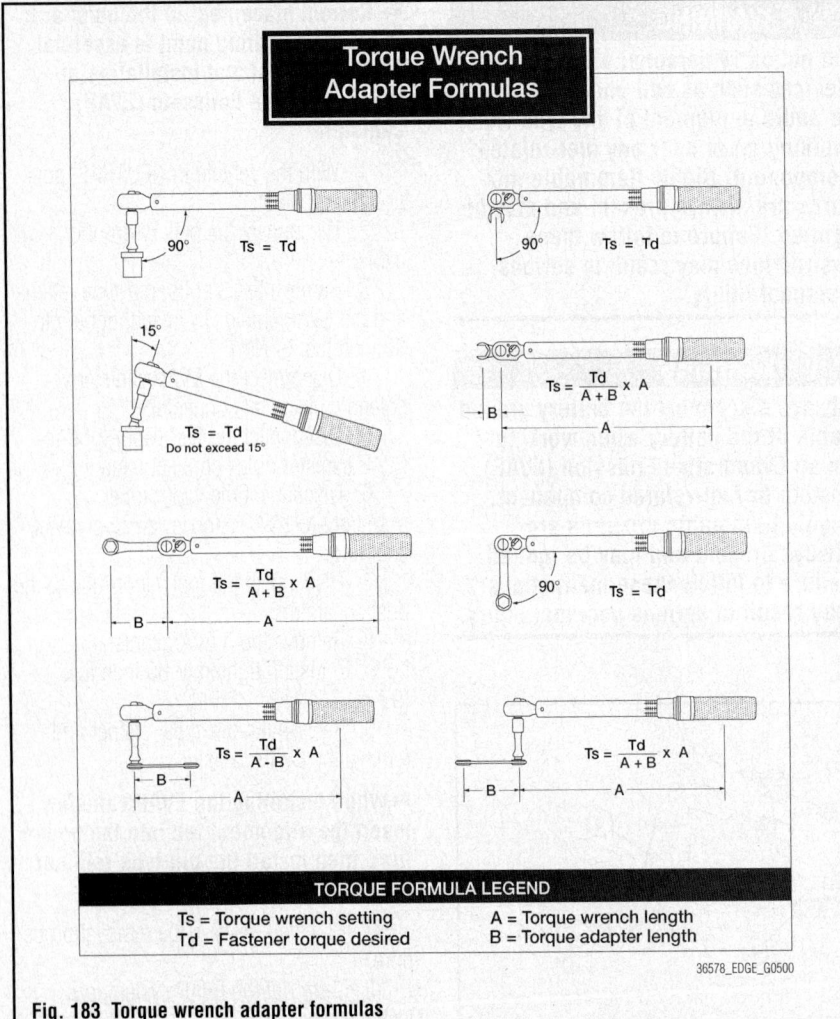

Fig. 183 Torque wrench adapter formulas

Torque Wrench Adapter Formulas

90°   Ts = Td

90°   Ts = Td

15°   Ts = Td
Do not exceed 15°

$$Ts = \frac{Td}{A+B} \times A$$

$$Ts = \frac{Td}{A+B} \times A$$

90°   Ts = Td

$$Ts = \frac{Td}{A-B} \times A$$

$$Ts = \frac{Td}{A+B} \times A$$

TORQUE FORMULA LEGEND

Ts = Torque wrench setting   A = Torque wrench length
Td = Fastener torque desired   B = Torque adapter length

36578_EDGE_G0500

KNOCK SENSOR (KS)

REMOVAL & INSTALLATION

See Figure 184.

→ Early build vehicle (built before January 19, 2009) cooling systems are filled with Motorcraft® Premium Gold Engine Coolant. Late build vehicle (built on or after January 19, 2009)

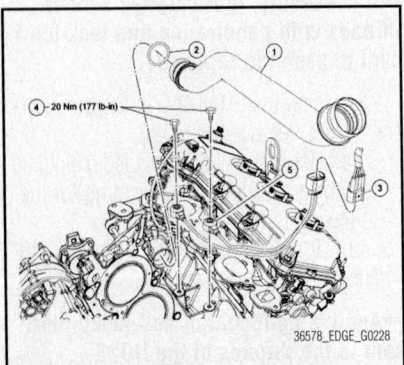

Fig. 184 Identifying Knock Sensor (KS) and related components

36578_EDGE_G0228

cooling systems are filled with Motorcraft® Specialty Green Engine Coolant. Mixing coolant types degrades the corrosion protection of the coolant. Do not mix coolant types. Failure to follow these instructions may result in engine or cooling system damage.

1. Remove the thermostat housing.
2. Remove the lower intake manifold.
3. Remove the coolant tube. Discard the O-ring.
4. Disconnect the Knock Sensor (KS). To install, tighten to 15 ft. lbs. (20 Nm).
5. To install, reverse the removal procedure. Lubricate the new o-ring seal with clean engine coolant.

MASS AIR FLOW (MAF) SENSOR (HOT WIRE)

REMOVAL & INSTALLATION

See Figure 185.

1. Disconnect the Mass Air Flow (MAF) sensor electrical connector.

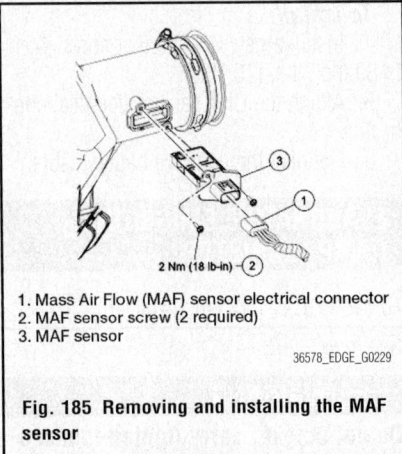

1. Mass Air Flow (MAF) sensor electrical connector
2. MAF sensor screw (2 required)
3. MAF sensor

2 Nm (18 lb-in)

36578_EDGE_G0229

Fig. 185 Removing and installing the MAF sensor

2. Remove the 2 screws and the MAF sensor. To install, tighten to 18 inch lbs. (2 Nm).
3. To install, reverse the removal procedure.

OUTPUT SHAFT SPEED (OSS) SENSOR

REMOVAL & INSTALLATION

See Figures 186 through 195.

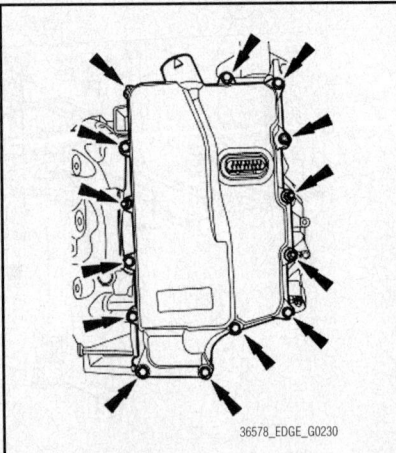

36578_EDGE_G0230

Fig. 186 Removing the main control cover

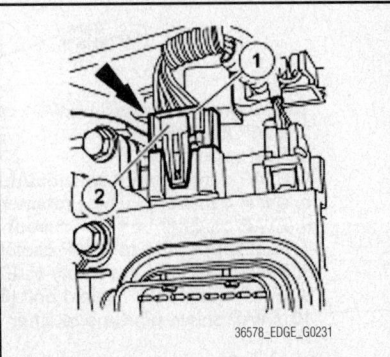

36578_EDGE_G0231

Fig. 187 Disconnecting the TR sensor electrical connector

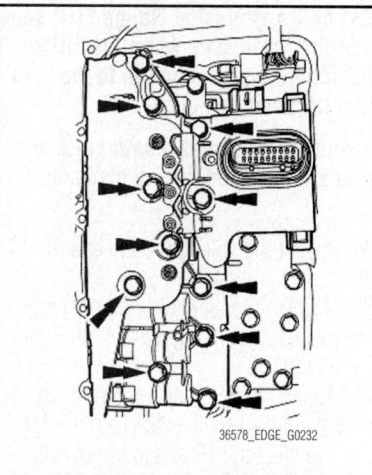

Fig. 188 Removing the solenoid body

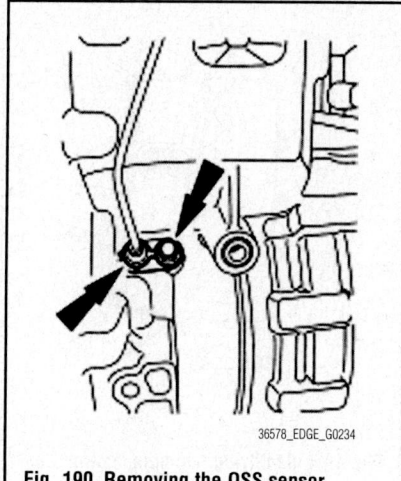

Fig. 190 Removing the OSS sensor

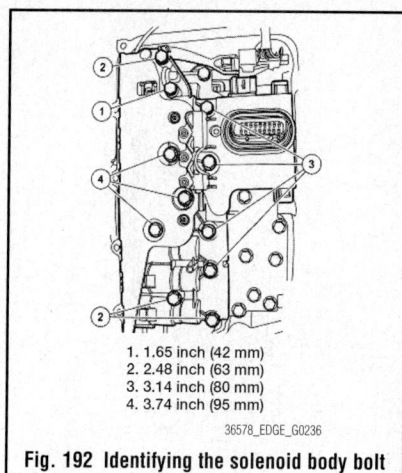

1. 1.65 inch (42 mm)
2. 2.48 inch (63 mm)
3. 3.14 inch (80 mm)
4. 3.74 inch (95 mm)

Fig. 192 Identifying the solenoid body bolt lengths

➡The use of any transmission fluid other than what is recommended for this transaxle will cause transaxle damage. Refer to the Material specification and/or the transmission fluid level indicator for the correct fluid. Use only clean transmission fluid designated for this transaxle and torque converter being serviced.

➡Do not mix Mercon®V or Mercon® LV transmission fluid. This may cause erratic shift feel, erratic shift timing and/or transmission failure.

➡Transmission fluid application:

- Early build vehicles require MERCON® V
- Late build vehicle require MERCON® LV

1. Position the vehicle on a hoist.
2. Disconnect the Mass Air Flow (MAF) sensor electrical connector and the wiring harness fastener from the Air Cleaner (ACL) assembly.

3. Disconnect the brake booster vacuum hose from the ACL outlet pipe.
4. Disconnect the engine breather from the ACL assembly.
5. Remove the ACL assembly bracket bolt.
6. Loosen the ACL outlet pipe clamp at the Throttle Body (TB) and remove the ACL and ACL outlet pipe assembly.
7. Remove the transmission fluid drain plug and allow the transmission fluid to drain.
8. Install the transmission fluid drain plug. Tighten to 80 inch lbs. (9 Nm).
9. Disconnect the selector lever cable end from the manual control lever.

➡The coolant hoses do not need to be removed from the engine.

10. Remove the coolant hoses from the transmission fluid filler tube and position aside.

➡The coolant hoses have been removed for clarity.

11. Remove the transmission fluid level indicator.

➡The coolant hoses have been removed for clarity.

12. Remove the nut, rotate the transmission fluid filler tube counterclockwise 90 degrees and remove the transmission fluid filler tube.
13. Loosen the transmission fluid cooler tube fitting from the thermal bypass valve.
14. Remove and discard the transmission fluid cooler tube bolt and remove the transmission fluid cooler tube.
15. Inspect the transaxle case to make sure that the transmission fluid cooler tube seal and backing ring were removed with the transmission fluid cooler tube and are not stuck in the transaxle case. If the transmission fluid cooler tube seal or backing ring are stuck in the transaxle case, remove the seal and backing ring.
16. Remove the nut and the manual control lever.

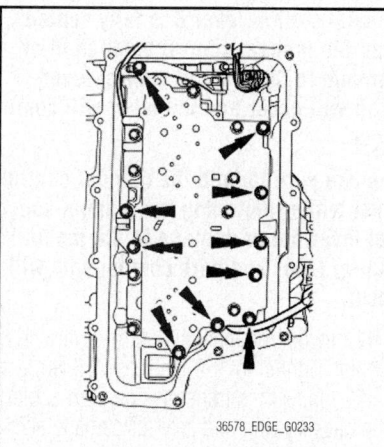

Fig. 189 Removing the TR sensor detent spring and main control valve body

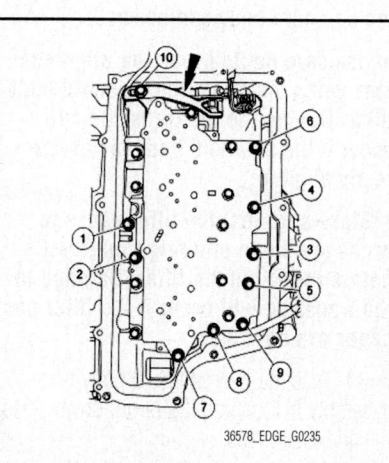

Fig. 191 Identifying the TR sensor bolt tightening sequence

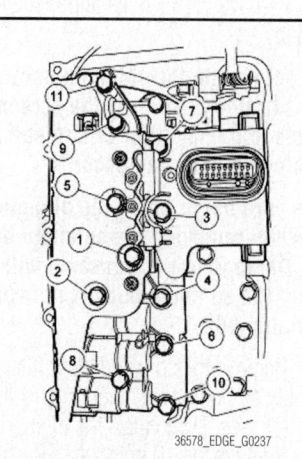

Fig. 193 Identifying the solenoid body bolt tightening sequence

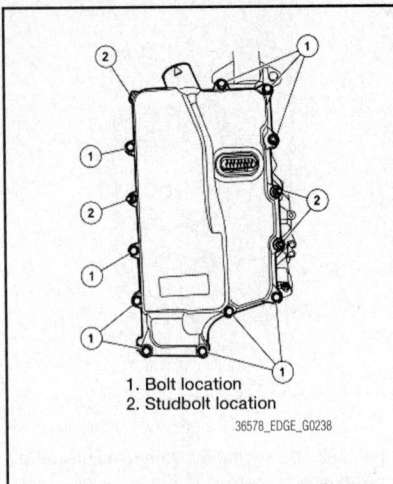

1. Bolt location
2. Studbolt location

36578_EDGE_G0238

Fig. 194 Installing the main control cover

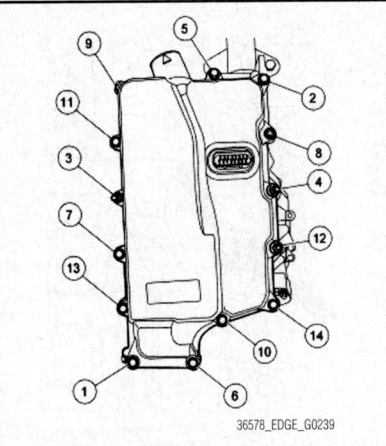

36578_EDGE_G0239

Fig. 195 Identifying the main control cover bolt tightening sequence

17. Disconnect the transaxle electrical connector.

18. Remove the 2 nuts, pull the transmission fluid cooler thermal bypass valve straight up and position it aside.

➡Note the location of the stud bolts for assembly.

19. Remove the 14 bolts and the main control cover.

20. Disconnect the Transmission Range (TR) sensor electrical connector.
    a. Slide the lock over.
    b. Press the tab and disconnect the connector.

21. Disconnect the Turbine Shaft Speed (TSS) and Output Shaft Speed (OSS) sensor electrical connectors.

➡The solenoid body should be handled with care or damage to the solenoid body may occur.

➡ Note the location of the different length bolts for assembly.

22. Remove the 11 bolts and the solenoid body.

➡Do not handle the solenoid body in the leadframe area or by the screens of the solenoid body filter or damage to the solenoid body can occur.

➡Use care not to break the alignment tabs when removing the solenoid body filter. Damage to the transaxle will occur if the solenoid body is not correctly aligned.

23. Remove the solenoid body filter assembly by pulling it straight up from the alignment tabs. Disconnect the filter.

24. Remove the 10 bolts, the TR sensor detent spring and the main control valve body.

25. Remove the bolt and the OSS sensor.

To install:
26. Install the OSS sensor and bolt. Tighten the bolt to 106 inch lbs. (12 Nm).

➡Make sure that the manual pin (part of the TR sensor) is correctly installed in the manual valve.

27. Position the TSS, OSS and TR sensor wiring harness aside and install the main control valve body.

28. Inspect the manual pin to make sure it is correctly installed in the manual valve. If it is not, pull the valve body off the transaxle case. Correctly install the manual pin in the manual valve and position the valve body in place.

29. Install the TR sensor detent spring and the 10 bolts. Tighten the bolts in the sequence shown. Tighten to 106 inch lbs. (12 Nm).

➡Do not handle the solenoid body in the leadframe area or by the screens of the solenoid body filter or damage to the solenoid body can occur.

➡Use care not to break the alignment tabs when installing the solenoid body filter. Damage to the transaxle will occur if the solenoid body is not correctly aligned.

➡Make sure that the filter passage areas are clean of foreign material before installing the filter. Damage to the transaxle will occur if the filter passages are not clean.

30. Install a new solenoid body filter assembly by pushing it straight down on to the alignment tabs.

➡Make sure not to pinch the Turbine Shaft Speed (TSS), Output Shaft Speed (OSS) or Transmission Range (TR) sensor wiring harnesses when installing the solenoid body. Damage to the wiring harness will occur.

➡Install the different length bolts in the locations noted during disassembly.

31. Install the solenoid body and the 11 bolts.

32. Tighten the solenoid body bolts in the sequence shown. Tighten to 106 inch lbs. (12 Nm).

33. Route the OSS sensor wiring harness and connect the electrical connector.

34. Connect the TR sensor electrical connector. Connect the electrical connector. Slide the locking tab over.

35. Connect the TSS sensor electrical connector.

36. Inspect the transaxle side cover seal for damage and install new if necessary.

➡Inspect the 20-pin solenoid body connector seal to make sure that the seal is on the inside of the main control cover or a transmission fluid leak will occur.

➡Install the studbolts in the locations noted during disassembly.

37. Install the main control cover and loosely install the 14 bolts.

38. Tighten the main control cover bolts in the sequence shown. Tighten to 106 inch lbs. (12 Nm).

39. Position the transmission fluid cooler thermal bypass valve and transmission fluid cooler tube assembly in place and install the 2 transmission fluid cooler tube bracket nuts. Tighten to 80 inch lbs. (9 Nm).

40. Connect the transaxle electrical connector.

➡Make sure that when installing the manual control lever it is fully seated onto the manual control lever shaft or damage to the manual control lever shaft will occur and the lever will come loose.

➡Make sure to hold the manual control lever while tightening the manual control lever nut or damage to the manual control lever and park components will occur.

41. Install the manual control lever and the nut. Tighten to 159 inch lbs. (18 Nm).

42. Inspect the transmission fluid cooler tube backing ring and seal for damage and install a new backing ring or seal if necessary. Lubricate the transmission fluid cooler tube seal with clean transmission fluid and

install the backing ring and seal on the transmission fluid cooler tube.

43. Position the transmission fluid cooler tube in place and install a new bolt. Tighten to 80 inch lbs. (9 Nm).

44. Tighten the transmission fluid cooler tube fitting. Tighten to 18 ft. lbs. (25 Nm).

45. Install the transmission fluid filler tube and the nut. Tighten to 97 inch lbs. (11 Nm).

46. Install the transmission fluid level indicator.

47. Route the coolant hoses in the transmission fluid filler tube.

48. Place the manual control lever in DRIVE. Rotate the manual control lever clockwise until it stops. Rotate the manual control lever counterclockwise one detent until it stops.

49. Unlock the selector lever cable adjuster by sliding the locking tab over.

50. Slide the cable end forward or backward to align it with the manual control lever.

51. With the adjuster locking tab released, connect the selector lever cable end to the manual control lever.

52. Slide the release tab back to lock the adjuster.

53. Position the ACL assembly in place and install the bolt. Tighten to 97 inch lbs. (11 Nm).

54. Tighten the ACL outlet pipe clamp at the TB. Tighten to 44 inch lbs. (5 Nm).

55. Connect the engine breather to the ACL assembly.

56. Connect the brake booster vacuum hose to the ACL assembly.

57. Connect the MAF sensor electrical connector and connect the electrical harness fastener.

58. Fill with clean transmission fluid to the correct level.

POSITIVE CRANKCASE VENTILATION (PCV) VALVE

REMOVAL & INSTALLATION

See Figure 196.

1. Disconnect the crankcase ventilation tube from the PCV valve.

➡**A new positive crankcase ventilation (PCV) valve must be installed if removed from the valve cover. During removal, damage will occur to the locking mechanism on the PCV valve.**

➡**To install, apply clean engine oil to the O-ring seal.**

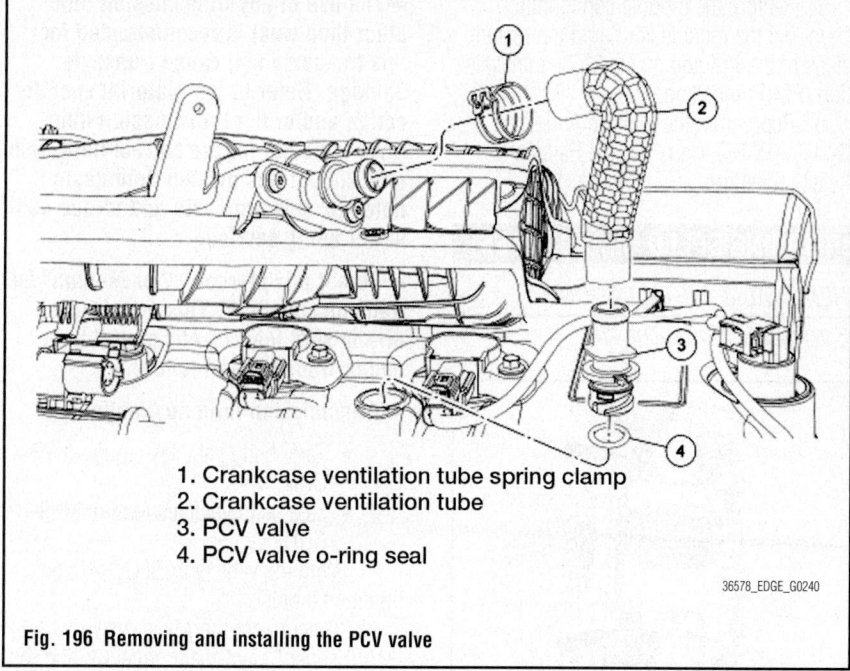

1. Crankcase ventilation tube spring clamp
2. Crankcase ventilation tube
3. PCV valve
4. PCV valve o-ring seal

36578_EDGE_G0240

Fig. 196 Removing and installing the PCV valve

2. Rotate the PCV valve counterclockwise and remove it from the valve cover. Discard the PCV valve.

3. To install, reverse the removal procedure. Install a new PCV valve.

POWERTRAIN CONTROL MODULE (PCM)

REMOVAL & INSTALLATION

See Figure 197.

➡**PCM replacement DOES NOT require new keys or programming of keys.**

1. Retrieve the module configuration. Carry out the module configuration retrieval steps of the Programmable Module Installation (PMI) procedure.

2. Disconnect the 3 PCM electrical connectors.

3. Remove the 2 nuts and the PCM. Remove the gasket.

To install:

4. Install the gasket and the PCM.

5. Install the 2 PCM nuts. Tighten to 44 inch lbs. (5 Nm).

6. Connect the 3 PCM electrical connectors.

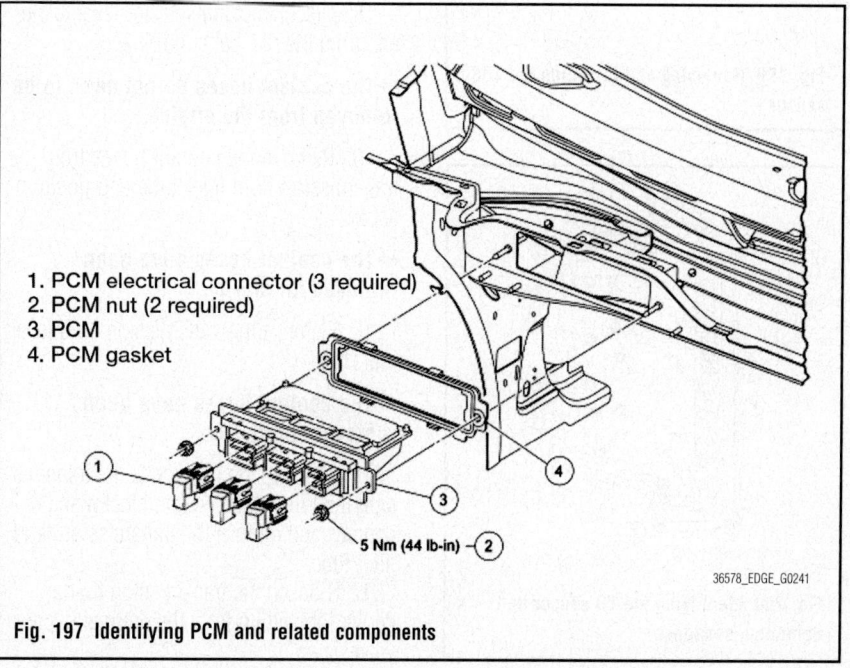

1. PCM electrical connector (3 required)
2. PCM nut (2 required)
3. PCM
4. PCM gasket

5 Nm (44 lb-in)

36578_EDGE_G0241

Fig. 197 Identifying PCM and related components

7. Restore the module configuration. Carry out the module configuration restore steps of the Programmable Module Installation (PMI) procedure.

8. Reprogram the Passive Anti-Theft System (PATS). Carry out the Parameter Reset procedure.

TURBINE SPEED SENSOR (TSS)

REMOVAL & INSTALLATION

See Figures 198 through 204.

36578_EDGE_G0242

Fig. 198 Disconnecting the TSS and OSS sensor electrical connectors

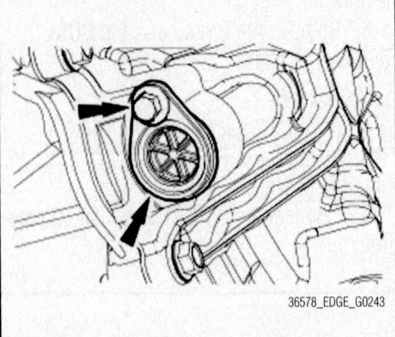

36578_EDGE_G0243

Fig. 199 Removing and installing the TSS sensor

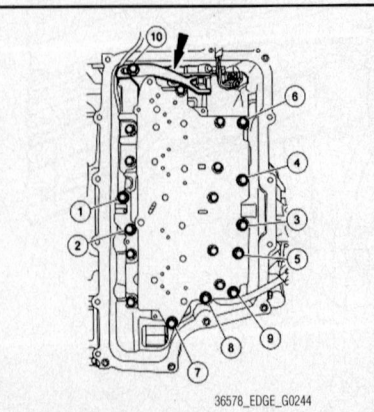

36578_EDGE_G0244

Fig. 200 Identifying the TR sensor bolt tightening sequence

➡The use of any transmission fluid other than what is recommended for this transaxle will cause transaxle damage. Refer to the Material specification and/or the transmission fluid level indicator for the correct fluid. Use only clean transmission fluid designated for this transaxle and torque converter being serviced.

➡Do not mix Mercon® V or Mercon® LV transmission fluid. This may cause erratic shift feel, erratic shift timing and/or transmission failure.

➡Transmission fluid application:

- Early build vehicles require MERCON® V
- Late build vehicles require MERCON® LV

1. With the vehicle in NEUTRAL, position it on a hoist.

2. Disconnect the Mass Air Flow (MAF) sensor electrical connector and the wiring harness fastener from the Air Cleaner (ACL) assembly. Disconnect the brake booster vacuum hose from the ACL outlet pipe.

3. Disconnect the engine breather from the ACL assembly.

4. Remove the ACL assembly bracket bolt.

5. Loosen the ACL outlet pipe clamp at the Throttle Body (TB) and remove the ACL and ACL outlet pipe assembly.

6. Remove the transmission fluid drain plug and allow the transmission fluid to drain.

7. Install the transmission fluid drain plug. Tighten to 80 inch lbs. (9 Nm).

8. Disconnect the selector lever cable end from the manual control lever.

➡The coolant hoses do not need to be removed from the engine.

9. Remove the coolant hoses from the transmission fluid filler tube and position aside.

➡The coolant hoses have been removed for clarity.

10. Remove the transmission fluid level indicator.

➡The coolant hoses have been removed for clarity.

11. Remove the nut, rotate the transmission fluid filler tube counterclockwise 90 degrees and remove the transmission fluid filler tube.

12. Loosen the transmission fluid cooler tube fitting from the thermal bypass valve.

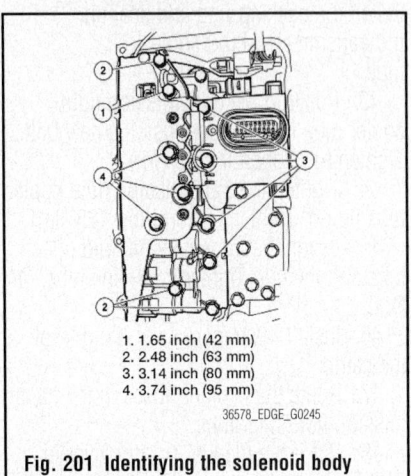

1. 1.65 inch (42 mm)
2. 2.48 inch (63 mm)
3. 3.14 inch (80 mm)
4. 3.74 inch (95 mm)

36578_EDGE_G0245

Fig. 201 Identifying the solenoid body bolts and lengths

13. Remove and discard the transmission fluid cooler tube bolt and remove the transmission fluid cooler tube.

14. Inspect the transaxle case to make sure that the transmission fluid cooler tube seal and backing ring were removed with the transmission fluid cooler tube and are not stuck in the transaxle case. If the transmission fluid cooler tube seal or backing ring are stuck in the transaxle case, remove the seal and backing ring.

15. Remove the nut and the manual control lever.

16. Disconnect the transaxle electrical connector.

17. Remove the 2 nuts, pull the transmission fluid cooler thermal bypass valve straight up and position it aside.

➡ **Note the location of the stud bolts for assembly.**

18. Remove the 14 bolts and the main control cover.

19. Disconnect the Transmission Range (TR) sensor electrical connector. Slide the

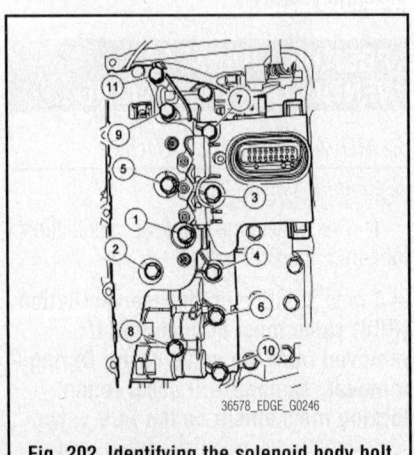

36578_EDGE_G0246

Fig. 202 Identifying the solenoid body bolt tightening sequence

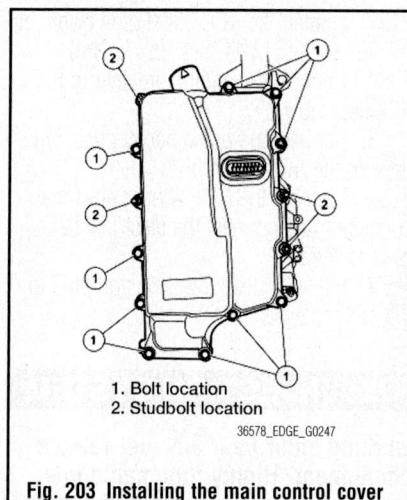

1. Bolt location
2. Studbolt location

36578_EDGE_G0247

Fig. 203 Installing the main control cover

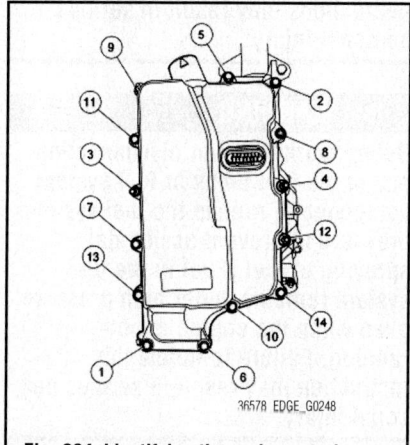

36578_EDGE_G0248

Fig. 204 Identifying the main control cover bolt tightening sequence

lock over. Press the tab and disconnect the connector.

20. Disconnect the Turbine Shaft Speed (TSS) and Output Shaft Speed (OSS) sensor electrical connectors.

➡**The solenoid body should be handled with care, damage to the solenoid body may occur.**

➡**Note the location of the different length bolts for assembly.**

21. Remove the 11 bolts and the solenoid body.

➡**Do not handle the solenoid body in the leadframe area or by the screens of the solenoid body filter or damage to the solenoid body can occur.**

➡**Use care not to break the alignment tabs when installing the solenoid body filter. Damage to the transaxle will occur if the solenoid body is not correctly aligned.**

22. Remove the solenoid body filter

assembly by pulling it straight up from the alignment tabs. Discard the filter.

23. Remove the 10 bolts, the TR sensor detent spring and the main control valve body.

24. Remove the bolt and the TSS sensor.

To install:

25. Route the TSS sensor wiring harness through the cover and the transaxle case. Tighten to 106 inch lbs. (12 Nm).

26. Install the TSS sensor in the cover and install the bolt. Tighten to 106 inch lbs. (12 Nm).

➡**Make sure that the manual pin (part of the TR sensor) is correctly installed in the manual valve.**

27. Position the TSS, OSS and TR sensor wiring harness aside and install the main control valve body.

28. Inspect the manual pin to make sure it is correctly installed in the manual valve. If it is not, pull the valve body off the transaxle case. Correctly install the manual pin in the manual control valve and position the valve body in place.

29. Install the TR sensor detent spring and the 10 bolts. Tighten the bolts in the sequence shown. Tighten to 106 inch lbs. (12 Nm).

➡**Do not handle the solenoid body in the leadframe area or by the screens of the solenoid body filter or damage to the solenoid body can occur.**

➡**Use care not to break the alignment tabs when installing the solenoid body filter. Damage to the transaxle will occur if the solenoid body is not correctly aligned.**

➡**Make sure that the filter passage areas are clean of foreign material before installing the filter. Damage to the transaxle will occur if the filter passages are not clean.**

30. Install a new solenoid body filter assembly by pushing it straight down on to the alignment tabs.

➡**Make sure not to pinch the Turbine Shaft Speed (TSS), Output Shaft Speed (OSS) or Transmission Range (TR) sensor wiring harnesses when installing the solenoid body. Damage to the wiring harness will occur.**

➡**Install the different length bolts in the locations noted during disassembly.**

31. Install the solenoid body and the 11 bolts.

32. Tighten the solenoid body bolts in

the sequence shown. Tighten to 106 inch lbs. (12 Nm).

33. Route the OSS sensor wiring harness and connect the electrical connector.

34. Connect the TR sensor electrical connector. Connect the electrical connector. Slide the locking tab over.

35. Connect the TSS sensor electrical connector.

36. Inspect the transaxle side cover seal for damage and install new if necessary.

➡**Inspect the 20-pin solenoid body connector seal to make sure that the seal is on the inside of the main control cover or a transmission fluid leak will occur.**

➡**Install the studbolts in the locations noted during disassembly.**

37. Install the main control cover and install the 14 bolts.

38. Tighten the main control cover bolts in the sequence shown. Tighten to 106 inch lbs. (12 Nm).

39. Position the transmission fluid cooler thermal bypass valve and transmission fluid cooler tube assembly in place and install the 2 transmission fluid cooler line bracket nuts. Tighten to 80 inch lbs. (9 Nm).

40. Connect the transaxle electrical connector.

➡**Make sure that when installing the manual control lever it is fully seated onto the manual control lever shaft or damage to the manual control lever shaft will occur and the lever will come loose.**

➡**Make sure to hold the manual control lever while tightening the manual control lever nut or damage to the manual control lever and park components will occur.**

41. Install the manual control lever and the nut. Tighten to 159 inch lbs. (18 Nm).

42. Inspect the transmission fluid cooler tube backing ring and seal for damage and install a new backing ring or seal if necessary. Lubricate the transmission fluid cooler tube seal with clean transmission fluid and install the backing ring and seal on the transmission fluid cooler tube.

43. Position the transmission fluid cooler tube in place and install a new bolt. Tighten to 80 inch lbs. (9 Nm).

44. Tighten the transmission fluid cooler tube fitting and tighten to 97 inch lbs. (11 Nm).

45. Install the transmission fluid level indicator.

46. Route the coolant hoses in the transmission fluid filler tube.

47. Place the manual control lever in DRIVE. Rotate the manual control lever clockwise until it stops. Rotate the manual control lever counterclockwise one detent until it stops.

48. Unlock the selector lever cable adjuster by sliding the locking tab over.

49. Slide the cable end forward or backward to align it with the manual control lever.

50. With the adjuster locking tab released, connect the selector lever cable end to the manual control lever.

51. Slide the release tab back to lock the adjuster.

52. Position the ACL assembly in place and install the bolt. Tighten to 97 inch lbs. (11 Nm).

53. Tighten the ACL outlet pipe clamp at the TB. Tighten to 44 inch lbs. (5 Nm).

54. Connect the engine breather to the ACL assembly.

55. Connect the brake booster vacuum hose to the ACL assembly.

56. Connect the MAF sensor electrical connector and connect the electrical harness fastener.

57. Fill with clean transmission fluid to the correct level.

FUEL — GASOLINE FUEL INJECTION SYSTEM

FUEL SYSTEM SERVICE PRECAUTIONS

Safety is the most important factor when performing not only fuel system maintenance but any type of maintenance. Failure to conduct maintenance and repairs in a safe manner may result in serious personal injury or death. Maintenance and testing of the vehicle's fuel system components can be accomplished safely and effectively by adhering to the following rules and guidelines.

• To avoid the possibility of fire and personal injury, always disconnect the negative battery cable unless the repair or test procedure requires that battery voltage be applied.

• Always relieve the fuel system pressure prior to disconnecting any fuel system component (injector, fuel rail, pressure regulator, etc.), fitting or fuel line connection. Exercise extreme caution whenever relieving fuel system pressure to avoid exposing skin, face and eyes to fuel spray. Please be advised that fuel under pressure may penetrate the skin or any part of the body that it contacts.

• Always place a shop towel or cloth around the fitting or connection prior to loosening to absorb any excess fuel due to spillage. Ensure that all fuel spillage (should it occur) is quickly removed from engine surfaces. Ensure that all fuel soaked cloths or towels are deposited into a suitable waste container.

• Always keep a dry chemical (Class B) fire extinguisher near the work area.

• Do not allow fuel spray or fuel vapors to come into contact with a spark or open flame.

• Always use a back-up wrench when loosening and tightening fuel line connection fittings. This will prevent unnecessary stress and torsion to fuel line piping.

• Always replace worn fuel fitting O-rings with new. Do not substitute fuel hose or equivalent where fuel pipe is installed.

Before servicing the vehicle, make sure to also refer to the precautions in the beginning of this section as well.

RELIEVING FUEL SYSTEM PRESSURE

See Figure 205.

✳✳ WARNING

Do not smoke, carry lighted tobacco or have an open flame of any type when working on or near any fuel-related component. Highly flammable mixtures are always present and may be ignited. Failure to follow these instructions may result in serious personal injury.

✳✳ WARNING

Do not carry personal electronic devices such as cell phones, pagers or audio equipment of any type when working on or near any fuel-related component. Highly flammable mixtures are always present and may be ignited. Failure to follow these instructions may result in serious personal injury.

✳✳ WARNING

Before working on or disconnecting any of the fuel tubes or fuel system components, relieve the fuel system pressure to prevent accidental spraying of fuel. Fuel in the fuel system remains under high pressure, even when the engine is not running. Failure to follow this instruction may result in serious personal injury.

1. Remove the LR quarter trim panel.

➡ The Inertia Fuel Shutoff (IFS) switch is located behind a shield and requires the use of a small screwdriver to release the electrical connector.

2. Disconnect the IFS switch electrical connector.

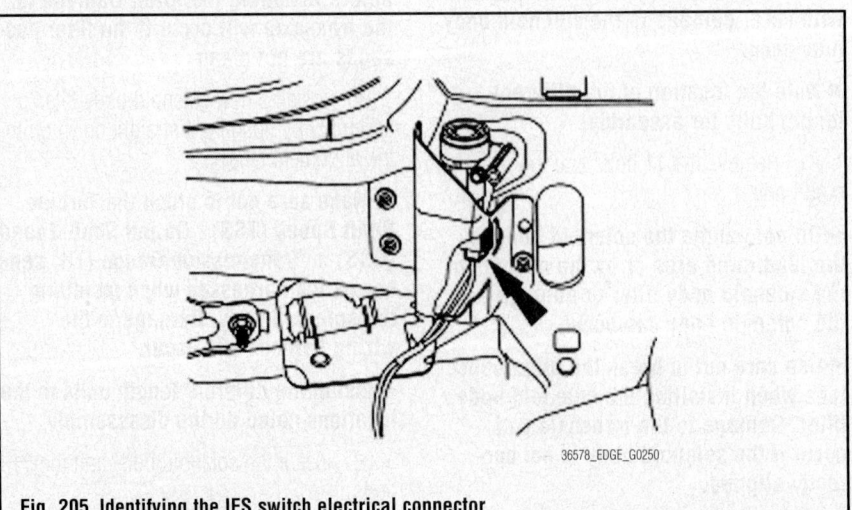

Fig. 205 Identifying the IFS switch electrical connector

36578_EDGE_G0250

3. Start the engine and allow to idle until the engine stalls.

4. After the engine stalls, crank the engine for approximately 5 seconds to make sure the fuel injector supply manifold pressure has been released.

5. Turn the ignition switch to the OFF position.

6. When the fuel system service is complete, connect the IFS switch electrical connector.

→It may take more than one key cycle to pressurize the fuel system. Cycle the ignition key and wait 3 seconds to pressurize the fuel system. Check for leaks prior to starting the engine.

7. Start the vehicle and check the fuel system for leaks.

FUEL LEVEL SENDING UNIT

✳✳ WARNING

Do not smoke, carry lighted tobacco or have an open flame of any type when working on or near any fuel-related component. Highly flammable mixtures are always present and may be ignited. Failure to follow these instructions may result in serious personal injury.

✳✳ WARNING

Do not carry personal electronic devices such as cell phones, pagers or audio equipment of any type when working on or near any fuel-related component. Highly flammable mixtures are always present and may be ignited. Failure to follow these instructions may result in serious personal injury.

✳✳ WARNING

When handling fuel, always observe fuel handling precautions and be prepared in the event of fuel spillage. Spilled fuel may be ignited by hot vehicle components or other ignition sources. Failure to follow these instructions may result in serious personal injury.

✳✳ WARNING

Always disconnect the battery ground cable at the battery when working on an evaporative emission (EVAP) system or fuel-related component. Highly flammable mixtures are always present and may be ignited. Failure to follow these instructions may result in serious personal injury.

REMOVAL & INSTALLATION

See Figures 206 and 207.

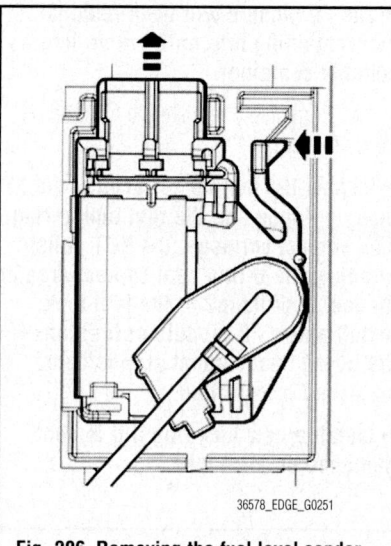

36578_EDGE_G0251

Fig. 206 Removing the fuel level sender

1. Remove the Fuel Pump (FP) module.
2. Disconnect the fuel level sender electrical connector.
3. Depress the lock tab and slide the fuel level sender upwards and remove.
4. To install, reverse the removal procedure.

FUEL PUMP MODULE

REMOVAL & INSTALLATION

✳✳ WARNING

Do not smoke, carry lighted tobacco or have an open flame of any type when working on or near any fuel-related component. Highly flammable mixtures are always present and may be ignited. Failure to follow these instructions may result in serious personal injury.

✳✳ WARNING

Do not carry personal electronic devices such as cell phones, pagers or audio equipment of any type when working on or near any fuel-related component. Highly flammable mixtures are always present and may be ignited. Failure to follow these instructions may result in serious personal injury.

✳✳ WARNING

Before working on or disconnecting any of the fuel tubes or fuel system components, relieve the fuel system pressure to prevent accidental spraying of fuel. Fuel in the fuel system remains under high pressure, even when the engine is not running. Failure to follow this instruction may result in serious personal injury.

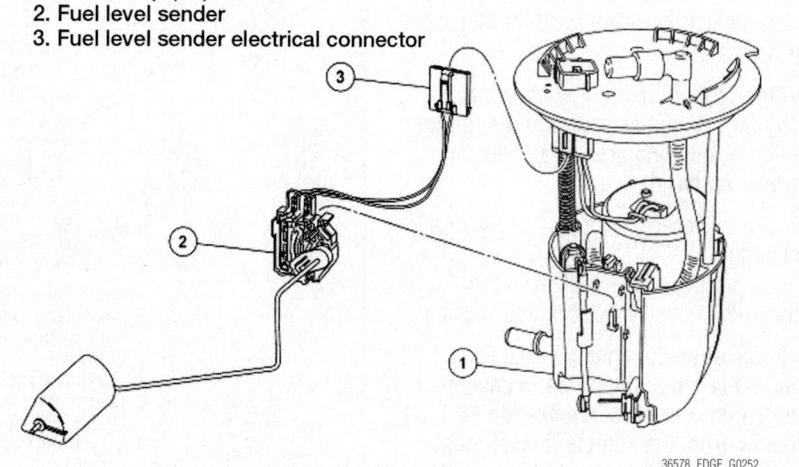

1. Fuel Pump (FP) module
2. Fuel level sender
3. Fuel level sender electrical connector

36578_EDGE_G0252

Fig. 207 Identifying the fuel level sender and related components

⁑ **WARNING**

When handling fuel, always observe fuel handling precautions and be prepared in the event of fuel spillage. Spilled fuel may be ignited by hot vehicle components or other ignition sources. Failure to follow these instructions may result in serious personal injury.

⁑ **WARNING**

Always disconnect the battery ground cable at the battery when working on an Evaporative Emission (EVAP) system or fuel-related component. Highly flammable mixtures are always present and may be ignited. Failure to follow these instructions may result in serious personal injury.

➡ The Fuel Pump (FP) module has a serviceable fuel level sender.

1. Release the fuel pressure.
2. Disconnect the battery ground cable. Carefully turn the fuel tank filler cap counterclockwise approximately ¼ turn until the thread disengages and position aside.
3. Insert a suitable semi-rigid fuel drain tube (approximately 120 inches long) into the fuel tank filler pipe until it enters the fuel tank.

➡ If the fuel tank is completely full, this step will lower the fuel level below the FP module mounting flange.

4. Attach the Fuel Storage Tanker to the fuel drain tube and drain ⅛ of a tank (approximately 3 gallons) of the fuel from a full tank.
5. Remove the rear seat.
6. Remove the 4 bolts and the FP module access cover.

➡ Clean the FP module connection, coupling, flange surface and the immediate surrounding area of any dirt or foreign material.

7. Disconnect the FP module electrical connector.
8. Disconnect the fuel tank jumper tube-to-FP module quick connect coupling.

➡ Place absorbent pads on the floor pan in the immediate area in case of fuel spills. Carefully remove the FP module from the vehicle to avoid fuel spillage inside the vehicle.

9. Using the Fuel Tanks Sender Unit Wrench, remove the FP module lock ring.

10. AWD vehicles, perform the following:

➡ The FP module must be handled carefully to avoid damage to the float arm.

a. Carefully lift the FP module out of the fuel tank enough to access and disconnect the internal fuel tube-to-FP module quick connect coupling.

➡ The FP module will have residual fuel remaining internally, drain into a suitable container.

11. Completely remove the FP module from the fuel tank.

➡ Inspect the mating surfaces of the FP module flange and the fuel tank o-ring seal contact surfaces. DO NOT polish or adjust the o-ring seal contact area of the fuel tank flange or the fuel tank. Install a new FP module or fuel tank if the o-ring seal contact area is bent, scratched or corroded.

➡ Install a new lock ring if it is bent, damaged or corroded.

➡ To install, apply clean engine oil to the O-ring seal.

12. Remove the FP module O-ring seal.

➡ Make sure the alignment tab on the FP module and the fuel tank meet before tightening the FP module lock ring.

13. To install, reverse the removal procedure. Install a FP module o-ring seal.

FUEL RAIL & INJECTORS

REMOVAL & INSTALLATION

See Figure 208.

⁑ **CAUTION**

Observe all applicable safety precautions when working around fuel. Whenever servicing the fuel system, always work in a well ventilated area. Do not allow fuel spray or vapors to come in contact with a spark or open flame. Keep a dry chemical fire extinguisher near the work area. Always keep fuel in a con-

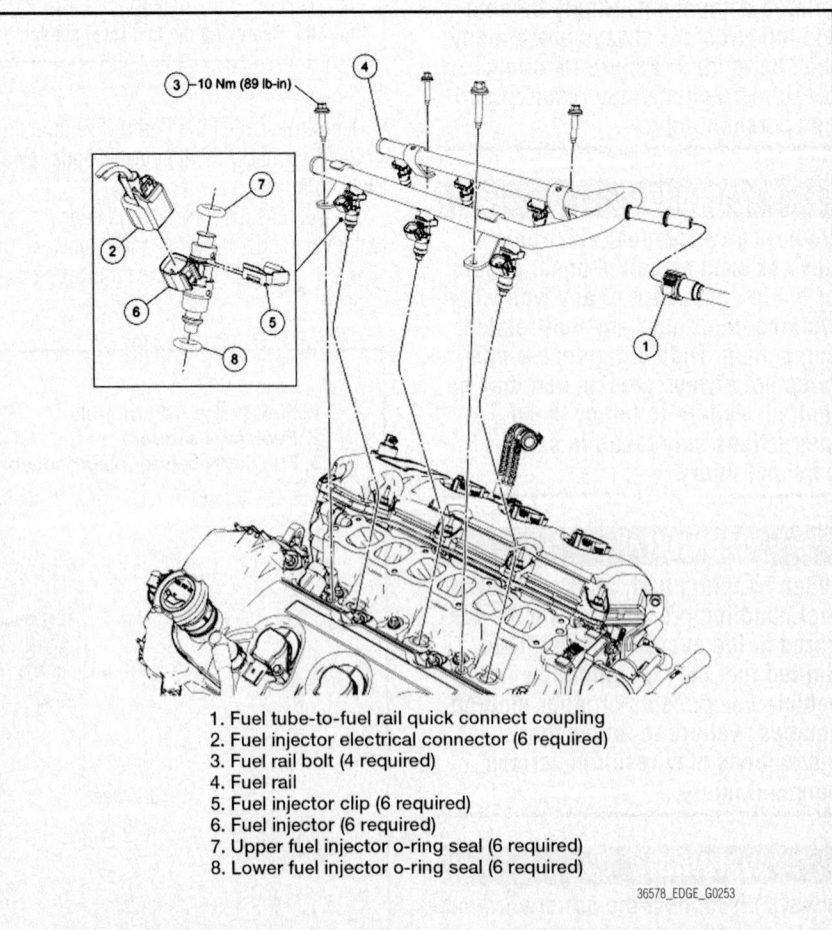

1. Fuel tube-to-fuel rail quick connect coupling
2. Fuel injector electrical connector (6 required)
3. Fuel rail bolt (4 required)
4. Fuel rail
5. Fuel injector clip (6 required)
6. Fuel injector (6 required)
7. Upper fuel injector o-ring seal (6 required)
8. Lower fuel injector o-ring seal (6 required)

36578_EDGE_G0253

Fig. 208 Fuel rail and injector exploded view

tainer specifically designed for fuel storage; also, always properly seal fuel containers to avoid the possibility of fire or explosion.

1. Disconnect the negative battery cable.
2. Relieve the fuel system pressure, as outlined in this section.
3. Remove the upper intake manifold. Refer to the Intake Manifold procedure in the Engine Mechanical Section.
4. Disconnect the fuel tube-to-fuel rail quick connect coupling.
5. Disconnect the 6 fuel injector electrical connectors.
6. Remove the 4 fuel rail bolts.
7. Remove the fuel rail and injectors as an assembly.
8. Remove the 6 fuel injector clips and the 6 fuel injectors.
9. Remove and discard the 12 fuel injector O-ring seals.

To install:

✸✸ WARNING

Only use O-ring seals that are made of special fuel-resistant material. Using regular O-rings can cause the fuel system to leak. Do not reuse the O-ring seals.

✸✸ WARNING

The upper and lower O-ring seals are not interchangeable.

➡️**Install new fuel injector O-ring seals and lubricate them with clean engine oil.**

10. Install the 6 fuel injectors and the 6 fuel injector clips into the fuel rail.
11. Install the fuel rail and fuel injectors as an assembly.
12. Install the 4 fuel rail bolts. Tighten to 10 Nm (89 inch lbs.).
13. Connect the 6 fuel injector electrical connectors.
14. Connect the fuel tube-to-fuel rail quick connect coupling.
15. Install the upper intake manifold.
16. Connect the negative battery cable.

FUEL TANK

REMOVAL & INSTALLATION

1. Disconnect the battery ground cable.
2. Drain the fuel tank.
3. AWD vehicles perform the following:
   a. Remove the muffler and tailpipe.
   b. Remove the driveshaft.

4. Disconnect the fuel tank wiring harness electrical connectors.
5. Disconnect the Fuel Tank Pressure (FTP) electrical connector and release the pin-type wire harness retainer from the fuel tank.
6. Disconnect the fuel vapor tube assembly-to-fuel tank quick connect coupling.
7. Release the clamp and disconnect the fuel tank filler pipe hose from the fuel tank. To install, tighten to 35 inch lbs. (4 Nm).
8. disconnect the fuel tank jumper tube-to-fuel tube quick connect coupling.
9. Remove the 2 bracket bolts and position parking brake cables aside. To install, tighten to 17 ft. lbs. (23 Nm).
10. Install the powertrain lift under the fuel tank.

➡️**Remove all bolts prior to lowering the fuel tank. Fuel tank damage can occur if all the bolts are not removed.**

11. Remove the 2 fuel tank bracket bolts and the 4 fuel tank bolts. To install, tighten to 18 ft. lbs. (25 Nm).
12. Completely lower and remove the fuel tank from the vehicle.

13. To install, reverse the removal procedure.

IDLE SPEED

ADJUSTMENT

Idle speed is maintained by the Powertrain Control Module (PCM). No adjustment is necessary or possible.

THROTTLE BODY

REMOVAL & INSTALLATION

See Figure 209.

1. Remove the air cleaner outlet pipe.
2. Disconnect the electronic throttle control electrical connector.
3. Remove the 4 bolts and the throttle body. Discard the throttle body gasket.

To install:

4. Install a new throttle body gasket.
5. Install the throttle body and tighten to 89 inch lbs. (10 Nm).
6. Attach the electronic throttle control electrical connector.
7. Install the air cleaner outlet pipe.

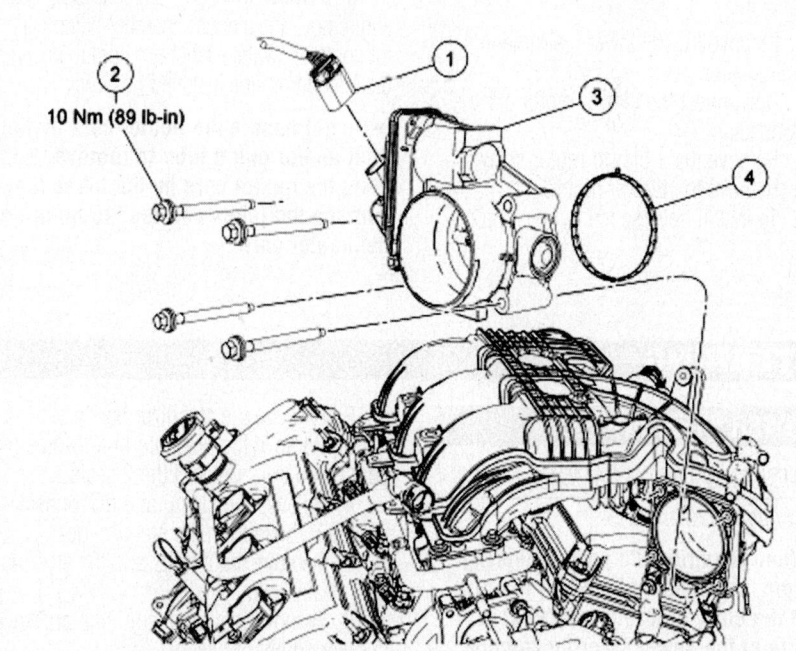

1. Electronic throttle control electrical connector
2. Throttle Body (TB) bolt (4 required)
3. TB
4. TB gasket

36578_EDGE_G0254

Fig. 209 Exploded view of the throttle body and related components

HEATING & AIR CONDITIONING SYSTEM

BLOWER MOTOR

REMOVAL & INSTALLATION

See Figure 210.

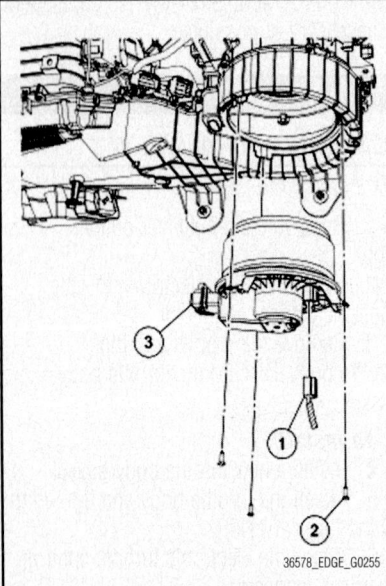

Fig. 210 Removing and installing the blower motor

1. Remove the RH lower instrument panel insulator.
2. Disconnect the blower motor electrical connector.
3. Remove the 3 blower motor screws.
4. Remove the blower motor.
5. To install, reverse the removal procedure.

HEATER CORE

REMOVAL & INSTALLATION

See Figure 211.

➡If a heater core leak is suspected, the heater core must be pressure leak tested before it is removed from the vehicle.

1. Remove the heater core and evaporator core housing.
2. Remove the 6 floor duct screws and the floor duct.
3. Remove the heater core tube dash panel seal.
4. Remove the heater tube bracket screw and the heater tube bracket.
5. Remove the 5 fresh air inlet duct screws and the fresh air inlet duct.
6. Disconnect the wire harness from the plenum chamber.
7. Remove the 7 lower facing plenum chamber screws.
8. Orient the heater core and evaporator core housing with the plenum chamber upright.
9. Remove the upper facing plenum chamber screw.
10. Remove the 2 plenum chamber clips and remove the plenum chamber being careful not to allow the evaporator core to become dislodged from the installed position.

➡Do not handle the heater core by the inlet and/or outlet tube to remove. Handling the heater core by the tubes may damage the joints and lead to failure of the heater core.

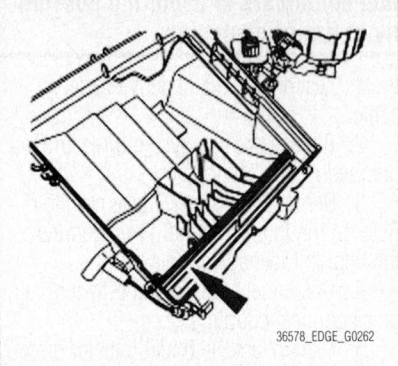

Fig. 211 Verifying the drain seal position

11. Remove the heater core in the following sequence.
   a. Grasp the heater core by the core-side of the heater tube connections and partially remove it from the plenum chamber.
   b. Grasp the heater core by the top of the core and remove it from the plenum chamber.

➡It is not necessary to carry out this step if the evaporator core has not become dislodged from the installed position during this procedure.

12. If the evaporator core has been moved at any point during heater core removal, remove the evaporator core, verify that the drain seal is installed in the correct position and install the evaporator core in the correct position.

To install:
To install, reverse the removal procedure.

STEERING

POWER STEERING GEAR

REMOVAL & INSTALLATION

See Figures 212 and 213.

➡When repairing the power steering system, care should be taken to prevent the entry of foreign material or failure of the power steering components may result.

➡Use a steering wheel holding device (such as Hunter® 28-75-1 or equivalent).

1. Using a suitable holding device, hold the steering wheel in the straight-ahead position.

2. Remove the stabilizer bar.
3. Remove the pressure line-to-steering gear banjo bolt. Discard the 2 seals.
4. Release the clamp and disconnect the return hose from the steering gear.
5. Remove the 2 bolts and the steering gear heat shield.
6. Remove the 3 pressure line bracket-to-steering gear bolts.
7. Remove and discard the 4 steering gear bolts. Remove the steering gear.

To install:

➡When installing a new steering gear, install a new steering gear turn tube heat wrap.

8. Position the steering gear and tighten the 4 steering gear bolts to 76 ft. lbs. (103 Nm) in the sequence shown.

➡New seals must be installed any time the pressure line is disconnected from the power steering pump and/or the steering gear or a fluid leak may occur.

9. Install the pressure line-to-steering gear banjo bolt. Tighten to 35 ft. lbs. (48 Nm).
10. Install the 3 pressure line bracket-to-steering gear bolts. Tighten to 80 inch lbs. (9 Nm).
11. Release the clamp and connect the return hose to the steering gear.

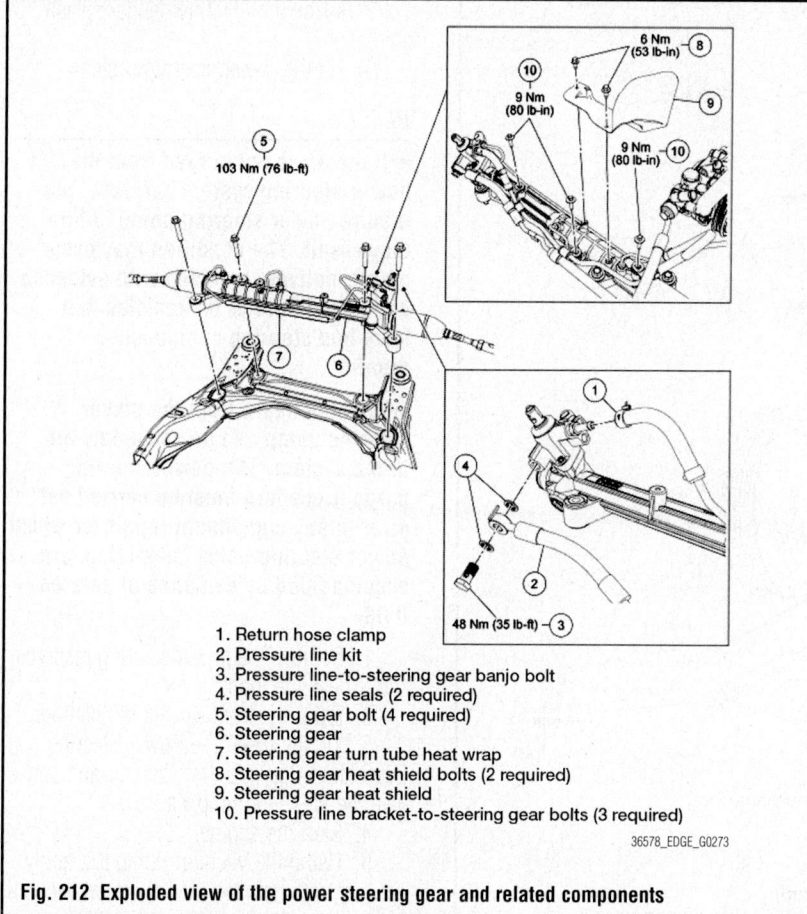

1. Return hose clamp
2. Pressure line kit
3. Pressure line-to-steering gear banjo bolt
4. Pressure line seals (2 required)
5. Steering gear bolt (4 required)
6. Steering gear
7. Steering gear turn tube heat wrap
8. Steering gear heat shield bolts (2 required)
9. Steering gear heat shield
10. Pressure line bracket-to-steering gear bolts (3 required)

36578_EDGE_G0273

Fig. 212 Exploded view of the power steering gear and related components

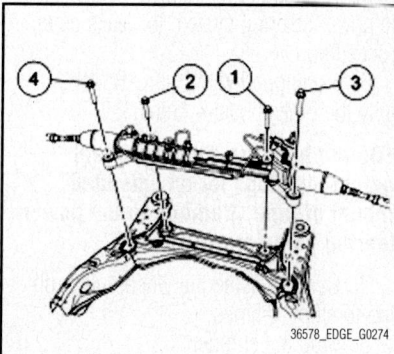

36578_EDGE_G0274

Fig. 213 Identifying steering gear bolt tightening sequence

12. Install the steering gear heat shield and the 2 bolts. Tighten to 53 inch lbs. (6 Nm).
13. Install the stabilizer bar.
14. Fill the power steering system.

POWER STEERING PUMP

REMOVAL & INSTALLATION

See Figures 214 through 217.

➡**While repairing the power steering system, care should be taken to pre-**

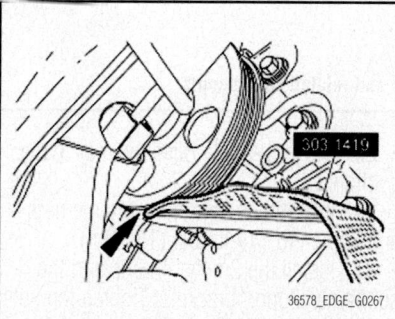

36578_EDGE_G0267

Fig. 214 Positioning the Stretchy Belt Remover on the power steering pulley belt

vent the entry of foreign material or failure of the power steering components may result.

1. With the vehicle in NEUTRAL, position it on a hoist.
2. Using a suitable suction device, remove the power steering fluid from the fluid reservoir.
3. Remove the RH inner fender splash shield.
4. Position the Stretchy Belt Remover on the power steering pump pulley belt as shown.

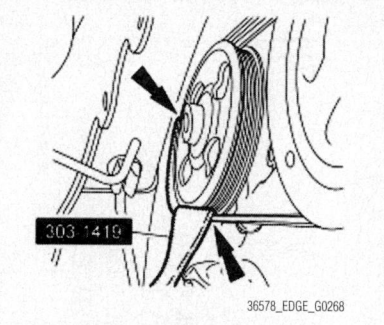

36578_EDGE_G0268

Fig. 215 Positioning the Stretchy Belt Remover on the power steering pump pulley

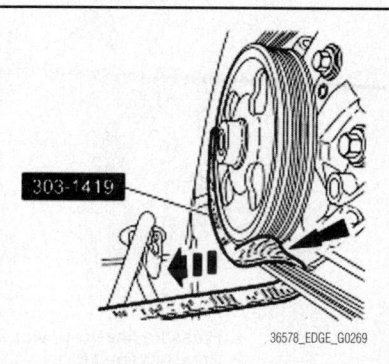

36578_EDGE_G0269

Fig. 216 Removing the power steering pump belt

➡**Feed the Stretchy Belt Remover on to the power steering pump pulley approximately 5.984 inch (152 mm).**

5. Turn the crankshaft clockwise nd feel the Stretchy Belt Remover evenly on the power steering pump pulley as shown.
6. Remove the power steering pump bolt.
   a. Fold the Stretchy Belt Remover under the inside of the power steering pump belt as shown.
   b. In one quick motion, firmly pull the Stretchy Belt Remover out of the RH fender well, removing the power steering pump belt.
7. AWD vehicles, remove the 4 bolts and position the driveshaft aside.
8. Using a suitable jack, support the rear of the subframe.
9. Remove the 2 nuts, 4 bolts and the subframe support brackets.
10. Remove the 2 middle subframe nuts.
11. Lower the rear of the subframe.
12. Release the clamp and disconnect the power steering pump supply hose from the power steering pump.
13. Disconnect the Power Steering Pressure (PSP) switch electrical connector.

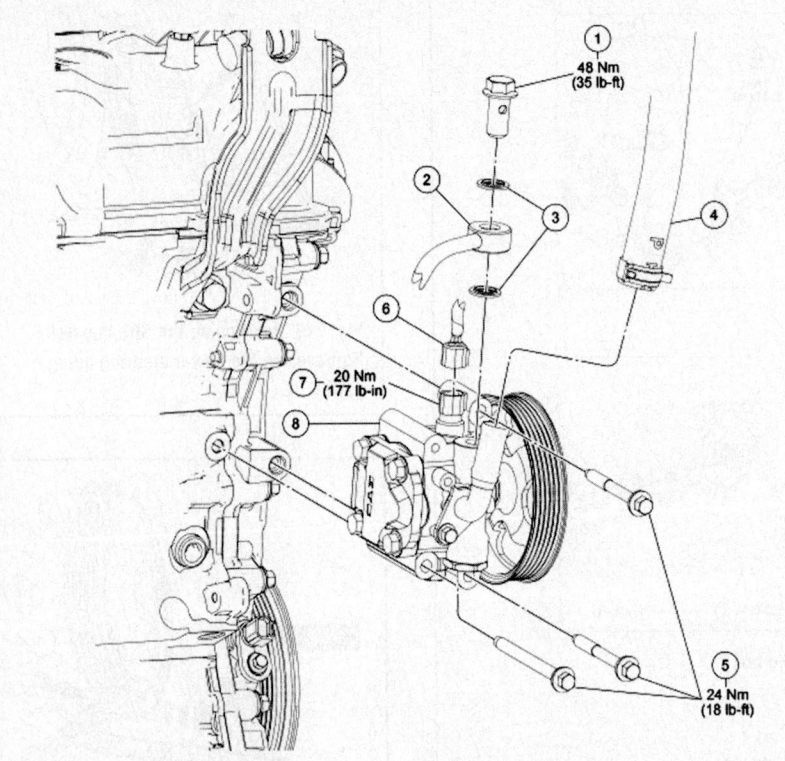

1. Pressure line-to-power steering pump banjo bolt
2. Pressure line kit
3. Pressure line seals (2 required)
4. Power steering pump supply hose
5. Power steering pump bolts (3 required)
6. Power Steering Pressure (PSP) switch electrical connector
7. PSP switch
8. Power steering pump

36578_EDGE_G0270

Fig. 217 Exploded view of the power steering pump and related components

14. Remove the pressure line-to-power steering pump banjo bolt and disconnect the pressure line from the pump. Discard the 2 seals.

15. Remove the 3 power steering pump bolts and the pump.

To install:

16. Position the power steering pump and install the 3 bolts. Tighten to 18 ft. lbs. (24 Nm).

➡**New seals must be installed any time the power steering pressure line is disconnected from the power steering pump, or a fluid leak may occur.**

17. Position the pressure line and install the pressure line-to-power steering pump banjo bolt and seals. Tighten to 35 ft. lbs. (48 Nm).

18. Connect the PSP switch electrical connector.

19. Connect the power steering pump supply hose and secure the clamp.

20. Using the jack, raise the rear of the subframe.

21. Install the 2 middle subframe nuts and tighten to 111 ft. lbs. (150 Nm).

22. Install the 2 nuts, 4 bolts and the subframe support brackets. Tighten the nuts to 111 ft. lbs. (150 Nm). Tighten the bolts to 76 ft. lbs. (103 Nm).

23. AWD vehicles, position the driveshaft and install the 4 bolts. Tighten to 52 ft. lbs. (70 Nm).

➡**After installation, make sure the belt is correctly seated on the crankshaft and power steering pulley or damage to the belt may occur.**

24. Using the Power Steering Belt Installation Tool, install the power steering belt onto the power steering pump pulley. Position the belt around the Power Steering Belt Installation Tool and the power steering pump pulley. Make sure that the belt is engaged with the pulley and rotate the crankshaft clockwise to install the belt.

25. Install the RH inner fender splash shield.

26. Fill the power steering system.

BLEEDING

➡**If the air is not purged from the power steering system correctly, premature power steering pump failure may result. The condition may occur on pre-delivery vehicles with evidence of aerated fluid or on vehicles that have had steering component repairs.**

➡**A whine heard from the power steering pump can be caused by air in the system. The power steering purge procedure must be carried out prior to any component repair for which power steering noise complaints are accompanied by evidence of aerated fluid.**

1. Remove the power steering reservoir cap. Check the fluid.

2. Raise the front wheels off the floor.

3. Tightly insert the Power Steering Evacuation Cap into the reservoir and connect the Vacuum Pump Kit.

4. Start the engine.

5. Using the Vacuum Pump Kit, apply vacuum and maintain the maximum vacuum of 20-25 in-Hg (68-85 kPa). If the Vacuum Pump Kit does not maintain vacuum, check the power steering system for leaks before proceeding.

6. If equipped with Hydro-Boost®, apply the brake pedal 4 times.

➡**Do not hold the steering wheel against the stops for an extended amount of time. Damage to the power steering pump may occur.**

7. Cycle the steering wheel fully from stop to stop 10 times.

8. Stop the engine.

9. Release the vacuum and remove the Vacuum Pump Kit and the Power Steering Evacuation Cap.

➡**DO NOT overfill the reservoir.**

10. Fill the reservoir. Use approved transmission fluid.

11. Start the engine.

12. Install the Power Steering Evacuation Cap and the Vacuum Pump Kit. Apply and maintain the maximum vacuum of 20-25 in-Hg (68-85 kPa).

➡**Do not hold the steering wheel against the stops for an extended amount of time. Damage to the power steering pump may occur.**

13. Cycle the steering wheel fully from stop-to-stop 10 times.

14. Stop the engine, release the vacuum and remove the Vacuum Pump Kit and the Power Steering Evacuation Cap.

➡ **Do not overfill the reservoir.**

15. Fill the reservoir as needed and install the reservoir cap.

16. Visually inspect the power steering system for leaks.

➡ **Do not overfill the reservoir.**

17. Fill the reservoir as needed and visually inspect the power steering system for leaks.

18. Install the reservoir cap.

SUSPENSION   FRONT SUSPENSION

LOWER CONTROL ARM

REMOVAL & INSTALLATION

See Figure 218.

➡ **Suspension fasteners are critical parts because they affect performance of vital components and systems and their failure may result in major service expense. New parts must be installed with the same part numbers or equivalent part, if replacement is necessary. Do not use a replacement part of lesser quality or substitute design. Torque values must be used as specified during reassembly to make sure correct retention of these parts.**

1. Remove the wheel and tire.

2. Remove and discard the stabilizer bar link lower nut.

3. Remove and discard the lower ball joint nut and bolt.

4. Remove the lower arm-to-frame forward bolt and spacer. Discard the bolt.

5. Remove the 2 lower arm-to-frame rearward bolts and the lower arm. Discard the 2 bolts.

To install:

➡ **Do not tighten the bolt at this time. Position the lower arm and loosely install the 2 new lower arm-to-frame rearward bolts.**

➡ **Do not tighten the bolts at this time.**

6. Loosely install the new lower arm-to-frame forward bolt and install the spacer.

7. Install the new lower arm ball joint bolt and nut.

8. Tighten to 41 ft. lbs. (55 Nm).

9. Install the new stabilizer bar link lower nut. Tighten to 66 ft. lbs. (90 Nm).

10. Install the wheel and tire.

11. With the weight of the vehicle resting on the wheels and tires, tighten the lower arm-to-frame forward bolts to 111 ft. lbs. (150 Nm).

12. With the weight of the vehicle resting on the wheels and tires, tighten the 2 lower arm-to-frame rearward bolts to 59 ft. lbs. (80 Nm).

13. Check and, if necessary, align the front end.

SHOCK ABSORBERS

REMOVAL & INSTALLATION

See Figure 219.

➡ **Suspension fasteners are critical parts because they affect performance of vital components and systems and their failure may result in major service expense. New parts must be installed with the same part numbers or equivalent part, if replacement is necessary. Do not use a replacement part of lesser quality or substitute design. Torque values must be used as specified during reassembly to make sure correct retention of these parts.**

1. Remove and discard the 4 shock absorber upper mount nuts. To install, tighten the new nuts to 26 ft. lbs. (35 Nm).

2. Remove the wheel and tire.

3. Remove the brake flexible hose bracket bolt and disconnect the hose from the shock absorber. To install, tighten to 15 ft. lbs. (20 Nm).

4. Disconnect the wheel speed sensor harness from the shock absorber bracket.

5. Remove the shock absorber lower nuts, flag bolts and the shock absorber and spring assembly.

6. Discard the nuts and flag bolts. To install, tighten the new nuts to 166 ft. lbs. (225 Nm).

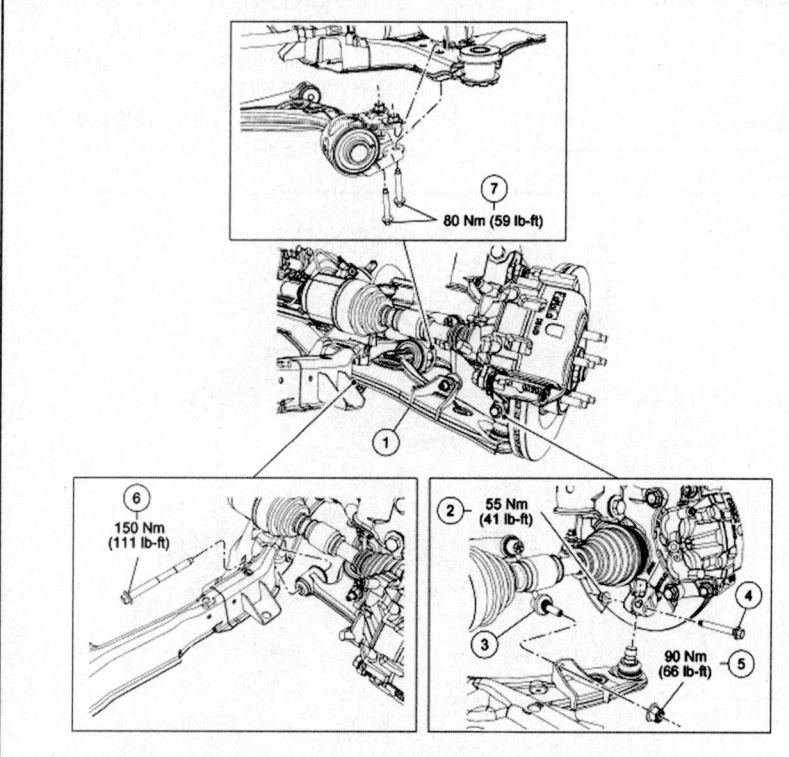

1. Lower arm
2. Lower ball joint nut
3. Stabilizer bar link
4. Lower ball joint bolt
5. Stabilizer bar link nut
6. Lower arm-to-frame forward bolt
7. Lower arm-to-frame rearward bolts (2 required)

36578_EDGE_G0275

Fig. 218 Exploded view of the lower control arm

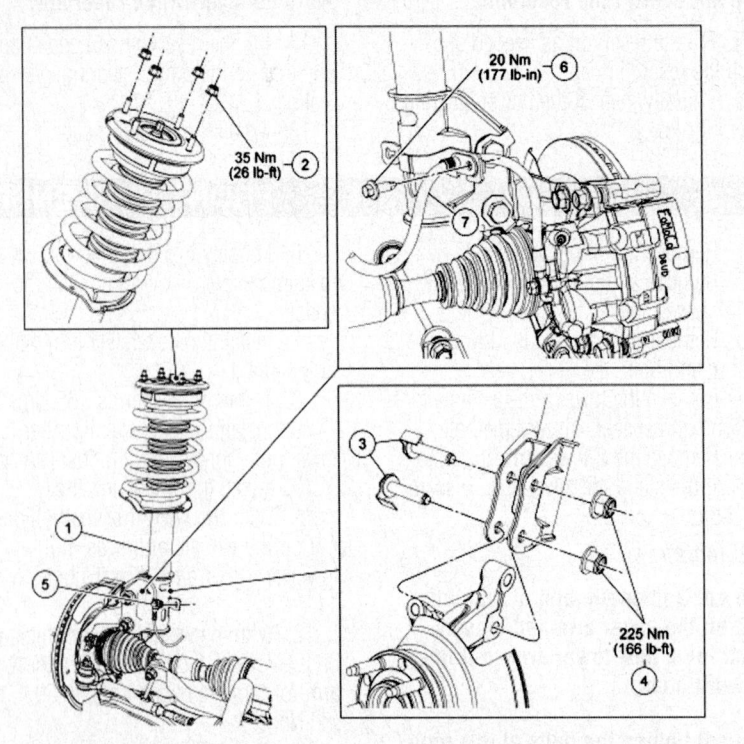

1. Shock absorber and spring assembly
2. Shock absorber upper mount nut (4 required)
3. Shock absorber lower flag bolts (2 required)
4. Shock absorber lower nuts (2 required)
5. Wheel speed sensor harness clip
6. Brake flexible hose bracket bolt
7. Brake flexible hose

36578_EDGE_G0276

Fig. 219 Exploded view of the shock absorber and spring assembly

To install:

7. To install, reverse the removal procedure.

8. Check and, if necessary, align the front end.

STABILIZER BAR

REMOVAL & INSTALLATION

See Figures 220 through 223.

➡Suspension fasteners are critical parts because they affect performance of vital components and systems and their failure may result in major service expense. New parts must be installed with the same part numbers or equivalent part, if replacement is necessary. Do not use a replacement part of lesser quality or substitute design. Torque values must be used as specified during reassembly to make sure correct retention of these parts.

➡If replacing only the stabilizer bar bushings, proceed to Step 23 of this procedure. All vehicles

➡Do not allow the steering column to rotate while the steering column shaft is disconnected, or damage to the clockspring may occur. If there is evidence that the steering column has rotated, the clockspring must be removed and recentered.

➡Use a steering wheel holding device (such as Hunter®28-75-1 or equivalent).

1. Using a suitable holding device, hold the steering wheel in the straight-ahead position.

2. Remove the wheel and tire.

3. Remove the steering column shaft bolt and disconnect the shaft from the steering gear. To install, tighten to 18 ft. lbs (25 Nm).

4. Index-mark the relationship of the front subframe to the underbody at the mounting locations.

5. Remove the 4 pin-type retainers and the RH fender splash shield.

6. Remove the 3 pushpin fasteners, the 7 screws and the front splash shield.

7. Remove the 3 RH front lower bumper-to-subframe nuts.

8. Remove the 3 LH front lower bumper-to-subframe nuts and separate the lower bumper from the subframe.

9. Remove the power steering fluid cooler hose bracket bolt.

10. Loosen the Y-pipe clamp and disconnect the 2 exhaust hangers.

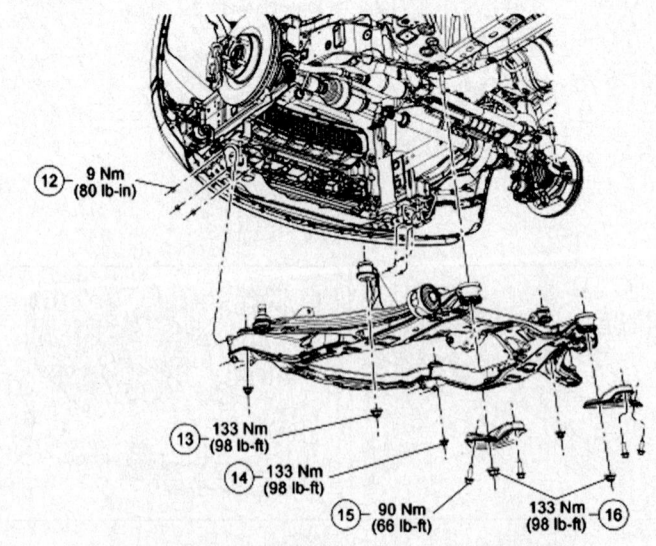

12. Front lower bumper-to-subframe nut (6 required)
13. Front subframe mounting nut (2 required)
14. Front subframe mounting nut (2 required)
15. Subframe support bracket bolt (4 required)
16. Subframe support bracket nuts (2 required)

36578_EDGE_G0278

Fig. 220 Exploded view of the subframe

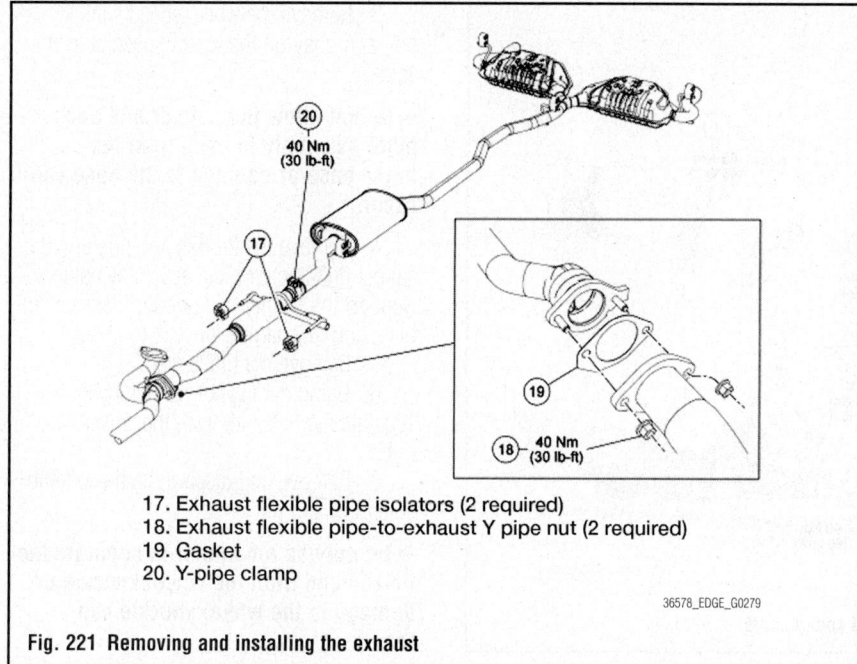

17. Exhaust flexible pipe isolators (2 required)
18. Exhaust flexible pipe-to-exhaust Y pipe nut (2 required)
19. Gasket
20. Y-pipe clamp

36578_EDGE_G0279

Fig. 221 Removing and installing the exhaust

11. Remove the 2 nuts and separate the flex pipe from the Y-pipe assembly.

12. AWD vehicles, index mark the driveshaft, remove the 4 bolts and position the driveshaft aside.

➡**Use the holding feature to prevent the ball stud from turning while removing or installing the stabilizer bar link nuts.**

13. Remove the stabilizer link upper and lower nuts and the stabilizer links. Discard the nuts.

14. Remove the 2 outer tie-rod end nuts.

15. Using the Tie-Rod End Remover, separate the outer tie rod ends from the wheel knuckles.

16. Remove the 2 lower ball joint bolts and nuts and separate the lower ball joints from the wheel knuckles. Discard the bolts and nuts.

17. Remove the upper nut, loosen the lower nut and remove the engine roll restrictor heat shield.

18. Remove the engine roll restrictor-to-subframe bolt.

19. Using a suitable jack, support the subframe. Support the subframe in the center rear area of the subframe.

20. Remove the 2 nuts, 4 bolts and the subframe support bracket. Discard the nuts and bolts.

21. Remove and discard the 4 subframe nuts.

22. Using the jack, lower the subframe approximately 3 inches (76.2 mm).

23. Remove the 4 bolts, 2 stabilizer bar brackets and bushings. Discard the bolts.

24. Remove the stabilizer bar.

To install:

25. Check and, if necessary, align the front end.

26. Install the stabilizer bar.

27. Install the 4 bolts and 2 stabilizer bar brackets and bushings. Tighten the new bolts to 46 ft. lbs. (63 Nm).

28. Install and tighten the 4 new subframe nuts to 98 ft. lbs. (133 Nm).

➡**During installation, the subframe brackets are loosely installed with the support bracket bolts. Align the index marks made in Step 2, then tighten the rear subframe nuts prior to tightening the support bracket bolts.**

29. Install the 4 bolts, 2 nuts and the subframe support bracket. Tighten the new nuts to 98 ft. lbs. (133 Nm). Tighten the new bolts to 66 ft. lbs. (90 Nm).

30. Install the engine roll restrictor-to-subframe bolt and tighten to 76 ft. lbs. (103 Nm).

31. Install the engine roll restrictor heat shield and tighten to 97 inch lbs. (11 Nm).

32. Install the 2 lower ball joint bolts and nuts and connect the lower ball joints on the wheel knuckles. Tighten to 41 ft. lbs. (55 Nm).

33. Install the 2 outer tie-rod end nuts and tighten to 35 ft. lbs. (48 Nm).

34. Install the stabilizer link and the upper and lower nuts. Tighten the new nuts to 66 ft. lbs. (90 Nm).

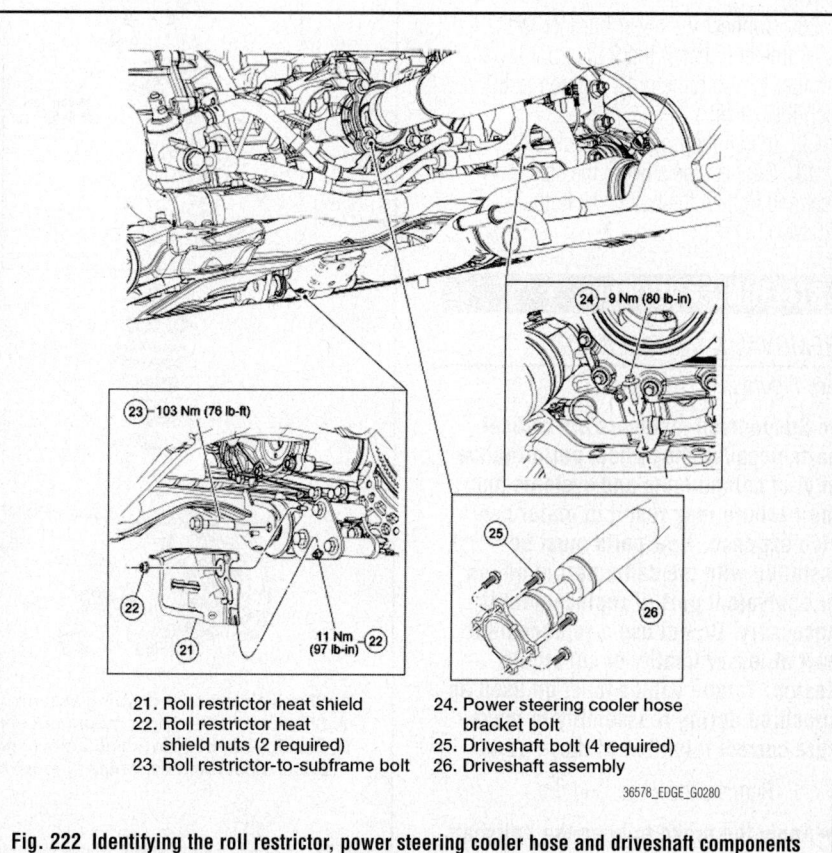

21. Roll restrictor heat shield
22. Roll restrictor heat shield nuts (2 required)
23. Roll restrictor-to-subframe bolt
24. Power steering cooler hose bracket bolt
25. Driveshaft bolt (4 required)
26. Driveshaft assembly

36578_EDGE_G0280

Fig. 222 Identifying the roll restrictor, power steering cooler hose and driveshaft components

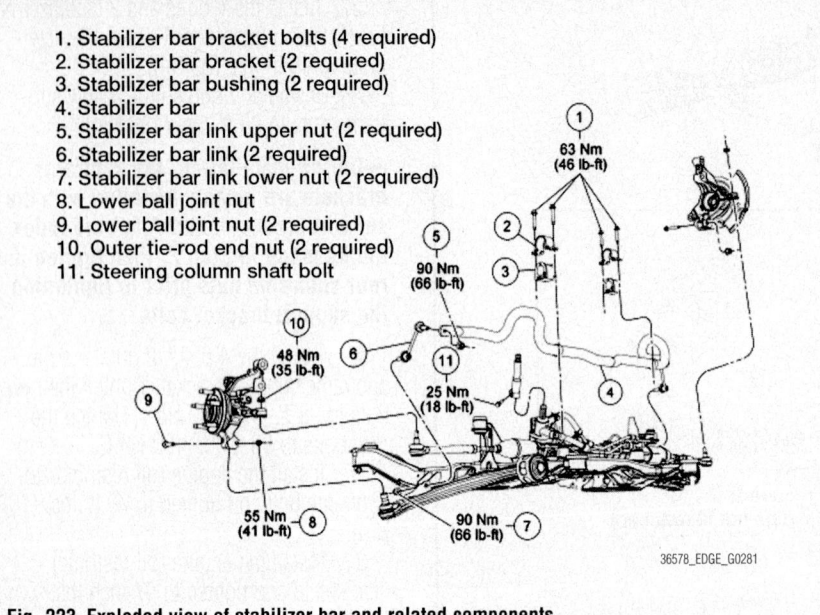

1. Stabilizer bar bracket bolts (4 required)
2. Stabilizer bar bracket (2 required)
3. Stabilizer bar bushing (2 required)
4. Stabilizer bar
5. Stabilizer bar link upper nut (2 required)
6. Stabilizer bar link (2 required)
7. Stabilizer bar link lower nut (2 required)
8. Lower ball joint nut
9. Lower ball joint nut (2 required)
10. Outer tie-rod end nut (2 required)
11. Steering column shaft bolt

63 Nm (46 lb-ft)
90 Nm (66 lb-ft)
48 Nm (35 lb-ft)
25 Nm (18 lb-ft)
55 Nm (41 lb-ft)
90 Nm (66 lb-ft)

36578_EDGE_G0281

Fig. 223 Exploded view of stabilizer bar and related components

35. AWD vehicles, install the driveshaft. Tighten to 52 ft. lbs. (70 Nm).

36. Connect the flex pipe and Y-pipe assembly. Tighten to 30 ft. lbs. (40 Nm).

37. Connect the 2 exhaust hangers and tighten to 30 ft. lbs. (40 Nm).

Install the power steering fluid cooler hose bracket bolt and tighten to 80 inch lbs. (9 Nm).

38. Connect the lower bumper to the subframe and install the 3 LH front lower bumper to subframe nuts. Tighten to 80 inch lbs. (9 Nm).

39. Install the front splash shield.

40. Connect the shaft to the steering gear and tighten the bolt to 18 ft. lbs. (25 Nm).

STEERING KNUCKLE

REMOVAL & INSTALLATION

See Figure 224.

➡ Suspension fasteners are critical parts because they affect performance of vital components and systems and their failure may result in major service expense. New parts must be installed with the same part numbers or equivalent part, if replacement is necessary. Do not use a replacement part of lesser quality or substitute design. Torque values must be used as specified during reassembly to make sure correct retention of these parts.

1. Remove the wheel and tire.

➡Apply the brake to keep the halfshaft from rotating.

➡Do not discard the wheel hub nut and washer at this time.

2. Remove the wheel hub nut and washer and the halfshaft hub seal. Discard the seal.

3. Remove the wheel speed sensor bolt and position the wheel speed sensor aside.

➡Do not allow the caliper and anchor plate assembly to hang from the brake hose or damage to the hose can occur.

4. Remove the 2 bolts and position the caliper and anchor plate assembly aside. Support the caliper and anchor plate assembly using mechanic's wire.

5. Remove the brake disc.

6. Using the Front Hub Remover, separate the halfshaft from the wheel hub.

7. Remove and discard the tie-rod end cotter pin and nut.

➡Do not use a hammer to separate the tie-rod end from the wheel knuckle or damage to the wheel knuckle can result.

8. Using the Tie-Rod End Remover, separate the tie-rod end from the wheel knuckle.

9. Remove the shock absorber lower nuts and flag bolts. Discard the nuts and flag bolts.

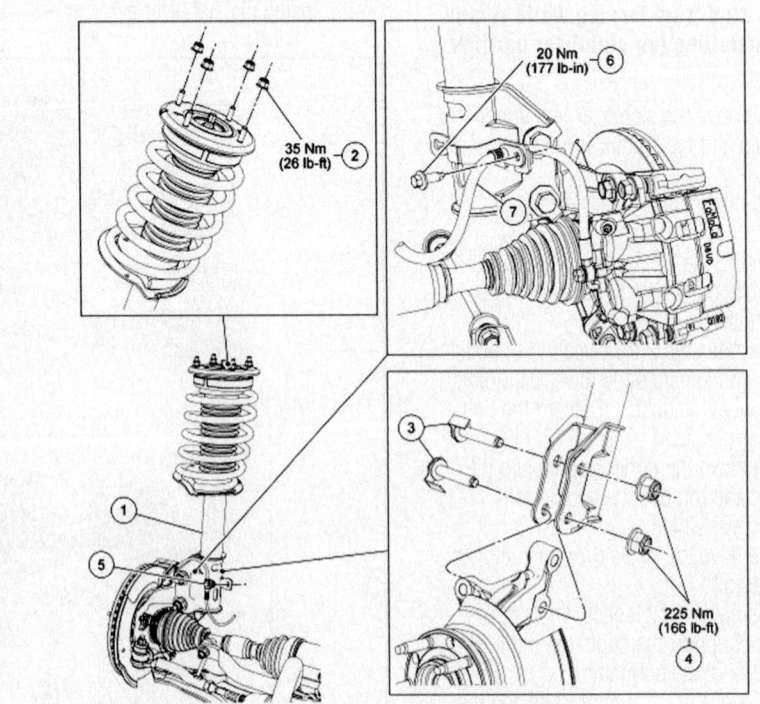

35 Nm (26 lb-ft)
20 Nm (177 lb-in)
225 Nm (166 lb-ft)

1. Shock absorber and spring assembly
2. Shock absorber upper mount nut (4 required)
3. Shock absorber lower flag bolts (2 required)
4. Shock absorber lower nuts (2 required)
5. Wheel speed sensor harness clip
6. Brake flexible hose bracket bolt
7. Brake flexible hose

36578_EDGE_G0276

Fig. 224 Exploded view of the wheel knuckle and related components

10. Remove the lower ball joint bolt, nut and the wheel knuckle. Discard the bolt and nut.

To install:

11. Position the wheel knuckle and install the new lower ball joint bolt and nut. Tighten the nut to 41 ft. lbs. (55 Nm).

12. Install the new shock absorber lower nuts and flag bolts. Tighten to 166 ft. lbs. (225 Nm).

13. Position the tie-rod end and install the new nut and cotter pin. Tighten to 35 ft. lbs. (48 Nm).

14. Position the wheel speed sensor and install the bolt. Tighten to 62 inch lbs. (7 Nm).

15. Install the brake disc.

16. Position the brake caliper and anchor plate assembly and install the 2 bolts. Tighten to 98 ft. lbs. (133 Nm).

➡️ **Do not tighten the front wheel hub nut with the vehicle on the ground. The nut must be tightened to specification before the vehicle is lowered onto the wheels. Wheel bearing damage will occur if the bearing is loaded with the weight of the vehicle applied.**

➡️ **Apply the brake to keep the halfshaft from rotating.**

17. Position the halfshaft in the hub and use the previously removed wheel hub nut and washer to seat the halfshaft. Tighten to 258 ft. lbs. (350 Nm). Remove and discard the wheel hub nut and washer.

➡️ **The wheel hub nut contains a one-time locking chemical that is activated by the heat created when it is tightened. Install and tighten the new wheel hub nut to specification within 5 minutes of starting it on the threads. Always install a new wheel hub nut after loosening or when not tightening within the specified time or damage to the components may occur.**

➡️ **Apply the brake to keep the halfshaft from rotating.**

18. Install a new wheel hub nut and washer. Tighten to 258 ft. lbs. (350 Nm).

19. Install the wheel and tire.

20. Check and, if necessary, align the front end.

WHEEL HUB & BEARING

REMOVAL & INSTALLATION

See Figures 225 through 227.

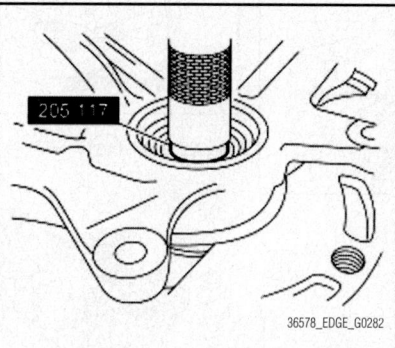

Fig. 225 Removing the wheel hub from the wheel bearing

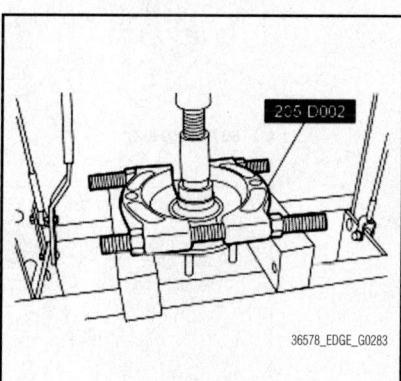

Fig. 226 Removing the inner wheel bearing race from the wheel hub

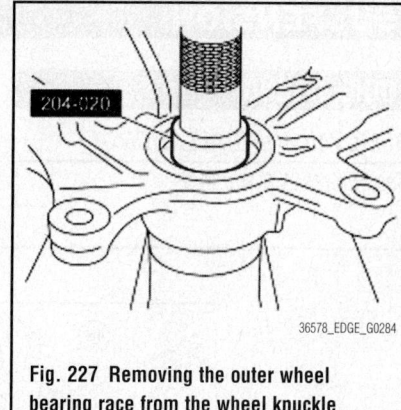

Fig. 227 Removing the outer wheel bearing race from the wheel knuckle

➡️ **If removing the wheel hub, the wheel bearing must be replaced.**

1. Remove the wheel knuckle.

2. Using the Step Plate and a suitable press, remove the wheel hub from the wheel bearing.

➡️ **This step may not be necessary if the inner wheel bearing race remains in the wheel knuckle after removing the wheel hub.**

3. Using the Pinion Bearing Cone Remover and a suitable press, remove the inner wheel bearing race from the wheel hub.

4. Remove the snap ring.

5. Using the Wheel Hub Cup Remover/Installer and a suitable press, remove the outer wheel bearing race from the wheel knuckle.

To install:

6. Using the Wheel Hub Bearing Cup Installer and a suitable press, install the wheel bearing into the wheel knuckle.

7. Install the snap ring.

8. Using the Wheel Hub Bearing Cup Installer, Step Plate and a suitable press, install the wheel hub into the wheel bearing.

9. Install the wheel knuckle.

COIL SPRING

REMOVAL & INSTALLATION

See Figures 228 and 229.

➡Suspension fasteners are critical parts because they affect performance of vital parts and systems and their failure can result in major service expense. A new part with the same part number must be installed if installation becomes necessary. Do not use a replacement part of lesser quality or substitute design. Torque values must be used as specified during reassembly

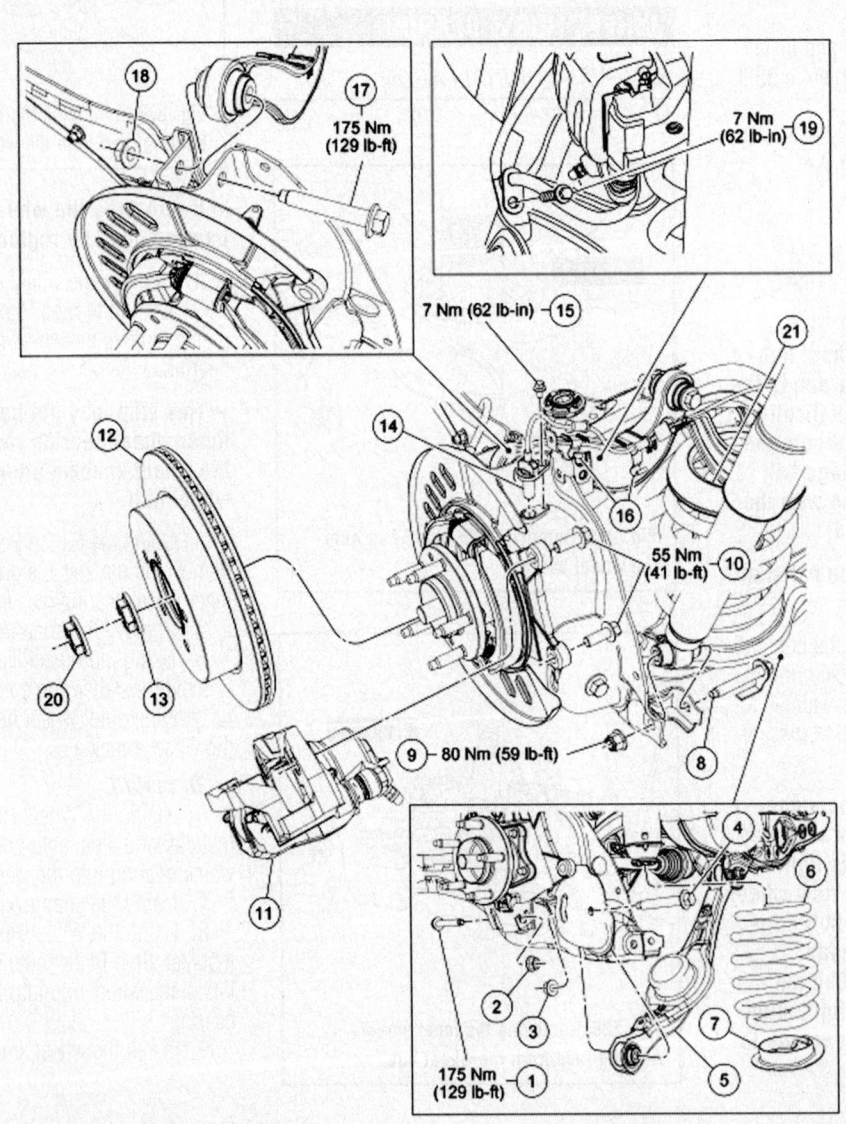

1. Toe link outboard bolt
2. Toe link outboard nut
3. Lower arm outboard nut
4. Lower arm outboard bolt
5. Lower arm
6. Spring
7. Spring lower seat
8. Shock absorber lower flag bolt
9. Shock absorber lower nut
10. Brake caliper anchor plate bolts (2 required)
11. Brake caliper and anchor plate assembly
12. Brake disc
13. Wheel hub (inner) AWD
14. Wheel speed sensor AWD
15. Wheel speed sensor bolt AWD
16. Wheel speed sensor harness clips (2 required) AWD
17. Upper arm outboard bolt
18. Upper arm outboard nut
19. Wheel speed sensor bolt AWD
20. Wheel hub nut (outer) AWD
21. Spring upper seat

36578_EDGE_G0285

Fig. 228 Exploded view of coil spring and related components

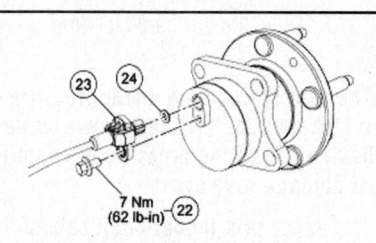

22. Wheel speed sensor bolt
23. Wheel speed sensor
24. O-ring seal

36578_EDGE_G0286

Fig. 229 Identifying FWD vehicles wheel speed sensor and o-ring seal

to make sure of correct retention of these parts.

➡**Suspension bushing fasteners must be tightened with the weight of the vehicle resting on the wheel and tires or incorrect clamp load and bushing damage may occur.**

1. Remove the wheel and tire.

➡**Do not allow the brake caliper and anchor plate assembly to hang from the brake hose or damage to the hose can occur.**

2. Remove the 2 anchor plate bolts and position the brake caliper and anchor plate assembly aside. Support the brake caliper and anchor plate assembly using mechanic's wire.

3. Remove the brake disc.

4. Remove the nut and disconnect the stabilizer bar link and parking brake cable bracket from the wheel knuckle. Discard the nut.

5. Remove the bolt and position the wheel speed sensor aside. If equipped, unclip the 2 retainers from the upper arm.

6. Remove the brake hose bracket bolt and position the hose aside.

7. AWD vehicles only, perform the following steps:

➡**Do not discard the wheel hub nuts at this time.**

a. Remove the outer and inner wheel hub nuts.

b. Using the Front Hub Remover, separate the halfshaft from the hub and bearing.

8. Position a suitable jackstand under the lower arm.

9. Remove and discard the shock absorber lower nut and flag bolt.

10. Remove and discard the upper arm outboard bolt and nut.

11. Remove and discard the toe link outboard bolt and nut.

12. Remove and discard the lower arm outboard bolt and nut.

13. AWD vehicles only, position the halfshaft through the wheel knuckle opening and secure the halfshaft aside.

✳✳ WARNING

The coil spring is under extreme load. Care must be taken at all times when removing or installing a loaded spring. Failure to follow this instruction may result in serious personal injury.

14. Pull outward on the wheel knuckle while lowering the jackstand and remove the spring. Inspect the spring upper and lower seats, remove and discard seats as necessary.

To install:

15. If removed, position a new lower seat into the lower arm with the recess in the seat aligned with the projection on the lower arm.

16. Position the spring onto the lower arm with the end of the spring 0-0.39 inch (0-10 mm) from the step on the spring seat.

✳✳ WARNING

The coil spring is under extreme load. Care must be taken at all times when removing or installing a loaded spring. Failure to follow this instruction may result in serious personal injury.

17. Pull outward on the wheel knuckle and install the spring.

18. AWD vehicles, position the halfshaft into the wheel bearing and wheel hub.

19. Raise the jackstand and loosely install the new lower arm outboard bolt and nut.

20. Position the toe link and loosely install the new toe link outboard bolt and nut.

21. Position the upper arm and loosely install the new upper arm outboard bolt and nut.

22. Loosely install the new lower shock nut and flag bolt.

23. Lower and remove the jackstand.

24. AWD vehicles, perform the following:

➡**Do not tighten the rear wheel hub nut with the vehicle on the ground. The nut must be tightened to specification before the vehicle is lowered onto the**

wheels. Wheel bearing damage will occur if the bearing is loaded with the weight of the vehicle applied.

➡**Apply the brake to keep the halfshaft from rotating.**

a. Position the halfshaft in the hub and use the previously removed wheel hub nut to seat the halfshaft. Tighten to 203 ft. lbs. (275 Nm). Remove and discard the wheel hub nut.

➡**The wheel hub nut contains a one-time locking chemical that is activated by the heat created when it is tightened. Install and tighten the new wheel hub nut to specification within 5 minutes of starting it on the threads. Always install a new wheel hub nut after loosening or when not tightening within the specified time or damage to the components may occur.**

➡**Apply the brake to keep the halfshaft from rotating.**

b. Install a new inner wheel hub nut. Tighten to 203 ft. lbs. (275 Nm).

c. Install a new outer wheel hub nut. Tighten to 129 ft. lbs. (175 Nm).

25. Install the brake hose bracket bolt and tighten to 62 inch lbs. (7 Nm).

26. Position the wheel speed sensor and install the bolt. Tighten to 62 inch lbs. (7 Nm). If equipped, clip the 2 retainers to the upper arm.

27. Connect the parking brake cable bracket and stabilizer bar link to the wheel knuckle and install the nut. Tighten the nut to 30 ft. lbs. (40 Nm).

28. Install the brake disc.

29. Position the brake caliper and anchor plate assembly and install the 2 anchor plate bolts. Tighten the bolts to 41 ft. lbs. (55 Nm).

30. Install the wheel and tire.

31. With the weight of the vehicle on the wheel and tire, tighten the lower shock nut to 58 ft. lbs. (80 Nm).

32. With the weight of the vehicle on the wheel and tire, tighten the upper arm outboard bolt to 129 ft. lbs. (175 Nm).

33. With the weight of the vehicle on the wheel and tire, tighten the toe link outboard bolt to 129 ft. lbs. (175 Nm).

34. With the weight of the vehicle on the wheel and tire, tighten the lower arm outboard bolt in the following sequence:

a. Tighten to 59 ft. lbs. (80 Nm).

b. Tighten an additional 90°.

35. Check and if necessary, align the vehicle.

CONTROL ARMS/LINKS

REMOVAL & INSTALLATION

Lower Arm

See Figure 230.

1. Remove the spring.
2. Remove the cam adjuster nut, cam adjuster and cam bolt. Discard the cam bolt and nut. To install, tighten the new nut to 111 ft. lbs. (150 Nm).

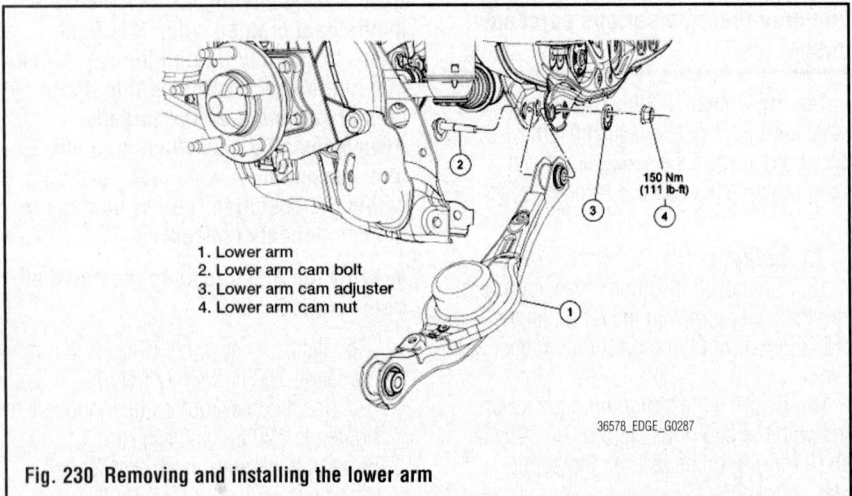

1. Lower arm
2. Lower arm cam bolt
3. Lower arm cam adjuster
4. Lower arm cam nut

36578_EDGE_G0287

Fig. 230 Removing and installing the lower arm

3. To install, reverse the removal procedure.

Upper Arm

See Figures 231 and 232.

➡Suspension fasteners are critical parts because they affect performance of vital components and systems and their failure may result in major service expense. New parts must be installed with the same part numbers or equivalent part, if replacement is necessary. Do not use a replacement part of lesser quality or substitute design. Torque values must be used as specified during reassembly to make sure correct retention of these parts.

➡Suspension bushing fasteners must be tightened with the weight of the vehicle resting on the wheel and tires or incorrect clamp load and bushing damage may occur.

1. Remove the wheel and tire.
2. Position a suitable jackstand under the lower arm and raise the suspension.
3. AWD vehicles, remove the bolt, unclip the 2 retainers and position aside the wheel speed sensor.
4. Remove the brake hose bracket bolt.

5. Remove and discard the upper arm outboard bolt and nut.
6. Carefully lower the lower arm and remove the jackstand.
7. Position the jackstand under the subframe.

➡The upper arm inboard bolt cannot be removed without first lowering the subframe.

8. Remove and discard the 2 subframe bushing brace bolts.

9. Remove the subframe forward nut.

➡The rear springs are under pressure. The jack must be lowered slowly while relieving the spring pressure or component damage may occur.

➡The upper arm inboard bolt cannot be removed without first lowering the subframe.

10. Remove the subframe rearward nut and lower the jackstand.
11. Remove and discard the upper arm inboard bolt and nut and remove the upper arm.

To install:

➡Do not tighten the bolt at this time.

12. Position the upper arm and loosely install the new upper arm inboard bolt and nut.
13. Raise the jackstand and install the subframe rearward nut. Tighten to 66 ft. lbs. (90 Nm).
14. Install the subframe forward nut. Tighten to 66 ft. lbs. (90 Nm).
15. Install the 2 subframe bushing brace bolts. Tighten to 18 ft. lbs. (25 Nm).

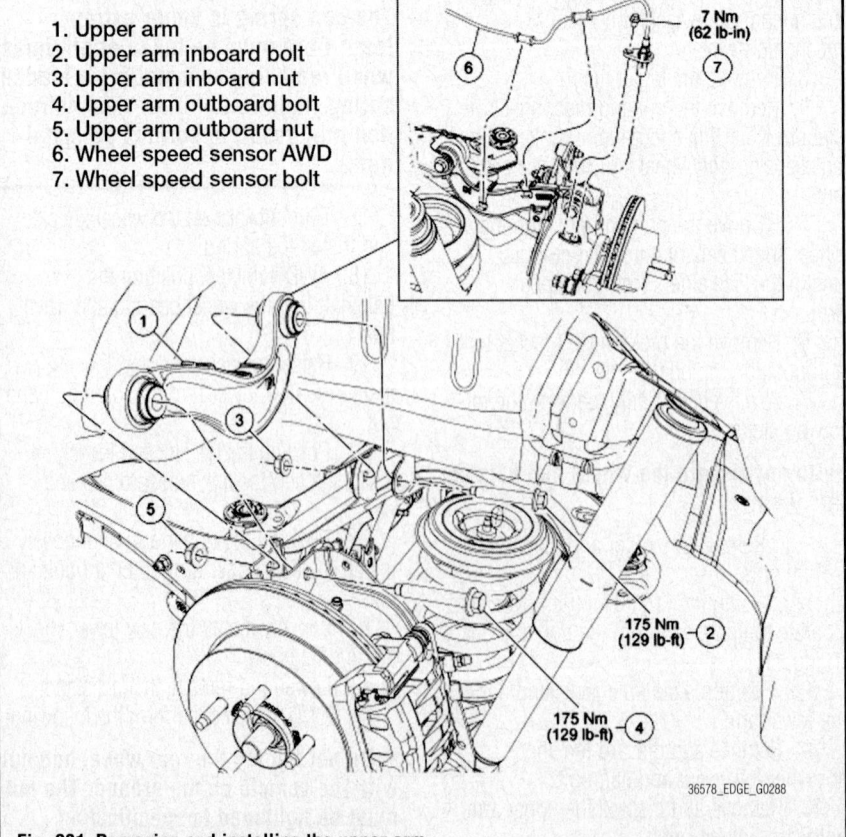

1. Upper arm
2. Upper arm inboard bolt
3. Upper arm inboard nut
4. Upper arm outboard bolt
5. Upper arm outboard nut
6. Wheel speed sensor AWD
7. Wheel speed sensor bolt

36578_EDGE_G0288

Fig. 231 Removing and installing the upper arm

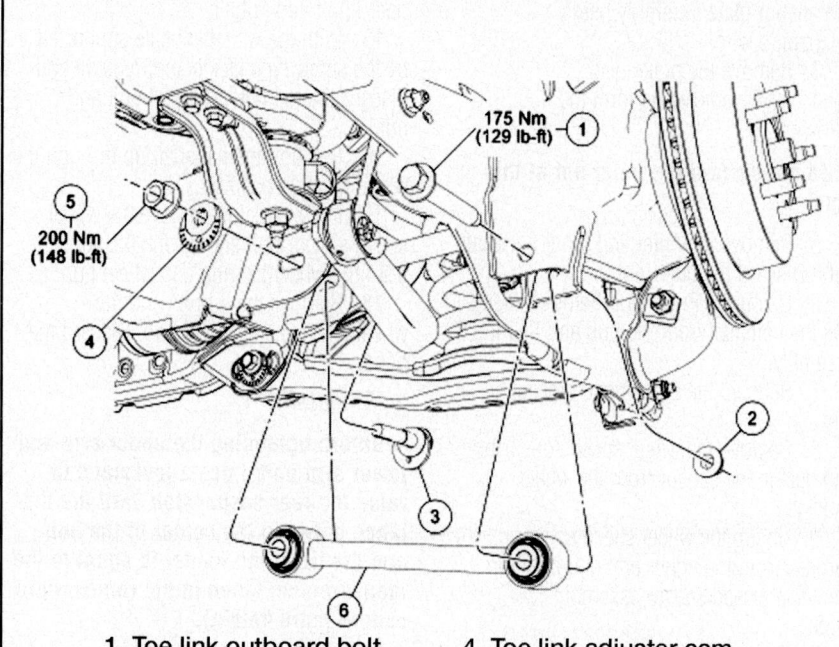

1. Toe link outboard bolt
2. Toe link outboard nut
3. Toe link inboard cam bolt
4. Toe link adjuster cam
5. Toe link inboard nut
6. Toe link

36578_EDGE_G0289

Fig. 232 Exploded view of the toe link and related components

16. Reposition the jack under the lower arm and raise the jack.

17. Loosely install the new upper arm outboard bolt and nut.

18. Remove the jackstand.

19. Install the wheel and tire.

20. AWD vehicles, position the wheel speed sensor, clip the 2 retainers to the upper arm and install the bolt. Tighten the bolt to 62 inch lbs. (7 Nm).

21. Install the brake hose bracket bolt.

22. With the weight of the vehicle on the wheel and tire, tighten the upper arm outboard bolt to 129 ft. lbs. (175 Nm).

23. With the weight of the vehicle on the wheel and tire, tighten the upper arm inboard bolt to 129 ft. lbs. (175 Nm).

Toe Link

➡Suspension fasteners are critical parts because they affect performance of vital components and systems and their failure may result in major service expense. New parts must be installed with the same part numbers or equivalent part, if replacement is necessary. Do not use a replacement part of lesser quality or substitute design. Torque values must be used as specified during reassembly to make sure correct retention of these parts.

➡Suspension bushing fasteners must be tightened with the weight of the vehicle resting on the wheel and tires or incorrect clamp load and bushing damage may occur.

1. Remove the wheel and tire.

2. Remove and discard the toe link inboard nut, cam adjuster and cam bolt.

3. Remove and discard the toe link outboard bolt and nut then remove the toe link.

To install:

➡Do not tighten the bolt at this time.

4. Position the toe link and loosely install the new toe link outboard bolt and nut.

➡Do not tighten the bolt at this time.

5. Loosely install the new toe link inboard bolt and nut.

6. Install the wheel and tire.

7. With the weight of the vehicle on the wheel and tire, tighten the toe link outboard bolt to 129 ft. lbs. (175 Nm).

8. With the weight of the vehicle on the wheel and tire, tighten the toe link inboard nut to 148 ft. lbs. (200 Nm).

SHOCK ABSORBER

REMOVAL & INSTALLATION

See Figure 233.

➡Suspension fasteners are critical parts because they affect performance of vital components and systems and their failure may result in major service expense. New parts must be installed with the same part numbers or equivalent part, if replacement is necessary. Do not use a replacement part of lesser quality or substitute design. Torque values must be used as specified during reassembly to make sure correct retention of these parts.

➡Suspension bushing fasteners must be tightened with the weight of the vehicle resting on the wheel and tires or incorrect clamp load and bushing damage may occur.

➡The new shock absorber is shipped with a strap securing it in the compressed position.

1. Remove the quarter trim panel.

2. Remove and discard the shock absorber upper nuts.

3. Remove the wheel and tire.

4. Position a suitable jackstand under the lower arm.

5. Remove the shock absorber lower bolt, flagnut and shock absorber. Discard the bolt and flagnut.

To install:

➡Do not tighten the bolt at this time.

6. Position the shock absorber and loosely install the new shock absorber lower bolt and flagnut.

7. Remove the jackstand.

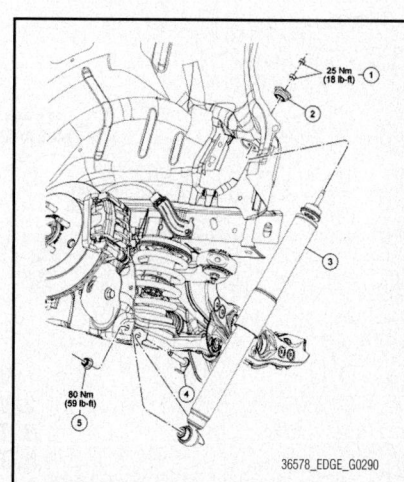

36578_EDGE_G0290

Fig. 233 Removing and installing the shock absorber

8. Install the wheel and tire.

9. With the weight of the vehicle on the wheel and tire, tighten the shock absorber lower bolt to 59 ft. lbs. (80 Nm).

10. Install the new shock absorber upper nuts. Tighten to 18 ft. lbs. (25 Nm).

11. Install the quarter trim panel.

WHEEL HUB & BEARING

REMOVAL & INSTALLATION

See Figures 234 through 236.

➡Suspension fasteners are critical parts because they affect performance of vital components and systems and their failure may result in major service expense. New parts must be installed with the same part numbers or equivalent part, if replacement is necessary. Do not use a replacement part of lesser quality or substitute design. Torque values must be used as specified during reassembly to make sure correct retention of these parts.

1. Remove the wheel and tire.

➡Do not allow the brake caliper and anchor plate assembly to hang from the brake hose or damage to the hose can occur.

2. Remove the 2 anchor plate bolts and position the brake caliper and anchor plate assembly aside. Support the brake caliper and anchor plate assembly using mechanic's wire.

3. Remove the brake disc.

4. AWD vehicles perform the following:

➡Do not discard the inner nut at this time.

5. Remove the outer and inner halfshaft nuts. Discard the outer nut.

6. Using the Front Hub Remover, separate the halfshaft from the hub and bearing assembly.

7. Remove the brake hose bracket bolt.

8. Remove the wheel speed sensor bolt and detach the sensor from the wheel knuckle.

9. Unclip the wheel speed sensor harness from the upper arm and position the wheel speed sensor assembly aside.

10. Remove and discard the upper arm outboard bolt and nut. Separate the upper arm from the wheel knuckle.

11. Position a suitable screw type jack stand under the lower arm.

12. Remove and discard the shock absorber lower bolt and nut.

13. Remove and discard the stabilizer bar link upper nut.

14. Remove and discard the toe link outboard bolt and nut.

15. With the wheel knuckle supported by the screw type jack stand, remove and discard the toe link outboard bolt and nut.

16. Position the halfshaft up through the wheel knuckle opening.

17. FWD vehicles, remove the wheel speed sensor bolt and detach the sensor from the wheel bearing and wheel hub.

18. Remove the 4 bolts and the wheel bearing and wheel hub. Discard the bolts.

To install:

➡Before tightening the upper arm and lower arm bolts, use a jackstand to raise the rear suspension until the distance between the center of the hub and the lip of the fender is equal to the measurement taken in the removal procedure (curb height).

19. Position the wheel bearing and wheel hub and install 4 new bolts. Tighten to 98 ft. lbs. (133 Nm).

20. AWD vehicles, position the halfshaft through the wheel knuckle and into the wheel bearing and wheel hub.

21. Position the wheel knuckle onto the toe link and lower arm.

22. Loosely install the new toe link outboard bolt and nut.

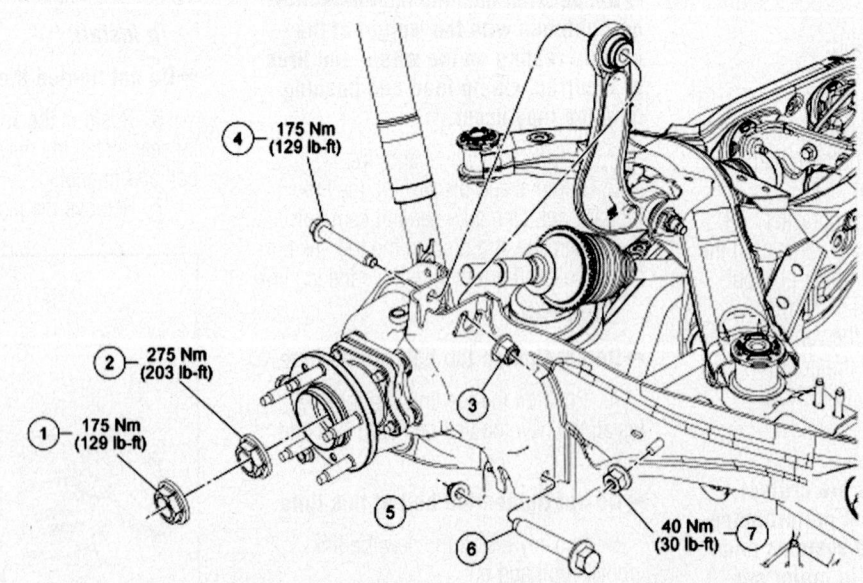

1. Wheel hub nut (outer)
2. Wheel hub nut (inner)
3. Toe link outboard nut
4. Toe link outboard bolt
5. Lower arm outboard nut
6. Lower arm outboard bolt
7. Stabilizer bar link upper nut

36578_EDGE_G0291

Fig. 234 Exploded view of the wheel bearing and wheel hub (AWD) vehicles—(1of 2)

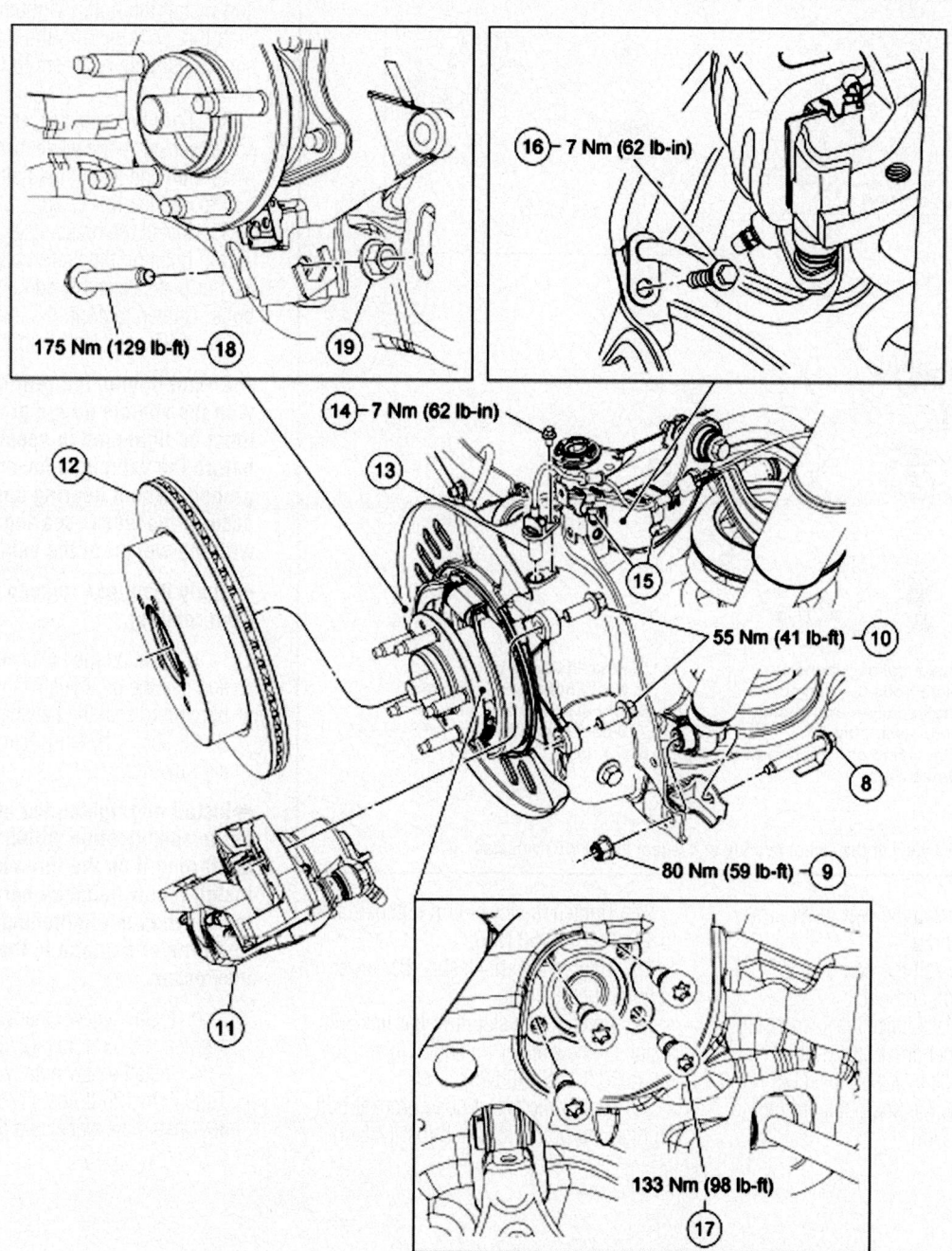

16 — 7 Nm (62 lb-in)

175 Nm (129 lb-ft) — 18   19

14 — 7 Nm (62 lb-in)

12   13   15

55 Nm (41 lb-ft) — 10

8

80 Nm (59 lb-ft) — 9

11

133 Nm (98 lb-ft)
17

1. Shock absorber lower flag bolt
2. Shock absorber lower nut
3. Brake caliper anchor plate bolts (2 required)
4. Brake caliper and anchor plate assembly
5. Brake disc
6. Wheel speed sensor
7. Wheel speed sensor bolt
8. Wheel speed sensor harness clips
9. Brake hose bracket bolt
10. Wheel bearing and wheel hub bolt (4 required)
11. Toe link outboard bolt
12. Toe link outboard nut

36578_EDGE_G0292

Fig. 235 Exploded view of the wheel bearing and wheel hub (AWD) vehicles—(2of 2)

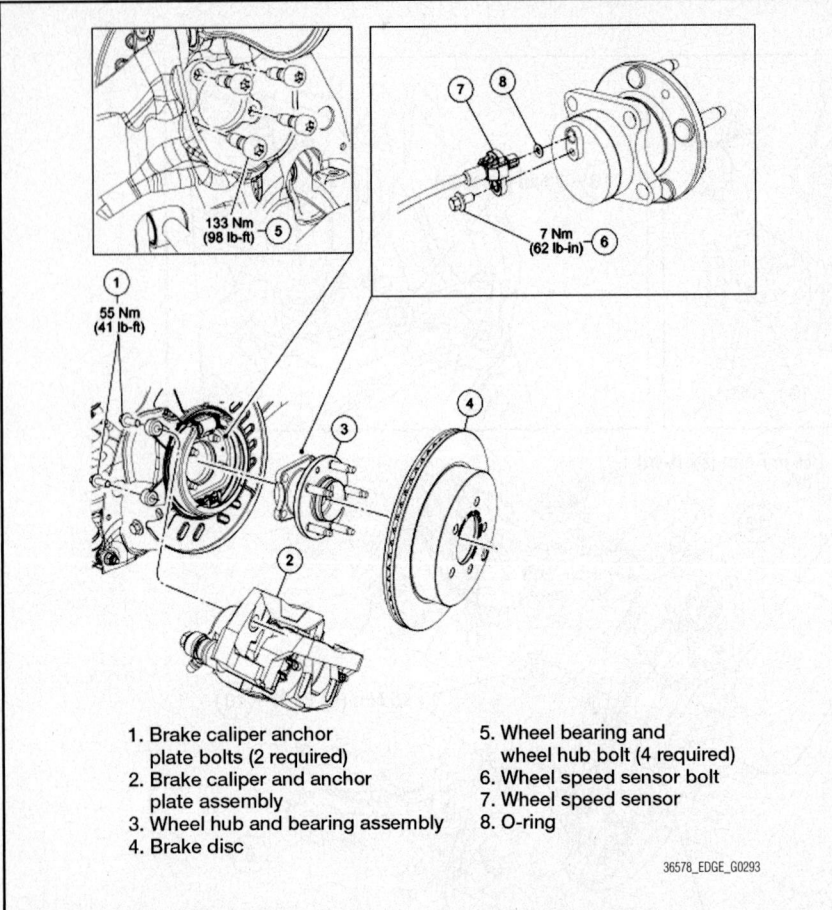

1. Brake caliper anchor plate bolts (2 required)
2. Brake caliper and anchor plate assembly
3. Wheel hub and bearing assembly
4. Brake disc
5. Wheel bearing and wheel hub bolt (4 required)
6. Wheel speed sensor bolt
7. Wheel speed sensor
8. O-ring

36578_EDGE_G0293

Fig. 236 Exploded view of the wheel bearing and wheel hub (FWD) vehicles

23. Loosely install the new lower arm outboard bolt and nut.

24. Loosely install the new shock absorber lower bolt and nut.

25. Using the jack, raise the suspension and install the upper arm outboard bolt and nut. Tighten the bolt to 129 ft. lbs. (175 Nm).

26. Tighten the toe link outboard bolt to (129 ft. lbs. (175 Nm).

27. Tighten the lower arm outboard bolt to 111 ft. lbs. (150 Nm).

28. Tighten the shock absorber lower nut to 59 ft. lbs. (80 Nm).

29. Position the stabilizer bar link and install the new upper link nut. Tighten the nut to 30 ft. lbs. (40 Nm).

30. Install the brake hose bracket bolt. Tighten the bolt to 62 inch lbs. (7 Nm).

31. Position the wheel speed sensor and install the bolts. Tighten the bolt to 62 inch lbs. (7 Nm). Clip the 2 wheel speed sensor harness retainers to the upper arm.

32. For FWD vehicles, attach the wheel speed sensor to the wheel bearing and wheel hub and install the bolt. Tighten the bolt to 62 inch lbs. (7 Nm).

33. Install the brake disc.

34. Position the brake caliper and anchor plate assembly and install the 2 bolts. Tighten to 41 ft. lbs. (55 Nm).

35. AWD vehicles, perform the following:

➡ **Do not tighten the rear halfshaft nut with the vehicle on the ground. The nut must be tightened to specification before the vehicle is lowered to the ground. Wheel bearing damage will occur if the wheel bearing is loaded with the weight of the vehicle applied.**

➡ **Apply the brake to keep the halfshaft from rotating.**

a. Position the halfshaft in the hub and use the previously removed wheel hub nut to seat the halfshaft. Tighten to 203 ft. lbs. (275 Nm). Remove and discard the nut.

➡ **Install and tighten the new halfshaft nut to specification within five minutes of starting it on the threads. Always install a new halfshaft nut after loosening or when not tightening within specified time or damage to the components may occur.**

b. Install a new inner wheel hub nut. Tighten to 203 ft. lbs. (275 Nm).

c. Install a new outer wheel hub nut. Tighten to 129 ft. lbs. (175 Nm).

36. Install the wheel and tire.

FORD

E-150 • E-250 • E-350

3

SPECIFICATIONS AND MAINTENANCE CHARTS

ENGINE AND VEHICLE IDENTIFICATION

Engine								Model Year	
Code ①	Liters (cc)	Cu. In.	Cyl.	Fuel Sys.	Type	Eng. Mfg.		Code ②	Year
L	5.4 (5409)	330	8	EFI	SOHC	Ford		8	2008
P	6.0 (5921)	365	8	TDI	OHV	Navistar		9	2009
S	6.8 (6802)	415	10	EFI	SOHC	Ford			
W	4.6 (4588)	280	8	EFI	SOHC	Ford			

MFI: Multi-port Fuel Injection

TDI: Direct Injection Turbo-Diesel

EFI: Electronic Fuel Injection

SFI: Sequential Fuel Injection

OHV: Overhead Valve

SOHC: Single Overhead Camshaft

① 8th digit of the Vehicle Identification Number (VIN)

② 10th digit of the Vehicle Identification Number (VIN)

36578_ETRK_C0001

GENERAL ENGINE SPECIFICATIONS

Year	Model	Engine Displ. Liters	Engine VIN	Net Horsepower @ rpm	Net Torque @ rpm (ft. lbs.)	Bore x Stroke (in.)	Com-pression Ratio	Oil Pressure @ rpm
2008	E-150	4.6	W	225@4800	286@3500	3.55x3.54	9.4:1	40-75@2000
		5.4	L	255@4500	350@2500	3.55x4.16	9.0:1	40-75@2000
	E-250	4.6	W	225@4800	286@3500	3.55x3.54	9.4:1	40-75@2000
		5.4	L	255@4500	350@2500	3.55x4.16	9.0:1	40-75@2000
	E-350	5.4	L	255@4500	350@2500	3.55x4.16	9.0:1	40-75@2000
		6.0	P	235@3150	440@1600	3.74x4.13	18.0:1	45@1800
		6.8	S	305@4250	420@3250	3.55x4.16	9.0:1	40-75@2000
2009	E-150	4.6	W	225@4800	286@3500	3.55x3.54	9.4:1	40-75@2000
		5.4	L	255@4500	350@2500	3.55x4.16	9.0:1	40-75@2000
	E-250	4.6	W	225@4800	286@3500	3.55x3.54	9.4:1	40-75@2000
		5.4	L	255@4500	350@2500	3.55x4.16	9.0:1	40-75@2000
	E-350	5.4	L	255@4500	350@2500	3.55x4.16	9.0:1	40-75@2000
		6.0	P	235@3150	440@1600	3.74x4.13	18.0:1	45@1800
		6.8	S	305@4250	420@3250	3.55x4.16	9.0:1	40-75@2000

36578_ETRK_C0002

GASOLINE ENGINE TUNE-UP SPECIFICATIONS

Year	Engine Displacement Liters	Engine VIN	Spark Plug Gap (in.)	Ignition Timing (deg.) ① MT	AT	Fuel Pump (psi) ②	Idle Speed (rpm) MT	AT	Valve Clearance In.	Ex.
2008	4.6	W	0.052-0.056	—	10B	28-45	—	③	HYD	HYD
	5.4	L	0.052-0.056	—	10B	28-45	—	③	HYD	HYD
	6.8	S	0.052-0.056	—	10B	28-45	—	③	HYD	HYD
2009	4.6	W	0.043-0.047	—	10B	28-45	—	③	HYD	HYD
	5.4	L	0.050-0.057	—	10B	28-45	—	③	HYD	HYD
	6.8	S	0.052-0.056	—	10B	55-65	—	③	HYD	HYD

NOTE: The Vehicle Emission Control Information label often reflects specification changes changes made during production. The label figures must be used if they differ from this chart.

B: Before top dead center

HYD: Hydraulic

① Ignition timing is preset and cannot be adjusted

② With engine running

③ Idle speed is electronically controlled and cannot be adjusted

36578_ETRK_C0003

DIESEL ENGINE TUNE-UP SPECIFICATIONS

Year	Engine Displ. Liters	Engine VIN	Valve Clearance Intake (in.)	Exhaust (in.)	Injection Pump Setting (deg.)	Injection Nozzle Pressure (psi) New	Used	Idle Speed (rpm)	Cranking Compression Pressure (psi)
2008	6.0	P	HYD	HYD	①	②	②	③	NA
2009	6.0	P	HYD	HYD	①	②	②	③	NA

NOTE: The Vehicle Emission Control Information label often reflects specification changes made during production. The label figures must be used if they differ from those in this chart.

NA: Not Available

① PCM controlled

② Pump output pressure: 450-4,000 psi

③ See underhood emission label

36578_ETRK_C0004

CAPACITIES

Year	Model	Engine Displ. Liters	Engine VIN	Engine Oil with Filter (qts.)	Transmission (pts.)		Transfer Case (pts.)*	Drive Axle		Fuel Tank (gal.)	Cooling System (qts.)
					MT	Auto.		Front (pts.)	Rear (pts.)		
2008	E-150	4.6	W	6.0	—	①	—	—	②	35.0	③
		5.4	L	6.0	—	①	—	—	②	35.0	④
	E-250	4.6	W	6.0	—	①	—	—	②	35.0	③
		5.4	L	6.0	—	①	—	—	②	35.0	④
	E-350	5.4	L	6.0	—	①	—	—	②	37.0	④
		6.0	P	15.0	—	①	—	—	②	37.0	⑤
		6.8	S	6.9	—	①	—	—	②	37.0	⑥
2009	E-150	4.6	W	6.0	—	①	—	—	②	35.0	③
		5.4	L	6.0	—	①	—	—	②	35.0	④
	E-250	4.6	W	6.0	—	①	—	—	②	35.0	③
		5.4	L	6.0	—	①	—	—	②	35.0	④
	E-350	5.4	L	6.0	—	①	—	—	②	35.0	④
		6.0	P	15.0	—	①	—	—	②	35.0	⑤
		6.8	S	6.9	—	①	—	—	②	35.0	⑥

NA: Information not available

NOTE: All capacities are approximate. Add fluid gradually and check to be sure a proper fluid level is obtained.

* Overhaul

① 4R70E/4R75E: 27.8 pts.
TorqShift: 38.4 pts.

② Model 60: 5.9 pts.
Model 70-2U: 6.6 pts.
Model 70TR: 8.2 pts.
Model 60 Limited slip includes 7 oz. of friction modifier

③ 4.6L without rear heat: 23.8 qts.
4.6L with rear heat: 26.0 qts.

④ 5.4L without rear heat: 28.8 qts.
5.4L with rear heat: 30.8 qts.

⑤ 6.0L without rear heat: 24.4 qts.
6.0L with rear heat: 26.0 qts.

⑥ 6.8L without rear heat: 30.4 qts.
6.8L with rear heat: 32.6 qts.

36578_ETRK_C0005

VALVE SPECIFICATIONS

Year	Engine Displ. Liters	Engine VIN	Seat Angle (deg.)	Face Angle (deg.)	Spring Test Pressure (lbs. @ in.)	Spring Installed Height (in.)	Stem-to-Guide Clearance (in.)		Stem Diameter (in.)	
							Intake	Exhaust	Intake	Exhaust
2008	4.6	W	45.5	45.25-45.75	132@1.103	1.563-1.586	0.0008-0.0027	0.0018-0.0037	0.2746-0.2754	0.2736-0.2744
	5.4	L	45.5	45.25-45.75	171@1.34	1.6654-1.6890	0.0008-0.0027	0.0018-0.0037	0.2746-0.2754	0.2736-0.2744
	6.0	P	①	①	191@1.51	1.820	0.0055 max.	0.0055 max.	0.2720-0.2735	0.2720-0.2735
	6.8	S	45.5	45.25-45.75	161.9-179.8 @1.10	1.6654-1.6890	0.0008-0.0027	0.0018-0.0037	0.2746-0.2754	0.2736-0.2744
2009	4.6	W	45.5	45.25-45.75	132@1.103	1.5630-1.5866	0.0008-0.0027	0.0018-0.0037	0.2746-0.2754	0.2736-0.2744
	5.4	L	45.5	45.25-45.75	171@1.339	1.6654-1.6890	0.0008-0.0027	0.0018-0.0037	0.2746-0.2754	0.2736-0.2744
	6.0	P	①	①	191@1.51	NA	0.0055 max.	0.0055 max.	0.2720-0.2735	0.2720-0.2735
	6.8	S	45.5	45.25-45.75	171@1.130	NA	0.0007-0.0027	0.0017-0.0037	0.2746-0.2754	0.2736-0.2744

NA: Information not available

① Intake: 30 degrees

   Exhaust: 37.5 degrees

② Intake: 1.767 in.

   Exhaust: 1.833 in.

36578_ETRK_C0006

CAMSHAFT AND BEARING SPECIFICATIONS CHART

All measurements are given in inches.

Year	Engine Displ. Liters	Engine VIN	Journal Dia.	Brg. Oil Clearance	Shaft End-play	Runout	Journal Bore	Lobe Lift	
								Intake	Exhaust
2008	4.6	W	1.0605-1.0615	0.0010-0.0030	0.0035-0.0075	0.0020	1.0625-1.0635	0.2560	0.2560
	5.4	L	1.0605-1.0615	0.0010-0.0030	0.0011-0.0075	0.0012	1.0625-1.0635	0.2799	0.2952
	6.0	P	2.4400-2.4410	0.0015-0.0060	0.0020-0.0080	NA	2.4430-2.4460	0.2261	0.2296
	6.8	S	1.0605-1.0615	0.0010-0.0030	0.0011-0.0075	0.0012	1.0625-1.0635	0.2799	0.2952
2009	4.6	W	1.0605-1.0615	0.0010-0.0030	0.0010-0.0070	0.0020	1.0605-1.0615	0.2560	0.2560
	5.4	L	1.0605-1.0615	0.0010-0.0030	0.0010-0.0070	0.0012	1.0625-1.0635	0.2799	0.2952
	6.0	P	2.4400-2.4410	0.0015-0.0060	0.0020-0.0080	NA	2.4430-2.4460	0.2261	0.2296
	6.8	S	1.0600-1.0620	0.0010-0.0030	0.0010-0.0070	0.0035	1.0620-0.0630	0.2790	0.2950

NA: Information not available

① Intake: 1.8532-1.8542 in.

   Exhaust: 1.5635-1.5645 in.

36578_ETRK_C0007

CRANKSHAFT AND CONNECTING ROD SPECIFICATIONS

All measurements are given in inches.

Year	Engine Displ. Liters	Engine VIN	Crankshaft Main Brg. Journal Dia.	Crankshaft Main Brg. Oil Clearance	Crankshaft Shaft End-play	Crankshaft Thrust on No.	Connecting Rod Journal Dia.	Connecting Rod Oil Clearance	Connecting Rod Side Clearance
2008	4.6	W	2.4803	0.0011-0.0026	0.0051-0.0120	5	2.0861-2.0867	0.0010-0.0027	0.0006-0.0177
	5.4	L	2.6568-2.6576	0.0009-0.0019	0.0030-0.0148	5	2.0859-2.0867	0.0010-0.0025	0.0049-0.0187
	6.0	P	2.6568-2.6576	0.0009-0.0019	0.0030-0.0148	NA	2.0877-2.0885	0.0010-0.0025	0.0049-0.0187
	6.8	S	2.6568-2.6576	0.0009-0.0019	0.0015-0.0030	5	2.0859-2.0867	0.0010-0.0025	0.0006-0.0177
2009	4.6	W	2.6568-2.6576	0.0011-0.0026	0.0051-0.0120	5	2.0861-2.0867	0.0010-0.0027	0.0006-0.0177
	5.4	L	2.6568-2.6576	0.0009-0.0019	0.0030-0.0148	5	2.0859-2.0867	0.0010-0.0025	0.0049-0.0187
	6.0	P	3.1884-3.1894	0.0008-0.0034	0.0197	NA	2.0877-2.0885	0.0008-0.0033	0.0118-0.0236
	6.8	S	2.6568-2.6576	0.0009-0.0019	0.0015-0.0030	5	2.0859-2.0867	0.0010-0.0025	0.0006-0.0177

NA: Information not available

36578_ETRK_C0008

PISTON AND RING SPECIFICATIONS

All measurements are given in inches.

Year	Engine Displ. Liters	Engine VIN	Piston Clearance	Ring Gap Top Compression	Ring Gap Bottom Compression	Ring Gap Oil Control	Ring Side Clearance Top Compression	Ring Side Clearance Bottom Compression	Ring Side Clearance Oil Control
2008	4.6	W	0.0001-0.0005	0.0090-0.0190	0.0090-0.0190	0.0020-0.0260	0.0012-0.0028	0.0012-0.0028	0.0018-0.0077
	5.4	L	0.0000-0.0001	0.0006-0.0012	0.0098-0.0197	0.0059-0.0256	0.0012-0.0032	0.0007-0.0028	NA
	6.0	P	0.0000-0.0001	0.0006-0.0012	0.0598-0.0606	0.1193-0.1201	0.0012-0.0032	0.0007-0.0028	NA
	6.8	S	0.0000-0.0001	0.0006-0.0012	0.0098-0.0197	0.0006-0.0256	0.0012-0.0032	0.0007-0.0028	NA
2009	4.6	W	0.0007-0.0019	0.0090-0.0190	0.0090-0.0190	0.0020-0.0260	0.0012-0.0028	0.0012-0.0028	0.0018-0.0077
	5.4	L	0.0010-0.0018	0.0006-0.0012	0.0098-0.0197	0.0059-0.0256	0.0012-0.0032	0.0007-0.0028	NA
	6.0	P	0.0017-0.0036	0.0114-0.0217	0.0598-0.0606	0.0094-0.0196	0.0012-0.0032	0.0007-0.0028	NA
	6.8	S	0.0010-0.0018	0.0059-0.0118	0.0098-0.0196	0.0059-0.0256	0.0012-0.0020	0.0012-0.0031	NA

NA: Information not available

36578_ETRK_C0017

TORQUE SPECIFICATIONS
All readings in ft. lbs.

	Engine Displ. Liters	Engine VIN	Cylinder Head Bolts	Main Bearing Bolts	Rod Bearing Bolts	Crankshaft Damper Bolts	Flywheel Bolts	Manifold Intake *	Manifold Exhaust	Spark Plugs	Oil Pan Drain Plug
2008	4.6	W	①	②	③	④	⑤	⑥	15	13	17
	5.4	L	⑦	⑧	⑨	⑩	⑤	⑥	18	13	17
	6.0	P	⑪	⑫	⑬	⑭	⑮	⑯	28	—	32
	6.8	S	⑦	⑧	⑨	⑩	⑤	⑤	18	13	17
2009	4.6	W	①	②	③	④	⑤	⑥	15	10	17
	5.4	L	⑦	⑧	⑨	⑩	⑤	⑥	18	10	17
	6.0	P	⑪	⑫	⑬	⑭	⑮	⑯	28	—	32
	6.8	S	⑦	⑧	⑨	⑩	⑤	⑤	18	10	17

NA: Information not available

* NOTE: Applies to Lower Manifold only. For Upper Manifold, see the text.

① Step 1: 30 ft. lbs.
  Step 2: Plus 90 degrees
  Step 3: Loosen one full turn
  Step 4: 30 ft. lbs.
  Step 5: Plus 90 degrees
  Step 6: Plus 90 degrees

② Vertical bolts:
  Step 1: 30 ft. lbs.
  Step 2: Plus 90 degrees
  Jack screws:
  Step 1: 44 inch lbs.
  Step 2: 89 inch lbs.
  Side bolts: 15 ft. lbs.

③ Step 1: 17 ft. lbs.
  Step 2: 32 ft. lbs.
  Step 3: Plus 105 degrees

④ Step 1: 89 ft. lbs.
  Step 2: Loosen 1 full turn
  Step 3: 37 ft. lbs.
  Step 4: Plus 90 deg.

⑤ Step 1: 15 ft. lbs.
  Step 2: 59 ft. lbs.

⑥ Step 1: 18 inch lbs.
  Step 2: 18 ft. lbs.

⑦ Step 1: 30 ft. lbs.
  Step 2: Plus 90 degrees
  Step 3: Plus 90 degrees

⑧ Vertical bolts:
  Step 1: 30 ft. lbs.
  Step 2: plus 90 degrees
  Side bolts:
  Step 1: 22 ft. lbs.
  Step 2: plus 90 degrees

⑨ Step 1: 32 ft. lbs.
  Step 2: Plus 105 degrees

⑩ Step 1: 66 ft. lbs.
  Step 2: loosen 1 full turn
  Step 3: 37 ft. lbs.
  Step 4: Plus 90 degrees

⑪ See the procedure in the text

⑫ Step 1: 90 ft. lbs.
  Step 2: 120 ft. lbs.
  Step 3: 170 ft. lbs.

⑬ Step 1: 33 ft. lbs.
  Step 2: 50 ft. lbs.

⑭ Step 1: 50 ft. lbs.
  Step 2: plus 90 degrees

⑮ Step 1: 44 inch lbs.
  Step 2: 69 ft. lbs.

⑯ Step 1: 97 inch lbs.
  Step 2: 97 inch lbs.

36578_ETRK_C0009

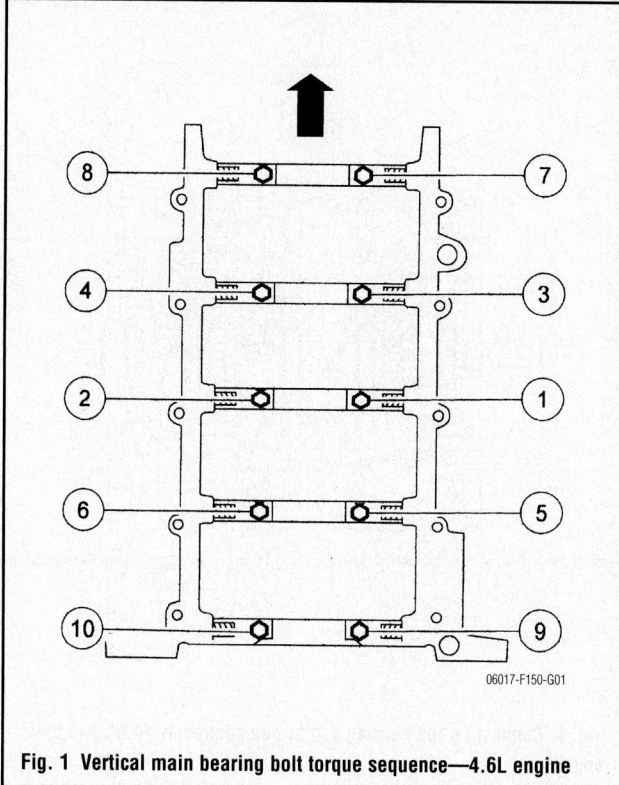

06017-F150-G01

Fig. 1 Vertical main bearing bolt torque sequence—4.6L engine

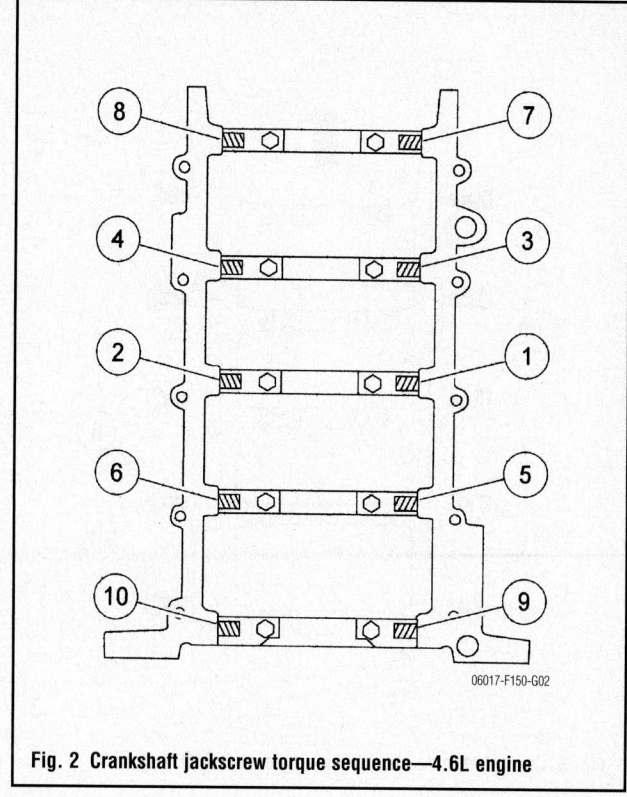

06017-F150-G02

Fig. 2 Crankshaft jackscrew torque sequence—4.6L engine

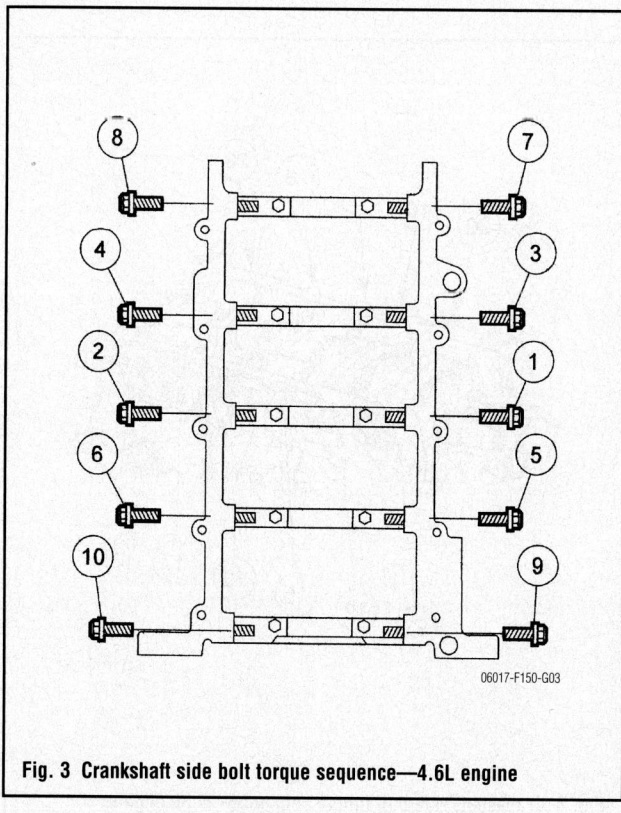

06017-F150-G03

Fig. 3 Crankshaft side bolt torque sequence—4.6L engine

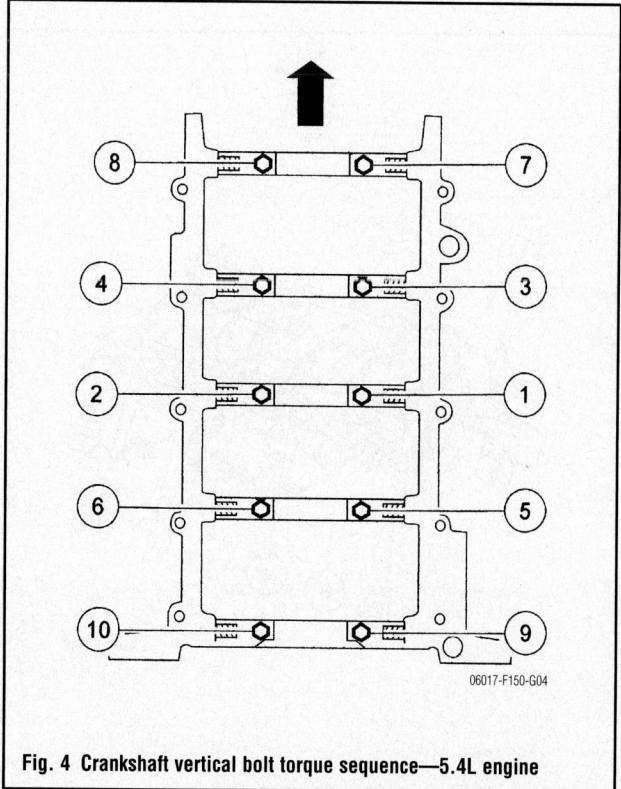

06017-F150-G04

Fig. 4 Crankshaft vertical bolt torque sequence—5.4L engine

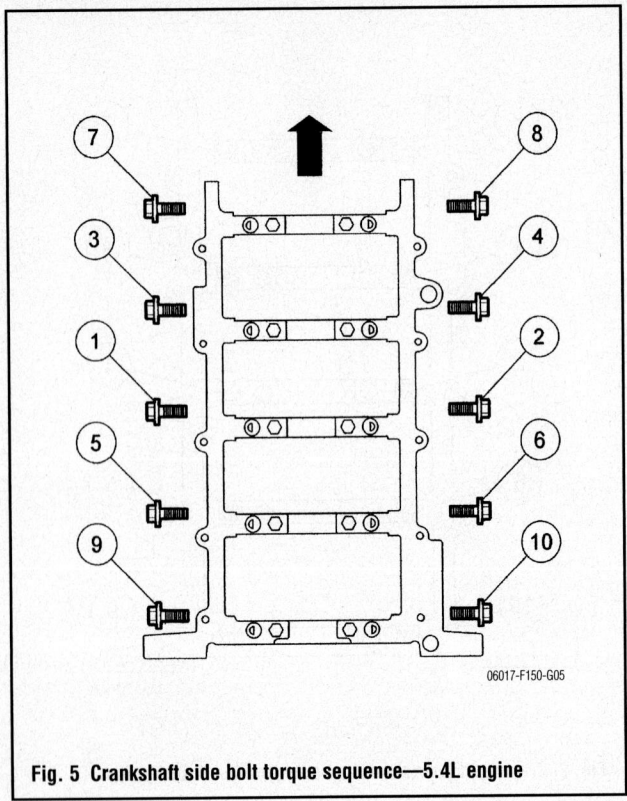

06017-F150-G05

Fig. 5 Crankshaft side bolt torque sequence—5.4L engine

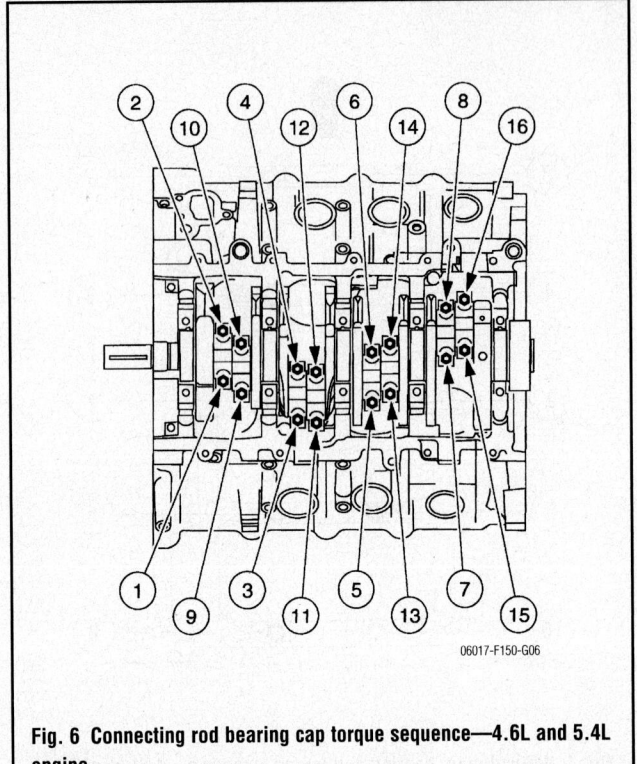

06017-F150-G06

Fig. 6 Connecting rod bearing cap torque sequence—4.6L and 5.4L engine

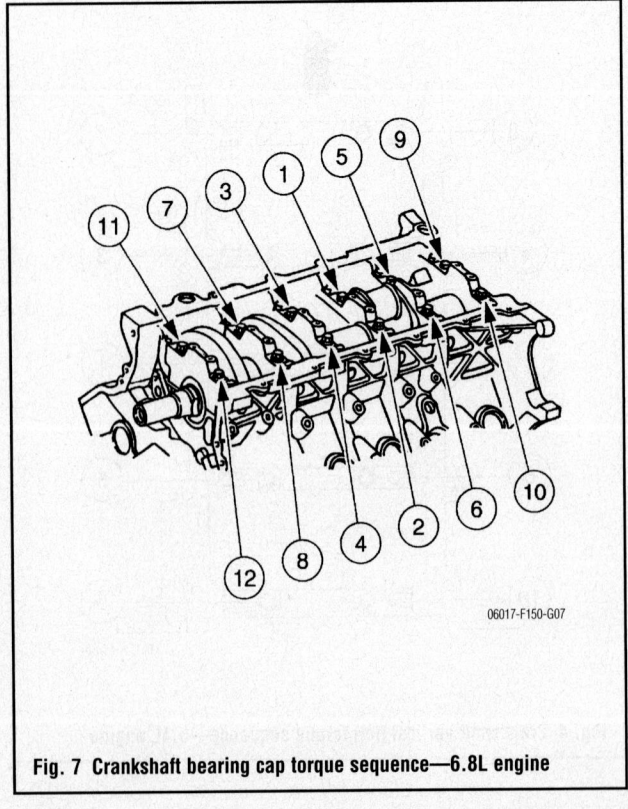

06017-F150-G07

Fig. 7 Crankshaft bearing cap torque sequence—6.8L engine

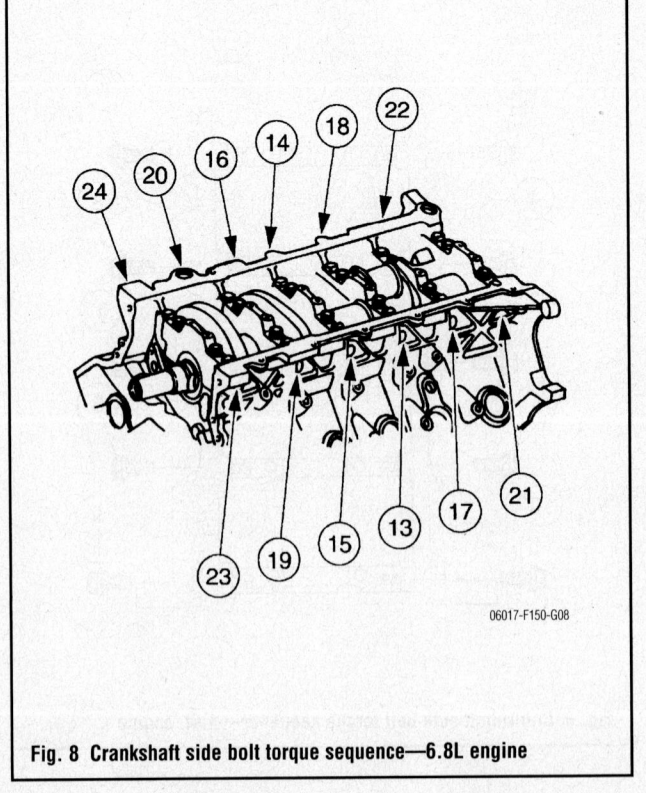

06017-F150-G08

Fig. 8 Crankshaft side bolt torque sequence—6.8L engine

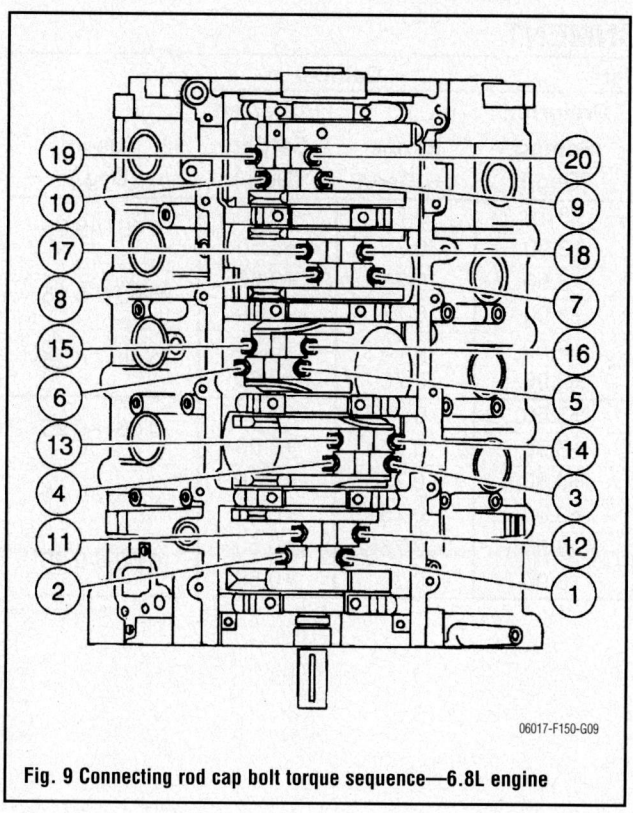

Fig. 9 Connecting rod cap bolt torque sequence—6.8L engine

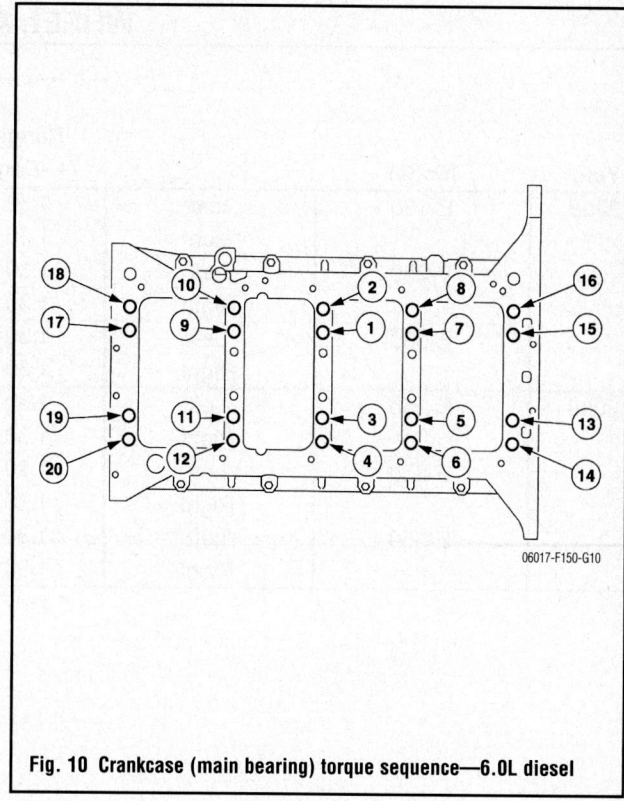

Fig. 10 Crankcase (main bearing) torque sequence—6.0L diesel

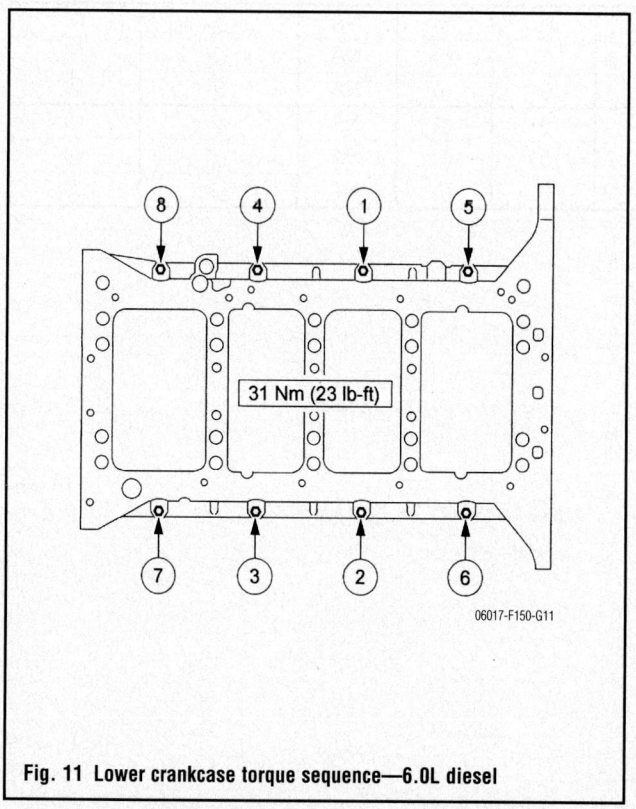

Fig. 11 Lower crankcase torque sequence—6.0L diesel

WHEEL ALIGNMENT

Year	Model			Caster Range (+/-Deg.)	Caster Preferred Setting (Deg.)	Camber Range (+/-Deg.)	Camber Preferred Setting (Deg.)	Toe-in (Deg.)
2008	E-150		Left	1.30	+3.50	0.75	+0.50	0.06+/-0.25
			Right	1.30	+3.90	0.75	+0.50	
	E-250		Left	1.30	+3.50	0.75	+0.50	0.06+/-0.25
			Right	1.30	+3.90	0.75	+0.50	
	E-350		Left	1.30	+3.50	0.75	+0.50	0.06+/-0.25
			Right	1.30	+3.90	0.75	+0.50	
2009	E-150		Left	1.30	+3.50	0.75	+0.50	0.06+/-0.25
			Right	1.30	+3.90	0.75	+0.50	
	E-250		Left	1.30	+3.50	0.75	+0.50	0.06+/-0.25
			Right	1.30	+3.90	0.75	+0.50	
	E-350		Left	1.30	+3.50	0.75	+0.50	0.06+/-0.25
			Right	1.30	+3.90	0.75	+0.50	

36578_ETRK_C0010

TIRE, WHEEL AND BALL JOINT SPECIFICATIONS

Year	Model	OEM Tires Standard	OEM Tires Optional	Tire Pressures (psi) Front	Tire Pressures (psi) Rear	Wheel Size	Ball Joint Inspection	Lug Nut Torque (ft. lbs.)
2008	E-150	P225/75R16	none	①	①	NA	②	③
	E-250	LT225/75R16E	none	①	①	NA	②	③
	E-350	LT245/75R16E	none	①	①	NA	②	③
2009	E-150	P225/75R16	none	①	①	NA	②	③
	E-250	LT225/75R16E	none	①	①	NA	②	③
	E-350	LT245/75R16E	none	①	①	NA	②	③

NA: Information not available

OEM: Original Equipment Manufacturer

PSI: Pounds Per Square Inch

① See placard on vehicle

② Upper: 0.040 in.
   Lower: 0.024 in.

③ Single Rear Wheel: 148 ft. lbs.
   Dual Rear Wheel: 140 ft. lbs.

36578_ETRK_C0011

BRAKE SPECIFICATIONS

All measurements in inches unless noted

| Year | Model | | Brake Disc | | | Minimum Lining Thickness | Brake Caliper | |
			Original Thickness	Minimum Thickness	Maximum Runout		Bracket Bolts (ft. lbs.)	Mounting Bolts (ft. lbs.)
2008	E-150	F	NA	1.511	NA	0.118	195	27
		R	NA	1.354	NA	0.118	166	45
	E-250	F	NA	1.511	NA	0.118	195	27
		R	NA	1.354	NA	0.118	166	45
	E-350	F	NA	1.511	NA	0.118	195	27
		R	NA	1.354	NA	0.118	166	45
2009	E-150	F	NA	1.511	NA	0.118	195	27
		R	NA	1.354	NA	0.118	166	45
	E-250	F	NA	1.511	NA	0.118	195	27
		R	NA	1.354	NA	0.118	166	45
	E-350	F	NA	1.511	NA	0.118	195	27
		R	NA	1.354	NA	0.118	166	45

F: Front

R: Rear

NA: Information not available

36578_ETRK_C0013

SCHEDULED MAINTENANCE INTERVALS
2008-09 E-Series with the 6.0L Diesel Engine

TO BE SERVICED	TYPE OF SERVICE	VEHICLE MILEAGE INTERVAL (x1000)												
		7.5	15	22.5	30	37.5	45	52.5	60	67.5	75	82.5	90	97.5
Engine oil & filter	R	✓	✓	✓	✓	✓	✓	✓	✓	✓	✓	✓	✓	✓
Tires	Rotate	✓	✓	✓	✓	✓	✓	✓	✓	✓	✓	✓	✓	✓
Air filter minder	I ①	✓	✓	✓	✓	✓	✓	✓	✓	✓	✓	✓	✓	✓
Wheels	I ②	✓	✓	✓	✓	✓	✓	✓	✓	✓	✓	✓	✓	✓
Brake pads, hoses, etc.	I		✓		✓		✓		✓		✓		✓	
Coolant hoses	I		✓		✓		✓		✓		✓		✓	
Steering linkage and suspension	I/L		✓		✓		✓		✓		✓		✓	
Cabin air filter	R						✓							
Ball joints	L		✓		✓		✓		✓		✓		✓	
Driveshaft	I/L		✓		✓		✓		✓		✓		✓	
Exhaust system and heat shields	I		✓		✓		✓		✓		✓		✓	
Engine air filter	R		✓		✓		✓		✓		✓		✓	
Fuel filters ③	R		✓		✓		✓		✓		✓		✓	
Auto trans fluid ④	I				✓				✓				✓	
Auto trans fluid (Torqshift)	R								✓					
Front wheel bearings	L								✓					
Front wheel bearing grease seals	R								✓					
Accessory drive belts	I												✓	
Rear differential fluid ⑤	R													✓
Coolant (Premium Gold)	R	every 105,000 miles												
Accessory drive belts	R	every 150,000 miles, if not previously done so												

R: Replace   S: Service   I: Inspect   L: Lubricate   Adj: adjust

① Reset after new filter is installed
② Inspect for end play and noise
③ Frame-mounted and engine
④ Including external and in-line filters
⑤ Dana axles using non-synthetic fluid only

Special Operating Condition Requirements

When towing a trailer or using a camper or car-top carrier:

Change engine oil and install a new oil filter every 5,000 miles, 6 months or 200 hours of engine operation (whichever occurs first).

Inspect and lubricate U-joints as required.

During extensive idling and/or low speed driving for long distances, as in heavy commercial use such as delivery, taxi, patrol car or livery:

Change engine oil and install a new oil filter every 5,000 miles, 6 months or 200 hours of engine operation (whichever occurs first).

Lube front lower control arm and steering linkage ball joints with zerk fittings (if equipped) every 4,800 km (3,000 miles) or 3 months.

Inspect brake system and check battery electrolyte level (Patrol cars) every 8,000 km (5,000 miles).

Install a new fuel filter every 24,000 km (15,000 miles).

Change automatic transmission fluid, lubricate 4x2 wheel bearings, install new grease seals and adjust bearings every 48,000 km (30,000 miles). If equipped, change the in-line service installed transmission fluid filter.

Install a new cabin air filter as required.

When operating in dusty conditions such as unpaved or dusty roads:

Change engine oil and install a new oil filter every 5,000 miles or 6 months.

Install a new fuel filter every 24,000 km (15,000 miles).

Change automatic transmission fluid every 48,000 km (30,000 miles). If equipped, change the in-line service installed transmission fluid filter.

Install a new engine air filter as required.

Install a new cabin air filter as required.

When operating in off-road conditions:

Change automatic transmission fluid every 48,000 km (30,000 miles). If equipped, change the in-line service installed transmission fluid filter.

Install a new cabin air filter as required.

Inspect and lubricate U-joints.

Inspect and lubricate steering linkage ball joints with zerk fittings.

SCHEDULED MAINTENANCE INTERVALS
2008-09 E-Series with Gasoline Engines

TO BE SERVICED	TYPE OF SERVICE	VEHICLE MILEAGE INTERVAL (x1000)												
		7.5	15	22.5	30	37.5	45	52.5	60	67.5	75	82.5	90	97.5
Engine oil & filter	R	✓	✓	✓	✓	✓	✓	✓	✓	✓	✓	✓	✓	✓
Tires	Rotate	✓	✓	✓	✓	✓	✓	✓	✓	✓	✓	✓	✓	✓
Cabin air filter	R		✓		✓		✓		✓		✓		✓	
Wheels	I ①	✓	✓	✓	✓	✓	✓	✓	✓	✓	✓	✓	✓	✓
Engine air filter	I						✓				✓			
Engine air filter	R				✓				✓				✓	
Auto trans. fluid	I		✓		✓		✓		✓		✓		✓	
Steering linkage	L		✓		✓		✓		✓		✓		✓	
Suspension	L		✓		✓		✓		✓		✓		✓	
4WD front axle shaft U-joints	L		✓		✓		✓		✓		✓		✓	
Brake pads & rotors	I		✓		✓		✓		✓		✓		✓	
Coolant hoses	S/I		✓		✓		✓		✓		✓		✓	
Exhaust system	I		✓		✓		✓		✓		✓		✓	
Auto trans fluid (Torqshift)	R								✓					
Trans filter (Torqshift)	R								✓					
Front wheel bearings grease seal	R								✓					
Spark plugs	R												✓	
Rear drive axle fluid	R	every 105,000 miles												
Accessory drive belts	I	every 120,000 miles												
PCV valve ②	R	every 120,000 miles												
Premium Gold coolant	R	every 3 years or 100,000 miles												
Auto trans fluid (all exc. 4R100 and TorqShift)	R	every 150,000 miles												
PCV valve (5.4L 3v)	I	every 150,000 miles												
Front wheel bearings	R	at 150,000 miles, if not previously done so												
Accessory drive belts	R	every 150,000 miles, if not previously done so												

R: Replace   S: Service   I: Inspect   L: Lubricate

NGV: Natural gas vehicle

① Inspect for end play and noise

② Vehicles under 6,000 lbs. GVW, exc. 5.4L 3v engines

Special Operating Condition Requirements

When towing a trailer or using a camper or car-top carrier:

Change engine oil and install a new oil filter every 5,000 miles, 6 months or 200 hours of engine operation (whichever occurs first).

Inspect and lubricate U-joints as required.

During extensive idling and/or low speed driving for long distances, as in heavy commercial use such as delivery, taxi, patrol car or livery:

Change engine oil and install a new oil filter every 5,000 miles, 6 months or 200 hours of engine operation (whichever occurs first).

Lube front lower control arm and steering linkage ball joints with zerk fittings (if equipped) every 4,800 km (3,000 miles) or 3 months.

Inspect brake system and check battery electrolyte level (Patrol cars) every 8,000 km (5,000 miles).

Change automatic transmission fluid, lubricate 4x2 wheel bearings, install new grease seals and adjust bearings every 48,000 km (30,000 miles). If equipped, change the in-line service installed transmission fluid filter.

Install new spark plugs every 96,000 km (60,000 miles).

Install a new cabin air filter as required.

SCHEDULED MAINTENANCE INTERVALS
2008-09 E-Series with Gasoline Engines (footnotes cont.)

When operating in dusty conditions such as unpaved or dusty roads:

Change engine oil and install a new oil filter every 5,000 miles or 6 months.

Change automatic transmission fluid every 48,000 km (30,000 miles). If equipped, change the in-line service installed transmission fluid filter.

Install a new engine air filter as required.

Install a new cabin air filter as required.

When operating in off-road conditions:

Change automatic transmission fluid every 48,000 km (30,000 miles). If equipped, change the in-line service installed transmission fluid filter.

Install a new cabin air filter as required.

Inspect and lubricate U-joints.

Inspect and lubricate steering linkage ball joints with zerk fittings.

Short trips in cold operating conditions:

Inspect and lubricate 4x2 ball joints and steering idler arms every 8,000 km (5,000 miles).

36578_ETRK_C0016

PRECAUTIONS

Before servicing any vehicle, please be sure to read all of the following precautions, which deal with personal safety, prevention of component damage, and important points to take into consideration when servicing a motor vehicle:

• Never open, service or drain the radiator or cooling system when the engine is hot; serious burns can occur from the steam and hot coolant.

• Observe all applicable safety precautions when working around fuel. Whenever servicing the fuel system, always work in a well-ventilated area. Do not allow fuel spray or vapors to come in contact with a spark, open flame, or excessive heat (a hot drop light, for example). Keep a dry chemical fire extinguisher near the work area. Always keep fuel in a container specifically designed for fuel storage; also, always properly seal fuel containers to avoid the possibility of fire or explosion. Refer to the additional fuel system precautions later in this section.

• Fuel injection systems often remain pressurized, even after the engine has been turned **OFF**. The fuel system pressure must be relieved before disconnecting any fuel lines. Failure to do so may result in fire and/or personal injury.

• Brake fluid often contains polyglycol ethers and polyglycols. Avoid contact with the eyes and wash your hands thoroughly after handling brake fluid. If you do get brake fluid in your eyes, flush your eyes with clean, running water for 15 minutes. If eye irritation persists, or if you have taken brake fluid internally, IMMEDIATELY seek medical assistance.

• The EPA warns that prolonged contact with used engine oil may cause a number of skin disorders, including cancer. You should make every effort to minimize your exposure to used engine oil. Protective gloves should be worn when changing oil. Wash your hands and any other exposed skin areas as soon as possible after exposure to used engine oil. Soap and water, or waterless hand cleaner should be used.

• All new vehicles are now equipped with an air bag system, often referred to as a Supplemental Restraint System (SRS) or Supplemental Inflatable Restraint (SIR) system. The system must be disabled before performing service on or around system components, steering column, instrument panel components, wiring and sensors. Failure to follow safety and disabling procedures could result in accidental air bag deployment, possible personal injury and unnecessary system repairs.

• Always wear safety goggles when working with, or around, the air bag system. When carrying a non-deployed air bag, be sure the bag and trim cover are pointed away from your body. When placing a non-deployed air bag on a work surface, always face the bag and trim cover upward, away from the surface. This will reduce the motion of the module if it is accidentally deployed. Refer to the additional air bag system precautions later in this section.

• Clean, high quality brake fluid from a sealed container is essential to the safe and proper operation of the brake system. You should always buy the correct type of brake fluid for your vehicle. If the brake fluid becomes contaminated, completely flush the system with new fluid. Never reuse any brake fluid. Any brake fluid that is removed from the system should be discarded. Also, do not allow any brake fluid to come in contact with a painted surface; it will damage the paint.

• Never operate the engine without the proper amount and type of engine oil; doing so WILL result in severe engine damage.

• Timing belt maintenance is extremely important. Many models utilize an interference-type, non-freewheeling engine. If the timing belt breaks, the valves in the cylinder head may strike the pistons, causing potentially serious (also time-consuming and expensive) engine damage. Refer to the maintenance interval charts for the recommended replacement interval for the timing belt, and to the timing belt section for belt replacement and inspection.

• Disconnecting the negative battery cable on some vehicles may interfere with the functions of the on-board computer system(s) and may require the computer to undergo a relearning process once the negative battery cable is reconnected.

• When servicing drum brakes, only disassemble and assemble one side at a time, leaving the remaining side intact for reference.

• Only an MVAC-trained, EPA-certified automotive technician should service the air conditioning system or its components.

BRAKES
ANTI-LOCK BRAKE SYSTEM (ABS)

GENERAL INFORMATION

PRECAUTIONS

• Certain components within the ABS system are not intended to be serviced or repaired individually.

• Do not use rubber hoses or other parts not specifically specified for and ABS system. When using repair kits, replace all parts included in the kit. Partial or incorrect repair may lead to functional problems and require the replacement of components.

• Lubricate rubber parts with clean, fresh brake fluid to ease assembly. Do not use shop air to clean parts; damage to rubber components may result.

• Use only DOT 3 brake fluid from an unopened container.

• If any hydraulic component or line is removed or replaced, it may be necessary to bleed the entire system.

• A clean repair area is essential. Always clean the reservoir and cap thoroughly before removing the cap. The slightest amount of dirt in the fluid may plug an orifice and impair the system function. Perform repairs after components have been thoroughly cleaned; use only denatured alcohol to clean components. Do not allow ABS components to come into contact with any substance containing mineral oil; this includes used shop rags.

• The Anti-Lock control unit is a microprocessor similar to other computer units in the vehicle. Ensure that the ignition switch is **OFF** before removing or installing controller harnesses. Avoid static electricity discharge at or near the controller.

• If any arc welding is to be done on the vehicle, the control unit should be unplugged before welding operations begin.

BLEEDING THE ABS SYSTEM

1. Follow the Manual Bleeding procedure steps to bleed the brake system. For additional information, refer to "Bleeding The Brake System, Bleeding Procedure.

2. Connect a scan tool and follow the ABS Service Bleed instructions.

3. Repeat the manual bleeding procedure steps to bleed the system.

WHEEL SPEED SENSORS

REMOVAL & INSTALLATION

Front

1. Remove the brake rotor.
2. Disconnect the wheel speed sensor harness connector.
3. Disconnect the wheel speed sensor wire from the front brake hose.
4. Remove the wheel speed sensor harness bolt.
5. Remove the speed sensor assembly mounting bolts.
6. Installation is the reverse order of assembly. Tighten the wheel speed sensor bolts to 80 inch lbs. (9 Nm).

Rear

1. Raise and safely support the vehicle.
2. Disconnect the wheel speed sensor electrical connector.
3. Disconnect the wheel speed sensor harness clips.
4. Remove the wheel speed sensor bolt, spacer, then remove the sensor.
5. Installation is the reverse order of removal. Tighten the sensor bolt to 18 ft. lbs. (25 Nm).

BRAKES   BLEEDING THE BRAKE SYSTEM

BLEEDING PROCEDURE

Pressure Bleeding

> ❋❋ **WARNING**
>
> **Do not use any fluid other than clean brake fluid meeting manufacturer's specification. Additionally, do not use brake fluid that has been previously drained. Following these instructions will help prevent system contamination, brake component damage and the risk of serious personal injury.**

> ❋❋ **WARNING**
>
> **Do not allow the brake master cylinder to run dry during the bleeding operation. Master cylinder may be damaged if operated without fluid, resulting in degraded braking performance. Failure to follow this instruction may result in serious personal injury.**

1. Clean all dirt from and remove the brake master cylinder filler cap and fill the brake master cylinder reservoir with clean, specified brake fluid.
2. Install the bleeder adapter to the brake master cylinder reservoir and attach the bleeder tank hose to the fitting on the adapter.
3. Remove the RH rear bleeder cap and place a box-end wrench on the bleeder screw. Attach a rubber drain tube to the RH rear bleeder screw and submerge the free end of the tube in a container partially filled with clean, specified brake fluid.
4. Open the valve on the bleeder tank.
5. Loosen the RH rear bleeder screw. Leave open until clear, bubble-free brake fluid flows, then tighten the RH rear bleeder screw and remove the rubber hose.
6. Continue bleeding the system, going in order from the LH rear bleeder screw to the RH front bleeder screw ending with the LH front bleeder screw.
7. Release the bleeder tank pressure and close the bleeder tank valve. Remove the tank hose from the adapter and remove the adapter from the brake fluid reservoir.

Manual Bleeding

> ❋❋ **WARNING**
>
> **Do not allow the brake master cylinder reservoir to run dry during the bleeding operation. Keep the brake master cylinder reservoir filled with the specified brake fluid. Never reuse the brake fluid that has been drained from the hydraulic system.**

1. Fill the brake master cylinder reservoir with brake fluid.
2. Connect a clear tube to the right rear disc brake caliper bleeder screw and the other end in a container partially filled with recommended brake fluid.
3. Have an assistant pump the brake pedal and then hold firm pressure on the brake pedal.
4. Loosen the disc brake caliper bleeder screw until a stream of brake fluid comes out. Have an assistant maintain pressure on the brake pedal while tightening the disc brake caliper bleeder screw. Repeat until clear, bubble-free fluid comes out. Refill the brake master cylinder reservoir as necessary.
5. Tighten the disc brake caliper bleeder screw.
6. Repeat Steps 1 through 5 for the three remaining brake calipers, going in order from the left rear disc brake caliper to the right front disc brake caliper ending with the left front disc brake caliper.
7. If the brake pedal feels spongy, repeat the bleed procedure.

Anti-Lock Brake System Hydraulic Control Unit Bleeding

➡ **This procedure is only required when a new hydraulic control unit is installed.**

8. Connect diagnostic tool Worldwide Diagnostic System (WDS) 418-F224, New Generation STAR (NGS) Tester 418-F052, or equivalent diagnostic tool and follow the ABS system bleed instructions.
9. Use the gravity bleed or manual bleed procedure(s) to bleed the system. Begin at the right rear caliper.

BRAKES

BRAKE CALIPER

REMOVAL & INSTALLATION

1. Raise and safely support the vehicle.
2. Remove the front wheel.
3. Release the wheel speed sensor wiring harness from the brake flexible hose.
4. Remove the brake caliper flow bolt and position the brake flexible hose aside. Discard the copper washers.
5. Remove the brake caliper guide pin bolts and the brake caliper.

To install:

6. Install the brake caliper and tighten the 27 ft. lbs. (37 Nm).
7. Install the brake hose with new copper washers and tighten the flow bolt to 30 ft. lbs. (40 Nm).
8. Attach the speed sensor wiring harnesses to the brake hose.

9. Bleed the brake system.
10. Install the front wheel.

DISC BRAKE PADS

REMOVAL & INSTALLATION

1. Raise and safely support the vehicle.
2. Remove the front wheel.
3. Release the wheel speed sensor wiring harness from the brake flexible hose.
4. Remove the brake caliper guide pin bolts and positing the caliper aside.

➡**Do not disconnect the brake hose.**

✳ WARNING

Do not allow the disc brake caliper to hang from the front brake hose. Use wire to support the disc brake caliper from a convenient underbody component.

5. Remove the brake pads from the caliper and discard the four retraction clips.

To install:

6. Install the brake pads with new anti-rattle clips into the anchor plate.

➡**Ensure the anti-rattle clips are correctly seated into the anchor plate.**

7. Using a C-clamp and a worn brake pad, compress the brake caliper pistons into the caliper.
8. Fill the rubber caliper sleeve boots with suitable grease and install the brake pads
9. Attach the wheel speed sensor wiring harness to the brake hose.
10. Install the brake caliper into position and tighten the guide pin bolts and tighten to 27 ft. lbs. (37 Nm).
11. Install the front wheel.

BRAKES

BRAKE CALIPER

REMOVAL & INSTALLATION

1. Before servicing the vehicle, refer to the Precautions Section.
2. Remove the wheel and tire assembly.
3. Remove the brake hose flow bolt and position the brake hose aside. Discard the copper washers.
4. Remove the caliper pin bolts.
5. Remove the rear disc brake caliper.

➡**Use new copper washers on the brake hose flow bolt.**

6. Bleed the brake system.
7. To install, reverse the removal procedure.

8. Observe the following torques:
   - Flow bolt: 26 ft. lbs. (35 Nm)
   - Caliper pin bolts: 24 ft. lbs. (32 Nm)

DISC BRAKE PADS

REMOVAL & INSTALLATION

1. Before servicing the vehicle, refer to the Precautions Section.
2. Remove the brake master cylinder filler cap. Check the brake fluid level in the brake master cylinder reservoir. Remove fluid until the brake master cylinder reservoir is half full.
3. Raise and safely support the vehicle.
4. Remove the rear wheel.

5. Using a C-clamp, compress the caliper pistons into the caliper.
6. Remove the brake caliper anchor plate bolts and position the caliper assembly aside.

✳ WARNING

Do not allow the disc brake caliper to hang from the front brake hose. Use wire to support the disc brake caliper from a convenient underbody component.

7. Remove the brake pads and anti-rattle clips from the caliper assembly.
8. Installation is the reverse order of removal. Tighten the brake caliper support bracket bolts to 166 ft. lbs. (225 Nm).

BRAKES
PARKING BRAKE

PARKING BRAKE SHOES

REMOVAL & INSTALLATION

1. Before servicing the vehicle, refer to the Precautions Section.
2. Raise and safely support the vehicle.
3. Remove the rear brake rotor.
4. Remove the park brake shoe adjusting screw.
5. Remove the park brake shoe adjusting screw spring.
6. Remove the park brake shoe hold-down spring retainers, springs and pins.
7. Position the park brake shoes apart and remove the brake shoes and the retracting spring from the axle.

To install:

8. Install the retraction spring and position the parking brake shoe assembly on the axle.
9. Position the 2 hold-down pins and install the 2 brake shoe hold-down springs and retainers.
10. Install the brake shoe adjusting screw spring.
11. Position the brake shoe adjusting screw.
12. Adjust the parking brake shoes. For additional information, refer to "Parking Brake Shoes, Adjustment."
13. The remainder of the installation is the reverse order of removal.

ADJUSTMENT

1. Before servicing the vehicle, refer to the Precautions Section.
2. Raise and safely support the vehicle.
3. Remove the rear brake rotor.
4. Using the Brake Adjusting Gauge, measure the inside diameter of the drum portion of the rear brake disc and set the locking screw. Record the measurement.
5. Place the Brake Adjusting Gauge over the widest diameter of the parking brake shoes.
6. Adjust the parking brake shoe clearance to 0.023 inches (0.6 mm) less than the inside diameter of the drum portion of the rear brake disc.
7. Reinstall the rear brake rotor and test the parking brake for proper operation.

CHASSIS ELECTRICAL
AIR BAG (SUPPLEMENTAL RESTRAINT SYSTEM)

GENERAL INFORMATION

SERVICE PRECAUTIONS

Always deplete the backup power supply before repairing or installing any new front or side air bag supplemental restraint system (SRS) component and before servicing, removing, installing, adjusting or striking components near the front or side impact sensors or the Restraints Control Module (RCM). Nearby components include doors, instrument panel, console, door latches, strikers, seats and hood latches.\

Make sure no one is in the vehicle and there is nothing blocking or placed in front of any air bag module when the battery is connected. Failure to follow these instructions may result in serious personal injury in the event of an accidental deployment.

Always wear eye protection when servicing a vehicle. Failure to follow this instruction may result in serious personal injury.

Never probe the electrical connectors on safety belt buckle/retractor pretensioners or adaptive load limiting retractors. Failure to follow this instruction may result in the accidental deployment of the safety belt pretensioners or adaptive load limiting retractors, which increases the risk of serious personal injury or death.

Never probe the electrical connectors on air bag, Safety Canopy® or side air curtain modules. Failure to follow this instruction

may result in the accidental deployment of these modules, which increases the risk of serious personal injury or death.

To reduce the risk of accidental deployment, do not use any memory saver devices. Failure to follow this instruction may result in serious personal injury or death.

DESCRIPTION AND OPERATION

The Restraints Control Module (RCM) continuously receives/monitors inputs from the following Supplemental Restraint System (SRS) components:
- Front impact severity sensor (left frontal restraints sensor)
- Driver safety belt buckle switch
- Passenger Air Bag Deactivation (PAD) switch

If the RCM detects sudden vehicle deceleration and/or lateral deceleration based on all the information received from all sensors and switches and determines that deployment is required, the RCM sends voltage and current to deploy the appropriate SRS components.

During a frontal crash, the RCM may deploy the following SRS components, based on crash severity and impact sensor input:
- Safety belt buckle pretensioner(s)
- Driver/passenger single-stage air bag

The fact that the safety belt buckle pretensioners or air bags did not activate for both front seat occupants in a collision does not mean that something is wrong with the system.

The RCM performs a self-test of the

complete SRS during each startup. If a SRS fault exists, the air bag warning indicator will illuminate and remain illuminated for the rest of the ignition cycle. In addition to the self-test at start up, the RCM continuously monitors all of its SRS components and circuitry for correct operation.

DISARMING THE SYSTEM

1. Turn all vehicle accessories OFF.
2. Turn the ignition OFF.
3. At the Smart Junction Box (SJB), located below the LH side of the instrument panel, remove the cover and the RCM fuse from the SJB.
4. Turn the ignition ON and monitor the air bag warning indicator for at least 30 seconds. The air bag warning indicator will remain lit continuously (no flashing) if the correct RCM fuse has been removed. If the air bag warning indicator does not remain lit continuously, remove the correct RCM fuse before proceeding.
5. Turn the ignition OFF.
6. Disconnect the battery ground cable and wait at least one minute.

ARMING THE SYSTEM

1. Turn the ignition from OFF to ON.
2. At the Smart Junction Box (SJB), located below the LH side of the instrument panel, remove the cover and install the Restraints Control Module (RCM) fuse and reinstall the cover.
3. Turn the ignition from ON to OFF. Wait 10 seconds, then turn the ignition

back ON and monitor the air bag warning indicator with all SRS components installed and connected. The air bag warning indicator will light continuously for approximately 6 seconds and then turn off.

CLOCKSPRING CENTERING

1. Hold the clockspring outer housing stationary.

✳✳ WARNING

Do not over-rotate the clockspring inner rotor. The internal ribbon wire is connected to the clockspring rotor. The internal ribbon wire acts as a stop and can be broken from its internal connection. Failure to follow this instruction may result in component damage and/or system failure.

---

2. While turning the rotor clockwise, carefully feel for the ribbon wire to run out of length and for a slight resistance. Stop turning at this point.

3. Turn the clockspring counterclockwise approximately 2 ¼ turns. This is the center point of the clockspring.

4. Do not allow the rotor to turn from this position.

DRIVE TRAIN

AUTOMATIC TRANSMISSION ASSEMBLY

REMOVAL & INSTALLATION

4R70E/4R75E Transmission

See Figures 12 through 14.

1. Before servicing the vehicle, refer to the Precautions Section.
2. Disconnect the negative battery cable.
3. Remove the air intake assembly.
4. Remove the transmission oil dipstick.
5. Remove the engine appearance cover.
6. Raise and safely support the vehicle.
7. Remove the transmission fluid filler tube.
8. Disconnect the electrical connectors.
9. Remove the torque converter housing-to-engine retaining bolts. Position the fuel and electrical harness brackets aside.
10. Disconnect the transmission fluid cooler tubes. Plug all fittings and position the transmission fluid cooler tubes aside.

➡**The case fittings must be held in place to prevent them from moving.**

11. Mark the driveshaft flange and the rear pinion flange for correct alignment during assembly.

➡**The output shaft and driveshaft are a balanced assembly.**

12. Remove the four driveshaft flange bolts.
13. Matchmark the driveshaft and extension housing. Slide the driveshaft back enough to index-mark the driveshaft output shaft and the extension housing. Separate the driveshaft from the transmission
14. Remove the gear selector lever cable and cable bracket.
15. Remove the torque converter access plug.
16. Remove the starter motor. For additional information, refer to "Starter, Removal & Installation."
17. Remove the fasteners and the front A/C deflector assembly, if equipped.
18. Remove and discard the 4 torque converter-to-flexplate retaining nuts.
19. Remove the flexplate inspection plate.
20. Disconnect the catalyst monitoring sensor harness connectors.
21. Remove the bolts.

22. Secure the high lift transmission jack to the transmission.
23. Remove the crossmember-to-frame nuts.
24. Remove the stud brackets.
25. Support the crossmember, then remove the transmission insulator and retainer-to-crossmember nuts and the crossmember.
26. Remove the lower bell housing bolts.
27. Separate and back the transmission away from the engine, positioning the extension housing above the exhaust

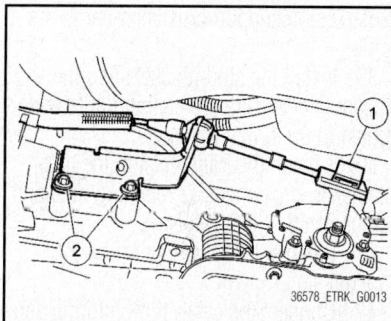

36578_ETRK_G0013

Fig. 13 Disconnect the clip (1) and remove the bolts (2) to remove the gear selector cable—4R70E/4R75E Transmission

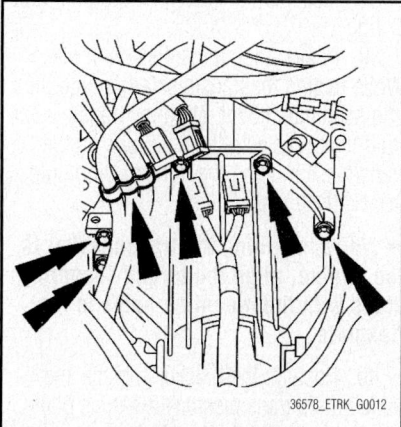

36578_ETRK_G0012

Fig. 12 Remove the torque converter housing-to-engine retaining bolts—4R70E/4R75E Transmission

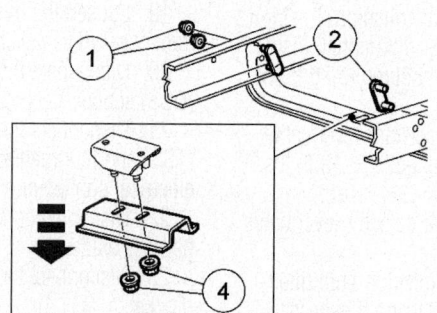

1. Crossmember-to-frame nuts
2. Stud brackets
3. Crossmember
4. Retainer-to-crossmember nuts

36578_ETRK_G0014

Fig. 14 Removing the crossmember—4R70E/4R75E Transmission

crossover pipe. Remove the transmission from the vehicle.

28. Remove any electrical connectors necessary.

To install:

29. Raise the transmission into the vehicle.

30. Align the torque converter studs with the mounting holes in the flexplate. Install the transmission to the engine.

31. Install and alternately tighten the torque converter housing-to-engine retaining bolts to 44 ft. lbs. (59 Nm).

32. Install four torque converter nuts to 27 ft. lbs. (36 Nm).

33. Position the transmission inspection cover into place and tighten the bolts to 26 ft. lbs. (35 Nm).

34. Install the torque converter access plug.

35. Reconnect the electrical connectors.

36. Install the front A/C deflector assembly with the fasteners, if equipped.

37. Install the transmission support crossmember onto the transmission retainer and insulator studs. Install the retaining nuts hand-tight.

38. Raise the transmission, aligning the transmission support crossmember to the frame.

39. Install the stud brackets and the crossmember-to-frame retaining nuts and tighten to 60 ft. lbs. (81 Nm).

40. Tighten the transmission insulator retainer-to-crossmember retaining nuts and tighten to 66 ft. lbs. (90 Nm).

41. Remove the jack supporting the transmission.

42. Connect the catalyst monitoring sensor harness connectors.

43. Install the exhaust heat shield-to-crossmember retaining bolts and tighten to 133 inch lbs. (15 Nm).

44. Install the starter.

45. Align the index marks and position the driveshaft on the transmission. Position the driveshaft to the rear differential. Install the driveshaft bolts and tighten to 76 ft. lbs. (103 Nm).

46. Install the gear selector lever cable and bracket. Tighten the bolts to 18 ft. lbs. (25 Nm).

47. Connect the gear selector lever cable to the manual lever.

48. Install the transmission fluid filler tube. Replace the tube O-ring if necessary. Tighten the bolts as follows:
- 4.6L Engine: 89 inch lbs. (10 Nm)
- 5.4L Engine: 21 ft. lbs. (28 Nm)

49. Remove the plugs and connect the transmission fluid cooler tubes. Tighten to 20 ft. lbs. (27 Nm).

50. Install the transmission bolts and tighten to 44 ft. lbs. (59 Nm).

51. The remainder of the installation is the reverse order of removal.

52. Ensure the transmission is filled with fluid to the correct level.

TorqShift Transmission

1. Before servicing the vehicle, refer to the Precautions Section.

2. Disconnect the negative battery cable.

3. Remove the transmission fluid level indicator.

4. Raise and safely support the vehicle.

5. Remove the driveshaft. For additional information, refer to "Driveshaft, Removal & Installation."

6. Drain the transmission fluid and reinstall the drain plug. Tighten the plug to 18 ft. lbs. (25 Nm).

7. Support the transmission assembly with a suitable transmission jack.

8. Remove the two wiring harness retainers from the crossmember and position them aside.

9. Remove the transmission fluid cooler inlet tube.

10. Remove the transmission fluid cooler tubes from the bracket.

11. Disconnect the selector lever cable from the manual control lever.

12. Disconnect the wire harness from the selector lever cable bracket.

13. Remove the bolts and position the selector lever cable and bracket aside.

14. Remove the heat shield screws from the crossmember.

15. Remove the center heat shield screws.

16. Remove the center heat shield screw.

17. Remove the forward RH heat shield screw.

18. Remove the forward RH heat shield screws from the frame.

19. Loosen the bolt and disconnect the transmission vehicle harness connector.

20. Disconnect the Output Shaft Speed (OSS) sensor electrical connector.

21. Disconnect the Turbine Shaft Speed (TSS) and intermediate shaft speed sensor electrical connector.

22. Disconnect and position the wire harness aside.

23. Disconnect the wire harness from the bracket.

24. Remove the cylinder block opening cover in order to gain access to the torque converter nuts.

25. Use the Strap Wrench to rotate the crankshaft in order to gain access to the torque converter to flexplate nuts.

26. Remove and discard the 6 torque converter to flexplate nuts.

27. Remove the starter motor. For additional information, refer to Section 303-06A.

28. Remove the screws and torque converter cover.

29. Remove the LH crossmember nuts and bracket.

30. Remove the RH crossmember nuts and bracket.

31. Remove the transmission insulator and retainer nuts and remove the crossmember.

32. Remove the bolts and the transmission insulator and retainer from the extension housing.

33. Remove the 9 transmission-to-engine mounting bolts and position the bracket aside.

34. Slide the transmission back and install the Torque Converter Retainer.

To install:

35. Lubricate the torque converter pilot hub with multi-purpose grease.

✹✦ WARNING

Prior to the installation of the assembly, the torque converter pilot hub must be lubricated or damage to the torque converter or the engine crankshaft can occur.

36. Rotate the torque converter so the orange or green paint daub is in the 12 o'clock position.

37. If the Torque Converter Retainer has not been installed during the assembly of the transmission, install the Torque Converter Retainer to hold the torque converter in place while moving and positioning the transmission in place. Once the transmission is in place, prior to bolting it to the engine, remove the Torque Converter Retainer.

38. Install a transmission fluid filler tube O-ring.

39. Position the transmission in place. While raising the transmission up into the engine compartment, align the transmission fluid filler tube with the stub tube on the transmission using the transmission fluid level indicator as a guide.

➡**While installing the transmission to the engine, align the torque converter studs with the mounting holes in the flexplate.**

40. Position the bracket in place and install the 9 transmission-to-engine bolts and tighten to 35 ft. lbs. (48 Nm).

41. Using the strap wrench, rotate the crankshaft to gain access to the torque converter studs.

42. Install the new torque converter-to-flexplate nuts and tighten to 35 ft. lbs. (48 Nm).

43. Install the cylinder block opening cover.

44. Install the torque converter cover and tighten to 26 ft. lbs. (35 Nm).

45. Install the transmission insulator and transmission insulator bolts and tighten to 69 ft. lbs. (94 Nm).

46. Position the crossmember to the transmission insulator and loosely install the transmission insulator nut.

47. Install the LH crossmember bracket and tighten the nuts to 60 ft. lbs. (81 Nm).

48. Install the RH crossmember bracket and tighten the crossmember nuts to 60 ft. lbs. (81 Nm).

49. Tighten the transmission insulator nuts to 69 ft. lbs. (94 Nm).

50. If equipped, connect the transmission fluid cooler tubes onto the bracket.

51. Install the transmission fluid cooler inlet tube while holding the case fitting and tighten to 30 ft. lbs. (40 Nm).

52. Install the transmission fluid cooler outlet tube while holding the case fitting and tighten to 30 ft. lbs. (40 Nm).

53. Connect the wire harness to the bracket.

54. Connect the wire harness on the LH and RH side of the transmission.

55. Install the starter motor.

56. Connect the Output Shaft Speed (OSS) sensor connector.

57. Connect the Turbine Shaft Speed (TSS) and intermediate shaft speed sensor connector.

58. Connect the transmission vehicle harness connector

59. Install the selector lever cable and selector lever cable bracket onto the transmission.

60. Position the selector lever cable bracket and tighten to 35 ft. lbs. (48 Nm).

61. Connect the selector lever cable onto the manual control lever and connect the wire harness onto the selector lever cable bracket.

62. Install the selector lever cable onto the routing clip, if equipped.

63. Install the heat shield and tighten the screws to the frame to 15 ft. lbs. (20 Nm).

64. If equipped, install the wire harness and install the 2 retaining clips to the rear of the crossmember.

65. Install the rear driveshaft.

66. Prior to lowering the vehicle, install a new transmission fluid in-line filter or a filter kit.

67. Connect the battery ground cable.

68. Adjust the selector lever cable. Verify that the vehicle starts in PARK and NEUTRAL and the reverse lamps illuminate in REVERSE.

69. Install the transmission fluid level indicator.

70. Ensure the transmission is filled with fluid to the correct level.

REAR AXLE HOUSING

REMOVAL & INSTALLATION

See Figure 15.

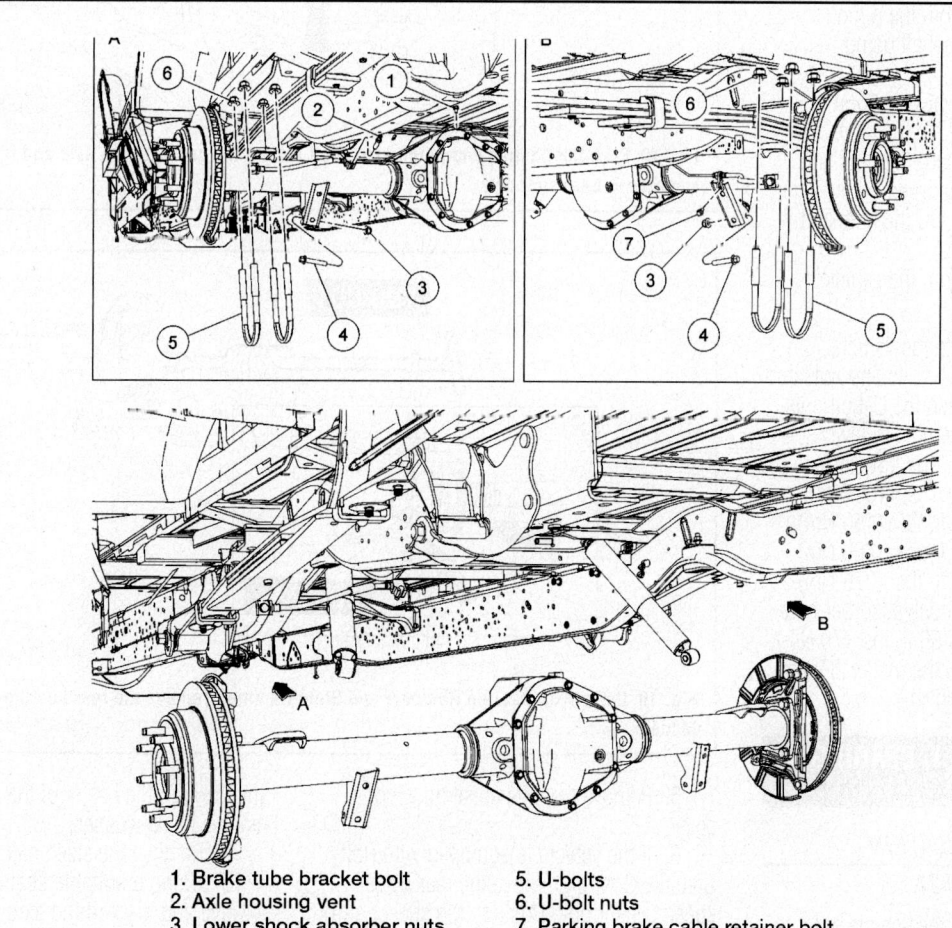

1. Brake tube bracket bolt
2. Axle housing vent
3. Lower shock absorber nuts
4. Lower shock absorber bolts
5. U-bolts
6. U-bolt nuts
7. Parking brake cable retainer bolt

36578_ETRK_G0015

Fig. 15 Exploded view of the rear axle assembly—E-Series Models

1. Before servicing the vehicle, refer to the Precautions Section.

2. Raise and safely support the vehicle.

3. Remove the rear wheels.

4. Remove the two brake caliper anchor plate bolts and support the caliper assembly using mechanic's wire.

5. Disconnect the parking brake cable from the parking brake. Repeat for the opposite side. Position the cables aside.

6. Disconnect the axle vent tube.

7. Remove the axle vent.

8. Remove the brake tube bracket bolt.

9. Remove the parking brake cable retainer bolt.

10. Disconnect the wheel speed sensor harness clips, if equipped.

11. Remove the rear wheel speed sensor bolt, spacer and the sensor, if equipped.

12. Position the brake tube, harness and cable aside.

13. To maintain driveline balance, matchmark the driveshaft flange yoke and the pinion flange. Remove the four driveshaft flange bolts.

14. Using a suitable tool, disconnect the driveshaft flange yoke from the pinion flange. Support the driveshaft using mechanic's wire.

15. Using a suitable jack, support the axle at the differential.

16. Remove and discard the nuts and bolts retaining shock absorbers to the axle.

17. Remove and discard the nuts and axle U-bolts.

18. Lower the axle from the vehicle.

To install:

19. Raise the axle into the vehicle.

20. Install new axle U-bolts and nuts and tighten until snug. Tighten the U-bolt nuts evenly in an X-type pattern as follows:

   a. Tighten to 37 ft. lbs. (50 Nm).

   b. Tighten to 74 ft. lbs. (100 Nm).

   c. Tighten to 111 ft. lbs. (150 Nm).

   d. Tighten to 148 ft. lbs. (200 Nm).

   e. Tighten to 166 ft. lbs. (225 Nm).

21. Install the new shock absorber nuts and bolts and tighten to 58 ft. lbs. (79 Nm).

22. The remainder of the installation is the reverse order of removal.

REAR AXLE SHAFT, BEARING & SEAL

REMOVAL & INSTALLATION

See Figures 16 through 21.

1. Before servicing the vehicle, refer to the Precautions Section.

2. Raise and safely support the vehicle.

3. Remove the rear wheels.

4. Remove the brake rotor.

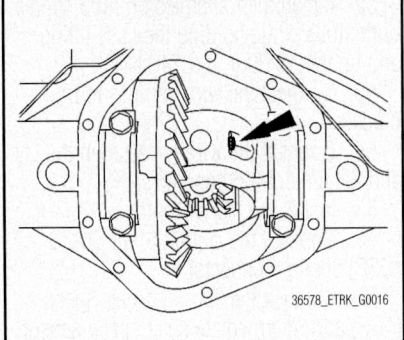

Fig. 16 Removing the lock screw—E-Series Models

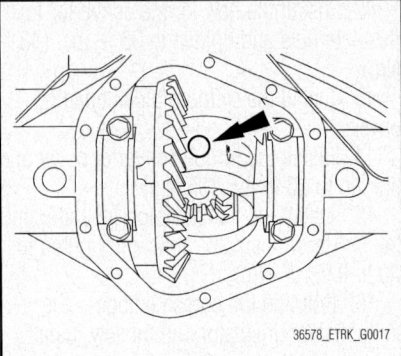

Fig. 17 Removing the differential pinion shaft—E-Series Models

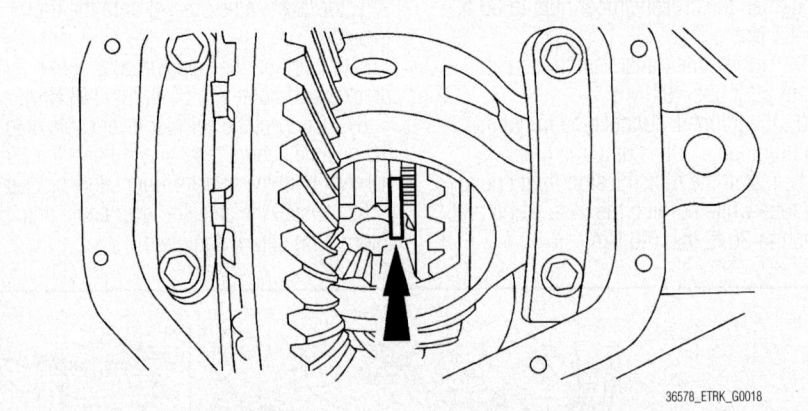

Fig. 18 Push the flanged end of the axle shaft toward the center of the axle and remove the U-washer—E-Series Models

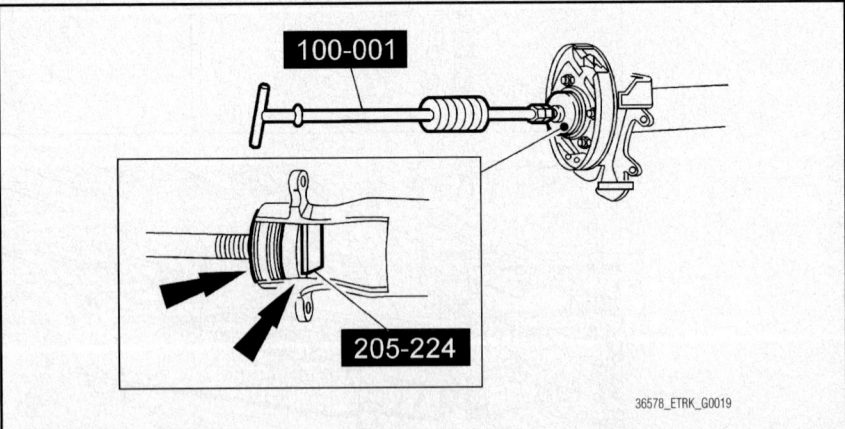

Fig. 19 Using Axle Bearing Remover and Slide Hammer, remove the rear bearing—E-Series Models

5. Remove the differential housing cover.

6. If the vehicle is equipped with Roll-Stability Control, remove the rear wheel speed sensor bolt. Position the spacer and sensor aside.

7. Remove the lock screw and remove the differential pinion shaft.

8. Push the flanged end of the axle shaft toward the center of the axle and remove the U-washer.

9. Remove the axle shaft.

10. Using a suitable seal remover, remove and discard the axle shaft oil seal.

11. Using an Axle Bearing Remover and Slide Hammer, remove the rear bearing.

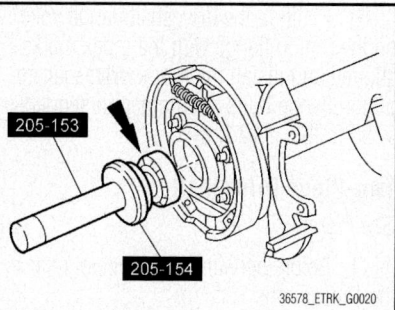

Fig. 20 Use a bearing installer and handle to install the rear wheel bearing—E-Series Models

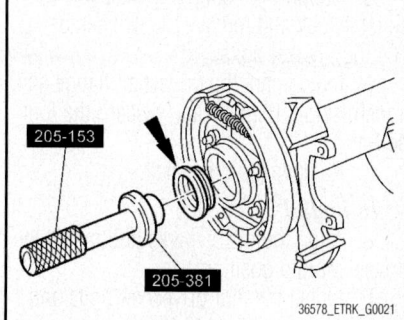

Fig. 21 Use a suitable seal installer to install a new axle shaft oil seal—E-Series Models

To install:

12. Lubricate the new rear wheel bearing with axle lubricant.

13. Using the Rear Axle Bearing Installer and Handle, install the rear wheel bearing.

14. Lubricate the lip of the new axle shaft oil seal with grease.

15. Using the Rear Axle Oil Seal Installer and Handle, install the new axle shaft oil seal.

16. Push the axle shaft into the axle tube and engage the differential side gear with the shaft splines.

17. Push the axle shaft toward the center of the axle and install the U-washer. Pull the axle shaft outward until the U-washer locks into the differential side gear.

18. Align the differential pinion shaft lock screw hole with the hole in the differential case. Correctly position the differential pinion thrust washers. Install the differential pinion shaft.

19. Install a new lock screw and tighten to 20 ft. lbs. (27 Nm).

20. The remainder of the installation is the reverse order of removal.

REAR PINION SEAL

REMOVAL & INSTALLATION

See Figures 22 through 24.

1. Before servicing the vehicle, refer to the Precautions Section.

2. Raise and safely support the vehicle.

3. Remove the driveshaft. For additional information, refer to "Driveshaft, Removal & Installation."

4. Matchmark the pinion flange to the pinion shaft.

5. Using a drive pinion flange holding tool, remove the locknut and washer.

6. Using a suitable puller, remove the pinion flange.

7. Using the Bushing Remover and slide hammer, remove the pinion seal.

To install:

8. Lubricate the pinion seal rubber lips with the specified lubricant.

9. Using a suitable driver, install the pinion seal.

➡ **After installation, verify that the garter spring did not pop out of the seal. If the garter spring popped out, install a new pinion seal.**

10. Coat the inside of the pinion flange with a small amount of the specified lubricant.

11. Install the pinion flange.

12. Using a drive pinion flange holding tool to prevent the flange from turning, tighten the pinion nut to 250 ft. lbs. (339 Nm).

13. Install the driveshaft aligning the matchmarks.

14. Refill the differential with fluid to the correct level.

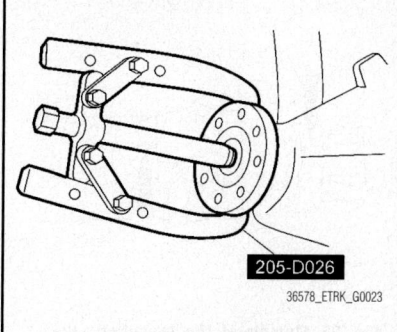

Fig. 23 Remove the pinion flange using a suitable 2-jaw puller—E-Series Models

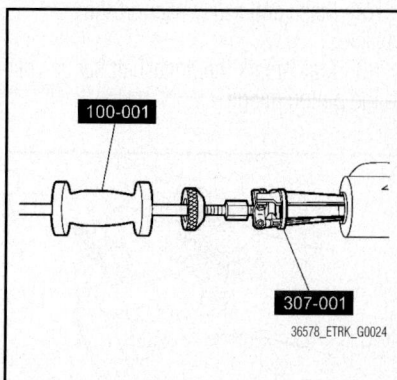

Fig. 24 Using the Bushing Remover and slide hammer, remove the pinion seal—E-Series Models

DRIVESHAFT

REMOVAL & INSTALLATION

One-Piece Driveshaft

See Figures 25 through 27.

1. Before servicing the vehicle, refer to the Precautions Section.

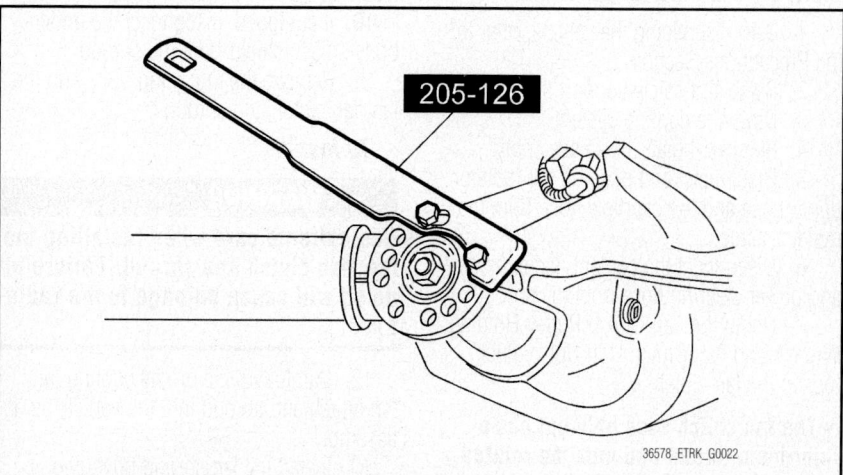

Fig. 22 Remove the locknut while using a flange holding tool to prevent the flange from turning—E-Series Models

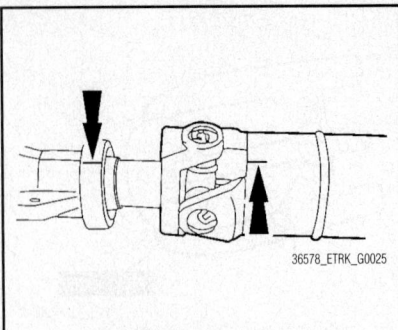

Fig. 25 Matchmark the driveshaft yoke to the transmission tailshaft—E-Series one-piece driveshaft

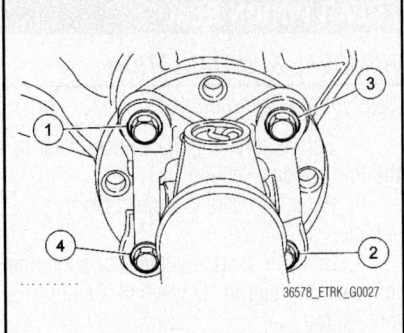

Fig. 27 Driveshaft-to-pinion flange bolt torque sequence—E-Series Models

10. Position the driveshaft flange yoke on the pinion flange with the index marks aligned and install the 4 new driveshaft-to-pinion flange bolts and tighten in sequence to 83 ft. lbs. (112 Nm).

Two-Piece Driveshaft

See Figure 27.

1. Before servicing the vehicle, refer to the Precautions Section.
2. Raise and safely support the vehicle.
3. Matchmark the driveshaft to the rear axle pinion flange.
4. Remove and discard the four bolts and disconnect the rear driveshaft section.
5. Support the coupling shaft with a suitable jack and remove the two center bearing bracket bolts.
6. Matchmark the driveshaft flange and transmission. Remove and discard the four bolts.
7. Remove the driveshaft.

To install:

8. Align the matchmarks and install the driveshaft into position.
9. Install the four driveshaft bolts and tighten to 76 ft. lbs. (103 Nm).
10. Support the coupling shaft, install the center bearing bracket and tighten the mounting bolts to 46 ft. lbs. (63 Nm).
11. Install the rear driveshaft section, position the flange yoke on the pinion shaft and tighten the flange bolts in sequence to 83 ft. lbs. (112 Nm).

2. Raise and safely support the vehicle.
3. Matchmark the driveshaft flange yoke to the pinion flange.

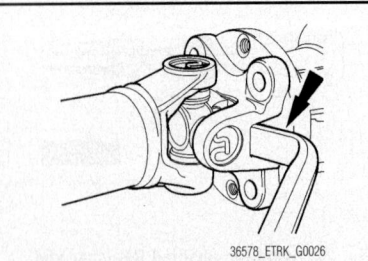

Fig. 26 Using a suitable pry bar, disconnect the driveshaft flange yoke from the pinion flange—E-Series one-piece driveshaft

4. Matchmark the driveshaft yoke to the transmission tailshaft.
5. Remove the four driveshaft-to-pinion flange bolts.
6. Using a suitable pry bar, disconnect the driveshaft flange yoke from the pinion flange.
7. Lower the driveshaft and slide it of the output shaft.

To install:

8. Lubricate the slip-yoke spline with grease.
9. Check to see if a paint mark is present on the front of the driveshaft and on the end of the transmission output shaft. Align the factory-made paint marks on the output shaft and driveshaft and position the driveshaft in the transmission. Align your matchmarks if the factory marks are not present.

ENGINE COOLING

ENGINE FAN

REMOVAL & INSTALLATION

4.6L, 5.4L & 6.8L Engines

1. Before servicing the vehicle, refer to the Precautions Section.
2. Raise and safely support the vehicle.
3. Drain the cooling system.
4. Remove the air intake assembly.
5. Disconnect and position the radiator upper hose and the overflow hose from the radiator aside.
6. Disconnect the coolant degas bottle and power steering hose from the shroud.
7. Using the Fan Clutch Pulley Holding Wrench and Fan Clutch Hub Nut Wrench, loosen the fan clutch.

➡The fan clutch assembly nut has a right-hand thread and must be rotated counterclockwise to remove it.

8. Carefully rotate the fan and fan clutch assembly counterclockwise until the assembly is free from the coolant pump. Place the fan and fan clutch into the shroud opening.
9. Disconnect the lower radiator hose retaining clamp from the shroud.
10. If equipped, disconnect the underbody splash shield from the shroud.
11. Remove the mounting bolts and the fan, fan clutch and shroud.

To install:

❋❋ WARNING

Use extreme care when installing the fan, fan clutch and shroud. Failure to do so will cause damage to the radiator.

12. Carefully position the cooling fan, fan clutch and shroud into the vehicle as an assembly.
13. Install the fan shroud bolts and tighten to 53 ft. lbs. (6 Nm).
14. Using the Fan Clutch Pulley Holding Wrench and the Fan Clutch Hub Nut

Wrench, install the cooling fan and tighten the nut as follows:
- 4.6L and 5.4L Engines: 41 ft. lbs. (55 Nm)
- 6.8L Engines: 98 ft. lbs. (133 Nm).

15. Connect the lower radiator hose retaining clamp to the shroud.
16. If equipped, connect the underbody splash shield to the shroud.
17. Connect the radiator upper hose and the overflow hose to the radiator.

❋❋ WARNING

The coolant hose must be mounted in the lower hole and power steering hose in the upper hole or damage to the hoses may occur.

18. Connect the coolant degas bottle and power steering hose to the shroud.
19. Install the air intake assembly.
20. Refill the cooling system to the correct level.

6.0L Engine

See Figures 28 and 29.

1. Before servicing the vehicle, refer to the Precautions Section.

2. Remove the radiator. For additional information, refer to "Radiator, Removal & Installation."

3. Disconnect the electrical connector. Release the wiring from the stator.

➡**Use a hole in the fan hub to prevent the fan from turning.**

4. Using the special tool, loosen the fan clutch by turning the wrench counterclockwise. Remove the cooling fan and clutch.

5. Remove the bolts and cooling fan stator assembly.

6. To install, reverse the removal procedure. Torque the stator bolts to 40 Nm (30 ft. lbs.) and the fun clutch to 133 Nm (98 ft. lbs.).

RADIATOR

REMOVAL & INSTALLATION

4.6L, 5.4L & 6.8L Engines

1. Before servicing the vehicle, refer to the Precautions Section.

2. Disconnect the negative battery cable.

3. Drain the engine cooling system.

4. Remove the engine fan. For additional information, refer to "Engine Fan, Removal & Installation."

5. Remove the engine splash shield, if equipped.

6. Disconnect the transmission oil cooler hoses and plug the lines.

7. Disconnect the lower radiator hose.

8. Remove the radiator support brackets.

9. Remove the radiator from the vehicle.

To install:

10. Install the radiator into the vehicle.

11. Install the radiator support brackets and tighten the bolts to 15 ft. lbs. (20 Nm).

12. Connect the lower radiator hose.

13. The remainder of the installation is the reverse order of removal.

14. Refill the cooling system to the correct level.

6.0L Engine

See Figures 30 through 32.

1. Before servicing the vehicle, refer to the Precautions Section.

2. Disconnect the negative battery cable.

3. Drain the engine cooling system.

4. Remove the six pushpin retainers and upper air deflector.

5. Remove the four bolts for the power steering reservoir bracket.

6. Remove the three bolts and power steering fluid indicator. Remove the power steering reservoir mounting bracket. Install the power steering fluid indicator and position aside.

7. Disconnect the coolant hoses from the Air Cleaner (ACL) outlet tube.

8. Loosen the 2 clamps and remove the ACL outlet pipe.

9. Disconnect the Mass Air Flow (MAF) sensor electrical connector. Disconnect the 3 clips and remove the ACL cover.

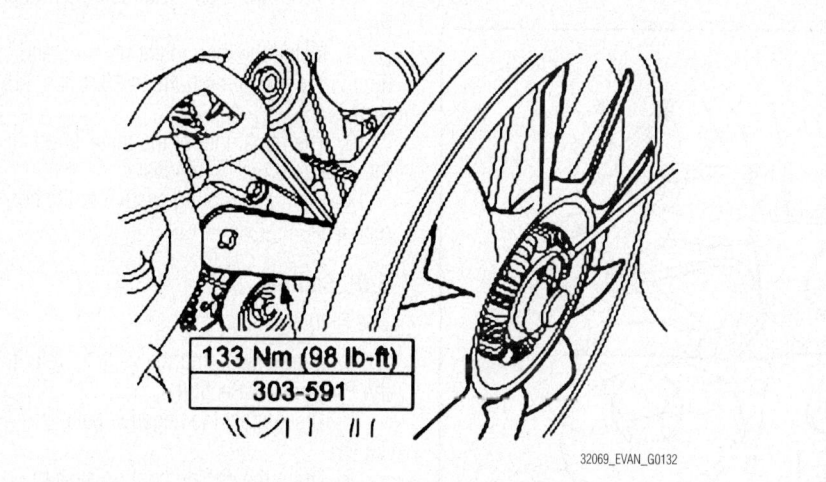

Fig. 28 Using the special tool, loosen the fan clutch by turning the wrench counterclockwise—6.0L engine

133 Nm (98 lb-ft)
303-591

32069_EVAN_G0132

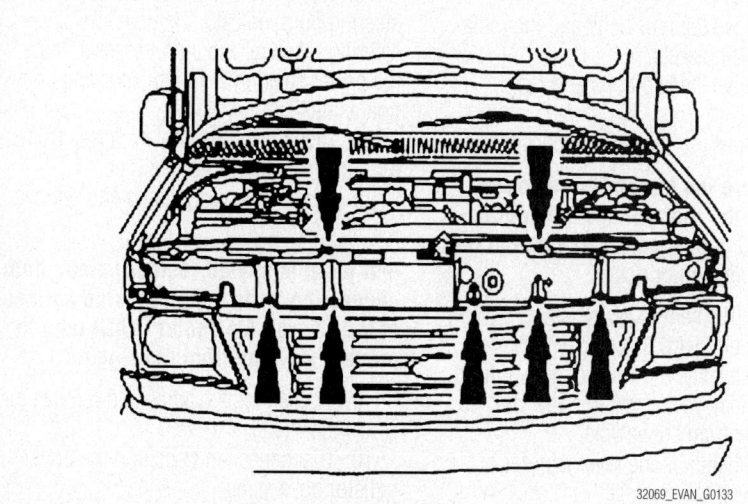

Fig. 29 Remove the bolts and cooling fan stator assembly

32069_EVAN_G0133

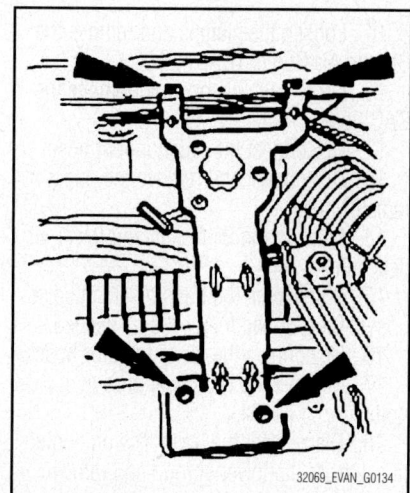

Fig. 30 Remove the bolts for the power steering reservoir bracket—6.0L Engine

32069_EVAN_G0134

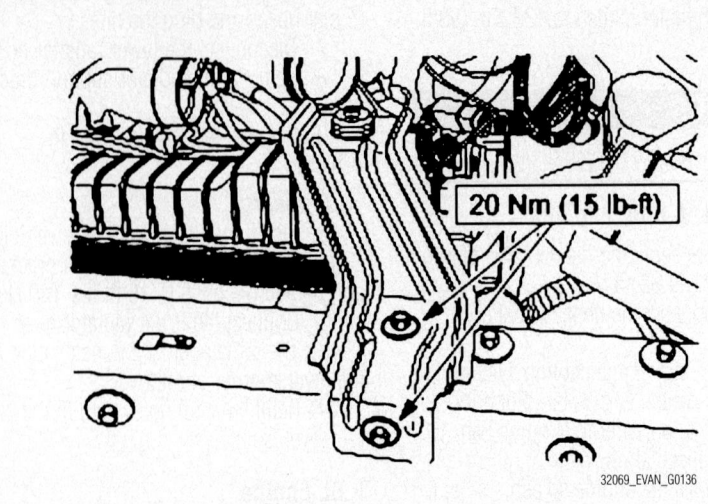

Fig. 31 Remove the bolts and the radiator mounting brackets—6.0L Engine

20 Nm (15 lb-ft)

32069_EVAN_G0136

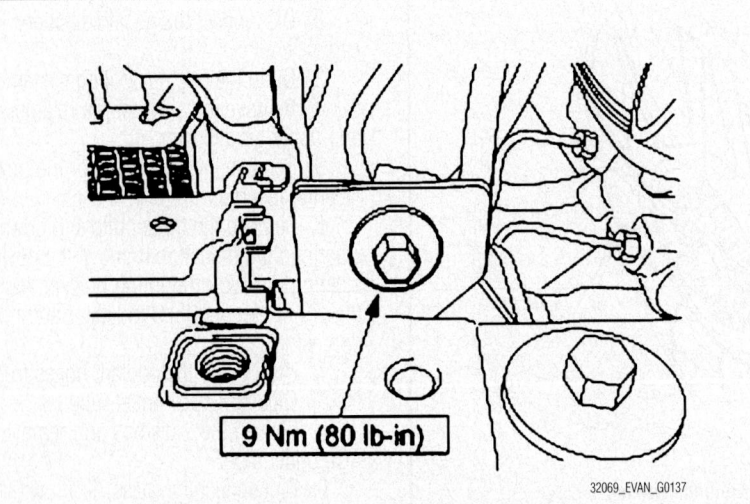

Fig. 32 Remove the two bolts and position the A/C condenser forward—6.0L Engine

9 Nm (80 lb-in)

32069_EVAN_G0137

10. Loosen the clamps and remove the Charge Air Cooler (CAC) tube.

11. Loosen the clamps and remove the CAC hose.

12. Disconnect the radiator vent hose.

13. Disconnect and remove the upper radiator hose.

14. Remove the four bolts and lower air deflector.

15. Disconnect the transmission cooler hoses. Plug or cap the hoses as needed.

16. Disconnect the lower radiator hose.

17. Remove the two lower shroud bolts.

18. Disconnect the transmission cooler hoses from the lower shroud and remove the lower shroud.

19. Remove the two pushpin retainers and the closeout.

20. Remove the four bolts and the radiator mounting brackets.

21. Remove the two bolts and fan shroud.

22. Remove the two A/C condenser bolts.

➡ **Make sure the transmission cooler fittings on the radiator are not contacting the A/C condenser or damage to the A/C condenser may occur.**

23. With the help of an assistant, raise the radiator and CAC as an assembly enough to separate the A/C condenser from the CAC . Remove the radiator and CAC as an assembly from the vehicle.

24. Installation is the reverse order of removal.

25. Refill the cooling system to the correct level.

THERMOSTAT

REMOVAL & INSTALLATION

4.6L, 5.4L & 6.8L Engines

See Figure 33.

1. Before servicing the vehicle, refer to the Precautions Section.

2. Disconnect the negative battery cable.

3. Drain the engine cooling system.

4. Remove the air intake assembly.

5. Disconnect the upper radiator hose for access if necessary.

6. Remove the mounting bolts and position the thermostat housing aside.

7. Remove the thermostat and discard the O-ring.

To install:

8. Install the thermostat using a new O-ring.

9. Install the thermostat housing and tighten the mounting bolts to 18 ft. lbs. (25 Nm).

10. The remainder of the installation is the reverse order of removal.

11. Refill the cooling system to the correct level.

6.0L Engine

See Figure 34.

1. Before servicing the vehicle, refer to the Precautions Section.

2. Disconnect the negative battery cable.

3. Drain the engine cooling system.

4. Remove the six pushpin retainers and upper air deflector.

5. Remove the four bolts for the power steering reservoir bracket.

6. Remove the three bolts and power steering fluid indicator. Remove the power steering reservoir mounting bracket. Install the power steering fluid indicator and position aside.

7. Disconnect the coolant hoses from the Air Cleaner (ACL) outlet pipe.

8. Loosen the two clamps and remove the ACL outlet pipe.

➡ **If there is any oil residue, clean both connecting ports and the inside surface of the Charge Air Cooler (CAC) tube to prevent the tube from blowing off.**

9. Loosen the 2 clamps and remove the CAC tube.

10. Disconnect and position the upper radiator hose aside.

11. Remove the nut and position the fuel line retainer aside.

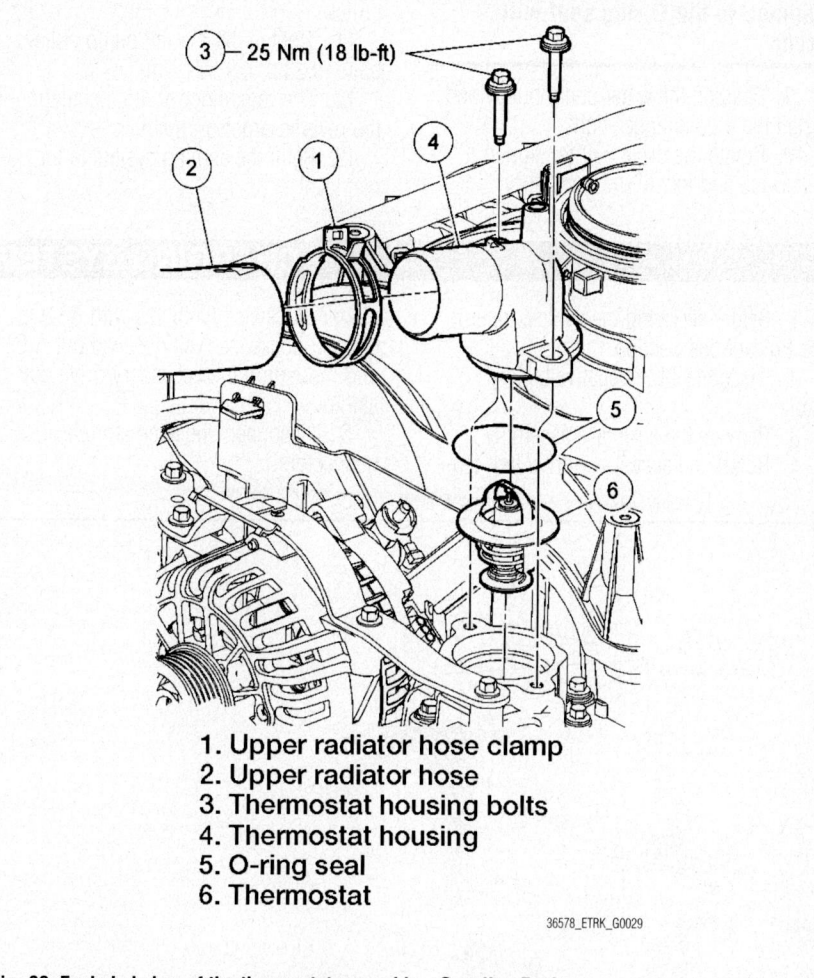

1. Upper radiator hose clamp
2. Upper radiator hose
3. Thermostat housing bolts
4. Thermostat housing
5. O-ring seal
6. Thermostat

36578_ETRK_G0029

Fig. 33 Exploded view of the thermostat assembly—Gasoline Engines

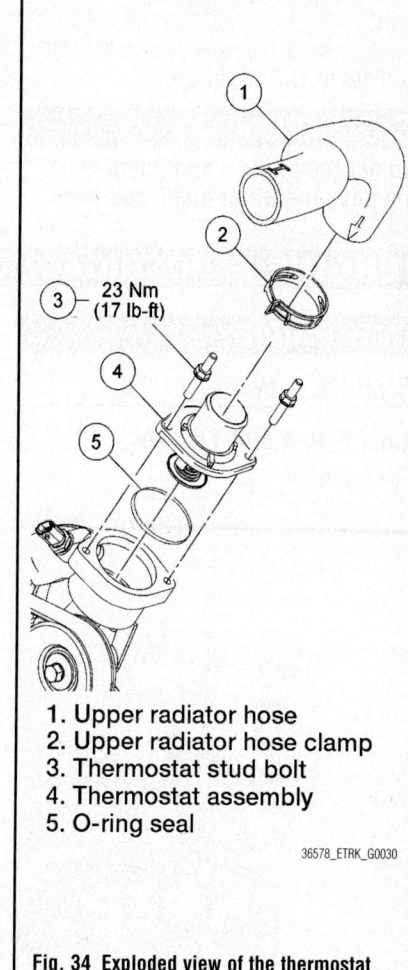

1. Upper radiator hose
2. Upper radiator hose clamp
3. Thermostat stud bolt
4. Thermostat assembly
5. O-ring seal

36578_ETRK_G0030

Fig. 34 Exploded view of the thermostat assembly—6.0L Engine

12. Remove the two stud bolts, thermostat assembly and discard the O-ring seal.

13. Installation is the reverse order of removal. Tighten the housing mounting bolts to 17 ft. lbs. (23 Nm).

WATER PUMP

REMOVAL & INSTALLATION

4.6L, 5.4L & 6.8L Engines

1. Before servicing the vehicle, refer to the Precautions Section.
2. Disconnect the negative battery cable.
3. Remove the engine fan. For additional information, refer to "Engine Fan, Removal & Installation."
4. Loosen the water pump pulley bolts.
5. Rotate the tensioner clockwise and remove the accessory drive belt from the coolant pulley.
6. Remove the four bolts and the water pump pulley.
7. Remove the four water pump mount-

ing bolts and the water pump. Discard the O-ring seal.

To install:

8. Install a new O-ring on the water pump.

➡**Lubricate the new O-ring seal with clean engine coolant prior to installation into the cylinder block.**

9. Position the water pump into place and tighten the mounting bolts to 18 ft. lbs. (25 Nm).

✳✳ WARNING

Do not rotate the coolant pump housing once the coolant pump has been positioned in the cylinder block. Damage to the O-ring seal will occur.

10. Position the water pump pulley onto the coolant pump and install the bolts finger-tight.
11. Rotate the tensioner clockwise and install the accessory drive belt onto the water pump pulley.

12. Tighten the water pump pulley bolts to 18 ft. lbs. (25 Nm).

13. The remainder of the installation is the reverse order of removal.

14. Refill the cooling system to the correct level.

6.0L Engine

1. Before servicing the vehicle, refer to the Precautions Section.
2. Disconnect the negative battery cable.
3. Loosen the four water pump pulley bolts.
4. Rotate the drive belt tensioner clockwise and remove the accessory drive belt from the water pump pulley.
5. Remove the four bolts and the water pump pulley.
6. Remove the 4 bolts and the water pump. Discard the O-ring seal.

To install:

➡**Lubricate the new O-ring seal with clean engine water prior to installation.**

7. Install a new O-ring on the water pump.

8. Position the water pump and tighten the bolts to 17 ft. lbs. (23 Nm).

✲✲ WARNING

Do not rotate the water pump housing once the water pump has been positioned in the cylinder block. Damage to the O-ring seal will occur.

9. Position the water pump pulley and install the 4 bolts finger-tight.

10. Rotate the drive belt tensioner clockwise and install the accessory drive belt onto the water pump pulley.

11. Tighten the 4 water pump pulley bolts to 23 ft. lbs. (31 Nm).

12. The remainder of the installation is the reverse order of removal.

13. Refill the cooling system to the correct level.

ENGINE ELECTRICAL

ALTERNATOR

REMOVAL & INSTALLATION

4.6L, 5.4L & 6.8L Engines

See Figure 35.

CHARGING SYSTEM

1. Before servicing the vehicle, refer to the Precautions Section.

2. Disconnect the negative battery cable.

3. Remove the air intake assembly.

4. Rotate the accessory drive belt tensioner clockwise (vehicles with A/C) or counterclockwise (vehicles without A/C) and reposition the accessory drive belt aside.

5. Disconnect the alternator electrical connectors.

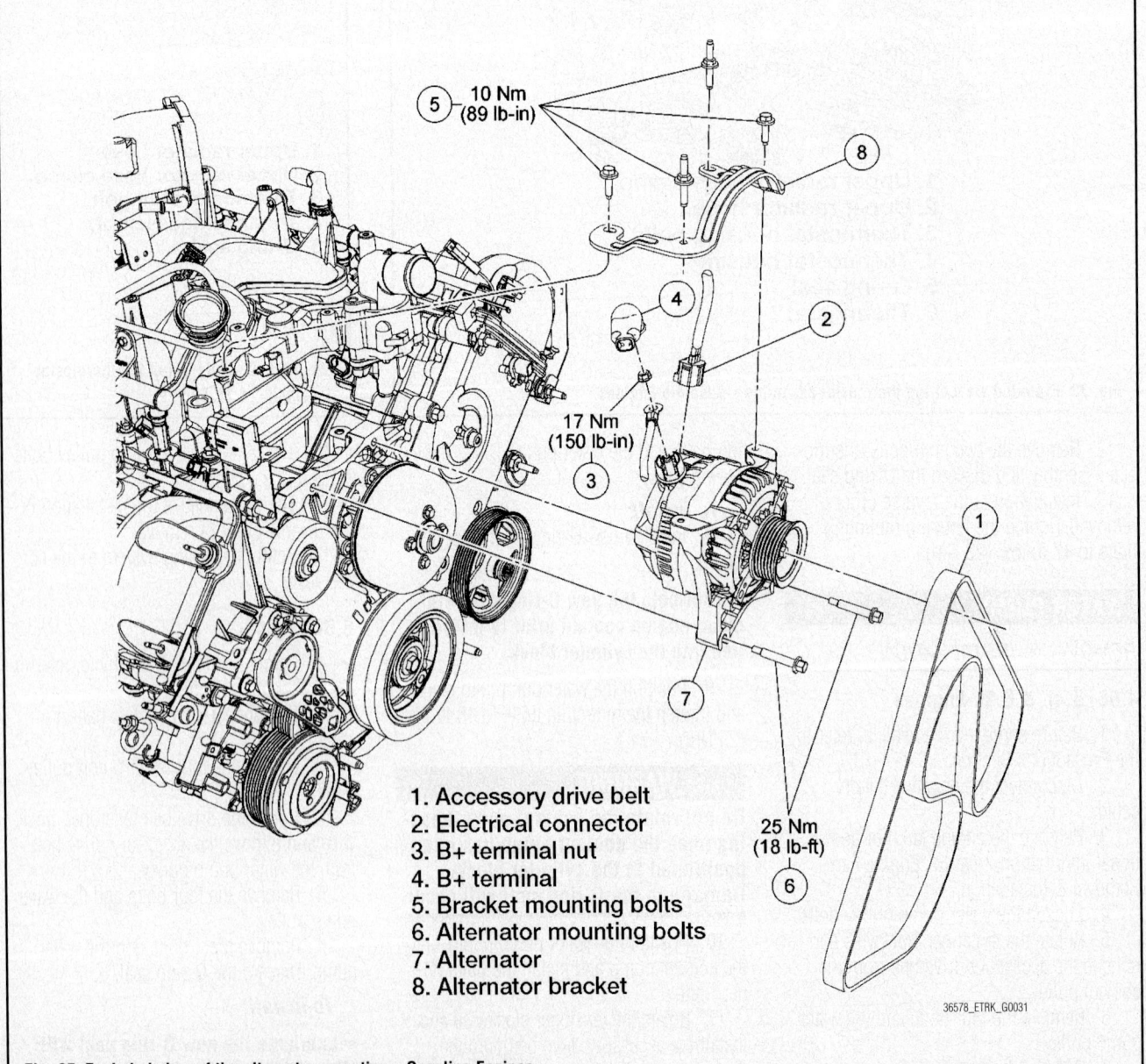

1. Accessory drive belt
2. Electrical connector
3. B+ terminal nut
4. B+ terminal
5. Bracket mounting bolts
6. Alternator mounting bolts
7. Alternator
8. Alternator bracket

36578_ETRK_G0031

Fig. 35 Exploded view of the alternator mounting—Gasoline Engines

6. Position the alternator B+ protective cover aside, remove the B+ terminal nut and position the B+ terminal aside.

7. Remove the four mounting bolts and the alternator bracket.

8. Remove the two mounting bolts and the alternator.

9. Installation is the reverse order of removal. Tighten the alternator mounting bolts to 18 ft. lbs. (25 Nm) and bracket mounting bolts to 89 inch lbs. (10 Nm).

6.0L Engine, Single Alternator

1. Before servicing the vehicle, refer to the Precautions Section.

2. Disconnect the negative battery cable.

3. Remove the bolt and position the Manifold Absolute Pressure (MAP) sensor aside.

4. Remove the bolt and position the ground strap aside.

5. Remove the two bolts and position the power steering fluid reservoir bracket aside.

6. Remove the three bolts and position the cowl wiring harness aside.

7. Remove the three bracket screws from the Charge Air Cooler (CAC) tube bracket.

8. Remove the two stud nuts and the CAC tube bracket.

9. Loosen the two clamps and remove the CAC tube.

10. Rotate the accessory drive belt tensioner clockwise and position the accessory drive belt aside.

11. Remove the nut from the alternator

stud bolt and position the transmission level indicator tube bracket aside.

12. Disconnect the alternator electrical connector.

13. Position the alternator B+ protective cover aside, remove the B+ terminal nut and position the B+ terminal aside.

14. Remove the 3 bolts, the ground strap and the alternator.

15. Installation is the reverse order of removal. Tighten the alternator mounting bolts to 35 ft. lbs. (47 Nm).

6.0L Engine, Dual Alternator

1. Before servicing the vehicle, refer to the Precautions Section.

2. Disconnect the negative battery cable.

3. Remove the bolt and position the ground strap aside.

4. Remove the two bolts and position the power steering fluid reservoir bracket aside.

5. Remove the three bolts and position the cowl wiring harness aside.

6. Remove the three bracket screws from the Charge Air Cooler (CAC) tube bracket.

7. Remove the two stud nuts and the CAC tube bracket.

8. Loosen the two clamps and remove the CAC tube.

9. Rotate the secondary accessory drive belt tensioner clockwise and position the accessory drive belt aside.

10. Disconnect the alternator electrical connector.

11. Position the alternator B+ protective

cover aside, remove the B+ terminal nut and position the B+ terminal aside.

12. Remove the 3 bolts and the alternator.

13. Installation is the reverse order of removal. Tighten the alternator mounting bolts to 35 ft. lbs. (47 Nm).

VOLTAGE REGULATOR

REMOVAL & INSTALLATION

1. Before servicing the vehicle, refer to the Precautions Section.

2. Remove the alternator. For additional information, refer to "Alternator, Removal & Installation."

3. Remove the 4 generator brush and terminal holder - voltage regulator screws and position the generator brush and terminal holder - voltage regulator aside.

4. Remove the test terminal A screw cap, the 2 generator brush and terminal holder screws and separate the generator brush and terminal holder from the generator voltage regulator.

To install:

5. Install the 2 screws and the brush and terminal holder on the generator voltage regulator.

6. Press the brushes in and insert a wire to hold the brushes during installation.

7. Position the generator brush and terminal holder - voltage regulator.

8. Install the 4 generator brush and terminal holder - voltage regulator screws.

9. Remove the wire.

10. Install the alternator.

ENGINE ELECTRICAL   IGNITION SYSTEM

FIRING ORDERS

See Figures 36 through 38.

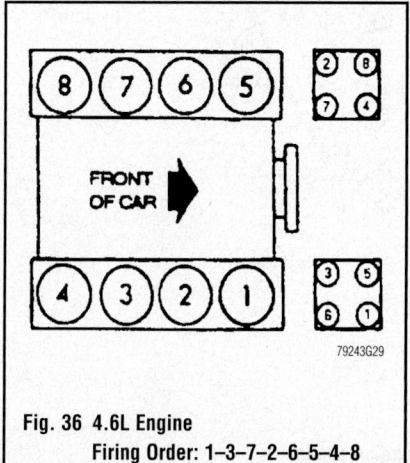

Fig. 36 4.6L Engine
Firing Order: 1–3–7–2–6–5–4–8

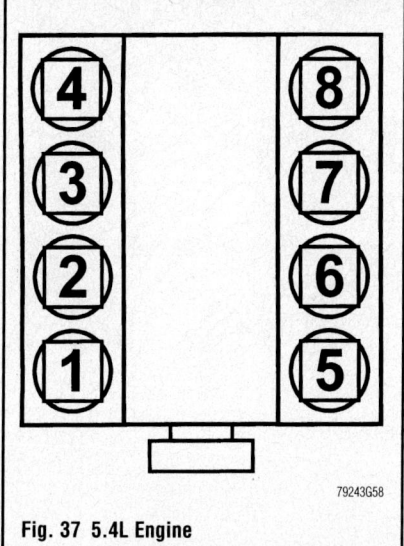

Fig. 37 5.4L Engine
Firing Order: 1–3–7–2–6–5–4–8

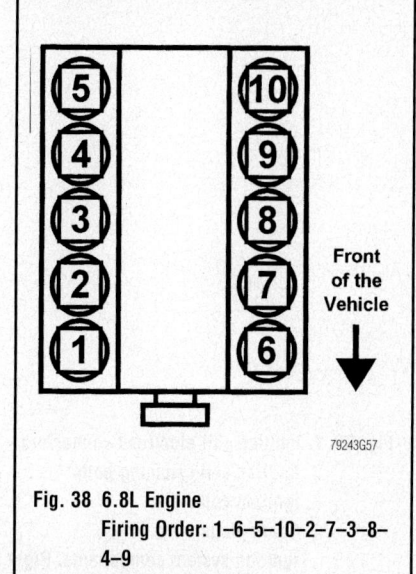

Fig. 38 6.8L Engine
Firing Order: 1–6–5–10–2–7–3–8–4–9

IGNITION COIL

REMOVAL & INSTALLATION

4.6L, 5.4L & 6.8L Engines

See Figures 39 and 40.

1. Before servicing the vehicle, refer to the Precautions Section.
2. Disconnect the negative battery cable.
3. Release the engine cover latches and remove the engine cover.
4. Remove the air intake assembly.
5. Disconnect the ignition coil electrical connector.
6. Remove the mounting bolt and remove the ignition coil.

➡Verify that the ignition coil spring is correctly located inside the ignition coil boot and that there is no damage to the tip of the boot.

7. Installation is the reverse order of removal. Tighten the ignition coil mounting bolt to 53 inch lbs. (6 Nm).

IGNITION TIMING

ADJUSTMENT

The injection timing is controlled by the Powertrain Control Module (PCM). No adjustment is necessary or possible.

SPARK PLUGS

REMOVAL & INSTALLATION

4.6L, 5.4L & 6.8L Engines

1. Before servicing the vehicle, refer to the Precautions Section.
2. Disconnect the negative battery cable.
3. Remove the ignition coil. For additional information, refer to "Ignition Coil, Removal & Installation."
4. Remove the spark plugs.

➡If an original spark plug is used, make sure it is installed in the same cylinder from which it was taken. New spark plugs can be used in any cylinder.

5. Installation is the reverse order. Tighten the spark plug to 10 ft. lbs. (14 Nm).

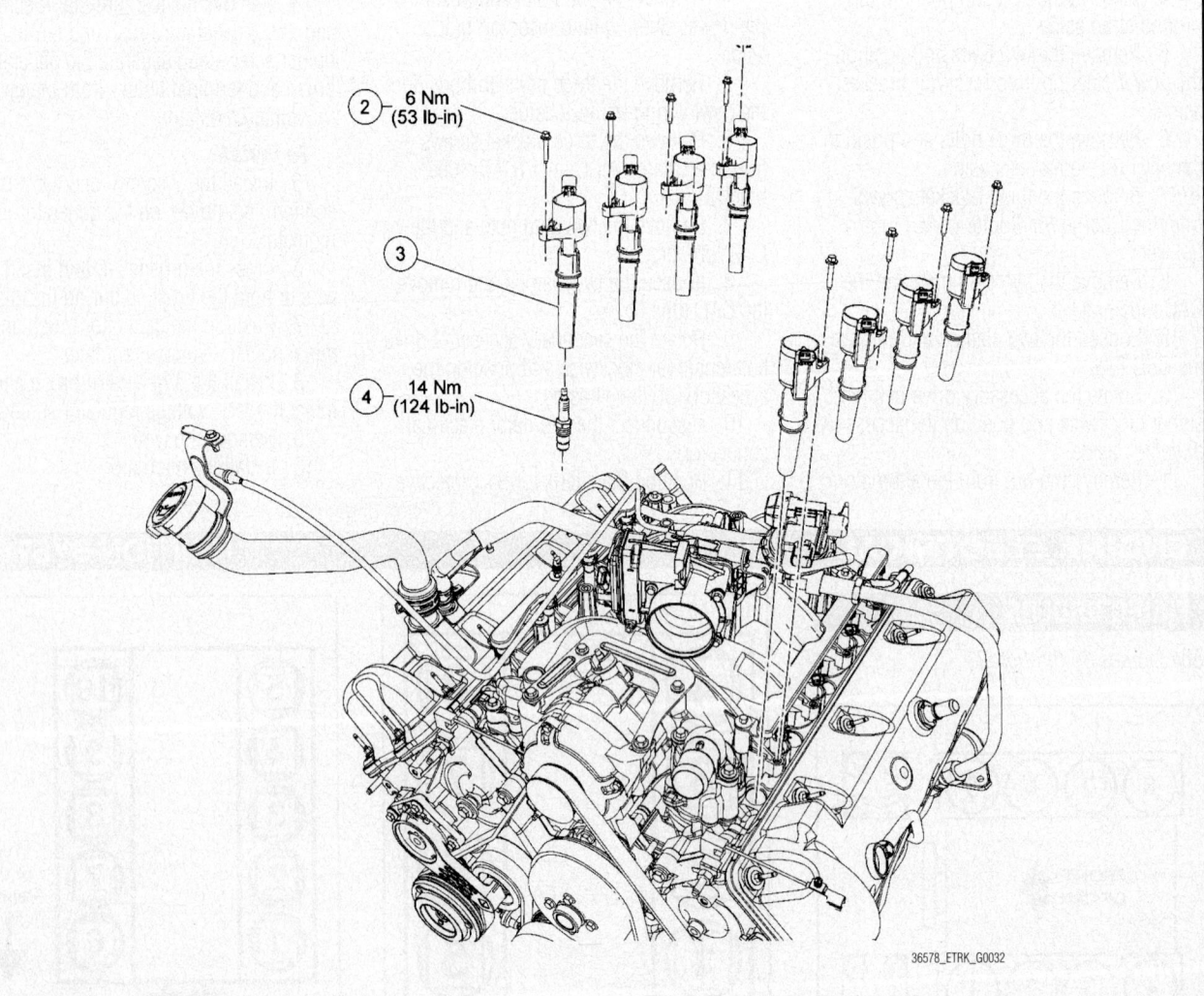

36578_ETRK_G0032

Fig. 39 1. Ignition coil electrical connectors
2. Ignition coil retaining bolts
3. Ignition coils
4. Spark plugs
Ignition system components. Right side shown; left side similar—4.6L Engine shown, 5.4L Engine similar

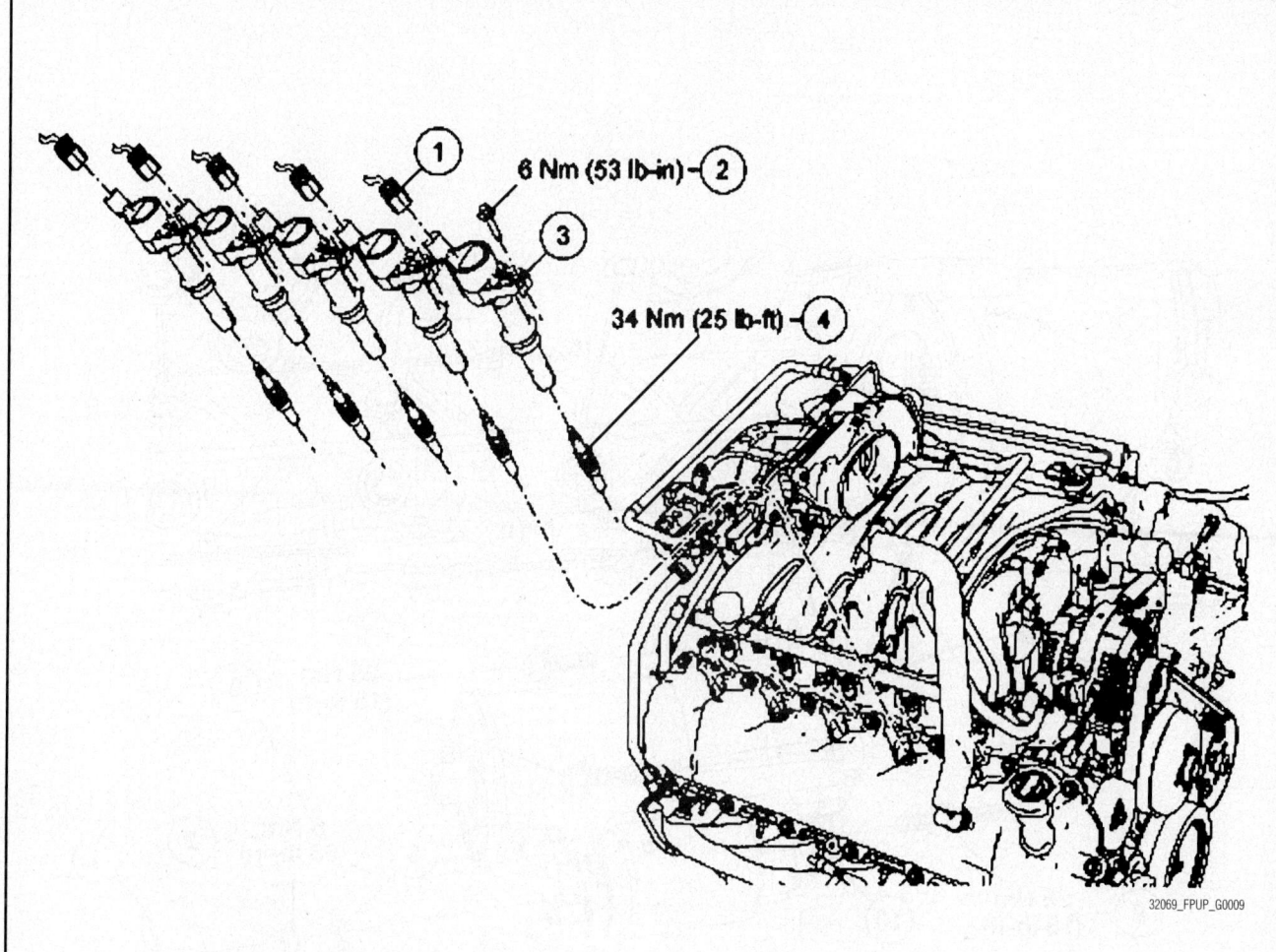

Fig. 40 1. Ignition coil electrical connectors
2. Ignition coil retaining bolts
3. Ignition coils
4. Spark plugs
Ignition system components. Right side shown; left side similar—6.8L Engine

ENGINE ELECTRICAL   STARTING SYSTEM

STARTER

REMOVAL & INSTALLATION

4.6L, 5.4L & 6.8L Engines
See Figure 41.

1. Before servicing the vehicle, refer to the Precautions Section.
2. Disconnect the negative battery cable.
3. Detach the starter motor solenoid terminal cover.
4. Remove the starter solenoid S-terminal nut and disconnect the S-terminal.

5. Remove the starter solenoid B-terminal nut and disconnect the B-terminal.
6. Remove the starter motor ground cable nut and disconnect the ground table.
7. Remove the mounting bolts, stud bolt and the starter.
8. Installation is the reverse order of removal. Tighten the starter upper bolt before the lower fasteners to 18 ft. lbs. (25 Nm).

6.0L Engine
See Figure 42.

1. Before servicing the vehicle, refer to the Precautions Section.

2. Disconnect the negative battery cable from the frame.
3. Raise and safely support the vehicle.
4. Remove the cable bracket nut and position the cable bracket aside.
5. Remove the starter solenoid protective cap.
6. Disconnect the starter electrical connections.
7. Remove the mounting bolts, stud bolt and the starter.
8. Installation is the reverse order of removal.

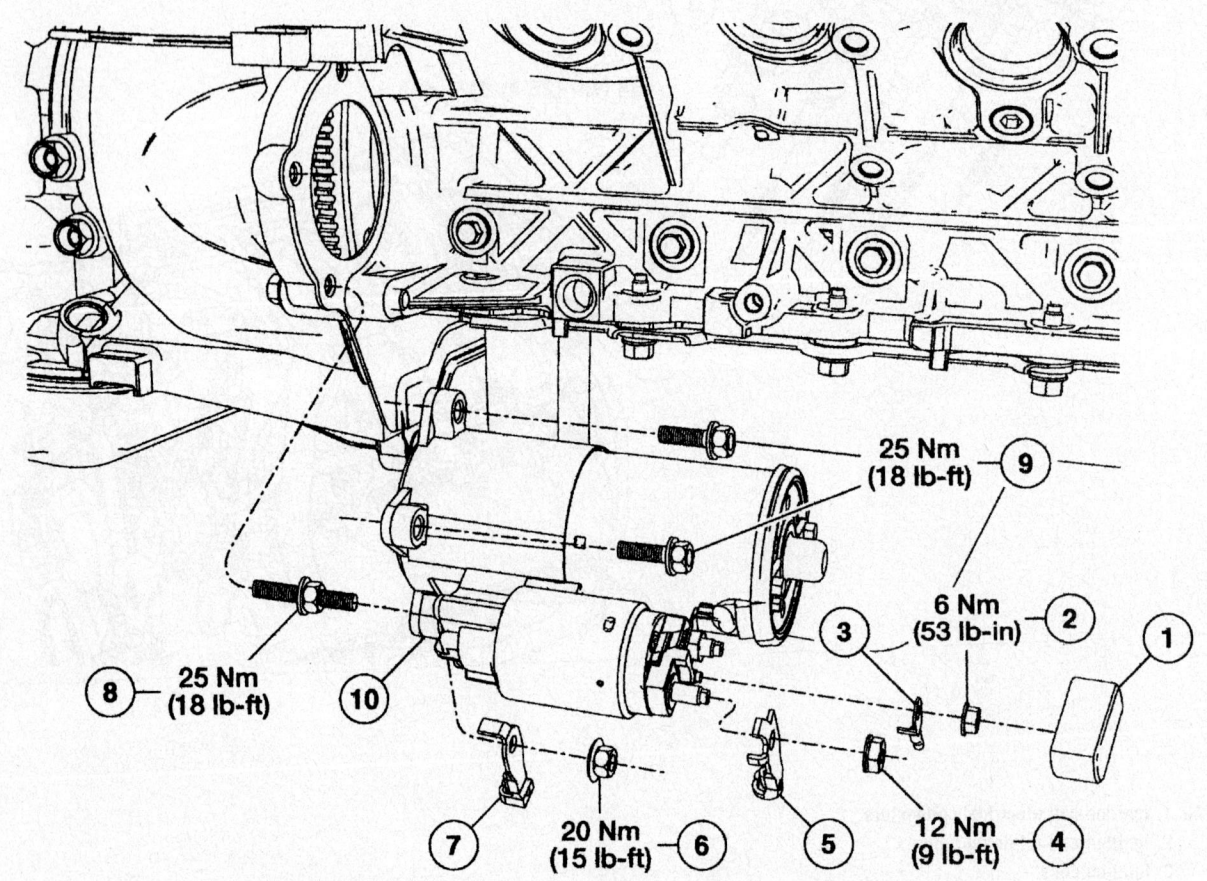

1 Terminal cover
2 Starter solenoid S-terminal nut
3 Starter solenoid S-terminal eyelet
4 Starter solenoid B-terminal nut
5 Starter solenoid B-terminal eyelet
6 Starter motor ground cable nut
7 Starter motor ground cable eyelet
8 Starter motor mounting stud bolt
9 Starter motor mounting bolt (2 required)
10 Starter motor

06017-F150-G87

Fig. 41 Starter and related parts—4.6L, 5.4L and 6.8L engines

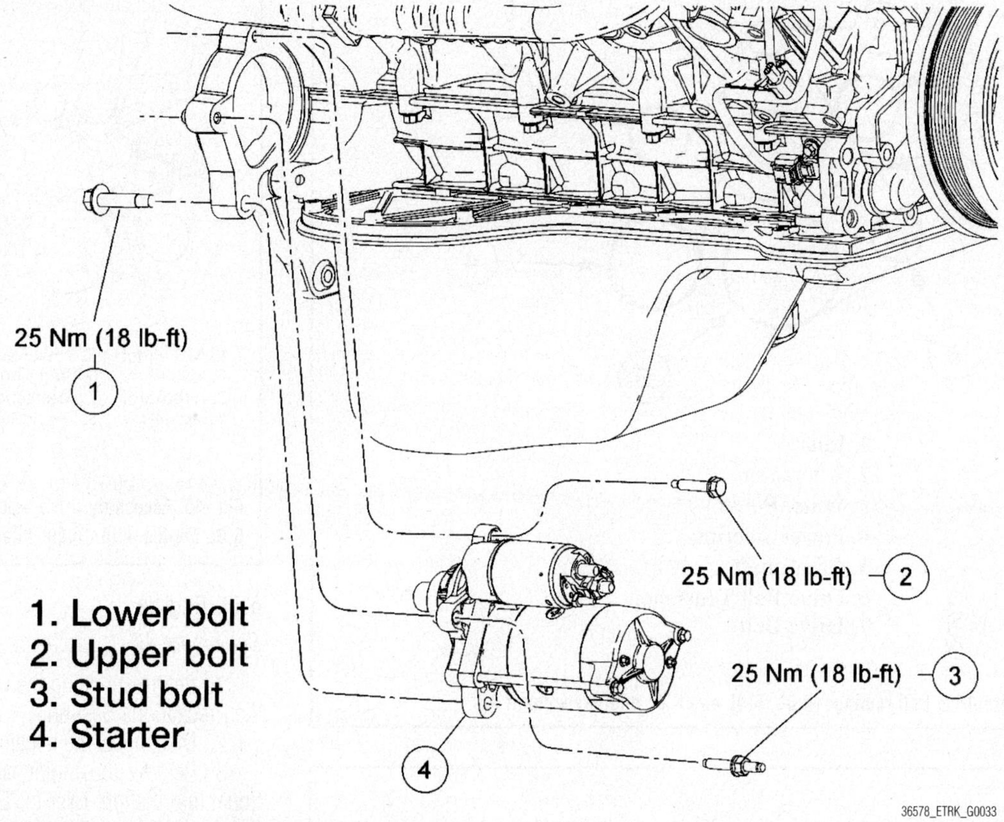

25 Nm (18 lb-ft)
1

25 Nm (18 lb-ft) — **2**

25 Nm (18 lb-ft) — **3**

1. Lower bolt
2. Upper bolt
3. Stud bolt
4. Starter

4

36578_ETRK_G0033

Fig. 42 Exploded view of the starter mounting—6.0L Engines

ENGINE MECHANICAL

ACCESSORY DRIVE BELTS

ACCESSORY BELT ROUTING

See Figures 43 through 46.

INSPECTION

Inspect the drive belt for signs of glazing or cracking. A glazed belt will be perfectly smooth from slippage, while a good belt will have a slight texture of fabric visible. Cracks will usually start at the inner edge of the belt and run outward. All worn or damaged drive belts should be replaced immediately.

ADJUSTMENT

The accessory drive belt tension is control by an automatic belt tensioner. Check that the belt length indicator, if equipped, on the belt tensioner is in the acceptable belt installation and wear range. If the indicator is in the belt replacement range, either an incorrect belt is installed or the belt is worn beyond the service limit. Install a new belt as necessary.

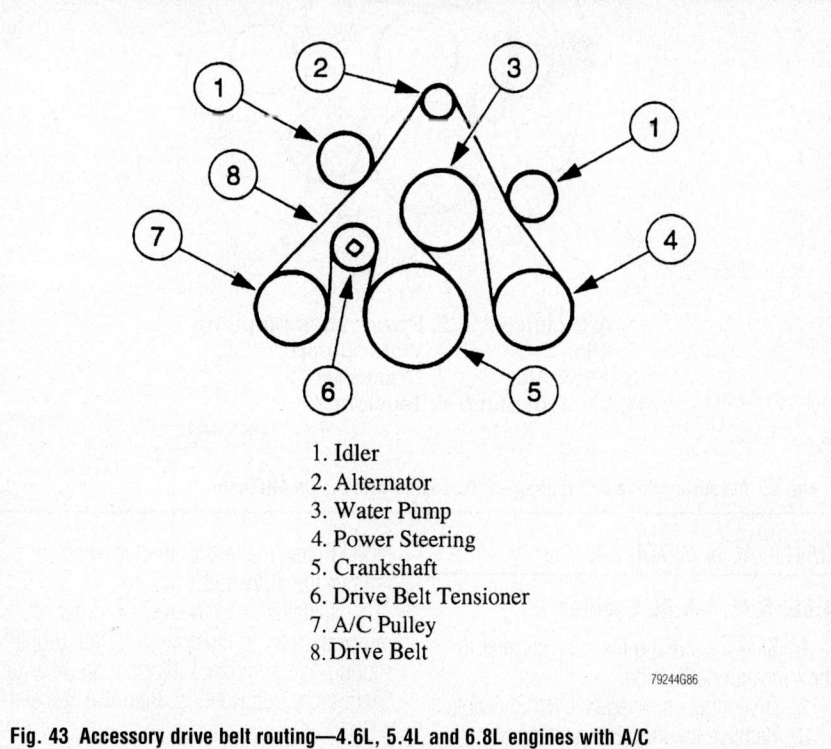

1. Idler
2. Alternator
3. Water Pump
4. Power Steering
5. Crankshaft
6. Drive Belt Tensioner
7. A/C Pulley
8. Drive Belt

79244G86

Fig. 43 Accessory drive belt routing—4.6L, 5.4L and 6.8L engines with A/C

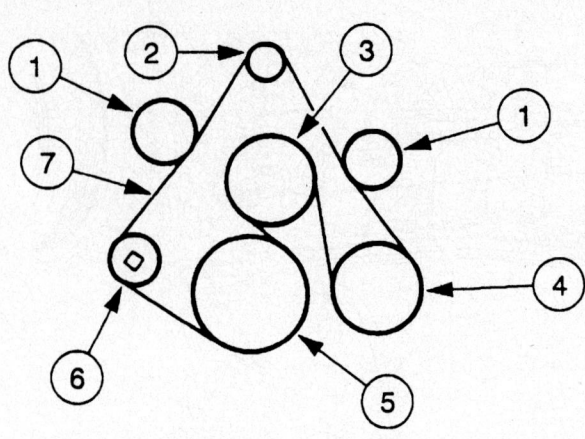

1. Idler
2. Alternator
3. Water Pump
4. Power Steering
5. Crankshaft
6. Drive Belt Tensioner
7. Drive Belt

79244G87

Fig. 44 Accessory drive belt routing—4.6L, 5.4L and 6.8L engines without A/C

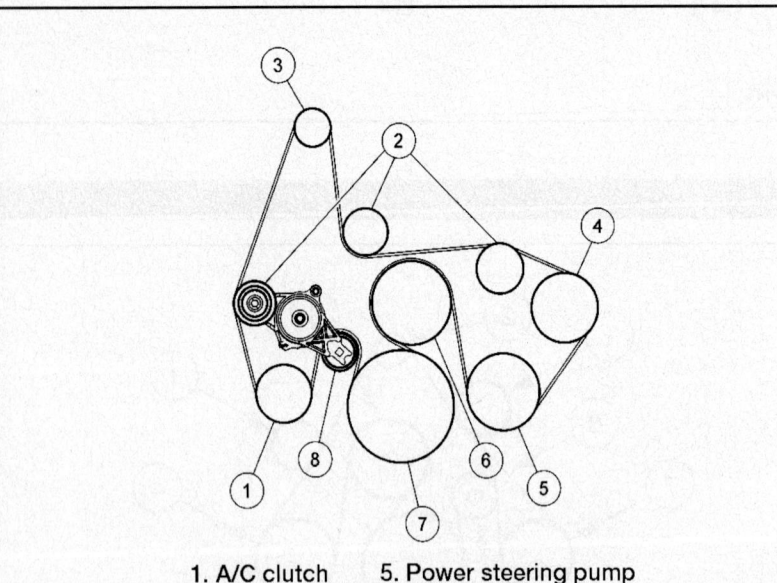

1. A/C clutch	5. Power steering pump
2. Idler	6. Water pump
3. Alternator	7. Crankshaft
4. Vacuum pump	8. Tensioner

36578_ETRK_G0034

Fig. 45 Accessory drive belt routing—6.0L Engine with Single Alternator

REMOVAL & INSTALLATION

4.6L, 5.4L & 6.8L Engines

1. Before servicing the vehicle, refer to the Precautions Section.
2. Disconnect the negative battery cable.
3. Remove the air intake assembly.
4. Rotate the tensioner clockwise and remove the drive belt.
5. Installation is the reverse order of removal. Refer to illustration for the proper routing. For additional information, refer to "Accessory Belt Routing, Removal & Installation."

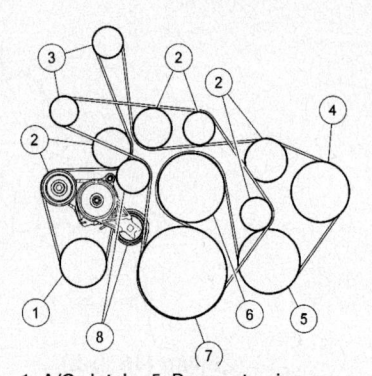

1. A/C clutch	5. Power steering pump
2. Idler	6. Water pump
3. Alternator	7. Crankshaft
4. Vacuum	8. Tensioners

36578_ETRK_G0035

Fig. 46 Accessory drive belt routing—6.0L Engine with Single Alternator

6.0L Engine

See Figure 47.

1. Before servicing the vehicle, refer to the Precautions Section.
2. Disconnect the negative battery cable.
3. Remove the engine fan. For additional information, refer to "Engine Fan, Removal & Installation."
4. Rotate the tensioner clockwise and remove the accessory drive belt.
5. Installation is the reverse order of removal.

36578_ETRK_G0036

Fig. 47 Rotate the tensioner clockwise and remove the accessory drive belt— 6.0L Engines

CAMSHAFT AND VALVE LIFTERS

REMOVAL & INSTALLATION

4.6L, 5.4L & 6.8L Engines

See Figures 48 through 54.

1. Before servicing the vehicle, refer to the Precautions Section.

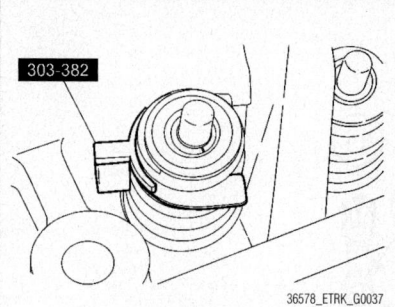

Fig. 48 Install the Valve Spring Compressor Spacer between the valve spring coils to protect the valve stem seal from damage—4.6L, 5.4L & 6.8L Engines

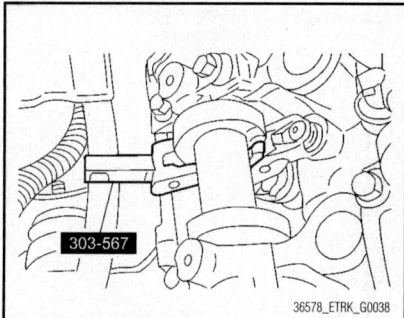

Fig. 49 Using a valve spring compressor, compress the valve spring and remove the camshaft roller follower—4.6L, 5.4L & 6.8L Engines

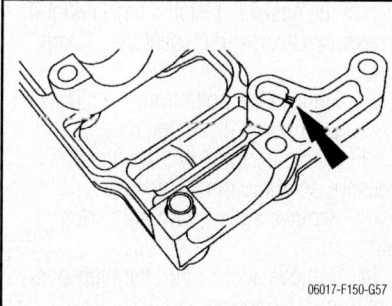

Fig. 50 One of the bearing caps contains an oil flow restriction groove—4.6L engine

2. Disconnect the negative battery cable.

3. Remove the valve cover. For additional information, refer to "Valve Covers, Removal & Installation."

4. Position the piston of the cylinder being repaired at the bottom of the stroke.

5. Install the Valve Spring Compressor Spacer between the valve spring coils to protect the valve stem seal from damage

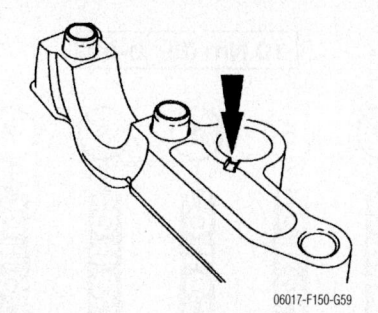

Fig. 51 One of the bearing caps contains an oil flow restriction groove—5.4L Engine

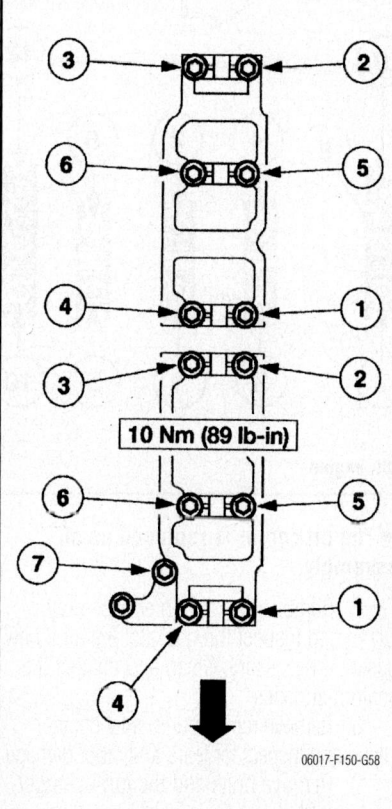

Fig. 52 Camshaft bearing cap torque sequence—4.6L engine

6. Using a valve spring compressor, compress the valve spring and remove the camshaft roller follower.

7. Remove the timing chains. For additional information, refer to "Timing Chain & Sprockets, Removal & Installation."

8. Remove the camshaft sprocket by removing the bolt.

9. Remove the 13 bolts, bearing caps and the camshaft.

➡**Camshaft bearing caps must be installed in their original location. Keep all drivetrain components in order so for installation is their original location.**

To install:

10. Lubricate the camshaft journals with clean engine oil.

11. Install the camshaft with the bearing caps in their original locations. Lubricate the camshaft bearing caps with clean engine oil before installation. Loosen install the bearing cap bolts.

12. Tighten the bolts in the sequence shown to 89 inch lbs. (10 Nm).

13. Install the timing chain.

14. Install the Valve Spring Compressor Spacer between the valve spring coils to protect the valve stem seal from damage.

✸✸ WARNING

The camshaft roller followers must be installed in their original locations. Failure to follow these instructions may result in engine damage.

➡**Do not allow the valve keepers to fall off the valve or the valve may drop into the cylinder. If a valve drops into the cylinder, the cylinder head must be removed.**

➡**It may be necessary to push the valve down while compressing the spring.**

15. Lubricate the camshaft roller follower with clean engine oil. Using the Valve Spring Compressor, compress the valve spring and install the camshaft roller follower.

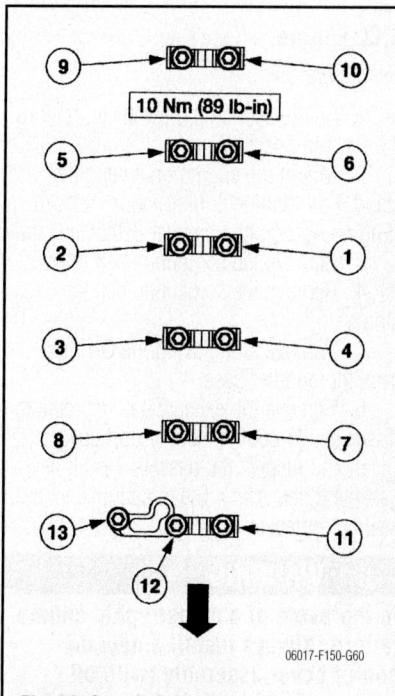

Fig. 53 Camshaft bearing torque sequence—5.4L Engine

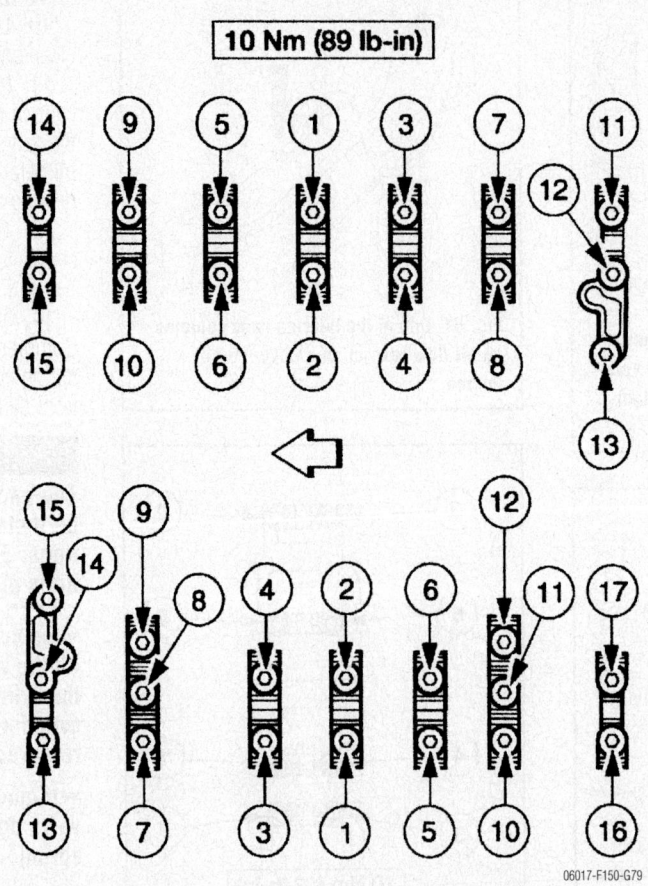

10 Nm (89 lb-in)

06017-F150-G79

Fig. 54 Camshaft bearing cap torque sequence—6.8L engine

16. Install the valve cover.
17. Connect the negative battery cable.

6.0L Engine

See Figure 55.

1. Before servicing the vehicle, refer to the Precautions Section.

2. Mount the engine on an engine stand. For additional information, refer to "Engine Assembly, Removal & Installation."

3. Remove the serpentine belt idler.

4. Remove the serpentine belt tensioner.

5. Remove and discard the O-rings from the oil filter base.

6. Remove the exhaust gas recirculation (EGR) cooler coolant supply port cover. Clean and inspect the gaskets. Install new gaskets if necessary. Clean and inspect the sealing surfaces.

✷✷ WARNING

In the event of a catastrophic engine failure, always install a new oil cooler cover assembly (with oil cooler). Foreign material cannot be removed from the oil cooler.

➡ **The oil cooler is replaced as an assembly.**

7. Remove the oil cooler assembly. Clean and inspect the gaskets. Install a new gasket if necessary. Clean and inspect the sealing surfaces.

8. Remove the oil pump inlet strainer. Clean and inspect for tears and other damage.

9. Remove bolts and the turbocharger heat shield.

10. Remove the high-pressure oil pump cover. Use a thin gasket scraper to separate

the cover from the crankcase. Clean and inspect the gaskets. Install a new gasket if necessary. Clean and inspect the sealing surfaces.

11. Remove the bolts from the high-pressure oil pump discharge pipe.

12. Disconnect and remove the high-pressure oil pump discharge pipe.

13. Remove and discard the D-ring seal.

14. Remove and discard the high-pressure pump O-ring seal.

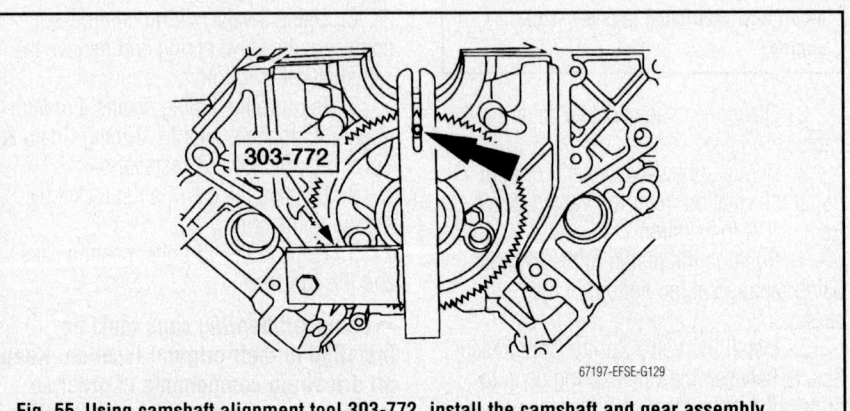

67197-EFSE-G129

Fig. 55 Using camshaft alignment tool 303-772, install the camshaft and gear assembly

15. Remove the bolts and the high-pressure oil pump.

16. Remove and discard the lower O-ring seal.

17. Remove the glow plug buss bar.

18. Remove the eight glow plugs.

➡**Mark the location of the stud bolts.**

19. Remove the valve covers. Clean and inspect the gaskets. Install a new gasket if necessary. Clean and inspect the sealing surfaces.

20. Remove the bolts and the coolant pump pulley.

21. Remove the coolant pump.

22. If equipped, remove the bolts and the dual alternator pulley.

23. Prior to removing the crankshaft damper, check the crankshaft vibration damper runout.

➡**Pry the crankshaft forward at the same point to eliminate possible error caused by crankshaft end play.**

24. Rotate the crankshaft 90 degrees. Pry the crankshaft forward. Record the measurement. Repeat every 90 degrees. If the runout exceeds 0.002 inch, install a new crankshaft vibration damper.

✳✳ WARNING

To prevent engine damage, you must always replace all four bolts when installing the vibration damper.

✳✳ CAUTION

To avoid personal injury, support the vibration damper during mounting bolt removal. The damper can slide off the nose of the crankshaft very easily.

25. Remove the bolts and the crankcase vibration damper. Discard the bolts.

26. Punch two holes in the seal. Remove the crankshaft seal with a slide hammer.

➡**Production engine will not have a wear sleeve. If equipped, remove the crankshaft damper wear sleeve.**

27. Remove the oil pump body. Remove and discard the O-ring seal.

➡**Mark the front of each drive rotor for correct reassembly orientation.**

28. Remove the inner and outer oil pump drive rotors.

29. Remove the engine front cover. Clean and inspect the gaskets. Install new gaskets if necessary. Clean and inspect the sealing surfaces.

30. Using a quick-disconnect tool, disconnect the high-pressure oil rail supply line at the high-pressure oil rail.

31. Remove the bolts and the high pressure oil rail. Disconnect and remove the high-pressure oil supply line.

✳✳ WARNING

Do not attempt to put battery voltage to the fuel injector or damage to the fuel injector will occur.

32. Using a 19 mm socket, push the fuel injector electrical connector out of the rocker arm carrier.

✳✳ WARNING

To prevent engine damage, do not use air tools to remove the fuel injectors. The clip that extracts the injector can dislodge and fall into the oil drain hole.

➡**If engine oil is found in the engine coolant or engine coolant is found in the combustion chambers, new injector sleeve may need to be installed.**

33. Remove the bolt, the fuel injector hold down and the fuel injector.

34. Remove and discard the crankcase-to-head tube assembly.

35. Remove the inner head bolts from both cylinder heads.

36. Remove the 16 bolts and the rocker arm assemblies.

37. Remove the rocker arm carrier from the cylinder head. Clean and inspect the gaskets. Install new gaskets if necessary. Clean and inspect the sealing surfaces.

➡**Mark the location of the valve bridges before removing.**

38. Remove the 16 valve bridges.

✳✳ WARNING

To prevent engine damage, keep the push rods in the order in which they were removed. Install all push rods back in their original positions.

39. Mark the location and remove the 16 push rods.

40. Remove the 10 outer head bolts.

41. Remove the cylinder heads.

42. Remove and discard the cylinder head gasket.

43. Remove and discard the four cylinder head dowel sleeves.

44. Remove the bolts from the rear engine tube assembly.

45. Remove the bolt and the rear engine tube assembly.

✳✳ WARNING

To prevent engine damage, keep the cam followers in the order in which they were removed. Install all cam followers back in their original positions.

46. Remove the bolts and the roller follower guides. Remove the hydraulic cam followers.

47. Install the special tool and measure the camshaft gear backlash. Install a new camshaft gear if backlash is not within specification.

48. Install a dial indicator and measure the camshaft end play. Install a new camshaft thrust plate if end play is not within 0.002–0.008 inch.

49. Remove the bolt and the camshaft position (CMP) sensor.

✳✳ WARNING

Do not knick or scratch the camshaft bearings with the camshaft lobes or engine damage will occur.

50. Remove the thrust plate mounting bolts and remove the camshaft and gear.

To install:

➡**Check alignment of the oil holes after installing the bearings.**

51. If removed, install the camshaft bearings.

✳✳ WARNING

Do not nick or scratch the camshaft bearings with the camshaft lobes or engine damage can occur.

➡**Apply clean engine oil to the camshaft prior to installing.**

52. Using camshaft alignment tool 303-772, install the camshaft and gear assembly. Aligning it with the crankshaft. Install the thrust plate mounting bolts. Torque to 23 ft. lbs. (31 Nm).

53. The remainder of installation is the reverse of removal.

CATALYTIC CONVERTER

REMOVAL & INSTALLATION

4.6L, 5.4L & 6.8L Engines

1. Before servicing the vehicle, refer to the Precautions Section.

2. Raise and safely support the vehicle.

3. Support the muffler and tail pipe assembly with a suitable jack.

4. Release the front muffler and tail pipe assembly and, if equipped, the extension pipe hanger isolators.

5. Loosen the muffler and tail pipe assembly or, if equipped, the extension pipe-to-catalytic converter Torca® clamp.

6. Remove the muffler and tail pipe and, if equipped, the extension pipe from the catalytic converter.

7. Disconnect the Catalyst Monitor Sensor (CMS) electrical connector.

8. Remove the three exhaust Y-pipe-to-catalytic converter nuts and discard. Remove the exhaust Y-pipe-to-catalytic converter support bracket.

9. Remove the catalytic converter from the exhaust Y-pipe and discard the gasket.

10. Installation is the reverse order of removal. Tighten the bolts as follows:
- Y-pipe-to-catalytic convert nuts: 30 ft. lbs. (40 Nm)
- Extension pipe-to-catalytic converter clamp: 41 ft. lbs. (55 Nm).

6.0L Engines

1. Before servicing the vehicle, refer to the Precautions Section.

2. Raise and safely support the vehicle.

3. Support the muffler and tail pipe assembly with a suitable jack.

4. Release the front muffler and tail pipe assembly and, if equipped, the extension pipe hanger insulator(s).

5. Loosen the muffler and tail pipe assembly or, if equipped, the extension pipe-to-catalytic converter Torca® clamp.

6. Remove the muffler and tail pipe assembly and, if equipped, the extension pipe from the catalytic converter.

7. Release the catalytic converter hanger isolator.

8. Remove the two exhaust downpipe-to-catalytic converter nuts and discard.

9. Remove the catalytic converter from the exhaust downpipe.

10. Installation is the reverse order of removal. Tighten the bolts as follows:
- Downpipe-to-catalytic convert nuts: 30 ft. lbs. (40 Nm)
- Extension pipe-to-catalytic converter clamp: 41 ft. lbs. (55 Nm).

CRANKSHAFT DAMPER

REMOVAL & INSTALLATION

4.6L, 5.4L and 6.8L Engines

See Figures 56 and 57.

1. Before servicing the vehicle, refer to the Precautions Section.

2. Disconnect the negative battery cable.

3. Raise and safely support the vehicle.

4. Remove the engine fan and shroud. For additional information, refer to "Engine Fan, Removal & Installation."

5. Remove the accessory drive belt. For additional information, refer to "Accessory Drive Belt, Removal & Installation."

6. Using a suitable strap wrench to hold the pulley, remove the crankshaft pulley bolt and washer.

7. Use a Crankshaft Vibration damper Remover to remove the crankshaft pulley.

To install:

8. Apply silicone gasket and sealant to the Woodruff key slot on the crankshaft pulley.

➡If not secured within 4 minutes, the sealant must be removed and the sealing area cleaned. To clean the sealing area, use silicone gasket remover and metal surface prep. Follow the directions on the packaging. Failure to follow this procedure can cause future oil leakage.

9. Lubricate the crankshaft pulley sealing area with clean engine oil prior to installation.

10. Using the Crankshaft Vibration Damper Installer, install the crankshaft pulley.

11. Using a new crankshaft pulley bolt, install the pulley bolt and washer. Using a

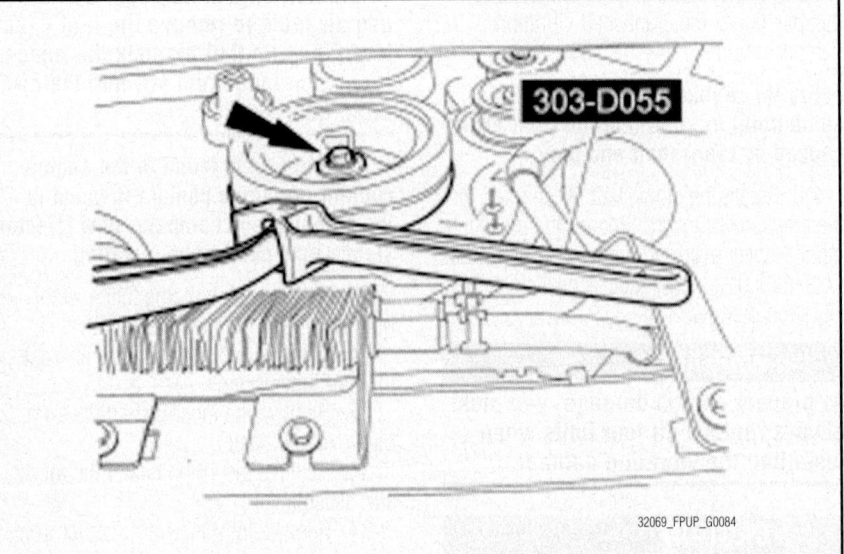

Fig. 56 Using a strap wrench, remove the bolt and washer and discard the bolt—4.6L, 5.4L and 6.8L engine

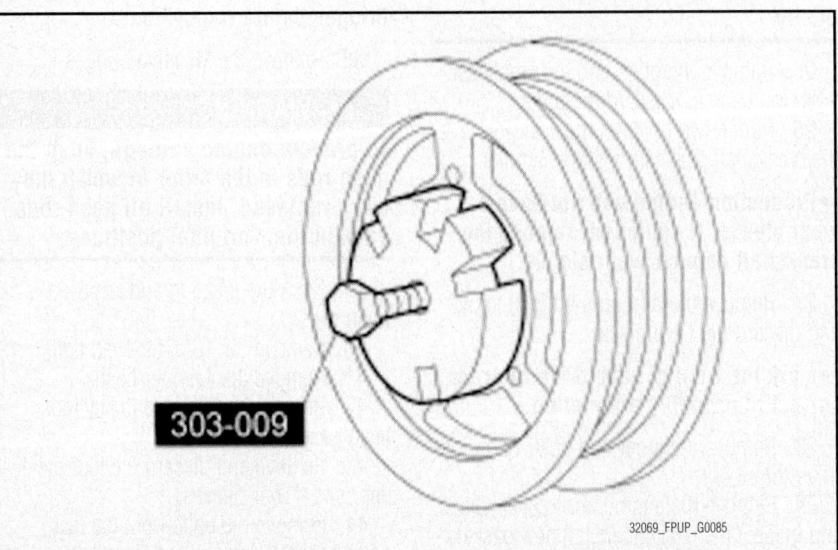

Fig. 57 Use the Special Tool 303-009 or equivalent to remove the crankshaft pulley—4.6L, 5.4L and 6.8L engine

strap wrench to hold the crankshaft pulley, tighten the bolt as follows:

- Step 1: 4.6L—89 ft. lbs. (120 Nm), 5.4L & 6.8L—66 ft. lbs. (90 Nm)
- Step 2: Loosen one full turn
- Step 3: Tighten to 37 ft. lbs. (50 Nm)
- Step 4: Tighten an additional 90 degrees

12. Install the accessory drive belt.
13. Install the engine fan and shroud.
14. Connect the negative battery cable.

6.0L Engine

See Figure 58.

1. Before servicing the vehicle, refer to the Precautions Section.
2. Disconnect the negative battery cable.
3. Raise and safely support the vehicle.
4. Remove the engine fan. For additional information, refer to "Engine Fan, Removal & Installation."
5. Remove the accessory drive belt. For additional information, refer to "Accessory Drive Belt, Removal & Installation."
6. Check the crankshaft vibration damper runout as follows:
  a. Remove the paint from the face of the crankshaft vibration damper at four points 90 degrees apart.
  b. Attach the special tool to the cylinder block. Position the special tool on one of the unpainted surfaces.
  c. Using a suitable tool, pry the crankshaft forward. Zero the dial indicator.

➡**Pry the crankshaft forward only to eliminate possible error caused by crankshaft end play.**

7. Rotate the crankshaft 90 degrees. Pry the crankshaft forward. Record the measurement. Repeat at each unpainted surface. If the runout exceeds specification, install a new crankshaft vibration damper.

❋ CAUTION

To avoid personal injury, support the vibration damper during mounting bolt removal. The damper can slide off the nose of the crankshaft very easily.

8. Remove the bolts and the crankshaft vibration damper. Discard the bolts.

To install:

❋ WARNING

To prevent engine damage, you must always install four new bolts

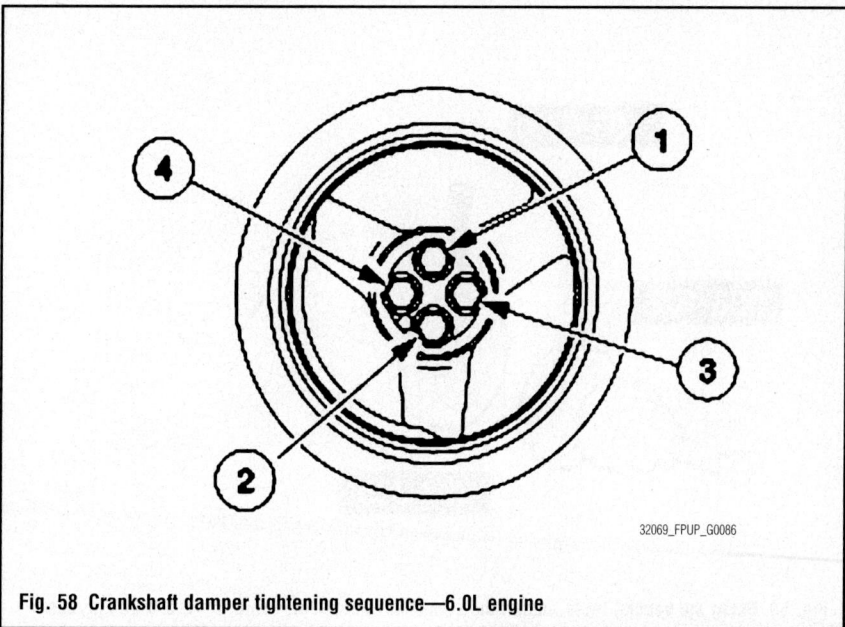

Fig. 58 Crankshaft damper tightening sequence—6.0L engine

when installing the vibration damper.

➡**Do not use anti-seize compounds, grease or any lubricants. Lubricants have an adverse effect on the torque results.**

9. Install the crankshaft vibration damper and bolts. Tighten in the sequence shown.
- Step 1: Tighten to 68 Nm (50 ft. lbs.).
- Step 2: Tighten an additional 90 degrees.
10. Install the accessory drive belt.
11. Install the engine fan.
12. Connect the negative battery cable.

CRANKSHAFT FRONT SEAL

REMOVAL & INSTALLATION

4.6L, 5.4L and 6.8L Engines

See Figures 59 and 60.

1. Before servicing the vehicle, refer to the Precautions Section.
2. Disconnect the negative battery cable.
3. Remove the crankshaft pulley. For additional information, refer to "Crankshaft Damper, Removal & Installation."
4. Using the Crankshaft Front Oil Seal Remover, remove and discard the crankshaft front seal.

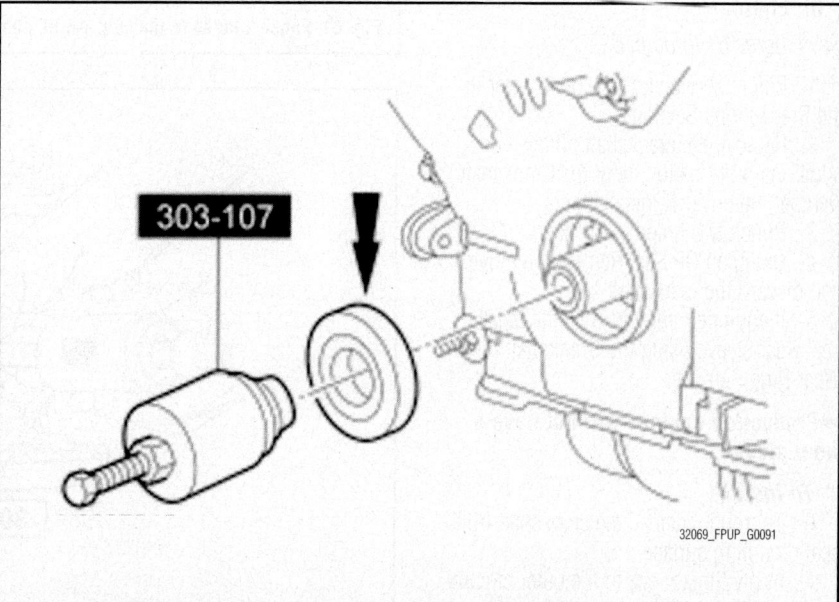

Fig. 59 Using the special tool, remove the crankshaft front seal—4.6L, 5.4L and 6.8L Engines

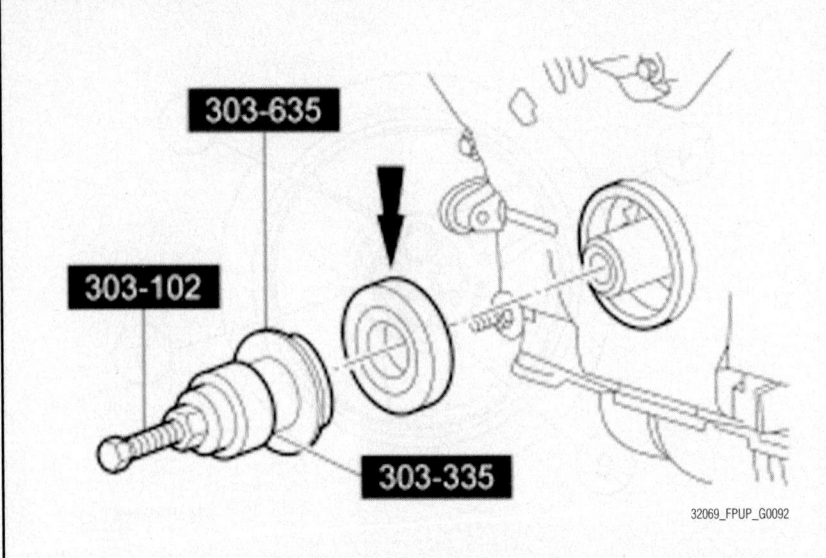

Fig. 60 Using the special tools, install the crankshaft front seal—4.6L, 5.4L & 6.8L Engines

To install:

5. Lubricate the engine front cover and the crankshaft front seal inner lip with clean engine oil.

6. Using the Crankshaft Front Oil Seal Installer, Front Cover Oil Seal Installer and Crankshaft Vibration Damper Installer, install a new crankshaft front seal.

7. Install the crankshaft pulley.

8. Install the accessory drive belt. For additional information, refer to "Accessory Drive Belt, Removal & Installation."

9. Install the engine fan. For additional information, refer to "Engine Fan, Removal & Installation."

10. Connect the negative battery cable.

6.0L Engine

See Figures 61 through 63.

1. Before servicing the vehicle, refer to the Precautions Section.

2. Remove the crankshaft pulley. For additional information, refer to "Crankshaft Damper, Removal & Installation."

3. Punch two holes in the seal.

4. Using an Oil Seal Remover, remove and discard the crankshaft seal.

5. If equipped, remove the crankshaft seal wear sleeve using the Crankshaft Front Wear Ring Remover.

➡ **Production engines will not have a wear sleeve.**

To install:

6. Thoroughly clean the crankshaft front seal mounting surface.

7. Apply thread lock to the outer circumference of the leading edge of the crankshaft.

8. Using the Crankshaft Front Seal and Wear Ring Installer, install the new oil seal and wear sleeve assembly.

9. Install the crankshaft pulley.

CYLINDER HEAD

REMOVAL & INSTALLATION

4.6L & 5.4L Engines

See Figures 64 through 80.

1. Before servicing the vehicle, refer to the Precautions Section.

2. Remove the engine assembly. For additional information, refer to "Engine Assembly, "Removal & Installation."

3. Lower the engine onto wooden blocks.

✳✳ WARNING

Use care when lowering the engine, to prevent damage to the oil pan.

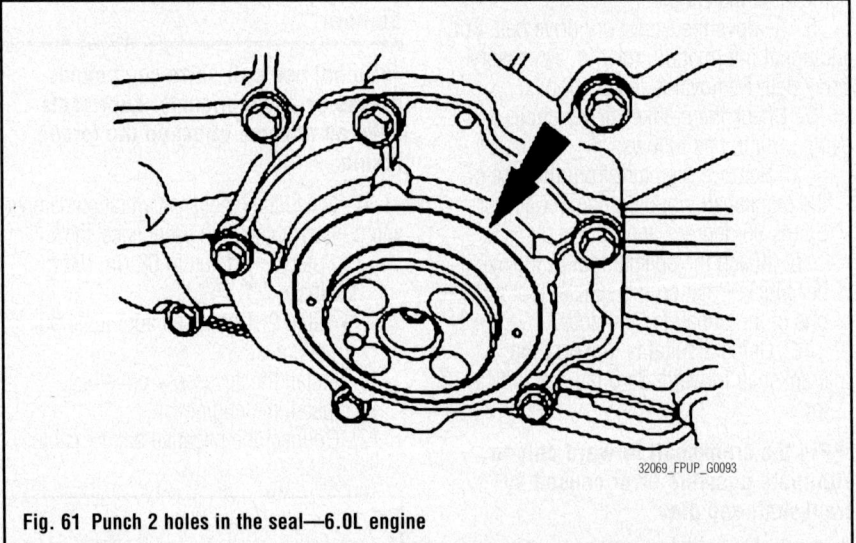

Fig. 61 Punch 2 holes in the seal—6.0L engine

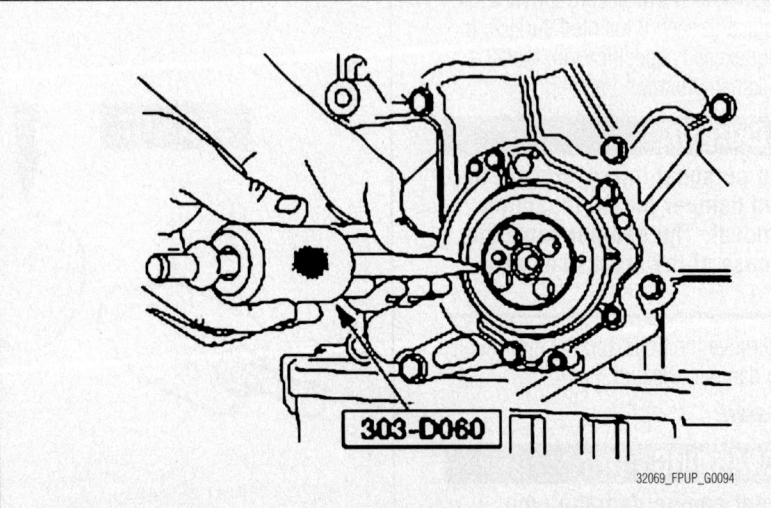

Fig. 62 Using the special tool, remove the crankshaft seal—6.0L engine

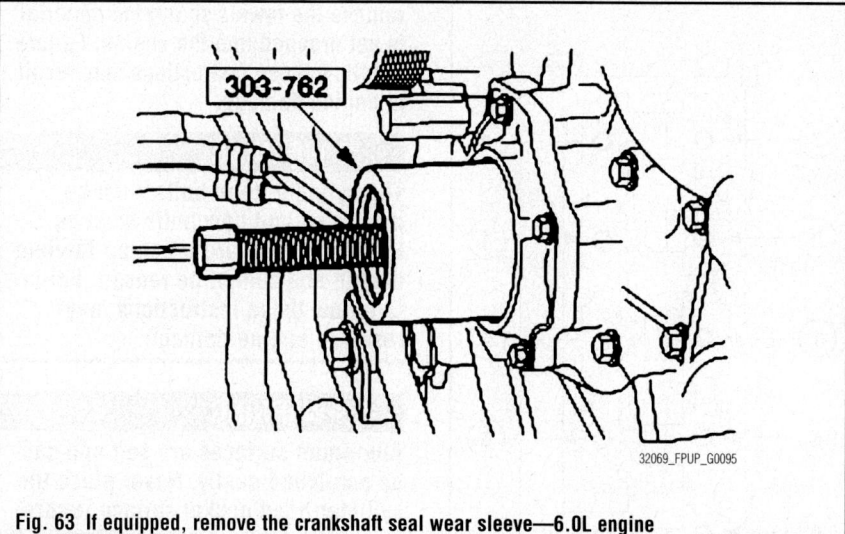

Fig. 63 If equipped, remove the crankshaft seal wear sleeve—6.0L engine

4. Remove the engine lift bracket. Install the engine lifting bracket set and mount the engine on a suitable work stand.

5. If equipped with cylinder block drain plugs, remove the 3 bolts and the right hand engine support insulator.

6. If equipped, remove the cylinder block drain plugs and drain the coolant in a suitable container.

7. Disconnect the left-hand radio frequency interference capacitor and Cylinder Head Temperature (CHT) sensor electrical connectors.

8. Disconnect the Camshaft Position (CMP) sensor electrical connector.

9. Disconnect the right-hand radio frequency interference capacitor electrical connector.

10. Disconnect the Knock Sensor (KS) electrical connector.

11. Disconnect the Engine Oil Pressure (EOP) switch electrical connector and wiring harness retainer.

12. Disconnect all of the harness routing clips and connector retainers. Remove the engine control sensor wiring harness.

13. Remove the two nuts and the two radio interference capacitors.

14. Remove the oil level indicator tube support bracket nut.

15. Remove the bolt and the oil level indicator and tube and discard the O-ring seal.

➡**Do not use metal scrapers, wire brushes, power abrasive discs or other abrasive means to clean the sealing surfaces. These tools cause scratches and gouges which make leak paths. Use a plastic scraping tool to remove all traces of old sealant.**

16. Fully loosen the fasteners and remove the valve covers.

➡**The fasteners are part of the valve cover and should not be removed.**

17. Remove the bolt and the CMP sensor.

18. Remove the bolt and the accessory drive belt idler pulley.

19. Remove the four bolts and the water pump pulley.

20. Remove the bolt and the Crankshaft Position (CKP) sensor.

21. Remove the crankshaft pulley bolt and washer.

22. Discard the crankshaft pulley bolt.

23. Using the Crankshaft Vibration Damper Remover, remove the crankshaft pulley.

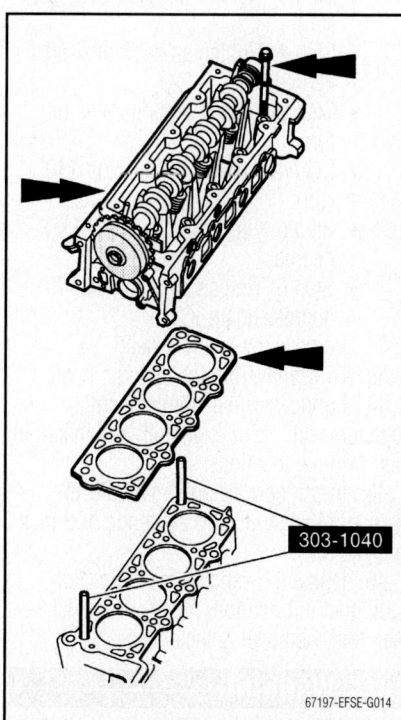

Fig. 64 Use the Cylinder Head Alignment Pins to position the cylinder head gaskets and cylinder heads —4.6L & 5.4L Engines

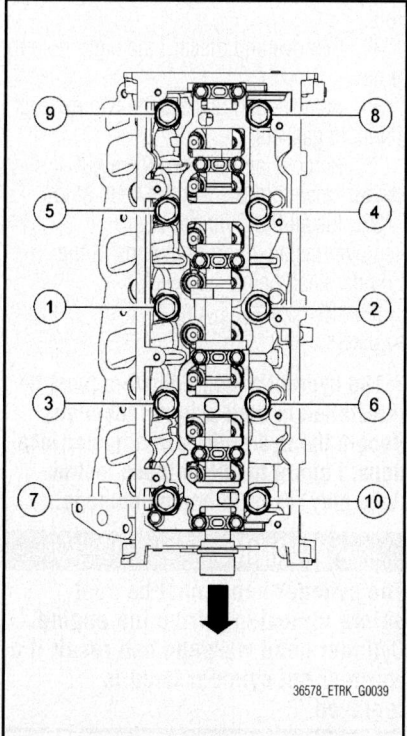

Fig. 65 Left hand cylinder head torque sequence—4.6L Engines

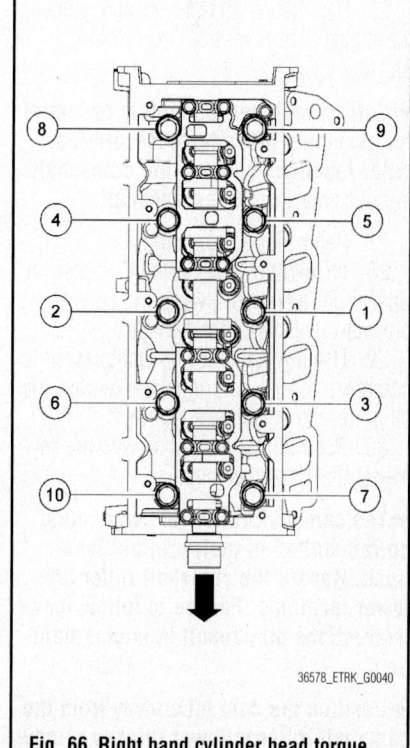

Fig. 66 Right hand cylinder head torque sequence—4.6L Engines

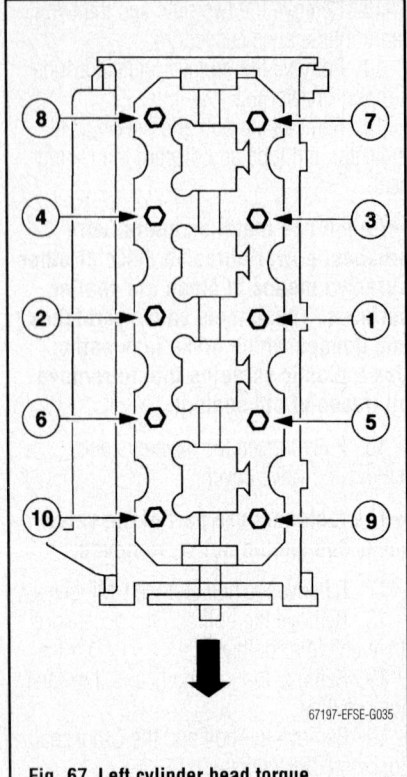

Fig. 67 Left cylinder head torque sequence—5.4L engine

67197-EFSE-G035

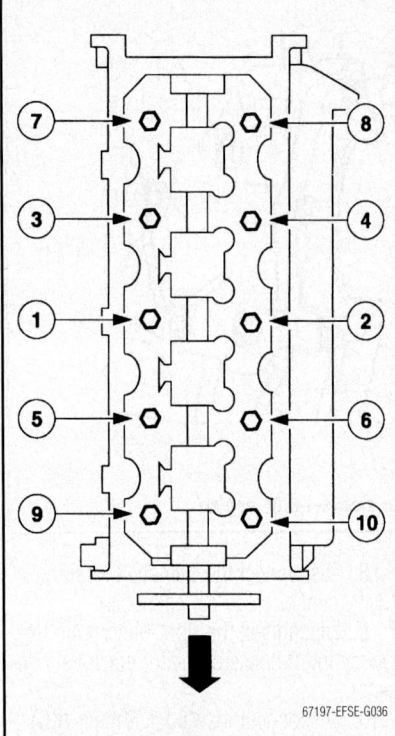

Fig. 68 Right cylinder head torque sequence—5.4L engine

67197-EFSE-G036

24. Using the Crankshaft Front Oil Seal Remover, remove and discard the crankshaft front seal.

25. Remove the four front oil pan bolts.

26. Remove the 15 fasteners and remove the engine front cover from the cylinder block.

➡**Correct fastener location is essential for assembly procedure. Record fastener location. Remove the crankshaft sensor ring from the crankshaft.**

27. Remove the spark plugs.

28. Install the Valve Spring Compressor Spacer between the valve spring coils to prevent valve stem seal damage.

29. Use the Valve Spring Compressor to compress the valve springs and remove the all of the camshaft roller followers.

30. Position the crankshaft with the keyway at the 12 o'clock position.

➡**The camshaft roller followers must be reinstalled in their original locations. Record the camshaft roller follower locations. Failure to follow these instructions may result in engine damage.**

➡**Position the cam lobe away from the camshaft roller follower prior to removing each camshaft roller follower.**

31. Remove the timing chain tensioning system from both timing chains.

32. Remove the timing chains and crankshaft sprocket.

33. Remove the applicable exhaust manifold.

34. Remove and discard the eight nuts to remove.

35. Remove and discard the two exhaust manifold gaskets.

36. Remove and discard the eight exhaust manifold-to-cylinder head studs.

37. Install the Cylinder Head Remover/Installers on both ends of the cylinder head being serviced.

38. Remove the hydraulic lash adjusters.

➡**The hydraulic lash adjusters must be reinstalled in their original locations. Record the hydraulic lash adjuster locations. Failure to follow these instructions may result in engine damage.**

> ❊❊ **WARNING**
>
> The cylinder head must be cool before removing it from the engine. Cylinder head warpage can result if a warm or hot cylinder head is removed.

➡**Place clean shop towels over exposed engine cavities. Carefully**

remove the towels so foreign material is not dropped into the engine. Failure to follow these instructions may result in engine damage.

> ❊❊ **WARNING**
>
> The cylinder head bolts must be discarded and new bolts must be installed. They are a tighten-to-yield design and cannot be reused. Failure to follow these instructions may result in engine damage.

> ❊❊ **WARNING**
>
> Aluminum surfaces are soft and can be scratched easily. Never place the cylinder head gasket surface, unprotected, on a bench surface. Failure to follow these instructions may result in engine damage.

39. Remove the bolts and the cylinder head.

40. Discard the cylinder head gasket and cylinder head bolts.

To install:

41. Using the Cylinder Head Alignment Pins, position the cylinder head gaskets and cylinder heads over the dowels and loosely install the new cylinder head bolts.

42. Tighten the cylinder head bolts as follows in the sequence shown:
- Step 1: Tighten to 30 ft. lbs. (40 Nm)
- Step 2: Tighten an additional 90 degrees
- Step 3: Loosen all bolts one full turn
- Step 4: Tighten to 30 ft. lbs. (40 Nm)
- Step 5: Tighten an additional 90 degrees
- Step 6: Tighten an additional 90 degrees again

43. Remove the cylinder head remover/installer from the cylinder head.

44. Lubricate the hydraulic lash adjusters with clean engine oil and install in their original locations.

45. Install new exhaust manifold-to-cylinder head studs and tighten to 106 inch lbs. (12 Nm).

46. Install the exhaust manifold. For additional information, refer to "Exhaust Manifold, Removal & Installation."

> ❊❊ **WARNING**
>
> Timing chain procedures must be followed exactly or damage to valves and pistons will result.

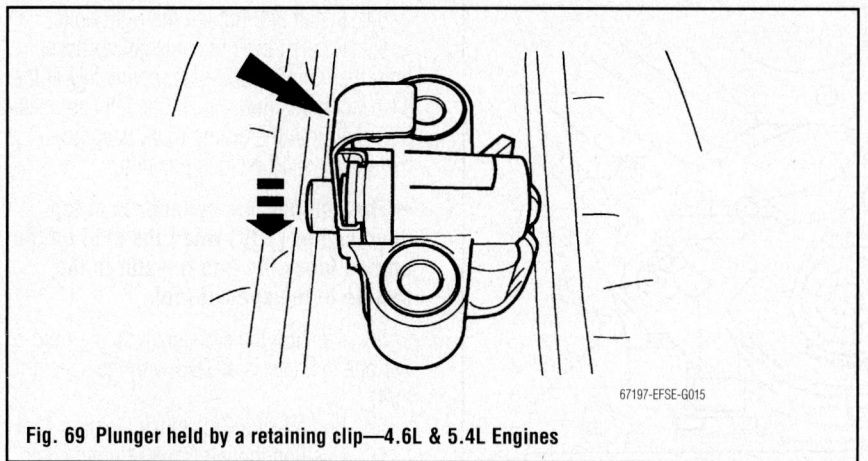

Fig. 69 Plunger held by a retaining clip—4.6L & 5.4L Engines

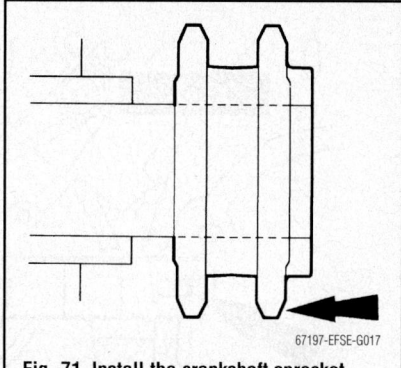

Fig. 71 Install the crankshaft sprocket, making sure the flange faces forward—4.6L & 5.4L Engines

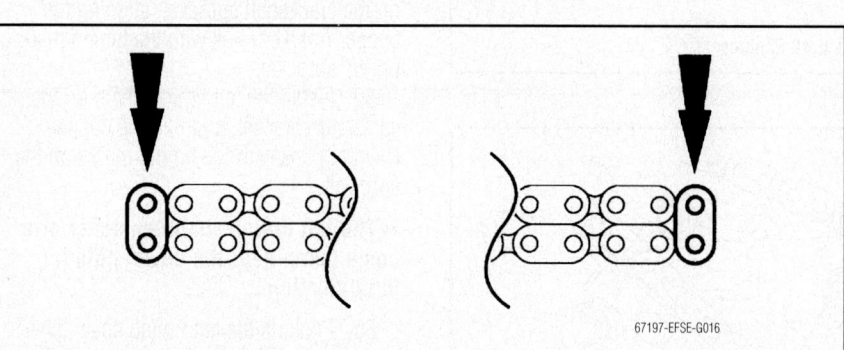

Fig. 70 If the copper links are not visible, mark one link on one end and one link on the other end, and use as timing marks—4.6L & 5.4L Engines

47. Compress the tensioner plunger, using a vise.

48. Install a retaining clip on the tensioner to hold the plunger in during installation.

49. Remove the tensioner from the vise. If the copper links are not visible, mark one link on one end and one link on the other end, and use as timing marks.

50. Install the crankshaft sprocket, making sure the flange faces forward.

51. Position the left timing chain guide.

52. Install and tighten the left bolts.

53. Position the right timing chain guide.

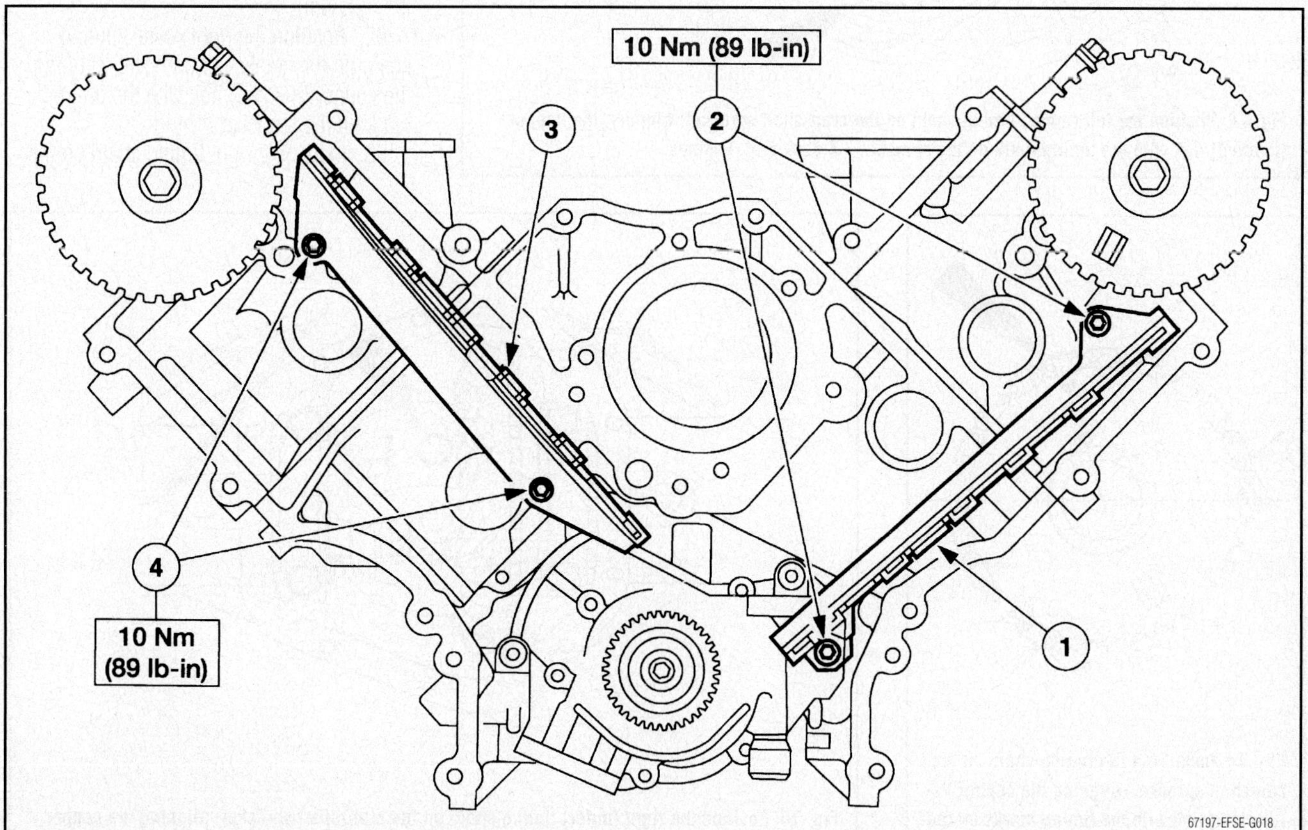

10 Nm (89 lb-in)

10 Nm (89 lb-in)

Fig. 72 Timing chain guide installation—4.6L & 5.4L Engines

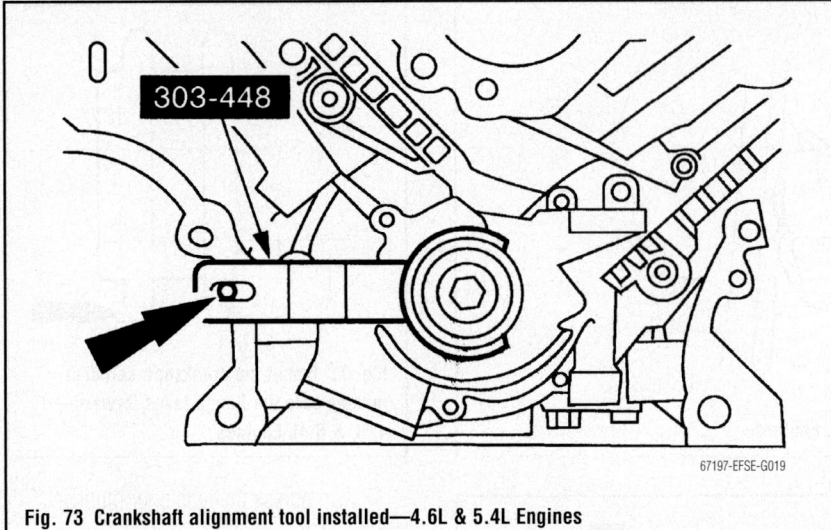

Fig. 73 Crankshaft alignment tool installed—4.6L & 5.4L Engines

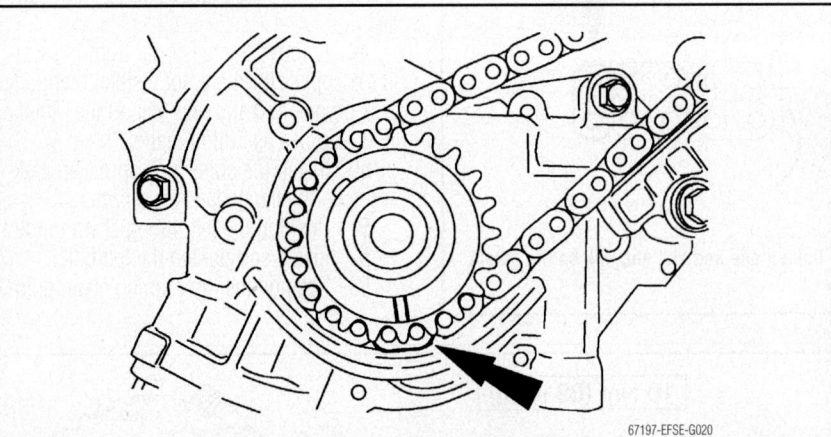

Fig. 74 Position the left (inner) timing chain on the crankshaft sprocket, aligning the copper (marked) link with the timing mark on the sprocket—4.6L & 5.4L Engines

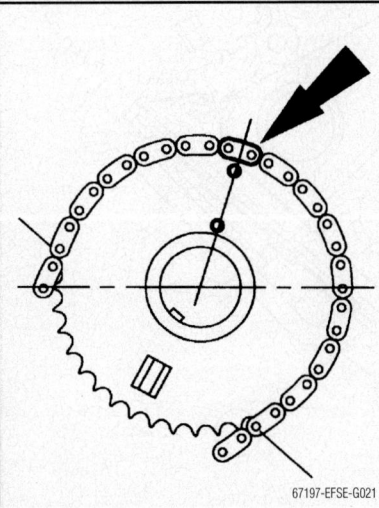

Fig. 75 Install the left timing chain on the camshaft sprocket, aligning the copper (marked) link with the timing marks on the sprocket—4.6L & 5.4L Engines

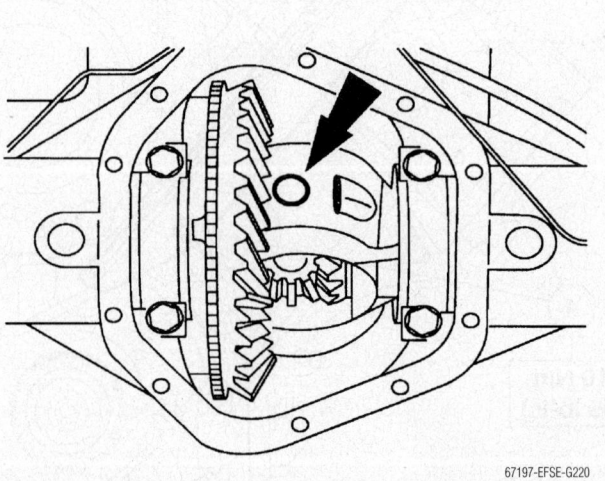

Fig. 76 Position the right (outer) timing chain on the crankshaft sprocket, aligning the copper (marked) link with the timing mark on the sprocket—4.6L & 5.4L Engines

54. Install and tighten the right bolts.

55. Rotate the right camshaft sprocket until the timing mark is approximately at the 11 o'clock position. Rotate the left camshaft sprocket until the timing mark is approximately at the 12 o'clock position.

➡ **The number one cylinder is at top dead center (TDC) when the stud on the engine block fits into the slot in the handle of the special tool.**

56. Position the crankshaft so the number one cylinder is at TDC with the special tool.

57. Remove the Crankshaft Holding Tool.

58. Position the left (inner) timing chain on the crankshaft sprocket, aligning the copper (marked) link with the timing mark on the sprocket.

59. Install the left timing chain on the camshaft sprocket, aligning the copper (marked) link with the timing marks on the sprocket.

➡ **The left timing chain tensioner arm has a bump near the dowel hole for identification.**

60. Position the left timing chain tensioner arm on the dowel pin and install the left timing chain tensioner.

61. Remove the retaining clip from the left timing chain tensioner. Tighten to 18 ft. lbs. (25 Nm).

62. Position the right (outer) timing chain on the crankshaft sprocket, aligning the copper (marked) link with the timing mark on the sprocket.

63. Install the right timing chain on the

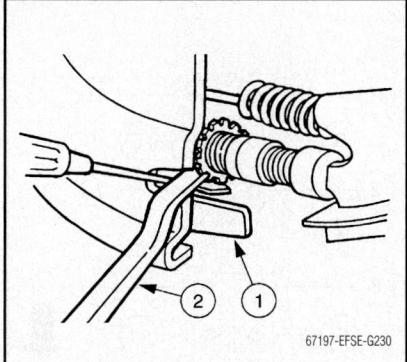

Fig. 77 Install the right timing chain on the camshaft sprocket, aligning the copper (marked) link with the timing marks on the sprocket—4.6L & 5.4L Engines

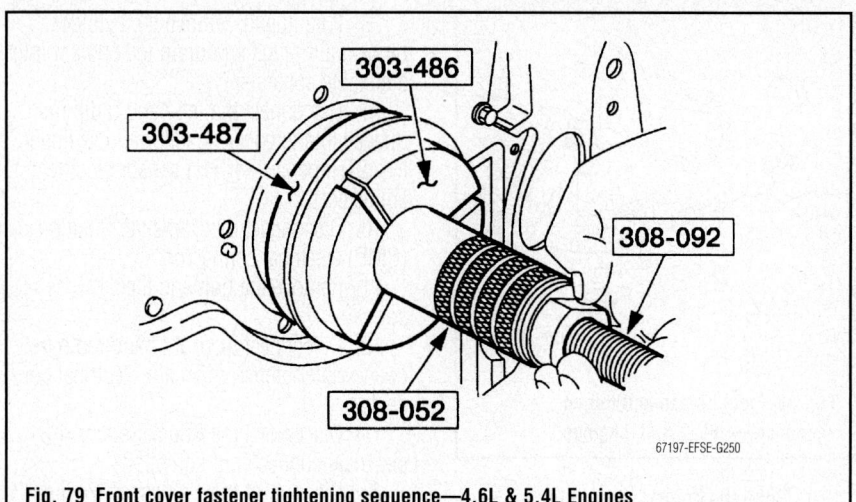

Fig. 79 Front cover fastener tightening sequence—4.6L & 5.4L Engines

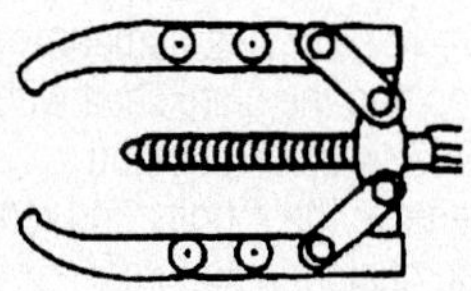

2-Jaw Puller or equivalent	
Installer, Drive Pinion Flange	
Holding Fixture, Drive Pinion Flange	
Installer, Drive Pinion Oil Seal	

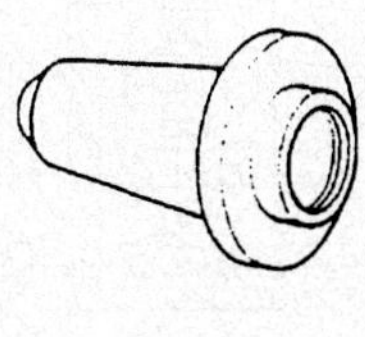

67197-EFSE-G240

Fig. 78 Apply a bead of silicone gasket and sealant along the cylinder head-to-cylinder block surface and the oil pan-to-cylinder block surface, at the locations shown—4.6L & 5.4L Engines

camshaft sprocket, aligning the copper (marked) link with the timing marks on the sprocket.

64. Position the right timing chain tensioner arm on the dowel pin and install the right timing chain tensioner. Torque to 18 ft. lbs. (25 Nm).

65. Remove the retaining clip from the right timing chain tensioner. Make sure that the copper (marked) chain links are lined up with the dots on the crankshaft sprockets and the camshaft sprocket.

66. Install the crankshaft sensor ring on the crankshaft.

67. Install the Valve Spring Compressor Spacer between the valve spring coils to prevent valve stem seal damage

68. Use the Valve Spring Compressor to compress the valve springs, and install the camshaft roller follower.

69. Install the spark plugs.

70. Apply a bead of silicone gasket and sealant along the cylinder head-to-cylinder block surface and the oil pan-to-cylinder block surface, at the locations shown.

71. Install a new engine front cover gasket on the engine front cover. Position the engine front cover. Install the fasteners finger-tight. Then tighten the bolts in sequence to 18 ft. lbs. (25 Nm).

72. Install the front four oil pan bolts and tighten the bolts in sequence as follows:
- Step 1: Tighten to 15 ft. lbs. (20 Nm)
- Step 2: Tighten an additional 60 degrees

73. Install the valve cover. For additional information, refer to "Valve Covers, Removal & Installation."

74. Install the accessory drive belt idler pulley and tighten the bolt to 18 ft. lbs. (25 Nm).

75. The remainder of the installation is the reverse order of removal.

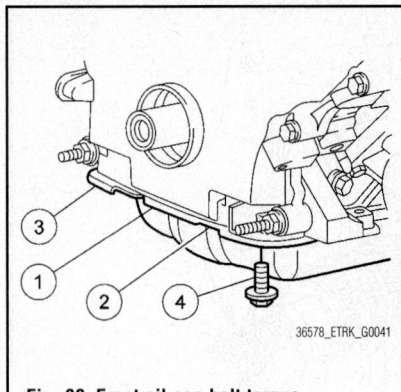

Fig. 80 Front oil pan bolt torque sequence—4.6L & 5.4L Engines

76. Refill the engine with oil to the correct level.

77. Refill the cooling system to the correct level.

6.8L Engines

See Figures 81 through 88.

1. Before servicing the vehicle, refer to the Precautions Section.

2. Remove the engine assembly. For additional information, refer to "Engine Assembly, "Removal & Installation."

3. Remove the flexplate. For additional information, refer to "Flexplate, Removal & Installation."

4. Lower the engine onto wooden blocks and remove the engine lifting bracket.

5. Install the engine lifting brackets from the engine lifting bracket set.

6. Mount the engine on a suitable work stand.

7. If equipped with cylinder block drain plugs, remove the 4 bolts and the right hand engine support insulator.

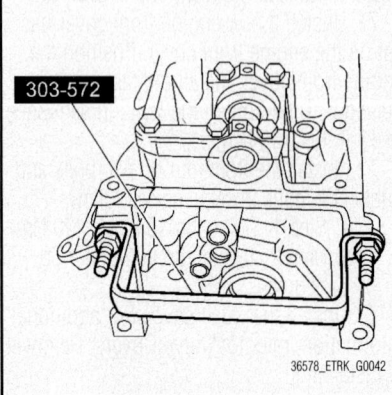

Fig. 81 Install the Cylinder Head Remover/Installer on both ends of the cylinder head being removed—6.8L Engine

8. If equipped, remove the cylinder block drain plugs and drain the coolant into a suitable container.

9. Disconnect the left hand radio frequency interference capacitor and Cylinder Head Temperature (CHT) sensor electrical connectors.

10. Disconnect the Camshaft Position (CMP) electrical connector.

11. Remove the bolt and the CMP sensor.

12. Disconnect the right hand radio frequency interference capacitor electrical connector.

13. Disconnect the Knock Sensor (KS) electrical connector, if equipped.

14. Disconnect the Crankshaft Position (CKP) sensor electrical connector.

15. Remove the bolt and the CKP sensor.

16. Disconnect the Engine Oil Pressure (EOP) switch electrical connector.

17. Disconnect all of the engine control sensor wiring harness routing clips and connector retainers. Remove the engine control sensor wiring harness.

18. Remove the two nuts and the two radio frequency interference capacitors.

19. Remove the nut attaching the oil level indicator tube to the front of the engine.

20. Remove the bolt attaching the oil level indicator tube to the left hand cylinder head.

21. Position the oil level indicator tube aside.

22. Remove the valve cover. For additional information, refer to "Valve Covers, Removal & Installation."

23. Remove the idler pulley.

24. Remove the four bolts and remove the water pump pulley.

25. Remove the crankshaft pulley. For additional information, refer to "Crankshaft Pulley, Removal & Installation."

26. Remove the crankshaft front seal. For additional information, refer to "Crankshaft Front Seal, Removal & Installation."

27. Remove the three bolts and the power steering pump.

28. Remove the four front oil pan bolts.

29. Remove the engine front cover bolts and remove the engine front cover.

➡ **The front cover bolts are different sizes. Keep them in order for reinstallation.**

30. Remove the crankshaft sensor ring from the crankshaft.

31. Remove the six bolts and remove the balance shaft bearing caps and remove the balance shaft.

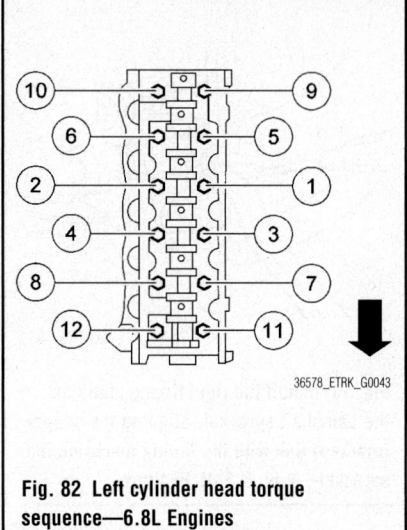

Fig. 82 Left cylinder head torque sequence—6.8L Engines

32. Remove the spark plugs.

33. Install the Valve Spring Compressor Spacer between the valve spring coils to prevent valve stem seal damage.

34. Position the crankshaft with the keyway at the 12 o'clock position.

35. Remove the 4 bolts and remove the two timing chain tensioners.

36. Remove the 2 timing chain tensioner arms.

37. Remove the 2 timing chains and the crankshaft sprocket.

38. Remove the mounting bolts and remove the timing chain guides.

39. Remove the cylinder head insert, if removing the left cylinder head.

40. Remove the exhaust manifold.

41. Remove and discard the exhaust manifold studs.

42. Install the Cylinder Head Remover/Installer on both ends of the cylinder head being removed.

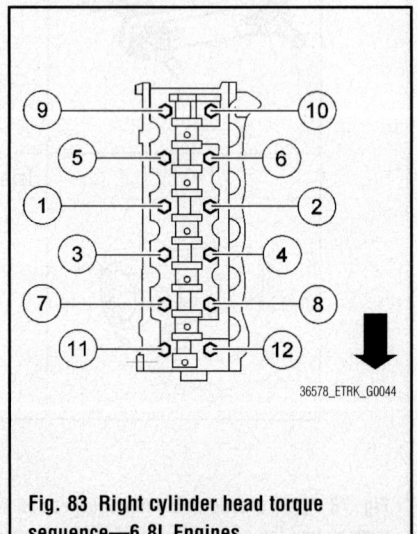

Fig. 83 Right cylinder head torque sequence—6.8L Engines

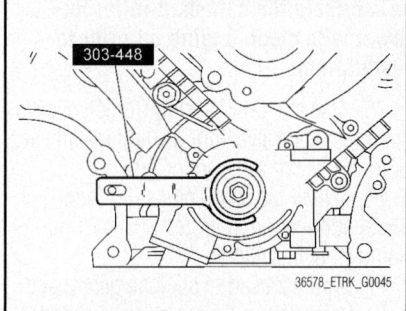

Fig. 84 Position the crankshaft with the Crankshaft Holding Tool, then remove the tool—6.8L Engine

43. Remove the hydraulic last adjusters.
44. Remove the cylinder head mounting bolts.
45. Remove the cylinder head.
46. Discard the bolts and the cylinder head gasket.

To install:

➡Make sure all coolant residue and foreign material is cleaned from the block surface and the cylinder bore.

➡The use of sealing aids is not permitted. The gasket must be installed dry.

➡The new gasket has a film coating which is crucial to the gasket's ability to seal properly. Do not scratch the gasket.

47. Using the Cylinder Head Alignment Pins, position the cylinder head gaskets and cylinder heads over the dowels and install the cylinder head bolts loosely.
48. Tighten the bolts in sequence as follows:
• Tighten to 30 ft. lbs. (40 Nm)
• Tighten an additional 90 degrees
• Tighten another 90 degrees

49. Lubricate the hydraulic lash adjusters with clean engine oil. Install the 20 hydraulic lash adjusters in their original locations.
50. Install new exhaust manifold studs and tighten to 106 inch lbs. (12 Nm).
51. Install the insert into cylinder head, left cylinder only.
52. Using a new gasket, install the exhaust manifold and tighten the new nuts to 18 ft. lbs. (25 Nm).

➡Timing chain procedures must be followed exactly or damage to valves and pistons will result.

➡Prior to installation, inspect the tensioner-sealing bead for seal integrity. If cracks, tears, separation from the tensioner body or permanent compression

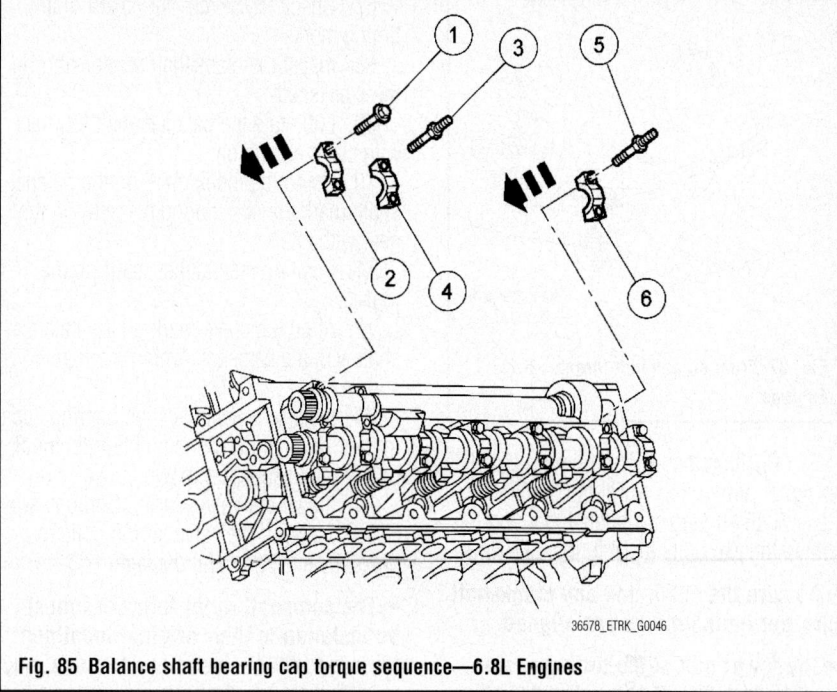

Fig. 85 Balance shaft bearing cap torque sequence—6.8L Engines

of the seal bead is observed, install a new tensioner or engine damage may occur.

53. Compress the tensioner plunger, using a vise.
54. Install a retaining clip on the tensioner to hold the plunger in during installation.

➡There are 61 links in each timing chain.

55. If copper links are not visible, mark 2 links on one end and one link on the other end, and use as timing marks.
56. Install the timing chain guides and tighten the four bolts to 89 inch lbs. (10 Nm).
57. Preposition the left hand camshaft until the timing mark is approximately at 12 o'clock and preposition the right hand

camshaft until the timing mark is approximately at 11 o'clock.
58. Position the crankshaft with the Crankshaft Holding Tool, then remove the tool.
59. Install the crankshaft sprocket, making sure the flange faces forward.
60. Install the lower end of the left hand timing chain, aligning the timing marks.

➡Be sure the upper half of the timing chain is below the tensioner guide dowel.

61. Install the left hand timing chain on the camshaft sprocket with the 2 chain (marked) links and the timing marks aligned.

➡The left hand timing chain tensioner arm has a bump near the dowel hole for identification.

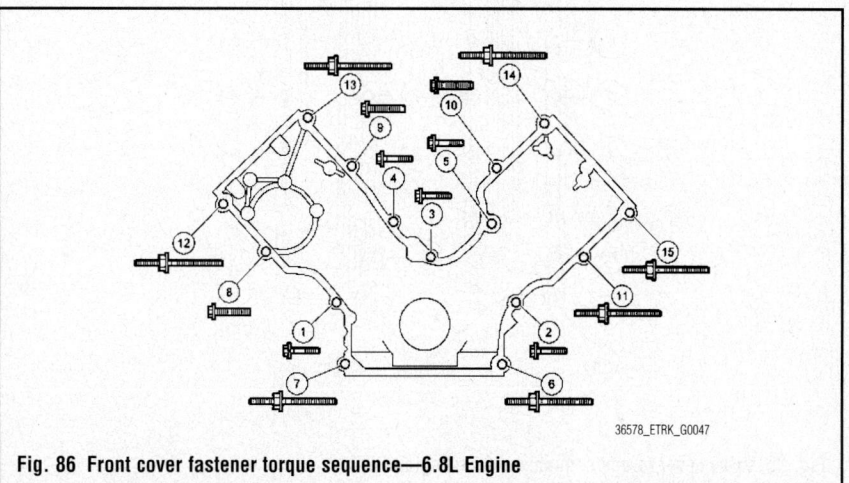

Fig. 86 Front cover fastener torque sequence—6.8L Engine

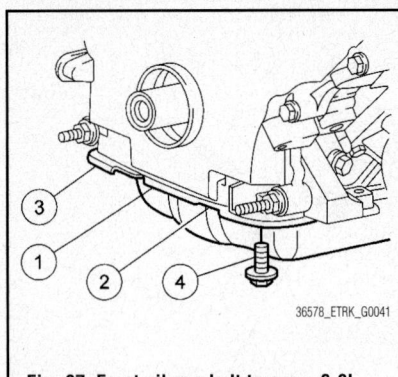

Fig. 87 Front oil pan bolt torque—6.8L Engines

62. Position the left hand timing chain tensioner arm on the dowel pin and install the left hand timing chain tensioner and tighten the two bolts to 18 ft. lbs. (25 Nm).

➡**Be sure the chain link and crankshaft sprocket timing marks are aligned.**

➡**The lower half of the timing chain must be positioned above the dowel.**

63. Install the right hand (outer) timing chain on the crankshaft sprocket.

64. Position the timing chain on the camshaft sprocket. Make sure the 2 copper-colored (marked) links align with the camshaft sprocket timing mark.

65. Position the right hand timing chain tensioner arm on the dowel pin and install the right hand timing chain tensioner and tighten the two bolts to 18 ft. lbs. (25 Nm).

66. Remove the retaining clips from the right hand and left hand timing chain tensioners.

67. Check for correct alignment of all timing marks.

68. Install the crankshaft sensor ring on the crankshaft.

69. Lubricate the balance shaft journals with clean engine oil.

70. Using the index mark on the balance shaft, mark the corresponding teeth on the gear with chalk.

71. Position the balance shaft on the journals.

72. Align the chalk mark on the balance shaft with the camshaft timing mark as shown.

73. Install the balance shaft bearing caps in their original locations and tighten the 6 bolts in the sequence shown.

74. Install the Valve Spring Compressor Spacer between the valve spring coils to prevent valve stem seal damage.

➡**The camshaft roller followers must be installed in their original locations. Failure to follow these instructions may result in engine damage.**

➡**Do not allow the valve keepers to fall off the valve or the valve may drop into the cylinder. If a valve drops into the cylinder, the cylinder head must be removed. For additional information, refer to Cylinder Head in this section.**

➡**It may be necessary to push the valve down while compressing the spring.**

➡**Position the cam lobe away from the camshaft roller follower prior to installing each camshaft roller follower.**

➡**Lubricate the camshaft roller follower with clean engine oil prior to installation.**

75. Use the Valve Spring Compressor to compress the valve springs, and install each of the camshaft roller followers.

76. Install the spark plugs. For additional information, refer to "Spark Plugs, Removal & Installation."

77. Apply a bead of silicone gasket and sealant along the cylinder head-to-cylinder block surface and the oil pan-to-cylinder block surface.

78. Install a new front cover gasket on the engine front cover. Position the engine front cover.

79. Install the front cover fasteners in sequence in two stages as follows:
- Step 1: Fasteners 1—5 to 18 ft. lbs. (25 Nm)
- Step 2: Fasteners 6—15 to 35 ft. lbs. (48 Nm)

80. Loosely install the four front oil pan bolts, then tighten the bolts in two stages, in the sequence shown:
- Stage 1: Tighten the 15 ft. lbs. (20 Nm)
- Stage 2: Tighten an additional 60 degrees

81. Apply instant gel adhesive completely around the gasket groove in the valve covers. Install the new valve cover gaskets.

82. Apply silicone gasket and sealant in two places where the engine front cover meets the cylinder head.

83. Position the valve covers and tighten the 14 fasteners to 89 inch lbs. (10 Nm) for each valve cover in the sequence shown.

84. Position the accessory drive belt idler pulley and tighten the bolt to 18 ft. lbs. (25 Nm).

85. Lubricate the engine front cover and the crankshaft front seal inner lip with clean engine oil.

86. Install a new crankshaft front seal. For additional information, refer to "Crankshaft Front Seal, Removal & Installation."

87. Install the crankshaft pulley. For additional information, refer to "Crankshaft Damper, Removal & Installation."

88. Put the power steering pump back into position and tighten the three mounting bolts to 18 ft. lbs. (25 Nm).

89. Position the oil level indicator tube and tighten bolt to the left cylinder head to 89 inch lbs. (10 Nm). Tighten the bracket support nut to 18 ft. lbs. (25 Nm).

90. The remainder of the installation is the reverse order of removal.

91. Install the engine into the vehicle.

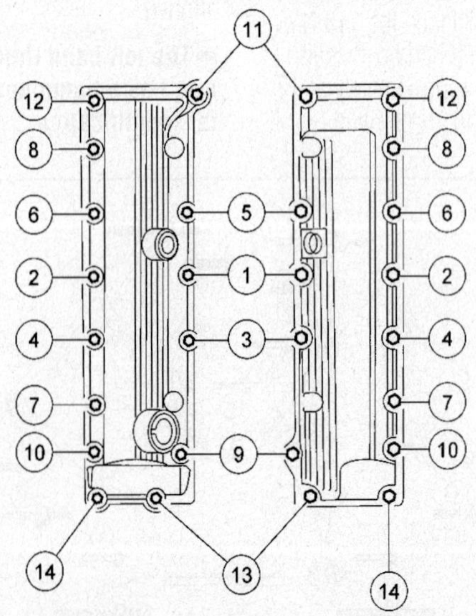

Fig. 88 Valve cover torque sequence—6.8L Engines

For additional information, refer to "Engine Assembly, Removal & Installation."

6.0L Engine

See Figures 89 through 91.

1. Before servicing the vehicle, refer to the Precautions Section.

2. Remove the engine assembly. For additional information, refer to "Engine Assembly, "Removal & Installation."

3. Remove the flexplate. For additional information, refer to "Flexplate, Removal & Installation."

4. Mount the engine on a suitable engine stand.

5. Unplug the glow plug harnesses and remove the glow plugs.

➡**Prior to removing the exhaust manifolds, inspect the exhaust manifold for warpage with a feeler gauge between the manifold and cylinder head. Record the measurement and compare with the specification.**

6. Remove the exhaust manifolds.

7. Remove the cylinder head banjo fitting and fuel line, left side only.

8. Remove the three bolts and turbocharger heat shield, left side only.

9. Remove the protective cover from the cylinder, left side only.

10. Remove the valve cover, right side only.

11. Remove the high pressure oil rail-to-valve cover gasket, right side only.

12. Disconnect the fuel injector electrical connectors.

13. Remove the crankcase-to-head tube(s).

⁂ WARNING

Do not remove the oil rail end plugs or acoustic wave attenuator port fitting. Service parts are not available to support the components.

14. Remove the 18 bolts and the high-pressure oil rails.

15. If the crankcase-to-head tube separated, using the High Pressure Supply Tube Remover, remove the lower crankcase-to-head tube.

16. Using the Injector Connector Release Tool, push the fuel injector electrical connectors out of the rocker arm carrier.

17. Prior to removing the injector assembly, insert clean shop towels in the oil drain holes adjacent to each glow plug.

18. Loosen the bolt and remove the bolt and fuel injector hold-down assembly and the fuel injector. Remove and discard the O-ring seals and copper washer.

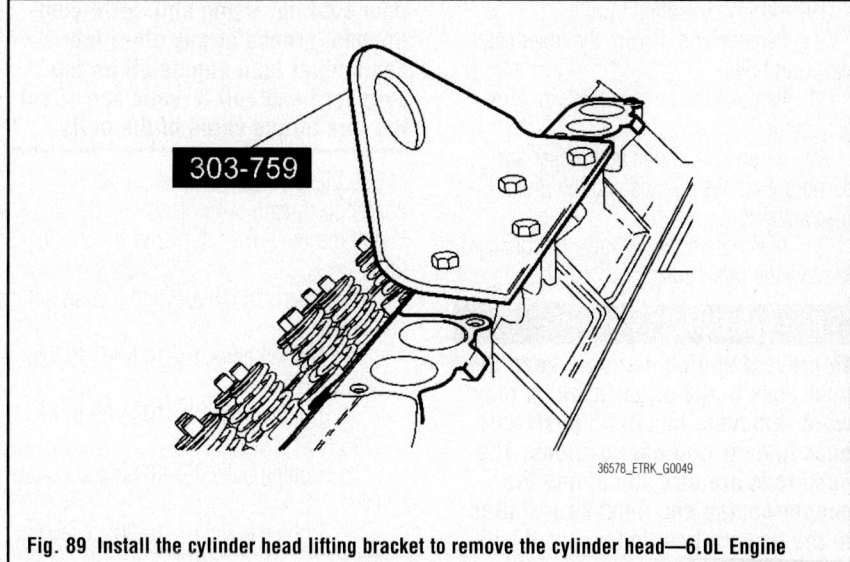

Fig. 89 Install the cylinder head lifting bracket to remove the cylinder head—6.0L Engine

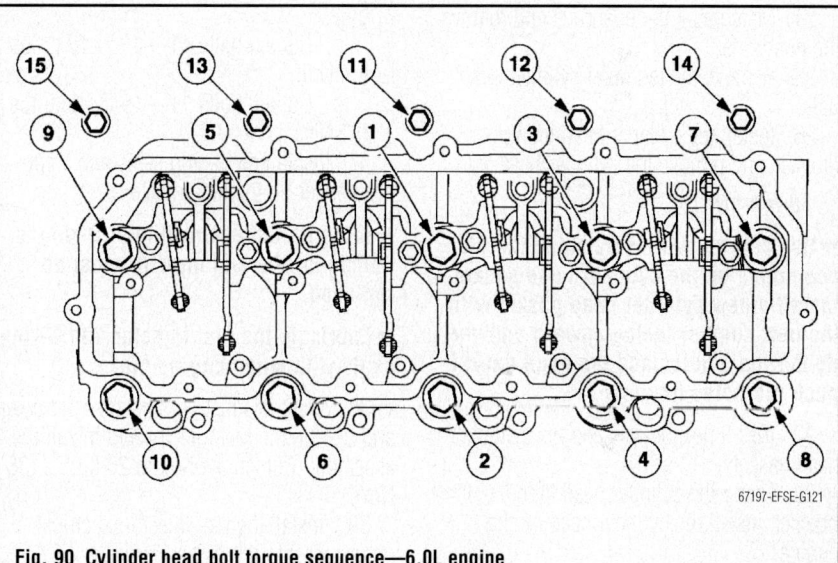

Fig. 90 Cylinder head bolt torque sequence—6.0L engine

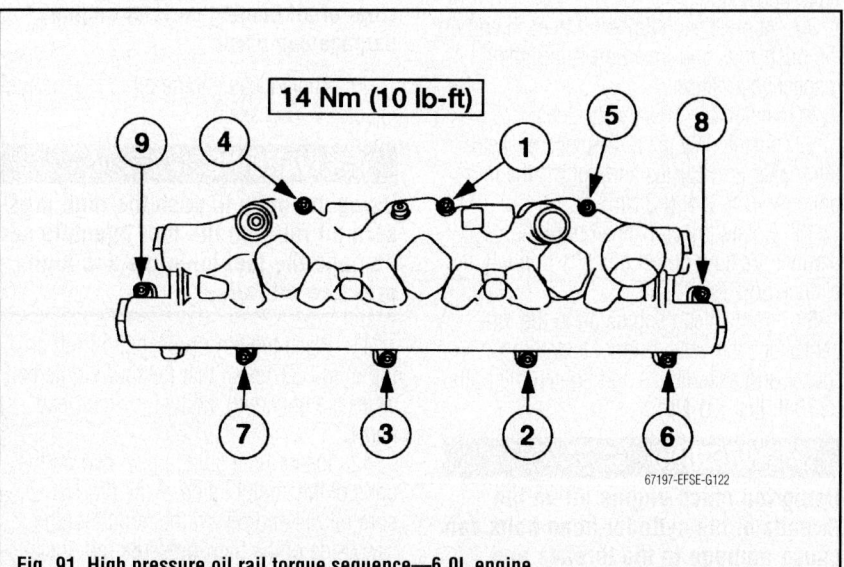

Fig. 91 High pressure oil rail torque sequence—6.0L engine

19. Remove the shop towels.
20. Remove and discard the inner cylinder head bolts.
21. Remove the bolts and rocker arm assemblies.
22. Remove the bolts and rocker arm carriers. Remove and discard the press-in-place gaskets.
23. Matchmark the 16 valve bridges and remove the pushrods.

✷✷ WARNING

To prevent engine damage, keep the push rods in the order in which they were removed. Install all push rods back in their original positions. The push rods are directional and the copper-coated end must be installed in the upward position where it will contact the rocker arm.

24. Matchmark the pushrods and remove the pushrods.
25. Remove the ten outer cylinder head bolts.
26. Install the cylinder head lifting bracket, and remove the cylinder head.

To install:

➡ **Use care to avoid scratching the blue compound on the cylinder head gasket. Install a new cylinder head gasket with the part number facing upward and verify the top 5 holes and the head gasket push rod holes line up.**

27. Install new dowels and the cylinder head gaskets.
28. Using the cylinder head lifting bracket, install the cylinder head on the engine.
29. Install the ten outer cylinder head bolts finger tight.
30. Apply clean engine oil to each end of the push rods and insert them into their respective positions.
31. Install the 16 valve bridges.
32. Install new press-in-place gaskets, the rocker arm carries and tighten the four bolts to 46 ft. lbs. (62 Nm).
33. Rotate the crankshaft until the damper locating dowel notch is in the 6 o'clock position.
34. Apply clean engine oil to the top center of each valve bridge. Install the rocker arm assemblies and tighten the bolts to 23 ft. lbs. (31 Nm).

✷✷ WARNING

Using too much engine oil on the threads of the cylinder head bolts can cause damage to the threads and

poor sealing. Using anti-seize compounds, grease or any other lubricants other than engine oil on the cylinder head bolt threads can affect the true torque value of the bolts.

35. Lightly lubricate the cylinder head bolt threads with clean engine oil. Install the inner cylinder head bolts finger tight.
36. Tighten the inner cylinder head bolts as follows:
   a. Tighten bolts 1—10 to 65 ft. lbs. (88 Nm).
   b. Tighten bolts 1—10 to 85 ft. lbs. (115 Nm).
   c. Tighten bolts 1—10 an additional 90°.
   d. Tighten bolts 1—10 90° a second time.
   e. Tighten bolts 1—10 90° a third time.
   f. Tighten bolts 11—15 to 18 ft. lbs. (24 Nm).
   g. Tighten bolts 11—15 to 23 ft. lbs. (31 Nm).
37. Install new O-ring seals and a copper washer on the fuel injectors.

➡ **If the fuel injector oil inlet D-ring is damaged, the fuel injector must be replaced.**

➡ **Lubricate the fuel injector and O-ring seals with clean engine oil.**

38. Assemble the fuel injector hold down and bolt on the fuel injector and install the assembly. Tighten the bolt to 26 ft. lbs. (35 Nm).
39. Install the fuel injector electrical connector into the rocker carrier.

➡ **Make sure the injector wiring is clear of all moving parts or engine damage can occur.**

40. Apply clean engine oil to the top fuel injector O-ring seals.

✷✷ WARNING

Using the bolts to push the high pressure oil rail into the fuel injectors can damage the fuel injectors and high pressure oil rail.

41. Place the high-pressure oil rail on top of the carrier so that the four single ball tubes are engaging the fuel injector lead angle.
42. Insert three guide bolts, two on the ends of the straight side of the high-pressure oil rail and one in the middle of the wavy side of the high-pressure rail. Install the guide studs 6 to 7 turns.

43. Manually press the high-pressure oil rail into the fuel injectors.
44. Inspect that the high-pressure oil rail mounting feet are flat against the mounting surface.
45. Loosely install the six bolts.
46. Remove the three guide bolts, and install the remaining bolts and tighten the nine bolts to 115 inch lbs. (13 Nm) in the sequence shown.
47. Apply clean engine oil to the D-ring seals and reassemble the crankcase-to-head tube if necessary. Install the crankcase-to-head tube(s) and tighten to 60 ft. lbs. (82 Nm).
48. Connect the fuel injector electrical connectors.
49. Install the high-pressure oil rail-to-valve cover gasket, right cylinder head only.
50. Position the right hand valve cover gasket, right hand valve cover, and tighten the six stud bolts and five bolts to 80 inch lbs. (9 Nm).
51. Install the right hand exhaust manifold, 8 spacers and tighten the eight new bolts to 28 ft. lbs. (38 Nm). For additional information, refer to "Exhaust Manifold, Removal & Installation."
52. Cover the left hand cylinder head with an appropriate covering.
53. Install the turbocharger heat shield. For additional information, refer to "Turbocharger, Removal & Installation."
54. Install the left-hand cylinder head fuel line and tighten to 28 ft. lbs. (38 Nm).
55. Install the left hand exhaust manifold, spacers and tighten the eight new bolts to 28 ft. lbs. (38 Nm). For additional information, refer to "Exhaust Manifold, Removal & Installation."
56. Install the glow plugs and tighten to 14 ft. lbs. (19 Nm).
57. Using the Glow Plug Connector Installer tool, install the glow plug harnesses.
58. The remainder of the installation is the reverse order of removal.
59. Install the engine assembly. For additional information, refer to "Engine Assembly, Removal & Installation."

ENGINE ASSEMBLY

REMOVAL & INSTALLATION

4.6L, 5.4L & 6.8L Engines

1. Disconnect the negative battery cable.
2. Raise and safely support the vehicle.
3. Properly recover the A/C system.
4. Remove the intake manifold. For additional information, refer to "Intake Manifold, Removal & Installation."

5. Remove the accessory drive belt, except 6.8L engine. For additional information, refer to "Accessory Drive Belt, Removal & Installation."

6. Remove the starter. For additional information, refer to "Starter, Removal & Installation."

7. Remove the front bumper.

8. Disconnect the lower radiator hose from the radiator.

9. Disconnect the transmission cooler hoses and drain the fluid into a suitable container.

10. Remove the 4 exhaust Y-pipe flange nuts.

11. Remove the oil drain plug and drain the engine oil. Install the drain plug when finished.

12. Disconnect the oil cooler coolant hoses and position aside.

13. Remove and discard the oil filter.

14. Loosen the threaded insert and remove and discard the oil cooler.

15. If equipped, disconnect the block heater electrical connector and two wiring harness retainers.

16. Remove the two bolts and the flexplate inspection cover.

17. Remove the cylinder block opening cover.

18. Rotate the crankshaft to access all of the torque converter nuts. Discard the torque converter nuts.

19. Remove the two transmission-to-engine bolts and position the shifter cable support bracket, mounting bracket and cable aside.

20. Remove the right hand lower transmission-to-engine bolt.

21. Remove the four engine support insulator-to-crossmember nuts.

22. Disconnect the power steering reservoir hose and the power steering pressure tube at the power steering pump.

23. Remove the nut and position aside the transmission cooler tube support bracket and the starter wiring harness support bracket.

24. Disconnect the A/C compressor electrical connector and the wiring harness retainer.

25. Disconnect the Crankshaft Position (CKP) sensor electrical connector.

26. If equipped, remove the 3 bolts and position the A/C compressor aside.

27. Remove the radiator grille support.

28. Disconnect the upper radiator and the degas bottle coolant hoses from the radiator.

29. Using the Fan Pulley Holding Wrench and the Fan Clutch Nut Wrench, remove the cooling fan assembly.

30. Disconnect the degas bottle hose and power steering hose retainers from the fan shroud.

31. Remove the fan shroud, fan and fan clutch.

32. Remove the four bolts and the radiator support brackets.

33. Remove the radiator from the vehicle.

34. If equipped, disconnect the A/C pressure cutoff switch electrical connector.

35. If equipped, remove the nut and disconnect the compressor suction tube.

36. If equipped, remove the nuts and disconnect the compressor discharge tube and the condenser-to-evaporator tube from the A/C condenser core.

37. Remove the A/C condenser core.

38. Set the hood latch aside. Remove the 2 hood latch bolts and disengage the cable routing clip.

39. Remove the three bolts and position the power steering reservoir aside.

40. Remove the nut and the battery feed cable at the Power Distribution Box (PDB).

41. Disengage the harness routing clips and position aside the battery feed wiring harness.

42. If equipped, disconnect the air temperature sensor electrical connector.

43. Disconnect the front impact severity sensor electrical connector.

44. Disconnect the horn electrical connector.

45. Disconnect the transmission fluid cooler hose retainers.

46. Remove the bolt and position the transmission fluid cooler aside.

47. Remove the pin-type retainers and the right hand and left hand air deflectors.

48. Remove the four bolts and the two upper radiator support plates.

49. Remove the eight bolts and the upper radiator support.

50. Remove the bolt and disconnect the 2 headlamp wiring harness retainers.

51. Disconnect the 4 wiring harness retainers and position the wiring harness aside.

52. Remove the 12 bolts and the lower radiator support.

53. Disconnect the lower radiator coolant hose and position aside.

54. Remove the 3 bolts and the power steering pump.

55. Disconnect the alternator electrical connections.

56. Remove the 2 bolts and the generator.

57. Disconnect the quick connect coupling and remove the crankcase ventilation tube.

58. Disconnect the electrical connector.

59. Disconnect the engine wiring harness retainer and the two PCM electrical connectors.

60. Disconnect the 2 generator wiring harness retainers and position the wiring harness aside.

61. Disconnect the electrical connector, electrical connector retainer and remove the nut, ground strap and mounting bracket.

62. Remove the engine oil filler tube support strap bolt.

63. Remove the fluid level indicator and disconnect the attachments at the transmission fluid filler tube.

64. Disconnect the oil fill tube from the right hand valve cover.

65. Disconnect the coolant hose from the heater outlet tube and remove the heater outlet tube stud, 4.6L engines only.

66. Disconnect the Knock Sensor (KS) electrical connector and engine wiring harness retainers, 5.4L engine only.

67. Disconnect the coolant hose from the heater outlet tube, 5.4L engine only.

68. Remove the 2 heater outlet tube studs, 5.4L engine only.

69. Remove the heater outlet tube and discard the O-ring seals.

70. Remove the bolt and the ground strap and disconnect the right hand HO2S electrical connector and retainer.

71. Disconnect the transmission wiring harness retainers from the engine wiring harness.

72. Disconnect the left hand HO2S sensor electrical wiring harness retainer from the rear of the left hand cylinder head.

73. Disconnect the transmission wiring harness retainer and position the transmission wiring harness aside.

74. Disconnect the left hand HO2S sensor electrical connector and retainer.

75. Remove the 4 upper transmission-to-engine bolts and position the fuel tube support bracket aside.

76. Install the Engine Lifting Bracket.

77. Support the transmission with a jack.

78. Using a suitable floor crane, remove the engine assembly from the vehicle.

To install:

79. Position the engine assembly into the vehicle.

80. Remove the floor jack and supporting the transmission.

81. Position the shifter cable support bracket and tighten the two transmission-to-engine bolts to 44 ft. lbs. (60 Nm).

82. Install the right hand lower transmission-to-engine bolt and tighten to 44 ft. lbs. (60 Nm).

83. Install the four engine support insulator-to-support insulator bracket nuts and tighten to 66 ft. lbs. (90 Nm).

84. Position the shift cable mounting bracket, tighten the two bolts to 18 ft. lbs. (25 Nm) and connect the shift cable.

85. Install four new torque converter nuts and tighten to 26 ft. lbs. (35 Nm).

86. Install the cylinder block opening cover.

87. Position the flexplate inspection cover and tighten the two bolts to 25 ft. lbs. (34 Nm).

88. If equipped, install the A/C compressor and tighten the three bolts to 18 ft. lbs. (25 Nm).

89. Connect the A/C compressor electrical connector and the wiring harness retainer.

90. Connect the Crankshaft Position (CKP) sensor electrical connector.

91. Position the exhaust Y-pipe and tighten the four nuts to 30 ft. lbs. (40 Nm).

92. Position a new oil cooler on the oil filter adapter and install the threaded insert. Tighten to 43 ft. lbs. (58 Nm).

✳✳ WARNING

The oil cooler must be replaced or severe damage to the engine can occur.

➡**Make sure the tab on the oil filter adapter nests into the notch in the oil cooler.**

93. Install a new oil filter

94. Connect the two oil cooler coolant hoses.

95. Position the power steering pump and tighten the three bolts to 18 ft. lbs. (25 Nm).

96. Using the Teflon Seal Installer Set, install a new Teflon® seal on the power steering pressure tube.

97. Connect the Power Steering Pressure (PSP) tube and the power steering reservoir hose to the power steering pump and tighten to 15 ft. lbs. (20 Nm).

98. Connect the lower radiator coolant hose to the oil filter adapter coolant inlet.

99. Position the fuel tube support bracket and tighten the four upper transmission-to-engine bolts to 44 ft. lbs. (60 Nm).

100. Position the ground strap, install the bolt and connect the right hand HO2S electrical connector and retainer.

101. Connect the left hand Heated Oxygen Sensor (HO2S) sensor electrical connector and retainer.

102. Position the transmission wiring harness and connect the transmission wiring harness retainer.

103. Connect the left hand HO2S sensor electrical wiring harness retainer to the rear of the left hand cylinder head.

104. Connect the transmission wiring harness retainers to the engine wiring harness.

105. Insert the heater outlet tube over the new seals.

➡**Do not reuse the O-ring seals. Lubricate the new O-ring seals with clean engine coolant before installing the heater outlet tube.**

106. Connect the coolant hose to the heater outlet tube and tighten the heater outlet tube stud to 18 ft. lbs. (25 Nm), 4.6L engines only.

107. Tighten the two heater outlet tube studs to 30 ft. lbs. (40 Nm), 5.4L engine only.

108. Connect the coolant hose to the heater outlet tube, 5.4L engine only.

109. Connect the KS electrical connector and engine wiring harness retainers, 5.4L engine only.

110. Position the transmission cooler tube support bracket and the starter wiring harness support bracket and install the nut.

111. Connect the oil fill tube to the right hand valve cover.

112. Install the engine oil filler tube support strap bolt.

113. Position the engine wiring harness support bracket, install the ground strap and nut, and connect the electrical connector to the bracket and tighten to 18 ft. lbs. (25 Nm).

114. Position the generator wiring harness and connect the two generator wiring harness retainers.

115. Connect the engine wiring harness retainer and the two PCM electrical connectors.

116. Connect the electrical connector.

117. Position the crankcase ventilation tube and connect the quick connect coupling.

118. Install the alternator and connect the electrical connector.

119. Position the lower radiator support and tighten the 12 bolts to 15 ft. lbs. (20 Nm).

120. Position the wiring harness and connect the 4 wiring harness retainers.

121. Connect the two headlamp wiring harness retainers and position the ground wire and tighten the bolt to 89 inch lbs. (10 Nm).

122. Position the upper radiator support and tighten the eight bolts to 15 ft. lbs. (20 Nm).

123. Position the two upper radiator support plates and tighten the four bolts to 15 ft. lbs. (20 Nm).

124. Position the right hand and left hand air deflectors and install the pin-type retainers.

125. Position the transmission fluid cooler and tighten the bolt to 89 inch lbs. (10 Nm).

126. Connect the transmission fluid cooler hose retainers.

127. Connect the horn electrical connector.

128. Connect the front impact severity sensor electrical connector.

129. If equipped, connect the air temperature sensor electrical connector.

130. Route the battery feed wiring harness to the Power Distribution Box (PDB) and insert the routing clips.

131. Install the battery feed cable to the PDB and the nuts.

132. Position the power steering reservoir and tighten the three bolts to 15 ft. lbs. (20 Nm).

133. Position the hood latch, connect the cable position retainer and tighten the bolts to 106 inch lbs. (12 Nm).

134. If equipped, install the A/C condenser core in the vehicle.

135. If equipped, connect the compressor discharge tube and the condenser-to-evaporator tube to the A/C condenser core and tighten the nuts to 11 ft. lbs. (15 Nm).

136. If equipped, connect the compressor suction tube and tighten the nut to 11 ft. lbs. (15 Nm).

137. If equipped, connect the A/C pressure cutoff switch electrical connector.

138. Position the radiator in the vehicle.

139. Position the radiator support brackets and tighten the four bolts to 15 ft. lbs. (20 Nm).

140. Position the fan shroud and the fan and fan clutch in the vehicle, and tighten the two bolts to 53 inch lbs. (6 Nm).

141. Connect the degas bottle hose and power steering hose retainers to the fan shroud.

142. Using the Fan Pulley Holding Wrench and Fan Clutch Nut Wrench, install the fan blade and the fan clutch. Tighten to 133 Nm (98 lb-ft).

143. Connect the upper radiator coolant hose and the degas bottle coolant hose to the radiator.

144. Install the radiator grille support.

145. Connect the transmission cooler tubes.

146. Connect the lower radiator hose to the radiator.

147. Install the front bumper.

148. Install the starter.

149. Install the intake manifold.

150. Refill the engine with oil to the correct level.

151. Refill the transmission with fluid to the correct level.

152. Fill and bleed the power steering system.

153. Start the engine and check for leaks.

154. Evacuate and recharge the air conditioning system

6.0L Engine

1. Before servicing the vehicle, refer to the Precautions Section.

2. Disconnect the negative battery cable.

3. Remove the radiator assembly. For additional information, refer to "Radiator, Removal & Installation."

4. Remove the front bumper.

5. Remove the two pushpin retainers and the front bumper shields.

6. Remove the radiator grille support.

7. Remove the six pushpin retainers and the side shields.

8. Matchmark the hood latch location. Disconnect the cable retainer. Remove the two bolts and position the hood latch aside.

9. Disconnect the pushpin retainers and the transmission cooler hose. Remove the bolt and the transmission cooler.

10. Disconnect the horn electrical connector.

11. Remove the four bolts and the radiator upper support brackets.

12. Remove the eight bolts and the radiator upper support.

13. Disconnect the front impact severity sensor electrical connector.

14. Remove the bolt for the ground wire. Disconnect the pushpin retainers and position aside the headlamp wire harness.

15. Remove the four pushpins and the side shields. Position the power steering cooler aside.

16. Remove the 12 bolts and the lower radiator support.

17. Remove the intake manifold. For additional information, refer to "Intake Manifold, Removal & Installation."

18. Remove the right hand fan stator stand-off. Remove the bolt and position the cable aside.

19. Disconnect the A/C electrical connector.

20. Remove and discard the O-ring seal and gasket. Cap or plug the A/C openings as needed.

21. Remove the bolt and disconnect the A/C pressure switch electrical connector.

22. Remove the three bolts and A/C compressor.

23. Disconnect the heater hose and position the heater hose aside.

24. Remove the bolt and idler pulley.

25. Remove the two nuts and the coolant hose shield.

26. Loosen the clamp and disconnect the engine coolant fill hose.

27. Disconnect the vacuum pump hose.

28. Remove the three stud bolts and the vacuum pump.

29. Remove the 2 power steering upper mounting bolts.

30. Remove the left hand fan stator stand-off.

31. Remove the 2 bolts and position the power steering pump aside.

32. Remove the lower radiator hose.

33. Disconnect the fuel tube spring lock couplings.

34. Disconnect the Crankshaft Position (CKP) sensor electrical connector and retaining clips.

35. Disconnect the Injection Control Pressure (ICP) sensor electrical connector. Disconnect the glow plug electrical connector and wire retainers.

36. Disconnect the Camshaft Position (CMP) sensor electrical connector and retaining clips.

37. Disconnect the electrical connector and wire retainers at the transmission.

38. Disconnect the glow plug module electrical connectors.

39. Disconnect the Exhaust Pressure (EP) sensor electrical connector and push-pin retainer.

40. Disconnect the left hand glow plug electrical connector.

41. Disconnect the engine-to-vehicle electrical connectors.

42. Disconnect the two PCM electrical connectors and position the engine wiring harness aside.

43. Remove the three bolts and the oil filter assembly.

44. Remove the engine-to-transmission bolt for the transmission cooler tubes.

45. Remove the nut and remove the transmission cooling tubes support bracket off the stud.

46. Remove the torque converter cover.

47. Remove and discard the 6 torque converter nuts.

48. Disconnect the block heater electrical connector.

49. Remove the nut. Disconnect the battery cable bracket at the starter and position aside.

50. Remove the starter solenoid protective cap.

51. Disconnect the starter motor electrical connections.

52. Remove the one stud bolt, two bolts and the starter motor.

53. Remove the right and left cylinder block drain plugs and drain the coolant from the block.

54. Apply clean engine oil to the O-ring seals and reinstall the cylinder block drain plugs and tighten to 15 ft. lbs. (20 Nm).

55. Remove the four engine mount nuts.

56. Remove the two lower engine-to-transmission bolts.

57. Remove the two mounting bolts from the lifting bracket and remove the tubes.

58. Disconnect the glow plug wire retainer and remove the nut and the oil indicator and tube and discard the O-ring seal.

59. Disconnect the EP tube at the exhaust manifold.

60. Remove the two nuts and glow plug module.

61. Remove the three nuts and the glow plug module mounting bracket.

62. Remove the left hand valve cover.

63. Remove the ICP sensor and plug the opening.

64. Install the engine lifting adapters.

65. Install the engine lifting attachment and heavy duty floor crane.

66. Drain the engine oil.

67. Remove the mounting bolts and position back the oil pan until the oil pickup tube bolts are accessible.

68. Remove the 2 bolts and let the oil pickup tube go into the oil pan. Remove the oil pan and remove the press-in-place gasket and discard.

69. Remove and discard the oil pickup tube O-ring seal.

70. Position a suitable transmission jack under the transmission.

71. Remove the four upper engine-to-transmission bolts.

72. Raise the engine.

73. Remove the mounting bolts and the left engine mount.

74. Remove the mounting bolts and the right engine mount.

75. Remove the engine from the vehicle.

➡ **The engine must be moved to the driver side for removal.**

To install:

76. Raise the engine high enough to clear the No. 1 crossmember and position the engine into the vehicle.

77. Position the engine mounts in the vehicle.

78. Align the torque converter studs with the holes in the flywheel and push the engine in. Install the top four

engine-to-transmission bolts and tighten to 35 ft. lbs. (47 Nm).

79. Lower the engine until it is just above the motor mounts and install the four right hand engine mounting bolts and tighten to 59 ft. lbs. (80 Nm).

80. Install the left hand engine mounting bolts and tighten to 59 ft. lbs. (80 Nm).

81. Remove the transmission jack.

82. Install a new O-ring seal on the oil pickup tube and position the oil pickup tube in the oil pan.

83. Install a new press-in-place gasket into the upper oil pan.

84. Position the oil pan in the vehicle and install the oil pickup tube and tighten the two bolts to 115 inch lbs. (13 Nm).

85. Install the oil pan and tighten the mounting bolts. For additional information, refer to "Oil Pan, Removal & Installation."

86. Install the oil pan drain plug and tighten to 32 ft. lbs. (44 Nm).

87. Lower the engine.

88. Install the factor engine lifting bracket.

89. Install the ground strap and tighten the bolt to 106 inch lbs. (12 Nm).

90. Loosely install the turbocharger exhaust pipe.

91. Install the ICP sensor and tighten to 106 inch lbs. (12 Nm).

92. Remove any protective covering that was placed over the cylinder head.

93. Install the left hand valve cover and gasket. Tighten the mounting bolts to 80 inch lbs. (9 Nm).

94. Install the glow plug module mounting bracket and tighten the nuts to 71 inch lbs. (8 Nm).

95. Connect the EP tube to the exhaust manifold and tighten to 22 ft. lbs. (30 Nm).

96. Position the oil indicator and tube, install the retaining nut and connect the glow plug wire retainer.

97. Position the fuel tubes and install the two mounting bolts for the fuel tube bracket.

98. Install the two lower engine-to-transmission bolts and tighten to 35 ft. lbs. (47 Nm).

99. Install the four engine mount-to-crossmember nuts and tighten to 66 ft. lbs. (90 Nm).

100. Install the starter. For additional information, refer to "Starter, Removal & Installation."

101. Connect the block heater electrical connector.

102. Install the torque converter nuts and tighten to 26 ft. lbs. (35 Nm). Install the torque converter cover.

103. Position the transmission cooler tube support bracket on the stud and tighten the nut to 106 inch lbs. (12 Nm).

104. Install the engine-to-transmission bolt for the transmission cooler tubes and tighten to 35 ft. lbs. (47 Nm).

105. Install the oil filter assembly and tighten the bolts to 18 ft. lbs. (24 Nm).

106. Position the engine wiring harness and connect the PCM electrical connectors.

107. Connect the 2 engine-to-vehicle electrical connectors.

108. Connect the left hand glow plug electrical connector.

109. Connect the pushpin retainer and EP sensor electrical connector.

110. Connect the electrical connector and wire retainers at the transmission.

111. Connect the glow plug module electrical connectors.

112. Connect the Camshaft Position (CMP) sensor electrical connector and retaining clips.

113. Position the wiring and connect the glow plug and ICP sensor electrical connectors.

114. Connect the Crankshaft Position (CKP) sensor electrical connector and retaining clips.

115. Connect the fuel tube spring lock couplings and install the retaining clips.

116. Install the lower radiator hose.

117. Install the power steering pump and tighten the bolts to 18ft. lbs. (25 Nm).

118. Install the left hand fan stator stand-off and tighten the bolts to 35 ft. lbs. (47 Nm).

119. Tighten the two power steering upper mounting bolts to 18 ft. lbs. (25 Nm).

120. Position the vacuum pump and tighten the three stud bolts to 35 ft. lbs. (47 Nm).

121. Connect the vacuum pump hose.

122. Connect the engine coolant fill hose and tighten the clamp.

123. Position the coolant hose shield and tighten the nuts to 53 inch lbs. (6 Nm).

124. Install the idler pulley and tighten the bolt to 35 ft. lbs. (47 Nm).

125. Connect the heater hose.

126. Install the A/C compressor and tighten the bolts to 18 ft. lbs. (25 Nm).

127. Connect the A/C pressure switch electrical connector and tighten the bolt to 21 ft. lbs. (28 Nm).

128. Connect the A/C fitting and tighten the nut to 133 inch lbs. (15 Nm).

129. Connect the A/C compressor electrical connector.

130. Position back the cable and install the bolt. Install the right hand fan stator stand-off.

131. Install the intake manifold. For additional information, refer to "Intake Manifold, Removal & Installation."

132. Install the lower radiator support and tighten the bolts to 15 ft. lbs. (20 Nm).

133. Position back the power steering cooler. Position back the side deflectors and install the 4 pushpin retainers.

134. Position the headlamp wire harness and connect the pushpin retainers. Install the bolt for the ground wire.

135. Connect the front impact severity sensor electrical connector.

136. Install the radiator upper support and tighten the eight bolts to 15 ft. lbs. (20 Nm).

137. Install the radiator upper support brackets and tighten the four bolts to 106 inch lbs. (12 Nm).

138. Connect the horn electrical connector.

139. Position the transmission cooler and loosely install a bolt.

140. Connect the transmission cooler hose and the pushpin retainers.

141. Position the hood latch and tighten the four bolts to 106 inch lbs. (12 Nm). Connect the cable retainer.

142. Position the side shields and install the six pushpin retainers.

143. Install the radiator grille support.

144. Install the front bumper shields and two pushpin retainers.

145. Install the front bumper.

146. Install the radiator assembly.

147. Refill the engine with oil to the correct level.

148. Ensure the engine cooling system is filled to the correct level.

149. Check and top off the transmission fluid level.

150. Connect the negative battery cable.

EXHAUST MANIFOLD

REMOVAL & INSTALLATION

4.6L, 5.4L & 6.8L Engines

Left Side

See Figures 92 through 94.

1. Before servicing the vehicle, refer to the Precautions Section.

2. Remove the engine cover.

3. Disconnect the upper and lower fitting and remove the EGR system module-to-exhaust manifold tube, 4.6L engine only.

4. Remove the four exhaust Y-pipe flange nuts.

5. Remove and discard the nuts and the exhaust manifold.

6. Remove and discard the exhaust manifold gasket.

7. Remove and discard the exhaust manifold-to-cylinder head studs.

To install:

8. Install new exhaust manifold-to-cylinder head studs and tighten to 106 inch lbs. (12 Nm).

9. Using new exhaust manifold gaskets, position the exhaust manifold and tighten the new nuts in sequence as follows:

- 4.6L engine: 15 ft. lbs. (20 Nm)
- 5.4L & 6.8L engines: 18 ft. lbs. (25 Nm)

10. Install the Y-pipe and tighten the new nuts to 30 ft. lbs. (40 Nm).

11. If equipped with 4.6L engine, install the EGR system module-to-exhaust manifold

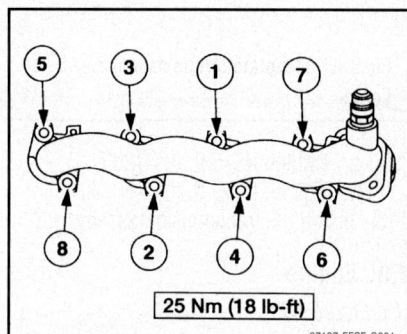

Fig. 92 Left exhaust manifold torque sequence—4.6L engine

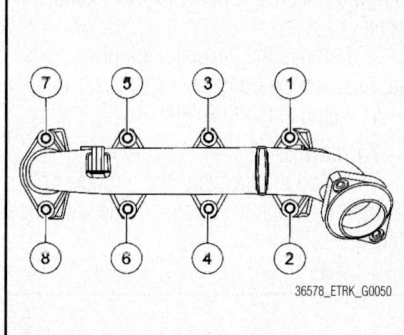

Fig. 93 Left exhaust manifold torque sequence—5.4L engine

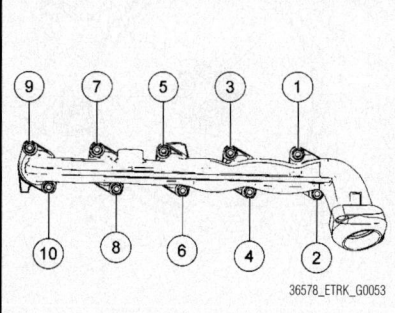

Fig. 94 Left exhaust manifold torque sequence—6.8L engine

tube and tighten the upper and lower fittings in 2 stages:

   a. Connect the upper and lower fittings and hand-tighten.

   b. Tighten to 31 ft. lbs. (42 Nm).

12. Install the engine cover.

Right Side

See Figures 95 through 97.

1. Before servicing the vehicle, refer to the Precautions Section.

2. Disconnect the negative battery cable.

3. Raise and safely support the vehicle.

4. Remove the four exhaust Y-pipe flange nuts.

5. Remove and discard the nuts and the exhaust manifold.

6. Remove the exhaust manifold and discard the gaskets.

7. Remove and discard the exhaust manifold-to-cylinder head studs.

To install:

8. Install new exhaust manifold-to-cylinder head studs and tighten to 106 inch lbs. (12 Nm).

9. Using new exhaust manifold gaskets, position the exhaust manifold and tighten the new nuts in sequence as follows:

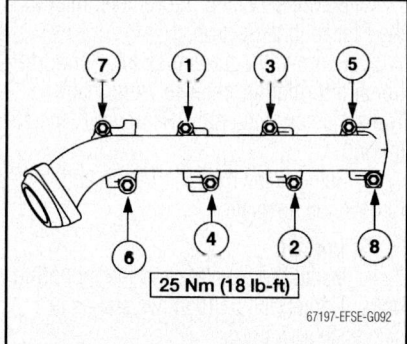

Fig. 95 Right exhaust manifold torque sequence—4.6L engine

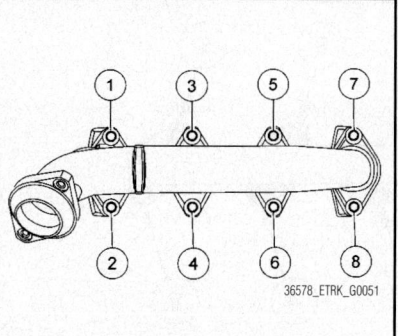

Fig. 96 Right exhaust manifold torque sequence—5.4L engine

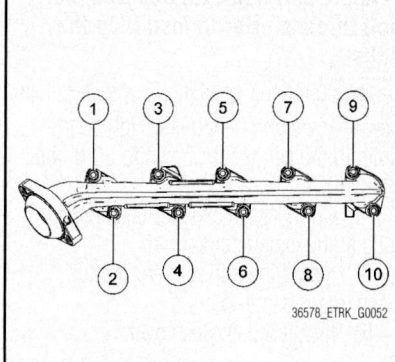

Fig. 97 Right exhaust manifold torque sequence—6.8L engine

- 4.6L engine: 15 ft. lbs. (20 Nm)
- 5.4L & 6.8L engine: 18 ft. lbs. (25 Nm)

10. Install the Y-pipe and tighten the new nuts to 30 ft. lbs. (40 Nm).

11. Connect the negative battery cable.

6.0L Engine

Left Side

See Figure 98.

1. Before servicing the vehicle, refer to the Precautions Section.

2. Raise and safely support the vehicle.

3. Remove the engine cover.

4. Remove the left bolts for the turbocharger adapter pipe.

5. Disconnect the exhaust back pressure tube.

6. Remove the bolts and the left exhaust manifold.

To install:

➡ Start installing the bolts with the second bolt from the rear on the top. The hole diameter is smaller, therefore allowing alignment of the remaining bolts.

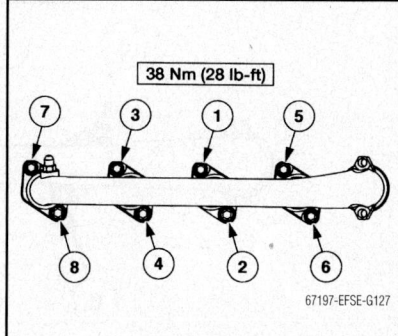

Fig. 98 Left exhaust manifold torque sequence—6.0L engine

➡ **Apply anti-seize lubricant to the bolt threads prior to installing the bolts.**

7. Install the left exhaust manifold with new spacers and new bolts. Tighten the bolts in the sequence shown to 28 ft. lbs. (38 Nm).

8. Connect the exhaust back pressure tube at the exhaust manifold.

9. Install the left bolts for the turbocharger adapter pipe.

10. Install the engine cover.

Right Side

See Figure 99.

1. Before servicing the vehicle, refer to the Precautions Section.

2. Raise and safely support the vehicle.

3. Disconnect the battery ground cable.

4. Remove the engine cover.

5. Remove the right bolts for the turbocharger adapter pipe.

6. Remove the bolts and the right exhaust manifold.

To install:

➡ **Start installing the bolts with the second bolt from the rear on the top. The hole diameter is smaller, therefore allowing alignment of the remaining bolts.**

➡ **Apply anti-seize lubricant to the bolt threads prior to installing the bolts.**

7. Install the right exhaust manifold with new spacers and new bolts. Tighten the bolts in the sequence shown to 28 ft. lbs. (38 Nm).

8. Install the right bolts for the turbocharger adapter pipe.

9. Install the engine cover.

10. Connect the battery ground cable.

FLEXPLATE

REMOVAL & INSTALLATION

4.6L, 5.4L & 6.8L Engine

See Figures 100 through 102.

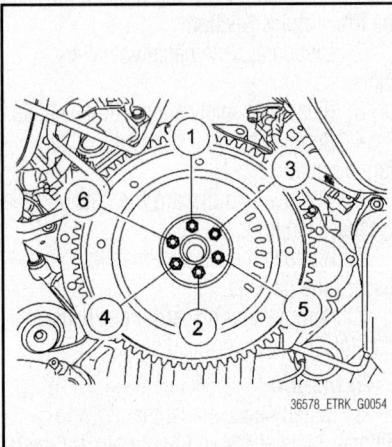

Fig. 100 Flexplate torque sequence—4.6L Engine

1. Before servicing the vehicle, refer to the Precautions Section.

2. Remove the transmission. For additional information, refer to "Automatic Transmission Assembly, Removal & Installation."

3. Remove the mounting bolts and remove the flexplate.

To install:

4. Install the flexplate and the mounting bolts. Tighten the bolts in two stages in sequence as follows:

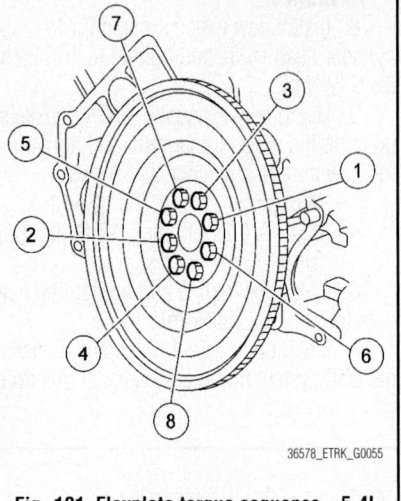

Fig. 101 Flexplate torque sequence—5.4L Engine

   a. Tighten to 15 ft. lbs. (20 Nm).
   b. Tighten to 59 ft. lbs. (80 Nm).

5. Install the transmission assembly.

6.0L Engine

See Figure 103.

1. Before servicing the vehicle, refer to the Precautions Section.

2. Remove the engine assembly. For additional information, refer to "Engine Assembly, Removal & Installation."

3. Remove the flexplate mounting bolts and discard the bolts.

4. Remove the flexplate.

To install:

5. Install the flexplate and ten new bolts. Tighten the bolts in 2 steps, in the sequence shown:

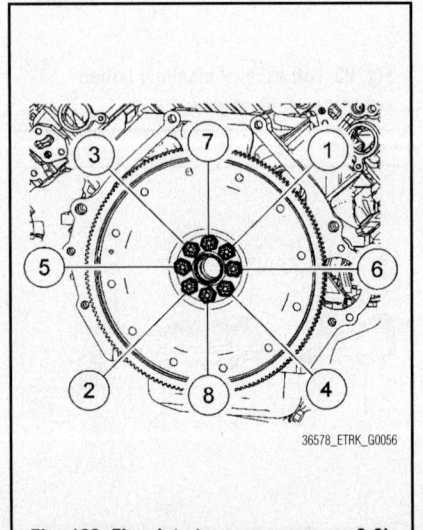

Fig. 102 Flexplate torque sequence—6.8L Engine

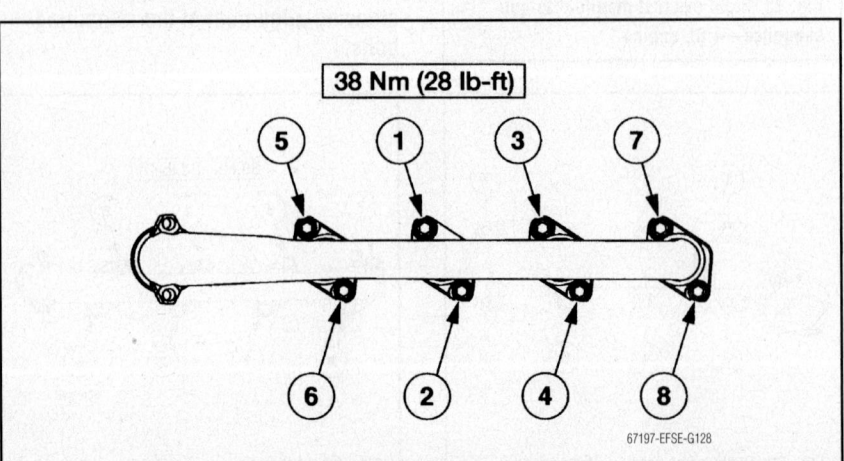

Fig. 99 Right exhaust manifold torque sequence—6.0L engine

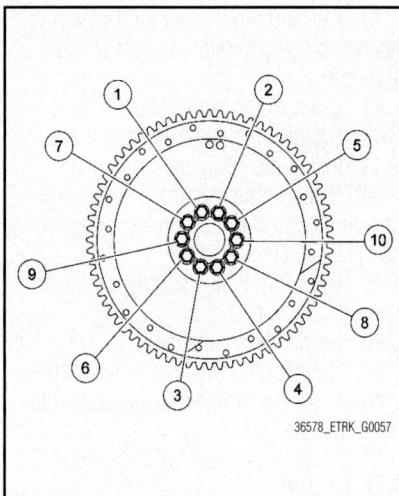

Fig. 103 Flexplate torque sequence—6.0L Engine

  a. Tighten to 44 inch lbs. (5 Nm).
  b. Tighten to 69 ft. lbs. (94 Nm).
6. Install the engine assembly.

INTAKE MANIFOLD

REMOVAL & INSTALLATION

4.6L Engine

See Figure 104.

1. Before servicing the vehicle, refer to the Precautions Section.
2. Disconnect the negative battery cable.
3. Release the engine cover latches and remove the engine cover.
4. Remove the air intake assembly.
5. Drain the engine cooling system.

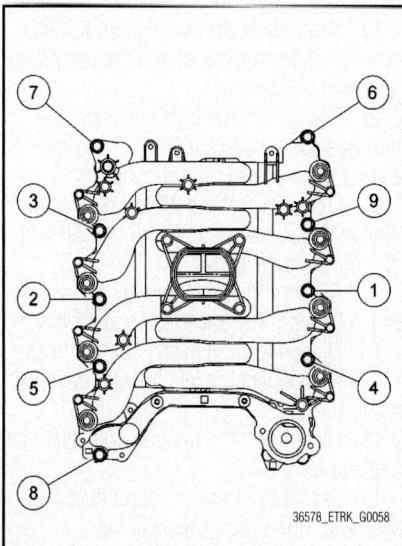

Fig. 104 Intake manifold torque sequence—4.6L Engine

6. Disconnect the fuel supply line.
7. Disconnect the PCV tube.
8. Remove the front transmission fluid filler tube support bracket bolt.
9. Remove bolt and position the transmission fluid filler tube aside.
10. Disconnect the auxiliary heater hoses and position them aside, if equipped.
11. Disconnect the Electronic Throttle Control (ETC) and the PCV heater element electrical connectors and the wiring harness retainer.
12. Remove the throttle body mounting bolts, throttle body and discard the gasket.
13. Disconnect the electrical connector and the Evaporative Emission (EVAP) canister-to- EVAP canister purge valve tube quick connect coupling from the EVAP purge valve.
14. Disconnect the brake booster vacuum hose from the intake manifold.
15. Disconnect the EGR system module vacuum connector and position the vacuum tube assembly aside.
16. Disconnect the EGR system module electrical connector.
17. Disconnect the upper and lower fittings and remove the exhaust manifold-to-EGR system module tube.
18. Remove the two bolts and the EGR system module.
19. Discard the EGR system module gasket.
20. Remove the ignition coils.
21. Remove the four bolts and the generator support bracket.
22. Disconnect the heater coolant hose and position aside.
23. Disconnect the fuel injector electrical connectors.
24. Disconnect the Knock Sensor (KS) electrical connector, electrical connector retainer and the 2 engine wiring harness retainers from the rear of the intake manifold.
25. Disconnect the upper radiator coolant hose and position aside.
26. Remove the 2 thermostat housing bolts and the thermostat housing and discard the O-ring seal.
27. Remove the thermostat.
28. Remove the intake manifold mounting bolts.
29. Remove the intake manifold through the passenger compartment and discard the RH and LH intake manifold gaskets.

To install:

30. Clean the mating surfaces of the cylinder head and the intake manifold with metal surface prep and silicone gasket remover.

31. Install new intake manifold gaskets and position the intake manifold. Loosely install the 9 intake manifold bolts.
32. Tighten the intake manifold mounting bolts in the sequence shown to 89 inch lbs. (10 Nm).
33. Install the thermostat, seal and tighten the thermostat housing bolts to 18 ft. lbs. (25 Nm).
34. Connect the upper radiator coolant hose.
35. Connect the KS electrical connector, electrical connector retainer and the 2 engine wiring harness retainers to the rear of the intake manifold.
36. Connect the fuel injector electrical connectors.
37. Connect the heater coolant hose.
38. Position the alternator support bracket and tighten the bolts to 89 inch lbs. (10 Nm).
39. Install the ignition coils.
40. Carefully clean both sealing surfaces and install a new EGR system module gasket with the side with the raised ring facing the intake manifold.
41. Install the EGR system module and tighten the bolts to 18 ft. lbs. (25 Nm) plus 90°.
42. Position the exhaust manifold-to-EGR system module tube and connect the upper and lower fittings.
43. Position the vacuum tube assembly and connect the EGR system module vacuum connector.
44. Connect the EGR system module electrical connector.
45. Connect the brake booster vacuum hose to the intake manifold.
46. Connect the electrical connector and the EVAP canister-to- EVAP canister purge valve tube quick connect coupling to the EVAP purge valve.
47. Install the throttle body with a new gasket and tighten the bolts to 80 inch lbs. (9 Nm) plus 90°.
48. Connect the auxiliary heater hose quick connect couplings, if equipped.
49. Install the transmission fluid filler tube and tighten the bolt to 89 inch lbs. (10 Nm).
50. Install the front transmission fluid filler tube support bracket bolt and tighten to 21 ft. lbs. (28 Nm).
51. Position the PCV tube and connect the quick connect couplings.
52. Connect the fuel supply tube quick connect coupling.
53. Install the engine cover.
54. Install the air intake assembly.
55. Connect the battery ground cable.
56. Refill the engine cooling system to the correct level.

5.4L Engine

See Figure 105.

1. Before servicing the vehicle, refer to the Precautions Section.

2. Disconnect the negative battery cable.

3. Release the engine cover latches and remove the engine cover.

4. Remove the air intake assembly.

5. Drain the engine cooling system.

6. Disconnect the fuel supply line.

7. Disconnect the quick connect coupling and remove the crankcase ventilation tube from the LH valve cover.

8. Remove the throttle body spacer. For additional information, refer to "Throttle Body, Removal & Installation."

9. Disconnect the upper radiator hose.

10. Disconnect the heater coolant hose.

11. Disconnect the Electronic Throttle Control (ETC) wiring harness retainer.

12. Disconnect the generator wiring harness retainer from the generator support bracket stud bolt.

13. Remove the 2 bolts, the 2 stud bolts and the alternator upper support bracket.

14. Remove the front transmission fluid filler tube support bracket bolt.

15. Remove the rear transmission fluid filler tube support bracket nut and position the transmission fluid filler tube aside.

16. Disconnect the electrical connector and the Evaporative Emission (EVAP) canister-to- EVAP canister purge valve tube quick connect coupling from the EVAP purge valve.

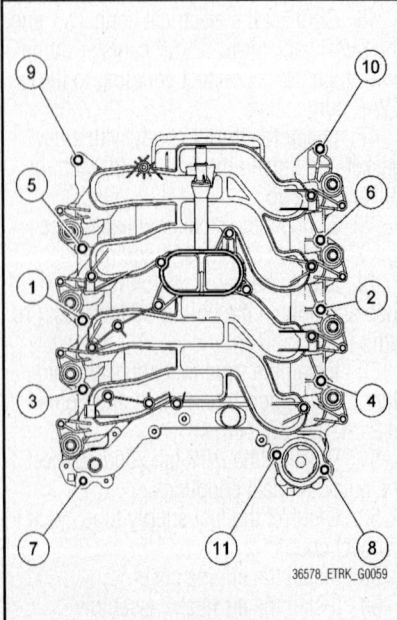

Fig. 105 Intake manifold torque sequence—5.4L Engine

36578_ETRK_G0059

17. Remove the bolt and the EVAP canister purge valve.

18. Disconnect the auxiliary heater hoses and position aside, if equipped.

19. Disconnect the quick connect coupling and remove the PCV tube from the RH valve cover.

20. Disconnect the fuel injector electrical connectors.

21. Disconnect the ignition coil electrical connectors.

22. Remove the ignition coils.

23. Remove the bolts, the thermostat housing and the thermostat and discard the O-ring seal.

24. Remove the mounting bolts, the intake manifold assembly and discard the intake manifold gaskets.

To install:

25. Clean the mating surfaces of the cylinder head and the intake manifold with metal surface prep and silicone gasket remover.

26. Install new intake manifold gaskets and position the intake manifold. Loosely install the intake manifold bolts.

27. Using a new O-ring seal, install the thermostat. Loosely install the thermostat housing and bolts.

28. Tighten the intake manifold bolts in two stages, in the sequence shown as follows:

    a. Tighten to 18 inch lbs. (2 Nm).

    b. Tighten to 18 ft. lbs. (25 Nm).

29. Install the ignition coils.

30. Connect the ignition coil electrical connectors.

31. Connect the fuel injector electrical connectors.

32. Position the PCV tube and connect the quick connect couplings.

33. Connect the auxiliary heater hoses, if equipped.

34. Install the EVAP canister purge valve and tighten the bolt to 89 inch lbs. (10 Nm).

35. Connect the electrical connector and the EVAP canister-to- EVAP canister purge valve tube quick connect coupling to the EVAP purge valve.

36. Position the transmission fluid filler tube and tighten the rear retaining nut to 21 ft. lbs. (28 Nm).

37. Install the transmission fluid filler tube front support bracket bolt and tighten to 89 inch lbs. (10 Nm).

38. Position the generator support bracket and tighten the two bolts and the two stud bolts to 89 inch lbs. (10 Nm).

39. Connect the generator wiring harness retainer to the generator support bracket stud bolt.

40. Connect the ETC wiring harness retainer to the generator support bracket stud bolt.

41. Connect the heater coolant hose.

42. Connect the upper radiator hose.

43. Install the TB spacer.

44. Position the crankcase ventilation tube and connect quick connect coupling to the LH valve cover.

45. Connect the fuel supply tube quick connect coupling.

46. Install the engine cover.

47. Connect the negative battery cable.

48. Refill the engine cooling system to the correct level.

6.8L Engine

See Figure 106.

1. Before servicing the vehicle, refer to the Precautions Section.

2. Disconnect the negative battery cable.

3. Drain the engine cooling system.

4. Remove the air intake assembly.

5. Disconnect the fuel supply hose.

6. Disconnect the alternator wiring harnesses.

7. Remove the mounting bolts and remove the alternator support bracket.

8. Compress and slide the hose clamp and disconnect the coolant hose.

9. Disconnect the Electronic Throttle Control (ETC) electrical connector.

10. Disconnect the Throttle Position (TP) sensor electrical connector.

➡The red clip must be pulled out before disconnecting the electrical connectors.

11. Disconnect the quick connect couplings and remove the PCV tube

12. Disconnect the two coolant heated PCV fitting coolant hoses and the body vacuum tube connector.

13. Disconnect the brake booster vacuum hose and the Evaporative Emission (EVAP) hose quick connect coupling.

14. Disconnect the electrical connector, remove the bolt and position the EVAP canister purge valve aside.

15. Remove the bolts and the Throttle Body (TB) and TB spacer as an assembly.

16. Disconnect the heater coolant hose.

17. Disconnect the fuel injector electrical connectors.

18. Disconnect the ignition coil electrical connectors.

19. Remove the transmission fluid indicator and tube support bracket nut.

20. Remove the transmission fluid level indicator tube support bracket nut and position the tube aside.

21. Disconnect the RH engine wiring harness retainers and position the harness aside.

22. Disconnect the LH engine wiring harness retainers and position the harness aside.

23. Remove the bolt and position the engine wiring harness support bracket aside.

24. Remove the bolts and the ignition coils.

25. Remove the bolts, thermostat housing and thermostat. Discard the O-ring seal.

26. Remove the mounting bolts, the intake manifold and the intake manifold gaskets. Discard the gaskets.

To install:

27. Clean the mating surfaces of the cylinder head and the intake manifold with metal surface prep and silicone gasket remover.

28. Install new intake manifold gaskets and position the intake manifold. Loosely install the intake manifold bolts.

29. Using a new O-ring seal, install the thermostat. Loosely install the thermostat housing and bolts.

30. Tighten the intake manifold bolts in two stages, in the sequence shown as follows:
   a. Tighten to 18 inch lbs. (2 Nm).
   b. Tighten to 18 ft. lbs. (25 Nm).

31. Install the ignition coils.

32. Connect the pushpin retainer to the intake manifold bracket.

33. Position the engine harness and connect the three LH engine wiring harness retainers.

34. Position the engine harness and connect the two RH engine wiring harness retainers.

35. Position back the transmission fluid level indicator tube and tighten the nut to 21 ft. lbs. (28 Nm).

36. Connect the 10 ignition coil electrical connectors.

37. Connect the 10 fuel injector electrical connectors.

38. Connect the heater coolant hose.

39. Install the throttle body assembly. For additional information, refer to "Throttle Body, Removal & Installation."

40. Position the EVAP canister purge valve and install the bolt and the electrical connector.

41. Connect the brake booster vacuum hose and the EVAP hose quick connect coupling.

42. Connect the 2 coolant heated PCV fitting coolant hoses and the body vacuum tube connector.

43. Position the PCV tube and connect the quick connect couplings.

44. Connect the TP sensor electrical connector and wiring harness retainer.

45. Connect the ETC electrical connector.

46. Install the upper radiator hose.

47. Position the alternator harness and the generator B+ terminal and install the nut and protective boot.

48. Connect the alternator electrical wiring harness retainer and the alternator electrical connector.

49. Connect the fuel hose quick connect coupling.

50. Install the air intake assembly.

51. Install the engine cover.

52. Connect the negative battery cable.

53. Refill the engine cooling system to the correct level.

6.0L Engine

See Figures 107 and 108.

1. Before servicing the vehicle, refer to the Precautions Section.

2. Disconnect the battery ground cable.

3. Remove the cooling fan stator.

4. Remove the turbocharger pedestal.

Vehicles with dual alternator

5. Remove the accessory drive belt.

6. Remove the bolt and the accessory drive belt tensioner.

7. Remove the accessory drive belt.

8. Remove the bolts, bracket and accessory drive belt idler pulley.

9. Remove the bolts and the accessory drive belt tensioner.

10. Disconnect the alternator electrical connector and the B+ wire.

11. Remove the bolts and the alternator with mounting bracket.

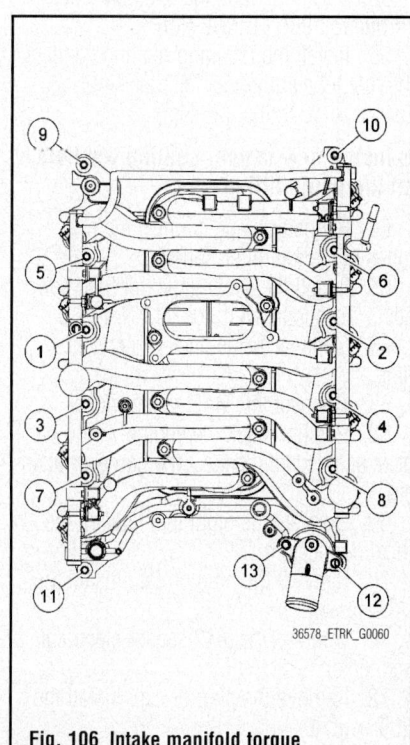

Fig. 106 Intake manifold torque sequence—6.8L Engine

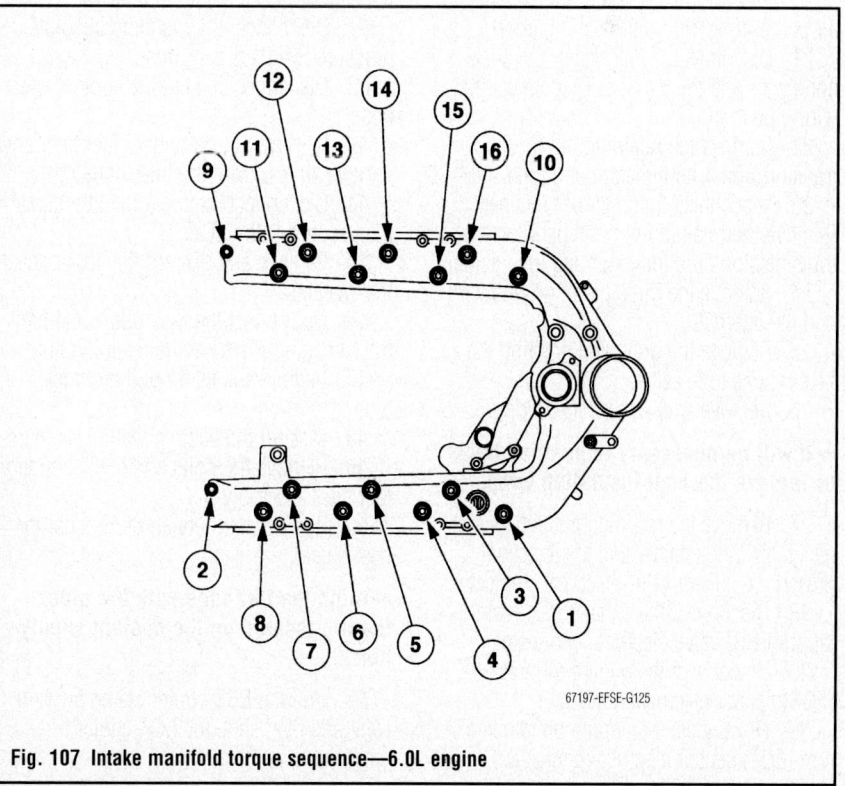

Fig. 107 Intake manifold torque sequence—6.0L engine

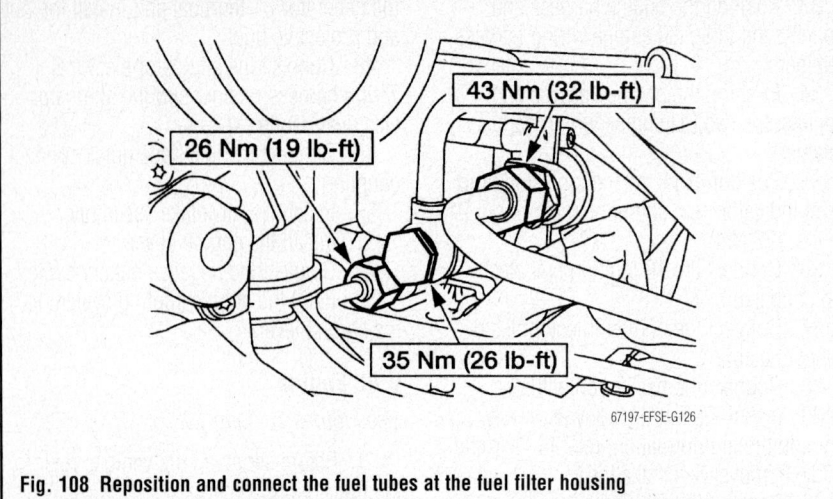

Fig. 108 Reposition and connect the fuel tubes at the fuel filter housing

Vehicles with single alternator
12. Remove the accessory drive belt.

All vehicles
13. Remove the bolt and position the ground wire aside. Disconnect the electrical connector push pin.

14. Remove the conduit and position the wiring aside.

15. Disconnect the locking tab.

16. Remove the bolts.

17. Disconnect the push pin and remove the wiring harness from the conduit.

18. Remove the bolts for the charge air cooler tube and oil fill tube.

19. Disconnect the oil fill tube at the valve cover.

20. Remove the retaining nuts, charge air cooler tube, oil fill tube and bracket.

21. Disconnect the alternator electrical connector and the B+ wire. Disconnect the wiring push pin.

22. Remove the retaining nut for the transmission fluid indicator and tube.

23. Disconnect the push pin retainer. Remove the retaining nut and position the transmission fluid indicator and tube aside.

24. Remove the three bolts, ground wire and the alternator.

25. Remove the bolts and position the heater hose tube aside.

26. Remove and discard the O-ring.

➡It will be necessary to position back or remove the heat insulating wrap.

27. Remove the retaining nut and disconnect the wiring retainer and the injection pressure regulator valve electrical connector.

28. Disconnect the exhaust gas recirculation (EGR) valve electrical connector.

29. Disconnect the engine oil pressure (EOP) sensor electrical connector.

30. Disconnect the engine oil temperature (EOT) sensor electrical connector.

31. Disconnect the EGR throttle position control module electrical connector.

32. Disconnect the EGR throttle position sensor electrical connector.

33. Disconnect the pin-type retainer and engine coolant temperature (ECT) sensor.

34. Remove the ECT sensor.

35. Plug or cap the opening as needed.

36. Disconnect the Intake Air Temperature (IAT2) sensor electrical connector.

37. Remove the IAT2 sensor.

38. Plug or cap the opening as needed.

39. Disconnect the eight fuel injector electrical connectors and wiring connectors.

40. Disconnect the harness retainers. Position the engine wiring harness as needed for intake manifold removal.

41. Disconnect the manifold absolute pressure (MAP) sensor hose.

42. Disconnect the engine coolant vent hose.

43. Remove the secondary fuel filter and remove all fuel from the filter housing.

44. Disconnect the fuel tube fittings at the secondary fuel filter.

45. Remove and discard the copper sealing washers.

46. Disconnect the fuel tube at the fuel filter housing. Remove the retaining nut.

47. Remove the banjo bolt and fuel tube.

48. Discard the copper sealing washers.

49. Remove the bolts and the secondary fuel filter assembly.

50. Remove the nuts and turbocharger heat shield.

➡Align the flat edge with the index feature located on the coolant supply port.

51. Pull the EGR cooler clamp forward, twist and then slide the EGR cooler hose rearward to remove.

52. Remove the bolts and the intake manifold.

53. Remove the intake manifold gaskets.

54. Clean and inspect the gaskets. Install new gaskets if necessary.

55. Clean and inspect the sealing surfaces.

56. Remove and discard the front module O-ring seal.

To install:

➡The locating tabs on the gaskets must be positioned upward and toward the center of the engine, or a leak will occur.

57. Install the intake manifold gaskets. Install a new front module O-ring seal.

58. Install the intake manifold and bolts and tighten in the following sequence.

    a. Loosely install bolts 1–8.

    b. Tighten bolts 9–16 to 11 Nm (8 ft. lbs.).

    c. Tighten all bolts to 11 Nm (8 ft. lbs.).

59. Slide the EGR cooler hose forward and rotate the flat to lock.

60. Install the turbocharger heat shield and nuts.

61. Install the secondary fuel filter assembly and bolts. Toque to 18 ft. lbs. (25 Nm).

➡Install new copper sealing washers.

62. Install the fuel line and banjo bolt. Torque to 28 ft. lbs. (38 Nm).

63. Install the retaining nut and connect the fuel tube at the fuel filter assembly. Torque to 19 ft. lbs. (26 Nm).

➡Install new copper sealing washers on the banjo fitting.

64. Reposition and connect the fuel tubes at the fuel filter housing.

65. Install the secondary fuel filter and cover. Torque to 10 ft. lbs. (14 Nm).

66. Connect the engine coolant vent hose.

67. Connect the MAP sensor hose.

68. Position back the engine wiring harness as needed. Connect the harness retainers.

69. Connect the eight fuel injector electrical connectors.

70. Remove the plug or cap. Install the IAT2 sensor.

71. Connect the IAT2 sensor electrical connector.

72. Remove the plug or cap. Install the ECT sensor.

73. Connect the ECT sensor electrical connector and the pin-type retainer.

74. Connect the EGR throttle position sensor electrical connector.

75. Connect the EGR throttle position control module electrical connector.

76. Connect the EOT sensor electrical connector.

77. Connect the EOP sensor electrical connector.

78. Connect the EGR valve electrical connector.

79. Connect the injector pressure regulator valve electrical connector and position back the heat insulating wrap. Install the wiring retainer and retaining nut.

➡**Install a new O-ring seal and apply clean engine coolant**

80. Install the heater tube and bolts.

81. Install the alternator, ground wire and the three bolts.

82. Position back the transmission fluid indicator and tube and install the retaining nut.

83. Connect the push pin retainer.

84. Install the retaining nut for the transmission fluid indicator and tube.

85. Connect the alternator B+ wire and electrical connector. Position back the boot. Connect the wiring push pin.

86. Position the charge air cooler tube, oil fill tube and bracket. Install the retaining nuts.

87. Connect the oil fill tube at the valve cover.

88. Install the bolts for the charge air cooler tube and oil fill tube.

89. Install the conduit and bolts.

90. Install the wiring harness into the conduit and connect the push pin.

91. Install the bolts.

92. Connect the locking tab.

93. Connect the electrical connector push pin. Position back the ground wire and install the bolt.

Vehicles with single alternator

94. Install the accessory drive belt.

Vehicles with dual alternator

95. Install the alternator with mounting bracket and bolts.

96. Connect the alternator B+ wire and electrical connector. Position the boot.

97. Install the accessory drive belt tensioner and bolts.

98. Position the accessory drive belt idler pulley. Install the bracket and bolts.

99. Install the accessory drive belt.

100. Install the accessory drive belt tensioner and bolt.

101. Install the accessory drive belt.

All vehicles

102. Install the cooling fan stator.

103. Install the turbocharger pedestal and turbocharger.

104. Connect the battery ground cable.

OIL PAN

REMOVAL & INSTALLATION

4.6L, 5.4L & 6.8L Engines

See Figures 109 through 115.

1. Before servicing the vehicle, refer to the Precautions Section.

2. Disconnect the negative battery cable.

3. Raise and safely support the vehicle.

4. Remove the intake manifold. For additional information, refer to "Intake Manifold, Removal & Installation."

5. Remove the fan shroud and engine cooling fan. For additional information, refer to "Engine Fan, Removal & Installation."

6. Disconnect the alternator electrical connectors.

7. Loosen the mounting bolts and position the alternator aside.

8. Remove the retainers and the shield.

9. Disconnect the coolant hose from the heater outlet tube and remove the heater outlet tube stud, 4.6L engine only.

10. Disconnect the Knock Sensor (KS) electrical connector and engine wiring harness retainers, 5.4L Engine only.

11. Disconnect the heater coolant hose from the heater outlet tube, 5.4L Engine only.

12. Remove the 2 heater outlet tube studs, 5.4L Engine only.

13. Remove the heater outlet tube and discard the O-ring seals.

14. Remove the two upper transmission-to-engine bolts.

15. Assemble the Engine Lifting Bracket and the Modular Engine Lift Bar Adapter.

16. Install the Engine Lifting Bracket and the Modular Engine Lift Bar Adapter.

17. Install the Engine Support Bar and support the engine.

18. Drain the engine oil, remove and discard the oil filter.

19. Remove the nut and position aside the transmission cooler tube support

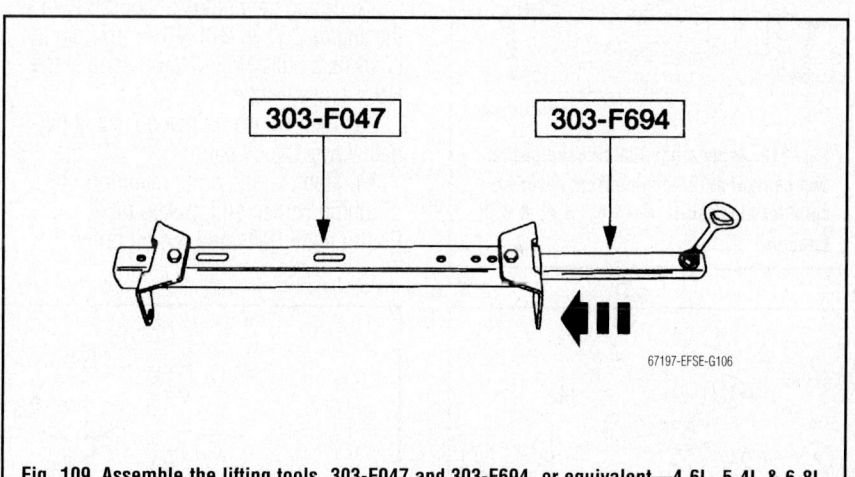

Fig. 109 Assemble the lifting tools, 303-F047 and 303-F694, or equivalent—4.6L, 5.4L & 6.8L Engines

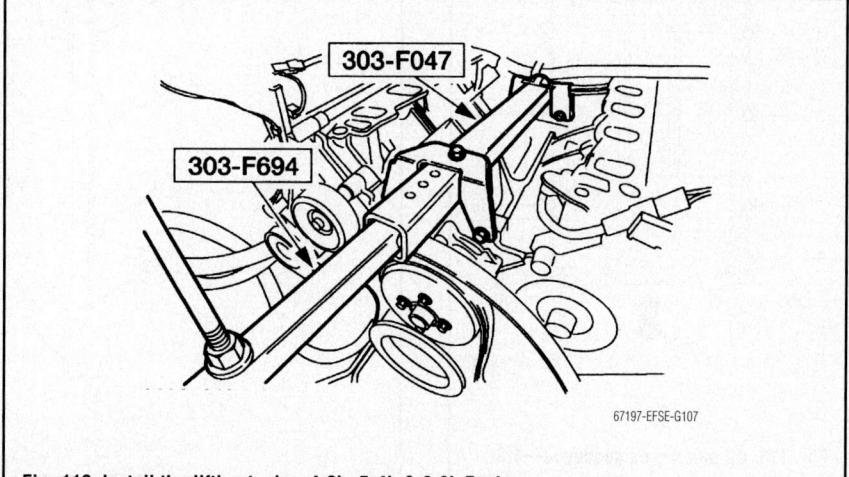

Fig. 110 Install the lifting tools—4.6L, 5.4L & 6.8L Engines

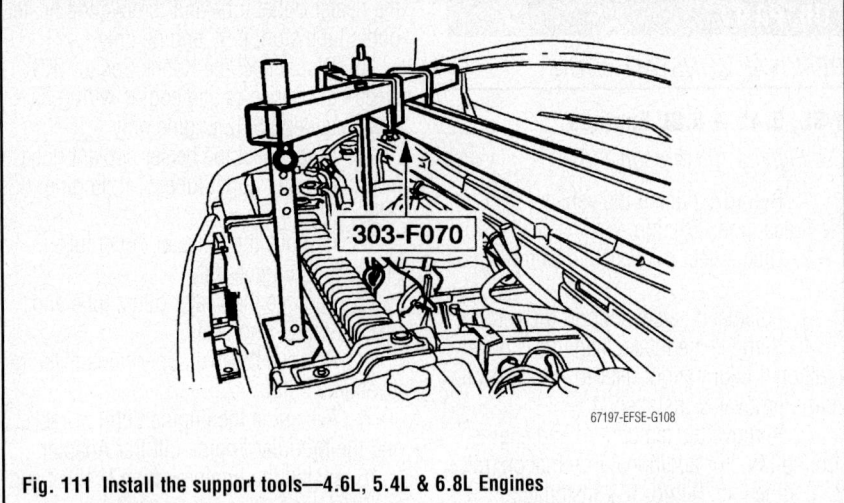

Fig. 111 Install the support tools—4.6L, 5.4L & 6.8L Engines

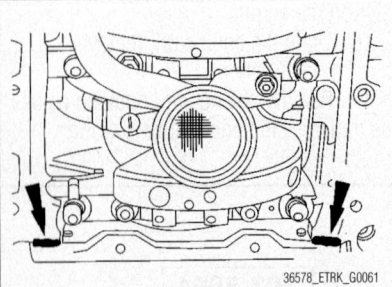

Fig. 112 Apply a bead of silicone gasket and sealant at the engine front cover-to-cylinder block surface—4.6L, 5.4L & 6.8L Engines

bracket and the starter wiring harness support bracket.

20. Remove the four engine support insulator-to-crossmember nuts.

21. Remove the two bolts and the flexplate inspection plate.

22. Using the Engine Support Bar, raise the engine 260.35 mm (10.25 in) from the crankshaft pulley to the lower edge of the No. 1 crossmember.

23. Remove the oil pan bolts and partially lower the oil pan.

24. Remove the bolts retaining the oil pump screen and pickup tube. Position the bolts and the oil pump screen and pickup tube in the oil pan.

25. Remove the oil pan from the rear of the engine. Discard the oil pan gasket.

To install:

❊❊ WARNING

Make sure the O-ring is in place and not damaged. A missing or damaged O-ring can cause foam in the lubrication system, low oil pressure and severe engine damage.

➡ Clean and inspect the mating surfaces and install a new O-ring. Lubricate the O-ring with clean engine oil.

26. Install the oil pump screen and pickup tube. Tighten the tube base bolts to 89 inch lbs. (10 Nm); the bracket bolt to 18 ft. lbs. (25 Nm).

➡ If not secured within four minutes, the sealant must be removed and the sealing area cleaned. To clean the sealing area, use silicone gasket remover and metal surface prep. Follow the directions on the packaging. Failure to follow this procedure can cause future oil leakage.

27. Apply a bead of silicone gasket and sealant at the crankshaft rear seal retainer-to-cylinder block surface.

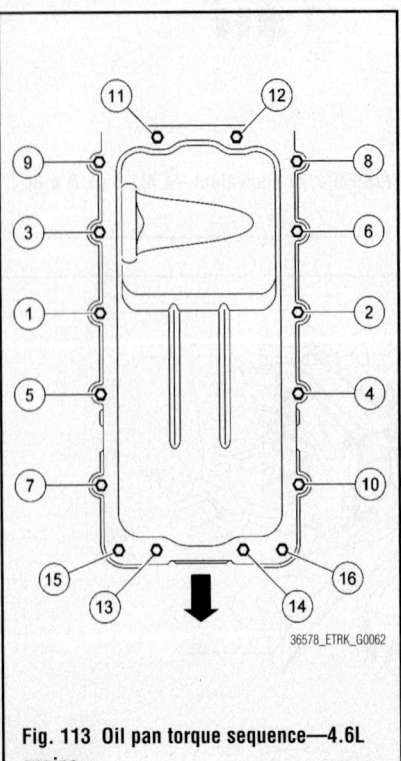

Fig. 113 Oil pan torque sequence—4.6L engine

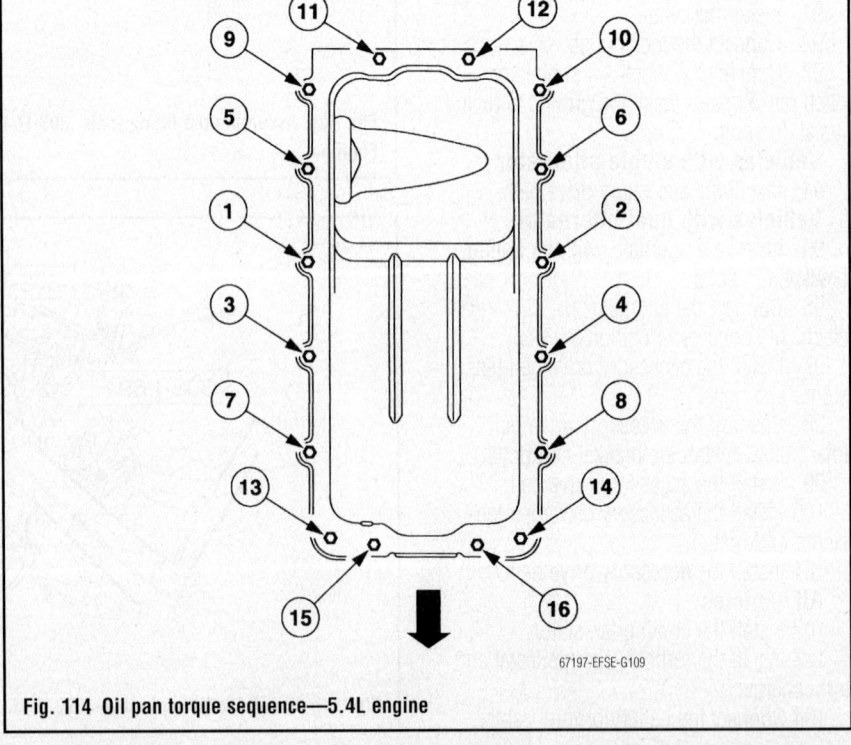

Fig. 114 Oil pan torque sequence—5.4L engine

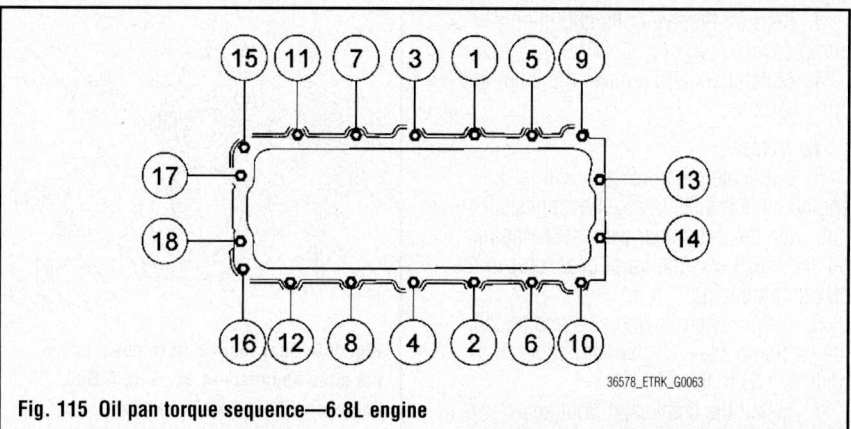

Fig. 115 Oil pan torque sequence—6.8L engine

36578_ETRK_G0063

28. Apply a bead of silicone gasket and sealant at the engine front cover-to-cylinder block surface.

29. Position the pan. Tighten the bolts in three steps, in the sequence shown.
   a. Tighten to 18 inch lbs. (2 Nm).
   b. Tighten to 15 ft. lbs. (20 Nm).
   c. Tighten an additional 90 degrees.

30. Install a new oil filter.

31. Lower the engine and remove the special tools.

32. Install the four engine mount nuts. Torque to 66 ft. lbs. (90 Nm).

33. Install the flexplate inspection plate. Torque to 25 ft. lbs. (34 Nm).

34. Lower the vehicle.

35. Install the transmission-to-engine bolts. Torque to 44 ft. lbs. (60 Nm).

➡ **Do not reuse the O-ring seals. Lubricate the new O-ring seals with clean engine coolant before installing the heater outlet tube.**

36. Insert the heater outlet tube over the new seals.

37. Install the heater outlet tube studs, 4.6L engine only.

38. Position the transmission fluid filler tube and install the nut, 4.6L engine only.

39. Install the heater outlet tube studs, 5.4L engine only.

40. Position the transmission fluid filler tube and install the nut, 5.4L engine only.

41. Connect the hose to the heater outlet tube.

42. Install the wiring retainers in the heater outlet tube bracket.

43. Install the knock sensor electrical connector retainer.

44. Install the engine harness routing clip retainer.

45. Install the retainers and the shield.

46. Install the fan shroud and the engine cooling fan.

47. Install the intake manifold.

❄❄ **WARNING**

The oil pump must be primed prior to starting the engine.

48. Fill the engine with clean engine oil.

49. Start the engine and check for leaks.

6.0L Engine

Lower Pan

1. Before servicing the vehicle, refer to the Precautions Section.

2. Raise and safely support the vehicle.

3. Disconnect the negative battery cable.

4. Release the engine cover latches and remove the engine cover.

5. Remove the engine fan. For additional information, refer to "Engine Fan, Removal & Installation."

6. Remove the A/C compressor. For additional information, refer to "A/C Compressor, Removal & Installation."

7. Remove the power steering pump upper mounting bolt.

8. Remove the left fan stator stand-off.

9. Remove the bolts and position the power steering pump aside.

➡ **The front bolt will remain in the power steering pump.**

10. Remove the oil pan drain plug.

11. Loosen the exhaust pipe retaining nuts.

12. Remove the motor mount retaining nuts.

13. Remove the right fan stator stand-off. Remove the bolt and position the cable aside.

14. Install the engine lifting adapters.

15. Install the engine lifting attachment and floor crane.

❄❄ **CAUTION**

Use care when raising the engine to avoid engine or body damage

16. Raise the engine.

17. Remove the bolts and position back the oil pan until the oil pick up tube bolts are accessible.

18. Remove the bolts and let the oil pick-up tube go into the oil pan. Remove the oil pan.

19. Remove and discard the oil pick-up tube O-ring seal.

20. Remove the press-in-place gasket and discard.

21. Clean and inspect the sealing surfaces.

To install:

22. Install a new press-in-place gasket into the upper oil pan.

23. Install a new O-ring seal on the oil pick-up tube and position the oil pick-up tube in the oil pan.

24. Position the oil pan in the vehicle.

25. Install the oil pan pick-up tube and tighten the bolts to 115 inch lbs. (13 Nm).

26. Install the oil pan and bolts as follows:
   a. Install the five longer oil pan bolts.
   b. Install the remaining oil pan bolts.
   c. Tighten all bolts to 115 inch lbs. (13 Nm).

27. Lower the engine.

28. Remove the floor crane and engine lifting attachment.

29. Remove the special tools.

30. Position back the cable and install the bolt. Install the right fan stator stand-off.

➡ **Tighten the top retaining nut first.**

31. Install the motor mount retaining nuts.

32. Tighten the exhaust pipe retaining nuts.

33. Clean and inspect the oil pan drain plug and gasket. Install new, if necessary.

34. Install the oil drain plug.

35. Reposition the power steering pump and install the power steering pump bolts.

36. Install the left fan stator stand-off.

37. Install the upper power steering mounting bolt.

38. Fill the engine with clean engine oil.

39. Install the engine cover.

40. Connect the battery ground cable.

41. Install the A/C compressor.

42. Install the cooling fan stator.

43. Run the engine and check for leaks.

Upper Pan

1. Before servicing the vehicle, refer to the Precautions Section.

2. Raise and safely support the vehicle.

3. Remove the lower oil pan.

4. Remove the mounting bolts and the upper oil pan.

5. Remove and discard the gasket.

To install:

6. Install a new press-in-place gasket.

7. Install the upper oil pan and tighten the bolts to 115 inch lbs. (13 Nm).

8. Install the lower oil pan. For additional information, refer to "Oil Pan, Removal & Installation, Lower Pan."

OIL PUMP

REMOVAL & INSTALLATION

4.6L, 5.4L & 6.8L Engines

See Figure 116.

1. Before servicing the vehicle, refer to the Precautions Section.

2. Raise and safely support the vehicle.

3. Remove the oil pan. For additional information, refer to "Oil Pan, Removal & Installation."

4. Remove the crankshafts sprocket. For additional information, refer to "Timing Chain and Sprockets, Removal & Installation."

5. Remove the bolts and oil pump.

To install:

6. Clean and inspect the mating surfaces, lubricate the new O-ring with clean engine oil and install a new O-ring seal.

7. Install the oil pump and tighten bolts in sequence to 89 inch lbs. (10 Nm).

8. Install the crankshaft sprocket.

9. Install the oil pan.

10. Start the engine and check for leaks.

6.0L Engine

1. Before servicing the vehicle, refer to the Precautions Section.

2. Remove the crankshaft front seal. For additional information, refer to "Crankshaft Front Seal, Removal & Installation."

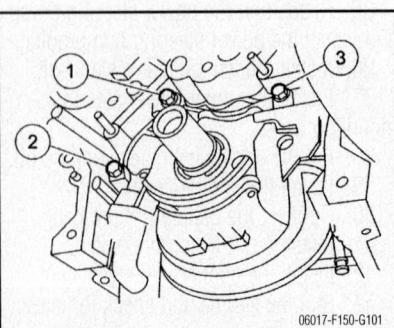

Fig. 116 Oil pump mounting bolt torque sequence—4.6L, 5.4L & 6.8L Engines

3. Remove the five bolts and the oil pump cover.

4. Matchmark and remove the inner and outer gerotors.

To install:

5. Lubricate the inner gear with clean engine oil and install onto the crankshaft. Lubricate the outer gear with clean engine oil and mesh with the inner gear rotor in the oil pump housing.

6. Install a new O-ring seal and install the oil pump cover. Tighten the mounting bolts to 115 ft. lbs. (13 Nm).

7. Install the crankshaft front seal.

PISTON AND RING

POSITIONING

See Figure 117.

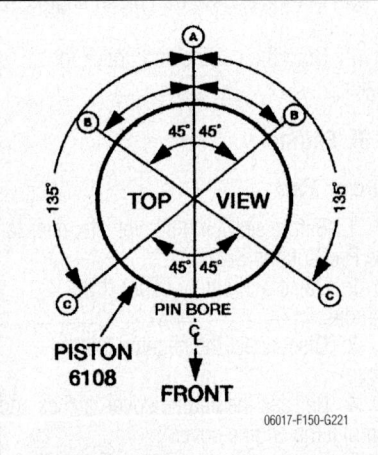

Fig. 117 Piston ring arrangement—all gasoline engines

REAR MAIN SEAL

REMOVAL & INSTALLATION

4.6L, 5.4L & 6.8L Engines

Without Retainer Plate

See Figure 118.

1. Before servicing the vehicle, refer to the Precautions Section.

2. Remove the flexplate. For additional information, refer to "Flexplate, Removal & Installation."

3. Remove the engine rear cover plate.

4. Using the Slide Hammer and Crankshaft Rear Oil Slinger Remover, remove the crankshaft oil slinger. Discard the oil slinger.

5. Using the slide hammer and crankshaft rear oil seal remover, remove the crankshaft rear seal.

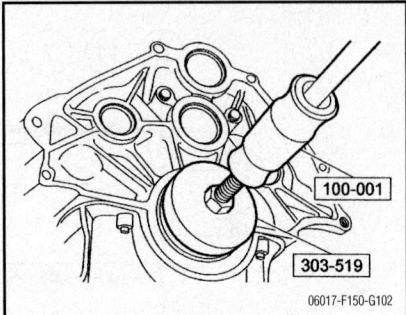

Fig. 118 Rear main seal removal using the slide hammer—4.6L, 5.4L & 6.8L Engines without Retainer Plate

To install:

6. Lubricate the inner lip of the crankshaft rear seal with clean engine oil. Using the Crankshaft Rear Oil Seal Installers, install a new crankshaft rear seal.

7. Using the Crankshaft Rear Oil Seal Installers and Crankshaft Rear Oil Slinger Installer, install a new crankshaft rear oil slinger.

8. Install the engine rear cover plate.

9. Install the flexplate.

With Retainer Plate

See Figure 119.

1. Before servicing the vehicle, refer to the Precautions Section.

2. Remove the flexplate. For additional information, refer to "Flexplate, Removal & Installation."

3. Remove the engine rear cover plate.

4. Using the Slide Hammer and Crankshaft Rear Oil Slinger Remover, remove the crankshaft oil slinger. Discard the oil slinger.

5. Using the slide hammer and crankshaft rear oil seal remover, remove the crankshaft rear seal.

6. Remove the crankshaft rear seal retainer plate.

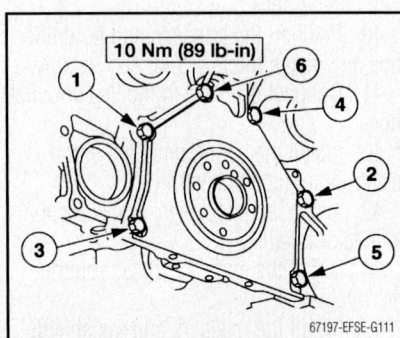

Fig. 119 Retainer plate torque sequence—4.6L, 5.4L & 6.8L Engines with Retainer Plate

To install:

7. Apply a bead of gasket maker to the rear crankshaft seal retainer plate mating surface on the engine block.

➡The rear crankshaft seal retainer plate does not have a sealant groove. Gasket maker must be applied to the rear crankshaft seal retainer plate mating surface on the engine block.

8. Install the retainer plate and tighten the bolts in sequence to 89 inch lbs. (10 Nm).

9. Lubricate the inner lip of the crankshaft rear seal with clean engine oil. Using the Crankshaft Rear Oil Seal Installers, install a new crankshaft rear seal.

10. Using the Crankshaft Rear Oil Seal Installers and Crankshaft Rear Oil Slinger Installer, install a new crankshaft rear oil slinger.

11. Install the engine rear cover plate.

12. Install the flexplate.

6.0L Engine

See Figures 120 and 121.

1. Before servicing the vehicle, refer to the Precautions Section.

2. Remove the transmission assembly. For additional information, refer to "Automatic Transmission Assembly, Removal & Installation."

3. Remove the flexplate. For additional information, refer to "Flexplate, Removal & Installation."

➡Use extreme care when removing the flywheel front adapter to prevent damage to the alignment dowel pin.

4. Remove the flywheel front adapter.

✳✳ CAUTION

To prevent engine damage, do not remove the rear primary crankshaft flange bolts under any circum-

stances. If the flange is removed and reinstalled, it will result in engine vibration and premature transmission component wear.

5. Using a center punch, mark a location for 2 holes 180 degrees apart, 0.37 inches (9.53 mm) from the outer diameter of the crankshaft flange. Using a drill bit of the appropriate size for the slide hammer being used, drill a hole on each side of the crankshaft rear seal as shown. Drill the holes to a depth of 0.34 inches (8.76 mm) to capture the metal case of the crankshaft seal as well as the wear sleeve.

6. Using the 2 drilled holes, the Slide Hammer and a commercially available body dent puller attachment, walk the seal out of the rear cover by alternating from side to side to remove the crankshaft rear seal.

7. Using the puller tool 100-001, remove the rear main seal.

➡Production engines will not have a wear sleeve.

8. If equipped with a crankshaft wear sleeve, use the tool 303-771 to remove the crankshaft rear wear sleeve.

9. Clean and inspect the crankshaft sealing surface.

To install:

➡The crankshaft rear oil seal and wear sleeve are installed as an assembly.

➡ Lubricate the outer diameter of the rubber seal with a solution of dish soap and water (approximately 50/50 mix) prior to assembly. Do not use any other type of lubricant.

10. Apply a bead of Threadlock 262® around the circumference of the outer rear edge of the secondary crankshaft flange.

11. Using tool 303-770, install crankshaft rear oil seal.

12. Install the flywheel front adapter.

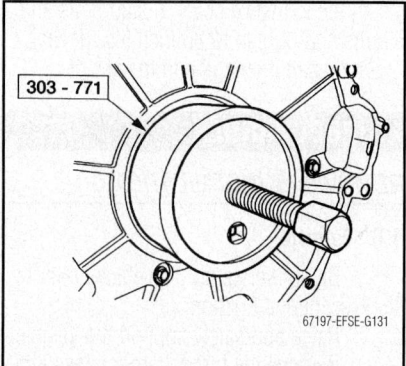

Fig. 120 Rear main seal wear sleeve removal—6.0L engine

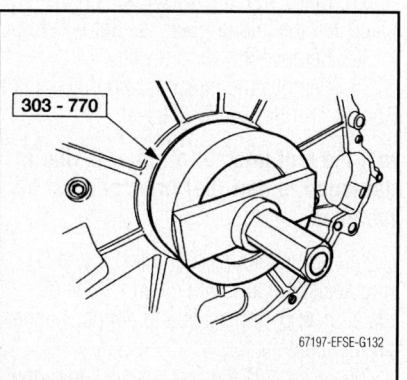

Fig. 121 Rear main seal installation—6.0L engine

13. Install the flexplate or flywheel.

14. Install the transmission.

ROCKER ARMS/SHAFTS

REMOVAL & INSTALLATION

6.0L Engine

1. Before servicing the vehicle, refer to the Precautions Section.

2. Remove the engine from the vehicle. For additional information, refer to "Engine Assembly, Removal & Installation."

3. Remove the right hand valve cover.

4. Remove the right hand high-pressure oil rail-to-valve cover gasket.

5. If replacing rocker arms on the LH side, remove the protective covering from the LH cylinder head.

6. Locate the dowel hole in the vibration damper. The hole is located between 2 of the 4 bolts that attach the damper to the front of the crankshaft.

7. Rotate the crankshaft until the dowel hole is at the 12 o'clock position. The No. 1 piston should be on the compression stroke. Wiggle the rocker on the No. 1 cylinder to verify both intake and exhaust rocker arms are able to move freely. If the intake and exhaust rocker arms do not move freely, rotate the crankshaft one complete revolution. The rocker arms for cylinders 1, 2, 7 and 8 are now positioned for service.

➡If servicing all rocker arms, or any of the rocker arms for cylinders 1, 2, 7 and 8, the remainder of this procedure must be performed before rotating the crankshaft to prepare the engine-to-service cylinders 3, 4, 5 and 6.

8. If not servicing cylinders 1, 2, 7 and 8 or if service to those cylinders has been completed, rotate the crankshaft one complete revolution to service the rocker arms for cylinders 3, 4, 5 and 6. Complete the rest of this procedure for rocker arms on cylinders 3, 4, 5 and 6.

9. Remove the crankcase-to-head tube(s).

✳✳ WARNING

Do not remove the oil rail end plugs or acoustic wave attenuator port fitting. Service parts are not available to support these components.

10. Remove the 9 bolts and the high-pressure oil rail.

11. If the crankcase-to-head tube separated, using the High Pressure Supply Tube Remover, remove the lower crankcase-to-head tube.

12. Inspect the D-ring seals for damage (nicks, cuts and gouges). If damaged, replace the crankcase-to-head tube.

> ※※ **WARNING**
> Do not attempt to apply battery voltage to the fuel injector or damage to the fuel injector may occur.

13. Using the Injector Connector Release Tool, push the fuel injector electrical connector out of the rocker arm carrier.

14. Prior to removing the injector assembly, insert clean shop towels in the oil drain holes adjacent to each glow plug.

> ※※ **WARNING**
> To prevent engine damage, do not use air tools to remove the fuel injectors.

15. Loosen the bolt and remove the bolt and fuel injector hold-down assembly and the fuel injector. Remove and discard the O-ring seals and copper washer.

➡ **The bolt is part of the fuel injector hold-down assembly.**

16. Insert the injector hold-down clamp into the Rocker Arm Service Tool base.

➡ **Make sure the notch in the base is aligned in the hold-down clamp.**

17. Install the injector hold-down clamp and Rocker Arm Service Tool base in between the bridges as if installing a fuel injector.

> ※※ **WARNING**
> While centering the base between the 2 bridges, snug the hold-down bolt only. Do not tighten it or engine damage can occur.

18. Install the Rocker Arm Service Tool plate on top of the bridges with the small point of the plate in between the exhaust rocker and bridge. Install the Rocker Arm Service Tool bolt and compress the valve springs until the plate contacts the top of the tool base.

➡ **If the rocker arm is severely worn, insert a small pry bar between the exhaust rocker arm and bridge to gain clearance by compressing the valves slightly.**

19. Disengage the rocker arm from the push rod. Then rotate the rocker arm out while compressing down on the rocker arm retaining clip. Remove and discard the rocker arm retaining clip. Repeat the step for the other rocker arm.

➡**When removing the rocker arm, be careful not to drop the ball from the fulcrum plate or rocker arm socket.**

20. Remove the push rod.

> ※※ **WARNING**
> To prevent engine damage, keep the push rods in the order in which they were removed. Install the push rods back in their original positions. The push rods are directional and the copper-coated end must be installed in the upward position where it will contact the rocker arm.

21. With the rocker arms removed, remove the Rocker Arm Service Tool bolt and the Rocker Arm Service Tool plate to gain access to the valve bridges.

22. Matchmark the location of the valve bridges and remove the valve bridges.

To install:

23. Apply clean engine oil on the valve stems and install the valve bridges.

24. Install the Rocker Arm Service Tool plate and bolt. Tighten the bolt until the plate contacts the top of the Rocker Arm Service Tool base.

25. Apply clean engine oil to each end of the push rods and insert them into their respective positions.

26. Place a dab of multi-purpose grease in the fulcrum socket to hold the ball in place while installing the rocker arms.

27. Apply clean engine oil to the top center of the valve bridges prior to installing the rocker arms.

28. Insert the rocker arm under the fulcrum and ball, rotate the rocker arm into place and position onto the push rod. Install a new rocker arm retaining clip.

29. Repeat the step for the other rocker arm.

30. Remove the Rocker Arm Service Tool bolt and plate.

31. Make sure the rocker arms remain in place and the fulcrum ball has not fallen out.

32. Remove the shop towels.

33. Remove the injector hold down and Rocker Arm Service Tool base.

➡**If the fuel injector oil inlet D-ring is damaged, a new fuel injector must be installed.**

34. Lubricate the fuel injector and O-ring seals liberally with clean engine oil. Install new O-ring seals and copper washer on the fuel injector.

35. Assemble the fuel injector hold down and bolt on the fuel injector and install the assembly.

> ※※ **WARNING**
> Be sure the injector wiring is clear of all moving parts or engine damage can occur.

36. Install the fuel injector electrical connector into the rocker arm carrier.

> ※※ **WARNING**
> Using the bolts to push the high-pressure oil rail into the fuel injectors can damage the fuel injectors and high-pressure oil rail.

37. Apply clean engine oil to the top fuel injector O-ring seals and position the high-pressure oil rail on the injectors.

38. Place the high-pressure oil rail on top of the carrier so that the 4 single ball tubes are engaging the fuel injector lead angle.

39. Insert 3 guide bolts, 2 on the ends of the straight side of the high-pressure oil rail and one in the middle of the wavy side of the high pressure oil rail. Install the guide studs 6 to 7 turns.

40. Manually press the high-pressure oil rail into the fuel injectors.

41. Inspect that the high-pressure oil rail mounting feet are flat against the mounting surface.

42. Loosely install the 6 bolts.

43. Remove the 3 guide bolts.

44. Loosely install the 3 remaining bolts.

45. Tighten the 9 bolts in the sequence shown to 13 Nm (115 lb-in).

46. Apply clean engine oil to the D-ring seals and reassemble the crankcase-to-head tube if necessary. Install the crankcase-to-head tube(s). and tighten to 60 ft. lbs. (82 Nm).

47. If removed, cover the LH cylinder head with an appropriate covering.

48. Install the RH high-pressure oil rail-to-valve cover gasket.

49. Position the RH valve cover gasket. Install the RH valve cover, 6 stud bolts and 5 bolts and tighten to 80 inch lbs. (9 Nm).

50. Install the engine in the vehicle.

TURBOCHARGER

REMOVAL & INSTALLATION

6.0L Engine

1. Before servicing the vehicle, refer to the Precautions Section.

2. Raise and safely support the vehicle.

3. Remove the turbocharger intake tube.

4. Loosen the turbocharger outlet clamp.

5. Remove the bolt and position the ground wire aside. Disconnect the electrical connector pushpin.

6. Remove the conduit and position the wiring aside.

7. Remove the three bolts for the Charge Air Cooler (CAC) tube.

8. Remove the two nuts, CAC tube and bracket.

9. Remove the turbocharger outlet clamp.

10. Remove and discard the 2 nuts. Position the exhaust downpipe aside.

11. Remove the LH nuts and bolts for the exhaust tube-to-exhaust manifold flange. Discard the nuts.

12. Remove the RH nuts and bolts for the exhaust tube-to-exhaust manifold flange. Discard the nuts.

13. Remove the EGR cooler clamp.

14. Remove the turbocharger inlet clamp and turbocharger adapter pipe.

15. Disconnect the turbocharger variable vane hydraulic control valve electrical connector and remove the wiring harness from the retaining clip.

16. Remove the bolt for the turbocharger oil feed tube.

17. Remove the bolts and the turbocharger oil feed tube.

18. Remove and discard the gasket and O-ring seal.

19. Remove the RH turbocharger mounting bolt.

20. Remove the LH turbocharger mounting bolts.

✳✳ WARNING

Use care not to damage the turbocharger outlet hose when removing the turbocharger.

21. Position the turbocharger to remove the turbocharger drain tube. Remove the turbocharger from the vehicle through the passenger compartment. Remove and discard the O-ring seals.

To install:

22. Position the turbocharger in the vehicle. Install the turbocharger drain tube and turbocharger.

➡Apply anti-seize lubricant to the bolt threads prior to installation.

23. Install the turbocharger mounting bolts and tighten to 23 ft. lbs. (31 Nm).

24. Lubricate the oil inlet hole of the turbocharger assembly with clean engine oil and spin the compressor wheel several times to coat the bearings with oil.

25. Use a new gasket and O-ring seal when installing the oil feed tube. Position

back the turbocharger oil feed tube and install a new gasket and tighten the bolts to 17 ft. lbs. (23 Nm).

26. Install the bolt for the turbocharger oil feed tube and tighten to 89 inch lbs. (10 Nm).

27. Connect the turbocharger variable vane hydraulic control valve electrical connector and install the wiring harness into the retaining clip.

28. Position the turbocharger adapter pipe and install the turbocharger inlet clamp.

29. Install the EGR cooler clamp.

30. Install the RH bolts and new nuts for the exhaust tube-to-exhaust manifold flange and tighten to 20 ft. lbs. (27 Nm).

31. Install the LH bolts and new nuts for the exhaust tube-to-exhaust manifold flange and tighten to 20 ft. lbs. (27 Nm).

32. Position the exhaust downpipe. Install the turbocharger exhaust clamp.

33. Install the new retaining nuts at the exhaust clamp and tighten to 35 ft. lbs. (47 Nm).

34. Position the CAC tube and bracket and install the retaining nuts.

35. Install the bolts for the CAC tube and oil fill tube.

36. Install the wiring harness conduit and mounting bolts.

37. Connect the electrical connector pushpin. Position the ground wire and install the bolt.

38. Tighten the turbocharger outlet clamp to 106 inch lbs. (12 Nm).

39. Install the turbocharger intake tube.

TIMING CHAIN COVER AND SEAL

REMOVAL & INSTALLATION

4.6L, 5.4L & 6.8L Engines

See Figures 122 and 123.

1. Before servicing the vehicle, refer to the Precautions Section.

2. Raise and safely support the vehicle.

3. Remove the radiator. For additional information, refer to "Radiator, Removal & Installation."

4. Remove the valve covers. For additional information, refer to "Valve Covers, Removal & Installation."

5. Drain the engine oil and reinstall the drain plug.

6. Remove the nut and position the LH radio interference capacitor aside.

7. Remove the nut and position the RH radio interference capacitor aside.

8. Loosen the water pump pulley bolts.

9. Rotate the tensioner clockwise and remove the accessory drive belt.

10. Remove the water pump pulley bolts and the water pump pulley.

11. Remove the bolt and the accessory drive belt idler pulley.

12. Remove the bolts and position the power steering pump aside.

13. Disconnect the A/C compressor electrical connector.

14. Disconnect the Crankshaft Position (CKP) sensor electrical connector.

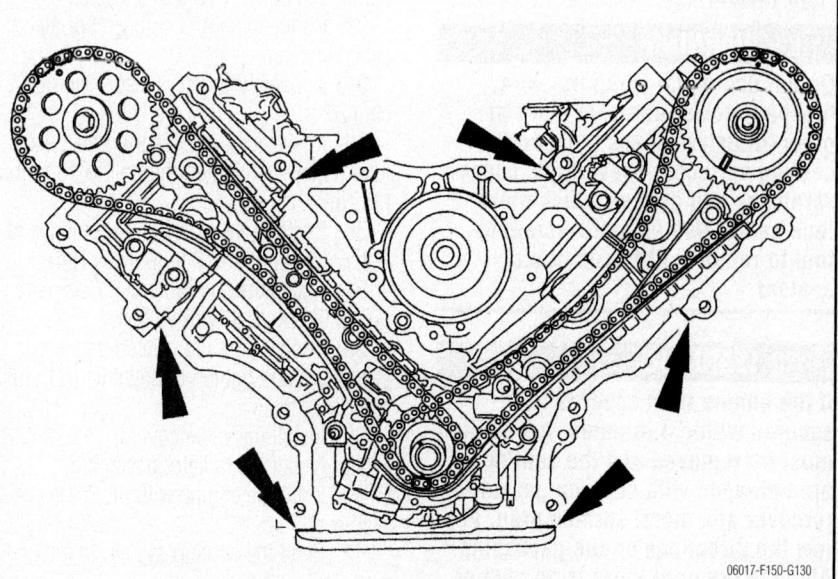

06017-F150-G130

Fig. 122 Apply a bead of silicone gasket and sealant along the cylinder head-to-cylinder block surface and the oil pan-to-cylinder block surface, at the locations indicated—4.6L, 5.4L & 6.8L Engines

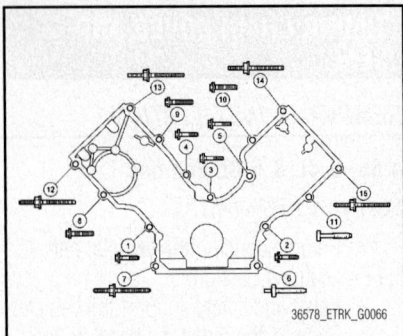

Fig. 123 Engine front cover torque sequence—4.6L, 5.4L & 6.8L Engines

15. Remove the nut and position aside the transmission cooler tube support bracket and the starter wiring harness support bracket.

16. Disconnect the Camshaft Position (CMP) sensor electrical connector.

17. Remove the bolt and the CMP sensor.

18. Remove the crankshaft pulley. For additional information, refer to "Crankshaft Damper, Removal & Installation."

19. Remove the crankshaft front seal. For additional information, refer to "Crankshaft Front Seal, Removal & Installation."

20. Remove the front 4 oil pan bolts.

21. Remove the 15 engine front cover fasteners.

22. Remove the engine front cover from the front cover-to-cylinder block dowel.

23. Remove and discard the front cover gaskets.

To install:

⁕⁕ WARNING

Do not use metal scrapers, wire brushes, power abrasive discs or other abrasive means to clean the sealing surfaces. These tools cause scratches and gouges which make leak paths. Use a plastic scraping tool to remove all traces of old sealant.

⁕⁕ WARNING

If the engine front cover is not secured within 4 minutes, the sealant must be removed and the sealing area cleaned with silicone gasket remover and metal surface prep. Follow the directions on the packaging. Allow to dry until there is no sign of wetness, or 4 minutes, whichever is longer. Failure to follow this procedure can cause future oil leakage.

24. Apply a bead of silicone gasket and sealant along the cylinder head-to-cylinder block surface and the oil pan-to-cylinder block surface, at the locations shown.

25. Install the engine front cover with the engine front cover gasket on the front cover-to-cylinder block dowel and loosely install the bolts.

26. Tighten the front cover fasteners in the sequence shown as follows:
   a. 4.6L Engines
   • 18 ft. lbs. (25 Nm).
   b. 5.4L Engines
   • Step 1: Fasteners 1—5 to 18 ft. lbs. (25 Nm)
   • Step 2: Fasteners 6—7 to 35 ft. lbs. (48 Nm)
   • Step 3: Fasteners 8—15 to 35 ft. lbs. (48 Nm)
   c. 6.8L Engines
   • Step 1: 15 ft. lbs. (20 Nm)
   • Step 2: Tighten an additional 60°

27. Install the front oil pan bolts to 15 ft. lbs. (20 Nm) plus 60°.

28. Install the crankshaft front seal.

29. Install the crankshaft pulley.

30. Install the CMP sensor and tighten the bolt to 89 inch lbs. (10 Nm). Connect the sensor electrical connector.

31. Position the transmission cooler tube support bracket and the starter wiring harness support bracket and install the nut and tighten as follows:
   a. 4.6L Engines to 89 inch lbs. (10 Nm).
   b. 5.4L Engines to 21 ft. lbs. (28 Nm).

32. Install the power steering pump and tighten the bolts to 18 ft. lbs. (25 Nm).

33. Connect the A/C compressor electrical connector.

34. Connect the CKP sensor electrical connector.

35. Position the accessory drive belt idler pulley and tighten the bolt to 18 ft. lbs. (25 Nm).

36. Position the water pump pulley and tighten the bolts to 18 ft. lbs. (25 Nm).

37. Rotate the tensioner clockwise and install the accessory drive belt.

38. Position the radio interference capacitors and tighten the nuts to 18 ft. lbs. (25 Nm).

39. Install the valve covers.

40. Install the radiator assembly.

41. Refill the engine with oil to the correct level.

42. Refill the cooling system to the correct level.

43. Using a suitable scan tool, perform the Misfire Monitor Neutral Profile Correction procedure, following the on-screen instructions.

TIMING CHAIN AND SPROCKETS

REMOVAL & INSTALLATION

4.6L & 5.4L Engine
See Figures 124 through 135.

1. Before servicing the vehicle, refer to the Precautions Section.

2. Remove the engine front cover. For additional information, refer to "Timing Chain Cover & Seal, Removal & Installation."

3. Remove the crankshaft sensor ring from the crankshaft.

4. Rotate the crankshaft until the timing mark on the RH camshaft sprocket is approximately at the 11 o'clock position and the timing mark on the LH camshaft sprocket is approximately at the 1 o'clock position.

5. Install the Camshaft Aligner and Camshaft Pulley Aligner on the camshaft.

⁕⁕ WARNING

If one or both of the tensioner mounting bolts are loosened or removed, the tensioner-sealing bead must be inspected for seal integrity. If cracks, tears or separation from the tensioner body or permanent compression of the seal bead is observed, install a new tensioner or engine damage may occur.

6. Remove the bolts, timing chain tensioners and timing chain tensioner arms.

7. Remove the timing chains and crankshaft sprocket.

8. Remove the mounting bolts and remove the timing chain guides.

To install:

⁕⁕ WARNING

Timing chain procedures must be followed exactly or damage to valves and pistons will result.

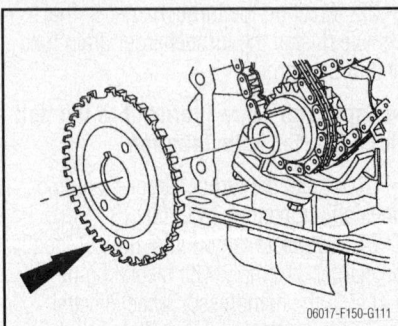

Fig. 124 Crankshaft sensor ring—4.6L & 5.4L Engine

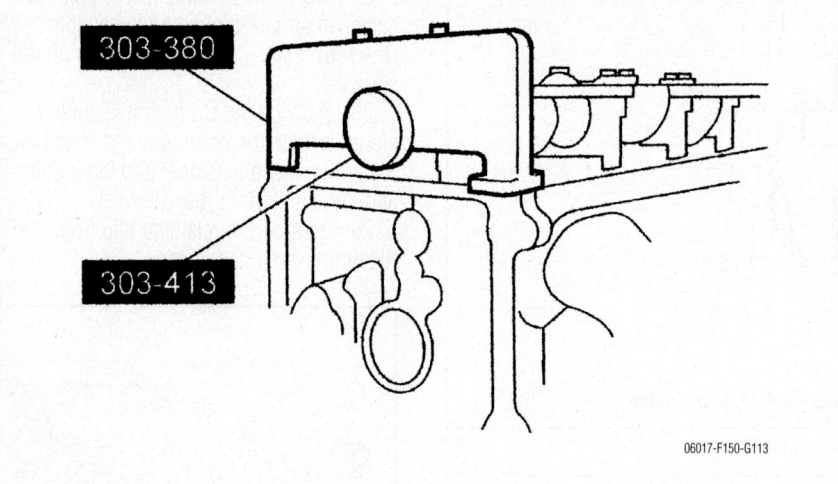

06017-F150-G113

Fig. 125 Install the Camshaft Aligner and Camshaft Pulley Aligner on the camshaft—4.6L & 5.4L Engine

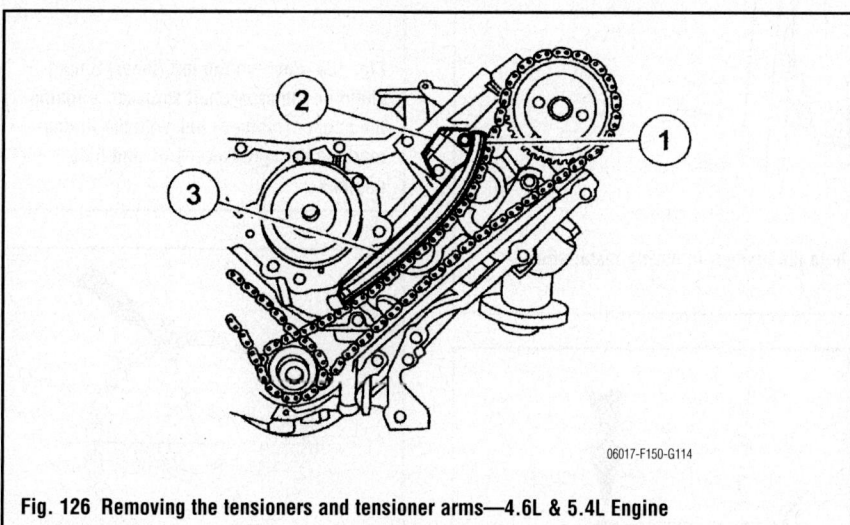

06017-F150-G114

Fig. 126 Removing the tensioners and tensioner arms—4.6L & 5.4L Engine

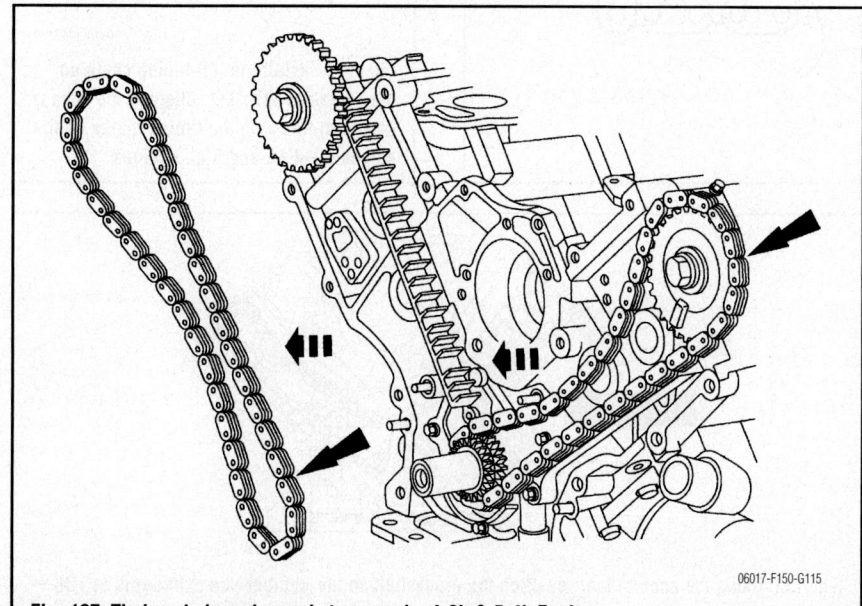

06017-F150-G115

Fig. 127 Timing chain and sprocket removal—4.6L & 5.4L Engine

✳✳ **WARNING**

Prior to installation, inspect the tensioner-sealing bead for seal integrity. If cracks, tears, separation from the tensioner body or permanent compression of the seal bead is observed, install a new tensioner.

9. Compress the tensioner plunger, using a vise.

10. Install a retaining clip on the tensioner to hold the plunger in during installation.

11. If the copper links are not visible, mark one link on one end and one link on the other end, and use as timing marks.

12. Install the crankshaft sprocket, making sure the flange faces forward.

13. Position the left timing chain guide.

14. Install and tighten the left bolts. Tighten to 89 inch lbs. (10 Nm).

15. Position the right timing chain guide.

16. Install and tighten the right bolts. Tighten to 89 inch lbs. (10 Nm).

✳✳ **WARNING**

Unless otherwise instructed, do not rotate either the crankshaft or the camshafts, when the timing chains are removed and the cylinder heads are installed. Severe piston and valve damage will occur.

➡The number one cylinder is at top dead center (TDC) when the stud on the engine block fits into the slot in the handle of the special tool.

17. Using the Crankshaft Holding Tool, position the crankshaft so the No. 1 cylinder is at TDC .

18. Remove the Crankshaft Holding Tool.

19. Position the LH (inner) timing chain on the crankshaft sprocket, aligning the copper (marked) link with the timing mark on the sprocket.

20. Install the LH timing chain on the camshaft sprocket, aligning the copper (marked) link with the timing marks on the sprocket.

21. Position the LH timing chain tensioner arm on the dowel pin and install the LH timing chain tensioner and the 2 bolts and tighten to 18 ft. lbs. (25 Nm).

22. Remove the retaining clip from the LH timing chain tensioner.

23. Position the RH (outer) timing chain on the crankshaft sprocket, aligning the copper (marked) link with the timing mark on the sprocket.

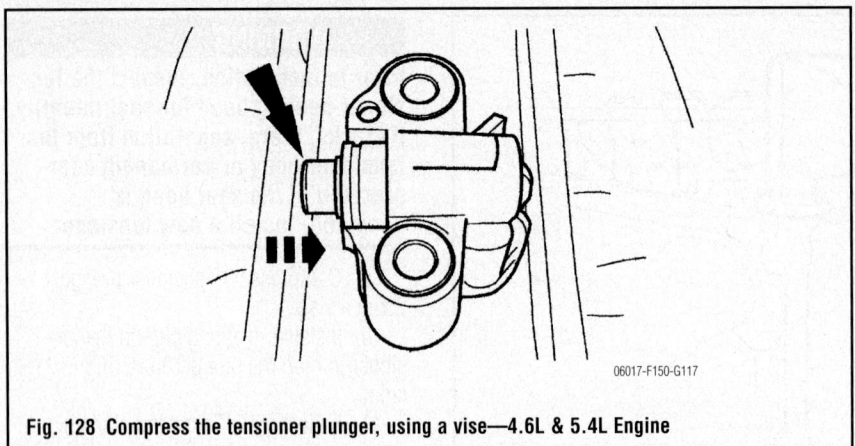

Fig. 128 Compress the tensioner plunger, using a vise—4.6L & 5.4L Engine

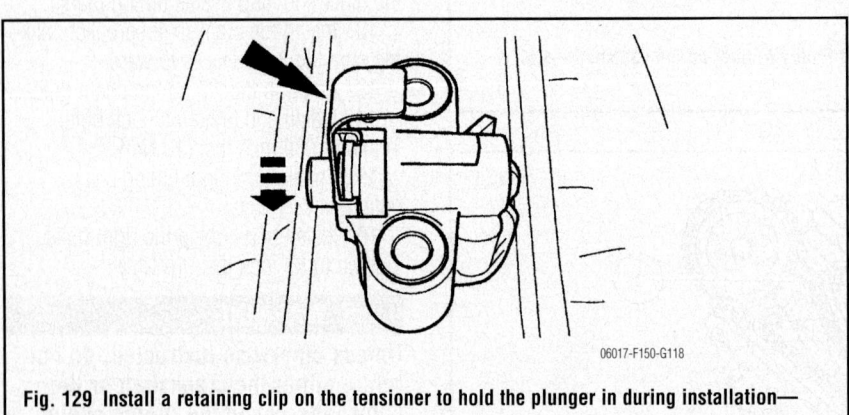

Fig. 129 Install a retaining clip on the tensioner to hold the plunger in during installation—4.6L & 5.4L Engine

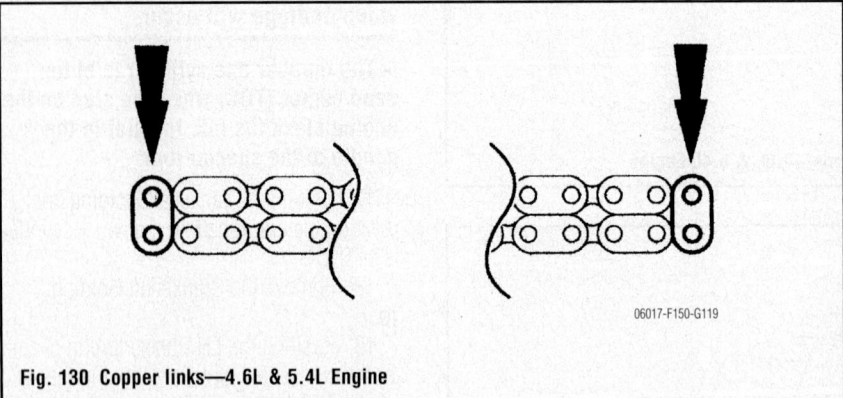

Fig. 130 Copper links—4.6L & 5.4L Engine

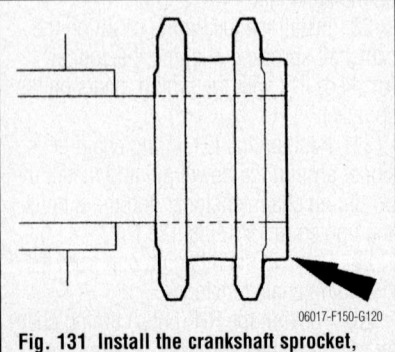

Fig. 131 Install the crankshaft sprocket, making sure the flange faces forward—4.6L & 5.4L Engine

24. Install the RH timing chain on the camshaft sprocket, aligning the copper (marked) link with the timing marks on the sprocket.

25. Position the RH timing chain tensioner arm on the dowel pin and install the RH timing chain tensioner and the 2 bolts and tighten to 18 ft. lbs. (25 Nm).

26. Remove the retaining clip from the RH timing chain tensioner.

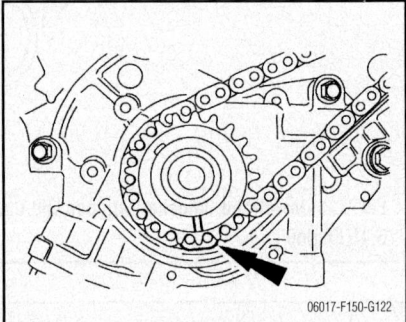

Fig. 133 Position the left (inner) timing chain on the crankshaft sprocket, aligning the copper (marked) link with the timing mark on the sprocket—4.6L and 5.4L engines

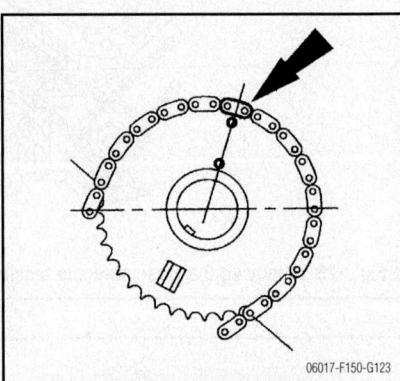

Fig. 134 Install the left timing chain on the camshaft sprocket, aligning the copper (marked) link with the timing marks on the sprocket—4.6L and 5.4L engines

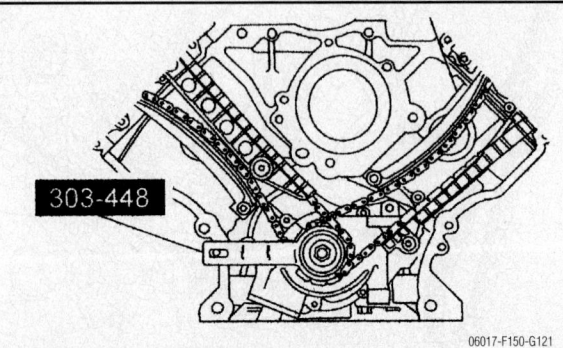

Fig. 132 Using the special tool, position the crankshaft so the number one cylinder is at TDC—4.6L and 5.4L engines

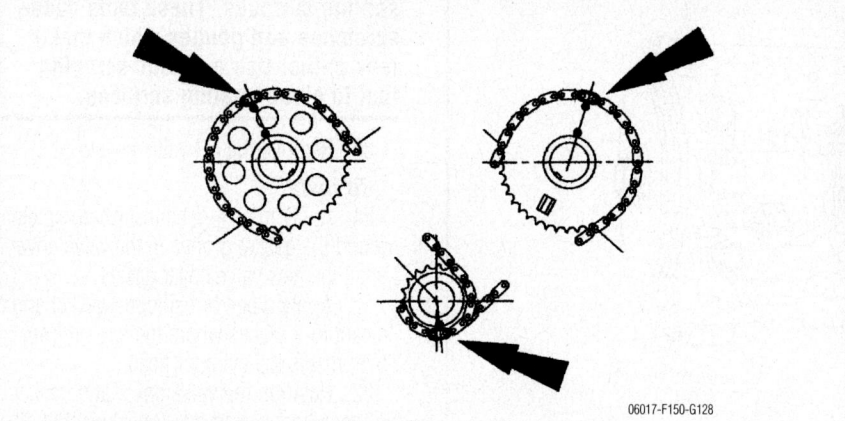

Fig. 135 Make sure that the copper (marked) chain links are lined up with the dots on the crankshaft sprockets and the camshaft sprocket—4.6L and 5.4L engines

27. Make sure that the copper (marked) chain links are lined up with the dots on the crankshaft sprockets and the camshaft sprocket.

28. Remove the Camshaft Aligner and Camshaft Pulley Aligner from the camshaft.

29. Install the crankshaft sensor ring on the crankshaft.

30. Install the engine front cover.

31. Refill the engine with oil to the correct level.

32. Start the engine and check for leaks.

6.8L Engine

See Figures 136 and 137.

1. Before servicing the vehicle, refer to the Precautions Section.

2. Remove the engine front cover. For additional information, refer to "Timing Chain Cover & Seal, Removal & Installation."

3. Remove the crankshaft sensor ring from the crankshaft.

4. Remove the balance shaft. For additional information, refer to "Balance Shaft, Removal & Installation."

5. Position the crankshaft with the keyway at the 12 o'clock position.

6. Install and carefully tighten the Camshaft Position Aligner on the camshafts.

7. Remove the 2 bolts, the LH timing chain tensioner and tensioner arm.

8. Remove the 2 bolts, the RH timing chain tensioner and tensioner arm.

9. Remove the LH and RH timing chains and the crankshaft sprockets.

10. Remove the 4 bolts and the timing chain guides.

11. Remove the 2 bolts, flat washers, camshaft sprockets and RH camshaft spacer.

To install:

> ⁑ **WARNING**
>
> Timing chain procedures must be followed exactly or damage to valves and pistons will result.

12. Compress the tensioner plunger, using a vise.

13. Install a retaining clip on the tensioner to hold the plunger in during installation.

14. If copper links are not visible, mark 2 links on one end and 1 link on the other end, and use as timing marks.

15. Install the RH camshaft spacer ring, both camshaft sprockets, flat washers and tighten the bolts in 2 stages.

    a. Tighten to 30 ft. lbs. (40 Nm).

    b. Tighten an additional 90°

16. Install the timing chain guides and tighten the bolts to 89 inch lbs. (10 Nm).

17. Preposition the camshafts:

    a. Rotate the LH camshaft until the timing mark is approximately at 12 o'clock.

    b. Tighten the Camshaft Position Aligner to maintain camshaft prepositioning.

    c. Rotate the RH camshaft until the timing mark is approximately at 11 o'clock.

    d. Tighten the Camshaft Position Aligner to maintain camshaft prepositioning.

18. Position the crankshaft with the Crankshaft Holding Tool, then remove the tool.

19. Install the crankshaft sprocket, making sure the flange faces forward.

20. Install the lower end of the LH timing chain, aligning the timing marks.

21. Install the LH timing chain on the camshaft sprocket with the 2 chain (marked) links and the timing marks aligned.

> ⁑ **WARNING**
>
> The camshaft sprocket can jump time causing engine damage if the Crankshaft Holding Tool is not secured.

➡ Be sure the chain link and crankshaft sprocket timing marks are aligned.

➡ The lower half of the timing chain must be positioned above the dowel.

22. Install the RH (outer) timing chain on the crankshaft sprocket.

23. Position the timing chain on the camshaft sprocket. Make sure the 2 copper-colored (marked) links align with the camshaft sprocket timing mark.

➡ The LH timing chain tensioner arm has a bump near the dowel hole, for identification.

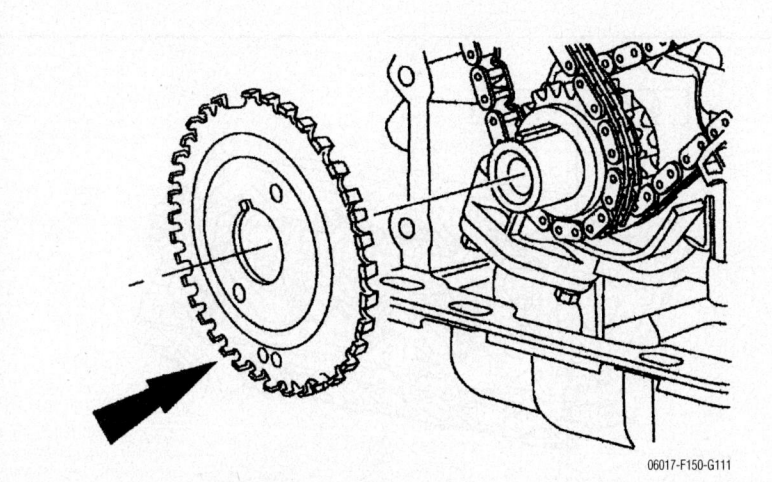

Fig. 136 Crankshaft sensor ring—6.8L Engine

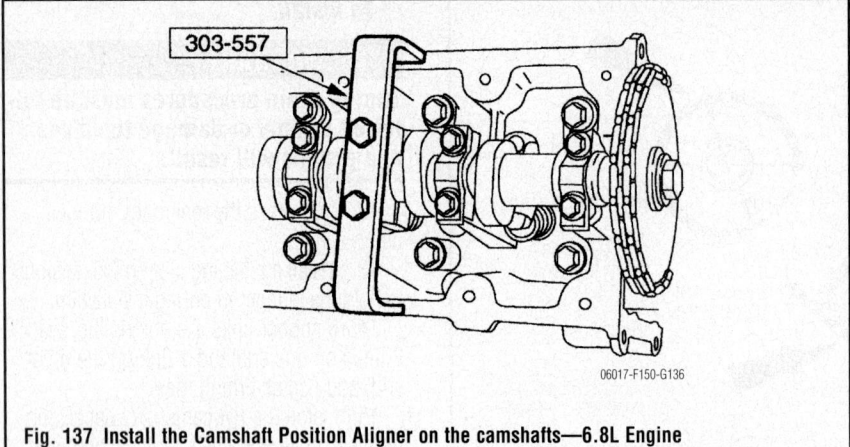

Fig. 137 Install the Camshaft Position Aligner on the camshafts—6.8L Engine

24. Position the LH and RH timing chain tensioner arms on the dowel pins and install the timing chain tensioners and tighten the bolts to 18 ft. lbs. (25 Nm).

25. Remove the retaining clips from the RH and LH timing chain tensioners.

26. Check for correct alignment of all timing marks.

27. Remove the Camshaft Position Aligner from the camshafts.

28. Install the crankshaft sensor ring on the crankshaft.

29. Install the balance shaft.

30. Install engine front cover.

VALVE COVERS

REMOVAL & INSTALLATION

4.6L Engine

Left Side

See Figures 138 and 139.

1. Before servicing the vehicle, refer to the Precautions Section.

2. Disconnect the negative battery cable.

3. Unfasten the latches and remove the engine cover.

4. Remove the air intake assembly.

5. Disconnect the crankcase ventilation tube quick connect coupling from the valve cover.

6. Remove the oil level indicator and tube support bracket net.

7. Disconnect the upper and lower fittings and remove the EGR system module tube.

8. Disconnect the LH fuel injector electrical connectors, ignition coil electrical connectors and the wire harness retainers.

9. Disconnect the wiring harness retainer and position the engine control wiring harness aside.

10. Disconnect the electrical connector.

11. Disconnect the engine wiring harness retainer and the 2 PCM electrical connectors.

12. Disconnect the transmission wiring harness retainers from the engine wiring harness and position both the engine and transmission wiring harness aside.

13. Remove the 2 bolts and position the cooling fan shroud onto the cooling fan.

14. Remove the 4 exhaust Y-pipe flange nuts and discard the flange nuts.

15. Remove the 4 engine support insulator-to-crossmember nuts.

16. Using a jack positioned on the RH rear of the cylinder block, raise the engine 25.4 mm (1 in).

17. Remove the engine support insulator-to-crossmember bracket nut.

18. Remove the 2 nuts and the engine support insulator-to-crossmember bracket.

19. Using the jack positioned on the RH rear of the cylinder block, lower the engine 51 mm (2 in).

❊❊ WARNING

Do not use metal scrapers, wire brushes, power abrasive discs or other abrasive means to clean the

sealing surfaces. These tools cause scratches and gouges which make leak paths. Use a plastic scraping tool to clean sealing surfaces.

20. Remove the LH valve cover.

To install:

21. Apply instant gel adhesive completely around the gasket groove in the valve cover. Install the new valve cover gasket.

22. Apply a bead of silicone gasket and sealant in 2 places where the engine front cover meets the cylinder head.

23. Position the valve cover and gasket on the cylinder head and loosely install all of the fasteners.

24. Tighten the fasteners in sequence to 89 inch lbs. (10 Nm).

25. Using the jack positioned on the RH rear of the cylinder block, raise the engine 51 mm (2 in).

26. Position the RH engine support insulator-to-crossmember bracket and tighten the nuts to 66 ft. lbs. (90 Nm).

27. Install the engine support insulator-to-crossmember bracket nut and tighten to 66 ft. lbs. (90 Nm).

28. Using the jack positioned on the RH rear of the cylinder block, lower the engine.

29. Install the 4 engine support insulator nuts and tighten to 66 ft. lbs. (90 Nm).

30. Install the new 4 exhaust Y-pipe flange nuts.

31. Position the radiator fan shroud and install the 2 bolts.

32. Position both the engine and transmission wiring harness and connect the transmission wiring harness retainers to the engine wiring harness.

33. Connect the engine wiring harness retainer and the 2 PCM electrical connectors.

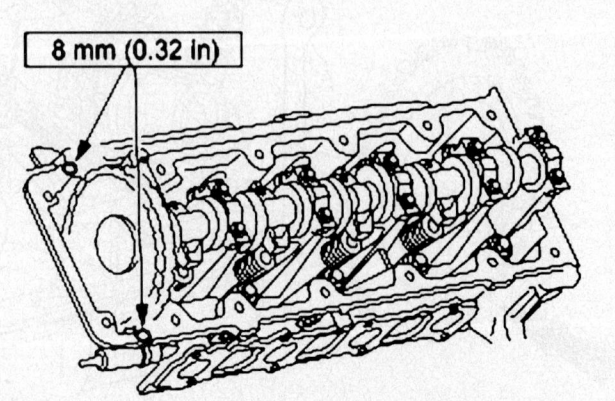

Fig. 138 Apply a bead of silicone gasket and sealant in two places where the engine front cover meets the cylinder head—4.6L Engine

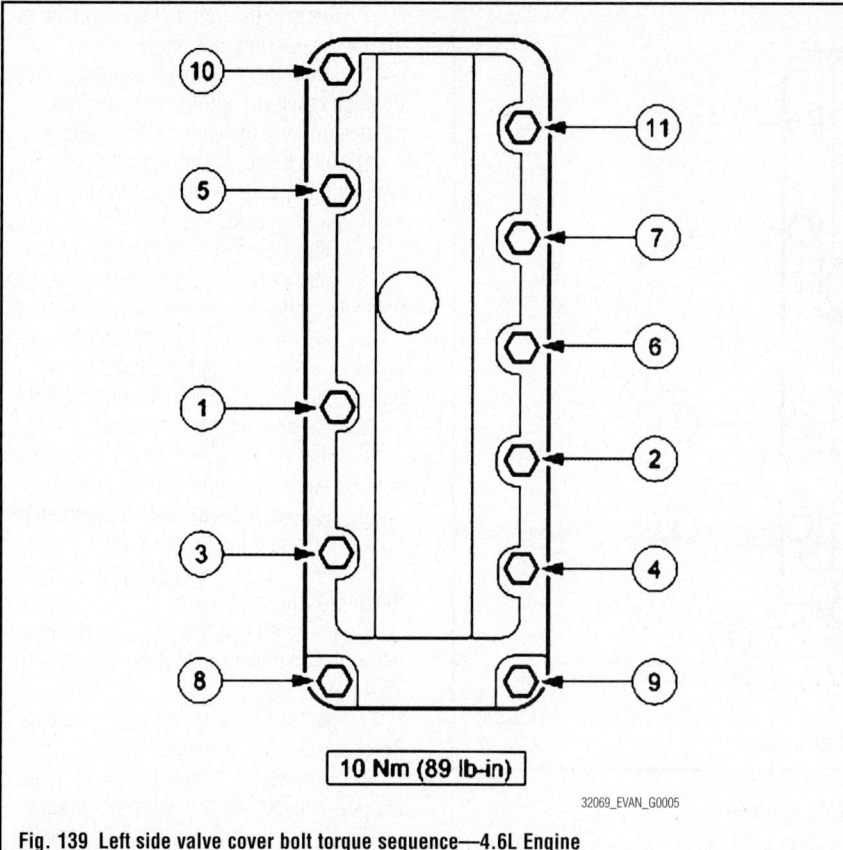

10 Nm (89 lb-in)

32069_EVAN_G0005

Fig. 139 Left side valve cover bolt torque sequence—4.6L Engine

34. Connect the electrical connector.

35. Position the engine control wiring harness retainer onto the valve cover stud.

36. Connect the LH ignition coil and fuel injector electrical connectors and the wiring harness retainers.

37. Install the EGR tube and tighten the fittings to 31 ft. lbs. (42 Nm).

38. Position the oil level indicator and tube and tighten the bolt to 89 inch lbs. (10 Nm).

39. Install the oil level indicator and tighten the tube support bracket nut to 89 inch lbs. (10 Nm).

40. Position the crankcase ventilation tube and connect the quick connect coupling to the valve cover.

41. Install the air intake assembly.

42. Install the engine cover.

43. Connect the negative battery cable.

Right Side

See Figures 140 and 141.

1. Before servicing the vehicle, refer to the Precautions Section.

2. Disconnect the negative battery cable.

3. Unfasten the latches and remove the engine cover.

4. Remove the air intake assembly.

5. Disconnect the quick connect couplings and remove the PCV tube.

6. Disconnect the PCV valve electrical connector, rotate the PCV valve counterclockwise and remove from the valve cover.

7. Remove the oil fill tube support bracket bolt.

8. Remove the clamp and the oil filler tube.

9. Disconnect the 2 generator wiring harness retainers and position the wiring harness aside.

10. Disconnect the electrical connector, remove the nut and ground strap.

11. Remove the fuel charging wiring harness from the valve cover studs and position the wiring harness and support bracket aside.

12. Remove the fluid level indicator and disconnect the attachments at the transmission fluid filler tube.

13. Remove the bolt, nut and position the transmission fluid filler tube aside.

14. Remove the 2 bolts and position the cooling fan shroud onto the cooling fan.

15. Remove the 4 exhaust Y-pipe flange nuts and discard the nuts.

16. Remove the 4 engine support insulator-to-crossmember nuts.

17. Using a suitable jack positioned on the LH rear of the cylinder block, raise the engine 1 inch (25.4 mm).

18. Remove the 3 nuts and the engine support insulator-to-crossmember bracket.

19. Using the jack positioned on the LH rear of the cylinder block, lower the engine 2 inches (51 mm).

20. Remove the RH valve cover.

To install:

21. Apply instant gel adhesive completely around the gasket groove in the valve cover. Install the new valve cover gasket.

22. Apply a bead of silicone gasket and sealant in 2 places where the engine front cover meets the cylinder head.

23. Install the valve cover and tighten the fasteners in sequence to 89 inch lbs. (10 Nm).

24. Using a suitable jack positioned on the LH rear of the cylinder block, raise the engine 2 inches (51 mm).

25. Position the LH engine support insulator-to-crossmember bracket and tighten the 3 nuts to 66 ft. lbs. (90 Nm).

26. Using the suitable jack positioned on the LH rear of the cylinder block, lower the engine.

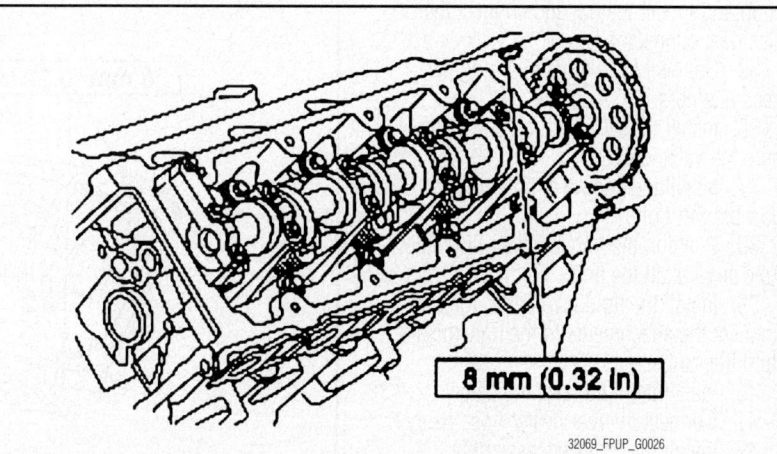

8 mm (0.32 in)

32069_FPUP_G0026

Fig. 140 Apply the silicone gasket and sealant in 2 places where the engine front cover meets the cylinder head—4.6L engine

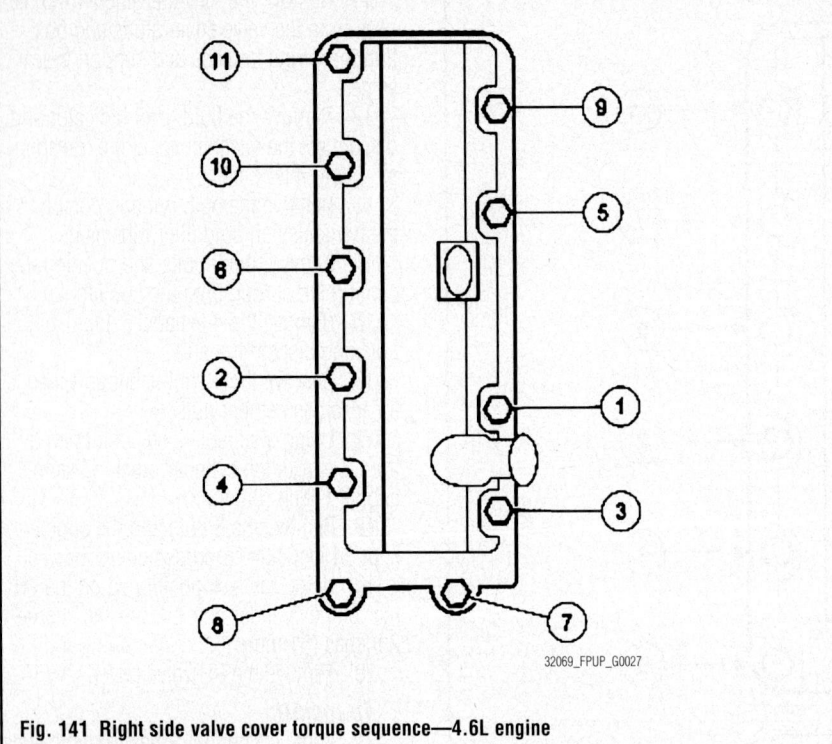

Fig. 141 Right side valve cover torque sequence—4.6L engine

27. Tighten the engine support insulator nuts to 66 ft. lbs. (90 Nm).

28. Install the new exhaust Y-pipe flange nuts and tighten to 3 ft. lbs. (40 Nm).

29. Position the radiator fan shroud and tighten the 2 bolts to 53 inch lbs. (6 Nm).

30. Install the PCV valve.

31. Connect the PCV electrical connector.

32. Position the PCV tube and connect the quick connect couplings.

33. Position the fuel charging wiring harness and connect the retainers to the valve cover studs.

34. Position the support bracket, ground strap and install the nut and connect the electrical connector.

35. Connect the alternator wiring harness retainers.

36. Install the oil filler tube and clamp onto the valve cover.

37. Install the engine oil filler tube support bracket bolt.

38. Position the transmission fluid filler tube and install the bolt.

39. Install the fluid level indicator and connect the attachments to the transmission fluid filler tube.

40. Install the fluid level indicator.

41. Connect the rear heater hose hanger.

42. Install the air intake assembly.

43. Install the engine cover.

44. Connect the negative battery cable.

5.4L Engine

Left Side

See Figures 142 and 143.

1. Before servicing the vehicle, refer to the Precautions Section.

2. Disconnect the negative battery cable.

3. Unfasten the latches and remove the engine cover.

4. Remove the air intake assembly.

5. Disconnect the crankcase ventilation tube quick connect coupling from the valve cover.

6. Remove the oil level indicator and tube support bracket nut.

7. Remove the bolt and position the oil level indicator and tube aside.

8. Disconnect the LH fuel injector electrical connectors, ignition coil electrical connectors and the wire harness retainers.

9. Disconnect the wiring harness retainer and position the engine control wiring harness aside.

10. Disconnect the electrical connector.

11. Disconnect the engine wiring harness retainer and the 2 PCM electrical connectors.

12. Disconnect the transmission wiring harness retainers from the engine wiring harness and position both the engine and transmission wiring harness aside.

13. Remove the 2 bolts and position the cooling fan shroud onto the cooling fan.

14. Remove the 4 exhaust Y-pipe flange nuts and discard the flange nuts.

15. Remove the 4 engine support insulator-to-crossmember nuts.

16. Using a jack positioned on the RH rear of the cylinder block, raise the engine 25.4 mm (1 in).

17. Remove the engine support insulator-to-crossmember bracket nut.

18. Remove the 2 nuts and the engine support insulator-to-crossmember bracket.

19. Using the jack positioned on the RH rear of the cylinder block, lower the engine 51 mm (2 in).

✳✳ WARNING

Do not use metal scrapers, wire brushes, power abrasive discs or other abrasive means to clean the sealing surfaces. These tools cause scratches and gouges which make leak paths. Use a plastic scraping tool to clean sealing surfaces.

20. Remove the LH valve cover.

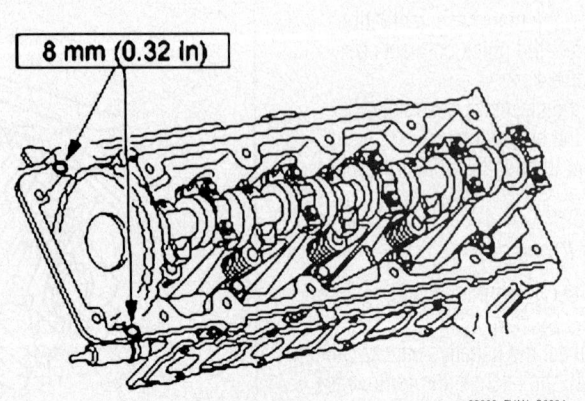

Fig. 142 Apply a bead of silicone gasket and sealant in two places where the engine front cover meets the cylinder head— 5.4L Engine

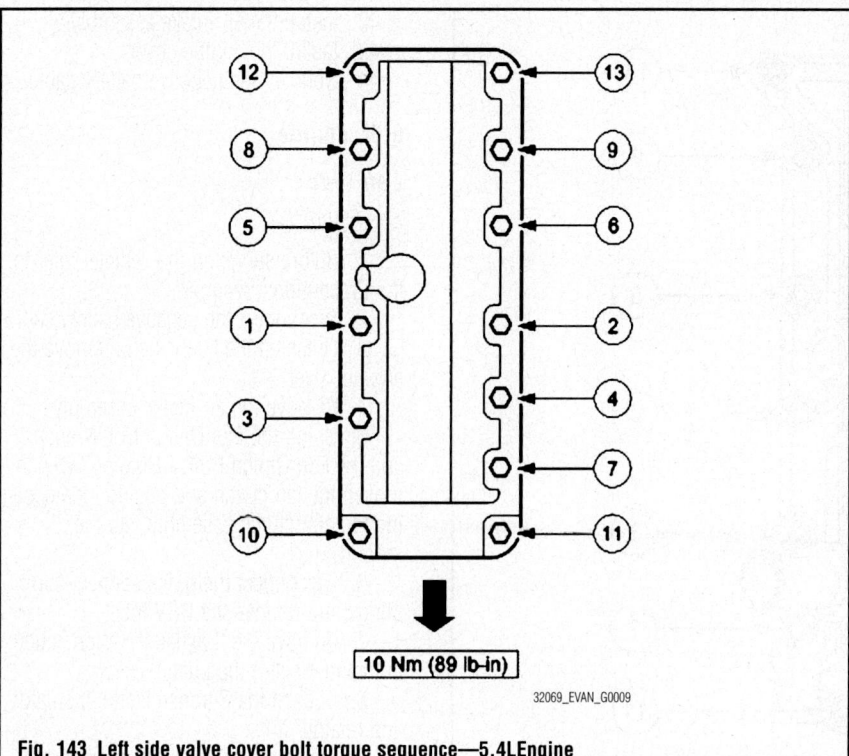

Fig. 143 Left side valve cover bolt torque sequence—5.4L Engine

10 Nm (89 lb-in)

32069_EVAN_G0009

To install:

21. Apply instant gel adhesive completely around the gasket groove in the valve cover. Install the new valve cover gasket.

22. Apply a bead of silicone gasket and sealant in 2 places where the engine front cover meets the cylinder head.

23. Position the valve cover and gasket on the cylinder head and loosely install all of the fasteners.

24. Tighten the fasteners in sequence to 89 inch lbs. (10 Nm).

25. Using the jack positioned on the RH rear of the cylinder block, raise the engine 2 inches. (51 mm).

26. Position the RH engine support insulator-to-crossmember bracket and tighten the nuts to 66 ft. lbs. (90 Nm).

27. Install the engine support insulator-to-crossmember bracket nut and tighten to 66 ft. lbs. (90 Nm).

28. Using the jack positioned on the RH rear of the cylinder block, lower the engine.

29. Install the 4 engine support insulator nuts and tighten to 66 ft. lbs. (90 Nm).

30. Install the new 4 exhaust Y-pipe flange nuts.

31. Position the radiator fan shroud and install the 2 bolts.

32. Position both the engine and transmission wiring harness and connect the transmission wiring harness retainers to the engine wiring harness.

33. Connect the engine wiring harness retainer and the 2 PCM electrical connectors.

34. Connect the electrical connector.

35. Position the engine control wiring harness retainer onto the valve cover stud.

36. Connect the LH ignition coil and fuel injector electrical connectors and the wiring harness retainers.

37. Position the oil level indicator and tube and tighten the bolt to 89 inch lbs. (10 Nm).

38. Install the oil level indicator and tighten the tube support bracket nut to 18 ft. lbs. (25 Nm).

39. Position the crankcase ventilation tube and connect the quick connect coupling to the valve cover.

40. Install the air intake assembly.

41. Install the engine cover.

42. Connect the negative battery cable.

Right Side

See Figures 144 and 145.

1. Before servicing the vehicle, refer to the Precautions Section.

2. Disconnect the negative battery cable.

3. Unfasten the latches and remove the engine cover.

4. Remove the air intake assembly.

5. Disconnect the quick connect couplings and remove the PCV tube.

6. Disconnect the PCV valve electrical connector, rotate the PCV valve counterclockwise and remove from the valve cover.

7. Remove the oil fill tube support bracket bolt.

8. Remove the clamp and the oil filler tube.

9. Disconnect the 2 generator wiring harness retainers and position the wiring harness aside.

10. Disconnect the electrical connector, remove the nut and ground strap.

11. Remove the fuel charging wiring harness from the valve cover studs and position the wiring harness and support bracket aside.

12. Remove the fluid level indicator and disconnect the attachments at the transmission fluid filler tube.

13. Remove the bolt, nut and position the transmission fluid filler tube aside.

14. Remove the 2 bolts and position the cooling fan shroud onto the cooling fan.

15. Remove the 4 exhaust Y-pipe flange nuts and discard the nuts.

16. Remove the 4 engine support insulator-to-crossmember nuts.

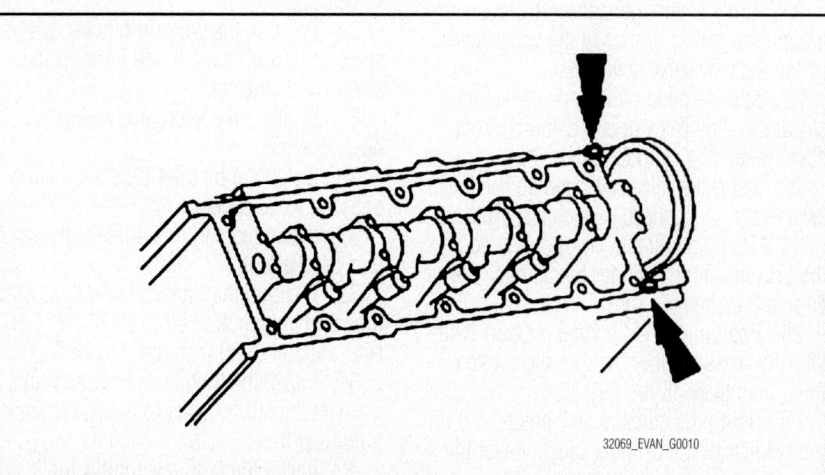

Fig. 144 Apply a bead of silicone gasket and sealant in two places where the engine front cover meets the cylinder head—5.4L Engine

32069_EVAN_G0010

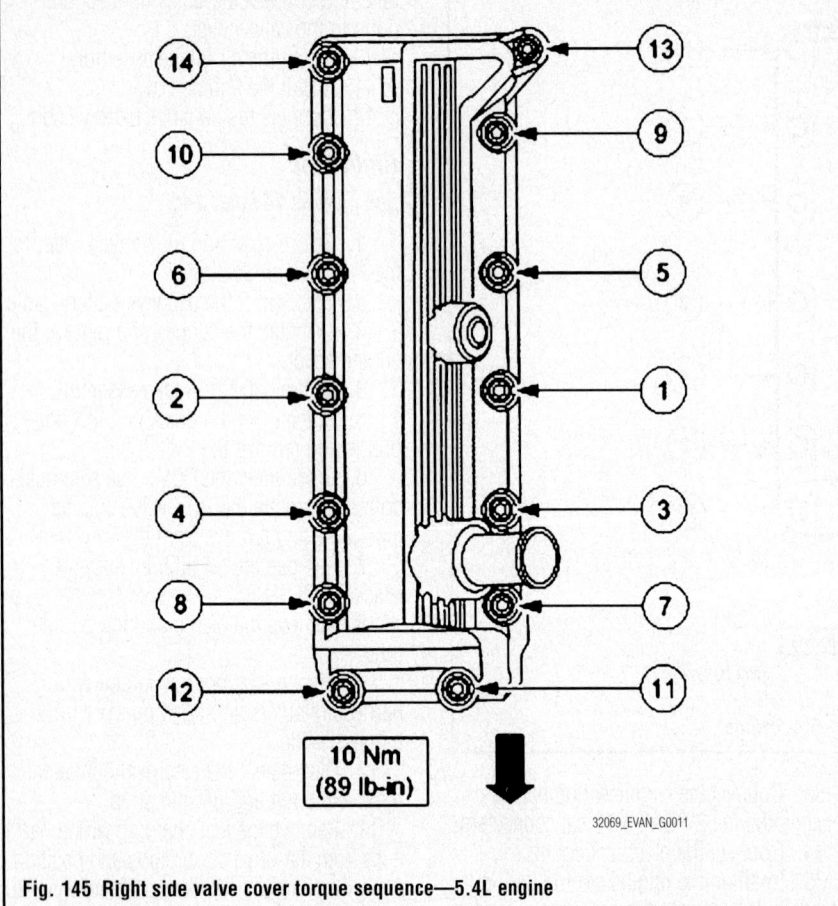

10 Nm
(89 lb-in)

32069_EVAN_G0011

Fig. 145 Right side valve cover torque sequence—5.4L engine

17. Using a suitable jack positioned on the LH rear of the cylinder block, raise the engine 1 inch (25.4 mm).

18. Remove the 3 nuts and the engine support insulator-to-crossmember bracket.

19. Using the jack positioned on the LH rear of the cylinder block, lower the engine 2 inches (51 mm).

20. Remove the RH valve cover.

To install:

21. Apply instant gel adhesive completely around the gasket groove in the valve cover. Install the new valve cover gasket.

22. Apply a bead of silicone gasket and sealant in 2 places where the engine front cover meets the cylinder head.

23. Install the valve cover and tighten the fasteners in sequence to 89 inch lbs. (10 Nm).

24. Using a suitable jack positioned on the LH rear of the cylinder block, raise the engine 2 inches (51 mm).

25. Position the LH engine support insulator-to-crossmember bracket and tighten the 3 nuts to 66 ft. lbs. (90 Nm).

26. Using the suitable jack positioned on the LH rear of the cylinder block, lower the engine.

27. Tighten the engine support insulator nuts to 66 ft. lbs. (90 Nm).

28. Install the new exhaust Y-pipe flange nuts and tighten to 3 ft. lbs. (40 Nm).

29. Position the radiator fan shroud and tighten the 2 bolts to 53 inch lbs. (6 Nm).

30. Install the PCV valve.

31. Connect the PCV electrical connector.

32. Position the PCV tube and connect the quick connect couplings.

33. Position the fuel charging wiring harness and connect the retainers to the valve cover studs.

34. Position the support bracket, ground strap and install the nut and connect the electrical connector.

35. Connect the alternator wiring harness retainers.

36. Install the oil filler tube and clamp onto the valve cover.

37. Install the engine oil filler tube support bracket bolt.

38. Position the transmission fluid filler tube and tighten the bolt to 21 ft. lbs. (28 Nm) and nut to 89 inch lbs. (10 Nm).

39. Install the fluid level indicator and connect the attachments to the transmission fluid filler tube.

40. Install the fluid level indicator.

41. Connect the rear heater hose hanger.

42. Install the air intake assembly.

43. Install the engine cover.

44. Connect the negative battery cable.

6.8L Engine

Left Side

See Figure 146.

1. Before servicing the vehicle, refer to the Precautions Section.

2. Disconnect the negative battery cable.

3. Unfasten the latches and remove the engine cover.

4. Remove the air intake assembly.

5. Using the Fan Clutch Nut Wrench and the Fan Clutch Pulley Holding Wrench, loosen the fan clutch and position the cooling fan and clutch assembly into the shroud.

6. Disconnect the quick connect couplings and remove the PCV tube.

7. Remove the 4 exhaust Y-pipe flange nuts and discard the nuts.

8. Loosen the 2 transmission insulator and retainer nuts.

9. Loosen the 2 LH engine support insulator nuts.

10. Remove the 2 RH engine support insulator nuts.

11. Using a utility stand positioned on the RH rear of the cylinder block, raise the engine 25.4 mm (1 in).

12. Remove the 2 RH engine support insulator-to-crossmember bracket nuts.

13. Remove the nut and the RH engine support insulator-to-crossmember bracket.

14. Using the utility stand positioned on the RH rear of the cylinder block, lower the engine 38 mm (1.5 in).

15. Disconnect the 2 PCM electrical connectors and the wiring harness retainer.

16. Disconnect the 3 LH engine wiring harness retainers.

17. Disconnect the engine wiring harness retainer from the LH valve cover stud bolt.

18. Disconnect the Camshaft Position (CMP) sensor electrical connector.

19. Disconnect the engine wiring harness retainer from the engine front cover stud bolt.

20. Disconnect the LH 5 fuel injector electrical connectors.

21. Disconnect the LH 5 ignition coil electrical connectors and position the engine wiring harness aside.

22. Remove the oil level indicator and tube support bracket nut.

23. Remove the bolt and position the oil level indicator and tube aside.

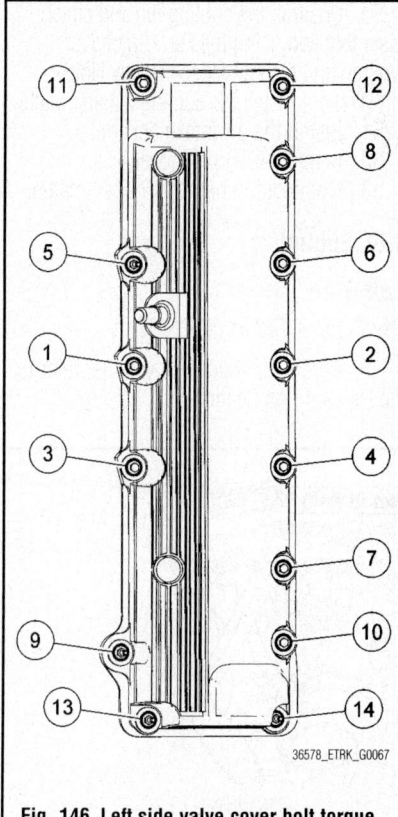

Fig. 146 Left side valve cover bolt torque sequence—6.8L Engine

24. Disconnect the quick connect coupling and remove the crankcase vent tube.
25. Remove the LH valve cover.

※※ WARNING

The fasteners are part of the valve cover and should not be removed.

To install:

26. Apply instant gel adhesive completely around the gasket groove in the valve cover. Install the new valve cover gasket.
27. Apply a bead of silicone gasket and sealant in 2 places where the engine front cover meets the cylinder head.
28. Install the valve cover and tighten the bolts in sequence to 89 inch lbs. (10 Nm).
29. Position back the oil level indicator and tube and tighten the bolt to 89 inch lbs. (10 Nm).
30. Tighten the oil level indicator and tighten the tube support bracket nut to 18 ft. lbs. (25 Nm).
31. Position back the engine wiring harness and connect the 3 wiring harness retainers.
32. Connect the LH 5 fuel injector electrical connectors.
33. Connect the LH 5 ignition coil electrical connectors.

34. Connect the CMP sensor electrical connector.
35. Connect the engine wiring harness retainer to the engine front cover stud bolt.
36. Connect the engine wiring harness retainer to the LH valve cover stud bolt.
37. Position the crankcase vent tube and connect the quick connect coupling.
38. Connect the 2 PCM electrical connectors and the wiring harness retainer.
39. Using the utility stand positioned on the RH rear of the cylinder block, raise the engine 1 ½ (38 mm).
40. Position the engine support insulator-to-crossmember bracket and install the nut finger-tight.
41. Install the 2 engine support insulator-to-crossmember bracket nuts and tighten to 66 ft. lbs. (90 Nm).
42. Using a utility stand positioned on the RH rear of the cylinder block, lower the engine.
43. Tighten the engine support insulator nuts to 66 ft. lbs. (90 Nm).
44. Tighten the 2 transmission insulator and retainer nuts to 66 ft. lbs. (90 Nm).
45. Install the 4 exhaust Y-pipe flange nuts and tighten to 30 ft. lbs. (40 Nm).
46. Position the PCV valve tube and connect the quick connect couplings.
47. Position the cooling fan and clutch assembly and using the Fan Clutch Nut Wrench and the Fan Clutch Pulley Holding Wrench, install the cooling fan and clutch.
48. Install the air intake assembly.
49. Install the engine cover.
50. Connect the negative battery cable.

Right Side

See Figure 147.

1. Before servicing the vehicle, refer to the Precautions Section.
2. Disconnect the negative battery cable.
3. Unfasten the latches and remove the engine cover.
4. Remove the air intake assembly.
5. Using the Fan Clutch Nut Wrench and the Fan Clutch Pulley Holding Wrench, loosen the fan clutch and position the cooling fan and clutch assembly into the shroud.
6. Remove the 4 exhaust Y-pipe flange nuts and discard the nuts.
7. Loosen the 2 transmission insulator and retainer nuts.
8. Loosen the 2 LH engine support insulator nuts.
9. Remove the 2 RH engine support insulator nuts.

10. Using a utility stand positioned on the RH rear of the cylinder block, raise the engine 25.4 mm (1 in).
11. Disconnect the alternator wiring harness retainer from the engine front cover stud bolt.
12. Disconnect the 2 electrical connectors.
13. Disconnect the electrical connector position retainers, remove the nut, ground strap and mounting bracket.
14. Disconnect the oil fill tube.
15. Remove the bolt and the oil fill tube.
16. If equipped, disconnect the PCV valve electrical connector.
17. Disconnect the quick connect couplings and rotate the PCV valve counterclockwise and remove the PCV tube.
18. Disconnect the wiring harness retainer from the front RH valve cover stud bolt.
19. Remove the nut for the transmission fluid indicator and tube.
20. Remove the nut and position the transmission fluid indicator and tube aside.
21. Disconnect the RH 5 ignition coil electrical connectors.
22. Disconnect the RH 5 fuel injector electrical connectors.

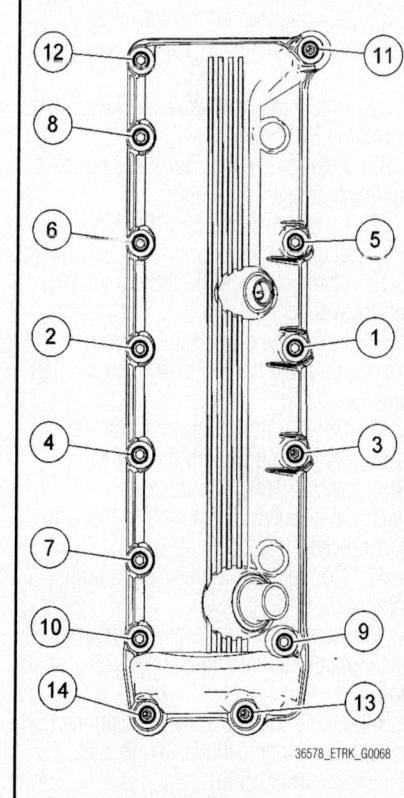

Fig. 147 Right side valve cover bolt torque sequence—6.8L Engine

23. Disconnect the 2 retainers and position the engine wiring harness aside.

24. Remove the 5 bolts and the 5 RH ignition coils.

25. Remove the RH valve cover.

➡ **The fasteners are part of the valve cover and should not be removed.**

To install:

26. Apply instant gel adhesive completely around the gasket groove in the valve cover. Install the new valve cover gasket.

27. Apply a bead of silicone gasket and sealant in 2 places where the engine front cover meets the cylinder head.

28. Install the valve cover and tighten the bolts in sequence to 89 inch lbs. (10 Nm).

29. Install the ignition coils and tighten the bolts to 53 inch lbs. (6 Nm).

30. Position the engine wiring harness and connect the 2 retainers.

31. Connect the 5 RH fuel injector electrical connectors.

32. Connect the 5 RH ignition coil electrical connectors.

33. Position back the transmission fluid indicator and tube and tighten the nut to 21 ft. lbs. (28 Nm).

34. Install the transmission fluid indicator and tube support bracket nut.

35. Connect the wiring harness retainer to the front RH valve cover stud bolt.

36. Rotate the PCV valve clockwise and install the PCV valve.

37. Position the PCV tube and connect the quick connect couplings.

38. If equipped, connect the PCV valve electrical connector.

39. Connect the oil fill tube to the RH valve cover.

40. Install the oil fill tube support bracket bolt and tighten to 89 inch lbs. (10 Nm).

41. Position the mounting bracket, ground strap and tighten the nut to 18 ft. lbs. (25 Nm). Connect the electrical connector retainers to the support bracket.

42. Connect the 2 electrical connectors.

43. Connect the generator wiring harness retainer to the engine front cover stud bolt.

44. Using the utility stand positioned on the LH rear of the cylinder block, raise the engine 38 mm (1.5 in).

45. Position the LH engine support insulator-to-crossmember bracket and tighten the 3 nuts to 66 ft. lbs. (90 Nm).

46. Using a utility stand positioned on the LH rear of the cylinder block, lower the engine.

47. Install the remaining engine support insulator nuts to 66 ft. lbs. (90 Nm).

48. Tighten the 2 transmission insulator and retainer nuts to 66 ft. lbs. (90 Nm).

49. Install the exhaust Y-pipe flange nuts and tighten to 30 ft. lbs. (40 Nm).

➡ **The clutch assembly nut has a right-hand thread and must be rotated clockwise to install it.**

50. Position the cooling fan and clutch assembly and using the Fan Clutch Nut Wrench and the Fan Clutch Pulley Holding Wrench, install the cooling fan and clutch.

51. Install the air intake assembly.

52. Install the engine cover.

53. Connect the negative battery cable.

6.0L Engine

Left Side

See Figures 148 through 152.

1. Before servicing the vehicle, refer to the Precautions Section.

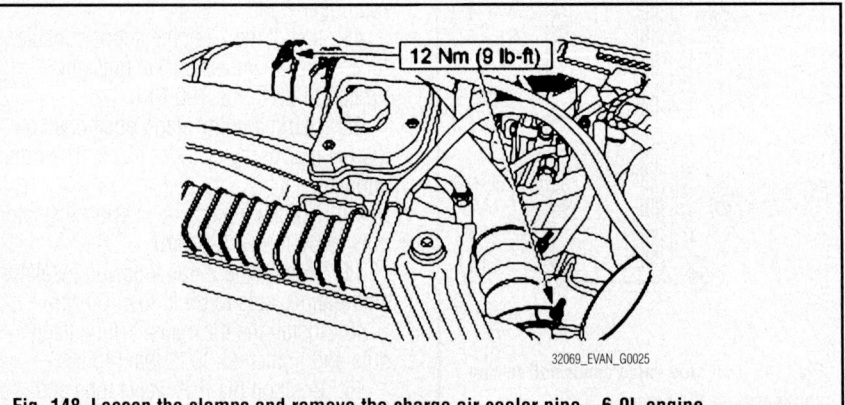

Fig. 148 Loosen the clamps and remove the charge air cooler pipe—6.0L engine

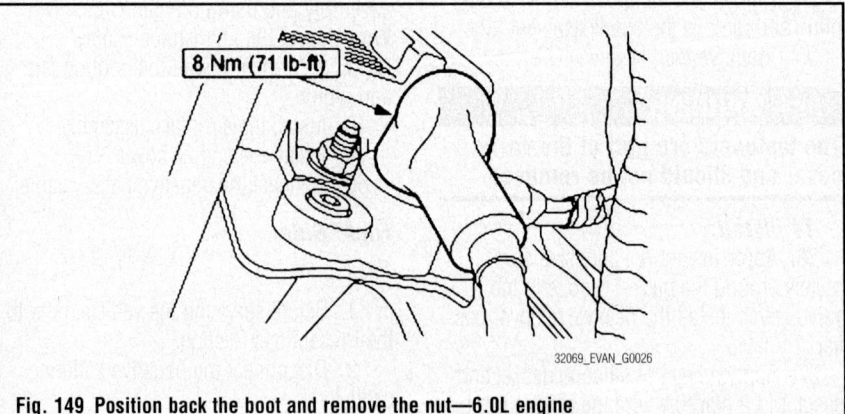

Fig. 149 Position back the boot and remove the nut—6.0L engine

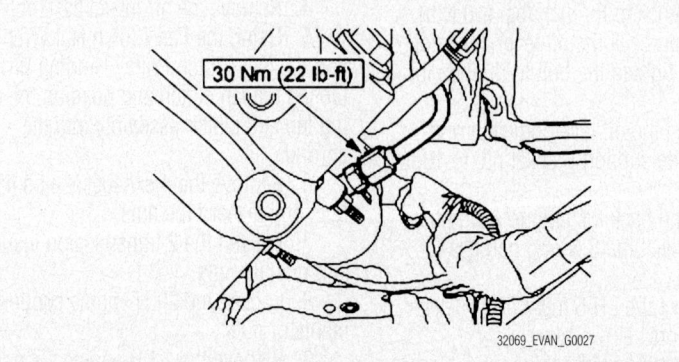

Fig. 150 Disconnect the exhaust back pressure tube at the exhaust manifold—6.0L engine

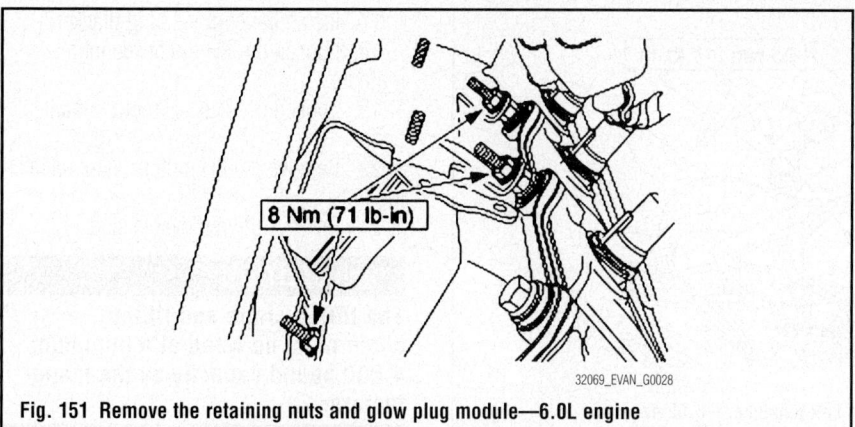

Fig. 151 Remove the retaining nuts and glow plug module—6.0L engine

2. Disconnect the negative battery cable.

3. Unfasten the latches and remove the engine cover.

4. Remove the turbocharger inlet tube.

➡️**If there is any oil residue, clean both connecting ports and the inside surface of the charge air cooler duct to prevent the duct from blowing off.**

5. Loosen the clamps and remove the charge air cooler pipe.

6. Disconnect the oil level indicator and tube from the stator.

7. Disconnect the glow plug wire retainer. Remove the nut and position the oil level indicator and tube aside.

8. Disconnect the glow plug module electrical connectors.

⁂ **WARNING**

Do not use power tools when removing or installing the nut. Use care not to overtighten the nut during installation.

9. Position back the boot and remove the nut. Disconnect the cables.

10. Disconnect the exhaust back pressure electrical connector and pushpin retainer.

11. Disconnect the exhaust back pressure tube at the exhaust manifold.

12. Remove the retaining nuts and glow plug module.

13. Remove the three retaining nuts and the glow plug module mounting bracket.

⁂ **WARNING**

To prevent engine damage, do not use air powered tools when installing the valve cover.

➡️**Mark the position of the valve cover bolts for valve cover bolt installation.**

14. Remove the 11 retainers and the valve cover. Clean and inspect the valve cover gasket.

15. Installation is the reverse order of removal. Torque the valve cover bolts to 80 inch lbs. (9 Nm).

Right Side

See Figures 153 through 168.

1. Before servicing the vehicle, refer to the Precautions Section.

2. With the vehicle in NEUTRAL, position it on a hoist.

3. Disconnect the negative battery cable.

4. Unfasten the latches and remove the engine cover.

5. Remove the engine fan. For additional information, refer to "Engine Fan, Removal & Installation."

Vehicles with dual alternator:

6. Remove the accessory drive belt.

7. Remove the bolt and the accessory drive belt tensioner.

8. Remove the accessory drive belt.

9. Remove the bolts, bracket and accessory drive belt idler pulley.

10. Remove the bolts and the accessory drive belt tensioner.

11. Disconnect the alternator electrical connector and the B+ wire.

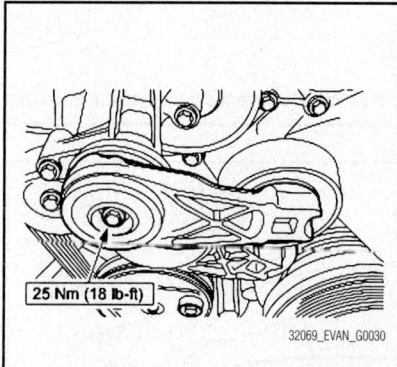

Fig. 153 Remove the bolt and the accessory drive belt tensioner—6.0L engine

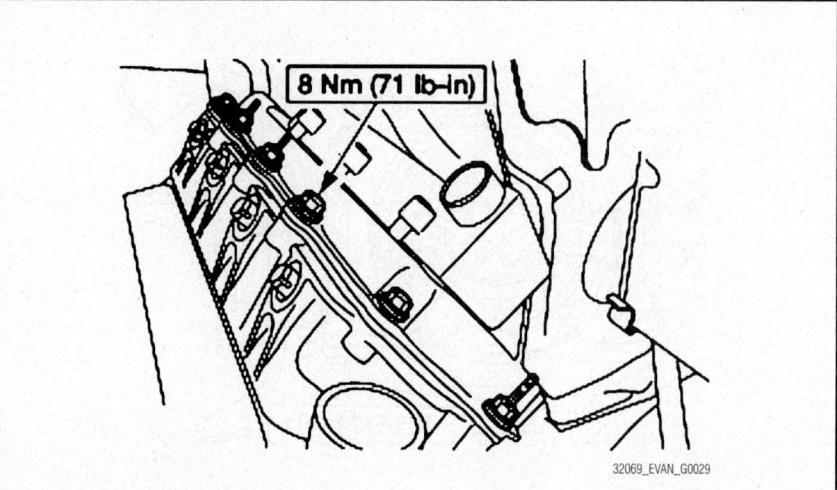

Fig. 152 Valve cover retainers—6.0L engine

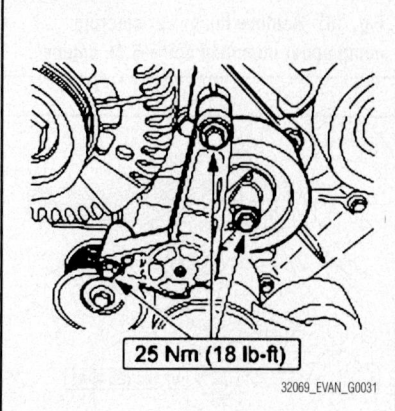

Fig. 154 Remove the bolts, bracket and accessory drive belt idler pulley—6.0L engine

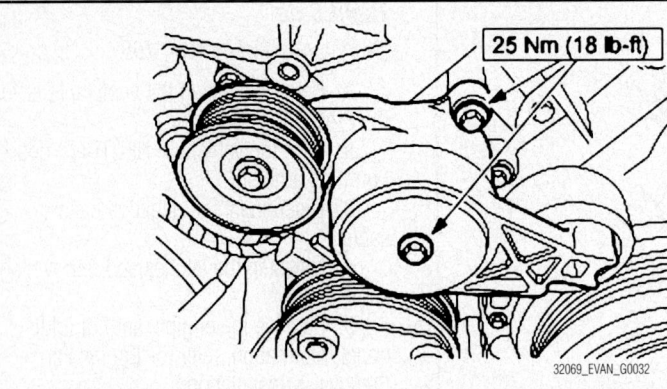

Fig. 155 Remove the bolts and the accessory drive belt tensioner—6.0L engine

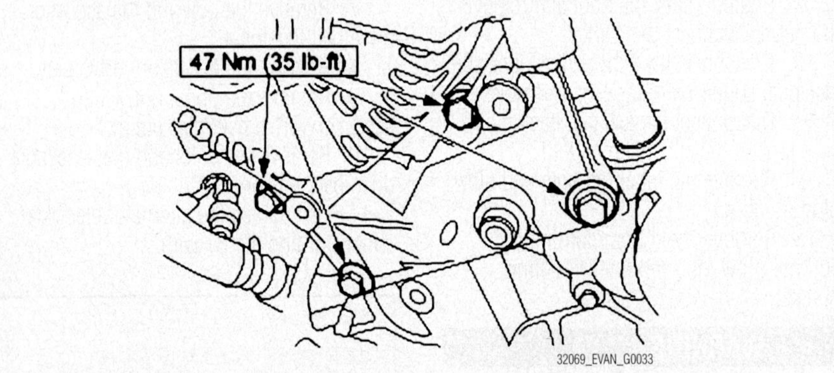

25 Nm (18 lb-ft)

47 Nm (35 lb-ft)

Fig. 156 Remove the bolts and the alternator with mounting bracket—6.0L engine

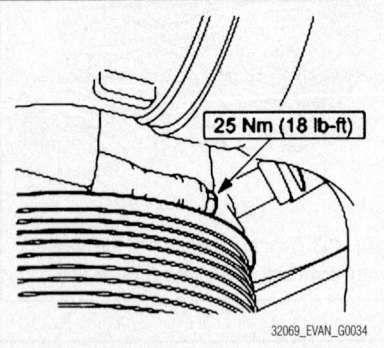

25 Nm (18 lb-ft)

Fig. 157 Remove the power steering pump upper mounting bolt—6.0L engine

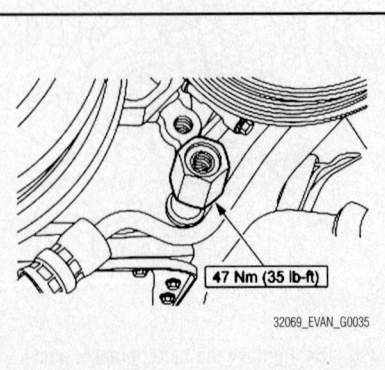

47 Nm (35 lb-ft)

Fig. 158 Remove the LH fan stator stand-off—6.0L engine

12. Remove the bolts and the alternator with mounting bracket.
Vehicles with single alternator:
13. Remove the accessory drive belt.
All vehicles:
14. Remove the power steering pump upper mounting bolt.
15. Remove the LH fan stator stand-off.
16. Remove the power steering pump bolts and position the power steering pump aside.

17. Install the engine lifting bracket.
18. Loosen the RH motor mount retaining nuts.
19. Loosen the four LH motor mount bolts.
20. Remove the LH motor mount retaining nuts.
21. Remove the removable stud.

✳✳ CAUTION

The lifting crane and lifting chain must be rated at a minimum 4,000 pound capacity by the manufacturer.

22. Connect a suitable lifting crane and lifting chain to the engine lifting bracket and raise the engine as needed to remove the motor mount. Remove the four bolts and the LH motor mount. Carefully lower the engine.
23. Remove the retaining nut and disconnect the push pin retainer.
24. Remove the retaining nut for the transmission fluid level indicator and tube. Position the tube aside.
25. Remove the bolt for the oil fill tube.
26. Disconnect the oil fill tube.
27. Disconnect the injection control pressure (ICP) sensor electrical connector and wire retainers.
28. Remove the ICP sensor. Plug or cap the opening as needed.
29. Position the wiring away from the valve cover as needed.

✳✳ WARNING

To prevent engine damage, do not use air powered tools when installing the valve cover.

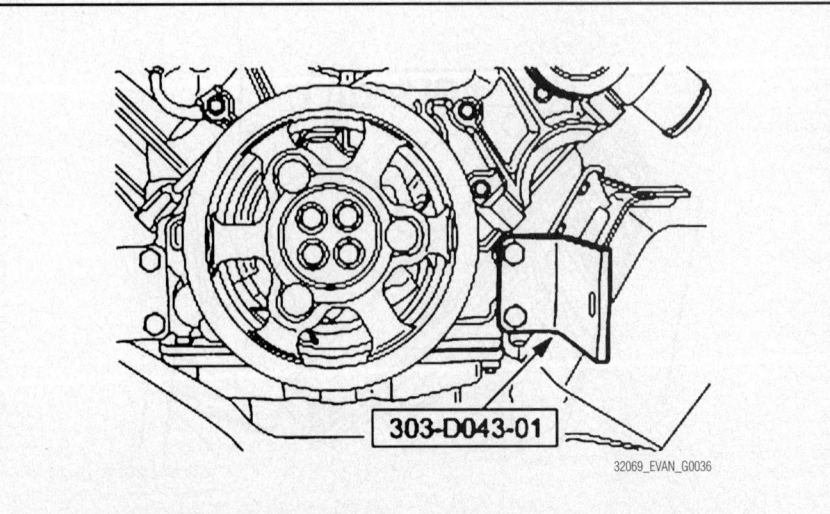

303-D043-01

Fig. 159 Install the engine lifting bracket—6.0L engine

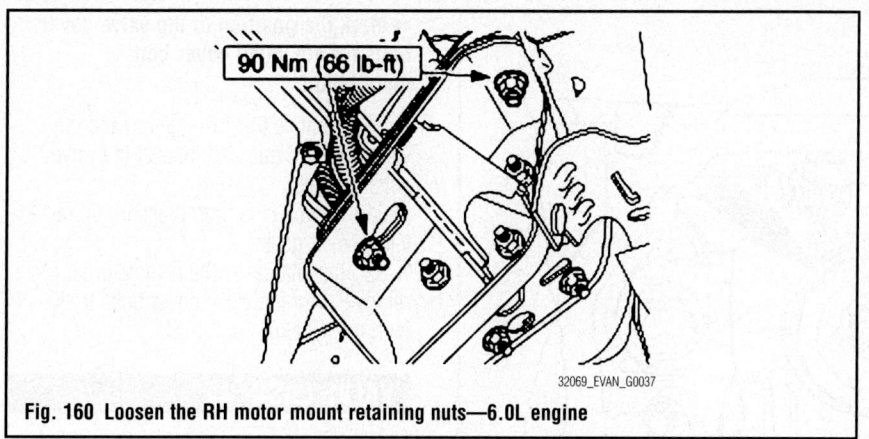

90 Nm (66 lb-ft)

32069_EVAN_G0037

Fig. 160 Loosen the RH motor mount retaining nuts—6.0L engine

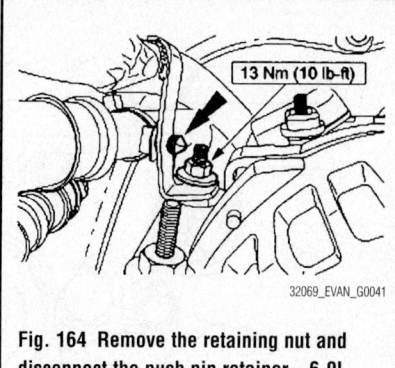

13 Nm (10 lb-ft)

32069_EVAN_G0041

Fig. 164 Remove the retaining nut and disconnect the push pin retainer—6.0L engine

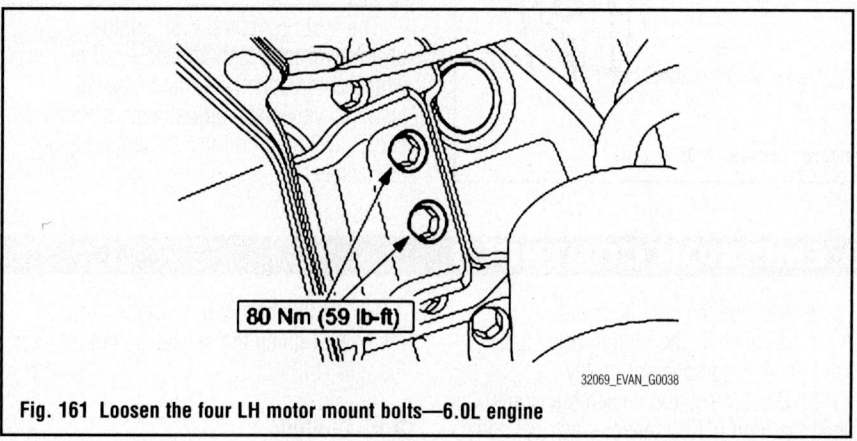

80 Nm (59 lb-ft)

32069_EVAN_G0038

Fig. 161 Loosen the four LH motor mount bolts—6.0L engine

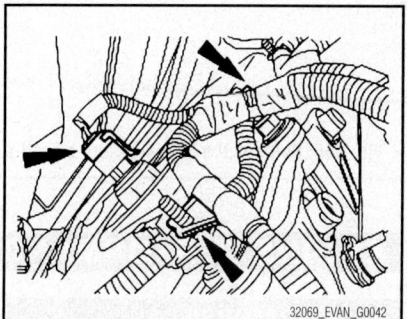

32069_EVAN_G0042

Fig. 165 Disconnect the injection control pressure (ICP) sensor electrical connector and wire retainers—6.0L engine

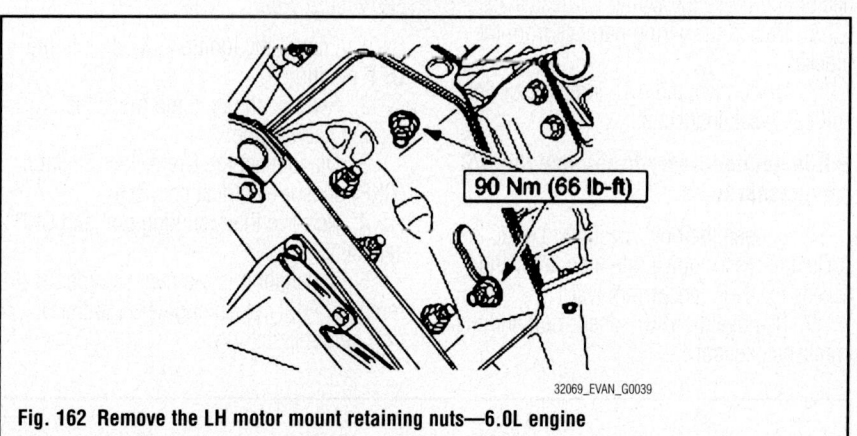

90 Nm (66 lb-ft)

32069_EVAN_G0039

Fig. 162 Remove the LH motor mount retaining nuts—6.0L engine

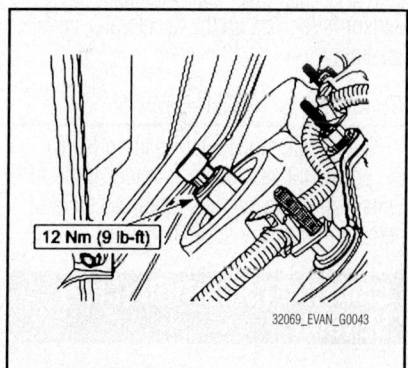

12 Nm (9 lb-ft)

32069_EVAN_G0043

Fig. 166 Remove the ICP sensor—6.0L engine

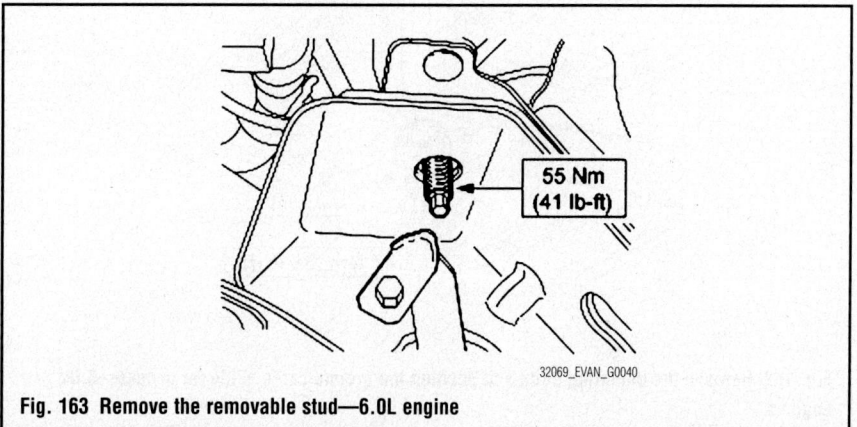

55 Nm
(41 lb-ft)

32069_EVAN_G0040

Fig. 163 Remove the removable stud—6.0L engine

8 Nm (71 lb-in)

32069_EVAN_G0045

Fig. 167 Remove the 11 retainers and the valve cover—6.0L engine

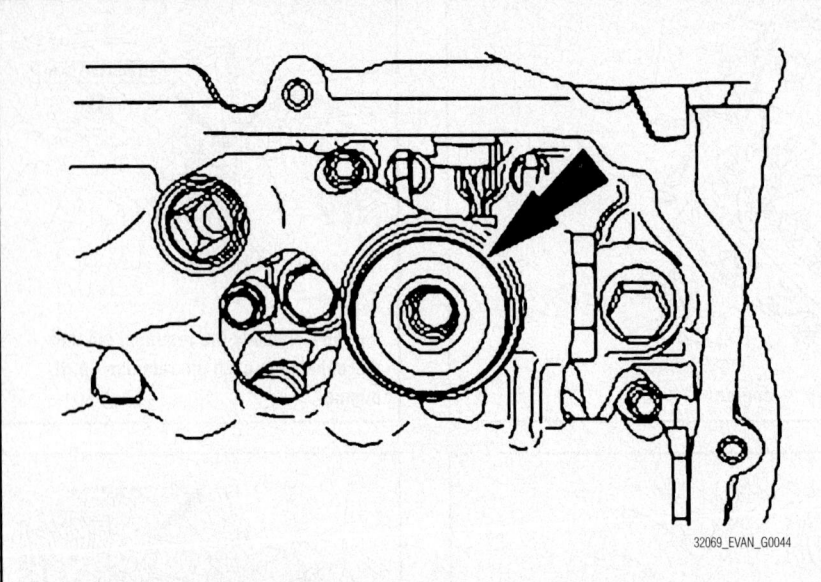

Fig. 168 Remove the high pressure oil rail-to-valve cover gasket—6.0L engine

→ Mark the position of the valve cover bolts for the valve cover bolt installation.

30. Remove the 11 retainers and the valve cover. Clean and inspect the valve cover gasket.

31. Remove the high pressure oil rail-to-valve cover gasket.

32. Installation is the reverse order of removal. Tighten valve cover bolts to 80 inch lbs. (9 Nm).

VALVE LASH

ADJUSTMENT

The 4.6L, 5.4L and 6.8L engines utilize hydraulic lash adjusters, all of which automatically adjust the valve lash. No valve lash adjustment is necessary. Valve lash on the 6.0L engine is not adjustable.

ENGINE PERFORMANCE & EMISSION CONTROLS

ACCELERATOR PEDAL POSITION (APP) SENSOR

LOCATION

The Accelerator Pedal Position (APP) Sensor is located on the accelerator pedal assembly.

REMOVAL & INSTALLATION

The Accelerator Pedal Position (APP) Sensor is not serviced separately. If the APP Sensor requires service, a new accelerator pedal and shaft must be installed.

CAMSHAFT POSITION (CMP) SENSOR

REMOVAL & INSTALLATION

1. Disconnect the negative battery cable.
2. Disconnect the Camshaft Position (CMP) sensor electrical connector.
3. Remove the mounting bolt and CMP sensor.
4. Installation is the reverse order of removal.

CRANKSHAFT POSITION (CKP) SENSOR

REMOVAL & INSTALLATION

4.6L, 5.4L & 6.8L Engines

1. Disconnect the negative battery cable.
2. Raise and safely support the vehicle.

3. Remove the splash shield.
4. Remove the accessory drive belt from the A/C compressor pulley.
5. Disconnect and detach the Crankshaft Position (CKP) sensor electrical connector and move the wiring harness aside.
6. Detach the wiring harness from the bracket.
7. Disconnect the A/C compressor field coil electrical connector.

→ It is not necessary to remove the A/C compressor bolts.

8. Loosen the bolts enough to slide the A/C compressor down one inch, allowing access for CKP sensor removal.
9. Remove the CKP sensor bolt and the crankshaft sensor.

10. Installation is the reverse order of removal. Tighten the sensor bolt to 89 inch lbs. (10 Nm).

6.0L Engine

See Figure 169.

1. Ensure the ignition switch is in the **OFF** position.
2. Remove the bolt and move the ground cable aside.
3. Disconnect the Crankshaft Position (CKP) sensor electrical connector.
4. Remove the mounting bolt and CKP sensor.
5. Installation is the reverse order of removal. Apply clean engine oil to the O-ring before installing.

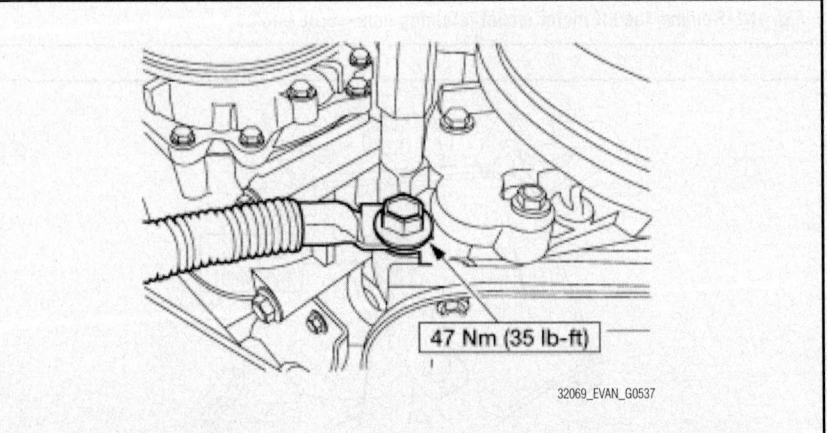

Fig. 169 Remove the mounting bolts and position the ground cable aside for access—6.0L Engines

47 Nm (35 lb-ft)

ENGINE COOLANT TEMPERATURE (ECT) SENSOR

REMOVAL & INSTALLATION

4.6L, 5.4L & 6.8L Engines

1. Disconnect the negative battery cable.
2. Drain the cooling system.
3. Disconnect the electrical connector and remove the Engine Coolant Temperature (ECT) sensor.
4. Installation is the reverse order of removal. Tighten the sensor to 15 ft. lbs. (20 Nm).
5. Refill the cooling system to the correct level.

6.0L Engine

See Figure 170.

1. Turn the ignition switch to the **OFF** position.
2. Partially drain the cooling system.
3. Remove the retainers and air deflector.
4. Remove the power steering reservoir bracket retainers.
5. Remove the power steering fluid indicator and retainers. Remove the power steering reservoir bracket. Install the power steering indicator and position aside.
6. Disconnect the coolant hoses from the air cleaner outlet pipe.
7. Loosen the clamps and remove the air cleaner outlet pipe.

➡**If there is any oil residue, clean both connecting ports and the inside surface of the charge air cooler pipe to prevent the pipe from blowing off.**

8. Loosen the clamps and remove the charge air cooler (CAC) pipe.
9. Disconnect the engine coolant temperature (ECT) electrical connector.
10. Remove the ECT sensor.
11. Installation is the reverse order of removal.

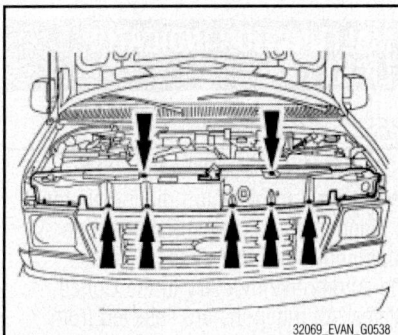

32069_EVAN_G0538

Fig. 170 Remove the retainers and air deflector—6.0L Engines

ENGINE OIL TEMPERATURE (EOT) SENSOR

LOCATION

6.0L Engine

See Figure 171.

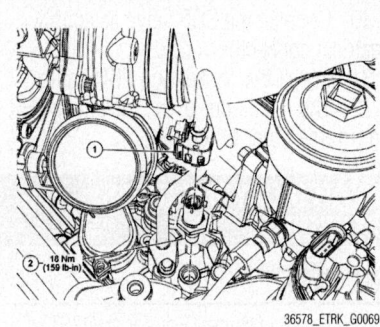

36578_ETRK_G0069

Fig. 171 Engine Oil Temperature sensor location—6.0L Engine

REMOVAL & INSTALLATION

6.0L Engine

1. Disconnect the negative battery cable.
2. Release the latches and remove the engine cover.
3. Loose the charge air cooler tube clamps.
4. Remove the bolt and position the ground wire aside. Disconnect the electrical connector pushpin.
5. Remove the bolt and position the Manifold Absolute Pressure (MAP) assembly aside.
6. Remove the 3 bolts and position the wiring aside.
7. Remove the 3 bolts for the CAC tube and the oil fill tube.
8. Disconnect and remove the oil fill tube at the valve cover.
9. Remove the 2 nuts, CAC tube, oil fill tube and bracket.
10. Disconnect the Engine Oil Temperature (EOT) sensor.
11. Remove the EOT sensor.
12. Installation is the reverse order of removal. Tighten the EOT sensor to 13 ft. lbs. (18 Nm).

EVAPORATIVE EMISSIONS (EVAP) CANISTER

LOCATION

The EVAP canister is located above the spare tire for midship fuel tanks and on the left hand frame rail for aft-of-axle fuel tanks.

REMOVAL & INSTALLATION

Aft-of-Axle Fuel Tank Models

1. Disconnect the negative battery cable.
2. Raise and safely support the vehicle.
3. Disconnect the fuel vapor tubes-to-Evaporative Emission (EVAP) canister quick connect couplings and fuel vapor tube pushpin retainer.
4. Disconnect the EVAP canister vent solenoid electrical connector.
5. Remove the EVAP canister assembly bracket-to-frame bolts.
6. Installation is the reverse order of removal. Tighten the bolts as follows:
   • Lower bolts to 53 ft. lbs. (6 Nm)
   • Upper bolts to 89 inch lbs. (10 Nm)

Midship Fuel Tank Models

1. Disconnect the negative battery cable.
2. Raise and safely support the vehicle.
3. Remove the spare tire.
4. Remove the Evaporative Emission (EVAP) canister assembly bracket-to-frame bolts.
5. Remove the EVAP canister-to-bracket bolts.
6. Slide the bracket out of the frame while support the EVAP canister assembly.
7. Disconnect the fresh air hose and the 2 fuel vapor tubes-to- EVAP canister quick connect couplings.
8. Disconnect the FVAP canister vent solenoid electrical connector and harness retainer(s) and remove the EVAP canister from the vehicle.
9. Installation is the reverse order of removal.

EXHAUST GAS RECIRCULATION (EGR) VALVE

LOCATION

6.0L Engine

See Figure 172.

REMOVAL & INSTALLATION

6.0L Engine

1. Disconnect the negative battery cable.
2. Remove the 6 pushpin retainers and upper air deflector.
3. Remove the 4 bolts for the power steering bracket.
4. Remove the 3 bolts and power steering fluid indicator. Remove the power steering reservoir mounting bracket. Install the power steering fluid indicator and position it aside.

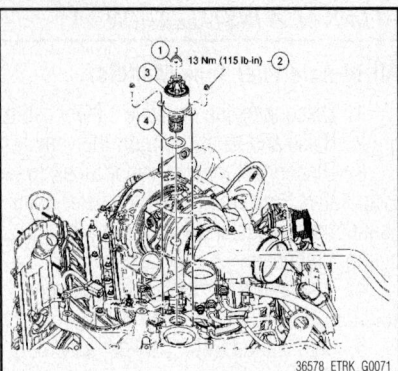

Fig. 172 Location of the EGR valve (3)—6.0L Engines

5. Disconnect the coolant hoses from the Air Cleaner (ACL) outlet pipe.

6. Loosen the clamps and remove the ACL outlet pipe.

7. Loosen the clamps and remove the Charge Air Cooler (CAC) tube.

8. Remove the 2 bolts and position the Manifold Absolute Pressure (MAP) sensor and the ground wire aside.

9. Remove the 3 bolts and disconnect the pushpin retainer. Position the cowl wiring harness aside.

10. Loosen the clamp for the CAC tube.

11. Remove the 3 bolts for the CAC tube and oil fill tube.

12. Remove the engine cover. For additional information, refer to Section 501-05 .

13. Loosen the clamp at the CAC tube.

14. Disconnect the oil fill tube at the valve cover.

15. Remove the 2 retaining nuts, CAC tube, oil fill tube and bracket.

16. Remove the 4 bolts and intake adapter.

17. Cover the opening after the intake adapter is removed.

18. Remove the EGR baffle and gasket.

19. Remove the secondary fuel filter and drain the housing. Install the fuel filter and cover.

20. Disconnect the fuel tubes at the secondary fuel filter and position them aside.

21. Remove the 2 bolts and position the secondary fuel filter assembly aside.

22. Disconnect the EGR valve assembly electrical connector.

23. Remove the 2 bolts and rotate the EGR valve counterclockwise.

24. Install the EGR Valve Remover and remove the EGR valve.

25. Remove and discard the O-ring seals and the EGR gasket.

To install:

26. Position the secondary fuel filter housing and tighten the bolts to 18 ft. lbs. (24 Nm).

27. Connect the fuel tubes at the secondary fuel filter and tighten to 19 ft. lbs. (26 Nm).

28. Install a new EGR gasket. Install new O-ring seals and lubricate with clean engine oil.

29. Position the EGR valve and install the 2 bolts. Tighten to 115 inch lbs. (13 Nm).

30. Connect the EGR valve assembly electrical connector.

31. Install the gasket and EGR baffle.

32. The remainder of the installation is the reverse order of removal.

HEATED OXYGEN (HO2S) SENSOR

LOCATION

The Heated Oxygen Sensor (HO2S) is located in the downpipe off the exhaust manifold.

REMOVAL & INSTALLATION

1. Disconnect the negative battery cable.

2. Raise and safely support the vehicle.

3. Disconnect the Heated Oxygen Sensor (HO2S) electrical connector.

4. Using a suitable oxygen sensor socket, remove the HO2S.

5. Installation is the reverse order of removal. Tighten the HO2S to 34 ft. lbs. (46 Nm).

INTAKE AIR TEMPERATURE (IAT) SENSOR

REMOVAL & INSTALLATION

6.0L Engines
See Figure 173.

1. Turn the ignition switch to the **OFF** position.

2. Remove the retainers and air deflector.

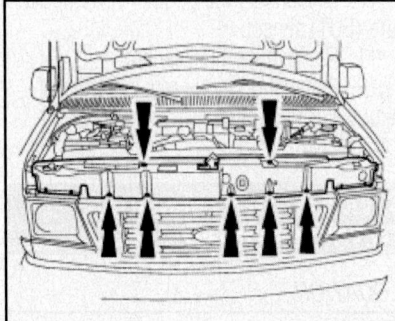

Fig. 173 Remove the retainers and air deflector—6.0L Engines

3. Remove the power steering reservoir bracket retainers.

4. Remove the power steering fluid indicator and retainers. Remove the power steering reservoir bracket. Install the power steering indicator and position aside.

5. Disconnect the coolant hoses from the air cleaner outlet pipe.

6. Loosen the clamps and remove the air cleaner outlet pipe.

➡If there is any oil residue, clean both connecting ports and the inside surface of the charge air cooler pipe to prevent the pipe from blowing off.

7. Loosen the clamps and remove the charge air cooler (CAC) pipe.

8. Disconnect Intake Air Temperature (IAT) sensor electrical connector.

9. Remove the IAT sensor.

10. Installation is the reverse order of removal. Tighten the IAT sensor to 13 ft. lbs. (17 Nm).

KNOCK SENSOR (KS)

LOCATION

4.6L, 5.4L & 6.8L Engines

The knock sensor is located directly under the intake manifold.

REMOVAL & INSTALLATION

4.6L, 5.4L & 6.8L Engines

1. Remove the intake manifold. For additional information, refer to "Intake Manifold, Removal & Installation."

2. Disconnect the Knock Sensor (KS) electrical connector.

3. Remove the mounting bolt and remove the KS.

4. Installation is the reverse order of removal. Tighten the mounting bolt to 18 ft. lbs. (25 Nm).

MALFUNCTION INDICATOR LIGHT (MIL)

RESET PROCEDURE

The Malfunction Indicator Light is reset using an off-board diagnostic tool. A diagnostic tool has certain generic capabilities that are standard across the automotive industry in the United States. All functions are selected from a menu. Refer to the instruction manual provided by the tool manufacturer.

MASS AIR FLOW (MAF) SENSOR (HOT WIRE)

LOCATION

The Mass Air Flow (MAF) sensor is located in the air intake assembly.

REMOVAL & INSTALLATION

➡The Mass Air Flow (MAF) sensor and body are calibrated and serviced as a unit.

1. Disconnect the negative battery cable.
2. Remove the air intake assembly.
3. Release the air cleaner clamp. Separate the inlet side from the outlet side of the air cleaner.
4. Remove the MAF assembly.
5. Disconnect the MAF sensor electrical connector.
6. Remove the nuts and separate the MAF sensor from the MAF sensor plate.
7. Installation is the reverse order of removal. Tighten the nuts to 89 inch lbs. (10 Nm).

MANIFOLD ABSOLUTE PRESSURE (MAP) SENSOR

REMOVAL & INSTALLATION

6.0L Engine

See Figure 175.

1. Move the ignition switch to the **OFF** position.
2. Disconnect the pressure hose.
3. Disconnect the Manifold Absolute Pressure (MAP) sensor electrical connector.
4. Remove the mounting screws and remove the MAP sensor.

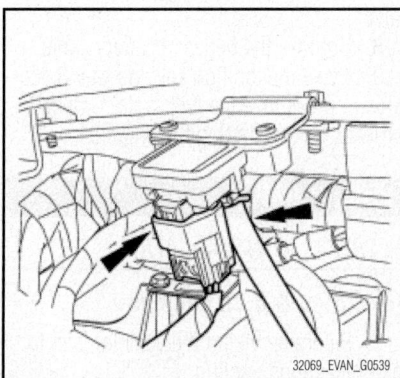

Fig. 175 Disconnect the MAP sensor electrical connector before removing the MAP sensor—6.0L Engines

5. Installation is the reverse order of removal.

OUTPUT SHAFT SPEED (OSS) SENSOR

LOCATION

The output shaft speed sensor is mounted on the side of transmission assembly.

REMOVAL & INSTALLATION

1. Raise and safely support the vehicle.
2. Disconnect the Output Shaft Speed (OSS) sensor electrical connector.
3. Remove the OSS sensor bolt and sensor.
4. Installation is the reverse order of removal. Tighten the sensor bolt to 106 inch lbs. (12 Nm).

POSITIVE CRANKCASE VENTILATION (PCV) VALVE

LOCATION

See Figures 176 and 177.

REMOVAL & INSTALLATION

1. Disconnect the negative battery cable.
2. Release the latches and remove the engine cover.

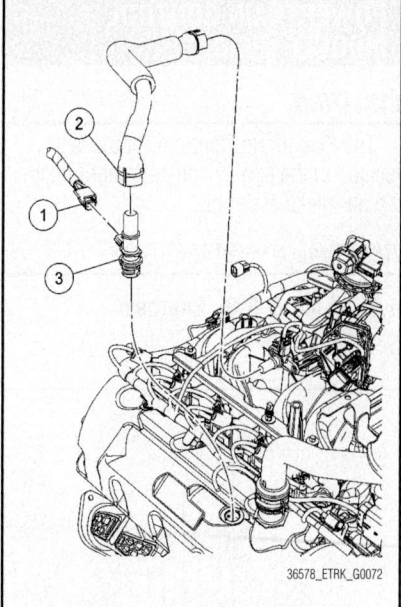

Fig. 176 PCV Valve (3) location—4.6L & 6.8L Engine

3. Disconnect the PCV valve electrical connector.
4. Disconnect the PCV valve tube quick-connect fitting and position the PCV tube aside
5. Rotate the PCV valve counterclockwise and remove the PCV valve.
6. Installation is the reverse order of removal using a new PCV valve.

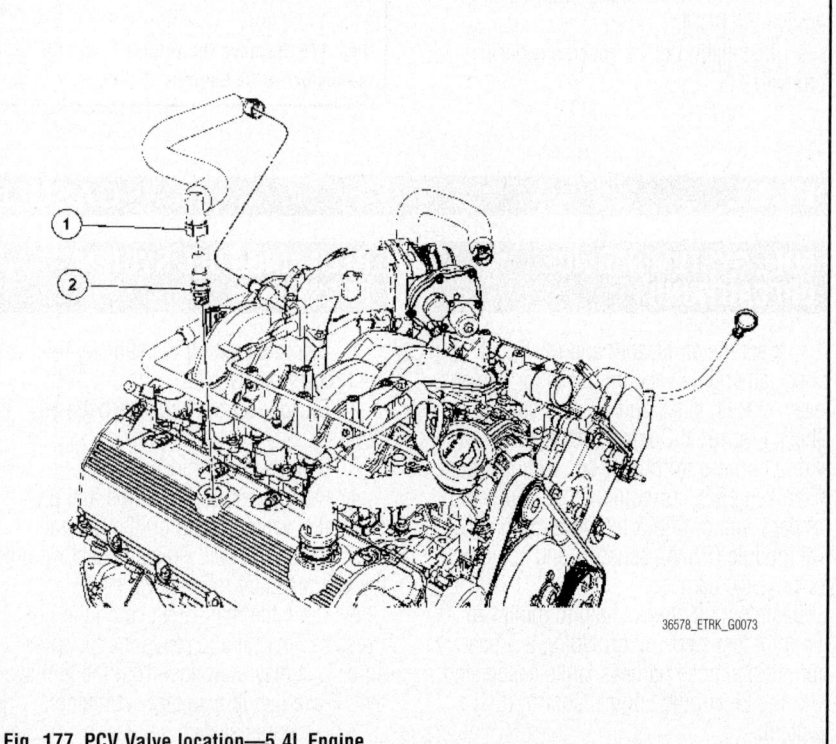

Fig. 177 PCV Valve location—5.4L Engine

POWERTRAIN CONTROL MODULE (PCM)

LOCATION

The Powertrain Control Module is located in the engine compartment under the air intake assembly.

REMOVAL & INSTALLATION

4.6L, 5.4L & 6.8L Engines

See Figure 178.

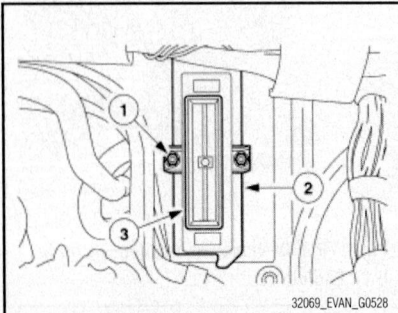

Fig. 178 Remove the nuts (1) and cover (2) to remove the PCM (3)—Gasoline Engines

1. Disconnect the negative battery cable.
2. Remove the air intake assembly.
3. Disconnect the Powertrain Control Module (PCM) electrical connector.
4. Remove the retaining nuts, cover and remove the PCM.
5. Installation is the reverse order of removal.

6.0L Engines

See Figure 179.

1. Turn the ignition switch to the **OFF** position.
2. Remove the retainers and air deflector.
3. Remove the power steering reservoir bracket retainers.
4. Remove the power steering fluid indicator and retainers. Remove the power steering reservoir bracket. Install the power steering indicator and position aside.
5. Disconnect the coolant hoses from the air cleaner outlet pipe.
6. Loosen the clamps and remove the air cleaner outlet pipe.
7. Unlatch and disconnect the Powertrain Control Module (PCM) electrical connectors.
8. Remove and mounting bolt and remove the PCM.
9. Installation is the reverse order of removal. Tighten the mounting bolt to 80 inch lbs. (9 Nm).

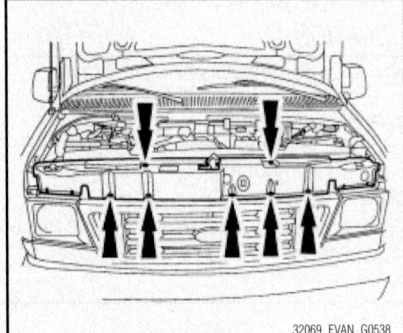

Fig. 179 Remove the retainers and air deflector—6.0L Engines

RESET PROCEDURE

1. Connect the Integrated Diagnostic System (IDS) and identify the vehicle as normal.
2. From the Toolbox icon, select Module Programming and press the check mark.
3. Select Programmable Module Installation.
4. Select the module that is being replaced.
5. Follow the on-screen instructions, turn the ignition key to the OFF position, and press the check mark.
6. Install the new module and press the check mark.
7. Follow the on-screen instructions, turn the ignition key to the ON position, and press the check mark.
8. The IDS downloads the data into the new module and displays Module Configuration Complete.
9. Test module for correct operation.

THROTTLE POSITION SENSOR (TPS)

LOCATION

The Throttle Position sensor is located on the throttle body assembly.

REMOVAL & INSTALLATION

4.6L, 5.4L & 6.8L Engines

1. Disconnect the negative battery cable.
2. Remove the air intake assembly.
3. Disconnect the Throttle Position Sensor (TPS) electrical connector.
4. Remove the mounting screws and TPS.
5. Installation is the reverse order of removal.

FUEL

GASOLINE FUEL INJECTION SYSTEM

FUEL SYSTEM SERVICE PRECAUTIONS

Inspect the air cleaner and inlet duct. Check all engine vacuum hoses for damage, leaks, cracks, kinks and proper routing. Check Electronic Control (EC) system wiring harness for proper connections, bent or broken pins, corrosion, loose wires and proper routing. Check the powertrain control module (PCM), sensors, and actuators for physical damage.

Basic circuit checks help to minimize pinpoint test steps by providing a procedure to diagnose harness faults associated with the Electronic Engine Control (EC) System:

RELIEVING FUEL SYSTEM PRESSURE

1. Before servicing the vehicle, refer to the Precautions Section.
2. Disconnect the negative battery cable.
3. Remove the engine cover.
4. Remove the cap from the fuel pressure relief valve located on the fuel rail.
5. Install the Fuel Pressure Test Kit onto the fuel pressure relief valve.
6. Open the manual valve on the Fuel Pressure Test Kit and relive the fuel pressure. This may drain fuel from the fuel system. Place fuel in a suitable container.
7. Once fuel system service is complete,

install the cap on the fuel pressure relief valve.
8. Connect the negative battery cable.
9. Cycle the ignition key and wait 3 seconds to pressurize the fuel system. Check for leaks before starting the engine.

FUEL PUMP

REMOVAL & INSTALLATION

4.6L, 5.4L & 6.8L Engines

1. Before servicing the vehicle, refer to the Precautions Section.
2. Disconnect the negative battery cable.
3. Properly relieve the fuel system pressure.

4. Remove the fuel tank. For additional information, refer to "Fuel Tank, Removal & Installation."

5. Disconnect the fuel vapor tube-to-Fuel Pump (FP) quick connect coupling, if equipped with midship fuel tank.

6. Using the Fuel Tank Sender Unit Wrench, remove the FP module lock ring.

7. Remove the fuel pump assembly and fuel pump O-ring seal.

8. Installation is the reverse order of removal using a new fuel pump O-ring seal.

FUEL RAIL & INJECTORS

REMOVAL & INSTALLATION

4.6L Engine
See Figure 180.

1. Before servicing the vehicle, refer to the Precautions Section.

2. Disconnect the negative battery cable.

3. Properly relieve the fuel system pressure.

4. Remove the air intake assembly.

5. Disconnect fuel supply hose quick connect coupling.

6. Disconnect the Evaporative Emission (EVAP) purge valve tube quick connect coupling from the intake manifold.

7. Disconnect the EVAP canister purge valve electrical connector.

8. Disconnect the EVAP canister-to-EVAP canister purge valve tube quick connect coupling.

9. Remove the bolt and the EVAP canister purge valve.

10. Disconnect the quick connect couplings and remove the PCV tube.

11. Disconnect the fuel injector electrical connectors.

12. Remove the fuel rail bolts.

13. Separate the fuel rail from the fuel injectors and remove the fuel rail.

14. Remove the fuel injectors from the intake manifold and discard the O-rings.

15. Installation is the reverse order of removal. Lubricate new O-rings with clean engine oil before installation.

5.4L Engine
See Figure 181.

1. Before servicing the vehicle, refer to the Precautions Section.

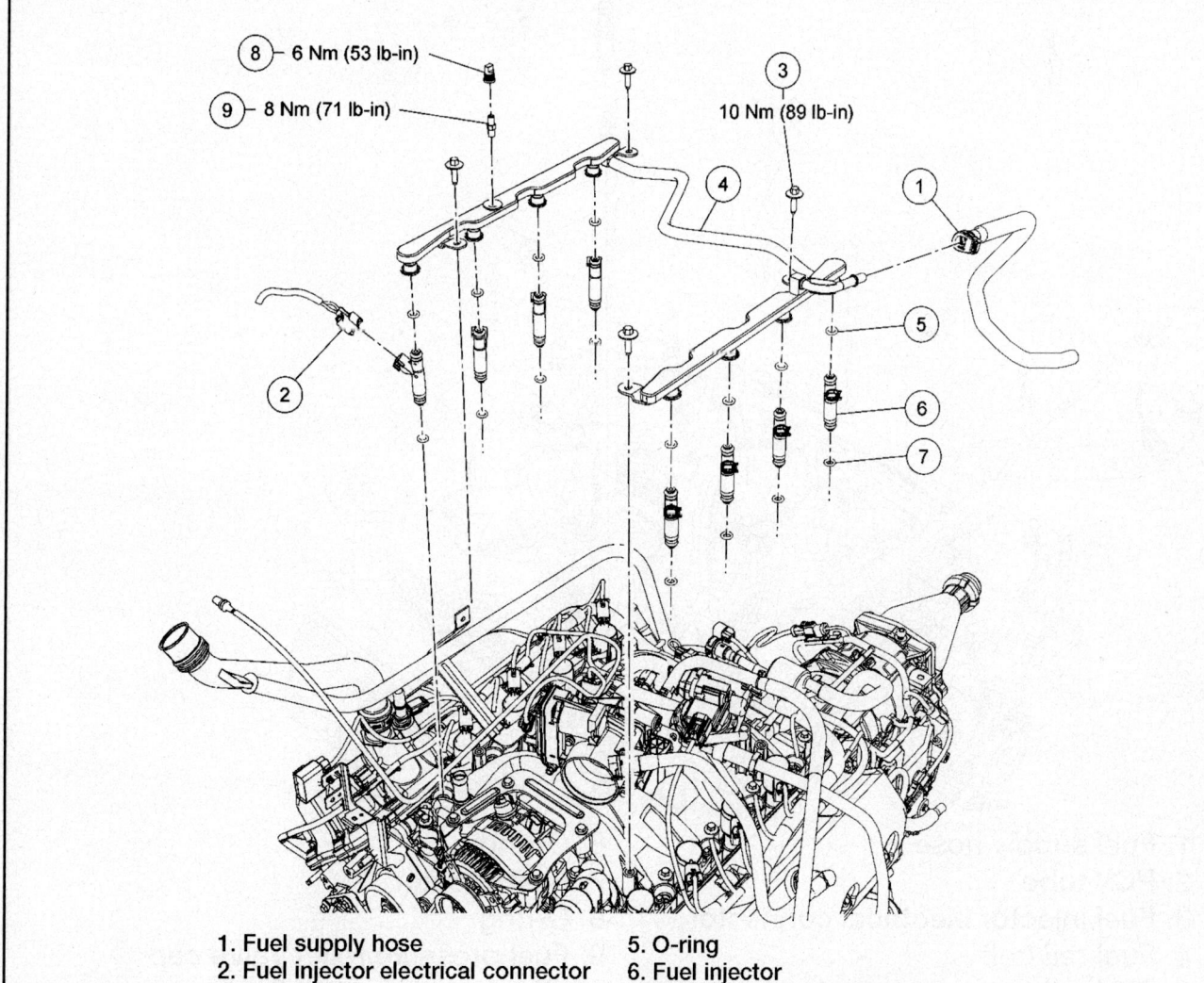

8 — 6 Nm (53 lb-in)
9 — 8 Nm (71 lb-in)
3
10 Nm (89 lb-in)

1. Fuel supply hose
2. Fuel injector electrical connector
3. Fuel rail bolt
4. Fuel rail
5. O-ring
6. Fuel injector
7. Fuel pressure relief valve cap
8. Fuel pressure relief valve

36578_ETRK_G0074

Fig. 180 Exploded view of the fuel rail and injectors—4.6L Engine

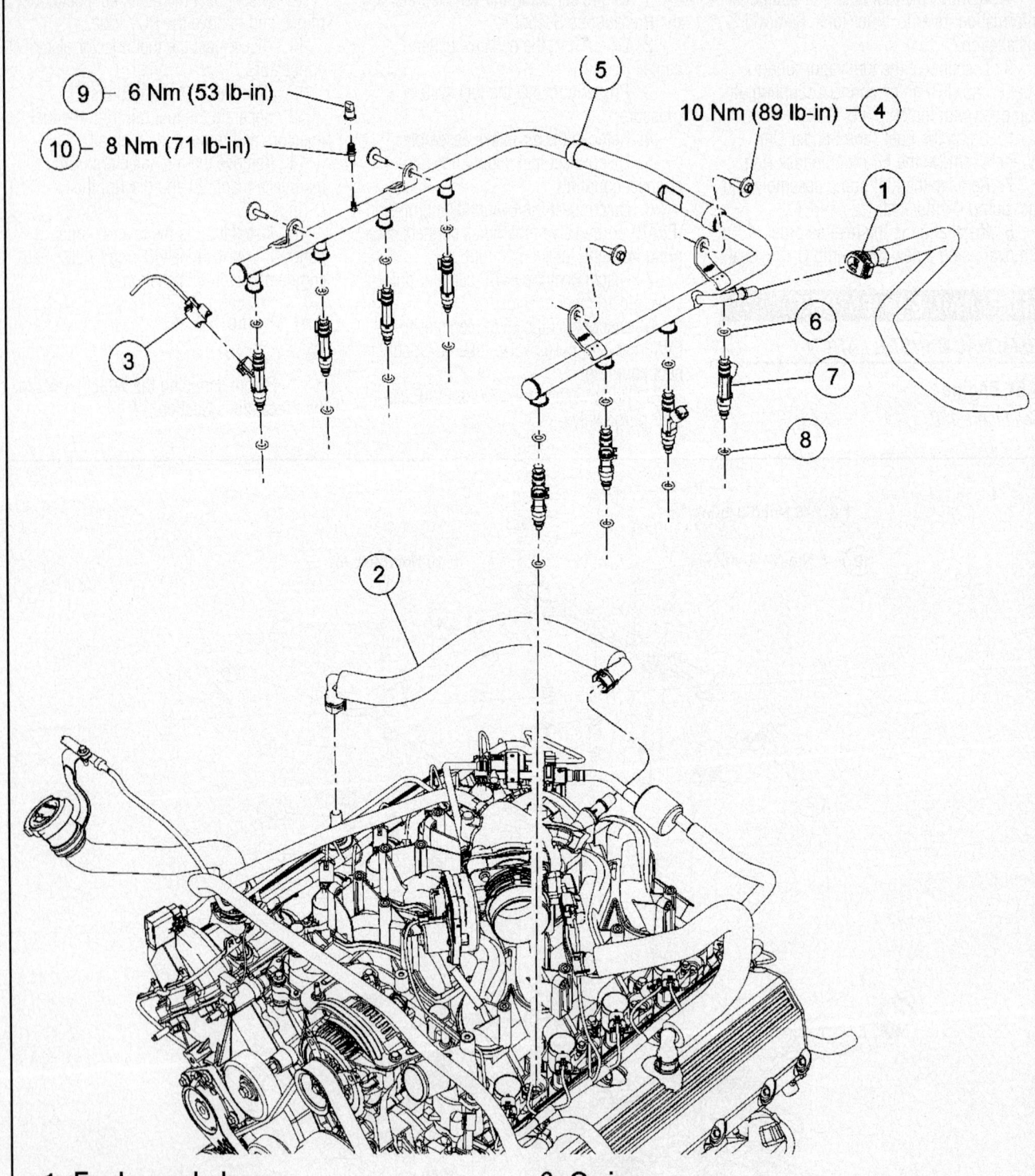

9 — 6 Nm (53 lb-in)

10 — 8 Nm (71 lb-in)

5

10 Nm (89 lb-in) — 4

1

3

6

7

8

2

1. Fuel supply hose
2. PCV tube
3. Fuel injector electrical connector
4. Fuel rail bolt
5. Fuel rail
6. O-ring
7. Fuel injector
8. O-ring
9. Fuel pressure relief valve cap
10. Fuel pressure relief valve

36578_ETRK_G0075

Fig. 181 Exploded view of the fuel rail and injectors—5.4L Engine

2. Disconnect the negative battery cable.

3. Release the latches and remove the engine cover.

4. Properly relieve the fuel system pressure.

5. Remove the air intake assembly.

6. Disconnect fuel supply hose quick connect coupling.

7. Disconnect the quick connect couplings and remove the PCV tube.

8. Disconnect the fuel injector electrical connectors.

9. Remove the fuel rail bolts.

10. Separate the fuel rail from the fuel injectors and remove the fuel rail.

11. Remove the fuel injectors from the intake manifold and discard the O-rings.

12. Installation is the reverse order of removal. Lubricate new O-rings with clean engine oil before installation.

6.8L Engine

1. Before servicing the vehicle, refer to the Precautions Section.

2. Disconnect the negative battery cable.

3. Release the latches and remove the engine cover.

4. Properly relieve the fuel system pressure.

5. Remove the air intake assembly.

6. Disconnect fuel supply hose quick connect coupling.

7. Disconnect the transmission wiring harness retainers from the engine wiring harness. Position the transmission wiring harness aside.

8. Disconnect the Throttle Position (TP) sensor electrical connector and the wiring harness retainer.

9. Disconnect the fuel injector electrical connectors.

10. Disconnect the ignition coil electrical connectors.

11. Disconnect the quick connect couplings and remove the PCV tube.

12. Disconnect the engine wiring harness retainer from the rear of the intake manifold.

13. Disconnect the right hand engine wiring harness retainers and position the wiring harness away from the fuel rail.

14. Disconnect the left hand engine wiring harness retainers and position the wiring harness away from the fuel rail.

➡ **When removing the fuel rail, leave the fuel injectors in the intake manifold to ease removal of the fuel rail.**

15. Remove the bolts, separate the fuel rail from the 10 fuel injectors and remove the fuel rail.

16. Remove the fuel injectors from the intake manifold and discard the upper and lower fuel injector O-ring seals.

To install:

17. Lubricate new O-rings with clean engine oil and install the O-rings onto the fuel injectors.

18. Install the fuel injectors into the intake manifold.

19. Install the fuel rail onto the fuel injectors and tighten the mounting bolts to 89 inch lbs. (10 Nm).

20. Position the engine wiring harness and connect the 3 LH engine wiring harness retainers.

21. Position the engine wiring harness and connect the 2 RH engine wiring harness retainers.

22. Connect the engine wiring harness retainer to the rear of the intake manifold.

23. Position the PCV tube and connect the quick connect couplings.

24. Connect the ignition coil electrical connectors.

25. Connect the fuel injector electrical connectors.

26. Connect the TP sensor electrical connector and wiring harness retainer.

27. Position the transmission wiring harness and connect harness retainers to the engine wiring harness.

28. Connect the fuel tube quick connect coupling.

29. Install the ACL and the ACL outlet tube.

30. Install the engine cover.

31. Connect the battery ground cable.

FUEL TANK

REMOVAL & INSTALLATION

Aft-Axle Tank Mounting

See Figure 182.

1. Before servicing the vehicle, refer to the Precautions Section.

2. Properly relieve the fuel system pressure.

3. Disconnect the negative battery cable.

4. Drain any remaining fuel from the tank.

5. Raise and safely support the vehicle.

6. Disconnect the fuel tank filler pipe and filler vent tube from the fuel tank.

7. Position a suitable jack under the fuel tank.

8. Remove the fuel tank support strap retaining bolts and nuts.

9. Remove the fuel tank support straps.

10. Partially lower the fuel tank.

11. Disconnect the fuel tubes from the fuel pump.

12. Disconnect the fuel pump and fuel tank sending unit electrical connector.

13. Disconnect the hose(s) from the evaporative emission valve.

14. Disconnect the fuel tank pressure sensor electrical connector.

15. Lower and remove the fuel tank assembly.

16. Installation is the reverse order of removal.

17. Tighten the support strap retaining nuts to 56–75 ft. lbs. (77–103 Nm) and support strap bolts to 64–88 ft. lbs. (87–119 Nm).

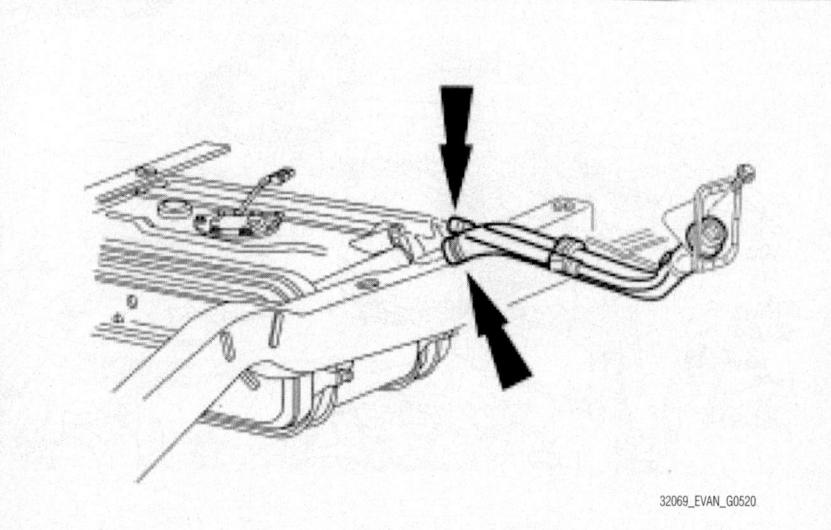

32069_EVAN_G0520

Fig. 182 Disconnect the filler pipe and filler vent tube from the fuel tank—Aft-Axle Tank Mounting

Midship Tank Mounting

1. Before servicing the vehicle, refer to the Precautions Section.

2. Properly relieve the fuel system pressure.

3. Disconnect the negative battery cable.

4. Drain any remaining fuel from the tank.

5. Disconnect the fuel pump/fuel sender electrical connector.

6. Disconnect the fuel tank filler pipe hose.

7. Disconnect the evaporative emissions (EVAP) tube connector, gasoline engines only.

8. Position a suitable jack under the fuel tank.

9. Remove the nut and the front fuel tank support strap.

10. Remove the nut and the rear fuel tank support strap.

11. Partially lower the fuel tank.

12. Disconnect the fuel tube spring lock coupling. For additional information, refer to Section 310-00 .

13. Disconnect the fuel tank vent tube connector., gasoline engines only.

14. Lower the fuel tank.

15. Installation is the reverse order of removal.

IDLE SPEED

ADJUSTMENT

Idle speed is maintained by the Powertrain Control Module (PCM). No adjustment is necessary or possible.

THROTTLE BODY

REMOVAL & INSTALLATION

4.6L Engine

See Figure 183.

1. Before servicing the vehicle, refer to the Precautions Section.

2. Disconnect the negative battery cable.

3. Remove the air intake assembly.

4. Disconnect the electronic throttle control electrical connector.

5. Remove the Throttle Body (TB) bolts and the TB and discard the gasket.

6. Installation is the reverse order of removal. Install a new TB gasket. To install, tighten to 89 inch lbs. (10 Nm). Tighten an additional 90°.

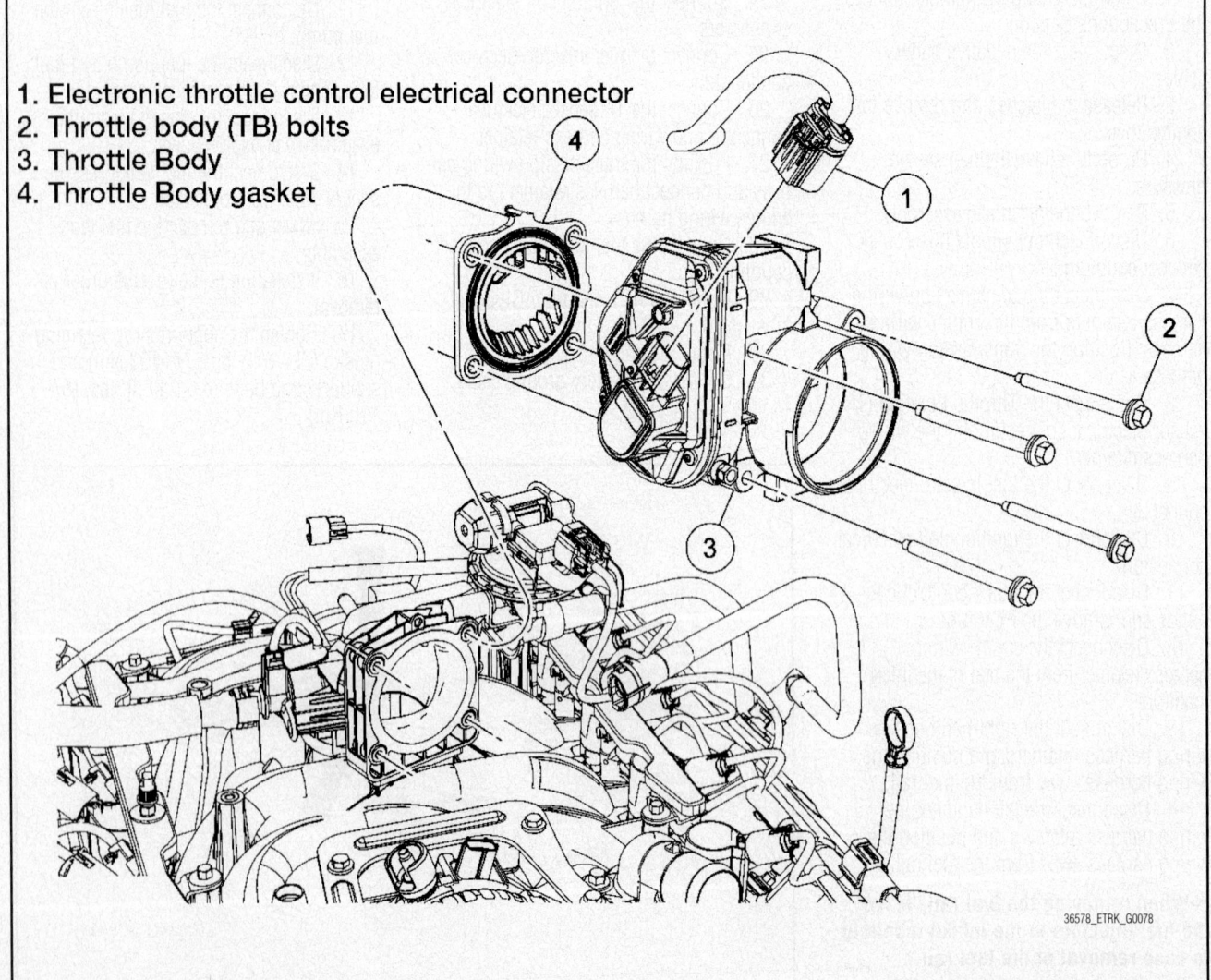

1. Electronic throttle control electrical connector
2. Throttle body (TB) bolts
3. Throttle Body
4. Throttle Body gasket

36578_ETRK_G0078

Fig. 183 Throttle body assembly—4.6L engine

5.4L Engine

See Figure 184.

1. Before servicing the vehicle, refer to the Precautions Section.

2. Disconnect the negative battery cable.

3. Remove the air cleaner and air cleaner intake pipe.

4. Disconnect the electronic throttle control electrical connector.

5. Disconnect the throttle position (TP) sensor electrical connector.

6. Remove the 4 throttle body (TB) bolts and the TB and discard the TB O-ring seal.

7. To install, reverse the removal procedure. Install a new TB gasket. To install, tighten to 80 inch lbs. (9 Nm) plus 90°

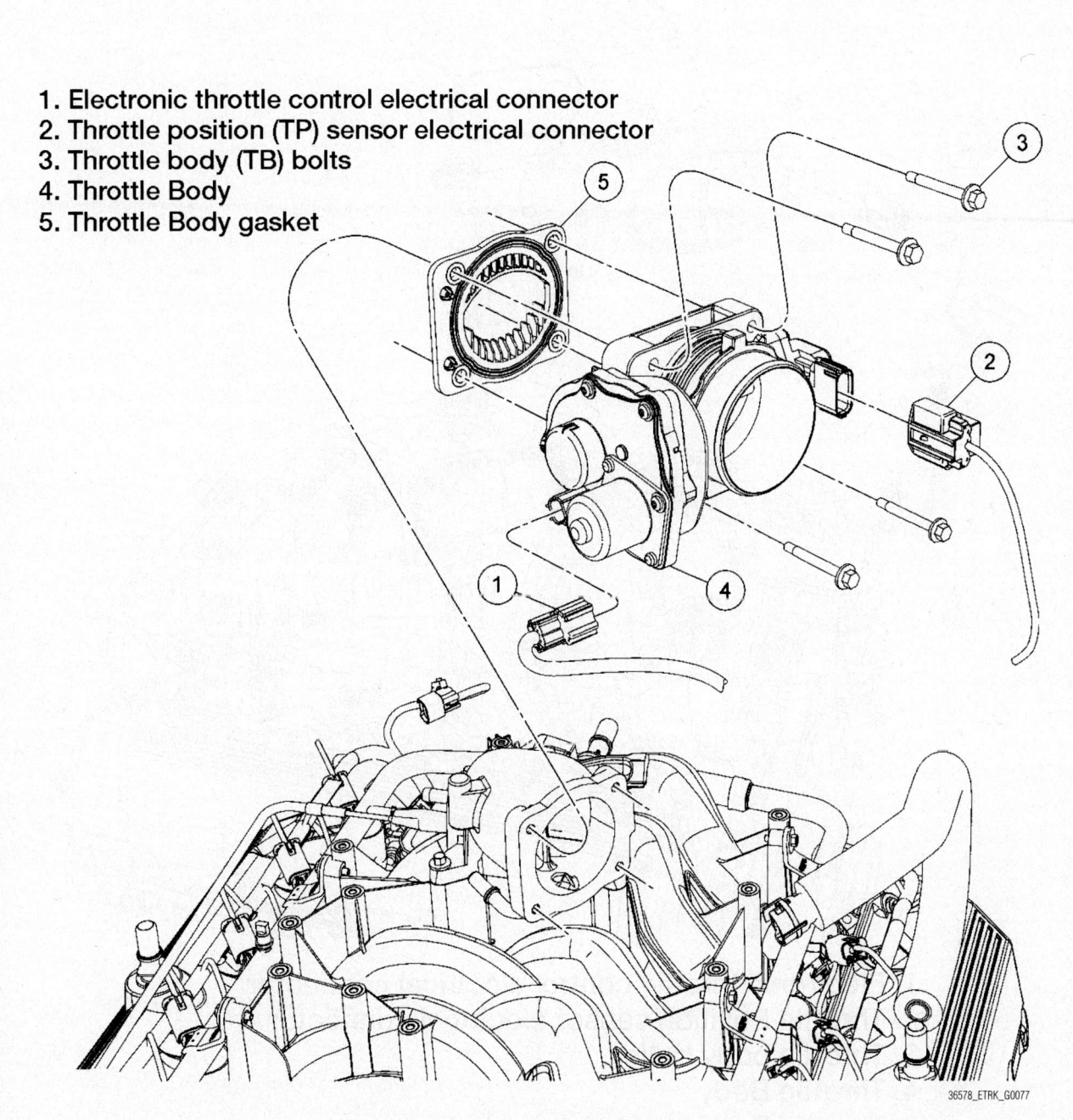

1. **Electronic throttle control electrical connector**
2. **Throttle position (TP) sensor electrical connector**
3. **Throttle body (TB) bolts**
4. **Throttle Body**
5. **Throttle Body gasket**

36578_ETRK_G0077

Fig. 184 Throttle body assembly—5.4L engine

6.8L Engine

See Figure 185.

1. Before servicing the vehicle, refer to the Precautions Section.

2. Disconnect the negative battery cable.

3. Remove the air intake assembly.

4. Disconnect the electronic throttle control electrical connector.

5. Disconnect the TP sensor electrical connector.

6. Remove the throttle body bolts and the throttle body and discard the throttle body gasket.

7. Installation is the reverse order of removal. To install, tighten to 80 inch lbs. (9 Nm) plus an additional 90°.

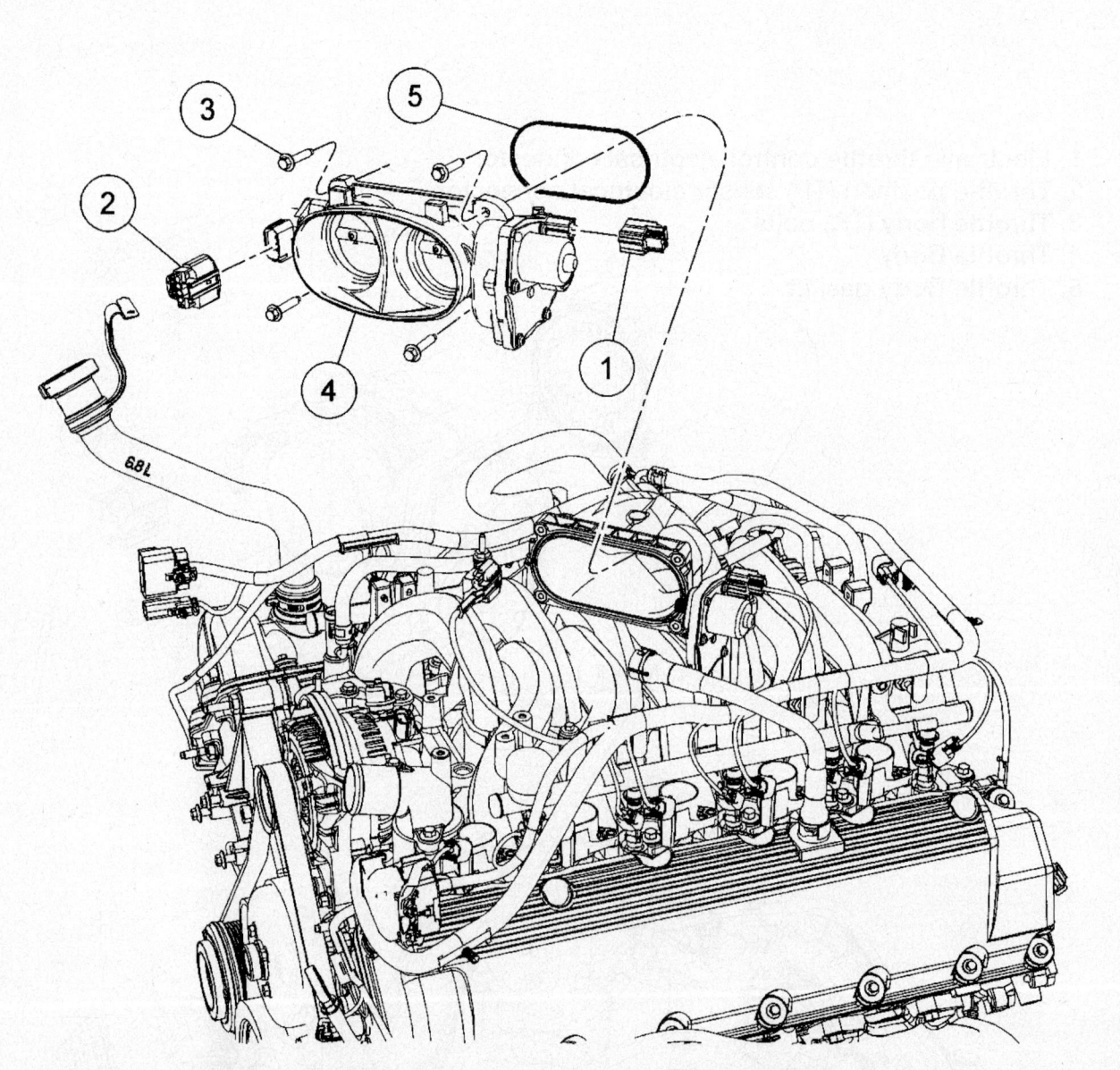

1. **Electronic throttle control electrical connector**
2. **Throttle Position sensor electrical connector**
3. **Throttle body bolts**
4. **Throttle Body**
5. **Throttle Body gasket**

36578_ETRK_G0079

Fig. 185 Throttle body assembly—6.8L engine

FUEL

FUEL SYSTEM SERVICE PRECAUTIONS

Safety is the most important factor when performing not only fuel system maintenance but any type of maintenance. Failure to conduct maintenance and repairs in a safe manner may result in serious personal injury or death. Maintenance and testing of the vehicle's fuel system components can be accomplished safely and effectively by adhering to the following rules and guidelines.

• To avoid the possibility of fire and personal injury, always disconnect the negative battery cable unless the repair or test procedure requires that battery voltage be applied.

• Always relieve the fuel system pressure prior to disconnecting any fuel system component (injector, fuel rail, pressure regulator, etc.), fitting or fuel line connection. Exercise extreme caution whenever relieving fuel system pressure to avoid exposing skin, face and eyes to fuel spray. Please be advised that fuel under pressure may penetrate the skin or any part of the body that it contacts.

• Always place a shop towel or cloth around the fitting or connection prior to loosening to absorb any excess fuel due to spillage. Ensure that all fuel spillage (should it occur) is quickly removed from engine surfaces. Ensure that all fuel soaked cloths or towels are deposited into a suitable waste container.

• Always keep a dry chemical (Class B) fire extinguisher near the work area.

• Do not allow fuel spray or fuel vapors to come into contact with a spark or open flame.

• Always use a back-up wrench when loosening and tightening fuel line connection fittings. This will prevent unnecessary stress and torsion to fuel line piping.

• Always replace worn fuel fitting O-rings with new. Do not substitute fuel hose or equivalent where fuel pipe is installed.

Before servicing the vehicle, make sure to also refer to the precautions in the beginning of this section as well.

RELIEVING FUEL SYSTEM PRESSURE

See Figure 186.

1. Before servicing the vehicle, refer to the Precautions Section.
2. Raise and safely support the vehicle.

3. Disconnect both battery ground cables.
4. Open the fuel/water separator drain valve to release the fuel pressure.

FUEL CONDITIONING MODULE

REMOVAL & INSTALLATION
See Figure 187.

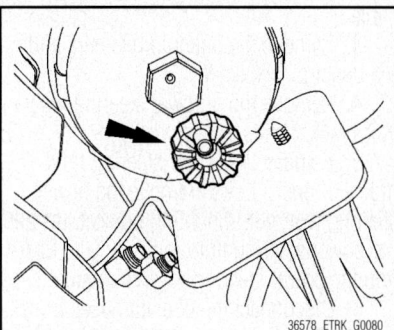

Fig. 186 Open the fuel/water separator drain valve to release the fuel pressure—6.0L Engine

1. Before servicing the vehicle, refer to the Precautions Section.
2. Properly relieve the fuel system pressure.
3. Disconnect the negative battery cable.
4. Disconnect the fuel conditioning module electrical connectors.
5. Disconnect the fuel hose spring lock couplings.
6. Disconnect the wiring pushpin. Remove the 2 mounting bolts and the fuel conditioning module.
7. Installation is the reverse order of removal.

FUEL FILTER

REMOVAL & INSTALLATION

1. Before servicing the vehicle, refer to the Precautions Section.
2. Disconnect the negative battery cable.
3. Detach the coolant hoses from the Air Cleaner (ACL) outlet pipe.
4. Loosen the clamps and remove the air cleaner outlet pipe.
5. Loosen the clamp on the Charge Air Cooler (CAC) tube at the intake manifold adapter.
6. Loosen the clamp on the CAC tube at the CAC.
7. Remove and position the CAC tube aside.

8. Remove the secondary fuel filter cap by turning the cap counterclockwise and remove the secondary fuel filter.
9. Installation is the reverse order of removal. Tighten the fuel filter cap to 124 inch lbs. (14 Nm).

FUEL INJECTION PRESSURE REGULATOR

REMOVAL & INSTALLATION

1. Before servicing the vehicle, refer to the Precautions Section.
2. Disconnect the negative battery cable.
3. Release the latches and remove the engine cover.
4. Disconnect the wiring harness from the oil filter tube bracket. Loosen the retaining nut and position the oil tube clamp aside.
5. Remove the bolts and position aside the rear heat shield.
6. Disconnect the Fuel Injection Pressure Regulator (IPR) valve electrical connector.
7. Using the Injector Pressure Regulator Socket, remove the IPR valve.
8. Installation is the reverse order of removal. Tighten the IPR valve to 37 ft. lbs. (50 Nm) using new O-ring seals.

FUEL PRESSURE REGULATOR

REMOVAL & INSTALLATION
See Figure 188.

1. Before servicing the vehicle, refer to the Precautions Section.
2. Disconnect the negative battery cable.
3. Remove the pushpin retainers and the upper air deflector.
4. Remove the power steering reservoir bracket bolts.

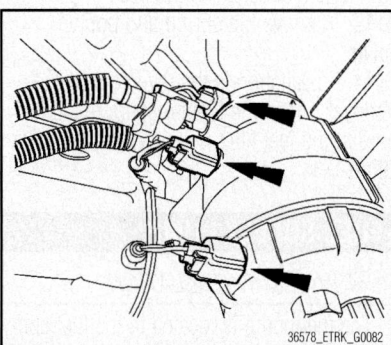

Fig. 187 Disconnect the fuel conditioning module electrical connectors—6.0L Engine

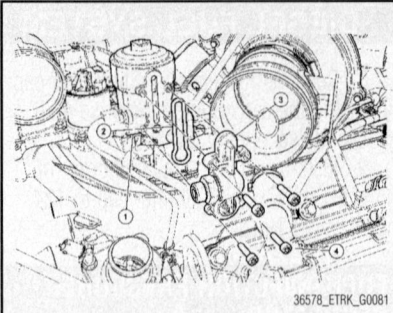

Fig. 188 Fuel filter body (1), O-ring seal (2), fuel pressure regulator cover (3) and mounting screws (4)—6.0L Engine

5. Remove the power steering fluid indicator and 3 bolts. Remove the power steering reservoir mounting bracket. Install the power steering fluid indicator and position the power steering reservoir aside.

6. Disconnect the coolant hoses from the Air Cleaner (ACL) outlet pipe.

7. Loosen the clamps and remove the ACL outlet pipe.

8. Loosen the clamps and remove the CAC tube.

9. Remove the secondary fuel filter and remove all fuel from the filter housing.

10. Disconnect the fuel return tube from the regulator cover.

※※ WARNING

Clean all fuel residue from the engine compartment. If not removed, fuel residue may ignite when the engine is returned to operation. Failure to follow this instruction may result in serious personal injury.

11. Remove the screws and the fuel pressure regulator cover.

12. Remove and discard the fuel pressure regulator cover O-ring seal.

13. Remove the spring and poppet valve.

14. Installation is the reverse order of removal. Clean the fuel pressure regulator bore in the fuel filter housing before installation.

FUEL SUPPLY PUMP

REMOVAL & INSTALLATION

The fuel pump is located in the fuel conditioning module. For additional information, refer to "Fuel Conditioning Module, Removal & Installation."

GLOW PLUGS

REMOVAL & INSTALLATION

6.0L Engine

➡Only the No. 2 glow plug is accessed from under the hood.

No. 2 Glow Plug

1. Before servicing the vehicle, refer to the Precautions Section.

2. Disconnect the negative battery cable.

3. Remove the pushpin retainers and the upper air deflector.

4. Remove the 4 power steering reservoir bracket bolts.

5. Remove the power steering fluid indicator and 3 bolts. Remove the power steering reservoir mounting bracket. Install the power steering fluid indicator and position the power steering reservoir aside.

6. Disconnect the coolant hoses from the Air Cleaner (ACL) outlet pipe.

7. Loosen the clamps and remove the ACL outlet pipe.

8. Disconnect the PCM electrical connectors.

9. Remove the bolt and PCM.

※※ WARNING

Do not pull on the wiring to remove the glow plug connector or damage may occur.

➡Only one glow plug connector shown.

10. Using the Glow Plug Connector Remover/Installer, remove the glow plug harness as needed.

11. Remove the glow plug.

To install:

12. Install the glow plug and tighten to 14 ft. lbs. (19 Nm).

13. Clean and apply clean engine oil to the O-ring seals prior to installation.

14. Using the Glow Plug Connector Remover/Installer, install the glow plug harness.

15. Install the PCM and tighten the bolt to 80 inch lbs. (9 Nm).

16. Connect the PCM electrical connectors.

17. Install the ACL outlet pipe and tighten the clamps.

18. Connect the coolant hoses to the ACL outlet pipe.

19. Remove the power steering fluid indicator. Position the power steering reservoir mounting bracket.

20. Install the bolts and power steering fluid indicator.

21. Install the power steering reservoir bracket bolts.

22. Position the upper air deflector and install the 6 pushpin retainers.

No. 7 & 8 Glow Plugs

1. Before servicing the vehicle, refer to the Precautions Section.

2. Disconnect the negative battery cable.

3. Release the latches and remove the engine cover.

4. Using the Glow Plug Connector Remover/Installer, remove the glow plug harness as needed.

5. Remove the glow plug.

To install:

6. Install the glow plug and tighten to 14 ft. lbs. (19 Nm).

7. Clean and apply clean engine oil to the O-ring seals prior to installation.

8. Using the Glow Plug Connector Remover/Installer, install the glow plug harness.

9. Install the engine cover.

10. Connect the negative battery cable.

No. 1, 3 & 5 Glow Plugs

➡The No. 1, 3 and 5 glow plugs are accessed through the wheel well.

1. Before servicing the vehicle, refer to the Precautions Section.

2. Disconnect the negative battery cable.

3. Raise and safely support the vehicle.

4. Using the Glow Plug Connector Remover/Installer, remove the glow plug harness as needed.

5. Remove the glow plug.

To install:

6. Install the glow plug and tighten to 14 ft. lbs. (19 Nm).

7. Clean and apply clean engine oil to the O-ring seals prior to installation.

8. Using the Glow Plug Connector Remover/Installer, install the glow plug harness.

No. 4 & 6 Glow Plugs

1. Before servicing the vehicle, refer to the Precautions Section.

2. Disconnect the negative battery cable.

3. Remove the left exhaust manifold. For additional information, refer to "Exhaust Manifold, Removal & Installation."

4. Using the Glow Plug Connector Remover/Installer, remove the glow plug harness as needed.

5. Remove the glow plug.

To install:

6. Install the glow plug and tighten to 14 ft. lbs. (19 Nm).

7. Clean and apply clean engine oil to the O-ring seals prior to installation.

8. Using the Glow Plug Connector Remover/Installer, install the glow plug harness.

9. Install the left exhaust manifold.

HIGH PRESSURE OIL PUMP DRIVE GEAR

REMOVAL & INSTALLATION

See Figure 189.

1. Before servicing the vehicle, refer to the Precautions Section.

2. Disconnect the negative battery cable.

3. Remove the turbocharger. For additional information, refer to "Turbocharger, Removal & Installation."

4. Remove the plug and drain the oil filter assembly and tubes.

5. Disconnect the wiring pushpin retainer.

6. Remove the bolt and retaining clamp at the oil filter adapter.

7. Remove the bolt and retaining clamp at the oil filter assembly.

8. Remove the bolt and retaining clamp. Remove the oil filter tubes.

9. Remove the bolts and turbocharger pedestal.

10. Position back the heat insulating wrap and disconnect the fuel Injection Pressure Regulator (IPR) valve electrical connector.

11. Using the Injector Pressure Regulator Socket, remove the IPR valve.

12. Remove and discard the O-ring seals.

➡Use care when removing the pump cover. The 3 bolts remaining in the pump cover under the EGR cooler can fall out of the pump cover and into the engine under the high-pressure pump.

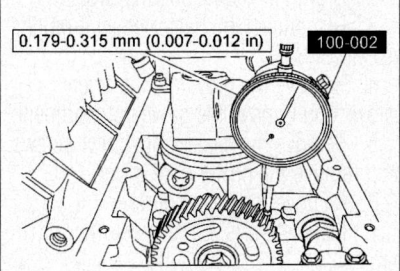

0.179-0.315 mm (0.007-0.012 in)   100-002

36578_ETRK_G0083

Fig. 189 Position the Dial Indicator Gauge with Holding Fixture and check the oil pump drive gear backlash—6.0L Engine

13. Remove or loosen the 8 bolts as needed.

14. Use a thin gasket scraper to separate the cover from the crankcase at the rear cover seam. Remove the high-pressure oil pump cover.

15. Remove and discard the press-in-place gasket.

16. Position the Dial Indicator Gauge with Holding Fixture and check the oil pump drive gear backlash.

17. Loosen the bolts on the high-pressure tube assembly.

18. Remove the bolts and the high-pressure oil pump.

19. Remove and discard the lower O-ring seals.

20. Remove and discard the high-pressure oil pump O-ring seal.

To install:

21. Install a new O-ring seal on the high-pressure oil pump.

22. Install new lower O-ring seals.

23. Install the high-pressure pump and tighten the bolts to 23 ft. lbs. (31 Nm).

24. Tighten the high-pressure tube assembly bolts to 97 inch lbs. (11 Nm).

25. Position the Dial Indicator Gauge with Holding Fixture and check the oil pump drive gear backlash.

26. Install a new press-in-place gasket in the high-pressure pump cover.

27. Clean the cover mounting surface and apply sealer at the seams.

✳✳ WARNING

To prevent engine damage, the high-pressure oil pump cover must be firmly seated on the O-ring seal to prevent cracking the cover plate.

28. Apply clean engine oil to the new high-pressure oil pump O-ring seal prior to installing the high-pressure pump cover. Install the high-pressure oil pump cover and tighten the remaining bolts to 97 inch lbs. (11 Nm).

29. Using the Injector Pressure Regulator Socket, install the IPR valve and tighten to 37 ft. lbs. (50 Nm).

30. Connect the IPR valve electrical connector.

31. Position back the heat insulating wrap.

32. Install the turbocharger.

INJECTION TIMING

ADJUSTMENT

The injection timing is controlled by the Powertrain Control Module (PCM). No adjustment is necessary or possible.

INJECTORS

REMOVAL & INSTALLATION

See Figures 190 and 191.

1. Before servicing the vehicle, refer to the Precautions Section.

2. Disconnect the negative battery cable.

3. Remove the valve covers. For additional information, refer to "Valve Covers, Removal & Installation."

4. Disconnect the fuel injector electrical connector.

5. Loosen the crankcase-to-head tube(s).

6. Position the crankcase-to-head tube and separate the tube.

7. Remove the 9 bolts and the high-pressure oil rail.

✳✳ WARNING

Do not remove the oil rail end plugs or acoustic wave attenuator port fitting. Service parts are not available to support these components.

8. If the crankcase-to-head tube separated, using the High Pressure Supply Tube Remover, remove the lower crankcase-to-head tube.

9. Inspect the D-ring seals for damage (nicks, cuts and gouges). If damaged, replace the crankcase-to-head tube.

10. Using the Injector Connector Release Tool, push the fuel injector electrical connector out of the rocker arm carrier.

11. Prior to removing the injector assembly, insert clean shop towels in the oil drain holes adjacent to each glow plug.

12. Loosen the bolt and remove the bolt and fuel injector hold-down assembly and the fuel injector. Remove and discard the O-ring seals and copper washer.

To install:

13. Install new O-ring seals and a copper washer on the fuel injector.

14. Assemble the fuel injector hold down and bolt on the fuel injector and install the assembly. Tighten the hold down bolt to 26 ft. lbs. (35 Nm).

15. Remove the shop towels.

➡Make sure the injector wiring is clear of all moving parts or engine damage can occur.

16. Install the fuel injector electrical connector into the rocker carrier.

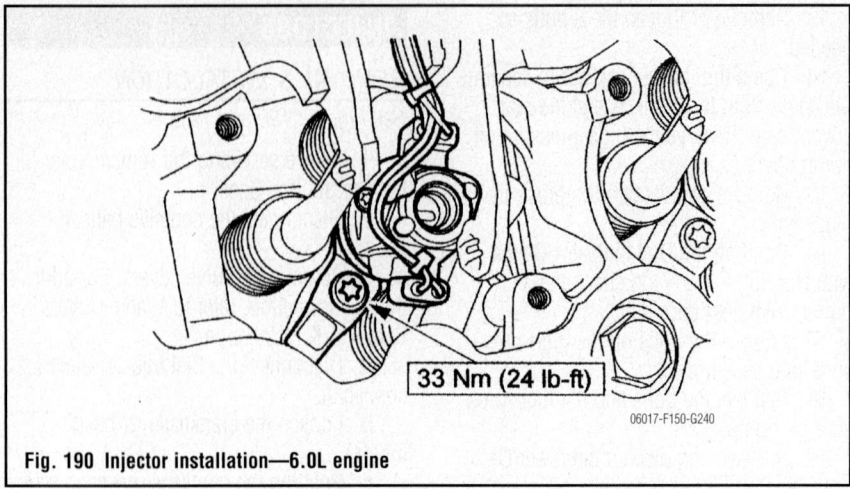

Fig. 190 Injector installation—6.0L engine

33 Nm (24 lb-ft)

06017-F150-G240

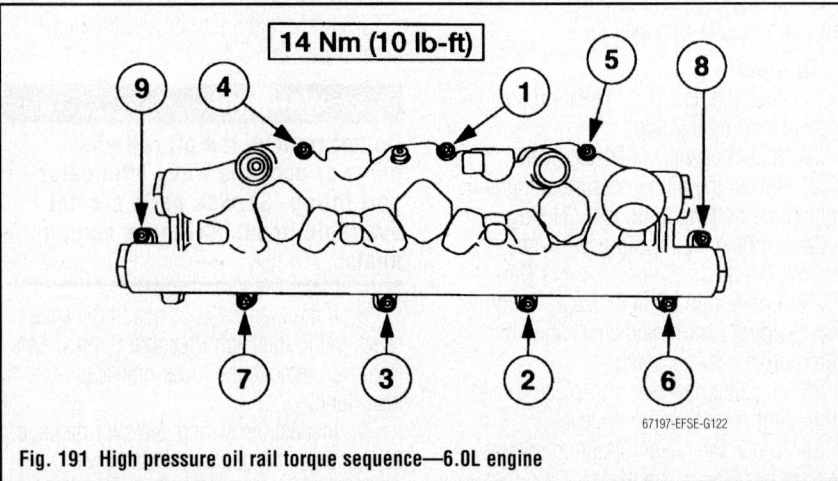

14 Nm (10 lb-ft)

67197-EFSE-G122

Fig. 191 High pressure oil rail torque sequence—6.0L engine

17. Apply clean engine oil to the top fuel injector O-ring seals.

18. Position the lower section of the crankcase-to-head tube in the engine.

19. Position the high-pressure oil rail on the injectors.

20. Place the high-pressure oil rail on top of the carrier so that the 4 single ball tubes are engaging the fuel injector lead angle.

21. Insert the guide bolts, 2 on the ends of the straight side of the high-pressure oil rail and 1 in the middle of the wavy side of the high-pressure rail. Install the guide studs 6 to 7 turns.

22. Manually press the high-pressure oil rail into the fuel injectors.

23. Inspect that the high-pressure oil rail mounting feet are flat against the mounting surface.

24. Loosely install the 6 high-pressure oil rail bolts.

25. Remove the 3 guide bolts, install the remaining high-pressure oil rail bolts and tighten the bolts in the sequence shown to 115 inch lbs. (13 Nm).

26. Apply clean engine oil to the D-ring seals and reassemble the crankcase-to-head tube. Tighten the crankcase-to-head tube(s) to 60 ft. lbs. (82 Nm).

27. Connect the fuel injector electrical connector.

28. Install the valve covers.

HEATING & AIR CONDITIONING SYSTEM

BLOWER MOTOR

REMOVAL & INSTALLATION

See Figure 192.

1. Before servicing the vehicle, refer to the Precautions Section.

2. Remove the battery and battery tray, Gasoline Engines only.

3. Remove the junction box mounting bolts and position the junction box aside, Diesel Engines only.

4. If equipped with air conditioning, loosen and move the suction accumulator/drier to access the blower motor. It is not necessary to discharge the refrigerant system.

5. Disconnect the blower motor electrical connector.

6. Remove the blower motor vent tube.

7. Remove four screws.

8. Remove the retaining clip.

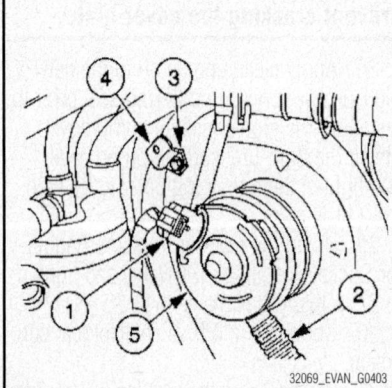

32069_EVAN_G0403

Fig. 192 Blower Motor electrical connector (1), tube (2), screws (3), retaining clip (4) and blower motor (5)—E-Series Models

9. Remove the blower motor.

10. Installation is the reverse order of removal.

HEATER CORE

REMOVAL & INSTALLATION

1. Before servicing the vehicle, refer to the Precautions Section.

2. Drain the engine cooling system.

3. Disconnect the heater hoses from the heater core.

4. Remove the glove compartment screws and remove the glove compartment.

5. Remove the heater core cover screws, then remove the heater core cover.

6. Remove the heater core.

7. Installation is the reverse order of removal.

8. Refill the engine cooling system to the correct level.

AUXILIARY HEATING & AIR CONDITIONING SYSTEM

BLOWER MOTOR

REMOVAL & INSTALLATION

See Figure 193.

1. Before servicing the vehicle, refer to the Precautions Section.

2. Remove the rear seats to access the LH rear quarter trim panel.

3. Remove the body side trim finish panel.

4. Disconnect the powerpoint electrical connector, if equipped.

5. Pry the rear seat shoulder strap covers from the upper trim panels.

6. Pull the rear door weatherstrip off at the rear door opening to access the trim panel pin-type retainers.

7. Remove the rear upper quarter trim panel and lower quarter trim panel.

8. Remove the window latches.

9. Disconnect the blower motor electrical connector.

10. Remove the blower motor vent tube.

11. Remove the blower motor screws.

12. Remove the blower motor.

13. Installation is the reverse order of removal.

HEATER CORE

REMOVAL & INSTALLATION

See Figure 194.

1. Before servicing the vehicle, refer to the Precautions Section.

2. Drain the engine cooling system.

3. Remove the rear seats to access the LH rear quarter trim panel.

4. Remove the body side trim finish panel.

5. Disconnect the powerpoint electrical connector, if equipped.

6. Pry the rear seat shoulder strap covers from the upper trim panels.

7. Pull the rear door weatherstrip off at the rear door opening to access the trim panel pin-type retainers.

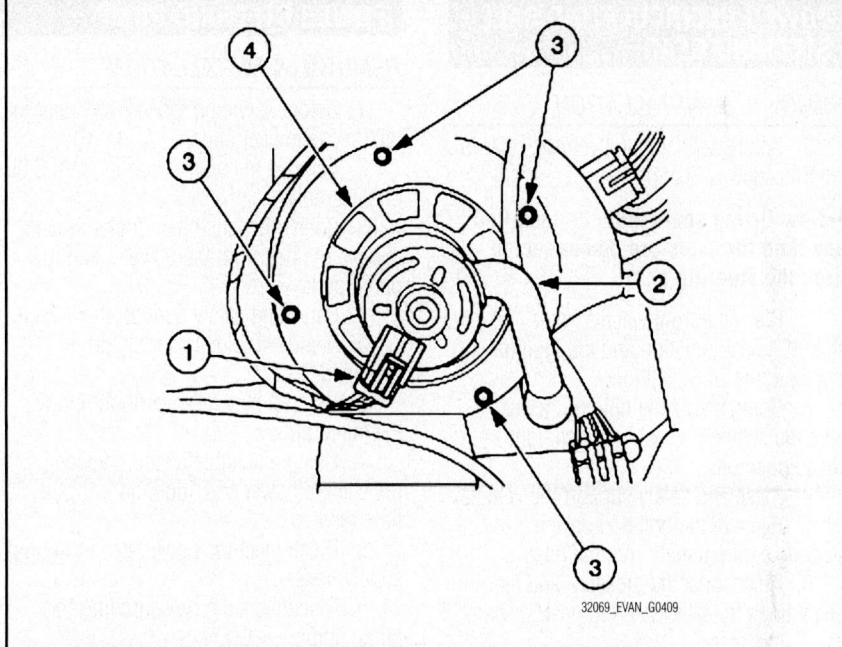

Fig. 193 Electrical Connector (1), Housing Tube (2), Mounting Screws (3), Blower Motor (4)—E-Series Models

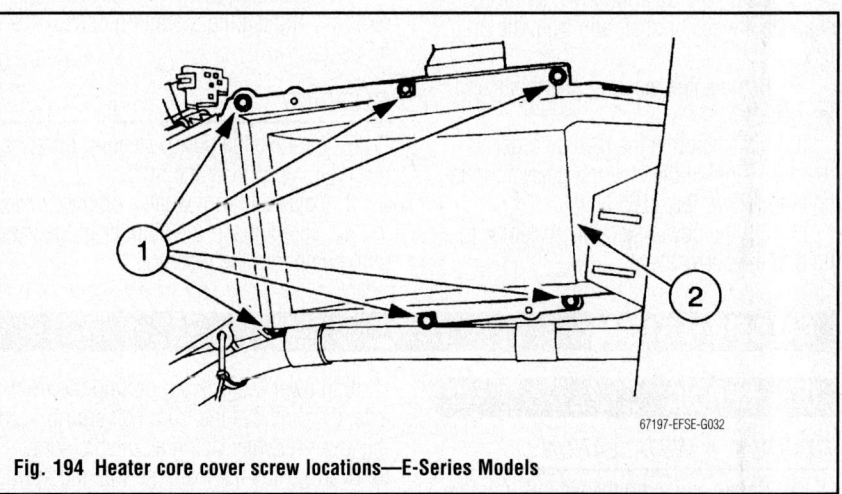

Fig. 194 Heater core cover screw locations—E-Series Models

8. Remove the rear upper quarter trim panel and lower quarter trim panel.

9. Remove the window latches.

10. Remove the heater core cover.

11. Release the clamps and disconnect the heater hoses from the heater core.

12. Remove the heater core case seal.

13. Remove the heater core.

14. Installation is the reverse order of removal.

15. Refill the engine cooling system to the correct level.

STEERING

POWER RECIRCULATING BALL STEERING GEAR

REMOVAL & INSTALLATION

1. Before servicing the vehicle, refer to the Precautions Section.

➡ **New O-ring seals must be installed any time the lines are disconnected from the steering gear.**

2. Place the front wheels in the straight-ahead position and the ignition switch in the OFF position.

3. Using a suitable holding device, hold the steering wheel in the straight-ahead position.

4. Raise and safely support the vehicle.

5. Remove the bolt and detach the steering column shaft from the gear.

6. Disconnect the pressure and returns line fittings from the steering gear. Discard the O-ring seals.

7. Remove the drag link-to-sector shaft arm cotter pin, nut retainer and nut.

8. Using the Steering Arm Remover, separate the sector shaft arm from the drag link.

9. Remove the steering gear bolts and the gear.

10. Installation is the reverse order of removal. Tighten the steering gear mounting bolts to 122 ft. lbs. (165 Nm).

11. Fill the power steering system with fluid to the correct level.

POWER STEERING PUMP

REMOVAL & INSTALLATION

1. Before servicing the vehicle, refer to the Precautions Section.

2. Remove the engine cooling fan, 6.0L Engines only.

3. Rotate the tensioner clockwise and remove the belt from the power steering pump pulley.

4. Raise and safely support the vehicle.

5. Remove the deflector shield, if equipped.

6. Using pulley remover tool, remove the pump pulley.

7. Using a suitable suction device, remove the power steering fluid from the fluid reservoir.

8. Disconnect the power steering pump supply hose.

9. Disconnect the pressure line-to-pump fitting.

10. Remove the power steering pump mounting bolts and remove the pump.

11. Installation is the reverse order of removal. Tighten the mounting bolts to 19 ft. lbs. (26 Nm).

BLEEDING

1. Remove the power steering pump reservoir cap. Check the fluid.

2. Raise the front wheels off the floor.

3. Tightly insert the stopper of the vacuum pump into the reservoir.

4. Start the engine.

5. Install the vacuum pump, apply vacuum, and maintain the maximum vacuum of 68-85 kPa (20-25 in-Hg).

6. If equipped with Hydro-Boost®, apply the brake pedal twice.

✳✳ CAUTION

Do not hold the steering wheel against the stops for more than 3 to 5 seconds at a time. Damage to the power steering pump can occur.

7. Cycle the steering wheel fully from stop-to-stop 10 times.

8. Stop the engine.

9. Release the vacuum and remove the vacuum pump.

10. Fill the reservoir.

11. Start the engine.

12. Install the vacuum pump. Apply and maintain the maximum vacuum of 68-85 kPa (20-25 in-Hg).

13. Cycle the steering wheel fully from stop-to-stop 10 times.

14. Stop the engine, release the vacuum and remove the vacuum pump.

15. Fill the reservoir as needed and install the reservoir cap.

16. Visually inspect the power steering system for leaks.

17. Install the reservoir cap.

SUSPENSION

COIL SPRING

REMOVAL & INSTALLATION

1. Before servicing the vehicle, refer to the Precautions Section.

2. Remove the stabilizer bar.

✳✳ WARNING

The axle must be supported throughout the procedure to prevent strain on the front brake hose.

3. Using a suitable jack, support the front axle.

4. Loosen the shock absorber upper nut. Loosen the nut to the top of the threads.

5. Remove the front spring upper retainer bolt and the upper spring retainer.

➡ **It may be necessary to loosen the radius arm-to-axle nut to remove the spring.**

6. Lower the jack supporting the front axle, then remove the front coil spring from the lower retainer. Using a suitable spray lubricant, spray the lower spring and spring retainer. Rotate the spring 180 degrees counterclockwise, tilt the spring outward and remove.

7. To install, reverse the removal procedure. Tighten the upper spring retainer to 17 ft. lbs. (23 Nm). Tighten the upper shock nut to 46 ft. lbs. (63 Nm).

CONTROL LINKS

REMOVAL & INSTALLATION

LOWER BALL JOINT

REMOVAL & INSTALLATION

1. Before servicing the vehicle, refer to the Precautions Section.

FRONT SUSPENSION

2. Remove the wheel knuckle assembly. For additional information, refer to "Steering Knuckle, Removal & Installation."

3. Remove the lower ball joint grease plug.

4. Position the steering knuckle assembly in a vise and remove the snap ring from the lower ball joint.

5. Using the C-Frame and Screw Installer/Remover and Ball Joint Installer/Remover, remove the lower ball joint.

To install:

6. Clean the knuckle ball joint bores.

7. Using the C-Frame and Screw Installer/Remover and Ball Joint Installer/Remover, install the lower ball joint.

8. Install the snap ring in the groove at the bottom of the lower ball joint.

9. Install the lower ball joint grease plug.

10. Install the wheel knuckle assembly.

RADIUS ARM

REMOVAL & INSTALLATION

1. Before servicing the vehicle, refer to the Precautions Section.

2. Remove the front coil spring.

3. Remove and discard the shock absorber lower nut and disconnect the shock absorber from the radius arm.

4. Remove and discard the radius arm rearward nut and flag bolt.

5. Remove the radius arm-to-axle nut and bolt, the spring retainer and the insulator.

➡**Inspect the bushings and install new as necessary.**

6. Installation is the reverse order of removal. Tighten the bolts as follows:

- Radius arm-to-axle nut to 295 ft. lbs. (400 Nm)
- Radius arm rearward nut and flag bolt: 258 ft. lbs. (350 Nm)

SHOCK ABSORBERS

REMOVAL & INSTALLATION

1. Before servicing the vehicle, refer to the Precautions Section.

2. If equipped with a 6.8L engine, remove the RH side heat shield bolt and heat shield.

3. Remove and discard the shock absorber upper nut, washer and bushing assembly.

4. Raise and safely support the vehicle.

5. Remove and discard the shock absorber lower nut and washer.

6. Remove the shock absorber.

To install:

7. Position the shock absorber and loosely install the new lower nut and washer, but do not tighten.

8. Position the shock absorber assembly up into the frame hole and install the new shock absorber upper nut washer and

bushing assembly and tighten to 46 ft. lbs. (63 Nm).

9. Tighten the lower shock absorber lower nut to 59 ft. lbs. (80 Nm).

10. Install the right hand heat shield, if removed.

STEERING KNUCKLE

REMOVAL & INSTALLATION

1. Before servicing the vehicle, refer to the Precautions Section.

2. Raise and safely support the vehicle.

3. Remove the brake rotor.

4. Remove the wheel speed sensor bolt and position the sensor aside.

5. Remove the wheel speed sensor harness bracket bolt.

6. Remove the outer tie-rod end cotter pin, retainer and nut. Discard the cotter pin.

7. Using the Ball Joint Separator, disconnect the outer tie-rod end.

8. Remove and discard the upper ball joint bolt.

9. Remove and discard the lower ball joint cotter pin and nut.

10. Strike the lower end of the axle to loosen the ball joint. Remove the wheel knuckle.

11. Installation is the reverse order of removal. Tighten the bolts as follows:

- Lower ball joint nut: 111 ft. lbs. (150 Nm)
- Upper ball joint bolt: 76 ft. lbs. (103 Nm)
- Outer tie-rod nut: 76 ft. lbs. (103 Nm)

STABILIZER BAR

REMOVAL & INSTALLATION

1. Before servicing the vehicle, refer to the Precautions Section.

2. Raise and safely support the vehicle.

3. Remove the two stabilizer bar link lower nuts.

4. Remove the two stabilizer bar bracket rear bolts.

5. Remove the two stabilizer bar bracket forward bolts and bar brackets.

6. Remove the stabilizer bar.

7. Installation is the reverse order of removal. Tighten the bolts as follows:

- Stabilizer bar bracket forward bolts: 111 ft. lbs. (150 Nm)
- Stabilizer bar bracket rear bolts: 18 ft. lbs. (25 Nm)

UPPER BALL JOINT

REMOVAL & INSTALLATION

1. Before servicing the vehicle, refer to the Precautions Section.

2. Remove the wheel knuckle assembly. For additional information, refer to "Steering Knuckle, Removal & Installation."

3. Remove the lower ball joint grease plug.

4. Position the steering knuckle assembly in a vise and remove the snap ring from the lower ball joint.

5. Using the C-Frame and Screw Installer/Remover and Ball Joint Installer/Remover, remove the upper ball joint.

To install:

6. Clean the knuckle ball joint bores.

7. Using the C-Frame and Screw Installer/Remover and Ball Joint Installer/Remover, install the upper ball joint.

8. Install the snap ring in the groove at the bottom of the lower ball joint, if removed.

9. Install the lower ball joint grease plug, if removed.

10. Install the wheel knuckle assembly.

SUSPENSION   **REAR SUSPENSION**

FULL FLOATING REAR AXLE BEARINGS

REMOVAL, REPACKING & INSTALLATION

1. Before servicing the vehicle, refer to the Precautions Section.
2. Raise and safely support the vehicle.
3. Remove the rear wheel.
4. Remove the 2 brake caliper anchor plate bolts and position the brake caliper and anchor plate assembly aside. Support the caliper and anchor plate assembly using mechanic's wire.
5. Remove the brake rotor.
6. Remove the axle shaft. For additional information, refer to "Axle Shaft, Removal & Installation."
7. Using the Wheel Hub Nut Socket, remove the hub nut.
8. Remove the rear hub.

To install:
9. Slide the rear hub over the axle housing spindle.
10. Grease and install the outer rear wheel bearing.
11. Start the hub nut making sure that the tab aligns correctly in the keyway prior to thread engagement.
12. To adjust the bearings, using the Wheel Hub Nut Socket, tighten the nut to 70 ft. lbs. (95 Nm).
13. Back off the nut 90 degrees.
14. Using the Wheel Hub Nut Socket, tighten the nut to 18 ft. lbs. (24 Nm).
15. Install the axle shaft.
16. Install the brake rotor.
17. Install the wheel.

LEAF SPRING

REMOVAL & INSTALLATION

1. Before servicing the vehicle, refer to the Precautions Section.

2. Raise and safely support the vehicle.
3. Remove the rear wheel.
4. Support the rear axle with a suitable jack.
5. Remove and discard the shock absorber lower nut and bolt.
6. Remove and discard the 4 U-bolt nuts, the plate and the 2 U-bolts.
7. Remove and discard the leaf spring front bracket bolt and flagnut.
8. Remove and discard the leaf spring shackle-to-bracket bolt and flagnut, then remove the leaf spring assembly.
9. Remove the shackle-to-leaf spring nut, bolt and shackle.

To install:
10. Position the leaf spring shackle and install the new bolt and nut.
11. Tighten until snug.
12. Position the rear spring and install the new shackle-to-rear bracket bolt and flag nut until snug.
13. Install the new spring-to-front bracket bolt and flag nut until snug.
14. Position the spring upper plate and install the U-bolts and nuts.
15. Install the new shock absorber lower nut and bolt.
16. Tighten until snug.
17. Install the wheel and tire.
18. Lower the vehicle until the weight of the vehicle is resting on the wheel.
19. Tighten the new shackle-to-rear bracket bolt to 98 ft. lbs. (133 Nm).
20. Tighten the shackle-to-leaf spring nut to 98 ft. lbs. (133 Nm).
21. Tighten the spring-to-front bracket bolt to 258 ft. lbs. (350 Nm).
22. Tighten the U-bolt nuts evenly in an X-type pattern as follows:
   • Tighten to 37 ft. lbs. (50 Nm).
   • Tighten to 74 ft. lbs. (100 Nm).
   • Tighten to 111 ft. lbs. (150 Nm).
   • Tighten to 148 ft. lbs. (200 Nm).
   • Tighten to 166 ft. lbs. (225 Nm).

23. Tighten the shock absorber lower nut to 76 ft. lbs. (103 Nm).

SHOCK ABSORBER

REMOVAL & INSTALLATION

1. Before servicing the vehicle, refer to the Precautions Section.
2. Raise and safely support the vehicle.
3. Support the rear axle using a suitable jack.
4. Remove the lower shock absorber bolt.
5. Remove the upper shock absorber bolt.
6. Installation is the reverse order of removal. Tighten the upper bolt to 30 ft. lbs. (40 Nm) and lower bolt to 76 ft. lbs. (103 Nm).

WHEEL BEARINGS

REMOVAL & INSTALLATION

1. Before servicing the vehicle, refer to the Precautions Section.
2. Remove the axle shaft. For additional information, refer to "Axle Shaft, Removal & Installation."
3. Using a suitable seal remover, remove and discard the axle shaft oil seal.
4. Inspect the rear wheel bearing and axle shaft for wear or damage.
5. Using the Axle Bearing Remover and Slide Hammer, remove the rear wheel bearing.

To install:
6. Lubricate the new rear wheel bearing with axle lubricant.
7. Using the Rear Axle Bearing Installer and Handle, install the rear wheel bearing.
8. Lubricate the lip of the new axle shaft oil seal with grease.
9. Using the Rear Axle Oil Seal Installer and Handle, install the new axle shaft oil seal.
10. Install the axle shaft.

FORD AND MERCURY

Escape • Mariner

4

SPECIFICATIONS AND MAINTENANCE CHARTS

ENGINE AND VEHICLE IDENTIFICATION

		Engine						Model Year	
Code ①	Liters	Cu. In.	Cyl.	Fuel Sys.	Engine Type	Eng. Mfg.		Code ②	Year
Z	2.3	140	4	SFI	DOHC	Ford		8	2008
7	2.5	153	4	SFI	DOHC	Ford		9	2009
1	3.0	182	6	SFI	DOHC	Ford			
G	3.0	182	6	SFI	DOHC	Ford			

SFI: Multi-port Fuel Injection

DOHC: Double Overhead Camshafts

① 8th digit of VIN

② 10th digit of VIN

36578_ESCA_C0001

GENERAL ENGINE SPECIFICATIONS

Year	Model	Engine Displacement Liters	Engine VIN	Net Horsepower @ rpm	Net Torque @ rpm (ft. lbs.)	Bore x Stroke (in.)	Compression Ratio	Oil Pressure @ rpm
2008	Escape/Mariner	2.3	Z	153@5800	152@4250	3.44x3.70	9.7:1	29-39@2000
	Escape/Mariner	3.0	1	200@5500	200@4500	3.50x3.13	10.0:1	11@1500 ①
2009	Escape/Mariner	2.5	7	171@6000	171@4500	3.50x3.93	10.0:1	29-39@2000
	Escape/Mariner	3.0	G	240@6550	223@4300	3.50x3.13	10.3:1	11@1500 ①

① Minimum with engine warmed up after 10 minutes of idling.

36578_ESCA_C0002

ENGINE TUNE-UP SPECIFICATIONS

Year	Engine Displacement Liters	Engine VIN	Spark Plug Gap (in.)	Ignition Timing (deg.) MT	Ignition Timing (deg.) AT	Fuel Pump (psi) ①	Idle Speed (rpm) MT	Idle Speed (rpm) AT	Valve Clearance Intake	Valve Clearance Exhaust
2008	2.3	Z	0.049-0.053	N/A	N/A	39	②	②	HYD.	HYD.
	3.0	1	0.052-0.056	N/A	N/A	39	②	②	HYD.	HYD.
2009	2.5	7	0.042-0.046	N/A	N/A	55	②	②	HYD.	HYD.
	3.0	G	0.045-0.048	N/A	N/A	55	②	②	HYD.	HYD.

HYD: Hydraulic lash adjusters

NA: Information not available

① Key on; engine off

② Refer to Vehicle Emission Control Information Label

36578_ESCA_C0003

CAPACITIES

Year	Model	Engine Displacement Liters	Engine VIN	Engine Oil with Filter (qts.)	Transmission (pts.) Manual	Transmission (pts.) Auto ①	Transfer Case (pts.)	Drive Axle Front (pts.)	Drive Axle Rear (pts.)	Fuel Tank (gal.)	Cooling System (qts.)
2008	Escape/Mariner	2.3	Z	4.5	5.0	20.0	0.75	N/A	2.43	16.5	②
	Escape/Mariner	3.0	1	6.0	5.0	20.0	0.75	N/A	2.43	16.5	10.5
2009	Escape/Mariner	2.5	7	4.5	5.0	18.0	0.75	N/A	2.43	16.5	②
	Escape/Mariner	3.0	G	6.0	5.0	18.0	0.75	N/A	2.43	16.5	10.5

N/A: Non Aplicable

NOTE: All capacities are approximate. Add fluid gradually and check to be sure a proper fluid level is obtained.

① Dry fill

② With manual transaxle: 6.9 qts; with automatic transaxle: 8.0 qts.

36578_ESCA_C0004

FLUID SPECIFICATIONS

Year	Model	Engine Displacement Liters (VIN)	Engine Oil	Auto. Trans.	Manual Trans.	Drive Axle ①	Transfer Case	Brake Master Cylinder	Engine Coolant
2008	Escape/ Mariner	2.3 (Z)	5W-20	Mercon® V	75W-90	75W-140	80W-90	DOT 3	Motorcraft Gold
		3.0 (1)	5W-20	Mercon® V	75W-90	75W-140	80W-90	DOT 3	Motorcraft Gold
2009	Escape/ Mariner	2.5 (7)	5W-20	Mercon® LV	75W-90	75W-140	80W-90	DOT 3	Motorcraft Gold
		3.0 (G)	5W-20	Mercon® LV	75W-90	75W-140	80W-90	DOT 3	Motorcraft Gold

DOT: Department Of Transpotation

®: Registerd Trademark

① 80W-90 is recommended for manual trans axles, both system use synthetic fluids.

36578_ESCA_C0005

VALVE SPECIFICATIONS

Year	Engine Displacement Liters	Engine VIN	Seat Angle (deg.)	Face Angle (deg.)	Spring Test Pressure (lbs. @ in.)	Spring Installed Height (in.)	Stem-to-Guide Clearance (in.) Intake	Stem-to-Guide Clearance (in.) Exhaust	Stem Diameter (in.) Intake	Stem Diameter (in.) Exhaust
2008	2.3	Z	45	45	38.6@1.49	1.492	0.0010	0.0011	0.2153-0.2159	0.2151-0.2157
	3.0	1	44.75	45.5	153@ 1.18	1.57	0.0007-0.0027	0.0017-0.0037	0.2343-0.2350	0.2350-0.2358
2009	2.5	7	45	45	38.6@1.49	1.492	0.0010	0.0011	0.2153-0.2159	0.2151-0.2157
	3.0	G	44.75	45.5	153@ 1.18	1.67	0.0007-0.0027	0.0017-0.0037	0.2352-0.2360	0.2343-0.2350

36578_ESCA_C0006

CAMSHAFT AND BEARING SPECIFICATIONS CHART

All measurements are given in inches.

Year	Engine Displacement Liters	Engine ID/VIN	Journal Dia.	Brg. Oil Clearance	Shaft End-play	Runout	Journal Bore	Lobe Height Intake	Lobe Height Exhaust
2008	2.3	Z	0.982-0.983	0.001-0.003	0.003-0.009	0.001	0.001-0.003	0.324	0.307
	3.0	1	1.061-1.060	0.001-0.00029	0.00748	N/A	1.063-1.062	0.189	0.189
2009	2.5	7	0.982-0.983	0.001-0.003	0.003-0.009	0.001	0.001-0.003	0.324	0.307
	3.0	G	1.061-1.060	0.001-0.00029	0.00748	N/A	1.063-1.062	0.189	0.189

N/A: Information not available

36578_ESCA_C0007

CRANKSHAFT AND CONNECTING ROD SPECIFICATIONS

All measurements are given in inches.

Year	Engine Displacement Liters	Engine VIN	Crankshaft Main Brg. Journal Dia.	Main Brg. Oil Clearance	Shaft End-play	Thrust on No.	Connecting Rod Journal Diameter	Oil Clearance	Side Clearance
2008	2.3	Z	2.0460-2.0470	0.0006-0.0015	0.0070-0.0180	NA	1.8490-1.8500	0.001-0.002	0.0760-0.1200
	3.0	1	2.4670-2.4790	0.0010-0.0018	0.0050-0.0010	3	2.0872-2.0879	0.0010-0.0025	0.0039-0.0118
2009	2.5	7	2.0460-2.0470	0.0006-0.0015	0.0070-0.0180	NA	2.0460-2.0470	0.001-0.002	0.0760-0.1200
	3.0	G	2.4791-2.4800	0.0010-0.0018	0.0030-0.0010	3	2.0872-2.0879	0.0010-0.0025	0.0039-0.0118

NA: Not Available

36578_ESCA_C0008

PISTON AND RING SPECIFICATIONS

All measurements are given in inches.

Year	Engine Displacement Liters	Engine VIN	Piston Clearance	Ring Gap Top Compression	Bottom Compression	Oil Control	Ring Side Clearance Top Compression	Bottom Compression	Oil Control
2008	2.3	Z	0.0009-0.0017	0.0060-0.0120	0.0120-0.0180	0.0070-0.0270	N/A	N/A	N/A
	3.0	1	0.0005-0.0009	0.0039-0.0098	0.0106-0.0165	0.0059-0.0255	0.0016-0.0030	0.0016-0.0033	N/A
2009	2.5	7	0.0009-0.0017	0.0060-0.0120	0.0120-0.0180	0.0070-0.0270	N/A	N/A	N/A
	3.0	G	0.0005-0.0009	0.0039-0.0098	0.0106-0.0165	0.0059-0.0256	0.0016-0.0030	0.0016-0.0033	N/A

N/A: Not Available

36578_ESCA_C0009

TORQUE SPECIFICATIONS

All readings in ft. lbs.

Year	Engine Displacement Liters	Engine VIN	Cylinder Head Bolts	Main Bearing Bolts	Rod Bearing Bolts	Crankshaft Damper Bolts	Flywheel Bolts	Manifold Intake	Manifold Exhaust	Spark Plugs	Oil Pan Drain Plug
2008	2.3	Z	①	N/A	N/A	②	③ ④	13	35	11	21
	3.0	1	⑤	⑥	⑦	⑧	59	⑨	15	11	19
2009	2.5	7	①	N/A	N/A	②	④	13	35	11	21
	3.0	G	⑤	⑥	⑦	⑧	③ ④	⑨	15	11	19

NA: Information not available

① Step 1: 44 inch lbs.
  Step 2: 11 ft. lbs.
  Step 3: 33 ft. lbs.
  Step 4: Plus 90 degrees
  Step 5: Plus an additional 90 degrees
② Step2: 74 ft. lbs.
  Step 2: Plus 90 degrees
③ For flexplate: refer to flywheel bolts
④ Step 1: 37 ft. lbs.
  Step 2: 59 ft. lbs.
  Step 3: 83 ft. lbs.

⑤ Step 1: 30 ft. lbs. (40 Nm).
  Step 2: Tighten the bolts 90 degrees.
  Step 3: Loosen the bolts one full turn.
  Step 4: 30 ft. lbs. (40 Nm).
  Step 5: Tighten the bolts 90 degrees.
  Step 6: Tighten the bolts 90 degrees.
⑥ Step 1: Fasteners 1-8: 18 ft. lbs.
  Step 2: Fasteners 9-19: 30 ft. lbs.
  Step 3: Fasteners 1-16: +90 degrees
  Step 4: Fasteners 17-22: 18 ft. lbs.

⑦ Step 1: 17 ft. lbs.
  Step 2: 32 ft. lbs.
⑧ Step1: 86 ft lbs
  Step 2: Loosen 1 full turn
  Step 3: 37 ft. lbs.
  Step 4: Plus 90 degrees
⑨ Upper and Lower 89 inch lbs.

36578_ESCA_C0010

WHEEL ALIGNMENT

Year	Model		Caster Range (+/-Deg.)	Caster Preferred Setting (Deg.)	Camber Range (+/-Deg.)	Camber Preferred Setting (Deg.)	Toe-in (in.)
2008	Escape/Mariner	F	0.50	+1.60	0.50	-0.84	0.23+/-0.23
		R	N/A	N/A	0.75	0.00	-0.18+/-0.20
2009	Escape/Mariner	F	0.50	+1.60	0.50	-0.84	0.23+/-0.23
		R	N/A	N/A	0.70 ①	0.00	-0.18+/-0.20

N/A: Not Available

① Left side: +/- 0.60

36578_ESCA_C0011

TIRE, WHEEL AND BALL JOINT SPECIFICATIONS

Year	Model	OEM Tires Standard	OEM Tires Optional	Tire Pressures (psi) Front	Tire Pressures (psi) Rear	Wheel Size	Ball Joint Inspection	Lug Nuts (ft. lbs.)
2008	Escape	P235/70R16	none	①	①	N/A	0.008 in.	100
	Mariner	P235/70R16	none	①	①	N/A	0.008 in.	100
2009	Escape	P235/70R16	none	①	①	N/A	0.008 in.	100
	Mariner	P235/70R16	none	①	①	N/A	0.008 in.	100

N/A: Not Available

OEM: Original Equipment Manufacturer

PSI: Pounds Per Square Inch

① See safety certification on driver's door jam

36578_ESCA_C0012

BRAKE SPECIFICATIONS
All measurements in inches unless noted

Year	Model		Brake Disc Original Thickness	Brake Disc Minimum Thickness	Brake Disc Maximum Run-out	Brake Drum Original Inside Diameter	Brake Drum Maximum Machine Diameter	Minimum Lining Thickness	Brake Caliper Bracket Bolts (ft. lbs.)	Brake Caliper Mounting Bolts (ft. lbs.)
2008	Escape/Mariner	F	NA	0.944	0.004	N/A	N/A	0.118	129	37
		R	NA	0.430	0.004	N/A	N/A	0.118	N/A	26
2009	Escape/Mariner	F	NA	0.944	0.004	N/A	N/A	0.118	129	37
		R	NA	0.430	0.004	N/A	10.090	0.039	N/A	N/A

NA: Not Available

36578_ESCA_C0013

SCHEDULED MAINTENANCE INTERVALS
2008-09 Ford Escape/Mercury Mariner

TO BE SERVICED	OF SERVIC	VEHICLE MILEAGE INTERVAL (x1000)												
		7.5	15	22.5	30	37.5	45	52.5	60	67.5	75	82.5	90	97.5
Air cleaner filter	R			✓			✓			✓			✓	
Auto. Trans. fluid level	I		✓		✓		✓		✓		✓		✓	
Auto. Trans. Fluid	R				✓				✓				✓	
Accessory drive belt	I ①	✓	✓	✓	✓	✓	✓	✓	✓	✓	✓	✓	✓	
Brake system ②	S/I		✓		✓		✓		✓		✓		✓	
Cabin air filter	R				✓				✓				✓	
Cooling system hoses and clamps	S/I		✓		✓		✓		✓		✓		✓	
Driveshafts & halfshafts	S/I		✓		✓		✓		✓		✓		✓	
Engine coolant	R	At 6 years or 100,000 miles; then every 3 years or 50,000 miles												
Engine oil & filter	R	✓	✓	✓	✓	✓	✓	✓	✓	✓	✓	✓	✓	✓
Exhaust system & heat shields	I		✓		✓		✓		✓		✓		✓	
Man. Trans. Fluid	R	Every 120,000 miles												
Fuel filter	R				✓				✓				✓	
PCV valve	S/I	Every 150,000 miles												
Rear axle lubricant (4wd)	R	Every 150,000 miles												
Rear (high voltage) battery A/C filter	I	✓	✓	✓	✓	✓	✓	✓	✓	✓	✓	✓	✓	
Rear (high voltage) battery A/C filter	R		✓		✓		✓		✓		✓		✓	
Tires	Rotate	Every 7,500 miles												
Steering linkage	S/I		✓		✓		✓		✓		✓		✓	
Spark plugs	R	Every 90,000 miles												
Suspension components and ball joints	S/I		✓		✓		✓		✓		✓		✓	
Multi-Point inspection	③	✓	✓	✓	✓	✓	✓	✓	✓	✓	✓	✓	✓	✓

R: Replace   S/I: Inspect and service, if necessary   L: Lubricate   A: Adjust   C: Clean

① Replace at 150,000 miles, if not previously done

② Inspect the reservoir fluid level, rotor and or drum, brake lines, hoses, calipers and or wheel cylinders

Monthly Checks

Check each of the following items every month:

All interior and exterior lights

Tires for wear and correct air pressure, including spare tire

Engine oil fluid level

Windshield washer solvent fluid level

Six Month Checks

Check each of the following items at least every 6 months:

Lap/shoulder belts and seat latches for wear and function

External mounted spare is stowed correctly (tight to body)

Parking brake for correct operation

Safety warning lamps (brake, ABS, air bag, safety belt) for correct operation

Clutch fluid level (if equipped)

Engine coolant system fluid level and correct strength

Power steering fluid

Battery 12-volt connections. Clean if necessary

Windshield washer spray, wiper operation, clean all wiper blades

Lubricate all hinges, latches and outside locks. Inspect for correct operation

Lubricate door rubber weatherstrips. Inspect for excessive wear

Clean body and door drain holes. Inspect for clogs and obstructions

SCHEDULED MAINTENANCE INTERVALS
2008-09 Ford Escape/Mercury Mariner
(Footnotes continued)

③ **Multi-Point inspection**

The following inspections are recommended at every service interval:

Check and top off brake, coolant, manual and automatic transmission fluid power steering and washer fluid

Inspect tires for wear and correct air pressure, including spare tire

Check exhaust system for leaks, damage, loose parts and foreign material

Check battery performance

Check operation of horn, exterior lamps, turn signals and hazard warning lights

Check radiator, coolers, heater and air conditioning hoses

Inspect tires for wear and correct air pressure, including spare tire

Inspect windshield wiper spray and wiper operation

Check windshield for cracks, chips and pitting

Inspect for oil and fluid leaks

Inspect air filter

Inspect halfshaft dust boots

Check shocks struts and other suspension components for leaks and damage

Inspect steering linkage

Inspect accessory drive belts

Inspect clutch operation (if equipped)

When operating in dusty conditions such as unpaved or dusty roads:

Change engine oil and install a new oil filter every 4,800 km (3,000 miles) or 3 months.

Install a new fuel filter every 24,000 km (15,000 miles).

Change automatic transmission fluid every 48,000 km (30,000 miles).

Change transfer case fluid every 96,000 km (60,000 miles).

Install a new engine air filter as required.

Install a new cabin air filter as required.

When operating in off-road conditions:

Change automatic transmission fluid every 48,000 km (30,000 miles).

Change transfer case fluid every 96,000 km (60,000 miles).

Install a new cabin air filter as required.

Inspect and lubricate U-joints.

Inspect and lubricate steering linkage ball joints with zerk fittings.

Special Operating Condition Requirements

When towing a trailer or using a camper or car-top carrier:

Change engine oil and install a new oil filter every 8,000 km (5,000 miles) or 3 months.

Change automatic transmission fluid every 48,000 km (30,000 miles). (not required on 6R60/6R75 transmissions).

Inspect and rotate tires 8,000 km (5,000 miles)

Change transfer case fluid every 96,000 km (60,000 miles).

Change manual transmission fluid as required.

Inspect and lubricate U-joints and half shafts as required.

During extensive idling and/or low speed driving for long distances, as in heavy commercial use such as delivery, taxi, patrol car or livery:

Change engine oil and install a new oil filter, lube front lower control arm and steering linkage ball joints with

zerk fittings (if equipped) every 8,000 km (5,000 miles) or 3 months.

Inspect brake system and check battery electrolyte level (Patrol cars) every 8,000 km (5,000 miles).

Install a new fuel filter every 24,000 km (15,000 miles).

Change automatic transmission fluid, lubricate 4x2 wheel bearings,

Lubricate rear wheel drive (RWD) front wheel bearings, install new grease seals and adjust every 48,000 km (30,000 miles).

Install new spark plugs and change transfer case fluid every 96,000 km (60,000 miles).

Install a new cabin air filter as required.

36578_ESCA_C0015

PRECAUTIONS

Before servicing any vehicle, please be sure to read all of the following precautions, which deal with personal safety, prevention of component damage, and important points to take into consideration when servicing a motor vehicle:

• Never open, service or drain the radiator or cooling system when the engine is hot; serious burns can occur from the steam and hot coolant.

• Observe all applicable safety precautions when working around fuel. Whenever servicing the fuel system, always work in a well-ventilated area. Do not allow fuel spray or vapors to come in contact with a spark, open flame, or excessive heat (a hot drop light, for example). Keep a dry chemical fire extinguisher near the work area. Always keep fuel in a container specifically designed for fuel storage; also, always properly seal fuel containers to avoid the possibility of fire or explosion. Refer to the additional fuel system precautions later in this section.

• Fuel injection systems often remain pressurized, even after the engine has been turned**OFF**. The fuel system pressure must be relieved before disconnecting any fuel lines. Failure to do so may result in fire and/or personal injury.

• Brake fluid often contains polyglycol ethers and polyglycols. Avoid contact with the eyes and wash your hands thoroughly after handling brake fluid. If you do get brake fluid in your eyes, flush your eyes with clean, running water for 15 minutes. If eye irritation persists, or if you have taken brake fluid internally, IMMEDIATELY seek medical assistance.

• The EPA warns that prolonged contact with used engine oil may cause a number of skin disorders, including cancer. You should make every effort to minimize your exposure to used engine oil. Protective gloves should be worn when changing oil. Wash your hands and any other exposed skin areas as soon as possible after exposure to used engine oil. Soap and water, or waterless hand cleaner should be used.

• All new vehicles are now equipped with an air bag system, often referred to as a Supplemental Restraint System (SRS) or Supplemental Inflatable Restraint (SIR) system. The system must be disabled before performing service on or around system components, steering column, instrument panel components, wiring and sensors. Failure to follow safety and disabling procedures could result in accidental air bag deployment, possible personal injury and unnecessary system repairs.

• Always wear safety goggles when working with, or around, the air bag system. When carrying a non-deployed air bag, be sure the bag and trim cover are pointed away from your body. When placing a non-deployed air bag on a work surface, always face the bag and trim cover upward, away from the surface. This will reduce the motion of the module if it is accidentally deployed. Refer to the additional air bag system precautions later in this section.

• Clean, high quality brake fluid from a sealed container is essential to the safe and proper operation of the brake system. You should always buy the correct type of brake fluid for your vehicle. If the brake fluid becomes contaminated, completely flush the system with new fluid. Never reuse any brake fluid. Any brake fluid that is removed from the system should be discarded. Also, do not allow any brake fluid to come in contact with a painted surface; it will damage the paint.

• Never operate the engine without the proper amount and type of engine oil; doing so WILL result in severe engine damage.

• Timing belt maintenance is extremely important. Many models utilize an interference-type, non-freewheeling engine. If the timing belt breaks, the valves in the cylinder head may strike the pistons, causing potentially serious (also time-consuming and expensive) engine damage. Refer to the maintenance interval charts for the recommended replacement interval for the timing belt, and to the timing belt section for belt replacement and inspection.

• Disconnecting the negative battery cable on some vehicles may interfere with the functions of the on-board computer system(s) and may require the computer to undergo a relearning process once the negative battery cable is reconnected.

• When servicing drum brakes, only disassemble and assemble one side at a time, leaving the remaining side intact for reference.

• Only an MVAC-trained, EPA-certified automotive technician should service the air conditioning system or its components.

BRAKES

GENERAL INFORMATION

PRECAUTIONS

• Certain components within the ABS system are not intended to be serviced or repaired individually.

• Do not use rubber hoses or other parts not specifically specified for and ABS system. When using repair kits, replace all parts included in the kit. Partial or incorrect repair may lead to functional problems and require the replacement of components.

• Lubricate rubber parts with clean, fresh brake fluid to ease assembly. Do not use shop air to clean parts; damage to rubber components may result.

• Use only DOT 3 brake fluid from an unopened container.

• If any hydraulic component or line is removed or replaced, it may be necessary to bleed the entire system.

• A clean repair area is essential. Always clean the reservoir and cap thoroughly before removing the cap. The slightest amount of dirt in the fluid may plug an orifice and impair the system function. Perform repairs after components have been thoroughly cleaned; use only denatured alcohol to clean components. Do not allow ABS components to come into contact with any substance containing mineral oil; this includes used shop rags.

• The Anti-Lock control unit is a microprocessor similar to other computer units in the vehicle. Ensure that the ignition switch is**OFF**before removing or installing

ANTI-LOCK BRAKE SYSTEM (ABS)

controller harnesses. Avoid static electricity discharge at or near the controller.

• If any arc welding is to be done on the vehicle, the control unit should be unplugged before welding operations begin.

WHEEL SPEED SENSORS

REMOVAL & INSTALLATION

Front Sensor

See Figure 1.

1. Before servicing the vehicle, refer to the Precautions Section.

2. Raise and safely support the vehicle.

➡**The harness connector is located in the engine compartment.**

3. Disconnect the electrical connector.

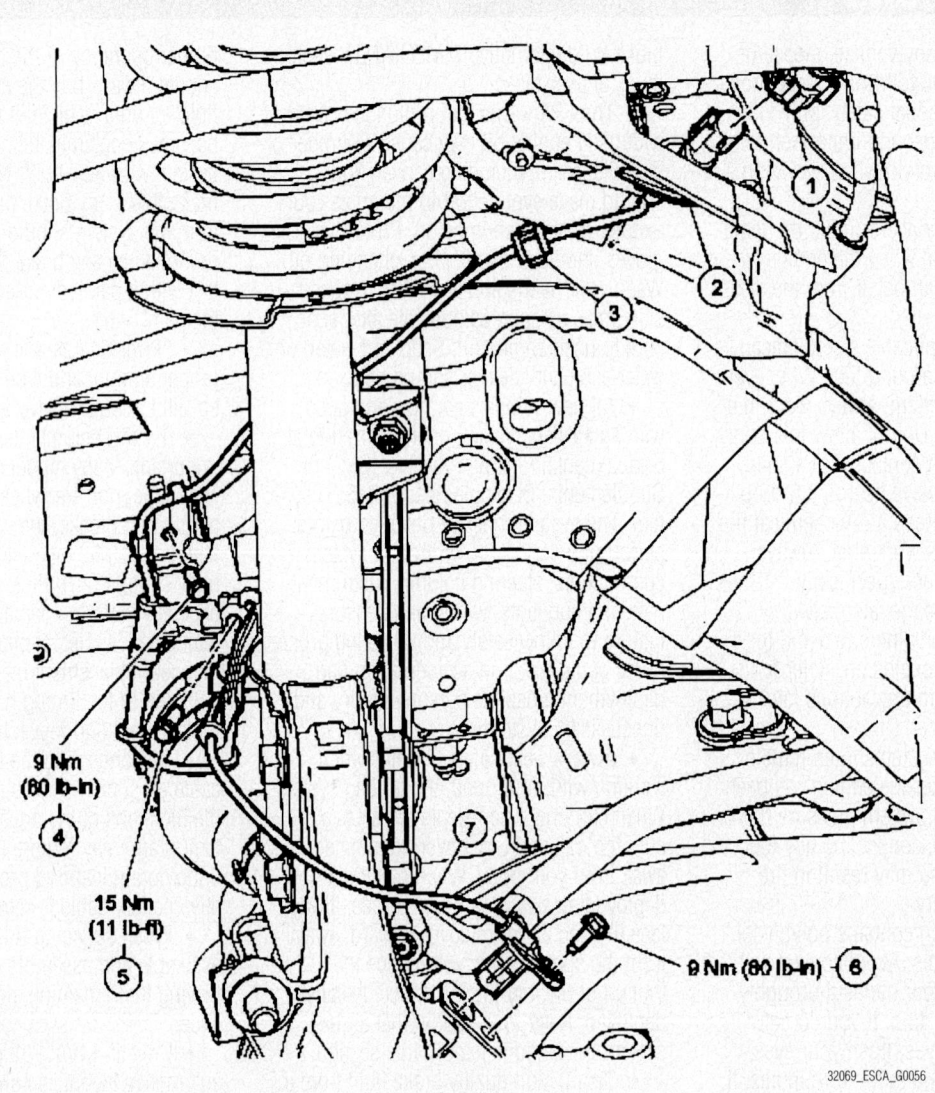

Fig. 1 View of the front wheel speed sensor wire connector (1), grommet (2), front wheel speed sensor wire retainer (3), front wheel speed sensor wire-to-body bolts (4), front wheel speed sensor bolts (5, 6) and front wheel speed sensor (7)

※※ **WARNING**

Care must be taken during the removal of the plug to prevent damage. If the plug is damaged, a new sensor may need to be installed, even though the sensor is functional in all other aspects.

4. Remove the grommet from the body.

5. When removing the body plug, rotate the plug into a position which allows the use of a small screwdriver to release the tabs on the underside of the body plug. These 2 tabs are located at right angles to the sensor wire.

6. Remove the front wheel speed sensor wire from the retainer.

7. Remove the front wheel speed sensor wire-to-body bolt.

8. Remove the front wheel speed sensor wire bolt.

9. Remove the front wheel speed sensor bolt from the wheel knuckle.

➡ Clean off any foreign material that may have collected around the sensor before removal.

10. Remove the front wheel speed sensor.

➡ Thoroughly clean the mounting surface.

11. Installation is the reverse of the removal procedure, noting the following tightening specifications:

- Front wheel speed sensor-to-knuckle bolt: 80 inch lbs. (9 Nm)
- Front wheel speed sensor wire bolt: 11 ft. lbs. (15 Nm)
- Front wheel speed sensor wire-to-body bolt: 80 inch lbs. (9 Nm)

Rear Sensor

See Figure 2.

1. Remove the wheel and tire.

※※ **WARNING**

Care must be taken during the removal of the plug to prevent damage. If the plug is damaged, a new sensor may need to be installed even though the sensor is functional in all other aspects.

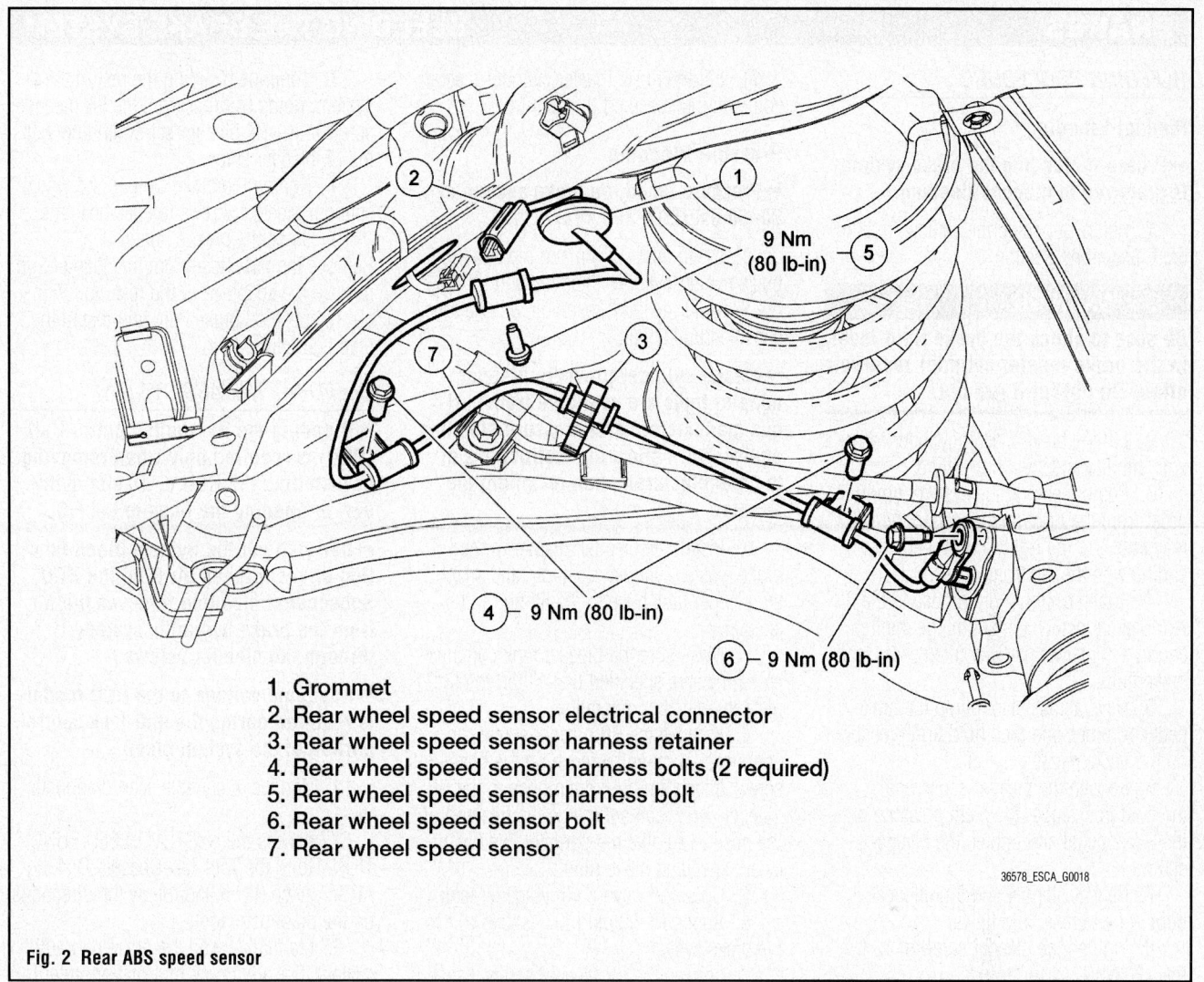

9 Nm
(80 lb-in)

4 — 9 Nm (80 lb-in)

6 — 9 Nm (80 lb-in)

1. Grommet
2. Rear wheel speed sensor electrical connector
3. Rear wheel speed sensor harness retainer
4. Rear wheel speed sensor harness bolts (2 required)
5. Rear wheel speed sensor harness bolt
6. Rear wheel speed sensor bolt
7. Rear wheel speed sensor

36578_ESCA_G0018

Fig. 2 Rear ABS speed sensor

2. Remove the grommet from the body.

3. When removing the body plug, rotate the plug into a position which allows the use of a small screwdriver to release the tabs on the underside of the body plug. These 2 tabs are located at right angles to the sensor wire.

4. Disconnect the rear wheel speed sensor electrical connector.

5. Remove the rear wheel speed sensor harness from the harness retainer.

6. Remove the 3 rear wheel speed sensor harness bolts.

➡**Clean off any dirt that may have collected around the sensor before removal.**

7. Remove the rear wheel speed sensor bolt from the wheel knuckle.

8. Remove the rear wheel speed sensor.

➡**Thoroughly clean the mounting surface.**

9. Installation is the reverse of the removal procedure.

10. Tighten all retaining bolts to 80 inch lbs. (9 Nm).

BRAKES | BLEEDING THE BRAKE SYSTEM

BLEEDING PROCEDURE

Manual Bleeding

➡️**Pressure bleeding the brake system is preferred to manual bleeding.**

1. Before servicing the vehicle, refer to the Precautions Section.

✳ WARNING

Be sure to check the brake fluid level in the brake master cylinder reservoir often. Do not let it run dry.

2. Fill the brake master cylinder reservoir with the specified brake fluid.
3. Begin bleeding the system, going in order from the right rear wheel, to the left rear wheel, to the right front wheel, and ending with the left front wheel.
4. Attach a rubber drain hose to the rear bleeder screw and submerge the free end in a container partially filled with clean brake fluid.
5. Have an assistant pump the brake pedal 10 times and then hold firm pressure on the brake pedal.
6. Loosen the bleeder screw until the fluid flow stops. Maintain pressure on the brake pedal and tighten the bleeder screw.
7. Repeat Steps 4 and 5 until clear, bubble-free brake fluid flows.
8. Tighten the bleeder screw to 12 ft. lbs. (16 Nm).
9. Refill the brake master cylinder reservoir as necessary.
10. Continue bleeding the brake hydraulic system at each wheel.

11. Fill the brake master cylinder reservoir with the specified brake fluid.

Pressure Bleeding

➡️**Pressure bleed the brake system at 30–50 psi (207–345 kPa).**

1. Clean all dirt from and remove the brake master cylinder filler cap and fill the brake master cylinder reservoir with clean, specified brake fluid.

➡️**Master cylinder pressure bleeder adapter tools are available from various manufacturers of pressure bleeding equipment. Follow the instructions of the manufacturer when installing the adapter.**

2. Install the bleeder adapter to the brake master cylinder reservoir, and attach the bleeder tank hose to the fitting on the adapter.
3. Make sure the bleeder tank contains enough clean, specified brake fluid to complete the bleeding operation.
4. Remove the RR bleeder screw cap and place a box-end wrench on the bleeder screw. Attach a rubber drain hose to the RR bleeder screw and submerge the free end of the hose in a container partially filled with clean, specified brake fluid.
5. Open the valve on the bleeder tank.
6. Apply 30–50 psi (207–345 kPa).) to the brake system.
7. Loosen the RR bleeder screw. Leave open until clear, bubble-free brake fluid flows, then tighten the RR bleeder screw to specifications. Refer to Specifications in this section. Remove the rubber hose.

8. Continue bleeding the rest of the system, going in order from the LR bleeder screw to the RF bleeder screw, ending with the LF bleeder screw.
9. Tighten the brake caliper and wheel cylinder bleeder screws to specifications.
10. Close the bleeder tank valve. Remove the tank hose from the adapter and remove the adapter. Fill the reservoir with clean, specified brake fluid and install the reservoir cap.

BLEEDING THE ABS SYSTEM

➡️**Bleeding the Hydraulic Control Unit (HCU) is required only when removing or installing the HCU or master cylinder, or opening the lines to the HCU.**

➡️**Carrying out the System Bleed function drives trapped air from the HCU. Subsequent bleeding removes the air from the brake hydraulic system through the bleeder screws.**

➡️**Adequate voltage to the HCU module is required during the anti-lock control portion of the system bleed.**

1. Connect a suitable scan/diagnostic tool.
2. Access the SYSTEM BLEED FUNCTION. Go to the Tool Tab-Chassis-Braking-ABS Service Bleed and follow the directions on the diagnostic tool.
3. Manually bleed the brake hydraulic system. For additional information, refer to Manual Bleed in this section.
4. Repeat the procedure carrying out a total of two diagnostic tool cycles and two manual bleed cycles.

BRAKES | FRONT DISC BRAKES

BRAKE CALIPER

REMOVAL & INSTALLATION

See Figures 3 through 5.

✳ CAUTION

Dust and dirt accumulating on brake parts during normal use may contain asbestos fibers from production or aftermarket brake linings. Breathing excessive concentrations of asbestos fibers can cause serious bodily harm. Exercise care when servicing brake parts. Do not sand or grind brake lining unless equipment used is designed to contain the dust residue. Do not clean brake parts with compressed air or by dry brushing. Cleaning should be done by dampening the brake components with a fine mist of water, then wiping the brake components clean with a dampened cloth. Dispose of cloth and all residue containing asbestos fibers in an impermeable container with the appropriate label. Follow practices prescribed by the Occupational Safety and Health Administration (OSHA) and the Environmental Protection Agency (EPA) for the handling, processing, and disposing of dust or debris that may contain asbestos fibers.

1. Before servicing the vehicle, refer to the Precautions Section.
2. The following steps must be followed to prevent the accumulator from charging and pressurizing the brake system:
   - Disconnect the battery.
   - Remove the battery junction box (BJB) fuses 9 (50A) and 18 (50A).
3. Remove the wheel and tire assembly.
4. Safely raise the vehicle.
5. For the LH brake caliper, release the lower portion of the brake pad anti-rattle spring.
6. Apply force to the center of the spring and pull outward at the bottom of the spring to remove it from the lower brake caliper cavity.

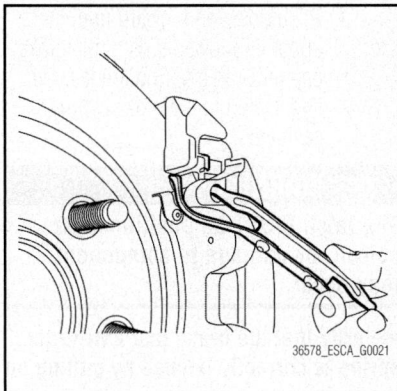

Fig. 3 For the LH brake caliper, rotate the spring upward and remove it from the brake caliper

7. Rotate the spring upward and remove it from the brake caliper.

8. For the RH brake caliper, release the upper portion of the brake pad anti-rattle spring.

9. Apply force to the center of the spring and pull outward at the top of the spring to remove it from the upper brake caliper cavity.

10. Rotate the spring downward and remove it from the brake caliper.

➡ **The brake caliper and brake flexible hose are removed as an assembly.**

11. Disconnect the brake tube fitting from the brake flexible hose.

12. Remove and discard the retainer clip from the brake flexible hose.

13. Remove the 2 guide pin bushing caps and the 2 brake caliper guide pin bolts, position the caliper aside. Support the caliper using mechanic's wire.

14. Remove the front brake caliper from the vehicle.

15. Remove the brake flexible hose from the brake caliper.

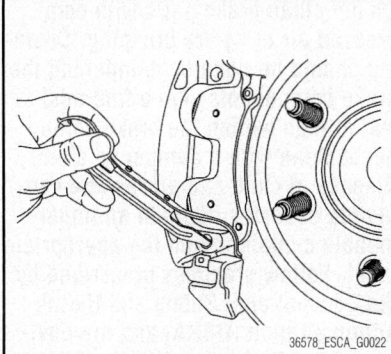

Fig. 4 For the RH brake caliper, rotate the spring downward and remove it from the brake caliper

Fig. 5 Brake pad anti-rattle spring correct installation shown

To install:

16. Install the brake pads onto the caliper and position the brake caliper onto the anchor plate.

17. Install the 2 brake caliper guide pin bolts and tighten to 37 ft. lbs. (50 Nm).

18. Install the 2 bushing caps.

➡ **If present, the 2-tabbed end of the brake pad anti-rattle spring must be installed first.**

19. Install the brake pad anti-rattle spring using the following procedure:
   • Insert the tab of the spring into the brake caliper cavity.
   • Twist the tab into the cavity (LH side in the upper brake caliper cavity, RH side in the lower brake caliper cavity).

20. Rotate the brake pad anti-rattle spring and position the upper portion onto the anchor plate.

21. Position the lower portion of the brake pad anti-rattle spring onto the anchor plate.

22. Push down and inward until the upper and lower ends of the brake pad anti-rattle spring are latched and seated in the brake caliper cavities.

23. Verify that the brake pad anti-rattle spring is correctly latched by pulling on the spring.

➡ **Make sure that the brake flexible hose is not twisted.**

24. Install the brake flexible hose to the brake caliper. Tighten the hose to 177 inch lbs. (20 Nm).

25. Position the brake flexible hose and install a new retainer clip.

26. Attach the brake tube fitting to the brake flexible hose and tighten to 159 inch lbs. (18 Nm).

27. Bleed the brake caliper.

28. Install the wheel and tire.

29. Lower the vehicle.

30. Install the battery junction box (BJB) fuses 9 (50A) and 18 (50A).

31. Connect the battery.

32. Check the brake fluid level and add as needed.

DISC BRAKE PADS

REMOVAL & INSTALLATION

✳✳ CAUTION

Dust and dirt accumulating on brake parts during normal use may contain asbestos fibers from production or aftermarket brake linings. Breathing excessive concentrations of asbestos fibers can cause serious bodily harm. Exercise care when servicing brake parts. Do not sand or grind brake lining unless equipment used is designed to contain the dust residue. Do not clean brake parts with compressed air or by dry brushing. Cleaning should be done by dampening the brake components with a fine mist of water, then wiping the brake components clean with a dampened cloth. Dispose of cloth and all residue containing asbestos fibers in an impermeable container with the appropriate label. Follow practices prescribed by the Occupational Safety and Health Administration (OSHA) and the Environmental Protection Agency (EPA) for the handling, processing, and disposing of dust or debris that may contain asbestos fibers.

1. Before servicing the vehicle, refer to the Precautions Section.

2. With the vehicle in NEUTRAL, position it on a hoist.

3. The following steps must be followed to prevent the accumulator from charging and pressurizing the brake system:
   • Disconnect the battery.
   • Remove the battery junction box (BJB) fuses 9 (50A) and 18 (50A).

4. Remove the tire and wheel assembly.

5. Safely raise the vehicle.

6. For the LH brake caliper, release the lower portion of the brake pad anti-rattle spring.

7. Apply force to the center of the spring and pull outward at the bottom of the spring to remove it from the lower brake caliper cavity.

8. Rotate the spring upward and remove it from the brake caliper.

9. For the RH brake caliper, release the upper portion of the brake pad anti-rattle spring.

10. Apply force to the center of the spring and pull outward at the top of the spring to remove it from the upper brake caliper cavity.

11. Rotate the spring downward and remove it from the brake caliper.

12. Remove the 2 guide pin bushing caps and the 2 brake caliper guide pin bolts, position the caliper aside.

13. Support the caliper using mechanic's wire.

14. Remove the 2 brake pads from the caliper.

15. Use a suitable tool to protect the brake caliper piston and compress the brake caliper piston into the brake caliper.

16. Inspect the brake disc and resurface or install new as necessary

To install:

17. Clean, dry and inspect the brake caliper anchor plate. Apply a light coat of specified lubricant to the 4 brake pad

➡**Make sure that the brake flexible hose is not twisted.**

18. Install the brake pads onto the caliper and position the brake caliper onto the anchor plate.

19. Install the 2 brake caliper guide pin bolts and tighten to 37 ft. lbs. (50 Nm) install the 2 bushing caps.

➡**The 2-tabbed end of the brake pad anti-rattle spring must be installed first.**

20. Install the brake pad anti-rattle spring using the following procedure:
- Insert the tab of the spring into the brake caliper cavity.
- Twist the tab into the cavity (LH side in the upper brake caliper cavity, RH side in the lower brake caliper cavity).
- Rotate the brake pad anti-rattle spring and position the upper portion onto the anchor plate.
- Position the lower portion of the brake pad anti-rattle spring onto the anchor plate.

- Push down and inward until the upper and lower ends of the brake pad anti-rattle spring are latched and seated in the brake caliper cavities.

❊❊ WARNING
The latch MUST be positioned as shown, or damage to component may occur.

➡**Verify that the brake pad anti-rattle spring is correctly latched by pulling on the spring.**

21. Install the wheel and tire.
22. Install the battery junction box (BJB) fuses 9 (50A) and 18 (50A).
23. Connect the battery.
24. Install the tire and wheel assembly.
25. Lower the vehicle.
26. Fill the brake master cylinder reservoir with clean, specified brake fluid.
27. Apply brakes several times to verify correct brake operation.
28. Test the brakes for normal operation.

BRAKES

BRAKE CALIPER

REMOVAL & INSTALLATION
See Figure 6.

❊❊ CAUTION
Dust and dirt accumulating on brake parts during normal use may contain asbestos fibers from production or aftermarket brake linings. Breathing excessive concentrations of asbestos fibers can cause serious bodily harm. Exercise care when servicing brake parts. Do not sand or grind brake lining unless equipment used is designed to contain the dust residue. Do not clean brake parts with compressed air or by dry brushing. Cleaning should be done by dampening the brake components with a fine mist of water, then wiping the brake components clean with a dampened cloth. Dispose of cloth and all residue containing asbestos fibers in an impermeable container with the appropriate label. Follow practices prescribed by the Occupational Safety and Health Administration (OSHA) and the Environmental Protection Agency (EPA) for the handling, processing, and disposing of dust or debris that may contain asbestos fibers.

1. Before servicing the vehicle, refer to the Precautions Section.

2. The following steps must be followed to prevent the accumulator from charging and pressurizing the brake system:
- Disconnect the battery.
- Remove the battery junction box (BJB) fuses 9 (50A) and 18 (50A).

3. Safely raise the vehicle.
4. Remove the wheel and tire assembly.
5. Remove the brake flexible hose flow bolt and discard the 2 copper washers.
6. Remove the 2 brake caliper guide bolts.
7. Remove the rear brake caliper.
8. Remove the brake pads from the rear brake caliper.

To install:

9. Install the brake pads to the rear brake caliper.
10. Install the rear brake caliper.
11. Install the 2 brake caliper guide bolts and tighten to 26 ft. lbs. (25 Nm).
12. Install the flexible hose with new cooper washers, tighten the flow bolt to 26 ft. lbs. (25 Nm).
13. Bleed the brake caliper.
14. Install the tire and wheel assembly.
15. Lower the vehicle.
16. Install the battery junction box (BJB) fuses 9 (50A) and 18 (50A).
17. Connect the negative battery cable.

REAR DISC BRAKES

DISC BRAKE PADS

REMOVAL & INSTALLATION
See Figure 6.

❊❊ CAUTION
Dust and dirt accumulating on brake parts during normal use may contain asbestos fibers from production or aftermarket brake linings. Breathing excessive concentrations of asbestos fibers can cause serious bodily harm. Exercise care when servicing brake parts. Do not sand or grind brake lining unless equipment used is designed to contain the dust residue. Do not clean brake parts with compressed air or by dry brushing. Cleaning should be done by dampening the brake components with a fine mist of water, then wiping the brake components clean with a dampened cloth. Dispose of cloth and all residue containing asbestos fibers in an impermeable container with the appropriate label. Follow practices prescribed by the Occupational Safety and Health Administration (OSHA) and the Environmental Protection Agency (EPA) for the handling, processing, and disposing of dust or debris that may contain asbestos fibers.

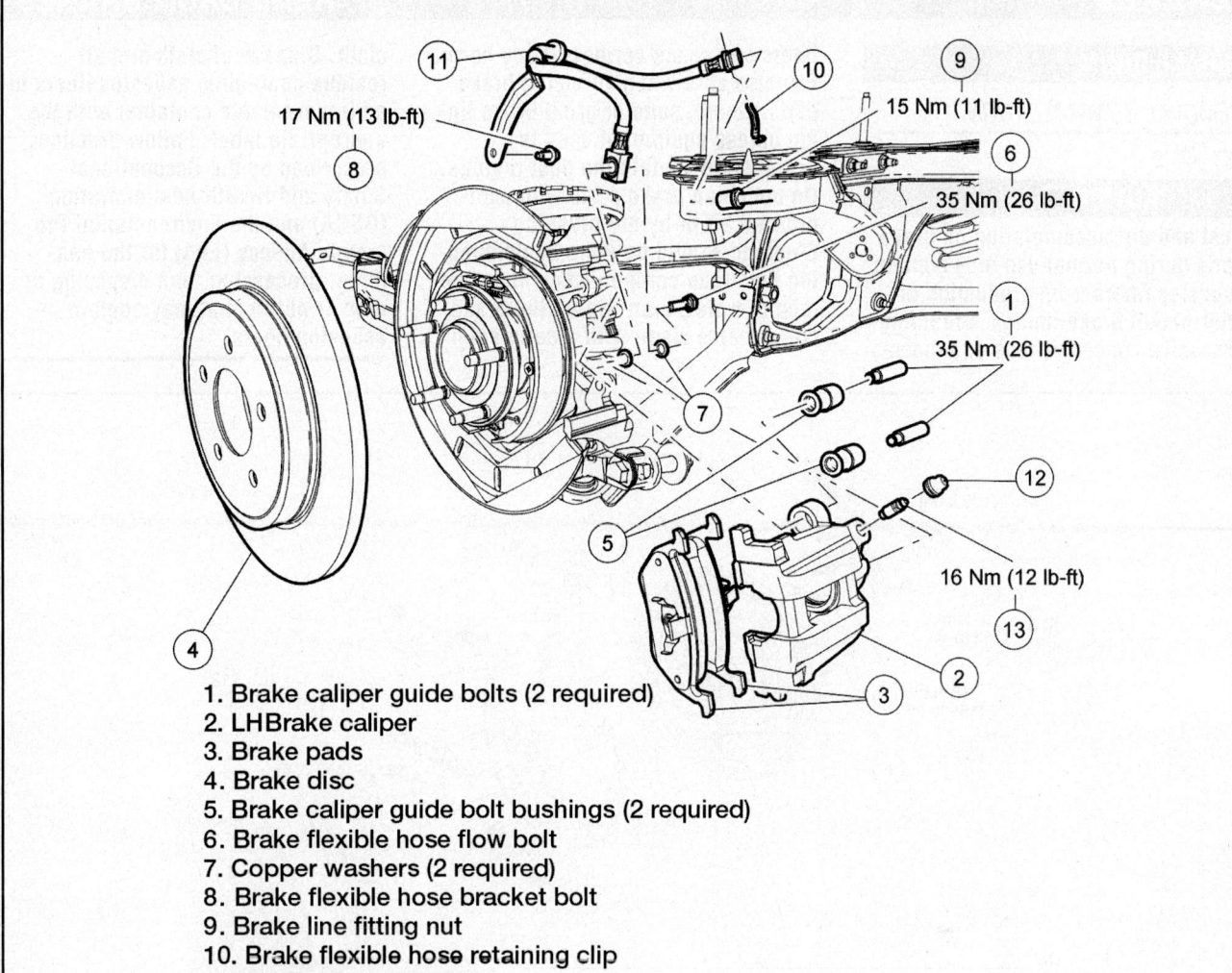

17 Nm (13 lb-ft)
15 Nm (11 lb-ft)
35 Nm (26 lb-ft)
35 Nm (26 lb-ft)
16 Nm (12 lb-ft)

1. Brake caliper guide bolts (2 required)
2. LH Brake caliper
3. Brake pads
4. Brake disc
5. Brake caliper guide bolt bushings (2 required)
6. Brake flexible hose flow bolt
7. Copper washers (2 required)
8. Brake flexible hose bracket bolt
9. Brake line fitting nut
10. Brake flexible hose retaining clip
11. LH Brake flexible hose
12. Bleeder screw cap
13. Bleeder screw

36578_ESCA_G0024

Fig. 6 Rear disc brake system—exploded view

1. Before servicing the vehicle, refer to the Precautions Section.

2. The following steps must be followed to prevent the accumulator from charging and pressurizing the brake system:
   - Disconnect the battery.
   - Remove the battery junction box (BJB) fuses 9 (50A) and 18 (50A)

3. Safely raise the vehicle.

4. Remove the wheel and tire assembly.

5. Remove the 2 brake caliper guide pin bolts and position the caliper aside. Support the caliper using mechanic's wire.

6. Remove the brake pads from the brake caliper.

To install:

7. Install the brake pads to the brake caliper.

8. Install the brake caliper.

9. Install the brake caliper guide pins and tighten to 26 ft. lbs. (35 Nm).

10. Install the tire and wheel assembly.

11. Lower the vehicle.

12. Install the battery junction box (BJB) fuses 9 (50A) and 18 (50A).

13. Connect the negative battery cable.

14. Pump the brake pedal to seat and adjust pads.

BRAKES   **REAR DRUM BRAKES**

BRAKE DRUM

REMOVAL & INSTALLATION
See Figure 7.

> **✳✳ CAUTION**
>
> Dust and dirt accumulating on brake parts during normal use may contain asbestos fibers from production or aftermarket brake linings. Breathing excessive concentrations of asbestos fibers can cause serious bodily harm. Exercise care when servicing brake parts. Do not sand or grind brake lining unless equipment used is designed to contain the dust residue. Do not clean brake parts with compressed air or by dry brushing. Cleaning should be done by dampening the brake components with a fine mist of water, then wiping the brake components clean with a dampened cloth. Dispose of cloth and all residue containing asbestos fibers in an impermeable container with the appropriate label. Follow practices prescribed by the Occupational Safety and Health Administration (OSHA) and the Environmental Protection Agency (EPA) for the handling, processing, and disposing of dust or debris that may contain asbestos fibers.

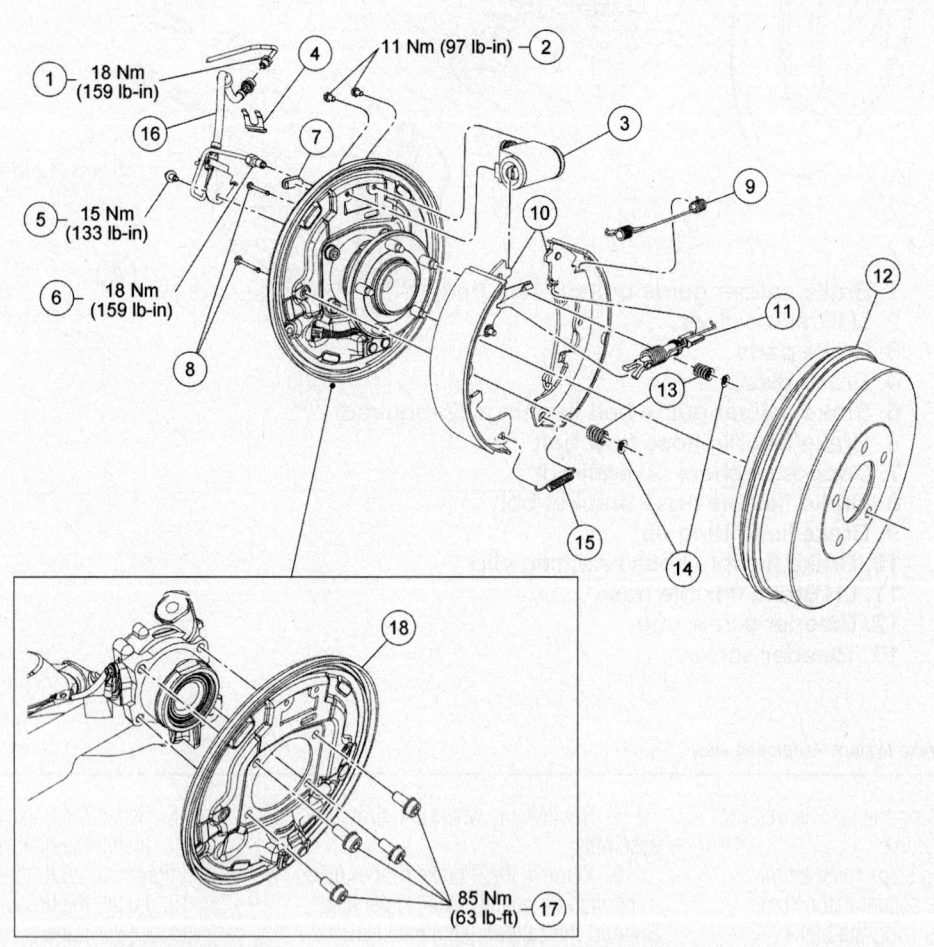

1. Brake tube fitting
2. Wheel cylinder bolts
3. Wheel cylinder
4. Brake flexible hose clip
5. Brake flexible hose bracket bolt
6. Brake flexible hose fitting
7. Plug
8. Brake shoe retaining pins
9. Upper return spring
10. Brake shoe (kit)
11. Self-adjuster assembly
12. Brake drum
13. Brake shoe retaining springs
14. Brake shoe retaining spring plates
15. Lower return spring
16. Brake flexible hose
17. Backing plate bolts
18. Backing plate

36578_ESCA_G0025

Fig. 7 Drum brake system—exploded view

1. Before servicing the vehicle, refer to the Precautions Section.

2. Remove the tire and wheel assembly.

✳✳ CAUTION

Use of a brake drum puller or a torch is not recommended. Brake drum distortion can result.

➡ **If the brake drum is rusted to the axle shaft pilot diameter, tap the center of the brake drum between the wheel studs.**

3. Remove the brake drum.

4. If equipped, remove the brake drum retaining clips.

5. If the brake drums will not come off, follow these steps.

6. Move the brake shoe adjusting lever off the brake adjuster screw.

7. Loosen the brake shoe adjuster screw nut by adjusting the nut upward.

8. Using the special tool, 134-R0191, measure the brake drum inside diameter.

9. Install a new brake drum if the maximum inside diameter exceeds the specification shown on the outside of the brake drum.

To install:

✳✳ WARNING

Whenever a wheel is installed, always remove any corrosion, dirt or foreign material present on the mounting surfaces of the wheel or the surface of the wheel hub, brake drum or brake disc that contacts the wheel. Installing wheels without correct metal-to-metal contact at the wheel mounting surfaces can cause the wheel nuts to loosen and the wheel to come off while the vehicle is in motion, causing loss of control. Failure to follow these instructions may result in personal injury.

10. Adjust the rear brakes.

11. Clean the wheel hub mounting surface and wheel pilot.

12. Position the brake drum on the vehicle.

13. Install the tire and wheel assembly.

BRAKE SHOES

REMOVAL & INSTALLATION

See Figure 7.

✳✳ CAUTION

Dust and dirt accumulating on brake parts during normal use may contain asbestos fibers from production or aftermarket brake linings. Breathing excessive concentrations of asbestos fibers can cause serious bodily harm. Exercise care when servicing brake parts. Do not sand or grind brake lining unless equipment used is designed to contain the dust residue. Do not clean brake parts with compressed air or by dry brushing. Cleaning should be done by dampening the brake components with a fine mist of water, then wiping the brake components clean with a dampened cloth. Dispose of cloth and all residue containing asbestos fibers in an impermeable container with the appropriate label. Follow practices prescribed by the Occupational Safety and Health Administration (OSHA) and the Environmental Protection Agency (EPA) for the handling, processing, and disposing of dust or debris that may contain asbestos fibers.

1. Before servicing the vehicle, refer to the Precautions Section.

2. Remove the tire and wheel assembly.

3. Remove the brake drum.

4. Use the Brake/Clutch/Service Vacuum to remove brake dust and dirt from the brake assemblies.

➡ **If new rear brake shoes and linings are being installed, resurface the brake drums to remove glazing and to ensure an equal friction surface from side-to-side. Resurfacing will also correct out-of-round and bell conditions.**

5. Remove the 2 brake shoe retaining springs and the 2 pins.

6. Remove the upper return spring.

7. Remove the self-adjuster and spring assembly.

8. Remove the lower return spring.

9. Remove the trailing brake shoe and parking brake actuator lever assembly.

10. Remove the leading brake shoe.

To install:

11. To install, reverse the removal procedure and note the following:

- Using specified brake parts cleaner, clean and dry the brake shoe contact points on the backing plate.
- Apply a thin coat of the specified silicone grease to the brake shoe contact points on the backing plate.
- Adjust the self-adjuster to the full retracted position to ease the installation of the brake drum.

12. Adjust the rear brake shoes.

13. Install the brake drum.

14. Install the tire and wheel assembly.

ADJUSTMENT

See Figures 8 and 9.

1. Remove the brake drum.

2. Using the special tool, 134-R0191, measure the brake drum inside diameter.

3. Position the special tool on the brake shoes and linings and adjust accordingly.

4. Install the brake drum

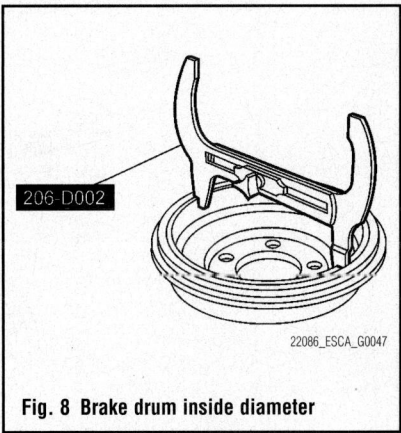

Fig. 8 Brake drum inside diameter

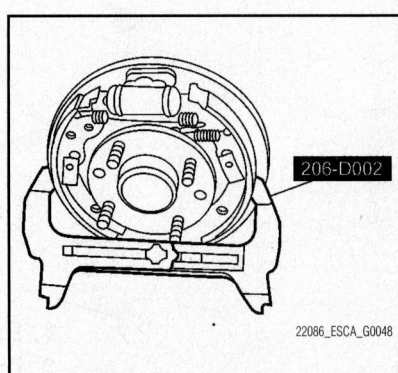

Fig. 9 Adjustment of brake shoes to drum inside diameter

PARKING BRAKE CABLES

ADJUSTMENT

If the parking brake needs to be adjusted, refer to the Parking Brake Shoes Adjustment in this section.

If the parking brake needs to be adjusted, refer to the Brake Shoes Adjustment in this section.

PARKING BRAKE SHOES

REMOVAL & INSTALLATION

With Rear Drum Brakes

The rear drum brake shoes serve as the parking brakes. Refer to the procedures under Rear Drum Brakes.

With Rear Disc Brakes

See Figure 10.

1. Before servicing the vehicle, refer to the Precautions Section.
2. Remove the rear brake disc.
3. Remove the parking brake shoe upper return spring.
4. Remove the 2 parking brake shoe retaining pins.
5. Remove the 2 parking brake shoe retaining springs.
6. Remove the parking brake shoe lower return spring.
7. Remove the parking brake shoe adjuster.
8. Remove the parking brake shoes.

To install:

9. To install, reverse the removal procedure.

- Using anti-seize lubricant, lubricate the parking brake shoe contact points before installation of the rear parking brake shoes.
- Lubricate the adjust screw threads with anti-seize lubricant.
- Adjust the parking brake shoes.
- Check the parking brake for normal operation.

ADJUSTMENT

See Figures 11 and 12.

1. Before servicing the vehicle, refer to the Precautions Section.
2. With the vehicle in NEUTRAL, position it on a hoist.

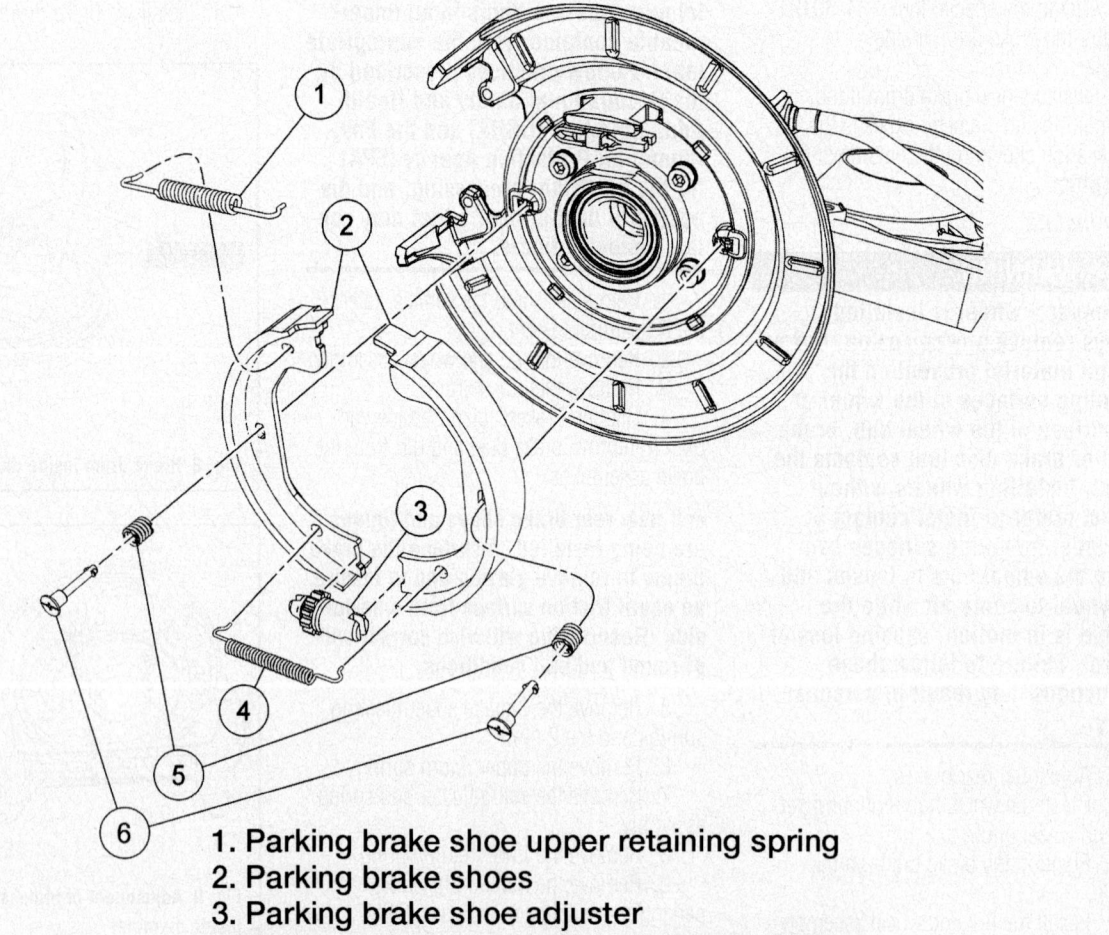

1. Parking brake shoe upper retaining spring
2. Parking brake shoes
3. Parking brake shoe adjuster
4. Parking brake shoe lower retaining spring
5. Parking brake shoe retaining springs (2 required)
6. Parking brake shoe retaining pins (2 required)

36578_ESCA_G0026

Fig. 10 Parking brake shoes

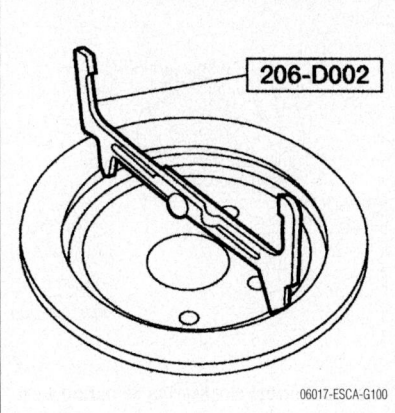

Fig. 11 Using the special tool, measure the inside diameter of the drum portion of the rear brake disc and set the locking screw

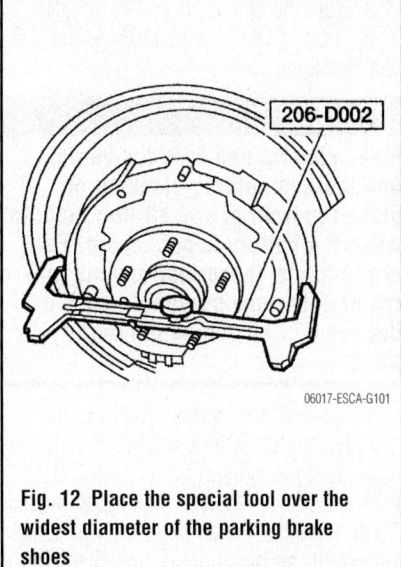

Fig. 12 Place the special tool over the widest diameter of the parking brake shoes

➡**Make sure the parking brake is fully released.**

3. Using the release handle, release the parking brake control.

4. Remove the rear brake disc.

5. Using the special tool, measure the inside diameter of the drum portion of the rear brake disc and set the locking screw. Record the measurement.

6. Place the special tool over the widest diameter of the parking brake shoes.

7. Adjust the parking brake shoe clearance to 0.01 inch (0.50 mm) less than the inside diameter of the drum portion of the rear brake disc. Rotate the parking brake shoe adjuster to achieve the correct parking brake shoe-to-brake disc clearance.

8. Install the rear brake disc.

9. Test the parking brake for normal operation.

CHASSIS ELECTRICAL

GENERAL INFORMATION

SERVICE PRECAUTIONS

Disconnect and isolate the battery negative cable before beginning any airbag system component diagnosis, testing, removal, or installation procedures. Allow system capacitor to discharge for two minutes before beginning any component service. This will disable the airbag system. Failure to disable the airbag system may result in accidental airbag deployment, personal injury, or death.

Do not place an intact undeployed airbag face down on a solid surface. The airbag will propel into the air if accidentally deployed and may result in personal injury or death.

When carrying or handling an undeployed airbag, the trim side (face) of the airbag should be pointing towards the body to minimize possibility of injury if accidental deployment occurs. Failure to do this may result in personal injury or death.

Replace airbag system components with OEM replacement parts. Substitute parts may appear interchangeable, but internal differences may result in inferior occupant protection. Failure to do so may result in occupant personal injury or death.

Wear safety glasses, rubber gloves, and long sleeved clothing when cleaning powder residue from vehicle after an airbag deployment. Powder residue emitted from a deployed airbag can cause skin irritation. Flush affected area with cool water if irritation is experienced. If nasal or throat irritation is experienced, exit the vehicle for fresh air until the irritation ceases. If irritation continues, see a physician.

Do not use a replacement airbag that is not in the original packaging. This may result in improper deployment, personal injury, or death.

The factory installed fasteners, screws and bolts used to fasten airbag components have a special coating and are specifically designed for the airbag system. Do not use substitute fasteners. Use only original equipment fasteners listed in the parts catalog when fastener replacement is required.

During, and following, any child restraint anchor service, due to impact event or vehicle repair, carefully inspect all mounting hardware, tether straps, and anchors for proper installation, operation, or damage. If a child restraint anchor is found damaged in any way, the anchor must be replaced. Failure to do this may result in personal injury or death.

Deployed and non-deployed airbags may or may not have live pyrotechnic material within the airbag inflator.

Do not dispose of driver/passenger/curtain airbags or seat belt tensioners unless you are sure of complete deployment. Refer to the Hazardous Substance Control System for proper disposal.

Dispose of deployed airbags and tensioners consistent with state, provincial, local, and federal regulations.

After any airbag component testing or service, do not connect the battery negative cable. Personal injury or death may result if the system test is not performed first.

AIR BAG (SUPPLEMENTAL RESTRAINT SYSTEM)

If the vehicle is equipped with the Occupant Classification System (OCS), do not connect the battery negative cable before performing the OCS Verification Test using the scan tool and the appropriate diagnostic information. Personal injury or death may result if the system test is not performed properly.

Never replace both the Occupant Restraint Controller (ORC) and the Occupant Classification Module (OCM) at the same time. If both require replacement, replace one, then perform the Airbag System test before replacing the other.

Both the ORC and the OCM store Occupant Classification System (OCS) calibration data, which they transfer to one another when one of them is replaced. If both are replaced at the same time, an irreversible fault will be set in both modules and the OCS may malfunction and cause personal injury or death.

If equipped with OCS, the Seat Weight Sensor is a sensitive, calibrated unit and must be handled carefully. Do not drop or handle roughly. If dropped or damaged, replace with another sensor. Failure to do so may result in occupant injury or death.

If equipped with OCS, the front passenger seat must be handled carefully as well. When removing the seat, be careful when setting on floor not to drop. If dropped, the sensor may be inoperative, could result in occupant injury, or possibly death.

If equipped with OCS, when the passenger front seat is on the floor, no one should sit in the front passenger seat. This uneven force may damage the sensing ability of the seat weight sensors. If sat on and damaged, the sensor may be inoperative, could result in occupant injury, or possibly death.

DISARMING THE SYSTEM

1. Before servicing the vehicle, refer to the Precautions Section.
2. Turn all vehicle accessories OFF.
3. Turn the ignition switch to OFF.
4. At the Smart Junction Box (SJB) located at the RH side of the center console, remove the cover and the RCM fuse 32 (10A) from the SJB See the Owner's Manual.
5. Turn the ignition ON and visually monitor the air bag indicator for at least 30 seconds. The air bag indicator will remain lit continuously (no flashing) if the correct RCM fuse has been removed. If the air bag indicator does not remain lit continuously, remove the correct RCM fuse before proceeding.
6. Turn the ignition OFF.

✳✳ CAUTION

To avoid accidental deployment and possible personal injury, the backup power supply must be depleted before repairing or replacing any front or side air bag Supplemental Restraint System (SRS) components and before servicing, replacing, adjusting or striking components near the front or side air bag sensors, such as doors, instrument panel, console, door latches, strikers, seats and hood latches.

➡To deplete the backup power supply energy, disconnect the battery ground cable and wait at least one minute. Be sure to disconnect auxiliary batteries and power supplies (if equipped).

7. Disconnect the battery ground cable and wait at least one minute

ARMING THE SYSTEM

1. Before servicing the vehicle, refer to the Precautions Section.

2. Turn the ignition from OFF to ON.
3. Install RCM fuse 32 (10A) to the SJB and install the cover.

✳✳ CAUTION

Make sure no one is in the vehicle and there is nothing blocking or placed in front of any air bag module when the battery is connected. Failure to follow these instructions may result in serious personal injury in the event of an accidental deployment.

4. Connect the battery ground cable. Prove out the SRS as follows:
5. Turn the ignition from ON to OFF. Wait 10 seconds, then turn the ignition back ON and monitor the air bag warning indicator with the air bag modules installed. The air bag indicator will light continuously for approximately 6 seconds and then turn off. If an air bag SRS fault is present, the air bag indicator will:
- Fail to light.
- Remain lit continuously.
- Flash.
6. The flashing might not occur until approximately 30 seconds after the ignition has been turned from the OFF to the ON position. This is the time required for the RCM to complete the testing of the SRS. If the air bag indicator is inoperative and a SRS fault exists, a chime will sound in a pattern of 5 sets of 5 beeps. If this occurs, the air bag warning indicator and any SRS fault discovered must be diagnosed and repaired.
7. Clear all continuous DTCs from the RCM using a scan tool.

CLOCKSPRING CENTERING

See Figure 13.

➡To prevent damage to the clockspring, make sure the road wheels are in the 12 o'clock position to install the steering wheel.

If a new clockspring was installed and the anti-rotation key has been removed

36578_ESCA_G0029

Fig. 13 Correct clockspring centering view

before the steering wheel is installed or the same clockspring is being installed, rotate the clockspring inner rotor counterclockwise and carefully feel for the ribbon wire to run out of length with slight resistance. Stop rotating the clockspring inner rotor at this point.

1. Starting with the clockspring inner rotor, wiring and connector in the 12 o'clock position, rotate the inner rotor clockwise through 4 revolutions to center the clockspring.
2. Verify that the clockspring is correctly centered by observing that after 4 revolutions:

- The clockspring rotor window is in the 4 o'clock position and the yellow indicator shows in the window.
- The 2 arrows located on the inner and outer rotor of the clockspring line up in the 6 o'clock position.
- The clockspring inner rotor, wiring and connector are in the 12 o'clock position.

✳✳ CAUTION

Do not over-rotate the clockspring inner rotor. The internal ribbon wire is connected to the clockspring rotor. The internal ribbon wire acts as a stop and can be broken from its internal connection. Failure to follow this instruction may result in component damage and/or system failure.

DRIVE TRAIN

AUTOMATIC TRANSAXLE ASSEMBLY

REMOVAL & INSTALLATION

2008—CD4E Transaxle

2.3L Engine

See Figures 14 through 17.

1. Before servicing the vehicle, refer to the Precautions Section.

All vehicles:

2. With the vehicle in NEUTRAL, position it on a hoist.

3. Remove the battery and the battery tray.

4. Remove the air cleaner as an assembly.

    a. Remove the bolt.

    b. Disconnect the Mass Air Flow (MAF) sensor electrical connector.

    c. Disconnect the brake booster vacuum hose.

    d. Disconnect the wiring harness retainer

    e. Disconnect the breather tube.

    f. Loosen the clamp and remove the air cleaner assembly.

AWD vehicles:

5. Disconnect the Power Transfer Unit (PTU) vent hose from the clip located on the fill tube.

All vehicles:

6. Remove the nut holding the wiring harness bracket and unplug the bulkhead electrical connector.

7. Remove the 2 bolts from the shift cable bracket and disconnect the shift cable from the manual lever.

8. Disconnect the Transmission Range (TR) sensor electrical connector.

9. Remove the 3 upper transaxle retaining bolts.

10. Install the suitable engine support tools.

11. Remove the LH transaxle mount through bolt.

12. Remove the 2 nuts, the bolt and the through bolt and remove the rear transaxle mount.

AWD vehicles:

13. Remove the 6 bolts holding the driveshaft to the PTO.

14. Remove the 2 center bearing nuts and position the driveshaft aside with mechanic's wire

All vehicles:

15. Remove the 4 bolts and remove the cross brace.

16. Remove the 7 retainers and the LH splash shield.

17. Remove the 5 retainers and the RH splash shield.

18. Remove the bolt for the mount and the 2 bolts from the cross brace.

19. Remove and discard the nut and remove the cross brace.

➡**If transmission disassembly or installation of a new transmission is necessary, the transmission fluid will need to be drained.**

20. Remove the drain plug and drain the fluid.

21. Remove and discard the LH front axle wheel hub nut.

22. Remove the frame bolt from the LH and RH control arms.

23. Using a suitable tool, separate the LH halfshaft from the front wheel knuckle.

24. Using a suitable tool, remove the LH halfshaft and disconnect the RH halfshaft from the intermediate shaft.

25. Remove the 2 intermediate shaft retaining nuts.

26. Remove the intermediate shaft.

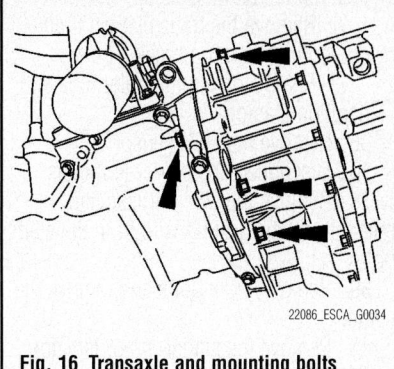

Fig. 16 Transaxle and mounting bolts shown

27. Remove the 2 bolts which hold the exhaust bracket to the intermediate shaft bracket.

28. Remove the 2 nuts on the other end of the exhaust-to-intermediate shaft bracket and remove the bracket.

29. Remove the 3 nuts and separate the flexpipe from the exhaust manifold.

AWD vehicles:

30. Remove the 6 bolts holding the engine bracket to the PTU and remove the bracket.

31. Remove the 3 bolts and the PTU assembly.

Front wheel drive (FWD) vehicles:

32. Remove the 3 bolts and the dampener.

All vehicles:

33. Remove the 3 bolts holding the transaxle front mount plate.

34. Remove the fluid cooler line.

35. Remove the fluid cooler tube.

    a. Disconnect the Output Shaft Sensor (OSS) sensor electrical connector (black).

    b. Disconnect the Transmission Shaft Sensor (TSS) sensor electrical connector (white).

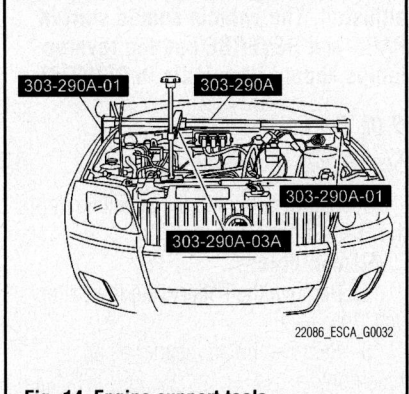

Fig. 14 Engine support tools

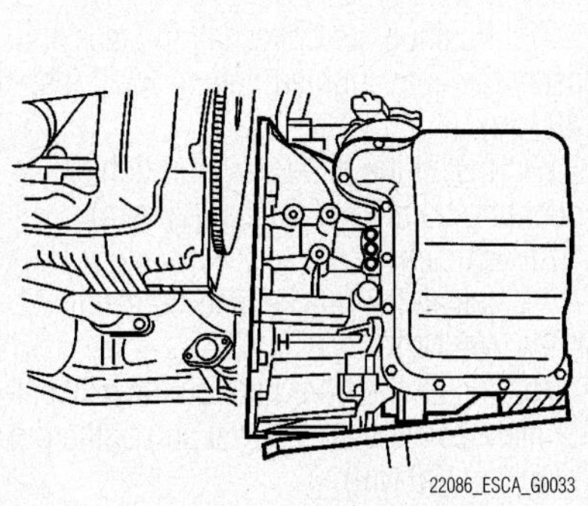

Fig. 15 Transaxle assembly removal

Fig. 17 LH upper transaxle through bolt shown

c. Disconnect the wiring harness retainer from the transmission case and position the harness aside

d. Remove the transmission fluid cooler line retaining bracket bolt.

e. Remove the fluid cooler tube and position it aside.

36. Remove the OSS sensor.

37. Disconnect the starter terminals.

38. Remove the wire harness clip retainer and the ground wire from the starter bolts.

39. Remove the 3 bolts and remove the starter.

40. Remove the starter motor isolator.

41. Remove and discard the 4 torque converter nuts.

42. Using a suitable tool, lower the transmission.

43. Push the converter back from the flexplate. Use a suitable transmission jack to support the transaxle and remove the 3 rear bell housing bolts.

44. Remove the 4 remaining transaxle-to-engine bolts.

➡The torque converter is heavy. Secure torque converter before lowering the transaxle.

45. Lower the transaxle from the engine compartment.

To install:

❊❊ WARNING

Carry out the transmission fluid cooler back flushing and cleaning if the transaxle is being overhauled or installing a new or remanufactured transaxle. Carry out the transmission fluid cooler flow test if the transaxle is being overhauled or installing a new or remanufactured transaxle.

All vehicles:

46. Lubricate the torque converter pilot hub with grease.

47. Rotate the torque converter to place the paint dot in the 6 o'clock position.

48. Position the transaxle in place.

49. Move the transaxle assembly toward the engine assembly and install the 4 bolts.

50. Tighten the transaxle mounting bolts to 30 ft. lbs. (40 Nm).

51. Install the transaxle retaining bolts and tighten to 30 ft. lbs. (40 Nm).

52. Install 4 new torque converter nuts and tighten to 30 ft. lbs. (40 Nm).

53. Install the transmission fluid cooler tube and tighten to 17 ft. lbs. (23 Nm).

54. Install the OSS sensor and tighten to 9 ft. lbs. (12 Nm).

55. Install the fluid cooler tube.

a. Connect the OSS sensor.

b. Connect the TSS sensor (white connector).

c. Connect the wiring harness retainer to the transmission case.

d. Install the fluid cooler tube and tighten to 17 ft. lbs. (23 Nm).

e. Install fluid cooler bolt and tighten to 10 ft. lbs. (13 Nm).

56. Install the starter motor isolator.

57. Install the starter motor and mounting bolts, tighten to 26 ft. lbs. (35 Nm).

58. Connect starter terminals and tighten nuts to 89 inch lbs. (10 Nm) for battery cable. And 62 inch lbs. (7 Nm). for solenoid wire nut.

59. Install the wire harness clip retainer and the ground wire to starter bolts.

60. Install the lower front mount bracket and tighten to 41 ft. lbs. (55 Nm).

61. Using a suitable tool, raise the transaxle.

62. Install the LH upper transaxle mount through bolt and tighten to 76 ft. lbs. (103 Nm).

63. Remove engine support tools.

64. Install the upper transaxle bolts and tighten to 30 ft. lbs. (40 Nm).

65. Connect the TR sensor electrical connector.

66. Connect the shift cable to the manual lever and install the 2 bolts then, tighten to 17 ft. lbs. (23 Nm).

67. Install the wire harness bracket nut and tighten to 89 inch lbs. (10 Nm). Plug in the bulkhead electrical connector.

68. Install the rear transmission mount and tighten to 59 ft. lbs. (80 Nm).

69. Install the rear transaxle mount through bolt and tighten to 89 ft. lbs. (120 Nm).

FWD vehicles:

70. Install the dampener and tighten bolts to 30 ft. lbs. (40 Nm).

AWD vehicles:

71. Install the PTU assembly and tighten to 33 ft. lbs. (45 Nm).

72. Position the driveshaft in place and install the nuts. Tighten nuts to 35 ft. lbs. (48 Nm).

73. Install the driveshaft and tighten mounting bolts to 15 ft. lbs. (20 Nm).

All vehicles

74. Install the bracket and tighten to 41 ft. lbs. (55 Nm).

75. Install the front nuts on the exhaust-to-intermediate shaft bracket and tighten to 22 ft. lbs. (30 Nm).

76. Install the bolts on the rear of the exhaust-to-intermediate shaft bracket and tighten to 22 ft. lbs. (30 Nm).

77. Install the flexpipe on the exhaust manifold, and tighten the mounting nuts to 18 ft. (25 Nm).

78. Install the intermediate shaft.

79. Install the intermediate shaft retaining nuts and tighten to 20 ft. lbs. (27 Nm).

80. Install the LH and RH halfshafts and frame bolts and tighten to 85 ft. lbs. (115 Nm).

81. Install the LH halfshaft into the wheel knuckle.

82. Install the LH hub nut and tighten to 214 ft. lbs. (290 Nm).

83. Install the cross brace and tighten rear nut to 129 ft. lbs. (175 Nm).

84. Tighten front cross brace bolts to 66 ft. lbs. (90 Nm).

85. Install the bolt for the mount and tighten to 85 ft. lbs. (115 Nm).

86. Install the cross brace and the 4 bolts, tighten bolts to 85 ft. lbs. (115 Nm).

87. Install the LH splash shield and the 7 retainers.

88. Install the RH splash shield and the 5 retainers.

AWD vehicles:

89. Install the vent tube to the fluid level indicator.

All vehicles:

90. Install the air cleaner assembly.

a. Install the bolt and tighten to 89 inch lbs. (10 Nm).

b. Reconnect the MAF sensor electrical connector.

c. Reconnect the brake booster vacuum hose.

d. Reconnect the wiring harness retainer.

e. Reconnect the breather tube.

f. Tighten the clamp and install the air cleaner assembly.

91. Install the battery tray.

92. Fill the transaxle with clean automatic transmission fluid.

93. Check the fluid level and correct as necessary.

➡Verify that the shift cable is correctly adjusted. The vehicle should start in PARK and REVERSE and the reverse lamps should illuminate in REVERSE.

3.0L Engine

See Figures 18 through 22.

1. Before servicing the vehicle, refer to the Precautions Section.

All vehicles:

2. Remove the battery and the battery tray.

3. Remove the air cleaner as an assembly.

a. Disconnect the breather tube.

b. Disconnect the Mass Air Flow (MAF) sensor electrical connector and the wiring harness fastener.

c. Remove the air intake tube.

d. Remove the air cleaner assembly retaining bolt.

e. Remove the air cleaner assembly

4. Disconnect the Transmission Range (TR) sensor.

5. Disconnect the transaxle harness connector, remove the wire harness bracket nut and position the harness bracket aside.

6. Remove the main control cover vent tube.

AWD vehicles:

7. Disconnect the Power Transfer Unit (PTU) vent hose from the transmission fluid filler tube.

All vehicles:

8. Disconnect the Power Transfer Unit (PTU) vent hose from the transmission fluid filler tube.

All vehicles:

9. Disconnect the wire harness from the battery tray hold-down bracket.

10. Disconnect the shift cable from the manual lever

11. Disconnect the wire harness retainer from the shift cable bracket, remove the 2 retaining bolts, and position the cable and bracket aside.

12. Remove the selector lever cable retainer from the transmission fluid filler tube

13. Disconnect the starter motor harness connector.

14. Disconnect the ground wire

15. Remove the 2 starter bolts and remove the starter motor.

16. Remove and disconnect both electrical connectors from the upper intake to gain access to the engine for installing the lifting bracket

17. Install suitable engine support system and secure engine with proper adapters.

18. Remove the 4 upper transaxle retaining bolts

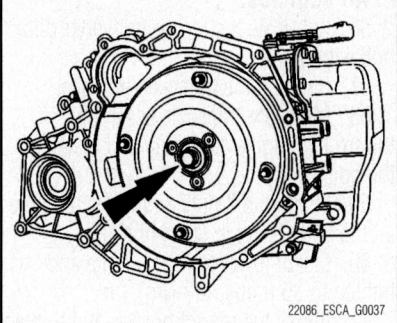
Fig. 19 Transaxle and torque converter pilot hub shown

19. Loosen, but do not remove, the 4 retaining nuts holding the bracket to the transaxle case. Remove the LH upper transaxle mount bolt.

20. Remove the RH upper engine mount bolt.

21. Remove the front wheels and tires.

22. Remove the 7 retainers and the LH splash shield.

23. Remove the 6 retainers and the RH splash shield.

24. If transaxle disassembly is necessary, remove the drain plug and drain the transmission fluid. After the fluid has drained, install the drain plug.

25. Disconnect the LH and RH suspension.

a. Disconnect the sway bar link.

b. Remove the tie-rod end retaining nut

c. Remove the lower control arm knuckle bolt.

26. Using a suitable tool, disconnect the LH and RH tie-rod end from the steering knuckle.

27. Carefully pry down on the LH and RH lower control arms and disconnect the steering knuckle from the lower ball joint and position the steering knuckle aside.

28. Remove the brake hose retainer and

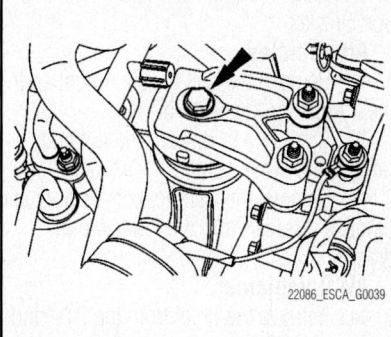
Fig. 21 RH engine mounting bolt view—3.0L engine

the ABS sensor retaining bolt from the RH strut.

29. Using a suitable tool, remove the RH halfshaft from the intermediate shaft and secure the halfshaft aside.

30. Remove the brake hose retainer and the ABS sensor retaining bolt from the LH strut.

31. Using a pry bar between the transaxle case and the LH halfshaft, carefully disconnect the halfshaft from the transaxle case and secure the halfshaft aside.

32. Disconnect the heated oxygen sensor (HO2S) connector and remove the 2 clips from the oil pan bolt studs.

33. Remove the 2 intermediate shaft retaining nuts.

34. Remove the intermediate shaft.

35. Remove the cross brace

36. Disconnect and remove the exhaust Y-pipe and hanger.

AWD vehicles:

37. Index the driveshaft to the yoke and remove the 6 bolts holding the driveshaft to the PTU

38. Remove the 2 center bearing nuts and position the driveshaft aside with mechanic's wire.

39. Remove the RH catalytic converter to gain access to the PTU bracket.

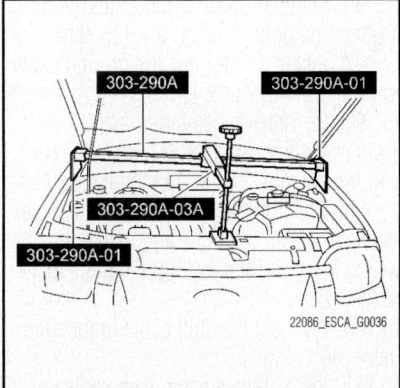
Fig. 18 Engine support system shown

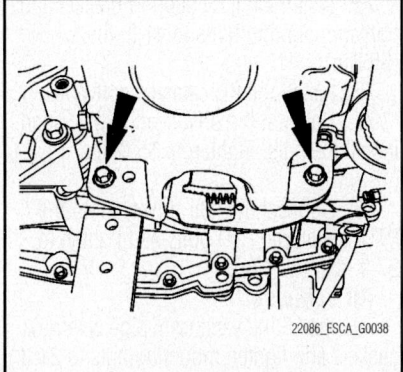
Fig. 20 Lower transaxle bolts shown

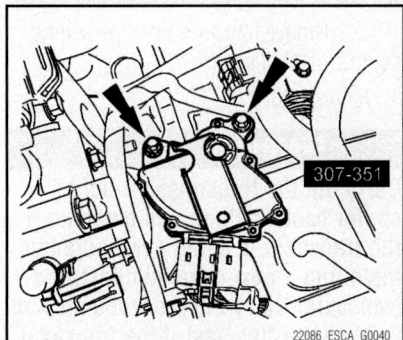
Fig. 22 Transmission range sensor tool 307-351 shown for alignment

40. Remove the bolts and the PTU support bracket.

All vehicles:

41. Remove the bolt for the mount and the 2 bolts for the cross brace.

42. Remove and discard the nut and remove the cross brace.

43. Remove the electrical connectors and harness fastener from the lower mount bracket.

AWD vehicles:

44. Remove the bolts from the PTU and remove the PTU.

All vehicles:

45. Remove the through bolt from the rear transaxle mount.

46. Disconnect the electrical connector and remove the bolt and output shaft speed (OSS) sensor.

➡ **It is necessary to raise the engine a couple of inches in order to remove the transaxle.**

47. Using the engine support system, raise the front of the engine.

➡ **It is necessary to lower the transaxle in order to clear the subframe to remove the transaxle.**

48. Lower the transaxle enough to clear the frame.

49. Remove the access cover.

50. Remove and discard the 4 torque converter nuts.

51. Remove the fluid cooler tube and position it aside.

52. Disconnect the turbine shaft speed (TSS) sensor and the harness retainers.

53. Support the transaxle with a high-lift jack.

54. Remove the remaining transaxle mounting bolts.

❊❊ WARNING

The torque converter is heavy. Secure the torque converter before lowering the transaxle.

55. Remove transaxle from the engine compartment of vehicle.

To install:

❊❊ WARNING

Carry out the transmission fluid cooler back flushing and cleaning if the transaxle is being overhauled or installing a new or remanufactured transaxle. Carry out the transmission fluid cooler flow test if the transaxle is being overhauled or installing a new or remanufactured transaxle.

All vehicles:

56. Lubricate the torque converter pilot hub with grease.

57. Position the transaxle in place.

58. Move the transaxle assembly toward the engine assembly and install the bolt.

59. Install the 2 nuts and the stud tighten all the bolts to 35 ft. lbs. (48 Nm).

60. Install lower transaxle bolts and tighten to 35 ft. lbs. (48 Nm).

61. Install the mount bracket and tighten to 41 ft. lbs. (55 Nm).

62. Loosely install the rear transaxle mount bolt.

63. Install the LH transaxle mount through bolt

64. Tighten the rear transaxle mount bolt to 89 ft. lbs. (120 Nm).

65. Install the transmission fluid cooler tubes and tighten to 18 ft. lbs. (25 Nm).

66. Install the output shaft speed (OSS) sensor and tighten the bolt to 9 ft. lbs. (12 Nm).

67. Connect the OSS speed sensor and the turbine shaft speed (TSS) sensor electrical connectors and connect the wiring harness fasteners.

68. Install 4 new torque converter nuts and tighten to 30 ft. lbs. (40 Nm).

69. Install the access cover.

AWD vehicles:

70. Position the Power Transfer Unit (PTU) in place and install the bolt and tighten to 35 ft. lbs. (37 Nm).

71. Install the PTU-to-transaxle bolts and tighten to 52 ft. lbs. (70 Nm).

All vehicles:

72. Connect the electrical connector fasteners to the lower mount bracket.

73. Install the cross brace and the rear nut. Tighten the rear nut to 129 ft. lbs. (175 Nm). and the front bolts to 66 ft. lbs. (90 Nm).

74. Install the bolt for the mount and tighten to 85 ft. lbs. (115 Nm).

AWD vehicles:

75. Install the PTU support bracket and tighten mounting bolts to 41 ft. lbs. (55 Nm).

76. Install the RH catalytic converter.

77. Position the driveshaft in place and install the nuts. Tighten to 35 ft. lbs. (48 Nm).

78. Connect the rear driveshaft to the PTU. Install the PTU bolts and tighten to 27 ft. lbs. (37 Nm).

All vehicles:

79. Install the exhaust Y-pipe with new gaskets and tighten mounting nuts to 21 ft. lbs. (29 Nm).

80. Install the exhaust rubber hanger.

81. Install the cross brace and tighten to 85 ft. lbs. (115 Nm).

82. Install the intermediate shaft and retaining nuts. Tighten nuts to 20ft. lbs. (27 Nm).

83. Connect the heated oxygen sensor (HO2S) wire to the oil pan bolt studs and connect the connector.

84. Install the LH halfshaft into the transaxle and the RH halfshafts in the intermediate shaft and install the ball joints in the knuckles

85. Install the LH and RH brake hose retainer and the ABS sensor bolt. Tighten bolt to 11 ft. lbs. (15 Nm).

86. Reconnect the LH and RH suspension.

   a. Reconnect the sway bar link and tighten nuts to 46 ft. lbs. (63 Nm).

   b. Install the tie-rod end retaining nut and tighten to 41 ft. lbs. (55 Nm).

   c. Install the lower control arm knuckle bolt and tighten to 46 ft. lbs. (63 Nm).

87. Install the LH splash shield, the retainer and the 5 bolts.

88. Install the RH splash shield, the retainer and the 5 bolts.

89. Install the front wheels and tires.

90. Using the engine support system, lower the engine onto the RH engine mount.

91. Install the bolt for the RH engine mount and tighten to 89 ft. lbs. (120 Nm).

92. Tighten the LH upper transaxle mount assembly.

   a. Tighten the 4 nuts for the bracket to 30 ft. lbs. (40 Nm).

   b. Tighten the through bolt to 76 ft. lbs. (104 Nm).

93. Install the upper transaxle retaining bolts and tighten to 35 ft. lbs. (48 Nm).

94. Remove the engine support system tool.

95. Connect the electrical connectors together and then connect them to the upper intake manifold.

96. Install the starter motor and bolts. Tighten the bolts to 18 ft. lbs. (25 Nm).

97. Install and tighten the ground cable to 20 ft. lbs. (27 Nm).

98. Reconnect the starter cables. Tighten battery cable to 20 ft. lbs. (27 Nm), and the solenoid nut to 44 inch lbs. (5 Nm).

99. Position the shift cable and bracket in place, install the bolts and install the wiring harness retainer. Tighten bolts to 17 ft. lbs. (23 Nm).

100. Connect the shift cable to the manual lever.

101. Install the selector lever cable retainer on the transmission fluid filler tube.

102. Connect the wire harness to the battery hold-down bracket.

AWD vehicles:

103. Connect the evaporative emissions (EVAP) and PTU vent hose to the transmission filler tube bracket.

All vehicles:

104. Install the main control cover vent tube.

105. Position the bracket in place and install and tighten the nut to 18 ft. lbs. (25 Nm). Connect the transaxle harness connector.

106. Connect the Transmission Range (TR) sensor.

➡ **If installing an exchange transaxle, the digital TR sensor must be aligned.**

107. Using the special tool, align the digital TR sensor.

108. Install the air cleaner as an assembly.

    a. Install the air cleaner assembly.

    b. Connect the air intake tube.

    c. Install the retaining bolt and tighten to 89 inch lbs. (10 Nm).

    d. Install the breather tube

    e. Connect the MAF sensor electrical connector.

➡ **Before installing the battery tray, check the vent tube hose for any obstructions, kinks or incorrect routing position**

109. Install the battery tray.

110. Fill the transaxle with clean automatic transmission fluid.

111. Verify that the shift cable is correctly adjusted. The vehicle should start in PARK and NEUTRAL and the reverse lamps should illuminate in REVERSE.

112. Check the fluid level and correct as necessary.

2009—6F35 Transaxle

2.5L Engine

See Figures 23 through 29.

➡ **Carry out the transmission fluid cooler back flushing and cleaning if the transaxle is being overhauled or if installing a new or remanufactured transaxle.**

➡ **Carry out the transmission fluid cooler flow test if the transaxle is being overhauled or if installing a new or remanufactured transaxle.**

All vehicles:

1. Before servicing the vehicle, refer to the Precautions Section.

2. With the vehicle in NEUTRAL, position it on a hoist.

3. Remove the battery and the battery tray. Refer to Battery Removal & Installation in the Engine Electrical section.

4. Remove the Air Cleaner (ACL) and outlet pipe assembly.

AWD vehicles:

5. Disconnect the Power Transfer Unit (PTU) vent hose from the clip located on the transmission fluid filler tube.

All vehicles:

6. Disconnect the selector lever cable from the manual control lever.

7. Remove the 2 retaining bolts and position the selector lever cable and bracket aside.

8. Remove the selector lever cable retainer from the transmission fluid filler tube bracket.

9. Remove the 3 upper transaxle retaining bolts.

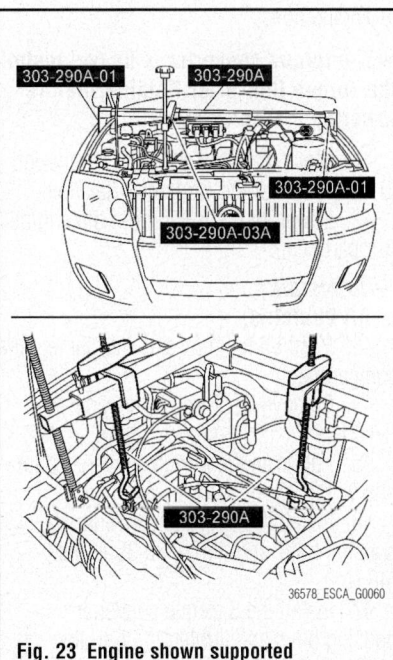

Fig. 23 Engine shown supported

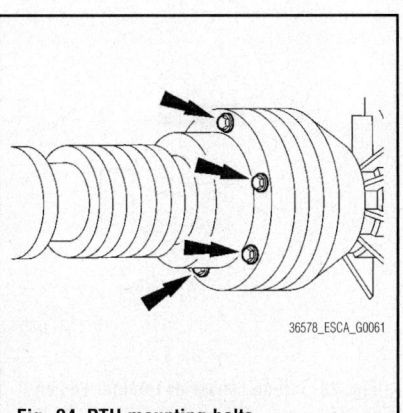

Fig. 24 PTU mounting bolts

10. Install the Engine Support Bar and Adapters and support the engine and transaxle.

11. Remove the LH support insulator through bolt.

12. Remove the 4 nuts and the support insulator bracket.

13. Remove the front wheels and tires

14. Remove the 7 retainers and the LH splash shield.

15. Remove the starter motor. Refer to Starter Removal & Installation in the Engine Electrical section.

16. Remove the LH front halfshaft and RH intermediate shaft. Refer to Halfshaft Removal & Installation in this section.

17. Remove the lower support insulator as follows:

- Remove the lower support insulator through bolt.
- Remove the lower support insulator bolt and 2 nuts.
- Remove the lower support insulator.

AWD vehicles:

18. Index the driveshaft to the yoke and remove the 6 bolts holding the driveshaft to the PTU.

All vehicles:

19. Remove the 4 bolts and remove the cross brace.

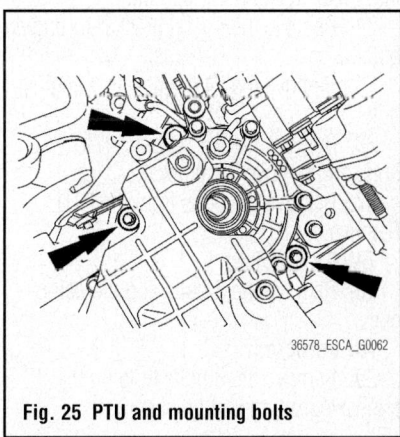

Fig. 25 PTU and mounting bolts

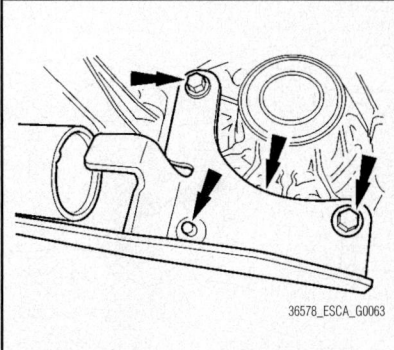

Fig. 26 FWD vehicles remove the 3 bolts and the dampener

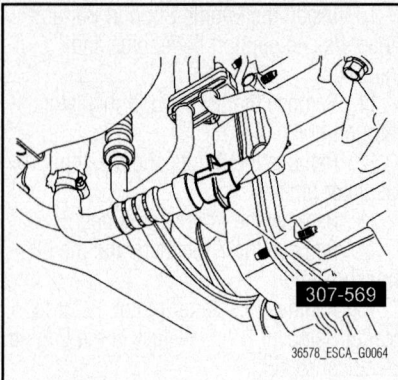

307-569

36578_ESCA_G0064

Fig. 27 Transaxle cooler line removal with disconnect tool

20. Remove the lower front support insulator through bolt for the mount and the 2 bolts from the cross brace.

21. Remove and discard the nut and remove the rear cross brace.

➡️**If transmission disassembly or installation of a new transmission is necessary, the transmission fluid will need to be drained.**

22. Remove the drain plug and drain the transmission fluid.

AWD vehicles:

23. Remove the 2 exhaust bracket-to-intermediate shaft bracket bolts.

24. Remove the 4 PTU bracket-to-engine bolts.

25. Remove the PTU bracket-to-engine bolt.

26. Remove the 2 PTU bracket-to-PTU bolts and remove the bracket.

27. Remove the bolts from the PTU. Remove the PTU.

FWD vehicles:

28. Remove the 3 bolts and the dampener.

All vehicles:

29. Remove the 3 bolts holding the transaxle front mount bracket.

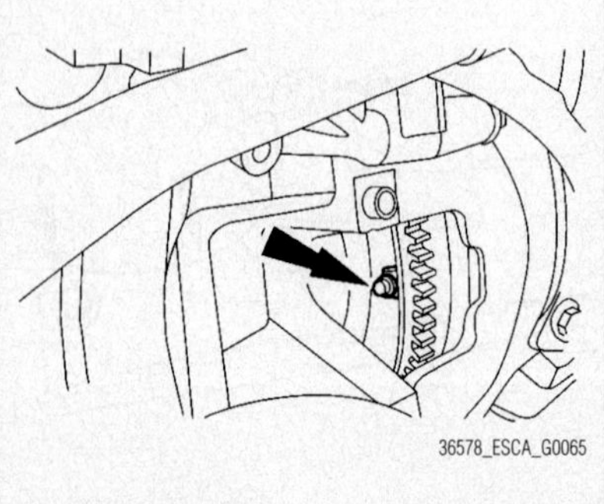

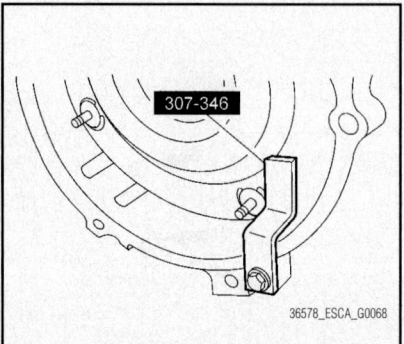

36578_ESCA_G0065

Fig. 28 Torque converter nut view after isolator removal

30. Remove the 2 secondary latches from the transaxle fluid cooler tubes.

31. Using the Transaxle Cooler Line Disconnect Tool, disconnect the 2 transaxle fluid cooler tubes.

32. Disconnect the transaxle electrical connector.

33. Disconnect the Turbine Shaft Speed (TSS) sensor electrical connector.

34. Remove the transaxle electrical wiring harness retainers from the transmission fluid pan stud bolts.

35. Remove the starter motor isolator.

36. Remove and discard the 4 torque converter nuts.

37. Using the Engine Support Bar, lower the transmission.

38. Push the torque converter back from the flexplate.

39. Use a suitable transmission jack to support the transaxle and remove the 3 rear bellhousing bolts.

40. Remove the 4 remaining transaxle-to-engine bolts.

➡️**The torque converter is heavy. Install the Torque Converter Retainer before lowering the transaxle.**

41. Move the transaxle back far enough to install the Torque Converter Retainer.

42. Lower the transaxle from the engine compartment.

To install:

All vehicles:

43. Position the transaxle into the engine compartment.

44. Remove the Torque Converter Retainer.

45. Lubricate the torque converter pilot hub with grease.

46. Install the 4 torque converter housing bolts and tighten to 35 ft. lbs. (48 Nm).

47. Install the 3 torque converter housing bolts and tighten to 35 ft. lbs. (48 Nm).

307-346

36578_ESCA_G0068

Fig. 29 Torque converter retainer shown installed

48. Position the transaxle support insulator bracket in place and install the 4 nuts. Tighten to 30 ft. lbs. (40 Nm).

49. Using the Engine Support Bar and Adapters, raise the transaxle until the transaxle support insulator bracket lines up with the transaxle support insulator and install the through bolt. Tighten the through bolt to 76 ft. lbs. (103 Nm).

50. Remove the Engine Support Bar and Adapters.

51. Install the 4 new torque converter nuts and tighten to 30 ft. lbs. (40 Nm).

52. Install the starter motor isolator.

53. Install the starter motor and tighten the mounting bolts to 26 ft. lbs. (53 Nm).

54. Connect the Turbine Shaft Speed (TSS) sensor electrical connector.

55. Connect the transaxle electrical connector.

56. Connect the transaxle electrical wiring harness retainers.

57. Position the transmission fluid cooler tubes in place. Install the transmission fluid cooler tubes in the transaxle by inserting the tube into the fitting until a click is heard/felt. Pull back to confirm connection is secure and install the secondary latches.

FWD vehicles:

58. Install the dampener and the 3 dampener bolts, 2 from the RH side of the transaxle and 1 from the LH side. Tighten the bolts to 30 ft. lbs. (40 Nm).

AWD vehicles:

59. Install the Power Transfer Unit (PTU) and install the mounting bolts. Tighten the mounting bolts to 52 ft. lbs. (70 Nm).

60. Install the PTU bracket and the 2 PTU bracket bolts. Tighten the bracket bolts to 33 ft. lbs. (45 Nm).

61. Install the PTU bracket-to-engine bolts and tighten to 30 ft. lbs. (40 Nm).

62. Install the 2 catalytic converter support bracket bolts and tighten to 177 inch lbs. (20 Nm).

All vehicles:

63. Install the front mount bracket and 3 nuts. Tighten the nuts to 41 ft. lbs. (55 Nm).

64. Install the engine support cross brace and new cross brace nut. Tighten the nut to 129 ft. lbs. (175 Nm).

65. Install the 2 bolts for the cross brace and the front roll restrictor bolt.

66. Tighten the 2 cross brace bolts to 66 ft. lbs. (90 Nm).

67. Tighten the lower support insulator through bolt to 83 ft. lbs. 115 Nm).

68. Install the rear cross brace and the 4 bolts. Tighten to 83 ft. lbs. 115 Nm).

69. Install the LH front halfshaft and the intermediate shaft.

AWD vehicles:

70. Position the driveshaft to the PTU and install the 6 driveshaft bolts. Tighten the drive shaft bolts to 27 ft. lbs. (37 Nm).

All vehicles:

71. Install the lower support insulator.

72. Install the lower support insulator bolt and 2 nuts. Tighten to 59 ft. lbs. (80 Nm).

73. Install the lower support insulator through bolt and tighten to 85 ft. lbs. (115 Nm).

74. Install the LH splash shield and 7 retainers.

75. Install the RH splash shield and 6 retainers.

76. Install the front wheels and tires.

77. Install the 3 upper torque converter housing bolts and tighten to 35 ft. lbs. (48 Nm).

78. Install the selector lever cable retainer to the transmission fluid filler tube bracket.

79. Position the selector lever cable and bracket in place and install the 2 retaining bolts. Tighten the retaining bolts to 106 inch lbs. (12 Nm).

80. Connect the selector lever cable end to the manual control lever with the manual control lever and selector lever in DRIVE. Check selector lever cable adjustment

81. Install the Air Cleaner (ACL) and outlet pipe assembly.

82. Install the battery tray and battery.

83. Fill with clean transmission fluid to the correct level.

3.0L Engine

See Figures 25, 27, 29, 00, 30 through 32.

➡Carry out the transmission fluid cooler back flushing and cleaning if the transaxle is being overhauled or if installing a new or remanufactured transaxle.

➡Carry out the transmission fluid cooler flow test if the transaxle is being overhauled or if installing a new or remanufactured transaxle.

All vehicles:

1. Before servicing the vehicle, refer to the Precautions Section.

2. With the vehicle in NEUTRAL, position it on a hoist.

3. Remove the battery and the battery tray. Refer to Battery Removal & Installation in the Engine Electrical section.

4. Remove the Air Cleaner (ACL) and outlet pipe assembly.

AWD vehicles:

5. Disconnect the Power Transfer Unit

(PTU) vent hose from the clip located on the transmission fluid filler tube.

All vehicles:

6. Disconnect the selector lever cable from the manual control lever.

7. Remove the 2 retaining bolts and position the selector lever cable and bracket aside.

8. Remove the selector lever cable retainer from the transmission fluid filler tube bracket.

9. Remove the starter motor. Refer to Starter Removal & Installation in the Engine Electrical section.

10. Remove the 4 upper transaxle retaining bolts.

11. Install the Engine Lifting Bracket and the Universal Adapter Brackets on both cylinder heads.

Install the Engine Support Bar, Support Leg and Adapters.

12. Install the Engine Lifting Chain and Adapter and support the engine and transaxle.

13. Remove the LH support insulator through bolt.

14. Remove the 4 nuts and the support insulator bracket.

15. Remove the front wheels and tires.

16. Remove the 7 retainers and the LH splash shield.

17. Remove the 6 retainers and the RH splash shield.

18. Remove the LH front halfshaft and RH intermediate shaft. Refer to Halfshaft Removal & Installation in this section.

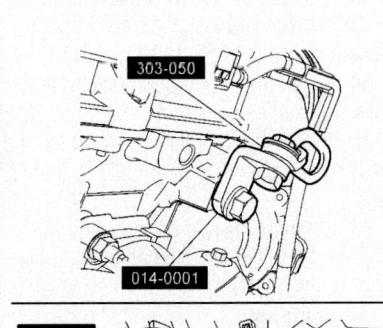
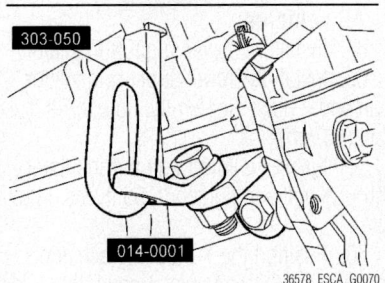

Fig. 30 Brackets shown installed on cylinder heads

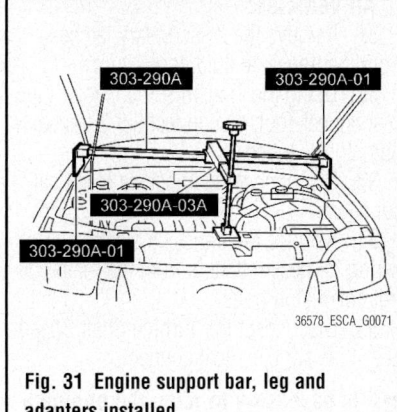

Fig. 31 Engine support bar, leg and adapters installed

AWD vehicles:

➡**Index-mark the drive shaft flange and PTU flange for installation.**

19. Remove and discard the 6 front driveshaft-to-PTU bolts and washers. Position the driveshaft aside and support with mechanic's wire.

All vehicles:

20. Remove the 4 bolts and remove the cross brace.

21. Remove the lower front support insulator through bolt for the mount and the 2 bolts from the cross brace.

22. Remove and discard the nut and remove the rear cross brace.

23. Remove the lower support insulator as follows:
- Remove the lower support insulator through bolt.
- Remove the lower support insulator bolt and 2 nuts.
- Remove the lower support insulator.

➡**If transmission disassembly or installation of a new transmission is necessary, the transmission fluid will need to be drained.**

24. Remove the drain plug and drain the transmission fluid.

25. Install the transmission fluid drain plug.

26. Disconnect the LH and RH Catalyst Monitor Sensor (CMS) electrical connector.

27. Remove and discard the 6 exhaust Y-pipe nuts and remove the Y-pipe.

AWD vehicles:

28. Remove the 3 nuts and the RH catalytic converter.

29. Remove the bolts and the PTU support bracket.

30. Remove the retaining bolts from the PTU and remove the PTU.

All vehicles:

31. Remove the 2 secondary latches from the transaxle fluid cooler tubes.

32. Using the Transmission Cooler Line Disconnect Tool, disconnect the 2 transaxle fluid cooler tubes.

33. Disconnect the transaxle electrical connector.

34. Remove the transaxle electrical wiring harness retainers from the main control cover stud bolts.

35. Disconnect the Turbine Shaft Speed (TSS) sensor electrical connector.

➡ **It is necessary to raise the engine a couple of inches in order to remove the transaxle.**

36. Using the Engine Lifting Chain and Adapter, raise the front of the engine.

➡ **It is necessary to lower the transaxle in order to clear the subframe to remove the transaxle.**

37. Lower the transaxle enough to clear the frame using the Engine Lifting Chain and Adapter.

38. Remove the torque converter access cover and remove the 4 torque converter nuts.

39. Support the transaxle with a high-lift jack.

40. Remove the 2 oil pan-to-transaxle bolts.

41. Remove the 2 nuts and the transaxle-to-engine stud.

42. Remove the transaxle converter housing bolt.

➡ **The torque converter is heavy. Install the Torque Converter Retainer before lowering the transaxle.**

43. Move the transaxle back far enough to install the Torque Converter Retainer.

44. Lower the transaxle from the engine compartment.

45. If it is necessary to install a new transaxle, remove the mount bracket and reuse the 3 bolts and the mount bracket on the new transaxle.

To install:
All vehicles:

46. Lubricate the torque converter pilot hub with grease.

47. Install the torque converter retainer.

48. Position the transaxle in place.

49. Once the transaxle is in place, before bolting it to the engine, remove the torque converter retainer.

50. Move the transaxle assembly toward the engine assembly and install the transaxle converter housing bolt. Tighten the bolt to 35 ft. lbs. (48 Nm).

51. Install the torque converter housing

nut and the stud. Tighten to 35 ft. lbs. (48 Nm).

52. Install the 2 oil pan-to-transaxle bolts and tighten to 35 ft. lbs. (48 Nm).

53. Position the transmission fluid cooler tubes in place. Install the transmission fluid cooler tubes in the transaxle by inserting the tube into the fitting until a click is heard/felt. Pull back to confirm connection is secure and install the secondary latches.

54. Connect the Turbine Shaft Speed (TSS) sensor electrical connector.

55. Connect the transaxle electrical connector.

56. Connect the transaxle electrical wiring harness retainers to the main control cover stud bolts.

57. Install 4 new torque converter nuts and tighten to 30 ft. lbs. (40 Nm).

58. Install the access cover.

59. Position the transaxle support insulator bracket in place and install the 4 nuts. Tighten the nuts to 30 ft. lbs. (40 Nm).

60. Using the Engine Support Bar and Adapters, raise the transaxle until the transaxle support insulator bracket lines up with the transaxle support insulator and install the through bolt. Tighten the through bolt to 76 ft. lbs. (103 Nm).

61. Remove the Engine Support Bar and Adapters.

62. Remove the Engine Lifting Brackets and the Universal Adapter Brackets from the cylinder heads.

AWD vehicles:

63. Position the Power Transfer Unit (PTU) in place and install the PTU bolts. Tighten the bolts to 52 ft. lbs. (70 Nm).

64. Install the PTU support bracket and bolts. Tighten the bolts to 41 ft. lbs. (55 Nm).

65. Install the RH catalytic converter and the 3 nuts. Tighten the nuts to 27 ft. lbs. (37 Nm).

66. Connect the rear driveshaft to the PTU. Install the driveshaft bolts and tighten to 27 ft. lbs. (37 Nm).

All vehicles:

67. Install the lower support insulator.

68. Install the lower support insulator bolt and 2 nuts. Tighten the nuts to 59 ft. lbs. (80 Nm).

69. Install the lower support insulator through bolt and tighten to 85 ft. lbs. (115 Nm).

70. Position the Y-pipe in place and install 6 new Y-pipe nuts. Tighten the nuts to 18 ft. lbs. (25 Nm).

71. Connect the LH and RH Catalyst Monitor Sensor (CMS) electrical connectors.

72. Install the transaxle front mount bracket and tighten the nuts to 41 ft. lbs. (55 Nm).

73. Position the cross brace in place and install the nut. Tighten the nut to 129 ft. lbs. (175 Nm).

74. Install the 2 bolts for the cross brace and the front roll restrictor bolt.

75. Tighten the cross brace bolts to 66 ft. lbs. (90 Nm).

76. Tighten the lower support insulator through bolt to 85 ft. lbs. (115 Nm).

77. Install the rear cross brace and 4 bolts. Tighten the bolts to 85 ft. lbs. (115 Nm).

78. Install the LH front halfshaft and intermediate shaft.

79. Install the LH and RH splash shields, the retainers and the bolts.

80. Install the front wheels and tires.

81. Install the 4 upper transaxle torque converter housing bolts and tighten to 35 ft. lbs. (48 Nm).

82. Install the starter motor.

83. Position the selector lever cable and bracket in place and install the 2 retaining bolts. Tighten the retaining bolts to 106 inch lbs. (12 Nm).

84. Connect the selector lever cable end to the manual control lever.

85. Install the selector lever cable retainer on the transmission fluid filler tube.

AWD vehicles:

86. Connect the PTU vent hose to the transmission filler tube bracket.

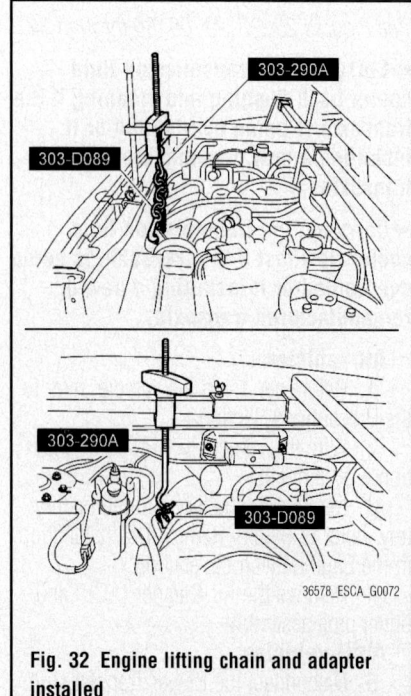

Fig. 32 Engine lifting chain and adapter installed

All vehicles:

87. Install the Air Cleaner (ACL) and outlet pipe.

88. Install the battery tray and battery.

89. Fill the transaxle with clean transmission fluid.

90. Verify that the selector lever cable is correctly adjusted. The vehicle should start in PARK and NEUTRAL and the reverse lamps should illuminate in REVERSE.

91. Check the transmission fluid level and correct as necessary.

MANUAL TRANSAXLE ASSEMBLY

REMOVAL & INSTALLATION

See Figures 33 through 36.

1. Before servicing the vehicle, refer to the Precautions Section.

2. With the vehicle in NEUTRAL, position it on a hoist.

3. Remove the air cleaner assembly.

4. Remove the battery and battery tray. Refer to Battery Removal & Installation in the Engine Electrical Section.

5. Remove the wiring harness bracket nut.

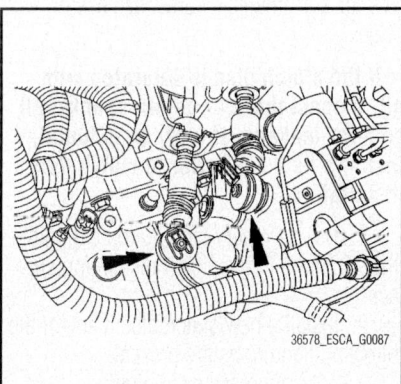

Fig. 33 Disconnect the shift cables

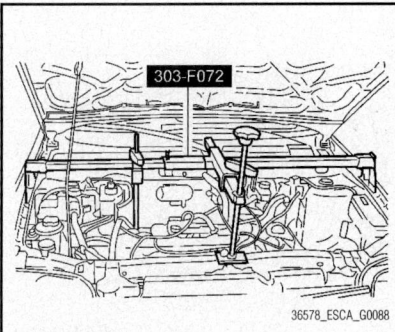

Fig. 34 Engine support bar shown installed

6. Disconnect the reverse switch and Vehicle Speed Sensor (VSS) connectors.

7. Disconnect the shift cables.

8. Remove the 3 shift cable bracket bolts. Position the bracket and shift cables aside.

➡**Do not spill brake fluid on painted or plastic surfaces or damage to the surface may occur. If brake fluid is spilled onto a painted or plastic surface, immediately wash the surface with water.**

9. Remove the clutch hydraulic tube bracket-to-transaxle bolt.

10. Disconnect the clutch hydraulic tube from the clutch slave cylinder.

11. Plug the hydraulic tube.

12. Position the clutch hydraulic tube aside.

13. Using the engine support bar, support the engine.

14. Remove the 3 LH transaxle support insulator bracket nuts. Loosen, but do not remove the through bolt.

15. Remove the transaxle rear support insulator bolt and the 2 nuts.

16. Remove the RH engine mount bolt.

17. Remove the 3 upper transaxle-to-engine bolts.

18. Remove the wheel and tires.

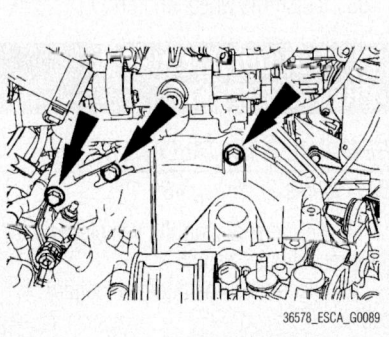

Fig. 35 3 upper transaxle-to-engine bolts shown

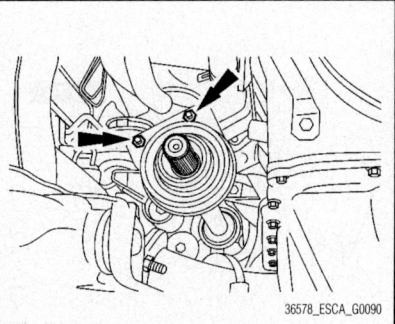

Fig. 36 Remove the intermediate shaft retaining nuts

19. Remove the 6 LH splash shield screws.

20. Remove the LH lower splash shield.

21. Remove the crossmember bolts and crossmember.

22. Remove the 3 front-to-aft crossmember bolts.

23. Remove the LH transaxle support insulator through bolt.

24. Remove the front-to-aft crossmember and the LH transaxle support insulator.

25. Remove the transaxle right support insulator through bolt and the mount.

26. Remove the starter motor assembly.

27. Disconnect the LH stabilizer bar link.

28. Using the ball joint separator, disconnect the LH tie-rod end.

29. Remove the pinch bolt and nut and separate the lower ball joint from the wheel knuckle.

30. Remove the clip, then disconnect the brake hose.

31. Remove the bolt and position the ABS wire aside.

32. Using the slide hammer with the halfshaft (Plate) remover, remove the LH front drive halfshaft from the differential. Support the halfshaft with a length of mechanic's wire.

33. Disconnect the RH stabilizer bar link.

34. Using the ball joint separator, disconnect the RH tie-rod end.

35. Remove the pinch bolt and nut and separate the lower ball joint from the wheel knuckle.

36. Remove the clip, then disconnect the brake hose.

37. Remove the bolt and position the ABS wire aside.

38. Using a brass drift to strike the RH halfshaft in the indicated area, separate and remove the halfshaft from the intermediate shaft. Support the halfshaft with a length of mechanic's wire.

39. Remove the 2 intermediate shaft retaining nuts. Remove the intermediate shaft.

40. Working in the engine compartment, use the engine support bar to raise the engine up 1.0 inches (25.4 mm), lowering the transaxle side downward.

41. Remove 2 lower transaxle-to-engine bolts.

✳✳ WARNING

Secure the assembly to the jack. Avoid any obstructions while lowering and raising the jack. Contact with obstructions may cause the assembly to fall off the jack, which may result in serious personal injury.

42. Position the transmission jack under the transaxle.

43. Remove the remaining 4 transaxle-to-engine bolts.

44. Remove the transaxle.

To install:

45. Raise and position the transaxle to the engine.

46. Install the 2 short transaxle-to-engine bolts and tighten to 35 ft. lbs. (47 Nm).

47. Install the LH transaxle support insulator bracket. Raise the transaxle, aligning the bracket to the insulator. Install the 3 nuts and tighten to 30 ft. lbs. (40 Nm).

48. Install the rear transaxle support insulator. Install the nuts, the bolt and through bolt. Tighten the through bolt to specification. Do not tighten the nuts and bolt at this time.

49. Remove the transmission jack.

50. Install 4 long transaxle-to-engine bolts and tighten to 35 ft. lbs. (47 Nm).

51. Install the front transaxle mount through bolt and tighten to 85 ft. lbs. (115 Nm).

52. Tighten the LH transaxle mount through bolt to 76 ft. lbs. (103 Nm).

53. Tighten the transaxle rear support insulator fasteners to 59 ft. lbs. (80 Nm).

54. Remove the engine support bar that was installed during the removal procedure.

55. Install the RH engine support bolt and tighten to 66 ft. lbs. (90 Nm).

56. Install the 3 upper transaxle-to-engine bolts and tighten to 35 ft. lbs. (47 Nm).

57. Install the intermediate shaft and the 2 retaining nuts. Tighten the nuts to 20 ft. lbs. (27 Nm).

58. Install the RH halfshaft onto the intermediate shaft.

59. Connect the RH ball joints. Tighten the pinch bolts to 46 ft. lbs. (63 Nm).

60. Connect the RH stabilizer bar link. Tighten to 41 ft. lbs. (55 Nm).

61. Connect the RH tie-rod end and tighten to 41 ft. lbs. (55 Nm).

62. Install the brake hose and the clip.

63. Position the ABS wire then install the bolt.

64. Install the LH halfshaft.

65. Connect the LH ball joint. Tighten the pinch bolts to 46 ft. lbs. (63 Nm).

66. Connect the LH stabilizer bar link. Tighten to 41 ft. lbs. (55 Nm).

67. Connect the RH tie-rod end and tighten to 41 ft. lbs. (55 Nm).

68. Connect the brake hose and install the clip.

69. Position the ABS wire then install the bolt.

70. Install the starter motor assembly.

71. Install the front-to-aft crossmember as follows:
- Position the crossmember.
- Install the 2 bolts and a nut.
- Tighten the bolts to 66 ft. lbs. (90 Nm).
- Tighten the new nut to 129 ft. lbs. (175 Nm).

72. Install the crossmember and tighten the retaining bolts to 85 ft. lbs. (115 Nm).

73. Connect and tighten the clutch hydraulic tube to the clutch slave cylinder.

74. Install the clutch hydraulic tube bracket-to-transaxle bolt and tighten to 22 inch lbs. (2.5 Nm).

75. Install the shift cable bracket. Install the 3 retaining bolts and tighten to 16 ft. lbs. (22 Nm).

76. Connect the shift cables.

77. Connect the reverse switch and Vehicle Speed Sensor (VSS) connectors.

78. Install the wiring harness bracket nut and tighten to 106 inch lbs. (12 Nm).

79. Install the battery tray and battery.

80. Install the air cleaner assembly.

81. Fill and bleed the clutch system.

82. Install the LH side splash shield and screws.

83. Install the wheel and tire.

CLUTCH DRIVEN DISC & PRESSURE PLATE

REMOVAL & INSTALLATION

See Figures 37 through 39.

1. Before servicing the vehicle, refer to the Precautions Section.

2. Disconnect the negative battery cable.

3. Remove the transaxle. Refer to Manual Transaxle Assembly Removal & Installation in this section.

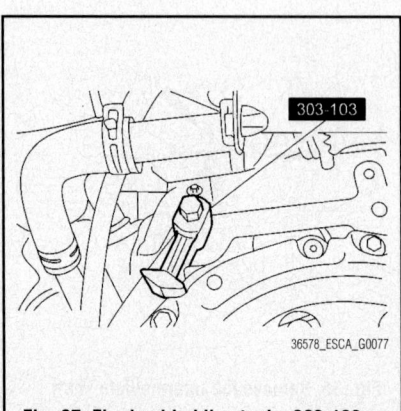

Fig. 37 Flywheel holding tool—303-103

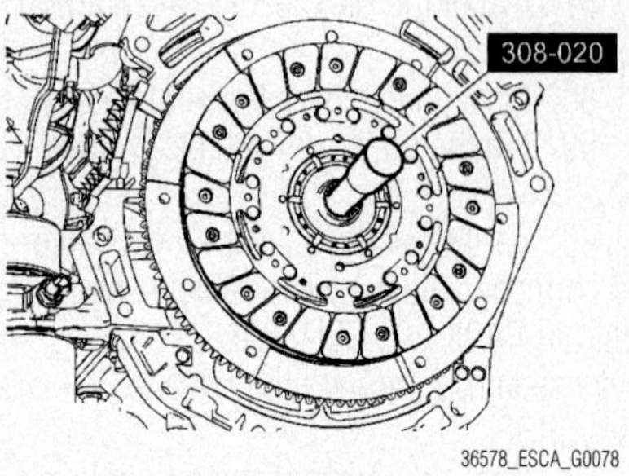

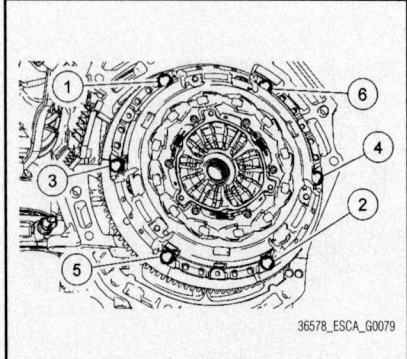

Fig. 38 Clutch disc installed with the alignment tool—308-020

4. Using the flywheel holding tool, lock the flywheel to the engine.

➡**The clutch disc and clutch pressure plate are heavy and may fall if not held when the bolts are removed. Failure to follow this instruction may result in serious personal injury.**

5. Remove the 6 bolts, clutch pressure plate and clutch disc. Loosen the bolts evenly to prevent pressure plate damage.

6. Use a suitable cleaning solution to remove any oil film from the clutch pressure plate friction surface.

7. Inspect the clutch pressure plate surface for burn marks, scores, flatness or ridges.

➡**If the clutch disc is saturated with oil, inspect the rear engine crankshaft seal for leakage. If leakage is found, install a new seal prior to clutch disc installation.**

8. Use an emery cloth to remove minor imperfections in the clutch disc lining surface.

9. Install a new clutch disc if any of the following conditions are present:
- Oil or grease saturation
- Worn or loose facings

Fig. 39 Pressure plate tightening sequence

- Warpage or loose rivets at the hub
- Wear or rust on the splines

10. Check the flywheel runout and wear.

➡**The flywheel cannot be machined and must be replaced.**

To install:

11. Using the clutch aligner, position the clutch disc on the flywheel.

12. Position the clutch pressure plate on the flywheel and install the 6 clutch pressure plate bolts.

13. Tighten the bolts in the sequence shown to 21 ft. lbs. (29 Nm).

14. Install the transaxle.

15. Connect the negative battery cable.

ADJUSTMENTS

The clutch is hydraulically driven and therefore no adjustment is required.

CLUTCH MASTER CYLINDER

REMOVAL & INSTALLATION

See Figure 40.

1. Before servicing the vehicle, refer to the Precautions Section.

✳✳ WARNING

Brake fluid is harmful to painted and plastic surfaces. If brake fluid is spilled onto a painted or plastic surface, wash it immediately with water.

2. Disconnect the clutch master cylinder hose from the brake master cylinder.

3. Plug the brake master cylinder.

4. Plug the clutch master cylinder hose.

5. Remove the 2 clutch master cylinder nuts.

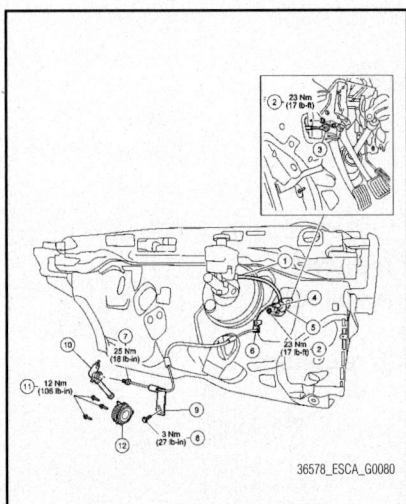

Fig. 40 Clutch controls—exploded view

6. Disconnect the clutch master cylinder push rod.

7. Disconnect the clutch hydraulic fluid tube fitting.

8. Plug the clutch hydraulic fluid tube.

9. Remove the clutch master cylinder.

10. To install, reverse the removal procedure.

11. Bleed the air from the system.

CLUTCH SLAVE CYLINDER

REMOVAL & INSTALLATION

See Figure 40.

1. Before servicing the vehicle, refer to the Precautions Section.

✳✳ WARNING

Brake fluid is harmful to painted and plastic surfaces. If brake fluid is spilled onto a painted or plastic surface, wash it immediately with water.

2. Remove the transaxle.

3. Disconnect the clutch slave cylinder-to-clutch hydraulic fluid tube adapter.

4. Remove the 3 clutch slave cylinder bolts and the clutch slave cylinder.

5. To install, reverse the removal procedure. Tighten the 3 clutch slave cylinder bolts to 106 inch lbs. (12 Nm)

6. Bleed the air from the system.

CLUTCH HYDRAULIC SYSTEM BLEEDING

See Figure 41.

✳✳ WARNING

Do not spill brake fluid on painted or plastic surfaces or damage to the surface may occur. If brake fluid is spilled onto a painted or plastic surface, immediately wash the surface with water.

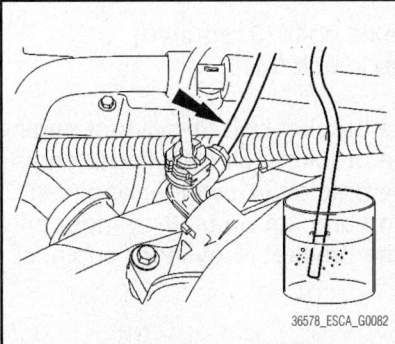

Fig. 41 Bleeding air from hydraulic clutch system shown

1. Before servicing the vehicle, refer to the Precautions Section.

2. With the vehicle in NEUTRAL, position it on a hoist.

3. Check the fluid level of the brake/clutch reservoir. Fill the reservoir with the specified fluid to the MAX mark.

4. Remove the 7 splash shield bolts and the pushpin, then remove the splash shield.

5. Remove the bleeder screw cover and attach a rubber hose to the bleeder screw. Place the other end of the rubber hose into a clear container partially filled with the specified brake fluid.

6. Have an assistant depress and release the clutch pedal 5 to 7 times. Fully depress the clutch pedal to the floor and hold down.

7. With the clutch pedal depressed, loosen the bleeder screw until fluid and air escape the system. With the clutch being held to the floor, tighten the bleeder screw. Repeat Steps 5 and 6 until no air comes from the rubber hose

8. Tighten the bleeder screw to 71 inch lbs. (8 Nm).

9. Install the bleeder screw cover.

10. Position the splash shield and install the 7 bolts and the pushpin.

11. Check the fluid level of the reservoir. Fill the reservoir with the specified fluid to the MAX mark. Install the reservoir cap

12. Depress and release the clutch pedal several times.

13. Test the clutch system for normal operation.

TRANSFER CASE ASSEMBLY

REMOVAL & INSTALLATION

See Figure 42.

The Transfer case is referred to as the Power Transfer Unit (PTU) for this model vehicle.

1. Before servicing the vehicle, refer to the Precautions Section.

All vehicles

2. With the vehicle in NEUTRAL, position it on a hoist

3. Drain the Power Transfer Unit (PTU).

4. Remove the front RH intermediate shaft. Refer to Intermediate Shaft Removal & Installation in the Drive Train section.

5. Remove the driveshaft. Refer to Driveshaft Removal & Installation in the Drive Train section.

6. Remove the 4 bolts and the crossmember brace.

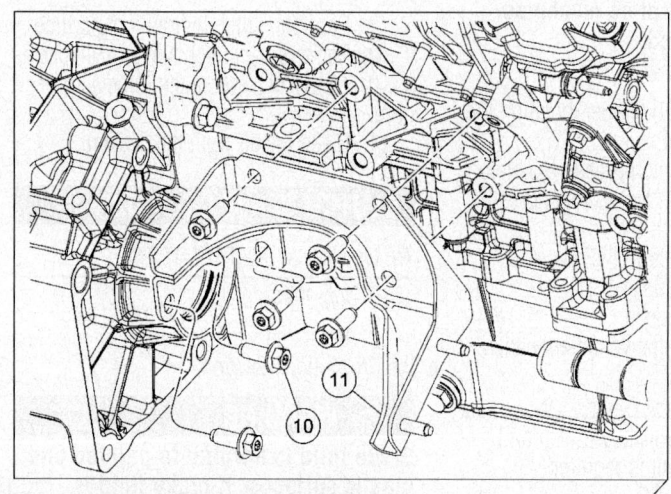

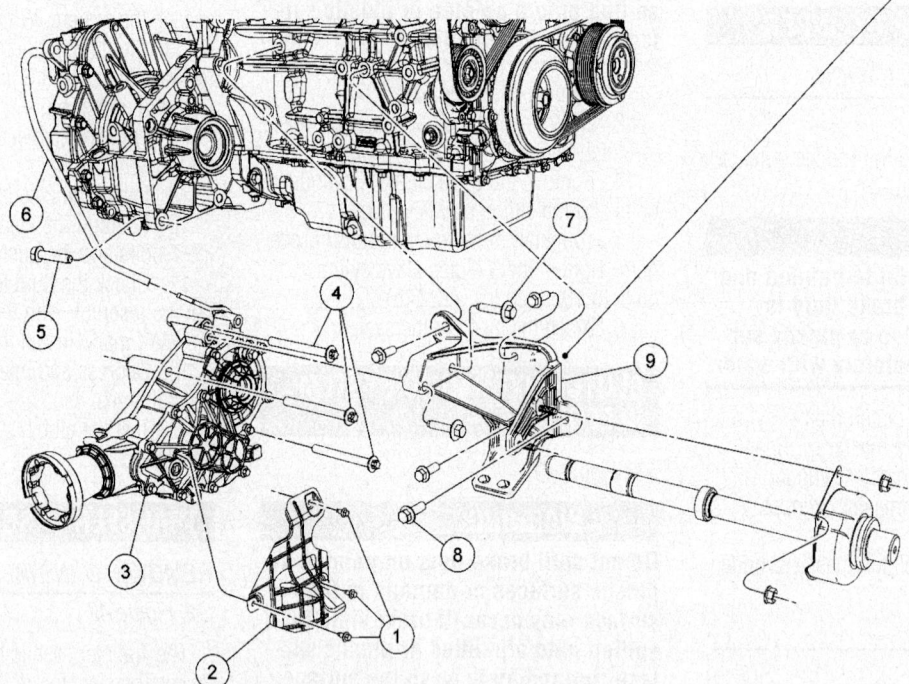

1. Power Transfer Unit (PTU) heat shield bolts (3 required)
2. PTU heat shield
3. PTU
4. PTU -to-transaxle bolts (3 required)
5. PTU -to-transaxle bolt (M10)
6. Vent tube
7. PTU -to-engine bracket bolt (4-cylinder engines) (2 required)
8. PTU -to-engine bracket bolt (4-cylinder engines) (4 required)
9. PTU -to-engine bracket (4-cylinder engines)
10. PTU -to-engine bracket bolts (6-cylinder engines) (6 required)
11. PTU -to-engine bracket (6-cylinder engines)

36578_ESCA_G0103

Fig. 42 Power Transfer Unit (PTU)

Vehicles equipped with 3.0L Engines

7. Remove the RH catalytic converter. Refer to Catalytic Converter Removal & Installation in the Engine Mechanical section.

All vehicles

8. Remove the 3 PTU heat shield bolts and the PTU heat shield.

9. Remove the 2 exhaust bracket nuts.

10. Remove the 6 PTU-to-engine bracket bolts and the bracket.

11. Disconnect the PTU vent tube and position it aside.

12. Remove the 3 PTU-to-transaxle bolts.

13. Remove the PTU.

To install:
All vehicles

14. If necessary, install a new RH differential fluid seal.

15. Position the Power Transfer Unit (PTU) to the transaxle.

16. Install the 3 PTU-to-transaxle bolts and tighten to 52 ft. lbs. (70 Nm).

17. Install the PTU-to-transaxle bolt (M10) and tighten to 35 ft. lbs. (48 Nm).

18. Connect the PTU vent tube.

19. Install the PTU-to-engine bracket and the 6 bracket bolts and 2 exhaust bracket bolts. Tighten the bolts to 35 ft. lbs. (48 Nm).

20. Install the PTU heat shield and the 3 PTU heat shield bolts. Tighten the bolts to 97 inch lbs. (11 Nm).

Vehicles equipped with 3.0L Engines

21. Install the RH catalytic converter.

All vehicles

22. Install the crossmember brace and the 4 bolts. Tighten the bolts to 30 ft. lbs. (40 Nm).

23. Install the driveshaft.

24. Install the front RH intermediate shaft.

25. Install the exhaust as required.

26. Fill the PTU with the correct fluid.

27. The PTU on an automatic transaxle vehicle uses 12 oz (0.35L) of Motorcraft® SAE 75W-140 synthetic lubricant. The PTU on a manual transaxle vehicle uses 12 oz (0.35L) of Motorcraft® 80W-90 synthetic lubricant.

FRONT HALFSHAFTS

REMOVAL & INSTALLATION

See Figures 43 through 45.

All halfshafts

1. Before servicing the vehicle, refer to the Precautions Section.

2. With the vehicle in NEUTRAL, position it on a hoist.

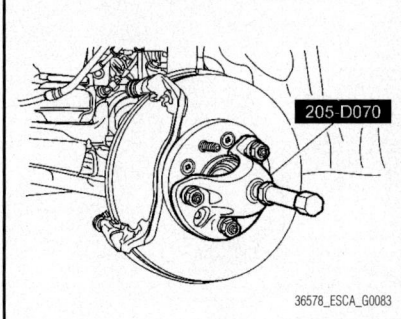

Fig. 43 Front hub remover installed to separate halfshaft from the wheel hub

3. Remove the front tire and wheel.

4. Remove and discard the front wheel hub nut.

5. Remove the ABS wheel speed sensor bolt and position the sensor aside.

6. Remove the lower arm pinch bolt and nut from the lower arm.

➡ **Do not allow the ball joint stud to contact the CV joint boot.**

7. Separate the lower arm from the front wheel knuckle.

8. Using the front hub remover, separate the halfshaft from the wheel hub.

Left halfshaft

Using the halfshaft remover and slide hammer, remove the LH halfshaft from the differential.

Right halfshaft

9. Using a brass drift to strike the RH halfshaft in the indicated area, separate and remove the halfshaft.

To install:
Left halfshaft

➡ **When seated correctly, the halfshaft bearing retainer circlip can be felt as it snaps into the differential side gear groove Position the LH halfshaft so the splines line up with the differential**

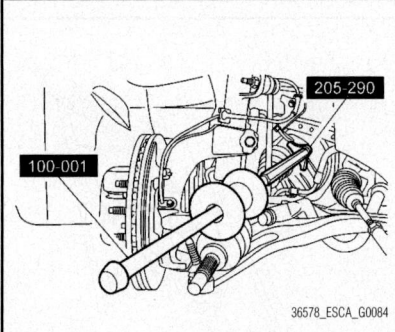

Fig. 44 Left halfshaft removal with slide hammer and adapter

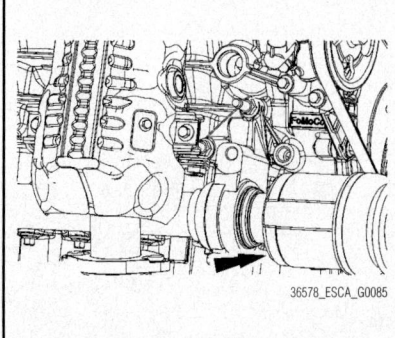

Fig. 45 Strike the RH in the area shown to remove the halfshaft

side gear splines. Push the halfshaft into the differential side gear.

Right halfshaft

10. Align the RH halfshaft with the splines of the intermediate shaft and push the halfshaft in until the circlip locks the shafts together.

11. Apply a thin coat of the specified grease to the splines of the intermediate shaft.

All halfshaft

12. Using the Halfshaft Installer, install the halfshaft into the front wheel hub.

13. Position the lower arm into the front wheel knuckle.

14. Install the new lower ball joint bolt and nut. Tighten to 46 ft. lbs. (63 Nm).

15. Install the ABS wheel speed sensor and bolt and tighten to 80 inch lbs. (9 Nm).

➡ **Do not tighten the front wheel hub nut with the vehicle on the ground. The nut must be tightened to specification before the vehicle is lowered onto the wheels. Wheel bearing damage will occur if the wheel bearing is loaded with the weight of the vehicle applied.**

16. Apply the brake to keep the halfshaft from rotating.

17. Install new front wheel hub nut and tighten to 222 ft. lbs. (300 Nm).

18. Install the front tires and wheels.

19. Check and fill the transaxle fluid as necessary.

INTERMEDIATE SHAFT

REMOVAL & INSTALLATION

See Figure 46.

➡ **If removing the intermediate shaft in order to repair a separate component, it should only be removed as an assembly with the RH front drive halfshaft.**

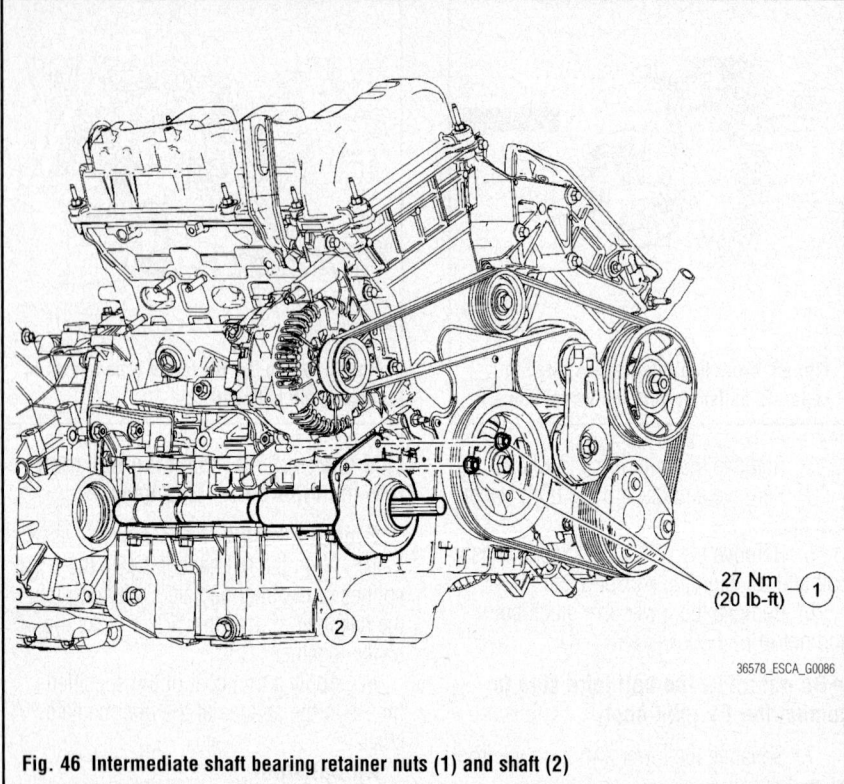

Fig. 46 Intermediate shaft bearing retainer nuts (1) and shaft (2)

27 Nm
(20 lb-ft) — 1

36578_ESCA_G0086

1. Before servicing the vehicle, refer to the Precautions Section.

2. Remove the RH halfshaft. Refer to halfshaft Removal & Installation in this section.

3. Remove the 2 intermediate shaft bearing retainer nuts.

4. Remove the intermediate shaft.

➡ **On All-Wheel Drive (AWD) vehicles, the Power Transfer Unit (PTU) seal must be replaced every time the intermediate shaft is removed.**

To install:

5. Install a new PTU seal for AWD models.

6. Install the intermediate shaft.

7. Install the 2 intermediate shaft bearing retainer nuts. Tighten the retaining nuts to 20 ft. lbs. (27 Nm).

8. Apply a thin coat of the specified grease to the splines of the intermediate shaft.

9. Install the RH halfshaft.

10. Check and fill the transaxle fluid as necessary.

REAR AXLE HOUSING

REMOVAL & INSTALLATION

See Figures 47 through 49.

1. Before servicing the vehicle, refer to the Precautions Section.

2. With the vehicle in NEUTRAL, position it on a hoist.

3. Index-mark the driveshaft flange and the pinion flange.

4. Remove and discard the 4 driveshaft-to-drive pinion bolts and position aside the rear driveshaft. Support the driveshaft.

5. Remove the rear halfshafts. Refer to Halfshaft Removal & Installation in this section.

6. Position a suitable transmission hydraulic jack to the axle housing. Securely strap the jack to the housing.

7. Disconnect the active torque coupling electrical connector.

8. Remove the 4 differential housing-to-front insulator bracket bolts.

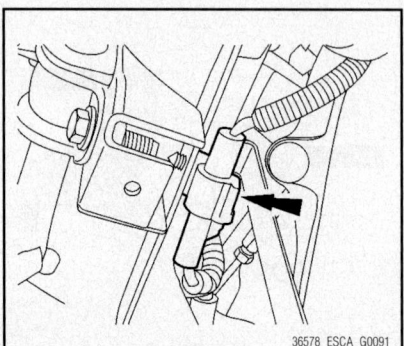

Fig. 47 Active torque coupling electrical connector

36578_ESCA_G0091

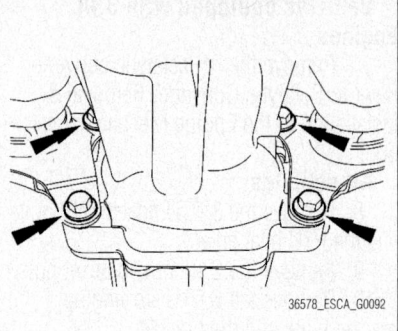

36578_ESCA_G0092

Fig. 48 Remove the 4 differential housing-to-front insulator bracket bolts

9. Remove and discard the LH front insulator bracket-to-subframe bolt and rotate the bracket aside.

10. Remove and discard the RH front insulator bracket-to-subframe bolt and the bracket.

11. Remove the 3 LH side insulator bracket-to-rear axle differential bolts.

12. Lower the rear axle assembly.

To install:

13. Position a suitable transmission hydraulic jack to the axle housing. Securely strap the jack to the housing.

14. Install the rear axle assembly.

15. Install the 3 LH side insulator bracket-to-rear axle differential bolts and tighten to 66 ft. lbs. (90 Nm).

16. Install the RH front insulator bracket and tighten the new bracket-to-subframe bolt to 66 ft. lbs. (90 Nm).

17. Install LH front insulator bracket and tighten the new bracket-to-subframe bolt to 66 ft. lbs. (90 Nm).

18. Install the 4 differential housing-to-front insulator bracket bolts and tighten to 66 ft. lbs. (90 Nm).

19. Connect the active torque coupling electrical connector.

20. Remove the transmission jack.

21. Install the rear halfshafts.

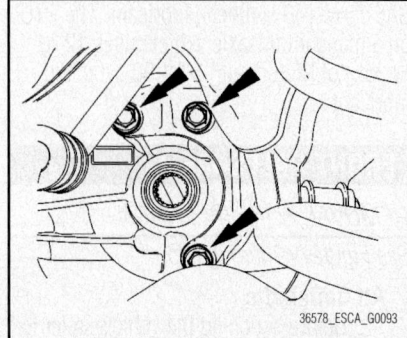

36578_ESCA_G0093

Fig. 49 Remove the 3 LH side insulator bracket-to-rear axle differential bolts

22. Install the rear drive shaft. Install 4 new driveshaft-to-drive pinion bolts and tighten to 30 ft. lbs. (40 Nm).

23. Lower the vehicle.

REAR HALFSHAFTS

REMOVAL & INSTALLATION

See Figures 50 through 53.

1. Before servicing the vehicle, refer to the Precautions Section.
2. Place the selector lever in NEUTRAL.
3. Raise and support the vehicle.

✳✳ WARNING

Do not loosen the rear axle wheel hub retainer until after the wheel and tire assembly are removed from the vehicle. Wheel bearing damage will occur if the wheel bearing is unloaded with the weight of the vehicle applied.

4. Remove the rear brake drum or brake disc.
5. Remove the rear coil spring. Refer to Coil Spring Removal & Installation in the Rear Suspension section.
6. Remove and discard the rear wheel hub nut.
7. Remove the anti-lock brake sensor harness-to-body retainer bolt.
8. Remove the nut and separate the lower ball joint.

✳✳ WARNING

Do not damage the oil seal when removing the axle halfshaft from the differential.

9. Using the special tool, remove the halfshaft from the differential.
10. Using the special tool, separate the halfshaft from the rear axle hub assembly.
11. Remove the rear halfshaft.

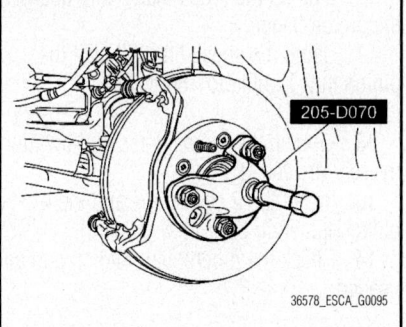

Fig. 51 Halfshaft separation with special tool

To install:

12. Using the halfshaft installer, pull the outer halfshaft end into the hub assembly.
13. Using the axle seal protector, install the halfshaft into the differential.
14. If the axle is equipped with the oil seal protector, make sure the oil seal lip and seal protector are correctly aligned.
15. Position the lower ball joint and install the lower ball joint nut. Tighten the lower ball joint nut to 76 ft. lbs. (103 Nm).
16. Install the rear coil spring.
17. Install the anti-lock brake sensor harness-to-body bolt and tighten to 80 inch lbs. (9 Nm).

➡**Do not tighten the rear wheel hub nut with the vehicle on the ground. The nut must be tightened to specification before the vehicle is lowered onto the wheels. Wheel bearing damage will occur if the wheel bearing is loaded with the weight of the vehicle applied.**

18. Apply the brake to keep the halfshaft from rotating.
19. Install the rear wheel hub nut and tighten to 222 ft. lbs. (300 Nm).

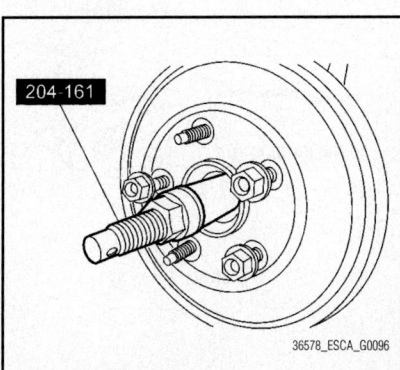

Fig. 52 Halfshaft pulled into the hub with the installation tool

20. Check the differential fluid an add as needed.

REAR PINION SEAL

REMOVAL & INSTALLATION

See Figures 54 through 57.

1. Before servicing the vehicle, refer to the Precautions Section.
2. With the vehicle in NEUTRAL, position it on a hoist.
3. Index-mark the pinion and pinion flange to the rear of the driveshaft.
4. Remove the 4 bolts and the 2 cap straps. Disconnect and support the driveshaft.

➡**Discard the nut after removing it. Install a new nut during installation.**

5. Using the special tool, hold the pinion flange while removing the nut. Remove the nut.

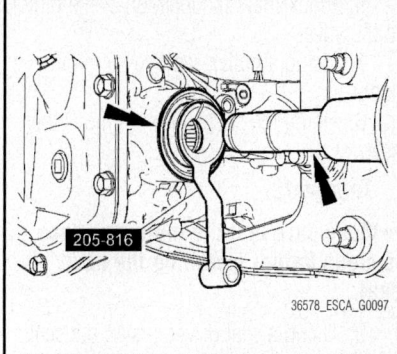

Fig. 53 Install the halfshaft into the differential using the seal protector

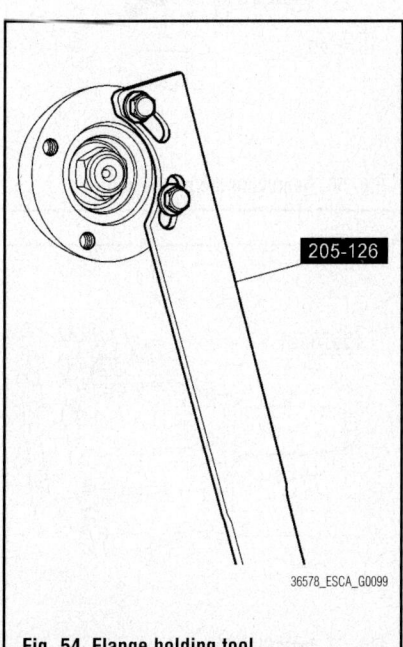

Fig. 54 Flange holding tool

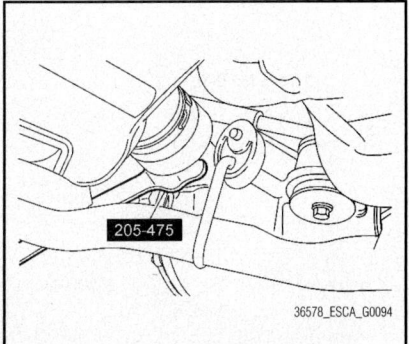

Fig. 50 Halfshaft removal with special tool

6. Index-mark the location of the pinion to the yoke.

7. Using a puller, remove the pinion flange.

8. Using the special tool, remove the seal.

To install:

➡Make sure that the mating surface is clean before installing the new seal.

9. Using a seal driver, install the seal.

➡Lubricate the pinion flange with premium long-life grease.

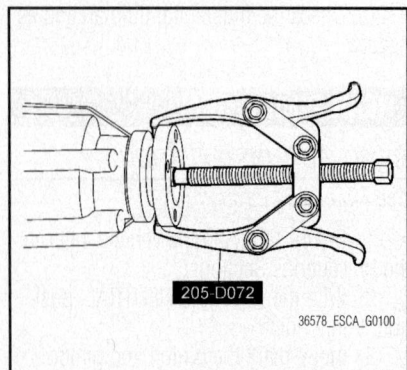

205-D072

36578_ESCA_G0100

Fig. 55 Removing the pinion flange

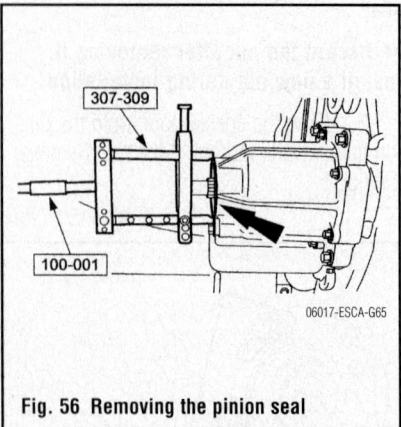

307-309

100-001

06017-ESCA-G65

Fig. 56 Removing the pinion seal

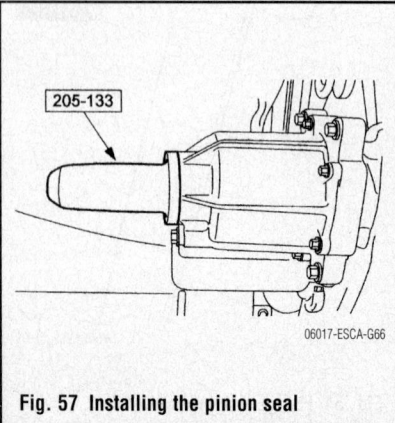

205-133

06017-ESCA-G66

Fig. 57 Installing the pinion seal

10. Line up the index marks and position the pinion flange.

11. Using the special tool, install the pinion nut. Tighten to 180 ft. lbs. (244 Nm).

12. Line up the index marks and position the rear driveshaft.

13. Install the 2 cap straps and the 4 bolts. Tighten to 52 ft. lbs. (70 Nm).

14. Check the differential fluid an add as needed.

REAR DRIVESHAFT

REMOVAL & INSTALLATION
See Figure 58.

1. Before servicing the vehicle, refer to the Precautions Section.

❊❊ CAUTION

The normal operating temperature of the exhaust system is very high. Never attempt to remove any part of the system until it has cooled. Be especially careful when working around the catalytic converters. The temperature of the converter rises to a high level after only a few minutes of engine operation. Failure to follow these instructions may result in personal injury.

➡Do not swap driveshaft assembles from different vehicles. The Escape Hybrid drive shaft is longer than the driveshaft in the Escape/Mariner and is not interchangeable. With the vehicle in NEUTRAL, position it on a hoist.

2. Remove the ground strap bolt.

❊❊ WARNING

Do not reuse the CV-joint bolts and washers. Install new bolts and washers or damage to the vehicle may occur.

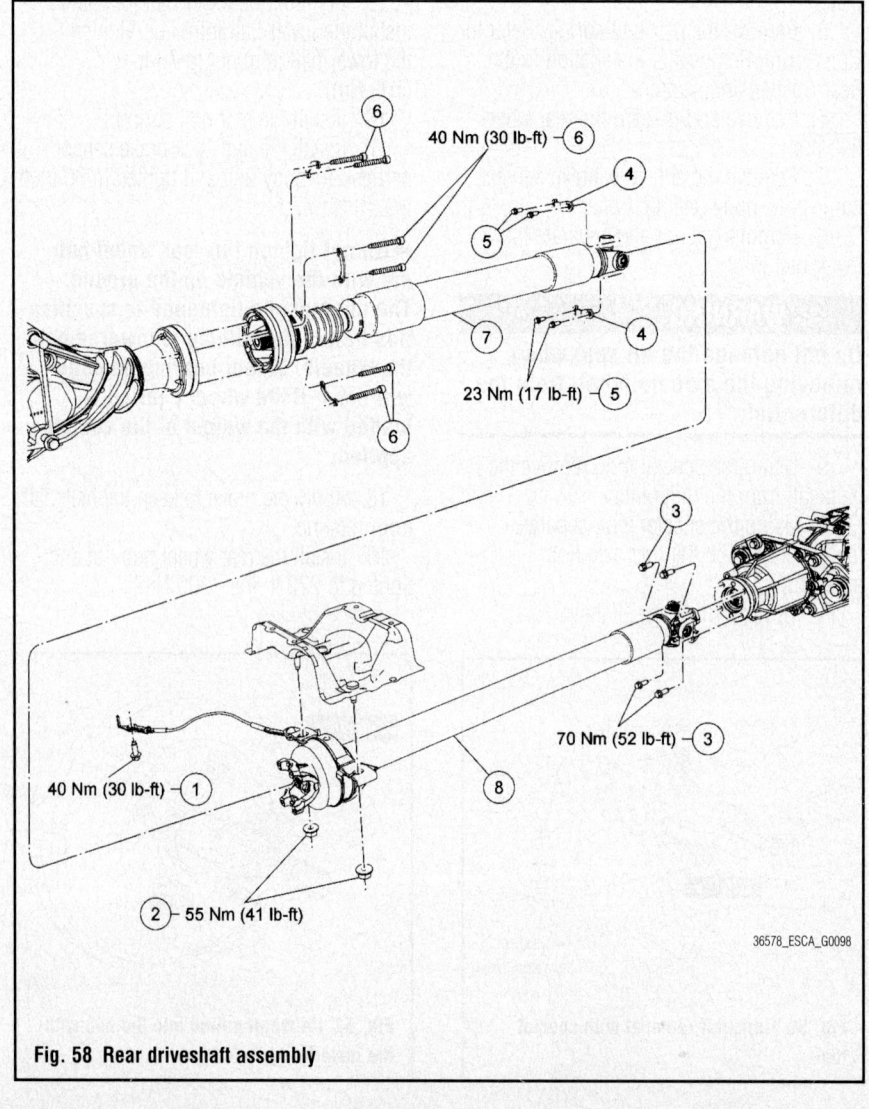

6   40 Nm (30 lb-ft)   6
4
5
7
4
23 Nm (17 lb-ft)   5
6
3
70 Nm (52 lb-ft)   3
40 Nm (30 lb-ft)   1
8
2   55 Nm (41 lb-ft)

36578_ESCA_G0098

Fig. 58 Rear driveshaft assembly

3. Remove and discard the 6 front driveshaft-to-transfer case bolts and washers.

4. Index-mark the front driveshaft to the center bearing.

> **❋❋ WARNING**
>
> **Do not reuse the bolts and cap straps for the center U-joint. Install new bolts and cap straps or damage to the vehicle may occur.**

➡ **There is a difference in the length of the head of the replacement cap strap bolts from the production bolts. The longer head pinion bolts can be used in either location.**

5. Remove and discard the 4 universal joint cap strap bolts and 2 cap straps and remove the front driveshaft.

6. Index-mark the pinion and yoke to the driveshaft.

> **❋❋ WARNING**
>
> **Do not reuse the bolts and cap straps for the rear U-joint. Install new bolts and cap straps.**

➡ **There is a difference in the length of the head of the replacement strap bolts from the production bolts. The longer head pinion bolts can be used in either location.**

7. Remove and discard the 4 universal joint cap bolts and 2 cap straps from the rear driveshaft universal joint.

8. With the help of an assistant, remove the center bearing support nuts and the driveshaft.

To install:

9. To install, reverse the removal procedure. Observe the following torques:

- Center bearing support nuts: 41 ft. lbs. (55 Nm)
- Rear universal joint cap bolts: 52 ft. lbs. (70 Nm)
- Front universal joint cap strap bolts: 17 ft. lbs. (23 Nm)
- The 6 front driveshaft-to-transfer case bolts: 30 ft. lbs. (40 Nm)
- Ground strap bolt: 30 ft. lbs. (40 Nm)

10. If a driveshaft is installed and driveshaft vibration is encountered after installation, index the driveshaft.

a. With the vehicle in NEUTRAL, position it on a hoist.

> **❋❋ WARNING**
>
> **Do not reuse the CV-joint bolts and washers. Install new bolts and washers or damage to the vehicle may occur.**

11. Remove and discard the 6 front driveshaft-to-transfer case bolts and washers.

12. Rotate the flange 60 degrees.

13. Connect the front driveshaft and install the 6 new bolts and washers. Tighten to 30 ft. lbs. (40 Nm).

> **❋❋ WARNING**
>
> **Do not reuse the bolts and cap straps for the pinion yoke. Install new bolts and cap straps or damage to the vehicle may occur.**

14. Disconnect the rear driveshaft universal joint. Discard the 4 bolts and the 2 cap straps.

15. Rotate the rear pinion 180 degrees.

16. Connect the rear driveshaft and install 4 new bolts and 2 new cap straps. Tighten to 52 ft. lbs. (70 Nm).

17. Lower the vehicle and test drive.

18. Repeat the procedure if necessary.

ENGINE COOLING

ENGINE FAN

REMOVAL & INSTALLATION

2008 Models

See Figure 59.

1. Before servicing the vehicle, refer to the Precautions Section.

2. With vehicle in NEUTRAL, position it on a hoist.

3. Drain the cooling system for 2.3L engines.

4. Remove the front bumper cover.

5. Remove the front impact severity sensor

6. Remove the 2 pin-type retainers.

7. Remove the 4 bolts and the 2 radiator brackets.

➡ **Mark the hood latch position prior to removal of the bolts.**

8. Loosen the nut, remove the 2 bolts and position aside the hood latch.

9. Remove the 2 wiring harness retainers from the front bumper bracket

10. Remove the center support bolt.

11. For 2.3L engines, perform the following:

- Disconnect the cooling fan resistor electrical connector.
- Disconnect the coolant recovery hose from the radiator and position it aside.

12. For 3.0L engines, detach the lower degas bottle hose from the cooling fan motor and shroud.

13. Disconnect the cooling fan electrical connectors.

14. Remove the 2 cooling fan bolts and the cooling fan motor and shroud.

To install:

15. To install, reverse the removal procedure and note the following:

- Tighten the cooling fan bolts, the cooling fan motor and shroud bolts to 71 inch. lbs (8 Nm).
- Tighten the center support bolt to 89 inch lbs. (10 Nm).
- Tighten the hood latch bolts to 80 inch lbs. (9 Nm).
- Tighten the radiator bracket bolts to 89 inch lbs. (10 Nm).

2009 Models

See Figure 59.

All vehicles

1. Before servicing the vehicle, refer to the Precautions Section.

2. With vehicle in NEUTRAL, position it on a hoist.

2.5L vehicles

3. Drain the cooling system.

All vehicles

4. Remove the front bumper cover.

5. Remove the 2 front impact severity sensors.

6. Remove the 2 pin-type retainers.

7. Remove the 4 bolts and the 2 radiator brackets.

8. Mark the hood latch position prior to removal of the bolts.

9. Loosen the nut, remove the 2 bolts and position aside the hood latch.

10. Remove the 2 wiring harness retainers from the radiator support.

11. Remove the center support bolt.

2.5L vehicles

12. Disconnect the cooling fan resistor electrical connector.

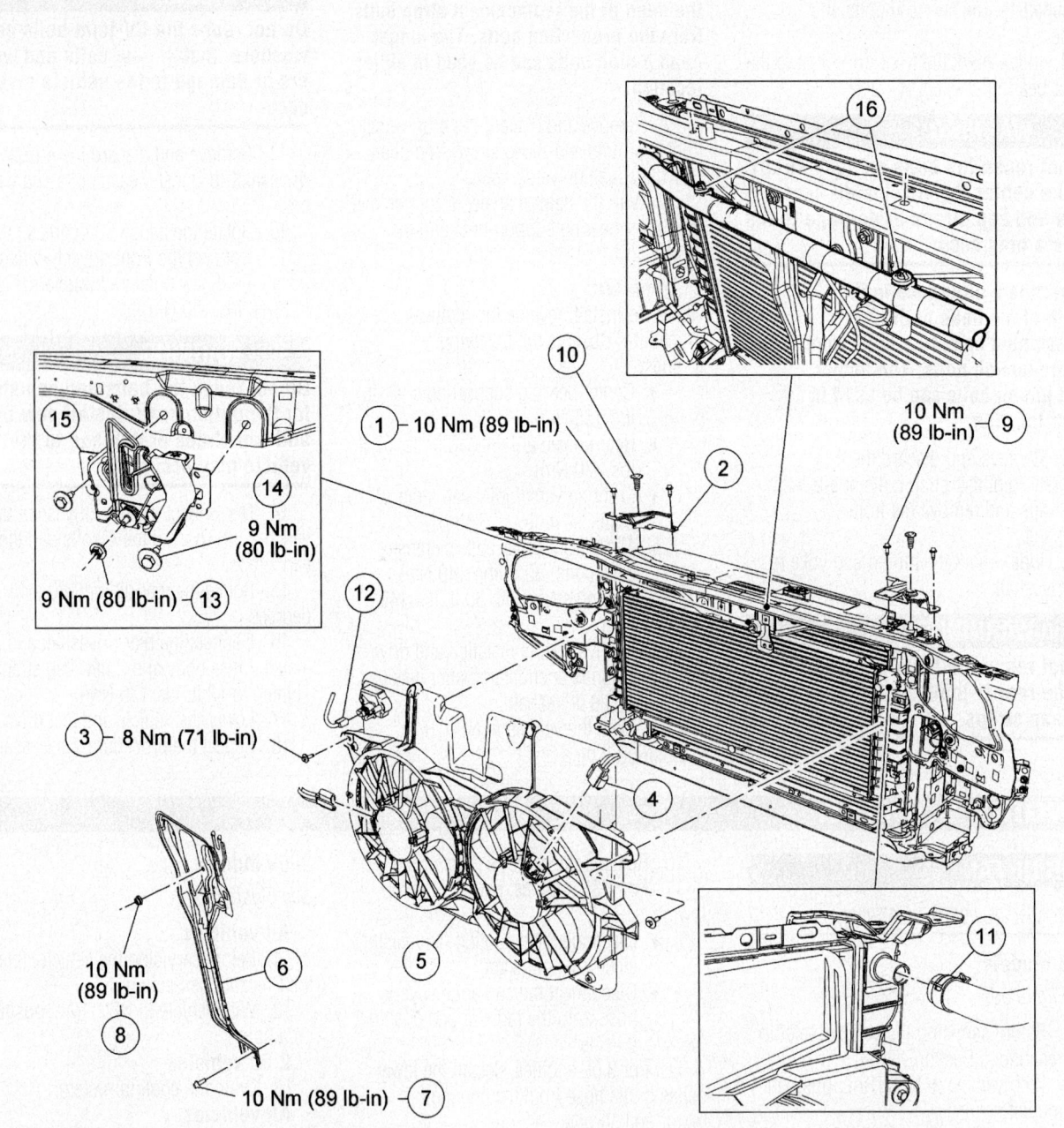

1. Radiator bracket bolt (4 required)
2. Radiator bracket (2 required)
3. Cooling fan bolt (2 required)
4. Cooling fan electrical connector (2 required)
5. Cooling fan motor and shroud
6. Center support
7. Center support lower bolt
8. Center support nut

9. Front grille bolt (2 required)
10. Pin-type retainer (2 required
11. Coolant recovery hose (2.3L only)
12. Cooling fan resistor electrical connector (2.3L only)
13. Hood latch nut
14. Hood latch bolt (2 required)
15. Hood latch
16. Wiring harness retainers (2 required)

22086_ESCA_G0021

Fig. 59 Cooling fan motor and shroud—2008 models

13. Disconnect the coolant recovery hose from the radiator and position it aside.

All vehicles

14. Disconnect the 2 cooling fan electrical connectors and wire harness retainers.

15. Remove the 2 cooling fan bolts and the cooling fan motor and shroud.

To install:

16. To install, reverse the removal procedure and note the following:
- 2.5L vehicles, fill and bleed the cooling system.
- Tighten the cooling fan bolts, the cooling fan motor and shroud bolts to 71 inch. lbs (8 Nm).
- Tighten the center support bolt to 89 inch lbs. (10 Nm).
- Tighten the hood latch bolts to 80 inch lbs. (9 Nm).
- Tighten the radiator bracket bolts to 89 inch lbs. (10 Nm).

RADIATOR

REMOVAL & INSTALLATION

4 Cylinder Engines

See Figure 60.

1. Before servicing the vehicle, refer to the Precautions Section.
2. With vehicle In NEUTRAL, position it on a hoist.
3. Remove the cooling fan motor and shroud.
4. Disconnect the upper radiator hose from the radiator.
5. Disconnect the lower degas bottle-to-radiator hose from the radiator.
6. Disconnect the lower radiator hose from the radiator.
7. Remove the 2 A/C condenser-to-radiator bolts and position aside the A/C condenser from the radiator.
8. Remove the radiator.

To install:

9. To install, reverse the removal procedure.
10. Tighten the A/C condenser-to-radiator bolts to 71 inch lbs. (8 Nm).
11. Fill and bleed the cooling system.

6 Cylinder Engines

See Figure 61.

1. With vehicle in NEUTRAL, position it on a hoist.
2. Drain the cooling system.
3. Remove the cooling fan motor and shroud.

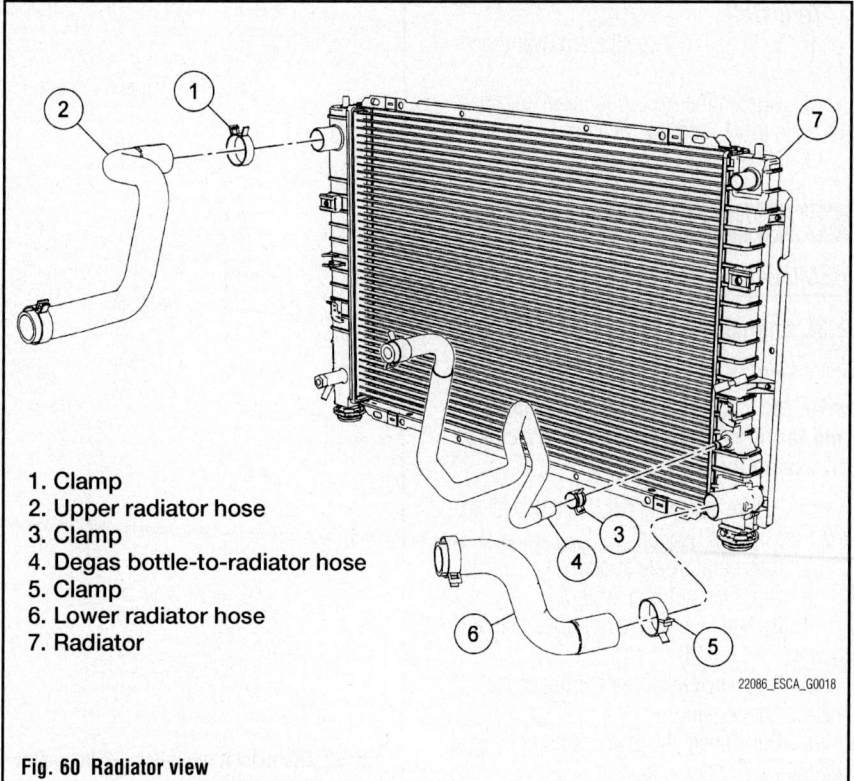

1. Clamp
2. Upper radiator hose
3. Clamp
4. Degas bottle-to-radiator hose
5. Clamp
6. Lower radiator hose
7. Radiator

22086_ESCA_G0018

Fig. 60 Radiator view

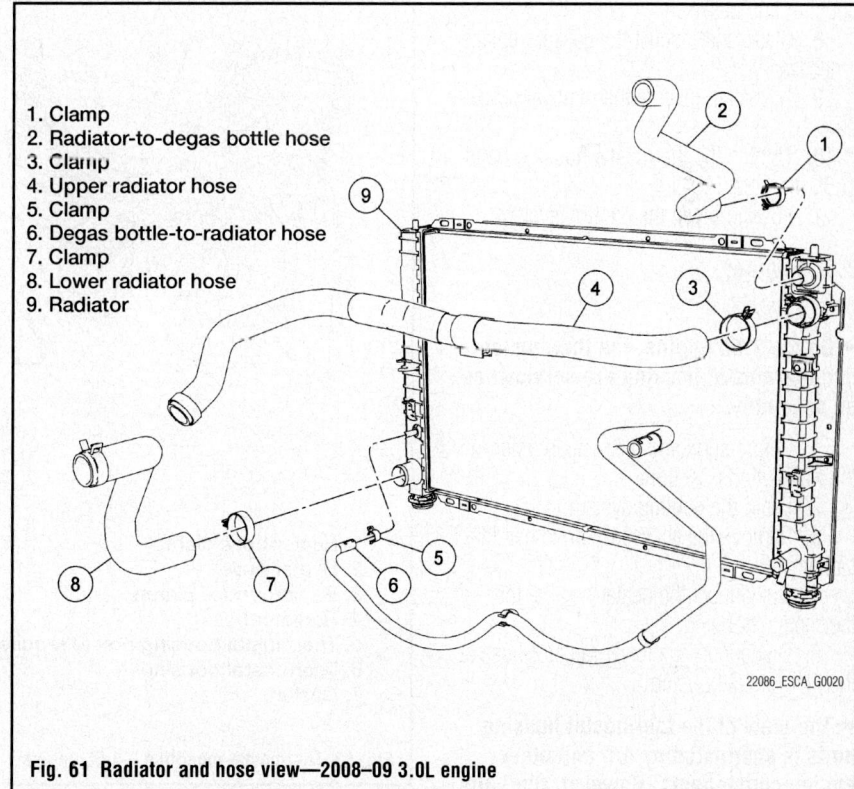

1. Clamp
2. Radiator-to-degas bottle hose
3. Clamp
4. Upper radiator hose
5. Clamp
6. Degas bottle-to-radiator hose
7. Clamp
8. Lower radiator hose
9. Radiator

22086_ESCA_G0020

Fig. 61 Radiator and hose view—2008–09 3.0L engine

4. Disconnect the radiator-to-degas bottle hose and upper radiator hose from the radiator.

5. Disconnect the lower degas bottle-to-radiator hose from the radiator.

6. Disconnect the lower radiator hose from the radiator.

7. Remove the 2 A/C condenser-to-radiator bolts and position aside the A/C condenser from the radiator.

8. Remove the radiator.

To install:

9. To install, reverse the removal procedure.

10. Tighten the A/C condenser-to-radiator bolts to 71 inch lbs. (8 Nm).

11. Fill and bleed the cooling system

THERMOSTAT

REMOVAL & INSTALLATION

2.3L Engine

See Figure 62.

➡ **On the 2.3L engine, the thermostat and thermostat housing are serviced as an assembly.**

1. Before servicing the vehicle, refer to the Precautions Section.

2. Raise and safely support the vehicle.

3. Drain the cooling system.

4. Remove the accessory drive belt tensioner.

5. Disconnect the heater hose at the thermostat housing.

6. Disconnect the lower radiator hose at the thermostat housing.

7. Remove the 3 bolts, thermostat housing and gasket.

8. Clean and inspect the gasket, replace if necessary.

9. To install, reverse the removal procedure.

10. Tighten the thermostat housing bolts to 89 inch lbs. (10 Nm).

11. Fill and bleed the cooling system.

2.5L Engine

See Figure 63.

➡ **On the 2.5L engine, the thermostat and thermostat housing are serviced as an assembly.**

1. Before servicing the vehicle, refer to the Precautions Section.

2. Drain the cooling system.

3. Remove the accessory drive belt tensioner.

4. Disconnect the heater hose at the thermostat housing.

5. Disconnect the lower radiator hose at the thermostat housing.

➡ **The view of the thermostat housing bolts is obstructed by A/C and other engine components. However, the bolts can be removed by using ¼ inch drive hand tools.**

6. Remove the 3 bolts, thermostat housing and gasket.

7. Clean and inspect the gasket, replace if necessary.

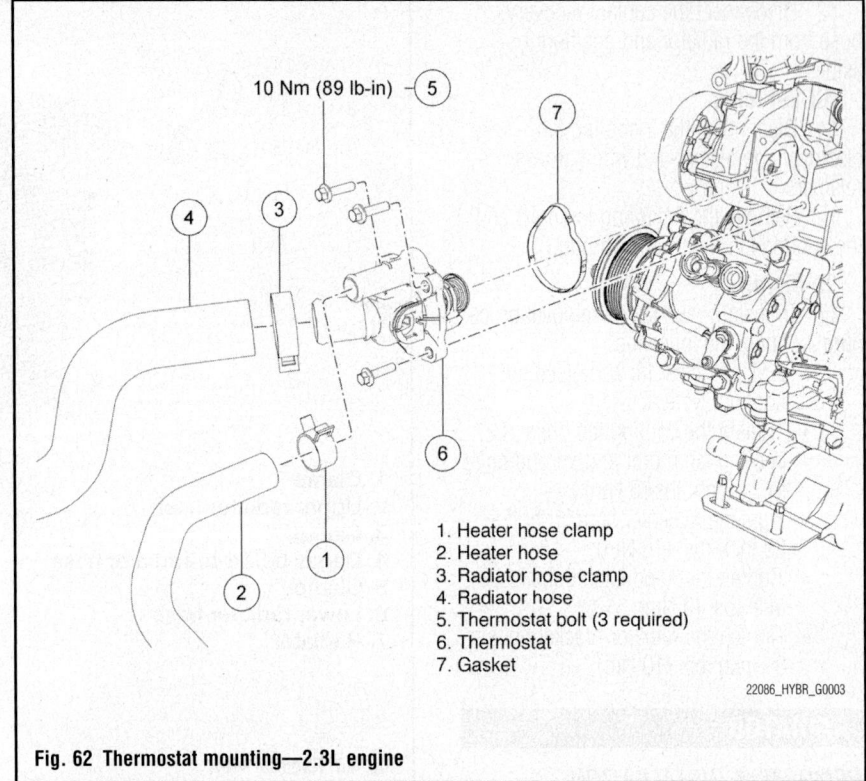

1. Heater hose clamp
2. Heater hose
3. Radiator hose clamp
4. Radiator hose
5. Thermostat bolt (3 required)
6. Thermostat
7. Gasket

22086_HYBR_G0003

Fig. 62 Thermostat mounting—2.3L engine

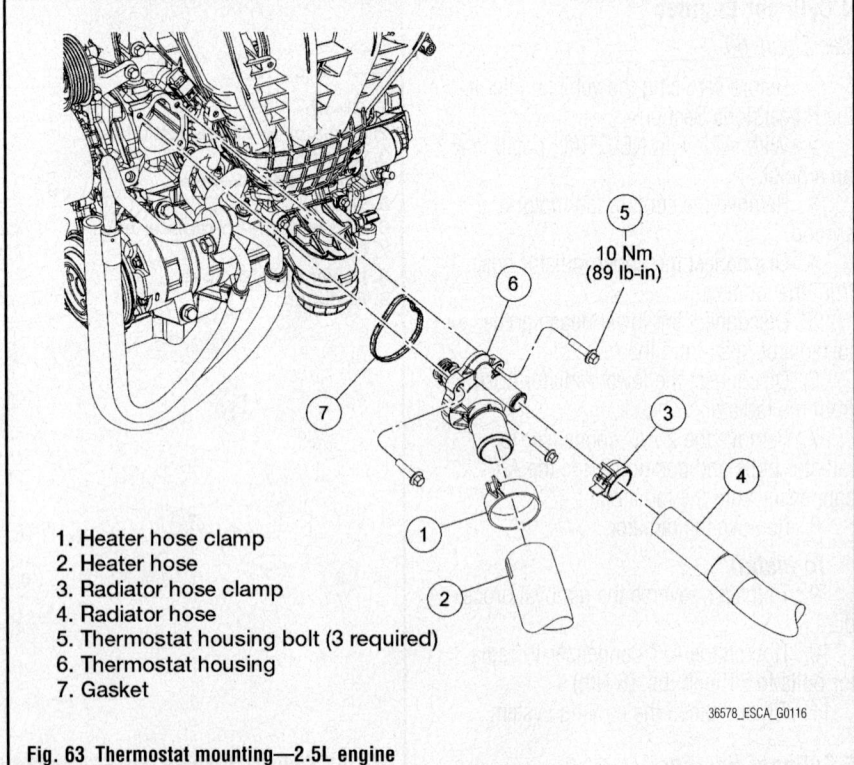

1. Heater hose clamp
2. Heater hose
3. Radiator hose clamp
4. Radiator hose
5. Thermostat housing bolt (3 required)
6. Thermostat housing
7. Gasket

36578_ESCA_G0116

Fig. 63 Thermostat mounting—2.5L engine

8. To install, reverse the removal procedure.

9. Tighten the thermostat housing bolts to 89 inch lbs. (10 Nm).

10. Fill and bleed the cooling system.

3.0L Engine

2008 Models

See Figure 64.

1. Before servicing the vehicle, refer to the Precautions Section.

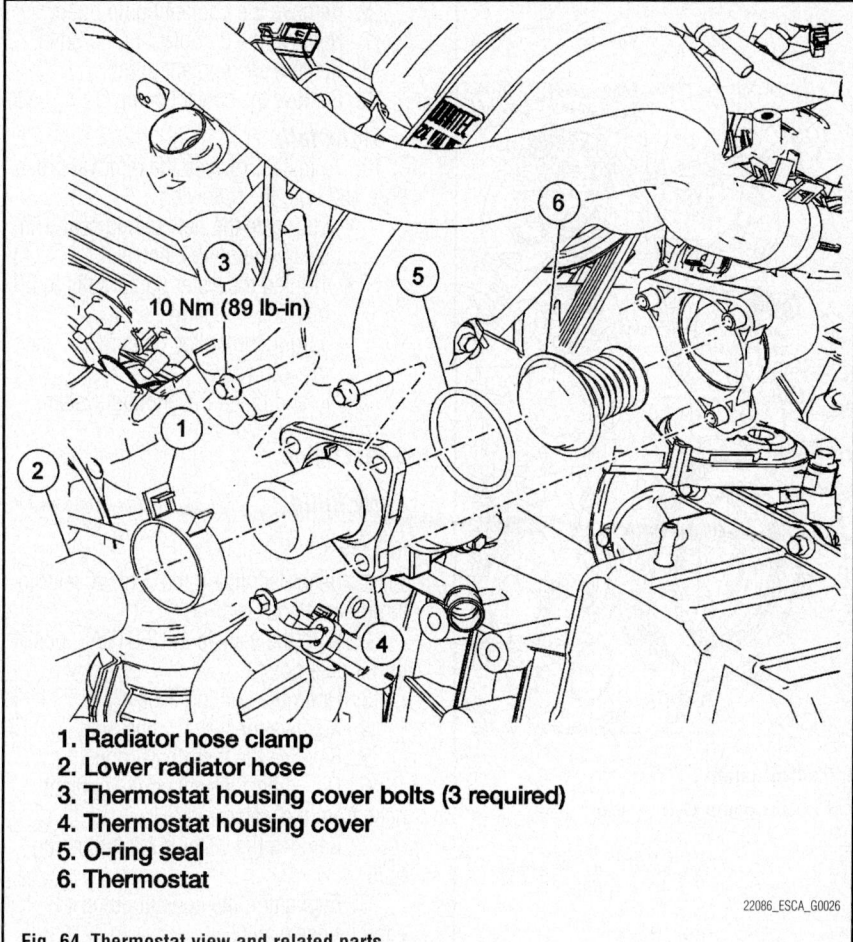

1. Radiator hose clamp
2. Lower radiator hose
3. Thermostat housing cover bolts (3 required)
4. Thermostat housing cover
5. O-ring seal
6. Thermostat

22086_ESCA_G0026

Fig. 64 Thermostat view and related parts

2. With the vehicle in NEUTRAL, position it on a hoist.
3. Drain the cooling system.
4. Remove the air cleaner outlet pipe.
5. Disconnect the lower radiator hose from the thermostat housing.
6. Remove the 3 bolts, thermostat housing cover, O-ring seal and thermostat.

To install:

7. Install thermostat a new O-ring seal.
8. Install thermostat housing and mounting bolts tighten to 89 inch lbs. (10 Nm).

➡ **To install, lubricate the thermostat housing O-ring seal with clean engine coolant**

9. Reconnect lower radiator hose.
10. Install air cleaner outlet pipe.
11. Fill and bleed the cooling system.

2009 Models

See Figure 65.

1. Before servicing the vehicle, refer to the Precautions Section.
2. With the vehicle in NEUTRAL, position it on a hoist.
3. Drain the cooling system.

4. Disconnect the lower radiator hose from the thermostat housing.
5. Remove the 3 bolts, thermostat housing cover, O-ring seal and thermostat.

To install:

6. Install thermostat a new O-ring seal.
7. Install thermostat housing and mounting bolts tighten to 89 inch lbs. (10 Nm).

➡ **To install, lubricate the thermostat housing O-ring seal with clean engine coolant**

8. Reconnect lower radiator hose.
9. Fill and bleed the cooling system.

WATER PUMP

REMOVAL & INSTALLATION

2.3L Engine
See Figure 66.

1. Before servicing the vehicle, refer to the Precautions Section.
2. With the vehicle in NEUTRAL, position it on a hoist.
3. Drain the cooling system.
4. Remove the accessory drive belt.
5. Remove the coolant pump pulley bolts.
6. Remove the coolant pump pulley.
7. Remove the coolant pump bolts.
8. Remove the coolant pump.
9. Remove the coolant pump O-ring seal.

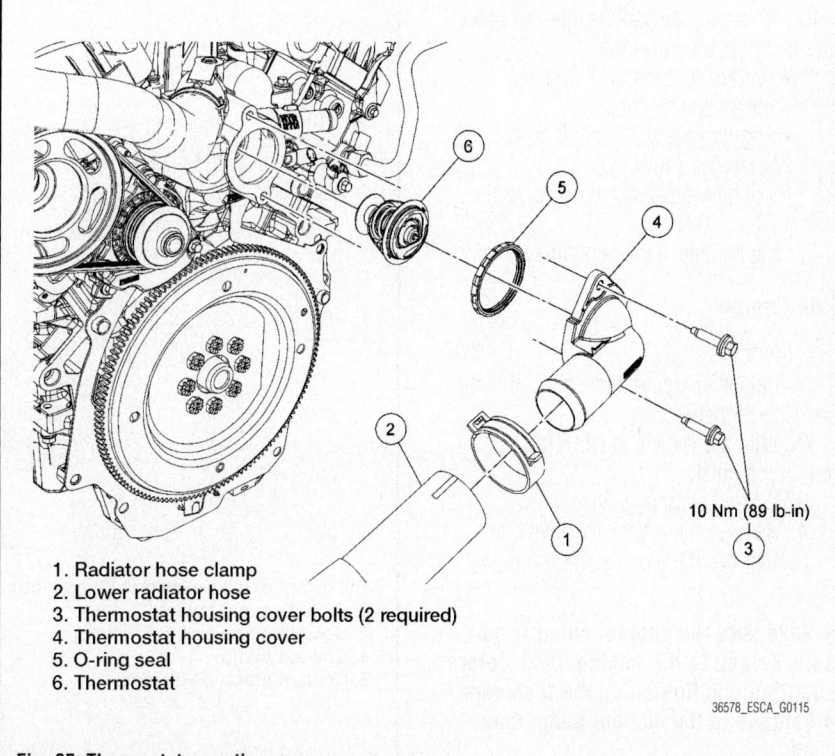

1. Radiator hose clamp
2. Lower radiator hose
3. Thermostat housing cover bolts (2 required)
4. Thermostat housing cover
5. O-ring seal
6. Thermostat

36578_ESCA_G0115

Fig. 65 Thermostat mounting

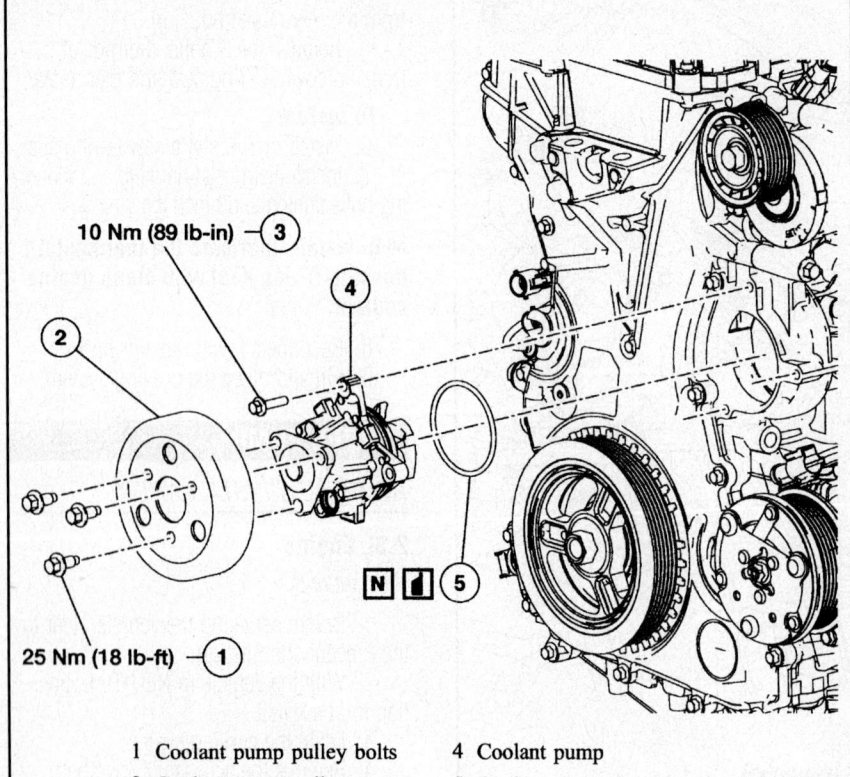

1. Coolant pump pulley bolts
2. Coolant pump pulley
3. Coolant pump bolts
4. Coolant pump
5. Coolant pump O-ring seal

67197-ESCA-G03

Fig. 66 Water pump mounting—2.3L engine

To install:

10. To install, reverse the removal procedure and note the following:

- Lubricate the new O-ring seal with clean engine coolant.
- Tighten the water pump bolts to 89 inch lbs. (10 Nm).
- Tighten the pulley bolts to 15 ft. lbs. (20 Nm).

11. Fill and bleed the cooling system.

2.5L Engine

See Figure 67.

1. Before servicing the vehicle, refer to the Precautions Section.

2. With the vehicle in NEUTRAL, position it on a hoist.

3. Drain the cooling system.

4. Remove the accessory drive belt.

5. Remove the 3 coolant pump pulley bolts.

➡Make sure the coolant pump is correctly seated to the engine block before installing and tightening the fasteners, or damage to the coolant pump may occur.

6. Remove the coolant pump pulley.
7. Remove the 3 coolant pump bolts.
8. Remove the coolant pump.
9. Remove the coolant pump O-ring seal.

To install:

10. To install, reverse the removal procedure and note the following:

- Lubricate the new O-ring seal with clean engine coolant.
- Tighten the water pump bolts to 89 inch lbs. (10 Nm).
- Torque the pulley bolts to 177 inch lbs. (20 Nm).

11. Fill and bleed the cooling system.

3.0L Engine

Early Build

See Figure 68.

1. Before servicing the vehicle, refer to the Precautions Section.

2. With the vehicle in NEUTRAL, position it on a hoist.

3. Drain the cooling system

4. Remove the water pump belt.

5. Remove the thermostat housing.

6. Disconnect the oil cooler coolant hose from the water pump.

7. Remove the water pump mounting bolts.

8. Reposition the coolant pump-to-engine hose clamp.

9. Remove the water pump.

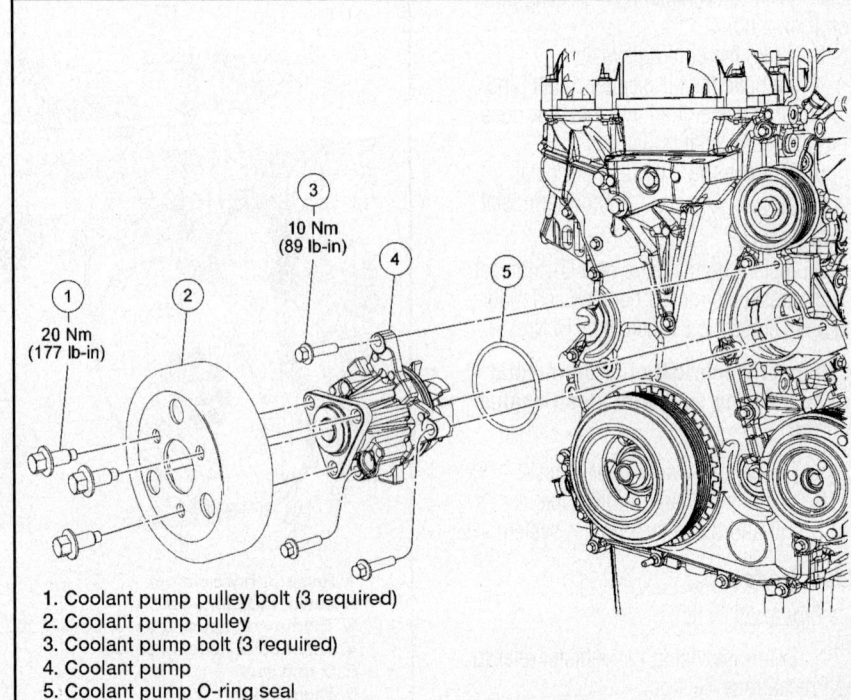

1. Coolant pump pulley bolt (3 required)
2. Coolant pump pulley
3. Coolant pump bolt (3 required)
4. Coolant pump
5. Coolant pump O-ring seal

36578_ESCA_G0117

Fig. 67 Water pump mounting—2.5L engine

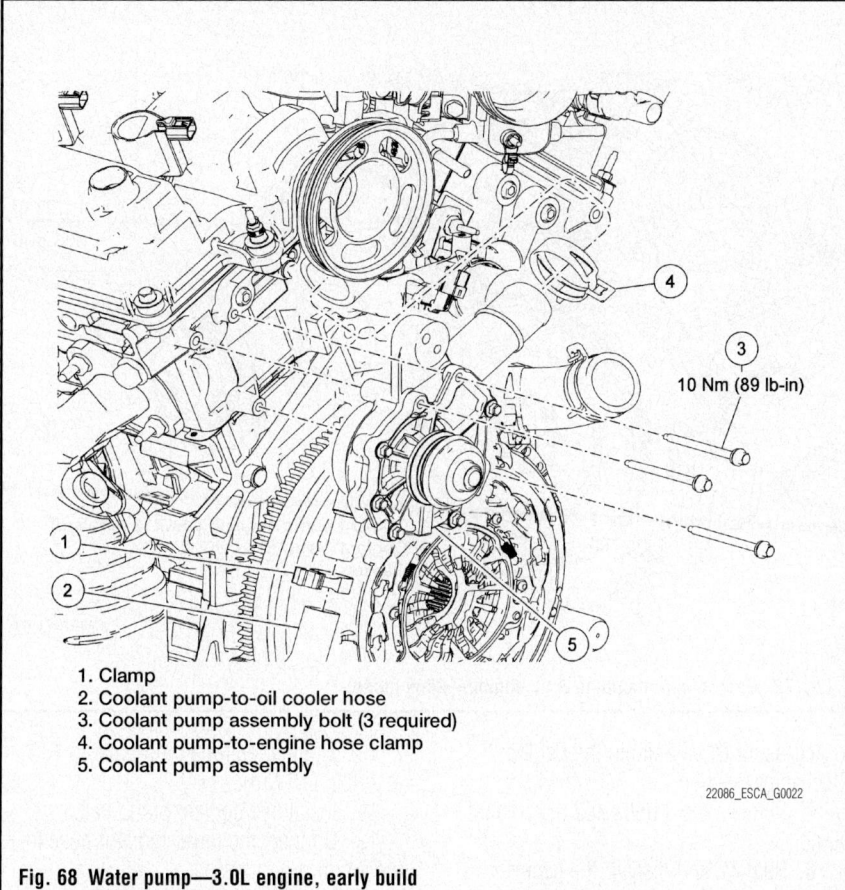

1. Clamp
2. Coolant pump-to-oil cooler hose
3. Coolant pump assembly bolt (3 required)
4. Coolant pump-to-engine hose clamp
5. Coolant pump assembly

22086_ESCA_G0022

10 Nm (89 lb-in)

Fig. 68 Water pump—3.0L engine, early build

To install:

10. To install, reverse the removal procedure and note the following:

    a. Tighten water pump mounting bolts to 89 inch. lbs (10 Nm).

    b. Tighten the water pump mounting bolts an additional 90 degrees.

11. Fill and bleed the cooling system.

Late Build

See Figures 69 through 71.

1. Before servicing the vehicle, refer to the Precautions Section.

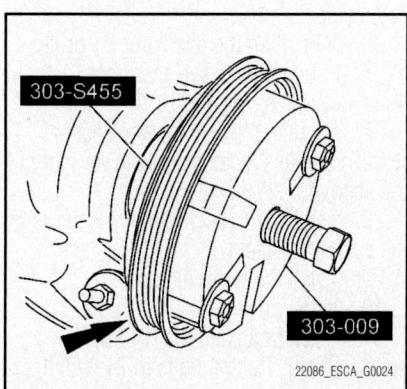

303-S455

303-009

22086_ESCA_G0024

Fig. 69 Water pump drive pulley and puller shown

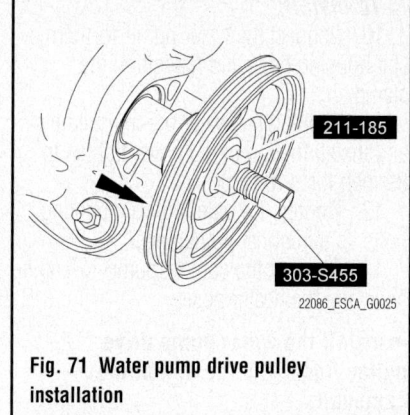

211-185

303-S455

22086_ESCA_G0025

Fig. 71 Water pump drive pulley installation

2. With the vehicle in NEUTRAL, position it on a hoist.

3. Drain the cooling system.

4. Disconnect the crankcase vent tube and position it aside.

5. Remove the water pump belt.

6. Using a suitable tool, remove the water pump drive pulley.

7. Disconnect the water pump-to-engine hose and position aside.

8. Remove the 3 mounting bolts from the water pump assembly.

9. Reposition the water pump-to-thermostat housing hose clamp and remove the coolant pump and hose as an assembly.

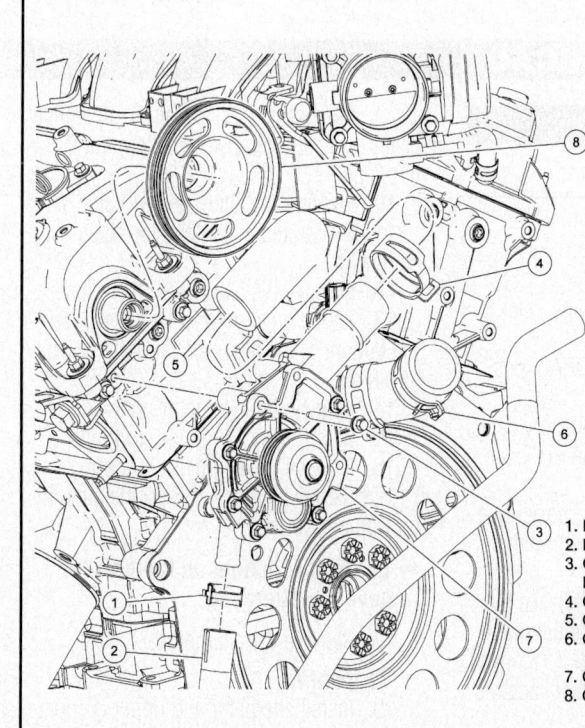

1. Heater hose clamp
2. Heater hose
3. Coolant pump assembly bolt (3 required)
4. Coolant pump-to-engine hose clamp
5. Coolant pump-to-engine hose
6. Coolant pump-to-thermostat housing hose clamp
7. Coolant pump assembly
8. Coolant pump drive pulley

22086_ESCA_G0023

Fig. 70 Water pump—3.0L engine, late build

To install:

10. Connect the water pump-to-thermostat housing hose and reposition the clamp.

11. Position the water pump assembly and install the mounting bolts, tighten to 89 inch lbs. (10 Nm).

12. Tighten the water pump mounting bolts an additional 90 degrees.

13. Connect the coolant pump-to-engine hose and the heater hose.

➡**Install the water pump drive pulley flush with the end of the camshaft.**

14. Using a suitable tool, install the coolant pump drive pulley.

15. Install the coolant pump belt.

16. Connect the crankcase vent tube.

17. Fill and bleed the cooling system.

3.0L Engine

See Figure 72.

1. Before servicing the vehicle, refer to the Precautions Section.

2. With the vehicle in NEUTRAL, position it on a hoist.

3. Drain the cooling system.

4. Remove the Air Cleaner (ACL) outlet pipe.

5. Disconnect the lower radiator hose from the thermostat housing.

6. Remove the coolant pump belt. Refer

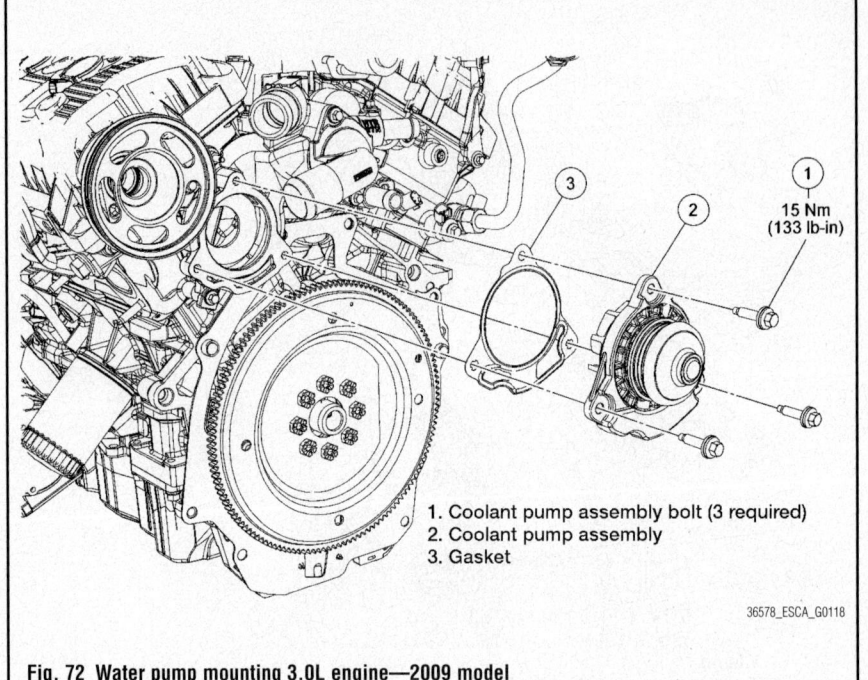

1. Coolant pump assembly bolt (3 required)
2. Coolant pump assembly
3. Gasket

36578_ESCA_G0118

Fig. 72 Water pump mounting 3.0L engine—2009 model

to Accessory Drive Belts in the Engine Mechanical section.

7. Remove the 3 bolts and the coolant pump.

8. Remove and discard the gasket.

To install:

9. Using a new gasket, install the coolant pump and the 3 bolts.

10. Tighten the mounting bolts to 133 inch lbs. (15 Nm).

11. Install the coolant pump belt.

12. Connect the lower radiator hose to the thermostat housing.

13. Install the ACL outlet pipe.

14. Fill and bleed the cooling system.

ENGINE ELECTRICAL

CHARGING SYSTEM

ALTERNATOR

REMOVAL & INSTALLATION

2.3L Engine

See Figure 73.

1. Before servicing the vehicle, refer to the Precautions Section.

2. With the vehicle in NEUTRAL, position it on a hoist.

3. Disconnect the negative battery cable.

4. Remove the bolts and the RH lower splash shield.

5. Rotate the front end accessory drive belt tensioner clockwise and position the accessory drive belt aside.

6. Press the locking tab to release the alternator lower air duct from the alternator and remove the lower air duct.

7. Remove the battery harness locators from the alternator shield.

8. Remove the heated oxygen sensor (HO2S) harness locator from the lower part of the alternator. shield.

9. Position the alternator B+ protective cover aside and remove the alternator B+ terminal nut.

10. Position the alternator B+ cable aside

11. Disconnect the alternator electrical connector.

12. Remove the alternator shield nuts.

13. Remove the pin-type retainer from the bottom of the alternator and the alternator shield.

14. Remove the alternator bolt.

15. Remove the alternator stud nuts.

16. Remove the alternator studs.

17. Remove the screws and the alternator upper air duct.

➡ **Lower the vehicle on the hoist to remove the alternator.**

18. Remove the alternator..

To install:

19. Install alternator and upper air duct screws tighten screws to 35 inch. lbs (4 Nm).

20. Install and tighten alternator studs to 18 ft. lbs. (25 Nm).

21. Install alternator stud nuts and tighten to 35 ft. lbs. (47 Nm).

22. Install alternator bolt and tighten to 35 ft. lbs. (47 Nm).

23. Install pin-type retainers to bottom of alternator and shield.

24. Install alternator shield nuts and tighten to 15 ft. lbs. (20 Nm).

25. Reconnect the alternator electrical connector.

26. Reposition the alternator B+ protective cover and tighten the alternator B+ terminal nut to 9 ft. lbs. (12 Nm).

27. Install the heated oxygen sensor (HO2S) harness locator to the lower part of the alternator shield.

28. Install the battery harness locators to the alternator shield.

29. Install the lower air duct.

30. Install drive belt

31. Install bolts and the RH lower splash shield. Tighten bolts to 71 inch lbs. (8 Nm).

32. Connect the negative battery cable.

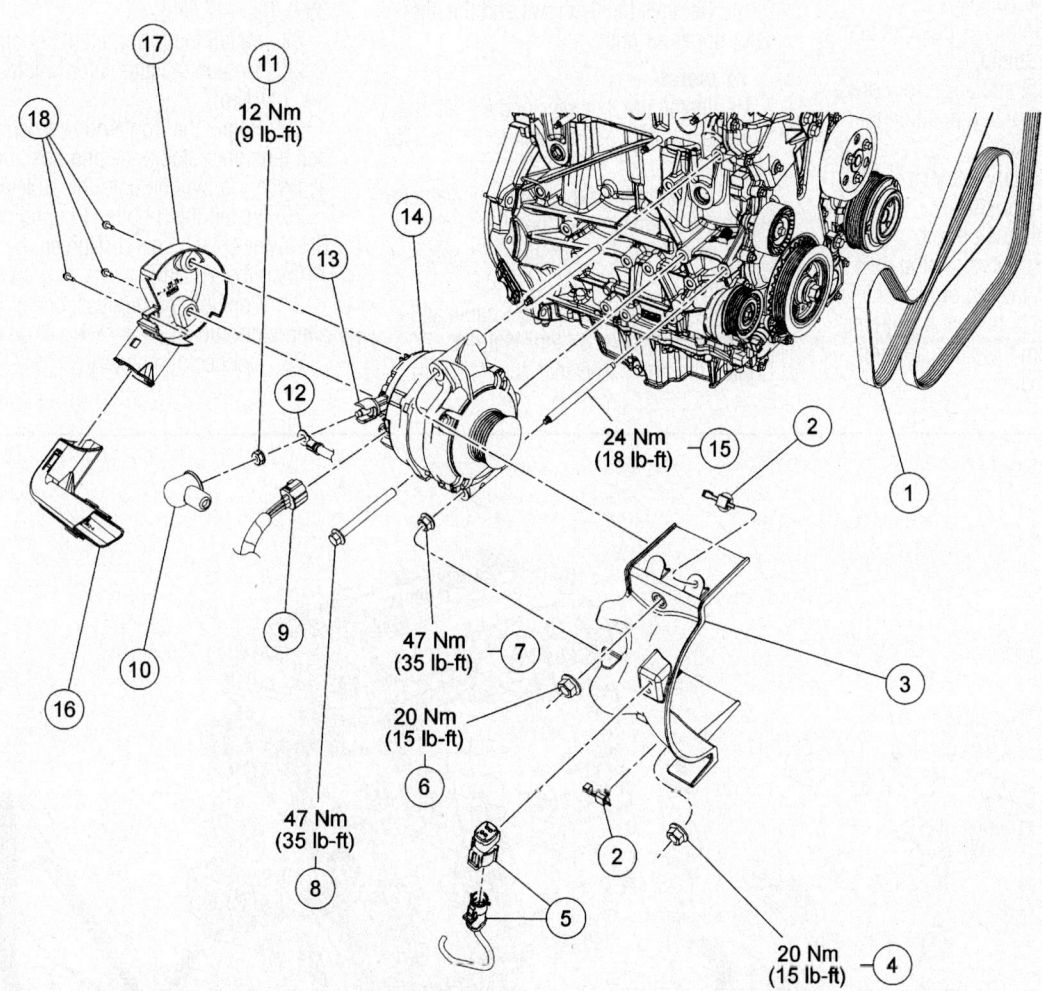

12 Nm
(9 lb-ft)

24 Nm
(18 lb-ft)

47 Nm
(35 lb-ft)

20 Nm
(15 lb-ft)

47 Nm
(35 lb-ft)

20 Nm
(15 lb-ft)

1. Front end accessory drive belt
2. Harness locators
3. Generator shield
4. Generator shield nut
5. Heated oxygen sensor
   (HO2S) harness connector/harness locator
6. Generator shield nut
7. Generator stud nut
8. Generator bolt
9. Generator electrical connector
10. B+ protective cover
11. Generator B+ terminal nut
12. Generator B+ cable
13. Generator B+ terminal
14. Generator
15. Generator stud (2 required-upper/lower)
16. Generator lower air duct
17. Generator upper air duct
18. Generator upper air duct screws
    (3 required)

22086_ESCA_G0002

Fig. 73 Alternator mounting—2.3L engine

2.5L Engine

See Figure 74.

1. Before servicing the vehicle, refer to the Precautions Section.

2. With the vehicle in NEUTRAL, position it on a hoist.

3. Disconnect the battery.

4. Remove the 5 bolts, 1 pushpin and the RH lower splash shield.

5. Rotate the front end accessory drive belt tensioner clockwise and position the accessory drive belt aside.

6. Remove the battery harness locator from the lower alternator stud.

7. Remove the alternator bolt.

8. Remove the 2 alternator stud nuts.

9. Working from the top of the vehicle, press the locking tab to release the alternator lower air duct from the alternator and remove the lower air duct.

10. Position the alternator B+ protective cover aside and remove the alternator B+ terminal nut.

11. Position the alternator B+ cable aside.

12. Disconnect the alternator electrical connector.

13. Remove the alternator.

14. Remove the 3 screws and the alternator upper air duct.

To install:

15. Install the 3 screws and the alternator upper air duct and tighten to 35 inch lbs. (4 Nm).

16. Working from the top of the vehicle, install the alternator and the alternator stud.

17. Install the 2 alternator stud nuts hand-tight.

18. Install the alternator B+ cable and install the alternator B+ terminal nut. Tighten the nut to 106 inch lbs. (12 Nm).

19. Connect the alternator electrical connector.

20. Position the alternator B+ protective cover on the B+ terminal.

21. Working from under the vehicle, install the lower alternator bolt hand-tight.

22. Tighten the 2 alternator stud nuts to 35 ft. lbs. (47 Nm).

23. Install the lower alternator air duct.

24. Tighten the alternator bolt to 35 ft. lbs. (47 Nm).

25. Rotate the front end accessory drive belt tensioner clockwise and position the accessory drive belt onto the pulleys.

26. Install the 5 bolts, 1 pushpin and the RH lower splash shield. Tighten the bolts to 71 inch lbs. (8 Nm).

27. Position the harness locator on the alternator stud.

28. Connect the battery.

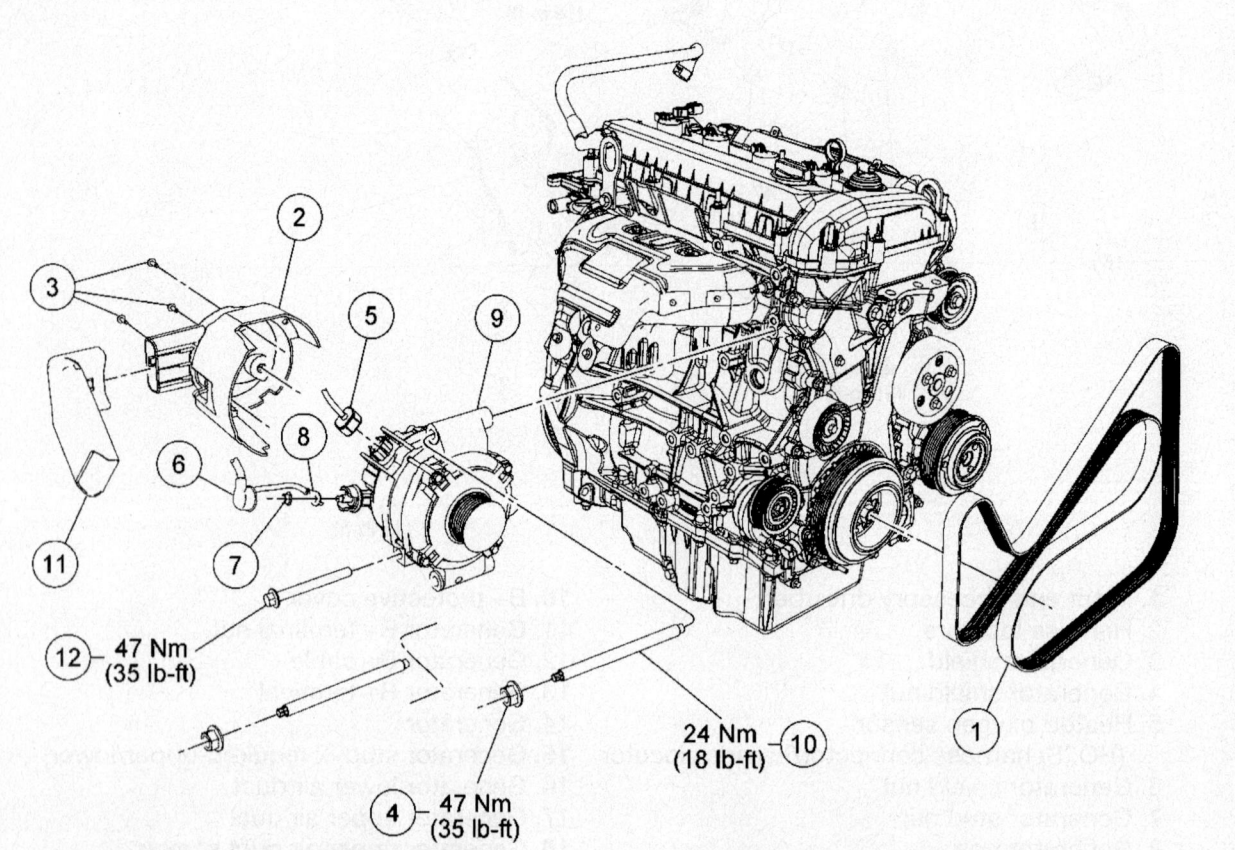

1. Front end accessory drive belt
2. Alternator upper air duct
3. Alternator upper air duct screws (3 required)
4. Alternator stud nut (2 required)
5. Alternator electrical connector
6. B+ protective cover
7. Alternator B+ terminal nut
8. Alternator B+ cable
9. Alternator
10. Alternator stud (2 required)
11. Alternator lower air duct
12. Alternator bolt

36578_ESCA_G0120

Fig. 74 Alternator mounting—2.5L engine

3.0L Engine

2008 Models

See Figure 75.

✳✳ WARNING

Do not allow any metal object to come in contact with the alternator housing and internal diode cooling fins. A short circuit may result and burn out the diodes. Failure to follow this instruction may result in component damage.

1. Before servicing the vehicle, refer to the Precautions Section.
2. Disconnect the negative battery cable.
3. Remove the lower splash shield bolts and the pin-type retainers.

➡ **The LH lower splash shield must be removed before the RH lower splash shield.**

4. Remove the lower splash shields.
5. Rotate the front end accessory drive tensioner counterclockwise and position the accessory drive belt aside
6. Disconnect the alternator electrical connector.
7. Position the alternator B+ protective cover aside and remove the alternator B+ terminal nut.
8. Remove the A/C compressor bolts. Use a tie-strap and position A/C compressor aside.
9. Loosen the alternator nuts.
10. Remove the lower alternator studs.
11. Remove the upper alternator bolt and the alternator.

To install:

12. Install alternator and upper bolt.
13. Tighten upper bolt to 35 ft. lbs. (47 Nm) with the vehicle on the ground.
14. Install the lower alternator studs and tighten to 62 inch lbs. (7 Nm).
15. Install and tighten the alternator nuts to 35 ft. lbs. (47 Nm).
16. Reposition and install A/C compressor bolts. Tighten to 18 ft. lbs. (25 Nm).
17. Reposition the alternator B+ protective cover and tighten terminal nut to 9 ft. lbs. (12 Nm).
18. Reconnect the alternator electrical connector.
19. Install accessory drive belt.
20. Install the splash shields and bolts and the 2 pin-type retainers.
21. Tighten the splash shield bolts to 71 inch lbs. (8 Nm).
22. Connect the negative battery cable.

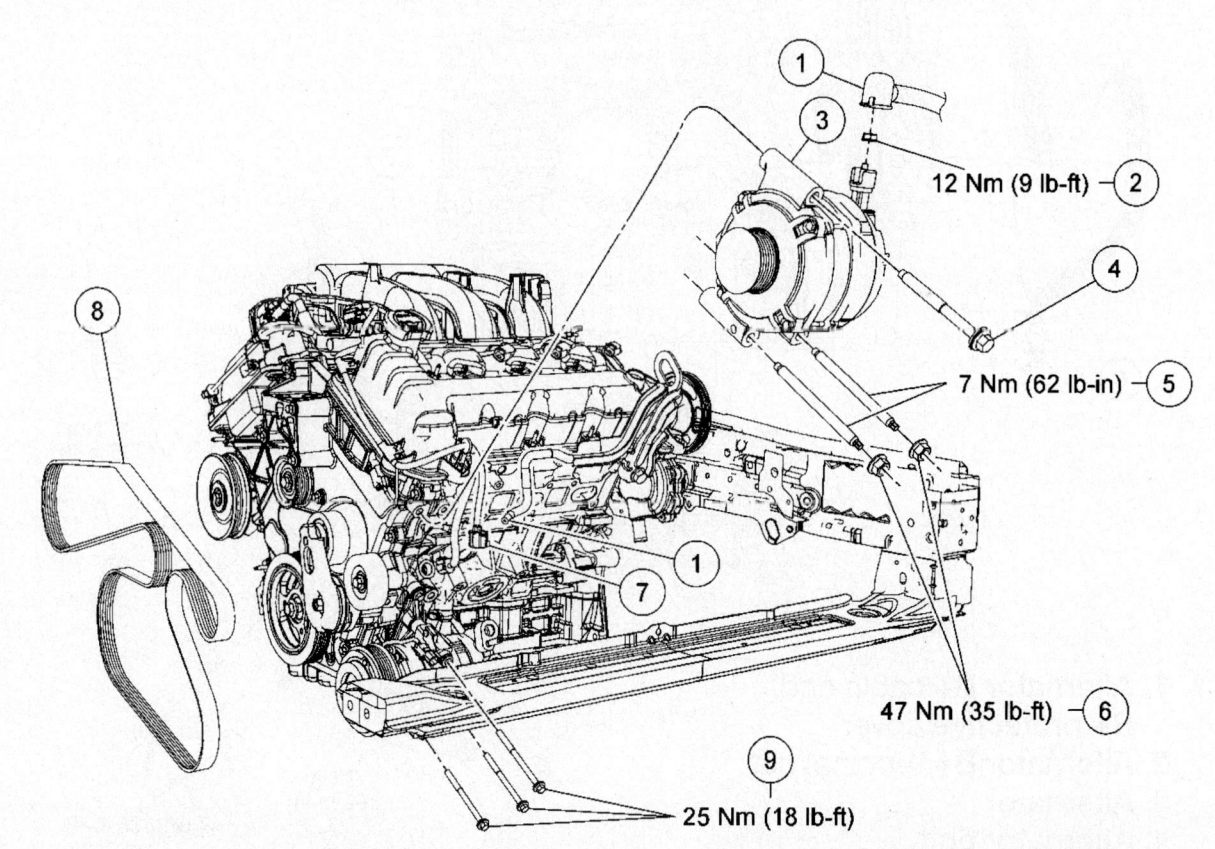

1. Alternator B+ cable and B+ protective cover
2. Alternator B+ terminal nut
3. Alternator
4. Alternator bolt
5. Alternator studs (2 required)
6. Alternator stud nuts (2 required)
7. Alternator electrical connector
8. Front end accessory drive belt
9. Air conditioning (A/C) compressor bolts (3 required)

36578_ESCA_G0121

Fig. 75 Alternator mounting—2008 3.0L engine

2009 Models

See Figure 76.

☀☀ WARNING

Do not allow any metal object to come in contact with the alternator housing and internal diode cooling fins. A short circuit may result and burn out the diodes. Failure to follow this instruction may result in component damage.

1. Before servicing the vehicle, refer to the Precautions Section.
2. Disconnect the negative battery cable.
3. Remove the 5 RH lower splash shield bolts and the 1 pin-type retainer.
4. Remove the RH lower splash shields.
5. Rotate the front end accessory drive tensioner counterclockwise and position the accessory drive belt aside
6. Disconnect the alternator electrical connector.

7. Position the alternator B+ protective cover aside and remove the alternator B+ terminal nut.
8. Remove the A/C compressor bolts. Use a tie-strap and position A/C compressor aside.
9. Loosen the 2 alternator nuts.
10. Remove the 2 lower alternator studs.
11. Remove the upper alternator bolt and the alternator.

To install:

12. Install alternator and upper bolt.

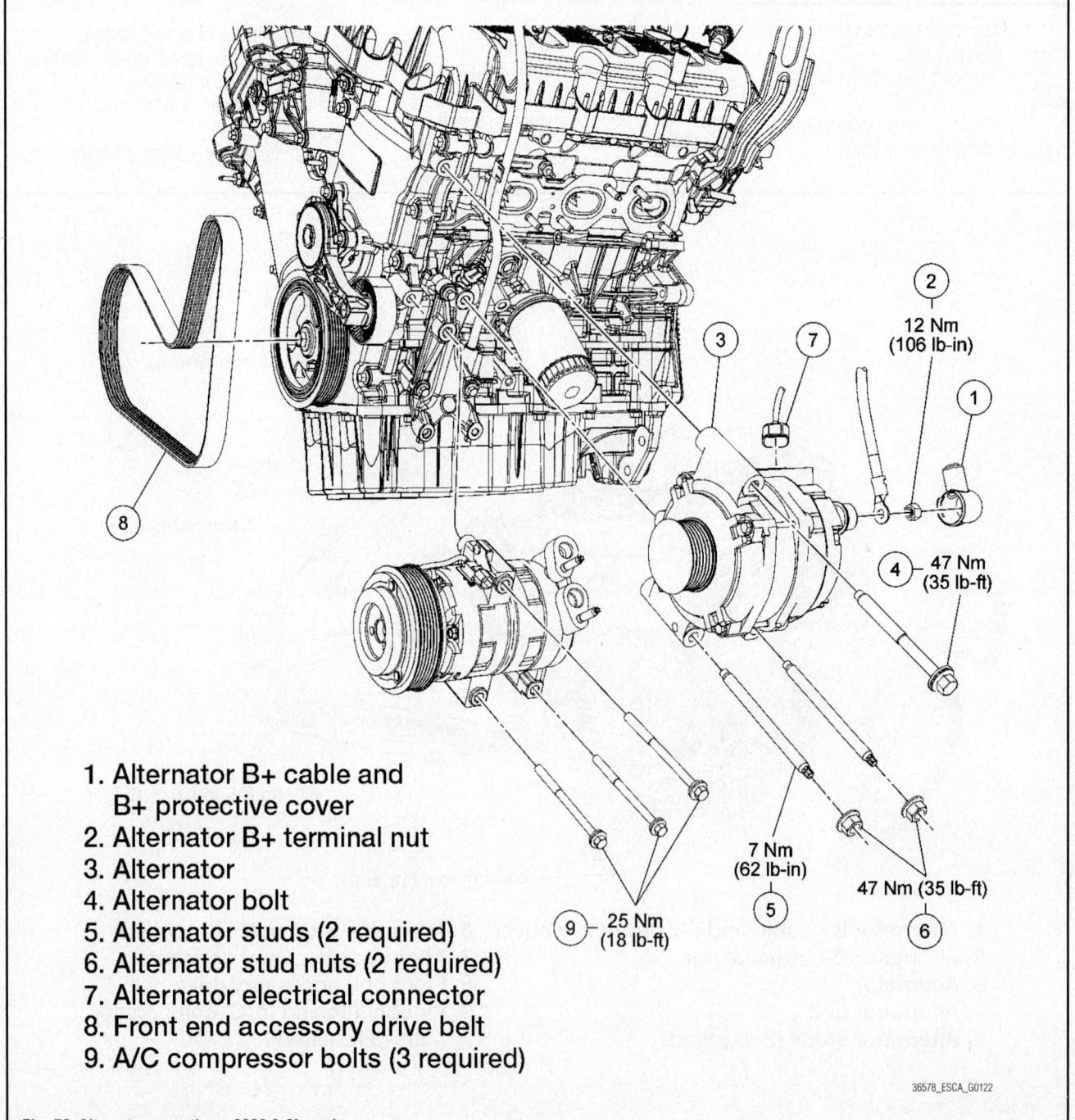

1. Alternator B+ cable and B+ protective cover
2. Alternator B+ terminal nut
3. Alternator
4. Alternator bolt
5. Alternator studs (2 required)
6. Alternator stud nuts (2 required)
7. Alternator electrical connector
8. Front end accessory drive belt
9. A/C compressor bolts (3 required)

36578_ESCA_G0122

Fig. 76 Alternator mounting—2009 3.0L engine

13. Tighten upper bolt to 35 ft. lbs. (47 Nm) with the vehicle on the ground.

14. Install the 2 lower alternator studs and tighten to 62 inch lbs. (7 Nm).

15. Install and tighten the 2 alternator nuts to 35 ft. lbs. (47 Nm).

16. Reposition and install A/C compressor bolts. Tighten to 18 ft. lbs. (25 Nm).

17. Reposition the alternator B+ protective cover and tighten terminal nut to 9 ft. lbs. (12 Nm).

18. Reconnect the alternator electrical connector.

19. Install accessory drive belt.

20. Install the splash shields and bolts and the 2 pin-type retainers.

21. Tighten the splash shield bolts to 71 inch lbs. (8 Nm).

22. Connect the negative battery cable.

VOLTAGE REGULATOR

REMOVAL & INSTALLATION

The voltage regulator is integral with the alternator and is not replaceable. If the voltage regulator is bad, the alternator must be replaced.

ENGINE ELECTRICAL

FIRING ORDERS

See Figures 77 through 79.

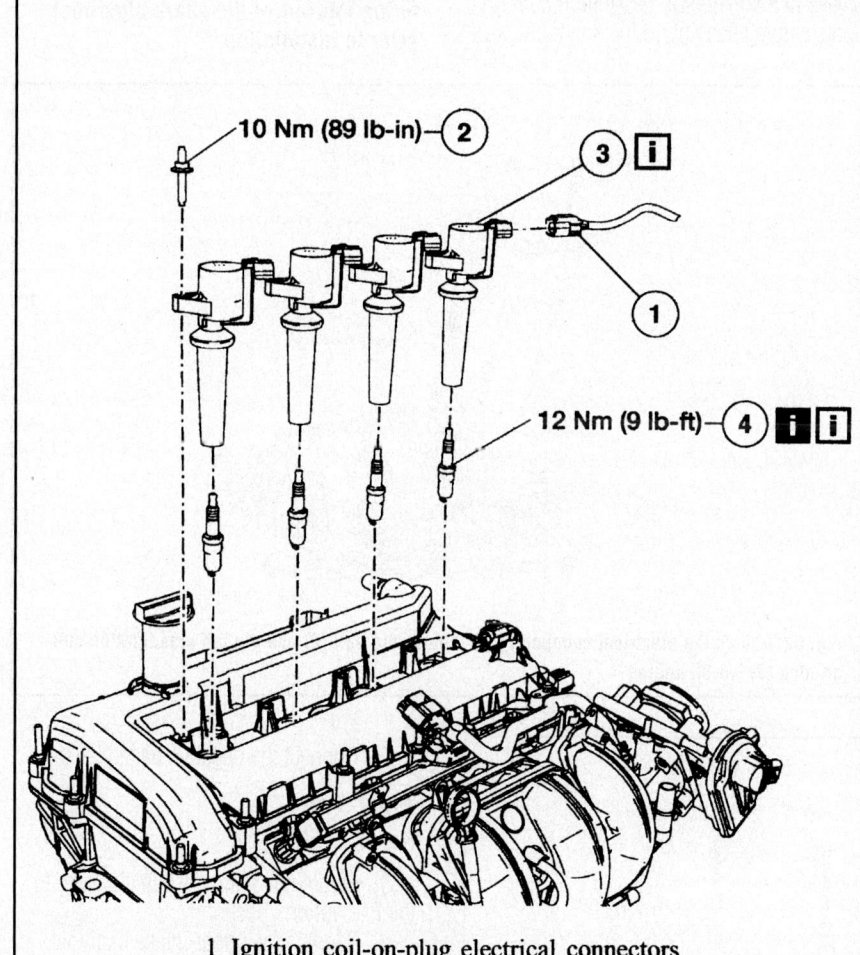

1 Ignition coil-on-plug electrical connectors
2 Ignition coil-to-valve cover bolts
3 Ignition coils
4 Spark plugs

67197-ESCA-G61

Fig. 77 Coil and spark plug arrangement—2.3L engine

IGNITION SYSTEM

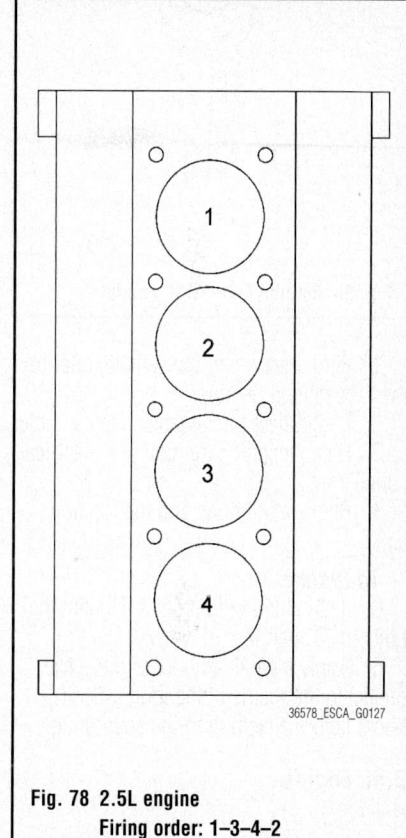

36578_ESCA_G0127

Fig. 78 2.5L engine
Firing order: 1–3–4–2

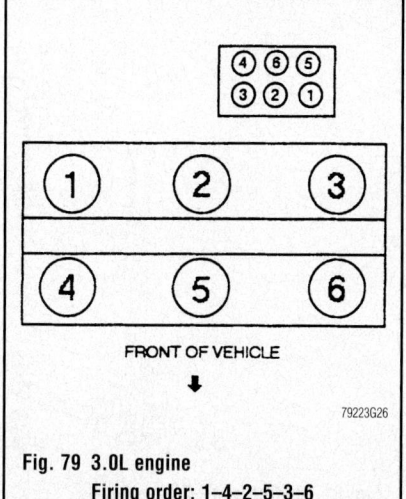

FRONT OF VEHICLE

79223G26

Fig. 79 3.0L engine
Firing order: 1–4–2–5–3–6

IGNITION COIL

REMOVAL & INSTALLATION

2.3L Engine

See Figure 80.

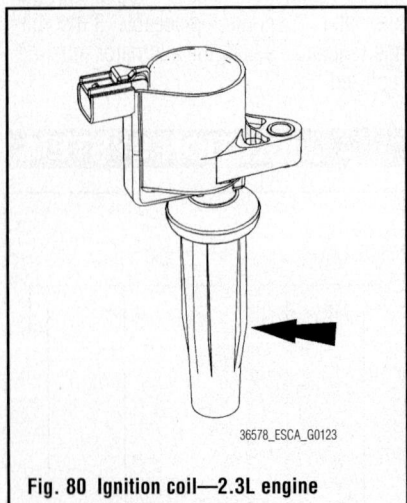

36578_ESCA_G0123

Fig. 80 Ignition coil—2.3L engine

1. Before servicing the vehicle, refer to the Precautions Section.
2. Disconnect the negative battery cable.
3. Disconnect the ignition coil electrical connectors.
4. Remove the bolts and the ignition coils.

To install:

5. Install the ignition coils. Tighten the bolts to 71 inch lbs. (8 Nm).
6. Apply a small amount of dielectric grease to the inside of the ignition coil boots before attaching to the spark plugs.

2.5L Engine

See Figure 81.

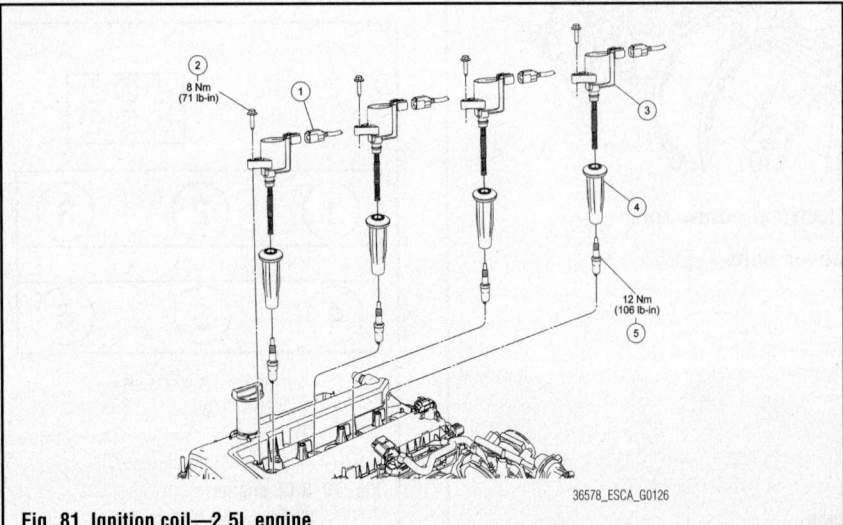

36578_ESCA_G0126

Fig. 81 Ignition coil—2.5L engine

1. Before servicing the vehicle, refer to the Precautions Section.
2. Disconnect the negative battery cable.

➡ **When removing the ignition coil-on-plugs, a slight twisting motion will break the seal and ease removal.**

3. Disconnect the 4 ignition coil electrical connectors.
4. Remove the bolts and the ignition coils.

➡ **Inspect the coil seals for rips, nicks or tears. Remove and discard any damaged coil seals.**

To install:

5. Install the ignition coils. Tighten the bolts to 71 inch lbs. (8 Nm).
6. Apply a small amount of dielectric grease to the inside of the ignition coil boots before attaching to the spark plugs.

3.0L Engine

Left Side

See Figure 82.

1. Before servicing the vehicle, refer to the Precautions Section.
2. Disconnect the negative battery cable.
3. Disconnect the ignition coil-on-plug electrical connector.
4. Remove the bolt, then remove the coil-on-plug.

To install:

5. Install the coil-on-plug. Tighten the coil-on-plug bolt to 62 inch lbs. (7 Nm).
6. Attach the electrical connector.

➡ **Apply a light film of silicone brake caliper grease and dielectric compound to the interior of the spark plug boot prior to installation.**

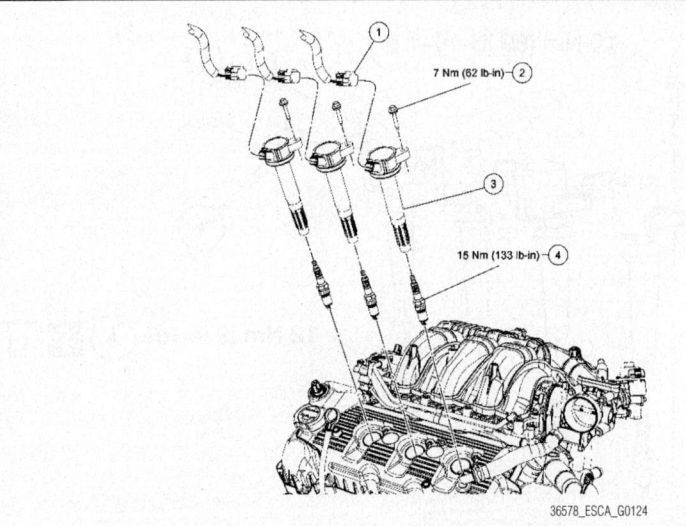

36578_ESCA_G0124

Fig. 82 Detach the electrical connector (1), remove the bolt (2) and the left side ignition coil-on-plug (3)—3.0L engine

7. Connect the negative battery cable.

Right Side

See Figure 83.

1. Before servicing the vehicle, refer to the Precautions Section.
2. Remove the upper intake manifold. Refer to Upper Intake Manifold in the Engine Mechanical Section.
3. Disconnect the electrical connector.
4. Remove the bolt, then remove the coil-on-plug.

To install:

5. Install the coil-on-plug. Tighten the coil-on-plug bolt to 62 inch lbs. (7 Nm).

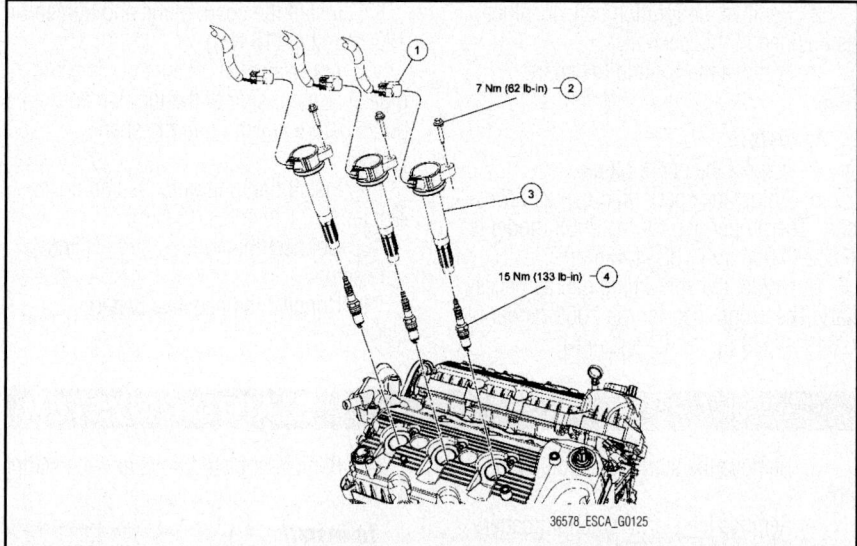

Fig. 83 View of the right side ignition coil-on-plug (3), electrical connector (1) and bolt (2)—3.0L engine

6. Attach the electrical connector.

➡ **Apply a light film of silicone brake caliper grease and dielectric compound to the interior of the spark plug boot prior to installation.**

7. Install the upper intake manifold.
8. Connect the negative battery cable.

IGNITION TIMING

ADJUSTMENT

The ignition timing is controlled by the Powertrain Control Module (PCM). No adjustment is necessary or possible.

SPARK PLUGS

REMOVAL & INSTALLATION

2.3L Engine

See Figure 84.

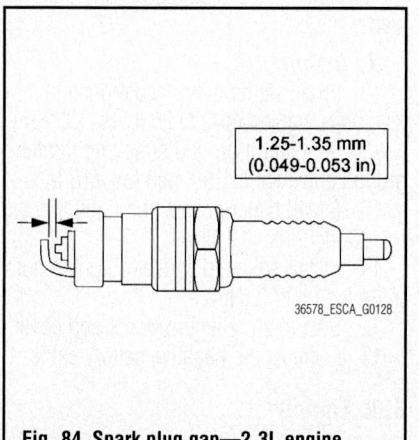

Fig. 84 Spark plug gap—2.3L engine

1. Before servicing the vehicle, refer to the Precautions Section.
2. Disconnect the negative battery cable.
3. Disconnect the ignition coil electrical connectors.
4. Remove the bolts and the ignition coils.

➡ **Use compressed air to remove any foreign material in the spark plug well before removing the spark plugs.**

5. Remove the spark plugs.

To install:
6. Inspect the spark plugs.
7. Adjust the spark plug gap as necessary. The proper gap is 0.049–0.053 in. (1.25–1.35mm).
8. Install the spark plugs and tighten to 106 inch lbs. (12 Nm).
9. Apply a small amount of dielectric grease to the inside of the ignition coil boots before attaching to the spark plugs.
10. Install the ignition coils and bolts. Tighten to 71 inch lbs. (8 Nm).
11. Connect the ignition coil electrical connectors.
12. Connect the negative battery cable.

2.5L Engine

See Figure 85.

1. Before servicing the vehicle, refer to the Precautions Section.
2. Disconnect the negative battery cable.
3. Disconnect the ignition coil electrical connectors.

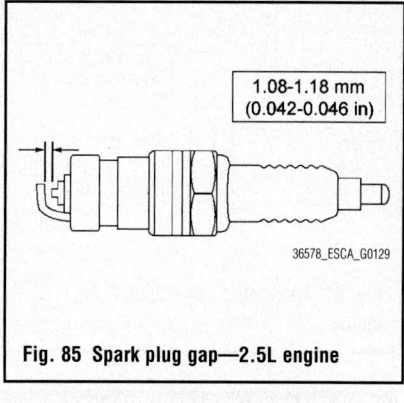

Fig. 85 Spark plug gap—2.5L engine

4. Remove the bolts and the ignition coils.

➡ **Use compressed air to remove any foreign material in the spark plug well before removing the spark plugs.**

5. Remove the spark plugs.

To install:
6. Inspect the spark plugs.
7. Adjust the spark plug gap as necessary. The proper gap is 0.042–0.046 in. (1.08–1.18mm).
8. Install the spark plugs and tighten to 106 inch lbs. (12 Nm).
9. Apply a small amount of dielectric grease to the inside of the ignition coil boots before attaching to the spark plugs.
10. Install the ignition coils and bolts. Tighten to 71 inch lbs. (8 Nm).
11. Connect the ignition coil electrical connectors.
12. Connect the negative battery cable.

3.0L Engine

See Figures 86 and 87.

1. Before servicing the vehicle, refer to the Precautions Section.

➡ **The upper intake manifold must be removed to access the RH spark plugs only.**

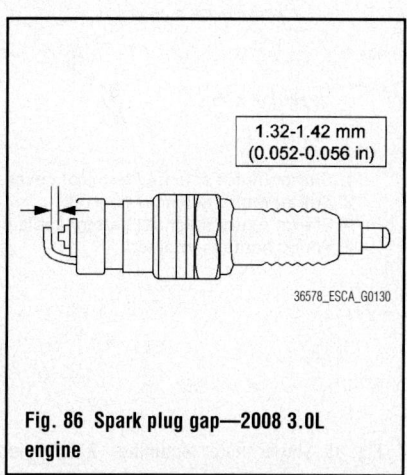

Fig. 86 Spark plug gap—2008 3.0L engine

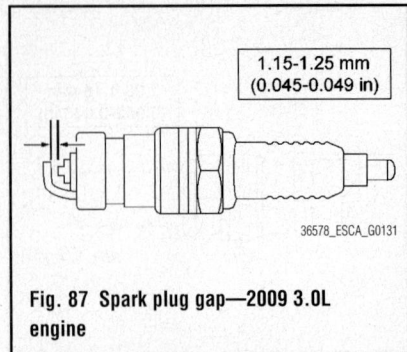

Fig. 87 Spark plug gap—2009 3.0L engine

2. Remove the ignition coil-on-plugs, as outlined in this section.

3. Remove the LH and RH spark plugs.

To install:

4. Inspect the spark plugs.

5. Adjust the spark plug gap as necessary. The proper gap for the 2008 model is 0.052–0.056 in. (1.32–1.42mm).

6. Adjust the spark plug gap as necessary. The proper gap for the 2009 model is 0.045–0.049 in. (1.32–1.42mm).

7. Install the spark plugs and tighten to 133 inch lbs. (15 Nm).

8. Apply a small amount of dielectric grease to the inside of the ignition coil boots before attaching to the spark plugs.

9. Install the ignition coils and bolts. Tighten to 71 inch lbs. (8 Nm).

10. Connect the ignition coil electrical connectors.

11. Connect the negative battery cable.

ENGINE ELECTRICAL

STARTING SYSTEM

STARTER

REMOVAL & INSTALLATION

2.3L Engine

See Figure 88.

1. With the vehicle in NEUTRAL, position it on a hoist.

2. Disconnect the negative battery cable.

3. Remove the starter solenoid wire nut.

4. Remove the starter solenoid battery cable nut and disconnect the starter motor solenoid terminal cover and cables.

5. Disconnect the wiring harness retainer and position aside the wiring harness.

6. Remove the ground strap nut and position aside the strap.

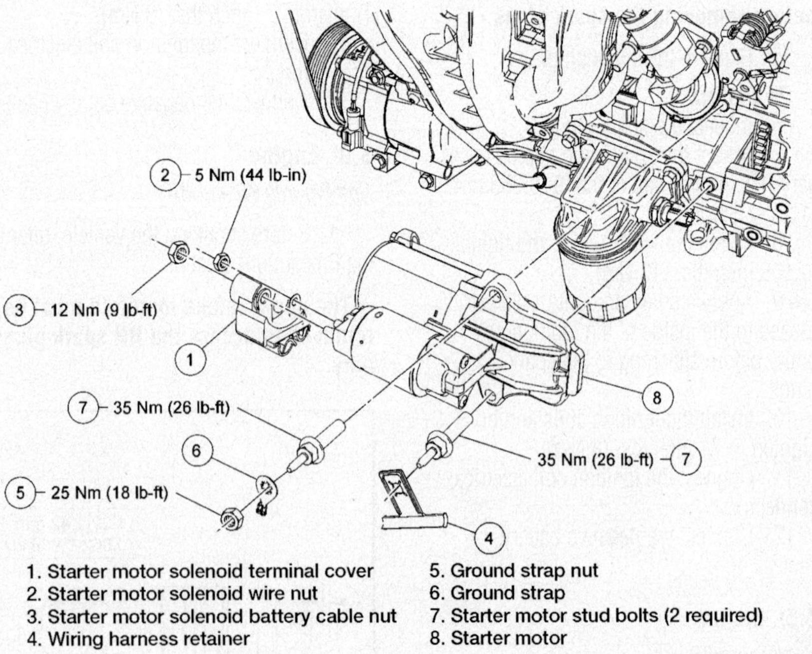

7. Remove the stud bolts and the starter motor.

To install:

8. Install starter motor and mounting stud bolts, tighten bolts to 26 ft. lbs. (35 Nm).

9. Reposition ground strap and tighten ground strap nut to 18 ft. lbs. (25 Nm).

10. Install battery cable and tighten nut to 106 inch lbs. (12 Nm).

11. Install solenoid wire and tighten nut to 44 inch lbs. (5 Nm).

12. Secure all retainers, wires and cover.

13. Connect the negative battery cable.

2.5L Engine

See Figure 89.

1. With the vehicle in NEUTRAL, position it on a hoist.

2. Disconnect the battery ground cable.

3. Remove the 5 bolts, the pin-type retainer and the RH splash shield.

4. Remove the starter solenoid wire nut.

5. Remove the starter solenoid battery cable nut and disconnect the starter motor solenoid terminal cover and cables.

6. Remove the ground wire nut and position aside the ground wire.

7. Remove the 2 stud bolts and the starter motor.

To install:

8. Install starter motor and mounting stud bolts, tighten bolts to 26 ft. lbs. (35 Nm).

9. Reposition ground strap and tighten ground strap nut to 159 inch lbs. (18 Nm).

10. Install battery cable and tighten nut to 106 inch lbs. (12 Nm).

11. Install solenoid wire and tighten nut to 44 inch lbs. (5 Nm).

12. Secure all retainers, wires and cover.

13. Connect the negative battery cable.

3.0L Engine

See Figure 90.

② — 5 Nm (44 lb-in)

③ — 12 Nm (9 lb-ft)

⑦ — 35 Nm (26 lb-ft)

⑤ — 25 Nm (18 lb-ft)

35 Nm (26 lb-ft) — ⑦

1. Starter motor solenoid terminal cover
2. Starter motor solenoid wire nut
3. Starter motor solenoid battery cable nut
4. Wiring harness retainer
5. Ground strap nut
6. Ground strap
7. Starter motor stud bolts (2 required)
8. Starter motor

Fig. 88 Starter motor mounting—2.3L engine

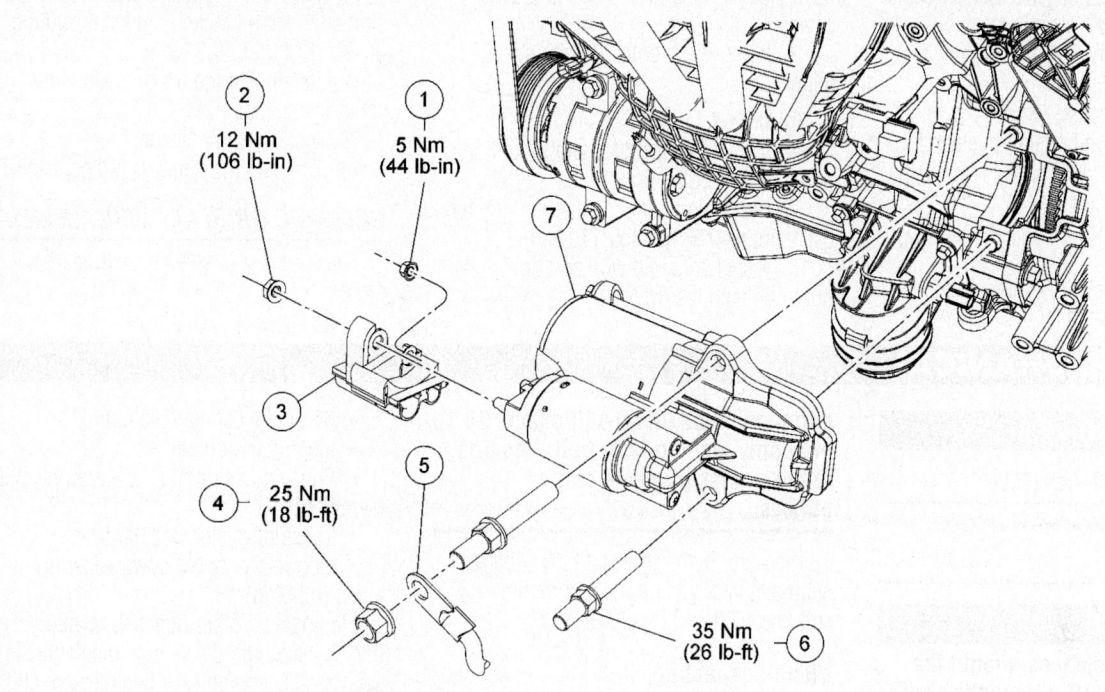

1. Starter motor solenoid wire nut
2. Starter motor solenoid battery cable nut
3. Starter motor solenoid terminal cover
4. Ground wire nut
5. Ground wire
6. Starter motor stud bolt (2 required)
7. Starter motor

36578_ESCA_G0134

Fig. 89 Starter motor mounting—2.5L engine

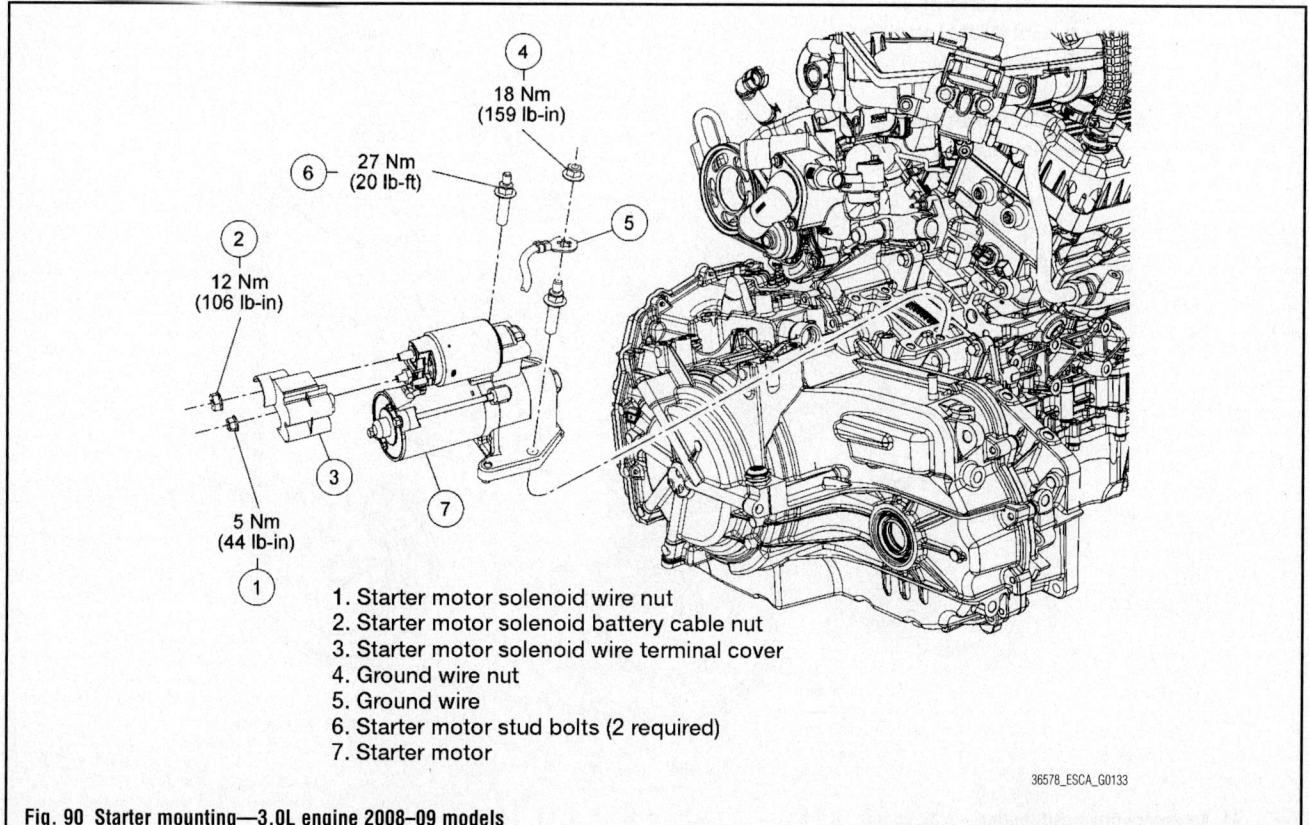

1. Starter motor solenoid wire nut
2. Starter motor solenoid battery cable nut
3. Starter motor solenoid wire terminal cover
4. Ground wire nut
5. Ground wire
6. Starter motor stud bolts (2 required)
7. Starter motor

36578_ESCA_G0133

Fig. 90 Starter mounting—3.0L engine 2008–09 models

1. Disconnect the negative battery cable.
2. Remove the air cleaner.
3. Disconnect the transmission shift cable-to-manual lever.
4. For 2008 models, remove the transmission cable bracket bolts and detach the wire harness retainer and position aside the transmission cable and bracket.
5. Remove the starter motor solenoid wire nut.
6. Remove the starter motor solenoid battery cable nut and position aside the cables.
7. Remove the bolts and the starter motor.

To install:

8. Install starter motor and mounting bolts, tighten bolts to 20 ft. lbs. (27 Nm).
9. Reposition battery cable and tighten cable nut to 106 inch lbs. (12 Nm).
10. Install solenoid wire and tighten nut to 44 inch lbs. (5 Nm).
11. For 2008 models, install transmission shift cable bracket, tighten mounting bolts to17 ft. lbs. (23 Nm).
12. Reconnect the transmission shift cable-to-manual lever.
13. Install the air cleaner.
14. Connect the negative battery cable.

SOLENOID OR RELAY REPLACEMENT

The solenoid is serviced with starter motor.

ENGINE MECHANICAL

ACCESSORY DRIVE BELTS

ACCESSORY BELT ROUTING

See Figures 91 through 94.

INSPECTION

❋❋ WARNING

Under no circumstances should the accessory drive belt, tensioner or pulleys be lubricated as potential damage to the belt material and tensioner damping mechanism will occur. Do not apply any fluids or belt dressing to the accessory drive belt or pulleys.

The water pump drive belt is on back of engine. It is driven off the rear cam pulley and doesn't have any adjustments.

Visual Inspection

Visually inspect the belt for obvious signs of mechanical damage:
• Drive belt cracking/chunking/wear
• Belt/pulley contamination
• Incorrectly routed belt
• Pulley misalignment or excessive pulley runout
• Loose or mislocated hardware
• Incorrectly routed power steering tubes (rubbing)

Eliminate all other non-belt related noises that could cause belt misdiagnosis, such as A/C compressor engagement chirp, power steering cavitations at low temperatures, variable camshaft timing (VCT) tick or alternator whine.

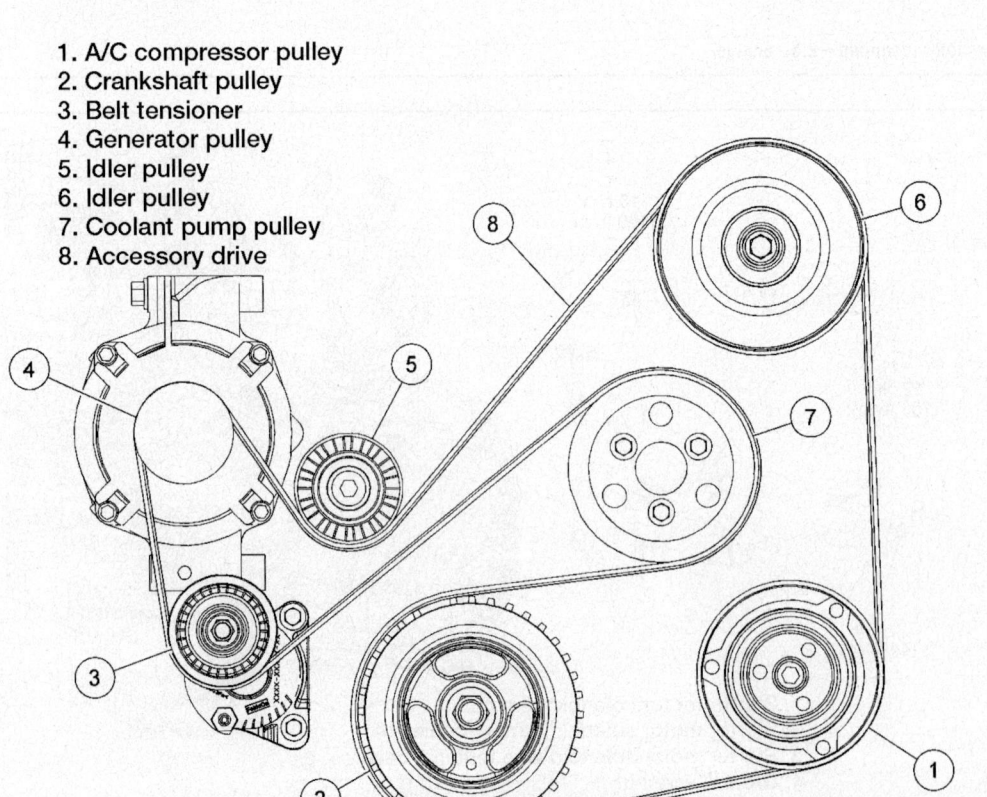

1. A/C compressor pulley
2. Crankshaft pulley
3. Belt tensioner
4. Generator pulley
5. Idler pulley
6. Idler pulley
7. Coolant pump pulley
8. Accessory drive

36578_ESCA_G0135

Fig. 91 Accessory drive belt routing—2.3L engine

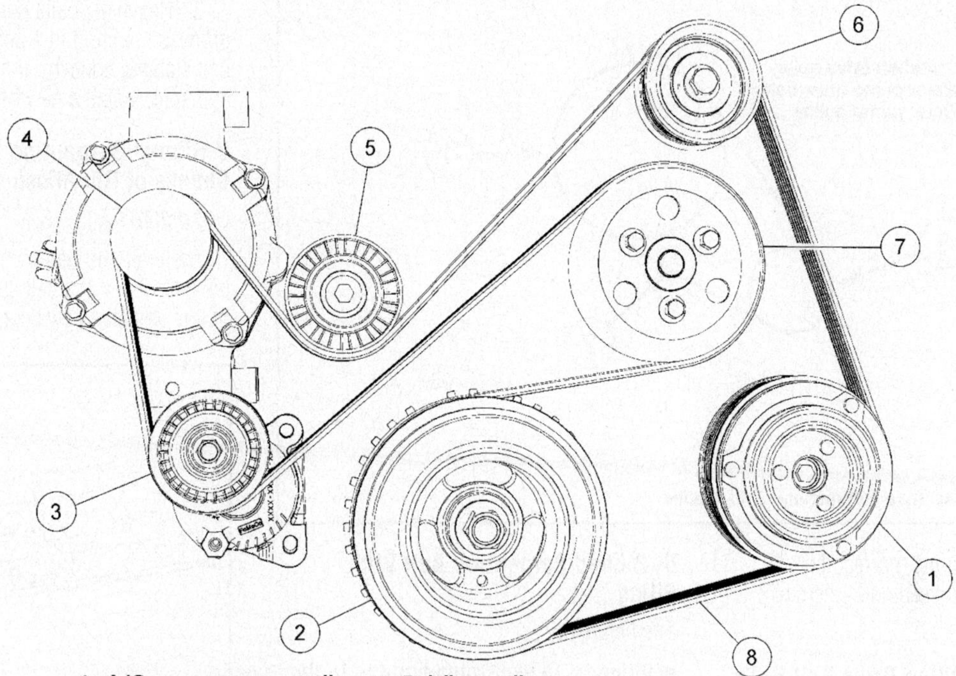

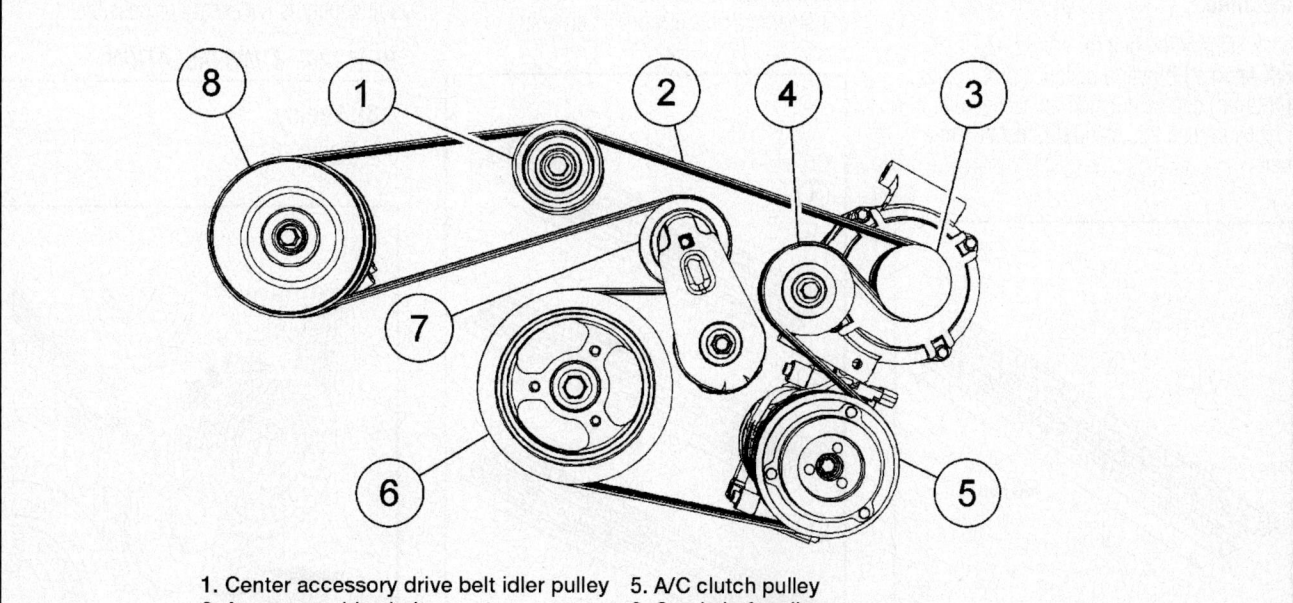

1. A/C compressor pulley
2. Crankshaft pulley
3. Belt tensioner
4. Generator pulley
5. Idler pulley
6. Idler pulley
7. Coolant pump pulley
8. Accessory drive belt

36578_ESCA_G0138

Fig. 92 Accessory drive belt routing—2.5L engine

1. Center accessory drive belt idler pulley
2. Accessory drive belt
3. Generator pulley
4. LH accessory drive belt idler pulley
5. A/C clutch pulley
6. Crankshaft pulley
7. Accessory drive belt tensioner
8. RH accessory drive belt idler pulley and bracket

36578_ESCA_G0136

Fig. 93 Accessory drive belt routing 2008–09—3.0L engine

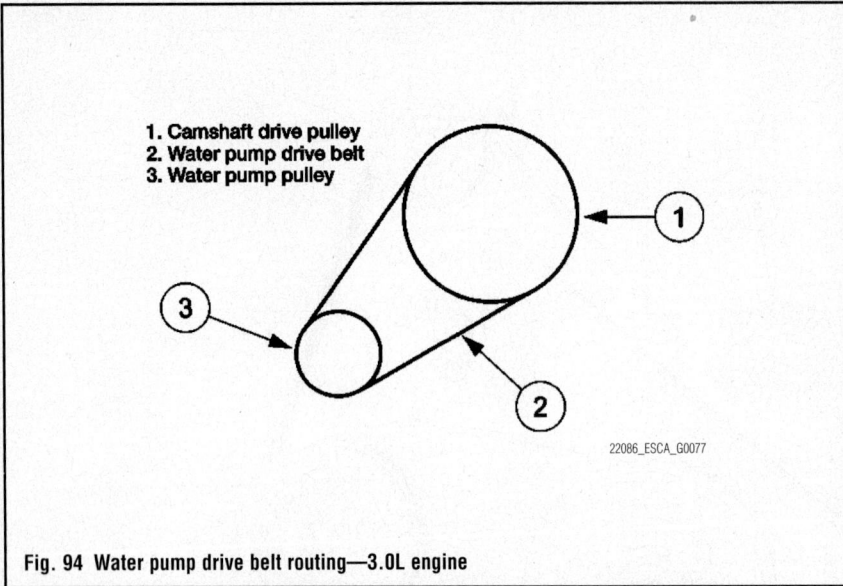

1. Camshaft drive pulley
2. Water pump drive belt
3. Water pump pulley

22086_ESCA_G0077

Fig. 94 Water pump drive belt routing—3.0L engine

If a concern is found, correct the condition before proceeding to the next section.

V-Ribbed Serpentine Drive Belt With Cracks Across Ribs

See Figure 95.

➡**Up to 15 cracks in a rib over a distance of 4 inches (100mm) can be considered acceptable. If damage exceeds the acceptable limit or any chunks are found to be missing from the ribs, a new belt must be installed.**

1. Check the belt for cracks. Up to 15 cracks in a rib over a distance of 4 inches (100mm) can be considered acceptable. If cracks exceed this standard, install a new belt.

V- Ribbed Serpentine Belt With Piling

See Figure 96.

➡**Piling is an excessive buildup in the V-grooves of the belt.**

The condition of the V-ribbed drive belt should be compared against the illustration and appropriate action taken.

1. Small scattered deposits of rubber material. This is not a concern, therefore, installation of a new belt is not required.
2. Longer deposit areas building up to 50 percent of the rib height. This is not considered a concern but it can result in

excessive noise. If noise is apparent, install a new belt.

3. Heavy deposits building up along the grooves resulting in a possible noise and belt stability concern. If heavy deposits are apparent, install a new belt.

V-Ribbed Serpentine Belt With Chunks of Rib Missing

See Figure 97.

There should be no chunks missing from the belt ribs. If the belt shows any evidence of this, install a new accessory drive belt.

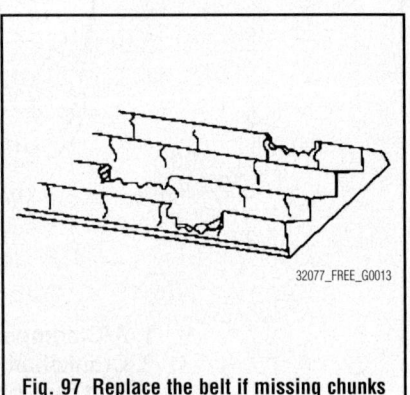

32077_FREE_G0013

Fig. 97 Replace the belt if missing chunks are found during inspection

ADJUSTMENT

The belts used on these vehicle are equipped with automatic (spring load) tensioners which maintain tension. No adjustment is necessary or possible.

REMOVAL & INSTALLATION

2.3L Engine

See Figure 98.

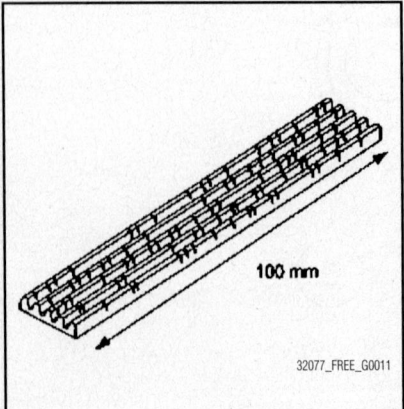

100 mm

32077_FREE_G0011

Fig. 95 Up to 15 cracks in a rib over a distance of 4 inches (100mm) can be considered acceptable. If cracks exceed this standard, install a new belt

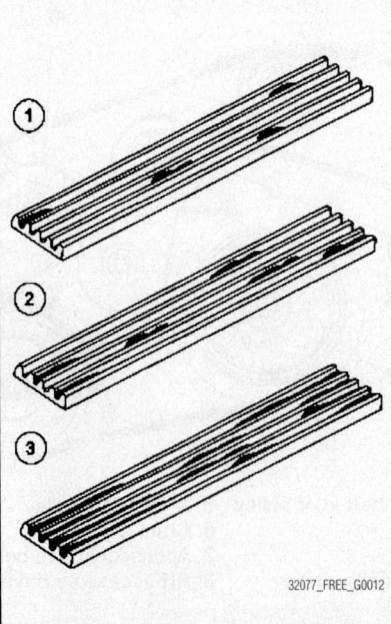

32077_FREE_G0012

Fig. 96 Compare the condition of the belt with the accompanying text

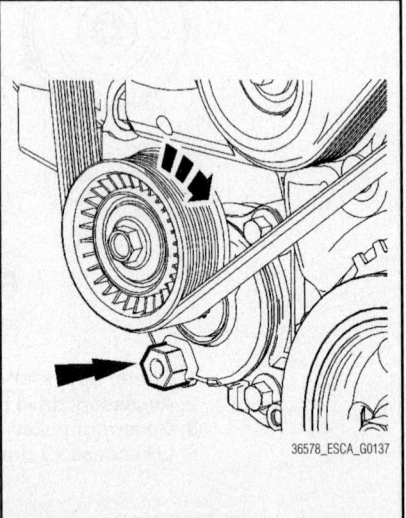

36578_ESCA_G0137

Fig. 98 Using the hex feature, rotate the accessory drive belt tensioner clockwise

1. Raise and safely support the vehicle..

2. Remove the pin-type retainer, 5 bolts and the RH splash shield.

3. Using the hex feature, rotate the accessory drive belt tensioner clockwise and remove the accessory drive belt from the coolant pump pulley.

To install:

4. Install the accessory drive belt. Make sure it is routed correctly.

5. Install the pin-type retainer, RH splash shield and tighten the retaining bolts to 80 inch lbs. (9 Nm).

3.0L Engine

See Figure 93.

1. With the vehicle in NEUTRAL, position it on a hoist.

2. Remove the pin-type retainer, 5 bolts and the RH lower splash shield.

3. Using a suitable belt tensioner release tool, rotate the accessory drive belt tensioner counterclockwise and remove the accessory drive belt.

4. Installation is the reverse of the removal procedure. Make sure the belt is properly routed.

Water Pump Belt

See Figures 99 through 101.

1. With the vehicle in NEUTRAL, position it on a hoist.

2. Position the stretchy belt remover under the coolant pump belt.

➡ **Feed the stretchy belt remover on to the camshaft coolant pump pulley approximately 90 degrees.**

➡ **It a stretchy belt remover is not available simply cut the belt to remove.**

3. With the help of an assistant, turn the crankshaft clockwise and feed the stretchy belt remover evenly on the camshaft coolant pump pulley as shown.

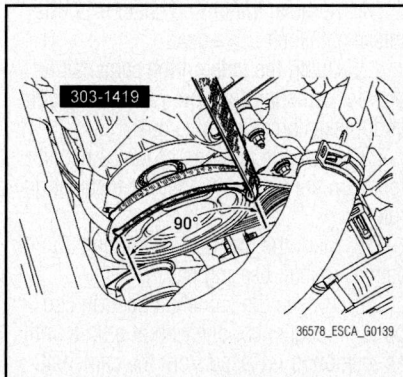

Fig. 99 Stretchy belt remover shown

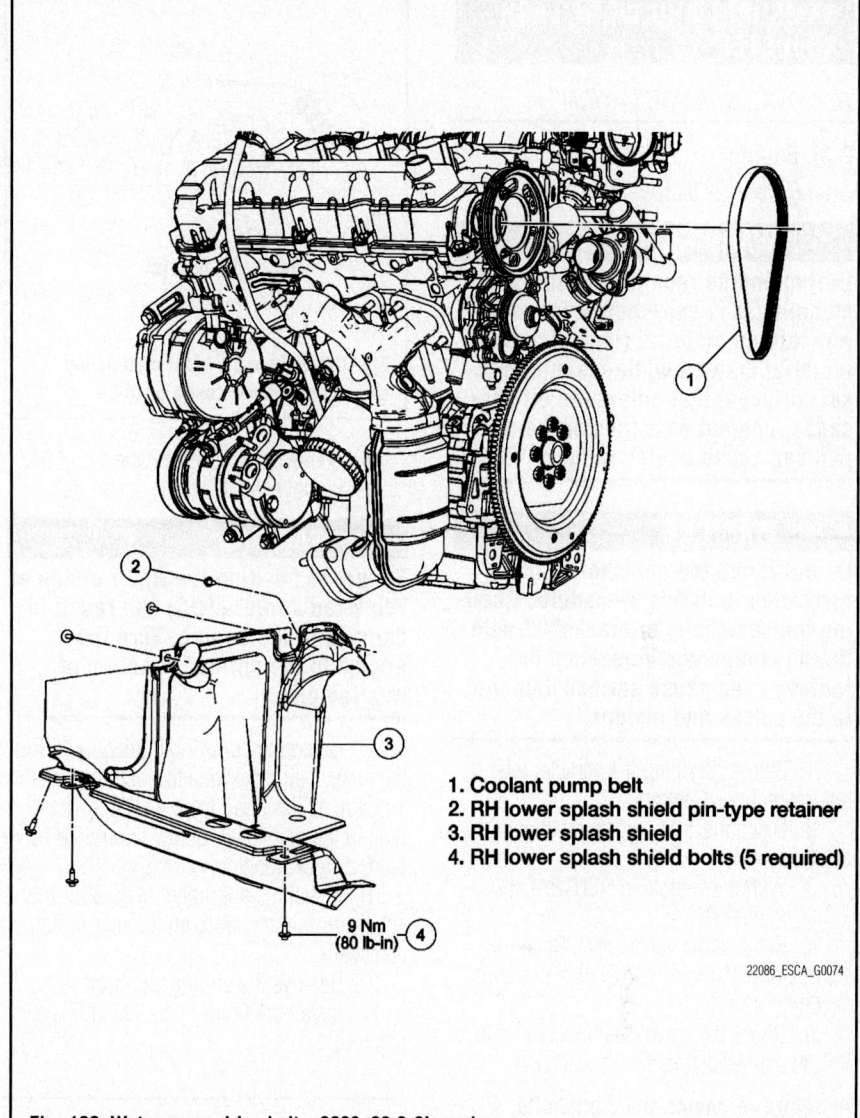

1. Coolant pump belt
2. RH lower splash shield pin-type retainer
3. RH lower splash shield
4. RH lower splash shield bolts (5 required)

9 Nm
(80 lb-in)

22086_ESCA_G0074

Fig. 100 Water pump drive belt—2008–09 3.0L engine

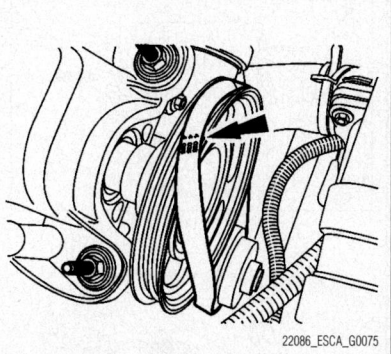

22086_ESCA_G0075

Fig. 101 Water pump belt position for installation

4. Fold the Stretchy Belt Remover over the top of the coolant pump belt.

5. In one quick motion, pull the stretchy belt remover up and toward the RH front of the vehicle removing the coolant pump belt.

To install:

6. Install the coolant pump belt on the coolant pump pulley and position it on the camshaft pulley.

➡ **This belt does not have any adjustments.**

❊❊ WARNING

Do not use any screwdrivers, pliers or other metal objects that could cause damage to the belt or camshaft pulley while installing the belt.

7. Remove the pin-type retainer, 5 bolts and the RH lower splash shield. Tighten the bolts to 80 inch lbs. (9 Nm).

8. Rotate the crankshaft clockwise to seat the coolant pump belt on the camshaft pulley.

CAMSHAFT AND VALVE LASH ADJUSTER

REMOVAL & INSTALLATION

2.3L Engine

See Figures 102 through 107.

> ✳✳ **WARNING**
>
> During engine repair procedures, cleanliness is extremely important. Any foreign material (including any material created while cleaning gasket surfaces) that enters the oil passages, coolant passages or the oil pan can cause engine failure.

> ✳✳ **WARNING**
>
> Do not rotate the camshafts unless instructed to in this procedure. Rotating the camshafts or crankshaft with timing components loosened or removed can cause serious damage to the valves and pistons.

1. Before servicing the vehicle, refer to the Precautions Section.
2. Disconnect the negative battery cable.
3. With the vehicle in NEUTRAL, position it on a hoist.
4. Remove the valve cover. Refer to Valve Cover Removal & Installation in this section.
5. Check the valve clearance. Refer to Valve Lash Adjustment in this section.

➡ Before removing the camshafts, measure the clearance of each valve at base circle, with the lobe pointed away from the tappet. Failure to measure all clearances prior to removing the camshafts will necessitate repeated removal and installation and wasted labor time.

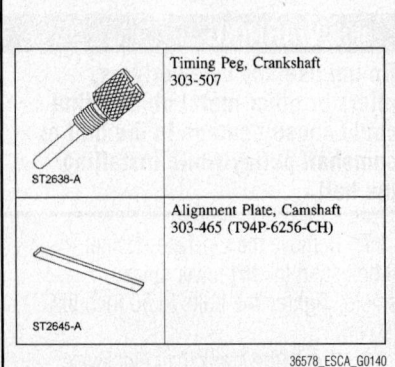

	Timing Peg, Crankshaft 303-507
ST2638-A	
	Alignment Plate, Camshaft 303-465 (T94P-6256-CH)
ST2645-A	

36578_ESCA_G0140

Fig. 102 Special tools required

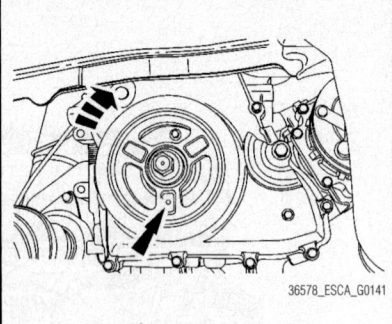

36578_ESCA_G0141

Fig. 103 Hole in the crankshaft pulley should be in the 6 o'clock position

6. Remove the front RH wheel and tire.
7. Remove the accessory drive belt.

> ✳✳ **WARNING**
>
> Failure to position the No. 1 piston at Top Dead Center (TDC) can result in damage to the engine. Turn the engine in the normal direction of rotation only.

8. Using the crankshaft pulley bolt, turn the crankshaft clockwise to position the No. 1 piston at Top Dead Center (TDC). The hole in the crankshaft pulley should be in the 6 o'clock position.
9. Install the alignment plate 303-465 special tool in the slots on the rear of both camshafts.
10. Remove the engine plug bolt.
11. Install the timing peg 303-507 special tool.

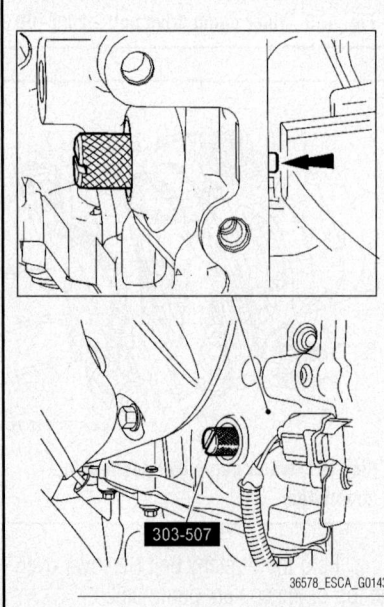

303-507

36578_ESCA_G0143

Fig. 104 Timing peg 303-507 special tool installed

➡ The timing peg special tool will contact the crankshaft and prevent it from turning past top dead center (TDC). However, the crankshaft can still be rotated in the counterclockwise direction. The crankshaft must remain at the TDC position during the camshaft removal and installation.

12. Install a standard 0.23 inch (6 mm) x 0.7 inch (18 mm) bolt through the crankshaft pulley and thread it into the front cover.
13. Remove the lower front cover timing hole plug from the engine front cover.
14. Remove the upper front cover timing hole plug from the engine front cover.
15. Reposition the alignment plate 303-465 special tool to the slot on the rear of the intake camshaft only.

➡ Releasing the ratcheting mechanism in the timing chain tensioner allows the plunger to collapse and create slack in the timing chain. Installing an 1.18 inch (M6 x 30 mm) bolt into the upper front cover timing hole will hold the tensioner arm in a retracted position and allow enough slack in the timing chain for removal of the exhaust camshaft gear.

16. Using a small pick tool, unlock the chain tensioner ratchet through the lower front cover timing hole.
17. Using the flats of the camshaft, have an assistant rotate the exhaust camshaft clockwise to collapse the timing chain tensioner plunger.
18. Insert an 1.18 inch (M6 x 30 mm) bolt into the upper front cover timing hole to hold the tensioner arm in the retracted position.
19. Remove the alignment plate 303-465 special tool.
20. Using the flats on the camshaft to prevent camshaft rotation, remove the bolt and exhaust camshaft drive gear.
21. Remove the timing chain from the intake camshaft drive gear.
22. Using the flats on the camshaft to prevent camshaft rotation, remove the bolt and intake camshaft drive gear.
23. Mark the position of the camshaft lobes on the No. 1 cylinder for installation reference.
24. Mark the location and orientation of each camshaft bearing cap.
25. Loosen the camshaft bearing cap bolts, in sequence, one turn at a time until all tension is released from the camshaft bearing caps.

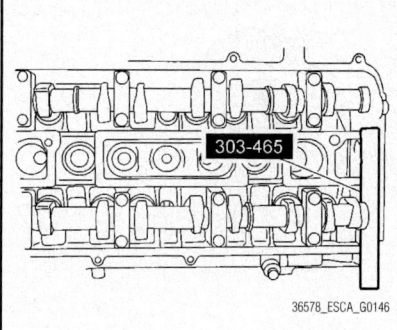

Fig. 105 Reposition the alignment plate 303-465 special tool to the slot on the rear of the intake camshaft

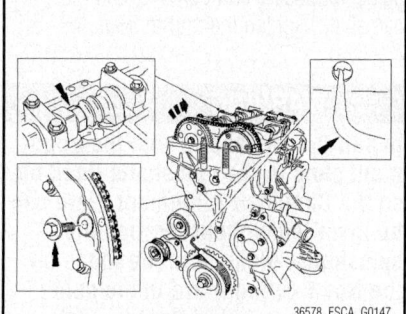

Fig. 106 Using a small pick tool, unlock the chain tensioner ratchet through the lower front cover timing hole

26. Remove the bolts and the camshaft bearing caps.
27. Remove the camshafts.

To install:

> ❊❊ **WARNING**
>
> **Install the camshafts with the alignment slots in the camshafts lined up so the Camshaft Alignment Plate can be installed without rotating the camshafts. Make sure the lobes on the No. 1 cylinder are in the same position as noted in the removal procedure. Rotating the camshafts when the timing chain is removed, or installing the camshafts 180 degrees out of position can cause severe damage to the valves and pistons.**

28. Lubricate the camshaft journals and bearing caps with clean engine oil.
29. Install the camshafts and bearing caps in their original location and orientation. Tighten the bearing caps in the sequence shown in 3 stages:
  - Stage 1: Tighten the camshaft bearing cap bolts one turn at a time, until finger tight.

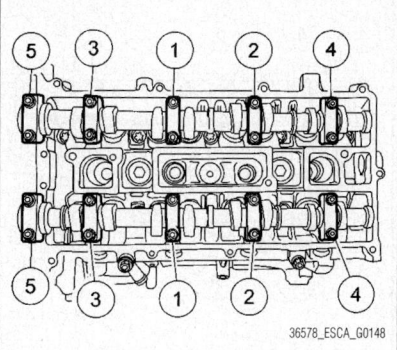

Fig. 107 Camshaft bearing cap tightening sequence

  - Stage 2: Tighten to 62 inch lbs. (7 Nm).
  - Stage 3: Tighten to 12 ft. lbs. (16 Nm).
30. Install the alignment plate 303-465 special tool.
31. Install the intake camshaft drive gear and hand-tighten the bolt.
32. Install the timing chain on the intake camshaft drive gear.

➡ **The timing chain must be correctly engaged on the teeth of the crankshaft timing sprocket and the intake camshaft drive gear in order to install the exhaust camshaft drive gear onto the exhaust camshaft.**

33. Position the exhaust camshaft drive gear in the timing chain and install the gear and bolt on the exhaust camshaft.
34. Hand-tighten the bolt.

➡ **Releasing the tensioner arm will remove the slack from the timing chain release.**

35. Remove the M6 x 30 mm bolt from the upper front cover timing hole to release the tensioner arm.

➡ **The special tool 303-465 is for camshaft alignment only. Using this tool to prevent engine rotation can result in engine damage.**

36. Using the flats on the camshafts to prevent camshaft rotation, tighten the bolts to 53 ft. lbs. (72 Nm).
37. Remove the alignment plate 303-465 special tool.
38. Remove the 0.23 inch (6 mm) x 0.7 inch (18 mm) bolt.
39. Remove the timing peg special tool.
40. Install the upper front cover timing hole plug and tighten to 89 inch lbs. (10 Nm).

41. Apply silicone gasket and sealant to the threads of the lower front cover timing hole plug.
42. Install the plug and tighten to 9 ft. lbs. (12 Nm).
43. Install the engine plug bolt and tighten to 15 ft. lbs. (20 Nm).
44. Install the accessory drive belt.
45. Install the front RH wheel and tire.
46. Install the valve cover.
47. Connect the negative battery cable.

2.5L Engine

See Figures 102, 104 through 110.

> ❊❊ **WARNING**
>
> **During engine repair procedures, cleanliness is extremely important. Any foreign material (including any material created while cleaning gasket surfaces) that enters the oil passages, coolant passages or the oil pan can cause engine failure.**

> ❊❊ **WARNING**
>
> **Do not rotate the camshafts unless instructed to in this procedure. Rotating the camshafts or crankshaft with timing components loosened or removed can cause serious damage to the valves and pistons.**

1. Before servicing the vehicle, refer to the Precautions Section.
2. Disconnect the negative battery cable.
3. With the vehicle in NEUTRAL, position it on a hoist.
4. Remove the valve cover. Refer to Valve Cover Removal & Installation in this section.
5. Check the valve clearance. Refer to Valve Lash Adjustment in this section.

➡ **Before removing the camshafts, measure the clearance of each valve at base circle, with the lobe pointed away from the tappet. Failure to measure all clearances prior to removing the camshafts will necessitate repeated removal and installation and wasted labor time.**

6. Remove the front RH wheel and tire.
7. Remove the accessory drive belt.

> ❊❊ **WARNING**
>
> **Failure to position the No. 1 piston at Top Dead Center (TDC) can result in damage to the engine. Turn the engine in the normal direction of rotation only.**

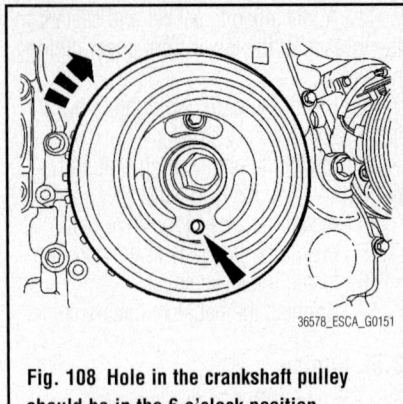

Fig. 108 Hole in the crankshaft pulley should be in the 6 o'clock position

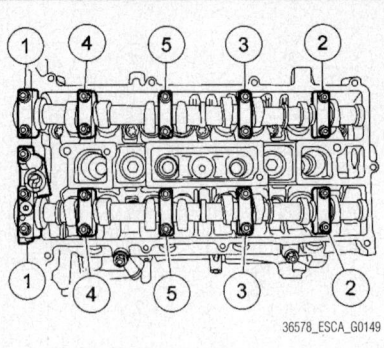

Fig. 109 Camshaft bearing cap loosening sequence

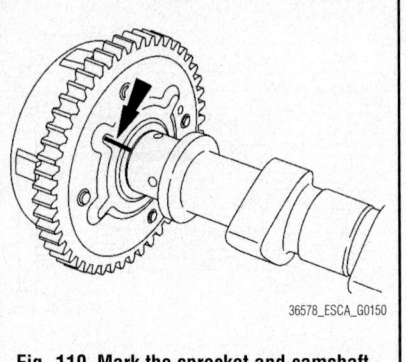

Fig. 110 Mark the sprocket and camshaft for reference during installation

8. Using the crankshaft pulley bolt, turn the crankshaft clockwise to position the No. 1 piston at Top Dead Center (TDC). The hole in the crankshaft pulley should be in the 6 o'clock position.

9. Install the alignment plate 303-465 special tool in the slots on the rear of both camshafts.

10. Remove the engine plug bolt.

11. Install the timing peg 303-507 special tool.

➡️The timing peg special tool will contact the crankshaft and prevent it from turning past top dead center (TDC). However, the crankshaft can still be rotated in the counterclockwise direction. The crankshaft must remain at the TDC position during the camshaft removal and installation.

12. Install a standard 0.23 inch (6 mm) x 0.7 inch (18 mm) bolt through the crankshaft pulley and thread it into the front cover.

13. Remove the lower front cover timing hole plug from the engine front cover.

14. Remove the upper front cover timing hole plug from the engine front cover.

15. Reposition the alignment plate 303-465 special tool to the slot on the rear of the intake camshaft only.

➡️Releasing the ratcheting mechanism in the timing chain tensioner allows the plunger to collapse and create slack in the timing chain. Installing an 1.18 inch (M6 x 30 mm) bolt into the upper front cover timing hole will hold the tensioner arm in a retracted position and allow enough slack in the timing chain for removal of the exhaust camshaft gear.

16. Using a small pick tool, unlock the chain tensioner ratchet through the lower front cover timing hole.

17. Using the flats of the camshaft, have an assistant rotate the exhaust camshaft clockwise to collapse the timing chain tensioner plunger.

18. Insert an 1.18 inch (M6 x 30 mm) bolt into the upper front cover timing hole to hold the tensioner arm in the retracted position.

19. Remove the alignment plate 303-465 special tool.

20. Using the flats on the camshaft to prevent camshaft rotation, remove the bolt and exhaust camshaft drive gear.

21. Remove the timing chain from the intake camshaft drive gear.

22. Using the flats on the camshaft to prevent camshaft rotation, remove the bolt and intake camshaft drive gear.

23. Mark the position of the camshaft lobes on the No. 1 cylinder for installation reference.

24. Mark the location and orientation of each camshaft bearing cap.

25. Loosen the camshaft bearing cap bolts, in sequence, one turn at a time until all tension is released from the camshaft bearing caps.

26. Remove the bolts and the camshaft bearing caps.

27. Remove the camshafts.

28. If removal of the camshaft phaser and sprocket is necessary, mark the sprocket and camshaft for reference during installation. If necessary, place the camshaft in a soft-jawed vise. Remove the bolt and the camshaft phaser and sprocket.

To install:

➡️If new parts are installed, transfer the reference marks made during disassembly to the new parts.

29. If necessary, position the camshaft in a soft-jawed vise and install the camshaft phaser and sprocket and the bolt.

30. Align the reference marks on the camshaft phaser and sprocket and the camshaft. Tighten the bolt to 53 ft. lbs. (72 Nm).

✳️ WARNING

Install the camshafts with the alignment slots in the camshafts lined up so the Camshaft Alignment Plate can be installed without rotating the camshafts. Make sure the lobes on the No. 1 cylinder are in the same position as noted in the removal procedure. Rotating the camshafts when the timing chain is removed, or installing the camshafts 180 degrees out of position can cause severe damage to the valves and pistons.

31. Lubricate the camshaft journals and bearing caps with clean engine oil.

32. Install the camshafts and bearing caps in their original location and orientation. Tighten the bearing caps in the sequence shown in 3 stages:
- Stage 1: Tighten the camshaft bearing cap bolts one turn at a time, until finger tight.
- Stage 2: Tighten to 62 inch lbs. (7 Nm).
- Stage 3: Tighten to 12 ft. lbs. (16 Nm).

33. Install the alignment plate 303-465 special tool.

34. Install the intake camshaft drive gear and hand-tighten the bolt.

35. Install the timing chain on the intake camshaft drive gear.

➡️The timing chain must be correctly engaged on the teeth of the crankshaft timing sprocket and the intake camshaft drive gear in order to install the exhaust camshaft drive gear onto the exhaust camshaft.

36. Position the exhaust camshaft drive gear in the timing chain and install the gear and bolt on the exhaust camshaft.

37. Hand-tighten the bolt.

➡**Releasing the tensioner arm will remove the slack from the timing chain release.**

38. Remove the M6 x 30 mm bolt from the upper front cover timing hole to release the tensioner arm.

➡**The special tool 303-465 is for camshaft alignment only. Using this tool to prevent engine rotation can result in engine damage.**

39. Using the flats on the camshafts to prevent camshaft rotation, tighten the bolts to 53 ft. lbs. (72 Nm).

40. Remove the alignment plate 303-465 special tool.

41. Remove the 0.23 inch (6 mm) x 0.7 inch (18 mm) bolt.

42. Remove the timing peg special tool.

43. Install the upper front cover timing hole plug and tighten to 89 inch lbs. (10 Nm).

44. Apply silicone gasket and sealant to the threads of the lower front cover timing hole plug.

45. Install the plug and tighten to 9 ft. lbs. (12 Nm).

46. Install the engine plug bolt and tighten to 15 ft. lbs. (20 Nm).

47. Install the accessory drive belt.

48. Install the front RH wheel and tire.

49. Install the valve cover.

50. Connect the negative battery cable.

3.0L Engine

See Figures 111 through 116.

1. Before servicing the vehicle, refer to the Precautions Section.

2. Disconnect the negative battery cable.

3. Remove the timing drive components.

4. Using the water pump pulley plate, water pump shaft protector and the crankshaft vibration damper remover, remove the coolant pump pulley.

➡**Do not scratch the camshaft sealing surface while removing the camshaft oil seal. If scratched, camshaft oil seal leakage may occur.**

5. Using the oil seal remover, remove and discard the camshaft oil seal.

6. Remove the 2 bolts and the camshaft oil seal retainer. Discard the press-in-place gasket.

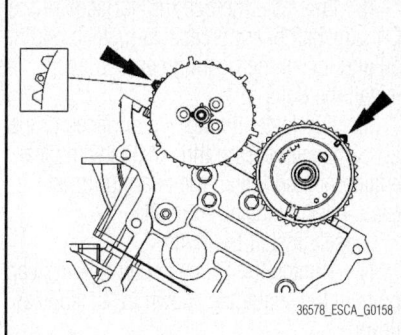

Fig. 111 LH camshafts in the neutral position

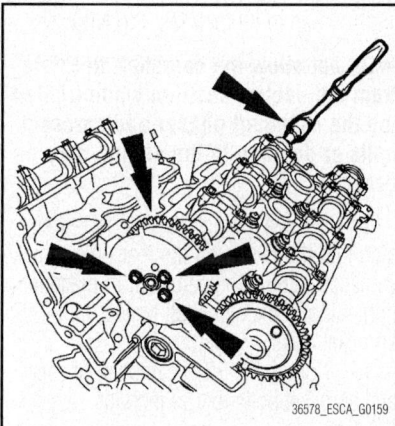

Fig. 112 Holding camshaft in place for removal of the camshaft phaser and sprocket bolts

➡**The camshafts must be in the neutral position before removing the bearing caps or damage to the engine may occur.**

7. Verify the LH camshafts are in the neutral position.

➡**Do not allow the camshaft to rotate from the neutral position while removing the camshaft phaser and sprocket or damage to the engine may occur.**

8. Install a ⅜ inch ratchet and extension into the D-slot on the rear of the intake camshaft to hold the camshaft in place for removal of the camshaft phaser and sprocket bolts.

9. Remove the 3 bolts and the LH camshaft phaser and sprocket.

➡**Cylinder head camshaft bearing caps must be assembled in their original positions. Some engines have factory markings on the camshaft bearing caps (as shown in illustration). Engines that do not have the factory markings must be marked for correct position and ori-**

entation prior to removal. Failure to install the camshaft bearing caps in their original positions may result in severe engine damage.

10. If necessary, mark the camshaft bearing cap position and orientation as shown in the illustration.

➡**After loosening all of the camshaft bearing cap bolts, remove the front camshaft bearing thrust caps (1L and 5L) first, or damage to the thrust caps may occur. 2008 model front caps may be marked (1L and 6L).**

➡**Make sure the camshaft bearing caps are marked as instructed in the previous step.**

11. Loosen the bolts evenly in the sequence shown as follows:
   - Remove the camshaft bearing front thrust caps (1L and 5L). Or (1L and 6L) for 2008 models.
   - Remove the remaining camshaft bearing caps.
   - Remove the camshafts from the cylinder head.

To install:

12. Position the camshaft phaser and sprocket onto the intake camshaft. Install the 3 bolts finger-tight.

13. Lubricate the LH camshafts with clean engine oil and carefully position the camshafts onto the cylinder head.

14. Align the LH camshafts as shown.

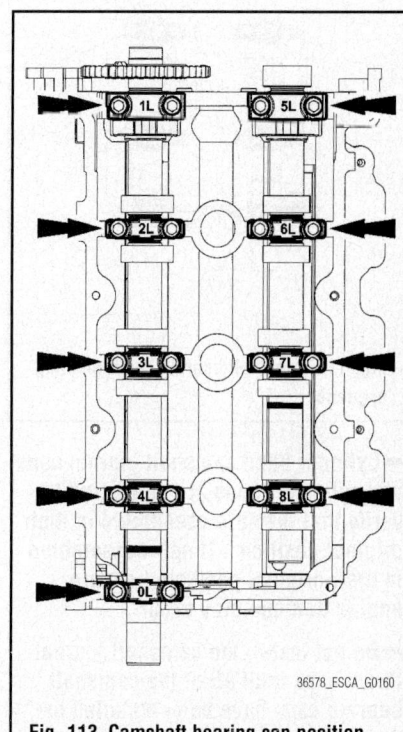

Fig. 113 Camshaft bearing cap position

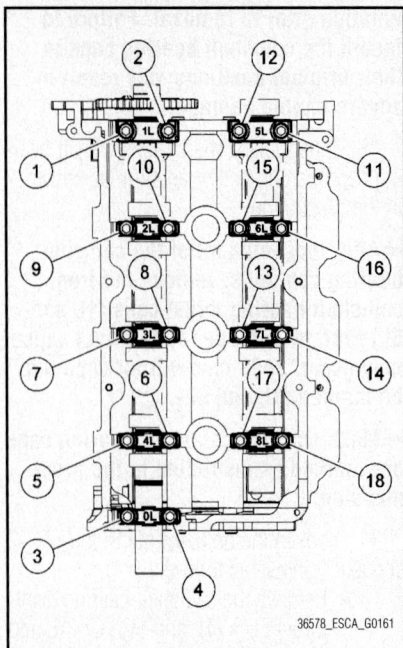

Fig. 114 Camshaft bearing cap removal sequence

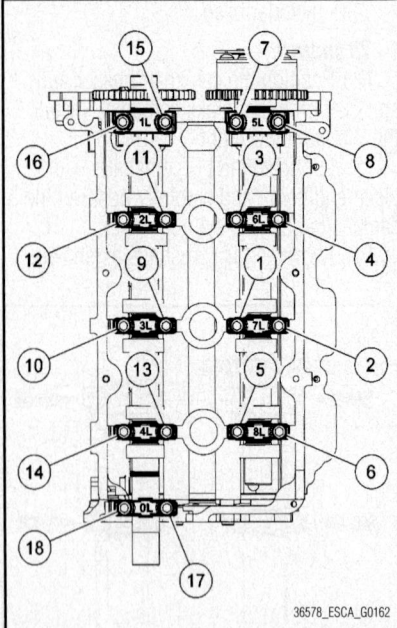

Fig. 115 Camshaft bearing cap tightening sequence

➡**Cylinder head camshaft journal caps and cylinder heads are numbered to verify that they are assembled in their original positions. If not reassembled in their original positions, severe engine damage may occur**

➡**Do not install the camshaft journal thrust caps until all of the camshaft bearing caps have been installed or damage to the thrust caps can occur.**

15. Lubricate the bearing surfaces of the LH camshaft bearing caps with clean engine oil and install the bearing caps. Loosely install the bolts.

16. Lubricate the bearing surfaces of the LH camshaft bearing thrust caps with clean engine oil and install the bearing thrust caps. Loosely install the bolts.

Loosely install the bolts.

17. Tighten the LH camshaft bearing cap bolts in the sequence shown in 2 stages as flows:

- Stage 1: Tighten to 89 inch lbs. (10 Nm).
- Stage 2: Individually loosen and then tighten each camshaft bearing cap to 89 inch lbs. (10 Nm).

➡**Do not allow the camshaft to rotate from the neutral position while tightening the camshaft phaser and sprocket bolts or damage to the engine may occur.**

18. Install a ⅜ inch ratchet and extension into the D-slot on the rear of the intake camshaft to hold the camshaft in place for tightening of the camshaft phaser and sprocket bolts.

19. Tighten the 3 LH camshaft phaser and sprocket bolts to 159 inch lbs. (18 Nm).

20. Clean the sealing surfaces with metal surface prep before installing a new press-in-place gasket.

21. Install the camshaft oil seal retainer and the 2 bolts.

22. Lubricate the camshaft oil seal with clean engine oil.

23. Using the camshaft oil seal installer, camshaft oil seal protector and the power steering pump pulley installer, install the camshaft oil seal.

24. Install the camshaft pulley installer in the camshaft as shown in the illustration.

25. Adjust the collar on the camshaft pulley Installer screw to get the best thread engagement in the rear of the camshaft.

26. Position the coolant pump pulley over the previously installed camshaft pulley installer and on the end of the camshaft. Install the camshaft pulley installer, power steering pump pulley installer and the water pump pulley spacer as shown in the illustration.

27. Using the camshaft pulley installer, power steering pump pulley installer and the water pump pulley spacer, install a new service coolant pump pulley flush with the end of the camshaft.

28. Install the timing drive components.

29. Install the coolant pump belt.

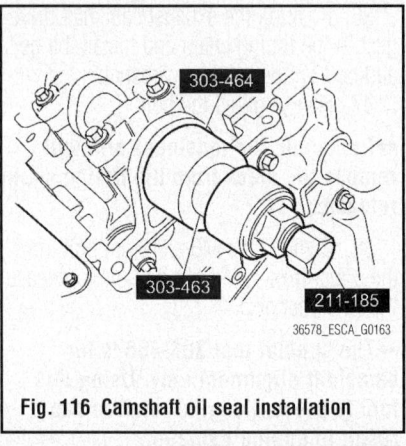

Fig. 116 Camshaft oil seal installation

CATALYTIC CONVERTER

REMOVAL & INSTALLATION

2008 Models

1. Before servicing the vehicle, refer to the Precautions Section.

2. With the vehicle in NEUTRAL, position it on a hoist.

3. Remove and discard the 2 exhaust catalytic converter nuts.

4. Remove and discard the U-bolt clamp assembly from the muffler.

5. Remove and discard the 2 resonator nuts.

6. Remove and discard the catalytic converter exhaust hanger.

7. Remove the exhaust catalytic converter and the muffler from the vehicle as an assembly. Discard the catalytic converter gasket.

8. Separate the converter from the muffler.

To install:

9. Install the converter into the muffler.

10. Thoroughly clean the sealing surfaces of the flanges using a finishing pad.

11. Install the 2 new front and rear gaskets.

12. Install the exhaust catalytic converter and the muffler assembly to the vehicle.

13. Install the exhaust hangers.

14. Tighten the front and rear flange retaining nuts to 35 ft. lbs. (47 Nm).

15. Adjust and tighten the U-bolt clamp to 35 ft. lbs. (47 Nm).

16. Start the vehicle and check for exhaust leaks.

2009 Models

See Figures 117 and 118.

➡**If replacement is not required, the production catalytic converter and muffler assembly can be removed and installed as one piece. It is only necessary to cut the production exhaust to** enable the service section to be fitted. Before cutting any part of the exhaust system, check that the position of the cut is correct in comparison to the service section being installed.

All Vehicles

1. Before servicing the vehicle, refer to the Precautions Section.

2. With the vehicle in NEUTRAL, position it on a hoist.

2.5L Engine Vehicles

3. Disconnect the Catalyst Monitor Sensor (CMS) electrical connector.

4. Remove the CMS.

All Vehicles

5. Remove and discard the two 10 mm exhaust catalytic converter-to-exhaust intermediate pipe/exhaust Y-pipe spring nuts.

6. Remove and discard the two 8-mm resonator-to-muffler spring nuts.

7. Detach the 3 exhaust hangers and remove the catalytic converter and muffler assembly.

8. Remove and discard the gaskets.

9. Cut the exhaust system 5.90 inches (150 mm) as indicated in illustration.

To install:

10. Thoroughly clean the sealing surfaces of the flanges using a finishing pad.

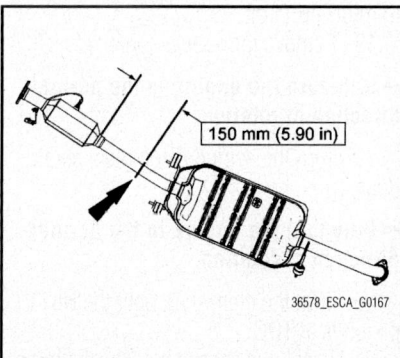

Fig. 117 Cut the exhaust system 5.90 inches (150 mm)

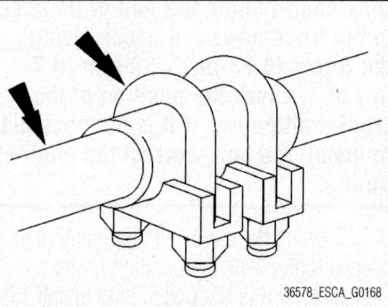

Fig. 118 Install the catalytic converter section and service clamp onto the muffler section

11. Install the service clamp onto the catalytic converter section. Do not tighten the service clamp at this time.

12. Install the catalytic converter section and service clamp onto the muffler section.

13. Inspect the exhaust intermediate pipe/exhaust Y-pipe and resonator flange studs for damage.

14. Attach the catalytic converter and muffler assembly to the 3 exhaust hangers.

2.5L Engine Vehicles

15. Install the Catalyst Monitor Sensor (CMS).

All Vehicles

16. Thoroughly clean the sealing surfaces of the flanges using a finishing pad. Inspect the cleaned sealing surface for nicks and scratches and replace as necessary.

17. Install a new resonator-to-muffler gasket by hand.

18. Install the 2 new 8-mm resonator-to-muffler spring nuts and alternately tighten RH side to LH side in sequence in 3 stages:
- Stage 1: Tighten to 44 inch lbs. (5 Nm).
- Stage 2: Tighten to 89 inch lbs. (10 Nm).
- Stage 3: Tighten to 150 inch lbs. (17 Nm).

19. Install a new converter-to-exhaust intermediate/exhaust Y-pipe gasket by hand.

20. Install the 2 new 10-mm catalytic converter-to-exhaust intermediate/exhaust Y-pipe spring nuts and alternately tighten RH side to LH side in sequence in 3 stages:
- Stage 1: Tighten to 44 inch lbs. (5 Nm).
- Stage 2: Tighten to 89 inch lbs. (10 Nm).
- Stage 3: Tighten to 150 inch lbs. (17 Nm).

21. Tighten the 4 service clamp nuts to 35 ft. lbs. (47 Nm).

2.5L Engine Vehicles

22. Connect the CMS electrical connector.

CRANKSHAFT DAMPER

REMOVAL & INSTALLATION

2.3L Engine—2008 Model

See Figures 108, 119 through 122.

➡**The following special tools, or their equivalents, are required for this procedure. Camshaft Alignment Plate**

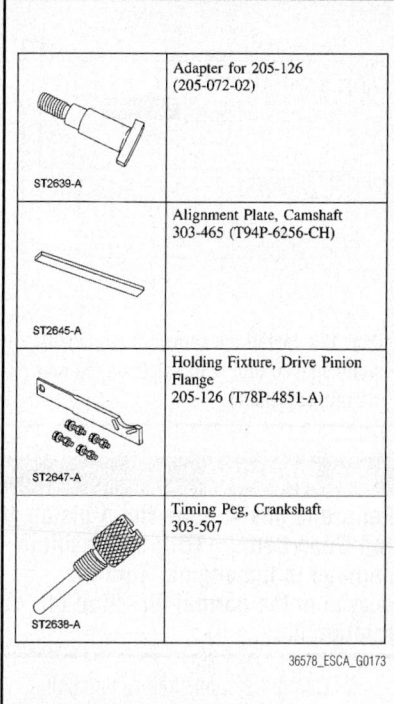

Fig. 119 Special tools required

303-465 (T94P-6256-CH), Crankshaft Timing Peg 303-057, Drive Pinion Flange Holding Fixture 205-126 (T78P-4851-A), Adapter for 205-126 (205-072-02).

✳✳ WARNING

During engine repair procedures, cleanliness is extremely important. Any foreign material, including any material created while cleaning gasket surfaces, which enters the oil passages, coolant passages or the oil pan can cause engine failure.

✳✳ WARNING

The crankshaft, the crankshaft sprocket and the pulley are fitted together by friction, using diamond washers between the flange faces on each part. For that reason, the crankshaft sprocket is also unfastened if you loosen the pulley. Therefore, the engine must be retimed each time the damper is removed. Otherwise severe engine damage can occur.

1. Before servicing the vehicle, refer to the Precautions Section.

2. Raise and safely support the vehicle.

3. Remove the front RH wheel and tire.

4. Remove the accessory drive belt.

5. Remove the valve cover, as outlined in this section.

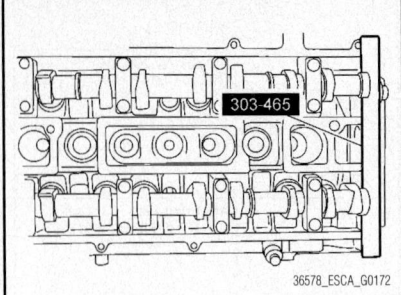

Fig. 120 Install the camshaft alignment plate special tool in the slots on the rear of both camshafts

✳✳ WARNING

Failure to position the No. 1 piston at Top Dead Center (TDC) can result in damage to the engine. Turn the engine in the normal direction of rotation only.

6. Using the crankshaft pulley bolt, turn the crankshaft clockwise to position the No. 1 piston at TDC. The hole in the crankshaft pulley should be in the 6 o'clock position.

✳✳ WARNING

The special tool 303-465 is for camshaft alignment only. Using this tool to prevent engine rotation can result in engine damage.

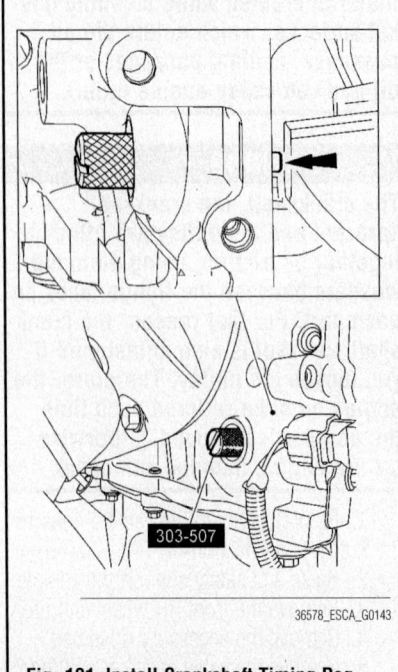

Fig. 121 Install Crankshaft Timing Peg 303-057 or equivalent special tool

➥The camshaft timing slots are offset. If the special tool cannot be installed, rotate the crankshaft one complete revolution clockwise to correctly position the camshafts.

7. Install camshaft alignment plate 303-465, or equivalent special tool in the slots on the rear of both camshafts.

8. Remove the engine plug bolt.

➥The special tool will contact the crankshaft and prevent it from turning past TDC. However, the crankshaft can still be rotated in the counterclockwise direction. The crankshaft must remain at the TDC position during the crankshaft pulley removal and installation.

9. Install Crankshaft Timing Peg 303-057 or equivalent special tool.

10. Install Drive Pinion Flange Holding Fixture 205-126 (T78P-4851-A) and Adapter for 205-126 (205-072-02) or equivalent special tools.

✳✳ WARNING

Failure to hold the crankshaft pulley in place while loosening the bolt can result in damage to the engine.

✳✳ WARNING

If the crankshaft sprocket diamond washer comes off with the crankshaft pulley it must be installed back onto the crankshaft.

11. Remove the crankshaft pulley bolt and washer. Discard the bolt.

12. Remove the crankshaft pulley.

To install:

➥Do not reuse the crankshaft pulley bolt.

➥Apply clean engine oil on the seal area before installing.

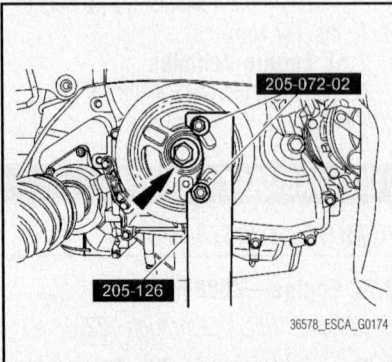

Fig. 122 Install Drive Pinion Flange Holding Fixture and Adapter special tools

13. Install the crankshaft pulley and hand-tighten the bolt.

✳✳ WARNING

Only hand-tighten the bolt or damage to the front cover can occur.

➥The following 2 steps will correctly align the crankshaft pulley to the crankshaft.

14. Install a standard 6-mm (0.23-in.) x 18-mm (0.7-in.) bolt through the crankshaft pulley and thread it into the front cover.

15. Rotate the pulley as necessary to align the bolt holes.

✳✳ WARNING

Failure to hold the crankshaft pulley in place while tightening the bolt can cause damage to the engine front cover.

16. Using the special tools to hold the crankshaft pulley in place, tighten the crankshaft pulley bolt in 2 stages:
   • Stage 1: Tighten to 74 ft. lbs. (100 Nm).
   • Stage 2: Tighten an additional 90 degrees (1/4 turn).

17. Remove the 6-mm (0.23-in.) x 18-mm (0.7-in.) bolt.

18. Remove the special tools.

➥Only turn the engine in the normal direction of rotation.

19. Turn the engine 2 complete revolutions.

➥Only turn the engine in the normal direction of rotation.

20. Turn the crankshaft until the No. 1 piston is at TDC.

21. Install the special crankshaft timing peg tool.

✳✳ WARNING

Only hand-tighten the bolt or damage to the front cover can occur. Using the 6-mm (0.23-in.) x 18-mm (0.7-in.) bolt, check the position of the crankshaft pulley. If it is not possible to install the bolt, correct the engine timing.

22. Using the camshaft alignment plate special tool, check the position of the camshafts. If it is not possible to install the special tool, correct the engine timing.

23. Remove the 6-mm (0.23-in.) x 18-mm (0.7-in.) bolt.

24. Install the engine plug bolt and tighten to 15 ft. lbs. (20 Nm).

25. Install the accessory drive belt.

26. Install the valve cover.

2.5L Model

See Figures 123 and 124.

1. Before servicing the vehicle, refer to the Precautions Section.

✳✳ WARNING

Do not loosen or remove the crankshaft pulley bolt without first installing the special tools as instructed in this procedure. The crankshaft pulley and the crankshaft timing sprocket are not keyed to the crankshaft. The crankshaft, the crankshaft sprocket and the pulley are fitted together by friction, using diamond washers between the flange faces on each part. For that reason, the crankshaft sprocket is also unfastened if the pulley bolt is loosened. Before any repair requiring loosening or removal of the crankshaft pulley bolt, the crankshaft and camshafts must be locked in place by the special service tools, otherwise severe engine damage can occur.

➡During engine repair procedures, cleanliness is extremely important. Any foreign material (including any mate-rial created while cleaning gasket surfaces) that enters the oil passages, coolant passages or the oil pan can cause engine failure.

2. With the vehicle in NEUTRAL, position it on a hoist.

3. Remove the front RH wheel and tire.

4. Remove the accessory drive belt.

5. Remove the valve cover.

➡Failure to position the No. 1 piston at Top Dead Center (TDC) can result in damage to the engine. Turn the engine in the normal direction of rotation only.

➡Using the crankshaft pulley bolt, turn the crankshaft clockwise to position the No. 1 piston at Top Dead Center (TDC). The hole in the crankshaft pulley should be in the 6 o'clock position.

➡The camshaft alignment plate is for camshaft alignment only. Using this tool to prevent engine rotation can result in engine damage.

➡The camshaft timing slots are offset. If the camshaft alignment plate cannot be installed, rotate the crankshaft one complete revolution clockwise to correctly position the camshafts.

6. Install the camshaft alignment plate in the slots on the rear of both camshafts.

7. Remove the engine plug bolt.

➡The crankshaft TDC timing peg will contact the crankshaft and prevent it from turning past TDC. However, the crankshaft can still be rotated in the counterclockwise direction. The crankshaft must remain at the TDC position during the crankshaft pulley removal and installation.

8. Install the crankshaft TDC timing peg.

Fig. 124 Crankshaft damper holding tool installed

➡The crankshaft must remain in the Top Dead Center (TDC) position during removal of the pulley bolt or damage to the engine can occur. Therefore, the crankshaft pulley must be held in place with the crankshaft damper holding tool, and the bolt should be removed using an air impact wrench (1/2-in drive minimum).

➡The crankshaft sprocket diamond washer may come off with the crankshaft pulley. The diamond washer must be replaced. Remove and discard the diamond washer. If the diamond washer is not installed, engine damage may occur.

9. Use the crankshaft damper holding tool and a suitable ½ inch drive hand tool to hold the crankshaft pulley. Use an air impact wrench to remove the crankshaft pulley bolt.

10. Remove and discard the crankshaft pulley bolt and washer.

11. Remove the crankshaft pulley.

12. Remove the diamond washer and discard.

To install:

13. Install a new diamond washer.

➡Do not install the crankshaft pulley bolt at this time.

➡Apply clean engine oil on the seal area before installing.

14. Position the crankshaft pulley onto the crankshaft with the hole in the pulley at the 6 o'clock position.

➡This step will correctly align the crankshaft pulley to the crankshaft.

15. Install a 6 mm x 18 mm bolt through the crankshaft pulley and thread it into the front cover. Only hand-tighten the 6 mm x 18 mm bolt or damage to the front cover can occur.

✳✳ WARNING

The crankshaft must remain in the Top Dead Center (TDC) position during installation of the pulley bolt or damage to the engine can occur. Therefore, the crankshaft pulley must be held in place with the Crankshaft Damper Holding Tool and the bolt should be installed using hand tools only.

16. Install a new crankshaft pulley bolt. Use the Crankshaft Damper Holding Tool and a suitable ½ inch drive hand tool to hold the crankshaft pulley, tighten the crankshaft pulley bolt in 2 stages:

Alignment Plate, Camshaft 303-465 (T94P-6256-CH)	ST2645-A
Holding Tool, Crankshaft Damper 303-1416	ST3054-A
Timing Peg, Crankshaft TDC 303-507	ST2638-A
Vehicle Communication Module (VCM) and Integrated Diagnostic System (IDS) software with appropriate hardware, or equivalent scan tool	ST2834-A

36578_ESCA_G0175

Fig. 123 Special tool required

- Stage 1: Tighten to 100 Nm (74 lb-ft).
- Stage 2: Tighten an additional 90 degrees.

17. Remove the 6 mm x 18 mm bolt.

18. Remove the crankshaft TDC timing peg.

19. Remove the camshaft alignment plate.

➡**Only turn the engine in the normal direction of rotation.**

20. Turn the crankshaft clockwise one and three-fourths turns.

21. Install the crankshaft TDC Timing Peg.

22. Turn the crankshaft clockwise until the crankshaft contacts the crankshaft TDC timing peg.

23. Using the 6 mm x 18 mm bolt, check the position of the crankshaft pulley.

24. If it is not possible to install the bolt, the engine valve timing must be corrected by repeating this procedure.

25. Install the camshaft alignment plate to check the position of the camshafts.

26. If it is not possible to install the Camshaft Alignment Plate, the engine valve timing must be corrected by repeating this procedure.

27. Remove the Camshaft Alignment Plate.

28. Remove the 6 mm x 18 mm bolt.

29. Remove the Crankshaft TDC Timing Peg.

30. Install the engine plug bolt and tighten to 177 inch lbs. (20 Nm).

31. Install the accessory drive belt.

32. Install the front RH wheel and tire.

33. Install the valve cover.

34. Using the scan tool, perform the Misfire Monitor Neutral Profile Correction procedure, following the on-screen instructions.

3.0L Engine

2008 Models

See Figures 125 through 128.

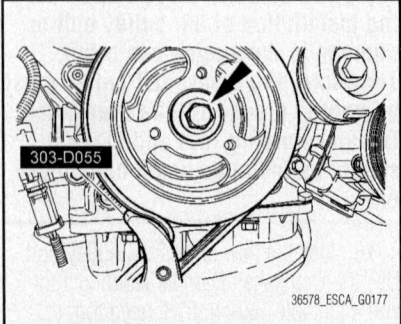

36578_ESCA_G0177

Fig. 125 Install the strap wrench to hold the crankshaft pulley stationary

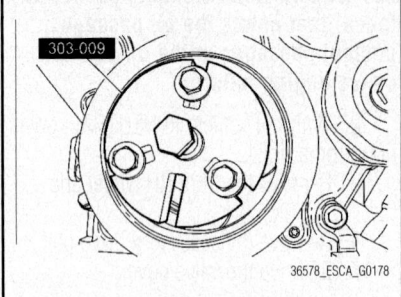

36578_ESCA_G0178

Fig. 126 Using the Crankshaft Vibration Damper Remover tool to remove the crankshaft pulley

1. Before servicing the vehicle, refer to the Precautions Section.

2. Remove the accessory drive belt.

3. Remove the splash shield.

4. Install the Strap Wrench 303-D055 (D85L-6000-A), or equivalent special tool.

5. Remove the crankshaft pulley bolt and washer.

6. Using the Crankshaft Vibration Damper Remover 303-009 (T58P-6316-D) or equivalent special tool, remove the crankshaft pulley.

To install:

➡**Clean the keyway and slot using metal surface cleaner before applying silicone gasket and sealer.**

➡**The crankshaft pulley must be installed and the bolt tightened within four minutes of applying the silicone gasket and sealer.**

7. Apply silicone gasket and sealant to the end of the keyway slot.

➡**Lubricate the outside diameter sealing surface of the crankshaft pulley with clean engine oil.**

8. Using Crankshaft Vibration Damper Installer 303-102 (T74P-6316-B) or equivalent special tool, install the crankshaft pulley.

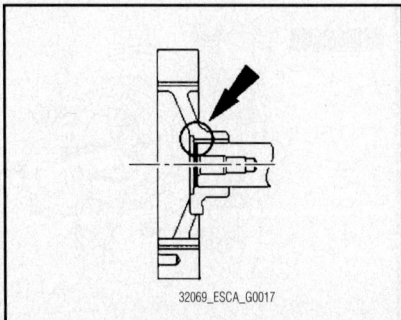

32069_ESCA_G0017

Fig. 127 Apply silicone gasket and sealant to the end of the keyway slot

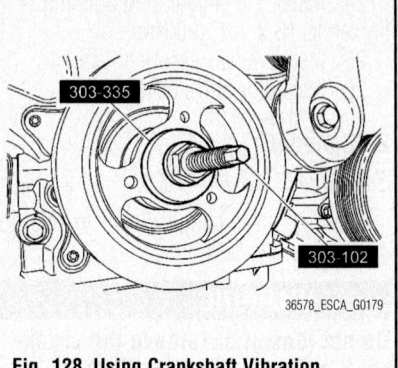

36578_ESCA_G0179

Fig. 128 Using Crankshaft Vibration Damper Installer 303-102 (T74P-6316-B) or equivalent special tool, install the crankshaft pulley

➡**Use an appropriate strap wrench to hold the crankshaft pulley.**

9. Install the bolt and the washer and tighten in four stages:

- Stage 1: Tighten to 89 ft. lbs. (120 Nm).
- Stage 2: Loosen 360 degrees.
- Stage 3: Tighten to 37 ft. lbs. (50 Nm).
- Stage 4: Tighten an additional 90 degrees.

10. Install RH front inner splash shield. Tighten the retainers to 80 inch lbs. (9 Nm).

11. Install the accessory drive belt.

2009 Models

See Figures 129 and 130.

1. Before servicing the vehicle, refer to the Precautions Section

2. With the vehicle in NEUTRAL, position it on a hoist.

3. Remove the accessory drive belt.

4. Remove the crankshaft pulley bolt and washer. Discard the crankshaft pulley bolt.

5. Using the 3 Jaw Puller, remove the crankshaft pulley.

To install:

6. Lubricate the crankshaft front seal inner lip with clean engine oil.

➡**Clean the keyway and slot using metal surface prep before applying silicone gasket and sealant. The crankshaft pulley must be installed and the bolt tightened within 4 minutes of applying the silicone gasket and sealant.**

7. Apply silicone gasket and sealant to the end of the keyway slot.

8. Lubricate the outside diameter sealing surface with clean engine oil.

9. Using the crankshaft vibration damper installer, install the crankshaft pulley.

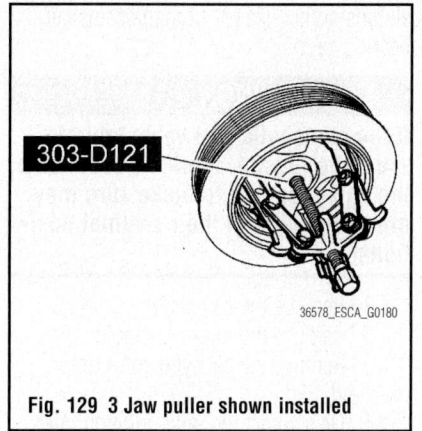

Fig. 129 3 Jaw puller shown installed

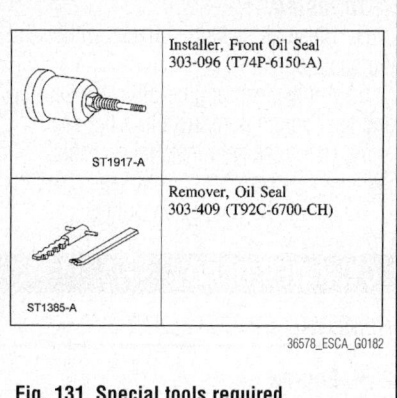

Fig. 131 Special tools required

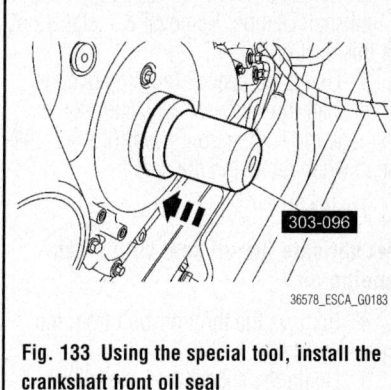

Fig. 133 Using the special tool, install the crankshaft front oil seal

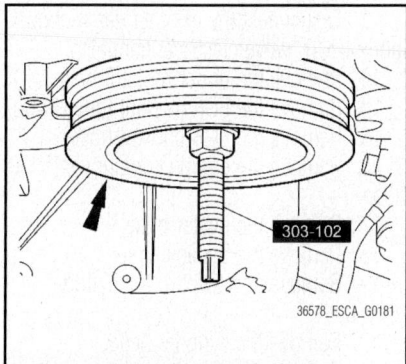

Fig. 130 Crankshaft vibration damper shown installed

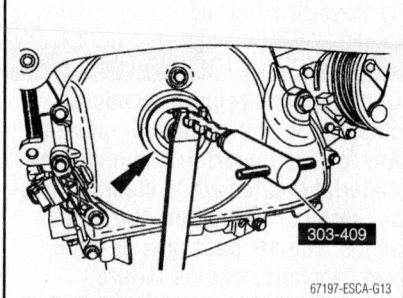

Fig. 132 Using the special tool, remove the crankshaft front oil seal—2.3L engine

10. Install the bolt and washer.
11. Tighten the bolt in 4 stages:
   • Stage 1: Tighten to 120 Nm (89 lb-ft).
   • Stage 2: Loosen one full turn.
   • Stage 3: Tighten to 50 Nm (37 lb-ft).
   • Stage 4: Tighten an additional 90 degrees.
12. Install the accessory drive belt.

CRANKSHAFT FRONT SEAL

REMOVAL & INSTALLATION

2.3L Engine

See Figures 131 through 133.

✳✳ WARNING

Do not loosen or remove the crankshaft pulley bolt without first installing the special tools as instructed in this procedure. The crankshaft pulley and the crankshaft timing sprocket are not keyed to the crankshaft. The crankshaft, the crankshaft sprocket and the pulley are fitted together by friction, using diamond washers between the flange faces on each part. For that reason,

the crankshaft sprocket is also unfastened if you loosen the pulley bolt. Before any repair requiring loosening or removal of the crankshaft pulley bolt, the crankshaft and camshafts must be locked in place by the special service tools, otherwise severe engine damage can occur.

✳✳ WARNING

During engine repair procedures, cleanliness is extremely important. Any foreign material (including any material created while cleaning gasket surfaces) that enters the oil passages, coolant passages or the oil pan can cause engine failure.

1. Before servicing the vehicle, refer to the Precautions Section.
2. Remove the crankshaft pulley. Refer to Crankshaft Damper Removal & Installation in this section.
3. Using the special tool, remove the crankshaft front oil seal. Use care not to damage the engine front cover or the crankshaft when removing the seal.

To install:

➡ Lubricate the oil seal with clean engine oil.

4. Remove the through-bolt from the special tool.
5. Using the special tool, install the crankshaft front oil seal.
6. Install the crankshaft pulley.

2.5L Engine

See Figures 131 through 133.

✳✳ WARNING

Do not loosen or remove the crankshaft pulley bolt without first installing the special tools as instructed in this procedure. The crankshaft pulley and the crankshaft timing sprocket are not keyed to the crankshaft. The crankshaft, the crankshaft sprocket and the pulley are fitted together by friction, using diamond washers between the flange faces on each part. For that reason, the crankshaft sprocket is also unfastened if you loosen the pulley bolt. Before any repair requiring loosening or removal of the crankshaft pulley bolt, the crankshaft and camshafts must be locked in place by the special service tools, otherwise severe engine damage can occur.

✳✳ WARNING

During engine repair procedures, cleanliness is extremely important. Any foreign material (including any material created while cleaning gasket surfaces) that enters the oil passages, coolant passages or the oil pan can cause engine failure.

1. Before servicing the vehicle, refer to the Precautions Section.

2. Remove the crankshaft pulley. Refer to Crankshaft Damper Removal & Installation in this section.

3. Using the special tool, remove the crankshaft front oil seal. Use care not to damage the engine front cover or the crankshaft when removing the seal.

To install:

➡ **Lubricate the oil seal with clean engine oil.**

4. Remove the through-bolt from the special tool.

5. Using the special tool, install the crankshaft front oil seal.

6. Install the crankshaft pulley.

3.0L Engine

See Figures 134 and 135.

1. Before servicing the vehicle, refer to the Precautions Section.

2. With the vehicle in NEUTRAL, position it on a hoist.

3. Remove the crankshaft pulley. Refer to Crankshaft Damper Removal & Installation in this section.

4. Using the seal remover tool, remove and discard the crankshaft front seal.

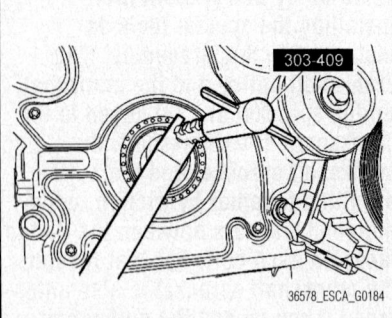

Fig. 134 Using the seal remover tool, remove and discard the crankshaft front seal

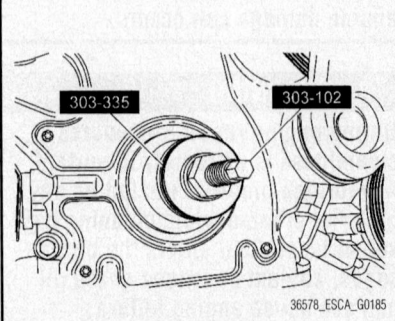

Fig. 135 Using the seal installation tools, install a new crankshaft front seal

To install:

5. Clean all sealing surfaces with metal surface prep.

6. Apply clean engine oil to the seal lip and seal bore before installing the seal.

7. Using the seal installation tools, install a new crankshaft front seal.

8. Install the crankshaft pulley.

CYLINDER HEAD

REMOVAL & INSTALLATION

2.3L Engine

See Figures 136 through 138.

1. Before servicing the vehicle, refer to the Precautions Section.

✳✳ WARNING

During engine repair procedures, cleanliness is extremely important. Any foreign material, including any material created while cleaning gasket surfaces that enters the oil passages, coolant passages or the oil pan can cause engine failure.

✳✳ WARNING

The crankshaft, the crankshaft sprocket and the pulley are fitted together by friction, using diamond washers between the flange faces on each part. For that reason, the crankshaft sprocket is also unfastened if you loosen the pulley. Therefore, the engine must be retimed each time the damper is removed. Otherwise severe engine damage can occur.

✳✳ WARNING

Do not loosen or remove the crankshaft pulley bolt without first installing the special tools as instructed in the timing chain section. The crankshaft pulley and the crankshaft timing sprocket are not keyed to the crankshaft.

2. With the vehicle in NEUTRAL, position it on a hoist.

3. Release the fuel system pressure.

4. Drain the engine cooling system.

5. Remove the timing drive components. For additional information, refer to Timing Drive Components in this section.

6. Mark the position of the camshaft lobes on the No. 1 cylinder for installation reference.

7. Loosen the camshaft bearing cap bolts, in sequence, one turn at a time until

all tension is released from the camshaft bearing caps.

✳✳ WARNING

If the camshafts and valve tappets are to be reused, mark the location of the valve tappets to make sure they are assembled in their original positions.

8. Remove the camshafts.

9. Remove the intake manifold.

10. Remove the catalytic converter/manifold.

11. Disconnect the radio ignition interference capacitor electrical connector

12. Disconnect the exhaust gas recirculation (EGR) valve electrical connector

13. Remove the upper radiator hose.

14. Remove the EGR coolant tube clamp.

15. Remove the EGR coolant hose.

16. Remove the engine coolant vent hose.

17. Remove the heater hose.

18. Remove the bypass hose.

19. Remove and discard the cylinder head bolts.

20. Remove the cylinder head.

21. Remove the cylinder head gasket.

22. Inspect the cylinder head for distortion.

✳✳ WARNING

Do not use metal scrapers, wire brushes, power abrasive discs or other abrasive means to clean the sealing surfaces. These tools cause scratches and gouges that make leak paths. Use a plastic scraping tool to remove all traces of the head gasket.

✳✳ WARNING .

Observe all warnings or cautions and follow all application directions contained on the packaging of the silicone gasket remover and the metal surface prep.

➡ **If there is no residual gasket material present, metal surface prep can be used to clean and prepare the surfaces.**

23. Clean the cylinder head-to-cylinder block mating surface of both the cylinder head and the cylinder block.

24. Remove any large deposits of silicone or gasket material with a plastic scraper.

25. Apply silicone gasket remover, following package directions, and allow to set for several minutes.

26. Remove the silicone gasket remover

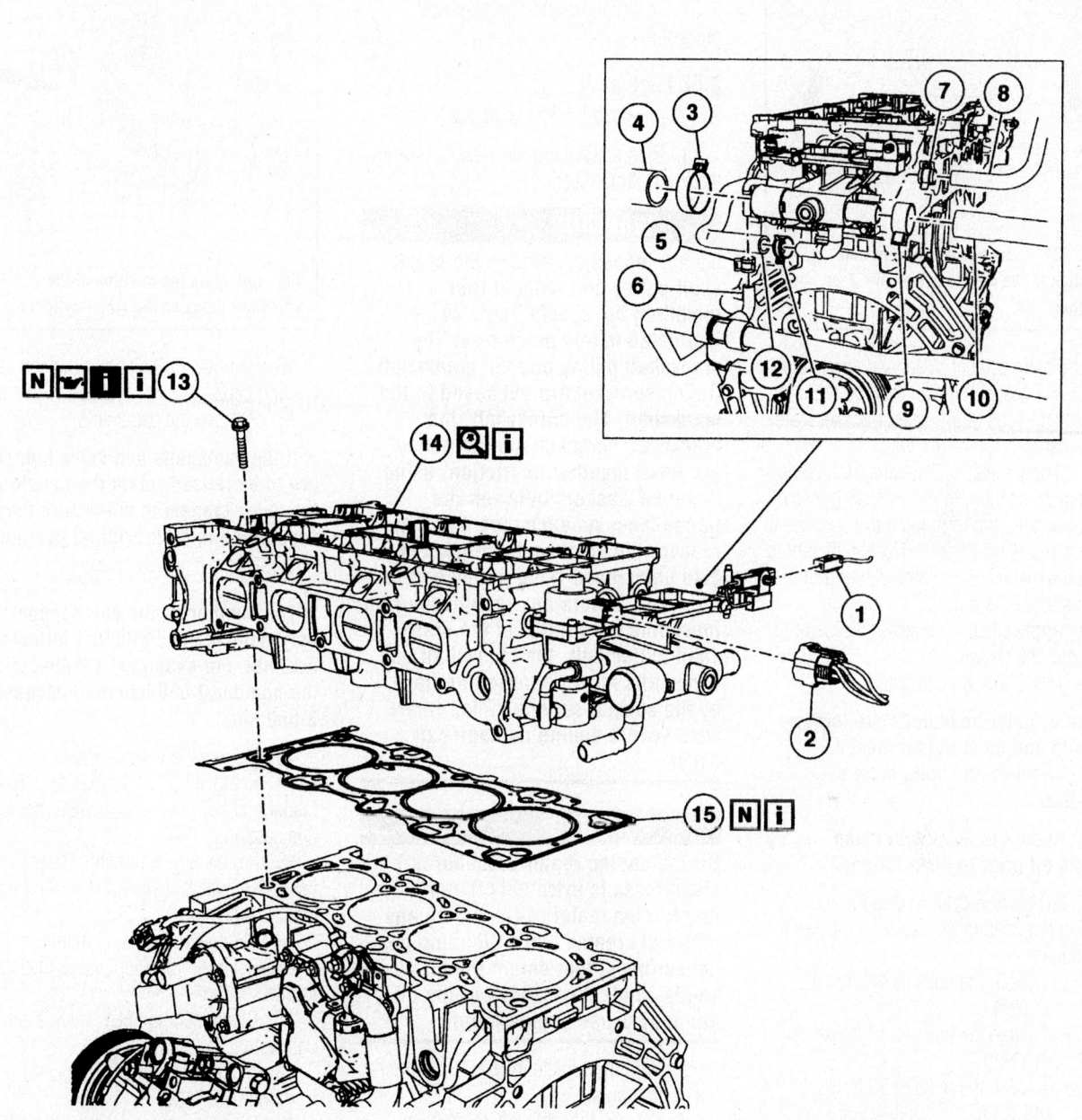

1 Radio ignition interference capacitor electrical connector
2 Exhaust gas recirculation (EGR) valve electrical connector
3 Upper radiator hose clamp
4 Upper radiator hose (position aside)
5 EGR coolant tube clamp
6 EGR coolant hose (part of heater hose) (position aside)
7 Engine coolant vent hose clamp
8 Engine coolant vent hose (position aside)

9 Heater hose clamp
10 Heater hose (position aside)
11 Bypass hose clamp
12 Bypass hose (position aside)
13 Cylinder head bolt
14 Cylinder head
15 Cylinder head gasket

67197-ESCA-G04

Fig. 136 Cylinder head removal—2.3L engine

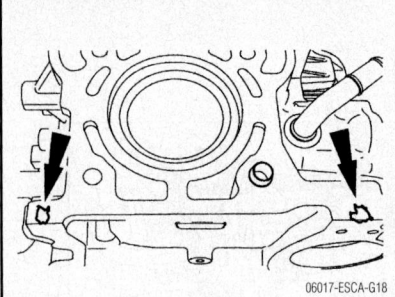

Fig. 137 Apply silicone gasket and sealant to the locations shown—2.3L engine

with a plastic scraper. A second application of silicone gasket remover may be required if residual traces of silicone or gasket material remain.

27. Apply metal surface prep, following package directions, to remove any traces of oil or coolant, and to prepare the surfaces to bond with the new gasket. Do not attempt to make the metal shiny. Some staining of the metal surfaces is normal.

28. Apply silicone gasket and sealant to the locations shown.

29. Install a new head gasket.

➡ **The cylinder head bolts are torque-to-yield and must not be reused. New cylinder head bolts must be installed.**

➡ **Lubricate the bolts with clean engine oil prior to installation.**

30. Install new cylinder head bolts. Tighten the bolts in the sequence shown in five stages:
- Tighten the bolts to 44 inch lbs. (5 Nm).
- Tighten the bolts to 11 ft. lbs. (15 Nm).
- Tighten the bolts to 33 ft. lbs. (45 Nm).
- Turn the bolts 90 degrees.

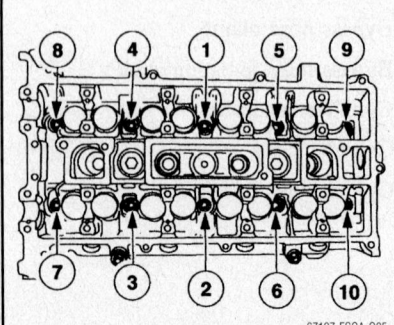

Fig. 138 Cylinder head bolt torque sequence—2.3L engine

- Turn the bolts an additional 90 degrees.
31. To install, reverse the removal procedure.

2.5L Engine

See Figures 120, 138, 139 through 141.

1. Before servicing the vehicle, refer to the Precautions Section.

✳✳ WARNING

Do not loosen or remove the crank-shaft pulley bolt without first installing the special tools as instructed in this procedure. The crankshaft pulley and the crankshaft timing sprocket are not keyed to the crankshaft. The crankshaft, the crankshaft sprocket and the pulley are fitted together by friction, using diamond washers between the flange faces on each part. For that reason, the crankshaft sprocket is also unfastened if the pulley bolt is loosened. Before any repair requiring loosening or removal of the crank-shaft pulley bolt, the crankshaft and camshafts must be locked in place by the special service tools, other-wise severe engine damage can occur.

✳✳ WARNING

During engine repair procedures, cleanliness is extremely important. Any foreign material (including any material created while cleaning gasket surfaces) that enters the oil passages, coolant passages or the oil pan may cause engine failure.

2. With the vehicle in NEUTRAL, position it on a hoist.

3. Release the fuel system pressure. Refer to the Fuel System section.

4. Drain the engine cooling system.

5. Remove the timing drive components. Refer to Timing Chain Cover, Chain and Sprockets in this section.

6. Remove the camshaft alignment plate.

7. Mark the position of the camshaft lobes on the No. 1 cylinder for installation reference.

8. Mark the location and orientation of each camshaft bearing cap.

9. Loosen the camshaft bearing cap bolts, in sequence, one turn at a time until all tension is released from the camshaft bearing caps.

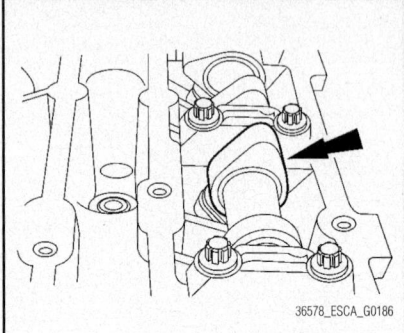

Fig. 139 Mark the position of the camshaft lobes on the No. 1 cylinder

10. Remove the bolts and the camshaft bearing caps.

11. Remove the camshafts.

➡ **If the camshafts and valve tappets are to be reused, mark the location of the valve tappets to make sure they are assembled in their original positions.**

12. Remove the valve tappets.

➡ **The number on the valve tappets only reflects the digits that follow the decimal. For example, a tappet with the number 0.650 has the thickness of 3.650 mm.**

13. Inspect the valve tappets.

14. Remove the intake manifold. Refer to Intake Manifold Removal & Installation in this section.

15. Remove the alternator. Refer to Alternator Removal & Installation in the Engine Electrical section.

16. Remove the exhaust manifold. Refer to Exhaust Manifold Removal & Installation in this section.

17. Disconnect the EGR valve electrical connector.

18. Disconnect the EGR coolant hose from the EGR valve.

19. Disconnect the upper radiator hose, coolant bypass hose, heater hose and coolant vent hose from the engine coolant outlet.

20. Remove the 10 bolts and the cylinder head. Discard the bolts and the cylinder head gasket.

To install:

✳✳ WARNING

Do not use metal scrapers, wire brushes, power abrasive discs or other abrasive means to clean the sealing surfaces. These tools cause scratches and gouges that make leak paths. Use a plastic scraping tool to remove all traces of the head gasket.

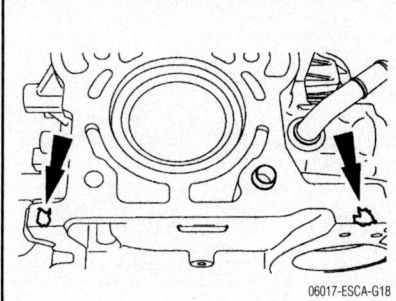

Fig. 140 Apply silicone gasket and sealant to the locations shown—2.5L engine

21. Clean the cylinder head-to-cylinder block mating surface of both the cylinder head and the cylinder block in the following sequence:
- Remove any large deposits of silicone or gasket material with a plastic scraper.
- Apply silicone gasket remover, following package directions, and allow to set for several minutes.
- Remove the silicone gasket remover with a plastic scraper. A second application of silicone gasket remover may be required if residual traces of silicone or gasket material remain.
- Apply metal surface prep, following package directions, to remove any traces of oil or coolant, and to prepare the surfaces to bond with the new gasket. Do not attempt to make the metal shiny. Some staining of the metal surfaces is normal.

22. Support the cylinder head on a bench with the head gasket side up. Check the cylinder head distortion and the cylinder block distortion.

23. Clean the cylinder head bolt holes in the cylinder block. Make sure all coolant, oil or other foreign material is removed.

24. Apply silicone gasket and sealant to the locations shown.

25. Install a new head gasket.

※※ WARNING

The cylinder head bolts are torque-to-yield and must not be reused. New cylinder head bolts must be installed.

26. Lubricate the bolts with clean engine oil prior to installation.

27. Install the cylinder head and 10 new bolts. Tighten the bolts in the sequence shown in 5 stages:

28. Install new cylinder head bolts.

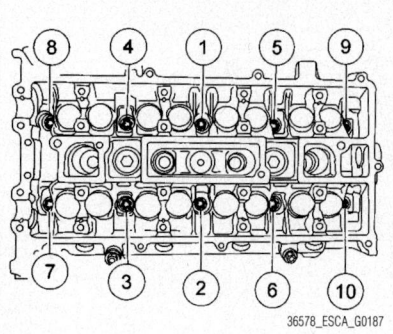

Fig. 141 Bearing cap tightening sequence

Tighten the bolts in the sequence shown in five stages:
- Tighten the bolts to 44 inch lbs. (5 Nm).
- Tighten the bolts to 11 ft. lbs. (15 Nm).
- Tighten the bolts to 33 ft. lbs. (45 Nm).
- Turn the bolts 90 degrees.
- Turn the bolts an additional 90 degrees.

29. Connect the upper radiator hose, coolant bypass hose, heater hose and coolant vent hose to the engine coolant outlet.

30. Connect the EGR coolant hose to the EGR valve.

31. Connect the EGR valve electrical connector.

32. Install the exhaust manifold.

33. Install the alternator.

34. Install the intake manifold.

35. Lubricate the valve tappets with clean engine oil.

36. Install the valve tappets in their original positions.

➡Install the camshafts with the alignment notches in the camshafts lined up so the camshaft alignment plate can be installed. Make sure the lobes on the No. 1 cylinder are in the same position as noted in the removal procedure. Failure to follow this procedure can cause severe damage to the valves and pistons.

37. Lubricate the camshaft journals and bearing caps with clean engine oil.
Install the camshafts and bearing caps in their original location and orientation. Tighten the bearing caps in the sequence shown in 3 stages:
- Stage 1: Tighten the camshaft bearing cap bolts, one turn at a time, until finger tight.
- Stage 2: Tighten to (62 inch (7 Nm).

- Stage 3: Tighten to 142 inch lbs. (16 Nm).

38. Install the camshaft alignment plate.

39. Install the timing drive components.

40. Fill and bleed the engine cooling system.

3.0L Engine

See Figures 142 through 144.

※※ WARNING

During engine repair procedures, cleanliness is extremely important. Any foreign material (including any material created while cleaning gasket surfaces) that enters the oil passages, coolant passages or the oil pan may cause engine failure.

1. Before servicing the vehicle, refer to the Precautions Section.

2. With the vehicle in NEUTRAL, position it on a hoist.

3. Remove the lower intake manifold.

4. Remove the coolant pump housing.

5. Remove the RH camshafts. Refer to Camshaft Removal & Installation in this section.

➡The camshaft roller followers and hydraulic lash adjusters must be installed in their original positions. If not reassembled in their original positions, severe engine damage may occur.

6. Remove the camshaft roller followers.

7. Remove the hydraulic lash adjusters.

8. Remove the RH exhaust manifold. Refer to Exhaust Manifold Removal & Installation in this section.

※※ WARNING

New cylinder head bolts must be installed. They are torque-to-yield designed and cannot be reused.

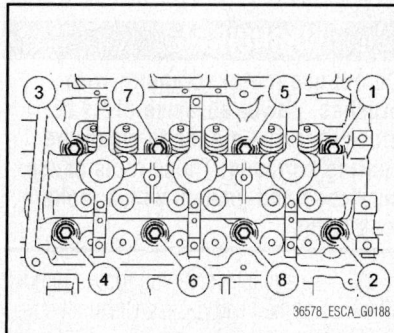

Fig. 142 Cylinder head bolt removal sequence

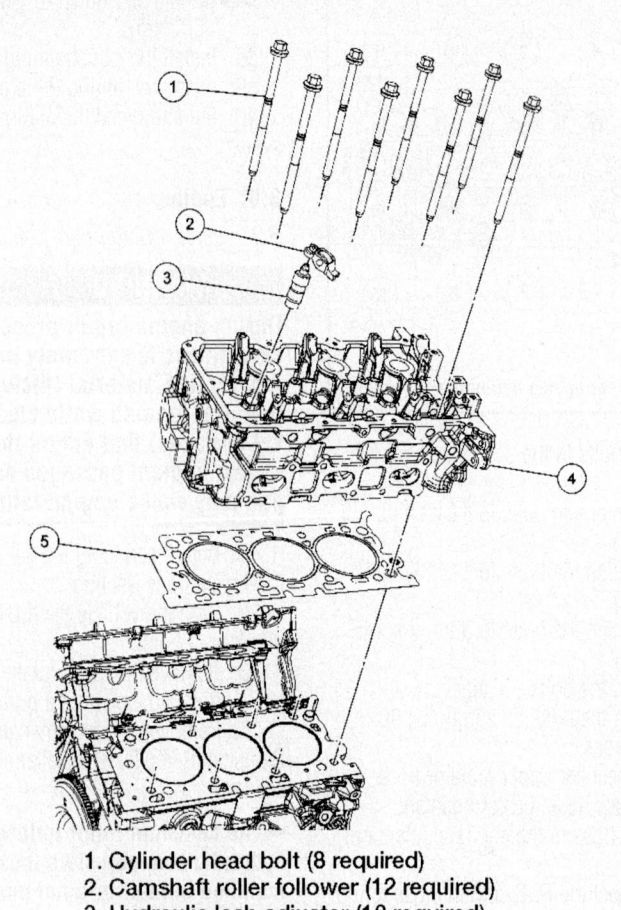

1. Cylinder head bolt (8 required)
2. Camshaft roller follower (12 required)
3. Hydraulic lash adjuster (12 required)
4. Cylinder head
5. Cylinder head gasket

36578_ESCA_G0189

Fig. 143 3.0L Engine—RH cylinder head

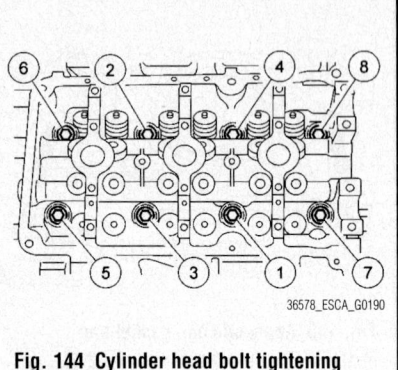

36578_ESCA_G0190

Fig. 144 Cylinder head bolt tightening sequence

21. Install the RH camshafts.
22. Install the coolant pump housing.
23. Install the lower intake manifold.
24. Fill and bleed the engine cooling system.

ENGINE ASSEMBLY

REMOVAL & INSTALLATION

4 Cylinder Engines

Manual Transaxle

See Figure 145.

1. Before servicing the vehicle, refer to the Precautions Section.
2. With the vehicle in NEUTRAL, position it on a hoist.
3. Release the fuel system pressure.
4. Remove the engine air cleaner and air cleaner outlet pipe.
5. Remove the battery tray.
6. Drain the engine oil.
7. Remove the front wheels and tires.
8. Drain the cooling system.
9. Remove the exhaust flexible pipe.
10. Disconnect the heated oxygen sensor (HO2S) and the catalyst monitor sensor electrical connectors.
11. Remove the accessory drive belt and tensioner.
12. Press the 2 locking tabs (1 shown) to release the lower air duct from the upper air duct
13. Detach the wire retainers from the alternator shield and remove the nut and pin-type retainer, remove shield.
14. Remove the 4 bolts and the lateral support crossmember.
15. Remove the brake hose retainer and the ABS sensor retaining bolt from the LH strut.
16. Disconnect the LH stabilizer bar link.
17. Remove the LH tie rod end retaining nut.

9. Remove the bolts in the sequence shown.
10. Remove the cylinder head. Discard the bolts and gasket.
11. Remove the RH cylinder head.
12. Support the cylinder head on a bench with the head gasket side up. Check the cylinder head distortion and the cylinder block distortion.

✳✳ WARNING

Do not use metal scrapers, wire brushes, power abrasive discs or other abrasive means to clean the sealing surfaces. These tools cause scratches and gauges which make leak paths.

13. Use a plastic scraping tool to remove all traces of the head gasket. Clean all surfaces with metal surface prep.
14. Position a new gasket and the cylinder head.

15. Install the new bolts and tighten in 6 stages in the sequence shown:
   - Stage 1: Tighten to 30 ft. (40 Nm).
   - Stage 2: Tighten 90 degrees.
   - Stage 3: Loosen one full turn.
   - Stage 4: Tighten to 30 ft. (40 Nm).
   - Stage 5: Tighten 90 degrees.
   - Stage 6: Tighten 90 degrees.
16. Install the RH exhaust manifold.

➡**The camshaft roller followers and hydraulic lash adjusters must be installed in their original positions. If not reassembled in their original positions, severe engine damage may occur.**

17. Install the hydraulic lash adjusters.
18. Lubricate the hydraulic lash adjusters with clean engine oil.
19. Install the camshaft roller followers.
20. Lubricate the camshaft roller followers with clean engine oil.

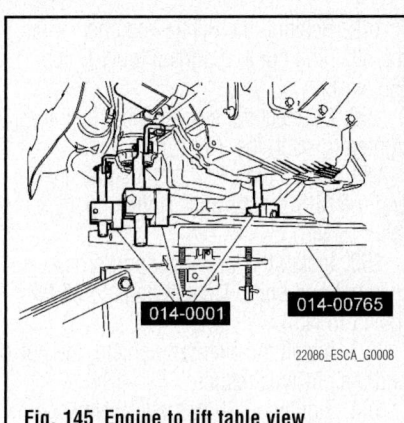

014-0001   014-00765

22086_ESCA_G0008

Fig. 145 Engine to lift table view

18. Remove the LH lower control arm knuckle bolt.

19. Remove the brake hose retainer and the ABS sensor retaining bolt from the RH strut

20. Disconnect the RH stabilizer bar link.

21. Remove the RH tie rod end retaining nut.

22. Remove the RH lower control arm knuckle bolt.

23. Using Removal tool, disconnect the LH and RH tie rod end from the steering knuckle.

24. Separate the LH and RH lower control arms and disconnect the steering knuckle from the lower ball joint and position the steering knuckle aside.

25. Using a suitable tool, separate the LH halfshaft from the transaxle and secure the halfshaft aside.

26. Using the suitable tools, remove the RH halfshaft from the intermediate shaft and secure the halfshaft aside.

27. Remove the 2 intermediate shaft retaining nuts.

28. Remove the intermediate shaft

29. Remove the Power Distribution Box (PDB) cover.

30. Remove the nut and the cable from the PDB.

31. Disconnect the electrical connector from the PDB.

32. Remove the bolt and ground strap.

33. Disconnect the 34-pin electrical connector.

34. Detach the wiring harness retainers from the battery tray bracket and position the wiring harness aside

35. Position the clutch hydraulic line aside.

36. Remove the clutch hydraulic line bracket-to-transaxle bolt.

37. Disconnect the clutch hydraulic line from the clutch slave cylinder.

38. Plug the hydraulic line.

39. Position the clutch hydraulic line aside.

40. Remove the wiring harness bracket nut and position aside

41. Disconnect the vehicle speed sensor (VSS) electrical connector and pin-type retainers

42. Disconnect the reversing lamp indicator switch.

43. Disconnect the shift cables.

44. Remove the 3 shift cable bracket bolts.

45. Position the bracket aside.

46. If equipped, disconnect the block heater electrical connector.

47. Detach all the block heater wiring harness retainers and position the wiring harness aside.

48. Disconnect the upper radiator hose.

49. Detach the heater hose support strap from the stud.

50. Disconnect the heater hoses from the heater core.

51. Remove the retainers and the accelerator cable snow shield

52. Disconnect the accelerator cable and speed control cable (if equipped).

53. Disconnect the accelerator and speed control cable (if equipped) from the throttle body.

54. Remove the bolts from the accelerator cable bracket.

55. Remove the nut from the accelerator control cable bracket.

56. Position the accelerator control cable and bracket assembly aside.

57. Remove the nut from the accelerator control cable bracket.

58. Disconnect the vacuum supply tube and position aside.

59. Disconnect the fuel vapor return tube and position aside.

60. Disconnect the fuel supply tube.

61. Detach the electrical connector retainers.

62. Remove the bolt and detach the ground wire.

63. Disconnect the PCM electrical connectors.

64. Remove the wiring harness retainer nut.

65. Disconnect the lower radiator hose from the radiator.

66. Disconnect the A/C compressor electrical connector and remove the 3 bolts.

67. Position the A/C compressor aside and support the compressor with a length of mechanic's wire.

68. Remove the front roll restrictor bolt and the 2 bolts for the engine support crossmember.

69. Remove the rear nut and the engine support crossmember.

➡**The transaxle-to-engine bolts differ in length. Mark the bolts for correct installation.**

70. Remove the transaxle-to-engine bolts.

71. Remove the engine-to-transaxle bolts

72. Using the special tools, secure the engine to the lift table

73. Remove the engine mount bracket bolt.

74. Remove the nuts and the engine mount bracket.

75. Remove the bolt from the transaxle rear mount.

76. Remove bolt from the LH transaxle mount.

77. Lower the engine and transaxle from the vehicle.

78. Remove the battery cable nut.

79. Remove the starter solenoid terminal nut.

80. Remove the wire harness clip retainer and the ground wire from the starter bolts.

81. Remove the 2 stud bolts and remove the starter.

82. Using the engine crane and spreader bar, remove the engine and transaxle from the lift table.

➡**The transaxle-to-engine bolts differ in length. Mark the bolts for correct installation.**

83. Remove the remaining 5 engine-to-transaxle bolts and separate the engine and transaxle.

To install:

84. Using the engine crane and spreader bar, position the engine and transaxle together. Install the 5 transaxle-to-engine bolts.

85. Using the engine crane and spreader bar, position the engine and transaxle onto the lift table.

86. Using the special tools, secure the engine to the lift table.

87. Install the starter motor and tighten bolts to 26 ft. lbs. (35 Nm).

88. Install the starter motor harness connector.

89. Install the starter motor solenoid battery nut and tighten to 9 ft. lbs. (12 Nm).

90. Install the starter motor solenoid nut and tighten to 44 inch. lbs (5 Nm).

91. Install the wire harness clip retainer and the ground wire and nut to the starter bolts tighten to 18 ft. lbs. (25 Nm).

92. Raise the engine and transaxle into the vehicle.

93. Install the bolt in the LH transaxle mount and tighten to 76 ft. lbs. (23 Nm).

94. Install the bolt in the rear transaxle mount and tighten to 85 ft. lbs. (115 Nm).

95. Install the engine mount bracket and nuts tighten to 85 ft. lbs. (115 Nm).

96. Install the engine mount bracket bolt and tighten to 85 ft. lbs. (115 Nm).

97. Install the 2 engine-to-transaxle bolts and tighten to 35 ft. lbs. (48 Nm).

98. Install the 2 transaxle-to-engine bolts and tighten to 35 ft. lbs. (48 Nm).

99. Install the engine support crossmember and new nut, tighten to 129 ft. lbs. (175 Nm).

100. Install the 2 bolts for the engine support crossmember and the front roll restrictor bolt.

101. Tighten the engine support crossmember bolts to 66 ft. lbs. (90 Nm).

102. Tighten the front roll restrictor bolt to 85 ft. lbs. (115 Nm).

103. Position the A/C compressor and install the bolts.

104. Tighten the bolts to 18 ft. lbs. (25 Nm).

105. Connect the A/C compressor electrical connector.

106. Connect the lower radiator hose to the radiator.

107. Connect the PCM electrical connectors.

108. Position the harness, install the nut and tighten to 53 inch. lbs (6 Nm).

109. Install the ground wire and bolt, tighten to 89 inch. lbs (10 Nm).

110. Attach the electrical connector retainers.

111. Connect the fuel supply tube quick connect coupling.

112. Connect the fuel vapor return tube and retainer.

113. Connect the vacuum supply tube.

114. Position the accelerator control cable and bracket and install the nut.

115. Tighten the bracket nut to 53 inch. lbs (6 Nm).

116. Install the accelerator cable and speed control cable (if equipped).

117. Connect the accelerator and speed control cable (if equipped) to the throttle body.

118. Install the accelerator cable bracket and bolts. Tighten to 89 inch. lbs (10 Nm).

119. Install the accelerator cable snow shield and retainers. Tighten to 35 inch. lbs (4 Nm).

120. Connect the heater hoses to the heater core.

121. Attach the heater hose support strap to the stud.

122. Connect the upper radiator hose.

123. If equipped, route the block heater wiring harness and attach all retainers.

124. Connect the block heater electrical connector.

125. Install the shift cable bracket and tighten mounting bolts to 16 ft. lbs. (22 Nm).

126. Connect the shift cables.

127. Connect the reversing lamp indicator switch.

128. Connect the vehicle speed sensor (VSS) electrical connector and pin-type retainer.

129. Install the wiring harness bracket nut and tighten to 9 ft. lbs. (12 Nm).

130. Connect the clutch hydraulic line to the clutch slave cylinder and tighten to 18 ft. lbs. (25 Nm).

131. Install the clutch hydraulic line bracket-to-transaxle bolt and tighten to 27 inch lbs. (3 Nm).

132. Attach the wiring harness retainers to the battery tray bracket.

133. Connect the 34-pin electrical connector.

134. Install the ground strap and bolt. Tighten to 89 inch lbs. (10 Nm).

135. Connect the electrical connector to the power distribution box (PDB).

136. Connect the cable to the PDB and install and tighten the nut to 9 ft. lbs. (12 Nm).

137. Install the PDB cover.

138. Install the intermediate shaft.

139. Install the intermediate shaft retaining nuts and tighten to 20 ft. lbs. (27 Nm).

140. Install the LH half shaft in the transaxle and the RH half shaft to the intermediate shaft.

141. Install the ball joints in the knuckles.

142. Install the LH lower ball joint-to-knuckle bolt and tighten to 46 ft. lbs. (63 Nm).

143. Position the RH tie-rod end, install the retaining nut and tighten to 41 ft. lbs. (55 Nm).

144. Connect the stabilizer bar link and tighten to 46 ft. lbs. (63 Nm).

145. Install the RH brake hose retainer and the anti-lock brake system (ABS) sensor bolt. Tighten to 11 ft. lbs. (15 Nm).

146. Install the RH half shaft in the transaxle and the RH half shaft to the intermediate shaft.

147. Install the ball joints in the knuckles.

148. Install the RH lower ball joint-to-knuckle bolt and tighten to 46 ft. lbs. (63 Nm).

149. Position the RH tie-rod end, install the retaining nut and tighten to 41 ft. lbs. (55 Nm).

150. Connect the stabilizer bar link and tighten to 46 ft. lbs. (63 Nm).

151. Install the LH brake hose retainer and the ABS sensor bolt. Tighten to 11 ft. lbs. (15 Nm).

152. Install the lateral support crossmember and bolts. Tighten bolts to 85 ft. lbs. (115 Nm).

153. Install the alternator shield, the nut and the pin-type retainer.

154. Tighten to 15 ft. lbs. (20 Nm).

155. Attach the wire retainers.

156. Install the lower air duct.

157. Install the accessory drive belt tensioner

158. Connect the heated oxygen sensor (HO2S) and the catalyst monitor sensor electrical connectors.

159. Install the exhaust flexible pipe.

160. Install the front wheels and tires.

161. Install the battery tray.

162. Install the engine air cleaner and air cleaner outlet pipe.

163. Fill the engine with clean engine oil.

164. Fill and bleed the cooling system.

165. Bleed the clutch system.

Automatic Transaxle

See Figure 146.

All vehicles:

1. Before servicing the vehicle, refer to the Precautions Section.

2. Disconnect the negative battery cable.

3. With the vehicle in NEUTRAL, position it on a hoist.

4. Release the fuel system pressure.

5. Remove the engine air cleaner and air cleaner outlet pipe.

6. Remove the battery tray.

7. Drain the engine oil.

8. Remove the front wheels and tires.

9. Drain the cooling system.

10. Remove the exhaust flexible pipe.

11. Remove the accessory drive belt and tensioner.

12. Press the 2 locking tabs to release the lower air duct from the upper air duct.

13. Detach the wire retainers from the alternator shield and remove the nut and pin-type retainer.

14. Remove the alternator shield.

15. Remove the bolts and the lateral support crossmember.

16. Remove the brake hose retainer and the ABS sensor retaining bolt from the LH strut

17. Disconnect the LH stabilizer bar link.

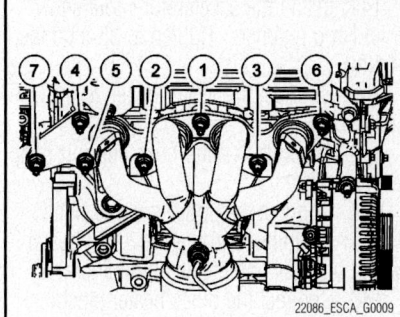

Fig. 146 Manifold tightening sequence—2008–09 engines

18. Remove the LH tie rod end retaining nut.

19. Remove the LH lower control arm knuckle bolt.

20. Remove the brake hose retainer and the ABS sensor retaining bolt from the RH strut.

21. Disconnect the RH stabilizer bar link.

22. Remove the RH tie rod end retaining nut.

23. Remove the RH lower control arm knuckle bolt.

24. Using a suitable tool, disconnect the LH and RH tie rod end from the steering knuckle.

25. Separate the LH and RH lower control arms from the lower ball joints and position the steering knuckles aside.

26. Using a suitable tool, separate the LH halfshaft from the transaxle and secure the halfshaft aside.

27. Using the suitable tools, remove the RH halfshaft from the intermediate shaft and secure the halfshaft aside.

28. Remove the 2 intermediate shaft retaining nuts.

29. Remove the intermediate shaft.

AWD vehicles:

➡ **Index-mark the driveshaft to the yoke for installation.**

30. Remove the 6 bolts holding the driveshaft to the PTU and position aside with mechanic's wire.

All vehicles:

31. If equipped, remove the bolt and ground eyelet.

32. Remove the Power Distribution Box (PDB) cover.

33. Remove the nut and disconnect the cable from the PDB.

34. Disconnect the electrical connector from the PDB.

35. Remove the bolt and the ground strap.

36. Disconnect the 34-pin electrical connector.

37. Detach the wiring harness retainers from the battery tray bracket.

38. Detach the transaxle vent tube retaining clip from the engine wiring harness.

39. Remove the nut holding the wiring harness bracket and unplug the transaxle electrical connector.

40. Disconnect the shift cable from the transaxle manual lever.

41. Detach the wiring harness pin-type retainer and remove the 2 bolts.

42. Position the transaxle cable and bracket aside.

43. Disconnect the transaxle range sensor electrical connector.

44. Disconnect the front transaxle fluid cooler tube.

45. Disconnect the rear transaxle fluid cooler tube.

46. Disconnect the transaxle fluid cooler tube.

47. Disconnect the Output Shaft Speed (OSS) sensor electrical connector (black).

48. Disconnect the Turbine Shaft Speed (TSS) sensor electrical connector (white).

49. Disconnect the wiring harness retainer from the transaxle case and position the harness aside.

50. Remove the transaxle fluid cooler retaining bracket bolt.

51. Position the fluid cooler tube aside.

52. Remove the bolt and the OSS sensor.

53. If equipped, disconnect the block heater electrical connector.

54. Detach all the block heater wiring harness retainers and position the wiring harness aside.

55. Disconnect the upper radiator hose.

56. Detach the heater hose support strap from the stud.

57. Disconnect the heater hoses from the heater core.

58. Remove the retainers and the accelerator cable snow shield.

59. Disconnect the accelerator and speed control cable (if equipped) from the throttle body.

60. Remove the bolts from the accelerator cable bracket.

61. Remove the nut from the accelerator control cable bracket.

62. Remove the nut from the accelerator control cable bracket.

63. Disconnect the vacuum supply tube and position aside.

64. Disconnect the fuel vapor return tube and retainer and position aside.

65. Disconnect the fuel supply tube quick connect coupling.

66. Detach the electrical connector retainers.

67. Remove the bolt and detach the ground wire.

68. Disconnect the Power Control Module (PCM) electrical connectors.

69. Remove the wiring harness retainer nut.

70. Disconnect the lower radiator hose from the radiator.

71. Disconnect the A/C compressor electrical connector and remove the 4 bolts.

72. Position the A/C compressor aside and support the compressor with a length of mechanic's wire.

73. Remove the front roll restrictor bolt and the 2 bolts for the engine support crossmember.

74. Remove the rear nut and the engine support crossmember.

Front wheel drive (FWD) vehicles:

75. Remove the 3 bolts and the damper.

All vehicles:

➡ **The transaxle-to-engine bolts differ in length. Mark the bolts for correct installation.**

76. Remove the 4 transaxle-to-engine bolts.

77. Using the suitable tools, secure the engine to the lift table.

78. Remove the engine mount bracket bolt.

79. Remove the nuts and the engine mount bracket

80. Remove the bolt from the transaxle rear mount.

81. Remove the bolt from the LH transaxle mount.

82. Lower the engine and transaxle from the vehicle.

83. Disconnect the starter battery cable, solenoid wire nuts and remove.

84. Remove the wire harness clip retainer and the ground wire from the starter bolts.

85. Remove the 2 stud bolts and remove the starter.

86. Remove the starter motor isolator.

AWD vehicles:

87. Remove the 2 lower catalytic converter bolts.

88. Remove the 6 bolts and the catalytic converter heat shield.

89. Remove and discard the 7 exhaust manifold nuts.

90. Remove the catalytic converter and discard the exhaust manifold gasket.

91. Remove and discard the 7 exhaust manifold studs.

92. Remove the 3 PTU bracket-to-engine bolts.

93. Remove the 2 PTU bracket-to-PTU bolts and remove the bracket.

94. Detach the PTU vent hose retainer.

95. Remove the transaxle-to-PTU bolt.

96. Remove the 3 PTU-to-transaxle bolts and the PTU.

All vehicles:

97. Remove and discard the 4 torque converter nuts.

98. Using the engine crane and spreader bar, remove the engine and transaxle from the lift table.

➡ **The transaxle-to-engine bolts differ in length. Mark the bolts for correct installation.**

99. Remove the remaining 6 engine-to-transaxle bolts and separate the engine and transaxle.

To install:
All vehicles:

100. Using the engine crane and spreader bar, position the engine and transaxle together. Install the 6 transaxle-to-engine bolts and tighten to 35 ft. lbs. (48 Nm).

101. Using the engine crane and spreader bar, position the engine and transaxle onto the lift table.

102. Using suitable tools, secure the engine to the lift table.

103. Install new torque converter nuts and tighten to 26 ft. lbs. (35 Nm).

AWD vehicles:

104. Install the Power Transfer Unit (PTU) and the 3 PTU-to-transaxle bolts. Tighten bolts to 52 ft. lbs. (70 Nm).

105. Install the 1 transaxle-to-PTU bolt and tighten to 35 ft. lbs. (48 Nm).

106. Attach the PTU vent hose.

107. Install the PTU bracket and the 2 bolts and tighten to 33 ft. lbs. (45 Nm).

108. Install the 3 PTU bracket-to-engine bolts and tighten to 30 ft. lbs. (40 Nm).

109. Install 7 new exhaust manifold studs in the cylinder head and tighten to 13 ft. lbs. (17 Nm).

110. Position the catalytic converter and tighten the 7 new exhaust manifold nuts in 2 stages:

a. Snug all nuts down evenly.

b. Tighten nuts to 35 ft. lbs. (47 Nm).

111. Install the heat shield and the 6 bolts and tighten to 89 inch lbs. (10 Nm).

112. Install the 2 lower catalytic converter bolts and tighten to 18 ft. lbs. (25 Nm).

All vehicles:

113. Install the starter motor isolator.

114. Install the starter motor tighten mounting bolts to 26 ft. lbs. (35 Nm).

115. Install starter cable harness tighten battery cable nut to 9 ft. lbs (12 Nm).

116. Tighten solenoid wire nut to 44 inch lbs. (5 Nm).

117. Install the wire harness clip retainer and the ground wire and nut to the starter bolts. Tighten nut to 18 ft. lbs. (25 Nm).

118. Raise the engine and transaxle into the vehicle.

119. Install the bolt in the LH transaxle mount and tighten to 76 ft. lbs. (103 Nm).

120. Install the bolt in the rear transaxle mount and tighten to 85 ft. lbs. (115 Nm).

121. Install the engine mount bracket and nuts. Tighten to 85 ft. lbs. (115 Nm).

122. Install the engine mount bracket bolt and tighten to 85 ft. lbs. (115 Nm).

123. Install the 4 transaxle-to-engine bolts and tighten to 35 ft. lbs. (38 Nm).

FWD vehicles:

124. Install the damper and the 3 bolts. Tighten to 30 ft. lbs. (40 Nm).

All vehicles:

125. Install the engine support crossmember and new nut. Tighten to 129 ft. lbs. (175 Nm).

126. Install the 2 bolts for the engine support crossmember and the front roll restrictor bolt.

a. Tighten the engine support crossmember bolts to 66 ft. lbs. (90 Nm).

b. Tighten the front roll restrictor bolt to 85 ft. lbs. (115 Nm).

127. Install the A/C compressor and connect the A/C compressor electrical connector.

128. Tighten A/C bolts to 18 ft. lbs. (25 Nm).

129. Connect the lower radiator hose to the radiator.

130. Connect the PCM electrical connectors.

131. Position the harness and install the nut. Tighten nut to 53 inch lbs. (6 Nm).

132. Install the ground wire and bolt. Tighten to 89 inch lbs. (10 Nm).

133. Attach the electrical connector retainers.

134. Connect the fuel supply tube quick connect coupling.

135. Connect the fuel vapor return tube and retainer.

136. Connect the vacuum supply tube.

137. Position the accelerator control cable and bracket and install the nut. Tighten nut to 53 inch lbs. (6 Nm).

138. Install the accelerator cable and speed control cable (if equipped).

139. Connect the accelerator and speed control cable (if equipped) to the throttle body.

140. Install the accelerator cable bracket and bolts. Tighten to 89 inch lbs. (10 Nm).

141. Install the accelerator cable snow shield and retainers. Tighten to 35 inch lbs. (4 Nm).

142. Connect the heater hoses to the heater core.

143. Attach the heater hose support strap to the stud.

144. Connect the upper radiator hose.

145. If equipped, route the block heater wiring harness and attach all retainers.

146. Connect the block heater electrical connector.

147. Install the Output Shaft Speed (OSS) sensor tighten mounting bolt to 10 ft. lbs. (13 Nm).

148. Install the fluid cooler tube.

a. Connect the OSS sensor.

b. Connect the turbine shaft speed (TSS) sensor (white connector).

c. Connect the wiring harness retainer to the transaxle case.

d. Position the bracket and install the bolt. Tighten to 10 ft. lbs. (13 Nm).

e. Install the fluid cooler tube fitting and tighten to 17 ft. lbs. (23 Nm).

149. Connect the rear transaxle fluid cooler tube and tighten to 17 ft. lbs. (23 Nm).

150. Connect the front transaxle fluid cooler tube and tighten to 17 ft. lbs. (23 Nm).

151. Connect the transaxle range sensor electrical connector.

152. Install the transaxle control cable, bracket and tighten bolts to 14 ft. lbs. (19 Nm).

153. Attach the wiring harness pin-type retainers.

154. Connect the shift cable to the transaxle manual lever.

155. Install the transaxle wiring harness bracket and nut and connect the transaxle electrical connector. Tighten bracket nut to 89 inch lbs. (10 Nm).

156. Attach the transaxle vent tube retaining clip to the engine wiring harness.

157. Attach the wiring harness retainers to the battery tray bracket.

158. Connect the 34-pin electrical connector.

159. Install the ground strap and tighten bolt to 89 inch lbs. (10 Nm).

160. Connect the electrical connector to the Power Distribution Box (PDB).

161. Connect the cable to the PDB and install and tighten the nut to 9 ft. lbs. (12 Nm).

162. Install the PDB cover.

163. If equipped, install the ground eyelet and bolt. Tighten to 89 inch lbs. (10 Nm).

AWD vehicles:

164. Align index mark and position the driveshaft to the PTU and install the 6 bolts.

165. Tighten driveshaft mounting bolts to 27 ft. lbs. (37 Nm).

All vehicles:

166. Install the intermediate shaft.

167. Install the intermediate shaft retaining nuts and tighten to 20 ft. lbs. (27 Nm).

168. Install the LH halfshaft in the transaxle and the RH halfshaft to the intermediate shaft.

169. Install the ball joints in the knuckles.

170. Install the RH lower ball joint-to-knuckle bolt and tighten to 46 ft. lbs. (63 Nm).

171. Position the RH tie-rod end and install the retaining nut. Tighten to 41 ft. lbs. (55 Nm).

172. Connect the RH stabilizer bar link and tighten to 46 ft. lbs. (63 Nm).

173. Install the RH brake hose retainer and the ABS sensor bolt. Tighten to 11 ft. lbs. (15 Nm).

174. Install the LH lower ball joint-to-knuckle bolt and tighten to 46 ft. lbs. (63 Nm).

175. Position the LH tie-rod end and install the retaining nut. Tighten to 41 ft. lbs. (55 Nm).

176. Connect the LH stabilizer bar link and tighten to 46 ft. lbs. (63 Nm).

177. Install the LH brake hose retainer and the ABS sensor bolt. Tighten to 11 ft. lbs. (15 Nm).

178. Install the lateral support crossmember and tighten bolts to 85 ft. lbs. (115 Nm).

179. Install the alternator shield and the pin-type retainer, tighten the nut to 15 ft. lbs. (20 Nm).

180. Install the lower air duct.

181. Install the accessory drive belt and tensioner.

182. Connect the heated oxygen sensor (HO2S) and the catalyst monitor sensor electrical connectors.

183. Install the exhaust flexible pipe.

184. Install the front wheels and tires.

185. Install the battery tray.

186. Install the engine air cleaner and air cleaner outlet pipe.

187. Fill the engine with clean engine oil.

188. Fill and bleed the cooling system.

6 Cylinder Engines

See Figures 147 through 149.

1. Before servicing the vehicle, refer to the Precautions Section.

2. Disconnect the negative battery cable.

3. With the vehicle in NEUTRAL, position it on a hoist.

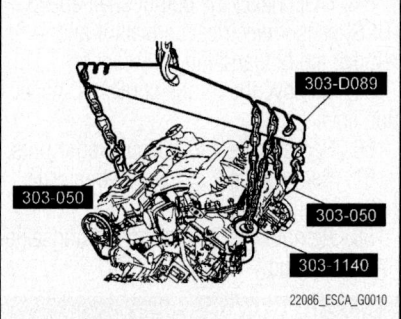

Fig. 147 6 Cylinder engine removal— 2008–09 models

4. Release the fuel system pressure.

5. Remove the battery tray.

6. Remove the air cleaner outlet pipe and air cleaner.

7. Remove the front wheels and tires.

8. Remove the lower splash shields.

9. Disconnect the catalyst monitor sensor electrical connector and the 2 wiring harness retainers.

10. Remove the 4 bolts and the lateral support crossmember.

11. Remove and discard the 6 exhaust Y-pipe-to-catalytic converter nuts.

12. Detach the exhaust hanger and remove the exhaust Y-pipe.

13. Remove the LH and RH brake hose retainers and ABS sensor wiring harness bolts.

14. Remove the LH and RH stabilizer link-to-strut nuts.

15. Remove the LH and RH tie-rod end nuts.

16. Using the suitable tool, separate the LH and RH tie-rod ends from the steering knuckles.

17. Remove the LH and RH lower ball joint pinch bolts and nuts.

18. Separate the steering knuckles from the lower ball joints.

19. Using a suitable tool, separate the LH halfshaft from the transaxle.

20. Support the halfshaft with a length of mechanic's wire.

21. Using the special tools, separate the RH halfshaft from the intermediate shaft.

22. Support the halfshaft with a length of mechanic's wire.

23. Remove the 2 intermediate shaft retaining nuts.

24. Remove the intermediate shaft.

All wheel drive (AWD) vehicles

✳✳ WARNING

Do not reuse the driveshaft flange bolts and washers. Install new bolts and washers or damage to the vehicle may occur.

➡Index-mark the drive shaft flange and Power Transfer Unit (PTU) flange for installation.

25. Remove and discard the 6 front driveshaft-to-PTU bolts and washers.

26. Position the driveshaft aside and support with mechanic's wire.

27. Rotate the accessory drive belt tensioner counterclockwise and remove the accessory drive belt.

28. Drain the engine coolant.

29. Drain the engine oil and install the drain plug.

30. Disconnect the A/C clutch field coil electrical connector.

31. Remove the 3 bolts and position the A/C compressor aside.

32. Remove the 3 accessory drive belt idler pulley assembly bolts.

33. Detach the wiring harness retainer and remove the idler pulley assembly.

34. Remove the front roll restrictor bolt and the 2 bolts for the engine support cross brace.

35. Remove the rear nut and the engine support crossmember.

36. Disconnect the 2 transmission cooler tubes (1 shown).

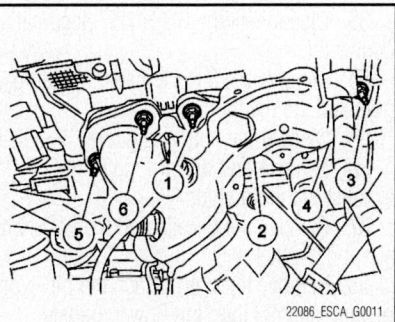

Fig. 148 Manifold tightening sequence— 2008–09 3.0L engine

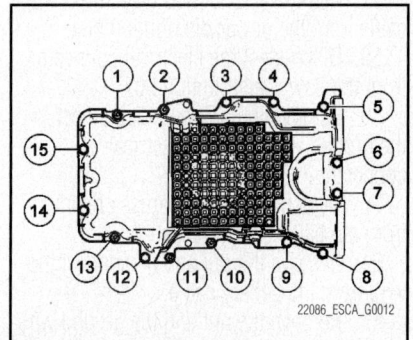

Fig. 149 Oil pan tightening sequence— 2008 3.0L engine

37. Loosen the transaxle cooler tube fitting.

38. Remove the bracket bolt and the transaxle cooler tube.

39. Disconnect the EGR tube fitting from the converter.

40. Remove the 2 bolts and the accelerator cable snow shield.

41. Disconnect the accelerator cable and the speed control actuator cable.

42. Remove the 2 accelerator cable bracket bolts.

43. Remove the bolt and position the cables and brackets aside.

44. Disconnect the upper and lower radiator hoses.

45. Disconnect the heater hoses and the throttle body coolant hose.

46. Detach the transaxle vent tube retainer from the throttle body.

47. Disconnect the fuel supply tube quick connect coupling.

48. Disconnect the gearshift cable from the transaxle.

49. Disconnect the wire harness retainer from the shift cable bracket, remove the 2 remaining bolts, and position the cable and bracket aside.

50. Disconnect the differential pressure feedback EGR sensor electrical connector and detach the pin-type retainer.

51. Disconnect the EGR tube fitting and remove the EGR tube and the differential pressure feedback EGR sensor as an assembly.

52. Disconnect the evaporative emissions (EVAP) canister purge valve tube from the intake manifold.

53. Disconnect the brake booster vacuum tube from the intake manifold.

54. Disconnect the manifold absolute pressure (MAP) sensor vacuum tube and electrical connector.

55. Disconnect the PCM electrical connectors and remove the nut.

56. Remove the bolt and detach the ground wire.

57. Remove the nut and disconnect the cable from the power distribution box.

58. Disconnect the electrical connector from the power distribution box.

59. Remove the bolt and disconnect the ground wire and the electrical connector.

60. Detach the wiring harness retainers from the battery tray bracket

61. Remove the nut and disconnect the wire from the battery cable.

62. Remove the nut and the ground wire from the engine mount stud.

63. If equipped, disconnect the engine block heater electrical connector.

64. Disconnect the output shaft speed (OSS) sensor electrical connector and remove the bolt and the OSS sensor.

65. Remove the torque converter inspection cover.

66. Remove the 4 torque converter nuts.

67. Remove the 2 oil pan-to-transaxle bolts.

68. Remove the 2 nuts and the transaxle-to-engine stud.

❉❉ WARNING

Do not allow the engine oil pan to rest on the power train lift. Doing so may cause damage to the oil pan.

69. Using the suitable tools, secure the engine and transaxle to the powertrain lift.

➡ **The next 5 steps must be carried out with the vehicle raised and the powertrain lift in position.**

70. Remove the RH transaxle support insulator bolt.

71. Remove the bolt, nuts and the RH transaxle support insulator.

72. Remove the rear transaxle support bolt.

73. Remove the 3 engine support bracket nuts and the bolt.

74. Remove the engine support bracket.

75. Lower the powertrain from the vehicle.

76. Disconnect the LH Heated Exhaust Gas Oxygen (HEGO) sensor and LH catalyst monitor sensor electrical connectors.

77. Detach the 3 pin-type retainers from the transaxle support bracket.

78. Disconnect the transmission range (TR) sensor electrical connector

79. Disconnect the transaxle electronic control switch electrical connector.

80. Detach the wiring harness from the bracket.

81. Disconnect the turbine speed sensor (TSS) electrical connector.

82. Detach the 2 wiring harness retainer.

AWD vehicles:

83. Disconnect the RH HO2S electrical connector

84. Remove the 6 RH exhaust manifold nuts and the manifold.

85. Discard the nuts and gasket.

86. Remove and discard the 6 RH exhaust manifold studs.

87. Remove the 6 bolts and the halfshaft support bracket.

88. Remove the bolt, detach the pin-type retainer and position the Power Transfer Unit (PTU) vent tube aside.

89. Remove the 3 PTU bolts.

90. Remove the bolt and the PTU.

All vehicles:

91. Remove the nut and detach wiring harness retainer.

92. Remove the 2 stud bolts and position the EGR regulator aside.

93. Install engine lifting brackets to engine.

94. Using the suitable tools and a suitable engine crane, remove the engine and transaxle from the lift table.

95. Remove the 5 remaining transaxle-to-engine bolts.

96. Using the suitable tools and a suitable engine crane, separate the engine and transaxle.

To install:
All vehicles:

97. Using the special tools, align the engine with the transaxle.

98. Install the 5 transaxle-to-engine bolts and tighten to 35 ft. lbs. (48 Nm).

99. Using the suitable tools, secure the engine and transaxle to the powertrain lift.

100. Install the EGR regulator and the 2 stud bolts. Tighten to 53 inch lbs. (6 Nm).

101. Attach the wiring harness retainer and install the nut. Tighten to 53 inch lbs. (6 Nm).

AWD vehicles:

102. Position the Power Transfer Unit (PTU) and install the bolt. Tighten to 33 ft. lbs. (45 Nm).

103. Install the 3 PTU bolts and tighten to 33 ft. lbs. (45 Nm).

104. Install the PTU vent tube, the pin-type retainer and the bolt. Tighten to 20 ft. lbs. (14 Nm).

105. Install the halfshaft support bracket and the 6 bolts. Tighten bolts to 35 ft. lbs. (48 Nm).

106. Install 6 new RH exhaust manifold studs and tighten to 9 ft. lbs. (12 Nm).

107. Using a new gasket, install the RH exhaust manifold and 6 new nuts.

108. Tighten the manifold nuts to 15 ft. lbs. (20 Nm).

109. Connect the RH heated oxygen sensor (HO2S) electrical connector.

All vehicles:

110. Connect the turbine speed sensor (TSS) electrical connector.

111. Attach the wiring harness retainer.

112. Attach the transaxle control harness to the bracket.

113. Connect the transaxle wiring harness electronic control switch electrical connector.

114. Connect the transmission range (TR) sensor electrical connector

115. Attach the pin-type retainers to the transaxle support bracket and connect the

HO2S and catalyst monitor sensor electrical connectors.

116. Position the powertrain into the vehicle

117. Install the engine support bracket, the bolt and the 3 nuts. Tighten the nuts to 56 ft. lbs. (41 Nm). And the bolts to 66 ft. lbs. (90 Nm).

118. Install the rear transaxle support through bolt and tighten to 76 ft. lbs. (103 Nm).

119. Position the RH transaxle support insulator and install the bolt and nuts. Tighten to 59 ft. lbs. (80 Nm).

120. Install the RH transaxle support insulator through bolt and tighten to 85 ft. lbs. (115 Nm).

121. Install the transaxle-to-engine stud and 2 nuts. Tighten to 35 ft. lbs. (48 Nm).

➡**Clean and degrease all sealing surfaces with metal surface cleaner. The oil pan must be installed and the bolts tightened within 4 minutes of the sealant application.**

122. Apply a 10 mm (0.39 in) dot of silicone gasket and sealant to the front cover-to-cylinder block sealing surface.

123. Install a new oil pan gasket.

124. Position the oil pan and gasket and loosely install the bolts and stud bolts.

125. Install the 2 oil pan-to-transaxle bolts. Tighten to 30 ft. lbs. (40 Nm).

126. Tighten the oil pan bolts in sequence to 18 ft. lbs. (25 Nm).

127. Install the 4 torque converter nuts and tighten to 30 ft. lbs. (40 Nm).

128. Install the torque converter inspection cover.

129. Install the output shaft speed (OSS) sensor and the bolt and connect the electrical connector. Tighten mounting bolt to 10 ft. lbs. (13 Nm).

130. If equipped, connect the engine block heater electrical connector.

131. Install the ground wire eyelet and nut to the engine mount stud. Tighten to 18 ft. lbs. (25 Nm).

132. Install the wire and nut to the battery cable. Tighten to 89 inch lbs. (10 Nm).

133. Attach the wiring harness retainers from the battery tray bracket.

134. Position the ground strap and the electrical connector and install the bolts. Tighten to 89 inch lbs. (10 Nm).

135. Connect the electrical connector to the power distribution box.

136. Install the cable and the nut. Tighten to 9 ft. lbs. (12 Nm).

137. Attach the ground wire and install the bolt. Tighten to 89 inch lbs. (10 Nm).

138. Position the wiring and install the nut. Tighten to 71 inch lbs. (8 Nm). Connect the PCM electrical connectors.

139. Connect the manifold absolute pressure (MAP) sensor electrical connector and vacuum tube.

140. Connect the brake booster vacuum tube

141. Connect the evaporative emissions (EVAP) purge valve tube to the intake manifold.

142. Position the EGR tube and loosely install the fittings.

143. Tighten the EGR tube-to-EGR valve fitting to 30 ft. lbs. (40 Nm).

144. Connect the differential pressure feedback EGR sensor electrical connector and attach the pin-type retainer.

145. Position the shift cable and bracket in place, install the bolts and tighten to 17 ft. lbs. (23 Nm). Install the wiring harness retainer.

146. Connect the gearshift cable to the transaxle.

147. Attach the wiring harness pin-type retainer to the gearshift cable bracket.

148. Connect the fuel supply tube quick connect coupling at the fuel rail

149. Attach the transaxle vent tube retainer to the throttle body.

150. Connect the heater hoses and the throttle body coolant hose

151. Connect the upper and lower radiator hoses.

152. Position the accelerator and speed control cables and bracket. Install the nut and tighten to 89 inch lbs. (10 Nm).

153. Position the bracket and install and tighten the bolts to 89 inch lbs. (10 Nm).

154. Connect the accelerator cable and the speed control actuator cable

155. Position the accelerator cable snow shield, install and tighten the bolts to 89 inch lbs. (10 Nm).

156. Tighten the EGR tube-to-RH catalytic converter fitting to 30 ft. lbs. (40 Nm).

157. Install the transaxle cooler tube and the bracket bolt.

158. Tighten the bolt to 10 ft. lbs. (13 Nm), tighten the fitting to 17 ft. lbs. (23 Nm).

159. Connect the 2 transmission cooler tubes.

160. Install the cross brace and the new nut finger tight.

161. Install the 2 bolts for the cross brace and the bolt for the front roll restrictor.

a. Tighten the 2 cross brace bolts to 66 ft. lbs. (90 Nm).

b. Tighten the front roll restrictor bolt to 85 ft. lbs. (115 Nm).

162. Tighten the cross brace nut to 129 ft. lbs. (175 Nm).

163. Position the RH accessory drive belt idler pulley and bracket and attach the wiring harness retainer. Install the bolts and tighten to 18 ft. lbs. (25 Nm).

164. Install the A/C compressor and bolts, tighten to 18 ft. lbs. (25 Nm).

165. Connect the A/C clutch field coil electrical connector

166. Rotate the accessory drive belt tensioner counterclockwise and install the accessory drive belt.

AWD vehicles:

✳✳ WARNING

Do not reuse the driveshaft flange bolts and washers. Install new bolts and washers or damage to the vehicle may occur.

167. Align the index-marks made during removal and install 6 new front driveshaft-to-PTU bolts and washers. Tighten to 27 ft. lbs. (37 Nm).

All vehicles:

168. Install the intermediate shaft and the 2 nuts. Tighten to 20 ft. lbs. (27 Nm).

169. Install the RH halfshaft onto the intermediate shaft.

170. Install the LH halfshaft into the transaxle.

171. Attach the LH and RH lower ball joints to the steering knuckles and install the pinch bolts and nuts. Tighten to 46 ft. lbs (63 Nm).

172. Install the LH and RH tie-rod ends and nuts. Tighten to 41 ft. lbs. (55 Nm).

173. Install the LH and RH stabilizer link-to-strut nuts. Tighten to 46 ft. lbs (63 Nm).

174. Install the LH and RH brake hose retainers and ABS sensor wiring harness bolts. Tighten to 11 ft. lbs. (15 Nm).

175. Install the Y-pipe and the 2 exhaust flange-to-RH catalytic converter nuts. Tighten to 21 ft. lbs. (29 Nm).

176. Install the 2 exhaust flange-to-LH catalytic converter nuts. Tighten to 21 ft. lbs. (29 Nm).

177. Attach the Y-pipe to the rear catalytic converter.

178. Attach the exhaust hanger.

179. Install the 2 exhaust flange-to-rear catalytic converter nuts and tighten to 21 ft. lbs. (29 Nm).

180. Install the lateral support cross-member and the 4 bolts. Tighten to 85 ft. lbs. (115 Nm).

181. Connect the catalyst monitor sensor electrical connector and the 2 wiring harness retainers

182. Install the lower splash shields.

183. Install the front wheels and tires.

184. Install the air cleaner outlet pipe and air cleaner

185. Install the battery tray.

186. Fill the engine with clean engine oil.

187. Fill and bleed the cooling system.

188. Connect the negative battery cable.

EXHAUST MANIFOLD

REMOVAL & INSTALLATION

2.3L Engine

See Figure 150.

1. Before servicing the vehicle, refer to the Precautions Section.

2. Raise and safely support the vehicle.

3. Remove the exhaust flexible pipe.

4. Remove the 2 catalytic converter bracket bolts.

5. Remove the 6 heat shield bolts and the heat shield.

6. Disconnect the Heated Oxygen Sensor (HO2S) and the catalyst monitor sensor electrical connectors.

7. Remove and discard the 7 catalytic converter manifold nuts.

8. Remove the catalytic converter from the vehicle. Discard the catalytic converter manifold gasket.

9. Remove and discard the 7 catalytic converter manifold studs.

To install:

10. Install the 7 new catalytic converter studs and tighten to 13 ft. lbs. (17 Nm).

11. Position a new catalytic converter manifold gasket on the engine.

➡Failure to tighten the catalytic converter nuts to specification before installing the converter bracket bolts will cause the converter to develop an exhaust leak.

12. Position the catalytic converter and tighten the 7 exhaust manifold nuts in 2 stages in the sequence shown:
- Stage 1: Tighten to 35 ft. lbs. (47 Nm).
- Stage 2: Tighten to 35 ft. lbs. (47 Nm).

13. Connect the HO2S and the catalyst monitor sensor electrical connectors.

14. Position the heat shield and install the 6 heat shield bolts. Tighten the heat shield bolts to 89 inch lbs. (10 Nm).

15. Install the 2 catalytic converter bracket bolts and tighten to 18 ft. lbs. (25 Nm).

16. Install the exhaust flexible pipe. Install a new gasket and tighten the flex pipe-to-converter nuts to 35 ft. lbs. (47 Nm).

17. Lower the vehicle.

18. Check the exhaust system for leaks.

2.5L Engine

See Figure 151.

1. Before servicing the vehicle, refer to the Precautions Section.

2. With the vehicle in NEUTRAL, position it on a hoist.

3. Remove and discard the 3 exhaust intermediate pipe-to-exhaust down pipe nuts.

4. Remove and discard the two 10-mm catalytic converter-to-exhaust intermediate pipe spring nuts and remove the intermediate pipe.

5. Remove the 2 exhaust bracket bolts.

6. Remove the 2 exhaust down pipe-to-exhaust manifold nuts and the exhaust down pipe.

7. Disconnect the Heated Oxygen Sensor (HO2S) electrical connector.

8. Remove the 4 exhaust manifold heat shield bolts and the heat shield.

9. Remove and discard the 7 exhaust manifold nuts.

10. Remove the exhaust manifold and discard the exhaust manifold gasket.

11. Remove and discard the 7 exhaust manifold studs.

12. Clean and inspect the exhaust manifold.

To install:

13. Install the 7 new exhaust manifold studs and tighten to 150 inch lbs. (17 Nm).

➡Failure to tighten the catalytic converter nuts to specification before installing the converter bracket bolts will cause the converter to develop an exhaust leak.

14. Install a new exhaust manifold gasket, the exhaust manifold and 7 new nuts in the sequence shown in 2 stages:
- Stage 1: Tighten to 35 ft. lbs. (48 Nm).
- Stage 2: Tighten to 35 ft. lbs. (48 Nm).

15. Install the exhaust manifold heat shield and the 4 bolts. Tighten the heat shield bolts to 89 inch lbs. (10 Nm).

16. Connect the HO2S electrical connector.

17. Install the down pipe with a new gasket, tighten the down pipe-to-exhaust manifold nuts to 30 ft. lbs. (40 Nm).

18. Install and tighten the exhaust bracket bolts to 18 ft. lbs. (25 Nm).

➡Thoroughly clean the sealing surfaces of the flanges using a finishing pad. Inspect the cleaned sealing surface for nicks and scratches and replace as necessary.

19. Install a new converter-to-exhaust intermediate pipe gasket by hand.

20. Install the 2 new 10-mm catalytic converter-to-exhaust intermediate pipe spring nuts and alternately tighten RH side to LH side in sequence in 3 stages:
- Stage 1: Tighten to 44 inch lbs. (5 Nm).
- Stage 2: Tighten to 133 inch lbs. (15 Nm).
- Stage 3: Tighten to 18 ft. lbs. (25 Nm).

21. Install 3 new exhaust intermediate pipe-to-exhaust down pipe nuts. Tighten the nuts to 18 ft. lbs. (25 Nm).

22. Start the engine and check for exhaust leaks, repair as needed.

3.0L Engine—2008 Models

Catalytic Converter—LH Manifold

See Figures 152 and 153.

1. Before servicing the vehicle, refer to the Precautions Section.

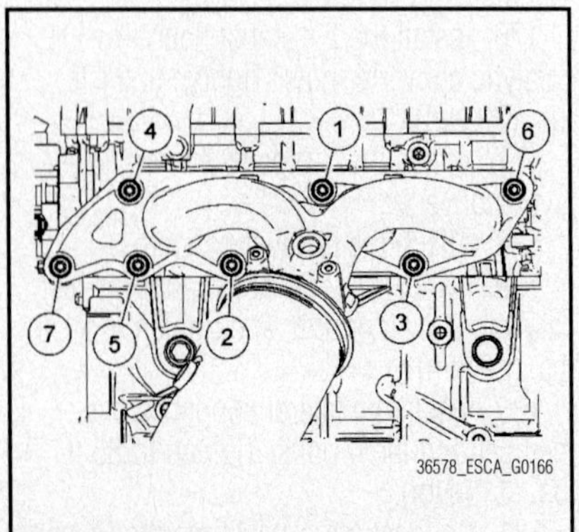

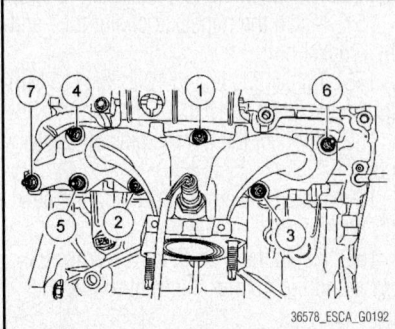

Fig. 150 Manifold tightening sequence—2.3L engine

36578_ESCA_G0166

Fig. 151 Exhaust manifold tightening sequence—2.5L engine

36578_ESCA_G0192

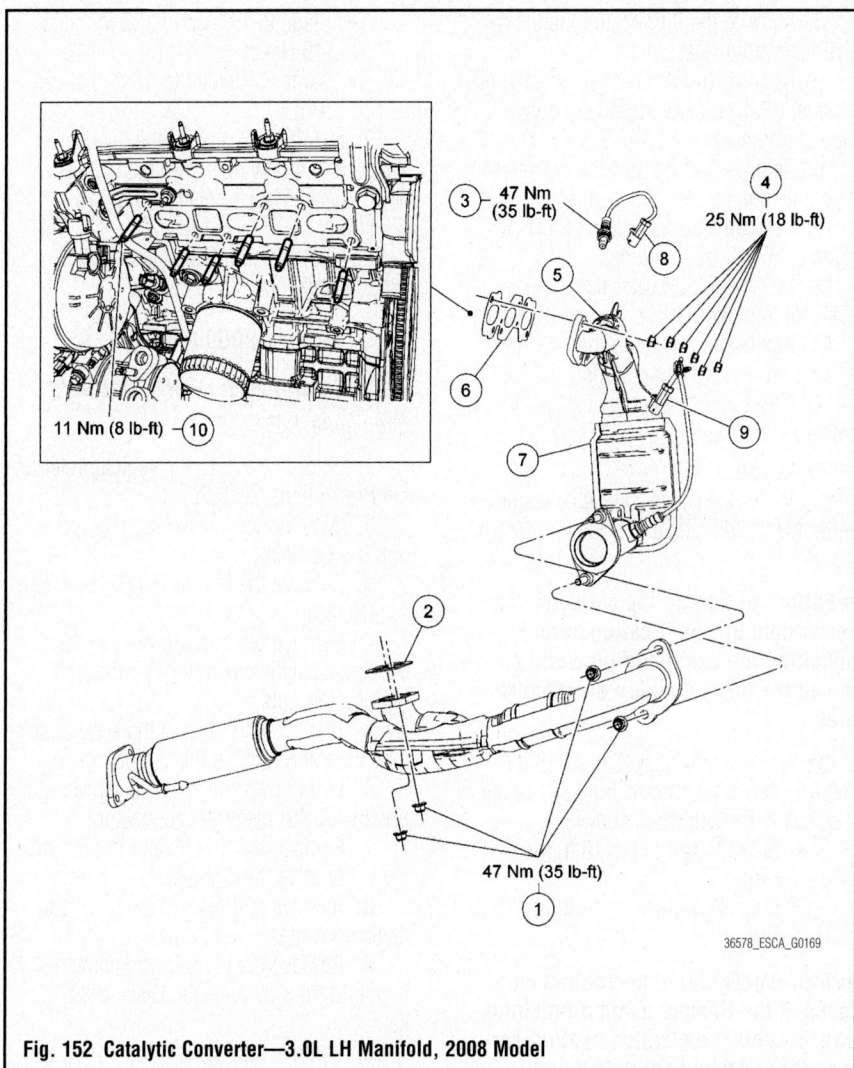

11 Nm (8 lb-ft) — ⑩

47 Nm (35 lb-ft)

③ 47 Nm (35 lb-ft)

④ 25 Nm (18 lb-ft)

Fig. 152 Catalytic Converter—3.0L LH Manifold, 2008 Model

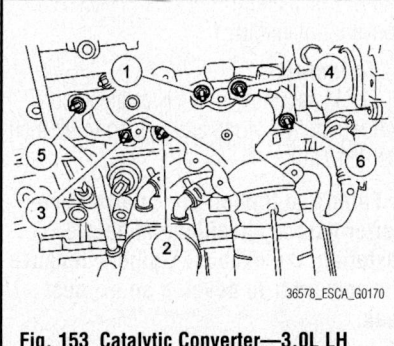

Fig. 153 Catalytic Converter—3.0L LH Manifold tightening sequence—2008 Model

2. With the vehicle in NEUTRAL, position it on a hoist

3. Remove the 5 bolts and the passenger side splash shield.

4. Disconnect the LH Heated Oxygen Sensor (HO2S) and the LH catalyst monitor sensor electrical connectors.

5. Using the HO2S socket, remove the HO2S.

➡**Do not allow the exhaust Y-pipe to hang from the flexible end. Support the exhaust Y-pipe or damage to the exhaust system may occur.**

6. Remove and discard the 4 exhaust Y-pipe nuts and position the exhaust Y-pipe aside. Discard the gasket.

7. Remove and discard the 6 LH catalytic converter manifold nuts.

8. Remove the LH catalytic converter from the vehicle. Discard the LH catalytic converter manifold gasket.

9. Remove and discard the 6 LH catalytic converter manifold studs.

To install:

10. Install the 6 new LH catalytic converter manifold studs and tighten to 97 inch lbs. (11 Nm).

11. Position a new LH catalytic converter manifold gasket.

➡**Failure to tighten the catalytic converter nuts to specification before installing the converter bracket bolts**

will cause the converter to develop an exhaust leak.

12. Position the LH catalytic converter and tighten the 6 exhaust manifold nuts in 2 stages in the sequence shown:
   - Stage 1: Tighten to 18 ft. lbs. (25 Nm).
   - Stage 2: Tighten to 18 ft. lbs. (25 Nm).

13. Position the exhaust Y-pipe gasket.

14. Position the exhaust Y-pipe and install the 4 new exhaust Y-pipe nuts and tighten to 35 ft. lbs. (47 Nm).

➡**Make sure to apply anti-seize lubricant to the threads of the HO2S before installation.**

15. Using the HO2S socket, install the HO2S and tighten to 35 ft. lbs. (47 Nm).

16. Install the passenger side splash shield and the 5 bolts.

17. Connect the LH HO2S and catalyst monitor sensor electrical connectors.

18. Start the engine and check for exhaust leaks, repair as needed.

Catalytic Converter—RH Manifold

See Figure 154.

1. Before servicing the vehicle, refer to the Precautions Section.

2. Remove and discard the 4 exhaust Y-pipe nuts and position the exhaust Y-pipe aside. Discard the gasket.

3. Disconnect the RH Heated Oxygen Sensor (HO2S) electrical connector.

4. Disconnect the EGR tube nut from the RH catalytic converter.

5. Remove and discard the 6 RH catalytic converter manifold nuts.

6. Remove the RH catalytic converter from the vehicle. Discard the RH catalytic converter manifold gasket.

7. Remove and discard the 6 RH catalytic converter manifold studs.

Fig. 154 Catalytic Converter—3.0L RH Manifold tightening sequence—2008 Model

8. Clean and inspect the RH catalytic converter manifold.

To install:

9. Install the 6 new RH catalytic converter manifold studs and tighten to 97 inch lbs. (11 Nm).

10. Position a new RH catalytic converter manifold gasket.

➡**Failure to tighten the catalytic converter nuts to specification before installing the converter bracket bolts will cause the converter to develop an exhaust leak.**

11. Position the RH catalytic converter and tighten the 6 exhaust manifold nuts in 2 stages in the sequence shown:
- Stage 1: Tighten to 18 ft. lbs. (25 Nm).
- Stage 2: Tighten to 18 ft. lbs. (25 Nm).

12. Connect the EGR tube nut to the RH catalytic converter. Tighten the tube nut to 30 ft. lbs. (40 Nm).

13. Connect the HO2S electrical connector.

14. Position the exhaust Y-pipe gasket.

15. Position the exhaust Y-pipe and install the 4 new exhaust Y-pipe nuts and tighten to 35 ft. lbs. (47 Nm).

➡**Make sure to apply anti-seize lubricant to the threads of the HO2S before installation.**

16. Install the passenger side splash shield and the 5 bolts.

17. Connect the LH HO2S and catalyst monitor sensor electrical connectors.

18. Start the engine and check for exhaust leaks, repair as needed.

3.0L Engine—2009 Models

Catalytic Converter—LH Manifold

See Figure 155.

1. Before servicing the vehicle, refer to the Precautions Section.

2. With the vehicle in NEUTRAL, position it on a hoist.

3. Remove the 6 retainers and the passenger side splash shield.

4. Remove the LH Heated Oxygen Sensor (HO2S).

5. Rotate the accessory drive belt tensioner counterclockwise and remove the accessory drive belt.

6. Disconnect the A/C compressor electrical connector.

7. Remove the 3 bolts and position the A/C compressor aside.

8. Remove the 3 bolts and the LH catalytic converter heat shield.

9. Remove and discard the two 10-mm exhaust catalytic converter-to-exhaust Y-pipe spring nuts.

10. Remove and discard the 4 exhaust Y-pipe nuts and remove the Y-pipe.

11. Remove and discard the 6 LH catalytic converter manifold nuts.

12. Remove the LH catalytic converter manifold from the vehicle. Discard the gasket.

13. Remove and discard the 6 LH catalytic converter manifold studs.

14. Clean and inspect the LH catalytic converter manifold.

To install:

15. Install the 6 new LH catalytic converter manifold studs and tighten to 97 inch lbs. (11 Nm).

➡**Failure to tighten the catalytic converter nuts to specification before installing the exhaust Y-pipe will cause the converter to develop an exhaust leak.**

16. Using a new gasket, install the LH catalytic converter and the 6 nuts. Tighten in 2 stages in the sequence shown:
- Stage 1: Tighten to 18 ft. lbs. (25 Nm).
- Stage 2: Tighten to 18 ft. lbs. (25 Nm).

➡**Thoroughly clean the sealing surfaces of the flanges using a finishing pad. Inspect the cleaned sealing surface for nicks and scratches and replace as necessary.**

17. Install a new converter-to-exhaust Y-pipe gasket.

18. Install the 2 new 10-mm catalytic converter-to-exhaust Y-pipe spring nuts and alternately tighten RH side to LH side in sequence in 3 stages:
- Stage 1: Tighten to 44 inch lbs. (5 Nm).

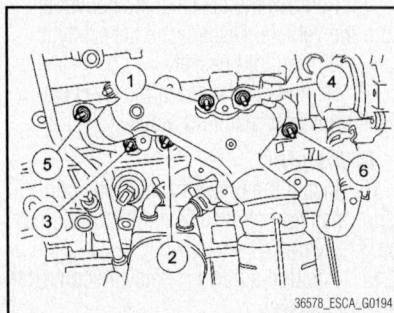

36578_ESCA_G0194

Fig. 155 Catalytic Converter—3.0L LH Manifold tightening sequence—2009 Model

- Stage 2: Tighten to 133 inch lbs. (15 Nm).
- Stage 3: Tighten to 18 ft. lbs. (25 Nm).

19. Install new gaskets, the exhaust Y-pipe and 4 new nuts. Tighten the 4 new exhaust Y-pipe nuts to 18 ft. lbs. (25 Nm).

20. Start the engine and check for exhaust leaks, repair as needed.

3.0L Engine—2009 Models

Catalytic Converter—RH Manifold

See Figure 156.

1. Before servicing the vehicle, refer to the Precautions Section.

2. With the vehicle in NEUTRAL, position it on a hoist.

3. Remove the LH Heated Oxygen Sensor (HO2S).

4. Remove and discard the two 10-mm exhaust catalytic converter-to-exhaust Y-pipe spring nuts.

5. Remove and discard the 4 exhaust Y-pipe nuts and remove the Y-pipe.

6. Disconnect the RH Catalyst Monitor Sensor (CMS) electrical connector.

7. Remove the 3 bolts and the RH catalytic converter heat shield.

8. Remove and discard the 6 RH catalytic converter manifold nuts.

9. Remove the LH catalytic converter manifold from the vehicle. Discard the gasket.

10. Remove and discard the 6 RH catalytic converter manifold studs.

11. Clean and inspect the RH catalytic converter manifold.

To install:

12. Install the 6 new RH catalytic converter manifold studs and tighten to 97 inch lbs. (11 Nm).

➡**Failure to tighten the catalytic converter nuts to specification before installing the exhaust Y-pipe will cause the converter to develop an exhaust leak.**

13. Using a new gasket, install the RH catalytic converter and the 6 nuts. Tighten the nuts in sequence in 2 stages:
- Stage 1: Tighten to 18 ft. lbs. (25 Nm).
- Stage 2: Tighten to 18 ft. lbs. (25 Nm).

➡**Thoroughly clean the sealing surfaces of the flanges using a finishing pad. Inspect the cleaned sealing surface for nicks and scratches and replace as necessary.**

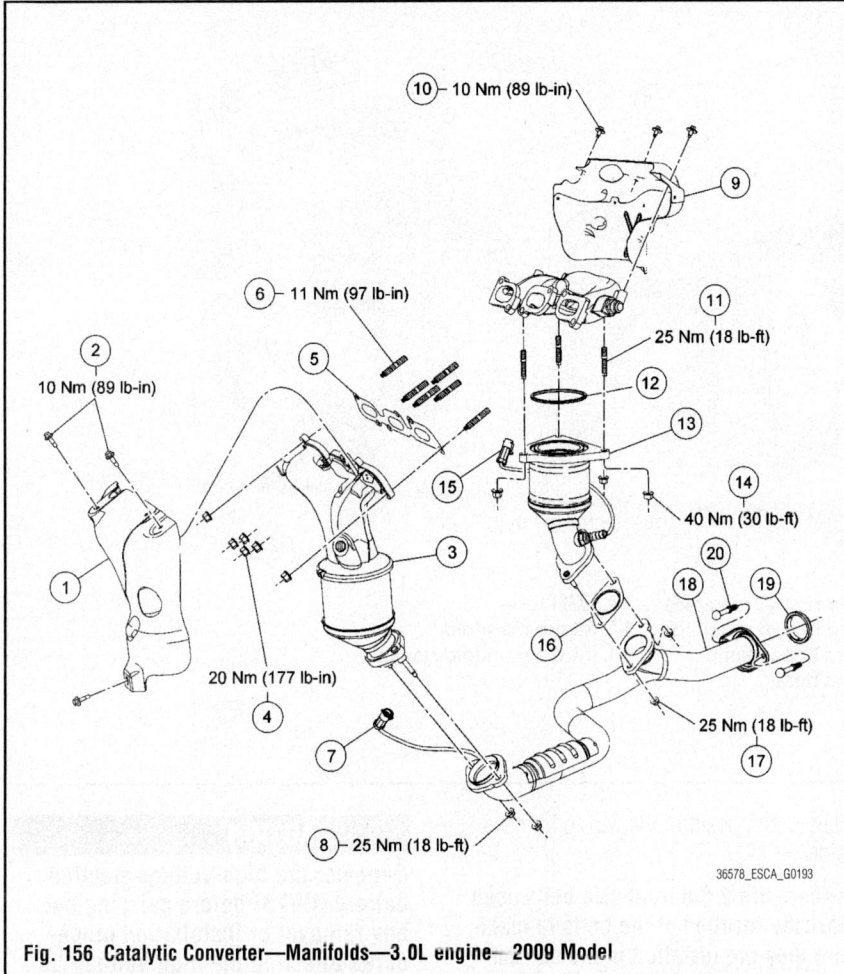

Fig. 156 Catalytic Converter—Manifolds—3.0L engine—2009 Model

14. Install a new converter-to-exhaust Y-pipe gasket.

15. Install the 2 new 10-mm catalytic converter-to-exhaust Y-pipe spring nuts and alternately tighten RH side to LH side in sequence in 3 stages:

- Stage 1: Tighten to 44 inch lbs. (5 Nm).
- Stage 2: Tighten to 133 inch lbs. (15 Nm).
- Stage 3: Tighten to 18 ft. lbs. (25 Nm).

16. Install new gaskets, the exhaust Y-pipe and 4 new nuts. Tighten the 4 new exhaust Y-pipe nuts to 18 ft. lbs. (25 Nm).

17. Start the engine and check for exhaust leaks, repair as needed.

FLYWHEEL

REMOVAL & INSTALLATION

See Figure 157.

1. With the vehicle in NEUTRAL, position it on a hoist.

2. Remove the manual transaxle and clutch. Refer to the Drive Train Section.

3. Remove the 6 bolts and the flywheel.

To install:

➡**Special bolts are used for installation. Do not use standard bolts.**

4. Install the flywheel and tighten the bolts in the sequence shown in 3 stages.

a. Stage 1: Tighten to 37 ft. lbs. (50 Nm).

b. Stage 2: Tighten to 50 ft. lbs. (80 Nm).

c. Stage 3: Tighten to 83 ft. lbs. (112 Nm).

5. Install the manual transaxle and clutch.

FLEXPLATE

REMOVAL & INSTALLATION

4 Cylinder Engine

1. Raise and safely support the vehicle.

2. Remove the automatic transaxle. Refer to the Drive Train Section.

3. Remove the 6 bolts and the flexplate.

To install:

➡**Special bolts are used for installation. Do not use standard bolts.**

4. Install the flexplate and tighten the bolts in the sequence shown in 3 stages:

- Stage 1: Tighten to 37 ft. lbs. (50 Nm).
- Stage 2: Tighten to 50 ft. lbs. (80 Nm).
- Stage 3: Tighten to 83 ft. lbs. (112 Nm).

5. Install the automatic transaxle.

6 Cylinder Engine

1. Remove the transaxle. Refer to the Drive Train Section.

2. Remove the bolts and the flexplate.

To install:

3. Install the flywheel. Tighten the bolts, in a criss-cross pattern to 59 ft. lbs. (80 Nm).

4. Install the transaxle.

INTAKE MANIFOLD

REMOVAL & INSTALLATION

2.3L Engine

See Figure 158.

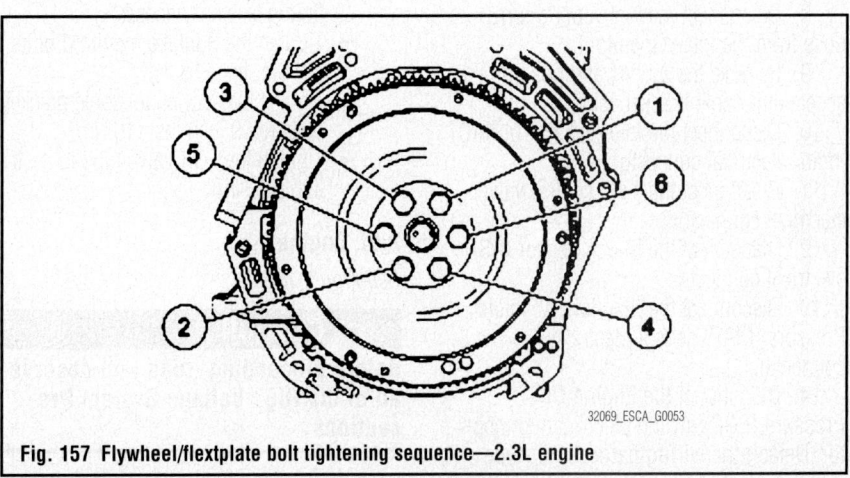

Fig. 157 Flywheel/flexplate bolt tightening sequence—2.3L engine

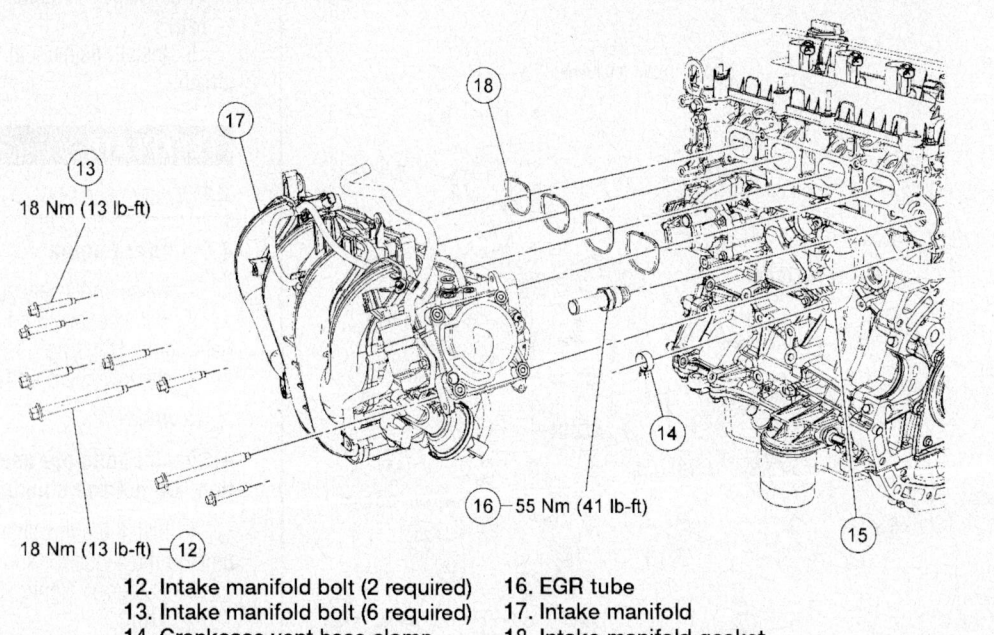

18 Nm (13 lb-ft)

18 Nm (13 lb-ft) — 12

16 — 55 Nm (41 lb-ft)

12. Intake manifold bolt (2 required)
13. Intake manifold bolt (6 required)
14. Crankcase vent hose clamp
15. Crankcase vent hose
16. EGR tube
17. Intake manifold
18. Intake manifold gasket

36578_ESCA_G0196

Fig. 158 Intake manifold—2.3L engine

1. Before servicing the vehicle, refer to the Precautions Section.
2. With the vehicle in NEUTRAL, position it on a hoist.
3. Properly relieve the fuel system pressure.
4. Remove the fuel rail. Refer to the Fuel System section.
5. Remove the throttle body. Refer to the Fuel System section.
6. Remove the oil level indicator and tube.
7. Disconnect the power brake booster vacuum tube as follows:
   • Depress the quick release locking ring.
   • Pull the vacuum tube out of the quick release fitting.
8. Disconnect the fuel vapor return hose from the intake manifold.
9. Remove the 3 bolts and position the accelerator cable bracket aside.
10. Disconnect the Idle Air Control (IAC) motor electrical connector.
11. Disconnect the swirl control valve electrical connector.
12. Disconnect the Knock Sensor (KS) electrical connector.
13. Disconnect the Manifold Absolute Pressure (MAP) sensor electrical connector.
14. Disconnect the Engine Oil Pressure (EOP) switch electrical connector. Detach the wiring harness pin-type

retainer and position the wiring harness aside.

➡**There are 2 different size bolts used. Mark the location of the bolts to make sure they are installed in the correct location.**

15. Remove the 8 bolts and position the intake manifold aside to access the crankcase vent hose clamp and the EGR tube.
16. Release the clamp and disconnect the crankcase vent hose.
17. Remove the EGR tube.
18. Remove the intake manifold and gaskets.
19. To install, reverse the removal procedure, note the following:
   • Inspect and install new intake manifold gaskets if necessary.
   • Tighten the 8 intake manifold bolts to 13 ft. lbs. (18 Nm).
   • Tighten the accelerator cable bracket bolts to 89 inch lbs. (10 Nm).
   • Tighten the EGR valve tube to 41 ft. lbs. (55 Nm).

2.5L Engine
See Figure 159.

❋❋ CAUTION
Before proceeding, read and observe all of the High Voltage System Precautions.

❋❋ CAUTION
Depower the high-voltage traction battery (HVTB) before carrying out any removal or installation procedures affecting the high-voltage battery system. Failure to follow this instruction may result in serious personal injury or death.

1. With vehicle in NEUTRAL, position it on a hoist.
2. With vehicle in NEUTRAL, position it on a hoist.

➡**Before removing the high voltage cables, the vehicle electrical system must be completely shut down for at least 5 minutes to allow for the high voltage capacitors to discharge.**

3. Disable the vehicle high voltage electrical system.
4. Remove the fuel rail.
5. Remove the Throttle Body (TB).
6. Remove the accessory drive belt tensioner.
7. Disconnect the Engine Oil Pressure (EOP) switch electrical connector.
8. Disconnect the Manifold Absolute Pressure (MAP) sensor electrical connector.
9. Disconnect the Evaporative Emission (EVAP) canister purge valve electrical connector.

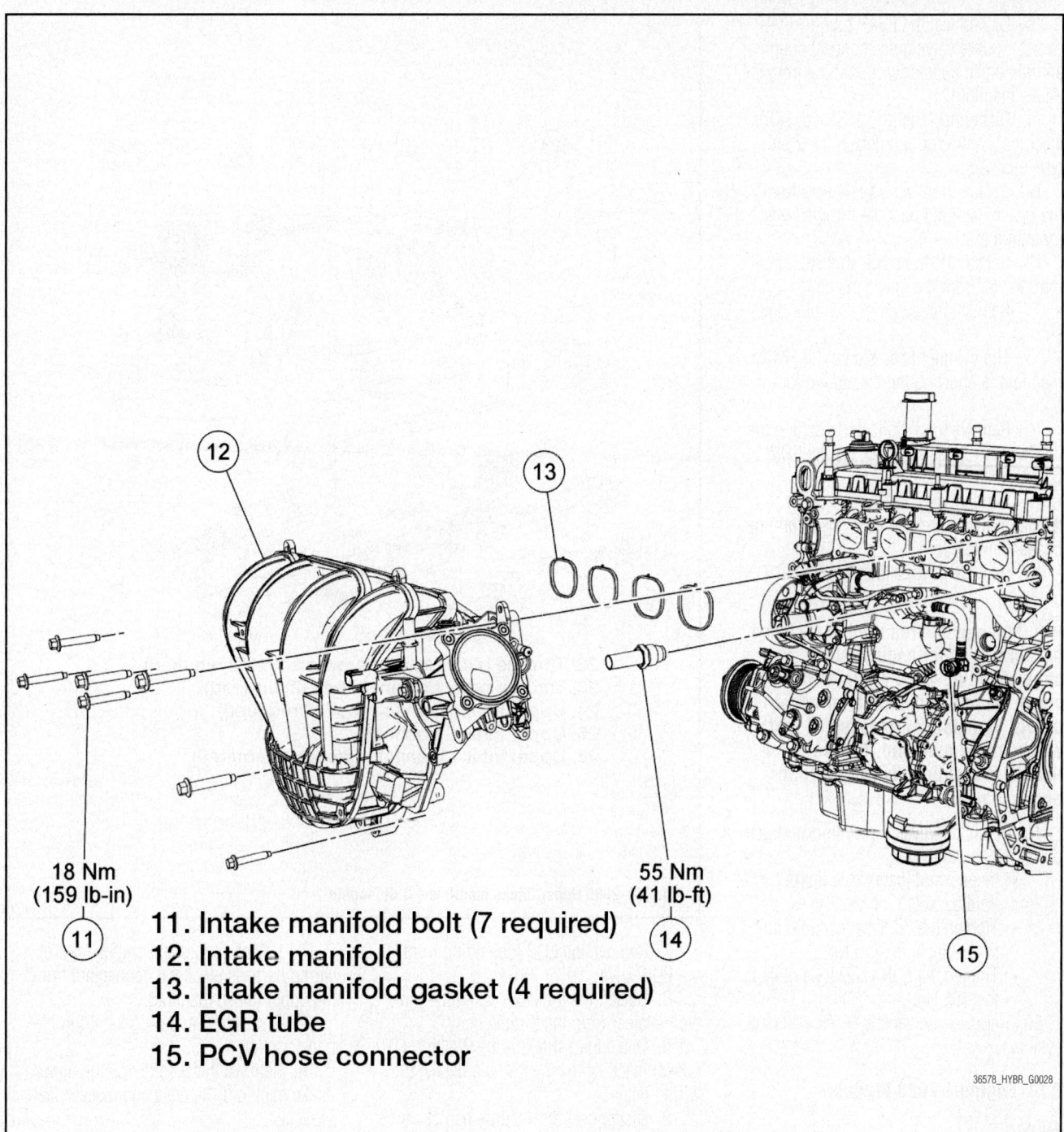

18 Nm
(159 lb-in)

55 Nm
(41 lb-ft)

11. Intake manifold bolt (7 required)
12. Intake manifold
13. Intake manifold gasket (4 required)
14. EGR tube
15. PCV hose connector

36578_HYBR_G0028

Fig. 159 Intake manifold—2.5L engine

10. Disconnect the EVAP tube-to-EVAP canister purge valve quick connect coupling and the brake booster vacuum tube from the intake manifold.

11. Disconnect the Knock Sensor (KS) electrical connector and detach the 2 pin-type retainers.

12. Detach the 2 wiring retainers from the intake manifold near the throttle body mounting area.

13. Detach the transaxle shift cable routing retainer from the intake manifold.

14. Remove the cooling fan motor and shroud.

15. The cylinder head side of the intake manifold is showing the location of the 7 bolts.

16. Remove the 7 bolts and position the intake manifold aside to access the PCV hose connector.

17. Squeeze the 2 PCV hose connector tabs and disconnect the PCV hose from the intake manifold.

18. Remove the intake manifold and gaskets.

➡**If the engine is repaired or replaced because of upper engine failure, typically including valve or piston damage, check the intake manifold for metal debris. If metal debris is found, install a new intake manifold. Failure to follow these instructions can result in engine damage.**

19. To install, reverse the removal procedure, note the following:
  • Inspect and install new intake manifold gaskets if necessary.
  • Tighten the 7 intake manifold bolts to 159 inch lbs. (18 Nm).
  • Tighten the EGR valve tube to 41 ft. lbs. (55 Nm).

20. Repower the vehicle HVTB electrical system.

3.0L Engine—2008 Models

Upper

See Figures 160 and 161.

1. Before servicing the vehicle, refer to the Precautions Section.

2. With the vehicle in NEUTRAL, position it on a hoist.

3. Remove the air cleaner outlet pipe.

4. Remove the 2 bolts and the accelerator cable snow shield.

5. Detach the speed control and accelerator cables from the throttle body.

6. Remove the 3 accelerator/speed control cable bracket bolts. Position the cables and brackets aside.

7. Remove the EGR tube fitting from the EGR valve.

8. Detach the transaxle vent tube pin-type retainer from the throttle body.

9. Disconnect the Throttle Position (TP) sensor electrical connector and detach the wiring retainer.

10. Disconnect the vacuum harness tube fittings from the EGR valve and the EGR vacuum regulator.

11. Disconnect the Evaporative Emissions (EVAP) tube from the upper intake manifold.

12. Disconnect the Idle Air Control (IAC) valve electrical connector.

13. Disconnect the EGR vacuum regulator electrical connector.

14. Remove the nut from the EGR vacuum regulator stud bolt and detach the wiring retainer.

15. Disconnect the PCV, brake booster and vacuum harness tubes from the upper intake manifold.

16. Detach the 2 main engine control wiring harness electrical connectors from the upper intake manifold.

17. Disconnect and plug the 2 throttle body coolant hoses.

18. Remove the 8 bolts and the upper intake manifold. Remove and discard the gaskets.

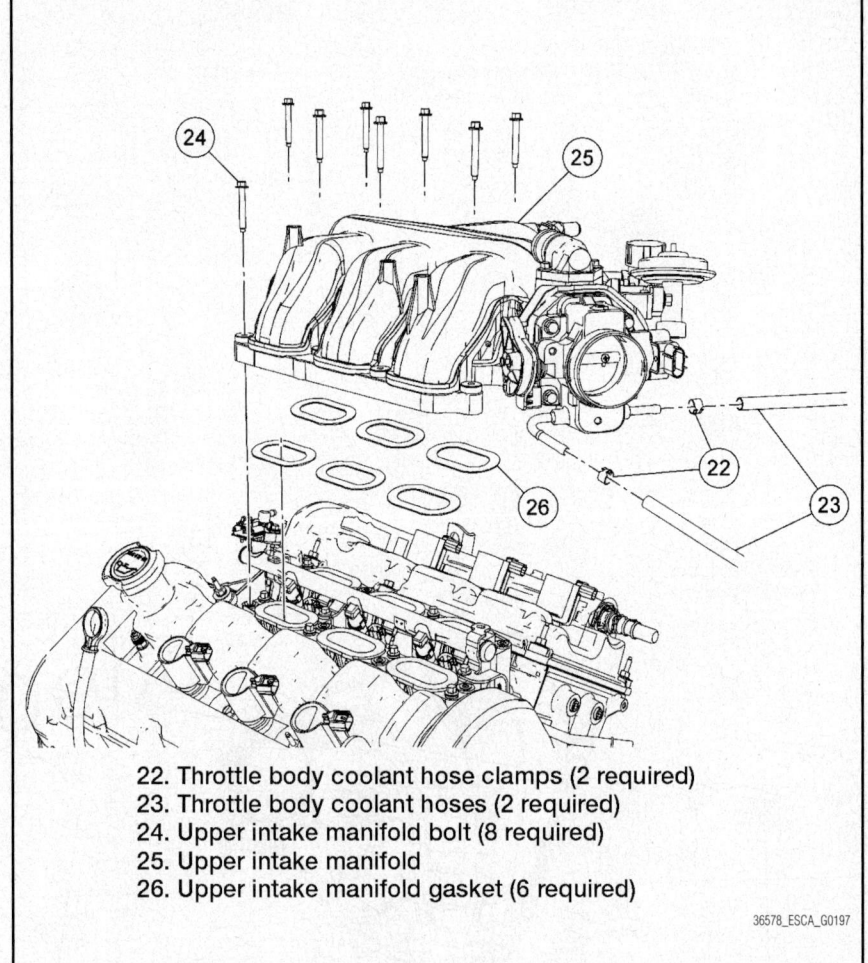

22. Throttle body coolant hose clamps (2 required)
23. Throttle body coolant hoses (2 required)
24. Upper intake manifold bolt (8 required)
25. Upper intake manifold
26. Upper intake manifold gasket (6 required)

36578_ESCA_G0197

Fig. 160 2008 Upper intake manifold—3.0L engine

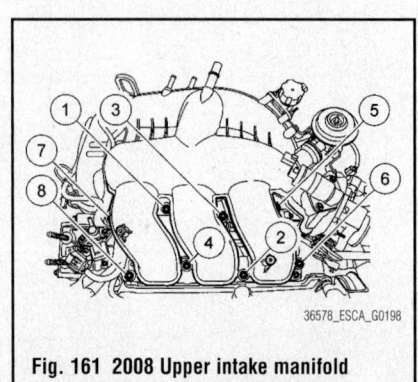

36578_ESCA_G0198

Fig. 161 2008 Upper intake manifold tightening sequence—3.0L engine

To install:

19. Clean and inspect all sealing surfaces. Install new gaskets.

20. Position the upper intake manifold and install the bolts.

21. Tighten the bolts in sequence to 89 inch lbs. (10 Nm).

22. Connect the 2 throttle body coolant hoses.

23. Attach the 2 main engine control wiring harness electrical connectors to the upper intake manifold.

24. Connect the PCV, brake booster and vacuum harness tubes to the upper intake manifold.

25. Attach the wiring retainer to the EGR vacuum regulator stud bolt and install the nut. Tighten the nut to 53 inch lbs. (6 Nm).

26. Connect the EGR vacuum regulator electrical connector.

27. Connect the IAC valve electrical connector and wiring harness retainer.

28. Connect the EVAP tube to the upper intake manifold.

29. Connect the vacuum harness tube fittings to the EGR valve and the EGR vacuum regulator.

30. Connect the TP sensor electrical connector and attach the wiring retainer.

31. Attach the transaxle vent tube pin-type retainer to the throttle body.

32. Install the EGR tube fitting to the EGR valve and tighten to 30 ft. lbs. (40 Nm).

33. Position the accelerator/speed control cables and brackets and install the 3 bolts. Tighten the 3 bolts to 89 inch lbs. (10 Nm).

34. Attach the speed control and accelerator cables to the throttle body.

35. Install the accelerator cable snow shield and the 2 bolts. Tighten the 2 bolts to 89 inch lbs. (10 Nm).

36. Install the air cleaner outlet pipe.

Lower

See Figures 162 and 163.

> **❊❊ CAUTION**
>
> **Do not smoke, carry lighted tobacco or have an open flame of any type when working on or near any fuel-related component. Highly flammable mixtures are always present and may be ignited. Failure to follow these instructions may result in serious personal injury.**

1. Before servicing the vehicle, refer to the Precautions Section.

2. Release the fuel system pressure.

3. Disconnect the battery ground cable.

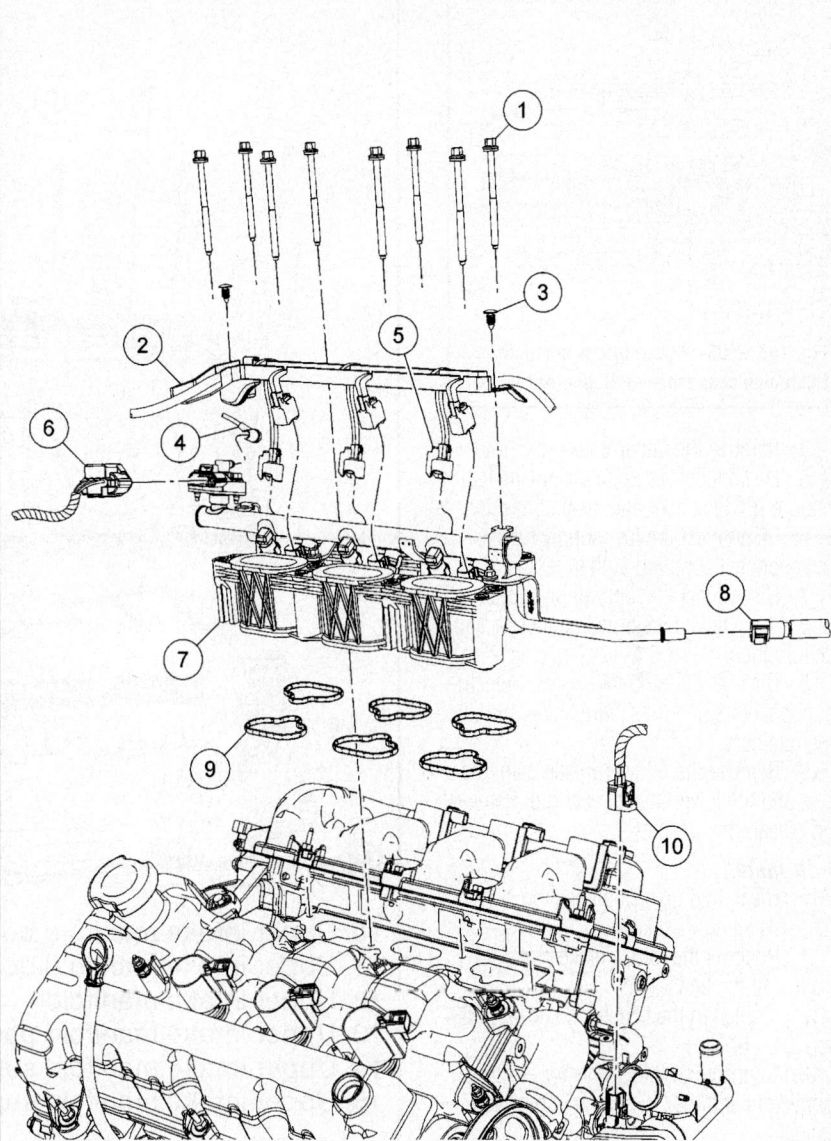

1. Lower intake manifold bolt (8 required)
2. Wire shield
3. Wire shield pin-type retainer (2 required)
4. Fuel rail pressure and temperature sensor vacuum tube fitting
5. Fuel injector electrical connector (6 required)
6. Fuel rail pressure and temperature sensor electrical connector
7. Lower intake manifold
8. Fuel tube
9. Lower intake manifold gasket (6 required)
10. Engine coolant temperature (ECT) sensor electrical connector

36578_ESCA_G0199

Fig. 162 2008—Lower intake manifold—3.0L engine

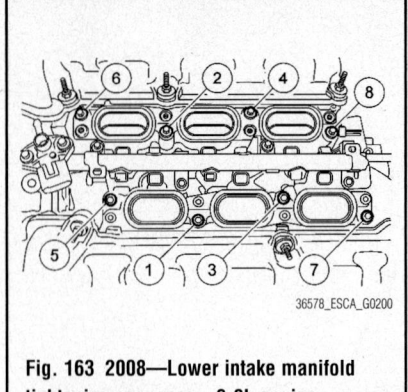

Fig. 163 2008—Lower intake manifold tightening sequence—3.0L engine

4. Remove the upper intake manifold.

5. Disconnect the Engine Coolant Temperature (ECT) sensor electrical connector.

6. Disconnect the fuel supply tube quick connect coupling at the fuel rail.

7. Disconnect the fuel rail pressure and temperature sensor electrical connector and vacuum tube.

8. Disconnect the 6 fuel injector electrical connectors and the 2 wire shield pin-type retainers.

9. Remove the 8 lower intake manifold bolts and the lower intake manifold. Remove and discard the gaskets.

To install:

10. Clean and inspect all sealing surfaces. Install new gaskets.

11. Position the lower intake manifold and install the bolts.

12. Tighten in the sequence shown to 89 inch lbs. (10 Nm).

13. Connect the 6 fuel injector electrical connectors and the 2 wire shield pin-type retainers.

14. Connect the fuel rail pressure and temperature sensor electrical connector and vacuum tube.

15. Connect the fuel supply tube quick connect coupling at the fuel rail

16. Connect the ECT sensor electrical connector.

17. Install the upper intake manifold.

18. Connect the battery ground cable.

3.0L Engine—2009 model

Upper

See Figures 164 and 165.

1. Before servicing the vehicle, refer to the Precautions Section.

2. Remove the Air Cleaner (ACL) outlet pipe and the ACL.

3. Remove the EGR tube fitting from the EGR valve.

4. Disconnect the electronic throttle control electrical connector.

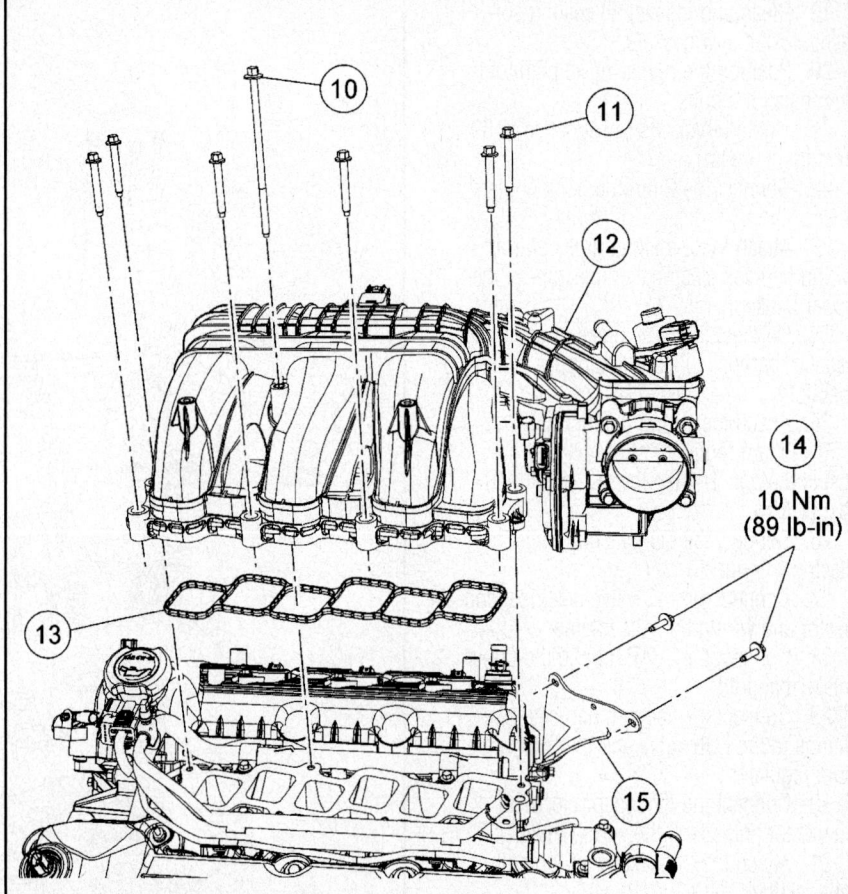

10. Upper intake manifold bolt
11. Upper intake manifold bolt (6 required)
12. Upper intake manifold
13. Upper intake manifold gasket
14. Upper intake manifold support bracket bolts (2 required)
15. Upper intake manifold support bracket

Fig. 164 2009—Upper intake manifold—3.0L engine

5. Disconnect the Evaporative Emission (EVAP) canister purge valve electrical connector.

6. Disconnect the EGR regulator electrical connector and detach the wiring retainer.

7. Disconnect the EVAP tube-to-EVAP canister purge valve quick connect coupling and the brake booster vacuum tube from the upper intake manifold.

8. Detach the engine control wiring harness retainer from the upper intake manifold.

9. Disconnect the PCV tube from the upper intake manifold.

10. Disconnect the Manifold Absolute Pressure (MAP) electrical connector and detach the wiring retainer.

11. Remove the 2 upper intake manifold support bracket bolts from the upper intake manifold.

12. Remove the 7 bolts and the upper intake manifold. Remove and discard the gaskets.

To install:

13. Clean and inspect all sealing surfaces. Install new gaskets.

14. Position the upper intake manifold and install the 7 bolts.

15. Tighten the bolts in 2 stages in the sequence shown:
- Stage 1: Tighten to 89 inch lbs. (10 Nm).
- Stage 2: Tighten an additional 45 degrees.

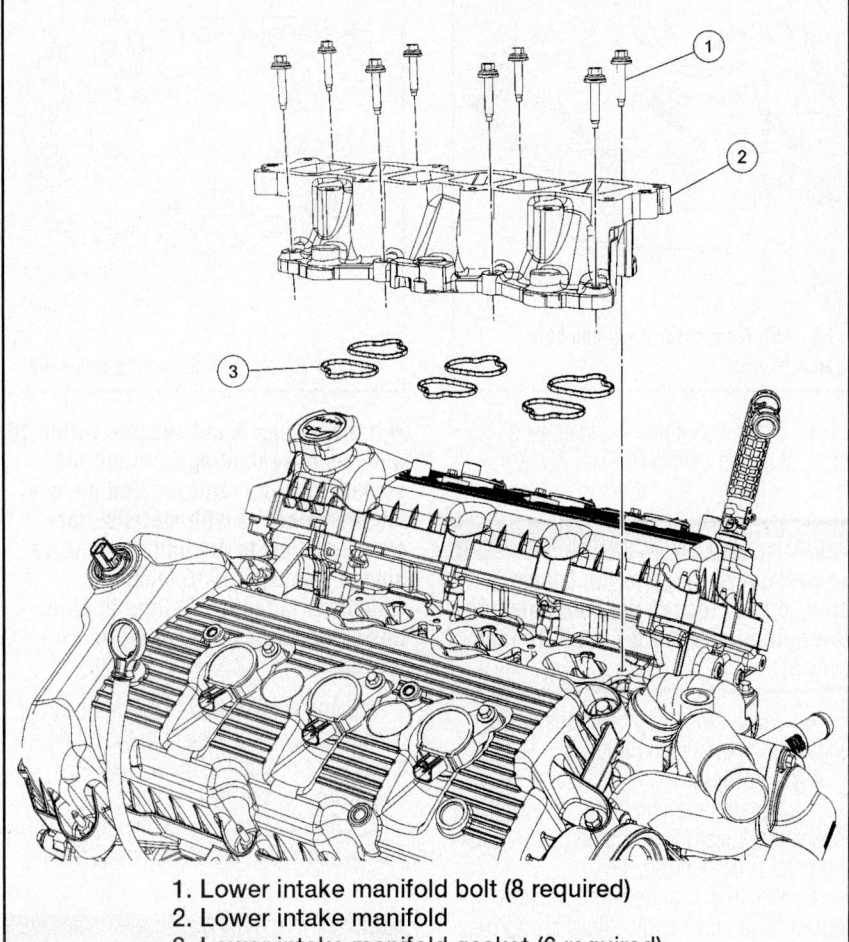

Fig. 165 2009—Upper intake manifold tightening sequence—3.0L engine

16. Install the 2 upper intake manifold support bracket bolts and tighten to 89 inch lbs. (10 Nm).

17. Connect the MAP electrical connector and attach the wiring retainer.

18. Connect the PCV tube to the upper intake manifold.

19. Attach the engine control wiring harness retainer to the upper intake manifold.

20. Connect the EVAP tube-to-EVAP canister purge valve quick connect coupling and the brake booster vacuum tube to the upper intake manifold.

21. Connect the EGR regulator electrical connector and attach the wiring retainer.

22. Connect the EVAP canister purge valve electrical connector.

23. Connect the electronic throttle control electrical connector.

24. Install the EGR tube fitting to the EGR valve. Tighten the fitting to 30 ft. lbs. (40 Nm).

25. Install the ACL outlet pipe and the ACL.

Lower

See Figures 166 and 167.

> **✳✳ CAUTION**
>
> **Do not smoke, carry lighted tobacco or have an open flame of any type when working on or near any fuel-related component. Highly flammable mixtures are always present and may be ignited. Failure to follow these instructions may result in serious personal injury.**

1. Before servicing the vehicle, refer to the Precautions Section.

2. Remove the upper intake manifold.

3. Release the fuel system pressure.

4. Disconnect the battery ground cable.

5. Remove the fuel rail.

1. Lower intake manifold bolt (8 required)
2. Lower intake manifold
3. Lower intake manifold gasket (6 required)

Fig. 166 Lower intake manifold—2008 3.0L engine

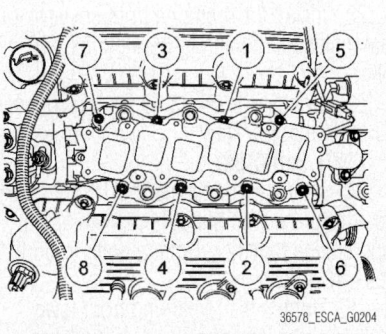

Fig. 167 Lower intake manifold tightening sequence—2009 3.0L engine

6. Remove the 8 lower intake manifold bolts and the lower intake manifold. Remove and discard the gaskets.

To install:

7. Clean and inspect all sealing surfaces. Install new gaskets.

8. Position the lower intake manifold and install the 8 bolts.

9. Tighten in the sequence shown to 89 inch lbs. (10 Nm).

10. Install the fuel rail.

11. Install the upper intake manifold.

12. Connect the battery ground cable.

OIL PAN

REMOVAL & INSTALLATION

4 Cylinder Engine

See Figures 168 and 169.

All vehicles:

1. Before servicing the vehicle, refer to the Precautions Section.

2. Disconnect the negative battery cable.

3. With the vehicle in NEUTRAL, position it on a hoist.

4. Remove the air cleaner outlet pipe.

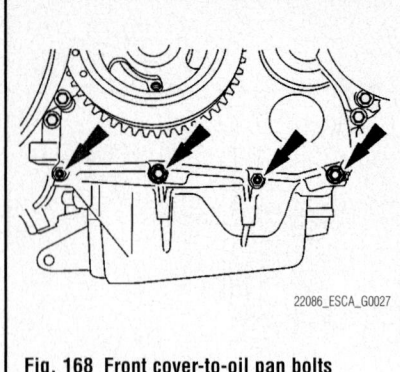

Fig. 168 Front cover-to-oil pan bolts shown

5. Drain the engine oil, then install the drain plug and tighten to 21 ft. lbs. (28 Nm).

✳✳ WARNING

To prevent damage to the transmission, do not loosen the transmission-to-engine bolts more than 0.19 inch (5mm).

6. Loosen the 2 top bell housing-to-engine bolts 0.19 inch (5mm).

AWD vehicles:

7. Working from the top of the vehicle, loosen the 2 rear lower engine-to-bell housing bolts 0.19 inch (5mm).

8. Working from under the vehicle, loosen the 2 upper engine bracket-to-Power Transfer Unit (PTU) bolts 0.19 inch (5mm).

All vehicles:

9. Remove the 7 retainers and the LH splash shield.

10. Remove the oil level indicator and tube

11. Loosen the 2 front lower bell housing-to-engine bolts 0.19 inch (5mm).

FWD vehicles:

12. Loosen the 1 (manual transmission) and 2 (automatic transmission) rear lower engine-to-bell housing bolt 0.19 inch (5mm).

All vehicles:

13. Remove the 2 oil pan-to-bell housing bolts.

14. Remove the 2 bell housing-to-oil pan bolt.

15. Slide the transmission rearward 5 mm (0.19 in).

16. Drain the engine oil.

17. Remove the 4 engine front cover-to-oil pan bolts.

18. Remove the 13 bolts and the oil pan.

To install:

All vehicles:

19. Clean and inspect all mating surfaces.

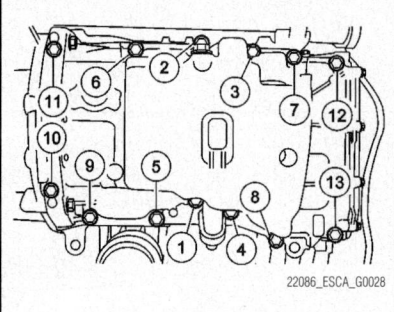

Fig. 169 Oil pan bolt tightening sequence

➡If the oil pan is not secured within 10 minutes of sealant application, the sealant must be removed and the sealing area cleaned with metal surface cleaner. Allow to dry until there is no sign of wetness, or 10 minutes, whichever is longer. Failure to follow this procedure can cause future oil leakage.

20. Apply a 0.09 inch (2.5mm) bead of silicone gasket and sealant to the oil pan-to-engine block and to the oil pan-to-engine front cover mating surface.

21. Position the oil pan onto the engine and install the oil pan bolts finger-tight.

✳✳ WARNING

The engine front cover-to-oil pan bolts must be tightened first to align the front surface of the oil pan flush with the front surface of the engine block.

22. Install the 4 engine front cover-to-oil pan bolts and tighten to 89 inch lbs. (10 Nm).

23. Tighten the oil pan bolts in sequence to 18 ft. lbs. (25 Nm).

FWD vehicles:

24. Alternate tightening the 1 front and 1 rear lower bolts to slide the transmission and engine together. Tighten bolts to 35 ft. lbs. (48 Nm).

25. Tighten the remaining front lower bolt and rear lower bolt (automatic transmission) to 35 ft. lbs. (48 Nm).

AWD vehicles:

26. Alternate tightening the 1 upper engine-to-PTU bracket bolt and 1 front lower bolt to slide transmission and engine together.

27. Tighten the PTU bracket bolt to 33 ft. lbs. (45 Nm).

28. Tighten the front lower bolt to 33 ft. lbs. (45 Nm).

29. Tighten the remaining upper engine-to-PTU bracket bolt to 33 ft. lbs. (45 Nm).

30. Tighten the remaining front lower bolt to 33 ft. lbs. (45 Nm).

All vehicles:

31. Install the 2 bell housing-to-oil pan bolts to 33 ft. lbs. (45 Nm).

32. Install the 2 oil pan-to-bell housing bolts to 33 ft. lbs. (45 Nm).

33. Install the oil level indicator and tube.

34. Install the LH splash shield and the 7 retainers. Tighten to 80 inch. lbs (90 Nm).

AWD vehicles:

35. Working from the top of vehicle, tighten the 2 rear lower engine-to-bell housing bolts to 35 ft. lbs. (48 Nm).

All vehicles:

36. Tighten the 2 top bell housing-to-engine bolts to 35 ft. lbs. (48 Nm).

37. Install the air cleaner outlet pipe.

38. Connect the negative battery cable.

39. Fill the engine with clean engine oil.

40. Recheck for leaks.

6 Cylinder Engine

See Figure 170.

✳✳ WARNING

During engine repair procedures, cleanliness is extremely important. Any foreign material (including any material created while cleaning gasket surfaces) that enters the oil passages, coolant passages or the oil pan may cause engine failure.

1. Before servicing the vehicle, refer to the Precautions Section.

2. Disconnect the negative battery cable.

3. With the vehicle in NEUTRAL, position it on a hoist.

4. Remove the exhaust Y-pipe.

5. Drain the engine oil and install the drain plug. Tighten to 19 ft. lbs (26 Nm).

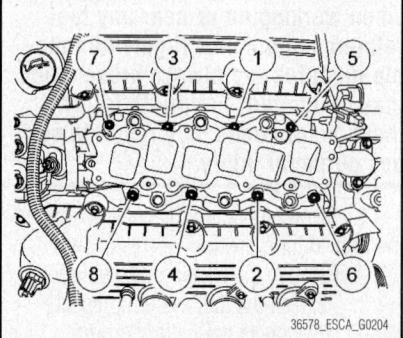

Fig. 170 Oil pan tightening sequence—2.3L engine

6. Remove and discard the oil filter.
7. Remove the access cover.
8. Remove the 2 oil pan-to-transaxle bolts.

➡**For reference during installation, mark the location of the stud bolts.**

9. Remove the 10 bolts, 5 stud bolts and the oil pan.
10. Remove and discard the oil pan gasket.

To install:

☀ WARNING

Do not use metal scrapers, wire brushes, power abrasive discs or other abrasive means to clean the sealing surfaces. These tools cause scratches and gouges which make leak paths.

11. Use a plastic scraping tool to remove all traces of the oil pan gasket.
12. Clean all sealing surfaces with metal surface prep and install a new oil pan gasket.

➡**The oil pan must be installed and the bolts tightened within 4 minutes of sealant application.**

13. Apply a 0.40 inch (10 mm) diameter dot of silicone sealant to the areas indicated.
14. Position the oil pan and loosely install the bolts and stud bolts.
15. Install the 2 oil pan-to-transaxle bolts and tighten to 30 ft. lbs. (40 Nm).
16. Tighten the oil pan-to-engine bolts and stud bolts in the sequence shown to 18 ft. lbs. (25 Nm).
17. Lubricate the engine oil filter gasket with clean engine oil prior to installing.
18. Install a new oil filter. Tighten to 44 inch lbs. (5 Nm) and then rotate an additional 180 degrees.
19. Install the exhaust Y-pipe.
20. Connect the negative battery cable.
21. Fill the engine with clean engine oil.
22. Start the engine and check for leaks.

OIL PUMP

REMOVAL & INSTALLATION

4 Cylinder Engine
See Figures 168, 169, 171 and 172.

☀ WARNING

During engine repair procedures, cleanliness is extremely important. Any foreign material, including any material created while cleaning

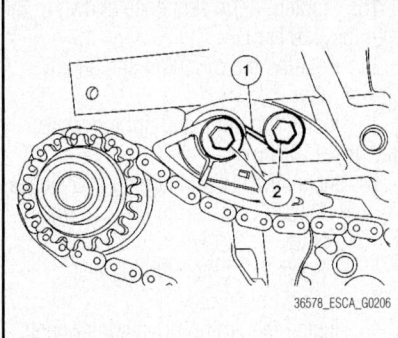
Fig. 171 Release the tension on the spring (1) and remove the shoulder bolts (2) to remove the tensioner

gasket surfaces that enters the oil passages, coolant passages or the oil pan, may cause engine failure.

1. Before servicing the vehicle, refer to the Precautions Section.
2. With the engine in NEUTRAL, position it on a hoist.
3. Remove the engine front cover.
4. Drain the engine oil, then install the drain plug and tighten to 21 ft. lbs. (28 Nm).
5. Remove the 4 oil pan-to-bellhousing bolts.
6. Remove the 13 bolts and the oil pan.
7. Discard the gasket and clean and inspect the gasket mating surfaces.
8. Remove the 2 bolts and the oil pump screen and pickup tube.
9. Release the tension on the tensioner spring.
10. Remove the 2 shoulder bolts and the tensioner.
11. Remove the chain from the oil pump sprocket.
12. Remove the bolt and oil pump sprocket.
13. Remove the 4 bolts and the oil pump

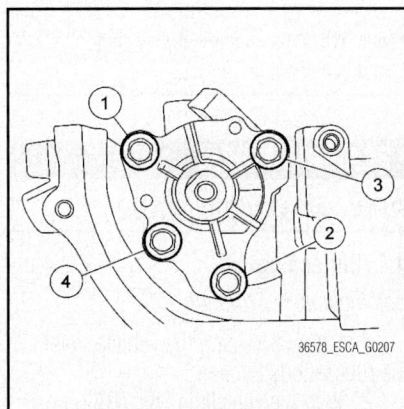
Fig. 172 Oil pump tightening sequence

To install:
14. Clean the oil pump and cylinder block mating surfaces with metal surface prep.
15. Install the oil pump assembly. Tighten the 4 bolts in the sequence shown in 2 stages:
• Stage 1: Tighten to 89 inch lbs. (10 Nm).
• Stage 2: Tighten to 177 inch lbs. (20 Nm).
16. Install the oil pump sprocket and bolt. Tighten the bolt to 18 ft. lbs. (25 Nm).
17. Install the chain onto the oil pump sprocket.
18. Install the oil pump drive chain tensioner shoulder bolt. Tighten the bolt to 89 inch lbs. (10 Nm).
19. Install the oil pump drive chain tensioner and bolt. Hook the tensioner spring around the shoulder bolt. Tighten to 89 inch lbs. (10 Nm).
20. Install the oil pump screen and pickup tube and the 2 bolts. Tighten the bolts to 89 inch lbs. (10 Nm).
21. Clean and inspect all mating surfaces.

➡**If the oil pan is not secured within 10 minutes of sealant application, the sealant must be removed and the sealing area cleaned with metal surface cleaner. Allow to dry until there is no sign of wetness, or 10 minutes, whichever is longer. Failure to follow this procedure can cause future oil leakage.**

22. Apply a 0.09 inch. (2.5mm) bead of silicone gasket and sealant to the oil pan-to-engine block and to the oil pan-to-engine front cover mating surface.
23. Position the oil pan onto the engine and install the oil pan bolts finger-tight.
24. Using a suitable straight edge, align the front surface of the oil pan flush with the front surface of the engine block.

☀ WARNING

The engine front cover-to-oil pan bolts must be tightened first to align the front surface of the oil pan flush with the front surface of the engine block.

25. Install the 4 engine front cover-to-oil pan bolts and tighten to 89 inch lbs. (10 Nm).
26. Tighten the oil pan bolts in sequence to 18 ft. lbs. (25 Nm).
27. Install the 4 oil pan-to-bellhousing bolts and tighten to 35 ft. lbs. (48 Nm).
28. Install the engine front cover.
29. Fill the engine with clean engine oil.

6 Cylinder Engine

See Figures 173 and 174.

1. Before servicing the vehicle, refer to the Precautions Section

2. With the vehicle in NEUTRAL, position it on a hoist.

3. Drain the engine oil and install the drain plug. Tighten to 19 ft. lbs. (26 Nm).

4. Remove the timing drive components.

5. Remove the oil pan.

6. Remove the oil pump screen and pickup tube mounting bolts.

7. Remove the oil pump screen and pickup tube.

8. Remove the oil pump bolts in the sequence shown.

To install:

9. Position the oil pump and install the bolts.

Fig. 173 Remove the oil pump bolts in the sequence

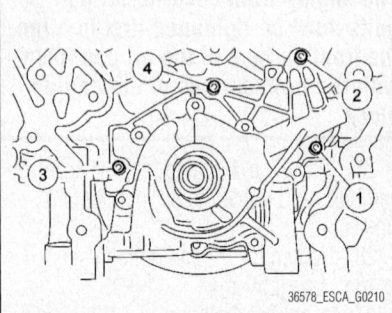

Fig. 174 Oil pump bolt tightening sequence

10. Tighten in the sequence shown to 89 inch lbs. (10 Nm).

11. Position the oil pump screen and pickup tube.

12. Install the bolts and tighten to 89 inch lbs. (10 Nm).

13. Install the nut and tighten in 2 stages:
   - Stage 1: Tighten to 44 inch lbs. (5 Nm).
   - Stage 2: Tighten 45 degrees.

14. Install the oil pan.

15. Install the timing drive components.

16. Fill the engine with clean engine oil.

PISTON AND RING

POSITIONING

See Figures 175 and 176.

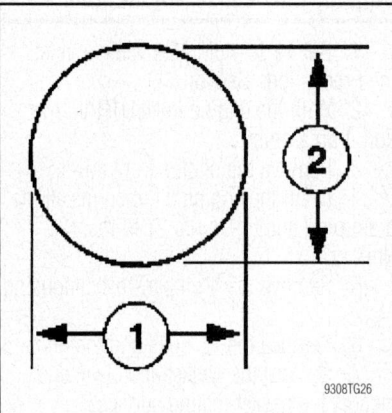

Fig. 175 2.3L engine—piston ring end-gap spacing

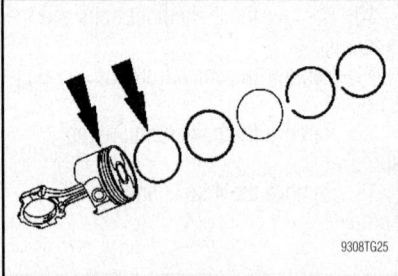

Fig. 176 3.0L engine—piston ring end-gap spacing

REAR MAIN SEAL

REMOVAL & INSTALLATION

4 Cylinder Engine

See Figures 177 through 179.

1. Before servicing the vehicle, refer to the Precautions Section.

2. With the vehicle in NEUTRAL, position it on a hoist.

3. If equipped, remove the automatic transaxle.

4. If equipped, remove the manual transaxle and clutch.

5. Remove the flexplate or flywheel.

6. Drain the engine oil, install drain plug and tighten to 21 ft. lbs. (28 Nm).

7. Remove the oil pan.

➡If the oil pan is not removed, damage to the rear oil seal retainer joint can occur.

8. Remove the crankshaft rear oil seal with retainer plate.

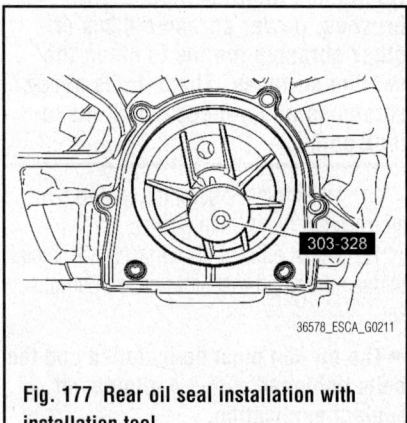

Fig. 177 Rear oil seal installation with installation tool

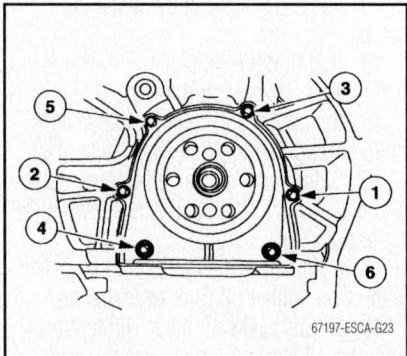

Fig. 178 Retainer plate torque sequence—L4 engine

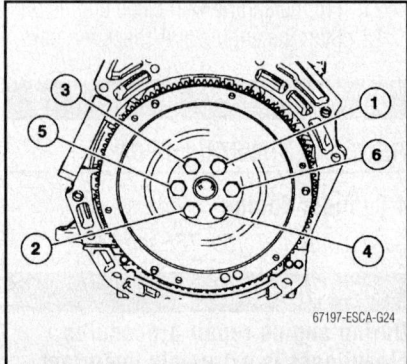

Fig. 179 Flywheel torque sequence—L4 engine

To install:

9. Using a seal installer, position the crankshaft rear oil seal with retainer plate onto the crankshaft.

10. Install the crankshaft rear oil seal with retainer plate. Tighten the bolts in the sequence shown to 89 inch lbs. (10 Nm).

11. Install the oil pan.

➡ **Special bolts are used for installation. Do not use standard bolts.**

12. Install the flywheel/flexplate.

13. Tighten the bolts in the sequence shown in three stages:
- Stage 1: Tighten to 37 ft. lbs. (50 Nm).
- Stage 2: Tighten to 50 ft. lbs. (80 Nm).
- Stage 3: Tighten to 83 ft. lbs. (112 Nm).

14. Fill the engine with clean engine oil.

6 Cylinder Engine

See Figures 180 and 181.

1. Before servicing the vehicle, refer to the Precautions Section.

2. Remove or disconnect the following:
- Negative battery cable
- Transaxle
- Flexplate

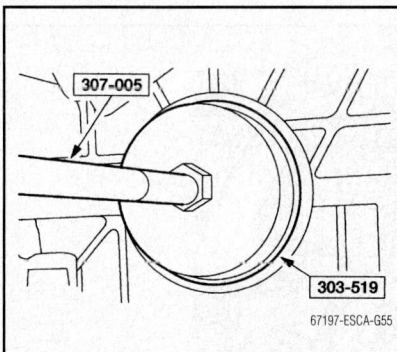

Fig. 180 Rear main seal removal—V6 engine

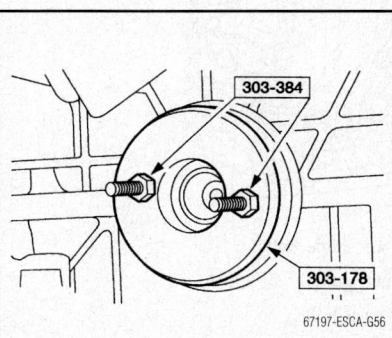

Fig. 181 Rear main seal installation—V6 engine

3. Using the Slide Hammer and the crankshaft rear oil seal remover, remove and discard the crankshaft rear oil seal.

To install:

4. Apply clean engine oil to the seal lip and seal bore before installing the seal.

5. Using the crankshaft rear main oil seal installer bolts and the crankshaft rear main oil seal installer, install the crankshaft rear oil seal.

6. Install or connect the following:
- Crankshaft rear oil seal
- Flywheel
- Transaxle
- Negative battery cable

TIMING CHAIN, GEARS, FRONT COVER & SEAL

REMOVAL & INSTALLATION

2.3L Engine

See Figures 182 through 190.

1. Before servicing the vehicle, refer to the Precautions Section.

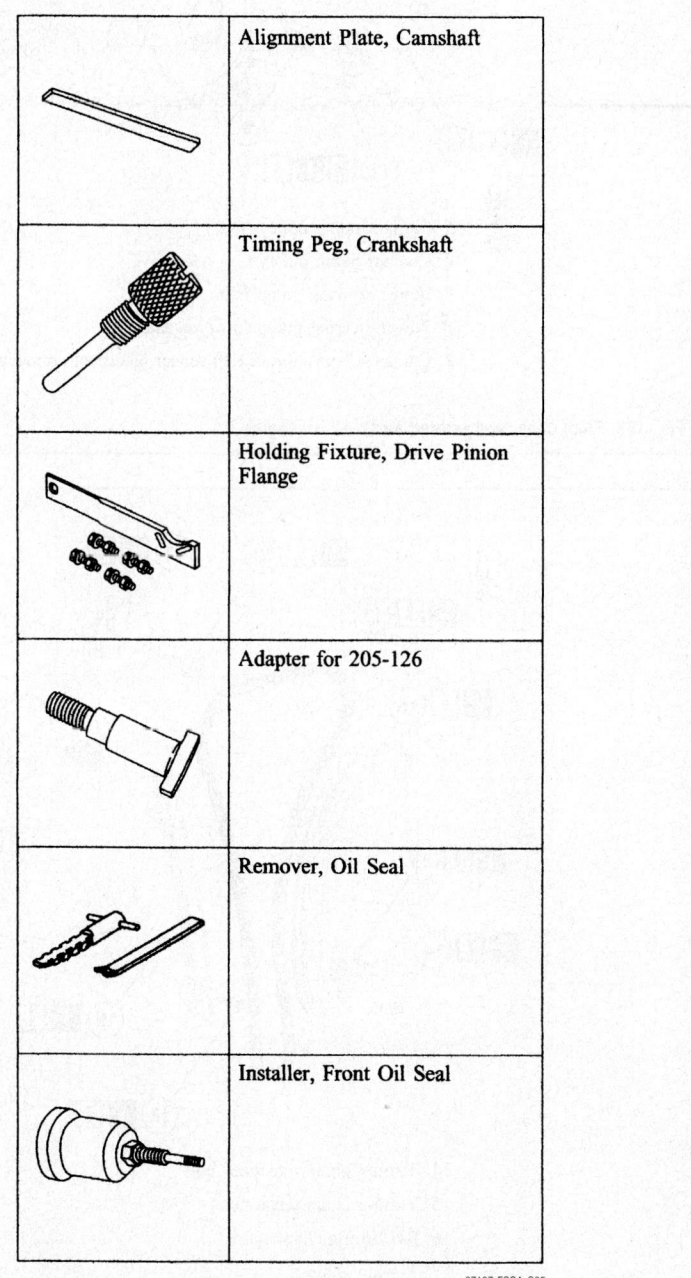

Fig. 182 Tools needed for timing chain and gears replacement—2.3L engine

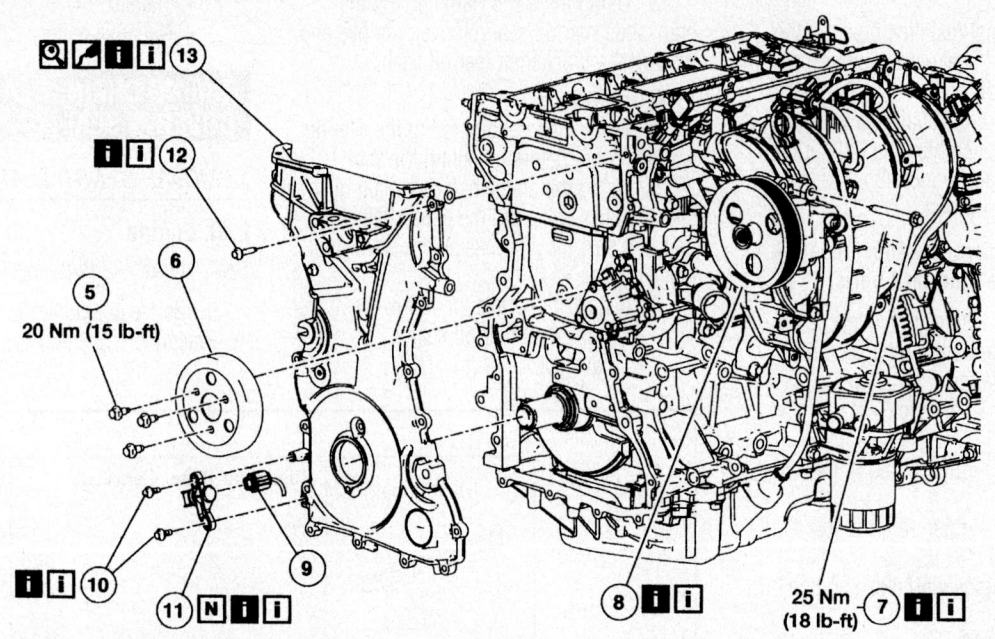

5 Coolant pump pulley bolt
6 Coolant pump pulley
7 Power steering pump bolt
8 Power steering pump (position aside)
9 Crankshaft position (CKP) sensor electrical connector

10 CKP sensor bolts
11 CKP sensor
12 Engine front cover bolt
13 Engine front cover

67197-ESCA-G26

Fig. 183 Front cover and related parts—2.3L engine

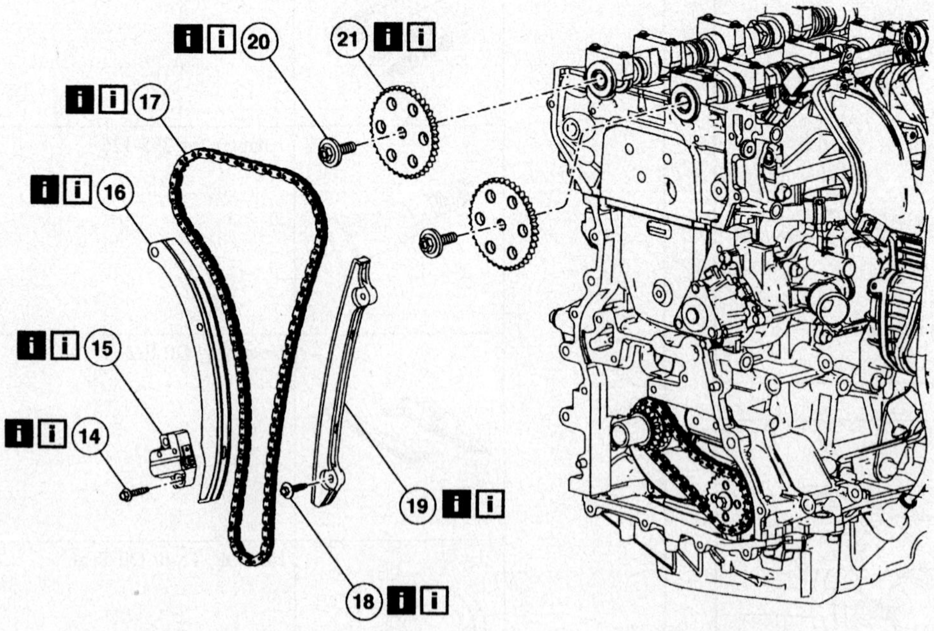

14 Timing chain tensioner bolt
15 Timing chain tensioner
16 RH timing chain guide
17 Timing chain

18 LH timing chain guide bolt
19 LH timing chain guide
20 Camshaft sprocket bolt
21 Camshaft sprocket

67197-ESCA-G27

Fig. 184 Timing chain and related parts—2.3L engine

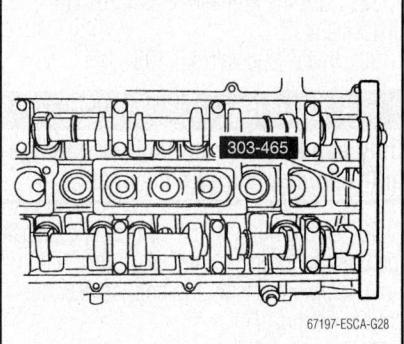

Fig. 185 Install special tool 303-465 in the slots on the rear of both camshafts—2.3L engine

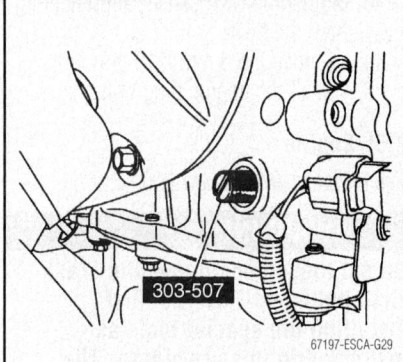

Fig. 186 Install special tool 303-507—2.3L engine

⚹⚹ **CAUTION**

During engine repair procedures, cleanliness is extremely important. Any foreign material, including any material created while cleaning gasket surfaces that enters the oil passages, coolant passages or the oil pan can cause engine failure.

⚹⚹ **CAUTION**

The crankshaft, the crankshaft sprocket and the pulley are fitted together by friction, using diamond washers between the flange faces on each part. For that reason, the crankshaft sprocket is also unfastened if you loosen the pulley. Therefore, the engine must be retimed each time the damper is removed. Otherwise severe engine damage can occur.

2. With the vehicle in NEUTRAL, position it on a hoist.
3. Remove the accessory drive belt and idler pulleys.

4. Remove the engine mount.
5. Remove the valve cover.

⚹⚹ **CAUTION**

Failure to position the No. 1 piston at top dead center (TDC) can result in damage to the engine. Turn the engine in the normal direction of rotation only.

6. Using the crankshaft pulley bolt, turn the crankshaft clockwise to position the No. 1 piston at TDC.

⚹⚹ **CAUTION**

The special tool 303-465 is for camshaft alignment only. Using this tool to prevent engine rotation can result in engine damage.

➡The camshaft timing slots are offset. If the special tool cannot be installed, rotate the crankshaft one complete revolution clockwise to correctly position the camshafts.

7. Install special tool 303-465 in the slots on the rear of both camshafts.
8. Remove the engine plug bolt.

➡Only turn the engine in the normal direction of rotation.

➡Installing the special tool in this step will prevent the engine from being rotated in the clockwise direction.

9. Install special tool 303-507.
10. Install the special tools 205-126 and 205-072-02.

⚹⚹ **CAUTION**

Failure to hold the crankshaft pulley in place while loosening the bolt can result in damage to the engine.

11. Remove the crankshaft pulley bolt and washer.
12. Remove the crankshaft pulley.
13. Remove the crankshaft front seal.
14. Remove the coolant pump pulley.
15. Remove the power steering pump and position it aside.

➡The bolt under the power steering pressure tube will remain with the power steering pump.

16. Remove the CKP sensor.

➡Whenever the crankshaft position (CKP) sensor is removed, a new one must be installed, using the alignment jig supplied with the new part.

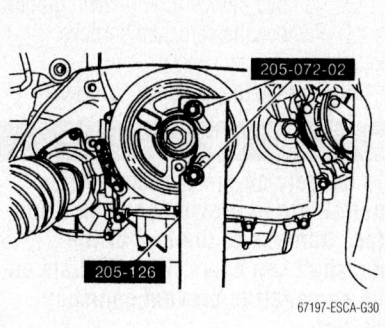

Fig. 187 Install the special tools 205-126 and 205-072-02—2.3L engine

17. Remove the engine front cover bolts (there are 22).
18. Remove the engine front cover.
19. Remove the timing chain tensioner. Compress the timing chain tensioner, and insert a paper clip into the hole to retain the tensioner.
20. Remove the right timing chain guide.

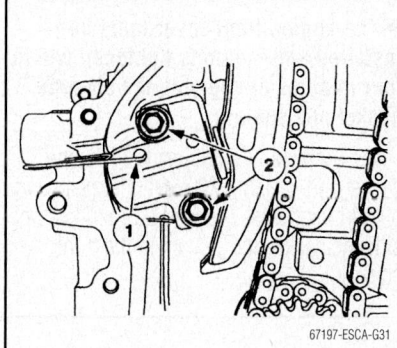

Fig. 188 Compress the timing chain tensioner, and insert a paper clip into the hole to retain the tensioner—2.3L engine

Fig. 189 Use the flats on the camshaft to prevent camshaft rotation—2.3L engine

21. Remove the timing chain.
22. Remove the left timing chain guide.
23. Remove the camshaft sprocket bolts.
24. Remove the camshaft sprockets.

✳✳ CAUTION

Do not rely on the Camshaft Alignment Plate to prevent camshaft rotation. Damage to the tool or the camshaft can occur. Use the flats on the camshaft to prevent camshaft rotation.

To install:

25. Installation is the reverse of removal. Note the following:

✳✳ CAUTION

Do not use metal scrapers, wire brushes, power abrasive disks or other abrasive means to clean sealing surfaces. These tools cause scratches and gouges which make leak paths.

26. Clean and inspect the mounting surfaces of the engine and the front cover.

➡**The engine front cover must be installed and the bolts tightened within four minutes of applying the silicone gasket and sealant.**

27. Apply a 2.5 mm bead of silicone gasket and sealant to the cylinder head and oil pan joint areas. Apply a 2.5 mm bead of silicone gasket and sealant to the front cover.

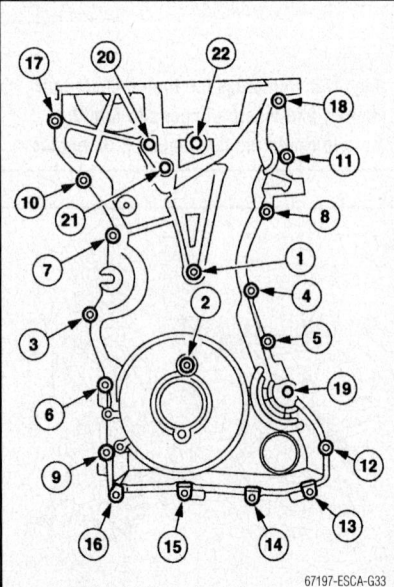

Fig. 190 Front cover bolt torque sequence—2.3L engine

67197-ESCA-G33

28. Install the engine front cover. Tighten the bolts in the sequence shown, to the following specifications:
   a. Tighten the 8 mm bolts to 89 inch lbs. (10 Nm).
   b. Tighten the 13 mm bolts to 35 ft. lbs. (48 Nm).
29. Position the power steering pump and install the bolts.

➡**Remove the through-bolt from the special tool.**

➡**Lubricate the oil seal with clean engine oil.**

30. Using a seal driver, install the crankshaft front oil seal.

➡**Do not reuse the crankshaft damper bolt.**

➡**Apply clean engine oil on the seal area before installing.**

31. Install the crankshaft pulley and hand-tighten the bolt.

✳✳ CAUTION

Only hand-tighten the bolt or damage to the front cover can occur.

➡**This step will correctly align the crankshaft pulley to the crankshaft.**

32. Install a standard 6 mm x 18 mm bolt through the crankshaft pulley and thread it into the front cover. Rotate the pulley as necessary to align the bolt holes.

✳✳ CAUTION

Failure to hold the crankshaft pulley in place while tightening the bolt can cause damage to the engine front cover.

33. Using the special tools to hold the crankshaft pulley in place, tighten the crankshaft pulley bolt in two stages:
   a. Stage 1: Tighten to 74 ft. lbs. (100 Nm).
   b. Stage 2: Tighten an additional 90 degrees (¼ turn).
34. Remove the 6 mm x 18 mm bolt.
35. Remove special tool 303-507.
36. Remove special tool 303-465.

➡**Only turn the engine in the normal direction of rotation.**

37. Turn the engine two complete revolutions.

➡**Only turn the engine in the normal direction of rotation.**

38. Turn the crankshaft until the No. 1 piston is at TDC.
39. Install special tool 303-507.

✳✳ CAUTION

Only hand-tighten the bolt or damage to the front cover can occur.

40. Using the 6 mm x 18 mm bolt, check the position of the crankshaft pulley. If it is not possible to install the bolt, correct the engine timing.
41. Using special tool 303-465, check the position of the camshafts. If it is not possible to install the special tool, correct the engine timing.
42. Install the CKP sensor. Do not tighten the bolts at this time.
43. Adjust the CKP sensor alignment jig and tighten the bolts.
44. Remove the 6 mm x 18 mm bolt.
45. Install the engine plug bolt.

2.5L Engine

See Figures 191 through 200.

✳✳ WARNING

Do not loosen or remove the crankshaft pulley bolt without first installing the special tools as instructed in this procedure. The crankshaft pulley and the crankshaft timing sprocket are not keyed to the crankshaft. The crankshaft, the crankshaft sprocket and the pulley are fitted together by friction, using diamond washers between the flange faces on each part. For that reason, the crankshaft sprocket is also unfastened if the pulley bolt is loosened. Before any repair requiring loosening or removal of the crankshaft pulley bolt, the crankshaft and camshafts must be locked in place by the special service tools, otherwise severe engine damage can occur. Refer to Crankshaft Damper in this section.

➡**During engine repair procedures, cleanliness is extremely important. Any foreign material, including any material created while cleaning gasket surfaces, which enters the oil passages, coolant passages or the oil pan can cause engine failure.**

1. With the vehicle in NEUTRAL, position it on a hoist.
2. Remove the accessory drive belt and the smooth idler pulley.
3. Disconnect the Crankshaft Position (CKP) sensor electrical connector.

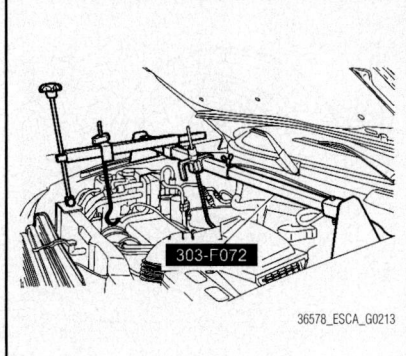

Fig. 191 Engine support bar shown installed on 2.5L engine

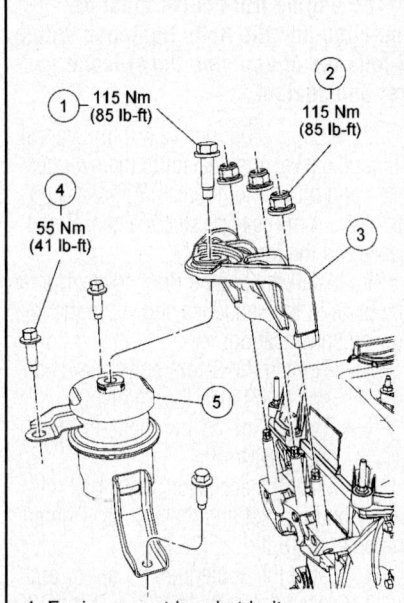

1. Engine mount bracket bolt
2. Engine mount bracket nut (3 required)
3. Engine mount bracket
4. Engine mount bolt (3 required)
5. Engine mount

Fig. 192 Engine support mount—2.5L engine

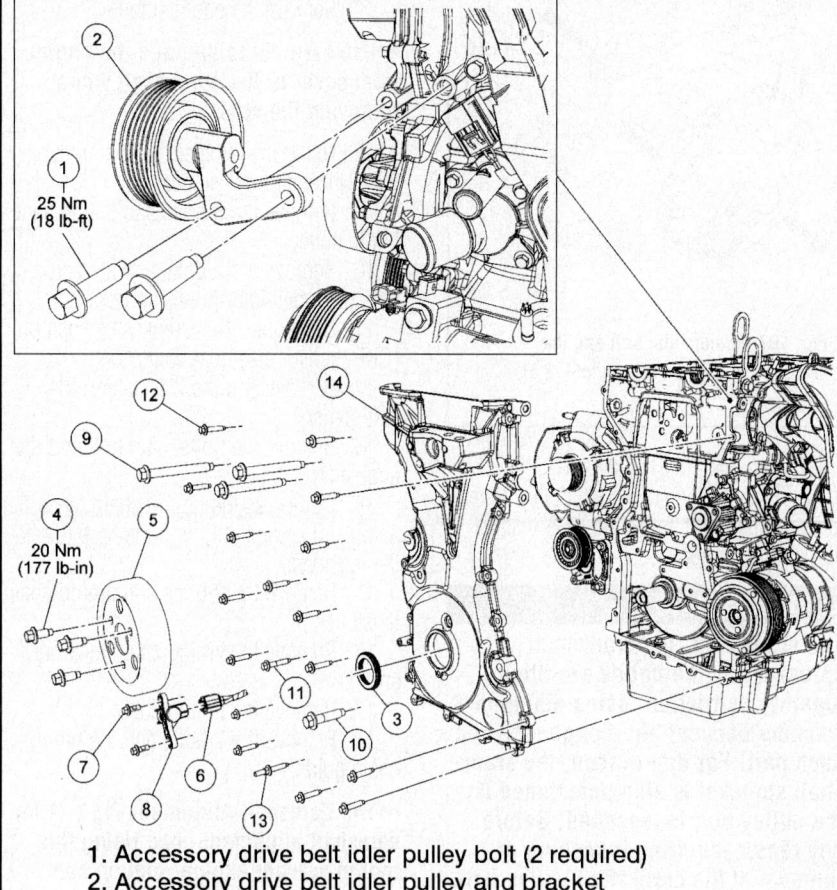

1. Accessory drive belt idler pulley bolt (2 required)
2. Accessory drive belt idler pulley and bracket
3. Crankshaft front seal
4. Coolant pump pulley bolt (3 required)
5. Coolant pump pulley
6. Crankshaft Position (CKP) sensor electrical connector
7. CKP sensor bolt (2 required)
8. CKP sensor
9. Engine front cover bolt (3 required)
10. Engine front cover bolt
11. Engine front cover bolt
12. Engine front cover bolt (16 required)
13. Engine front cover stud bolt
14. Engine front cover

Fig. 194 Engine front cover—2.5L engine

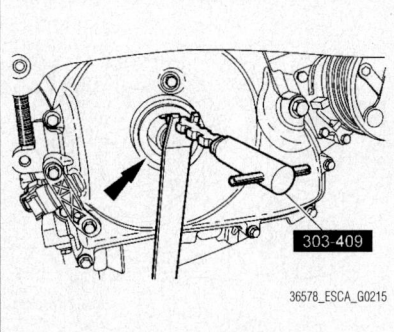

Fig. 193 Front oil seal removal—2.5L engine

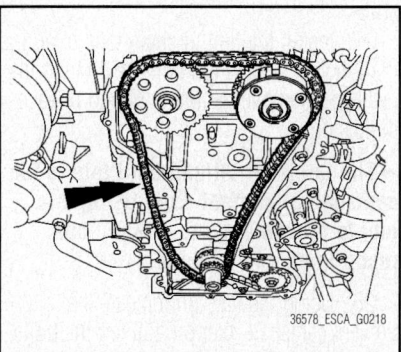

Fig. 195 Remove the timing chain—2.5L engine

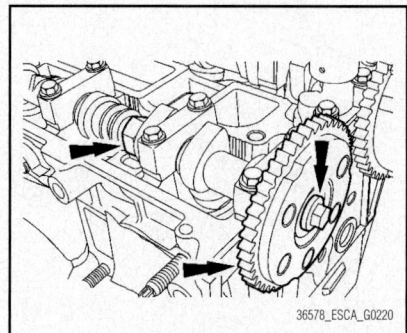

Fig. 196 Remove the bolt and the exhaust camshaft sprocket—2.5L engine

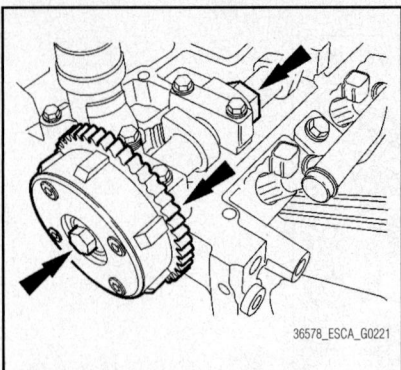

Fig. 197 Remove the bolt and the camshaft phaser and sprocket—2.5L engine

4. Remove the CKP sensor.

5. Remove the crankshaft pulley. Refer to Crankshaft Damper Removal & Installation in this section.

✳✳ WARNING

The crankshaft, the crankshaft sprocket and the pulley are fitted together by friction, using diamond washers between the flange faces on each part. For that reason, the crankshaft sprocket is also unfastened if the pulley bolt is loosened. Before any repair requiring loosening or removal of the crankshaft pulley bolt, the crankshaft and camshafts must be locked in place by the special service tools, otherwise severe engine damage can occur.

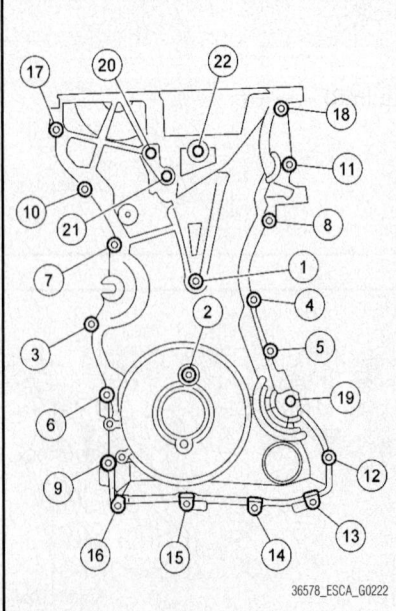

Fig. 198 Timing cover tightening sequence—2.5L engine

6. Install the engine support bar.

7. Remove the engine mount.

➥Use care not to damage the engine front cover or the crankshaft when removing the seal.

8. Using the oil seal remover, remove the crankshaft front oil seal.

9. Remove the 3 bolts and the coolant pump pulley.

10. Remove the 2 bolts and the accessory drive belt idler pulley and bracket.

11. Disconnect the Crankshaft Position (CKP) sensor electrical connector.

12. Remove and the 2 bolts and the CKP sensor.

13. Remove the bolts, stud bolt and the engine front cover.

14. Compress the timing chain tensioner and insert a paper clip into the hole to retain the tensioner.

15. Remove the 2 bolts and timing chain tensioner.

16. Remove the timing chain tensioner arm.

17. Remove the timing chain.

18. Remove the 2 bolts and the timing chain guide.

➥The Camshaft Alignment Plate is for camshaft alignment only. Using this tool to prevent engine rotation can result in engine damage.

19. Using the flats on the camshaft to prevent camshaft rotation, remove the bolt and the exhaust camshaft sprocket.

20. Using the flats on the camshaft to prevent camshaft rotation, remove the bolt and the camshaft phaser and sprocket.

To install:

21. Install the camshaft sprockets and the bolts. Do not tighten the bolts at this time.

22. Install the timing chain guide and the 2 bolts. Tighten to 89 inch lbs. (10 Nm).

23. Install the timing chain.

24. Install the timing chain tensioner arm.

25. Install the timing chain tensioner and the 2 bolts. Tighten the bolts to 89 inch lbs. (10 Nm). Remove the paper clip to release the piston.

➥The Camshaft Alignment Plate is for camshaft alignment only. Using this tool to prevent engine rotation can result in engine damage.

26. Using the flats on the camshafts to prevent camshaft rotation, tighten the bolts to 53 ft. lbs. (72 Nm).

27. Clean and inspect the mounting surfaces of the engine and the front cover.

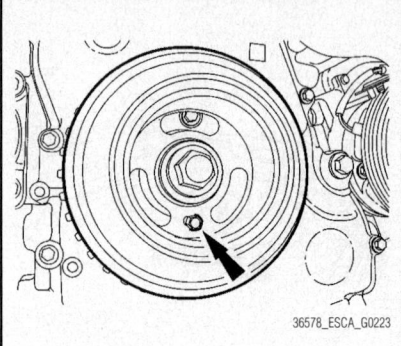

Fig. 199 Install a 6 mm x 18 mm bolt through the crankshaft pulley and thread it into the front cover

➥The engine front cover must be installed and the bolts tightened within 4 minutes of applying the silicone gasket and sealant.

28. Apply a 0.09 inch (2.5 mm) bead of silicone gasket and sealant to the cylinder head and oil pan joint areas. Apply a 0.09 inch (2.5 mm) bead of silicone gasket and sealant to the front cover.

29. Install the engine front cover. Tighten the bolts in the sequence shown, to the following specifications:

- Tighten the 8-mm bolts and stud bolt to 89 inch lbs. (10 Nm).
- Tighten the 13-mm bolts to 35 ft. lbs. (48 Nm).

30. Install the accessory drive belt idler pulley and bracket and the 2 bolts. Tighten the bolts to 18 ft. lbs. (25 Nm).

31. Install the coolant pump pulley and bolts. Tighten the bolts to 177 inch lbs. (20 Nm).

32. Using the Camshaft Front Oil Seal Installer, install the crankshaft front oil seal.

33. Install the engine support mount, refer to the graphic for correct torque specifications.

34. Remove the engine support bar.

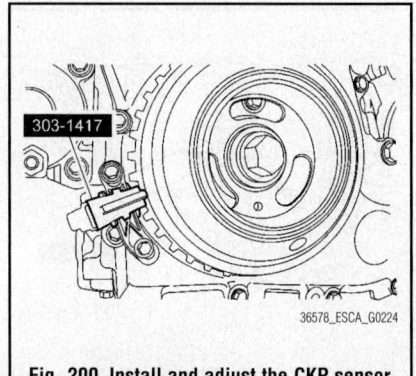

Fig. 200 Install and adjust the CKP sensor with the special tool

35. Install the front crankshaft damper pulley. Refer to Crankshaft Damper in this section.

✳✳ WARNING

The crankshaft, the crankshaft sprocket and the pulley are fitted together by friction, using diamond washers between the flange faces on each part. For that reason, the crankshaft sprocket is also unfastened if the pulley bolt is loosened. Before any repair requiring loosening or removal of the crankshaft pulley bolt, the crankshaft and camshafts must be locked in place by the special service tools, otherwise severe engine damage can occur. Refer to Crankshaft Damper in this section.

36. Install a 6 mm x 18 mm bolt through the crankshaft pulley and thread it into the front cover.

37. Install the CKP sensor and the 2 bolts. Using the crankshaft sensor aligner, adjust the CKP sensor. Tighten the bolts to 62 inch lbs. (7 Nm).

38. Connect the CKP sensor electrical connector.

39. Remove the 6 mm x 18 mm bolt.

40. Install the accessory drive belt and smooth idler pulley.

3.0L Engine

2008 Models

See Figures 201 through 212.

1. Before servicing the vehicle, refer to the Precautions Section.

2. Remove or disconnect the following:
   - Negative battery cable
   - Engine front cover

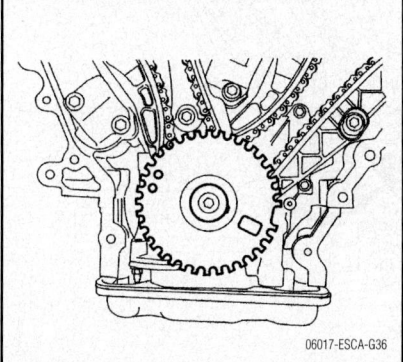

Fig. 201 Ignition pulse wheel—3.0L engine

➡This pulse wheel is used in several different engines. Install the pulse wheel with the keyway in the slot stamped "30" or "30RFF" (orange in color).

   - Ignition pulse wheel and install the damper bolt
   - Spark plugs

3. Rotate the crankshaft clockwise to position the keyway at the 11 o'clock posi-

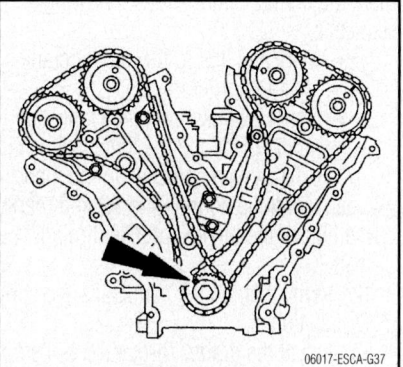

Fig. 202 Rotate the crankshaft clockwise to position the keyway at the 11 o'clock position—3.0L engine

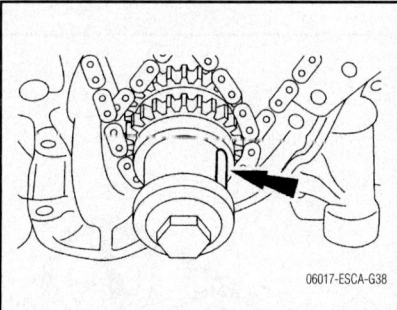

Fig. 203 Rotate the crankshaft clockwise 120 degrees to the 3 o'clock position to locate the right side camshafts in the neutral position—3.0L engine

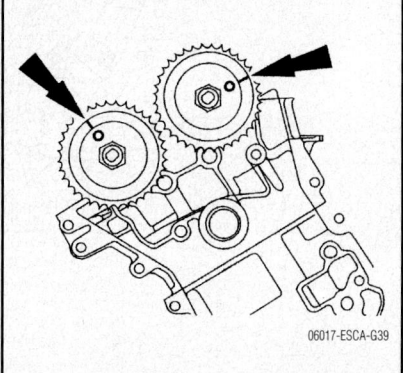

Fig. 204 Verify that the right camshafts are in the neutral position—3.0L engine

tion and the camshafts in the correct positions. The No. 1 cylinder will be at Top Dead Center (TDC).

4. Rotate the crankshaft clockwise 120 degrees to the 3 o'clock position to locate the right side camshafts in the neutral position. Verify that the right camshafts are in the neutral position.

5. Remove or disconnect the following:
   - Right side timing chain and tensioner
   - Tensioner arm and timing chain guide

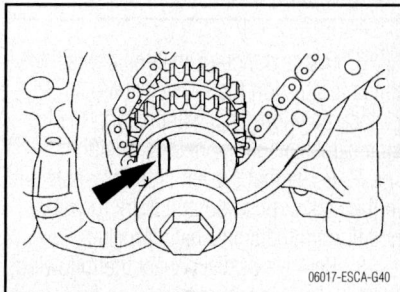

Fig. 205 Rotate the crankshaft clockwise 1⅔ times to position the keyway at the 11 o'clock position—3.0L engine

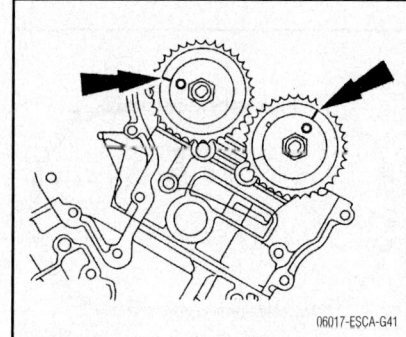

Fig. 206 Verify that the left side camshafts are in the neutral position—3.0L engine

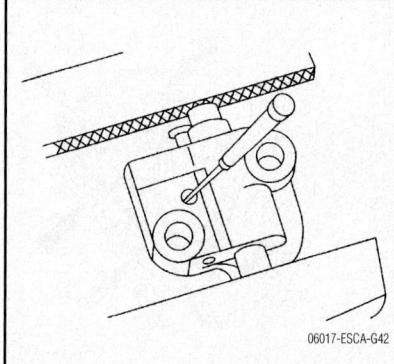

Fig. 207 Hold the ratchet lock mechanism away from the ratchet stem—3.0L engine

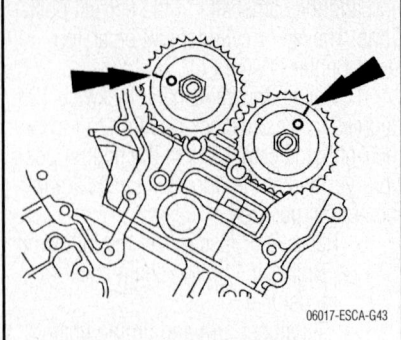

Fig. 208 Verify that the left camshafts are correctly positioned–3.0L engine

6. Rotate the crankshaft clockwise 1⅔ times to position the keyway at the 11 o'clock position. This will position the left side camshafts in the neutral position.

7. Verify that the left side camshafts are in the neutral position and mark the link position on the crankshaft sprocket.

8. Remove or disconnect the following:
- Left side timing chain and tensioner
- Tensioner arm and timing chain guide
- Damper bolt and crankshaft sprockets

To install:

9. Install the crankshaft sprockets.

10. Position the timing chain tensioner in a soft jaw vise. Hold the ratchet lock mechanism away from the ratchet stem and slowly compress the timing chain tensioner. Retain the piston with a 1.5mm wire or paper clip.

11. If the timing marks on the chain are not visible, use a permanent marker to mark the left and right side timing chains. Mark the timing chains in the following sequence:
- Mark any link to use as the crankshaft timing mark.
- Count 29 links from the crankshaft timing mark and mark the link as the exhaust cam sprocket timing mark.

a. Continue counting to 42 and mark the link as the intake sprocket timing mark.

12. Verify that the left camshafts are correctly positioned.

13. Install the guide. Torque the bolts to 18 ft. lbs. (25 Nm).

14. Install the left side timing chain and align the chain in the following sequence:
- Mark any link to use as the crankshaft timing mark.

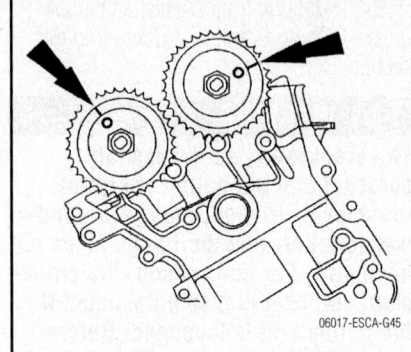

Fig. 211 Verify that the right camshafts are correctly positioned–3.0L engine

- Count 29 links from the crankshaft timing mark and mark the link as the exhaust cam sprocket timing mark.
- Continue counting to 42 and mark the link as the intake sprocket timing mark

15. Install or connect the following:
- Left side timing chain and tensioner arm. Torque the bolts to 18 ft. lbs. (25 Nm).
- Crankshaft damper bolt and rotate the keyway to the 3 o'clock position.

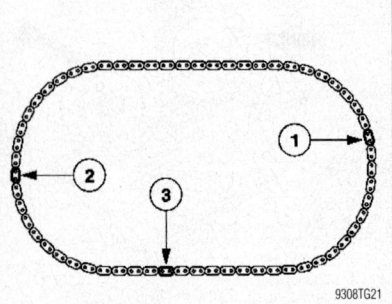

Fig. 209 Mark the timing chain in the proper sequence–3.0L engine

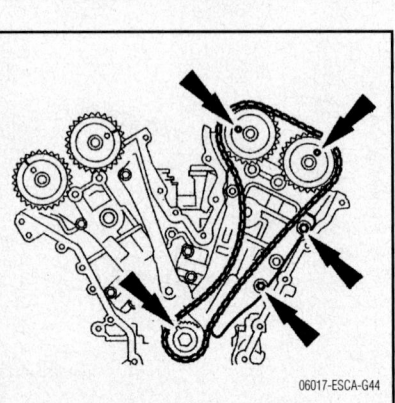

Fig. 210 Left side timing chain installed–3.0L engine

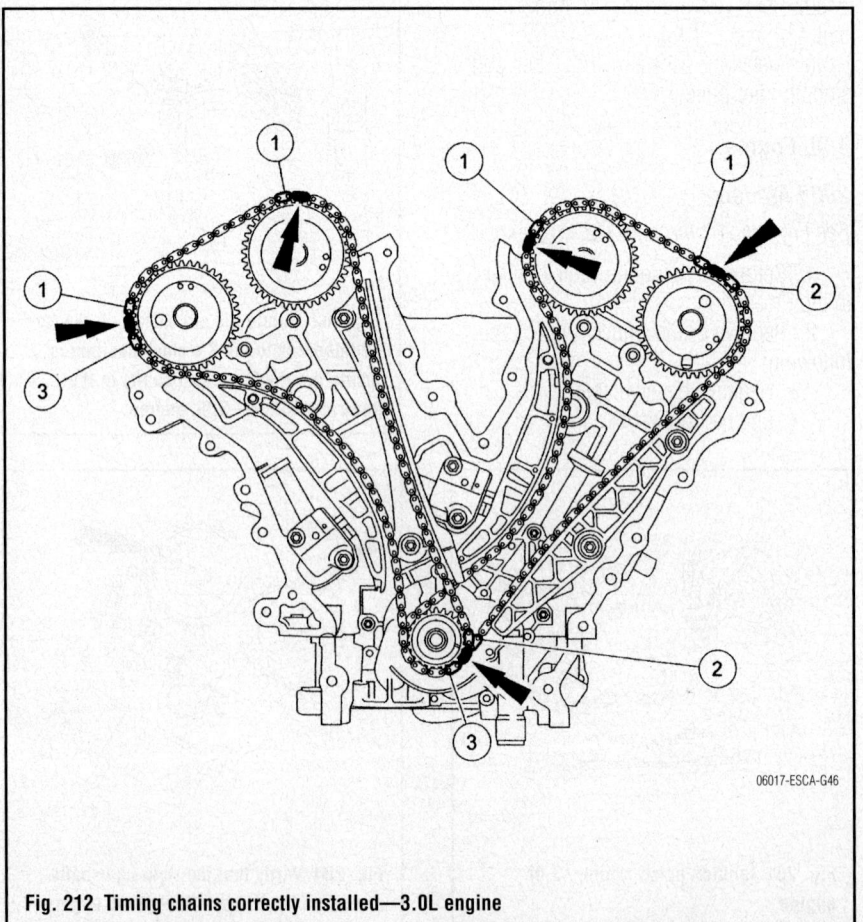

Fig. 212 Timing chains correctly installed–3.0L engine

16. Verify that the right side camshafts are properly positioned and install the right side timing chain and guide. Torque the bolts to 18 ft. lbs. (25 Nm).

17. Make certain that the timing chain aligns with the marks on the camshaft and crankshaft sprockets

✳✳ CAUTION

Install the pulse wheel with the keyway in the slot stamped 20–25–34Y–30M (Color Blur).

18. Install or connect the following:
- Right side timing chain tensioner and arm. Torque the bolts to 18 ft. lbs. (25 Nm) and remove the damper bolt
- Ignition pulse wheel
- Spark plugs
- Engine front cover
- Negative battery cable

2009 Models

See Figures 213 through 224.

✳✳ WARNING

During engine repair procedures, cleanliness is extremely important. Any foreign material (including any material created while cleaning gasket surfaces) that enters the oil passages, coolant passages or the oil pan may cause engine failure.

✳✳ WARNING

Failure to verify correct timing drive component alignment will result in severe engine damage.

1. Before servicing the vehicle, refer to the Precautions Section.

2. With the vehicle in NEUTRAL, position it on a hoist.

3. Drain the cooling system.

4. Disconnect the battery ground cable.

5. Remove the drive belt.

6. Remove the crankshaft damper. Refer to Crankshaft Damper Removal & Installation in this section.

7. Remove the crankshaft front seal.

8. Remove the alternator bolt and the 2 nuts

9. Remove the stud and position the generator away from the engine.

10. Remove the 3 bolts and the accessory drive belt tensioner.

11. Detach the wiring harness retainer from the engine front cover stud bolt.

12. Disconnect the Crankshaft Position (CKP) sensor electrical connector.

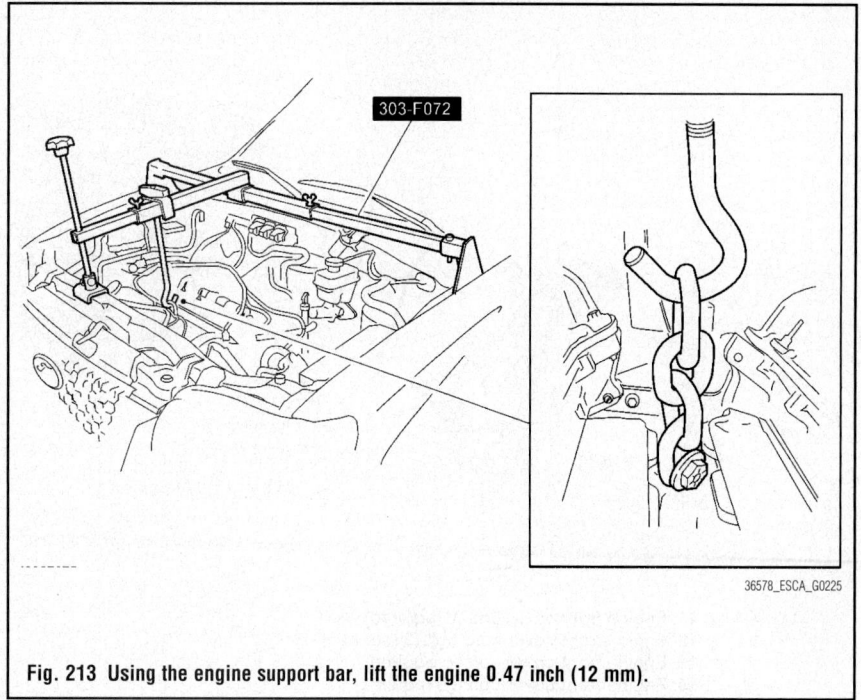

Fig. 213 Using the engine support bar, lift the engine 0.47 inch (12 mm).

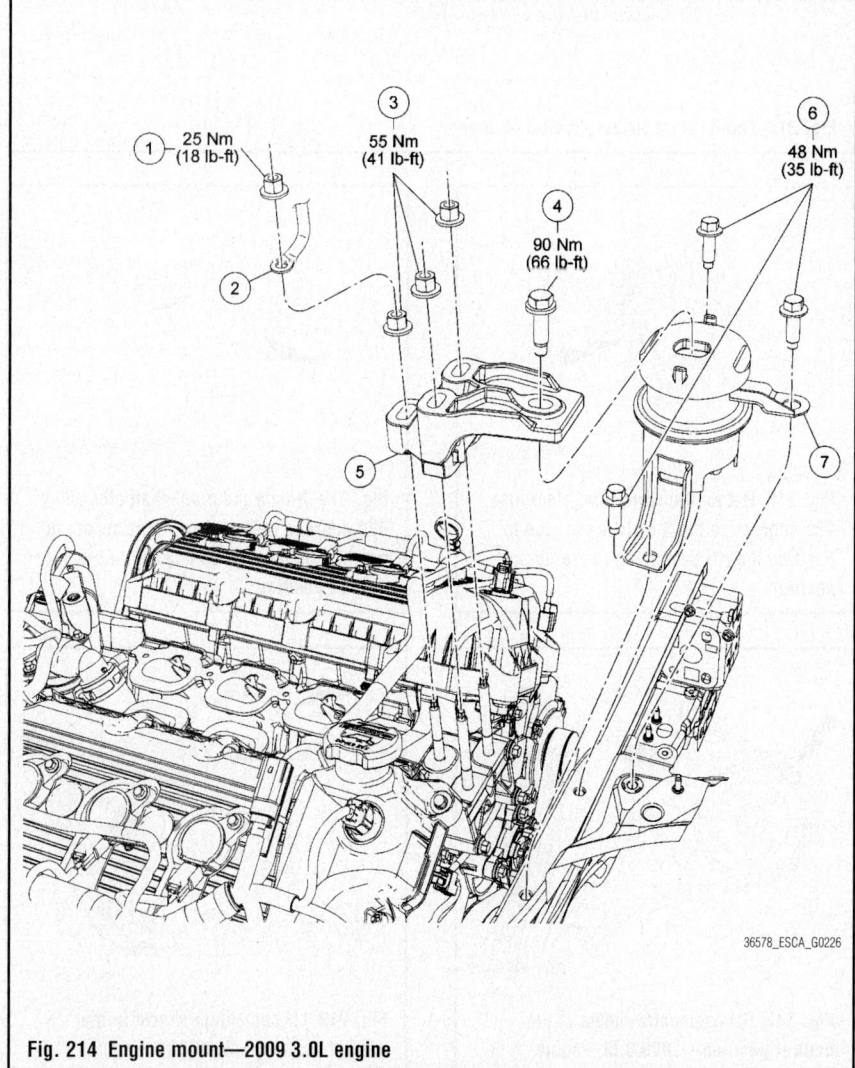

Fig. 214 Engine mount—2009 3.0L engine

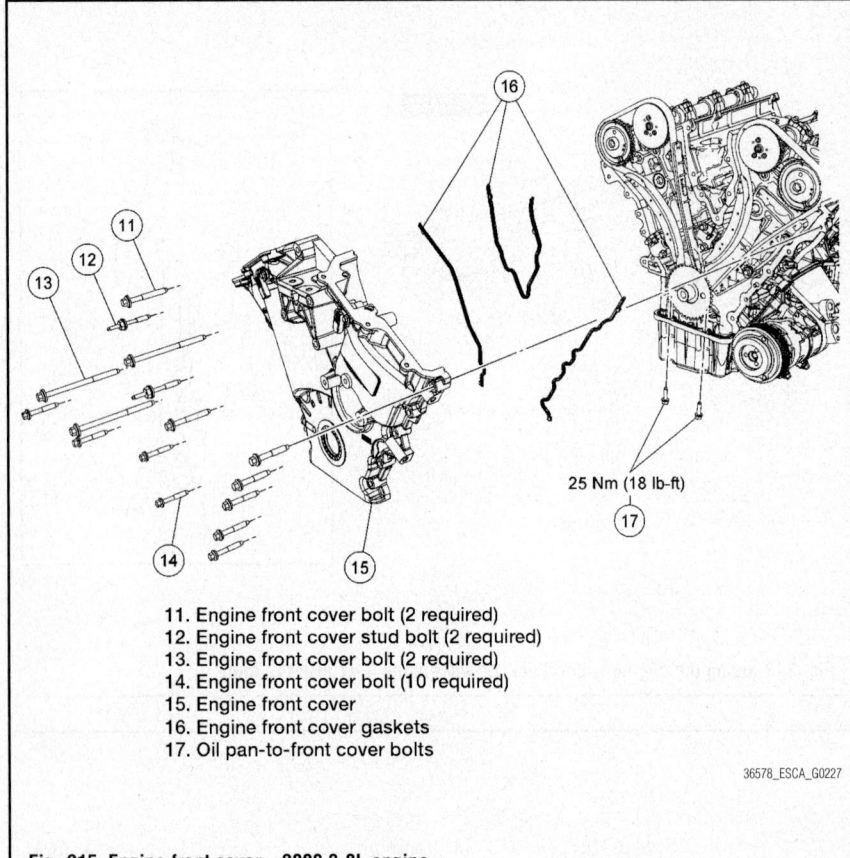

11. Engine front cover bolt (2 required)
12. Engine front cover stud bolt (2 required)
13. Engine front cover bolt (2 required)
14. Engine front cover bolt (10 required)
15. Engine front cover
16. Engine front cover gaskets
17. Oil pan-to-front cover bolts

36578_ESCA_G0227

Fig. 215 Engine front cover—2009 3.0L engine

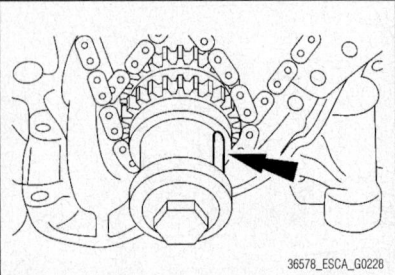

36578_ESCA_G0228

Fig. 216 Rotate the crankshaft clockwise 120 degrees to the 3 o'clock position to position the RH camshafts in the neutral position

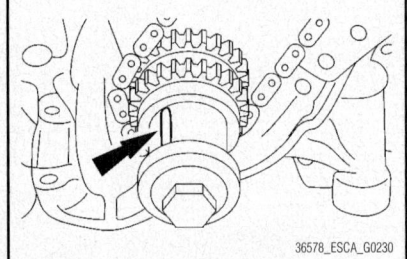

36578_ESCA_G0230

Fig. 218 Rotate the crankshaft clockwise 600 degrees (one and two-third turns) to position the crankcase keyway in the 11 o'clock position

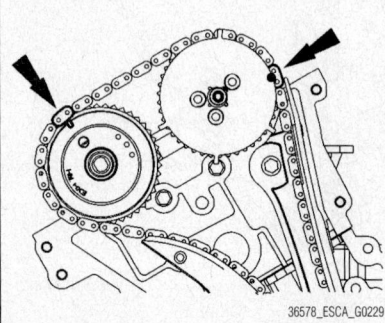

36578_ESCA_G0229

Fig. 217 RH camshafts shown in the neutral position—2009 3.0L engine

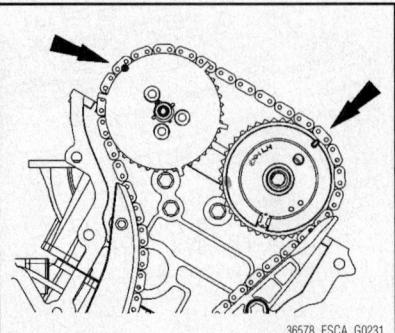

36578_ESCA_G0231

Fig. 219 LH camshafts shown in the neutral position—2009 3.0L engine

13. Disconnect the 2 Camshaft Position (CMP) sensor electrical connectors and detach the wiring harness retainer from the engine front cover stud bolt.

14. Remove the valve covers.

15. Remove the LH and RH Variable Camshaft Timing (VCT) oil control solenoids. Refer to the Engine Performance & Emission Controls section.

16. Remove the upper and lower intake manifold.

17. Remove the engine support insulator as follows:
- Remove the engine support insulator bracket bolt.
- Install the engine support bar, universal adapter brackets and a suitable piece of chain.
- Using the engine support bar, lift the engine 0.47 inch (12 mm).
- Remove the engine support mount.

18. Remove the 2 oil pan-to-front cover bolts.

19. Remove the 14 bolts, 2 stud bolts and the engine front cover. Remove and discard the gaskets.

20. Remove the 2 oil pan-to-front cover bolts.

21. Remove the 14 bolts, 2 stud bolts and the engine front cover.

22. Remove the LH and RH spark plugs.

➡**This pulse wheel is used in several different engines. Install the pulse wheel with the keyway in the slot stamped "30RFF" (orange in color).**

23. Remove the ignition pulse wheel.

24. Install the crankshaft pulley bolt and washer.

25. Rotate the crankshaft clockwise to position the crankshaft keyway in the 11 o'clock position and position the camshafts in the correct position. This will position the No. 1 cylinder at Top Dead Center (TDC).

26. Verify that the camshafts are correctly located. If not, rotate the crankshaft one additional turn and recheck.

27. Rotate the crankshaft clockwise 120 degrees to the 3 o'clock position to position the RH camshafts in the neutral position.

28. Verify that the RH camshafts are in the neutral position.

29. Remove the RH timing chain tensioner arm as follows:
- Remove the 2 bolts.
- Remove the tensioner.
- Remove the tensioner arm.

30. Remove the 2 bolts and the RH timing chain guide.

31. Remove the RH timing chain from the engine.

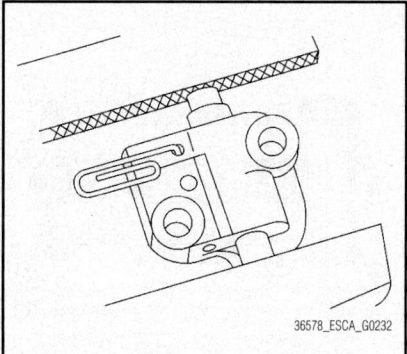

Fig. 220 Retaining the tensioner piston with a paper clip

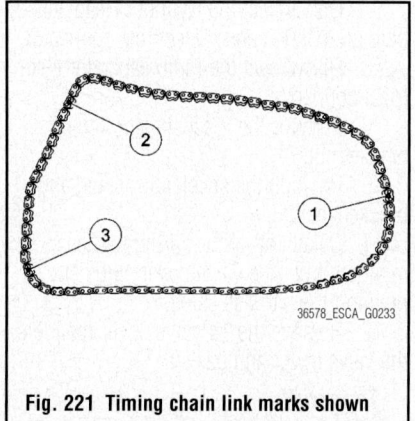

Fig. 221 Timing chain link marks shown

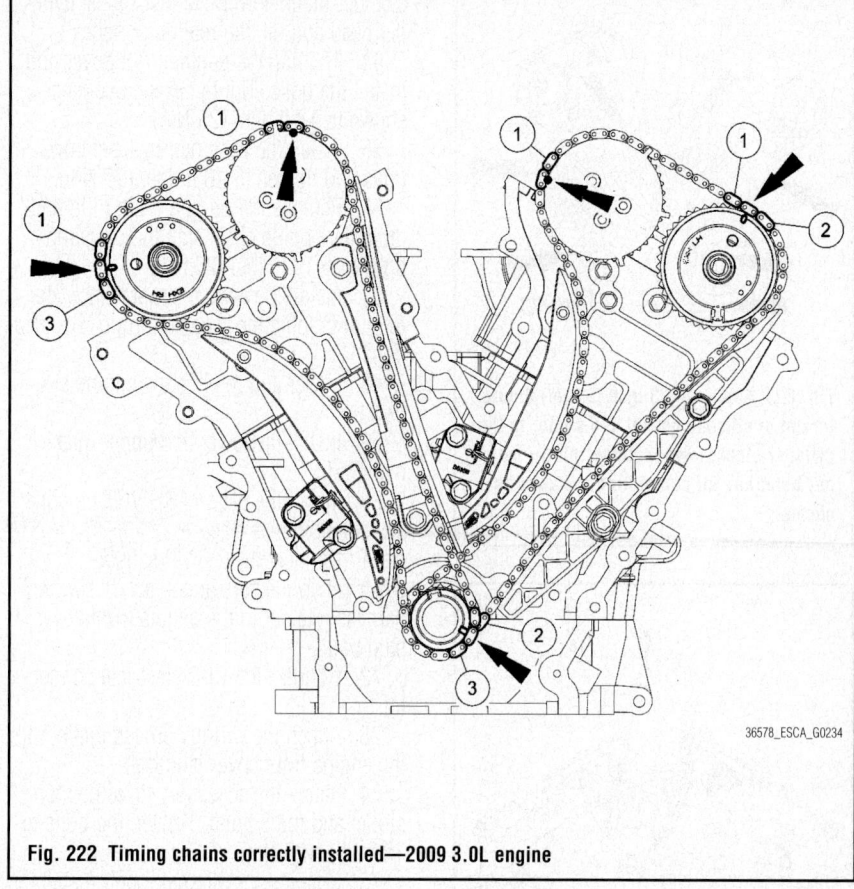

Fig. 222 Timing chains correctly installed—2009 3.0L engine

32. Rotate the crankshaft clockwise 600 degrees (one and two-third turns) to position the crankcase keyway in the 11 o'clock position. This will position the LH camshafts in the neutral position.

33. Verify the LH camshafts are in the neutral position.

34. Remove the LH timing chain tensioner arm as follows:
   - Remove the 2 bolts.
   - Remove the tensioner.
   - Remove the tensioner arm.

35. Remove the 2 bolts and the LH timing chain guide.

36. Remove the LH timing chain from the engine.

37. Remove the crankshaft pulley bolt and the crankshaft sprocket.

To install:

38. Install the crankshaft sprockets with the timing marks out.

39. Position the LH and RH chain tensioners in a soft-jawed vise and slowly collapse the tensioner ratchet.

40. Hold the chain tensioner ratchet lock mechanism away from the ratchet stem with a small pick.

41. Retain the tensioner piston with a 1.5 mm (0.06 in) diameter wire or paper clip.

42. If timing marks in the timing chains are not evident, use a permanent-type marker to mark the crankshaft and camshaft timing marks on the LH and RH timing chains.

43. Mark any link to use as the crankshaft timing mark.

44. Starting with the crankshaft timing mark, count 29 links and mark the link.

45. Continue counting to link 42 and mark the link.

46. Position the LH timing chain and guide and install the bolts. Tighten the bolts to 18 ft. lbs. (25 Nm).

47. Align the marks on the timing chain with the marks on the camshaft and crankshaft sprockets.

48. Install the LH timing chain tensioner arm and the LH timing chain tensioner. Tighten the mounting bolts to 18 ft. lbs. (25 Nm).

49. Install the crankshaft pulley bolt and rotate the crankshaft clockwise 120 degrees until the crankshaft keyway is in the 3 o'clock position.

50. Verify that the RH camshafts are correctly positioned.

51. Install the RH timing chain and chain guide and install the bolts. Tighten the bolts to 18 ft. lbs. (25 Nm).

52. Install the RH timing chain tensioner and tensioner arm. Tighten the bolts to 18 ft. lbs. (25 Nm).

53. Remove the LH and RH timing chain tensioner piston retaining wires.

54. Rotate the crankshaft counterclockwise 120 degrees to TDC.

✸✸ WARNING

Failure to verify correct timing drive component alignment will result in severe engine damage.

55. Verify the timing with the following steps:

56. There should be 12 chain links between the camshaft timing marks.

57. There should be 27 chain links between the camshaft and the crankshaft timing marks.

58. There should be 30 chain links between the camshaft and the crankshaft timing marks.

59. Remove the crankshaft pulley bolt and washer.

➡This pulse wheel is used in several different engines. Install the pulse wheel with the keyway in the slot stamped "30RFF" only (orange in color).

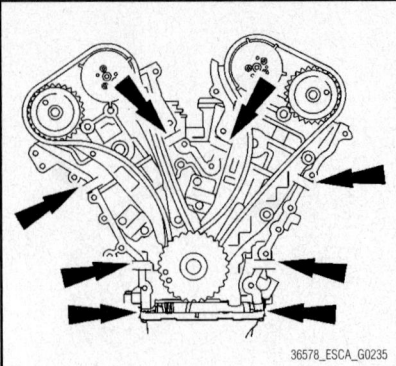

Fig. 223 Apply a 0.23 inch (6 mm) diameter dot of silicone gasket and sealer to the cylinder block, lower cylinder block, cylinder head and oil pan mating surfaces as shown

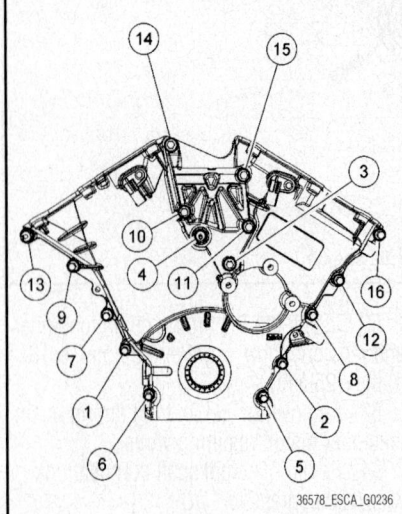

Fig. 224 Engine front cover tightening sequence—2009 3.0L engine

60. Install the ignition pulse wheel.
61. Install the LH and RH spark plugs.

➡Do not use metal scrapers, wire brushes, power abrasive discs or other abrasive means to clean the sealing surfaces. These tools cause scratches and gouges which make leak paths.

➡Use a plastic scraping tool to remove all traces of sealant. Clean all sealing surfaces with metal surface prep and install new gaskets.

➡The engine front cover must be installed and the bolts tightened within 4 minutes of applying sealant.

62. Install the front cover gaskets.
63. Apply a 0.23 inch (6 mm) diameter dot of silicone gasket and sealer to the

cylinder block, lower cylinder block, cylinder head and oil pan mating surfaces.
64. Position the engine front cover and install the bolts. Tighten in the sequence shown to 18 ft. lbs. (25 Nm).
65. Install the 2 oil pan-to-front cover bolts and tighten to 18 ft. lbs. (25 Nm).
66. Remove the oil pan drain plug and drain the engine oil. Install the plug and tighten to 19 ft. lbs. (26 Nm).
67. Install the engine support insulator, refer to graphic for specific torque specifications.
68. Lower and remove the engine support bar.
69. Install the lower and upper intake manifold.
70. Install the LH and RH VCT oil control solenoids.
71. Connect the 2 CMP sensor electrical connectors and attach the wiring harness retainer to the engine front cover stud bolt.
72. Connect the CKP electrical connector.
73. Attach the wiring harness retainer to the engine front cover stud bolt.
74. Install the accessory drive belt tensioner and the 3 bolts. Tighten the bolts to 18 ft. lbs. (25 Nm).
75. Position the alternator and install the stud. Tighten the stud to 71 inch lbs. (8 Nm).
76. Install the alternator bolt and 2 nuts. Tighten to 35 ft. lbs. (47 Nm).
77. Install the crankshaft front seal.
78. Fill the engine with clean engine oil.
79. Refill and bleed the cooling system.
80. Connect the battery ground cable.
81. Start the engine and check for leaks.

VALVE COVERS

REMOVAL & INSTALLATION

2.3L Engine
See Figure 225.

1. Before servicing the vehicle, refer to the Precautions Section.
2. With the vehicle in NEUTRAL, position it on a hoist.
3. Remove the ignition coil-on-plugs.
4. Disconnect the crankcase vent hose.
5. Disconnect the Camshaft Position (CMP) sensor electrical connector.
6. Disconnect the fuel rail pressure and temperature sensor electrical connector.

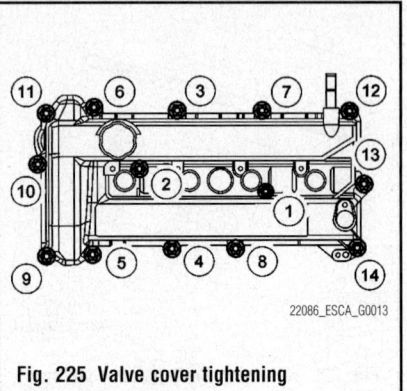

Fig. 225 Valve cover tightening sequence—2.3L engine

7. Disconnect the Cylinder Head Temperature (CHT) sensor electrical connector.
8. Disconnect the radio capacitor electrical connector.
9. Remove the 2 accelerator cable bracket nuts.
10. Position the accelerator cable and brackets aside.
11. Detach all of the wiring harness retainers from the valve cover studs and position the harness aside.
12. Remove the 14 valve cover retainers, the valve cover and gasket.

To install:

✱✱ WARNING

Do not use metal scrapers, wire brushes, power abrasive discs or other abrasive means to clean the sealing surfaces. These tools cause scratches and gouges which make leak paths.

13. Clean and inspect the sealing surfaces
14. Install the valve cover, gasket and retainers.
15. Tighten in sequence to 89 inch lbs. (10 Nm).
16. Position the wiring harness and attach all of the wiring harness retainers to the valve cover studs.
17. Install the accelerator control cable brackets and tighten nuts to 53 inch lbs. (6 Nm).
18. Connect the radio capacitor electrical connector.
19. Connect the CHT sensor electrical connector.
20. Connect the fuel rail pressure and temperature sensor electrical connector
21. Connect the CMP sensor electrical connector.
22. Connect the crankcase vent hose.
23. Install the ignition coil-on-plugs. Tighten to 71 inch lbs. (8 Nm).

2.5L Engine

See Figures 226 and 227.

❈❈ WARNING

During engine repair procedures, cleanliness is extremely important. Any foreign material, including any material created while cleaning gasket surfaces, which enters the oil passages, coolant passages or the oil pan can cause engine failure.

1. Before servicing the vehicle, refer to the Precautions Section.
2. With the vehicle in NEUTRAL, position it on a hoist.
3. Remove the oil level indicator.
4. Remove the ignition coil-on-plugs.
5. Disconnect the crankcase vent hose.
6. Disconnect the Cylinder Head Temperature (CHT) sensor electrical connector.
7. Disconnect the Camshaft Position (CMP) sensor electrical connector.
8. Disconnect the radio capacitor electrical connector.
9. Disconnect the Variable Camshaft Timing (VCT) solenoid electrical connector.
10. Detach all of the wiring harness retainers from the valve cover studs and position the harness aside.

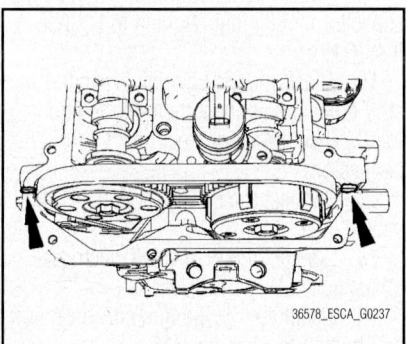

36578_ESCA_G0237

Fig. 226 Apply silicone gasket and sealant to the locations shown

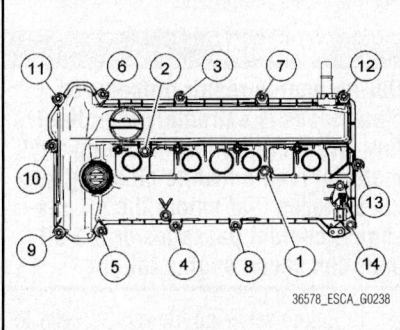

36578_ESCA_G0238

Fig. 227 Valve cover tightening sequence—2.5L engine

11. Remove the 14 valve cover retainers, the valve cover and gasket.

To install:

➡Do not use metal scrapers, wire brushes, power abrasive discs or other abrasive means to clean the sealing surfaces. These tools cause scratches and gouges which make leak paths.

12. Clean and inspect the sealing surfaces.

➡The valve cover must be secured within 4 minutes of silicone gasket application. If the valve cover is not secured within 4 minutes, the sealant must be removed and the sealing area cleaned with metal surface prep.

13. Apply silicone gasket and sealant to the locations shown.
14. Clean and inspect the gasket. Install a new gasket, if necessary.
15. Install the valve cover, gasket and retainers.
16. Tighten in the sequence shown to 89 inch lbs. 10 Nm).
17. Position the wiring harness and attach all of the wiring harness retainers to the valve cover studs.
18. Connect the VCT solenoid electrical connector.
19. Connect the radio capacitor electrical connector.
20. Connect the CMP sensor electrical connector.
21. Connect the CHT sensor electrical connector.
22. Connect the crankcase vent hose.
23. Install the ignition coil-on-plugs.
24. Install the oil level indicator.

3.0L Engine—2008 Model

Left Side

See Figures 228 and 229.

❈❈ WARNING

During engine repair procedures, cleanliness is extremely important. Any foreign material, including any material created while cleaning gasket surfaces that enters the oil passages, coolant passages or the oil pan, can cause engine failure.

1. Before servicing the vehicle, refer to the Precautions Section.
2. Remove the LH ignition coil-on-plugs.
3. Remove the Power Steering Pressure (PSP) tube bracket nut and position the PSP tube and bracket aside.

4. If equipped, remove the bolt and the engine lift bracket.
5. Remove the 2 bolts and the accelerator cable snow shield.

❈❈ WARNING

Do not disconnect the crankcase ventilation tube from the valve cover or damage to the ventilation tube may occur.

6. Disconnect the crankcase ventilation tube from the air cleaner outlet pipe.
7. Detach the 5 wiring retainers from the valve cover stud bolts.

➡Inspect the crankcase ventilation tube and valve cover sealing area. If either a new valve cover or crankcase ventilation tube is required, both components must be installed new.

8. Remove the 2 bolts, 9 stud bolts and the valve cover.
9. Remove and discard the gasket.

To install:

10. Clean the valve cover, cylinder head and front cover sealing surfaces with metal surface cleaner and install a new valve cover gasket.

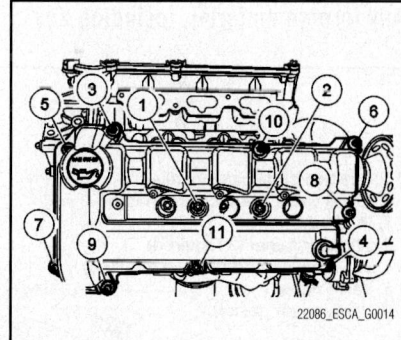

22086_ESCA_G0014

Fig. 228 Early build valve cover tightening sequence

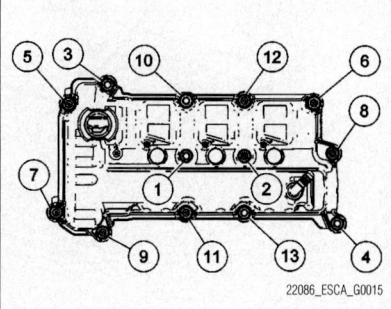

22086_ESCA_G0015

Fig. 229 Late build valve cover tightening sequence

➡️The valve cover must be installed and the bolts and stud bolts tightened within 4 minutes of sealant application.

11. Apply a 19 inch. (5mm) dot of silicone gasket sealant to the front cover-to-cylinder head joints.

12. Position the valve cover and install the bolts and stud bolts. Tighten to 89 inch lbs. (10 Nm).

13. Attach the wiring retainers to the valve cover stud bolts.

14. Attach the crankcase ventilation tube to the air cleaner outlet pipe

15. Install the accelerator cable snow shield and the 2 bolts. Tighten to 89 inch lbs. (10 Nm).

16. If equipped, install the engine lift bracket and the bolt. Tighten to 87 ft. lbs. (118 Nm).

17. Position the PSP tube and bracket and install the nut. Tighten to 18 ft. lbs. (25 Nm).

18. Install the LH ignition coil-on-plugs and tighten to 11 ft. lbs. (15 Nm).

Right Side

See Figures 230 and 231.

✳✳ WARNING

During engine repair procedures, cleanliness is extremely important. Any foreign material, including any material created while cleaning gasket surfaces that enters the oil passages, coolant passages or the oil pan, can cause engine failure.

1. Before servicing the vehicle, refer to the Precautions Section.
2. Remove the upper intake manifold.
3. Remove the RH ignition coil-on-plugs.
4. Disconnect the Positive Crankcase Ventilation (PCV) valve electrical connector.
5. Disconnect the PCV tube from the PCV valve and position it aside.

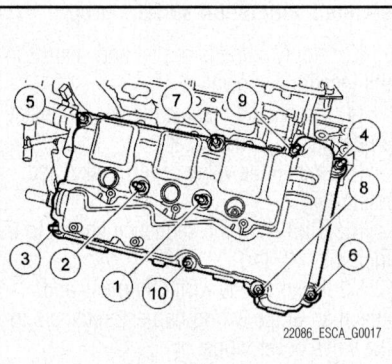

22086_ESCA_G0017

Fig. 231 Right valve cover tightening sequence 3.0L engine

6. Disconnect the radio ignition interference capacitor electrical connector and detach the 3 wiring retainers from the stud bolts.
7. Remove the nut and the radio ignition interference capacitor.
8. Remove the 2 nuts and position the engine control harness aside.
9. Remove the bolt, 9 stud bolts and the valve cover.
10. Remove and discard the gasket.

To install:

11. Clean the valve cover, cylinder head and front cover sealing surfaces with metal surface cleaner and install a new valve cover gasket.

➡️The valve cover must be installed and the bolts and stud bolts tightened within 4 minutes of sealant application. Apply a 19 inch. (5mm) dot of silicone gasket sealant to the front cover-to-cylinder head joints.

12. Position the valve cover and install the stud bolts.

13. Tighten in sequence to 89 inch lbs. (10 Nm).

14. Position the engine control harness and install the nuts. Tighten to 53 inch lbs. (6 Nm).

15. Install the radio ignition interference capacitor and the nut. Tighten to 53 inch lbs. (6 Nm).

16. Attach the wiring retainers to the stud bolts and connect the radio ignition interference capacitor electrical connector.

17. Connect the PCV tube to the PCV valve.

18. Connect the PCV valve electrical connector.

19. Install the RH ignition coil-on-plugs and tighten to 11 ft. lbs. (15 Nm).

3.0L Engine—2009 Model

Left Side

See Figures 232 and 233.

✳✳ WARNING

During engine repair procedures, cleanliness is extremely important. Any foreign material, including any material created while cleaning gasket surfaces that enters the oil passages, coolant passages or the oil pan, can cause engine failure.

1. Before servicing the vehicle, refer to the Precautions Section.
2. Remove the LH ignition coil-on-plugs.

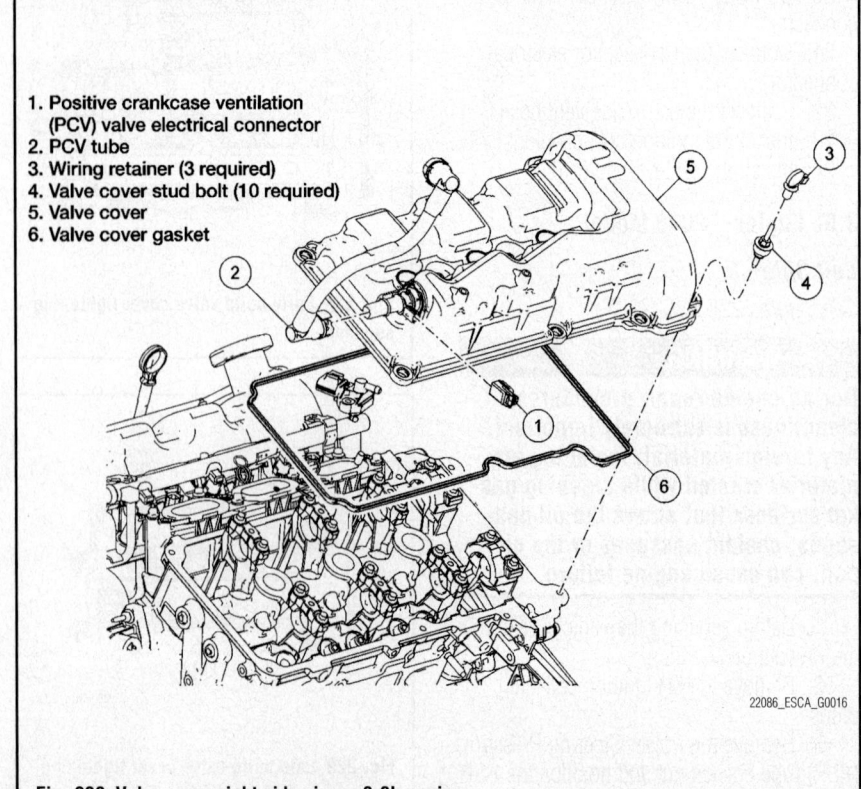

1. Positive crankcase ventilation (PCV) valve electrical connector
2. PCV tube
3. Wiring retainer (3 required)
4. Valve cover stud bolt (10 required)
5. Valve cover
6. Valve cover gasket

22086_ESCA_G0016

Fig. 230 Valve cover right side view—3.0L engine

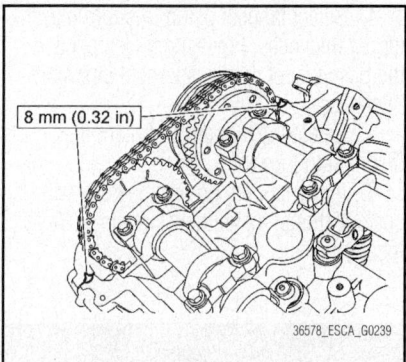

Fig. 232 Apply a bead of silicone gasket and sealant in 2 places shown

3. Detach the upper radiator hose from the 2 retainers on the cooling fan shroud and position the hose aside.

4. Detach the 2 wiring retainers from the valve cover.

5. Detach the 2 wiring retainers from the valve cover stud bolts.

6. Disconnect the Variable Camshaft Timing (VCT) electrical connector.

7. Disconnect the Heated Oxygen Sensor (HO2S) electrical connector.

➡Inspect the crankcase ventilation tube and valve cover sealing area. If either a new valve cover or crankcase ventilation tube is required, both components must be installed new.

8. Remove the 8 bolts, 6 stud bolts and the valve cover. Remove and discard the gasket.

To install:

➡If the valve cover is not secured within 4 minutes, the sealant must be removed and the sealing area cleaned with metal surface prep. Failure to follow this procedure can cause future oil leakage.

9. Apply a bead of silicone gasket and sealant in 2 places where the engine front cover meets the cylinder head.

10. Position the valve cover and install the bolts and stud bolts.

11. Tighten in the sequence shown to 89 inch lbs. (10 Nm).

12. Connect the HO2S electrical connector.

13. Connect the VCT electrical connector.

14. Attach the 2 wiring retainers to the valve cover stud bolts.

15. Attach the 2 wiring retainers to the valve cover.

16. Attach the upper radiator hose to the 2 retainers on the cooling fan shroud.

17. Install the LH ignition coil-on-plugs.

Right Side

See Figure 234.

✳✳ WARNING

During engine repair procedures, cleanliness is extremely important. Any foreign material, including any material created while cleaning gasket surfaces that enters the oil passages, coolant passages or the oil pan, can cause engine failure.

1. Before servicing the vehicle, refer to the Precautions Section.

2. Remove the upper intake manifold, Refer to Intake Manifold Removal & Installation in this section.

3. Remove the RH ignition coil-on-plugs.

4. Detach the 4 main engine control wiring harness retainers from the valve cover stud bolts.

5. Detach the 3 main engine control wiring harness retainers from the valve cover.

6. Disconnect the Variable Camshaft Timing (VCT) electrical connector.

7. Detach the Crankshaft Position (CKP) wiring harness retainer from the stud.

8. Remove the 11 bolts, 3 stud bolts and the valve cover. Remove and discard the gasket.

To install:

➡If the valve cover is not secured within 4 minutes, the sealant must be removed and the sealing area cleaned with metal surface prep. Failure to follow this procedure can cause future oil leakage.

9. Apply a bead of silicone gasket and sealant in 2 places where the engine front cover meets the cylinder head.

10. Position the valve cover and install the bolts and stud bolts.

11. Tighten in the sequence shown to 89 inch lbs. (10 Nm).

12. Attach the CKP wiring harness retainer on the stud.

13. Connect the VCT electrical connector.

14. Attach the 3 main engine control wiring harness retainers to the valve cover.

15. Attach the 4 main engine control wiring harness retainers to the valve cover stud bolts.

16. Install the RH ignition coil-on-plugs.

VALVE LASH

ADJUSTMENT

4 Cylinder Engine
See Figure 235.

1. Before servicing the vehicle, refer to the Precautions Section.

➡Before removing the camshafts, measure the clearance of each valve at base circle, with the lobe pointed away from the tappet. Failure to measure all

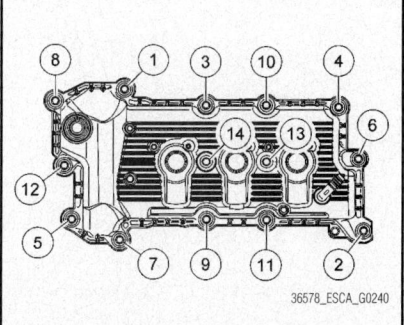

Fig. 233 LH valve cover tightening sequence—2009 3.0L engine

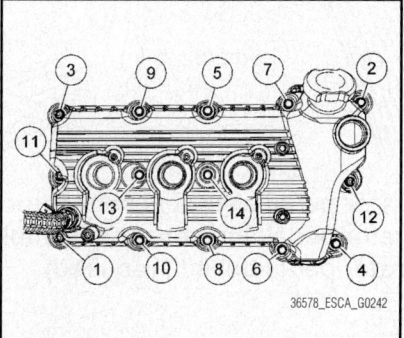

Fig. 234 RH valve cover tightening sequence—2009 3.0L engine

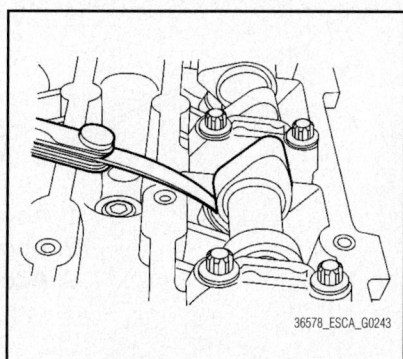

Fig. 235 Using a feeler gauge to measure the clearance

clearances prior to removing the camshafts will necessitate repeated removal and installation and wasted labor time.

2. Use a feeler gauge to measure the clearance of each valve and record its location.

➡ The number on the valve tappet only reflects the digits that follow the decimal. For example, a tappet with the number 0.650 has the thickness of 3.650 mm.

3. A midrange clearance is the most desirable:
- Intake: 0.22–0.28 mm (0.008–0.011 inch)
- Exhaust: 0.27–0.33 mm (0.010–0.013 inch)

4. Select tappets using this formula: tappet thickness = measured clearance + the base tappet thickness–most desirable thickness.

5. Select the tappets and mark the installation location.

6. If any tappets do not measure within specifications, install new tappets in these locations.

ENGINE PERFORMANCE & EMISSION CONTROLS

ACCELERATOR PEDAL POSITION (APP) SENSOR

LOCATION

See Figure 236.

The Accelerator Pedal Position (APP) Sensor is located inside the vehicle and is integral to the accelerator pedal.

REMOVAL & INSTALLATION

1. Disconnect the accelerator pedal electrical connector.

➡ The accelerator pedal bracket and bolts on the 2.5L and 3.0L vehicles are similar but not interchangeable with the 2.5L Hybrid vehicles.

2. Remove the 3 bolts and the accelerator pedal and sensor assembly.

3. To install, reverse the removal procedure and note the following:
- To install, tighten to 89 inch lbs, (10 Nm) on 2.5L and 3.0L vehicles.

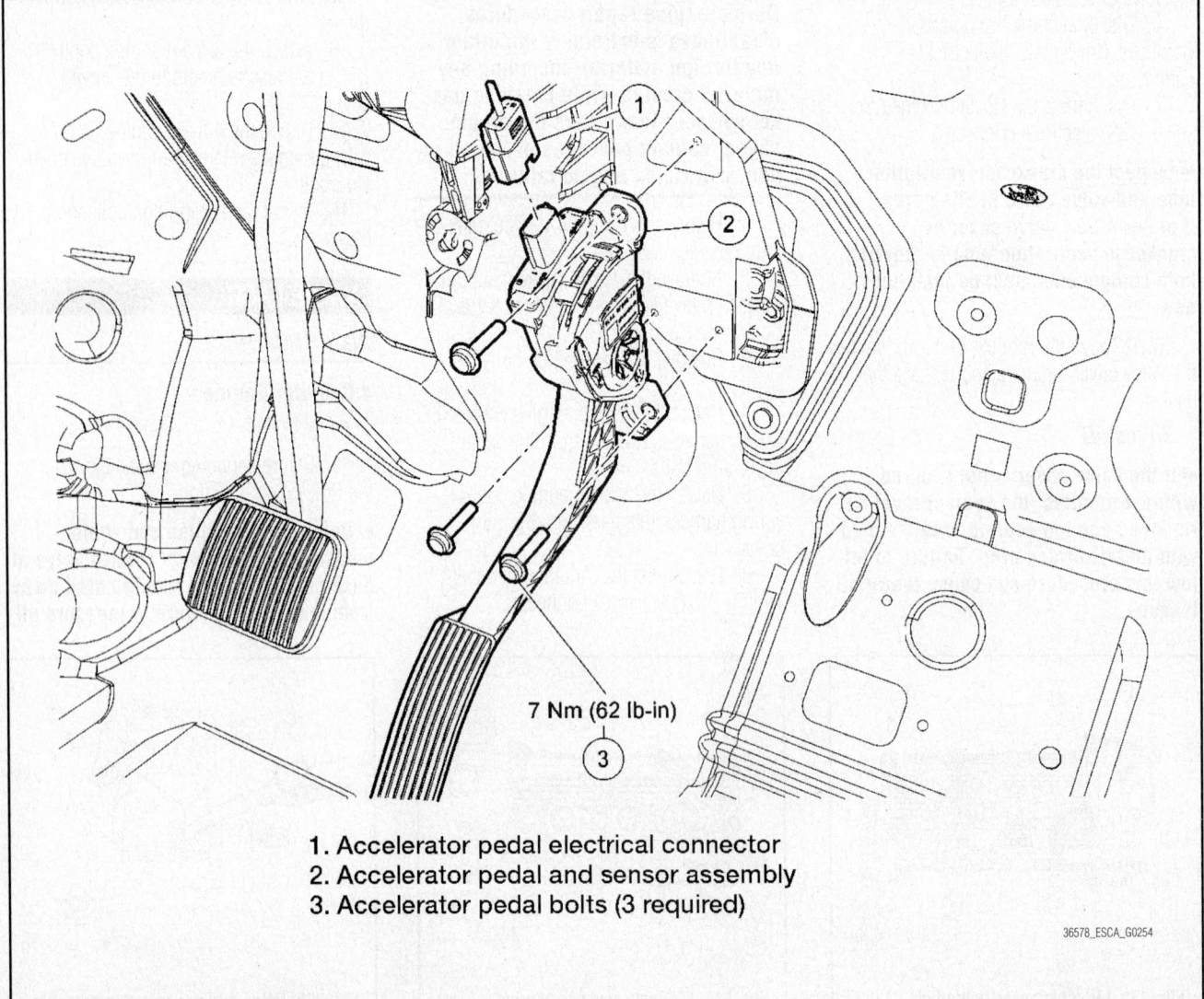

7 Nm (62 lb-in)

1. Accelerator pedal electrical connector
2. Accelerator pedal and sensor assembly
3. Accelerator pedal bolts (3 required)

36578_ESCA_G0254

Fig. 236 Accelerator Pedal Position (APP) Sensor location view

CAMSHAFT POSITION (CMP) SENSOR

LOCATION

2.3L Engine

See Figure 237.

The Camshaft Position (CMP) sensor is located on top the valve cover towards the front of the vehicle.

2.5L Engine

See Figure 238.

The Camshaft Position (CMP) sensor is located on top the valve cover towards the front of the vehicle.

3.0L Engine

2008 Models

See Figure 239.

The Camshaft Position (CMP) sensor is located on left cylinder head just below the valve cover.

2009 Models

See Figure 240.

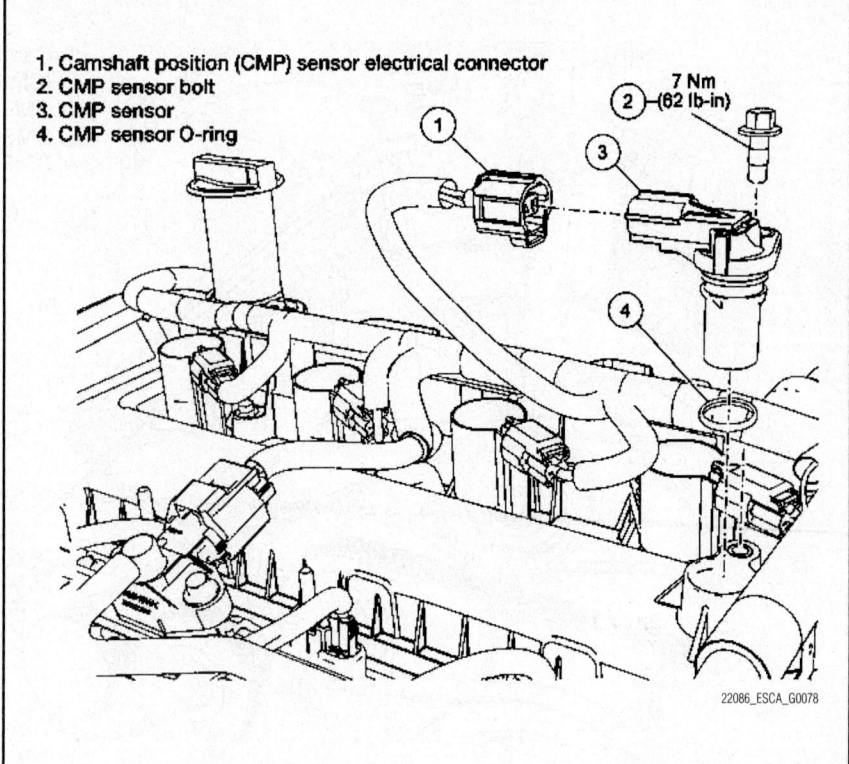

1. Camshaft position (CMP) sensor electrical connector
2. CMP sensor bolt
3. CMP sensor
4. CMP sensor O-ring

7 Nm (62 lb-in)

22086_ESCA_G0078

Fig. 237 Camshaft Position (CMP) sensor location—2.3L engine—2008 model

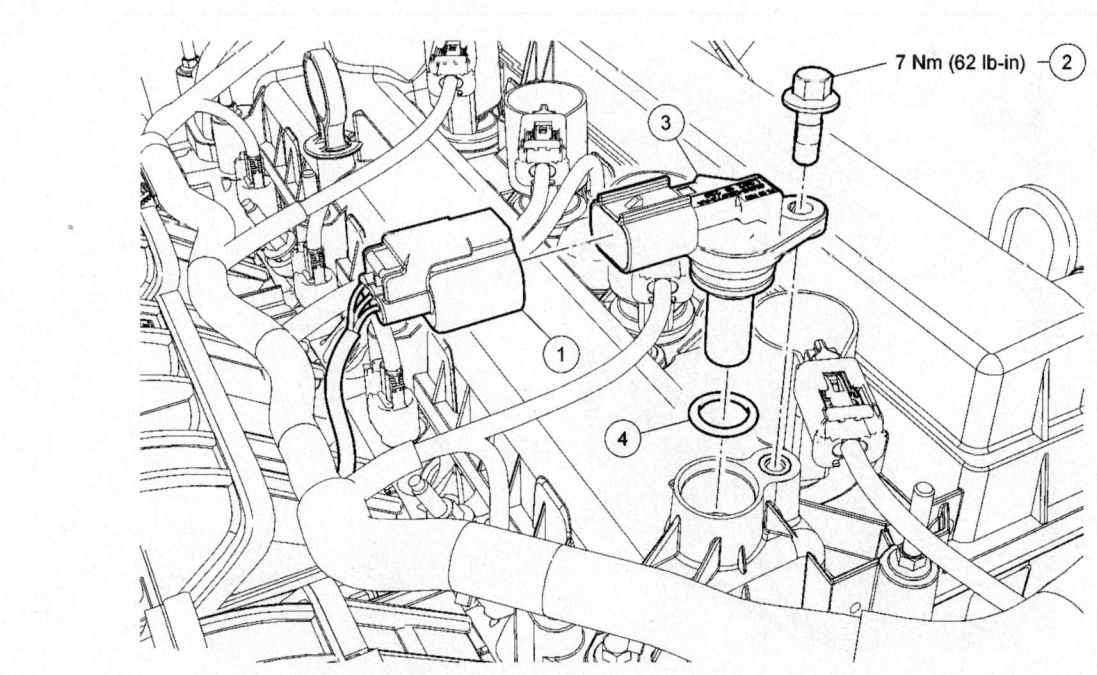

7 Nm (62 lb-in)

1. Camshaft Position (CMP) sensor electrical connector
2. CMP sensor bolt
3. CMP sensor
4. CMP sensor O-ring

36578_ESCA_G0262

Fig. 238 Camshaft Position (CMP) sensor location—2.5L engine—2009 model

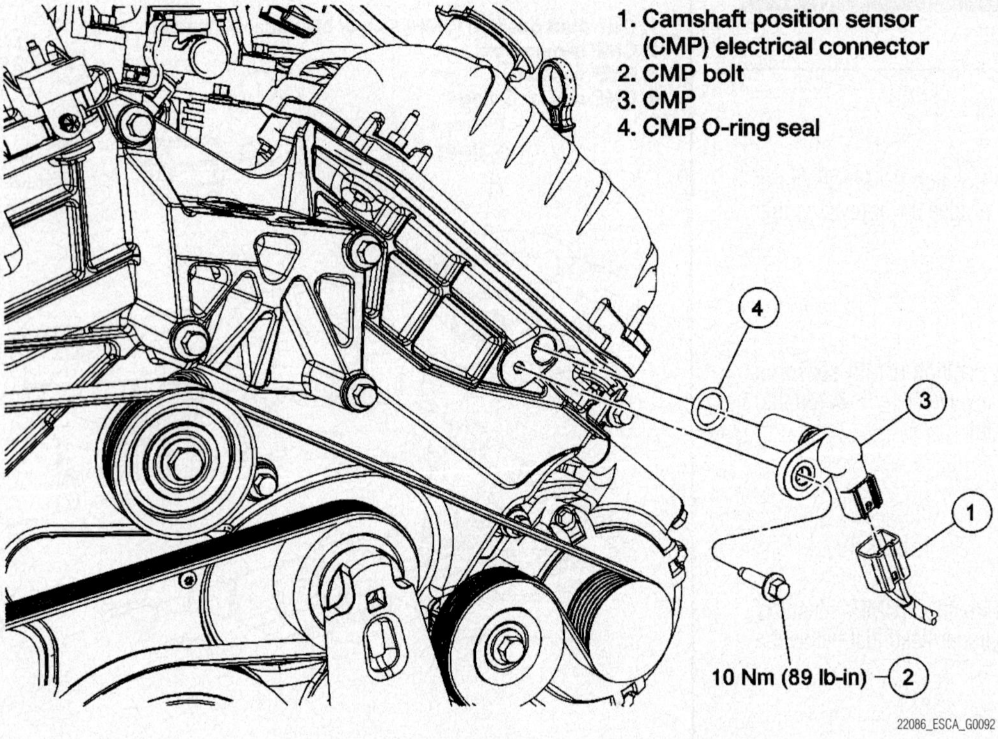

1. Camshaft position sensor (CMP) electrical connector
2. CMP bolt
3. CMP
4. CMP O-ring seal

10 Nm (89 lb-in)

22086_ESCA_G0092

Fig. 239 Camshaft Position (CMP) sensor location—3.0L engine

4
3
2
10 Nm (89 lb-in)
1
7
8
10 Nm (89 lb-in)
6
5

1. Camshaft Position (CMP) sensor electrical connector
2. CMP sensor bolt — LH
3. CMP sensor — LH
4. CMP sensor O-ring seal — LH
5. CMP sensor electrical connector
6. CMP sensor bolt — RH
7. CMP sensor — RH
8. CMP sensor O-ring seal — RH

36578_ESCA_G0261

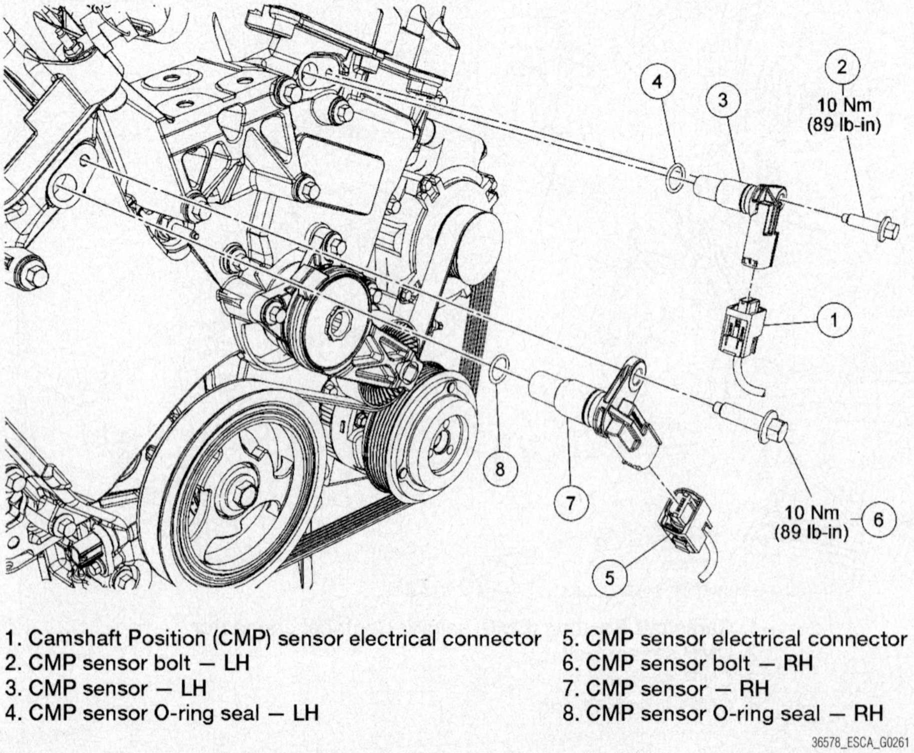

Fig. 240 Camshaft Position (CMP) sensor location—3.0L engine—2009 model

The Camshaft Position (CMP) sensors are located on the left and right cylinder head just below the valve cover.

OPERATION

Component Description

The Camshaft Position (CMP) Sensor is a permanent magnet output coil device that operates within a 5 volt DC reference range, and monitors the speed and position of the camshaft. A reluctor is attached directly to the camshaft, and is used to generate a digital signal as it passes the magnetic coil; the alternating lines of magnetic flux are used by the sensor to produce a digital pulse. The CMP signal is used by the Powertrain Control Module (PCM) to calculate ignition timing, firing order, fuel injector timing, and misfire diagnostics.

REMOVAL & INSTALLATION

4 Cylinder Engine

1. Disconnect the Camshaft Position (CMP) sensor electrical connector.
2. Remove the bolt and the CMP sensor.

To install:

➡**Lubricate the CMP sensor O-ring seal with clean engine oil.**

3. To install, reverse the removal procedure.
4. Tighten the mounting bolt to 62 inch lbs. (7 Nm)

6 Cylinder Engine

1. Disconnect the Camshaft Position (CMP) sensor electrical connector.
2. Remove the bolt and the CMP sensor.

To install:

➡**Lubricate the CMP O-ring seal with clean engine oil.**

3. To install, reverse the removal procedure and tighten the mounting bolt to 89 inch lbs. (10 Nm).

CRANKSHAFT POSITION (CKP) SENSOR

LOCATION

4 Cylinder Engine

See Figure 241.

The Crankshaft Position (CKP) sensor is located to the left of the crankshaft pulley.

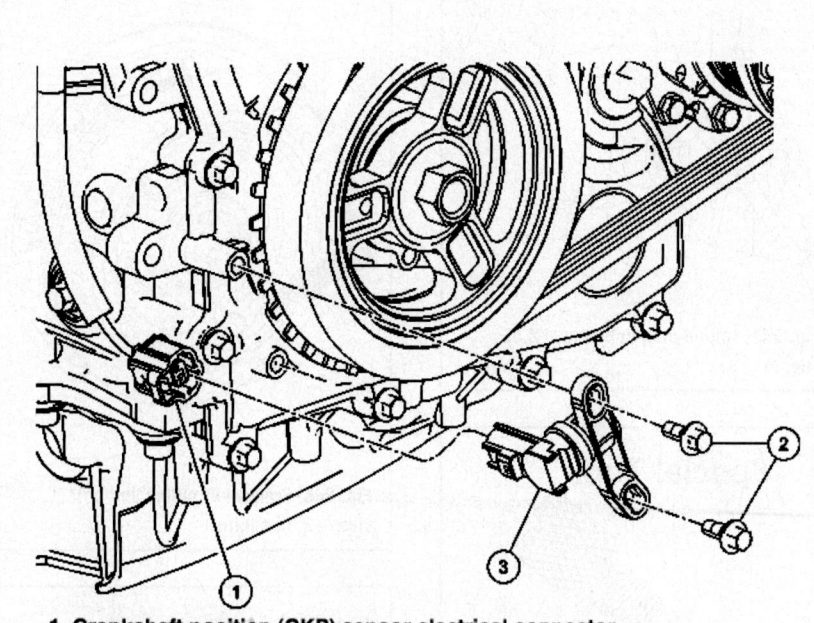

1. Crankshaft position (CKP) sensor electrical connector
2. CKP sensor screws (2 required)
3. CKP sensor

22086_ESCA_G0079

Fig. 241 Crankshaft Position (CKP) sensor location—4 cylinder engine

6 Cylinder Engine

See Figure 242.

The Crankshaft Position (CKP) sensor is located just behind the crankshaft pulley on engine block.

REMOVAL & INSTALLATION

4 Cylinder Engine

See Figures 243 through 247.

1. With the vehicle in NEUTRAL, position it on a hoist.

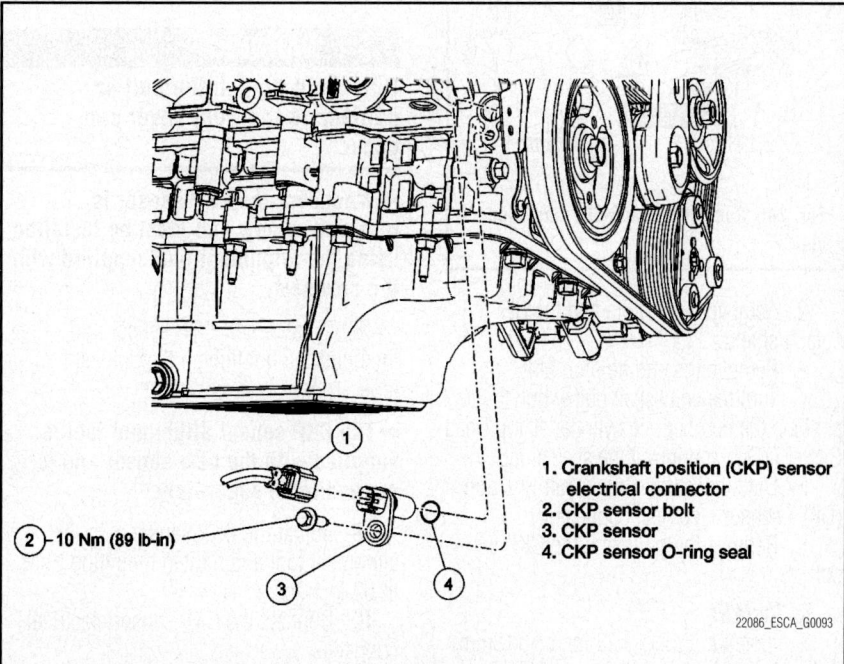

1. Crankshaft position (CKP) sensor electrical connector
2. CKP sensor bolt
3. CKP sensor
4. CKP sensor O-ring seal

2 — 10 Nm (89 lb-in)

22086_ESCA_G0093

Fig. 242 Crankshaft Position (CKP) sensor location—3.0L engine

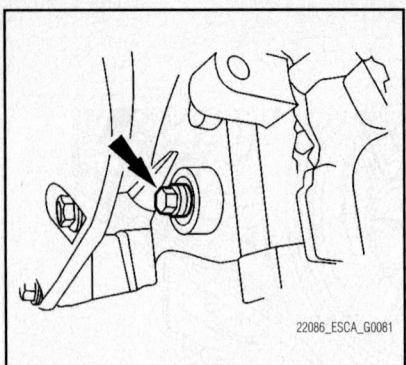

Fig. 243 Engine plug bolt view—2.3L engine

Special Tool

ST2638-A

Fig. 244 Special tool 303-507 timing peg, crankshaft

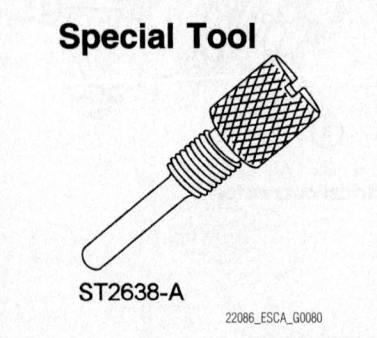

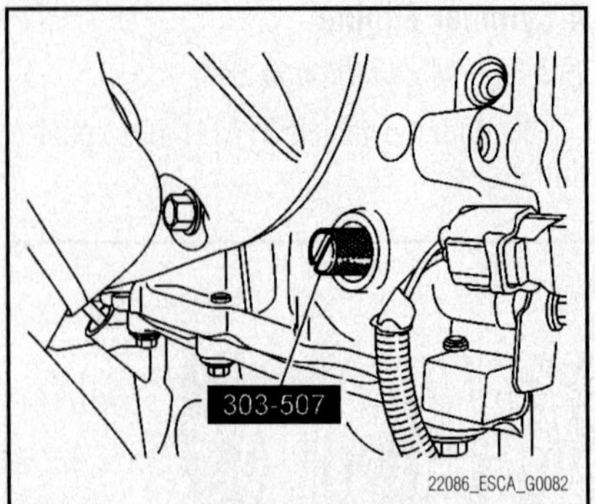

303-507

Fig. 245 Special tool 303-507, installed view

2. Remove the 5 bolts and the RH splash shield.

3. Remove the engine plug bolt.

4. Turn the crankshaft pulley bolt to position the number one cylinder at Top Dead Center (TDC) and install the special tool.

5. Disconnect the Crankshaft Position (CKP) sensor electrical connector.

6. Remove the bolts and the CKP sensor.

To install:

7. Install a (6mm) 0.23 inch. x (18mm) 0.7 inch standard bolt in the crankshaft pulley.

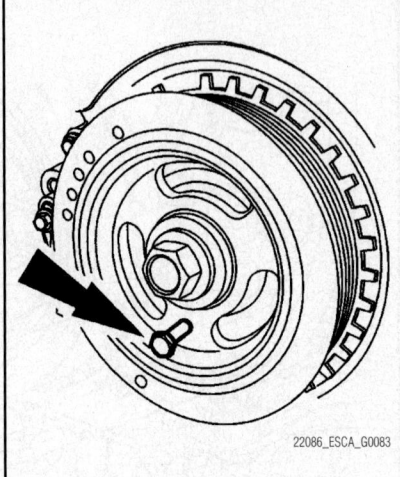

Fig. 246 Crankshaft pulley and bolt view—2.3L engine

Fig. 247 Crankshaft sensor and alignment tool shown—2.3L engine

✳✳ WARNING

Only hand-tighten the bolt or damage to the front cover can occur.

➡**Whenever the CKP sensor is removed, a new one must be installed using the alignment tool supplied with the new part.**

8. Install a new CKP sensor and the bolts. Do not tighten the bolts at this time.

➡**The CKP sensor alignment tool is supplied with the new sensor and is not available separately.**

9. Adjust the CKP sensor with the alignment tool and tighten mounting bolts to 62 inch lbs. (7 Nm).

10. Connect the CKP sensor electrical connector.

11. Remove the (6mm) 0.23 inch bolt from the crankshaft pulley.

12. Install the engine plug bolt and tighten to 15 ft. lbs. (20 Nm).

13. Install the RH splash shield and tighten the bolts to 80 inch lbs. (9 Nm).

6 Cylinder Engine

1. With the vehicle in NEUTRAL, position it on a hoist.

2. Remove the 5 bolts and the RH splash shield.

3. Disconnect the Crankshaft Position (CKP) sensor electrical connector.

4. Remove the bolt and the CKP sensor.

➡**Lubricate the CKP sensor O-ring seal with clean engine oil.**

5. To install, reverse the removal procedure and tighten sensor mounting bolt to 89 inch lbs. (10 Nm).

CYLINDER HEAD TEMPERATURE (CHT) SENSOR

LOCATION

4 Cylinder Engine

See Figure 248.

The Cylinder Head Temperature (CHT) sensor is located between the two center ignition coils.

6 Cylinder Engine

See Figure 249.

The Cylinder Head Temperature (CHT) sensor is located at the front of the right cylinder head.

REMOVAL & INSTALLATION

4 Cylinder Engine

1. Detach the Cylinder Head Temperature (CHT) sensor cover and position aside.

2. Disconnect the CHT sensor electrical connector.

3. Remove and discard the CHT sensor.

4. To install, reverse the removal procedure and tighten the CHT sensor to 106 inch lbs. (12 Nm).

6 Cylinder Engine

➡**If the cylinder head is being replaced, the CHT must be replaced.**

1. Disconnect the Cylinder Head Temperature (CHT) sensor electrical connector.

2. Remove the CHT sensor.

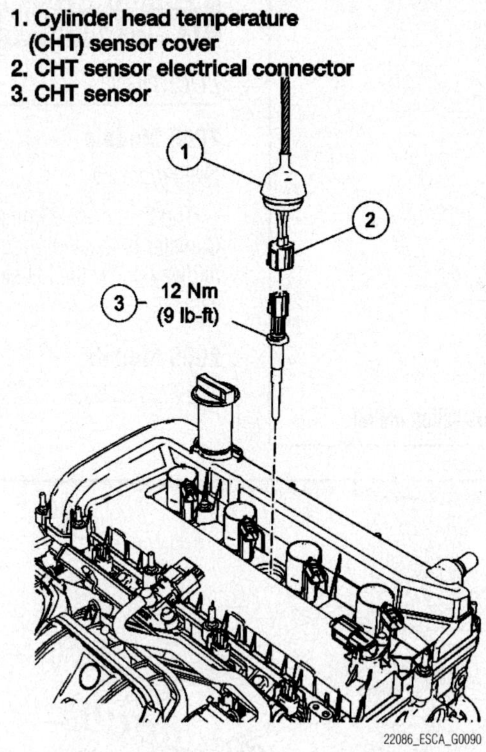

1. Cylinder head temperature (CHT) sensor cover
2. CHT sensor electrical connector
3. CHT sensor

12 Nm (9 lb-ft)

22086_ESCA_G0090

Fig. 248 Cylinder Head Temperature (CHT) sensor location—4 Cylinder engines 2008–09 models

3. To install, reverse the removal procedure and not the following:
4. Tighten the CHT sensor to 97 inch lbs. (11 Nm).

ENGINE COOLANT TEMPERATURE (ECT) SENSOR

LOCATION

6 Cylinder Engine

See Figure 250.

The Engine Coolant Temperature (ECT) sensor is located on the front of left cylinder head, just under valve cover.

REMOVAL & INSTALLATION

6 Cylinder Engine

1. Drain the cooling system.
2. Disconnect the Engine Coolant Temperature (ECT) sensor electrical connector.
3. To remove the ECT sensor, pull up on locking tab and rotate the sensor clockwise.
4. To install, reverse the removal procedure.

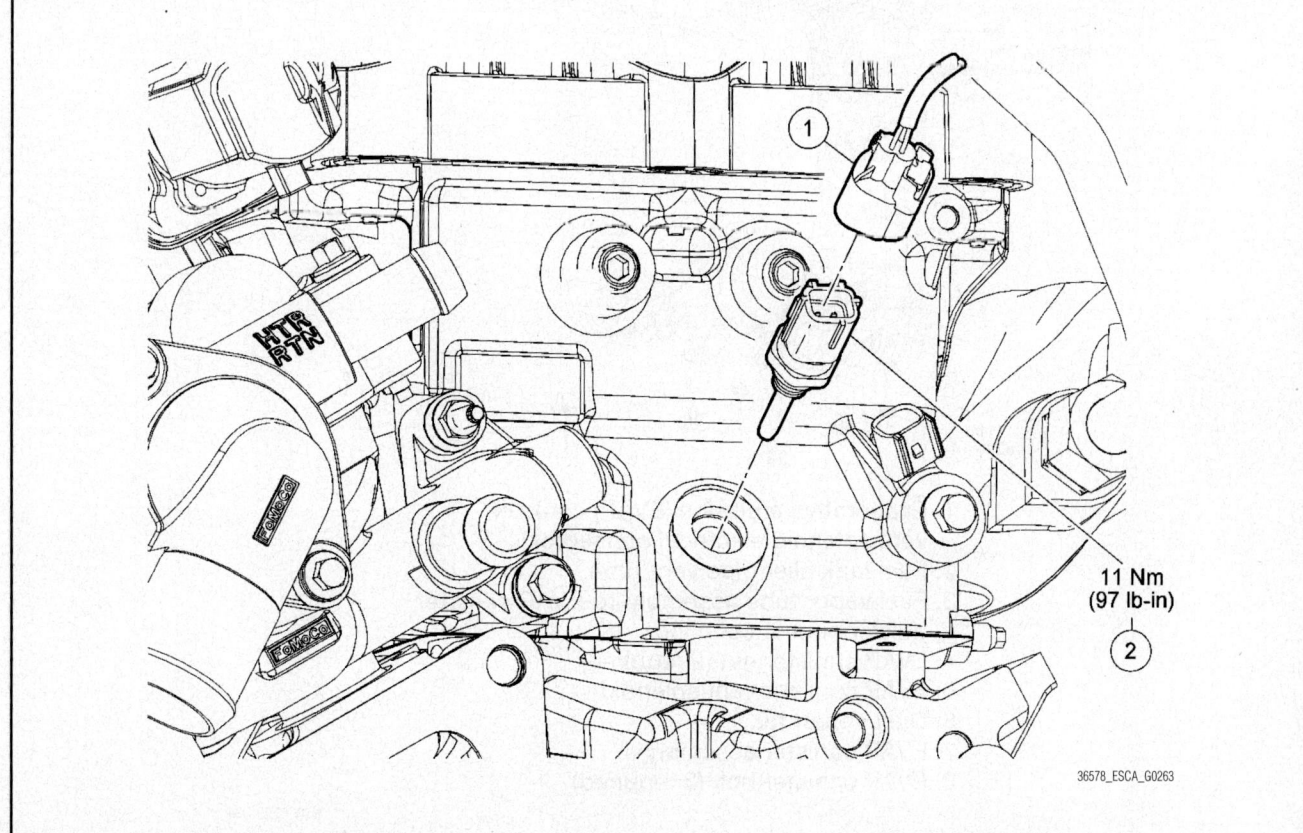

11 Nm (97 lb-in)

36578_ESCA_G0263

Fig. 249 Cylinder Head Temperature (CHT) sensor location—3.0L engine—2009 models

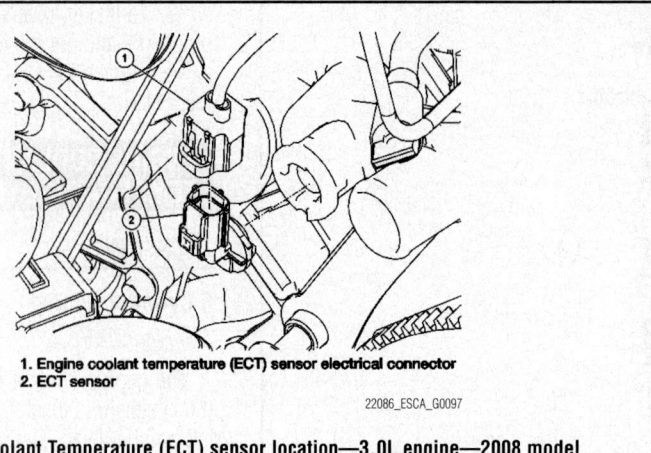

1. Engine coolant temperature (ECT) sensor electrical connector
2. ECT sensor

22086_ESCA_G0097

Fig. 250 Engine Coolant Temperature (ECT) sensor location—3.0L engine—2008 model

EVAPORATIVE EMISSIONS (EVAP) CANISTER

LOCATION

2008 Models

See Figure 251.

The Evaporative Emissions (EVAP) Canister is located under the vehicle midway under the LH side of the vehicle.

2009 Models

See Figure 252.

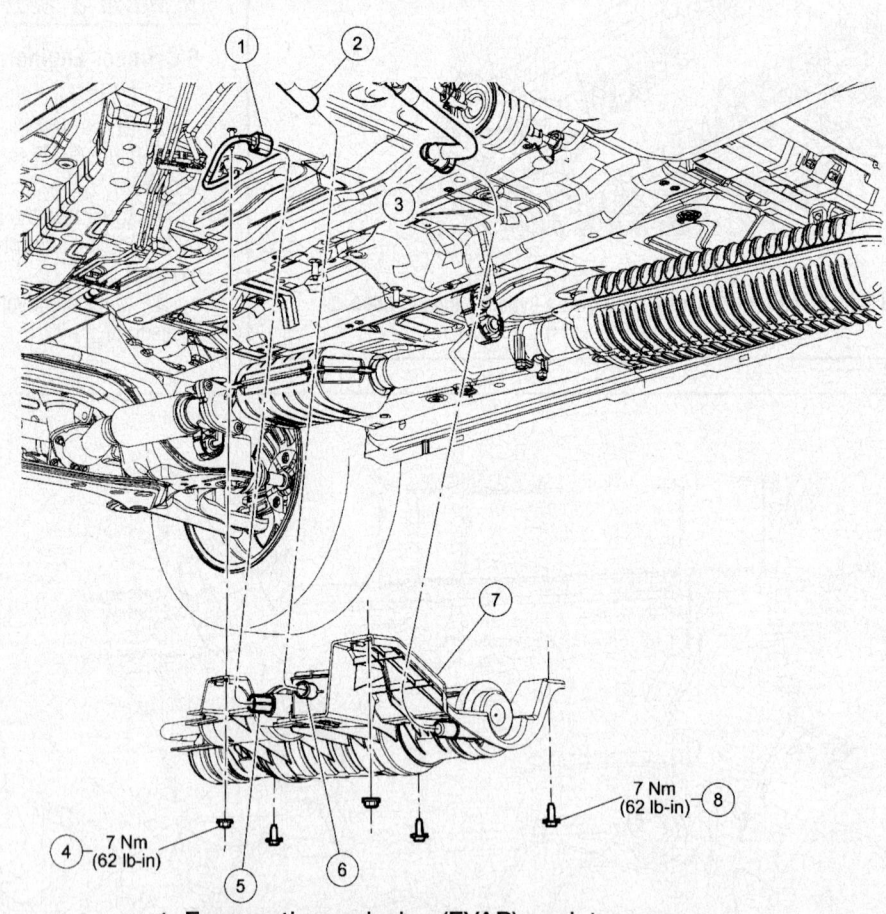

7 Nm (62 lb-in)

7 Nm (62 lb-in)

1. Evaporative emission (EVAP) canister vent solenoid electrical connector
2. Fuel tank filler pipe vent tube
3. Fuel vapor tube assembly-to-EVAP canister quick connect coupling
4. EVAP canister nut (2 required)
5. EVAP canister vent solenoid
6. Dust separator
7. EVAP canister assembly
8. EVAP canister bolt (3 required)

36578_ESCA_G0269

Fig. 251 Evaporative Emissions (EVAP) Canister—2008 model

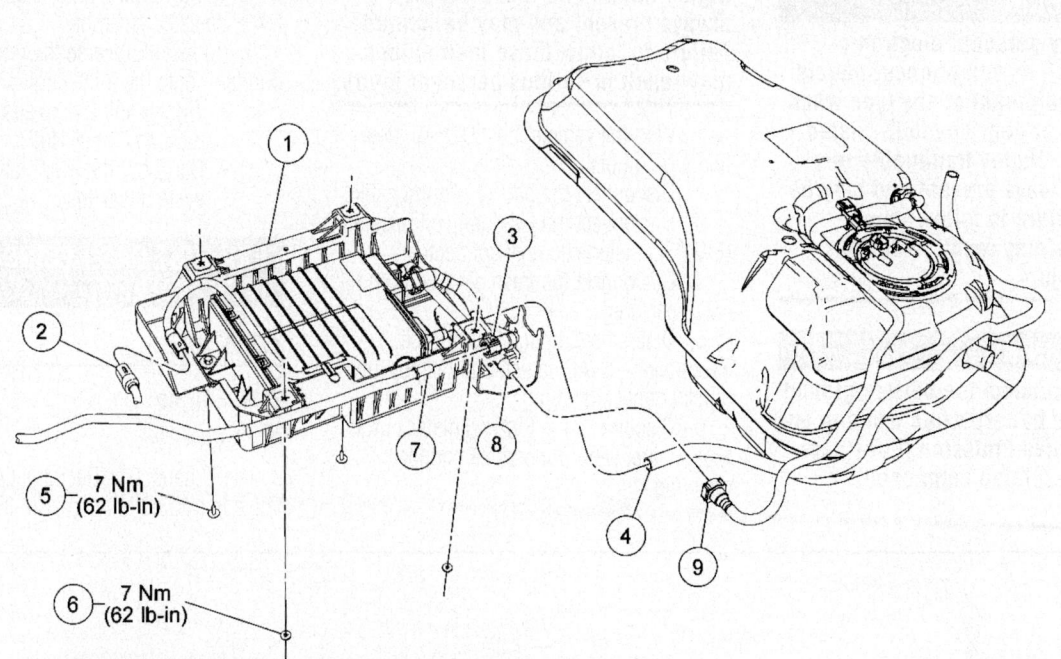

1. Evaporative Emission (EVAP) canister assembly
2. EVAP canister electrical connector
3. EVAP canister purge tube quick connect coupling
4. Fresh air tube
5. EVAP canister bolt (2 required)
6. EVAP canister nut (2 required)
7. Fuel vapor tube
8. EVAP canister fuel vapor tube
9. Fuel vapor tube assembly-to- EVAP canister fuel vapor tube quick connect coupling

36578_ESCA_G0264

Fig. 252 Evaporative Emissions (EVAP) Canister—2009 model

The Evaporative Emissions (EVAP) Canister is located under the vehicle midway under the LH side of the vehicle.

REMOVAL & INSTALLATION

2008 Models

See Figure 251.

> ❈❈ **WARNING**
>
> **Do not smoke, carry lighted tobacco or have an open flame of any type when working on or near any fuel-related component. Highly flammable mixtures are always present and may be ignited. Failure to follow these instructions may result in serious personal injury.**

> ❈❈ **WARNING**
>
> **Do not carry personal electronic devices such as cell phones, pagers or audio equipment of any type when working on or near any fuel-related**

component. **Highly flammable mixtures are always present and may be ignited. Failure to follow these instructions may result in serious personal injury.**

> ❈❈ **WARNING**
>
> **Always disconnect the battery ground cable at the battery when working on an Evaporative Emission (EVAP) system or fuel-related component. Highly flammable mixtures are always present and may be ignited. Failure to follow these instructions may result in serious personal injury.**

1. With the vehicle in NEUTRAL, position it on a hoist.
2. Disconnect the battery ground cable.
3. Disconnect the evaporative emission (EVAP) canister vent solenoid electrical connector.
4. Disconnect the fuel tank filler pipe vent tube from the dust separator.

5. Release the fuel vapor tube assembly-to-EVAP canister quick connect coupling.
6. Remove the 2 nuts, 3 bolts and the EVAP canister assembly.
7. To install, reverse the removal procedure and note the following:
   - Tighten the 2 nuts and 3 bolts to 62 inch lbs. (7 Nm).
   - Carry out the evaporative emission system leak test.

2009 Models

See Figure 252.

> ❈❈ **WARNING**
>
> **Do not smoke, carry lighted tobacco or have an open flame of any type when working on or near any fuel-related component. Highly flammable mixtures are always present and may be ignited. Failure to follow these instructions may result in serious personal injury.**

Highly flammable mixtures are always present and may be ignited. Failure to follow these instructions may result in serious personal injury.

1. With the vehicle in NEUTRAL, position it on a hoist.
2. Disconnect the battery ground cable.
3. Disconnect the Evaporative Emission (EVAP) canister electrical connector.
4. Disconnect the fresh air tube from the EVAP canister.
5. Disconnect the fuel vapor tube assembly-to-EVAP canister fuel vapor tube quick connect coupling.
6. Disconnect the EVAP canister purge tube-to-fuel vapor tube quick connect coupling.

7. Remove the 2 nuts, 2 bolts and the EVAP canister assembly.
8. To install, reverse the removal procedure and note the following:
- Tighten the 2 nuts and 2 bolts to 62 inch lbs. (7 Nm).
- Carry out the evaporative emission system leak test.

EXHAUST GAS RECIRCULATION (EGR) VALVE

LOCATION

2.3L Engine
See Figure 253.

The Exhaust Gas Recirculation (EGR) Valve is located at the rear of the engine and

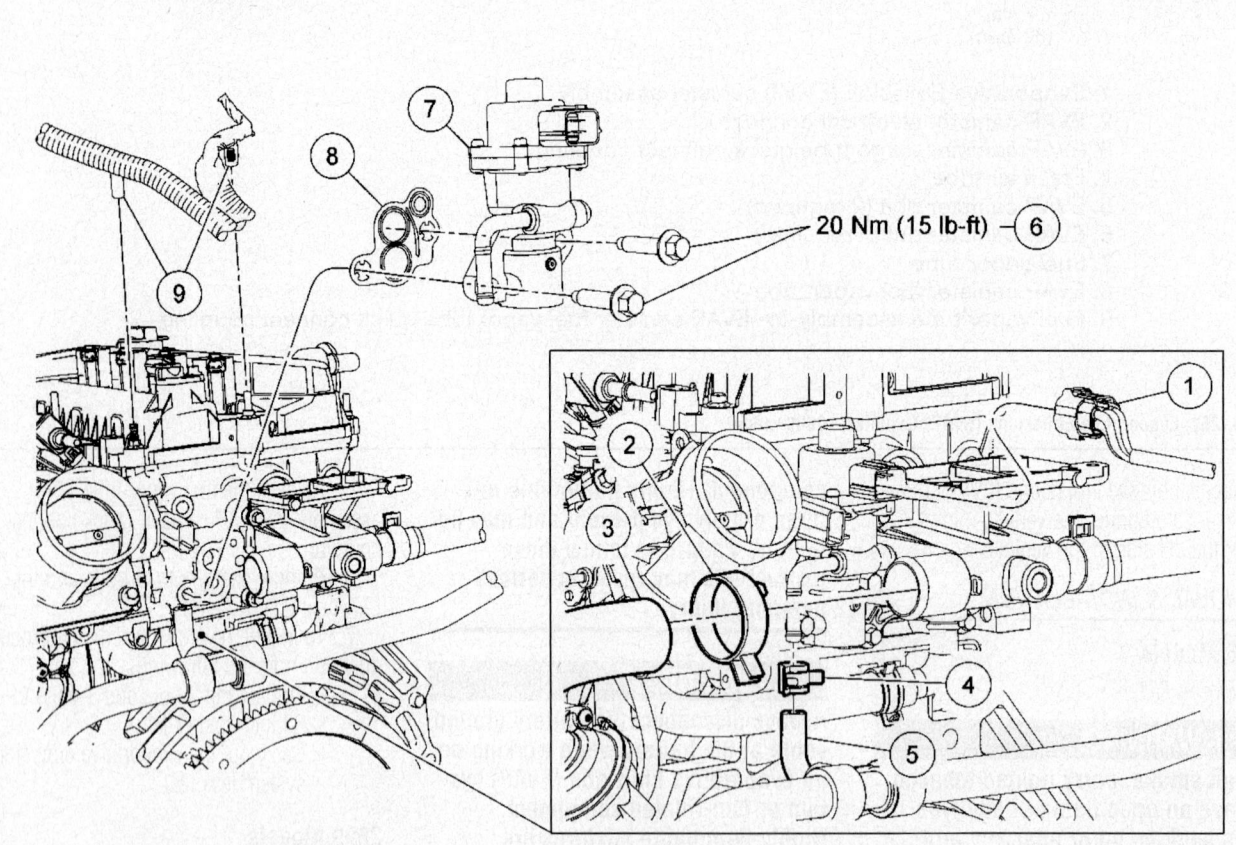

1. EGR valve electrical connector
2. Upper radiator hose clamp
3. Upper radiator hose
4. EGR coolant hose clamp
5. EGR coolant hose
6. EGR valve bolts (2 required)
7. EGR valve
8. EGR valve gasket
9. Engine wiring harness retainer clips

36578_ESCA_G0271

Fig. 253 Exhaust Gas Recirculation (EGR) Valve

is mounted to the cylinder head next to the valve body.

2.5L Engine

See Figure 254.

The Exhaust Gas Recirculation (EGR) Valve is located at the rear of the engine and is mounted to the cylinder head next to the valve body.

3.0L Engine

2008 Models

See Figure 255.

The Exhaust Gas Recirculation (EGR) Valve is located at the rear of the engine and is mounted to the upper intake manifold next to the valve body.

2009 Models

See Figure 256.

The Exhaust Gas Recirculation (EGR) Valve is located at the rear of the engine and is mounted to the upper intake manifold.

REMOVAL & INSTALLATION

2.3L Engine

See Figure 253.

1. Drain the cooling system.
2. Remove the air cleaner outlet pipe.
3. Detach the 2 engine wiring harness retainer clips from the studs.
4. Disconnect the EGR valve electrical connector.

5. Release the clamp and remove the upper radiator hose from the coolant outlet.
6. Release the clamp and remove the coolant hose from the EGR valve.
7. Remove the 2 bolts and the EGR valve.

> ✶✶ **WARNING**
>
> **Do not use metal scrapers, wire brushes, power abrasive discs or other abrasive means to clean the sealing surfaces. These tools cause scratches and gouges that make leak paths. Use a plastic scraping tool to remove all traces of the Exhaust Gas Recirculation (EGR) valve gasket.**

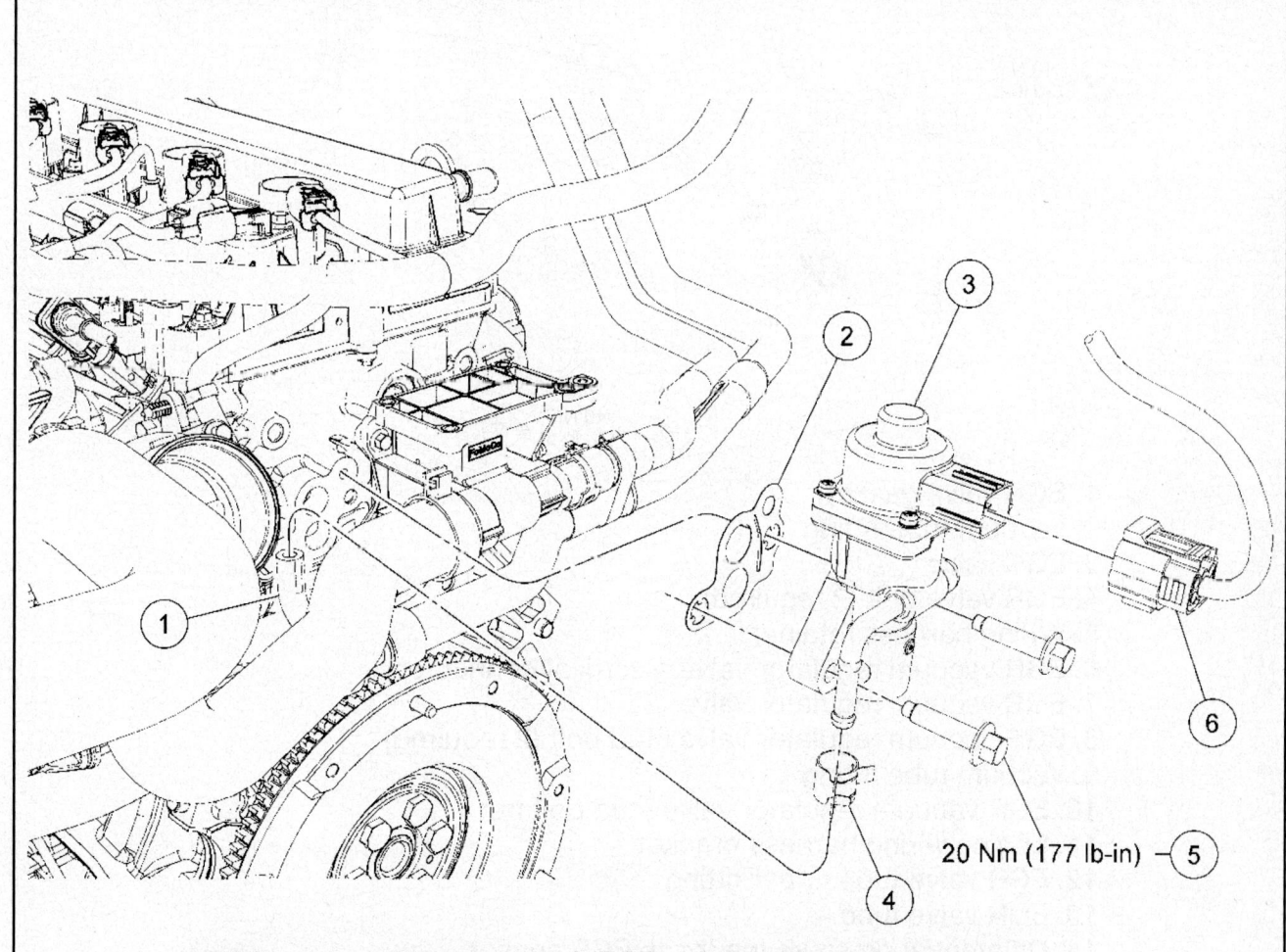

1. EGR valve coolant hose
2. EGR valve gasket
3. EGR valve
4. EGR valve coolant hose clamp
5. EGR valve bolt (2 required)
6. EGR valve electrical connector

20 Nm (177 lb-in)

36578_ESCA_G0273

Fig. 254 Exhaust Gas Recirculation (EGR) Valve—2.5L engine

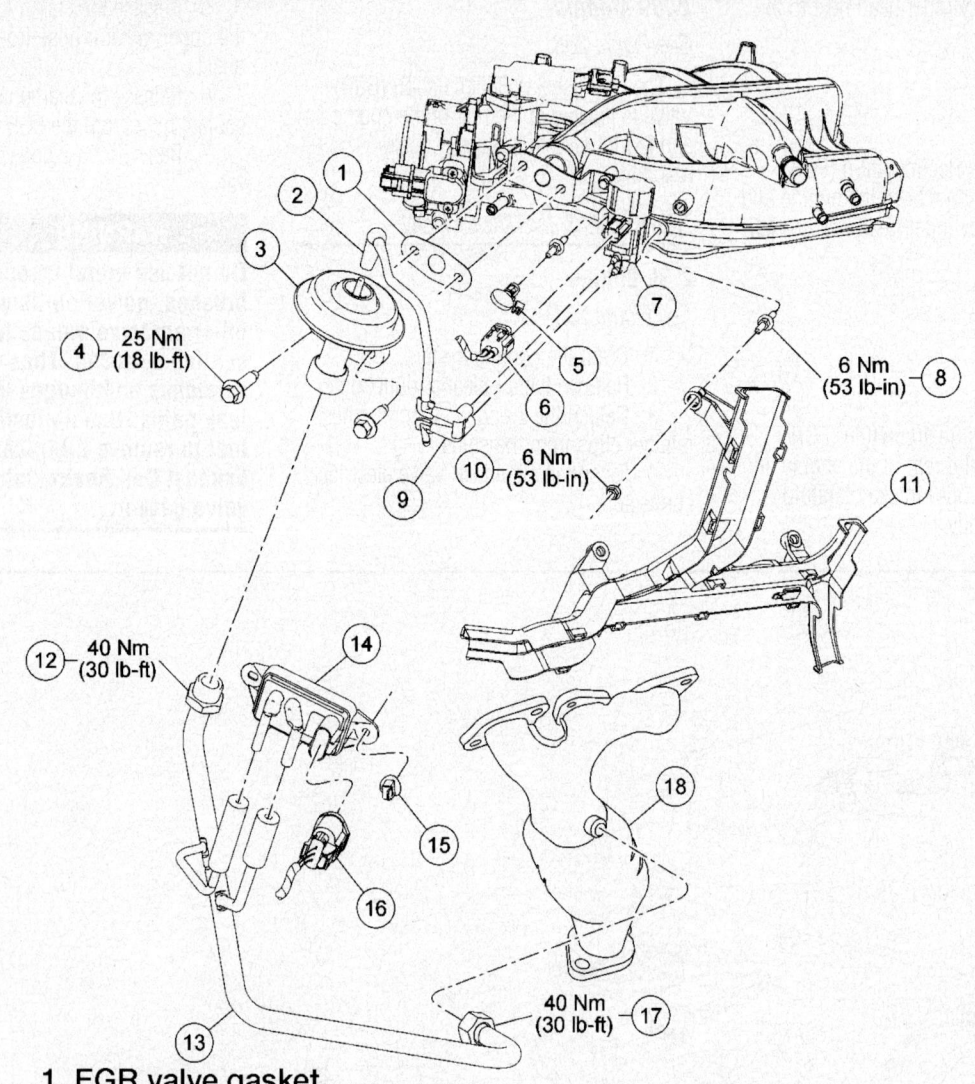

1. EGR valve gasket
2. Vacuum tube fitting
3. EGR valve
4. EGR valve bolt (2 required)
5. Wiring harness retainer
6. EGR vacuum regulator valve electrical connector
7. EGR vacuum regulator valve
8. EGR vacuum regulator valve stud bolt (2 required)
9. Vacuum tube fitting
10. EGR vacuum regulator valve stud bolt nut
11. Engine wiring harness bracket
12. EGR valve tube upper fitting
13. EGR valve tube
14. Differential pressure feedback EGR sensor
15. Wiring harness retainer
16. Differential pressure feedback EGR sensor electrical connector
17. EGR valve tube lower fitting
18. Catalytic converter (RH)

36578_ESCA_G0272

Fig. 255 Exhaust Gas Recirculation (EGR) Valve—2008 model

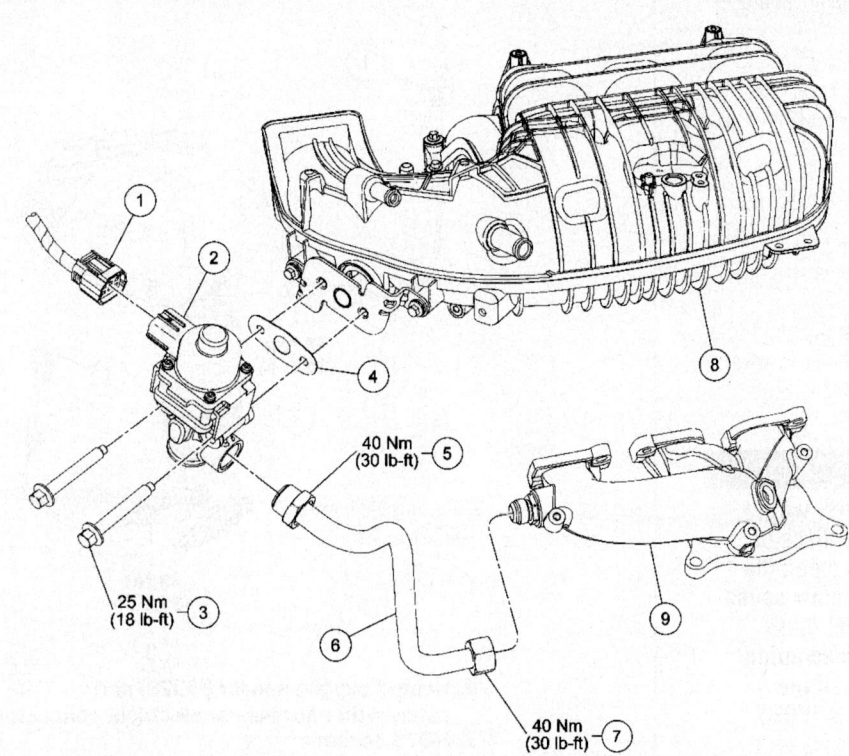

1. EGR valve electrical connector
2. EGR valve
3. EGR valve bolt (2 required)
4. EGR valve gasket
5. Exhaust manifold-to-EGR valve tube fitting
6. Exhaust manifold-to-EGR valve tube
7. Exhaust manifold-to-EGR valve tube fitting
8. Intake manifold
9. RH catalytic converter

36578_ESCA_G0274

Fig. 256 Exhaust Gas Recirculation (EGR) Valve—3.0L engine—2009 model

➡If there is no residual gasket material present, metal surface prep can be used to clean and prepare the surfaces.

8. Remove and discard the EGR valve gasket.

9. Clean and inspect the EGR gasket mating surfaces.

10. To install, reverse the removal procedure and note the following:
   • Fill and bleed the cooling system.
   • Tighten the 2 EGR valve bolts to 15 ft. lbs. (20 Nm).

2.5L Engine

See Figure 254.

1. Drain the cooling system.

2. Remove the air cleaner outlet pipe.

3. Detach the 2 engine wiring harness retainer clips from the studs.

4. Disconnect the EGR valve electrical connector.

5. Release the clamp and remove the upper radiator hose from the coolant outlet.

6. Release the clamp and remove the coolant hose from the EGR valve.

7. Remove the 2 bolts and the EGR valve.

✳✳ WARNING

Do not use metal scrapers, wire brushes, power abrasive discs or other abrasive means to clean the sealing surfaces. These tools cause scratches and gouges that make leak paths. Use a plastic scraping tool to remove all traces of the Exhaust Gas Recirculation (EGR) valve gasket.

➡If there is no residual gasket material present, metal surface prep can be used to clean and prepare the surfaces.

8. Remove and discard the EGR valve gasket.

9. Clean and inspect the EGR gasket mating surfaces.

10. To install, reverse the removal procedure and note the following:
   • Fill and bleed the cooling system.
   • Tighten the 2 EGR valve bolts to 177 inch lbs. (20 Nm).

3.0L Engine

2008 Models

See Figure 255.

1. Disconnect the EGR valve tube-to-EGR valve upper fitting.

2. Disconnect the vacuum tube fitting from the EGR valve.

3. Remove the 2 bolts and the EGR valve.

✳✳ WARNING

Do not use metal scrapers, wire brushes, power abrasive discs or other abrasive means to clean the sealing surfaces. These tools cause scratches and gouges that make leak paths. Use a plastic scraping tool to remove all traces of the Exhaust Gas Recirculation (EGR) valve gasket.

➡If there is no residual gasket material present, metal surface prep can be used to clean and prepare the surfaces.

4. Remove and discard the EGR valve gasket.

5. To install, reverse the removal procedure and note the following:
- Tighten the 2 EGR valve bolts to 18 ft. lbs. (25 Nm).
- Tighten the EGR valve tube nut to 30 ft. lbs. (40 Nm).

2009 Models

See Figure 256.

1. Disconnect the EGR valve electrical connector.

2. Disconnect the exhaust manifold-to-EGR valve tube fitting from the EGR valve.

3. Remove the 2 bolts and the EGR valve.

☀☀ WARNING

Do not use metal scrapers, wire brushes, power abrasive discs or other abrasive means to clean the sealing surfaces. These tools cause scratches and gouges that make leak paths. Use a plastic scraping tool to remove all traces of the Exhaust Gas Recirculation (EGR) valve gasket.

➡ **If there is no residual gasket material present, metal surface prep can be used to clean and prepare the surfaces**

4. Remove and discard the EGR valve gasket.

5. To install, reverse the removal procedure and note the following:
- Tighten the 2 EGR valve bolts to 18 ft. lbs. (25 Nm).
- Tighten the EGR valve tube nut to 30 ft. lbs. (40 Nm).

HEATED OXYGEN (HO2S) SENSOR

LOCATION

2.3L Engine

See Figure 257.

The Heated Oxygen Sensor (HO2S) is located just below exhaust manifold shield. The Catalyst Monitor Sensor (CMS) is located after the front Heated Oxygen Sensor (HO2S).

2.5L Engine

See Figure 258.

The Heated Oxygen Sensor (HO2S) is located just below the exhaust manifold shield. The Catalyst Monitor Sensor (CMS) is located after the front Heated Oxygen Sensor (HO2S).

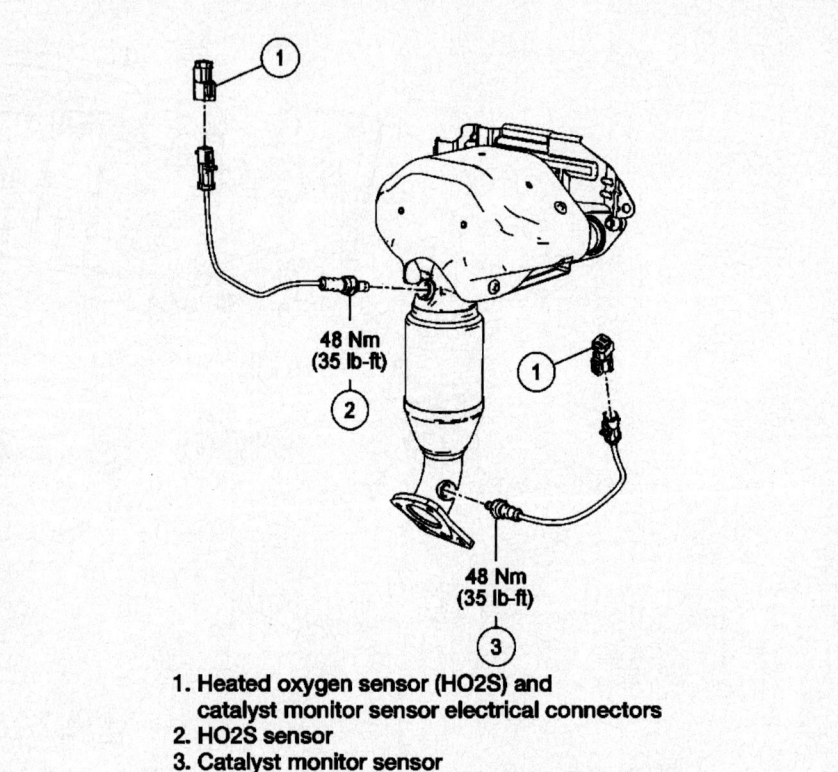

48 Nm (35 lb-ft)

48 Nm (35 lb-ft)

1. Heated oxygen sensor (HO2S) and catalyst monitor sensor electrical connectors
2. HO2S sensor
3. Catalyst monitor sensor

22086_ESCA_G0089

Fig. 257 Heated Oxygen Sensor (HO2S) and Catalyst Monitor Sensor (CMS) locations—2.3L engine

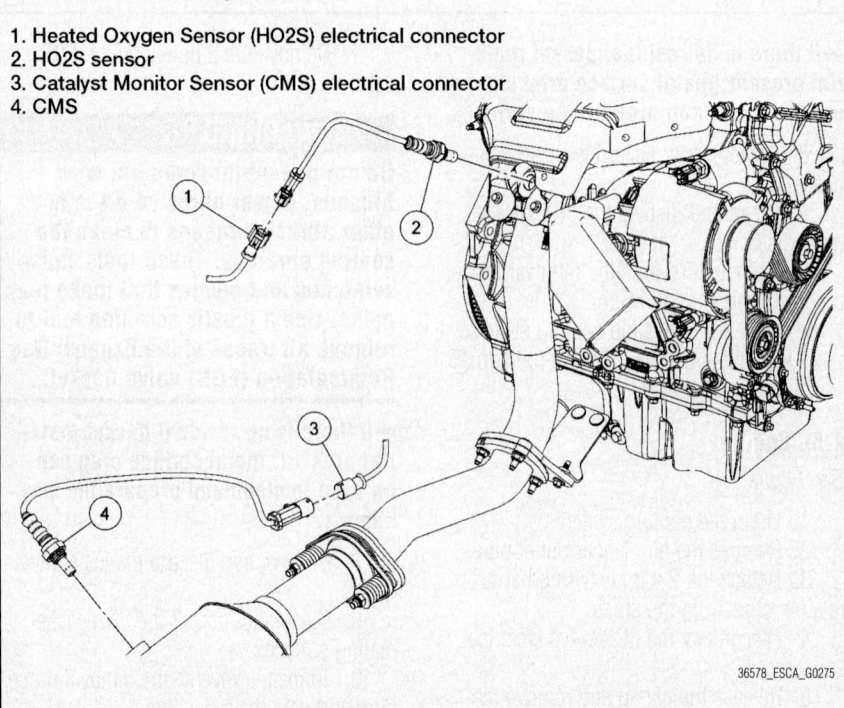

1. Heated Oxygen Sensor (HO2S) electrical connector
2. HO2S sensor
3. Catalyst Monitor Sensor (CMS) electrical connector
4. CMS

36578_ESCA_G0275

Fig. 258 Heated Oxygen Sensor (HO2S) and Catalyst Monitor Sensor (CMS) locations—2.5L engine

3.0L Engine

2008 Models

See Figure 259.

The Heated Oxygen Sensors (HO2S) are located at the top of the LH and RH converters. The Catalyst Monitor Sensor (CMS) is located after the front Heated Oxygen Sensor (HO2S).

2009 Models

See Figure 260.

The Heated Oxygen Sensors (HO2S) are located at the top of the LH and RH manifold converters. The Catalyst Monitor Sensors (CMS) are located after the front Heated Oxygen Sensor (HO2S).

REMOVAL & INSTALLATION

4 Cylinder Engine

See Figure 261.

1. With the vehicle in NEUTRAL, position it on a hoist.
2. Disconnect the Heated Oxygen Sensor (HO2S) electrical connector.
3. Using a suitable tool, remove the HO2S.

➡**Apply a light coat of anti-seize lubricant to the threads of the HO2S.**

4. To install, reverse the removal procedure and tighten HO2S to 35 ft. lbs. (48 Nm).

➡**Use the above procedure for the rear Catalyst Monitor Sensor (CMS).**

6 Cylinder Engine

See Figure 262.

1. With the vehicle in NEUTRAL, position it on a hoist.
2. Remove the 7 bolts (5 shown) and the LH splash shield. (Front LH sensor only)
3. Disconnect the Heated Oxygen Sensor (HO2S) electrical connector.

➡**If necessary, lubricate the sensor threads with penetrating and lock lubricant to assist in removal.**

4. Using a suitable tool, remove the HO2S.

➡**Apply a light coat of anti-seize lubricant to the threads of the HO2S.**

5. To install, reverse the removal procedure and tighten HO2S to 35 ft. lbs. (48 Nm).

➡**Use the above procedure for the rear Catalyst Monitor Sensor (CMS).**

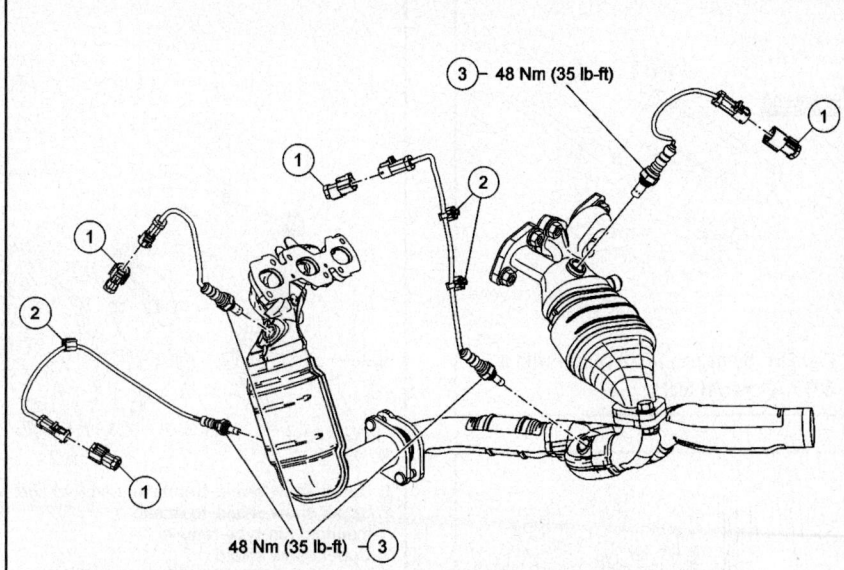

1. Heated oxygen sensor (HO2S) and catalyst monitor sensor electrical connectors
2. HO2S and catalyst monitor sensor wiring retainers (3 required)
3. HO2S and catalyst monitor sensors

22086_ESCA_G0098

Fig. 259 Heated Oxygen Sensor (HO2S) and Catalyst Monitor Sensor (CMS) locations—3.0L engine—2008 model

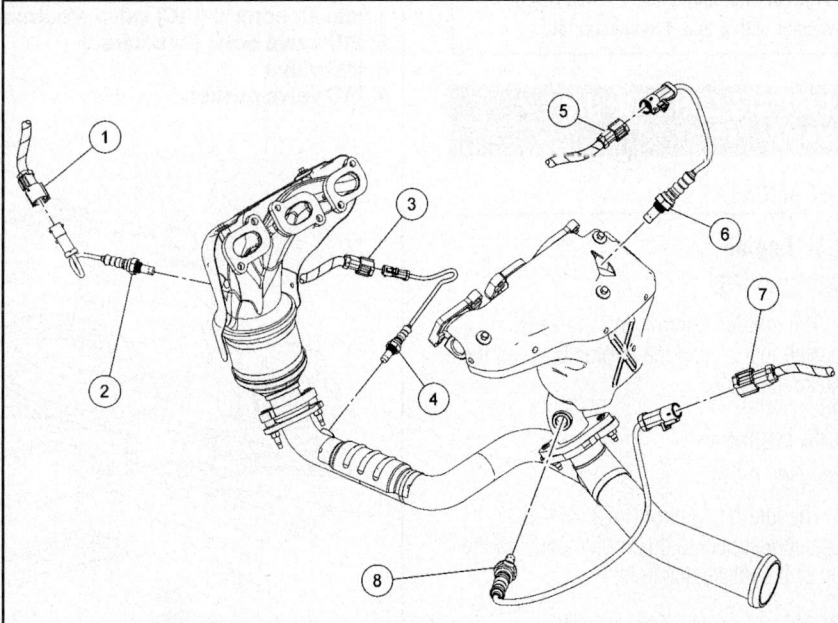

1. Heated Oxygen Sensor (HO2S) electrical connector — LH
2. HO2S — LH
3. Catalyst Monitor Sensor (CMS) electrical connector — LH
4. CMS — LH
5. HO2S electrical connector — RH
6. HO2S — RH
7. CMS electrical connector — RH
8. CMS — RH

36578_ESCA_G0278

Fig. 260 Heated Oxygen Sensor (HO2S) and Catalyst Monitor Sensor locations (CMS)—3.0L engine—2009 model

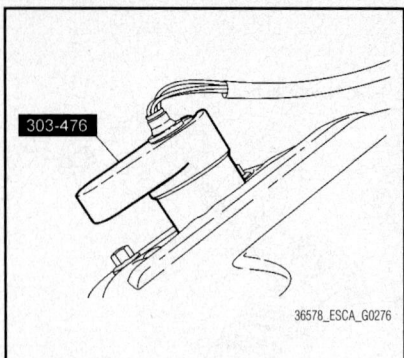

Fig. 261 Removing HO2S sensor with a 303-476 special tool

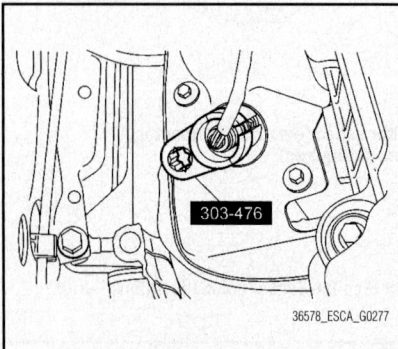

Fig. 262 Removing the LH side HO2S sensor with a 303-476 special tool

IDLE AIR CONTROL (IAC) VALVE

LOCATION

2.3L Engine

See Figure 263.

The Idle Air Control (IAC) valve is located just behind the throttle body on the intake manifold.

3.0L Engine

See Figure 264.

The Idle Air Control (IAC) valve is located just behind the throttle body on the top of the intake manifold.

REMOVAL & INSTALLATION

2.3L Engine

See Figure 263.

1. Remove the 3 screws, the pin-type retainer and the upper and lower snow shield.
2. Disconnect the Idle Air Control (IAC) valve electrical connector.
3. Remove the 2 bolts and the IAC valve.
4. To install, reverse the removal procedure and tighten IAC mounting bolts to 89 inch lbs. (10 Nm).

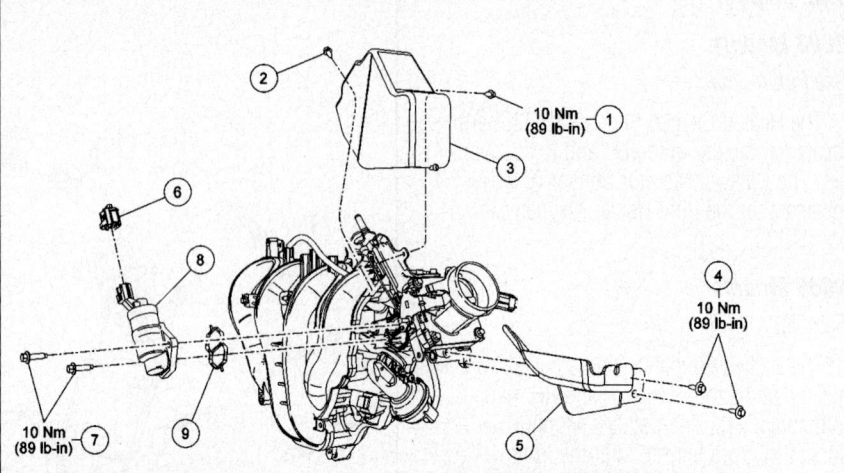

1. Upper snow shield-to-intake manifold screw
2. Upper snow shield-to-intake manifold pin-type retainer
3. Upper snow shield
4. Lower snow shield-to-intake manifold screws (2 required)
5. Lower snow shield
6. Idle air control (IAC) valve electrical connector
7. IAC valve bolts (2 required)
8. IAC valve
9. IAC valve gasket

Fig. 263 Idle Air Control (IAC) valve location—2.3L engine—2008 model

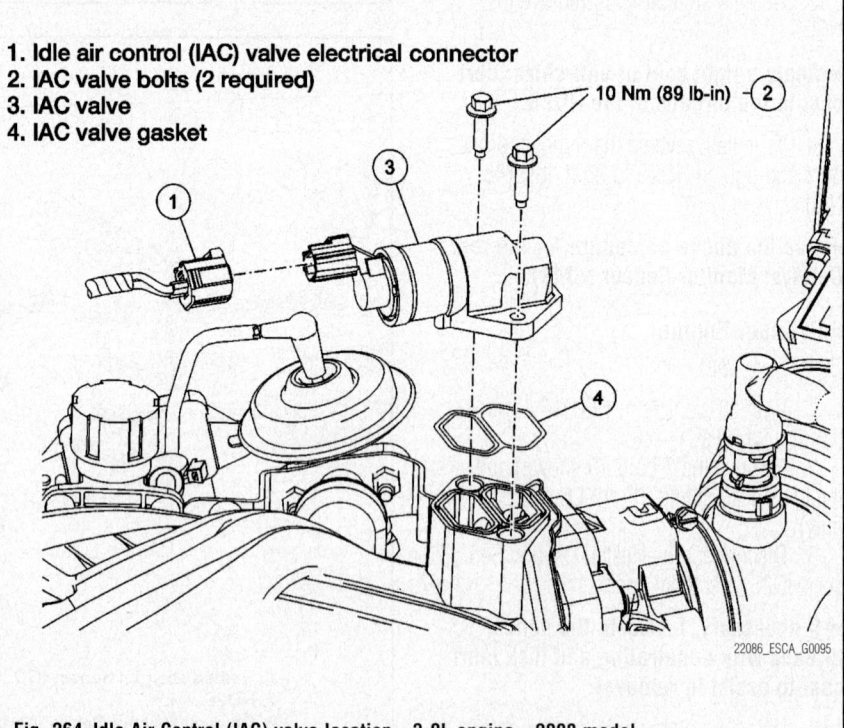

1. Idle air control (IAC) valve electrical connector
2. IAC valve bolts (2 required)
3. IAC valve
4. IAC valve gasket

Fig. 264 Idle Air Control (IAC) valve location—3.0L engine—2008 model

➡Inspect the gasket and install new as necessary.

3.0L Engine

See Figure 264.

1. Disconnect the Idle Air Control (IAC) valve electrical connector.

2. Remove the 2 bolts and the IAC valve and discard the gasket.
3. To install, reverse the removal procedure.
4. Clean and inspect all sealing surfaces. Install new gasket.
5. Tighten IAC mounting bolts to 89 inch lbs. (10 Nm).

INTAKE AIR TEMPERATURE (IAT) SENSOR

LOCATION

The Intake Air Temperature (IAT) sensor is incorporated in the Mass Air Flow assembly. Refer to the Mass Air Flow (MAF) sensor in this section.

OPERATION

The Intake Air Temperature (IAT) Sensor is a Negative Temperature Coefficient (NTC) Thermistor that monitors the intake air temperature. The IAT Sensor operates within a 5 volt DC reference range, and provides a linear input signal to the Powertrain Control Module (PCM) that is based upon the measured engine intake air temperature. The PCM uses data from the IAT Sensor to calculate air-fuel mixture, ignition timing, and fuel injector pulse width. The IAT Sensor is sometimes integrated with the Mass Air Flow (MAF) Sensor as a physical component.

REMOVAL & INSTALLATION

Refer to the Mass Air Flow (MAF) sensor in this section.

KNOCK SENSOR (KS)

LOCATION

4 Cylinder Engine

See Figure 265.

The Knock Sensor (KS) is located behind the intake manifold to the rear of engine block.

6 Cylinder

See Figures 266 and 267.

The 3.0L engine uses two Knock Sensors (KS), one is located at the cylinder head and one is located under the intake manifold mounted to the engine block.

REMOVAL & INSTALLATION

4 Cylinder Engine

See Figure 265.

1. With the vehicle in NEUTRAL, position it on a hoist.

2. Remove the intake manifold. Refer to Intake Manifold Removal & Installation in the Engine Mechanical section.

3. Remove the bolt and the Knock Sensor (KS).

4. To install, reverse the removal procedure and tighten the sensor mounting bolt to 15ft. lbs. (20 Nm).

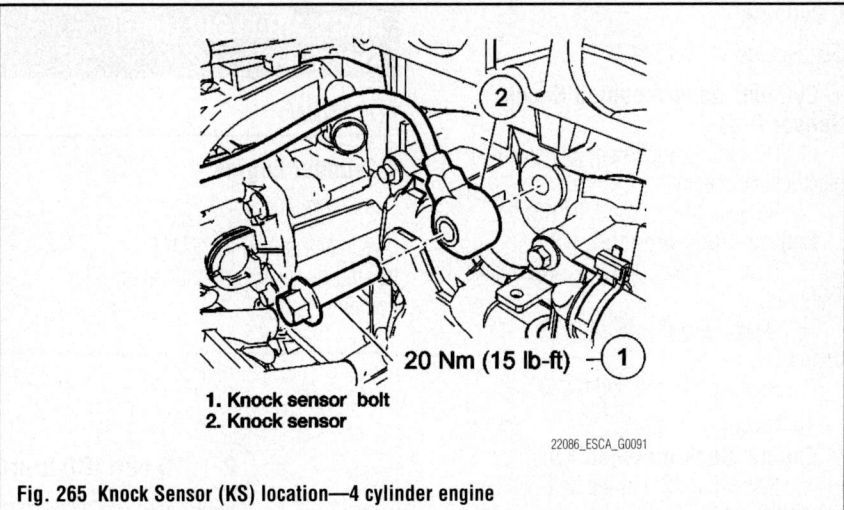

20 Nm (15 lb-ft) — 1
1. Knock sensor bolt
2. Knock sensor

22086_ESCA_G0091

Fig. 265 Knock Sensor (KS) location—4 cylinder engine

25 Nm (18 lb-ft)
1. Knock Sensor (KS) electrical connector
2. KS bolt
3. KS

36578_ESCA_G0279

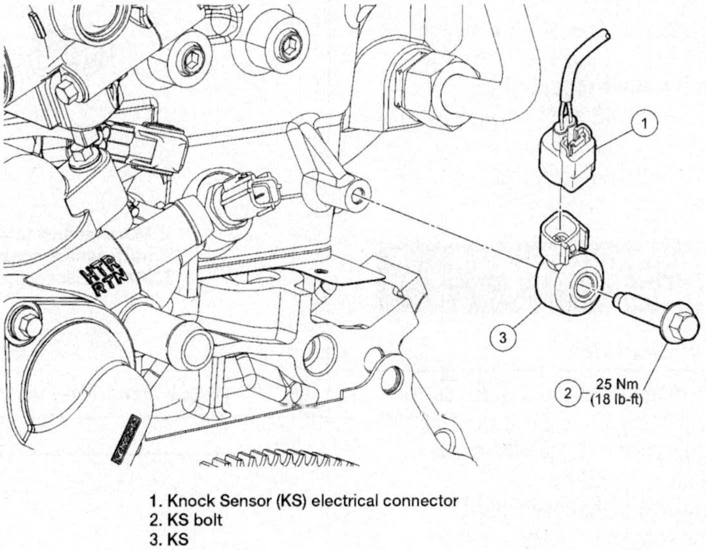

Fig. 266 Cylinder head mounted KS—3.0L engine

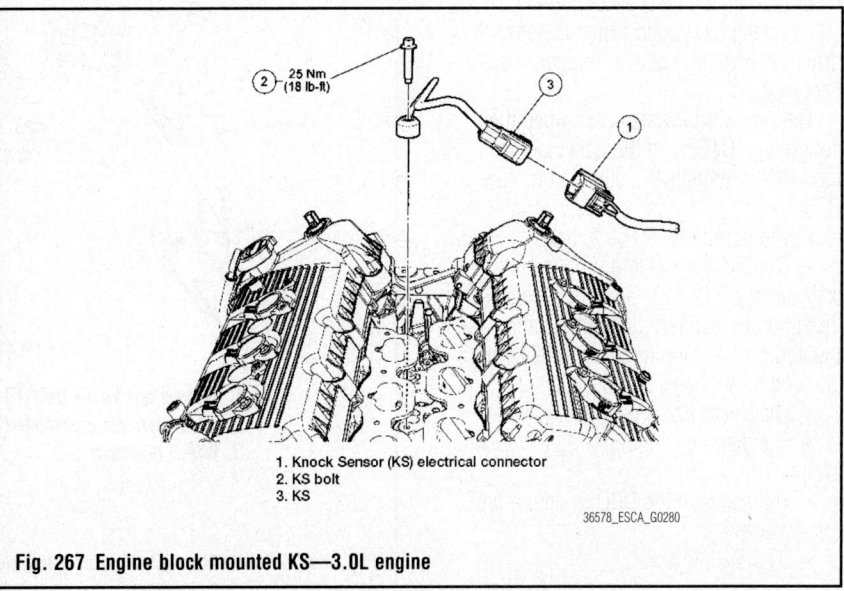

25 Nm (18 lb-ft)
1. Knock Sensor (KS) electrical connector
2. KS bolt
3. KS

36578_ESCA_G0280

Fig. 267 Engine block mounted KS—3.0L engine

6 Cylinder

See Figures 266 and 267.

Cylinder head-mounted Knock Sensor (KS)

1. Disconnect the Knock Sensor (KS) electrical connector.
2. Remove the bolt and the KS.

Engine block-mounted KS

3. Remove the upper and lower intake manifold.
4. Disconnect the KS electrical connector.
5. Remove the bolt and the KS.

To install:

Engine block-mounted KS

6. Install the KS and the bolt. Tighten the bolt to 18 ft. lbs. (25 Nm).
7. Connect the KS electrical connector.
8. Install the upper and lower intake manifold.

Cylinder head-mounted KS

9. Install the KS and the bolt. Tighten the bolt to 18 ft. lbs. (25 Nm).
10. Connect the KS electrical connector.

MALFUNCTION INDICATOR LIGHT (MIL)

RESET PROCEDURE

All On Board Diagnostics (OBD) scan tools support the clearing of continuous DTCs and resetting of emission monitors information in the PCM.

The clearing of the continuous DTCs allows the scan tool to command the PCM to clear/reset all emission-related diagnostic information. While carrying out this operation DTC P1000 is stored in the PCM until all the OBD system monitors or components have been tested to satisfy a drive cycle without any other concerns occurring.

The following events occur when the continuous DTCs and the emission monitors information is cleared from the PCM:

• The number of DTCs is reset
• The DTCs are cleared (on vehicles with permanent DTCs, additional vehicle operation is required to complete and pass the appropriate monitors to complete the clearing of permanent DTCs)
• The freeze frame data is cleared
• The diagnostic monitoring test results are reset
• The status of the OBD system monitors is reset
• DTC P1000 is set

MASS AIR FLOW (MAF) SENSOR

LOCATION

4 Cylinder Engine

See Figure 268.

The Mass Air Flow (MAF) sensor is located on air supply tube at air filter housing.

6 Cylinder Engine

See Figure 269.

The Mass Air Flow (MAF) sensor is located on air supply tube before throttle body.

REMOVAL & INSTALLATION

2.3L Engine

See Figure 268.

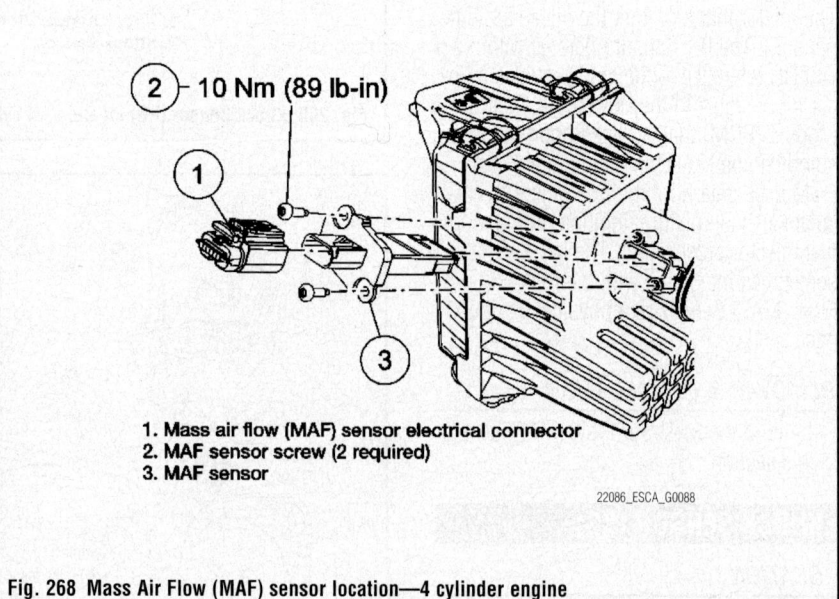

1. Mass air flow (MAF) sensor electrical connector
2. MAF sensor screw (2 required)
3. MAF sensor

22086_ESCA_G0088

Fig. 268 Mass Air Flow (MAF) sensor location—4 cylinder engine

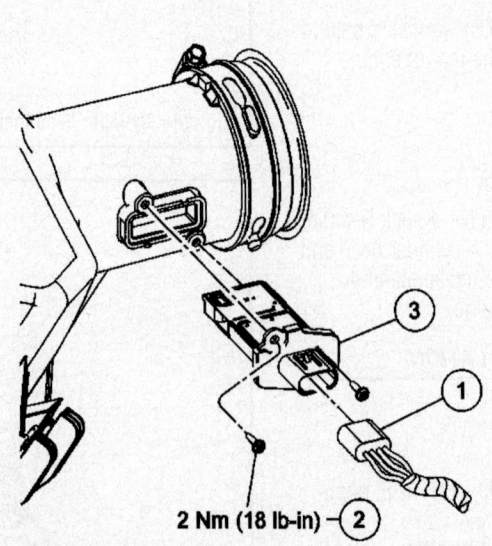

1. Mass air flow (MAF) sensor electrical connector
2. MAF sensor screw (2 required)
3. MAF sensor

22086_ESCA_G0096

Fig. 269 Mass Air Flow (MAF) sensor location—6 cylinder engine

1. Disconnect the Mass Air Flow (MAF) sensor electrical connector.

2. Remove the 2 screws and the MAF sensor.

3. To install, reverse the removal procedure and tighten MAF sensor mounting screws to 89 inch lbs. (10 Nm).

3.0L Engine

See Figure 269.

1. Disconnect the Mass Air Flow (MAF) sensor electrical connector.

2. Remove the 2 screws and the MAF sensor.

3. To install, reverse the removal procedure and tighten screws to 18 inch lbs. (2 Nm).

MANIFOLD ABSOLUTE PRESSURE (MAP) SENSOR

LOCATION

4 Cylinder Engine

See Figure 270.

The Manifold Absolute Pressure (MAP) Sensor is located at the intake manifold just below the throttle body.

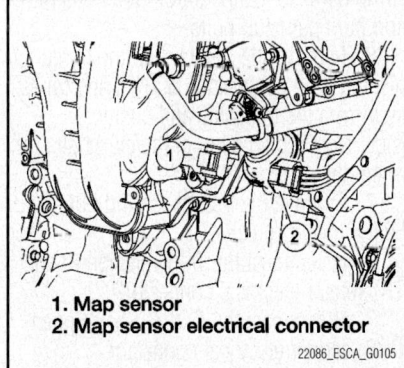

1. Map sensor
2. Map sensor electrical connector

22086_ESCA_G0105

Fig. 270 Manifold Absolute Pressure (MAP) sensor location—4 cylinder engine

6 Cylinder Engine

2008 Models

See Figure 271.

The Manifold Absolute Pressure (MAP) Sensor is located at the firewall mounted just to the left of the Power Control Module (PCM).

2009 Models

See Figure 272.

The Manifold Absolute Pressure (MAP) Sensor is located at the top of the intake manifold.

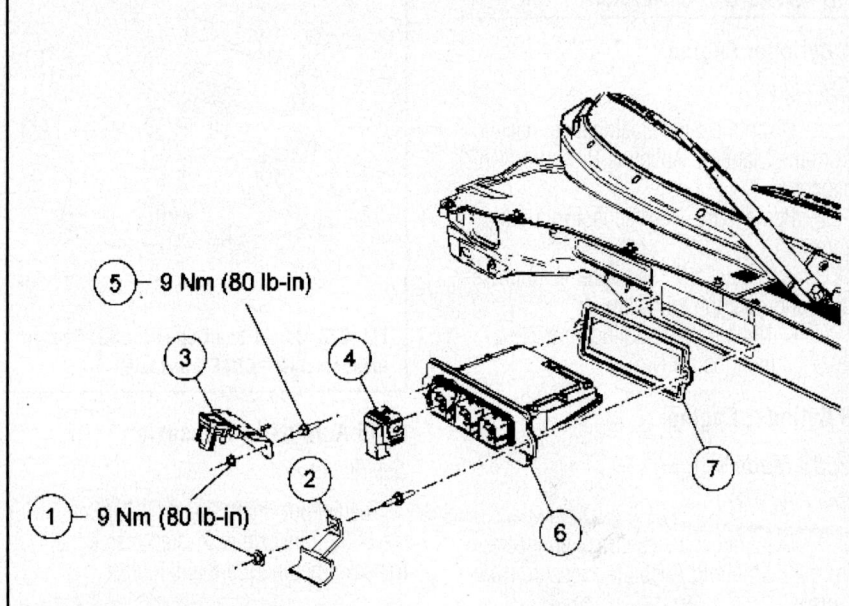

1. PCM-to-dash stud bolt nuts (2 required)
2. Wiring harness retainer
3. Manifold absolute pressure (MAP) sensor and bracket
4. PCM electrical connector
5. PCM-to-cowl stud bolt (2 required)
6. PCM
7. PCM cowl seal

36578_ESCA_G0294

Fig. 271 Manifold Absolute Pressure (MAP) Sensor location view—2008—3.0L engine

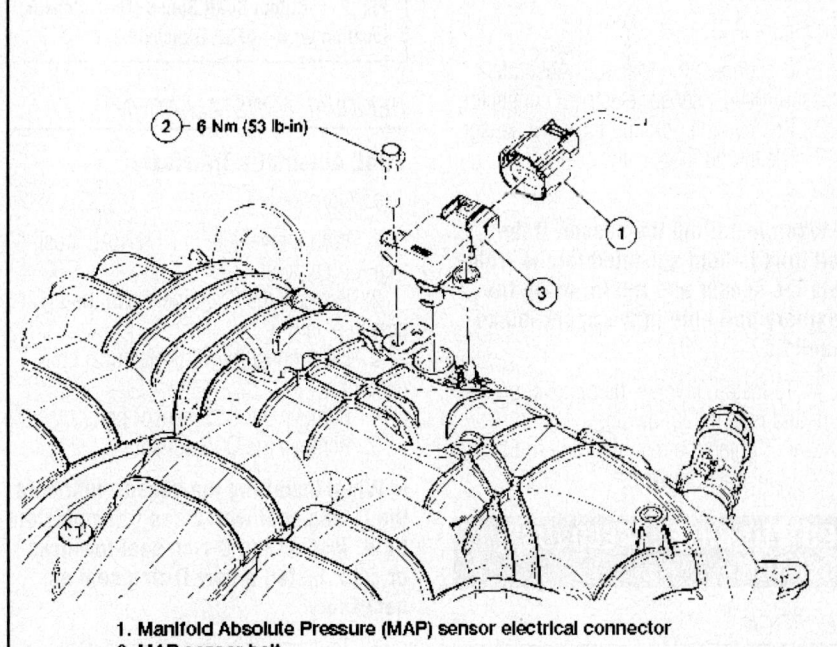

1. Manifold Absolute Pressure (MAP) sensor electrical connector
2. MAP sensor bolt
3. MAP sensor

36578_ESCA_G0281

Fig. 272 Manifold Absolute Pressure (MAP) sensor location—6 cylinder engine

REMOVAL & INSTALLATION

4 Cylinder Engine

See Figure 270.

1. Disconnect the electrical connector from the Manifold Absolute Pressure (MAP) sensor.
2. Remove the MAP sensor mounting screws.
3. To install, reverse the removal procedure and note the following:
   - Tighten the retaining screw to 27 inch lbs. (3 Nm).

6 Cylinder Engine

2008 Models

See Figure 271.

1. Disconnect the electrical connector from the Manifold Absolute Pressure (MAP) sensor.
2. Remove the MAP sensor mounting bracket nut.
3. Gently twist the vacuum hose and remove it from the MAP sensor.
4. Remove the MAP sensor from the mounting bracket.
5. To install, reverse the removal procedure and note the following:
   - Tighten the MAP sensor mounting bracket nut to 80 inch lbs. (9 Nm).

2009 Models

See Figure 272.

1. Disconnect the Manifold Absolute Pressure (MAP) sensor electrical connector.
2. Remove the bolt and the MAP sensor.
3. Clean and inspect the sealing surface.

➡When installing the sensor, if the bolt fails to hold specified torque, relocate the sensor and retain, using the auxiliary bolt hole in the upper intake manifold.

4. To install, reverse the removal procedure and note the following:
   - Tighten the retaining bolt to 53 inch lbs. (6 Nm).

OUTPUT SHAFT SPEED (OSS) SENSOR

LOCATION

CD4E Automatic Transaxle

See Figure 273.

The Output Shaft Speed (OSS) Sensor for the CD4E transaxle is located at the left side of the transaxle.

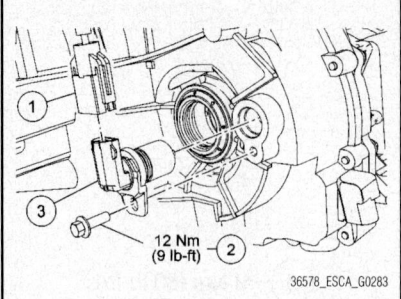

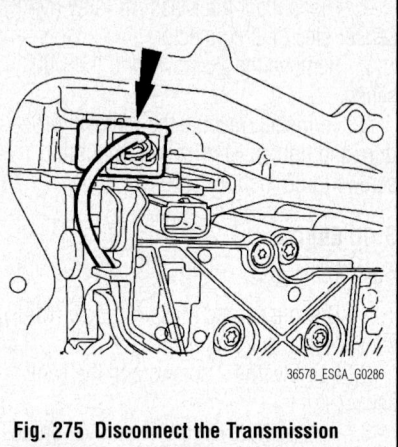

Fig. 273 Output Shaft Speed (OSS) Sensor location view—CD4E Transaxle

6F35 Automatic Transaxle

See Figure 274.

The Output Shaft Speed (OSS) Sensor for the 6F35 transaxle is located inside the transaxle behind the main control.

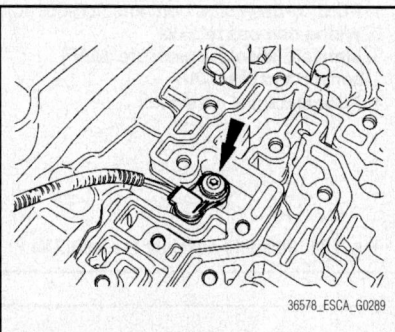

Fig. 274 Output Shaft Speed (OSS) Sensor location view—6F35 Transaxle

REMOVAL & INSTALLATION

CD4E Automatic Transaxle

See Figure 273.

1. With the vehicle in NEUTRAL, position it on a hoist.
2. Remove the 7 retainers and the LH splash shield.
3. Disconnect the OSS electrical connector.
4. Remove the OSS sensor bolt.
5. Remove the OSS sensor.

➡When installing the sensor, lubricate the O-ring seal with clean transmission fluid. Inspect the O-ring seal for nicks or cuts. Install a new O-ring seal as necessary.

6. To install, reverse the removal procedure and note the following:
   - Tighten the OSS retaining bolt to 106 inch lbs. (12 Nm).

6F35 Automatic Transaxle

See Figures 274 through 277.

Fig. 275 Disconnect the Transmission Range (TR) sensor electrical connector

1. With the vehicle in NEUTRAL, position it on a hoist.
2. Remove the retainers and the LH splash shield. For 3.0L engines remove the RH splash shield.
3. Remove the transmission fluid drain plug and allow the transmission fluid to drain. Tighten the drain plug to 106 inch lbs. (12 Nm).
4. Disconnect the transaxle electrical connector.
5. Remove the transaxle electrical wiring harness retainers from the transmission fluid pan stud bolts.
6. Remove the 2 nuts, pull the transmission fluid cooler tube bracket and tubes away from the transaxle and position it aside. Note the location of the stud bolts for assembly.
7. Remove the 8 bolts, 5 stud bolts and the main control cover.
8. Disconnect the Transmission Range (TR) sensor electrical connector.
9. Disconnect the Output Shaft Speed (OSS) sensor electrical connector.
10. Remove the main control-to-main control cover grommet.

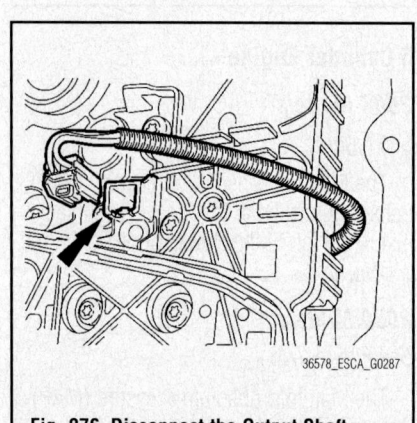

Fig. 276 Disconnect the Output Shaft Speed (OSS) sensor electrical connector

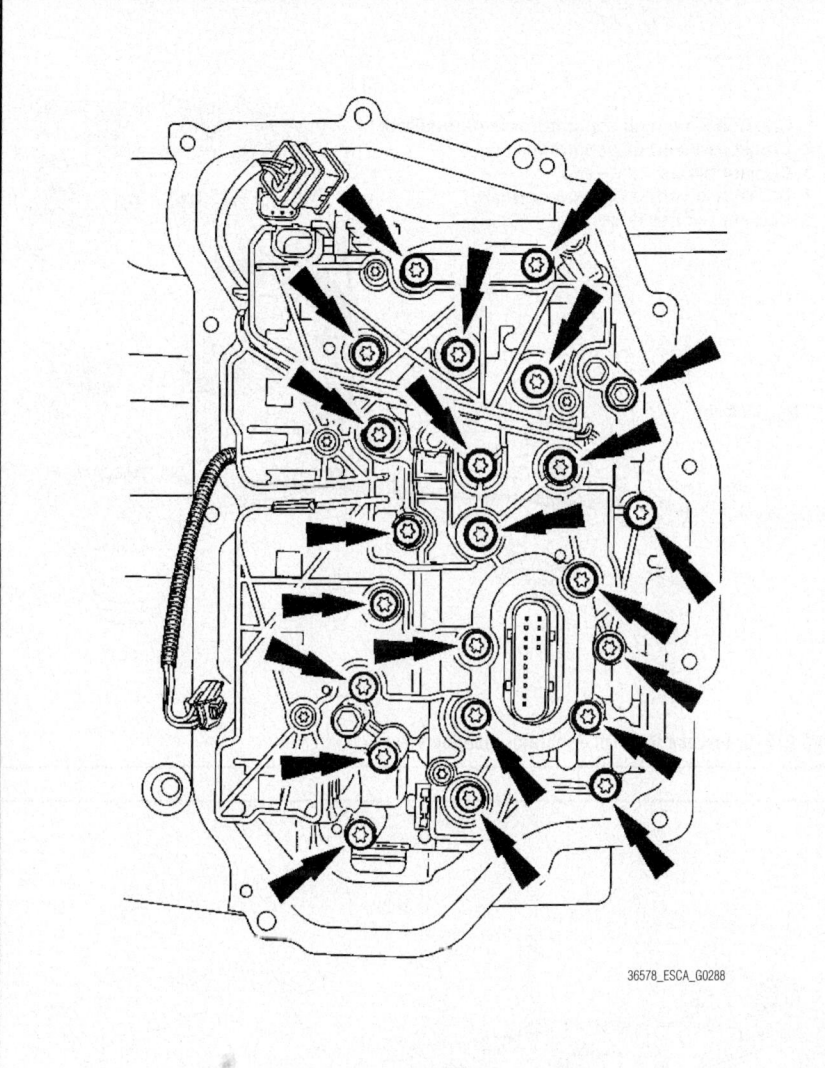

Fig. 277 Remove the nut, 22 bolts and the main control

➡ **The main control should be handled with care, damage to the main control may occur.**

11. Remove the nut, 22 bolts and the main control. Note the location of the different length bolts for assembly.

12. Remove the main control-to-transaxle separator plate.

13. Remove the bolt and the OSS sensor.

To install:

14. Install the OSS sensor and tighten the bolt to 89 inch lbs. (10 Nm).

15. Position the OSS and TR sensor wiring harnesses aside and install the main control-to-transaxle separator plate.

➡**Make sure that the manual lever pin (part of the TR sensor) is correctly installed in the manual valve.**

16. Install the main control.

✳✳ WARNING

Make sure not to pinch the Output Shaft Speed (OSS) or Transmission Range (TR) sensor wiring harnesses when installing the main control.

17. Install the different length bolts in the locations noted during disassembly.

18. Install the main control and the nut and 22 bolts. Tighten in a crisscross pattern to 89 inch lbs. (10 Nm).

19. Route the OSS sensor wiring harness and connect the electrical connector.

20. Connect the TR sensor electrical connector.

21. Install the main control-to-main control cover grommet.

22. Clean the main control cover sealing surface and inspect for damage. Replace if needed.

23. Apply silicone to the main control sealing surface of the transaxle case.

24. Position the main control cover in place.

➡**Inspect the main control-to-main control cover grommet to make sure that the seal is on the inside of the main control cover or a transmission fluid leak will occur.**

25. Install the stud bolts in the locations noted during disassembly. Tighten in a crisscross pattern to 106 inch lbs. (12 Nm).

26. Position the transmission fluid cooler tube bracket and transmission fluid cooler tube assembly in place and install the 2 nuts. Tighten the nuts to 80 inch lbs. (9 Nm).

27. Connect the transaxle electrical connector.

28. Connect the transaxle electrical wiring harness retainers to the transmission fluid pan stud bolts.

29. Install the LH splash shield and the retainers. (Install the LH splash shield and the retainers for 3.0L engine.

30. Fill with clean transmission fluid to the correct level.

POSITIVE CRANKCASE VENTILATION (PCV) VALVE

LOCATION

2.3L Engine

See Figure 278.

The PCV valve is located under the intake manifold mounted in the crankcase vent oil separator

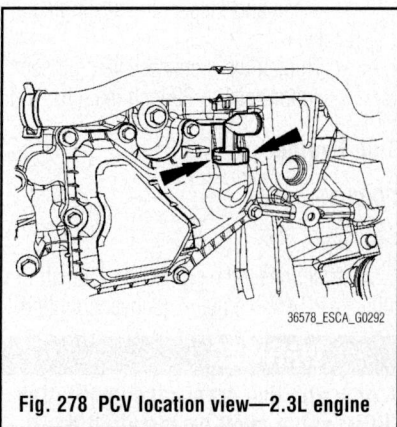

Fig. 278 PCV location view—2.3L engine

2.5L Engine

See Figure 279.

The 2.5L engine uses a Crankcase Vent Oil Separator in place of a conventional PCV valve. The Crankcase Vent Oil Separator is located under the intake manifold and mounted to the engine block.

3.0L Engine

2008 Models

See Figure 280.

The PCV valve is located at the rear of the RH valve cover.

2009 Models

See Figure 281.

The electric PCV valve is located at the rear of the RH valve cover.

REMOVAL & INSTALLATION

2.3L Engine

See Figure 278.

1. Remove the intake manifold. Refer to Intake Manifold, Removal & Installation in the Engine Mechanical section.
2. Depress the 2 release tabs and remove the PCV valve.

➡**Clean and inspect the crankcase oil vent separator gasket and install a new gasket if necessary.**

3. To install, reverse the removal procedure.

2.5L Engine

See Figure 279.

1. Remove the intake manifold.
2. Release the coolant bypass hose from the clip.
3. Remove the 8 bolts, the crankcase vent oil separator and gasket.
4. To install, reverse the removal procedure and note the following:
   - Clean and inspect the sealing surfaces.
   - Tighten the crankcase vent oil separator bolts to 89 inch lbs. (10 Nm).

3.0L Engine

2008 Models

See Figure 280.

1. Disconnect the crankcase ventilation tube-to-PCV valve quick connect coupling.

❈❈ WARNING

A new positive crankcase ventilation (PCV) valve must be installed if removed from the valve cover. Damage will occur to the locking mechanism on the PCV valve upon removal.

2. Rotate the PCV valve counterclockwise and remove it from the valve cover.
3. To install, reverse the removal procedure.

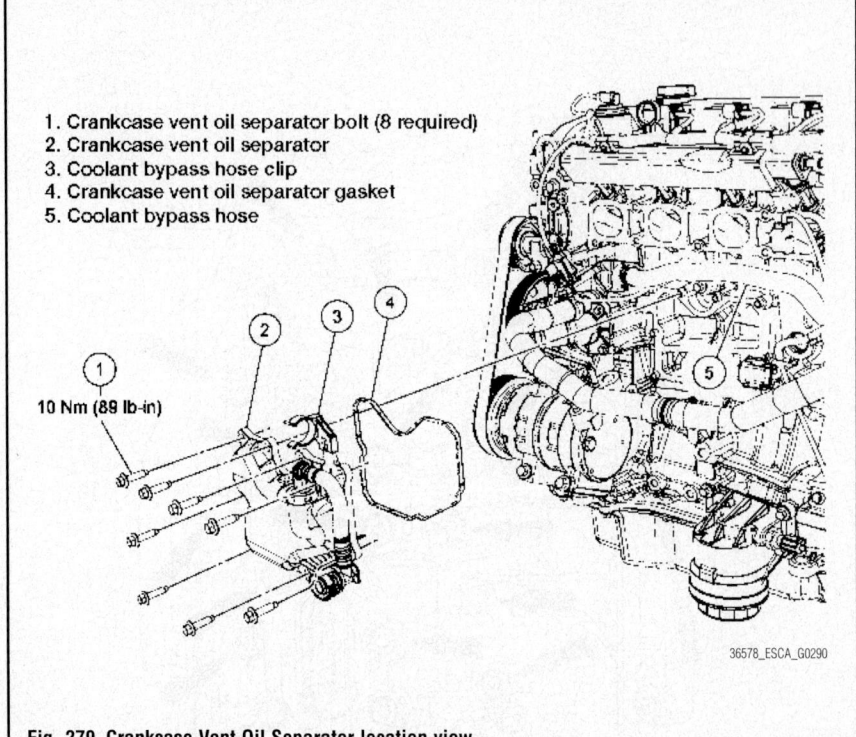

1. Crankcase vent oil separator bolt (8 required)
2. Crankcase vent oil separator
3. Coolant bypass hose clip
4. Crankcase vent oil separator gasket
5. Coolant bypass hose

10 Nm (89 lb-in)

36578_ESCA_G0290

Fig. 279 Crankcase Vent Oil Separator location view

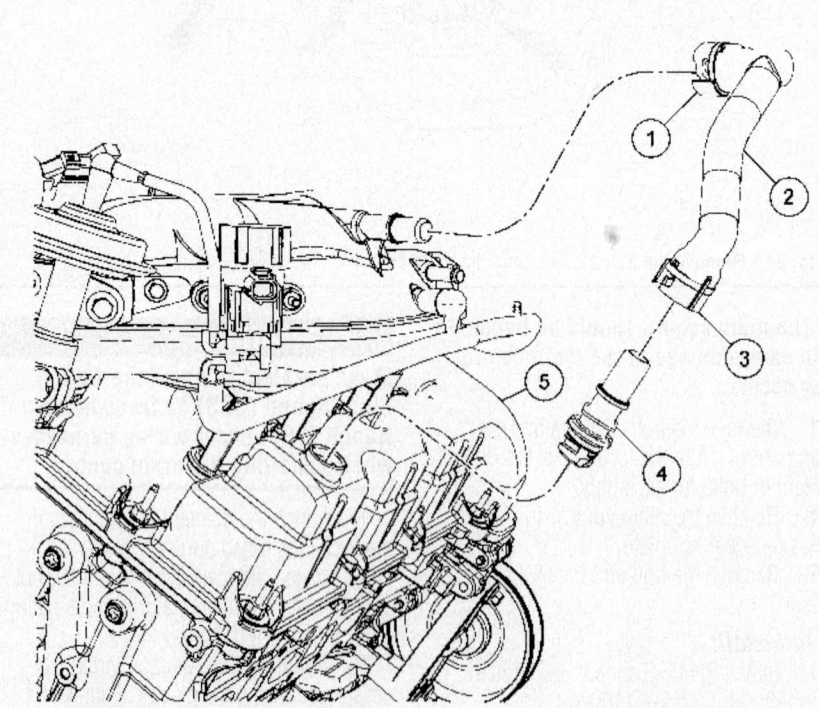

1. Crankcase ventilation tube-to-intake manifold quick connect coupling
2. Crankcase ventilation tube
3. Crankcase ventilation tube-to-PCV valve quick connect coupling
4. PCV valve
5. Valve cover

36578_ESCA_G0293

Fig. 280 PCV valve location view—3.0L engine—2008 model

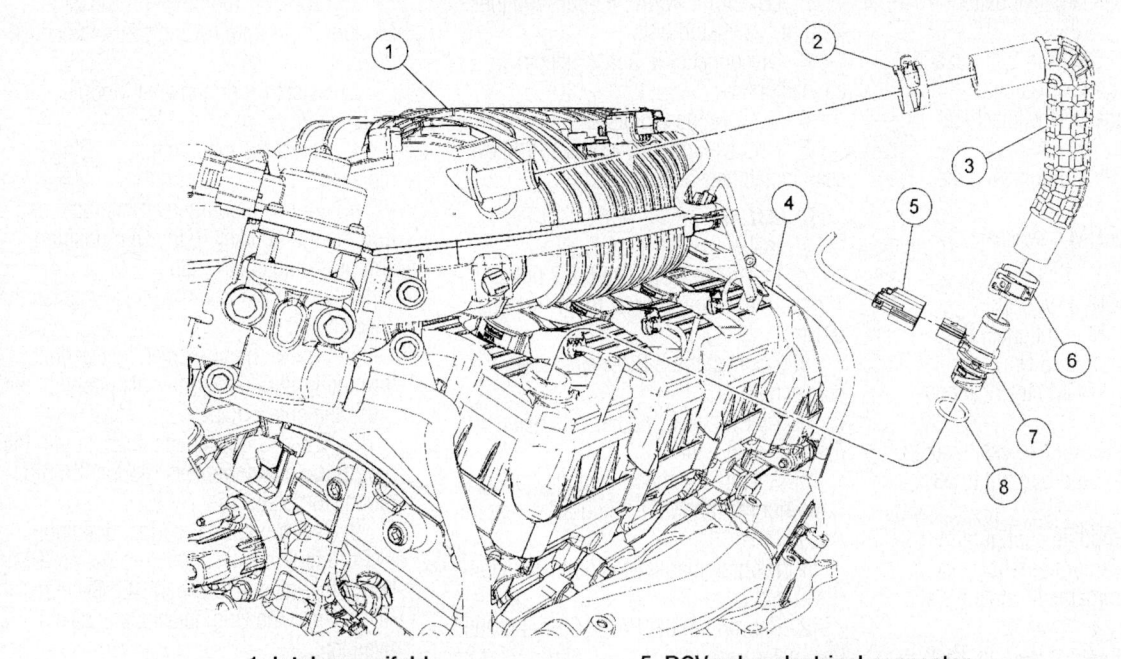

1. Intake manifold
2. Crankcase ventilation tube clamp
3. Crankcase ventilation tube
4. RH valve cover
5. PCV valve electrical connector
6. Crankcase ventilation tube clamp
7. PCV valve
8. PCV valve O-ring seal

36578_ESCA_G0291

Fig. 281 Electric PCV valve location view—3.0L engine—2009 model

2009 Models

See Figure 281.

1. Disconnect the Positive Crankcase Ventilation (PCV) valve electrical connector.

2. Release the clamp and disconnect the crankcase ventilation tube from the PCV valve.

➡ **A new PCV valve must be installed if removed from the valve cover. Damage will occur to the locking mechanism on the PCV valve.**

❋ WARNING

When installing, make sure the PCV valve electrical connector is pointing in the correct position to allow the wiring harness to be connected. Incorrect installation would require removal and replacement of the valve.

3. Rotate the PCV valve counterclockwise and remove it from the valve cover.

4. To install, reverse the removal procedure.

POWERTRAIN CONTROL MODULE (PCM)

LOCATION

See Figure 282.

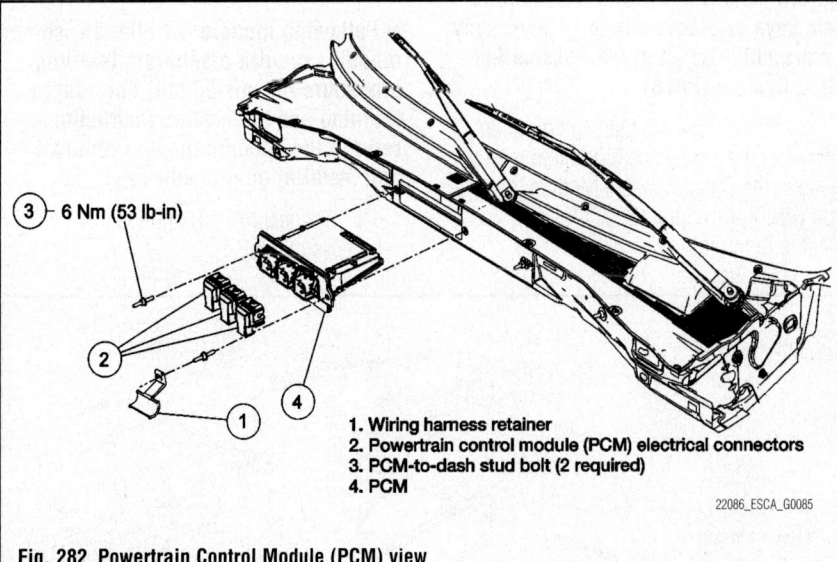

3 — 6 Nm (53 lb-in)

1. Wiring harness retainer
2. Powertrain control module (PCM) electrical connectors
3. PCM-to-dash stud bolt (2 required)
4. PCM

22086_ESCA_G0085

Fig. 282 Powertrain Control Module (PCM) view

For Escape and Mariner, the Powertrain Control Module (PCM) is located behind the instrument panel (cowl), center to both driver and passenger sides (access from the engine compartment).

REMOVAL & INSTALLATION

2008 Models

See Figure 282.

➡ **Any Powertrain Control Module (PCM) replacement will require that ALL customer keys are available to be programmed at the time of installation. PCM replacement DOES NOT require new keys.**

1. Retrieve the module configuration. Carry out the module configuration retrieval steps of the Programmable Module Installation procedure.

2. Disconnect the negative battery cable.

3. Remove the PCM stud bolt nut and position the wiring harness aside.

4. Disconnect the 3 PCM electrical connectors.

5. Remove the 2 stud bolts and the PCM

6. Remove the PCM cowl seal.

To install:

7. Install the PCM cowl seal.

8. Install the PCM and tighten the 2 stud bolts to 53 inch lbs. (6 Nm).

9. Connect the 3 PCM electrical connectors.

10. Position the wiring harness. Install and tighten the PCM stud bolt nut to 53 inch lbs. (6 Nm).

11. Restore the module configuration. Carry out the module configuration restore steps of the Programmable Module Installation procedure.

12. Reprogram the Passive Anti-Theft System (PATS). Carry out the Key Programming Using Two Programmed Keys procedure.

2009 Models

See Figure 283.

➡**PCM installation DOES NOT require new keys or programming of keys, only a Parameter Reset of the Passive Anti-Theft System (PATS).**

1. Retrieve the module configuration. Carry out the module configuration retrieval steps of the Programmable Module Installation (PMI) procedure. (Specialized equipment is required)

2. Detach the wiring harness retainer from the cowl stud bolt.

3. Disconnect the 3 PCM electrical connectors.

4. Remove the 2 bolts and the PCM.

5. Remove and inspect the PCM cowl seal; install new if damaged.

To install:

6. Install the PCM cowl seal.

7. Install the PCM and the 2 bolts. Tighten the retaining bolts to 71 inch lbs. (8 Nm).

8. Connect the 3 PCM electrical connectors.

9. Attach the wiring harness retainer to the cowl stud bolt.

10. Restore the module configuration. Carry out the module configuration restore steps of the

11. Programmable Module Installation (PMI) procedure.

12. Reprogram the PATS. Carry out the Parameter Reset procedure.

PROGRAMMABLE MODULE INSTALLATION (PMI) PROCEDURE

Programmable Module Installation (PMI) Using the Integrated Diagnostic System (IDS) When the Original Module is Available.

➡**Following module installation, some modules require a separate learning procedure be carried out. For adaptive learning and calibration instructions, refer to the specific module removal and installation procedures.**

1. Connect the IDS and identify the vehicle as normal.

2. From the Toolbox icon, select Module Programming and press the check mark.

3. Select Programmable Module Installation.

4. Select the module that is being replaced.

5. Follow the on-screen instructions, turn the ignition key to the OFF position, and press the check mark.

6. Install the new module and press the check mark.

7. Follow the on-screen instructions, turn the ignition key to the ON position, and press the check mark.

8. The IDS downloads the data into the new module and displays Module Configuration Complete.

9. Test module for correct operation.

Programmable Module Installation (PMI) Using the Integrated Diagnostic System (IDS) When the Original Module is NOT Available.

➡**Following module installation, some modules require a separate learning procedure be carried out. For adaptive learning and calibration instructions, refer to the specific module removal and installation procedures.**

10. Install the new module.

11. Connect the IDS and identify the vehicle as normal.

12. From the Toolbox icon, select Module Programming and press the check mark.

13. Select Programmable Module Installation.

14. Select the module that was replaced.

15. Follow the on-screen instructions, turn the ignition key to the OFF position, and press the check mark.

16. Follow the on-screen instructions, turn the ignition key to the ON position, and press the check mark.

17. If the data is not available, the IDS displays a screen stating to contact the As-Built Data Center. Retrieve the data from the technician service publication website at this time and press the check mark.

18. Enter the module data and press the check mark.

19. The IDS downloads the data into the new module and displays Module Configuration Complete.

20. Test module for correct operation.

PASSIVE ANTI-THEFT SYSTEM (PATS) PARAMETER RESET

➡**When using the Integrated Diagnostic System (IDS), the Instrument Cluster (IC) and the PCM parameters are reset at the same time**

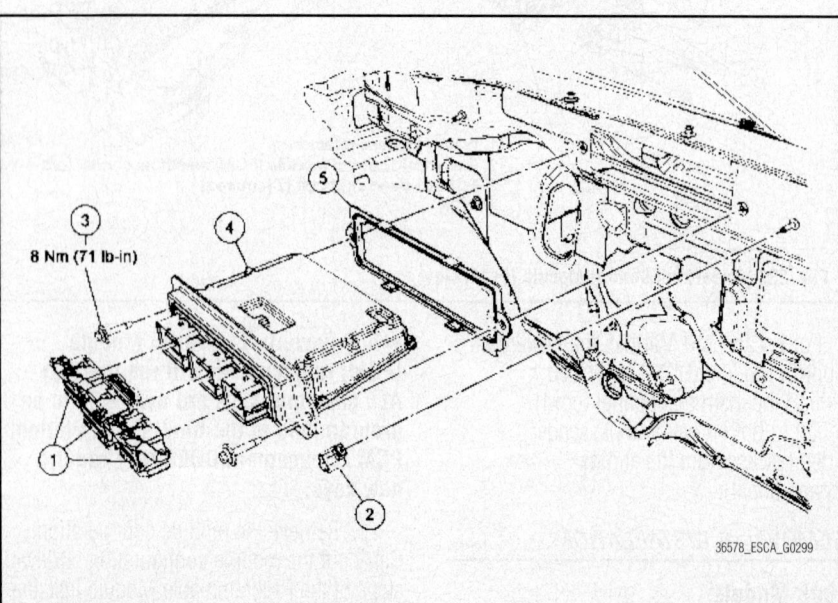

8 Nm (71 lb-in)

36578_ESCA_G0299

Fig. 283 Powertrain Control Module (PCM) view

→Once security access has been granted, multiple security access commands should be executed (if necessary) prior to exiting the command menu. This avoids an additional security access procedure and the associated 10 minute time delay.

1. Turn the key from the OFF position to the ON position.

2. From the scan tool, enter TOOLBOX. Select BODY-SECURITY-PATS Functions and follow the on-screen instructions to ENTER SECURITY ACCESS.

3. From the scan tool, select: Parameter Reset and follow the IDS on-screen instructions.

→If the IC was replaced, follow Steps 4–9. If the IC and the PCM were replaced, follow Steps 4–9. If only the PCM was replaced, cycle the key off, then back on, to complete the procedure.

→If steps 4–9 are followed, 2 keys must be present.

4. From the scan tool, select: Ignition Key Code Erase and follow the IDS on-screen instructions.

5. Turn the key to the OFF position and disconnect the scan tool.

→Integrated Key head Transmitter (IKT) keys require a 6–second programming time frame for the Remote Keyless Entry (RKE) data transfer to take place, while standard Passive Anti-Theft System (PATS) keys only require a minimum of 3 seconds.

6. Turn the key to the ON position for a minimum of 6 seconds (if it is an IKT key).

7. Turn the key to the OFF position and remove it from the ignition lock cylinder.

8. Insert the second key and turn it to the ON position for a minimum of 6 seconds (if it is an IKT key).

9. Both keys will now start the vehicle and will also operate the RKE functions of the vehicle (if they are IKT keys).

→The RKE data transfer will take place between the key and the IC first. After both keys are programmed into the IC, the RKE data will transfer from the IC to the Smart Junction Box (SJB). Until the final data transfer takes place into the SJB , the RKE functions will not operate.

THROTTLE POSITION SENSOR (TPS)

LOCATION

2.3L Engine
See Figure 284.

3.0L Engine
See Figure 285.

The Throttle Position Sensor (TPS) is located to the right of throttle plate.

The Throttle Position Sensor (TPS) is located on the throttle body just behind the EGR valve tube.

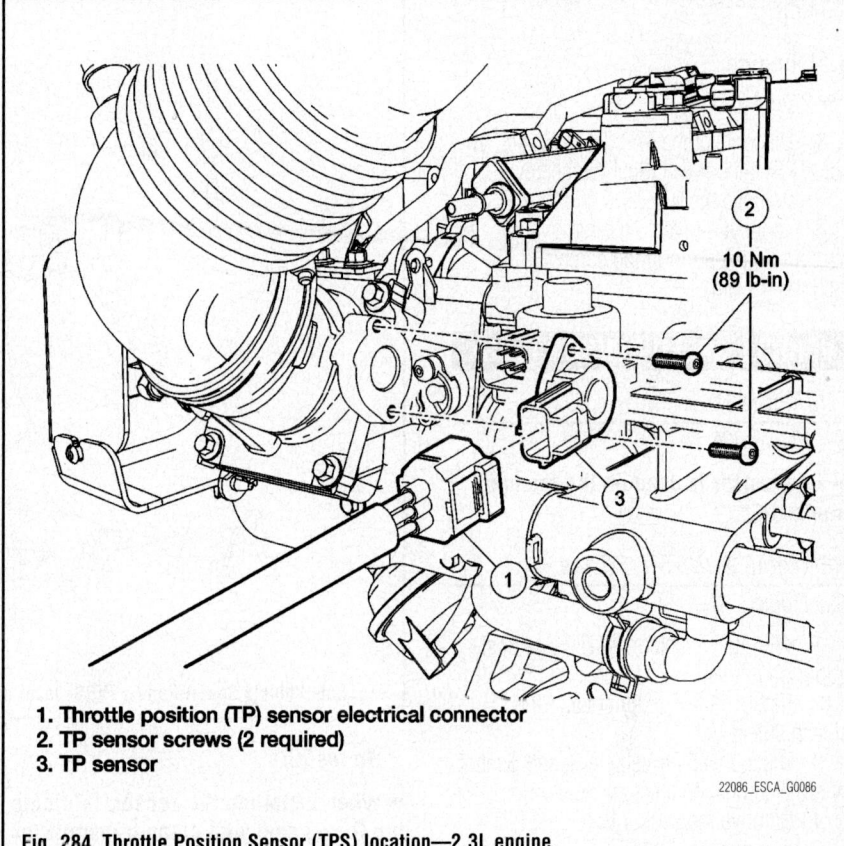

1. Throttle position (TP) sensor electrical connector
2. TP sensor screws (2 required)
3. TP sensor

22086_ESCA_G0086

Fig. 284 Throttle Position Sensor (TPS) location—2.3L engine

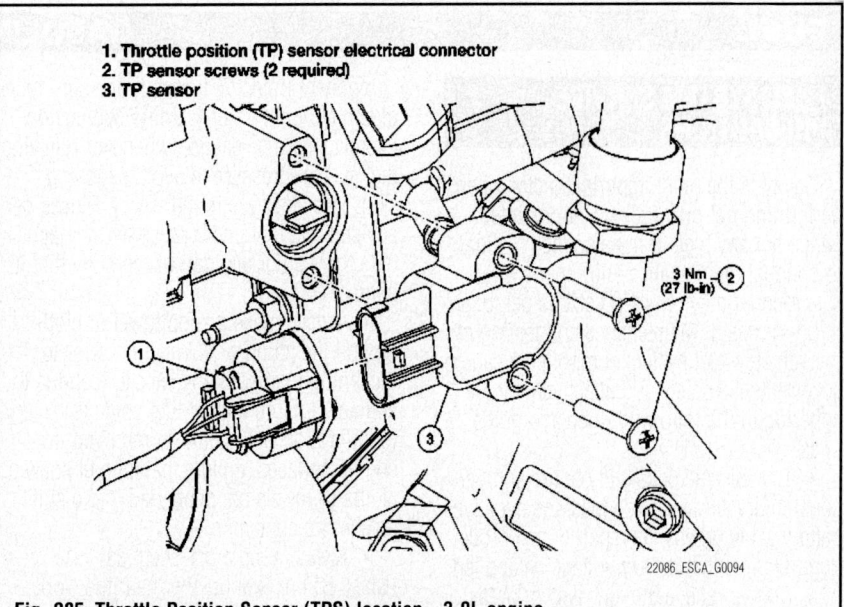

1. Throttle position (TP) sensor electrical connector
2. TP sensor screws (2 required)
3. TP sensor

22086_ESCA_G0094

Fig. 285 Throttle Position Sensor (TPS) location—3.0L engine

REMOVAL & INSTALLATION

2.3L Engine

See Figure 284.

1. Disconnect the Throttle Position Sensor (TPS) electrical connector.
2. Remove the 2 screws and the TPS.
3. To install, reverse the removal procedure and tighten TPS screws to 89 inch lbs. (10 Nm).

3.0L Engine

See Figure 285.

1. Disconnect the Throttle Position Sensor (TPS) sensor electrical connector.
2. Remove the 2 screws and the TPS.
3. To install, reverse the removal procedure and tighten mounting screws to 27 inch lbs. (3 Nm).

VEHICLE SPEED SENSOR (VSS)

LOCATION

See Figure 286.

➡ **This sensor is used on the manual transaxle.**

REMOVAL & INSTALLATION

See Figure 286.

1. With the vehicle in NEUTRAL, position it on a hoist.
2. Remove the 7 retainers and the LH splash shield.
3. Disconnect the Vehicle Speed Sensor (VSS) electrical connector.
4. Remove the sensor bolt.
5. Remove the sensor.

1. Vehicle speed sensor (VSS) bolt
2. VSS
3. VSS electrical connector

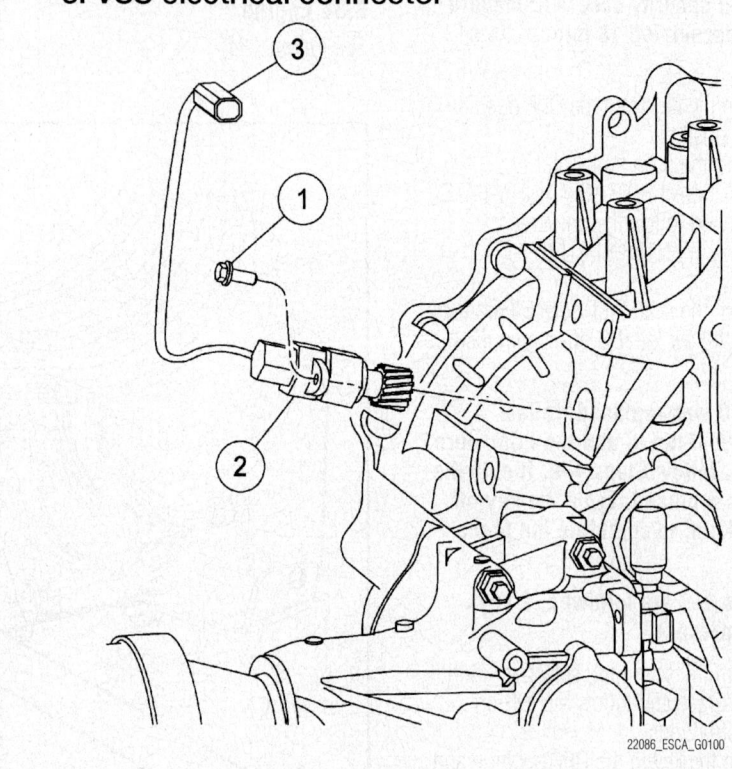

22086_ESCA_G0100

Fig. 286 Vehicle Speed Sensor (VSS) location—manual transaxle

To install:

➡ **When installing the sensor, lubricate the O-ring seal with clean transmission fluid.**

6. To install, reverse the removal procedure and note the following:
   • Tighten the sensor mounting bolt to 9 ft. lbs. (12 Nm).

FUEL
GASOLINE FUEL INJECTION SYSTEM

FUEL SYSTEM SERVICE PRECAUTIONS

Safety is the most important factor when performing not only fuel system maintenance but any type of maintenance. Failure to conduct maintenance and repairs in a safe manner may result in serious personal injury or death. Maintenance and testing of the vehicle's fuel system components can be accomplished safely and effectively by adhering to the following rules and guidelines.

• To avoid the possibility of fire and personal injury, always disconnect the negative battery cable unless the repair or test procedure requires that battery voltage be applied.
• Always relieve the fuel system pressure prior to disconnecting any fuel system component (injector, fuel rail, pressure regulator, etc.), fitting or fuel line connection. Exercise extreme caution whenever relieving fuel system pressure to avoid exposing skin, face and eyes to fuel spray. Please be advised that fuel under pressure may penetrate the skin or any part of the body that it contacts.

• Always place a shop towel or cloth around the fitting or connection prior to loosening to absorb any excess fuel due to spillage. Ensure that all fuel spillage (should it occur) is quickly removed from engine surfaces. Ensure that all fuel soaked cloths or towels are deposited into a suitable waste container.
• Always keep a dry chemical (Class B) fire extinguisher near the work area.

• Do not allow fuel spray or fuel vapors to come into contact with a spark or open flame.
• Always use a back-up wrench when loosening and tightening fuel line connection fittings. This will prevent unnecessary stress and torsion to fuel line piping.
• Always replace worn fuel fitting O-rings with new. Do not substitute fuel hose or equivalent where fuel pipe is installed.
• Do not carry personal electronic devices such as cell phones, pagers or audio equipment of any type when working on or near any fuel-related component. Highly flammable mixtures are always present and may be ignited. Failure to follow these instructions may result in serious personal injury

• Do not smoke, carry lighted tobacco or have an open flame of any type when working on or near any fuel-related component. Highly flammable mixtures are always present and may be ignited. Failure to follow these instructions may result in serious personal injury.

Before servicing the vehicle, make sure to also refer to the precautions in the beginning of this section as well.

RELIEVING FUEL SYSTEM PRESSURE

2008 Model

See Figure 287.

> **✳✳ CAUTION**
>
> **Do not carry personal electronic devices such as cell phones, pagers or audio equipment of any type when working on or near any fuel-related component. Highly flammable mixtures are always present and may be ignited. Failure to follow these instructions may result in serious personal injury.**

> **✳✳ CAUTION**
>
> **Do not smoke, carry lighted tobacco or have an open flame of any type when working on or near any fuel-related component. Highly flammable mixtures are always present and may be ignited. Failure to follow these instructions may result in serious personal injury.**

1. Before servicing the vehicle, refer to the Precautions Section.
2. With the vehicle in NEUTRAL, position it on a hoist.
3. Disconnect the Fuel Pump (FP) driver module electrical connector.

4. Start the engine and allow it to idle until it stalls.
5. After the engine stalls, crank the engine for approximately 5 seconds to make sure the fuel injection supply manifold pressure has been released.
6. Turn the ignition switch to the OFF position.
7. When fuel system service is complete, connect the FP driver module electrical connector.
8. It may take more than one key cycle to pressurize the fuel system.
9. Cycle the ignition key and wait 3 seconds to pressurize the fuel system. Check for leaks before starting the engine.
10. Start the vehicle and check the fuel system for leaks.

2009 Model

See Figure 288.

> **✳✳ CAUTION**
>
> **Do not carry personal electronic devices such as cell phones, pagers or audio equipment of any type when working on or near any fuel-related component. Highly flammable mixtures are always present and may be ignited. Failure to follow these instructions may result in serious personal injury.**

> **✳✳ CAUTION**
>
> **Do not smoke, carry lighted tobacco or have an open flame of any type when working on or near any fuel-related component. Highly flammable mixtures are always present and may be ignited. Failure to follow these instructions may result in serious personal injury.**

1. Before servicing the vehicle, refer to the Precautions Section.

2. Remove the fuel pump fuse that is located in the Battery Junction Box (BJB), location 22.
3. Start the engine and allow it to idle until it stalls.
4. After the engine stalls, crank the engine for approximately 5 seconds to make sure the fuel injection supply manifold pressure has been released.
5. Turn the ignition switch to the OFF position.
6. When the fuel system service is complete, install the FP fuse.
7. Carry out a Key ON Engine OFF (KOEO) visual inspection for leaks prior to starting the engine.
8. Start the vehicle and check the fuel system for leaks.

FUEL FILTER

REMOVAL & INSTALLATION

2008 Model

See Figure 289.

> **✳✳ CAUTION**
>
> **Do not carry personal electronic devices such as cell phones, pagers or audio equipment of any type when working on or near any fuel-related component. Highly flammable mixtures are always present and may be ignited. Failure to follow these Instructions may result In serlous personal injury.**

> **✳✳ CAUTION**
>
> **Do not smoke, carry lighted tobacco or have an open flame of any type when working on or near any fuel-related component. Highly flammable mixtures are always present and may be ignited. Failure to follow these instructions may result in serious personal injury.**

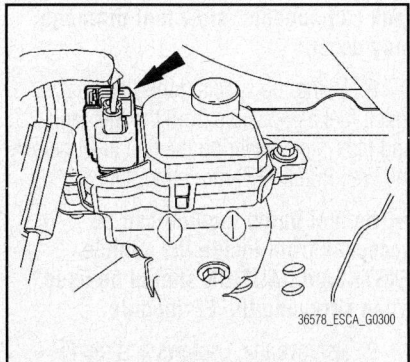

36578_ESCA_G0300

Fig. 287 Fuel Pump (FP) driver module

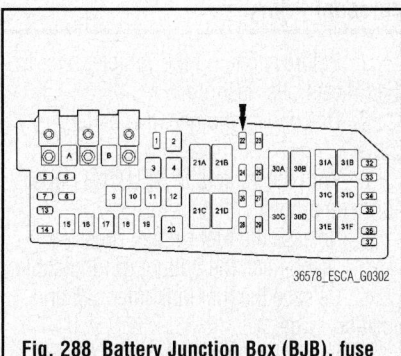

36578_ESCA_G0302

Fig. 288 Battery Junction Box (BJB), fuse location 22 shown

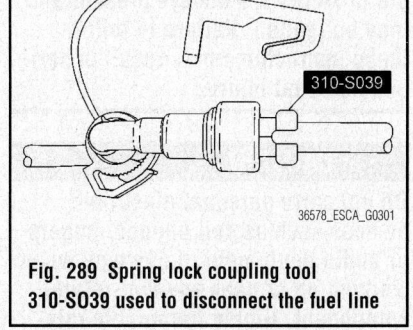

310-S039

36578_ESCA_G0301

Fig. 289 Spring lock coupling tool 310-SO39 used to disconnect the fuel line

1. Before servicing the vehicle, refer to the Precautions Section.

2. Properly relieve the fuel system pressure.

➡**Some residual fuel may remain in the fuel filter after releasing the fuel system pressure. Upon disconnecting or removing the fuel filter, carefully drain any residual fuel into a suitable container.**

3. Disconnect the fuel supply tube-to-fuel filter inlet spring lock coupling.

4. Disconnect the fuel supply tube-to-fuel filter outlet spring lock coupling.

5. Release the fuel filter clamp and remove the fuel filter.

6. To install, reverse the removal procedure and tighten the fuel filter retaining clamp to 35 inch lbs. (4 Nm).

2009 Model

The 2009 model has a lifetime fuel filter (serviced as part of the fuel pump module).

FUEL PUMP MODULE

REMOVAL & INSTALLATION
See Figure 290.

❉ CAUTION

Do not carry personal electronic devices such as cell phones, pagers or audio equipment of any type when working on or near any fuel-related component. Highly flammable mixtures are always present and may be ignited. Failure to follow these instructions may result in serious personal injury.

❉ CAUTION

Do not smoke, carry lighted tobacco or have an open flame of any type when working on or near any fuel-related component. Highly flammable mixtures are always present and may be ignited. Failure to follow these instructions may result in serious personal injury.

❉ CAUTION

Do not carry personal electronic devices such as cell phones, pagers or audio equipment of any type when working on or near any fuel-related component. Highly flammable mix-

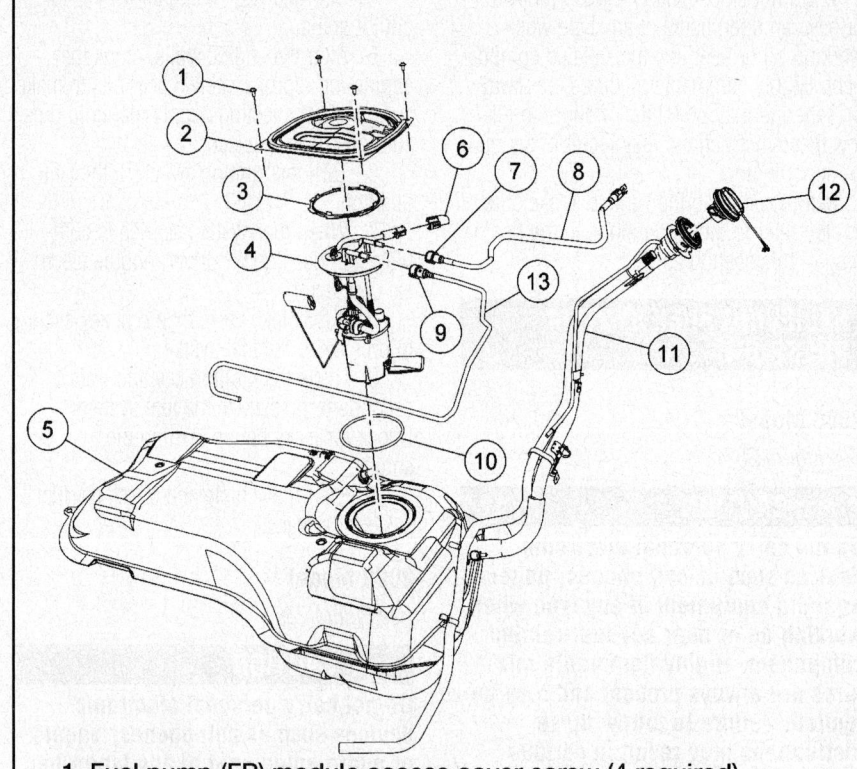

1. Fuel pump (FP) module access cover screw (4 required)
2. FP module access cover
3. FP module lock ring
4. FP module
5. Fuel tank
6. FP module electrical connector
7. Fuel vapor tube-to-FP module quick connect coupling
8. Fuel vapor tube
9. Fuel supply tube assembly-to-fuel tank quick connect coupling
10. FP module O-ring seal
11. Fuel tank filler pipe
12. Fuel tank filler cap
13. Fuel supply tube

36578_ESCA_G0306

Fig. 290 Fuel Pump (FP) module and related components

tures are always present and may be ignited. Failure to follow these instructions may result in serious personal injury.

1. Before servicing the vehicle, refer to the Precautions Section.

2. Disconnect the negative battery cable.

3. With the vehicle in NEUTRAL, position it on a hoist.

4. Release the fuel system pressure.

5. Disconnect the battery ground cable.

6. Release the fuel tank filler cap and position aside.

7. Insert the special tool into the fuel tank filler pipe until it opens the fuel tank level shutoff valve located at the inlet of the fuel tank.

➡**Due to the internal design of the fuel tank components, slow fuel drainage may occur.**

8. Using the special tools, drain as much fuel as possible from the fuel tank and filler pipe, lowering the fuel level below the Fuel Pump (FP) mounting flange.

➡**The fuel pump module can be accessed from inside the vehicle EXSTREAM CAUTION should be used when servicing the FP module.**

9. Remove the 4 screws and the FP module access cover. (If Applicable)

➡Clean the FP module connection, couplings, mounting flange and the immediate surrounding area of any dirt or foreign material.

10. Disconnect the FP module electrical connector. Place absorbent toweling in the immediate surrounding area in case of fuel spills.

11. Disconnect the fuel supply tube and fuel vapor recirculation tube-to-FP module quick connect couplings.

❄❄ WARNING

The fuel pump (FP) module must be handled carefully to avoid damage to the float arm and the filter.

12. Carefully remove the FP module lock ring and verify that enough fuel has been drained to avoid spillage.

13. Drain any residual in the FP module into a suitable container.

14. Using a suitable FP module lock ring remover, rotate the lock ring counterclockwise and remove the FP module.

15. Inspect the surfaces of the FP module flange and fuel tank seal contact surfaces. Do not polish or adjust the seal contact area of the FP module flange or fuel tank. Install a new FP module or fuel tank if the seal contact area is bent, scratched or corroded.

16. Remove and discard the FP module O-ring seal.

17. Apply clean engine oil to the FP module O-ring seal.

18. To install, reverse the removal procedure.

FUEL RAIL & INJECTORS

REMOVAL & INSTALLATION

2.3L Engine

See Figures 291 and 292.

❄❄ CAUTION

Do not carry personal electronic devices such as cell phones, pagers or audio equipment of any type when working on or near any fuel-related component. Highly flammable mixtures are always present and may be ignited. Failure to follow these instructions may result in serious personal injury.

❄❄ CAUTION

Do not smoke or carry lighted tobacco or open flame of any type

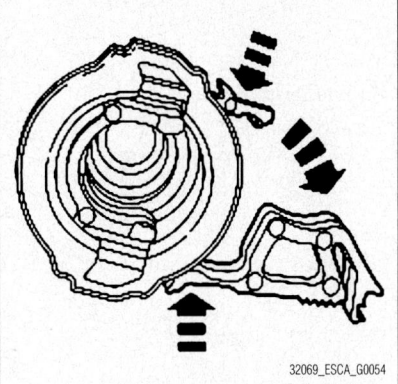

Fig. 291 Rotate the primary locking tab to the fully opened position and squeeze the secondary locking tabs to release the locking mechanism

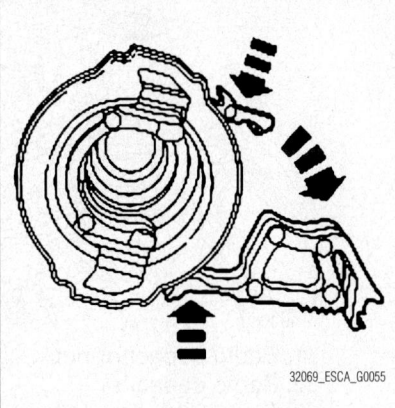

Fig. 292 Push the locking mechanism outward and release the tube

when working on or near any fuel-related components. Highly flammable mixtures are always present and may be ignited. Failure to follow these instructions can result in personal injury.

❄❄ CAUTION

Fuel in the fuel system remains under high pressure even when the engine is not running. Before working on or disconnecting any of the fuel tubes or fuel system components, the fuel system pressure must be relieved. Failure to follow these instructions can result in personal injury.

1. Before servicing the vehicle, refer to the Precautions Section.

2. Release the fuel pressure.

3. Disconnect the negative battery cable.

❄❄ WARNING

When reusing liquid or vapor tube connectors, make sure to use compressed air to remove any foreign material from the connector retaining clip area before separating the tube.

➡Carefully release the locking tabs to avoid breakage.

4. Release the fuel tube-to-fuel rail quick release coupling primary locking tab.

5. Rotate the primary locking tab to the fully opened position and squeeze the secondary locking tabs to release the locking mechanism.

6. Push the locking mechanism outward and release the tube.

7. Disconnect the fuel rail pressure and temperature vacuum tube and electrical connector.

8. Disconnect the 4 fuel injector electrical connectors.

9. Remove the 2 fuel rail bolts and detach the wiring retainers from the fuel rail.

10. Remove the fuel rail and injectors as an assembly and then remove the spacers.

11. Remove the 4 fuel injector retainer clips and the fuel injectors.

12. Remove and discard the 8 fuel injector O-ring seals.

To install:

❄❄ WARNING

Use O-ring seals that are made of special fuel-resistant material. Use of ordinary O-rings can cause the fuel system to leak. Do not reuse the O-ring seals.

➡Install new fuel injector O-ring seals and lubricate them with clean engine oil.

13. Install the fuel injectors and the retainer clips.

14. Position the fuel rail spacers and the fuel rail.

15. Install the fuel rail bolts and attach the wiring retainers. Tighten to 23 Nm (17 lb-ft).

16. Connect the fuel injector electrical connectors.

17. Connect the fuel rail pressure and temperature vacuum tube and electrical connector.

➡Make sure the collar on the fuel tube is inserted fully into the quick release coupling before the locking tang is locked.

➡Apply clean engine oil to the end of the tube before inserting a tube into the connector.

18. Connect the fuel tube quick release coupling:

    a. Connect the quick lock coupling to the tube.

    b. Press the quick connect coupling locking tangs into position.

    c. Pull on the fitting to make sure it is fully engaged.

19. Connect the negative battery cable.

2.5L Engine

See Figure 293.

> **⁂ CAUTION**
>
> **Do not carry personal electronic devices such as cell phones, pagers or audio equipment of any type when working on or near any fuel-related component. Highly flammable mixtures are always present and may be ignited. Failure to follow these instructions may result in serious personal injury.**

> **⁂ CAUTION**
>
> **Do not smoke or carry lighted tobacco or open flame of any type when working on or near any fuel-related components. Highly flammable mixtures are always present and may be ignited. Failure to follow these instructions may result in personal injury.**

> **⁂ CAUTION**
>
> **Fuel in the fuel system remains under high pressure even when the engine is not running. Before working on or disconnecting any of the fuel lines or fuel system components, the fuel system pressure must be relieved. Failure to follow these instructions may result in personal injury.**

1. Before servicing the vehicle, refer to the Precautions Section.

2. Release the fuel pressure.

3. Disconnect the battery ground cable.

4. Disconnect the fuel supply tube-to-fuel quick connect coupling.

5. Disconnect the 4 fuel injector electrical connectors.

6. Remove the nut and position the radio capacitor aside.

7. Detach the 2 pin-type wire harness retainers from the fuel rail.

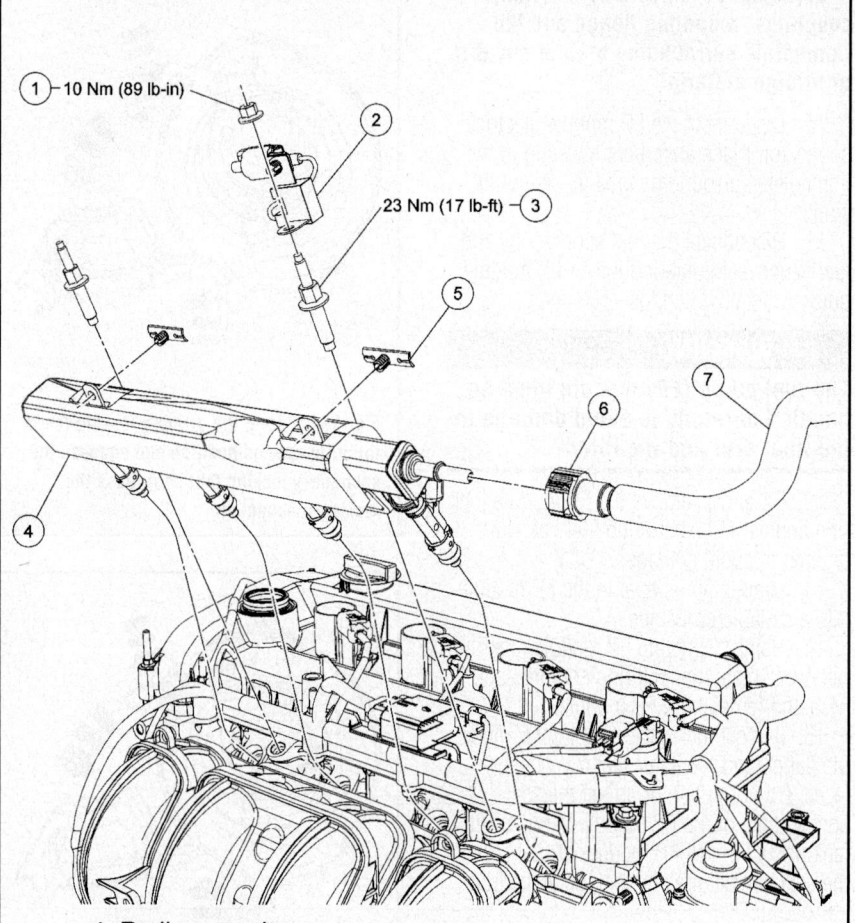

1. Radio capacitor nut
2. Radio capacitor
3. Fuel rail stud bolt (2 required)
4. Fuel rail
5. Wire harness pin-type retainer (2 required)
6. Fuel supply tube-to-fuel rail quick connect coupling
7. Fuel supply tube

36578_ESCA_G0308

Fig. 293 Fuel rail—2.5L engine

8. Remove the 2 fuel rail stud bolts.

9. Remove the fuel rail and injectors as an assembly.

10. Remove the 4 fuel injector retainer clips and the 4 fuel injectors.

11. Remove and discard the 8 fuel injector O-ring seals.

To install:

➡**Use O-ring seals that are made of special fuel-resistant material. Use of ordinary O-rings can cause the fuel system to leak. Do not reuse the O-ring seals.**

12. Install 8 new fuel injector O-ring seals and lubricate them with clean engine oil.

13. Install the 4 fuel injectors and the 4 retainer clips on the fuel rail.

14. Install the fuel rail and injectors as an assembly.

15. Install the 2 fuel rail stud bolts and tighten to 17 ft lbs. (23 Nm).

16. Attach the 2 pin-type wire harness retainers to the fuel rail.

17. Position the radio capacitor and install and tighten the nut to 89 inch lbs. (10 Nm).

18. Connect the 4 fuel injector electrical connectors.

19. Connect the fuel supply tube-to-fuel rail quick connect coupling.

20. Connect the battery ground cable.

3.0L Engine

2008 Models

See Figure 294.

> ❊❊ **CAUTION**
>
> Do not carry personal electronic devices such as cell phones, pagers or audio equipment of any type when working on or near any fuel-related component. Highly flammable mixtures are always present and may be ignited. Failure to follow these instructions may result in serious personal injury.

> ❊❊ **CAUTION**
>
> Do not smoke or carry lighted tobacco or open flame of any type when working on or near any fuel-related components. Highly flammable mixtures are always present and may be ignited. Failure to follow these instructions may result in personal injury.

> ❊❊ **CAUTION**
>
> Fuel in the fuel system remains under high pressure even when the engine is not running. Before working on or disconnecting any of the fuel lines or fuel system components, the fuel system pressure must be relieved. Failure to follow these instructions may result in personal injury.

1. Before servicing the vehicle, refer to the Precautions Section.
2. Remove the upper intake manifold. Refer to the Engine Mechanical Section.
3. Disconnect the fuel line.
4. Disconnect the six fuel injector electrical connectors and release the wiring harness locators from the fuel injection supply manifold.

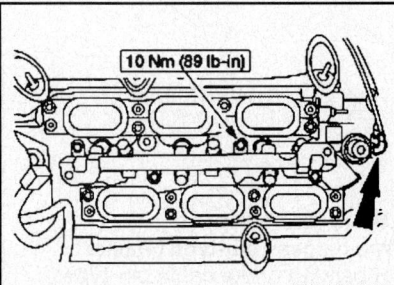

Fig. 294 Tighten the fuel injection supply manifold bolts to 89 inch lbs. (10 Nm)

5. Remove the vacuum hose.
6. Remove the bolts and the fuel injection supply manifold.

➡Lubricate the fuel injector O-ring seals with clean engine oil to aid installation.

7. Installation is the reverse of the removal procedure. Tighten the fuel injection supply manifold bolts to 89 inch lbs. (10 Nm).

2009 Models

See Figure 295.

> ❊❊ **CAUTION**
>
> Do not carry personal electronic devices such as cell phones, pagers or audio equipment of any type when working on or near any fuel-related component. Highly flammable mixtures are always present and may be ignited. Failure to follow these instructions may result in serious personal injury.

> ❊❊ **CAUTION**
>
> Do not smoke or carry lighted tobacco or open flame of any type when working on or near any fuel-related components. Highly flammable mixtures are always present and may be ignited. Failure to follow these instructions may result in personal injury.

> ❊❊ **CAUTION**
>
> Fuel in the fuel system remains under high pressure even when the engine is not running. Before working on or disconnecting any of the fuel lines or fuel system components, the fuel system pressure must be relieved. Failure to follow these instructions may result in personal injury.

1. Before servicing the vehicle, refer to the Precautions Section.
2. Release the fuel system pressure.

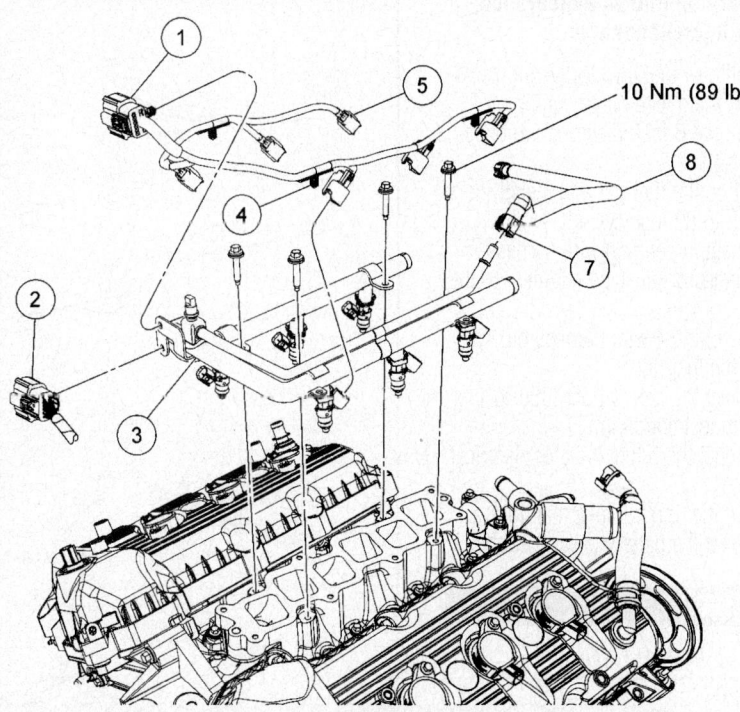

1. Fuel charging wire harness electrical connector
2. Engine wire harness electrical connector pin-type retainer
3. Fuel rail
4. Wire harness pin-type retainer (4 required)
5. Fuel injector electrical connector (6 required)
6. Fuel rail bolt (4 required)
7. Fuel jumper tube-to-fuel rail quick connect coupling
8. Fuel jumper tube

Fig. 295 Explode view of the fuel rail and injectors—2009 3.0L engine

3. Disconnect the battery ground cable.

4. Remove the upper intake manifold.

5. Disconnect the fuel jumper tube-to-fuel rail quick connect coupling.

6. Release the 4 wire harness pin-type retainers from the fuel rail.

7. Release the engine wire harness electrical connector pin-type retainer from the fuel rail.

8. Disconnect the 6 fuel injector electrical connectors.

9. Remove the 4 fuel rail bolts.

10. Remove the fuel rail and injectors as an assembly.

11. Remove the 6 clips and the fuel injectors.

12. Remove and discard the 12 fuel injector O-ring seals.

To install:

➡ Use O-ring seals that are made of special fuel-resistant material. Use of ordinary O-rings can cause the fuel system to leak. Do not reuse the O-ring seals.

➡ The upper and lower fuel injector O-ring seals are similar in appearance, but are not interchangeable.

13. Install new fuel injector O-ring seals and lubricate them with clean engine oil.

14. Install the 6 fuel injectors and clips on the fuel rail.

15. Position the fuel rail and install the bolts, tighten to 89 inch lbs. (10 Nm).

16. Connect the engine wire harness electrical connector pin-type retainers to the fuel rail.

17. Connect the 4 wire harness pin-type retainers to the fuel rail.

18. Connect the fuel jumper tube-to-fuel rail quick connect coupling.

19. Connect the 6 fuel injector electrical connectors.

20. Install the upper intake manifold.

21. Connect the battery ground cable

FUEL TANK

REMOVAL & INSTALLATION

See Figure 296.

✳✳ CAUTION

Do not carry personal electronic devices such as cell phones, pagers or audio equipment of any type when working on or near any fuel-related component. Highly flammable mixtures are always present and may be ignited. Failure to follow these instructions may result in serious personal injury.

✳✳ CAUTION

Do not smoke or carry lighted tobacco or open flame of any type when working on or near any fuel-related components. Highly flammable mixtures are always present and may be ignited. Failure to follow these instructions may result in personal injury.

✳✳ CAUTION

Fuel in the fuel system remains under high pressure even when the engine is not running. Before working on or disconnecting any of the fuel lines or fuel system components, the fuel system pressure must be relieved. Failure to follow these instructions may result in personal injury.

1. Before servicing the vehicle, refer to the Precautions Section.

2. With the vehicle in NEUTRAL, position it on a hoist.

3. Drain the fuel tank.

4. Remove the exhaust muffler and resonator.

5. For AWD vehicles remove the rear driveshaft. Refer to Drive Shaft Removal & Installation in the Drive Train section.

6. Release the clamp and remove the fuel tank filler pipe hose from the fuel tank.

7. Position a suitable lifting device under the fuel tank.

8. Detach the parking brake cable pin-type retainer from the LH fuel tank strap.

9. Detach the wire harness pin-type retainer from the LH fuel tank strap.

10. Remove the 2 bolts and position the 2 fuel tank straps aside.

11. To install, tighten to 41 ft. lbs. (55 Nm).

12. Partially lower the fuel tank enough to disconnect the fuel vapor tube assembly-to-fuel tank quick connect coupling.

13. Completely lower and remove the fuel tank from the vehicle.

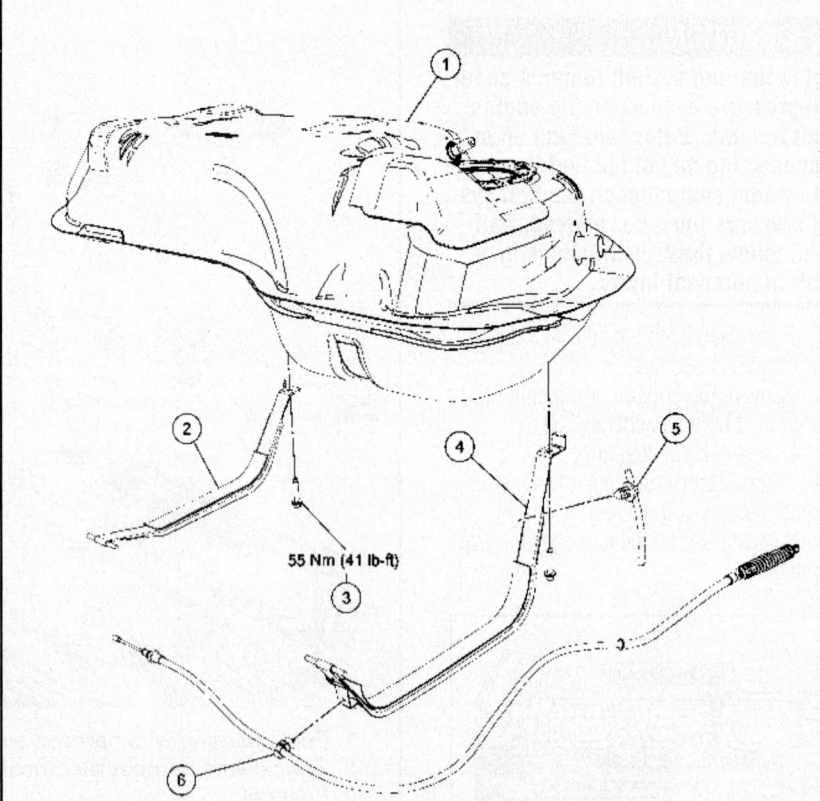

55 Nm (41 lb-ft)

1. Fuel tank
2. RH fuel tank strap
3. Fuel tank strap bolt (2 required)
4. LH fuel tank strap
5. Wire harness pin-type retainer
6. LH parking brake cable pin-type retainer

36578_ESCA_G0310

Fig. 296 Fuel tank

14. To install, reverse the removal procedure and note the following:
- Tighten the filler pipe hose clamp to 35 inch lbs (4 Nm).
- tighten the fuel tank strap retaining bolts to 41 ft. lbs (55 Nm).

IDLE SPEED

ADJUSTMENT

Idle speed is maintained by the Powertrain Control Module (PCM). No adjustment is necessary or possible.

THROTTLE BODY

REMOVAL & INSTALLATION

2.3L Engine

See Figure 297.

1. Before servicing the vehicle, refer to the Precautions Section.

✶✶ WARNING

Throttle body bore and plate area have a special coating and cannot be cleaned, or possible damage to the throttle body can occur.

2. Disconnect the negative battery cable.
3. Remove the air cleaner outlet pipe.
4. Remove the upper snow shield screw and pin-type retainer.
5. Remove the upper snow shield.
6. Detach the accelerator and speed control cables from the throttle body.
7. Disconnect the throttle position sensor electrical connector.
8. Remove the 4 bolts and the throttle body.
9. Inspect the throttle body gasket and install new as necessary.

To install:

10. To install, reverse the removal procedure. Note the following tightening specifications:
- Throttle body bolts: 89 inch lbs. (10 Nm).
- Upper snow shield: 89 inch lbs. (10 Nm).

2.5L Engine

See Figure 298.

1. Before servicing the vehicle, refer to the Precautions Section.
2. Remove the Air Cleaner (ACL) outlet pipe.
3. Disconnect the electrical throttle control electrical connector.

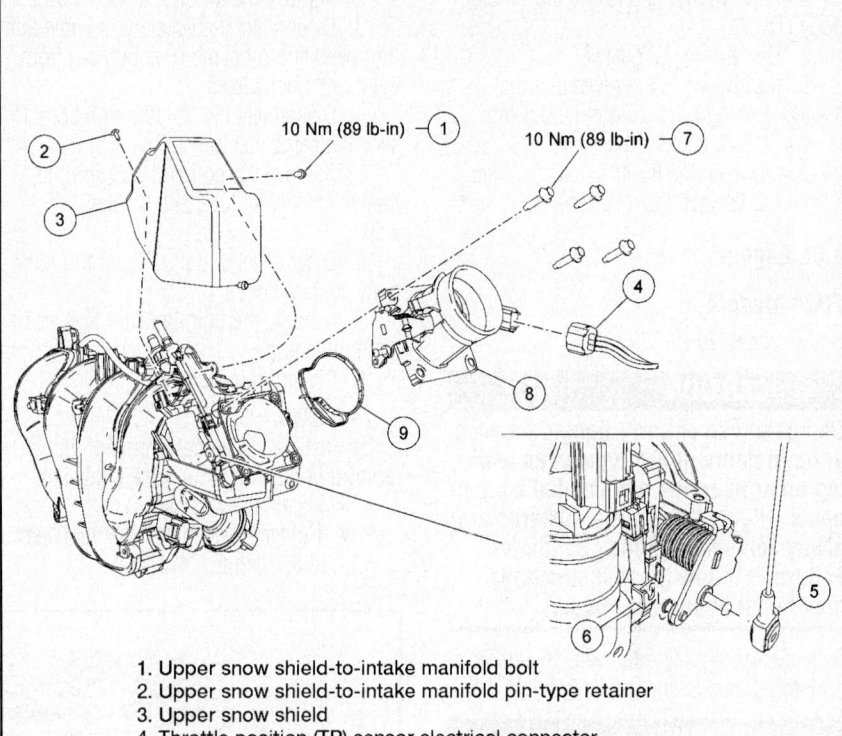

1. Upper snow shield-to-intake manifold bolt
2. Upper snow shield-to-intake manifold pin-type retainer
3. Upper snow shield
4. Throttle position (TP) sensor electrical connector
5. Accelerator cable
6. Speed control cable
7. Throttle body-to-upper intake manifold bolt (4 required)
8. Throttle body
9. Gasket

36578_ESCA_G0313

Fig. 297 Throttle Body (TB)—2.3L engine

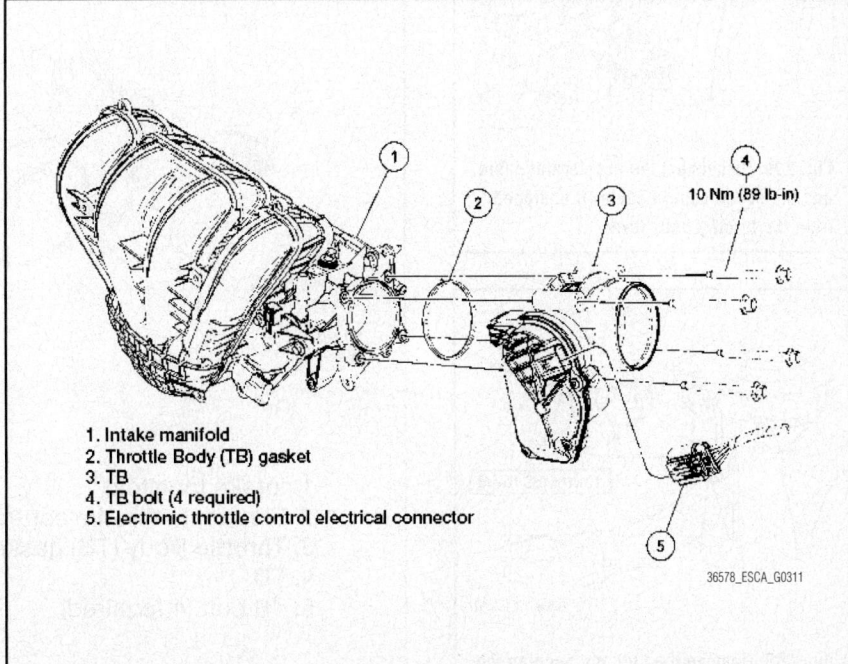

1. Intake manifold
2. Throttle Body (TB) gasket
3. TB
4. TB bolt (4 required)
5. Electronic throttle control electrical connector

36578_ESCA_G0311

Fig. 298 Throttle Body (TB)—2.5L engine

4. Remove the 4 bolts and the Throttle Body (TB).

5. Discard the TB gasket.

6. Installation is the reverse of the removal procedure, noting the following:
- Install a new gasket
- Tighten the throttle body retainers to 89 inch lbs. (10 Nm).

3.0L Engine

2008 Models

See Figures 299 and 300.

> ✴✴ **CAUTION**
>
> **Do not smoke or carry lighted tobacco or open flame of any type when working on or near any fuel-related components. Highly flammable mixtures are always present and may be ignited. Failure to follow these instructions may result in personal injury.**

1. Before servicing the vehicle, refer to the Precautions Section.

> ✴✴ **WARNING**
>
> **Throttle body bore and plate area have a special coating and should not be cleaned.**

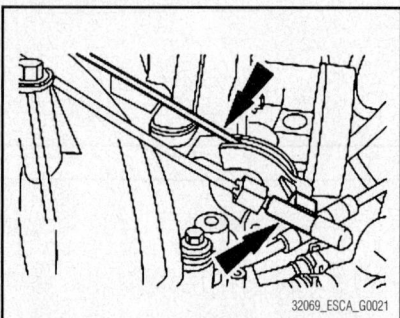

32069_ESCA_G0021

Fig. 299 Disconnect the accelerator cable and the speed control cable (if equipped) from the throttle body lever

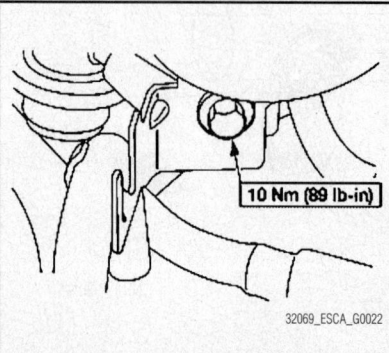

10 Nm (89 lb-in)

32069_ESCA_G0022

Fig. 300 Remove the bolt and position the transmission vent tube and bracket aside

2. Remove the air cleaner outlet tube.

3. Disconnect the accelerator cable and the speed control cable (if equipped) from the throttle body lever.

4. Disconnect the Throttle Position (TP) sensor electrical connector.

5. Remove the bolt and position the transmission vent tube and bracket aside.

6. Disconnect and plug the 2 throttle body coolant hoses.

7. Remove the bolt, the stud bolt and the throttle body.

8. Discard the gasket.

To install:

9. Installation is the reverse of the removal procedure, noting the following:
- Install a new gasket
- Tighten the throttle body retainers to 89 inch lbs. (10 Nm).

- Tighten the transmission vent tube and bracket bolt to 89 inch lbs. (10 Nm).

2009 Models

See Figure 301.

1. Before servicing the vehicle, refer to the Precautions Section.

2. Remove the Air Cleaner (ACL) outlet pipe.

3. Disconnect the electronic throttle control electrical connector.

4. Remove the 4 bolts and the Throttle Body (TB).

5. Discard the TB gasket.

6. Installation is the reverse of the removal procedure, noting the following:
- Install a new gasket
- Tighten the throttle body retainers to 89 inch lbs. (10 Nm).

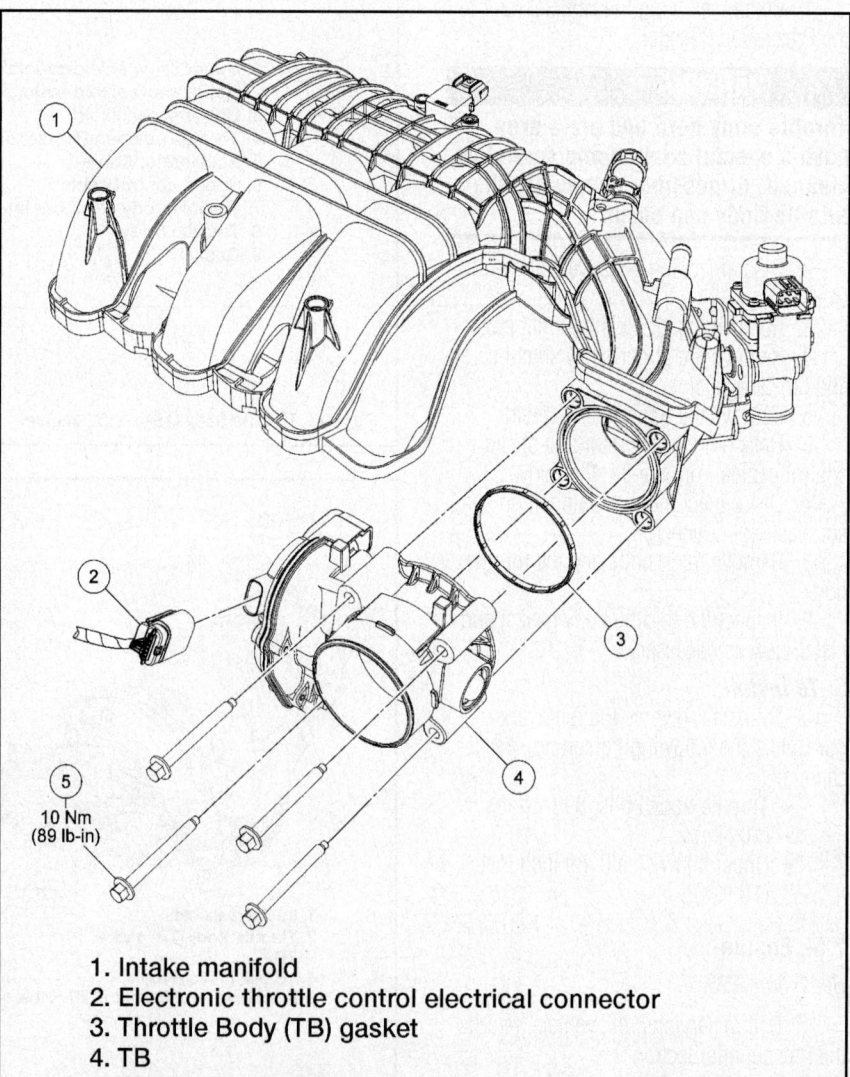

5
10 Nm
(89 lb-in)

1. Intake manifold
2. Electronic throttle control electrical connector
3. Throttle Body (TB) gasket
4. TB
5. TB bolt (4 required)

36578_ESCA_G0312

Fig. 301 Throttle Body (TB)—3.0L engine—2009 model

HEATING & AIR CONDITIONING SYSTEM

BLOWER MOTOR

REMOVAL & INSTALLATION

See Figure 302.

1. Disconnect the blower motor electrical connector.
2. Release the 2 blower motor vent tube clips and pull the vent tube down until it is disengaged from the heater core and evaporator core housing.
3. The carpet below the blower motor must be slightly repositioned to remove the blower motor.
4. Rotate the blower motor counterclockwise to disengage it from the housing and remove the blower motor.
5. To install, reverse the removal procedure.

HEATER CORE

REMOVAL & INSTALLATION

See Figure 303.

1. Before beginning this procedure, refer to the precautions section.

➡ **If a heater core leak is suspected, the heater core must be leak tested before the heater core is removed.**

2. Use only the approved coolant for this vehicle.
3. Remove the heater core and evaporator core housing. Refer to Heater Core & Evaporator Core Housing in this section.
4. Remove the dash panel seal.
5. Remove the heater core bracket screw and the heater core bracket.

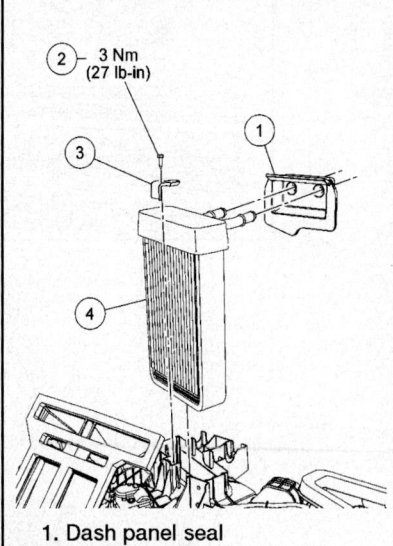

1. Dash panel seal
2. Heater core bracket screw
3. Heater core bracket
4. Heater core

36578_ESCA_G0321

Fig. 303 Heater core mounting

6. Remove the heater core.
7. To install, reverse the removal procedure and note the following:
   • Clean out any antifreeze from the housing.
   • Tighten the heater core bracket retaining screw to 27 inch lbs. (3 Nm).

HEATER CORE & EVAPORATOR CORE HOUSING

REMOVAL & INSTALLATION

See Figures 304 and 305.

1. Before servicing the vehicle, refer to the Precautions Section.
2. Drain the engine coolant.
3. Recover the refrigerant.
4. Position the seats forward and remove the 2 floor console rear bolts
5. Position the seats rearward.
6. Remove the transmission selector lever trim ring.
7. Remove the floor console storage bin.
8. Remove the floor console finish panel.
9. Remove the 8 floor console bolts and remove the floor console.
10. Disarm the supplemental restraint system (SRS).

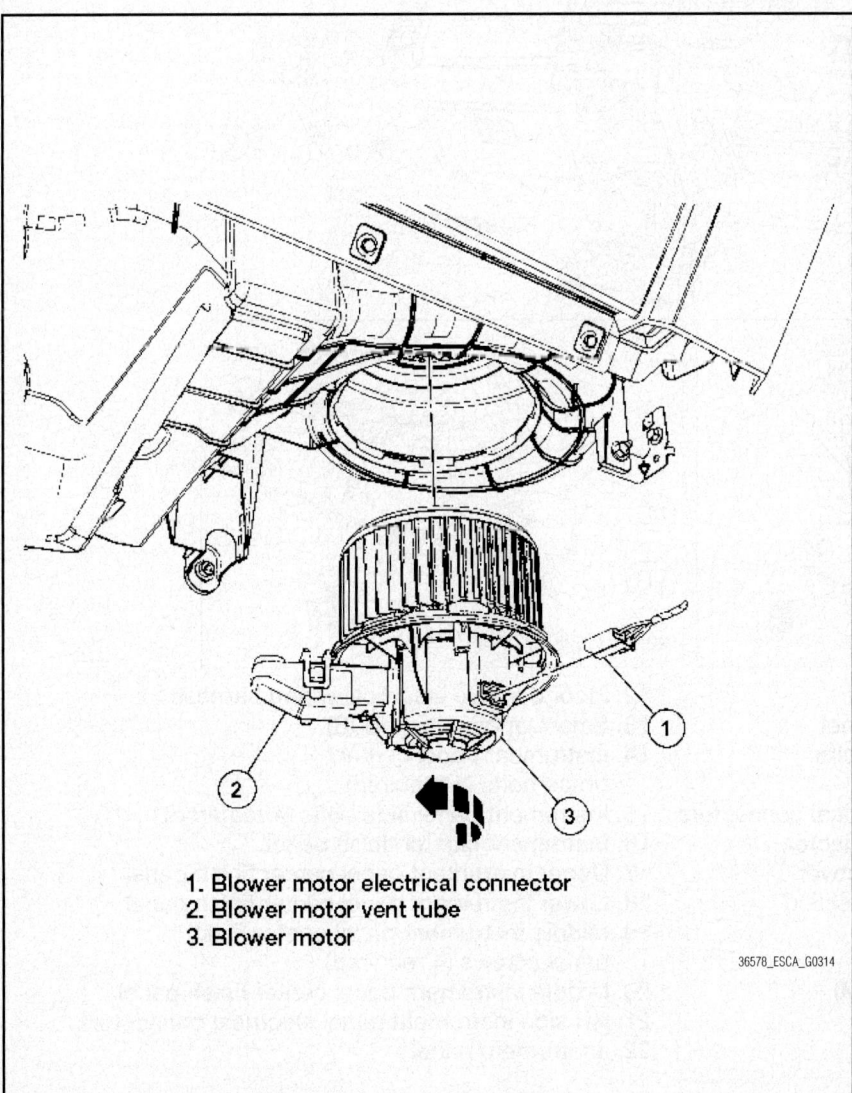

1. Blower motor electrical connector
2. Blower motor vent tube
3. Blower motor

36578_ESCA_G0314

Fig. 302 Blower motor mounting

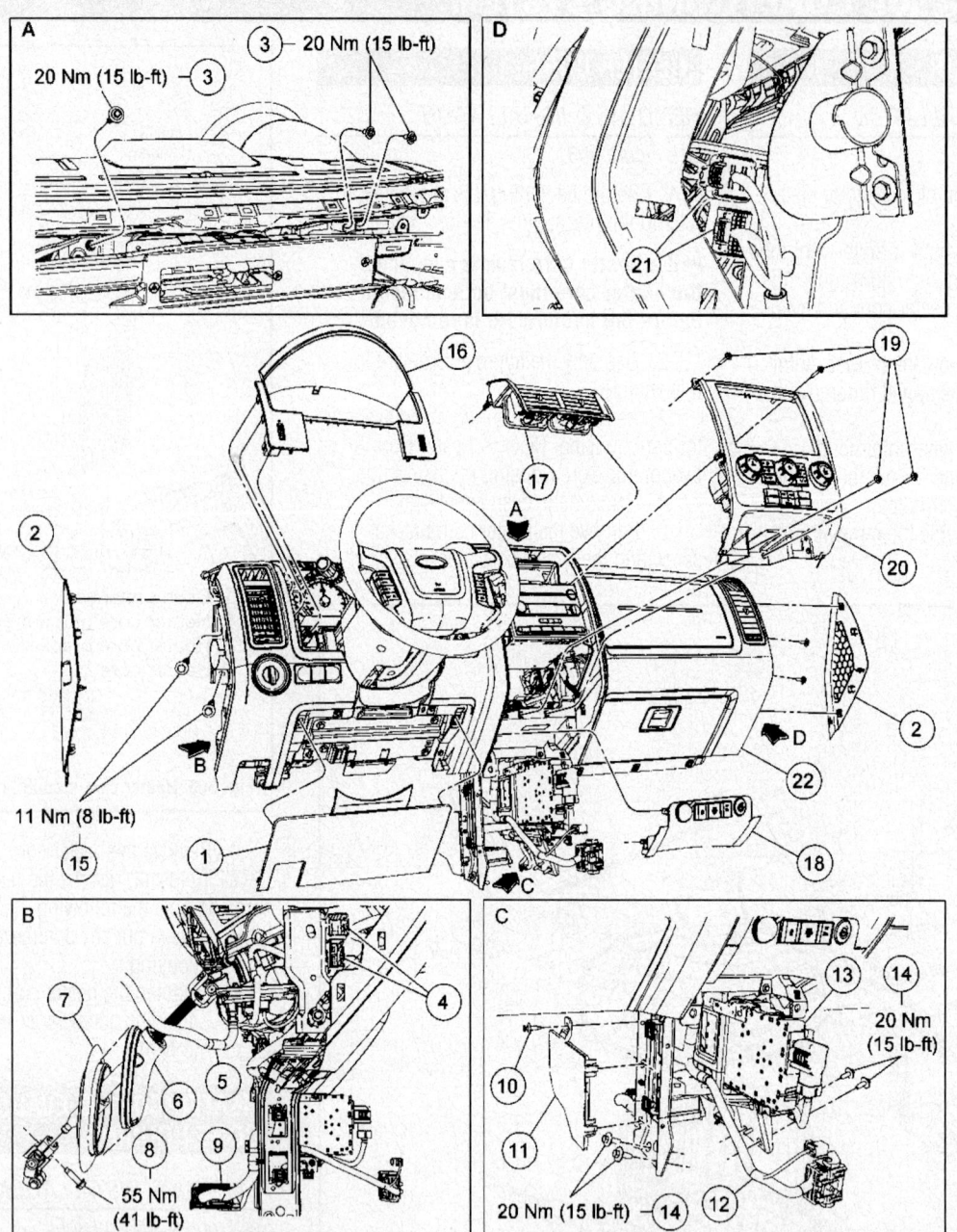

1. Steering column opening cover
2. Instrument panel side finish panel
3. Instrument panel upper cowl bolts
   (3 required)
4. LH side instrument panel electrical connectors
5. Steering module electrical connector
6. Steering column shaft access cover
7. Steering column shaft weather shield
8. Steering column intermediate
   shaft-to-coupling bolt
9. Restraints control module (RCM)
   electrical wiring harness
10. Scrivet
11. RCM access cover
12. Floor console electrical wiring harness
13. Smart junction box (SJB)
14. Instrument panel center
    brace bolts (4 required)
15. Instrument panel side bolts (4 required)
16. Instrument cluster finish panel
17. Upper instrument panel center finish panel
18. Lower instrument panel center finish panel
19. Middle instrument panel center finish
    panel screws (4 required)
20. Middle instrument panel center finish panel
21. RH side instrument panel electrical connectors
22. Instrument panel

22086_ESCA_G0049

Fig. 304 Instrument panel exploded view

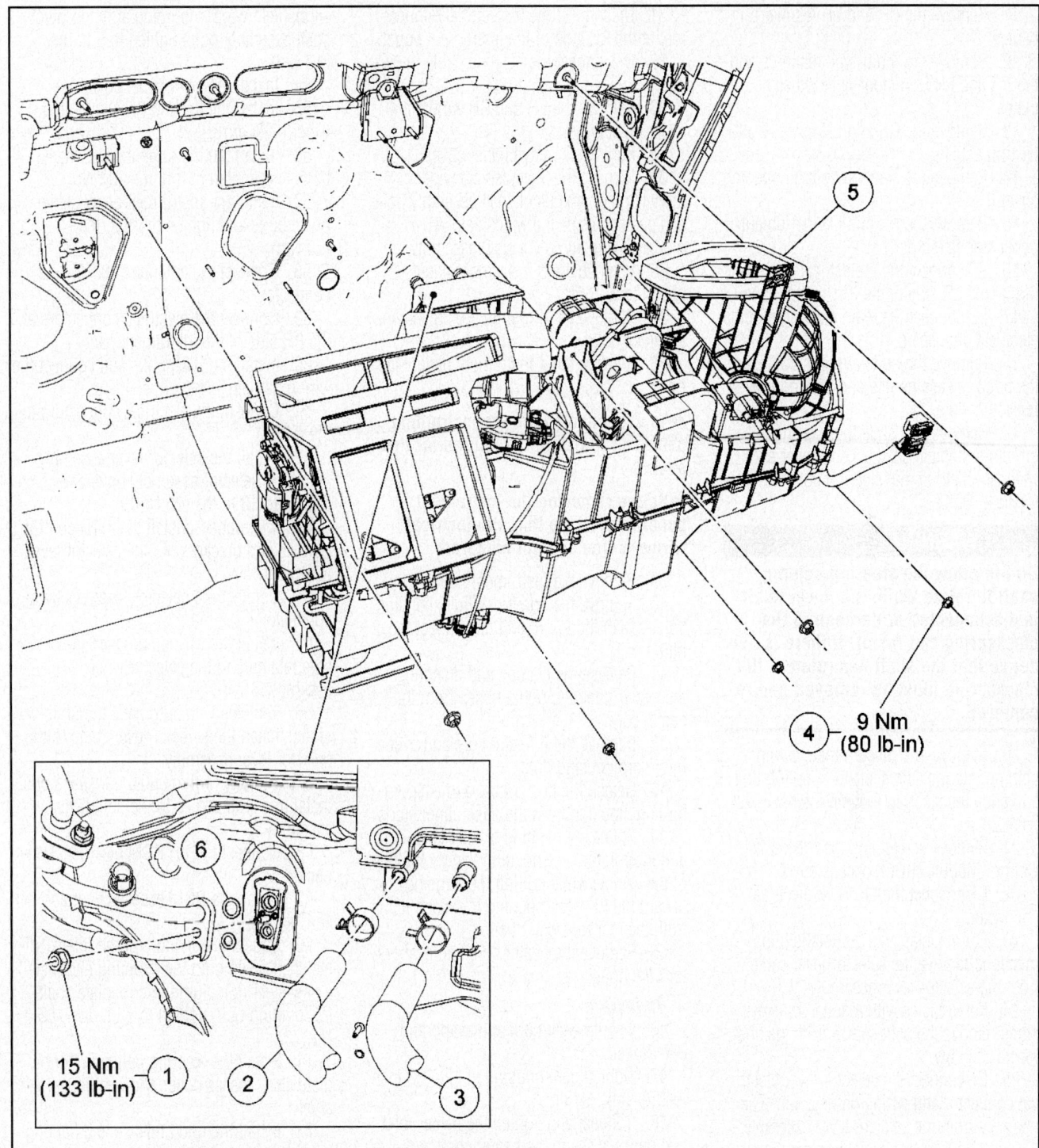

1. Thermostatic Expansion Valve (TXV) fitting nut
2. Heater core inlet hose
3. Heater core outlet hose
4. Heater core and evaporator core housing nut (6 required)
5. Heater core and evaporator core housing
6. TXV fitting gasket seal kit (2 pieces from kit required)

36578_ESCA_G0324

Fig. 305 Heater Core And Evaporator Core Housing

11. Remove the RH and LH A-pillar trim panels.

12. Remove the 4 pin-type retainers and the RH and LH front door opening scuff plates.

13. Remove the RH and LH lower A-pillar trim panels.

14. Remove the steering column opening cover.

15. Remove the RH and LH instrument panel side finish panels.

16. Disconnect the 2 electrical connectors at the LH side of the instrument panel.

17. Disconnect the main steering module electrical connector.

18. Remove the bolts and position aside the hood release handle and parking brake release handle.

19. Remove and slide the steering column intermediate shaft access cover and weather shield up the steering column intermediate shaft.

✳✳ WARNING

Do not allow the steering column shaft to rotate while the lower shaft is disconnected or damage to the clockspring can result. If there is evidence that the shaft has rotated, the clockspring must be removed and re-centered.

20. Remove and discard the steering column intermediate shaft-to-coupling bolt and slide the steering column intermediate shaft up.

21. Remove scrivet and the Restraints Control Module (RCM) access cover.

22. Disconnect the LH RCM electrical connector.

23. For vehicles with automatic transmissions remove the selector lever cable from the selector lever assembly.

24. For vehicles with manual transmissions remove the shift cables from the shift lever assembly.

25. Disconnect the selector lever electrical connector and wiring harness pin-type retainers from the selector lever assembly.

26. If equipped, remove and position aside the Four Wheel Drive (4WD) control module and bracket from the selector lever assembly.

27. Remove the 4 selector lever assembly bolts and remove the selector lever assembly.

28. Disconnect the electrical connectors from the Smart Junction Box (SJB).

29. Disconnect the wiring harness pin-type retainers.

30. Remove the SJB lower bolts and the SJB.

31. Disconnect the 2 electrical connectors at the RH side of the instrument panel.

32. Disconnect the antenna cable in-line connector

33. Remove the LH and RH windshield wiper pivot arms.

34. Remove the cowl panel cover

35. Remove the 3 windshield wiper mounting arm and pivot shaft assembly bolts and position aside the windshield wiper mounting arm and pivot shaft assembly.

36. Remove the 3 instrument panel upper cowl bolts.

37. Remove the 4 instrument panel center brace bolts

38. Remove the 4 instrument panel side bolts.

➡**To avoid damage to the instrument panel, an assistant is required for this step.**

➡**Before removing the instrument panel, make sure that all electrical wiring is free and not hindered**

39. Remove the instrument panel.

40. Remove the Thermostatic Expansion Valve (TXV) fitting nut and disconnect the fitting.

41. Release the clamps and disconnect the heater inlet and outlet hoses from the heater core.

42. Remove the 6 heater core and evaporator core housing nuts.

43. Detach the heater core and evaporator core housing from the dash panel studs.

44. Rotate the RH side of the heater core and evaporator core housing toward the rear of the vehicle while pulling the housing toward the RH door opening to detach it from the rear foot well duct.

45. Remove the heater core and evaporator core housing

To install:

46. Install heater core and evaporator core housing.

47. Tighten core housing nuts to 80 inch lbs. (9 Nm).

48. Connect and tighten the heater inlet and outlet hoses to the heater core.

49. Install the thermostatic expansion valve (TXV) fitting nut and disconnect the fitting.

50. Install the instrument panel.

51. Install 2 instrument panel side bolts, one on each side, to hold the instrument panel in place.

52. Install the 3 instrument panel upper cowl bolts and tighten to 15 ft. lbs. (20 Nm).

53. Install the windshield wiper mounting arm and pivot shaft assembly and the 3

windshield wiper mounting arm and pivot shaft assembly bolts tighten to 9 ft. lbs. (12 Nm).

54. Install the cowl panel cover.

55. Install the LH and RH windshield wiper pivot arms.

56. Install the instrument panel side bolts and tighten to 8 ft. lbs. (11 Nm).

57. Install the instrument panel center brace bolts and tighten to 15 ft. lbs. (20 Nm).

58. Connect the antenna cable in-line connector.

59. Connect the electrical connectors at the RH side of the instrument panel

60. Install the SJB, bolts and connect the wiring harness pin-type retainers.

61. Connect the electrical connectors to the SJB.

62. Install the selector lever assembly and the 4 selector assembly bolts and tighten to 18 ft. lbs (25 Nm).

63. If equipped, install the 4WD control module and bracket onto the selector lever assembly.

64. Connect the selector lever electrical connector.

65. Install the wiring harness pin-type retainers to the selector lever assembly.

66. Vehicles with automatic transmissions, install the selector lever cable to the selector lever assembly.

67. Vehicles with manual transmissions, install the shift cables to the shift lever assembly.

68. Connect the LH RCM electrical connector

69. Install the RCM access cover and scrivet

70. Slide the steering column intermediate shaft down onto the coupling and install a new steering column intermediate shaft-to-coupling bolt, tighten to 42 ft. lbs. (55 Nm).

71. Install the steering column intermediate shaft access cover and weather shield.

72. Install the hood release and parking brake release handles and bolts.

73. Connect the main steering module electrical connector.

74. Connect the electrical connectors at the LH side of the instrument panel

75. Install the RH and LH instrument panel side finish panels

76. Install the steering column opening cover.

77. Install the RH and LH lower A-pillar trim panels.

78. Install the RH and LH A-pillar trim panels

79. Install the RH and LH front door opening scuff plates and the 4 pin-type retainers.
80. Rearm the SRS.
81. Install the 8 floor console bolts and the floor console.

82. Install the floor console finish panel.
83. Install the floor console storage bin.
84. Install the transmission selector lever trim ring.

85. Install and tighten the floor console rear bolts to 62 inch. lbs (7 Nm).
86. Evacuate, leak test and charge the refrigerant system.
87. Refill and bleed cooling system.

STEERING

MANUAL RACK & PINION STEERING GEAR

REMOVAL & INSTALLATION

See Figures 306 and 307.

➡The rack and pinion steering gear that is used with the Electronic Power Assist Steering (EPAS) system is a manual (non-hydraulic) steering gear that is contained within a 1-piece die cast aluminum housing. The power assist is provided by a 12-volt, 65 amp brush-less motor, mounted to the steering column. The steering column and motor/module are serviced as an assembly.

1. Before servicing the vehicle, refer to the Precautions Section.
2. Remove the front wheels and tires.
3. Turn the ignition key to the OFF position. Remove the ignition key.

❊ WARNING

Do not allow the steering wheel to rotate while the intermediate shaft is disconnected or damage to the clockspring can result. If there is evidence that the shaft has rotated, the clockspring must be removed and re-centered

4. Remove and discard the steering column coupling-to-steering gear bolt and disconnect the coupling from the steering gear.

5. From the engine compartment, loosen the 2 steering gear bolts.
6. If equipped, remove the 3 pin-type retainers and the steering gear shield.
7. Remove and discard the 2 outer tie-rod end nuts.
8. Do not use a hammer to separate the tie-rod end from the wheel knuckle or damage to the wheel knuckle can result.
9. Using a suitable tool, separate the tie-rod ends from the wheel knuckles.
10. For AWD vehicles, remove the rear transaxle insulator through bolt.

11. For FWD vehicles with the 2.3L engine and an automatic transaxle, remove the 3 transmission damper bolts and the transmission damper.
12. Remove and discard the 2 steering gear bolts.

➡**For All Wheel Drive (AWD) vehicles, it is necessary to grasp the driveshaft by hand and apply slight downward pressure to obtain clearance for the removal of the steering gear.**

13. Remove the steering gear from the LH side of the vehicle.

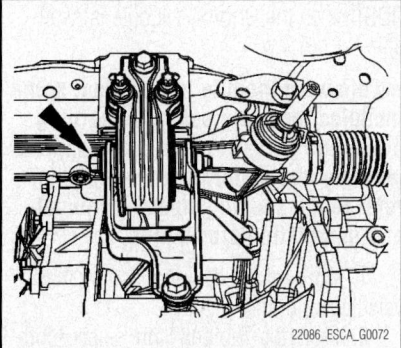

Fig. 306 Rear transaxle insulator and through bolt

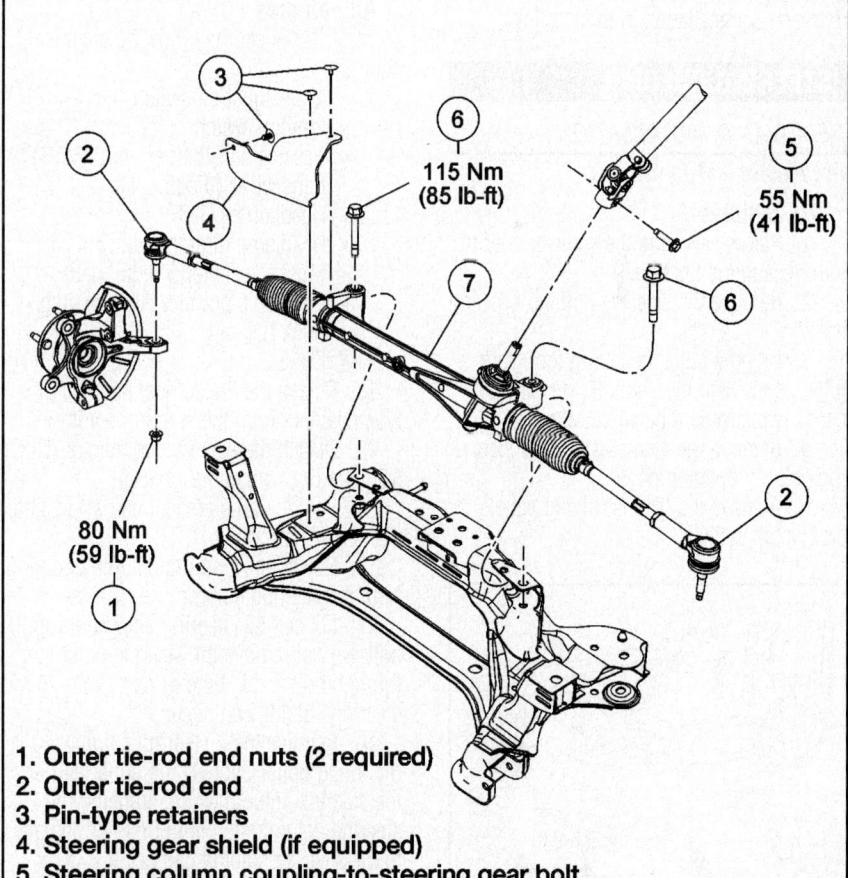

1. Outer tie-rod end nuts (2 required)
2. Outer tie-rod end
3. Pin-type retainers
4. Steering gear shield (if equipped)
5. Steering column coupling-to-steering gear bolt
6. Steering gear bolts (2 required)
7. Steering gear

Fig. 307 Steering gear exploded view—2008–models

To install:

14. To install, reverse the removal procedure and note the following:

    a. Install a new steering column coupling-to-steering gear bolt and tighten to 41 ft. lbs. (55 Nm).

    b. Install and tighten the 2 steering gear bolts to 85 ft. lbs. (115 Nm).

    c. Install new outer tie-rod end nuts and tighten to 59 ft. lbs. (80 Nm).

    d. Tighten rear transaxle insulator through bolt to 66 ft. lbs. (90 Nm).

    e. Tighten transmission damper bolts to 30 ft. lbs. (40 Nm). (2.3L engines)

15. Check and, if necessary, align the front end.

POWER STEERING PUMP

REMOVAL & INSTALLATION

The power assist is provided by a 12-volt, 65 amp brush-less motor, mounted to the steering column. The steering column and motor/module are serviced as an assembly. Refer to Steering Column Removal & Installation in this section.

STEERING COLUMN

REMOVAL & INSTALLATION

See Figures 308 and 309.

All vehicles

1. Before servicing the vehicle, refer to the Precautions Section.

2. Remove the steering column opening trim.

3. Using a suitable cutting tool, carefully cut through the 2 cutoff lines and discard the instrument panel cutoff panel.

4. Remove the 4 screws and the steering column opening panel.

5. Remove the LH instrument panel side finish panel.

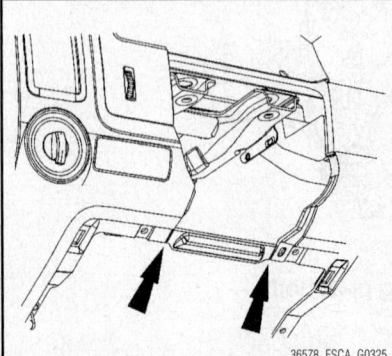

36578_ESCA_G0325

Fig. 308 Carefully cut through the 2 cutoff lines and discard the instrument panel cutoff panel.

6. Through the side finish panel opening, remove the ground wire eyelet bolt. Position the 2 ground wire eyelets and wires aside.

7. Through the side finish panel opening, disconnect the 2 instrument panel wiring harness electrical connectors and, if equipped, the battery high-voltage jumper switch electrical connector. Position the harnesses and connectors aside.

8. Turn the ignition switch to the ON position and rotate the steering wheel clockwise until the steering column coupling-to-steering column bolt is accessible.

9. Through the side finish panel opening, remove and discard the steering column coupling-to-steering column bolt.

10. Remove the clockspring. Refer to Clockspring Removal & Installation in the Chassis Electrical section.

Vehicles with manual transmission

11. Rotate the Clutch Pedal Position (CPP) switch clockwise and position the switch aside.

All vehicles

12. Disconnect the following electrical connectors:

- Multi-function switch
- Ignition switch
- Passive anti-theft system (PATS) transceiver (if equipped)
- Headlamp switch
- Headlamp dimmer adjuster
- Message center (if equipped)
- Electronic power assist steering (EPAS) 6-pin
- EPAS 2-pin

13. Detach the 2 electrical harness pin-type retainers from the steering column.

14. Detach the data link connector (DLC) from the DLC mounting bracket.

15. Position all electrical harnesses and connector's aside.

16. Detach the steering column coupling from the steering column.

17. Loosen the steering column through bolt. Do not remove the steering column through bolt at this time or damage to the steering column can occur.

18. Remove the 2 steering column mounting bolts. Support the upper end of the steering column while removing the 2 steering column mounting bolts or damage to the steering column can occur.

✳✳ WARNING

Do not release the tilting mechanism while lowering the steering column or damage to the steering column can occur.

19. Carefully lower the upper end of the steering column.

20. Remove the steering column through bolt and carefully remove the steering column through the steering column opening. Support the lower end of the steering column while removing the through bolt or damage to the steering column can occur.

✳✳ WARNING

Do not allow the steering column upper and lower halves to become separated. If the column halves become separated, make sure that the upper and lower column shaft master (larger) splines are correctly aligned. Once the splines are correctly aligned, the column halves will slide together easily using hands only. Do not force the upper and lower column halves together or damage to the column may occur.

21. To install, reverse the removal procedure and note the following:

- Tighten the steering column through bolt 18 ft. lbs. (25 Nm).
- Tighten the 2 steering column mounting bolts to 21 ft. lbs. (28 Nm).
- Tighten the steering column coupling-to-steering column bolt to 41 ft. lbs. (55 Nm).
- Tighten the steering column opening panel screws to (71 inch lbs. (8 Nm).

22. Reconfigure the EPAS module. For additional information refer to Programmable Module Installation.

Calibrate the steering wheel position sensor. For additional information, refer to Steering Wheel Position Sensor Calibration.

PROGRAMMABLE MODULE INSTALLATION (PMI) PROCEDURE

Programmable Module Installation (PMI) Using the Integrated Diagnostic System (IDS) When the Original Module is Available.

➡**Following module installation, some modules require a separate learning procedure be carried out. For adaptive learning and calibration instructions, refer to the specific module removal and installation procedures.**

1. Connect the IDS and identify the vehicle as normal.

2. From the Toolbox icon, select Module Programming and press the check mark.

3. Select Programmable Module Installation.

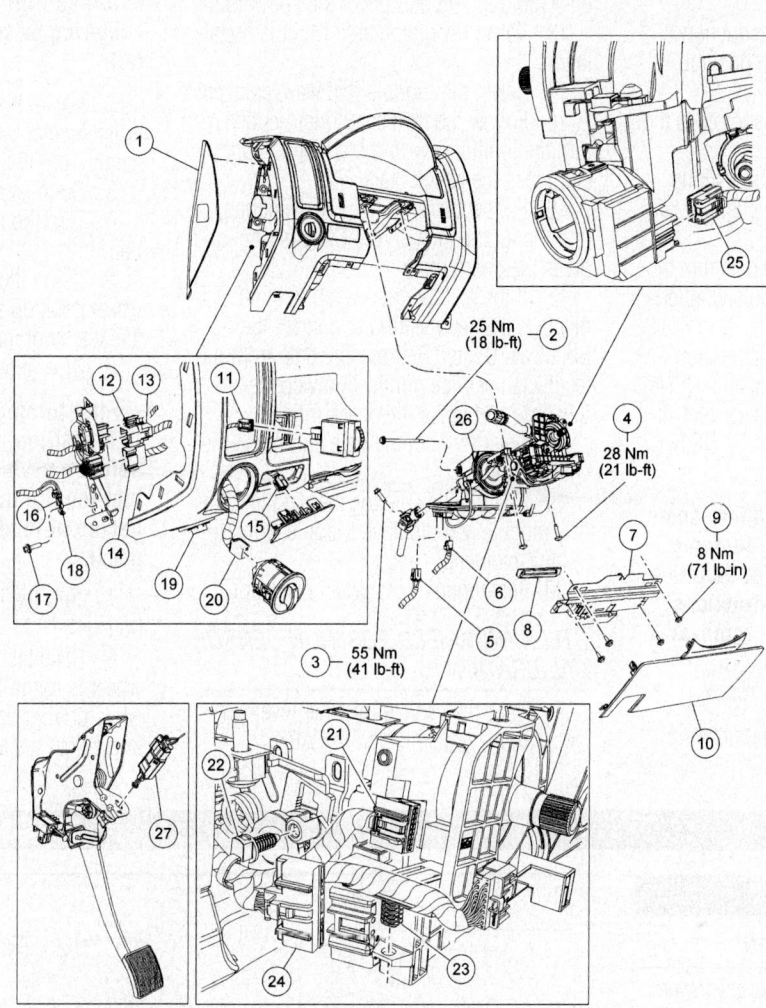

25 Nm
(18 lb-ft)

28 Nm
(21 lb-ft)

8 Nm
(71 lb-in)

55 Nm
(41 lb-ft)

1. Instrument panel side finish panel
2. Steering column through bolt
3. Steering column coupling-to-steering column bolt
4. Steering column mounting bolt (2 required)
5. Electronic power assist steering (EPAS) 2-pin electrical connector
6. EPAS 6-pin electrical connector
7. Steering column opening panel
8. Instrument panel cutoff panel
9. Steering column opening panel bolt (4 required)
10. Steering column opening trim
11. Headlamp dimmer adjuster switch electrical connector
12. Battery high-voltage jumper switch electrical connector (if equipped)
13. Instrument panel wiring harness electrical connector
14. Instrument panel wiring harness electrical connector
15. Message center electrical connector (if equipped)
16. Ground wire eyelet bolt
17. Ground wire eyelet
18. Ground wire eyelet
19. Data link connector (DLC)
20. Headlamp switch electrical connector
21. Multi-function switch electrical connector
22. Pin-type harness retainer
23. Pin-type harness retainer
24. Ignition switch electrical connector
25. Passive anti-theft system (PATS) transceiver electrical connector
26. Steering column assembly
27. Clutch pedal position (CPP) switch

36578_ESCA_G0326

Fig. 309 Steering Column

4. Select the module that is being replaced.

5. Follow the on-screen instructions, turn the ignition key to the OFF position, and press the check mark.

6. Install the new module and press the check mark.

7. Follow the on-screen instructions, turn the ignition key to the ON position, and press the check mark.

8. The IDS downloads the data into the new module and displays Module Configuration Complete.

9. Test module for correct operation Programmable Module Installation (PMI) Using the Integrated Diagnostic System (IDS) When the Original Module is NOT Available.

➡**Following module installation, some modules require a separate learning procedure be carried out. For adaptive learning and calibration instructions, refer to the specific module removal and installation procedures.**

10. Install the new module.

11. Connect the IDS and identify the vehicle as normal.

12. From the Toolbox icon, select Module Programming and press the check mark.

13. Select Programmable Module Installation.

14. Select the module that was replaced.

15. Follow the on-screen instructions, turn the ignition key to the OFF position, and press the check mark.

16. Follow the on-screen instructions, turn the ignition key to the ON position, and press the check mark.

17. If the data is not available, the IDS displays a screen stating to contact the As-Built Data Center. Retrieve the data from the technician service publication website at this time and press the check mark.

18. Enter the module data and press the check mark.

19. The IDS downloads the data into the new module and displays Module Configuration Complete.

20. Test module for correct operation.

STEERING WHEEL POSITION SENSOR CALIBRATION

1. Place the vehicle on a flat level surface with the transmission in PARK.

➡**Make sure that the steering wheel is turned from right to left before centering or sensor calibration will fail.**

2. Rotate the steering wheel from right to left, center the steering wheel and remove hands from the wheel.

3. Connect the scan tool to the vehicle.

4. Turn the ignition key to the RUN position.

5. Using the scan tool, select steering wheel position sensor calibration and follow the scan tool instructions.

6. Clear any PSCM DTCs.

➡**After turning the ignition key to the OFF position, wait at least 25 seconds before carrying out any procedures that require the battery to be disconnected or module memory loss may occur.**

7. Turn the ignition key to the OFF position.

8. Road test the vehicle. If the steering wheel is not in the straight ahead position while driving on a flat road surface, check and adjust the alignment as necessary.

SUSPENSION   FRONT SUSPENSION

LOWER BALL JOINT

REMOVAL & INSTALLATION

The lower ball joint is part of the lower control arm assembly.

LOWER CONTROL ARM

REMOVAL & INSTALLATION

See Figure 310.

➡**Suspension fasteners are critical parts because they affect performance of vital components and systems and their failure may result in major service expense. New parts must be installed with the same part numbers or equivalent part, if replacement is necessary. Do not use a replacement part of lesser quality or substitute design. Torque values must be used as specified during reassembly to make sure correct retention of these parts.**

1. Before servicing the vehicle, refer to the Precautions Section.

2. Record the ride height.

➡**For reference during the installation of the lower arm, measure the distance between the center of the wheel hub and the lip of the fender with the**

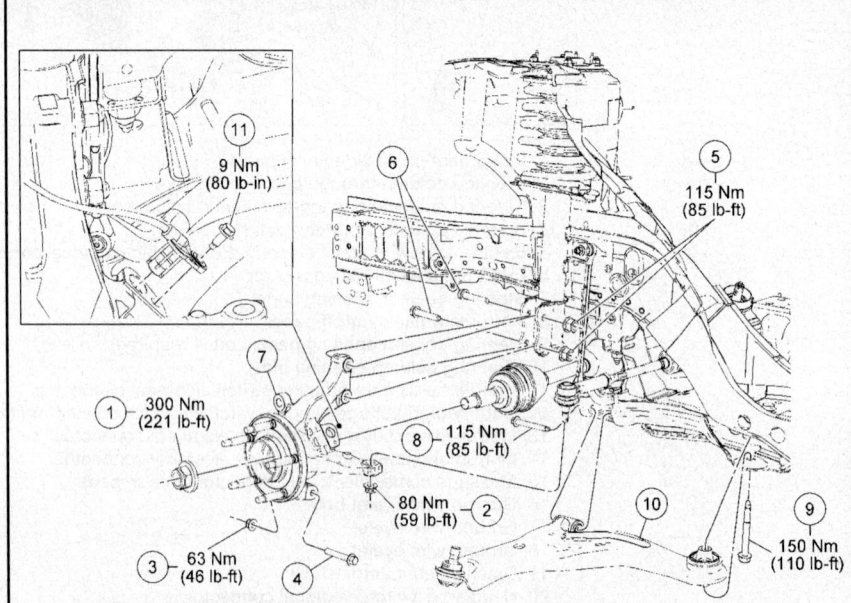

1. Wheel hub nut
2. Tie-rod end nut
3. Lower ball joint nut
4. Lower ball joint pinch bolt
5. Strut-to-knuckle nuts (2 required)
6. Strut-to-knuckle bolts (2 required)
7. Wheel knuckle
8. Lower arm forward bolt
9. Lower arm rearward bolt
10. Lower arm
11. Wheel speed sensor bolt

36578_ESCA_G0331

Fig. 310 Front suspension—exploded view

weight of the vehicle resting on the wheel and tire assemblies.

3. Remove the wheel and tire.

4. Remove and discard the lower ball joint nut and bolt.

5. Separate the lower ball joint from the wheel knuckle.

6. Remove and discard the lower arm forward bolt.

7. Using a suitable jackstand, support the subframe.

8. Remove the lower arm rearward bolt and the lower arm.

To install:

9. Position the lower arm and loosely install the new front and rear lower arm bolts.

10. Remove the jackstand.

11. Position the wheel knuckle on the lower ball joint and install the new lower ball joint bolt and nut. Tighten to 46 ft. lbs. (63 Nm).

12. Position a floor jack under the lower ball joint and raise it until the previously recorded ride height is achieved.

13. Tighten the lower arm forward bolt to 85 ft. lbs. (115 Nm).

14. Tighten the lower arm rearward bolt to 110 ft. lbs. (150 Nm).

15. Check and, if necessary, align the front end.

STABILIZER BAR

REMOVAL & INSTALLATION

See Figure 311.

➡Suspension fasteners are critical parts because they affect performance of vital components and systems and their failure may result in major service expense. New parts must be installed with the same part numbers or equivalent part, if replacement is necessary. Do not use a replacement part of lesser quality or substitute design. Torque values must be used as specified during reassembly to make sure correct retention of these parts.

1. Before servicing the vehicle, refer to the Precautions Section.

2. Remove the stabilizer bar bushing bracket bolts.

3. Remove the tires.

➡Use the hex holding feature to prevent the ball stud from turning while removing or installing the stabilizer link nut.

4. Remove the 2 lower stabilizer bar link nuts.

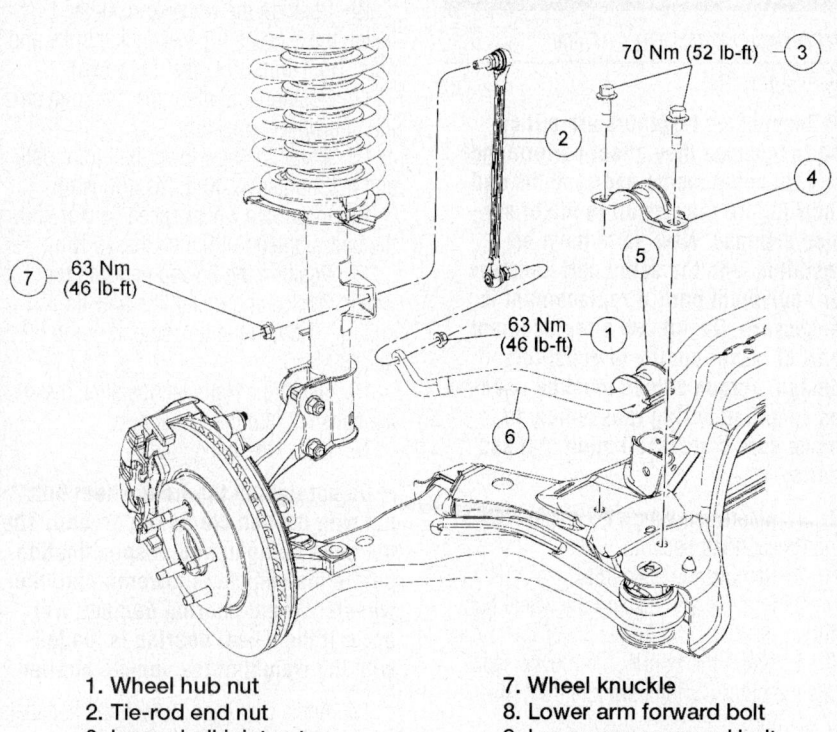

1. Wheel hub nut
2. Tie-rod end nut
3. Lower ball joint nut
4. Lower ball joint pinch bolt
5. Strut-to-knuckle nuts (2 required)
6. Strut-to-knuckle bolts (2 required)
7. Wheel knuckle
8. Lower arm forward bolt
9. Lower arm rearward bolt
10. Lower arm
11. Wheel speed sensor bolt

36578_ESCA_G0332

Fig. 311 Front suspension—exploded view

➡Access the stabilizer bar through the left wheel opening.

5. Remove the stabilizer bar.

6. To install, reverse the removal procedure. Observe the following torques:
- Link nuts: 46 ft. lbs. (63 Nm)
- Bushing bracket bolts: 52 ft. lbs. (70 Nm)

➡When installing the stabilizer link to the stabilizer bar, make sure the stabilizer bar is perpendicular to the stabilizer link when tightening the link nut or the link nut may not seat properly.

STABILIZER LINKS

REMOVAL & INSTALLATION

See Figure 311.

➡Suspension fasteners are critical parts because they affect performance of vital components and systems and their failure may result in major service expense. New parts must be installed with the same part numbers or equivalent part, if replacement is necessary. Do not use a replacement part of lesser quality or substitute design. Torque values must be used as specified during reassembly to make sure correct retention of these parts.

1. Before servicing the vehicle, refer to the Precautions Section.

2. Raise and support vehicle

3. Remove the wheel and tire.

➡Use the hex holding feature to prevent the ball stud from turning while removing or installing the stabilizer bar link nut.

4. Remove the upper stabilizer bar link nut.

5. Remove the lower stabilizer bar link nut.

6. Remove the stabilizer bar link.

7. Inspect the stabilizer bar link ball joints and boots for wear. If necessary, install new parts.

To install:

8. Install the stabilizer bar link.

9. Tighten the upper and lower stabilizer bar link nut to 46 ft. lbs. (63 Nm).

10. Install the wheel and tire.

11. Lower vehicle

STEERING KNUCKLE

REMOVAL & INSTALLATION

See Figure 312.

➡Suspension fasteners are critical parts because they affect performance of vital components and systems and their failure may result in major service expense. New parts must be installed with the same part numbers or equivalent part, if replacement is necessary. Do not use a replacement part of lesser quality or substitute design. Torque values must be used as specified during reassembly to make sure correct retention of these parts.

1. Before servicing the vehicle, refer to the Precautions Section.
2. Remove the brake disc.
3. Remove and discard the wheel hub nut.
4. Using the front hub remover, separate the outer CV joint spindle from the wheel hub.

✳✳ WARNING

Do not use a hammer to separate the tie-rod end from the wheel knuckle or damage to the wheel knuckle can result. Do not damage the tie-rod end boot while installing the special tool.

5. Separate the tie-rod from the wheel knuckle.
6. Remove the lower ball joint pinch bolt nut and the pinch bolt.
7. Remove the wheel speed sensor bolt and position the sensor aside.
8. Separate the lower ball joint from the wheel knuckle.
9. Remove the 2 strut-to-knuckle nuts, bolts and the wheel knuckle.

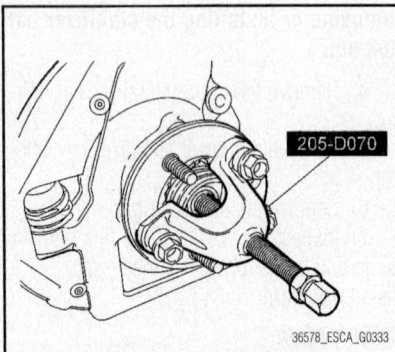

205-D070

36578_ESCA_G0333

Fig. 312 Using the front hub remover, separate the outer CV joint spindle from the wheel hub

To install:

10. Position the wheel knuckle and install the 2 new strut-to-knuckle bolts and nuts. Tighten to 85 ft. lbs. (115 Nm).
11. Position and align the ball joint stud into the wheel knuckle.
12. Install the new lower ball joint bolt and nut, tighten to 46 ft. lbs. (63 Nm).
13. Install the wheel speed sensor and the bolt, tighten to 80 inch lbs. (9 Nm).
14. Position the tie-rod end into the wheel knuckle and install the new tie-rod end nut. Tighten the tie-rod end nut to 59 ft. lbs. (80 Nm).
15. Using the Halfshaft Installer, install the halfshaft into the wheel hub.
16. Install the brake disc.

➡Do not tighten the front wheel hub nut with the vehicle on the ground. The nut must be tightened to specification before the vehicle is lowered onto the wheels. Wheel bearing damage will occur if the wheel bearing is loaded with the weight of the vehicle applied.

17. Apply the brake to keep the halfshaft from rotating. Install the new front wheel hub nut and tighten to 221 ft. lbs. (300 Nm).
18. Check and, if necessary, align the front end.

STRUT

REMOVAL & INSTALLATION

See Figure 313.

➡Suspension fasteners are critical parts because they affect performance of vital components and systems and their failure may result in major service expense. New parts must be installed with the same part numbers or equivalent part, if replacement is necessary. Do not use a replacement part of lesser quality or substitute design. Torque values must be used as specified during reassembly to make sure correct retention of these parts.

1. Before servicing the vehicle, refer to the Precautions Section.
2. Verify the steering wheel is in the unlocked position before removal.
3. Remove the wheel and tire.
4. Remove the brake jounce hose clip.
5. Pull the brake jounce hose downward slightly to remove the hose from the bracket and position the brake jounce hose aside.
6. Remove the wheel speed sensor harness bolt.

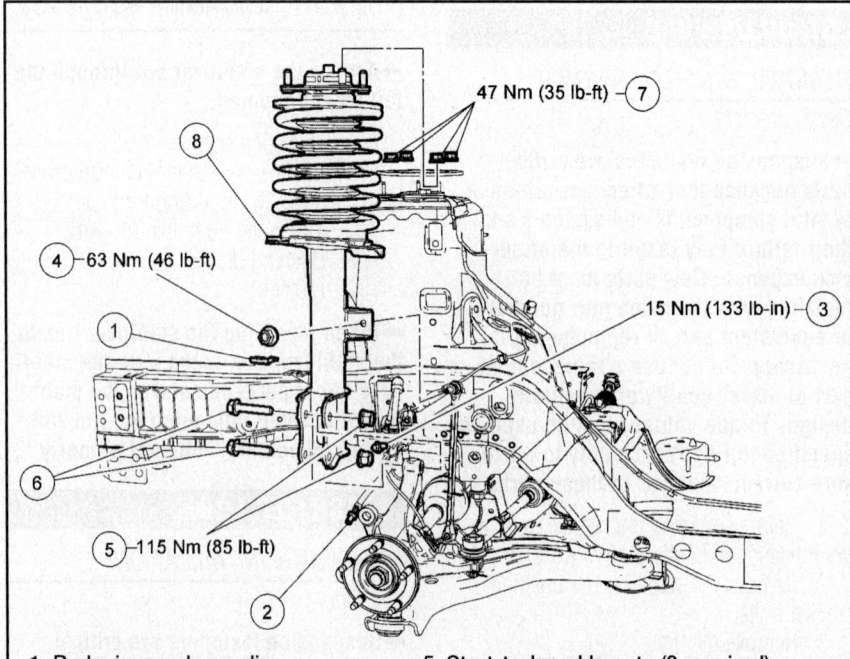

1. Brake jounce hose clip
2. Brake jounce hose (LH/RH)
3. Wheel speed sensor harness bolt
4. Upper stabilizer bar link nut
5. Strut-to-knuckle nuts (2 required)
6. Strut-to-knuckle bolts (2 required)
7. Strut upper bushing nuts (4 required)
8. Strut and spring assembly

36578_ESCA_G0334

Fig. 313 Strut and spring assembly

➡Use the hex-holding feature to prevent the ball stud from turning while removing or installing the stabilizer bar link nut.

7. Remove and discard the upper stabilizer bar link nut.

8. Remove and discard the 2 strut-to-knuckle nuts and bolts.

9. Reference mark the 4 strut upper bushing plate nuts.

10. Remove and discard the 4 strut upper bushing nuts.

➡Do not allow the axle shaft to move outboard. Over-extension of the tripod Constant Velocity (CV) joint can result in the separation of internal parts, causing failure of the axle shaft.

11. Remove the strut and spring assembly.

To install:

12. Position the strut and spring assembly upper mounting plate into the inner fender.

13. Align the 4 new strut upper bushing nuts to the reference marks and tighten to 35 ft. lbs. (47 Nm).

14. Install the 2 new strut-to-knuckle bolts and nuts. Tighten to 85 ft. lbs. (115 Nm).

15. Install the new upper stabilizer bar link nut and tighten to 46 ft. lbs. (63 Nm).

16. Install the wheel speed sensor harness bolt and tighten to 133 inch lbs. (15 Nm).

17. Position the brake jounce hose to the bracket and install the brake jounce hose clip.

18. Check the front end alignment and adjust as necessary.

WHEEL BEARINGS

REMOVAL & INSTALLATION

See Figures 314 through 319.

➡If removing the wheel hub, a new wheel bearing must be installed.

1. Before servicing the vehicle, refer to the Precautions Section.

➡If removing the wheel hub, the wheel bearing must be replaced.

2. Remove the wheel knuckle.

3. Using the special tool, press the wheel hub from the wheel bearing.

➡This step may not be necessary if the inner wheel bearing race remains in the wheel knuckle after removing the wheel hub.

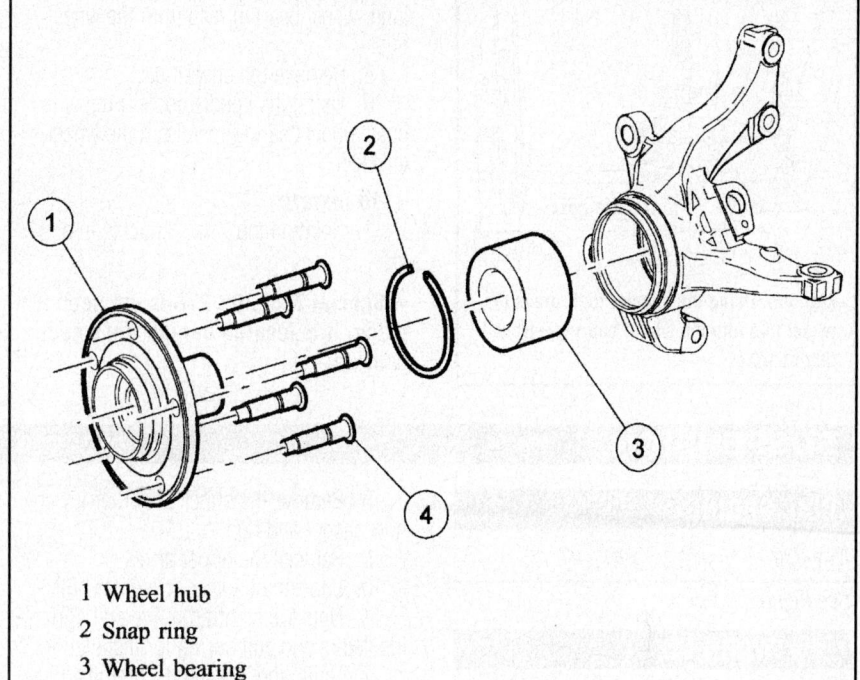

1 Wheel hub
2 Snap ring
3 Wheel bearing
4 Wheel studs (5 required)

06017-ESCA-G86

Fig. 314 Front hub and bearing

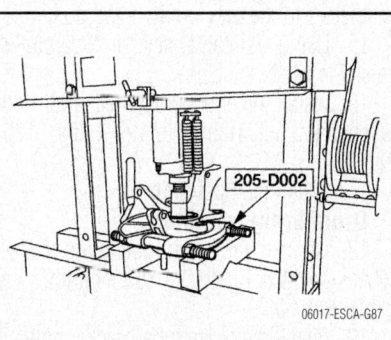

06017-ESCA-G87

Fig. 315 Using the special tool, press the wheel hub from the wheel bearing—front hub/bearing

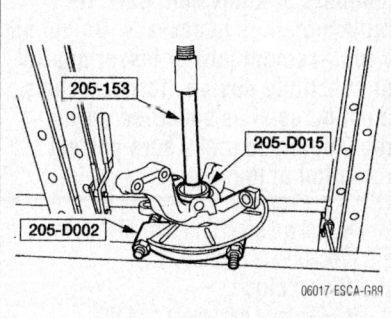

06017-ESCA-G89

Fig. 317 Using the special tools, press the outer wheel bearing race from the wheel knuckle—front hub/bearing

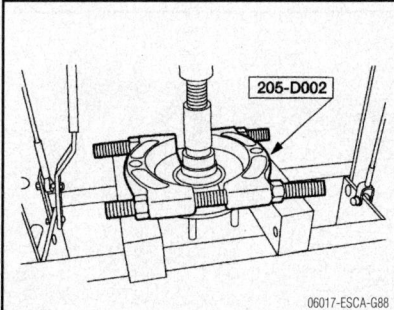

06017-ESCA-G88

Fig. 316 Using the special tool, press the inner wheel bearing race from the wheel hub—front hub/bearing

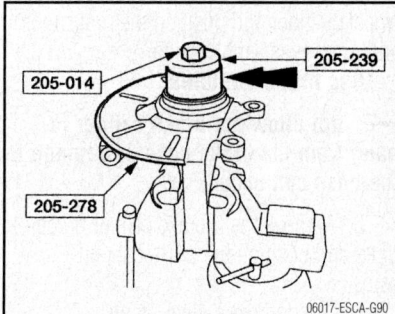

06017-ESCA-G90

Fig. 318 Using the special tools, install the wheel bearing into the wheel knuckle—front hub/bearing

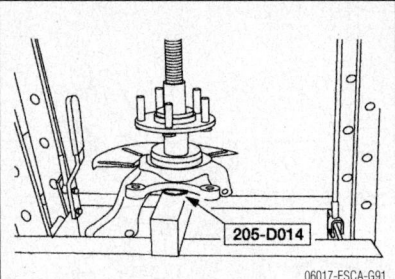

Fig. 319 Using the special tool, press the wheel hub into the wheel bearing—front hub/bearing

4. Using the special tool, press the inner wheel bearing race from the wheel hub.

5. Remove the snapring.

6. Using the special tools, press the outer wheel bearing race from the wheel knuckle.

To install:

7. Position the wheel knuckle in a vise.

➡Special Tool 205-278 is not seen in place. It is located behind the wheel knuckle.

8. Using the special tools, install the wheel bearing into the wheel knuckle.

9. Install the snapring.

10. Using the special tool, press the wheel hub into the wheel bearing.

11. Install the wheel knuckle.

ADJUSTMENT

No adjustment is required or possible.

1. If the tire and wheel (hub) is loose on the spindle, does not rotate freely, or has a rough feeling when spun, install a new wheel bearing.

SUSPENSION

COIL SPRING

REMOVAL & INSTALLATION

See Figure 320.

> **❋❋ WARNING**
>
> **Suspension fasteners are critical parts because they affect performance of vital components and systems and their failure may result in major service expense. New parts must be installed with the same part numbers or equivalent part, if replacement is necessary. Do not use a replacement part of lesser quality or substitute design. Torque values must be used as specified during reassembly to make sure correct retention of these parts.**

1. Before servicing the vehicle, refer to the Precautions Section.

All vehicles

2. Remove the wheel and tire assembly.

3. Remove the brake cable bracket bolt.

Drum brake vehicles

4. Disconnect the brake tube from the wheel cylinder and position the brake tube and bracket assembly aside.

Disc brake vehicles

➡Do not allow the brake caliper to hang from the brake hose or damage to the hose can occur.

5. Remove the 2 brake caliper guide bolts and position the brake caliper aside.

6. Support the caliper using mechanic's wire.

All vehicles

7. Using a suitable jackstand, support the wheel knuckle.

8. Remove the shock absorber lower nut, washer and bolt.

9. Remove the upper arm.

10. Loosen the lower arm inner bolt.

11. Note the position of the coil spring insulators and coil spring for installation.

12. Using the jackstand, carefully lower the wheel knuckle.

13. Remove the coil spring.

To install:
All vehicles

14. Align the coil spring and coil spring insulators to the previously noted position.

15. Using a suitable jackstand, carefully raise the wheel knuckle.

16. Install the shock absorber lower bolt, washer and nut. Tighten to 129 ft. lbs. (175 Nm).

17. Install the upper arm.

Drum brake vehicles

18. Connect the brake tube fitting to the wheel cylinder. Tighten to 150 inch lbs. (150 Nm).

19. Install the brake tube bracket bolt. Tighten to 16 ft. lbs. (22 Nm).

20. Install the brake cable bracket bolt. Tighten to 16 ft. lbs. (22 Nm).

21. Bleed the rear wheel cylinder.

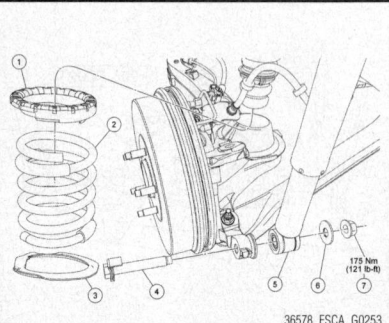

Fig. 320 Rear coil spring—drum brake shown disc similar

REAR SUSPENSION

Disc brake vehicles

22. Position the brake caliper and install the 2 caliper guide bolts. Tighten to 26 ft. lbs. (35 Nm).

All vehicles

23. Install the brake cable bracket bolt. Tighten to 16 ft. lbs. (22 Nm).

Drum brake vehicles

24. Bleed the rear wheel cylinder.

All vehicles

25. Install the wheel and tire assembly.

CONTROL ARMS/LINKS

REMOVAL & INSTALLATION

Upper

See Figure 321.

1. Before servicing the vehicle, refer to the Precautions Section.

2. Remove the wheel and tire.

➡It may be necessary to hold the ball joint stud to keep it from turning while removing the nut.

3. Separate the upper arm from the wheel knuckle. Remove the upper ball joint nut.

4. Remove the upper arm inner bolt.

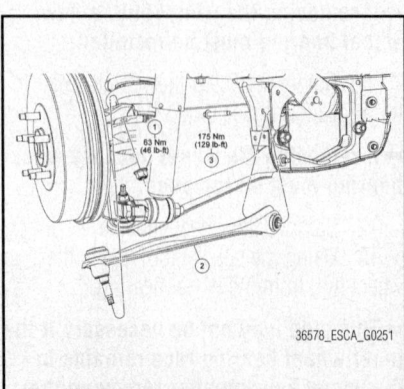

Fig. 321 Rear suspension upper arm—2008–09 models

5. Remove the upper arm.

6. To install, reverse the removal procedure and note the following:
- Ball joint nut: 46 ft. lbs. (63 Nm)
- Upper arm inner bolt: 129 ft. lbs. (175 Nm)

Lower

See Figure 322.

1. Before servicing the vehicle, refer to the Precautions Section.

2. Remove the wheel and tire.

3. Remove and discard the lower ball joint nut and separate the lower ball joint from the wheel knuckle.

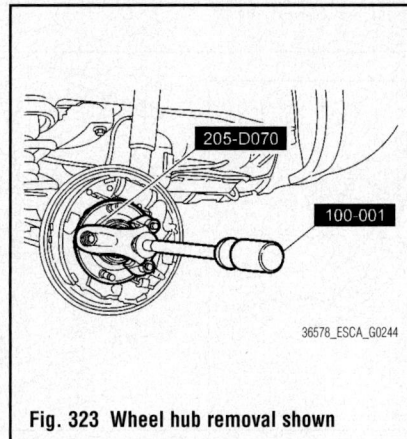

Fig. 323 Wheel hub removal shown

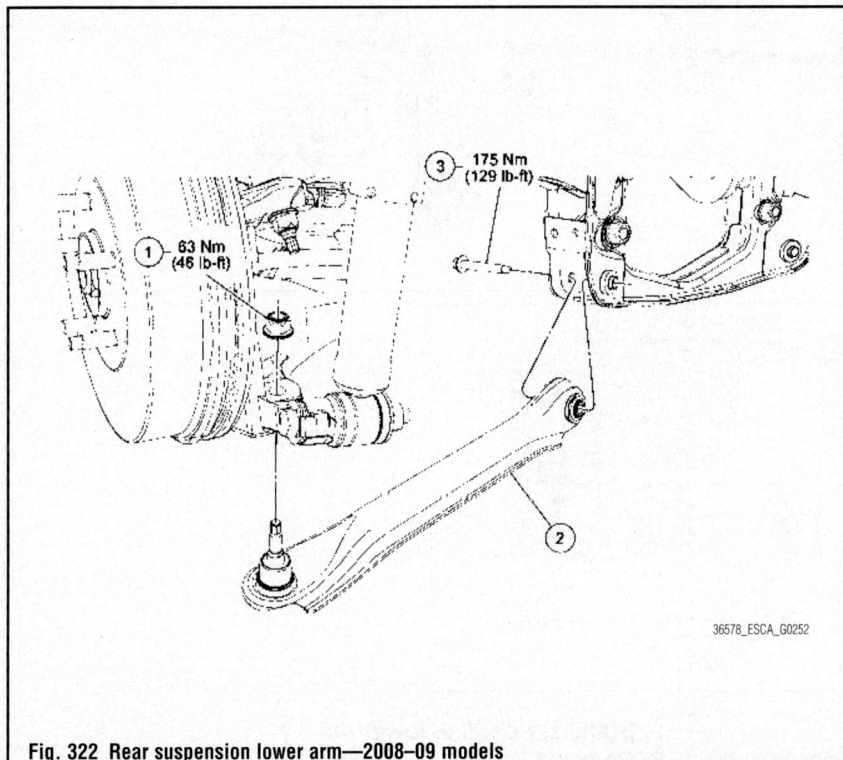

Fig. 322 Rear suspension lower arm—2008–09 models

➡**Tighten the lower arm inner bolt with the weight of the vehicle on the wheels and tires.**

4. Remove the lower arm inner bolt and the lower arm.

5. To install, reverse the removal procedure and note the following:
- Ball joint nut: 46 ft. lbs. (63 Nm)
- Lower arm inner bolt: 129 ft. lbs. (175 Nm)

WHEEL KNUCKLE

REMOVAL & INSTALLATION

FWD Vehicles

See Figures 323 and 324.

☀ **WARNING**

Suspension fasteners are critical parts because they affect performance of vital components and systems and their failure may result in major service expense. New parts must be installed with the same part numbers or equivalent part, if replacement is necessary. Do not use a replacement part of lesser quality or substitute design. Torque values must be used as specified during reassembly to make sure correct retention of these parts.

1. Before servicing the vehicle, refer to the Precautions Section.

All vehicles

2. Remove the wheel and tire.

➡**Apply the brake to keep the wheel hub from rotating.**

3. Remove and discard the wheel hub nut.

4. Remove the wheel speed sensor ring.

Vehicles with drum brakes

5. Remove the brake drum.

6. Using the Front Hub Remover or equivalent and the Impact Slide Hammer or equivalent, remove the wheel hub.

7. Remove the brake shoes.

8. Disconnect the brake tube fitting from the wheel cylinder and remove the brake flexible hose bracket bolt.

9. Remove the parking brake cable bracket bolt.

10. Unclip the wheel speed harness retainer from the parking brake cable and disconnect the cable from the brake backing plate.

Disc brake vehicles

11. Remove the parking brake shoes.

12. Release the parking brake cable end from the parking brake actuator lever and compress the cable conduit locking tabs.

13. Remove the brake flexible hose bracket bolt.

14. Using the Front Hub Remover and Impact Slide Hammer or equivalent tools, remove the wheel hub.

All vehicles

➡**This step may not be necessary if the inner wheel bearing race remains in the wheel knuckle after removing the wheel hub.**

15. Using a suitable press and the Pinion Bearing Cone Remover or equivalent, press the inner bearing race from the wheel hub.

16. Remove the wheel speed sensor bolt and the 2 wheel speed sensor harness bolts.

17. Disconnect the wheel speed sensor from the wheel knuckle, and position the sensor and harness aside.

18. Remove the coil spring.

19. Remove and discard the lower ball joint nut.

20. Index-mark the notch on the cam nut adjustment cam.

21. Remove and discard the wheel knuckle bolt and cam nut.

22. Remove the wheel knuckle.

23. Remove the wheel bearing.

To install:
All vehicles

24. Install the wheel bearing.

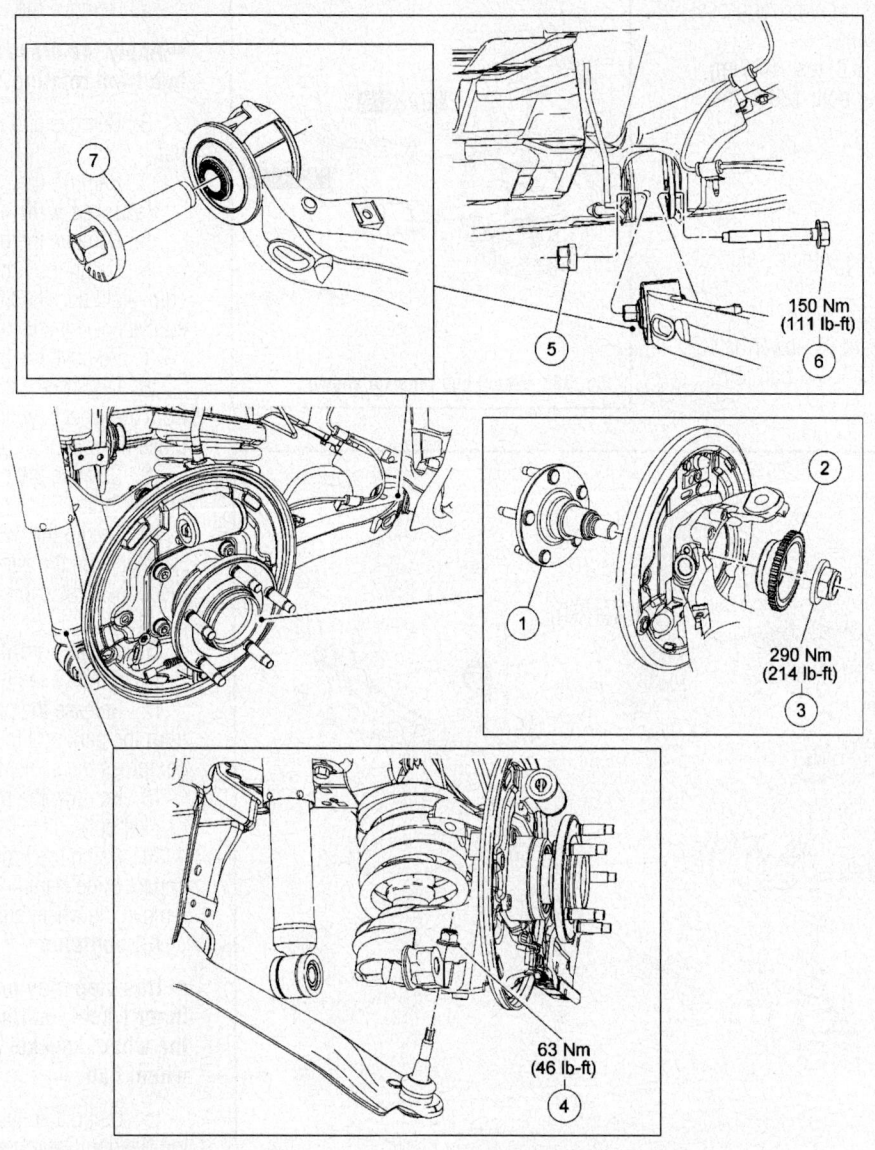

1. Wheel hub
2. Wheel speed sensor ring
3. Wheel hub nut
4. Lower ball joint nut
5. Stabilizer bar link lower nut
6. Cam nut
7. Wheel knuckle bolt
8. Cam sleeve

36578_ESCA_G0336

Fig. 324 Wheel knuckle—exploded view—FWD models

➡**The joint area must be free of foreign material to make sure of correct clamping.**

25. Align the notch on the cam nut with the index marks.

26. Position the wheel knuckle and install a new wheel knuckle bolt and cam nut.

27. Using a suitable tool, hold the cam nut stationary while tightening the new wheel knuckle bolt. Tighten the wheel knuckle bolt to 92 ft. lbs. (125 Nm).

28. Position the lower ball joint into the wheel knuckle and install the new lower ball joint nut. Tighten the ball joint nut to 46 ft. lbs. (63 Nm).

29. Install the coil spring.

30. Position the wheel speed sensor harness and the sensor.

31. Install the wheel speed sensor bolt and the 2 wheel speed sensor harness bolts.

Vehicles with drum brakes

32. Connect the brake tube to the wheel cylinder. Tighten to 11 ft. lbs. (15 Nm).

33. Install the brake flexible hose bracket bolt. Tighten to 13 ft. lbs. (17 Nm).

34. Connect the parking brake cable to the brake backing plate and install the parking brake cable bracket bolt. Tighten to 17 ft. lbs. (23 Nm).

35. Install the brake shoes and brake drum.

36. Bleed the brake system.

Disc brake vehicles

37. Install the parking brake cable onto the actuator lever and insert the cable conduit to secure the locking tabs.

38. Install the parking brake shoes.

39. Install the brake flexible hose bracket bolt and tighten to 16 ft. lbs. (22 Nm).

All vehicles

➡️**Apply the brake to keep the wheel hub from rotating.**

40. Install a new wheel hub nut and tighten to 214 ft. lbs (290 Nm).

41. Check and, if necessary, align the rear end

AWD Vehicles

See Figures 323, 325 and 326.

> ❊❊ **WARNING**
>
> **Suspension fasteners are critical parts because they affect performance of vital components and systems and their failure may result in major service expense. New parts must be installed with the same part numbers or equivalent part, if replacement is necessary. Do not use a replacement part of lesser quality or substitute design. Torque values must be used as specified during reassembly to make sure correct retention of these parts.**

1. Before servicing the vehicle, refer to the Precautions Section.
   All vehicles
2. Remove the wheel and tire.

➡️**Apply the brake to keep the halfshaft from rotating.**

3. Remove and discard the wheel hub nut.

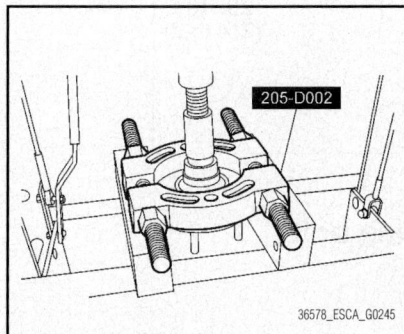

Fig. 325 Pressing the inner bearing race from the bearing hub

Vehicles with drum brakes
4. Remove the brake drum.
5. Using the Front Hub Remover or equivalent, separate the CV joint from the wheel hub. Using the Front Hub Remover or equivalent and the Impact Slide Hammer or equivalent, remove the wheel hub.
6. Remove the brake shoes.
7. Disconnect the brake tube fitting from the wheel cylinder and remove the brake flexible hose bracket bolt
8. Remove the parking brake cable bracket bolt.
9. Unclip the wheel speed harness retainer from the parking brake cable and disconnect the cable from the brake backing plate.

Vehicles with disc brakes

10. Remove the parking brake shoes.
11. Remove the parking brake cable bolt.
12. Release the parking brake cable end from the parking brake actuator lever and compress the cable conduit locking tabs.
13. Remove the flexible brake tube bracket bolt.
14. Using the Front Hub Remover equivalent, separate the outer CV joint from the wheel hub. Using the Front Hub Remover or equivalent and Impact Slide Hammer or equivalent, remove the wheel hub.

All vehicles

15. This step may not be necessary if the inner wheel bearing race remains in the wheel knuckle after removing the wheel hub.
16. Using a suitable press and the Pinion Bearing Cone Remover or equivalent, press the inner bearing race from the wheel hub.
17. Remove the wheel speed sensor bolt and the 2 wheel speed sensor harness bolts.
18. Disconnect the wheel speed sensor from the wheel knuckle, and position the sensor and harness aside.
19. Remove the coil spring.
20. Remove and discard the lower ball joint nut.
21. Index-mark the notch on the cam nut adjustment cam.
22. Remove and discard the wheel knuckle bolt and cam nut.
23. Remove the wheel knuckle.
24. Remove the wheel bearing.

To install:

All vehicles

25. Install the wheel bearing.

➡️**The joint area must be free of foreign material to make sure of correct clamping.**

26. Align the notch on the cam nut with the index marks.
27. Do not tighten the wheel knuckle bolt at this time.
28. Position the halfshaft into the wheel hub and install the wheel knuckle.
29. Hold the cam nut stationary and loosely install a new wheel knuckle bolt and cam nut.
30. Position the lower ball joint into the wheel knuckle and install the new lower ball joint nut. Tighten to 46 ft. lbs. (63 Nm).
31. Install the coil spring.
32. Position the wheel speed sensor harness and the sensor.
33. Install the wheel speed sensor bolt and the 2 wheel speed sensor harness bolts. Tighten the bolts to 80 inch lbs. (9 Nm).

Vehicles with drum brakes

34. Connect the brake tube fitting to the wheel cylinder and install the brake flexible hose bracket bolt.
35. Tighten the brake tube fitting to 11 ft. lbs. (15 Nm).
36. Tighten the brake flexible hose bracket bolt to 13 ft. lbs. (17 Nm).
37. Connect the parking brake cable to the brake backing plate and install the parking brake cable bracket bolt. Tighten to 17 ft. lbs. (23 Nm).
38. Install the brake shoes.
39. Bleed the brake system.
40. Using the Halfshaft Installer, install the halfshaft into the wheel hub.

Vehicles with disc brakes

41. Install the parking brake cable onto the actuator lever and insert the cable conduit to secure the locking tabs.
42. Install the brake tube bracket bolt and tighten to 16 ft. lbs. (22 Nm).
43. Install the parking brake cable bracket bolt and tighten to 17 ft. lbs. (23 Nm).
44. Install the parking brake shoes.
45. Using the Halfshaft Installer, install the halfshaft into the wheel hub.

All vehicles

➡️**Apply the brake to keep the halfshaft from rotating.**

46. Install a new wheel hub nut and tighten to 214 ft. lbs. (290 Nm).
47. With the weight of the vehicle on the wheel and tire, tighten the wheel knuckle bolt to 92 ft. lbs. (125 Nm).
48. Check and, if necessary, align the rear end.

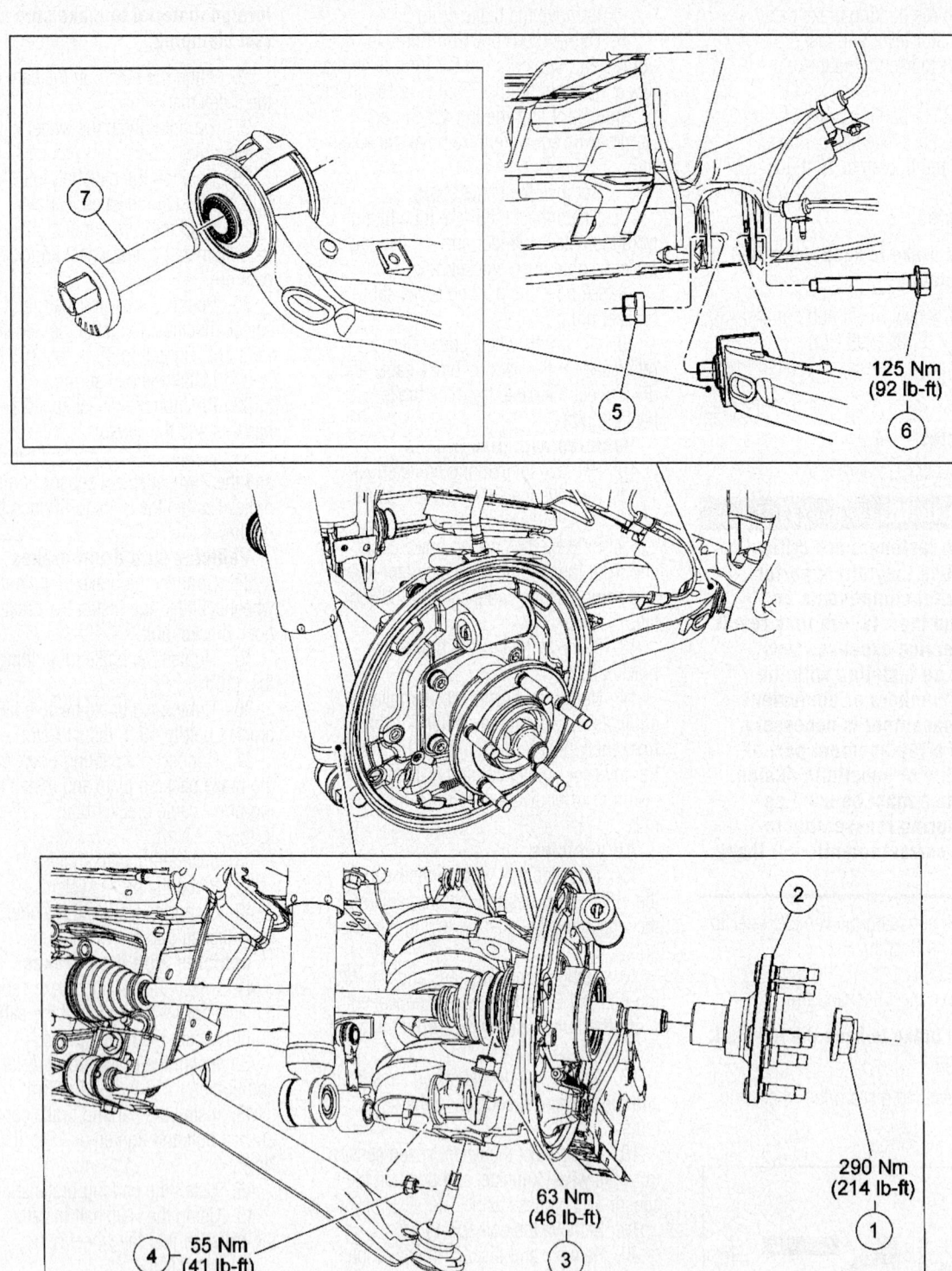

1. Wheel hub nut
2. Wheel hub
3. Lower ball joint nut
4. Stabilizer bar link lower nut
5. Cam nut
6. Wheel knuckle bolt
7. Cam sleeve

36578_ESCA_G0335

Fig. 326 Wheel knuckle—exploded view—AWD models

SHOCK ABSORBER

REMOVAL & INSTALLATION

See Figure 327.

1. Remove the wheel and tire assemblies.
2. Remove the rear quarter trim panel.
3. Remove the upper shock absorber nut, bushing and washer.
4. Remove the lower shock absorber nut, bolt and washer.
5. Remove the shock absorber and bushing.
6. To install, reverse the removal procedure.
7. Tighten the upper nut to 30 ft. lbs. (40 Nm)
8. Tighten the lower nut to 129 ft. lbs. (175 Nm).

WHEEL BEARINGS

REMOVAL & INSTALLATION

FWD Vehicles

See Figures 323, 325, 328 through 330.

1. Before servicing the vehicle, refer to the Precautions Section.

❋❋ CAUTION

Suspension fasteners are critical parts because they affect performance of vital components and systems and their failure may result in major service expense. New parts must be installed with the same part numbers or equivalent part, if replacement is necessary. Do not use a replacement part of lesser quality or substitute design. Torque values must be used as specified during reassembly to make sure correct retention of these parts.

2. Safely raise the vehicle.
3. Remove the wheel and tire assembly.
4. Apply the brake to keep the halfshaft from rotating.
5. Remove and discard the wheel hub nut.
6. Remove the wheel speed sensor ring.
7. Remove the brake drum or brake disc.
8. Using the front hub remover and impact slide hammer or equivalent tools, remove the wheel hub.

➡This step may not be necessary if the inner wheel bearing race remains in the wheel knuckle after removing the wheel hub.

9. Using a suitable press and the pinion bearing cone remover or equivalent, press the inner bearing race from the wheel hub.
10. Remove and discard the wheel bearing snap ring.
11. Using the impact slide hammer or equivalent and the axle bearing remover, remove the bearing from the wheel knuckle.

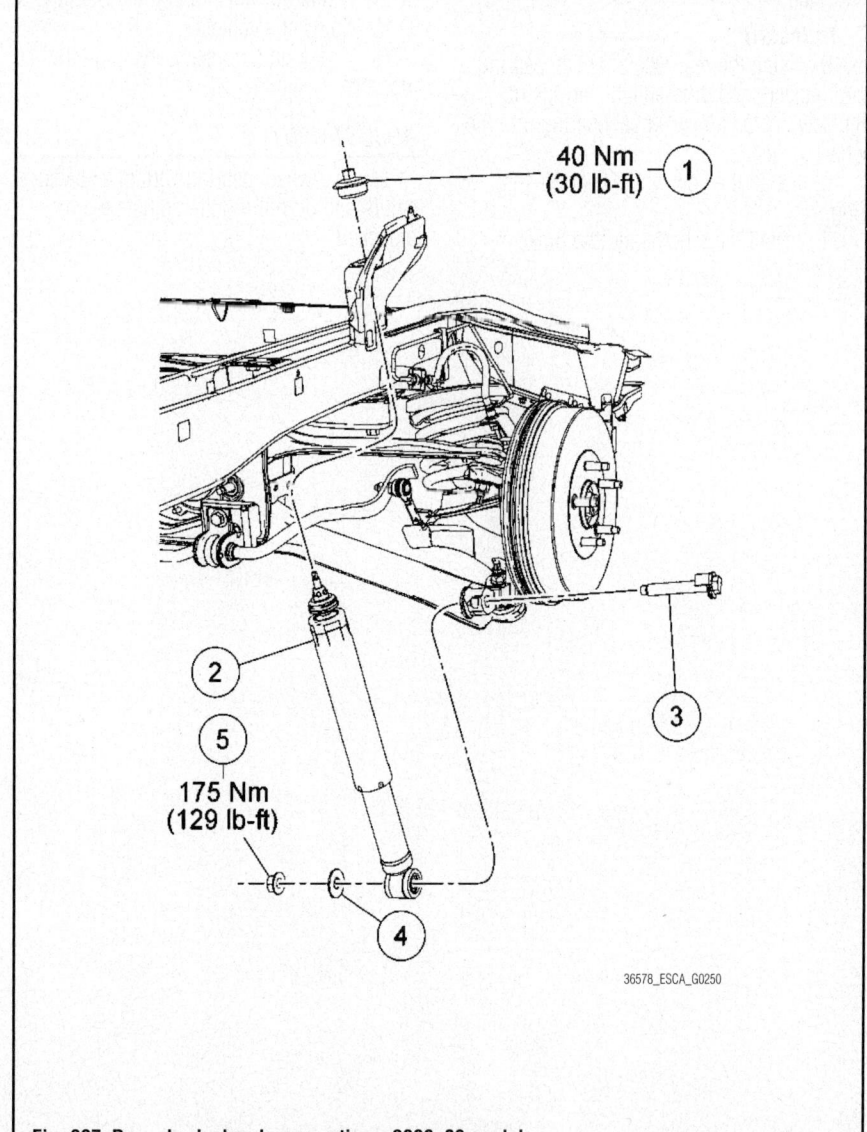

Fig. 327 Rear shock absorber mounting—2008–09 models

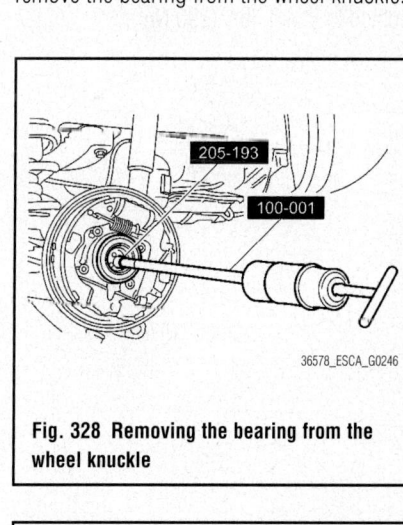

Fig. 328 Removing the bearing from the wheel knuckle

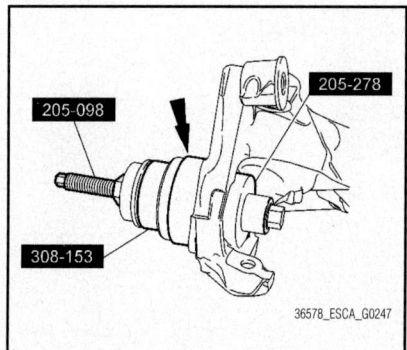

Fig. 329 Installing the wheel bearing into the rear knuckle

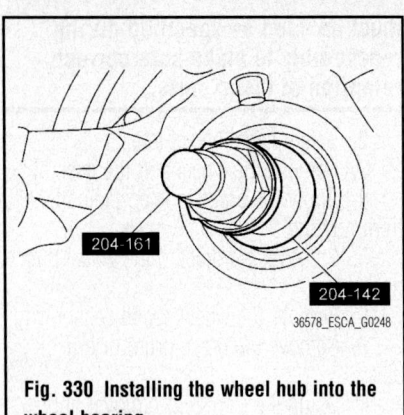

Fig. 330 Installing the wheel hub into the wheel bearing

To install:

12. Using the rear axle drawbar, bearing cup replacer and differential Bearing Cup replacer, install a new wheel bearing into the wheel knuckle.

13. Install the new wheel bearing snap ring.

14. Using the half shaft installer and receiver adapter, install the wheel hub into the wheel bearing.

15. Install the wheel speed sensor ring.

16. Apply the brake to keep the halfshaft from rotating.

17. Install the new wheel hub nut and tighten to 214 ft. lbs. (290 Nm).

18. Install the brake drum or disc.

19. Install the wheel and tire assembly.

AWD Vehicles

See Figures 329 through 331.

1. Before servicing the vehicle, refer to the Precautions Section.

2. Safely raise the vehicle.

3. Remove the wheel and tire assembly.

4. Remove the wheel knuckle.

5. Remove the wheel bearing snap ring.

6. Remove the 4 bolts and the brake drum backing plate.

7. Position the wheel knuckle on a suitable press.

8. Using the PTO driven gear oil seal installer, the handle and the pinion bearing cone remover or equivalent, position the wheel knuckle on a suitable press and press the wheel bearing from the wheel knuckle.

To install:

9. Using the rear axle drawbar, bearing cup replacer and differential bearing cup replacer, install a new wheel bearing into the wheel knuckle.

10. Install the new wheel bearing snap ring.

11. Install the 4 bolts and the brake

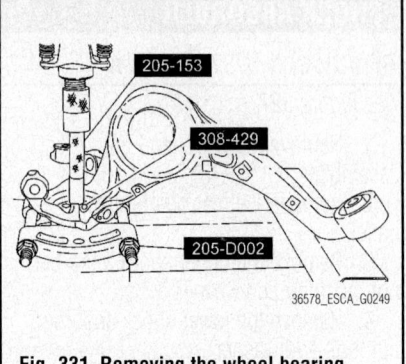

Fig. 331 Removing the wheel bearing from the wheel knuckle

drum backing plate. Tighten to 63 ft. lbs. (85 Nm).

12. Using the Halfshaft Installer and Receiver Adapter, install the wheel hub into the wheel bearing.

13. Install the wheel knuckle.

14. Install the wheel and tire assembly.

15. Lower the vehicle.

16. Check and, if necessary, align the rear end.

ADJUSTMENT

The rear wheel bearings are of a sealed nature and do not require adjustment or repacking.

FORD AND MERCURY

SPECIFICATIONS AND MAINTENANCE CHARTS

ENGINE AND VEHICLE IDENTIFICATION

Engine							Model Year	
Code ①	Liters	Cu. In.	Cyl.	Fuel Sys.	Engine Type	Eng. Mfg.	Code ②	Year
H	2.3	137	4	SFI/Hybrid	DOHC	Ford	8	2008
3	2.5	153	4	SFI/Hybrid	DOHC	Ford	9	2009

SFI: Multi-port Fuel Injection

DOHC: Double Overhead Camshafts

① 8th digit of VIN

② 10th digit of VIN

36578_HYBR_C0001

GENERAL ENGINE SPECIFICATIONS

Year	Model	Engine Displacement Liters	Engine VIN	Net Horsepower @ rpm	Net Torque @ rpm (ft. lbs.)	Bore x Stroke (in.)	Com-pression Ratio	Oil Pressure @ rpm
2008	Escape Hybrid	2.3	H	133@6000	129@4500	3.44x3.70	12.3:1	29-39@2000
	Mariner Hybrid	2.3	H	133@6000	129@4500	3.44x3.70	12.3:1	29-39@2000
2009	Escape Hybrid	2.5	3	153@6000	136@4500	3.50x3.93	12.5:1	29-39@2000
	Mariner Hybrid	2.5	3	153@6000	136@4500	3.50x3.93	12.5:1	29-39@2000

36578_HYBR_C0002

ENGINE TUNE-UP SPECIFICATIONS

Year	Engine Displacement Liters	Engine VIN	Spark Plug Gap (in.)	Ignition Timing (deg.) MT	AT	Fuel Pump (psi) ①	Idle Speed (rpm) MT	AT	Valve Clearance Intake	Exhaust
2008	2.3	H	0.049-0.053	N/A	N/A	39	②	②	HYD	HYD
2009	2.5	3	0.042-0.046	N/A	N/A	55	②	②	HYD	HYD

N/A: Not Available

HYD: Hydraulic lash adjusters

① Key on; engine off

② Refer to Vehicle Emission Control Information Label

36578_HYBR_C0003

CAPACITIES

Year	Model	Engine Displacement Liters	Engine VIN	Engine Oil with Filter (qts.)	Transmission (pts.) Manual	Transmission (pts.) Auto ①	Transfer Case (pts.)	Rear Diff. (pts.)	Fuel Tank (gal.)	Cooling System (qts.)	Hybrid Motor Electronics (qts.)
2008	Escape Hybrid	2.3	H	4.5	N/A	10.6	0.75	2.4	15.0	8.5	3.7
	Mariner Hybrid	2.3	H	4.5	N/A	10.6	0.75	2.4	15.0	8.5	3.7
2009	Escape Hybrid	2.5	3	4.5	N/A	8.6	0.75	2.4	15.0	8.5	3.7
	Escape Hybrid	2.5	3	4.5	N/A	8.6	0.75	2.4	15.0	8.5	3.7

N/A: Non Aplicable

NOTE: All capacities are approximate. Add fluid gradually and check to be sure a proper fluid level is obtained.

① Dry fill

36578_HYBR_C0004

FLUID SPECIFICATIONS

Year	Model	Engine Displacement Liters	Engine ID/VIN	Engine Oil	Auto. Trans.	Drive Axle	Transfer Case ①	Engine Coolant	Brake Master Cylinder
2008	Escape Hybrid	2.3	H	5W-20	Mercon®LV	80W-90	75W-140	Motorcraft Gold	DOT 3
	Mariner Hybrid	2.3	H	5W-20	Mercon®LV	80W-90	75W-140	Motorcraft Gold	DOT 3
2009	Escape Hybrid	2.5	3	5W-20	Mercon®LV	80W-90	75W-140	Motorcraft Gold	DOT 3
	Mariner Hybrid	2.5	3	5W-20	Mercon®LV	80W-90	75W-140	Motorcraft Gold	DOT 3

DOT: Department Of Transpotation

® Registerd Trademark

① Synthetic fluid is recommended.

36578_HYBR_C0005

VALVE SPECIFICATIONS

Year	Engine Displacement Liters	Engine VIN	Seat Angle (deg.)	Face Angle (deg.)	Spring Test Pressure (lbs. @ in.)	Spring Installed Height (in.)	Stem-to-Guide Clearance (in.) Intake	Stem-to-Guide Clearance (in.) Exhaust	Stem Diameter (in.) Intake	Stem Diameter (in.) Exhaust
2008	2.3	H	45	45	38.6@1.49	1.492	0.0010	0.0011	0.2153-0.2159	0.2151-0.2157
2009	2.5	3	45	45	38.6@1.49	1.492	0.0010	0.0011	0.2153-0.2159	0.2151-0.2157

36578_HYBR_C0006

CAMSHAFT AND BEARING SPECIFICATIONS

All measurements are given in inches.

Year	Engine Displacement Liters	Engine ID/VIN	Journal Dia.	Brg. Oil Clearance	Shaft End-play	Runout	Journal Bore	Lobe Height Intake	Lobe Height Exhaust
2008	2.3	H	0.9820-0.9830	N/A	0.0016-0.0035	0.001	0.001-0.0030	N/A	0.3070
2009	2.5	3	0.9820-0.9830	N/A	0.0016-0.0035	0.001	0.001-0.0030	0.3240	0.3070

N/A: Not Available

36578_HYBR_C0007

CRANKSHAFT AND CONNECTING ROD SPECIFICATIONS

All measurements are given in inches.

Year	Engine Displacement Liters	Engine VIN	Crankshaft Main Brg. Journal Dia.	Crankshaft Main Brg. Oil Clearance	Crankshaft Shaft End-play	Crankshaft Thrust on No.	Connecting Rod Journal Diameter	Connecting Rod Oil Clearance	Connecting Rod Side Clearance
2008	2.3	H	2.0460-2.0470	0.0006-0.0015	0.0080-0.0160	N/A	1.9673-1.9681	0.0011-0.0026	0.0760-0.1200
	2.3	H	2.0460-2.0470	0.0006-0.0015	0.0080-0.0160	N/A	1.9673-1.9681	0.0011-0.0026	0.0760-0.1200
2009	2.5	3	2.0460-2.0470	0.0006-0.0015	0.0080-0.0160	N/A	1.9673-1.9681	0.0011-0.0026	0.0760-0.1200
	2.5	3	2.0460-2.0470	0.0006-0.0015	0.0080-0.0160	N/A	1.9673-1.9681	0.0011-0.0026	0.0760-0.1200

N/A: Not Available

36578_HYBR_C0008

PISTON AND RING SPECIFICATIONS

All measurements are given in inches.

Year	Engine Displacement Liters	Engine VIN	Piston Clearance	Ring Gap Top Compression	Ring Gap Bottom Compression	Ring Gap Oil Control	Ring Width Top Compression	Ring Width Bottom Compression	Ring Width Oil Control
2008	2.3	H	0.0009-0.0017	0.0060-0.0120	0.0120-0.0180	0.0070-0.0270	0.0460-0.0466	0.0471-0.0472	0.093-0.0960
	2.3	H	0.0009-0.0017	0.0060-0.0120	0.0120-0.0180	0.0070-0.0270	0.0460-0.0466	0.0471-0.0472	0.093-0.0960
2009	2.5	3	0.0009-0.0017	0.0060-0.0100	0.0120-0.0180	0.0070-0.0270	0.0460-0.0466	0.0471-0.0472	0.093-0.0960
	2.5	3	0.0009-0.0017	0.0060-0.0100	0.0120-0.0180	0.0070-0.0270	0.0460-0.0466	0.0471-0.0472	0.093-0.0960

NA: Not Available

36578_HYBR_C0009

TORQUE SPECIFICATIONS
All readings in ft. lbs.

Year	Engine Displacement Liters	Engine VIN	Cylinder Head Bolts	Main Bearing Bolts	Rod Bearing Bolts	Crankshaft Damper Bolts	Flywheel Bolts	Manifold Intake	Manifold Exhaust	Spark Plugs	Oil Pan Drain Plug
2008	2.3	H	①	N/A	N/A	②	③	13	35	④	21
	2.3	H	①	N/A	N/A	②	③	13	35	④	21
2009	2.5	3	①	NIA	NIA	②	③	13	35	④	21
	2.5	3	①	N/A	N/A	②	③	13	35	④	21

N/A: Not Available

① Step 1: 44 inch lbs.

   Step 2: 11 ft. lbs.

   Step 3: 33 ft. lbs.

   Step 4: Plus 90 degrees

   Step 5: Plus an additional 90 degrees

② Step 1: 74 ft. lbs.

   Step 2: Plus 90 degrees

③ Step 1: 37 ft. lbs.

   Step 2: 59 ft. lbs.

   Step 2: 83 ft. lbs.

④ 106 inch lbs.

36578_HYBR_C0010

WHEEL ALIGNMENT

Year	Model		Caster Range (+/-Deg.)	Caster Preferred Setting (Deg.)	Camber Range (+/-Deg.)	Camber Preferred Setting (Deg.)	Toe-in (in.)
2008	Escape/Mariner	F	0.50	+1.60	0.50	-0.84	0.23+/-0.23
	Hybrid	R	N/A	N/A	0.75	0.00	-0.12+/-0.20
2009	Escape/Mariner	F	0.50	+1.60	0.50	-0.84	0.23+/-0.23
	Hybrid	R	N/A	N/A	0.70 ①	0.01	-0.12+/-0.20

N/A: Not Available

① Left side: +/- 0.60

36578_HYBR_C0011

TIRE, WHEEL AND BALL JOINT SPECIFICATIONS

Year	Model	OEM Tires Standard	OEM Tires Optional	Tire Pressures (psi) Front	Tire Pressures (psi) Rear	Wheel Size	Ball Joint Inspection	Lug Nuts (ft. lbs.)
2008	Escape Hybrid	P235/70R16	none	①	①	N/A	0.008 in.	100
	Mariner Hybrid	P235/70R16	none	①	①	N/A	0.008 in.	100
2009	Escape Hybrid	P235/70R16	none	①	①	N/A	0.008 in.	100
	Mariner Hybrid	P235/70R16	none	①	①	N/A	0.008 in.	100

N/A: Not Available

PSI: Pounds Per Square Inch

① See safety cirtification on drivers door jam

36578_HYBR_C0012

BRAKE SPECIFICATIONS
All measurements in inches unless noted

| Year | Model | | Brake Disc | | | Brake Drum | | Minimum Lining Thickness | Brake Caliper | |
			Original Thickness	Minimum Thickness	Maximum Run-out	Original Inside Diameter	Maximum Machine Diameter		Bracket Bolts (ft. lbs.)	Mounting Bolts (ft. lbs.)
2008	Escape Hybrid/	F	NA	0.944	0.004	N/A	N/A	0.118	129	37
	Mariner Hybrid	R	NA	0.430	0.004	N/A	N/A	0.118	N/A	26
2009	Escape Hybrid/	F	NA	0.944	0.004	N/A	N/A	0.118	129	37
	Mariner Hybrid	R	NA	0.430	0.004	N/A	10.090	0.039	N/A	N/A

N/A: Non Aplicable

36578_HYBR_C0013

SCHEDULED MAINTENANCE INTERVALS
2008-09 Ford Escape Hybrid/Mercury Mariner Hybrid

TO BE SERVICED	TYPE OF SERVICE	Vehicle mileage intervals (x1000)											
		10	20	30	40	50	60	70	80	90	100	110	120
Air cleaner filter	R			✓			✓			✓			✓
Accessory drive belt	I ①										✓		
Brake system ②	S/I		✓		✓		✓		✓		✓		✓
Cooling system hoses and clamps	S/I		✓		✓		✓		✓		✓		✓
Motor/electrical cooling system and hoses	S/I		✓		✓		✓		✓		✓		✓
Driveshafts & halfshafts	S/I		✓		✓		✓		✓		✓		✓
Engine coolant	R	At 6 years or 100,000 miles; then every 3 years or 80,000 miles											
Motor/electrical system coolant	R	At 6 years or 100,000 miles; then every 3 years or 80,000 miles											
Engine oil & filter	R	✓	✓	✓	✓	✓	✓	✓	✓	✓	✓	✓	✓
Exhaust system & heat shields					✓				✓				✓
Fuel filter	R										✓		
PCV valve	S/I	Every 150,000 miles											
Rear axle lubricant (4wd)	R	Every 150,000 miles											
Rear (high voltage) battery A/C filter	I	✓	✓	✓	✓	✓	✓	✓	✓	✓	✓	✓	✓
Rear (high voltage) battery A/C filter	R		✓		✓		✓		✓		✓		✓
Tires	Rotate	First 5000 miles than every 10,000 miles after											
Steering linkage	S/I		✓		✓		✓		✓		✓		✓
Spark plugs	R										✓		
Suspension components and ball joints	S/I		✓		✓		✓		✓		✓		✓
Multi-Point inspection	③	✓	✓	✓	✓	✓	✓	✓	✓	✓	✓	✓	✓

R: Replace   S/I: Inspect and service, if necessary   L: Lubricate   A: Adjust   C: Clean

① Replace at 150,000 miles, if not previously done

② Inspect the reservoir fluid level, rotor and or drum, brake lines, hoses, calipers and or wheel cylinders

Monthly Checks

Check each of the following items every month:

   All interior and exterior lights

   Tires for wear and correct air pressure, including spare tire

   Engine oil fluid level

   Windshield washer solvent fluid level

Six Month Checks

Check each of the following items at least every 6 months:

   Lap/shoulder belts and seat latches for wear and function

   Parking brake for correct operation

   Safety warning lamps (brake, ABS, air bag, safety belt) for correct operation

   Engine coolant system fluid level and correct strength

   Motor/electrical cooling system fluid level and correct strength

   Battery 12-volt connections. Clean if necessary

   Windshield washer spray, wiper operation, clean all wiper blades

   Lubricate all hinges, latches and outside locks. Inspect for correct operation

   Lubricate door rubber weatherstrips. Inspect for excessive wear

   Clean body and door drain holes. Inspect for clogs and obstructions

36578_HYBR_C0014

SCHEDULED MAINTENANCE INTERVALS
2008-09 Ford Escape Hybrid/Mercury Mariner Hybrid
(Footnotes continued)

③ **Multi-Point inspection**

The following inspections are recommended at every service interval:

Check and top off brake, coolant, manual and automatic transmission fluid power steering and washer fluid

Inspect tires for wear and correct air pressure, including spare tire

Check exhaust system for leaks, damage, loose parts and foreighn material

Check low voltage (under the hood) battery performance

Check operation of horn, exterior lamps, turn signals and hazard warning lights

Check radiator, coolers, heater and airconditioning hoses

Inspect tires for wear and correct air pressure, including spare tire

Inspect windshield wiper spray and wiper operation

Check windshield for cracks, chips and pitting

Inspect for oil and fluid leaks

Inspect air filter

Inspect halfshaft dust boots

Check shocks struts and other suspension components for leaks and damage

Inspect steering linkage

Inspect accesory drive belts

When operating in dusty conditions such as unpaved or dusty roads:

Change engine oil and install a new oil filter every 8,000 km (5,000 miles) or 12 months or 200 hours of engine operation.

Install a new high voltage battery A/C filter as required

Inspect and rotate tires every 8,000 km (5,000 miles)

Install a new engine air filter as required.

Install a new cabin air filter as required.

When operating in off-road conditions:

Change engine oil and install a new oil filter every 8,000 km (5,000 miles) or 12 months or 200 hours of engine operation.

Inspect and rotate tires every 8,000 km (5,000miles).

Install a new engine air filter as required.

Install a new cabin air filter as required.

Install a new high voltage battery A/C filter as required

Inspect and lubricate U-joints.

Inspect and lubricate steering linkage ball joints with zerk fittings.

Special Operating Condition Requirements

When towing a trailer or using a camper or car-top carrier:

Change engine oil and install a new oil filter every 8,000 km (5,000 miles) or 12months or 200 hours of engine operation.

Inspect and rotate tires 8,000 km (5,000 miles)

Change manual transmission fluid as required.

Inspect and lubricate U-joints and half shafts as required.

During extensive idling and/or low speed driving for long distances, as in heavy commercial use such as delivery, taxi, patrol car or delivery:

Change engine oil and install a new oil filter, lube front lower control arm and steering linkage ball joints with

zerk fittings (if equipped) every 8,000 km (5,000 miles) or 12 months or 200 hours of engine operation.

Inspect brake system and check battery electrolyte level (Patrol cars) every 8,000 km (5,000 miles).

Install a new fuel filter every 24,000 km (15,000 miles).

Install new spark plugs and change transfer case fluid every 96,000 km (60,000 miles).

Install a new cabin air filter as required.

36578_HYBR_C0015

PRECAUTIONS

Before servicing any vehicle, please be sure to read all of the following precautions, which deal with personal safety, prevention of component damage, and important points to take into consideration when servicing a motor vehicle:

• Never open, service or drain the radiator or cooling system when the engine is hot; serious burns can occur from the steam and hot coolant.

• Observe all applicable safety precautions when working around fuel. Whenever servicing the fuel system, always work in a well-ventilated area. Do not allow fuel spray or vapors to come in contact with a spark, open flame, or excessive heat (a hot drop light, for example). Keep a dry chemical fire extinguisher near the work area. Always keep fuel in a container specifically designed for fuel storage; also, always properly seal fuel containers to avoid the possibility of fire or explosion. Refer to the additional fuel system precautions later in this section.

• Fuel injection systems often remain pressurized, even after the engine has been turned **OFF**. The fuel system pressure must be relieved before disconnecting any fuel lines. Failure to do so may result in fire and/or personal injury.

• Brake fluid often contains polyglycol ethers and polyglycols. Avoid contact with the eyes and wash your hands thoroughly after handling brake fluid. If you do get brake fluid in your eyes, flush your eyes with clean, running water for 15 minutes. If eye irritation persists, or if you have taken

brake fluid internally, IMMEDIATELY seek medical assistance.

• The EPA warns that prolonged contact with used engine oil may cause a number of skin disorders, including cancer. You should make every effort to minimize your exposure to used engine oil. Protective gloves should be worn when changing oil. Wash your hands and any other exposed skin areas as soon as possible after exposure to used engine oil. Soap and water, or waterless hand cleaner should be used.

• All new vehicles are now equipped with an air bag system, often referred to as a Supplemental Restraint System (SRS) or Supplemental Inflatable Restraint (SIR) system. The system must be disabled before performing service on or around system components, steering column, instrument panel components, wiring and sensors. Failure to follow safety and disabling procedures could result in accidental air bag deployment, possible personal injury and unnecessary system repairs.

• Always wear safety goggles when working with, or around, the air bag system. When carrying a non-deployed air bag, be sure the bag and trim cover are pointed away from your body. When placing a non-deployed air bag on a work surface, always face the bag and trim cover upward, away from the surface. This will reduce the motion of the module if it is accidentally deployed. Refer to the additional air bag system precautions later in this section.

• Clean, high quality brake fluid from a sealed container is essential to the safe and

proper operation of the brake system. You should always buy the correct type of brake fluid for your vehicle. If the brake fluid becomes contaminated, completely flush the system with new fluid. Never reuse any brake fluid. Any brake fluid that is removed from the system should be discarded. Also, do not allow any brake fluid to come in contact with a painted surface; it will damage the paint.

• Never operate the engine without the proper amount and type of engine oil; doing so WILL result in severe engine damage.

• Timing belt maintenance is extremely important. Many models utilize an interference-type, non-freewheeling engine. If the timing belt breaks, the valves in the cylinder head may strike the pistons, causing potentially serious (also time-consuming and expensive) engine damage. Refer to the maintenance interval charts for the recommended replacement interval for the timing belt, and to the timing belt section for belt replacement and inspection.

• Disconnecting the negative battery cable on some vehicles may interfere with the functions of the on-board computer system(s) and may require the computer to undergo a relearning process once the negative battery cable is reconnected.

• When servicing drum brakes, only disassemble and assemble one side at a time, leaving the remaining side intact for reference.

• Only an MVAC-trained, EPA-certified automotive technician should service the air conditioning system or its components.

BRAKES

GENERAL INFORMATION

PRECAUTIONS

• Certain components within the ABS system are not intended to be serviced or repaired individually.

• Do not use rubber hoses or other parts not specifically specified for and ABS system. When using repair kits, replace all parts included in the kit. Partial or incorrect repair may lead to functional problems and require the replacement of components.

• Lubricate rubber parts with clean, fresh brake fluid to ease assembly. Do not use shop air to clean parts; damage to rubber components may result.

• Use only DOT 3 brake fluid from an unopened container.

• If any hydraulic component or line is removed or replaced, it may be necessary to bleed the entire system.

• A clean repair area is essential. Always clean the reservoir and cap thoroughly before removing the cap. The slightest amount of dirt in the fluid may plug an orifice and impair the system function. Perform repairs after components have been thoroughly cleaned; use only denatured alcohol to clean components. Do not allow ABS components to come into contact with any substance containing mineral oil; this includes used shop rags.

• The Anti-Lock control unit is a microprocessor similar to other computer units in the vehicle. Ensure that the ignition switch is **OFF** before removing or installing

ANTI-LOCK BRAKE SYSTEM (ABS)

controller harnesses. Avoid static electricity discharge at or near the controller.

• If any arc welding is to be done on the vehicle, the control unit should be unplugged before welding operations begin.

WHEEL SPEED SENSORS

REMOVAL & INSTALLATION

Front Sensor

See Figure 1.

1. Before servicing the vehicle, refer to the Precautions Section.
2. Raise and safely support the vehicle.

➡**The harness connector is located in the engine compartment.**

3. Disconnect the electrical connector.

⁂ WARNING

Care must be taken during the removal of the plug to prevent damage. If the plug is damaged, a new sensor may need to be installed, even though the sensor is functional in all other aspects.

4. Remove the grommet from the body.

5. When removing the body plug, rotate the plug into a position which allows the use of a small screwdriver to release the tabs on the underside of the body plug. These 2 tabs are located at right angles to the sensor wire.

6. Remove the front wheel speed sensor wire from the retainer.

7. Remove the front wheel speed sensor wire-to-body bolt.

8. Remove the front wheel speed sensor wire bolt.

9. Remove the front wheel speed sensor bolt from the wheel knuckle.

➡ **Clean off any foreign material that may have collected around the sensor before removal.**

10. Remove the front wheel speed sensor.

➡ **Thoroughly clean the mounting surface.**

11. Installation is the reverse of the removal procedure, noting the following tightening specifications:

- Front wheel speed sensor-to-knuckle bolt: 80 inch lbs. (9 Nm)
- Front wheel speed sensor wire bolt: 11 ft. lbs. (15 Nm)
- Front wheel speed sensor wire-to-body bolt: 80 inch lbs. (9 Nm)

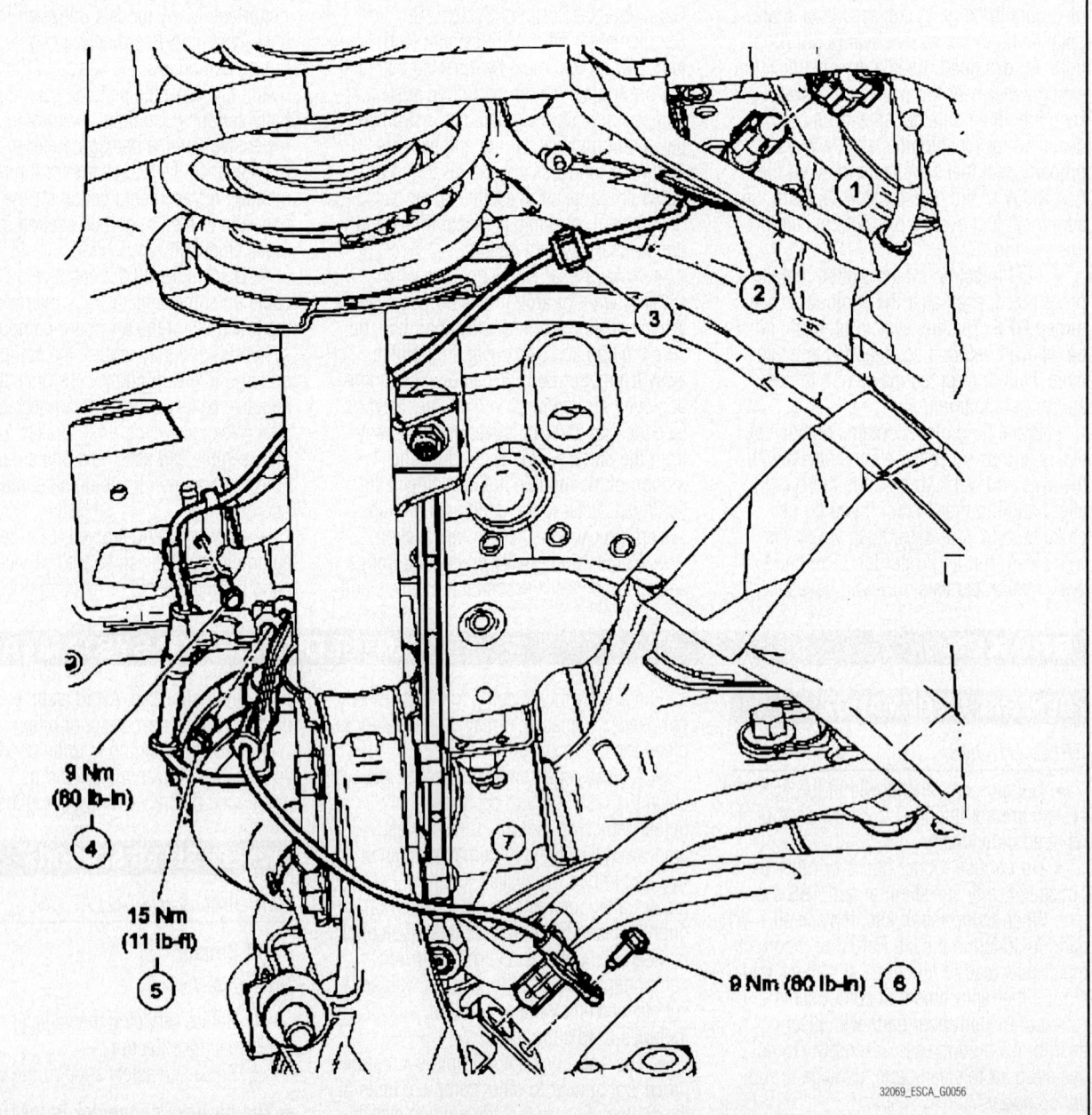

32069_ESCA_G0056

Fig. 1 View of the front wheel speed sensor wire connector (1), grommet (2), front wheel speed sensor wire retainer (3), front wheel speed sensor wire-to-body bolts (4), front whyeel speed sensor bolts (5, 6) and front wheel speed sensor (7)

Rear Sensor

See Figure 2.

1. Remove the wheel and tire.

☀☀ WARNING

Care must be taken during the removal of the plug to prevent damage. If the plug is damaged, a new sensor may need to be installed even though the sensor is functional in all other aspects.

2. Remove the grommet from the body.

3. When removing the body plug, rotate the plug into a position which allows the use of a small screwdriver to release the tabs on the underside of the body plug. These 2 tabs are located at right angles to the sensor wire.

4. Disconnect the rear wheel speed sensor electrical connector.

5. Remove the rear wheel speed sensor harness from the harness retainer.

6. Remove the 3 rear wheel speed sensor harness bolts.

➡ **Clean off any dirt that may have collected around the sensor before removal.**

7. Remove the rear wheel speed sensor bolt from the wheel knuckle.

8. Remove the rear wheel speed sensor.

➡ **Thoroughly clean the mounting surface.**

9. Installation is the reverse of the removal procedure.

10. Tighten all retaining bolts to 80 inch lbs. (9 Nm).

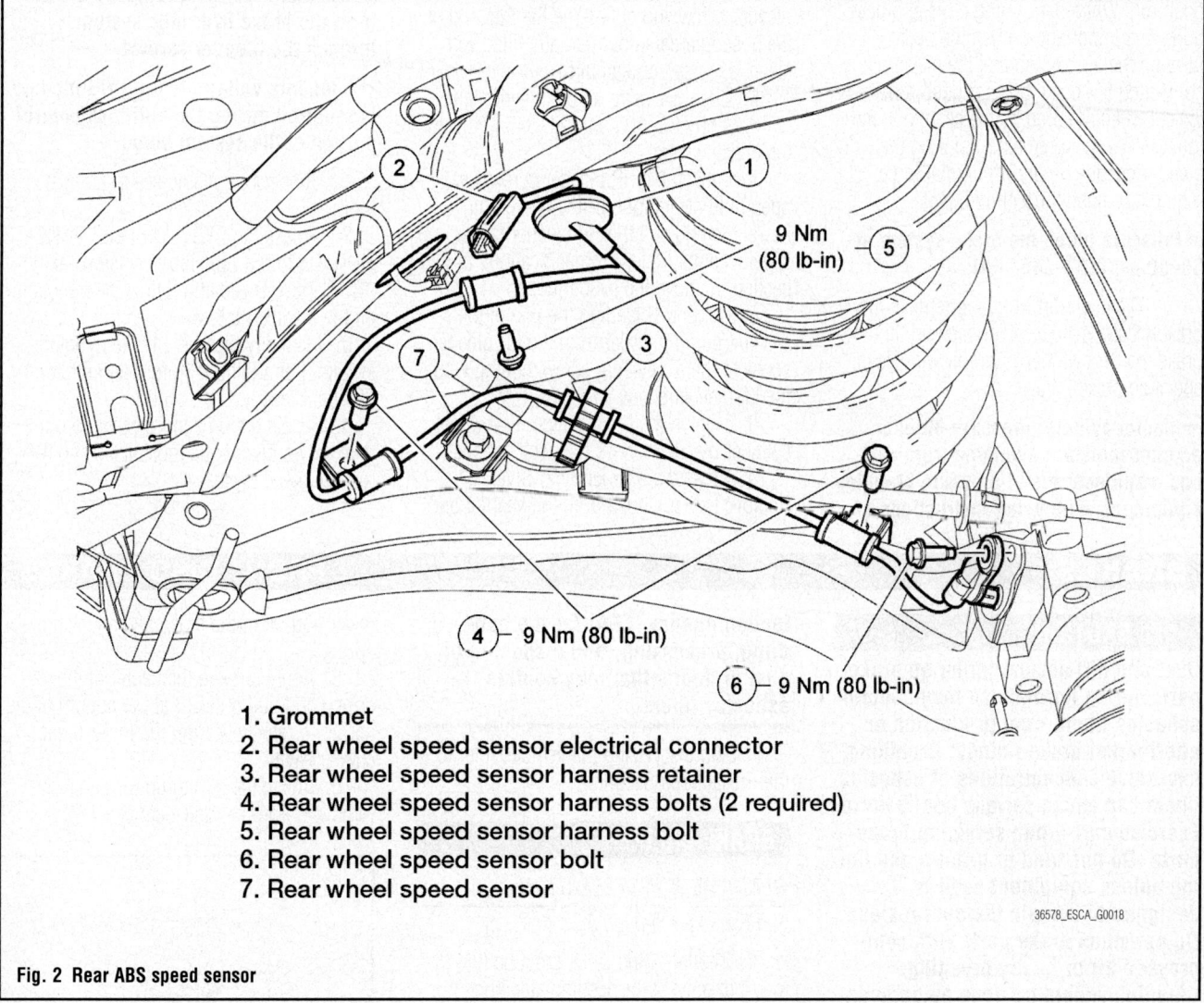

1. Grommet
2. Rear wheel speed sensor electrical connector
3. Rear wheel speed sensor harness retainer
4. Rear wheel speed sensor harness bolts (2 required)
5. Rear wheel speed sensor harness bolt
6. Rear wheel speed sensor bolt
7. Rear wheel speed sensor

36578_ESCA_G0018

Fig. 2 Rear ABS speed sensor

BRAKES

BLEEDING THE BRAKE SYSTEM

BLEEDING PROCEDURE

Pressure Bleeding

Due to the complexity of the fluid path within the hybrid brake system, it is necessary to pressure bleed this system. On hybrid vehicles, the brake booster push rod has an elongated slot that attaches to the brake pedal with a clevis pin. The elongated slot allows for a small amount of pedal travel (free play) to occur without the brake pedal applying pressure on the booster push rod. When performing a bleed procedure, it is important to push the pedal through the air gap, so that the clevis pin is contacting the brake booster push rod. Except when required by the scan tool, the ignition key must remain off during the bleed procedure to allow minimal force required to push through the gap.

➡**Pressure bleed the brake system at 30–50 psi (207–345 kPa).**

1. Clean all dirt from and remove the brake master cylinder filler cap and fill the brake master cylinder reservoir with clean, specified brake fluid.

➡**Master cylinder pressure bleeder adapter tools are available from various manufacturers of pressure bleeding equipment. Follow the instructions of**

the manufacturer when installing the adapter.

2. Install the bleeder adapter to the brake master cylinder reservoir, and attach the bleeder tank hose to the fitting on the adapter.

3. Make sure the bleeder tank contains enough clean, specified brake fluid to complete the bleeding operation.

4. Remove the RR bleeder screw cap and place a box-end wrench on the bleeder screw. Attach a rubber drain hose to the RR bleeder screw and submerge the free end of the hose in a container partially filled with clean, specified brake fluid.

5. Open the valve on the bleeder tank.

6. Apply 30–50 psi (207–345 kPa).) to the brake system.

7. Loosen the RR bleeder screw. Leave open until clear, bubble-free brake fluid flows, then tighten the RR bleeder screw to specifications. Refer to Specifications in this section. Remove the rubber hose.

8. Continue bleeding the rest of the system, going in order from the LR bleeder screw to the RF bleeder screw, ending with the LF bleeder screw.

9. Tighten the brake caliper and wheel cylinder bleeder screws to specifications.

10. Close the bleeder tank valve. Remove the tank hose from the adapter and

remove the adapter. Fill the reservoir with clean, specified brake fluid and install the reservoir cap.

BLEEDING THE ABS SYSTEM

➡**Bleeding the Hydraulic Control Unit (HCU) is required only when removing or installing the HCU or master cylinder, or opening the lines to the HCU.**

➡**Carrying out the System Bleed function drives trapped air from the HCU. Subsequent bleeding removes the air from the brake hydraulic system through the bleeder screws.**

➡**Adequate voltage to the HCU module is required during the anti-lock control portion of the system bleed.**

1. Connect a suitable scan/diagnostic tool.

2. Access the SYSTEM BLEED FUNCTION. Go to the Tool Tab-Chassis-Braking-ABS Service Bleed and follow the directions on the diagnostic tool.

3. Manually bleed the brake hydraulic system. For additional information, refer to Manual Bleed in this section.

4. Repeat the procedure carrying out a total of two diagnostic tool cycles and two manual bleed cycles.

BRAKES

FRONT DISC BRAKES

✳✳ CAUTION

Dust and dirt accumulating on brake parts during normal use may contain asbestos fibers from production or aftermarket brake linings. Breathing excessive concentrations of asbestos fibers can cause serious bodily harm. Exercise care when servicing brake parts. Do not sand or grind brake lining unless equipment used is designed to contain the dust residue. Do not clean brake parts with compressed air or by dry brushing. Cleaning should be done by dampening the brake components with a fine mist of water, then wiping the brake components clean with a dampened cloth. Dispose of cloth and all residue containing asbestos fibers in an impermeable container with the appropriate label. Follow practices prescribed by the Occupational Safety and Health Administration (OSHA) and the Environmental Pro-

tection Agency (EPA) for the handling, processing, and disposing of dust or debris that may contain asbestos fibers.

1. Before servicing the vehicle, refer to the Precautions Section.

BRAKE CALIPER

REMOVAL & INSTALLATION
See Figures 3 through 5.

1. The following steps must be followed to prevent the accumulator from charging and pressurizing the brake system:
   • Disconnect the battery.
   • Remove the battery junction box (BJB) fuses 9 (50A) and 18 (50A).

2. Remove the wheel and tire assembly.

3. Safely raise the vehicle.

4. For the LH brake caliper, release the

lower portion of the brake pad anti-rattle spring.

5. Apply force to the center of the spring and pull outward at the bottom of the spring to remove it from the lower brake caliper cavity.

6. Rotate the spring upward and remove it from the brake caliper.

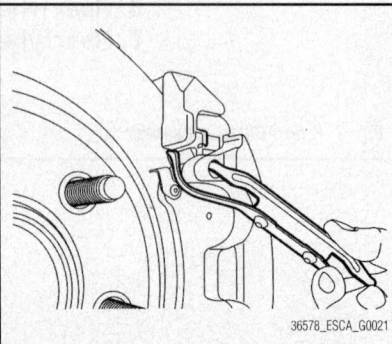

36578_ESCA_G0021

Fig. 3 For the LH brake caliper, rotate the spring upward and remove it from the brake caliper

7. For the RH brake caliper, release the upper portion of the brake pad anti-rattle spring.

8. Apply force to the center of the spring and pull outward at the top of the spring to remove it from the upper brake caliper cavity.

9. Rotate the spring downward and remove it from the brake caliper.

➡️**The brake caliper and brake flexible hose are removed as an assembly.**

10. Disconnect the brake tube fitting from the brake flexible hose.

11. Remove and discard the retainer clip from the brake flexible hose.

12. Remove the 2 guide pin bushing caps and the 2 brake caliper guide pin bolts, position the caliper aside. Support the caliper using mechanic's wire.

13. Remove the front brake caliper from the vehicle.

14. Remove the brake flexible hose from the brake caliper.

To install:

15. Install the brake pads onto the caliper and position the brake caliper onto the anchor plate.

16. Install the 2 brake caliper guide pin bolts and tighten to 37 ft. lbs. (50 Nm).

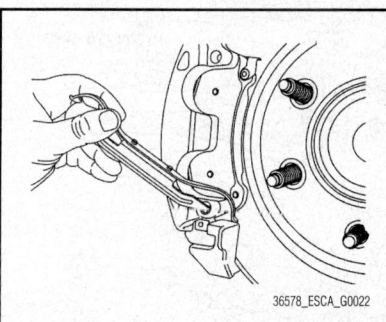

Fig. 4 For the RH brake caliper, rotate the spring downward and remove it from the brake caliper

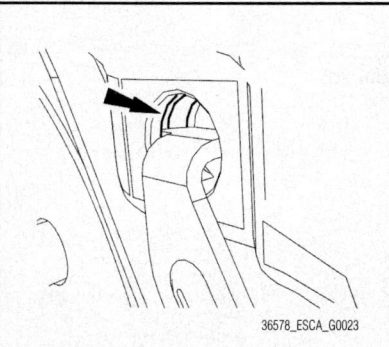

Fig. 5 Brake pad anti-rattle spring correct installation shown

17. Install the 2 bushing caps.

➡️**If present, the 2-tabbed end of the brake pad anti-rattle spring must be installed first.**

18. Install the brake pad anti-rattle spring using the following procedure:
*   Insert the tab of the spring into the brake caliper cavity.
*   Twist the tab into the cavity (LH side in the upper brake caliper cavity, RH side in the lower brake caliper cavity).

19. Rotate the brake pad anti-rattle spring and position the upper portion onto the anchor plate.

20. Position the lower portion of the brake pad anti-rattle spring onto the anchor plate.

21. Push down and inward until the upper and lower ends of the brake pad anti-rattle spring are latched and seated in the brake caliper cavities.

22. Verify that the brake pad anti-rattle spring is correctly latched by pulling on the spring.

➡️**Make sure that the brake flexible hose is not twisted.**

23. Install the brake flexible hose to the brake caliper. Tighten the hose to 177 inch lbs. (20 Nm).

24. Position the brake flexible hose and install a new retainer clip.

25. Attach the brake tube fitting to the brake flexible hose and tighten to 159 inch lbs. (18 Nm).

26. Bleed the brake caliper.

27. Install the wheel and tire.

28. Lower the vehicle.

29. Install the battery junction box (BJB) fuses 9 (50A) and 18 (50A).

30. Connect the battery.

31. Check the brake fluid level and add as needed.

DISC BRAKE PADS

REMOVAL & INSTALLATION

1. Before servicing the vehicle, refer to the Precautions Section.

2. With the vehicle in NEUTRAL, position it on a hoist.

3. The following steps must be followed to prevent the accumulator from charging and pressurizing the brake system:
*   Disconnect the battery.
*   Remove the battery junction box (BJB) fuses 9 (50A) and 18 (50A).

4. Remove the tire and wheel assembly.

5. Safely raise the vehicle.

6. For the LH brake caliper, release the

lower portion of the brake pad anti-rattle spring.

7. Apply force to the center of the spring and pull outward at the bottom of the spring to remove it from the lower brake caliper cavity.

8. Rotate the spring upward and remove it from the brake caliper.

9. For the RH brake caliper, release the upper portion of the brake pad anti-rattle spring.

10. Apply force to the center of the spring and pull outward at the top of the spring to remove it from the upper brake caliper cavity.

11. Rotate the spring downward and remove it from the brake caliper.

12. Remove the 2 guide pin bushing caps and the 2 brake caliper guide pin bolts, position the caliper aside.

13. Support the caliper using mechanic's wire.

14. Remove the 2 brake pads from the caliper.

15. Use a suitable tool to protect the brake caliper piston and compress the brake caliper piston into the brake caliper.

16. Inspect the brake disc and resurface or install new as necessary

To install:

17. Clean, dry and inspect the brake caliper anchor plate. Apply a light coat of specified lubricant to the 4 brake pad

➡️**NOTE: Make sure that the brake flexible hose is not twisted.**

18. Install the brake pads onto the caliper and position the brake caliper onto the anchor plate.

19. Install the 2 brake caliper guide pin bolts and tighten to 37 ft. lbs. (50 Nm) install the 2 bushing caps.

➡️**The 2-tabbed end of the brake pad anti-rattle spring must be installed first.**

20. Install the brake pad anti-rattle spring using the following procedure:
*   Insert the tab of the spring into the brake caliper cavity.
*   Twist the tab into the cavity (LH side in the upper brake caliper cavity, RH side in the lower brake caliper cavity).
*   Rotate the brake pad anti-rattle spring and position the upper portion onto the anchor plate.
*   Position the lower portion of the brake pad anti-rattle spring onto the anchor plate.
*   Push down and inward until the upper and lower ends of the brake

pad anti-rattle spring are latched and seated in the brake caliper cavities.

✳✳ WARNING

The latch MUST be positioned as shown, or damage to component may occur.

BRAKES

✳✳ CAUTION

Dust and dirt accumulating on brake parts during normal use may contain asbestos fibers from production or aftermarket brake linings. Breathing excessive concentrations of asbestos fibers can cause serious bodily harm. Exercise care when servicing brake parts. Do not sand or grind brake lining unless equipment used is designed to contain the dust residue. Do not clean brake parts with compressed air or by dry brushing. Cleaning should be done by dampening the brake components with a fine mist of water, then wiping the brake components clean with a dampened cloth. Dispose of cloth and all residue containing asbestos fibers in an impermeable container with the appropriate label. Follow practices prescribed by the Occupational Safety and Health Administration (OSHA) and the Environmental Protection Agency (EPA) for the handling, processing, and disposing of dust or debris that may contain asbestos fibers.

BRAKE CALIPER

REMOVAL & INSTALLATION

See Figure 6.

1. Before servicing the vehicle, refer to the Precautions Section.
2. The following steps must be followed to prevent the accumulator from charging and pressurizing the brake system:
   - Disconnect the battery.
   - Remove the battery junction box (BJB) fuses 9 (50A) and 18 (50A)
3. Safely raise the vehicle.
4. Remove the wheel and tire assembly.
5. Remove the brake flexible hose flow bolt and discard the 2 copper washers.
6. Remove the 2 brake caliper guide bolts.
7. Remove the rear brake caliper.

8. Remove the brake pads from the rear brake caliper.

To install:

9. Install the brake pads to the rear brake caliper.
10. Install the rear brake caliper.
11. Install the 2 brake caliper guide bolts and tighten to 26 ft. lbs. (25 Nm).
12. Install the flexible hose with new cooper washers, tighten the flow bolt to 26 ft. lbs. (25 Nm).

→Verify that the brake pad anti-rattle spring is correctly latched by pulling on the spring.

21. Install the wheel and tire.
22. Install the battery junction box (BJB) fuses 9 (50A) and 18 (50A).
23. Connect the battery.
24. Install the tire and wheel assembly.

25. Lower the vehicle.
26. Fill the brake master cylinder reservoir with clean, specified brake fluid.
27. Apply brakes several times to verify correct brake operation.
28. Test the brakes for normal operation.

REAR DISC BRAKES

13. Bleed the brake caliper.
14. Install the tire and wheel assembly.
15. Lower the vehicle.
16. Install the battery junction box (BJB) fuses 9 (50A) and 18 (50A).
17. Connect the negative battery cable.

DISC BRAKE PADS

REMOVAL & INSTALLATION

See Figure 6.

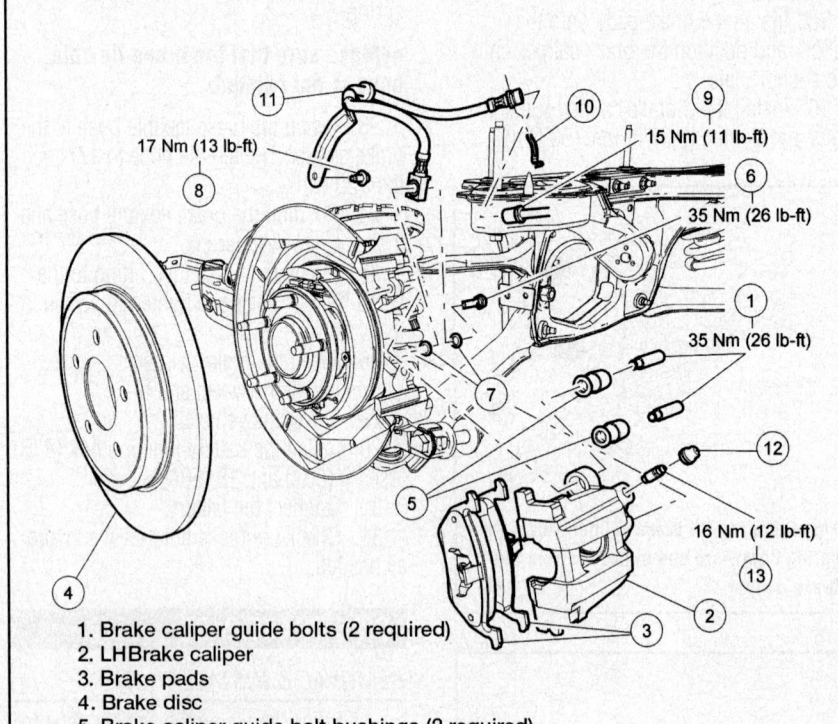

17 Nm (13 lb-ft)
15 Nm (11 lb-ft)
35 Nm (26 lb-ft)
35 Nm (26 lb-ft)
16 Nm (12 lb-ft)

1. Brake caliper guide bolts (2 required)
2. LH Brake caliper
3. Brake pads
4. Brake disc
5. Brake caliper guide bolt bushings (2 required)
6. Brake flexible hose flow bolt
7. Copper washers (2 required)
8. Brake flexible hose bracket bolt
9. Brake line fitting nut
10. Brake flexible hose retaining clip
11. LH Brake flexible hose
12. Bleeder screw cap
13. Bleeder screw

36578_ESCA_G0024

Fig. 6 Rear disc brake system—exploded view

1. Before servicing the vehicle, refer to the Precautions Section.

2. The following steps must be followed to prevent the accumulator from charging and pressurizing the brake system:
   - Disconnect the battery.
   - Remove the battery junction box (BJB) fuses 9 (50A) and 18 (50A)

3. Safely raise the vehicle.

4. Remove the wheel and tire assembly.

5. Remove the 2 brake caliper guide pin bolts and position the caliper aside. Support the caliper using mechanic's wire.

6. Remove the brake pads from the brake caliper.

To install:

7. Install the brake pads to the brake caliper.

8. Install the brake caliper.

9. Install the brake caliper guide pins and tighten to 26 ft. lbs. (35 Nm).

10. Install the tire and wheel assembly.

11. Lower the vehicle.

12. Install the battery junction box (BJB) fuses 9 (50A) and 18 (50A).

13. Connect the negative battery cable.

14. Pump the brake pedal to seat and adjust pads.

BRAKES   REAR DRUM BRAKES

BRAKE DRUM

REMOVAL & INSTALLATION

See Figure 7.

✳✳ CAUTION

Dust and dirt accumulating on brake parts during normal use may contain asbestos fibers from production or aftermarket brake linings. Breathing excessive concentrations of asbestos fibers can cause serious bodily harm. Exercise care when servicing brake parts. Do not sand or grind brake lining unless equipment used is designed to contain the dust residue. Do not clean brake parts with compressed air or by dry brushing. Cleaning should be done by dampening the brake components with a fine mist of water, then wiping the brake components clean with a dampened cloth. Dispose of cloth and all residue containing asbestos fibers in an impermeable container with the appropriate label. Follow practices prescribed by the Occupational Safety and Health Administration (OSHA) and the Environmental Protection Agency (EPA) for the handling, processing, and disposing of dust or debris that may contain asbestos fibers.

1. Before servicing the vehicle, refer to the Precautions Section.

2. Remove the tire and wheel assembly.

✳✳ CAUTION

Use of a brake drum puller or a torch is not recommended. Brake drum distortion can result.

➡ If the brake drum is rusted to the axle shaft pilot diameter, tap the center of the brake drum between the wheel studs.

3. Remove the brake drum.

4. If equipped, remove the brake drum retaining clips.

5. If the brake drums will not come off, follow these steps.

6. Move the brake shoe adjusting lever off the brake adjuster screw.

7. Loosen the brake shoe adjuster screw nut by adjusting the nut upward.

8. Using the special tool, 134-R0191, measure the brake drum inside diameter.

9. Install a new brake drum if the maximum inside diameter exceeds the

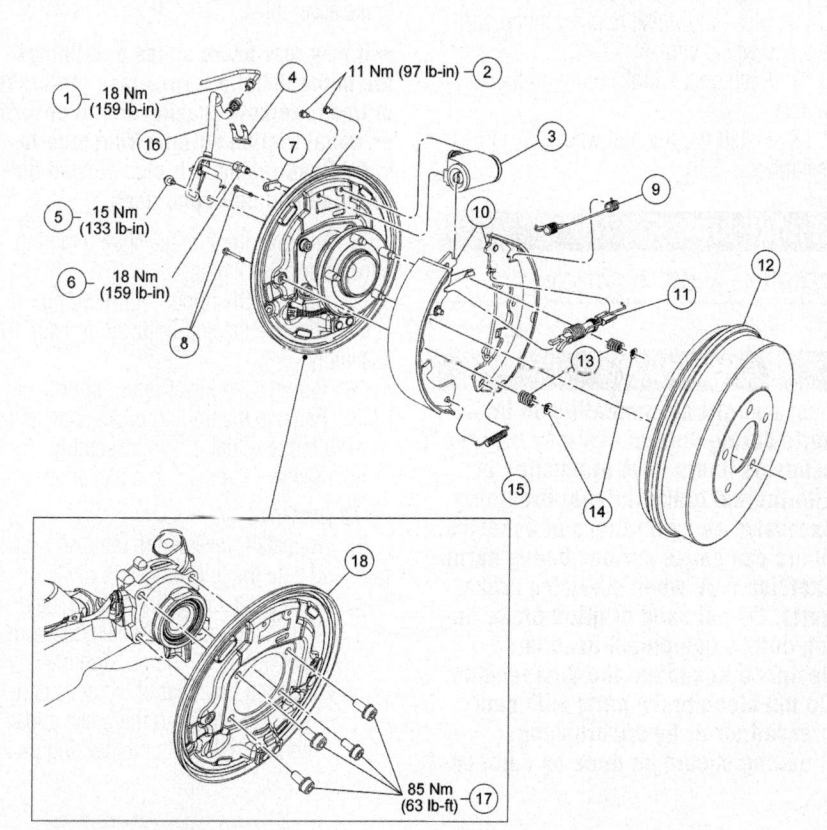

1. Brake tube fitting
2. Wheel cylinder bolts
3. Wheel cylinder
4. Brake flexible hose clip
5. Brake flexible hose bracket bolt
6. Brake flexible hose fitting
7. Plug
8. Brake shoe retaining pins
9. Upper return spring
10. Brake shoe (kit)
11. Self-adjuster assembly
12. Brake drum
13. Brake shoe retaining springs
14. Brake shoe retaining spring plates
15. Lower return spring
16. Brake flexible hose
17. Backing plate bolts
18. Backing plate

Fig. 7 Drum brake system—exploded view

36578_ESCA_G0025

specification shown on the outside of the brake drum.

To install:

> ### ✷ WARNING
>
> **Whenever a wheel is installed, always remove any corrosion, dirt or foreign material present on the mounting surfaces of the wheel or the surface of the wheel hub, brake drum or brake disc that contacts the wheel. Installing wheels without correct metal-to-metal contact at the wheel mounting surfaces can cause the wheel nuts to loosen and the wheel to come off while the vehicle is in motion, causing loss of control. Failure to follow these instructions may result in personal injury.**

10. Adjust the rear brakes.
11. Clean the wheel hub mounting surface and wheel pilot.
12. Position the brake drum on the vehicle.
13. Install the tire and wheel assembly.

BRAKE SHOES

REMOVAL & INSTALLATION
See Figure 7.

> ### ✷ CAUTION
>
> **Dust and dirt accumulating on brake parts during normal use may contain asbestos fibers from production or aftermarket brake linings. Breathing excessive concentrations of asbestos fibers can cause serious bodily harm. Exercise care when servicing brake parts. Do not sand or grind brake lining unless equipment used is designed to contain the dust residue. Do not clean brake parts with compressed air or by dry brushing. Cleaning should be done by dampen-**

ing the brake components with a fine mist of water, then wiping the brake components clean with a dampened cloth. Dispose of cloth and all residue containing asbestos fibers in an impermeable container with the appropriate label. Follow practices prescribed by the Occupational Safety and Health Administration (OSHA) and the Environmental Protection Agency (EPA) for the handling, processing, and disposing of dust or debris that may contain asbestos fibers.

1. Before servicing the vehicle, refer to the Precautions Section.
2. Remove the tire and wheel assembly.
3. Remove the brake drum.
4. Use the Brake/Clutch/Service Vacuum to remove brake dust and dirt from the brake assemblies.

➡ **If new rear brake shoes and linings are being installed, resurface the brake drums to remove glazing and to ensure an equal friction surface from side-to-side. Resurfacing will also correct out-of-round and bell conditions.**

5. Remove the 2 brake shoe retaining springs and the 2 pins.
6. Remove the upper return spring.
7. Remove the self-adjuster and spring assembly.
8. Remove the lower return spring.
9. Remove the trailing brake shoe and parking brake actuator lever assembly.
10. Remove the leading brake shoe.

To install:
11. To install, reverse the removal procedure and note the following:
- Using specified brake parts cleaner, clean and dry the brake shoe contact points on the backing plate.
- Apply a thin coat of the specified silicone grease to the brake shoe contact points on the backing plate.

- Adjust the self-adjuster to the full retracted position to ease the installation of the brake drum.
12. Adjust the rear brake shoes.
13. Install the brake drum.
14. Install the tire and wheel assembly.

ADJUSTMENT

See Figures 8 and 9.

1. Remove the brake drum.
2. Using the special tool, 134-R0191, measure the brake drum inside diameter.
3. Position the special tool on the brake shoes and linings and adjust accordingly.
4. Install the brake drum

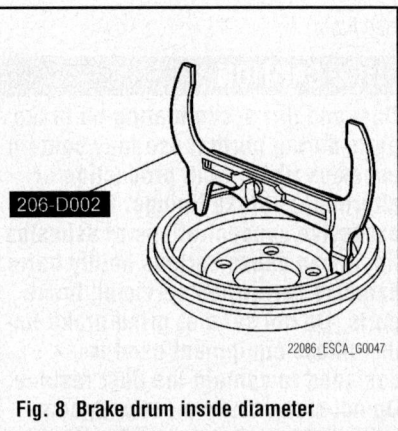

Fig. 8 Brake drum inside diameter

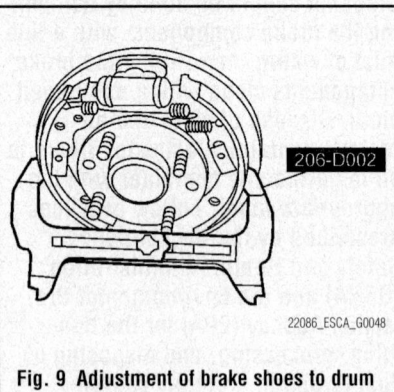

Fig. 9 Adjustment of brake shoes to drum inside diameter

BRAKES   **PARKING BRAKE**

PARKING BRAKE CABLES

ADJUSTMENT

If the parking brake needs to be adjusted, refer to the Parking Brake Shoes Adjustment in this section.

If the parking brake needs to be adjusted, refer to the Brake Shoes Adjustment in this section.

PARKING BRAKE SHOES

REMOVAL & INSTALLATION

With Rear Drum Brakes

The rear drum brake shoes serve as the parking brakes. Refer to the procedures under Rear Drum Brakes.

With Rear Disc Brakes

See Figure 10.

1. Before servicing the vehicle, refer to the Precautions Section.
2. Remove the rear brake disc.
3. Remove the parking brake shoe upper return spring.
4. Remove the 2 parking brake shoe retaining pins.
5. Remove the 2 parking brake shoe retaining springs.
6. Remove the parking brake shoe lower return spring.
7. Remove the parking brake shoe adjuster.
8. Remove the parking brake shoes.

To install:

9. To install, reverse the removal procedure.

- Using anti-seize lubricant, lubricate the parking brake shoe contact points before installation of the rear parking brake shoes.

- Lubricate the adjust screw threads with anti-seize lubricant.
- Adjust the parking brake shoes.
- Check the parking brake for normal operation.

ADJUSTMENT

See Figures 11 and 12.

1. Before servicing the vehicle, refer to the Precautions Section.
2. With the vehicle in NEUTRAL, position it on a hoist.

➡ **Make sure the parking brake is fully released.**

3. Using the release handle, release the parking brake control.
4. Remove the rear brake disc.
5. Using the special tool, measure the inside diameter of the drum portion of the

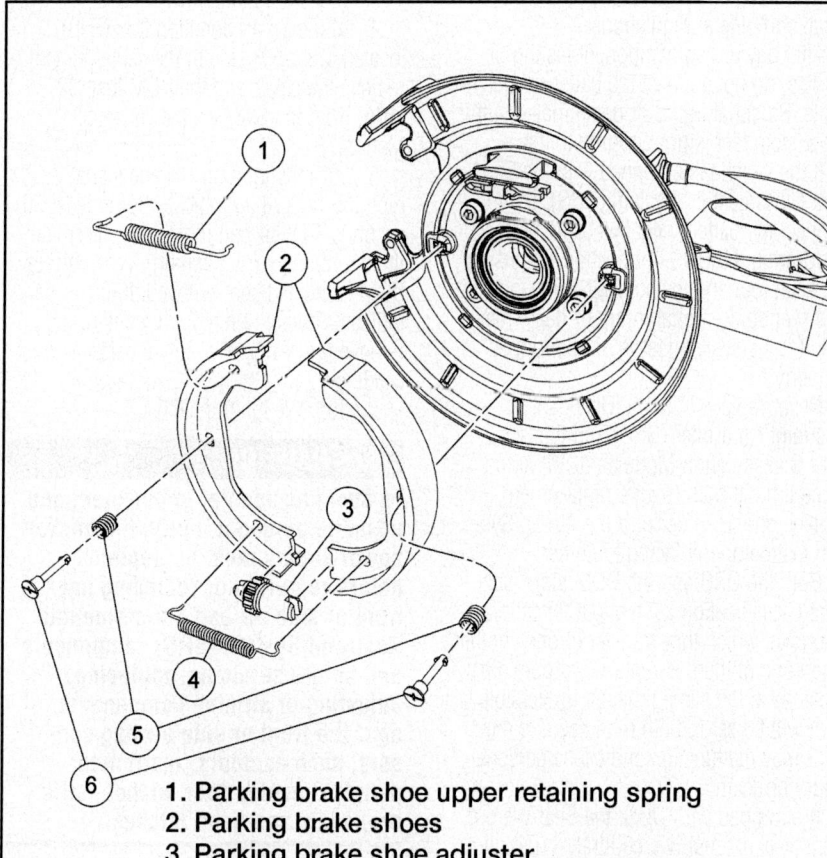

1. Parking brake shoe upper retaining spring
2. Parking brake shoes
3. Parking brake shoe adjuster
4. Parking brake shoe lower retaining spring
5. Parking brake shoe retaining springs (2 required)
6. Parking brake shoe retaining pins (2 required)

36578_ESCA_G0026

Fig. 10 Parking brake shoes

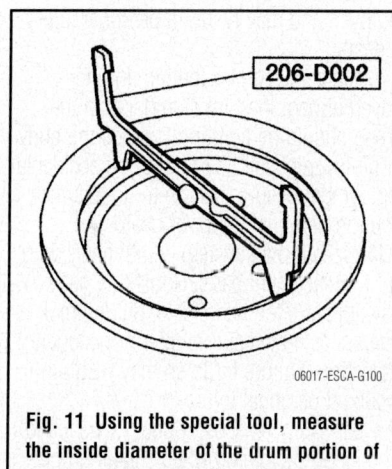

206-D002

06017-ESCA-G100

Fig. 11 Using the special tool, measure the inside diameter of the drum portion of the rear brake disc and set the locking screw

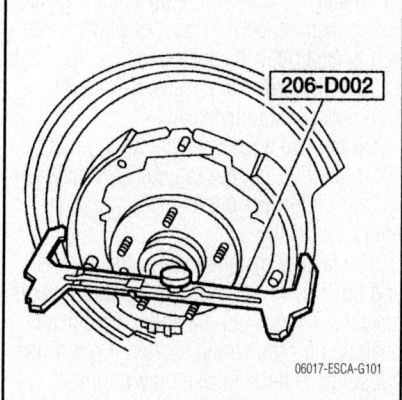

206-D002

06017-ESCA-G101

Fig. 12 Place the special tool over the widest diameter of the parking brake shoes

rear brake disc and set the locking screw. Record the measurement.

6. Place the special tool over the widest diameter of the parking brake shoes.

7. Adjust the parking brake shoe clearance to 0.01 inch (0.50 mm) less than the inside diameter of the drum portion of the rear brake disc. Rotate the parking brake shoe adjuster to achieve the correct parking brake shoe-to-brake disc clearance.

8. Install the rear brake disc.

9. Test the parking brake for normal operation.

CHASSIS ELECTRICAL

AIR BAG (SUPPLEMENTAL RESTRAINT SYSTEM)

GENERAL INFORMATION

SERVICE PRECAUTIONS

Disconnect and isolate the battery negative cable before beginning any airbag system component diagnosis, testing, removal, or installation procedures. Allow system capacitor to discharge for two minutes before beginning any component service. This will disable the airbag system. Failure to disable the airbag system may result in accidental airbag deployment, personal injury, or death.

Do not place an intact undeployed airbag face down on a solid surface. The airbag will propel into the air if accidentally deployed and may result in personal injury or death.

When carrying or handling an undeployed airbag, the trim side (face) of the airbag should be pointing towards the body to minimize possibility of injury if accidental deployment occurs. Failure to do this may result in personal injury or death.

Replace airbag system components with OEM replacement parts. Substitute parts may appear interchangeable, but internal differences may result in inferior occupant protection. Failure to do so may result in occupant personal injury or death.

Wear safety glasses, rubber gloves, and long sleeved clothing when cleaning powder residue from vehicle after an airbag deployment. Powder residue emitted from a deployed airbag can cause skin irritation. Flush affected area with cool water if irritation is experienced. If nasal or throat irritation is experienced, exit the vehicle for fresh air until the irritation ceases. If irritation continues, see a physician.

Do not use a replacement airbag that is not in the original packaging. This may result in improper deployment, personal injury, or death.

The factory installed fasteners, screws and bolts used to fasten airbag components have a special coating and are specifically designed for the airbag system. Do not use substitute fasteners. Use only original equipment fasteners listed in the parts catalog when fastener replacement is required.

During, and following, any child restraint anchor service, due to impact event or vehicle repair, carefully inspect all mounting hardware, tether straps, and anchors for proper installation, operation, or damage. If a child restraint anchor is found damaged in any way, the anchor must be replaced. Failure to do this may result in personal injury or death.

Deployed and non-deployed airbags may or may not have live pyrotechnic material within the airbag inflator.

Do not dispose of driver/passenger/curtain airbags or seat belt tensioners unless you are sure of complete deployment. Refer to the Hazardous Substance Control System for proper disposal.

Dispose of deployed airbags and tensioners consistent with state, provincial, local, and federal regulations.

After any airbag component testing or service, do not connect the battery negative cable. Personal injury or death may result if the system test is not performed first.

If the vehicle is equipped with the Occupant Classification System (OCS), do not connect the battery negative cable before performing the OCS Verification Test using the scan tool and the appropriate diagnostic information. Personal injury or death may result if the system test is not performed properly.

Never replace both the Occupant Restraint Controller (ORC) and the Occupant Classification Module (OCM) at the same time. If both require replacement, replace one, then perform the Airbag System test before replacing the other.

Both the ORC and the OCM store Occupant Classification System (OCS) calibration data, which they transfer to one another when one of them is replaced. If both are replaced at the same time, an irreversible fault will be set in both modules and the OCS may malfunction and cause personal injury or death.

If equipped with OCS, the Seat Weight Sensor is a sensitive, calibrated unit and must be handled carefully. Do not drop or handle roughly. If dropped or damaged, replace with another sensor. Failure to do so may result in occupant injury or death.

If equipped with OCS, the front passenger seat must be handled carefully as well.

When removing the seat, be careful when setting on floor not to drop. If dropped, the sensor may be inoperative, could result in occupant injury, or possibly death.

If equipped with OCS, when the passenger front seat is on the floor, no one should sit in the front passenger seat. This uneven force may damage the sensing ability of the seat weight sensors. If sat on and damaged, the sensor may be inoperative, could result in occupant injury, or possibly death.

DISARMING THE SYSTEM

1. Before servicing the vehicle, refer to the Precautions Section.

2. Turn all vehicle accessories OFF.

3. Turn the ignition switch to OFF.

4. At the Smart Junction Box (SJB) located at the RH side of the center console, remove the cover and the RCM fuse 32 (10A) from the SJB See the Owner's Manual.

5. Turn the ignition ON and visually monitor the air bag indicator for at least 30 seconds. The air bag indicator will remain lit continuously (no flashing) if the correct RCM fuse has been removed. If the air bag indicator does not remain lit continuously, remove the correct RCM fuse before proceeding.

6. Turn the ignition OFF.

✳✳ CAUTION

To avoid accidental deployment and possible personal injury, the backup power supply must be depleted before repairing or replacing any front or side air bag Supplemental Restraint System (SRS) components and before servicing, replacing, adjusting or striking components near the front or side air bag sensors, such as doors, instrument panel, console, door latches, strikers, seats and hood latches.

➡To deplete the backup power supply energy, disconnect the battery ground cable and wait at least one minute. Be sure to disconnect auxiliary batteries and power supplies (if equipped).

7. Disconnect the battery ground cable and wait at least one minute

ARMING THE SYSTEM

1. Before servicing the vehicle, refer to the Precautions Section.
2. Turn the ignition from OFF to ON.
3. Install RCM fuse 32 (10A) to the SJB and install the cover.

> **❊❊ CAUTION**
>
> **Make sure no one is in the vehicle and there is nothing blocking or placed in front of any air bag module when the battery is connected. Failure to follow these instructions may result in serious personal injury in the event of an accidental deployment.**

4. Connect the battery ground cable. Prove out the SRS as follows:
5. Turn the ignition from ON to OFF. Wait 10 seconds, then turn the ignition back ON and monitor the air bag warning indicator with the air bag modules installed. The air bag indicator will light continuously for approximately 6 seconds and then turn off. If an air bag SRS fault is present, the air bag indicator will:
- Fail to light.
- Remain lit continuously.
- Flash.
6. The flashing might not occur until approximately 30 seconds after the ignition has been turned from the OFF to the ON position. This is the time required for the RCM to complete the testing of the SRS. If the air bag indicator is inoperative and a SRS fault exists, a chime will sound in a pattern of 5 sets of 5 beeps. If this occurs, the air bag warning indicator and any SRS fault discovered must be diagnosed and repaired.
7. Clear all continuous DTCs from the RCM using a scan tool.

CLOCKSPRING CENTERING
See Figure 13.

➡**To prevent damage to the clockspring, make sure the road wheels are in the 12 o'clock position to install the steering wheel.**

If a new clockspring was installed and the anti-rotation key has been removed before the steering wheel is installed or the same clockspring is being installed, rotate the clockspring inner rotor counterclockwise and carefully feel for the ribbon wire to run out of length with slight resistance. Stop rotating the clockspring inner rotor at this point.

1. Starting with the clockspring inner rotor, wiring and connector in the 12 o'clock position, rotate the inner rotor clockwise through 4 revolutions to center the clockspring.
2. Verify that the clockspring is correctly centered by observing that after 4 revolutions:
- The clockspring rotor window is in the 4 o'clock position and the yellow indicator shows in the window.
- The 2 arrows located on the inner and outer rotor of the clockspring line up in the 6 o'clock position.
- The clockspring inner rotor, wiring and connector are in the 12 o'clock position.

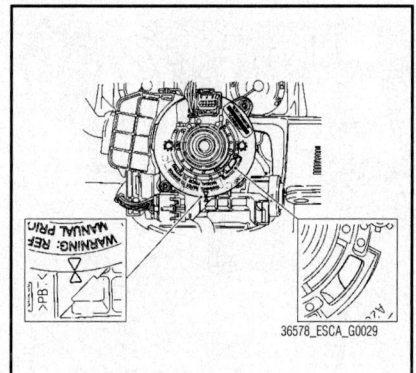

36578_ESCA_G0029

Fig. 13 Correct clockspring centering view

> **❊❊ CAUTION**
>
> **Do not over-rotate the clockspring inner rotor. The internal ribbon wire is connected to the clockspring rotor. The internal ribbon wire acts as a stop and can be broken from its internal connection. Failure to follow this instruction may result in component damage and/or system failure.**

DRIVE TRAIN

AUTOMATIC TRANSAXLE ASSEMBLY

REMOVAL & INSTALLATION

Refer to Engine Electrical section for the Hybrid Transaxle.

TRANSFER CASE ASSEMBLY

REMOVAL & INSTALLATION
See Figure 14.

The Transfer case is referred to as the Power Transfer Unit (PTU) for this model vehicle.

1. Before servicing the vehicle, refer to the Precautions Section.

All vehicles
2. With the vehicle in NEUTRAL, position it on a hoist
3. Drain the Power Transfer Unit (PTU).
4. Remove the front RH intermediate shaft. Refer to Intermediate Shaft Removal & Installation in the Drive Train section.
5. Remove the driveshaft. Refer to Driveshaft Removal & Installation in the Drive Train section.
6. Remove the 4 bolts and the cross-member brace.

All vehicles
7. Remove the 3 PTU heat shield bolts and the PTU heat shield.
8. Remove the 2 exhaust bracket nuts.
9. Remove the 6 PTU-to-engine bracket bolts and the bracket.
10. Disconnect the PTU vent tube and position it aside.
11. Remove the 3 PTU-to-transaxle bolts.
12. Remove the PTU.

To install:
All vehicles
13. If necessary, install a new RH differential fluid seal.
14. Position the Power Transfer Unit (PTU) to the transaxle.

15. Install the 3 PTU-to-transaxle bolts and tighten to 52 ft. lbs. (70 Nm).
16. Install the PTU-to-transaxle bolt (M10) and tighten to 35 ft. lbs. (48 Nm).
17. Connect the PTU vent tube.
18. Install the PTU-to-engine bracket and the 6 bracket bolts and 2 exhaust bracket bolts. Tighten the bolts to 35 ft. lbs. (48 Nm).
19. Install the PTU heat shield and the 3 PTU heat shield bolts. Tighten the bolts to 97 inch lbs. (11 Nm).
All vehicles
20. Install the crossmember brace and the 4 bolts. Tighten the bolts to 30 ft. lbs. (40 Nm).
21. Install the driveshaft.
22. Install the front RH intermediate shaft.
23. Install the exhaust as required.
24. Fill the PTU with Motorcraft® SAE 75W-140 synthetic lubricant.
25. Check the transaxle fluid level.

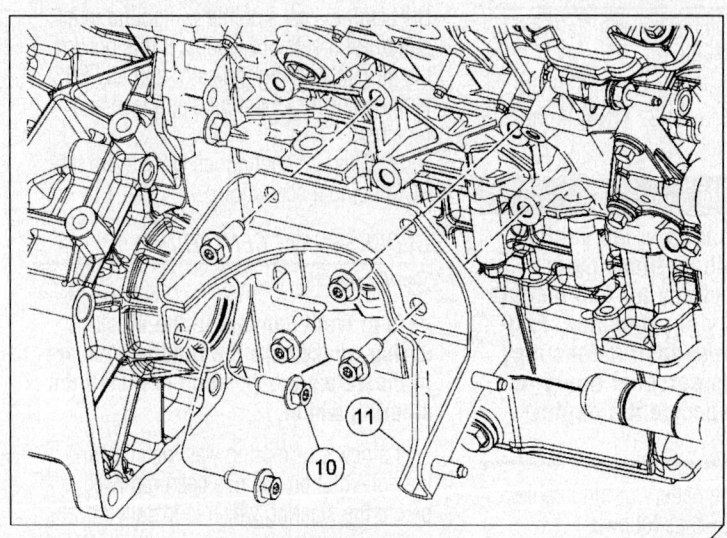

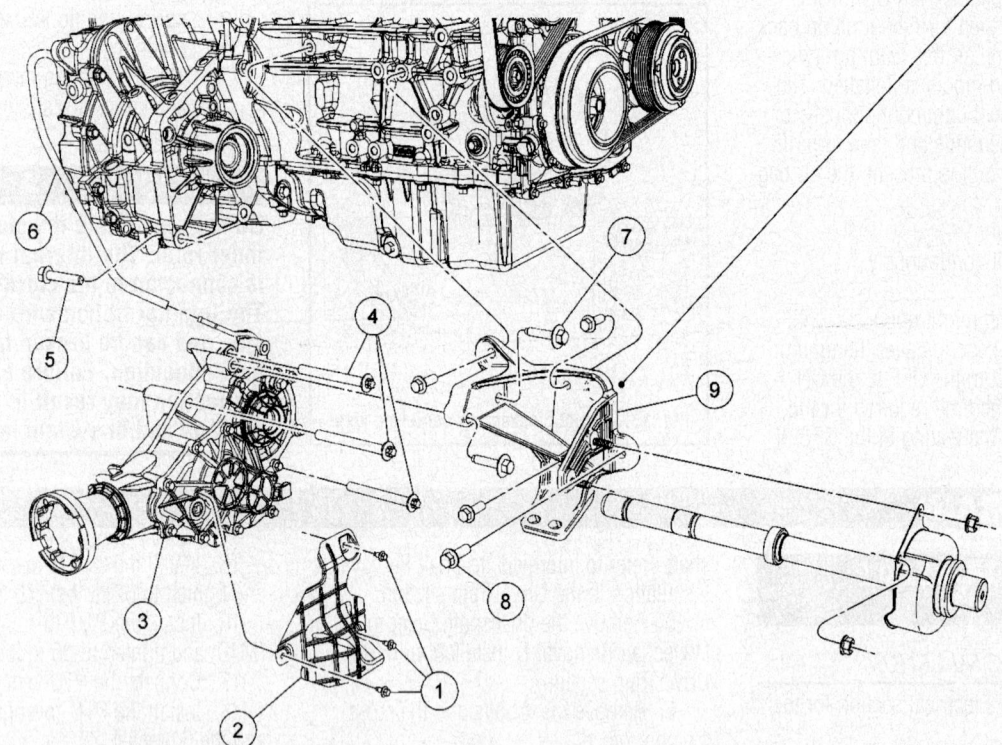

1. Power Transfer Unit (PTU) heat shield bolts (3 required)
2. PTU heat shield
3. PTU
4. PTU -to-transaxle bolts (3 required)
5. PTU -to-transaxle bolt (M10)
6. Vent tube
7. PTU -to-engine bracket bolt (4-cylinder engines) (2 required)
8. PTU -to-engine bracket bolt (4-cylinder engines) (4 required)
9. PTU -to-engine bracket (4-cylinder engines)
10. PTU -to-engine bracket bolts (6-cylinder engines) (6 required)
11. PTU -to-engine bracket (6-cylinder engines)

36578_ESCA_G0103

Fig. 14 Power Transfer Unit (PTU)

FRONT HALFSHAFTS

REMOVAL & INSTALLATION

See Figures 15 through 17.

All halfshafts

1. Before servicing the vehicle, refer to the Precautions Section.
2. With the vehicle in NEUTRAL, position it on a hoist.
3. Remove the front tire and wheel.
4. Remove and discard the front wheel hub nut.
5. Remove the ABS wheel speed sensor bolt and position the sensor aside.
6. Remove the lower arm pinch bolt and nut from the lower arm.

➡**Do not allow the ball joint stud to contact the CV joint boot.**

7. Separate the lower arm from the front wheel knuckle.
8. Using the front hub remover, separate the halfshaft from the wheel hub.

Left halfshaft

Using the halfshaft remover and slide hammer, remove the LH halfshaft from the differential.

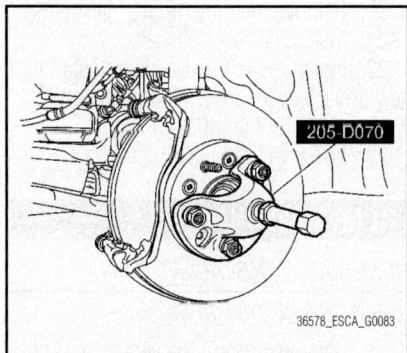

Fig. 15 Front hub remover installed to separate halfshaft from the wheel hub

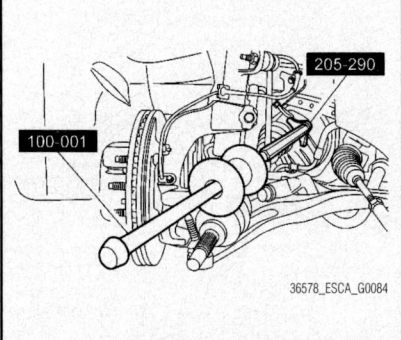

Fig. 16 Left halfshaft removal with slide hammer and adapter

Right halfshaft

9. Using a brass drift to strike the RH halfshaft in the indicated area, separate and remove the halfshaft.

To install:
Left halfshaft

➡**When seated correctly, the halfshaft bearing retainer circlip can be felt as it snaps into the differential side gear groove**

Position the LH halfshaft so the splines line up with the differential side gear splines. Push the halfshaft into the differential side gear.

Right halfshaft

10. Align the RH halfshaft with the splines of the intermediate shaft and push the halfshaft in until the circlip locks the shafts together.
11. Apply a thin coat of the specified grease to the splines of the intermediate shaft.

All halfshaft

12. Using the Halfshaft Installer, install the halfshaft into the front wheel hub.
13. Position the lower arm into the front wheel knuckle.
14. Install the new lower ball joint bolt and nut. Tighten to 46 ft. lbs. (63 Nm).
15. Install the ABS wheel speed sensor and bolt and tighten to 80 inch lbs. (9 Nm).

➡**Do not tighten the front wheel hub nut with the vehicle on the ground. The nut must be tightened to specification before the vehicle is lowered onto the wheels. Wheel bearing damage will occur if the wheel bearing is loaded with the weight of the vehicle applied.**

16. Apply the brake to keep the halfshaft from rotating.
17. Install new front wheel hub nut and tighten to 222 ft. lbs. (300 Nm).
18. Install the front tires and wheels.

19. Check and fill the transaxle fluid as necessary.

CV-BOOTS INSPECTION

1. With the vehicle in NEUTRAL, position it on a hoist.
➡Turn the wheels to inspect the entire boot.
2. Check the CV-boots for rips and tears.
3. Check for grease leaking from the CV-boots.
4. Check the boot bands for damage.
5. Replace any component if found to be defective.

INTERMEDIATE SHAFT

REMOVAL & INSTALLATION

See Figure 18.

➡**If removing the intermediate shaft in order to repair a separate component, it should only be removed as an assembly with the RH front drive halfshaft.**

1. Before servicing the vehicle, refer to the Precautions Section.
2. Remove the RH halfshaft. Refer to halfshaft Removal & Installation in this section.
3. Remove the 2 intermediate shaft bearing retainer nuts.
4. Remove the intermediate shaft.

➡**On All-Wheel Drive (AWD) vehicles, the Power Transfer Unit (PTU) seal must be replaced every time the intermediate shaft is removed.**

To install:
5. Install a new PTU seal for AWD models.
6. Install the intermediate shaft.
7. Install the 2 intermediate shaft bearing retainer nuts. Tighten the retaining nuts to 20 ft. lbs. (27 Nm).

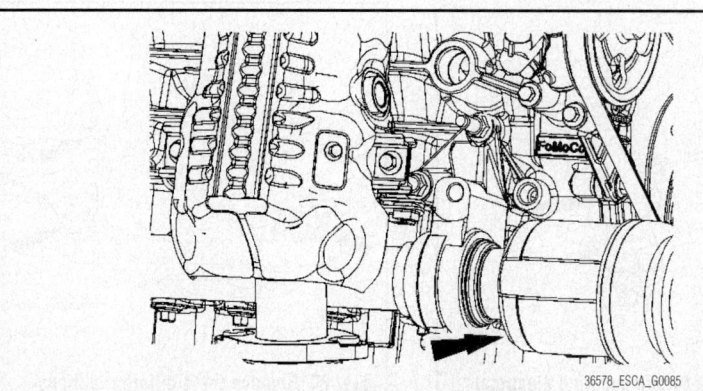

Fig. 17 Strike the RH in the area shown to remove the halfshaft

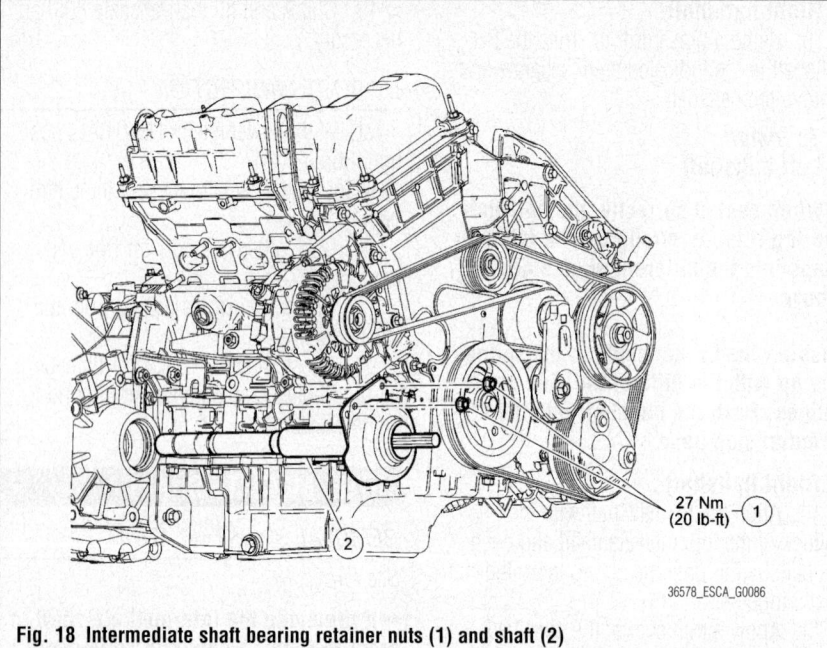

Fig. 18 Intermediate shaft bearing retainer nuts (1) and shaft (2)

8. Apply a thin coat of the specified grease to the splines of the intermediate shaft.

9. Install the RH halfshaft.

10. Check and fill the transaxle fluid as necessary.

REAR AXLE HOUSING

REMOVAL & INSTALLATION

See Figures 19 through 21.

1. Before servicing the vehicle, refer to the Precautions Section.

2. With the vehicle in NEUTRAL, position it on a hoist.

3. Index-mark the driveshaft flange and the pinion flange.

4. Remove and discard the 4 driveshaft-to-drive pinion bolts and position aside the rear driveshaft. Support the driveshaft.

5. Remove the rear halfshafts. Refer to

Halfshaft Removal & Installation in this section.

6. Position a suitable transmission hydraulic jack to the axle housing. Securely strap the jack to the housing.

7. Disconnect the active torque coupling electrical connector.

8. Remove the 4 differential housing-to-front insulator bracket bolts.

9. Remove and discard the LH front insulator bracket-to-subframe bolt and rotate the bracket aside.

10. Remove and discard the RH front insulator bracket-to-subframe bolt and the bracket.

11. Remove the 3 LH side insulator bracket-to-rear axle differential bolts.

12. Lower the rear axle assembly.

To install:

13. Position a suitable transmission hydraulic jack to the axle housing. Securely strap the jack to the housing.

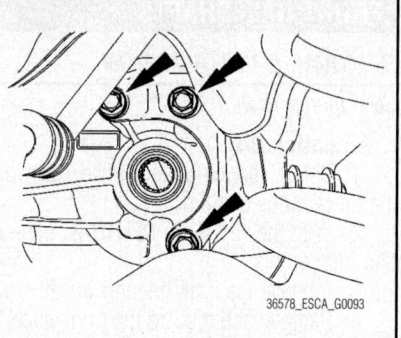

Fig. 21 Remove the 3 LH side insulator bracket-to-rear axle differential bolts

14. Install the rear axle assembly.

15. Install the 3 LH side insulator bracket-to-rear axle differential bolts and tighten to 66 ft. lbs. (90 Nm).

16. Install the RH front insulator bracket and tighten the new bracket-to-subframe bolt to 66 ft. lbs. (90 Nm).

17. Install LH front insulator bracket and tighten the new bracket-to-subframe bolt to 66 ft. lbs. (90 Nm).

18. Install the 4 differential housing-to-front insulator bracket bolts and tighten to 66 ft. lbs. (90 Nm).

19. Connect the active torque coupling electrical connector.

20. Remove the transmission jack.

21. Install the rear halfshafts.

22. Install the rear drive shaft. Install 4 new driveshaft-to-drive pinion bolts and tighten to 30 ft. lbs. (40 Nm).

23. Lower the vehicle.

REAR HALFSHAFTS

REMOVAL & INSTALLATION

See Figures 22 through 25.

1. Before servicing the vehicle, refer to the Precautions Section.

2. Place the selector lever in NEUTRAL.

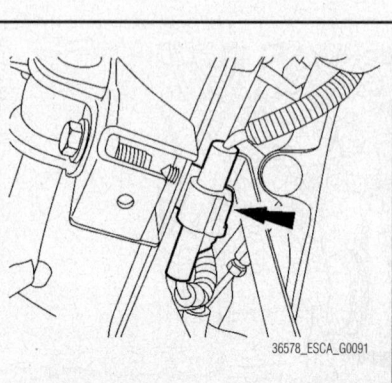

Fig. 19 Active torque coupling electrical connector

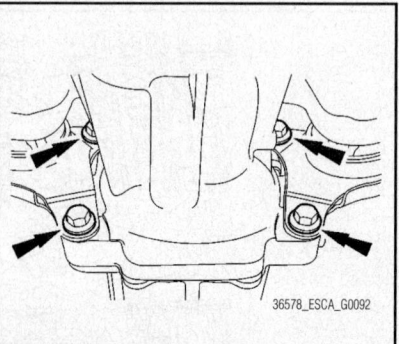

Fig. 20 Remove the 4 differential housing-to-front insulator bracket bolts

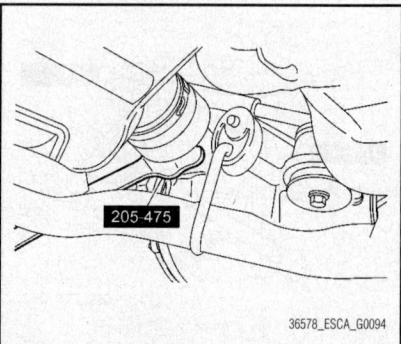

Fig. 22 Halfshaft removal with special tool

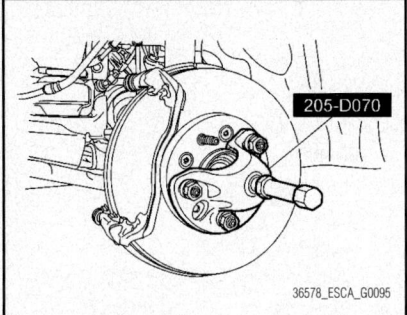

Fig. 23 Halfshaft separation with special tool

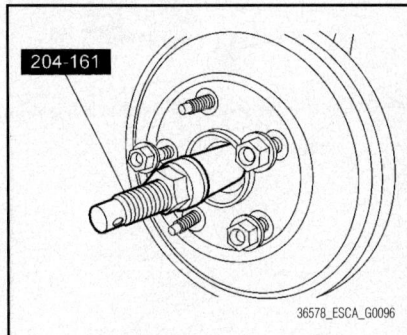

Fig. 24 Halfshaft pulled into the hub with the installation tool

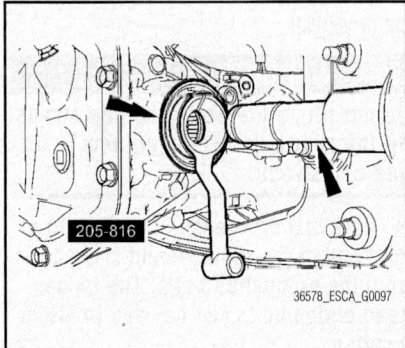

Fig. 25 Install the halfshaft into the differential using the seal protector

3. Raise and support the vehicle.

✻✻ WARNING

Do not loosen the rear axle wheel hub retainer until after the wheel and tire assembly are removed from the vehicle. Wheel bearing damage will occur if the wheel bearing is unloaded with the weight of the vehicle applied.

4. Remove the rear brake drum or brake disc.

5. Remove the rear coil spring. Refer to

Coil Spring Removal & Installation in the Rear Suspension section.

6. Remove and discard the rear wheel hub nut.

7. Remove the anti-lock brake sensor harness-to-body retainer bolt.

8. Remove the nut and separate the lower ball joint.

✻✻ WARNING

Do not damage the oil seal when removing the axle halfshaft from the differential.

9. Using the special tool, remove the halfshaft from the differential.

10. Using the special tool, separate the halfshaft from the rear axle hub assembly.

11. Remove the rear halfshaft.

To install:

12. Using the halfshaft installer, pull the outer halfshaft end into the hub assembly.

13. Using the axle seal protector, install the halfshaft into the differential.

14. If the axle is equipped with the oil seal protector, make sure the oil seal lip and seal protector are correctly aligned.

15. Position the lower ball joint and install the lower ball joint nut. Tighten the lower ball joint nut to 76 ft. lbs. (103 Nm).

16. Install the rear coil spring.

17. Install the anti-lock brake sensor harness-to-body bolt and tighten to 80 inch lbs. (9 Nm).

➥Do not tighten the rear wheel hub nut with the vehicle on the ground. The nut must be tightened to specification before the vehicle is lowered onto the wheels. Wheel bearing damage will occur if the wheel bearing is loaded with the weight of the vehicle applied.

18. Apply the brake to keep the halfshaft from rotating.

19. Install the rear wheel hub nut and tighten to 222 ft. lbs. (300 Nm).

20. Check the differential fluid an add as needed.

REAR PINION SEAL

REMOVAL & INSTALLATION

See Figures 26 through 29.

1. Before servicing the vehicle, refer to the Precautions Section.

2. With the vehicle in NEUTRAL, position it on a hoist.

3. Index-mark the pinion and pinion flange to the rear of the driveshaft.

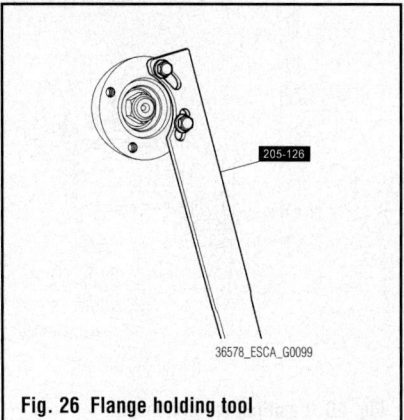

Fig. 26 Flange holding tool

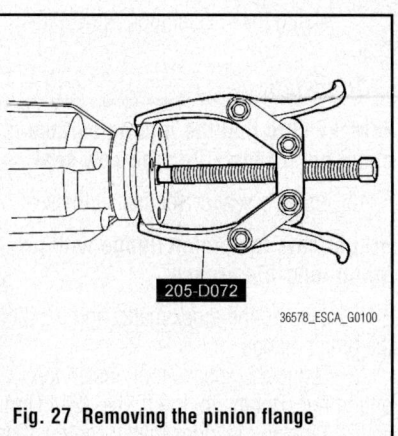

Fig. 27 Removing the pinion flange

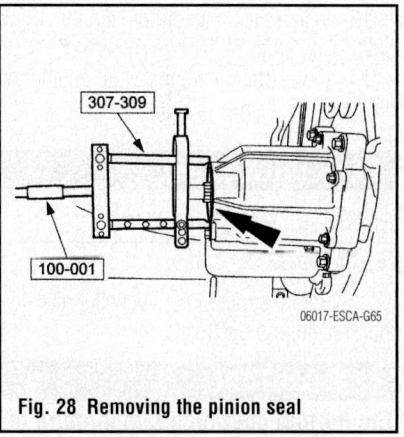

Fig. 28 Removing the pinion seal

4. Remove the 4 bolts and the 2 cap straps. Disconnect and support the driveshaft.

➥Discard the nut after removing it. Install a new nut during installation.

5. Using the special tool, hold the pinion flange while removing the nut. Remove the nut.

6. Index-mark the location of the pinion to the yoke.

7. Using a puller, remove the pinion flange.

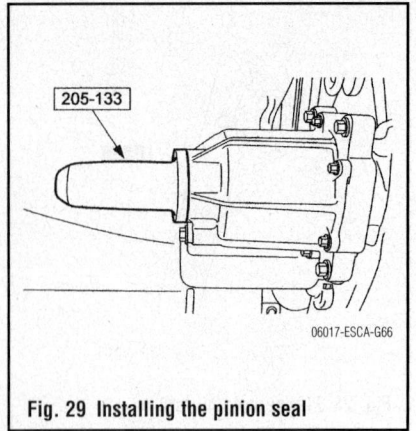

Fig. 29 Installing the pinion seal

8. Using the special tool, remove the seal.

To install:

➡ **Make sure that the mating surface is clean before installing the new seal.**

9. Using a seal driver, install the seal.

➡ **Lubricate the pinion flange with premium long-life grease.**

10. Line up the index marks and position the pinion flange.

11. Using the special tool, install the pinion nut. Tighten to 180 ft. lbs. (244 Nm).

12. Line up the index marks and position the rear driveshaft.

13. Install the 2 cap straps and the 4 bolts. Tighten to 52 ft. lbs (70 Nm).

14. Check the differential fluid an add as needed.

REAR DRIVESHAFT

REMOVAL & INSTALLATION

See Figure 30.

1. Before servicing the vehicle, refer to the Precautions Section.

❊❊ CAUTION

The normal operating temperature of the exhaust system is very high. Never attempt to remove any part of the system until it has cooled. Be especially careful when working around the catalytic converters. The temperature of the converter rises to a high level after only a few minutes of engine operation. Failure to follow these instructions may result in personal injury.

➡ **Do not swap driveshaft assembles from different vehicles. The Escape Hybrid drive shaft is longer than the driveshaft in the Escape/Mariner and is not interchangeable.**

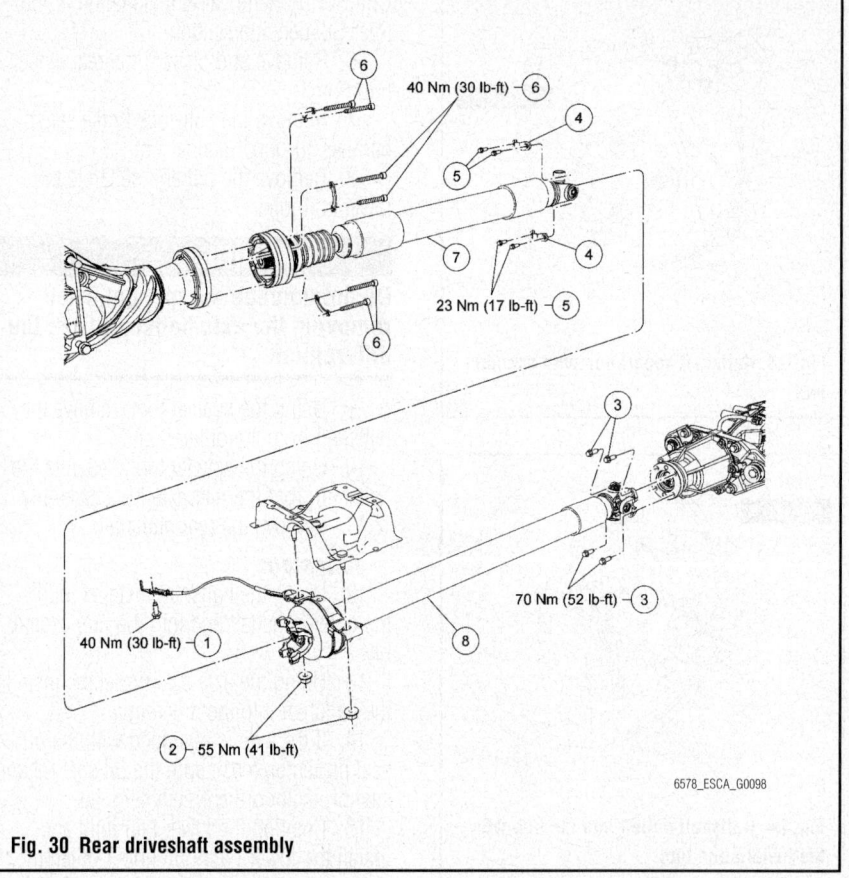

Fig. 30 Rear driveshaft assembly

With the vehicle in NEUTRAL, position it on a hoist.

2. Remove the ground strap bolt.

❊❊ WARNING

Do not reuse the CV-joint bolts and washers. Install new bolts and washers or damage to the vehicle may occur.

3. Remove and discard the 6 front driveshaft-to-transfer case bolts and washers.

4. Index-mark the front driveshaft to the center bearing.

❊❊ WARNING

Do not reuse the bolts and cap straps for the center U-joint. Install new bolts and cap straps or damage to the vehicle may occur.

➡ **There is a difference in the length of the head of the replacement cap strap bolts from the production bolts. The longer head pinion bolts can be used in either location.**

5. Remove and discard the 4 universal joint cap strap bolts and 2 cap straps and remove the front driveshaft.

6. Index-mark the pinion and yoke to the driveshaft.

❊❊ WARNING

Do not reuse the bolts and cap straps for the rear U-joint. Install new bolts and cap straps.

➡ **There is a difference in the length of the head of the replacement strap bolts from the production bolts. The longer head pinion bolts can be used in either location.**

7. Remove and discard the 4 universal joint cap bolts and 2 cap straps from the rear driveshaft universal joint.

8. With the help of an assistant, remove the center bearing support nuts and the driveshaft.

To install:

9. To install, reverse the removal procedure. Observe the following torques:
- Center bearing support nuts: 41 ft. lbs. (55 Nm)
- Rear universal joint cap bolts: 52 ft. lbs. (70 Nm)
- Front universal joint cap strap bolts: 17 ft. lbs. (23 Nm)
- The 6 front driveshaft-to-transfer case bolts: 30 ft. lbs. (40 Nm)

• Ground strap bolt: 30 ft. lbs. (40 Nm)

10. If a driveshaft is installed and drive-shaft vibration is encountered after installation, index the driveshaft.

    a. With the vehicle in NEUTRAL, position it on a hoist.

✲✲ WARNING

Do not reuse the CV-joint bolts and washers. Install new bolts and washers or damage to the vehicle may occur.

11. Remove and discard the 6 front drive-shaft-to-transfer case bolts and washers.

12. Rotate the flange 60 degrees.

13. Connect the front driveshaft and install the 6 new bolts and washers. Tighten to 30 ft. lbs. (40 Nm).

✲✲ WARNING

Do not reuse the bolts and cap straps for the pinion yoke. Install new bolts and cap straps or damage to the vehicle may occur.

14. Disconnect the rear driveshaft universal joint. Discard the 4 bolts and the 2 cap straps.

15. Rotate the rear pinion 180 degrees.

16. Connect the rear driveshaft and install 4 new bolts and 2 new cap straps. Tighten to 52 ft. lbs. (70 Nm).

17. Lower the vehicle and test drive.

18. Repeat the procedure if necessary.

ENGINE COOLING

ENGINE FAN

REMOVAL & INSTALLATION

See Figures 31 and 32.

1. Before servicing the vehicle, refer to the Precautions Section.

2. With vehicle in NEUTRAL, position it on a hoist.

3. Remove the front bumper cover.

4. Remove the 2 front impact severity sensors.

5. Remove the 4 bolts and the 2 radiator brackets.

6. Mark the hood latch position prior to removal of the bolts.

7. Loosen the nut, remove the 2 bolts and position aside the hood latch.

8. Remove the center support lower bolt.

9. Remove the bolt and the center support.

10. Remove the 2 bolts and position the auxiliary coolant pump aside.

11. Disconnect the cooling fan resistor electrical connector.

12. Disconnect the 2 cooling fan electrical connectors.

13. Remove the 6 cooling fan bolts.

➡**Remove the LH cooling fan first and slide the RH cooling fan to the left side to remove.**

14. Remove the LH and the RH cooling fans.

    To install:

15. To install, reverse the removal procedure and note the following:

• Tighten the 6 cooling fan bolts, the cooling fan motor and shroud bolts to 71 inch. lbs (8 Nm).

• Tighten the auxiliary coolant pump bolts to 62 inch. lbs (7 Nm).

• Tighten the center support bolts to 89 inch. lbs. (10 Nm).

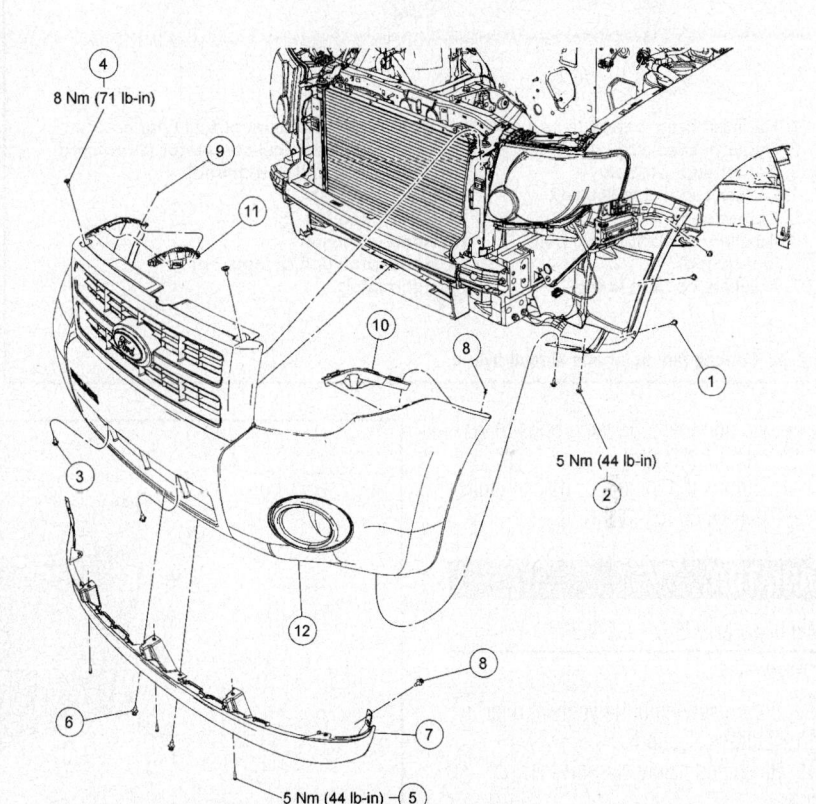

1. Fender splash shield scrivet (6 required)
2. Fender splash shield-to-air deflector bolt (4 required)
3. Front bumper cover center scrivet (2 required)
4. Front bumper cover upper bolt (2 required)
5. Front bumper cover air deflector bolt (3 required)
6. Front bumper cover air deflector pushpin (2 required)
7. Front bumper cover air deflector
8. Front bumper cover air deflector pushpins (2 required)
9. Front bumper cover mounting bracket pushpin (2 required)
10. Front bumper cover mounting bracket
11. Front bumper cover mounting bracket
12. Front bumper cover

36578_HYBR_G0003

Fig. 31 Front bumper—exploded view

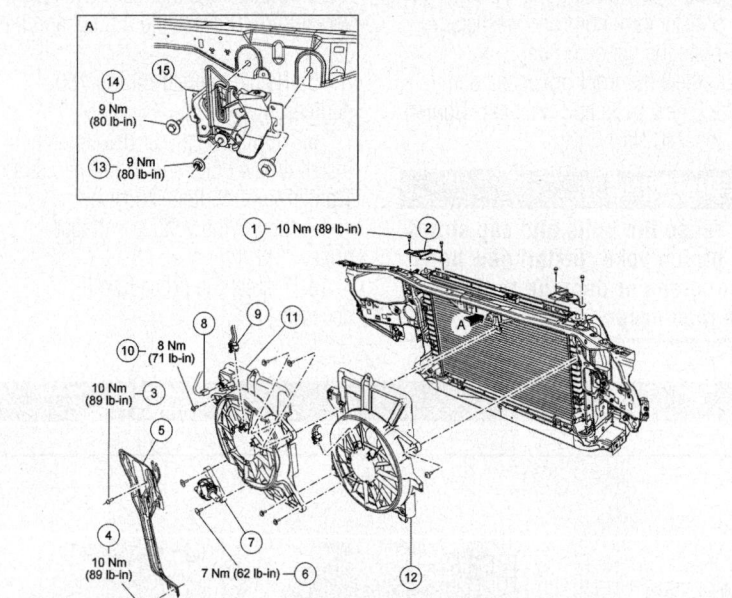

1. Radiator bracket bolt (4 required)
2. Radiator bracket (2 required)
3. Center support bolt
4. Center support lower bolt
5. Center support
6. Auxiliary coolant pump bolt (2 required)
7. Auxiliary coolant pump
8. Cooling fan resistor electrical connector
9. Cooling fan electrical connector (2 required)
10. Cooling fan bolt (6 required)
11. LH cooling fan
12. RH cooling fan
13. Hood latch nut
14. Hood latch bolt (2 required)
15. Hood latch

36578_HYBR_G0002

Fig. 32 Cooling fan motor and shroud hybrid

- Tighten the hood latch bolts to 80 inch lbs. (9 Nm).
- Tighten the 4 radiator bracket bolts to 89 inch lbs. (10 Nm).

RADIATOR

REMOVAL & INSTALLATION

See Figure 33.

1. Before servicing the vehicle, refer to the Precautions Section.
2. Raise and safely support the vehicle.
3. Drain the cooling system.
4. Drain the motor electronics cooling system, as follows:
   - With the vehicle in DRIVE, make sure the vehicle is raised and safely supported.
   - Turn the ignition to the OFF position.
   - Remove the LH splash shield.
   - Place a suitable container below the transaxle.
   - Loosen the hose clamps at the transaxle, then pull the hoses off to allow the coolant to drain.
5. Remove the cooling fan motor and shroud.

6. Disconnect the upper hose from the motor electronics radiator.
7. Remove the 2 motor electronics radiator-to-engine radiator bolts and position the motor electronics radiator aside.
8. Remove the 2 A/C condenser-to-radiator bolts and position the A/C condenser aside.
9. Disconnect the lower radiator hose from the radiator.
10. Disconnect the degas bottle return hose from the radiator.
11. Disconnect the engine coolant vent hose from the radiator.
12. Disconnect the upper radiator hose from the radiator.
13. Remove the radiator.

To install:

14. Installation is the reverse of the removal procedure, noting the following tightening specifications:
   - A/C condenser-to-radiator bolts: 89 inch lbs. (10 Nm)
   - Motor electronics radiator-to-engine radiator bolts: 53 inch lbs. (6 Nm).
15. Fill and bleed the cooling system.
16. Fill and bleed the motor electronics cooling system.

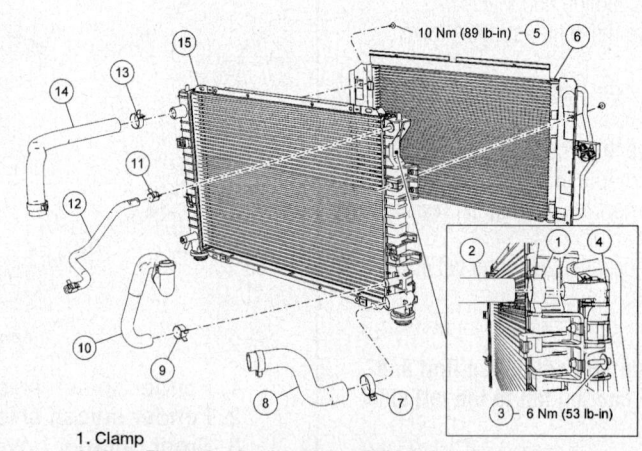

1. Clamp
2. Motor Electronics Cooling System (MECS) upper radiator hose
3. MECS radiator-to-engine radiator bolt (2 required)
4. MECS radiator
5. A/C condenser-to-radiator bolt (2 required)
6. A/C condenser
7. Clamp
8. Lower radiator hose
9. Clamp
10. Degas bottle return hose
11. Clamp
12. Engine coolant vent hose
13. Clamp
14. Upper radiator hose
15. Radiator

36578_HYBR_G0004

Fig. 33 Radiator and related components hybrid vehicle 2008–2009 models

THERMOSTAT

REMOVAL & INSTALLATION

See Figure 34.

➡ **The thermostat and thermostat housing are serviced as an assembly.**

1. Raise and safely support the vehicle.
2. Drain the cooling system.
3. Remove the accessory drive belt tensioner.
4. Disconnect the heater hose at the thermostat housing.
5. Disconnect the lower radiator hose at the thermostat housing.
6. Remove the 3 bolts, thermostat housing and gasket.
7. Clean and inspect the gasket, replace if necessary.
8. To install, reverse the removal procedure. Tighten the thermostat housing bolts to 89 inch lbs. (10 Nm).
9. Fill and bleed the cooling system.

WATER PUMP

REMOVAL & INSTALLATION

See Figure 35.

1. Before servicing the vehicle, refer to the Precautions Section.
2. With the vehicle in NEUTRAL, position it on a hoist.
3. Drain the cooling system.
4. Remove the accessory drive belt.
5. Remove the coolant pump pulley bolts.
6. Remove the coolant pump pulley.
7. Remove the coolant pump bolts.
8. Remove the coolant pump.
9. Remove the coolant pump O-ring seal.
10. To install, reverse the removal procedure and note the following:
    - Tighten the water pump bolts to 89 inch lbs. (10 Nm).
    - Tighten the pulley bolts to 15 ft. lbs. (20 Nm).
11. Fill and bleed the cooling system.

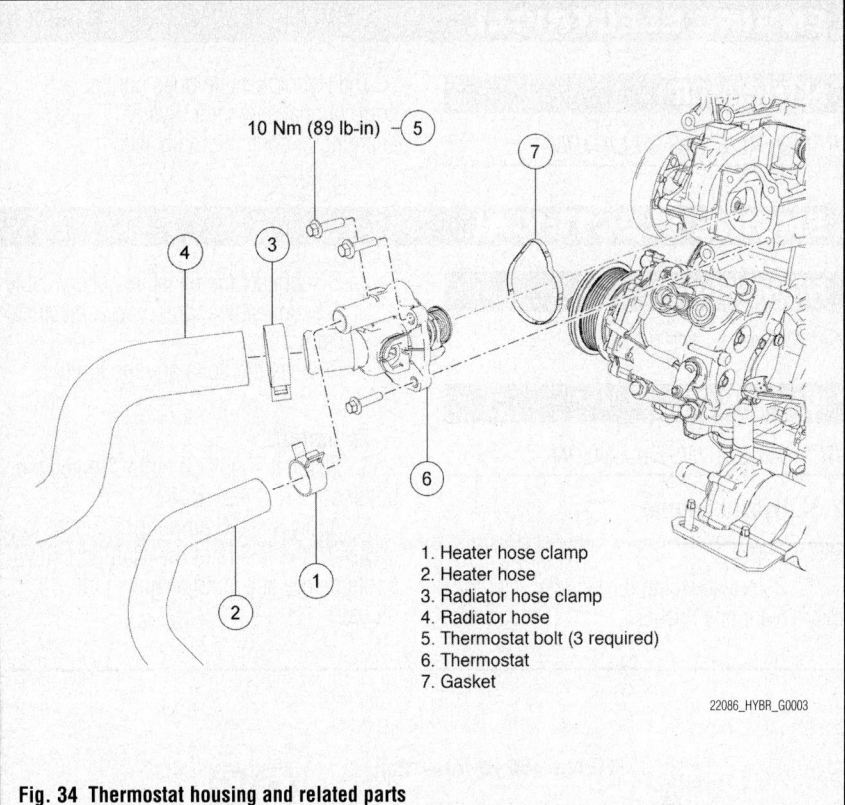

1. Heater hose clamp
2. Heater hose
3. Radiator hose clamp
4. Radiator hose
5. Thermostat bolt (3 required)
6. Thermostat
7. Gasket

22086_HYBR_G0003

Fig. 34 Thermostat housing and related parts

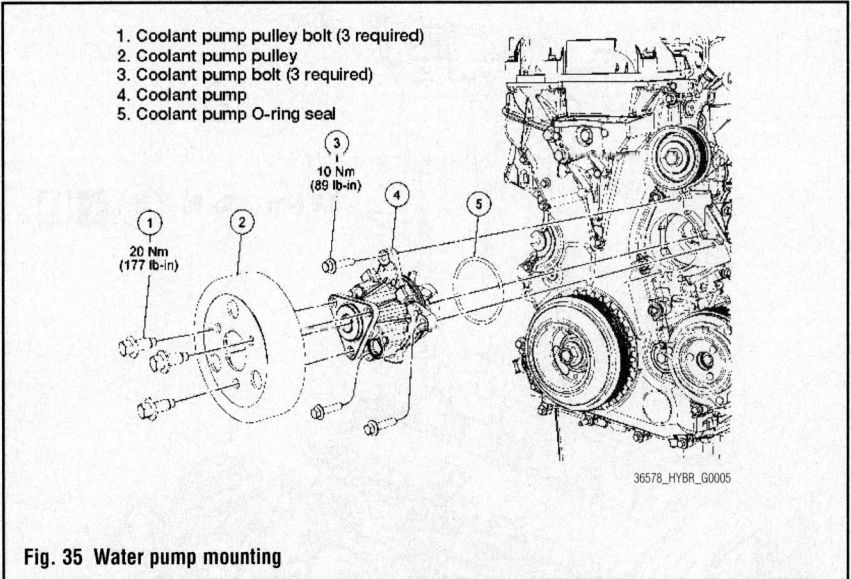

1. Coolant pump pulley bolt (3 required)
2. Coolant pump pulley
3. Coolant pump bolt (3 required)
4. Coolant pump
5. Coolant pump O-ring seal

36578_HYBR_G0005

Fig. 35 Water pump mounting

ENGINE ELECTRICAL

ALTERNATOR

REMOVAL & INSTALLATION

The Hybrid vehicle does not use a conventional alternator. System charging is done internally with the electric motor when it at as a generator.

CHARGING SYSTEM

ENGINE ELECTRICAL

FIRING ORDERS

See Figures 36 and 37.

IGNITION COIL

REMOVAL & INSTALLATION

2.3L Hybrid Engine
See Figure 38.

1. Before servicing the vehicle, refer to the Precautions Section.

2. Disconnect the negative battery cable.
3. Disconnect the ignition coil electrical connectors.
4. Remove the bolts and the ignition coils.

To install:
5. Install the ignition coils. Tighten the bolts to 71 inch lbs. (8 Nm).
6. Apply a small amount of dielectric grease to the inside of the ignition coil boots before attaching to the spark plugs.

IGNITION SYSTEM

2.5L Hybrid Engine
See Figure 39.

1. Before servicing the vehicle, refer to the Precautions Section.
2. Disconnect the negative battery cable.

➡**When removing the ignition coil-on-plugs, a slight twisting motion will break the seal and ease removal.**

3. Disconnect the 4 ignition coil electrical connectors.
4. Remove the bolts and the ignition coils.

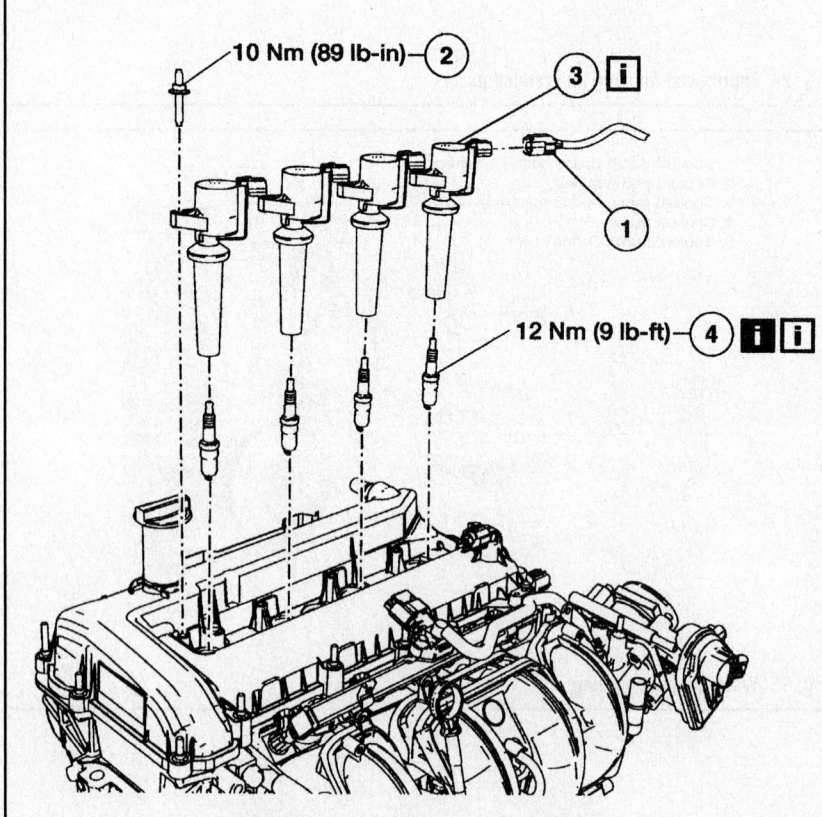

1 Ignition coil-on-plug electrical connectors
2 Ignition coil-to-valve cover bolts
3 Ignition coils
4 Spark plugs

67197-ESCA-G61

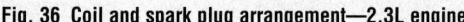

Fig. 36 Coil and spark plug arrangement—2.3L engine

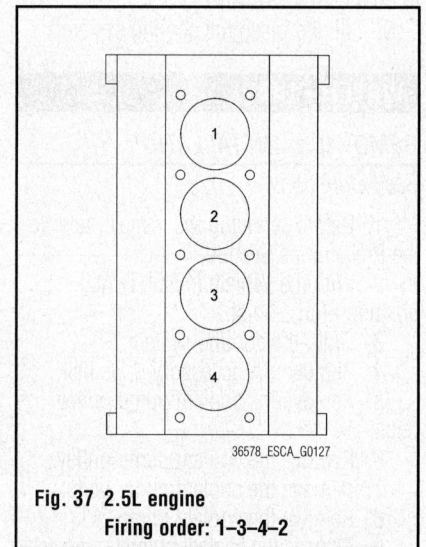

36578_ESCA_G0127

Fig. 37 2.5L engine
Firing order: 1–3–4–2

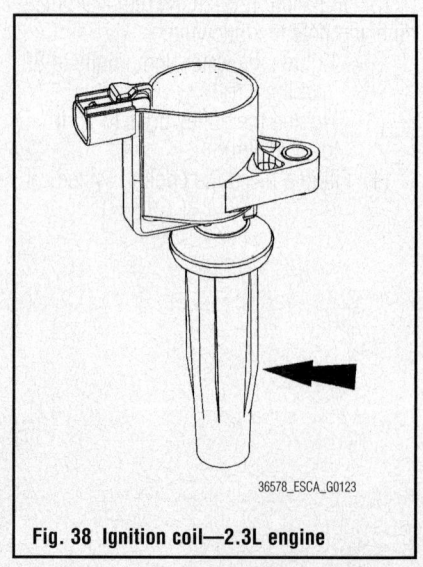

36578_ESCA_G0123

Fig. 38 Ignition coil—2.3L engine

8 Nm
(71 lb-in)
12 Nm
(106 lb-in)
36578_ESCA_G0126

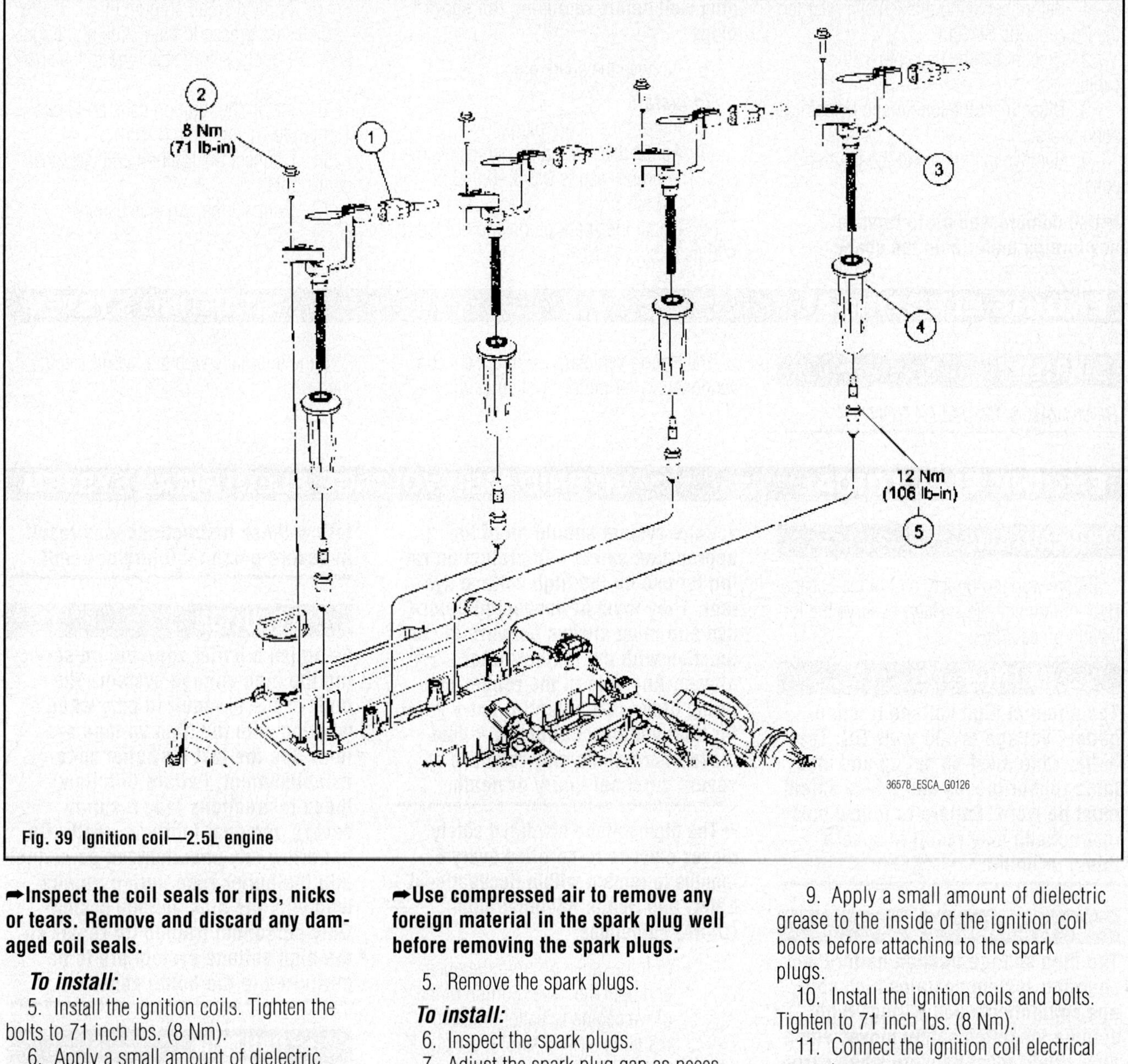

Fig. 39 Ignition coil—2.5L engine

➡Inspect the coil seals for rips, nicks or tears. Remove and discard any damaged coil seals.

To install:

5. Install the ignition coils. Tighten the bolts to 71 inch lbs. (8 Nm).

6. Apply a small amount of dielectric grease to the inside of the ignition coil boots before attaching to the spark plugs.

SPARK PLUGS

REMOVAL & INSTALLATION

2.3L Hybrid Engine

See Figure 40.

1. Before servicing the vehicle, refer to the Precautions Section.

2. Disconnect the negative battery cable.

3. Disconnect the ignition coil electrical connectors.

4. Remove the bolts and the ignition coils.

➡Use compressed air to remove any foreign material in the spark plug well before removing the spark plugs.

5. Remove the spark plugs.

To install:

6. Inspect the spark plugs.

7. Adjust the spark plug gap as necessary. The proper gap is 0.049–0.053 in. (1.25–1.35mm).

8. Install the spark plugs and tighten to 106 inch lbs. (12 Nm).

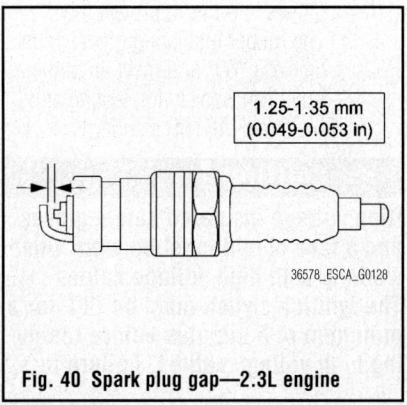

1.25-1.35 mm
(0.049-0.053 in)
36578_ESCA_G0128

Fig. 40 Spark plug gap—2.3L engine

9. Apply a small amount of dielectric grease to the inside of the ignition coil boots before attaching to the spark plugs.

10. Install the ignition coils and bolts. Tighten to 71 inch lbs. (8 Nm).

11. Connect the ignition coil electrical connectors.

12. Connect the negative battery cable.

2.5L Hybrid Engine

See Figure 41.

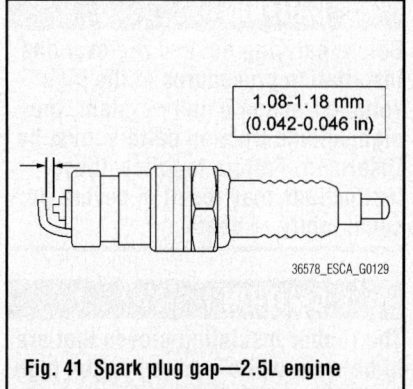

1.08-1.18 mm
(0.042-0.046 in)
36578_ESCA_G0129

Fig. 41 Spark plug gap—2.5L engine

1. Before servicing the vehicle, refer to the Precautions Section.

2. Disconnect the negative battery cable.

3. Disconnect the ignition coil electrical connectors.

4. Remove the bolts and the ignition coils.

➡ **Use compressed air to remove any foreign material in the spark plug well before removing the spark plugs.**

5. Remove the spark plugs.

To install:

6. Inspect the spark plugs.

7. Adjust the spark plug gap as necessary. The proper gap is 0.042–0.046 in. (1.08–1.18mm).

8. Install the spark plugs and tighten to 106 inch lbs. (12 Nm).

9. Apply a small amount of dielectric grease to the inside of the ignition coil boots before attaching to the spark plugs.

10. Install the ignition coils and bolts. Tighten to 71 inch lbs. (8 Nm).

11. Connect the ignition coil electrical connectors.

12. Connect the negative battery cable.

ENGINE ELECTRICAL

STARTER

REMOVAL & INSTALLATION

The Hybrid vehicle does not use a conventional starter motor. System starting is

STARTING SYSTEM

done internally with the hybrid electric motor.

ENGINE ELECTRICAL

HYBRID HIGH VOLTAGE ELECTRICAL SYSTEM

PRECAUTIONS

Before working on any part of the Escape Hybrid high voltage system, observe the following precautions:

✳✳ CAUTION

The nominal high voltage traction battery voltage is 330 volts DC. The buffer zone must be set up and insulated rubber gloves and a face shield must be worn. Failure to follow these instructions may result in severe injury or death.

✳✳ CAUTION

The high voltage traction battery and charging system contains high voltage components and wiring. High voltage insulated safety gloves and a face shield must be worn when carrying out any diagnostics on this vehicle. Failure to follow these instructions may result in severe personal injury or death.

✳✳ CAUTION

Before carrying out any removal and installation procedures of the high voltage traction battery system, the high voltage traction battery must be Disarmed. Failure to follow these instructions may result in severe personal injury or death.

✳✳ CAUTION

The rubber insulating gloves that are to be worn while working on the high

voltage system should be of the appropriate safety and protection rating for use on the high voltage system. They must be inspected before use and must always be worn in conjunction with the leather outer gloves. Any hole in the rubber insulating glove is a potential entry point for high voltage. Failure to follow these instructions may result in severe personal injury or death.

➡ The high voltage insulated safety gloves must be re-certified every 6 months to remain within Occupational Safety and Health Administration (OSHA) guidelines:

- Roll the glove up from the open end until the lower portion of the glove begins to balloon from the resulting air pressure. If the glove leaks any air, it must not be used.
- The gloves should not be used if they exhibit any signs of wear and tear.
- The leather gloves must always be worn over the rubber insulating gloves in order to protect them.
- The rubber insulating gloves must be class "00" and meet all of the American Society for Testing and Materials (ASTM) standards

✳✳ CAUTION

High voltage insulated safety gloves and a face shield must be worn when working with high voltage cables. The ignition switch must be OFF for a minimum of 5 minutes before removing high voltage cables. Failure to

follow these instructions may result in severe personal injury or death.

✳✳ CAUTION

Establish a buffer zone before servicing the high voltage system. The buffer zone is required only when working with the high voltage system. See the text for buffer zone establishment. Failure to follow these instructions may result in severe personal injury or death. Do not allow any unauthorized personnel into the buffer zone during repairs involving the high voltage system. Only personnel trained for repair on the high voltage system are to be permitted in the buffer zone.

✳✳ CAUTION

Disarm the high voltage traction battery (HVTB) before working on the high voltage system. See the text for the Disarming procedure. Failure to follow these instructions may result in severe personal injury or death.

ALTERNATING CURRENT POWERPOINT

REMOVAL & INSTALLATION
See Figure 42.

✳✳ CAUTION

Before proceeding, read and observe all of the High Voltage System Precautions.

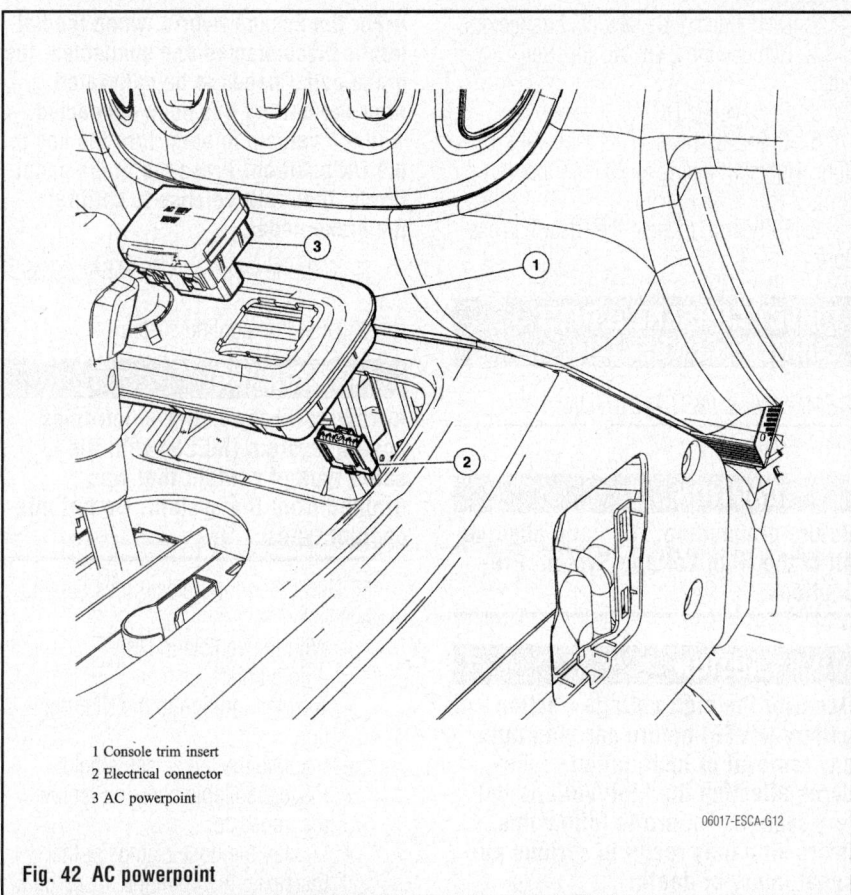

1 Console trim insert
2 Electrical connector
3 AC powerpoint

06017-ESCA-G12

Fig. 42 AC powerpoint

✳✳ CAUTION

Depower the high-voltage traction battery (HVTB) before carrying out any removal or installation procedures affecting the high-voltage battery system. Failure to follow this instruction may result in serious personal injury or death.

1. Disconnect the 12 volt battery.

➡For the Escape/Mariner Hybrid, when the battery is disconnected and connected, the brake pedal needs to be calibrated. After the battery has been connected, with the vehicle in park, turn the key to the ON position. Press the brake pedal firmly, then fully release to calibrate the brake pedal.

2. Remove the console trim insert.
3. Disconnect the electrical connector and remove the AC powerpoint.
4. To install, reverse the removal procedure.

BUFFER ZONE

See Figure 43.

1. Before servicing the vehicle, refer to the Precautions Section.

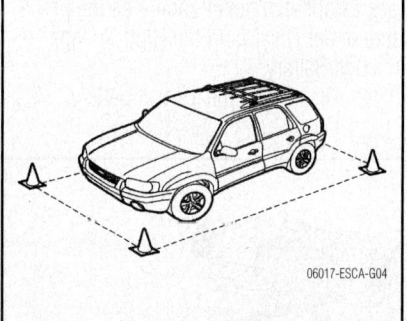

06017-ESCA-G04

Fig. 43 Buffer zone—Escape/Mariner Hybrid

✳✳ CAUTION

Before proceeding, read and observe all of the High Voltage System Precautions.

2. Establish a buffer zone around the vehicle:
   a. Position the vehicle in the repair bay.
   b. Position 4 orange cones at the corners of the vehicle to mark off a 1 m (3 ft.) perimeter around the vehicle.
   c. Do not allow any unauthorized personnel into the buffer zone during repairs

involving the high voltage system. Only personnel trained for repair on the high voltage system are to be permitted in the buffer zone.

DISARMING THE HIGH VOLTAGE TRACTION BATTERY

See Figure 44.

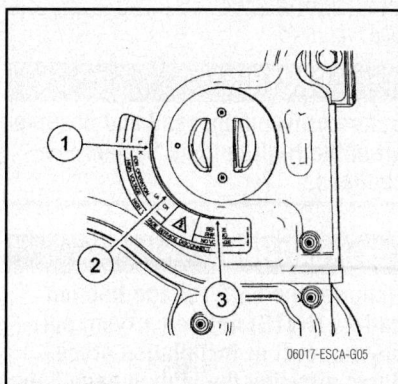

06017-ESCA-G05

Fig. 44 Rotate the service disconnect plug from the LOCK (1) position to the UNLOCK (2) position—Escape/Mariner Hybrid

1. Before servicing the vehicle, refer to the Precautions Section.

✳✳ CAUTION

Before proceeding, read and observe all of the High Voltage System Precautions.

2. Establish a buffer zone. See the procedure above. Do not allow any unauthorized personnel into the buffer zone during repairs involving the high voltage system. Only personnel trained for repair on the high voltage system are to be permitted in the buffer zone.

3. Disarm the high voltage traction battery (HVTB).
   a. Rotate the service disconnect plug from the LOCK (1) position to the UNLOCK (2) position.
   b. Remove the service disconnect plug and place in the SERVICING SHIPPING (3) position.

✳✳ WARNING

Place the service disconnect plug into the SERVICING SHIPPING position while the high voltage traction battery (HVTB) is being removed and/or while the high voltage system is having repairs carried out. If the service disconnect plug is left out and placed on the bench or toolbox, dirt or other contaminants may enter the HVTB, which can cause damage.

4. Insert the service disconnect plug into the SERVICING SHIPPING position. This disconnects the HVTB.

5. To Rearm, reverse the Disarm procedure.

DIRECT CURRENT/ALTERNATING CURRENT INVERTER

REMOVAL & INSTALLATION
See Figure 45.

✲✲ CAUTION

Before proceeding, read and observe all of the High Voltage System Precautions.

✲✲ CAUTION

Depower the high-voltage traction battery (HVTB) before carrying out any removal or installation procedures affecting the high-voltage battery system. Failure to follow this instruction may result in serious personal injury or death.

1. Disconnect the 12 volt battery.

➡ For the Escape Hybrid, when the battery is disconnected and connected, the brake pedal needs to be calibrated. After the battery has been connected, with the vehicle in park, turn the key to the ON position. Press the brake pedal firmly, then fully release to calibrate the brake pedal.

2. Disconnect the electrical connectors.
3. Remove the 2 DC/AC inverter nuts.
4. Remove the DC/AC inverter.
5. To install, reverse the removal procedure. Tighten the nuts to 80 inch lbs. (9 Nm).
6. To Rearm, reverse the Disarm procedure.

DIRECT CURRENT/DIRECT CURRENT CONVERTER

REMOVAL & INSTALLATION
See Figures 46 and 47.

✲✲ CAUTION

Before proceeding, read and observe all of the High Voltage System Precautions.

✲✲ CAUTION

Depower the high-voltage traction battery (HVTB) before carrying out any removal or installation procedures affecting the high-voltage battery system. Failure to follow this instruction may result in serious personal injury or death.

1. Disarm the high voltage traction battery. Establish a buffer zone. See the procedure under Disarming the High Voltage Traction Battery.
2. Disconnect the 12 volt battery.

➡ For the Escape Hybrid, when the battery is disconnected and connected, the brake pedal needs to be calibrated. After the battery has been connected, with the vehicle in park, turn the key to the ON position. Press the brake pedal firmly, then fully release to calibrate the brake pedal.

3. With the vehicle in NEUTRAL, position it on a hoist.
4. Drain the cooling system.

✲✲ WARNING

Always refill the motor electronics cooling system (MECS) with the same type of coolant that was drained from the system. Do not mix coolant types.

5. Drain the motor electronics cooling system:
   • With the vehicle in DRIVE, position it on a hoist.
   • Turn the ignition to the OFF position.
   • Remove the left splash shield.
   • Place a suitable container below the transaxle.
   • Loosen the hose clamps at the transaxle, then pull the hoses off to allow the coolant to drain.
6. Disconnect the motor electronics coolant vent hose.
7. Disconnect the 2 engine coolant vent hoses.
8. Remove the degas bottle bolt and nut.
9. Lift the degas bottle up and disconnect the engine coolant and motor electronics coolant return hoses.
10. Remove the degas bottle.
11. Disconnect the 2 female pin-type retainers.

➡ Press the locking clip to release the connector.

12. Disconnect the DC/DC converter high voltage connector.
13. Clamp the motor/electronics coolant (MECT) hoses to prevent coolant from leaking from the hoses during the repair.
14. Loosen the hose clamps and remove the MECT hoses from the DC/DC converter.
15. Remove the 2 DC/DC converter low voltage battery cable nuts and remove the low voltage battery cables.
16. Disconnect the DC/DC converter low voltage electrical connector.
17. Remove the 3 DC/DC converter nuts.
18. Remove the DC/DC converter assembly.

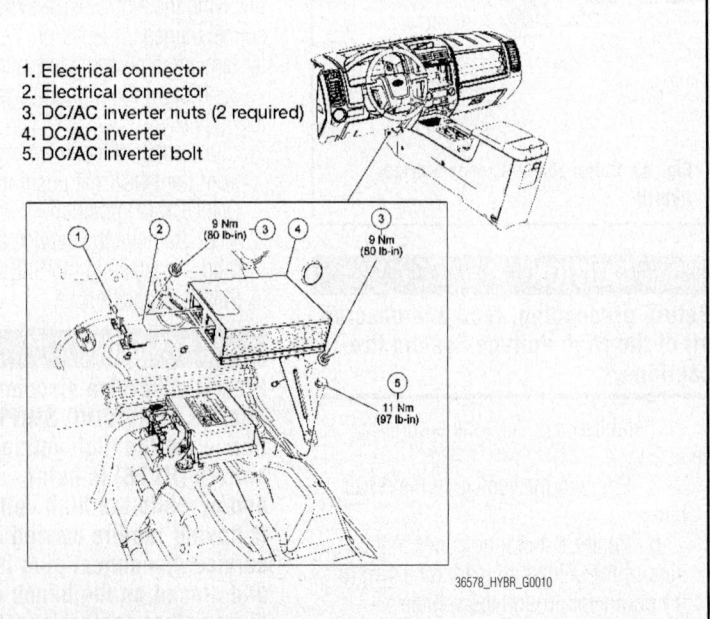

1. Electrical connector
2. Electrical connector
3. DC/AC inverter nuts (2 required)
4. DC/AC inverter
5. DC/AC inverter bolt

9 Nm
(80 lb-in)

9 Nm
(80 lb-in)

11 Nm
(97 lb-in)

36578_HYBR_G0010

Fig. 45 DC/AC Inverter—Escape/Mariner Hybrid

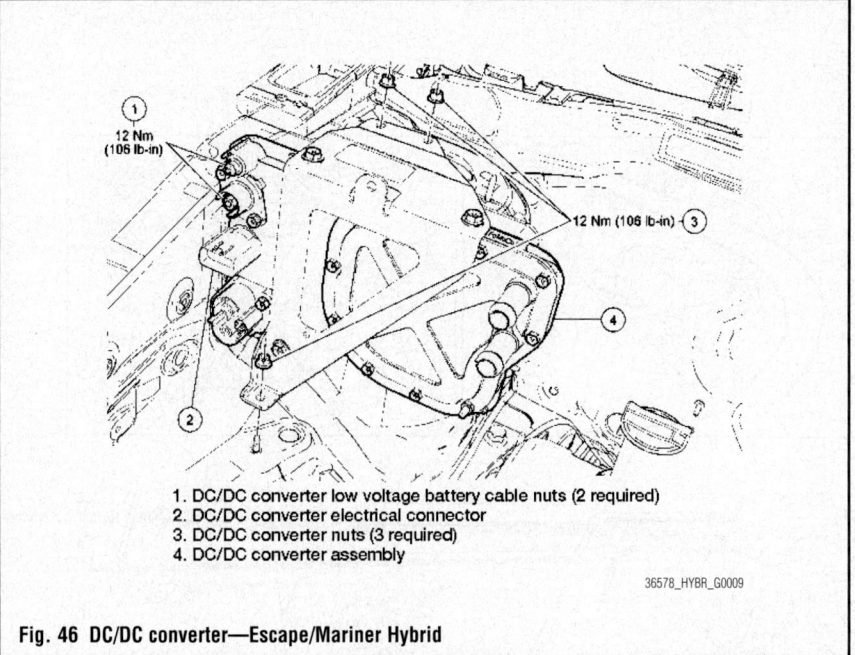

1. DC/DC converter low voltage battery cable nuts (2 required)
2. DC/DC converter electrical connector
3. DC/DC converter nuts (3 required)
4. DC/DC converter assembly

36578_HYBR_G0009

Fig. 46 DC/DC converter—Escape/Mariner Hybrid

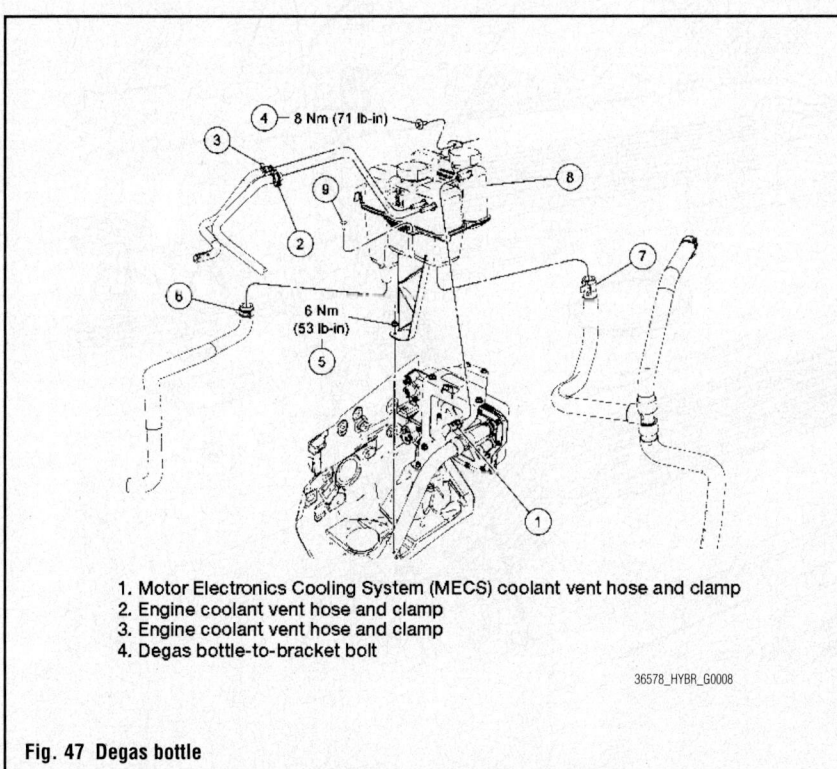

1. Motor Electronics Cooling System (MECS) coolant vent hose and clamp
2. Engine coolant vent hose and clamp
3. Engine coolant vent hose and clamp
4. Degas bottle-to-bracket bolt

36578_HYBR_G0008

Fig. 47 Degas bottle

19. To install, reverse the removal procedure. Rearm the high voltage battery. Observe the following torques:
   - The 3 DC/DC converter nuts: 106 inch lbs. (12 Nm)
   - The 2 DC/DC converter low voltage battery cable nuts: 106 inch lbs. (12 Nm)
   - The degas bottle bolt and nut: 53 inch lbs. (6 Nm)

20. Fill the Motor Electronics Cooling System as follows:

➡Vehicle cooling systems are filled with Motorcraft® Premium Gold Engine Coolant. Always fill the cooling system with the same coolant that is present in the system. Do not mix coolant types.

   - Connect the hoses to the transaxle and install the hose clamps.

✳✳ WARNING

Adhesives, stop-leak pellets or small debris in the Motor Electronics Cooling System (MECS) can cause poor performance or temporary blockage of the motor electronics pump. Only use clean, approved coolant when filling the system.

   - Loosen the bleed screw and fill the degas bottle with coolant until it begins to flow out of the bleed hole. Then, close the bleed screw.
   - Turn the ignition to the ON position to actuate the motor electronics cooling pump and continue to fill the degas bottle to the correct level.

➡Most of the MECS air bleeding occurs as a normal process at the degas bottle through the vent tube; very little occurs at the bleed screw.

   - To bleed air from the system, loosen the bleed screw and allow air to escape while the M/E coolant pump is operating.

21. To Rearm, reverse the Disarm procedure.

DIRECT CURRENT/DIRECT CURRENT CONVERTER WIRING HARNESS

REMOVAL & INSTALLATION
See Figure 48.

✳✳ CAUTION

Before proceeding, read and observe all of the High Voltage System Precautions.

✳✳ CAUTION

Depower the high-voltage traction battery (HVTB) before carrying out any removal or installation procedures affecting the high-voltage battery system. Failure to follow this instruction may result in serious personal injury or death.

1. Disarm the high voltage traction battery. Establish a buffer zone. See the procedure under Disarming the High Voltage Traction Battery.
2. Disconnect the 12 volt battery.

➡For the Escape Hybrid, when the battery is disconnected and connected, the

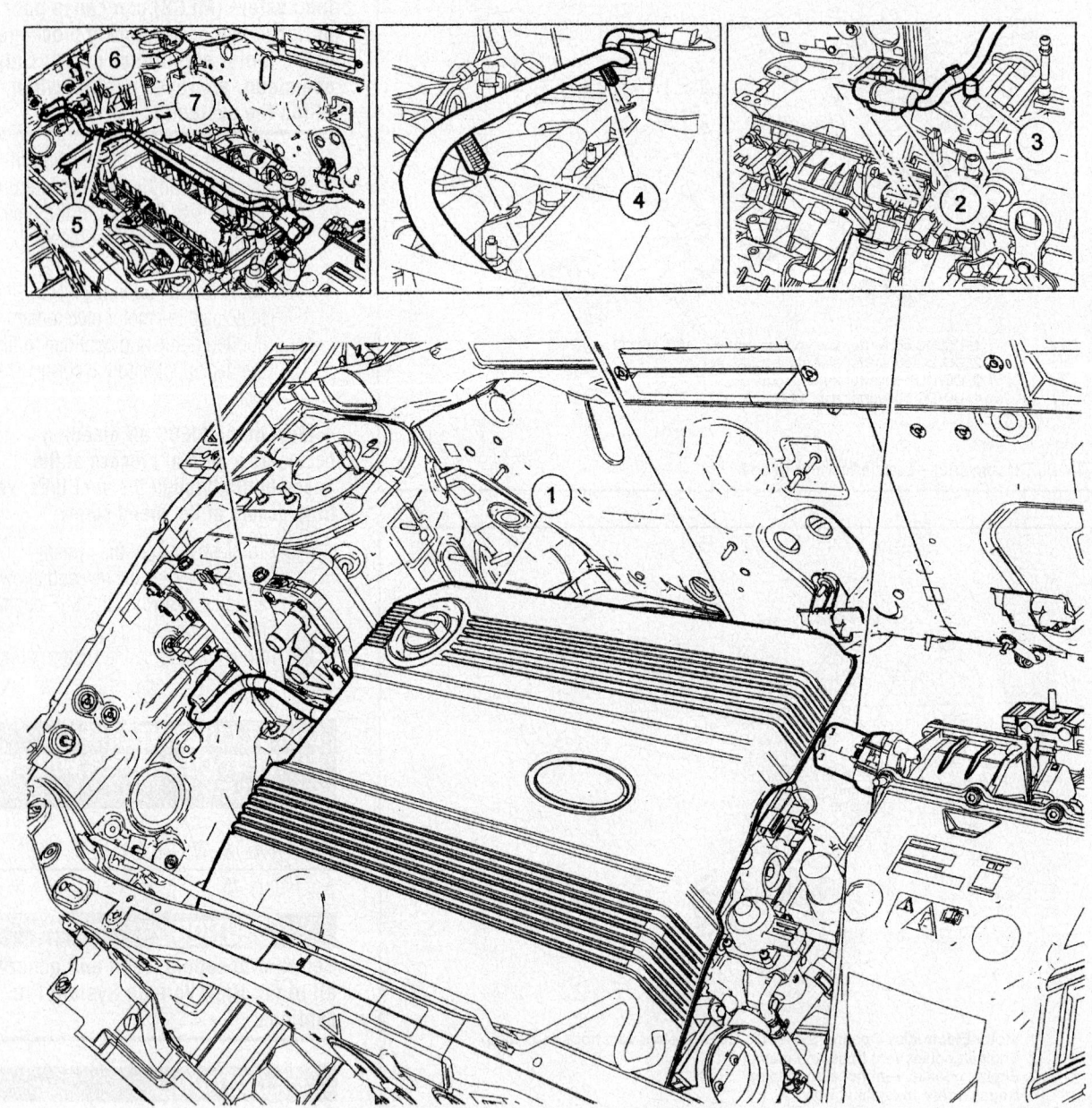

1 Engine cover

2 DC/DC converter high
voltage electrical connector

3 Plastic loop

4 Pin-type retainers (part of
14B323) (2 required)

5 Pin-type retainers (female)
(part of 14B323) (2 required)

6 DC/DC converter high
voltage electrical connector
(high voltage)

7 DC/DC converter wiring
harness

06017-ESCA-G11

Fig. 48 DC/DC converter wiring harness—Escape/Mariner Hybrid

brake pedal needs to be calibrated. After the battery has been connected, with the vehicle in park, turn the key to the ON position. Press the brake pedal firmly, then fully release to calibrate the brake pedal.

3. Remove the engine cover.

4. Disconnect the DC/DC converter harness connector from the electronically controlled continuously variable transaxle (ECVT).

5. Drain the cooling system.

> ❋❋ **WARNING**
>
> **Always refill the motor electronics cooling system (MECS) with the same type of coolant that was drained from the system. Do not mix coolant types.**

6. Drain the motor electronics cooling system:
   - With the vehicle in DRIVE, position it on a hoist.
   - Turn the ignition to the OFF position.
   - Remove the left splash shield.
   - Place a suitable container below the transaxle.
   - Loosen the hose clamps at the transaxle, then pull the hoses off to allow the coolant to drain.

7. Disconnect the motor electronics coolant vent hose.

8. Disconnect the 2 engine coolant vent hoses.

9. Remove the degas bottle bolt and nut.

10. Lift the degas bottle up and disconnect the engine coolant and motor electronics coolant return hoses.

11. Remove the degas bottle.

12. Disconnect the plastic loop.

13. Disconnect the 2 pin-type retainers.

14. Disconnect the 2 female pin-type retainers.

➡ **Press the locking clip to release the connector.**

15. Disconnect the DC/DC converter high voltage electrical connector.

16. Remove the DC/DC converter wiring harness.

17. To install, reverse the removal procedure. Rearm the high voltage battery.

18. Fill the Motor Electronics Cooling System as follows:

➡ **Vehicle cooling systems are filled with Motorcraft® Premium Gold Engine Coolant. Always fill the cooling system with the same coolant that is present in the system. Do not mix coolant types.**

- Connect the hoses to the transaxle and install the hose clamps.

> ❋❋ **WARNING**
>
> **Adhesives, stop-leak pellets or small debris in the Motor electronics cooling system (MECS) can cause poor performance or temporary blockage of the motor electronics pump. Only use clean, approved coolant when filling the system.**

- Loosen the bleed screw and fill the degas bottle with coolant until it begins to flow out of the bleed hole. Then, close the bleed screw.
- Turn the ignition to the ON position to actuate the motor electronics cooling pump and continue to fill the degas bottle to the correct level.

➡ **Most of the MECS air bleeding occurs as a normal process at the degas bottle through the vent tube; very little occurs at the bleed screw.**

- To bleed air from the system, loosen the bleed screw and allow air to escape while the M/E coolant pump is operating.

19. To Rearm, reverse the Disarm procedure.

HIGH VOLTAGE TRACTION BATTERY

REMOVAL & INSTALLATION
See Figure 49.

> ❋❋ **CAUTION**
>
> **Before proceeding, read and observe all of the High Voltage System Precautions.**

> ❋❋ **CAUTION**
>
> **Depower the high-voltage traction battery (HVTB) before carrying out any removal or installation procedures affecting the high-voltage battery system. Failure to follow this instruction may result in serious personal injury or death.**

1. Disarm the high voltage traction battery. Establish a buffer zone. See the procedure under Disarm the High Voltage Traction Battery.

2. Position the carpet aside.

➡ **When installing, tighten the screws on the HVTB first or an air flow loss to the HVTB may occur.**

3. Remove the 5 A/C return duct assembly screws.

4. Remove the A/C return duct assembly.

➡ **Due to clearance issues, the 6-pin connector must be disconnected first during the removal process and connected last during the installation process.**

5. From the left rear door opening, fold the left rear seat backrest down and disconnect the 6-pin low voltage electrical connector.

➡ **Due to clearance issues, the 40-pin connector must be disconnected last during the removal process and connected first during the installation process.**

6. Loosen the bolt and disconnect the 40-pin low voltage connector.

7. From the right rear door opening, fold the right rear seat cushion forward and remove the 2 high voltage cables shield nuts (access the shield nuts through the slotted opening in the carpet).

8. Fold the right rear seat backrest down and remove the high voltage cables shield bolt.

9. Remove the high voltage cables shield plastic rivet/screw.

10. Remove the high voltage cables shield.

11. Press the locking tab down and rotate the locking lever upward until the aligning dowels are disengaged from the locking lever to remove the high voltage cables electrical connector.

➡ **The attaching bolts have a conductive coating on them and are serrated under the head flange. These features ground the HVTB to the vehicle, which is required for electromagnetic compatibility (EMC). The serration also helps the grounding effect. If a bolt(s) is lost or damaged, it must be replaced with the identical type of bolt.**

12. Remove the 9 HVTB bolts.

➡ **The 2 front lift points are the eyelets on each front corner and the rear lift point is beneath the cap plug in the center rear of the HVTB.**

➡ **Remove the cap plug to expose the center (rear) lifting attachment point.**

➡ **Attach 3 M10 x 1.5 x 35 eyebolts to the 3 HVTB lift points. Obtain the eyebolts locally.**

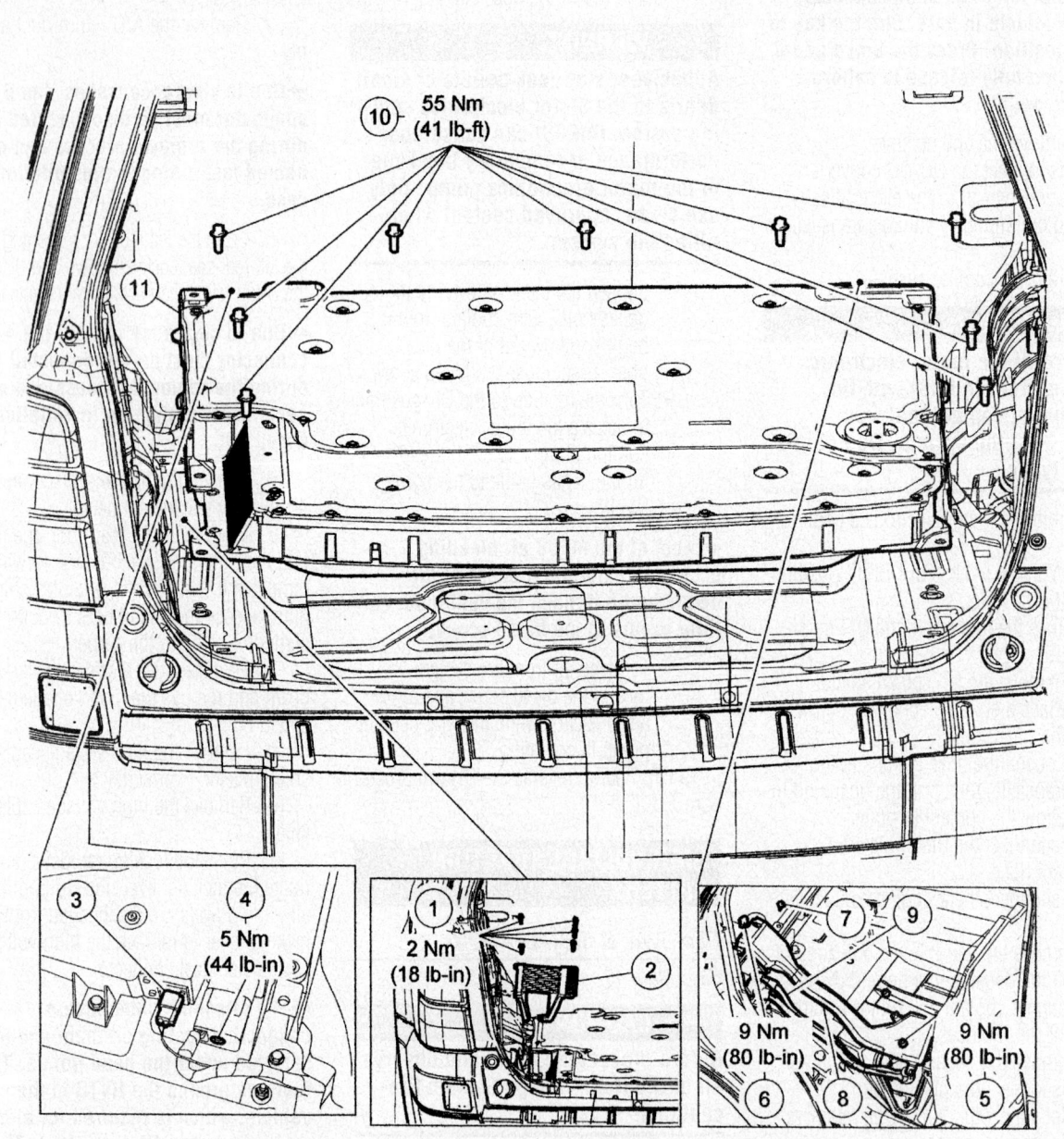

1 A/C return duct assembly
 screws (5 required)

2 A/C return duct assembly

3 6-pin low voltage electrical
 connector

4 40-pin low voltage electrical
 connector

5 High voltage cables shield
 nuts (2 required)

6 High voltage cables shield
 bolt

7 High voltage cables shield
 plastic rivet/screw

8 High voltage cables shield

9 High voltage cables electrical
 connector

10 High voltage traction battery
 bolts (9 required)

11 High voltage traction battery

06017-ESCA-G06

Fig. 49 High voltage traction battery — Escape/Mariner Hybrid

➡Make certain the HVTB does not mar or damage the interior panels during removal. There is only 6 mm (0.23 in) clearance on each side. Cover the battery mounting brackets with protective padding.

➡Do not strike the headliner with the HVTB (or floor crane) during removal.

➡Inspect the HVTB tray drain grommet. Replace it if necessary.

➡Inspect the 10 HVTB cushions for damage and proper placement. Replace them if necessary.

➡Failure to install the rear lift eye cap plug may result in noise, vibration, and harshness (NVH) issues.

13. With an assistant, attach a chain or suitable lifting device to the 3 lift points and lift the HVTB off the 2 alignment dowels using a floor crane. Remove the HVTB from the vehicle.

14. To install, reverse the removal procedure. To Rearm, reverse the Disarm procedure. Observe the following torques:

- The 9 HVTB bolts. Hand-start all of the bolts before tightening them to: 41 ft. lbs. (55 Nm)
- The high voltage cables shield bolt: 80 inch lbs. (9 Nm).
- The 2 high voltage cables shield nuts: 80 inch lbs. (9 Nm)
- The 40-pin low voltage connector: 44 inch lbs. (5 Nm)
- The 5 A/C return duct assembly screws: 18 inch lbs. (2 Nm)

15. To Rearm, reverse the Disarm procedure.

HIGH VOLTAGE CABLES

REMOVAL & INSTALLATION

See Figure 50.

✳✳ CAUTION

Before proceeding, read and observe all of the High Voltage System Precautions.

✳✳ CAUTION

Depower the high-voltage traction battery (HVTB) before carrying out any removal or installation procedures affecting the high-voltage battery system. Failure to follow this instruction may result in serious personal injury or death.

1. Disarm the high voltage traction battery. Establish a buffer zone. See the procedure under Disarming the High Voltage Traction Battery.

2. From the right rear door opening, fold the right rear seat cushion forward and remove the 2 high voltage cables shield nuts (access the shield nuts through the slotted opening in the carpet).

3. Fold the right rear seat backrest down and remove the high voltage cables shield bolt.

4. Remove the high voltage cables shield plastic rivet/screw.

5. Remove the high voltage cables shield.

6. Press the locking tab down and rotate the locking lever upward until the aligning dowels are disengaged from the locking lever to remove the high voltage cables electrical connector.

7. With the vehicle in NEUTRAL, position it on a hoist.

8. Remove the high voltage cables floor pan grommet.

9. Remove the 2 bolts and the park brake cable bracket.

10. Remove the 5 high voltage cables conduit nuts (right side inner frame rail and floor pan).

11. Lower the vehicle.

12. Remove the 2 high voltage cables bracket nuts (bulkhead). (Access the nuts through the engine compartment.)

13. Remove the nut and the eCVT shift cable.

14. Remove the high voltage cables-to-eCVT bolt.

15. Rotate the locking lever rearward until the alignment dowels are disengaged from the locking lever and remove the high voltage cables connection to the eCVT.

16. To install, reverse the removal procedure. Observe the following torques:

- The high voltage cables-to-eCVT bolt: 80 inch lbs. (9 Nm)
- The eCVT shift cable: 8 Nm (71 lb-in)
- The 2 high voltage cables bracket nuts: 71 inch lbs. (8 Nm)
- The 5 high voltage cables conduit nuts: 71 inch lbs. (8 Nm)
- The park brake cable bracket: 71 inch lbs. (8 Nm)
- The high voltage cables shield bolt: 80 inch lbs. (9 Nm)
- The 2 high voltage cables shield nuts: 80 inch lbs. (9 Nm)

17. To Rearm, reverse the Disarm procedure.

MOTOR ELECTRONICS RADIATOR

REMOVAL & INSTALLATION

See Figure 51.

✳✳ CAUTION

Before proceeding, read and observe all of the High Voltage System Precautions.

✳✳ CAUTION

Depower the high-voltage traction battery (HVTB) before carrying out any removal or installation procedures affecting the high-voltage battery system. Failure to follow this instruction may result in serious personal injury or death.

1. Drain the Motor Electronics Cooling System (MECS).

2. Remove the front bumper cover.

3. Loosen the hose clamp and disconnect the MECS radiator inlet hose.

4. Loosen the hose clamp and disconnect the MECS radiator outlet hose.

5. Remove the MECS radiator bolts.

6. Remove the MECS radiator.

To install:

7. Install the MECS radiator.

8. Install the MECS radiator mounting bolts and tighten to 53 inch lbs. (6 Nm).

9. Connect the MECS radiator outlet hose and clamp.

10. Connect the MECS radiator inlet hose and clamp.

11. Install the front bumper cover.

12. Refill and bleed the Motor Electronics Cooling System (MECS).

13. To Rearm, reverse the Disarm procedure.

MOTOR ELECTRONICS COOLANT PUMP

REMOVAL & INSTALLATION

See Figure 52.

✳✳ CAUTION

Before proceeding, read and observe all of the High Voltage System Precautions.

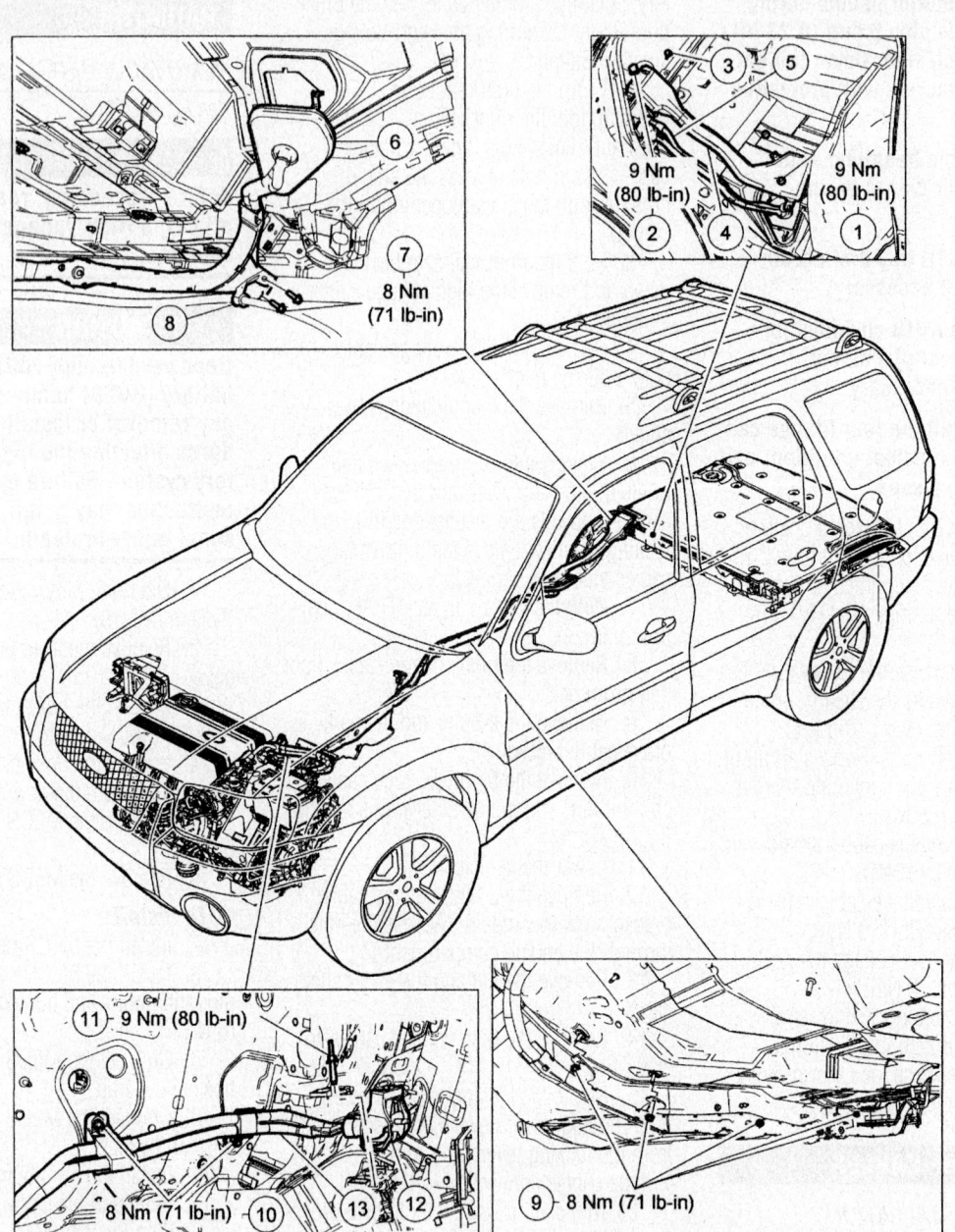

9 Nm
(80 lb-in)

9 Nm
(80 lb-in)

8 Nm
(71 lb-in)

11 - 9 Nm (80 lb-in)

8 Nm (71 lb-in)

9 - 8 Nm (71 lb-in)

1 High voltage cables shield
nuts (2 required)

2 High voltage cables shield
bolt

3 High voltage cables shield
plastic rivet/screw

4 High voltage cables shield

5 High voltage cables electrical
connector

6 High voltage cables floorpan
grommet

7 Park brake cable bracket bolts
(2 required)

8 Park brake cable bracket

9 High voltage cables conduit
nuts (right side inner frame
rail and floorpan) (5 required)

10 High voltage cables bracket
nuts (bulkhead) (2 required)

11 High voltage
cables-to-electronically
controlled continuously
variable transmission (eCVT)
bolt

12 High voltage cables
connection to eCVT

13 High voltage cables

Fig. 50 High Voltage Cables—Escape/Mariner Hybrid

06017-ESCA-G07

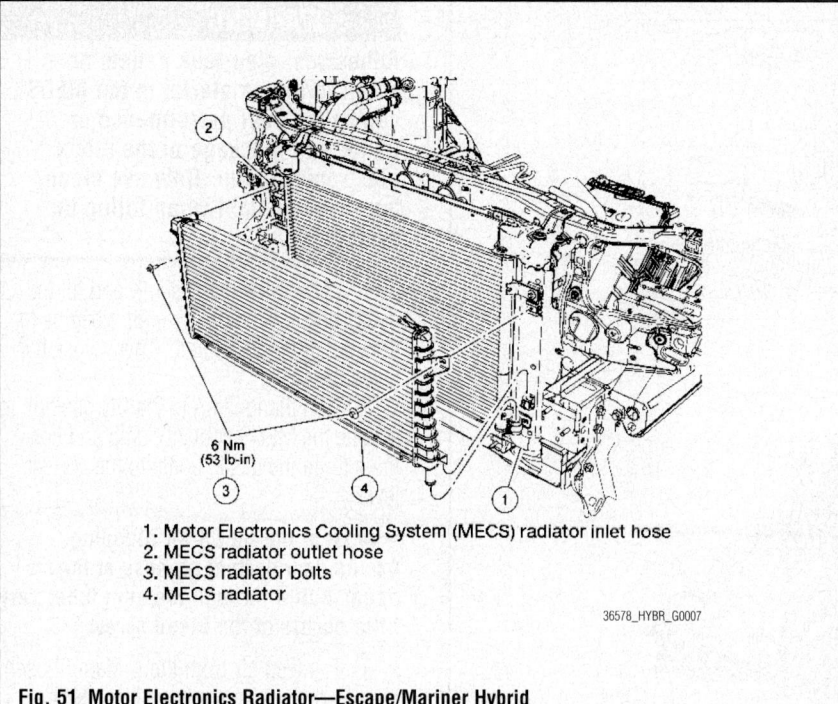

1. Motor Electronics Cooling System (MECS) radiator inlet hose
2. MECS radiator outlet hose
3. MECS radiator bolts
4. MECS radiator

36578_HYBR_G0007

Fig. 51 Motor Electronics Radiator—Escape/Mariner Hybrid

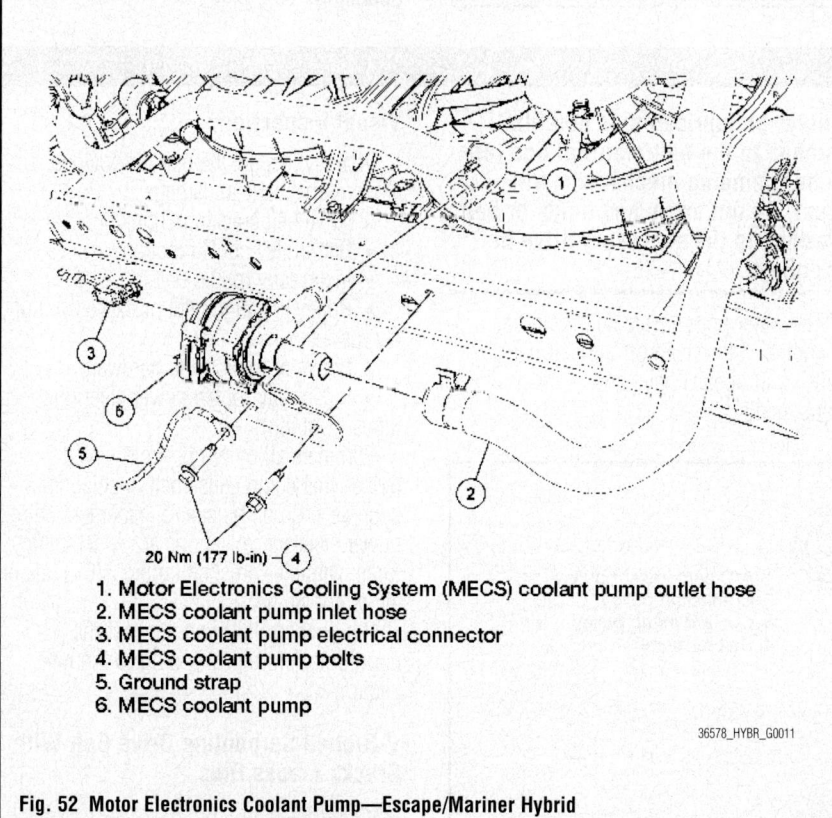

1. Motor Electronics Cooling System (MECS) coolant pump outlet hose
2. MECS coolant pump inlet hose
3. MECS coolant pump electrical connector
4. MECS coolant pump bolts
5. Ground strap
6. MECS coolant pump

36578_HYBR_G0011

Fig. 52 Motor Electronics Coolant Pump—Escape/Mariner Hybrid

> **✳✳ CAUTION**
>
> **Depower the high-voltage traction battery (HVTB) before carrying out any removal or installation procedures affecting the high-voltage battery system. Failure to follow this**

instruction may result in serious personal injury or death.

1. Drain the Motor Electronics Cooling System.
2. Disconnect the MECS coolant pump inlet and outlet hoses.

3. Remove the MECS coolant pump bolts and ground strap.
4. Remove the MECS coolant pump.

To install:
5. Install the MECS coolant pump.
6. Install the MECS coolant pump bolts and ground strap. Tighten the bolts to 177 inch lbs. (20 Nm).
7. Connect the MECS coolant pump inlet and outlet hoses and clamps
8. Refill and bleed the Motor Electronics Cooling System (MECS).
9. To Rearm, reverse the Disarm procedure

MOTOR ELECTRONICS COOLING SYSTEM DRAINING AND FILLING

DRAINING

See Figure 53.

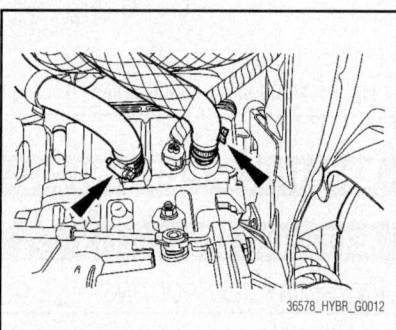

36578_HYBR_G0012

Fig. 53 Transaxle coolant hoses— Escape/Mariner Hybrid

> **✳✳ CAUTION**
>
> **Before proceeding, read and observe all of the High Voltage System Precautions.**

1. With the vehicle in NEUTRAL, position it on a hoist.
2. Turn the ignition to the OFF position.
3. Remove the LH splash shield.
4. Loosen the hose clamps at the transaxle, then pull the hoses off to allow the coolant to drain.
5. Connect the hoses to the transaxle and install the hose clamps.
6. Install the LH splash shield.

FILLING

See Figure 54.

➡Always refill the Motor Electronics Cooling System (MECS) with the same type of coolant that was drained from the system. Do not mix coolant types.

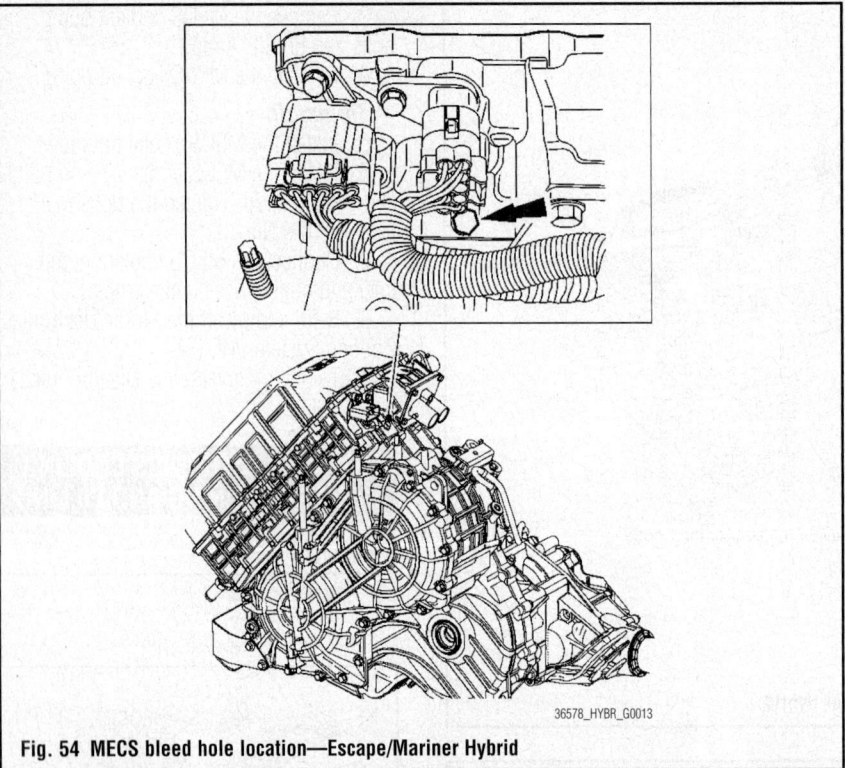

Fig. 54 MECS bleed hole location—Escape/Mariner Hybrid

⁂ WARNING

Adhesives, stop-leak pellets or small foreign material in the MECS can cause poor performance or temporary blockage of the motor electronics pump. Only use clean, approved coolant when filling the system.

1. Loosen the bleed screw and fill the degas bottle with coolant until it begins to flow out of the bleed hole. Then, close the bleed screw.

2. Turn the ignition to the ON position to actuate the MECS coolant pump and continue to fill the degas bottle to the correct level.

→Most of the MECS air bleeding occurs as a normal process at the degas bottle through the vent tube; very little occurs at the bleed screw

3. To bleed air from the system, loosen the bleed screw and allow air to escape while the MECS coolant pump is operating.

ENGINE MECHANICAL

ACCESSORY DRIVE BELTS

ACCESSORY BELT ROUTING

See Figure 55.

INSPECTION

⁂ WARNING

Under no circumstances should the accessory drive belt, tensioner or

pulleys be lubricated as potential damage to the belt material and tensioner damping mechanism will occur. Do not apply any fluids or belt dressing to the accessory drive belt or pulleys.

The water pump drive belt is on back of engine. It is driven off the rear cam pulley and doesn't have any adjustments.

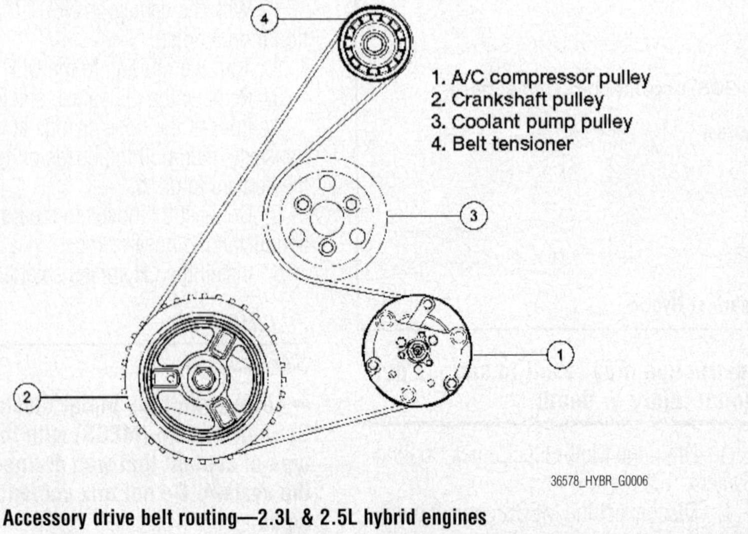

Visual Inspection

Visually inspect the belt for obvious signs of mechanical damage:
- Drive belt cracking/chunking/wear
- Belt/pulley contamination
- Incorrectly routed belt
- Pulley misalignment or excessive pulley runout
- Loose or mislocated hardware
- Incorrectly routed power steering tubes (rubbing)

Eliminate all other non-belt related noises that could cause belt misdiagnosis, such as A/C compressor engagement chirp, power steering cavitations at low temperatures, variable camshaft timing (VCT) tick or alternator whine.

If a concern is found, correct the condition before proceeding to the next section.

V-Ribbed Serpentine Drive Belt With Cracks Across Ribs

See Figure 56.

→Up to 15 cracks in a rib over a distance of 4 inches (100mm) can be considered acceptable. If damage exceeds the acceptable limit or any chunks are found to be missing from the ribs, a new belt must be installed.

1. A/C compressor pulley
2. Crankshaft pulley
3. Coolant pump pulley
4. Belt tensioner

Fig. 55 Accessory drive belt routing—2.3L & 2.5L hybrid engines

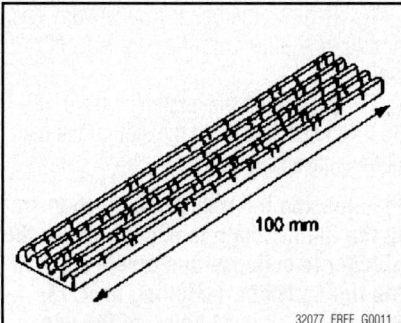

Fig. 56 Up to 15 cracks in a rib over a distance of 4 inches (100mm) can be considered acceptable. If cracks exceed this standard, install a new belt

1. Check the belt for cracks. Up to 15 cracks in a rib over a distance of 4 inches (100mm) can be considered acceptable. If cracks exceed this standard, install a new belt.

V- Ribbed Serpentine Belt With Piling

See Figure 57.

➡**Piling is an excessive buildup in the V-grooves of the belt.**

The condition of the V-ribbed drive belt should be compared against the illustration and appropriate action taken.

1. Small scattered deposits of rubber material. This is not a concern, therefore, installation of a new belt is not required.
2. Longer deposit areas building up to 50 percent of the rib height. This is not

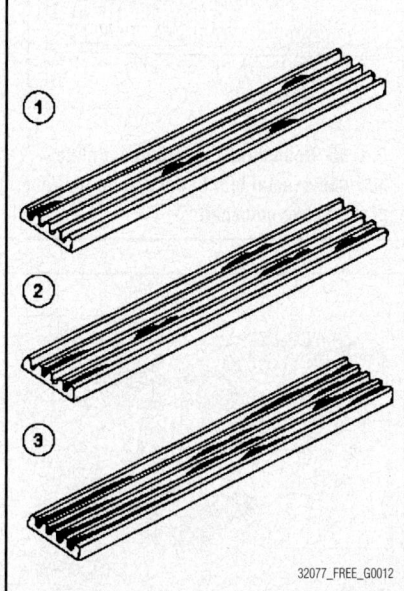

Fig. 57 Compare the condition of the belt with the accompanying text

considered a concern but it can result in excessive noise. If noise is apparent, install a new belt.

3. Heavy deposits building up along the grooves resulting in a possible noise and belt stability concern. If heavy deposits are apparent, install a new belt.

V-Ribbed Serpentine Belt With Chunks of Rib Missing

See Figure 58.

There should be no chunks missing from the belt ribs. If the belt shows any evidence of this, install a new accessory drive belt.

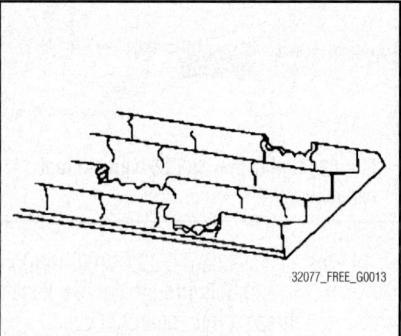

Fig. 58 Replace the belt if missing chunks are found during inspection

ADJUSTMENT

The belts used on these vehicle are equipped with automatic (spring load) tensioners which maintain tension. No adjustment is necessary or possible.

REMOVAL & INSTALLATION

See Figure 55.

1. Raise and safely support the vehicle..
2. Remove the pin-type retainer, 5 bolts and the RH splash shield.
3. Rotate the accessory drive belt tensioner clockwise and remove the accessory drive belt.

To install:
4. Install the accessory drive belt. Make sure it is routed correctly.
5. Install the pin-type retainer, RH splash shield and tighten the retaining bolts to 80 inch lbs. (9 Nm).

CAMSHAFT AND VALVE LASH ADJUSTER

REMOVAL & INSTALLATION

2.3L Hybrid Engine

See Figures 59 through 67.

✱✱ **CAUTION**

Before removing the high voltage cables, the vehicle electrical system must be completely shut down for at least 5 minutes to allow for the high voltage capacitors to discharge.

1. Depower the vehicle High Voltage Traction Battery (HVTB) electrical system.
2. Remove the degas bottle.
3. Remove the DC/DC converter.

✱✱ **WARNING**

During engine repair procedures, cleanliness is extremely important. Any foreign material (including any material created while cleaning gasket surfaces) that enters the oil passages, coolant passages or the oil pan can cause engine failure.

✱✱ **WARNING**

Do not rotate the camshafts unless instructed to in this procedure. Rotating the camshafts or crankshaft with timing components loosened or removed can cause serious damage to the valves and pistons.

4. Disconnect the negative battery cable.
5. With the vehicle in NEUTRAL, position it on a hoist.
6. Remove the valve cover, Refer to Valve Cover Removal & Installation in this section.
7. Check the valve clearance. Refer to Valve Lash Adjustment in this section.

➡**Before removing the camshafts, measure the clearance of each valve at base circle, with the lobe pointed away from the tappet. Failure to measure all clearances prior to removing the camshafts will necessitate repeated removal and installation and wasted labor time.**

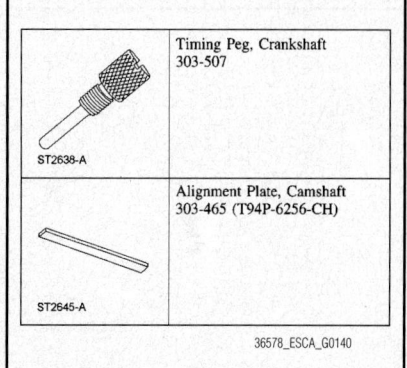

Fig. 59 Special tools required

8. Remove the front RH wheel and tire.
9. Remove the accessory drive belt.

✵✵ WARNING

Failure to position the No. 1 piston at Top Dead Center (TDC) can result in damage to the engine. Turn the engine in the normal direction of rotation only.

10. Using the crankshaft pulley bolt, turn the crankshaft clockwise to position the No. 1 piston at Top Dead Center (TDC). The hole in the crankshaft pulley should be in the 6 o'clock position.

11. Install the alignment plate 303-465 special tool in the slots on the rear of both camshafts.

12. Remove the engine plug bolt.

13. Install the timing peg 303-507 special tool.

➡The timing peg special tool will contact the crankshaft and prevent it from turning past top dead center (TDC). However, the crankshaft can still be rotated in the counterclockwise direction. The crankshaft must remain at the TDC position during the camshaft removal and installation.

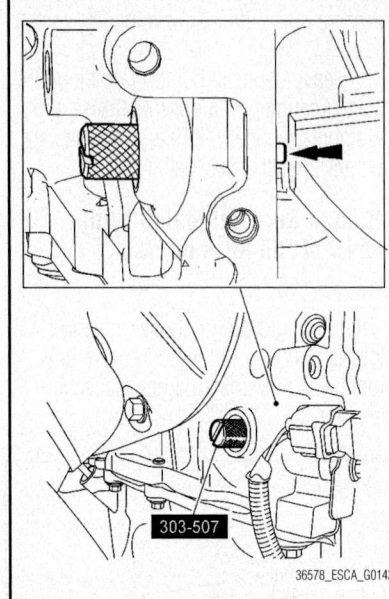

Fig. 62 Timing peg 303-507 special tool installed

14. Install a standard 0.23 inch (6 mm) x 0.7 inch (18 mm) bolt through the crankshaft pulley and thread it into the front cover.

15. Remove the lower front cover timing hole plug from the engine front cover.

16. Remove the upper front cover timing hole plug from the engine front cover.

17. Reposition the alignment plate 303-465 special tool to the slot on the rear of the intake camshaft only.

➡Releasing the ratcheting mechanism in the timing chain tensioner allows the plunger to collapse and create slack in the timing chain. Installing an 1.18 inch (M6 x 30 mm) bolt into the upper front cover timing hole will hold the tensioner arm in a retracted position and allow enough slack in the timing chain for removal of the exhaust camshaft gear.

18. Using a small pick tool, unlock the chain tensioner ratchet through the lower front cover timing hole.

19. Using the flats of the camshaft, have an assistant rotate the exhaust camshaft clockwise to collapse the timing chain tensioner plunger.

20. Insert an 1.18 inch (M6 x 30 mm) bolt into the upper front cover timing hole to hold the tensioner arm in the retracted position.

21. Remove the alignment plate 303-465 special tool.

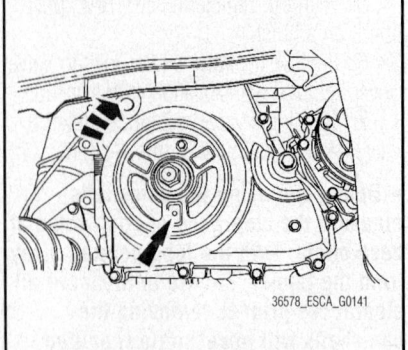

Fig. 60 Hole in the crankshaft pulley should be in the 6 o'clock position

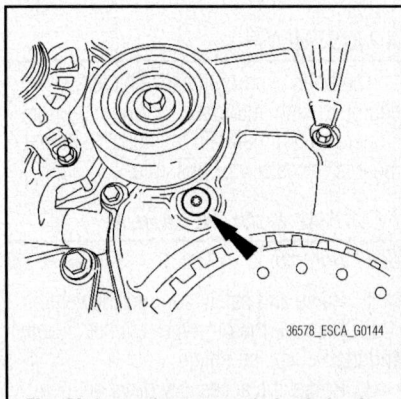

Fig. 63 Lower front cover timing hole plug

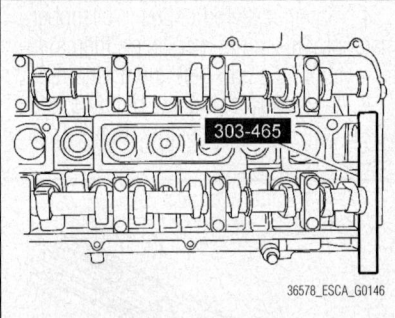

Fig. 65 Reposition the alignment plate 303-465 special tool to the slot on the rear of the intake camshaft

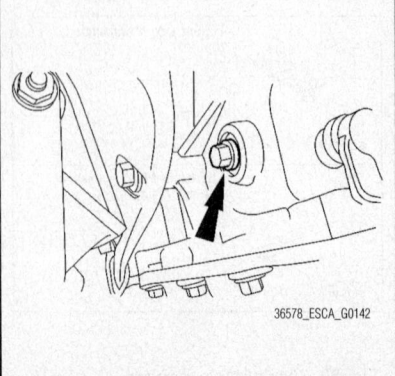

Fig. 61 Remove the engine plug bolt

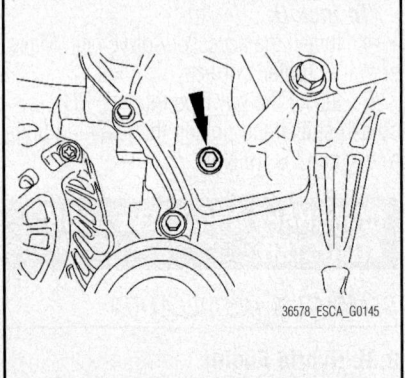

Fig. 64 Upper front cover timing hole plug

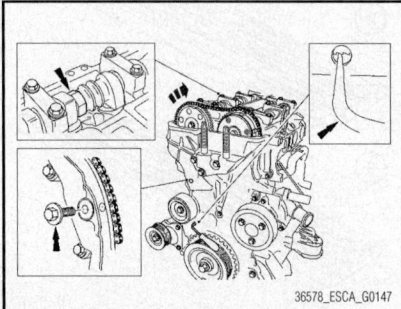

Fig. 66 Using a small pick tool, unlock the chain tensioner ratchet through the lower front cover timing hole

22. Using the flats on the camshaft to prevent camshaft rotation, remove the bolt and exhaust camshaft drive gear.

23. Remove the timing chain from the intake camshaft drive gear.

24. Using the flats on the camshaft to prevent camshaft rotation, remove the bolt and intake camshaft drive gear.

25. Mark the position of the camshaft lobes on the No. 1 cylinder for installation reference.

26. Mark the location and orientation of each camshaft bearing cap.

27. Loosen the camshaft bearing cap bolts, in sequence, one turn at a time until all tension is released from the camshaft bearing caps.

28. Remove the bolts and the camshaft bearing caps.

29. Remove the camshafts.

To install:

✳✳ WARNING

Install the camshafts with the alignment slots in the camshafts lined up so the Camshaft Alignment Plate can be installed without rotating the camshafts. Make sure the lobes on the No. 1 cylinder are in the same position as noted in the removal procedure. Rotating the camshafts when the timing chain is removed, or installing the camshafts 180 degrees out of position can cause severe damage to the valves and pistons.

30. Lubricate the camshaft journals and bearing caps with clean engine oil.

31. Install the camshafts and bearing caps in their original location and orientation. Tighten the bearing caps in the sequence shown in 3 stages:
- Stage 1: Tighten the camshaft bearing cap bolts one turn at a time, until finger tight.

- Stage 2: Tighten to 62 inch lbs. (7 Nm).
- Stage 3: Tighten to 12 ft. lbs. (16 Nm).

32. Install the alignment plate 303-465 special tool.

33. Install the intake camshaft drive gear and hand-tighten the bolt.

34. Install the timing chain on the intake camshaft drive gear.

➡ **The timing chain must be correctly engaged on the teeth of the crankshaft timing sprocket and the intake camshaft drive gear in order to install the exhaust camshaft drive gear onto the exhaust camshaft.**

35. Position the exhaust camshaft drive gear in the timing chain and install the gear and bolt on the exhaust camshaft.

36. Hand-tighten the bolt.

➡ **Releasing the tensioner arm will remove the slack from the timing chain release.**

37. Remove the M6 x 30 mm bolt from the upper front cover timing hole to release the tensioner arm.

➡ **The special tool 303-465 is for camshaft alignment only. Using this tool to prevent engine rotation can result in engine damage.**

38. Using the flats on the camshafts to prevent camshaft rotation, tighten the bolts to 53 ft. lbs. (72 Nm).

39. Remove the alignment plate 303-465 special tool.

40. Remove the 0.23 inch (6 mm) x 0.7 inch (18 mm) bolt.

41. Remove the timing peg special tool.

42. Install the upper front cover timing hole plug and tighten to 89 inch lbs. (10 Nm).

43. Apply silicone gasket and sealant to the threads of the lower front cover timing hole plug.

44. Install the plug and tighten to 12 Nm (9 lb-ft).

45. Install the engine plug bolt and tighten to 15 ft. lbs. (20 Nm).

46. Install the accessory drive belt.

47. Install the front RH wheel and tire.

48. Install the valve cover.

49. Install the DC/DC converter.

50. Install the degas bottle and refill with coolant.

51. Repower the vehicle HVTB electrical system.

52. Connect the negative battery cable.

2.5L Hybrid Engine

See Figures 59, 61, 62 through 70.

✳✳ CAUTION

Before removing the high voltage cables, the vehicle electrical system must be completely shut down for at least 5 minutes to allow for the high voltage capacitors to discharge.

1. Depower the vehicle High Voltage Traction Battery (HVTB) electrical system.
2. Remove the degas bottle.
3. Remove the DC/DC converter.

✳✳ WARNING

During engine repair procedures, cleanliness is extremely important. Any foreign material (including any material created while cleaning gasket surfaces) that enters the oil passages, coolant passages or the oil pan can cause engine failure.

✳✳ WARNING

Do not rotate the camshafts unless instructed to in this procedure. Rotating the camshafts or crankshaft with timing components loosened or removed can cause serious damage to the valves and pistons.

4. Disconnect the negative battery cable.
5. With the vehicle in NEUTRAL, position it on a hoist.
6. Remove the valve cover. Refer to Valve Cover Removal & Installation in this section.
7. Check the valve clearance. Refer to Valve Lash Adjustment in this section.

➡ **Before removing the camshafts, measure the clearance of each valve at base circle, with the lobe pointed away from the tappet. Failure to measure all clearances prior to removing the camshafts will necessitate repeated removal and installation and wasted labor time.**

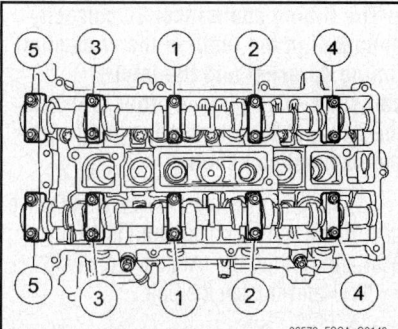

Fig. 67 Camshaft bearing cap tightening sequence

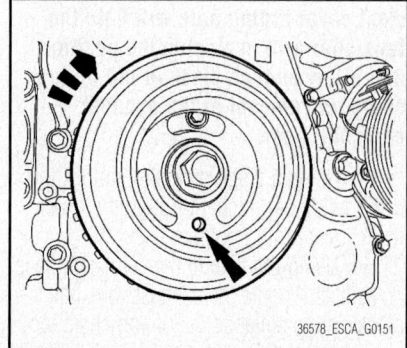

Fig. 68 Hole in the crankshaft pulley should be in the 6 o'clock position

8. Remove the front RH wheel and tire.

9. Remove the accessory drive belt.

⁕ WARNING

Failure to position the No. 1 piston at Top Dead Center (TDC) can result in damage to the engine. Turn the engine in the normal direction of rotation only.

10. Using the crankshaft pulley bolt, turn the crankshaft clockwise to position the No. 1 piston at Top Dead Center (TDC). The hole in the crankshaft pulley should be in the 6 o'clock position.

11. Install the alignment plate 303-465 special tool in the slots on the rear of both camshafts.

12. Remove the engine plug bolt.

13. Install the timing peg 303-507 special tool.

➡ The timing peg special tool will contact the crankshaft and prevent it from turning past top dead center (TDC). However, the crankshaft can still be rotated in the counterclockwise direction. The crankshaft must remain at the TDC position during the camshaft removal and installation.

14. Install a standard 0.23 inch (6 mm) x 0.7 inch (18 mm) bolt through the crankshaft pulley and thread it into the front cover.

15. Remove the lower front cover timing hole plug from the engine front cover.

16. Remove the upper front cover timing hole plug from the engine front cover.

17. Reposition the alignment plate 303-465 special tool to the slot on the rear of the intake camshaft only.

➡ Releasing the ratcheting mechanism in the timing chain tensioner allows the plunger to collapse and create slack in the timing chain. Installing an 1.18 inch (M6 x 30 mm) bolt into the upper front cover timing hole will hold the tensioner arm in a retracted position and allow enough slack in the timing chain for removal of the exhaust camshaft gear.

18. Using a small pick tool, unlock the chain tensioner ratchet through the lower front cover timing hole.

19. Using the flats of the camshaft, have an assistant rotate the exhaust camshaft clockwise to collapse the timing chain tensioner plunger.

20. Insert an 1.18 inch (M6 x 30 mm) bolt into the upper front cover timing hole

to hold the tensioner arm in the retracted position.

21. Remove the alignment plate 303-465 special tool.

22. Using the flats on the camshaft to prevent camshaft rotation, remove the bolt and exhaust camshaft drive gear.

23. Remove the timing chain from the intake camshaft drive gear.

24. Using the flats on the camshaft to prevent camshaft rotation, remove the bolt and intake camshaft drive gear.

25. Mark the position of the camshaft lobes on the No. 1 cylinder for installation reference.

26. Mark the location and orientation of each camshaft bearing cap.

27. Loosen the camshaft bearing cap bolts, in sequence, one turn at a time until all tension is released from the camshaft bearing caps.

28. Remove the bolts and the camshaft bearing caps.

29. Remove the camshafts.

30. If removal of the camshaft phaser and sprocket is necessary, mark the sprocket and camshaft for reference during installation. If necessary, place the camshaft in a soft-jawed vise. Remove the bolt and the camshaft phaser and sprocket.

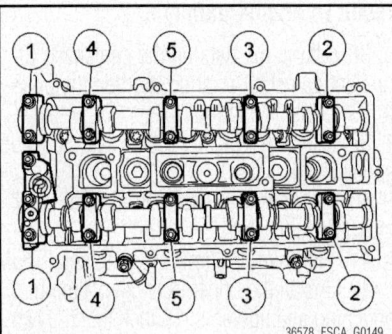

Fig. 69 Camshaft bearing cap loosening sequence

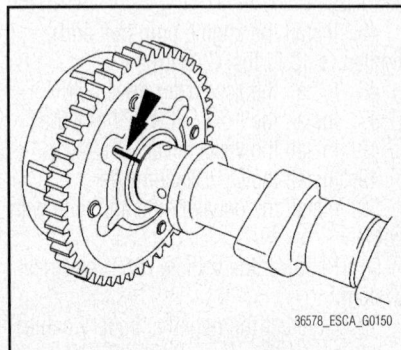

Fig. 70 Mark the sprocket and camshaft for reference during installation

To install:

➡ If new parts are installed, transfer the reference marks made during disassembly to the new parts.

31. If necessary, position the camshaft in a soft-jawed vise and install the camshaft phaser and sprocket and the bolt.

32. Align the reference marks on the camshaft phaser and sprocket and the camshaft. Tighten the bolt to 53 ft. lbs. (72 Nm).

⁕ WARNING

Install the camshafts with the alignment slots in the camshafts lined up so the Camshaft Alignment Plate can be installed without rotating the camshafts. Make sure the lobes on the No. 1 cylinder are in the same position as noted in the removal procedure. Rotating the camshafts when the timing chain is removed, or installing the camshafts 180 degrees out of position can cause severe damage to the valves and pistons.

33. Lubricate the camshaft journals and bearing caps with clean engine oil.

34. Install the camshafts and bearing caps in their original location and orientation. Tighten the bearing caps in the sequence shown in 3 stages:
- Stage 1: Tighten the camshaft bearing cap bolts one turn at a time, until finger tight.
- Stage 2: Tighten to 62 inch lbs. (7 Nm).
- Stage 3: Tighten to 12 ft. lbs. (16 Nm).

35. Install the alignment plate 303-465 special tool.

36. Install the intake camshaft drive gear and hand-tighten the bolt.

37. Install the timing chain on the intake camshaft drive gear.

➡ The timing chain must be correctly engaged on the teeth of the crankshaft timing sprocket and the intake camshaft drive gear in order to install the exhaust camshaft drive gear onto the exhaust camshaft.

38. Position the exhaust camshaft drive gear in the timing chain and install the gear and bolt on the exhaust camshaft.

39. Hand-tighten the bolt.

➡ Releasing the tensioner arm will remove the slack from the timing chain release.

40. Remove the M6 x 30 mm bolt from the upper front cover timing hole to release the tensioner arm.

➡**The special tool 303-465 is for camshaft alignment only. Using this tool to prevent engine rotation can result in engine damage.**

41. Using the flats on the camshafts to prevent camshaft rotation, tighten the bolts to 53 ft. lbs. (72 Nm).

42. Remove the alignment plate 303-465 special tool.

43. Remove the 0.23 inch (6 mm) x 0.7 inch (18 mm) bolt.

44. Remove the timing peg special tool.

45. Install the upper front cover timing hole plug and tighten to 89 inch lbs. (10 Nm).

46. Apply silicone gasket and sealant to the threads of the lower front cover timing hole plug.

47. Install the plug and tighten to 12 Nm (9 lb-ft).

48. Install the engine plug bolt and tighten to 15 ft. lbs. (20 Nm).

49. Install the accessory drive belt.

50. Install the front RH wheel and tire.

51. Install the valve cover.

52. Install the DC/DC converter.

53. Install the degas bottle and refill with coolant.

54. Repower the vehicle HVTB electrical system.

55. Connect the negative battery cable.

CATALYTIC CONVERTER

REMOVAL & INSTALLATION

2008 Models

See Figure 71.

> ❋❋ **CAUTION**
>
> **Before proceeding, read and observe all of the High Voltage System Precautions.**

1. With the vehicle in NEUTRAL, position it on a hoist.

2. Remove and discard the 2 exhaust catalytic converter nuts.

3. Remove and discard the U-bolt clamp assembly from the muffler.

4. Remove and discard the 2 resonator nuts.

5. Remove and discard the catalytic converter exhaust hanger.

6. Remove the exhaust catalytic converter and the muffler from the vehicle as an assembly. Discard the catalytic converter gasket.

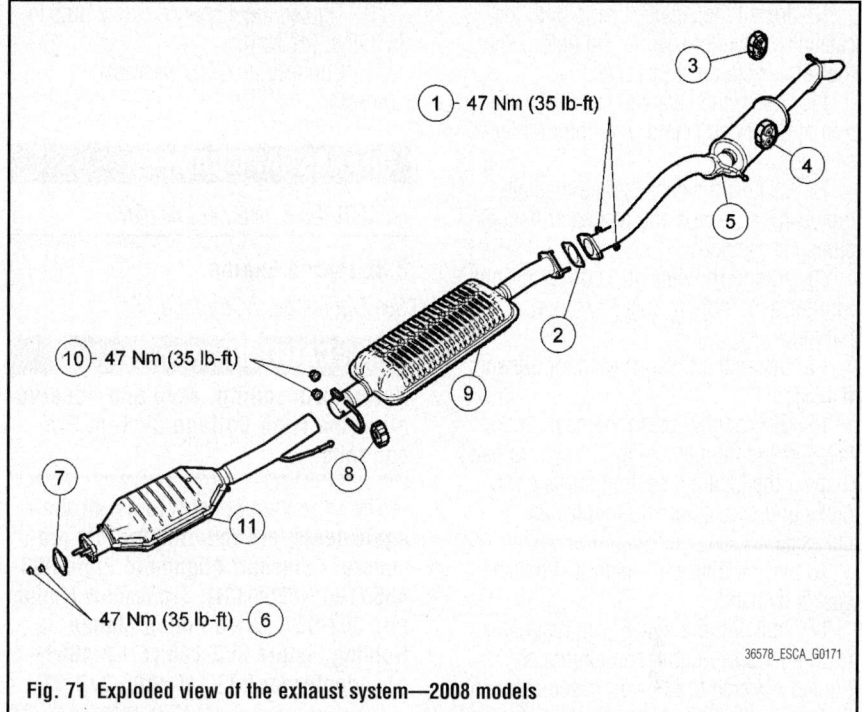

Fig. 71 Exploded view of the exhaust system—2008 models

7. Separate the converter from the muffler.

To install:

8. Install the converter into the muffler.

9. Thoroughly clean the sealing surfaces of the flanges using a finishing pad.

10. Install the 2 new front and rear gaskets.

11. Install the exhaust catalytic converter and the muffler assembly to the vehicle.

12. Install the exhaust hangers.

13. Tighten the front and rear flange retaining nuts to 35 ft. lbs. (47 Nm).

14. Adjust and tighten the U-bolt clamp to 35 ft. lbs. (47 Nm).

15. Start the vehicle and check for exhaust leaks.

2009 Models

See Figures 72 and 73.

➡**If replacement is not required, the production catalytic converter and muffler assembly can be removed and installed as one piece. It is only necessary to cut the production exhaust to enable the service section to be fitted. Before cutting any part of the exhaust system, check that the position of the cut is correct in comparison to the service section being installed.**

> ❋❋ **CAUTION**
>
> **Before proceeding, read and observe all of the High Voltage System Precautions.**

1. With the vehicle in NEUTRAL, position it on a hoist.

2. Disconnect the Catalyst Monitor Sensor (CMS) electrical connector.

3. Remove the CMS.

4. Remove and discard the two 10 mm exhaust catalytic converter-to-exhaust intermediate pipe/exhaust Y-pipe spring nuts.

5. Remove and discard the two 8-mm resonator-to-muffler spring nuts.

6. Detach the 3 exhaust hangers and remove the catalytic converter and muffler assembly.

7. Remove and discard the gaskets.

8. Cut the exhaust system 5.90 inches (150 mm) as indicated in illustration.

To install:

9. Thoroughly clean the sealing surfaces of the flanges using a finishing pad.

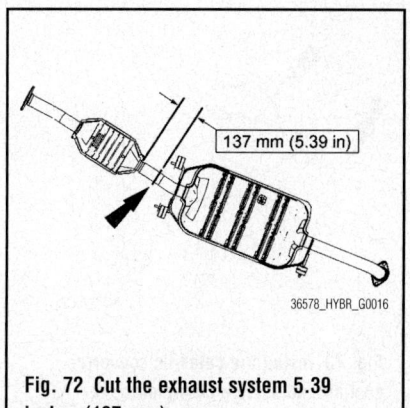

Fig. 72 Cut the exhaust system 5.39 inches (137 mm)

10. Install the service clamp onto the catalytic converter section. Do not tighten the service clamp at this time.

11. Install the catalytic converter section and service clamp onto the muffler section.

12. Inspect the exhaust intermediate pipe/exhaust Y-pipe and resonator flange studs for damage.

13. Attach the catalytic converter and muffler assembly to the 3 exhaust hangers.

14. Install the Catalyst Monitor Sensor (CMS).

15. Thoroughly clean the sealing surfaces of the flanges using a finishing pad. Inspect the cleaned sealing surface for nicks and scratches and replace as necessary.

16. Install a new resonator-to-muffler gasket by hand.

17. Install the 2 new 8-mm resonator-to-muffler spring nuts and alternately tighten RH side to LH side in sequence in 3 stages:
- Stage 1: Tighten to 44 inch lbs. (5 Nm).
- Stage 2: Tighten to 89 inch lbs. (10 Nm).
- Stage 3: Tighten to 150 inch lbs. (17 Nm).

18. Install a new converter-to-exhaust intermediate/exhaust Y-pipe gasket by hand.

19. Install the 2 new 10-mm catalytic converter-to-exhaust intermediate/exhaust Y-pipe spring nuts and alternately tighten RH side to LH side in sequence in 3 stages:
- Stage 1: Tighten to 44 inch lbs. (5 Nm).
- Stage 2: Tighten to 89 inch lbs. (10 Nm).
- Stage 3: Tighten to 150 inch lbs. (17 Nm).

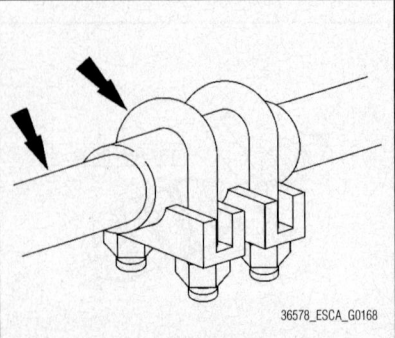

Fig. 73 Install the catalytic converter section and service clamp onto the muffler section

20. Tighten the 4 service clamp nuts to 35 ft. lbs. (47 Nm).

21. Connect the CMS electrical connector.

CRANKSHAFT DAMPER

REMOVAL & INSTALLATION

2.3L Hybrid Engine

See Figures 68, 74 through 77.

✳✳ CAUTION

Before proceeding, read and observe all of the High Voltage System Precautions.

➡**The following special tools, or their equivalents, are required for this procedure. Camshaft Alignment Plate 303-465 (T94P-6256-CH), Crankshaft Timing Peg 303-057, Drive Pinion Flange Holding Fixture 205-126 (T78P-4851-A), Adapter for 205-126 (205-072-02).**

✳✳ WARNING

During engine repair procedures, cleanliness is extremely important. Any foreign material, including any material created while cleaning gas-ket surfaces, which enters the oil passages, coolant passages or the oil pan can cause engine failure.

✳✳ WARNING

The crankshaft, the crankshaft sprocket and the pulley are fitted together by friction, using diamond washers between the flange faces on each part. For that reason, the crankshaft sprocket is also unfastened if you loosen the pulley. Therefore, the engine must be retimed each time the damper is removed. Otherwise severe engine damage can occur.

1. Before servicing the vehicle, refer to the Precautions Section.

2. Raise and safely support the vehicle.

3. Remove the front RH wheel and tire.

4. Remove the pin-type retainer, the 5 bolts and the RH splash shield.

5. Remove the accessory drive belt.

6. Remove the valve cover, as outlined in this section.

✳✳ WARNING

Failure to position the No. 1 piston at Top Dead Center (TDC) can result in

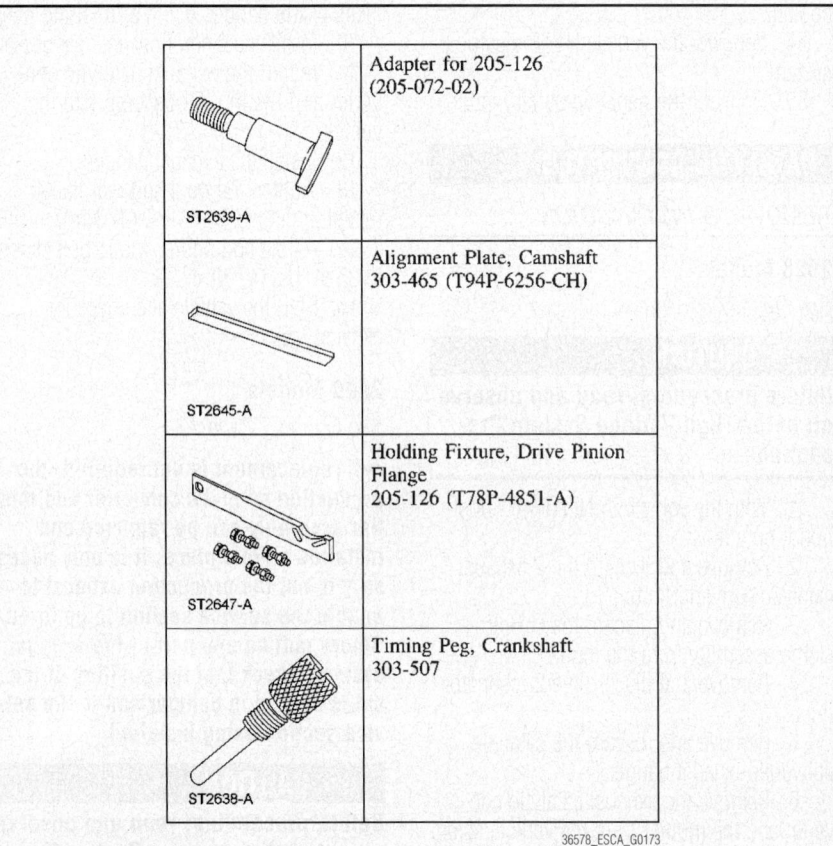

ST2639-A	Adapter for 205-126 (205-072-02)
ST2645-A	Alignment Plate, Camshaft 303-465 (T94P-6256-CH)
ST2647-A	Holding Fixture, Drive Pinion Flange 205-126 (T78P-4851-A)
ST2638-A	Timing Peg, Crankshaft 303-507

Fig. 74 Special tools required

damage to the engine. Turn the engine in the normal direction of rotation only.

7. Using the crankshaft pulley bolt, turn the crankshaft clockwise to position the No. 1 piston at TDC.

The hole in the crankshaft pulley should be in the 6 o'clock position.

※※ WARNING

The special tool 303-465 is for camshaft alignment only. Using this tool to prevent engine rotation can result in engine damage.

➡**The camshaft timing slots are offset. If the special tool cannot be installed, rotate the crankshaft one complete revolution clockwise to correctly position the camshafts.**

8. Install camshaft alignment plate 303-465, or equivalent special tool in the slots on the rear of both camshafts.

9. Remove the engine plug bolt.

➡**The special tool will contact the crankshaft and prevent it from turning past TDC. However, the crankshaft can still be rotated in the counterclockwise direction. The crankshaft must remain at the TDC position during the crankshaft pulley removal and installation.**

10. Install Crankshaft Timing Peg 303-057 or equivalent special tool.

11. Install Drive Pinion Flange Holding Fixture 205-126 (T78P-4851-A) and Adapter for 205-126 (205-072-02) or equivalent special tools.

※※ WARNING

Failure to hold the crankshaft pulley in place while loosening the bolt can result in damage to the engine.

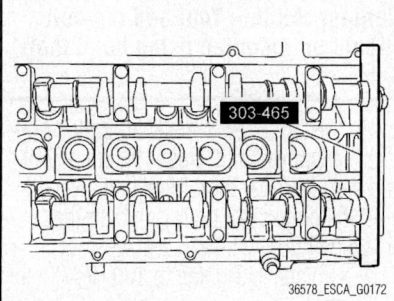

Fig. 75 Install the camshaft alignment plate special tool in the slots on the rear of both camshafts

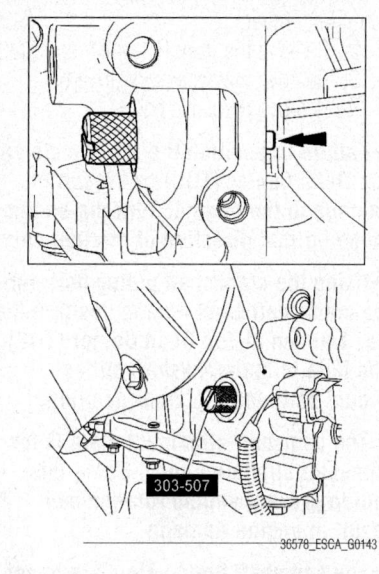

Fig. 76 Install Crankshaft Timing Peg 303-057 or equivalent special tool

※※ WARNING

If the crankshaft sprocket diamond washer comes off with the crankshaft pulley it must be installed back onto the crankshaft.

12. Remove the crankshaft pulley bolt and washer. Discard the bolt.

13. Remove the crankshaft pulley.

To install:

➡**Do not reuse the crankshaft pulley bolt.**

➡**Apply clean engine oil on the seal area before installing.**

14. Install the crankshaft pulley and hand-tighten the bolt.

※※ WARNING

Only hand-tighten the bolt or damage to the front cover can occur.

➡**The following 2 steps will correctly align the crankshaft pulley to the crankshaft.**

15. Install a standard 6-mm (0.23-in.) x 18-mm (0.7-in.) bolt through the crankshaft pulley and thread it into the front cover.

16. Rotate the pulley as necessary to align the bolt holes.

※※ WARNING

Failure to hold the crankshaft pulley in place while tightening the bolt can cause damage to the engine front cover.

17. Using the special tools to hold the crankshaft pulley in place, tighten the crankshaft pulley bolt in 2 stages:
- Stage 1: Tighten to 74 ft. lbs. (100 Nm).
- Stage 2: Tighten an additional 90 degrees (1/4 turn).

18. Remove the 6-mm (0.23-in.) x 18-mm (0.7-in.) bolt.

19. Remove the special tools.

➡**Only turn the engine in the normal direction of rotation.**

20. Turn the engine 2 complete revolutions.

➡**Only turn the engine in the normal direction of rotation.**

21. Turn the crankshaft until the No. 1 piston is at TDC.

22. Install the special crankshaft timing peg tool.

※※ WARNING

Only hand-tighten the bolt or damage to the front cover can occur. Using the 6-mm (0.23-in.) x 18-mm (0.7-in.) bolt, check the position of the crankshaft pulley. If it is not possible to install the bolt, correct the engine timing.

23. Using the camshaft alignment plate special tool, check the position of the camshafts.

If it is not possible to install the special tool, correct the engine timing.

24. Remove the 6-mm (0.23-in.) x 18-mm (0.7-in.) bolt.

25. Install the engine plug bolt and tighten to 15 ft. lbs. (20 Nm).

26. Install the front RH wheel and tire.

27. Install the pin-type retainer, the 5 bolts and the RH splash shield. Tighten the bolts to 80 inch lbs. (9 Nm).

28. Lower the vehicle.

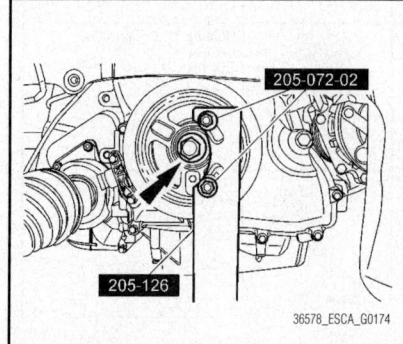

Fig. 77 Install Drive Pinion Flange Holding Fixture and Adapter special tools

29. Install the accessory drive belt.
30. Install the valve cover.

2.5L Hybrid Engine

See Figures 62, 68, 75, 78 and 79.

✳✳ CAUTION

Before proceeding, read and observe all of the High Voltage System Precautions.

✳✳ WARNING

Do not loosen or remove the crankshaft pulley bolt without first installing the special tools as instructed in this procedure. The crankshaft pulley and the crankshaft timing sprocket are not keyed to the crankshaft. The crankshaft, the crankshaft sprocket and the pulley are fitted together by friction, using diamond washers between the flange faces on each part. For that reason, the crankshaft sprocket is also unfastened if the pulley bolt is loosened. Before any repair requiring loosening or removal of the crankshaft pulley bolt, the crankshaft and camshafts must be locked in place by the special service tools, otherwise severe engine damage can occur.

➡During engine repair procedures, cleanliness is extremely important. Any foreign material (including any material created while cleaning gasket surfaces) that enters the oil passages, coolant passages or the oil pan can cause engine failure.

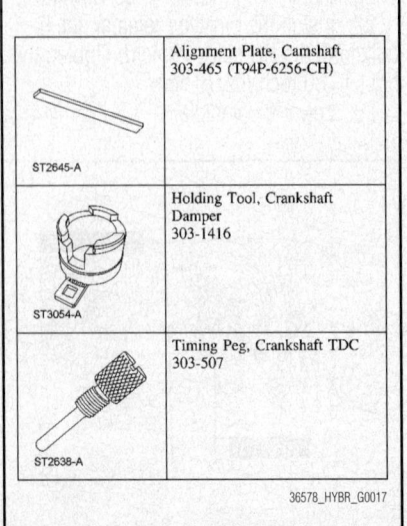

![ST2645-A]	Alignment Plate, Camshaft 303-465 (T94P-6256-CH)
![ST3054-A]	Holding Tool, Crankshaft Damper 303-1416
![ST2638-A]	Timing Peg, Crankshaft TDC 303-507

36578_HYBR_G0017

Fig. 78 Special tool required

1. With the vehicle in NEUTRAL, position it on a hoist.
2. Remove the front RH wheel and tire.
3. Remove the accessory drive belt.
4. Remove the valve cover.

➡**Failure to position the No. 1 piston at Top Dead Center (TDC) can result in damage to the engine. Turn the engine in the normal direction of rotation only.**

➡**Using the crankshaft pulley bolt, turn the crankshaft clockwise to position the No. 1 piston at Top Dead Center (TDC). The hole in the crankshaft pulley should be in the 6 o'clock position.**

➡**The camshaft alignment plate is for camshaft alignment only. Using this tool to prevent engine rotation can result in engine damage.**

➡**The camshaft timing slots are offset. If the camshaft alignment plate cannot be installed, rotate the crankshaft one complete revolution clockwise to correctly position the camshafts.**

5. Install the camshaft alignment plate in the slots on the rear of both camshafts.
6. Remove the engine plug bolt.

➡**The crankshaft TDC timing peg will contact the crankshaft and prevent it from turning past TDC. However, the crankshaft can still be rotated in the counterclockwise direction. The crankshaft must remain at the TDC position during the crankshaft pulley removal and installation.**

7. Install the crankshaft TDC timing peg.

➡**The crankshaft must remain in the Top Dead Center (TDC) position during removal of the pulley bolt or damage to the engine can occur. Therefore, the crankshaft pulley must be held in place with the crankshaft damper holding tool, and the bolt should be removed using an air impact wrench (1/2-in drive minimum).**

➡**The crankshaft sprocket diamond washer may come off with the crankshaft pulley. The diamond washer must be replaced. Remove and discard the diamond washer. If the diamond washer is not installed, engine damage may occur.**

8. Use the crankshaft damper holding tool and a suitable ½ inch drive hand tool to hold the crankshaft pulley. Use an air impact wrench to remove the crankshaft pulley bolt.

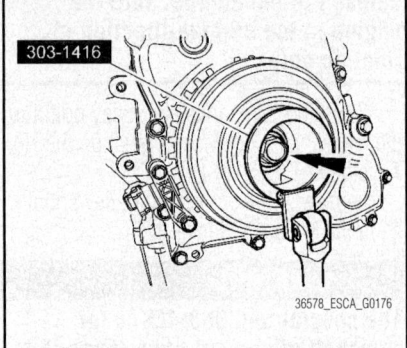

303-1416

36578_ESCA_G0176

Fig. 79 Crankshaft damper holding tool installed

9. Remove and discard the crankshaft pulley bolt and washer.
10. Remove the crankshaft pulley.
11. Remove the diamond washer and discard.

To install:

12. Install a new diamond washer.

➡**Do not install the crankshaft pulley bolt at this time.**

➡**Apply clean engine oil on the seal area before installing.**

13. Position the crankshaft pulley onto the crankshaft with the hole in the pulley at the 6 o'clock position.

➡**This step will correctly align the crankshaft pulley to the crankshaft.**

14. Install a 6 mm x 18 mm bolt through the crankshaft pulley and thread it into the front cover. Only hand-tighten the 6 mm x 18 mm bolt or damage to the front cover can occur.

✳✳ WARNING

The crankshaft must remain in the Top Dead Center (TDC) position during installation of the pulley bolt or damage to the engine can occur. Therefore, the crankshaft pulley must be held in place with the Crankshaft Damper Holding Tool and the bolt should be installed using hand tools only.

15. Install a new crankshaft pulley bolt. Use the Crankshaft Damper Holding Tool and a suitable ½ inch drive hand tool to hold the crankshaft pulley, tighten the crankshaft pulley bolt in 2 stages:
   - Stage 1: Tighten to 100 Nm (74 lb-ft).
   - Stage 2: Tighten an additional 90 degrees.
16. Remove the 6 mm x 18 mm bolt.

17. Remove the crankshaft TDC timing peg.

18. Remove the camshaft alignment plate.

➡️**Only turn the engine in the normal direction of rotation.**

19. Turn the crankshaft clockwise one and three-fourths turns.

20. Install the crankshaft TDC Timing Peg.

21. Turn the crankshaft clockwise until the crankshaft contacts the crankshaft TDC timing peg.

22. Using the 6 mm x 18 mm bolt, check the position of the crankshaft pulley.

23. If it is not possible to install the bolt, the engine valve timing must be corrected by repeating this procedure.

24. Install the camshaft alignment plate to check the position of the camshafts.

25. If it is not possible to install the Camshaft Alignment Plate, the engine valve timing must be corrected by repeating this procedure.

26. Remove the Camshaft Alignment Plate.

27. Remove the 6 mm x 18 mm bolt.

28. Remove the Crankshaft TDC Timing Peg.

29. Install the engine plug bolt and tighten to 177 inch lbs. (20 Nm).

30. Install the accessory drive belt.

31. Install the front RH wheel and tire.

32. Install the valve cover.

CRANKSHAFT FRONT SEAL

REMOVAL & INSTALLATION

2.3L Hybrid Engine
See Figures 80 through 82.

> ❋❋ **WARNING**
>
> Do not loosen or remove the crankshaft pulley bolt without first installing the special tools as instructed in this procedure. The crankshaft pulley and the crankshaft timing sprocket are not keyed to the crankshaft. The crankshaft, the crankshaft sprocket and the pulley are fitted together by friction, using diamond washers between the flange faces on each part. For that reason, the crankshaft sprocket is also unfastened if you loosen the pulley bolt. Before any repair requiring loosening or removal of the crankshaft pulley bolt, the crankshaft and camshafts must be locked in place by the spe-

cial service tools, otherwise severe engine damage can occur.

> ❋❋ **WARNING**
>
> During engine repair procedures, cleanliness is extremely important. Any foreign material (including any material created while cleaning gasket surfaces) that enters the oil passages, coolant passages or the oil pan can cause engine failure.

> ❋❋ **CAUTION**
>
> Before proceeding, read and observe all of the High Voltage System Precautions.

1. Remove the crankshaft pulley. Refer to Crankshaft Damper Removal & Installation in this section.

2. Using the special tool, remove the crankshaft front oil seal. Use care not to damage the engine front cover or the crankshaft when removing the seal.

To install:

➡️**Lubricate the oil seal with clean engine oil.**

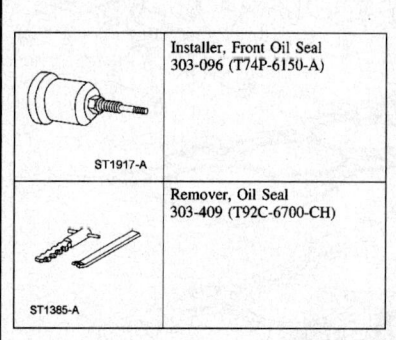

	Installer, Front Oil Seal 303-096 (T74P-6150-A)
ST1917-A	
	Remover, Oil Seal 303-409 (T92C-6700-CH)
ST1385-A	

36578_ESCA_G0182

Fig. 80 Special tools required

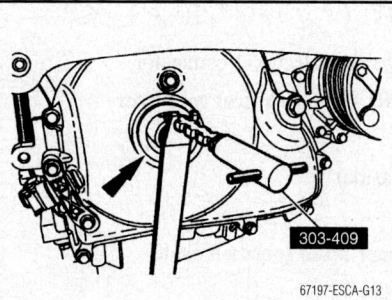

303-409

67197-ESCA-G13

Fig. 81 Using the special tool, remove the crankshaft front oil seal—2.3L engine

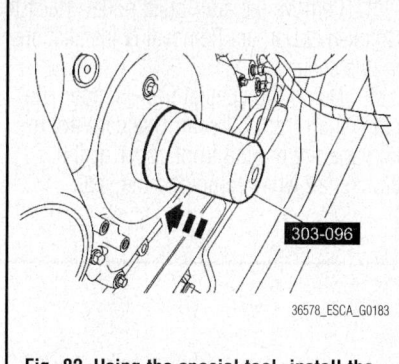

303-096

36578_ESCA_G0183

Fig. 82 Using the special tool, install the crankshaft front oil seal

3. Remove the through-bolt from the special tool.

4. Using the special tool, install the crankshaft front oil seal.

5. Install the crankshaft pulley.

2.5L Hybrid Engine
See Figures 80 through 82.

> ❋❋ **WARNING**
>
> Do not loosen or remove the crankshaft pulley bolt without first installing the special tools as instructed in this procedure. The crankshaft pulley and the crankshaft timing sprocket are not keyed to the crankshaft. The crankshaft, the crankshaft sprocket and the pulley are fitted together by friction, using diamond washers between the flange faces on each part. For that reason, the crankshaft sprocket is also unfastened if you loosen the pulley bolt. Before any repair requiring loosening or removal of the crankshaft pulley bolt, the crankshaft and camshafts must be locked in place by the special service tools, otherwise severe engine damage can occur.

> ❋❋ **WARNING**
>
> During engine repair procedures, cleanliness is extremely important. Any foreign material (including any material created while cleaning gasket surfaces) that enters the oil passages, coolant passages or the oil pan can cause engine failure.

> ❋❋ **CAUTION**
>
> Before proceeding, read and observe all of the High Voltage System Precautions.

1. Remove the crankshaft pulley. Refer to Crankshaft Damper Removal & Installation in this section.

2. Using the special tool, remove the crankshaft front oil seal. Use care not to damage the engine front cover or the crankshaft when removing the seal.

To install:

➡️**Lubricate the oil seal with clean engine oil.**

3. Remove the through-bolt from the special tool.

4. Using the special tool, install the crankshaft front oil seal.

5. Install the crankshaft pulley.

CYLINDER HEAD

REMOVAL & INSTALLATION

2.3L Hybrid Engine
See Figures 83 through 85.

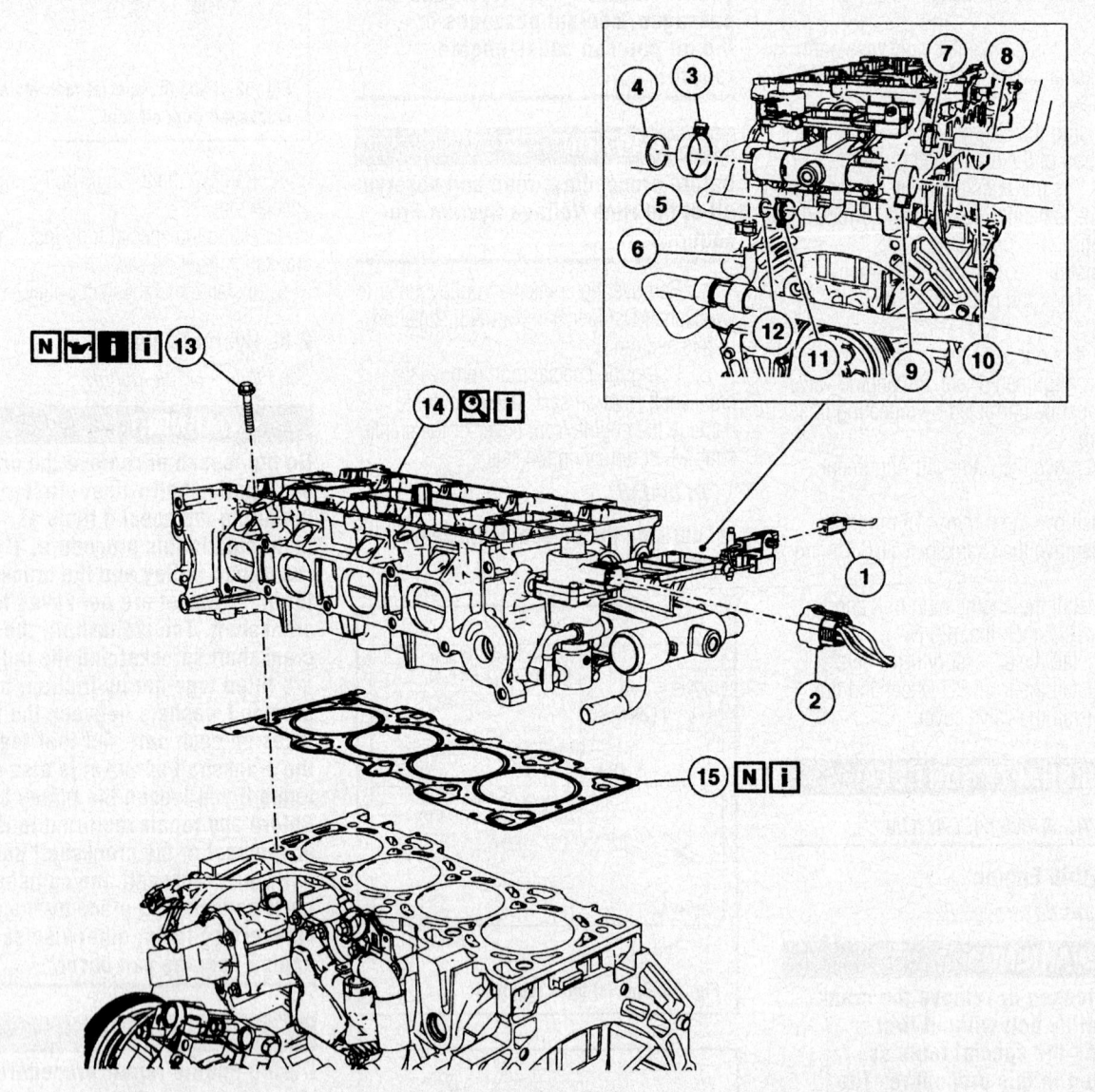

1   Radio ignition interference capacitor electrical connector

2   Exhaust gas recirculation (EGR) valve electrical connector

3   Upper radiator hose clamp

4   Upper radiator hose (position aside)

5   EGR coolant tube clamp

6   EGR coolant hose (part of heater hose) (position aside)

7   Engine coolant vent hose clamp

8   Engine coolant vent hose (position aside)

9   Heater hose clamp

10   Heater hose (position aside)

11   Bypass hose clamp

12   Bypass hose (position aside)

13   Cylinder head bolt

14   Cylinder head

15   Cylinder head gasket

67197-ESCA-G04

Fig. 83 Cylinder head removal—2.3L engine

⁂ CAUTION

Before proceeding, read and observe all of the High Voltage System Precautions.

⁂ WARNING

During engine repair procedures, cleanliness is extremely important. Any foreign material, including any material created while cleaning gasket surfaces that enters the oil passages, coolant passages or the oil pan can cause engine failure.

⁂ WARNING

The crankshaft, the crankshaft sprocket and the pulley are fitted together by friction, using diamond washers between the flange faces on each part. For that reason, the crankshaft sprocket is also unfastened if you loosen the pulley. Therefore, the engine must be retimed each time the damper is removed. Otherwise severe engine damage can occur.

⁂ WARNING

Do not loosen or remove the crankshaft pulley bolt without first installing the special tools as instructed in the timing chain section. The crankshaft pulley and the crankshaft timing sprocket are not keyed to the crankshaft.

1. With the vehicle in NEUTRAL, position it on a hoist.
2. Release the fuel system pressure.
3. Drain the engine cooling system.
4. Remove the timing drive components. For additional information, refer to Timing Drive Components in this section.
5. Mark the position of the camshaft lobes on the No. 1 cylinder for installation reference.
6. Loosen the camshaft bearing cap bolts, in sequence, one turn at a time until all tension is released from the camshaft bearing caps.

⁂ WARNING

If the camshafts and valve tappets are to be reused, mark the location of the valve tappets to make sure they are assembled in their original positions.

7. Remove the camshafts.
8. Remove the intake manifold.

9. Remove the catalytic converter/manifold.
10. Disconnect the radio ignition interference capacitor electrical connector
11. Disconnect the exhaust gas recirculation (EGR) valve electrical connector
12. Remove the upper radiator hose.
13. Remove the EGR coolant tube clamp.
14. Remove the EGR coolant hose.
15. Remove the engine coolant vent hose.
16. Remove the heater hose.
17. Remove the bypass hose.
18. Remove and discard the cylinder head bolts.
19. Remove the cylinder head.
20. Remove the cylinder head gasket.
21. Inspect the cylinder head for distortion.

⁂ WARNING

Do not use metal scrapers, wire brushes, power abrasive discs or other abrasive means to clean the sealing surfaces. These tools cause scratches and gouges that make leak paths. Use a plastic scraping tool to remove all traces of the head gasket.

⁂ WARNING

Observe all warnings or cautions and follow all application directions contained on the packaging of the silicone gasket remover and the metal surface prep.

➡ **If there is no residual gasket material present, metal surface prep can be used to clean and prepare the surfaces.**

22. Clean the cylinder head-to-cylinder block mating surface of both the cylinder head and the cylinder block.
23. Remove any large deposits of silicone or gasket material with a plastic scraper.
24. Apply silicone gasket remover, following package directions, and allow to set for several minutes.
25. Remove the silicone gasket remover with a plastic scraper. A second application of silicone gasket remover may be required if residual traces of silicone or gasket material remain.
26. Apply metal surface prep, following package directions, to remove any traces of oil or coolant, and to prepare the surfaces to bond with the new gasket. Do not attempt to make the metal shiny. Some staining of the metal surfaces is normal.
27. Apply silicone gasket and sealant to the locations shown.

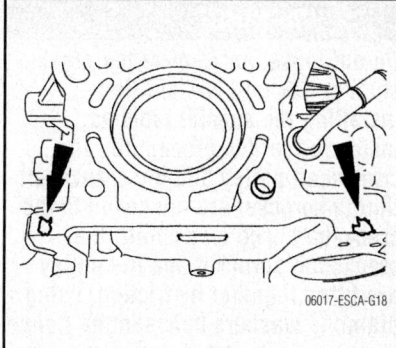

Fig. 84 Apply silicone gasket and sealant to the locations shown

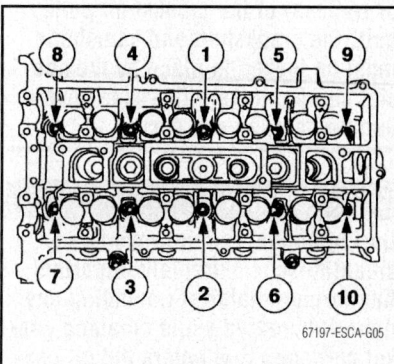

Fig. 85 Cylinder head bolt torque sequence—2.3L engine

28. Install a new head gasket.

➡ **The cylinder head bolts are torque-to-yield and must not be reused. New cylinder head bolts must be installed.**

➡ **Lubricate the bolts with clean engine oil prior to installation.**

29. Install new cylinder head bolts. Tighten the bolts in the sequence shown in five stages:
- Tighten the bolts to 44 inch lbs. (5 Nm).
- Tighten the bolts to 11 ft. lbs. (15 Nm).
- Tighten the bolts to 33 ft. lbs. (45 Nm).
- Turn the bolts 90 degrees.
- Turn the bolts an additional 90 degrees.

30. To install, reverse the removal procedure.

2.5L Hybrid Engine

See Figures 75 and 84 through 87.

⁂ CAUTION

Before proceeding, read and observe all of the High Voltage System Precautions.

✳✳ WARNING

Do not loosen or remove the crankshaft pulley bolt without first installing the special tools as instructed in this procedure. The crankshaft pulley and the crankshaft timing sprocket are not keyed to the crankshaft. The crankshaft, the crankshaft sprocket and the pulley are fitted together by friction, using diamond washers between the flange faces on each part. For that reason, the crankshaft sprocket is also unfastened if the pulley bolt is loosened. Before any repair requiring loosening or removal of the crankshaft pulley bolt, the crankshaft and camshafts must be locked in place by the special service tools, otherwise severe engine damage can occur.

✳✳ WARNING

During engine repair procedures, cleanliness is extremely important. Any foreign material (including any material created while cleaning gasket surfaces) that enters the oil passages, coolant passages or the oil pan may cause engine failure.

1. With the vehicle in NEUTRAL, position it on a hoist.
2. Release the fuel system pressure. Refer to the Fuel System section.
3. Drain the engine cooling system.
4. Remove the timing drive components. Refer to Timing Chain Cover, Chain and Sprockets in this section.
5. Remove the camshaft alignment plate.
6. Mark the position of the camshaft lobes on the No. 1 cylinder for installation reference.
7. Mark the location and orientation of each camshaft bearing cap.

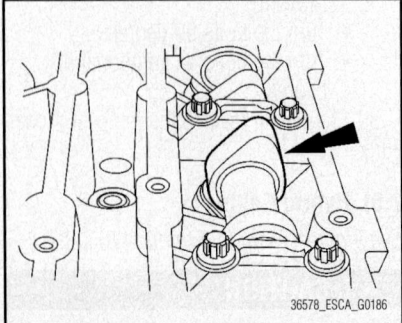

36578_ESCA_G0186

Fig. 86 Mark the position of the camshaft lobes on the No. 1 cylinder

8. Loosen the camshaft bearing cap bolts, in sequence, one turn at a time until all tension is released from the camshaft bearing caps.
9. Remove the bolts and the camshaft bearing caps.
10. Remove the camshafts.

➡If the camshafts and valve tappets are to be reused, mark the location of the valve tappets to make sure they are assembled in their original positions.

11. Remove the valve tappets.

➡The number on the valve tappets only reflects the digits that follow the decimal. For example, a tappet with the number 0.650 has the thickness of 3.650 mm.

12. Inspect the valve tappets.
13. Remove the intake manifold. Refer to Intake Manifold Removal & Installation in this section.
14. Remove the alternator. Refer to Alternator Removal & Installation in the Engine Electrical section.
15. Remove the exhaust manifold. Refer to Exhaust Manifold Removal & Installation in this section.
16. Disconnect the EGR valve electrical connector.
17. Disconnect the EGR coolant hose from the EGR valve.
18. Disconnect the upper radiator hose, coolant bypass hose, heater hose and coolant vent hose from the engine coolant outlet.
19. Remove the 10 bolts and the cylinder head. Discard the bolts and the cylinder head gasket.

To install:

✳✳ WARNING

Do not use metal scrapers, wire brushes, power abrasive discs or other abrasive means to clean the sealing surfaces. These tools cause scratches and gouges that make leak paths. Use a plastic scraping tool to remove all traces of the head gasket.

20. Clean the cylinder head-to-cylinder block mating surface of both the cylinder head and the cylinder block in the following sequence:
   - Remove any large deposits of silicone or gasket material with a plastic scraper.
   - Apply silicone gasket remover, following package directions, and allow to set for several minutes.
   - Remove the silicone gasket remover with a plastic scraper. A

second application of silicone gasket remover may be required if residual traces of silicone or gasket material remain.
   - Apply metal surface prep, following package directions, to remove any traces of oil or coolant, and to prepare the surfaces to bond with the new gasket. Do not attempt to make the metal shiny. Some staining of the metal surfaces is normal.

21. Support the cylinder head on a bench with the head gasket side up. Check the cylinder head distortion and the cylinder block distortion.
22. Clean the cylinder head bolt holes in the cylinder block. Make sure all coolant, oil or other foreign material is removed.
23. Apply silicone gasket and sealant to the locations shown.
24. Install a new head gasket.

✳✳ WARNING

The cylinder head bolts are torque-to-yield and must not be reused. New cylinder head bolts must be installed.

25. Lubricate the bolts with clean engine oil prior to installation.
26. Install the cylinder head and 10 new bolts. Tighten the bolts in the sequence shown in 5 stages:
27. Install new cylinder head bolts. Tighten the bolts in the sequence shown in five stages:
   - Tighten the bolts to 44 inch lbs. (5 Nm).
   - Tighten the bolts to 11 ft. lbs. (15 Nm).
   - Tighten the bolts to 33 ft. lbs. (45 Nm).
   - Turn the bolts 90 degrees.
   - Turn the bolts an additional 90 degrees.

28. Connect the upper radiator hose, coolant bypass hose, heater hose and coolant vent hose to the engine coolant outlet.
29. Connect the EGR coolant hose to the EGR valve.
30. Connect the EGR valve electrical connector.
31. Install the exhaust manifold.
32. Install the alternator.
33. Install the intake manifold.
34. Lubricate the valve tappets with clean engine oil.
35. Install the valve tappets in their original positions.

➡Install the camshafts with the alignment notches in the camshafts lined up

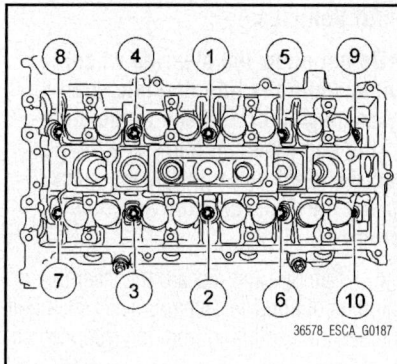

Fig. 87 Bearing cap tightening sequence

so the camshaft alignment plate can be installed. Make sure the lobes on the No. 1 cylinder are in the same position as noted in the removal procedure. Failure to follow this procedure can cause severe damage to the valves and pistons.

36. Lubricate the camshaft journals and bearing caps with clean engine oil.

Install the camshafts and bearing caps in their original location and orientation. Tighten the bearing caps in the sequence shown in 3 stages:

- Stage 1: Tighten the camshaft bearing cap bolts, one turn at a time, until finger tight.
- Stage 2: Tighten to (62 inch (7 Nm).
- Stage 3: Tighten to 142 inch lbs. (16 Nm).

37. Install the camshaft alignment plate.
38. Install the timing drive components.
39. Fill and bleed the engine cooling system.

ENGINE ASSEMBLY

REMOVAL & INSTALLATION
See Figures 88 through 96.

✳✳ CAUTION

Before removing the high voltage cables, the vehicle electrical system must be completely shut down for at least 5 minutes to allow for the high voltage capacitors to discharge.

✳✳ CAUTION

Before proceeding, read and observe all of the High Voltage System Precautions.

✳✳ CAUTION

Depower the high-voltage traction battery (HVTB) before carrying out

any removal or installation procedures affecting the high-voltage battery system. Failure to follow this instruction may result in serious personal injury or death.

All Vehicles

1. With the vehicle in NEUTRAL, position it on a hoist.
2. Release the fuel system pressure.
3. Place the steering wheel in the straight-ahead position and the ignition key in the OFF position.
4. Disconnect the battery ground cable.
5. Disarm the high voltage traction battery. Establish a buffer zone.
6. Drain the cooling system.
7. Drain the motor electronics cooling system.
8. Remove the engine coolant degas bottle.
9. Remove the accessory drive belt.
10. Disconnect the fuel supply tube.
11. Remove the front wheels and tires.
12. Remove the bolts and the lateral support crossmember.
13. Remove the catalytic converter.
14. Remove the brake hose retainer and the ABS sensor retaining bolt from the LH and RH strut.
15. Disconnect the LH and RH suspension as follows:
- Remove the nut and disconnect the stabilizer bar link.
- Remove the tie-rod end retaining nut.
- Remove the lower control arm knuckle bolt.
16. Separate the LH and RH lower control arms from the lower ball joints and position the steering knuckles aside.
17. Drain the transmission fluid.
18. Using the Halfshaft Remover and Slide Hammer, remove the LH front drive halfshaft from the differential and secure aside.

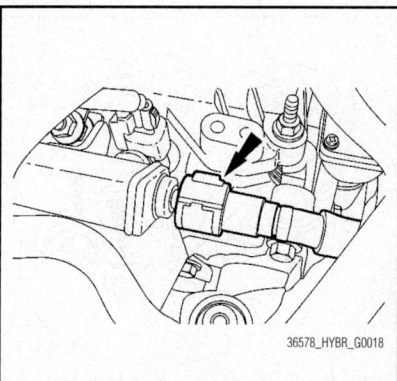

Fig. 88 Disconnect the fuel supply tube

19. Using a brass drift to strike the RH halfshaft in the indicated area, separate the halfshaft from the intermediate shaft and secure aside.
20. Remove the 2 intermediate shaft retaining nuts.

➡ **A new Power Transfer Unit (PTU) intermediate shaft seal must be installed whenever the intermediate shaft or PTU is removed from the vehicle.**

21. Remove the intermediate shaft.
AWD Vehicles
22. Remove the driveshaft
23. Remove the 3 PTU heat shield bolts and the PTU heat shield.
24. Remove the bolts and the PTU-to-engine bracket.
25. Disconnect the PTU vent hose and position it aside.
26. Remove the 4 PTU-to-transaxle bolts and remove the PTU.
27. Using the Halfshaft Oil Seal Remover and Slide Hammer, remove the intermediate shaft seal.

All Vehicles
28. Remove the oil filter element.
29. Drain the engine oil.
30. Disconnect the heater hoses from the heater core.
31. Detach the heater hose retaining clip from the transaxle mount stud.
32. Disconnect the upper radiator and coolant vent hoses.
33. Disconnect the PCM electrical connector. Remove the wiring harness retainer nut.

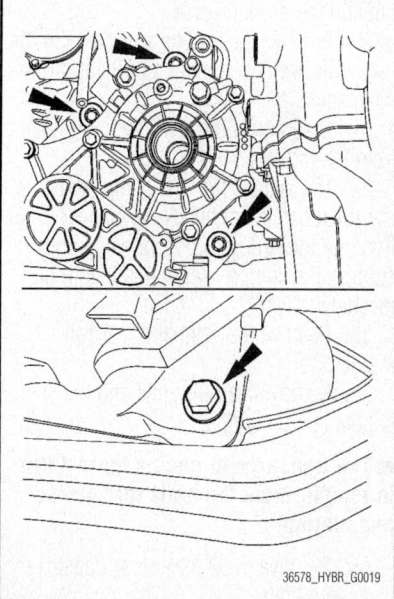

Fig. 89 Remove the 4 PTU-to-transaxle bolts and remove the PTU

34. Disconnect the engine control harness electrical connector.

35. Disconnect the upper evaporative emissions (EVAP) tube quick connect coupling from the purge valve.

36. Remove the selector lever cable fasteners from the stud bolts on the transaxle.

37. Remove the stud bolt and disconnect the transaxle harness electrical connector.

38. Disconnect the 2 low voltage electrical connectors and the engine harness-to-body harness retainer.

39. Disconnect the DC-to-DC converter electrical connector and 2 wire harness retainers.

40. Remove the 3 nuts and position aside the DC-to-DC converter.

41. If equipped, disconnect the block heater electrical connector.

42. Remove the 2 bolts and disconnect the auxiliary coolant pump electrical connector. Position the auxiliary coolant pump aside.

43. Remove the bolts and the transaxle control snow shield.

44. Disconnect the transaxle control cable.

45. Release the transaxle control cable from the control lever.

46. Remove the nuts from the transaxle control cable bracket.

47. Disconnect the transaxle coolant temperature sensor electrical connector and pin-type retainer.

48. Disconnect the transaxle coolant hoses.

49. Remove the 2 harness fasteners, the nut and the ground cable.

50. Remove the 2 bolts and position the motor electronics coolant pump and ground strap aside.

51. Disconnect the lower radiator hose from the radiator.

52. Disconnect the A/C compressor electrical connector and remove the 3 bolts. Position the A/C compressor aside and support the compressor with a length of mechanic's wire.

53. Remove the front and rear roll restrictor bolt.

54. Remove the nut, bolts and the engine support crossmember.

➡ **The transaxle-to-engine bolts differ in length. Mark the bolts for correct installation.**

55. Remove the 2 lower rear transaxle-to-engine bolts.

56. Remove the 2 lower front transaxle-to-engine bolts.

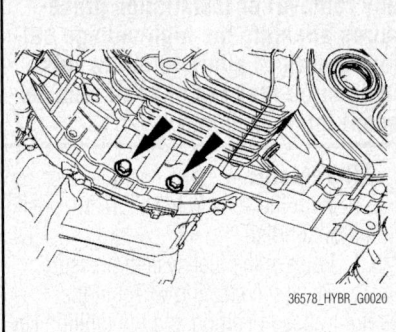

Fig. 90 Remove the 2 lower rear transaxle-to-engine bolts

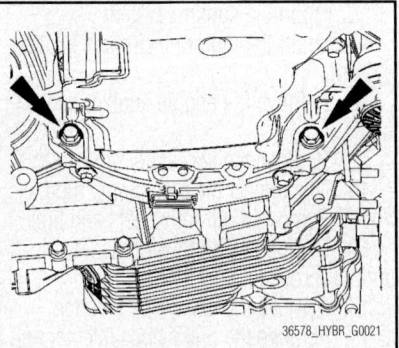

Fig. 91 Remove the 2 lower front transaxle-to-engine bolts

Early Build

57. Remove the RH transaxle mount bracket nut.

58. Remove the 3 bolts and the rear transaxle mount bracket.

Late Build

59. Remove the lower support insulator through bolt.

60. Remove the 2 lower support insulator nuts and 1 bolt.

61. Remove the 2 lower support insulator studs.

62. Remove the lower support insulator.

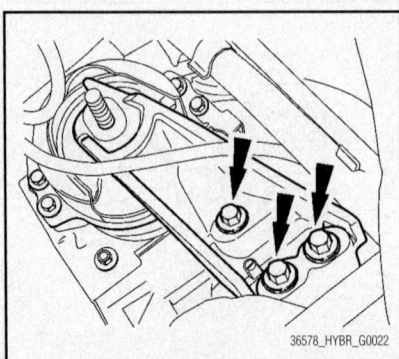

Fig. 92 Remove the 3 bolts and the rear transaxle mount bracket

All Vehicles

➡ **Do not allow the steering wheel to rotate while the intermediate shaft is disconnected or damage to the clockspring can result. If there is evidence that the shaft has rotated, the clockspring must be removed and recentered.**

63. Remove and discard the steering column coupling-to-steering gear pinch bolt and separate coupling from the steering gear.

64. Remove the 2 bolts and the roll restrictor bracket.

65. Using a suitable lift table, support the subframe.

➡ **Do not allow the front sub-frame rear bolts to come out of the lower control arm bushing.**

66. Loosen the 2 sub-frame bolts.

67. Remove the 2 sub-frame nuts and lower the sub-frame.

68. Remove the sub-frame from the lift table.

➡ **Due to the weight of the transaxle, special care should be taken to mount the powertrain securely to the lift table.**

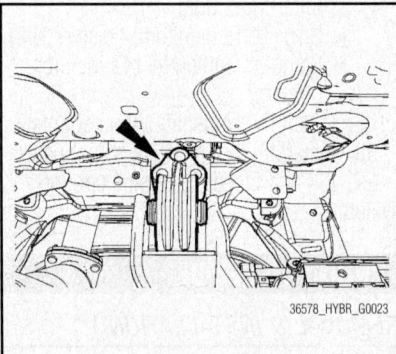

Fig. 93 Remove the lower support insulator

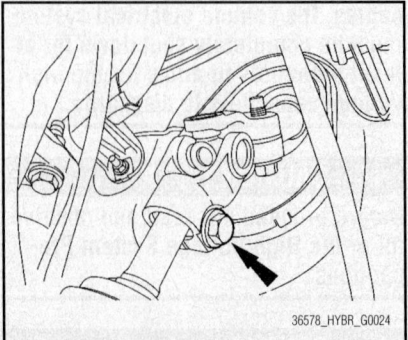

Fig. 94 Remove the pinch bolt and separate coupling from the steering gear

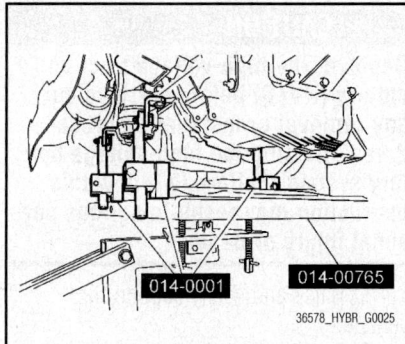

Fig. 95 Using the special tools, secure the engine to the lift table

69. Using the special tools, secure the engine to the lift table.

70. Remove the engine mount bracket bolt.

71. Remove the nuts and the engine mount bracket.

72. Remove the bolt, nut and the rear transaxle mount brace.

73. Remove the nuts, bolt and rear transaxle mount.

74. Lower the engine and transaxle from the vehicle.

75. Using the engine crane and spreader bar, remove the engine and transaxle from the lift table.

76. Disconnect the high voltage wiring harness electrical connector.

77. Remove the remaining 6 engine-to-transaxle bolts and separate the engine and transaxle. Mark the bolts for correct installation.

➡**The damper contains a clutch which is designed to slip briefly during vehicle operation. It is essential that no grease, oil or cleaning solvents be allowed to contaminate the slip**

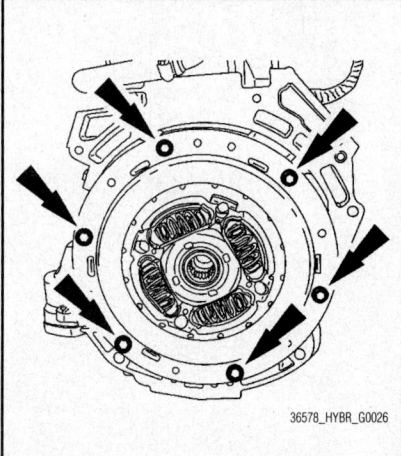

Fig. 96 Remove the bolts and the transaxle damper

clutch. **Do not use grease on transmission input shaft. Should the damper become contaminated, it must be replaced.**

78. Remove the bolts and the transaxle damper.

To install:
All Vehicles
79. Install the transaxle damper and tighten the bolts to 21 ft. lbs. (29 Nm).

➡**When positioning the engine to the transaxle, care must be taken to maintain alignment of the damper spline with the transaxle input shaft.**

80. Using the engine crane and spreader bar, position the engine and transaxle together. Install the 6 transaxle-to-engine bolts. Tighten the bolts to 35 ft. lbs. (48 Nm).

81. Connect the high voltage wiring harness electrical connector.

82. Using the engine crane and spreader bar, position the engine and transaxle onto the lift table.

83. Using the special tools, secure the engine to the lift table.

84. Raise the engine and transaxle into the vehicle.

85. Install the rear transaxle mount. Tighten the nuts to 66 ft. lbs. (90 Nm). Tighten the bolt to 76 ft. lbs. (103 Nm).

86. Install the rear transaxle mount brace and tighten to 18 ft. lbs. (25 Nm).

87. Install the engine mount bracket and tighten to 85 ft. lbs. (115 Nm).

88. Install the engine mount through bracket bolt and tighten to 85 ft. lbs. (115 Nm).

89. Using the lift table, raise the subframe into position and install the 2 nuts. Tighten to 111 ft. lbs. (150 Nm).

90. When installing the subframe bolts, make sure both of the subframe bolts are fully engaged in their cage nuts before tightening to specification.

91. Tighten the 2 sub-frame bolts to 129 ft. lbs. (175 Nm).

92. Install the roll restrictor bracket and bolts. Tighten the bolts to 85 ft. lbs. (115 Nm).

93. Connect the steering column coupling-to-steering gear and install the new pinch bolt. Tighten to 30 ft. lbs. (40 Nm).

Early Build
94. Install the RH transaxle mount bracket and the 3 bolts. Tighten the bolts to 66 ft. lbs. (90 Nm).

95. Install the RH transaxle mount bracket nut and tighten to 66 ft. lbs. (90 Nm).

Late Build
96. Install the lower support insulator.

97. Install the 2 lower support insulator studs and tighten to 9 ft. lbs. (12 Nm).

98. Install the 2 lower support insulator nuts and 1 lower support insulator bolt. Tighten nuts and bolt to 58 ft. lbs. (80 Nm).

99. Install lower support insulator through bolt and tighten to 85 ft. lbs. (115 Nm).

All Vehicles
100. Install the 2 front lower transaxle-to-engine bolts and tighten to 35 ft. lbs. (48 Nm).

101. Install the 2 rear lower transaxle-to-engine bolts and tighten to 35 ft. lbs. (48 Nm).

102. Install the engine support cross-member. Tighten the bolts to 66 ft. lbs. (90 Nm). Tighten the new nut to 129 ft. lbs. (175 Nm).

103. Install the front and rear roll restrictor bolt and tighten to 66 ft. lbs. (90 Nm).

104. Install the A/C compressor and connect the A/C compressor electrical connector. Tighten the mounting bolts to 18 ft. lbs. (25 Nm).

105. Connect the lower radiator hose to the radiator.

106. Position the motor electronics coolant pump and the ground strap. Install the 2 bolts and tighten to 15 ft. lbs. (20 Nm).

107. Install the wiring harness fasteners, the ground cable and nut. Tighten the nut to 15 ft. lbs. (20 Nm).

108. Connect the transaxle coolant hoses.

109. Connect the transaxle coolant temperature sensor electrical connector and pin type retainer.

110. Install the transaxle control cable bracket and the 2 nuts finger tight.

111. Attach the transaxle control cable to the control lever.

112. Position the control lever between the 2 casting ribs on the transaxle case.

113. Place the gear selector lever in the D position.

114. Tighten the transaxle control cable bracket nuts to 16 ft. lbs. (22 Nm).

➡**To verify the correct cable adjustment, observe the control lever on the transaxle while an assistant shifts the gear selector lever to each range position ending in the D position.**

115. Install the transaxle control snow shield. Tighten the retainers to 89 inch lbs. (10 Nm).

116. Install the auxiliary coolant pump and tighten the retainers to 89 inch lbs. (10 Nm). Connect the electrical connector.

117. If equipped, connect the block heater electrical connector.

118. Position the DC-to-DC converter in place and install the 3 nuts. Tighten the nuts to 106 inch lbs. (9 Nm).

119. Connect the DC-to-DC converter electrical connector and 2 wire harness retainer.

120. Connect the 2 low voltage electrical connectors and the engine harness-to-body harness retainer.

121. Connect the transaxle harness electrical connector and install the stud bolt. Tighten to 89 inch lbs. (10 Nm).

122. Install the selector lever cable fasteners on the transaxle stud bolts.

123. Connect the upper evaporative emissions (EVAP) tube quick connect coupling to the purge valve.

124. Connect the engine control harness electrical connector.

125. Connect the PCM electrical connector. Position the harness and install and tighten the nut to 53 inch lbs. (6 Nm).

126. Connect the upper radiator and coolant vent hoses.

127. Attach the heater hose retaining clip to the transaxle mount stud.

128. Connect the heater hoses to the heater core.

AWD Vehicles

129. Using the Handle and PTO Driven Gear Oil Seal Installer, install the intermediate shaft seal.

130. Position the Power Transfer Unit (PTU) in place and install the 4 bolts. Tighten the bolts to 33 ft. lbs. (45 Nm).

131. Connect the PTU vent hose.

132. Position the PTU-to-engine support bracket and install and tighten the bolts to 30 ft. lbs. (40 Nm).

133. Install the PTU heat shield and the bolts. Tighten the bolts to 10 ft. lbs. (14 Nm).

134. Install the driveshaft.

All Vehicles

135. Install the intermediate shaft and nuts, tighten the retaining nuts to 20 ft. lbs. (27 Nm).

136. Install the LH halfshafts in the transaxle and the RH halfshaft in the intermediate shaft and install the ball joints in the knuckles.

137. Connect the RH and LH suspension as follows:
- Install the lower ball joint-to-knuckle bolt and tighten to 46 ft. lbs. (63 Nm).
- Position the tie-rod end and install the retaining nut, tighten to 41 ft. lbs. (55 Nm).
- Connect the stabilizer bar link and

install the nut, tighten to 46 ft. lbs. (63 Nm).

138. Install the RH and LH brake hose retainer and the ABS sensor bolt. Tighten to 11 ft. lbs. (15 Nm).

139. Install the catalytic converter. Install the lateral support crossmember and tighten the mounting bolts to 85 ft. lbs. (115 Nm).

140. Install the oil filter element.

141. Install the front wheels and tires.

142. Connect the fuel supply tube.

143. Install the accessory drive belt.

144. Install the engine coolant degas bottle.

145. Install the engine air cleaner.

146. Fill the engine with clean engine oil.

147. Enable the vehicle high voltage electrical system.

148. Connect the battery ground cable.

149. Fill and bleed the motor electronics cooling system.

150. Fill and bleed the cooling system.

151. Fill the transaxle

152. Start engine and check for leaks.

EXHAUST MANIFOLD

REMOVAL & INSTALLATION

2.3L Hybrid Engine

See Figures 97 and 98.

❋❋ CAUTION

Before proceeding, read and observe all of the High Voltage System Precautions.

❋❋ CAUTION

Depower the high-voltage traction battery (HVTB) before carrying out any removal or installation procedures affecting the high-voltage battery system. Failure to follow this instruction may result in serious personal injury or death.

1. Raise and safely support the vehicle.

2. Remove the exhaust flexible pipe.

3. Remove the 2 catalytic converter bracket bolts.

4. Remove the 6 heat shield bolts and the heat shield.

5. Disconnect the Heated Oxygen Sensor (HO2S) and the catalyst monitor sensor electrical connectors.

6. Remove and discard the 7 catalytic converter manifold nuts.

7. Remove the catalytic converter from the vehicle. Discard the catalytic converter manifold gasket.

8. Remove and discard the 7 catalytic converter manifold studs.

To install:

9. Install the 7 new catalytic converter studs and tighten to 13 ft. lbs. (17 Nm).

10. Position a new catalytic converter manifold gasket on the engine.

➡**Failure to tighten the catalytic converter nuts to specification before installing the converter bracket bolts will cause the converter to develop an exhaust leak.**

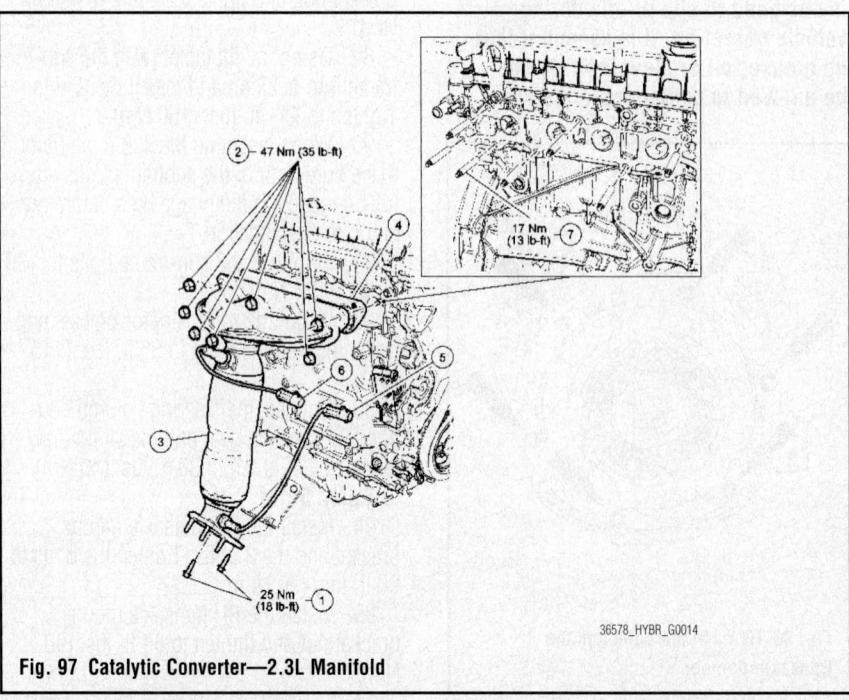

Fig. 97 Catalytic Converter—2.3L Manifold

36578_HYBR_G0014

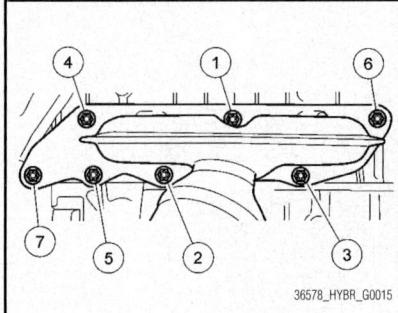

Fig. 98 Manifold tightening sequence—2.3L Hybrid

11. Position the catalytic converter and tighten the 7 exhaust manifold nuts in 2 stages in the sequence shown:
- Stage 1: Tighten to 35 ft. lbs. (47 Nm).
- Stage 2: Tighten to 35 ft. lbs. (47 Nm).

12. Connect the HO2S and the catalyst monitor sensor electrical connectors.

13. Position the heat shield and install the 6 heat shield bolts. Tighten the heat shield bolts to 89 inch lbs. (10 Nm).

14. Install the 2 catalytic converter bracket bolts and tighten to 18 ft. lbs. (25 Nm).

15. Install the exhaust flexible pipe. Install a new gasket and tighten the flex pipe-to-converter nuts to 35 ft. lbs. (47 Nm).

16. Lower the vehicle.

17. Check the exhaust system for leaks.

2.5L Hybrid Engine

See Figure 98.

> ✷✷ **CAUTION**
>
> **Before proceeding, read and observe all of the High Voltage System Precautions.**

> ✷✷ **CAUTION**
>
> **Depower the high-voltage traction battery (HVTB) before carrying out any removal or installation procedures affecting the high-voltage battery system. Failure to follow this instruction may result in serious personal injury or death.**

1. Remove the exhaust intermediate pipe.

2. Remove the 2 exhaust bracket bolts.

3. Disconnect the Heated Oxygen Sensor (HO2S) and the Catalyst Monitor Sensor (CMS) electrical connectors.

4. Remove and discard the 7 catalytic converter manifold nuts.

5. Remove the catalytic converter mani-

fold from the vehicle. Discard the catalytic converter manifold gasket.

6. Remove and discard the 7 catalytic converter manifold studs.

7. Install the 7 new catalytic converter manifold studs. And tighten to 150 inch lbs. (17 Nm).

➡ **Failure to tighten the catalytic converter manifold nuts to specification before installing the converter bracket bolts will cause the converter to develop an exhaust leak.**

➡ **Failure to tighten the catalytic converter manifold nuts to specification a second time will cause the converter to develop an exhaust leak.**

8. Using a new gasket, install the catalytic converter and the 7 exhaust manifold nuts. Tighten in 2 stages in the sequence shown:
- Stage 1: Tighten to 35 ft. lbs. (47 Nm).
- Stage 2: Tighten to 35 ft. lbs. (47 Nm).

9. Connect the HO2S and the CMS electrical connectors.

10. Install the 2 exhaust bracket bolts and tighten to 18 ft. lbs. (25 Nm).

11. Install the exhaust intermediate pipe and tighten to 18 ft. lbs. (25 Nm).

FLYWHEEL

REMOVAL & INSTALLATION

See Figure 99.

1. With the vehicle in NEUTRAL, position it on a hoist.

2. Remove the engine.

3. Remove the 6 bolts and the flywheel.

To install:

➡ **Special bolts are used for installation. Do not use standard bolts.**

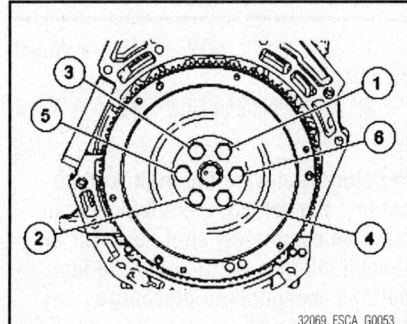

Fig. 99 Flywheel bolt tightening sequence—Hybrid

4. Install the flywheel and tighten the bolts in the sequence shown in 3 stages.
   a. Stage 1: Tighten to 37 ft. lbs. (50 Nm).
   b. Stage 2: Tighten to 50 ft. lbs. (80 Nm).
   c. Stage 3: Tighten to 83 ft. lbs. (112 Nm).

5. Install the engine.

INTAKE MANIFOLD

REMOVAL & INSTALLATION

2.3L Hybrid Engine

See Figure 100.

> ✷✷ **CAUTION**
>
> **Before proceeding, read and observe all of the High Voltage System Precautions.**

> ✷✷ **CAUTION**
>
> **Depower the high-voltage traction battery (HVTB) before carrying out any removal or installation procedures affecting the high-voltage battery system. Failure to follow this instruction may result in serious personal injury or death.**

1. With vehicle in NEUTRAL, position it on a hoist.

2. Release the fuel pressure.

➡ **Before removing the high voltage cables, the vehicle electrical system must be completely shut down for at least 5 minutes to allow for the high voltage capacitors to discharge.**

3. Disable the vehicle high voltage electrical system.

4. Remove the fuel rail.

5. Remove the throttle body.

6. Remove the accessory drive belt tensioner.

7. Remove the oil level indicator and tube.

8. Disconnect the Engine Oil Pressure (EOP) switch electrical connector.

9. Disconnect the Manifold Absolute Pressure (MAP) sensor electrical connector.

10. If equipped, disconnect the block heater electrical harness connector.

11. Disconnect the Knock Sensor (KS) electrical connector and detach the pin-type retainer.

12. Disconnect the fuel vapor return hose from the intake manifold.

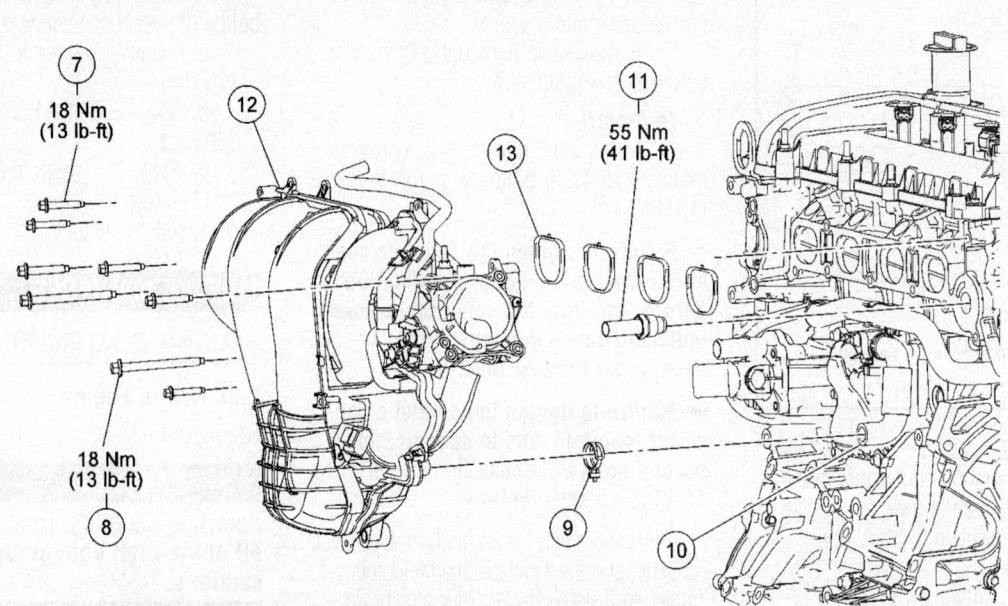

7. Intake manifold bolt (6 required)
8. Intake manifold bolt (2 required)
9. Crankcase vent hose clamp
10. Crankcase vent hose
11. Exhaust gas recirculation (EGR) tube
12. Intake manifold
13. Intake manifold gasket

36578_HYBR_G0027

Fig. 100 Intake manifold—2.3L Hybrid

➡**There are 2 different size bolts used. Mark the location of the bolts to make sure they are installed in the correct location.**

13. Remove the 8 bolts and position the intake manifold aside to access the crankcase vent hose clamp and the Exhaust Gas Recirculation (EGR) tube.

14. Release the clamp and disconnect the crankcase vent hose.

15. Remove the EGR tube.

16. Remove the intake manifold and gaskets.

➡**If the engine is repaired or replaced because of upper engine failure, typically including valve or piston damage, check the intake manifold for metal debris. If metal debris is found, install a new intake manifold. Failure to follow these instructions can result in engine damage.**

17. To install, reverse the removal procedure, note the following:
- Inspect and install new intake manifold gaskets if necessary.
- Tighten the 8 intake manifold bolts to 13 ft. lbs. (18 Nm).
- Tighten the EGR valve tube to 41 ft. lbs. (55 Nm).

18. Repower the vehicle HVTB electrical system.

2.5L Hybrid Engine
See Figure 101.

⁜ **CAUTION**

Before proceeding, read and observe all of the High Voltage System Precautions.

⁜ **CAUTION**

Depower the high-voltage traction battery (HVTB) before carrying out any removal or installation procedures affecting the high-voltage battery system. Failure to follow this instruction may result in serious personal injury or death.

1. With vehicle in NEUTRAL, position it on a hoist.

2. With vehicle in NEUTRAL, position it on a hoist.

➡**Before removing the high voltage cables, the vehicle electrical system must be completely shut down for at least 5 minutes to allow for the high voltage capacitors to discharge.**

3. Disable the vehicle high voltage electrical system.

4. Remove the fuel rail.

5. Remove the Throttle Body (TB).

6. Remove the accessory drive belt tensioner.

7. Disconnect the Engine Oil Pressure (EOP) switch electrical connector.

8. Disconnect the Manifold Absolute Pressure (MAP) sensor electrical connector.

9. Disconnect the Evaporative Emission (EVAP) canister purge valve electrical connector.

10. Disconnect the EVAP tube-to-EVAP canister purge valve quick connect coupling and the brake booster vacuum tube from the intake manifold.

11. Disconnect the Knock Sensor (KS) electrical connector and detach the 2 pin-type retainers.

12. Detach the 2 wiring retainers from the intake manifold near the throttle body mounting area.

13. Detach the transaxle shift cable routing retainer from the intake manifold.

14. Remove the cooling fan motor and shroud.

15. The cylinder head side of the intake manifold is showing the location of the 7 bolts.

16. Remove the 7 bolts and position the intake manifold aside to access the PCV hose connector.

17. Squeeze the 2 PCV hose connector tabs and disconnect the PCV hose from the intake manifold.

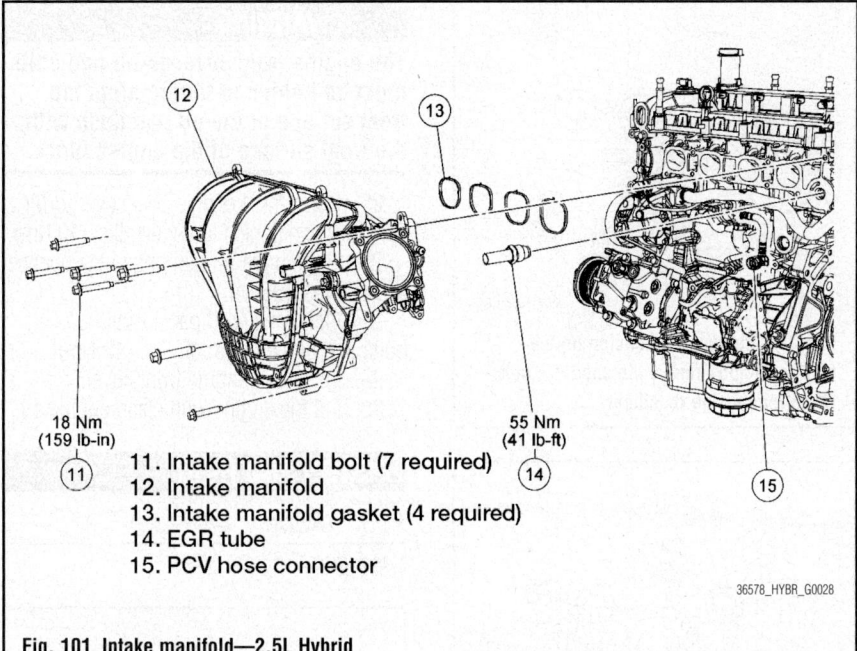

18 Nm
(159 lb-in)

55 Nm
(41 lb-ft)

11. Intake manifold bolt (7 required)
12. Intake manifold
13. Intake manifold gasket (4 required)
14. EGR tube
15. PCV hose connector

36578_HYBR_G0028

Fig. 101 Intake manifold—2.5L Hybrid

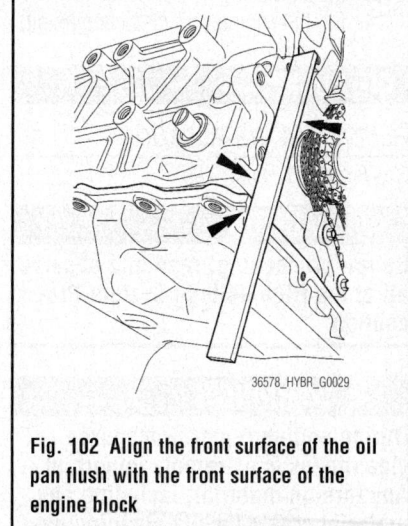

36578_HYBR_G0029

Fig. 102 Align the front surface of the oil pan flush with the front surface of the engine block

18. Remove the intake manifold and gaskets.

➡️**If the engine is repaired or replaced because of upper engine failure, typically including valve or piston damage, check the intake manifold for metal debris. If metal debris is found, install a new intake manifold. Failure to follow these instructions can result in engine damage.**

19. To install, reverse the removal procedure, note the following:
   • Inspect and install new intake manifold gaskets if necessary.
   • Tighten the 7 intake manifold bolts to 159 inch lbs. (18 Nm).
   • Tighten the EGR valve tube to 41 ft. lbs. (55 Nm).
20. Repower the vehicle HVTB electrical system.

OIL PAN

REMOVAL & INSTALLATION
See Figures 102 and 103.

❄ CAUTION

Before proceeding, read and observe all of the High Voltage System Precaution.

1. With the vehicle in NEUTRAL, position it on a hoist.
2. Drain the engine oil, then install the drain plug and tighten to 21 ft. lbs. (21 Nm).
3. Remove the engine front cover.

4. Remove the 4 oil pan-to-bellhousing bolts.
5. Remove the 13 bolts and the oil pan.

To install:

❄ WARNING

Do not use metal scrapers, wire brushes, power abrasive discs or other abrasive means to clean the sealing surfaces. These tools cause scratches and gouges, which make leak paths. Use a plastic scraping tool to remove traces of sealant.

6. Clean and inspect all mating surfaces.

➡️**If the oil pan is not secured within 4 minutes of sealant application, the sealant must be removed and the sealing area cleaned with metal surface prep. Allow to dry until there is no sign of wetness, or 4 minutes, whichever is longer. Failure to follow this procedure can cause future oil leakage**

7. Apply a 0.09 inch (2.5 mm) bead of silicone gasket and sealant to the oil pan.
8. Position the oil pan and install the 2 rear oil pan bolts finger-tight.
9. Using a suitable straightedge, align the front surface of the oil pan flush with the front surface of the engine block.
10. Install the remaining oil pan bolts.
11. Tighten in the sequence shown to 18 ft. lbs. (25 Nm).
12. Install the 4 oil pan-to-bellhousing bolts, tighten to 35 ft. lbs. (48 Nm).

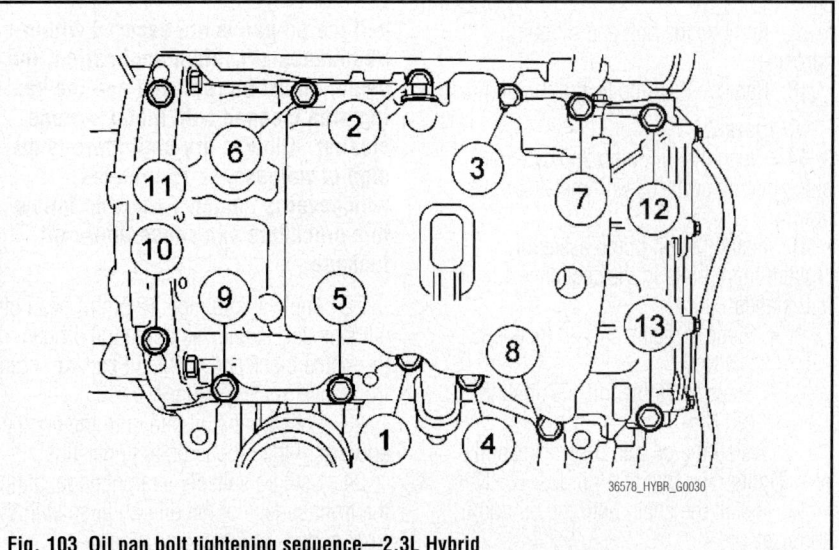

36578_HYBR_G0030

Fig. 103 Oil pan bolt tightening sequence—2.3L Hybrid

13. Install the engine front cover.
14. Fill the engine with clean engine oil.

OIL PUMP

REMOVAL & INSTALLATION

See Figures 104 and 105.

✳✳ CAUTION

Before proceeding, read and observe all of the High Voltage System Precaution.

✳✳ WARNING

During engine repair procedures, cleanliness is extremely important. Any foreign material, including any material created while cleaning gasket surfaces that enters the oil passages, coolant passages or the oil pan, may cause engine failure.

1. Before servicing the vehicle, refer to the Precautions Section.
2. With the engine in NEUTRAL, position it on a hoist.
3. Remove the engine front cover.
4. Drain the engine oil, then install the drain plug and tighten to 21 ft. lbs. (28 Nm).
5. Remove the 4 oil pan-to-bellhousing bolts.
6. Remove the 13 bolts and the oil pan.
7. Discard the gasket and clean and inspect the gasket mating surfaces.
8. Remove the 2 bolts and the oil pump screen and pickup tube.
9. Release the tension on the tensioner spring.
10. Remove the 2 shoulder bolts and the tensioner.
11. Remove the chain from the oil pump sprocket.
12. Remove the bolt and oil pump sprocket.
13. Remove the 4 bolts and the oil pump

To install:

14. Clean the oil pump and cylinder block mating surfaces with metal surface prep.
15. Install the oil pump assembly. Tighten the 4 bolts in the sequence shown in 2 stages:
- Stage 1: Tighten to 89 inch lbs. (10 Nm).
- Stage 2: Tighten to 177 inch lbs. (20 Nm).
16. Install the oil pump sprocket and bolt. Tighten the bolt to 18 ft. lbs. (25 Nm).
17. Install the chain onto the oil pump sprocket.

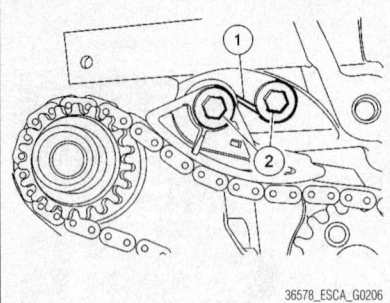

Fig. 104 Release the tension on the spring (1) and remove the shoulder bolts (2) to remove the tensioner

36578_ESCA_G0206

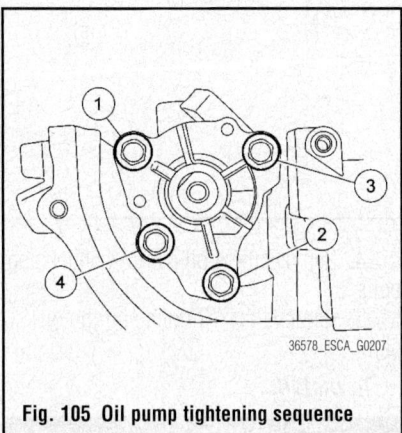

36578_ESCA_G0207

Fig. 105 Oil pump tightening sequence

18. Install the oil pump drive chain tensioner shoulder bolt. Tighten the bolt to 89 inch lbs. (10 Nm).
19. Install the oil pump drive chain tensioner and bolt. Hook the tensioner spring around the shoulder bolt. Tighten to 89 inch lbs. (10 Nm).
20. Install the oil pump screen and pickup tube and the 2 bolts. Tighten the bolts to 89 inch lbs. (10 Nm).
21. Clean and inspect all mating surfaces.

➡If the oil pan is not secured within 10 minutes of sealant application, the sealant must be removed and the sealing area cleaned with metal surface cleaner. Allow to dry until there is no sign of wetness, or 10 minutes, whichever is longer. Failure to follow this procedure can cause future oil leakage.

22. Apply a 0.09 inch. (2.5mm) bead of silicone gasket and sealant to the oil pan-to-engine block and to the oil pan-to-engine front cover mating surface.
23. Position the oil pan onto the engine and install the oil pan bolts finger-tight.
24. Using a suitable straight edge, align the front surface of the oil pan flush with the front surface of the engine block.

✳✳ WARNING

The engine front cover-to-oil pan bolts must be tightened first to align the front surface of the oil pan flush with the front surface of the engine block.

25. Install the 4 engine front cover-to-oil pan bolts and tighten to 89 inch lbs. (10 Nm).
26. Tighten the oil pan bolts in sequence to 18 ft. lbs. (25 Nm).
27. Install the 4 oil pan-to-bellhousing bolts and tighten to 35 ft. lbs. (48 Nm).
28. Install the engine front cover.
29. Fill the engine with clean engine oil.

PISTON AND RING

POSITIONING

See Figure 106.

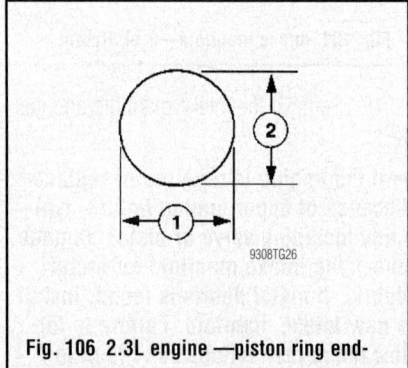

9308TG26

Fig. 106 2.3L engine —piston ring end-gap spacing

REAR MAIN SEAL

REMOVAL & INSTALLATION

See Figures 107 through 110.

✳✳ CAUTION

Before proceeding, read and observe all of the High Voltage System Precaution.

1. With the vehicle in NEUTRAL, position it on a hoist.
2. If equipped, remove the automatic transaxle.
3. If equipped, remove the manual transaxle and clutch.
4. Remove the flexplate or flywheel.
5. Drain the engine oil, install drain plug and tighten to 21 ft. lbs. (28 Nm).
6. Remove the oil pan.

➡If the oil pan is not removed, damage to the rear oil seal retainer joint can occur.

7. Remove the crankshaft rear oil seal with retainer plate.

To install:

8. Using a seal installer, position the crankshaft rear oil seal with retainer plate onto the crankshaft.

9. Install the crankshaft rear oil seal with retainer plate. Tighten the bolts in the sequence shown to 89 inch lbs. (10 Nm).

10. Install the oil pan.

➡**Special bolts are used for installation. Do not use standard bolts.**

11. Install the flywheel/flexplate.

12. Tighten the bolts in the sequence shown in three stages:
   • Stage 1: Tighten to 37 ft. lbs. (50 Nm).

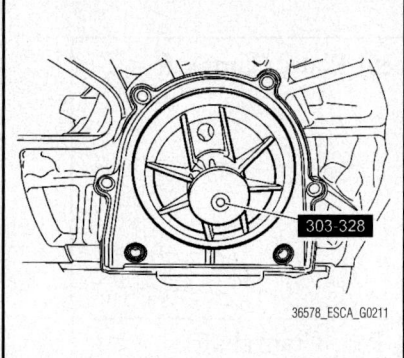

Fig. 108 Rear oil seal installation with installation tool

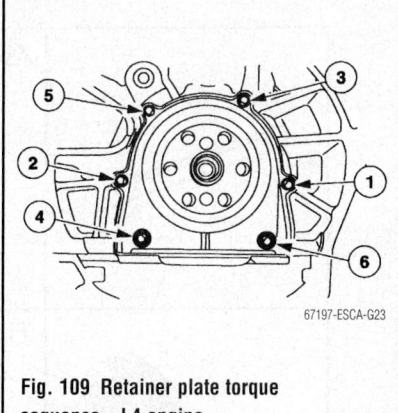

Fig. 109 Retainer plate torque sequence—L4 engine

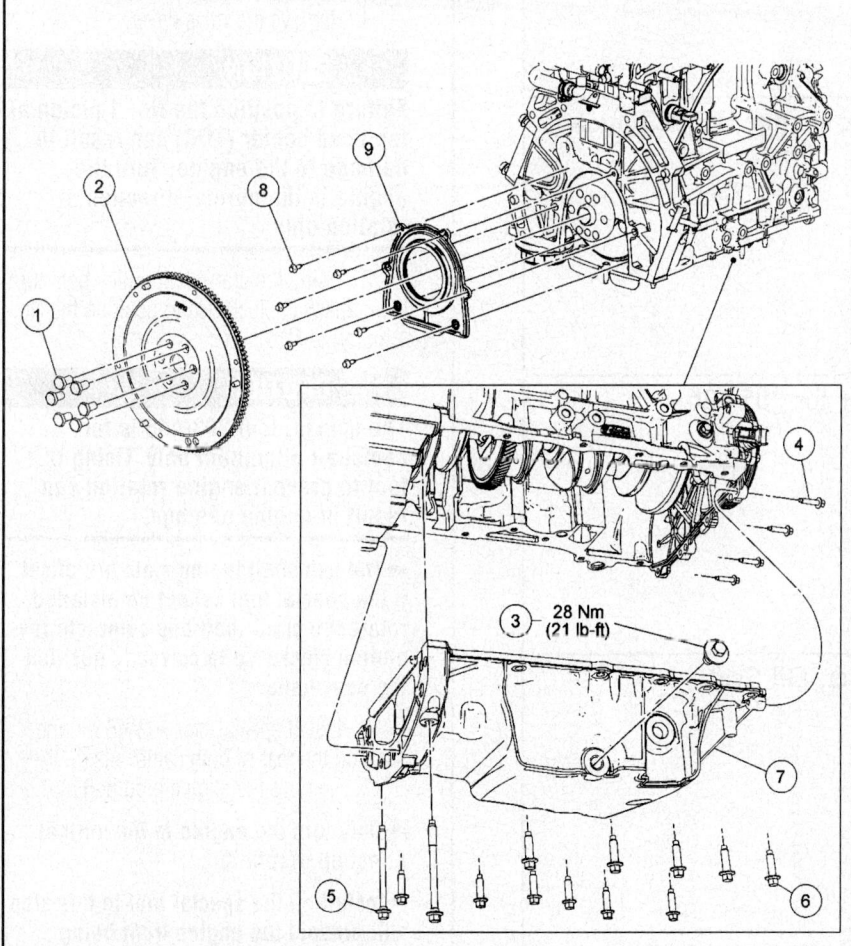

1. Flexplate or flywheel bolt (6 required)
2. Flexplate or flywheel
3. Oil pan drain plug
4. Engine front cover bolt (4 required)
5. Oil pan bolt (2 required)
6. Oil pan bolt (11 required)
7. Oil pan
8. Crankshaft rear oil seal with retainer plate bolt (6 required)
9. Crankshaft rear oil seal with retainer plate

Fig. 107 Exploded view—flexplate/flywheel and crankshaft rear seal

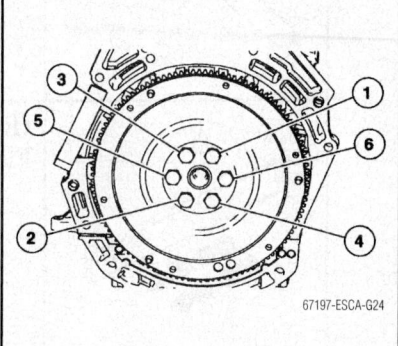

Fig. 110 Flywheel torque sequence—L4 engine

   • Stage 2: Tighten to 50 ft. lbs. (80 Nm).
   • Stage 3: Tighten to 83 ft. lbs. (112 Nm).

13. Fill the engine with clean engine oil.

TIMING CHAIN, GEARS, FRONT COVER & SEAL

REMOVAL & INSTALLATION

2.3L Hybrid Engine
See Figures 111 through 119.

✻✻ CAUTION

Before proceeding, read and observe all of the High Voltage System Precaution.

✻✻ CAUTION

During engine repair procedures, cleanliness is extremely important. Any foreign material, including any material created while cleaning gasket surfaces that enters the oil passages, coolant passages or the oil pan can cause engine failure.

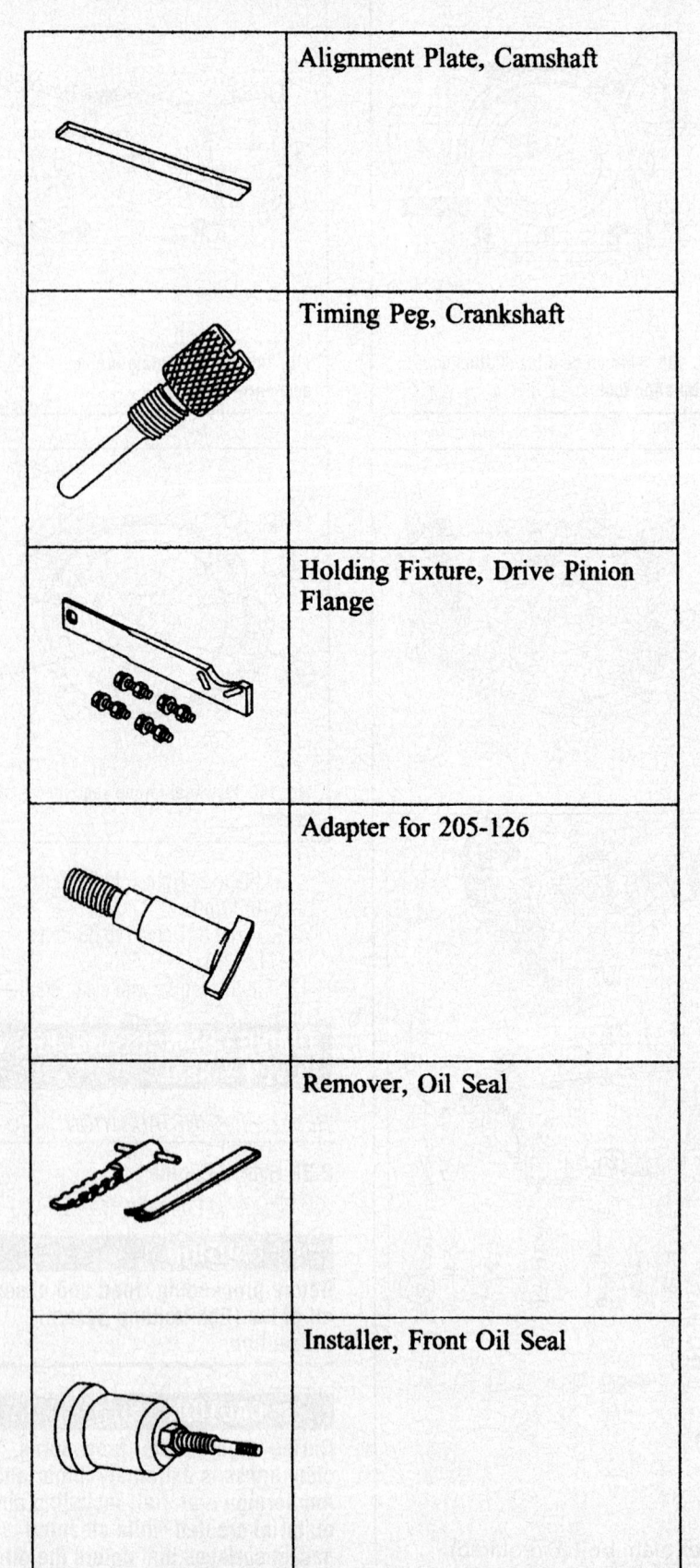

	Alignment Plate, Camshaft
	Timing Peg, Crankshaft
	Holding Fixture, Drive Pinion Flange
	Adapter for 205-126
	Remover, Oil Seal
	Installer, Front Oil Seal

67197-ESCA-G25

Fig. 111 Tools needed for timing chain and gears replacement—2.3L engine

✳✳ CAUTION

The crankshaft, the crankshaft sprocket and the pulley are fitted together by friction, using diamond washers between the flange faces on each part. For that reason, the crankshaft sprocket is also unfastened if you loosen the pulley. Therefore, the engine must be retimed each time the damper is removed. Otherwise severe engine damage can occur.

  1. With the vehicle in NEUTRAL, position it on a hoist.
  2. Remove the accessory drive belt and idler pulleys.
  3. Remove the engine mount.
  4. Remove the valve cover.

✳✳ CAUTION

Failure to position the No. 1 piston at top dead center (TDC) can result in damage to the engine. Turn the engine in the normal direction of rotation only.

  5. Using the crankshaft pulley bolt, turn the crankshaft clockwise to position the No. 1 piston at TDC.

✳✳ CAUTION

The special tool 303-465 is for camshaft alignment only. Using this tool to prevent engine rotation can result in engine damage.

➡ The camshaft timing slots are offset. If the special tool cannot be installed, rotate the crankshaft one complete revolution clockwise to correctly position the camshafts.

  6. Install special tool 303-465 in the slots on the rear of both camshafts.
  7. Remove the engine plug bolt.

➡ Only turn the engine in the normal direction of rotation.

➡ Installing the special tool in this step will prevent the engine from being rotated in the clockwise direction.

  8. Install special tool 303-507.
  9. Install the special tools 205-126 and 205-072-02.

✳✳ CAUTION

Failure to hold the crankshaft pulley in place while loosening the bolt can result in damage to the engine.

  10. Remove the crankshaft pulley bolt and washer.

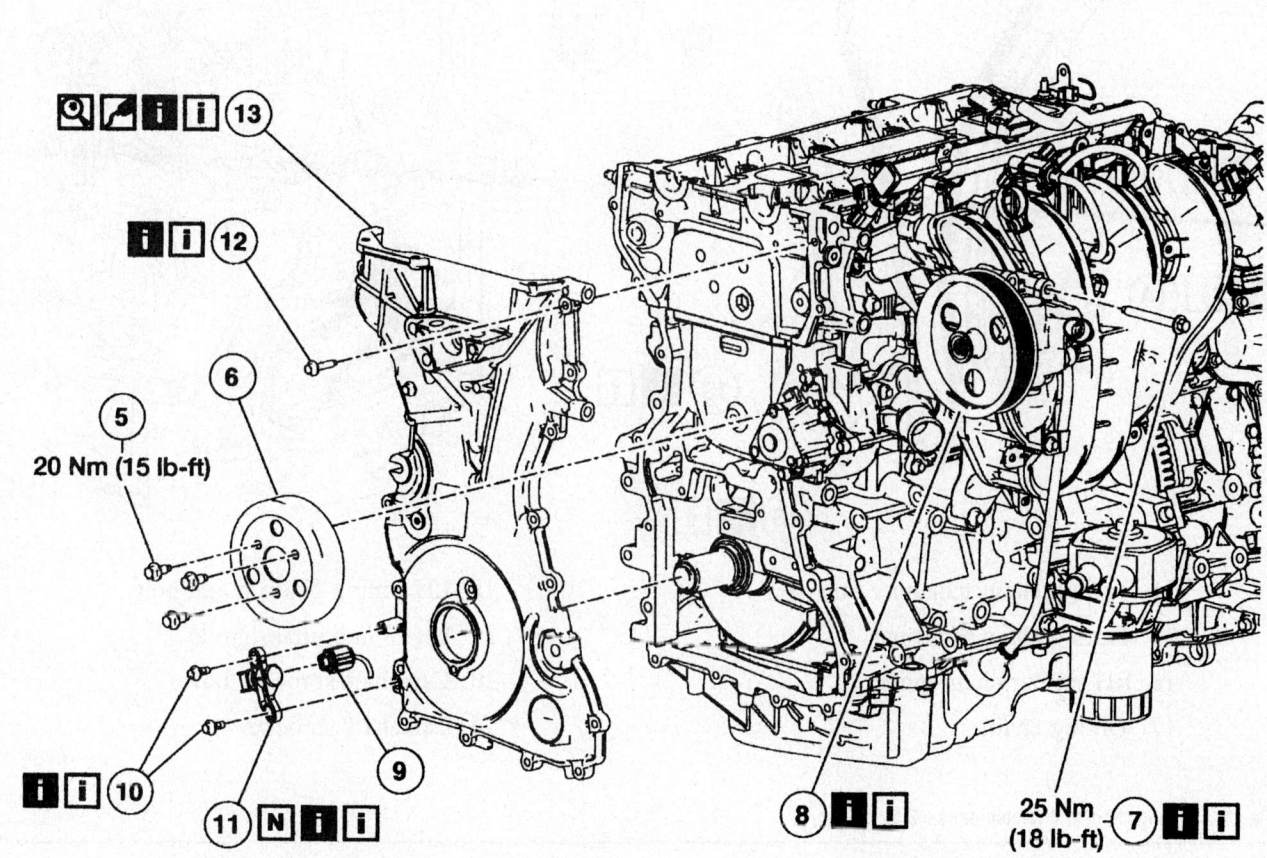

20 Nm (15 lb-ft)

25 Nm
(18 lb-ft)

5   Coolant pump pulley bolt

6   Coolant pump pulley

7   Power steering pump bolt

8   Power steering pump (position aside)

9   Crankshaft position (CKP) sensor electrical connector

10 CKP sensor bolts

11 CKP sensor

12 Engine front cover bolt

13 Engine front cover

67197-ESCA-G26

Fig. 112 Front cover and related parts—2.3L engine

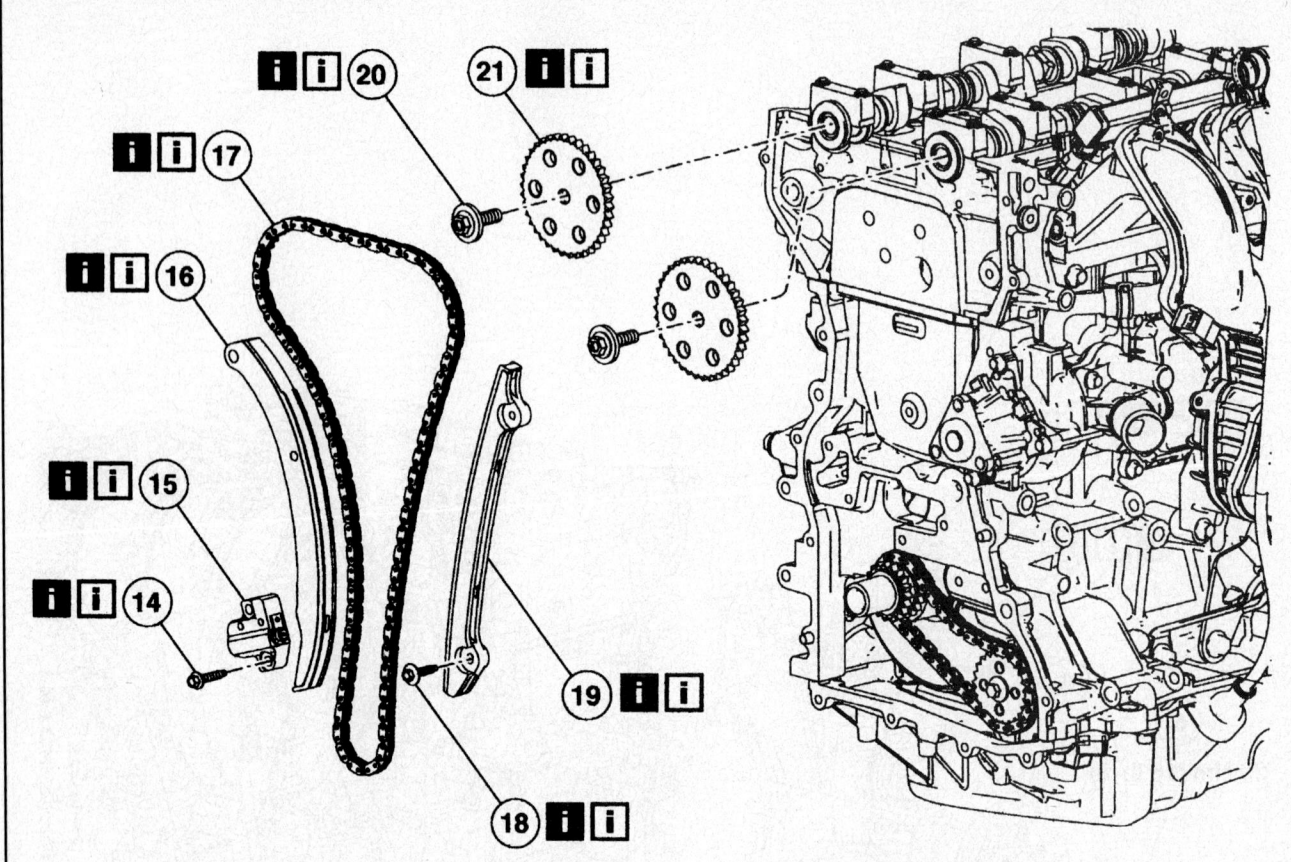

14 Timing chain tensioner bolt

15 Timing chain tensioner

16 RH timing chain guide

17 Timing chain

18 LH timing chain guide bolt

19 LH timing chain guide

20 Camshaft sprocket bolt

21 Camshaft sprocket

67197-ESCA-G27

Fig. 113 Timing chain and related parts—2.3L engine

11. Remove the crankshaft pulley.
12. Remove the crankshaft front seal.
13. Remove the coolant pump pulley.
14. Remove the power steering pump and position it aside.

➡ The bolt under the power steering pressure tube will remain with the power steering pump.

15. Remove the CKP sensor.

➡ Whenever the crankshaft position (CKP) sensor is removed, a new one must be installed, using the alignment jig supplied with the new part.

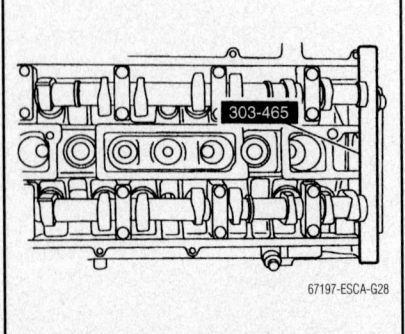

67197-ESCA-G28

Fig. 114 Install special tool 303-465 in the slots on the rear of both camshafts— 2.3L engine

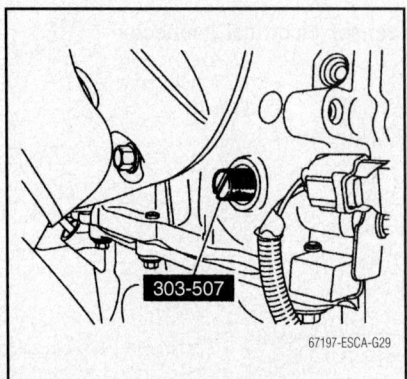

67197-ESCA-G29

Fig. 115 Install special tool 303-507— 2.3L engine

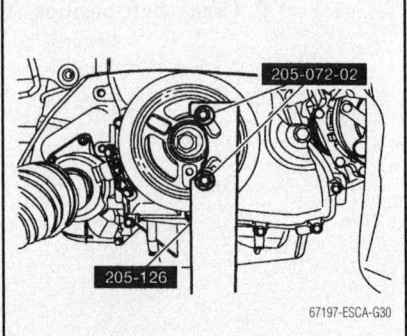

67197-ESCA-G30

Fig. 116 Install the special tools 205-126 and 205-072-02—2.3L engine

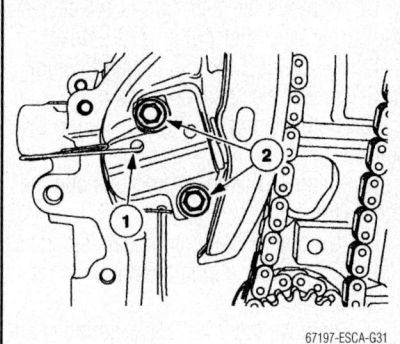

Fig. 117 Compress the timing chain tensioner, and insert a paper clip into the hole to retain the tensioner—2.3L engine

16. Remove the engine front cover bolts (there are 22).

17. Remove the engine front cover.

18. Remove the timing chain tensioner. Compress the timing chain tensioner, and insert a paper clip into the hole to retain the tensioner.

19. Remove the right timing chain guide.

20. Remove the timing chain.

21. Remove the left timing chain guide.

22. Remove the camshaft sprocket bolts.

23. Remove the camshaft sprockets.

✳✳ CAUTION

Do not rely on the Camshaft Alignment Plate to prevent camshaft rotation. Damage to the tool or the camshaft can occur. Use the flats on the camshaft to prevent camshaft rotation.

To install:

24. Installation is the reverse of removal. Note the following:

✳✳ CAUTION

Do not use metal scrapers, wire brushes, power abrasive disks or

Fig. 118 Use the flats on the camshaft to prevent camshaft rotation—2.3L engine

other abrasive means to clean sealing surfaces. These tools cause scratches and gouges which make leak paths.

25. Clean and inspect the mounting surfaces of the engine and the front cover.

➡ **The engine front cover must be installed and the bolts tightened within four minutes of applying the silicone gasket and sealant.**

26. Apply a 2.5 mm bead of silicone gasket and sealant to the cylinder head and oil pan joint areas. Apply a 2.5 mm bead of silicone gasket and sealant to the front cover.

27. Install the engine front cover. Tighten the bolts in the sequence shown, to the following specifications:

- Tighten the 8 mm bolts to 89 inch lbs. (10 Nm).
- Tighten the 13 mm bolts to 35 ft. lbs. (48 Nm).

28. Position the power steering pump and install the bolts.

➡ **Remove the through-bolt from the special tool.**

➡ **Lubricate the oil seal with clean engine oil.**

29. Using a seal driver, install the crankshaft front oil seal.

➡ **Do not reuse the crankshaft damper bolt.**

➡ **Apply clean engine oil on the seal area before installing.**

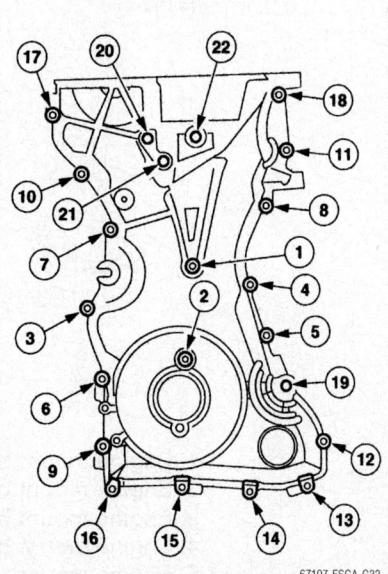

Fig. 119 Front cover bolt torque sequence—2.3L engine

30. Install the crankshaft pulley and hand-tighten the bolt.

✳✳ CAUTION

Only hand-tighten the bolt or damage to the front cover can occur.

➡ **This step will correctly align the crankshaft pulley to the crankshaft.**

31. Install a standard 6 mm x 18 mm bolt through the crankshaft pulley and thread it into the front cover. Rotate the pulley as necessary to align the bolt holes.

✳✳ CAUTION

Failure to hold the crankshaft pulley in place while tightening the bolt can cause damage to the engine front cover.

32. Using the special tools to hold the crankshaft pulley in place, tighten the crankshaft pulley bolt in two stages:

- Stage 1: Tighten to 74 ft. lbs. (100 Nm).
- Stage 2: Tighten an additional 90 degrees (¼ turn).

33. Remove the 6 mm x 18 mm bolt.

34. Remove special tool 303-507.

35. Remove special tool 303-465.

➡ **Only turn the engine in the normal direction of rotation.**

36. Turn the engine two complete revolutions.

➡ **Only turn the engine in the normal direction of rotation.**

37. Turn the crankshaft until the No. 1 piston is at TDC.

38. Install special tool 303-507.

✳✳ CAUTION

Only hand-tighten the bolt or damage to the front cover can occur.

39. Using the 6 mm x 18 mm bolt, check the position of the crankshaft pulley. If it is not possible to install the bolt, correct the engine timing.

40. Using special tool 303-465, check the position of the camshafts. If it is not possible to install the special tool, correct the engine timing.

41. Install the CKP sensor. Do not tighten the bolts at this time.

42. Adjust the CKP sensor alignment jig and tighten the bolts.

43. Remove the 6 mm x 18 mm bolt.

44. Install the engine plug bolt.

2.5L Hybrid Engine

See Figures 120 through 130.

✷✷ CAUTION

Before proceeding, read and observe all of the High Voltage System Precaution.

✷✷ WARNING

Do not loosen or remove the crankshaft pulley bolt without first installing the special tools as instructed in this procedure. The crankshaft pulley and the crankshaft timing sprocket are not keyed to the crankshaft. The crankshaft, the crankshaft sprocket and the pulley are fitted together by friction, using diamond washers between the flange faces on each part. For that reason, the crankshaft sprocket is also unfastened if the pulley bolt is loosened. Before any repair requiring loosening or removal of the crankshaft pulley bolt, the crankshaft and camshafts must be locked in place by the special service tools, otherwise severe engine damage can occur. Refer to Crankshaft Damper in this section.

➡During engine repair procedures, cleanliness is extremely important. Any foreign material, including any material created while cleaning gasket surfaces, which enters the oil passages, coolant passages or the oil pan can cause engine failure.

1. With the vehicle in NEUTRAL, position it on a hoist.
2. Remove the accessory drive belt and the smooth idler pulley.
3. Disconnect the Crankshaft Position (CKP) sensor electrical connector.
4. Remove the CKP sensor.
5. Remove the crankshaft pulley. Refer to Crankshaft Damper Removal & Installation in this section.

✷✷ WARNING

The crankshaft, the crankshaft sprocket and the pulley are fitted together by friction, using diamond washers between the flange faces on each part. For that reason, the crankshaft sprocket is also unfastened if the pulley bolt is loosened. Before any repair requiring loosening or removal of the crankshaft pulley bolt, the crankshaft fond camshafts must be locked in place by the special ser-

vice tools, otherwise severe engine damage can occur.

6. Install the engine support bar.
7. Remove the engine mount.

➡Use care not to damage the engine front cover or the crankshaft when removing the seal.

8. Using the oil seal remover, remove the crankshaft front oil seal.
9. Remove the 3 bolts and the coolant pump pulley.

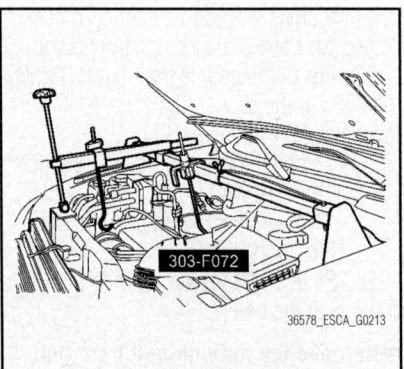

36578_ESCA_G0213

Fig. 120 Engine support bar shown installed on—2.5L engine

10. Remove the 2 bolts and the accessory drive belt idler pulley and bracket.
11. Disconnect the Crankshaft Position (CKP) sensor electrical connector.
12. Remove and the 2 bolts and the CKP sensor.
13. Remove the bolts, stud bolt and the engine front cover.
14. Compress the timing chain tensioner and insert a paper clip into the hole to retain the tensioner.
15. Remove the 2 bolts and timing chain tensioner.

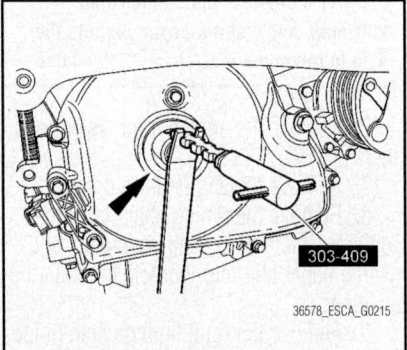

36578_ESCA_G0215

Fig. 122 Front oil seal removal—2.5L engine

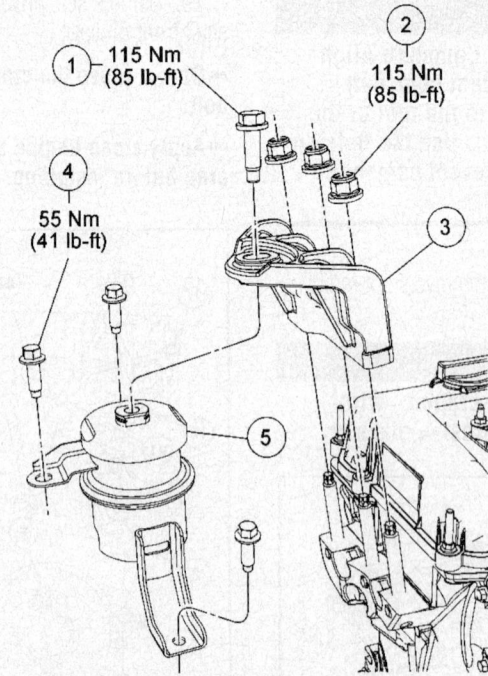

1. Engine mount bracket bolt
2. Engine mount bracket nut (3 required)
3. Engine mount bracket
4. Engine mount bolt (3 required)
5. Engine mount

36578_ESCA_G0214

Fig. 121 Engine support mount—2.5L engine

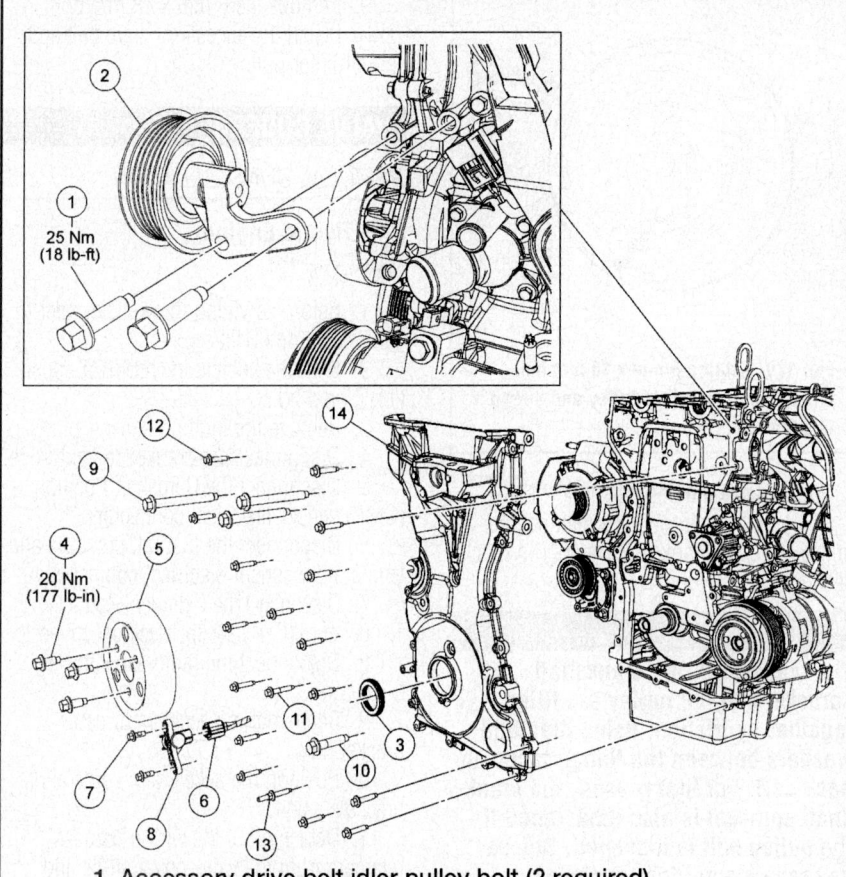

1. Accessory drive belt idler pulley bolt (2 required)
2. Accessory drive belt idler pulley and bracket
3. Crankshaft front seal
4. Coolant pump pulley bolt (3 required)
5. Coolant pump pulley
6. Crankshaft Position (CKP) sensor electrical connector
7. CKP sensor bolt (2 required)
8. CKP sensor
9. Engine front cover bolt (3 required)
10. Engine front cover bolt
11. Engine front cover bolt
12. Engine front cover bolt (16 required)
13. Engine front cover stud bolt
14. Engine front cover

36578_ESCA_G0216

Fig. 123 Engine front cover—2.5L engine

16. Remove the timing chain tensioner arm.

17. Remove the timing chain.

18. Remove the 2 bolts and the timing chain guide.

➡ **The Camshaft Alignment Plate is for camshaft alignment only. Using this tool to prevent engine rotation can result in engine damage.**

19. Using the flats on the camshaft to prevent camshaft rotation, remove the bolt and the exhaust camshaft sprocket.

20. Using the flats on the camshaft to prevent camshaft rotation, remove the bolt and the camshaft phaser and sprocket.

To install:

21. Install the camshaft sprockets and the bolts. Do not tighten the bolts at this time.

22. Install the timing chain guide and the 2 bolts. Tighten to 89 inch lbs. (10 Nm).

23. Install the timing chain.

24. Install the timing chain tensioner arm.

25. Install the timing chain tensioner and the 2 bolts. Tighten the bolts to 89 inch lbs. (10 Nm). Remove the paper clip to release the piston.

➡ **The Camshaft Alignment Plate is for camshaft alignment only. Using this tool to prevent engine rotation can result in engine damage.**

26. Using the flats on the camshafts to prevent camshaft rotation, tighten the bolts to 53 ft. lbs. (72 Nm).

27. Clean and inspect the mounting surfaces of the engine and the front cover.

➡ **The engine front cover must be installed and the bolts tightened within 4 minutes of applying the silicone gasket and sealant.**

28. Apply a 0.09 inch (2.5 mm) bead of silicone gasket and sealant to the cylinder

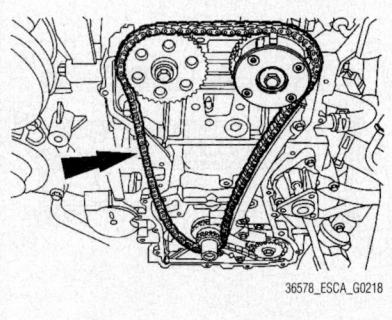

36578_ESCA_G0218

Fig. 124 Remove the timing chain—2.5L engine

36578_ESCA_G0219

Fig. 125 Remove the 2 bolts and the timing chain guide—2.5L engine

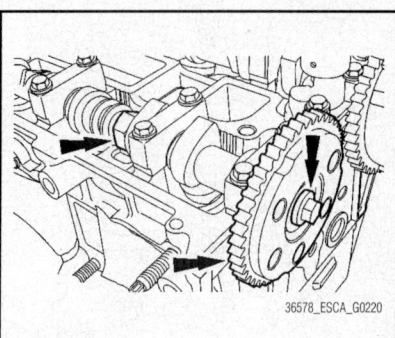

36578_ESCA_G0220

Fig. 126 Remove the bolt and the exhaust camshaft sprocket—2.5L engine

head and oil pan joint areas. Apply a 0.09 inch (2.5 mm) bead of silicone gasket and sealant to the front cover.

29. Install the engine front cover. Tighten the bolts in the sequence shown, to the following specifications:
   - Tighten the 8-mm bolts and stud bolt to 89 inch lbs. (10 Nm).
   - Tighten the 13-mm bolts to 35 ft. lbs. (48 Nm).

30. Install the accessory drive belt idler pulley and bracket and the 2 bolts. Tighten the bolts to 18 ft. lbs. (25 Nm).

31. Install the coolant pump pulley and bolts. Tighten the bolts to 177 inch lbs. (20 Nm).

32. Using the Camshaft Front Oil Seal Installer, install the crankshaft front oil seal.

33. Install the engine support mount, refer to the graphic for correct torque specifications.

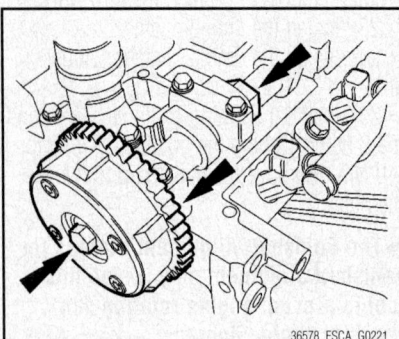

Fig. 127 Remove the bolt and the camshaft phaser and sprocket —2.5L engine

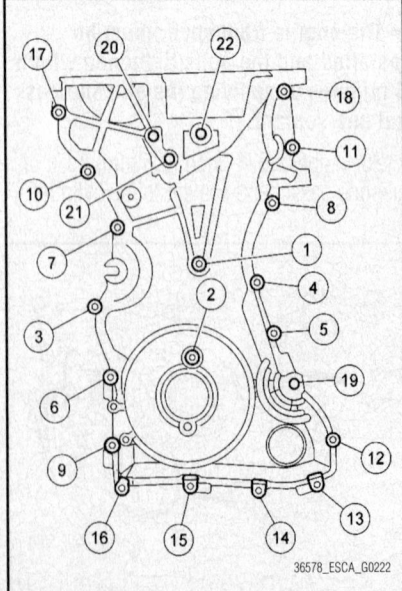

Fig. 128 Timing cover tightening sequence—2.5L engine

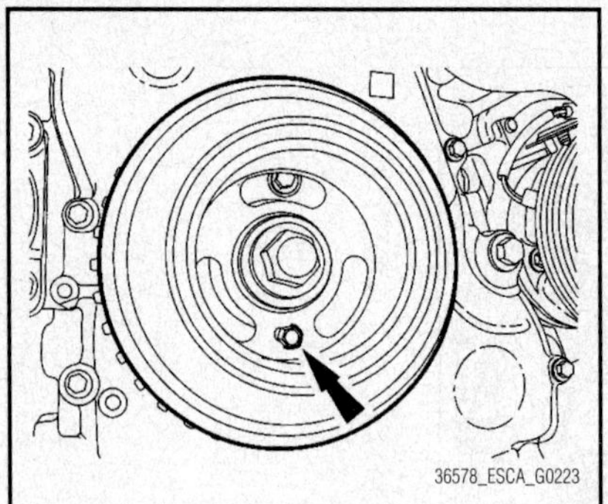

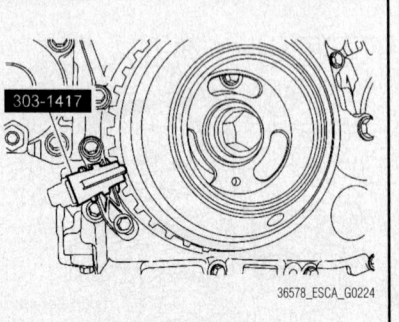

Fig. 129 Install a 6 mm x 18 mm bolt through the crankshaft pulley and thread it into the front cover

34. Remove the engine support bar.

35. Install the front crankshaft damper pulley. Refer to Crankshaft Damper in this section.

✻✻ WARNING

The crankshaft, the crankshaft sprocket and the pulley are fitted together by friction, using diamond washers between the flange faces on each part. For that reason, the crankshaft sprocket is also unfastened if the pulley bolt is loosened. Before any repair requiring loosening or removal of the crankshaft pulley bolt, the crankshaft and camshafts must be locked in place by the special service tools, otherwise severe engine damage can occur. Refer to Crankshaft Damper in this section.

36. Install a 6 mm x 18 mm bolt through the crankshaft pulley and thread it into the front cover.

37. Install the CKP sensor and the 2 bolts. Using the crankshaft sensor aligner, adjust the CKP sensor. Tighten the bolts to 62 inch lbs. (7 Nm).

38. Connect the CKP sensor electrical connector.

Fig. 130 Install and adjust the CKP sensor with the special tool

39. Remove the 6 mm x 18 mm bolt.

40. Install the accessory drive belt and smooth idler pulley.

VALVE COVERS

REMOVAL & INSTALLATION

2.3L Hybrid Engine

See Figure 131.

1. Before servicing the vehicle, refer to the Precautions Section.

2. With the vehicle in NEUTRAL, position it on a hoist.

3. Remove the ignition coil-on-plugs.

4. Disconnect the crankcase vent hose.

5. Disconnect the Camshaft Position (CMP) sensor electrical connector.

6. Disconnect the fuel rail pressure and temperature sensor electrical connector.

7. Disconnect the Cylinder Head Temperature (CHT) sensor electrical connector.

8. Disconnect the radio capacitor electrical connector.

9. Remove the 2 accelerator cable bracket nuts.

10. Position the accelerator cable and brackets aside.

11. Detach all of the wiring harness retainers from the valve cover studs and position the harness aside.

12. Remove the 14 valve cover retainers, the valve cover and gasket.

To install:

✻✻ WARNING

Do not use metal scrapers, wire brushes, power abrasive discs or other abrasive means to clean the sealing surfaces. These tools cause scratches and gouges which make leak paths.

13. Clean and inspect the sealing surfaces

14. Install the valve cover, gasket and retainers.

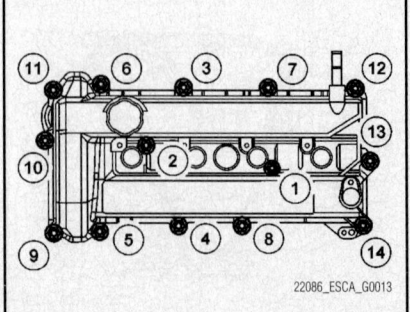

Fig. 131 Valve cover tightening sequence 2.3L engine

15. Tighten in sequence to 89 inch lbs. (10 Nm).

16. Position the wiring harness and attach all of the wiring harness retainers to the valve cover studs.

17. Install the accelerator control cable brackets and tighten nuts to 53 inch lbs. (6 Nm).

18. Connect the radio capacitor electrical connector.

19. Connect the CHT sensor electrical connector.

20. Connect the fuel rail pressure and temperature sensor electrical connector

21. Connect the CMP sensor electrical connector.

22. Connect the crankcase vent hose.

23. Install the ignition coil-on-plugs. Tighten to 71 inch lbs. (8 Nm).

2.5L Hybrid Engine
See Figures 132 and 133.

※ WARNING

During engine repair procedures, cleanliness is extremely important. Any foreign material, including any material created while cleaning gasket surfaces, which enters the oil passages, coolant passages or the oil pan can cause engine failure.

1. Before servicing the vehicle, refer to the Precautions Section.

2. With the vehicle in NEUTRAL, position it on a hoist.

3. Remove the oil level indicator.

4. Remove the ignition coil-on-plugs.

5. Disconnect the crankcase vent hose.

6. Disconnect the Cylinder Head Temperature (CHT) sensor electrical connector.

7. Disconnect the Camshaft Position (CMP) sensor electrical connector.

8. Disconnect the radio capacitor electrical connector.

9. Disconnect the Variable Camshaft Timing (VCT) solenoid electrical connector.

10. Detach all of the wiring harness retainers from the valve cover studs and position the harness aside.

11. Remove the 14 valve cover retainers, the valve cover and gasket.

To install:

→Do not use metal scrapers, wire brushes, power abrasive discs or other abrasive means to clean the sealing surfaces. These tools cause scratches and gouges which make leak paths.

12. Clean and inspect the sealing surfaces.

→The valve cover must be secured within 4 minutes of silicone gasket application. If the valve cover is not secured within 4 minutes, the sealant must be removed and the sealing area cleaned with metal surface prep.

13. Apply silicone gasket and sealant to the locations shown.

14. Clean and inspect the gasket. Install a new gasket, if necessary.

15. Install the valve cover, gasket and retainers.

16. Tighten in the sequence shown to 89 inch lbs. 10 Nm).

17. Position the wiring harness and attach all of the wiring harness retainers to the valve cover studs.

18. Connect the VCT solenoid electrical connector.

19. Connect the radio capacitor electrical connector.

20. Connect the CMP sensor electrical connector.

21. Connect the CHT sensor electrical connector.

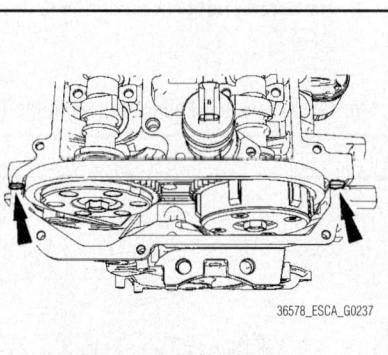

Fig. 132 Apply silicone gasket and sealant to the locations shown

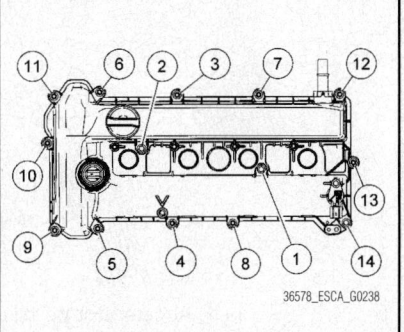

Fig. 133 Valve cover tightening sequence—2.5L engine

22. Connect the crankcase vent hose.

23. Install the ignition coil-on-plugs.

24. Install the oil level indicator.

VALVE LASH

ADJUSTMENT

See Figure 134.

1. Before servicing the vehicle, refer to the Precautions Section.

→Before removing the camshafts, measure the clearance of each valve at base circle, with the lobe pointed away from the tappet. Failure to measure all clearances prior to removing the camshafts will necessitate repeated removal and installation and wasted labor time.

2. Use a feeler gauge to measure the clearance of each valve and record its location.

→The number on the valve tappet only reflects the digits that follow the decimal. For example, a tappet with the number 0.650 has the thickness of 3.650 mm.

3. A midrange clearance is the most desirable:

- Intake: 0.22–0.28 mm (0.008–0.011 inch)
- Exhaust: 0.27–0.33 mm (0.010 0.013 inch)

4. Select tappets using this formula: tappet thickness = measured clearance + the base tappet thickness–most desirable thickness.

5. Select the tappets and mark the installation location.

6. If any tappets do not measure within specifications, install new tappets in these locations.

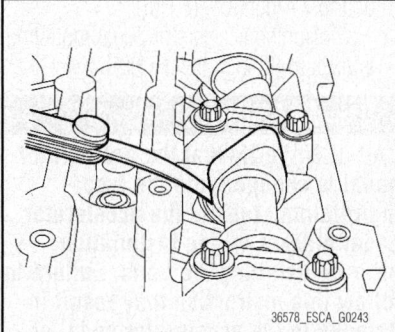

Fig. 134 Using a feeler gauge to measure the clearance

ENGINE PERFORMANCE & EMISSION CONTROLS

ACCELERATOR PEDAL POSITION (APP) SENSOR

LOCATION

2.3L Hybrid Engine

See Figure 135.

The Accelerator Pedal Position (APP) sensor is inside of the vehicle and is part of the pedal assembly.

2.5L Hybrid Engine

See Figure 136.

REMOVAL & INSTALLATION

2.3L Hybrid Engine

See Figure 135.

1. Disconnect the accelerator pedal electrical connector.
2. Remove the 3 bolts and release the accelerator pedal from the locating/retaining tabs on the lower RH corner of the accelerator pedal mounting bracket.
3. Remove the accelerator pedal bracket bolt.
4. Remove the 2 bolts and remove the accelerator pedal bracket.

➡️If installing a new accelerator edal and sensor assembly, the accelerator pedal bracket may also require replacement due to a different mounting bolt pattern between the original and replacement service parts.

To install:

5. To install, reverse the removal procedure and note the following:
  a. Tighten accelerator pedal bracket bolts to 80 inch lbs. (9 Nm).
  b. Tighten accelerator pedal bracket bolt to 71 inch lbs. (8 Nm).
  c. Tighten accelerator pedal mounting bracket to 80 inch lbs. (9 Nm).

✳✳ WARNING

CAUTION: Verify that the accelerator pedal is engaged into the locating/retaining tabs of the accelerator pedal bracket during installation, prior to installing the bolts. Failure to follow this instruction may result in damage to the accelerator pedal or accelerator pedal bracket.

2.5L Hybrid Engine

See Figure 136.

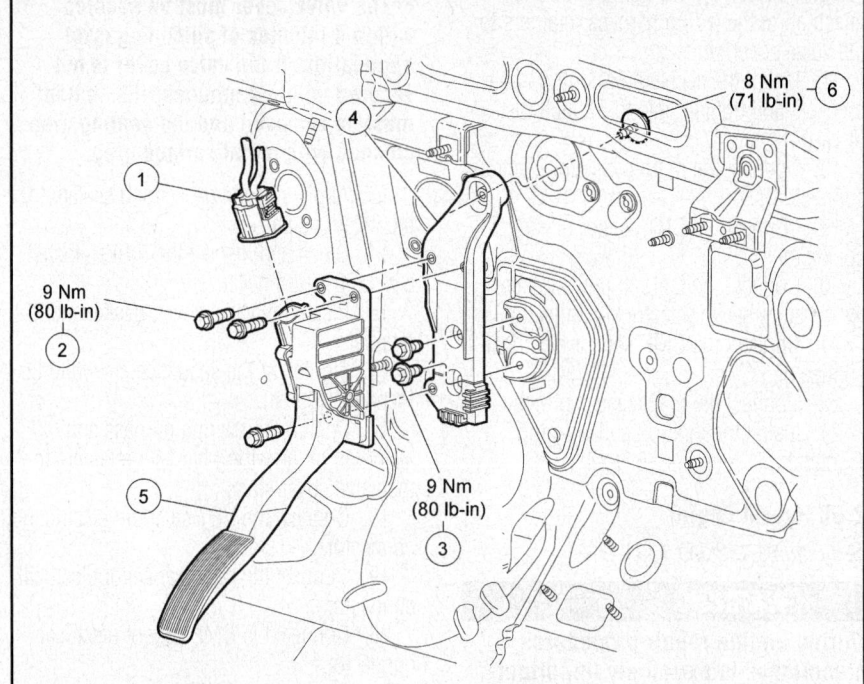

1. Accelerator pedal electrical connector
2. Accelerator pedal bolt (3 required)
3. Accelerator pedal bracket bolt (2 required)
4. Accelerator pedal bracket
5. Accelerator pedal
6. Accelerator pedal bracket bolt

22086_HYBR_G0058

Fig. 135 Accelerator Pedal Position (APP)—2.3L hybrid engine

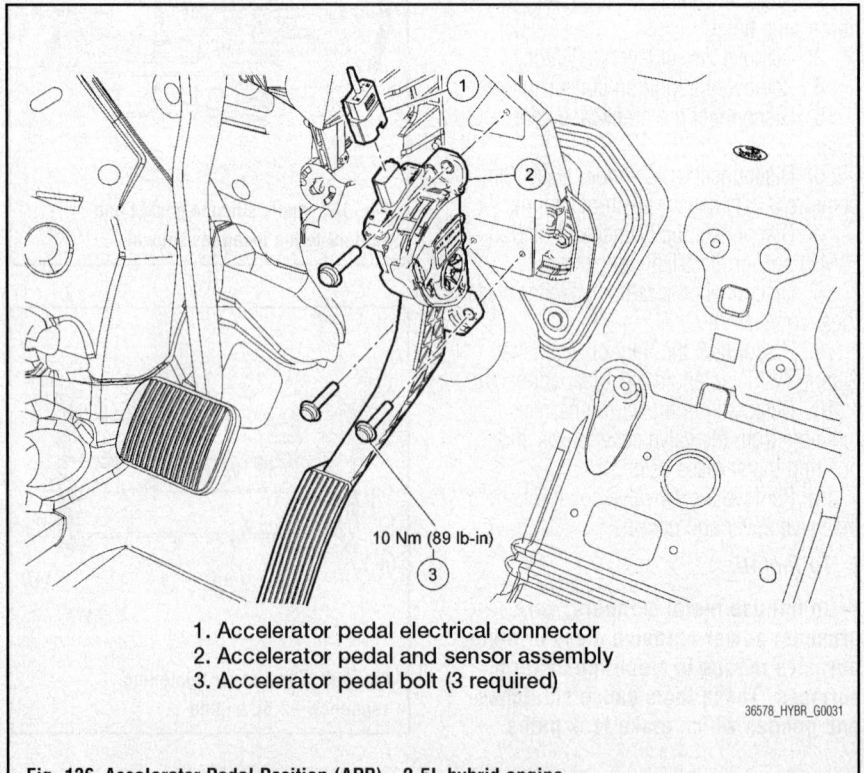

1. Accelerator pedal electrical connector
2. Accelerator pedal and sensor assembly
3. Accelerator pedal bolt (3 required)

36578_HYBR_G0031

Fig. 136 Accelerator Pedal Position (APP)—2.5L hybrid engine

1. Disconnect the accelerator pedal electrical connector.

➡**The accelerator pedal bracket and bolts on the 2.5L and 3.0L vehicles are similar but not interchangeable with the 2.5L Hybrid vehicles.**

2. Remove the 3 bolts and the accelerator pedal and sensor assembly.

3. To install, reverse the removal procedure and note the following:

4. To install, tighten to 62 inch lbs. (7 Nm) on 2.5L Hybrid vehicles.

CAMSHAFT POSITION (CMP) SENSOR

LOCATION

2.3L Hybrid Engine

See Figure 137.

The Camshaft Position (CMP) sensor is located on top the valve cover towards the front of the vehicle.

2.5L Hybrid Engine

The Camshaft Position (CMP) sensor is located on top the valve cover towards the front of the vehicle.

REMOVAL & INSTALLATION

See Figure 138.

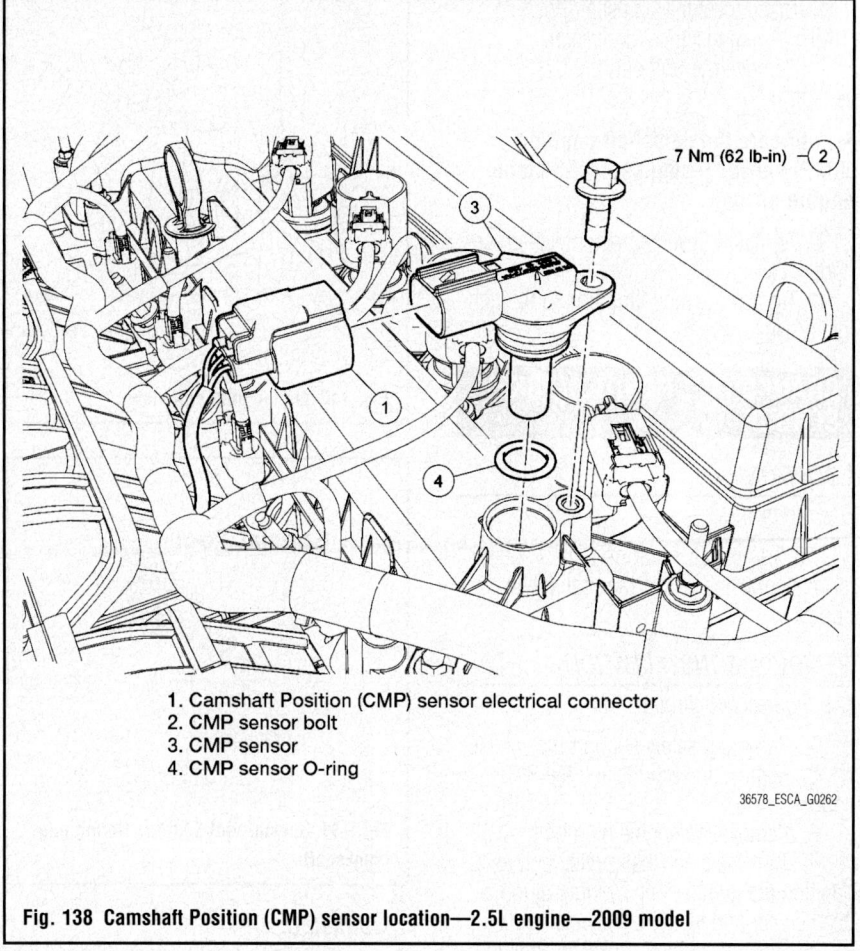

1. Camshaft Position (CMP) sensor electrical connector
2. CMP sensor bolt
3. CMP sensor
4. CMP sensor O-ring

36578_ESCA_G0262

Fig. 138 Camshaft Position (CMP) sensor location—2.5L engine—2009 model

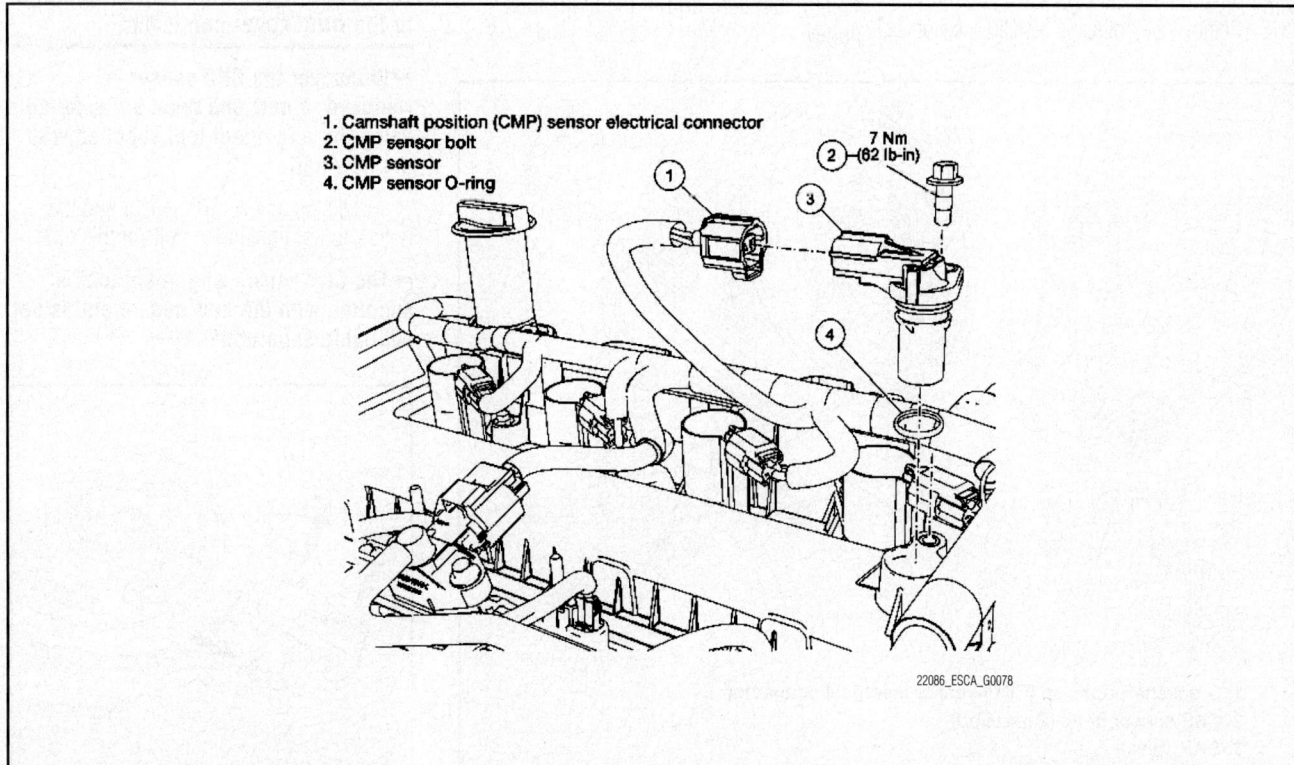

1. Camshaft position (CMP) sensor electrical connector
2. CMP sensor bolt
3. CMP sensor
4. CMP sensor O-ring

7 Nm (62 lb-in)

22086_ESCA_G0078

Fig. 137 Camshaft Position (CMP) sensor location—2.3L engine—2008 model

1. Disconnect the Camshaft Position (CMP) sensor electrical connector.
2. Remove the bolt and the CMP sensor.

➡ **Lubricate the camshaft position (CMP) sensor O-ring seal with clean engine oil.**

3. To install, reverse the removal procedure.
4. Tighten the mounting bolt to 62 inch lbs. (7 Nm)

CRANKSHAFT POSITION (CKP) SENSOR

LOCATION

See Figure 139.

The Crankshaft Position (CKP) sensor is located to the left of the crankshaft pulley.

REMOVAL & INSTALLATION

See Figures 140 through 144.

1. Raise and safely support the vehicle.
2. Remove the 5 bolts and the RH splash shield.
3. Remove the engine plug bolt.
4. Turn the crankshaft pulley bolt to position the number one cylinder at top dead center and install the special tool.
5. Disconnect the Crankshaft Position (CKP) sensor electrical connector.
6. Remove the bolts and the CKP sensor.

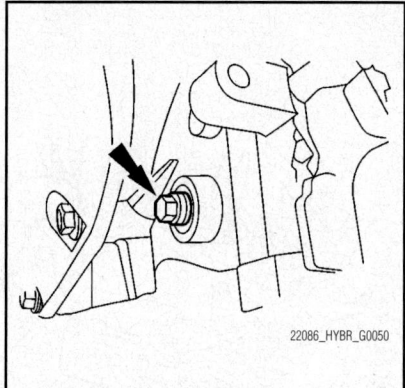

Fig. 140 Engine plug bolt view

22086_HYBR_G0050

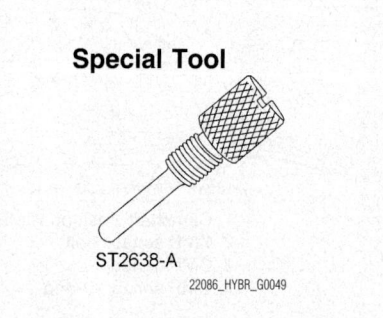

Special Tool

ST2638-A

22086_HYBR_G0049

Fig. 141 Special tool 303-507 timing peg, crankshaft

To install:

7. Install a 0.23 x 0.7 inch (6mm x 18mm) standard bolt in the crankshaft pulley.

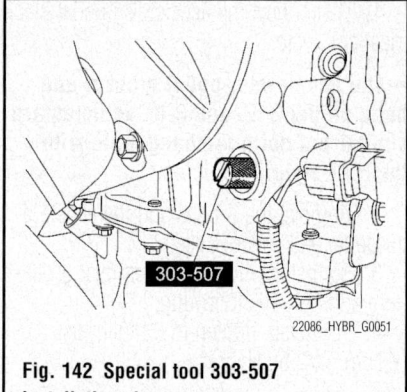

303-507

22086_HYBR_G0051

Fig. 142 Special tool 303-507 installation view

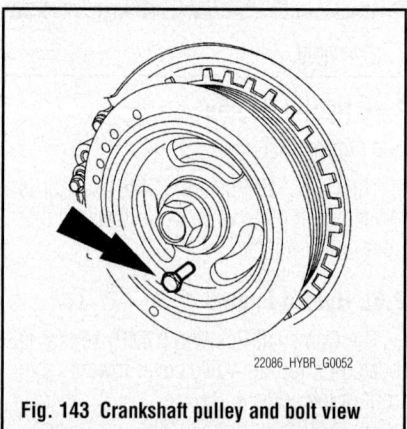

22086_HYBR_G0052

Fig. 143 Crankshaft pulley and bolt view

✳✳ WARNING

Only hand-tighten the bolt or damage to the front cover can occur.

➡ **Whenever the CKP sensor is removed, a new one must be installed using the alignment tool supplied with the new part.**

8. Install a new CKP sensor and the bolts. Do not tighten the bolts at this time.

➡ **The CKP sensor alignment tool is supplied with the new sensor and is not available separately.**

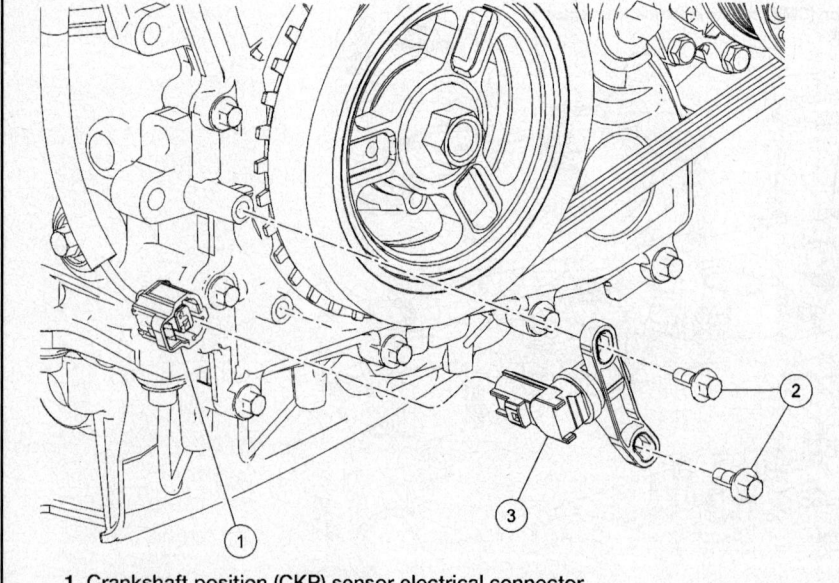

1. Crankshaft position (CKP) sensor electrical connector
2. CKP sensor bolts (2 required)
3. CKP sensor

22086_HYBR_G0048

Fig. 139 Crankshaft position sensor location

22086_HYBR_G0053

Fig. 144 Crankshaft sensor and alignment tool shown

9. Adjust the CKP sensor with the alignment tool and tighten mounting bolts to 62 inch lbs. (7 Nm).

10. Connect the CKP sensor electrical connector.

11. Remove the bolt from the crankshaft pulley.

12. Install the engine plug bolt and tighten to 15 ft. lbs. (20 Nm).

13. Install the RH splash shield and tighten the bolts to 80 inch lbs. (9 Nm).

EVAPORATIVE EMISSIONS (EVAP) CANISTER

LOCATION

2.3L Hybrid Engine

See Figure 145.

The Evaporative Emissions (EVAP) Canister is located under the vehicle midway under the LH side of the vehicle.

2.5L Hybrid Engine

See Figure 146.

The Evaporative Emissions (EVAP) Canister is located under the vehicle midway under the LH side of the vehicle.

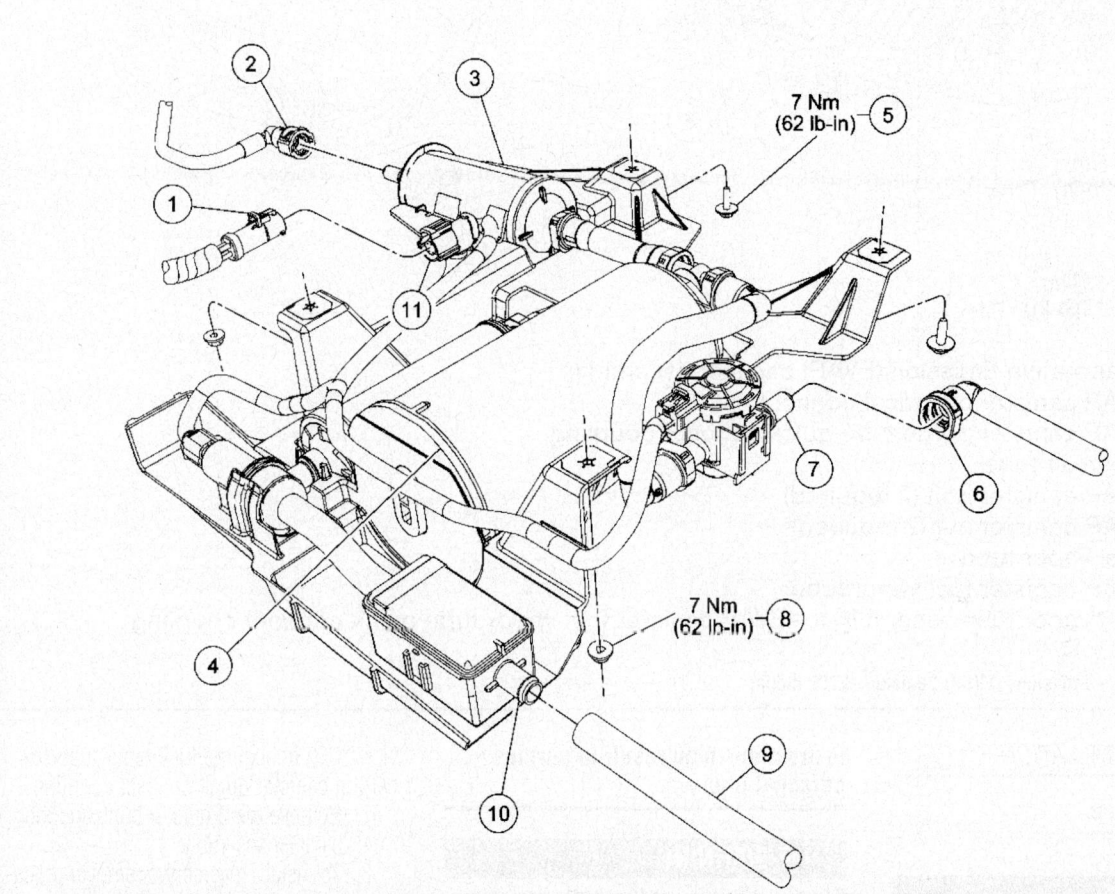

1. Evaporative emissions (EVAP) canister harness electrical connector
2. Fuel vapor tube-to-carbon canister quick connect coupling
3. EVAP carbon canister
4. EVAP canister assembly
5. EVAP canister bolt (2 required)
6. Fuel vapor tube assembly-to-fuel vapor vent valve quick connect coupling
7. Fuel vapor vent valve
8. EVAP canister nut (2 required)
9. Fuel tank filler pipe vent tube
10. Dust separator
11. EVAP canister wiring harness

36578_HYBR_G0035

Fig. 145 Evaporative Emissions (EVAP) Canister—2008 model

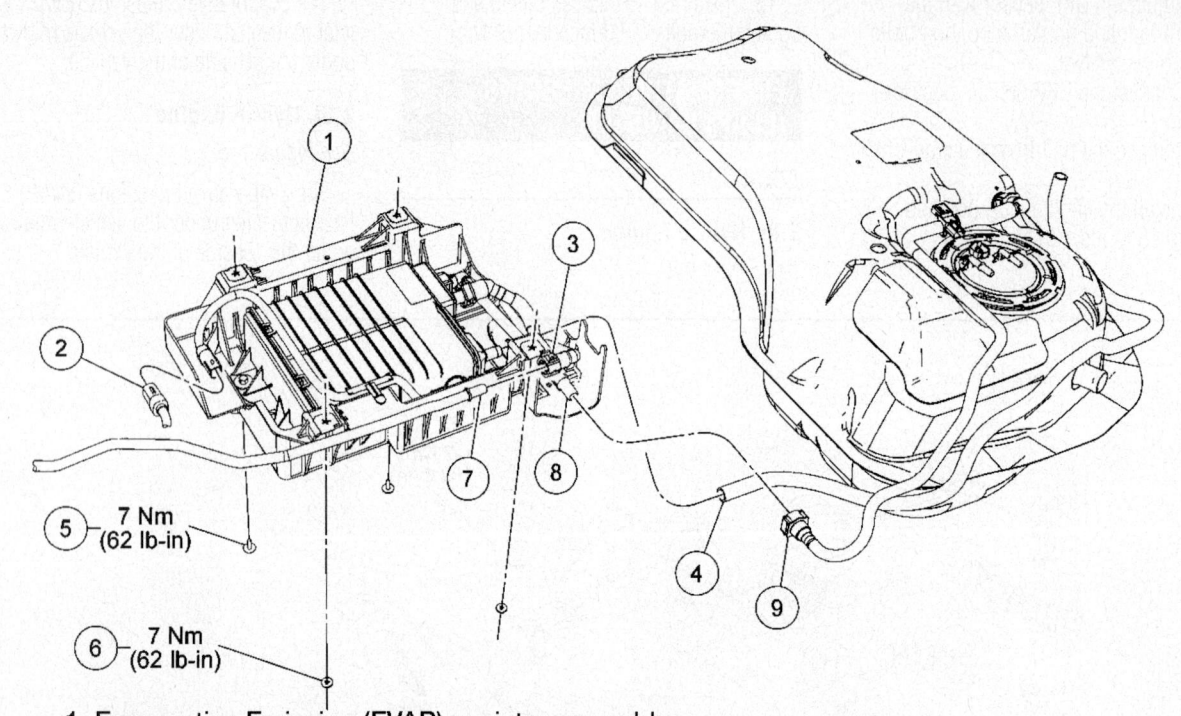

1. Evaporative Emission (EVAP) canister assembly
2. EVAP canister electrical connector
3. EVAP canister purge tube quick connect coupling
4. Fresh air tube
5. EVAP canister bolt (2 required)
6. EVAP canister nut (2 required)
7. Fuel vapor tube
8. EVAP canister fuel vapor tube
9. Fuel vapor tube assembly-to- EVAP canister fuel vapor tube quick connect coupling

36578_ESCA_G0264

Fig. 146 Evaporative Emissions (EVAP) Canister—2009 model

REMOVAL & INSTALLATION

2.3L Hybrid Engine

See Figure 145.

✳✳ WARNING

Do not smoke, carry lighted tobacco or have an open flame of any type when working on or near any fuel-related component. Highly flammable mixtures are always present and may be ignited. Failure to follow these instructions may result in serious personal injury.

✳✳ WARNING

Do not carry personal electronic devices such as cell phones, pagers or audio equipment of any type when working on or near any fuel-related component. Highly flammable mixtures are always present and may be ignited. Failure to follow these instructions may result in serious personal injury.

✳✳ WARNING

Always disconnect the battery ground cable at the battery when working on an Evaporative Emission (EVAP) system or fuel-related component. Highly flammable mixtures are always present and may be ignited. Failure to follow these instructions may result in serious personal injury.

1. With the vehicle in NEUTRAL, position it on a hoist.
2. Disconnect the battery ground cable.
3. Disconnect the evaporative emission (EVAP) canister harness electrical connector.
4. Disconnect the fuel tank filler pipe vent tube from the dust separator.
5. Disconnect the fuel vapor tube assembly-to-fuel vapor vent valve quick connect coupling.

6. Disconnect the fuel vapor tube-to-carbon canister quick connect coupling.
7. Remove the 2 nuts, 2 bolts and the EVAP canister assembly.
8. To install, reverse the removal procedure and note the following:
   • Tighten the 2 mounting nuts and bolts to 62 inch lbs. (7 Nm).
   • Carry out the evaporative emission system leak test.

2.5L Hybrid Engine

See Figure 146.

✳✳ WARNING

Do not smoke, carry lighted tobacco or have an open flame of any type when working on or near any fuel-related component. Highly flammable mixtures are always present and may be ignited. Failure to follow these instructions may result in serious personal injury.

1. With the vehicle in NEUTRAL, position it on a hoist.
2. Disconnect the battery ground cable.
3. Disconnect the Evaporative Emission (EVAP) canister electrical connector.
4. Disconnect the fresh air tube from the EVAP canister.
5. Disconnect the fuel vapor tube assembly-to-EVAP canister fuel vapor tube quick connect coupling.
6. Disconnect the EVAP canister purge tube-to-fuel vapor tube quick connect coupling.
7. Remove the 2 nuts, 2 bolts and the EVAP canister assembly.
8. To install, reverse the removal procedure and note the following:
   - Tighten the 2 nuts and 2 bolts to 62 inch lbs. (7 Nm).
   - Carry out the evaporative emission system leak test.

EXHAUST GAS RECIRCULATION (EGR) VALVE

LOCATION

2.3L Hybrid Engine

See Figure 147.

The Exhaust Gas Recirculation (EGR) Valve is located at the rear of the engine and is mounted to the cylinder head next to the valve body.

2.5L Hybrid Engine

See Figure 148.

The Exhaust Gas Recirculation (EGR) Valve is located at the rear of the engine and is mounted to the cylinder head next to the valve body.

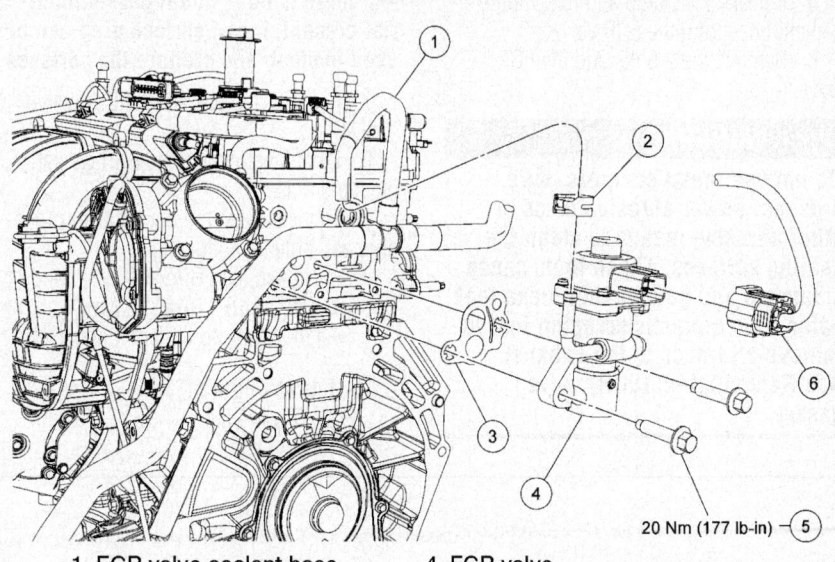

1. EGR valve coolant hose
2. EGR valve coolant hose clamp
3. EGR valve gasket
4. EGR valve
5. EGR valve bolt (2 required)
6. EGR valve electrical connector

20 Nm (177 lb-in)

36578_HYBR_G0038

Fig. 147 Exhaust Gas Recirculation (EGR) Valve—2.3L engine

REMOVAL & INSTALLATION

2.3L Hybrid Engine

See Figure 148.

1. Drain the cooling system.
2. Remove the air cleaner outlet pipe.
3. Detach the 2 engine wiring harness retainer clips from the studs.
4. Disconnect the EGR valve electrical connector.

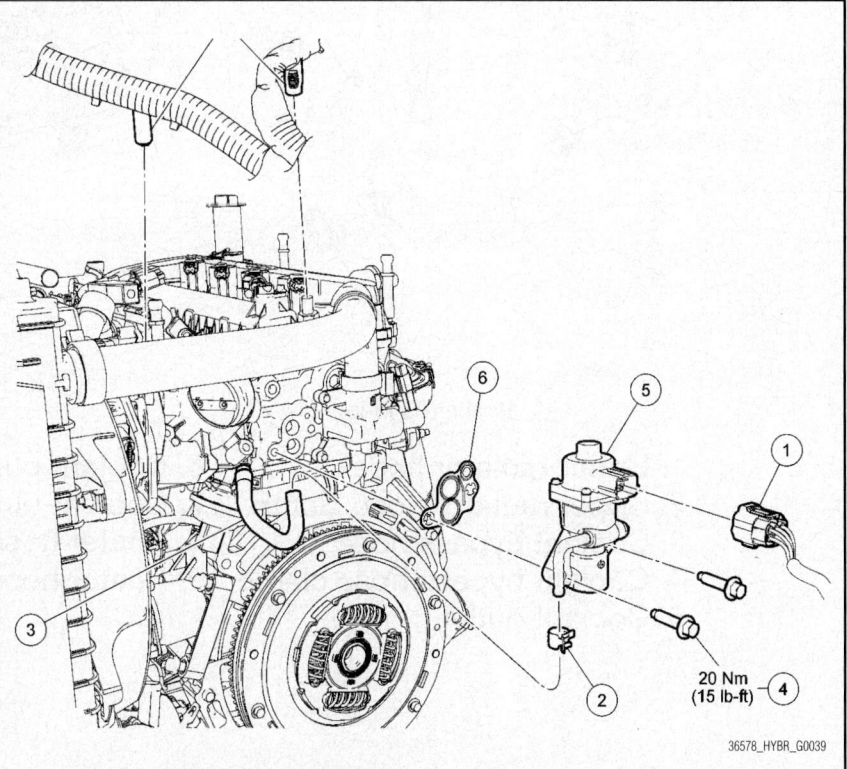

20 Nm (15 lb-ft)

36578_HYBR_G0039

Fig. 148 Exhaust Gas Recirculation (EGR) Valve—2.5L engine

5. Release the clamp and remove the coolant hose from the EGR valve.

6. Remove the 2 bolts and the EGR valve.

❋❋ WARNING

Do not use metal scrapers, wire brushes, power abrasive discs or other abrasive means to clean the sealing surfaces. These tools cause scratches and gouges that make leak paths. Use a plastic scraping tool to remove all traces of the Exhaust Gas Recirculation (EGR) valve gasket.

➡ **If there is no residual gasket material present, metal surface prep can be used to clean and prepare the surfaces**

7. Remove and discard the EGR valve gasket.

8. Clean and inspect the EGR gasket mating surfaces.

9. To install, reverse the removal procedure and note the following:
- Tighten the EGR valve mounting bolts to 15 ft. lbs. (20 Nm).
- Fill and bleed the cooling system.

2.5L Hybrid Engine
See Figures 148 through 149.

1. Drain the cooling system.

2. Remove the Air Cleaner (ACL) outlet pipe.

3. Release the clamp and remove the upper radiator hose from the coolant outlet.

4. Release the clamp and remove the coolant bypass hose from the coolant outlet.

5. Release the clamp and remove the heater hose from the coolant outlet.

6. Remove the 4 bolts and the coolant outlet and gasket.

7. Disconnect the EGR valve electrical connector.

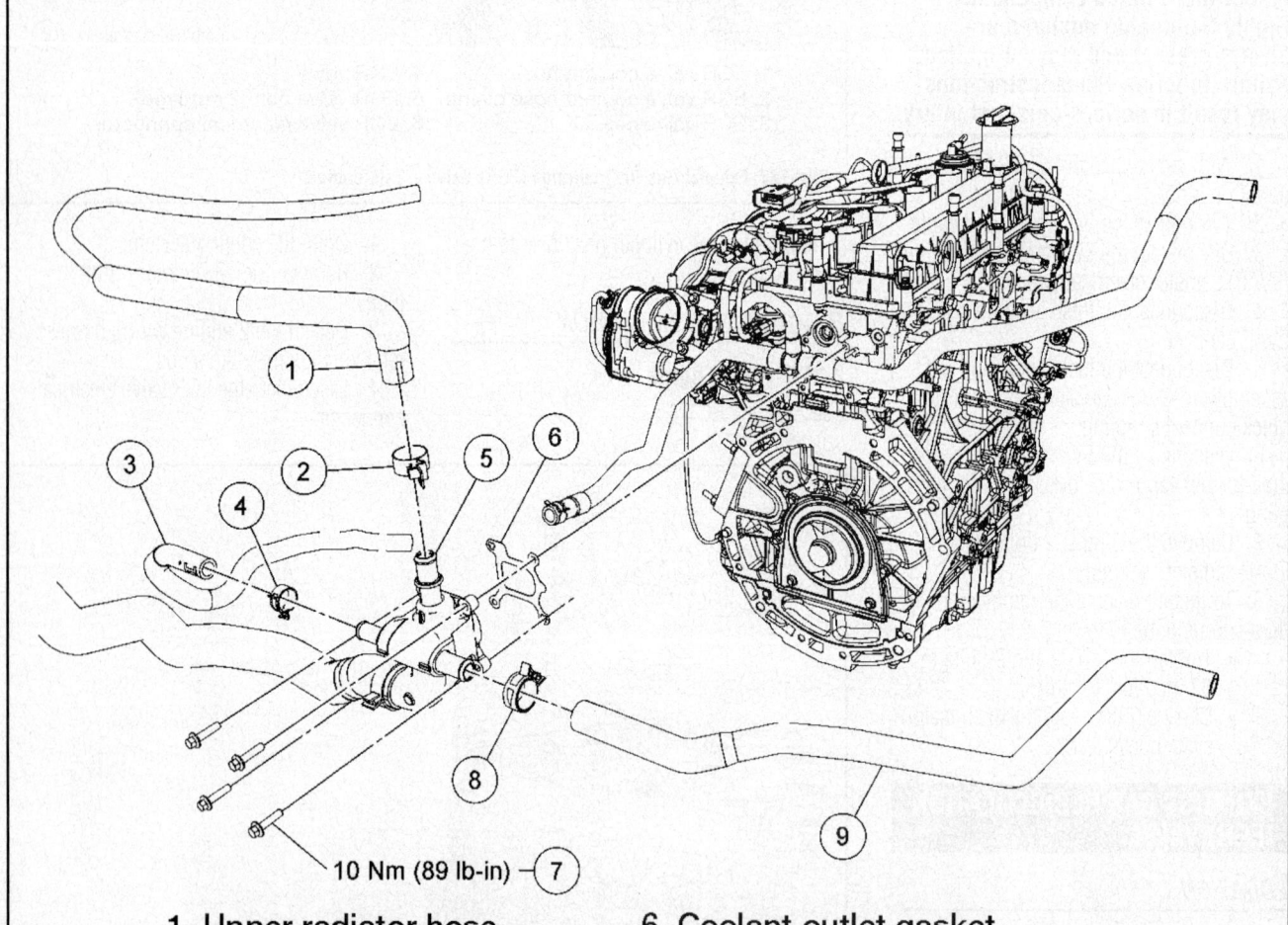

10 Nm (89 lb-in) — ⑦

1. Upper radiator hose
2. Upper radiator hose clamp
3. Coolant bypass hose
4. Coolant bypass hose clamp
5. Coolant outlet
6. Coolant outlet gasket
7. Coolant outlet bolt (4 required)
8. Heater hose clamp
9. Heater hose

36578_HYBR_G0037

Fig. 149 Coolant outlet and related hoses

8. Release the clamp and remove the coolant hose from the EGR valve.

9. Remove the 2 bolts and the EGR valve.

❋❋ WARNING

Do not use metal scrapers, wire brushes, power abrasive discs or other abrasive means to clean the sealing surfaces. These tools cause scratches and gouges that make leak paths. Use a plastic scraping tool to remove all traces of the Exhaust Gas Recirculation (EGR) valve gasket.

➥**If there is no residual gasket material present, metal surface prep can be used to clean and prepare the surfaces.**

10. Remove and discard the EGR valve gasket.

11. Clean and inspect the EGR gasket mating surfaces.

12. Install a new EGR valve and coolant outlet gaskets.

13. To install, reverse the removal procedure and note the following:
- Tighten the 2 EGR valve bolts to 177 inch lbs. (20 Nm).
- Tighten the 4 coolant outlet bolts to 89 inch lbs. (10 Nm).
- Fill and bleed the cooling system

HEATED OXYGEN SENSOR (HO2S)

LOCATION

See Figure 150.

The Heated Oxygen Sensor (HO2S) is located just below exhaust manifold shield. The Catalyst Monitor Sensor (CMS) is located after the front Heated Oxygen Sensor (HO2S).

REMOVAL & INSTALLATION

See Figure 151.

1. With the vehicle in NEUTRAL, position it on a hoist.

2. Disconnect the Heated Oxygen Sensor (HO2S) electrical connector.

3. Using a suitable tool, remove the HO2S.

➥**Apply a light coat of anti-seize lubricant to the threads of the HO2S.**

4. To install, reverse the removal procedure and tighten HO2S to 35 ft. lbs. (48 Nm).

➥**Use the above procedure for the rear Catalyst Monitor Sensor (CMS).**

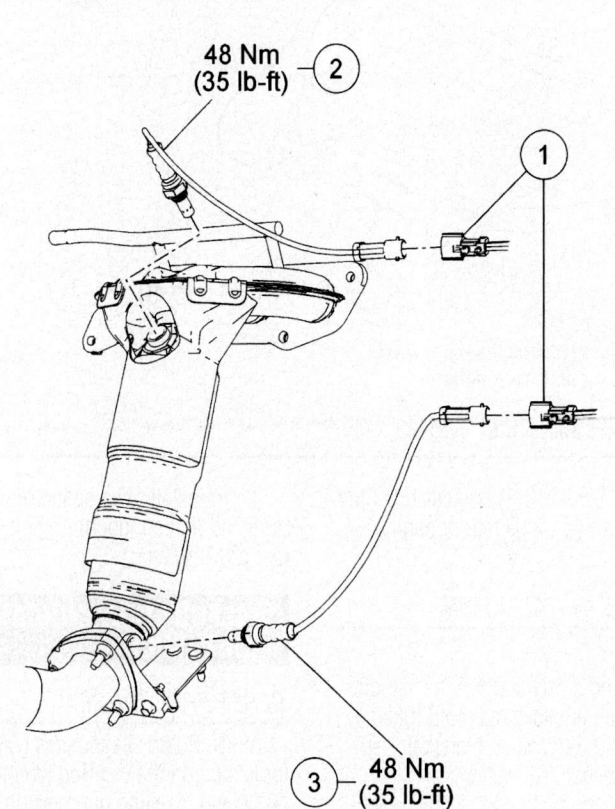

48 Nm
(35 lb-ft) ②

①

③ 48 Nm
(35 lb-ft)

1. Heated oxygen sensor (HO2S) and catalyst monitor sensor electrical connectors
2. HO2S
3. Catalyst monitor sensor

22086_HYBR_G0056

Fig. 150 Heated Oxygen Sensor (HO2S) location—2.3L engine

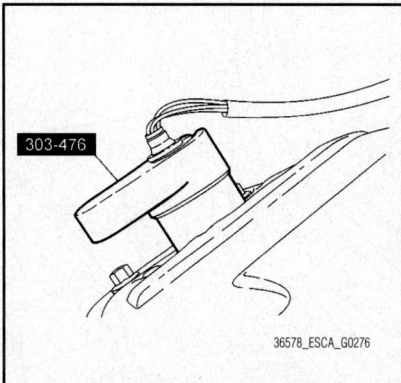

303-476

36578_ESCA_G0276

Fig. 151 Removing HO2S sensor with a 303-476 special tool

INTAKE AIR TEMPERATURE (IAT) SENSOR

LOCATION

The Intake Air Temperature (IAT) sensor is part of the Mass Air Flow (MAF) sensor.

REMOVAL & INSTALLATION

Refer to Mass Air Flow (MAF) sensor in this section.

KNOCK SENSOR (KS)

LOCATION

See Figure 152.

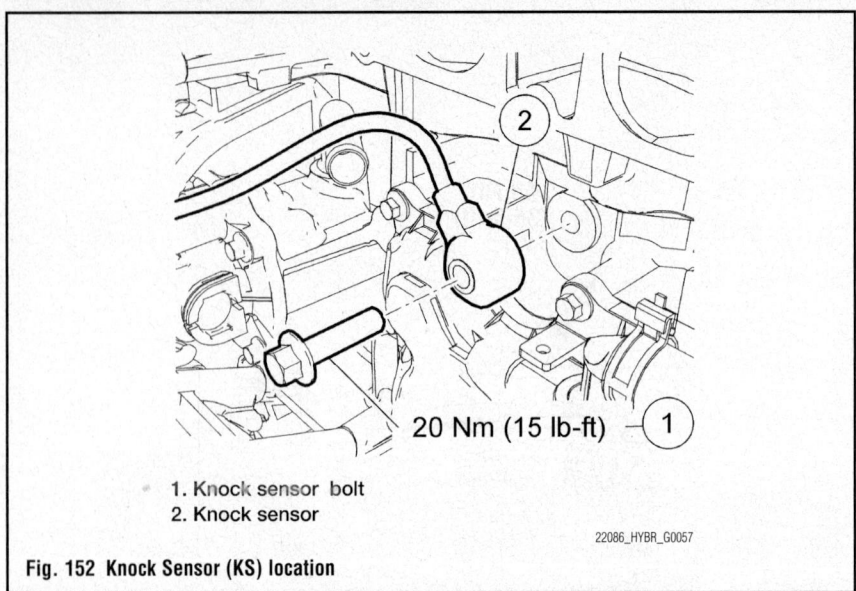

1. Knock sensor bolt
2. Knock sensor

22086_HYBR_G0057

Fig. 152 Knock Sensor (KS) location

The Knock Sensor (KS) is located behind the intake manifold to the rear of engine block.

REMOVAL & INSTALLATION

See Figure 152.

1. Raise and safely support the vehicle.
2. Remove the intake manifold. Refer to Intake Manifold Removal & Installation in the Engine Mechanical section.
3. Remove the bolt and the Knock Sensor (KS).

4. To install, reverse the removal procedure and tighten mounting bolt to 177 inch lbs. (20 Nm).

MALFUNCTION INDICATOR LIGHT (MIL)

RESET PROCEDURE

All On Board Diagnostics (OBD) scan tools support the clearing of continuous DTCs and resetting of emission monitors information in the PCM.

The clearing of the continuous DTCs allows the scan tool to command the PCM to clear/reset all emission-related diagnostic information. While carrying out this operation DTC P1000 is stored in the PCM until all the OBD system monitors or components have been tested to satisfy a drive cycle without any other concerns occurring.

The following events occur when the continuous DTCs and the emission monitors information is cleared from the PCM:

- The number of DTCs is reset
- The DTCs are cleared (on vehicles with permanent DTCs, additional vehicle operation is required to complete and pass the appropriate monitors to complete the clearing of permanent DTCs)
- The freeze frame data is cleared
- The diagnostic monitoring test results are reset
- The status of the OBD system monitors is reset
- DTC P1000 is set

MASS AIR FLOW (MAF) SENSOR

LOCATION

See Figure 153.

The Mass Air Flow (MAF) sensor is located in air filter housing lid.

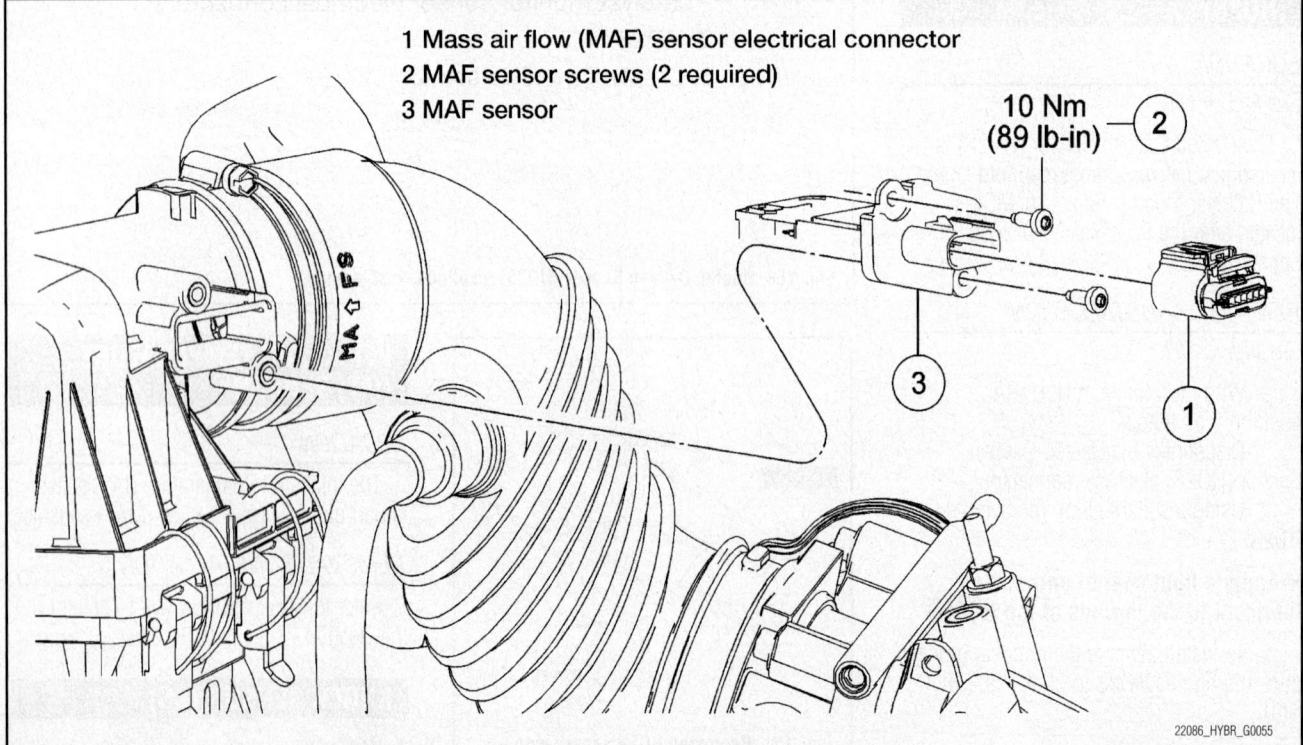

1 Mass air flow (MAF) sensor electrical connector
2 MAF sensor screws (2 required)
3 MAF sensor

10 Nm (89 lb-in)

22086_HYBR_G0055

Fig. 153 Mass Air Flow (MAF) sensor location

REMOVAL & INSTALLATION

See Figure 153.

1. Disconnect the Mass Air Flow (MAF) sensor electrical connector.
2. Remove the 2 screws and the MAF sensor.
3. To install, reverse the removal procedure and tighten mounting screws to 89 inch lbs. (10 Nm

MANIFOLD ABSOLUTE PRESSURE (MAP) SENSOR

LOCATION

See Figure 154.

REMOVAL & INSTALLATION

See Figure 154.

1. Disconnect the electrical connector from the Manifold Absolute Pressure (MAP) sensor.
2. Remove the mounting screws, then remove the MAP sensor.
3. To install, reverse the removal procedure.

POSITIVE CRANKCASE VENTILATION (PCV) VALVE

LOCATION

2.3L Hybrid Engine

See Figure 155.

The PCV valve is located under the intake manifold mounted in the crankcase vent oil separator

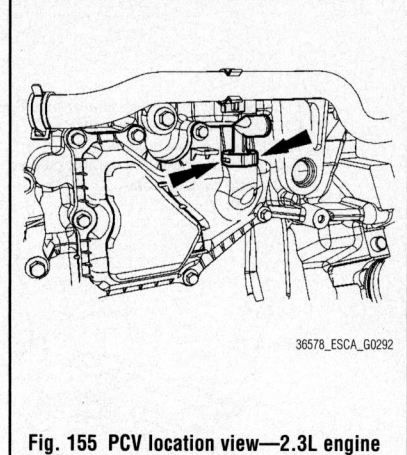

36578_ESCA_G0292

Fig. 155 PCV location view—2.3L engine

2.5L Hybrid Engine

See Figure 156.

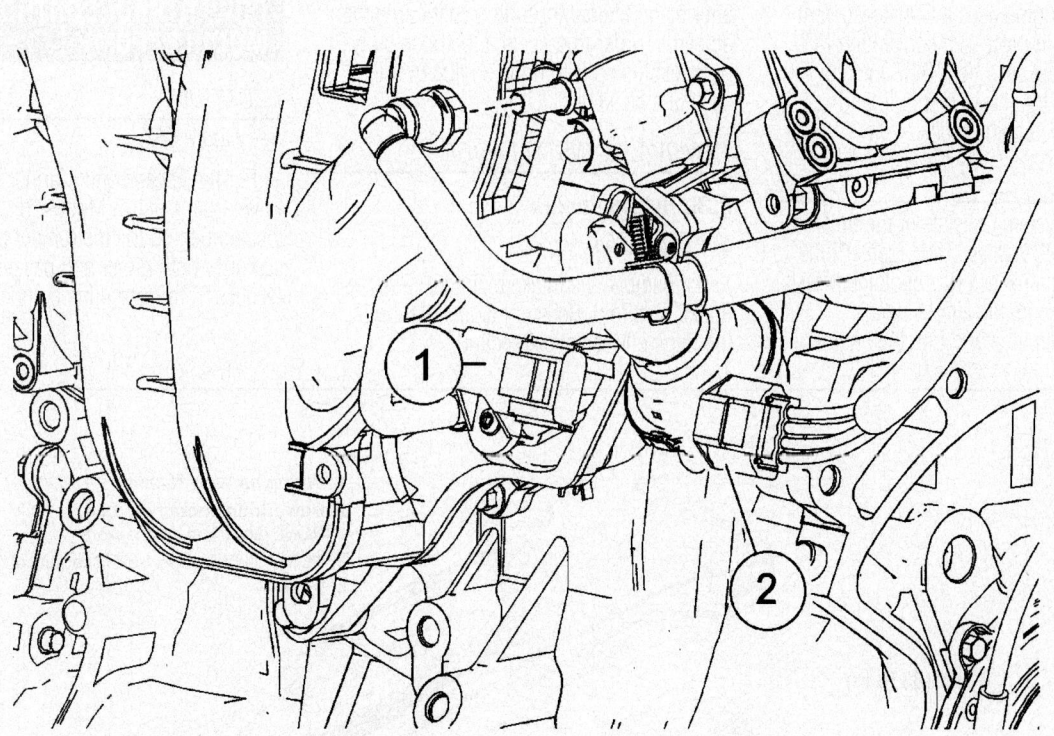

1. Map sensor
2. Map sensor electrical connector

22086_HYBR_G0061

Fig. 154 Manifold Absolute Pressure (MAP) sensor

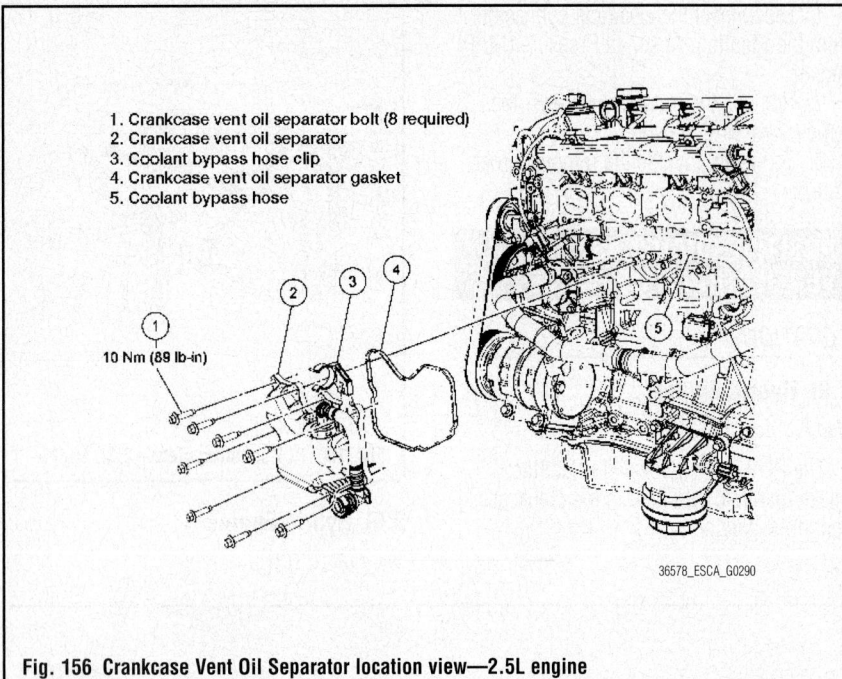

1. Crankcase vent oil separator bolt (8 required)
2. Crankcase vent oil separator
3. Coolant bypass hose clip
4. Crankcase vent oil separator gasket
5. Coolant bypass hose

10 Nm (89 lb-in)

36578_ESCA_G0290

Fig. 156 Crankcase Vent Oil Separator location view—2.5L engine

The 2.5L engine uses a Crankcase Vent Oil Separator in place of a convention PCV valve. The Crankcase Vent Oil Separator is located under the intake manifold and mounted to the engine block.

OPERATION

The PCV system consists of the breather tube and the PCV valve. The breather tube connects the crankcase to a contained fresh air source such as the air cleaner. Air passes into this tube and into the engine after being filtered through a spark arrestor screen in order to prevent a the possibility of an explosion within the engine in the case of a backfire.

REMOVAL & INSTALLATION

2.3L Hybrid Engine

See Figure 155.

1. Remove the intake manifold. Refer to Intake Manifold, Removal & Installation in the Engine Mechanical section.

2. Depress the 2 release tabs and remove the PCV valve.

➡**Clean and inspect the crankcase oil vent separator gasket and install a new gasket if necessary.**

3. To install, reverse the removal procedure.

2.5L Hybrid Engine

See Figure 156.

1. Remove the intake manifold.
2. Release the coolant bypass hose from the clip.
3. Remove the 8 bolts, the crankcase vent oil separator and gasket.
4. To install, reverse the removal procedure and note the following:
   - Clean and inspect the sealing surfaces.
   - Tighten the crankcase vent oil separator bolts to 89 inch lbs. (10 Nm).

POWERTRAIN CONTROL MODULE (PCM)

LOCATION

See Figure 157.

For the Escape and Mariner hybrids, the Powertrain Control Module (PCM) is located behind the instrument panel (cowl), center to both driver and passenger sides (access from the engine compartment).

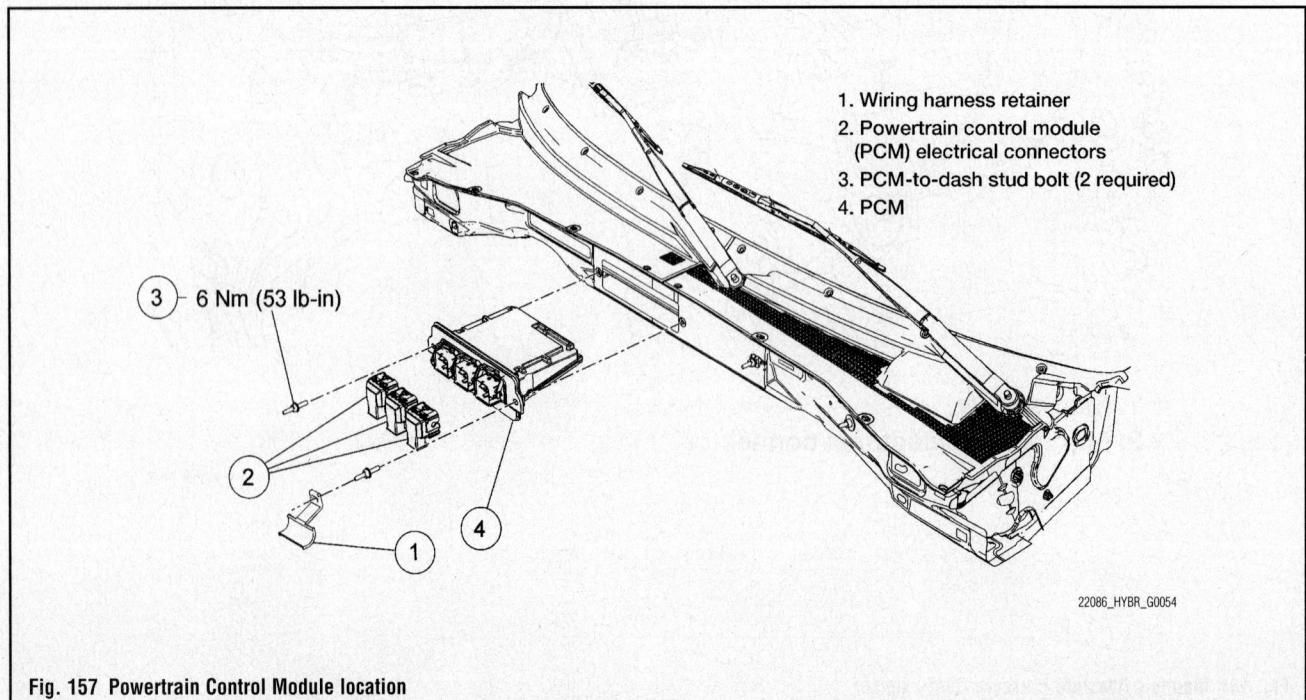

1. Wiring harness retainer
2. Powertrain control module (PCM) electrical connectors
3. PCM-to-dash stud bolt (2 required)
4. PCM

3 — 6 Nm (53 lb-in)

22086_HYBR_G0054

Fig. 157 Powertrain Control Module location

REMOVAL & INSTALLATION

See Figure 157.

➡**Any Powertrain Control Module (PCM) replacement will require that ALL customer keys are available to be programmed at the time of installation. PCM replacement DOES NOT require new keys.**

1. Retrieve the module configuration. Carry out the module configuration retrieval steps of the Programmable Module Installation procedure.
2. Disconnect the negative battery cable.
3. Remove the PCM stud bolt nut and position the wiring harness aside.
4. Disconnect the 3 PCM electrical connectors.
5. Remove the 2 stud bolts and the PCM
6. Remove the PCM cowl seal.

To install:

7. Install the PCM cowl seal.
8. Install the PCM and tighten the 2 stud bolts to 53 inch lbs. (6 Nm).
9. Connect the 3 PCM electrical connectors.
10. Position the wiring harness. Install and tighten the PCM stud bolt nut to 53 inch lbs. (6 Nm).
11. Restore the module configuration. Carry out the module configuration restore steps of the Programmable Module Installation procedure.
12. Reprogram the Passive Anti-Theft System (PATS). Carry out the Key Programming Using Two Programmed Keys procedure.

THROTTLE POSITION SENSOR (TPS)

LOCATION

The Throttle Position Sensor (TPS) is integral to the electronic throttle body.

REMOVAL & INSTALLATION

Refer to Throttle Body, Removal & Installation in the Fuel System section.

FUEL

GASOLINE FUEL INJECTION SYSTEM

FUEL SYSTEM SERVICE PRECAUTIONS

Safety is the most important factor when performing not only fuel system maintenance but any type of maintenance. Failure to conduct maintenance and repairs in a safe manner may result in serious personal injury or death. Maintenance and testing of the vehicle's fuel system components can be accomplished safely and effectively by adhering to the following rules and guidelines.

• To avoid the possibility of fire and personal injury, always disconnect the negative battery cable unless the repair or test procedure requires that battery voltage be applied.

• Always relieve the fuel system pressure prior to disconnecting any fuel system component (injector, fuel rail, pressure regulator, etc.), fitting or fuel line connection. Exercise extreme caution whenever relieving fuel system pressure to avoid exposing skin, face and eyes to fuel spray. Please be advised that fuel under pressure may penetrate the skin or any part of the body that it contacts.

• Always place a shop towel or cloth around the fitting or connection prior to loosening to absorb any excess fuel due to spillage. Ensure that all fuel spillage (should it occur) is quickly removed from engine surfaces. Ensure that all fuel soaked cloths or towels are deposited into a suitable waste container.

• Always keep a dry chemical (Class B) fire extinguisher near the work area.

• Do not allow fuel spray or fuel vapors to come into contact with a spark or open flame.

• Always use a back-up wrench when loosening and tightening fuel line connection fittings. This will prevent unnecessary stress and torsion to fuel line piping.

• Always replace worn fuel fitting O-rings with new. Do not substitute fuel hose or equivalent where fuel pipe is installed.

• Do not carry personal electronic devices such as cell phones, pagers or audio equipment of any type when working on or near any fuel-related component. Highly flammable mixtures are always present and may be ignited. Failure to follow these instructions may result in serious personal injury

• Do not smoke, carry lighted tobacco or have an open flame of any type when working on or near any fuel-related component. Highly flammable mixtures are always present and may be ignited. Failure to follow these instructions may result in serious personal injury.

Before servicing the vehicle, make sure to also refer to the precautions in the beginning of this section as well.

RELIEVING FUEL SYSTEM PRESSURE

2008 Models

See Figure 158.

✳✳ CAUTION

Do not carry personal electronic devices such as cell phones, pagers or audio equipment of any type when working on or near any fuel-related component. Highly flammable mixtures are always present and may be ignited. Failure to follow these instructions may result in serious personal injury.

✳✳ CAUTION

Do not smoke, carry lighted tobacco or have an open flame of any type when working on or near any fuel-related component. Highly flammable mixtures are always present and may be ignited. Failure to follow these instructions may result in serious personal injury.

1. Before servicing the vehicle, refer to the Precautions Section.
2. With the vehicle in NEUTRAL, position it on a hoist.
3. Disconnect the Fuel Pump (FP) driver module electrical connector.
4. Start the engine and allow it to idle until it stalls.
5. After the engine stalls, crank the engine for approximately 5 seconds to make sure the fuel injection supply manifold pressure has been released.

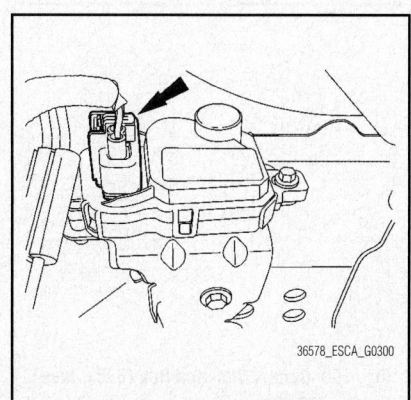

36578_ESCA_G0300

Fig. 158 Fuel Pump (FP) driver module

6. Turn the ignition switch to the OFF position.

7. When fuel system service is complete, connect the FP driver module electrical connector.

8. It may take more than one key cycle to pressurize the fuel system.

9. Cycle the ignition key and wait 3 seconds to pressurize the fuel system. Check for leaks before starting the engine.

10. Start the vehicle and check the fuel system for leaks.

2009 Models

See Figure 159.

> ✳✳ **CAUTION**
>
> **Do not carry personal electronic devices such as cell phones, pagers or audio equipment of any type when working on or near any fuel-related component. Highly flammable mixtures are always present and may be ignited. Failure to follow these instructions may result in serious personal injury.**

> ✳✳ **CAUTION**
>
> **Do not smoke, carry lighted tobacco or have an open flame of any type when working on or near any fuel-related component. Highly flammable mixtures are always present and may be ignited. Failure to follow these instructions may result in serious personal injury.**

1. Before servicing the vehicle, refer to the Precautions Section.

2. Remove the fuel pump fuse that is located in the Battery Junction Box (BJB), location 22.

3. Start the engine and allow it to idle until it stalls.

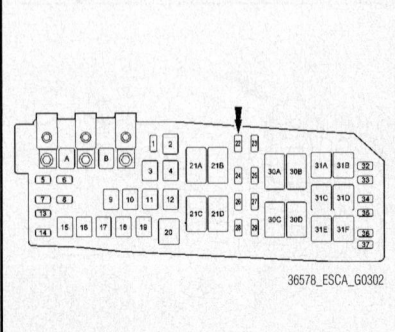

36578_ESCA_G0302

Fig. 159 Battery Junction Box (BJB), fuse location 22 shown

4. After the engine stalls, crank the engine for approximately 5 seconds to make sure the fuel injection supply manifold pressure has been released.

5. Turn the ignition switch to the OFF position.

6. When the fuel system service is complete, install the FP fuse.

7. Carry out a Key ON Engine OFF (KOEO) visual inspection for leaks prior to starting the engine.

8. Start the vehicle and check the fuel system for leaks.

FUEL FILTER

REMOVAL & INSTALLATION

2008 Models

See Figure 160.

> ✳✳ **CAUTION**
>
> **Do not carry personal electronic devices such as cell phones, pagers or audio equipment of any type when working on or near any fuel-related component. Highly flammable mixtures are always present and may be ignited. Failure to follow these instructions may result in serious personal injury.**

> ✳✳ **CAUTION**
>
> **Do not smoke, carry lighted tobacco or have an open flame of any type when working on or near any fuel-related component. Highly flammable mixtures are always present and may be ignited. Failure to follow these instructions may result in serious personal injury.**

1. Before servicing the vehicle, refer to the Precautions Section.

2. Properly relieve the fuel system pressure.

➡ Some residual fuel may remain in the fuel filter after releasing the fuel system pressure. Upon disconnecting or removing the fuel filter, carefully drain any residual fuel into a suitable container.

3. Disconnect the fuel supply tube-to-fuel filter inlet spring lock coupling.

4. Disconnect the fuel supply tube-to-fuel filter outlet spring lock coupling.

5. Release the fuel filter clamp and remove the fuel filter.

6. To install, reverse the removal procedure and tighten the fuel filter retaining clamp to 35 inch lbs. (4 Nm).

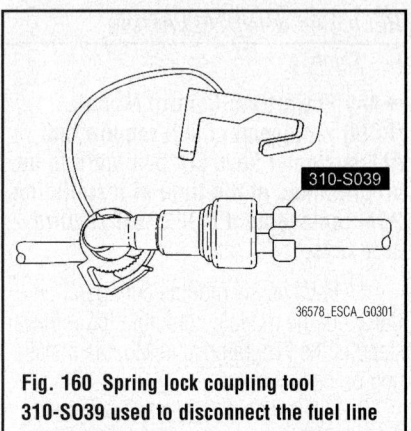

310-S039

36578_ESCA_G0301

Fig. 160 Spring lock coupling tool 310-SO39 used to disconnect the fuel line

2009 Models

The 2009 model has a lifetime fuel filter (serviced as part of the fuel pump module).

FUEL PUMP MODULE

REMOVAL & INSTALLATION

See Figure 161.

> ✳✳ **CAUTION**
>
> **Do not carry personal electronic devices such as cell phones, pagers or audio equipment of any type when working on or near any fuel-related component. Highly flammable mixtures are always present and may be ignited. Failure to follow these instructions may result in serious personal injury.**

> ✳✳ **CAUTION**
>
> **Do not smoke, carry lighted tobacco or have an open flame of any type when working on or near any fuel-related component. Highly flammable mixtures are always present and may be ignited. Failure to follow these instructions may result in serious personal injury.**

> ✳✳ **CAUTION**
>
> **Do not carry personal electronic devices such as cell phones, pagers or audio equipment of any type when working on or near any fuel-related component. Highly flammable mixtures are always present and may be ignited. Failure to follow these instructions may result in serious personal injury.**

1. Before servicing the vehicle, refer to the Precautions Section.

2. Disconnect the negative battery cable.

3. With the vehicle in NEUTRAL, position it on a hoist.

4. Release the fuel system pressure.

5. Disconnect the battery ground cable.

6. Release the fuel tank filler cap and position aside.

7. Insert the special tool into the fuel tank filler pipe until it opens the fuel tank level shutoff valve located at the inlet of the fuel tank.

➡ **Due to the internal design of the fuel tank components, slow fuel drainage may occur.**

8. Using the special tools, drain as much fuel as possible from the fuel tank and filler pipe, lowering the fuel level below the Fuel Pump (FP) mounting flange.

➡ **The fuel pump module can be accessed from inside the vehicle EXSTREAM CAUTION should be used when servicing the FP module.**

9. Remove the 4 screws and the FP module access cover. (If Applicable)

➡ **Clean the FP module connection, couplings, mounting flange and the immediate surrounding area of any dirt or foreign material.**

10. Disconnect the FP module electrical connector. Place absorbent toweling in the immediate surrounding area in case of fuel spills.

11. Disconnect the fuel supply tube and fuel vapor recirculation tube-to-FP module quick connect couplings.

✳✳ WARNING

The fuel pump (FP) module must be handled carefully to avoid damage to the float arm and the filter.

12. Carefully remove the FP module lock ring and verify that enough fuel has been drained to avoid spillage.

13. Drain any residual in the FP module into a suitable container.

14. Using a suitable FP module lock ring remover, rotate the lock ring counterclockwise and remove the FP module.

15. Inspect the surfaces of the FP module flange and fuel tank seal contact surfaces. Do not polish or adjust the seal contact area of the FP module flange or fuel tank. Install a new FP module or fuel tank if the seal contact area is bent, scratched or corroded.

16. Remove and discard the FP module O-ring seal.

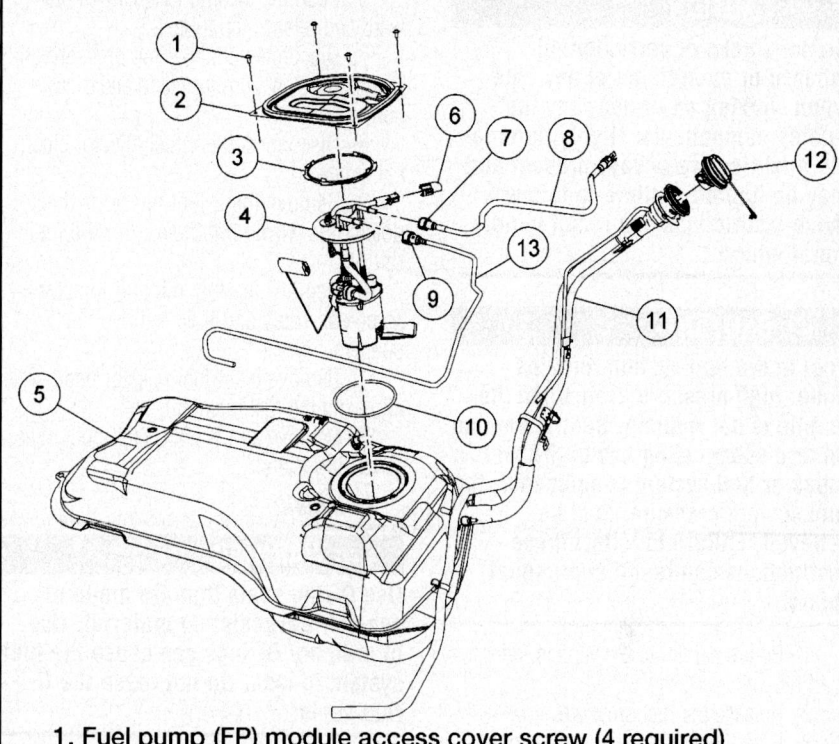

1. Fuel pump (FP) module access cover screw (4 required)
2. FP module access cover
3. FP module lock ring
4. FP module
5. Fuel tank
6. FP module electrical connector
7. Fuel vapor tube-to-FP module quick connect coupling
8. Fuel vapor tube
9. Fucl supply tube assembly-to-fuel tank quick connect coupling
10. FP module O-ring seal
11. Fuel tank filler pipe
12. Fuel tank filler cap
13. Fuel supply tube

36578_ESCA_G0306

Fig. 161 Fuel Pump (FP) module and related components

17. Apply clean engine oil to the FP module O-ring seal.

18. To install, reverse the removal procedure.

FUEL RAIL & INJECTORS

REMOVAL & INSTALLATION

2.3L Hybrid Engine
See Figures 162 and 163.

✳✳ CAUTION

Do not carry personal electronic devices such as cell phones, pagers or audio equipment of any type when working on or near any fuel-related component. Highly flammable mixtures are always present and may be ignited. Failure to follow these

instructions may result in serious personal injury.

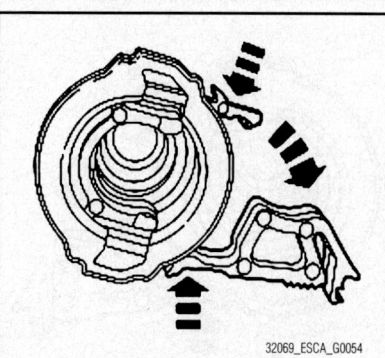

32069_ESCA_G0054

Fig. 162 Rotate the primary locking tab to the fully opened position and squeeze the secondary locking tabs to release the locking mechanism

❋❋ CAUTION

Do not smoke or carry lighted tobacco or open flame of any type when working on or near any fuel-related components. Highly flammable mixtures are always present and may be ignited. Failure to follow these instructions can result in personal injury.

❋❋ CAUTION

Fuel in the fuel system remains under high pressure even when the engine is not running. Before working on or disconnecting any of the fuel tubes or fuel system components, the fuel system pressure must be relieved. Failure to follow these instructions can result in personal injury.

1. Before servicing the vehicle, refer to the Precautions Section.
2. Release the fuel pressure.
3. Disconnect the negative battery cable.

❋❋ WARNING

When reusing liquid or vapor tube connectors, make sure to use compressed air to remove any foreign material from the connector retaining clip area before separating the tube.

➡ Carefully release the locking tabs to avoid breakage.

4. Release the fuel tube-to-fuel rail quick release coupling primary locking tab.
5. Rotate the primary locking tab to the fully opened position and squeeze the secondary locking tabs to release the locking mechanism.

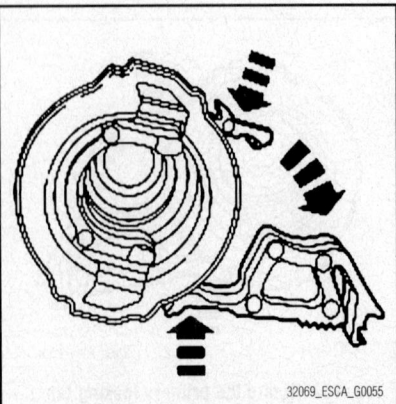

Fig. 163 Push the locking mechanism outward and release the tube

6. Push the locking mechanism outward and release the tube.
7. Disconnect the fuel rail pressure and temperature vacuum tube and electrical connector.
8. Disconnect the 4 fuel injector electrical connectors.
9. Remove the 2 fuel rail bolts and detach the wiring retainers from the fuel rail.
10. Remove the fuel rail and injectors as an assembly and then remove the spacers.
11. Remove the 4 fuel injector retainer clips and the fuel injectors.
12. Remove and discard the 8 fuel injector O-ring seals.

To install:

❋❋ WARNING

Use O-ring seals that are made of special fuel-resistant material. Use of ordinary O-rings can cause the fuel system to leak. Do not reuse the O-ring seals.

➡ Install new fuel injector O-ring seals and lubricate them with clean engine oil.

13. Install the fuel injectors and the retainer clips.
14. Position the fuel rail spacers and the fuel rail.
15. Install the fuel rail bolts and attach the wiring retainers. Tighten to 23 Nm (17 lb-ft).
16. Connect the fuel injector electrical connectors.
17. Connect the fuel rail pressure and temperature vacuum tube and electrical connector.

➡ Make sure the collar on the fuel tube is inserted fully into the quick release coupling before the locking tang is locked.

➡ Apply clean engine oil to the end of the tube before inserting a tube into the connector.

18. Connect the fuel tube quick release coupling:
    a. Connect the quick lock coupling to the tube.
    b. Press the quick connect coupling locking tangs into position.
    c. Pull on the fitting to make sure it is fully engaged.
19. Connect the negative battery cable.

2.5L Hybrid Engine

See Figure 164.

❋❋ CAUTION

Do not carry personal electronic devices such as cell phones, pagers or audio equipment of any type when working on or near any fuel-related component. Highly flammable mixtures are always present and may be ignited. Failure to follow these instructions may result in serious personal injury.

❋❋ CAUTION

Do not smoke or carry lighted tobacco or open flame of any type when working on or near any fuel-related components. Highly flammable mixtures are always present and may be ignited. Failure to follow these instructions may result in personal injury.

❋❋ CAUTION

Fuel in the fuel system remains under high pressure even when the engine is not running. Before working on or disconnecting any of the fuel lines or fuel system components, the fuel system pressure must be relieved. Failure to follow these instructions may result in personal injury.

1. Before servicing the vehicle, refer to the Precautions Section.
2. Release the fuel pressure.
3. Disconnect the battery ground cable.
4. Disconnect the fuel supply tube-to-fuel quick connect coupling.
5. Disconnect the 4 fuel injector electrical connectors.
6. Remove the nut and position the radio capacitor aside.
7. Detach the 2 pin-type wire harness retainers from the fuel rail.
8. Remove the 2 fuel rail stud bolts.
9. Remove the fuel rail and injectors as an assembly.
10. Remove the 4 fuel injector retainer clips and the 4 fuel injectors.
11. Remove and discard the 8 fuel injector O-ring seals.

To install:

➡ Use O-ring seals that are made of special fuel-resistant material. Use of ordinary O-rings can cause the fuel system to leak. Do not reuse the O-ring seals.

12. Install 8 new fuel injector O-ring seals and lubricate them with clean engine oil.

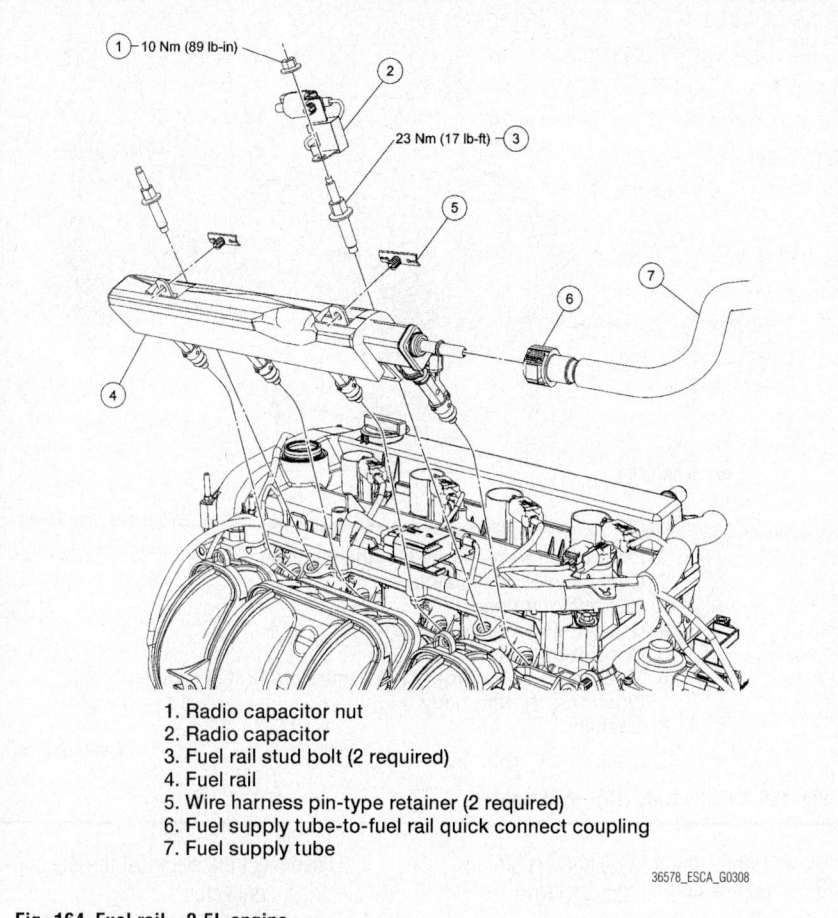

1. Radio capacitor nut
2. Radio capacitor
3. Fuel rail stud bolt (2 required)
4. Fuel rail
5. Wire harness pin-type retainer (2 required)
6. Fuel supply tube-to-fuel rail quick connect coupling
7. Fuel supply tube

36578_ESCA_G0308

Fig. 164 Fuel rail—2.5L engine

tures are always present and may be ignited. Failure to follow these instructions may result in serious personal injury.

1. Before servicing the vehicle, refer to the Precautions Section.
2. With the vehicle in NEUTRAL, position it on a hoist.
3. Drain the fuel tank.

13. Install the 4 fuel injectors and the 4 retainer clips on the fuel rail.
14. Install the fuel rail and injectors as an assembly.
15. Install the 2 fuel rail stud bolts and tighten to 17 ft lbs. (23 Nm).
16. Attach the 2 pin-type wire harness retainers to the fuel rail.
17. Position the radio capacitor and install and tighten the nut to 89 inch lbs. (10 Nm).
18. Connect the 4 fuel injector electrical connectors.
19. Connect the fuel supply tube-to-fuel rail quick connect coupling.
20. Connect the battery ground cable.

FUEL TANK

REMOVAL & INSTALLATION
See Figure 165.

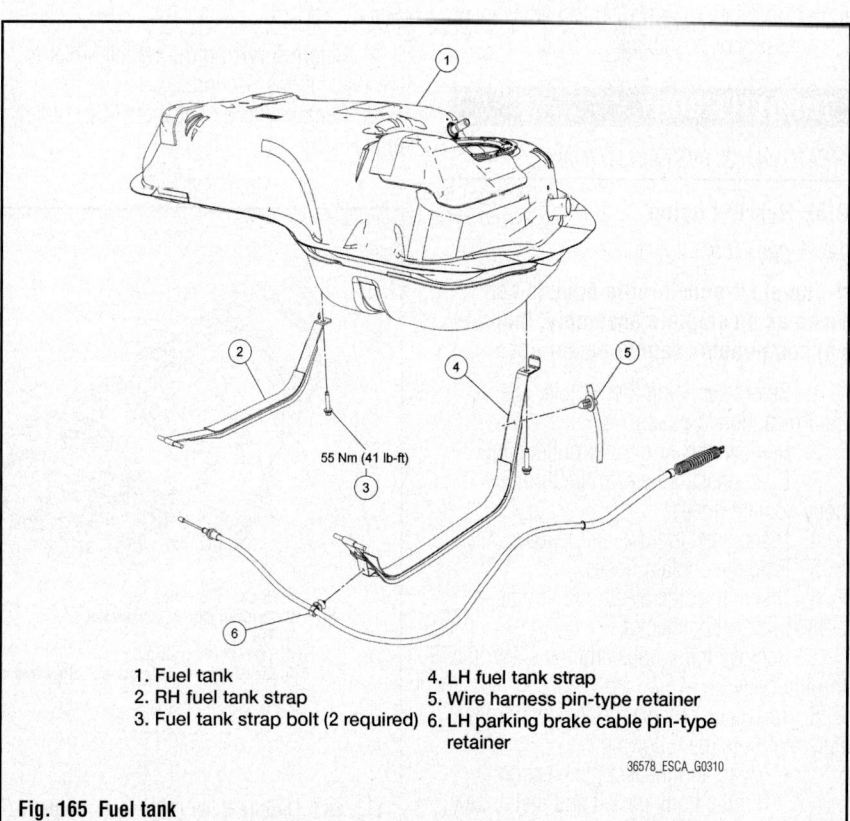

55 Nm (41 lb-ft)

1. Fuel tank
2. RH fuel tank strap
3. Fuel tank strap bolt (2 required)
4. LH fuel tank strap
5. Wire harness pin-type retainer
6. LH parking brake cable pin-type retainer

36578_ESCA_G0310

Fig. 165 Fuel tank

4. Remove the exhaust muffler and resonator.

5. For AWD vehicles remove the rear driveshaft. Refer to Drive Shaft Removal & Installation in the Drive Train section.

6. Release the clamp and remove the fuel tank filler pipe hose from the fuel tank.

7. Position a suitable lifting device under the fuel tank.

8. Detach the parking brake cable pin-type retainer from the LH fuel tank strap.

9. Detach the wire harness pin-type retainer from the LH fuel tank strap.

10. Remove the 2 bolts and position the 2 fuel tank straps aside.

11. To install, tighten to 41 ft. lbs. (55 Nm).

12. Partially lower the fuel tank enough to disconnect the fuel vapor tube assembly-to-fuel tank quick connect coupling.

13. Completely lower and remove the fuel tank from the vehicle.

14. To install, reverse the removal procedure and note the following:
- Tighten the filler pipe hose clamp to 35 inch lbs (4 Nm).
- Tighten the fuel tank strap retaining bolts to 41 ft. lbs (55 Nm).

IDLE SPEED

ADJUSTMENT

Idle speed is maintained by the Powertrain Control Module (PCM). No adjustment is necessary or possible.

THROTTLE BODY

REMOVAL & INSTALLATION

2.3L Hybrid Engine

See Figure 166.

➡**The electronic throttle body is serviced as a complete assembly. Individual components cannot be serviced.**

1. Before servicing the vehicle, refer to the Precautions Section.

2. Remove the air cleaner outlet pipe.

3. Disconnect the electronic throttle body coolant hoses.

4. Disconnect the coolant hoses.

5. Plug the coolant hoses.

6. Disconnect the electronic throttle body electrical connector.

7. Remove the 4 bolts and the electronic throttle body.

8. To install, reverse the removal procedure and note the following:
- Clean and inspect the electronic throttle body gasket and install new if necessary.

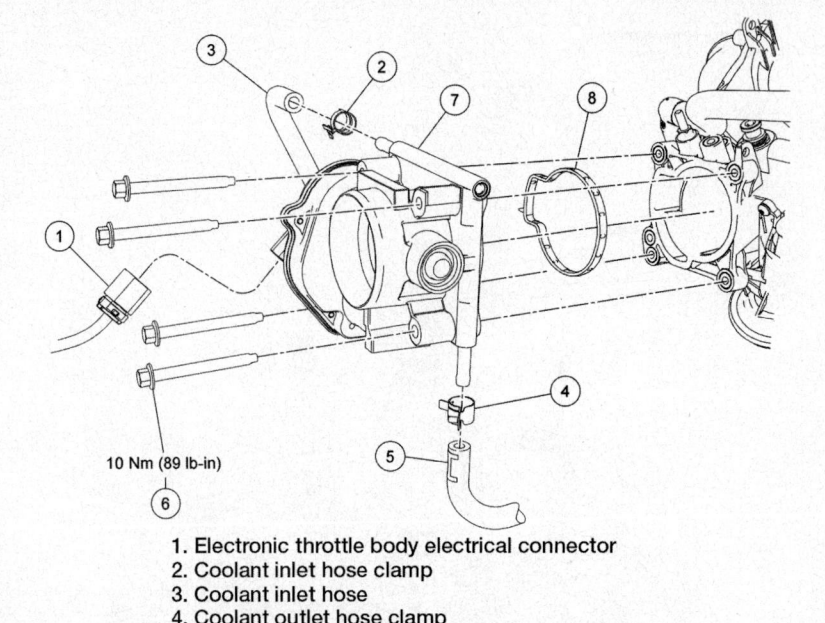

10 Nm (89 lb-in)

1. Electronic throttle body electrical connector
2. Coolant inlet hose clamp
3. Coolant inlet hose
4. Coolant outlet hose clamp
5. Coolant outlet hose
6. Throttle body-to-upper intake manifold bolt (4 required)
7. Electronic throttle body
8. Gasket

36578_HYBR_G0040

Fig. 166 Throttle body (TB)—2.3L engine

- Tighten the throttle body retaining bolts to 89 inch lbs. (10 Nm).

2.5L Hybrid Engine

See Figure 167.

1. Before servicing the vehicle, refer to the Precautions Section.

2. Remove the Air Cleaner (ACL) outlet pipe.

3. Disconnect the electrical throttle control electrical connector.

4. Remove the 4 bolts and the Throttle Body (TB).

5. Discard the TB gasket.

6. Installation is the reverse of the removal procedure, noting the following:
- Install a new gasket
- Tighten the throttle body retainers to 89 inch lbs. (10 Nm).

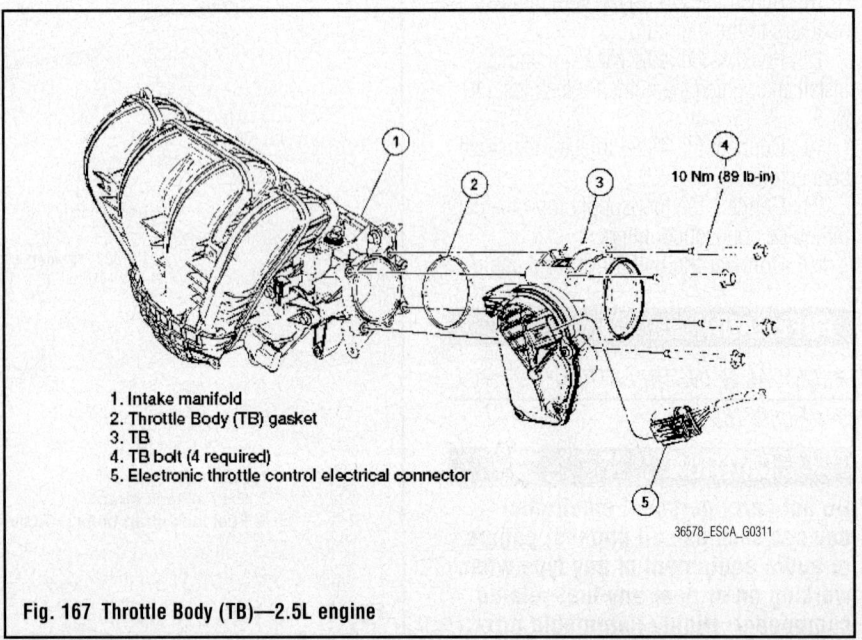

10 Nm (89 lb-in)

1. Intake manifold
2. Throttle Body (TB) gasket
3. TB
4. TB bolt (4 required)
5. Electronic throttle control electrical connector

36578_ESCA_G0311

Fig. 167 Throttle Body (TB)—2.5L engine

HEATING & AIR CONDITIONING SYSTEM

BLOWER MOTOR

REMOVAL & INSTALLATION

See Figure 168.

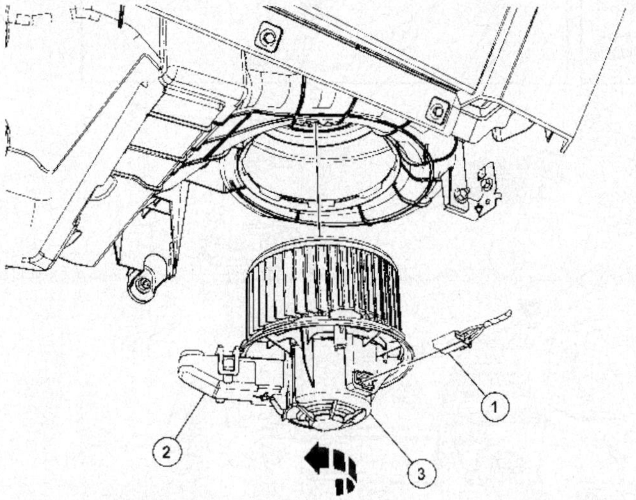

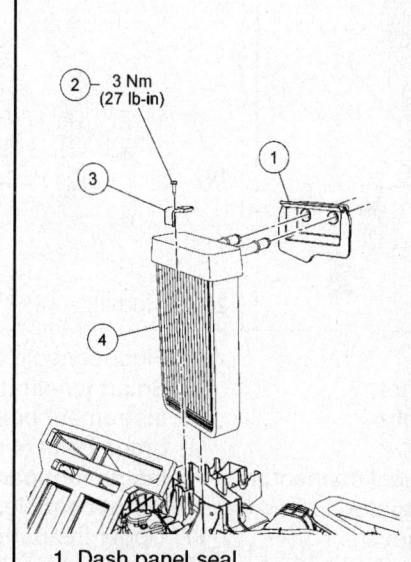

1. Blower motor electrical connector
2. Blower motor vent tube
3. Blower motor

36578_ESCA_G0314

Fig. 168 Blower motor mounting

1. Before beginning this procedure, refer to the precautions section.
2. Disconnect the blower motor electrical connector.
3. Release the 2 blower motor vent tube clips and pull the vent tube down until it is disengaged from the heater core and evaporator core housing.
4. The carpet below the blower motor must be slightly repositioned to remove the blower motor.
5. Rotate the blower motor counter-clockwise to disengage it from the housing and remove the blower motor.
6. To install, reverse the removal procedure.

HEATER CORE

REMOVAL & INSTALLATION

See Figure 169.

1. Before beginning this procedure, refer to the precautions section.

➡**If a heater core leak is suspected, the heater core must be leak tested before the heater core is removed.**

2. Use only the approved coolant for this vehicle.

3. Remove the heater core and evaporator core housing. Refer to Heater Core & Evaporator Core Housing in this section.

2 — 3 Nm
(27 lb-in)

1. Dash panel seal
2. Heater core bracket screw
3. Heater core bracket
4. Heater core

36578_ESCA_G0321

Fig. 169 Heater core mounting

4. Remove the dash panel seal.
5. Remove the heater core bracket screw and the heater core bracket.
6. Remove the heater core.
7. To install, reverse the removal procedure and note the following:
   • Clean out any antifreeze from the housing.
   • Tighten the heater core bracket retaining screw to 27 inch lbs. (3 Nm).

HEATER CORE & EVAPORATOR CORE HOUSING

REMOVAL & INSTALLATION

See Figures 170 and 171.

1. Before servicing the vehicle, refer to the Precautions Section.
2. Drain the engine coolant.
3. Recover the refrigerant.
4. Position the seats forward and remove the 2 floor console rear bolts
5. Position the seats rearward.
6. Remove the transmission selector lever trim ring.
7. Remove the floor console storage bin.
8. Remove the floor console finish panel.
9. Remove the 8 floor console bolts and remove the floor console.
10. Disarm the supplemental restraint system (SRS).
11. Remove the RH and LH A-pillar trim panels.
12. Remove the 4 pin-type retainers and the RH and LH front door opening scuff plates.
13. Remove the RH and LH lower A-pillar trim panels.
14. Remove the steering column opening cover.
15. Remove the RH and LH instrument panel side finish panels.
16. Disconnect the 2 electrical connectors at the LH side of the instrument panel.
17. Disconnect the main steering module electrical connector.
18. Remove the bolts and position aside the hood release handle and parking brake release handle.
19. Remove and slide the steering column intermediate shaft access cover and weather shield up the steering column intermediate shaft.

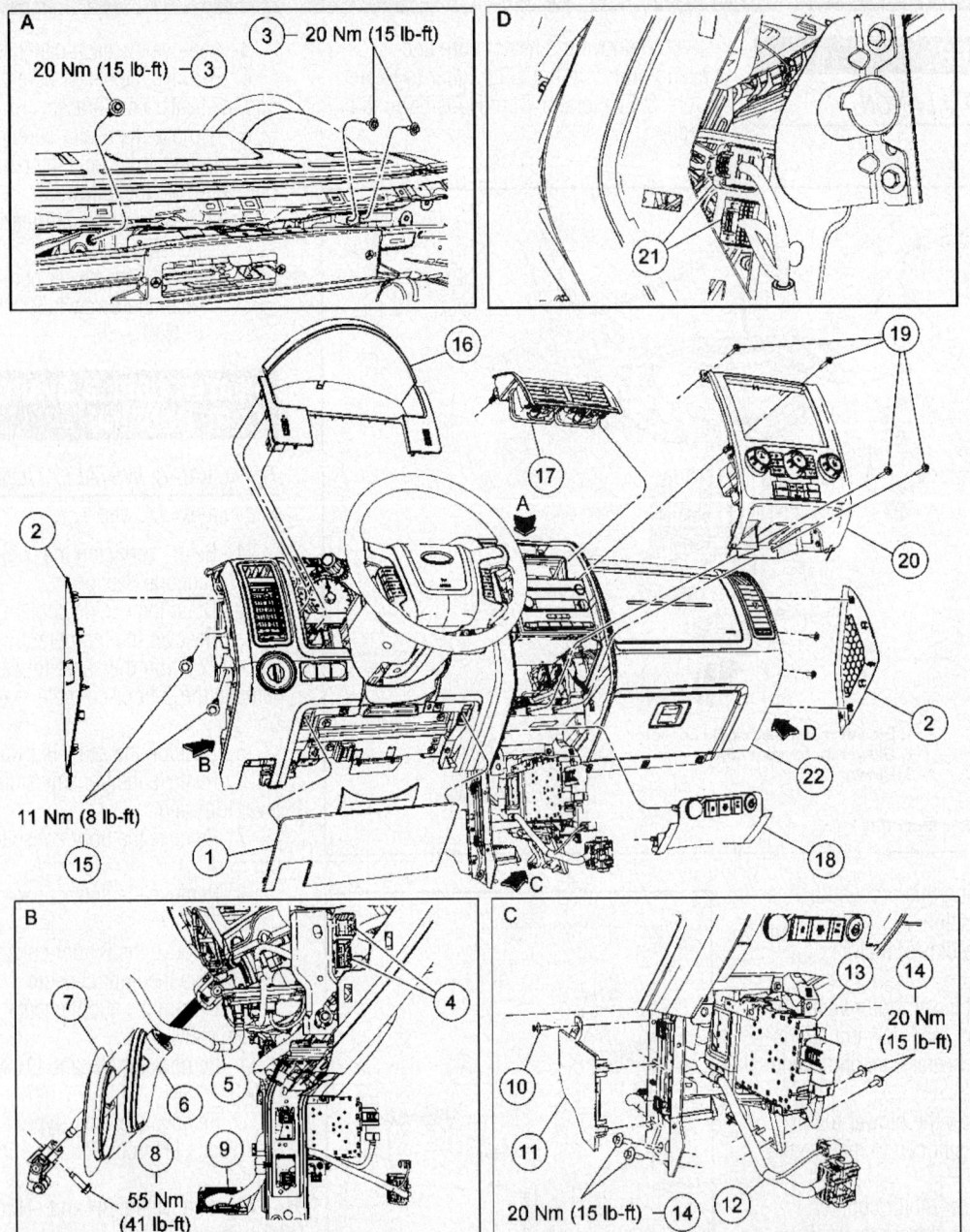

1. Steering column opening cover
2. Instrument panel side finish panel
3. Instrument panel upper cowl bolts
   (3 required)
4. LH side instrument panel electrical connectors
5. Steering module electrical connector
6. Steering column shaft access cover
7. Steering column shaft weather shield
8. Steering column intermediate
   shaft-to-coupling bolt
9. Restraints control module (RCM)
   electrical wiring harness
10. Scrivet
11. RCM access cover

12. Floor console electrical wiring harness
13. Smart junction box (SJB)
14. Instrument panel center
    brace bolts (4 required)
15. Instrument panel side bolts (4 required)
16. Instrument cluster finish panel
17. Upper instrument panel center finish panel
18. Lower instrument panel center finish panel
19. Middle instrument panel center finish
    panel screws (4 required)
20. Middle instrument panel center finish panel
21. RH side instrument panel electrical connectors
22. Instrument panel

Fig. 170 Instrument panel exploded view

22086_ESCA_G0049

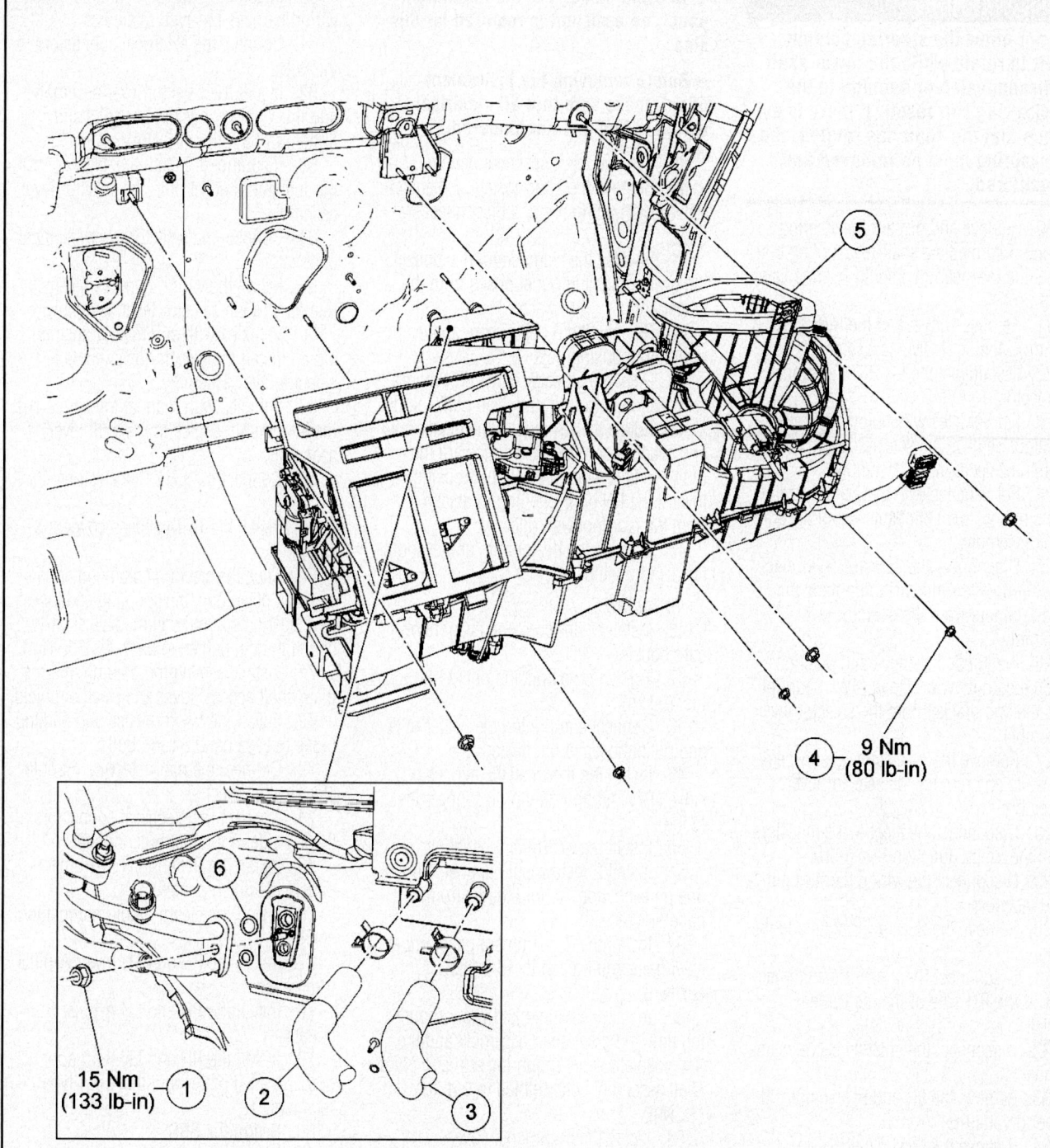

1. Thermostatic Expansion Valve (TXV) fitting nut
2. Heater core inlet hose
3. Heater core outlet hose
4. Heater core and evaporator core housing nut (6 required)
5. Heater core and evaporator core housing
6. TXV fitting gasket seal kit (2 pieces from kit required)

36578_ESCA_G0324

Fig. 171 Heater Core And Evaporator Core Housing

⁑ WARNING

Do not allow the steering column shaft to rotate while the lower shaft is disconnected or damage to the clockspring can result. If there is evidence that the shaft has rotated, the clockspring must be removed and re-centered.

20. Remove and discard the steering column intermediate shaft-to-coupling bolt and slide the steering column intermediate shaft up.

21. Remove scrivet and the Restraints Control Module (RCM) access cover.

22. Disconnect the LH RCM electrical connector.

23. For vehicles with automatic transmissions remove the selector lever cable from the selector lever assembly.

24. For vehicles with manual transmissions remove the shift cables from the shift lever assembly.

25. Disconnect the selector lever electrical connector and wiring harness pin-type retainers from the selector lever assembly.

26. If equipped, remove and position aside the Four Wheel Drive (4WD) control module and bracket from the selector lever assembly.

27. Remove the 4 selector lever assembly bolts and remove the selector lever assembly.

28. Disconnect the electrical connectors from the Smart Junction Box (SJB).

29. Disconnect the wiring harness pin-type retainers.

30. Remove the SJB lower bolts and the SJB.

31. Disconnect the 2 electrical connectors at the RH side of the instrument panel.

32. Disconnect the antenna cable in-line connector

33. Remove the LH and RH windshield wiper pivot arms.

34. Remove the cowl panel cover

35. Remove the 3 windshield wiper mounting arm and pivot shaft assembly bolts and position aside the windshield wiper mounting arm and pivot shaft assembly.

36. Remove the 3 instrument panel upper cowl bolts.

37. Remove the 4 instrument panel center brace bolts

38. Remove the 4 instrument panel side bolts.

➡ To avoid damage to the instrument panel, an assistant is required for this step.

➡ Before removing the instrument panel, make sure that all electrical wiring is free and not hindered

39. Remove the instrument panel.

40. Remove the Thermostatic Expansion Valve (TXV) fitting nut and disconnect the fitting.

41. Release the clamps and disconnect the heater inlet and outlet hoses from the heater core.

42. Remove the 6 heater core and evaporator core housing nuts.

43. Detach the heater core and evaporator core housing from the dash panel studs.

44. Rotate the RH side of the heater core and evaporator core housing toward the rear of the vehicle while pulling the housing toward the RH door opening to detach it from the rear foot well duct.

45. Remove the heater core and evaporator core housing

To install:

46. Install heater core and evaporator core housing.

47. Tighten core housing nuts to 80 inch lbs. (9 Nm).

48. Connect and tighten the heater inlet and outlet hoses to the heater core.

49. Install the thermostatic expansion valve (TXV) fitting nut and disconnect the fitting.

50. Install the instrument panel.

51. Install 2 instrument panel side bolts, one on each side, to hold the instrument panel in place.

52. Install the 3 instrument panel upper cowl bolts and tighten to 15 ft. lbs. (20 Nm).

53. Install the windshield wiper mounting arm and pivot shaft assembly and the 3 windshield wiper mounting arm and pivot shaft assembly bolts tighten to 9 ft. lbs. (12 Nm).

54. Install the cowl panel cover.

55. Install the LH and RH windshield wiper pivot arms.

56. Install the instrument panel side bolts and tighten to 8 ft. lbs. (11 Nm).

57. Install the instrument panel center brace bolts and tighten to 15 ft. lbs. (20 Nm).

58. Connect the antenna cable in-line connector.

59. Connect the electrical connectors at the RH side of the instrument panel

60. Install the SJB, bolts and connect the wiring harness pin-type retainers.

61. Connect the electrical connectors to the SJB.

62. Install the selector lever assembly and the 4 selector assembly bolts and tighten to 18 ft. lbs (25 Nm).

63. If equipped, install the 4WD control module and bracket onto the selector lever assembly.

64. Connect the selector lever electrical connector.

65. Install the wiring harness pin-type retainers to the selector lever assembly.

66. Vehicles with automatic transmissions, install the selector lever cable to the selector lever assembly.

67. Vehicles with manual transmissions, install the shift cables to the shift lever assembly.

68. Connect the LH RCM electrical connector

69. Install the RCM access cover and scrivet

70. Slide the steering column intermediate shaft down onto the coupling and install a new steering column intermediate shaft-to-coupling bolt, tighten to 42 ft. lbs. (55 Nm).

71. Install the steering column intermediate shaft access cover and weather shield.

72. Install the hood release and parking brake release handles and bolts.

73. Connect the main steering module electrical connector.

74. Connect the electrical connectors at the LH side of the instrument panel

75. Install the RH and LH instrument panel side finish panels

76. Install the steering column opening cover.

77. Install the RH and LH lower A-pillar trim panels.

78. Install the RH and LH A-pillar trim panels

79. Install the RH and LH front door opening scuff plates and the 4 pin-type retainers.

80. Rearm the SRS.

81. Install the 8 floor console bolts and the floor console.

82. Install the floor console finish panel.

83. Install the floor console storage bin.

84. Install the transmission selector lever trim ring.

85. Install and tighten the floor console rear bolts to 62 inch. lbs (7 Nm).

86. Evacuate, leak test and charge the refrigerant system.

87. Refill and bleed cooling system.

STEERING

MANUAL RACK & PINION STEERING GEAR

REMOVAL & INSTALLATION

See Figures 172 and 173.

➡ The rack and pinion steering gear that is used with the Electronic Power Assist Steering (EPAS) system is a manual (non-hydraulic) steering gear that is contained within a 1-piece die cast aluminum housing. The power assist is provided by a 12-volt, 65 amp brush-less motor, mounted to the steering column. The steering column and motor/module are serviced as an assembly.

1. Before servicing the vehicle, refer to the Precautions Section.
2. Remove the front wheels and tires.
3. Turn the ignition key to the OFF position. Remove the ignition key.

❋❋ WARNING

Do not allow the steering wheel to rotate while the intermediate shaft is disconnected or damage to the clock-spring can result. If there is evidence that the shaft has rotated, the clock-spring must be removed and re-centered

4. Remove and discard the steering column coupling-to-steering gear bolt and disconnect the coupling from the steering gear.
5. From the engine compartment, loosen the 2 steering gear bolts.
6. If equipped, remove the 3 pin-type retainers and the steering gear shield.
7. Remove and discard the 2 outer tie-rod end nuts.

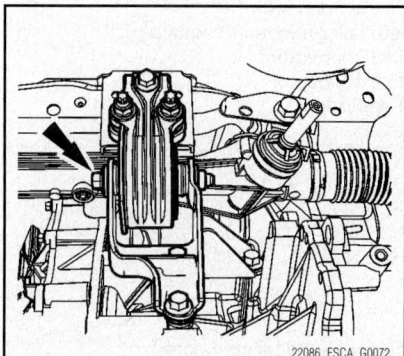

Fig. 172 Rear transaxle insulator and through bolt

8. Do not use a hammer to separate the tie-rod end from the wheel knuckle or damage to the wheel knuckle can result.
9. Using a suitable tool, separate the tie-rod ends from the wheel knuckles.
10. For AWD vehicles, remove the rear transaxle insulator through bolt.
11. For FWD vehicles with the 2.3L engine and an automatic transaxle, remove the 3 transmission damper bolts and the transmission damper.
12. Remove and discard the 2 steering gear bolts.

➡ **For All Wheel Drive (AWD) vehicles, it is necessary to grasp the driveshaft by hand and apply slight downward pressure to obtain clearance for the removal of the steering gear.**

13. Remove the steering gear from the LH side of the vehicle.

To install:
14. To install, reverse the removal procedure and note the following:

- Install a new steering column coupling-to-steering gear bolt and tighten to 41 ft. lbs. (55 Nm).
- Install and tighten the 2 steering gear bolts to 85 ft. lbs. (115 Nm).
- Install new outer tie-rod end nuts and tighten to 59 ft. lbs. (80 Nm).
- Tighten rear transaxle insulator through bolt to 66 ft. lbs. (90 Nm).
- Tighten transmission damper bolts to 30 ft. lbs. (40 Nm). (2.3L engines)
- Check and, if necessary, align the front end.

POWER STEERING PUMP

REMOVAL & INSTALLATION

The power assist is provided by a 12-volt, 65 amp brush-less motor, mounted to the steering column. The steering column and motor/module are serviced as an assembly. Refer to Steering Column Removal & Installation in this section.

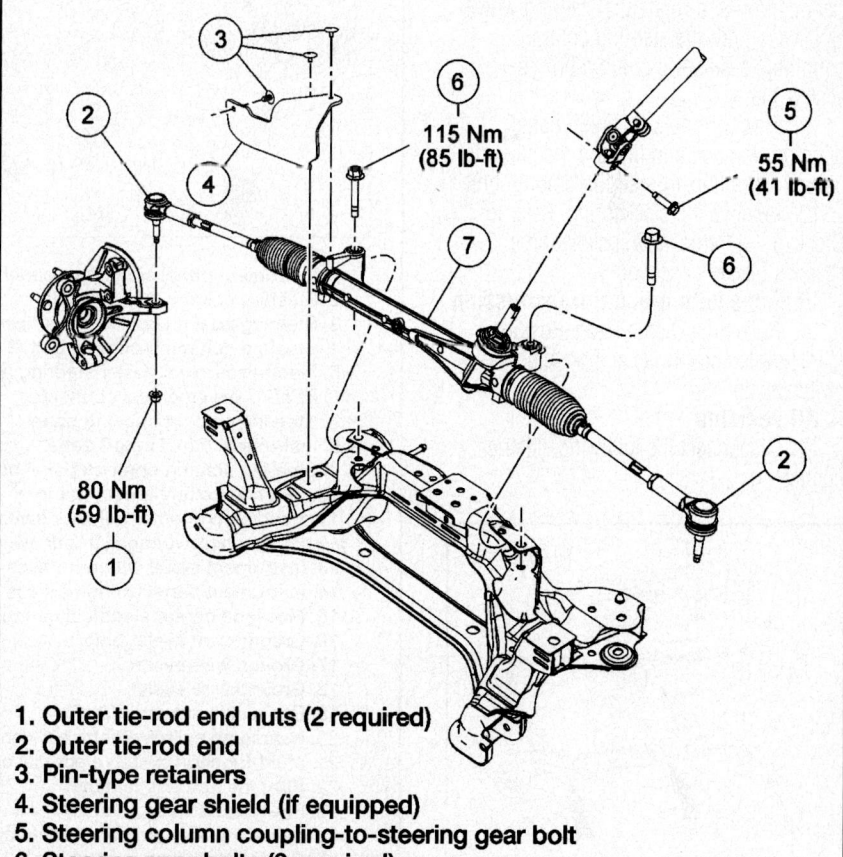

1. Outer tie-rod end nuts (2 required)
2. Outer tie-rod end
3. Pin-type retainers
4. Steering gear shield (if equipped)
5. Steering column coupling-to-steering gear bolt
6. Steering gear bolts (2 required)
7. Steering gear

Fig. 173 Steering gear exploded view—2008–09 models

STEERING COLUMN

REMOVAL & INSTALLATION

See Figures 174 and 175.

All vehicles

1. Before servicing the vehicle, refer to the Precautions Section.

2. Remove the steering column opening trim.

3. Using a suitable cutting tool, carefully cut through the 2 cutoff lines and discard the instrument panel cutoff panel.

4. Remove the 4 screws and the steering column opening panel.

5. Remove the LH instrument panel side finish panel.

6. Through the side finish panel opening, remove the ground wire eyelet bolt. Position the 2 ground wire eyelets and wires aside.

7. Through the side finish panel opening, disconnect the 2 instrument panel wiring harness electrical connectors and, if equipped, the battery high-voltage jumper switch electrical connector. Position the harnesses and connectors aside.

8. Turn the ignition switch to the ON position and rotate the steering wheel clockwise until the steering column coupling-to-steering column bolt is accessible.

9. Through the side finish panel opening, remove and discard the steering column coupling-to-steering column bolt.

10. Remove the clockspring. Refer to Clockspring Removal & Installation in the Chassis Electrical section.

Vehicles with manual transmission

11. Rotate the Clutch Pedal Position (CPP) switch clockwise and position the switch aside.

All vehicles

12. Disconnect the following electrical connectors:

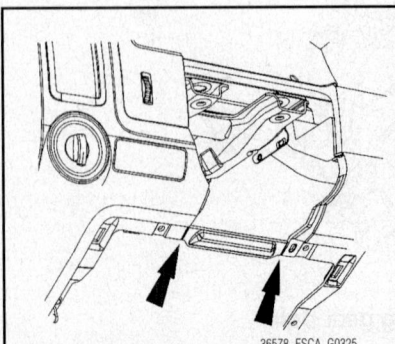

Fig. 174 Carefully cut through the 2 cutoff lines and discard the instrument panel cutoff panel.

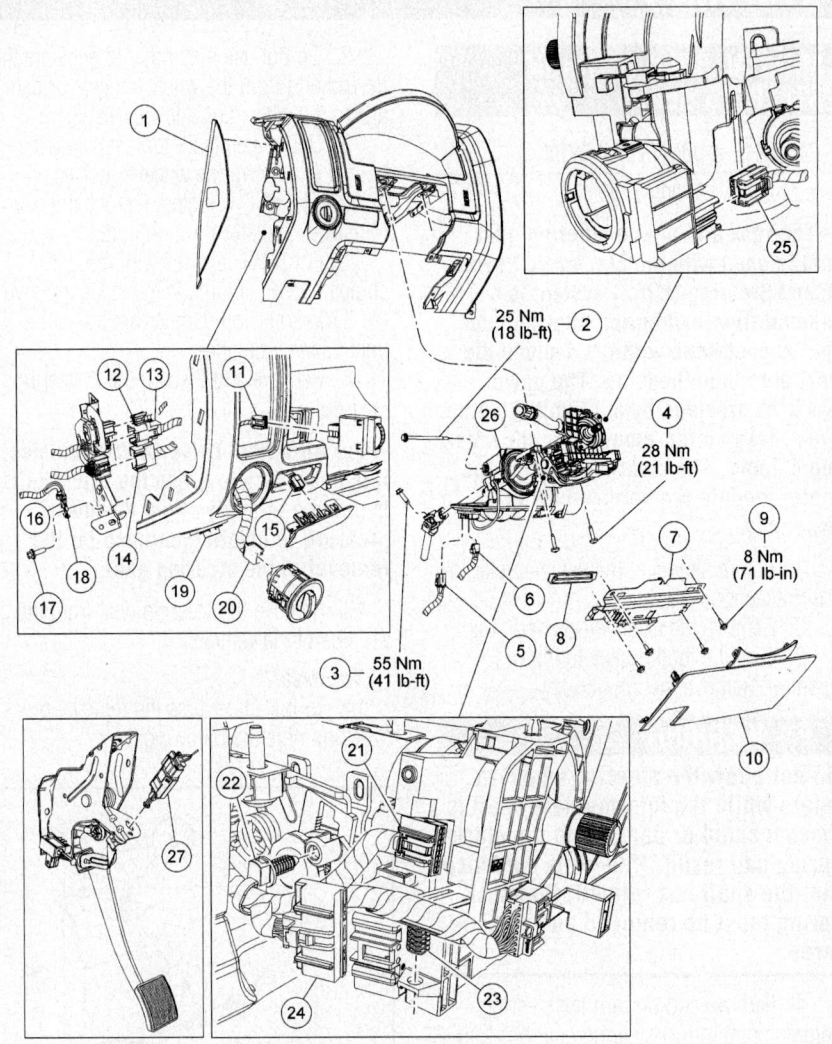

1. Instrument panel side finish panel
2. Steering column through bolt
3. Steering column coupling-to-steering column bolt
4. Steering column mounting bolt (2 required)
5. Electronic power assist steering (EPAS) 2-pin electrical connector
6. EPAS 6-pin electrical connector
7. Steering column opening panel
8. Instrument panel cutoff panel
9. Steering column opening panel bolt (4 required)
10. Steering column opening trim
11. Headlamp dimmer adjuster switch electrical connector
12. Battery high-voltage jumper switch electrical connector (if equipped)
13. Instrument panel wiring harness electrical connector
14. Instrument panel wiring harness electrical connector
15. Message center electrical connector (if equipped)
16. Ground wire eyelet bolt
17. Ground wire eyelet
18. Ground wire eyelet
19. Data link connector (DLC)
20. Headlamp switch electrical connector
21. Multi-function switch electrical connector
22. Pin-type harness retainer
23. Pin-type harness retainer
24. Ignition switch electrical connector
25. Passive anti-theft system (PATS) transceiver electrical connector
26. Steering column assembly
27. Clutch pedal position (CPP) switch

Fig. 175 Steering Column

- Multi-function switch
- Ignition switch
- Passive anti-theft system (PATS) transceiver (if equipped)
- Headlamp switch
- Headlamp dimmer adjuster
- Message center (if equipped)
- Electronic power assist steering (EPAS) 6-pin
- EPAS 2-pin

13. Detach the 2 electrical harness pin-type retainers from the steering column.

14. Detach the data link connector (DLC) from the DLC mounting bracket.

15. Position all electrical harnesses and connector's aside.

16. Detach the steering column coupling from the steering column.

17. Loosen the steering column through bolt. Do not remove the steering column through bolt at this time or damage to the steering column can occur.

18. Remove the 2 steering column mounting bolts. Support the upper end of the steering column while removing the 2 steering column mounting bolts or damage to the steering column can occur.

❊❊ WARNING

Do not release the tilting mechanism while lowering the steering column or damage to the steering column can occur.

19. Carefully lower the upper end of the steering column.

20. Remove the steering column through bolt and carefully remove the steering column through the steering column opening. Support the lower end of the steering column while removing the through bolt or damage to the steering column can occur.

❊❊ WARNING

Do not allow the steering column upper and lower halves to become separated. If the column halves become separated, make sure that the upper and lower column shaft master (larger) splines are correctly aligned. Once the splines are correctly aligned, the column halves will slide together easily using hands only. Do not force the upper and lower column halves together or damage to the column may occur.

21. To install, reverse the removal procedure and note the following:

- Tighten the steering column through bolt 18 ft. lbs. (25 Nm).
- Tighten the 2 steering column mounting bolts to 21 ft. lbs. (28 Nm).
- Tighten the steering column coupling-to-steering column bolt to 41 ft. lbs. (55 Nm).
- Tighten the steering column opening panel screws to (71 inch lbs. (8 Nm).

22. Reconfigure the EPAS module. For additional information refer to Programmable Module Installation.

Calibrate the steering wheel position sensor. For additional information, refer to Steering Wheel Position Sensor Calibration.

PROGRAMMABLE MODULE INSTALLATION (PMI) PROCEDURE

Programmable Module Installation (PMI) Using the Integrated Diagnostic System (IDS) When the Original Module is Available.

➡**Following module installation, some modules require a separate learning procedure be carried out. For adaptive learning and calibration instructions, refer to the specific module removal and installation procedures.**

1. Connect the IDS and identify the vehicle as normal.

2. From the Toolbox icon, select Module Programming and press the check mark.

3. Select Programmable Module Installation.

4. Select the module that is being replaced.

5. Follow the on-screen instructions, turn the ignition key to the OFF position, and press the check mark.

6. Install the new module and press the check mark.

7. Follow the on-screen instructions, turn the ignition key to the ON position, and press the check mark.

8. The IDS downloads the data into the new module and displays Module Configuration Complete.

9. Test module for correct operation Programmable Module Installation (PMI) Using the Integrated Diagnostic System (IDS) When the Original Module is NOT Available.

➡**Following module installation, some modules require a separate learning procedure be carried out. For adaptive learning and calibration instructions, refer to the specific module removal and installation procedures.**

10. Install the new module.

11. Connect the IDS and identify the vehicle as normal.

12. From the Toolbox icon, select Module Programming and press the check mark.

13. Select Programmable Module Installation.

14. Select the module that was replaced.

15. Follow the on-screen instructions, turn the ignition key to the OFF position, and press the check mark.

16. Follow the on-screen instructions, turn the ignition key to the ON position, and press the check mark.

17. If the data is not available, the IDS displays a screen stating to contact the As-Built Data Center. Retrieve the data from the technician service publication website at this time and press the check mark.

18. Enter the module data and press the check mark.

19. The IDS downloads the data into the new module and displays Module Configuration Complete.

20. Test module for correct operation.

STEERING WHEEL POSITION SENSOR CALIBRATION

1. Place the vehicle on a flat level surface with the transmission in PARK.

➡**Make sure that the steering wheel is turned from right to left before centering or sensor calibration will fail.**

2. Rotate the steering wheel from right to left, center the steering wheel and remove hands from the wheel.

3. Connect the scan tool to the vehicle.

4. Turn the ignition key to the RUN position.

5. Using the scan tool, select steering wheel position sensor calibration and follow the scan tool instructions.

6. Clear any PSCM DTCs.

➡**After turning the ignition key to the OFF position, wait at least 25 seconds before carrying out any procedures that require the battery to be disconnected or module memory loss may occur.**

7. Turn the ignition key to the OFF position.

8. Road test the vehicle. If the steering wheel is not in the straight ahead position while driving on a flat road surface, check and adjust the alignment as necessary.

SUSPENSION

LOWER BALL JOINT

REMOVAL & INSTALLATION

The lower ball joint is part of the lower control arm assembly.

LOWER CONTROL ARM

REMOVAL AND & INSTALLATION

See Figure 176.

➡️**Suspension fasteners are critical parts because they affect performance of vital components and systems and their failure may result in major service expense. New parts must be installed with the same part numbers or equivalent part, if replacement is necessary. Do not use a replacement part of lesser quality or substitute design. Torque values must be used as specified during reassembly to make sure correct retention of these parts.**

1. Before servicing the vehicle, refer to the Precautions Section.
2. Record the ride height.

➡️**For reference during the installation of the lower arm, measure the distance** between the center of the wheel hub and the lip of the fender with the weight of the vehicle resting on the wheel and tire assemblies.

3. Remove the wheel and tire.
4. Remove and discard the lower ball joint nut and bolt.
5. Separate the lower ball joint from the wheel knuckle.
6. Remove and discard the lower arm forward bolt.
7. Using a suitable jackstand, support the subframe.
8. Remove the lower arm rearward bolt and the lower arm.

To install:

9. Position the lower arm and loosely install the new front and rear lower arm bolts.
10. Remove the jackstand.
11. Position the wheel knuckle on the lower ball joint and install the new lower ball joint bolt and nut. Tighten to 46 ft. lbs. (63 Nm).
12. Position a floor jack under the lower ball joint and raise it until the previously recorded ride height is achieved.
13. Tighten the lower arm forward bolt to 85 ft. lbs. (115 Nm).

14. Tighten the lower arm rearward bolt to 110 ft. lbs. (150 Nm).
15. Check and, if necessary, align the front end.

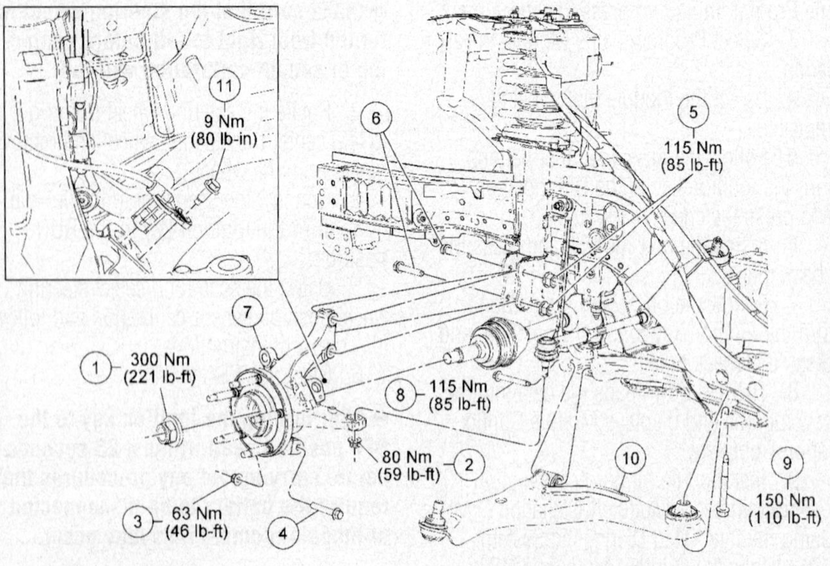

FRONT SUSPENSION

STABILIZER BAR

REMOVAL & INSTALLATION

See Figure 177.

➡️**Suspension fasteners are critical parts because they affect performance of vital components and systems and their failure may result in major service expense. New parts must be installed with the same part numbers or equivalent part, if replacement is necessary. Do not use a replacement part of lesser quality or substitute design. Torque values must be used as specified during reassembly to make sure correct retention of these parts.**

1. Before servicing the vehicle, refer to the Precautions Section.
2. Remove the stabilizer bar bushing bracket bolts.
3. Remove the tires.

➡️**Use the hex holding feature to prevent the ball stud from turning while removing or installing the stabilizer link nut.**

4. Remove the 2 lower stabilizer bar link nuts.

➡️**Access the stabilizer bar through the left wheel opening.**

5. Remove the stabilizer bar.
6. To install, reverse the removal procedure. Observe the following torques:
   - Link nuts: 46 ft. lbs. (63 Nm)
   - Bushing bracket bolts: 52 ft. lbs. (70 Nm)

➡️**When installing the stabilizer link to the stabilizer bar, make sure the stabilizer bar is perpendicular to the stabilizer link when tightening the link nut or the link nut may not seat properly.**

STABILIZER LINKS

REMOVAL & INSTALLATION

See Figure 177.

➡️**Suspension fasteners are critical parts because they affect performance of vital components and systems and their failure may result in major service expense. New parts must be installed with the same part numbers**

1. Wheel hub nut
2. Tie-rod end nut
3. Lower ball joint nut
4. Lower ball joint pinch bolt
5. Strut-to-knuckle nuts (2 required)
6. Strut-to-knuckle bolts (2 required)
7. Wheel knuckle
8. Lower arm forward bolt
9. Lower arm rearward bolt
10. Lower arm
11. Wheel speed sensor bolt

36578_ESCA_G0331

Fig. 176 Front suspension—exploded view

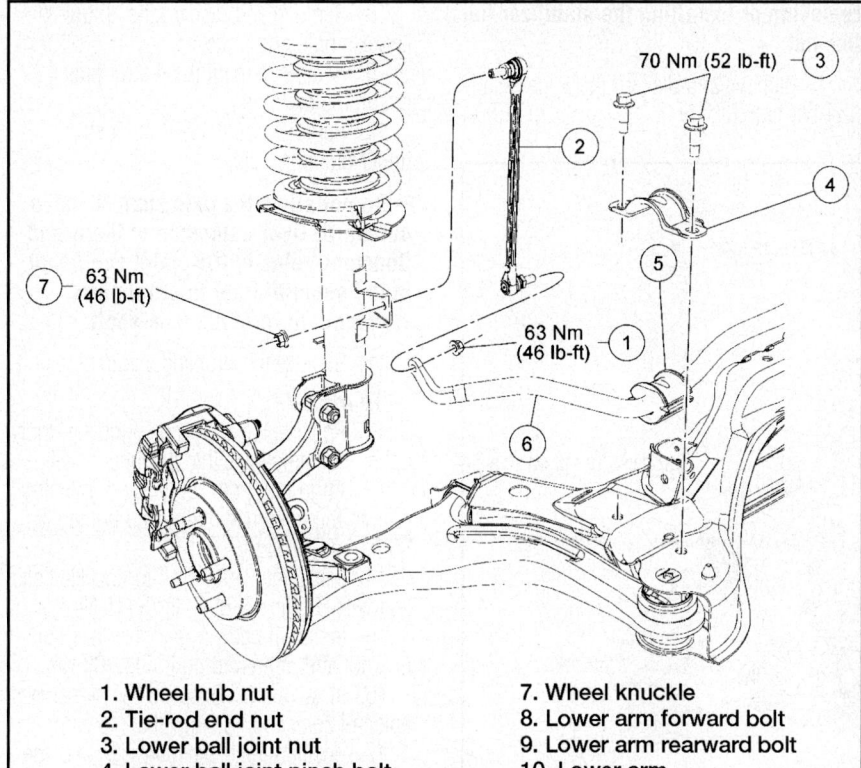

Fig. 177 Front suspension—exploded view

1. Wheel hub nut
2. Tie-rod end nut
3. Lower ball joint nut
4. Lower ball joint pinch bolt
5. Strut-to-knuckle nuts (2 required)
6. Strut-to-knuckle bolts (2 required)
7. Wheel knuckle
8. Lower arm forward bolt
9. Lower arm rearward bolt
10. Lower arm
11. Wheel speed sensor bolt

36578_ESCA_G0332

or equivalent part, if replacement is necessary. Do not use a replacement part of lesser quality or substitute design. Torque values must be used as specified during reassembly to make sure correct retention of these parts.

1. Before servicing the vehicle, refer to the Precautions Section.
2. Raise and support vehicle
3. Remove the wheel and tire.

➡Use the hex holding feature to prevent the ball stud from turning while removing or installing the stabilizer bar link nut.

4. Remove the upper stabilizer bar link nut.
5. Remove the lower stabilizer bar link nut.
6. Remove the stabilizer bar link.
7. Inspect the stabilizer bar link ball joints and boots for wear. If necessary, install new parts.

To install:
8. Install the stabilizer bar link.
9. Tighten the upper and lower stabilizer bar link nut to 46 ft. lbs. (63 Nm).
10. Install the wheel and tire.
11. Lower vehicle

STEERING KNUCKLE

REMOVAL & INSTALLATION
See Figure 178.

➡Suspension fasteners are critical parts because they affect performance of vital components and systems and their failure may result in major service expense. New parts must be installed with the same part numbers or equivalent part, if replacement is necessary. Do not use a replacement part of lesser quality or substitute

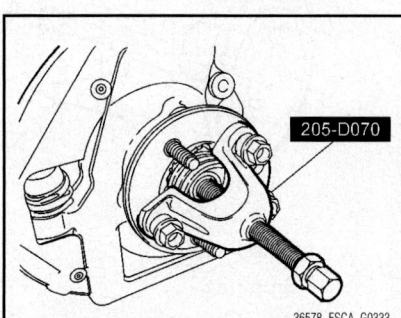

205-D070

36578_ESCA_G0333

Fig. 178 Using the front hub remover, separate the outer CV joint spindle from the wheel hub

design. Torque values must be used as specified during reassembly to make sure correct retention of these parts.

1. Before servicing the vehicle, refer to the Precautions Section.
2. Remove the brake disc.
3. Remove and discard the wheel hub nut.
4. Using the front hub remover, separate the outer CV joint spindle from the wheel hub.

✳✳ WARNING

Do not use a hammer to separate the tie-rod end from the wheel knuckle or damage to the wheel knuckle can result. Do not damage the tie-rod end boot while installing the special tool.

5. Separate the tie-rod from the wheel knuckle.
6. Remove the lower ball joint pinch bolt nut and the pinch bolt.
7. Remove the wheel speed sensor bolt and position the sensor aside.
8. Separate the lower ball joint from the wheel knuckle.
9. Remove the 2 strut-to-knuckle nuts, bolts and the wheel knuckle.

To install:
10. Position the wheel knuckle and install the 2 new strut-to-knuckle bolts and nuts. Tighten to 85 ft. lbs. (115 Nm).
11. Position and align the ball joint stud into the wheel knuckle.
12. Install the new lower ball joint bolt and nut, tighten to 46 ft. lbs. (63 Nm).
13. Install the wheel speed sensor and the bolt, tighten to 80 inch lbs. (9 Nm).
14. Position the tie-rod end into the wheel knuckle and install the new tie-rod end nut. Tighten the tie-rod end nut to 59 ft. lbs. (80 Nm).
15. Using the Halfshaft Installer, install the halfshaft into the wheel hub.
16. Install the brake disc.

➡Do not tighten the front wheel hub nut with the vehicle on the ground. The nut must be tightened to specification before the vehicle is lowered onto the wheels. Wheel bearing damage will occur if the wheel bearing is loaded with the weight of the vehicle applied.

17. Apply the brake to keep the halfshaft from rotating. Install the new front wheel hub nut and tighten to 221 ft. lbs. (300 Nm).
18. Check and, if necessary, align the front end.

STRUT

REMOVAL & INSTALLATION

See Figure 179.

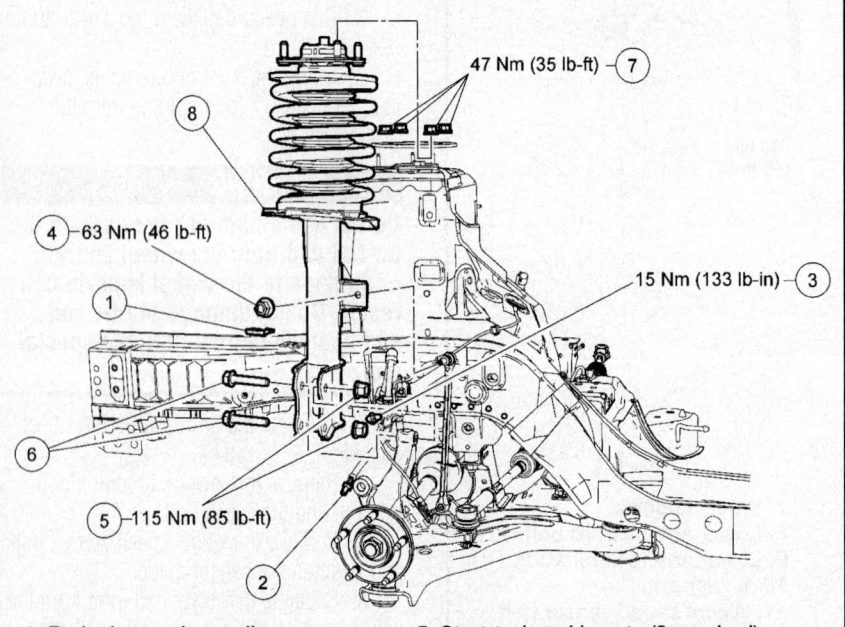

1. Brake jounce hose clip
2. Brake jounce hose (LH/RH)
3. Wheel speed sensor harness bolt
4. Upper stabilizer bar link nut
5. Strut-to-knuckle nuts (2 required)
6. Strut-to-knuckle bolts (2 required)
7. Strut upper bushing nuts (4 required)
8. Strut and spring assembly

36578_ESCA_G0334

Fig. 179 Strut and spring assembly

➡**Suspension fasteners are critical parts because they affect performance of vital components and systems and their failure may result in major service expense. New parts must be installed with the same part numbers or equivalent part, if replacement is necessary. Do not use a replacement part of lesser quality or substitute design. Torque values must be used as specified during reassembly to make sure correct retention of these parts.**

1. Before servicing the vehicle, refer to the Precautions Section.
2. Verify the steering wheel is in the unlocked position before removal.
3. Remove the wheel and tire.
4. Remove the brake jounce hose clip.
5. Pull the brake jounce hose downward slightly to remove the hose from the bracket and position the brake jounce hose aside.
6. Remove the wheel speed sensor harness bolt.

➡**Use the hex-holding feature to prevent the ball stud from turning while**

removing or installing the stabilizer bar link nut.

7. Remove and discard the upper stabilizer bar link nut.

8. Remove and discard the 2 strut-to-knuckle nuts and bolts.
9. Reference mark the 4 strut upper bushing plate nuts.
10. Remove and discard the 4 strut upper bushing nuts.

➡**Do not allow the axle shaft to move outboard. Over-extension of the tripod Constant Velocity (CV) joint can result in the separation of internal parts, causing failure of the axle shaft.**

11. Remove the strut and spring assembly.

To install:

12. Position the strut and spring assembly upper mounting plate into the inner fender.
13. Align the 4 new strut upper bushing nuts to the reference marks and tighten to 35 ft. lbs. (47 Nm).
14. Install the 2 new strut-to-knuckle bolts and nuts. Tighten to 85 ft. lbs. (115 Nm).
15. Install the new upper stabilizer bar link nut and tighten to 46 ft. lbs. (63 Nm).
16. Install the wheel speed sensor harness bolt and tighten to 133 inch lbs. (15 Nm).
17. Position the brake jounce hose to the bracket and install the brake jounce hose clip.
18. Check the front end alignment and adjust as necessary.

WHEEL HUB & BEARING

REMOVAL & INSTALLATION

See Figures 180 through 185.

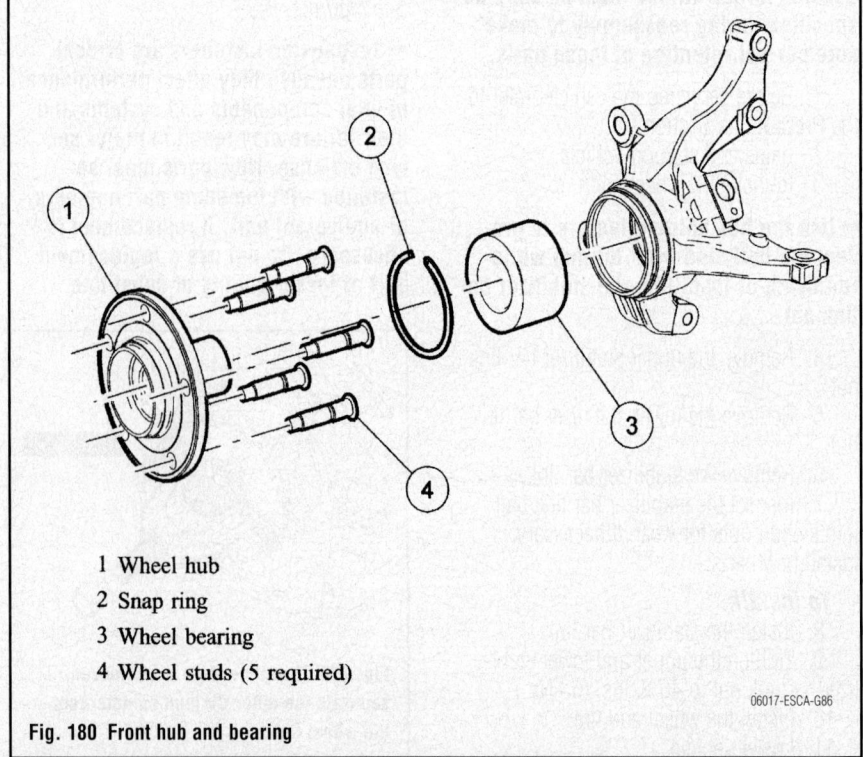

1 Wheel hub
2 Snap ring
3 Wheel bearing
4 Wheel studs (5 required)

06017-ESCA-G86

Fig. 180 Front hub and bearing

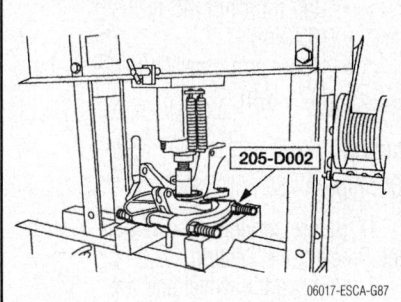

Fig. 181 Using the special tool, press the wheel hub from the wheel bearing—front hub/bearing

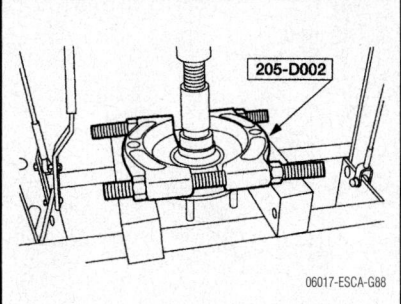

Fig. 182 Using the special tool, press the inner wheel bearing race from the wheel hub—front hub/bearing

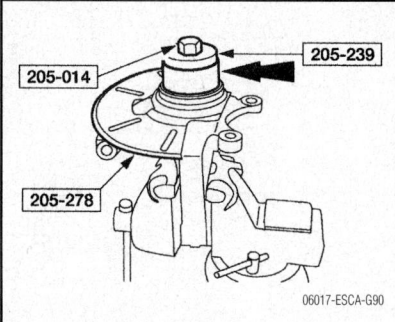

Fig. 184 Using the special tools, install the wheel bearing into the wheel knuckle—front hub/bearing

➡ If removing the wheel hub, a new wheel bearing must be installed.

1. Before servicing the vehicle, refer to the Precautions Section.

➡ If removing the wheel hub, the wheel bearing must be replaced.

2. Remove the wheel knuckle.
3. Using the special tool, press the wheel hub from the wheel bearing.

➡ This step may not be necessary if the inner wheel bearing race remains in the wheel knuckle after removing the wheel hub.

4. Using the special tool, press the inner wheel bearing race from the wheel hub.
5. Remove the snapring.
6. Using the special tools, press the outer wheel bearing race from the wheel knuckle.

To install:
7. Position the wheel knuckle in a vise.

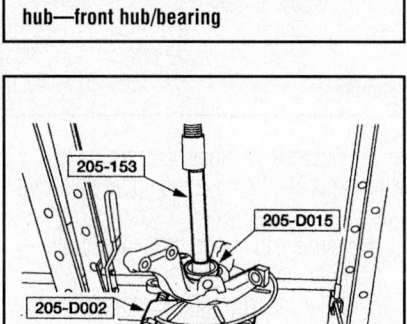

Fig. 183 Using the special tools, press the outer wheel bearing race from the wheel knuckle—front hub/bearing

➡ Special Tool 205-278 is not seen in place. It is located behind the wheel knuckle.

8. Using the special tools, install the wheel bearing into the wheel knuckle.
9. Install the snapring.
10. Using the special tool, press the wheel hub into the wheel bearing.

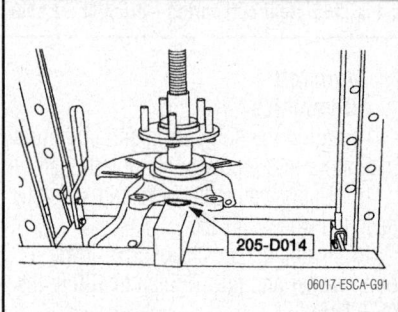

Fig. 185 Using the special tool, press the wheel hub into the wheel bearing—front hub/bearing

11. Install the wheel knuckle.

ADJUSTMENT

No adjustment is required or possible.
1. If the tire and wheel (hub) is loose on the spindle, does not rotate freely, or has a rough feeling when spun, install a new wheel bearing.

SUSPENSION

COIL SPRING

REMOVAL & INSTALLATION
See Figure 186.

✳✳ WARNING

Suspension fasteners are critical parts because they affect performance of vital components and systems and their failure may result in major service expense. New parts must be installed with the same part numbers or equivalent part, if replacement is necessary. Do not use a replacement part of lesser quality or substitute design. Torque values must be used as specified during

reassembly to make sure correct retention of these parts.

1. Before servicing the vehicle, refer to the Precautions Section.
All vehicles
2. Remove the wheel and tire assembly.
3. Remove the brake cable bracket bolt.
Drum brake vehicles
4. Disconnect the brake tube from the wheel cylinder and position the brake tube and bracket assembly aside.
Disc brake vehicles

➡ Do not allow the brake caliper to hang from the brake hose or damage to the hose can occur.

REAR SUSPENSION

5. Remove the 2 brake caliper guide bolts and position the brake caliper aside.
6. Support the caliper using mechanic's wire.
All vehicles
7. Using a suitable jackstand, support the wheel knuckle.
8. Remove the shock absorber lower nut, washer and bolt.
9. Remove the upper arm.
10. Loosen the lower arm inner bolt.
11. Note the position of the coil spring insulators and coil spring for installation.
12. Using the jackstand, carefully lower the wheel knuckle.
13. Remove the coil spring.

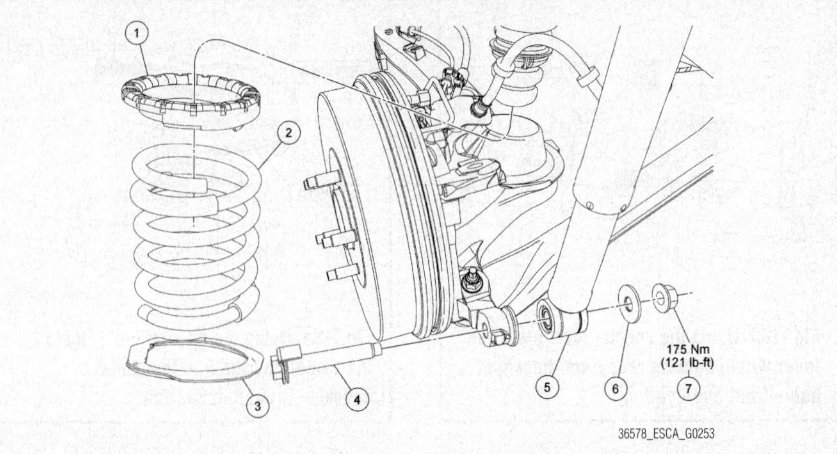

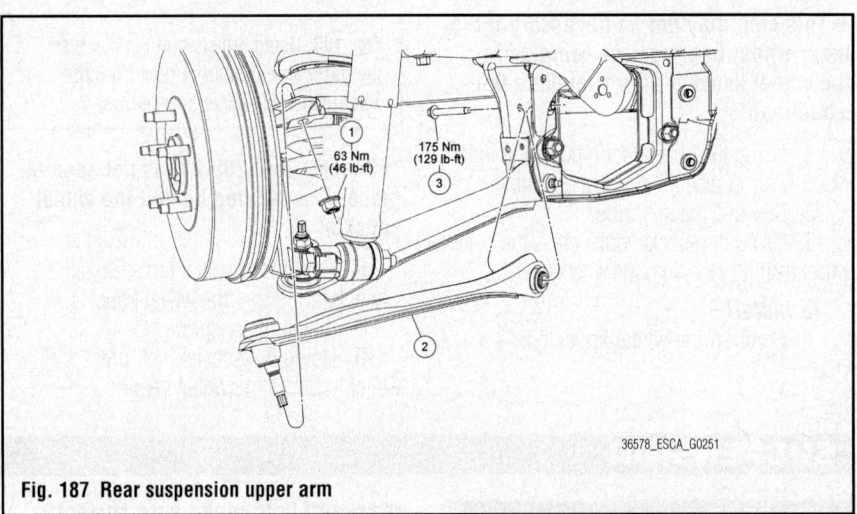

Fig. 186 Rear coil spring—drum brake shown disc similar

To install:
All vehicles
14. Align the coil spring and coil spring insulators to the previously noted position.

15. Using a suitable jackstand, carefully raise the wheel knuckle.

16. Install the shock absorber lower bolt, washer and nut. Tighten to 129 ft. lbs. (175 Nm).

17. Install the upper arm.
Drum brake vehicles
18. Connect the brake tube fitting to the wheel cylinder. Tighten to 150 inch lbs. (150 Nm).

19. Install the brake tube bracket bolt. Tighten to 16 ft. lbs. (22 Nm).

20. Install the brake cable bracket bolt. Tighten to 16 ft. lbs. (22 Nm).

21. Bleed the rear wheel cylinder.
Disc brake vehicles
22. Position the brake caliper and install the 2 caliper guide bolts. Tighten to 26 ft. lbs. (35 Nm).
All vehicles
23. Install the brake cable bracket bolt. Tighten to 16 ft. lbs. (22 Nm).
Drum brake vehicles
24. Bleed the rear wheel cylinder.
All vehicles
25. Install the wheel and tire assembly.

CONTROL ARMS/LINKS

REMOVAL & INSTALLATION

Upper
See Figure 187.

1. Before servicing the vehicle, refer to the Precautions Section.

2. Remove the wheel and tire.

➡**It may be necessary to hold the ball joint stud to keep it from turning while removing the nut.**

3. Separate the upper arm from the wheel knuckle. Remove the upper ball joint nut.

4. Remove the upper arm inner bolt.

5. Remove the upper arm.

6. To install, reverse the removal procedure and note the following:

- Ball joint nut: 46 ft. lbs. (63 Nm)
- Upper arm inner bolt: 129 ft. lbs. (175 Nm)

Lower
See Figure 188.

1. Before servicing the vehicle, refer to the Precautions Section.

2. Remove the wheel and tire.

3. Remove and discard the lower ball joint nut and separate the lower ball joint from the wheel knuckle.

➡**Tighten the lower arm inner bolt with the weight of the vehicle on the wheels and tires.**

4. Remove the lower arm inner bolt and the lower arm.

5. To install, reverse the removal procedure and note the following:
- Ball joint nut: 46 ft. lbs. (63 Nm)
- Lower arm inner bolt: 129 ft. lbs. (175 Nm)

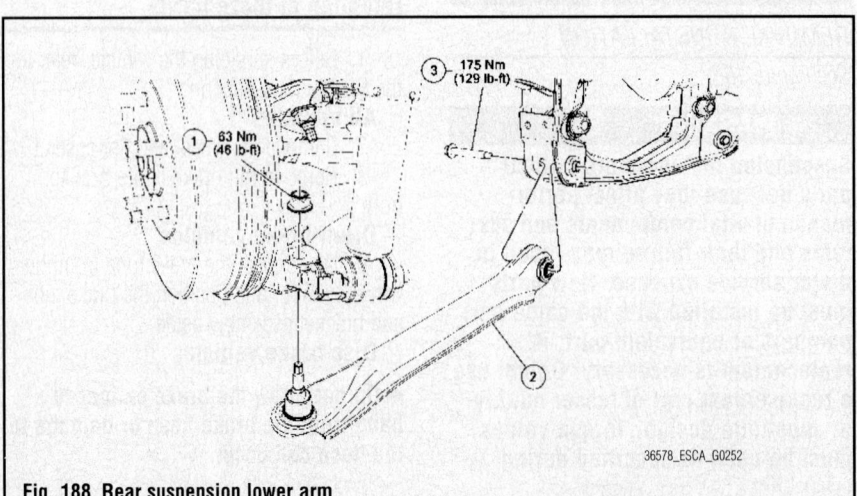

Fig. 187 Rear suspension upper arm

Fig. 188 Rear suspension lower arm

WHEEL KNUCKLE

REMOVAL & INSTALLATION

FWD Vehicles

See Figures 189 and 190.

✳✳ WARNING

Suspension fasteners are critical parts because they affect performance of vital components and systems and their failure may result in major service expense. New parts must be installed with the same part numbers or equivalent part, if replacement is necessary. Do not use a replacement part of lesser quality or substitute design. Torque values must be used as specified during reassembly to make sure correct retention of these parts.

1. Before servicing the vehicle, refer to the Precautions Section.

All vehicles

2. Remove the wheel and tire.

➡️**Apply the brake to keep the wheel hub from rotating.**

3. Remove and discard the wheel hub nut.

4. Remove the wheel speed sensor ring.

Vehicles with drum brakes

5. Remove the brake drum.

6. Using the Front Hub Remover or equivalent and the Impact Slide Hammer or equivalent, remove the wheel hub.

7. Remove the brake shoes.

8. Disconnect the brake tube fitting from the wheel cylinder and remove the brake flexible hose bracket bolt.

9. Remove the parking brake cable bracket bolt.

10. Unclip the wheel speed harness retainer from the parking brake cable and disconnect the cable from the brake backing plate.

Disc brake vehicles

11. Remove the parking brake shoes.

12. Release the parking brake cable end from the parking brake actuator lever and compress the cable conduit locking tabs.

13. Remove the brake flexible hose bracket bolt.

14. Using the Front Hub Remover and Impact Slide Hammer or equivalent tools, remove the wheel hub.

All vehicles

➡️**This step may not be necessary if the inner wheel bearing race remains in the wheel knuckle after removing the wheel hub.**

15. Using a suitable press and the Pinion Bearing Cone Remover or equivalent, press the inner bearing race from the wheel hub.

16. Remove the wheel speed sensor bolt and the 2 wheel speed sensor harness bolts.

17. Disconnect the wheel speed sensor from the wheel knuckle, and position the sensor and harness aside.

18. Remove the coil spring.

19. Remove and discard the lower ball joint nut.

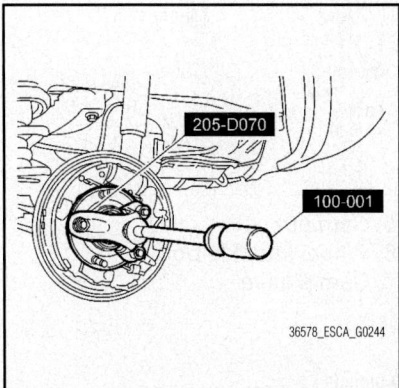

Fig. 189 Wheel hub removal shown

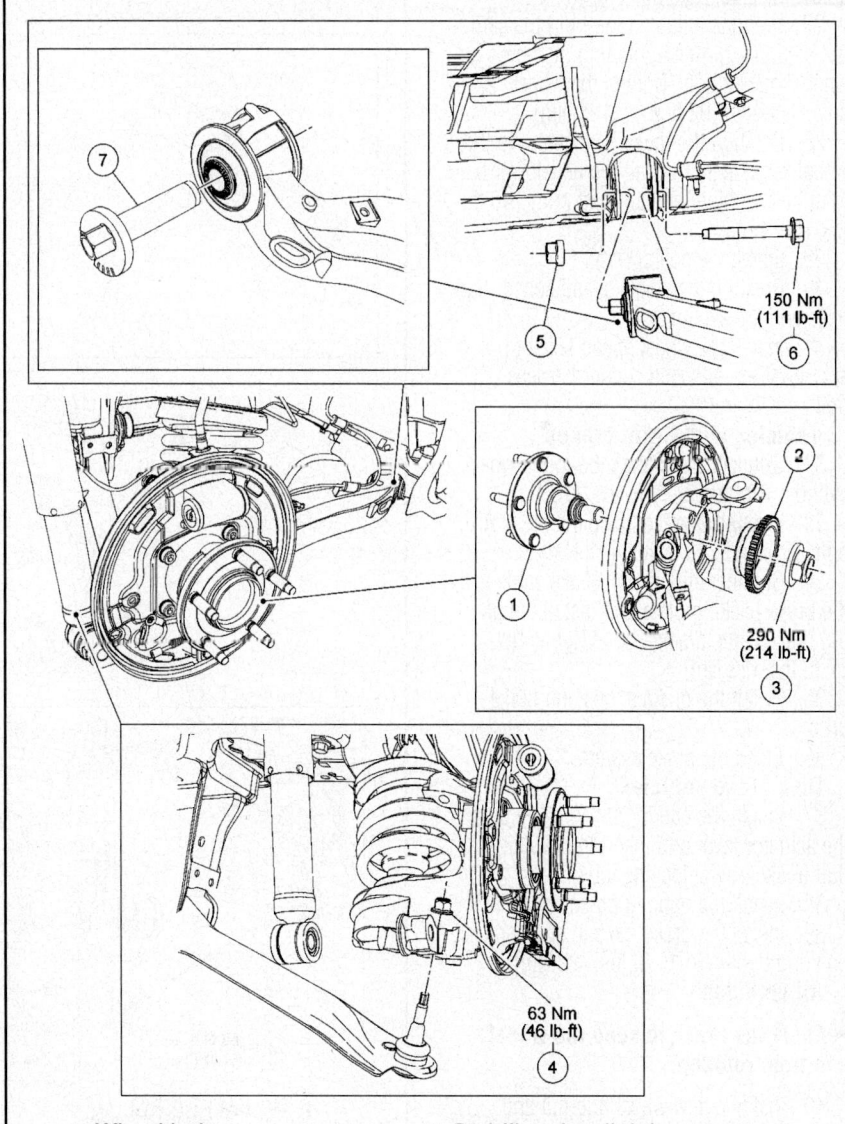

1. Wheel hub
2. Wheel speed sensor ring
3. Wheel hub nut
4. Lower ball joint nut
5. Stabilizer bar link lower nut
6. Cam nut
7. Wheel knuckle bolt
8. Cam sleeve

Fig. 190 Wheel knuckle —exploded view—FWD models

20. Index-mark the notch on the cam nut adjustment cam.

21. Remove and discard the wheel knuckle bolt and cam nut.

22. Remove the wheel knuckle.

23. Remove the wheel bearing.

To install:
All vehicles
24. Install the wheel bearing.

➤ **The joint area must be free of foreign material to make sure of correct clamping.**

25. Align the notch on the cam nut with the index marks.

26. Position the wheel knuckle and install a new wheel knuckle bolt and cam nut.

27. Using a suitable tool, hold the cam nut stationary while tightening the new wheel knuckle bolt. Tighten the wheel knuckle bolt to 92 ft. lbs. (125 Nm).

28. Position the lower ball joint into the wheel knuckle and install the new lower ball joint nut. Tighten the ball joint nut to 46 ft. lbs. (63 Nm).

29. Install the coil spring.

30. Position the wheel speed sensor harness and the sensor.

31. Install the wheel speed sensor bolt and the 2 wheel speed sensor harness bolts.

Vehicles with drum brakes
32. Connect the brake tube to the wheel cylinder. Tighten to 11 ft. lbs. (15 Nm).

33. Install the brake flexible hose bracket bolt. Tighten to 13 ft. lbs. (17 Nm).

34. Connect the parking brake cable to the brake backing plate and install the parking brake cable bracket bolt. Tighten to 17 ft. lbs. (23 Nm).

35. Install the brake shoes and brake drum.

36. Bleed the brake system.

Disc brake vehicles
37. Install the parking brake cable onto the actuator lever and insert the cable conduit to secure the locking tabs.

38. Install the parking brake shoes.

39. Install the brake flexible hose bracket bolt and tighten to 16 ft. lbs. (22 Nm).

All vehicles

➤ **Apply the brake to keep the wheel hub from rotating.**

40. Install a new wheel hub nut and tighten to 214 ft. lbs (290 Nm).

41. Check and, if necessary, align the rear end

AWD Vehicles
See Figures 189, 191.

✳✳ WARNING
Suspension fasteners are critical parts because they affect performance of vital components and systems and their failure may result in major service expense. New parts must be installed with the same part numbers or equivalent part, if replacement is necessary. Do not use a replacement part of lesser quality or substitute design. Torque values must be used as specified during reassembly to make sure correct retention of these parts.

1. Before servicing the vehicle, refer to the Precautions Section.
   All vehicles
2. Remove the wheel and tire.

➤ **Apply the brake to keep the halfshaft from rotating.**

3. Remove and discard the wheel hub nut.
   Vehicles with drum brakes
4. Remove the brake drum.

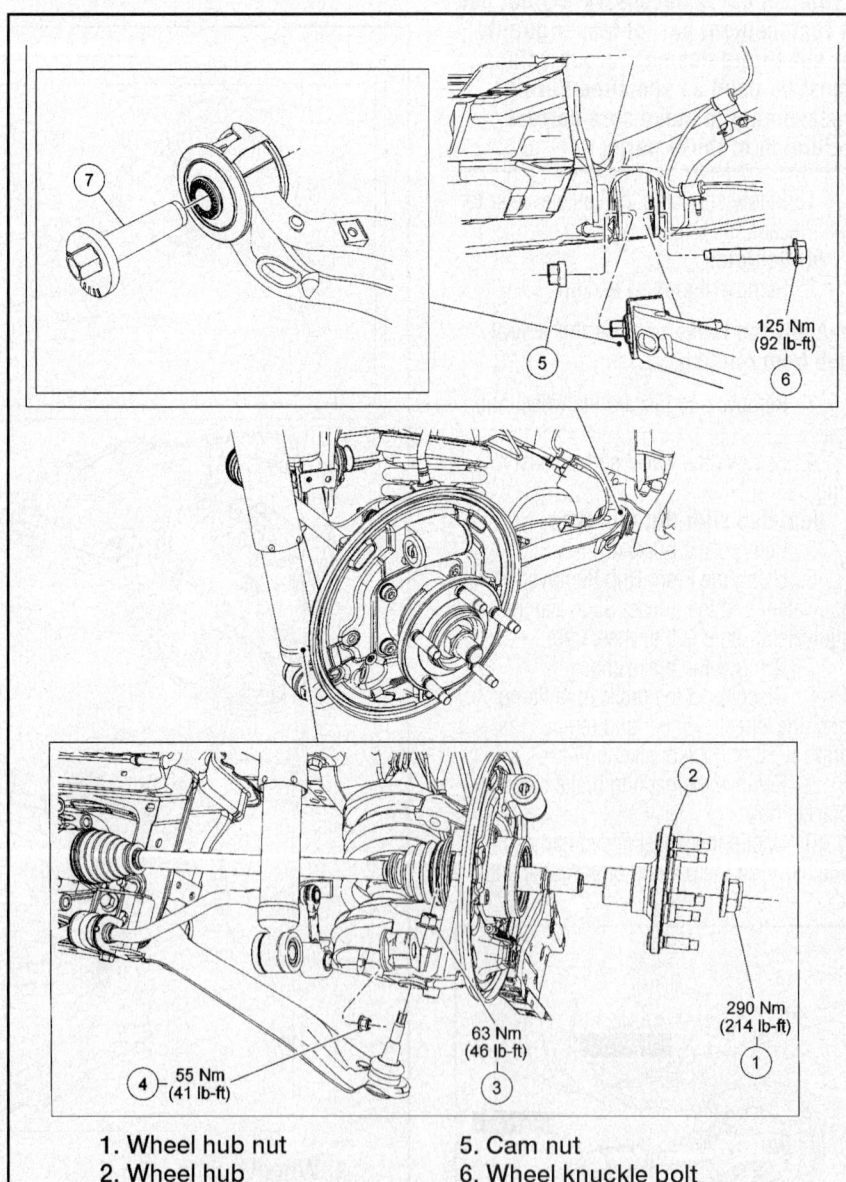

1. Wheel hub nut
2. Wheel hub
3. Lower ball joint nut
4. Stabilizer bar link lower nut
5. Cam nut
6. Wheel knuckle bolt
7. Cam sleeve

36578_ESCA_G0335

Fig. 191 Exploded view of the wheel knuckle—AWD models

5. Using the Front Hub Remover or equivalent, separate the CV joint from the wheel hub.

Using the Front Hub Remover or equivalent and the Impact Slide Hammer or equivalent, remove the wheel hub.

6. Remove the brake shoes.

7. Disconnect the brake tube fitting from the wheel cylinder and remove the brake flexible hose bracket bolt

8. Remove the parking brake cable bracket bolt.

9. Unclip the wheel speed harness retainer from the parking brake cable and disconnect the cable from the brake backing plate.

Vehicles with disc brakes

10. Remove the parking brake shoes.

11. Remove the parking brake cable bolt.

12. Release the parking brake cable end from the parking brake actuator lever and compress the cable conduit locking tabs.

13. Remove the flexible brake tube bracket bolt.

14. Using the Front Hub Remover equivalent, separate the outer CV joint from the wheel hub.

Using the Front Hub Remover or equivalent and Impact Slide Hammer or equivalent, remove the wheel hub.

All vehicles

15. This step may not be necessary if the inner wheel bearing race remains in the wheel knuckle after removing the wheel hub.

16. Using a suitable press and the Pinion Bearing Cone Remover or equivalent, press the inner bearing race from the wheel hub.

17. Remove the wheel speed sensor bolt and the 2 wheel speed sensor harness bolts.

18. Disconnect the wheel speed sensor from the wheel knuckle, and position the sensor and harness aside.

19. Remove the coil spring.

20. Remove and discard the lower ball joint nut.

21. Index-mark the notch on the cam nut adjustment cam.

22. Remove and discard the wheel knuckle bolt and cam nut.

23. Remove the wheel knuckle.

24. Remove the wheel bearing.

To install:
All vehicles

25. Install the wheel bearing.

➥**The joint area must be free of foreign material to make sure of correct clamping.**

26. Align the notch on the cam nut with the index marks.

27. Do not tighten the wheel knuckle bolt at this time.

28. Position the halfshaft into the wheel hub and install the wheel knuckle.

29. Hold the cam nut stationary and loosely install a new wheel knuckle bolt and cam nut.

30. Position the lower ball joint into the wheel knuckle and install the new lower ball joint nut. Tighten to 46 ft. lbs. (63 Nm).

31. Install the coil spring.

32. Position the wheel speed sensor harness and the sensor.

33. Install the wheel speed sensor bolt and the 2 wheel speed sensor harness bolts. Tighten the bolts to 80 inch lbs. (9 Nm).

Vehicles with drum brakes

34. Connect the brake tube fitting to the wheel cylinder and install the brake flexible hose bracket bolt.

35. Tighten the brake tube fitting to 11 ft. lbs. (15 Nm).

36. Tighten the brake flexible hose bracket bolt to 13 ft. lbs. (17 Nm).

37. Connect the parking brake cable to the brake backing plate and install the parking brake cable bracket bolt. Tighten to 17 ft. lbs. (23 Nm).

38. Install the brake shoes.

39. Bleed the brake system.

40. Using the Halfshaft Installer, install the halfshaft into the wheel hub.

Vehicles with disc brakes

41. Install the parking brake cable onto the actuator lever and insert the cable conduit to secure the locking tabs.

42. Install the brake tube bracket bolt and tighten to 16 ft. lbs. (22 Nm).

43. Install the parking brake cable bracket bolt and tighten to 17 ft. lbs. (23 Nm).

44. Install the parking brake shoes.

45. Using the Halfshaft Installer, install the halfshaft into the wheel hub.

All vehicles

➥**Apply the brake to keep the halfshaft from rotating.**

46. Install a new wheel hub nut and tighten to 214 ft. lbs. (290 Nm).

47. With the weight of the vehicle on the wheel and tire, tighten the wheel knuckle bolt to 92 ft. lbs. (125 Nm).

48. Check and, if necessary, align the rear end.

SHOCK ABSORBER

REMOVAL & INSTALLATION

See Figure 192.

1. Remove the wheel and tire assemblies.

2. Remove the rear quarter trim panel.

3. Remove the upper shock absorber nut, bushing and washer.

4. Remove the lower shock absorber nut, bolt and washer.

5. Remove the shock absorber and bushing.

6. To install, reverse the removal procedure.

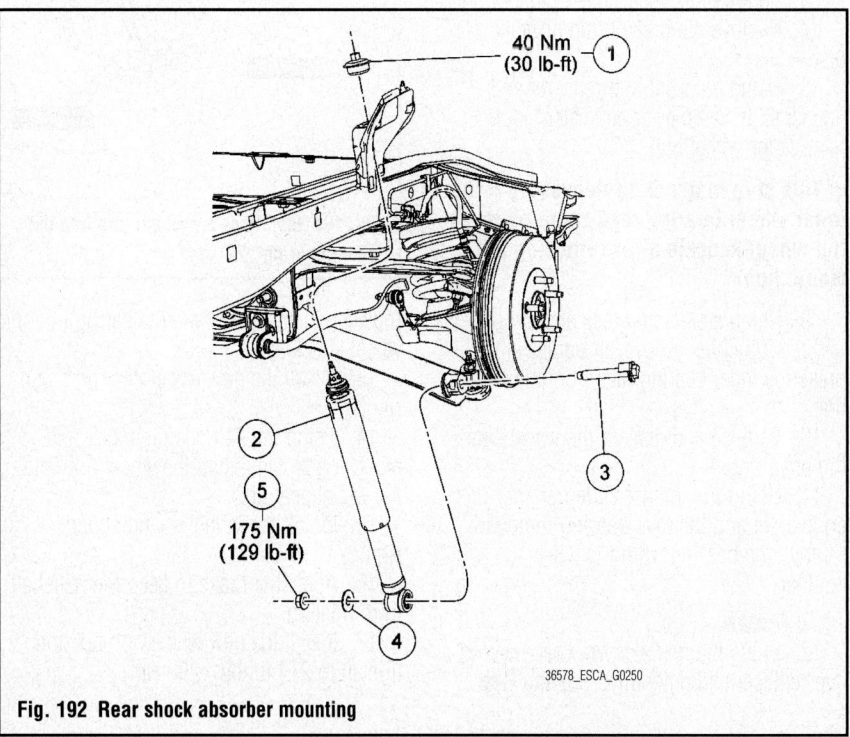

36578_ESCA_G0250

Fig. 192 Rear shock absorber mounting

7. Tighten the upper nut to 30 ft. lbs. (40 Nm)

8. Tighten the lower nut to 129 ft. lbs. (175 Nm).

WHEEL BEARINGS

REMOVAL & INSTALLATION

FWD Vehicles

See Figures 189, 193 through 195.

1. Before servicing the vehicle, refer to the Precautions Section.

✳✳ CAUTION

Suspension fasteners are critical parts because they affect performance of vital components and systems and their failure may result in major service expense. New parts must be installed with the same part numbers or equivalent part, if replacement is necessary. Do not use a replacement part of lesser quality or substitute design. Torque values must be used as specified during reassembly to make sure correct retention of these parts.

2. Safely raise the vehicle.

3. Remove the wheel and tire assembly.

4. Apply the brake to keep the halfshaft from rotating.

5. Remove and discard the wheel hub nut.

6. Remove the wheel speed sensor ring.

7. Remove the brake drum or brake disc.

8. Using the front hub remover and impact slide hammer or equivalent tools, remove the wheel hub.

➡ **This step may not be necessary if the inner wheel bearing race remains in the wheel knuckle after removing the wheel hub.**

9. Using a suitable press and the pinion bearing cone remover or equivalent, press the inner bearing race from the wheel hub.

10. Remove and discard the wheel bearing snap ring.

11. Using the impact slide hammer or equivalent and the axle bearing remover, remove the bearing from the wheel knuckle.

To install:

12. Using the rear axle drawbar, bearing cup replacer and differential Bearing Cup

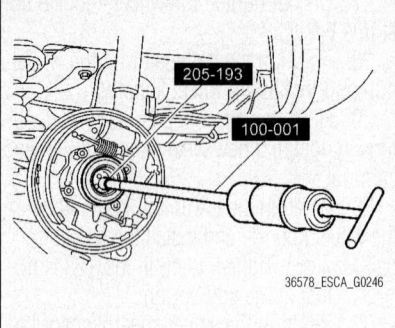

Fig. 193 Removing the bearing from the wheel knuckle

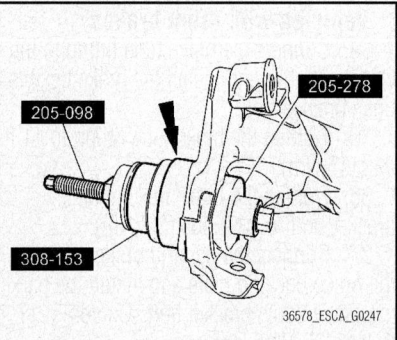

Fig. 194 Installing the wheel bearing into the rear knuckle

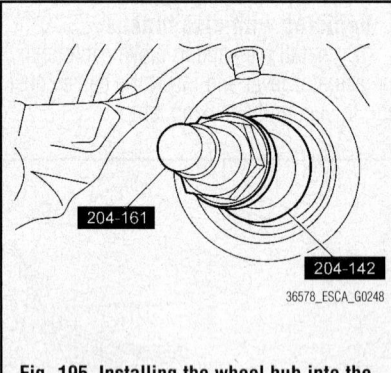

Fig. 195 Installing the wheel hub into the wheel bearing

replacer, install a new wheel bearing into the wheel knuckle.

13. Install the new wheel bearing snap ring.

14. Using the half shaft installer and receiver adapter, install the wheel hub into the wheel bearing.

15. Install the wheel speed sensor ring.

16. Apply the brake to keep the halfshaft from rotating.

17. Install the new wheel hub nut and tighten to 214 ft. lbs. (290 Nm).

18. Install the brake drum or disc.

19. Install the wheel and tire assembly.

AWD Vehicles

See Figure 196.

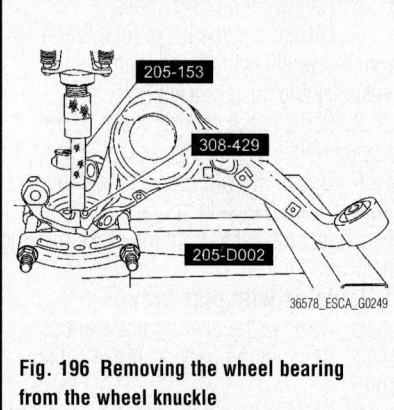

Fig. 196 Removing the wheel bearing from the wheel knuckle

1. Before servicing the vehicle, refer to the Precautions Section.

2. Safely raise the vehicle.

3. Remove the wheel and tire assembly.

4. Remove the wheel knuckle.

5. Remove the wheel bearing snap ring.

6. Remove the 4 bolts and the brake drum backing plate.

7. Position the wheel knuckle on a suitable press.

8. Using the PTO driven gear oil seal installer, the handle and the pinion bearing cone remover or equivalent, position the wheel knuckle on a suitable press and press the wheel bearing from the wheel knuckle.

To install:

9. Using the rear axle drawbar, bearing cup replacer and differential bearing cup replacer, install a new wheel bearing into the wheel knuckle.

10. Install the new wheel bearing snap ring.

11. Install the 4 bolts and the brake drum backing plate. Tighten to 63 ft. lbs. (85 Nm).

12. Using the Halfshaft Installer and Receiver Adapter, install the wheel hub into the wheel bearing.

13. Install the wheel knuckle.

14. Install the wheel and tire assembly.

15. Lower the vehicle.

16. Check and, if necessary, align the rear end.

ADJUSTMENT

The rear wheel bearings are of a sealed nature and do not require adjustment or repacking.

FORD AND LINCOLN

6

Expedition • Navigator

SPECIFICATIONS AND MAINTENANCE CHARTS

ENGINE AND VEHICLE IDENTIFICATION

Engine							Model Year	
Code ①	Liters (cc)	Cu. In.	Cyl.	Fuel Sys.	Type	Eng. Mfg.	Code ②	Year
5	5.4 (5409)	330	8	EFI	SOHC	Ford	8	2008
							9	2009

EFI: Electronic Fuel Injection

SOHC: Single Overhead Camshaft

① 8th digit of the Vehicle Identification Number (VIN)

② 10th digit of the Vehicle Identification Number (VIN)

36578_EXPD_C0001

GENERAL ENGINE SPECIFICATIONS

Year	Model	Engine Displacement Liters (VIN)	Net Horsepower @ rpm	Net Torque @ rpm (ft. lbs.)	Bore x Stroke (in.)	Com- pression Ratio	Oil Pressure @ rpm
2008	Expedition	5.4 (5)	300@5000	365@3750	3.55X4.17	9.8:1	75@2000
	Navigator	5.4 (5)	300@5000	365@3750	3.55X4.17	9.8:1	75@2000
2009	Expedition	5.4 (5)	300@5000	365@3750	3.55X4.17	9.8:1	75@2000
	Navigator	5.4 (5)	300@5000	365@3750	3.55X4.17	9.8:1	75@2000

36578_EXPD_C0002

GASOLINE ENGINE TUNE-UP SPECIFICATIONS

Year	Engine Displacement Liters	Engine ID/VIN	Spark Plug Gap (in.)	Ignition Timing (deg.) ①	Fuel Pump (psi) ①	Idle Speed (rpm)	Valve Clearance In.	Valve Clearance Ex.
2008	5.4	5	0.040-0.050	10B	28-45	②	HYD	HYD
2009	5.4	5	0.040-0.050	10B	62-69	②	HYD	HYD

NOTE: The Vehicle Emission Control Information label often reflects specification changes changes made during production. The label figures must be used if they differ from those in this chart.

HYD: Hydraulic

① With engine running

② Idle speed and timing are electronically controlled and cannot be adjusted

36578_EXPD_C0003

CAPACITIES

Year	Model	Engine Displacement Liters (VIN)	Engine Oil with Filter (qts.)	Transmission (pts.)	Transfer Case (pts.)	Drive Axle Front (pts.)	Drive Axle Rear (pts.)	Fuel Tank (gal.)	Cooling System (qts.)
2008	Expedition	5.4 (5)	7.0	①	3.5	3.6	②	28.0	③
	Navigator	5.4 (5)	7.0	①	3.5	3.6	②	28.0	③
2009	Expedition	5.4 (5)	7.0	④	3.5	3.6	②	28.0	③
	Navigator	5.4 (5)	7.0	④	3.5	3.6	②	28.0	③

NOTE: All capacities are approximate. Add fluid gradually and check to be sure a proper fluid level is obtained.

① With 4R70W: 28 pts.
With 4R100: 32.0 pts.
With E40D: 32.0 pts.
2005 Expedition with 4R70/75: 28 pts.
2005 Navigator : 32 pts.

② 8.8 inch covential axle: 4.0 pts.
9.75 inch covential axle: 4.5 pts.
8.8 inch limited slip axle: 3.75 pts.
9.75 inch limited slip axle: 4.25 pts.

③ Base radiator without aux rear heat: 19.4
Heavy duty radiator without aux rear heat: 19.4
Base radiator with aux rear heat: 20.7
Heavy duty radiator with aux rear heat: 20.9

④ With 4R75E: 28 pts
With ZF6HP26: 17 pts
With6R75: 21pts

36578_EXPD_C0004

FLUID SPECIFICATIONS

Year	Model	Engine Displacement Liters	Engine ID/VIN	Engine Oil	Auto. Trans.	Drive Axle	Power Steering Fluid	Brake Master Cylinder
2008	Expedition	5.4	5	5W-20	Mercon® LV	①	Mercon® V	DOT 3
	Navigator	5.4	5	5W-20	Mercon® LV	①	Mercon® V	DOT 3
2009	Expedition	5.4	5	5W-20	Mercon® LV	①	Mercon® V	DOT 3
	Navigator	5.4	5	5W-20	Mercon® LV	①	Mercon® V	DOT 3

DOT: Department Of Transportation
① Front: 80W-90
Rear: 75W-140 (Synthetic)
Add Additive Friction Modifier: XL-3 (4.5 oz)

36578_EXPD_C0011

VALVE SPECIFICATIONS

Year	Engine Displacement Liters (VIN)	Seat Angle (deg.)	Face Angle (deg.)	Spring Test Pressure (lbs. @ in.)	Spring Installed Height (in.)	Stem-to-Guide Clearance (in.) Intake	Stem-to-Guide Clearance (in.) Exhaust	Stem Diameter (in.) Intake	Stem Diameter (in.) Exhaust
2008	5.4 (5)	44.5-45.0	45.5	79@1.66	1.660	0.0010-0.0020	0.0030-0.0040	0.2350-0.2360	0.2340-0.2350
2009	5.4 (5)	44.5-45.0	45.5	79@1.66	1.660	0.0010-0.0020	0.0030-0.0040	0.2350-0.2360	0.2340-0.2350

36578_EXPD_C0005

CAMSHAFT AND BEARING SPECIFICATIONS CHART

All measurements are given in inches.

Year	Engine Displacement Liters (VIN)	Journal Dia.	Brg. Oil Clearance	Shaft End-play	Runout	Journal Bore	Lobe Height	
							Intake	Exhaust
2008	5.4 (5)	1.126-1.127	0.001-0.003	0.003-0.007	0.001	1.128-1.129-	0.2170	0.2170
2009	5.4 (5)	1.126-1.127	0.001-0.003	0.003-0.007	0.001	1.128-1.129-	0.2170	0.2170

36578_EXPD_C0006

CRANKSHAFT AND CONNECTING ROD SPECIFICATIONS

All measurements are given in inches.

Year	Engine Displacement Liters (VIN)	Crankshaft				Connecting Rod		
		Main Brg. Journal Dia.	Main Brg. Oil Clearance	Shaft End-play	Thrust on No.	Journal Diameter	Oil Clearance	Side Clearance
2008	5.4 (5)	2.6567-2.6576	NA	0.0030-0.0148	5	2.0885-2.0877	0.0010-0.0025	0.0187-0.0049
2009	5.4 (5)	2.6567-2.6576	NA	0.0030-0.0148	5	2.0885-2.0877	0.0010-0.0025	0.0187-0.0049

NA: Not Available

36578_EXPD_C0008

PISTON AND RING SPECIFICATIONS

All measurements are given in inches.

Year	Engine Displacement Liters (VIN)	Piston Clearance	Ring Gap			Ring Side Clearance		
			Top Compression	Bottom Compression	Oil Control	Top Compression	Bottom Compression	Oil Control
2008	5.4 (5)	0.0010-0.0018	0.006-0.012	0.0098-0.0197	0.0059-0.0256	0.0008-0.0031	0.0012-0.0028	NA
2009	5.4 (5)	0.0010-0.0018	0.006-0.012	0.0098-0.0197	0.0059-0.0256	0.0008-0.0031	0.0012-0.0028	NA

NA: Not Available

36578_EXPD_C0007

TORQUE SPECIFICATIONS
All readings in ft. lbs.

Engine Displacement Liters (VIN)	Cylinder Head Bolts	Main Bearing Bolts	Rod Bearing Bolts	Crankshaft Damper Bolts	Flywheel Bolts	Manifold Intake	Manifold Exhaust	Spark Plugs	Oil Pan Drain Plug
2008	5.4 (5)	①	②	③	④	59	⑤	18	25	10
2009	5.4 (5)	①	②	③	④	59	⑤	18	25	10

① Step 1: 30 ft. lbs.

  Step 2: Plus 90 degrees

  Step 3: Plus 90 degrees

② Vertical mounted bolts:

  Step 1: 30 ft. lbs.

  Step 2: Plus 90 degrees

  Side Bolts:

  Step 1: 22 ft. lbs.

  Step 2: plus 90 degrees

③ Step 1: 32 ft. lbs.

  Step 2: Plus 105 degrees

④ Step 1: 66 ft. lbs.

  Step 2: Loosen bolt

  Step 3: 37 ft. lbs.

  Step 4: Plus 90 degrees

⑤ Step 1: 18 inch lbs.

  Step 2: 18 ft. lbs.

36578_EXPD_C0009

WHEEL ALIGNMENT

Year	Model	Suspension Type	Caster Range (+/-Deg.)	Caster Preferred Setting (Deg.)	Camber Range (+/-Deg.)	Camber Preferred Setting (Deg.)	Toe-in (in.)
2008	Expedition	Coil spring	1.00	+5.3	0.75	-0.30	0.14+/-0.20
	Navigator	Air	1.00	+5.5	0.75	-0.60/-0.30	0.14+/-0.20
2009	Expedition	Coil spring	1.00	+4.3	0.75	-0.30	0.14+/-0.20
	Navigator	Air	1.00	+4.3	0.75	-0.30	0.14+/-0.20

36578_EXPD_C0010

TIRE, WHEEL AND BALL JOINT SPECIFICATIONS

Year	Model	OEM Tires Standard	OEM Tires Optional	Tire Pressures (psi) Front	Tire Pressures (psi) Rear	Wheel Size	Ball Joint Inspection	Lug Nut (ft. lbs.)
2008	Expedition							
	Eddie Bauer 4x2	P265/70R17	P255/70R18	35	35	8J/8.5J	0.030 in. ①	②
	Eddie Bauer 4x4	P265/70R17	P255/70R18	35	35	8J/8.5J	0.030 in. ①	②
	20" Tire Option	P275/55R20		35	35	8.5J	0.030 in. ①	②
	Eddie Bauer EL	P255/70R18	P275/55R20	35	35	8.5J	0.030 in. ①	②
	Limited	P255/70R18	P275/55R20	35	35	8.5J	0.030 in. ①	②
	Limited EL	P255/70R18	P275/55R20	35	35	8.5J	0.030 in. ①	②
	SSV	P265/70R17	—	35	35	8.5J	0.030 in. ①	②
	XLT	P265/70R17	P255/70R18	35	35	8.5J	0.030 in. ①	②
	Navigator	P255/70R18	—	35	35	8.5J	0.030 in. ①	②
	20" Tire Option	P275/55R20	—	35	35	8.5J	0.030 in. ①	②
2009	Expedition							
	Eddie Bauer 4x2	P265/70R17	P255/70R18	35	35	8J/8.5J	0.030 in. ①	②
	Eddie Bauer 4x4	P265/70R17	P255/70R18	35	35	8J/8.5J	0.030 in. ①	②
	20" Tire Option	P275/55R20		35	35	8.5J	0.030 in. ①	②
	Eddie Bauer EL	P255/70R18	P275/55R20	35	35	8.5J	0.030 in. ①	②
	Limited	P255/70R18	P275/55R20	35	35	8.5J	0.030 in. ①	②
	Limited EL	P255/70R18	P275/55R20	35	35	8.5J	0.030 in. ①	②
	SSV	P265/70R17	—	35	35	8.5J	0.030 in. ①	②
	XLT	P265/70R17	P255/70R18	35	35	8.5J	0.030 in. ①	②
	Navigator	P255/70R18	—	35	35	8.5J	0.030 in. ①	②
	20" Tire Option	P275/55R20	—	35	35	8.5J	0.030 in. ①	②

OEM: Original Equipment Manufacturer

PSI: Pounds Per Square Inch

STD: Standard

OPT: Optional

① Both upper and lower

② 12mm nuts 100 ft. lbs.

   14mm nuts 150 ft. lbs.

36578_EXPD_C0012

BRAKE SPECIFICATIONS

All measurements in inches unless noted

Year	Model		Brake Disc Original Thickness	Brake Disc Minimum Thickness	Brake Disc Maximum Runout	Brake Drum Diameter Original Inside Diameter	Brake Drum Diameter Max. Wear Limit	Brake Drum Diameter Max. Machine Diameter	Minimum Lining Thickness	Brake Caliper Bracket Bolts (ft. lbs.)	Brake Caliper Mounting Bolts (ft. lbs.)
2008	Expedition	F	1.023	0.106	0.0025	—	—	—	0.118	148	41
		R	0.700	0.074	0.0250	—	—	—	0.039	140	20
	Navigator	F	1.023	0.106	0.0025	—	—	—	0.118	148	41
		R	0.700	0.074	0.0250	—	—	—	0.039	140	20
2009	Expedition	F	1.023	0.106	0.0025	—	—	—	0.118	148	41
		R	0.700	0.075	0.0250	—	—	—	0.039	140	20
	Navigator	F	1.023	0.106	0.0025	—	—	—	0.118	148	41
		R	0.700	0.075	0.0250	—	—	—	0.039	140	20

NOTE: Due to changes made during production, refer to manufacturer's specifications if they differ from those in this chart

F: Front

R: Rear

36578_EXPD_C0013

SCHEDULED MAINTENANCE INTERVALS
FORD EXPEDITION & LINCOLN NAVIGATOR

TO BE SERVICED	TYPE OF SERVICE	VEHICLE MILEAGE INTERVAL (x1000)												
		5	10	15	20	25	30	35	40	45	50	55	60	65
Engine oil & filter	R	✓	✓	✓	✓	✓	✓	✓	✓	✓	✓	✓	✓	✓
Tires	Rotate	✓	✓	✓	✓	✓	✓	✓	✓	✓	✓	✓	✓	✓
Wheels	I ①	✓	✓	✓	✓	✓	✓	✓	✓	✓	✓	✓	✓	✓
Auto trans. fluid	I			✓			✓			✓			✓	
Brake pads/shoes	I			✓			✓			✓			✓	
Coolant hoses	S/I			✓			✓			✓			✓	
Steering linkage	I			✓			✓			✓			✓	
(Navigator) seat cushion filters (if equipped)	R						✓						✓	
Cabin air filter	R			✓			✓			✓			✓	
Ball joints (2wd)	L			✓			✓			✓			✓	
Exhaust system	I						✓						✓	
Engine air filter	R						✓						✓	
Fuel filter	R						✓						✓	
Auto trans fluid ②	R						✓						✓	
Front wheel bearings (2wd)	R	at 150,000 miles, if not previously done so												
Spark plugs	R	every 100,000 miles												
PCV valve	R	every 120,000 miles												
Spark plugs	R	every 100,000 miles												
PCV valve	R	every 120,000 miles												
Premium Gold coolant	R	every 5 years or 100,000 miles												
Auto trans fluid (all exc. 4R100)	R	every 150,000 miles												
Differential fluid	R	every 150,000 miles												
Transfer case fluid	R	every 150,000 miles												
Accessory drive belts	R	every 150,000 miles, if not previously done so												

R: Replace   S: Service   I: Inspect   L: Lubricate

① Inspect for end play and noise

② Change transmission fluid on 4R100 and Torqshift transmissions. Replace in-linr filters if equipped.

Special Operating Condition Requirements:

When towing a trailer or using a camper or car-top carrier:

Change engine oil and install a new oil filter every 4,800 km (3,000 miles), 3 months or 200 hours of engine operation (whichever occurs first).

Change transfer case fluid every 96,000 km (60,000 miles).

Change manual transmission fluid as required.

Inspect and lubricate U-joints as required.

During extensive idling and/or low speed driving for long distances, as in heavy commercial use such as delivery, taxi, patrol car or livery:

Change engine oil and install a new oil filter every 4,800 km (3,000 miles), 3 months or 200 hours of engine operation (whichever occurs first).

Lube front lower control arm and steering linkage ball joints with zerk fittings (if equipped) every 4,800 km (3,000 miles) or 3 months.

Inspect brake system and check battery electrolyte level (Patrol cars) every 8,000 km (5,000 miles).

Install a new fuel filter every 24,000 km (15,000 miles).

Change automatic transmission fluid, lubricate 4x2 wheel bearings, install new grease seals and adjust bearings every 48,000 km (30,000 miles). If equipped, change the in-line service installed transmission fluid filter.

Install new spark plugs and change transfer case fluid every 96,000 km (60,000 miles).

Install a new cabin air filter as required.

36578_EXPD_C0014

SCHEDULED MAINTENANCE INTERVALS
FORD EXPEDITION & LINCOLN NAVIGATOR
(Footnotes Continued)

When operating in dusty conditions such as unpaved or dusty roads:

Change engine oil and install a new oil filter every 4,800 km (3,000 miles) or 3 months.

Install a new fuel filter every 24,000 km (15,000 miles).

Change automatic transmission fluid every 48,000 km (30,000 miles). If equipped, change the in-line service installed transmission fluid filter.

Change transfer case fluid every 96,000 km (60,000 miles).

Install a new engine air filter as required.

Install a new cabin air filter as required.

When operating in off-road conditions:

Change automatic transmission fluid every 48,000 km (30,000 miles). If equipped, change the in-line service installed transmission fluid filter.

Change transfer case fluid every 96,000 km (60,000 miles).

Install a new cabin air filter as required.

Inspect and lubricate U-joints.

Inspect and lubricate steering linkage ball joints with zerk fittings.

36578_EXPD_C0015

PRECAUTIONS

Before servicing any vehicle, please be sure to read all of the following precautions, which deal with personal safety, prevention of component damage, and important points to take into consideration when servicing a motor vehicle:

• Never open, service or drain the radiator or cooling system when the engine is hot; serious burns can occur from the steam and hot coolant.

• Observe all applicable safety precautions when working around fuel. Whenever servicing the fuel system, always work in a well-ventilated area. Do not allow fuel spray or vapors to come in contact with a spark, open flame, or excessive heat (a hot drop light, for example). Keep a dry chemical fire extinguisher near the work area. Always keep fuel in a container specifically designed for fuel storage; also, always properly seal fuel containers to avoid the possibility of fire or explosion. Refer to the additional fuel system precautions later in this section.

• Fuel injection systems often remain pressurized, even after the engine has been turned **OFF**. The fuel system pressure must be relieved before disconnecting any fuel lines. Failure to do so may result in fire and/or personal injury.

• Brake fluid often contains polyglycol ethers and polyglycols. Avoid contact with the eyes and wash your hands thoroughly after handling brake fluid. If you do get brake fluid in your eyes, flush your eyes with clean, running water for 15 minutes. If eye irritation persists, or if you have taken brake fluid internally, IMMEDIATELY seek medical assistance.

• The EPA warns that prolonged contact with used engine oil may cause a number of skin disorders, including cancer. You should make every effort to minimize your exposure to used engine oil. Protective gloves should be worn when changing oil. Wash your hands and any other exposed skin areas as soon as possible after exposure to used engine oil. Soap and water, or waterless hand cleaner should be used.

• All new vehicles are now equipped with an air bag system, often referred to as a Supplemental Restraint System (SRS) or Supplemental Inflatable Restraint (SIR) system. The system must be disabled before performing service on or around system components, steering column, instrument panel components, wiring and sensors. Failure to follow safety and disabling procedures could result in accidental air bag deployment, possible personal injury and unnecessary system repairs.

• Always wear safety goggles when working with, or around, the air bag system. When carrying a non-deployed air bag, be sure the bag and trim cover are pointed away from your body. When placing a non-deployed air bag on a work surface, always face the bag and trim cover upward, away from the surface. This will reduce the motion of the module if it is accidentally deployed. Refer to the additional air bag system precautions later in this section.

• Clean, high quality brake fluid from a sealed container is essential to the safe and proper operation of the brake system. You should always buy the correct type of brake fluid for your vehicle. If the brake fluid becomes contaminated, completely flush the system with new fluid. Never reuse any brake fluid. Any brake fluid that is removed from the system should be discarded. Also, do not allow any brake fluid to come in contact with a painted surface; it will damage the paint.

• Never operate the engine without the proper amount and type of engine oil; doing so WILL result in severe engine damage.

• Timing belt maintenance is extremely important. Many models utilize an interference-type, non-freewheeling engine. If the timing belt breaks, the valves in the cylinder head may strike the pistons, causing potentially serious (also time-consuming and expensive) engine damage. Refer to the maintenance interval charts for the recommended replacement interval for the timing belt, and to the timing belt section for belt replacement and inspection.

• Disconnecting the negative battery cable on some vehicles may interfere with the functions of the on-board computer system(s) and may require the computer to undergo a relearning process once the negative battery cable is reconnected.

• When servicing drum brakes, only disassemble and assemble one side at a time, leaving the remaining side intact for reference.

• Only an MVAC-trained, EPA-certified automotive technician should service the air conditioning system or its components.

BRAKES

GENERAL INFORMATION

PRECAUTIONS

• Certain components within the ABS system are not intended to be serviced or repaired individually.

• Do not use rubber hoses or other parts not specifically specified for and ABS system. When using repair kits, replace all parts included in the kit. Partial or incorrect repair may lead to functional problems and require the replacement of components.

• Lubricate rubber parts with clean, fresh brake fluid to ease assembly. Do not use shop air to clean parts; damage to rubber components may result.

• Use only DOT 3 brake fluid from an unopened container.

• If any hydraulic component or line is removed or replaced, it may be necessary to bleed the entire system.

• A clean repair area is essential. Always clean the reservoir and cap thoroughly before removing the cap. The slightest amount of dirt in the fluid may plug an orifice and impair the system function. Perform repairs after components have been thoroughly cleaned; use only denatured alcohol to clean components. Do not allow ABS components to come into contact with any substance containing mineral oil; this includes used shop rags.

• The Anti-Lock control unit is a microprocessor similar to other computer units in the vehicle. Ensure that the ignition switch is **OFF** before removing or installing controller harnesses. Avoid static electricity discharge at or near the controller.

• If any arc welding is to be done on the vehicle, the control unit should be unplugged before welding operations begin.

ANTI-LOCK BRAKE SYSTEM (ABS)

WHEEL SPEED SENSORS

REMOVAL & INSTALLATION

Front Speed Sensor

See Figures 1 and 2.

1. Before servicing the vehicle, refer to the precautions section.

➡**If equipped, turn the air suspension switch to the OFF position.**

2. With the vehicle in NEUTRAL, position it on a hoist

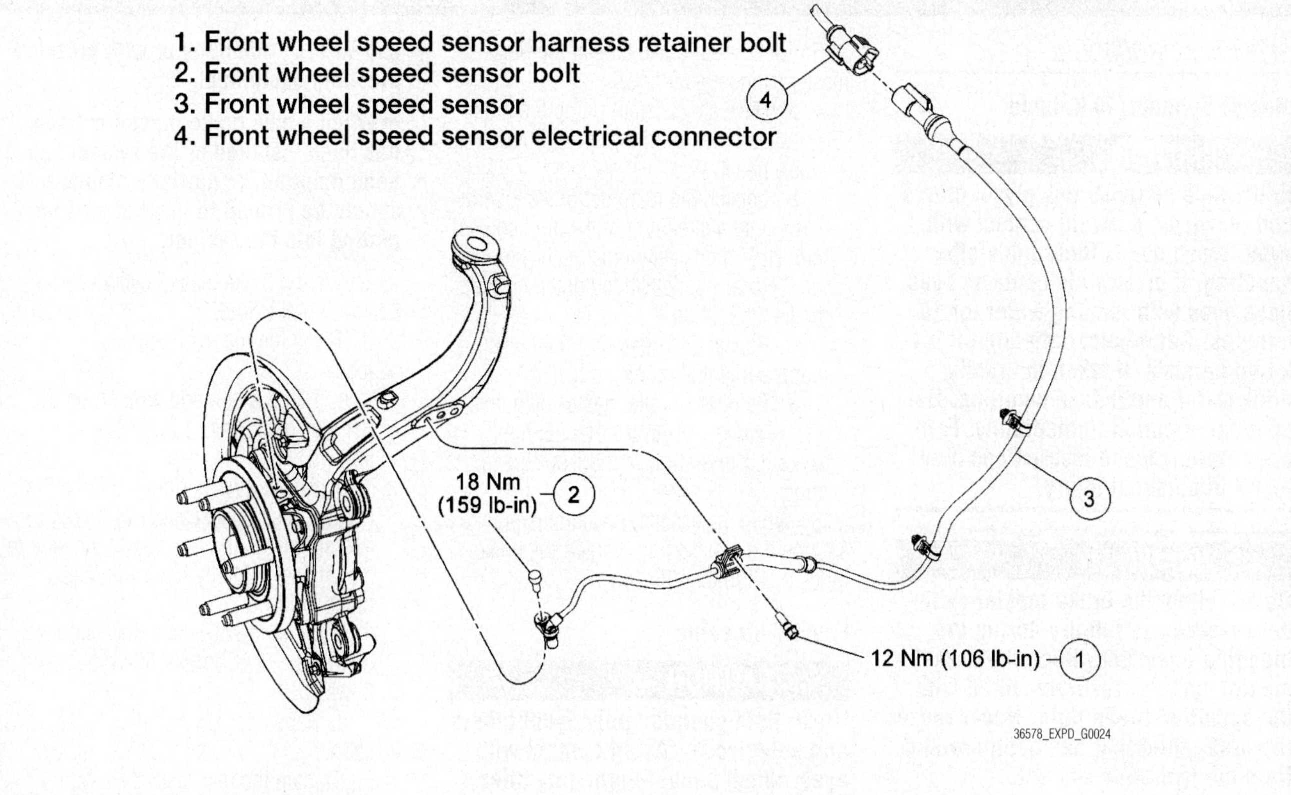

1. Front wheel speed sensor harness retainer bolt
2. Front wheel speed sensor bolt
3. Front wheel speed sensor
4. Front wheel speed sensor electrical connector

18 Nm
(159 lb-in)

12 Nm (106 lb-in)

36578_EXPD_G0024

Fig. 1 View of the front wheel speed sensor

3. Disconnect the wheel speed sensor electrical connector.

4. Remove the wheel speed sensor harness retainer bolt and the retainers.

☼☼ WARNING

Do not allow the caliper to hang from the brake hose or damage to the hose can result.

5. Remove the bolts and position the caliper, pads and anchor plate aside.

6. Remove the brake disc.

7. Remove the bolt and the front wheel speed sensor.

8. Installation is the reverse of the removal procedure. Please note the following tightening specifications:

  a. Front wheel speed sensor bolt: 13 ft. lbs. (18 Nm)

  b. Caliper anchor plate mounting bolts: 148 ft. lbs. (200 Nm)

  c. Wheel speed sensor harness retainer: 9 ft. lbs. (12 Nm)

Rear speed sensor

See Figure 2.

1. Before servicing the vehicle, refer to the precautions section.

2. Remove the parking brake shoes, as outlined in this section.

3. Disconnect the wheel speed sensor wire from the retaining clips.

4. Remove the bolt and the rear wheel speed sensor.

5. Installation is the reverse of the removal procedure. Tighten the rear wheel speed sensor retaining bolt to 13 ft. lbs. (18 Nm).

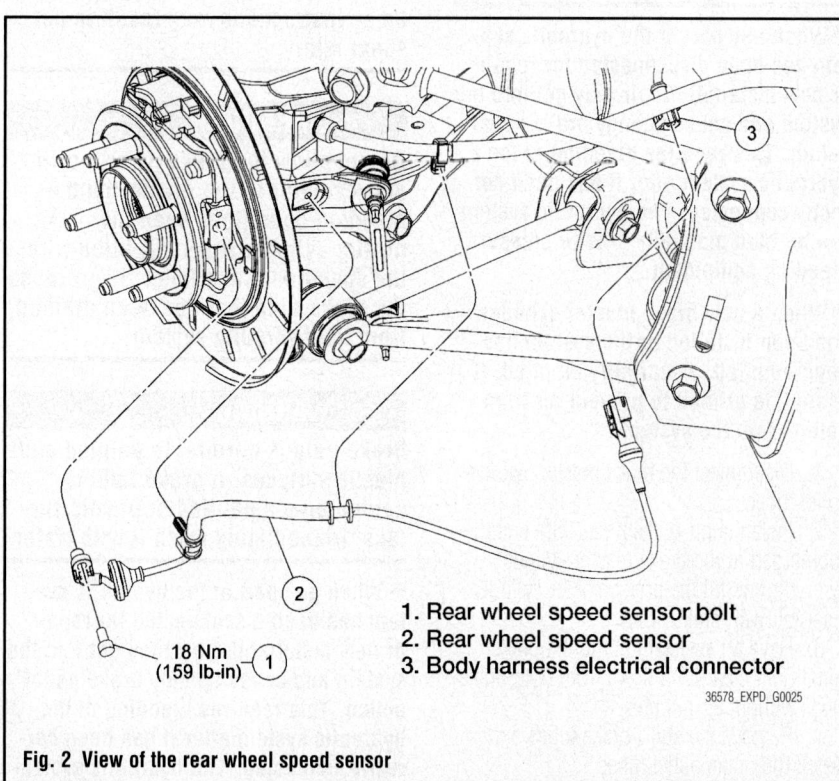

18 Nm
(159 lb-in)

1. Rear wheel speed sensor bolt
2. Rear wheel speed sensor
3. Body harness electrical connector

36578_EXPD_G0025

Fig. 2 View of the rear wheel speed sensor

BRAKES   BLEEDING THE BRAKE SYSTEM

BLEEDING PROCEDURE

Master Cylinder, In Vehicle

❋❋ CAUTION

Brake fluid contains polyglycol ethers and polyglycols. Avoid contact with eyes. Wash hands thoroughly after handling. If brake fluid contacts eyes, flush eyes with running water for 15 minutes. Get medical attention if irritation persists. If taken internally, drink water and induce vomiting. Get medical attention immediately. Failure to follow these instructions may result in personal injury.

❋❋ WARNING

Do not allow the brake master cylinder reservoir to run dry during the bleeding operation. Keep the brake master cylinder reservoir filled with the specified brake fluid. Never reuse the brake fluid that has been drained from the hydraulic system.

❋❋ WARNING

Brake fluid is harmful to painted and plastic surfaces. If brake fluid is spilled onto a painted or plastic surface, immediately wash it with water.

➡When any part of the hydraulic system has been disconnected for repair or new installation, air may get into the system and cause spongy brake pedal action. This requires bleeding of the hydraulic system after it has been correctly connected. The hydraulic system can be bled manually or with pressure bleeding equipment.

➡When a new brake master cylinder has been installed or the system has been emptied, or partially emptied, it should be primed to prevent air from getting into the system.

1. Disconnect the brake master cylinder outlet tubes.
2. Install short brake tubes with ends submerged in the brake master cylinder reservoir and fill the brake master cylinder reservoir with brake fluid.
3. Have an assistant pump the brake pedal until clear fluid flows from both brake tubes without air bubbles.
4. Remove the short brake tubes and install the brake outlet tubes.

5. Bleed each brake tube at the brake master cylinder as follows:
   a. Have an assistant pump the brake pedal and then hold firm pressure on the brake pedal.
   b. Loosen the rearmost brake tube fittings until a stream of brake fluid comes out. Have an assistant maintain pressure on the brake pedal while tightening the brake tube fitting.
   c. Repeat this operation until clear, bubble-free fluid comes out.
   d. Refill the brake master cylinder reservoir as necessary. Repeat the bleeding operation at the front brake tube.
6. While the assistant maintains pressure on the brake pedal, tighten the brake tubes to 18 ft. lbs. (25 Nm).

Gravity Bleeding

❋❋ CAUTION

Brake fluid contains polyglycol ethers and polyglycols. Avoid contact with eyes. Wash hands thoroughly after handling. If brake fluid contacts eyes, flush eyes with running water for 15 minutes. Get medical attention if irritation persists. If taken internally, drink water and induce vomiting. Get medical attention immediately. Failure to follow these instructions may result in personal injury.

❋❋ WARNING

Do not allow the brake master cylinder reservoir to run dry during the bleeding operation. Keep the brake master cylinder reservoir filled with the specified brake fluid. Never reuse the brake fluid that has been drained from the hydraulic system.

❋❋ WARNING

Brake fluid is harmful to painted and plastic surfaces. If brake fluid is spilled onto a painted or plastic surface, immediately wash it with water.

➡When any part of the hydraulic system has been disconnected for repair or new installation, air may get into the system and cause spongy brake pedal action. This requires bleeding of the hydraulic system after it has been correctly connected. The hydraulic system

can be bled manually or with pressure bleeding equipment.

➡When a new brake master cylinder has been installed or the system has been emptied, or partially emptied, it should be primed to prevent air from getting into the system.

1. Fill the brake master cylinder reservoir with brake fluid.
2. Bleed the rear disc brake calipers.
   a. Place a box end wrench on the RH rear disc brake caliper bleeder screw.
   b. Attach a rubber drain tube to the RH rear disc brake caliper bleeder screw and submerge the free end of the tube in a container partially filled with clean brake fluid.
   c. Open the bleeder screw and leave open until clear bubble-free brake fluid flows.
   d. Repeat for LH rear disc brake caliper.
3. Tighten the rear disc brake caliper bleeder screws to 11 ft. lbs. (15 Nm).
4. Bleed the front disc brake calipers.
   a. Place a box end wrench on the RH front disc brake caliper bleeder screw.
   b. Attach a rubber drain tube to the RH front disc brake caliper bleeder screw and submerge the free end of the tube in a container partially filled with clean brake fluid.
   c. Open the bleeder screw and leave open until clear bubble-free brake fluid flows.
   d. Repeat for LH front disc brake caliper.
5. Tighten the front disc brake caliper bleeder screws to 11 ft. lbs. (15 Nm).

Manual Bleeding

❋❋ CAUTION

Brake fluid contains polyglycol ethers and polyglycols. Avoid contact with eyes. Wash hands thoroughly after handling. If brake fluid contacts eyes, flush eyes with running water for 15 minutes. Get medical attention if irritation persists. If taken internally, drink water and induce vomiting. Get medical attention immediately. Failure to follow these instructions may result in personal injury.

Do not allow the brake master cylinder reservoir to run dry during the bleeding operation. Keep the brake master cylinder reservoir filled with the specified brake fluid. Never reuse the brake fluid that has been drained from the hydraulic system.

Brake fluid is harmful to painted and plastic surfaces. If brake fluid is spilled onto a painted or plastic surface, immediately wash it with water.

➡When any part of the hydraulic system has been disconnected for repair or new installation, air may get into the system and cause spongy brake pedal action. This requires bleeding of the hydraulic system after it has been correctly connected. The hydraulic system can be bled manually or with pressure bleeding equipment.

1. Place a box end wrench on the RH rear disc brake caliper bleeder screw. Attach a rubber drain tube to the RH rear disc brake caliper bleeder screw and submerge the free end of the tube in a container partially filled with clean brake fluid.

2. Have an assistant pump the brake pedal and then hold firm pressure on the brake pedal.

3. Loosen the RH rear disc brake caliper bleeder screw until a stream of brake fluid comes out. Have an assistant maintain pressure on the brake pedal while tightening the RH rear disc brake caliper bleeder screw.

   a. Repeat until clear, bubble-free fluid comes out.

   b. Refill the brake master cylinder reservoir as necessary.

4. Tighten the RH rear disc brake caliper bleeder screw to 11 ft. lbs. (15 Nm).

5. Repeat Steps 1, 2, 3, and 4 for the LH rear disc brake caliper.

6. Place a box end wrench on the RH front disc brake caliper bleeder screw. Attach a rubber drain tube to the RH front disc brake caliper bleeder screw and submerge the free end of the tube in a container partially filled with clean brake fluid.

7. Have an assistant pump the brake pedal and then hold firm pressure on the brake pedal.

8. Loosen the RH front disc brake caliper bleeder screw until a stream of brake fluid comes out. Have an assistant maintain pressure on the brake pedal while tightening the RH front disc brake caliper bleeder screw.

   a. Repeat until clear, bubble-free fluid comes out.

   b. Refill the brake master cylinder reservoir as necessary.

9. Tighten the RH front disc brake caliper bleeder screw to 11 ft. lbs. (15 Nm).

10. Repeat Steps 6, 7, 8, and 9 for the LH front disc brake caliper bleeder screw.

11. If necessary, bleed the brake master cylinder.

Pressure Bleeding

Brake fluid contains polyglycol ethers and polyglycols. Avoid contact with eyes. Wash hands thoroughly after handling. If brake fluid contacts eyes, flush eyes with running water for 15 minutes. Get medical attention if irritation persists. If taken internally, drink water and induce vomiting. Get medical attention immediately. Failure to follow these instructions may result in personal injury.

Do not allow the brake master cylinder reservoir to run dry during the bleeding operation. Keep the brake master cylinder reservoir filled with the specified brake fluid. Never reuse the brake fluid that has been drained from the hydraulic system.

Brake fluid is harmful to painted and plastic surfaces. If brake fluid is spilled onto a painted or plastic surface, immediately wash it with water.

➡When any part of the hydraulic system has been disconnected for repair or new installation, air may get into the system and cause spongy brake pedal action. This requires bleeding of the hydraulic system after it has been correctly connected. The hydraulic system can be bled manually or with pressure bleeding equipment.

➡Bleed the longest line first. Be sure the bleeder tank contains enough specified brake fluid to complete the bleeding operation.

1. Clean all dirt from and remove the brake master cylinder filler cap and fill the brake master cylinder reservoir with the specified brake fluid.

➡Master cylinder pressure bleeder adapter tools are available from various manufacturers of pressure bleeding equipment. Follow the instructions of the manufacturer when installing the adapter.

2. Install the bleeder adapter to the brake master cylinder reservoir and attach the bleeder tank hose to the fitting on the adapter.

3. Place a box end wrench on the RH rear disc brake caliper bleeder screw. Attach a rubber drain tube to the RH rear disc brake caliper bleeder screw and submerge the free end of the tube in a container partially filled with clean brake fluid.

4. Open the valve on the bleeder tank.

5. Loosen the rear disc brake caliper bleeder screw. Leave open until clear, bubble-free brake fluid flows, then tighten rear disc brake caliper bleeder screw to 11 ft. lbs. (15 Nm) and remove the rubber hose.

6. Continue bleeding the rest of the system, going in order from the LH rear disc brake caliper to the RH front disc brake caliper ending with the LH front disc brake caliper.

7. Close the bleeder tank valve and remove the tank hose from the adapter and remove the adapter.

8. Fill the brake master cylinder reservoir and install the brake master cylinder filler cap.

Master Cylinder, Bench Bleeding

Brake fluid contains polyglycol ethers and polyglycols. Avoid contact with eyes. Wash hands thoroughly after handling. If brake fluid contacts eyes, flush eyes with running water for 15 minutes. Get medical attention if irritation persists. If taken internally, drink water and induce vomiting. Get medical attention immediately. Failure to follow these instructions may result in personal injury.

Do not allow the brake master cylinder reservoir to run dry during the bleeding operation. Keep the brake master cylinder reservoir filled with the specified brake fluid. Never reuse the brake fluid that has been drained from the hydraulic system.

❊❊ WARNING

Brake fluid is harmful to painted and plastic surfaces. If brake fluid is spilled onto a painted or plastic surface, immediately wash it with water.

→When any part of the hydraulic system has been disconnected for repair or new installation, air may get into the system and cause spongy brake pedal action. This requires bleeding of the hydraulic system after it has been correctly connected. The hydraulic system can be bled manually or with pressure bleeding equipment.

1. Support the brake master cylinder body in a vise and fill the brake master cylinder reservoir with specified brake fluid. Make sure to use clean brake fluid.

2. Install short brake tubes with the ends submerged in the brake master cylinder reservoir.

3. Slowly depress the primary piston until clear fluid flows from both brake tubes, without air bubbles.

4. Remove the short brake tubes.

BLEEDING THE ABS SYSTEM

❊❊ CAUTION

Brake fluid contains polyglycol ethers and polyglycols. Avoid contact with eyes. Wash hands thoroughly after handling. If brake fluid contacts eyes, flush eyes with running water for 15 minutes. Get medical attention if irritation persists. If taken internally, drink water and induce vomiting. Get medical attention immediately. Failure to follow these instructions may result in personal injury.

❊❊ WARNING

Do not allow the brake master cylinder reservoir to run dry during the bleeding operation. Keep the brake master cylinder reservoir filled with the specified brake fluid. Never reuse the brake fluid that has been drained from the hydraulic system.

❊❊ WARNING

Brake fluid is harmful to painted and plastic surfaces. If brake fluid is spilled onto a painted or plastic surface, immediately wash it with water.

→When any part of the hydraulic system has been disconnected for repair or new installation, air may get into the system and cause spongy brake pedal action. This requires bleeding of the hydraulic system after it has been correctly connected. The hydraulic system can be bled manually or with pressure bleeding equipment.

→This procedure must be performed if the 4 wheel anti-lock brake (4WABS) hydraulic control unit (HCU) has been installed new.

→One conventional pressure bleed cycle consists of advancing the brake pedal to its depressed position, opening the disc brake caliper bleeder screw, allowing fluid to be released into the waste container, closing the disc brake caliper bleeder screw and releasing the brake pedal.

→Performing the diagnostic program routine drives entrapped air from the otherwise inaccessible lower section of the 4WABS valve into the upper sections (accessible by bleeding the brakes). Subsequent bleedings remove the air from the system.

→Add recommended brake fluid as necessary throughout the procedure.

1. Connect a clear waste line to the RH rear disc brake caliper bleeder screw and the other end in a container partially filled with recommended brake fluid.

2. Have an assistant pump the brake pedal and then hold firm pressure on the brake pedal.

3. Loosen the RH rear disc brake caliper bleeder screw until a stream of brake fluid comes out. Have an assistant maintain pressure on the brake pedal while tightening the RH rear disc brake caliper bleeder screw.

   a. Repeat until clear, bubble-free fluid comes out.

   b. Refill the brake master cylinder reservoir as necessary.

4. Tighten the RH rear disc brake caliper bleeder screw to 11 ft. lbs. (15 Nm).

5. Repeat Steps 1, 2, 3, and 4 for the LH rear disc brake caliper bleeder screw, RH front disc brake caliper bleeder screw, and the LH front disc brake caliper bleeder screw. Tighten to 11 ft. lbs. (15 Nm).

→Go to the Help menu in the diagnostic tool.

6. Connect the diagnostic tool DCL cable adapter into the vehicle data link connector (DLC) under the dash and follow the diagnostic tool instructions.

7. Repeat the conventional bleed procedure as outlined in Steps 1 through 5.

8. If the brake pedal feels spongy, repeat the diagnostic tool service bleed procedure.

BRAKES

FRONT DISC BRAKES

❋❋ CAUTION

Dust and dirt accumulating on brake parts during normal use may contain asbestos fibers from production or aftermarket brake linings. Breathing excessive concentrations of asbestos fibers can cause serious bodily harm. Exercise care when servicing brake parts. Do not sand or grind brake lining unless equipment used is designed to contain the dust residue. Do not clean brake parts with compressed air or by dry brushing. Cleaning should be done by dampening the brake components with a fine mist of water, then wiping the brake components clean with a dampened cloth. Dispose of cloth and all residue containing asbestos fibers in an impermeable container with the appropriate label. Follow practices prescribed by the Occupational Safety and Health Administration (OSHA) and the Environmental Protection Agency (EPA) for the handling, processing, and disposing of dust or debris that may contain asbestos fibers.

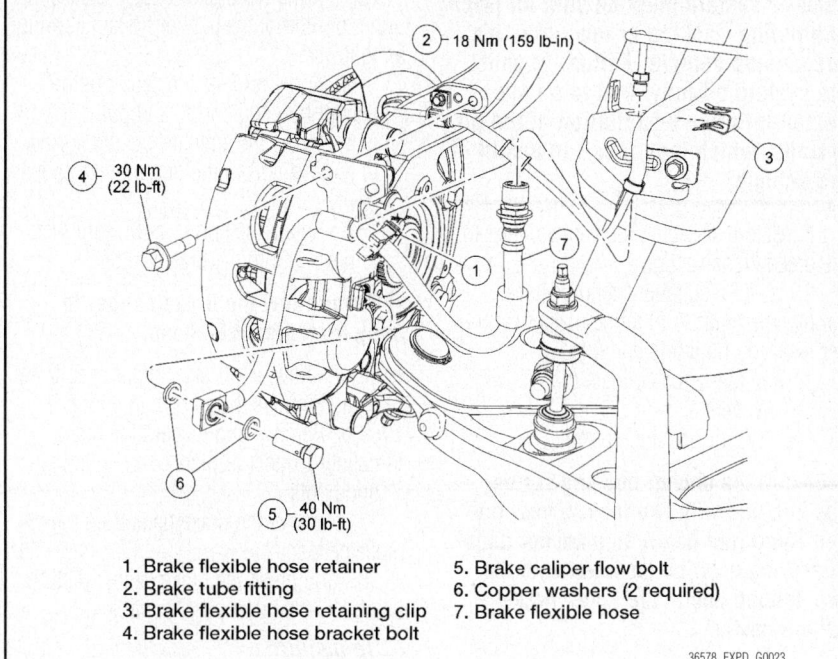

1. Brake flexible hose retainer
2. Brake tube fitting
3. Brake flexible hose retaining clip
4. Brake flexible hose bracket bolt
5. Brake caliper flow bolt
6. Copper washers (2 required)
7. Brake flexible hose

36578_EXPD_G0023

Fig. 4 Front disc brake assembly components

BRAKE CALIPER

REMOVAL & INSTALLATION
See Figures 3 and 4.

❋❋ WARNING

The electrical power to the air suspension system must be shut off prior to hoisting, jacking or towing an air suspension vehicle. Failure to shut the system off may lead to an unexpected inflation or deflation of the air springs, which may result in a shift of the vehicle.

1. Before servicing the vehicle, refer to the precautions section.
2. Remove or disconnect the following:
   - Wheels
   - Brake pads
   - Front brake hose bolt and the copper washers and plug the front brake hose
   - 2 front disc brake caliper bolts, then lift the caliper off of the front caliper anchor plate

To install:
3. Install or connect the following:
   - 2 front disc brake caliper bolts, tighten the bolts to 41 ft. lbs. (55 Nm)
   - Front brake hose to the brake caliper, using new copper washers. Tighten the retaining bolt to 26 ft. lbs. (35 Nm).
   - Brake pads
   - Wheels

1. Brake disc
2. Brake disc shield screws (3 required)
3. Brake disc shield
4. Brake caliper anchor plate
5. Brake pad slide clip (4 required)
6. Brake pad
7. Anchor housing spring
8. Brake caliper anchor plate bolts
9. Brake caliper assembly
10. Brake caliper guide pin bushing (2 required)
11. Bleeder screw cap
12. Brake caliper guide pin (2 required)
13. Brake caliper guide pin bushing cap (2 required)

36578_EXPD_G0022

Fig. 3 Exploded view of the front disc brake assembly

DISC BRAKE PADS

REMOVAL & INSTALLATION
See Figures 3 and 4.

✳✳ WARNING

The electrical power to the air suspension system must be shut off prior to hoisting, jacking or towing an air suspension vehicle. Failure to shut the system off may lead to an unexpected inflation or deflation of the air springs, which may result in a shift of the vehicle.

1. Before servicing the vehicle, refer to the precautions section.

2. Using a suitable suction device, remove the brake fluid in the master cylinder reservoir until it is half filled.

3. Remove or disconnect the following:
   • Wheels
   • Anchor housing spring.

➡Ensure the anchor housing spring has one end with two tabs. If yes, the Left Hand (left hand) side anchor housing spring must be installed with the two–tabbed end in the upper brake caliper cavity.

4. On the left hand brake caliper, release the lower portion of the anchor housing spring as follows:

   a. Apply force at the center of the anchor housing spring and pull outward at the bottom of the anchor housing spring to remove it from the lower brake caliper cavity.

   b. Rotate the spring upward then remove it from the brake caliper.

➡On the Right Hand (RH) side, the anchor housing spring must be installed with the two–tabbed end in the lower brake caliper cavity.

5. For the RH brake caliper, release the upper portion of the anchor housing spring as follows:

   a. Apply force at the center of the anchor housing spring and pull outward at the top of the anchor housing spring to remove it from the upper brake caliper cavity.

   b. Rotate the spring downward then remove it from the brake caliper.

➡Never allow the brake caliper to hang from the brake hose.

6. Remove the brake caliper as follows:
   a. Remove the zero-drag spring.
   b. Remove and discard the brake caliper-to-anchor plate bolts, guide pins and boots.

7. Remove the brake pads from the brake caliper.

8. Compress the brake caliper pistons using a C-clamp or other suitable tool.

To install:

9. Clean the inner surfaces of the brake caliper where the brake pads attach.

10. Install new brake hardware as follows:

   a. Install the guide pin bushings into the caliper bores.

   b. Apply grease to the inside of the guide pin bushing. Do not apply grease to the guide pin threads.

   c. Push the guide pins into the bushing.

11. Install or connect the following:

   • Inboard brake pad into the brake caliper.
   • Outboard brake pad into the brake caliper
   • Brake caliper on the brake disc. Tighten the guide pins and install the dust caps.
   • Zero-drag spring

➡If present, the 2-tabbed end of the anchor housing spring must be installed first.

12. Install the anchor housing spring as follows:

   a. Insert tab of the anchor housing spring into the brake caliper cavity.

   b. Twist tab into the brake caliper cavity (left hand side-upper brake caliper cavity/RH side-lower brake caliper cavity).

   c. Rotate the anchor housing spring and position the upper portion onto the anchor plate.

   d. Position the other anchor housing spring portion onto the brake caliper anchor plate.

   e. Push down and inward until the upper and lower ends of the anchor housing spring are latched and seated in the brake caliper cavities.

13. Verify that the anchor housing spring is correctly latched.

14. Bleed the brake system, filling the brake master cylinder reservoir as required.

15. Install the wheels.

16. Make sure that the brakes are operating correctly.

BRAKES

✳✳ CAUTION

Dust and dirt accumulating on brake parts during normal use may contain asbestos fibers from production or aftermarket brake linings. Breathing excessive concentrations of asbestos fibers can cause serious bodily harm. Exercise care when servicing brake parts. Do not sand or grind brake lining unless equipment used is designed to contain the dust residue. Do not clean brake parts with compressed air or by dry brushing. Cleaning should be done by dampening the brake components with a fine mist of water, then wiping the brake components clean with a dampened cloth. Dispose of cloth and all residue containing asbestos fibers in an impermeable container with the appropriate label. Follow practices prescribed by the Occupational Safety and Health Administration (OSHA) and the Environmental Protection Agency (EPA) for the handling, processing, and disposing of dust or debris that may contain asbestos fibers.

BRAKE CALIPER

REMOVAL & INSTALLATION
See Figure 5.

✳✳ WARNING

The electrical power to the air suspension system must be shut off prior to hoisting, jacking or towing an air suspension vehicle. Failure to shut the system off may lead to an unex-

REAR DISC BRAKES

pected inflation or deflation of the air springs, which may result in a shift of the vehicle.

1. Before servicing the vehicle, refer to the precautions section.

2. Remove or disconnect the following:
   • Wheels
   • 2 rear disc brake caliper bolts and caps, then lift the caliper off of the front caliper anchor plate
   • Rear brake hose bolt and the copper washers and plug the front brake hose

To install:

3. Install or connect the following:
   • 2 rear disc brake caliper bolts and caps. Tighten the bolts to 26 ft. lbs. (35 Nm).

- Rear brake hose to the brake caliper, using new copper washers. Tighten the retaining bolts to 26 ft. lbs. (35 Nm).
- Brake pads
- Wheels

4. Bleed the brake system, filling the brake master cylinder reservoir as required.

5. Road-test the vehicle and check for proper brake system operation.

DISC BRAKE PADS

REMOVAL & INSTALLATION

See Figure 5.

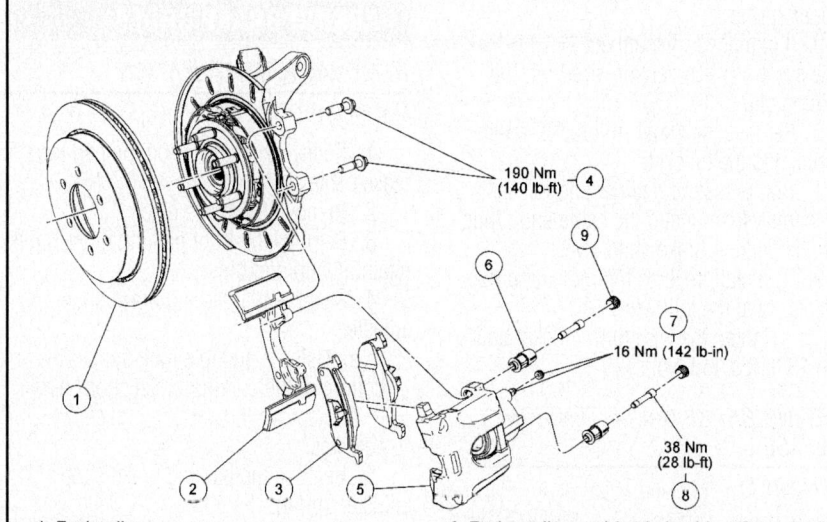

1. Brake disc
2. Brake caliper anchor plate kit
3. Brake pad
4. Brake caliper anchor plate bolts (2 required)
5. Brake caliper
6. Brake caliper guide pin bushing (2 required)
7. Bleeder screw and cap
8. Brake caliper guide pin (2 required)
9. Brake caliper guide pin cap (2 required)

190 Nm (140 lb-ft) — 4
16 Nm (142 lb-in)
38 Nm (28 lb-ft)

36578_EXPD_G0026

Fig. 5 Exploded view of the rear disc brake assembly

✳✳ WARNING

The electrical power to the air suspension system must be shut off prior to hoisting, jacking or towing an air suspension vehicle. Failure to shut the system off may lead to an unexpected inflation or deflation of the air springs, which may result in a shift of the vehicle.

1. Before servicing the vehicle, refer to the precautions section.

2. Remove enough brake fluid from the brake master cylinder reservoir until it is ½ full.

3. Remove or disconnect the following:
- Wheels
- Anchor housing spring by squeezing at the center of the spring until it unlatches from the brake caliper at both ends, then rotate the spring to remove it from the caliper housing
- Caps and brake caliper bolts
- Brake caliper without disconnecting the brake hose
- Brake pads

4. Thoroughly clean the areas of the caliper and caliper support assembly which contact each other during the sliding action of the caliper.

To install:

5. Compress the caliper piston using a C-clamp or other suitable tool.

6. Install or connect the following:
- Brake shoes on the disc brake caliper support bracket
- Anchor housing spring by placing the upper anchor housing spring end into the brake caliper cavity, then rotate the anchor housing spring and position the lower arm onto the anchor plate
- Upper arm onto the anchor plate, then press down and inward until it is correctly seated and latched into the brake caliper cavities
- Rear disc brake caliper onto the rear support bracket
- Brake caliper caps and bolts, tighten pin bolts to 26 ft. lbs. (35 Nm).

7. Bleed the brake system, filling the brake master cylinder reservoir as required.
- Front wheels

8. Make sure that the brakes are operating correctly.

BRAKES **PARKING BRAKE**

PARKING BRAKE CABLES

REMOVAL & INSTALLATION

Front Cable

1. Before servicing the vehicle, refer to the precautions section.
2. Remove the parking brake control.
3. If equipped, turn the air suspension switch to the OFF position.
4. With the vehicle in NEUTRAL, position it on a hoist.
5. Remove the front park brake cable P-clip-to-frame bolt.
6. Pry the rubber seal from the front floor pan.
7. Compress the retainer and release the conduit from the bracket
8. Remove the front cable and conduit from the cable union.
9. To install, reverse the removal procedure and tighten the P-clip-to-frame bolt to 13 ft. lbs. (18 Nm).

Right Rear Cable

1. Before servicing the vehicle, refer to the precautions section.
2. Relieve the tension on the parking brake cable system.
3. With the vehicle in NEUTRAL, position it on a hoist
4. Disconnect the RH rear cable from the cable union.
5. Compress the 2 tabs and release the conduit from the equalizer.
6. Remove the RH rear cable from the retaining clip
7. Remove the bolt and the wire form bracket from the LH side of the vehicle.
8. Remove the rear park brake cable-to-crossmember bolt.
9. Remove the bolt and the wire form bracket from the RH side of the vehicle.
10. Compress the 2 tabs and release the conduit, then unclip the cable end fitting from the parking brake shoe lever
To install, reverse the removal procedure and note the following:
   a. Tighten the left wire form bracket bolt to 13 ft. lbs. (18 Nm).
   b. Tighten the rear park brake cable-to-crossmember bolt to 80 inch lbs. (90 Nm).
   c. Tighten the right wire form bracket bolt to 13 ft. lbs. (18 Nm).

Left Rear Cable

1. Before servicing the vehicle, refer to the precautions section.

2. Relieve the tension on the parking brake cable system.
3. With the vehicle in NEUTRAL, position it on a hoist.
4. Separate the LH rear cable from the equalizer.
5. Compress the 2 tabs.
6. Remove the conduit from the bracket.

➡**Be sure to correctly install the park brake cable retainer spring and route cables between suspension links.**

7. Remove the LH rear cable from the retaining clip.
8. Disconnect the park brake cable retainer spring.
9. If equipped, disconnect the anti-lock brake system (ABS) sensor wire from the retaining clip
10. Remove the wireform bracket retaining bolt and the bracket.
11. Compress the retainer and release the conduit, then unclip the cable end fitting from the parking brake shoe lever
12. To install, reverse the removal procedure and note the following:
   a. Tighten the wire form bracket bolt to 13 ft. lbs. (18 Nm).

PARKING BRAKE CABLE TENSION RELEASE

See Figure 6.

1. Remove the LH cowl side trim panel.
2. With the help of an assistant, release the parking brake cable tension by pulling

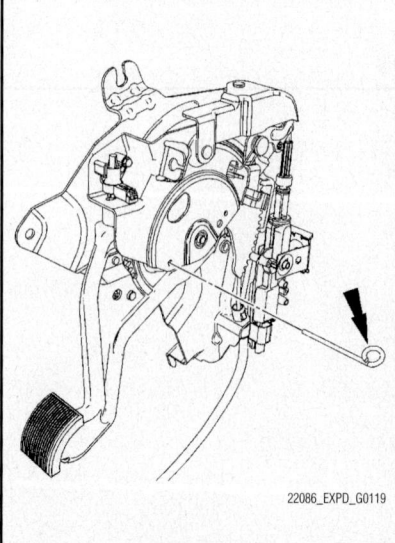

22086_EXPD_G0119

Fig. 6 Insert the retainer pin as shown

down on the intermediate cable at the cable-to-cable connector clip until the parking brake control sector rotates to its stop and a 4 mm (0.15 in) x 150 mm (5.9 in) retainer pin can be inserted.

3. Disconnect the cable-to-cable connector clip.
4. To reload the tension on the parking brake cable, follow the release procedure in reverse.
5. Make sure the cable-to-cable connector clip is connected to the front and rear cable before removing the brake control retaining pin, and the cable tension is reloaded slowly.

PARKING BRAKE SHOES

REMOVAL & INSTALLATION

See Figure 7.

1. Relieve the tension on the parking brake cable system.
2. Remove the brake disc.
3. Remove the front parking brake shoe retaining clip and pin.
4. Remove the parking brake shoe adjuster.
   a. Using a suitable tool, spread the bottom of the parking brake shoes apart.
   b. Remove the parking brake shoe adjuster.
5. Remove the parking brake shoe adjuster spring.
6. Slide the front parking brake shoe up and out of the guide flange.
7. Remove the front parking brake shoe.
   a. Rotate the front parking brake shoe outward.
   b. Remove the parking brake shoe return spring.
8. Remove the rear parking brake shoe.
   a. Remove the retaining clip and pin.
   b. Remove the rear parking brake shoe.
9. Inspect the components for excessive wear or damage and install new parts as required.

To install:

➡**Apply the grease only where indicated, do not apply the grease to the parking brake shoes. The grease will contaminate the brake shoe linings and damage to the linings will result.**

10. Apply a light coat of the specified grease to the 6 parking brake shoe contact points on the disc brake shield.
11. Install the rear parking brake shoe.

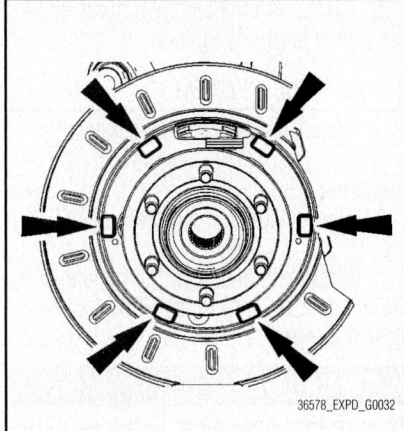

Fig. 7 Greasing the 6 parking brake shoe contact points

a. Hold the rear parking brake shoe in position.
b. Install the retaining pin and clip.
12. Install the front parking brake shoe.
a. Install the parking brake shoe return spring to the rear parking brake

shoe and to the front parking brake shoe.
b. Rotate the front parking brake shoe into the guide flange.
13. Slide the front parking brake shoe down into position on the flange.
14. Install the front parking brake shoe retaining pin and clip.
15. Install the parking brake shoe adjuster spring.
16. Install the parking brake shoe adjuster.
a. Using a suitable tool, spread the bottom of the parking brake shoes apart.
b. Install the parking brake shoe adjuster.
17. Adjust the parking brake shoes

→**This step will require the aid of an assistant.**

18. Enable the parking brake cable system.
a. Pull down on the front parking brake cable at the coupler.
b. Remove the retaining pin from the parking brake lever.

19. Check the parking brake for correct operation.

ADJUSTMENT

1. Make sure the parking brake is fully released.
2. Using the release handle, release the parking brake control.
3. Remove the rear brake disc.
4. Using the Brake Adjusting Gauge, measure the inside diameter of the drum portion of the rear brake disc and set the locking screw. Record the measurement
5. Place the Brake Adjusting Gauge over the widest diameter of the parking brake shoes.
6. Adjust the parking brake shoe clearance to 0.45 mm (0.02 in) less than the inside diameter of the drum portion of the rear brake disc.
7. Rotate the parking brake shoe adjuster to achieve the correct parking brake shoe-to-brake disc clearance.
8. Install the rear brake disc.
9. Test the parking brake for normal operation.

CHASSIS ELECTRICAL

GENERAL INFORMATION

✳✳ CAUTION

Some vehicles are equipped with an air bag system. The system must be disarmed before performing service on, or around, system components, the steering column, instrument panel components, wiring and sensors. Failure to follow the safety precautions and the disarming procedure could result in accidental air bag deployment, possible injury and unnecessary system repairs.

SERVICE PRECAUTIONS

Disconnect and isolate the battery negative cable before beginning any airbag system component diagnosis, testing, removal, or installation procedures. Allow system capacitor to discharge for two minutes before beginning any component service. This will disable the airbag system. Failure to disable the airbag system may result in accidental airbag deployment, personal injury, or death.

Do not place an intact undeployed airbag face down on a solid surface. The airbag will propel into the air if accidentally deployed and may result in personal injury or death.

AIR BAG (SUPPLEMENTAL RESTRAINT SYSTEM)

When carrying or handling an undeployed airbag, the trim side (face) of the airbag should be pointing towards the body to minimize possibility of injury if accidental deployment occurs. Failure to do this may result in personal injury or death.

Replace airbag system components with OEM replacement parts. Substitute parts may appear interchangeable, but internal differences may result in inferior occupant protection. Failure to do so may result in occupant personal injury or death.

Wear safety glasses, rubber gloves, and long sleeved clothing when cleaning powder residue from vehicle after an airbag deployment. Powder residue emitted from a deployed airbag can cause skin irritation. Flush affected area with cool water if irritation is experienced. If nasal or throat irritation is experienced, exit the vehicle for fresh air until the irritation ceases. If irritation continues, see a physician.

Do not use a replacement airbag that is not in the original packaging. This may result in improper deployment, personal injury, or death.

The factory installed fasteners, screws and bolts used to fasten airbag components have a special coating and are specifically designed for the airbag system. Do not use substitute fasteners. Use only original equipment fasteners listed in the

parts catalog when fastener replacement is required.

During, and following, any child restraint anchor service, due to impact event or vehicle repair, carefully inspect all mounting hardware, tether straps, and anchors for proper installation, operation, or damage. If a child restraint anchor is found damaged in any way, the anchor must be replaced. Failure to do this may result in personal injury or death.

Deployed and non-deployed airbags may or may not have live pyrotechnic material within the airbag inflator.

Do not dispose of driver/passenger/curtain airbags or seat belt tensioners unless you are sure of complete deployment. Refer to the Hazardous Substance Control System for proper disposal.

Dispose of deployed airbags and tensioners consistent with state, provincial, local, and federal regulations.

After any airbag component testing or service, do not connect the battery negative cable. Personal injury or death may result if the system test is not performed first.

If the vehicle is equipped with the Occupant Classification System (OCS), do not connect the battery negative cable before performing the OCS Verification Test using the scan tool and the appropriate diagnostic information. Personal injury or death may result if the system test is not performed properly.

Never replace both the Occupant Restraint Controller (ORC) and the Occupant Classification Module (OCM) at the same time. If both require replacement, replace one, then perform the Airbag System test before replacing the other.

Both the ORC and the OCM store Occupant Classification System (OCS) calibration data, which they transfer to one another when one of them is replaced. If both are replaced at the same time, an irreversible fault will be set in both modules and the OCS may malfunction and cause personal injury or death.

If equipped with OCS, the Seat Weight Sensor is a sensitive, calibrated unit and must be handled carefully. Do not drop or handle roughly. If dropped or damaged, replace with another sensor. Failure to do so may result in occupant injury or death.

If equipped with OCS, the front passenger seat must be handled carefully as well. When removing the seat, be careful when setting on floor not to drop. If dropped, the sensor may be inoperative, could result in occupant injury, or possibly death.

If equipped with OCS, when the passenger front seat is on the floor, no one should sit in the front passenger seat. This uneven force may damage the sensing ability of the seat weight sensors. If sat on and damaged, the sensor may be inoperative, could result in occupant injury, or possibly death.

DISARMING THE SYSTEM

❋❋ WARNING

Always wear safety glasses when repairing an air bag Supplemental Restraint System (SRS) vehicle and when handling an air bag module. This will reduce the risk of injury in the event of an accidental deployment.

❋❋ WARNING

Never probe the connectors on the air bag module. Doing so can result in air bag deployment, which can result in personal injury.

❋❋ WARNING

To reduce the risk of personal injury, do not use any memory saver devices.

➡The air bag warning lamp illuminates when the restraints control module (RCM) fuse is removed and the ignition switch is ON. This is normal operation and does not indicate a Supplemental Restraint System (SRS) fault.

➡The SRS must be fully operational and free of faults before releasing the vehicle to the customer.

1. Turn all vehicle accessories OFF.
2. Turn the ignition switch to OFF.
3. At the smart power distribution junction box (SPDJB), located in the RH lower kick panel, remove the cover and the restraints control module (RCM) fuse 32 (10A) from the SPDJB.
4. Turn the ignition ON and visually monitor the air bag warning indicator for at least 30 seconds. The air bag warning indicator will remain lit continuously (no flashing) if the correct RCM fuse has been removed. If the air bag warning indicator does not remain lit continuously, remove the correct RCM fuse before proceeding.
5. Turn the ignition switch to OFF.

❋❋ CAUTION

To avoid accidental deployment and possible personal injury, the backup power supply must be depleted before repairing or replacing any front or side air bag Supplemental Restraint System (SRS) components and before servicing, replacing, adjusting or striking components near the front or side air bag sensors, such as doors, instrument panel, console, door latches, strikers, seats and hood latches.

➡The front impact severity sensor is located on the bottom of the radiator support bracket.

➡The front door side impact sensors (if equipped) are located in the first row doors, behind the door trim panel.

➡The C-pillar side impact sensors (if equipped) are located on the C-pillar.

➡To deplete the backup power supply energy, disconnect the battery ground cable and wait at least one minute. Be sure to disconnect auxiliary batteries and power supplies (if equipped). Failure to follow these instructions may increase the risk of personal injury or death in a crash.

6. Disconnect the battery ground cable and wait at least one minute

ARMING THE SYSTEM

1. Make sure that all Supplemental Restraint System (SRS) components are connected.
2. Turn the ignition switch from OFF to ON.
3. Install restraints control module (RCM) fuse 32 (10A) to the SPDJB and close the cover.

❋❋ CAUTION

Be sure that nobody is in the vehicle and that there is nothing blocking or set in front of any air bag module when the battery ground cable is connected. Failure to follow these instructions may increase the risk of personal injury or death in a crash.

4. Connect the battery ground cable.
5. Prove out the SRS as follows:
6. Turn the ignition key from ON to OFF. Wait 10 seconds, then turn the key back to ON and visually monitor the air bag warning indicator with the air bag modules installed. The air bag warning indicator will light continuously for approximately 6 seconds and then turn off. If an air bag SRS fault is present, the air bag warning indicator will either:
   a. Fail to light.
   b. Remain lit continuously.
   c. Flash.
   d. The air bag warning indicator may not illuminate until approximately 30 seconds after the ignition switch has been turned from the OFF to the ON position. This is the time required for the RCM to complete the testing of the SRS. If the air bag warning indicator is inoperative and an SRS fault exists, a chime will sound in a pattern of 5 sets of 5 beeps. If this occurs, the air bag warning indicator will need to be repaired before diagnosis can continue.

Clear all continuous memory DTCs from the restraints control module using a scan tool.

CLOCKSPRING CENTERING

❋❋ WARNING

Overturning will destroy the clockspring. The internal ribbon wire acts as the stop and can be broken from its internal connection. Make sure the road wheels are in the straight-ahead position.

1. Centralize the clockspring.
2. Hold the clockspring outer housing stationary.
3. While holding the clockspring locking tab in the released position, turn the rotor counterclockwise, carefully feeling for the ribbon wire to run out of length and a slight resistance to be felt. Stop turning at this point.
4. While holding the clockspring locking tab in the released position, turn the clockspring clockwise approximately 2.25 turns. This is the center point of the clockspring.
5. Do not allow the rotor to turn from this position.

DRIVE TRAIN

AUTOMATIC TRANSMISSION ASSEMBLY

REMOVAL & INSTALLATION

6R80 Transmission

2WD Models

See Figures 8 through 11.

1. Before servicing the vehicle, refer to the precautions section.
2. Disconnect the battery ground cable
3. Remove the driveshaft.
4. Remove the fluid fill plug fluid level indicator assembly located on the passenger side front portion of the transmission case. Removal of the plug will relieve any vacuum that might have built up in the transmission. This will aid in allowing the fluid pan to be easily removed when the bolts are removed.

➡ **If transmission disassembly or installation of a new transmission is necessary, the transmission fluid will need to be drained.**

5. Remove the transmission fluid pan and allow the fluid to drain.
6. Install the fluid pan and tighten the bolts in a crisscross pattern.
7. If equipped, remove the heat shield.

➡ **To prevent selector lever cable damage, do not apply force to the selector lever cable between the manual control lever and the selector lever cable bracket.**

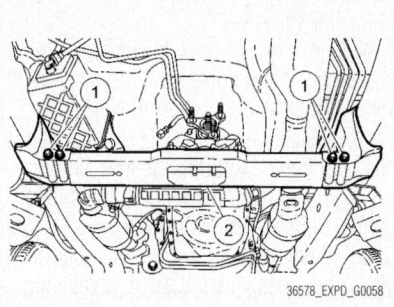

Fig. 9 Removing the 4 crossmember bolts and nuts and crossmember

8. Move the locking tab up and disconnect the selector lever cable from the manual lever ball stud.
9. Remove the selector lever bracket bolts and remove the bracket.
10. Remove the flexplate inspection cover bolts and the inspection cover.
11. Remove the rubber torque converter nut access plug.
12. Remove and discard the 4 flexplate-to-torque converter nuts.
13. Remove the transmission cooler tube bracket bolt.
14. Remove the transmission case bolt.
15. Remove the transmission fluid cooler tube bracket nut and position the bracket and tubes aside.
16. Remove the plastic starter motor electrical connector cap.
17. Remove the starter motor electrical connectors.

18. Remove the ground wire from the stud.
19. Remove the starter motor bolts and the starter motor.
20. Remove the RH exhaust heat shield bolt.
21. Remove the LH exhaust heat shield and evaporative emissions canister assembly bolts.
22. Disconnect the RH and LH heated oxygen sensors (HO2S) and the catalyst monitor sensor (CMS) electrical connectors.
23. Remove the fuel line bracket bolt and position the bracket and lines aside.

➡ **Make sure that the transmission jack makes contact on the outer ribs of the fluid pan. And that the transmission is securely fastened to the transmission jack.**

24. Position a suitable high-lift transmission jack under the transmission.
25. Remove the 2 rear crossmember nuts.
26. Remove the 4 crossmember bolts and nuts.
27. Remove the rear crossmember.
28. Remove the 3 bolts and remove the insulator.
29. Remove the RH and LH exhaust flange nuts.
30. Remove the 2 dual converter Y-pipe bolts and the dual converter Y-pipe.

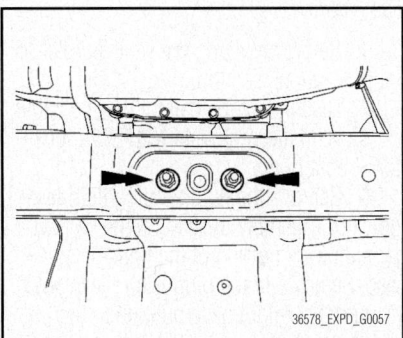

Fig. 8 Removing the 2 rear crossmember nuts

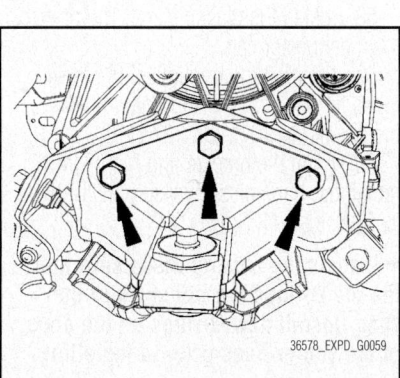

Fig. 10 Removing the 3 insulator bolts and insulator

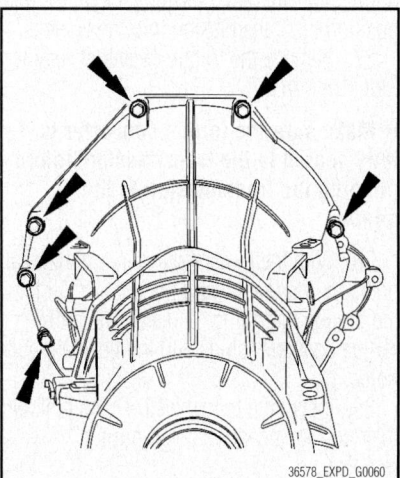

Fig. 11 Locating the remaining transmission housing bolts

31. Disconnect the wire harness from the top of the transmission

32. Disconnect the main transmission electrical harness by twisting the outer shell and pulling back on the connector

➡The top 2 transmission-to-engine bolts need to be removed prior to removing the rest of the bolts. The top left bolt secures the fuel line bracket to the transmission case.

33. Remove the 6 remaining transmission case bolts.

34. Slide the transmission back far enough to install the torque converter retainer tool 307-346. This holds the torque converter in place.

35. Remove the transmission from the vehicle.

✱✱ WARNING

If the transmission is to be overhauled or if installing a new transmission, carry out transmission fluid cooler back flushing and cleaning. Make sure the cooler is not restricted. If you have poor cooler flow replace with a new transmission cooler.

To install:

✱✱ WARNING

The converter housing is piloted into position by dowels in the rear of the engine block. The torque converter must rest squarely against the flexplate. This indicates that the converter pilot is not binding in the engine crankshaft.

36. Position and secure the transmission on the high-lift transmission jack. Raise and position the transmission into the vehicle.

37. Remove the torque converter retainer tool 307-346.

➡Make sure the torque converter is fully seated in the transmission before aligning the transmission to the engine.

38. With the transmission in a horizontal position, move it toward the engine. Align the orange balancing marks between the torque converter studs and the flexplate bolt holes.

39. Install the transmission case bolts in their correct locations noted during removal.

➡The top 2 transmission case bolts need to be installed prior to installing the rest of the bolts. The top left bolt is

inserted through the fuel line bracket first, then through the transmission case.

40. Install 6 of the 7 transmission case bolts and tighten to 35 ft. lbs. (48 Nm).

41. Connect the main transmission electrical harness by pushing it in and twisting the outer shell to lock it in place.

42. Connect the wire harness to the top of the transmission.

43. Position the dual converter Y-pipe in place. Install and tighten the 2 dual converter Y-pipe to 30 ft. lbs. (40 Nm).

44. Install the LH and RH exhaust flange nuts and tighten to 30 ft. lbs. (40 Nm).

45. Install the 3 bolts and the insulator, tighten to 66 ft. lbs. (90 Nm).

46. Position the rear crossmember in place and loosely install the transmission insulator nuts.

47. Install the crossmember.

48. Install the 4 crossmember bolts and nuts and tighten to 66 ft. lbs. (90 Nm).

49. Tighten the transmission insulator nuts to 76 ft. lbs. (103 Nm).

50. Install the fuel line bracket tighten the mounting bolt to 18 ft. lbs. (25 Nm).

51. Connect the RH and LH heated oxygen sensors (HO2S) electrical connectors and the CMS electrical connectors.

52. Install the LH exhaust heat shield and evaporative emissions canister assembly bolts. Tighten the bolts to 11 ft. lbs.(15 Nm).

53. Install the RH exhaust heat shield bolt and tighten to 11 ft. lbs.(15 Nm).

54. Position the starter motor in place, install and tighten the 3 starter motor bolts to 19 ft. lbs. (26 Nm).

55. Install the ground wire on the stud, install and tighten the ground wire nut to 17 ft. lbs. 23 (Nm).

56. Install the starter motor electrical connectors. Tighten main power cable to 9 ft. lbs. (15 Nm).

57. Tighten the smaller solenoid feed wire to 53 inch. (6 Nm).

58. Install the plastic starter motor electrical connector cap.

59. Position the transmission cooler tubes in place, install and tighten the bracket nut to 20 ft. lbs. (27 Nm).

60. Align the bracket and install the remaining transmission case bolt. Tighten to 35 ft. lbs. (48 Nm).

➡Inspect the case to make sure that the old O-rings are not stuck in the case. Install new O-rings on the ends of the cooler lines prior to installing.

61. Install new O-rings on the transmission fluid cooler tubes.

62. Install the transmission cooler tubes and tighten the bracket bolt to 17 ft. lbs. (23 Nm).

63. Install 4 new flexplate-to-torque converter nuts. Tighten the nuts to 26 ft. lbs. (35 Nm).

64. Install the rubber access plug.

65. Install the flexplate inspection cover and tighten the flexplate inspection cover bolts to 26 ft. lbs. (35 Nm).

66. Install the selector lever bracket and tighten the bolts to 35 ft. lbs. (48 Nm).

➡When installing the selector lever cable, make sure that the selector lever cable locking tabs are locked in place and the cable end is snapped onto the ball stud. Press the selector lever cable into the bracket and listen for the cable to click into place. Pull back on the selector lever cable to make sure that it is locked into the bracket. Also, make sure that the selector lever cable end is correctly installed onto the ball stud. Pull back on the selector lever cable to make sure that the cable end is correctly installed.

67. With the manual lever in NEUTRAL, connect the selector lever cable onto the manual lever ball stud and move the locking tab down. Listen for the audible click.

68. Pull back on the selector lever cable to make sure that it is correctly installed.

69. If equipped, install the heat shield.

70. Install the driveshaft.

71. Connect the battery ground cable.

72. Verify that the selector lever cable is correctly adjusted.

73. Reflash the transmission control module (TCM) to the latest level of software.

74. Fill the transmission with clean automatic transmission fluid.

75. Test drive and check for leaks.

4WD Models

See Figure 12.

1. Before servicing the vehicle, refer to the precautions section.

2. Disconnect the battery ground cable.

3. With the vehicle in NEUTRAL, position it on a hoist.

4. Remove the fluid fill plug fluid level indicator assembly located on the passenger side front portion of the transmission case. Removal of the plug will relieve any vacuum that might have built up in the transmission. This will aid in allowing the fluid pan to be easily removed when the bolts are removed.

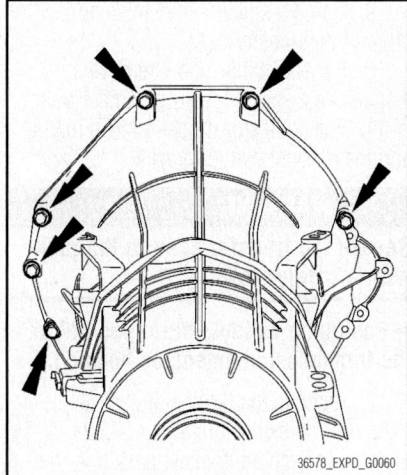

Fig. 12 Locating the remaining transmission housing bolts

➡️**If transmission disassembly or installation of a new transmission is necessary, the transmission fluid will need to be drained.**

5. Remove the transmission fluid pan and allow the fluid to drain

6. Install the fluid pan and tighten the bolts in a crisscross pattern.

7. Remove the transfer case.

8. Remove the fuel line bracket bolt and position the bracket and lines aside.

9. If equipped, remove the heat shield.

10. Move the locking tab up and disconnect the selector lever cable from the manual lever ball stud.

11. Remove the selector lever bracket bolts and remove the bracket.

12. Remove the flexplate inspection cover bolts and the inspection cover.

13. Remove the rubber torque converter nut access plug.

14. Remove and discard the 4 flexplate-to-torque converter nuts.

15. Remove the transmission cooler tube bracket bolt.

16. Remove the transmission case bolt.

17. Remove the transmission fluid cooler tube bracket nut and position the bracket and tubes.

18. Remove the plastic starter motor electrical connector cap.

19. Remove the starter motor electrical connectors.

20. Remove the ground wire from the stud.

21. Remove the 3 starter motor bolts and the starter motor.

22. Disconnect the wiring harness from the top of the transmission.

23. Disconnect the main transmission electrical harness by twisting the outer shell and pulling back on the connector.

➡️ **The top 2 transmission-to-engine bolts need to be removed prior to removing the rest of the bolts. The top left bolt secures the fuel line bracket to the transmission case.**

24. Remove the 6 remaining transmission case bolts.

25. Leaving the transmission in a horizontal position, slide it back far enough to install the torque converter holding tool 307-346.

26. Make sure that the torque converter holding tool 307-346 is in place and the transmission is securely fastened to the transmission jack before tilting the transmission.

27. Remove the transmission from the vehicle.

To install:

⁕ WARNING

The converter housing is piloted into position by dowels in the rear of the engine block. The torque converter must rest squarely against the flexplate. This indicates that the converter pilot is not binding in the engine crankshaft.

28. Position and secure the transmission on the high-lift transmission jack. Raise and position the transmission into the vehicle.

29. Remove the torque converter retainer tool 307-346.

➡️**Make sure the torque converter is fully seated in the transmission before aligning the transmission to the engine.**

30. With the transmission in a horizontal position, move it toward the engine. Align the orange balancing marks between the torque converter studs and the flexplate bolt holes.

31. Install the transmission case bolts in their correct locations noted during removal.

➡️**The top 2 transmission case bolts need to be installed prior to installing the rest of the bolts. The top left bolt is inserted through the fuel line bracket first, then through the transmission case.**

32. Install 6 of the 7 transmission case bolts and tighten to 35 ft. lbs. (48 Nm).

33. Connect the main transmission electrical harness by pushing it in and twisting the outer shell to lock it in place

34. Connect the wire harness to the top of the transmission.

35. Position the starter motor in place, install and tighten the 3 starter motor bolts to 19 ft. lbs. (26 Nm).

36. Install the ground wire on the stud, install and tighten the ground wire nut to 17 ft. lbs. 23 (Nm).

37. Install the starter motor electrical connectors. Tighten main power cable to 9 ft. lbs. (15 Nm).

38. Tighten the smaller solenoid feed wire to 53 inch. (6 Nm).

39. Install the plastic starter motor electrical connector cap.

40. Position the transmission cooler tubes in place, install and tighten the bracket nut to 20 ft. lbs. (27 Nm).

41. Align the bracket and install the remaining transmission case bolt. Tighten to 35 ft. lbs. (48 Nm).

➡️**Inspect the case to make sure that the old O-rings are not stuck in the case. Install new O-rings on the ends of the cooler lines prior to installing.**

42. Install new O-rings on the transmission fluid cooler tubes.

43. Install the transmission cooler tubes and tighten the bracket bolt to 17 ft. lbs. (23 Nm).

44. Install 4 new flexplate-to-torque converter nuts. Tighten the nuts to 26 ft. lbs. (35 Nm).

45. Install the rubber access plug.

46. Install the flexplate inspection cover and tighten the inspection cover bolts to 26 ft. lbs. (35 Nm).

47. Install the selector lever bracket and tighten the bolts to 35 ft. lbs. (48 Nm).

➡️**When installing the selector lever cable, make sure that the selector lever cable locking tabs are locked in place and the cable end is snapped onto the ball stud. Press the selector lever cable into the bracket and listen for the cable to click into place. Pull back on the selector lever cable to make sure that it is locked into the bracket. Also, make sure that the selector lever cable end is correctly installed onto the ball stud. Pull back on the selector lever cable to make sure that the cable end is correctly installed.**

48. With the manual lever in NEUTRAL, connect the selector lever cable onto the manual lever ball stud and move the locking tab down. Listen for the audible click.

49. Pull back on the selector lever cable to make sure that it is correctly installed.

50. If equipped, install the heat shield.

51. Install the fuel line bracket and tighten the mounting bolt to 18 ft. lbs. (25 Nm).

52. Install the transfer case.

53. Connect the battery ground cable.

54. Verify that the selector lever cable is correctly adjusted.

55. Reflash the transmission control module (TCM) to the latest level of software.

56. Fill the transmission with clean automatic transmission fluid.

57. Test drive and check for leaks.

TRANSFER CASE ASSEMBLY

REMOVAL & INSTALLATION

See Figure 13.

1. Before servicing the vehicle, refer to the precautions in the beginning of this section.

2. With the vehicle in NEUTRAL, position it on a hoist.

3. Drain the fluid if the transfer case is to be disassembled. Install the drain plug when finished draining.

4. Remove the 2 nuts and the front driveshaft shield.

➡**Index-mark Both of the driveshaft's to maintain initial driveshaft balance during installation.**

5. Remove the front driveshaft.

6. Remove the rear driveshaft.

7. Disconnect the electrical connector.

8. Disconnect the vent hose.

9. Using a suitable transmission jack, support the transfer case.

10. For Navigator model remove the 2 exhaust heat shield-to-crossmember bolts.

11. For Navigator model remove the bolt and the exhaust hanger bracket.

✳✳ WARNING

Secure the transfer case to the jack with a safety strap.

➡**Position a suitable drain pan below the transmission extension housing.**

12. Remove the 6 transfer case-to-transmission extension housing bolts.

13. Separate the transfer case from the transmission extension housing, move the transfer case rearward off the output shaft,

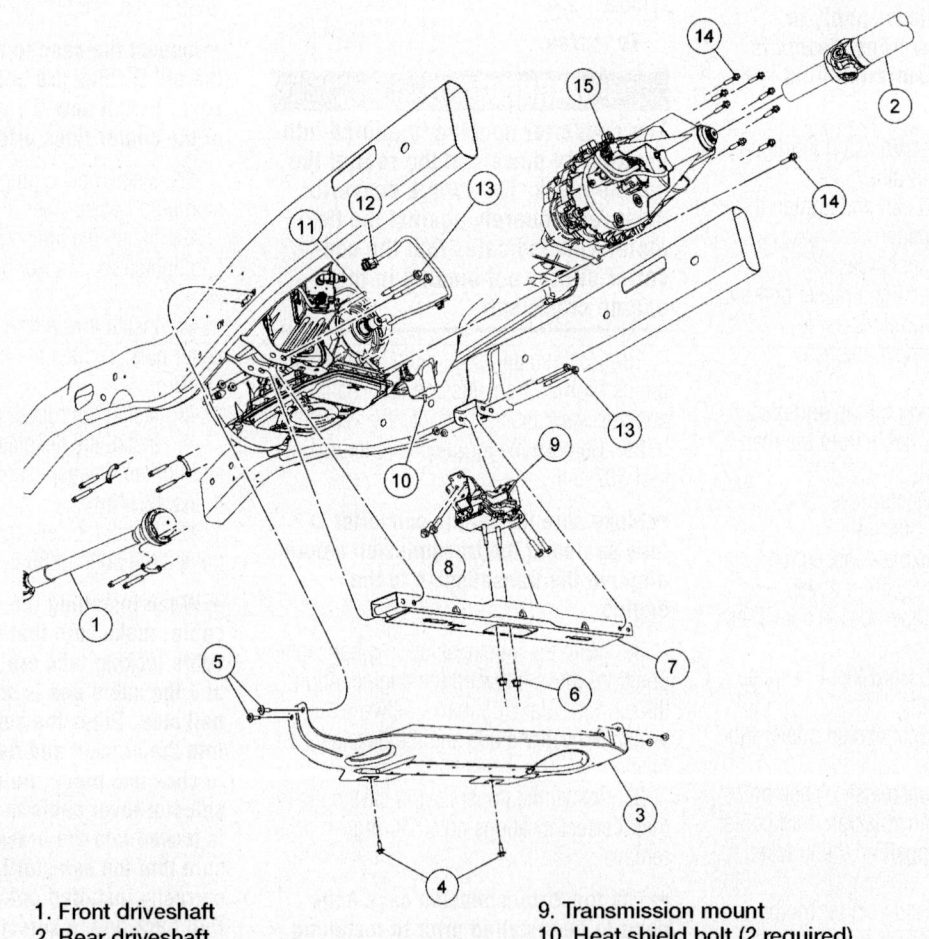

1. Front driveshaft
2. Rear driveshaft
3. Skid plate
4. Skid plate-to-crossmember bolts (2 required)
5. Skid plate-to-frame bolts (4 required)
6. Transmission mount nut (2 required)
7. Crossmember
8. Transmission mount bolt (4 required)
9. Transmission mount
10. Heat shield bolt (2 required)
11. Vent hose
12. Shift motor electrical connector
13. Crossmember bolts (4 required)
14. Transfer case bolts (9 required)
15. Transfer case

36578_EXPD_G0067

Fig. 13 Exploded view of the transfer case

then lower the transfer case from the vehicle.

14. Remove the transfer case-to-transmission gasket and clean the mating surfaces.

To install:

To install, reverse the removal procedure and note the following:

a. Tighten the transfer case-to-transmission bolts evenly in a star pattern.

b. Tighten the transfer case-to-transmission bolts to 35 ft. lbs. (47 Nm).

c. Navigator model tighten the transfer case-to-transmission bolts to 30 ft. lbs. (40 Nm).

d. Navigator model tighten the 2 exhaust heat shield-to-crossmember bolts to 30 ft. lbs. (40 Nm).

e. Navigator model tighten the exhaust hanger bracket to 30 ft. lbs. (40 Nm).

f. Tighten the front drive shaft shield nuts to 13 ft. lbs. (18 Nm).

g. Install a new transfer case-to-transmission gasket.

h. Adjust the transmission selector lever cable.

i. Fill the transfer case if previously drained. Refer to Specifications in this section for the correct type and quantity of fluid.

j. Tighten drain plug to 11 ft. lbs. (15 Nm).

FRONT AXLE ASSEMBLY

REMOVAL & INSTALLATION

See Figure 14.

1. Before servicing the vehicle, refer to the precautions section.

2. With the transmission in NEUTRAL, raise and support the vehicle

3. Index-mark the front driveshaft to the universal joint drive pinion flange.

Fig. 14 Four crossmember bolts shown

4. Disconnect and support the front driveshaft.

➡**Do not allow the driveshaft to hang unsupported.**

5. Remove the bolts, and disconnect both front drive halfshafts from the front axle shaft.

6. Remove the 4 crossmember bolts and the crossmember.

7. Use a high-lift jack to support the axle assembly.

8. Remove the axle housing isolator nut and bolts.

9. Remove the front mounting isolator bolt.

10. Remove the bolt from the lower steering shaft-to-steering gear and disconnect the coupler from the rack.

11. Remove the upper mounting isolator bolt.

12. Carefully lower the front drive axle assembly.

13. Disconnect the vent hose from the axle vent barbed fitting.

To install:

14. To install, reverse the removal procedure and not the following:

a. Tighten axle housing isolator bolts and nut to 85 ft. lbs. (115 Nm).

b. Tighten housing isolator bolts and nut to 111 ft. lbs. (150 Nm).

c. Tighten crossmember bolts to 66 ft. lbs. (90 Nm).

d. Tighten halfshaft mounting bolts to 60 ft. lbs. (82 Nm).

e. Tighten front drive shaft mounting bolts to 83 ft. lbs. (112 Nm).

f. Tighten the bolt from the lower steering shaft-to-steering gear to 22 ft. lbs. (22 Nm).

FRONT HALFSHAFTS

REMOVAL & INSTALLATION

See Figure 15.

1. Before servicing the vehicle, refer to the precautions section.

➡**Whenever a halfshaft is removed, a new circlip and stub shaft pilot bearing seal must be installed.**

2. With the vehicle in NEUTRAL, position it on a hoist.

3. Disable the air suspension system.

4. Remove the dust cap.

5. Remove and discard the axle nut.

6. Remove the vacuum/vent line at the vacuum/vent port of the Integrated Wheel End (IWE) disconnect.

7. Remove the 3 IWE retaining bolts to the steering knuckle.

8. Disconnect the tie-rod end from the steering knuckle.

9. Discard the tie-rod end nut.

10. Disconnect the upper ball joint from the steering knuckle.

11. Discard the upper ball joint nut.

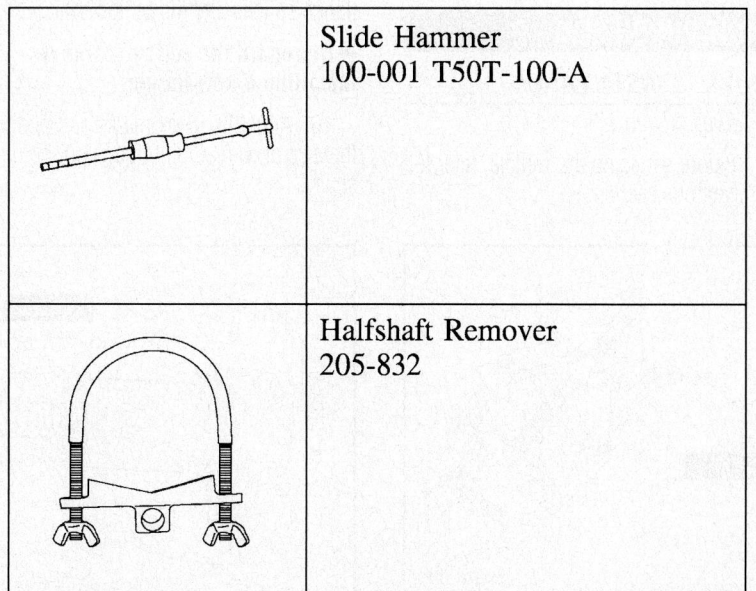

Special Tools

Slide Hammer 100-001 T50T-100-A	
Halfshaft Remover 205-832	

Fig. 15 Special tools, slide hammer and halfshaft remover

✳✳ WARNING

Do not damage the hub seal.

→Allow the steering knuckle to swing outboard while keeping the constant velocity (CV) shaft pushed inboard.

12. Once clearance is available, remove the CV shaft joint outboard end and IWE disconnect from the steering knuckle hub bearing.

13. Remove the IWE disconnect from the outboard CV joint housing.

14. Using special tools 205-832 and 100-001, remove the halfshaft from the differential and the intermediate shaft.

15. Remove and discard the circlip and the stub shaft seal.

✳✳ WARNING

Verify the spline engagement by checking for spline lash before installing the halfshaft nut.

To install:

16. To install, reverse the removal procedure.

a. Install a new axle nut, tie-rod end nut and an upper ball joint nut.

b. Install the tie rod and use a new nut. Tighten the nut to 111 ft. lbs. (150 Nm).

c. Install the ball joint and use a new nut. Tighten the nut to 111 ft. lbs. (150 Nm).

d. Tighten the 3 IWE retaining bolts to 9 ft. lbs. (12 Nm).

e. Install a new axle nut and tighten to 20 ft. lbs. (27 Nm).

FRONT PINION SEAL

REMOVAL & INSTALLATION

See Figures 16 and 17.

1. Before servicing the vehicle, refer to the precautions section.

2. Position the vehicle on a hoist.

→Remove the front brake caliper to prevent drag during the drive pinion bearing preload adjustment.

3. Remove the front brake calipers. Wire the caliper aside.

4. Index-mark the front driveshaft to the axle universal joint flange

5. Remove and discard the 6 bolts and 3 washers.

6. Carefully disconnect and support the front driveshaft

7. Using a Nm (inch/pound) torque wrench, measure the torque necessary to maintain pinion rotation. Record the measurement for reference during installation.

8. Install special tool 205-126 and remove the pinion nut

9. Index-mark the axle universal joint flange to the pinion stem.

10. Using special tool 205-D072, separate the axle universal joint flange from the pinion gear.

11. Remove the flange.

12. Inspect the axle universal joint flange for burrs, the nut counterbore and the seal contact surface for nicks, and the bearing cone contact area for damage. Install a new flange if necessary.

13. Check the pinion stem splines for burrs. If burrs are evident, remove them with a fine crocus cloth.

To install:

14. Clean the pinion seal bore and use an oil seal installer to install the pinion seal.

15. Lubricate the axle universal joint flange splines and the pinion seal

→Disregard the scribe marks if installing a new flange.

16. Align the index marks and position the axle universal joint flange on the pinion shaft.

→Rotate the pinion gear occasionally to make sure the pinion bearings seat correctly.

17. Using special tool 205-002, install the axle universal joint flange.

18. Install the special tool, and tighten the pinion nut.

a. Rotate the pinion gear occasionally to make sure the pinion bearings are seating correctly.

b. Take frequent pinion bearing torque preload readings by rotating the pinion gear with a (Nm)inch/pound torque wrench.

c. If the preload recorded prior to disassembly is lower than the specification for used bearings, then tighten the pinion nut to the specification 29 inch lbs. (1.8-3.3 Nm).

d. If the preload recorded prior to disassembly is higher than the specification for used bearings, then tighten the pinion nut to the original reading as recorded.

19. Align the index-marks then attach the front driveshaft and tighten the 6 flange bolts to 41 ft. lbs. (55 Nm).

20. Inspect and, if necessary, fill the differential.

21. Lower the vehicle.

REAR AXLE HOUSING

REMOVAL & INSTALLATION

With Rear Air Suspension
See Figure 18.

1. Before servicing the vehicle, refer to the precautions section.

2. Deflate the rear air springs.:
- Make sure that the air suspension switch is in the ON position.
- Make sure that a battery voltage of at least 11 volts is maintained while carrying out this procedure.

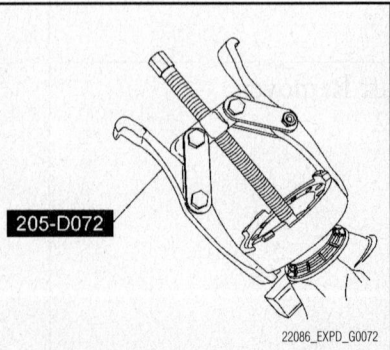

22086_EXPD_G0072

Fig. 16 Flange removal with special tool 205-D072

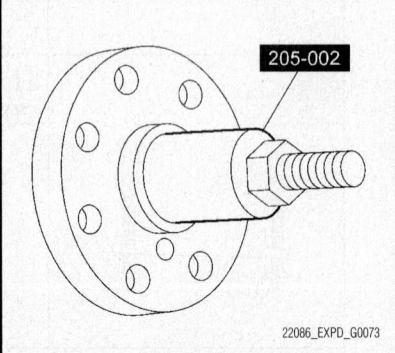

22086_EXPD_G0073

Fig. 17 Axle flange installation with special tool 205-002

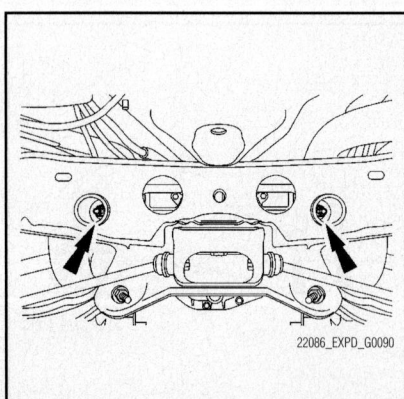

22086_EXPD_G0090

Fig. 18 Upper housing stud nut view

- Turn the ignition switch to the ON position.
- Connect the diagnostic tool to the Data Link Connector (DLC).
- Select Air Suspension Control Module under Active Command Mode.
- Follow the diagnostic tool directions to lift or vent the rear suspension.

3. With the vehicle in NEUTRAL, position the vehicle on a hoist.

4. Remove the rear wheel and tire assemblies.

5. Remove the rear driveshaft assembly.

6. Remove the axle halfshafts.

7. Remove the lower rear sway bar links.

8. Remove the 4 bracket bolts and remove the rear sway bar.

9. Using a suitable jack, support the axle housing

10. Remove the upper axle housing stud nuts.

11. Remove the front torque arm bolt.

➡**Move the axle housing forward to clear the rear mounting studs from the bushings.**

12. Lower the axle housing from the vehicle.

13. To install, reverse the removal procedure and note the following:

   a. Tighten the lower rear sway bar link nuts to 66 ft. lbs. (90 Nm).

   b. Tighten the 4 bracket bolts to 30 ft. lbs. (40 Nm).

   c. Tighten the upper axle housing stud nuts to 100 ft. lbs. (135 Nm).

   d. Tighten the front torque arm bolt to 100 ft. lbs. (135 Nm).

   e. Reactivate rear air suspension.

With Rear Coil Suspension

1. Before servicing the vehicle, refer to the precautions section.

2. With the vehicle in NEUTRAL, position the vehicle on a hoist.

3. Remove the rear wheel and tire assemblies.

4. Remove the rear driveshaft assembly.

5. Remove the axle halfshafts.

6. Remove the lower rear sway bar links.

7. Remove the 4 bracket bolts and remove the rear sway bar.

8. Using a suitable jack, support the axle housing

9. Remove the upper axle housing stud nuts.

10. Remove the front torque arm bolt.

➡**Move the axle housing forward to clear the rear mounting studs from the bushings.**

11. Lower the axle housing from the vehicle.

12. To install, reverse the removal procedure and note the following:

   a. Tighten the lower rear sway bar link nuts to 66 ft. lbs. (90 Nm).

   b. Tighten the 4 bracket bolts to 30 ft. lbs. (40 Nm).

   c. Tighten the upper axle housing stud nuts to 100 ft. lbs. (135 Nm).

   d. Tighten the front torque arm bolt to 100 ft. lbs. (135 Nm).

REAR HALFSHAFTS

REMOVAL & INSTALLATION

See Figures 19 and 20.

✷✷ WARNING

Do not loosen the rear axle wheel hub retainer until after the wheel and tire assembly is removed from the vehicle. Wheel bearing damage will occur if the wheel bearing is unloaded with the weight of the vehicle applied.

1. Before servicing the vehicle, refer to the precautions section.

2. With the vehicle in NEUTRAL, raise and support the vehicle.

➡**Have an assistant press the brake pedal to keep the axle from rotating.**

3. Remove and discard the rear axle wheel hub retainer and the washer.

4. Using a suitable hub puller, separate the halfshaft from the knuckle

5. Remove the brake disc rotor.

6. Remove the upper trailing arm bolt.

7. Remove the upper trailing arm-to-wheel knuckle nut.

8. Using the special tool 204-592, separate the upper arm from the wheel knuckle.

9. Remove the stabilizer bar link.

10. Remove the toe link-to-knuckle bolt.

11. Disconnect the anti-lock brake sensor at the connector and open the wire retaining clips

12. Compress the spring, depress the retaining tabs and detach the parking brake cable from the wheel knuckle.

13. Remove the 2 lower trailing arm-to-wheel knuckle bolts.

14. Remove the lower ball joint nut.

15. Using the special tool 204-592, separate the lower ball joint from the wheel knuckle.

16. Rotating the top of the knuckle assembly outboard, remove the knuckle assembly.

➡**A circlip retains the inboard CV joint housing to the differential side gear in the axle.**

17. Using the special tool 205-529 and 205-123, disengage the inboard CV joint housing from the differential side gear.

18. Remove the halfshaft assembly from the vehicle.

19. Remove and discard the halfshaft retainer circlip.

✷✷ WARNING

Always install a new differential stub shaft seal, a new retainer circlip and a new rear axle wheel hub retainer.

20. To install, reverse the removal procedure and note the following:

   a. Tighten the rear axle wheel hub retainer 254 ft. lbs. (345 Nm).

   b. Tighten the upper trailing arm bolt to 184 ft. lbs. (250 Nm).

   c. Tighten the upper trailing arm-to-wheel knuckle nut to 76 ft. lbs. (103 Nm).

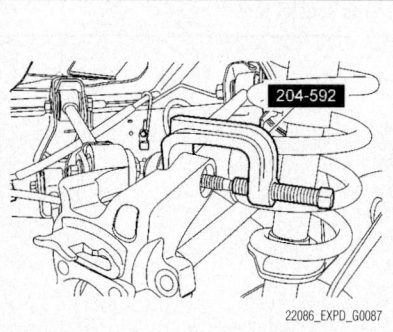

22086_EXPD_G0087

Fig. 19 Separating the upper arm from the wheel knuckle using the special tools

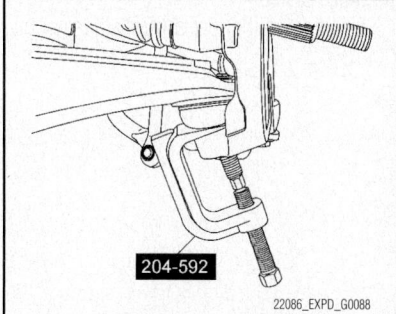

22086_EXPD_G0088

Fig. 20 Separating the lower ball joint from the wheel knuckle using the special tools

d. Tighten the stabilizer bar link nut to 46 ft. lbs. (63 Nm).

e. Tighten the toe link-to-knuckle bolt to 166 ft. lbs. (225 Nm).

f. Tighten the 2 lower trailing arm-to-wheel knuckle bolts to 76 ft. lbs. (103 Nm).

g. Tighten the lower ball joint nut to 111 ft. lbs. (150 Nm).

REAR PINION SEAL

REMOVAL & INSTALLATION

See Figures 21 and 22.

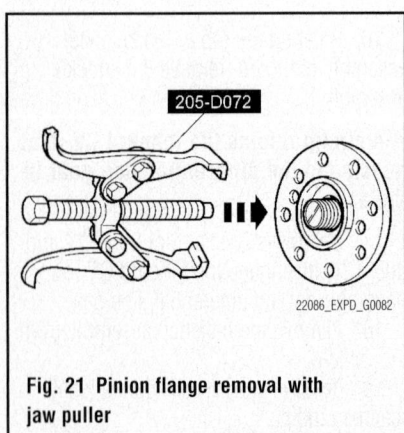

Fig. 21 Pinion flange removal with jaw puller

1. Before servicing the vehicle, refer to the precautions section.

➡️ If equipped, turn the air suspension switch to the OFF position.

➡️ The rear wheels and brake calipers must be removed to prevent brake drag during drive pinion bearing preload adjustment.

2. With the vehicle in NEUTRAL, position the vehicle on a hoist.

3. Remove the rear wheel and tire assemblies.

4. Remove the rear brake calipers and the brake discs.

5. Remove the rear driveshaft assembly.

6. Install a Nm (lb-in) torque wrench on the nut and record the torque necessary to maintain rotation of the drive pinion gear through several revolutions

✳️ WARNING

After removing the pinion nut, discard it. Use a new nut for installation.

7. Use the special tool to hold the pinion flange while removing the pinion nut.

8. Index-mark the drive pinion flange and the drive pinion gear stem to maintain initial balance during installation.

9. Using the special tool 205-D072, remove the drive pinion flange.

10. Force up on the metal flange of the drive pinion seal. Install gripping pliers and strike with a hammer until the pinion seal is removed.

To install:

11. Lubricate the lips of the new drive pinion seal with grease.

12. Using the special tool 205-208, install the drive pinion seal.

13. Lubricate the drive pinion flange splines with rear axle lubricant

14. Position the drive pinion flange.

15. Using the special tool 205-233, install the drive pinion flange.

16. Position the new drive pinion nut

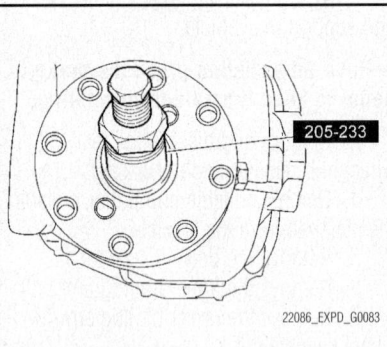

Fig. 22 Drive pinion flange installation with special tool

✳️ WARNING

Do not under any circumstance loosen the nut to reduce preload. If it is necessary to reduce preload, install a new drive pinion collapsible spacer and nut.

17. Use the special tool 205-126 to hold the pinion flange while tightening the nut.

- Rotate the pinion occasionally to make sure the pinion bearings seat correctly. Take frequent pinion bearing torque preload readings by rotating the drive pinion gear with a Nm (lb-in) torque wrench
- If the preload recorded prior to disassembly is lower than the specification for used bearings, tighten the nut to 16-29 inch lbs. (1.8-3.3 mm).
- If the preload recorded prior to disassembly is higher than the specification for used bearings, tighten the nut to the original reading as recorded.

➡️ Install the driveshaft with new bolts. If new bolts are not available, apply sealer to the threads of the original bolts.

18. Align the index marks.

➡️ The driveshaft flange yoke fits tightly on the pinion flange pilot. To make sure that the yoke seats squarely on the flange, tighten the bolts evenly in a cross pattern as shown.

19. Install the rear driveshaft.

20. Install the rear brake discs and the brake calipers.

21. Check fluid level and add if needed.

22. Install the rear wheel and tire assemblies.

23. Lower the vehicle.

24. If equipped with air suspension, reactivate the system.

ENGINE COOLING

ENGINE FAN

REMOVAL & INSTALLATION
See Figure 23.

1. With the vehicle in NEUTRAL, position it on a hoist.
2. Disconnect the cooling fan electronic clutch electrical connector.
3. Remove the nut and the cooling fan electronic clutch harness support bracket from the stud bolt.
4. Release the cooling fan shroud position tab and rotate the shroud upwards until the lower tab locks into position.
5. Using the special tools 303-214 and 303-239, remove the cooling fan assembly.
6. To install, reverse the removal procedure and note the following:
    a. Tighten the cooling fan electronic clutch harness support bracket nut to 10 ft. lbs. (13 Nm).

b. Tighten fan assembly to 41 ft. lbs. (55 Nm).

RADIATOR

REMOVAL & INSTALLATION
See Figure 24.

1. Before servicing the vehicle, refer to the precautions section.
2. With the vehicle in NEUTRAL, position it on a hoist.
3. Remove the RH and LH headlamp assemblies.
4. Remove the cooling fan shroud.
5. Remove the 2 radiator-to-radiator support bolts.
6. Remove the 2 bolts and position the degas bottle aside.
7. Disconnect the electrical connector and remove the bolt and the horn assembly.

8. Remove the 6 LH and RH air deflector-to-condenser core pin-type retainers.
9. Disconnect the 2 transmission fluid cooler-to-radiator hoses.

➡ **The cooling module must be positioned rearward to raise and detach the 4 condenser mounts from the radiator.**

10. Depress the retaining tabs on the 2 lower condenser mounting brackets and raise the condenser assembly until the 4 condenser mounting brackets detach from the radiator.
11. Remove the radiator.
12. To install, reverse the removal procedure and note the following:
    a. Tighten radiator-to-radiator support bolts to 11 ft. lbs.(15 Nm).
    b. Tighten degas bottle mounting bolts to 11 ft. lbs.(15 Nm).
    c. Tighten horn assembly mounting bolt to 89 inch lbs. (10 Nm).

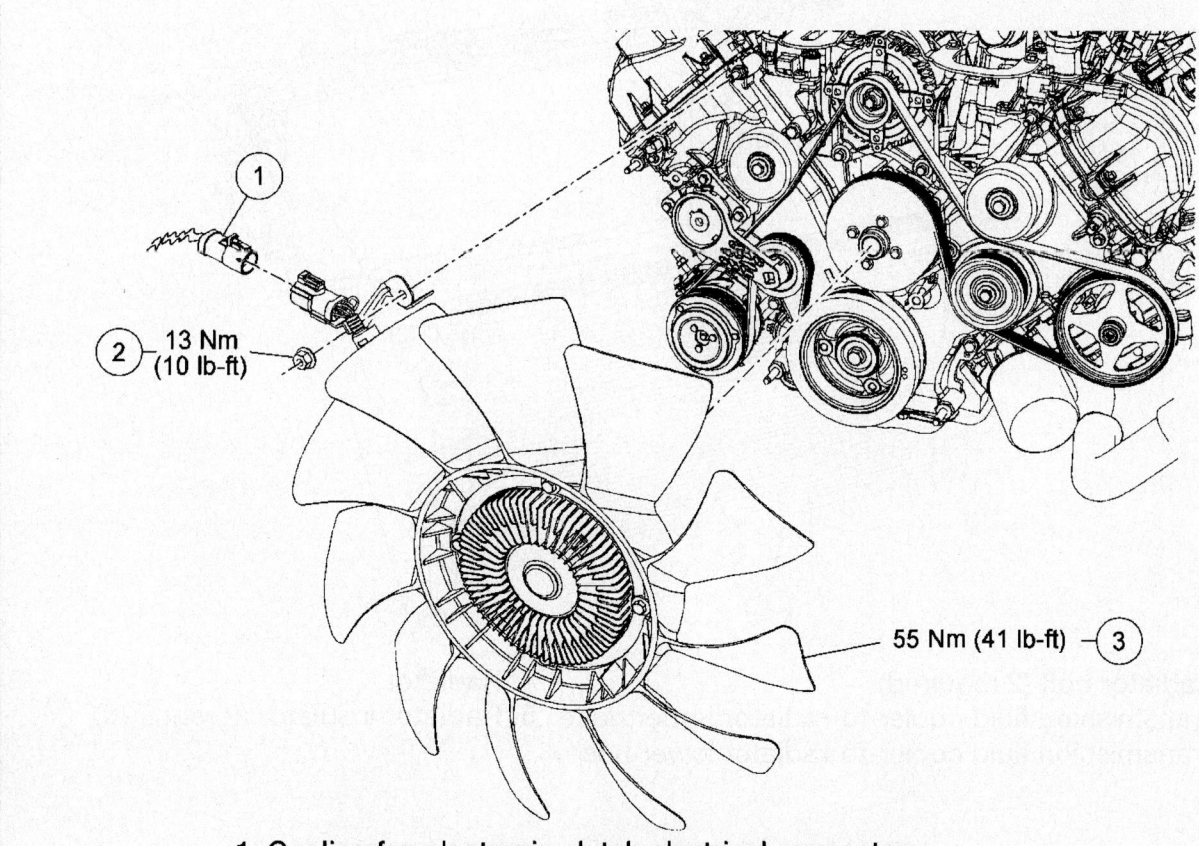

1. Cooling fan electronic clutch electrical connector
2. Cooling fan electronic clutch wiring harness support bracket nut
3. Cooling fan and clutch assembly

22086_EXPD_G0025

Fig. 23 View of cooling fan and clutch assembly

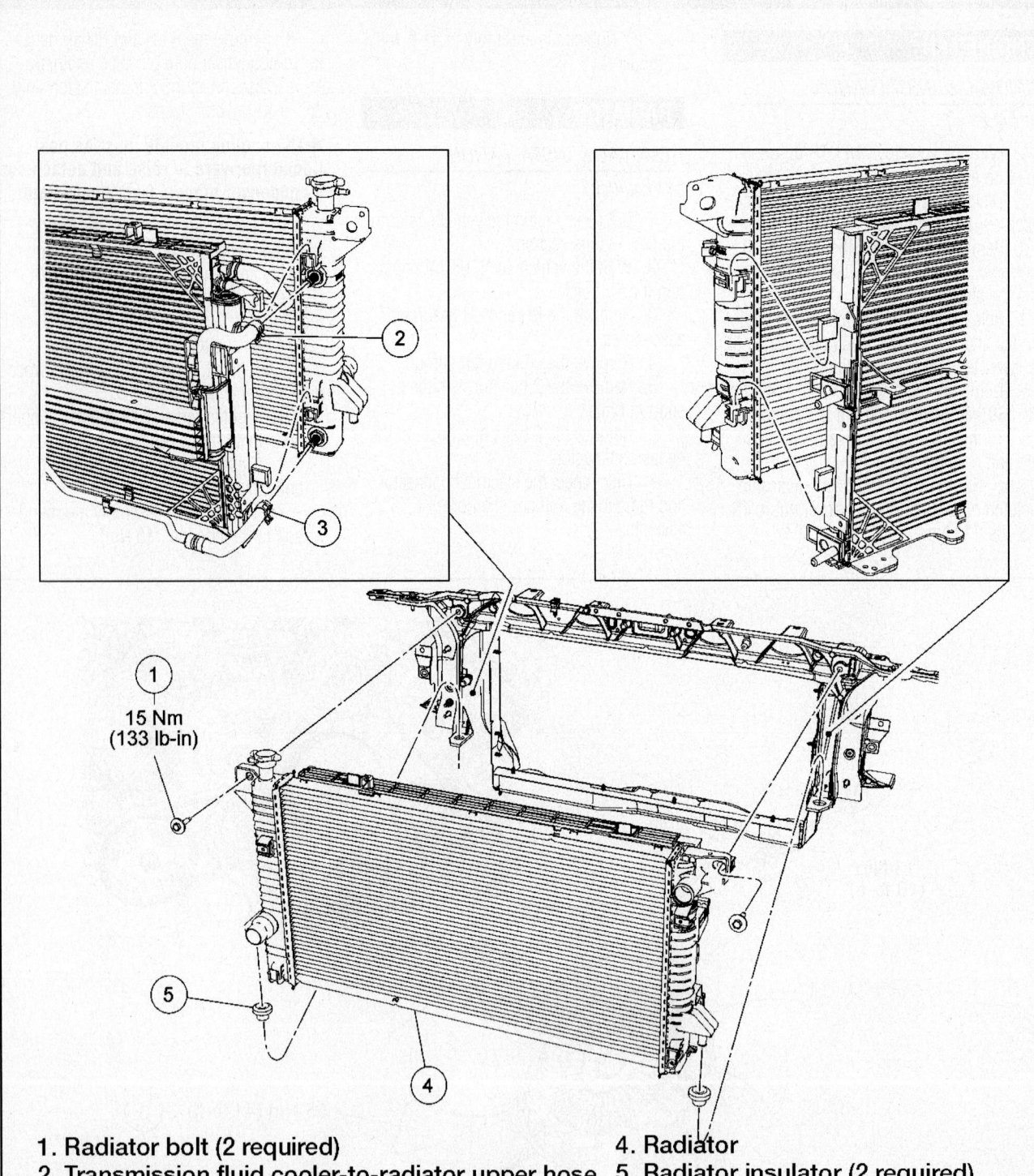

1. Radiator bolt (2 required)
2. Transmission fluid cooler-to-radiator upper hose
3. Transmission fluid cooler-to-radiator lower hose
4. Radiator
5. Radiator insulator (2 required)

36578_EXPD_G0073

Fig. 24 Exploded view of radiator and components

THERMOSTAT

REMOVAL & INSTALLATION

See Figure 25.

1. Before servicing the vehicle, refer to the precautions section.

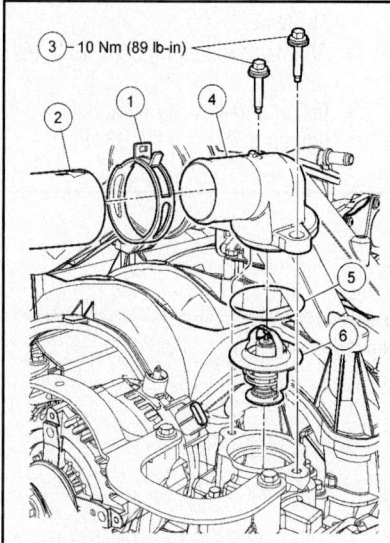

1. Upper radiator hose clamp
2. Upper radiator hose
3. Thermostat housing bolts (2 required)
4. Thermostat housing
5. Thermostat O-ring seal
6. Thermostat

36578_EXPD_G0076

Fig. 25 View of thermostat and housing

2. Partially drain the cooling system to a level below the thermostat.
3. Disconnect the upper radiator hose.
4. Remove the 2 bolts, the thermostat housing and the thermostat. Discard the O-ring seal.
5. Inspect the mating surfaces. Clean the sealing surfaces with metal surface prep and silicone gasket remover. Follow the directions on the packaging.
6. If necessary, install a new thermostat with the spring facing down.
7. Install a new O-ring seal.
8. Make sure the thermostat housing is seated evenly by hand tightening the 2 thermostat housing bolts prior to final tightening.
9. To install, reverse the removal procedure. Tighten thermostat housing bolts to 89 inch lbs. (10 Nm).

WATER PUMP

REMOVAL & INSTALLATION

See Figures 26 and 27.

1. Before servicing the vehicle, refer to the precautions section.
2. Drain the engine cooling system.
3. Remove the cooling fan.
4. Loosen the 4 coolant pump pulley bolts.
5. Rotate the belt tensioner clockwise

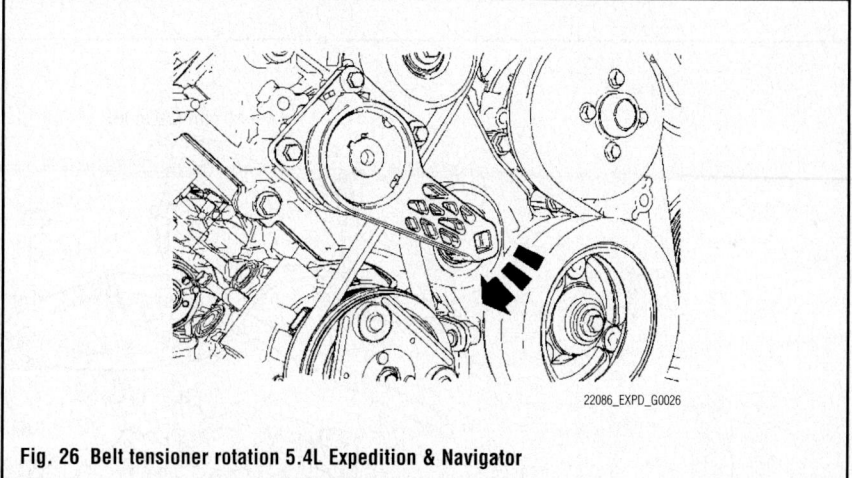

22086_EXPD_G0026

Fig. 26 Belt tensioner rotation 5.4L Expedition & Navigator

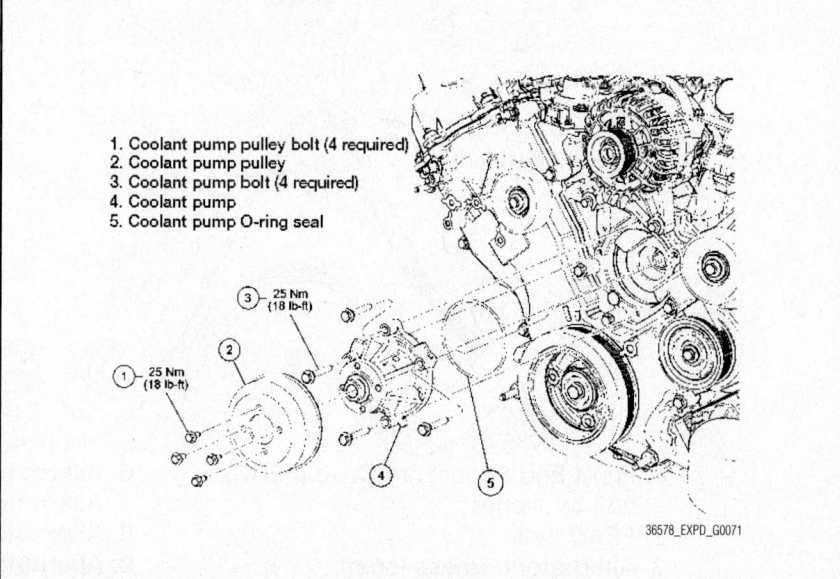

1. Coolant pump pulley bolt (4 required)
2. Coolant pump pulley
3. Coolant pump bolt (4 required)
4. Coolant pump
5. Coolant pump O-ring seal

3. 25 Nm (18 lb-ft)
1. 25 Nm (18 lb-ft)

36578_EXPD_G0071

Fig. 27 Exploded view of water pump and components

and disconnect the accessory drive belt from the coolant pump pulley.

6. Remove the 4 bolts and the coolant pump pulley.
7. Remove the 4 bolts and the coolant pump. Discard the O-ring seal.
8. To install, reverse the removal procedure and note the following:

a. Tighten water pump pulley bolts and water pump mounting bolts to 18 ft. lbs. (25 Nm).

ENGINE ELECTRICAL   **CHARGING SYSTEM**

ALTERNATOR

REMOVAL & INSTALLATION

See Figure 28.

1. Disconnect the negative battery cable.
2. For Navigator, release the 2 retainers and remove the engine cover.
3. Remove the air cleaner intake pipe.
4. Rotate the front end accessory drive belt tensioner counterclockwise and position the accessory drive belt aside.
5. Remove the harness locator from the alternator bracket.
6. Remove the 4 bolts and the alternator bracket.
7. Remove the 2 bolts and position the alternator aside
8. Disconnect the alternator electrical connector.
9. Position the alternator B+ protective cover aside, remove and discard the nut, then position the generator B+ terminal aside.
10. Remove the alternator.
11. To install, reverse the removal procedure and note the following:

- Alternator bracket bolts 89 inch lbs. (10 Nm).
- Alternator mounting bolts 18 ft. lbs. (25 Nm).
- Install a new B+ terminal nut; tighten to 71 inch lbs. (8 Nm).

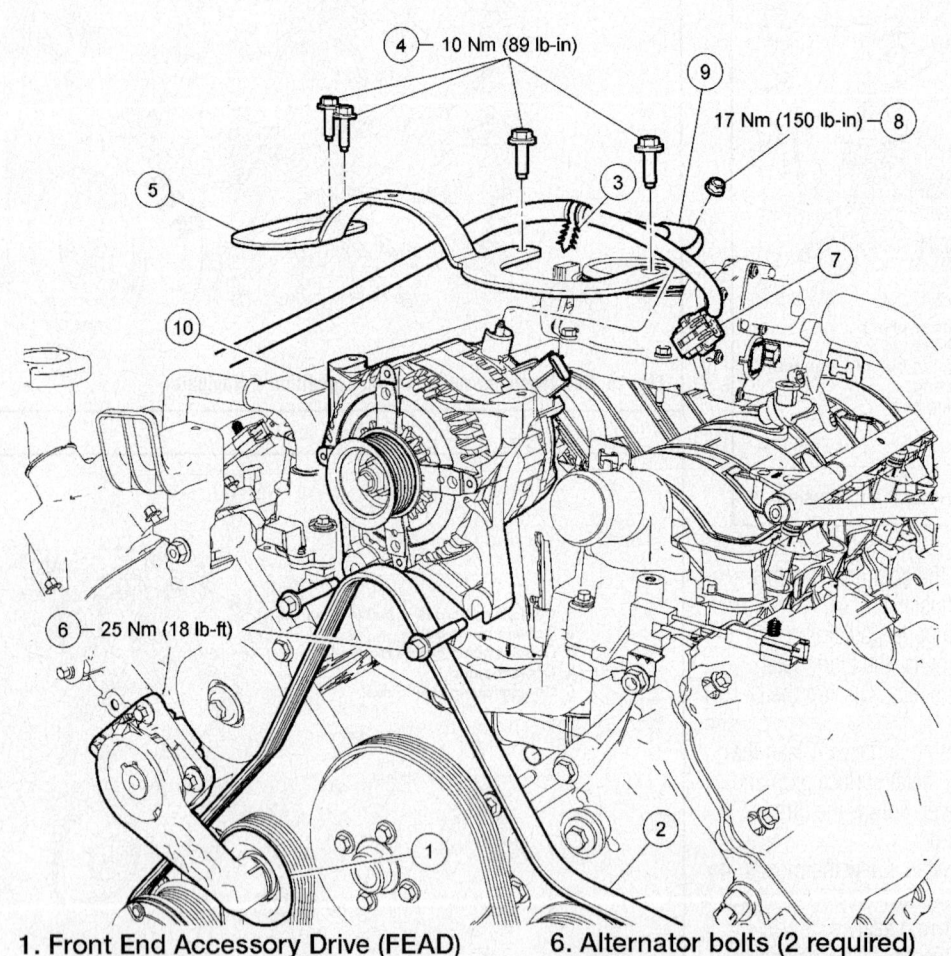

1. Front End Accessory Drive (FEAD) belt tensioner
2. FEAD belt
3. Alternator harness locator
4. Alternator bracket bolts (4 required)
5. Alternator bracket
6. Alternator bolts (2 required)
7. Alternator electrical connector
8. Alternator B+ terminal nut
9. Alternator B+ terminal
10. Alternator

36578_EXPD_G0079

Fig. 28 Exploded view of the alternator and components

ENGINE ELECTRICAL   **DISTRIBUTORLESS SYSTEM**

FIRING ORDERS

See Figure 29.

Fig. 29 5.4L Engines
Firing order: 1–3–7–2–6–5–4–8
Distributorless ignition system
(one coil on each cylinder)

IGNITION COIL

REMOVAL & INSTALLATION

See Figures 30 and 31.

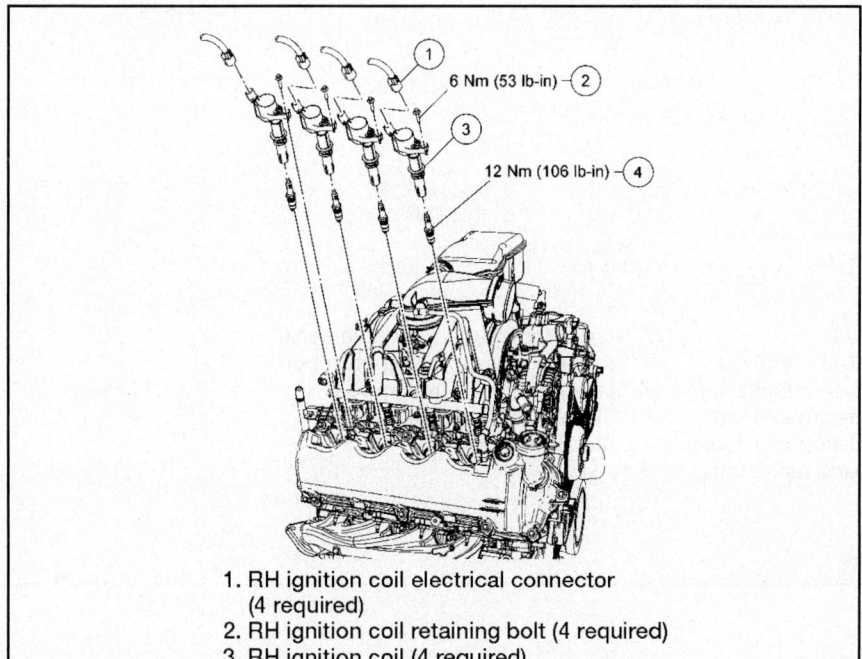

1. RH ignition coil electrical connector
   (4 required)
2. RH ignition coil retaining bolt (4 required)
3. RH ignition coil (4 required)
4. RH spark plug (4 required)

36578_EXPD_G0080

Fig. 30 Exploded view of the engine ignition components–RH

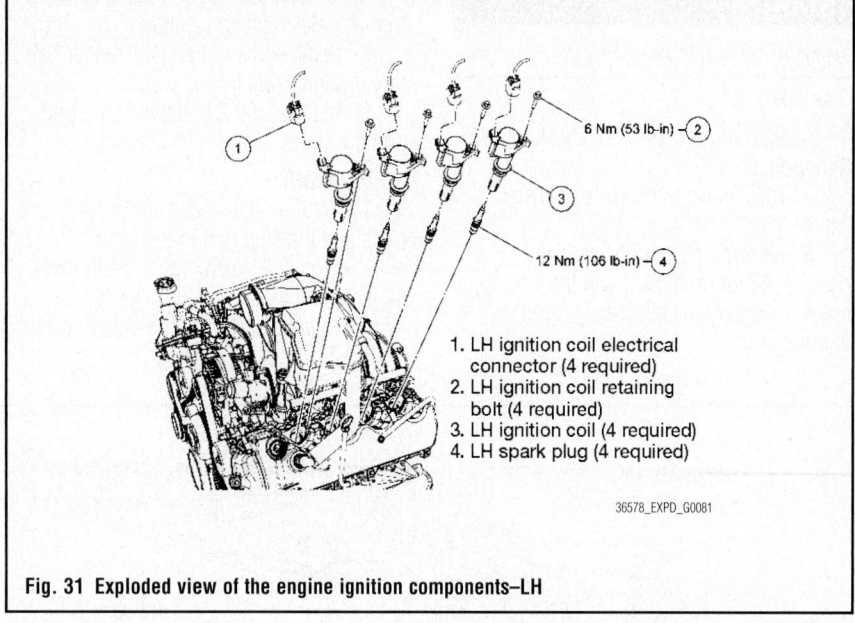

1. LH ignition coil electrical
   connector (4 required)
2. LH ignition coil retaining
   bolt (4 required)
3. LH ignition coil (4 required)
4. LH spark plug (4 required)

36578_EXPD_G0081

Fig. 31 Exploded view of the engine ignition components–LH

1. Before servicing the vehicle, refer to the precautions section.
2. Disconnect the negative battery cable.
3. Remove the bolts and the ignition coil cover.
4. Disconnect the electrical connector from the ignition coil.
5. Remove the ignition coils.
6. Installation is the reverse of the removal procedure. Tighten the ignition coil cover bolts to 9 ft. lbs. (12 Nm).

IGNITION TIMING

ADJUSTMENT

Base timing for distributorless ignition engines is set at the factory at 10 degrees Before Top Dead Center (BTDC) and is not adjustable.

SPARK PLUGS

REMOVAL & INSTALLATION

See Figures 30 and 31.

1. Before servicing the vehicle, refer to the precautions section.
2. Disconnect the negative battery cable.
3. Remove the coil on plugs as outlined under Ignition Coil in this section.

➡**Remove any foreign material from the spark plug wells with compressed air before removing the spark plugs.**

4. Remove the spark plugs.
5. Inspect the spark plugs
6. Adjust the spark plug gap as necessary. Proper gap is 0.52–0.56 in. (1.32–1.42mm).

To install:

7. Install the spark plugs and tighten them to 25 ft. lbs. (34 Nm).
9. Install the coil on plugs.
10. Connect the negative battery cable.

ENGINE ELECTRICAL

STARTER

REMOVAL & INSTALLATION

See Figure 32.

1. With the vehicle in NEUTRAL, position it on a hoist.

2. Disconnect the negative battery cable.

3. Remove the starter terminal cover and remove the nut and the solenoid S-terminal electrical connection.

4. Remove the nut and the solenoid B-terminal electrical connection.

5. Remove the nut and the starter battery ground cable from the stud.

6. Remove the 2 bolts, the stud bolt and the starter motor.

To install:

7. Position the starter and install the 2 bolts and the stud bolt in 3 stages.
   - Stage 1: Install the 2 starter bolts and the stud bolt finger tight.
   - Stage 2: Tighten the upper bolt to 18 ft. lbs. (25 Nm).
   - Tighten the lower bolt and stud bolt to 18 ft. lbs. (25 Nm).

8. Position the starter battery ground cable onto the stud and install the nut. Tighten to 18 ft. lbs. (25 Nm).

9. Connect the solenoid B-terminal electrical connection and install the nut. Tighten to 9 ft. lbs. (12 Nm).

10. Connect the solenoid S-terminal electrical connection and install the nut and the starter terminal cover. Tighten to 56 inch lbs. (6 Nm).

11. Connect the negative battery cable.

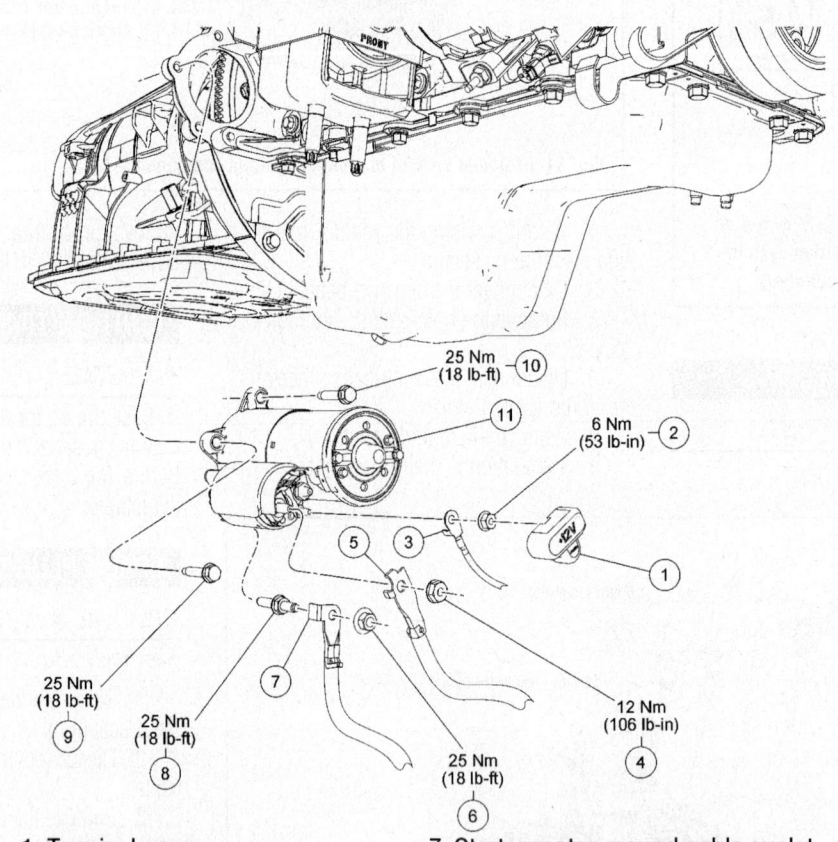

1. Terminal cover
2. Starter solenoid S-terminal nut
3. Starter solenoid S-terminal eyelet
4. Starter solenoid B-terminal nut
5. Starter solenoid B-terminal eyelet
6. Starter motor ground cable nut
7. Starter motor ground cable eyelet
8. Starter motor mounting stud bolt
9. Starter motor mounting bolt
10. Starter motor mounting bolt
11. Starter motor

36578_EXPD_G0082

Fig. 32 Exploded view of the starter and components

ENGINE MECHANICAL

ACCESSORY DRIVE BELTS

ACCESSORY BELT ROUTING

See Figure 33.

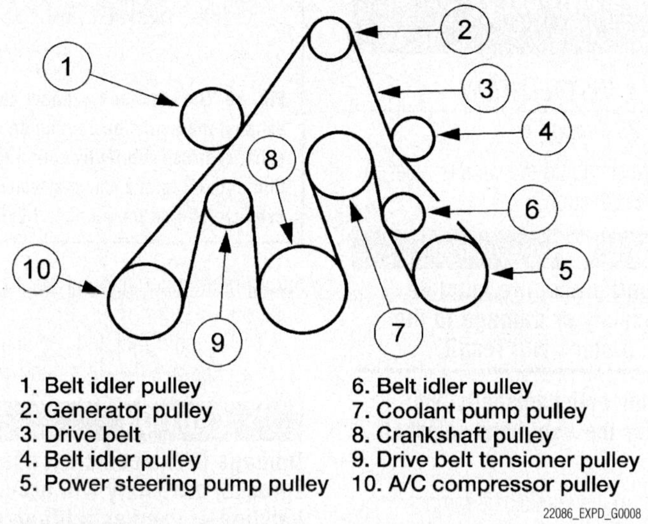

Fig. 33 Accessory serpentine belt routing—5.4L engines with A/C

1. Belt idler pulley
2. Generator pulley
3. Drive belt
4. Belt idler pulley
5. Power steering pump pulley
6. Belt idler pulley
7. Coolant pump pulley
8. Crankshaft pulley
9. Drive belt tensioner pulley
10. A/C compressor pulley

22086_EXPD_G0008

INSPECTION

> ✴✴ **WARNING**
>
> **Under no circumstances should the accessory drive belt, tensioner or pulleys be lubricated as potential damage to the belt material and tensioner damping mechanism will occur. Do not apply any fluids or belt dressing to the accessory drive belt or pulleys.**

Visual Inspection

Visually inspect the belt for obvious signs of mechanical damage:
- Drive belt cracking/chunking/wear
- Belt/pulley contamination
- Incorrectly routed belt
- Pulley misalignment or excessive pulley runout
- Loose or mislocated hardware
- Incorrectly routed power steering tubes (rubbing)

Eliminate all other non-belt related noises that could cause belt misdiagnosis, such as A/C compressor engagement chirp, power steering cavitations at low temperatures, variable camshaft timing (VCT) tick or generator whine.

If a concern is found, correct the condition before proceeding to the next section.

V-Ribbed Serpentine Drive Belt With Cracks Across Ribs

See Figure 34.

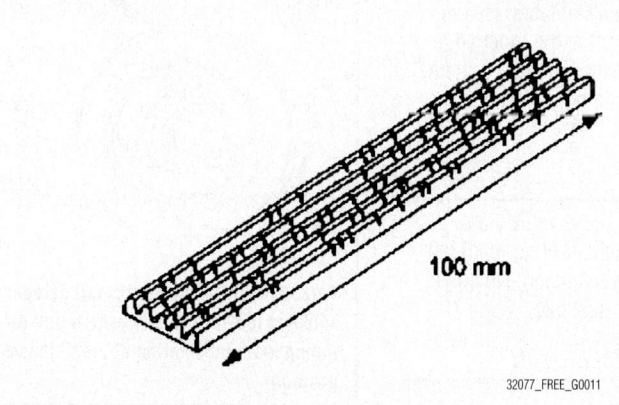

Fig. 34 Up to 15 cracks in a rib over a distance of 4 inches (100mm) can be considered acceptable. If cracks exceed this standard, install a new belt

100 mm

32077_FREE_G0011

➡ **Up to 15 cracks in a rib over a distance of 4 inches (100mm) can be considered acceptable. If damage exceeds the acceptable limit or any chunks are found to be missing from the ribs, a new belt must be installed.**

1. Check the belt for cracks. Up to 15 cracks in a rib over a distance of 4 inches (100mm) can be considered acceptable. If cracks exceed this standard, install a new belt.

V- Ribbed Serpentine Belt With Piling

See Figure 35.

➡ **Piling is an excessive buildup in the V-grooves of the belt.**

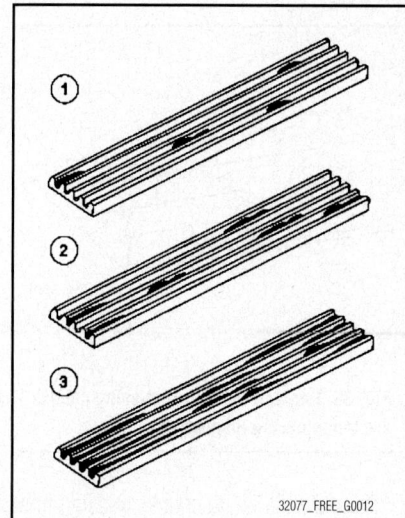

32077_FREE_G0012

Fig. 35 Compare the condition of the belt with the accompanying text

The condition of the V-ribbed drive belt should be compared against the illustration and appropriate action taken.

1. Small scattered deposits of rubber material. This is not a concern, therefore, installation of a new belt is not required.

2. Longer deposit areas building up to 50 percent of the rib height. This is not considered a concern but it can result in excessive noise. If noise is apparent, install a new belt.

3. Heavy deposits building up along the

grooves resulting in a possible noise and belt stability concern. If heavy deposits are apparent, install a new belt.

V-Ribbed Serpentine Belt With Chunks of Rib Missing

See Figure 36.

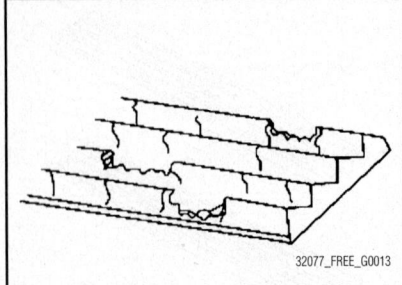

Fig. 36 Replace the belt if missing chunks are found during inspection

There should be no chunks missing from the belt ribs. If the belt shows any evidence of this, install a new accessory drive belt.

Inspect the drive belt for signs of glazing or cracking. A glazed belt will be perfectly smooth from slippage, while a good belt will have a slight texture of fabric visible. Cracks will usually start at the inner edge of the belt and run outward. All worn or damaged drive belts should be replaced immediately.

ADJUSTMENT

The belts used on these vehicle are equipped with automatic (spring load) tensioners which maintain tension. No adjustment is necessary or possible.

REMOVAL & INSTALLATION

See Figures 33 and 37.

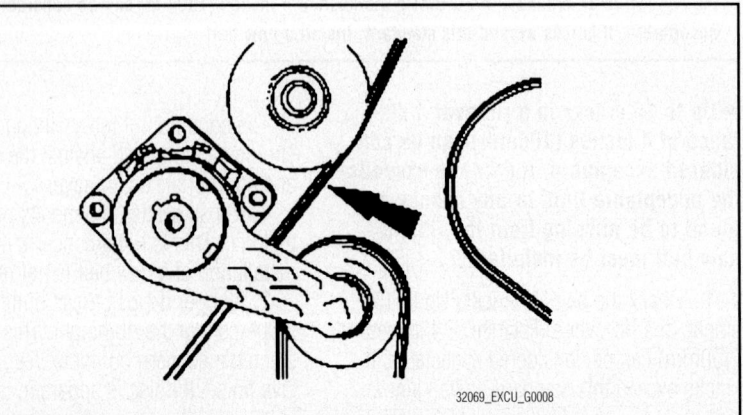

Fig. 37 Rotate the drive belt tensioner clockwise and remove the drive belt

1. Remove the air cleaner outlet pipe.
2. Rotate the drive belt tensioner clockwise and remove the drive belt.

To install:
3. Installation is the reverse of the removal procedure. Make sure the belt is routed properly.

CAMSHAFT AND VALVE LIFTERS

REMOVAL & INSTALLATION

See Figures 38 through 48.

1. Before servicing the vehicle, refer to the precautions section.

> ※※ **WARNING**
>
> **The camshaft procedure must be followed exactly or damage to the valves and pistons will result.**

➡ **If removing both camshafts, you must remove the right hand camshaft first.**

2. Position the crankshaft damper spoke at the 12 o'clock position and the

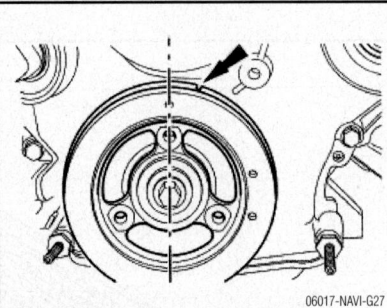

Fig. 38 Position the crankshaft damper spoke at the 12 o'clock position and the timing mark indentation at the 1 o'clock position

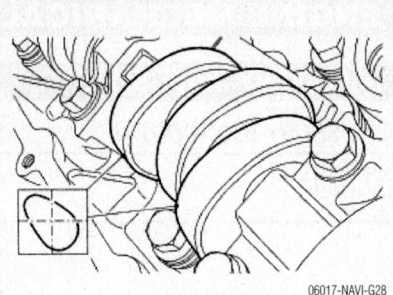

Fig. 39 The number 1 cylinder camshaft exhaust lobe must be coming up on the exhaust stroke. Verify by noting the position of the 2 intake camshaft lobes and the exhaust lobe on the number 1 cylinder

timing mark indentation at the 1 o'clock position.

3. For the right hand camshaft:
   a. Remove the right hand valve cover.

> ※※ **CAUTION**
>
> **Damage to the camshaft phaser sprocket assembly will occur if mishandled or used as a lifting or leveraging device.**

   b. Loosen and back off the right hand camshaft phaser bolt 1 full turn.
   c. Disconnect the right hand Camshaft Position (CMP) sensor connector.
   d. Remove the bolt and the right hand CMP sensor.

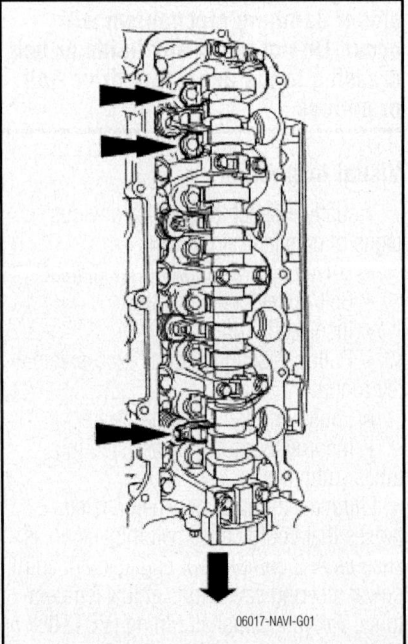

Fig. 40 Remove only the 3 roller followers shown from the right hand cylinder head

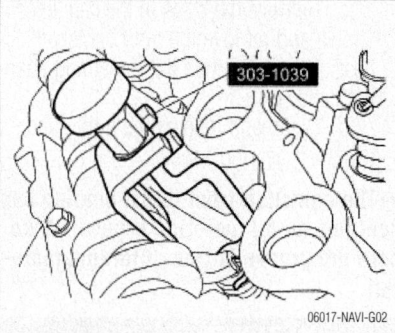

Fig. 41 Using the tool illustrated, remove the 3 designated roller followers

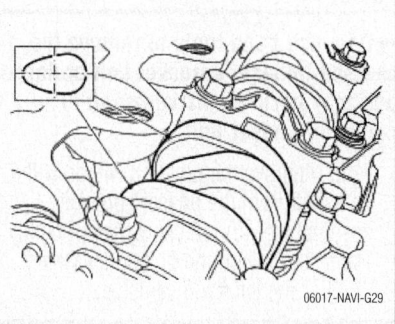

Fig. 42 The number 5 cylinder camshaft lobe must be coming up on the exhaust stroke. Verify by noting the position of the 2 intake camshaft lobes and the exhaust lobe on the number 5 cylinder

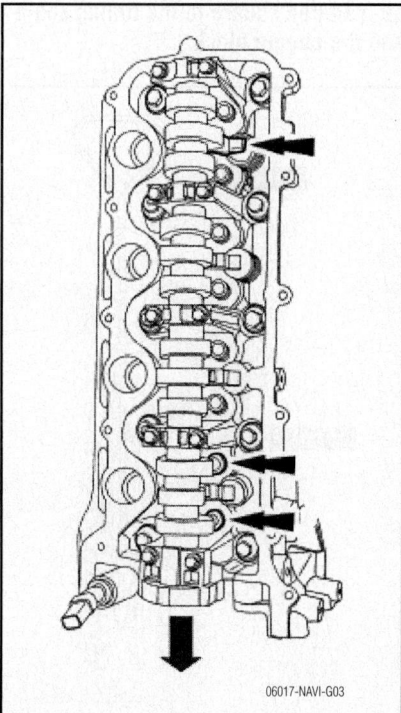

Fig. 43 Remove only the 3 roller followers shown from the left hand cylinder head

➡️If the camshaft lobes are not exactly positioned as shown, the crankshaft will require 1 full additional rotation to 12 o'clock.

  e. The number 1 cylinder camshaft exhaust lobe must be coming up on the exhaust stroke. Verify by noting the position of the 2 intake camshaft lobes and the exhaust lobe on the number 1 cylinder.

Fig. 44 Rotate the crankshaft clockwise, as viewed from the front, positioning the crankshaft damper spoke at the 6 o'clock position and the timing mark indentation at the 7 o'clock position

4. Remove only the 3 roller followers shown in the illustration.

✳✳ WARNING

Do not allow the valve keepers to fall off the valve or the valve may drop into the cylinder.

➡️The camshaft roller followers must be installed in their original locations. Record camshaft roller follower locations. It may be necessary to push the valve down while compressing the spring.

  a. Using the tool illustrated, remove the 3 designated roller followers in the previous step from the right hand cylinder head.

5. For the left hand camshaft:
  a. Remove the left hand valve cover.

✳✳ WARNING

Damage to the camshaft phaser sprocket assembly will occur if mishandled or used as a lifting or leveraging device.

  b. Loosen and back off the left hand camshaft phaser bolt 1 full turn.

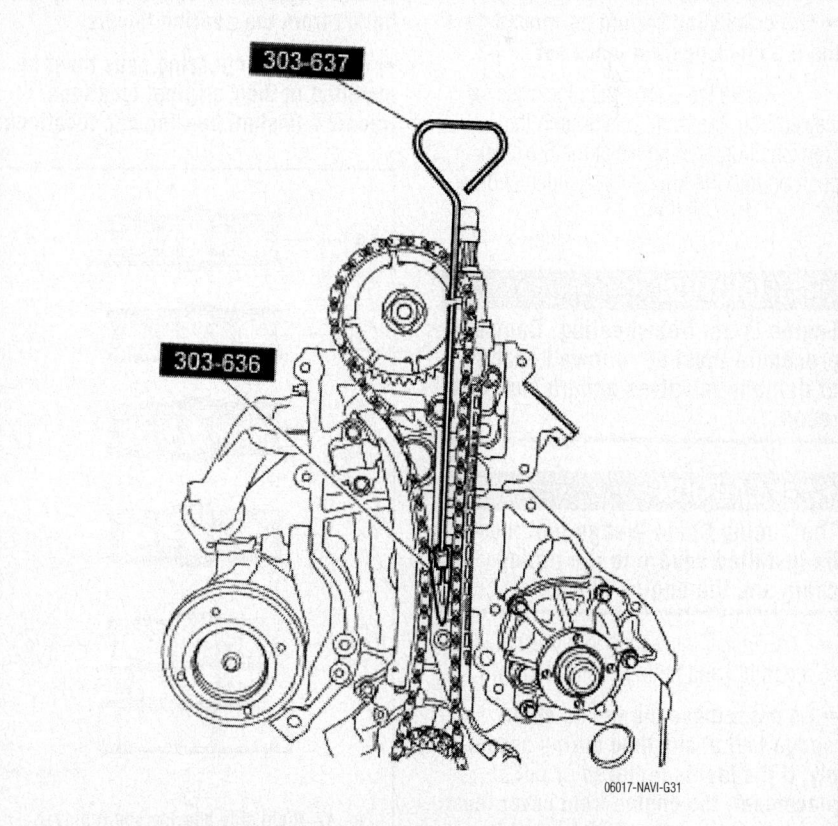

Fig. 45 Install the wedge tool illustrated in the right hand timing chain

c. Disconnect the left hand Camshaft Position (CMP) sensor connector.

d. Remove the left hand CMP sensor and the bolt.

➡ **If servicing both camshafts, do not rotate the crankshaft. As camshaft position has been established.**

➡ **If the camshaft lobes are not exactly positioned as shown, the crankshaft keyway will require one full additional rotation to 12 o'clock.**

e. The number 5 cylinder camshaft lobe must be coming up on the exhaust stroke. Verify by noting the position of the 2 intake camshaft lobes and the exhaust lobe on the number 5 cylinder.

f. Remove only the 3 roller followers shown in the illustration from the left hand cylinder head.

➡ **The camshaft roller followers must be installed in their original locations. Record camshaft roller follower locations.**

➡ **It may be necessary to push the valve down while compressing the spring.**

g. Using the tool illustrated, remove the 3 designated roller followers in the previous step from the left hand cylinder head.

➡ **The crankshaft cannot be moved past the 6 o'clock position once set.**

6. Rotate the crankshaft clockwise, as viewed from the front, positioning the crankshaft damper spoke at the 6 o'clock position and the timing mark indentation at the 7 o'clock position.

7. For the right hand camshaft:

✳✳ CAUTION

Engine is not freewheeling. Camshaft procedure must be followed exactly or damage to valves and pistons will result.

✳✳ CAUTION

The Timing Chain Wedge tool must be installed square to the timing chain and the engine block.

a. Install the wedge tool illustrated in the right hand timing chain as shown.

➡ **Do not remove the timing chain wedge tool at any time during assembly. If the tool is removed or out of placement, the engine front cover must be removed and the engine must be retimed.**

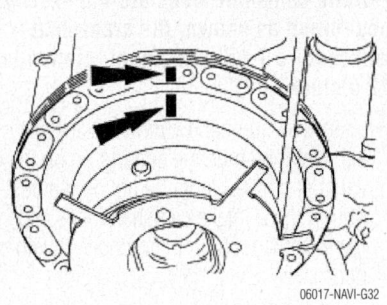
Fig. 46 Scribe a location mark on the timing chain and the camshaft phaser sprocket assembly, right side shown, left side similar

✳✳ WARNING

The timing chain must be installed in its original position onto the camshaft phaser sprocket using the scribed marks, or damage to valves and pistons will result.

b. Scribe a location mark on the timing chain and the camshaft phaser sprocket assembly.

➡ **When removing the front thrust camshaft bearing cap, use care as the cap may be damaged from sideloading when removing the cam unequally in height from the bearing towers.**

➡ **The camshaft bearing caps must be installed in their original locations. Record camshaft bearing cap locations.**

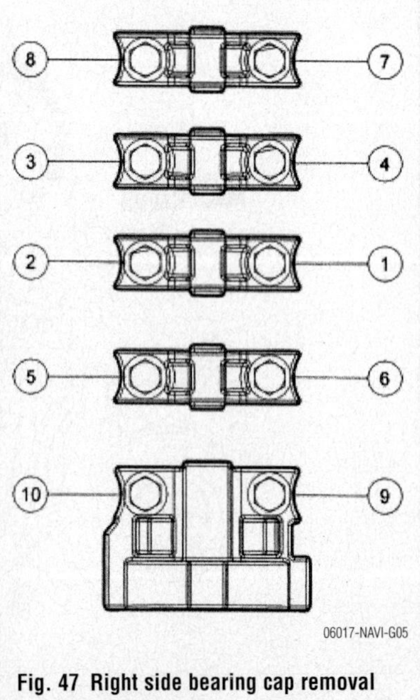

Fig. 47 Right side bearing cap removal and tightening sequence, left side similar

c. Remove the bolts in the sequence shown and remove the front camshaft bearing cap and then the remaining bearing caps.

d. Clean and inspect the right hand camshaft bearing caps.

➡ **The camshaft front thrust bearing cap contains an oil metering groove. Make sure the groove is free of foreign material.**

✳✳ WARNING

Damage to the camshaft phaser sprocket assembly will occur if mishandled or used as a lifting or leveraging device.

➡ **Only use hand tools to remove the camshaft phaser sprocket bolt or damage may occur to the camshaft or camshaft phaser unit.**

e. Remove the bolt and withdraw the camshaft from the phaser sprocket assembly leaving the sprocket assembly in place. Discard the bolt and washer.

8. For the left hand camshaft:

✳✳ WARNING

Engine is not freewheeling. Camshaft procedure must be followed exactly or damage to valves and pistons will result.

➡ **The Timing Chain Wedge tool must be installed square to the timing chain and the engine block.**

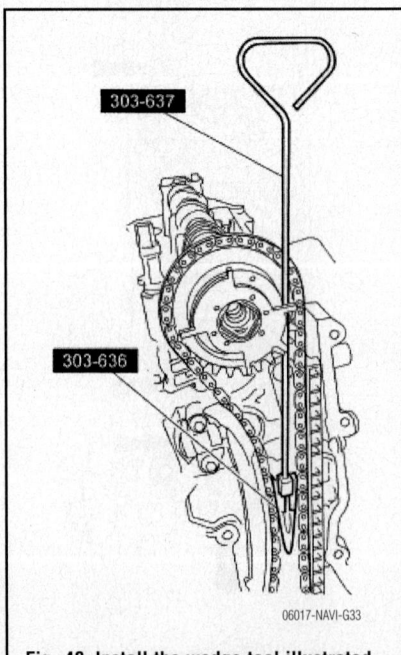
Fig. 48 Install the wedge tool illustrated in the left hand timing chain

a. Install the wedge tool illustrated in the left hand timing chain as shown.

➡Do not remove the timing chain wedge tool at any time during assembly. If the special tool is removed or out of placement, the engine front cover must be removed and the engine must be retimed.

✳✳ WARNING

The timing chain must be installed in its original position onto the camshaft phaser sprocket using the scribed marks, or damage to valves and pistons will result.

b. Scribe a location mark on the timing chain and the camshaft phaser sprocket assembly.

➡When removing the front thrust camshaft bearing cap, use care as the cap may be damaged from sideloading when removing the cam unequally in height from the bearing towers.

➡The camshaft bearing caps must be installed in their original locations. Record camshaft bearing cap locations.

c. Remove the bolts in the sequence shown and remove the front camshaft bearing cap and then the remaining bearing caps.

d. Clean and inspect the left hand camshaft bearing caps.

➡The camshaft front thrust bearing cap contains an oil metering groove. Make sure the groove is free of foreign material.

✳✳ WARNING

Damage to the camshaft phaser sprocket assembly will occur if mishandled or used as a lifting or leveraging device.

➡Only use hand tools to remove the camshaft phaser sprocket bolt or damage may occur to the camshaft or camshaft phaser unit.

✳✳ WARNING

Do not remove the timing chain wedge tool at any time during assembly. If the special tool is removed or out of placement, the engine front cover must be removed and the engine must be retimed.

e. Remove the bolt and withdraw the camshaft from the phaser sprocket assembly leaving the sprocket assembly in place. Discard the bolt and washer.

To install:

9. Lubricate the camshaft and camshaft journals with clean engine oil.

10. For the right hand camshaft:

➡Damage to the camshaft phaser sprocket assembly will occur if mishandled or used as a lifting or leveraging device.

➡Do not allow the roller followers to move out of position when installing the camshaft.

a. Install the camshaft into the camshaft phaser sprocket assembly and onto the head. Install a new camshaft phaser bolt finger tight.

✳✳ WARNING

Do not remove the timing chain wedge tool at any time during assembly. If the special tool is removed or out of placement, the engine front cover must be removed and the engine must be retimed.

✳✳ WARNING

The timing chain must be installed in its original position onto the camshaft phaser sprocket using the scribed marks, or damage to valves and pistons will result.

b. Verify the camshaft phaser sprocket and timing chain scribe marks are still in alignment.

✳✳ CAUTION

Do not allow the roller followers to move out of position when installing the camshaft.

c. Lubricate the camshaft bearing caps with clean engine oil.

d. Install the camshaft bearing caps in their original locations.

e. Install the bolts loosely, then tighten the bolts in the sequence illustrated to 89 inch lbs. (10 Nm).

f. Remove the wedge tools.

11. For the left hand camshaft:

➡Damage to the camshaft phaser sprocket assembly will occur if mishandled or used as a lifting or leveraging device.

➡Do not allow the roller followers to move out of position when installing the camshaft.

a. Install the camshaft into the camshaft phaser sprocket assembly and onto the head. Install a new camshaft phaser bolt finger tight.

✳✳ WARNING

Do not remove the timing chain wedge tool at any time during assembly. If the special tool is removed or out of placement, the engine front cover must be removed and the engine must be retimed.

✳✳ WARNING

The timing chain must be installed in its original position onto the camshaft phaser sprocket using the scribed marks, or damage to valves and pistons will result.

b. Verify the camshaft phaser sprocket and timing chain scribe marks are still in alignment.

➡Do not allow the roller followers to move out of position when installing the camshaft.

c. Lubricate the camshaft bearing caps with clean engine oil.

d. Install the camshaft bearing caps in their original locations. Install the bolts loosely.

e. Tighten the bolts in the sequence illustrated to 89 inch lbs. (10 Nm).

f. Remove the wedge tools.

g. Rotate the crankshaft a half turn counterclockwise and position the crankshaft damper spoke at the 12 o'clock position and the timing mark indentation at the 1 o'clock position.

12. For the right hand camshaft:

a. Verify correct cam position by noting the position of the number 1 cylinder intake and exhaust camshaft lobes.

b. Using the tool 303-1039, install the 3 originally removed roller followers.

c. Install the CMP sensor and the bolt.

d. Connect the CMP connector.

✳✳ WARNING

Only use hand tools to install the camshaft phaser sprocket assembly or damage may occur to the camshaft or camshaft phaser unit.

➡Damage to the camshaft phaser sprocket assembly will occur if mishandled or used as a lifting or leveraging device.

e. Tighten the camshaft phaser bolt in 2 steps: Tighten to 30 ft. lbs. (40 Nm), then tighten an additional 90 degrees.

f. Install the right hand valve cover.

13. For the left hand camshaft:

a. Verify correct cam position by noting the position of the number 5 cylinder intake and exhaust camshaft lobes.

b. Using the tool 303-1039, install the 3 originally removed roller followers.

c. Install the CMP sensor and the bolt.

d. Connect the CMP connector.

✳✳ WARNING

Damage to the camshaft phaser sprocket assembly will occur if mishandled or used as a lifting or leveraging device.

e. Tighten the camshaft phaser bolt in 2 steps. Tighten to 30 ft. lbs. (40 Nm), then tighten an additional 90 degrees.

f. Install the left hand valve cover.

CATALYTIC CONVERTER

REMOVAL & INSTALLATION

See Figures 49 and 50.

➡ Do not use oil or grease-based lubricants on isolators as they deteriorate the rubber.

➡ The exhaust Y-pipe dual catalytic converter is a 2-piece assembly. The RH and LH converters can be serviced separately as needed.

1. Before servicing the vehicle, refer to the precautions section.

2. With the vehicle in NEUTRAL, position it on a hoist.

3. Disconnect the Heated Oxygen Sensor (HO2S) and Catalyst Monitor Sensor (CMS) electrical connectors.

4. Remove the transmission support crossmember.

5. Loosen the exhaust and transmission mounting bracket cap bolt.

6. On RWD vehicles, remove the 3 bolts and then slide off the exhaust and transmission mounting bracket from the exhaust Y-pipe dual catalytic converter.

➡ On Four-Wheel Drive (4WD) vehicles, the exhaust and transmission mounting bracket will not slide off the exhaust Y-pipe dual catalytic converter until the exhaust Y-pipe dual catalytic converter is removed from the vehicle.

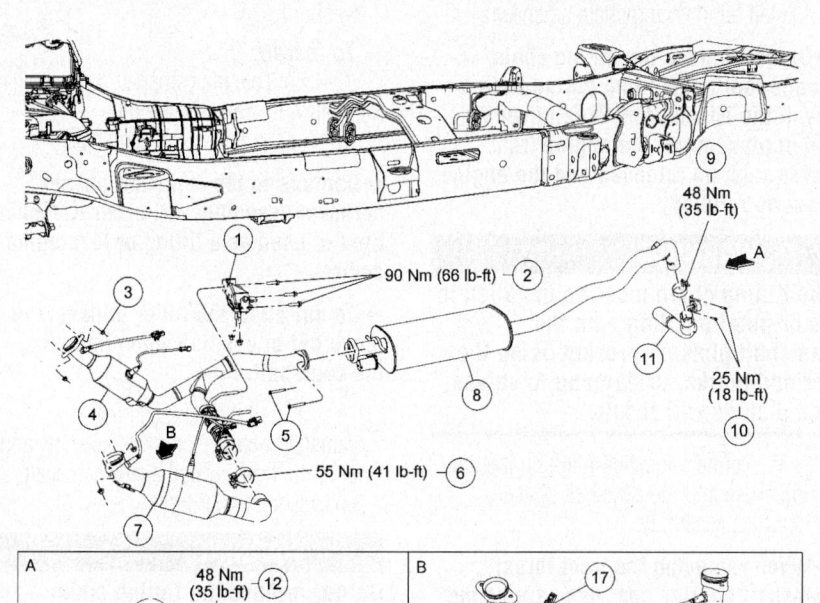
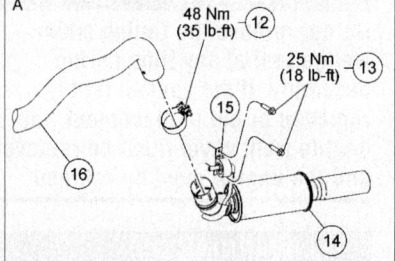
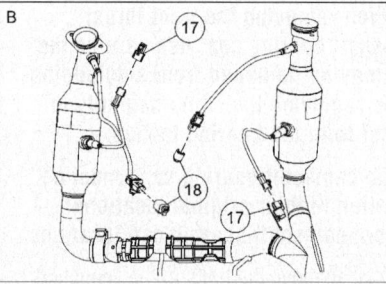

1. Exhaust and transmission mounting bracket
2. Exhaust and transmission mount bolts (3 required)
3. Exhaust Y-pipe dual catalytic converter-to-exhaust manifold nut (4 required)
4. RH catalytic converter
5. RH catalytic converter-to-muffler assembly bolts (2 required)
6. RH catalytic converter-to-LH catalytic converter Torca® clamp
7. LH catalytic converter
8. Muffler assembly
9. Muffler assembly-to-resonator Torca® clamp
10. Isolator and bracket assembly bolts (2 required)
11. Tail pipe
12. Muffler assembly-to-tail pipe Torca® clamp
13. Isolator and bracket assembly bolts (2 required)
14. Resonator
15. Isolator and bracket assembly
16. Muffler assembly
17. Catalyst Monitor Sensor (CMS) sensor electrical connectors
18. Heated Oxygen Sensor (HO2S) electrical connector

36578_EXPD_G0084

Fig. 49 Exploded view of the exhaust system–RWD shown, 4WD similar

7. On 4WD vehicles, remove the 4 bolts from the exhaust and transmission mounting bracket.

8. On all vehicles, remove the 2 exhaust Y-pipe dual catalytic converter-to-muffler assembly bolts.

9. Remove the 4 exhaust Y-pipe dual catalytic converter-to-exhaust manifold nuts and discard.

10. Remove the exhaust Y-pipe dual catalytic converter from the vehicle.

11. On 4WD vehicles, if necessary, remove the exhaust and transmission mounting bracket from the exhaust Y-pipe dual catalytic converter.

12. On all vehicles, if necessary, loosen the RH catalytic converter-to-LH catalytic converter Torca® clamp.

13. If necessary, separate the RH catalytic converter from the LH catalytic converter.

14. To install, reverse removal procedure. Refer to illustrations for torque specifications.

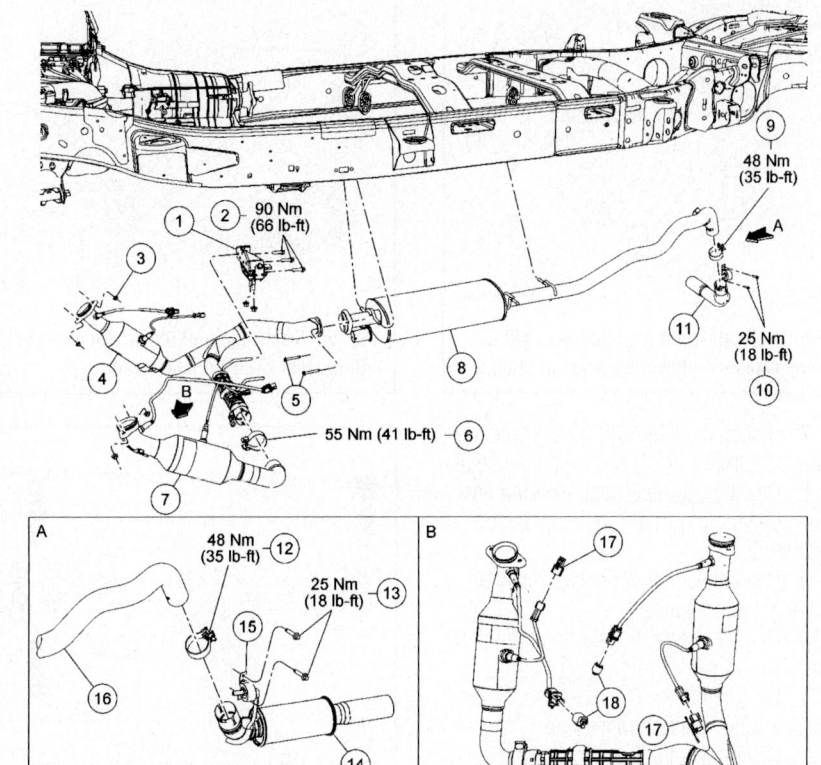

1. Exhaust and transmission mounting bracket
2. Exhaust and transmission mount bolts (3 required)
3. Exhaust Y-pipe dual catalytic converter-to-exhaust manifold nut (4 required)
4. RH catalytic converter
5. RH catalytic converter-to-muffler assembly bolts (2 required)
6. RH catalytic converter-to-LH catalytic converter Torca® clamp
7. LH catalytic converter
8. Muffler assembly
9. Muffler assembly-to-resonator Torca® clamp
10. Isolator and bracket assembly bolts (2 required)
11. Tail pipe
12. Muffler assembly-to-tail pipe Torca® clamp
13. Isolator and bracket assembly bolts (2 required)
14. Resonator
15. Isolator and bracket assembly
16. Muffler assembly
17. Catalyst Monitor Sensor (CMS) electrical connectors
18. Heated Oxygen Sensor (HO2S) electrical connectors

36578_EXPD_G0085

Fig. 50 Exploded view of the exhaust system—Expedition EL and Navigator L–RWD shown, 4WD similar

CRANKSHAFT DAMPER

REMOVAL & INSTALLATION

See Figure 51.

1. With the vehicle in NEUTRAL, position it on a hoist.
2. Remove the engine cooling fan lower shroud.
3. Rotate the tensioner clockwise and remove the accessory drive belt from the crankshaft pulley.

4. Remove the crankshaft pulley bolt and washer. Discard the crankshaft pulley bolt
5. Remove the crankshaft pulley using a suitable pulling tool.

To install:

6. Apply silicone gasket and sealant to the Woodruff key slot in the crankshaft pulley.

➡**If not secured within four minutes, the sealant must be removed and the sealing area cleaned. To clean the**

sealing area, use silicone gasket remover and metal surface prep. Follow the directions on the packaging. Failure to follow this procedure can cause future oil leakage.

7. Lubricate the crankshaft pulley sealing area with clean engine oil prior to installation
8. Using the special tool, install the crankshaft pulley.
9. Install the bolt and washer. Tighten the bolt in four stages.
    a. Stage 1: Tighten to 66 ft. lbs. (90 Nm)
    b. Stage 2: Loosen the bolt 360 degrees
    c. Stage 3: Tighten to 37 ft. lbs. (50 Nm)
    d. Stage 4: Tighten an additional 90 degrees.
10. Rotate the tensioner clockwise and install the accessory drive belt onto the crankshaft pulley.
11. Install the engine cooling fan lower shroud.

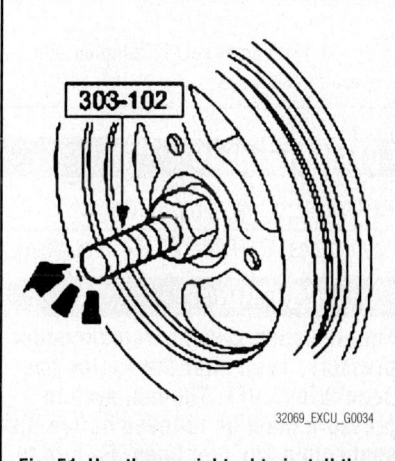

32069_EXCU_G0034

Fig. 51 Use the special tool to install the crankshaft pulley

CRANKSHAFT FRONT SEAL

REMOVAL & INSTALLATION

See Figures 52 and 53.

1. Remove the crankshaft pulley.
2. Using the special tool 303-107, remove the crankshaft front seal.

To install:

3. Lubricate the engine front cover and the crankshaft front seal inner lip with clean engine oil.
4. Using the special tools, install the crankshaft front seal into the engine front cover.
5. Install the crankshaft pulley.

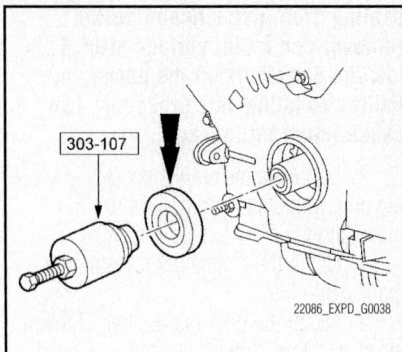

Fig. 52 Front crank seal removal with special tool

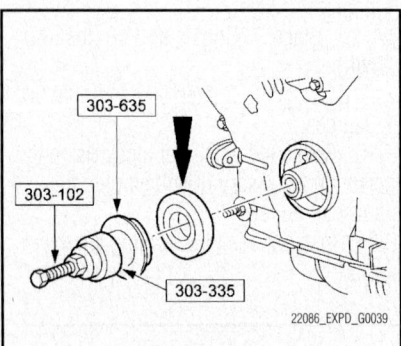

Fig. 53 Front crank seal installation with special tools

CYLINDER HEAD

REMOVAL & INSTALLATION

See Figures 40 and 41, 43, 54 through 73.

✳✳ CAUTION

Fuel injection systems remain under pressure, even after the engine has been turned OFF. The fuel system pressure must be relieved before disconnecting any fuel lines. Failure to do so may result in fire and/or personal injury.

➡️ **To correctly tighten the cylinder head bolts, an angle torque wrench is needed.**

1. Before servicing the vehicle, refer to the precautions section.
2. Remove the engine.
3. Remove the bolts and the flexplate.
4. Install the engine onto a suitable engine stand.
5. Disconnect the right hand Camshaft Position (CMP) sensor connector.
6. Remove the stud bolt and the right hand radio ignition interference capacitor.

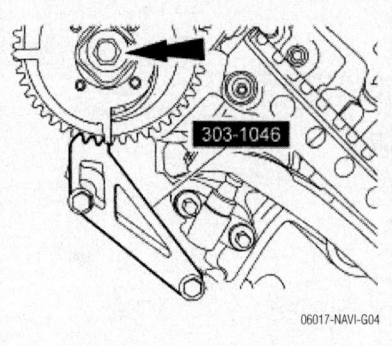

Fig. 54 Remove the bolt and the right hand camshaft phaser sprocket assembly

7. Disconnect the right hand Variable Camshaft Timing (VCT) solenoid connector.
8. Disconnect the 2 engine wiring harness retainers from the right hand valve cover studs.
9. Disconnect the connector retainer from the coolant tube.
10. Disconnect the 4 right hand ignition coil connectors.
11. Disconnect the Cylinder Head Temperature (CHT) sensor connector.
12. Disconnect the 2 engine wiring harness retainers from the left hand valve cover studs.
13. Disconnect the left hand VCT solenoid connector.
14. Disconnect the oil pressure sensor connector.
15. Disconnect the left hand CMP sensor connector.

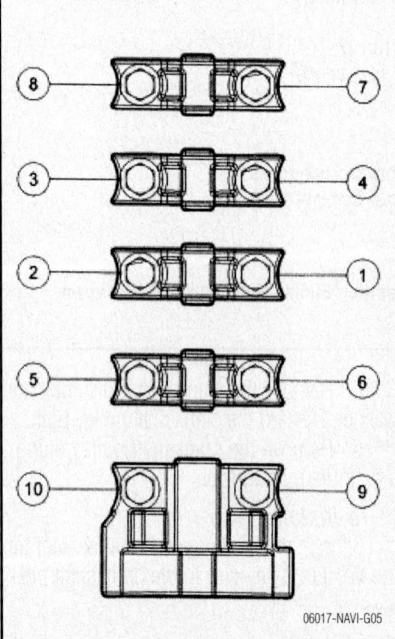

Fig. 55 Right side bearing cap removal and tightening sequence, left side similar

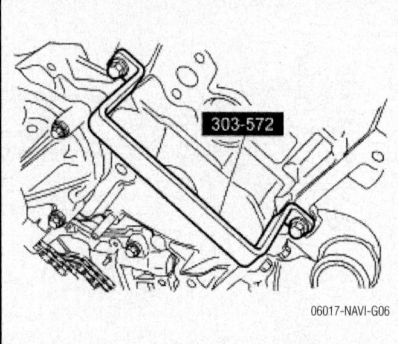

Fig. 56 Install the tool illustrated onto the left or right hand cylinder head

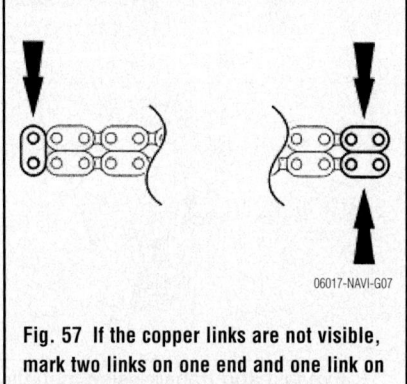

Fig. 57 If the copper links are not visible, mark two links on one end and one link on the other end, and use as timing marks

16. Remove the stud bolt and the left hand radio ignition interference capacitor.
17. Disconnect the 4 left hand ignition coil connectors.
18. Remove the 8 bolts and the 8 ignition coils.
19. Disconnect the Crankshaft Position (CKP) sensor connector.
20. Remove the engine wiring harness from the engine assembly.
21. Remove the bolt and the oil level indicator tube and discard the O-ring seal.
22. Remove the bolt and the right hand CMP sensor.
23. Remove the bolt and the left hand CMP sensor.
24. Remove the bolt and the CKP sensor.

✳✳ CAUTION

Do not use metal scrapers, wire brushes, power abrasive discs or other abrasive means to clean the sealing surfaces. These tools cause scratches and gouges which make leak paths. Use a plastic scraping tool to remove all traces of old sealant.

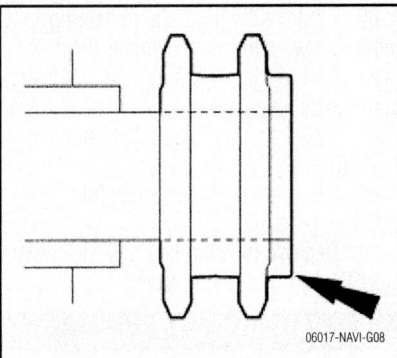

Fig. 58 Install the crankshaft sprocket, making sure the flange faces forward

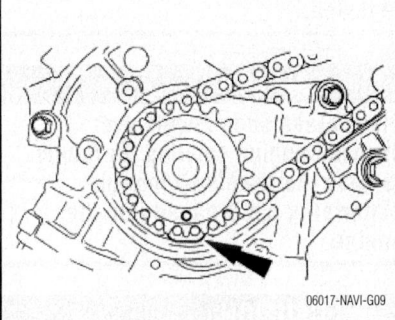

Fig. 59 Position the lower end of the left hand (inner) timing chain on the crankshaft sprocket, aligning the timing mark on the outer flange of the crankshaft sprocket with the single copper (marked) link on the chain

> ✳✳ **CAUTION**
>
> **When removing the valve cover, make sure to avoid damaging the variable camshaft timing (VCT) solenoid.**

➡ **The bolts are part of the valve cover and should not be removed.**

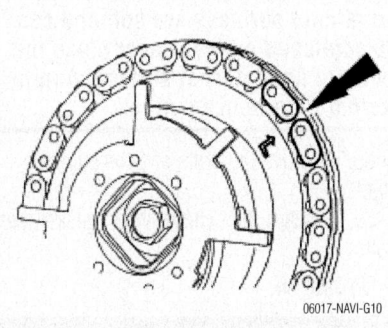

Fig. 60 Position the timing chain on the camshaft sprocket with the camshaft sprocket timing mark positioned between the two copper (marked) chain links

25. Remove the bolts and the valve covers.

26. Clean the valve cover mating surface of the cylinder head with silicone gasket remover and metal surface prep.

27. Inspect the valve cover gasket. If the gasket is damaged, remove and discard the gasket. Clean the valve cover gasket groove with soap and water or a suitable solvent.

28. Remove the bolts, the coolant pump pulley and the 3 accessory drive belt idler pulleys.

29. Remove the bolts and the accessory drive belt tensioner.

30. Remove and discard the crankshaft pulley bolt. Using tool 303-009, remove the crankshaft pulley.

31. Using the tool 303-107, remove the crankshaft seal.

32. Remove the front 4 oil pan bolts.

➡ **Correct fastener location is essential for assembly procedure. Record fastener location.**

33. Remove the engine front cover fasteners and the cover.

34. Remove the crankshaft sensor ring from the crankshaft.

35. Position the crankshaft keyway at the 12 o'clock position.

➡ **f the camshaft lobes are not exactly positioned at the 12 o'clock position, the crankshaft will require one full additional rotation to 12 o'clock. The number 1 cylinder camshaft exhaust lobe must be coming up on the exhaust stroke. Verify by noting the position of the 2 intake camshaft lobes and the exhaust lobe on the number 1 cylinder.**

➡ **If the components are to be reinstalled, they must be installed in the same positions. Mark the components for installation into the original locations.**

36. Remove only the 3 roller followers shown in the illustration from the right hand cylinder head.

> ✳✳ **CAUTION**
>
> **Do not allow the valve keepers to fall off the valve or the valve may drop into the cylinder.**

➡ **It may be necessary to push the valve down while compressing the spring.**

37. Using the tool illustrated, remove the 3 designated roller followers in the previous step from the right hand cylinder head.

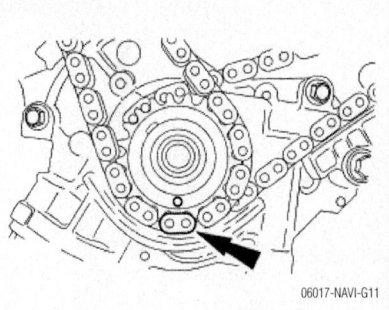

Fig. 61 Position the lower end of the right hand (outer) timing chain on the crankshaft sprocket, aligning the timing mark on the sprocket with the single copper (marked) chain link

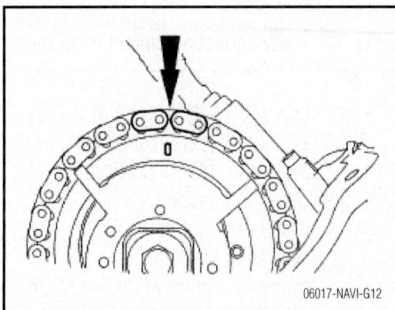

Fig. 62 Position the right hand timing chain on the camshaft sprocket. Make sure the camshaft sprocket timing mark is positioned between the two copper (marked) chain links

38. Remove only the 3 roller followers shown in the illustration from the left hand cylinder head.

39. Using the tool 303-1039, remove the 3 designated roller followers in the previous step from the left hand cylinder head.

40. The crankshaft cannot be moved past the 6 o'clock position once set.

41. Rotate the crankshaft clockwise and position the crankshaft keyway at the 6 o'clock position.

> ✳✳ **CAUTION**
>
> **If one or both of the tensioner mounting bolts are loosened or removed, the tensioner-sealing bead must be inspected for seal integrity. If cracks, tears, separation from the tensioner body or permanent compression of the seal bead is observed, install a new tensioner.**

42. Remove the bolts, the left hand timing chain tensioner and tensioner arm.

43. Remove the bolts, the right hand timing chain tensioner and tensioner arm.

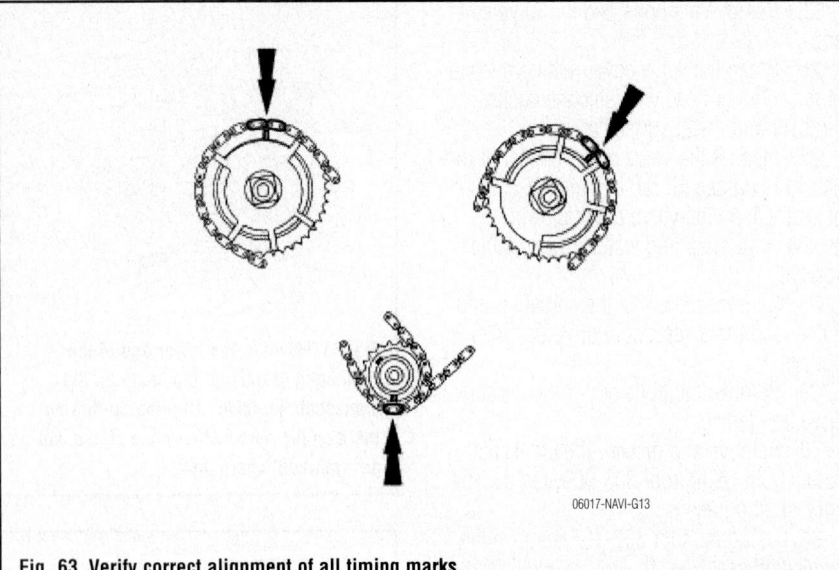

06017-NAVI-G13

Fig. 63 Verify correct alignment of all timing marks

44. Remove the right hand and left hand timing chains and the crankshaft sprocket.

45. Remove the right hand timing chain from the camshaft sprocket.

46. Remove the right hand timing chain from the crankshaft sprocket.

47. Remove the left hand timing chain from the camshaft sprocket.

48. Remove the left hand timing chain and crankshaft sprocket.

49. Remove the left hand and right hand timing chain guides.

❋❋ CAUTION

Damage to the camshaft phaser sprocket assembly will occur if mishandled or used as a lifting or leveraging device.

❋❋ CAUTION

Only use hand tools to remove the camshaft phaser sprocket assembly or damage may occur to the camshaft or camshaft phaser unit.

❋❋ CAUTION

Damage to the camshaft phaser sprocket assembly will occur if mishandled or used as a lifting or leveraging device.

50. Using the tool illustrated, remove the bolt and the right hand camshaft phaser sprocket assembly. Discard the camshaft phaser sprocket bolt.

51. Using tool 303-1046, remove the bolt and the left hand camshaft phaser sprocket assembly. Discard the camshaft phaser sprocket bolt.

❋❋ CAUTION

When removing the front thrust camshaft bearing cap, use care as the cap may be damaged from side loading when removing the cam unequally in height from the bearing towers.

➡ The camshaft bearing caps must be installed in their original locations. Record camshaft bearing cap locations.

52. Remove the bolts in the sequence shown and remove the right hand cylinder head front camshaft bearing cap and then the remaining bearing caps.

53. Clean and inspect the right hand camshaft bearing caps.

54. The camshaft front thrust bearing cap contains an oil metering groove. Make sure the groove is free of foreign material.

55. Remove the right hand camshaft.

56. Remove the bolts in the sequence shown and remove the left hand cylinder head front camshaft bearing cap and then the remaining bearing caps.

57. Clean and inspect the left hand camshaft bearing caps.

58. The camshaft front thrust bearing cap contains an oil metering groove. Make sure the groove is free of foreign material.

59. Remove the left hand camshaft.

❋❋ CAUTION

If the components are to be reinstalled, they must be installed in the same positions. Mark the components for installation into the original locations.

60. Remove the all of the remaining roller followers from the cylinder heads.

61. Remove the hydraulic lash adjusters from the cylinder heads.

62. Install the tool illustrated onto the cylinder head.

63. Remove the exhaust manifold. Discard the gasket.

64. Remove the stud bolt and the coolant tube. Discard the O-ring seals.

❋❋ CAUTION

The cylinder head must be cool before removing it from the engine. Cylinder head warpage can result if a warm or hot cylinder head is removed.

❋❋ CAUTION

Place clean shop towels over exposed engine cavities. Carefully remove the towels so foreign material is not dropped into the engine.

❋❋ CAUTION

The cylinder head bolts must be discarded and new bolts must be installed. They are tighten-to-yield designed and cannot be reused.

❋❋ CAUTION

Do not use metal scrapers, wire brushes, power abrasive discs or other abrasive means to clean the sealing surfaces. These tools cause scratches and gouges that make leak paths. Use a plastic scraping tool to remove all traces of the head gasket.

❋❋ CAUTION

Aluminum surfaces are soft and can be scratched easily. Never place the cylinder head gasket surface, unprotected, on a bench surface.

65. Remove the bolts and the cylinder head.

66. Discard the cylinder head gasket and bolts.

To install:

❋❋ CAUTION

Make sure all coolant residue and foreign material are cleaned from the block surface and cylinder bore.

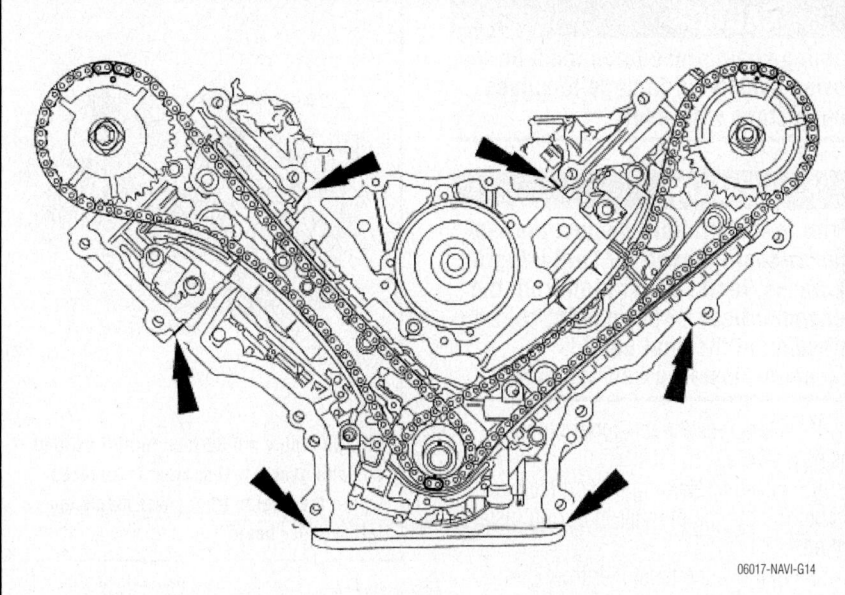

Fig. 64 Apply a bead of silicone gasket and sealant along the cylinder head-to-cylinder block surface and the oil pan-to-cylinder block surface, at the locations shown

camshaft bearing caps in their original locations.

77. Lubricate the camshaft bearing caps with clean engine oil.

78. Install the camshaft bearing cap. Position the remaining camshaft bearing caps. Install the bolts loosely, then tighten to 89 inch lbs. (10 Nm).

✳✳ CAUTION

Damage to the camshaft phaser sprocket assembly will occur if mishandled or used as a lifting or leveraging device.

79. Install the camshaft phaser sprockets and new camshaft phaser bolts finger tight.

✳✳ CAUTION

Only use hand tools to remove the camshaft phaser sprocket assembly or damage may occur to the camshaft or camshaft phaser unit.

✳✳ CAUTION

The use of sealing aids (aviation cement, copper spray, and glue) is not permitted. The gasket must be installed dry.

➡ Do not turn the crankshaft until instructed to do so.

67. Position the cylinder head gaskets and cylinder heads over the dowels and install the cylinder head bolts loosely.

68. Tighten the bolts in three steps, in the sequence shown as follows:

  a. Step 1: Tighten to 30 ft. lbs. (40 Nm).

  b. Step 2: Tighten an additional 90 degrees.

  c. Step 3: Tighten an additional 90 degrees.

69. Remove the tool from the left hand cylinder head.

70. Lubricate the hydraulic lash adjusters with clean engine oil prior to installation.

71. Install the hydraulic lash adjusters into the left hand cylinder head.

72. Using a new gasket, install the exhaust manifold.

73. Install the coolant tube and the stud bolt.

74. Lubricate the camshaft and camshaft journals with clean engine oil prior to installation.

75. Install the left hand and right hand camshafts.

76. Install the left hand and right hand

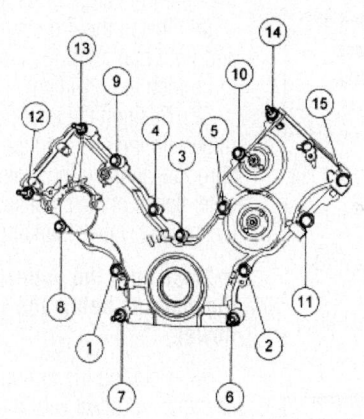

1	Bolt, Hex Flange Head Pilot, M8 x 1.25 x 50
2	Bolt, Hex Flange Head Pilot, M8 x 1.25 x 50
3	Bolt, Hex Flange Head Pilot, M8 x 1.25 x 50
4	Bolt, Hex Flange Head Pilot, M8 x 1.25 x 50
5	Bolts, Hex Flange Head Pilot, M8 x 1.25 x 50
6	Stud, Hex Head Pilot, M10 x 1.5 x 1.5 x 103
7	Stud, Hex Head Pilot, M10 x 1.5 x 1.5 x 103
8	Bolt, Hex Flange Head Pilot, M8 x 1.25 x 50
9	Bolt, Hex Flange Head Pilot, M8 x 1.25 x 50
10	Bolt, Hex Flange Head Pilot, M8 x 1.25 x 50
11	Bolt, Hex Flange Head Pilot, M8 x 1.25 x 50
12	Stud and Washer, Hex Head Pilot, M8 x 1.25 x 1.25 x 94
13	Stud and Washer, Hex Head Pilot, M8 x 1.25 x 1.25 x 94
14	Stud and Washer, Hex Head Pilot, M8 x 1.25 x 1.25 x 94
15	Bolt, Hex Head Pilot, M8 x 1.25 x 56

Fig. 65 Engine front cover fastener location and torque sequence

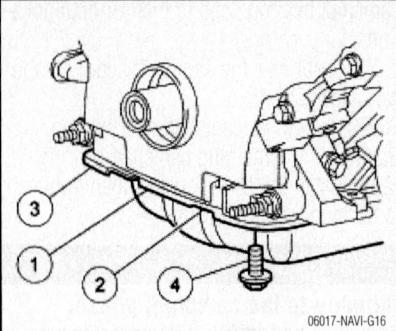

Fig. 66 Front oil pan bolts torque sequence

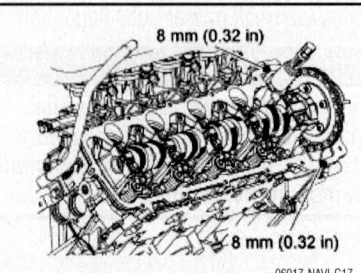

Fig. 67 Apply a 0.32 inch (8mm) bead of silicone gasket and sealant in 2 places where the engine front cover meets the right cylinder head

80. Using tool 303-1046, tighten the left hand and right hand camshaft phaser sprocket bolts in 2 steps:

    a. Step 1: Tighten to 30 ft. lbs. (40 Nm).

    b. Step 2: Tighten an additional 90 degrees.

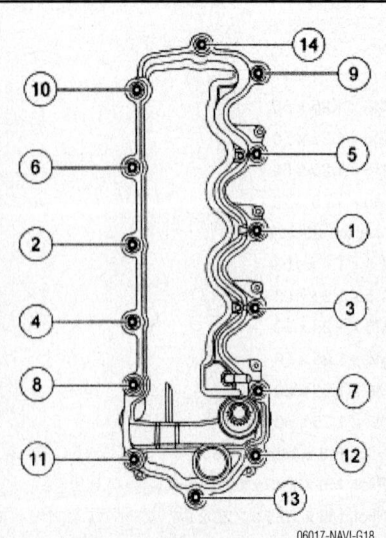

Fig. 68 Install the right hand valve cover and gasket on the cylinder head and tighten the bolts in sequence

✳✳ CAUTION

Timing chain procedures must be followed exactly or damage to valves and pistons will result.

✳✳ CAUTION

Prior to installation, inspect the tensioner-sealing bead for seal integrity. If cracks, tears, separation from the tensioner body or permanent compression of the seal bead is observed, install a new tensioner.

81. Compress the tensioner plunger, using a vise.

82. Install a retaining clip on the tensioner to hold the plunger in during installation.

83. Remove the tensioner from the vise.

84. If the copper links are not visible, mark two links on one end and one link on the other end, and use as timing marks.

85. Install the crankshaft sprocket, making sure the flange faces forward.

86. Install the 4 bolts and the left hand and right hand timing chain guides. Tighten to 89 inch lbs. (10 Nm).

87. Position the lower end of the left hand (inner) timing chain on the crankshaft sprocket, aligning the timing mark on the outer flange of the crankshaft sprocket with the single copper (marked) link on the chain.

➡**Make sure the upper half of the timing chain is below the tensioner arm dowel.**

88. Position the timing chain on the camshaft sprocket with the camshaft sprocket timing mark positioned between the two copper (marked) chain links.

➡**The left hand timing chain tensioner arm has a bump near the dowel hole for identification.**

89. Position the left hand timing chain tensioner arm on the dowel pin and install the left hand timing chain tensioner and bolts. Tighten the bolts to 18 ft. lbs. (25 Nm).

90. Remove the retaining clip from the left hand timing chain tensioner.

91. Position the lower end of the right hand (outer) timing chain on the crankshaft sprocket, aligning the timing mark on the sprocket with the single copper (marked) chain link.

➡**The lower half of the timing chain must be positioned above the tensioner arm dowel.**

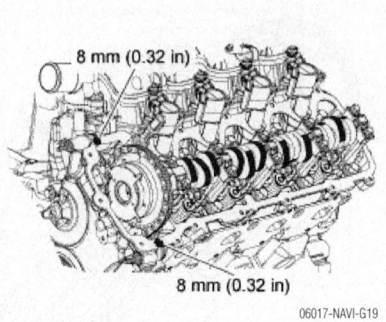

Fig. 69 Apply a 0.32 inch (8mm) bead of silicone gasket and sealant in 2 places where the engine front cover meets the left cylinder head

92. Position the right hand timing chain on the camshaft sprocket. Make sure the camshaft sprocket timing mark is positioned between the two copper (marked) chain links.

93. Position the right hand timing chain tensioner arm on the dowel pin and install the right hand timing chain tensioner and bolts. Tighten the bolts to 18 ft. lbs. (25 Nm).

94. Remove the retaining clip from the right hand timing chain tensioner.

95. As a final-check, verify correct alignment of all timing marks.

96. Install the crankshaft sensor ring on the crankshaft.

97. Lubricate the roller followers with clean engine oil prior to installation.

98. Using tool 303-1039, install all of the camshaft roller followers.

✳✳ CAUTION

Do not use metal scrapers, wire brushes, power abrasive discs or other abrasive means to clean the sealing surfaces. These tools cause scratches and gouges which make leak paths. Use a plastic scraping tool to remove all traces of old sealant.

➡**If the engine front cover is not secured within 4 minutes, the sealant must be removed and the sealing area cleaned. To clean the sealing area, use silicone gasket remover and metal surface prep. Failure to follow this procedure can cause future oil leakage.**

➡**Make sure that the engine front cover gasket is in place on the engine front cover before installation.**

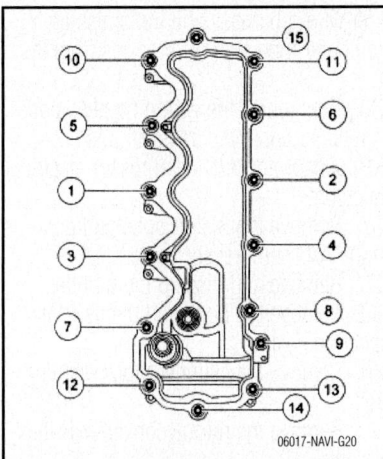

Fig. 70 Install the left hand valve cover and gasket on the cylinder head and tighten the bolts in sequence

99. Apply a bead of silicone gasket and sealant along the cylinder head-to-cylinder block surface and the oil pan-to-cylinder block surface, at the locations illustrated.

100. Install a new engine front cover gasket on the engine front cover. Position the engine front cover onto the dowels. Install the fasteners finger-tight.

101. Tighten the engine front cover fasteners in sequence in 2 steps:

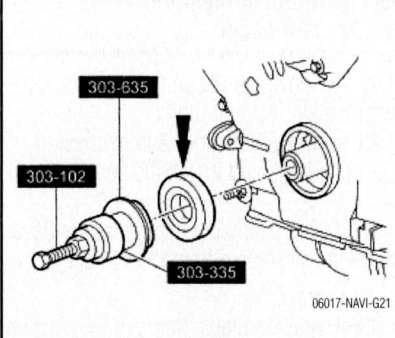

Fig. 71 Install the crankshaft seal into the engine front cover

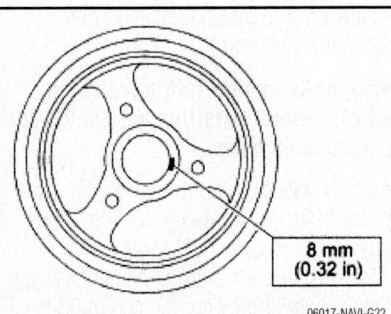

Fig. 72 Apply a 0.32 inch (8mm) bead of silicone gasket and sealant to the Woodruff key slot on the crankshaft pulley

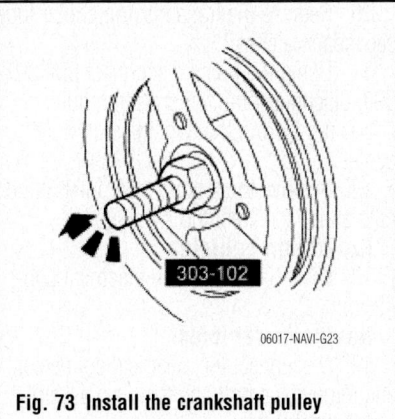

Fig. 73 Install the crankshaft pulley

   a. Step 1: Tighten fasteners 1 through 15 to 18 ft. lbs. (25 Nm).
   b. Step 2: Tighten fasteners 6 and 7 to 35 ft. lbs. (48 Nm).

> ❄❄ **CAUTION**
>
> **Do not use metal scrapers, wire brushes, power abrasive discs or other abrasive means to clean sealing surfaces. These tools cause scratches and gouges which make leak paths. Use a plastic scraping tool to remove all traces of old sealant.**

102. Clean the valve cover mating surface with silicone gasket remover and metal surface prep.

103. Install the 4 front oil pan bolts in the sequence shown in 2 steps.
   a. Step 1: Tighten to 15 ft. lbs. (20 Nm).
   b. Step 2: Tighten an additional 60 degrees.

➡ **If not secured within 4 minutes, the sealant must be removed and the sealing area cleaned. To clean the sealing area, use silicone gasket remover and metal surface prep. Failure to follow this procedure can cause future oil leakage.**

104. Apply a 0.32 inch (8mm) bead of silicone gasket and sealant in 2 places where the engine front cover meets the cylinder head.

> ❄❄ **CAUTION**
>
> **When installing the valve cover, make sure to avoid damaging the Variable Camshaft Timing (VCT) solenoid.**

105. Install the right hand valve cover and gasket on the cylinder head and tighten the bolts in the sequence shown and tighten to 89 inch lbs. (10 Nm).

➡ **If not secured within 4 minutes, the sealant must be removed and the sealing area cleaned. To clean the sealing area, use silicone gasket remover and metal surface prep. Failure to follow this procedure can cause future oil leakage.**

106. Apply a 0.32 inch (8mm) bead of silicone gasket and sealant in 2 places where the engine front cover meets the left cylinder head.

107. Install the left hand valve cover and gasket on the cylinder head and tighten the bolts in the sequence shown and tighten to 89 inch lbs. (10 Nm).

108. Lubricate the engine front cover and the crankshaft seal inner lip with clean engine oil.

109. Use the tools illustrated to install the crankshaft seal into the engine front cover.

➡ **If not secured within 4 minutes, the sealant must be removed and the sealing area cleaned. To clean the sealing area, use silicone gasket remover and metal surface prep. Failure to follow this procedure can cause future oil leakage.**

110. Apply a 0.32 inch (8mm) bead of silicone gasket and sealant to the Woodruff key slot on the crankshaft pulley.

111. Use the tool illustrated to install the crankshaft pulley.

112. Tighten the new crankshaft pulley bolt in 4 steps
   a. Step 1: Tighten to 66 ft. lbs. (90 Nm).
   b. Step 2: Loosen 360 degrees.
   c. Step 3: Tighten to 37 ft. lbs. (50 Nm).
   d. Step 4: Tighten an additional 90 degrees.

➡ **Lubricate the new O-ring seal with clean engine oil prior to installation.**

113. Install the left hand CMP sensor and the bolt.

➡ **Lubricate the new O-ring seal with clean engine oil prior to installation.**

114. Install the right hand CMP sensor and the bolt.

115. Install the CKP sensor and the bolt.

116. Install the accessory drive belt tensioner and install the 3 bolts. Tighten the bolts to 18 ft. lbs. (25 Nm).

117. Install the 3 accessory drive belt idler pulleys, the coolant pump pulley and the 7 bolts. Tighten the bolts to 18 ft. lbs. (25 Nm).

118. Position the electrical harness on the engine assembly and connect the engine wiring harness retainers to the valve cover studs.

119. Connect the CKP sensor connector.

120. Install the 8 ignition coils and the 8 bolts.

121. Connect the 4 left hand ignition coil connectors.

122. Install the left hand radio ignition interference capacitor and the stud bolt. Tighten the bolt to 18 ft. lbs. (25 Nm).

123. Connect the left hand CMP sensor connector.

124. Connect the engine oil pressure sensor connector.

125. Connect the left hand VCT solenoid connector.

126. Connect the 2 engine wiring harness retainers to the left hand valve cover studs.

127. Connect the CHT sensor connector.

128. Connect the 4 right hand ignition coil connectors.

129. Connect the connector retainer to the coolant tube.

130. Connect the 2 engine wiring harness retainers to the right hand valve cover studs.

131. Connect the right hand VCT solenoid connector.

132. Install the right hand radio ignition interference capacitor and the stud bolt. Tighten the bolt to 18 ft. lbs. (25 Nm).

133. Connect the right hand CMP sensor connector.

134. Using a suitable floor crane, remove the engine from the engine stand.

135. Install the flexplate and the 8 bolts in a star pattern. Tighten the bolts to 59 ft. lbs. (80 Nm).

136. Install the engine.

ENGINE ASSEMBLY

REMOVAL & INSTALLATION

See Figure 74.

1. Disconnect the negative battery cable.

2. Drain and the engine coolant.

3. Recover A/C system refrigerant.

4. Remove the RH and LH headlamp assemblies.

5. Remove the front fascia.

6. Remove the cooling fan shroud.

7. Remove the 2 hood latch assembly bolts.

8. Disconnect the cable position retainers and position the hood latch assembly aside.

9. Remove the pushpin and move the air deflector aside.

10. Remove the transmission cooler tube secondary latches.

11. Using the quick disconnect tool 307-309, disconnect the transmission fluid cooler tubes from the transmission fluid cooler hoses.

12. Remove the 2 condenser inlet fitting nuts and disconnect the 2 fittings.

Expedition vehicles

13. Disconnect the horn electrical connector.

Navigator vehicles

14. Disconnect the electrical connector and remove the bolt and the horn assembly

All vehicles

15. Disconnect the ambient temperature sensor electrical connector.

16. Remove the 6 radiator support bolts and remove the cooling module from the vehicle.

17. Remove the bypass tube.

18. If servicing the engine on a four wheel drive (4WD) vehicle, remove the front drive shaft

19. Remove the starter.

20. Remove the accessory drive belt.

21. Remove the nut and the ground cable and disconnect the wiring harness retainer.

22. Disconnect the powertrain control module (PCM) electrical connector.

23. Remove the bolt and the ground cable.

24. If equipped, disconnect the 2 auxiliary heat coolant hose quick connect couplings.

25. Disconnect the heater coolant hose quick connect coupling.

26. Disconnect and remove the 2 heater coolant hose quick connect couplings.

27. Remove the clip and disconnect the degas bottle coolant outlet hose quick connect coupling.

28. If equipped, disconnect the block heater electrical connector.

29. If equipped, disconnect the block heater wiring harness retainers.

30. Disconnect the wiring harness position retainer from the power steering pump stud bolt.

31. Disconnect the wiring harness position retainer and the engine oil pressure (EOP) switch electrical connector and position the wiring harness aside.

32. Remove the nut and the power steering pressure tube support bracket.

33. Remove the 2 bolts, the stud bolt and position the power steering pump aside.

34. Disconnect the starter wiring harness retainer.

35. Remove the nut and remove the starter wiring harness and transmission fluid cooler tube support brackets from the nut.

36. Disconnect the wiring harness position retainer and the crankshaft position (CKP) sensor and A/C compressor electrical connectors

37. Remove the 3 stud bolts and position the A/C compressor aside.

38. Remove and discard the oil filter.

39. Remove the bolts and the flexplate inspection cover.

40. Remove the cylinder block opening cover.

41. Remove the torque converter-to-flexplate nuts.

➡**The upper 2 transmission-to-engine bolts will be removed later.**

42. Remove the lower 5 transmission-to-engine bolts.

43. Disconnect the heated exhaust gas oxygen sensor (HO2S) electrical connectors.

44. Remove the 4 exhaust manifold flange nuts.

✳✳ WARNING

Only use hand tools when removing the engine support insulator through bolts or damage to the engine support insulator-to-cylinder block bracket can occur.

45. Remove the RH and LH engine support insulator through bolts.

46. Remove the upper 2 transmission-to-engine bolts and install the special tool.

47. Using a suitable floor crane, remove the engine assembly from the vehicle

To install:

48. Using a suitable floor crane, position the engine assembly into the vehicle.

49. Install the LH and RH engine support insulator bolts.

50. Apply Threadlock 262 to the bolt threads prior to installation and tighten to 258 ft. lbs. (350 Nm).

➡**Align the engine-to-transmission dowels before installing the engine-to-transmission bolts.**

51. Install the lower 5 transmission-to-engine bolts and tighten to 35 ft. lbs. (48 Nm).

52. Install the 4 exhaust manifold-to-catalytic converter nuts and tighten to 30 ft. lbs. (40 Nm).

53. Connect the heated exhaust gas oxygen sensor (HO2S) electrical connectors.

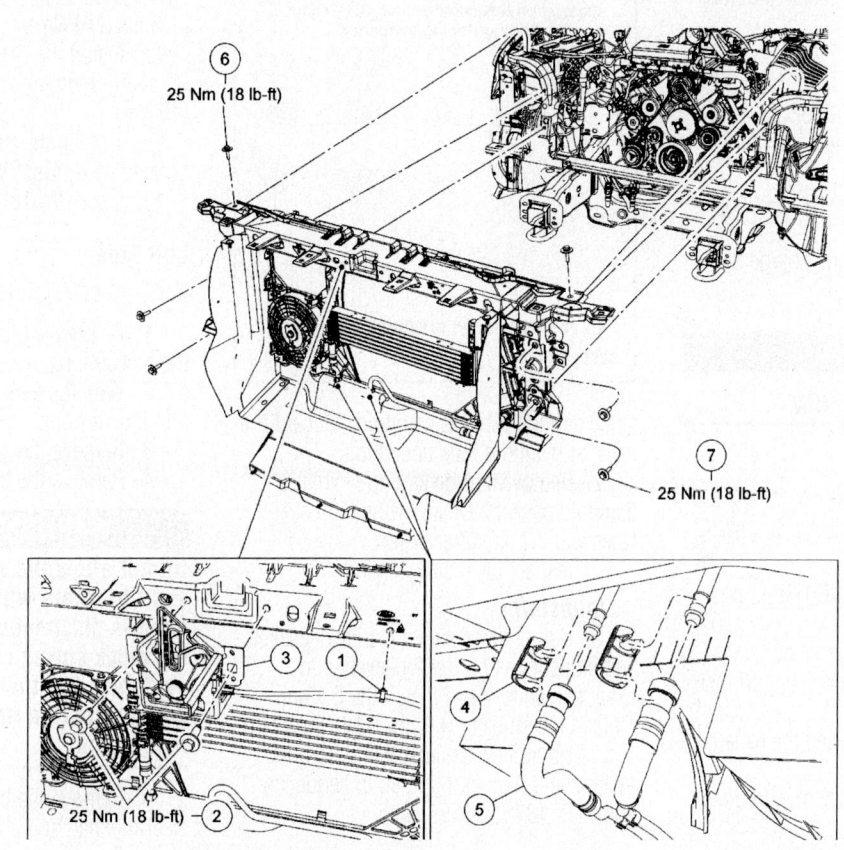

25 Nm (18 lb-ft) — 6

25 Nm (18 lb-ft) — 7

25 Nm (18 lb-ft) — 2

1. Hood latch assembly cable retainer
2. Hood latch assembly bolts (2 required)
3. Hood latch assembly
4. Transmission fluid cooler tube secondary latches (2 required)
5. Transmission fluid cooler tube (2 required)
6. Cooling module upper bolt (2 required)
7. Cooling module front bolt (4 required)

22086_EXPD_G0009

Fig. 74 Expedition & Navigator Cooling Module and related parts

54. Install new torque converter-to-flexplate nuts and tighten to 26 ft. lbs. (35 Nm).

55. Install the cylinder block opening cover.

56. Install the flexplate inspection cover and the bolts to 26 ft. lbs. (35 Nm).

57. Install the upper 2 transmission-to-engine bolts and tighten to 35 ft. lbs. (48 Nm).

58. Position the starter wiring harness and transmission fluid cooler tube support brackets and tighten the retaining nut to 89 inch lbs. (10 Nm).

59. Connect the starter wiring harness retainer.

60. Install a new oil filter.

61. Position the power steering pump and install the stud bolt and the 2 bolts. Tighten to 18 ft. lbs. (25 Nm).

62. Connect the wiring harness position

retainer to the power steering pump stud bolt.

63. Connect the wiring harness position retainer and the engine oil pressure (EOP) switch electrical connector.

64. Install the power steering pump support bracket and the nut. Tighten the nut to 89 inch lbs. (10 Nm).

65. If equipped, connect the block heater wiring harness retainers.

66. If equipped, connect the block heater electrical connector.

67. Position the A/C compressor and install the 3 stud bolts. Tighten to 18 ft. lbs. (25 Nm).

68. Connect the wiring harness position retainer and the crankshaft position (CKP) sensor and A/C compressor electrical connectors.

69. Install the clip and connect the degas bottle coolant outlet hose quick connect coupling.

70. Position the ground cable and install the bolt. Tighten to 89 inch lbs. (10 Nm).

71. Position the 2 heater coolant hoses and connect the quick connect couplings.

72. Connect the heater coolant hose quick connect coupling.

73. If equipped, connect the 2 auxiliary heat coolant hose quick connect couplings.

74. Connect the powertrain control module (PCM) electrical connector.

75. Connect the wiring harness retainer and ground cable and install the nut. Tighten to 89 inch lbs. (10 Nm).

76. Install the accessory drive belt.

77. Install the bypass tube.

78. Install the cooling module.

79. If servicing the engine on a four wheel drive (4WD) vehicle, install the front drive shaft.

80. Install the starter.

81. Install the hood.

82. Fill the crankcase with oil.

83. Fill and bleed the engine cooling system.

84. Fill and bleed the power steering system.

85. Evacuate, leak test and charge the refrigerant system.

EXHAUST MANIFOLD

REMOVAL & INSTALLATION

Right Side

See Figures 75 and 76.

1. Before servicing the vehicle, refer to the precautions section.

2. With the vehicle in NEUTRAL, position it on a hoist.

3. Remove the RH inner fender well.

4. Remove the RH engine support insulator.

5. Remove the 2 bolts and the exhaust manifold heat shield.

6. Remove the 8 exhaust manifold nuts,

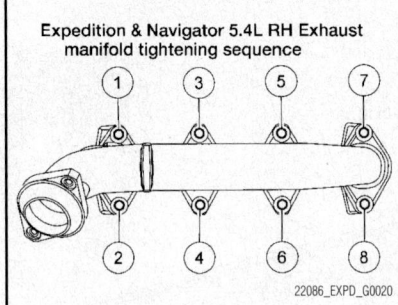

Expedition & Navigator 5.4L RH Exhaust manifold tightening sequence

Fig. 76 RH exhaust manifold tightening sequence

studs and the exhaust manifold. Discard the exhaust manifold nuts and studs.

7. Remove and discard the exhaust manifold gaskets. Clean the sealing surfaces with metal surface prep.

8. Inspect the exhaust manifold.

To install:

9. Using new exhaust manifold gaskets and studs, position the 2 gaskets and exhaust manifold and install the 8 studs. Tighten the studs to 9 ft. lbs. (12 Nm).

10. Using new exhaust manifold nuts, install the 8 nuts and tighten in sequence shown to 18 ft. lbs. (25 Nm).

11. Position the exhaust manifold heat shield and install the 2 bolts. Tighten to 89 inch lbs. (10 Nm).

12. Install the RH engine support insulator and tighten the 2 stud bolts to 11 ft. lbs. (15 Nm).

13. Tighten the RH insulator bracket bolts to 46 ft. lbs. (63 Nm).

14. Install the RH inner fender well.

Left Side

See Figures 77 through 79.

1. Before servicing the vehicle, refer to the precautions section.

2. With the vehicle in NEUTRAL, position it on a hoist.

3. Remove the air cleaner outlet tube.

4. Remove the degas bottle.

❊❊ WARNING

Do not allow the steering column shaft to rotate while the intermediate shaft is disconnected or damage to the clock spring can result. If there is evidence that the shaft has rotated, the clockspring must be removed and recentered.

5. Remove the bolt and disconnect the steering shaft and position aside.

6. Remove the 4 (2 LH and 2 RH) exhaust manifold-to-catalytic converter nuts.

7. Remove the 3 bolts and the exhaust manifold heat shield.

8. Four wheel drive (4WD) vehicles:
   a. Remove the front driveshaft.

9. All vehicles: Remove the 8 exhaust manifold nuts, studs and the exhaust manifold.

10. Remove and discard the exhaust manifold gaskets. Clean the sealing surfaces with metal surface prep.

11. Inspect the exhaust manifold.

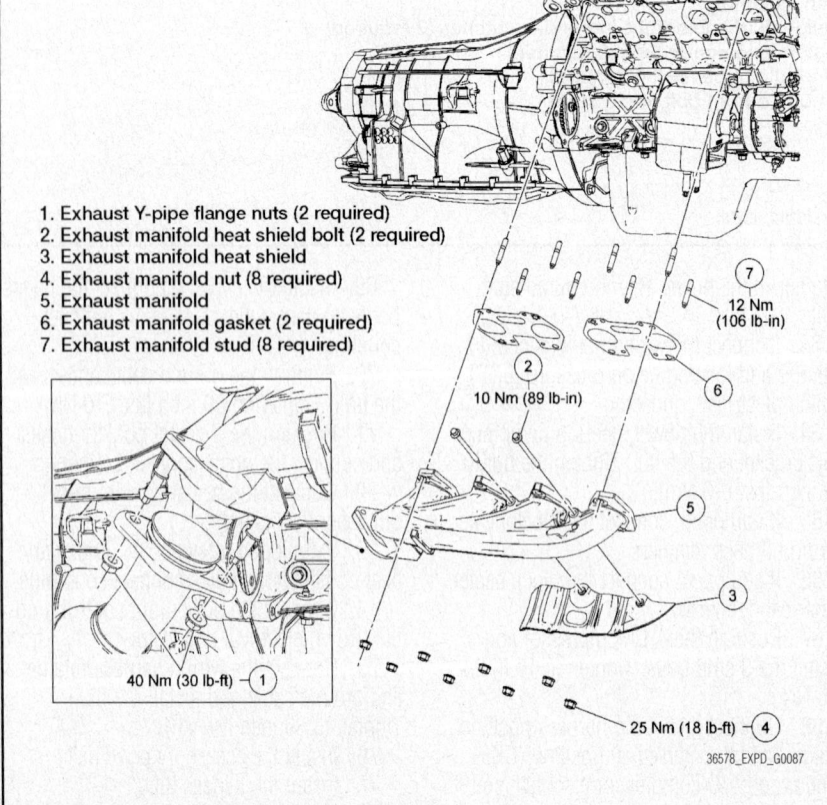

1. Exhaust Y-pipe flange nuts (2 required)
2. Exhaust manifold heat shield bolt (2 required)
3. Exhaust manifold heat shield
4. Exhaust manifold nut (8 required)
5. Exhaust manifold
6. Exhaust manifold gasket (2 required)
7. Exhaust manifold stud (8 required)

Fig. 75 Exploded view of the RH exhaust manifold

Fig. 77 Steering shaft and bolt view

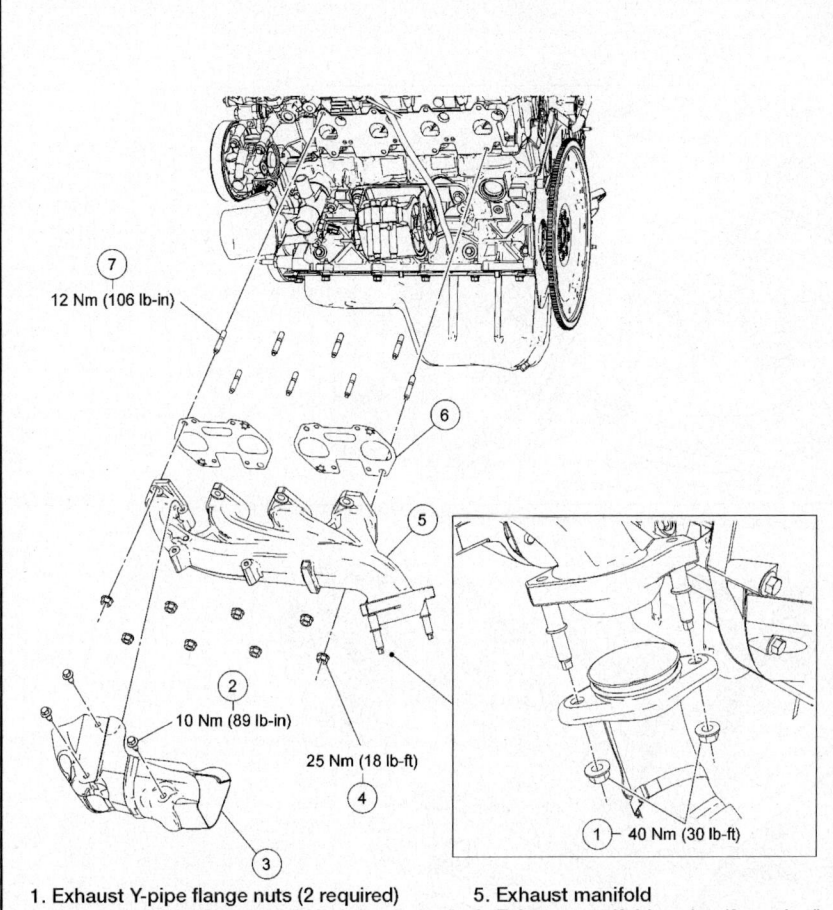

12 Nm (106 lb-in)

10 Nm (89 lb-in)

25 Nm (18 lb-ft)

1 — 40 Nm (30 lb-ft)

1. Exhaust Y-pipe flange nuts (2 required)
2. Exhaust manifold heat shield bolt (3 required)
3. Exhaust manifold heat shield
4. Exhaust manifold nut (8 required)
5. Exhaust manifold
6. Exhaust manifold gasket (2 required)
7. Exhaust manifold stud (8 required)

36578_EXPD_G0088

Fig. 78 Exploded view of the LH exhaust manifold

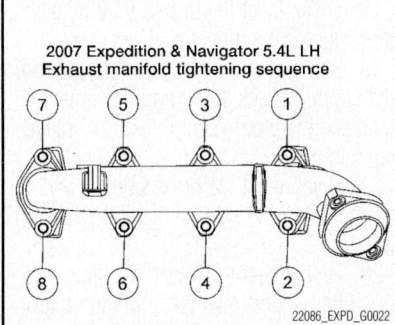

2007 Expedition & Navigator 5.4L LH
Exhaust manifold tightening sequence

22086_EXPD_G0022

Fig. 79 LH exhaust manifold tightening sequence

To install:

12. Using new exhaust manifold gaskets and studs, position the 2 gaskets and exhaust manifold and install the 8 studs. Tighten the studs to 9 ft. lbs. (12 Nm).

13. Using new exhaust manifold nuts, install the 8 nuts and tighten in sequence shown to 18 ft. lbs. (25 Nm).

14. For four wheel drive (4WD) vehicles:
    a. Install the front driveshaft.
    b. Connect the steering shaft, install and tighten bolt to 22 ft. lbs. (30 Nm).
    c. Install the 4 exhaust manifold-to-catalytic converter nuts.
    d. Position the exhaust manifold heat shield and install the 2 bolts. Tighten to 89 inch lbs. (10 Nm).
    e. Install the degas bottle.
    f. Install the air cleaner outlet tube.

FLEXPLATE

REMOVAL & INSTALLATION

See Figure 80.

1. Before servicing the vehicle, refer to the precautions section.

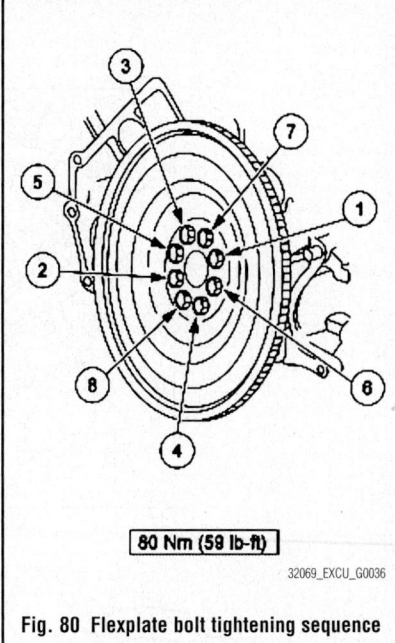

80 Nm (59 lb-ft)

32069_EXCU_G0036

Fig. 80 Flexplate bolt tightening sequence

2. Remove the transmission, as outlined in the Drive Train Section.

3. Remove the bolts and the flexplate.

To install:

4. Position the flexplate and install the bolts. Tighten the bolts in two stages:
    a. Stage 1: loosely install the bolts.
    b. Stage 2: tighten the bolts in sequence shown to 59 ft. lbs. (80 Nm).

5. Install the transmission.

INTAKE MANIFOLD

REMOVAL & INSTALLATION

See Figures 81 through 83.

✳✳ CAUTION

Fuel injection systems remain under pressure, even after the engine has been turned OFF. The fuel system pressure must be relieved before disconnecting any fuel lines. Failure to do so may result in fire and/or personal injury.

➡**When the battery is disconnected and reconnected, some abnormal drive symptoms may occur while the vehicle relearns its adaptive strategy. The vehicle may need to be driven 10 miles (16 km) or more to relearn the strategy.**

1. Before servicing the vehicle, refer to the precautions section.

2. Properly relieve the fuel system pressure.

3. Drain the cooling system.

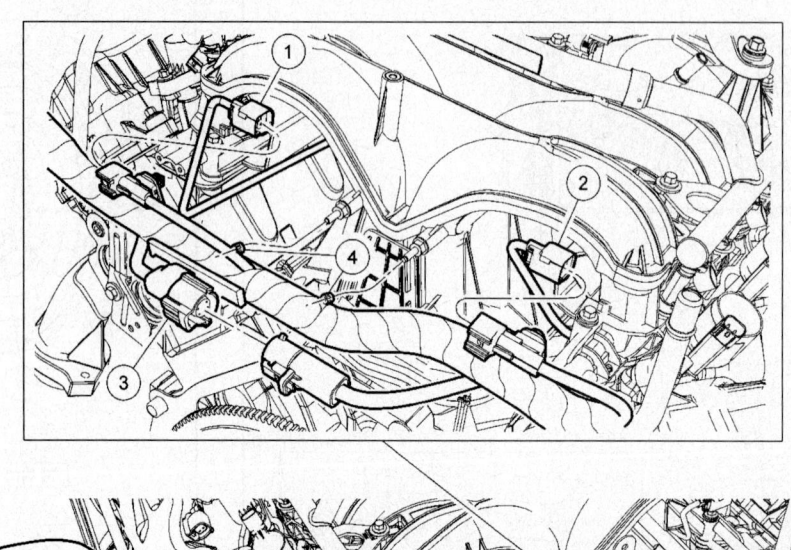

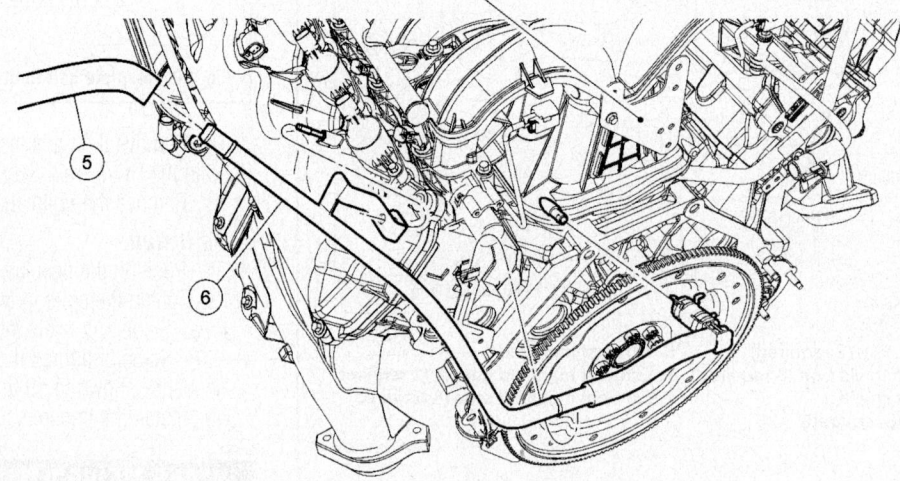

1. LH Knock Sensor (KS) electrical connector
2. RH KS electrical connector
3. Cylinder Head Temperature (CHT) electrical connector
4. Electrical wiring harness retainers
5. Brake booster vacuum hose
6. Intake manifold vacuum tube assembly

36578_EXPD_G0089

Fig. 81 View of the intake manifold vacuum tube assembly

4. Disconnect the battery ground cable.

5. Disconnect the fuel supply hose spring lock coupling from the fuel rail.

6. Remove the generator.

7. Remove the air cleaner outlet pipe.

8. Disconnect the crankcase ventilation tube quick connect coupling from the intake manifold.

9. Disconnect the quick connect coupling and remove the evaporative emissions system (EVAP) hose from the intake manifold.

10. Disconnect the EVAP hose position retainer from the intake manifold.

11. Remove the 4 bolts and the air cleaner outlet pipe-to-TB adapter

12. Disconnect the heater coolant hose from the coolant bypass tube.

13. Disconnect the quick connect couplings and remove the positive crankcase ventilation (PCV) tube. For additional information

14. Disconnect the 8 fuel injector electrical connectors.

15. Disconnect the 8 ignition coil electrical connectors.

16. Disconnect the Throttle Position Sensor (TPS) and electronic acceleration control electrical connectors

17. Disconnect the heated PCV intake fitting electrical connector.

18. Remove the intake manifold vacuum tube support bracket bolt and disconnect the intake manifold vacuum tube-to-intake manifold hose.

19. Disconnect the brake booster vacuum hose from the intake manifold vacuum tube.

20. Disconnect the intake manifold vacuum tube support retainer from the valve cover and position the intake manifold vacuum tube aside

21. Remove the 10 intake manifold bolts.

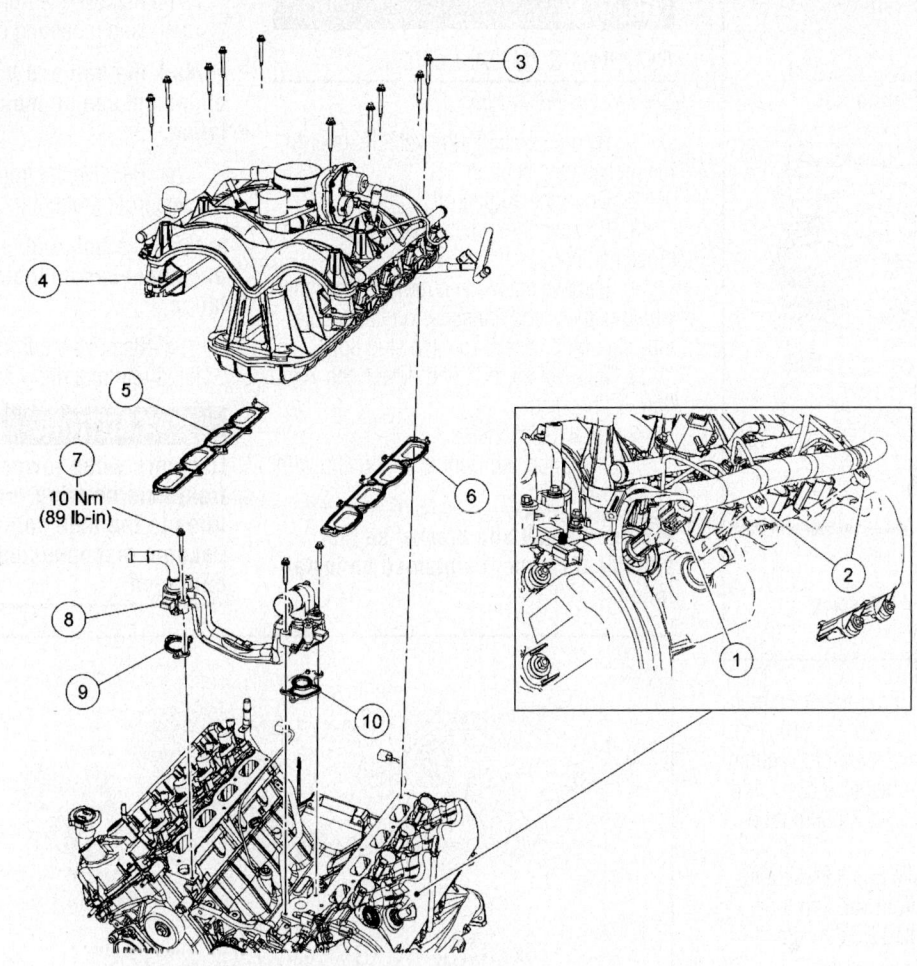

1. Variable Camshaft Timing (VCT) solenoid electrical connector
2. Engine wiring harness retainers (2 required)
3. Intake manifold bolt (10 required)
4. Intake manifold
5. RH intake manifold gasket
6. LH intake manifold gasket
7. Coolant crossover manifold assembly bolt (3 required)
8. Coolant crossover manifold assembly
9. RH coolant crossover manifold assembly gasket
10. LH coolant crossover manifold assembly gasket

36578_EXPD_G0090

Fig. 82 Exploded view of the intake manifold, coolant crossover manifold and gasket assembly

22. Disconnect the charge motion control valve (CMCV) electrical connector.

23. Disconnect the cylinder head temperature (CHT) sensor jumper harness electrical connector.

24. Disconnect the LH and RH knock sensor (KS) electrical connectors.

25. Remove the nut and disconnect the engine wiring harness retainer from the CMCV stud.

26. Remove the intake manifold and discard the gaskets.

27. Inspect and clean the sealing surfaces with silicone gasket remover and metal surface prep.

To install:

➡**Electrical and vacuum harnesses must not restrict movement of the CMCV control rods at rear of the intake manifold. Use extreme care on installation of the intake manifold to prevent any pinching of electrical and vacuum harnesses.**

28. Using new intake manifold gaskets, position the intake manifold.

29. Connect the engine wiring harness retainer to the CMCV stud and install the nut. Tighten nut to 89 inch lbs. (10 Nm).

30. Connect the CMCV electrical connector.

31. Connect the CHT sensor jumper harness electrical connector.

32. Connect the LH and RH KS electrical connectors.

33. Install the intake manifold bolts and tighten in 2 stages, in the sequence shown.

   a. Stage 1: Tighten to 18 inch lbs. (2 Nm).

   b. Stage 2: Tighten to 89 inch lbs. (10 Nm).

34. Install the intake manifold vacuum tube support bracket bolt and connect the

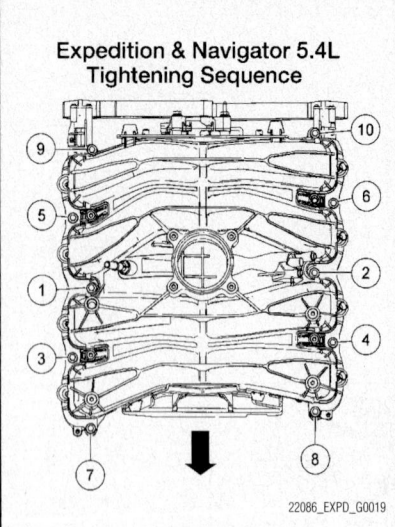

Expedition & Navigator 5.4L Tightening Sequence

22086_EXPD_G0019

Fig. 83 Intake manifold tightening sequence

intake manifold vacuum tube-to-intake manifold hose. Tighten to 89 inch lbs. (10 Nm).

35. Connect the intake manifold vacuum tube support retainer to the valve cover and position the intake manifold vacuum tube aside

36. Connect the brake booster vacuum hose to the intake manifold vacuum tube.

37. Connect the heated PCV intake fitting electrical connector.

38. Connect the TPS and electronic acceleration control electrical connectors.

39. Connect the 8 fuel injector electrical connectors.

40. Connect the 8 ignition coil electrical connectors.

41. Position the air cleaner outlet pipe-to-TB adapter and install the 4 bolts. Tighten to 89 inch lbs. (10 Nm).

42. Connect the crankcase ventilation tube quick connect coupling to the intake manifold.

43. Position the EVAP hose and connect the quick connect coupling to the intake manifold.

44. Connect the EVAP hose position retainer to the intake manifold.

45. Position the PCV tube and connect the quick connect couplings.

46. Connect the heater coolant hose to the coolant bypass.

47. Connect the fuel supply spring lock coupling to the fuel rail.

48. Install the generator.

49. Install the air cleaner outlet pipe.

50. Connect the battery ground cable.

51. Fill and bleed the engine cooling system.

OIL PAN

REMOVAL & INSTALLATION

See Figures 84 and 85.

1. Before servicing the vehicle, refer to the precautions section.

2. Drain the engine oil.

3. Remove the bolts and the frame crossmember.

4. Remove the nut and remove the starter wiring harness and transmission fluid cooler tube support brackets from the stud bolt.

5. Remove the bolt and detach the wire harness bracket.

6. On 4WD models:

a. Support the front axle housing with a jack stand.

➡**Mark the bolt and bracket so that alignment can be maintained on installation.**

b. Remove the front axle housing right hand mounting bolt.

➡**Mark the bolt and bracket so that alignment can be maintained on installation.**

c. Remove the front axle housing left hand front mounting bolt.

➡**Mark the bolt and bracket so that alignment can be maintained on installation**

d. Remove the front axle housing left hand rear mounting bolt.

✴✴ CAUTION

Use care when lowering the front axle housing, or the vacuum lines to the axle solenoid may become disconnected or damaged.

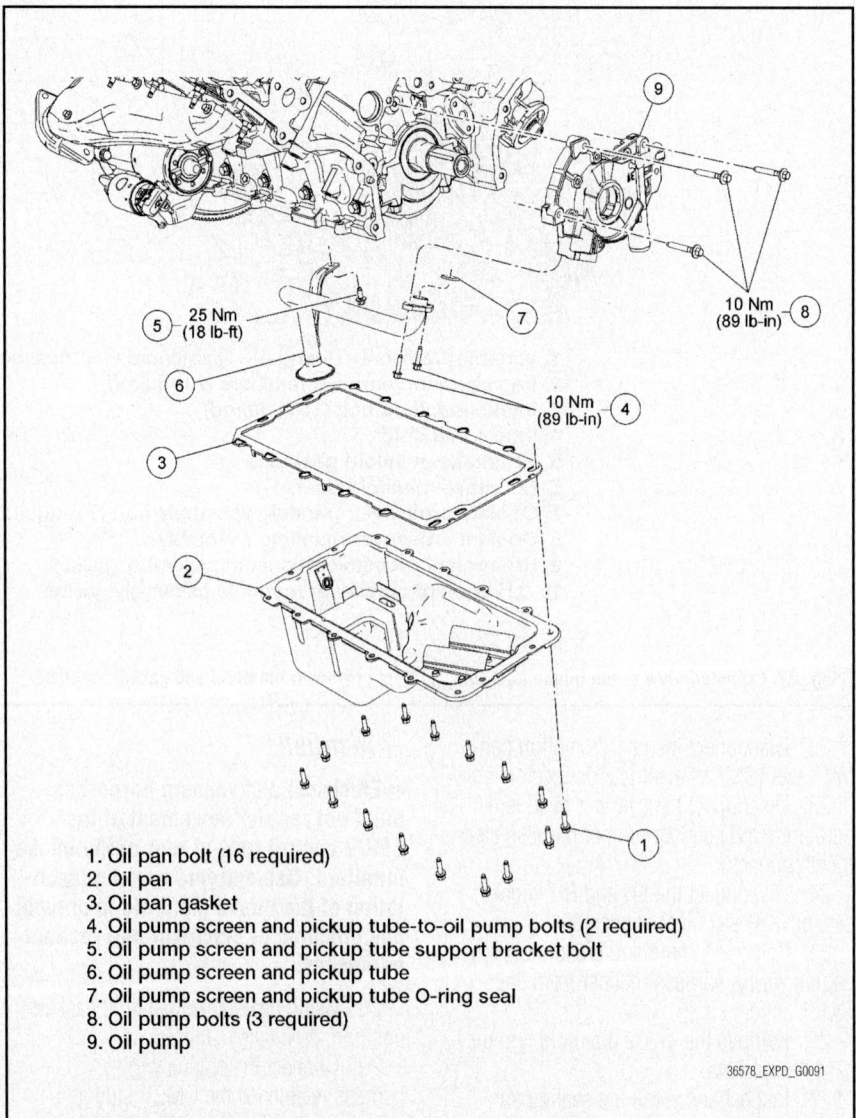

5 — 25 Nm (18 lb-ft)

10 Nm (89 lb-in) — 8

10 Nm (89 lb-in) — 4

1. Oil pan bolt (16 required)
2. Oil pan
3. Oil pan gasket
4. Oil pump screen and pickup tube-to-oil pump bolts (2 required)
5. Oil pump screen and pickup tube support bracket bolt
6. Oil pump screen and pickup tube
7. Oil pump screen and pickup tube O-ring seal
8. Oil pump bolts (3 required)
9. Oil pump

36578_EXPD_G0091

Fig. 84 Exploded view of the engine lubrication system assembly

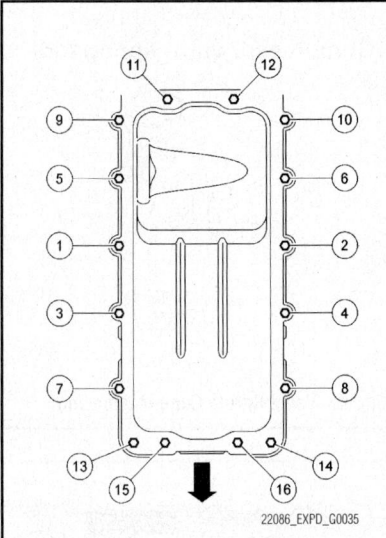

Fig. 85 Oil pan tightening sequence 5.4L engine

e. Lower the axle to allow clearance for the oil pan to be removed.

➡**Be careful when removing the oil pan gasket. It is reusable.**

7. Remove the 16 bolts, the oil pan and the gaskets. Inspect the oil pan gasket for damage.

8. If damaged, discard the oil pan gasket and the oil pan-to-oil pump gaskets.

To install:

※※ CAUTION

Do not use metal scrapers, wire brushes, power abrasive discs or other abrasive means to clean the sealing surfaces. These tools cause scratches and gouges, which make leak paths. Use a plastic scraping tool to remove all traces of old sealant.

9. Inspect the oil pan. Clean the mating surface for the oil pan with silicone gasket remover and metal surface prep.

➡**If not secured within four minutes, the sealant must be removed and the sealing area cleaned. To clean the sealing area, use silicone gasket remover and metal surface prep. Follow the directions on the packaging. Failure to follow this procedure can cause future oil leakage.**

10. Apply silicone gasket and sealant at the crankshaft rear seal retainer plate-to-cylinder block sealing surface.

11. Apply silicone gasket and sealant at the engine front cover-to-cylinder block sealing surface.

12. Install the oil pan gasket and the oil pan and loosely install the 16 bolts.

13. Tighten the bolts in 3 steps, in the sequence illustrated.

a. Step 1: Tighten to 18 inch lbs. (2 Nm)

b. Step 2: Tighten to 15 ft. lbs. (20 Nm).

c. Step 3: Tighten an additional 60 degrees.

14. On 4WD models:

※※ CAUTION

Use care when positioning the front axle housing, or the vacuum lines to the axle solenoid may become disconnected or damaged.

a. Position the front axle housing and loosely install the three bolts, aligning the bolt location marks made during removal.

b. Install the front axle housing right hand mounting bolt. Tighten to 66 ft. lbs. (89 Nm).

c. Install the front axle housing left hand front mounting bolt. Tighten to 66 ft. lbs. (89 Nm).

d. Install the front axle housing left hand rear mounting bolt. Tighten to 66 ft. lbs. (89 Nm).

15. Position the frame crossmember and the 4 bolts. Tighten to 75 ft. lbs. (102 Nm).

16. Install the wire harness bracket and the bolt. Tighten to 89 inch lbs. (10 Nm).

17. Fill the crankcase with clean engine oil.

OIL PUMP

REMOVAL & INSTALLATION
See Figure 86.

1. Before servicing the vehicle, refer to the precautions section.

2. Disconnect the negative battery cable.

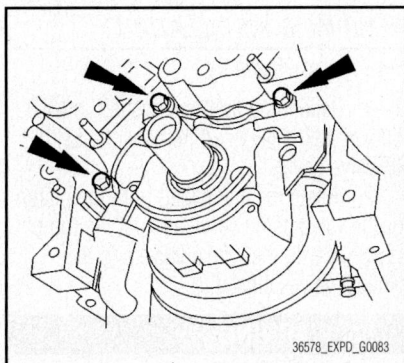

Fig. 86 Removing the 3 bolts and oil pump

3. Remove the timing drive components.

4. Remove the oil pan.

5. Remove the 3 bolts and the oil pump screen and pickup tube.

6. Remove the 3 bolts and the oil pump.

To install:

➡**Do not use metal scrapers, wire brushes, power abrasive discs or other abrasive means to clean the sealing surfaces. These tools cause scratches and gouges which make leak paths. Use a plastic scraping tool to remove all traces of old sealant.**

7. Clean the sealing surfaces with metal surface prep. Follow the directions on the packaging. Inspect the mating surfaces.

8. Position the oil pump and install the 3 bolts.

➡**Make sure the O-ring is in place and not damaged. A missing or damaged O-ring can cause foam in the lubrication system, low oil pressure and severe engine damage.**

➡**Clean and inspect the mating surfaces and install a new O-ring. Lubricate the O-ring with clean engine oil prior to installation.**

9. Position the oil pump screen and pickup tube and install the 3 bolts.

a. Tighten the 2 oil pump screen and pickup tube-to-oil pump bolts to 89 inch lbs. (10 Nm).

b. Tighten the oil pump screen and pickup tube-to-spacer bolt to 18 ft. lbs. (25 Nm).

10. Install the oil pan.

11. Install the timing drive components.

PISTON AND RING

POSITIONING
See Figure 87.

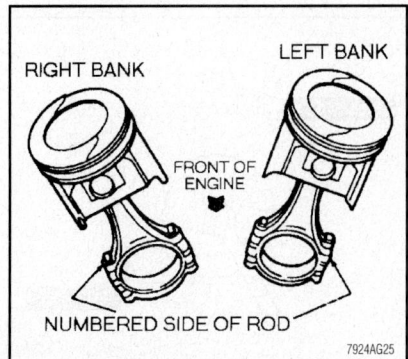

Fig. 87 Piston and connecting rod assembly positioning

REAR MAIN SEAL

REMOVAL & INSTALLATION

See Figures 88 through 92.

1. Before servicing the vehicle, refer to the precautions section.
2. Disconnect the negative battery cable.
3. Remove the transmission.
4. Remove the 8 bolts and the flexplate
5. Using the special tools 303-514 and 100-001, remove the crankshaft oil slinger.
6. Using the special tools 303-519 and 100-001, remove the crankshaft rear seal.

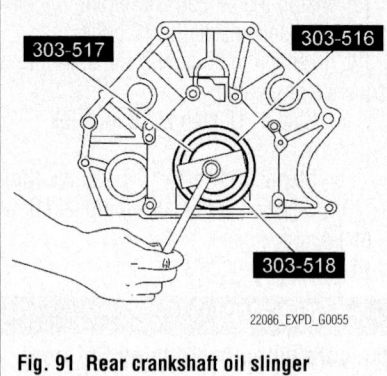

Fig. 91 Rear crankshaft oil slinger installation

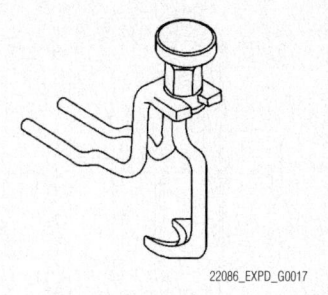

Compressor valve spring tool

Fig. 93 Valve Spring Compression Tool

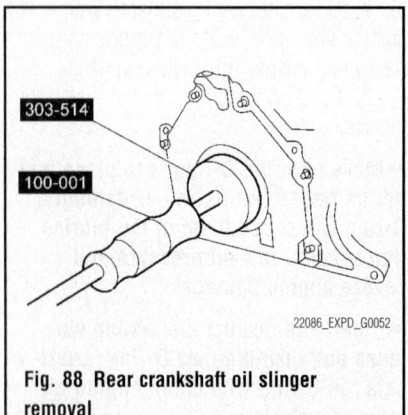

Fig. 88 Rear crankshaft oil slinger removal

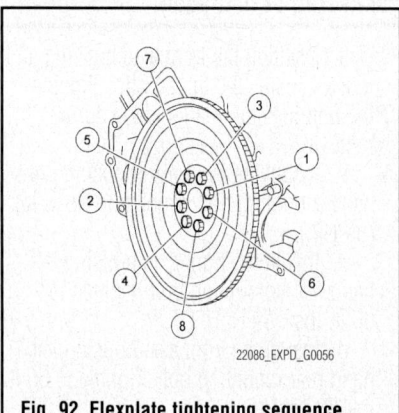

Fig. 92 Flexplate tightening sequence

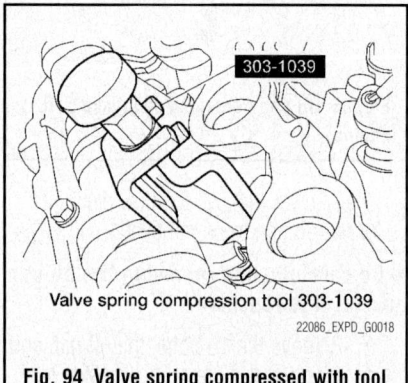

Valve spring compression tool 303-1039

Fig. 94 Valve spring compressed with tool 303-1039 shown

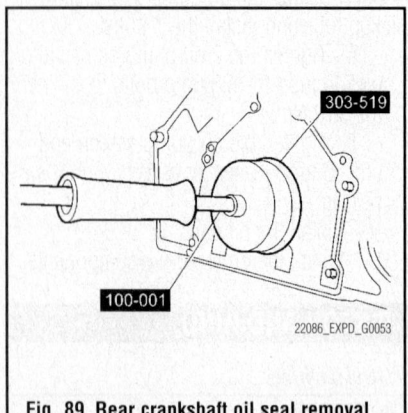

Fig. 89 Rear crankshaft oil seal removal

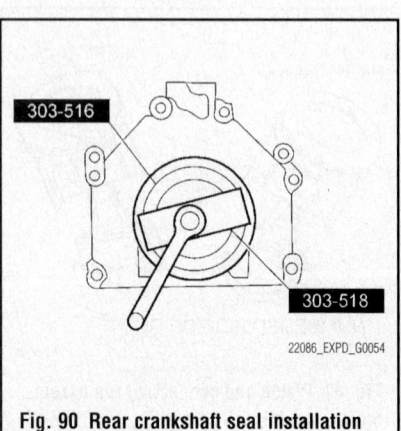

Fig. 90 Rear crankshaft seal installation

To install:

7. Lubricate the inner lip of the crankshaft rear seal with clean engine oil.
8. Using the special tools 303-516 and 303-518, install a new crankshaft rear seal.
9. Using the special tools 303-516, 303-517 and 303-518, install a new crankshaft rear oil slinger.
10. Install the flexplate and tighten the 8 bolts in the sequence shown to 59 ft. lbs. (80 Nm).
11. Install the transmission.

ROCKER ARMS/SHAFTS

REMOVAL & INSTALLATION

See Figures 93 and 94.

1. Depending on the camshaft roller follower being serviced, remove the LH or RH valve cover.
2. Rotate the crankshaft until the piston for the valve being serviced is at the top of its stroke with the intake valve and the exhaust valves closed.

❈❈ WARNING

If the components are to be reinstalled, they must be installed in the same position. Mark the components

for installation into the original location.

3. Using the special tool, compress the valve spring and remove the camshaft roller follower.
4. Repeat the previous 2 steps for each camshaft roller follower being serviced.
5. Inspect the camshaft roller follower.

To install:

→ Lubricate the camshaft roller followers with clean engine oil prior to installation.

6. Using the special tool, compress the valve spring and install the camshaft roller follower.
7. Repeat the previous step for each camshaft roller follower being serviced.
8. Depending on the camshaft roller follower being serviced, install the LH or RH valve cover.

TIMING CHAIN, SPROCKETS AND FRONT COVER

REMOVAL & INSTALLATION

See Figures 95 through 111.

1. Before servicing the vehicle, refer to the precautions section.

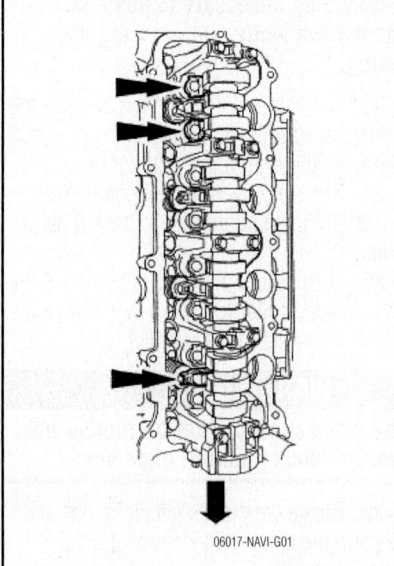

Fig. 95 Remove only the 3 roller followers shown from the right hand cylinder head

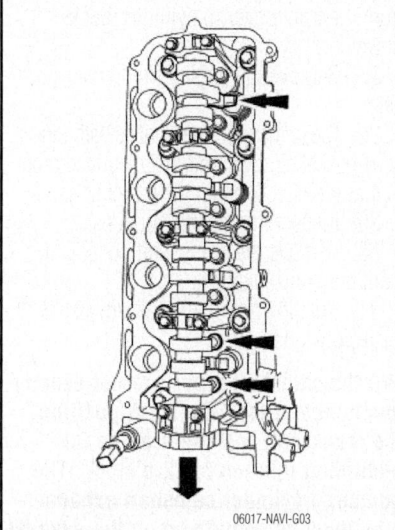

Fig. 97 Remove only the 3 roller followers shown from the left hand cylinder head

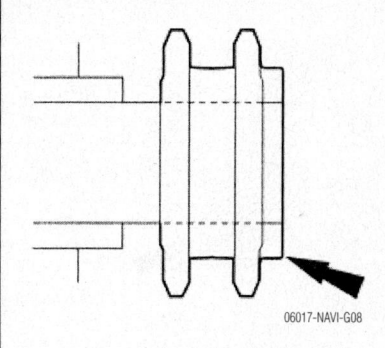

Fig. 99 Install the crankshaft sprocket, making sure the flange faces forward

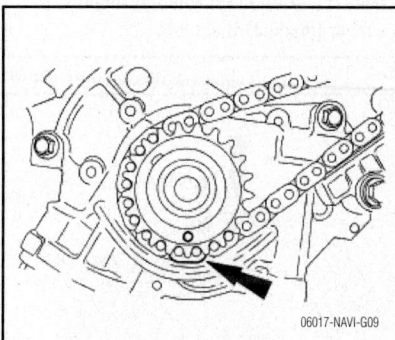

Fig. 100 Position the lower end of the left hand (inner) timing chain on the crankshaft sprocket, aligning the timing mark on the outer flange of the crankshaft sprocket with the single copper (marked) link on the chain

2. Drain the engine oil.

3. Remove the engine cooling fan.

4. Remove the valve covers.

5. Remove the accessory drive belt.

6. Remove the nut and the power steering pressure hose support bracket.

7. Remove the nut and the transmission cooler tube support bracket.

8. Remove the crankshaft pulley bolt and washer. Discard the crankshaft pulley bolt.

9. Using the tool 303-009, remove the crankshaft pulley.

10. Using the tool 303-107, remove the crankshaft front seal.

11. Remove the bolts and the accessory drive idler pulleys.

12. Remove the bolts and the coolant pump pulley.

13. Remove the bolts and the accessory drive belt tensioner.

14. Disconnect the right hand Camshaft Position (CMP) sensor. Discard the O-ring seal.

15. Disconnect the A/C compressor electrical connector.

16. Disconnect the radio ignition interference capacitor electrical connectors.

17. Remove the nut and the right hand radio ignition interference capacitor.

18. Disconnect the left CMP sensor. Discard the O-ring seal.

19. Remove the nut and the left hand radio ignition interference capacitor.

20. Remove the bolts and position the power steering pump assembly aside.

21. Disconnect the wiring harness position retainer and the engine oil pressure (EOP) switch electrical connector and position the wiring harness aside.

22. Disconnect the Crankshaft Position (CKP) sensor connector.

23. Remove the 4 front oil pan bolts.

24. Remove the bolt and the CKP sensor. Discard the O-ring seal.

25. Remove the bolts and the studs from the front cover.

✳✳ CAUTION

Do not use metal scrapers, wire brushes, power abrasive discs or other abrasive means to clean the sealing surfaces. These tools cause scratches and gouges which make leak paths. Use a plastic scraping tool to remove all traces of old sealant.

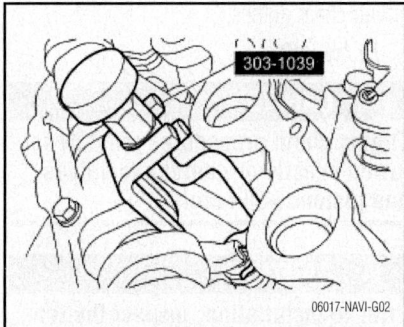

Fig. 96 Remove the 3 designated roller followers from the right hand cylinder head

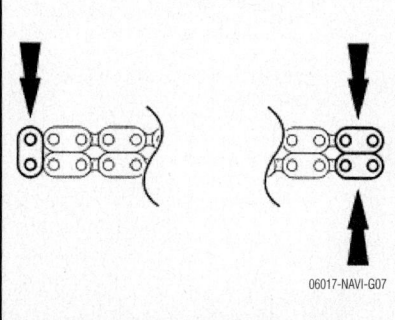

Fig. 98 If the copper links are not visible, mark two links on one end and one link on the other end, and use as timing marks

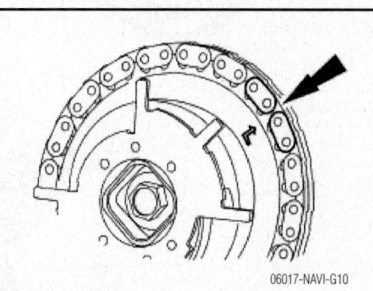

Fig. 101 Position the timing chain on the camshaft sprocket with the camshaft sprocket timing mark positioned between the two copper (marked) chain links

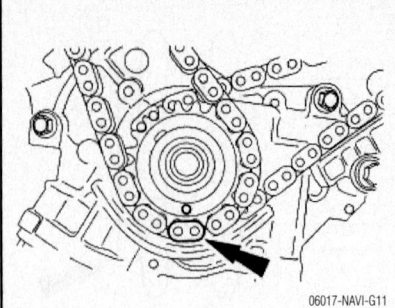

Fig. 102 Position the lower end of the right hand (outer) timing chain on the crankshaft sprocket, aligning the timing mark on the sprocket with the single copper (marked) chain link

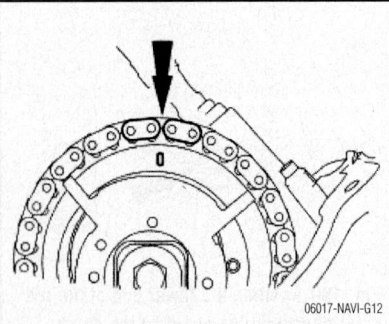

Fig. 103 Position the right hand timing chain on the camshaft sprocket. Make sure the camshaft sprocket timing mark is positioned between the two copper (marked) chain links

26. Remove the engine front cover from the front cover to cylinder block dowel.

27. Remove the engine front cover gaskets.

28. Clean the mating surfaces with silicone gasket remover and metal surface prep. Follow the directions on the packaging.

29. Inspect the mating surfaces.

30. Remove the crankshaft sensor ring from the crankshaft.

31. Position the crankshaft keyway at the 12 o'clock position.

➡️ If the camshaft lobes are not exactly positioned at the 12 o'clock position, the crankshaft will require one full additional rotation to 12 o'clock. The number 1 cylinder camshaft exhaust lobe must be coming up on the exhaust stroke. Verify by noting the position of the 2 intake camshaft lobes and the exhaust lobe on the number 1 cylinder.

➡️ If the components are to be reinstalled, they must be installed in the same positions. Mark the components for installation into the original locations.

32. Remove only the 3 roller followers shown in the illustration from the right hand cylinder head.

✳️ CAUTION

Do not allow the valve keepers to fall off the valve or the valve may drop into the cylinder.

➡️ It may be necessary to push the valve down while compressing the spring.

33. Using the tool illustrated, remove the 3 designated roller followers in the previous step from the right hand cylinder head.

34. Remove only the 3 roller followers shown in the illustration from the left hand cylinder head.

35. Using the tool 303-1039, remove the 3 designated roller followers in the previous step from the left hand cylinder head.

✳️ WARNING

The crankshaft cannot be moved past the 6 o'clock position once set.

36. Rotate the crankshaft clockwise and position the crankshaft keyway at the 6 o'clock position.

✳️ CAUTION

If one or both of the tensioner mounting bolts are loosened or removed, the tensioner-sealing bead must be inspected for seal integrity. If cracks, tears, separation from the tensioner body or permanent compression of the seal bead is observed, install a new tensioner.

37. Remove the bolts, the left hand timing chain tensioner and tensioner arm.

38. Remove the bolts, the right hand timing chain tensioner and tensioner arm.

39. Remove the right hand and left hand timing chains and the crankshaft sprocket.

40. Remove the right hand timing chain from the camshaft sprocket.

41. Remove the right hand timing chain from the crankshaft sprocket.

42. Remove the left hand timing chain from the camshaft sprocket.

43. Remove the left hand timing chain and crankshaft sprocket.

44. Remove the left hand and right hand timing chain guides.

To install:

✳️ CAUTION

Timing chain procedures must be followed exactly or damage to valves and pistons will result.

✳️ CAUTION

Prior to installation, inspect the tensioner-sealing bead for seal integrity. If cracks, tears, separation from the tensioner body or permanent com-

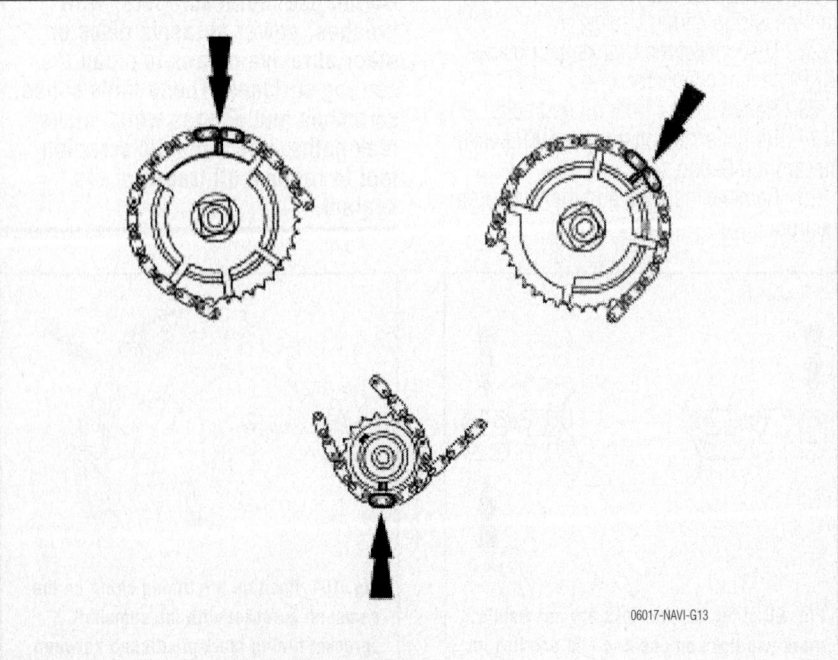

Fig. 104 Verify correct alignment of all timing marks

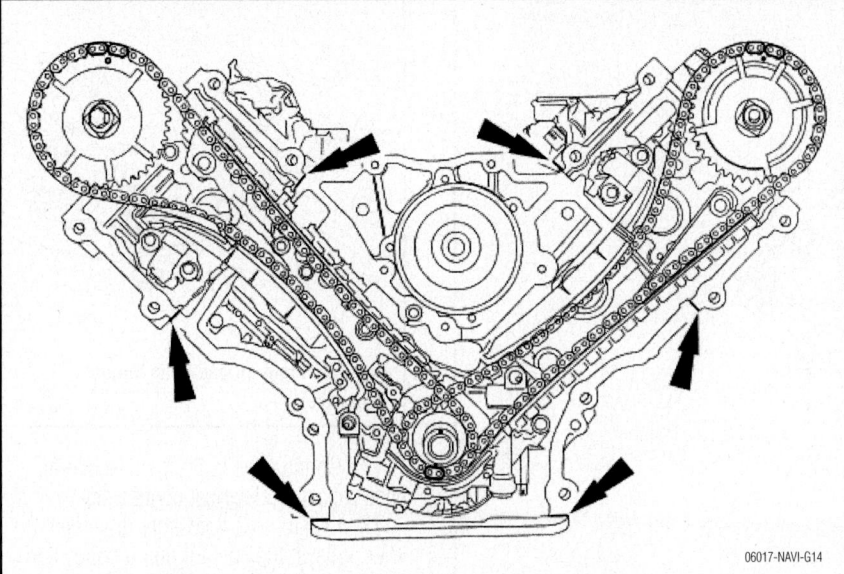

Fig. 105 Apply a bead of silicone gasket and sealant along the cylinder head-to-cylinder block surface and the oil pan-to-cylinder block surface, at the locations shown

06017-NAVI-G14

pression of the seal bead is observed, install a new tensioner.

45. Compress the tensioner plunger, using a vise.

46. Install a retaining clip on the tensioner to hold the plunger in during installation.

47. Remove the tensioner from the vise.

48. If the copper links are not visible, mark two links on one end and one link on the other end, and use as timing marks.

49. Install the crankshaft sprocket, making sure the flange faces forward.

50. Install the 4 bolts and the left hand and right hand timing chain guides. Tighten to 89 inch lbs. (10 Nm).

51. Position the lower end of the left hand (inner) timing chain on the crankshaft sprocket, aligning the timing mark on the outer flange of the crankshaft sprocket with the single copper (marked) link on the chain.

➡Make sure the upper half of the timing chain is below the tensioner arm dowel.

52. Position the timing chain on the camshaft sprocket with the camshaft sprocket timing mark positioned between the two copper (marked) chain links.

➡The left hand timing chain tensioner arm has a bump near the dowel hole for identification.

53. Position the left hand timing chain tensioner arm on the dowel pin and install the left hand timing chain tensioner and

bolts. Tighten the bolts to 18 ft. lbs. (25 Nm).

54. Remove the retaining clip from the left hand timing chain tensioner.

55. Position the lower end of the right hand (outer) timing chain on the crankshaft sprocket, aligning the timing mark on the sprocket with the single copper (marked) chain link.

➡The lower half of the timing chain must be positioned above the tensioner arm dowel.

56. Position the right hand timing chain on the camshaft sprocket. Make sure the camshaft sprocket timing mark is positioned between the two copper (marked) chain links.

57. Position the right hand timing chain tensioner arm on the dowel pin and install the right hand timing chain tensioner and bolts. Tighten the bolts to 18 ft. lbs. (25 Nm).

58. Remove the retaining clip from the right hand timing chain tensioner.

59. As a final-check, verify correct alignment of all timing marks.

60. Install the crankshaft sensor ring on the crankshaft.

61. Lubricate the roller followers with clean engine oil prior to installation.

62. Using tool 303-1039, install all of the camshaft roller followers.

❊❊ CAUTION

Do not use metal scrapers, wire brushes, power abrasive discs or other abrasive means to clean the

sealing surfaces. These tools cause scratches and gouges which make leak paths. Use a plastic scraping tool to remove all traces of old sealant.

➡If the engine front cover is not secured within 4 minutes, the sealant must be removed and the sealing area cleaned. To clean the sealing area, use silicone gasket remover and metal surface prep. Failure to follow this procedure can cause future oil leakage.

➡Make sure that the engine front cover gasket is in place on the engine front cover before installation.

63. Apply a bead of silicone gasket and sealant along the cylinder head-to-cylinder block surface and the oil pan-to-cylinder block surface, at the locations illustrated.

64. Install a new engine front cover gasket on the engine front cover. Position the engine front cover onto the dowels. Install the fasteners finger-tight.

65. Tighten the engine front cover fasteners in sequence in 2 steps:
   a. Step 1: Tighten fasteners 1 through 15 to 18 ft. lbs. (25 Nm).
   b. Step 2: Tighten fasteners 6 and 7 to 35 ft. lbs. (48 Nm).

66. Install the 4 front oil pan bolts in the sequence shown in 2 steps.
   a. Step 1: Tighten to 15 ft. lbs. (20 Nm).
   b. Step 2: Tighten an additional 60 degrees.

❊❊ CAUTION

Do not use metal scrapers, wire brushes, power abrasive discs or other abrasive means to clean sealing surfaces. These tools cause scratches and gouges which make leak paths. Use a plastic scraping tool to remove all traces of old sealant.

67. Connect the CKP sensor electrical connector.

68. Position the power steering pump assembly and install the bolts. Tighten to 18 ft. lbs. (25 Nm).

69. Position the power steering pressure hose support bracket and install the nut.

70. Position the transmission cooler tube support bracket and install the nut.

➡Lubricate the O-ring seal with clean engine oil prior to installation.

71. Using a new O-ring seal, install the right hand CMP sensor and the bolt.

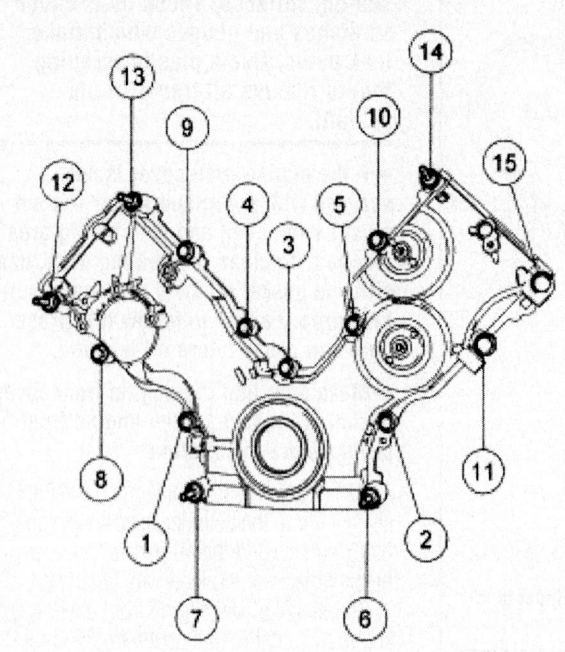

1 Bolt, Hex Flange Head Pilot, M8 x 1.25 x 50

2 Bolt, Hex Flange Head Pilot, M8 x 1.25 x 50

3 Bolt, Hex Flange Head Pilot, M8 x 1.25 x 50

4 Bolt, Hex Flange Head Pilot, M8 x 1.25 x 50

5 Bolts, Hex Flange Head Pilot, M8 x 1.25 x 50

6 Stud, Hex Head Pilot, M10 x 1.5 x 1.5 x 103

7 Stud, Hex Head Pilot, M10 x 1.5 x 1.5 x 103

8 Bolt, Hex Flange Head Pilot, M8 x 1.25 x 50

9 Bolt, Hex Flange Head Pilot, M8 x 1.25 x 50

10 Bolt, Hex Flange Head Pilot, M8 x 1.25 x 50

11 Bolt, Hex Flange Head Pilot, M8 x 1.25 x 50

12 Stud and Washer, Hex Head Pilot, M8 x 1.25 x 1.25 x 94

13 Stud and Washer, Hex Head Pilot, M8 x 1.25 x 1.25 x 94

14 Stud and Washer, Hex Head Pilot, M8 x 1.25 x 1.25 x 94

15 Bolt, Hex Head Pilot, M8 x 1.25 x 56

06017-NAVI-G15

Fig. 106 Engine front cover fastener location and torque sequence

72. Connect the right hand CMP sensor electrical connector.

73. Install the left hand radio ignition interference capacitor and the nut.

➡ **Lubricate the O-ring seal with clean engine oil prior to installation.**

74. Using a new O-ring seal, install the left hand CMP sensor and the bolt.

75. Connect the left hand CMP sensor electrical connector.

76. Install the right hand radio ignition interference capacitor and the nut.

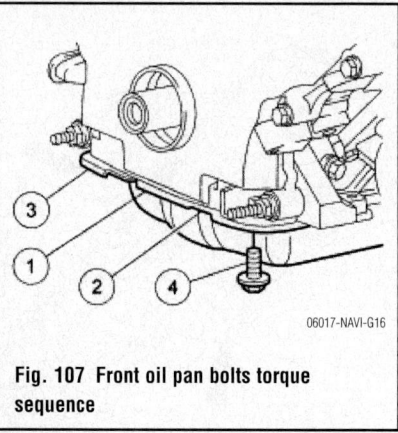

06017-NAVI-G16

Fig. 107 Front oil pan bolts torque sequence

77. Connect the radio ignition interference capacitor electrical connectors.

78. Install the 3 accessory drive belt idler pulleys, the coolant pump pulley and the 7 bolts. Tighten the bolts to 18 ft. lbs. (25 Nm).

79. Lubricate the engine front cover and the crankshaft seal inner lip with clean engine oil.

80. Use the tools illustrated to install the crankshaft seal into the engine front cover.

➡ **If not secured within 4 minutes, the sealant must be removed and the sealing area cleaned. To clean the sealing area, use silicone gasket remover and metal surface prep. Failure to follow this procedure can cause future oil leakage.**

81. Apply a 0.32 inch (8mm) bead of silicone gasket and sealant to the Woodruff key slot on the crankshaft pulley.

82. Use the tool illustrated to install the crankshaft pulley.

83. Tighten the new crankshaft pulley bolt in 4 steps:

   a. Step 1: Tighten to 66 ft. lbs. (90 Nm).

   b. Step 2: Loosen 360 degrees.

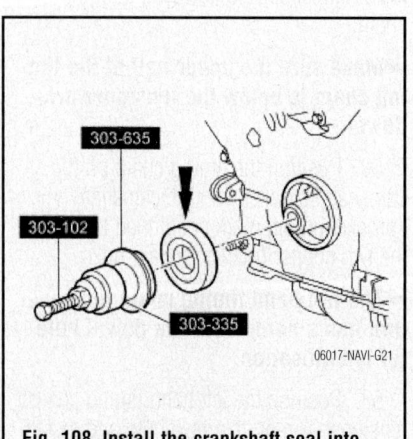

06017-NAVI-G21

Fig. 108 Install the crankshaft seal into the engine front cover

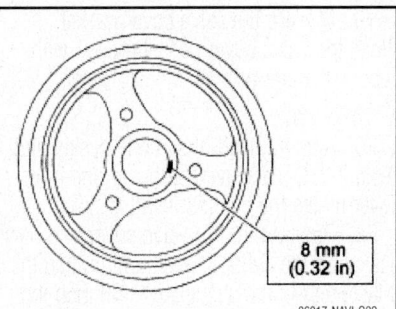

Fig. 109 Apply a 0.32 inch (8mm) bead of silicone gasket and sealant to the Woodruff key slot on the crankshaft pulley

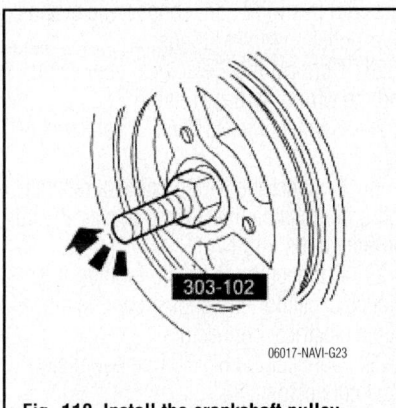

Fig. 110 Install the crankshaft pulley

c. Step 3: Tighten to 37 ft. lbs. (50 Nm).

d. Step 4: Tighten an additional 90 degrees.

84. Install the accessory drive belt.

85. Clean the valve cover mating surface with silicone gasket remover and metal surface prep.

➡If not secured within 4 minutes, the sealant must be removed and the sealing area cleaned. To clean the sealing area, use silicone gasket remover and

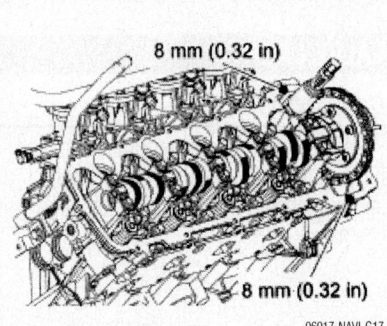

Fig. 111 Apply a 0.32 inch (8mm) bead of silicone gasket and sealant in 2 places where the engine front cover meets the right cylinder head

metal surface prep. Failure to follow this procedure can cause future oil leakage.

86. Apply a 0.32 inch (8mm) bead of silicone gasket and sealant in 2 places where the engine front cover meets the cylinder head.

☀☀ CAUTION

When installing the valve cover, make sure to avoid damaging the Variable Camshaft Timing (VCT) solenoid.

87. Install the right hand valve cover and gasket on the cylinder head and tighten the bolts in sequence and tighten to 89 inch lbs. (10 Nm).

➡If not secured within 4 minutes, the sealant must be removed and the sealing area cleaned. To clean the sealing area, use silicone gasket remover and metal surface prep. Failure to follow this procedure can cause future oil leakage.

88. Apply a 0.32 inch (8mm) bead of silicone gasket and sealant in 2 places where the engine front cover meets the left cylinder head.

89. Install the left hand valve cover and gasket on the cylinder head and tighten the bolts in sequence shown and tighten to 89 inch lbs. (10 Nm).

90. Install the engine cooling fan.

91. Fill the crankcase with clean engine oil.

92. Check steering and transmission fluid, top off if needed.

93. Check all connections for leaks

VALVE COVERS

REMOVAL & INSTALLATION

Left Side

See Figures 112 and 113.

1. Remove the air cleaner outlet pipe.

2. Remove the degas bottle.

3. Remove the LH ignition coils.

4. Disconnect the quick connect couplings and remove the positive crankcase ventilation (PCV) tube

5. Remove the bolt and position the oil level indicator tube aside.

6. Disconnect the LH radio ignition interference capacitor electrical connector.

7. Disconnect the LH variable camshaft timing (VCT) solenoid electrical connector and the wiring harness retainers.

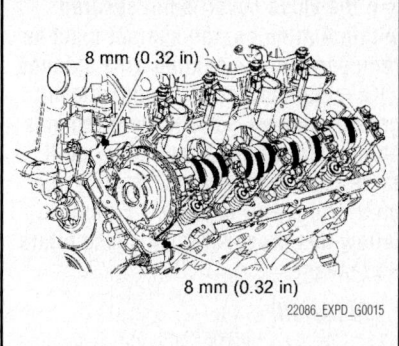

Fig. 112 Application points of silicone sealant

8. Disconnect the intake manifold vacuum tube hose from the brake booster.

9. Disconnect the intake manifold vacuum tube assembly from the support bracket and the valve cover stud and position aside.

☀☀ WARNING

When removing the valve cover, make sure to avoid damaging the VCT solenoid.

10. Fully loosen the fasteners and remove the LH valve cover and gasket.

11. Clean the valve cover mating surface of the cylinder head with silicone gasket remover and metal surface prep.

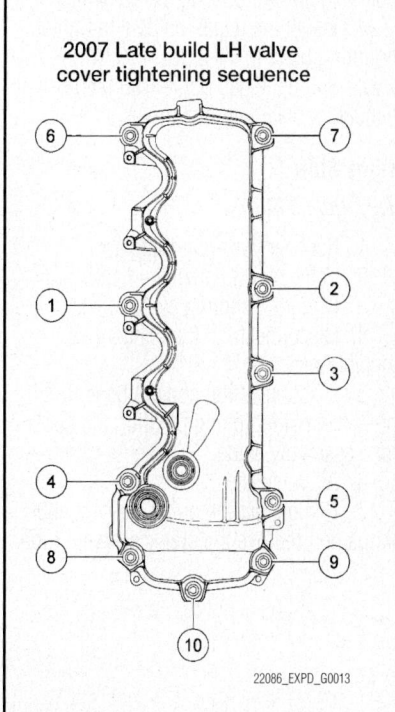

Fig. 113 LH Valve cover tightening sequence

➡If the valve cover is not secured within 4 minutes, the sealant must be removed and the sealing area cleaned with metal surface prep and silicone gasket remover. Follow the directions on the packaging. Allow to dry until there is no sign of wetness, or 4 minutes, whichever is longer. Failure to follow this procedure can cause future oil leakage.

To install:

12. Apply a bead of silicone gasket and sealant in 2 places where the engine front cover meets the cylinder head.

13. Position the LH valve cover and new gasket on the cylinder head and tighten the 10 fasteners in the sequence to 89 inch lbs. (10 Nm).

All vehicles

14. Position the intake manifold vacuum tube assembly onto the support bracket and the valve cover stud

15. Connect the intake manifold vacuum tube hose to the brake booster.

16. Connect the VCT solenoid electrical connector and the wiring harness retainers

17. Connect the radio ignition interference capacitor electrical connector.

18. Position the oil level indicator tube and install the bolt and tighten to 89 inch lbs. (10 Nm).

19. Position the PCV tube and connect the quick connect couplings.

20. Install the LH ignition coils and tighten mounting bolts to 53 inch lbs. (6 Nm).

21. Install the degas bottle and tighten mounting bolts to 11 ft. lbs. (15 Nm).

22. Fill the degas bottle with recommended coolant and mixture.

Right Side

See Figure 114.

1. Recover the A/C refrigerant.
2. Vehicles with auxiliary heat:
3. Drain the cooling system.
4. Disconnect the 2 auxiliary heat coolant hoses.
5. Disconnect the coolant hose from the intake manifold and position the coolant hose assembly aside.
6. All vehicles:
7. Disconnect the quick connect couplings and remove the crankcase vent tube.

8. Remove the nut and the ground cable and disconnect the wiring harness retainer.

9. Disconnect the powertrain control module (PCM) electrical connector.

10. Disconnect the 2 electrical connectors and the wiring harness retainer.

11. Disconnect the evaporator outlet and inlet fittings. Discard the O-ring seals

12. Disconnect the RH radio ignition interference capacitor and engine cooling fan clutch electrical connectors.

13. Remove the RH ignition coils.

14. Disconnect the RH variable camshaft timing (VCT) solenoid electrical connector

15. Disconnect the RH camshaft position (CMP) sensor electrical connector.

16. Disconnect the 2 engine wiring harness retainers from the RH valve cover studs.

➡The fasteners are part of the valve cover and should not be removed.

17. Fully loosen the fasteners and remove the RH valve cover and gasket.

18. Clean the valve cover mating surface of the cylinder head with silicone gasket remover and metal surface prep.

2007 Late build RH valve cover tightening sequence

22086_EXPD_G0016

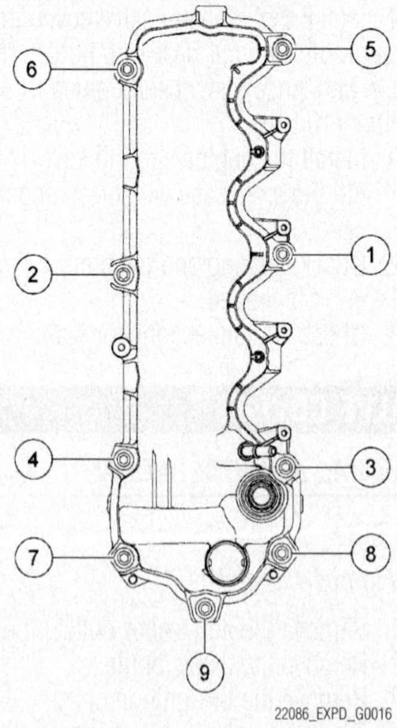

Fig. 114 RH Valve cover tightening sequence

19. Discard the valve cover gasket. Clean the valve cover gasket groove with soap and water or a suitable solvent.

To install:

20. Apply a bead of silicone gasket and sealant in 2 places where the engine front cover meets the cylinder head.

21. Position the LH valve cover and new gasket on the cylinder head and tighten the 9 fasteners in the sequence to 89 inch lbs. (10 Nm).

22. Install the RH ignition coils and tighten mounting bolts to 53 inch lbs. (6 Nm).

23. Install new O-ring seals, and lubricate with fresh PAG oil, connect the evaporator outlet and inlet fittings.

24. Connect the 2 electrical connectors and the wiring harness retainer

25. Connect the PCM electrical connector.

26. Connect the wiring harness retainer and ground cable, install and tighten the nut to 89 inch lbs. (10 Nm).

27. Connect the RH radio ignition interference capacitor and engine cooling fan clutch electrical connectors.

28. Connect the RH VCT solenoid electrical connector.

29. Connect the RH CMP sensor electrical connector.

30. Connect the wiring harness retainers to the valve cover.

31. Position the crankcase vent tube and connect the quick connect couplings.

Vehicles with auxiliary heat

32. Position the coolant hose assembly and connect the coolant hose to the intake manifold.

33. Connect the 2 auxiliary heat coolant hoses.

34. Fill and bleed the coolant system.

All vehicles

35. Evacuate, leak test and charge the refrigerant system.

VALVE LASH

ADJUSTMENT

These engines do not require valve lash adjusting, because they utilize hydraulic lash components in their valve actuation systems.

ENGINE PERFORMANCE & EMISSION CONTROLS

ACCELERATOR PEDAL POSITION (APP) SENSOR

LOCATION

See Figure 115.

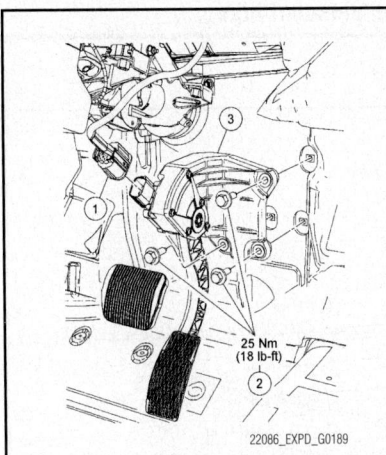

Fig. 115 The Accelerator Pedal Position (APP) Sensor location view

The Accelerator Pedal Position (APP) Sensor is located on the accelerator pedal and is serviced as an assembly.

REMOVAL & INSTALLATION

See Figure 115.

1. Disconnect the battery ground cable.
2. Disconnect the accelerator pedal position sensor electrical connector.
3. Remove the 3 bolts and the accelerator pedal assembly.

To install:

4. Install the 3 bolts and the accelerator pedal assembly.
5. Tighten the mounting bolts to 18 ft. lbs. (25 Nm).

CAMSHAFT POSITION (CMP) SENSOR

LOCATION

The Camshaft Position (CMP) Sensors are located on front of the engine. Just below valve covers.

REMOVAL & INSTALLATION

See Figure 116.

1. Disconnect the negative battery cable.
2. Disconnect the Camshaft Position (CMP) sensor electrical connector.

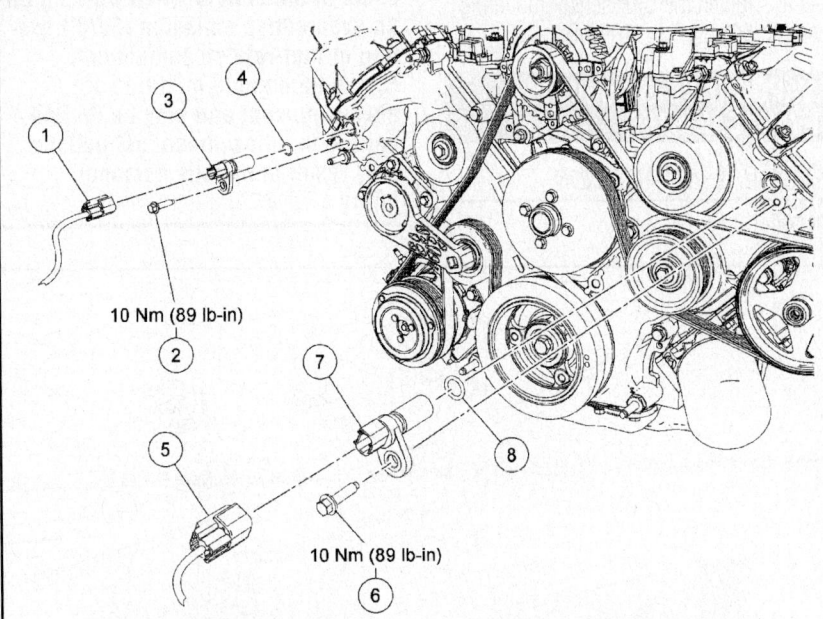

1. RH camshaft position (CMP) sensor electrical connector
2. RH CMP sensor bolt
3. RH CMP sensor
4. RH CMP sensor O-ring seal
5. LH camshaft position (CMP) sensor electrical connector
6. LH CMP sensor bolt
7. LH CMP sensor
8. LH CMP sensor O-ring seal

Fig. 116 Camshaft Position (CMP) sensor location view

3. For the left CMP sensor, remove the air cleaner inlet tube.
4. Remove the bolt and the CMP sensor.

To install:

5. To install, reverse the removal procedure and note the following:
   a. Tighten the CMP sensor mounting bolt to 89 inch lbs. (10 Nm).

CRANKSHAFT POSITION (CKP) SENSOR

LOCATION

The Crankshaft Position (CKP) Sensor is located to the left of the balancer pulley and behind the air conditioning compressor.

REMOVAL & INSTALLATION

See Figure 117.

1. Disconnect the battery ground cable.
2. Remove the accessory drive belt from the A/C compressor pulley.
3. Raise and support the vehicle.
4. Disconnect the wiring harness connector from the crankshaft position sensor.

5. Disconnect the A/C compressor field coil electrical connector.

➡**It is not necessary to remove the A/C compressor bolts**

6. Loosen the bolts enough for the compressor to slide down one inch, allowing access for crankshaft position (CKP) sensor removal.
8. Remove the bolt and the CKP sensor.

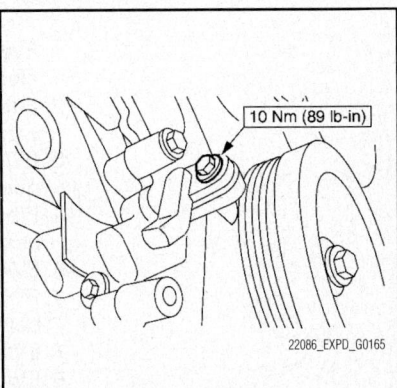

Fig. 117 Crankshaft Position (CKP) sensor view

To install:

9. To install, reverse the removal procedure and note the following:

a. Tighten the CKP sensor mounting bolt to 89 inch lbs. (10 Nm).

EVAPORATIVE EMISSIONS (EVAP) CANISTER

REMOVAL & INSTALLATION

See Figure 118.

⁂ WARNING

Always disconnect the battery ground cable at the battery when working on an evaporative emission (EVAP) system or fuel-related component. Highly flammable mixtures are always present and may be ignited. Failure to follow these instructions may result in serious personal injury.

⁂ WARNING

Do not smoke, carry lighted tobacco or have an open flame of any type when working on or near any fuel-related component. Highly flammable mixtures are always present and may be ignited. Failure to follow these instructions may result in serious personal injury.

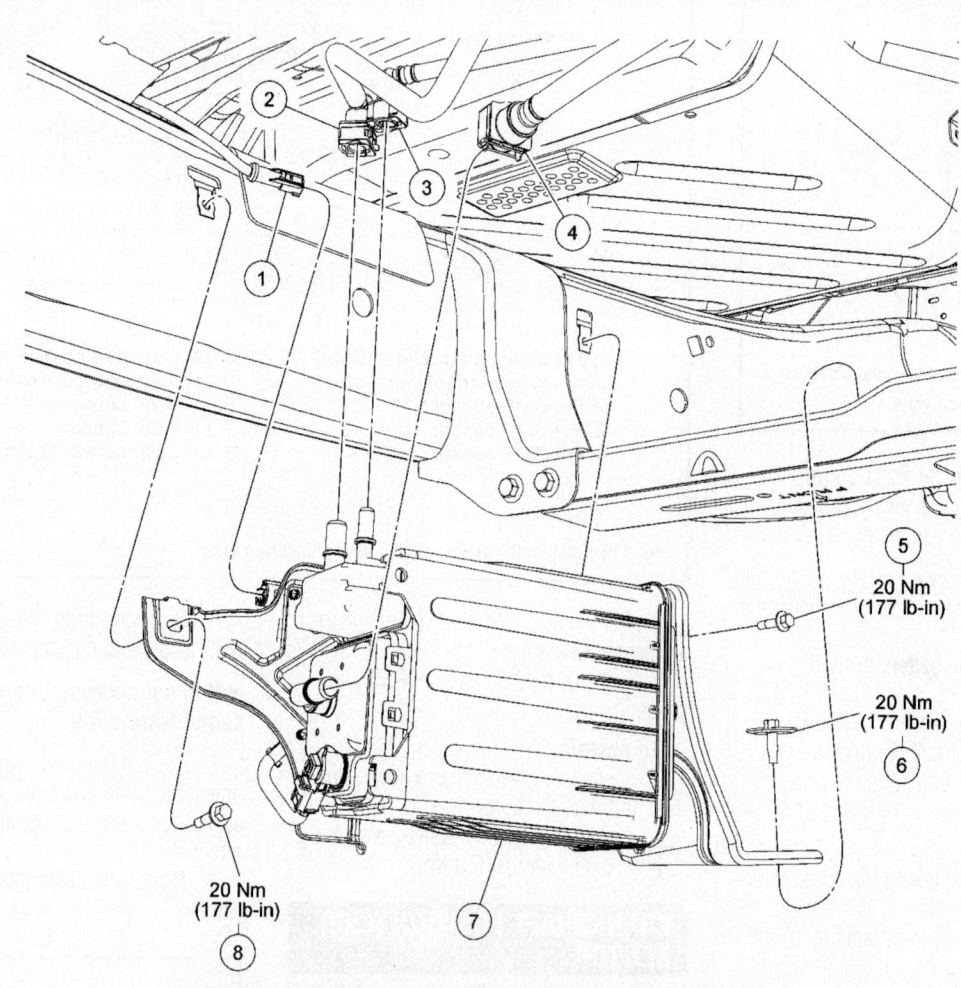

1. Evaporative Emission (EVAP) canister vent solenoid electrical connector
2. Fuel Tank Pressure (FTP) sensor and vapor tube assembly-to- EVAP canister quick connect coupling
3. EVAP canister purge valve vapor tube-to- EVAP canister quick connect coupling
4. Fresh air tube-to-canister vent solenoid and dust separator assembly quick connect coupling
5. EVAP canister assembly bracket-to-frame rail bolt
6. EVAP canister assembly bracket and exhaust Y-pipe dual catalytic converter heat shield-to-transmission crossmember bolt
7. EVAP canister assembly
8. EVAP canister assembly bracket-to-frame rail bolt

36578_EXPD_G0092

Fig. 118 View of the EVAP canister assembly

➡ The Evaporative Emission (EVAP) canister vent solenoid and dust separator are an assembly.

1. With the vehicle in NEUTRAL, position it on a hoist.
2. Disconnect the battery ground cable.
3. Disconnect the EVAP canister vent solenoid electrical jumper from the wiring harness.
4. Disconnect the Fuel Tank Pressure (FTP) sensor and vapor tube assembly-to-EVAP canister quick connect coupling.
5. Disconnect the EVAP canister purge valve vapor tube-to- EVAP canister quick connect coupling.
6. Disconnect the fresh air tube-to-canister vent solenoid and dust separator assembly quick connect coupling.
7. Remove the EVAP canister assembly bracket-to-frame rail bolt in the rear.
8. Remove the EVAP canister assembly bracket-to-frame rail bolt in the front.
9. Remove the EVAP canister assembly bracket and exhaust Y-pipe dual catalytic converter heat shield-to-transmission crossmember bolt and remove the EVAP canister assembly from the vehicle.
10. Disconnect the EVAP canister vent solenoid electrical connector.
11. Remove the 5 EVAP canister-to-EVAP canister assembly bracket bolts.
12. Remove the EVAP canister assembly from the EVAP canister assembly brackets.
13. Remove the canister vent solenoid and dust separator assembly from the EVAP canister.

➡ Inspect the EVAP canister heat shield and if damaged, install a new EVAP canister heat shield.

14. To install, reverse the removal procedure.
15. Carry out the Evaporative Emission System Leak Test.

HEATED OXYGEN SENSOR (HO2S)

LOCATION
See Figure 119.

The HO2S are located at the top of front pipe near exhaust manifolds.

REMOVAL & INSTALLATION
See Figure 119.

1. Disconnect the battery ground cable.
2. Disconnect the heated oxygen sensor (HO2S) electrical connector.

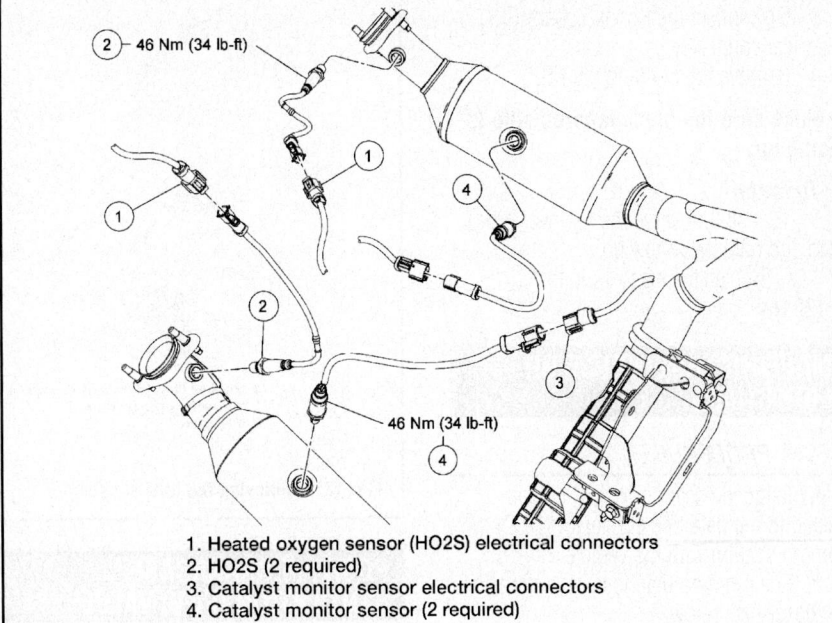

1. Heated oxygen sensor (HO2S) electrical connectors
2. HO2S (2 required)
3. Catalyst monitor sensor electrical connectors
4. Catalyst monitor sensor (2 required)

22086_EXPD_G0180

Fig. 119 HO2S sensor locations

3. Using a HO2S socket tool 303-476, remove the HO2S.

➡ If necessary, lubricate the HO2S with penetrating and lock lubricant to aid in removal.

To install:
4. To install, reverse the removal procedure and note the following:
   a. Tighten the HO2S sensor to 34 ft. lbs. (46 Nm).

➡ Apply a light coat of nickel anti-seize lubricant to the threads of the HO2S.

IDLE AIR CONTROL (IAC) VALVE

LOCATION

The Idle Air Control Valve is mounted on the intake manifold, just behind the throttle body.

REMOVAL & INSTALLATION

1. Disconnect the battery ground cable.
2. Disconnect the idle air control (IAC) valve electrical connector.
3. Disconnect the throttle bypass hose.
4. Remove the two bolts and the IAC valve.

To install:
5. Install the IAC valve and tighten the bolts in two stages:
   a. Stage 1: Tighten to 89 inch lbs. (10 Nm).

   b. Stage 2: Tighten an additional 90 degrees.
6. Connect the throttle bypass hose.
7. Connect the IAC electrical connector.
8. Connect the battery ground cable.

KNOCK SENSOR (KS)

LOCATION

1. The Knock Sensor (KS) is located under the intake manifold just about in the center.

REMOVAL & INSTALLATION
See Figure 120.

1. Disconnect the negative battery cable.

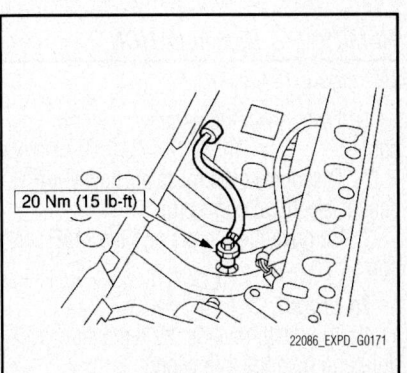

20 Nm (15 lb-ft)

22086_EXPD_G0171

Fig. 120 Knock Sensor (KS) View

2. Remove the upper intake manifold.
3. Disconnect the Knock Sensor (KS) electrical connector
4. Remove the bolt and the KS.

➡ **Make sure the black tapered side is facing up.**

To install:

5. To install, reverse the removal procedure and note the following:
   a. Tighten the KS to 15 ft. lbs. (20 Nm).

MALFUNCTION INDICATOR LIGHT (MIL)

RESET PROCEDURE

A diagnostic scan tool must be connected to the data link connector (DLC) for communication with the vehicle.

1. The required diagnostic tool functions are described below:
   • Diagnostic test modes; self-test, clear diagnostic trouble codes (DTCs)
   • Resetting keep alive memory (KAM)
   • On-board system readiness (OBD monitor completion status)
   • Diagnostic monitoring test results (mode 6) for on-board diagnostic (OBD) on-board monitors
   • Output test mode
   • Monitor, record, and playback of parameter identification (PIDs)
   • Freeze frame PID data

MASS AIR FLOW (MAF) SENSOR

LOCATION

The Mass Air Flow (MAF) is located between the air cleaner and the throttle body or inside the air cleaner assembly.

REMOVAL & INSTALLATION

See Figure 121.

1. Disconnect the negative battery cable.
2. Disconnect the mass air flow (MAF) sensor electrical connector.
3. Remove the 2 bolts and the MAF sensor.

To install:

4. To install, reverse the removal procedure and note the following:
   a. Tighten the MAF sensor mounting bolts to 62 inch lbs. (7 Nm).

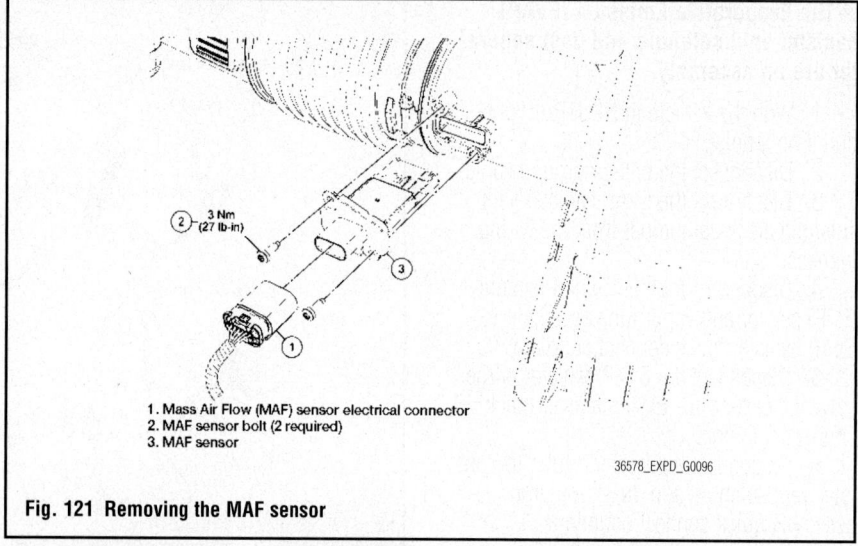

1. Mass Air Flow (MAF) sensor electrical connector
2. MAF sensor bolt (2 required)
3. MAF sensor

36578_EXPD_G0096

Fig. 121 Removing the MAF sensor

POSITIVE CRANKCASE VENTILATION (PCV) VALVE

LOCATION

The Positive Crankcase Ventilation (PCV) valve is located on the intake manifold to the left.

REMOVAL & INSTALLATION

See Figure 122.

1. Disconnect the negative battery cable.
2. Release the clamp and remove the bolt and the air intake resonator assembly.
3. Disconnect the quick connect couplings and remove the PCV tube.
4. Disconnect the PCV heater element electrical connector.
5. Remove the 2 bolts and the PCV heater element.

6. Discard the O-ring seal.
7. To install, reverse removal procedure. Lubricate the o-ring with clean engine oil prior to installation.

THROTTLE POSITION SENSOR (TPS)

LOCATION

The Throttle Position Sensor (TPS) is located on the throttle body.

REMOVAL & INSTALLATION

See Figure 123.

1. Disconnect the negative battery cable.
2. Remove the throttle body.

➡ **Do not put direct heat on the Throttle Position Sensor (TPS) or any other plastic parts because heat damage may**

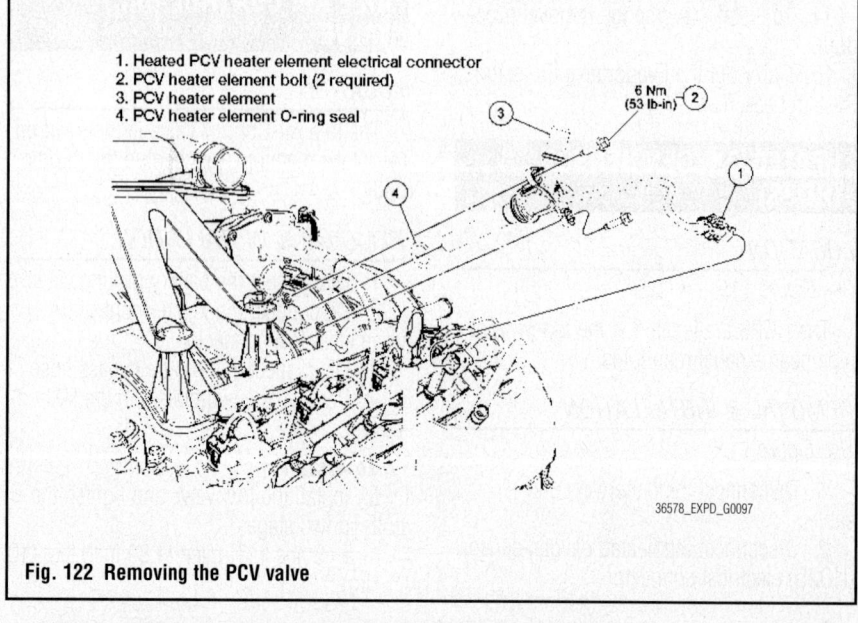

1. Heated PCV heater element electrical connector
2. PCV heater element bolt (2 required)
3. PCV heater element
4. PCV heater element O-ring seal

6 Nm (53 lb-in)

36578_EXPD_G0097

Fig. 122 Removing the PCV valve

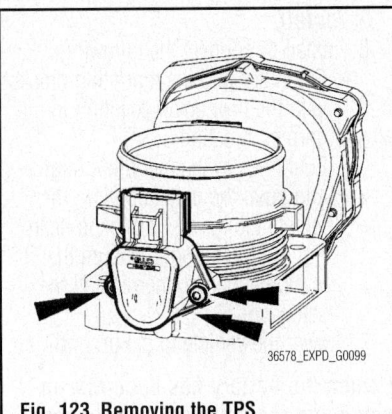

Fig. 123 Removing the TPS

occur. **Damage may also occur if Electronic Throttle Body (ETB) temperature exceeds 248°F (120°C).**

➡**Do not use power tools.**

3. Using a suitable heat gun, apply heat to the top of the Electronic Throttle Body (ETB) until the top TPS bolt ear reaches approximately 130°F (55°C), this should take no more than 3 minutes using an 1,100-watt heat gun. The heat gun should be about 25.4 mm (1 in) away from the ETB.

4. Monitor the temperature of the top TPS bolt ear on the ETB with a suitable temperature measuring device, such as a digital temperature laser or infrared thermometer, while heating the ETB.

5. Using hand tools, quickly remove the bolt farthest from the heat source first and discard.

6. Using hand tools, remove the remaining bolt and discard.

7. Remove and discard the TPS.

8. To install, reverse removal procedure.

VARIABLE CAMSHAFT TIMING OIL CONTROL SOLENOID

LOCATION

The Variable Camshaft Timing Oil Control Solenoid (VCT) is located under the valve cover.

REMOVAL & INSTALLATION

See Figure 124.

1. Remove the valve cover. Refer to valve cover removal in this section.

2. Remove the bolt and the variable camshaft timing (VCT) oil control solenoid.

To install:

3. To install, reverse the removal procedure and note the following:

a. Tighten the VCT to 44 inch lbs. (5 Nm).

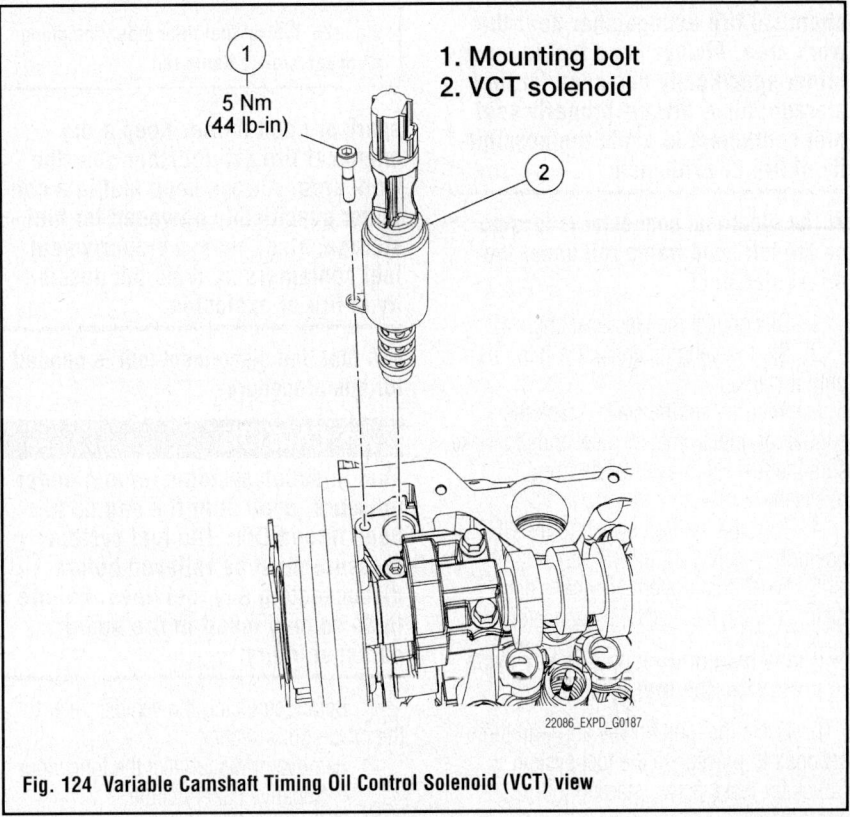

1. Mounting bolt
2. VCT solenoid

Fig. 124 Variable Camshaft Timing Oil Control Solenoid (VCT) view

---

FUEL
GASOLINE FUEL INJECTION SYSTEM

FUEL SYSTEM SERVICE PRECAUTIONS

Safety is the most important factor when performing not only fuel system maintenance but any type of maintenance. Failure to conduct maintenance and repairs in a safe manner may result in serious personal injury or death. Maintenance and testing of the vehicle's fuel system components can be accomplished safely and effectively by adhering to the following rules and guidelines.

• To avoid the possibility of fire and personal injury, always disconnect the negative battery cable unless the repair or test procedure requires that battery voltage be applied.

• Always relieve the fuel system pressure prior to disconnecting any fuel system component (injector, fuel rail, pressure regulator, etc.), fitting or fuel line connection. Exercise extreme caution whenever relieving fuel system pressure to avoid exposing skin, face and eyes to fuel spray. Please be advised that fuel under pressure may penetrate the skin or any part of the body that it contacts.

• Always place a shop towel or cloth around the fitting or connection prior to loosening to absorb any excess fuel due to spillage. Ensure that all fuel spillage (should it occur) is quickly removed from engine surfaces. Ensure that all fuel soaked cloths or towels are deposited into a suitable waste container.

• Always keep a dry chemical (Class B) fire extinguisher near the work area.

• Do not allow fuel spray or fuel vapors to come into contact with a spark or open flame.

• Always use a back-up wrench when loosening and tightening fuel line connection fittings. This will prevent unnecessary stress and torsion to fuel line piping.

• Always replace worn fuel fitting O-rings with new. Do not substitute fuel hose or equivalent where fuel pipe is installed.

Before servicing the vehicle, make sure to also refer to the precautions in the beginning of this section as well.

RELIEVING FUEL SYSTEM PRESSURE

✳✳ CAUTION

Observe all applicable safety precautions when working around fuel. Whenever servicing the fuel system, always work in a well ventilated area. Do not allow fuel spray or vapors to come in contact with a spark or open flame. Keep a dry chemical fire extinguisher near the work area. Always keep fuel in a container specifically designed for fuel storage; also, always properly seal fuel containers to avoid the possibility of fire or explosion.

➡The electrical connector is located on the left hand frame rail under the driver side door.

1. Disconnect the electrical connector.
2. Start the engine and allow it to idle until it stalls.
3. After the engine stalls, crank the engine for approximately 5 seconds to make sure the fuel rail pressure has been released.
4. Turn the ignition switch to the OFF position.
5. When fuel system service is complete, connect the electrical connector.

➡It may take more than one key cycle to pressurize the fuel system.

6. Cycle the ignition key and wait three seconds to pressurize the fuel system. Check for leaks before starting the engine.
7. Install the diagnostic tool. Turn the key ON with the engine OFF. Cycle the key OFF, then ON. Select the appropriate vehicle and engine qualifier. Clear all diagnostic trouble codes (DTCs) and carry out a PCM reset.
8. Start the vehicle and check the fuel system for leaks.

FUEL FILTER

REMOVAL & INSTALLATION
See Figure 125.

✳✳ CAUTION

Observe all applicable safety precautions when working around fuel. Whenever servicing the fuel system, always work in a well ventilated area. Do not allow fuel spray or vapors to come in contact with a

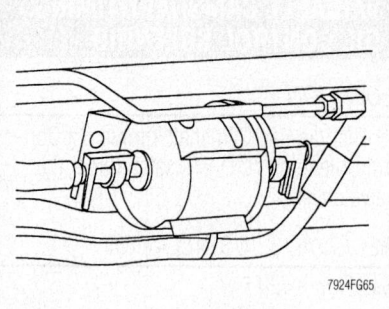

7924FG65

Fig. 125 Typical fuel filter mounting along an under-vehicle frame rail

spark or open flame. Keep a dry chemical fire extinguisher near the work area. Always keep fuel in a container specifically designed for fuel storage; also, always properly seal fuel containers to avoid the possibility of fire or explosion.

➡A fuel line disconnect tool is needed for this procedure.

✳✳ CAUTION

Fuel injection systems remain under pressure, even after the engine has been turned OFF. The fuel system pressure must be relieved before disconnecting any fuel lines. Failure to do so may result in fire and/or personal injury.

1. Before servicing the vehicle, refer to the precautions section.
2. Remove or disconnect the following:
   • Negative battery cable
3. Relieve the fuel system pressure.
   • Fuel lines from the fuel filter. Have a drain pan handy to catch any residual fuel once the lines are separated.
4. Disconnect the fuel lines from the filter as follows:
   • Safety clip from the male hose
   • Install and push the fuel line disconnect tool into the female fitting.
5. Remove or disconnect the following:
   • Male and female fittings from the filter

➡Inspect the fuel lines for any damage after the fuel is finished draining.

   • Fuel filter from the bracket and the retainer, if equipped. Note the direction of the flow arrow so the replacement filter can be installed correctly.

To install:

6. Install or connect the following:
   • Fuel filter into the mounting bracket with the flow arrow pointing in the correct direction.
   • Fuel lines to the fuel filter. Align and push the male tube into the female fitting until a click is heard. Pull on the fitting to ensure that it is fully engaged, then install the safety clip.
7. Lower the vehicle to the ground.

➡When the battery has been disconnected and reconnected, some abnormal drive symptoms may occur while the Powertrain Control Module (PCM) relearns its adaptive strategy. The vehicle may need to be driven 10 miles (16 km) or more to relearn the strategy.

8. Connect the negative battery cable.

FUEL PUMP MODULE

REMOVAL & INSTALLATION
See Figures 126 and 127.

✳✳ CAUTION

Observe all applicable safety precautions when working around fuel. Whenever servicing the fuel system, always work in a well ventilated area. Do not allow fuel spray or vapors to come in contact with a spark or open flame. Keep a dry chemical fire extinguisher near the work area. Always keep fuel in a container specifically designed for fuel storage; also, always properly seal fuel containers to avoid the possibility of fire or explosion.

✳✳ CAUTION

Fuel injection systems remain under pressure, even after the engine has been turned OFF. The fuel system pressure must be relieved before disconnecting any fuel lines. Failure to do so may result in fire and/or personal injury.

1. Before servicing the vehicle, refer to the precautions section.
2. Release the fuel system pressure.
3. Drain the fuel tank.
4. If equipped, remove the four nuts and the fuel tank skid plate.
5. Disconnect the two vapor tubes at the rear of the fuel tank.

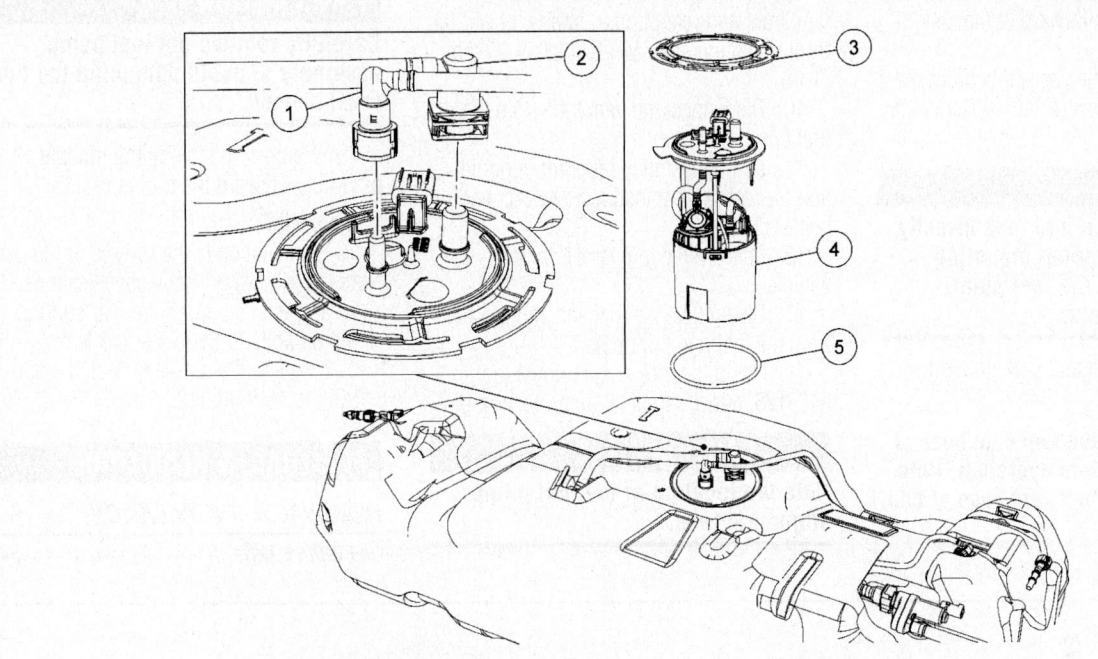

1. Fuel supply tube-to-Fuel Pump (FP) module quick connect coupling
2. Fuel Tank Pressure (FTP) sensor and vapor tube assembly-to- FP module quick connect coupling
3. FP module locking ring
4. FP pump module
5. FP module O-ring seal

36578_EXPD_G0100

Fig. 126 Exploded view of fuel pump module and components—28 gallon tank

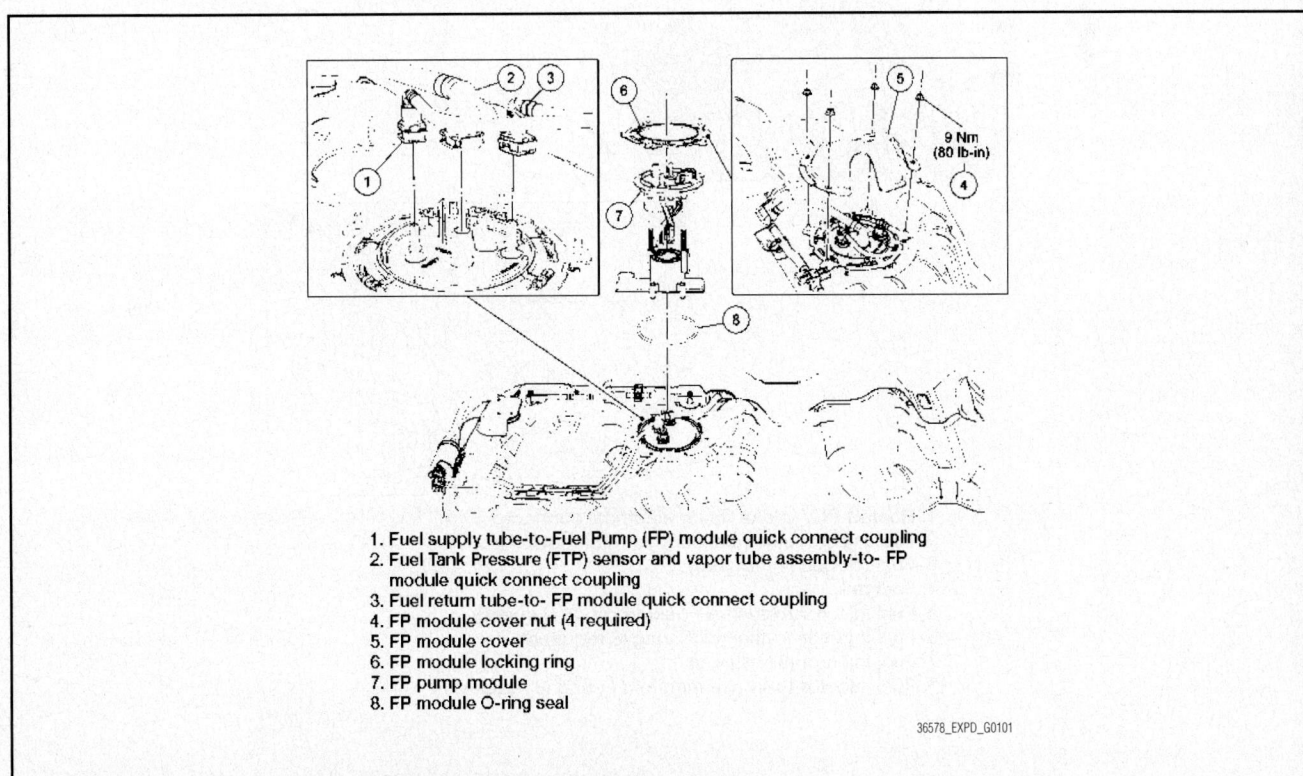

1. Fuel supply tube-to-Fuel Pump (FP) module quick connect coupling
2. Fuel Tank Pressure (FTP) sensor and vapor tube assembly-to- FP module quick connect coupling
3. Fuel return tube-to- FP module quick connect coupling
4. FP module cover nut (4 required)
5. FP module cover
6. FP module locking ring
7. FP pump module
8. FP module O-ring seal

36578_EXPD_G0101

Fig. 127 Exploded view of fuel pump module and components—33.5 gallon tank

6. Disconnect the vapor tube and the fuel filter outlet tube forward of the fuel tank.

7. Disconnect the vapor tube from the Evaporative Emissions (EVAP) system dust separator.

✳✳ CAUTION

Do not support the fuel tank directly beneath the fuel pump mounting area. Damage to the fuel pump assembly can occur.

8. Position a suitable jack under the fuel tank.

➡ **The location of the fuel vent hose is critical to fuel system operation. Note the routing of the fuel vent hose at this time.**

9. Remove the two bolts and the fuel tank front and rear support straps. Lower the front of the fuel tank approximately 25 mm (1 in).

10. Disconnect the vent tube from the fuel pump module.

11. Disconnect the fuel pump module and fuel pressure transducer electrical connectors.

12. Remove the fuel tank from the vehicle.

13. Disconnect the fuel and vapor tubes from the fuel pump module.

14. Using the lock ring removal tool 310-123, remove the fuel pump lock ring.

✳✳ CAUTION

Note the location of the fuel pump alignment tabs.

✳✳ CAUTION

Carefully remove the fuel pump assembly to avoid damaging the fuel level sensor.

15. Remove the fuel pump module assembly. Discard the O-ring seal

To install:

16. Installation is the reverse of removal. Note the following torque specifications:

   a. Fuel tank front and rear support straps bolts to 35 ft. lbs. (47 Nm).

   b. If equipped, fuel tank skid plate nuts to 15 ft. lbs. (20 Nm).

FUEL RAIL & INJECTORS

REMOVAL & INSTALLATION

See Figure 128.

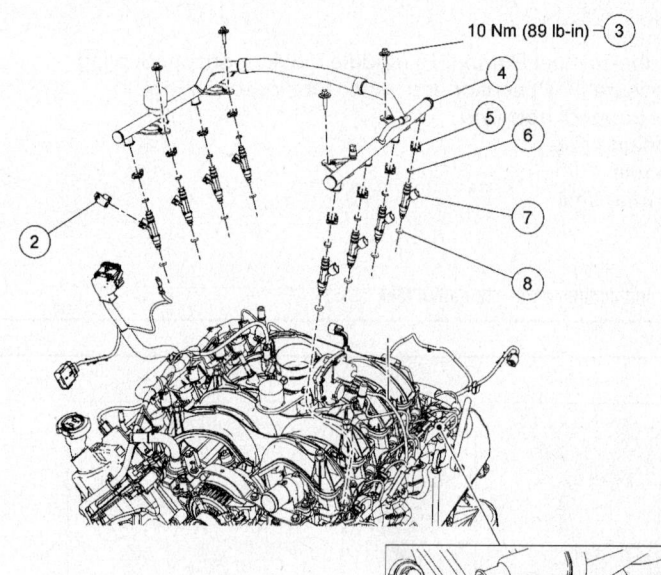
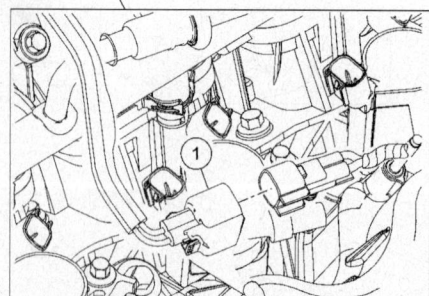

1. Heated PCV intake fitting electrical connector
2. Fuel injector electrical connector (8 required)
3. Fuel rail bolt (4 required)
4. Fuel rail
5. Fuel injector-to-fuel rail locking clip (8 required)
6. Fuel injector-to-fuel rail O-ring (8 required)
7. Fuel injector (8 required)
8. Fuel injector-to-intake manifold O-ring (8 required)

36578_EXPD_G0107

Fig. 128 Exploded view of the fuel rail and fuel injectors

✳✳ CAUTION

Fuel injection systems remain under pressure, even after the engine has been turned OFF. The fuel system pressure must be relieved before disconnecting any fuel lines. Failure to do so may result in fire and/or personal injury.

    1. Before servicing the vehicle, refer to the precautions section.
    2. Properly relieve the fuel system pressure.
    3. Disconnect the negative battery cable.
    4. Disconnect the fuel supply tube spring lock coupling.
    5. Remove the air cleaner outlet pipe.
    6. Disconnect the quick connect couplings and remove the crankcase vent tube.
    7. Disconnect the generator wiring harness retainer from the air cleaner outlet pipe-to-throttle body (TB) adapter.
    8. Remove the 4 bolts and the air cleaner outlet pipe-to-TB adapter.
    9. Disconnect the quick connect couplings and remove the positive crankcase ventilation (PCV) tube.
    10. Disconnect the electronic throttle control electrical connector
    11. Disconnect the Throttle Position Sensor (TPS) electrical connector.
    12. Disconnect the heated PCV intake fitting electrical connector.
    13. Disconnect the 8 fuel injector electrical connectors.
    14. Remove the 4 fuel rail bolts.
    15. Remove the fuel rail and fuel injectors as an assembly.
    16. Separate the fuel injectors from the fuel rail.

✳✳ WARNING

Use O-ring seals that are made of special fuel-resistant material. Use of ordinary O-rings can cause the fuel system to leak. Do not reuse the O-ring seals. Lubricate the O-ring seals with clean engine oil prior to installation.

    17. To install, reverse the removal procedure and note the following:
    • Lubricate the air cleaner outlet pipe-to-TB adapter seal with clean engine coolant prior to installation
    • Tighten the fuel rail retainers to 89 inch lbs. (10 Nm).
    • Tighten the 4 bolts to the air cleaner outlet pipe-to-TB adapter, to 89 inch lbs. (10 Nm).

FUEL TANK

REMOVAL & INSTALLATION

See Figure 129.

✳✳ CAUTION

Do not smoke or carry lighted tobacco or open flame of any type when working on or near any fuel-related components. Highly flammable mixtures are always present and may be ignited. Failure to follow these instructions may result in personal injury.

✳✳ CAUTION

Fuel in the fuel system remains under high pressure even when the engine is not running. Before working on or disconnecting any of the fuel lines or fuel system components, the fuel system pressure must be relieved. Failure to follow these instructions may result in personal injury.

✳✳ WARNING

Fuel injection equipment is manufactured to very precise tolerances and fine clearances. It is therefore essential that absolute cleanliness is observed when working with these components. Always install blanking plugs to any open orifices or tubes.

    1. Before servicing the vehicle, refer to the precautions section.
    2. With the vehicle in NEUTRAL, position it on a hoist.
    3. Release the fuel system pressure.
    4. Drain the fuel tank.
28 gal. (106 L) fuel tank
    5. If equipped, remove the 4 nuts and the fuel tank skid plate.

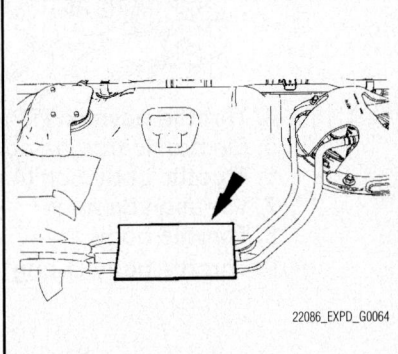

Fig. 129 Mastic patch location

22086_EXPD_G0064

33.5 gal. (127 L) fuel tank
    6. If equipped, remove the 5 nuts and the fuel tank skid plate.
All fuel tanks
    7. Disconnect the fuel tank filler pipe vapor tube from the evaporative emissions (EVAP) canister fresh air tube, and the fuel tank filler pipe vent tube-to-fuel tank pressure sensor and vapor tube assembly quick connect coupling in the rear of the fuel tank.
    8. Disconnect the fuel filter outlet tube-to-fuel tube spring lock coupling, EVAP canister fresh air tube-to-dust separator quick connect coupling and the fuel tank pressure sensor and vapor tube assembly-to-EVAP canister quick connect coupling in the front of the fuel tank.
    9. Remove the sway bar bracket nuts and let the sway bar hang down.
    10. Position a suitable jack under the fuel tank.

➡**Do not support the fuel tank directly beneath the fuel pump mounting area. Damage to the fuel pump assembly can occur.**

33.5 gal. (127 L) fuel tank
    11. Remove the center fuel tank support strap bolt.
All fuel tanks
    12. Remove the 2 bolts from the front and rear fuel tank support straps.
    13. Remove the front fuel tank support strap.
28 gal. (106 L) fuel tank
    14. Lower the fuel tank slightly and rotate the center fuel tank support strap aside.

➡**To assist in removing the center fuel tank support strap, you may have to push up slightly on the front of the tank to get the center fuel tank support strap to clear the fuel tank.**

All fuel tanks
    15. Rotate the rear fuel tank support strap aside.
    16. Lower the fuel tank slightly. Disconnect the fuel pump module and fuel tank pressure sensor electrical connectors.
    17. Remove the fuel tank from the vehicle.
33.5 gal. (127 L) fuel tank

✳✳ WARNING

When installing a new fuel supply tube, fuel return tube or a fuel tank, it is essential that a new mastic patch be installed over both fuel tubes. If a new mastic patch is not installed correctly, fuel tube damage will occur.

➡Clean the fuel supply tube, fuel return tube and the fuel tank of any dirt and foreign material before installing the new mastic patch.

➡If installing a new fuel supply tube, fuel return tube or a fuel tank, install a new mastic patch over both fuel tubes. Position the mastic patch over the fuel tubes as shown. If the patch is installed too far inboard, it can interfere with installation of the fuel tank.

18. If installing a new center fuel tank support strap, remove the center fuel tank support strap from the vehicle.

All fuel tanks

19. If installing a new rear fuel tank support strap, remove the rear fuel tank support strap from the vehicle.

20. To install, reverse the removal procedure and note the following:

21. Tighten fuel tank support strap bolt to 30 ft. lbs. (40 Nm).

22. Tighten sway bar bracket nuts to 35 ft. lbs. (48 Nm).

23. If removed, tighten the fuel tank skid plate nuts to 15 ft. lbs. (20 Nm).

IDLE SPEED

ADJUSTMENT

Idle speed is maintained by the Powertrain Control Module (PCM). No adjustment is necessary or possible.

THROTTLE BODY

REMOVAL & INSTALLATION

See Figures 130 and 131.

❋❋ CAUTION

Do not smoke or carry lighted tobacco or open flame of any type when working on or near any fuel-related components. Highly flammable mixtures are always present and may be ignited. Failure to follow these instructions may result in personal injury.

1. Before servicing the vehicle, refer to the precautions section.

2. Disconnect the negative battery cable.

3. Remove the air cleaner outlet pipe.

4. Disconnect the quick connect couplings and remove the crankcase vent tube.

5. Disconnect the generator wiring harness retainer from the air cleaner outlet pipe-to-throttle body (TB) adapter.

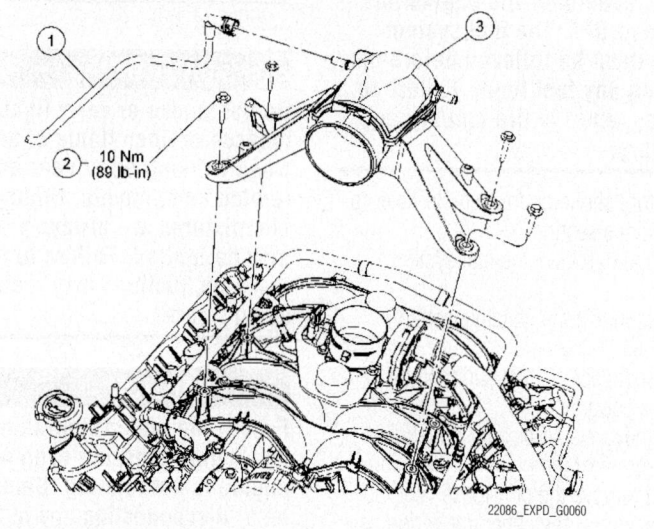

1. Crankcase ventilation tube
2. Air cleaner outlet pipe-to-throttle body adapter bolt (4 required)
3. Air cleaner outlet pipe-to-throttle body adapter

10 Nm
(89 lb-in)

22086_EXPD_G0060

Fig. 130 Air cleaner outlet pipe view

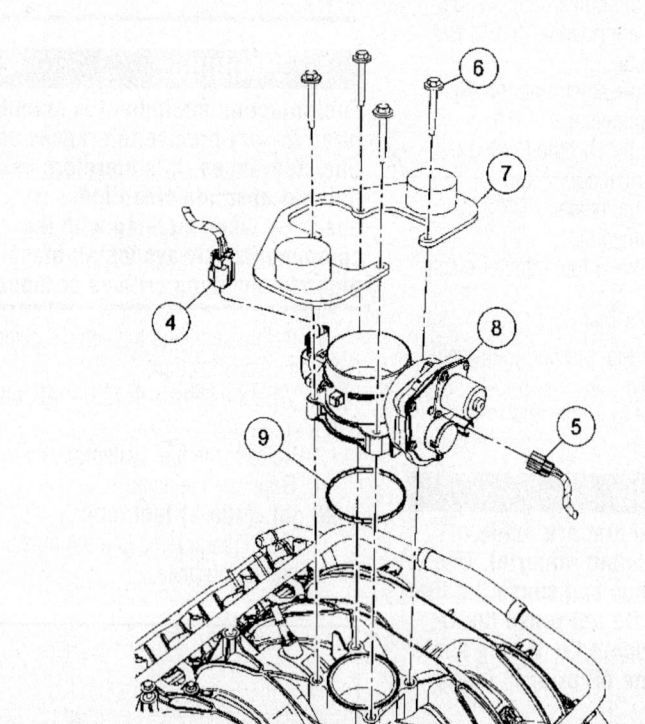

4. Throttle position (TP) sensor electrical connector
5. Electronic throttle control electrical connector
6. Throttle body bolt (4 required)
7. Vibration damper
8. Throttle body
9. Throttle body O-ring

22086_EXPD_G0059

Fig. 131 Throttle body

6. Remove the 4 bolts and position aside the air cleaner outlet tube-to-TB adapter.

7. Disconnect the electronic throttle control electrical connector

8. Disconnect the Throttle Position Sensor (TPS) electrical connector.

9. Remove the 4 bolts and the vibration damper

10. Remove the TB assembly.

To install:

11. Using a new O-ring seal, position the TB and vibration damper and tighten the 4 bolts in 2 stages.

- Stage 1: Tighten to 80 inch lbs. (9 Nm).
- Stage 2: Tighten an additional 90 degrees.

12. Connect the TPS electrical connector.

13. Connect the electronic throttle control electrical connector.

14. Lubricate the air cleaner outlet pipe-to-TB adapter seal with clean engine coolant prior to installation.

15. Position the air cleaner outlet pipe-to-TB adapter and install the 4 bolts.

16. Tighten bolts to 80 inch lbs. (9 Nm).

17. Connect the generator wiring harness retainer to the air cleaner outlet tube-to-TB adapter.

18. Position the crankcase vent tube and connect the quick connect couplings

19. Install the air cleaner outlet pipe.

20. Connect the negative battery cable.

HEATING & AIR CONDITIONING SYSTEM

BLOWER MOTOR

REMOVAL & INSTALLATION

See Figure 132.

1. Before servicing the vehicle, refer to the precautions section.

➡ The blower motor vent tube must be completely removed from the blower motor before it can be rotated and disengaged from the heater core and evaporator core housing.

2. Remove the RH lower instrument panel insulator (if equipped).

3. Remove the RH lower A-pillar junction box cover.

4. Position the carpet below the blower motor aside.

5. Release the 2 blower motor vent tube clips and remove the blower motor vent tube.

6. Disconnect the blower motor electrical connector.

➡ The blower motor will have to be carefully manipulated along the dash panel insulator, and the dash panel insulator will have to be slightly deflected to allow the blower motor to clear the heater core and evaporator core housing.

7. Rotate the blower motor counterclockwise to disengage it from the housing and remove the blower motor.

8. To install, reverse the removal procedure.

HEATER CORE

REMOVAL & INSTALLATION

Expedition

See Figures 133 and 134.

1. Before servicing the vehicle, refer to the precautions in the beginning of this section.

2. Depower the Supplemental Restraint System (SRS).

3. Disconnect the negative battery cable.

4. Recover the refrigerant.

5. Drain the engine coolant.

6. If equipped with adjustable pedals, move the pedals to the full forward position.

7. Place the gear shift lever in NEUTRAL and apply the parking brake.

8. Position the front seat forward.

9. Remove the 2 front floor console rear bolts.

10. Position the front seats rearward.

11. Remove the 2 front floor console front bolts.

12. Remove the 2 bolt covers.

13. Remove the shifter trim ring.

14. Position the gear shift lever indicator bezel aside.

15. Release the 4 retainers and position aside.

16. Remove the front floor console tray mat.

17. Remove the front floor console screw.

18. Disconnect the shifter cable.

19. Remove the floor console front screws.

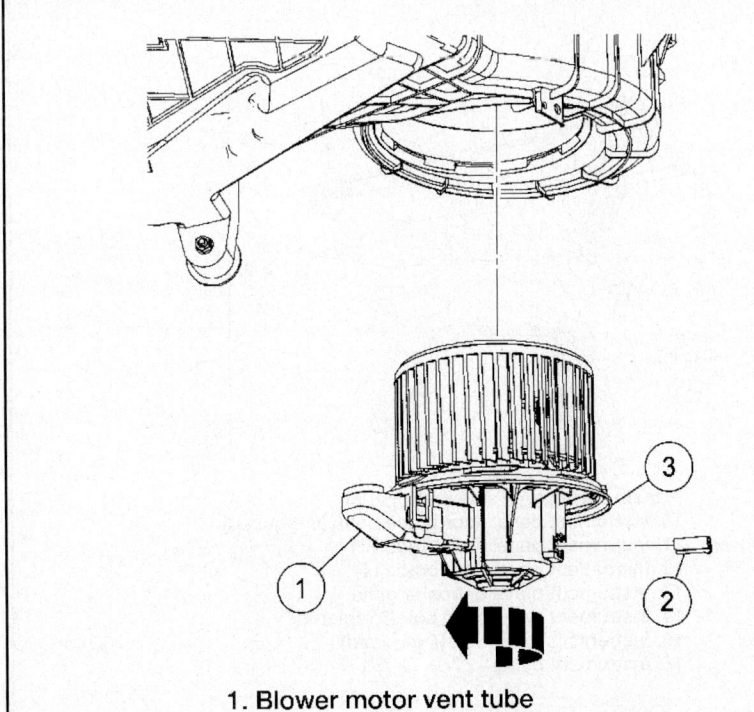

1. Blower motor vent tube
2. Blower motor electrical connector
3. Blower motor

22086_EXPD_G0122

Fig. 132 Blower motor view

20. Loosen the bulkhead electrical connector bolt.

21. Disconnect the bulkhead electrical connector

22. Disconnect the electrical connector.

23. Remove the front floor console.

24. Remove the instrument panel steering column cover.

25. Remove the screws.

26. Release the cover from the instrument panel.

27. Remove the hood release handle bolt and position aside.

28. Remove the instrument panel lower cover.

29. Remove the bolt from the parking brake handle and position aside

30. Remove the bolts and the steering column reinforcement panel.

31. Loosen the bolt and disconnect the LH instrument panel bulkhead connector.

32. Disconnect the LH electrical connectors

33. Disconnect the park brake indicator connector.

34. Disconnect the cruise control deacti-

vator and the brake on/off switch electrical connector

35. Disconnect the electrical connector located above the data link.

36. Disconnect the steering wheel position sensor electrical connector

37. Disconnect the steering column shift cable from the shift lever.

38. Remove the steering column shift cable and position aside.

39. Remove the shift cable from the bracket.

40. Remove the shift cable and retainer from the steering column.

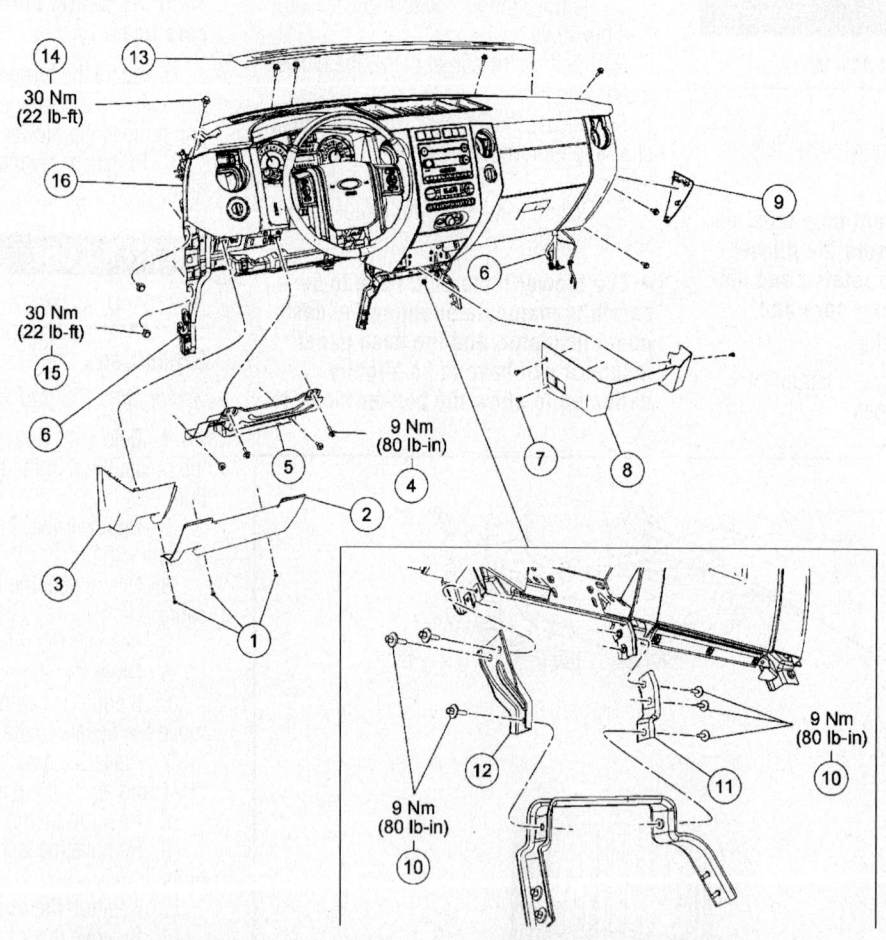

1. Instrument panel steering column cover screws (3 required)
2. Instrument panel steering column cover
3. Instrument panel lower cover
4. Steering column reinforcement panel bolt (4 required)
5. Steering column reinforcement panel
6. Instrument panel electrical wiring harness connectors
7. Pin-type retainer (3 required)
8. Valance panel
9. Instrument panel side finish panel
10. Instrument panel floor brace bolts (6 required)
11. Instrument panel floor brace RH
12. Instrument panel floor brace LH
13. Instrument panel defroster grille
14. Instrument panel cowl bolt (5 required)
15. Instrument panel bolt (4 required)
16. Instrument panel

22086_EXPD_G0124

Fig. 133 Expedition instrument panel exploded view

Secure the steering wheel to prevent any rotation or damage to the clockspring.

41. Remove the pinch bolt and separate the intermediate shaft from the steering column.

42. If equipped, remove the 3 pin-type retainers and the valance panel.

43. If equipped, disconnect the electronic automatic temperature control (EATC) hose from the evaporator case.

44. Disconnect the stability control sensor cluster electrical connector.

45. Disconnect the wiring harness from the console bracket

46. Remove the satellite radio antenna from the wiring harness, if equipped

47. Remove the RH instrument panel side finish panel.

48. Disconnect the RH instrument panel electrical connectors.

49. Remove the RH ground bolt.

50. Disconnect the in-line antenna connector.

51. Lower the glove compartment.

52. Disconnect the electrical connectors.

➡**There are 6 electrical connectors.**

53. Position the carpet aside, remove the bolts and the instrument panel floor brace.

54. Remove the instrument panel defroster grille.

55. Remove the instrument panel cowl bolts.

56. Remove the LH instrument panel bolts.

57. Remove the RH instrument panel bolts.

➡**This step requires an assistant.**

58. Remove the instrument panel.

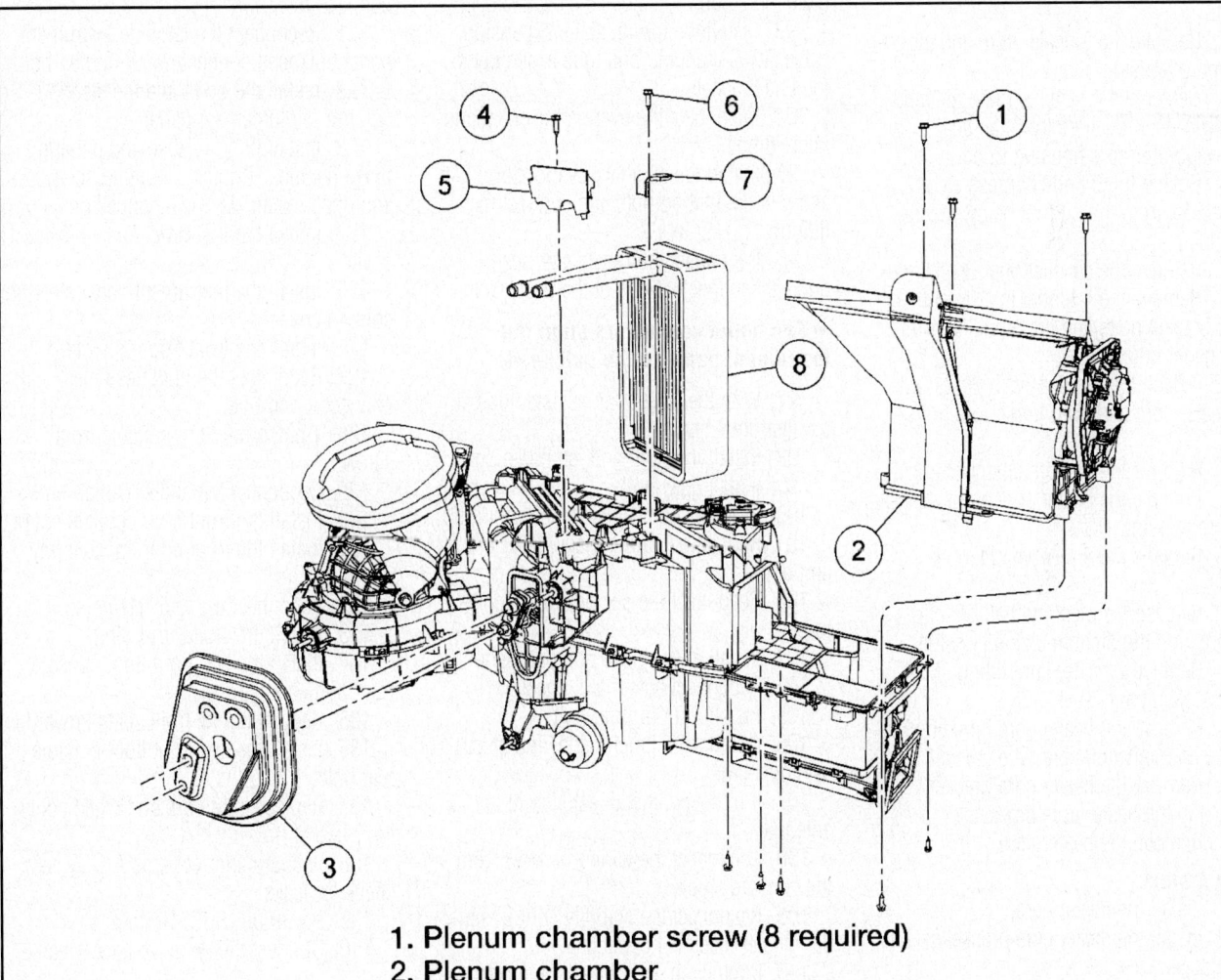

1. Plenum chamber screw (8 required)
2. Plenum chamber
3. Dash panel seal
4. Heater core tube bracket screw
5. Heater core tube bracket
6. Heater core bracket screw
7. Heater core bracket
8. Heater core

22086_EXPD_G0123

Fig. 134 Heater core and evaporator core housing heater core removal shown

➡**Two bullet connectors align the instrument panel to the bulkhead.**

59. Disconnect the 2 heater hose quick disconnect fittings at the heater core.

60. Remove the auxiliary evaporator outlet and inlet line fitting nuts and disconnect the fittings.

61. Disconnect the evaporator outlet and inlet fittings.

62. Detach the thermostatic expansion valve (TXV) manifold and tube assembly from the line 2 brackets.

63. Detach the TXV manifold and tube assembly bracket from the heater core and evaporator core housing stud at the dash panel.

64. Remove the 3 heater core and evaporator core housing nuts.

65. Detach the 4 satellite radio antenna cable pin-type retainers from the heater core and evaporator core housing (if equipped).

66. Detach the 3 body harness electrical connectors from the bracket below the air inlet duct.

67. Remove the air inlet duct bracket nut.

68. Remove the 4 tunnel instrument panel bracket bolts and the tunnel instrument panel bracket.

69. Detach the rear foot well duct from the heater core and evaporator core housing.

70. Remove the plenum chamber nut.

71. Remove the heater core and evaporator core housing.

72. Remove the 8 plenum chamber screws.

73. Release the plenum chamber clip and position the plenum chamber aside

74. Remove 2 heater core fitting clips and the dash panel seal.

75. Remove the heater core tube bracket screw and the heater core tube bracket.

76. Remove the heater core bracket screw and the heater core bracket.

77. Remove the heater core.

To install:

78. Install the heater core.

79. Install the heater core bracket screws and bracket.

80. Install the heater core tube bracket and screws.

81. Install the heater core fitting clips and dash panel seal.

82. Install the plenum chamber clip and reposition the plenum chamber.

83. Install the plenum chamber screws.

84. Install the heater core and evaporator core housing.

85. Install the plenum chamber nut.

86. Install the rear foot well duct from the heater core and evaporator core housing.

87. Install the four tunnel instrument panel bracket bolts and the tunnel instrument panel bracket

88. Install the air inlet duct bracket nut.

89. Reattach the three body harness electrical connectors to the bracket below the air inlet duct.

90. Install the four satellite radio antenna cable pin-type retainers to the heater core and evaporator core housing (if equipped).

91. Install the three heater core and evaporator core housing nuts.

92. Install the TXV manifold and tube assembly bracket to the heater core and evaporator core housing stud at the dash panel.

93. Install the thermostatic expansion valve (TXV) manifold and tube assembly to the line brackets.

94. Reconnect the evaporator outlet and inlet fittings.

95. Install the auxiliary evaporator outlet and inlet line fitting nuts and connect the fittings.

96. Reconnect the two heater hose quick disconnect fittings at the heater core.

➡**Two bullet connectors align the instrument panel to the bulkhead.**

97. With the help of an assistant install the instrument panel.

98. Install the right and left panel bolts.

99. Install cowl bolts.

100. Install instrument panel defroster grill.

101. Reposition carpet install floor brace and bolts.

102. Reconnect the six electrical connectors.

103. Install lower glove compartment.

104. Reconnect antenna connector.

105. Install right ground bolt.

106. Install right finish panel and electrical connector.

107. If removed. Install satellite radio antenna.

108. Reconnect the wiring harness from the console bracket.

109. Reconnect the stability control sensor cluster electrical connector.

110. If removed, Reconnect the electronic automatic temperature control (EATC) hose from the evaporator case.

111. If removed, install the three pin-type retainers and the valance panel.

112. Install the steering intermediate shaft pinch bolt.

✳✳ WARNING

Secure the steering wheel to prevent any rotation or damage to the clockspring.

113. Install the shift cable and retainer from the steering column.

114. Install the shift cable in the bracket.

115. Install the steering column shift cable into the shift lever.

116. Reconnect the steering wheel position sensor electrical connector.

117. Reconnect the electrical connector located above the data link.

118. Reconnect the cruise control deactivator and the brake on/off switch electrical connector.

119. Reconnect the park brake indicator connector.

120. Reconnect the left side electrical connectors.

121. Reconnect the left side instrument panel bulkhead connector and tighten bolt.

122. Install the bolts and the steering column reinforcement panel.

123. Install hood release and parking brake handles. Tighten mounting screws, if equipped install electrical connector.

124. Install the instrument panel lower cover.

125. Install the instrument panel steering column cover

126. Install the front floor console.

127. Reconnect the bulk head electrical connector and bolt.

128. Tighten the floor console front screws.

129. Reconnect the shifter cable.

130. Install the front floor console screw.

131. Install the front floor console tray mat.

132. Reconnect the four retainers.

133. Install the shifter trim ring.

134. Install the two front floor console front bolts and covers.

135. Reposition the front seats forward.

136. Install the two front floor console rear bolts.

137. Replace antifreeze and bleed cooling system.

138. Vacuum and recharge A/C system, check for leaks.

139. Power up (SRS) System.

140. Connect the negative battery cable.

Navigator

See Figures 134 and 135.

1. Before servicing the vehicle, refer to the precautions in the beginning of this section.

2. Depower the Supplemental Restraint System (SRS).

3. Disconnect the negative battery cable.

4. Recover the refrigerant.

5. Drain the engine coolant.

6. If equipped with adjustable pedals, move the pedals to the full forward position.

7. Place the shift lever in NEUTRAL and apply the parking brake.

8. Position the front seat forward

9. Remove the two front floor console rear bolts.

10. Position the front seats rearward.

11. Remove the shifter trim ring.

12. Remove the front floor console finish panel.

13. Pull upward on the rear of the finish panel to release the retainers.

14. Position the shifter lever indicator bezel aside.

15. Disconnect the shift cable.

16. Remove the front floor console front screws.

17. Loosen the bulkhead electrical connector bolt.

18. Disconnect the bulkhead electrical connector.

19. Disconnect the electrical connector.

20. Remove the left and right front floor console side finish panels.

21. If equipped, disconnect the electrical connector.

22. Remove the left and right front floor console front bolts and the floor console.

23. If equipped, remove the right instrument panel insulator.

24. Disconnect the instrument panel insulator lamp.

25. Remove the left and right cowl trim panels.

26. Remove the scuff plate.

27. Remove the cowl trim panel

28. Position the left and right door weather-strip seals aside.

29. Remove the left and right assist handles.

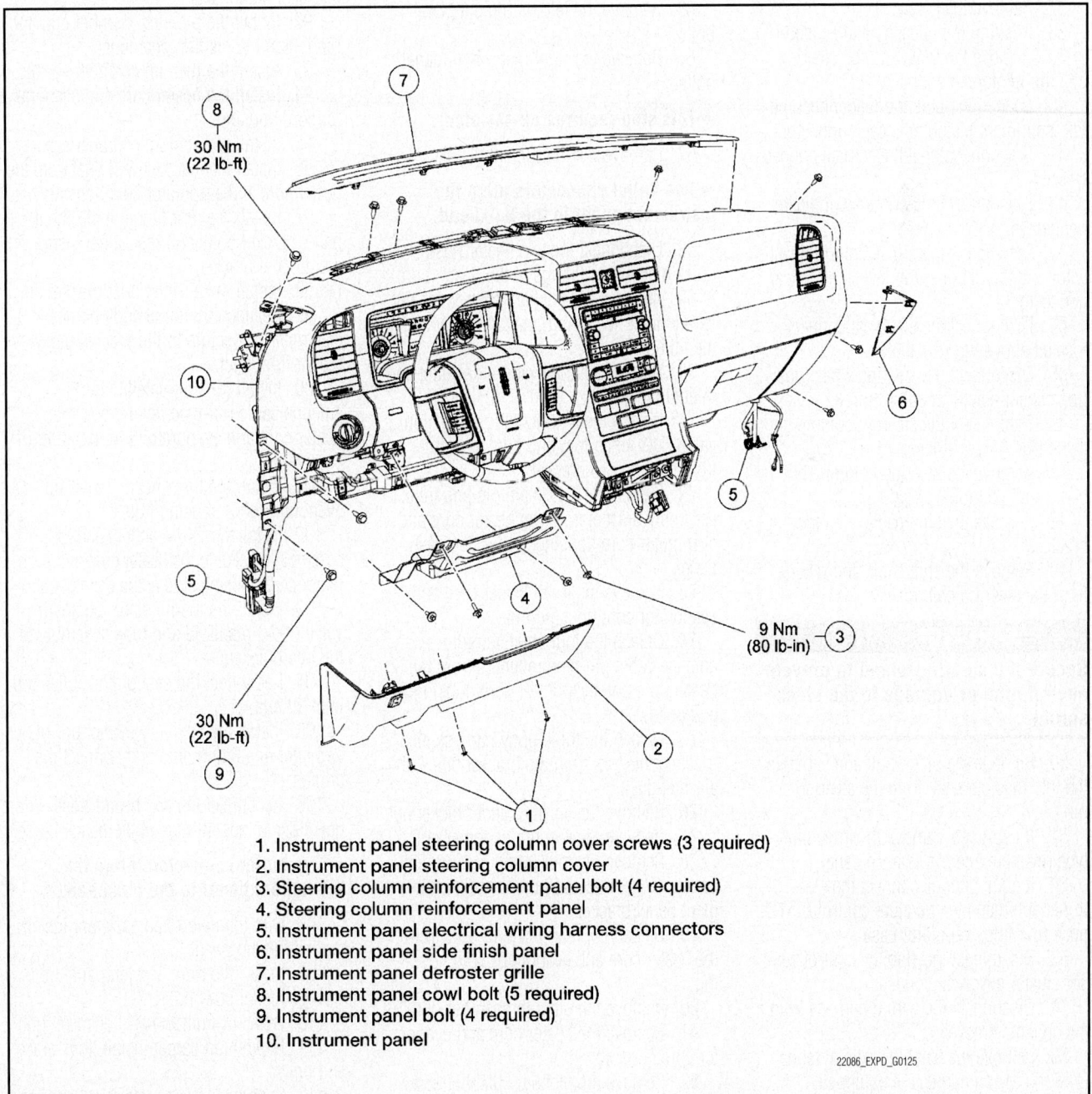

1. Instrument panel steering column cover screws (3 required)
2. Instrument panel steering column cover
3. Steering column reinforcement panel bolt (4 required)
4. Steering column reinforcement panel
5. Instrument panel electrical wiring harness connectors
6. Instrument panel side finish panel
7. Instrument panel defroster grille
8. Instrument panel cowl bolt (5 required)
9. Instrument panel bolt (4 required)
10. Instrument panel

22086_EXPD_G0125

Fig. 135 Navigator Instrument panel Exploded view

30. Remove the covers.
31. Remove the bolts.

➡ **Release the top attachments by pulling inboard first and then upward to release the lower hook.**

32. Remove the instrument panel steering column cover.
33. Remove the screws.
34. Release the cover from the instrument panel.
35. Disconnect the electrical connector, if equipped
36. Position the hood release and parking brake release handles aside.
37. Remove the screws.
38. Position the release handles aside.
39. Remove the bolts and the steering column reinforcement panel.
40. Loosen the bolt and disconnect the left instrument panel bulkhead connector.
41. Disconnect the left electrical connectors.
42. Disconnect the park brake indicator connector.
43. Disconnect the cruise control deactivator and the brake on/off switch electrical connector.
44. Disconnect the electrical connector located above the data link.
45. Disconnect the steering wheel position sensor electrical connector
46. Disconnect the steering column shift cable from the shift lever.
47. Remove the steering column shift cable and position aside.
48. Remove the shift cable from the bracket.
49. Remove the shift cable and retainer from the steering column.

❊❊ WARNING

Secure the steering wheel to prevent any rotation or damage to the clockspring.

50. Remove the pinch bolt and separate the intermediate shaft from the steering column.
51. If equipped, remove the three pin-type retainers and the valance panel.
52. If equipped, disconnect the electronic automatic temperature control (EATC) hose from the evaporator case.
53. Disconnect the stability control sensor cluster electrical connector.
54. Disconnect the wiring harness from the console bracket.
55. Remove the satellite radio antenna from the wiring harness, if equipped.
56. Remove the right instrument panel side finish panel.

57. Disconnect the right instrument panel electrical connectors.
58. Remove the right ground bolt.
59. Disconnect the in-line antenna connector.
60. Lower the glove compartment.
61. Disconnect the electrical connectors.

➡ **There are six electrical connectors.**

62. Position the carpet aside, remove the bolts and the instrument panel floor brace.
63. Remove the instrument panel defroster grille.
64. Remove the instrument panel cowl bolts.
65. Remove the left instrument panel bolts.
66. Remove the right instrument panel bolts.

➡ **This step requires an assistant.**

67. Remove the instrument panel.

➡ **Two bullet connectors align the instrument panel to the bulkhead.**

68. Disconnect the two heater hose quick disconnect fittings at the heater core.
69. Remove the auxiliary evaporator outlet and inlet line fitting nuts and disconnect the fittings
70. Disconnect the evaporator outlet and inlet fittings.
71. Detach the thermostatic expansion valve (TXV) manifold and tube assembly from the line two brackets.
72. Detach the TXV manifold and tube assembly bracket from the heater core and evaporator core housing stud at the dash panel.
73. Remove the three heater core and evaporator core housing nuts.
74. Detach the four satellite radio antenna cable pin-type retainers from the heater core and evaporator core housing (if equipped).
75. Detach the three body harness electrical connectors from the bracket below the air inlet duct.
76. Remove the air inlet duct bracket nut.
77. Remove the plenum chamber nut.
78. Remove the four tunnel instrument panel bracket bolts and the tunnel instrument panel bracket.
79. Detach the rear foot well duct from the heater core and evaporator core housing.
80. Remove the plenum chamber nut.
81. Remove the heater core and evaporator core housing.
82. Remove the plenum chamber screws.
83. Release the plenum chamber clip and position the plenum chamber aside

84. Remove the heater core fitting clips and the dash panel seal.
85. Remove the heater core tube bracket screw and the heater core tube bracket.
86. Remove the heater core bracket screw and the heater core bracket.
87. Remove the heater core.

To install:

88. Install the heater core.
89. Install the heater core bracket screws and bracket.
90. Install the heater core tube bracket and screws.
91. Install the heater core fitting clips and dash panel seal.
92. Install the plenum chamber clip and reposition the plenum chamber.
93. Install the plenum chamber screws.
94. Install the heater core and evaporator core housing.
95. Install the plenum chamber nut.
96. Install the rear foot well duct from the heater core and evaporator core housing.
97. Install the four tunnel instrument panel bracket bolts and the tunnel instrument panel bracket
98. Install the air inlet duct bracket nut.
99. Reattach the three body harness electrical connectors to the bracket below the air inlet duct.
100. Install the four satellite radio antenna cable pin-type retainers to the heater core and evaporator core housing (if equipped).
101. Install the three heater core and evaporator core housing nuts.
102. Install the TXV manifold and tube assembly bracket to the heater core and evaporator core housing stud at the dash panel.
103. Install the thermostatic expansion valve (TXV) manifold and tube assembly to the line brackets.
104. Reconnect the evaporator outlet and inlet fittings.
105. Install the auxiliary evaporator outlet and inlet line fitting nuts and connect the fittings.
106. Reconnect the two heater hose quick disconnect fittings at the heater core.

➡ **Two bullet connectors align the instrument panel to the bulkhead.**

107. with the help of an assistant install the instrument panel.
108. Install the right and left panel bolts.
109. Install cowl bolts.
110. Install instrument panel defroster grill.
111. Reposition carpet install floor brace and bolts.
112. Reconnect the six electrical connectors.

113. Install lower glove compartment.
114. Reconnect antenna connector.
115. Install right ground bolt.
116. Install right finish panel and electrical connector.
117. If removed. Install satellite radio antenna.
118. Reconnect the wiring harness from the console bracket.
119. Reconnect the stability control sensor cluster electrical connector.
120. If removed, Reconnect the electronic automatic temperature control (EATC) hose from the evaporator case.
121. If removed, install the three pin-type retainers and the valance panel.
122. Install the steering intermediate shaft pinch bolt.

�֍֍ WARNING

Secure the steering wheel to prevent any rotation or damage to the clockspring.

123. Install the shift cable and retainer from the steering column.
124. Install the shift cable in the bracket.
125. Install the steering column shift cable into the shift lever.

126. Reconnect the steering wheel position sensor electrical connector.
127. Reconnect the electrical connector located above the data link.
128. Reconnect the cruise control deactivator and the brake on/off switch electrical connector.
129. Reconnect the park brake indicator connector.
130. Reconnect the left side electrical connectors.
131. Reconnect the left side instrument panel bulkhead connector and tighten bolt.
132. Install the bolts and the steering column reinforcement panel.
133. Install hood release and parking brake handles. Tighten mounting screws, if equipped install electrical connector.
134. Install instrument panel cover and screws.
135. Install left and right assist handles, tighten bolts and replace covers.
136. Reposition the left and right door weather-strip seals.
137. Install the cowl trim panel.
138. Install the scuff plate.
139. Install the left and right cowl trim panels.

140. Reconnect the instrument panel insulator lamp.
141. If removed, install the right instrument panel insulator.
142. Install the left and right front floor console front bolts and the floor console.
143. Install the left and right front floor console side finish panels, if equipped reconnect electrical connector.
144. Reconnect the bulkhead electrical connector and bolt.
145. Install the front floor console front screws.
146. Reposition the shifter lever indicator bezel and reconnect the shift cable.
147. Install the front floor console finish panel.
148. Install the shifter trim ring.
149. Reposition the front seats.
150. Install the two front floor console rear bolts.
151. Replace antifreeze and bleed cooling system.
152. Vacuum and recharge A/C system, check for leaks.
153. Power up the SRS System.
154. Connect the negative battery cable.

AUXILIARY HEATING & AIR CONDITIONING SYSTEM

BLOWER MOTOR

REMOVAL & INSTALLATION

See Figure 136.

1. Before servicing the vehicle, refer to the precautions section.
2. On Expedition & Navigator models, remove the RH quarter trim panel.
3. Disconnect the blower motor electrical connector.
4. Remove the screws, then remove the blower motor.
5. On Expedition & Navigator models remove the wheel from the blower motor, as follows:
   a. Remove the push clip.
   b. Remove the wheel.
6. Installation is the reverse of the removal procedure. Use a new push clip to install the wheel onto the blower motor.

HEATER CORE

REMOVAL & INSTALLATION

Except Expedition EL & Navigator L Models

See Figure 137.

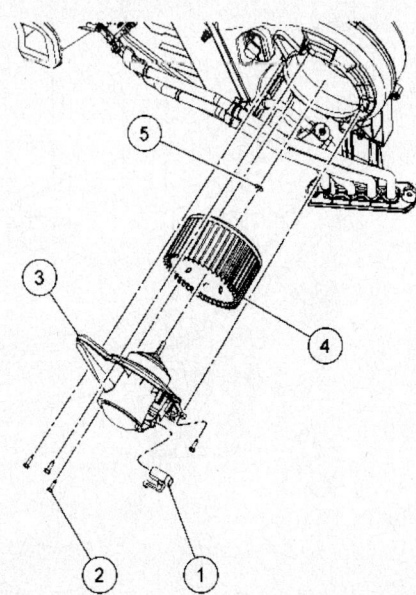

1. Blower motor electrical connector (Expedition or Navigator)
1. Blower motor electrical connector (Expedition EL or Navigator L)
2. Blower motor screw (Expedition or Navigator) (4 required)
2. Blower motor screw (Expedition EL or Navigator L) (3 required)
3. Blower motor
4. Blower motor wheel (Expedition or Navigator)
5. Blower motor wheel clip (Expedition or Navigator)

36578_EXPD_G0115

Fig. 136 Removing the blower motor

1. Before servicing the vehicle, refer to the precautions section.

2. With the vehicle in NEUTRAL, position it on a hoist.

3. Recover the refrigerant.

4. Drain the engine coolant.

➡**Allow any residual coolant to drain from the auxiliary heater core after disconnecting the auxiliary heater hose fittings.**

5. Position a suitable drain pan and disconnect the 2 auxiliary heater hose fittings at the floor pan connection.

6. Disconnect the 2 auxiliary evaporator line fittings at the floor pan connection. Discard the O-ring seals.

7. Remove the 2 floor pan bracket bolts.

8. Remove the auxiliary headliner duct pin-type retainer and disconnect the duct.

9. Disconnect the auxiliary mode door actuator electrical connector.

10. Disconnect the auxiliary temperature blend door actuator electrical connector.

11. Disconnect the auxiliary blower motor resistor electrical connector.

12. Disconnect the auxiliary blower motor electrical connector and detach the wire harness from the housing.

13. Remove the 2 auxiliary heater core and evaporator core housing bolts.

14. Remove the auxiliary heater core and evaporator core housing.

15. Release the clip and open the floor pan bracket.

16. Remove the heater core tube bracket screw and the heater core tube bracket.

17. Remove the 12 evaporator/heater core access cover screws.

18. Remove the evaporator/heater core access cover.

19. Remove the heater core.

20. To install, reverse the removal procedure and note the following:

    a. Vacuum and recharge A/C system.

    b. Refill and bleed the cooling system.

    c. Install new O-ring seals.

    d. Lubricate the refrigerant system with the correct amount of clean PAG oil.

    e. Tighten the 2 auxiliary heater core and evaporator core housing bolts to 71 inch lbs. (8 Nm).

Expedition EL & Navigator L Models

See Figure 138.

1. Before servicing the vehicle, refer to the precautions section.

➡**It is not necessary to install the new heater core tubes contained in the heater core service kit unless there is evidence of damage to the heater core tubes. New O-ring seals must be installed any time the heater core tubes are detached from the heater core.**

2. With the vehicle in NEUTRAL, position it on a hoist.

3. Drain the engine coolant.

4. Remove the RH quarter trim panel.

5. Position a suitable drain pan and disconnect the 2 auxiliary heater outlet and inlet line quick disconnect fittings at the floor pan connections to allow any residual

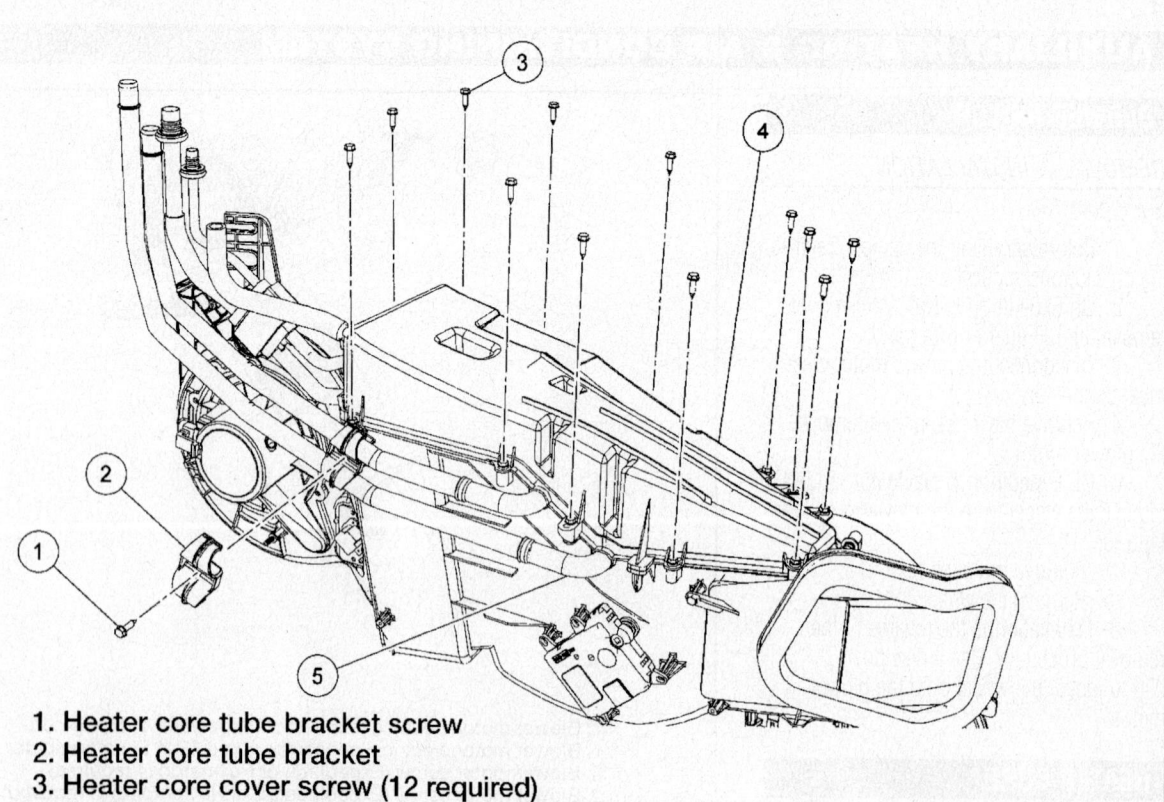

1. Heater core tube bracket screw
2. Heater core tube bracket
3. Heater core cover screw (12 required)
4. Evaporator/heater core access cover
5. Heater core

22086_EXPD_G0131

Fig. 137 Expedition and Navigator Auxiliary Heater Core

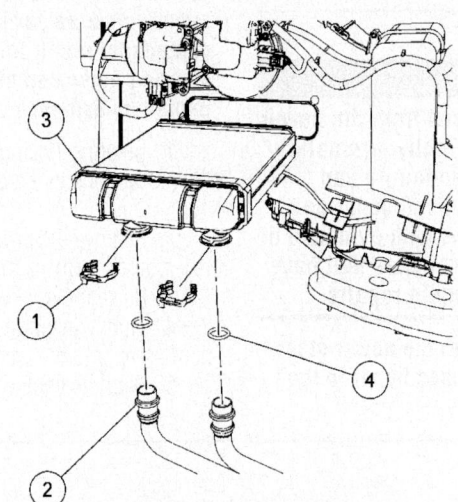

1 Auxiliary heater core tube
  fitting clip (2 required)
2 Auxiliary heater core tube
  (2 required)
3 Auxiliary heater core
4 O-ring seal (2 required)

22086_EXPD_G0132

Fig. 138 Expedition EL & Navigator L Auxiliary Heater Core.

coolant to drain from the auxiliary heater core.

6. Remove the heater core door screw.

7. Remove the 2 auxiliary heater core tube fitting clips.

8. Position the auxiliary heater core partially out of the housing.

9. Disconnect the auxiliary heater core inlet tube.

10. Disconnect the auxiliary heater core outlet tube. Discard the O-ring seals.

11. Remove the auxiliary heater core.

➡**Use only the O-ring seals contained in the auxiliary heater core service kit.**

12. Verify that the heater core tube fittings are completely seated in the heater core before installing the heater core tube fitting clips.

13. To install, reverse the removal procedure and note the following:

  a. Refill and bleed the cooling system.

STEERING

POWER RACK & PINION STEERING GEAR

REMOVAL & INSTALLATION

See Figure 139.

1. Before servicing the vehicle, refer to the precautions in the beginning of this section.

2. With the vehicle in NEUTRAL, position it on a hoist.

3. Hold the steering wheel in the straight ahead position using a suitable holding device.

✳✳ WARNING

Do not allow the steering column shaft to rotate while disconnected from the gear or damage to the clockspring can occur. if there is evidence that the steering column shaft has rotated, the clockspring must be recentered.

4. Remove and discard the tie-rod end nuts.

5. Using the special tool 204-592, disconnect the tie-rod ends from the wheel knuckles.

6. Release the lower cooling fan shroud tab and rotate the shroud upward.

7. Remove the 2 bolts and the oil drip shield.

8. Remove the steering column shaft-to-steering gear bolt and disconnect the steering column shaft from the steering gear.

9. Remove the steering line clamp plate bolt, rotate the clamp plate and disconnect the power steering lines

10. Remove the 2 steering gear bolts and remove the steering gear.

To install:

✳✳ WARNING

New O-ring seals must be installed any time the lines are disconnected from the steering gear.

➡**Make sure the LH steering gear bushing is seated correctly or failure of the steering gear may occur. The RH side bushing does not have locking tabs.**

11. Position the steering gear and install the 2 steering gear bolts. Tighten bolts to 325 ft. lbs. (440 Nm).

12. Connect the steering column shaft and install the bolt.

13. Connect the steering lines, rotate the clamp plate and install the clamp plate bolt. Tighten the bolt to 17 ft. lbs. (23 Nm).

14. Install the oil drip shield and tighten the 2 bolts to 8 ft. lbs. (11 Nm).

15. Release the lower cooling fan shroud tab and rotate the shroud downward.

16. Connect the tie-rod ends to the wheel knuckles, install and tighten the nuts to 85 ft. lbs. (115 Nm).

17. Fill the power steering system.

18. Check and, if necessary, align the front end.

POWER STEERING PUMP

REMOVAL & INSTALLATION

See Figure 140.

➡**While repairing the power steering system, care should be taken to prevent the entry of foreign material or failure of the power steering components may result.**

➡**A new Teflon® seal must be installed any time the line is disconnected from the power steering pump.**

1. Remove the power steering pump pulley.

2. Using a suitable suction device, remove the power steering fluid from the fluid reservoir.

3. Release the clamp and disconnect the power steering fluid reservoir-to-pump supply hose.

4. Remove the power steering pressure

line bracket-to-engine nut. Upon installation, tighten to 30 ft. lbs. (40 Nm).

5. Disconnect the power steering pressure line-to-power steering pump fitting. Discard the Teflon®seal. Upon installation, tighten to 48 ft. lbs. (65 Nm).

6. Remove the 3 bolts and the power steering pump. To install, tighten to 18 ft. lbs. (25 Nm).

7. To install, reverse the removal procedure.

8. Using the Teflon®Seal Installer Set (211–D027), install a new Teflon®seal on the pressure line-to-pump fitting.

BLEEDING

See Figure 141.

✳✳ WARNING

If the air is not purged from the power steering system correctly, premature power steering pump failure can result. The condition can occur on pre-delivery vehicles with evidence of aerated fluid or on vehicles that have had steering component repairs.

➡**A whine heard from the power steering pump can be caused by air in the** system. The power steering purge procedure must be carried out prior to any component repair for which power steering noise complaints are accompanied by evidence of aerated fluid.

1. Before servicing the vehicle, refer to the precautions in the beginning of this section.

2. Remove the power steering pump reservoir cap. Check the fluid.

3. Raise the front wheels off the floor.

4. Tightly insert the stopper of the vacuum pump into the reservoir.

5. Start the engine.

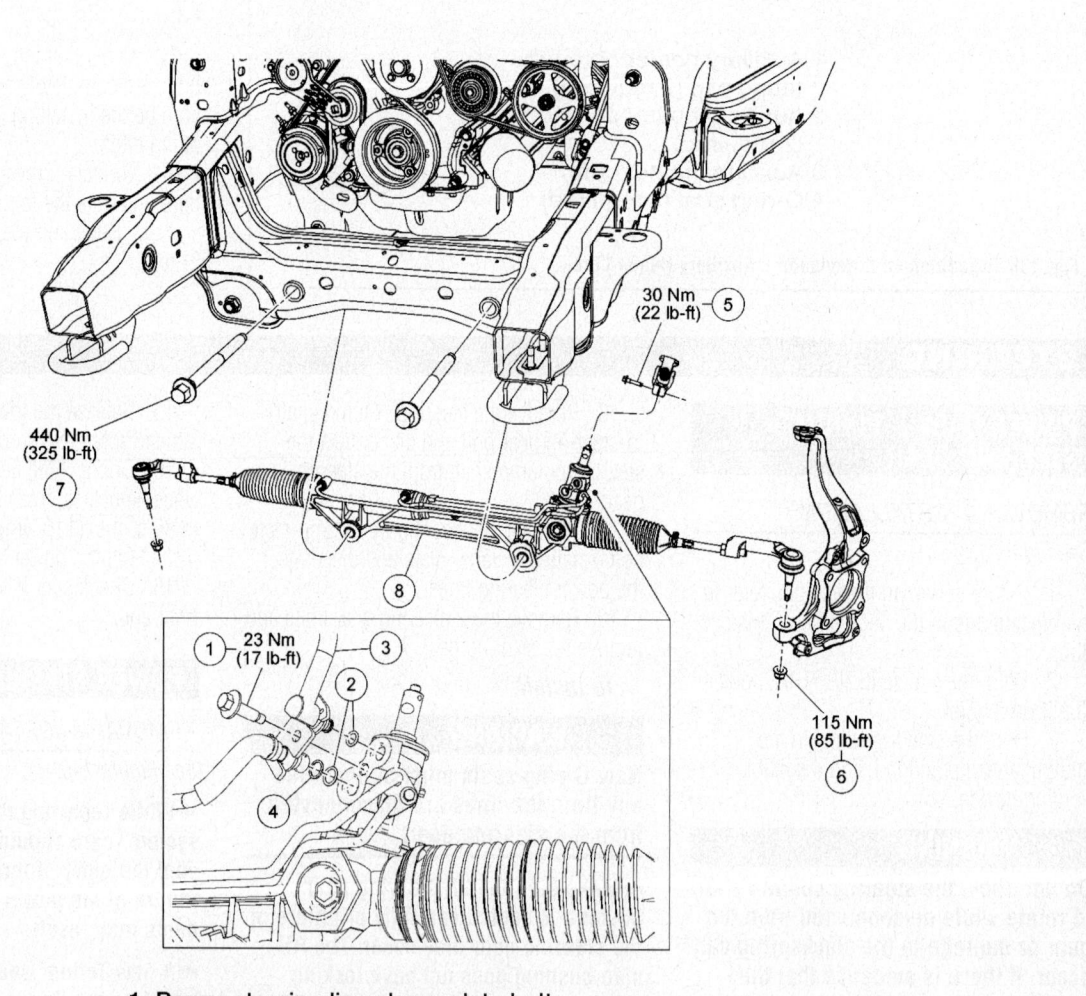

1. Power steering line clamp plate bolt
2. Power steering line O-ring seals (2 required)
3. Power steering return line
4. O-ring seal
5. Steering column shaft-to-steering gear bolt
6. Outer tie-rod end nut (2 required)
7. Steering gear-to-crossmember bolt (2 required)
8. Steering gear

36578_EXPD_G0117

Fig. 139 Exploded view of the power rack and pinion steering gear components

6. Install the vacuum pump, apply vacuum and maintain the maximum vacuum of 68-85 kPa (20-25 in-Hg).

7. If equipped with Hydro-Boost®, apply the brake pedal twice.

✳✳ WARNING

Do not hold the steering wheel against the stops for more than 3 to 5 seconds at a time. Damage to the power steering pump can occur.

8. Cycle the steering wheel fully from stop-to-stop 10 times.

9. Stop the engine
10. Release the vacuum and remove the vacuum pump.

✳✳ WARNING

Do not overfill the reservoir.

11. Fill the reservoir with approved transmission fluid.
12. Start the engine.
13. Install the vacuum pump. Apply and maintain the maximum vacuum of 68-85 kPa (20-25 in-Hg).
14. Cycle the steering wheel fully from stop-to-stop 10 times.

15. Fill the reservoir as needed and install the reservoir cap.
16. Visually inspect the power steering system for leaks.
17. Fill the reservoir as needed and visually inspect the power steering system for leaks.
18. Install the power steering reservoir cap.

FLUSHING

1. Before servicing the vehicle, refer to the precautions in the beginning of this section.

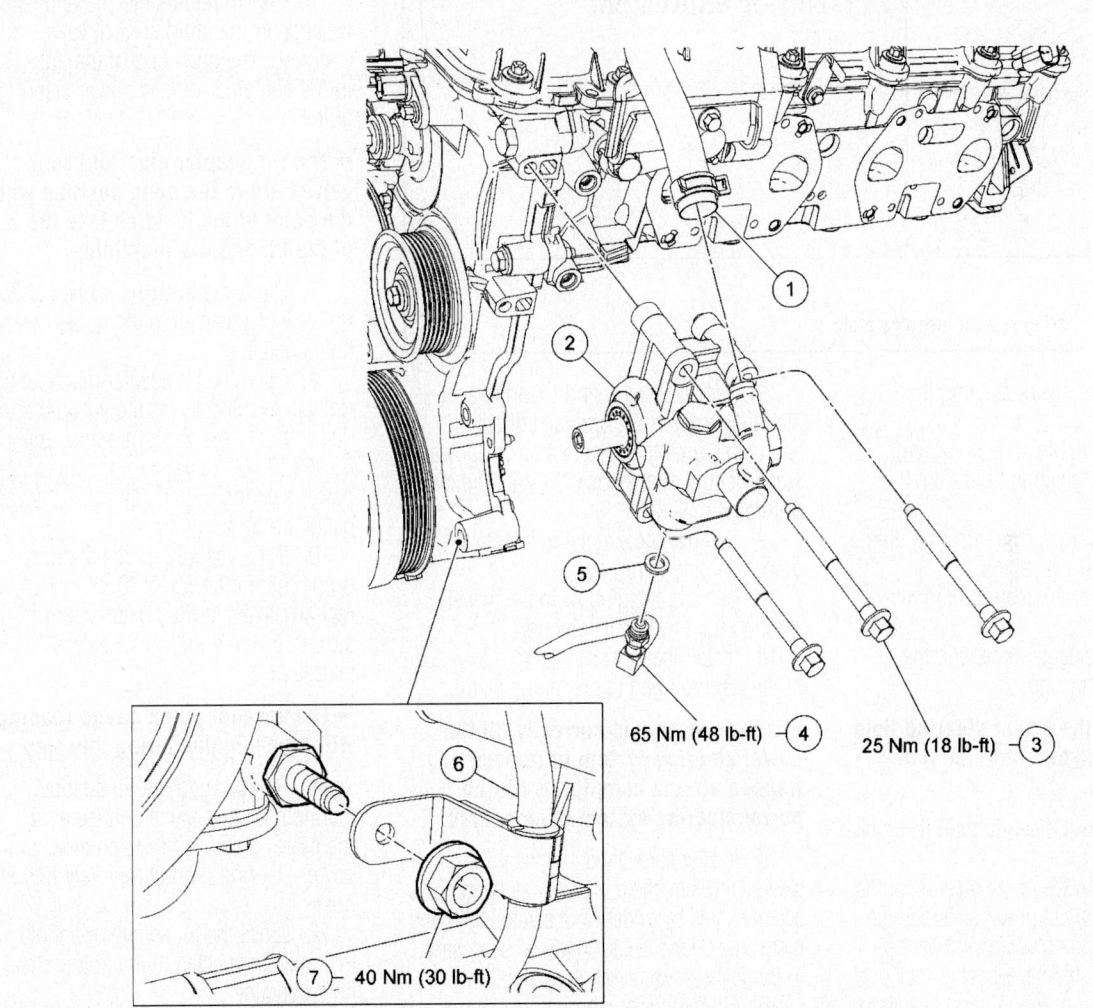

65 Nm (48 lb-ft) — 4   25 Nm (18 lb-ft) — 3

6

7 — 40 Nm (30 lb-ft)

1. Power steering fluid reservoir-to-pump supply hose
2. Power steering pump
3. Power steering pump bolt (3 required)
4. Power steering pressure line-to-power steering pump fitting
5. Power steering pressure line Teflon® seal
6. Power steering pressure line
7. Power steering pressure line bracket-to-engine nut

36578_EXPD_G0118

Fig. 140 View of the power steering pump and components

Required tools for power steering system bleeding

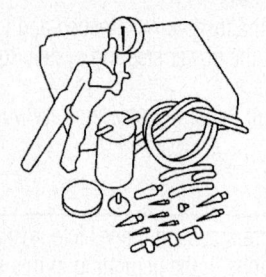	Vacuum Pump Kit 416-D002 (D95L-7559-A) or equivalent
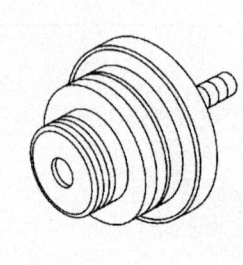	Evacuation Cap, Power Steering 211-265 or equivalent

22086_EXPD_G0117

Fig. 141 Power steering system bleeding tools

2. Remove the power steering fluid reservoir cap.

3. Using a suitable suction device, remove the power steering fluid from the reservoir.

4. Disconnect the power steering fluid return hose from the reservoir.

5. Plug the power steering fluid reservoir inlet port.

6. Attach an extension hose to the power steering return hose.

➡ **Do not reuse the power steering fluid that has been flushed from the power steering system.**

7. Fill the power steering fluid reservoir with new fluid.

8. Do not allow the power steering pump to run completely dry of power steering fluid.

9. Start the engine while simultaneously turning the steering wheel to lock and then immediately turn the ignition switch to the OFF position.

❊❊ WARNING

Avoid turning the steering wheel without the engine running as this may cause air to be pulled into the steering gear.

10. Fill the power steering fluid reservoir with the approved power steering fluid. Do not overfill.

11. Repeat Steps 8 and 9, turning the steering wheel in the opposite direction each time, until the fluid exiting the power steering fluid return hose is clean and clear of foreign material.

12. Remove the extension hose from the power steering return hose.

13. Remove the plug from the power steering fluid reservoir inlet port.

14. Install the power steering return hose to the reservoir and the retaining clamp.

➡ **It is necessary to correctly fill the power steering system to remove any trapped air and completely fill the power steering system components.**

15. If, after correctly filling the power steering system, there is power steering noise accompanied by evidence of aerated fluid and there are no fluid leaks, it may be necessary to purge the power steering system.

16. Fill the power steering system.

FILLING
See Figure 142.

1. Before servicing the vehicle, refer to the precautions in the beginning of this section.

❊❊ WARNING

If the air is not purged from the power steering system correctly, pre-

mature power steering pump failure can result. The condition can occur on pre-delivery vehicles with evidence of aerated fluid or on vehicles that have had steering component repairs.

2. Remove the power steering pump reservoir cap.

3. Tightly install the evacuation cap to the power steering pump reservoir.

4. Install the hose from the fill adapter manifold tee to the evacuation cap on the power steering pump reservoir.

5. Install the vacuum pump to the fill adapter manifold control valve.

6. Install the hose to the opposite fill adapter manifold control valve and submerge the open end of the hose into a container of new power steering fluid.

➡ **The fill adapter manifold control valves are in the open position when the point of the handles face the center of the fill adapter manifold.**

7. Close the fill adapter manifold control valve connected to the power steering fluid container.

8. Open the fill adapter manifold control valve connected to the vacuum pump

9. Using the vacuum pump, apply 68-85 kPa (20-25 in-Hg) of vacuum to the power steering system. Observe the vacuum gauge for 30 seconds.

10. If the vacuum gauge reading drops more than 3 kPa (0.88 in-Hg), correct any leaks in the power steering system or the filling tools before proceeding.

➡ **The vacuum pump gauge reading will drop slightly during this step.**

11. Slowly open the fill adapter manifold control valve connected to the power steering fluid container until power steering fluid completely fills the hose.

12. Close the fill adapter manifold control valve connected to the power steering fluid container.

13. Using the vacuum pump, apply 68-85 kPa (20-25 in-Hg) of vacuum to the power steering system

14. Close the fill adapter manifold control valve connected to the vacuum pump.

15. Slowly open the fill adapter manifold control valve connected to the power steering fluid container

16. When the power steering fluid has drained from the hose connected to the

Tools required for power steering filling

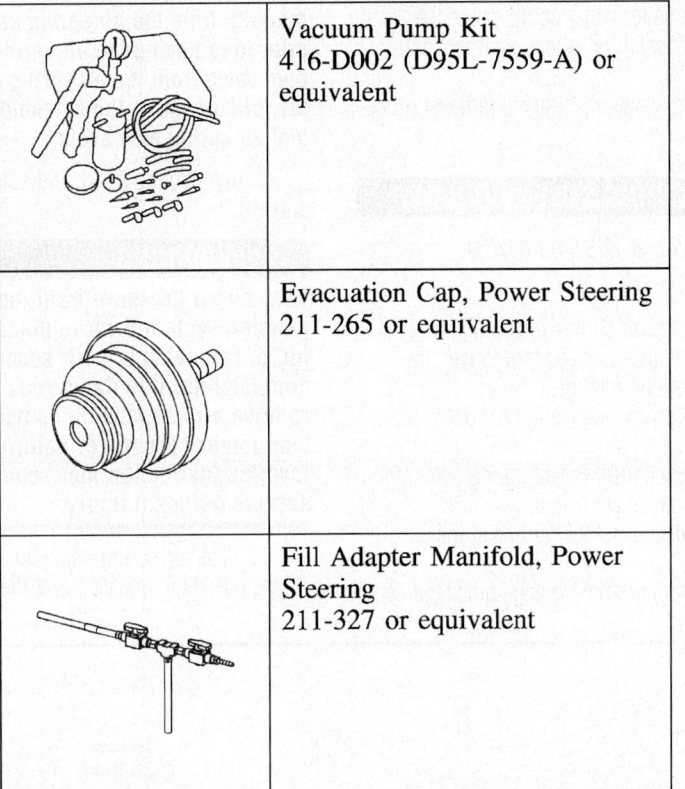	Vacuum Pump Kit 416-D002 (D95L-7559-A) or equivalent
	Evacuation Cap, Power Steering 211-265 or equivalent
	Fill Adapter Manifold, Power Steering 211-327 or equivalent

22086_EXPD_G0118

Fig. 142 Power steering fluid filling tools

power steering fluid container, close the fill adapter manifold control valve connected to the power steering fluid container.

17. Remove the tools from the vehicle.

18. Install the power steering reservoir cap.

> ❋❋ **WARNING**
> **Do not hold the steering wheel against the stops for more than 3 to 5 seconds at a time. Damage to the power steering pump can occur.**

➡ **There will be a slight drop in the power steering fluid level in the power steering fluid reservoir when the engine is started.**

19. Start the engine and turn the steering wheel from stop-to-stop.

20. If equipped with Hydro-Boost®, apply the brake pedal twice.

21. Turn the ignition switch to the OFF position.

> ❋❋ **WARNING**
> **Do not overfill the reservoir.**

22. Remove the power steering reservoir cap and fill the reservoir.

23. Install the power steering reservoir cap.

SUSPENSION

ADJUSTMENTS

> ❋❋ **WARNING**
> **The suspension ride height dimensions are for reference only. The vehicle attitude must be controlled by the correct dimensions to prevent vehicle damage.**

➡ **If one or both height sensors are installed new, both height sensors must be calibrated.**

➡ **Incorrect air suspension ride height can be caused by an air suspension system that is incorrectly set.**

➡ **The air suspension module has a preprogrammed trim height.**

➡ **The vehicle must be on a level surface, such as a drive on alignment hoist.**

1. Position the vehicle on a level surface.

2. Using the vehicle message center, verify that the air suspension is in the ON mode. For additional information, refer to Disable/Enable in this section.

3. Using the scan tool, run the accurate trim test.

4. Measure the ride height.

5. If the ride height is not within specification (3.9–4.2 inches), use the scan tool to vent or fill the air suspension to the correct dimension.

➡ **The air suspension height sensor sends a signal to the air suspension module. The output ranges from approximately 4.5 volts at minimum height (when the vehicle is low or in full jounce) to 0.5 volt at maximum height (when the vehicle is in high or in full rebound).**

6. Using the scan tool, monitor the 2 suspension height sensors voltage PIDs.

7. Using the scan tool, save the vehicle trim height for both sensors.

AIR SUSPENSION

DISABLING AND ENABLING

> ❋❋ **WARNING**
> **Shut off the electrical power to the air suspension system prior to hoisting or jacking an air suspension equipped vehicle. Failure to do so may result in unexpected inflation or deflation of the air springs, which may result in shifting of the vehicle during these operations. Failure to follow this instruction may result in serious personal injury.**

➡ **The message center is located on the instrument cluster and displays important information through a constant monitoring of vehicle systems. Select display features on the message center for a display of status proceeded by a brief chime. The system will also notify the driver of potential vehicle problems with a display of** system warnings followed by a long indicator chime. The message center is used to disable and enable the vehicle air suspension system. When the driver elects to disable the air suspension system, the message center sends a message over the High Speed Controller Area Network (HS-CAN) bus to the air suspension module. Once the message is received, the air suspension module will take no further action to inflate or deflate the air springs. The system will default to ON when the ignition key is cycled.

1. Turn the ignition to the ON position, close all doors and clear warnings.

2. Select the SETUP control function on the message center.

3. Select the AIR SUSPENSION function to display the current status of the air suspension system.

4. Press the RESET control to turn the air suspension OFF or ON.

AIR COMPRESSOR

REMOVAL & INSTALLATION

See Figure 143.

❊ WARNING

Vent all air pressure from the air suspension system prior to disconnecting or removing any air suspension components. It is dangerous to remove air suspension components while under pressure. Failure to follow this instruction may result in serious personal injury.

1. Remove the inner fender splash shield.

2. Disconnect the air line from the compressor drier. Compress the quick connect lock ring inward, then pull the line outward from the air drier.

3. Disconnect the air compressor air intake hose.

4. Disconnect the air compressor electrical connector.

5. Remove the 3 air compressor bracket bolts and remove the air compressor and bracket assembly.

6. When installing the air lines, make sure the white inner air line is fully inserted into the fitting for correct installation.

➥**Make sure that there are no objects trapped under or on the bracket.**

7. Make sure that the air compressor is not in contact with any surrounding components that could cause vibration noises.

➥**Make sure that the air compressor moves freely in the rubber isolators.**

8. Make sure that the bracket has no deformations that could cause the 3 rubber isolators to load against each other.

9. To install, reverse the removal procedure.

AIR SPRING SOLENOID VALVE

REMOVAL & INSTALLATION
See Figure 144.

1. If the air spring solenoid valve is functional, use the scan tool to vent the appropriate air spring(s).

2. With the vehicle in NEUTRAL, position it on a hoist.

3. Disconnect the air spring solenoid valve electrical connector.

4. Disconnect the air line at the air valve.

5. Compress the orange quick connect lock ring, then pull downward on the air supply line.

➥**Remove any dirt or other foreign material from the air spring assembly prior to removing the air spring solenoid valve from the air spring assembly, or damage to the solenoid valve and air spring may occur.**

6. Remove the air spring solenoid clip.

❊ WARNING

Vent all air pressure from the air suspension system prior to disconnecting or removing any air suspension components. It is dangerous to remove air suspension components while under pressure. Failure to follow this instruction may result in serious personal injury.

7. The air spring solenoid valve has a 2-stage release. Vent the

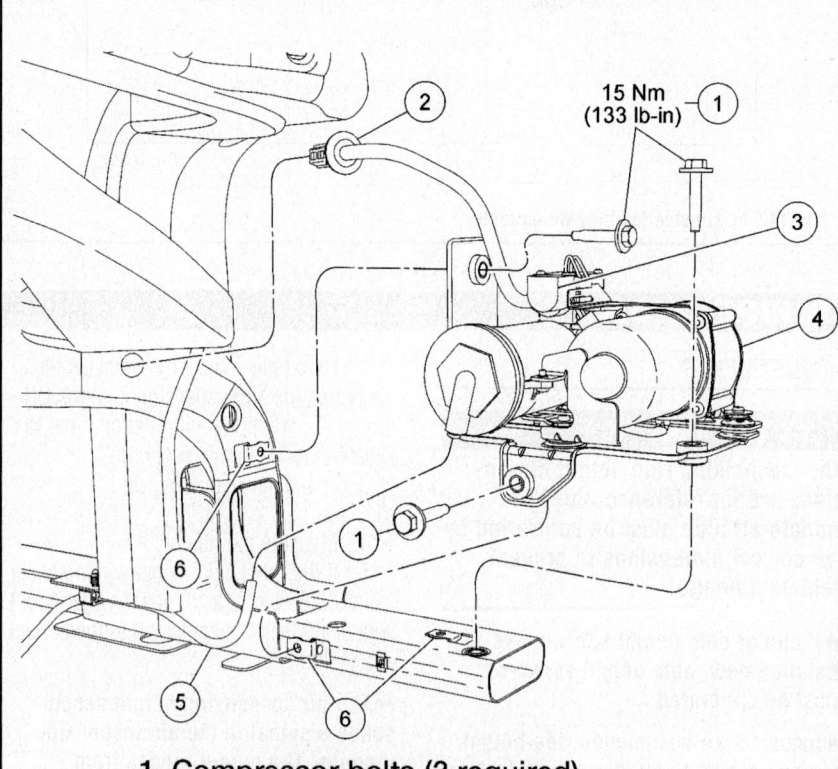

15 Nm
(133 lb-in)

1. Compressor bolts (3 required)
2. Compressor air intake hose
3. Compressor electrical connector
4. Compressor and bracket assembly
5. Air line
6. Clip nuts (3 required)

36578_EXPD_G0120

Fig. 143 View of air suspension compressor components

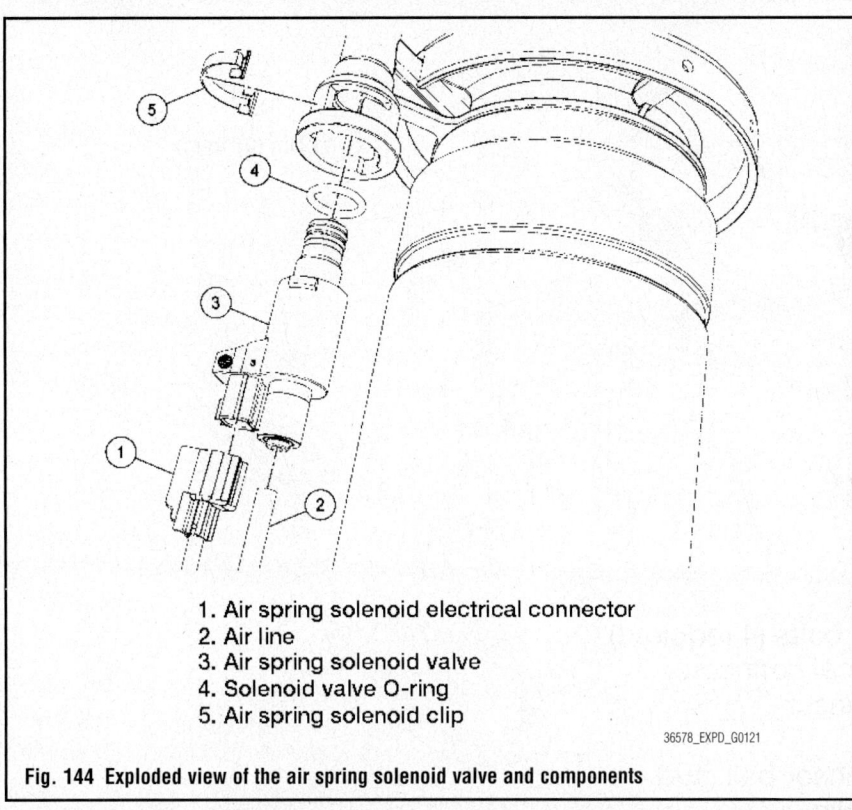

1. Air spring solenoid electrical connector
2. Air line
3. Air spring solenoid valve
4. Solenoid valve O-ring
5. Air spring solenoid clip

36578_EXPD_G0121

Fig. 144 Exploded view of the air spring solenoid valve and components

air spring using the following procedure:

a. Carefully rotate the air spring solenoid counterclockwise until it reaches the first stage and allow the air in the spring to completely vent.

b. Rotate the solenoid counterclockwise to the second stage and remove the solenoid.

8. Inspect the air spring O-ring for damage and install a new O-ring as necessary. Lightly lubricate the solenoid seal area with silicone grease.

9. After installing the solenoid, it is necessary to inflate the air suspension system. For additional information, refer to Ride Height Adjustments in this section.

10. When installing the air spring solenoid, make sure that the electrical connector is positioned away from the air spring.

11. When installing the air lines, make sure the air line is fully inserted into the fitting for correct installation.

12. To install, reverse the removal procedure.

SUSPENSION

AUTOMATIC LEVEL CONTROL

SENSOR

REMOVAL & INSTALLATION

See Figures 145 and 146.

1. With the vehicle in NEUTRAL, position it on a hoist.
2. Disconnect the height sensor harness from the sensor bracket.

3. Disconnect the height sensor electrical connector.
4. Disconnect the height sensor arm from the ball stud on the lower control arm.

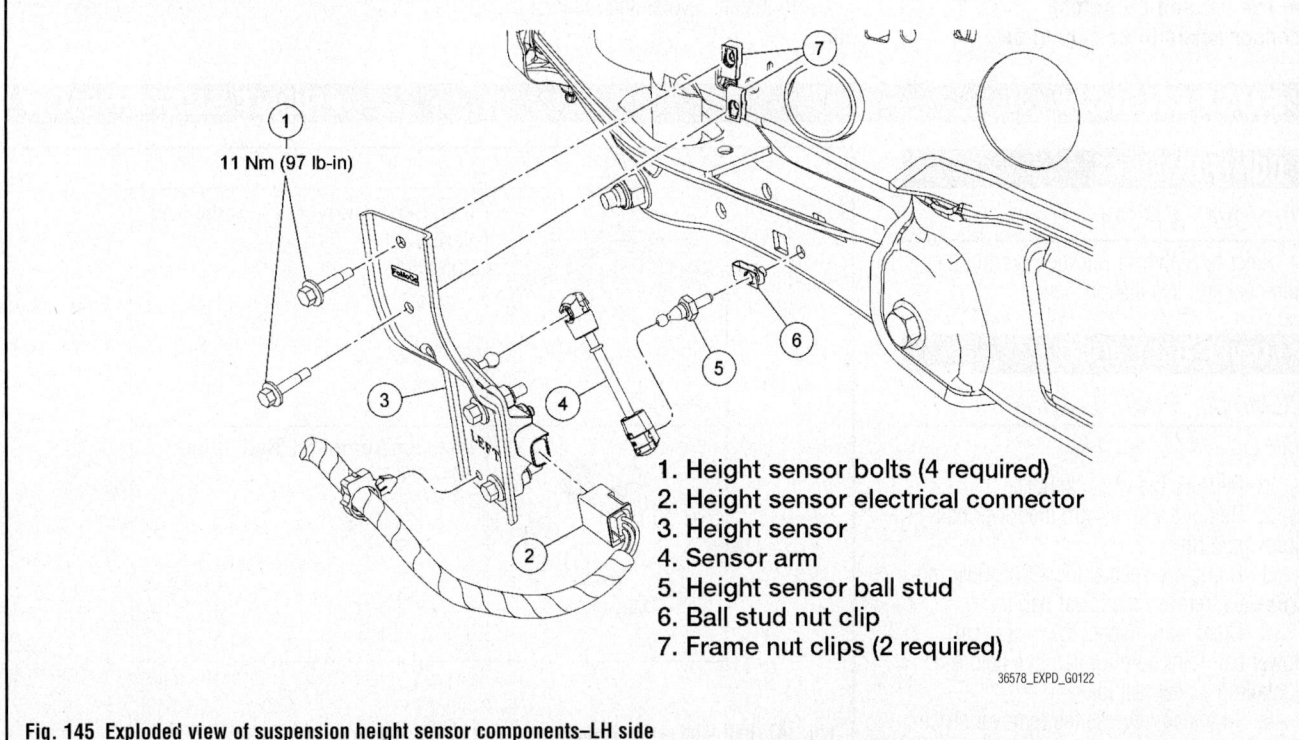

11 Nm (97 lb-in)

1. Height sensor bolts (4 required)
2. Height sensor electrical connector
3. Height sensor
4. Sensor arm
5. Height sensor ball stud
6. Ball stud nut clip
7. Frame nut clips (2 required)

36578_EXPD_G0122

Fig. 145 Exploded view of suspension height sensor components–LH side

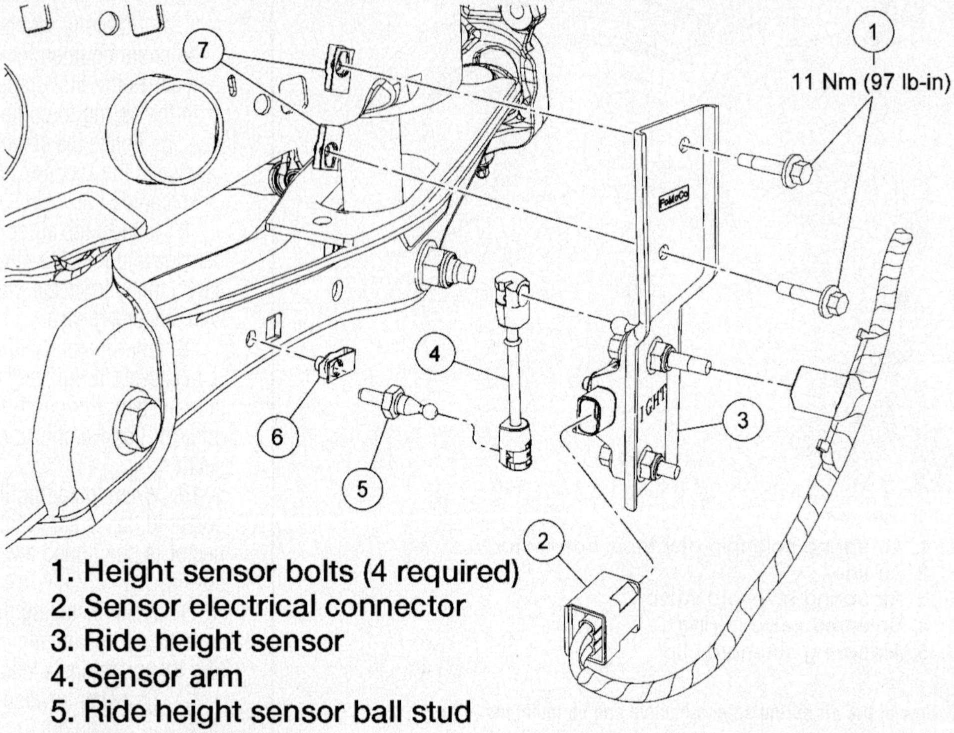

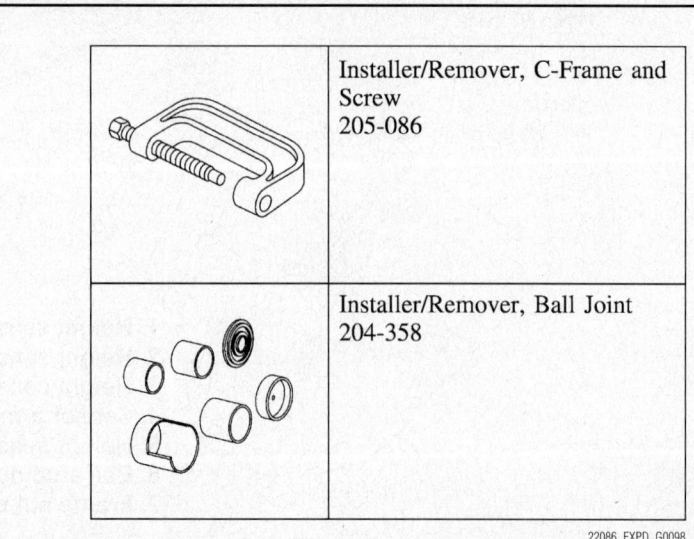

1. Height sensor bolts (4 required)
2. Sensor electrical connector
3. Ride height sensor
4. Sensor arm
5. Ride height sensor ball stud
6. Ball stud nut clip
7. Frame nut clips (2 required)

36578_EXPD_G0123

Fig. 146 Exploded view of suspension height sensor components–RH side

5. Remove and discard the 2 height sensor bolts.

➡**The RH and LH height sensor assemblies cannot be used on opposite sides of the vehicle.**

6. To install, reverse the removal procedure.

7. Calibrate the LH and RH height sensors. Refer to Air Suspension Adjustment.

SUSPENSION

FRONT SUSPENSION

CONTROL LINKS

REMOVAL & INSTALLATION

Refer to Stabilizer Bar for Control Links removal and installation.

LOWER BALL JOINT

REMOVAL & INSTALLATION

See Figures 147 and 148.

1. Remove the wheel knuckle.
2. Remove and discard the lower ball joint snap ring.
3. Using the special tools 205-086 and 204-358, remove the lower ball joint.
4. Clean and inspect the lower arm lower ball joint bore for damage before installing a new ball joint.
5. To install, reverse the removal procedure.

	Installer/Remover, C-Frame and Screw 205-086
	Installer/Remover, Ball Joint 204-358

22086_EXPD_G0098

Fig. 147 Ball joint removal tools

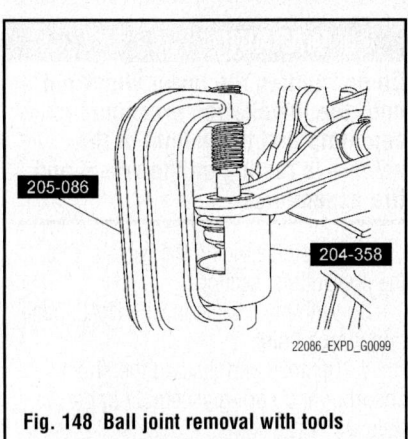

Fig. 148 Ball joint removal with tools

➡Make sure the lower ball joint is fully seated in the lower control arm, and new lower ball joint snap ring is fully seated.

✳✳ WARNING

Always install new nuts and cotter pins.

LOWER CONTROL ARM

REMOVAL & INSTALLATION

See Figure 149.

1. Before servicing the vehicle, refer to the precautions section.

✳✳ CAUTION

The electrical power to the air suspension system must be shut off prior to hoisting, jacking or towing an air suspension vehicle. This can be accomplished by turning off the air suspension switch located in the LH rear quarter trim panel. Failure to do so can result in unexpected inflation or deflation of the air springs, which can result in shifting of the vehicle during these operations. Failure to follow these instructions may result in personal injury.

✳✳ WARNING

Suspension fasteners are critical parts because they affect performance of vital parts and systems and their failure can result in major service expense. A new part with the same part number must be installed if installation becomes necessary. Do not use a replacement part of lesser quality or substitute design. Torque values must be used as specified during reassembly to make sure of correct retention of these parts.

2. If equipped, turn the air suspension switch to the OFF position.
3. With the vehicle in NEUTRAL, position it on a hoist.

➡**Use the hex holding feature to prevent the stud from turning while removing the nut.**

4. Remove and discard the stabilizer bar link lower nut.
5. Remove and discard the lower ball joint nut
6. Using the special tool, separate the ball joint from the knuckle.
7. Remove the lower arm rearward nut and bolt.
8. Remove the lower arm forward nut and bolt.
9. Remove the shock absorber lower nut, bolt and the lower arm.

✳✳ WARNING

Do not tighten the lower arm forward and rearward nuts and bolts until the installation procedure is complete and the weight of the vehicle is resting on the wheel and tire assemblies.

To install:

10. To install, reverse the removal procedure and note the following:

a. Tighten the stabilizer bar link lower nut to 59 ft. lbs. (80 Nm).
b. Tighten the lower ball joint nut to 148 ft. lbs. (200 Nm).
c. Tighten the lower rearward and forward arm, nut and bolt to 285 ft. lbs. (350 Nm).
d. Tighten the lower shock absorber nut and bolt to 350 ft. lbs. (475 Nm).
e. Check and, if necessary, align the front end.

MACPHERSON STRUT

REMOVAL & INSTALLATION

See Figures 150 and 151.

✳✳ WARNING

Suspension fasteners are critical parts because they affect performance of vital parts and systems and their failure can result in major service expense. A new part with the same part number must be installed if installation becomes necessary. Do not use a replacement part of lesser quality or substitute design. Torque values must be used as specified during reassembly to make sure of correct retention of these parts.

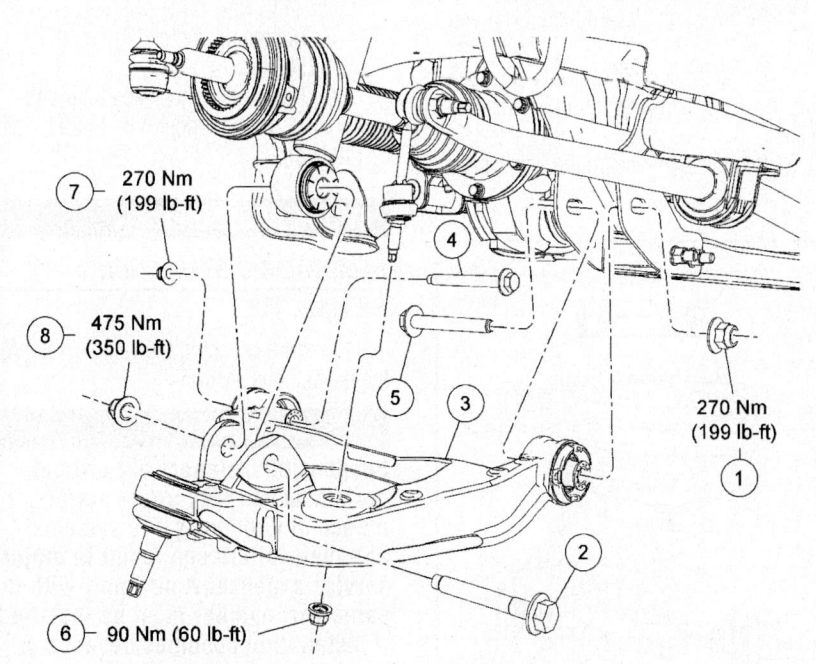

1. Lower arm rearward nut
2. Shock absorber lower bolt
3. Lower arm
4. Lower arm forward bolt
5. Lower arm rearward bolt
6. Stabilizer bar link lower nut
7. Lower arm forward nut
8. Shock absorber lower nut

Fig. 149 Exploded view of the front lower control arm and related parts

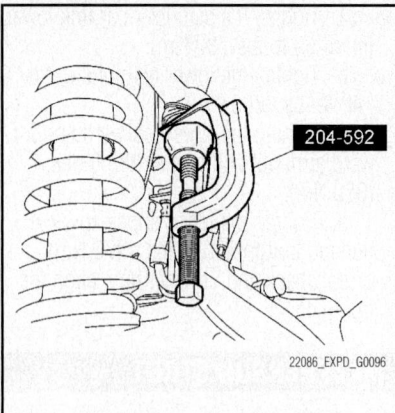

Fig. 150 Upper ball joint separation with special tool

✳✳ WARNING

Do not tighten the lower shock nut until the installation procedure is complete and the weight of the vehicle is resting on the wheel and tire assemblies.

1. Before servicing the vehicle, refer to the precautions section.
2. With the vehicle in NEUTRAL, position it on a hoist.
3. Remove and discard the shock absorber and spring assembly upper nuts.
4. Remove and discard the tie-rod end nut.
5. Using the special tool 204-592, separate the upper ball joint from the wheel knuckle.
6. Remove and discard the upper ball joint nut.

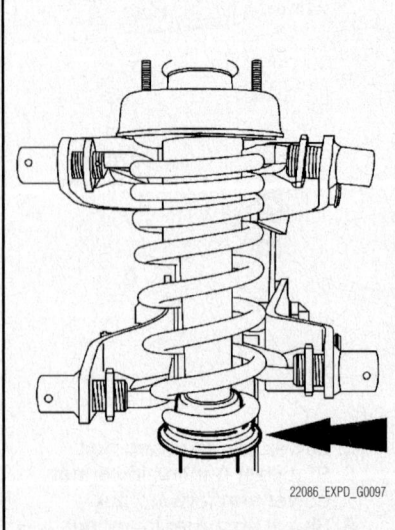

Fig. 151 Spring compression with spring compressor tool

7. Remove and discard the shock absorber and spring assembly lower nut and bolt
8. Using the special tool, disconnect the upper arm from the wheel knuckle and remove the shock absorber and spring assembly.

➡**For reference during assembly, index the upper mount, spring and shock absorber.**

9. Using a suitable spring compressor, compress the spring until the tension is released from the shock absorber.

➡**Use the hex holding feature to prevent the shock rod from turning while removing the nut.**

10. While holding the shock rod, remove the nut and the shock absorber. Discard the nut.
11. Remove the upper mount, dust boot and insulator
12. Remove coil spring.
13. To install, reverse the removal procedure and note the following:
   a. Tighten shock absorber nut to 41ft. lbs. (56 Nm).
   b. Tighten lower shock absorber nut and bolt to 295 ft. lbs. (475 Nm).
   c. Tighten upper ball joint nut to 85 ft. lbs. (115 Nm).
   d. Tighten tie-rod end nut to 111 ft lbs. (150 Nm).
   e. Tighten the shock absorber and spring assembly upper nuts to 30 ft. lbs. (40 Nm).

SHOCK ABSORBERS

REMOVAL & INSTALLATION
See Figure 152.

1. Before servicing the vehicle, refer to the precautions section.

✳✳ WARNING

Suspension fasteners are critical parts because they affect performance of vital parts and systems and their failure can result in major service expense. A new part with the same part number must be installed if installation becomes necessary. Do not use a replacement part of lesser quality or substitute design. Torque values must be used as specified during reassembly to make sure of correct retention of these parts.

✳✳ WARNING

Do not tighten the lower shock nut until the installation procedure is complete and the weight of the vehicle is resting on the wheel and tire assemblies.

2. Before servicing the vehicle, refer to the precautions section.
3. With the vehicle in NEUTRAL, position it on a hoist.
4. Remove and discard the shock absorber and spring assembly upper nuts.
5. Remove and discard the tie-rod end nut.
6. Using the special tool 204-592, separate the upper ball joint from the wheel knuckle.
7. Remove and discard the upper ball joint nut.
8. Remove and discard the shock absorber and spring assembly lower nut and bolt
9. Using the special tool, disconnect the upper arm from the wheel knuckle and remove the shock absorber and spring assembly.

To install:
10. To install, reverse the removal procedure and note the following:
   a. Tighten lower shock absorber nut and bolt to 295 ft. lbs. (475 Nm).
   b. Tighten upper ball joint nut to 85 ft. lbs. (115 Nm).
   c. Tighten tie-rod end nut to 111 ft lbs. (150 Nm).
   d. Tighten the shock absorber and spring assembly upper nuts to 30 ft. lbs. (40 Nm).

STEERING KNUCKLE

REMOVAL & INSTALLATION

2WD Models
See Figure 153.

✳✳ CAUTION

The electrical power to the air suspension system must be shut off prior to hoisting, jacking or towing an air suspension vehicle. This can be accomplished by turning off the air suspension switch located in the LH rear quarter trim panel. Failure to do so can result in unexpected inflation or deflation of the air springs, which can result in shifting of the vehicle during these operations.

1. Before servicing the vehicle, refer to the precautions section.

2. If equipped, turn the air suspension to the OFF position.

3. Remove the wheel speed sensor harness bolt and detach the harness from the retainers.

4. Remove the wheel hub and bearing, as outlined in this section.

➡**Use the hex holding feature to prevent the stud from turning while removing the nut.**

5. Remove the nut and detach the tie-rod from the wheel knuckle. Discard the nut.

6. Remove the bolt and position the brake hose aside.

➡**Use the hex holding feature to prevent the stud from turning while removing the nut.**

7. Remove and discard the stabilizer bar link lower nut. Discard the nut.

8. Remove the shock absorber-to-lower arm nut and bolt. Discard the nut.

➡**Use the hex holding feature to prevent the stud from turning while removing the nut.**

➡**To separate the ball joints from the wheel knuckle, use tool 204-592.**

9. Remove the nut and separate the ball joint from the knuckle. Discard the nut.

➡**Use the hex holding feature to prevent the stud from turning while removing the nut.**

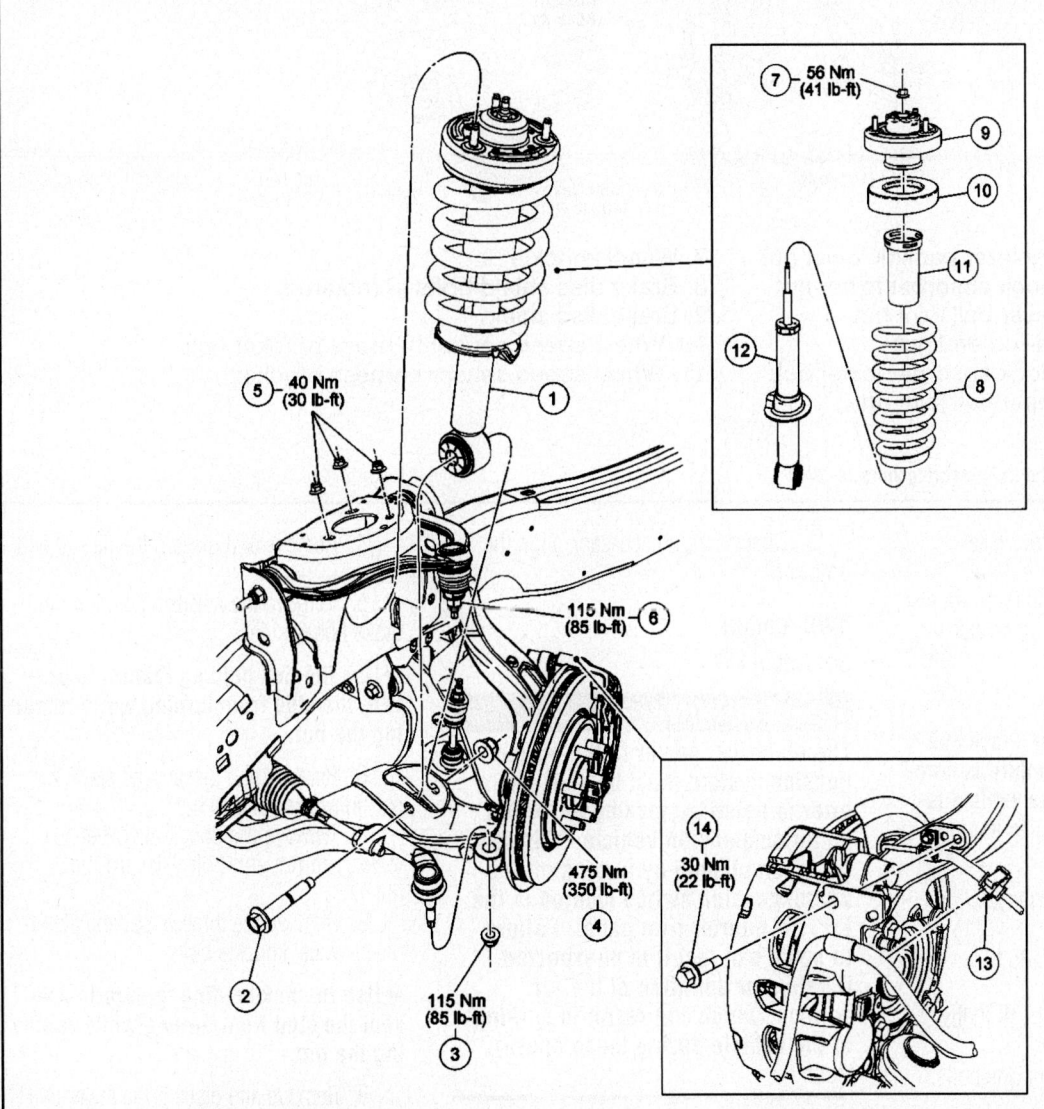

1. Shock absorber and spring assembly
2. Shock absorber lower bolt
3. Tie-rod end nut
4. Shock absorber lower nut
5. Shock absorber upper mount nuts (3 required)
6. Upper ball joint nut
7. Shock rod nut
8. Spring
9. Upper mount
10. Insulator
11. Dust boot
12. Shock absorber
13. Brake flexible hose retainer
14. Brake flexible hose bracket bolt

36578_EXPD_G0135

Fig. 152 Exploded view of the front shock absorber and components

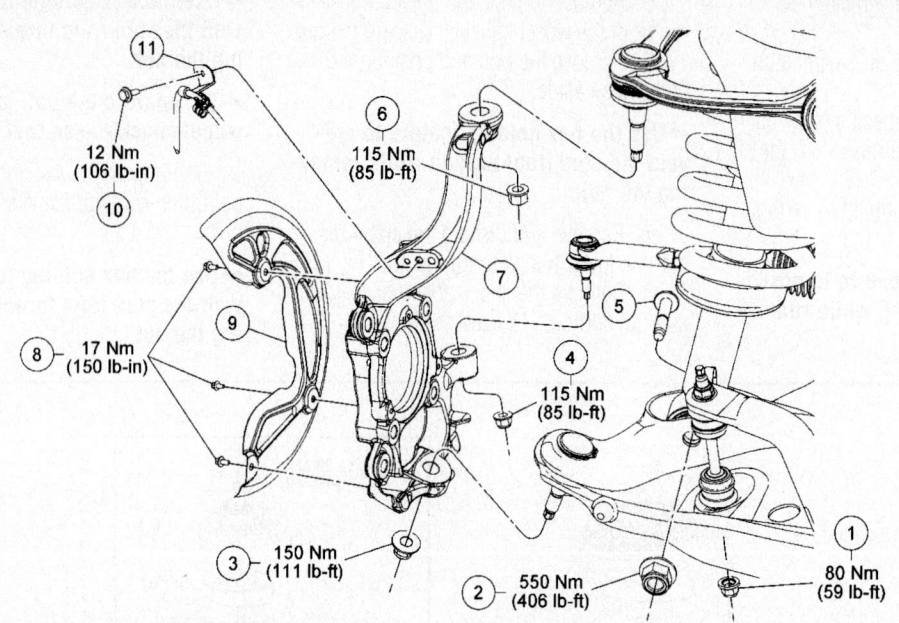

1. Stabilizer bar link lower nut
2. Shock absorber lower nut
3. Lower ball joint nut
4. Tie-rod end nut
5. Shock absorber lower bolt
6. Upper ball joint nut
7. Wheel knuckle
8. Brake disc shield bolts (3 required)
9. Brake disc shield
10. Wheel speed sensor harness bracket bolt
11. Wheel speed sensor harness bracket

36578_EXPD_G0124

Fig. 153 Exploded view of the front steering knuckle–2WD

10. Remove the nut and the wheel knuckle. Discard the nut.

11. If necessary, remove the 3 brake disc shield bolts and remove the brake disc shield.

To install:

→Do not tighten the lower shock nut until the installation procedure is complete and the weight of the vehicle is resting on the wheel and tire assemblies.

12. To install, reverse the removal procedure and note the following:

   a. Upper ball joint nut: 85 ft. lbs. (115 Nm).

   b. Lower ball joint nut: 148 ft. lbs. (200 Nm).

   d. Wheel bearing-to-knuckle bolts: 148 ft. lbs. (200 Nm).

   e. Shock absorber-to-lower control arm bolt and nut: 350 ft. lbs. (475 Nm).

   f. Stabilizer bar link-to-control arm nuts: 66 ft. lbs. (90 Nm).

   g. Brake hose bracket bolt: 9 ft. lbs. (12 Nm).

   h. Tie rod end nuts: 85 ft. lbs. (115 Nm).

   i. The brake disc shield bolts: 9 ft. lbs. (12 Nm).

13. Check and, if necessary, align the front end.

4WD Models

See Figure 154.

❄ **CAUTION**

The electrical power to the air suspension system must be shut off prior to hoisting, jacking or towing an air suspension vehicle. This can be accomplished by turning off the air suspension switch located in the LH rear quarter trim panel. Failure to do so can result in unexpected inflation or deflation of the air springs, which can result in shifting of the vehicle during these operations.

1. Before servicing the vehicle, refer to the precautions section.

2. If equipped, turn the air suspension to the OFF position.

3. Remove the wheel hub and bearing, as outlined in this section.

→Use the hex holding feature to prevent the stud from turning while removing the nut.

4. Remove and discard the tie rod end nut.

5. Remove the bolt and position the brake hose aside.

→Use the hex holding feature to prevent the stud from turning while removing the nut.

6. Remove and discard the stabilizer bar link-to-lower arm nut.

7. Remove the shock absorber-to-lower arm nut and bolt. Discard the nut.

8. Remove the three wheel end actuator-to-wheel knuckle bolts.

→Use the hex holding feature to prevent the stud from turning while removing the nut.

9. Remove and discard the lower ball joint nut.

→Use the hex holding feature to prevent the stud from turning while removing the nut.

→To separate the ball joints from the wheel knuckle, use tool 204-592.

10. Remove the upper ball joint nut and the wheel knuckle. Discard the nut.

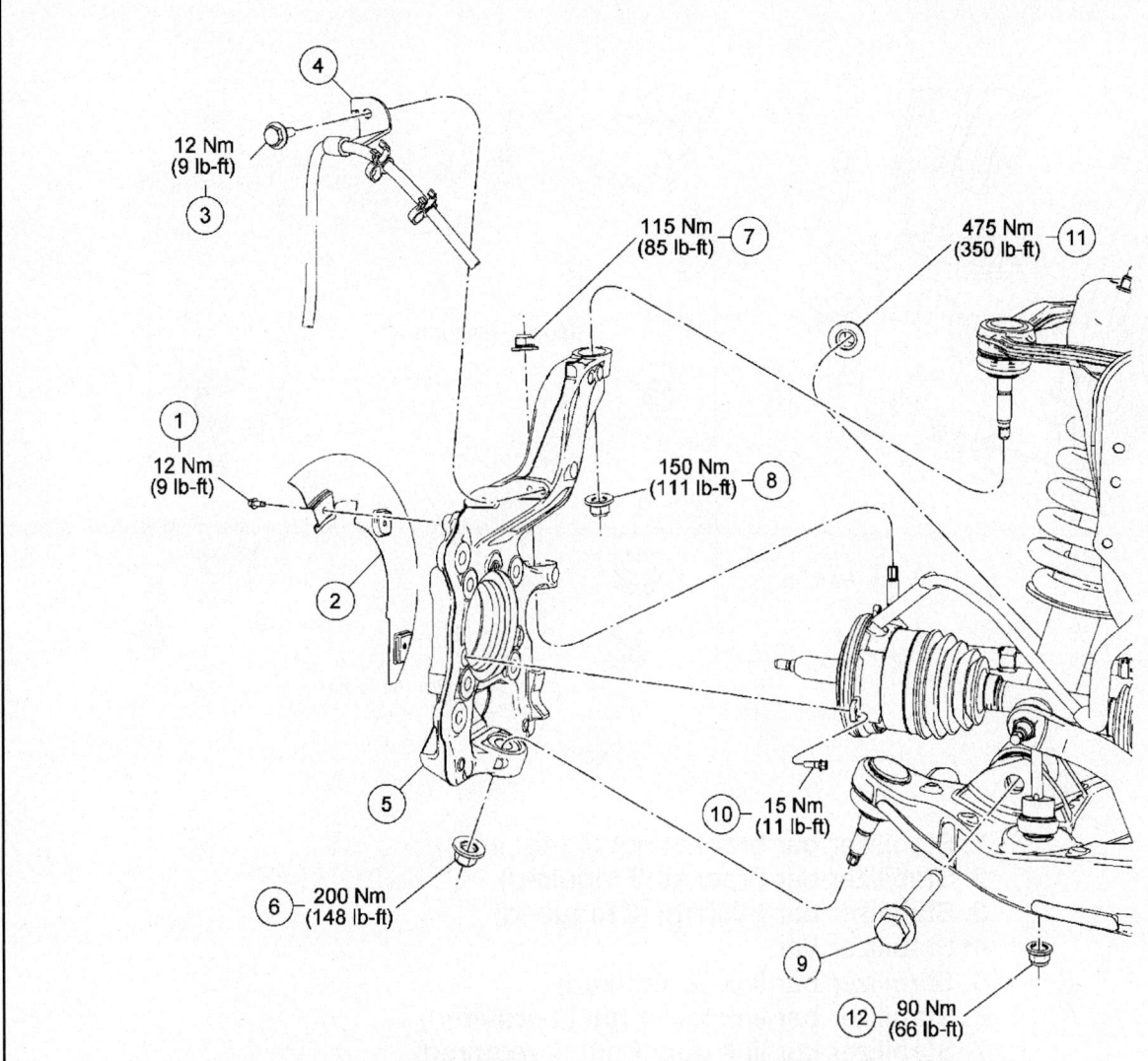

1. Brake disc shield bolt (3 required)
2. Brake disc shield
3. Brake hose bracket bolt
4. Brake hose bracket
5. Wheel knuckle
6. Lower ball joint nut
7. Tie-rod end nut
8. Upper ball joint nut
9. Shock absorber lower bolt
10. Integrated wheel end disconnect bolt (3 required)
11. Shock absorber lower nut
12. Stabilizer bar link lower nut

22086_EXPD_G0103

Fig. 154 Exploded view of the front steering knuckle—4WD

To install:

➡ Do not tighten the lower shock nut until the installation procedure is complete and the weight of the vehicle is resting on the wheel and tire assemblies.

11. To install, reverse the removal procedure and note the following:

a. Upper ball joint nut: 111 ft. lbs. (150 Nm).

b. Lower ball joint nut: 148 ft. lbs. (200 Nm).

d. Wheel end actuator-to-wheel knuckle bolts and shield: 9 ft. lbs. (12 Nm)

e. Shock absorber-to-lower arm nut and bolt: 350 ft. lbs. (475 Nm)

f. Stabilizer bar link-to-lower arm nut: 66 ft. lbs. (90 Nm)

g. Brake hose bracket bolt: 9 ft. lbs. (12 Nm)

h. Tie rod end nut: 85 ft. lbs. (115 Nm)

12. Check and, if necessary, align the front end.

STABILIZER BAR

REMOVAL & INSTALLATION

See Figure 155.

1. Before servicing the vehicle, refer to the precautions section.

2. With the vehicle in NEUTRAL, position it on a hoist.

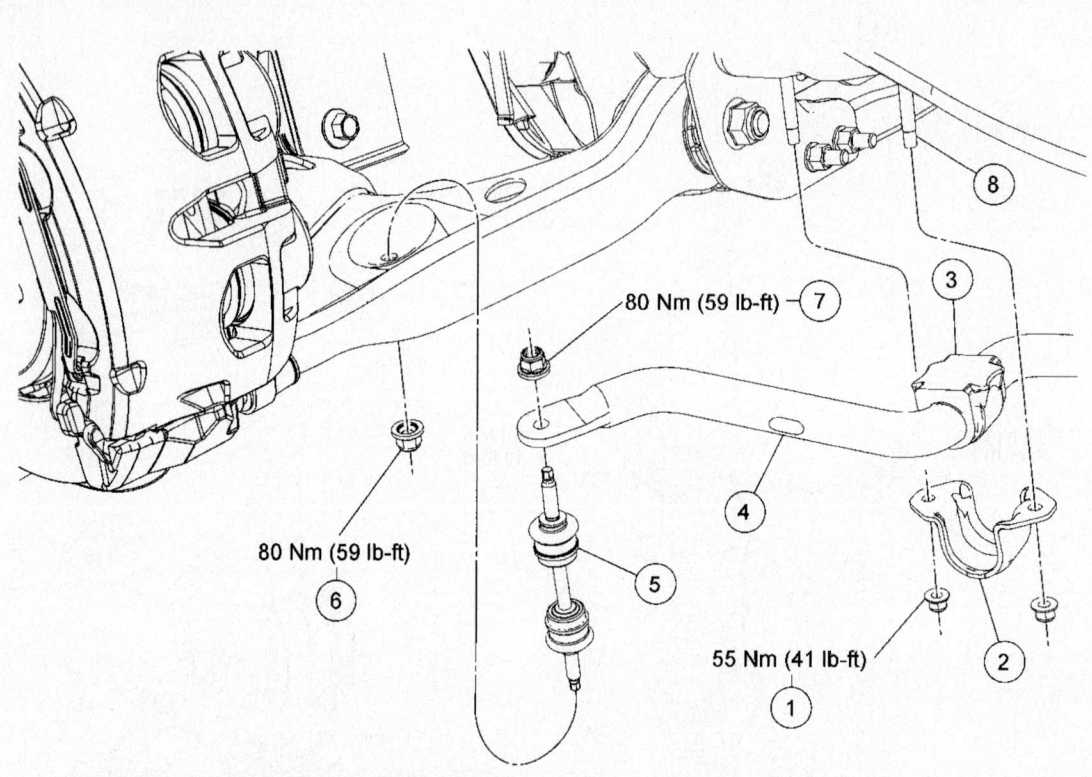

1. Stabilizer bar bracket nut (4 required)
2. Stabilizer bar bracket (2 required)
3. Stabilizer bar bushing (2 required)
4. Stabilizer bar
5. Stabilizer bar link (2 required)
6. Stabilizer bar link lower nut (2 required)
7. Stabilizer bar link upper nut (2 required)
8. Stabilizer bracket bolt plate

36578_EXPD_G0127

Fig. 155 Exploded view of the front stabilizer bar and control link

➡The hex holding feature can be used to prevent turning of the stud while removing the nut.

3. Remove and discard the 2 stabilizer bar link upper nuts.

4. Remove and discard the 2 stabilizer bar link lower nuts and remove the 2 stabilizer bar links.

5. Remove the 4 stabilizer bar bracket nuts, brackets and the stabilizer bar. Discard the nuts.

6. Remove and discard the stabilizer bracket bolt plates.

➡Make sure the stabilizer bar bushing upset is installed into the bracket groove

7. Inspect and, if necessary, install new stabilizer bar bushings.

To install:

8. To install, reverse the removal procedure and note the following:
   a. Tighten upper and lower link nuts to 59 ft. lbs. (80 Nm).
   b. Tighten the stabilizer bar bracket nuts to 41 ft. lbs. (55 Nm).

UPPER BALL JOINT

REMOVAL & INSTALLATION

The upper ball joints on these models are an integral part of the control am. If found to be defective the control arm must be

replaced. Refer to control arm removal and installation.

UPPER CONTROL ARM

REMOVAL & INSTALLATION
See Figure 156.

➡Before tightening any suspension bushing fasteners, use a suitable jack to raise the suspension until the distance between the center of the hub and the lip of the fender is equal to the measurement taken in Step 1 (curb height).

1. Measure the distance from the center of the hub to the lip of the fender with the

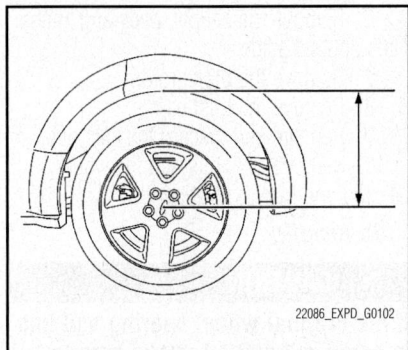

Fig. 156 Center of hub to fender lip measurement shown

vehicle in a level, static ground position (curb height).

2. Before servicing the vehicle, refer to the precautions section.

✳✳ CAUTION

The electrical power to the air suspension system must be shut off prior to hoisting, jacking or towing an air suspension vehicle. This can be accomplished by turning off the air suspension switch located in the LH rear quarter trim panel. Failure to do so can result in unexpected inflation or deflation of the air springs, which can result in shifting of the vehicle during these operations. Failure to follow these instructions may result in personal injury.

✳✳ WARNING

Suspension fasteners are critical parts because they affect performance of vital parts and systems and their failure can result in major service expense. A new part with the same part number must be installed if installation becomes necessary. Do not use a replacement part of lesser quality or substitute design. Torque values must be used as specified during reassembly to make sure of correct retention of these parts.

3. Raise and safely support the vehicle.

4. Remove the wheel and tire assembly.

5. Remove the shock absorber and spring assembly.

6. On models with an air suspension, detach the height sensor from the upper arm.

➡️**Use the hex holding feature to prevent the stud from turning while removing the nut.**

7. Remove and discard the upper ball joint nut.

8. Using the special tool 204-592, separate the upper ball joint from the wheel knuckle.

9. Remove the rearward upper arm-to-frame nut and bolt. Discard the nut.

10. Remove the forward upper arm-to-frame nut, bolt and the upper arm. Discard the nut.

To install:

11. To install, reverse the removal procedure and note the following:

   a. Tighten the control arm nuts/bolts to 111 ft. lbs. (150 Nm).

   b. Tighten the upper control arm nut to 85 ft. lbs. (115 Nm).

   c. Check and, if necessary, align the front end.

WHEEL HUB & BEARING

REMOVAL & INSTALLATION

2WD Models

See Figure 157.

✳✳ WARNING

The electrical power to the air suspension system must be shut off prior to hoisting, jacking or towing an air suspension vehicle. Failure to shut

the system off may lead to an unexpected inflation or deflation of the air springs, which may result in a shift of the vehicle.

1. Before servicing the vehicle, refer to the precautions in the beginning of this section.

2. If equipped, turn the air suspension switch to the OFF position.

3. Disconnect the wheel speed sensor electrical connector.

4. With the vehicle in NEUTRAL, position it on a hoist.

5. Remove the wheel and tire assembly.

6. Remove the bolt and detach the brake line retainers.

✳✳ CAUTION

Do not allow the caliper to hang from the brake hose or damage to the hose can result.

7. Remove the caliper, pads and anchor plate and set aside.

8. Remove the brake rotor.

9. Remove the bolts and the wheel bearing and hub assembly.

10. If installing a new wheel bearing and wheel hub, remove the wheel speed sensor bolt and the wheel speed sensor.

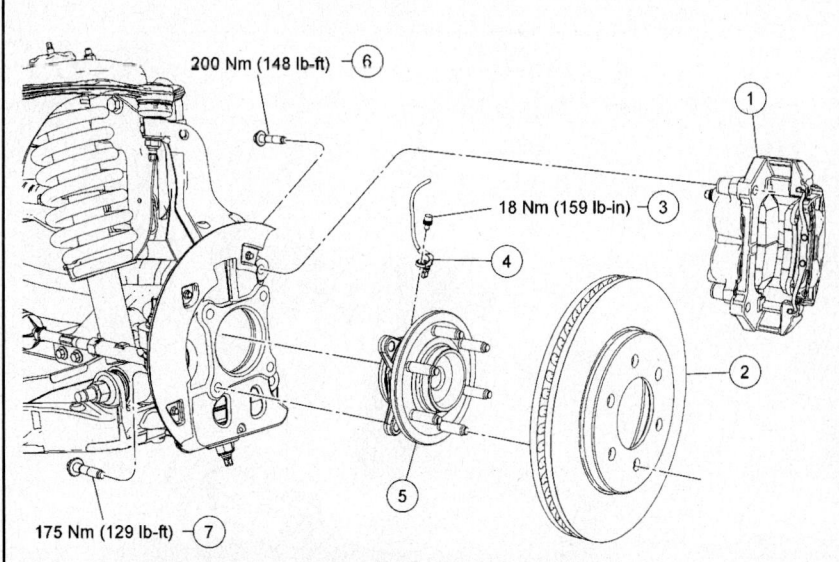

1. Brake caliper and anchor plate assembly
2. Brake disc
3. Wheel speed sensor bolt
4. Wheel speed sensor
5. Wheel bearing and wheel hub
6. Brake caliper anchor plate bolt (2 required)
7. Wheel bearing and wheel hub bolt (4 required)

Fig. 157 Exploded view of the front wheel bearing and wheel hub–2WD

To install:

➡ **If the original wheel bearing and hub is being reinstalled, make sure to install a new O-ring.**

11. To install, reverse the removal procedure and note the following:

    a. Wheel bearing/hub assembly bolts: 111 ft. lbs. (150 Nm).

    b. Brake anchor plate: 148 ft. lbs. (200 Nm).

    c. Speed sensor bolt: 13 ft. lbs. (18 Nm).

    d. Retainer bracket bolts: 9 ft. lbs. (12 Nm).

4WD Models

See Figure 158.

※ WARNING

The electrical power to the air suspension system must be shut off prior to hoisting, jacking or towing an air suspension vehicle. Failure to shut the system off may lead to an unexpected inflation or deflation of the air springs, which may result in a shift of the vehicle.

1. Before servicing the vehicle, refer to the precautions in the beginning of this section.

2. If equipped, turn the air suspension switch to the OFF position.

3. Disconnect the wheel speed sensor electrical connector.

4. Remove the wheel and tire assembly.

5. Remove the bolt and detach the brake line retainers.

※ CAUTION

Do not allow the caliper to hang from the brake hose or damage to the hose can result.

6. Remove the caliper, pads and anchor plate and set aside.

7. Remove the brake rotor.

8. Remove the dust cap.

9. Remove and discard the axle nut.

10. Remove the bolts and the wheel bearing and hub assembly.

To install:

※ CAUTION

If the original wheel bearing and hub is being reinstalled, make sure to install a new O-ring.

11. To install, reverse the removal procedure and note the following:

    a. Wheel bearing/hub assembly bolts: 148 ft. lbs. (200 Nm).

    b. Axle nut: 20 ft. lbs. (27 Nm).

    c. Brake anchor plate: 148 ft. lbs. (200 Nm).

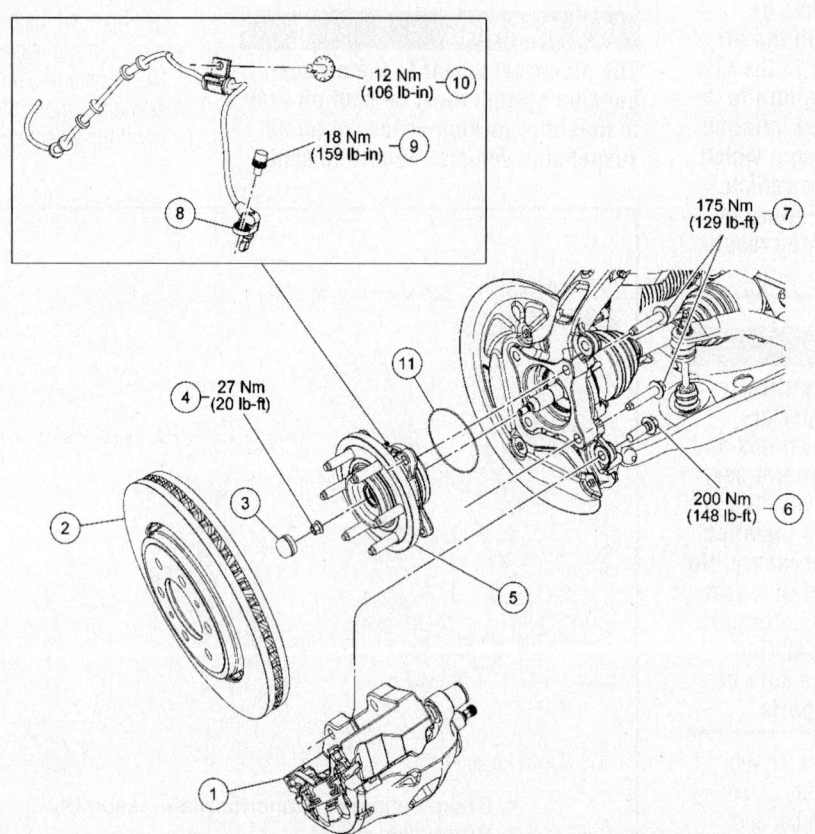

1. Brake caliper and anchor plate assembly
2. Brake disc
3. Dust cap
4. Halfshaft nut
5. Wheel bearing and wheel hub
6. Brake caliper anchor plate bolt (2 required)
7. Wheel bearing and wheel hub bolts (4 required)
8. Wheel speed sensor
9. Wheel speed sensor bolt
10. Wheel speed sensor harness bracket bolt
11. O-ring seal

36578_EXPD_G0125

Fig. 158 Exploded view of the front wheel bearing and wheel hub—4WD

SUSPENSION

REAR SUSPENSION

COIL SPRING

REMOVAL & INSTALLATION
See Figure 159.

✳✳ WARNING

Do not tighten the lower arm-to-frame bolt or shock absorber lower nut until the installation procedure is complete and the weight of the vehicle is resting on the wheel and tire assemblies.

✳✳ WARNING

Suspension fasteners are critical parts because they affect performance of vital parts and systems and their failure can result in major service expense. A new part with the same part number must be installed if installation becomes necessary. Do not use a replacement part of lesser quality or substitute design. Torque values must be used as specified during reassembly to make sure of correct retention of these parts.

1. Before servicing the vehicle, refer to the precautions section.
2. With the vehicle in NEUTRAL, position it on a hoist.
3. If equipped, disconnect the air suspension height sensor connecting link from the lower arm.
4. Remove and discard the shock absorber lower bolt and flagnut.
5. Remove and discard the lower arm-to-frame bolt and flagnut.

6. Remove and discard the lower ball joint nut.

✳✳ WARNING

Do not damage the ball joint boot while installing the special tool.

7. Using the special tool 204-592, separate the lower ball joint from the wheel knuckle.
8. Swing the lower arm to the rear of the vehicle and remove the lower arm
9. Remove and discard the upper mount nuts.
10. Remove the shock absorber and spring assembly.

➡**For reference during assembly, index the upper mount, spring and shock absorber.**

11. Using a suitable spring compressor, compress the spring until the tension is released from the shock absorber.
12. While holding the shock rod, remove the nut and washer.
13. Remove the shock absorber and discard the nut.
14. Remove the upper mount, dust boot and insulator.
15. To install, reverse the removal procedure and note the following:

   a. Tighten the new upper mount nuts to 30 ft. lbs. (40 Nm).
   b. Tighten the new shock absorber lower bolt and nut to 350 ft. lbs. (475 Nm).
   c. Tighten the new lower ball joint nut to 111 ft. lbs. (150 Nm).

   d. Tighten the new lower arm-to-frame bolt to 221 ft. lbs. (300 Nm).
   e. Tighten the new shock rod nut to 41 ft. lbs. (56 Nm).

CONTROL ARMS/LINKS

REMOVAL & INSTALLATION

Refer to Stabilizer Bar for control link removal and installation.

LOWER CONTROL ARM

REMOVAL & INSTALLATION
See Figures 160 and 161.

✳✳ WARNING

Suspension fasteners are critical parts because they affect performance of vital parts and systems and their failure can result in major service expense. A new part with the same part number must be installed if installation becomes necessary. Do not use a replacement part of lesser quality or substitute design. Torque values must be used as specified during reassembly to make sure of correct retention of these parts. Orientation of the suspension fasteners is important. Make sure the fasteners are installed in the same direction as they were in when removed.

1. Before servicing the vehicle, refer to the precautions section.
2. With the vehicle in NEUTRAL, position it on a hoist.

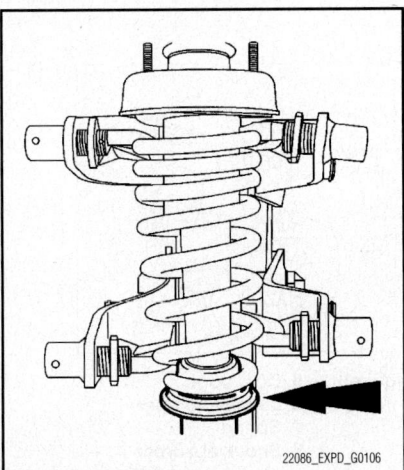

22086_EXPD_G0106

Fig. 159 Shock assembly view showing spring compression

Special Tool(s)

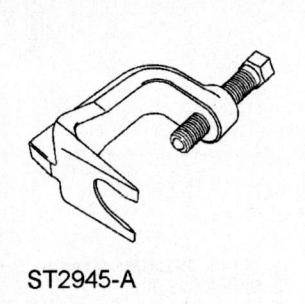

ST2945-A

Separator, Ball Joint
204-592

22086_EXPD_G0108

Fig. 160 Ball joint separator tool

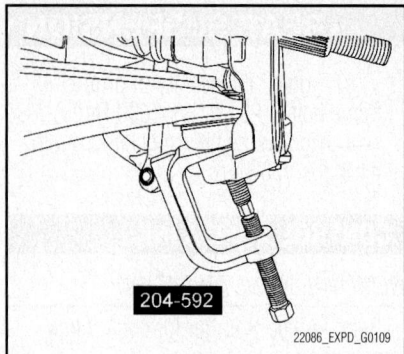

Fig. 161 Ball joint removal with separator tool

3. If equipped, disconnect the air suspension height sensor connecting link from the lower arm.

4. Remove and discard the shock absorber lower bolt and flagnut.

5. Remove and discard the lower arm-to-frame bolt and flagnut.

6. Remove and discard the lower ball joint nut.

✳✳ WARNING
Do not damage the ball joint boot while installing the special tool.

7. Using the special tool, separate the lower ball joint from the wheel knuckle.

8. Swing the lower arm to the rear of the vehicle and remove the lower arm.

To install:

9. Position the lower arm ball joint onto the wheel knuckle and install the lower ball joint nut, tighten the new nut to 111 ft. lbs. (150 Nm).

➡**Do not tighten the lower arm-to-frame bolt at this time.**

10. Install the lower arm-to-frame bolt and flagnut, tighten to 37 ft. lbs. (50 Nm).

➡**Do not tighten the shock absorber lower nut at this time.**

11. Position the lower arm and install a new shock absorber lower bolt and nut.

12. Lower the vehicle so that the weight of the vehicle is on the wheel and tire assemblies.

13. Tighten the lower arm-to-frame bolt to 221 ft. lbs. (300 Nm).

14. Tighten the shock absorber lower bolt to 350 ft. lbs. (475 Nm).

15. If equipped, connect the air suspension height sensor connecting link to the lower arm.

16. Check and, if necessary, align the rear end.

SHOCK ABSORBER

REMOVAL & INSTALLATION
See Figure 162.

✳✳ WARNING
Do not tighten the lower arm-to-frame bolt or shock absorber lower nut until the installation procedure is complete and the weight of the vehicle is resting on the wheel and tire assemblies.

✳✳ WARNING
Suspension fasteners are critical parts because they affect performance of vital parts and systems and their failure can result in major service expense. A new part with the same part number must be installed if installation becomes necessary. Do not use a replacement part of lesser quality or substitute design. Torque values must be used as specified during reassembly to make sure of correct retention of these parts.

1. Before servicing the vehicle, refer to the precautions section.

2. With the vehicle in NEUTRAL, position it on a hoist.

3. If equipped, disconnect the air suspension height sensor connecting link from the lower arm.

4. Remove and discard the shock absorber lower bolt and flagnut.

5. Remove and discard the lower arm-to-frame bolt and flagnut.

6. Remove and discard the lower ball joint nut.

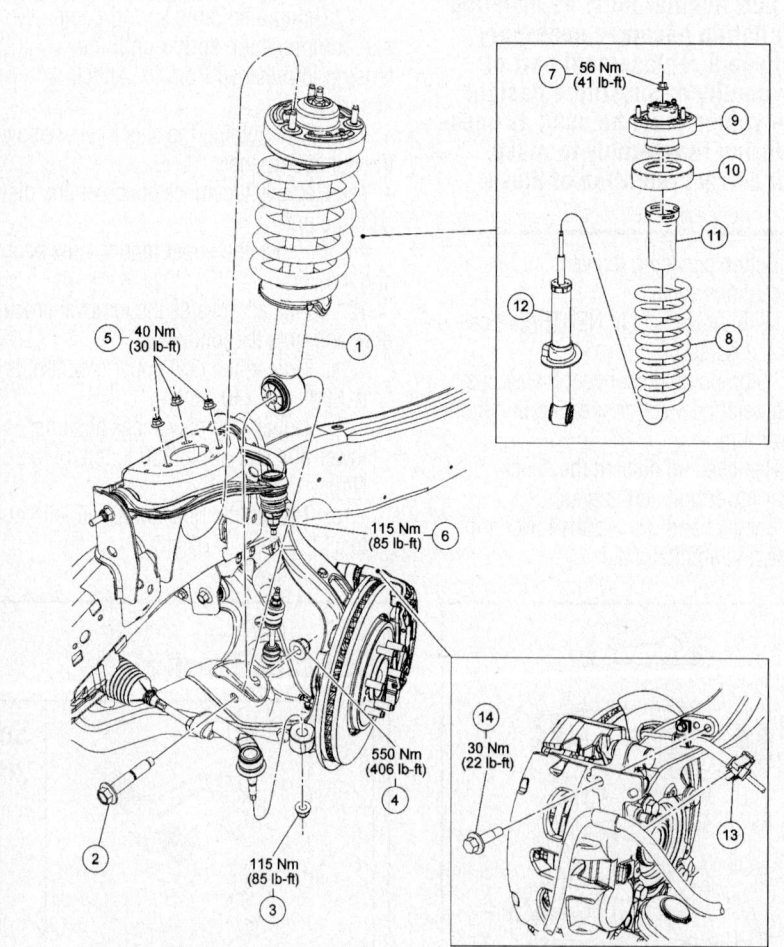

1. Shock absorber upper mount nut (3 required)
2. Shock rod nut
3. Upper mount
4. Insulator
5. Dust boot
6. Jounce bumper
7. Spring
8. Shock absorber

Fig. 162 Exploded view of the rear coil spring and shock absorber assembly

Do not damage the ball joint boot while installing the special tool.

7. Using the special tool 204-592, separate the lower ball joint from the wheel knuckle.

8. Swing the lower arm to the rear of the vehicle and remove the lower arm

9. Remove and discard the upper mount nuts.

10. Remove the shock absorber and spring assembly.

11. To install, reverse the removal procedure and note the following:

  a. Tighten the new upper mount nuts to 30 ft. lbs. (40 Nm).

  b. Tighten the shock absorber lower bolt to 350 ft. lbs. (475 Nm).

  c. Tighten the lower ball joint nut to 111 ft. lbs. (150 Nm).

  d. Tighten the lower arm-to-frame bolt to 221 ft. lbs. (300 Nm).

TOE LINK

REMOVAL & INSTALLATION

See Figure 163.

⁂ WARNING

Do not tighten the toe link-to-frame cam bolt or toe link-to-wheel knuckle bolt until the installation procedure is complete and the weight of the vehicle is resting on the wheel and tire assemblies.

1. Before servicing the vehicle, refer to the precautions section.

2. With the vehicle in NEUTRAL, position it on a hoist.

3. Index-mark the cam bolt and cam washer positions.

4. Remove and discard the bolt and washer.

5. Remove the toe link-to-frame cam bolt, cam washer and nut.

6. Remove the toe link.

➡ **Using the index marks, transfer the marks onto the new cam bolt and cam washer. Use these index marks when installing the toe link.**

7. To install, reverse the removal procedure and note the following:

  a. Tighten the cam bolt to 166 ft. lbs. (225 Nm).

  b. Tighten the toe link-to-frame cam bolt to 203 ft. lbs. (275 Nm).

  c. Check and, if necessary, adjust the rear toe.

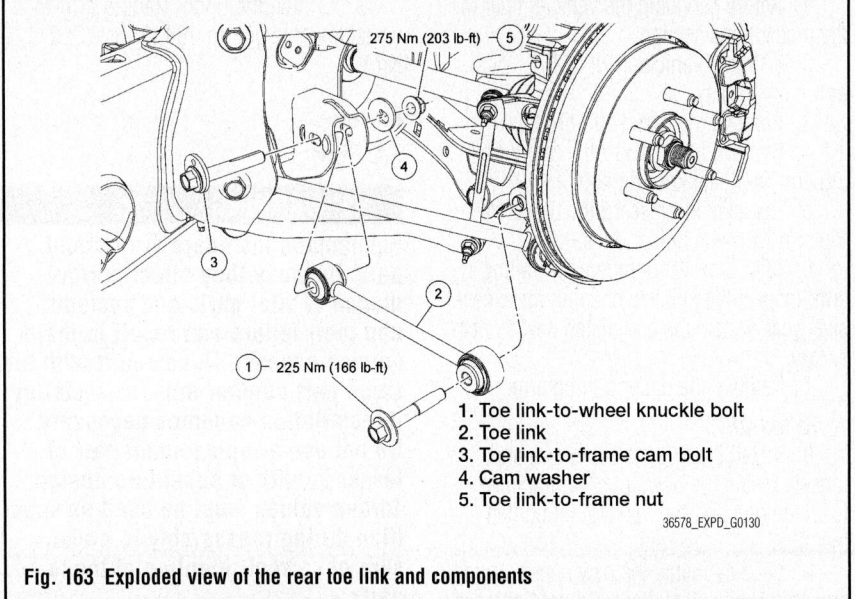

1. Toe link-to-wheel knuckle bolt
2. Toe link
3. Toe link-to-frame cam bolt
4. Cam washer
5. Toe link-to-frame nut

36578_EXPD_G0130

Fig. 163 Exploded view of the rear toe link and components

TRAILING ARM

REMOVAL & INSTALLATION

Upper

See Figure 164.

⁂ WARNING

Suspension fasteners are critical parts because they affect perfor- mance of vital parts and systems and their failure can result in major service expense. A new part with the same part number must be installed if installation becomes necessary. Do not use a replacement part of lesser quality or substitute design. Torque values must be used as specified during reassembly to make sure of correct retention of these parts.

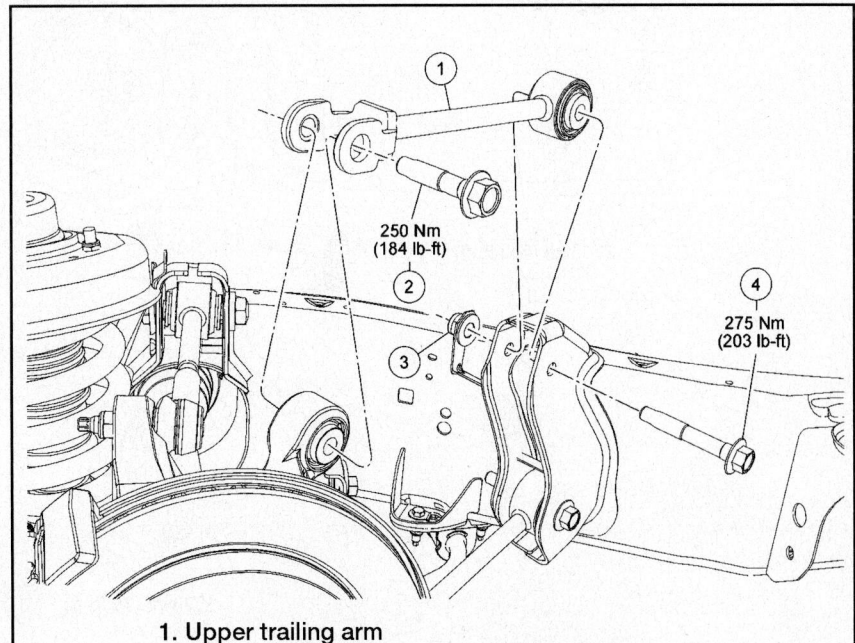

1. Upper trailing arm
2. Upper trailing arm-to-wheel knuckle bolt
3. Upper trailing arm-to-frame flagnut
4. Upper trailing arm-to-frame bolt

36578_EXPD_G0132

Fig. 164 Exploded view of the rear upper trailing arm

1. Before servicing the vehicle, refer to the precautions section.

2. With the vehicle in NEUTRAL, position it on a hoist.

3. Remove the wheel and tire.

4. Remove and discard the upper trailing arm-to-wheel knuckle bolt.

5. Remove and discard the upper trailing arm-to-frame bolt and flagnut.

6. After removal of the upper trailing arm, inspect the knuckle bushing for excessive wear or damage and install new as necessary.

7. Remove the upper trailing arm.

To install:

8. Install the upper trailing arm and loosely install the new upper trailing arm-to-frame bolt and flagnut. Do not tighten at this time.

9. Loosely install the new upper trailing arm-to-wheel knuckle bolt. Do not tighten at this time.

10. Install the wheel and tire.

11. Lower the vehicle so that the weight of the vehicle is resting on the wheel and tires.

12. Tighten the upper trailing arm-to-frame bolt and flagnut to 203 ft. lbs. (275 Nm).

13. Tighten the upper trailing arm-to-wheel knuckle bolt to 184 ft. lbs. (250 Nm).

Lower

See Figure 165.

> ❋❋ **WARNING**
>
> **Suspension fasteners are critical parts because they affect performance of vital parts and systems and their failure can result in major service expense. A new part with the same part number must be installed if installation becomes necessary. Do not use a replacement part of lesser quality or substitute design. Torque values must be used as specified during reassembly to make sure of correct retention of these parts.**

1. Before servicing the vehicle, refer to the precautions section.

2. With the vehicle in NEUTRAL, position it on a hoist.

3. Remove the wheel and tire.

4. Remove and discard the 2 lower trailing arm-to-wheel knuckle bolts.

5. Remove and discard the lower trailing arm-to-frame bolt and flagnut.

6. Remove the lower trailing arm.

To install:

7. Install the lower trailing arm and loosely install the new lower trailing arm-to-frame bolt and flagnut. Do not tighten at this time.

8. Loosely install the 2 new lower trailing arm-to-wheel knuckle bolt. Do not tighten at this time.

9. Install the wheel and tire.

10. Lower the vehicle so that the weight of the vehicle is resting on the wheel and tires.

11. Tighten the 2 lower trailing arm-to-wheel knuckle bolts to 76 ft. lbs. (103 Nm).

12. Tighten the lower trailing arm-to-frame bolt to 203 ft. lbs. (275 Nm).

UPPER CONTROL ARM

REMOVAL & INSTALLATION

See Figure 166.

> ❋❋ **WARNING**
>
> **Suspension fasteners are critical parts because they affect performance of vital parts and systems and their failure can result in major ser-**

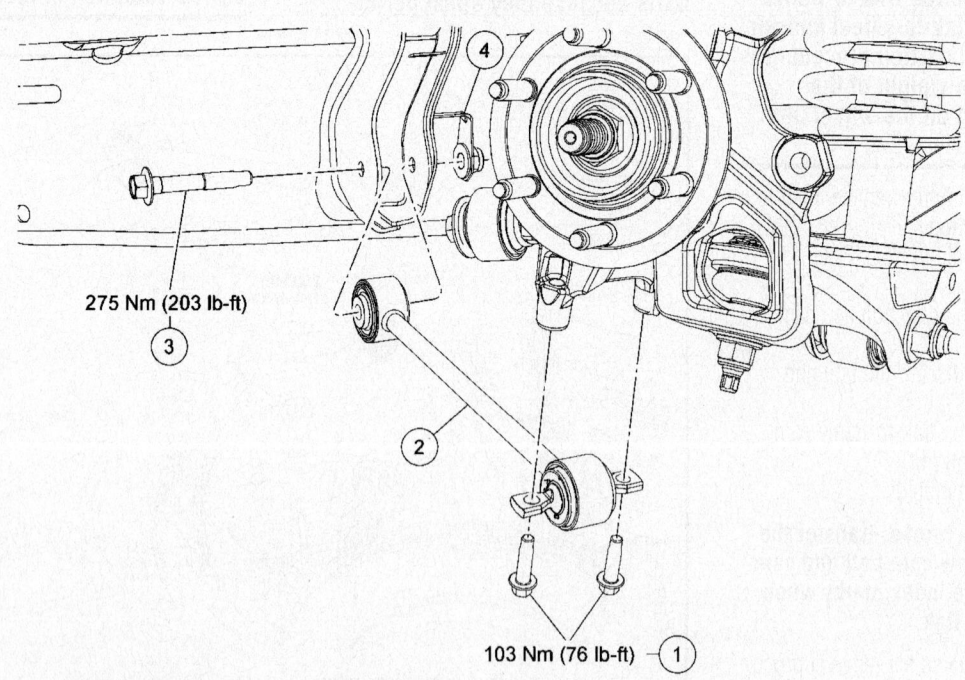

275 Nm (203 lb-ft)
3

2

103 Nm (76 lb-ft) — 1

1. **Lower trailing arm-to-wheel knuckle bolts (2 required)**
2. **Lower trailing arm**
3. **Lower trailing arm-to-frame bolt**
4. **Lower trailing arm-to-frame flagnut**

36578_EXPD_G0133

Fig. 165 Exploded view of the rear lower trailing arm

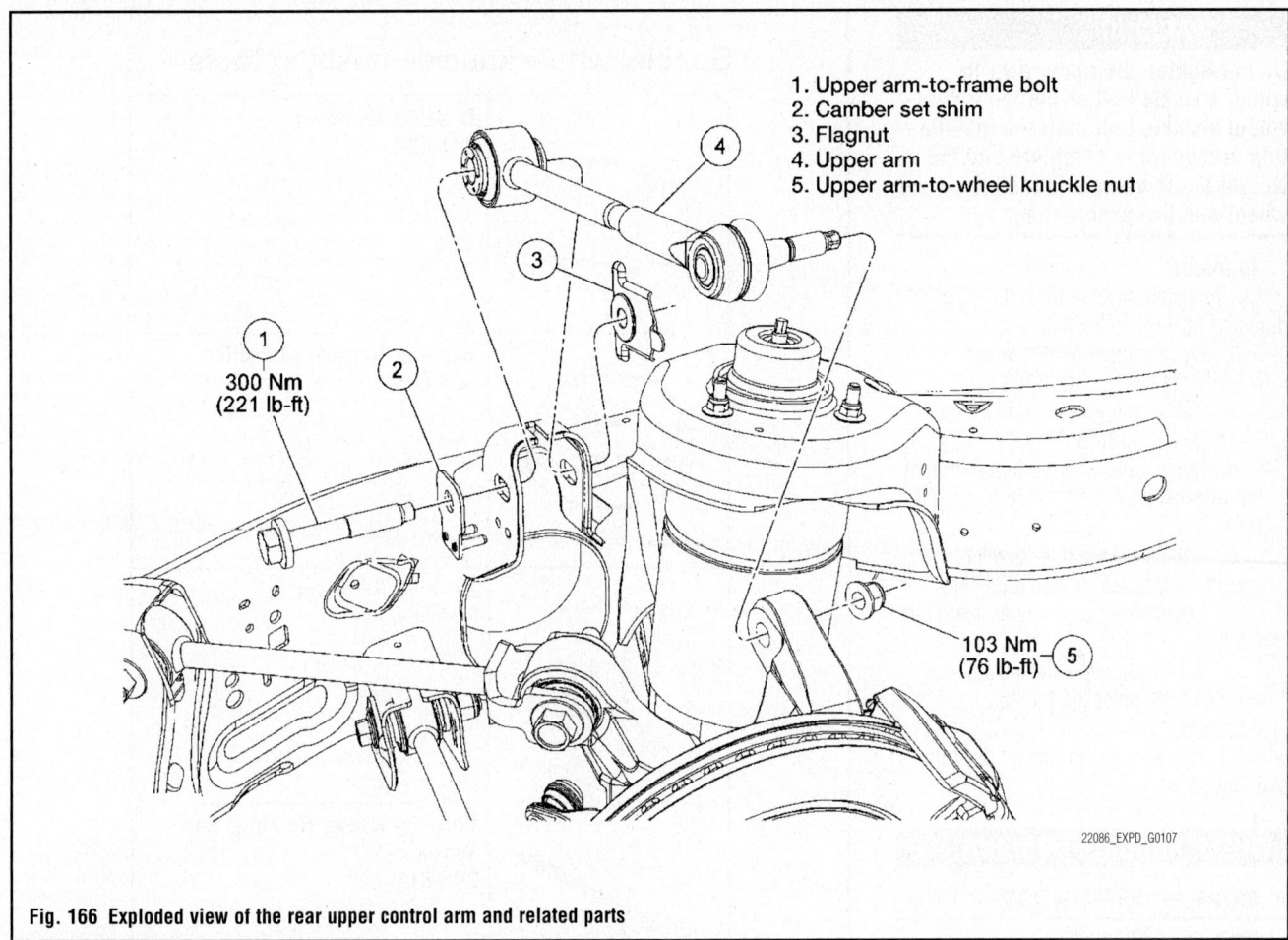

1. Upper arm-to-frame bolt
2. Camber set shim
3. Flagnut
4. Upper arm
5. Upper arm-to-wheel knuckle nut

300 Nm
(221 lb-ft)

103 Nm
(76 lb-ft)

22086_EXPD_G0107

Fig. 166 Exploded view of the rear upper control arm and related parts

vice expense. A new part with the same part number must be installed if installation becomes necessary. Do not use a replacement part of lesser quality or substitute design. Torque values must be used as specified during reassembly to make sure of correct retention of these parts.

❈❈ WARNING

Do not tighten the upper arm-to-frame bushing until the installation procedure is complete and the weight of the vehicle is resting on the wheel and tire assemblies.

1. Before servicing the vehicle, refer to the precautions section.
2. With the vehicle in NEUTRAL, position it on a hoist.
3. Remove and discard the upper arm-to-wheel knuckle nut.
4. Remove and discard the upper arm-to-frame bolt, washer, camber set shim and flagnut.
5. Remove the upper arm.
6. To install, reverse the removal procedure and note the following:

a. Tighten the upper arm-to-frame bolt to 221 ft. lbs. (300 Nm).
b. Tighten the upper arm-to-wheel knuckle nut to 76 ft. lbs. (103 Nm).

WHEEL KNUCKLE

REMOVAL & INSTALLATION

❈❈ WARNING

Suspension fasteners are critical parts because they affect performance of vital parts and systems and their failure can result in major service expense. A new part with the same part number must be installed if installation becomes necessary. Do not use a replacement part of lesser quality or substitute design. Torque values must be used as specified during reassembly to make sure of correct retention of these parts.

1. Before servicing the vehicle, refer to the precautions section.
2. Remove the wheel bearing and wheel hub assembly.

3. Remove the parking brake shoes.
4. Remove the brake disc shield.
5. Compress the spring and depress the retaining tabs and detach the parking brake cable from the wheel knuckle.
6. Remove and discard the upper arm-to-wheel knuckle nut
7. Using the special tool, separate the upper arm from the wheel knuckle.
8. Remove and discard the lower ball joint nut.
9. Using the special tool 204-592, separate the lower ball joint from the wheel knuckle
10. Remove and discard the 2 bolts and disconnect the lower trailing arm from the wheel knuckle.
11. Remove and discard the bolt and disconnect the toe link from the wheel knuckle.

➡**Use the hex holding feature to prevent the stud from turning while removing the nut.**

12. Remove the upper trailing arm-to-wheel knuckle bolt and the wheel knuckle. Discard the bolt.

✳✳ WARNING

Do not tighten the upper arm-to wheel knuckle bolt or the toe link-to-wheel knuckle bolt until the installation procedure is complete and the weight of the vehicle is resting on the wheel and tire assemblies.

To install:

13. To install, reverse the removal procedure and note the following:

a. Tighten upper arm-to-wheel knuckle nut to 76 ft. lbs. (103 Nm).

b. Tighten the lower ball joint nut to 111 ft. lbs. (150 Nm).

c. Tighten the lower trailing arm from the wheel knuckle bolts to 76 ft. lbs. (103 Nm).

d. Tighten the toe link-to-wheel knuckle bolt to 166 ft. lbs. (225 Nm).

e. Tighten the stabilizer bar link nut to 46 ft. lbs. (63 Nm).

f. Tighten the upper trailing arm-to-wheel knuckle bolt to 184 ft. lbs. (250 Nm).

14. Check and, if necessary, adjust the rear alignment.

WHEEL KNUCKLE BUSHING

REMOVAL & INSTALLATION

See Figures 167 through 170.

✳✳ WARNING

Do not tighten the upper trailing arm-to-knuckle bolt until the installation procedure is complete and the weight of the vehicle is resting on the wheel and tire assemblies.

1. Before servicing the vehicle, refer to the precautions section.

2. With the vehicle in NEUTRAL, position it on a hoist.

3. Remove and discard the upper trailing arm-to-wheel knuckle bolt.

4. Using the special tools 205-813, 204-608 and 204-034, remove the wheel knuckle bushing.

To install:

5. Clean and inspect the wheel knuckle bushing bore for damage or excessive wear.

6. Position the new wheel knuckle bushing with the larger void facing towards the upper trailing arm.

7. Install the special tools.

✳✳ WARNING

Do not use the forward forcing screw nut to install the bushing. The for-

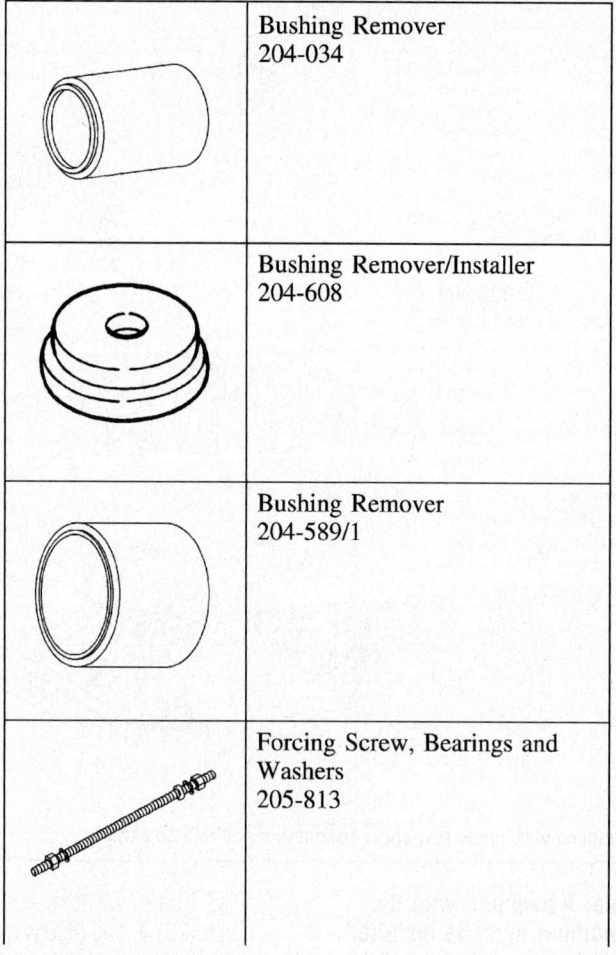

Special wheel knuckle bushing tools

	Bushing Remover 204-034
	Bushing Remover/Installer 204-608
	Bushing Remover 204-589/1
	Forcing Screw, Bearings and Washers 205-813

22086_EXPD_G0110

Fig. 167 Wheel knuckle bushing tools

ward forcing screw nut is only used to properly position and align the bushing for installation.

8. Hand tighten the forward forcing screw nut to align the bushing with the rearward side of the wheel knuckle bore.

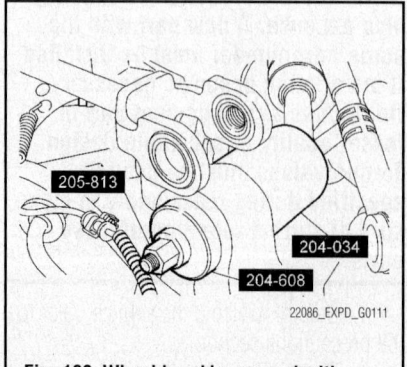

22086_EXPD_G0111

Fig. 168 Wheel knuckle removal with special tools

✳✳ WARNING

Use the rearward forcing screw nut to install the bushing or damage to the bushing and/or the wheel knuckle bushing bore can result.

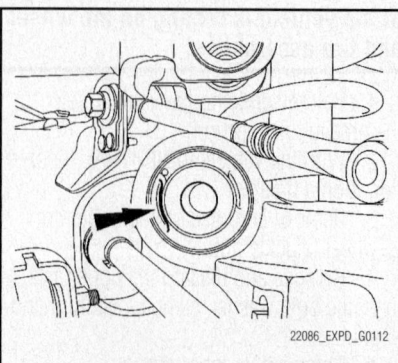

22086_EXPD_G0112

Fig. 169 Bushing with the larger void facing towards the upper trailing arm

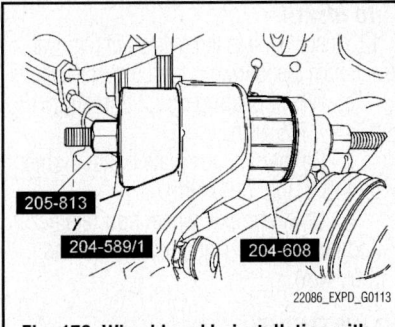

Fig. 170 Wheel knuckle installation with special tools

9. Tighten the rearward forcing screw nut and install the bushing until it is centered in the wheel knuckle.

➡**After installing the wheel knuckle bushing, make sure to**

measure the bushings position in the wheel knuckle bore. The measurement from the bushings outer metal surface to the machined face surface of knuckle bore should be **0.16 inch. (2.54 mm) +/– 0.01 inch. (0.25 mm).**

10. If necessary, use the special tool to adjust the bushing position in the wheel knuckle bushing bore.

11. Connect the upper trailing arm to the wheel knuckle.

12. Remove the jack stand from under the lower arm.

WHEEL HUB & BEARING

REMOVAL & INSTALLATION

See Figure 171.

✳✳ WARNING

The electrical power to the air suspension system must be shut off prior to hoisting, jacking or towing an air suspension vehicle. This can be accomplished by turning off the air suspension switch located in the left hand rear quarter trim panel. Failure to do so can result in unexpected inflation or deflation of the air springs, which can result in shifting of the vehicle during these operations.

1. Before servicing the vehicle, refer to the precautions section.
2. If equipped, turn the air suspension switch to the OFF position.
3. Remove the wheel and tire assembly.

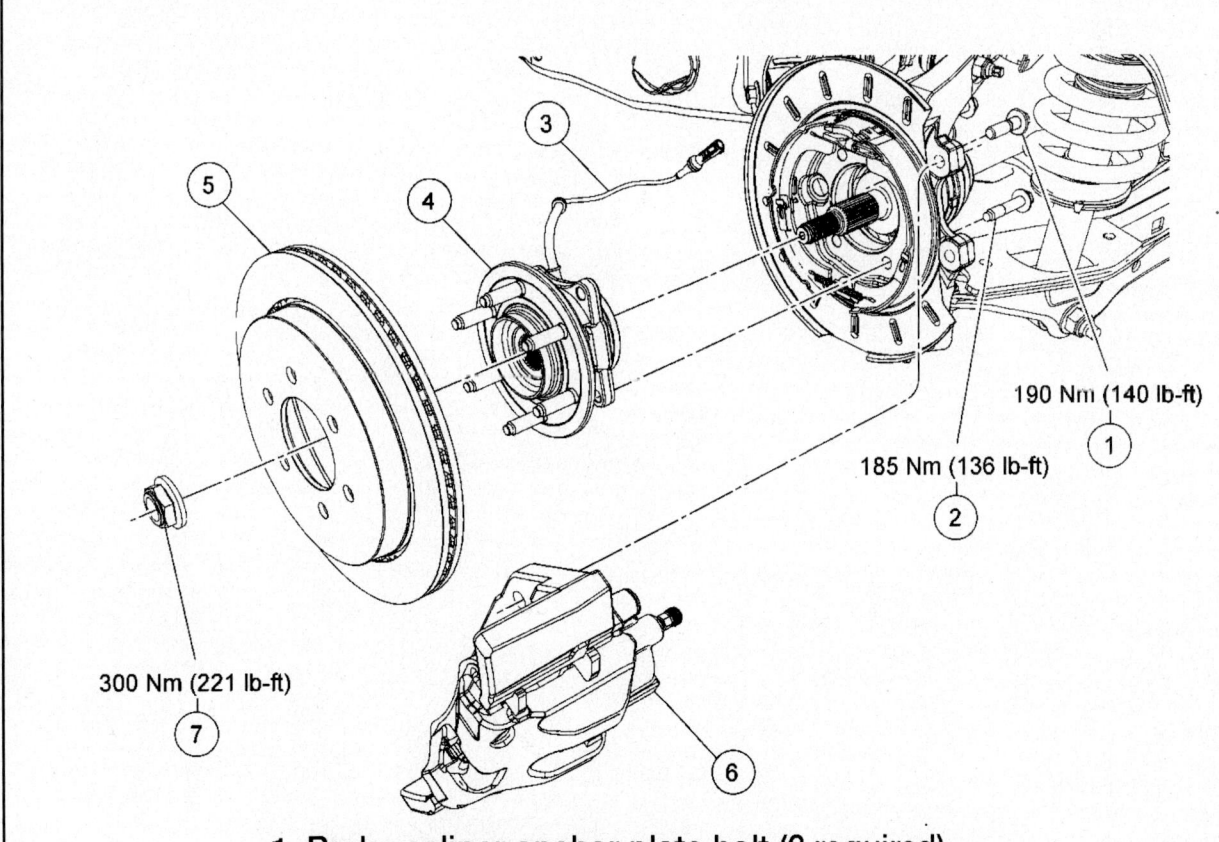

1. Brake caliper anchor plate bolt (2 required)
2. Wheel bearing and wheel hub bolt (4 required)
3. Rear wheel speed sensor bolt
4. Wheel bearing and wheel hub
5. Brake disc
6. Brake caliper and anchor plate assembly
7. Halfshaft nut

Fig. 171 Exploded view of the rear wheel bearing and wheel hub

➡**Have an assistant press the brake pedal to keep the axle from rotating.**

4. Remove and discard the rear axle wheel hub retainer and the washer.

5. Using a suitable hub puller, separate the outboard CV joint from the wheel hub.

✳✳ CAUTION

Do not allow the caliper to hang from the brake hose or damage to the hose can result.

6. Remove the caliper anchor plate bolts, and position the caliper, pads and anchor plate aside.

7. Remove the rotor.

8. Disconnect the wheel speed sensor electrical connector and detach the retainer.

9. Remove the bolt and detach brake line the retainers.

10. Remove the bolts, the wheel bearing and the wheel speed sensor as an assembly.

11. Route the sensor wiring through the access hole in the brake shield and discard the bolts.

To install:

12. Installation is the reverse of removal, please note the following torque specifications:

a. Wheel bearing bolts: tighten to 136 ft. lbs. (185 Nm).

b. Caliper anchor plate bolts: Tighten to 140 ft. lbs. (190 Nm).

c. New rear axle wheel hub retainer and the washer: Tighten to 221 ft. lbs. (300 Nm).

ADJUSTMENT

This is a sealed unit and no adjustment is required or possible.

FORD AND MERCURY

Explorer • Mountaineer • Sport Trac

7

SPECIFICATIONS AND MAINTENANCE CHARTS

ENGINE AND VEHICLE IDENTIFICATION

Engine							Model Year	
Code ①	Liters	Cu. In.	Cyl.	Fuel Sys.	Type	Eng. Mfg.	Code ②	Year
E	4.0	244	6	MFI	SOHC	Ford	8	2008
8	4.6	281	8	MFI	SOHC	Ford	9	2009

MFI: (Sequential) Multi-port Fuel Injection

SOHC: Single Overhead Camshaft

① 8th digit of the Vehicle Identification Number (VIN)

② 10th digit of the Vehicle Identification Number (VIN)

36578_EXPL_C0001

GENERAL ENGINE SPECIFICATIONS

Year	Model	Engine Displ. Liters	Engine VIN	Net Horsepower @ rpm	Net Torque @ rpm (ft. lbs.)	Bore x Stroke (in.)	Com- pression Ratio	Oil Pressure @ rpm
2008	Explorer/	4.0	E	210@5100	254@3700	3.95x3.32	9.7:1	15@2000
	Mountaineer	4.6	8	292@5700	315@4000	3.55x3.54	9.8:1	75@2000
2009	Explorer/	4.0	E	210@5100	254@3700	3.95x3.32	9.7:1	15@2000
	Mountaineer	4.6	8	292@5700	315@4000	3.55x3.54	9.8:1	75@2000

36578_EXPL_C0002

GASOLINE ENGINE TUNE-UP SPECIFICATIONS

Year	Engine Displacement Liters	Engine ID/VIN	Spark Plug Gap (in.)	Ignition Timing (deg.) ① MT	AT	Fuel Pressure (psi) ②	Idle Speed (rpm) MT	AT	Valve Clearance In.	Ex.
2008	4.0	K	0.052-0.056	—	10B	30-40	①	①	HYD	HYD
	4.6	8	0.039-0.043	—	10B	30-40	①	①	HYD	HYD
2009	4.0	K	0.052-0.056	—	10B	30-40	①	①	HYD	HYD
	4.6	8	0.039-0.043	—	10B	30-40	①	①	HYD	HYD

NOTE: The Vehicle Emission Control Information label often reflects specification changes changes made during production. The label figures must be used if they differ from those in this chart.

B: Before top dead center

HYD: Hydraulic

① Idle speed and ignition timing are electronically controlled and cannot be adjusted

② Key on; engine off

36578_EXPL_C0003

CAPACITIES

Year	Model	Engine Displ. Liters	Engine ID/VIN	Engine Oil with Filter (qts.)	Transmission (pts.) 5-Spd	Transmission (pts.) Auto. ①	Transfer Case (pts.)	Drive Axle Front (pts.)	Drive Axle Rear (pts.)	Fuel Tank (gal.)	Cooling System (qts.)
2008	Explorer/	4.0	K	5.0	—	①	3.0	2.70	3.50	22.5	②
	Mountaineer	4.6	8	6.5	—	①	3.0	2.70	3.50	22.5	③
2009	Explorer/	4.0	K	5.0	—	①	3.0	2.70	3.50	22.5	②
	Mountaineer	4.6	8	6.5	—	①	3.0	2.70	3.50	22.5	③

NOTE: All capacities are approximate. Add fluid gradually and check to be sure a proper fluid level is obtained.

① 5R55S A/T: 25.4 pts.
   6R80 A/T: 23.9 pts.

② w/o auxiliary heater: 12.2 qts.
   w/auxiliary heater: 14.0 qts.

③ w/o auxiliary heater: 14.0 qts.
   w/auxiliary heater: 15.7 qts.

36578_EXPL_C0004

FLUID SPECIFICATIONS

Year	Model	Engine Displacement Liters	Engine ID/VIN	Engine Oil	Auto. Trans. ①	Drive Axle	Power Steering Fluid	Brake Master Cylinder
2008	Explorer/	4.0L	K	5W-30	① ②	③	Mercon® V	DOT 3
	Mountaineer	4.6L	8	5W-20	① ②	③	Mercon® V	DOT 3
2009	Explorer/	4.0L	K	5W-30	① ②	③	Mercon® V	DOT 3
	Mountaineer	4.6L	8	5W-20	① ②	③	Mercon® V	DOT 3

DOT: Department Of Transpotation

① 5R55S: Mercon® V

② 6R80: Mercon® LV

③ Rear 75W-140 Synthetic Rear Axle Lubricant, Front 80W-90 Premium Lubricant

36578_EXPL_C0005

VALVE SPECIFICATIONS

Year	Engine Displ. Liters	Engine ID/VIN	Seat Angle (deg.)	Face Angle (deg.)	Spring Test Pressure (lbs. @ in.)	Spring Installed Height (in.)	Stem-to-Guide Clearance (in.) Intake	Stem-to-Guide Clearance (in.) Exhaust	Stem Diameter (in.) Intake	Stem Diameter (in.) Exhaust
2008	4.0	K	45	45	203-225@ 1.413-1.445	1.569-1.609	0.0010-0.0020	0.0010-0.0030	0.2740-0.2750	0.2730-0.2740
	4.6	8	44.5-45	45.5	163-179@ 1.22	1.660	0.0008-0.0027	0.0018-0.0037	0.2352-0.2360	0.2343-0.2351
2009	4.0	K	45	45	203-225@ 1.413-1.445	1.569-1.609	0.0010-0.0020	0.0010-0.0030	0.2740-0.2750	0.2730-0.2740
	4.6	8	44.5-45	45.5	163-179@ 1.22	1.660	0.0008-0.0027	0.0018-0.0037	0.2352-0.2360	0.2343-0.2351

36578_EXPL_C0006

CAMSHAFT AND BEARING SPECIFICATIONS CHART

All measurements are given in inches.

Year	Engine Displ. Liters	Engine VIN	Journal Dia.	Brg. Oil Clearance	Shaft End-play	Runout	Journal Bore	Lobe Height Intake	Lobe Height Exhaust
2008	4.0	K	1.099-1.101	0.002-0.004	0.003-0.007	0.002	1.102-1.104	0.259	0.259
	4.6	8	1.126-1.127	0.001-0.003	0.001-0.007	0.001	1.128-1.129	0.217	0.217
2009	4.0	K	1.099-1.101	0.002-0.004	0.003-0.007	0.002	1.102-1.104	0.259	0.259
	4.6	8	1.126-1.127	0.001-0.003	0.001-0.007	0.001	1.128-1.129	0.217	0.217

36578_EXPL_C0007

CRANKSHAFT AND CONNECTING ROD SPECIFICATIONS

All measurements are given in inches.

Year	Engine Displ. Liters	Engine ID/VIN	Crankshaft Main Brg. Journal Dia.	Crankshaft Main Brg. Oil Clearance	Crankshaft Shaft End-play	Crankshaft Thrust on No.	Connecting Rod Journal Diameter	Connecting Rod Oil Clearance	Connecting Rod Side Clearance
2008	4.0	K	2.2430-2.2440	0.0003-0.0024	0.0020-0.0126	3	2.1250-2.1260	0.0008-0.0012	0.0036-0.0125
	4.6	8	2.6567-2.6576	0.0009-0.0019	0.0030-0.0148	3	2.0859-2.0867	0.0009-0.0026	0.0060-0.0200
2009	4.0	K	2.2430-2.2440	0.0003-0.0024	0.0020-0.0126	3	2.1250-2.1260	0.0008-0.0012	0.0036-0.0125
	4.6	8	2.6567-2.6576	0.0009-0.0019	0.0030-0.0148	3	2.0859-2.0867	0.0009-0.0026	0.0060-0.0200

36578_EXPL_C0009

PISTON AND RING SPECIFICATIONS

All measurements are given in inches.

Year	Engine Displ. Liters	Engine ID/VIN	Piston Clearance	Ring Gap Top Compression	Ring Gap Bottom Compression	Ring Gap Oil Control	Ring Side Clearance Top Compression	Ring Side Clearance Bottom Compression	Ring Side Clearance Oil Control
2008	4.0	K	0.0012-0.0020	0.009-0.015	0.016-0.028	—	0.0016-0.0030	0.0012-0.0026	SNUG
	4.6	8	0.0007-0.0019	0.006-0.012	0.0098-0.0197	0.006-0.0256	0.0008-0.0020	0.0008-0.0020	SNUG
2009	4.0	K	0.0012-0.0020	0.009-0.015	0.016-0.028	—	0.0016-0.0030	0.0012-0.0026	SNUG
	4.6	8	0.0007-0.0019	0.006-0.012	0.0098-0.0197	0.006-0.0256	0.0008-0.0020	0.0008-0.0020	SNUG

36578_EXPL_C0008

TORQUE SPECIFICATIONS
All readings in ft. lbs.

Year	Engine Displ. Liters	Engine ID/VIN	Cylinder Head Bolts	Main Bearing Bolts	Rod Bearing Bolts	Crankshaft Damper Bolts	Flywheel Bolts	Manifold Intake *	Exhaust	Spark Plugs	Oil Pan Drain Plug
2008	4.0	K	①	72	②	③	④	8	16	13	19
	4.6	8	⑤	⑥	⑦	⑧	59	⑨	18	9	17
2008	4.0	K	①	72	②	③	④	8	16	13	19
	4.6	8	⑤	⑥	⑦	⑧	59	⑨	18	9	17

NA: Information not available

* NOTE: Applies to Lower Manifold only.

① Step 1: 12mm bolts: 9 ft. lbs.

Step 2: 12mm bolts: 18 ft. lbs.

Step 3: 8mm bolts: 24 ft. lbs.

Step 4: 12mm bolts: plus 90 degrees

Step 5: 12mm bolts: plus an additional 90 degrees

② Step 1: 15 ft. lbs.

Step 2: +90 degrees

③ Step 1: 41 ft. lbs.

Step 2: plus 85 degrees

④ Step 1: 37 ft. lbs.

Step 2: +90 degrees

⑤ Step 1: 30 ft. lbs.

Step 2: plus 90 degrees

Step 3: plus 90 additional degrees

⑥ Vertical Bolts:

Step 1: 30 ft. lbs.

Step 2: plus 90 degrees

Jack screws:

Step 1: 44 inch lbs.

Step 2: 89 inch lbs.

Cross bolts:

Step 1: 15 ft. lbs.

⑦ Step 1: 32 ft. lbs.

Step 2: plus 105 degrees

⑧ Step 1: 89 ft. lbs.

Step 2: back off 1 full turn

Step 3: 37 ft. lbs.

Step 4: plus 90 degrees

⑨ Step 1: 18 inch lbs.

Step 2: 89 inch lbs.

36578_EXPL_C0010

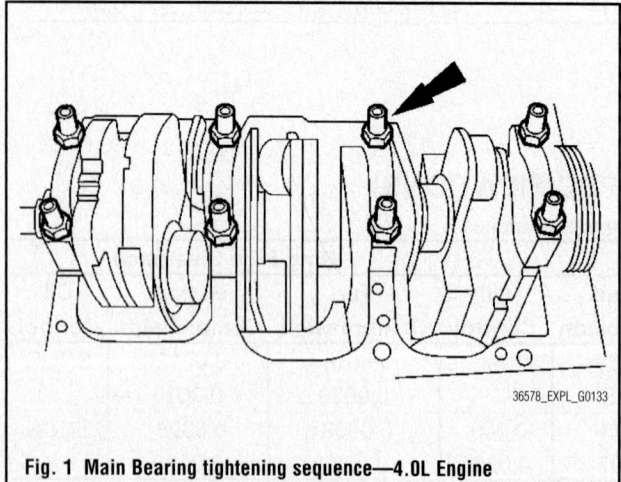

36578_EXPL_G0133

Fig. 1 Main Bearing tightening sequence—4.0L Engine

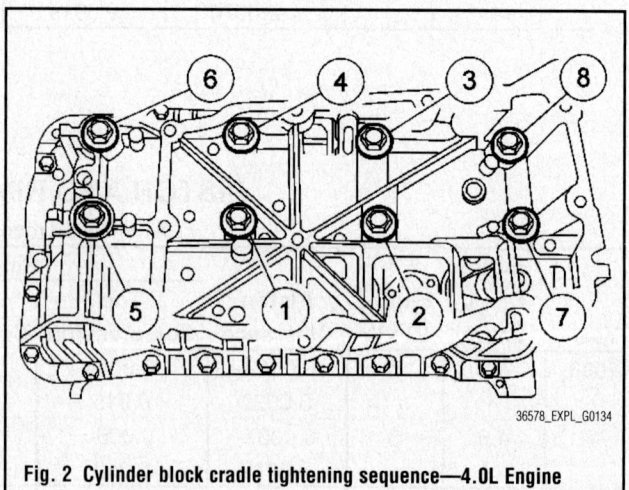

36578_EXPL_G0134

Fig. 2 Cylinder block cradle tightening sequence—4.0L Engine

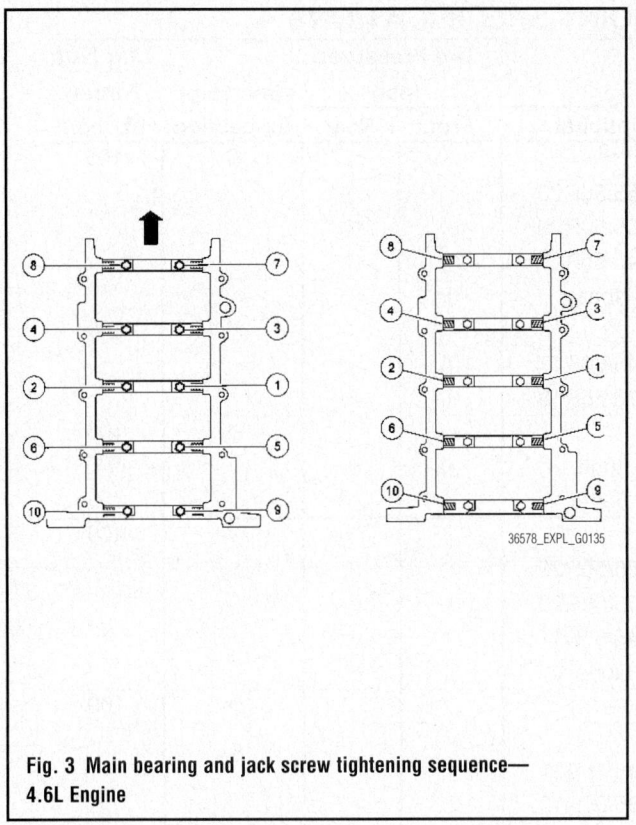

Fig. 3 Main bearing and jack screw tightening sequence—
4.6L Engine

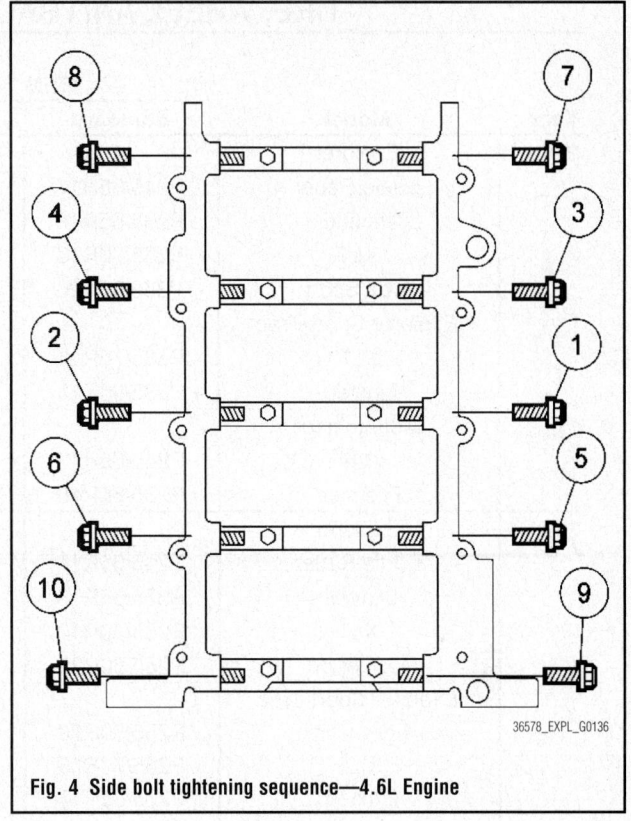

Fig. 4 Side bolt tightening sequence—4.6L Engine

WHEEL ALIGNMENT

Year	Model		Caster Range (+/-Deg.)	Caster Preferred Setting (Deg.)	Camber Range (+/-Deg.)	Camber Preferred Setting (Deg.)	Toe-in (in.)
2008	Explorer/	F	0.75	+4.6	0.75	-0.50	0.20+/-0.20
	Mountaineer	R	—	—	0.75	-0.50	0.10+/-0.20
	Sport Trac	F	0.75	RH +4.7, LH +4.5	0.75	-0.50	0.20+/-0.20
		R	—	—	0.75	-0.50	0.10+/-0.20
2009	Explorer/	F	0.75	+4.6	0.75	-0.50	0.20+/-0.20
	Mountaineer	R	—	—	0.75	-0.50	0.10+/-0.20
	Sport Trac	F	0.75	RH +4.7, LH +4.5	0.75	-0.50	0.20+/-0.20
		R	—	—	0.75	-0.50	0.10+/-0.20

36578_EXPL_C0012

TIRE, WHEEL AND BALL JOINT SPECIFICATIONS

Year	Model	OEM Tires Standard	OEM Tires Optional	Tire Pressures (psi) Front	Tire Pressures (psi) Rear	Ball Joint Inspection	Lug Nut Torque (ft. lbs.)
2008	Explorer					②	100
	Eddie Bauer	P245/65R17	P255/50R20	①	①		
	Limited	P235/65R18	P255/50R20	①	①		
	XLT	P235/70R16	P245/65R17	①	①		
	XLT Sport	P255/50R20	None	①	①		
	Explorer Sport-Trac					②	100
	XLT	P235/70R16	P245/65R17	①	①		
	Limited	P235/65R18	P235/65R18	①	①		
	Mountaineer					②	100
	V6	P245/65R17	none	①	①		
	Premier	P235/65R18	none	①	①		
2009	Explorer					②	100
	Eddie Bauer	P245/65R17	P255/50R20	①	①		
	Limited	P235/65R18	P255/50R20	①	①		
	XLT	P235/70R16	P245/65R17	①	①		
	XLT Sport	P255/50R20	None	①	①		
	Explorer Sport-Trac					②	100
	Adrenalin	P255/50R20					
	XLT	P235/70R16	P245/65R17	①	①		
	Limited	P235/65R18	P235/65R18	①	①		
	Mountaineer					②	100
	V6	P245/65R17	none	①	①		
	Premier	P235/65R18	none	①	①		

NS: Information not specified

OEM: Original Equipment Manufacturer

PSI: Pounds Per Square Inch

STD: Standard

OPT: Optional

① See placard on vehicle

② Upper: 0.008"; Lower: 0.32"

36578_EXPL_C0013

BRAKE SPECIFICATIONS

All measurements in inches unless noted

Year	Model		Brake Disc Original Thickness	Brake Disc Min. Thickness	Brake Disc Max. Runout	Brake Drum Diameter Original Inside Dia.	Brake Drum Diameter Max. Wear Limit	Brake Drum Diameter Max. Machine Dia.	Minimum Lining Thickness	Brake Caliper Bracket Bolts (ft. lbs.)	Brake Caliper Mounting Bolts (ft. lbs.)
2008	Explorer/	F	NA	1.122	NS	—	—	—	0.118	122	53
	Mountaineer	R	NA	0.433	NS	—	—	—	0.118	—	24
2009	Explorer/	F	NA	1.122	NS	—	—	—	0.118	122	53
	Mountaineer	R	NA	0.433	NS	—	—	—	0.118	—	24

NS: Information not supplied

36578_EXPL_C0011

SCHEDULED MAINTENANCE INTERVALS
Ford Explorer/Sport Trac and Mercury Mountaineer

TO BE SERVICED	TYPE OF SERVICE	VEHICLE MILEAGE INTERVAL (x1000)												
		7.5	15	22.5	30	37.5	45	52.5	60	67.5	75	82.5	90	97.5
Air cleaner filter	R				✓				✓				✓	
Auto. Trans. fluid level	I		✓		✓		✓		✓		✓		✓	
Auto. Trans. Fluid ①	R								✓					
Accessory drive belt ②	I	Every 150,000 miles												
Cabin air filter	R		✓		✓		✓		✓		✓		✓	
Cooling system hoses and clamps	S/I		✓		✓		✓		✓		✓		✓	
Driveshafts & halfshafts	S/I		✓		✓		✓		✓		✓		✓	
Engine coolant	R	At 6 years or 105,000 miles; then every 3 years or 45,000 miles												
Engine oil & filter	R	Every 7,500 miles												
Exhaust system & heat shields	I		✓		✓		✓		✓		✓		✓	
Fuel filter	R				✓				✓				✓	
Tires	Rotate	Every 7,500 miles												
Steering linkage	S/I		✓		✓		✓		✓		✓		✓	
Spark plugs	R	Every 90,000 miles												
Suspension components and ball joints ③	S/I		✓		✓		✓		✓		✓		✓	
Multi-Point inspection	④	✓	✓	✓	✓	✓	✓	✓	✓	✓	✓	✓	✓	✓

R: Replace   S/I: Inspect and service, if necessary   L: Lubricate   A: Adjust   C: Clean

① TorqShift fluid and filter change at 60,000 miles, if not previously done

② Replace at 150,000 miles, if not previously done

③ Replace front bearing grease and seal on RWD vehicles at 60,000 miles.

④ Inspect the reservoir fluid level, rotor and or drum, brake lines, hoses, calipers and or wheel cylinders

Monthly Checks

Check each of the following items every month:

    All interior and exterior lights

    Tires for wear and correct air pressure, including spare tire

    Engine oil fluid level

    Windshield washer solvent fluid level

Six Month Checks

Check each of the following items at least every 6 months:

    Lap/shoulder belts and seat latches for wear and function

    External mounted spare is stowed correctly (tight to body)

    Parking brake for correct operation

    Safety warning lamps (brake, ABS, air bag, safety belt) for correct operation

    Engine coolant system fluid level and correct strength

    Power steering fluid

    Battery 12-volt connections. Clean if necessary

    Windshield washer spray, wiper operation, clean all wiper blades

    Lubricate all hinges, latches and outside locks. Inspect for correct operation

    Lubricate door rubber weatherstrips. Inspect for excessive wear

    Clean body and door drain holes. Inspect for clogs and obstructions

36578_EXPL_C0014

SCHEDULED MAINTENANCE INTERVALS
2008-09 Ford Explorer/Sport Trac and Mercury Mountaineer

④ **Multi-Point inspection**

The following inspections are recommended at every service interval:

Check and top off brake, coolant, manual and automatic transmission fluid power steering and washer fluid

Inspect tires for wear and correct air pressure, including spare tire

Check exhaust system for leaks, damage, loose parts and foreign material

Check battery performance

Check operation of horn, exterior lamps, turn signals and hazard warning lights

Check radiator, coolers, heater and air conditioning hoses

Inspect windshield wiper spray and wiper operation

Check windshield for cracks, chips and pitting

Inspect for oil and fluid leaks

Inspect air filter

Inspect halfshaft dust boots

Check shocks struts and other suspension components for leaks and damage

Inspect steering linkage

Inspect accessory drive belts

When operating in dusty conditions such as unpaved or dusty roads:

Change engine oil and install a new oil filter every 8,000 km (5,000 miles) or 6 months.

Install a new fuel filter every 24,000 km (15,000 miles).

Rotate tires every 8,000 km (5,000 miles) or 6 months.

Inspect and lubricate control arms, steering linkage, and drivetrain zerk fittings every 8,000 km (5,000 miles) or 6 months.

Change non-TorqShift automatic transmission fluid every 48,000 km (30,000 miles).

Change transfer case fluid every 96,000 km (60,000 miles).

Install a new engine air filter as required.

Replace wheel bearing grease and seals every 48,000 km (30,000 miles).

Install a new cabin air filter as required.

When operating in off-road conditions:

Change engine oil and install a new oil filter every 8,000 km (5,000 miles) or 6 months.

Rotate tires every 8,000 km (5,000 miles) or 6 months.

Inspect and lubricate control arms, steering linkage, and drivetrain zerk fittings every 8,000 km (5,000 miles) or 6 months.

Change non-TorqShift automatic transmission fluid every 48,000 km (30,000 miles). (not required on 6R60/6R75 transmissions).

Change transfer case fluid every 96,000 km (60,000 miles).

Replace wheel bearing grease and seals every 48,000 km (30,000 miles).

Install a new cabin air filter as required.

Inspect and lubricate steering linkage ball joints with zerk fittings.

Special Operating Condition Requirements

When towing a trailer or using a camper or car-top carrier:

Change engine oil and install a new oil filter every 8,000 km (5,000 miles) or 3 months.

Change non-TorqShift automatic transmission fluid every 48,000 km (30,000 miles). (not required on 6R60/6R75 transmissions).

Inspect and rotate tires 8,000 km (5,000 miles)

Change transfer case fluid every 96,000 km (60,000 miles).

Inspect and lubricate steering linkage ball joints with zerk fittings.

During extensive idling and/or low speed driving for long distances, as in heavy commercial use such as delivery, taxi, patrol car or livery:

Change engine oil and install a new oil filter every 8,000 km (5,000 miles) or 6 months.

Install a new fuel filter every 24,000 km (15,000 miles).

Rotate tires every 8,000 km (5,000 miles) or 6 months.

Inspect and lubricate control arms, steering linkage, and drivetrain zerk fittings every 8,000 km (5,000 miles) or 6 months.

Change non-TorqShift automatic transmission fluid every 48,000 km (30,000 miles).

Change transfer case fluid every 96,000 km (60,000 miles).

Replace wheel bearing grease and seals every 48,000 km (30,000 miles).

Install a new cabin air filter as required.

PRECAUTIONS

Before servicing any vehicle, please be sure to read all of the following precautions, which deal with personal safety, prevention of component damage, and important points to take into consideration when servicing a motor vehicle:

• Never open, service or drain the radiator or cooling system when the engine is hot; serious burns can occur from the steam and hot coolant.

• Observe all applicable safety precautions when working around fuel. Whenever servicing the fuel system, always work in a well-ventilated area. Do not allow fuel spray or vapors to come in contact with a spark, open flame, or excessive heat (a hot drop light, for example). Keep a dry chemical fire extinguisher near the work area. Always keep fuel in a container specifically designed for fuel storage; also, always properly seal fuel containers to avoid the possibility of fire or explosion. Refer to the additional fuel system precautions later in this section.

• Fuel injection systems often remain pressurized, even after the engine has been turned **OFF**. The fuel system pressure must be relieved before disconnecting any fuel lines. Failure to do so may result in fire and/or personal injury.

• Brake fluid often contains polyglycol ethers and polyglycols. Avoid contact with the eyes and wash your hands thoroughly after handling brake fluid. If you do get brake fluid in your eyes, flush your eyes with clean, running water for 15 minutes. If eye irritation persists, or if you have taken

brake fluid internally, IMMEDIATELY seek medical assistance.

• The EPA warns that prolonged contact with used engine oil may cause a number of skin disorders, including cancer. You should make every effort to minimize your exposure to used engine oil. Protective gloves should be worn when changing oil. Wash your hands and any other exposed skin areas as soon as possible after exposure to used engine oil. Soap and water, or waterless hand cleaner should be used.

• All new vehicles are now equipped with an air bag system, often referred to as a Supplemental Restraint System (SRS) or Supplemental Inflatable Restraint (SIR) system. The system must be disabled before performing service on or around system components, steering column, instrument panel components, wiring and sensors. Failure to follow safety and disabling procedures could result in accidental air bag deployment, possible personal injury and unnecessary system repairs.

• Always wear safety goggles when working with, or around, the air bag system. When carrying a non-deployed air bag, be sure the bag and trim cover are pointed away from your body. When placing a non-deployed air bag on a work surface, always face the bag and trim cover upward, away from the surface. This will reduce the motion of the module if it is accidentally deployed. Refer to the additional air bag system precautions later in this section.

• Clean, high quality brake fluid from a sealed container is essential to the safe and

proper operation of the brake system. You should always buy the correct type of brake fluid for your vehicle. If the brake fluid becomes contaminated, completely flush the system with new fluid. Never reuse any brake fluid. Any brake fluid that is removed from the system should be discarded. Also, do not allow any brake fluid to come in contact with a painted surface; it will damage the paint.

• Never operate the engine without the proper amount and type of engine oil; doing so WILL result in severe engine damage.

• Timing belt maintenance is extremely important. Many models utilize an interference-type, non-freewheeling engine. If the timing belt breaks, the valves in the cylinder head may strike the pistons, causing potentially serious (also time-consuming and expensive) engine damage. Refer to the maintenance interval charts for the recommended replacement interval for the timing belt, and to the timing belt section for belt replacement and inspection.

• Disconnecting the negative battery cable on some vehicles may interfere with the functions of the on-board computer system(s) and may require the computer to undergo a relearning process once the negative battery cable is reconnected.

• When servicing drum brakes, only disassemble and assemble one side at a time, leaving the remaining side intact for reference.

• Only an MVAC-trained, EPA-certified automotive technician should service the air conditioning system or its components.

BRAKES

ANTI-LOCK BRAKE SYSTEM (ABS)

GENERAL INFORMATION

PRECAUTIONS

• Certain components within the ABS system are not intended to be serviced or repaired individually.

• Do not use rubber hoses or other parts not specifically specified for and ABS system. When using repair kits, replace all parts included in the kit. Partial or incorrect repair may lead to functional problems and require the replacement of components.

• Lubricate rubber parts with clean, fresh brake fluid to ease assembly. Do not use shop air to clean parts; damage to rubber components may result.

• Use only DOT 3 brake fluid from an unopened container.

• If any hydraulic component or line is

removed or replaced, it may be necessary to bleed the entire system.

• A clean repair area is essential. Always clean the reservoir and cap thoroughly before removing the cap. The slightest amount of dirt in the fluid may plug an orifice and impair the system function. Perform repairs after components have been thoroughly cleaned; use only denatured alcohol to clean components. Do not allow ABS components to come into contact with any substance containing mineral oil; this includes used shop rags.

• The Anti-Lock control unit is a microprocessor similar to other computer units in the vehicle. Ensure that the ignition switch is **OFF** before removing or installing controller harnesses. Avoid static electricity discharge at or near the controller.

• If any arc welding is to be done on the vehicle, the control unit should be unplugged before welding operations begin.

WHEEL SPEED SENSORS

REMOVAL & INSTALLATION

Front

See Figure 5.

1. Remove the front brake disc. See Rotor in Front Disc Brakes.
2. Disconnect the wheel speed sensor electrical connector.
3. Remove the wheel speed sensor harness bolt.
4. Remove the wheel speed sensor harness pin-type retainers.
5. Remove the wheel speed sensor bolt.

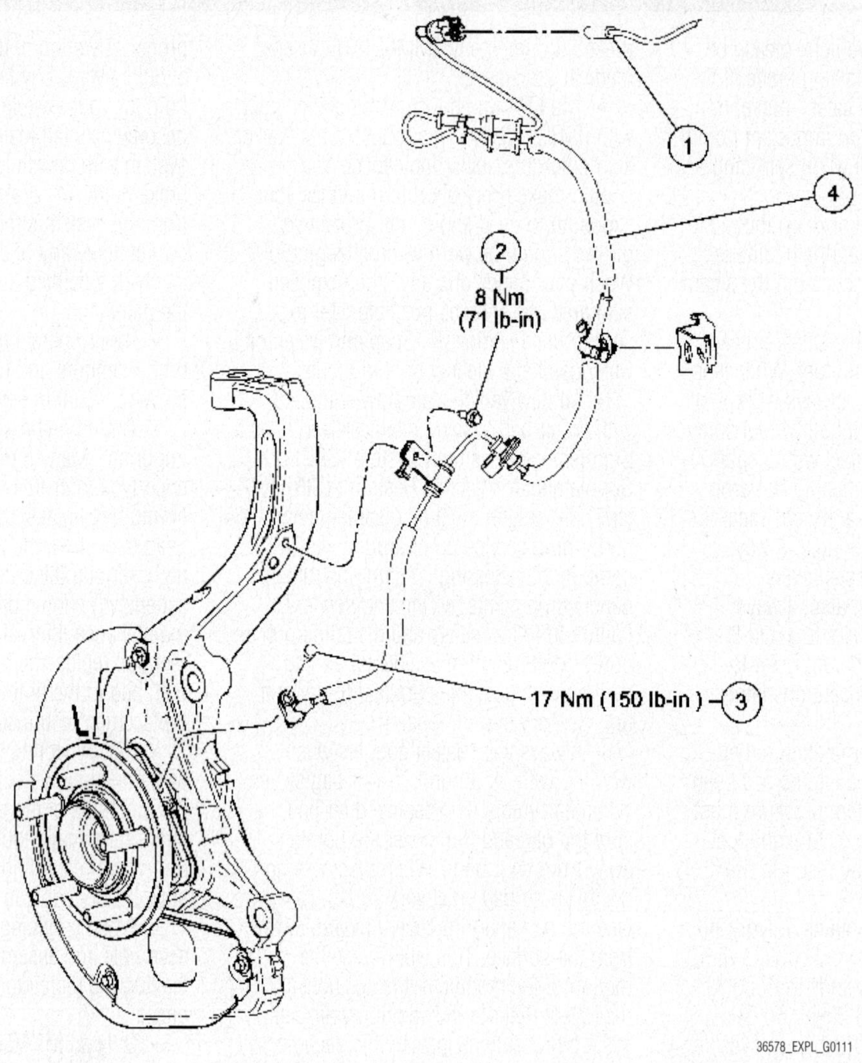

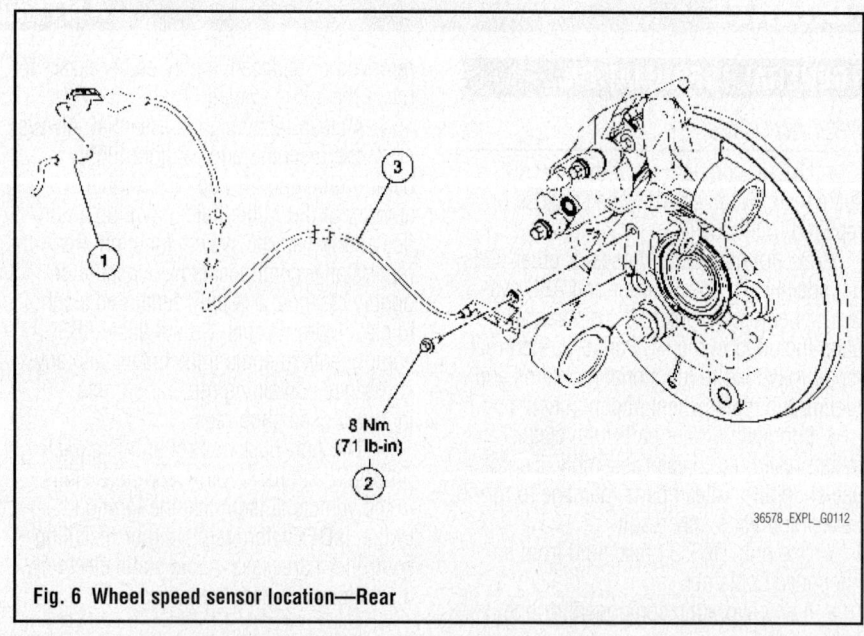

Fig. 5 Wheel speed sensor location—Front

6. Remove the wheel speed sensor and the harness.

To install:

7. Installation is the reverse of the removal procedure, tighten the wheel speed sensor bolt to 13 ft. lbs. (17 Nm).

Rear

See Figure 6.

1. With the vehicle in NEUTRAL, position it on a hoist.

2. Disconnect the wheel speed sensor electrical connector.

3. Disconnect the wheel speed harness from the retainers.

4. Remove the wheel speed sensor bolt and the wheel speed sensor.

To install:

5. Installation is the reverse of the removal procedure.

Fig. 6 Wheel speed sensor location—Rear

BRAKES   **BLEEDING THE BRAKE SYSTEM**

BLEEDING PROCEDURE

1. Before servicing, refer to Precautions.

> **※※ WARNING**
>
> **Do not allow the brake master cylinder reservoir to run dry during the bleeding operation. Keep the brake master cylinder reservoir filled with the specified brake fluid. Never reuse brake fluid that has been drained from the hydraulic system.**

> **※※ WARNING**
>
> **Brake fluid is harmful to painted and plastic surfaces. If brake fluid is spilled onto a painted or plastic surface, immediately wash it with water.**

When any part of the hydraulic system has been disconnected for repair or replacement, air may get into the lines and cause spongy pedal action (because air can be compressed and brake fluid cannot). To correct this condition, it is necessary to bleed the hydraulic system after it has been properly connected to be sure all air is expelled from the brake cylinders and lines.

When bleeding the brake system, bleed one brake cylinder at a time, beginning at the cylinder with the longest hydraulic line (farthest from the master cylinder) first. ALWAYS Keep the master cylinder reservoir filled with brake fluid during the bleeding operation. Never use brake fluid that has been drained from the hydraulic system, no matter how clean it is.

It will be necessary to centralize the pressure differential value after a brake system failure has been corrected and the hydraulic system has been bled.

The primary and secondary hydraulic brake systems are individual systems and are bled separately. During the entire bleeding operation, do not allow the reservoir to run dry. Keep the master cylinder reservoir filled with brake fluid.

Master Cylinder Bleeding

See Figure 7.

➡**When a new brake master cylinder has been installed or the system has been emptied or partially emptied, it should be primed to prevent air from getting into the system.**

1. Disconnect the brake master cylinder tubes from the side of the master cylinder.

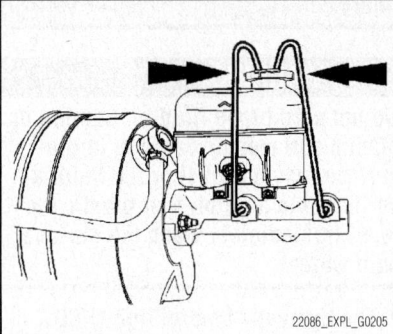

22086_EXPL_G0205

Fig. 7 Install the 2 short brake tubes with the ends submerged in the brake master cylinder reservoir and fill the brake master cylinder reservoir with DOT 3 motor vehicle brake fluid

➡**Original equipment lines are not intended to be used during this procedure.**

2. Install the 2 short brake tubes with the ends submerged in the brake master cylinder reservoir and fill the brake master cylinder reservoir with DOT 3 motor vehicle brake fluid.

3. Have an assistant pump the brake pedal until clear fluid flows from both brake tubes without air bubbles.

4. Remove the 2 short brake tubes and install the 2 master cylinder brake tube fittings.

5. Bleed each brake tube at the brake master cylinder as follows:

   a. Have an assistant pump the brake pedal and then hold firm pressure on the brake pedal.

   b. Loosen the rear brake tube fittings until a stream of brake fluid comes out. Have an assistant maintain pressure on the brake pedal while tightening the brake tube fitting.

   c. Repeat this operation until clear, bubble-free fluid comes out.

   d. Refill the brake master cylinder reservoir as necessary. REPEAT the bleeding operation at the front brake tube.

6. While the assistant maintains pressure on the brake pedal, tighten the master cylinder brake tubes to 13 ft. lbs. (18 Nm).

Brake Caliper Bleeding

See Figure 8.

➡**It is not necessary to bleed the entire brake system. It is possible to bleed only the opened part of the system.**

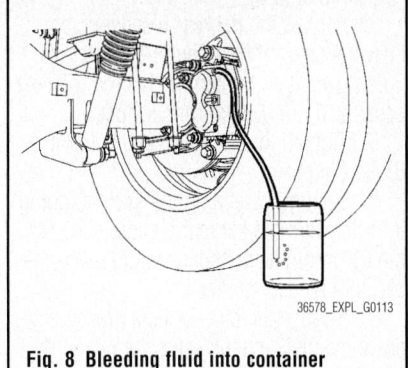

36578_EXPL_G0113

Fig. 8 Bleeding fluid into container

1. Connect one end of a clear flexible hose to the bleeder screw. Submerge the other end in a container partially filled with the specified brake fluid.

2. Have an assistant pump the brake pedal and then hold firm pressure on the brake pedal.

3. Open the caliper bleeder screw until brake fluid flows into the container.

4. When fluid stops flowing, close the bleeder screw. Tighten to 97 inch lbs. (11 Nm) for the front brake bleeder screw and 16 ft. lbs. (22 Nm) for the rear brake bleeder screw.

5. Repeat the previous steps until there are no air bubbles in the brake fluid.

Pressure Bleeding

➡**Pressure bleeding the brake system is preferred to manual bleeding.**

1. Clean all dirt from and remove the brake master cylinder filler cap and fill the brake master cylinder reservoir with clean, specified brake fluid.

➡**Master cylinder pressure bleeder adapter tools are available from various manufacturers of pressure bleeding equipment. Follow the instructions of the equipment manufacturer when installing the adapter.**

2. Install the bleeder adapter to the brake master cylinder reservoir and attach the bleeder tank hose to the fitting on the adapter.

➡**Make sure the bleeder tank contains enough clean, specified brake fluid to complete the bleeding operation.**

3. Remove the RH rear bleeder cap and place a box-end wrench on the bleeder screw. Attach a rubber drain tube to the RH rear bleeder screw and submerge the free end of the tube in a container partially filled with clean, specified brake fluid.

4. Open the valve on the bleeder tank.
   a. Set pressure to 30-50 psi (207-345 kPa).

5. Loosen the RH rear bleeder screw. Leave open until clear, bubble-free brake fluid flows, then tighten the RH rear bleeder screw and remove the rubber hose.

6. Tighten to specifications. Refer to Brake Caliper.

7. Continue bleeding the system, going in order from the LH rear bleeder screw to the RH front bleeder screw ending with the LH front bleeder screw.

8. Release the bleeder tank pressure and close the bleeder tank valve. Remove the tank hose from the adapter and remove the adapter from the brake fluid reservoir.

Manual Bleeding

> ## ✶✶ CAUTION
>
> **Do not allow the brake master cylinder to run dry during the bleeding operation. Master cylinder may be damaged if operated without fluid, resulting in degraded braking perfor-**

mance. Failure to follow this instruction may result in serious personal injury.

> ## ✶✶ WARNING
>
> **Do not spill brake fluid on painted or plastic surfaces or damage to the surface may occur. If brake fluid is spilled onto a painted or plastic surface, immediately wash the surface with water.**

➡ The Hydraulic Control Unit (HCU) bleeding procedure must be carried out if the HCU or any components upstream of the HCU are installed new.

➡ Pressure bleeding the brake system is preferred to manual bleeding.

1. Clean all dirt from and remove the brake master cylinder filler cap and fill the brake master cylinder reservoir with clean, specified brake fluid.

2. Remove the bleeder screw cap and place a box-end wrench on the RH rear

bleeder screw. Attach a rubber drain hose to the RH rear bleeder screw and submerge the free end of the hose in a container partially filled with clean, specified brake fluid.

3. Have an assistant pump the brake pedal at least 3 times and then hold firm pressure on the brake pedal.

4. Loosen the RH rear bleeder screw until a stream of brake fluid comes out. While the assistant maintains pressure on the brake pedal, tighten the RH rear bleeder screw.

5. Repeat until clear, bubble-free fluid comes out.

6. Refill the brake master cylinder reservoir as necessary.

7. Remove the rubber hose and tighten the bleeder screw to specifications. Refer to Brake Caliper.

8. Install the bleeder screw cap.

9. Repeat Steps 2 through 5 for the LH rear, RH front and LH front bleeder screws in this order.

BLEEDING THE ABS SYSTEM

Refer to Bleeding the Brake System.

BRAKES

BRAKE CALIPER

REMOVAL & INSTALLATION

See Figure 9.

1. Before servicing the vehicle, refer to Precautions.

2. With the vehicle in NEUTRAL, position it on a hoist.

3. Remove the front wheels.

4. Remove the brake hose flow bolt and position the brake hose aside. Discard the 2 copper washers. Cap the fluid ports.

5. Remove the 2 brake caliper bolts and the brake caliper.

> ## ✶✶ WARNING
>
> **Do not pry in the brake caliper sight hole to retract the pistons as this can damage the pistons and boots.**

6. If leaks or damaged boots are found, install a new brake caliper.

To install:

7. Position the brake caliper and install the 2 bolts. Tighten the bottom locator pin brake caliper bolt before tightening the top guide pin brake caliper bolt. Torque the bolts to 53 ft. lbs. (72 Nm).

8. Using 2 new copper washers, position the brake hose and install the brake hose flow bolt. Tighten the bolt to 26 ft. lbs. (35 Nm).

FRONT DISC BRAKES

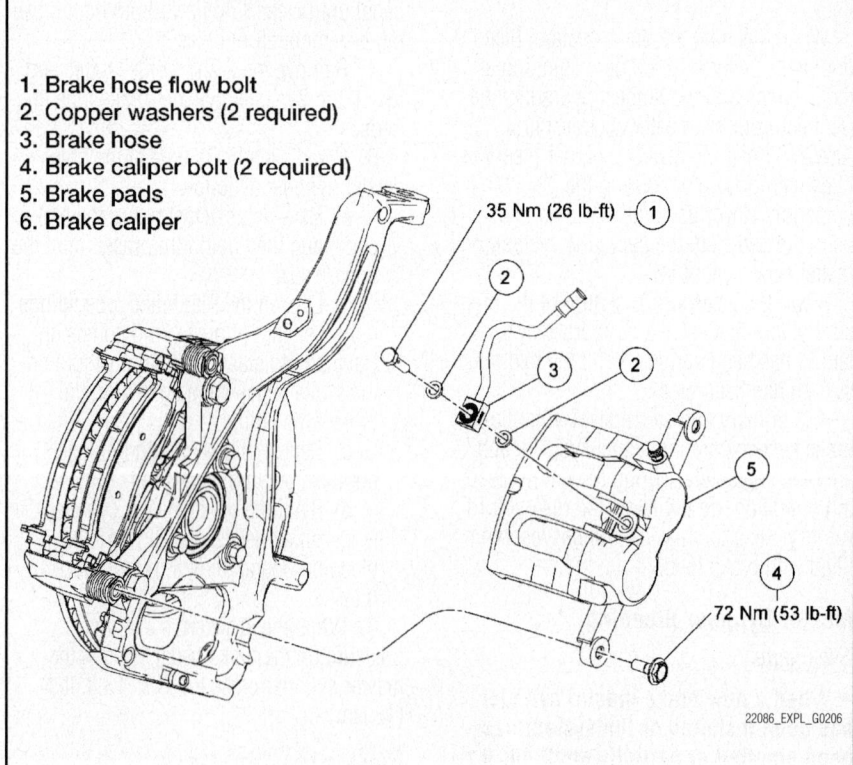

1. Brake hose flow bolt
2. Copper washers (2 required)
3. Brake hose
4. Brake caliper bolt (2 required)
5. Brake pads
6. Brake caliper

35 Nm (26 lb-ft) — 1

72 Nm (53 lb-ft)

22086_EXPL_G0206

Fig. 9 Showing the brake caliper mounting, brake hose bolt (1), washer (2), hose connection (3), caliper bolts (4) and the brake caliper (5)

9. Bleed the brake caliper. Refer to Bleeding the Brake System.

10. Install the wheels and lower the vehicle.

11. Test the brake system for normal operation.

DISC BRAKE PADS

REMOVAL & INSTALLATION

See Figure 10.

➡**Install new brake pads if they are worn past the specified thickness above the metal backing plate or rivets. Install new brake pads in complete axle sets.**

1. Before servicing the vehicle, refer to the Precautions.

2. Remove brake fluid in the master cylinder reservoir until the reservoir is half full.

3. Raise and support the vehicle.

4. Remove the wheel and tire assembly.

5. Remove the 2 brake caliper bolts and position the brake caliper aside. Support the caliper using mechanic's wire.

6. Inspect the brake pads for wear and contamination.

7. Inspect the brake disc, machine or install a new front brake disc as necessary.

8. Remove the brake pads and clips. Discard the clips.

To install:

9. Install the new brake pad clips and the brake pads.

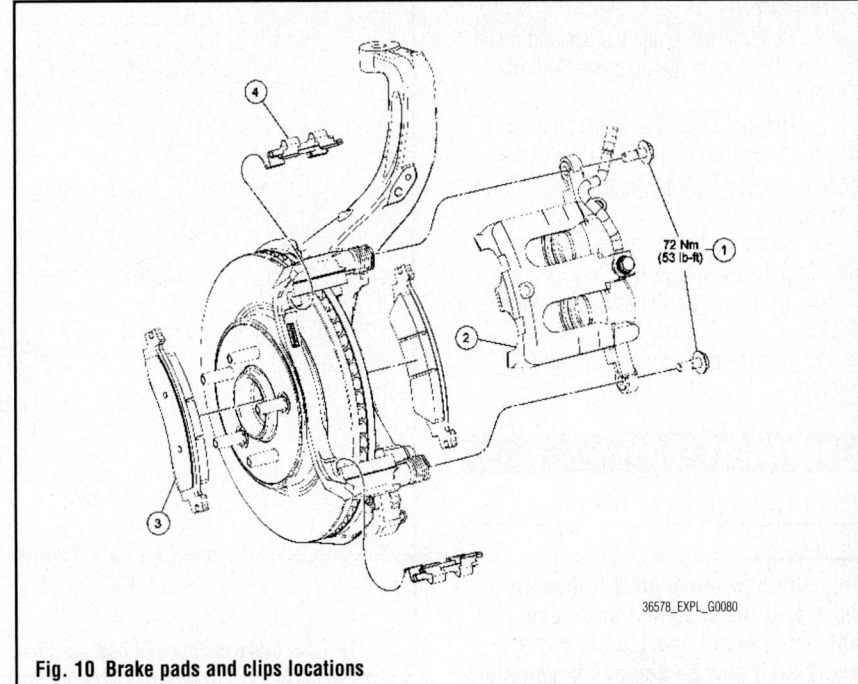

Fig. 10 Brake pads and clips locations

✳✳ WARNING

Protect the piston and boots when pushing the caliper piston into the caliper piston bores.

10. Using a suitable tool (C-clamp) and a worn brake pad, compress the disc brake caliper pistons into the caliper.

11. Position the brake caliper and install the 2 bolts. Tighten the lower bolt and then the upper bolt to 53 ft. lbs. (72 Nm).

12. Install the wheel and tire assembly and lower the vehicle.

13. Fill the brake master cylinder reservoir with clean brake fluid.

14. Test the brakes for normal operation.

BRAKES

REAR DISC BRAKES

BRAKE CALIPER

REMOVAL & INSTALLATION

See Figure 11.

1. Before servicing the vehicle, refer to Precautions.

2. With the vehicle in NEUTRAL, position it on a hoist.

3. Remove the rear wheels.

4. Remove the brake hose flow bolt and position the brake hose aside. Discard the 2 copper washers. Cap the fluid ports.

5. Remove the 2 brake caliper bolts and the brake caliper.

✳✳ WARNING

Do not pry in the brake caliper sight hole to retract the pistons as this can damage the pistons and boots.

6. If leaks or damaged boots are found, install a new brake caliper.

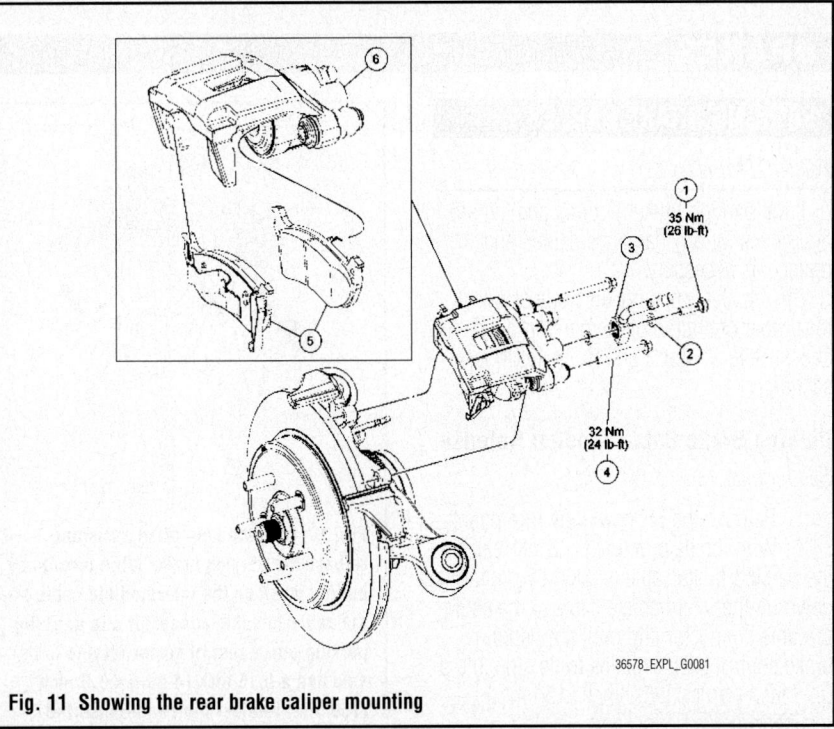

Fig. 11 Showing the rear brake caliper mounting

To install:

7. Position the brake caliper and install the 2 bolts. Torque the bolts to 24 ft. lbs. (32 Nm).

8. Using 2 new copper washers, position the brake hose and install the brake hose flow bolt. Tighten the bolt to 26 ft. lbs. (35 Nm).

9. Bleed the brake caliper. Refer to Bleeding the Brake System.

10. Install the wheels and lower the vehicle.

11. Test the brake system for normal operation.

DISC BRAKE PADS

REMOVAL & INSTALLATION

See Figure 12.

➡ **Install new brake pads if they are worn past the specified thickness above the metal backing plate or rivets. Install new brake pads in complete axle sets.**

1. Before servicing the vehicle, refer to the Precautions.

2. Remove brake fluid in the master cylinder reservoir until the reservoir is half full.

3. Raise and support the vehicle.

4. Remove the wheel and tire assembly.

5. Remove the 2 brake caliper bolts and position the brake caliper aside. Support the caliper using mechanic's wire.

6. Inspect the brake pads for wear and contamination.

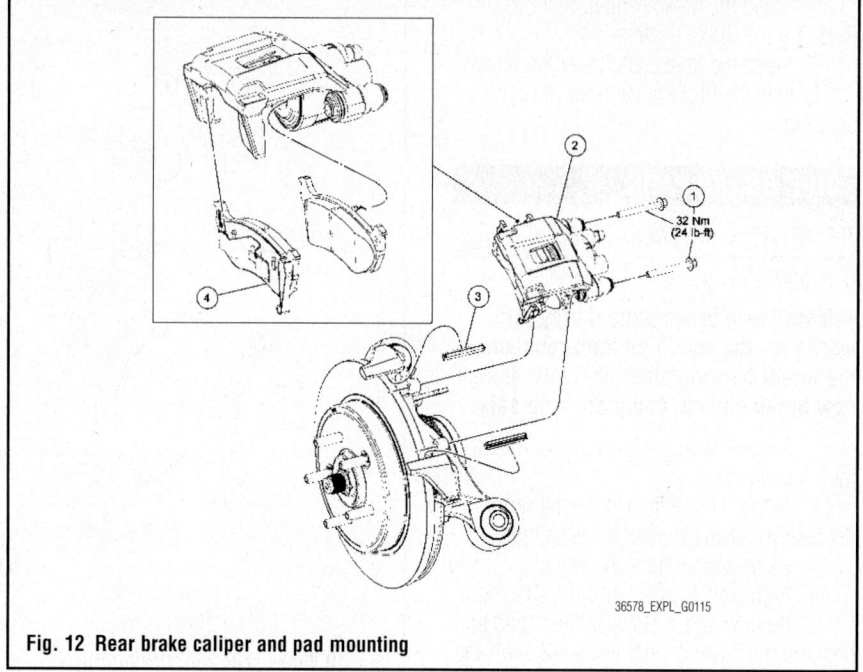

Fig. 12 Rear brake caliper and pad mounting

36578_EXPL_G0115

7. Inspect the brake disc, machine or install a new front brake disc as necessary.

8. Remove the brake pads and clips. Discard the clips.

To install:

9. Install the new brake pad clips and the brake pads.

✳✳ WARNING

Protect the piston and boots when pushing the caliper piston into the caliper piston bores.

10. Using a suitable tool (C-clamp) and a worn brake pad, compress the disc brake caliper pistons into the caliper.

11. Position the brake caliper and install the 2 bolts. Tighten the lower bolt and then the upper bolt to 24 ft. lbs. (32 Nm).

12. Install the wheel and tire assembly and lower the vehicle.

13. Fill the brake master cylinder reservoir with clean brake fluid.

14. Test the brakes for normal operation.

BRAKES

PARKING BRAKE

PARKING BRAKE CABLES

ADJUSTMENT

If the parking brake requires adjustment first check for any damaged cables and replace as necessary.

On vehicles with rear disc brakes check for proper operation of the parking brake shoes. Refer to the "Parking Brake Shoes" section.

Parking Brake Cable Tension Release

See Figures 13 and 14.

1. Remove the LH cowl side trim panel.

2. With the help of an assistant, release the parking brake cable tension by pulling down on the intermediate cable at the cable-to-cable connector clip until the parking brake control sector rotates to its stop and a 0.15 inch (4 mm) x 5.9 inch (150 mm) retainer pin can be inserted.

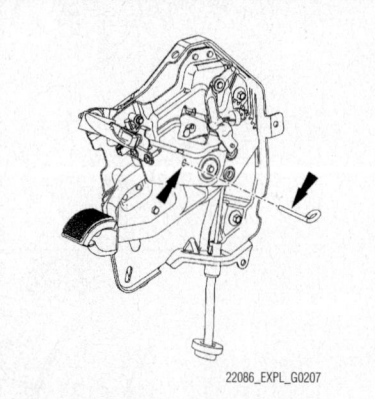

22086_EXPL_G0207

Fig. 13 With the help of an assistant, release the parking brake cable tension by pulling down on the intermediate cable at the cable-to-cable connector clip until the parking brake control sector rotates to its stop and a 0.15 inch (4 mm) x 5.9 inch (150 mm) retainer pin can be inserted

✳✳ WARNING

Make sure the cable-to-cable connector clip is connected to the front and rear cable before removing the brake

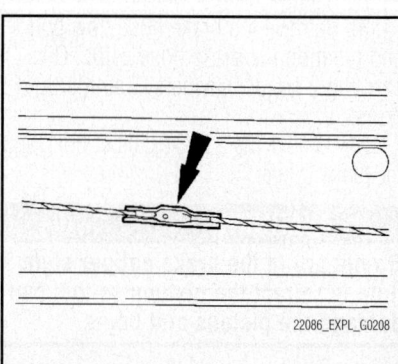

22086_EXPL_G0208

Fig. 14 Disconnect the cable-to-cable connector clip

control retaining pin, and the cable tension is reloaded slowly.

3. Disconnect the cable-to-cable connector clip.

4. To reload the tension on the parking brake cable, follow the release procedure in reverse.

PARKING BRAKE SHOES

REMOVAL & INSTALLATION

See Figures 15 and 16.

1. Before servicing the vehicle, refer to the Precautions.

2. Remove the rear brake disc.

3. Remove the parking brake shoe adjusting screw.

4. Remove the parking brake shoe adjusting screw spring.

5. Remove the 2 parking brake shoe hold-down springs and pins.

6. Remove the parking brake shoe retracting spring and the parking brake shoes.

To install:

7. Position the parking brake shoes and attach the retracting spring.

8. Install the 2 parking brake shoe hold-down pins and springs.

9. Install the parking brake shoe adjusting screw spring.

→**Completely retract the parking brake adjusting screw before installation.**

10. Install the brake shoe adjusting screw.

11. Use a brake adjusting gauge to measure the inside diameter of the parking brake drum.

12. Adjust the parking brake shoe clearance of 0.04 inch (1.07 mm) less than the inside diameter of the parking

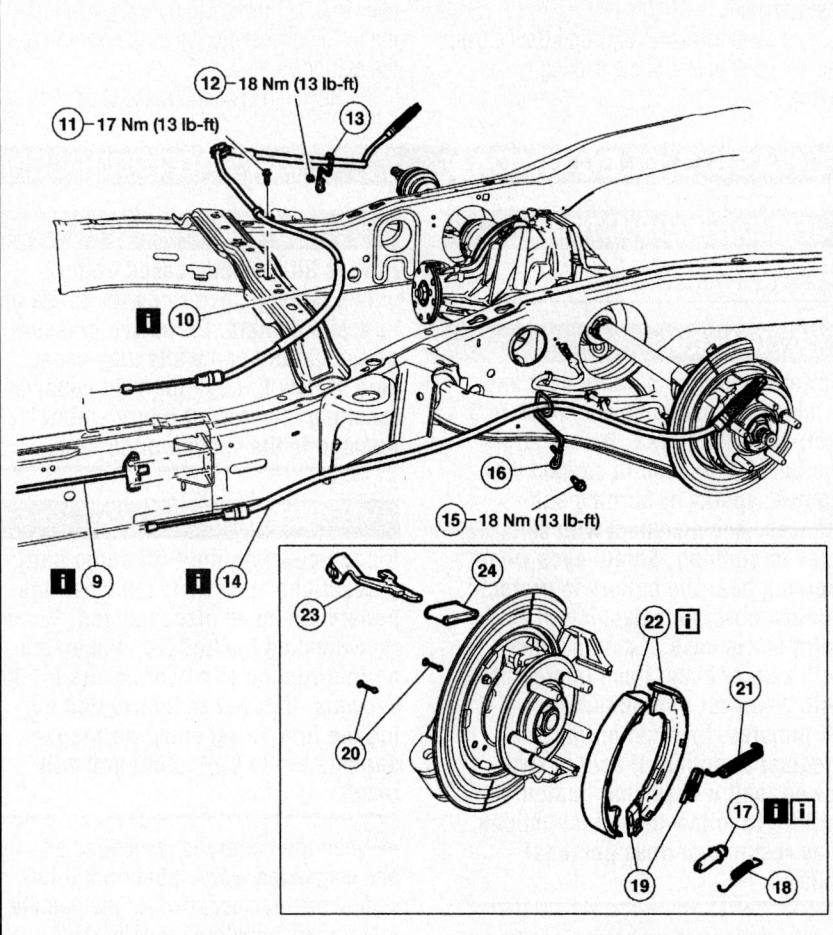

9	Intermediate parking brake cable	17	Brake shoe adjusting screw
10	Rear parking brake cable (RH)	18	Brake shoe adjusting screw spring
11	Rear parking brake cable bracket bolt	19	Brake shoe hold-down spring
12	Wire form retainer bolt	20	Brake shoe hold-down pins
13	Wire form retainer	21	Brake shoe retracting spring
14	Rear parking brake cable (LH)	22	Parking brake shoe kit (one kit required)
15	Wire form retainer bolt	23	Parking brake lever (RH/LH)
16	Wire form retainer	24	Parking brake lever boot

06017-EXPL-G164

Fig. 16 Parking brake shoes and related parts

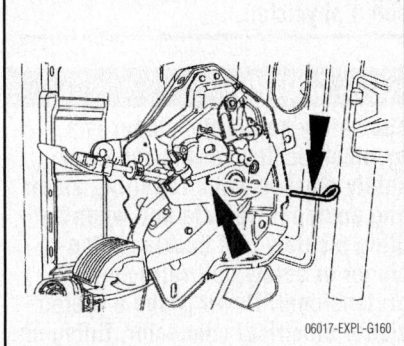

06017-EXPL-G160

Fig. 15 Parking brake control

brake drum. Make sure that the parking brake shoes are correctly centered and measure across the center point of the shoes. Rotate the parking brake shoe adjuster wheel to achieve the correct parking brake shoe-to-brake disc clearance.

13. Install the rear brake disc.

14. To reload the tension on the parking brake cable, follow the release procedure in reverse.

ADJUSTMENT

→**Make sure the parking brake is fully released.**

1. Using the release handle, release the parking brake control.

2. Remove the rear brake disc. Refer to Rotor in Rear Disc Brakes

3. Using the Brake Adjusting Gauge, measure the inside diameter of the drum portion of the rear brake disc and

set the locking screw. Record the measurement.

4. Place the Brake Adjusting Gauge over the widest diameter of the parking brake shoes.

5. Adjust the parking brake shoe clearance to 0.021 inches (0.54 mm) less than the inside diameter of the drum portion of the rear brake disc.

6. Rotate the parking brake shoe adjuster to achieve the correct parking brake shoe-to-brake disc clearance.

7. Install the rear brake disc.

8. Test the parking brake for normal operation.

CHASSIS ELECTRICAL

AIR BAG (SUPPLEMENTAL RESTRAINT SYSTEM)

GENERAL INFORMATION

SERVICE PRECAUTIONS

CAUTION

Batteries contain sulfuric acid and produce explosive gases. Work in a well-ventilated area. Do not allow the battery to come in contact with flames, sparks or burning substances. Avoid contact with skin, eyes or clothing. Shield eyes when working near the battery to protect against possible splashing of acid solution. In case of acid contact with skin or eyes, flush immediately with water for a minimum of 15 minutes, then get prompt medical attention. If acid is swallowed, call a physician immediately. Failure to follow these instructions may result in serious personal injury.

CAUTION

Always deplete the backup power supply before repairing or installing any new front or side air bag supplemental restraint system (SRS) component and before servicing, removing, installing, adjusting or striking components near the front or side impact sensors or the restraints control module (RCM). Nearby components include doors, instrument panel, console, door latches, strikers, seats and hood latches.

CAUTION

To deplete the backup power supply energy, disconnect the battery ground cable and wait at least 1 minute. Be sure to disconnect auxiliary batteries and power supplies (if equipped). Failure to follow these instructions may result in serious personal injury or death in the event of an accidental deployment.

CAUTION

Always lift a plastic-cased battery with a battery carrier or with hands on opposite corners. Excessive pressure on the battery end walls may cause acid to flow through the vent caps, resulting in personal injury and/or damage to the vehicle or battery.

WARNING

If equipped with the CD6 audio unit, precautions must be taken when the battery has been disconnected. When reconnecting the battery, make sure no interruption of power occurs for 30 seconds. If power is interrupted during the first 30 seconds, permanent damage to the CD6 audio unit will result.

➡When the battery is disconnected and connected, some abnormal drive symptoms may occur while the vehicle relearns its adaptive strategy. The vehicle may need to be driven to relearn its strategy.

➡When disconnecting the battery ground cable to interrupt power to the vehicle electrical system, disconnect the battery ground cable only. It is not necessary to disconnect the positive battery cable.

CAUTION

Disconnect and isolate the battery negative cable before beginning any airbag system component diagnosis, testing, removal, or installation procedures. Allow system capacitor to discharge for two minutes before beginning any component service. This will disable the airbag system. Failure to disable the airbag system may result in accidental airbag deployment, personal injury, or death.

CAUTION

Do not place an intact undeployed airbag face down on a solid surface. The airbag will propel into the air if accidentally deployed and may result in personal injury or death.

CAUTION

When carrying or handling an undeployed airbag, the trim side (face) of the airbag should be pointing away from the body to minimize possibility of injury if accidental deployment occurs. Failure to do this may result in personal injury or death.

CAUTION

Replace airbag system components with original equipment replacement parts. Substitute parts may appear interchangeable, but internal differences may result in inferior occupant protection. Failure to do so may result in occupant personal injury or death.

CAUTION

Wear safety glasses, rubber gloves, and long sleeved clothing when cleaning powder residue from vehicle after an airbag deployment. Powder residue emitted from a deployed airbag can cause skin irritation. Flush affected area with cool water if irritation is experienced. If nasal or throat irritation is experienced, exit the vehicle for fresh air until the irritation ceases. If irritation continues, see a physician.

CAUTION

The safety belt pretensioner is a pyrotechnic device. Always wear safety glasses when repairing an air bag equipped vehicle and when handling a safety belt buckle pretensioner or safety belt retractor pretensioner. Never probe a pretensioner electrical connector. Doing so could result in pretensioner or air bag deployment and could result in personal injury.

✳✳ CAUTION

Do not use a replacement airbag that is not in the original packaging. This may result in improper deployment, personal injury, or death.

✳✳ CAUTION

To reduce the risk of personal injury, do not use any memory saver devices.

✳✳ CAUTION

The factory installed fasteners, screws and bolts used to fasten airbag components have a special coating and are specifically designed for the airbag system. Do not use substitute fasteners. Use only original equipment fasteners listed in the parts catalog when fastener replacement is required.

✳✳ CAUTION

During, and following, any child restraint anchor service, due to impact event or vehicle repair, carefully inspect all mounting hardware, tether straps, and anchors for proper installation, operation, or damage. If a child restraint anchor is found damaged in any way, the anchor must be replaced. Failure to do this may result in personal injury or death.

✳✳ CAUTION

Never probe the connectors on the air bag module or safety canopy module. Doing so can result in air bag deployment, which can result in personal injury.

Deployed and non–deployed airbags may or may not have live pyrotechnic material within the airbag inflator.

Do not dispose of driver/passenger/curtain airbags or seat belt tensioners unless you are sure of complete deployment.

Dispose of deployed airbags and tensioners consistent with state, provincial, local, and federal regulations.

✳✳ CAUTION

Anytime the Safety Canopy® or side air curtain module has deployed, a new headliner and new A-, B-, C- and D-pillar upper trim panels and attaching hardware must be installed. Remove any other damaged components and hardware and install new components and hardware as needed. Failure to follow these instructions may result in the Safety Canopy® or side air curtain module deploying incorrectly and increases the risk of serious personal injury or death in a crash.

✳✳ CAUTION

Always carry or place a live Safety Canopy®, or side air curtain module, with the module and tear seam pointed away from your body. Failure to follow this instruction may result in serious personal injury or death in the event of an accidental deployment.

✳✳ CAUTION

Do not obstruct or place objects in the deployment path of the Safety Canopy® or side air curtain module. Failure to follow this instruction may result in the Safety Canopy® or side air curtain module deploying incorrectly and increases the risk of serious personal injury or death in a crash.

✳✳ CAUTION

Never probe the electrical connectors on air bag, Safety Canopy® or side air curtain modules. Failure to follow this instruction may result in the accidental deployment of these modules, which increases the risk of serious personal injury or death.

DISARMING THE SYSTEM

1. Before servicing the vehicle, refer to Precautions.

If a seat equipped with a seat mounted side air bag and/or a safety belt pretensioner (if equipped) system is being serviced, the supplemental restraint system (SRS) must be de-powered.

The air bag warning lamp illuminates when the RCM fuse is removed and the ignition switch is ON. This is normal operation and does not indicate a supplemental restraint system (SRS) fault.

2. Turn all vehicle accessories OFF.
3. Turn the ignition switch to OFF.
4. At the central junction box (CJB), located below the left side of the instrument panel, remove the restraints control module (RCM) fuse (10A) from the CJB.

5. Turn the ignition **ON** and visually monitor the air bag indicator for at least 30 seconds. The air bag indicator will remain lit continuously (no flashing) if the correct RCM fuse has been removed. If the air bag indicator does not remain lit continuously, remove the correct RCM fuse before proceeding.

6. Turn the ignition **OFF**.

✳✳ WARNING

To avoid accidental deployment and possible personal injury, the backup power supply must be depleted before repairing or replacing any front or side air bag supplemental restraint system (SRS) components and before servicing, replacing, adjusting or striking components near the front or side air bag sensors or RCM, such as doors, instrument panel, console, door latches, strikers, seats and hood latches. The side impact sensors (if equipped) are located at or near the base of the B-pillars and C-pillars.

✳✳ CAUTION

To deplete the backup power supply energy, disconnect the battery ground cable and wait at least one minute. Be sure to disconnect auxiliary batteries and power supplies (if equipped). Disconnect the battery ground cable and wait at least one minute.

ARMING THE SYSTEM

✳✳ CAUTION

The restraint system diagnostic tool is for restraint system service only. Remove from vehicle prior to road use. Failure to remove could result in injury and possible violation of vehicle safety standards. Make sure all restraint system diagnostic tool(s) that may have been installed during the repair have been removed from the vehicle and all SRS components are connected.

1. Before servicing the vehicle, refer to the Precautions.
2. Turn the ignition switch from **OFF** to **ON**.
3. Install the RCM fuse to the CJB.

❊❊ CAUTION

Be sure that nobody is in the vehicle and that there is nothing blocking or set in front of any air bag module when the battery ground cable is connected.

4. Connect the battery ground cable.

5. Prove out the supplemental restraint system (SRS) as follows:

a. Turn the ignition key from **ON** to **OFF**. Wait 10 seconds, then turn the key back to ON and visually monitor the air bag indicator with the air bag modules installed. The air bag indicator will light continuously for approximately 6 seconds and then turn off. If an air bag supplemental restraint system (SRS) fault is present, the air bag indicator will:

- Fail to light.
- Remain lit continuously.
- Flash.

b. The flashing might not occur until approximately 30 seconds after the ignition switch has been turned from the **OFF** to the **ON** position. This is the time required for the restraints control module (RCM) to complete the testing of the SRS. If the air bag indicator is inoperative and a SRS fault exists, a chime will sound in a pattern of 5 sets of 5 beeps. If this occurs, the air bag indicator and any SRS fault discovered must be diagnosed and repaired.

6. Clear all continuous DTCs from the restraints control module using a scan tool.

CLOCKSPRING CENTERING

See Figures 17 through 21.

1. Before servicing the vehicle, refer to Precautions.

2. Disarm the system. Refer to Disarming the System.

3. Make sure the road wheels are in the straight-ahead position.

4. Remove the 2 steering wheel back cover plugs.

5. Remove the 2 driver air bag module bolts.

6. Partially remove the driver air bag module from the steering wheel.

7. Disconnect the driver air bag module electrical connectors and carefully remove the airbag to a proper location.

❊❊ WARNING

The clockspring electrical connectors are unique and cannot be reversed when connected to the driver air bag module. Match the electrical connector key to the keyway in the driver air

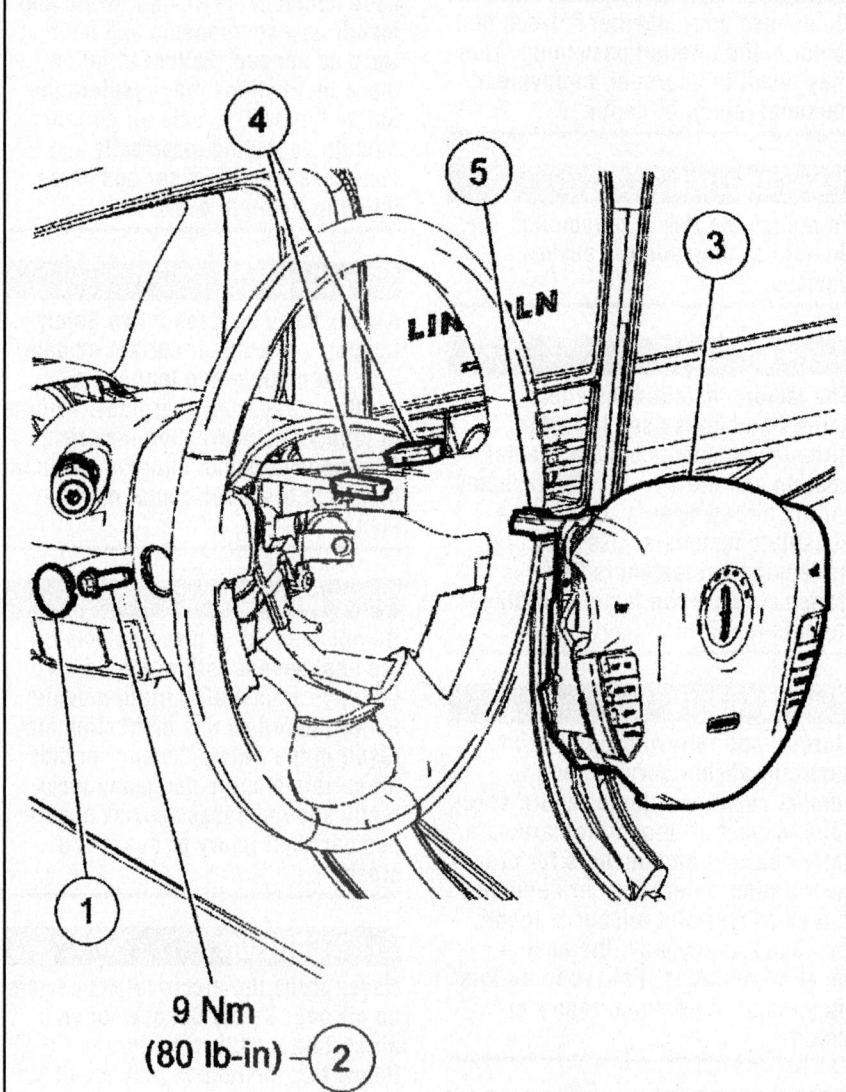

9 Nm
(80 lb-in) —②

1 Steering wheel back cover plug (2 required)

2 Driver air bag module bolt (2 required)

3 Driver air bag module

4 Driver air bag module electrical connectors

5 Horn switch electrical connector

06017-EXPL-G125

Fig. 17 Air bag module—generic shown most are similar

1 Steering wheel bolt
2 Steering wheel

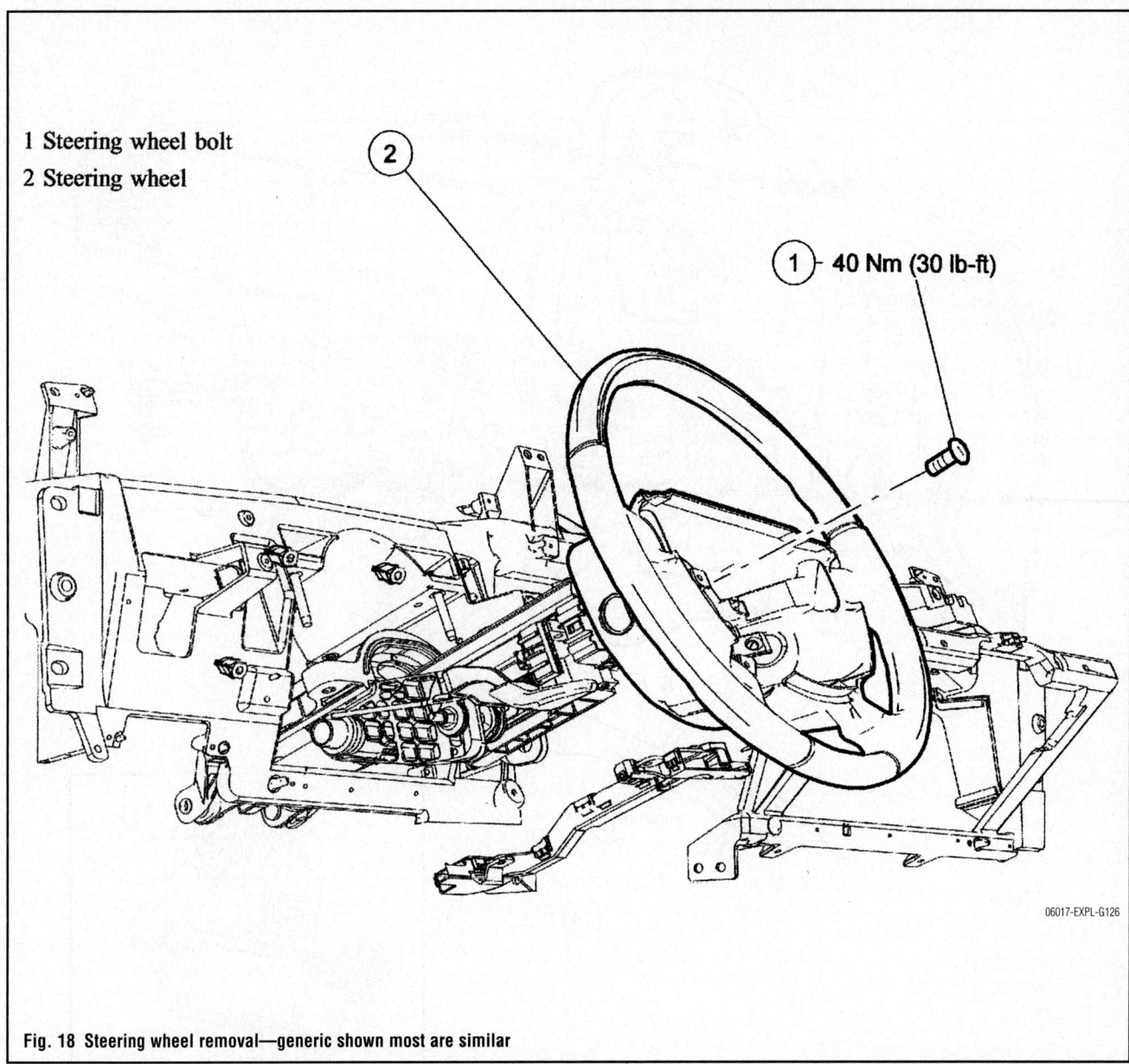

②

① 40 Nm (30 lb-ft)

06017-EXPL-G126

Fig. 18 Steering wheel removal—generic shown most are similar

bag module. **Do not force the electrical connectors into the driver air bag module.**

8. Disconnect the horn switch electrical connector and remove the driver air bag module.

9. Loosen the steering wheel bolt.

✳✳ WARNING

Removing the steering wheel without using a puller can damage the column bearings.

10. Using the special tool, separate the steering wheel from the steering column.

➡**A new bolt must be installed.**

11. Remove and discard the steering wheel bolt.

12. Remove the steering wheel.

13. Remove the 2 steering column opening cover screws.

14. Remove the steering column opening cover.

15. Remove the 3 lower steering column shroud screws.

16. Remove the lower steering column shroud.

17. Remove the upper steering column shroud. Lift where shown, releasing the retaining clips and rotate the upper steering column trim panel out of the instrument cluster finish panel. Remove the upper steering column shroud hard shell.

18. If installing the same clockspring, apply 2 strips of masking tape across the clockspring to prevent accidental rotation when the clockspring is removed.

19. Remove the multifunction switch screw.

20. While releasing the retaining tab at the top of the multifunction switch, slide the multifunction switch up and out of the way.

21. Remove the 2 clockspring screws.

➡**If the clockspring is to be reinstalled, do not allow the clockspring to turn from its removal position.**

22. Disconnect the 3 clockspring electrical connectors and remove the clockspring.

23. Remove the 3 clockspring mounting bracket screws and discard the clockspring mounting bracket if damaged.

To install:

24. Position the clockspring mounting bracket, if removed.

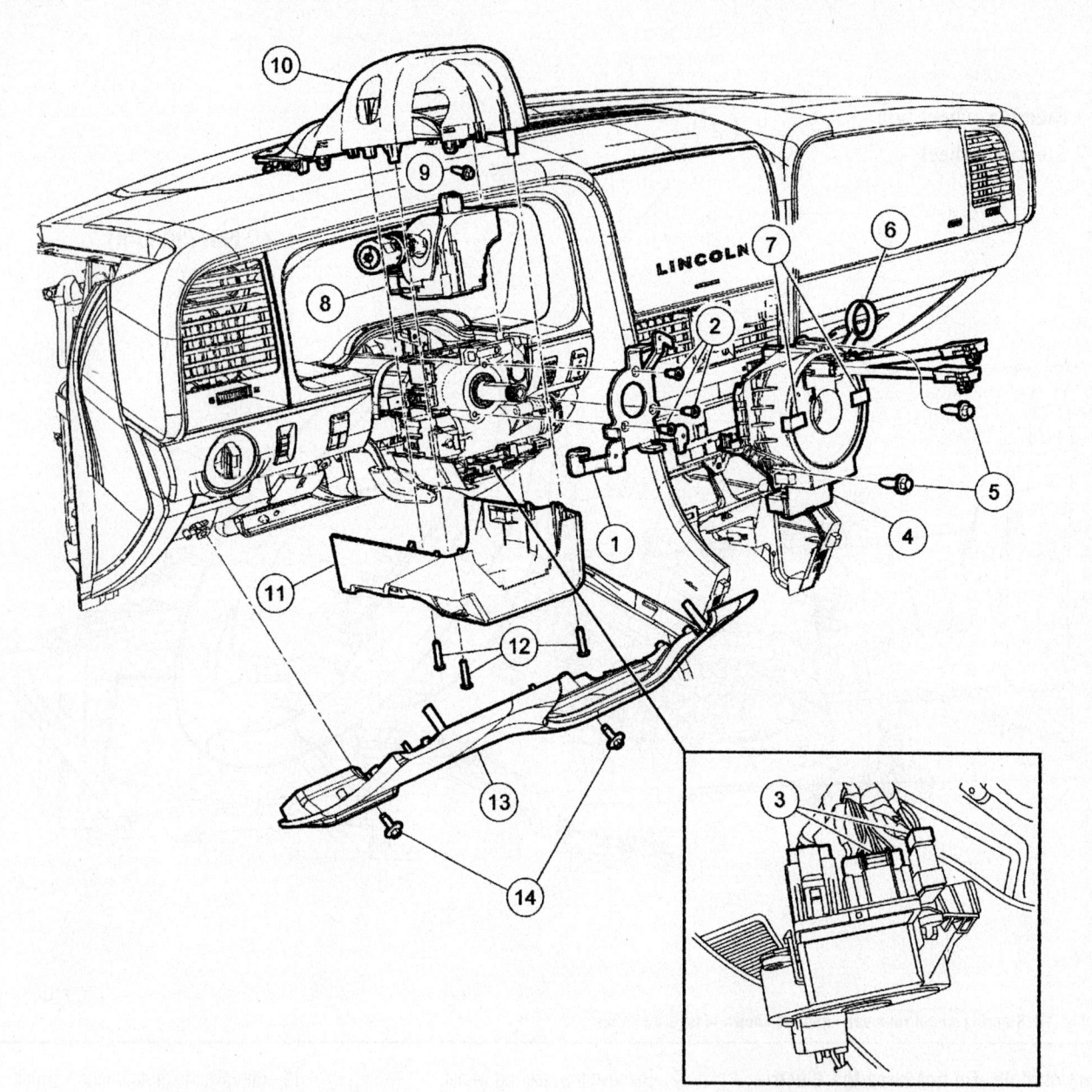

1 Clockspring mounting bracket

2 Clockspring mounting bracket
screws (3 required)

3 Clockspring electrical
connectors (3 required)

4 Clockspring

5 Clockspring screws
(2 required)

6 Retaining pin

7 Tape

8 Multi-function switch

9 Multi-function switch screw

10 Upper steering column shroud

11 Lower steering column
shroud

12 Lower steering column
shroud screws (3 required)

13 Lower steering column
opening cover

14 Lower steering column
opening cover screws (2
required)

06017-EXPL-G127

Fig. 19 Clockspring removal—generic shown most are similar

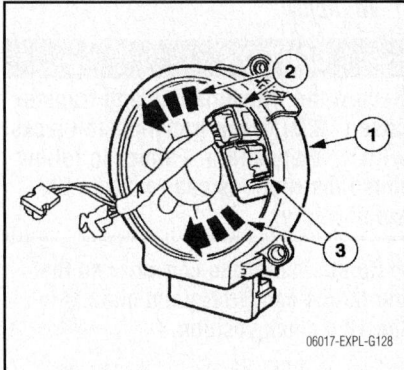

Fig. 20 Turn the clockspring rotor clockwise approximately 2 turns

25. Install the 3 clockspring mounting bracket screws.
26. Connect the 3 clockspring electrical connectors.

✳ CAUTION

Incorrect centralization may result in premature component failure. If in doubt when centralizing the clockspring, repeat the centralizing procedure. Failure to follow this instruction may result in personal injury.

✳ WARNING

Make sure the road wheels are in the straight-ahead position.

27. If the vehicle's clockspring has rotated out of the center position, follow these steps to center the clockspring.

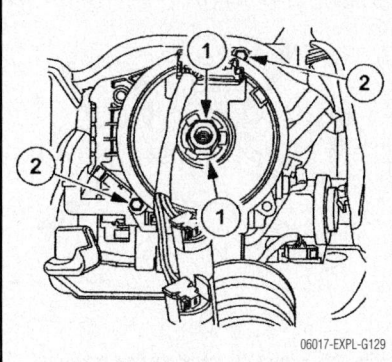

Fig. 21 Positioning the clockspring on the column

a. Hold the clockspring outer housing stationary.

✳ WARNING

Overturning will destroy the clockspring. The internal ribbon wire acts as the stop and can be broken from its internal connection.

b. While turning the clockspring rotor counterclockwise, carefully feel for the ribbon wire to run out of length and for a slight resistance. Stop turning at this point.
28. Starting with the clockspring inner rotor, wiring and connector in the 12 o'clock position, rotate the inner rotor clockwise through 2 revolutions to center the clockspring.
29. The clockspring inner rotor, wiring and connector must be in the 12 o'clock position.

✳ WARNING

To prevent damage to the clockspring, make sure the road wheels are in the straight-ahead position.

➡ The clockspring inner rotor, wiring and connector must be in the 12 o'clock position to install the steering wheel.

30. With the flats of the clockspring aligned to the flats of the steering column, slide the clockspring onto the steering column.
31. Install the 2 clockspring screws.
32. For vehicles receiving a new clockspring, remove the retaining pin.
33. For vehicles reusing the clockspring that was removed, remove the 2 pieces of tape from the clockspring.
34. Install the multifunction switch onto the steering column.
35. Install the multifunction switch screw.
36. Install the upper steering column shroud.
37. Install the lower steering column shroud.
38. Install the 3 lower steering column shroud screws.
39. Install the lower steering column opening cover.
40. Install the 2 lower steering column opening cover screws.
41. Install the steering wheel. Tighten to 30 ft. lbs. (40 Nm).
42. Install the driver air bag module. Tighten to 62 inch lbs. (7 Nm).
43. Arm the system. See "Arming the System" section.

DRIVE TRAIN

AUTOMATIC TRANSMISSION ASSEMBLY

REMOVAL & INSTALLATION

5R55S TRANSMISSION

See Figures 22 through 25.

1. Before servicing the vehicle, refer to Precautions.

➡ When the battery has been disconnected and reconnected, some abnormal drive symptoms can occur while the vehicle relearns its adaptive strategy. The customer needs to be notified that they can experience slightly different upshifts either (soft or firm) and that this is a temporary condition and will eventually return to normal operating condition.

2. Disconnect the battery ground cable.
3. Remove the coolant expansion tank bolts and position it aside.
4. Remove the fan shroud bolts. Do not remove the fan shroud.

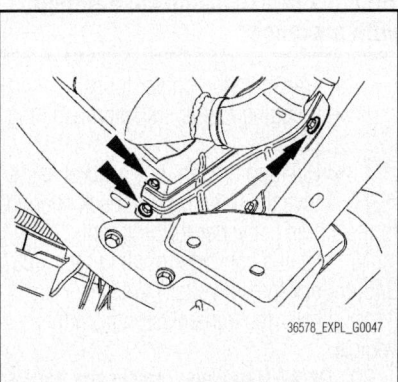

Fig. 22 Right heat shield locations

5. Raise and support the vehicle.
6. If transmission disassembly or installation of new transmission is necessary, drain the transmission fluid. Install the drain plug when finished.

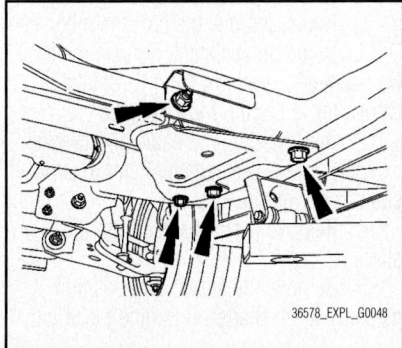

Fig. 23 RH crossmember bolts and nut locations

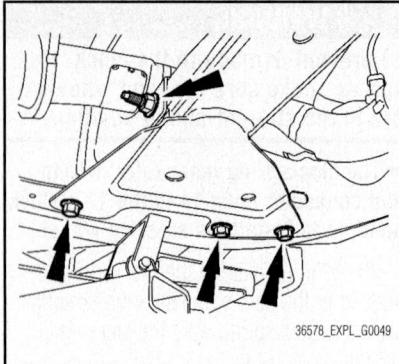

Fig. 24 LH crossmember bolts and nut locations

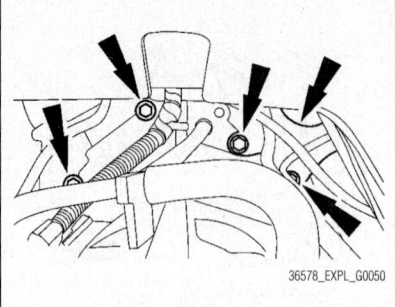

Fig. 25 Engine-to-transmission retaining bolts locations

7. Remove or disconnect the following:
- 2 RH heat shield bolts and position the right heat shield aside
- 2 heated oxygen sensor electrical connectors, refer to Heated Oxygen Sensor in Engine Performance & Emission Controls
- 2 catalyst monitor sensor electrical connectors
- 2 RH heat shield bolts
- RH heat shield bolt and remove the heat shield
- LH heat shield bolt
- Bolts, springs, flag nuts and separate the muffler from the converter
- 4 converter-to-manifold nuts; repeat for both sides, refer to Catalytic Converter in Engine Mechanical

8. On 2WD models, install a suitable jack stand under the transmission (2WD) or transfer case (4WD), securing with a safety chain.

9. Remove the RH and LH side crossmember bolts and nuts.

10. Remove or disconnect the following:
- 2 bolts and position the bracket aside (mounted on the side of the transmission)
- Transmission support insulator nuts; remove the crossmember

11. Using an assistant, remove the 3-way converter system. Refer to Catalytic Converter in Engine Mechanical.

12. Remove the shift cable and bracket.

13. Remove driveshafts. Refer to Driveshaft in Drivetrain.

14. Remove ground cable from the starter.

15. Remove the starter and position aside. Refer to Starter in Engine Electrical.

➡ **Make an identifying mark on the nut, stud and flexplate to allow for correct installation.**

16. Remove or disconnect the following:
- 4 torque converter nuts
- Lower transmission retaining bolts
- RH catalyst monitor connector and the fuel lines from the bracket
- RH heated oxygen sensor from the transmission
- If equipped, shift motor electrical connector
- LH heated oxygen sensor and the harness clip from the transmission
- LH catalyst monitor connector from the transmission
- Turbine shaft speed (TSS) sensor, Output Shaft Speed (OSS) sensor and Intermediate Shaft Speed (ISS) sensor electrical connectors.

➡ **Clean the area around connector to prevent contamination of the solenoid body connector.**

- Solenoid body connector
- Transmission range (TR) sensor electrical connector
- Wiring harness retainers from the side of the transmission

✳✳ WARNING

Do not damage the cooler tubes. Hold the transmission case fittings with a wrench.

- Transmission cooler tubes
- 6 engine-to-transmission retaining bolts
- Position the fuel line bracket aside

17. Move the transmission back enough to install the converter holding tool.

18. Install a converter holding tool, 303-346, to lock the converter in place.

19. Lower the transmission from the vehicle.

20. On 4WD models, remove the transfer case from the back of the transmission.

To install:

✳✳ CAUTION

Secure the transmission and transfer case (4WD) to the transmission jacks with a safety chain. Failure to follow these instructions can result in personal injury.

➡ **Rotate the torque converter so that the torque converter paint mark is in the 12 o'clock position.**

21. On 4WD, if removed, install the transfer case to the back of the transmission, install the bracket and connect the vent hose. Tighten retaining bolts to 30 ft. lbs. (41 Nm).

22. If removed, install the torque converter holding tool.

23. Raise and position the transmission to the back of the engine.

24. Remove the converter holding tool.

25. Position the fuel line bracket.

26. Install and torque the following fasteners:
- 6 engine-to-transmission retaining bolts: 35 ft. lbs. (48 Nm)
- 4 torque converter nuts: 32 ft. lbs. (44 Nm)
- Install the starter: 18 ft. lbs. (24 Nm)
- Starter motor ground cable nut: 10 ft. lbs. (13 Nm)
- 2 lower transmission retaining bolts: 35 ft. lbs. (48 Nm)

✳✳ CAUTION

Ensure transmission and (on 4WD) transfer case are properly supported on jacks and attached to the stand with safety chains.

- Transmission fluid cooler tubes: 30 ft. lbs. (40 Nm)

27. Install or connect the following:
- Wiring harness and retainers to side of transmission
- TR sensor electrical connector (restore rubber cover)
- LH heated oxygen sensor to the transmission; install retainer
- New O-ring seals on transmission connector; tighten connector
- LH catalyst monitor connector
- RH heated oxygen sensor to the transmission
- Fuel line and RH catalyst monitor connector to the bracket
- TSS sensor, OSS sensor and intermediate shaft speed sensor electrical connectors

- Shift cable and bracket; tighten to 30 ft. lbs. (40 Nm)
- Cable shield; if loose on the cable, replace the shield
- Transmission support insulator bolts to 66 ft. lbs. (90 Nm)
- 3-way catalytic converter; loosely install 4 converter-to-manifold nuts
- Both heated oxygen sensor connectors
- Both catalyst monitor sensor connectors

28. Position the crossmember and loosely install 2 nuts in the center of the crossmember.

29. Install the 4 RH crossmember bolts and 1 nut. Torque to 52 ft. lbs. (70 Nm).

30. Repeat for the LH crossmember side.

31. Tighten the rear transmission mount nuts to 66 ft. lbs. (90 Nm).

32. Remove the jack from under the transmission and (on 4WD) transfer case.

33. On 2WD models, install or connect the following:
- Cable bracket and 2 bolts to transmission; tighten to 30 ft. lbs. (40 Nm)
- RH and LH heat shield and bolts; tighten to 15 ft. lbs. (20 Nm)
- 4 converter-to-manifold nuts (on both sides); tighten to 30 ft. lbs. (40 Nm)
- Converter-to-pipe (with new gasket); tighten bolts to 30 ft. lbs. (40 Nm)

34. On 4WD models, install or connect the following:
- Rear transmission mount nuts; torque to 66 ft. lbs. (90 Nm)
- RH and LH heat shield and bolts; tighten to 15 ft. lbs. (20 Nm)
- 4 converter-to-manifold nuts (on both sides); tighten to 30 ft. lbs. (40 Nm)
- Converter-to-pipe (with new gasket); tighten bolts to 30 ft. lbs. (40 Nm)
- If equipped, shift motor electrical connector

35. Install driveshafts.

36. Use the following guidelines for installing the in-line transmission fluid filter:

a. If the transmission was overhauled and the vehicle was equipped with an in-line fluid filter, install a new in-line fluid filter.

b. If the transmission was overhauled and the vehicle was not equipped with an in-line fluid filter, install a new in-line fluid filter kit.

c. If the transmission is being installed for a non-internal repair, do not install an in-line filter or filter kit.

d. If installing a new or a Ford-authorized remanufactured transmission, install the in-line transmission fluid filter that is supplied.

37. If equipped, install skid plate and tighten bolts to 18 ft. lbs. (24 Nm).

38. Connect the negative battery cable.

39. Install the fan shroud and bolts.

40. Reposition the coolant expansion tank and install the bolts.

41. Refill the transmission with fluid.

42. Perform a complete fluid level check.

43. Ensure the shift cable is correctly adjusted.

44. Check for leaks.

6R80 TRANSMISSION

2WD Models

See Figures 26 through 35.

1. Before servicing the vehicle, refer to the precautions in the beginning of this section.

2. With the vehicle in NEUTRAL, position it on a hoist.

3. Disconnect the battery ground cable.

4. Remove the fluid fill plug fluid level indicator assembly located on the passenger side front portion of the transmission case. Removal of the plug will relieve any vacuum that might have built up in the transmission. This will aid in allowing the fluid pan to be easily removed when the bolts are removed.

5. If transmission disassembly or installation of a new transmission is necessary, remove the transmission fluid pan and allow the fluid to drain.

6. Install the fluid pan and tighten the bolts in a crisscross pattern to 10 ft. lbs. (14 Nm).

7. Mark the driveshaft flange with the output shaft flange for correct alignment during installation.

8. Remove the 4 bolts and position the driveshaft aside. Refer to Driveshaft in Drivetrain.

9. Mark the driveshaft flange with the differential flange for correct alignment during installation.

10. Remove the 4 bolts and the driveshaft.

11. Remove the fuel line bracket bolt from the bracket and position the bracket and lines aside.

12. Disconnect the shift cable end and remove the shift cable bracket bolts and position the cable and bracket aside.

13. Remove or disconnect the following:
- Flexplate inspection cover
- Rubber torque converter nut access plug
- 4 flexplate-to-torque converter nuts (discard nuts)
- Starter motor electrical connectors
- Ground wire from the stud near the starter

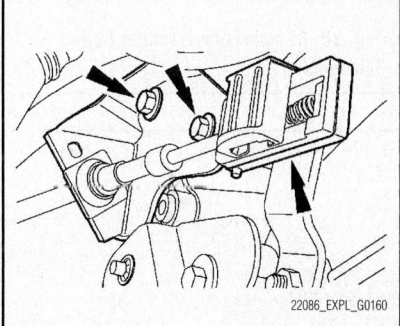

Fig. 27 Disconnect the shift cable end and remove the shift cable bracket bolts and position the cable and bracket aside—6R80 transmission with 2WD

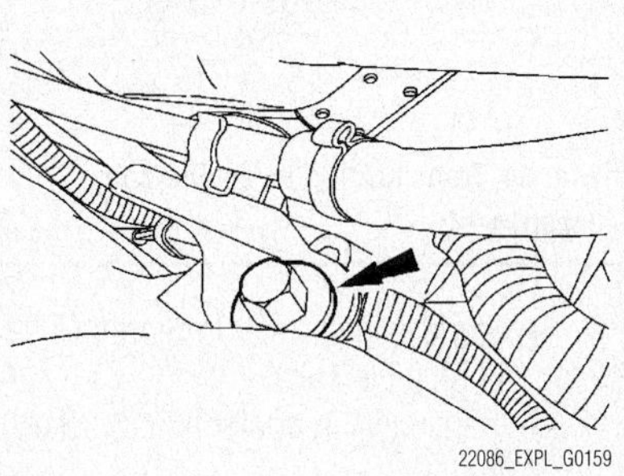

Fig. 26 Remove the fuel line bracket bolt from the bracket and position the bracket and lines aside—6R80 transmission with 2WD

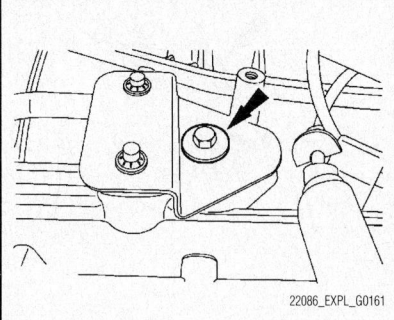

Fig. 28 Remove the transmission fluid cooler tube bracket nut and position the bracket and tubes aside

Fig. 29 Rear crossmember bolt locations

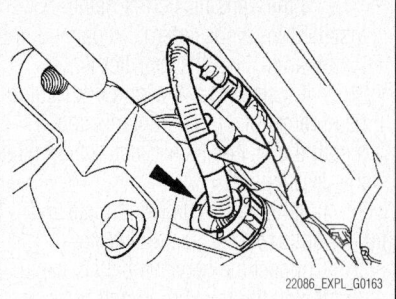

Fig. 32 Remove the main transmission electrical harness by twisting the outer shell and pulling back on the connector

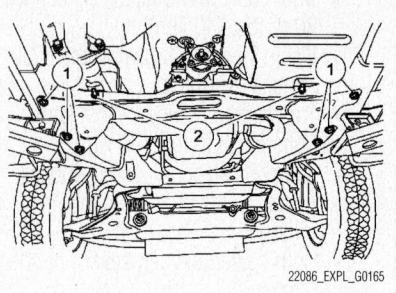

Fig. 35 Install the 8 crossmember bolts; tighten bolts "1" to 59 ft. lbs. (80 Nm) and bolts "2" to 66 ft. lbs. (90 Nm)

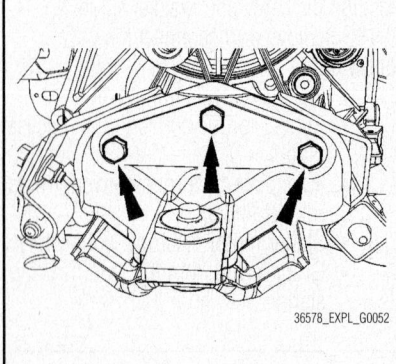

Fig. 30 Transmission insulator bolt locations

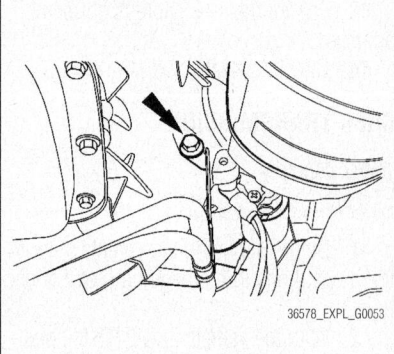

Fig. 33 Transmission-to-engine bolt location—

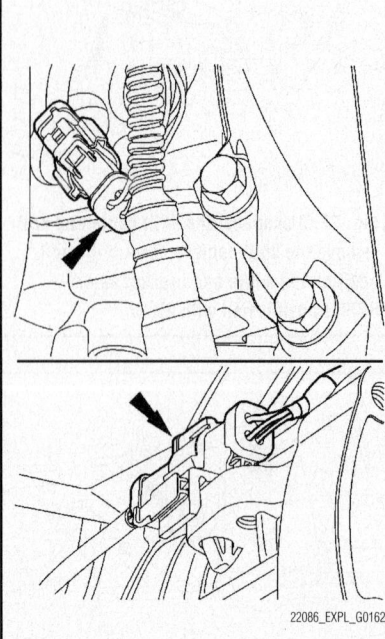

Fig. 31 Remove the RH and LH heated oxygen sensors (HO2S) and the catalyst monitor sensor (CMS) electrical connectors

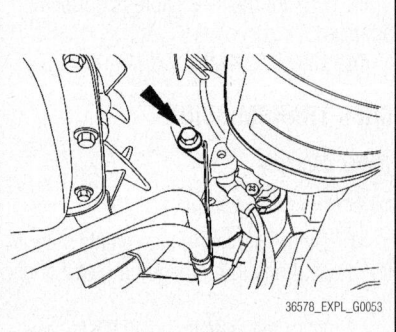

Fig. 34 Transmission-to-engine bolt location—2

- Starter motor, refer to Starter in Engine Electrical
- Transmission cooler tube bracket bolt
- Engine oil level sensor electrical connector
- Transmission fluid cooler tube bracket nut and position the bracket and tubes aside

- 3 bolts and the RH exhaust heat shield
- LH exhaust heat shield bolt

✳✳ CAUTION

Make sure that the transmission jack makes contact on the outer ribs of the fluid pan, and make sure that the transmission is securely fastened to the transmission jack.

14. Position a suitable high-lift transmission jack under the transmission.
15. Remove or disconnect the following:
- 8 rear crossmember bolts (4 at each end)
- 2 center rear crossmember nuts and the crossmember
- 3 bolts and the transmission insulator
- RH and LH heated oxygen sensors (HO2S) and the catalyst monitor sensor (CMS) electrical connectors
- RH and LH exhaust flange nuts
- 2 bolts and the dual converter Y-pipe
- CMS electrical connector from the LH side of the transmission
- Wire harness from the top of the transmission
- Main transmission electrical harness by twisting the outer shell and pulling back on the connector
16. Remove the 7 transmission-to-engine bolts.
17. Slide the transmission back far enough to install the converter locking tool.
18. Install the converter locking tool.
19. Remove the transmission from the vehicle.
20. Remove the 4 bolts and the transmission mount bracket.
21. If the transmission is to be overhauled or if installing a new transmission, carry out transmission fluid cooler backflushing and cleaning.

To install:

22. Install the converter locking tool, if it has been removed.

➡**The converter housing is piloted into position by dowels in the rear of the engine block. The torque converter must rest squarely against the flex-plate. This indicates that the converter pilot is not binding in the engine crankshaft.**

23. Position and secure the transmission on the high-lift transmission jack. Raise and position the transmission into the vehicle.

24. Remove the converter locking tool.

❊❊ WARNING

Make sure the torque converter is fully seated in the transmission before aligning the transmission to the engine.

25. With the transmission in a horizontal position, move it toward the engine. Align the orange balancing marks between the torque converter studs and the flexplate bolt holes.

26. Install the transmission bolts in their correct locations noted during removal.

27. Install the 7 transmission-to-engine bolts around the top of the housing, noting that the top 2 bolts need to be installed prior to installing the rest of the bolts. Torque the bolts to 35 ft. lbs. (48 Nm).

28. Install or connect the following:

- Main transmission electrical harness by pushing it in and twisting the outer shell to lock it in place
- Wire harness to the top of the transmission
- Catalyst monitor sensor (CMS) electrical connector to the LH side of the transmission
- Dual converter Y-pipe; torque the bolts to 30 ft. lbs. (40 Nm)
- LH and RH exhaust flange nuts; torque the nuts to 30 ft. lbs. (40 Nm)
- RH and LH heated oxygen sensors (HO2S) and the CMS electrical connectors
- Transmission insulator; torque the 3 bolts to 66 ft. lbs. (90 Nm)
- Rear crossmember in place and loosely install the transmission insulator nuts in the center
- 8 crossmember bolts; tighten bolts "1" to 59 ft. lbs. (80 Nm) and bolts "2" to 66 ft. lbs. (90 Nm), as shown
- Center crossmember transmission insulator nuts to 66 ft. lbs. (90 Nm)

- LH exhaust heat shield bolt and 2 RH exhaust heat shield bolts; torque to 11 ft. lbs. (15 Nm)
- Transmission cooler tubes in place and install the bracket nut; torque to 20 ft. lbs. (27 Nm)
- Oil level sensor electrical connector
- Transmission cooler tube bracket bolt; torque to 17 ft. lbs. (23 Nm)
- Starter motor; torque to 19 ft. lbs. (26 Nm)
- Ground wire on the stud near the starter; torque to 17 ft. lbs. (23 Nm)
- Starter motor electrical connectors
- Plastic starter motor electrical connector cap
- 4 new flexplate-to-torque converter nuts; torque to 26 ft. lbs. (35 Nm)
- Rubber access plug
- Flexplate inspection cover; torque to 26 ft. lbs. (35 Nm)
- Selector lever cable in place, install the bolts and connect the selector lever cable end; torque to 35 ft. lbs. (48 Nm)
- Fuel line in place and install the bolt; torque to 18 ft. lbs. (25 Nm)

➡**To maintain initial driveshaft balance, align the index marks made during removal.**

29. Install the rear driveshaft. Torque the bolts to 60 ft. lbs. (81 Nm).

30. Connect the battery ground cable.

31. Verify that the shift cable is correctly adjusted.

32. Re-flash the transmission control module (TCM) to the latest level of software. See Diagnostic Trouble Codes.

33. Using the refill procedure, fill the transmission with clean automatic transmission fluid.

4WD Models

See Figures 36 through 38.

1. Before servicing the vehicle, refer to the precautions in the beginning of this section.

2. With the vehicle in NEUTRAL, position it on a hoist.

3. Disconnect the battery ground cable.

4. Remove the fluid fill plug fluid level indicator assembly located on the passenger side front portion of the transmission case. Removal of the plug will relieve any vacuum that might have built up in the transmission. This will aid in allowing the fluid pan to be easily removed when the bolts are removed.

5. If transmission disassembly or installation of a new transmission is

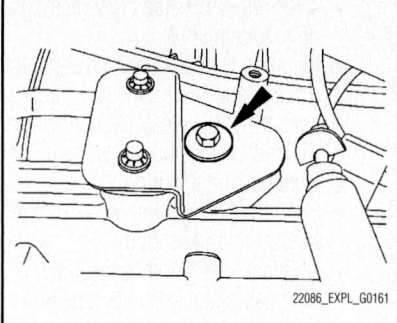

Fig. 36 Showing the location of the transmission cooler tube bracket bolt

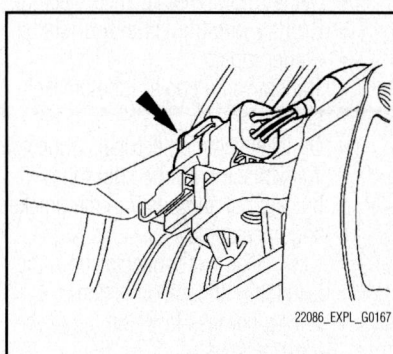

Fig. 37 Showing the location of the CMS electrical connector

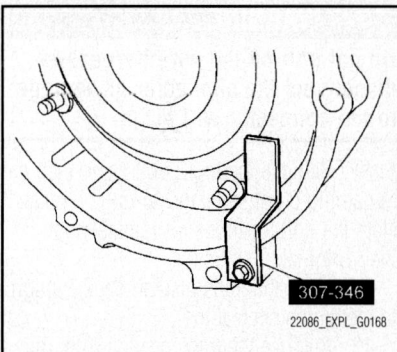

Fig. 38 Slide the transmission back enough to install the special converter locking tool

necessary, remove the transmission fluid pan and allow the fluid to drain.

6. Install the fluid pan and tighten the bolts in a crisscross pattern to 10 ft. lbs. (14 Nm).

7. Remove the transfer case. Refer to Transfer Case.

8. Position a suitable transmission jack to the transmission. Securely strap the transmission to the jack.

9. Remove or disconnect the following:

- LH and RH exhaust heat shield bolts

- 4 RH and 4 LH side crossmember bolts and the nut
- RH and LH heated oxygen sensors (HO2S) and the catalyst monitor sensor (CMS) electrical connectors
- RH and LH exhaust flange nuts
- Dual converter Y-pipe
- Fuel line bracket bolt; position the bracket and lines aside
- Shift cable end and remove the shift cable bracket bolts; position the cable and bracket aside
- Flexplate inspection cover
- Plastic starter motor electrical connector cap
- Starter motor electrical connectors
- Ground wire from stud near starter
- Starter motor
- Transmission cooler tube bracket bolt
- Oil level sensor electrical connector
- Transmission fluid cooler tube bracket nut and position the bracket and lines aside
- CMS electrical connector from the LH side of the transmission
- Wiring harness from the top of the transmission

10. Disconnect the main transmission electrical harness by twisting the outer shell and pulling back on the connector.

✳✳ WARNING

Do not pull on the wire harness to disconnect the connector or damage to the connector will occur.

11. Remove the top 2 bolts, and then the remaining 5 transmission-to-engine bolts. Note the bolt locations for reinstallation in their original positions.

12. Slide the transmission back enough to install the special tool.

13. Remove the transmission from the vehicle.

14. If the transmission is to be overhauled or if installing a new transmission, carry out transmission fluid cooler back-flushing and cleaning.

To install:

15. If removed, reinstall the special converter locking tool.

✳✳ WARNING

The converter housing is piloted into position by dowels in the rear of the engine block. The torque converter must rest squarely against the flexplate. This indicates that the converter pilot is not binding in the engine crankshaft.

16. Position and secure the transmission on the high-lift transmission jack. Raise and position the transmission into the vehicle.

17. Remove the converter locking tool.

✳✳ WARNING

Make sure the torque converter is fully seated in the transmission before aligning the transmission to the engine.

18. With the transmission in a horizontal position move it toward the engine. Align the orange balancing marks between the torque converter studs and the flexplate bolt holes.

19. Install the transmission bolts in their correct locations noted during removal. The top 2 bolts need to be installed prior to installing the rest of the bolts.

20. Torque the 7 transmission-to-engine bolts to 35 ft. lbs. (48 Nm).

21. Install or connect the following:
- Main transmission electrical harness by pushing it in and twisting the outer shell to lock it in place
- Catalyst monitor sensor (CMS) electrical connector to the LH side of the transmission
- Transmission cooler tubes in place and install the cooler tube bracket nut to 20 ft. lbs. (27 Nm)
- Engine oil level sensor electrical connector
- Transmission cooler tube bracket bolt to 17 ft. lbs. (23 Nm)
- Starter motor and the 3 bolts to 18 ft. lbs. (23 Nm)
- Ground wire on the stud; tighten the nut to 15 ft. lbs. (20 Nm)
- Starter motor electrical connectors; replace plastic cap
- 4 new torque converter nuts to 26 ft. lbs. (35 Nm)
- Flexplate inspection cover and bolts to 26 ft. lbs. (35 Nm)
- Selector lever bracket and connect the selector lever cable end; tighten retaining bolt to 18 ft. lbs. (25 Nm)
- Fuel line bracket bolt to 18 ft. lbs. (25 Nm)
- Dual converter Y-pipe in place and install the bolts to 30 ft. lbs. (40 Nm)
- LH and RH exhaust flange new nuts to 30 ft. lbs. (40 Nm)
- RH and LH heated oxygen sensors (HO2S) and the CMS electrical connectors
- 4 RH and LH side crossmember bolts and the nut; torque the verti-

cal bolts to 59 ft. lbs. and the horizontal bolts to 66 ft. lbs. (90 Nm)
- RH and LH exhaust heat shields

22. Install the transfer case. See "Transfer Case" section.

23. Connect the battery ground cable.

24. Verify that the shift cable is correctly adjusted.

25. Re-flash the transmission control module (TCM) to the latest level of software.

26. Using the refill procedure, fill the transmission with clean automatic transmission fluid.

TRANSFER CASE ASSEMBLY

REMOVAL & INSTALLATION

See Figures 39 and 40.

1. Before servicing the vehicle, refer to Precautions.

2. Place the transmission in **Neutral**.

3. Remove or disconnect the following:
- Negative battery cable
- Skid plate, if equipped

➡**Drain the transfer case if disassembly is necessary.**

➡**Match-mark the front and rear driveshaft yokes and pinion flange and the rear driveshaft yoke and rear output flange.**

- Rear driveshaft, refer to Driveshaft in Rear Drive Axle
- Front driveshaft, refer to Driveshaft in Front Drive Axle
- Vent tube
- Shift motor electrical connector

4. Using a suitable high lift jack, support the transfer case.

5. Remove or disconnect the following:
- Right crossmember cover, then the four bolts
- The four left crossmember bolts
- Heat shields from the crossmember
- Transmission mount nuts
- The seven bolts and separate the transfer case from the extension housing

6. Lower the transfer case from the vehicle.

7. Remove and discard the transfer case-to-extension housing gasket. Clean the gasket surfaces.

To install:

8. Installation is the reverse of the removal procedure.

9. Use a new transfer case gasket.

10. Replace aluminum transfer case-to-transmission bolts.

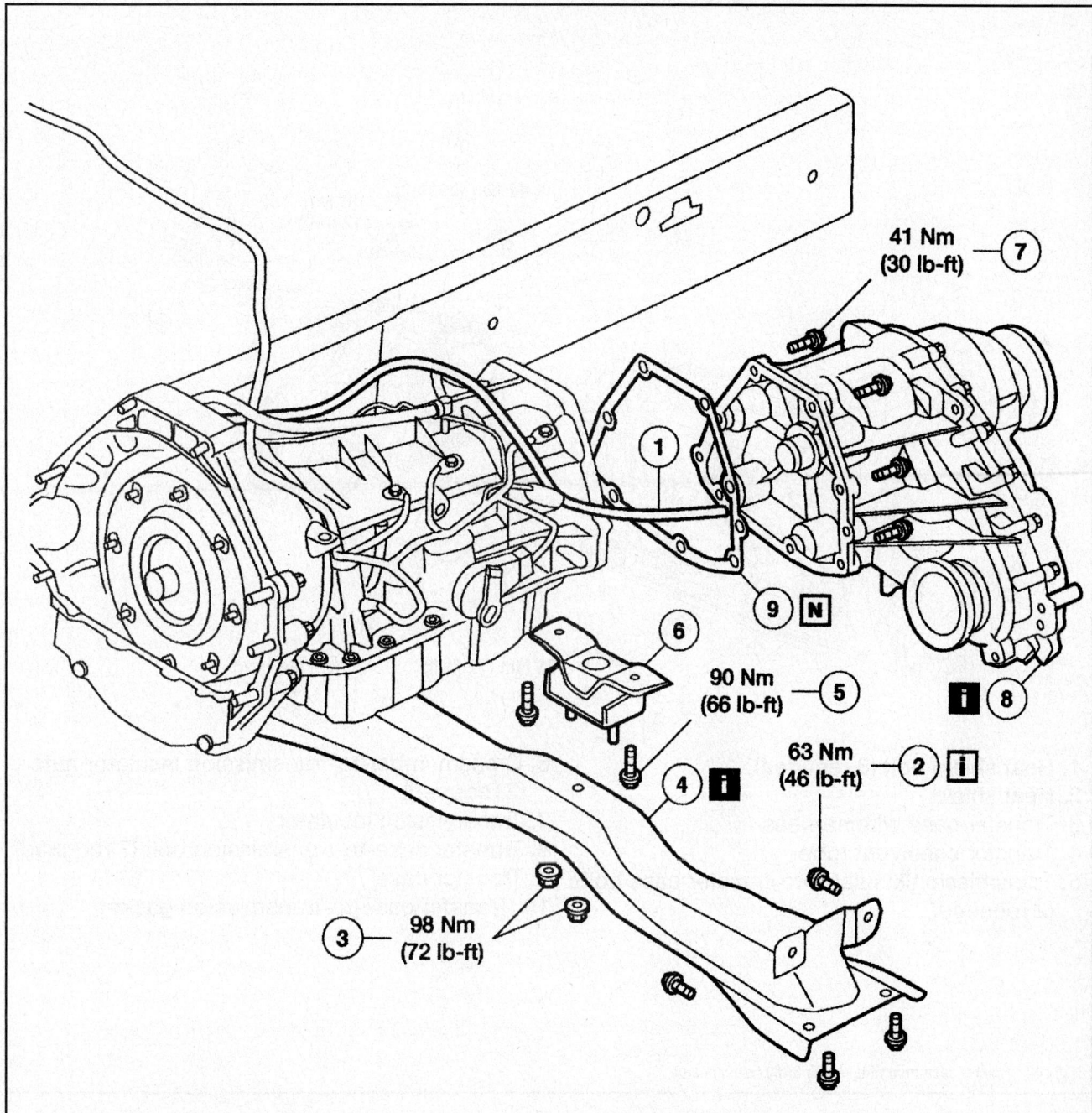

1 Vent hose

2 Crossmember bolt (8 required) Installation Note

3 Crossmember-to-transmission insulator nut (2 required)

4 Crossmember Removal Note

5 Transmission insulator-to-transfer case bolts (2 required)

6 Transmission insulator

7 Transfer case-to-transmission bolts (7 required)

8 Transfer case Removal Note

9 Transfer case-to-transmission gasket

06017-EXPL-G81

Fig. 39 Transfer case mounting—with 5R55 transmission

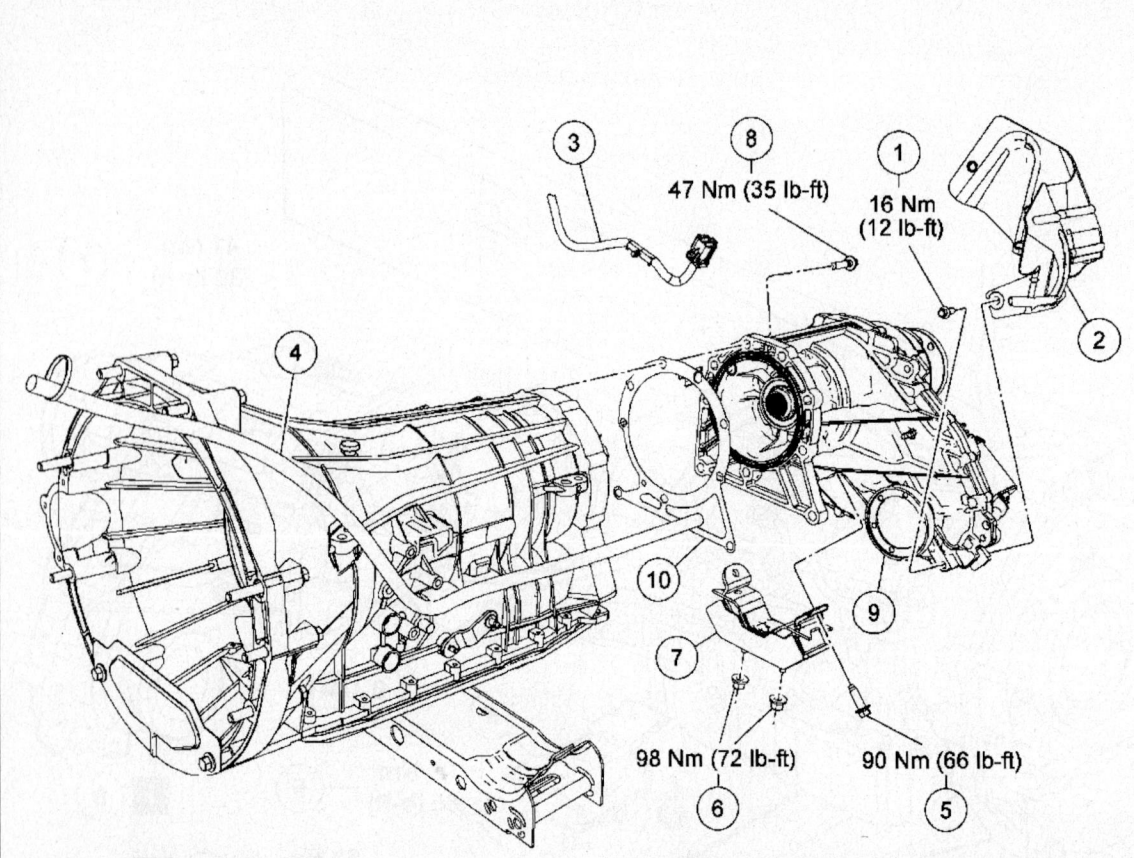

1. Heat shield bolt (3 required)
2. Heat shield
3. Transfer case wire harness
4. Transfer case vent tube
5. Transmission insulator-to-transfer case bolts (2 required)
6. Crossmember-to-transmission insulator nuts (2 required)
7. Transmission insulator
8. Transfer case-to-transmission bolt (7 required)
9. Transfer case
10. Transfer case-to-transmission gasket

22086_EXPL_G0169

Fig. 40 Transfer case mounting—with 6R80 transmission

11. Observe the following tightening specifications:
- Aluminum transfer case-to-transmission bolts 15 ft. lbs. (20 Nm).
- Transmission mount bolts 66 ft. lbs. (90 Nm).
- Crossmember bolts/nuts 72 ft. lbs. (98 Nm).

FRONT DRIVESHAFT

REMOVAL & INSTALLATION

See Figures 41 through 43.

1. Remove the following:
   a. If necessary, remove the transmission insulator.

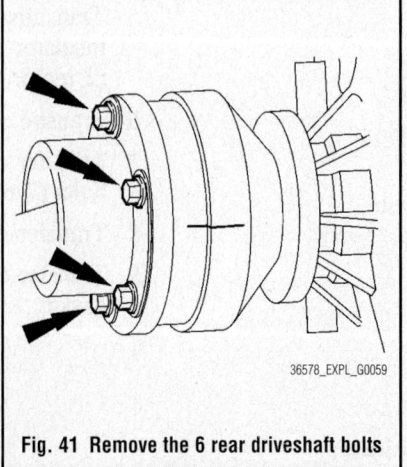

36578_EXPL_G0059

Fig. 41 Remove the 6 rear driveshaft bolts

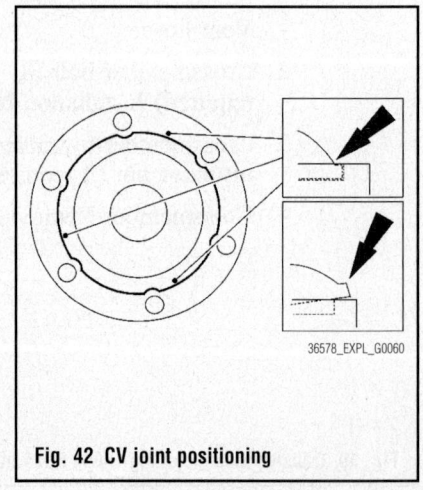

36578_EXPL_G0060

Fig. 42 CV joint positioning

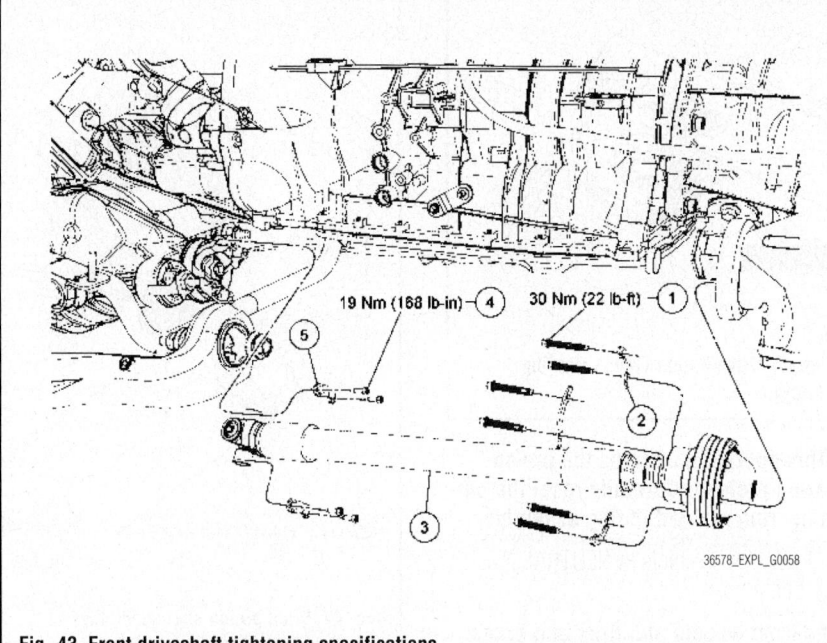

Fig. 43 Front driveshaft tightening specifications

b. Remove the cable shield by prying on the side of the shield closest to the boot, then sliding the shield away from the boot.

c. Remove the shift cable and bracket.

d. Index-mark the front differential pinion flange and the front driveshaft.

e. Remove and discard the front driveshaft bolts and universal joint retainers.

f. Index-mark the front output shaft assembly and the front driveshaft constant velocity (CV) joint.

g. Remove and discard the front driveshaft CV joint bolts and washers.

> ✳✳ **WARNING**
>
> **Always disconnect the front drive-shaft from the transfer case first. Otherwise, the weight of the driveshaft can pinch the boot between the shaft and the boot can and cause the boot to tear. Also, tape the bearing cups to the driveshaft to prevent them from falling off of the spider.**

h. Remove the driveshaft.

i. Mark the rear driveshaft pinion flange and the rear transfer case flange for correct alignment during assembly.

j. Remove the 6 rear driveshaft bolts.

k. Remove the rear driveshaft from the flange using a pry bar.

To install:

2. To install, reverse removal procedure.

➡**Tighten the Constant Velocity (CV) joint bolts evenly in a cross pattern or damage will occur to the CV joint. The can (domed CV joint housing cover) is pressed into the CV joint housing at the factory. When housed correctly, the can will appear as shown in the cut-away illustration (top box). Do not reseat the can in the CV joint housing if the can's flange is above the CV joint housing as shown in the cut-away illustration (bottom box), install a new driveshaft.**

FRONT HALFSHAFTS

REMOVAL & INSTALLATION

See Figure 44.

1. Before servicing the vehicle, refer to Precautions.

2. Remove or disconnect the following:

3. Loosen the front axle wheel hub retainer.

- Wheel and tire assembly
- Hub retainer and the washer. Discard the front axle wheel hub retainer.
- The two bolts and position the disc brake caliper aside. Refer to Caliper in Front Disc Brakes.
- Tie rod end from the knuckle. Discard the nut.
- Stabilizer bar link. Discard the nut. Refer to Stabilizer Bar in Suspension.

> ✳✳ **WARNING**
>
> **Do not allow the knuckle to hang freely. It is possible to overextend and internally separate each inner CV-joint from its housing.**

- Upper ball joint from the knuckle

> ✳✳ **WARNING**
>
> **Do not use a hammer to separate the outboard CV-joint from the hub. Damage to the threads and internal CV-joint components may result.**

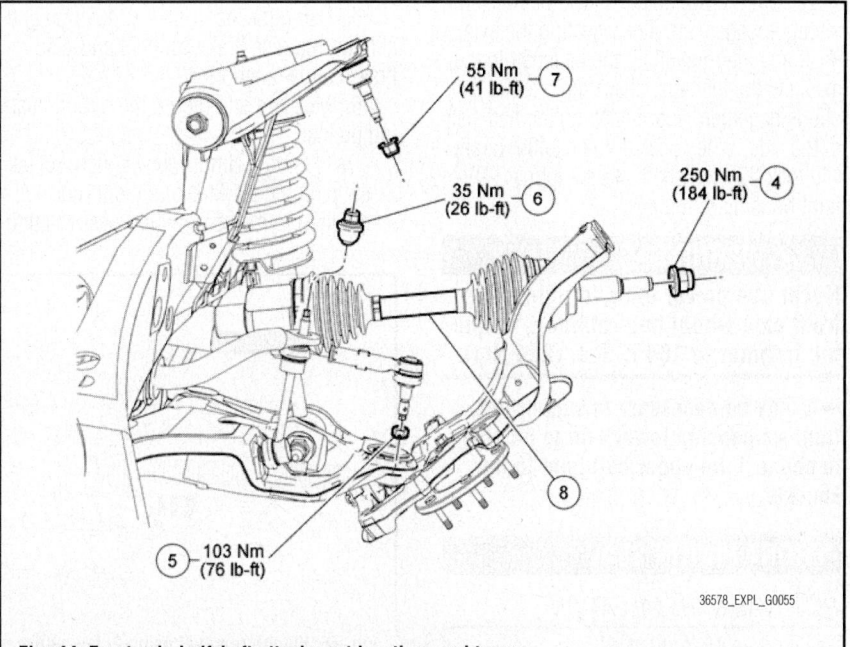

Fig. 44 Front axle halfshaft attachment locations and torques

4. Press the outboard CV-joint until it is loose in the hub.

5. Remove the outboard CV-joint from the hub.

✳✳ WARNING

Do not damage the axle shaft oil seal or the machined sealing surface on the inboard CV-joint housing.

➡**A circlip retains the inboard CV-joint housing to the differential side gear in the axle.**

6. On the left side, pry the left inboard CV-joint housing from the differential side gear.

7. On the right side, disengage the right inboard CV-joint housing from the axle tube.

8. Pull the halfshaft and the axle shaft away from the axle tube, and separate the inboard CV-joint housing from the axle shaft.

9. Remove the halfshaft assembly from the vehicle.

✳✳ WARNING

Do not damage the axle shaft oil seal, the machined sealing surface on the inboard CV-joint housing, or the axle shaft splines.

To install:

10. Installation is the reverse of the removal procedure.

11. Always install the halfshaft with a new retainer circlip and a new front axle wheel hub retainer.

12. On the right side, check the retainer circlip engagement after reseating the axle shaft and after installing the halfshaft in the axle. On the left side, check the retainer circlip engagement after installing the halfshaft in the axle. When seated, the retainer circlip will lock the axle shaft and the inboard CV-joint housing to the axle.

✳✳ WARNING

Never use power tools to tighten the front axle wheel hub retainer. Torque the retainer to 184 ft. lbs. (250 Nm).

➡**It may be necessary to support the front suspension lower arm to be able to connect the upper ball joint to the knuckle.**

FRONT PINION SEAL

REMOVAL & INSTALLATION

See Figures 45 through 47.

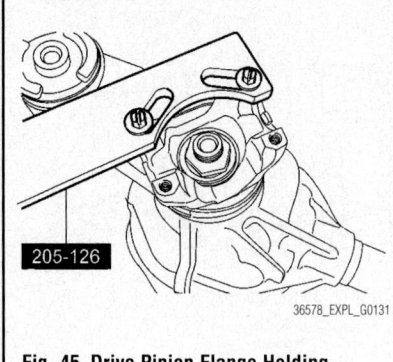

205-126

36578_EXPL_G0131

Fig. 45 Drive Pinion Flange Holding Fixture

➡**This operation disturbs the pinion bearing preload. Carefully reset the pinion bearing preload during assembly.**

1. With the vehicle in NEUTRAL, position it on a hoist.

➡**he front wheels and tires and brake calipers must be removed to prevent drag during the pinion bearing preload recording and adjustment.**

2. Remove the front tires and wheels.

3. Remove the front driveshaft.

✳✳ WARNING

When removing the disc brake caliper, never allow it to hang from the brake hose or damage to the component may occur.

4. Remove the 4 disc brake caliper anchor bolts, then remove the disc brake calipers and disc brake caliper anchors as an assembly.

5. Using mechanic's wire, position and support the disc brake calipers and disc brake caliper anchors.

6. Measure and record the pinion bearing preload.

a. Using a Nm torque wrench, rotate the pinion gear. Measure the torque required to maintain pinion gear rotation.

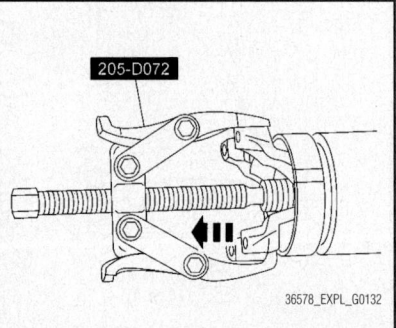

205-D072

36578_EXPL_G0132

Fig. 46 Flange removal using 2-Jaw puller

36578_EXPL_G0130

Fig. 47 Front pinion seal assembly

b. Index-mark the pinion flange and the pinion gear stem.

7. Using the Drive Pinion Flange Holding Fixture to hold the pinion flange, remove and discard the pinion nut.

8. Using the 2-Jaw Puller, remove the pinion flange.

9. Inspect the pinion flange for burrs and damage. Inspect the end of the pinion flange that contacts the pinion bearing cone, pinion nut counterbore and drive pinion oil seal surface for nicks. Discard the pinion flange if damaged.

10. Using gripping pliers and a hammer, remove the drive pinion oil seal.

11. Remove the drive pinion oil slinger and the outer pinion bearing.

12. Remove and discard the collapsible spacer.

13. Verify the splines on the pinion stem are free of burrs. If burrs are evident, remove them with a fine crocus cloth.

14. Clean the drive pinion oil seal bore.

To install:

15. Install a new collapsible spacer.

16. Install the outer pinion bearing and the drive pinion oil slinger.

➡**Lubricate the drive pinion oil seal lips with axle lubricant.**

17. Using the Drive Pinion Oil Seal Installer, install the drive pinion oil seal.

✳✳ WARNING

Never install the pinion flange with power tools or damage to the component may occur.

18. Align the index marks and using the special tool, install the pinion flange.

19. Install the new pinion nut. Only hand-tighten the pinion nut at this time.

✳✳ WARNING

Do not loosen the pinion nut to reduce pinion bearing preload. Install a new collapsible spacer and pinion nut if pinion bearing preload reduction is necessary or damage to the component may occur.

20. Using the Drive Pinion Flange Holding Fixture to hold the pinion flange, tighten the pinion nut to set the pinion bearing preload.

21. Tighten the pinion nut, rotating the pinion occasionally to make sure the pinion bearings are seating correctly. Take frequent pinion bearing preload readings by rotating the pinion gear with a Nm torque wrench. The final reading must be 5 inch lbs. (0.56 Nm) more than the initial reading taken during removal.

22. Install the disc brake calipers and disc brake caliper anchors as an assembly, then the 4 disc brake caliper anchor bolts and tighten to 80 ft. lbs. (108 Nm).

✳✳ WARNING

Always connect the front driveshaft to the axle first. Otherwise, the weight of the driveshaft may pinch the boot between the shaft and the flange and cause the boot to tear.

➡ **Install the driveshaft with new bolts and washers and new bolts and U-joint retainers. If new bolts are not available, coat the threads of the original bolts with threadlock and sealer.**

23. Install the front driveshaft.
24. Install the front tires and wheels.

REAR DRIVESHAFT

REMOVAL & INSTALLATION

One Piece

4.0L Engine

See Figure 48.

1. Perform the following:
   a. Index-mark the rear driveshaft flange and the rear pinion flange for proper realignment.
   b. Remove and discard the 4 rear driveshaft bolts.
   c. Remove and discard the bolts and universal joint retainers.

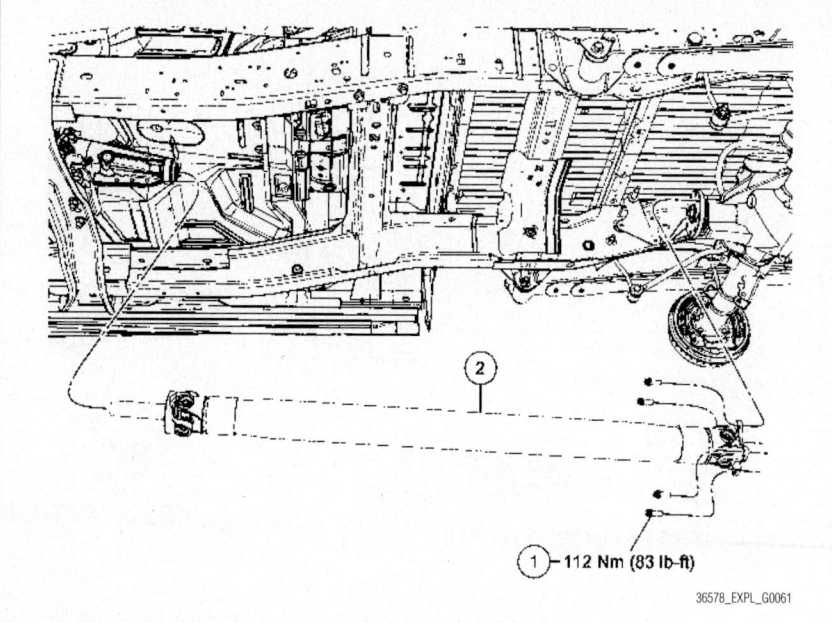

Fig. 48 Rear driveshaft with torques—One piece, 4.0L Engine

① -112 Nm (83 lb-ft)

36578_EXPL_G0061

   d. Remove the rear driveshaft from the flange, using a pry bar; do not hammer on the flange or driveshaft.

To install:

2. Installation is reverse of removal.

3. Tighten rear driveshaft to flange, with marks aligned; tighten the bolts to 83 ft. lbs. (112 Nm)

➡ **If new bolts to retain the driveshaft to the axle are not available, coat the threads of the original bolts with threadlock and sealer.**

✳✳ WARNING

The driveshaft flange fits tightly on the rear axle pinion flange pilot. To make sure that the driveshaft flange seats squarely on the pinion flange, tighten the bolts evenly in a cross pattern.

One Piece

4.6L Engine

See Figures 49 and 50.

1. With the vehicle in NEUTRAL, position it on a hoist.

2. If equipped, remove the skid plate.

3. Index-mark the driveshaft flange to the transfer case rear output flange to maintain driveshaft balance.

4. Index-mark the driveshaft flange to the pinion flange to maintain driveshaft balance.

5. Remove and discard the 4 driveshaft flange bolts.

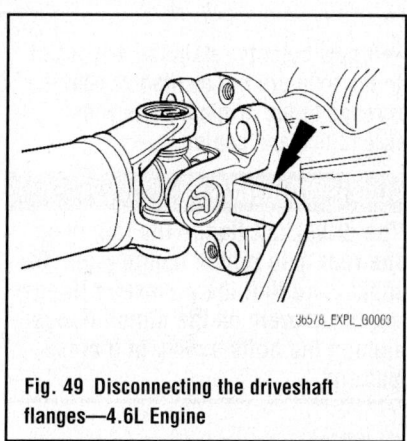

36578_EXPL_G0003

Fig. 49 Disconnecting the driveshaft flanges—4.6L Engine

6. Remove and discard the 4 transfer case rear output flange bolts.

✳✳ WARNING

The driveshaft flange fits tightly on the axle pinion flange pilot and the transfer case output flange. Never hammer on the driveshaft, or any of its components, to disconnect the driveshaft flanges from the mating flanges. Pry only in the area shown with a suitable tool.

7. Using a suitable tool as shown, disconnect the driveshaft flanges and remove the driveshaft.

To install:

8. Installation is reverse of removal.

9. Tighten rear driveshaft to flange, with marks aligned; tighten the bolts to 83 ft. lbs. (112 Nm)

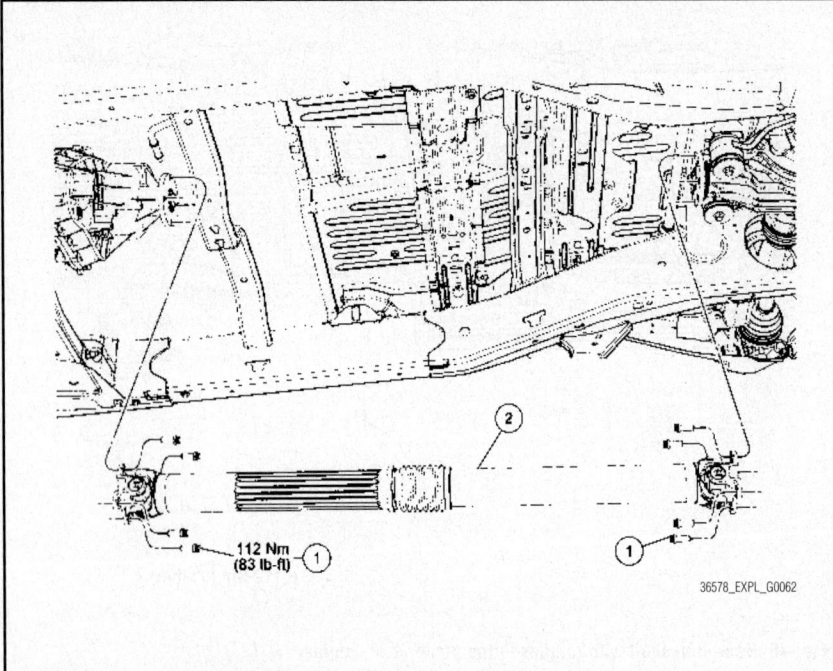

Fig. 50 Rear driveshaft with torques—One piece, 4.6L Engine

➡If new bolts to retain the driveshaft to the axle are not available, coat the threads of the original bolts with threadlock and sealer.

✳✳ WARNING

The driveshaft flange fits tightly on the rear axle pinion flange pilot. To make sure that the driveshaft flange seats squarely on the pinion flange, tighten the bolts evenly in a cross pattern.

Two Piece

2WD Models

See Figures 51 and 52.

1. With the vehicle in NEUTRAL, position it on a hoist.

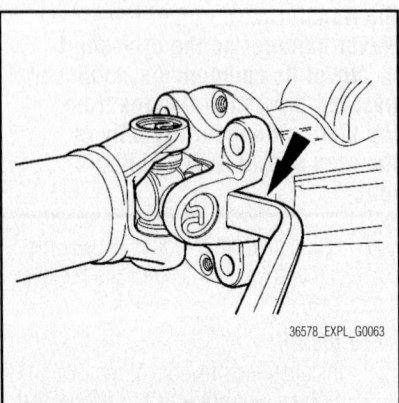

Fig. 51 Disconnecting the driveshaft flanges—Two Piece, 2WD

2. Remove the 2 nuts from the driveshaft center bearing bracket.

3. Index-mark the rear U-joint flange to the differential pinion flange.

➡For 4.0L engine place an index mark on the transmission output shaft that matches the transmission extension housing mark.

➡For 4.6L engine index-mark the front U-joint flange to the transmission output flange

➡If new flange bolts are not available and the originals are not damaged, they can be reused if the threads are coated with threadlock and sealer.

4. Remove and discard the 4 driveshaft flange bolts from the transmission output shaft flange.

✳✳ WARNING

The driveshaft flange fits tightly on the axle pinion flange pilot and the transfer case output flange. Never hammer on the driveshaft, or any of its components, to disconnect the driveshaft flanges from the mating flanges. Pry only in the area shown with a suitable tool.

5. Using a suitable tool as shown, disconnect the driveshaft flanges and remove the driveshaft.

6. Slide the driveshaft toward the rear of the vehicle, while maneuvering the front section over the top of the vehicle frame crossmember and remove the driveshaft.

To install:

7. Installation is reverse of removal.

8. Tighten center support bracket to 41 ft. lbs. (55 Nm).

9. Tighten front and rear driveshaft to flange, with marks aligned; tighten the bolts to 83 ft. lbs. (112 Nm)

➡If new bolts to retain the driveshaft to the axle are not available, coat the threads of the original bolts with threadlock and sealer.

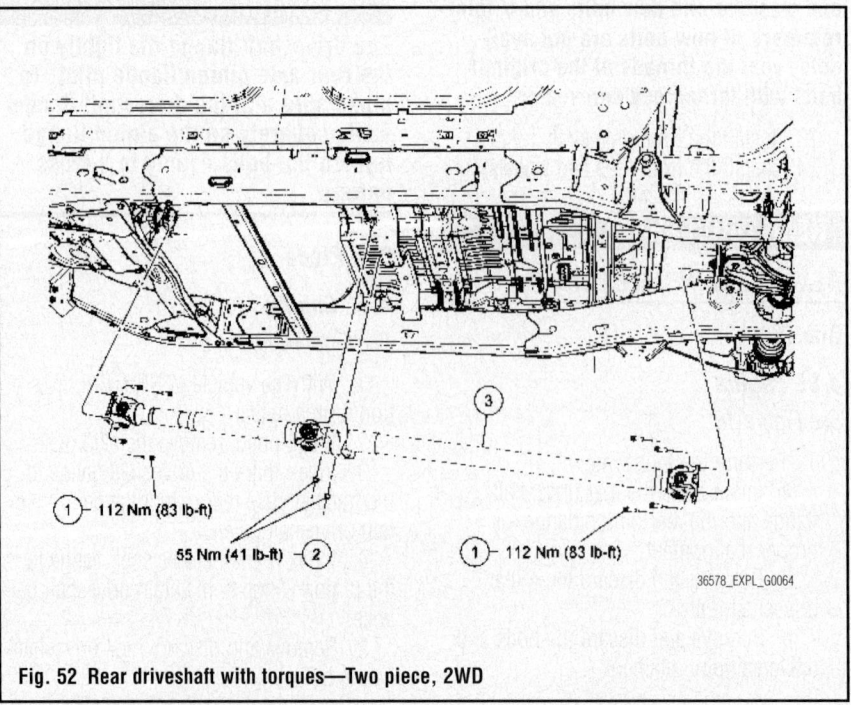

Fig. 52 Rear driveshaft with torques—Two piece, 2WD

※※ **WARNING**

The driveshaft flange fits tightly on the rear axle pinion flange pilot. To make sure that the driveshaft flange seats squarely on the pinion flange, tighten the bolts evenly in a cross pattern.

Two Piece

4WD Models

See Figures 53 and 54.

1. With the vehicle in NEUTRAL, position it on a hoist.
2. Remove the 2 nuts from the driveshaft center bearing bracket.
3. Index-mark the CV joint to the transfer case output flange.
4. Index-mark the rear U-joint flange to the differential pinion flange.

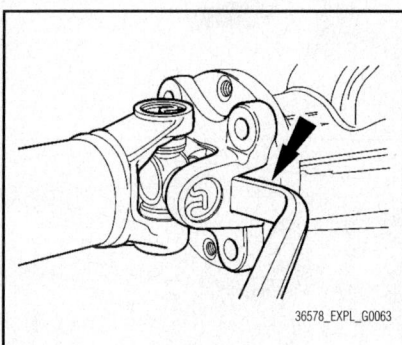

Fig. 53 Disconnecting the driveshaft flanges—Two piece, 4WD

5. Remove and discard the 6 CV joint bolts and 3 CV joint washers.
6. Remove and discard the 4 driveshaft flange bolts.

※※ **WARNING**

The driveshaft flange fits tightly on the axle pinion flange pilot and the transfer case output flange. Never hammer on the driveshaft, or any of its components, to disconnect the driveshaft flanges from the mating flanges. Pry only in the area shown with a suitable tool.

7. Using a suitable tool as shown, disconnect the driveshaft flanges and remove the driveshaft.
8. Slide the driveshaft toward the rear of the vehicle, while maneuvering the front section over the top of the vehicle frame crossmember and remove the driveshaft.

To install:

9. Installation is reverse of removal.
10. Tighten center support bracket to 41 ft. lbs. (55 Nm).
11. Tighten rear driveshaft to flange bolts to 83 ft. lbs. (112 Nm), with marks aligned.
12. Tighten front CV joint to the transfer case output flange bolts to 22 ft. lbs. (30 Nm), with marks aligned.

➡ **If new bolts to retain the driveshaft to the axle are not available, coat the threads of the original bolts with threadlock and sealer.**

※※ **WARNING**

The driveshaft flange fits tightly on the rear axle pinion flange pilot. To make sure that the driveshaft flange seats squarely on the pinion flange, tighten the bolts evenly in a cross pattern.

REAR HALFSHAFTS

REMOVAL & INSTALLATION

See Figures 55 through 60.

※※ **WARNING**

Do not loosen the rear axle wheel end nut until after the wheel and tire assembly are removed from the vehicle. Wheel bearing damage will occur if the wheel bearing is unloaded with the weight of the vehicle applied.

1. Before servicing the vehicle, refer to Precautions.
2. With the vehicle in NEUTRAL, position it on a hoist.
3. Remove the rear wheel and tire assembly.
4. Remove and discard the rear axle wheel end nut.

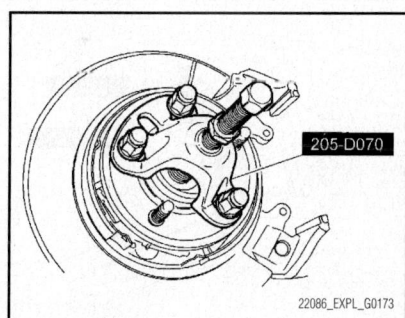

Fig. 55 Using the special tool, press the outboard CV joint until it is loose in the hub

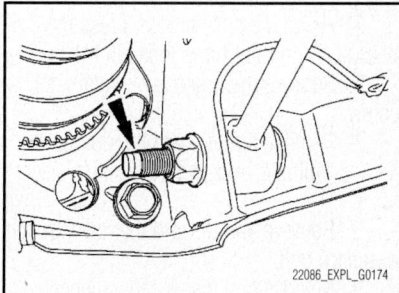

Fig. 56 Remove and discard the outboard toe link nut and back out the bolt for clearance

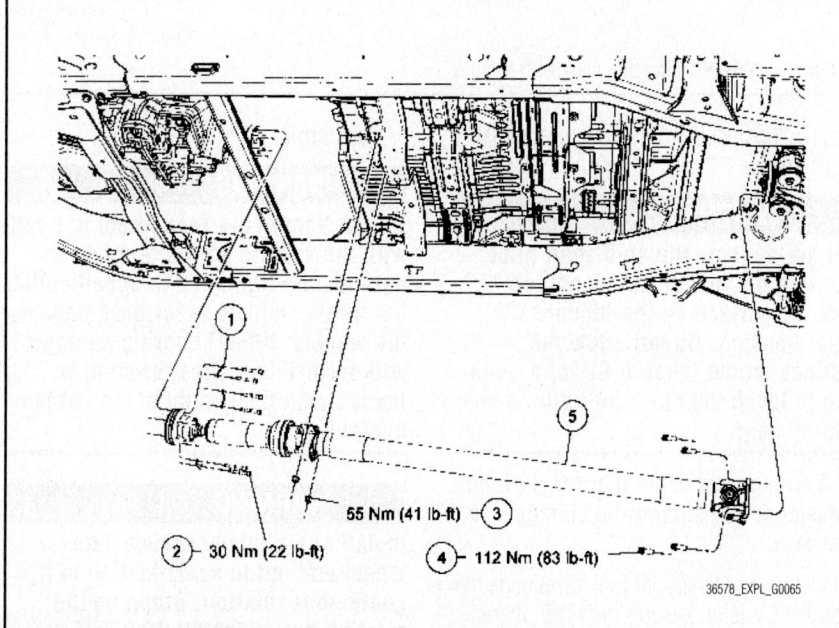

55 Nm (41 lb-ft) ③
② 30 Nm (22 lb-ft)
④ 112 Nm (83 lb-ft)

Fig. 54 Rear driveshaft with torques—Two piece, 4WD

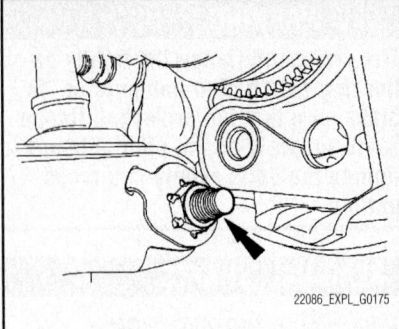

Fig. 57 Remove and discard the lower arm outboard bolt

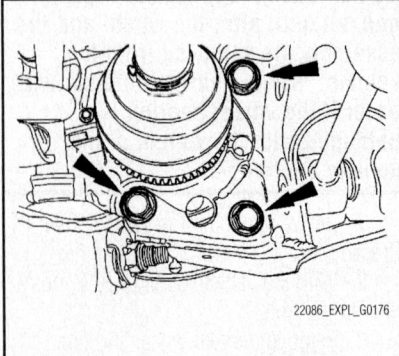

Fig. 58 Remove and discard the 3 wheel knuckle bolts

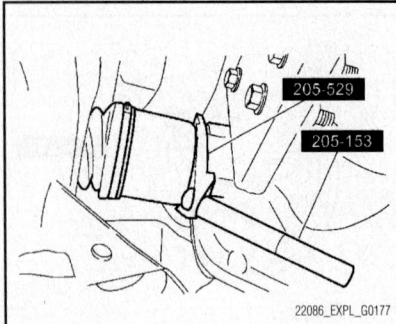

Fig. 59 Using the special tool, disengage the inboard CV joint housing from the differential side gear

5. Using the special tool, press the outboard CV joint until it is loose in the hub.

6. Remove the brake cable retainer screw.

7. Remove and discard the outboard toe link nut and back out the bolt for clearance.

8. Remove and discard the lower arm outboard bolt.

9. Remove and discard the 3 wheel knuckle bolts.

10. Pivot the wheel knuckle assembly upward on the upper arm outboard bolt.

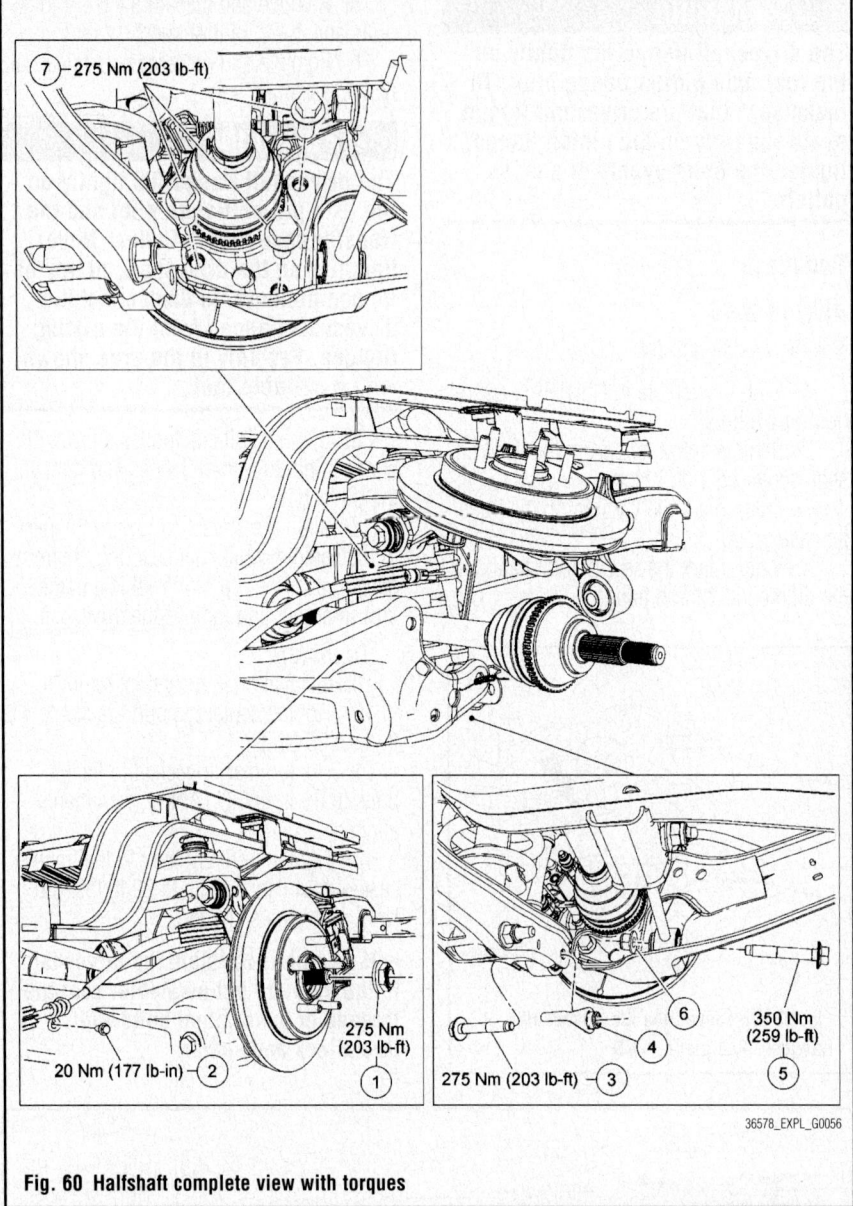

Fig. 60 Halfshaft complete view with torques

Loosen the upper arm bolt to prevent bushing damage.

❊❊ WARNING

Do not damage the stub shaft pilot bearing oil seal or the machined sealing surface on the inboard CV joint housing. Do not allow the splines on the inboard CV joint housing to touch the stub shaft pilot bearing oil seal.

➡ **A circlip retains the inboard CV joint housing to the differential side gear in the axle.**

11. Using the special tool, disengage the inboard CV joint housing from the differential side gear.

12. Remove the halfshaft assembly.

To install:

❊❊ WARNING

Do not tighten the rear wheel hub nut with the vehicle on the ground. The nut must be tightened to specification before the vehicle is lowered onto the wheels. Wheel bearing damage will occur if the wheel bearing is loaded with the weight of the vehicle applied.

❊❊ WARNING

Install and tighten the new axle wheel end nut to specification in a continuous rotation. Stopping the rotation during installation will cause the nylon lock to seat incorrectly.

This will cause incorrect torque readings while tightening the axle wheel end nut and lead to bearing failure. Always install a new axle wheel end nut, after loosening or when not tightened to specifications, in a continuous rotation.

✴✴ WARNING

Always install a new differential stub shaft seal whenever the halfshaft is removed.

13. Position the halfshaft in the vehicle.
14. Start one end of the circlip in the groove and work the circlip over the halfshaft and into the groove to prevent the circlip from over-expanding.

✴✴ WARNING

Make sure the halfshaft is completely seated in the differential side gear by pushing the halfshaft into the rear axle assembly until an audible click is heard or a leak can occur from the axle assembly.

15. Reposition the steering knuckle. Install the upper arm bolt finger-tight (final tightening will be done with vehicle resting on its full weight).
16. Install the 3 wheel knuckle bolts and torque to 203 ft. lbs. (275 Nm).
17. Install the lower arm outboard bolt; torque only snug at this time (final tightening will be done with the vehicle resting on its full weight).
18. Install a new outboard toe link nut. Tighten the bolt only snugly (final tightening will be done with the vehicle resting on its full weight).
19. Install the brake cable retainer screw. Torque to 15 ft. lbs. (20 Nm).
20. Check that the outboard CV joint is properly fit into the hub.
21. Install a new rear axle wheel end nut. Tighten the nut to 258 ft. lbs. (350 Nm).
22. Install the wheel and tire assembly.
23. Lower the vehicle to its full resting weight.
24. Tighten the fasteners as follows:
   a. Wheel lug nuts: 100 ft. lbs. (135 Nm)

   b. Outboard toe link bolt: 259 ft. lbs. (350 Nm)
   c. Lower arm outboard bolt: 203 ft. lbs. (275 Nm)
   d. Upper arm bolt: 203 ft. lbs. (275 Nm)

REAR PINION SEAL

REMOVAL & INSTALLATION
See Figure 61.

1. Before servicing the vehicle, refer to Precautions.
2. Drain the axle housing fluid.
3. Remove or disconnect the following:
   • Rear wheel and tire assemblies
   • Brake caliper and support bracket from the knuckle as an assembly. Wire the caliper and support bracket assembly out of the way.

➡**Matchmark the driveshaft flange and rear axle pinion flange to maintain initial balance during installation.**

4. Disconnect and position the driveshaft out of the way.
5. Install an inch/pound torque wrench on the nut and record the torque necessary to maintain rotation of the drive pinion gear through several revolutions.
6. Remove and discard the pinion flange nut.

➡**Matchmark the rear axle pinion flange and drive pinion gear stem to maintain initial balance during installation.**

7. Remove the rear axle pinion flange.
8. Force up on the metal flange of the rear axle drive pinion seal. Install gripping pliers and strike with a hammer until the rear axle drive pinion seal is removed.

To install:
9. Lubricate the new rear drive pinion seal with grease.

➡**If the rear axle drive pinion seal becomes misaligned during installation, remove the rear axle drive pinion seal and install a new seal.**

10. Drive in the rear axle drive pinion seal.
11. Inspect the rear axle pinion flange seal journal for rust, nicks and scratches prior to installing the flange. Polish the seal journal with fine crocus cloth, if necessary.

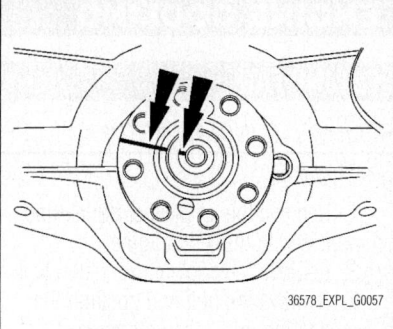

36578_EXPL_G0057

Fig. 61 Matchmark the rear axle pinion flange and drive pinion gear stem

12. Lubricate the rear axle pinion flange splines.
13. Install the rear axle pinion flange, aligning the matchmarks made during disassembly.

➡**Disregard the index marks if installing a new pinion flange.**

✴✴ WARNING

Do not under any circumstance loosen the nut to reduce preload. If it is necessary to reduce preload, install a new differential drive pinion collapsible spacer and nut.

14. Rotate the pinion occasionally to make sure the pinion bearings seat correctly. Take frequent pinion bearing torque preload readings by rotating the drive pinion gear with an inch/pound torque wrench.

➡**Rotational torque must be at least the recorded original torque plus a maximum of 5 inch-pounds.**

15. If the preload recorded prior to disassembly is lower than the specification for used bearings, then tighten the nut to specification. If the preload recorded prior to disassembly is higher than the specification for used bearings, then tighten the nut to the original reading as recorded.
   Pinion bearing preload: 16–29 inch lbs. (1.8–3.2 Nm).
16. Connect the driveshaft. Torque the bolts to 83 ft. lbs. (112 Nm).
17. Install the rear brake calipers. Torque the bolts to 24 ft. lbs. (32 Nm).
18. Install the rear wheel and tire assemblies.

ENGINE COOLING

ENGINE FAN

REMOVAL & INSTALLATION

See Figure 62.

1. Remove the air cleaner outlet tube, on models with the 4.6L engine.
2. Remove the coolant expansion tank.
3. Remove the bolt and position the power steering fluid reservoir aside.
4. Remove the bolts, then unclip the upper fan shroud from the lower fan shroud and remove the upper fan shroud.
5. Disconnect the fan clutch electrical connector.
6. Remove the fan clutch wiring harness bracket bolt.
7. Remove the cooling fan.

To install:

8. Installation is the reverse of the removal procedure.
9. Torque the cooling fan bolts to 41 ft. lbs. (55 Nm).
10. Torque the power steering reservoir bolt to 89 inch lbs. (10 Nm).

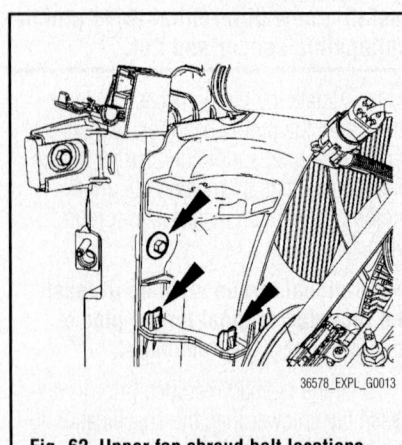

Fig. 62 Upper fan shroud bolt locations

RADIATOR

REMOVAL & INSTALLATION

See Figures 62 and 63.

1. Drain the cooling system.
2. Remove or disconnect the following:
   - Air cleaner outlet pipe (4.6L)
   - Coolant expansion tank
   - Power steering fluid reservoir; remove bolts and position aside
   - Upper and lower radiator hoses
   - Transmission cooling hose retainer from radiator support bracket
   - 4 lower radiator air deflector push pins

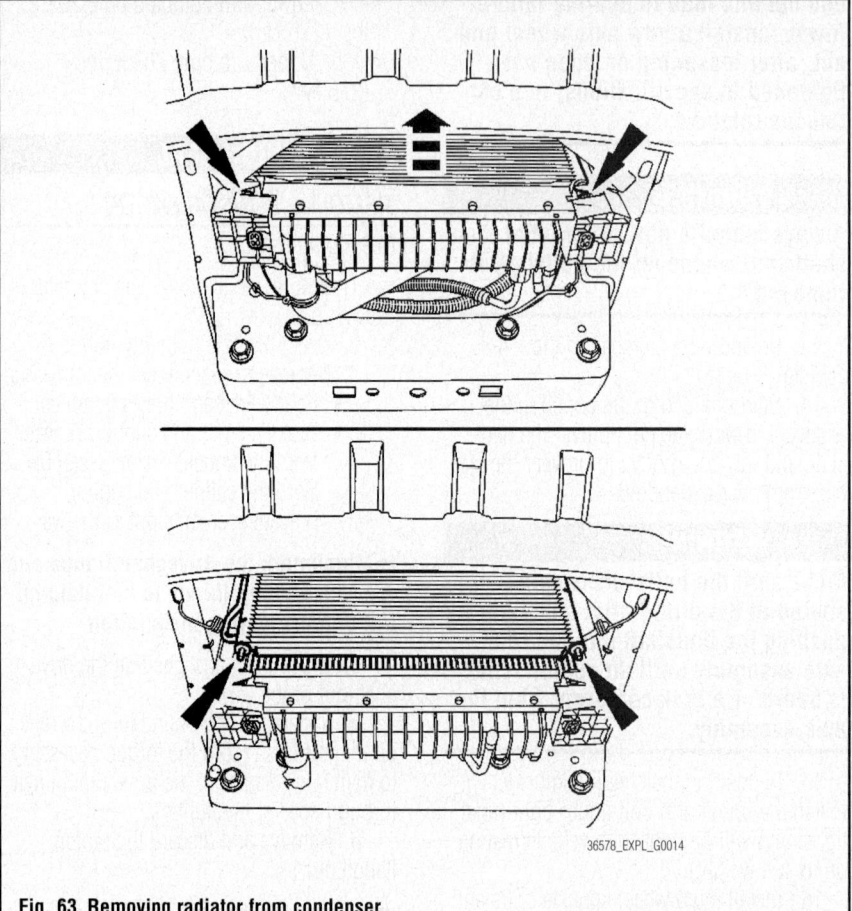

Fig. 63 Removing radiator from condenser

   - Latch assemblies from the transmission cooler tubes
   - Transmission cooler tubes, using special tool 307-569
   - Upper fan shroud
   - Fan clutch electrical connector
   - Fan clutch wiring harness bracket bolt
   - Cooling fan
   - Lower fan shroud
   - A/C tube from the upper retainer
   - Radiator support bracket-to-body bolts
   - Radiator top seal

3. Deflect the A/C condenser seals and remove the A/C condenser-to-radiator support bracket bolts.
4. Remove the radiator and the radiator support brackets as an assembly.
5. Remove the bolts and separate the radiator support brackets and the radiator.

To install:

6. Install or connect the following:
   - Support brackets to the radiator
   - Radiator into position; tighten the bolts to 9 ft. lbs. (12 Nm)
   - Reposition A/C condenser seals
   - Radiator top seal
   - Radiator support bracket-to-body bolts; tighten the bolts to 11 ft. lbs. (15 Nm)
   - A/C tube from the upper retainer
   - Lower fan shroud
   - Cooling fan; tighten the bolts to 41 ft. lbs. (55 Nm)
   - Fan clutch wiring harness bracket bolt
   - Fan clutch electrical connector
   - Upper fan shroud
   - Transmission cooler tubes
   - Upper and lower radiator hoses
   - Power steering fluid reservoir; tighten bolts to 89 inch lbs. (10 Nm)
   - Coolant expansion tank
   - Air cleaner outlet pipe (4.6L)

THERMOSTAT

REMOVAL & INSTALLATION

4.0L Engine

See Figure 64.

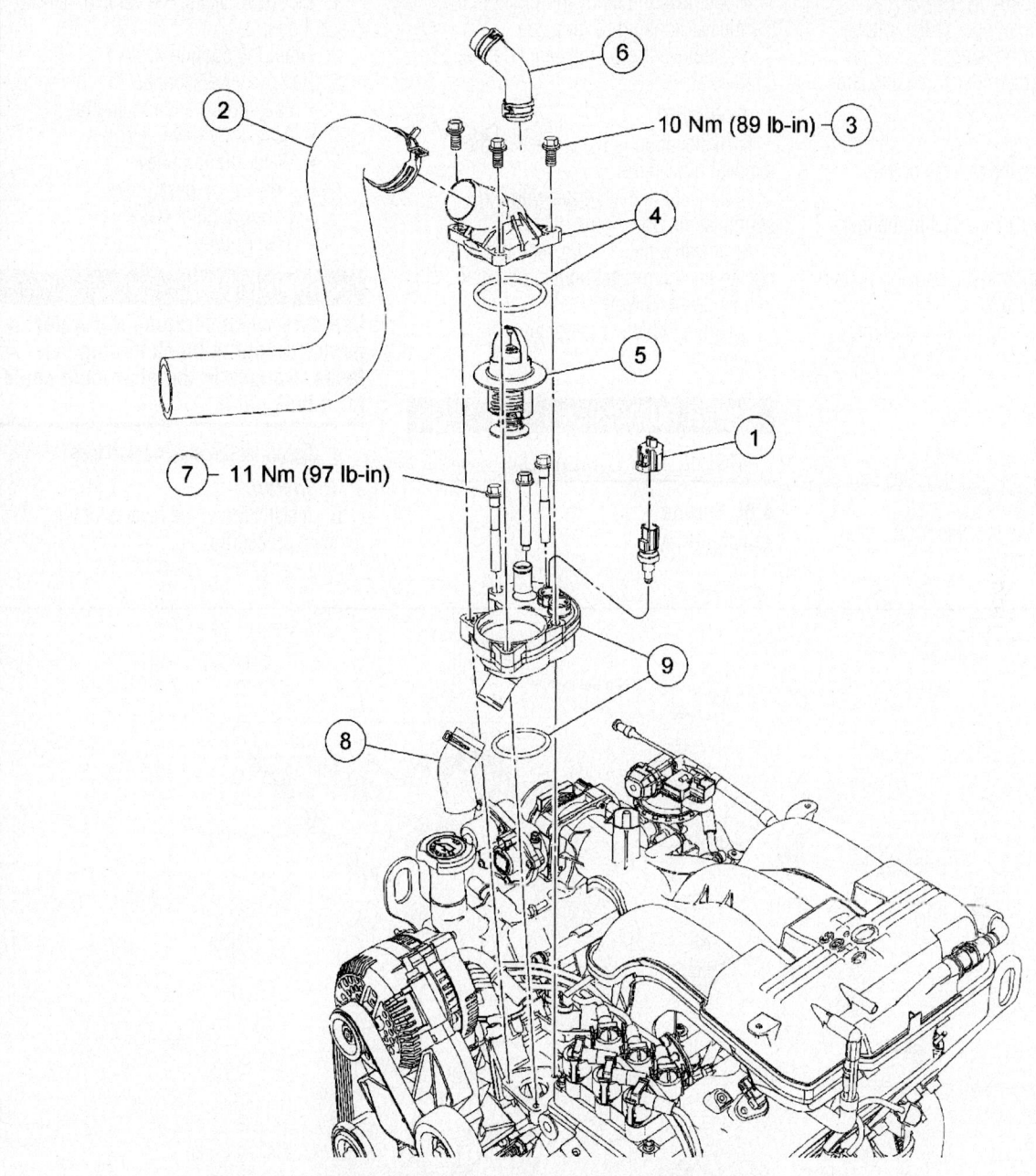

10 Nm (89 lb-in)

11 Nm (97 lb-in)

1. Engine Coolant Temperature (ECT) sensor electrical connector
2. Upper radiator hose
3. Thermostat housing cover bolt (3 required)
4. Thermostat housing cover with O-ring seal
5. Thermostat
6. Heater hose
7. Thermostat housing bolt (3 required)
8. Bypass hose
9. Thermostat housing with O-ring seal

36578_EXPL_G0206

Fig. 64 Thermostat housing assembly—4.0L Engine

1. Drain the cooling system.
2. Disconnect the upper radiator hose from the thermostat housing.
3. Remove the thermostat housing and the thermostat.

To install:

4. Installation is the reverse of the removal procedure.
5. Install a new O-ring seal in the thermostat housing.
6. Torque the thermostat housing bolts to 89 inch lbs. (10 Nm).
7. Fill and bleed the cooling system.

4.6L Engine

See Figure 65.

1. Drain the cooling system.
2. Remove the throttle body. See the "Fuel Systems" section.
3. Disconnect the fuel vapor tube near the thermostat housing.

4. Remove the bolts and position the thermostat housing cover aside.
5. Remove the O-ring seal and the thermostat.

To install:

6. Installation is the reverse of the removal procedure.
7. Install the thermostat with the spring facing downward.
8. Install a new O-ring seal and tighten the thermostat housing bolts to 89 inch lbs. (10 Nm).
9. Fill and bleed the cooling system.

WATER PUMP

REMOVAL & INSTALLATION

4.0L Engine

See Figure 66.

1. Before servicing the vehicle, refer to Precautions.
2. Drain the cooling system.
3. Remove or disconnect the following:
   - Fan shroud and cooling fan
   - Accessory drive belt
   - Water pump pulley
   - Coolant by-pass hose
   - Lower radiator hose
   - Water pump

❋❋ WARNING

Use care when scraping the water pump-to-engine block mating surfaces. Gouges in the aluminum could form leak paths.

4. Clean all the sealing surfaces.

To install:

5. Installation is the reverse of the removal procedure.

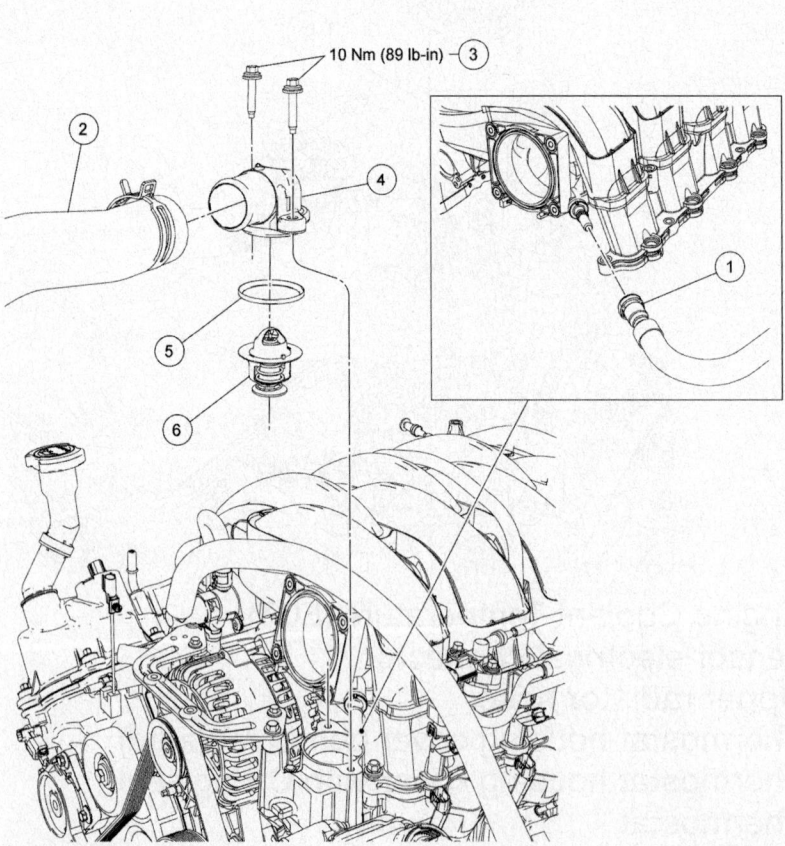

1. Fuel vapor tube
2. Upper radiator hose
3. Thermostat housing bolt (2 required)
4. Thermostat housing cover
5. Thermostat O-ring seal
6. Thermostat

36578_EXPL_G0015

Fig. 65 Thermostat bolt location—4.6L Engine

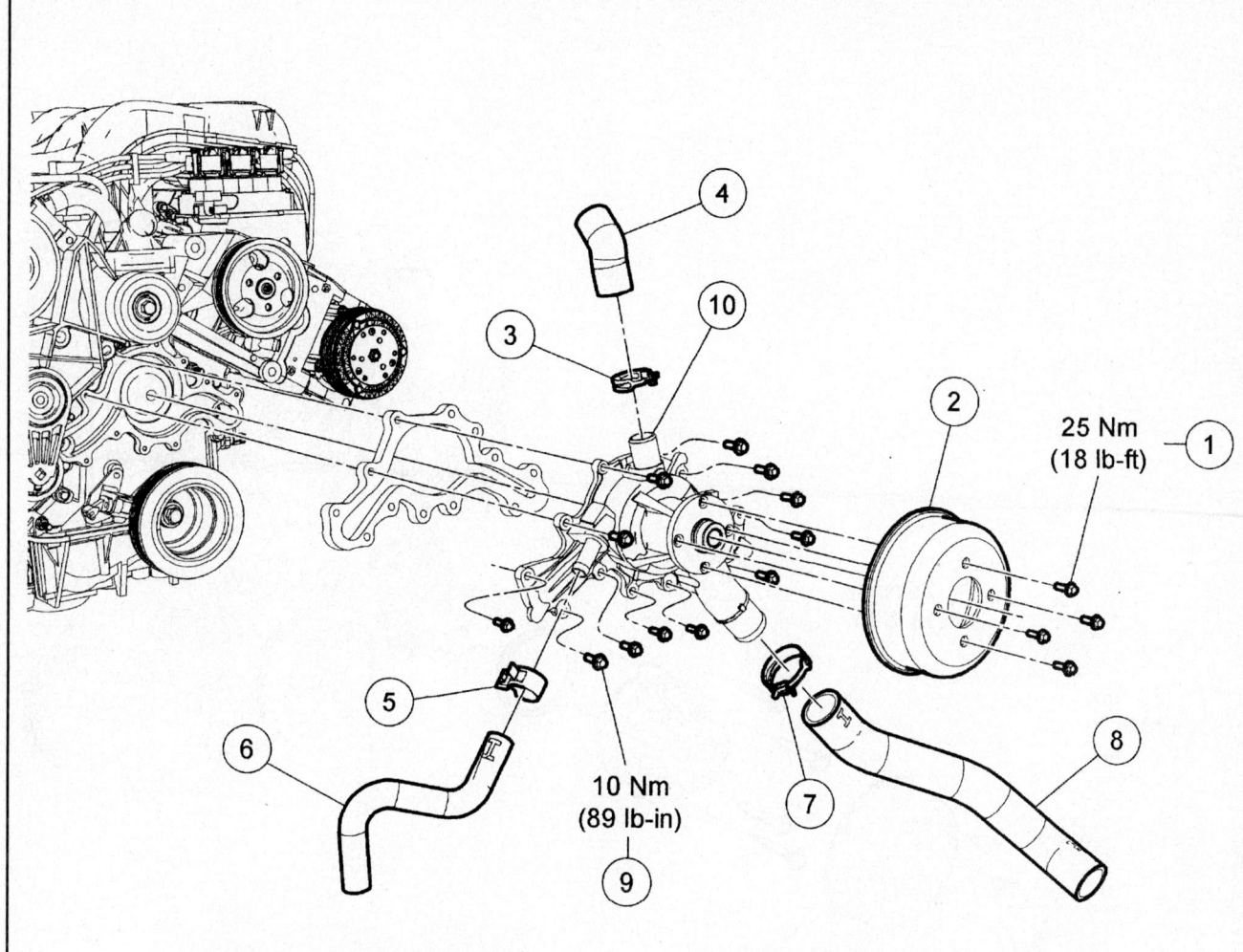

**25 Nm
(18 lb-ft)**

**10 Nm
(89 lb-in)**

1	Coolant pump pulley bolts (4 required)	6	Heater hose
2	Coolant pump pulley	7	Lower radiator hose clamp
3	Coolant pump bypass hose clamp	8	Lower radiator hose
4	Coolant pump bypass hose	9	Coolant pump bolts (12 required)
5	Heater hose clamp	10	Coolant pump

06017-EXPL-G09

Fig. 66 Typical water pump installation—4.0L engine

6. Observe the following tightening specifications:
- Water pump bolts: 89 inch lbs. (10 Nm)
- Pulley bolts: 18 ft. lbs. (25 Nm)

4.6L Engine

See Figure 67.

1. Before servicing the vehicle, refer to Precautions.

2. Drain the cooling system.
3. Remove or disconnect the following:
- Engine cooling fan
- Upper fan shroud
- Water pump pulley bolts (loosen only)
- Accessory drive belt
- Water pump pulley
- Water pump
4. Discard the O-ring seal.

To install:

5. Installation is the reverse of the removal procedure.
6. Install a new O-ring seal and lubricate with engine coolant.
7. Observe the following tightening specifications:
- Water pump mounting bolts: 18 ft. lbs. (25 Nm).
- Water pump pulley bolts: 18 ft. lbs. (25 Nm).

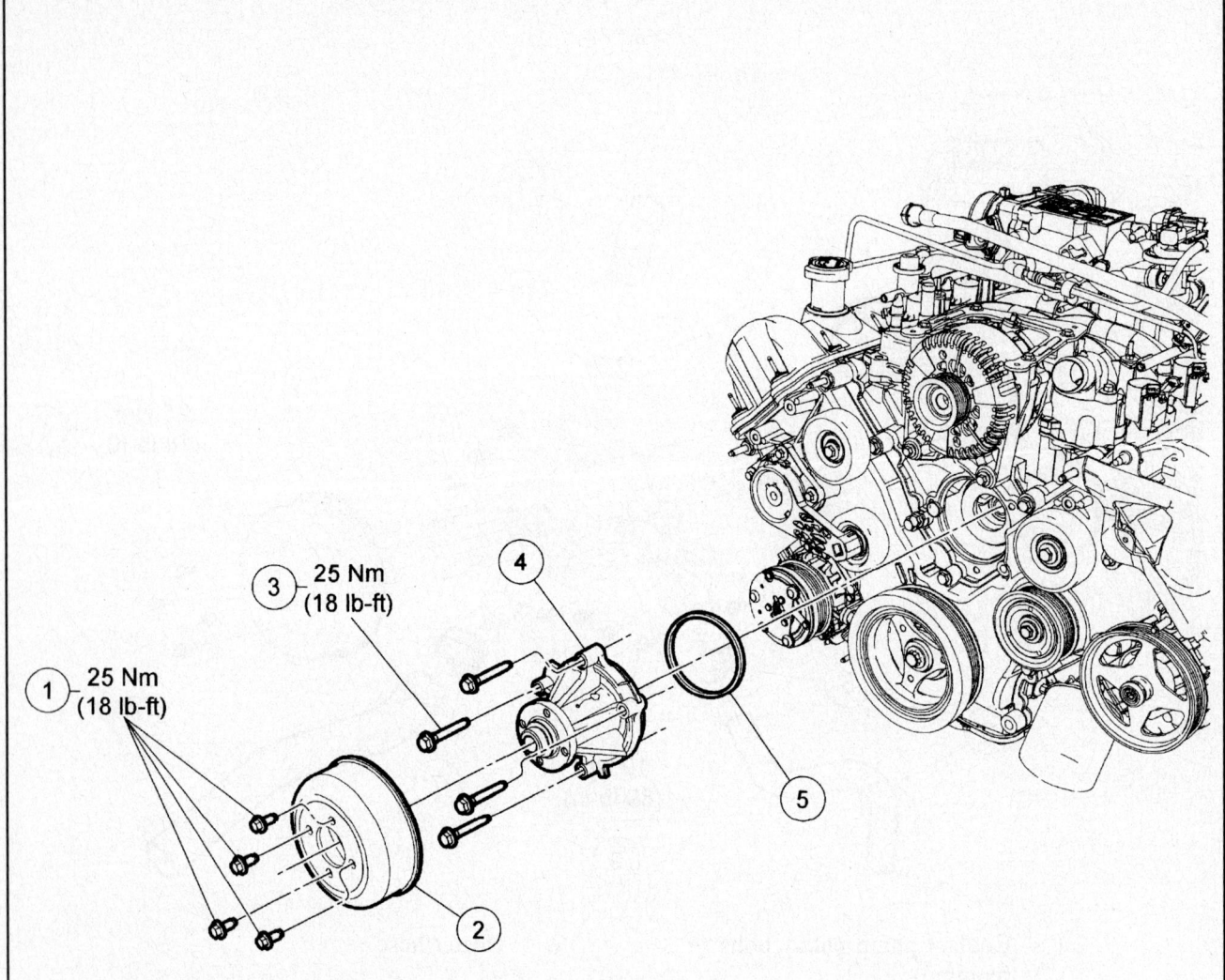

1   25 Nm
    (18 lb-ft)

3   25 Nm
    (18 lb-ft)

4

5

2

1   Coolant pump pulley bolts (4 required)
2   Coolant pump pulley
3   Coolant pump bolts (4 required)
4   Coolant pump
5   Coolant pump O-ring

06017-EXPL-G10

Fig. 67 Water pump installation—4.6L engine

ENGINE ELECTRICAL   CHARGING SYSTEM

ALTERNATOR

REMOVAL & INSTALLATION

4.0L Engine

See Figure 68.

1. Before servicing the vehicle, refer to the precautions in the beginning of this section.
2. Disconnect the battery.
3. Rotate the front end accessory drive belt tensioner counterclockwise and position the front end accessory drive belt aside.
4. Position the protective cover aside and remove the alternator B+ terminal nut.
5. Disconnect the alternator B+ terminal and the 2 electrical connectors.

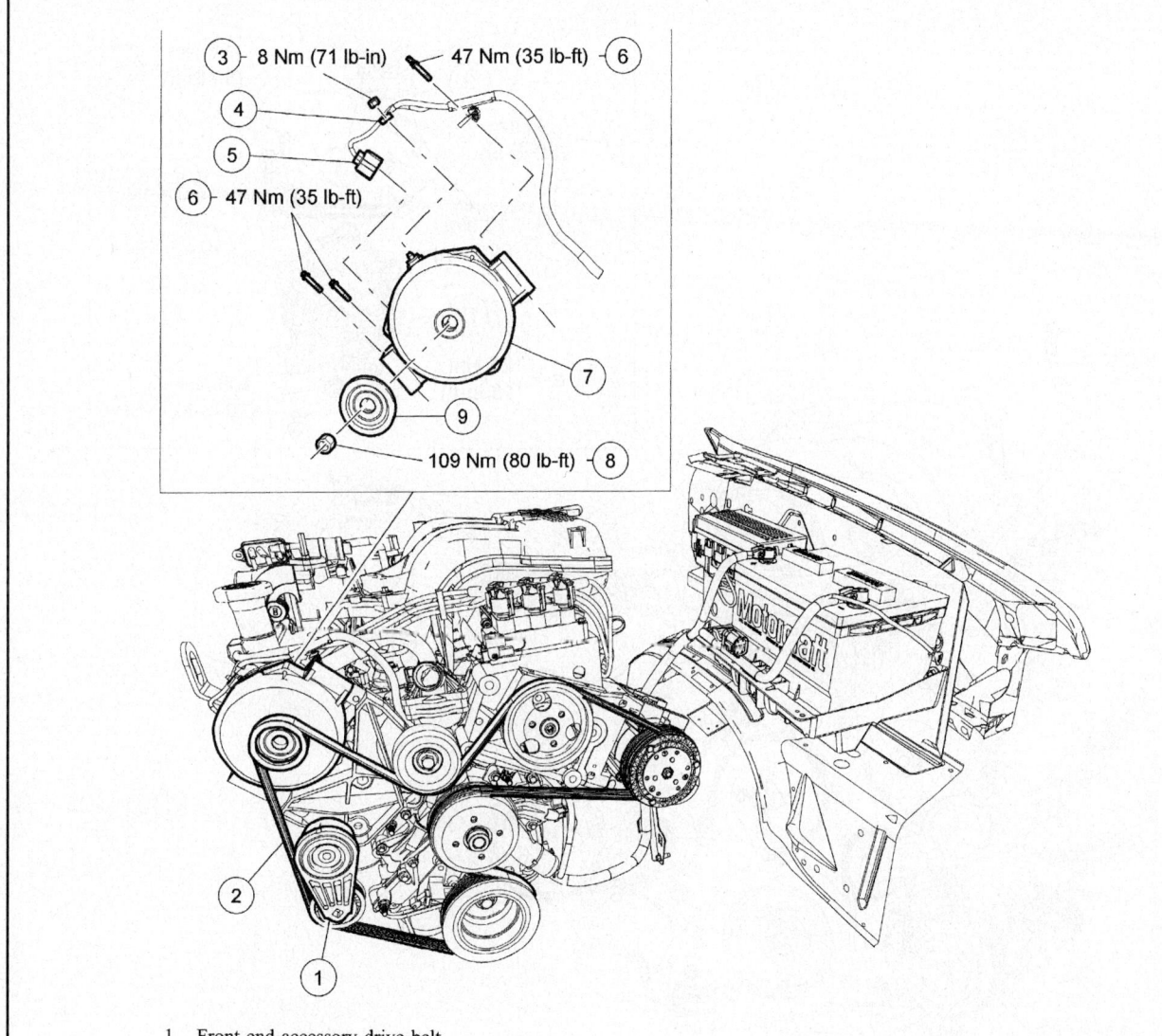

1. Front end accessory drive belt tensioner
2. Front end accessory drive belt
3. Generator B+ terminal nut
4. Generator B+ terminal
5. Generator electrical connectors
6. Generator bolts
7. Generator
8. Generator pulley nut
9. Generator pulley

06017-EXPL-G02

Fig. 68 Alternator mounting—4.0L engine

6. Remove the 3 bolts and the alternator.

7. If necessary, remove the nut and the alternator pulley.

To install:

8. If the alternator pulley was removed, install it and tighten the pulley bolt to 80 ft. lbs. (109 Nm).

9. Position the alternator and install the 3 mounting bolts. Tighten the mounting bolts to 35 ft. lbs. (47 Nm).

10. Connect the alternator B+ terminal and both electrical connectors.

11. Install the alternator B+ terminal nut. Tighten it to 80 inch lbs. (9 Nm).

12. Install the accessory drive belt and slowly release the tensioner.

13. Connect the battery cables.

4.6L Engine

See Figures 69 and 70.

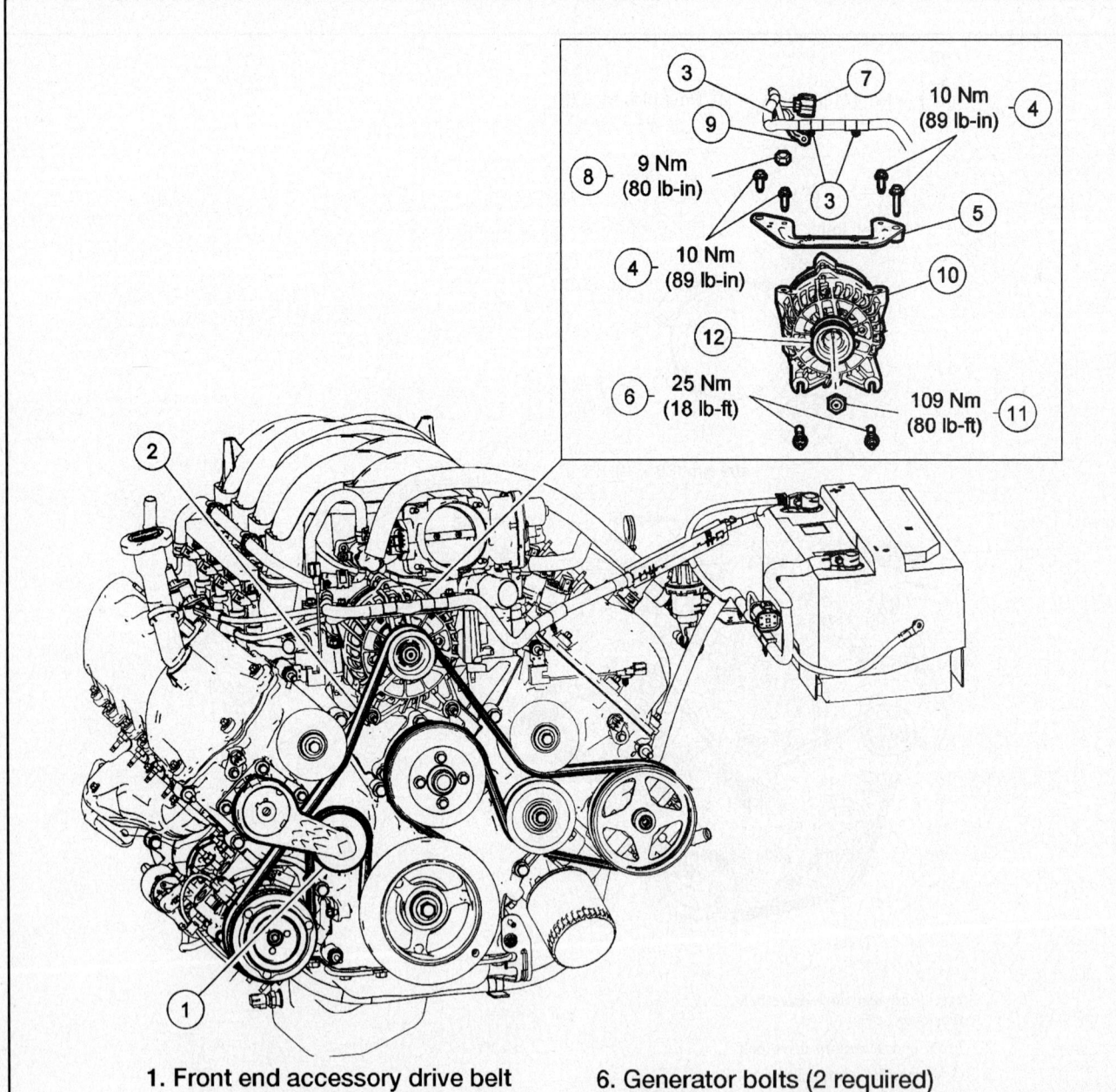

1. Front end accessory drive belt
2. Front end accessory drive belt
3. Generator harness locators (3 required)
4. Generator bracket bolts (4 required)
5. Generator bracket tensioner
6. Generator bolts (2 required)
7. Generator electrical connector
8. Generator B+ terminal nut
9. Generator B+ terminal
10. Generator
11. Generator pulley nut
12. Generator pulley

22086_EXPL_G0003

Fig. 69 A front engine view of the alternator mounting components and the accessory drive belt routing—4.6L engine

1. Before servicing the vehicle, refer to the precautions in the beginning of this section.

2. Disconnect the battery.

3. Remove the throttle body as follows:

   a. Remove the air cleaner outlet pipe.

   b. Disconnect the electronic throttle control and throttle position (TP) sensor electrical connectors.

   c. Remove the bolts, the throttle body, and the gasket. Discard the gasket.

4. Rotate the front end accessory drive belt tensioner clockwise and position the front end accessory drive belt aside.

5. Remove or disconnect the following:

   • 4 bolts and the alternator bracket

   • 2 bolts and position the alternator aside

   • Protective cover and nut; position the alternator B+ terminal aside

   • Remove the alternator.

   • If necessary, remove the pulley from the alternator.

To install:

6. If removed, install the pulley onto the alternator. Tighten the pulley nut to 80 ft. lbs. (109 Nm).

7. Position the alternator. Install the mounting bolts and tighten to 18 lb. ft. (25 Nm).

8. Install the alternator B+ terminal and nut; reposition the protective cover.

9. Install the alternator bracket. Tighten the 4 bolts to 89 inch lbs. (10 Nm).

10. Install the accessory drive belt and release the tensioner.

11. Install the throttle body as follows:

    a. Position the throttle body, with a new gasket. Install and tighten the mounting bolts to 89 inch lbs. (10 Nm).

    b. Connect the TP sensor and electronic throttle control connectors.

    c. Install the air cleaner outlet pipe.

12. Reconnect the battery.

VOLTAGE REGULATOR

ADJUSTMENT

The voltage regulator is an internal component of the alternator and cannot be serviced separately.

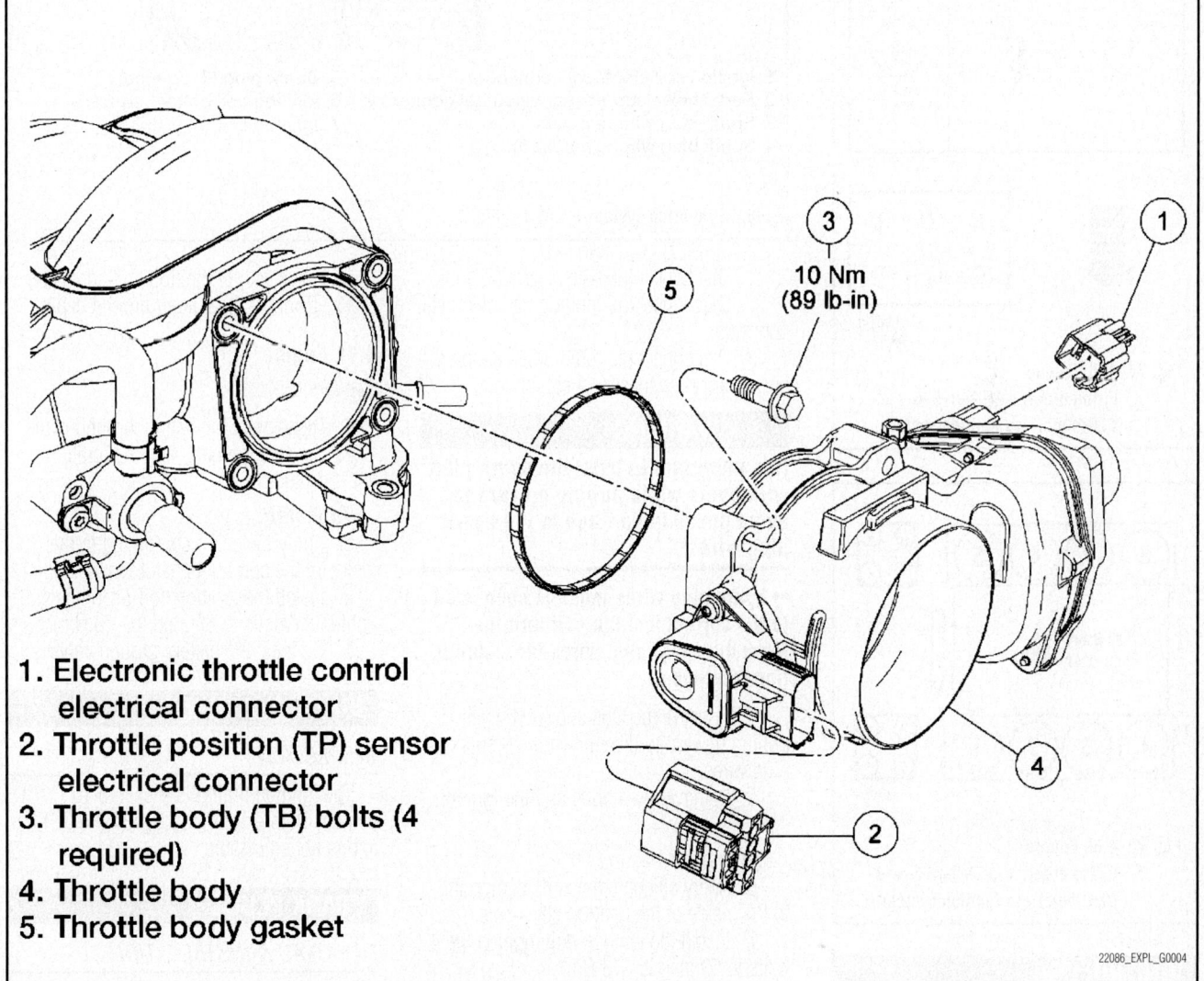

1. **Electronic throttle control electrical connector**
2. **Throttle position (TP) sensor electrical connector**
3. **Throttle body (TB) bolts (4 required)**
4. **Throttle body**
5. **Throttle body gasket**

3 10 Nm (89 lb-in)

22086_EXPL_G0004

Fig. 70 Exploded view of the throttle body—4.6L engine

ENGINE ELECTRICAL

IGNITION SYSTEM

FIRING ORDERS

See Figures 71 and 72.

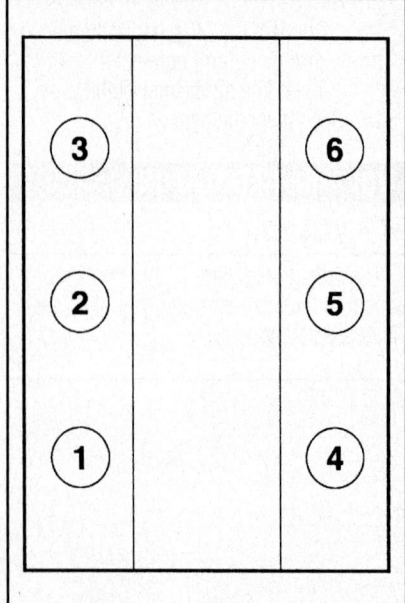

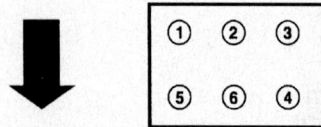

Fig. 71 4.0L Engine
Firing order: 1–4–2–5–3–6
Distributorless ignition system

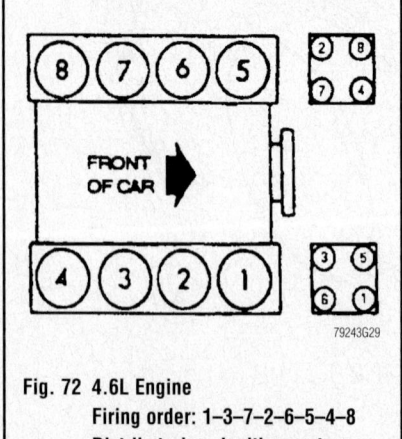

Fig. 72 4.6L Engine
Firing order: 1–3–7–2–6–5–4–8
Distributorless ignition system

IGNITION COIL

REMOVAL & INSTALLATION

4.0L Engine

See Figure 73.

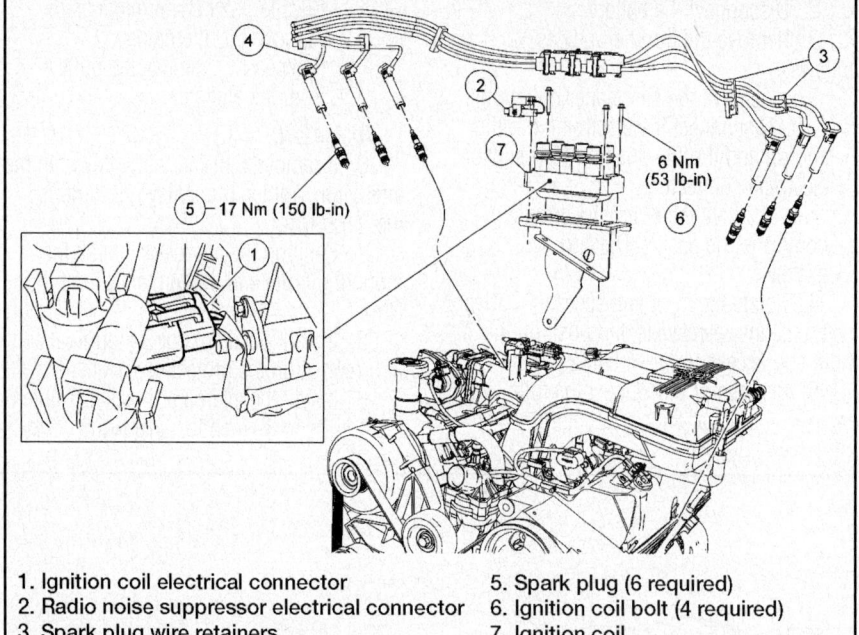

1. Ignition coil electrical connector
2. Radio noise suppressor electrical connector
3. Spark plug wire retainers
4. Spark plug wire (6 required)
5. Spark plug (6 required)
6. Ignition coil bolt (4 required)
7. Ignition coil

Fig. 73 Ignition system—4.0L Engine

1. Disconnect the battery ground cable.
2. Disconnect the ignition coil electrical connector.
3. Disconnect the radio noise suppressor electrical connector, if equipped.

※ WARNING

It is important to twist the spark plug wire boots while pulling upward to avoid possible damage to the spark plug wire.

➡Spark plug wires must be connected to the correct ignition coil terminal. Mark the spark plug wires for installation reference.

4. Squeeze the tabs and twist while pulling upward to disconnect the 6 spark plug wires.
5. Remove the 4 bolts and the ignition coil.

To install:

6. Apply silicone dielectric compound to the inside of the ignition coil boots.
7. Install the ignition coil; tighten the 4 bolts to 53 inch lbs. (6 Nm).
8. Install the spark plug wires to the correct spark plugs, as referenced during removal.
9. Connect the radio noise suppressor electrical connector, if equipped.

10. Connect the ignition coil connector.
11. Connect the battery ground cable.

4.6L Engine

See Figure 74.

1. Disconnect the battery ground cable.
2. Remove the bolts and the ignition coil-on-plugs.

To install:

3. Apply dielectric compound to the inside of the coil boots before installation.
4. Install the ignition coil-on-plugs and tighten the bolts to 53 inch lbs. (6 Nm).
5. Connect the battery ground cable.

IGNITION TIMING

INSPECTION

The ignition timing is preset to 10 degrees Before Top Dead Center (BTDC) and is not adjustable.

SPARK PLUGS

REMOVAL & INSTALLATION

4.0L Engine

➡Ford recommends replacing standard spark plugs every 100,000 miles.

When you're removing spark plugs,

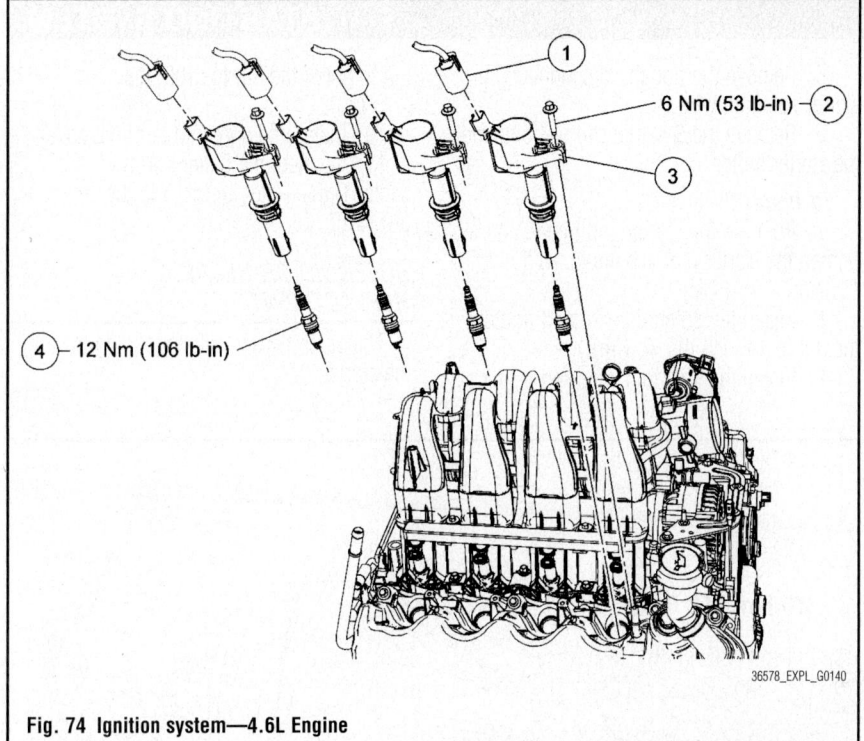

6 Nm (53 lb-in) — ②
③
④ — 12 Nm (106 lb-in)

36578_EXPL_G0140

Fig. 74 Ignition system—4.6L Engine

work on one at a time. Don't start by removing the plug wires all at once, because, unless you number them, they may become mixed up. Take a minute before you begin and number the wires with tape. Also, an anti-seize compound should be used before installing the plugs into the cylinder head.

1. Disconnect the negative battery cable, and if the vehicle has been run recently, allow the engine to thoroughly cool.

2. Carefully twist the spark plug wire boot to loosen it, then pull upward and remove the boot from the plug. Be sure to pull on the boot and not on the wire, otherwise the connector located inside the boot may become separated.

3. Using compressed air, blow any water or debris from the spark plug well to assure that no harmful contaminants are allowed to enter the combustion chamber when the spark plug is removed.

➡**Remove the spark plugs when the engine is cold, if possible, to prevent damage to the threads. If removal of the plugs is difficult, apply penetrating oil or spray to the area around the base of the plug, and allow it a few minutes to work.**

4. Using a spark plug socket that is equipped with a rubber insert to properly hold the plug, turn the spark plug counterclockwise to loosen and remove the spark plug from the bore.

❋❋ **WARNING**

Be sure not to use a flexible extension on the socket. Use of a flexible extension may allow a shear force to be applied to the plug. A shear force could break the plug off in the cylinder head, leading to costly and frustrating repairs.

To install:

5. Inspect the spark plug boot for tears or damage. If a damaged boot is found, the spark plug wire must be replaced.

➡**Coat the spark plug threads with an anti-seize compound before installing it into the cylinder head.**

6. Carefully thread the plug into the bore by hand. If resistance is felt before the plug

is almost completely threaded, back the plug out and begin threading again. In small, hard to reach areas, an old spark plug wire and boot could be used as a threading tool. The boot will hold the plug while you twist the end of the wire and the wire is supple enough to twist before it would allow the plug to cross-thread.

❋❋ **WARNING**

Do not use the spark plug socket to thread the plugs. Always carefully thread the plug by hand or using an old plug wire to prevent the possibility of cross-threading and damaging the cylinder head bore.

7. Carefully tighten the spark plug to 13 ft. lbs. (17 Nm).

8. Apply a small amount of silicone dielectric compound to the end of the spark plug lead or inside the spark plug boot to prevent sticking, then install the boot to the spark plug and push until it clicks into place. The click may be felt or heard, then gently pull back on the boot to assure proper contact.

4.6 Engine

See Figure 75.

1. Disconnect the 8 ignition coil electrical connectors.

2. Remove the 8 ignition coil bolts.

➡**When removing the ignition coils, a slight twisting motion will break the seal and ease removal.**

3. Remove the 8 ignition coils.

To install:

4. To install, reverse the removal procedure.

5. Apply a light film of brake caliper grease to the inside of the coil boots before installation.

   a. To install, tighten to 53 inch lbs. (6 Nm).

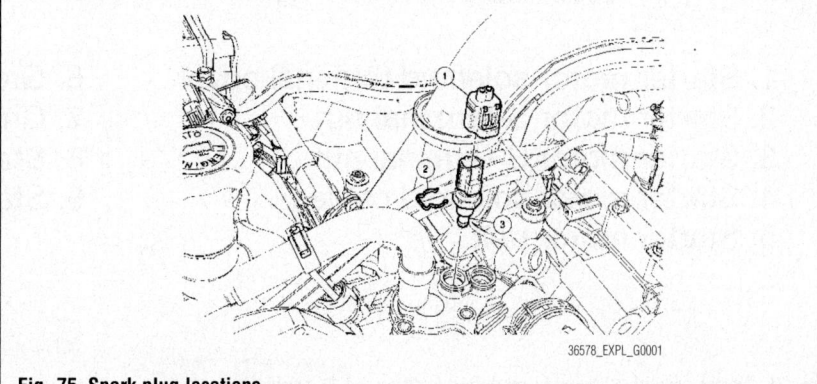

36578_EXPL_G0001

Fig. 75 Spark plug locations

ENGINE ELECTRICAL

STARTING SYSTEM

STARTER

REMOVAL & INSTALLATION

See Figures 76 and 77.

1. With the vehicle in NEUTRAL, raise vehicle on hoist.
2. Disconnect the battery ground cable.
3. Remove the starter solenoid terminal cover.
4. Remove the nut and disconnect the starter solenoid battery cable.

5. Remove the nut and disconnect the starter solenoid wire.
6. Remove the 3 starter motor bolts and the starter motor.

To install:

7. Position the starter and install and tighten the starter motor bolts to 18 ft. lbs. (25 Nm).
8. Install the solenoid wire and tighten the nut to 44 inch lbs. (6 Nm).
9. Install the solenoid wire and

nut. Tighten the nut to 10 ft. lbs. (13 Nm).
10. Install the solenoid terminal cover.
11. Connect the battery ground cable. Tighten the nut to 15 ft. lbs. (20 Nm).

SOLENOID OR RELAY REPLACEMENT

The solenoid and relay are integral with the starter.

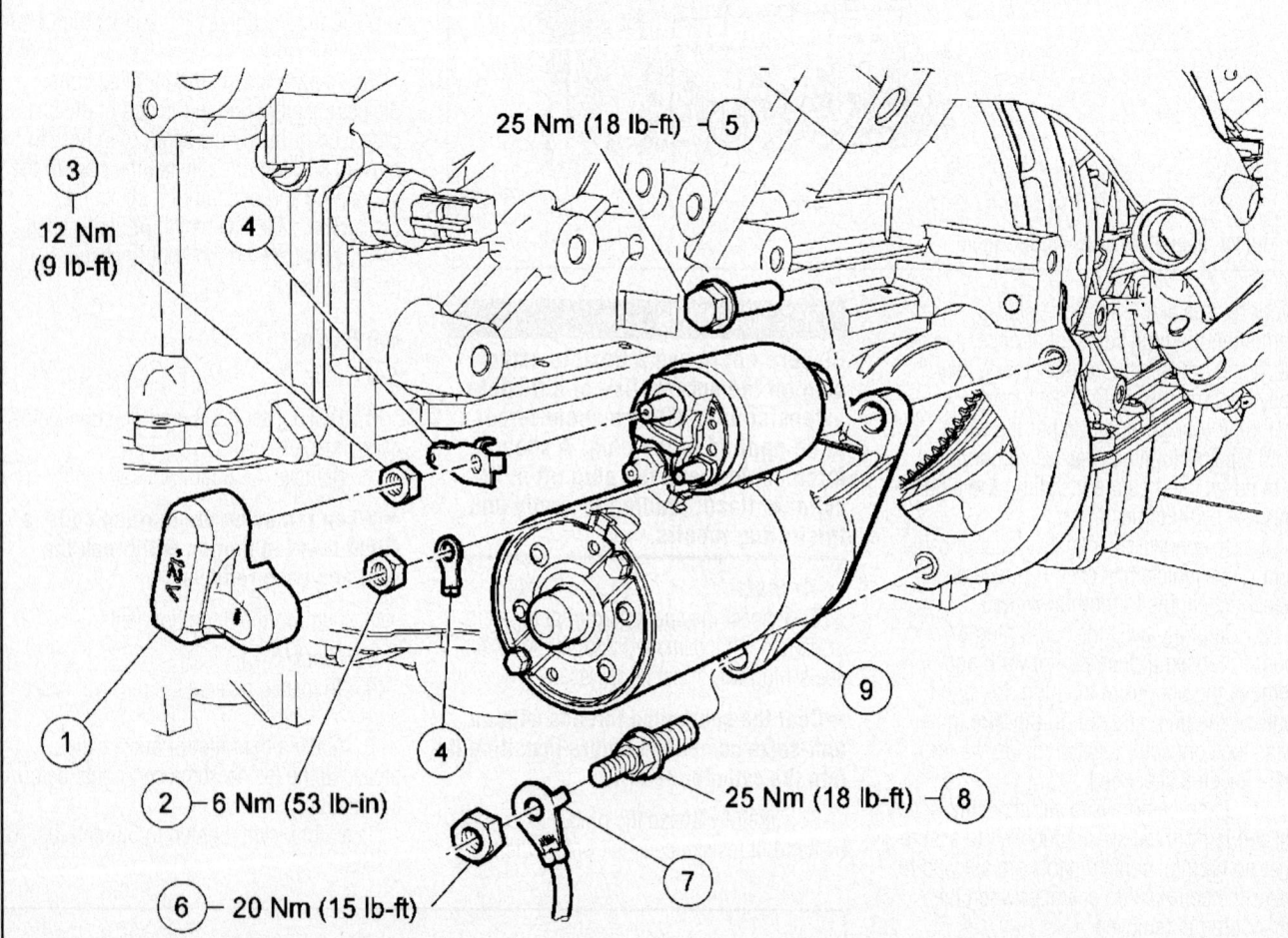

1. Starter motor solenoid terminal cover
2. Starter motor S-terminal nut
3. Starter motor B-terminal nut
4. Starter motor solenoid cables
5. Starter motor bolt
6. Ground cable nut
7. Ground cable
8. Starter motor stud bolt
9. Starter motor

22086_EXPL_G0008

Fig. 76 Starter assembly shown in mounting position—4.0L engine

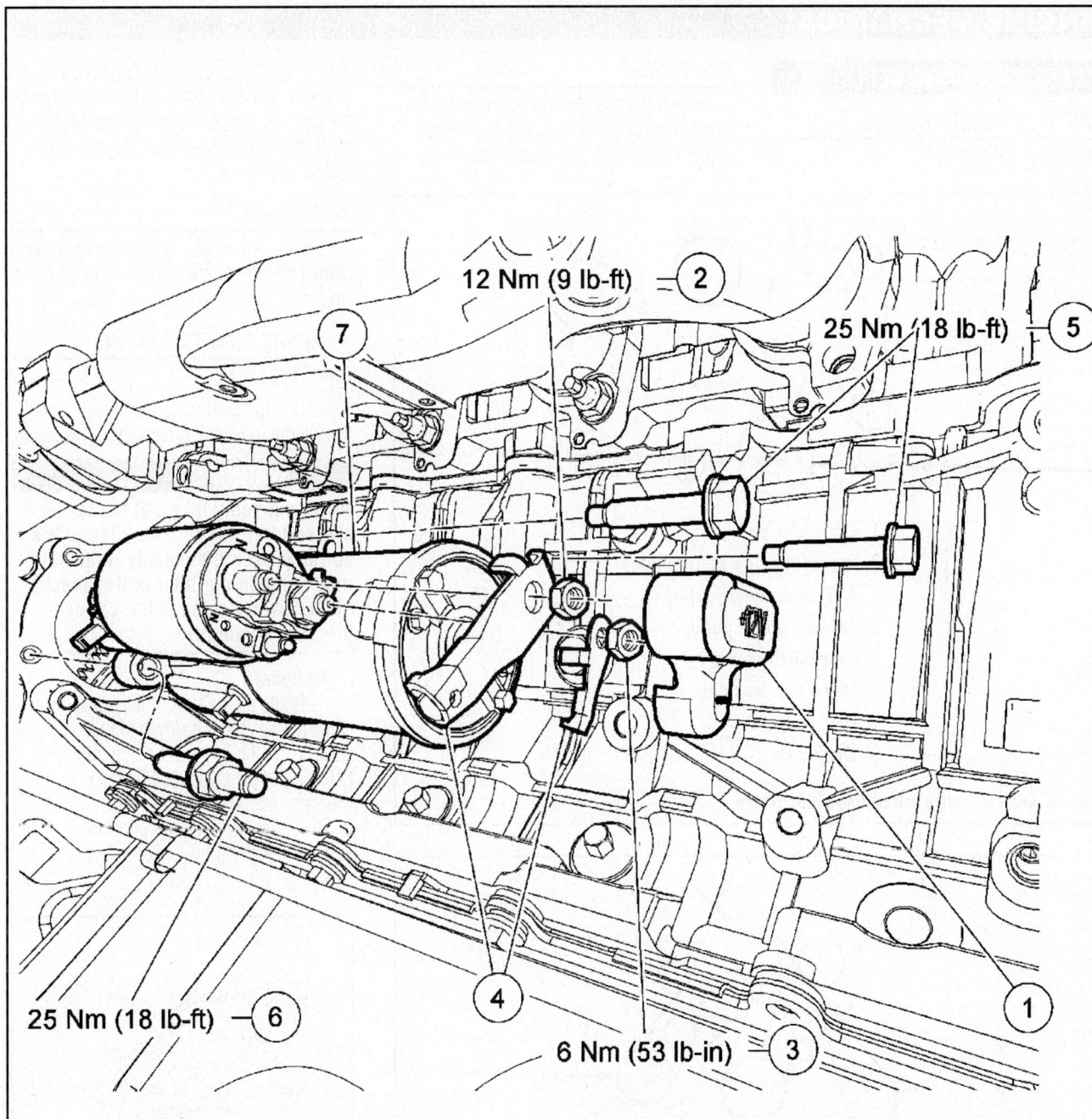

1. Starter motor solenoid terminal cover
2. B-terminal nut
3. S-terminal nut
4. Starter motor solenoid cables
5. Starter motor bolts (2 required)
6. Starter motor stud bolt
7. Starter motor

22086_EXPL_G0009

Fig. 77 Starter assembly shown in mounting position—4.6L engine

ENGINE MECHANICAL

ACCESSORY DRIVE BELTS

ACCESSORY BELT ROUTING

See Figures 78 and 79.

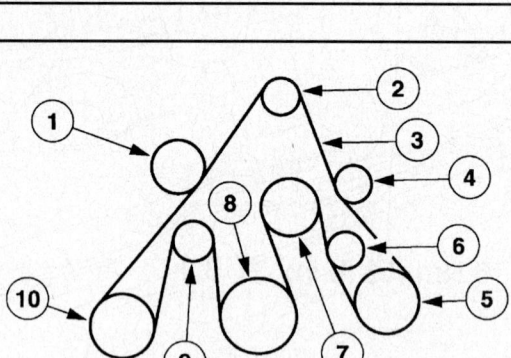

1 Generator pulley
2 Power steering pump pulley
3 A/C compressor pulley
4 Coolant pump pulley
5 Crankshaft damper
6 Drive belt tensioner pulley
7 Belt idler pulley
8 Drive belt

67197-EXPL-GCC

Fig. 78 Accessory drive belt routing—4.0L Engine

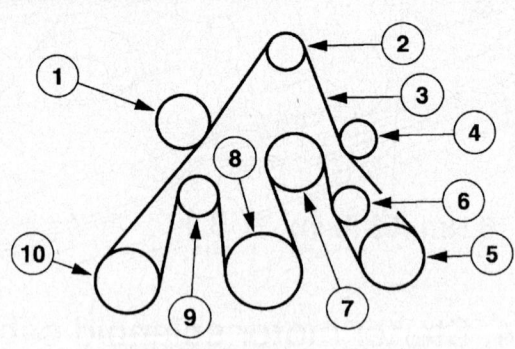

1 Belt idler pulley
2 Generator pulley
3 Drive belt
4 Belt idler pulley
5 Power steering pump pulley
6 Belt idler pulley
7 Coolant pump pulley
8 Crankshaft pulley
9 Drive belt tensioner pulley
10 A/C compressor pulley

67197-EXPL-GBB

Fig. 79 Accessory drive belt routing—4.6L Engine

INSPECTION

Inspect the drive belt for signs of glazing or cracking. A glazed belt will be perfectly smooth from slippage, while a good belt will have a slight texture of fabric visible. Cracks will usually start at the inner edge of the belt and run outward. All worn or damaged drive belts should be replaced immediately.

ADJUSTMENT

The belt tensioner automatically set the correct tension on the accessory drive belt. No further adjustment is necessary.

REMOVAL & INSTALLATION

See Figure 80.

1. Rotate the drive belt tensioner clockwise and remove the drive belt.

> ❊❊ **WARNING**
>
> **Never suddenly let go of the tensioned idler pulley. The force of the spring pressure suddenly released may damage the idler pulley mechanism. Always release the spring pressure gradually.**

To install:

2. Route the belt over the pulleys making sure all the grooves in the pulleys and the belt line up correctly. Refer to the accessory belt routing diagrams above.

3. Rotate belt tensioner clockwise and slip drive belt over idler pulley on tensioner.

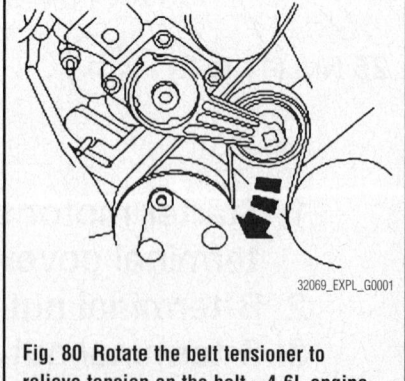

32069_EXPL_G0001

Fig. 80 Rotate the belt tensioner to relieve tension on the belt—4.6L engine shown, others similar

BALANCE SHAFT

REMOVAL & INSTALLATION

See Figures 81 through 87.

1. Remove timing chain and tensioner. Refer to Timing Chain and Tensioners.

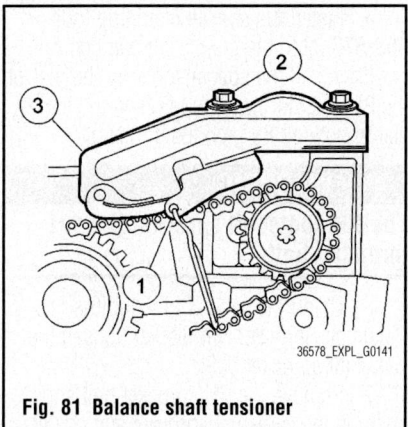

Fig. 81 Balance shaft tensioner

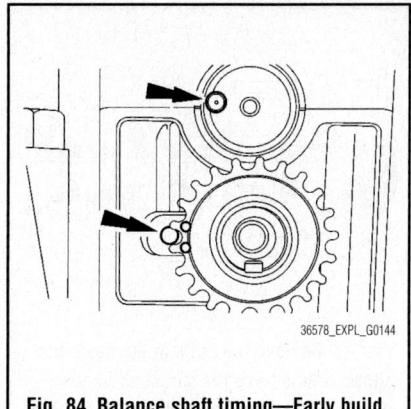

Fig. 84 Balance shaft timing—Early build

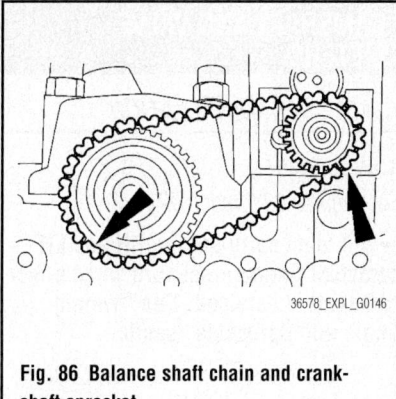

Fig. 86 Balance shaft chain and crankshaft sprocket

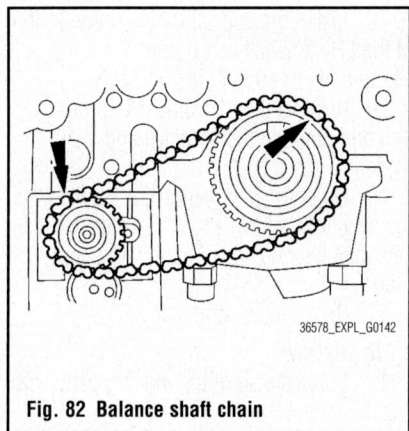

Fig. 82 Balance shaft chain

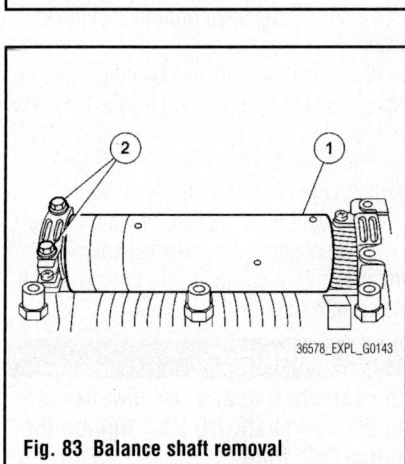

Fig. 83 Balance shaft removal

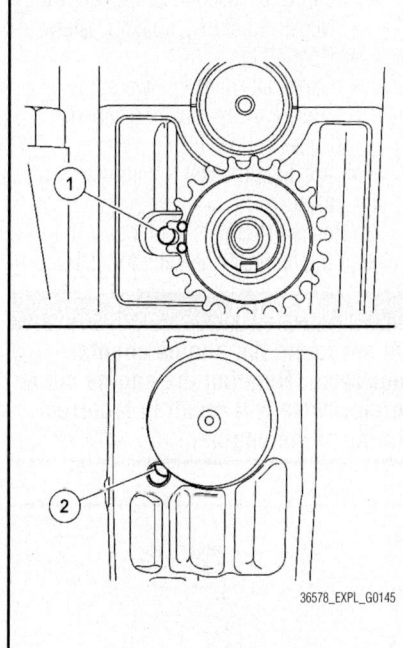

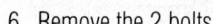

Fig. 85 Balance shaft timing—Late build

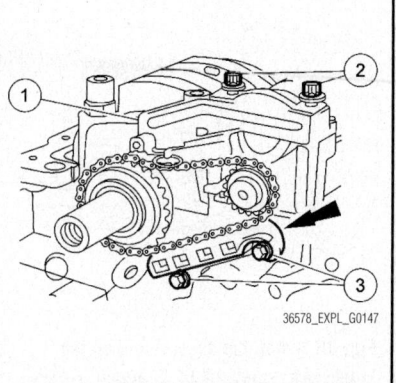

Fig. 87 Balance shaft tensioner and chain guide

2. Remove the balance shaft tensioner.
   a. Install a pin in the balance shaft tensioner.
   b. Remove the 2 bolts.
   c. Remove the balance shaft tensioner.
3. Remove the 2 bolts and the balance shaft chain guide.

➡**DO NOT remove the balance shaft sprocket bolt.**

4. Remove the balance shaft chain and crankshaft sprocket.
5. Remove the balance shaft.

6. Remove the 2 bolts.
7. Remove the balance shaft.

To install:
8. Install the balance shaft.
9. Install the balance shaft assembly.
10. Install the 2 bolts and tighten to 21 ft. lbs. (29 Nm).
Early build vehicles.

➡**Due to the gear ratio between the reversal shaft and the balance shaft, up to 7 complete turns of the balance shaft may be required to find the correct position.**

11. Align the timing marks.
12. Install a 0.16 inch (4 mm) pin to hold the shaft in place.
Late build vehicles.

➡**Due to the gear ratio between the reversal shaft and the balance shaft, up**

to 7 complete turns of the balance shaft may be required to find the correct position.

13. Align the timing marks.
14. Align the front balance shaft gear alignment marks with the hole in the balance shaft housing.
15. From the rear of the balance shaft, make sure the balance shaft gear alignment mark is visible through the hole in the balance shaft housing.
All vehicles
16. Install the balance shaft chain and crankshaft sprocket.
17. Install the balance shaft tensioner and chain guide.
   a. Install the balance shaft tensioner.
   b. Install the 2 bolts and tighten to 21 ft. lbs. (29 Nm).
   c. Position the balance shaft chain guide, install the 2 bolts and tighten to 89 inch lbs. (10 Nm).
   • Remove the pins from the tensioner and, if installed, the sprocket.
   • Install the crankshaft key.
18. Install timing chain and tensioner. Refer to Timing Chain and Tensioners.

CAMSHAFT AND VALVE LIFTERS

REMOVAL & INSTALLATION

4.0L Engine

See Figures 88 through 92.

➡ You must carry out the RH and LH camshaft timing procedure when either camshaft is serviced. See "Timing Chain and Sprockets" section.

1. Before servicing the vehicle, refer to Precautions.

Fig. 88 Install the special tool on the crankshaft pulley—4.0L Engine

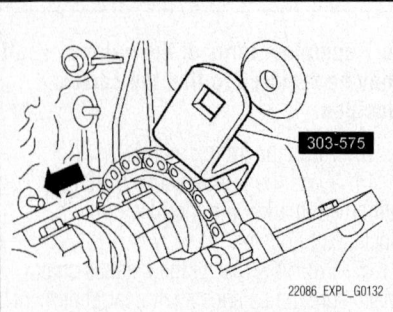

Fig. 89 Using the special tool with the Camshaft Sprocket Nut Socket 303-565, loosen the RH camshaft sprocket bolt—4.0L Engine

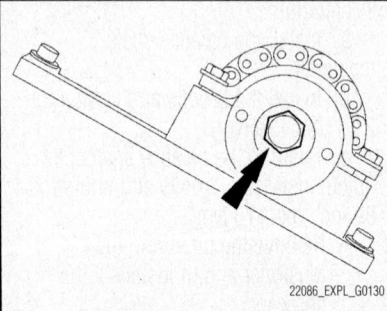

Fig. 90 Install the LH camshaft sprocket special holding tools—4.0L Engine

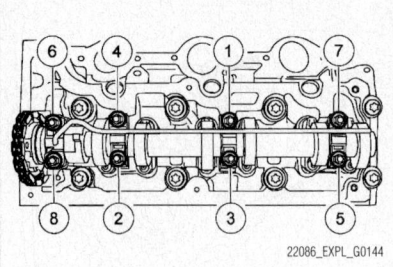

Fig. 91 Remove the bolts in the sequence shown and remove the camshaft bearing caps and the oil supply tube—4.0L Engine

2. Remove or disconnect the following:
   - Negative battery cable for safety
   - Cooling fan
   - Camshaft roller followers; see "Rocker Arms/Shafts (Camshaft Roller Followers)"
   - A/C tube bracket (position tube aside)

3. Rotate the crankshaft clockwise to position the number one cylinder at TDC.

✳✳ WARNING

Do not rotate the engine counterclockwise. Rotating the engine counterclockwise will result in incorrect timing of the engine.

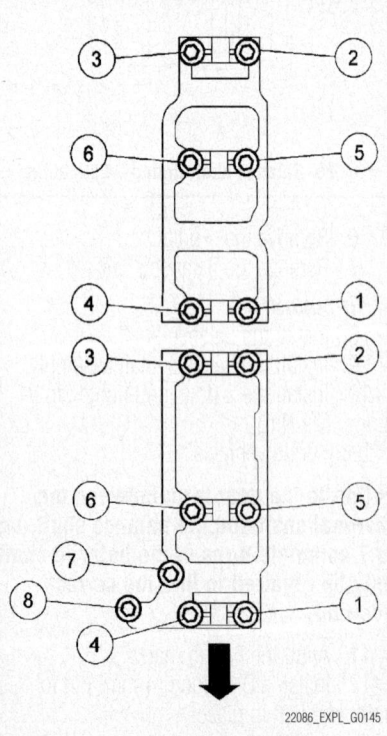

Fig. 92 Camshaft bearing cap torque sequence—4.0L Engine

4. Install the special clamping tool, 303-573, onto the crankshaft damper.

5. Install the special tools on the rear of the RH cylinder head and tighten the top 2 clamp bolts to 89 inch lbs. (10 Nm).

✳✳ WARNING

The RH camshaft sprocket is a LH threaded bolt.

6. Using the special tool and the Camshaft Sprocket Nut Socket, loosen the camshaft sprocket bolt.

7. Remove the RH sprocket bolt and position the camshaft sprocket and chain aside.

8. Install the special tools on the front of the LH camshaft and tighten the 2 top clamp bolts to 89 inch lbs. (10 Nm)

9. Remove the LH camshaft sprocket bolt and position the sprocket and chain aside.

10. On both sides, remove the bolts in the sequence shown and remove the camshaft bearing caps and the oil supply tube.

11. Remove the camshaft.

To install:

12. Lubricate all of the moving parts with clean engine oil.

13. Install camshaft onto the cylinder head.

14. Install the camshaft bearing caps, in their original locations, and torque the bolts in 2 steps:
   a. Step 1—53.5 inch lbs. (6 Nm).
   b. Step 2—12 ft. lbs. (16 Nm).

15. Install the camshaft oil supply tube.

16. Reposition the camshaft sprocket and chain, for each side, and loosely install the sprocket bolt.

✳✳ WARNING

The camshaft gear must turn freely on the camshaft. DO NOT tighten the bolt at this time.

17. Retime the camshafts. See the procedure in "Timing Chain and Sprocket" section.

18. Install or connect the following:
   - Camshaft roller followers
   - A/C tube and bracket
   - Valve covers
   - Cooling fan
   - Negative battery cable

19. Start the engine check for proper operation and leaks. Repair if necessary.

4.6L Engine

See Figure 93.

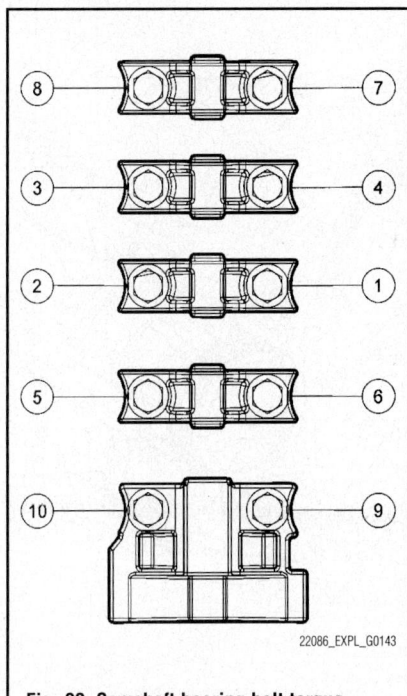

Fig. 93 Camshaft bearing bolt torque sequence—4.6L Engine

1. Before servicing the vehicle, refer to Precautions.
2. Remove or disconnect the following:

✳✳ WARNING

At no time, when the timing chains are removed and the cylinder heads are installed may the crankshaft or camshaft be rotated. Severe piston and valve damage will occur.

- Timing chains, refer to Timing Chain and Sprockets.
- Camshaft roller followers
- Camshaft sprocket
- Camshaft bearing cap bolts (keeping them marked for reinstallation to original locations)
- Camshaft from the cylinder head

To install:

3. Lubricate the camshaft journals with clean engine oil.
4. Install the camshaft onto the cylinder head.
5. Lubricate the camshaft bearing caps with clean engine oil.
6. Install the camshaft bearing caps and loosely install the bolts.
7. Tighten the bolts in the sequence shown.
8. Install the camshaft sprocket. Tighten the sprocket bolt in two stages.
- Step 1: Tighten to 30 ft. lbs. (40 Nm)
- Step 2: Tighten an additional 90 degrees.

9. Install the roller followers
10. Install the timing chains

CATALYTIC CONVERTER

REMOVAL & INSTALLATION
See Figures 94 and 95.

✳✳ WARNING

Do not use oil or grease-based lubricants on the isolators. These lubricants may cause deterioration of the rubber. This can lead to separation of the isolator from the exhaust hanger bracket during vehicle operation. Use only water-based lubricants on the isolators.

➡**Exhaust fasteners are of a prevailing torque design. Use only new fasteners with the same part number as the original. Torque values must be used as specified during reassembly to make sure of correct retention of exhaust components.**

1. With the vehicle in NEUTRAL, position it on a hoist.
2. Using a suitable jack, support the exhaust system.
3. Disconnect the Heated Oxygen Sensor (HO2S) and the Catalyst Monitor Sensor (CMS) electrical connectors.

4. Remove the 2 exhaust Y-pipe dual catalytic converter-to-muffler assembly bolts, 2 nuts and gasket.
5. Discard the exhaust Y-pipe dual catalytic converter-to-muffler assembly nuts and gasket.
6. Remove the transmission support crossmember.
7. Remove the exhaust Y-pipe dual catalytic converter-to-exhaust manifold nuts.

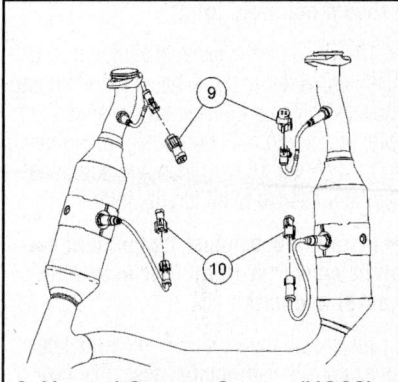

9. Heated Oxygen Sensor (HO2S) electrical connectors
10. Catalyst Monitor Sensor (CMS) electrical connectors

Fig. 95 Catalytic Converter locations

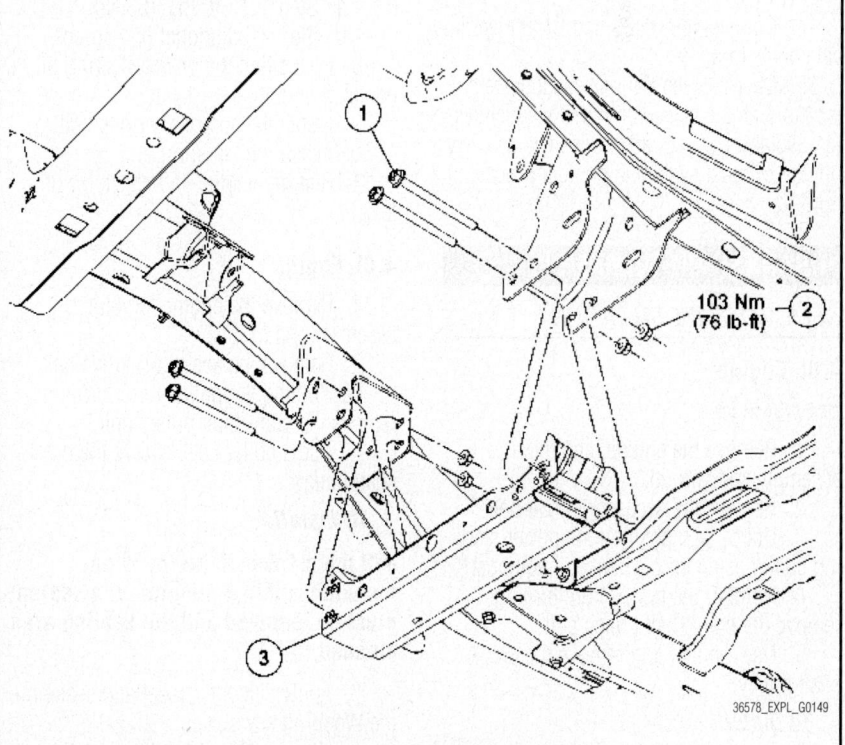

Fig. 94 Transmission support crossmember bolt locations

8. Discard the exhaust Y-pipe dual catalytic converter-to-exhaust manifold nuts.

9. Remove the exhaust Y-pipe dual catalytic converter.

To install:

➡️**Install new exhaust Y-pipe dual catalytic converter-to-exhaust manifold nuts.**

➡️**Do not fully tighten the exhaust Y-pipe dual catalytic converter-to-exhaust manifold joint.**

10. Position the exhaust Y-pipe dual catalytic converter to the exhaust manifold and loosely tighten all 4 new nuts to stiffen the joint enough to maintain position. Tighten to 71 inch lbs. (8 Nm) then add additional torque if needed to stiffen the joint.

➡️**Install new exhaust Y-pipe dual catalytic converter-to-muffler assembly gasket and nuts.**

11. Install the exhaust Y-pipe-dual catalytic converter-to-muffler assembly new gasket, 2 bolts and 2 new nuts and tighten to 30 ft. lbs. (40 Nm).

12. Tighten the 4 new exhaust Y-pipe dual catalytic converter-to-exhaust manifold nuts and tighten to 30 ft. lbs. (40 Nm).

13. Install the transmission support crossmember and tighten to 76 ft. lbs. (103 Nm).

14. Connect the HO2S and CMS electrical connectors.

15. Check to see if the exhaust system isolators are at zero load. If the exhaust system isolators are not at zero load, then carry out the exhaust system alignment procedure.

CRANKSHAFT DAMPER

REMOVAL & INSTALLATION

4.0L Engine

See Figure 96.

1. Remove the engine fan/clutch assembly and shroud.

2. Remove the accessory drive belt.

3. Unbolt and position the power steering cooler aside for clearance, if equipped.

4. Holding the pulley from turning, remove the crankshaft pulley bolt.

5. Use a puller and remove the crankshaft pulley.

To install:

6. Use a crankshaft pulley installation tool, press the pulley onto the crankshaft.

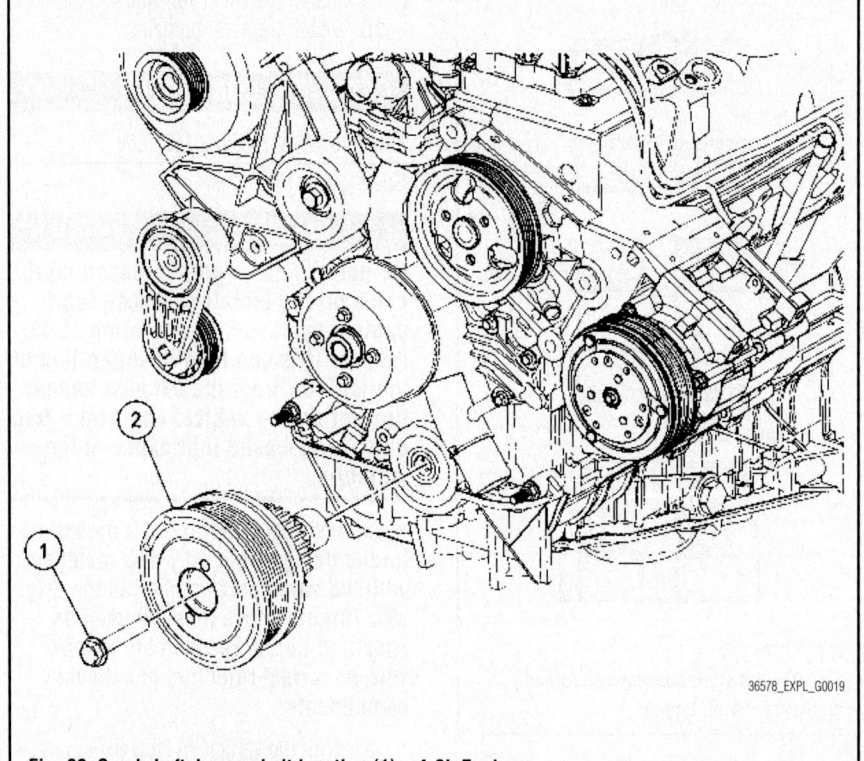

Fig. 96 Crankshaft damper bolt location (1)—4.0L Engine

36578_EXPL_G0019

➡️**Always use a new damper-to-crankshaft bolt. Do not attempt to re-use the old bolt.**

7. Install the damper-to-crankshaft snout and tighten to:
   a. Step 1: 41 ft. lbs. (55 Nm)
   b. Step 2: additional 85 degrees
8. Reposition the power steering oil cooler, if equipped.
9. Install the accessory drive belt.
10. Install the fan shroud.
11. Run the engine and check for oil leaks.

4.6L Engine

1. Remove the engine fan/clutch assembly and shroud.
2. Remove the accessory drive belt.
3. Holding the pulley from turning, remove the crankshaft pulley bolt.
4. Use a puller and remove the crankshaft pulley.

To install:

➡️**If the crankshaft pulley is not installed within 4 minutes, the sealant must be removed and the sealing area cleaned.**

5. Apply silicone gasket and sealant to the Woodruff key slot.
6. Use a crankshaft pulley installation tool, press the pulley onto the crankshaft.

➡️**Always use a new damper-to-crankshaft bolt. Do not attempt to re-use the old bolt.**

7. Install the crankshaft pulley and tighten the bolt as follows:
   a. Step 1: 89 ft. lbs. (120 Nm)
   b. Step 2: LOOSEN the bolt one full turn
   c. Step 3: 37 ft. lbs. (50 Nm)
   d. Step 4: additional 90 degrees (do not exceed 148 ft. lbs. or 200 Nm of torque)
8. Install the accessory drive belt.
9. Install the fan shroud.
10. Run the engine and check for oil leaks.

CRANKSHAFT FRONT SEAL

REMOVAL & INSTALLATION

4.0L Engine

See Figures 97 and 98.

1. Before servicing the vehicle, refer to Precautions.
2. Remove the crankshaft pulley. Refer to Crankshaft Damper.
3. Using a proper seal remover, remove the front crankshaft seal.

To install:

4. Installation is the reverse of the removal procedure.

Fig. 97 Front crankshaft seal (1)—4.0L Engine

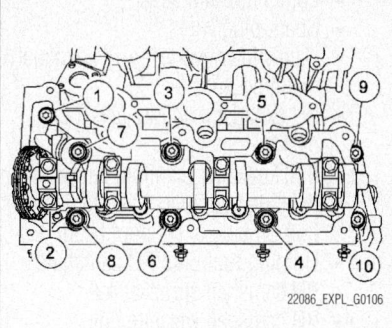

Fig. 101 Remove the cylinder head bolts in the sequence shown—4.0L Engine

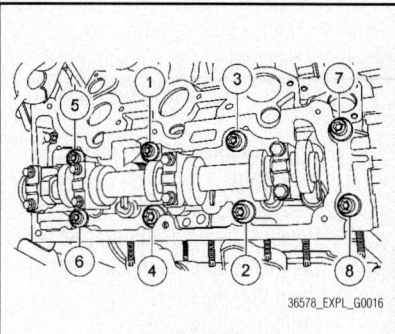

Fig. 102 Cylinder head 12mm bolt tightening sequence—4.0L Engine

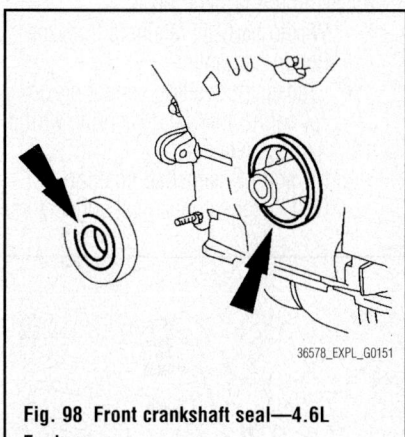

Fig. 98 Front crankshaft seal—4.6L Engine

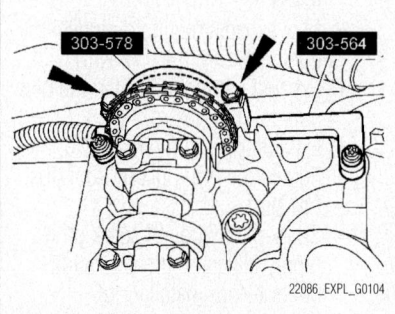

Fig. 99 Install a holding tool onto camshaft RH shown—4.0L Engine

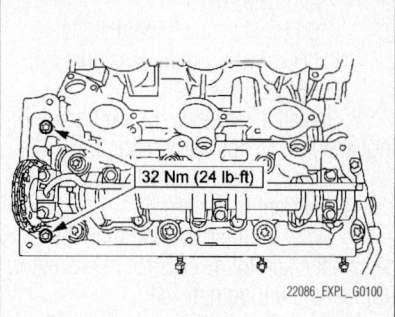

Fig. 103 Installing the 2 8mm cylinder head bolts—4.0L Engine

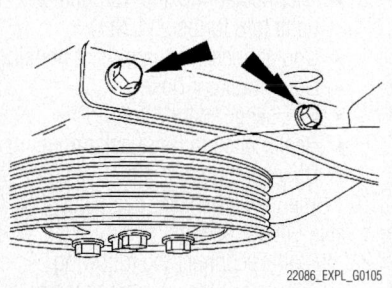

Fig. 100 Remove the 2 bolts as shown—4.0L Engine

5. Lubricate the new seal lip before installation.

4.6L Engine

1. Before servicing the vehicle, refer to Precautions.
2. Remove the crankshaft pulley. Refer to Crankshaft Damper.
3. Using a proper seal remover, remove the front crankshaft seal.

To install:

4. Installation is the reverse of the removal procedure.
5. Lubricate the new seal lip before installation.

CYLINDER HEAD

REMOVAL & INSTALLATION

4.0L Engine

See Figures 99 through 103.

1. Before servicing the vehicle, refer to Precautions.
2. Drain the cooling system.
3. Remove the camshaft roller followers. Refer to Rocker Arms/Shafts.
4. Remove the accessory drive belt.
5. On RH side cylinder head, remove or disconnect the following:

- Heater hose tube bracket (position aside)

- Battery ground cable
- Alternator electrical connections and disconnect the pushpin
- Accessory drive belt tensioner
- Alternator mounting bracket assembly
- Heater hose from the thermostat housing
- ECT sensor electrical connector
- Upper radiator hose
- Coolant bypass hose
- Thermostat housing
- Position the engine wiring harness aside

- Engine ground strap
- Spark plug wires
- Catalytic converter-to-RH exhaust manifold nuts
- RH exhaust manifold and the gasket
- 6 RH exhaust manifold studs
- RH side hydraulic chain tensioner bolt on side of cylinder head
- Holding tool onto RH camshaft
- RH camshaft sprocket nut
- RH camshaft cassette bolt
- RH camshaft sprocket

➡**Use a rubber band around the chain and cassette to hold the chain from falling.**

6. On the LH side cylinder head, remove or disconnect the following:
- Heater hose tube bracket (position aside)
- LH radio interference capacitor connector
- 2 bolts as shown
- Power steering pump bracket (position aside without disconnecting the pump lines)
- Ignition coil bracket
- Oil level indicator tube
- Exhaust pipe from LH exhaust manifold (discard nuts and gasket)
- LH exhaust manifold (discard nuts and gasket)
- 6 LH exhaust manifold studs
- LH camshaft chain tensioner bolt from side of head

7. Install a camshaft sprocket holding tool and remove the sprocket bolt.

8. Remove the LH camshaft cassette bolt in the front of the head.

9. Wrap a rubber band around the camshaft chain to the cassette to prevent it from falling during removal.

10. Remove the LH camshaft sprocket

✷✷ WARNING

To avoid damage to the camshaft cassette, an assistant will be required to lift the cylinder head from the vehicle. Watch the A/C tube on the RH side when lifting the head.

11. For either cylinder head, using the sequence shown, remove and discard the cylinder head bolts.

12. Lift the cylinder head(s) from the vehicle. Discard the gaskets.

To install:

➡**The installation procedure that follows is for either cylinder head, unless otherwise specified.**

13. Clean all mating surfaces. Clean the bolt holes.

14. Position the new cylinder head gasket on the block mating surface.

15. Carefully set the cylinder head into position, watching for any possible interference with engine components.

16. Install the new 12mm bolts and tighten in 2 stages, in the sequence shown:
   a. Stage 1: 9 ft. lbs. (12 Nm)
   b. Stage 2: 18 ft. lbs. (25 Nm)

17. Install the 2 8mm bolts near the front of the cylinder head. Tighten the bolts to 24 ft. lbs. (32 Nm).

18. Now, retighten the 8 12mm cylinder head bolts, in the same sequence as above, to the following:
   a. Stage 1: 90 degrees additional
   b. Stage 2: 90 degrees additional

19. Install or connect the following:
- Camshaft chain and sprocket
- Camshaft cassette bolt; tighten to 9 ft. lbs. (12 Nm)
- New exhaust manifold studs; tighten to 9 ft. lbs. (12 Nm)
- Exhaust manifold; tighten the new nuts to 16 ft. lbs. (22 Nm)
- Exhaust pipe to the manifold; tighten the new nuts to 30 ft. lbs. (40 Nm)
- Spark plug wires to spark plugs (apply dielectric grease inside boots before installation)
- Engine ground strap (RH side)
- Engine wiring harness retaining bolt to side of engine; tighten bolt to 35 ft. lbs. (47 Nm) (RH side)
- Thermostat housing; torque the bolts to 8 ft. lbs. (11 Nm)
- Coolant hose to thermostat housing
- Upper radiator hose
- ECT sensor connector
- Heater hose to thermostat housing
- Oil level indicator tube (LH side)

20. Time the camshafts. See "Camshaft and Valve Lifters" section.

21. Install or connect the following:
- Alternator bracket; tighten the bolts to 31 ft. lbs. (42 Nm)
- Accessory drive belt tensioner; tighten the bolt to 35 ft. lbs. (47 Nm)
- Alternator electrical connections; tighten to 71 inch lbs. (8 Nm)
- Heater hose tube bracket; rear bolt to 17 ft. lbs. (25 Nm) and front bolt to 25 ft. lbs. (34 Nm)
- Ignition coil bracket; tighten the bolts to 89 inch lbs. (10 Nm)
- A/C compressor and power steering pump; tighten mounting bolts to 31 ft. lbs. (42 Nm)

- Ignition coil bracket to accessory drive bracket; tighten bolts to 89 inch lbs. (10 Nm)
- Radio interference capacitor electrical connector
- Accessory drive belt

22. Fill and bleed the cooling system.

4.6L Engine

See Figures 104 through 113.

1. Before servicing the vehicle, refer to Precautions.

➡**Clean all mating surfaces as components are removed during this procedure.**

2. Remove the engine. Refer to Engine Assembly.

3. Transfer the engine to a proper workstand.

4. Remove or disconnect the following for access to the cylinder heads:
- Wiring harness retainers from the RH oil pan bolts
- Crankshaft position sensor electrical connector and detach the wiring harness retainer
- RH and LH camshaft position (CMP) sensor electrical connectors

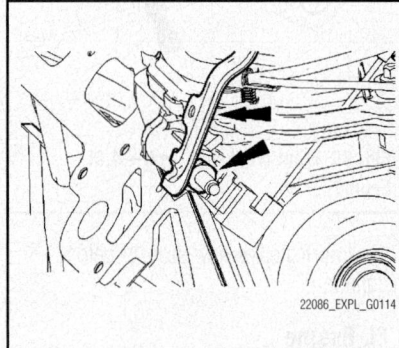

22086_EXPL_G0114

Fig. 104 Remove the cooling fan wiring harness bracket and the LH radio interference capacitor—4.6L Engine

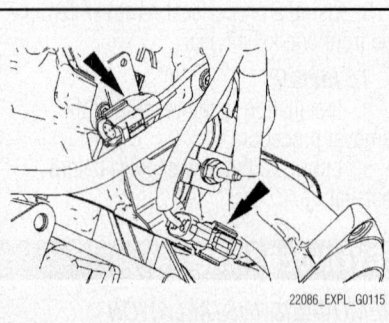

22086_EXPL_G0115

Fig. 105 Remove the electrical connector retainers and remove the engine wiring harness—4.6L Engine

- RH and LH variable camshaft timing (VCT) solenoid electrical connectors
- Wiring harness retainers from the front end of the engine
- RH radio ignition interference capacitor

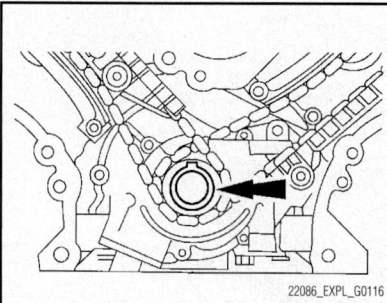

Fig. 106 Position the crankshaft keyway at the 12 o'clock position—4.6L Engine

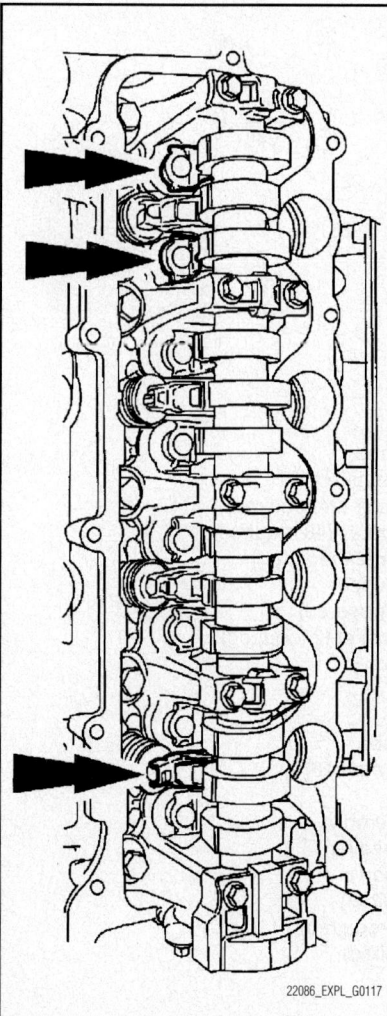

Fig. 107 Remove only the 3 roller followers, as indicated, from the RH cylinder head—4.6L Engine

- Oil pressure sensor electrical connector
- LH CMP sensor electrical connector and detach the wiring harness retainers
- Cooling fan wiring harness bracket
- LH radio interference capacitor
- Wiring harness retainers from the LH valve cover studs
- 4 RH and 4 LH ignition coil electrical connectors
- Wiring harness retainers from the RH valve cover studs
- Cylinder head temperature (CHT) sensor electrical connector
- Electrical connector retainers and remove the engine wiring harness
- Breather tube from the RH valve cover
- Positive crankcase ventilation (PCV) tube from the LH valve cover
- Oil filter

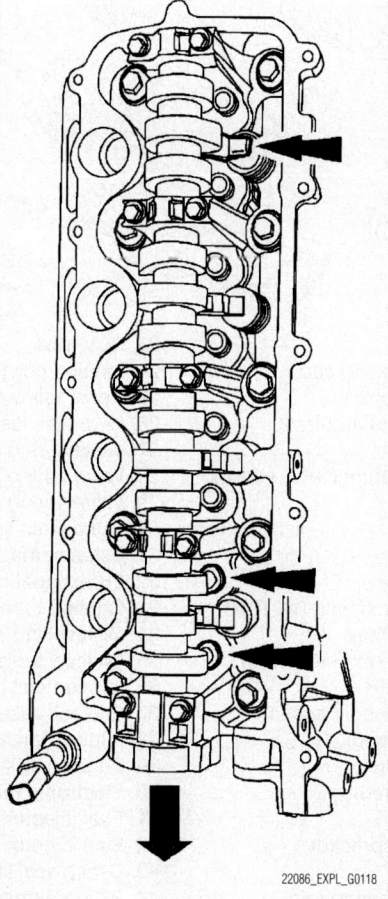

Fig. 108 Remove only the 3 roller followers, as indicated, from the LH cylinder head—4.6L Engine

- 8 ignition coils
- Position the oil level indicator aside
- Valve covers
- Coolant pump pulley and the RH side accessory drive belt idler pulley
- Crankshaft pulley (discard pulley bolt)
- Front crankshaft seal
- 4 oil pan-to-engine front cover bolts
- Engine front cover
- Crankshaft sensor ring from the crankshaft

5. Position the crankshaft keyway at the 12 o'clock position.

✱✱ WARNING

If the camshaft lobes are not exactly positioned as shown, the crankshaft will require one full additional rotation to the 12 o'clock position.

6. The No. 1 cylinder camshaft exhaust lobe must be coming up on the exhaust stroke. Verify by noting the position of the 2 intake lobes and the exhaust lobe on the No. 1 cylinder.

7. Remove only the 3 roller followers shown from the RH and LH cylinder heads.

8. Rotate the crankshaft clockwise and position the crankshaft keyway at the 6 o'clock position.

9. Remove the timing chains, guides and sprockets. See "Timing Chain and Sprockets" section.

10. Remove the camshafts. Refer to Camshaft and Valve Lifter.

11. Remove all of the camshaft roller followers and lash adjusters.

12. Install lifting handles on each end of the cylinder heads.

13. Remove the exhaust manifolds.

14. Remove the nut and ground strap from the RH cylinder head.

15. Remove the stud bolt and the heater supply tube and hoses as an assembly from between the cylinder heads.

16. Remove the bolts and lift off the cylinder heads. Remove and discard the gaskets.

To install:

17. Carefully clean all cylinder head mating surfaces and bolt holes.

18. Use a straightedge to check the cylinder head surface flatness. Any distortion must be within 0.0004 in. (0.010 mm) from end to end.

19. Inspect the areas shown for any signs of wear, corrosion or deep scratches.

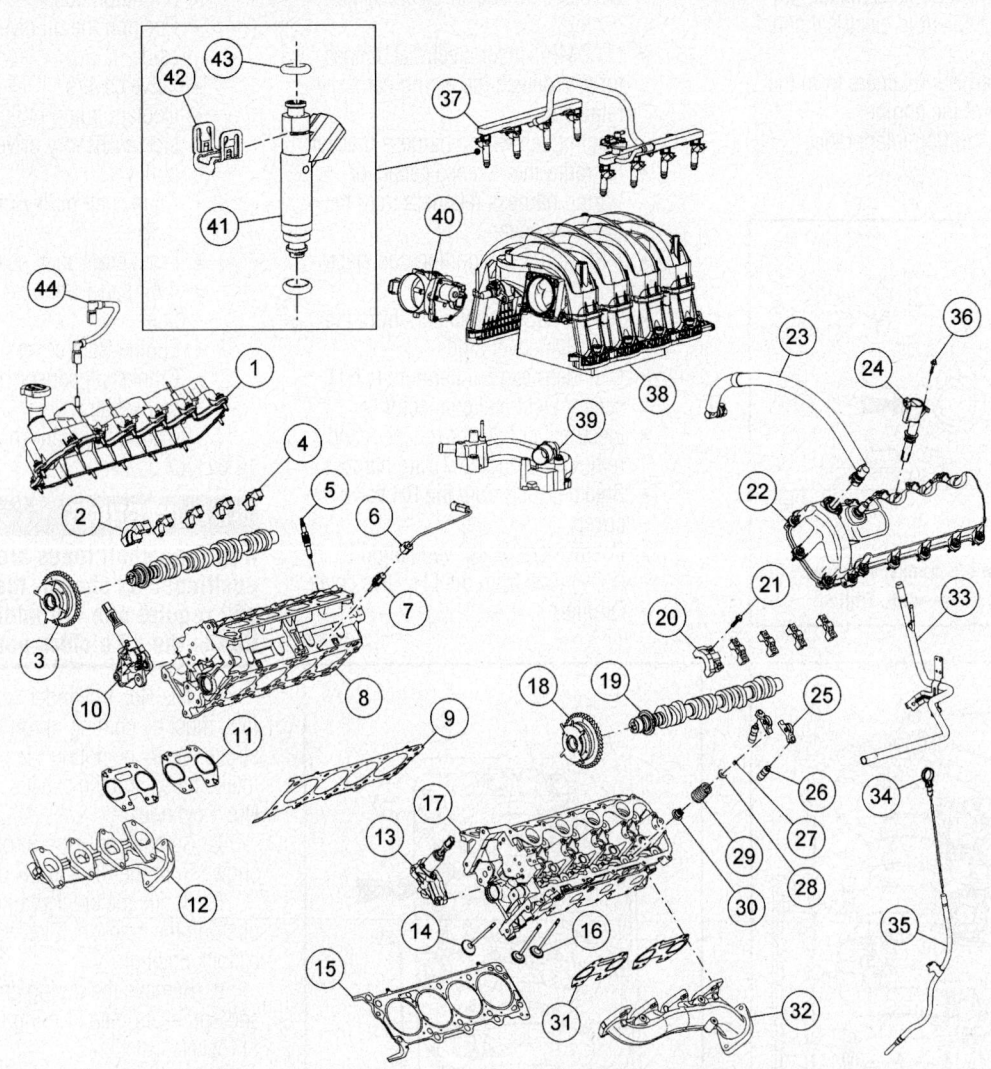

1. RH valve cover
2. RH camshaft thrust bearing cap
3. RH camshaft phaser sprocket
4. Camshaft bearing cap (8 required)
5. Spark plug (8 required)
6. Cylinder Head Temperature (CHT) sensor jumper harness
7. CHT sensor
8. RH cylinder head
9. RH cylinder head gasket
10. RH Variable Camshaft Timing (VCT) oil control solenoid assembly
11. Exhaust manifold gasket (2 required)
12. Exhaust manifold — RH
13. LH VCT oil control solenoid assembly
14. Exhaust valve (8 required)
15. LH cylinder head gasket
16. Intake valve (16 required)
17. LH cylinder head
18. LH camshaft phaser sprocket
19. LH camshaft
20. LH camshaft thrust bearing cap
21. Camshaft bearing cap bolt (20 required)
22. LH valve cover

23. PCV tube
24. Ignition coil (8 required)
25. Roller follower (24 required)
26. Hydraulic lash adjuster (24 required)
27. Valve spring retainer key (48 required)
28. Valve spring retainer (24 required)
29. Valve spring (24 required)
30. Valve stem seal (24 required)
31. Exhaust manifold gasket (2 required)
32. LH exhaust manifold
33. Coolant tube
34. Oil level indicator
35. Oil level indicator tube
36. Ignition coil bolt (8 required)
37. Fuel rail assembly
38. Intake manifold assembly
39. Engine coolant crossover
40. Electronic throttle body
41. Fuel injector (8 required)
42. Fuel injector clip (8 required)
43. O-ring seal (16 required)
44. PCV breather hose

36578_EXPL_G0018

Fig. 109 Cylinder head exploded view

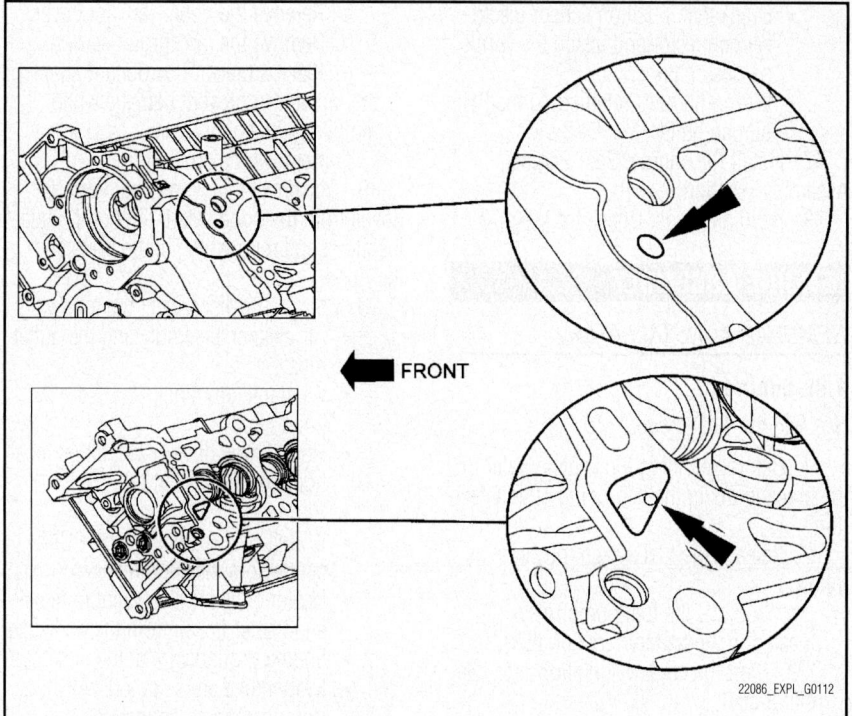

← FRONT

Fig. 110 Inspect the areas shown for any signs of wear, corrosion or deep scratches—4.6L Engine

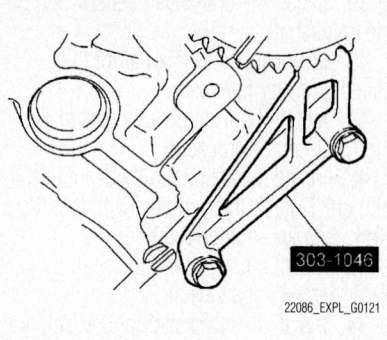

Fig. 113 Using the special tool, as shown, tighten the LH and RH camshaft phaser sprocket bolts—4.6L Engine

25. With a new O-ring seal, loosely install the oil level indicator tube.

26. With a new gasket, install the LH exhaust manifold. Refer to Exhaust Manifold for tightening sequence and specifications.

27. With new gaskets in place, carefully position the RH cylinder head into position. Use locator dowels, if necessary.

28. Install and tighten the cylinder head bolts, in the sequence shown.

29. Tighten the RH cylinder head bolts in 3 steps:

   a. Step 1: 30 ft. lbs. (40 Nm)
   b. Step 2: additional 90 degrees
   c. Step 3: additional 90 degrees

30. Remove the cylinder head lifting handles from the end of the cylinder head.

31. Lubricate and install the RH cylinder head lash adjusters in their original positions.

32. With a new gasket, install the RH exhaust manifold. Refer to Exhaust Manifold for tightening sequence and specifications.

33. Install or connect the following:

- Heater supply tube and the hoses as an assembly
- Ground strap
- LH and RH camshafts; refer to Camshafts and Valve Lifters.

34. Install the camshaft phaser sprockets and new camshaft phaser bolts finger-tight.

35. Using the special tool, as shown, tighten the LH and RH camshaft phaser sprocket bolts in 2 stages:

   a. Stage 1: 30 ft. lbs. (40 Nm)
   b. Stage 2: additional 90 degrees

36. Install the crankshaft sprocket, making sure the flange faces forward.

37. Rotate the crankshaft to position the crankshaft sprocket timing mark in the 6 o'clock position.

38. Install the camshaft sprockets and timing chains. Refer to Timing Chain and Sprockets.

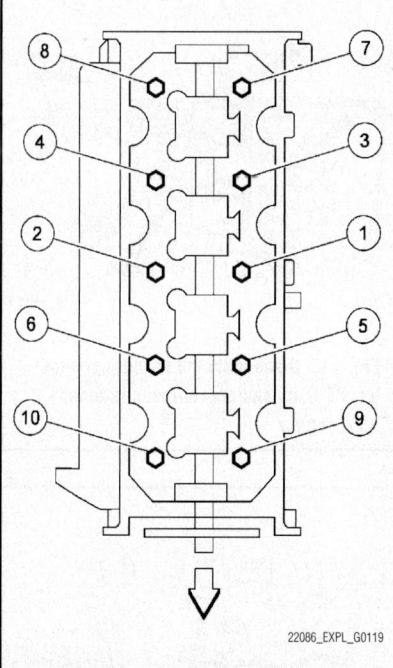

Fig. 111 Tighten the LH cylinder head bolts in the sequence shown—4.6L Engine

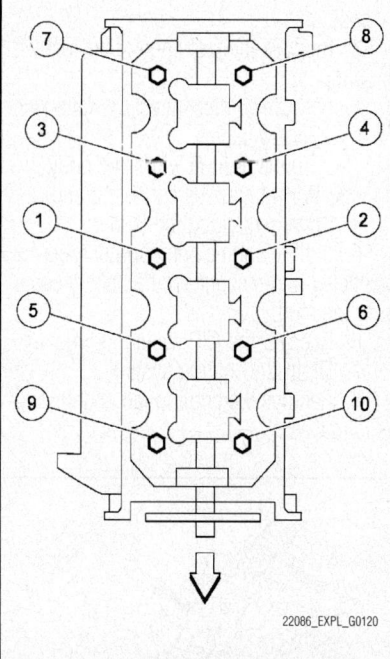

Fig. 112 Tighten the RH cylinder head bolts in the sequence shown—4.6L Engine

20. With new gaskets in place, carefully position the LH cylinder head into position. Use locator dowels, if necessary.

21. Install and tighten the cylinder head bolts, in the sequence shown.

22. Tighten the LH cylinder head bolts in 3 steps:

   a. Step 1: 30 ft. lbs. (40 Nm)
   b. Step 2: additional 90 degrees
   c. Step 3: additional 90 degrees

23. Remove the cylinder head lifting handles from the end of the cylinder head.

24. Lubricate and install the LH cylinder head lash adjusters in their original positions.

39. Install the crankshaft sensor ring on the crankshaft.

40. Lubricate and install all of the camshaft roller followers.

41. Install the front cover. Refer to Timing Chain and Sprockets.

42. Install the 4 bolts to the front of the oil pan. Tighten the bolts to 15 ft. lbs. (20 Nm), then an additional 60 degrees.

43. Install a new front crankshaft oil seal. Refer to Crankshaft Front Seal.

44. Install the crankshaft pulley. Apply silicone to the keyway prior to installation.

45. Tighten the new crankshaft pulley bolt in 4 steps:

    a. Step 1: 89 ft. lbs. (120 Nm)

    b. Step 2: LOOSEN 1 full turn (360 degrees)

    c. Step 3: 37 ft. lbs. (50 Nm)

    d. Step 4: additional 90 degrees

46. Install or connect the following:

- RH side accessory drive belt idler pulley, the coolant pump pulley and the 5 bolts; tighten the bolts to 18 ft. lbs. (25 Nm)
- Valve covers; refer to Valve Covers.
- Tighten the oil level indicator tube bolt to 89 inch lbs. (10 Nm)
- 8 ignition coils
- New oil filter
- Positive crankcase ventilation (PCV) hose to the LH valve cover
- Breather tube to the RH valve cover
- Engine wiring harness and attach the electrical connectors to the heater supply tube bracket
- Cylinder head temperature (CHT) sensor electrical connector
- Wiring harness retainers to the RH valve cover studs
- RH and LH ignition coil electrical connectors
- Wiring harness retainers to the LH valve cover studs
- LH radio interference capacitor; tighten the nut to 18 ft. lbs. (25 Nm)
- Cooling fan wiring harness; tighten the nut to 18 ft. lbs. (25 Nm)
- LH camshaft position sensor and attach the wiring harness retainers
- Oil pressure sensor electrical connector
- RH radio interference capacitor; tighten the nut to 18 ft. lbs. (25 Nm)
- Wiring harness retainers
- RH and LH variable camshaft timing (VCT) solenoid electrical connectors
- RH and LH camshaft position (CMP) sensor electrical connectors

- Crankshaft position sensor electrical connector and attach the wiring harness retainer
- Wiring harness retainers to the RH oil pan bolts

47. Install the engine. See "Engine Assembly" section.

48. Refill all fluids. Check for leaks.

ENGINE ASSEMBLY

REMOVAL & INSTALLATION

4.0L Engine

See Figures 114 through 118.

1. Before servicing the vehicle, refer to the precautions in the beginning of this section.

2. Release the fuel system pressure as follows:

    a. Remove the fuel pump relay (located in the battery junction box).

    b. Start the engine and allow it to idle until it stalls.

    c. After the engine stalls, crank the engine for approximately 5 seconds to make sure the fuel rail pressure has been released.

    d. Turn the ignition switch to the OFF position.

3. Remove the fuel line spring-lock coupling.

4. Remove or disconnect the following:

- Battery cables
- Engine ground wire from body
- Wiring harness connector and retainers along the fender

5. Lift the engine compartment relay box cover and disconnect the battery cable from the stud.

6. Recover the A/C system refrigerant.

7. Drain the cooling system.

8. Remove the cooling fan and shroud as follows:

a. Remove the upper radiator cover.

b. Remove the fan shroud screws.

c. Place a piece of cardboard against the radiator to prevent damage while removing the cooling fan.

d. Remove the cooling fan.

9. Disconnect the windshield washer hoses from the hood. Mark the hood hinge locations and remove the hinge bolts and the hood.

10. Remove or disconnect the following:

- Air cleaner assembly and the outlet pipe
- Windshield washer hose from the hood clips
- Hood hinge bolts (mark hinge locations for reinstallation)
- Hood
- Wiring harness connector, PCM connectors, harness retainer
- Heater control valve vacuum hose and heater hoses from the bulkhead
- Engine ground wire at the bulkhead
- Evaporative emissions (EVAP) tube from the engine connection and position it aside
- Upper radiator hose

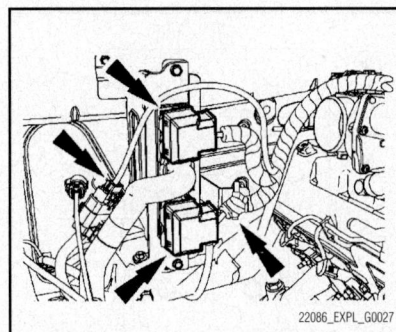

Fig. 115 Disconnect the harness connector, PCM connectors, harness retainer—4.0L engine

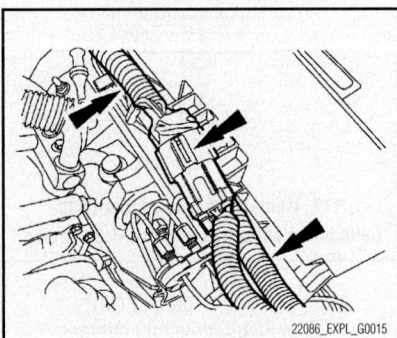

Fig. 114 Identifying the wiring harness connector and retainers to remove from fender—4.0L Engine

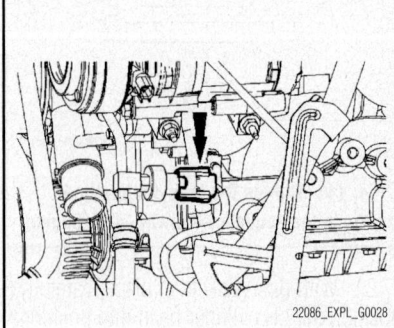

Fig. 116 Disconnect the PSP switch electrical connector—4.0L engine

- Power steering pump pulley bolts (loosen only)
- Accessory drive belt
- Power steering pump pulley
- Lower radiator hose
- PSP switch electrical connector, if necessary
- PSP hose and pump supply hose bracket bolts
- Power steering pump; position out of the way
- Brake booster vacuum hose from the cylinder head cover
- EVAP canister purge valve electrical connector
- EVAP hose
- A/C tubes from the compressor
- A/C high-pressure switch electrical connector
- High-pressure A/C tube from the condenser

11. Remove the transmission.
12. Remove or disconnect the following:
- Starter motor
- Oil filter
- Transmission cooler tube connector/bracket (suspend with wire)
- Battery cable harness bracket from the frame rail
- LH engine support through-bolt

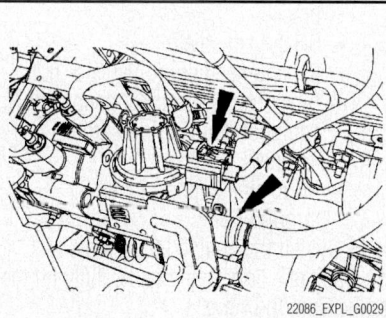

Fig. 117 Disconnect the EVAP purge valve electrical connector and EVAP hose—4.0L Engine

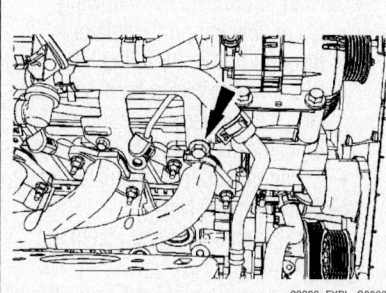

Fig. 118 Remove the heater tube bracket bolt—4.0L engine

- RH engine support nuts
- Block heater electrical connector and harness retainer (if equipped)
- Heater tube bracket bolt, if necessary

13. Install the lifting hangars on the LH and RH sides of the engine, using bolts on the exhaust manifolds to retain the hangars.
14. Attach the lifting sling, and with a floor crane, remove the engine.

To install:

15. Using the floor crane, carefully lower the engine into the vehicle.
16. Install the RH engine support insulator nuts, and tighten the nuts to 66 ft. lbs. (90 Nm).
17. Remove the lifting hangar from the RH side of the engine.
18. Install the heater tube bracket bolt and torque it to 25 ft. lbs. (34 Nm).
19. If equipped, connect the block heater connector and the wiring harness retainer.
20. Remove the LH engine lifting hangar.
21. Install the LH engine support through-bolt and tighten it to 76 ft. lbs. (103 Nm).
22. Install or connect the following:
- Battery cable harness bracket and nut; torque to 11 ft. lbs. (15 Nm)
- Transmission cooler tube bracket; torque nut to 17 ft. lbs. (23 Nm)
- Oil filter
- Transmission
- Starter and wiring
- A/C high-pressure tube to the condenser (with a new gasket and O-ring seal); tighten the fitting to 11 ft. lbs. (15 Nm)
- High-pressure cutoff switch electrical connector
- A/C tubes to the compressor (with new gaskets and new O-ring seals); tighten the tube fitting nuts to 11 ft. lbs. (15 Nm) and the bracket nut to 89 inch lbs. (10 Nm)
- EVAP hose to canister purge valve
- Purge valve electrical connector
- Brake booster vacuum hose to the cylinder head cover
- Power steering pump; torque the bolts to 18 ft. lbs. (25 Nm)
- Power steering pump-to-reservoir hoses
- PSP hose and PSP switch electrical connector
- Lower radiator hose
- Power steering pump pulley; install bolts only finger-tight
- Accessory drive belt
- Power steering pump pulley bolts to 18 ft. lbs. (25 Nm)

- Upper radiator hose
- EVAP hose to connector
- Engine ground wire at body attachment; torque the bolt to 89 inch lbs. (10 Nm)
- Heater hoses and heater valve vacuum hose at bulkhead
- Engine wiring harness-to-Powertrain Control Module (PCM) electrical connectors and the wiring harness electrical connector; wiring harness retainer
- Hood; torque bolts to 9 ft. lbs. (12 Nm)
- Windshield washer hose to hood clips
- Air cleaner and outlet pipe
- Engine cooling fan
- Battery cable connectors and nuts; torque to 9 ft. lbs. (12 Nm)
- Wiring harness connector and retainer at bulkhead
- Engine ground wire at bulkhead; torque nut to 80 inch lbs. (9 Nm)
- Battery cables
- Fuel supply tube spring-lock coupling

23. Refill the engine with clean engine oil.
24. Refill the cooling system.
25. Evacuate and recharge the A/C system.
26. Start the engine and check for leaks. Stop the engine and check all fluid levels.
27. Perform an A/C system leak test.
28. Check the transmission fluid level.

4.6L Engine

See Figures 119 through 125.

1. Before servicing the vehicle, refer to the precautions in the beginning of this section.
2. Disconnect the windshield washer hose from the hood.

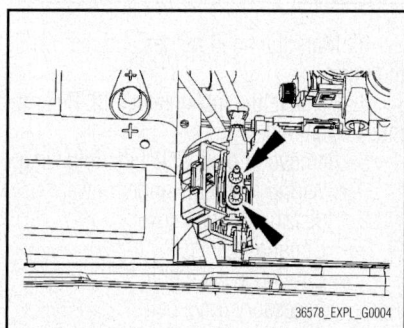

Fig. 119 Wiring terminals under power distribution box cover

Fig. 120 Heater hose removed from heater control valve

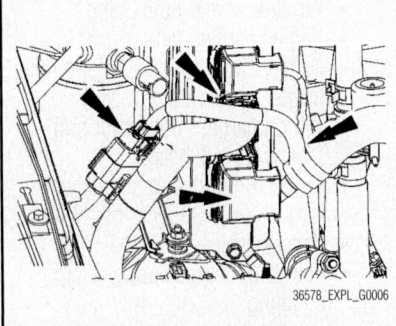

Fig. 121 Powertrain Control Module (PCM) electrical connectors

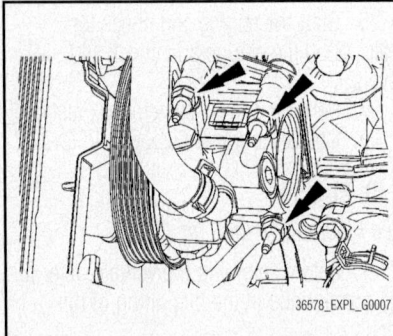

Fig. 122 Stud bolts and position of the power steering pump

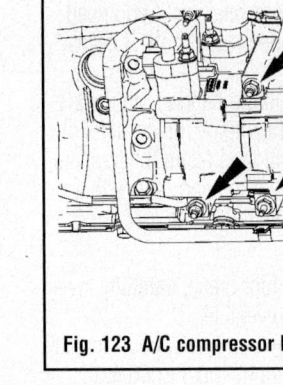

Fig. 123 A/C compressor bolt location

Fig. 124 RH engine support insulator nut location

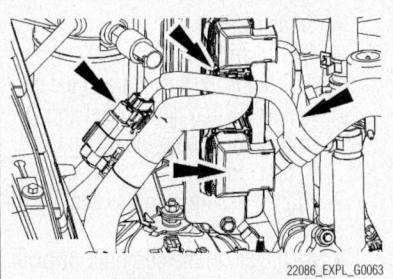

Fig. 125 Connect the wiring harness pin-type retainer, 2 Powertrain Control Module (PCM) electrical connectors and in-line electrical connector—4.6L Engine

3. Mark the hood hinges and remove the hood.

4. Remove the intake manifold. Refer to Intake Manifold.

5. Remove or disconnect the following:
- Wiring terminals under power distribution box cover
- Cooling fan
- Cooling system fluid
- Accessory drive belt
- Electrical connector beneath the A/C tube and A/C pressure switch
- Heated PCV fitting coolant hose

- Wiring harness retainer from the cooling fan wiring harness bracket
- Alternator
- Heater hose from heater control valve
- Upper radiator hose
- Coolant crossover manifold, the gaskets, the heated PCV fitting and the heated PCV fitting coolant hose as an assembly
- Evaporative emission (EVAP) canister purge valve electrical connector
- Heater hose retainer from the RH valve cover

- In-line electrical connector and the 2 Powertrain Control Module (PCM) electrical connectors, and detach the wiring harness pin-type retainer
- Heater hoses
- Engine ground wire from the body terminal
- Transmission; see "Transmission" section
- Inner fender splash shield
- Power steering pressure hose bracket
- Wiring harness brackets near the oil filter and pulley
- Wiring harness retainer from the power steering pump stud bolt
- Stud bolts and position the power steering pump aside
- Lower radiator hose from the oil filter adapter
- A/C clutch electrical connector and detach the wiring harness retainer; remove the nut and detach the A/C hose bracket
- A/C compressor aside
- Engine oil and filter; install the drain plug when finished
- Oil temperature sensor
- Wiring harness bracket from the RH engine support insulator bracket
- RH splash shield
- RH engine support insulator nuts
- Block heater electrical connector (if equipped) and wiring harness retainers
- LH engine support insulator through bolt

6. Install the engine lifting tools and use a suitable floor crane to carefully lift the engine from the vehicle.

To install:

7. Position the engine in the vehicle and remove the floor crane.

8. Remove the lifting tools from the engine.

9. Install or connect the following:
- LH engine support insulator through bolt to 76 ft. lbs. (103 Nm)
- Block heater wiring harness retainers (if equipped) and connect the block heater electrical connector
- RH engine support insulator nuts to 66 ft. lbs. (90 Nm)
- RH splash shield and install the pushpins
- Battery cable bracket on the RH engine support insulator bracket and install the bolt to 11 ft. lbs. (15 Nm)

- Oil temperature sensor to 11 ft. lbs. (15 Nm)
- A/C compressor; torque fasteners to 18 ft. lbs. (25 Nm)
- A/C hose bracket, wiring harness retainer and A/C clutch electrical connector
- Lower radiator hose to the oil filter adapter
- Power steering pump; tighten bolts to 18 ft. lbs. (25 Nm)
- Wiring harness retainer to the power steering pump stud bolt below heater hose connection
- Wiring harness brackets on block
- Power steering pressure hose bracket
- Inner fender splash shield
- Transmission; see "Transmission" section
- Ground wire to body stud
- Heater hoses at bulkhead
- Wiring harness pin-type retainer, 2 Powertrain Control Module (PCM) electrical connectors and in-line electrical connector
- Heater hose retainer to the RH valve cover
- EVAP canister purge valve electrical connector
- Coolant crossover, the heated positive crankcase ventilation (PCV) fitting and the heated PCV fitting hose as an assembly, with new gaskets; torque the bolts to 89 inch lbs. (10 Nm)
- Upper radiator hose
- Heater hose to control valve
- Alternator, alternator bracket and the wiring harness as an assembly; torque mounting nuts to 18 ft. lbs. (25 Nm)
- Wiring harness retainer to the cooling fan wiring harness bracket
- Heated PCV fitting coolant hose
- Electrical connector located beneath the A/C tube and A/C pressure switch
- Accessory drive belt
- Engine cooling fan
- Wiring harness terminals to power distribution center
- Intake manifold; refer to Intake Manifold.
- Hood; torque bolts to 9 ft. lbs. (12 Nm)
- Windshield washer hose to hood

10. Refill the engine with clean oil, using a new oil filter.

11. Fill and bleed the cooling system.

12. Evacuate and recharge the A/C system.

13. Start the engine and check for leaks; stop the engine and recheck all fluid levels.

14. Perform an A/C system leak check.

EXHAUST MANIFOLD

REMOVAL & INSTALLATION

4.0L Engine

See Figures 126 and 127.

1. Before servicing the vehicle, refer to Precautions.

2. Remove or disconnect the following:
- Negative battery cable
- EGR tube (RH manifold)
- Exhaust pipe attaching bolts
- Exhaust manifold and discard the gasket

To install:

3. Clean the gasket mating surfaces.

4. Install or connect the following:
- New gasket and the exhaust manifold. Torque the bolts to 16 ft. lbs. (22 Nm).

- Exhaust pipe-to-manifold attaching bolts. Torque the bolts to 30 ft. lbs. (40 Nm).
- EGR tube to the manifold. Torque the fastener to 30 ft. lbs. (40 Nm) (RH manifold)
- Negative battery cable

5. Start the vehicle and check for leaks, repair if necessary.

4.6L Engine

Right Side

See Figure 128.

1. With the vehicle in NEUTRAL, position it on a hoist.

2. Remove the 4 nuts and disconnect the dual converter Y-pipe from the exhaust manifolds.

3. Remove the 3 bolts and the RH exhaust manifold heat shield.

4. Remove the 5 pushpins and the RH splash shield.

5. Remove the 8 nuts, the RH exhaust manifold and the 2 gaskets.

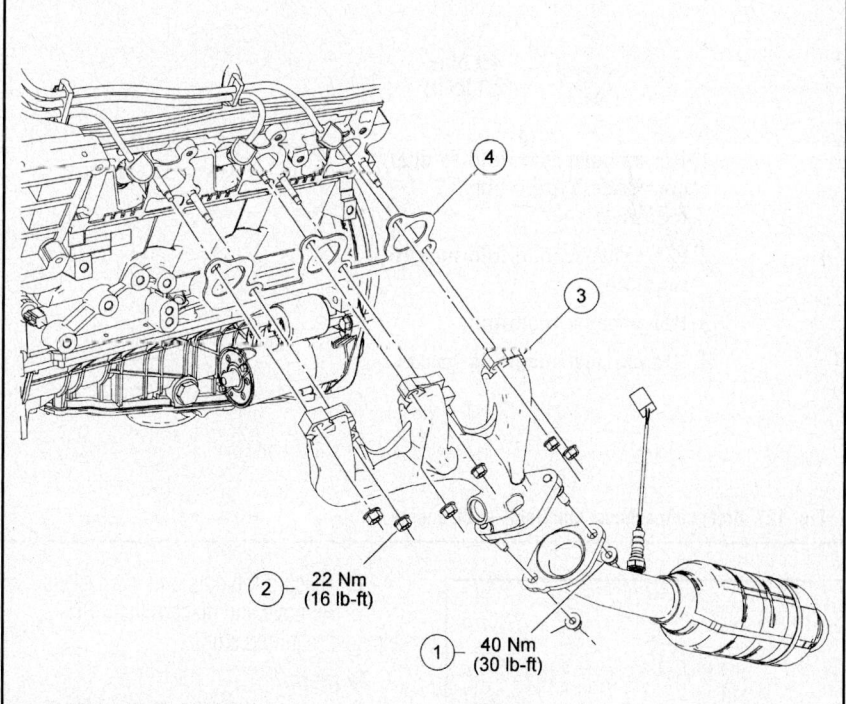

1 LH exhaust manifold-to-dual converter Y-pipe nuts (2 required)

2 LH exhaust manifold nut (6 required)

3 LH exhaust manifold

4 LH exhaust manifold gasket

06017-EXPL-G29

Fig. 12.6 Left side exhaust manifold—4.0L engine

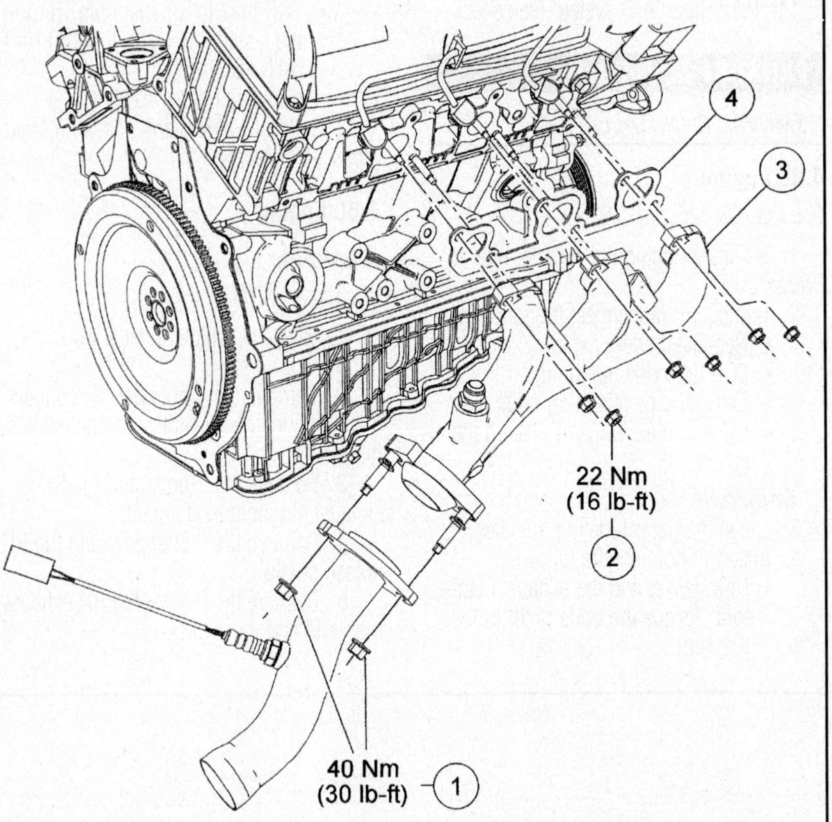

**22 Nm
(16 lb-ft)**

②

**40 Nm
(30 lb-ft)** ①

1 RH exhaust manifold-to-dual
converter Y-pipe nuts (2
required)

2 RH exhaust manifold nuts (6
required)

3 RH exhaust manifold

4 RH exhaust manifold gasket

06017-EXPL-G30

Fig. 127 Right side exhaust manifold—4.0L engine

Left Side

See Figure 129.

1. With the vehicle in NEUTRAL, position it on a hoist.
2. Detach the Evaporative Emission (EVAP) canister purge valve from the bracket and position the valve aside.

➡ **Do not allow the lower steering column shaft to rotate while it is disconnected from the gear or the clockspring may be damaged. If there is evidence that the lower steering column shaft has rotated, the clockspring must be removed and re-centered.**

3. Remove the intermediate steering shaft pinch bolt and disconnect the intermediate steering shaft from the lower steering column shaft.
4. Remove the 4 nuts and disconnect the dual converter Y-pipe from the exhaust manifolds.
5. Remove the 2 nuts and position the battery cable bracket aside.
6. Remove the 3 bolts and the LH exhaust manifold heat shield.
7. Remove and discard the pushpin.
8. Remove the 8 nuts, the LH exhaust manifold and the 2 gaskets.
9. Deflect the inner fender splash shield and remove the manifold between the splash shield and the frame rail.
10. Discard the nuts and the gaskets.
11. Remove and discard the 8 LH exhaust manifold studs.

To install:

12. Installation is the reverse of the removal procedure, noting the following:
   a. Tighten the nuts in the sequence shown as follows:
   • Studs—9 ft. lbs. (12 Nm); nuts—18 ft. lbs. (25 Nm)
13. Tighten the Y-pipe new nuts as follows:
   • 30 ft. lbs. (40 Nm)

6. Discard the nuts and the gaskets.
7. Remove and discard the 8 RH exhaust manifold studs.

To install:

8. Installation is the reverse of the removal procedure, noting the following:
   a. Tighten the nuts in the sequence shown as follows:
   • Studs—9 ft. lbs. (12 Nm); nuts—18 ft. lbs. (25 Nm)
9. Tighten the Y-pipe new nuts as follows:
   • 30 ft. lbs. (40 Nm)
10. Tighten the intermediate shaft pinch bolt to 35 ft. lbs. (48 Nm).

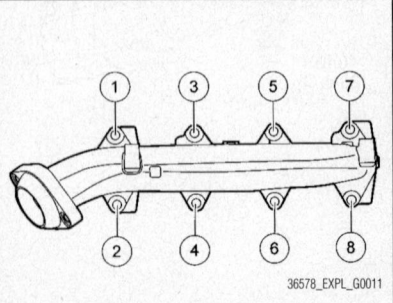

36578_EXPL_G0011

Fig. 128 Exhaust manifold tightening sequence RH—4.6L Engine

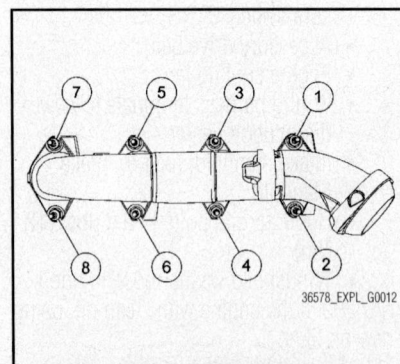

36578_EXPL_G0012

Fig. 129 Exhaust manifold tightening sequence LH—4.6L Engine

14. Tighten the intermediate shaft pinch bolt to 35 ft. lbs. (48 Nm).

FLEXPLATE

REMOVAL & INSTALLATION

See Figures 130 through 132.

1. Remove the transmission. Refer to Automatic Transmission.
2. Remove the flexplate attaching bolts and remove the flexplate.

To install:

3. Position the flexplate into position.
4. Select only the appropriate new bolts designed for flexplate application.
5. Install and tighten the bolts in sequence as shown:
   4.0L
   a. Stage 1: 37 ft. lbs. (51 Nm)
   b. Stage 2: Plus 90 degrees
   4.6L: 59 ft. lbs. (80 Nm)
6. Install the transmission. Refer to Automatic Transmission.

INTAKE MANIFOLD

REMOVAL & INSTALLATION

4.0L Engine

See Figures 133 and 134.

1. Before servicing the vehicle, refer to Precautions.
2. Release fuel system pressure.
3. Remove or disconnect the following:
   - Air cleaner outlet pipe
   - Knock sensor (KS) electrical connector from the intake manifold
   - PCV tube from the intake manifold
   - Brake booster vacuum hose from the intake manifold
   - Main vacuum harness fitting from the intake manifold
   - EVAP tube from the intake manifold
   - EGR system module electrical connector
   - Wiring harness retainer
   - EGR system module vacuum fitting
   - Exhaust manifold-to-EGR system module tube from the EGR system module
   - TP sensor electrical connector
   - Electronic Throttle Body (TB) electrical connector
   - Wiring harness bracket from the electronic TB
   - Intake manifold and the gaskets

To install:

4. Clean the sealing surfaces and inspect the gaskets. Install new gaskets if necessary.
5. Position the intake manifold and tighten the bolts to 8 ft. lbs. (11 Nm).
6. Install or connect the following:
   - Wiring harness bracket to the electronic TB
   - Electronic TB electrical connector
   - TP sensor electrical connector
   - Exhaust manifold-to-EGR system module tube to the EGR system module
   - EGR system module vacuum fitting
   - Wiring harness retainer
   - EGR system module electrical connector
   - EVAP tube to the intake manifold
   - Main vacuum harness fitting to the intake manifold
   - Brake booster vacuum hose to the intake manifold
   - PCV tube to the intake manifold
   - Knock sensor (KS) electrical connector to the intake manifold
   - Air cleaner outlet pipe

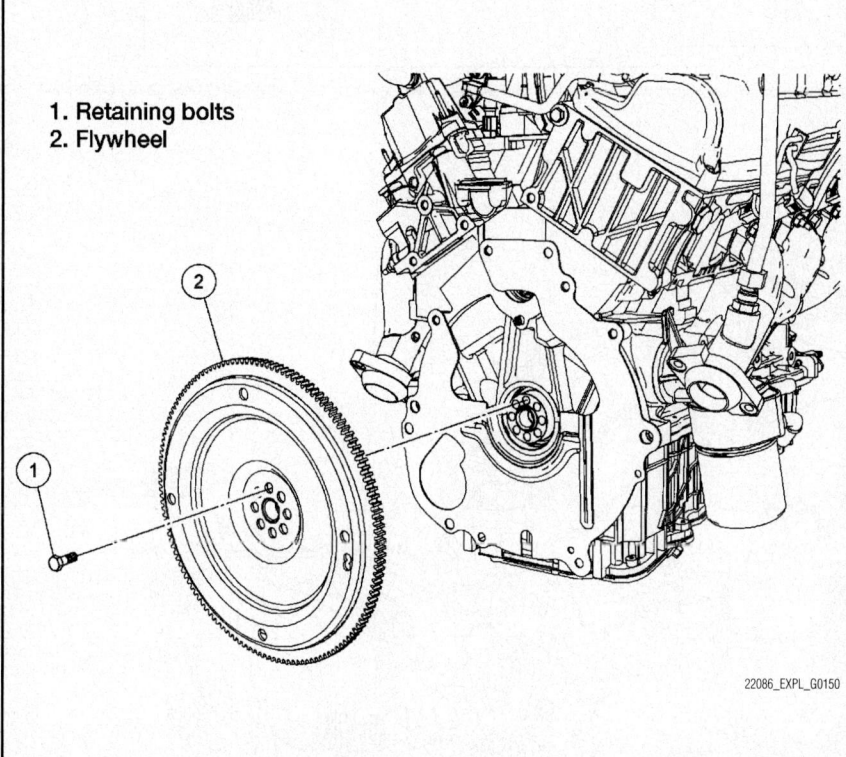

1. Retaining bolts
2. Flywheel

22086_EXPL_G0150

Fig. 130 Remove the flexplate attaching bolts (1) and remove the flexplate (2)—4.0L & 4.6L engine

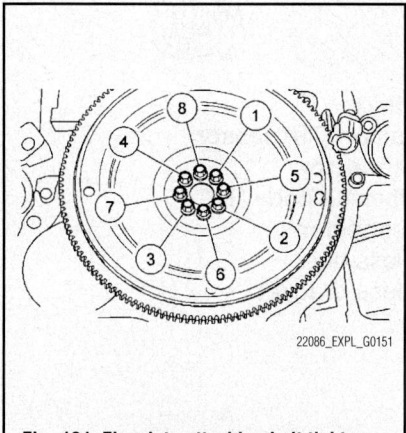

22086_EXPL_G0151

Fig. 131 Flexplate attaching bolt tightening sequence—4.0L engine

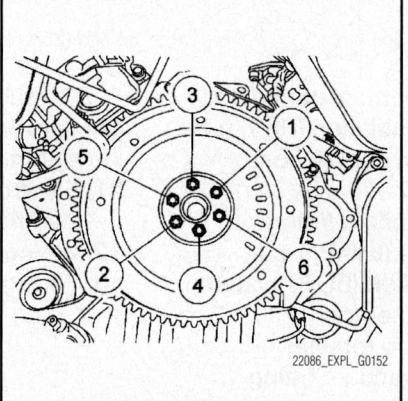

22086_EXPL_G0152

Fig. 132 Flywheel/flexplate attaching bolt tightening sequence—4.6L engine

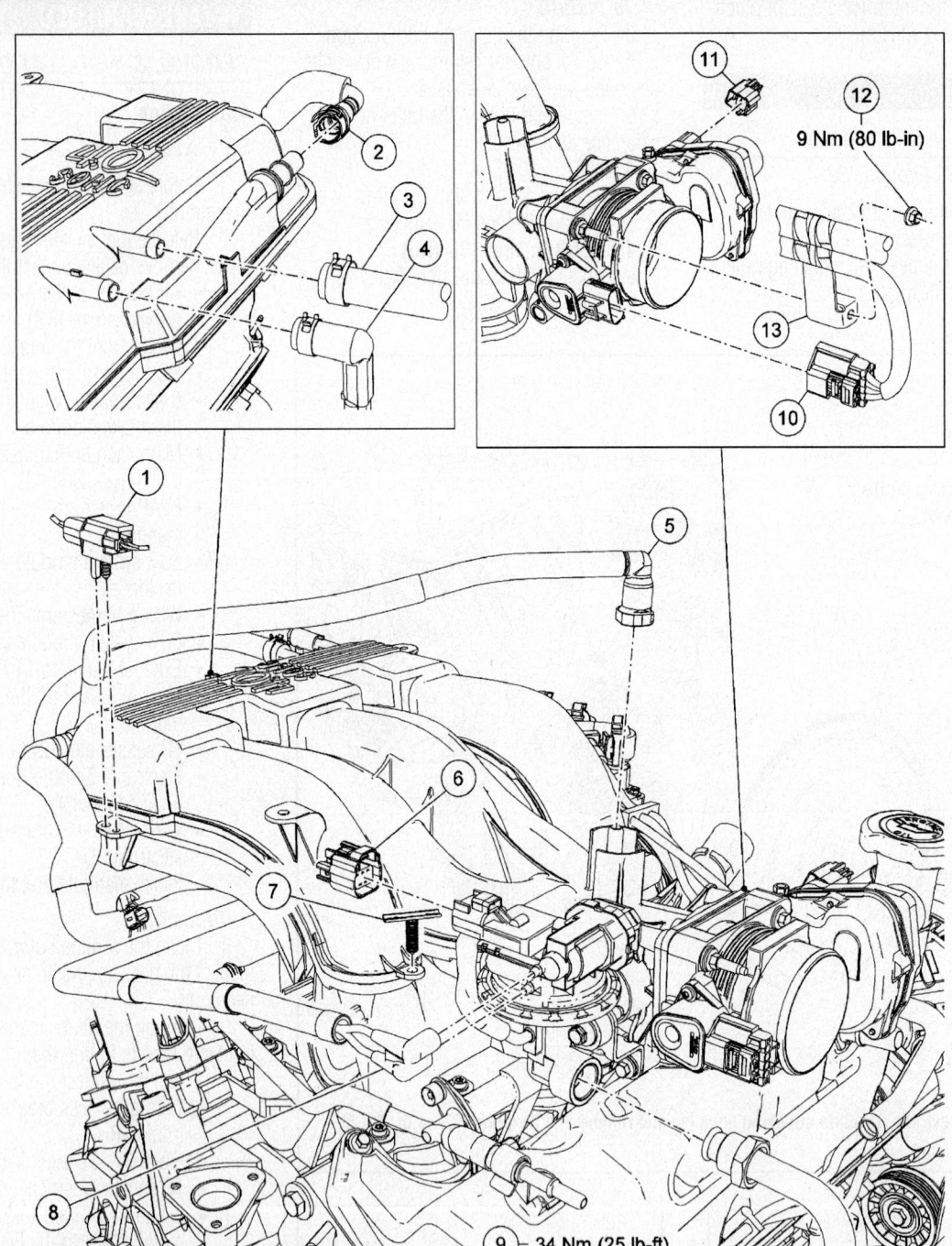

1. Knock sensor (KS) electrical connector
2. Positive crankcase ventilation (PCV) tube
3. Brake booster vacuum supply hose
4. Engine main vacuum harness-to-intake manifold fitting
5. Evaporative emissions (EVAP) tube
6. Exhaust gas recirculation (EGR) system module electrical connector
7. Wiring harness pin-type retainer
8. EGR system module vacuum fitting
9. EGR tube fitting
10. Throttle position (TP) sensor electrical connector
11. Electronic throttle body (TB) electrical connector
12. Wiring harness nut
13. Wiring harness bracket

22086_EXPL_G0081

Fig. 133 Exploded view of the external engine component to remove for intake manifold removal—4.0L engine

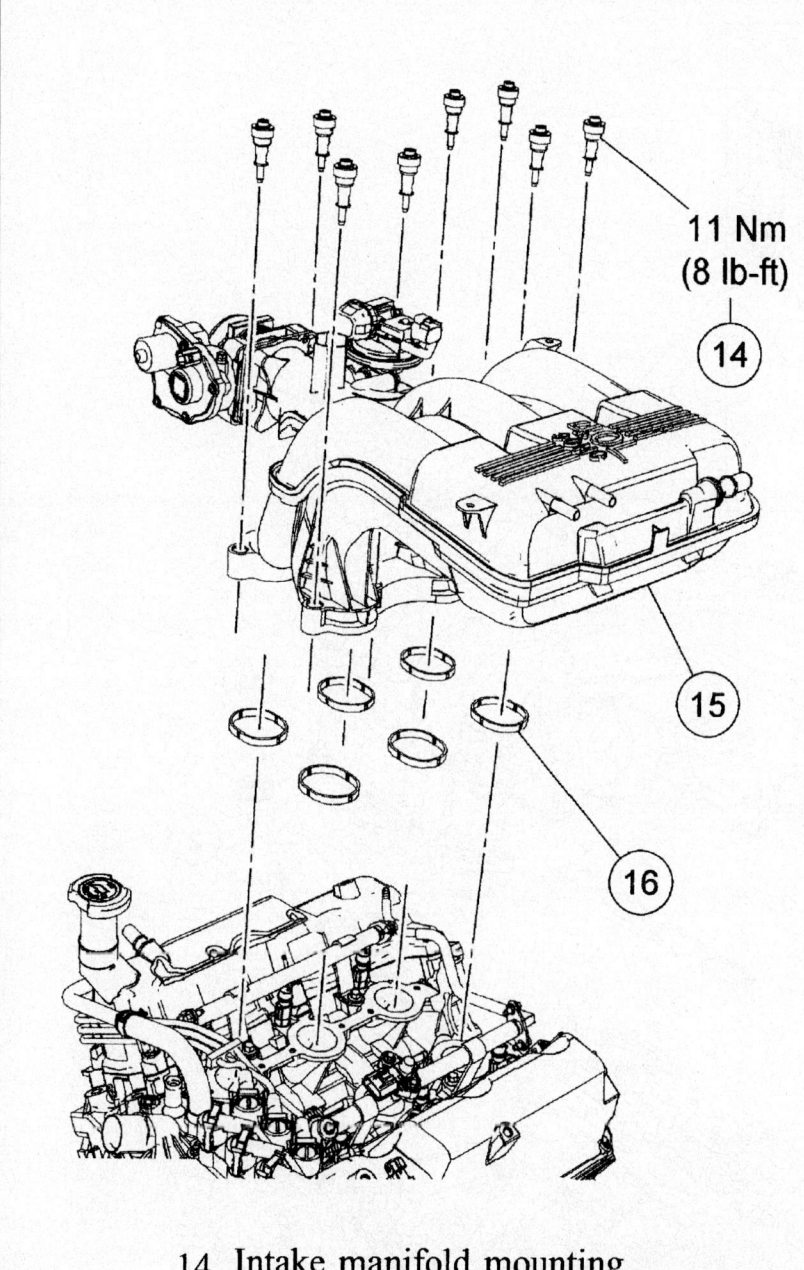

11 Nm
(8 lb-ft)

(14)

(15)

(16)

14 Intake manifold mounting bolts (8 required)

15 Intake manifold

16 Intake manifold gaskets

06017-EXPL-G27

Fig. 134 Intake manifold removal—4.0L engine

4.6L Engine

See Figures 135 and 136.

1. Before servicing the vehicle, refer to Precautions.

2. Relieve the fuel system pressure.

3. Remove or disconnect the following:
- Negative battery cable
- Air cleaner outlet pipe
- Fuel rail and injectors
- Electronic Throttle Body (TB) electrical connector
- EVAP tube from the intake manifold
- TP sensor electrical connector
- PCV hose from the heated PCV fitting on the intake manifold
- Position the heated PCV fitting aside
- Wiring harness retainers from the intake manifold
- Charge motion control valve (CMCV) electrical connector
- Intake manifold bolts and position the intake manifold forward
- Brake booster vacuum hose from the rear of the intake manifold
- Vacuum hose from the rear of the intake manifold

4. Remove the intake manifold and gaskets.

To install:

5. Clean and inspect the sealing surfaces.

❋❋ WARNING

Electrical and vacuum harnesses must not restrict movement of the CMCV control rods at the rear of the intake manifold. Use extreme care during the installation of the intake manifold to prevent any pinching of electrical and vacuum harnesses.

6. Using new intake manifold gaskets, position the intake manifold.

7. Connect the vacuum hose to the rear of the intake manifold.

8. Connect the brake booster hose to the rear of the intake manifold.

9. Install the intake manifold bolts and tighten the bolts in the sequence shown in 2 stages:
   a. Stage 1: 18 inch lbs. (2 Nm)
   b. State 2: 89 inch lbs. (10 Nm)

10. Install or connect the following:
- CMCV electrical connector
- Wiring harness retainers to the intake manifold
- New O-ring seal, position the heated PCV fitting and install the bolts
- PCV hose to the heated PCV fitting on the intake manifold
- TP sensor electrical connector
- EVAP hose to the intake manifold
- Electronic TB electrical connector
- Fuel rail and injectors
- Air cleaner outlet pipe
- Negative battery cable

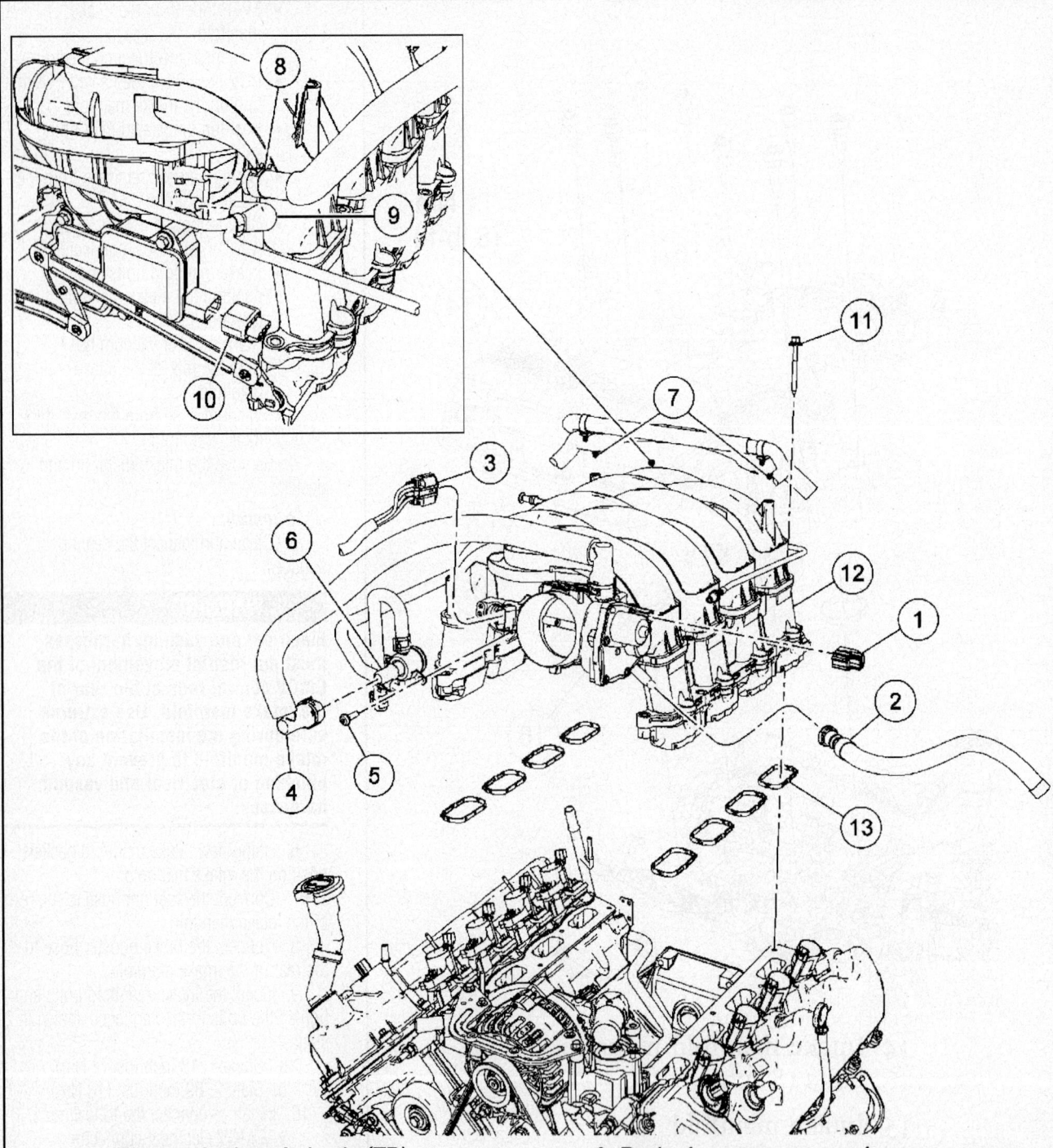

1. Electronic throttle body (TB) electrical connector
2. Evaporative emissions (EVAP) hose
3. Throttle position (TP) sensor electrical connector
4. Positive crankcase ventilation (PCV) hose
5. Heated PCV fitting bolt (2 required)
6. Heated PCV fitting
7. Wiring harness retainers
8. Brake booster vacuum hose
9. Vacuum hose
10. Charge motion control valve (CMCV) electrical connector
11. Intake manifold bolt (10 required)
12. Intake manifold
13. Intake manifold gasket

22086_EXPL_G0086

Fig. 135 Intake manifold and related components—4.6L engine

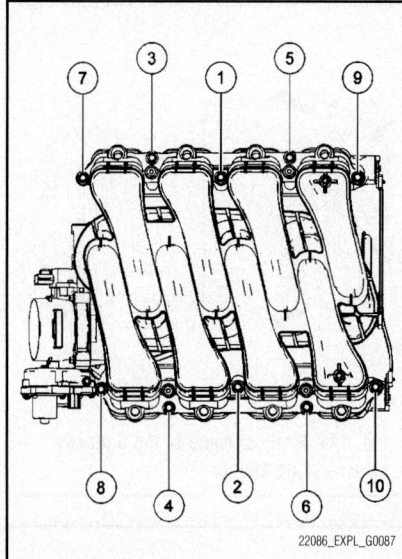

Fig. 136 Intake manifold bolt tightening sequence—4.6L engine

OIL PAN

REMOVAL & INSTALLATION

4.0L Engine

See Figure 137.

1. Before servicing the vehicle, refer to Precautions.
2. Raise the vehicle on a hoist.
3. Drain the engine oil.
4. Remove the oil pan bolts, oil pan and discard the gasket

To install:

➡ Do not use metal scrapers, wire brushes, power abrasive discs or other abrasive means to clean sealing surfaces. These tools cause scratches and gouges which make leak paths. Use a plastic scraping tool to remove all traces of the old oil pan gasket.

5. Clean the pan and block mating surfaces.

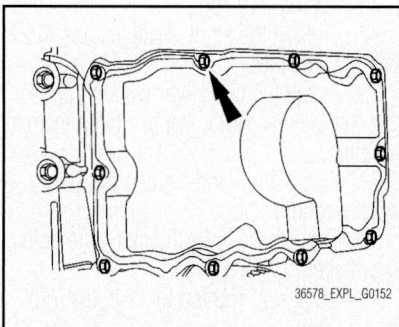

Fig. 137 Oil pan bolt location—4.0L engine

6. Install a new gasket.
7. Position the oil pan. Torque the bolts, in an alternating pattern, to 97 inch lbs. (11 Nm).
8. Torque the pan drain bolt to 19 ft. lbs. (26 Nm).
9. Fill the engine with clean oil.
10. Start the vehicle and check for leaks, repair if necessary.

4.6L Engine

See Figure 138.

1. Before servicing the vehicle, refer to Precautions.
2. With the vehicle in NEUTRAL position on a hoist.
3. Lower the front axle (4WD). Refer to Front Suspension in Suspension.
4. Remove the front stabilizer bar. Refer to Stabilizer Bar in Suspension.
5. Drain the engine oil.
6. Remove the nut and position the power steering pressure (PSP) hose bracket aside.
7. Remove the nut and position the battery cable bracket aside.
8. Disconnect the oil temperature sensor electrical connector.
9. Remove the bolts and the oil drain splash shield.
10. If equipped with a block heater, detach the block heater wiring harness retainer from the LH side oil pan bolt.

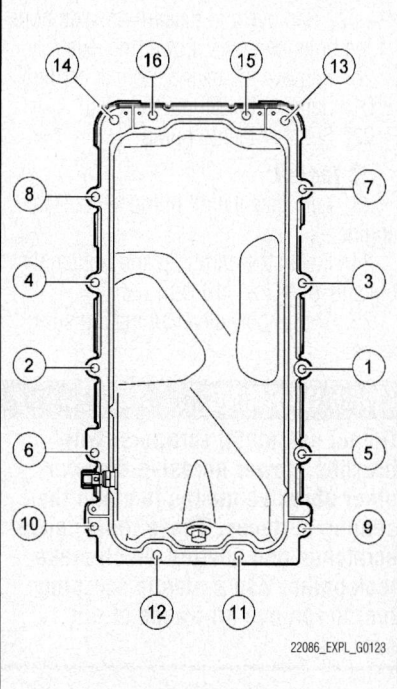

Fig. 138 Oil pan bolt tightening sequence—4.6L Engine

11. Remove the 16 bolts, the oil pan and the gasket.

To install:

❋❋ WARNING

Do not use metal scrapers, wire brushes, power abrasive discs, or other abrasive means to clean the sealing surfaces. These can cause scratches and gouges resulting in leak paths. Use a plastic scraper to clean the sealing surfaces.

12. Clean the sealing surfaces with metal surface cleaner.

➡ If the oil pan and gasket are not secured within four minutes of sealer application, the sealant must be removed and the sealing surfaces cleaned with metal surface cleaner.

13. Apply silicone gasket and sealant at the front corners and rear corners of the pan-to-block mating surface.
14. Install a new oil pan gasket, position the oil pan and tighten the pan bolts, in the sequence shown, in 3 steps:
    a. Step 1: 18 inch lbs. (2 Nm)
    b. Step 2: 15 ft. lbs. (20 Nm)
    c. Step 3: additional 60 degrees of turn
15. If equipped with a block heater, attach the block heater wiring harness retainer to the LH oil pan bolt.
16. Position the oil drain splash shield and install the bolts.
17. Attach the wiring harness retainers to the RH oil pan bolts.
18. Connect the oil temperature sensor electrical connector.
19. Attach the battery cable bracket and install the nut to 89 inch lbs. (10 Nm).
20. Attach the PSP hose bracket and install the nut to 89 inch lbs. (10 Nm).
21. Install the stabilizer bar. Tighten the stabilizer bar end nut to 26 ft. lbs. (35 Nm) and the clamp bolts to 41 ft. lbs. (55 Nm).
22. Install the front axle. Tighten the axle mounting insulator bolts to 74 ft. lbs. (100 Nm).
23. Refill the engine with new oil.

OIL PUMP

REMOVAL & INSTALLATION

4.0L Engine

See Figures 139 through 142.

1. Before servicing the vehicle, refer to Precautions.
2. With the vehicle in NEUTRAL, position it on a hoist.

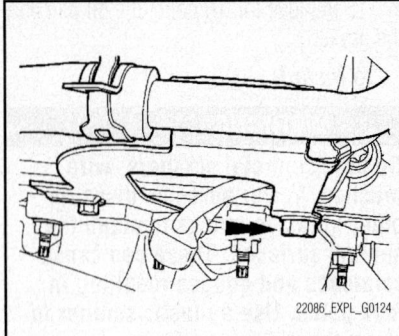

Fig. 139 Remove the heater hose bracket bolt as shown, then install a RH lifting eye, using the previously removed bolt—4.0L

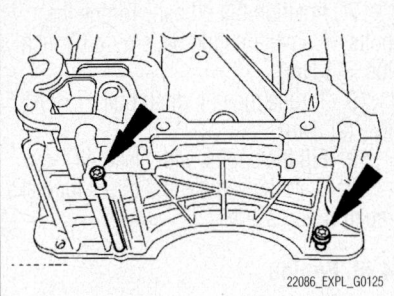

Fig. 140 Remove the 2 Torx® bolts at the rear of the block cradle—4.0L (shown with block cradle removed for clarity of location)

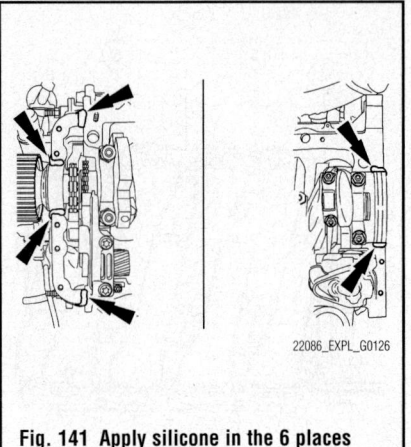

Fig. 141 Apply silicone in the 6 places shown—4.0L Engine

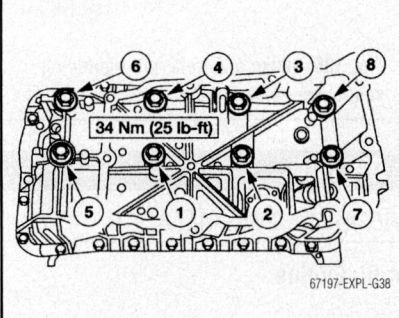

Fig. 142 Cylinder block cradle bolt torque sequence—4.0L Engine

3. Remove or disconnect the following:
 • Negative battery cable
 • Air cleaner outlet tube
 • Starter
 • Oil pan
 • Weatherstrip across front of engine compartment

4. Remove the bolt and position the power steering fluid reservoir aside.

5. Disconnect the coolant overflow hose. Remove the bolts and the coolant expansion tank.

6. On all models, remove the fan shroud.

7. Remove the heater hose bracket bolt as shown, then install a RH lifting eye, using the previously removed bolt.

➥This is not a typical setup. Only the right side of the engine will be raised.

8. Install the engine lifting tools.

9. On AWD models, remove the front stabilizer bar brackets (if equipped) and the crossmember.

10. On AWD models, remove the 4 bolts and the crossmember.

11. Remove the RH motor mount insulator nut.

12. Remove the LH motor mount insulator through-bolt.

13. Raise the engine.

14. Remove the 2 bell housing-to-cylinder block cradle bolts.

15. Remove the 2 Torx® bolts at the rear of the block cradle.

16. Remove the 20 bolts and 2 nuts along the outside of the cylinder block cradle. Mark the location of the 2 silver-colored bolts, with washer seals; these must be installed the same position, with new washer seals.

17. Remove the 8 cylinder block cradle inner bolts and 2 washer seals.

18. With the lifting device, raise the engine.

⁂ CAUTION

Secure the assembly to the jack. Avoid any obstructions while lowering and raising the jack. Contact with obstructions may cause the assembly to fall off the jack, which may result in serious personal injury.

19. On AWD models, perform the following:
 a. Support the front axle with a suitable jack stand and secure with a safety strap or chain.
 b. Disconnect the vent hose from the differential housing vent tube.
 c. Remove and discard the axle housing bolts and nuts. Lower the axle.

20. Remove the cylinder block cradle.

21. Remove the oil pump bolts.

22. Remove the oil pump.

To install:

23. Lubricate the oil pump with clean engine oil.

24. Install the oil pump and tighten the bolts to 14 ft. lbs. (19 Nm).

25. Thoroughly clean all mating surfaces.

⁂ WARNING

Do not use metal scrapers, wire brushes, power abrasive discs or other abrasive means to clean the sealing surfaces. These tools cause scratches and gouges which make leak paths. Use a plastic scraping tool to remove all traces of old sealant.

➥Failure to back off the set screws may result in damage to the cylinder block cradle.

26. Back the set screws off until they are below the cylinder block cradle boss.

➥If not secured within 4 minutes, the sealant must be removed and the sealing area cleaned.

27. Apply silicone in the 6 places shown.

28. Position a new gasket and the cylinder block cradle.

29. Install and hand-tighten the 2 rear Torx® bolts.

30. Install the 2 bell housing-to-cylinder block cradle bolts. Tighten the bolts to 35 ft. lbs. (47 Nm).

31. Tighten the outer 20 bolts and 2 nuts to 89 inch lbs. (10 Nm).

32. Tighten the eight cradle inserts to 27 inch lbs. (3 Nm).

33. Install the two silver-covered bolts and new washer seals. Hand-tighten them at this time.

34. Install and hand-tighten the six remaining inner bolts.

35. Tighten the lower block cradle bolts in two stages:
 • Stage 1: Tighten to 11 ft. lbs. (15 Nm).
 • Stage 2: Tighten to 25 ft. lbs. (34 Nm).

36. On AWD models, perform the following:

a. Raise the axle into position. Install new bolts and nuts and tighten to 49 ft. lbs. (66 Nm).

b. Connect the vent hose to the differential housing.

c. Install the front stabilizer bar brackets and torque the nuts to 41 ft. lbs. (55 Nm).

37. On all models, lower the engine and remove the lifting tools.

38. Install the LH engine support through-bolt and nut. Tighten to 76 ft. lbs. (103 Nm).

39. Install the RH engine support nut and tighten to 66 ft. lbs. (90 Nm).

40. Install the crossmember (AWD models). Tighten the retaining bolts to 76 ft. lbs. (103 Nm).

41. Install the oil pump screen and pickup tube.

42. Install the fan shroud and bolts.
43. Install the expansion tank.
44. Install the power steering reservoir.
45. Install the weatherstrip.
46. Install the air cleaner outlet pipe.
47. Connect the battery ground cable.
48. Fill the engine with clean engine oil.

4.6L Engine

See Figure 143.

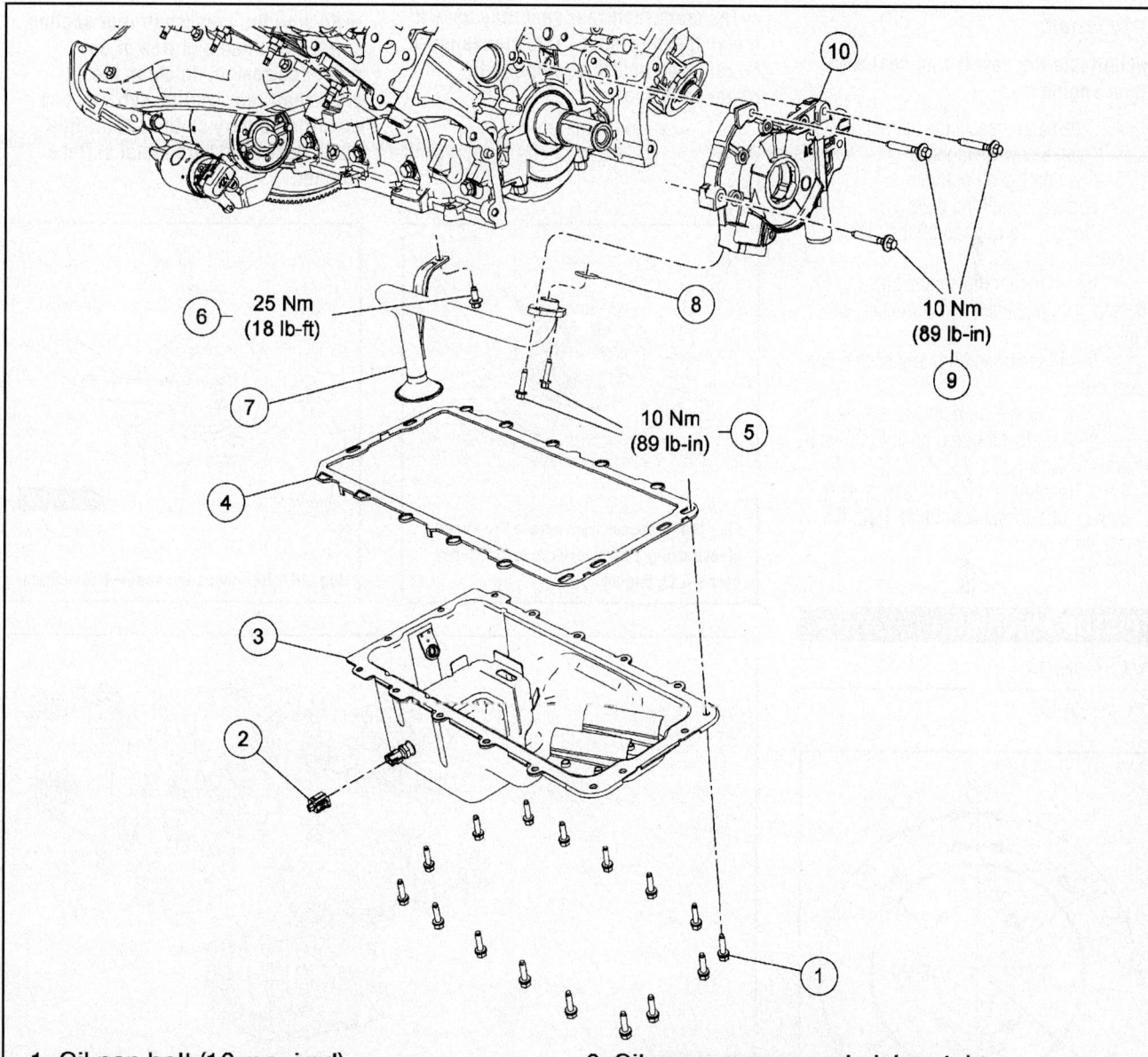

1. Oil pan bolt (16 required)
2. Oil temperature sensor electrical connector
3. Oil pan
4. Oil pan gasket
5. Oil pump screen and pickup tube-to-oil pump bolts (2 required)
6. Oil pump screen and pickup tube support bracket bolt
7. Oil pump screen and pickup tube
8. Oil pump screen and pickup tube O-ring seal
9. Oil pump bolts (3 required)
10. Oil pump

22086_EXPL_G0127

Fig. 143 Exploded view of the oil pan, oil pickup screen and tube, and the oil pump—4.6L Engine

1. Before servicing the vehicle, refer to Precautions.
2. Drain the engine oil.
3. Remove or disconnect the following:
   - Negative battery cable
   - Oil pan; refer to Oil Pan.
   - Three bolts and the oil pump screen cover and tube
   - Timing chains and sprockets; see "Timing Chain and Sprocket" section
   - Oil pump

To install:

➡**Lubricate the new O-ring seal with clean engine oil.**

4. Clean and inspect the mating surfaces. Install a new O-ring seal.
5. Position the oil pump.
6. Loosely install the bolts.
7. Tighten the bolts to 89 inch lbs. (10 Nm).
8. Install the timing chains and sprockets; see "Timing Chain and Sprocket" section.
9. Install the three oil pump screen and cover bolts.
   a. Tighten the oil pump screen and pickup tube-to-oil pump bolts to 89 inch lbs. (10 Nm).
   b. Tighten the oil pump screen and pickup tube-to-spacer bolt to 18 ft. lbs. (25 Nm).
10. Install the oil pan.

PISTON AND RING

POSITIONING
See Figure 144.

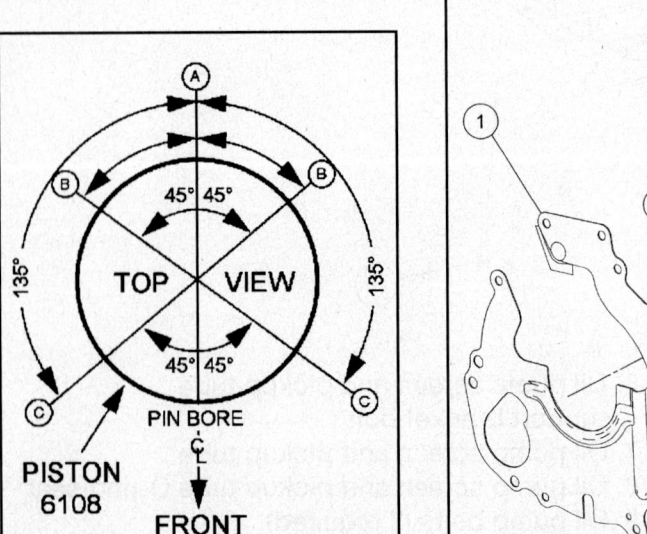

Fig. 144 Piston ring positioning—4.0L & 4.6L Engine

REAR MAIN SEAL

REMOVAL & INSTALLATION

4.0L Engine
See Figures 145 through 149.

1. Before servicing the vehicle, refer to Precautions.
2. Remove the flexplate.
3. Remove the spacer plate and the flexplate-to-crankshaft spacer.

➡**The crankshaft rear seal may have a metal speedy sleeve. This sleeve must be removed before attempting to remove the seal.**

4. If necessary, remove the speedy sleeve using 2 screwdrivers or small pry bars.

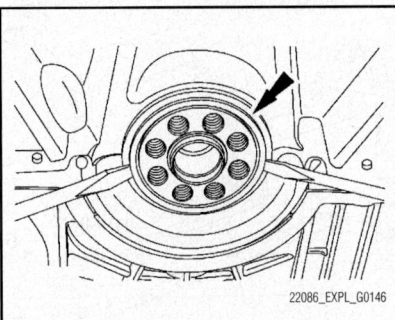

Fig. 145 If necessary, remove the speedy sleeve using 2 screwdrivers or small pry bars—4.0L Engine

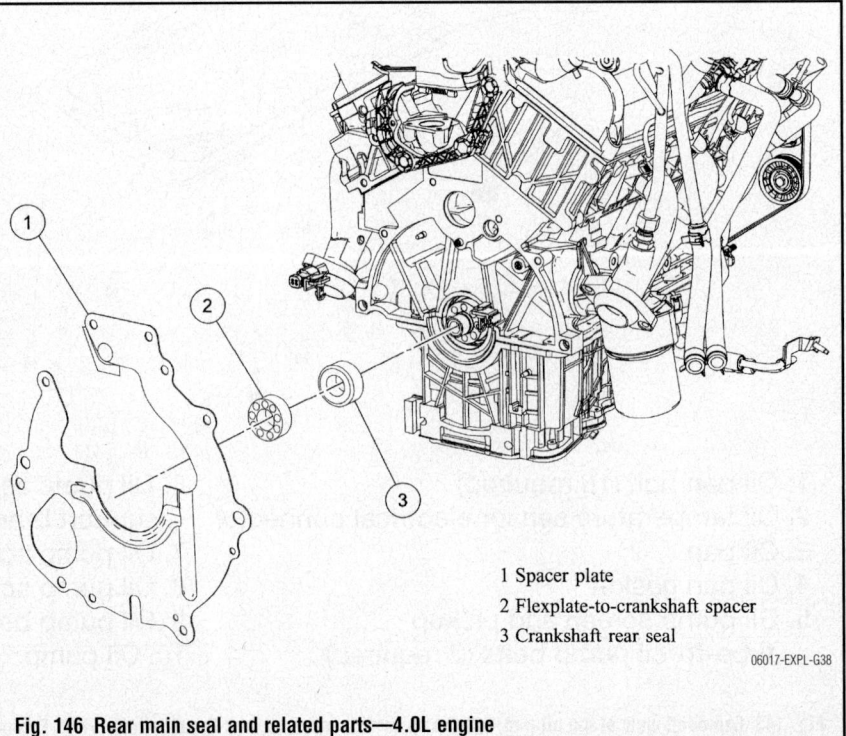

1 Spacer plate
2 Flexplate-to-crankshaft spacer
3 Crankshaft rear seal

Fig. 146 Rear main seal and related parts—4.0L engine

✳✳ WARNING

Avoid scratching or damaging the oil crankshaft seal running surface during removal of the crankshaft rear oil seal.

5. Using special tool, 303-514, remove the oil slinger.
6. Using special tool, 303-519, remove the crankshaft rear oil seal.

To install:

➡**Be sure the crankshaft rear sealing surface is clean and free of any rust or corrosion. To clean the crankshaft rear sealing surface, use extra-fine emery cloth or extra-fine 0000 steel wool with metal surface cleaner.**

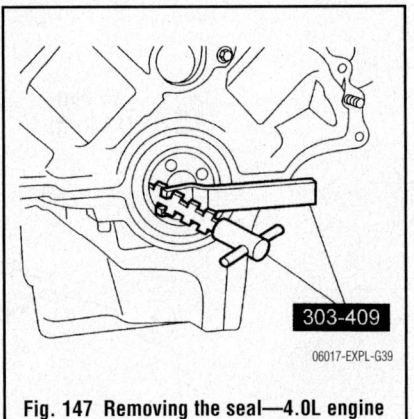

Fig. 147 Removing the seal—4.0L engine

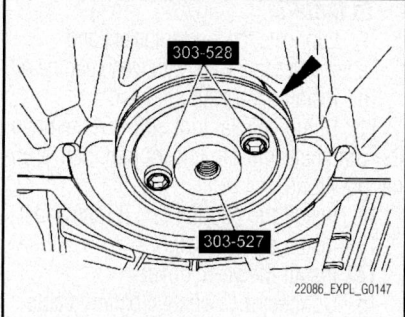

Fig. 148 Using special tool 303-527 and 303-528, position the crankshaft rear oil seal—4.0L Engine

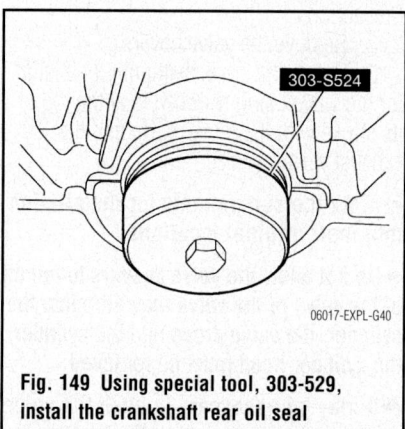

Fig. 149 Using special tool, 303-529, install the crankshaft rear oil seal

7. Lubricate the crankshaft rear oil seal with clean engine oil and install on the special tool.

8. Using special tool 303-527 and 303-528, position the crankshaft rear oil seal.

9. Install the flexplate or flexplate.

4.6L Engine

See Figures 150 through 152.

1. Before servicing the vehicle, refer to Precautions.

2. Remove or disconnect the following:
   - Flexplate
   - Crankshaft rear oil seal slinger with a slide hammer and proper removed tool
   - Rear oil seal with a slide hammer and proper remover tool

To install:

3. Installation is the reverse of the removal procedure. Note the following:
   - Lubricate the inner lip of the rear crankshaft seal with clean engine oil.
   - Use the two Crankshaft Rear Oil Seal Installers to install the rear oil seal.
   - Using the two Crankshaft Rear Oil Seal Installers and the Crankshaft Rear Oil Slinger Installer, install the crankshaft rear oil slinger.

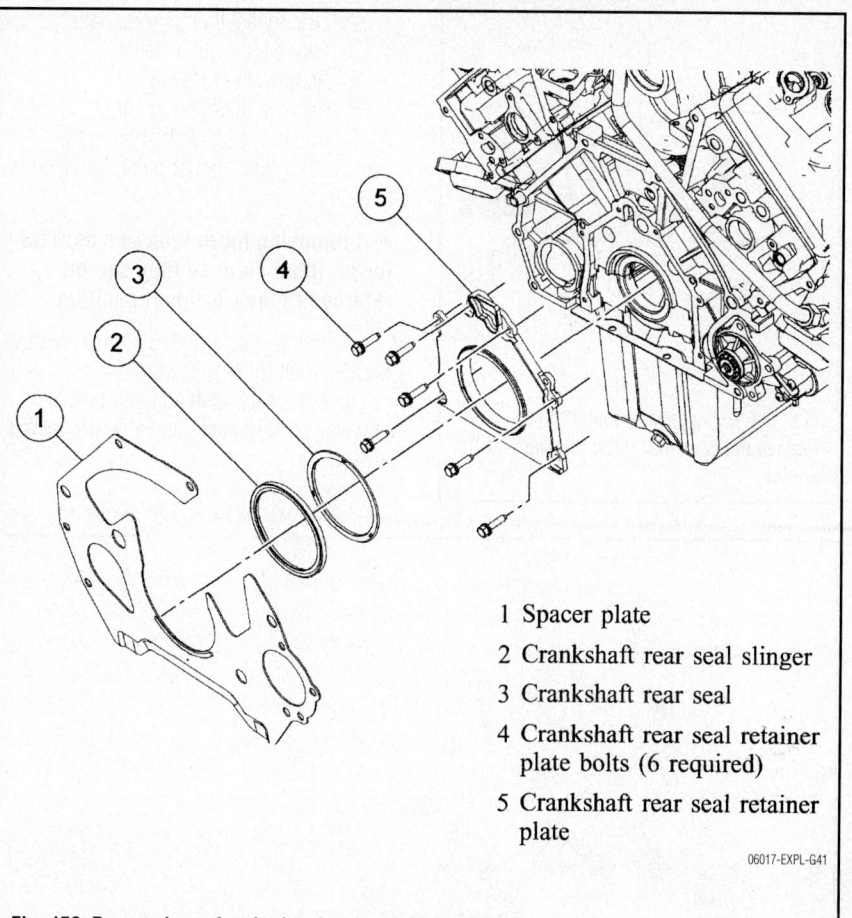

1 Spacer plate

2 Crankshaft rear seal slinger

3 Crankshaft rear seal

4 Crankshaft rear seal retainer plate bolts (6 required)

5 Crankshaft rear seal retainer plate

Fig. 150 Rear main seal and related parts—4.6L engine

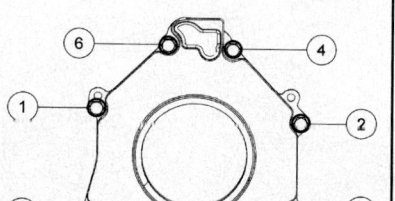

Fig. 151 Retainer plate removal and torque sequence—4.6L engine

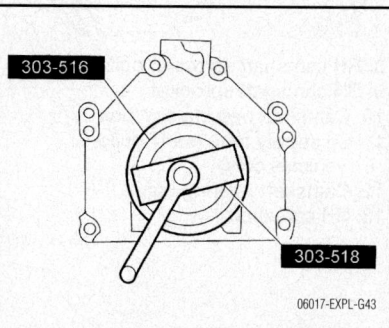

Fig. 152 Rear main seal installation—4.6L engine

ROCKER ARMS/SHAFTS

REMOVAL & INSTALLATION

This procedure covers the removal and installation of the Camshaft Roller Follower and Hydraulic Lash Adjusters.

4.0L Engine

See Figures 153 through 155.

1. Before servicing the vehicle, refer to Precautions.

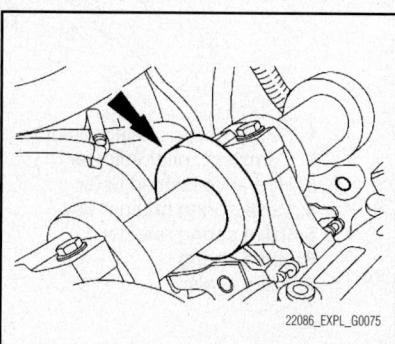

Fig. 153 Rotate the crankshaft until the camshaft for the cylinder being serviced is at base circle—4.0L engine

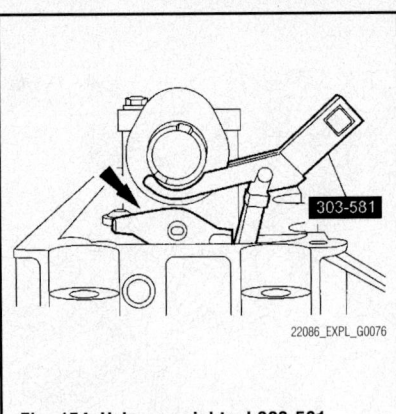

Fig. 154 Using special tool 303-581, remove the camshaft roller follower—4.0L engine

2. Disconnect the negative battery cable.

3. Remove the valve cover.

4. Remove the fuel rail.

5. Remove the cooling fan.

6. Rotate the crankshaft until the camshaft for the cylinder being serviced is at base circle.

➡**If removing more than one cam follower, label them so they can be returned to their original position.**

7. Using special tool 303-581, remove the camshaft roller followers.

8. Mark each lash adjuster before removal; remove each lash adjuster, as necessary.

To install:

9. Lubricate the lash adjusters and camshaft roller followers with clean engine oil.

10. Install each lash adjuster.

11. Using special tool 303-581, remove the camshaft roller followers into their original positions.

12. Install the cooling fan, if removed.

13. Install the fuel rail.

14. Install the valve cover.

15. Connect the negative battery cable.

4.6L Engine

See Figure 156.

1. Before servicing the vehicle, refer to Precautions.

2. Remove the valve covers.

3. Rotate the crankshaft until the piston for the valve being serviced is at the top of its stroke with the intake valve and the exhaust valves closed.

➡**Mark the components for installation into their original locations.**

➡**Do not allow the valve keepers to fall off of the valve or the valve may drop into the cylinder. If a valve drops into the cylinder, the cylinder head must be removed.**

➡**It may be necessary to push the valve down while compressing the spring.**

4. Using the Valve Spring Compressor, compress the valve spring and remove the camshaft roller follower.

5. Repeat the previous 2 steps for each roller follower being serviced.

6. Inspect the roller follower.

➡**If the components are to be reinstalled, they must be installed in their original positions. Mark the components for installation into their original locations. Failure to follow these instructions may result in engine damage.**

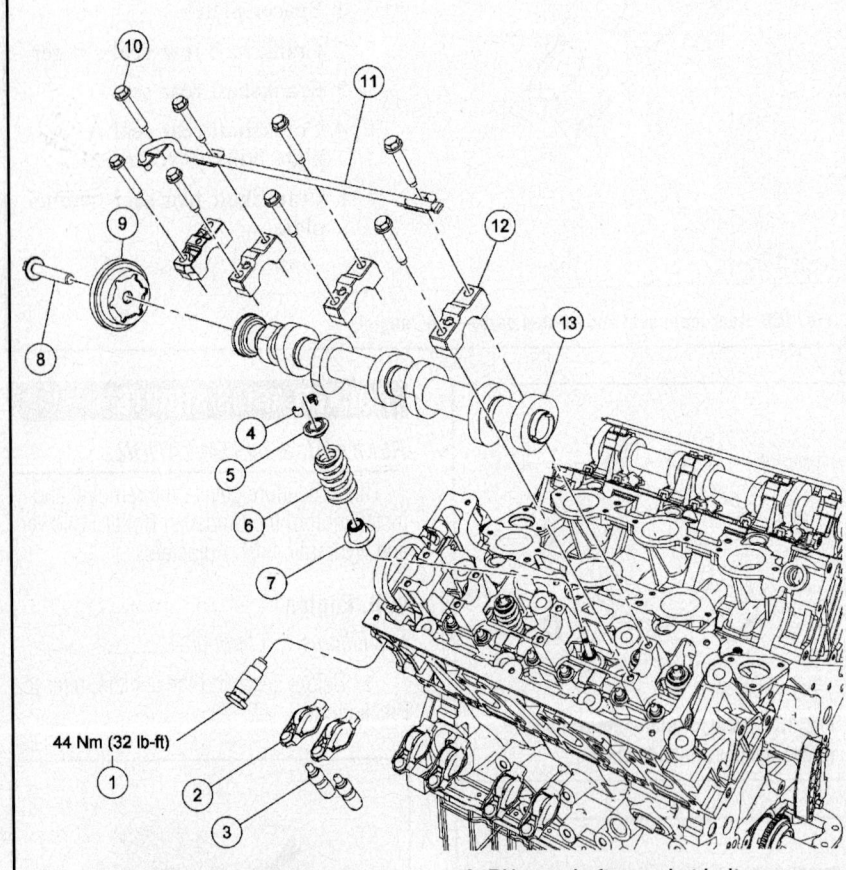

1. RH hydraulic chain tensioner
2. Camshaft roller follower
3. Hydraulic lash adjuster
4. Valve spring retainer key
5. Valve spring retainer
6. Valve spring
7. Valve seals
8. RH camshaft sprocket bolt
9. RH camshaft sprocket
10. Camshaft bearing cap bolt
11. Oil supply tube (early build vehicles only)
12. Camshaft bearing cap
13. RH camshaft

44 Nm (32 lb-ft)

Fig. 155 Exploded view of valve train components—4.0L engine (RH components shown; LH components similar)

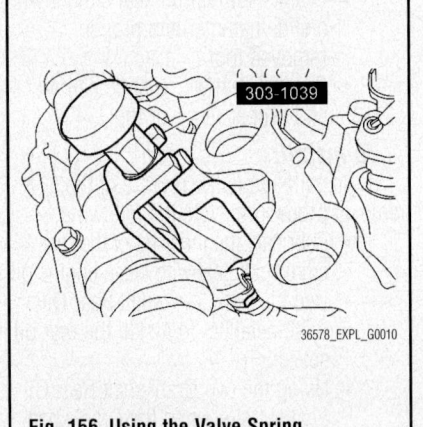

Fig. 156 Using the Valve Spring Compressor

To install:

➡**Lubricate the roller follower with clean engine oil.**

7. Using the Valve Spring Compressor, compress the valve spring and install the camshaft roller follower.

8. Repeat the previous step for each roller follower being serviced.

9. Depending on the valve being serviced, install the LH or RH valve cover.

TIMING CHAIN COVER AND SEAL

REMOVAL & INSTALLATION

4.0L Engine

See Figures 157 through 160.

1. Disconnect the battery ground cable.
2. Drain the cooling system.

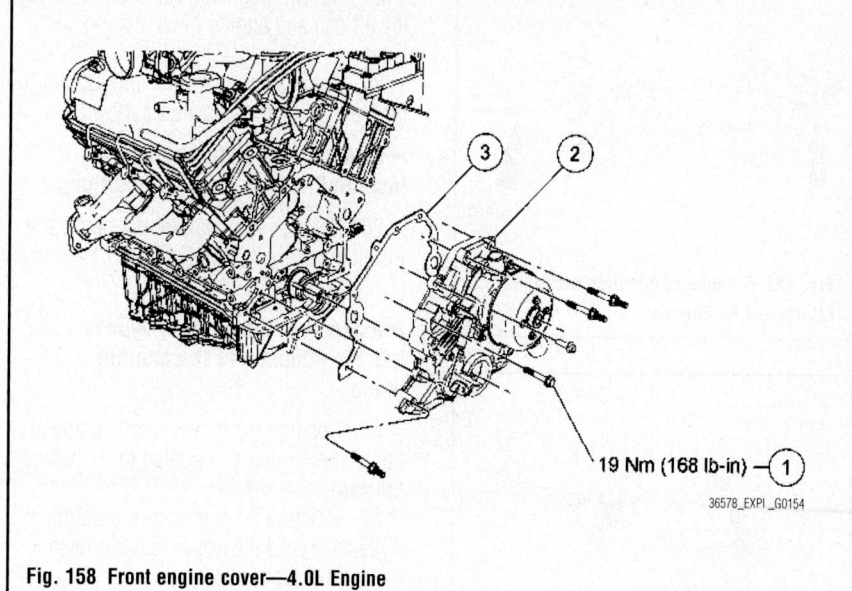

Fig. 158 Front engine cover—4.0L Engine

3. Remove the crankshaft front seal. Refer to Crankshaft Front Seal.

4. Remove the nut and detach the wiring harness bracket from the front cover.

5. Remove the 5 oil pan-to-front cover bolts.

6. Disconnect the lower radiator hose.

7. Remove the bolt and the drive belt tensioner.

8. Disconnect the heater hose from the coolant pump.

9. Disconnect the Crankshaft Position (CKP) sensor electrical connector.

10. Remove the nut and disconnect the generator B+ terminal.

11. Disconnect the generator electrical connector and detach the wiring harness retainer.

12. Remove the 3 generator bracket bolts and the generator bracket.

13. Remove the coil bracket-to-A/C compressor and power steering pump bracket bolt.

14. Remove the 4 bolts and the A/C compressor and power steering pump bracket.

15. Remove and discard the CKP sensor wiring harness retainers.

16. Disconnect the Engine Coolant Temperature (ECT) sensor electrical connector.

17. Disconnect the upper radiator hose from the thermostat housing.

18. Disconnect the heater hose from the thermostat housing.

➡**The bypass hose will be removed with the thermostat housing.**

19. Release the bypass hose clamp from the coolant pump end.

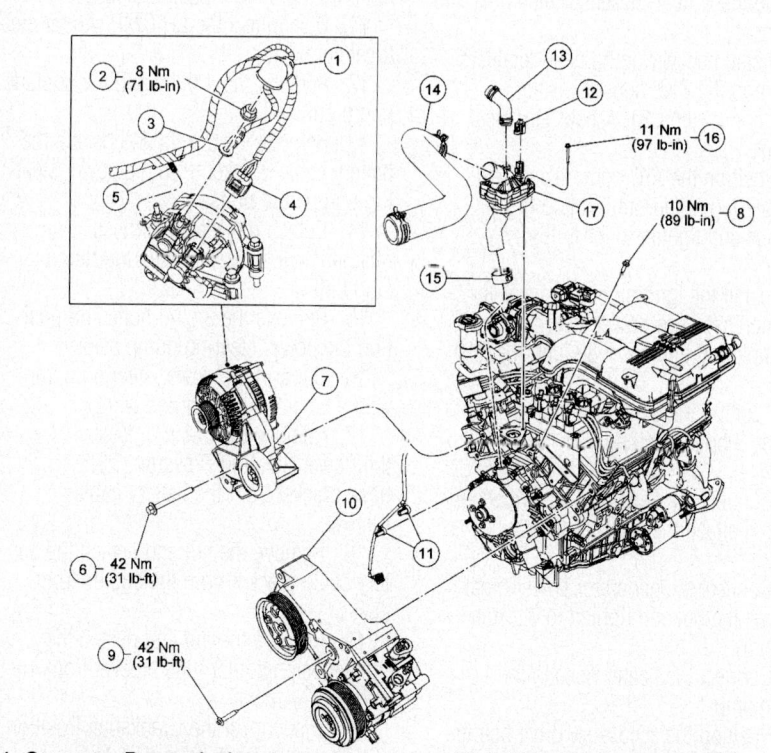

1. Generator B+ terminal cover
2. Generator B+ terminal nut
3. Generator B+ terminal
4. Generator electrical connector
5. Wiring harness retainer
6. Generator bracket bolt (3 required)
7. Generator bracket
8. Ignition coil bracket-to-A/C compressor and power steering pump bracket bolt
9. A/C compressor and power steering pump bracket bolt (4 required)
10. A/C compressor and power steering pump bracket
11. Wiring harness routing clips
12. Engine Coolant Temperature (ECT) sensor electrical connector
13. Heater hose
14. Upper radiator hose
15. Bypass hose clamp
16. Thermostat housing bolt (3 required)
17. Thermostat housing

Fig. 157 Front engine component locations—4.0L Engine

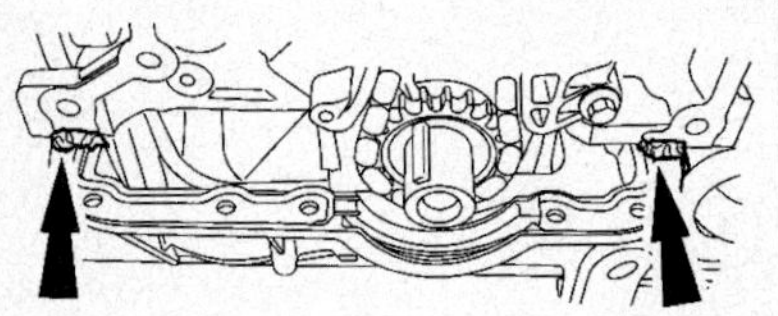

Fig. 159 Silicone application locations, oil pan—4.0L Engine

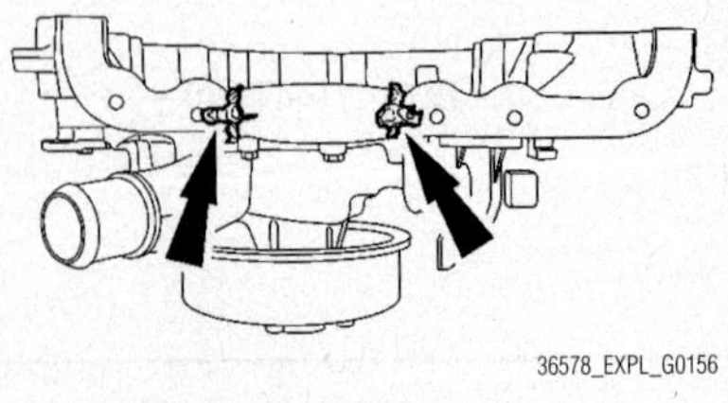

Fig. 160 Silicone application locations, front cover—4.0L Engine

20. Remove the 3 bolts and the thermostat housing.

➡**Note the positions of the stud bolts for installation reference.**

21. Remove the 10 bolts, the engine front cover and the gasket. Discard the gasket

To install:

⁂ WARNING

Do not use metal scrapers, wire brushes, power abrasive discs or other abrasive means to clean sealing surfaces. These tools cause scratches and gouges which make leak paths. Use a plastic scraping tool to remove all traces of the old front cover gasket and the silicone sealer.

22. Clean and inspect the gasket mating surfaces. Use silicone gasket remover and metal surface prep and a plastic scraping tool. Follow the directions on the packaging.
23. Position the front cover gasket.

⁂ WARNING

If not secured within 4 minutes, the sealant must be removed and the sealing area cleaned. To clean the sealing area, use silicone gasket remover and metal surface prep. Follow the directions on the packaging. Failure to follow this procedure can cause future oil leakage.

24. Apply silicone gasket and sealant to the oil pan and engine block mating surfaces.
25. Apply silicone gasket and sealant to the front cover in 2 places as shown.

➡**Make sure the stud bolts are installed in their original positions.**

26. Position the engine front cover and install the 10 bolts and tighten to 14 ft. lbs. (19 Nm).

➡**Make sure the coolant bypass hose is attached to the coolant pump.**

27. Position the thermostat housing and install the 3 bolts and tighten to 97 inch lbs. (11 Nm).
28. Position the bypass hose clamp.
29. Connect the upper radiator hose to the thermostat housing.
30. Connect the heater hose to the thermostat housing.
31. Connect the ECT sensor electrical connector.
32. Install new wiring harness retainers and position the CKP sensor wiring.
33. Connect the CKP sensor electrical connector.
34. Position the A/C compressor and power steering pump bracket and install the 4 bolts and tighten to 31 ft. lbs. (42 Nm).
35. Install the ignition coil bracket-to-A/C compressor and power steering pump bracket bolt and tighten to 89 inch lbs. (10 Nm).
36. Position the generator bracket and install the 3 bolts tighten to 31 ft. lbs. (42 Nm).
37. Connect the generator electrical connector and attach the wiring harness retainer.
38. Connect the generator B+ terminal and install the nut and tighten to 71 inch lbs. (8 Nm).
39. Connect the heater hose to the coolant pump.
40. Position the accessory drive belt tensioner and install the bolt and tighten to 35 ft. lbs. (47 Nm).
41. Connect the lower radiator hose.
42. Install the 5 cylinder block cradle-to-front cover bolts and tighten to 10 ft. lbs. (14 Nm).
43. Position the wiring harness bracket and install the nut and tighten to 15 ft. lbs. (20 Nm).
44. Install the crankshaft front seal. Refer to Crankshaft Front Seal.
45. Connect the battery ground cable.
46. Fill the engine cooling system.

4.6L Engine

See Figures 161 through 165.

1. With the vehicle in NEUTRAL, position it on a hoist.
2. Remove the drain plug and drain the engine oil. To install, tighten to 17 ft. lbs. (23 Nm).
3. Remove the cooling fan shroud. Refer to Cooling Fan in Engine Cooling.
4. Remove the RH side idler pulley.
5. Remove the RH valve cover. Refer to Valve Covers.
6. Remove the LH valve cover. Refer to Valve Covers.
7. Remove the nut and position the RH radio interference capacitor aside.
8. Disconnect the RH Camshaft Position (CMP) sensor electrical connector.
9. Remove the nut and the cooling fan wiring harness bracket.
10. Remove the nut and position the LH radio interference capacitor aside.
11. Disconnect the LH CMP sensor electrical connector.
12. Remove the 4 bolts and the coolant pump pulley.
13. Remove the 2 nuts and detach the battery cable bracket from the power steering pump stud bolts.
14. Detach the wiring harness retainer from the power steering pump stud bolt.
15. Remove the 3 stud bolts and position the power steering pump aside.
16. Support the power steering pump with a length of mechanic's wire.
17. Remove the nut and detach the Power Steering Pressure (PSP) hose bracket from the battery cable bracket.
18. Remove the nut and detach the battery cable bracket from the engine front cover.
19. Remove the nut and detach the transmission cooler tube bracket from the engine front cover.
20. Disconnect the Crankshaft Position (CKP) sensor electrical connector.
21. Remove the crankshaft pulley bolt and washer. Refer to Crankshaft Front Seal.
22. Remove the 4 oil pan-to-engine front cover bolts.
23. Remove the 15 engine front cover bolts and stud bolts.
24. Remove the engine front cover from the engine front cover-to-cylinder block dowel.
25. Remove and discard the engine front cover gaskets

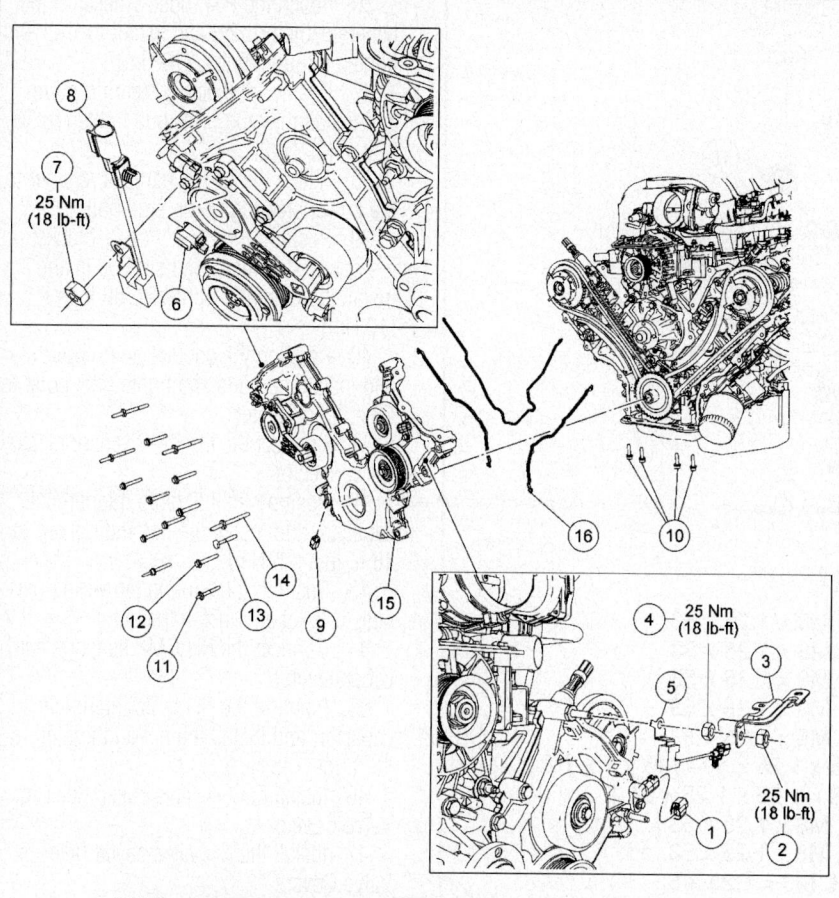

1. LH Camshaft Position (CMP) sensor electrical connector
2. Cooling fan wiring harness bracket nut
3. Cooling fan wiring harness bracket
4. LH radio interference capacitor nut
5. LH radio interference capacitor
6. RH CMP sensor electrical connector
7. RH radio interference capacitor nut
8. RH radio interference capacitor
9. Crankshaft Position (CKP) sensor electrical connector
10. Oil pan-to-engine front cover bolts (4 required)
11. Engine front cover stud bolt
12. Engine front cover bolt (8 required)
13. Engine front cover bolt
14. Engine front cover stud bolt (5 required)
15. Engine front cover
16. Engine front cover gasket (3 required

36578_EXPL_G0157

Fig. 161 Front cover bolt locations—4.6L Engine

To install:

❄❄ WARNING

Do not use metal scrapers, wire brushes, power abrasive discs or other abrasive means to clean the sealing surfaces. These tools cause scratches and gouges which make leak paths. Use a plastic scraping tool to remove all traces of old sealant.

26. Clean the mating surfaces with silicone gasket remover, metal surface prep and a plastic scraping tool. Follow the directions on the packaging.

❄❄ WARNING

Do not use metal scrapers, wire brushes, power abrasive discs or other abrasive means to clean the sealing surfaces. These tools cause scratches and gouges which make

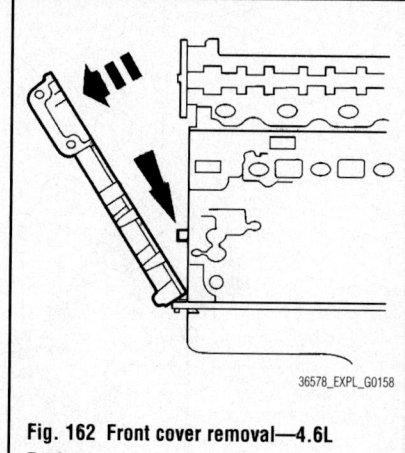

36578_EXPL_G0158

Fig. 162 Front cover removal—4.6L Engine

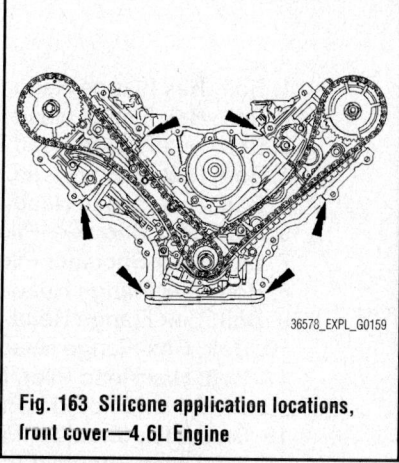

36578_EXPL_G0159

Fig. 163 Silicone application locations, front cover—4.6L Engine

leak paths. Use a plastic scraping tool to remove all traces of old sealant.

➡ If the engine front cover is not secured within 4 minutes, the sealant must be removed and the sealing area cleaned. To clean the sealing area, use silicone gasket remover and metal surface prep. Follow the directions on the packaging. Failure to follow this procedure can cause future oil leakage.

27. Apply a bead of silicone gasket and sealant along the cylinder head-to-cylinder block mating surface and the oil pan-to-cylinder block mating surface at the locations shown.

28. Install new engine front cover gaskets on the engine front cover. Position the engine front cover onto the dowels. Install the 15 fasteners finger-tight.

29. Tighten the 15 engine front cover fasteners in the sequence shown to 18 ft. lbs. (25 Nm).

30. Loosely install the 4 oil pan-to-

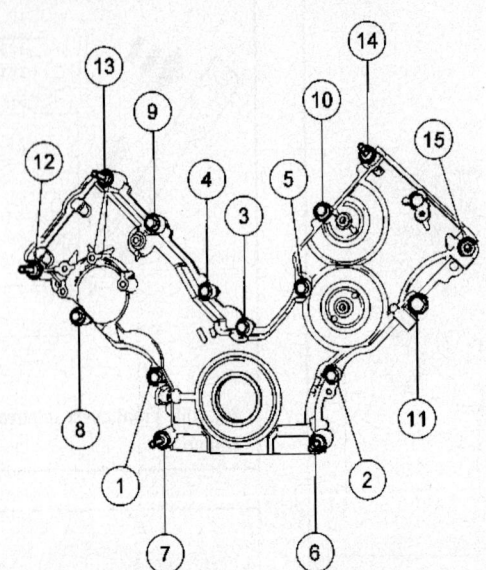

1. Bolt, Hex Flange Head Pilot, M8 x 1.25 x 53
2. Bolt, Hex Flange Head Pilot, M8 x 1.25 x 53
3. Bolt, Hex Flange Head Pilot, M8 x 1.25 x 53
4. Bolt, Hex Flange Head Pilot, M8 x 1.25 x 53
5. Bolt, Hex Flange Head Pilot, M8 x 1.25 x 53
6. Stud, Hex Shoulder Pilot, M8 x 1.25 x 50 - M6 x 1 x 10
7. Stud, Hex Shoulder Pilot, M8 x 1.25 x 1.25 x 91.1
8. Bolt, Hex Flange Head Pilot, M8 x 1.25 x 53
9. Bolt, Hex Flange Head Pilot, M8 x 1.25 x 53
10. Bolt, Hex Flange Head Pilot, M8 x 1.25 x 53
11. Bolt, Hex Head Pilot, M8 x 1.25 x 53
12. Stud, Hex Shoulder Pilot, M8 x 1.25 x 1.25 x 91.1
13. Stud, Hex Shoulder Pilot, M8 x 1.25 x 1.25 x 91.1
14. Stud, Hex Shoulder Pilot, M8 x 1.25 x 1.25 x 91.1
15. Stud, Hex Shoulder Pilot, M8 x 1.25 x 1.25 x 91.1

36578_EXPL_G0160

Fig. 164 Front cover bolt tightening sequence—4.6L Engine

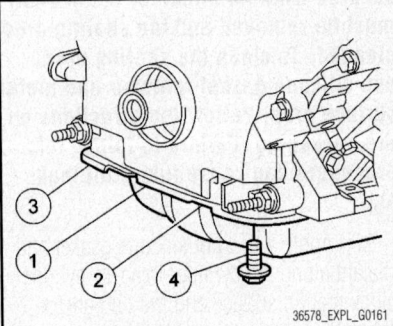

36578_EXPL_G0161

Fig. 165 Oil pan-to-engine front cover bolts —4.6L Engine

engine front cover bolts, then tighten the bolts in 2 stages in the sequence shown.

- Stage 1: Tighten to 15 ft. lbs. (20 Nm).
- Stage 2: Tighten an additional 60 degrees.

➡If not secured within 4 minutes, the sealant must be removed and the sealing area cleaned with silicone gasket remover and metal surface prep. Follow the directions on the packaging. Failure to follow this procedure can cause future oil leakage.

31. Apply silicone gasket sealant to the Woodruff key slot in the crankshaft pulley.

32. Install the crankshaft front oil seal and pulley. Refer to Crankshaft Front Oil Seal.

33. Connect the CKP sensor electrical connector.

34. Attach the transmission cooler tube bracket to the engine front cover and install the nut and tighten to 106 inch lbs. (12 Nm).

35. Attach the battery cable bracket to the front cover and install the nut and tighten to 89 inch lbs. (10 Nm).

36. Attach the PSP hose bracket to the battery cable bracket and install the nut and tighten to 89 inch lbs. (10 Nm).

37. Position the power steering pump and install the stud bolts and tighten to 18 ft. lbs. (25 Nm).

38. Attach the wiring harness retainer to the power steering pump stud bolt.

39. Position the battery cable bracket on the power steering pump stud bolts and install the nuts and tighten to 89 inch lbs. (10 Nm).

40. Position the coolant pump pulley and install the bolts and tighten the bolts to 18 ft. lbs. (25 Nm).

41. Connect the LH CMP sensor electrical connector.

42. Position the LH radio interference capacitor and install the nut and tighten to 18 ft. lbs. (25 Nm).

43. Position the cooling fan wiring harness bracket and install the nut.

44. Connect the RH CMP sensor electrical connector.

45. Position the RH radio interference capacitor and install the nut and tighten to 18 ft. lbs. (25 Nm).

46. Install the LH valve cover. Refer to Valve Covers.

47. Install the RH valve cover. Refer to Valve Covers.

48. Install the RH side idler pulley.

49. Install the cooling fan shroud.

50. Fill the engine with clean engine oil.

TIMING CHAIN AND SPROCKETS

REMOVAL & INSTALLATION

4.0L Engine

See Figures 166 through 170.

1. Before servicing the vehicle, refer to Precautions.

2. Remove the valve covers. Refer to Valve Covers.

3. Remove the fuel rail. Refer to Fuel System.

4. Remove the engine front cover. Refer to Front Cover and Seal.

5. Remove the thermostat housing.

6. Remove all of the roller followers.

a. Rotate the crankshaft until the camshaft for the cylinder being serviced is at base circle.

➡Mark each camshaft roller follower to make sure it is returned to its original position.

b. Using the Valve Spring Compressor, remove the camshaft roller followers.

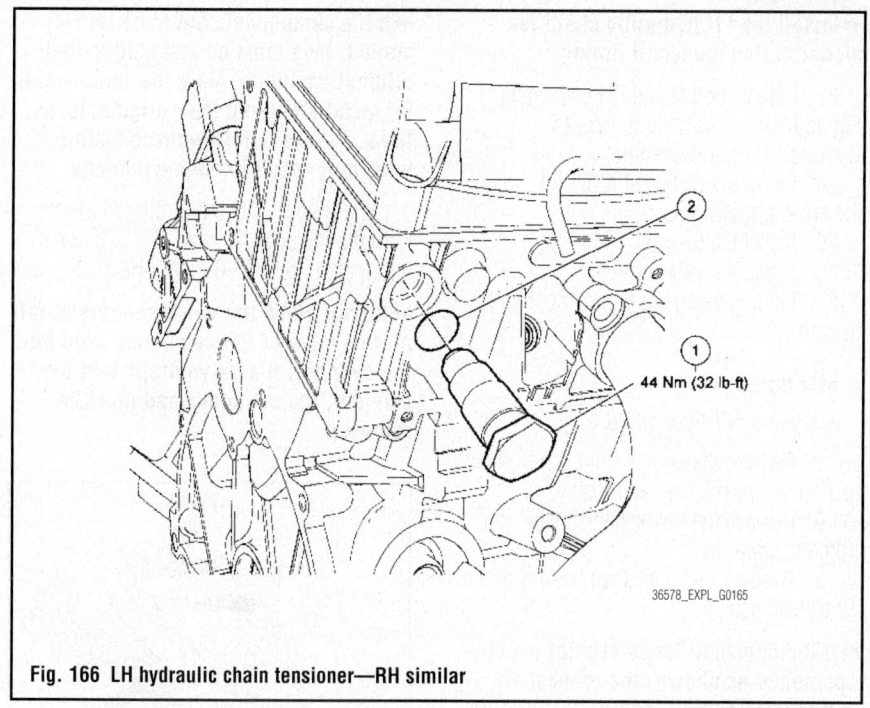

Fig. 166 LH hydraulic chain tensioner—RH similar

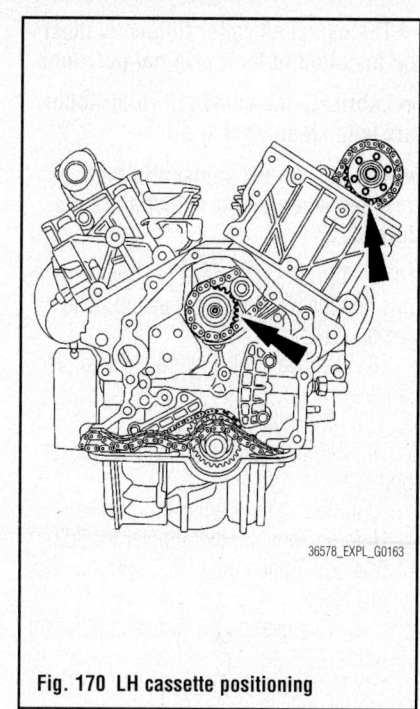

Fig. 170 LH cassette positioning

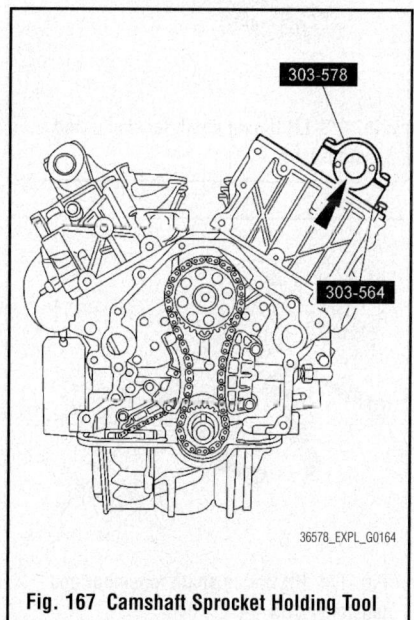

Fig. 167 Camshaft Sprocket Holding Tool

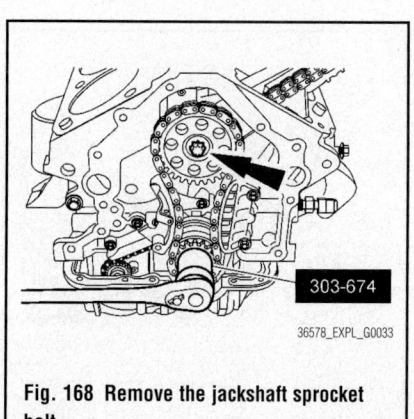

Fig. 168 Remove the jackshaft sprocket bolt

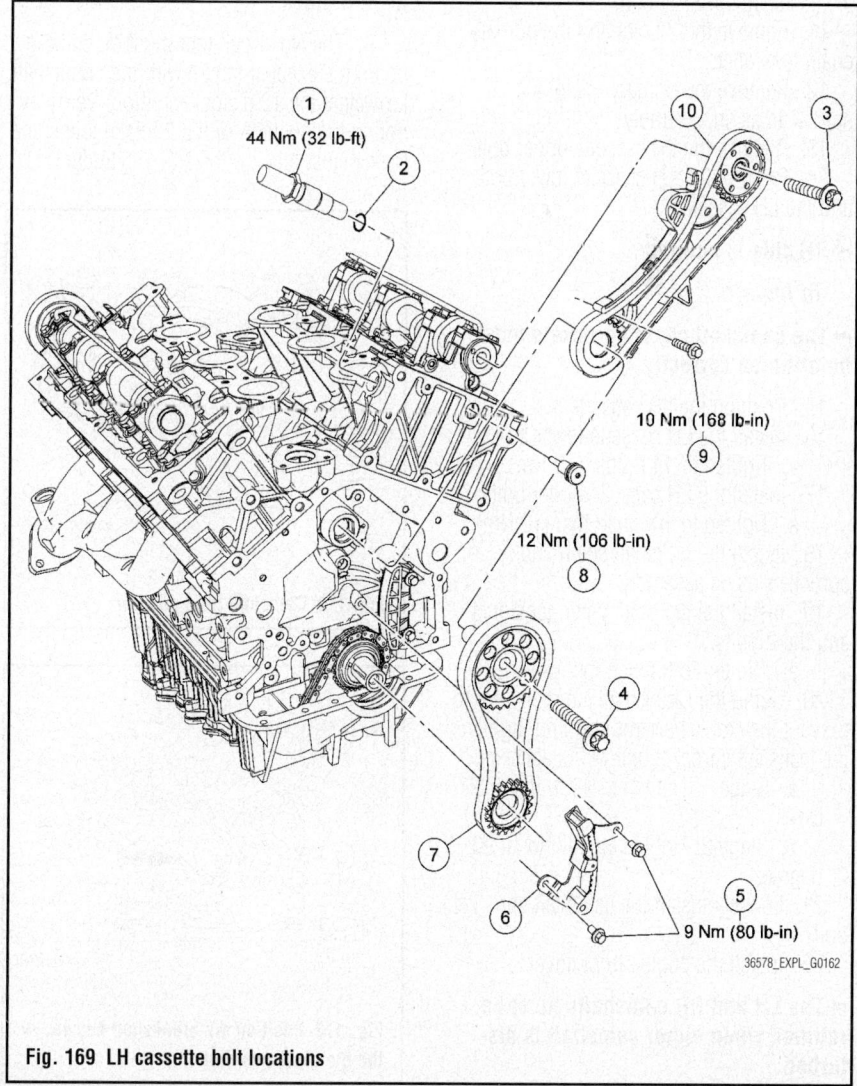

Fig. 169 LH cassette bolt locations

➡The camshaft roller followers must be installed in their original positions.

➡Lubricate the camshaft roller followers with clean engine oil

➡The LH and RH camshafts must be retimed when either camshaft is disturbed.

7. Turn the crankshaft clockwise to position the No. 1 cylinder at Top Dead Center (TDC).

8. Remove the LH hydraulic chain tensioner.

a. Discard the washer.

9. Remove the LH camshaft sprocket bolt.

a. Install the Camshaft Sprocket Holding Tool and the Adapter for 303-564 and tighten the bolts to 89 inch lbs. (10 Nm).

b. Remove the LH camshaft sprocket bolt.

10. Using the Crankshaft Holding Tool to prevent the crankshaft from turning, remove the jackshaft sprocket bolt.

11. Remove the 2 bolts and the primary chain tensioner.

12. Remove the primary chain and sprockets as an assembly.

13. Remove the LH cassette upper bolt.

14. Remove the LH cassette lower bolt and the LH cassette.

➡RH side is similar.

To install:

➡The camshaft chain sprockets must be oriented correctly.

15. Position the LH cassette.

16. Install the LH cassette lower bolt.

a. Tighten to 14 ft. lbs. (19 Nm).

17. Install the LH cassette upper bolt.

a. Tighten to 106 inch lbs. (12 Nm).

18. Install the jackshaft chain and sprockets as an assembly.

19. Install the jackshaft chain tensioner and the 2 bolts.

a. Tighten to 80 inch lbs. (9 Nm).

20. Using the Crankshaft Holding Tool to prevent the crankshaft from turning, tighten the jackshaft sprocket bolt in 2 stages.

a. Stage 1: Tighten to 33 ft. lbs. (45 Nm).

b. Stage 2: Tighten an additional 90 degrees.

21. Loosely install the camshaft sprocket bolt.

22. Install the engine front cover.

➡The LH and RH camshafts must be retimed when either camshaft is disturbed.

➡Install the LH hydraulic chain tensioner during camshaft timing.

23. Retime the LH and RH camshafts. For additional information, refer to Camshaft Timing Procedure.

24. Install the camshaft roller followers. Reversed removal procedure.

25. Install the fuel rail.

26. Install the valve covers.

27. Fill and bleed the engine cooling system.

4.6L Engine

See Figures 171 through 183.

1. Remove the engine front cover. Refer to Timing Chain Cover and Seal.

2. Remove the crankshaft sensor ring from the crankshaft.

3. Position the crankshaft keyway at the 12 o'clock position.

➡If the camshaft lobes are not exactly positioned as shown, the crankshaft will require one full additional rotation to 12 o'clock.

4. The No. 1 cylinder must be coming up on the exhaust stroke with the crankshaft keyway at the 12 o'clock position. Verify by noting the position of the 2 intake lobes and the exhaust lobe on the No. 1 cylinder.

➡If the components are to be reinstalled, they must be installed in their original positions. Mark the components for installation into their original locations. Failure to follow these instructions may result in engine damage.

5. Remove only the 3 roller followers from the RH cylinder head. For additional information, refer to Cylinder Head.

➡Do not allow the valve keepers to fall off the valve or the valve may drop into the cylinder. If a valve drops into the cylinder, the cylinder head must be removed.

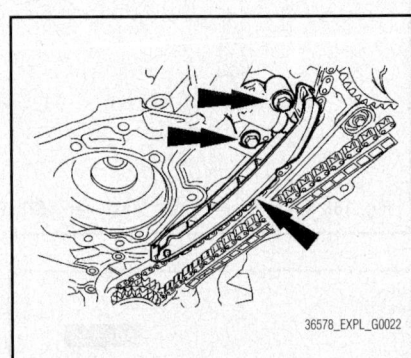

Fig. 173 LH timing chain tensioner and tensioner arm

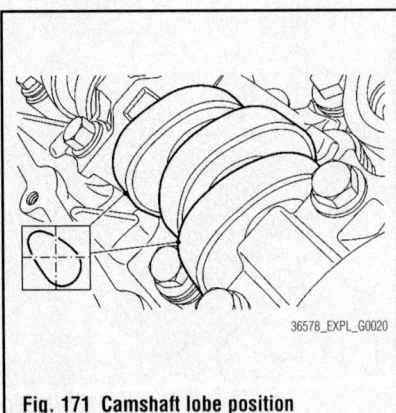

Fig. 171 Camshaft lobe position

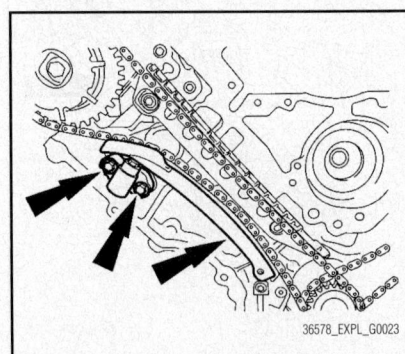

Fig. 174 RH timing chain tensioner and tensioner arm

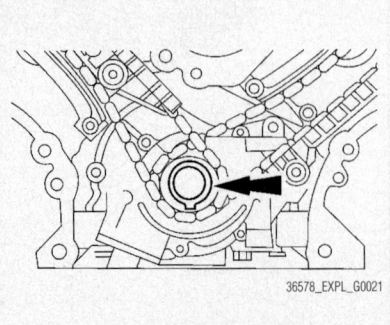

Fig. 172 Position the crankshaft keyway at the 6 o'clock position

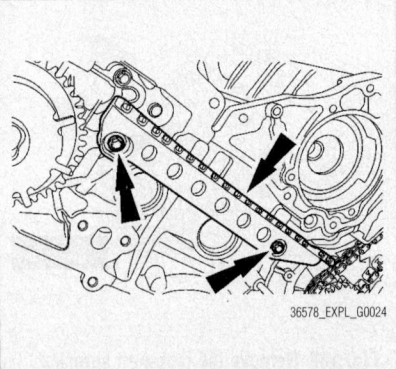

Fig. 175 LH and RH timing chain guides

➡️It may be necessary to push the valve down while compressing the spring.

6. Using the Valve Spring Compressor, remove the 3 roller followers designated in the previous step from the RH cylinder head. For additional information, refer to Cylinder Head.

➡️If the components are to be reinstalled, they must be installed in their

original positions. Mark the components for installation into their original locations. Failure to follow these instructions may result in engine damage.

7. Remove only the 3 roller followers shown in the illustration from the LH cylinder head. For additional information, refer to Cylinder Head.

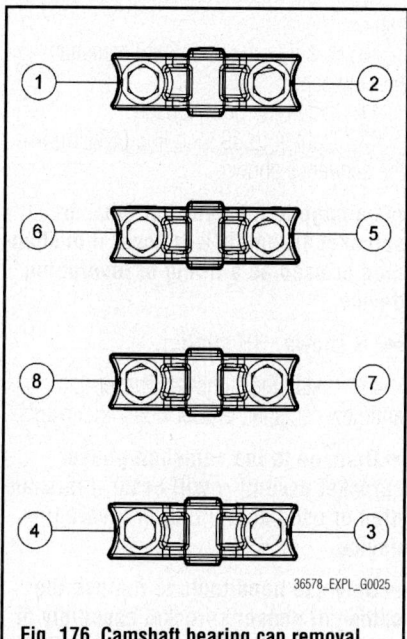

Fig. 176 Camshaft bearing cap removal sequence

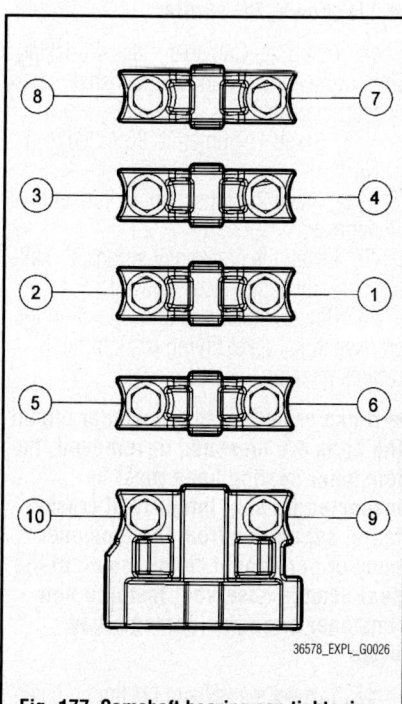

Fig. 177 Camshaft bearing cap tightening sequence

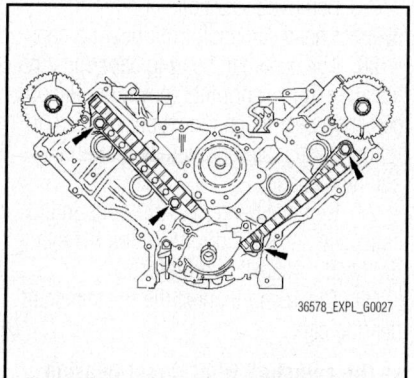

Fig. 178 LH and RH timing chain guide locations

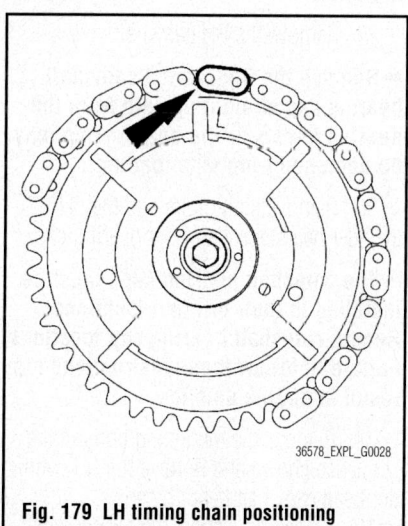

Fig. 179 LH timing chain positioning

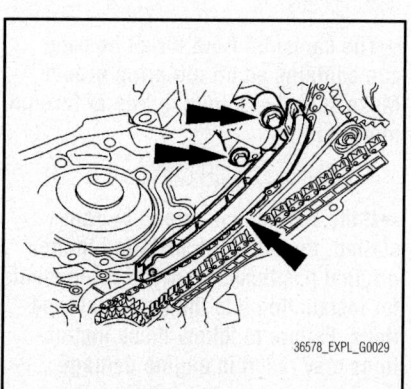

Fig. 180 LH timing chain tensioner

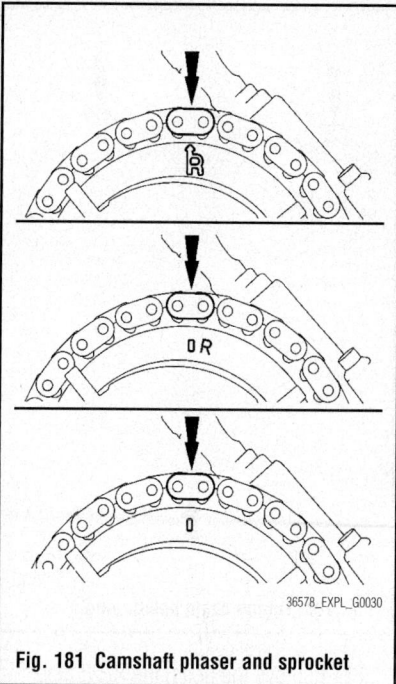

Fig. 181 Camshaft phaser and sprocket

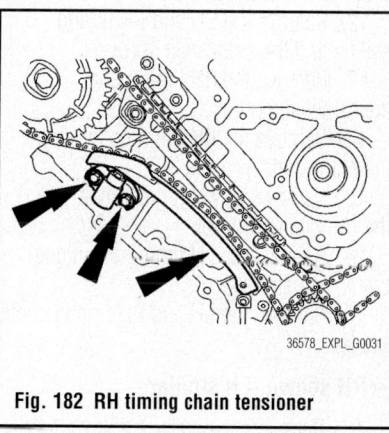

Fig. 182 RH timing chain tensioner

➡️Do not allow the valve keepers to fall off the valve or the valve may drop into the cylinder. If a valve drops into the cylinder, the cylinder head must be removed. For additional information, refer to Cylinder Head in this section.

➡️It may be necessary to push the valve down while compressing the spring.

8. Using the Valve Spring Compressor, remove the 3 roller followers designated in the previous step from the LH cylinder head.

➡️The crankshaft cannot be moved past the 6 o'clock position once set or engine damage may occur.

9. Rotate the crankshaft clockwise and position the crankshaft keyway at the 6 o'clock position.

10. Remove the bolts, the LH timing chain tensioner and tensioner arm.

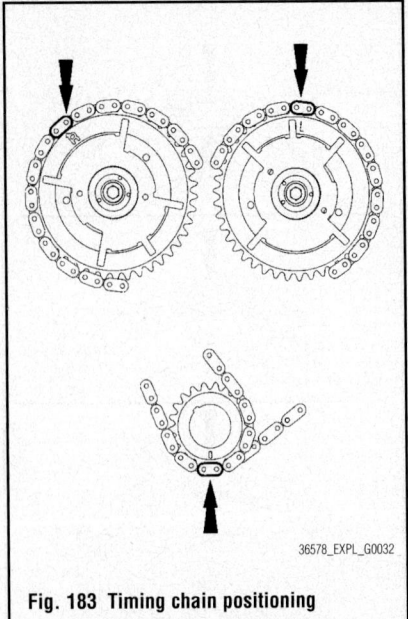

Fig. 183 Timing chain positioning

11. Remove the bolts, the RH timing chain tensioner and tensioner arm.

12. Remove the RH and LH timing chains and the crankshaft sprocket.

13. Remove the RH timing chain from the camshaft sprocket.

14. Remove the RH timing chain from the crankshaft sprocket.

15. Remove the LH timing chain from the camshaft sprocket.

16. Remove the LH timing chain and crankshaft sprocket.

17. Remove the LH and RH timing chain guides.

➡**RH shown, LH similar.**

18. Remove the bolts.

19. Remove both timing chain guides.

➡**Damage to the camshaft phaser sprocket assembly will occur if mishandled or used as a lifting or leveraging device.**

➡**Only use hand tools to remove the camshaft phaser sprocket assembly or damage may occur to the camshaft or camshaft phaser unit.**

20. Using the Camshaft Phaser Locking Tool, remove the bolt and the RH camshaft phaser sprocket assembly.

21. Discard the camshaft phaser sprocket bolt.

➡**Damage to the camshaft phaser sprocket assembly will occur if mishandled or used as a lifting or leveraging device.**

➡**Only use hand tools to remove the camshaft phaser sprocket assembly or**

damage may occur to the camshaft or camshaft phaser unit.

22. Using the Camshaft Phaser Locking Tool, remove the bolt and the LH camshaft phaser sprocket assembly.

23. Discard the camshaft phaser sprocket bolt.

24. Remove the front thrust camshaft bearing cap straight upward from the bearing towers or the bearing cap may be damaged from side loading.

25. Remove the 2 bolts and the RH cylinder head camshaft front bearing cap.

26. The camshaft bearing caps must be installed in their original locations. Record camshaft bearing cap locations. Failure to follow these instructions may result in engine damage.

27. Remove the remaining bolts in the sequence shown and remove the RH cylinder head camshaft bearing caps.

28. Clean and inspect the RH camshaft bearing caps.

➡**The camshaft front thrust bearing cap contains an oil metering groove. Make sure the groove is free of foreign material.**

29. Remove the RH camshaft.

➡**Remove the front thrust camshaft bearing cap straight upward from the bearing towers or the bearing cap may be damaged from side loading.**

30. Remove the 2 bolts and the LH cylinder head camshaft front bearing cap.

➡**The camshaft bearing caps must be installed in their original locations. Record camshaft bearing cap locations. Failure to follow these instructions may result in engine damage.**

31. Remove the remaining bolts in the sequence shown and remove the LH cylinder head camshaft bearing caps.

32. Clean and inspect the LH camshaft bearing caps.

➡**The camshaft front thrust bearing cap contains an oil metering groove. Make sure the groove is free of foreign material.**

33. Remove the LH camshaft.

➡**If the components are to be reinstalled, they must be installed in their original positions. Mark the components for installation into their original locations. Failure to follow these instructions may result in engine damage.**

34. Remove all of the remaining roller followers from the cylinder heads.

To install:

35. Install the LH and RH camshafts.

36. Lubricate the camshaft and camshaft journals with clean engine oil prior to installation.

➡**LH shown, RH similar.**

37. Install the LH and RH camshaft bearing caps in their original locations.

38. Lubricate the camshaft bearing caps with clean engine oil.

39. Position the front camshaft bearing cap.

40. Position the remaining camshaft bearing caps.

41. Install the bolts loosely.

42. Tighten to 89 inch lbs. (10 Nm) in the sequence shown.

➡**Damage to the camshaft phaser sprocket assembly will occur if mishandled or used as a lifting or leveraging device.**

➡**LH shown, RH similar.**

43. Install the camshaft phaser sprockets and new camshaft phaser bolts finger-tight.

➡**Damage to the camshaft phaser sprocket assembly will occur if mishandled or used as a lifting or leveraging device.**

➡**Only use hand tools to remove the camshaft phaser sprocket assembly or damage may occur to the camshaft or camshaft phaser unit.**

➡ **LH shown, RH similar.**

44. Using the Camshaft Phaser Locking Tool, tighten the LH and RH camshaft phaser sprocket bolts in 2 stages.

a. Stage 1: Tighten to 30 ft. lbs. (40 Nm).

b. Stage 2: Tighten an additional 90 degrees.

45. Install the crankshaft sprocket, making sure the flange faces forward.

46. Rotate the crankshaft to position the crankshaft sprocket timing mark in the 6 o'clock position.

➡**If one or both of the tensioner mounting bolts are loosened or removed, the tensioner-sealing bead must be inspected for seal integrity. If cracks, tears, separation from the tensioner body or permanent compression of the seal bead is observed, install a new tensioner or engine damage may occur.**

47. Inspect the RH and LH timing chain tensioners.

48. Install new tensioners as necessary.

➡Timing chain procedures must be followed exactly or damage to valves and pistons will result.

49. Compress the tensioner plunger, using a vise.

50. Install a retaining clip on the tensioner to hold the plunger in during installation.

51. Remove the tensioner from the vise.

52. If the colored links are not visible, mark one link on one end and one link on the other end and use as timing marks.

53. Install the 4 bolts and the LH and RH timing chain guides and tighten to 89 inch lbs. (10 Nm).

54. Position the lower end of the LH (inner) timing chain on the crankshaft sprocket, aligning the timing mark on the outer flange of the crankshaft sprocket with the single colored (marked) link on the chain.

➡Make sure the upper half of the timing chain is below the tensioner arm dowel.

55. Position the LH timing chain on the camshaft sprocket. Make sure the camshaft sprocket timing mark is aligned with the colored (marked) chain link.

➡The LH timing chain tensioner arm has a bump near the dowel hole for identification.

56. Position the LH timing chain tensioner arm on the dowel pin and install the LH timing chain tensioner and bolts and tighten to 89 inch lbs. (10 Nm).

57. Remove the retaining clip from the LH timing chain tensioner.

58. Position the lower end of the RH (outer) timing chain on the crankshaft sprocket, aligning the timing mark on the sprocket with the single colored (marked) chain link.

➡The camshaft phaser and sprocket will be stamped with one of the illustrated timing marks for the RH camshaft.

➡The lower half of the timing chain must be positioned above the tensioner arm dowel.

59. Position the RH timing chain on the camshaft sprocket. Make sure the camshaft sprocket timing mark is aligned with the colored (marked) chain link.

60. Position the RH timing chain tensioner arm on the dowel pin and install the RH timing chain tensioner and bolts and tighten to 89 inch lbs. (10 Nm).

61. Remove the retaining clip from the RH timing chain tensioner.

➡The RH and LH camshaft phaser sprockets are similar. Refer to the single timing mark to identify the RH camshaft phaser sprocket and the L timing mark to identify the LH camshaft phaser sprocket.

62. As a post-check, verify correct alignment of all timing marks. Make sure the timing marks on the sprockets correspond to the above note.

63. Install the crankshaft sensor ring on the crankshaft.

➡It is necessary to rotate the engine to position the camshaft lobes at base circle to install the roller followers.

64. Using the Valve Spring Compressor, install all of the camshaft roller followers.

65. Lubricate the roller followers with clean engine oil prior to installation.

66. Install the engine front cover.

CAMSHAFT TIMING PROCEDURE

4.0L Engine

See Figures 184 through 187.

➡You must retime both camshafts when either camshaft is disturbed.

1. If installed, remove the camshaft roller followers.

2. On the RH side, perform the following:
   a. Turn the crankshaft clockwise to position the number one cylinder at top dead center (TDC).
   b. Remove the retainer and position the A/C manifold tube aside.

❊❊ WARNING

Do not rotate the engine counterclockwise. Rotating the engine counterclockwise will result in incorrect timing of the engine.

Fig. 184 Install the special tool on the crankshaft pulley—4.0L Engine

➡The special tool must be installed on the damper and should contact the engine block, this positions the engine at TDC.

c. Install the special tool on the crankshaft pulley.

d. Install the special tools to the RH cylinder head and tighten the 2 top clamp bolts to 89 inch lbs. (10 Nm).

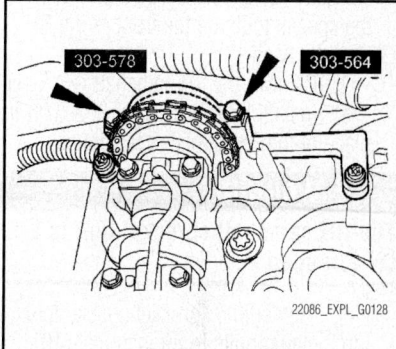

Fig. 185 Install the RH camshaft sprocket special holding tools—4.0L Engine

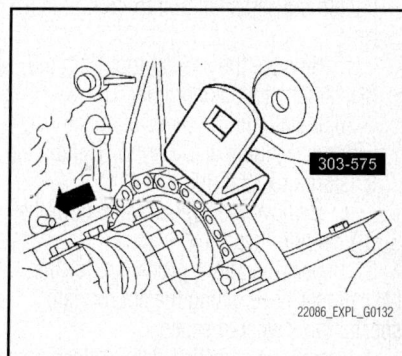

Fig. 186 Using the special tool with the Camshaft Sprocket Nut Socket 303-565, loosen the RH camshaft sprocket bolt—4.0L Engine

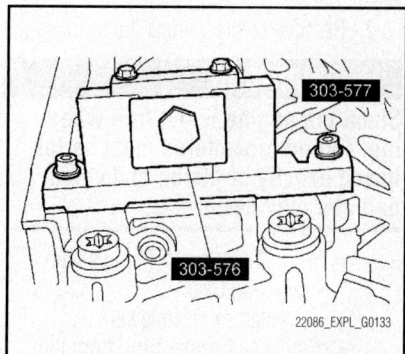

Fig. 187 Position the camshaft timing slots below the centerline of the camshaft to correctly fit the special tools and install the special tools on the front of the RH cylinder head—4.0L Engine

e. Using the special tool with the Camshaft Sprocket Nut Socket 303-565, loosen the RH camshaft sprocket bolt.

f. Loosen the top 2 special tool sprocket clamp bolts.

➡ **The camshaft timing slots are off-center.**

g. Position the camshaft timing slots below the centerline of the camshaft to correctly fit the special tools and install the special tools on the front of the RH cylinder head.

h. Remove the RH camshaft tensioner.

i. Install the special tool, 303-571, in place of the RH camshaft tensioner.

✳✳ WARNING

The RH camshaft sprocket bolt is a LH-threaded bolt.

j. Tighten the sprocket special tool top 2 clamp bolts to 89 inch lbs. (10 Nm).

k. Using the special tool with the Camshaft Sprocket Nut Socket 303-565, tighten the camshaft bolt to 45 ft. lbs. (61 Nm).

l. Remove the special tool from the RH camshaft tensioner hole.

m. Install the RH camshaft tensioner, with a new, lubricated O-ring. Tighten the tensioner to 32 ft. lbs. (44 Nm).

n. Remove the special tools from the RH cylinder head.

3. Repeat the above procedure for the LH cylinder head, using the appropriate special tools where needed.

4. Install the camshaft roller followers.

4.6L Engine

See Figures 188 through 196.

1. Before servicing the vehicle, refer to Precautions.

2. Remove or disconnect the following:

✳✳ WARNING

Since the engine is not free-wheeling, timing procedures must be followed exactly or piston and valve damage may occur.

- Front cover; see "Timing Chain Cover and Seal"
- Camshaft roller followers
- Crankshaft sensor ring from the crankshaft

✳✳ WARNING

If one or both of the tensioner mounting bolts are loosened or removed, the tensioner-sealing bead must be

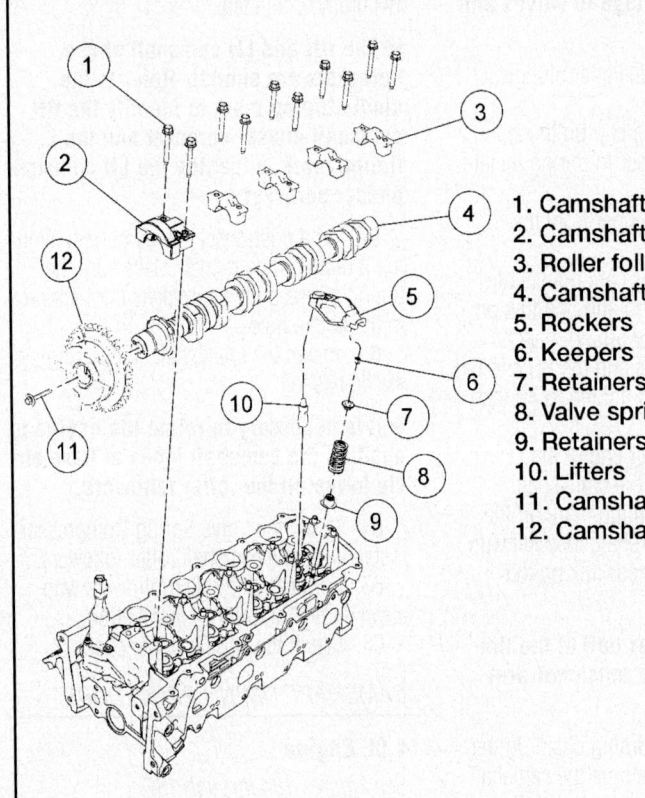

1. Camshaft bearing cap bolts
2. Camshaft bearing caps
3. Roller followers
4. Camshaft
5. Rockers
6. Keepers
7. Retainers
8. Valve springs
9. Retainers
10. Lifters
11. Camshaft sprocket bolt
12. Camshaft sprocket

22086_EXPL_G0134

Fig. 188 Exploded view of the timing components—4.6L Engine (LH head shown; RH head similar)

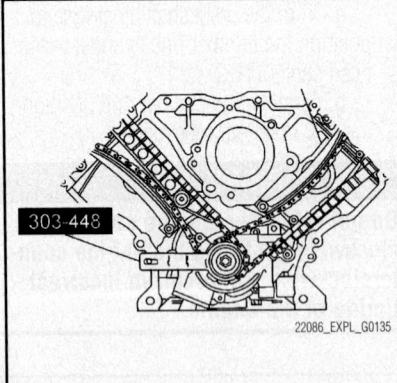

303-448

22086_EXPL_G0135

Fig. 189 Using the special tool, position the crankshaft—4.6L Engine

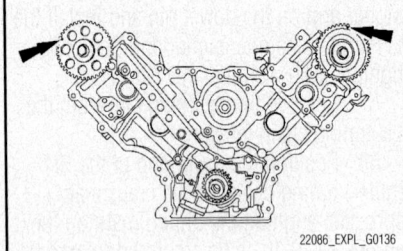

22086_EXPL_G0136

Fig. 190 Rotate the LH camshaft timing sprocket until the timing mark is approximately at the 12 o'clock position. Rotate the RH camshaft timing sprocket until the timing mark is at approximately the 11 o'clock position—4.6L Engine

inspected for seal integrity. If cracks, tears, separation from the tensioner body or permanent compression of the seal bead is observed, install a new tensioner.

3. Remove the following:
- 2 bolts and the RH timing chain tensioner
- RH timing chain tensioner arm

- 2 bolts and the LH timing chain tensioner
- LH timing chain tensioner arm
- 2 bolts and the RH timing chain guide
- RH timing chain
- 2 bolts and the LH timing chain guide
- LH timing chain
- Crankshaft sprocket

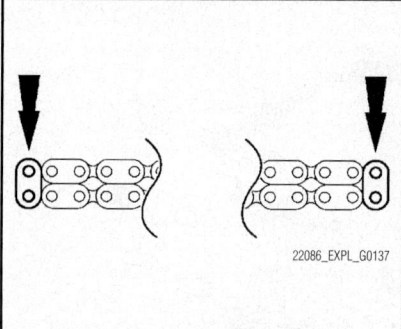

Fig. 191 If the copper links are not visible, mark one link on one end and one link on the other end and use as timing marks—4.6L Engine

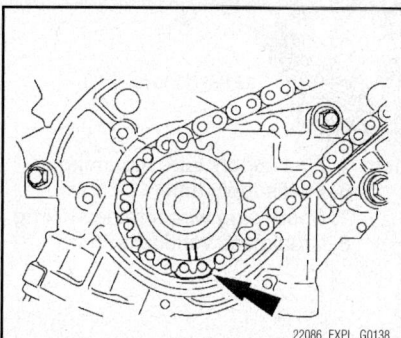

Fig. 192 Position the LH (inner) timing chain on the crankshaft sprocket, aligning the copper (marked) link with the timing mark on the sprocket—4.6L Engine

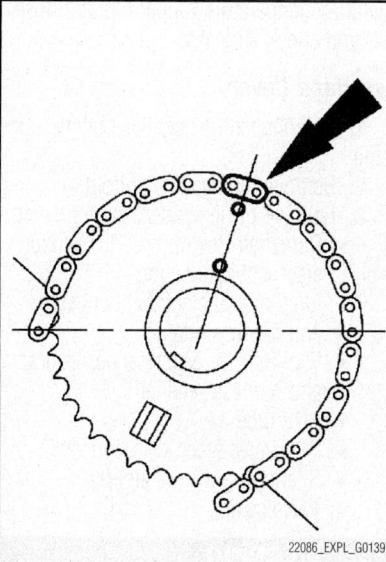

Fig. 193 Position the LH timing chain on the camshaft sprocket. Make sure the copper-colored link aligns with the camshaft sprocket timing mark—4.6L Engine

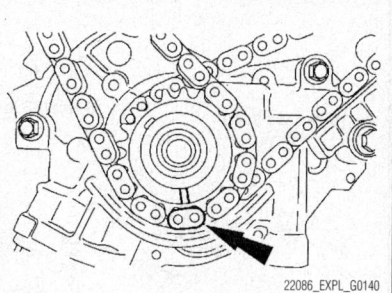

Fig. 194 Position the RH (outer) timing chain on the crankshaft sprocket, aligning the copper (marked) link with the timing mark on the sprocket—4.6L Engine

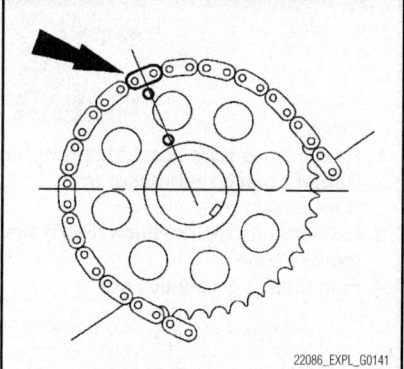

Fig. 195 Position the RH timing chain on the camshaft sprocket. Make sure the copper-colored link aligns with the camshaft sprocket timing mark—4.6L Engine

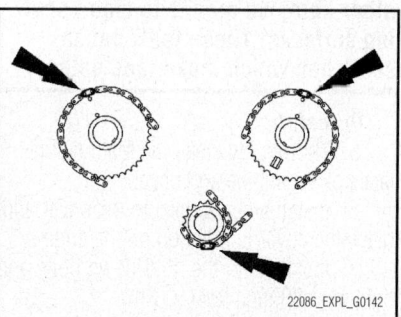

Fig. 196 As a post-check, verify correct alignment of all timing marks—4.6L Engine

To install:

> ✳✳ **WARNING**
>
> **Rotate the crankshaft counterclockwise only. Do not rotate past the position shown or severe piston and/or valve damage will occur.**

4. Using the special tool, position the crankshaft.

5. Install the crankshaft sprocket with the flange facing forward.

6. Rotate the LH camshaft timing sprocket until the timing mark is approximately at the 12 o'clock position. Rotate the RH camshaft timing sprocket until the timing mark is at approximately the 11 o'clock position.

7. Install the timing chain guides. Tighten the bolts to 89 inch lbs. (10 Nm).

8. If the copper links are not visible, mark one link on one end and one link on the other end and use as timing marks.

9. Position the LH (inner) timing chain on the crankshaft sprocket, aligning the copper (marked) link with the timing mark on the sprocket.

➡ **If necessary, adjust the camshaft sprocket slightly to obtain timing mark alignment.**

10. Position the LH timing chain on the camshaft sprocket. Make sure the copper-colored link aligns with the camshaft sprocket timing mark.

> ✳✳ **WARNING**
>
> **Prior to installation, inspect the tensioner-sealing bead for seal integrity. If cracks, tears, separation from the tensioner body or permanent compression of the seal bead is observed, install a new tensioner.**

11. Compress the LH tensioner plunger, using a vise.

12. Install a retaining clip on the LH tensioner to hold the plunger in during installation.

➡ **The LH timing chain tensioner arm has a bump near the dowel hole for identification.**

13. Position the LH timing chain tensioner arm on the dowel pin and install the LH timing chain tensioner and the bolts to 18 ft. lbs. (25 Nm).

14. Remove the retaining clip from the LH timing chain tensioner.

15. Position the RH (outer) timing chain on the crankshaft sprocket, aligning the copper (marked) link with the timing mark on the sprocket.

➡ **If necessary, adjust the camshaft sprocket slightly to obtain timing mark alignment.**

16. Position the RH timing chain on the camshaft sprocket. Make sure the copper-colored link aligns with the camshaft sprocket timing mark.

17. Compress the RH tensioner plunger, using a vise.

18. Install a retaining clip on the RH tensioner to hold the plunger in during installation.

19. Position the RH timing chain tensioner arm on the dowel pin and install the RH timing chain tensioner and the bolts to 18 ft. lbs. (25 Nm).

20. Remove the retaining clip from the RH timing chain tensioner.

21. As a post-check, verify correct alignment of all timing marks.

22. Install the sensor ring on the crankshaft.

23. Install the camshaft roller followers.

24. Install the engine front cover.

VALVE COVERS

REMOVAL & INSTALLATION

4.0L Engine

➡**Always use new gaskets when installing the valve covers.**

Right Hand Cover

See Figure 197.

1. Disconnect the negative battery cable.

2. Relieve the fuel system pressure and disconnect the fuel line supply tube spring-lock coupling.

3. Remove the intake manifold. Refer to Intake Manifold.

4. Remove or disconnect the following:
- Heater hose tube bracket rear bolt
- Heater hose tube bracket front bolt
- Exhaust manifold-to-exhaust gas recirculation (EGR) system module tube lower fitting and remove the tube
- Fuel supply tube-to-valve cover bracket bolt, the fuel supply tube-to-fuel rail bolts and the fuel supply tube
- Spark plug wire retainers and position the spark plug wires aside
- Crankcase ventilation tube
- Valve cover bolts and valve cover

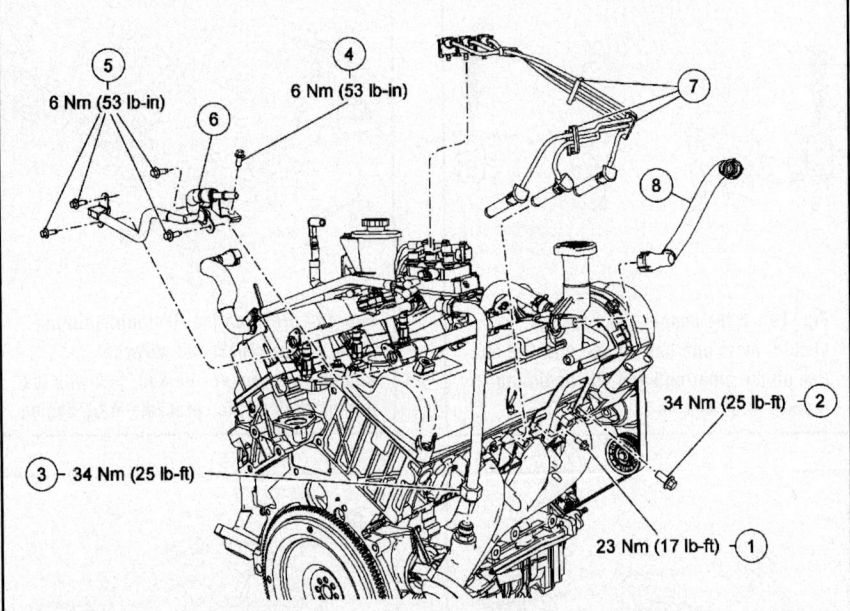

1. Heater hose tube bracket rear mounting bolt
2. Heater hose tube bracket front bolts (4 required)
3. Exhaust gas recirculation (EGR) system module tube
4. Fuel manifold-to-valve cover
5. Fuel supply tube mounting
6. Fuel supply tube
7. Spark plug wire retainers fitting
8. Crankcase ventilation tube

22086_EXPL_G0064

Fig. 197 Showing components for removal of the RH valve cover—4.0L engine

To install:

5. Thoroughly clean the mating surfaces of the engine and cover.

6. Install a new gasket to the cover and place the cover in position on the engine.

7. Install all of the hold-down bolts and tighten to 89 inch lbs (10 Nm).

8. Install or connect the following:
- Crankcase vent tube
- Spark plug cables to their wire looms and plugs
- Fuel supply tube-to-valve cover; use new O-ring seals
- EGR module tube; tighten the fasteners to 25 ft. lbs. (34 Nm)
- Coolant tube bracket front bolt to 25 ft. lbs. (34 Nm) and rear bolt to 17 ft. lbs. (23 Nm)

9. Install the intake manifold. See "Intake Manifold" in this section.

10. Reconnect the fuel supply line spring-lock coupling.

11. Refill the cooling system and run the engine.

12. Connect the negative battery cable.

13. Allow the engine to reach normal operating temperature (upper radiator hose hot) and check for leaks.

Left Hand Cover

1. Disconnect the negative battery cable.

2. Remove the intake manifold.

3. Remove or disconnect the following:
- Camshaft Position (CMP) sensor electrical connection
- Ignition coil electrical connector and harness retainer
- Fuel injector electrical connectors and harness retainer
- PCV tube
- PCV valve electrical connector
- Spark plug wire retainers
- Valve cover

To install:

4. Thoroughly clean the mating surfaces of the engine and cover.

5. Install a new gasket to the cover and place the cover in position on the engine.

6. Install or connect the following:
- Valve cover bolts to 89 inch lbs (10 Nm)
- Spark plug wire retainers
- PCV valve electrical connector
- PCV tube
- Fuel injector wiring and connectors
- Ignition coil wiring and connector
- CMP sensor electrical connector
- Intake manifold; refer to Intake Manifold

4.6L Engine

Right Hand Cover

See Figures 198 and 199.

1. Remove or disconnect the following:
- Air cleaner and the air cleaner outlet pipe
- RH ignition coils
- Wiring harness from the powertrain control module
- RH variable camshaft timing (VCT) oil control solenoid electrical connector
- 2 wiring harness retainers from the RH valve cover studs
- Wiring harness pin-type retainer from the front of the RH valve cover
- Heater hose retainer from the RH valve cover
- Crankcase breather tube from the RH valve cover
- RH valve cover bolts and remove the RH valve cover and the RH valve cover gasket

To install:

2. Clean the gasket mating surfaces and install a new gasket.

3. Apply a bead of silicone gasket and sealant in 2 places where the engine front cover meets the RH cylinder head.

4. Position the RH valve cover with a new gasket on the cylinder head and tighten the bolts in the sequence shown to 89 inch lbs. (10 Nm).

5. Install or connect the following:
- Crankcase breather tube to the RH valve cover
- Heater hose retainer to the RH valve cover
- Wiring harness pin-type retainer to the front of the RH valve cover
- Wiring harness retainers to the RH valve cover studs
- Engine wiring harness to the PCM

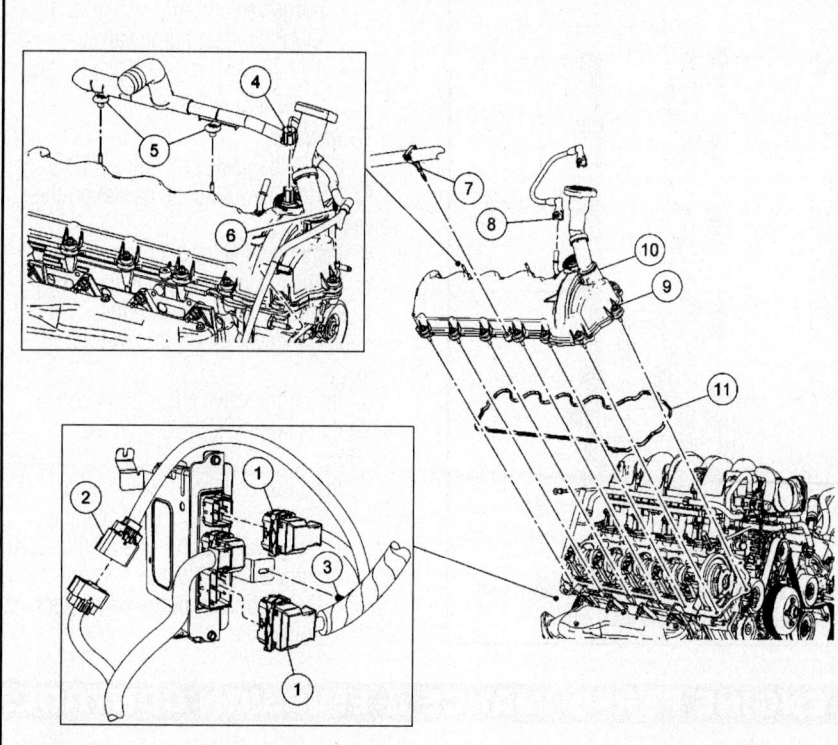

1. Engine wiring (VCT) oil control solenoid harness-to-powertrain control electrical connector
2. Engine wiring harness in-line electrical connector retainer
3. Wiring harness pin-type retainer
4. RH variable camshaft timing
5. Wiring harness retainers
7. Heater hose retainer retainer
8. Crankcase breather tube
9. RH valve cover bolts
10. RH valve cover
11. RH valve cover gasket

22080_EXPL_G0007

Fig. 198 Showing components to remove/install for valve cover—4.6L engine

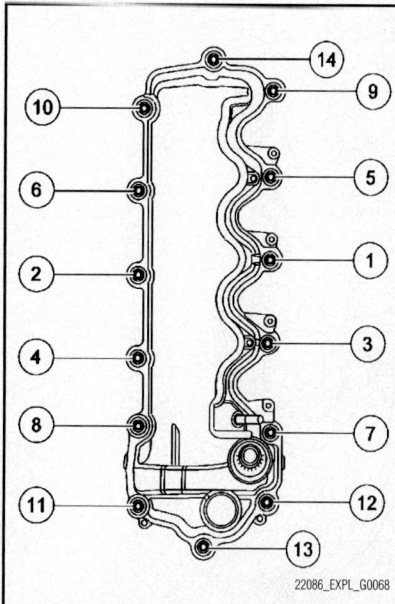

22086_EXPL_G0068

Fig. 199 Showing RH valve cover bolt tightening sequence—4.6L engine

- RH ignition coils
- Air cleaner and the air cleaner outlet pipe

Left Hand Cover

See Figure 200.

1. Remove or disconnect the following:
- LH ignition coils
- Oil level indicator and tube; position aside
- EVAP tube from the intake manifold
- PCV hose from the valve cover
- Fan wiring harness bracket; position aside
- 2 pin-type retainers from the valve cover
- Variable camshaft timing (VCT) solenoid electrical connector
- Wiring harness retainers from the valve cover studs
- EVAP canister purge valve electrical connector

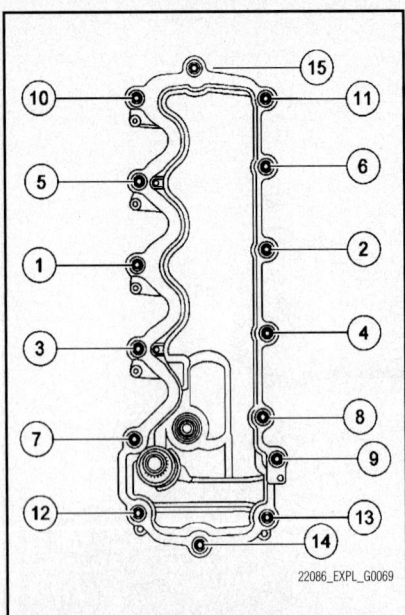

Fig. 200 Showing the LH valve cover bolt tightening sequence—4.6L engine

- EVAP canister-to-EVAP canister purge valve EVAP hose from the EVAP canister purge valve
- 15 bolts and remove the LH valve cover and gasket

To install:
2. Clean the gasket mating surfaces.
3. Form a new silicone gasket on the valve cover.
4. Install the LH valve cover.
5. Apply a bead of silicone gasket and sealant in 2 places where the engine front cover meets the cylinder head.
6. Install the valve cover bolts and tighten, in sequence, to 89 inch lbs. (10 Nm).
7. Install or connect the following:
- EVAP canister-to-EVAP canister purge valve EVAP hose to the EVAP canister purge valve
- EVAP canister purge valve electrical connector
- Wiring harness retainers to the valve cover studs
- Variable camshaft timing (VCT) solenoid electrical connector
- 2 pin-type retainers to the valve cover
- Fan wiring harness bracket
- PCV hose to the valve cover
- EVAP tube to the intake manifold
- Oil level indicator and tube
- LH ignition coils

VALVE LASH

ADJUSTMENT

The 4.0L and 4.6L engine are equipped with hydraulic lash adjusters. Valve lash is maintained by the hydraulic lifter or hydraulic lash adjuster eliminating the need for any additional manual adjustment. No further adjustment is possible.

ENGINE PERFORMANCE & EMISSION CONTROLS

ACCELERATOR PEDAL POSITION (APP) SENSOR

LOCATION
See Figure 201.

REMOVAL & INSTALLATION
See Figure 201.

1. From atop the accelerator pedal, disconnect the pedal electrical connector.
2. Remove the attaching screws.
3. Remove the accelerator pedal position sensor.

To install:
4. To install, reverse removal.

CAMSHAFT POSITION (CMP) SENSOR

LOCATION
See Figures 202 and 203.

REMOVAL & INSTALLATION

4.0L Engine
See Figure 202.

1. Disconnect the Camshaft Position (CMP) sensor electrical connector.
2. Remove the bolt and the CMP sensor.

To install:
3. To install, reverse the removal procedure and tighten bolt to 53 inch lbs. (6 Nm).

4.6L Engine
See Figure 203.

➡**For RH side remove the Air Cleaner (ACL) outlet pipe.**

1. Disconnect the Camshaft Position (CMP) sensor electrical connector.
2. Remove the bolt and the CMP sensor.

To install:
3. To install, reverse the removal procedure and tighten bolts to 89 inch lbs. (10 Nm).

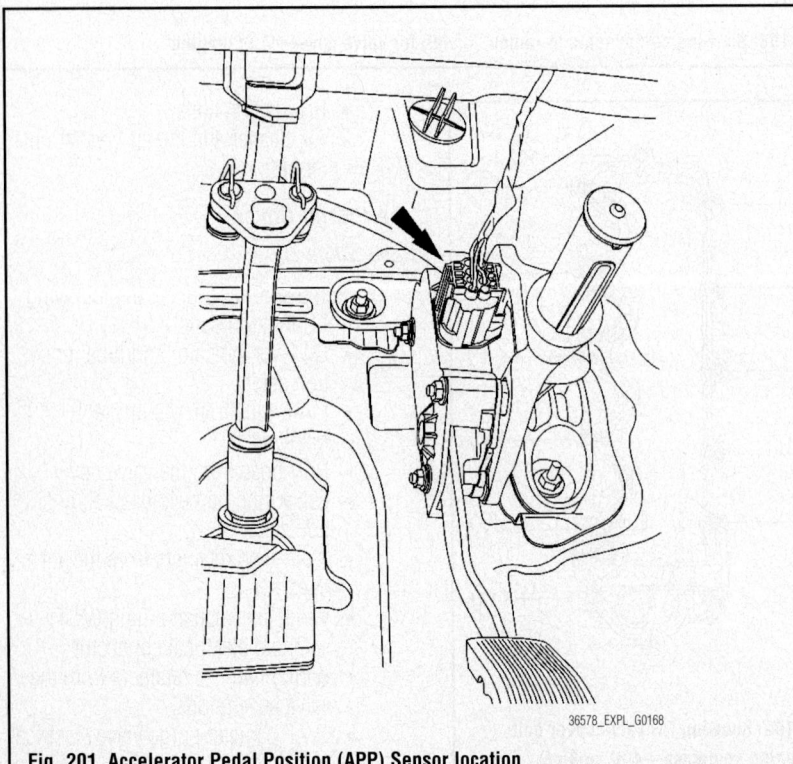

Fig. 201 Accelerator Pedal Position (APP) Sensor location

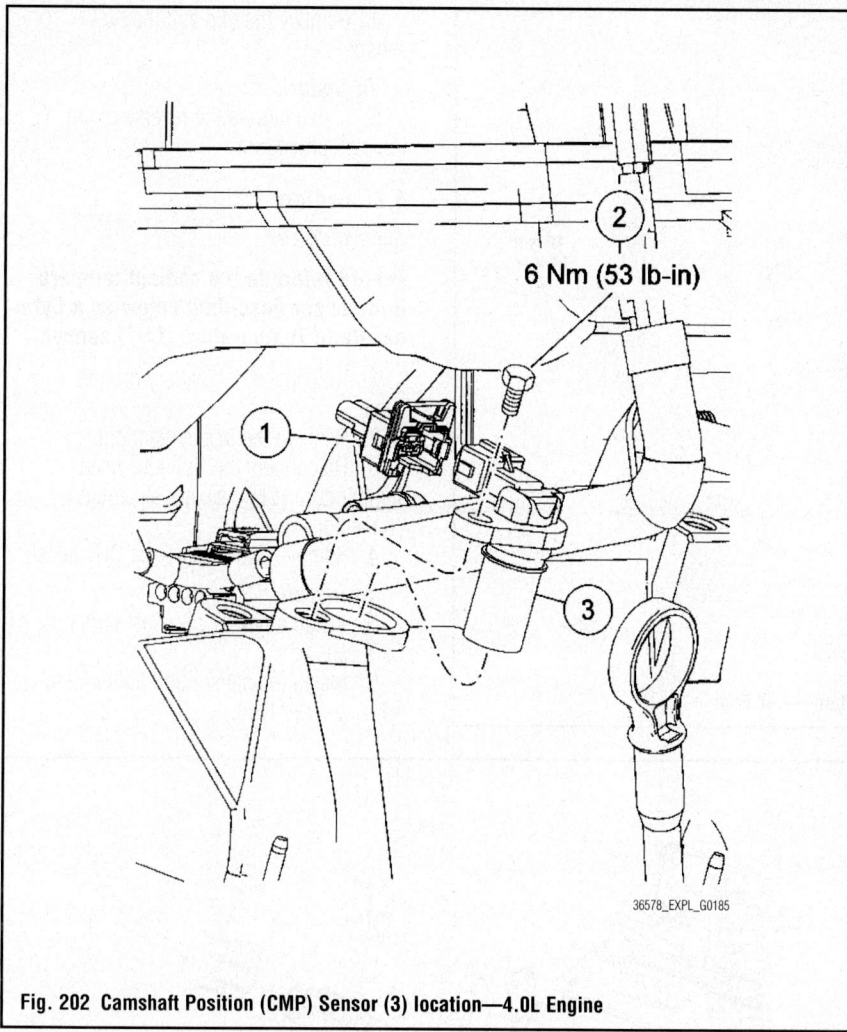

Fig. 202 Camshaft Position (CMP) Sensor (3) location—4.0L Engine

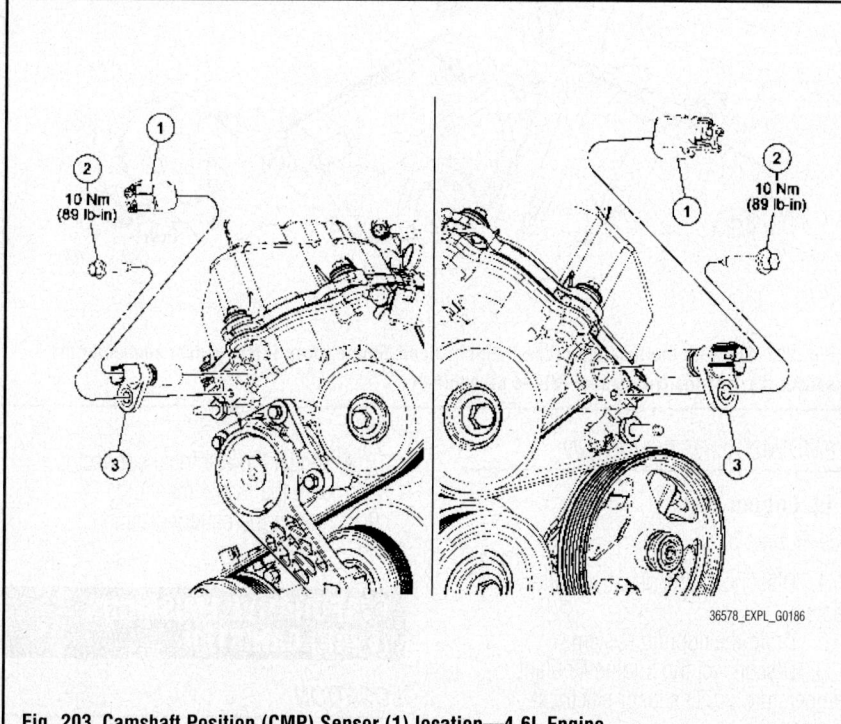

Fig. 203 Camshaft Position (CMP) Sensor (1) location—4.6L Engine

CRANKSHAFT POSITION (CKP) SENSOR

LOCATION

See Figures 204 and 205.

REMOVAL & INSTALLATION

4.0L Engine

See Figure 204.

1. With the vehicle in NEUTRAL, position it on a hoist.
2. Disconnect the Crankshaft Position (CKP) sensor electrical connector.
3. Remove the 2 bolts and the CKP sensor.

To install:

4. To install, reverse the removal procedure and tighten to 89 inch lbs. (10 Nm).

➡ **Be sure the sensor wiring is routed away from the battery cable.**

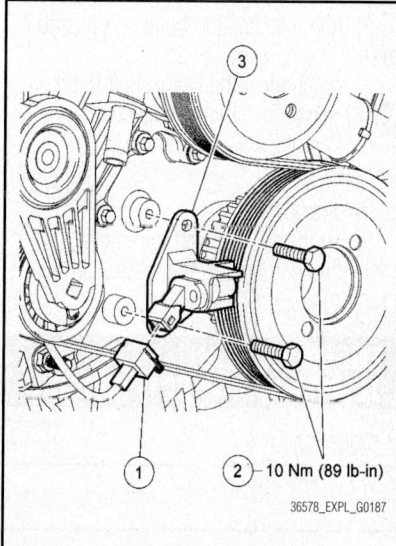

Fig. 204 Crankshaft Position (CMP) Sensor (3) location—4.0L Engine

4.6L Engine

See Figure 205.

1. With the vehicle in NEUTRAL, position it on a hoist.
2. Remove the accessory drive belt. Refer to Accessory Drive Belt in Engine Mechanical.
3. Disconnect the A/C compressor coil electrical connector.
4. Detach the battery cable retainer from the A/C compressor stud bolts.
5. Remove the nut and detach the A/C tube bracket.

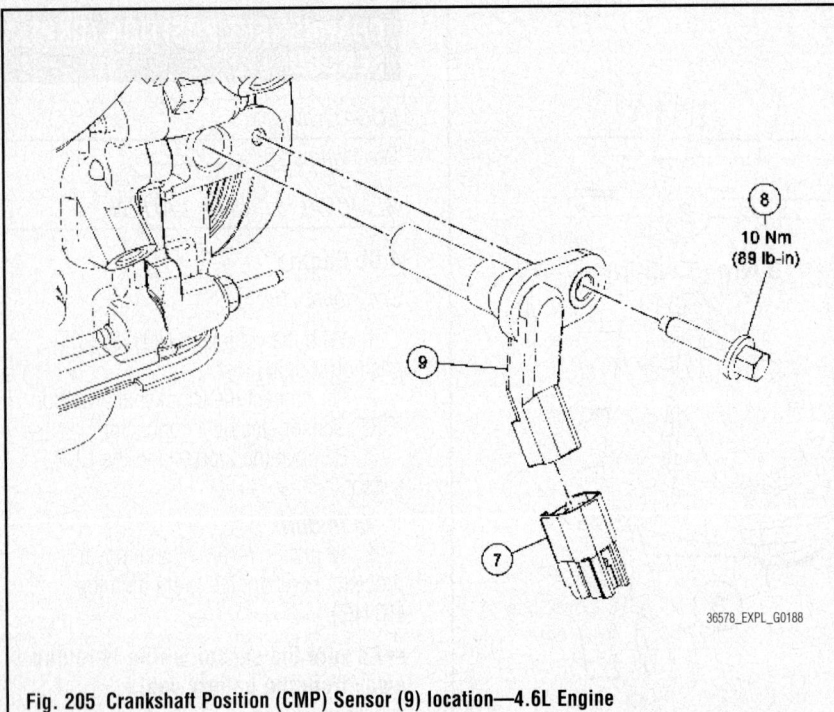

Fig. 205 Crankshaft Position (CMP) Sensor (9) location—4.6L Engine

36578_EXPL_G0188

6. Remove the stud bolts and position the A/C compressor aside.

7. Disconnect the Crankshaft Position (CKP) sensor electrical connector.

8. Remove the bolt and the CKP sensor.

To install:

9. To install, reverse the removal procedure and tighten bolt to 89 inch lbs. (10 Nm).

ENGINE COOLANT TEMPERATURE (ECT) SENSOR

LOCATION

See Figures 206 and 207.

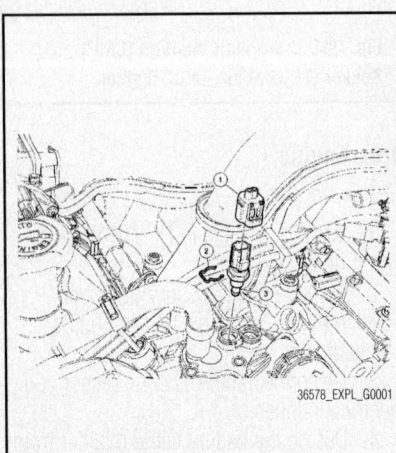

Fig. 206 Engine Coolant Temperature (ECT) Sensor—4.0L Engine

36578_EXPL_G0001

4. Remove the clip and the ECT sensor.

To install:

5. Installation is the reverse of the removal procedure.

4.6L Engine

See Figure 207.

➡ **Ford refers to the coolant temperature sensor described below as a Cylinder Head Temperature (CHT) sensor.**

1. Disconnect the battery ground cable.

2. Remove the intake manifold.

3. Disconnect the Cylinder Head Temperature (CHT) sensor electrical connector.

4. Remove and discard the CHT sensor.

To install:

5. Install a new O-ring seal on a new CHT sensor.

6. Install the sensor and tighten it to 19 ft. lbs. (26 Nm).

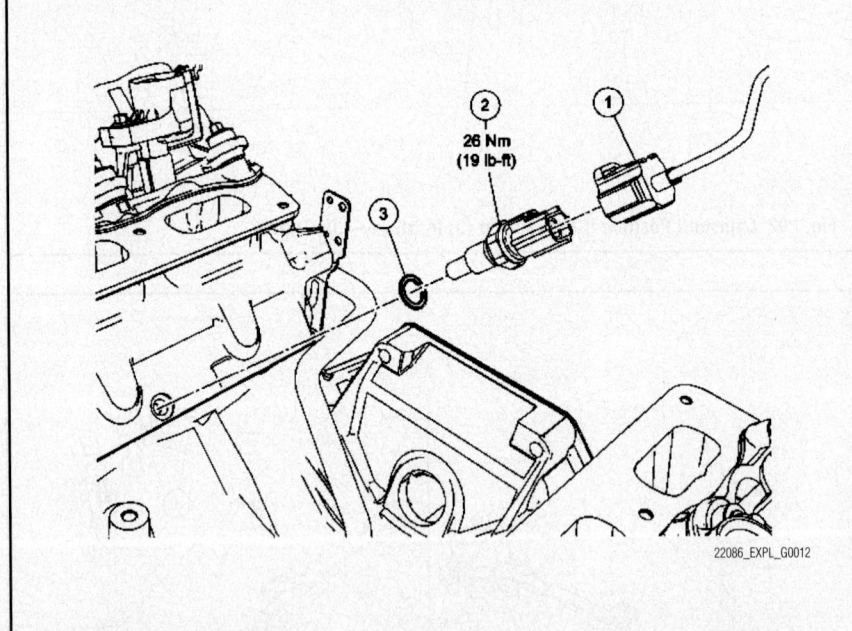

Fig. 207 Showing the location of the Cylinder Head Temperature (CHT) sensor connector (1), sensor (2), and the O-ring seal (3)—4.6L engine

22086_EXPL_G0012

REMOVAL & INSTALLATION

4.0L Engine

See Figure 75.

1. Disconnect the negative battery cable.

2. Drain the cooling system.

3. Disconnect the Engine Coolant Temperature (ECT) sensor electrical connector.

7. Connect the electrical connector.

8. Install the intake manifold.

9. Connect the battery ground cable.

EVAPORATIVE EMISSIONS (EVAP) CANISTER

LOCATION

See Figure 208.

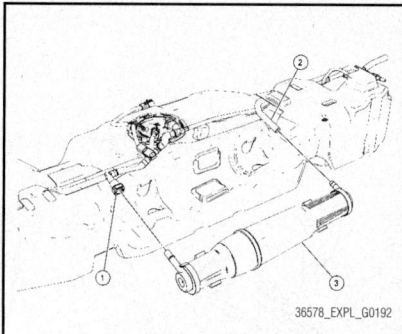

Fig. 208 Evaporative Emissions (EVAP) Canister location

REMOVAL & INSTALLATION

See Figure 208.

> ✳✳ **CAUTION**
>
> **Always disconnect the battery ground cable at the battery when working on an evaporative emission (EVAP) system or fuel-related component. Highly flammable mixtures are always present and may be ignited. Failure to follow these instructions may result in serious personal injury.**

> ✳✳ **CAUTION**
>
> **Do not smoke, carry lighted tobacco or have an open flame of any type when working on or near any fuel-related component. Highly flammable mixtures are always present and may be ignited. Failure to follow these instructions may result in serious personal injury.**

➡**Use only water-based lubricants on the vapor hoses.**

1. With the vehicle in NEUTRAL, position it on a hoist.
2. Disconnect the battery ground cable.
3. Remove the fuel tank. Refer to Fuel Tank in Fuel Systems.
4. Detach the Evaporative Emission (EVAP) canister from the fuel tank to gain access to the quick connect coupling.
5. Disconnect the Fuel Tank Pressure (FTP) sensor and vapor tube assembly quick connect coupling from the EVAP canister.
6. Disconnect the vapor hose from the EVAP canister.
7. Remove the EVAP canister.

To install:

8. To install, reverse the removal procedure.

9. Lubricate the vapor hoses with a water-based lubricant to ease installation.
10. Using a can tool, carry out the Evaporative Emission System Leak Test.

EXHAUST GAS RECIRCULATION (EGR) VALVE

LOCATION

See Figure 209.

REMOVAL & INSTALLATION

See Figure 209.

1. Disconnect the EGR system module electrical and vacuum connectors.
2. Disconnect the EGR system module-to-exhaust manifold tube upper fitting.

➡**When installing the new EGR module gasket, install with the side with the raised circle facing the intake manifold.**

3. Remove the 2 bolts, the EGR system module and the gasket. Discard the gasket.

➡**The EGR system module sealing surfaces are soft metals.**

4. Carefully clean the EGR system module sealing surfaces.

To install:

5. To install, reverse the removal procedure.
6. Install a new EGR system module gasket.

7. Install and tighten the module-to-exhaust manifold tube to 30 ft. lbs. (40 Nm).
8. Install and tighten the EGR system module to 18 ft. lbs. (25 Nm).

HEATED OXYGEN SENSOR (HO2S)

LOCATION

See Figure 210.

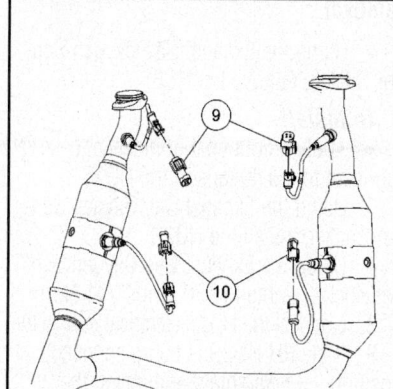

9. Heated Oxygen Sensor (HO2S) electrical connectors
10. Catalyst Monitor Sensor (CMS) electrical connectors

Fig. 210 Heated Oxygen Sensor (HO2S) locations

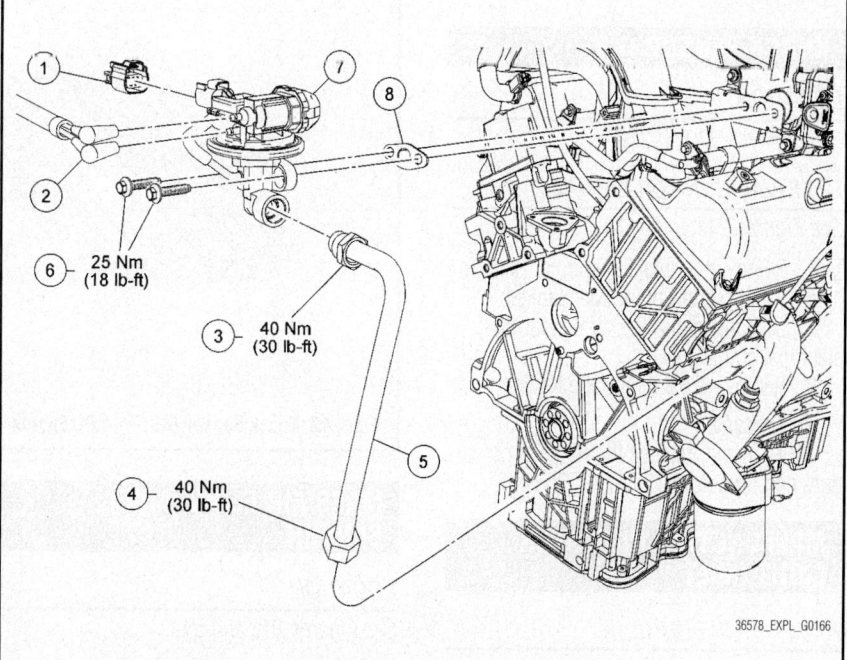

25 Nm (18 lb-ft)
40 Nm (30 lb-ft)
40 Nm (30 lb-ft)

Fig. 209 EGR system component locations—4.0L Engine

REMOVAL & INSTALLATION

See Figure 95.

1. With the vehicle in NEUTRAL, position it on a hoist.

2. If the RH Heated Oxygen Sensor (HO2S) is being serviced, remove the 2 bolts and position the heat shield aside.

3. Disconnect the HO2S electrical connector.

➡**If necessary, lubricate the HO2S with penetrating and lock lubricant to ease removal.**

4. Using the Exhaust Gas Oxygen Sensor Socket, remove the HO2S.

To install:

5. Apply a light coat of nickel anti-seize lubricant to the threads of the HO2S.

6. Using the Exhaust Gas Oxygen Sensor Socket, install the HO2S.

7. Using the Exhaust Gas Oxygen Sensor Socket, tighten to 30 ft. lbs. (41 Nm).

8. Connect the HO2S electrical connector.

9. If the RH HO2S is being serviced, position the heat shield and install the 2 bolts and tighten to 15 ft. lbs. (20 Nm).

INTAKE AIR TEMPERATURE (IAT) SENSOR

LOCATION

Refer to Mass Air Flow sensor.

REMOVAL & INSTALLATION

Refer to Mass Air Flow sensor.

KNOCK SENSOR (KS)

LOCATION

See Figures 211 and 212.

REMOVAL & INSTALLATION

See Figures 211 and 212.

1. Remove the intake manifold. Refer to Intake Manifold in Engine Mechanical.

2. Disconnect the Knock Sensor (KS) electrical connector.

3. Remove the bolt and the KS.

To install:

4. To install, reverse the removal procedure and tighten to 15 ft. lbs. (20 Nm).

MALFUNCTION INDICATOR LIGHT (MIL)

RESET PROCEDURE

Clearing Diagnostic Trouble Codes, resets MIL.

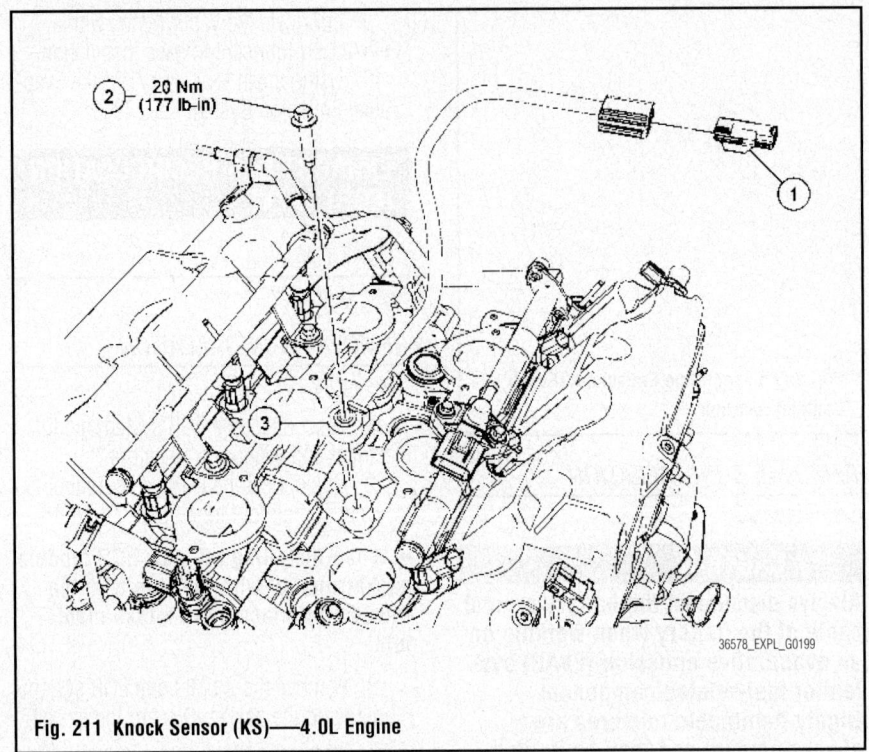

Fig. 211 Knock Sensor (KS)—4.0L Engine

36578_EXPL_G0199

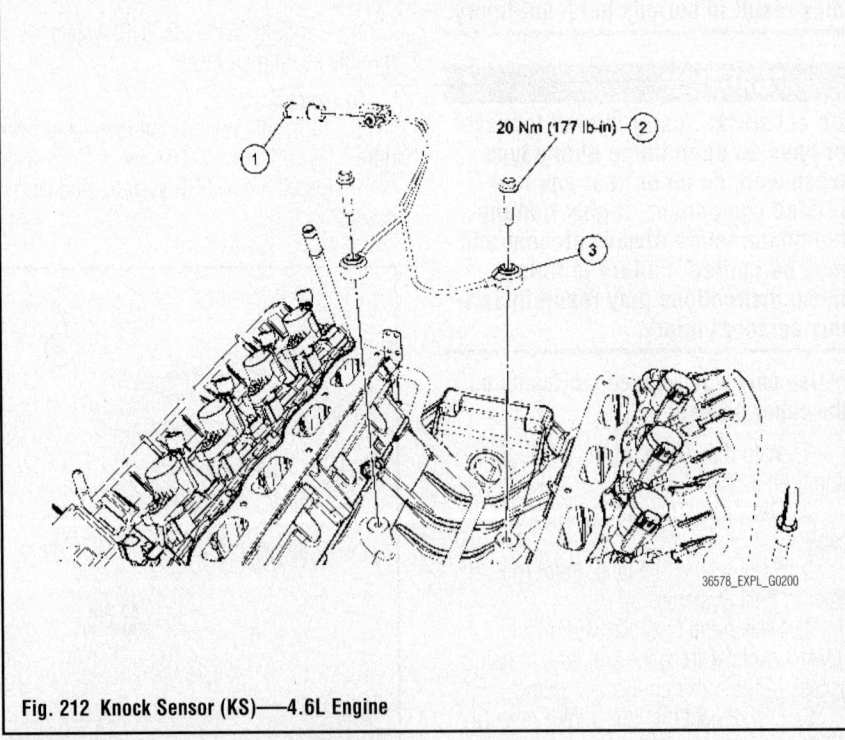

Fig. 212 Knock Sensor (KS)—4.6L Engine

36578_EXPL_G0200

MASS AIR FLOW (MAF) SENSOR

LOCATION

See Figures 213 and 214.

REMOVAL & INSTALLATION

See Figures 213 and 214.

1. Disconnect the Mass Air Flow (MAF) sensor electrical connector.

2. Remove the 2 bolts and the MAF sensor.

To install:

3. To install, reverse the removal procedure and tighten bolts to 18 inch lbs. (2 Nm).

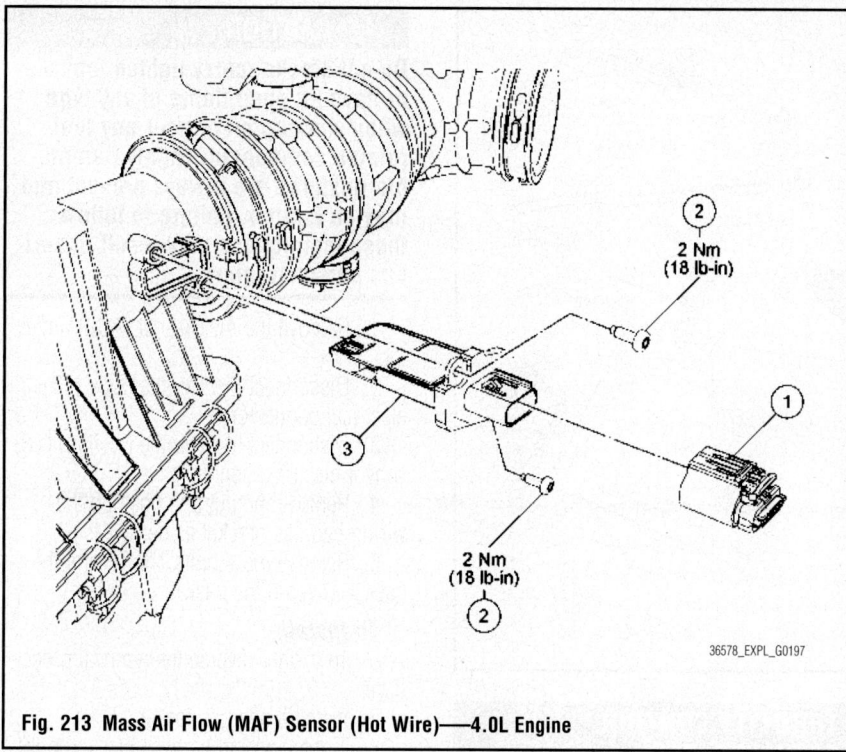

Fig. 213 Mass Air Flow (MAF) Sensor (Hot Wire)——4.0L Engine

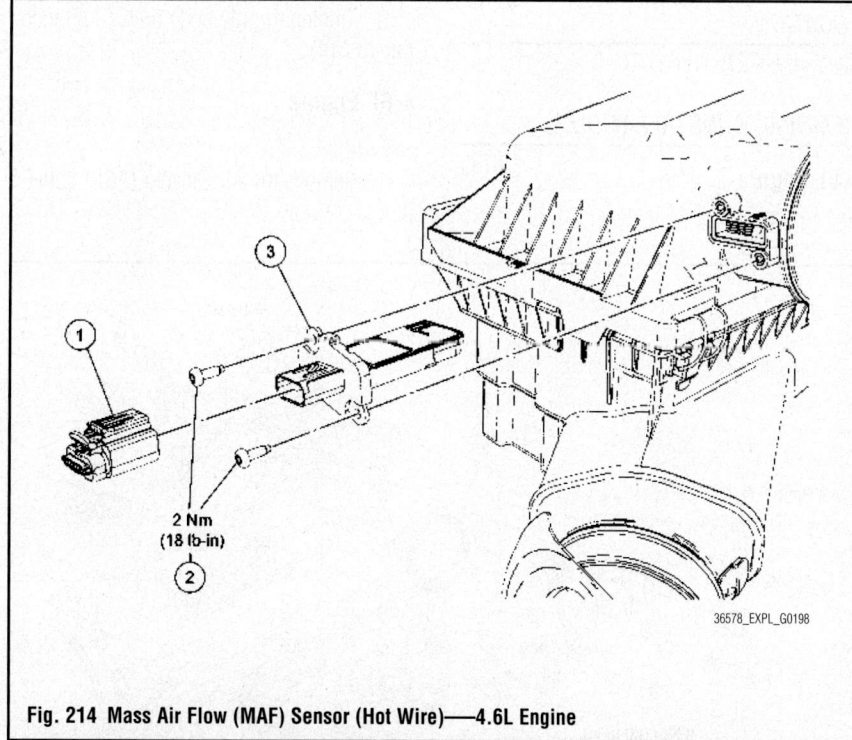

Fig. 214 Mass Air Flow (MAF) Sensor (Hot Wire)——4.6L Engine

POSITIVE CRANKCASE VENTILATION (PCV) VALVE

LOCATION
See Figure 215.

For 4.6L engine, the PCV valve is located on the LH valve cover.

REMOVAL & INSTALLATION
See Figure 215.

1. Disconnect the PCV valve electrical connector (if necessary).
2. Disconnect the PCV valve hose.

➡**If the PCV valve is removed from the valve cover, a new PCV valve must be installed.**

3. Rotate the PCV valve counterclockwise and remove it from the valve cover.

To install:
4. To install, reverse the removal procedure

POWERTRAIN CONTROL MODULE (PCM)

LOCATION
Passenger side, near side cowl, behind the glove compartment.

REMOVAL & INSTALLATION

➡**PCM installation DOES NOT require new keys.**

1. Retrieve the module configuration. Carry out the module configuration retrieval steps of the Programmable Module Installation (PMI) procedure:
   a. Connect the IDS and identify the vehicle as normal.
   b. From the Toolbox icon, select Module Programming and press the check mark.
   c. Select Programmable Module Installation.
   d. Select the module that is being replaced.
   e. Follow the on-screen instructions, turn the ignition key to the OFF position, and press the check mark.
   f. Install the new module and press the check mark.
   g. Follow the on-screen instructions, turn the ignition key to the ON position, and press the check mark.
   h. The IDS downloads the data into the new module and displays Module Configuration Complete.
   i. Test module for correct operation.
Vehicles equipped with a 4.6L (3V) engine
2. Remove the Air Cleaner (ACL). Disconnect the RH front wheel speed sensor electrical connector.
3. Remove the nut(s) and position the A/C tube bracket(s) and wiring harness aside.
4. Disconnect the PCM connectors.
5. Remove the 2 bolts and the PCM.

To install:
6. Install the PCM and the 2 bolts and tighten to 89 inch lbs. (10 Nm).
7. Connect the PCM electrical connectors.
8. Position the wiring harness and the A/C tube bracket(s) and install the nut(s).

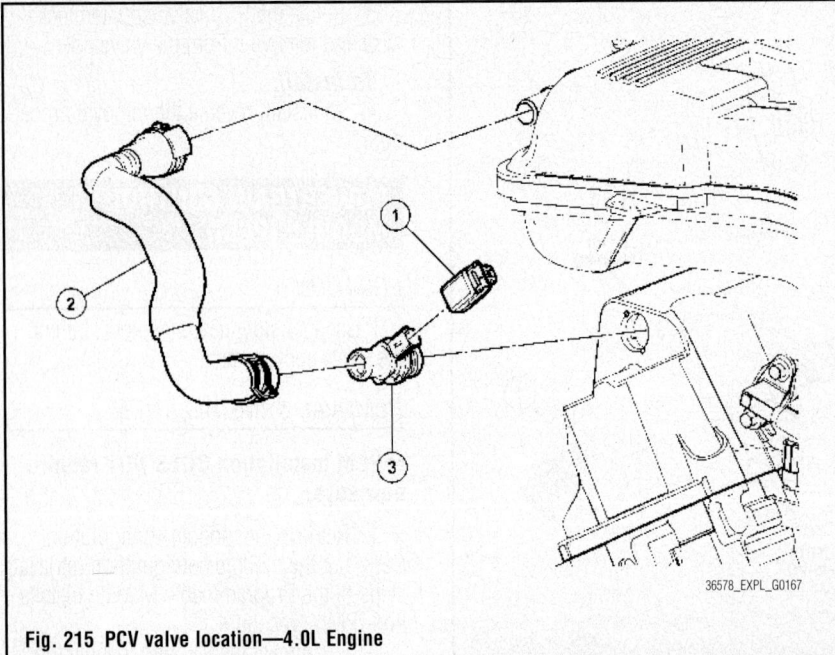

Fig. 215 PCV valve location—4.0L Engine

Connect the RH front wheel speed sensor electrical connector and tighten to 62 inch lbs. (7 Nm).

Vehicles equipped with a 4.6L (3V) engine

9. Install the air cleaner assembly
All vehicles

10. Restore the module configuration. Carry out the module configuration restore steps of the Programmable Module Installation (PMI) procedure.

11. Using scan tool, reprogram the Passive Anti-Theft System (PATS). Carry out the Parameter Reset procedure.

RESET PROCEDURE

a. Connect the IDS and identify the vehicle as normal.

b. From the Toolbox icon, select Module Programming and press the check mark.

c. Select Programmable Module Installation.

d. Select the module that is being replaced.

e. Follow the on-screen instructions, turn the ignition key to the OFF position, and press the check mark.

f. Install the new module and press the check mark.

g. Follow the on-screen instructions, turn the ignition key to the ON position, and press the check mark.

h. The IDS downloads the data into the new module and displays Module Configuration Complete.

i. Test module for correct operation.

THROTTLE CONTROL ACTUATOR (TAC)

LOCATION
See Figures 216 and 217.

REMOVAL & INSTALLATION

4.0L Engine
See Figure 216.

⁕⁕ CAUTION

Do not smoke, carry lighted tobacco or have an open flame of any type when working on or near any fuel-related component. Highly flammable mixtures are always present and may be ignited. Failure to follow these instructions may result in serious personal injury.

1. Remove the Air Cleaner (ACL) outlet tube.

2. Disconnect the Throttle Body (TB) electrical connector.

3. Disconnect the Throttle Position (TP) sensor electrical connector.

4. Remove the nut and position the wiring harness bracket aside.

5. Remove the 4 bolts, the TB and the gasket. Discard the gasket.

To install:

6. To install, reverse the removal procedure.

7. Install a new TB gasket.

8. Tighten wiring harness bracket to 80 inch lbs. (9 Nm).

9. Tighten throttle body bolts to 80 inch lbs. (9 Nm).

4.6L Engine
See Figure 217.

1. Remove the Air Cleaner (ACL) outlet pipe.

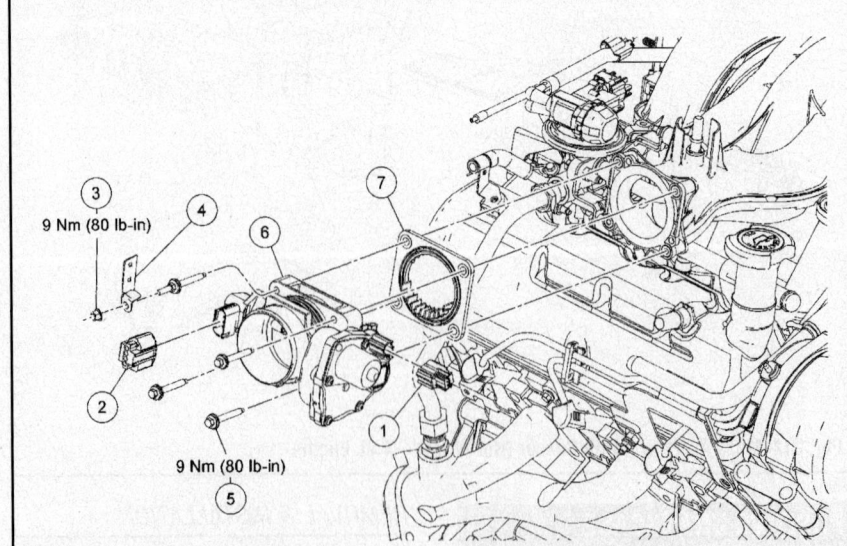

1. Throttle Body (TB) electrical connector
2. Throttle Position (TP) sensor electrical connector
3. Wiring harness bracket nut
4. Wiring harness bracket
5. TB bolt (4 required)
6. TB
7. TB gasket

9 Nm (80 lb-in)

9 Nm (80 lb-in)

Fig. 216 Throttle Control Actuator (TAC) location—4.0L Engine

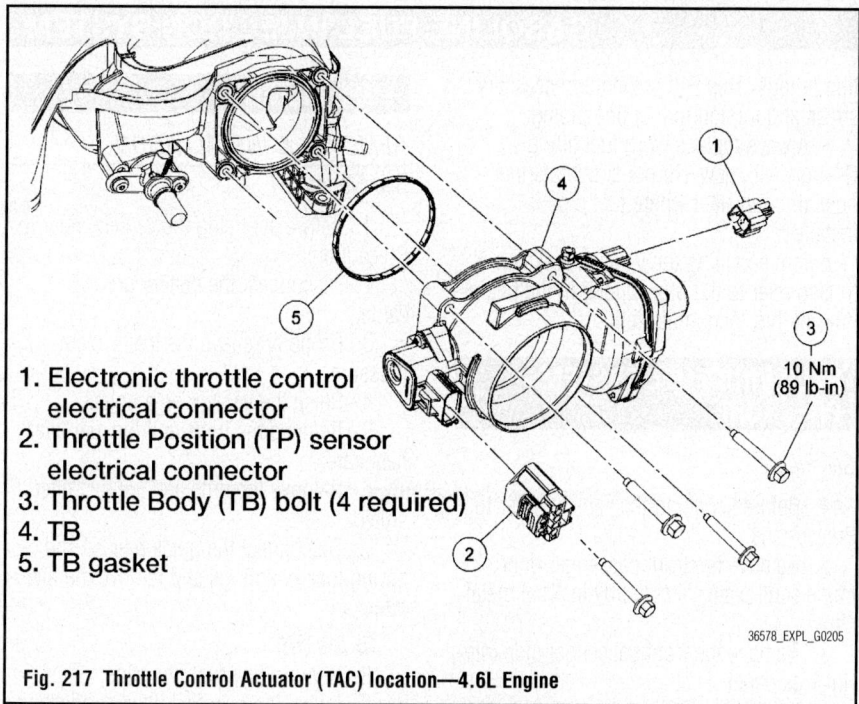

1. Electronic throttle control electrical connector
2. Throttle Position (TP) sensor electrical connector
3. Throttle Body (TB) bolt (4 required)
4. TB
5. TB gasket

10 Nm (89 lb-in)

36578_EXPL_G0205

Fig. 217 Throttle Control Actuator (TAC) location—4.6L Engine

2. Disconnect the electronic throttle control electrical connector.

3. Disconnect the Throttle Position (TP) sensor electrical connector.

4. Remove the 4 bolts, the Throttle Body (TB) and the TB gasket. Discard the gasket.

To install:

5. To install, reverse the removal procedure.

6. To install, tighten throttle body bolts to 89 inch lbs. (10 Nm).

THROTTLE POSITION SENSOR (TPS)

LOCATION

See Figure 218.

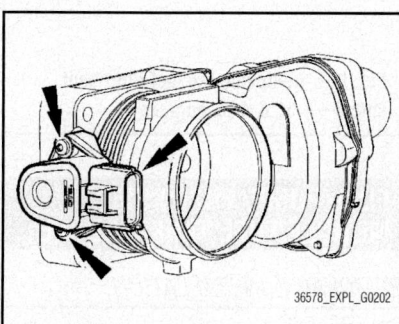

36578_EXPL_G0202

Fig. 218 Throttle Position Sensor (TPS) location

REMOVAL & INSTALLATION

See Figure 219.

All vehicles

1. Remove the Air Cleaner (ACL) outlet pipe.

2. Disconnect the Throttle Position (TP) sensor electrical connector.

Vehicles equipped with a 4.6L (3V) engine

3. Disconnect the PCV hose from the heated PCV fitting.

4. Disconnect the heated PCV fitting electrical connector.

5. Remove the 2 bolts and the heated PCV fitting.

6. Remove and discard the heated PCV fitting O-ring seal.

All vehicles

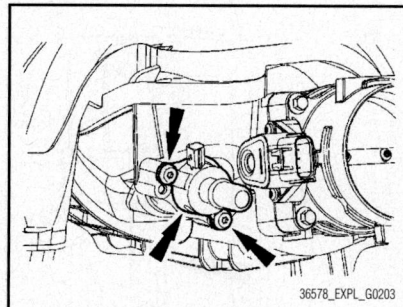

36578_EXPL_G0203

Fig. 219 2 bolts and the heated PCV fitting location—4.6L Engine

7. Remove the TP sensor.

8. Using a suitable heat gun, apply heat to the top of the Electronic Throttle Body (ETB) until the top TP sensor bolt ear reaches approximately 130°F (55°C), this should take no more than 3 minutes using a 1100-watt heat gun. The heat gun should be about an 25.4 mm (1 in) away from the ETB.

Monitor the temperature of the top TP sensor bolt ear on the ETB with a suitable temperature measuring device, such as a digital temperature laser or infrared thermometer, while heating the ETB.

9. Using hand tools, quickly remove the bolt farthest from the heat source first and discard.

10. Using hand tools, remove the remaining bolt and discard.

11. Remove and discard the TP sensor.

To install:

All vehicles

12. Install the new TP sensor.

13. Using hand tools, install the 2 new bolts and tighten to 27 inch lbs. (3 Nm).

Vehicles equipped with a 4.6L (3V) engine

14. Install a new O-ring seal and position the heated PCV fitting and install the 2 bolts.

15. Connect the heated PCV fitting electrical connector.

16. Connect the PCV hose to the heated PCV fitting.

All vehicles

17. Connect the TP sensor electrical connector.

18. Install the ACL outlet pipe.

FUEL **GASOLINE FUEL INJECTION SYSTEM**

FUEL SYSTEM SERVICE PRECAUTIONS

Safety is the most important factor when performing not only fuel system maintenance but any type of maintenance. Failure to conduct maintenance and repairs in a safe manner may result in serious personal injury or death. Maintenance and testing of the vehicle's fuel system components can be accomplished safely and effectively by adhering to the following rules and guidelines.

• To avoid the possibility of fire and personal injury, always disconnect the negative battery cable unless the repair or test procedure requires that battery voltage be applied.

• Always relieve the fuel system pressure prior to disconnecting any fuel system component (injector, fuel rail, pressure regulator, etc.), fitting or fuel line connection. Exercise extreme caution whenever relieving fuel system pressure to avoid exposing skin, face and eyes to fuel spray. Please be advised that fuel under pressure may penetrate the skin or any part of the body that it contacts.

• Immediately cap all open fittings to prevent contaminants from entering the fuel system during service.

• Fuel injection equipment is manufactured to very precise tolerances and fine clearances. It is therefore essential that absolute cleanliness is observed when working with these components. Always install blanking plugs to any open orifices or tubes.

• When reusing liquid or vapor tube connectors, make sure to use compressed air to remove any foreign material from the connector retaining clip area before separating from the tube.

• Always place a shop towel or cloth around the fitting or connection prior to loosening to absorb any excess fuel due to spillage. Ensure that all fuel spillage (should it occur) is quickly removed from engine surfaces. Ensure that all fuel soaked cloths or towels are deposited into a suitable waste container.

• Always keep a dry chemical (Class B) fire extinguisher near the work area.

• Do not allow fuel spray or fuel vapors to come into contact with a spark or open flame.

• Always use a back-up wrench when loosening and tightening fuel line connection fittings. This will prevent unnecessary stress and torsion to fuel line piping.

• Always replace worn fuel fitting O-rings with new. Do not substitute fuel hose or equivalent where fuel pipe is installed.

Before servicing the vehicle, make sure to also refer to the precautions in the beginning of this section as well.

RELIEVING FUEL SYSTEM PRESSURE

See Figure 220.

1. Before servicing the vehicle, refer to Precautions.
2. Remove the front passenger door frame scuff plate (retained by internal metal clips).
3. Remove the front passenger side interior kick panel.

➡**It may be necessary to reposition the lower end of the door jam weather stripping to remove the front passenger door side interior kick panel.**

4. Disconnect the Inertia Fuel Shutoff (IFS) switch electrical connector.
5. Start the engine and let it idle until it stalls.
6. After the engine stalls, crank it for 5 seconds to ensure all system pressure is relieved.
7. Turn the ignition switch to the OFF position.
8. When the fuel system maintenance and/or repair is complete, reconnect the IFS electrical connector.

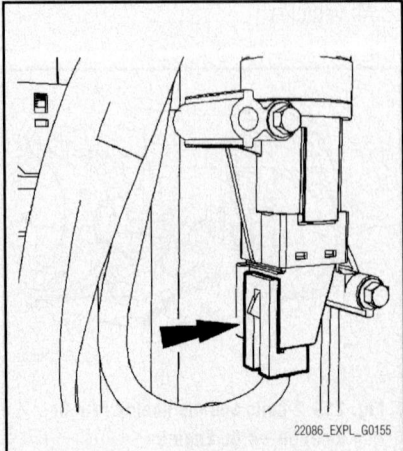

22086_EXPL_G0155

Fig. 220 Disconnect the Inertia Fuel Shutoff (IFS) switch electrical connector

FUEL FILTER

REMOVAL & INSTALLATION

See Figure 221.

1. Before servicing the vehicle, refer to Precautions.
2. Disconnect the battery ground cable.
3. Properly relieve the fuel system pressure.
4. Raise the vehicle on a hoist.
5. Remove the bolts and the fuel filter heat shield.
6. Remove the nuts and the fuel filter shield.
7. Disconnect the quick release and spring lock couplings and remove the fuel filter.

To install:

8. Remove any fuel line caps.
9. Install the new fuel filter, connecting the quick-release and spring-lock couplings.
10. Install the fuel filter shield.
11. Install the fuel filter heat shield. Torque the bolts to 15 ft. lbs. (20 Nm).
12. Reconnect the battery ground cable.
13. Lower the vehicle.
14. Start the vehicle, check for leaks and repair if necessary.

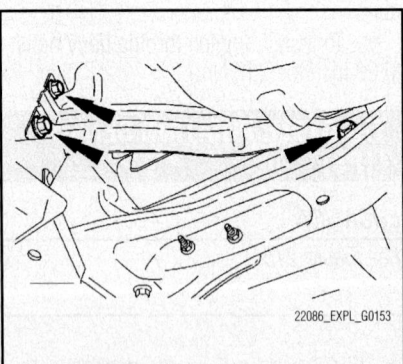

22086_EXPL_G0153

Fig. 221 Removing the fuel filter heat shield—4.0L & 4.6L engines

FUEL PUMP/ FUEL PUMP MODULE/FUEL TANK MODULE

REMOVAL & INSTALLATION

See Figure 222.

1. Before servicing the vehicle, refer to Precautions.
2. With the vehicle in NEUTRAL, position it on a hoist.
3. Release the fuel system pressure.

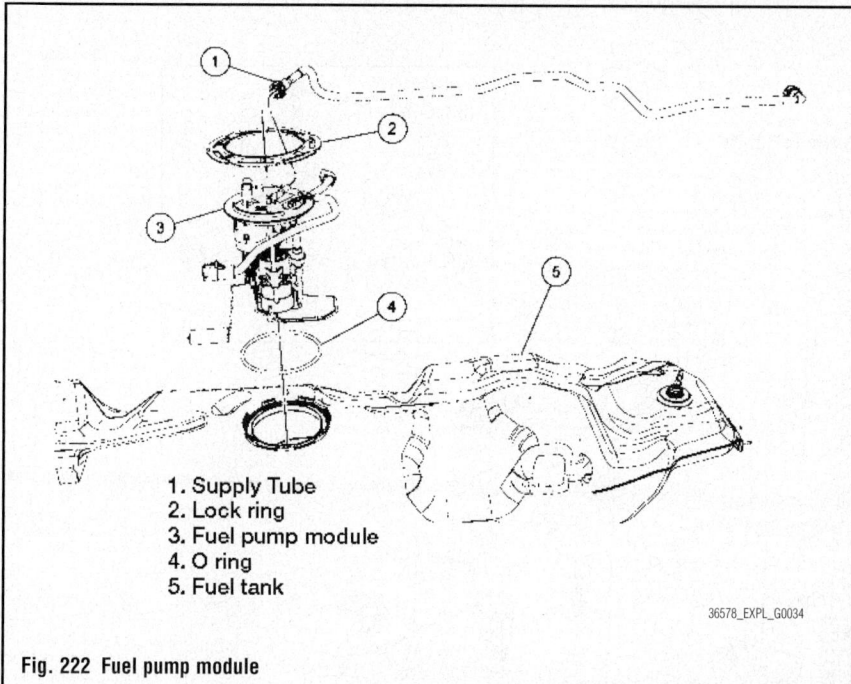

1. Supply Tube
2. Lock ring
3. Fuel pump module
4. O ring
5. Fuel tank

36578_EXPL_G0034

Fig. 222 Fuel pump module

4. Remove the fuel tank. Refer to Fuel Tank.

5. Remove the EVAP canister.

6. Remove the fuel tank shield.

7. Disconnect the fuel pressure sensor and vapor tube assembly-to-fuel pump and the fuel tank vapor valves quick connect couplings.

8. Disconnect the vapor tube fitting.

9. Disconnect the fuel supply tube-to-fuel pump quick connect coupling.

10. Remove the fuel supply tube.

11. Using the special tool, remove the fuel pump locking ring.

✳✳ WARNING

The fuel pump module must be handled carefully to avoid damage to the float arm and filter.

12. Remove the fuel pump module and the O-ring seal. Discard the O-ring seal.

To install:

13. Installation is the reverse of the removal procedure.

FUEL RAIL & INJECTORS

REMOVAL & INSTALLATION

4.0L Engine

See Figure 223.

✳✳ CAUTION

Fuel in the fuel system remains under high pressure even when the engine is not running. Before working on or

disconnecting any of the fuel lines or fuel system components, the fuel system pressure must be relieved. Failure to follow these instructions may result in personal injury.

✳✳ WARNING

If used as a leverage device, the fuel rail may be damaged. Care must be taken when working around the fuel rail.

1. Before servicing the vehicle, refer to Precautions.

2. Remove the intake manifold. Refer to Intake Manifold in Engine Mechanical.

3. Disconnect the spring lock coupling.

4. Remove the fuel supply tube bracket bolt.

5. Disconnect the fuel injector electrical connectors.

6. Disconnect the fuel pressure and temperature sensor electrical and vacuum connectors.

7. Remove the bolts and the fuel rail and injectors as an assembly.

✳✳ WARNING

O-ring seals are made of special fuel-resistant material. Use of ordinary O-ring seals can cause the fuel system to leak. Do not reuse O-ring seals.

➡Install new fuel injector-to-intake manifold O-ring seals and lubricate them with clean engine oil.

8. Remove the fuel injectors and the fuel injector O-ring seals.

✳✳ WARNING

O-ring seals are made of special fuel-resistant material. Use of ordinary O-ring seals can cause the fuel system to leak. Do not reuse O-ring seals.

➡Install new fuel injector-to-fuel rail O-ring seals and lubricate them with clean engine oil.

To install:

9. Installation is the reverse of the removal procedure. Observe the following tightening specifications:

- Fuel rail bolts to 17 ft. lbs. (23 Nm).
- Fuel supply bracket bolt to 71 inch lbs. (8 Nm).

4.6L Engine

See Figure 224.

1. Before servicing the vehicle, refer to Precautions.

2. Release the fuel system pressure.

3. Disconnect the fuel supply tube spring lock coupling.

4. Detach the 2 positive crankcase ventilation (PCV) coolant hose retainers from the fuel rail stud bolts and position the hose aside.

5. Disconnect the fuel rail pressure and temperature sensor electrical connector and vacuum hose.

6. Disconnect the 8 fuel injector electrical connectors.

7. Remove the fuel rail stud bolts.

8. Remove the fuel rail and fuel injectors as an assembly from the intake manifold.

9. Remove the retaining clips and fuel injectors from the fuel rail.

➡The fuel injector clip can be reused if it is not damaged during removal. If the clip is reused, the 2 sides of the clip should be squeezed back into shape by placing it between index finger and thumb.

10. Remove and discard the fuel injector O-ring seals.

To install:

11. Installation is the reverse of the removal procedure, noting the following:

a. Use new O-ring seals.

b. Use new fuel injector retaining clips, if needed.

c. Tighten the fuel rail stud bolts to 89 inch lbs. (10 Nm).

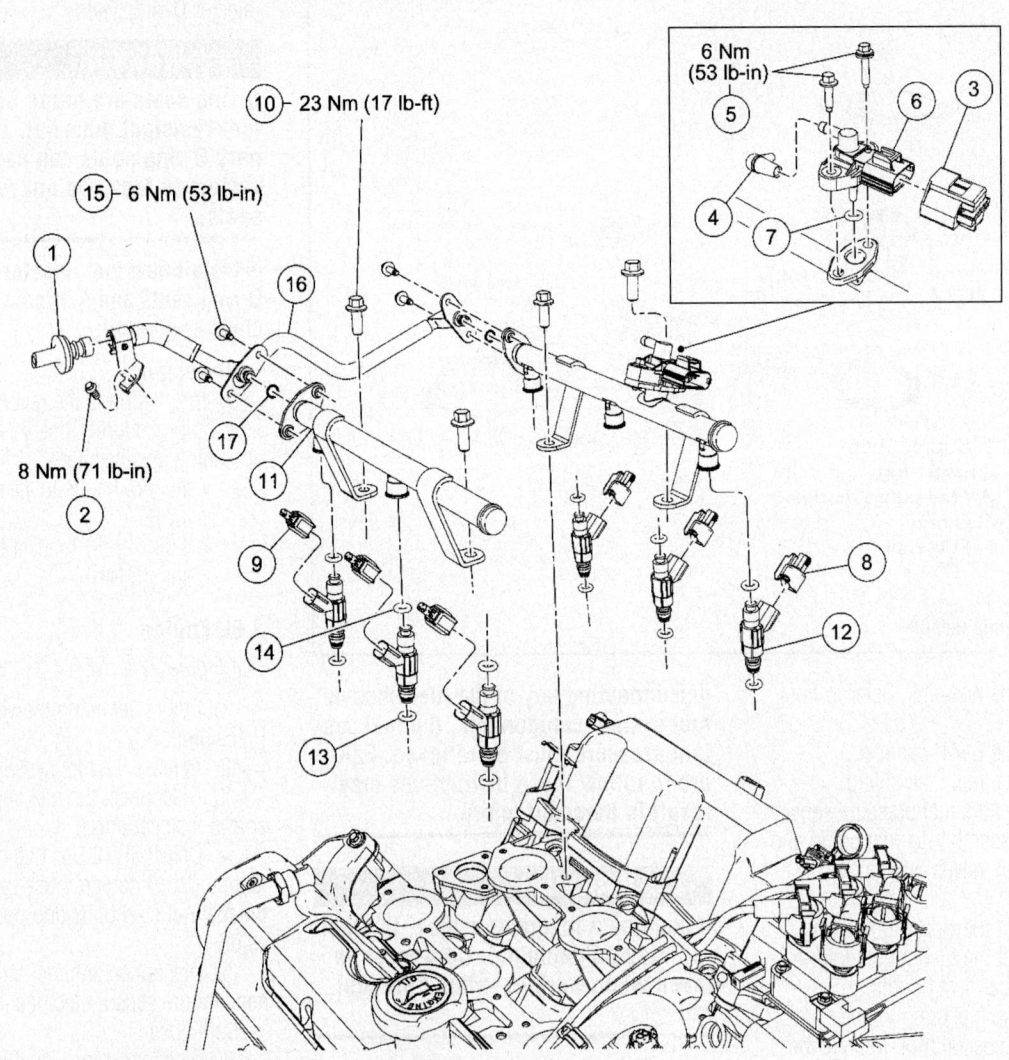

10 — 23 Nm (17 lb-ft)

15 — 6 Nm (53 lb-in)

8 Nm (71 lb-in)

6 Nm (53 lb-in)

1. Fuel tube spring lock coupling
2. Fuel supply tube bracket bolt
3. Fuel pressure and temperature sensor electrical connector
4. Fuel pressure and temperature sensor vacuum hose
5. Fuel rail pressure and temperature sensor bolts (2 required)
6. Fuel rail pressure and temperature sensor
7. Fuel rail pressure and temperature sensor O-ring seal
8. Fuel injector electrical connector (LH side) (3 required)
9. Fuel injector electrical connector (RH side) (3 required)
10. Fuel rail bolt (4 required)
11. Fuel rail
12. Fuel injector (6 required)
13. Fuel injector-to-cylinder head O-ring seal (6 required)
14. Fuel injector-to-fuel rail O-ring seal (6 required)
15. Fuel supply tube bolt (4 required)
16. Fuel supply tube
17. Fuel supply tube O-ring seal (2 required)

36578_EXPL_G0036

Fig. 223 Fuel rail, injectors and related parts—4.0L engine

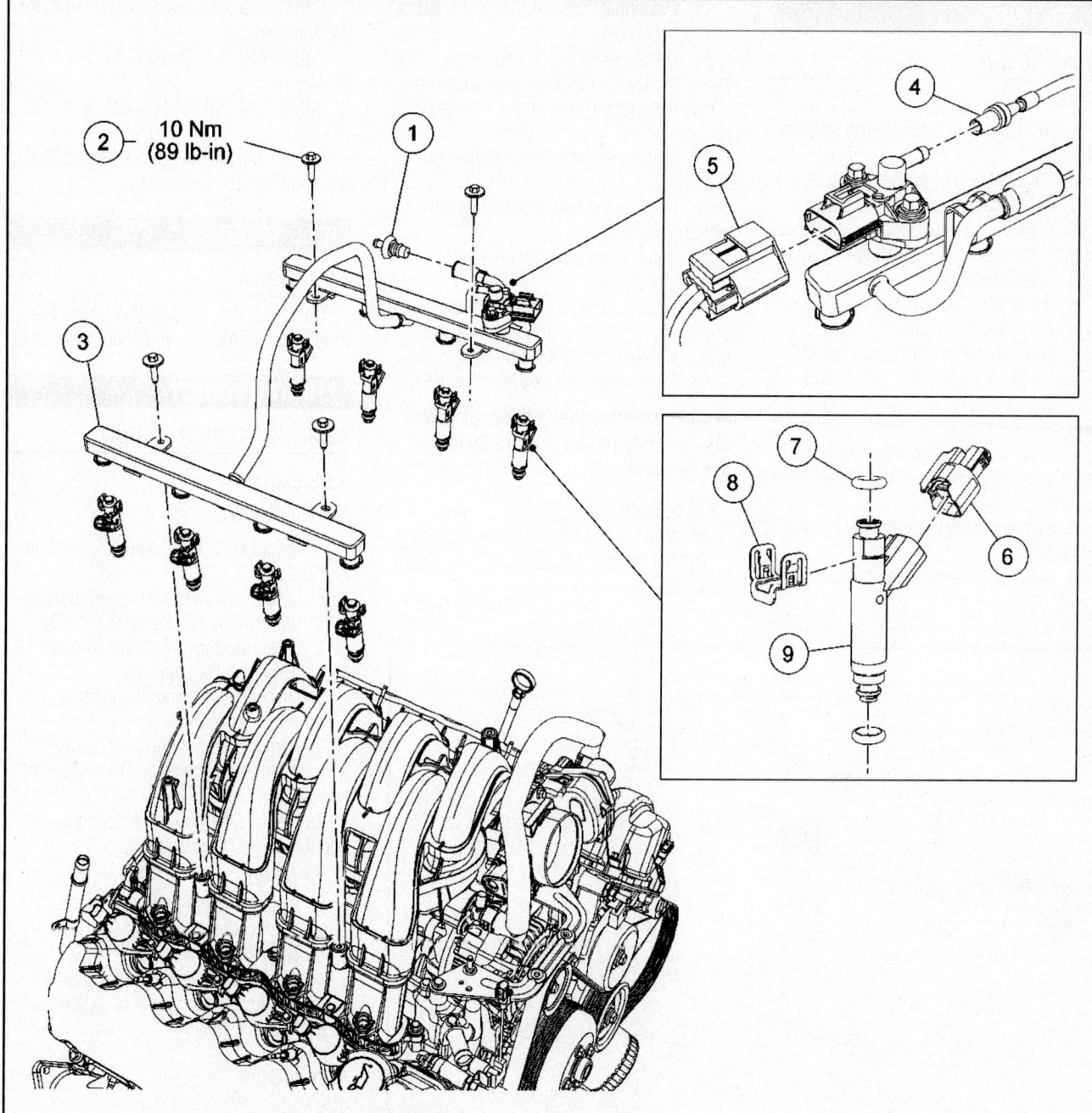

1. Fuel supply tube spring lock coupling
2. Fuel rail bolt (4 required)
3. Fuel rail
4. Vacuum hose
5. Fuel rail pressure and temperature sensor electrical connector
6. Fuel injector electrical connector (8 required)
7. O-ring seal (16 required)
8. Fuel injector retaining clip (8 required)
9. Fuel injector

36578_EXPL_G0037

Fig. 224 Exploded view of the fuel rail and injector components—4.6L engine

FUEL TANK

REMOVAL & INSTALLATION

See Figure 225.

1. Before servicing the vehicle, refer to Precautions.
2. Release the fuel system pressure.
3. Disconnect negative battery cable.
4. Remove the driveshaft. For additional information, refer to Driveshaft in Drivetrain.
5. Drain the fuel tank.
6. If equipped, remove the 4 bolts and the transfer case skid plate.
7. Disconnect the filler pipe vapor tube-to-Fuel Tank Pressure (FTP) sensor and vapor tube assembly quick connect coupling.
8. Disconnect the fuel vapor hose from the Evaporative Emission (EVAP) canister vent valve.
9. Remove the 3 bolts and the fuel filter heat shield.
10. Remove the 2 nuts and the fuel filter shield.

11. Disconnect the fuel filter outlet quick connect coupling.
12. Disconnect the FTP and tube assembly-to-vapor tube quick connect coupling.
13. If equipped, remove the 4 bolts, 1 nut and the fuel tank skid plate.
14. Using a suitable jack, support the fuel tank.
15. Remove the bolt and the fuel tank rear support strap.
16. Remove the nut and the fuel tank front support strap.
17. Lower the fuel tank far enough to access the Fuel Pump (FP) electrical connector and disconnect the connector.
18. Remove the fuel tank from the vehicle.

➡**Make sure the fuel and vapor tubes are correctly routed prior to installing the fuel tank.**

To install:

To install, reverse the removal procedure. Tighten transfer case skid plate to 30 ft. lbs. (40 Nm).

Tighten fuel filter heat shield to 15 ft. lbs. (20 Nm).
Tighten fuel filter shield to 53 inch lbs. (6 Nm).
Tighten fuel tank skid plate to 30 ft. lbs. (40 Nm).
Tighten fuel tank support straps to 35 ft. lbs. (48 Nm).

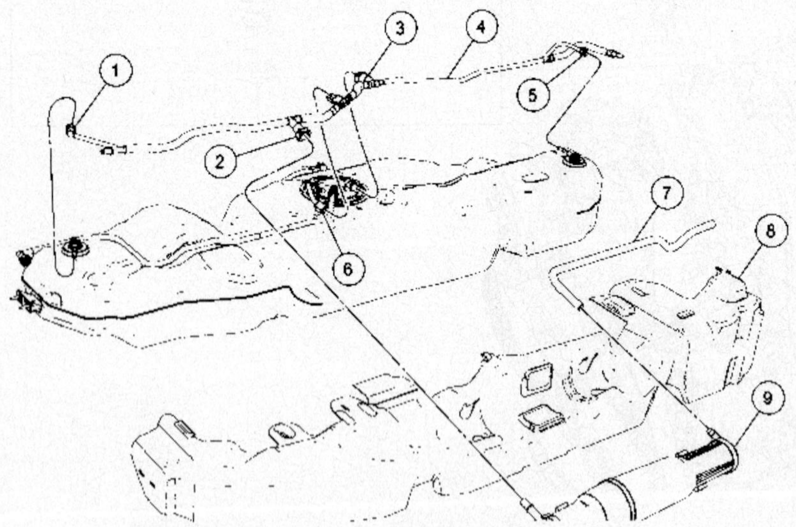

IDLE SPEED

ADJUSTMENT

The idle speed is controlled by the Electronic Control Module and is not adjustable.

THROTTLE BODY

REMOVAL & INSTALLATION

4.0L Engine

See Figure 226.

1. Before servicing the vehicle, refer to Precautions.
2. Disconnect the battery ground cable.
3. Remove the air cleaner outlet tube.
4. Disconnect the electronic throttle body (TB) electrical connector.
5. Disconnect the throttle position (TP) sensor electrical connector.
6. Remove the nut and position the wiring harness bracket aside (if needed for clearance).
7. Remove the bolts, the electronic TB and the gasket. Discard the gasket.

To install:

8. Installation is the reverse of the removal procedure.
9. Note the following:
   a. Use a new throttle body gasket.
   b. Tighten the throttle body screws to 80 inch lbs. (9 Nm).

4.6L Engine

See Figure 227.

1. Before servicing the vehicle, refer to Precautions.
2. Disconnect the battery ground cable.
3. Remove the air cleaner outlet tube.
4. Disconnect the electronic throttle body (TB) electrical connectors.
5. Disconnect the throttle position (TP) sensor electrical connector.
6. Remove the bolts, the electronic TB and the gasket. Discard the gasket.

To install:

7. Installation is the reverse of the removal procedure, noting the following:
   a. Use a new throttle body gasket.
   b. Tighten the throttle body bolts to 89 inch lbs. (10 Nm).

1. Fuel Tank Pressure (FTP) sensor and vapor tube assembly quick connect coupling
2. FTP sensor and vapor tube assembly quick connect coupling
3. FTP sensor and vapor tube assembly quick connect coupling
4. FTP sensor and vapor tube assembly
5. FTP sensor and vapor tube assembly quick connect coupling
6. FTP sensor electrical connector
7. Vapor hose
8. Fuel tank shield
9. Evaporative Emission (EVAP) canister

36578_EXPL_G0169

Fig. 225 Evaporative Emission (EVAP) canister vent valve location

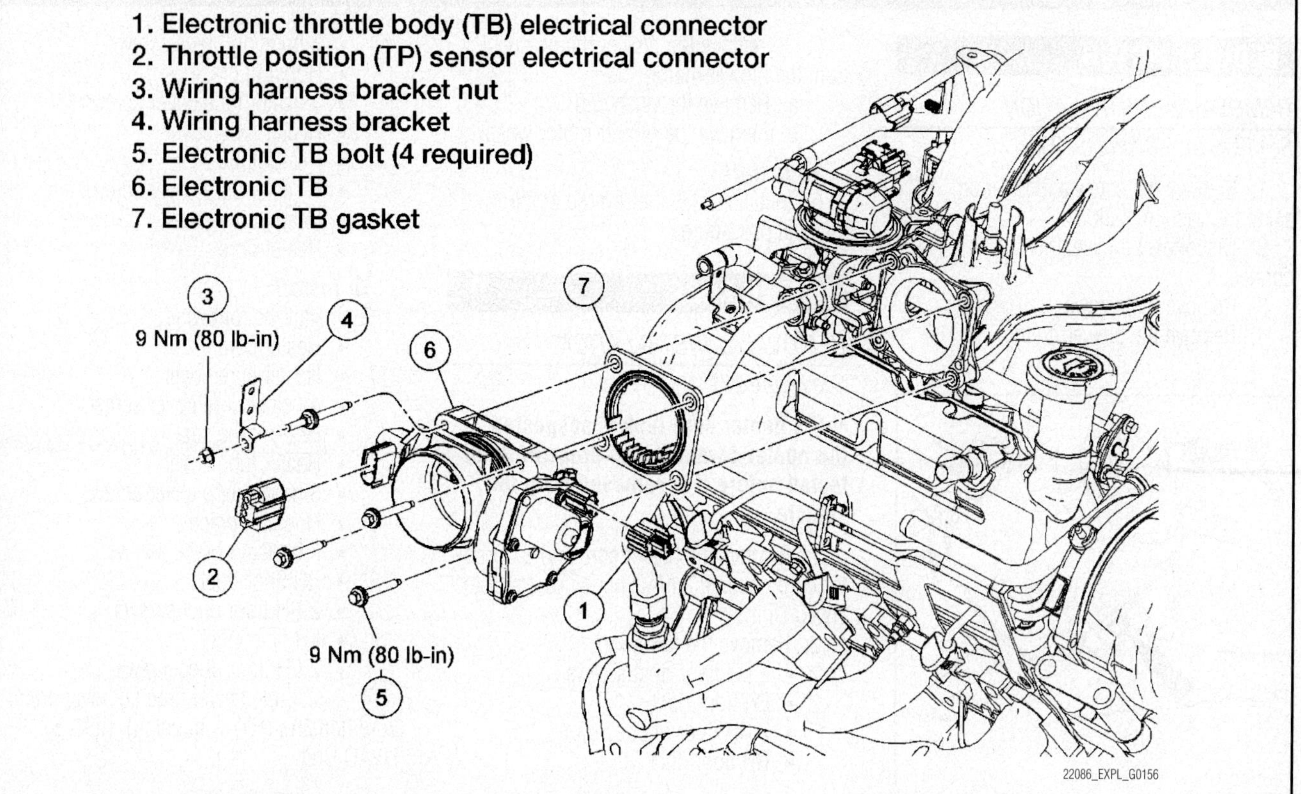

1. Electronic throttle body (TB) electrical connector
2. Throttle position (TP) sensor electrical connector
3. Wiring harness bracket nut
4. Wiring harness bracket
5. Electronic TB bolt (4 required)
6. Electronic TB
7. Electronic TB gasket

9 Nm (80 lb-in)

9 Nm (80 lb-in)

22086_EXPL_G0156

Fig. 226 Exploded view of the throttle body assembly—4.0L engine

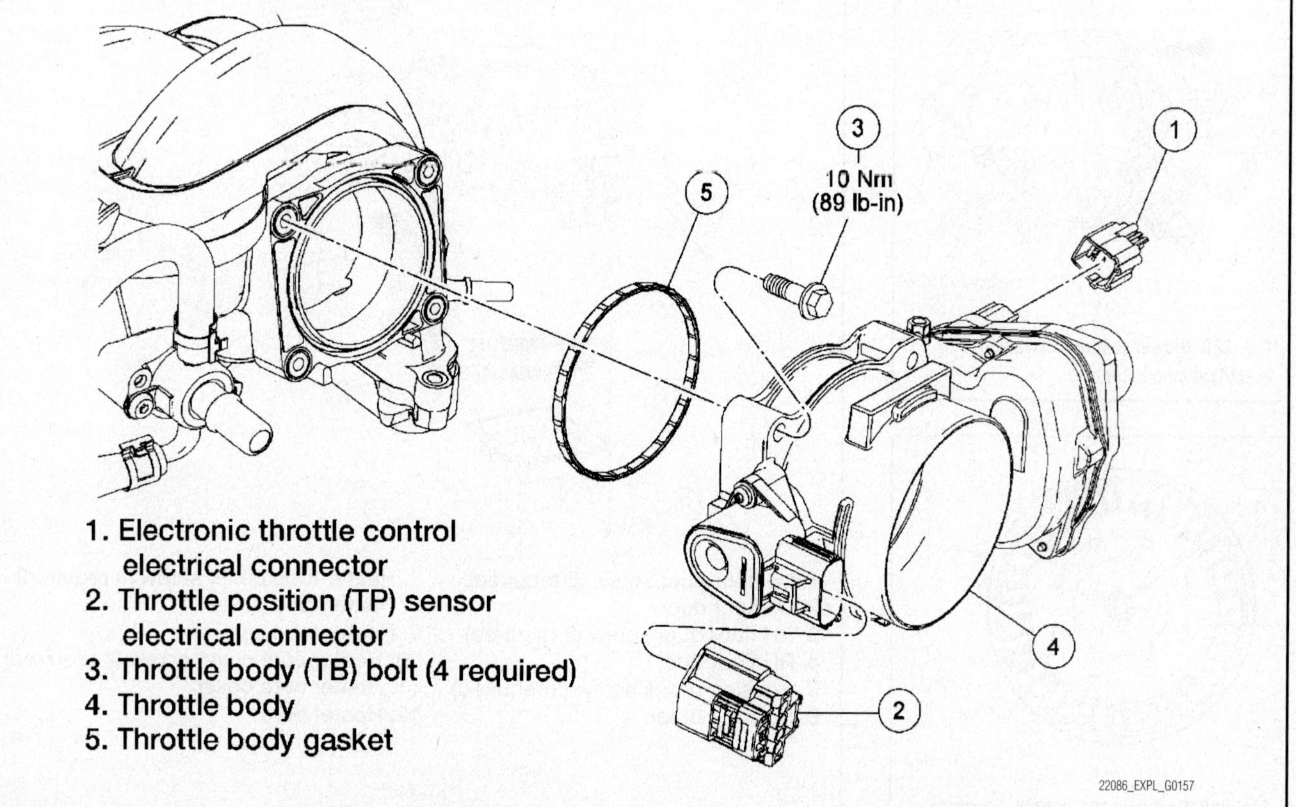

10 Nm
(89 lb-in)

1. Electronic throttle control
   electrical connector
2. Throttle position (TP) sensor
   electrical connector
3. Throttle body (TB) bolt (4 required)
4. Throttle body
5. Throttle body gasket

22086_EXPL_G0157

Fig. 227 Exploded view of the throttle body—4.6L engine

HEATING & AIR CONDITIONING SYSTEM

BLOWER MOTOR

REMOVAL & INSTALLATION

See Figures 228 through 230.

1. Remove the screw and position aside the vacuum tank.
2. Disconnect the electrical connector.
3. Remove the screws.
4. Remove the blower motor.

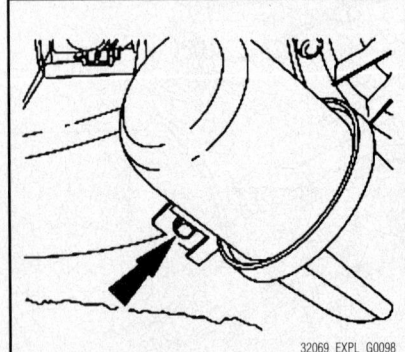

Fig. 228 Remove screw (arrow) from vacuum tank and position it aside

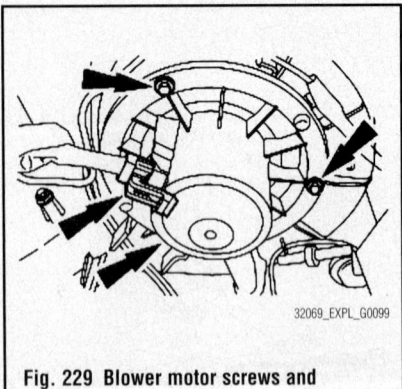

Fig. 229 Blower motor screws and electrical connector

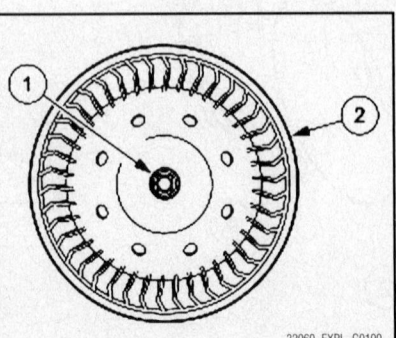

Fig. 230 Push clip (1) and blower motor wheel (2)

5. To remove the blower motor wheel from the blower motor:
   a. Remove the push clip.
   b. Remove the blower motor wheel.

To install:

6. Installation is the reverse of the removal procedure.

HEATER CORE

REMOVAL & INSTALLATION

See Figure 231.

➡ **If a heater core leak is suspected, the heater core must be pressure leak tested before it is removed from the vehicle.**

1. Remove the heater core and evaporator core housing (HVAC housing). Refer to HVAC Unit.
2. Remove the following:
   - 2 LH floor duct screws
   - LH floor duct
   - 2 RH floor duct screws
   - RH floor duct
   - 3 housing brace screws
   - Housing brace
   - 3 heater tube cover screws
   - Heater tube cover
   - Heater tube seal
   - 4 heater core cover screws
   - Heater core cover
   - Heater core

To install:

3. Install the following:
   - Heater core
   - Heater core cover
   - 4 heater core cover screws
   - Heater tube seal
   - Heater tube cover
   - 3 heater tube cover screws
   - Housing brace
   - 3 housing brace screws
   - RH floor duct
   - 2 RH floor duct screws
   - LH floor duct
   - 2 LH floor duct screws
4. Install the heater core and evaporator core housing (HVAC housing). Refer to HVAC Unit.

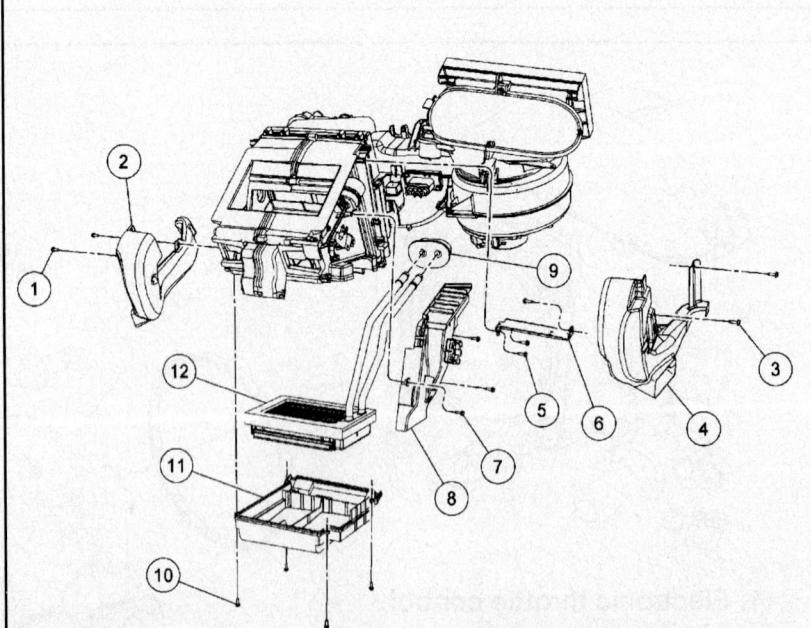

1. LH floor duct screw (2 required)
2. LH floor duct
3. RH floor duct screw (2 required)
4. RH floor duct
5. Housing brace screw (3 required)
6. Housing brace
7. Heater tube cover screw (3 required)
8. Heater tube cover
9. Heater tube seal
10. Heater core cover screw (4 required)
11. Heater core cover
12. Heater core

Fig. 231 Exploded view of the HVAC housing showing the heater core

HVAC UNIT

REMOVAL & INSTALLATION

See Figures 232 through 234.

➡ **If an evaporator core leak is suspected, the evaporator core must be vacuum leak tested before it is removed from the vehicle.**

➡ **Installation of a new suction accumulator is not required when repairing the air conditioning system, except when there is physical evidence of contamination from a failed A/C compressor or damage to the accumulator.**

➡ **Lubricate the coolant hoses with plain water only if needed.**

1. Recover the refrigerant.
2. Drain the engine coolant.
3. Remove the instrument panel.
4. Detach the wiring harness bracket (above the heater tube bracket) and position the harness aside.
5. Remove the heater tube bracket nut.
6. Remove the A/C line bracket nut at the dash panel.
7. Disconnect the 2 heater hose clamps at the heater core.
8. Disconnect the evaporator inlet fitting. Discard the O-ring seals.
9. Disconnect the evaporator outlet fitting. Discard the O-ring seals.
10. Disconnect the 2 vacuum connectors.
11. Detach the grommet and push the vacuum lines into the passenger compartment.
12. Remove the 4 HVAC housing nuts.
13. Disconnect the ground terminal bolt.
14. Remove the HVAC housing.

To install:

15. Position the HVAC housing into the vehicle.
16. Disconnect the ground terminal bolt.
17. Install the HVAC housing nuts. Tighten the nuts to 80 inch lbs. (9 Nm).
18. Position the grommet and vacuum lines back into the dash panel.
19. Connect the 2 vacuum connectors.
20. Install new O-ring seals and connect the evaporator inlet and outlet fittings.
21. Connect the heater hoses.
22. Install the A/C line bracket nut at the dash panel.
23. Install the heater tube bracket nut.
24. Attach the wiring harness bracket (above the heater tube bracket)
25. Install the instrument panel.
26. Evacuate and recharge the A/C system.
27. Refill the cooling system.
28. Perform an A/C system leak test.

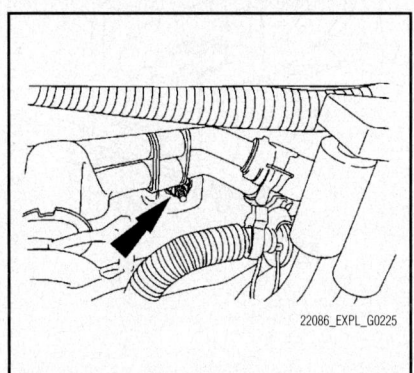

Fig. 232 Remove the heater tube bracket nut

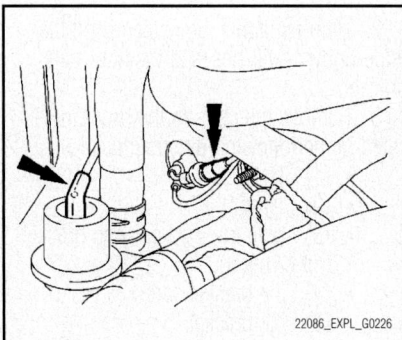

Fig. 233 Disconnect the 2 vacuum connectors

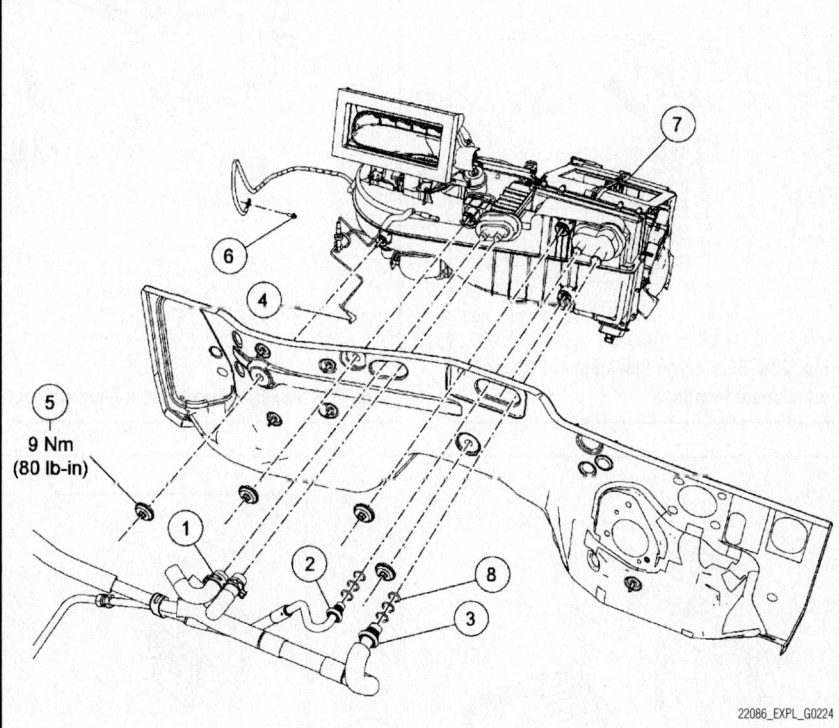

Fig. 234 Exploded view of the HVAC housing assembly: heater hoses (1), pressure hose (2), suction hose (3), vacuum connector (4), retaining nuts (5), screw (6), HVAC housing assembly (7), and O-ring seals (8)

AUXILIARY HEATING & AIR CONDITIONING SYSTEM

BLOWER MOTOR

REMOVAL & INSTALLATION

See Figures 235 through 237.

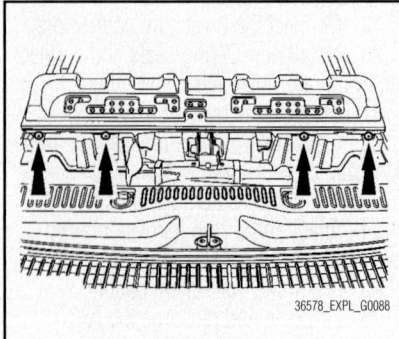

Fig. 235 Rear cargo management cover attachment locations

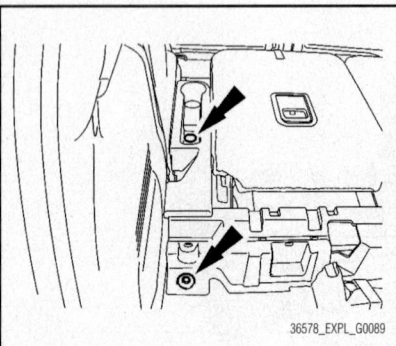

Fig. 236 Rear cargo management system attachment locations

1. Remove the bolts and the rear cargo management cover.
2. Remove the screw and pin-type retainer and remove the rear cargo management system.
3. Remove the access panel.
4. Remove the vent tube.
5. Disconnect the blower motor electrical connector.
6. Remove the 3 blower motor screws.
7. Remove the blower motor.
8. Remove the blower motor retainer.
9. Remove the blower motor wheel.

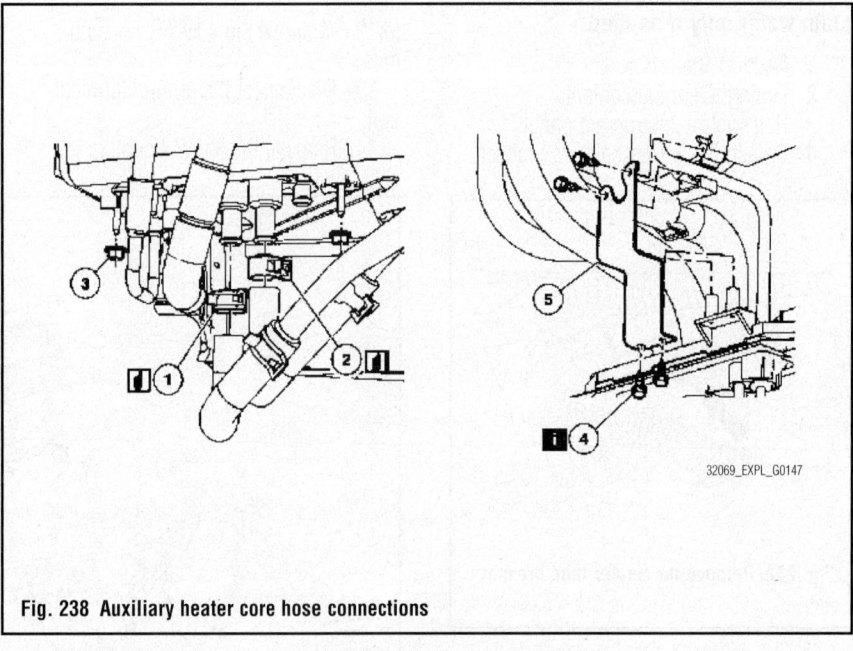

Fig. 238 Auxiliary heater core hose connections

To install:

10. To install, reverse the removal procedure.

HEATER CORE

REMOVAL & INSTALLATION

See Figures 238 through 240.

➡**Lubricate the coolant hoses with plain water only if needed.**

1. Position the vehicle on a hoist with the gear selector in NEUTRAL.

2. Using suitable tools, clamp-off the underbody heater hoses at the floor pan bracket.

3. Remove the parts in the order indicated in the following illustrations.
- (1) Clamp
- (2) Clamp
- (3) Auxiliary line floor pan bracket nut (2 req'd)
- (4) Line bracket screw (4 req'd)
- (5) Line bracket

➡**Item (4), the screw and line bracket are located inside the vehicle above the floor pan line bracket.**

- (6) Auxiliary harness electrical connector
- (7) Auxiliary housing bolt
- (8) Auxiliary housing bolt
- (9) Auxiliary housing nut
- (10) Blend door actuator electrical connector

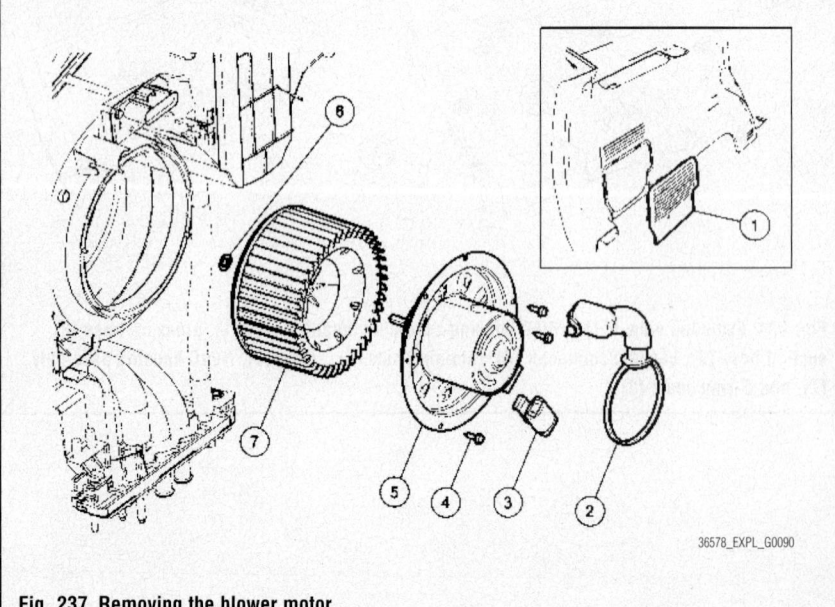

Fig. 237 Removing the blower motor

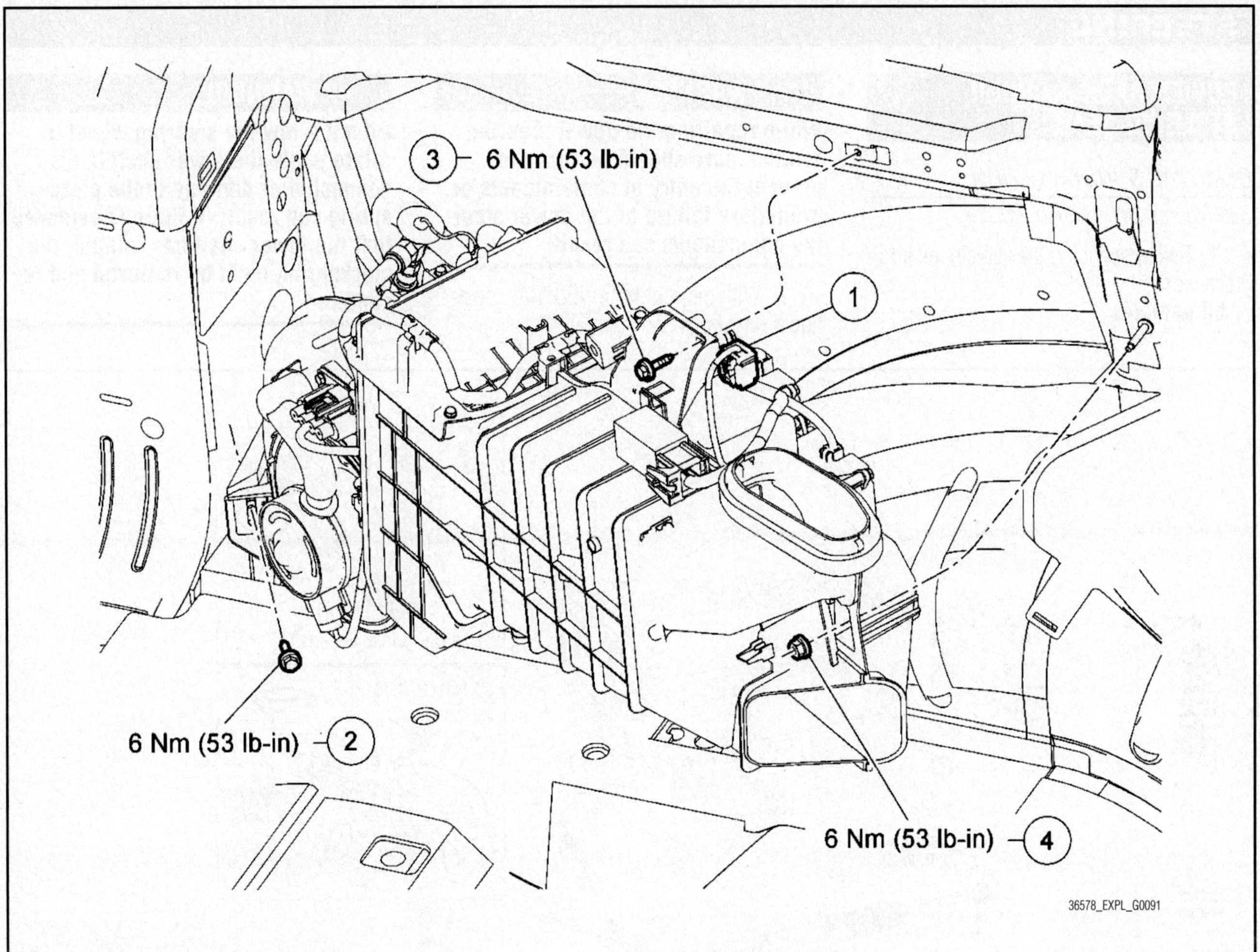

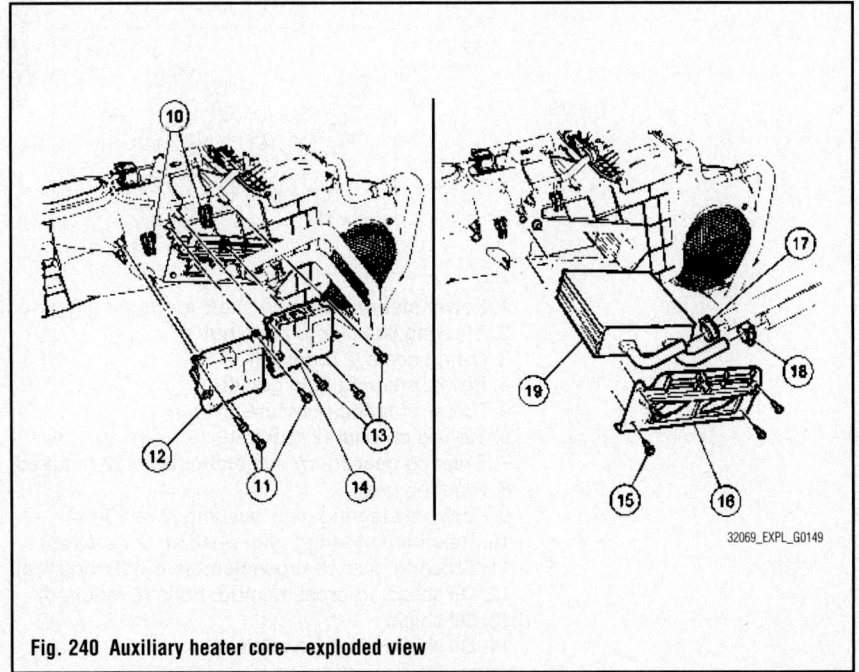

Fig. 239 Auxiliary heater core housing

- (11) Blend door actuator screw (3 req'd)
- (12) Auxiliary blend door actuator
- (13) Temperature blend door actuator screw (3 req'd)
- (14) Auxiliary temperature blend door actuator
- (15) Heater core cover screw (4 req'd)
- (16) Heater core cover
- (17) Clamp
- (18) Clamp
- (19) Auxiliary heater core

To install:
4. Installation is the reverse of the removal procedure.
5. Fill the engine cooling system.
6. Observe the following tightening specifications:
- Auxiliary housing bolts, 53 inch lbs (6 Nm)
- Auxiliary housing nut, 53 inch lbs (6 Nm)

Fig. 240 Auxiliary heater core—exploded view

STEERING

POWER RACK & PINION STEERING GEAR

REMOVAL & INSTALLATION

See Figures 241 through 243.

1. Before servicing the vehicle, refer to Precautions.

All vehicles

❋❋ WARNING

While repairing the power steering system, care should be taken to prevent the entry of contaminants or premature failure of the power steering components can result.

2. With the vehicle in NEUTRAL, position it on a hoist.

❋❋ WARNING

Do not allow the steering wheel to rotate while the lower shaft is disconnected or damage to the clockspring can result. If there is evidence that the lower shaft has rotated, the clockspring must be removed and re-centered.

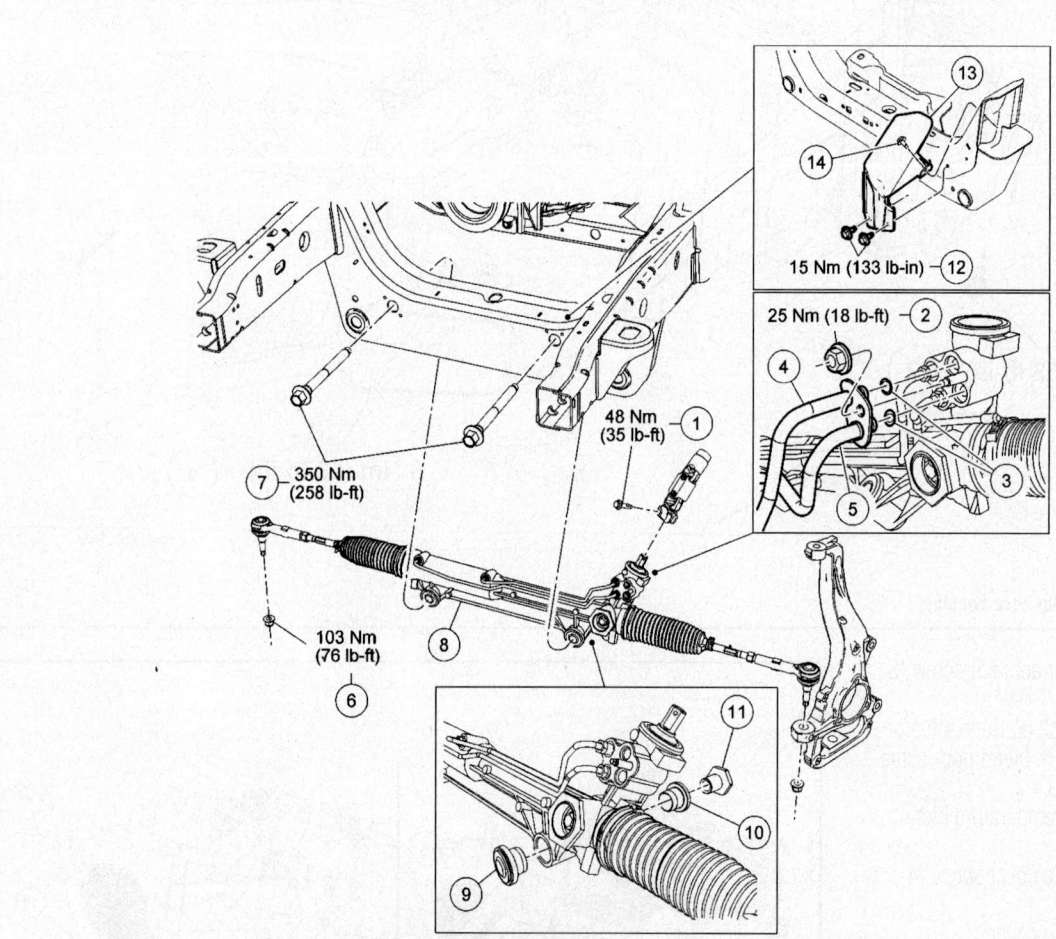

1. Lower steering column shaft-to-steering gear bolt
2. Steering line clamp plate nut
3. O-ring seals (2 required)
4. Power steering fluid cooler
5. Power steering pressure line
6. Tie-rod end nut (2 required)
7. Steering gear-to-crossmember bolts (2 required)
8. Steering gear
9. Forward steering gear bushing (2 required)
10. Rearward steering gear bushing (2 required)
11. Steering gear-to-crossmember nut (2 required)
12. Oil shield-to-crossmember bolts (2 required)
13. Oil shield
14. Oil shield pin-type retainer

36578_EXPL_G0079

Fig. 241 Steering gear and related parts

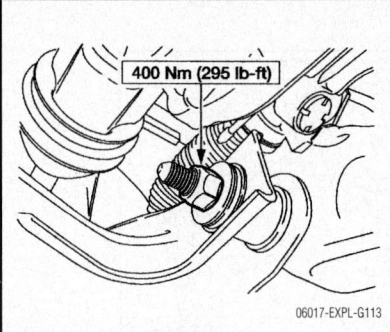

Fig. 242 Lower arm forward nut and flag bolt

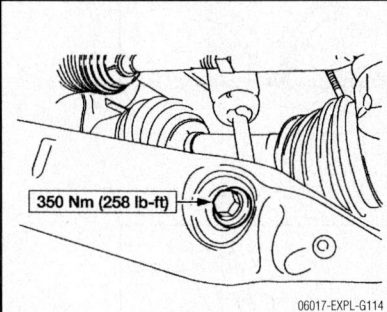

Fig. 243 Shock absorber-to-lower arm bolt and flag nut

3. Hold the steering wheel in the straight-ahead position using a suitable device.

4. Using a suitable suction device, drain the power steering fluid reservoir.

5. Remove the 2 bolts and the oil drip shield.

➡**Install a new lower shaft-to-steering gear bolt.**

6. Remove and discard the lower shaft-to-steering gear bolt.

7. Disconnect the lower shaft from the steering gear.

8. Remove the steering line clamp plate nut.

9. Rotate the steering line clamp plate and disconnect the power steering lines.

➡**New O-rings must be installed whenever the power steering lines are disconnected.**

10. Remove and discard the 2 O-rings.

➡**New cotter pins must be installed.**

11. Remove and discard the 2 cotter pins.

➡**New tie rod end nuts must be installed.**

12. Remove and discard the 2 tie rod end nuts.

✳✳ WARNING

Do not damage the tie rod end boot when installing the special tool.

13. Using the special tool, separate the 2 tie rod ends from the wheel knuckle.

14. Remove the 2 steering gear-to-crossmember nuts and bolts.

15. Remove the 2 bolts and remove the steering gear bracket.

4WD vehicles

➡**On 4WD vehicles, the following steps (left lower arm only) must be carried out to provide clearance to remove the steering gear.**

✳✳ WARNING

Do not tighten the left lower arm inboard mounting nuts until the installation procedure is complete and the weight of the vehicle is resting on the wheel and tire assemblies. Make sure to tighten the lower arm forward nut before tightening the lower arm-to-frame nuts.

➡**It is not necessary to disconnect the left lower ball joint.**

16. Remove the lower arm forward nut and flag bolt. Discard the nut.

17. Remove and discard the 2 lower arm-to-frame nuts.

18. Remove the shock absorber-to-lower arm bolt and flag nut. Discard the flag nut.

19. Remove the stabilizer bar connecting link nut and disconnect the link.

All vehicles

20. Remove the steering gear from the left side of the vehicle.

To install:

21. Installation is the reverse of the removal procedure.

22. Install 2 new O-rings. Fill the power steering system

23. Observe the following torque specifications:

- Oil drip shield: 11 ft. lbs. (15 Nm)
- Lower shaft-to-steering gear bolt: 35 ft. lbs. (48 Nm)
- Fluid line clamp bolt: 18 ft. lbs. (25 Nm)
- Tie rod end nuts: 76 ft. lbs. (103 Nm)
- Steering gear-to-crossmember nuts and bolts: 258 ft. lbs. (350 Nm)
- Steering gear bracket bolts: 52 ft. lbs. (70 Nm)

- Lower arm forward nut and flag bolt: 296 ft. lbs. (400 Nm)
- Lower arm rearward nut and flag bolt: 148 ft. lbs. (200 Nm)
- Shock absorber-to-lower arm bolt and flag nut: 258 ft. lbs. (350 Nm)
- Stabilizer bar connecting link nut: 26 ft. lbs. (35 Nm)

POWER STEERING PUMP

REMOVAL & INSTALLATION

4.0L Engine

See Figures 244 and 245.

✳✳ WARNING

While repairing the power steering system, care should be taken to prevent the entry of contaminants or premature failure of the power steering components can result.

1. Using a suitable suction device, drain the power steering fluid reservoir.

2. With the vehicle in NEUTRAL, position it on a hoist.

3. Remove the power steering pump pulley as follows:

a. Disconnect the fan clutch electrical connector.

b. Remove the fan clutch wiring harness bracket bolt and position harness aside.

c. Loosen the 3 power steering pump pulley bolts.

d. Rotate the tensioner and remove the engine accessory drive belt from the power steering pump pulley.

e. Remove the 3 bolts and the power steering pump pulley.

4. Remove the pressure line bracket-to-engine bolt.

5. Remove the power steering fluid reservoir-to-pump hose bracket bolt.

6. Release the reservoir-to-pump hose clamp and disconnect the hose.

7. Disconnect the pressure line-to-pump fitting. Remove and discard the Teflon® O-ring seal.

8. Remove the 3 bolts and the power steering pump.

To install:

9. Using the special tool, install a new Teflon® O-ring seal to the pressure line fitting.

10. Position the power steering pump and install the 3 bolts. Torque the bolts to 18 ft. lbs. (25 Nm).

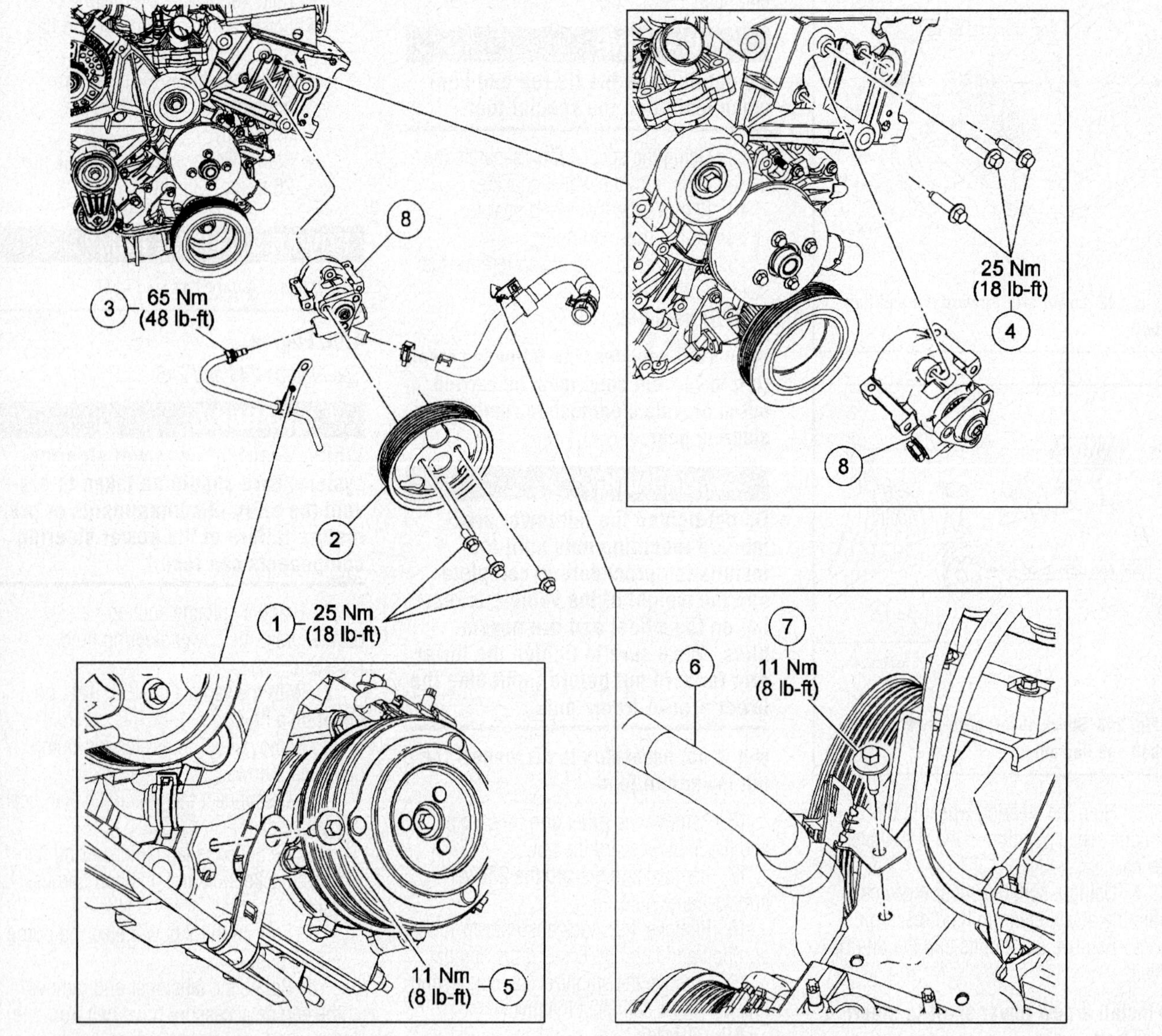

③ 65 Nm (48 lb-ft)

⑧

25 Nm (18 lb-ft) ④

⑧

① 25 Nm (18 lb-ft)

②

11 Nm (8 lb-ft) ⑤

⑥ ⑦ 11 Nm (8 lb-ft)

1. Power steering pump pulley bolts (3 required)
2. Power steering pump pulley
3. Pressure line-to-pump fitting
4. Power steering pump bolts (3 required)
5. Pressure line bracket-to-engine bolt
6. Power steering fluid reservoir-to-pump hose
7. Power steering fluid reservoir-to-pump hose bracket bolt
8. Power steering pump

22086_EXPL_G0202

Fig. 244 Showing the power steering pump, reservoir and related components—4.0L Engine

11. Connect the pressure line-to-pump fitting. Tighten the fitting to 48 ft. lbs. (65 Nm).

12. Connect the reservoir-to-pump hose.

13. Install the power steering fluid reservoir-to-pump hose bracket bolt to 8 ft. lbs. (11 Nm).

14. Install the pressure line bracket-to-engine bolt to 8 ft. lbs. (11 Nm).

15. Install the power steering pump pulley as follows:

a. Install the power steering pump pulley and loosely install the bolts.

b. Install the engine accessory drive belt to the power steering pump pulley.

c. Torque the 3 bolts for the power steering pump pulley to 18 ft. lbs. (25 Nm).

d. Install and tighten the fan clutch wiring harness bracket bolt.

e. Connect the fan clutch electrical connector.

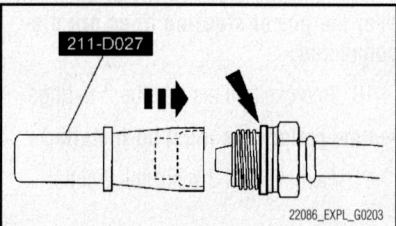

211-D027

22086_EXPL_G0203

Fig. 245 Using the special tool, install a new Teflon® O-ring seal to the pressure line fitting

16. Fill and bleed the power steering system. Refer to Bleeding.

4.6L Engine

See Figure 246.

1. Using a suitable suction device, drain the power steering fluid reservoir.

2. With the vehicle in NEUTRAL, position it on a hoist.

3. Remove the power steering pump pulley.

4. Remove the pressure line bracket-to-engine nut.

5. Compress the clamp and disconnect the reservoir-to-pump hose.

6. Disconnect the pressure line-to-pump fitting.

7. Remove and discard the Teflon® O-ring seal.

8. Remove the 2 engine wiring bracket nuts and position the wiring harness and ground cable aside.

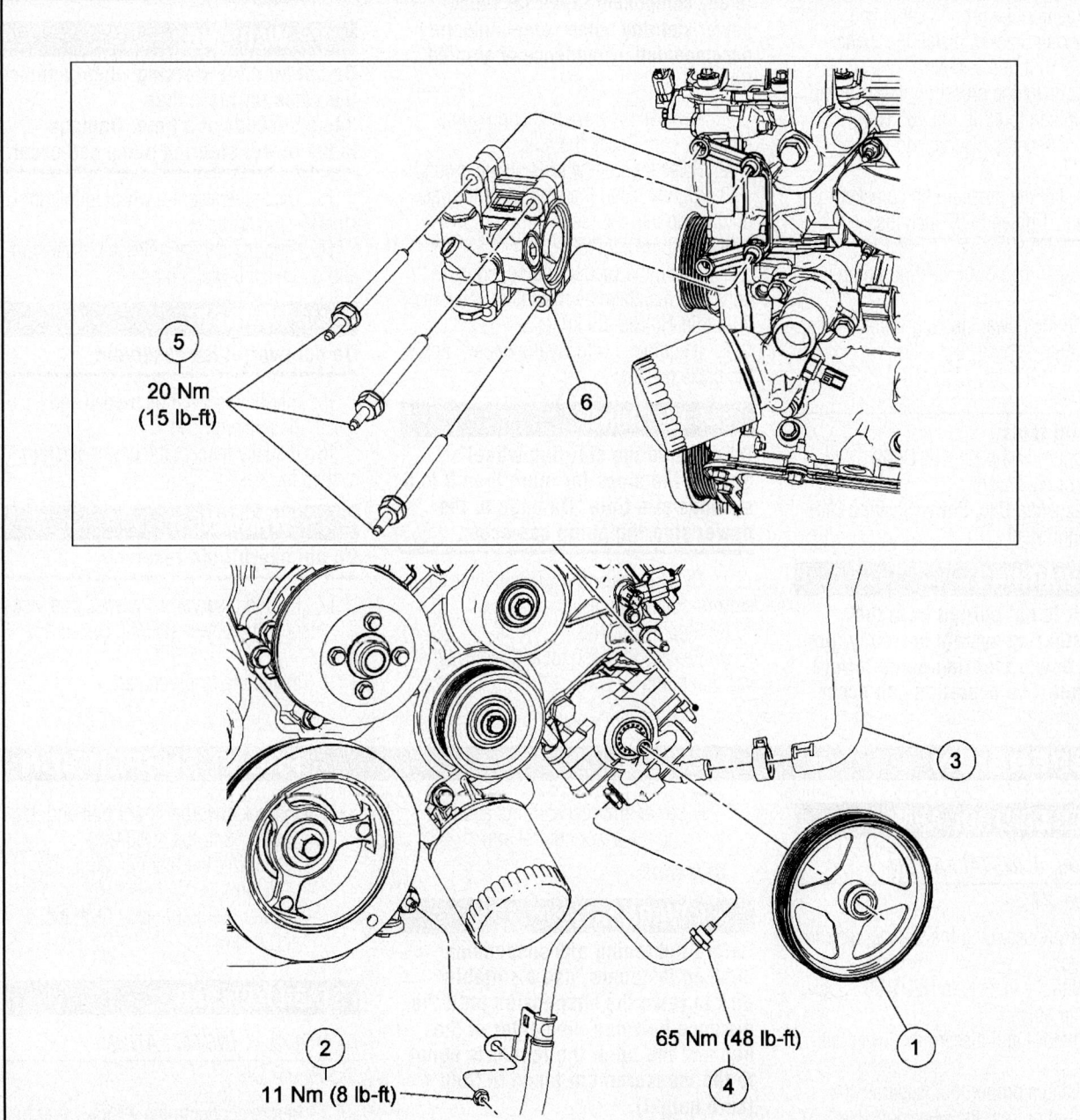

1. Power steering pump pulley
2. Pressure line bracket-to-engine nut
3. Power steering fluid reservoir-to-pump hose
4. Pressure line-to-pump fitting
5. Upper/ lower power steering pump bolts (3 required)
6. Power steering pump

22086_EXPL_G0256

Fig. 246 Showing the power steering pump, hoses and reservoir mounting—4.6L Engine

9. Remove the 3 bolts and the power steering pump.

To install:

10. Using the special tool, install a new Teflon® O-ring seal on the pressure line-to-pump fitting.

11. Position the power steering pump and install the 3 bolts. Tighten to 15 ft. lbs. (20 Nm).

12. Position the ground cable and engine wiring bracket. Install the 2 nuts. Tighten to 15 ft. lbs. (20 Nm).

13. Connect the pressure line-to-pump fitting. Tighten to 48 ft. lbs. (65 Nm).

14. Connect the reservoir-to-pump hose.

15. Install the pressure line bracket-to-engine nut. Tighten to 97 inch lbs. (11 Nm).

16. Install the power steering pump pulley.

17. Fill the power steering system. Refer to Bleeding.

BLEEDING

Special tools:
- Vacuum Pump Kit 416-D002 (D95L-7559-A) or equivalent
- Evacuation Cap, Power Steering 211-265 or equivalent

✳✳ WARNING

If the air is not purged from the power steering system correctly, premature power steering pump failure can result. The condition can occur

on pre-delivery vehicles with evidence of aerated fluid or on vehicles that have had steering component repairs.

➡ **A whine heard from the power steering pump can be caused by air in the system. The power steering purge procedure must be carried out prior to any component repair for which power steering noise complaints are accompanied by evidence of aerated fluid.**

1. Remove the power steering pump reservoir cap. Check the fluid.
2. Raise the front wheels off the ground.
3. Tightly insert the stopper of the vacuum pump into the reservoir.
4. Start the engine.
5. Install the vacuum pump, apply vacuum, and maintain the maximum vacuum of 20–25 in-Hg (68–85 kPa).
6. If equipped with Hydro-Boost®, apply the brake pedal twice.

✳✳ WARNING

Do not hold the steering wheel against the stops for more than 3 to 5 seconds at a time. Damage to the power steering pump can occur.

7. Cycle the steering wheel fully from stop-to-stop 10 times.
8. Stop the engine.
9. Release the vacuum and remove the vacuum pump.

✳✳ WARNING

Do not overfill the reservoir.

10. Fill the reservoir.
   a. Use approved transmission fluid.
11. Start the engine.
12. Install the vacuum pump. Apply and maintain the maximum vacuum of 20–25 in-Hg (68–85 kPa).

✳✳ WARNING

Do not hold the steering wheel against the stops for more than 3 to 5 seconds at a time. Damage to the power steering pump can occur.

13. Cycle the steering wheel fully from stop-to-stop 10 times.
14. Stop the engine, release the vacuum and remove the vacuum pump.

✳✳ WARNING

Do not overfill the reservoir.

15. Fill the reservoir as needed and install the reservoir cap.
16. Visually inspect the power steering system for leaks.

✳✳ WARNING

Do not overfill the reservoir.

17. Fill the reservoir as needed and visually inspect the power steering system for leaks.
18. Install the reservoir cap.

SUSPENSION

LOWER CONTROL ARM

REMOVAL & INSTALLATION

See Figure 247.

1. Before servicing the vehicle, refer to Precautions.
2. With the vehicle in NEUTRAL, position it on a hoist.
3. Remove and discard the lower ball joint nut.
4. Using a proper tool, separate the lower ball joint from the wheel knuckle.
5. Remove the following:
   - Stabilizer bar link nut (discard the nut)
   - Stabilizer bar link assembly
   - Shock absorber lower bolt and flag nut (discard the fasteners)
   - Lower arm forward nut and bolt (discard the fasteners)

- Lower arm rearward nut and bolt and the lower control arm

To install:

✳✳ WARNING

Before tightening any suspension bushing fasteners, use a suitable jack to raise the suspension until the distance between the center of the hub and the lip of the fender is equal to the measurement taken in Step 1 (curb height).

6. Installation is the reverse of the removal procedure, using new fasteners.
7. Note the following tightening specifications:
   - Lower control arm rearward nut and bolt: 148 ft. lbs. (200 Nm)
   - Lower arm forward nut and bolt: 296 ft. lbs. (400 Nm)

FRONT SUSPENSION

- Shock absorber lower bolt and flag nut: 258 ft. lbs. (350 Nm)
- Stabilizer bar link nut: 26 ft. lbs. (35 Nm)
- Lower ball joint nut: 111 ft. lbs. (150 Nm)

STABILIZER BAR

REMOVAL & INSTALLATION

See Figure 248.

1. Before servicing the vehicle, refer to Precautions.
2. Remove and discard the 2 stabilizer bar nut and grommets.
3. Remove the 2 stabilizer bar studs.
4. Remove the 2 stabilizer bar links.

➡ **Inspect and clean the mating surfaces and the internal threads. Make sure all mating surfaces are free of**

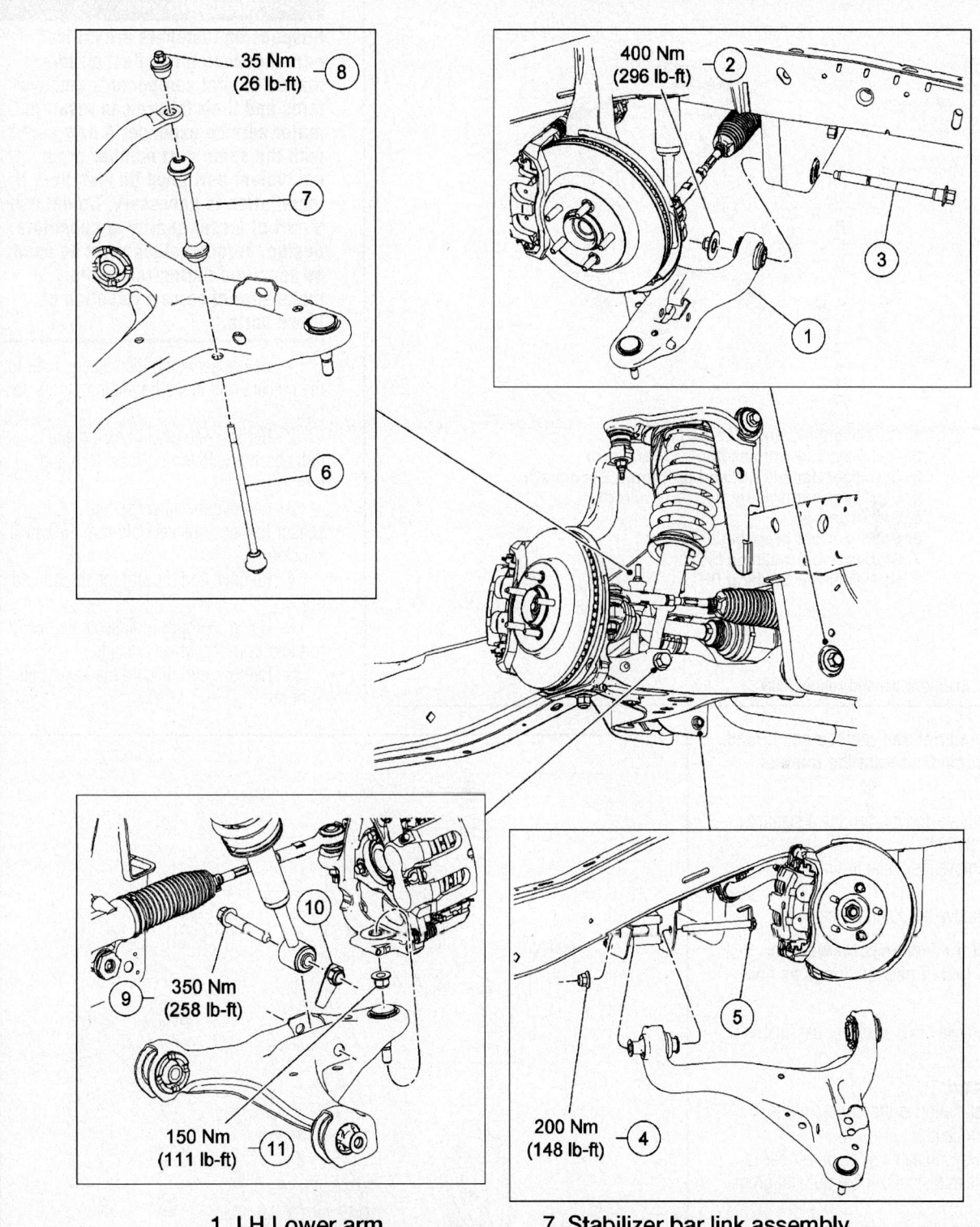

1. LH Lower arm
2. Lower arm forward nut
3. Lower arm forward bolt
4. Lower arm rearward nut
5. Lower arm rearward bolt
6. Stabilizer bar link stud
7. Stabilizer bar link assembly
8. Stabilizer bar link nut
9. Shock absorber lower bolt
10. Shock absorber lower flag nut
11. Lower ball joint nut

22086_EXPL_G0183

Fig. 247 Exploded view of the front suspension, showing the lower control arm and components

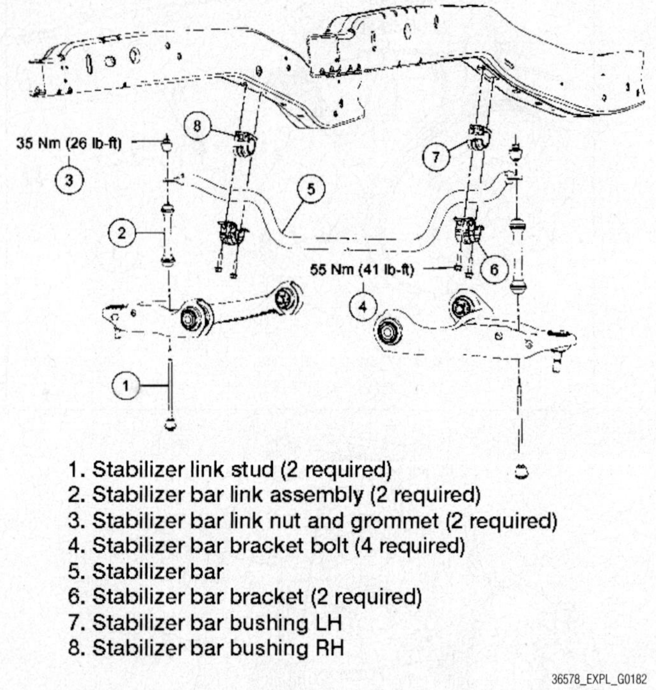

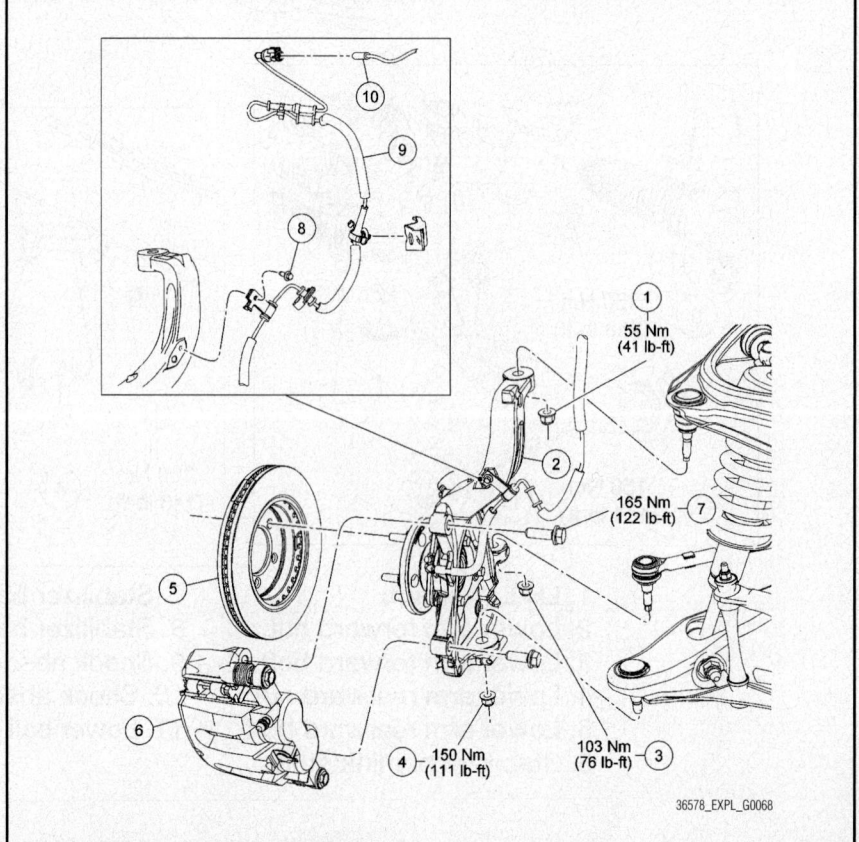

35 Nm (26 lb-ft)

55 Nm (41 lb-ft)

1. Stabilizer link stud (2 required)
2. Stabilizer bar link assembly (2 required)
3. Stabilizer bar link nut and grommet (2 required)
4. Stabilizer bar bracket bolt (4 required)
5. Stabilizer bar
6. Stabilizer bar bracket (2 required)
7. Stabilizer bar bushing LH
8. Stabilizer bar bushing RH

36578_EXPL_G0182

Fig. 248 Stabilizer bar and control links

✳✳ WARNING

Suspension fasteners are critical parts because they affect performance of vital components and systems and their failure can result in major service expense. A new part with the same part number or an equivalent part must be installed, if installation is necessary. Do not use a part of lesser quality or substitute design. Torque values must be used as specified during reassembly to make sure of correct retention of these parts.

1. Before servicing the vehicle, refer to the precautions in the beginning of this section.
2. Remove the wheel bearing and hub assembly. Refer to Wheel Hub and Bearing.
3. Remove the wheel speed sensor harness bracket bolt from the wheel knuckle.
4. Remove and discard the tie rod end nut.
5. Using a proper tool, separate the tie rod end from the wheel knuckle.
6. Remove and discard the lower ball joint nut.

foreign material and remove any thread locking compound from the internal threads.

5. Remove and discard the 4 stabilizer bar-to-frame bolts.
6. Remove the 2 stabilizer bar brackets.
7. Remove the stabilizer bar.

➡**Inspect the bushings for wear or damage. Install new bushings as necessary.**

8. Remove the 2 stabilizer bar bushings.

To install:

9. Installation is the reverse of the removal procedure
10. Always install new stabilizer bar-to-frame bolts and stabilizer bar nut and grommets.
11. Tighten the stabilizer bar bracket bolts to 41 ft. lbs. (55 Nm), with the vehicle at curb weight.

STEERING KNUCKLE

REMOVAL & INSTALLATION

See Figure 249.

55 Nm (41 lb-ft)

165 Nm (122 lb-ft)

150 Nm (111 lb-ft)

103 Nm (76 lb-ft)

36578_EXPL_G0068

Fig. 249 Steering knuckle exploded view

7. Using a proper tool, separate the lower arm ball joint from the wheel knuckle.

8. Remove and discard the upper ball joint nut.

9. Using a proper tool, separate the upper arm ball joint from the wheel knuckle.

10. Remove the wheel knuckle.

To install:

11. Installation is the reverse of the removal procedure.

12. Use new fasteners where indicated.

13. Note the following tightening specifications:

- Wheel speed sensor: 71 inch lbs. (8 Nm)
- Upper ball joint nut: 41 ft. lbs. (55 Nm)
- Lower ball joint nut: 111 ft. lbs. (150 Nm)
- Tie rod end nut: 76 ft. lbs. (103 Nm)

14. Check and, if necessary, align the front end.

STRUT

REMOVAL & INSTALLATION

See Figures 250 and 251.

❊❊ WARNING

All vehicles are equipped with gas-pressurized shock absorbers which will extend unassisted. Do not apply heat or flame to the shock absorbers during removal or component servicing. Failure to follow these instructions may result in personal injury.

1. Before servicing the vehicle, refer to Precautions.

2. Measure the distance from the center of the hub to the lip of the fender with the vehicle in a level, static ground position (curb height).

3. Remove and discard the 3 shock absorber upper mount nuts.

4. With the vehicle in NEUTRAL, position it on a hoist.

5. Using a suitable jack, support the lower control arm near the lower ball joint.

6. Remove and discard the stabilizer bar link nut and grommet and then remove the stabilizer bar link assembly.

7. Remove the shock absorber lower bolt and flag nut.

8. Remove and discard the upper ball joint nut.

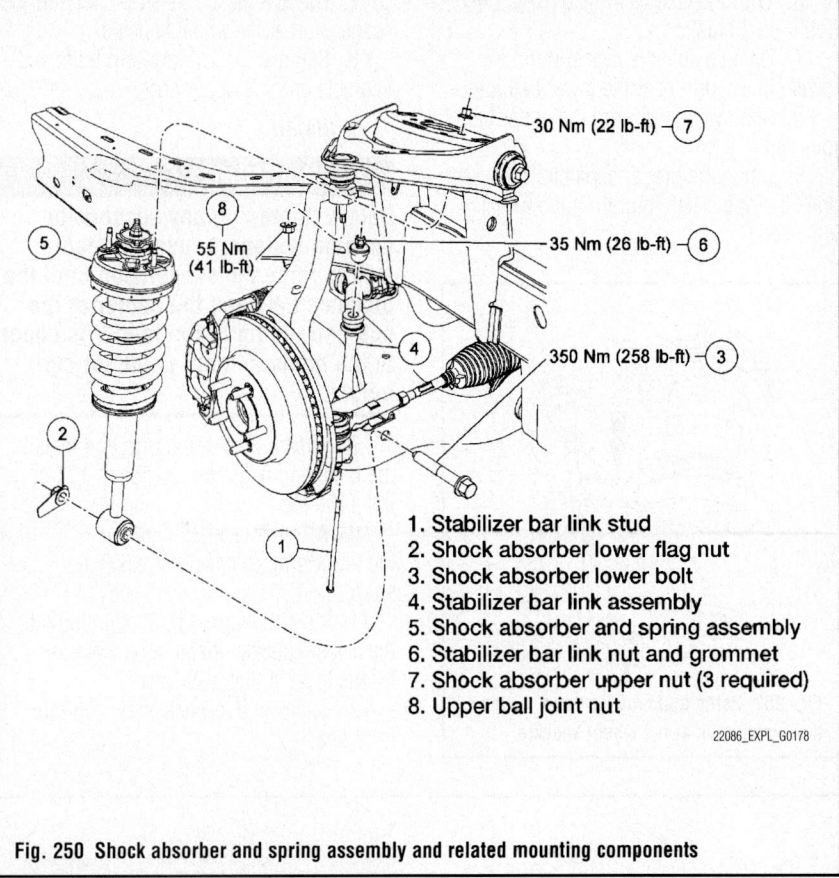

1. Stabilizer bar link stud
2. Shock absorber lower flag nut
3. Shock absorber lower bolt
4. Stabilizer bar link assembly
5. Shock absorber and spring assembly
6. Stabilizer bar link nut and grommet
7. Shock absorber upper nut (3 required)
8. Upper ball joint nut

30 Nm (22 lb-ft) — 7
35 Nm (26 lb-ft) — 6
350 Nm (258 lb-ft) — 3
55 Nm (41 lb-ft)

22086_EXPL_G0178

Fig. 250 Shock absorber and spring assembly and related mounting components

❊❊ WARNING

Do not use a hammer to separate the ball joint from the wheel knuckle or damage to the wheel knuckle can result.

9. Using the proper separator tool, separate the upper ball joint from the wheel knuckle.

10. While lowering the suspension, remove the shock and spring assembly.

To install:

➡**Before tightening any suspension bushing fasteners, use a suitable jack to raise the suspension until the distance between the center of the hub and the lip of the fender is equal to the measurement taken in Step 1 (curb height).**

11. Position the shock absorber and spring assembly and raise the suspension into normal position.

12. Install a new upper ball joint nut. Torque to 41 ft. lbs. (55 Nm).

13. Install the lower shock absorber bolt and flag nut. Torque to 258 ft. lbs. (350 Nm).

14. Install a new stabilizer bar link nut and grommet. Torque to 26 ft. lbs. (35 Nm).

15. Install 3 new upper shock mounting nuts. Torque to 22 ft. lbs. (30 Nm).

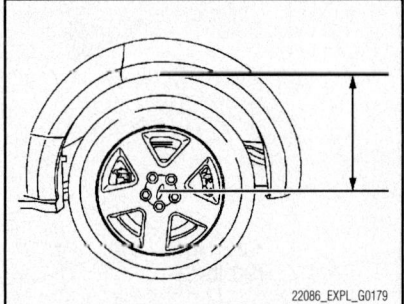

22086_EXPL_G0179

Fig. 251 Measure the distance from the center of the hub to the lip of the fender with the vehicle in a level, static ground position (curb height)

16. Lower the vehicle.

UPPER CONTROL ARM

REMOVAL & INSTALLATION

See Figures 251 and 252.

1. Before servicing the vehicle, refer to the precautions in the beginning of this section.

2. Measure the distance from the center of the hub to the lip of the fender with the vehicle in a level, static ground position (curb height).

3. With the vehicle in NEUTRAL, position it on a hoist.

4. Using a suitable jack support the lower control arm near the lower ball joint.

5. Remove and discard the upper ball joint nut.

6. Using the proper separator tool, separate the upper ball joint from the wheel knuckle.

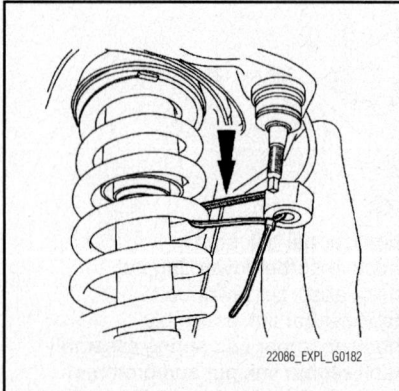

Fig. 252 Using a plastic tie strap, support the suspension at the wheel knuckle

7. Using a plastic tie strap, support the suspension at the wheel knuckle.

8. Remove the 2 upper arm bolts and flag nuts and the upper arm.

To install:

✳✳ WARNING

Before tightening any suspension bushing fasteners, use a suitable jack to raise the suspension until the distance between the center of the hub and the lip of the fender is equal to the measurement taken for curb height.

9. Position the upper arm and install the bolts and flag nuts. Torque to 111 ft. lbs. (150 Nm).

10. With the jack still under the lower arm, remove the plastic tie strap.

11. Insert the upper ball joint stud into the wheel knuckle. Install a new nut and torque to 41 ft. lbs. (55 Nm).

12. Check and, if necessary, align the front end.

WHEEL HUB & BEARING

REMOVAL & INSTALLATION

✳✳ WARNING

Suspension fasteners are critical parts because they affect performance of vital components and systems and their failure can result in major service expense. A new part with the same part number or an equivalent part must be installed, if installation is necessary. Do not use a part of lesser quality or substitute design. Torque values must be used as specified during reassembly to make sure of correct retention of these parts.

2WD Models
See Figure 253.

1. With the vehicle in NEUTRAL, position it on a hoist.

2. Remove the bolts and position the caliper, pads and anchor plate assembly

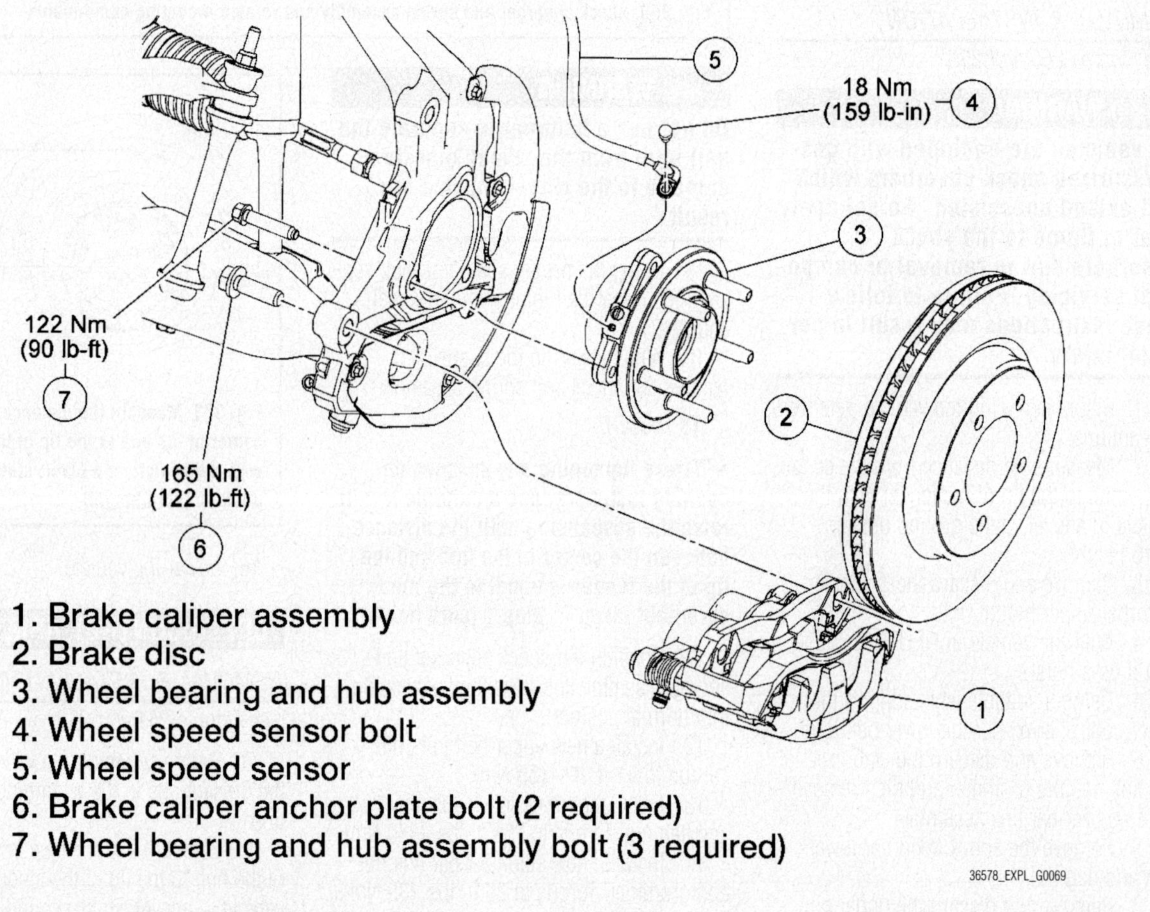

122 Nm
(90 lb-ft)
7

165 Nm
(122 lb-ft)
6

18 Nm
(159 lb-in)
4

5

3

2

1

1. Brake caliper assembly
2. Brake disc
3. Wheel bearing and hub assembly
4. Wheel speed sensor bolt
5. Wheel speed sensor
6. Brake caliper anchor plate bolt (2 required)
7. Wheel bearing and hub assembly bolt (3 required)

Fig. 253 Wheel hub and bearing with torques—Front, 2WD

aside. Discard the bolts. b. Support the caliper and anchor plate assembly using mechanic's wire.

3. Remove the brake disc.

4. Remove the wheel speed sensor bolt and disconnect the wheel speed sensor from the wheel bearing and hub assembly.

5. Remove the 3 bolts and the wheel bearing and hub assembly.

To install:

6. Install the wheel bearing and hub assembly. Tighten the 3 bolts to 90 ft. lbs. (122 Nm).

7. Install the wheel speed sensor to the wheel bearing and hub assembly. Connect the electrical connector and install the bolt. Tighten bolt to 159 inch lbs. (18 Nm).

8. Install the brake disc.

9. Install the caliper and anchor plate assembly. Tighten the bolts to 122 ft. lbs. (165 Nm).

4WD Models

See Figure 254.

1. With the vehicle in NEUTRAL, position it on a hoist.

2. Remove and discard the halfshaft nut and washer.

3. separate the outboard CV joint from the wheel hub.

4. Remove the bolts and position the caliper, pads and anchor plate assembly aside. Discard the bolts. Support the caliper and anchor plate assembly using mechanic's wire.

5. Remove the brake disc.

6. Remove the wheel speed sensor bolt and disconnect the wheel speed sensor from the wheel bearing and hub assembly.

7. Remove the 3 bolts and the wheel bearing and hub assembly.

To install:

8. Install the wheel bearing and hub assembly. Tighten the 3 bolts to 90 ft. lbs. (122 Nm).

9. Install the wheel speed sensor to the wheel bearing and hub assembly. Connect the electrical connector and install the bolt.

10. Install the brake disc.

11. Install the caliper and anchor plate assembly. Tighten the bolts to 122 ft. lbs. (165 Nm).

12. Install the outboard CV joint to the wheel hub.

13. Install a new nut and washer to the halfshaft. Tight the nut to 184 ft. lbs. (250 Nm).

14. Lower the vehicle.

ADJUSTMENT

No adjustments are possible or necessary

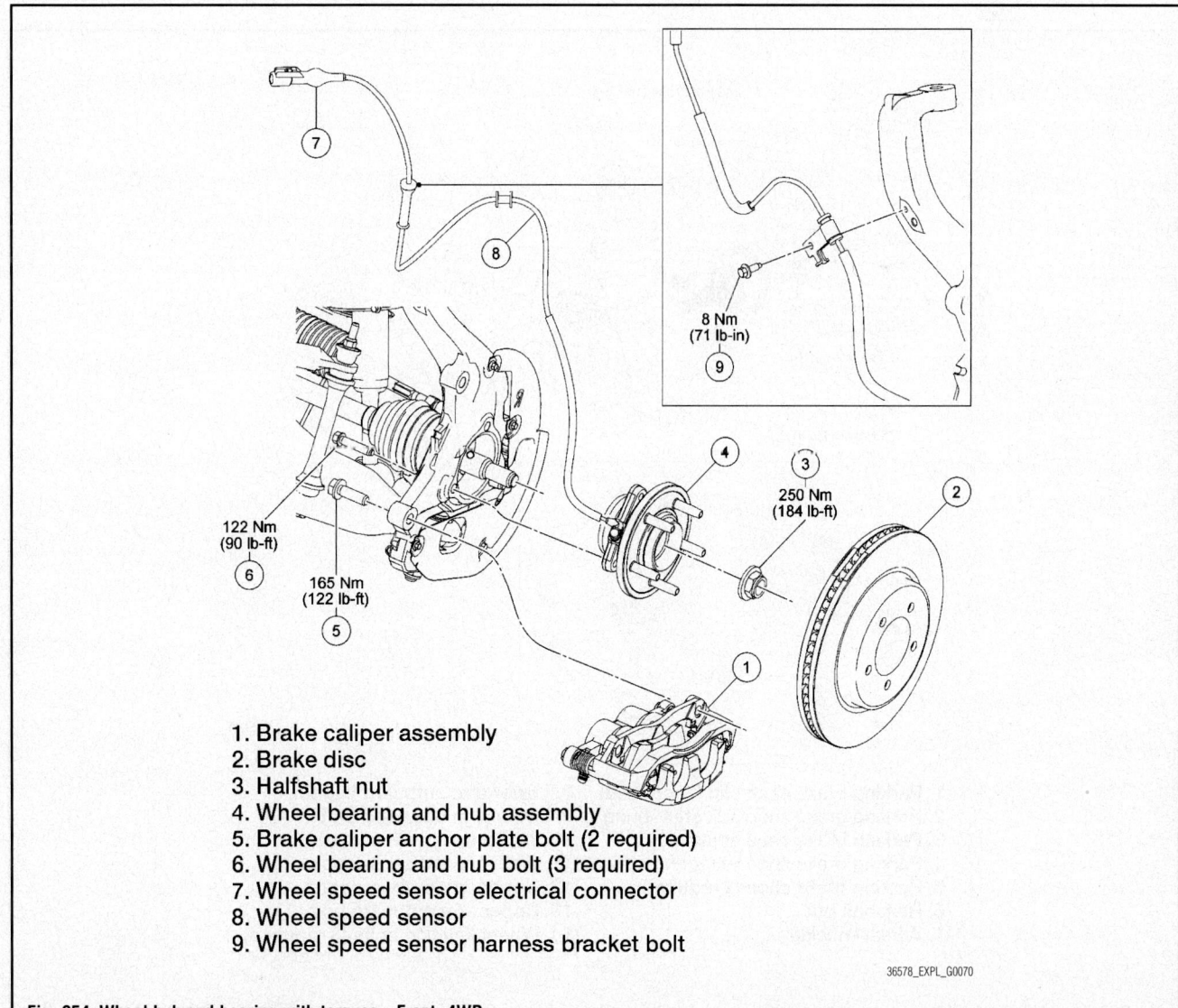

1. Brake caliper assembly
2. Brake disc
3. Halfshaft nut
4. Wheel bearing and hub assembly
5. Brake caliper anchor plate bolt (2 required)
6. Wheel bearing and hub bolt (3 required)
7. Wheel speed sensor electrical connector
8. Wheel speed sensor
9. Wheel speed sensor harness bracket bolt

36578_EXPL_G0070

Fig. 254 Wheel hub and bearing with torques—Front, 4WD

SUSPENSION

REAR SUSPENSION

KNUCKLE

REMOVAL & INSTALLATION

See Figures 255 through 258.

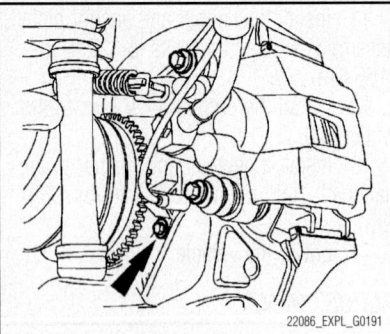

Fig. 255 Showing the location of the wheel speed sensor bolt

1. Before servicing the vehicle, refer to Precautions.
2. Measure the distance from the center of the hub to the lip of the fender with the vehicle in a level, static ground position (curb height).
3. If equipped, remove the wheel speed sensor bolt and position the sensor aside.

✵✵ WARNING

Do not loosen the halfshaft nut and washer until the wheel and tire are removed from the vehicle, as wheel bearing damage will occur if the wheel bearing is unloaded with the weight of the vehicle applied.

4. Remove the rear wheels.

5. Apply the brake to keep the halfshaft from rotating. Remove and discard the front wheel hub nut.
6. Remove the parking brake shoes.

Fig. 257 Showing the proper direction for the upper arm outboard bolt

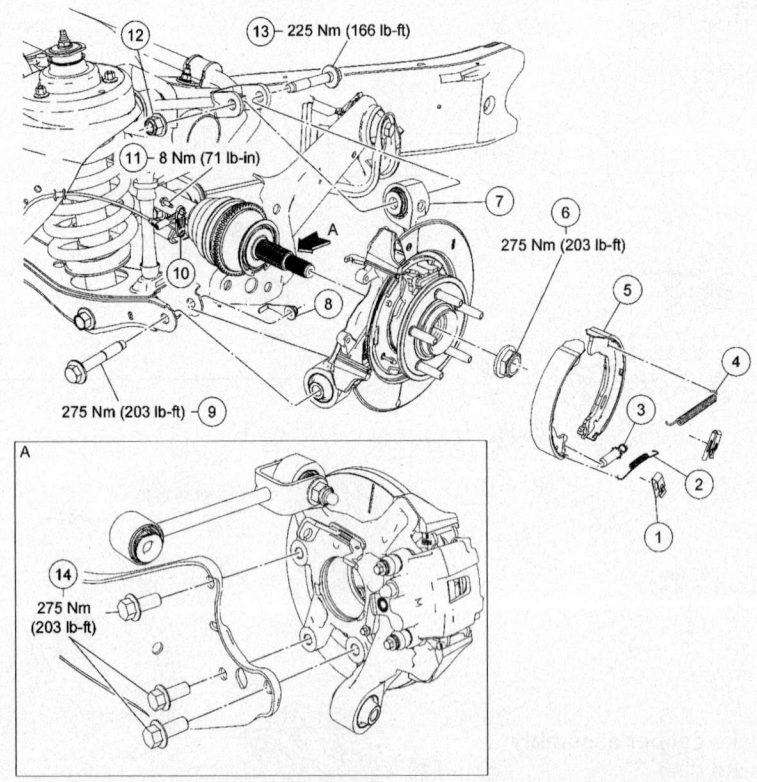

1. Parking brake shoe clip (2 required)
2. Parking brake shoe adjuster spring
3. Parking brake shoe adjuster
4. Parking brake shoe retracting spring
5. Parking brake shoe (2 required)
6. Halfshaft nut
7. Wheel knuckle
8. Lower arm outboard flagnut
9. Lower arm outboard bolt
10. Wheel speed sensor
11. Wheel speed sensor bolt
12. Upper arm outboard nut
13. Upper arm outboard bolt
14. Wheel knuckle bolts (3 required)

Fig. 256 Exploded view of the wheel knuckle, spindle, and related mounting components

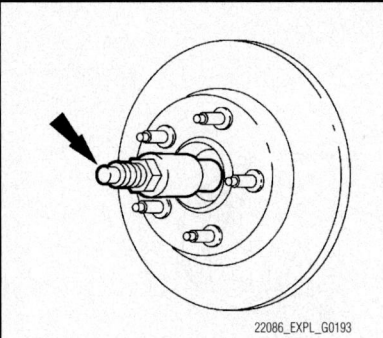

Fig. 258 Using a suitable halfshaft installer tool, install the halfshaft

7. Using a proper tool, press the half-shaft from the hub.

8. Position a suitable jack under the wheel knuckle and raise the suspension until the distance between the center of the hub and the lip of the fender is equal to the curb height measurement.

9. Remove and discard the following:
- toe link outboard nut and bolt
- upper arm outboard nut and bolt
- lower arm outboard nut and bolt
- 3 wheel knuckle bolts

10. Remove the wheel knuckle.

11. If a new wheel knuckle is being installed, remove the wheel bearing and wheel hub.

To install:

12. Position a suitable jack under the wheel knuckle and raise the suspension until the distance between the center of the hub and the lip of the fender is equal to the curb height measurement.

13. Position the wheel knuckle and install 3 new wheel knuckle bolts. Torque the bolts to 203 ft lbs. (275 Nm).

14. Install a new lower arm outboard bolt and flag nut. Torque the nut to 203 ft. lbs. (275 Nm).

※ WARNING

The upper arm outboard bolt must be installed with the bolt head toward the front of the vehicle or wheel damage can occur.

15. Install a new upper arm outboard bolt and nut with the bolt head toward the front of the vehicle. Torque the bolt to 166 ft. lbs. (225 Nm).

16. Position the toe link and install a new toe link outboard bolt and nut.

17. Lower the suspension and remove the jack.

18. Install the parking brake shoes. See "Parking Brake" section.

19. Position the wheel speed sensor and install the bolt.

20. Using a suitable halfshaft installer tool, install the halfshaft.

21. Have an assistant press the brake pedal to keep the axle from turning, then install a new halfshaft nut and washer. Torque the nut to 203 ft. lbs. (275 Nm).

LOWER CONTROL ARM

REMOVAL & INSTALLATION

See Figures 259 and 260.

1. Before servicing the vehicle, refer to Precautions.

※ WARNING

Orientation of the suspension fasteners is important. Make sure the fasteners are installed in the same direction as they were in when removed.

2. Measure the distance from the center of the hub to the lip of the fender with the vehicle in a level, static ground position (curb height).

3. With the vehicle in NEUTRAL, position it on a hoist.

4. Position a suitable jack under the wheel knuckle and raise the suspension until the distance between the center of the hub and the lip of the fender is equal to the curb height measurement.

5. Remove and discard the lower arm outboard bolt and flag nut.

6. Remove the stabilizer bar link nut and grommet, stud and link assembly. Discard the nut and grommet.

7. Lower the suspension and remove the jack.

8. Remove and discard the shock absorber lower nut and bolt.

9. Remove and discard the lower arm

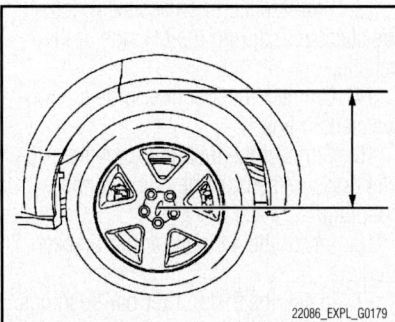

Fig. 259 Measure the distance from the center of the hub to the lip of the fender with the vehicle in a level, static ground position (curb height)

inboard nut and bolt and remove the lower arm.

To install:

10. Position the lower arm and install a new lower arm inboard bolt and nut. Hand-tighten only at this time.

11. Position the lower arm and install a new shock absorber lower bolt and nut. Hand-tighten only at this time.

12. Position a suitable jack under the wheel knuckle and raise the suspension until the distance between the center of the hub and the lip of the fender is equal to the curb height measurement.

13. Install the stabilizer link assembly, the link stud and a new nut and grommet. Torque the nut to 22 ft. lbs. (30 Nm).

14. Install a new lower arm outboard bolt and flag nut. Torque the nut to 203 ft. lbs. (275 Nm).

15. Tighten the lower arm inboard bolt to 185 ft. lbs. (250 Nm).

16. Tighten the shock absorber lower bolt to 203 ft. lbs. (275 Nm).

17. Lower the suspension and remove the jack

STABILIZER BAR

REMOVAL & INSTALLATION

Explorer and Mountaineer

See Figures 259 and 261.

1. Before servicing the vehicle, refer to Precautions.

2. Measure the distance from the center of the hub to the lip of the fender with the vehicle in a level, static ground position (curb height).

3. Remove the wheel and tire assemblies.

4. Remove and discard the outboard nut and bolt from both upper arms.

5. Remove the stabilizer bar link nut and grommet and the stabilizer bar link.

6. Discard the nut and grommet.

7. Remove and discard the 4 stabilizer bar bracket nuts.

8. Remove the 2 stabilizer bar brackets and the 2 stabilizer bar bushings.

9. Remove the 4 stabilizer bar bracket studs.

   a. For the front studs, push the stud down and slide the stud toward the rear of the vehicle.

   b. For the rear studs, push the stud down and slide the stud toward the front of the vehicle.

10. Disconnect the fuel filler pipe tube-to-fuel pressure sensor line quick connect coupling.

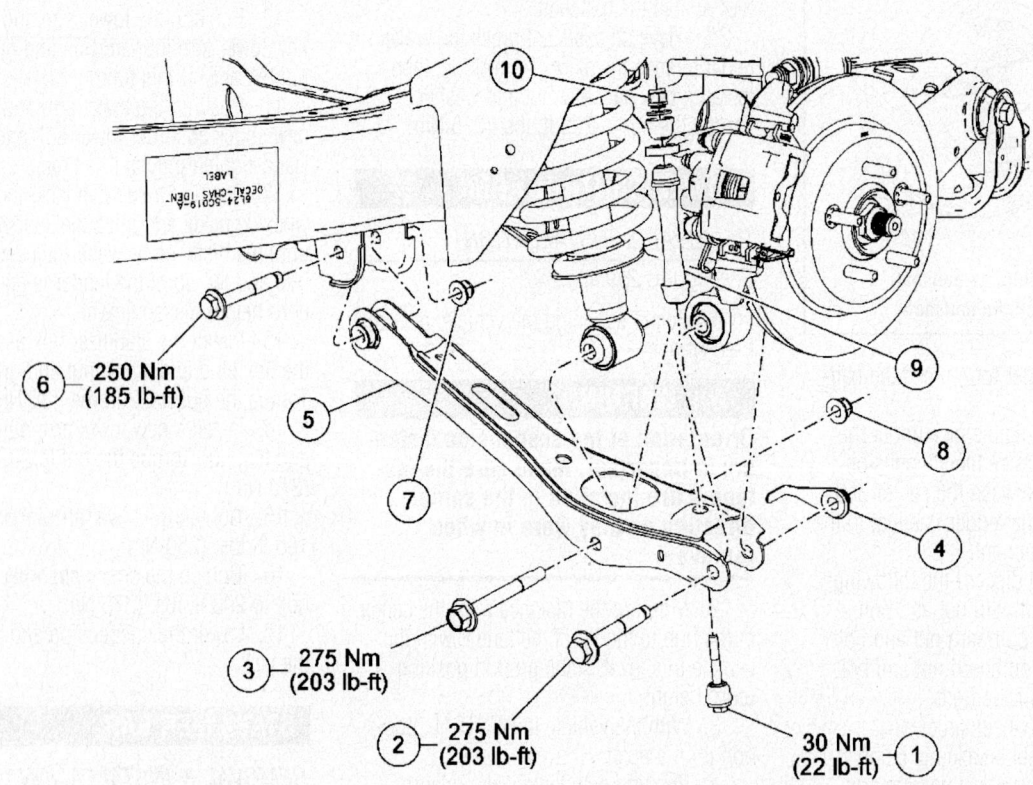

1. Stabilizer bar link stud
2. Lower arm outboard bolt
3. Shock absorber lower bolt
4. Lower arm outboard flag nut
5. Lower arm
6. Lower arm inboard bolt
7. Lower arm inboard nut
8. Shock absorber lower nut
9. Stabilizer bar link assembly
10. Stabilizer bar link nut and grommet

22086_EXPL_G0185

Fig. 260 Showing the lower arm and mounting components

11. Unclip the fuel filler pipe tube-to-fuel pressure sensor line from the fuel tank and position aside.

⁑ WARNING

Extreme care must be exercised when removing and installing the stabilizer bar on vehicles equipped with rear Air Conditioning (A/C) and/or rear heating or damage to the A/C lines and rear heater hoses can occur.

12. With the aid of an assistant, remove the stabilizer bar from the LH side of the vehicle.

To install:

13. With the aid of an assistant, install the stabilizer bar into the LH side of the vehicle.

14. Connect the fuel filler pipe tube-to-fuel sensor line.

15. Connect the fuel filler pipe tube-to-fuel pressure sensor line quick connect coupling.

16. Install the 4 stabilizer bar bracket studs.

17. Install the 2 stabilizer bar bushings and the 2 stabilizer bar brackets.

18. Install the 4 new stabilizer bar bracket nuts and tighten to 35 ft. lbs. (48 Nm).

19. Using the jack, raise the suspension until the distance between the center of the hub and the lip of the fender is equal to the measurement taken in Step 1 (curb height) in Removal.

20. Install the stabilizer bar link and new link nut and grommet and tighten the nut to 22 ft. lbs. (30 Nm).

⁑ WARNING

The upper arm outboard bolts must be installed with the bolt head toward the front of the vehicle or wheel damage may occur.

21. Install the 2 new upper arm outboard bolts and the 2 new upper arm outboard nuts and tighten to 166 ft. lbs. (225 Nm).

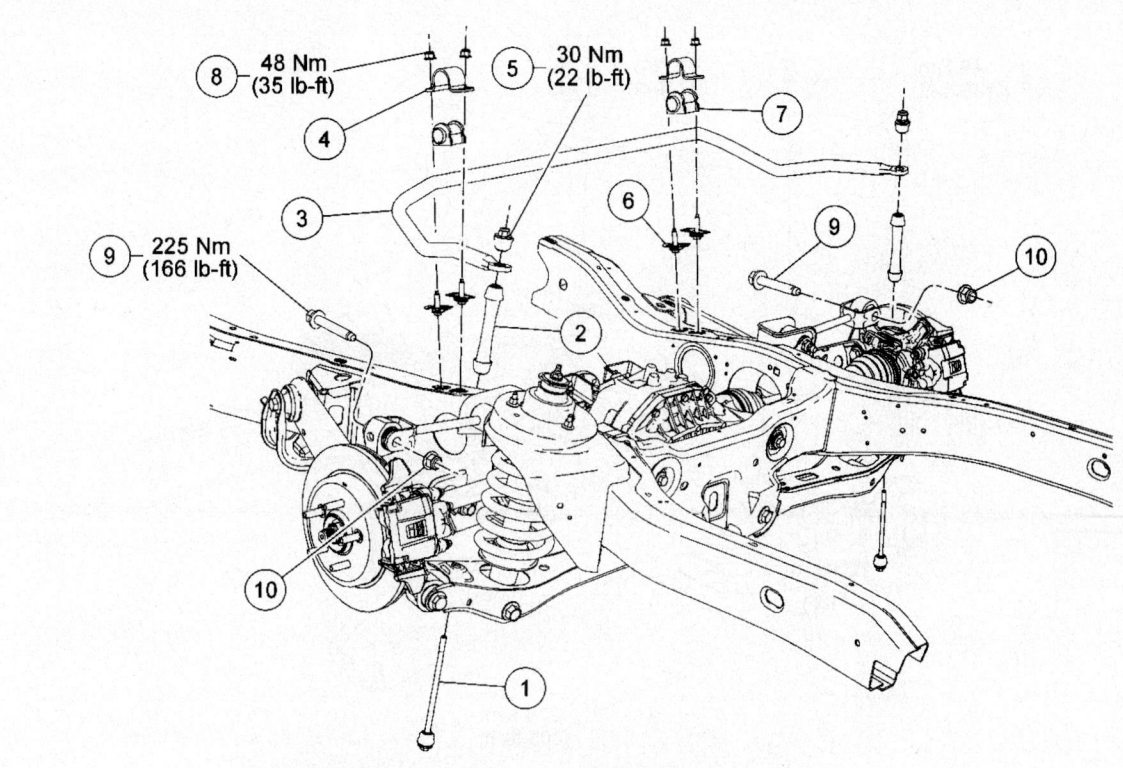

1. Stabilizer bar link stud (2 required)
2. Stabilizer bar link assembly (2 required)
3. Stabilizer bar
4. Stabilizer bar bracket (2 required)
5. Stabilizer bar link nut and grommet (2 required)
6. Stabilizer bar bracket stud (4 required)
7. Stabilizer bar bushing (2 required)
8. Stabilizer bar bracket nut (4 required)
9. Upper arm outboard bolts
10. Upper arm outboard nuts

36578_EXPL_G0073

Fig. 261 Rear suspension components with torques—Explorer and Mountaineer

22. Remove the jack.
23. Install the wheel and tire.

Explorer Sport-Trac

See Figures 251 and 262.

1. Before servicing the vehicle, refer to Precautions.
2. Measure the distance from the center of the hub to the lip of the fender with the vehicle in a level, static ground position (curb height).
3. Remove both upper arms. For additional information, refer to Upper Control Arm.

➡**Removal of the LH shock absorber lower bolt will allow more movement** of the wheel knuckle when installing the stabilizer bar.

4. Remove the LH shock absorber lower bolt.
5. Disconnect the Evaporative Emission (EVAP) canister vent valve electrical connector.
6. Unclip the wiring harness from the frame.
7. Remove the fuel tank filler pipe bracket bolt.
8. Loosen the fuel tank filler pipe hose clamps and disconnect the hose.
9. Remove the stabilizer bar link nut and grommet and the stabilizer bar link.
10. Discard the nut and grommet.

11. Remove the wiring harness retainer caps from the stabilizer bar bracket studs.
12. Remove and discard the 4 stabilizer bar bracket nuts.
13. Remove the 2 stabilizer bar brackets and the 2 stabilizer bar bushings.
14. Remove the 4 stabilizer bar bracket studs.
  a. For the front studs, push the stud down and slide the stud toward the rear of the vehicle.
  b. For the rear studs, push the stud down and slide the stud toward the front of the vehicle.
15. Disconnect the fuel filler pipe tube-to-fuel pressure sensor line quick connect coupling.

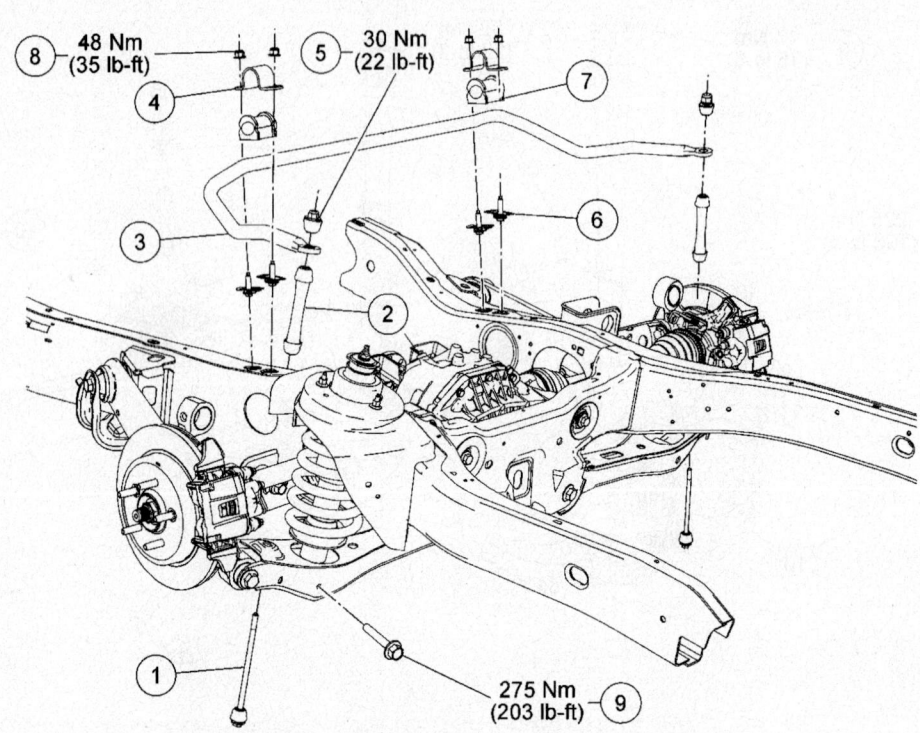

1. Stabilizer bar link stud (2 required)
2. Stabilizer bar link assembly (2 required)
3. Stabilizer bar
4. Stabilizer bar bracket (2 required)
5. Stabilizer bar link nut and grommet (2 required)
6. Stabilizer bar bracket stud (4 required)
7. Stabilizer bar bushing (2 required)
8. Stabilizer bar bracket nut (4 required)
9. Shock absorber lower bolt

36578_EXPL_G0074

Fig. 262 Rear suspension components with torques—Sport-Trac

16. Unclip the fuel filler pipe tube-to-fuel pressure sensor line from the fuel tank and position aside.

❊❊ WARNING

When removing the stabilizer bar, care must be taken to avoid damage to the wiring harness, fuel lines, fuel filler tube and body.

❊❊ WARNING

Extreme care must be exercised when removing and installing the stabilizer bar on vehicles equipped with rear Air Conditioning (A/C)

and/or rear heating, or damage to the A/C lines and rear heater hoses can occur.

17. With the aid of an assistant, remove the stabilizer bar from the LH side of the vehicle.

To install:

❊❊ WARNING

When installing the stabilizer bar, care must be taken to avoid damage to the wiring harness, fuel lines, fuel filler tube and body.

❊❊ WARNING

Extreme care must be exercised when removing and installing the stabilizer bar on vehicles equipped with rear Air Conditioning (A/C) and/or rear heating, or damage to the A/C lines and rear heater hose may occur.

18. With the aid of an assistant, install the stabilizer bar into the LH side of the vehicle.
19. Connect the fuel filler pipe tube-to-fuel sensor line.
20. Connect the fuel filler pipe tube-to-fuel pressure sensor line quick connect coupling.

21. Install the 4 stabilizer bar bracket studs.

22. Install the 2 stabilizer bar bushings and the 2 stabilizer bar brackets.

23. Install the 4 new stabilizer bar bracket nuts and tighten to 35 ft. lbs. (48 Nm).

24. Install the wiring harness retaining caps onto the stabilizer bar studs.

25. Use the jack to raise the suspension until the distance between the center of the hub and the lip of the fender is equal to the measurement taken in Step 1 of the Upper Control Arm procedure in this section.

26. Install the stabilizer bar link, the new link nut and the grommet and tighten to 22 ft. lbs. (30 Nm).

27. Connect the fuel tank filler hose and tighten the 2 filler pipe hose clamps to 27 inch (3 Nm).

28. Install the fuel tank filler pipe bracket bolt and tighten to 133 inch lbs. (15 Nm).

29. Connect the wiring harness clip to the frame.

30. Connect the EVAP canister vent electrical connector.

31. Install the new LH shock absorber lower bolt and tighten to 203 ft. lbs. (275 Nm).

32. Install both upper arms.

STRUTS

REMOVAL & INSTALLATION

See Figure 263.

1. Before servicing the vehicle, refer to Precautions.

2. Remove the lower arm. Refer to Control Arms/Links.

3. Remove and discard the 3 shock absorber upper mount nuts and remove the shock absorber and spring assembly.

To install:

4. Install the shock absorber and torque the upper mount nuts to 22 ft. lbs. (30 Nm).

5. Install the lower arm. See "Control Arms/Links" section.

TOE LINK

REMOVAL & INSTALLATION

See Figures 251 and 264.

1. Before servicing the vehicle, refer to Precautions.

✳✳ WARNING

Orientation of the suspension fasteners is important. Make sure the fasteners are installed in the same direction as they were in when removed.

2. Measure the distance from the center of the hub to the lip of the fender with the vehicle in a level, static ground position (curb height).

3. With the vehicle in NEUTRAL, position it on a hoist.

4. Position a suitable jack under the wheel knuckle and raise the suspension until the distance between the center of the hub and the lip of the fender is equal to the curb height measurement.

5. Index-mark the toe link cam bolt to the subframe.

6. Remove the toe link cam adjuster nut, cam adjuster and cam bolt. Discard the nut.

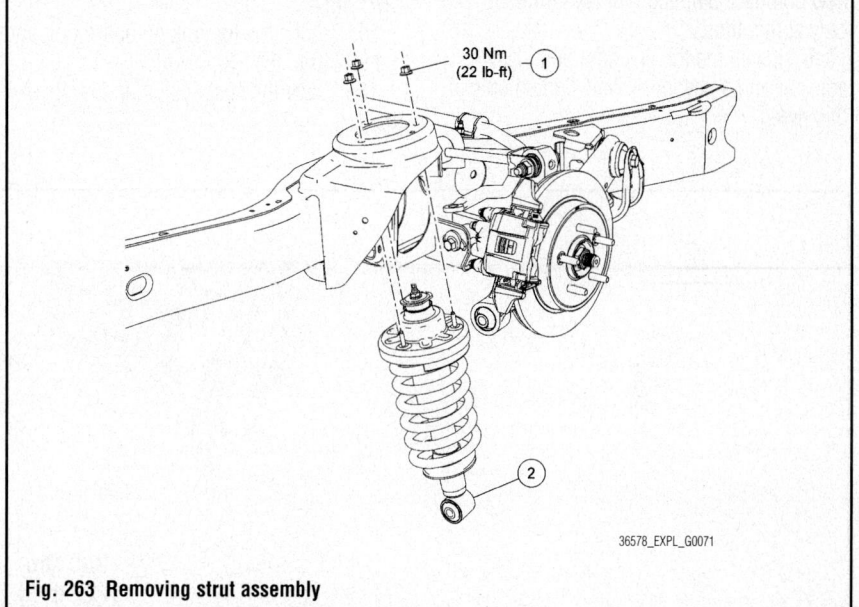

Fig. 263 Removing strut assembly

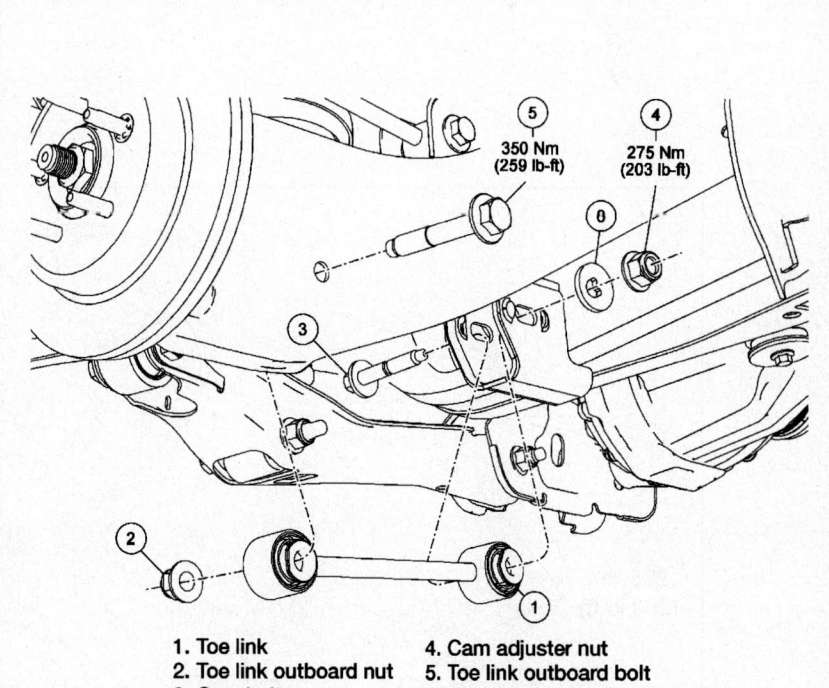

1. Toe link
2. Toe link outboard nut
3. Cam bolt
4. Cam adjuster nut
5. Toe link outboard bolt
6. Adjustment cam

Fig. 264 Showing the toe link and mounting components

7. Remove and discard the toe link outboard nut and bolt and remove the toe link.

To install:

8. If removed, install and raise the jack under the suspension to equal the curb height measurement.

9. Position the toe link and install a new outboard bolt and nut. Hand-tighten only at this time.

10. Install the toe link cam bolt, cam adjuster and a new nut. Hand-tighten only at this time.

11. If removed, install and raise the jack under the suspension to equal the curb height measurement.

12. Make sure the cam bolt and the adjustment cam are seated between the offsets before tightening the nut.

13. Align the index mark on the cam bolt with the index mark on the subframe and tighten the nut to 203 ft. lbs. (275 Nm).

14. Torque the toe link outboard bolt and nut to 240 ft. lbs. (325 Nm).

15. Lower the suspension and remove the jack.

16. Check and, if necessary, adjust the rear toe.

TRAILING ARM

REMOVAL & INSTALLATION

See Figure 265.

1. Remove the toe link. refer to Toe Link.
2. Remove the parking brake cable bracket bolt.
3. Remove and discard the trailing arm bolt.
4. Remove the 3 wheel knuckle bolts to the trailing arm bolts and discard the bolts.

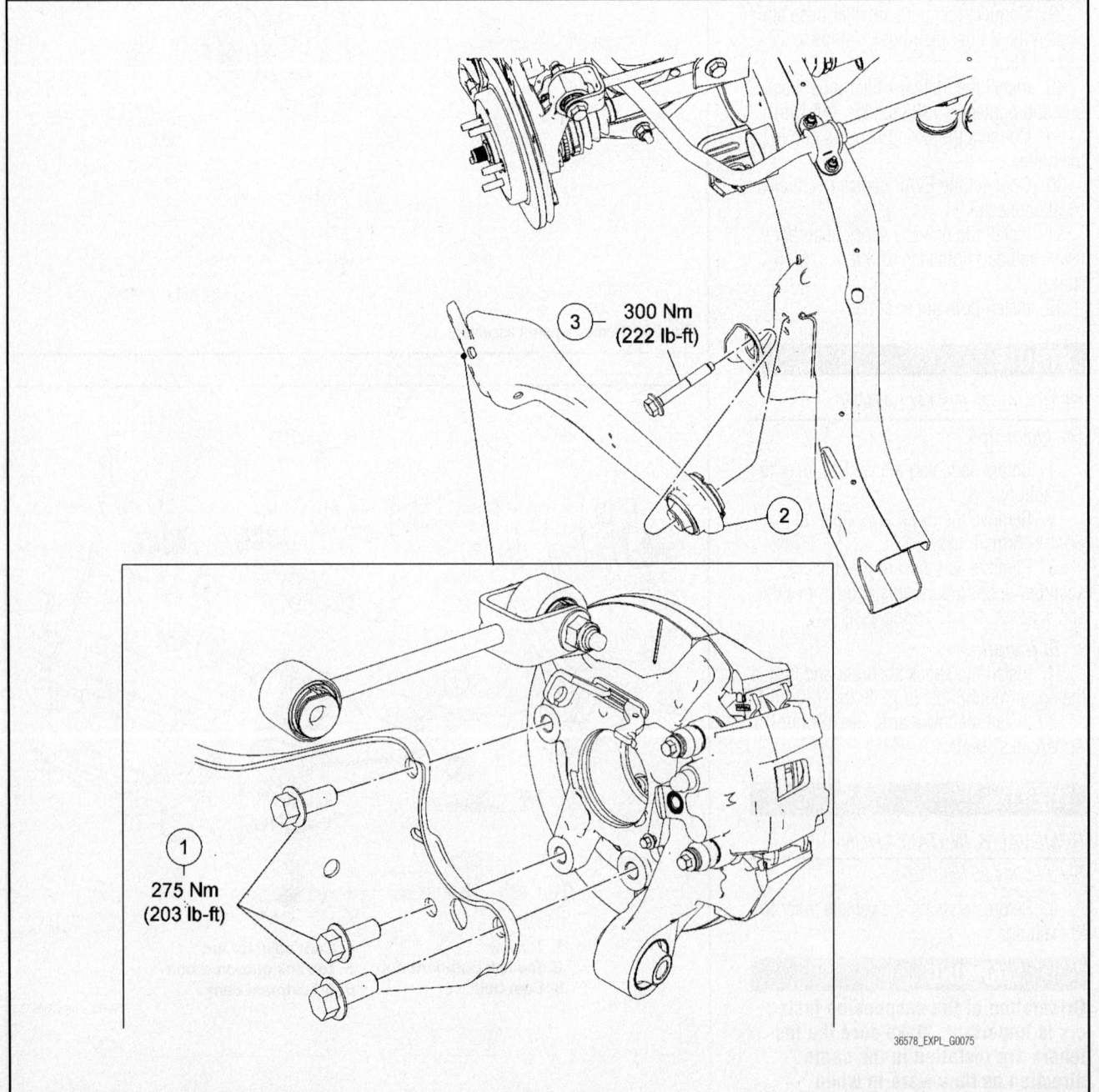

③ 300 Nm (222 lb-ft)

②

① 275 Nm (203 lb-ft)

Fig. 265 Trailing arm mounting components

36578_EXPL_G0075

To install:

5. To install, reverse the removal procedure.

6. Tighten parking brake cable bracket bolt to 89 inch lbs. (10 Nm).

7. Tighten new trailing arm bolt to 222 ft. lbs. (300 Nm) at curb height.

8. Tighten 3 new wheel knuckle bolts to 203 ft. lbs. (275 Nm).

UPPER CONTROL ARM

REMOVAL & INSTALLATION

See Figures 251 and 266.

1. Before servicing the vehicle, refer to Precautions.

2. Measure the distance from the center of the hub to the lip of the fender with the vehicle in a level, static ground position (curb height).

3. With the vehicle in NEUTRAL, position it on a hoist.

4. Position a suitable jack under the wheel knuckle and raise the suspension until the distance between the center of the hub and the lip of the fender is equal to the curb height measurement taken.

5. Remove and discard the upper arm outboard nut and bolt.

➡The inboard nut that is installed at the assembly plant is a flag nut. This flag nut is used to set and maintain the rear camber settings. Discard the flag nut and install a non-flag nut to allow the rear camber to be adjusted.

6. Remove and discard the upper arm inboard bolt and flag nut and remove the upper arm.

To install:

7. Ensure the jack is still properly positioned under the wheel knuckle.

8. Position the upper arm and install a new inboard bolt and non-flag nut. Torque the fasteners to 185 ft. lbs. (250 Nm).

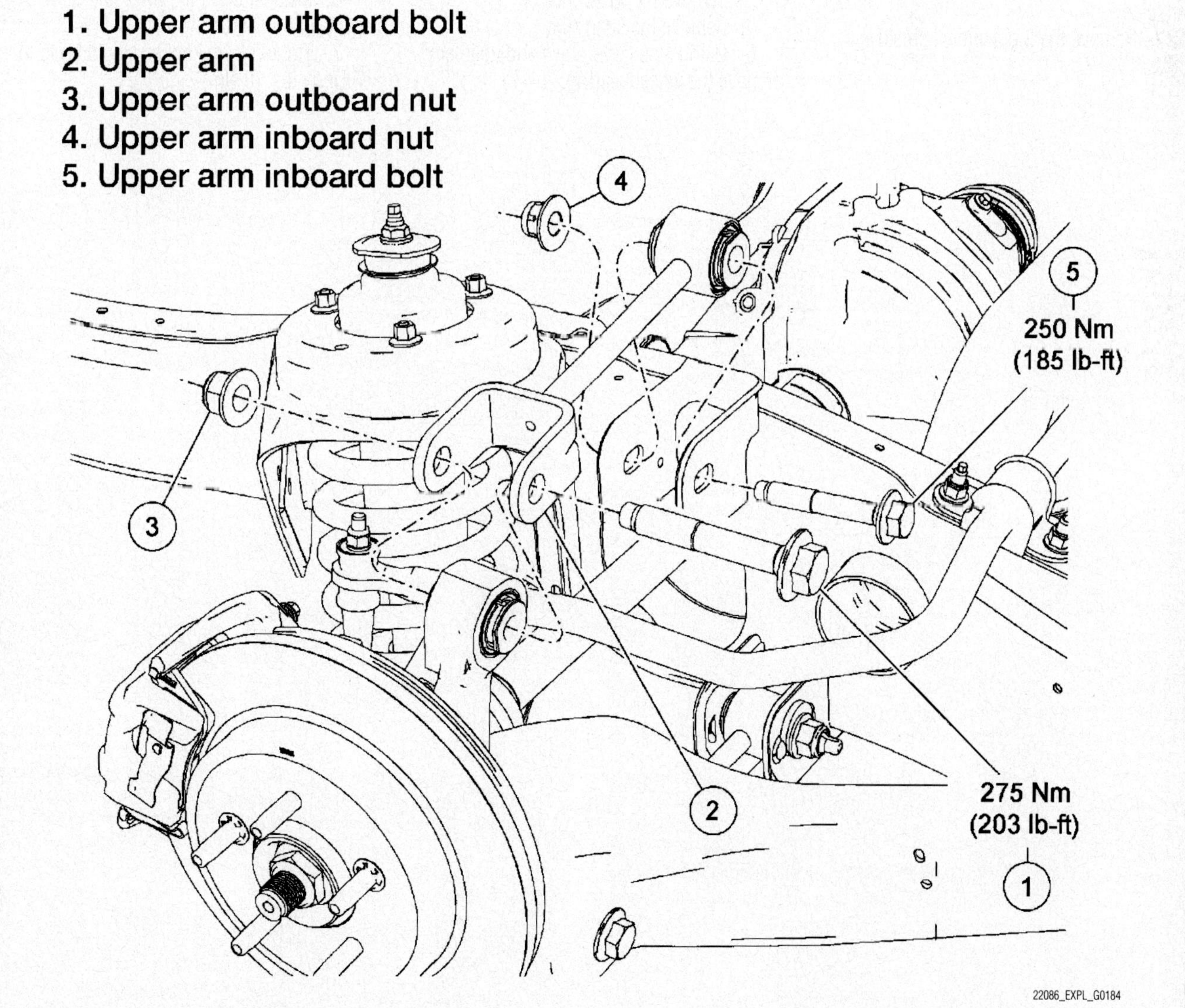

1. Upper arm outboard bolt
2. Upper arm
3. Upper arm outboard nut
4. Upper arm inboard nut
5. Upper arm inboard bolt

250 Nm
(185 lb-ft)

275 Nm
(203 lb-ft)

22086_EXPL_G0184

Fig. 266 Showing the upper arm and mounting components

✳✳ WARNING

The upper arm outboard bolt must be installed with the bolt head toward the front of the vehicle or wheel damage can occur.

9. Install a new outboard bolt and nut with the bolt head toward the front of the vehicle. Torque to 166 ft. lbs. (225 Nm).

10. Lower the suspension and remove the jack.

11. Check and, if necessary, align the rear end.

WHEEL HUB & BEARING

REMOVAL & INSTALLATION

See Figure 267.

1. Remove the wheel knuckle. Refer to Knuckle.

2. Remove the 3 brake disc shield bolts.

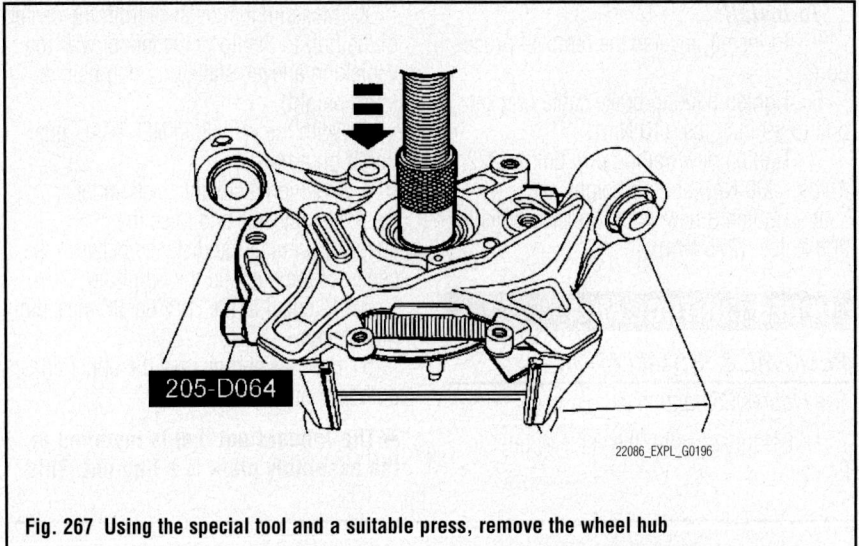

Fig. 267 Using the special tool and a suitable press, remove the wheel hub

3. Using the special tool and a suitable press, remove the wheel hub.

4. Remove the snap ring.

5. Using a suitable press and adapters, remove the wheel bearing.

To install:

6. Installation is the reverse of the removal procedure.

7. Tighten 3 brake disc shield bolts to 71 inch lbs. (8 Nm).

FORD AND LINCOLN

F-150 • Mark LT

8

SPECIFICATIONS AND MAINTENANCE CHARTS

ENGINE AND VEHICLE IDENTIFICATION

Code ①	Liters (cc)	Cu. In.	Cyl.	Fuel Sys.	Type	Eng. Mfg.	Code ②	Year
		Engine					Model Year	
2	4.2 (4195)	256	6	EFI	OHV	Ford	8	2008
W	4.6 (4588)	280	8	EFI	SOHC	Ford	9	2009
8 ③	4.6 (4588)	280	8	EFI	SOHC	Ford		
5 ③	5.4 (5409)	330	8	EFI	SOHC	Ford		
V ④	5.4 (5409)	330	8	EFI	SOHC	Ford		

EFI: Electronic Fuel Injection

OHV: Overhead Valve

SOHC: Single Overhead Camshaft

① 8th digit of the Vehicle Identification Number (VIN)

② 10th digit of the Vehicle Identification Number (VIN)

③ 3 valves per cylinder

④ 3 valves per cylinder Flex-Fuel engine

36578_FTRK_C0001

GENERAL ENGINE SPECIFICATIONS

Year	Model	Engine Displ. Liters	Engine VIN	Net Horsepower @ rpm	Net Torque @ rpm (ft. lbs.)	Bore x Stroke (in.)	Com- pression Ratio	Oil Pressure @ rpm
2008	F-150	4.2	2	202@4800	255@3400	3.81x3.74	9.3:1	40@2500
		4.6	W	210@4400	290@3250	3.55x3.54	9.3:1	40@2500
		5.4 ①	V	300@5000	365@3750	3.55x4.17	9.8:1	40@2000
		5.4	5 ②	300@5000	365@3750	3.55x4.17	9.8:1	75@2000
	Mark LT	5.4	5 ②	300@5000	365@3750	3.55x4.17	9.8:1	75@2000
2009	F-150	4.6	W	248@4750	294@4000	3.55x3.54	9.8:1	75@2000
		4.6	8 ① ②	248@4750	294@4000	3.55x3.54	9.8:1	75@2000
		5.4	V ① ②	300@5000	365@3750	3.55x4.17	9.8:1	75@2000

① Flex-Fuel

② 3 valves per cylinder

36578_FTRK_C0002

GASOLINE ENGINE TUNE-UP SPECIFICATIONS

Year	Engine Displacement Liters	Engine VIN	Spark Plug Gap (in.)	Ignition Timing (deg.) ① MT	AT	Fuel Pump (psi) ②	Idle Speed (rpm) MT	AT	Valve Clearance In.	Ex.
2008	4.2	2	0.052-0.056	NA	NA	28-45	④	④	HYD	HYD
	4.6	W	0.040-0.050	NA	NA	28-45	④	④	HYD	HYD
	5.4	5	0.040-0.050	NA	NA	28-45	④	④	HYD	HYD
	5.4	V ③	0.040-0.050	NA	NA	28-45	④	④	HYD	HYD
2009	4.6	W	0.040-0.050	NA	NA	55-60	④	④	HYD	HYD
	4.6	8 ③	0.040-0.050	NA	NA	55-60	④	④	HYD	HYD
	5.4	V ③	0.040-0.050	NA	NA	55-60	④	④	HYD	HYD

NOTE: The Vehicle Emission Control Information label often reflects specification changes changes made during production. The label figures must be used if they differ from this chart.

B: Before top dead center

HYD: Hydraulic

NA: Information not Available

① Ignition timing is preset and cannot be adjusted

② With engine running

③ Flex-fuel engine

④ Idle speed is electronically controlled and cannot be adjusted

36578_FTRK_C0003

CAPACITIES

Year	Model	Engine Displ. Liters	Engine VIN	Engine Oil with Filter (qts.)	Transmission (pts.) MT	Auto.	Transfer Case (pts.)	Drive Axle Front (pts.)	Rear (pts.)	Fuel Tank (gal.)	Cooling System (qts.)
2008	F-150	4.2	2	6.0	②	26.4	4.0	3.6	③	④	17.6
		4.6	W	6.0	②	26.4	4.0	3.6	③	④	20.5
		5.4	V ①	7.0	②	26.4	4.0	3.6	③	④	21.2
	F-150, Mark LT	5.4	5	7.0	②	26.4	4.0	3.6	③	④	21.2
2009	F-150	4.6	W	6.0	NA	⑤	3.0	3.6	5.5	⑥	16.3
		4.6	8 ①	6.0	NA	⑤	3.0	3.6	5.5	⑥	15.5
		5.4	V ①	7.0	NA	⑤	3.0	3.6	5.5	⑥	16.9

NOTE: All capacities are approximate. Add fluid gradually and check to be sure a proper fluid level is obtained.

① Flex-fuel engine

② Fill to bottom of oil fill hole.

③ 8.8 and 9.75 inch axles: 5.5 pts.

   10.25 inch axle: 7 pts.

④ Regular cab w/126 in. wheel base and 6.5 ft. bed: 26 gal.

   Super cab w/132 inch wheel base and 5.5 ft. bed: 26 gal

   Crew cab w/138 in. wheel base and 5.5 ft. bed: 30 gal.

   Regular cab w/144 in. wheel base and 8 ft. bed: 27.0

   SuperCab w/163 in. wheel base and 8 ft. bed: 27 gal.

   Optional for SuperCab w/144 in. wheel base and 6.5 ft. bed: 35.7 gal.

   Optional for Regular Cab w/144 in. wheel base and 8 ft. bed: 35.7 gal.

   Optional for SuperCab w/163 in. wheel base and 8 ft. bed: 35.7 gal.

⑤ For 4R70E/4R75E transmission: 28 pts.

   For 6R80 transmission: 24 pts.

⑥ Standard fuel tank: 26 gal.

   Optional long wheelbase fuel tank: 36 gal.

36578_FTRK_C0004

FLUID SPECIFICATIONS

Year	Model	Engine Displacement Liters	Engine ID/VIN	Engine Oil	Man. Trans.	Auto. Trans.	Drive Axle	Power Steering Fluid	Brake Master Cylinder
2008	F-150	4.2	2	5W-20	①	①	②	MERCON ATF	DOT 3
		4.6	W	5W-20	①	①	②	MERCON ATF	DOT 3
	F-150, Mark LT	5.4	5, V	5W-20	①	①	②	MERCON ATF	DOT 3
2009	F-150	4.6	W	5W-20	①	①	②	MERCON ATF	DOT 3
		4.6	8	5W-20	①	①	②	MERCON ATF	DOT 3
		5.4	V	5W-20	①	①	②	MERCON ATF	DOT 3

DOT: Department Of Transpotation

① MERCON Type XT-5-QM ATF

② Fluid type varies per axle type usage:

With Ford 8.8 in. and Ford 9.75 in.: Motorcraft SAE 75W-140 Synthetic Rear Axle Lubricant XY-75W140-QL (US); CXY-75W140-1L (Canada)

With Ford 10.25 in.: SAE 75W-140 High Performance Rear Axle Lubricant F1TZ-19580-B

36578_FTRK_C0005

VALVE SPECIFICATIONS

Year	Engine Displ. Liters	Engine VIN	Seat Angle (deg.)	Face Angle (deg.)	Spring Test Pressure (lbs. @ in.)	Spring Installed Height (in.)	Stem-to-Guide Clearance (in.) Intake	Stem-to-Guide Clearance (in.) Exhaust	Stem Diameter (in.) Intake	Stem Diameter (in.) Exhaust
2008	4.2	2	44.75	45.675	225@1.15	1.610	0.0008-0.0027	0.0015-0.0033	0.2738-0.2751	0.2728-0.2741
	4.6	W	45.5	45.25-45.75	132@1.103	1.5630-1.5866	0.0008-0.0027	0.0018-0.0037	0.2754-0.2746	0.2744-0.2736
	5.4	5, V	44.5-45	45.5	79@1.66	1.660	0.0010-0.0020	0.0030-0.0040	0.2350-0.2360	0.2340-0.2350
2009	4.6	W	45.5	45.25-45.75	132@1.103	1.5630-1.5866	0.0008-0.0027	0.0018-0.0037	0.2754-0.2746	0.2744-0.2736
	4.6	8	44.5-45	45.5	79@1.66	1.660	0.0010-0.0030	0.0020-0.0040	0.2350-0.2360	0.2340-0.2350
	5.4	V	44.5-45	45.5	79@1.66	1.660	0.0010-0.0020	0.0030-0.0040	0.2350-0.2360	0.2340-0.2350

36578_FTRK_C0006

CAMSHAFT AND BEARING SPECIFICATIONS

All measurements are given in inches.

Year	Engine Displacement Liters	Engine VIN	Journal Diameter	Brg. Oil Clearance	Shaft End-play	Runout	Journal Bore	Lobe Lift Intake	Lobe Lift Exhaust
2008	4.2	2	2.0505-2.0515	0.0010-0.0030	0.0010-0.0060	0.002	①	0.2449	0.2587
	4.6	W	1.0605-1.0615	0.0010-0.0030	0.0035-0.0075	0.002	1.0625-1.0635	0.2560	0.2560
	5.4	5	1.1260-1.1270	0.0010-0.0030	0.0035-0.0075	0.001	1.1280-1.1290	0.2173	0.2168
	5.4	V ②	1.1260-1.1270	0.0010-0.0030	0.0035-0.0075	0.001	1.1280-1.1290	0.2173	0.2168
2009	4.6	W	1.0605-1.0615	0.0010-0.0030	0.0010-0.0070	0.002	1.0625-1.0635	0.2560	0.2560
	4.6	8 ②	1.1260-1.1270	0.0010-0.0030	0.0010-0.0070	0.001	1.1280-1.1290	0.2170	0.2170
	5.4	V ②	1.1260-1.1270	0.0010-0.0030	0.0010-0.0070	0.001	1.1280-1.1290	0.2170	0.2170

① Intake: 1.8532-1.8542 in.

Exhaust: 1.5635-1.5645 in.

② Flex-fuel engine

36578_FTRK_C0009

CRANKSHAFT AND CONNECTING ROD SPECIFICATIONS

All measurements are given in inches.

Year	Engine Displ. Liters	Engine VIN	Crankshaft Main Brg. Journal Dia.	Crankshaft Main Brg. Oil Clearance	Crankshaft Shaft End-play	Crankshaft Thrust on No.	Connecting Rod Journal Dia.	Connecting Rod Oil Clearance	Connecting Rod Side Clearance
2008	4.2	2	2.5190-2.5198	0.0005-0.0023	0.004-0.0080	3	NA	0.0010-0.0014	0.0043-0.0193
	4.6	W	2.6570-2.6576	0.0011-0.0026	0.0051-0.0120	5	2.0859-2.0867	0.0010-0.0027	0.0006-0.0177
	5.4	5	2.6568-2.6576	0.0009-0.0019	0.0030-0.0148	5	2.0859-2.0867	0.0010-0.0025	0.0049-0.0187
	5.4	V ①	2.6568-2.6576	0.0009-0.0019	0.0030-0.0148	5	2.0859-2.0867	0.0010-0.0025	0.0049-0.0187
2009	4.6	W	2.65	0.0011-0.0026	0.0051-0.0120	5	2.0859-2.0867	NA	NA
	4.6	8 ①	2.65	0.0009-0.0019	0.0030-0.0148	5	2.0859-2.0867	NA	NA
	5.4	V ①	2.6568-2.6576	0.0009-0.0019	0.0030-0.0148	5	2.0859-2.0867	NA	NA

NA: Information not available

① Flex-fuel engine

36578_FTRK_C0008

PISTON AND RING SPECIFICATIONS
All measurements are given in inches.

Engine Displ. Liters	Engine VIN	Piston Clearance	Ring Gap			Ring Side Clearance		
			Top Compression	Bottom Compression	Oil Control	Top Compression	Bottom Compression	Oil Control
2008 4.2	2	0.0007-0.0017	0.0067-0.0130	0.0118-0.0217	0.006-0.026	0.0012-0.0032	0.0012-0.0031	SNUG
4.6	W	0.0005-0.0001	0.010-0.020	0.010-0.020	0.006-0.026	0.0012-0.0028	0.0012-0.0028	0.0018-0.0077
5.4	5	0.0010-0.0018	0.006-0.012	0.0098-0.0197	0.006-0.026	0.0008-0.0031	0.0012-0.0028	0.1193-0.1201
5.4	V ①	0.0010-0.0018	0.006-0.012	0.0098-0.0197	0.006-0.026	0.0008-0.0031	0.0012-0.0028	0.1193-0.1201
2009 4.6	W	0.0007-0.0017	0.010-0.020	0.010-0.020	0.006-0.026	0.0008-0.0020	0.0008-0.0020	0.0018-0.0077
4.6	8 ①	0.0007-0.0019	0.006-0.012	0.0098-0.0197	0.0059-0.0256	0.0008-0.0020	0.0008-0.0020	0.1193-0.1203
5.4	V ①	0.0010-0.0018	0.006-0.012	0.0098-0.0197	0.0059-0.0256	0.0008-0.0031	0.0012-0.0028	0.1193-0.1201

① Flex-fuel engine

36578_FTRK_C0007

TORQUE SPECIFICATIONS
All readings in ft. lbs.

	Engine Displ. Liters	Engine VIN	Cylinder Head Bolts	Main Bearing Bolts	Rod Bearing Bolts	Crankshaft Damper Bolts	Flywheel Bolts	Manifold Intake *	Exhaust	Spark Plugs	Oil Pan Drain Plug
2008	4.2	2	①	②	③	118	59	④	24	11	19
	4.6	W	⑤	⑥	⑦	⑧	59	⑨	18	11	10
	5.4	5	⑤	⑩	⑪	⑧	59	⑫	18	25	10
	5.4	V	⑤	⑩	⑪	⑧	59	⑫	18	25	10
2009	4.6	W	⑤	⑥	⑦	⑧	59	⑨	18	11	10
	4.6	8	⑤	⑩	⑪	⑧	59	⑫	18	25	10
	5.4	V	⑤	⑩	⑪	⑧	59	⑫	18	25	10

NA: Information not available

* NOTE: Applies to Lower Manifold only. For Upper Manifold, see the text.

① See the procedure in the text

② Step 1: 37 ft. lbs.
Step 2: Plus 120 degrees

③ Step 1: 18 ft. lbs.
Step 2: 33 ft. lbs.
Step 3: plus 90-120 degrees

④ Step 1: 44 inch lbs.
Step 2: 89 inch lbs.

⑤ Step 1: 30 ft. lbs.
Step 2: Plus 85-95 degrees
Step 3: Plus 85-95 degrees

⑥ Vertical bolts:
Step 1: 30 ft. lbs.
Step 2: Plus 90 degrees
Jack screws:
Step 1: 44 inch lbs.
Step 2: 89 inch lbs.
Side bolts: 15 ft. lbs.

⑦ Step 1: 32 ft. lbs.
Step 2: 105 degrees

⑧ Step 1: 66 ft. lbs.
Step 2: loosen 1 full turn
Step 3: 37 ft. lbs.
Step 4: + 90 deg. Without exceeding 148 ft. lbs.

⑨ 89 inch lbs.

⑩ Vertical bolts:
Step 1: 30 ft. lbs.
Step 2: plus 90 degrees
Side bolts:
Step 1: 22 ft. lbs.
Step 2: plus 90 degrees

⑪ Step 1: 18 ft. lbs.
Step 2: 33 ft. lbs.
Step 3: plus 90-120 degrees

⑫ Step 1: 18 inch lbs.
Step 2: 89 inch lbs.

36578_FTRK_C0010

WHEEL ALIGNMENT

Year	Model	Style	Caster Range (+/-Deg.)	Caster Preferred Setting (Deg.)	Camber Range (+/-Deg.)	Camber Preferred Setting (Deg.)	Toe-in Front (Deg.)
2008	F-150 & Mark LT Reg. Cab	4x2	1.00	①	0.75	0.0	0.20+/-0.20
	F-150 & Mark LT Super Cab	4x2	1.00	②	0.75	-0.2	0.20+/-0.20
	F-150 & Mark LT Crew Cab	4x2	1.00	③	0.75	-0.2	0.20+/-0.20
	F-150 & Mark LT Reg. Cab	4x4	1.00	④	0.75	-0.2	0.20+/-0.20
	F-150 & Mark LT Super Cab	4x4	1.00	⑤	0.75	-0.2	0.20+/-0.20
	F-150 & Mark LT Crew Cab	4x4	1.00	⑥	0.75	-0.2	0.20+/-0.20
2009	F-150 Reg. Cab	4x2	1.00	①	0.75	0.0	0.20+/-0.20
	F-150 Super Cab	4x2	1.00	②	0.75	-0.2	0.20+/-0.20
	F-150 Crew Cab	4x2	1.00	③	0.75	-0.2	0.20+/-0.20
	F-150 Reg. Cab	4x4	1.00	④	0.75	-0.2	0.20+/-0.20
	F-150 Super Cab	4x4	1.00	⑤	0.75	-0.2	0.20+/-0.20
	F-150 Crew Cab	4x4	1.00	⑥	0.75	-0.2	0.20+/-0.20

① Left: +4.1
Right: +4.5
② Left: 4.3
Right: 4.7
With 20 in. or 22 in. tires:
Left: 3.9
Right: 4.3
③ Left: 4.4
Right: 4.8
With 20 in. or 22 in. tires:
Left: 4.0
Right: 4.0

④ Left: 4.1
Right: 4.5
⑤ Left: 4.4
Right: 4.8
⑥ Left: 4.5
Right: 4.9

36578_FTRK_C0011

TIRE, WHEEL AND BALL JOINT SPECIFICATIONS

Year	Model	OEM Tires Standard	OEM Tires Optional	Tire Pressures (psi.) Front	Tire Pressures (psi.) Rear	Wheel Size	Ball Joint Inspection	Lug Nut Torque (ft. lbs.)
2008	F-150 4x2 ③	P235/70R17	①	②	②	NA	③	150
	F-150 4x4 ③	P235/75R17	①	②	②	NA	③	150
	Mark LT 4x2 ③	2wd P265/60R18	①	②	②	NA	0.060 in. ②	150
	Mark LT 4x4 ③	4wd P275/65R18	①	②	②	NA	0.060 in. ②	150
2009	F-150 4x2 ③	P235/70R17	①	②	②	NA	③	150
	F-150 4x4 ③	P235/75R17	①	②	②	NA	③	150

NA: Information not available
OEM: Original Equipment Manufacturer
PSI: Pounds Per Square Inch
① Multiple optional tires available; consult tire dealer.
② See placard on vehicle
③ Upper: 0.0.032 in.; Lower: 0.008 in.

36578_FTRK_C0012

BRAKE SPECIFICATIONS
All measurements in inches unless noted

Year	Model		Brake Disc Original Thickness	Brake Disc Minimum Thickness	Brake Disc Maximum Runout	Brake Drum Diameter Original Inside Diameter	Brake Drum Diameter Max. Wear Limit	Brake Drum Diameter Maximum Machine Diameter	Brake Caliper Bracket Bolts (ft. lbs.)	Brake Caliper Mounting Bolts (ft. lbs.)
2008	F-150, Mark LT	F	NA	1.12	NA	NA	NA	NA	148	55
		R	NA	0.72	NA	NA	NA	NA	60	22
2009	F-150	F	NA	1.12	NA	NA	NA	NA	148	55
		R	NA	0.72	NA	NA	NA	NA	60	22

NOTE: Due to changes made during production, refer to manufacturer's specifications if they differ from those in this chart

NA: Information not available

① Caliper support bolts: 101 ft. lbs.

Anchor plate bolts: 203 ft. lbs.

36578_FTRK_C0013

SCHEDULED MAINTENANCE INTERVALS
F-150 Series

TO BE SERVICED	TYPE OF SERVICE	VEHICLE MILEAGE INTERVAL (x1000)												
		5	10	15	20	25	30	35	40	45	50	55	60	65
Engine oil & filter	R	✓	✓	✓	✓	✓	✓	✓	✓	✓	✓	✓	✓	✓
Tires	Rotate	✓	✓	✓	✓	✓	✓	✓	✓	✓	✓	✓	✓	✓
Wheels	I ①			✓			✓			✓			✓	
Auto trans. fluid	I			✓			✓			✓			✓	
Brake pads/shoes	I			✓			✓			✓			✓	
Coolant hoses	S/I			✓			✓			✓			✓	
Steering linkage	I			✓			✓			✓			✓	
Suspension	I			✓			✓			✓			✓	
Driveshaft	I			✓			✓			✓			✓	
Cabin air filter	R			✓			✓			✓			✓	
Ball joints (2wd)	L			✓			✓			✓			✓	
Front drive axle U-joints	I/L			✓			✓			✓			✓	
NGV fuel filter	R					✓					✓			
Exhaust system	I						✓						✓	
Engine air filter	R						✓						✓	
Fuel filter	R						✓						✓	
Auto trans fluid (4R100 and	R						✓						✓	
Manual trans. fluid	R												✓	
Front wheel bearings (2wd)	L/Adj												✓	
Front wheel bearings grease	R												✓	
Accessory drive belts	I	every 100,000 miles												
Spark plugs	R	every 100,000 miles												
PCV valve ②	R	every 100,000 miles												
Premium Gold coolant	R	every 3 years or 100,000 miles												
Auto trans fluid (all exc. 4R100 and TorqShift)	R	every 120,000 miles												
PCV valve (5.4L 3v)	I	every 150,000 miles												
Front wheel bearings (2wd)	R	at 150,000 miles, if not previously done so												
Front drive axle needle bearings (F-Super Duty)	L	every 150,000 miles												
Fuel tank	I	every 150,000 miles												
Front drive axle fluid	R	every 150,000 miles												
Rear drive axle fluid	R	every 150,000 miles												
Transfer case fluid	R	every 150,000 miles												
Accessory drive belts	R	every 150,000 miles, if not previously done so												

NOTE: See next chart for footnotes.

SCHEDULED MAINTENANCE INTERVALS
F-150 Series
Footnotes

R: Replace   S: Service   I: Inspect   L: Lubricate

NGV: Natural gas vehicle

① Inspect for end play and noise

② Vehicles under 6,000 lbs. GVW, exc. 5.4L 3v engines

Special Operating Condition Requirements

When towing a trailer or using a camper or car-top carrier:

Change engine oil and install a new oil filter every 4,800 km (3,000 miles), 3 months or 200 hours of engine operation (whichever occurs first).

Change transfer case fluid every 96,000 km (60,000 miles).

Change manual transmission fluid as required.

Inspect and lubricate U-joints as required.

During extensive idling and/or low speed driving for long distances, as in heavy commercial use such as delivery, taxi, patrol car or livery:

Change engine oil and install a new oil filter every 4,800 km (3,000 miles), 3 months or 200 hours of engine operation (whichever occurs first).

Lube front lower control arm and steering linkage ball joints with zerk fittings (if equipped) every 4,800 km (3,000 miles) or 3 months.

Inspect brake system and check battery electrolyte level (Patrol cars) every 8,000 km (5,000 miles).

Install a new fuel filter every 24,000 km (15,000 miles).

Change automatic transmission fluid, lubricate 4x2 wheel bearings, install new grease seals and adjust bearings every 48,000 km (30,000 miles). If equipped, change the in-line service installed transmission fluid filter.

Install new spark plugs and change transfer case fluid every 96,000 km (60,000 miles).

Install a new cabin air filter as required.

When operating in dusty conditions such as unpaved or dusty roads:

Change engine oil and install a new oil filter every 4,800 km (3,000 miles) or 3 months.

Install a new fuel filter every 24,000 km (15,000 miles).

Change automatic transmission fluid every 48,000 km (30,000 miles). If equipped, change the in-line service installed transmission fluid filter.

Change transfer case fluid every 96,000 km (60,000 miles).

Install a new engine air filter as required.

Install a new cabin air filter as required.

When operating in off-road conditions:

Change automatic transmission fluid every 48,000 km (30,000 miles). If equipped, change the in-line service installed transmission fluid filter.

Change transfer case fluid every 96,000 km (60,000 miles).

Install a new cabin air filter as required.

Inspect and lubricate U-joints.

Inspect and lubricate steering linkage ball joints with zerk fittings.

Short trips in cold operating conditions:

Inspect and lubricate 4x2 ball joints and steering idler arms every 8,000 km (5,000 miles).

Change transfer case fluid every 96,000 km (60,000 miles).

SCHEDULED MAINTENANCE INTERVALS
Lincoln Mark LT

TO BE SERVICED	SERVIC	5	10	15	20	25	30	35	40	45	50	55	60	65
		\multicolumn{13}{c}{VEHICLE MILEAGE INTERVAL (x1000)}											
Engine oil & filter	R	✓	✓	✓	✓	✓	✓	✓	✓	✓	✓	✓	✓	✓
Tires	Rotate	✓	✓	✓	✓	✓	✓	✓	✓	✓	✓	✓	✓	✓
Wheels	I ①			✓			✓			✓			✓	
Brake fluid level	S/I	✓	✓	✓	✓	✓	✓	✓	✓	✓	✓	✓	✓	✓
Tire pressure and wear	S/I	✓	✓	✓	✓	✓	✓	✓	✓	✓	✓	✓	✓	✓
Auto trans. fluid	I			✓			✓			✓			✓	
Power steering fluid level	S/I	✓	✓	✓	✓	✓	✓	✓	✓	✓	✓	✓	✓	✓
Washer fluid level	S/I	✓	✓	✓	✓	✓	✓	✓	✓	✓	✓	✓	✓	✓
Battery performance	I		✓	✓	✓	✓	✓	✓	✓	✓	✓	✓	✓	✓
Exterior lights	I	✓	✓	✓	✓	✓	✓	✓	✓	✓	✓	✓	✓	✓
Brake pads/shoes	I			✓			✓			✓			✓	
Coolant hoses	S/I	✓	✓	✓	✓	✓	✓	✓	✓	✓	✓	✓	✓	✓
A/C hoses	I		✓	✓	✓	✓	✓	✓	✓	✓	✓	✓	✓	✓
Engine air filter	I	✓	✓	✓	✓	✓	✓	✓	✓	✓	✓	✓	✓	✓
Steering linkage	I			✓			✓			✓			✓	
Suspension	I/L			✓			✓			✓			✓	
Halfshafts	I			✓			✓			✓			✓	
Driveshaft	I			✓			✓			✓			✓	
Cabin air filter	R			✓			✓			✓			✓	
Ball joints (2wd)	L			✓			✓			✓			✓	
Front drive axle U-joints	I/L			✓			✓			✓			✓	
Exhaust system	I	✓	✓	✓	✓	✓	✓	✓	✓	✓	✓	✓	✓	✓
Engine air filter	R						✓						✓	
Fuel filter	R						✓						✓	
Climate controlled seat filters	R						✓						✓	
Front wheel bearings (2wd)	L/Adj									✓				
Accessory drive belts	I	\multicolumn{13}{c}{every 100,000 miles}											
Spark plugs	R	\multicolumn{13}{c}{every 100,000 miles}											
Premium Gold coolant	R	\multicolumn{13}{c}{every 5 years or 100,000 miles}											
PCV valve	R	\multicolumn{13}{c}{every 100,000 miles}											
Auto trans fluid	R	\multicolumn{13}{c}{every 150,000 miles}											
Front wheel bearings (2wd)	R	\multicolumn{13}{c}{at 150,000 miles, if not previously done so}											
Fuel tank	I	\multicolumn{13}{c}{every 150,000 miles}											
Front drive axle fluid	R	\multicolumn{13}{c}{every 150,000 miles}											
Rear drive axle fluid	R	\multicolumn{13}{c}{every 150,000 miles}											
Transfer case fluid	R	\multicolumn{13}{c}{every 150,000 miles}											
Accessory drive belts	R	\multicolumn{13}{c}{every 150,000 miles, if not previously done so}											

NOTE: See next chart for footnotes.

36578_FTRK_C0016

SCHEDULED MAINTENANCE INTERVALS
Lincoln Mark LT
Footnotes

R: Replace   S: Service   I: Inspect   L: Lubricate

NGV: Natural gas vehicle

① Inspect for end play and noise

Special Operating Condition Requirements

When towing a trailer or using a camper or car-top carrier:

Change engine oil and install a new oil filter every 4,800 km (3,000 miles), 3 months or 200 hours of engine operation (whichever occurs first).

Change transfer case fluid every 96,000 km (60,000 miles).

Change manual transmission fluid as required.

Inspect and lubricate U-joints as required.

During extensive idling and/or low speed driving for long distances, as in heavy commercial use such as delivery, taxi, patrol car or livery:

Change engine oil and install a new oil filter every 4,800 km (3,000 miles), 3 months or 200 hours of engine operation (whichever occurs first).

Lube front lower control arm and steering linkage ball joints with zerk fittings (if equipped) every 4,800 km (3,000 miles) or 3 months.

Inspect brake system and check battery electrolyte level (Patrol cars) every 8,000 km (5,000 miles).

Install a new fuel filter every 24,000 km (15,000 miles).

Change automatic transmission fluid, lubricate 4x2 wheel bearings, install new grease seals and adjust bearings every 48,000 km (30,000 miles). If equipped, change the in-line service installed transmission fluid filter.

Install new spark plugs and change transfer case fluid every 96,000 km (60,000 miles).

Install a new cabin air filter as required.

When operating in dusty conditions such as unpaved or dusty roads:

Change engine oil and install a new oil filter every 4,800 km (3,000 miles) or 3 months.

Install a new fuel filter every 24,000 km (15,000 miles).

Change automatic transmission fluid every 48,000 km (30,000 miles). If equipped, change the in-line service installed transmission fluid filter.

Change transfer case fluid every 96,000 km (60,000 miles).

Install a new engine air filter as required.

Install a new cabin air filter as required.

When operating in off-road conditions:

Change automatic transmission fluid every 48,000 km (30,000 miles). If equipped, change the in-line service installed transmission fluid filter.

Change transfer case fluid every 96,000 km (60,000 miles).

Install a new cabin air filter as required.

Inspect and lubricate U-joints.

Inspect and lubricate steering linkage ball joints with zerk fittings.

Short trips in cold operating conditions:

Inspect and lubricate 4x2 ball joints and steering idler arms every 8,000 km (5,000 miles).

Change transfer case fluid every 96,000 km (60,000 miles).

PRECAUTIONS

Before servicing any vehicle, please be sure to read all of the following precautions, which deal with personal safety, prevention of component damage, and important points to take into consideration when servicing a motor vehicle:

• Never open, service or drain the radiator or cooling system when the engine is hot; serious burns can occur from the steam and hot coolant.

• Observe all applicable safety precautions when working around fuel. Whenever servicing the fuel system, always work in a well-ventilated area. Do not allow fuel spray or vapors to come in contact with a spark, open flame, or excessive heat (a hot drop light, for example). Keep a dry chemical fire extinguisher near the work area. Always keep fuel in a container specifically designed for fuel storage; also, always properly seal fuel containers to avoid the possibility of fire or explosion. Refer to the additional fuel system precautions later in this section.

• Fuel injection systems often remain pressurized, even after the engine has been turned **OFF**. The fuel system pressure must be relieved before disconnecting any fuel lines. Failure to do so may result in fire and/or personal injury.

• Brake fluid often contains polyglycol ethers and polyglycols. Avoid contact with the eyes and wash your hands thoroughly after handling brake fluid. If you do get brake fluid in your eyes, flush your eyes with clean, running water for 15 minutes. If eye irritation persists, or if you have taken brake fluid internally, IMMEDIATELY seek medical assistance.

• The EPA warns that prolonged contact with used engine oil may cause a number of skin disorders, including cancer. You should make every effort to minimize your exposure to used engine oil. Protective gloves should be worn when changing oil. Wash your hands and any other exposed skin areas as soon as possible after exposure to used engine oil. Soap and water, or waterless hand cleaner should be used.

• All new vehicles are now equipped with an air bag system, often referred to as a Supplemental Restraint System (SRS) or Supplemental Inflatable Restraint (SIR) system. The system must be disabled before performing service on or around system components, steering column, instrument panel components, wiring and sensors. Failure to follow safety and disabling procedures could result in accidental air bag deployment, possible personal injury and unnecessary system repairs.

• Always wear safety goggles when working with, or around, the air bag system. When carrying a non-deployed air bag, be sure the bag and trim cover are pointed away from your body. When placing a non-deployed air bag on a work surface, always face the bag and trim cover upward, away from the surface. This will reduce the motion of the module if it is accidentally deployed. Refer to the additional air bag system precautions later in this section.

• Clean, high quality brake fluid from a sealed container is essential to the safe and proper operation of the brake system. You should always buy the correct type of brake fluid for your vehicle. If the brake fluid becomes contaminated, completely flush the system with new fluid. Never reuse any brake fluid. Any brake fluid that is removed from the system should be discarded. Also, do not allow any brake fluid to come in contact with a painted surface; it will damage the paint.

• Never operate the engine without the proper amount and type of engine oil; doing so WILL result in severe engine damage.

• Timing belt maintenance is extremely important. Many models utilize an interference-type, non-freewheeling engine. If the timing belt breaks, the valves in the cylinder head may strike the pistons, causing potentially serious (also time-consuming and expensive) engine damage. Refer to the maintenance interval charts for the recommended replacement interval for the timing belt, and to the timing belt section for belt replacement and inspection.

• Disconnecting the negative battery cable on some vehicles may interfere with the functions of the on-board computer system(s) and may require the computer to undergo a relearning process once the negative battery cable is reconnected.

• When servicing drum brakes, only disassemble and assemble one side at a time, leaving the remaining side intact for reference.

• Only an MVAC-trained, EPA-certified automotive technician should service the air conditioning system or its components.

BRAKES

GENERAL INFORMATION

PRECAUTIONS

• Certain components within the ABS system are not intended to be serviced or repaired individually.

• Do not use rubber hoses or other parts not specifically specified for and ABS system. When using repair kits, replace all parts included in the kit. Partial or incorrect repair may lead to functional problems and require the replacement of components.

• Lubricate rubber parts with clean, fresh brake fluid to ease assembly. Do not use shop air to clean parts; damage to rubber components may result.

• Use only DOT 3 brake fluid from an unopened container.

• If any hydraulic component or line is removed or replaced, it may be necessary to bleed the entire system.

• A clean repair area is essential. Always clean the reservoir and cap thoroughly before removing the cap. The slightest amount of dirt in the fluid may plug an orifice and impair the system function. Perform repairs after components have been thoroughly cleaned; use only denatured alcohol to clean components. Do not allow ABS components to come into contact with any substance containing mineral oil; this includes used shop rags.

• The Anti-Lock control unit is a microprocessor similar to other computer units in the vehicle. Ensure that the ignition switch is **OFF** before removing or installing controller harnesses. Avoid static

ANTI-LOCK BRAKE SYSTEM (ABS)

electricity discharge at or near the controller.

• If any arc welding is to be done on the vehicle, the control unit should be unplugged before welding operations begin.

WHEEL SPEED SENSORS

REMOVAL & INSTALLATION

Front

2WD Vehicles

See Figures 1 and 2.

1. Raise and safely support the vehicle.

➡**The harness connector is located in the engine compartment secured to the fender apron.**

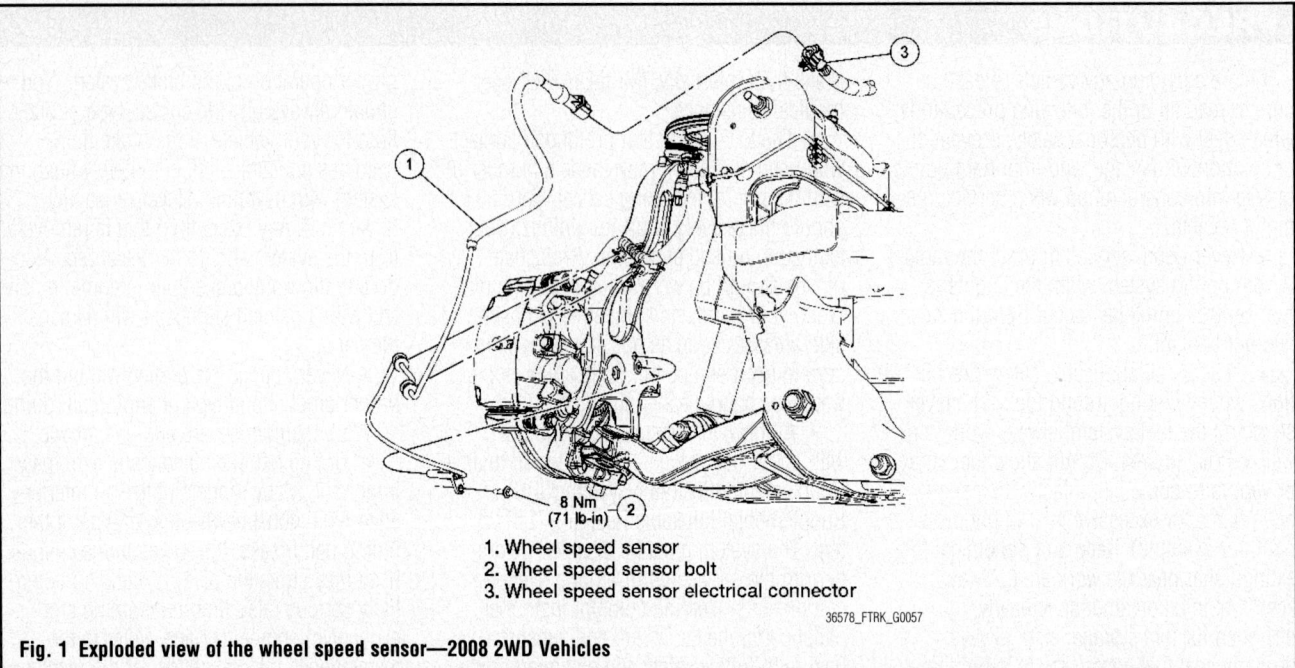

1. Wheel speed sensor
2. Wheel speed sensor bolt
3. Wheel speed sensor electrical connector

36578_FTRK_G0057

Fig. 1 Exploded view of the wheel speed sensor—2008 2WD Vehicles

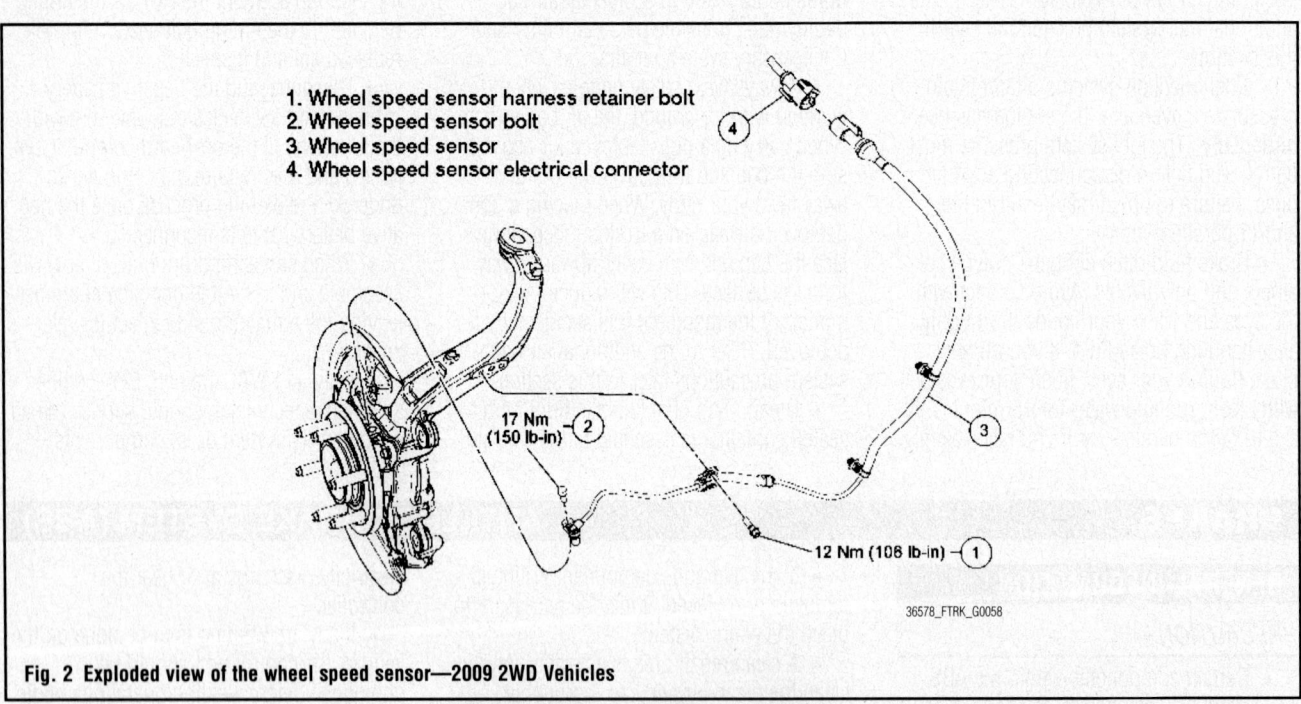

1. Wheel speed sensor harness retainer bolt
2. Wheel speed sensor bolt
3. Wheel speed sensor
4. Wheel speed sensor electrical connector

36578_FTRK_G0058

Fig. 2 Exploded view of the wheel speed sensor—2009 2WD Vehicles

2. Disconnect the wheel speed sensor electrical connector.

3. Remove the 2 wheel speed sensor harness retainers.

4. Remove the wheel speed sensor harness from the pushpin retainer.

5. Remove the bolt and the wheel speed sensor.

6. To install, reverse the removal procedure.

4WD Vehicles

See Figure 3.

⁂ **WARNING**

When removing the front disc brake components, never allow them to hang from the brake hose.

1. Raise and safely support the vehicle.

➡ **The harness connector is located in the engine compartment secured to the fender apron.**

2. Disconnect the wheel speed sensor electrical connector.

3. Remove the 4 wheel speed sensor harness retainers.

4. Remove the 2 bolts and position the front brake caliper assembly aside. See Brake Caliper R&I.

➡ **Match mark the front disc brake rotor and front wheel hub flange before removing the front disc brake rotor.**

5. Remove the brake disc.

6. Remove the bolt and the front wheel speed sensor.

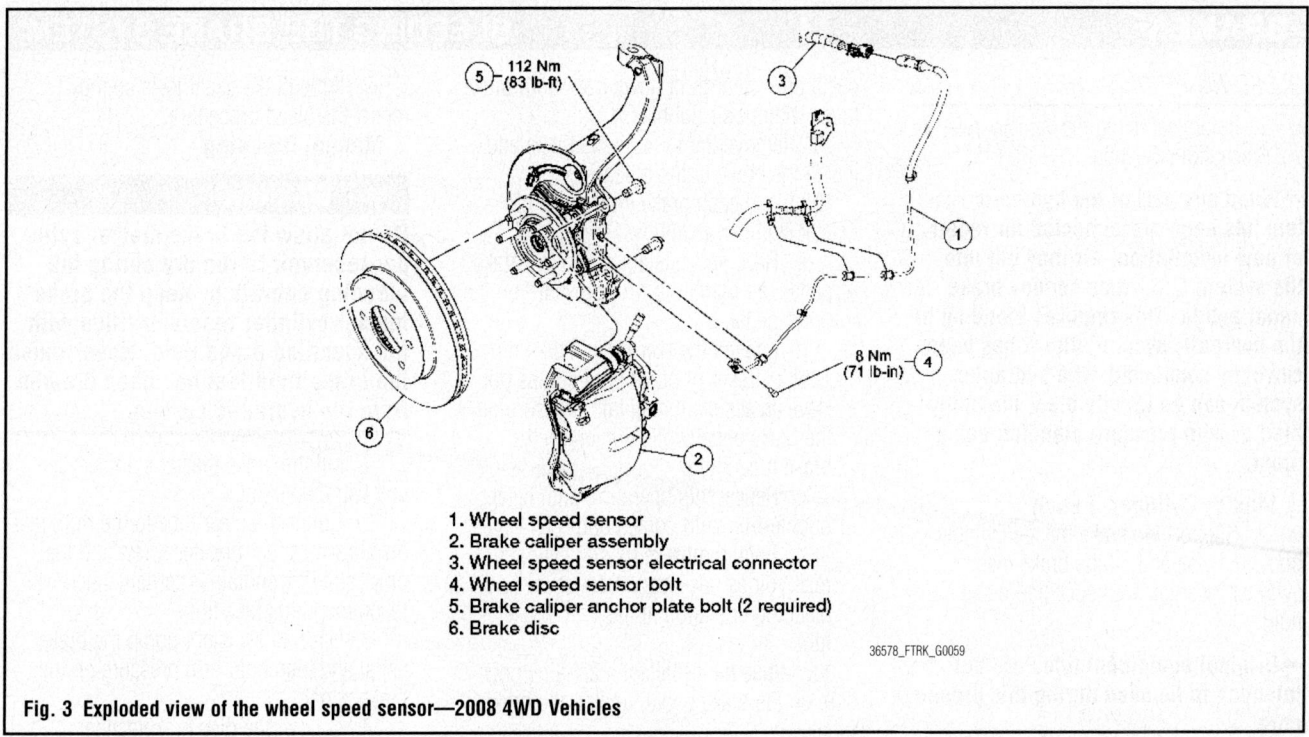

1. Wheel speed sensor
2. Brake caliper assembly
3. Wheel speed sensor electrical connector
4. Wheel speed sensor bolt
5. Brake caliper anchor plate bolt (2 required)
6. Brake disc

36578_FTRK_G0059

Fig. 3 Exploded view of the wheel speed sensor—2008 4WD Vehicles

7. To install, reverse the removal procedure.

Rear

See Figure 4.

1. Raise and safely support the vehicle.
2. Disconnect the rear axle speed sensor electrical connector.
3. Remove the rear axle speed sensor bolt.

➡**Install a new O-ring before installing the rear axle speed sensor.**

4. Remove the rear axle speed sensor.
5. To install, reverse the removal procedure. Tighten to 15 Nm (11 ft. lbs.).

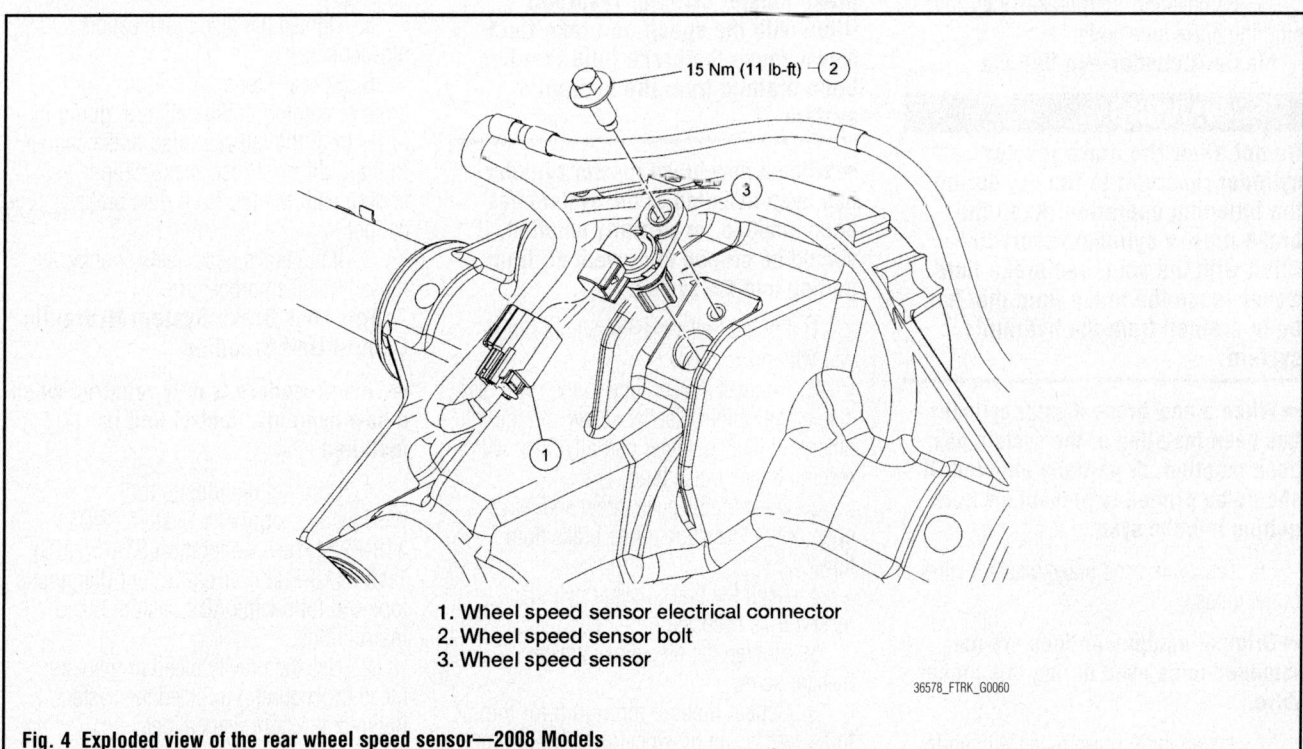

1. Wheel speed sensor electrical connector
2. Wheel speed sensor bolt
3. Wheel speed sensor

36578_FTRK_G0060

Fig. 4 Exploded view of the rear wheel speed sensor—2008 Models

BRAKES   **BLEEDING THE BRAKE SYSTEM**

BLEEDING PROCEDURE

1. Before servicing the vehicle, refer to the Precautions Section.

➡ **When any part of the hydraulic system has been disconnected for repair or new installation, air may get into the system and cause spongy brake pedal action. This requires bleeding of the hydraulic system after it has been correctly connected. The hydraulic system can be gravity bled, manually bled or with pressure bleeding equipment.**

Master Cylinder, Bench

2. Support the brake master cylinder body in a vise and fill the brake master cylinder reservoir with specified brake fluid.

➡ **Original equipment lines are not intended to be used during this procedure.**

3. Install short brake tubes with the ends submerged in the brake master cylinder reservoir.

4. Slowly press the primary piston until clear fluid flows from both brake tubes, without air bubbles.

5. Remove the short brake tubes and plug the brake tube ports.

Master Cylinder—In Vehicle

❋❋ **WARNING**

Do not allow the brake master cylinder reservoir to run dry during the bleeding operation. Keep the brake master cylinder reservoir filled with the specified brake fluid. Never reuse the brake fluid that has been drained from the hydraulic system.

➡ **When a new brake master cylinder has been installed or the system has been emptied, or partially emptied, it should be primed to prevent air from getting into the system.**

6. Disconnect the brake master cylinder outlet tubes.

➡ **Original equipment lines are not intended to be used during this procedure.**

7. Install short brake tubes with ends submerged in the brake master cylinder reservoir and fill the brake master cylinder reservoir with brake fluid.

8. Have an assistant pump the brake pedal until clear fluid flows from both brake tubes without air bubbles.

9. Remove the short brake tubes and install the brake outlet tubes.

10. Bleed each brake tube at the brake master cylinder as follows:

   a. Have an assistant pump the brake pedal and then hold firm pressure on the brake pedal.

   b. Loosen the rear brake tube fittings until a stream of brake fluid comes out. Have an assistant maintain pressure on the brake pedal while tightening the brake tube fitting.

   c. Repeat this operation until clear, bubble-free fluid comes out.

   d. Refill the brake master cylinder reservoir as necessary. Repeat the bleeding operation at the front brake tube.

11. While the assistant maintains pressure on the brake pedal, tighten the brake tubes.

Gravity Bleeding

❋❋ **WARNING**

Do not allow the brake master cylinder reservoir to run dry during the bleeding operation. Keep the brake master cylinder reservoir filled with the specified brake fluid. Never reuse the brake fluid that has been drained from the hydraulic system.

➡ **When a new brake master cylinder has been installed or the system has been emptied, or partially emptied, it should be primed to prevent air from getting into the system.**

1. Fill the brake master cylinder reservoir with brake fluid.

2. Connect a clear tube to the right rear disc brake caliper bleeder screw and the other end in a container partially filled with recommended brake fluid.

3. Open the bleeder screw and leave open until clear bubble-free brake fluid flows.

4. Refill the brake master cylinder reservoir as necessary.

5. Tighten the disc brake caliper bleeder screw.

6. Repeat Steps 2 through 5 for the three remaining brake calipers, going in order from the left rear disc brake caliper to the right front disc brake caliper ending with the left front disc brake caliper.

7. If the brake pedal feels spongy, repeat the bleed procedure.

Manual Bleeding

❋❋ **WARNING**

Do not allow the brake master cylinder reservoir to run dry during the bleeding operation. Keep the brake master cylinder reservoir filled with the specified brake fluid. Never reuse the brake fluid that has been drained from the hydraulic system.

1. Fill the brake master cylinder reservoir with brake fluid.

2. Connect a clear tube to the right rear disc brake caliper bleeder screw and the other end in a container partially filled with recommended brake fluid.

3. Have an assistant pump the brake pedal and then hold firm pressure on the brake pedal.

4. Loosen the disc brake caliper bleeder screw until a stream of brake fluid comes out. Have an assistant maintain pressure on the brake pedal while tightening the disc brake caliper bleeder screw. Repeat until clear, bubble-free fluid comes out. Refill the brake master cylinder reservoir as necessary.

5. Tighten the disc brake caliper bleeder screw.

6. Repeat Steps 1 through 5 for the three remaining brake calipers, going in order from the left rear disc brake caliper to the right front disc brake caliper ending with the left front disc brake caliper.

7. If the brake pedal feels spongy, repeat the bleed procedure.

Anti-Lock Brake System Hydraulic Control Unit Bleeding

➡ **This procedure is only required when a new hydraulic control unit is installed.**

1. Connect diagnostic tool Worldwide Diagnostic System (WDS) 418-F224, New Generation STAR (NGS) Tester 418-F052, or equivalent diagnostic tool and follow the ABS system bleed instructions.

2. Use the gravity bleed or manual bleed procedure(s) to bleed the system. Begin at the right rear caliper.

BLEEDING THE ABS SYSTEM

Anti-Lock Brake System (ABS) Hydraulic Control Unit Bleeding

→This procedure is required only when a new hydraulic control unit is installed. A diagnostic tool, or equivalent, is necessary.

→When any part of the hydraulic system has been disconnected for repair or new installation, air may get into the system and cause spongy brake pedal action. This requires bleeding of the hydraulic system after it has been correctly connected. See Bleeding the Brake System.

1. Connect the diagnostic tool and follow the ABS system bleed instructions.

2. Use the manual bleed procedure(s) to bleed the system. Begin at the right rear caliper.

BRAKES

FRONT DISC BRAKES

BRAKE CALIPER

REMOVAL & INSTALLATION

2008 Models

See Figure 5.

1. Before servicing the vehicle, refer to the Precautions Section.

2. Remove the wheel and tire assembly.

3. Remove the caliper bolts

4. Remove the brake caliper

> ※ **WARNING**
>
> **Do not allow the brake caliper to hang by the flexible brake hose.**

5. Support the caliper to the vehicle.

6. Remove the flow bolt

7. Remove the copper washers

8. Remove the brake line

9. To install, reverse the removal procedure. Tighten the bottom caliper bolt and then the top caliper bolt. Always use new copper washers.

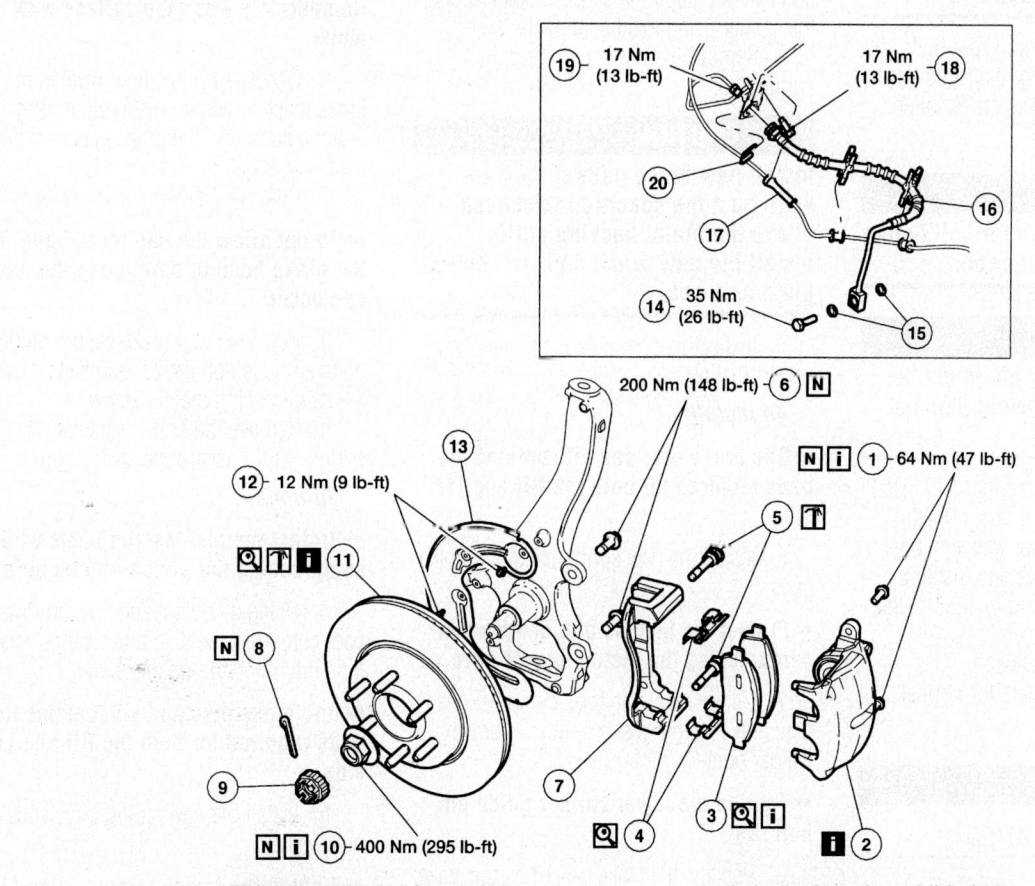

1 Caliper bolt (2 required for each side)
2 Brake caliper (RH/LH)
3 Brake disc pads (1 kit LH and RH)
4 Slippers
5 Guide pin and boot (2 required for each side)
6 Anchor bracket bolts (2 required for each side)
7 Anchor bracket
8 Cotter pin
9 Retainer
10 Spindle nut (1 each side)
11 Brake disc (heavy duty and light duty)
12 Dust shield bolts (3 required each side)
13 Dust shield (RH/LH)
14 Flow bolt
15 Copper washers (2 required each side)
16 Brake line (RH/LH)
17 Anti-lock brake sensor cable
18 Brake line bracket bolt
19 Brake line fitting
20 Retainer clip

67197-EFSE-G201

Fig. 5 Exploded view of the front disc brake components—2008 Models

10. Observe the following torques:
- Caliper mounting bolts: 47 ft. lbs. (64 Nm)
- Brake line flow bolt: 26 ft. lbs. (35 Nm)

11. Bleed the brake system.

2009 Models

1. Before servicing the vehicle, refer to the Precautions Section.
2. Raise and safely support the vehicle.
3. Remove the brake flexible hose flow bolt and position the brake flexible hose aside. Discard the 2 copper washers.

> **❊❊ WARNING**
>
> Do not pry in the caliper sight hole to retract the pistons as this can damage the pistons and boots.

4. Remove the 2 brake caliper bolts and the brake caliper. If leaks or damaged boots are found, install a new disc brake caliper.

To install:

> **❊❊ WARNING**
>
> Tighten the bottom caliper bolt before tightening the top caliper bolt.

> **❊❊ WARNING**
>
> Make sure the caliper pin boots are correctly seated to prevent damage to the guide pins.

5. Position the brake caliper and install the 2 bolts. Torque to 56 ft. lbs. (76 Nm).
6. Using 2 new copper washers, position the brake flexible hose and install the brake caliper flow bolt. Torque to 35 ft. lbs. (48 Nm).
7. Bleed the brake caliper.
8. Test the brake system for normal operation.

DISC BRAKE PADS

REMOVAL & INSTALLATION

2008 Models

See Figure 5.

> **❊❊ WARNING**
>
> Use of any other than approved DOT 3 motor vehicle brake fluid will cause permanent damage to brake components and will render the brakes inoperative. Failure to follow these instructions may result in personal injury.

> **❊❊ CAUTION**
>
> Brake fluid is harmful to painted and plastic surfaces. If brake fluid is spilled onto a painted or plastic surface, immediately wash it with water.

1. Check the brake fluid level in the brake master cylinder reservoir. If necessary, remove fluid until the brake master cylinder reservoir is half full.
2. With the vehicle in NEUTRAL, position it on a hoist.

> **❊❊ CAUTION**
>
> Do not allow the caliper to hang from the brake hose or damage to the hose can occur.

3. Remove the 2 brake caliper guide pin bolts and position the caliper aside. Support the caliper using mechanic's wire.
4. Remove the brake pads and the 2 spring clips.

> **❊❊ CAUTION**
>
> Install new brake pads if they are worn past the specified thickness, above the metal backing plate. Install the new brake pads in complete axle sets.

5. Inspect the brake pads for wear and contamination.

To install:

➡ One brake disc pad kit contains the pads required for both the RH and LH side.

6. Install the new spring clips and brake pads.

➡ Protect the pistons and boots when compressing the piston into its bore.

7. Using a suitable tool, compress the disc brake caliper pistons into the brake caliper bore.

➡ Tighten the lower caliper guide pin bolt first.

8. Position the brake caliper on the brake caliper anchor plate and install the 2 guide pin bolts. Tighten to 55 ft. lbs. (74 Nm).

2009 Models

See Figure 6.

> **❊❊ WARNING**
>
> Do not use any fluid other than clean brake fluid meeting manufacturer's specification. Additionally, do not use brake fluid that has been previ-

ously drained. Following these instructions will help prevent system contamination, brake component damage and the risk of serious personal injury.

> **❊❊ WARNING**
>
> Always install new brake shoes or pads at both ends of an axle to reduce the possibility of brakes pulling vehicle to one side. Failure to follow this instruction may result in uneven braking and serious personal injury.

➡ Do not spill brake fluid on painted or plastic surfaces or damage to the surface may occur. If brake fluid is spilled onto a painted or plastic surface, immediately wash the surface with water.

1. Check the brake fluid level in the brake master cylinder reservoir. If necessary, remove fluid until the brake master cylinder reservoir is half full.
2. Remove the wheel and tire

➡ Do not allow the caliper to hang from the brake hose or damage to the hose can occur.

3. Remove the 2 brake caliper guide pin bolts and position the caliper aside. Support the caliper using mechanic's wire.
4. Remove the brake pads and the 2 spring clips. Discard the spring clips.

To install:

➡ Protect the pistons and boots when compressing the piston into its bore.

5. Using a C-clamp and a worn brake pad, compress the disc brake caliper pistons into the brake caliper bore.

➡ One brake disc pad kit contains the pads required for both the RH and LH side.

6. Install the new spring clips and brake pads.

➡ Tighten the lower caliper guide pin bolt first.

7. Position the brake caliper on the brake caliper anchor plate and install the 2 guide pin bolts. Tighten to 55 ft. lbs. (74 Nm).

8. Install the wheel and tire.
9. Apply brakes several times to verify correct brake operation.
10. Fill the master cylinder with clean specified brake fluid.

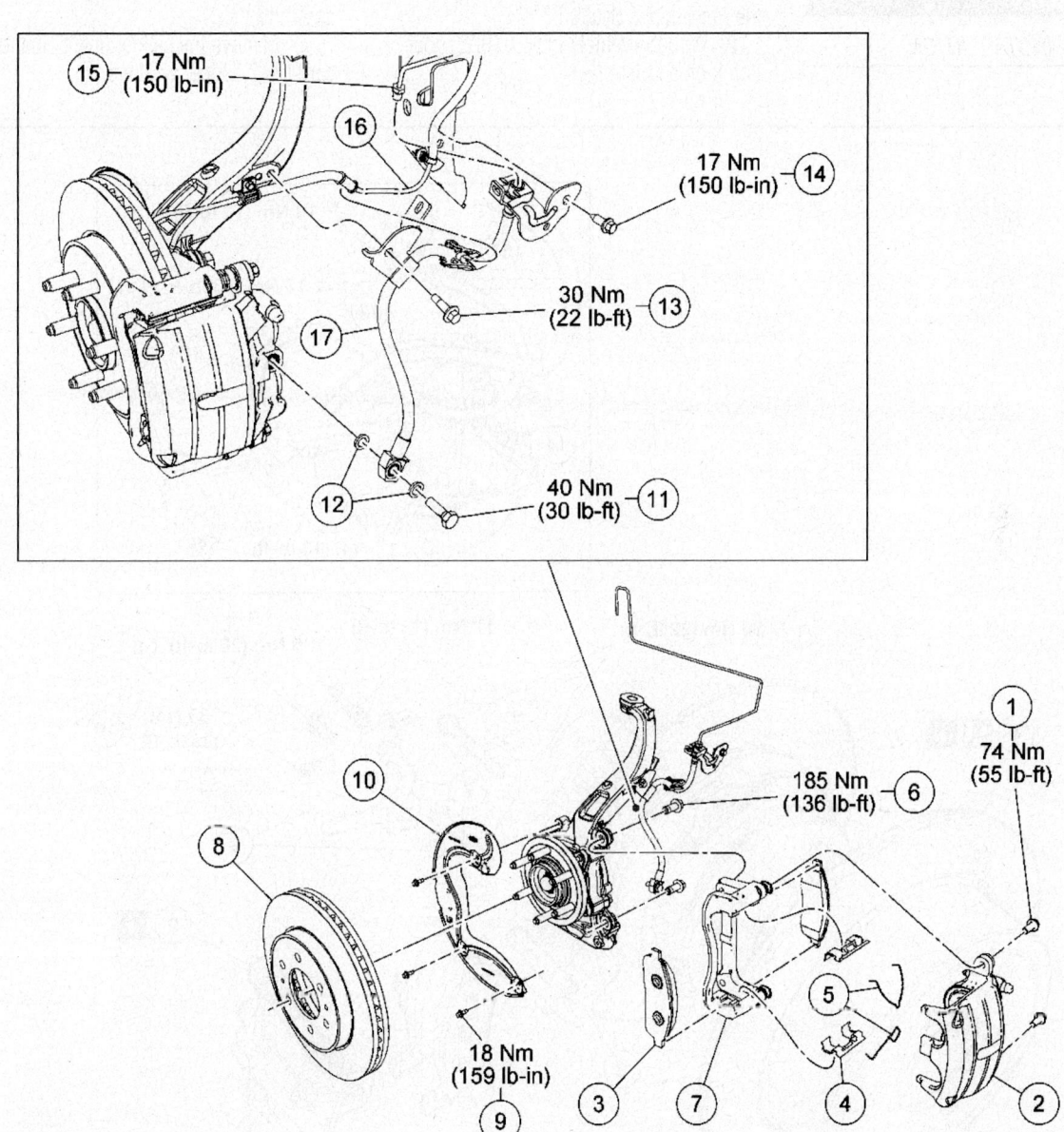

1. Brake caliper guide pin bolts
2. Brake caliper
3. Brake disc pad (2 required)
4. Spring clips
5. Brake pad retraction clip
6. Brake caliper anchor plate bolt (2 required)
7. Brake caliper anchor plate
8. Brake disc

9. Brake disc shield bolt (3 required)
10. Brake disc shield
11. Brake caliper flow bolt
12. Copper washers
13. Brake flexible hose bracket-to-spindle bolt
14. Brake flexible hose bracket-to-frame bolt
15. Brake tube fitting
16. Wheel speed sensor harness
17. Brake flexible hose

36578_FTRK_G0062

Fig. 6 Exploded view of the front disc brake components—2WD shown, 4WD similar—2009 Models

BRAKES **REAR DISC BRAKES**

BRAKE CALIPER

REMOVAL & INSTALLATION

See Figure 7.

1. Before servicing the vehicle, refer to the Precautions Section.
2. With the vehicle in NEUTRAL, position it on a hoist.
3. Remove the rear wheel and tire assembly.
4. Remove the caliper flow bolt and discard the 2 copper washers.

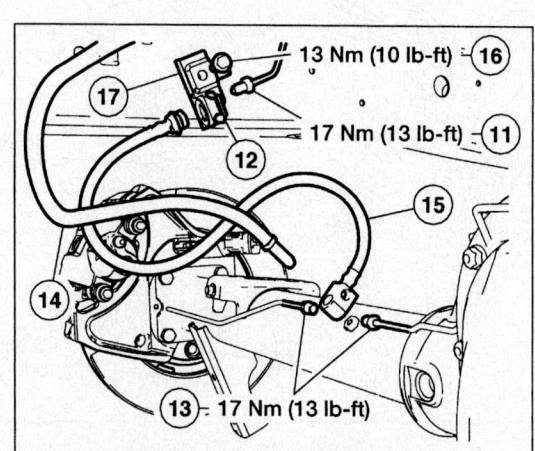

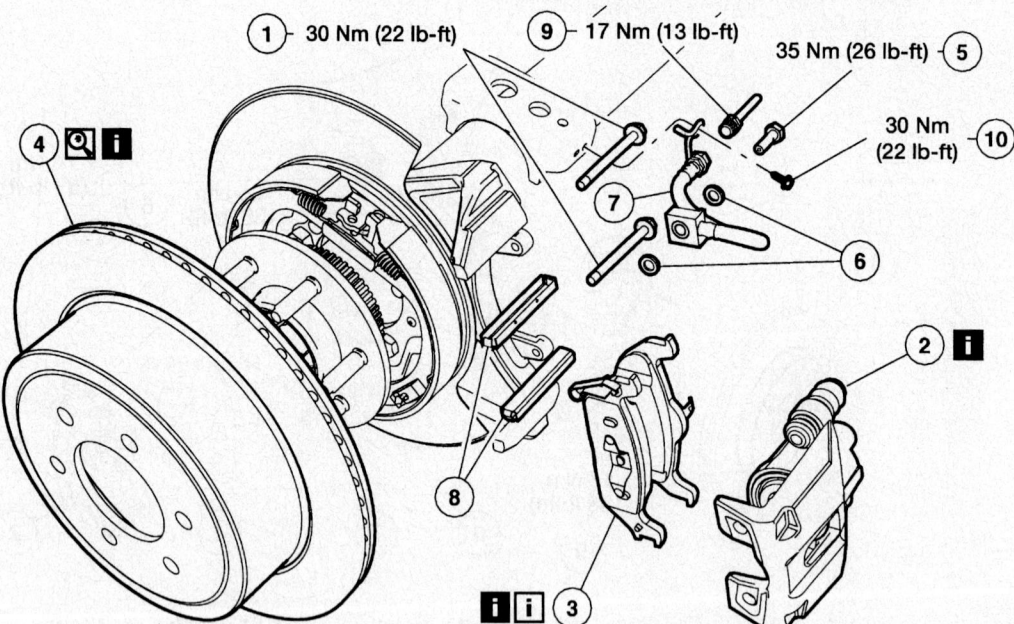

1 Caliper bolts (2 required each side)
2 Brake caliper
3 Disc brake pads (1 kit)
4 Brake disc
5 Flow bolt
6 Brass washers (2 required each side)
7 Brake hose
8 Slippers (2 required each side)
9 Brake line fitting
10 Rear brake hose bracket bolt
11 Brake line fitting
12 Retainer clip
13 Brake line fittings
14 Rear axle vent tube
15 Rear brake jounce hose
16 Rear brake jounce hose bracket bolt
17 Rear brake jounce hose bracket

67197-EFSE-G208

Fig. 7 Exploded view of the rear disc brake components

5. Remove the two guide pin bolts and the brake caliper.

6. To install, reverse the removal procedure. Observe the following torques:
- Caliper pin bolts: 22 ft. lbs. (30 Nm)
- Flow bolt: 26 ft. lbs. (35 Nm)

7. If the hydraulic system has been opened, bleed the brake system.

DISC BRAKE PADS

REMOVAL & INSTALLATION

See Figure 7.

1. Before servicing the vehicle, refer to the Precautions Section.

2. With the vehicle in NEUTRAL, position it on a hoist.

3. Check the brake fluid level in the brake master cylinder reservoir. If required, remove fluid until the brake master cylinder reservoir is half full.

❋❋ CAUTION

Do not allow the brake caliper to hang from the brake hose or damage to the hose can result.

4. Remove the 2 brake caliper guide pin bolts and position the brake caliper aside. Support the caliper using mechanic's wire.

5. Measure the brake disc thickness and install a new brake disc if it is not within specification.

6. Remove the brake pads and the 2 spring clips. Discard the spring clips.

❋❋ CAUTION

Install a new pad if it is worn past the specified thickness above the metal backing plate or rivets. Install new pads in complete axle sets.

7. Inspect the pads for wear and contamination.

8. Inspect the brake caliper anchor plate assembly.
   a. Check the guide pin boots for damage.
   b. Check the guide pins for binding and damage.
   c. Replace worn or damaged boots. Lubricate the guide pins.

To install:

❋❋ CAUTION

Protect the piston and boot when pushing the piston into the caliper bore.

9. Using a suitable tool and a worn brake pad, compress the caliper piston into the caliper.

❋❋ CAUTION

Do not allow grease, oil, brake fluid or other contaminants to contact the pad lining material. Do not install contaminated pads.

➡**Install all new hardware supplied with the pad kit and spring kit.**

10. Install the 2 new spring clips and brake pads.

11. Position the brake caliper and install the 2 guide pin bolts. Tighten to 30 Nm (22 lb-ft).

12. Test the brakes for normal operation.

BRAKES

PARKING BRAKE

PARKING BRAKE CABLES

ADJUSTMENT

The parking brake system utilizes an automatic adjuster. No adjustment is necessary.

PARKING BRAKE SHOES

REMOVAL & INSTALLATION

See Figure 8.

1. Before servicing the vehicle, refer to the Precautions Section.

➡**One parking brake shoe kit contains the linings required for both the left and right side.**

➡**Make sure the parking brake control is fully released.**

2. Relieve the tension on the parking brake cable.
   a. With the vehicle in NEUTRAL, position it on the hoist.
   b. Remove the left A-pillar lower trim panel.

   c. With an assistant, release the parking brake cable tension by pulling down on the intermediate cable at the cable-to-cable union until the parking brake control sector rotates to its stop and a 4 mm (0.15 in.) x 150 mm (5.9 in.) retainer pin can be inserted.
   d. Disconnect the cable at the cable-to-cable union.

3. Remove the rear brake disc.

4. Remove the brake shoe adjuster screw.

5. Remove the brake shoe adjuster screw spring.

6. Remove the 2 brake shoe hold down springs and 2 pins.

7. Remove the brake shoe retracting spring and the parking brake shoes.

To install:

➡**Lubricate the parking brake shoes where the shoe contacts the wear pad on the backing plate.**

8. Position the parking brake shoes and attach the retracting spring.

9. Install the 2 brake shoe hold-down pins and springs.

10. Install the brake shoe adjusting screw spring.

➡**Completely retract the parking brake adjusting screw before installation.**

11. Install the brake shoe adjusting screw.

12. Measure the inside diameter of the parking brake drum.

13. Adjust the parking brake shoe clearance to 0.6 mm (0.02 in.) less than the inside diameter of the parking brake drum.

14. Make sure that the parking brake shoes are correctly centered by measuring across the center point of the shoes.

15. Rotate the parking brake shoe adjuster wheel to achieve the correct parking brake shoe-to-brake disc clearance.

16. Install the rear brake disc.

17. Reload the tension on the parking brake cable.

ADJUSTMENT

Parking brake shoe adjustment is part of the parking brake shoe installation procedure.

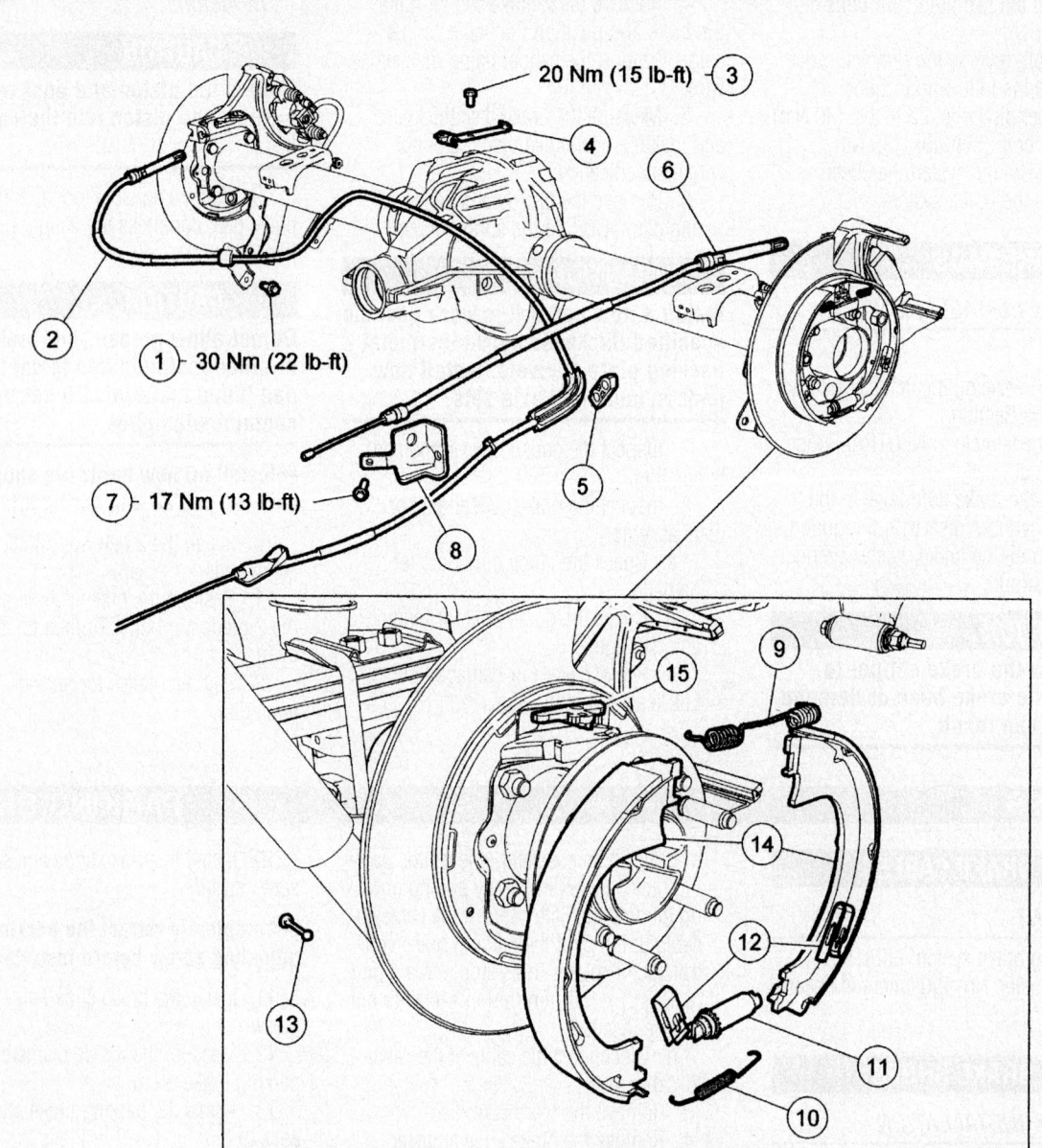

20 Nm (15 lb-ft) — 3

4

6

1 — 30 Nm (22 lb-ft)

2

7 — 17 Nm (13 lb-ft)

8

5

15

9

14

12

11

13

10

1 Parking brake cable bracket bolt (RH)	9 Parking brake shoe return spring
2 Rear parking brake cable (RH)	10 Parking brake shoe adjuster spring
3 Parking brake cable differential bracket bolt (RH)	11 Parking brake shoe adjuster
4 Parking brake cable differential bracket	12 Parking brake shoe retainer spring clip (2 required)
5 Double cable clamp	13 Parking brake shoe retainer pin (2 required)
6 Parking brake cable (LH)	14 Parking brake shoe kit (1 kit required)
7 Parking brake cable bracket bolt (LH)	15 Actuator lever kit (LH/RH)
8 Parking brake cable bracket (LH)	

06017-F150-G282

Fig. 8 Parking brake exploded view—2008 model shown, 2009 similar

CHASSIS ELECTRICAL   AIR BAG (SUPPLEMENTAL RESTRAINT SYSTEM)

✳✳ CAUTION

These vehicles are equipped with an air bag system. The system must be disarmed before performing service on, or around, system components, the steering column, instrument panel components, wiring and sensors. Failure to follow the safety precautions and the disarming procedure could result in accidental air bag deployment, possible injury and unnecessary system repairs.

GENERAL INFORMATION

SERVICE PRECAUTIONS

Disconnect and isolate the battery negative cable before beginning any airbag system component diagnosis, testing, removal, or installation procedures. Allow system capacitor to discharge for two minutes before beginning any component service. This will disable the airbag system. Failure to disable the airbag system may result in accidental airbag deployment, personal injury, or death.

Do not place an intact undeployed airbag face down on a solid surface. The airbag will propel into the air if accidentally deployed and may result in personal injury or death.

When carrying or handling an undeployed airbag, the trim side (face) of the airbag should be pointing towards the body to minimize possibility of injury if accidental deployment occurs. Failure to do this may result in personal injury or death.

Replace airbag system components with OEM replacement parts. Substitute parts may appear interchangeable, but internal differences may result in inferior occupant protection. Failure to do so may result in occupant personal injury or death.

Wear safety glasses, rubber gloves, and long sleeved clothing when cleaning powder residue from vehicle after an airbag deployment. Powder residue emitted from a deployed airbag can cause skin irritation. Flush affected area with cool water if irritation is experienced. If nasal or throat irritation is experienced, exit the vehicle for fresh air until the irritation ceases. If irritation continues, see a physician.

Do not use a replacement airbag that is not in the original packaging. This may result in improper deployment, personal injury, or death.

The factory installed fasteners, screws

and bolts used to fasten airbag components have a special coating and are specifically designed for the airbag system. Do not use substitute fasteners. Use only original equipment fasteners listed in the parts catalog when fastener replacement is required.

During, and following, any child restraint anchor service, due to impact event or vehicle repair, carefully inspect all mounting hardware, tether straps, and anchors for proper installation, operation, or damage. If a child restraint anchor is found damaged in any way, the anchor must be replaced. Failure to do this may result in personal injury or death.

Deployed and non-deployed airbags may or may not have live pyrotechnic material within the airbag inflator.

Do not dispose of driver/passenger/curtain airbags or seat belt tensioners unless you are sure of complete deployment. Refer to the Hazardous Substance Control System for proper disposal.

Dispose of deployed airbags and tensioners consistent with state, provincial, local, and federal regulations.

After any airbag component testing or service, do not connect the battery negative cable. Personal injury or death may result if the system test is not performed first.

If the vehicle is equipped with the Occupant Classification System (OCS), do not connect the battery negative cable before performing the OCS Verification Test using the scan tool and the appropriate diagnostic information. Personal injury or death may result if the system test is not performed properly.

Never replace both the Occupant Restraint Controller (ORC) and the Occupant Classification Module (OCM) at the same time. If both require replacement, replace one, then perform the Airbag System test before replacing the other.

Both the ORC and the OCM store Occupant Classification System (OCS) calibration data, which they transfer to one another when one of them is replaced. If both are replaced at the same time, an irreversible fault will be set in both modules and the OCS may malfunction and cause personal injury or death.

If equipped with OCS, the Seat Weight Sensor is a sensitive, calibrated unit and must be handled carefully. Do not drop or handle roughly. If dropped or damaged, replace with another sensor. Failure to do so may result in occupant injury or death.

If equipped with OCS, the front passen-

ger seat must be handled carefully as well. When removing the seat, be careful when setting on floor not to drop. If dropped, the sensor may be inoperative, could result in occupant injury, or possibly death.

If equipped with OCS, when the passenger front seat is on the floor, no one should sit in the front passenger seat. This uneven force may damage the sensing ability of the seat weight sensors. If sat on and damaged, the sensor may be inoperative, could result in occupant injury, or possibly death.

DISARMING THE SYSTEM

1. Before servicing the vehicle, refer to the Precautions Section.
2. Turn all vehicle accessories OFF.
3. Turn the ignition switch to OFF.
4. At the central junction box (CJB), located below the instrument panel, remove the trim panel, the cover, and the restraints control module (RCM) fuse from the CJB. See your Owner's Manual for fuse identification.
5. Turn the ignition ON and visually monitor the air bag indicator for at least 30 seconds. The air bag indicator will remain lit continuously (no flashing) if the correct RCM fuse has been removed. If the air bag indicator does not remain lit continuously, remove the correct RCM fuse before proceeding.
6. Turn the ignition OFF.

✳✳ CAUTION

To avoid accidental deployment and possible personal injury, the backup power supply must be depleted before repairing or replacing any front or side air bag supplemental restraint system (SRS) components and before servicing, replacing, adjusting or striking components near the front or side air bag sensors, such as doors, instrument panel, console, door latches, strikers, seats and hood latches.

7. To deplete the backup power supply energy, disconnect the battery ground cable and wait at least 1 minute. Be sure to disconnect auxiliary batteries and power supplies (if equipped).
8. Disconnect the battery ground cable and wait at least 1 minute.

ARMING THE SYSTEM

1. Before servicing the vehicle, refer to the Precautions Section.

2. Turn the ignition switch from OFF to ON.

3. Install the RCM fuse to the CJB and install the cover and trim panel.

> ❈❈ **CAUTION**
>
> **Be sure that nobody is in the vehicle and that there is nothing blocking or set in front of any air bag module when the battery ground cable is connected.**

4. Connect the battery ground cable.

5. Prove out the supplemental restraint system (SRS) as follows:

6. Turn the ignition key from ON to OFF. Wait 10 seconds, then turn the key back to ON and visually monitor the air bag indicator with the air bag modules installed. The air bag indicator will light continuously for approximately 6 seconds and then turn off. If an air bag supplemental restraint system (SRS) fault is present, the air bag indicator will either:

- Fail to light
- Remain lit continuously
- Flash

7. The flashing might not occur until approximately 30 seconds after the ignition switch has been turned from the OFF to the ON position. This is the time required for the restraints control module (RCM) to complete the testing of the SRS. If the air bag indicator is inoperative and a SRS fault exists, a chime will sound in a pattern of 5 sets of 5 beeps. If this occurs, the air bag indicator and any SRS fault discovered must be diagnosed and repaired.

8. Clear all continuous DTCs from the restraints control module using a diagnostic tool.

DRIVE TRAIN

AUTOMATIC TRANSMISSION ASSEMBLY

REMOVAL & INSTALLATION

4R70E/4R75E Transmission

2WD Models

See Figures 9 and 10.

1. Before servicing the vehicle, refer to the Precautions Section.

2. Disconnect the battery ground cable.

3. With the vehicle in **Neutral**, position it on a hoist

4. Remove the rear driveshaft.

5. Drain the transmission fluid.

6. Loosen the transmission fluid pan bolts and allow the fluid to drain. After the fluid has drained, remove the bolts.

7. Remove the transmission fluid pan and transmission fluid pan gasket. Drain the rest of the fluid from the pan.

➡**The transmission fluid pan gasket is reusable. Clean and inspect for damage. If not damaged, the gasket should be reused.**

8. Install the transmission fluid pan and gasket.

➡**If removing the transmission for a transmission related failure, it is not necessary to torque the transmission fluid pan back onto the transmission case. If removing the transmission for a non-related transmission failure it is necessary to re-torque the transmission fluid pan.**

9. Install the bolts.

10. Remove the starter motor solenoid terminal cover.

11. Disconnect the starter motor electrical connectors and the ground wire.

12. Remove the starter motor.

13. Remove the rubber plug to access the nuts.

14. Remove the four torque converter nuts. Rotate either the front of the crankshaft or the flexplate to access all of the torque converter retaining nuts.

15. Remove the transmission inspection cover.

16. Remove the shift cable and bracket.

17. Disconnect the transmission electrical connectors.

18. Disconnect the solenoid body assembly electrical connector.

19. Using a suitable transmission jack, support the transmission and secure the transmission to it with a safety strap.

20. Remove the left bolt retaining the heat shield to the transmission support crossmember.

21. Remove the right bolt retaining the heat shield to the transmission support crossmember.

22. Loosen, but do not remove, the transmission mount-to-crossmember nuts.

23. Remove the two bolts for the exhaust hanger.

24. Remove the four crossmember-to-frame nuts and bolts (two on each side).

25. Remove the transmission mount-to-crossmember nuts, and remove the crossmember.

26. Remove the two bolts and the rear transmission mount.

27. Remove the exhaust hanger.

28. Disconnect the transmission fluid cooler tubes.

29. Remove the seven transmission-to-engine bolts.

30. Position the fuel lines and bracket aside.

> ❈❈ **CAUTION**
>
> **The torque converter is heavy and can result in injury if it falls out of**

the transmission. Secure the torque converter in the transmission. If the torque converter is dropped, a new one must be installed.

31. Slide the transmission rearward enough to install the holding tool.

> ❈❈ **CAUTION**
>
> **The transmission must be secured with a safety chain or strap.**

➡**The front of the transmission must be lowered for the transmission to clear the exhaust system during removal.**

32. Continue moving the transmission rearward, while gradually lowering the front of the transmission. As the transmission jack is being lowered, move the transmission forward and remove it from the vehicle.

33. If the transmission is to be overhauled or if installing a new transmission, carry out transmission backflushing and cleaning.

To install:

> ❈❈ **WARNING**
>
> **The torque converter cover is piloted into position to the engine crankshaft by dowels in the rear of the engine block. The torque converter must rest squarely and loosely against the flexplate. This indicates that the torque converter pilot is not binding in the engine crankshaft.**

> ❈❈ **CAUTION**
>
> **The transmission must be secured with a safety chain or strap.**

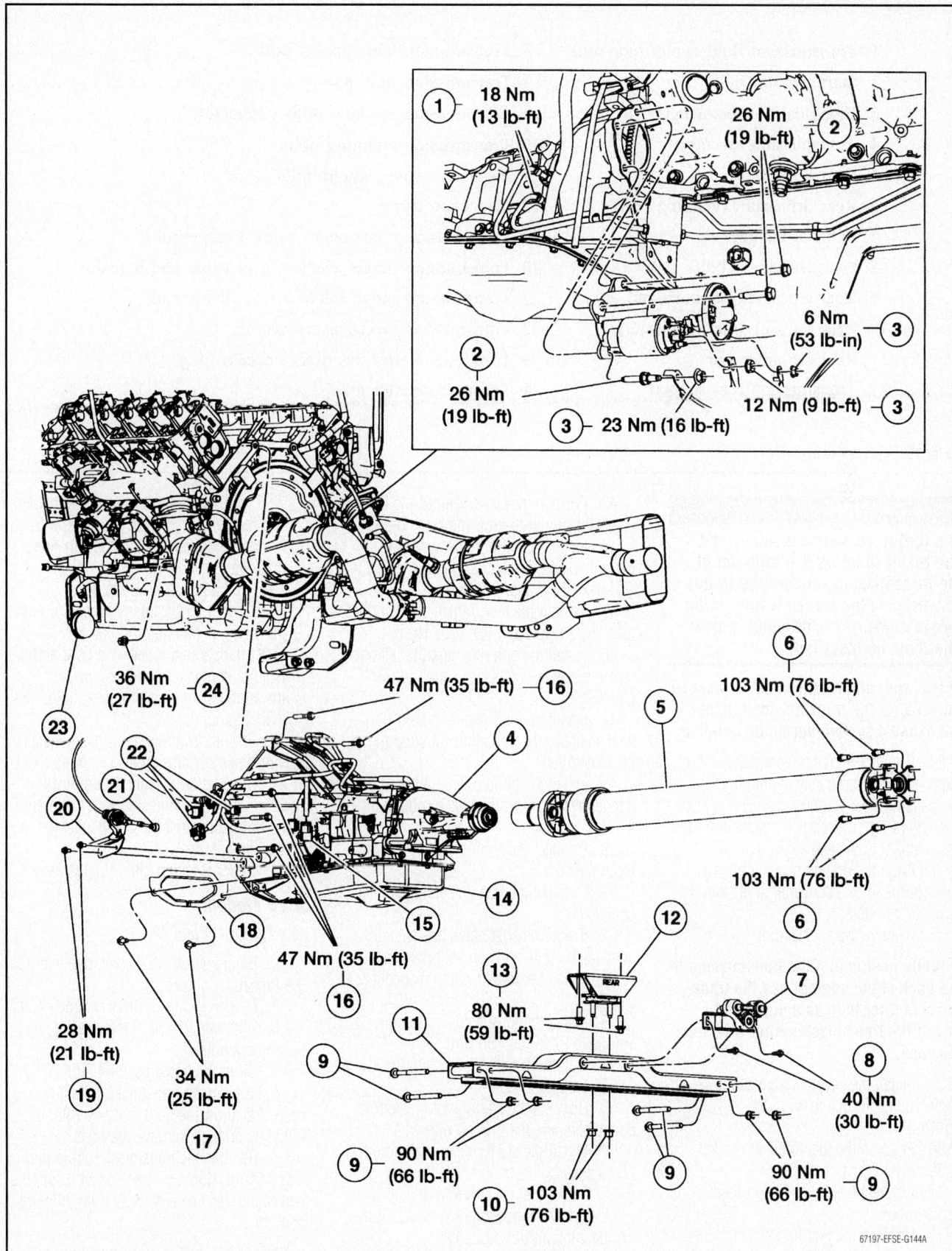

1 18 Nm (13 lb-ft)

2 26 Nm (19 lb-ft)

2 26 Nm (19 lb-ft)

3 23 Nm (16 lb-ft)

3 6 Nm (53 lb-in)

3 12 Nm (9 lb-ft)

23 36 Nm (27 lb-ft) **24**

16 47 Nm (35 lb-ft)

6 103 Nm (76 lb-ft)

5

4

14

15

22 21 20 18

16 47 Nm (35 lb-ft)

6 103 Nm (76 lb-ft)

19 28 Nm (21 lb-ft)

17 34 Nm (25 lb-ft)

9 90 Nm (66 lb-ft)

9

11

13 80 Nm (59 lb-ft)

12

10 103 Nm (76 lb-ft)

9 90 Nm (66 lb-ft)

7

8 40 Nm (30 lb-ft)

67197-EFSE-G144A

Fig. 9 4R70E/4R75E mounting (1 of 2)—2-wheel drive

1 Transmission fluid cooler tube nuts	13 Transmission rear support bolts
2 Starter motor bolts	14 Transmission fluid pan
3 Electrical connector nuts	15 Transmission solenoid body connector
4 Transmission assembly	16 Transmission retaining bolts
5 Rear driveshaft	17 Inspection cover shield bolts
6 Rear driveshaft retaining bolts	18 Inspection cover
7 Exhaust hanger	19 Transmission range selector lever cable bolts
8 Exhaust hanger bolts	20 Transmission range selector lever cable and bracket
9 Rear crossmember bolts and nuts	21 Transmission range selector lever cable end
10 Rear transmission mount nuts	22 Transmission electrical connectors
11 Rear crossmember	23 Torque converter nut rubber access plug
12 Transmission rear support	24 Torque converter nuts

67197-EFSE-G144B

Fig. 10 Keylist (2 of 2)

☀ CAUTION

The torque converter is heavy and can result in injury if it falls out of the transmission. Secure the torque converter in the transmission. If the torque converter is dropped, a new one must be installed.

➡**The front of the transmission must be lowered for the transmission to clear the exhaust system during installation.**

34. Continue moving the transmission rearward, while gradually raising the front of the transmission. As the transmission jack is being raised, move the transmission back and install it in the vehicle.

35. Align the orange balancing marks between the torque converter studs and the flexplate bolt holes.

36. Remove the special tool.

➡**While positioning the transmission to the back of the engine, use the transmission filler tube as a guide and install the transmission filler tube into the case.**

37. Install the seven transmission-to-engine bolts. Torque to 35 ft. lbs. (48 Nm).

38. Position the fuel line and bracket.

39. Install the bolts.

40. Connect the transmission fluid cooler tubes.

41. Position the rear transmission insulator and install the bolts. Torque to 59 ft. lbs. (80 Nm).

42. Install the exhaust hanger onto the exhaust crossover pipe.

43. Position the crossmember and loosely install the mount-to-crossmember nuts.

44. Install the four crossmember-to-frame nuts and bolts (two on each side). Torque to 66 ft. lbs. (90 Nm).

45. Tighten the rear transmission mount nuts. Torque to 76 ft. lbs. (103 Nm).

46. Install the bolt retaining the left heat shield to the transmission support crossmember.

47. Install the bolt retaining the right heat shield to the transmission support crossmember.

48. Install the bolts retaining the exhaust hanger to the crossmember. Torque to 30 ft. lbs. (40 Nm).

49. Connect the solenoid body assembly electrical connector.

50. Connect the transmission electrical connectors.

51. Install the shift cable bracket and connect the transmission shift linkage.

52. Install the transmission inspection cover.

53. Install the torque converter nuts. Torque to 27 ft. lbs. (36 Nm).

54. Install the rubber access plug.

55. Install the starter motor.

56. Connect the starter motor electrical connectors and the ground wire.

57. Install the starter motor solenoid terminal cover.

58. Install the rear driveshaft.

59. Use the following guidelines for the in-line transmission fluid filter:

 a. If the transmission was overhauled and the vehicle was equipped with an in-line fluid filter, install a new in-line fluid filter.

 b. If the transmission was overhauled and the vehicle was not equipped with an in-line fluid filter, install a new in-line fluid filter kit.

 c. If the transmission is being installed for a non-internal repair, do not install an in-line filter or filter kit.

 d. If installing a new or a Ford authorized remanufactured transmission, install the in-line transmission fluid filter that is supplied.

60. Prior to lowering the vehicle, install a new in-line transmission filter or a filter kit.

61. Connect the battery ground cable.

62. Fill the transmission with clean automatic transmission fluid and inspect for correct operation.

63. Check the fluid filter for any leaks.

4WD Models

See Figures 11 and 12.

1. Before servicing the vehicle, refer to the Precautions Section.

2. Disconnect the battery ground cable.

3. With the vehicle in **Neutral**, position it on a hoist.

4. Drain the transmission fluid.

5. Loosen the transmission fluid pan bolts and allow the fluid to drain. After the fluid has drained, remove the bolts.

6. Remove the transmission fluid pan and transmission fluid pan gasket. Drain the rest of the transmission fluid from the fluid pan.

➡**The transmission fluid pan gasket is reusable. Clean and inspect for damage. If not damaged, the gasket should be reused.**

7. Install the transmission fluid pan and gasket.

8. Position the transmission fluid pan gasket.

9. Position the transmission fluid pan.

➡**If removing the transmission for a transmission related failure, it is not necessary to torque the transmission fluid pan back onto the transmission case. If removing the transmission for a non-related transmission failure it is necessary to re-torque the transmission fluid pan.**

10. Install the bolts.

11. Using a suitable transmission jack, support the transmission and secure the transmission to it with a safety strap.

12. Index-mark the front flange of the front driveshaft.

13. Index-mark the rear flange of the front driveshaft at the transfer case.

14. Remove the front driveshaft shield.

15. Remove the transfer case.

16. Remove the front driveshaft.

17. Remove the left bolt retaining the heat shield to the transmission support crossmember.

18. Remove the right bolt retaining the heat shield to the transmission support crossmember.

19. Loosen, but do not remove, the transmission mount-to-crossmember nuts.

20. Remove the two bolts for the exhaust hanger.

21. Remove the four crossmember-to-frame nuts and bolts (two on each side).

22. Remove the transmission mount-to-crossmember nuts, and remove the cross-member.

23. Remove the two bolts and the rear transmission mount.

24. Remove the exhaust hanger.

25. Remove the starter motor solenoid terminal cover.

26. Disconnect the starter motor electrical connectors and the ground wire.

27. Remove the starter motor.

28. Remove the rubber plug to access the nuts.

29. Remove the four nuts. Rotate the crankshaft/flexplate assembly to access all the nuts.

30. Remove the transmission inspection cover.

31. Remove the shift cable and bracket.

32. Disconnect the solenoid body assembly electrical connector.

33. Disconnect the transmission electrical connectors.

34. Disconnect the transmission fluid cooler tubes.

35. Remove the seven transmission-to-engine bolts.

36. Position the fuel lines and bracket aside.

※ CAUTION

The torque converter is heavy and can result in injury if it falls out of the transmission. Secure the torque converter in the transmission. If the torque converter is dropped, a new one must be installed.

37. Slide the transmission rearward enough to install a torque converter holding tool.

※ CAUTION

The transmission must be secured with a safety chain or strap.

➡**The front of the transmission must be lowered for the transmission to clear the exhaust system during removal.**

38. Continue moving the transmission rearward, while gradually lowering the front of the transmission. As the transmission jack is being lowered, move the transmission forward and remove it from the vehicle.

39. If the transmission is to be overhauled or if installing a new transmission, carry out transmission backflushing and cleaning.

To install:

※ CAUTION

The torque converter cover is piloted into position to the engine crankshaft by dowels in the rear of the engine block. The torque converter must rest squarely and loosely against the flexplate. This indicates that the torque converter pilot is not binding in the engine crankshaft.

40. When installing a new transmission, install a torque converter holding tool.

※ CAUTION

The transmission must be secured with a safety chain or strap.

※ CAUTION

The torque converter is heavy and can result in injury if it falls out of the transmission. Secure the torque converter in the transmission. If the torque converter is dropped, a new one must be installed.

➡**The front of the transmission must be lowered for the transmission to clear the exhaust system during installation.**

41. Continue moving the transmission rearward, while gradually raising the front of the transmission. As the transmission jack is being raised, move the transmission back and install it in the vehicle.

42. Align the orange balancing marks between the torque converter studs and the flexplate bolt holes.

43. Remove the special tool.

➡**While positioning the transmission to the back of the engine use the transmission filler tube as a guide and install the transmission filler tube into the case.**

44. Install the seven transmission-to-engine bolts. Torque to 35 ft. lbs. (48 Nm).

45. Position the fuel line and bracket.

46. Install the bolts.

47. Connect the transmission fluid cooler tubes.

48. Install the exhaust hanger onto the exhaust crossover pipe.

49. Position the rear transmission insulator and install the bolts. Torque to 59 ft. lbs. (80 Nm).

50. Position the crossmember and loosely install the mount-to-crossmember nuts.

51. Install the four crossmember-to-frame nuts and bolts (two on each side). Torque to 66 ft. lbs. (90 Nm).

52. Tighten the rear transmission mount nuts. Torque to 76 ft. lbs. (103 Nm).

53. Install the bolt retaining the left heat shield to the transmission support cross-member.

54. Install the bolt retaining the right heat shield to the transmission support crossmember.

55. Install the bolts retaining the exhaust hanger to the crossmember.

56. Connect the solenoid body assembly electrical connector.

57. Connect the transmission electrical connectors.

58. Install the shift cable bracket and connect the transmission shift linkage.

59. Install the transmission inspection cover.

60. Install the torque converter nuts. Torque to 27 ft. lbs. (36 Nm).

61. Install the rubber access plug.

62. Install the starter motor.

63. Connect the starter motor electrical connectors and the ground wire.

64. Install the starter motor solenoid terminal cover.

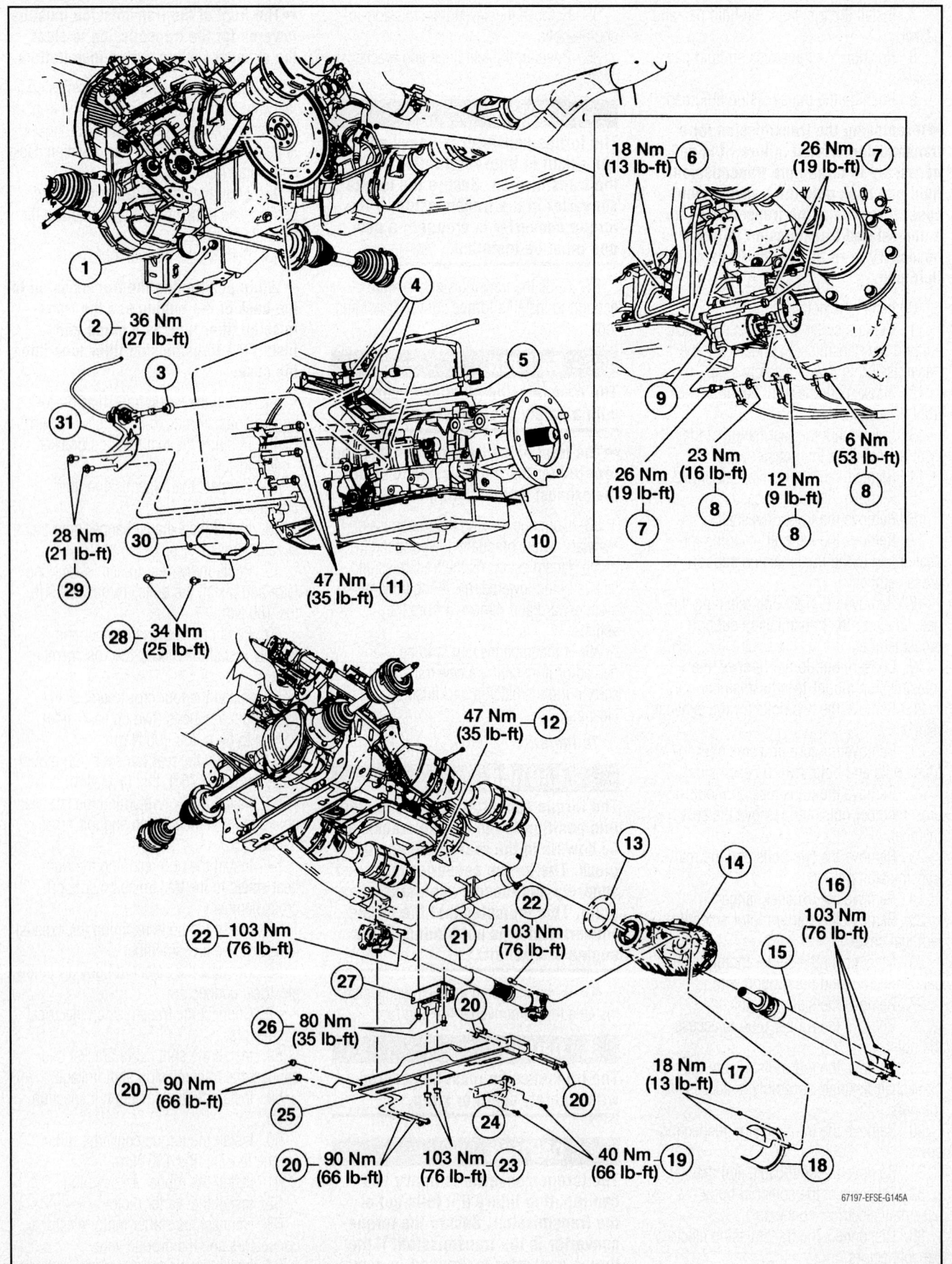

Fig. 11 4R70E/4R75E mounting (1 of 2)—4-wheel drive

67197-EFSE-G145A

1	Torque converter nut rubber access plug	17	Front driveshaft shield nuts
2	Torque converter nuts	18	Front driveshaft shield
3	Transmission range selector lever cable end	19	Exhaust hanger bolts
4	Transmission electrical connectors	20	Rear crossmember bolts and nuts
5	Transmission solenoid body connector	21	Front driveshaft
6	Transmission fluid cooler tube nuts	22	Front driveshaft retaining bolts
7	Starter motor bolts	23	Rear transmission mount nuts
8	Starter motor electrical connector nuts	24	Exhaust hanger
9	Starter motor	25	Rear crossmember
10	Transmission assembly	26	Transmission rear support bolts
11	Transmission retaining bolts	27	Transmission rear support
12	Transfer case retaining bolts	28	Inspection cover shield bolts
13	Transfer case gasket	29	Transmission range selector lever cable bracket bolts
14	Transfer case	30	Inspection cover shield
15	Rear driveshaft	31	Transmission range selector lever cable bracket
16	Rear driveshaft retaining bolts		

67197-EFSE-G145B

Fig. 12 Keylist (2 of 2)

65. Position the front driveshaft in place.
66. Install the transfer case.
67. Align the marks made during removal, install the front driveshaft flange and the four bolts.
68. Align the marks made during removal, install the rear driveshaft flange and the four bolts.
69. Install the front driveshaft shield.
70. Install the rear driveshaft.
71. Use the following guidelines for the in-line transmission fluid filter:
    a. If the transmission was overhauled and the vehicle was equipped with an in-line fluid filter, install a new in-line fluid filter.
    b. If the transmission was overhauled and the vehicle was not equipped with an in-line fluid filter, install a new in-line fluid filter kit.
    c. If the transmission is being installed for a non-internal repair, do not install an in-line filter or filter kit.
    d. If installing a new or a Ford authorized remanufactured transmission, install the in-line transmission fluid filter that is supplied.
72. Prior to lowering the vehicle, install a new in-line transmission filter or a filter kit.
73. Connect the battery ground cable.
74. Fill the transmission with clean automatic transmission fluid and inspect for correct operation.
75. Check the fluid filter for any leaks.

6R80 Transmission

2WD MODELS

See Figures 13 through 16.

1. Before servicing the vehicle, refer to the precautions section.
2. Disconnect the battery ground cable
3. Remove the driveshaft.
4. Remove the fluid fill plug fluid level indicator assembly located on the passenger side front portion of the transmission case. Removal of the plug will relieve any vacuum that might have built up in the transmission. This will aid in allowing the fluid pan to be easily removed when the bolts are removed.

➡ **If transmission disassembly or installation of a new transmission is necessary, the transmission fluid will need to be drained.**

5. Remove the transmission fluid pan and allow the fluid to drain.
6. Install the fluid pan and tighten the bolts in a crisscross pattern.
7. If equipped, remove the heat shield.

➡ **To prevent selector lever cable damage, do not apply force to the selector**

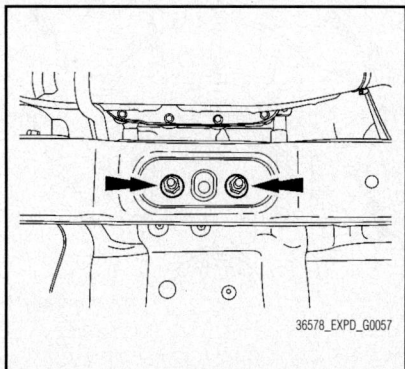

36578_EXPD_G0057

Fig. 13 Removing the 2 rear crossmember nuts

36578_EXPD_G0058

Fig. 14 Removing the 4 crossmember bolts and nuts and crossmember

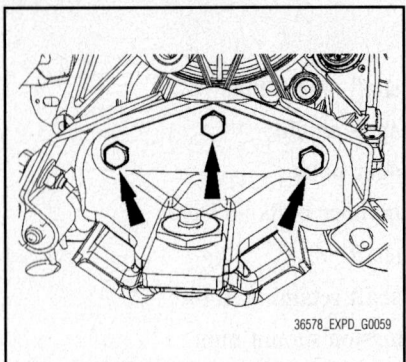

Fig. 15 Removing the 3 insulator bolts and insulator

lever cable between the manual control lever and the selector lever cable bracket.

8. Move the locking tab up and disconnect the selector lever cable from the manual lever ball stud.

9. Remove the selector lever bracket bolts and remove the bracket.

10. Remove the flexplate inspection cover bolts and the inspection cover.

11. Remove the rubber torque converter nut access plug.

12. Remove and discard the 4 flexplate-to-torque converter nuts.

13. Remove the transmission cooler tube bracket bolt.

14. Remove the transmission case bolt.

15. Remove the transmission fluid cooler tube bracket nut and position the bracket and tubes aside.

16. Remove the plastic starter motor electrical connector cap.

17. Remove the starter motor electrical connectors.

18. Remove the ground wire from the stud.

19. Remove the starter motor bolts and the starter motor.

20. Remove the RH exhaust heat shield bolt.

21. Remove the LH exhaust heat shield and evaporative emissions canister assembly bolts.

22. Disconnect the RH and LH heated oxygen sensors (HO2S) and the catalyst monitor sensor (CMS) electrical connectors.

23. Remove the fuel line bracket bolt and position the bracket and lines aside.

➡**Make sure that the transmission jack makes contact on the outer ribs of the fluid pan. And that the transmission is securely fastened to the transmission jack.**

24. Position a suitable high-lift transmission jack under the transmission.

25. Remove the 2 rear crossmember nuts.

26. Remove the 4 crossmember bolts and nuts.

27. Remove the rear crossmember.

28. Remove the 3 bolts and remove the insulator.

29. Remove the RH and LH exhaust flange nuts.

30. Remove the 2 dual converter Y-pipe bolts and the dual converter Y-pipe.

31. Disconnect the wire harness from the top of the transmission

32. Disconnect the main transmission electrical harness by twisting the outer shell and pulling back on the connector

➡**The top 2 transmission-to-engine bolts need to be removed prior to removing the rest of the bolts. The top left bolt secures the fuel line bracket to the transmission case.**

33. Remove the 6 remaining transmission case bolts.

34. Slide the transmission back far enough to install the torque converter retainer tool 307-346. This holds the torque converter in place.

35. Remove the transmission from the vehicle.

⁂ **WARNING**

If the transmission is to be overhauled or if installing a new transmission, carry out transmission fluid cooler back flushing and cleaning. Make sure the cooler is not restricted. If you have poor cooler flow replace with a new transmission cooler.

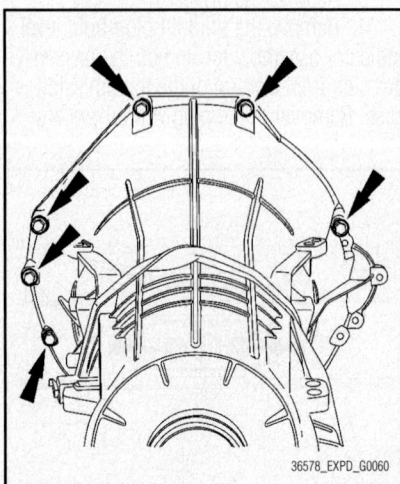

Fig. 16 Locating the remaining transmission housing bolts

To install:

⁂ **WARNING**

The converter housing is piloted into position by dowels in the rear of the engine block. The torque converter must rest squarely against the flexplate. This indicates that the converter pilot is not binding in the engine crankshaft.

36. Position and secure the transmission on the high-lift transmission jack. Raise and position the transmission into the vehicle.

37. Remove the torque converter retainer tool 307-346.

➡**Make sure the torque converter is fully seated in the transmission before aligning the transmission to the engine.**

38. With the transmission in a horizontal position, move it toward the engine. Align the orange balancing marks between the torque converter studs and the flexplate bolt holes.

39. Install the transmission case bolts in their correct locations noted during removal.

➡**The top 2 transmission case bolts need to be installed prior to installing the rest of the bolts. The top left bolt is inserted through the fuel line bracket first, then through the transmission case.**

40. Install 6 of the 7 transmission case bolts and tighten to 35 ft. lbs. (48 Nm).

41. Connect the main transmission electrical harness by pushing it in and twisting the outer shell to lock it in place.

42. Connect the wire harness to the top of the transmission.

43. Position the dual converter Y-pipe in place. Install and tighten the 2 dual converter Y-pipe to 30 ft. lbs. (40 Nm).

44. Install the LH and RH exhaust flange nuts and tighten to 30 ft. lbs. (40 Nm).

45. Install the 3 bolts and the insulator, tighten to 66 ft. lbs. (90 Nm).

46. Position the rear crossmember in place and loosely install the transmission insulator nuts.

47. Install the crossmember.

48. Install the 4 crossmember bolts and nuts and tighten to 66 ft. lbs. (90 Nm).

49. Tighten the transmission insulator nuts to 76 ft. lbs. (103 Nm).

50. Install the fuel line bracket tighten the mounting bolt to 18 ft. lbs. (25 Nm).

51. Connect the RH and LH heated oxygen sensors (HO2S) electrical connectors and the CMS electrical connectors.

52. Install the LH exhaust heat shield and evaporative emissions canister assembly bolts. Tighten the bolts to 11 ft. lbs.(15 Nm).

53. Install the RH exhaust heat shield bolt and tighten to 11 ft. lbs.(15 Nm).

54. Position the starter motor in place, install and tighten the 3 starter motor bolts to 19 ft. lbs. (26 Nm).

55. Install the ground wire on the stud, install and tighten the ground wire nut to 17 ft. lbs. 23 (Nm).

56. Install the starter motor electrical connectors. Tighten main power cable to 9 ft. lbs. (15 Nm).

57. Tighten the smaller solenoid feed wire to 53 inch. (6 Nm).

58. Install the plastic starter motor electrical connector cap.

59. Position the transmission cooler tubes in place, install and tighten the bracket nut to 20 ft. lbs. (27 Nm).

60. Align the bracket and install the remaining transmission case bolt. Tighten to 35 ft. lbs. (48 Nm).

➡ **Inspect the case to make sure that the old O-rings are not stuck in the case. Install new O-rings on the ends of the cooler lines prior to installing.**

61. Install new O-rings on the transmission fluid cooler tubes.

62. Install the transmission cooler tubes and tighten the bracket bolt to 17 ft. lbs. (23 Nm).

63. Install 4 new flexplate-to-torque converter nuts. Tighten the nuts to 26 ft. lbs. (35 Nm).

64. Install the rubber access plug.

65. Install the flexplate inspection cover and tighten the flexplate inspection cover bolts to 26 ft. lbs. (35 Nm).

66. Install the selector lever bracket and tighten the bolts to 35 ft. lbs. (48 Nm).

➡ **When installing the selector lever cable, make sure that the selector lever cable locking tabs are locked in place and the cable end is snapped onto the ball stud. Press the selector lever cable into the bracket and listen for the cable to click into place. Pull back on the selector lever cable to make sure that it is locked into the bracket. Also, make sure that the selector lever cable end is correctly installed onto the ball stud. Pull back on the selector lever cable to make sure that the cable end is correctly installed.**

67. With the manual lever in NEUTRAL, connect the selector lever cable onto the manual lever ball stud and move the locking tab down. Listen for the audible click.

68. Pull back on the selector lever cable to make sure that it is correctly installed.

69. If equipped, install the heat shield.

70. Install the driveshaft.

71. Connect the battery ground cable.

72. Verify that the selector lever cable is correctly adjusted.

73. Reflash the transmission control module (TCM) to the latest level of software.

74. Fill the transmission with clean automatic transmission fluid.

75. Test drive and check for leaks.

4WD Models

See Figure 16.

1. Before servicing the vehicle, refer to the precautions section.

2. Disconnect the battery ground cable.

3. With the vehicle in NEUTRAL, position it on a hoist.

4. Remove the fluid fill plug fluid level indicator assembly located on the passenger side front portion of the transmission case. Removal of the plug will relieve any vacuum that might have built up in the transmission. This will aid in allowing the fluid pan to be easily removed when the bolts are removed.

➡ **If transmission disassembly or installation of a new transmission is necessary, the transmission fluid will need to be drained.**

5. Remove the transmission fluid pan and allow the fluid to drain

6. Install the fluid pan and tighten the bolts in a crisscross pattern.

7. Remove the transfer case.

8. Remove the fuel line bracket bolt and position the bracket and lines aside.

9. If equipped, remove the heat shield.

10. Move the locking tab up and disconnect the selector lever cable from the manual lever ball stud.

11. Remove the selector lever bracket bolts and remove the bracket.

12. Remove the flexplate inspection cover bolts and the inspection cover.

13. Remove the rubber torque converter nut access plug.

14. Remove and discard the 4 flexplate-to-torque converter nuts.

15. Remove the transmission cooler tube bracket bolt.

16. Remove the transmission case bolt.

17. Remove the transmission fluid cooler tube bracket nut and position the bracket and tubes.

18. Remove the plastic starter motor electrical connector cap.

19. Remove the starter motor electrical connectors.

20. Remove the ground wire from the stud.

21. Remove the 3 starter motor bolts and the starter motor.

22. Disconnect the wiring harness from the top of the transmission.

23. Disconnect the main transmission electrical harness by twisting the outer shell and pulling back on the connector.

➡ **The top 2 transmission-to-engine bolts need to be removed prior to removing the rest of the bolts. The top left bolt secures the fuel line bracket to the transmission case.**

24. Remove the 6 remaining transmission case bolts.

25. Leaving the transmission in a horizontal position, slide it back far enough to install the torque converter holding tool 307-346.

26. Make sure that the torque converter holding tool 307-346 is in place and the transmission is securely fastened to the transmission jack before tilting the transmission.

27. Remove the transmission from the vehicle.

To install:

✳✳ WARNING

The converter housing is piloted into position by dowels in the rear of the engine block. The torque converter must rest squarely against the flexplate. This indicates that the converter pilot is not binding in the engine crankshaft.

28. Position and secure the transmission on the high-lift transmission jack. Raise and position the transmission into the vehicle.

29. Remove the torque converter retainer tool 307-346.

➡ **Make sure the torque converter is fully seated in the transmission before aligning the transmission to the engine.**

30. With the transmission in a horizontal position, move it toward the engine. Align the orange balancing marks between the torque converter studs and the flexplate bolt holes.

31. Install the transmission case bolts in their correct locations noted during removal.

➡The top 2 transmission case bolts need to be installed prior to installing the rest of the bolts. The top left bolt is inserted through the fuel line bracket first, then through the transmission case.

32. Install 6 of the 7 transmission case bolts and tighten to 35 ft. lbs. (48 Nm).

33. Connect the main transmission electrical harness by pushing it in and twisting the outer shell to lock it in place

34. Connect the wire harness to the top of the transmission.

35. Position the starter motor in place, install and tighten the 3 starter motor bolts to 19 ft. lbs. (26 Nm).

36. Install the ground wire on the stud, install and tighten the ground wire nut to 17 ft. lbs. 23 (Nm).

37. Install the starter motor electrical connectors. Tighten main power cable to 9 ft. lbs. (15 Nm).

38. Tighten the smaller solenoid feed wire to 53 inch. (6 Nm).

39. Install the plastic starter motor electrical connector cap.

40. Position the transmission cooler tubes in place, install and tighten the bracket nut to 20 ft. lbs. (27 Nm).

41. Align the bracket and install the remaining transmission case bolt. Tighten to 35 ft. lbs. (48 Nm).

➡Inspect the case to make sure that the old O-rings are not stuck in the case. Install new O-rings on the ends of the cooler lines prior to installing.

42. Install new O-rings on the transmission fluid cooler tubes.

43. Install the transmission cooler tubes and tighten the bracket bolt to 17 ft. lbs. (23 Nm).

44. Install 4 new flexplate-to-torque converter nuts. Tighten the nuts to 26 ft. lbs. (35 Nm).

45. Install the rubber access plug.

46. Install the flexplate inspection cover and tighten the inspection cover bolts to 26 ft. lbs. (35 Nm).

47. Install the selector lever bracket and tighten the bolts to 35 ft. lbs. (48 Nm).

➡When installing the selector lever cable, make sure that the selector lever cable locking tabs are locked in place and the cable end is snapped onto the ball stud. Press the selector lever cable into the bracket and listen for the cable to click into place. Pull back on the selector lever cable to make sure that it is locked into the bracket. Also, make sure that the selector lever cable end is correctly installed onto the ball stud. Pull back on the selector lever cable to make sure that the cable end is correctly installed.

48. With the manual lever in NEUTRAL, connect the selector lever cable onto the manual lever ball stud and move the locking tab down. Listen for the audible click.

49. Pull back on the selector lever cable to make sure that it is correctly installed.

50. If equipped, install the heat shield.

51. Install the fuel line bracket and tighten the mounting bolt to 18 ft. lbs. (25 Nm).

52. Install the transfer case.

53. Connect the battery ground cable.

54. Verify that the selector lever cable is correctly adjusted.

55. Reflash the transmission control module (TCM) to the latest level of software.

56. Fill the transmission with clean automatic transmission fluid.

57. Test drive and check for leaks.

MANUAL TRANSMISSION ASSEMBLY

REMOVAL & INSTALLATION

See Figure 17.

1. Before servicing the vehicle, refer to the Precautions Section.

2. Disconnect the battery ground cable.

3. Unclip the console cover, then slide the cover and boot assembly up.

4. Remove the gearshift lever nut.

5. Install the gearshift lever nut on the left side of the lever, then, tighten the nut to remove the eccentric stud out of the gearshift lever. Remove the upper gearshift lever.

6. Remove the 4 screws and the lower boot.

7. Remove the 4 bolts and the lower gearshift lever.

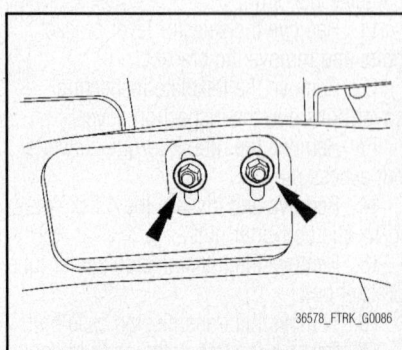

36578_FTRK_G0086

Fig. 17 Removing the 2 transmission mount nuts and the crossmember

8. Raise and safely support the vehicle.

9. If transmission disassembly is required, remove the drain plug and drain the transmission fluid. Install the drain plug after draining all the fluid. Tighten to 48 Nm (35 ft. lbs.).

10. Remove the right catalytic converter.

11. Remove the 2 starter motor bolts and the starter motor. Using mechanic's wire, position the starter motor aside.

12. Disconnect the wire harness from the transmission and disconnect both of the heated oxygen (HEGO) sensor electrical connectors.

13. Disconnect the reverse lamp switch electrical connector.

14. Disconnect the vehicle speed sensor (VSS) electrical connector.

15. Remove the front stabilizer bar.

16. Remove the 2 nuts and disconnect the fuel lines and the wire harness from the rear of the transmission. Position them aside.

17. Using the special tool, disconnect the clutch hydraulic line.

18. Position a suitable jack under the transmission. Secure the transmission to the jack with a safety strap.

19. Remove the 2 exhaust hanger bolts.

20. Remove the 2 exhaust heat shield bolts.

21. Remove the 4 crossmember bolts.

22. Remove the 2 transmission mount nuts and the crossmember.

23. Lower the transmission enough to gain access to the upper transmission-to-engine bolts.

24. Remove 9 transmission-to-engine bolts.

25. Pull the transmission rearward until the input shift is clear of the pressure plate, then lower the transmission from the vehicle.

26. To install, reverse the removal procedure. Note the following:

a. Before securing the engine to the transmission, connect the hydraulic line to the clutch slave cylinder.

b. Make sure the exhaust system is correctly aligned.

c. Align the index marks when installing the rear driveshaft.

d. Check and, if necessary, fill the transmission with the specified type and quantity of fluid.

27. Observe the following torques:

• Transmission-to-engine bolts: 60 Nm (44 ft. lbs.).

- Transmission mount nuts: 98 Nm (72 ft. lbs.).
- The 4 crossmember bolts: 90 Nm (66 ft. lbs.).
- The 2 exhaust heat shield bolts: 15 Nm (11 ft. lbs.).
- The 2 starter motor bolts: 33 Nm (24 ft. lbs.)

TRANSFER CASE ASSEMBLY

REMOVAL & INSTALLATION

2008 Models

See Figures 18 and 19.

1. Index-mark the driveshaft to maintain initial driveshaft balance during installation.
2. Remove the front driveshaft.

➡**To maintain initial driveshaft balance, index-mark the rear driveshaft.**

3. Remove the rear driveshaft.
4. Remove the 4 skid plate bolts and the skid plate, if equipped.
5. For electronic transfer cases, disconnect the transfer case shift motor electrical connector.
6. For electronic transfer cases, disconnect the transfer case shift motor wiring harness from the transfer case.
7. Drain the fluid if the transfer case is to be disassembled.
8. Disconnect the transfer case wire harness.

➡ **The transfer case shift linkage assembly is serviced as an assembly only. If any part is damaged or worn, install a new assembly.**

9. Using a 5/8-inch wrench, disconnect the shift linkage from the shift bracket.
10. Disconnect the vent tube.
11. Using a suitable jack, support the transfer case. Secure the transfer case to the jack with a safety strap.
12. Remove the 6 transfer case-to-transmission bolts and separate the transfer case from the transmission.
13. Lower the transfer case from the vehicle.
14. Remove the transfer case-to-transmission gasket and clean the mating surfaces.
15. To install, reverse the removal procedure.
16. Tighten the transmission-to-transfer case bolts evenly in a star pattern to 35 ft. lbs. (47 Nm).
17. Fill the transfer case.

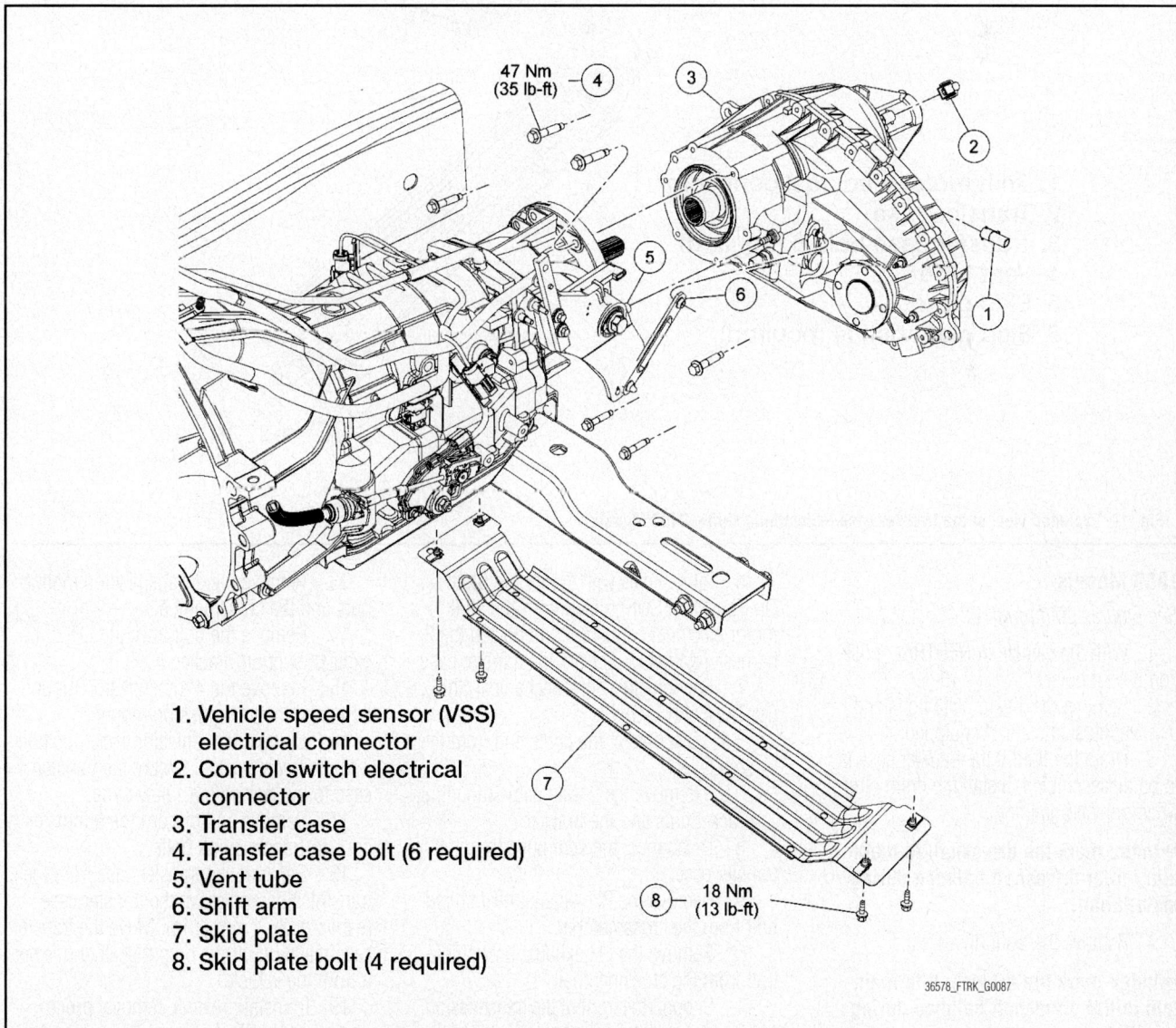

1. Vehicle speed sensor (VSS) electrical connector
2. Control switch electrical connector
3. Transfer case
4. Transfer case bolt (6 required)
5. Vent tube
6. Shift arm
7. Skid plate
8. Skid plate bolt (4 required)

36578_FTRK_G0087

Fig. 18 Exploded view of the transfer case—Mechanical shift—2008 Models

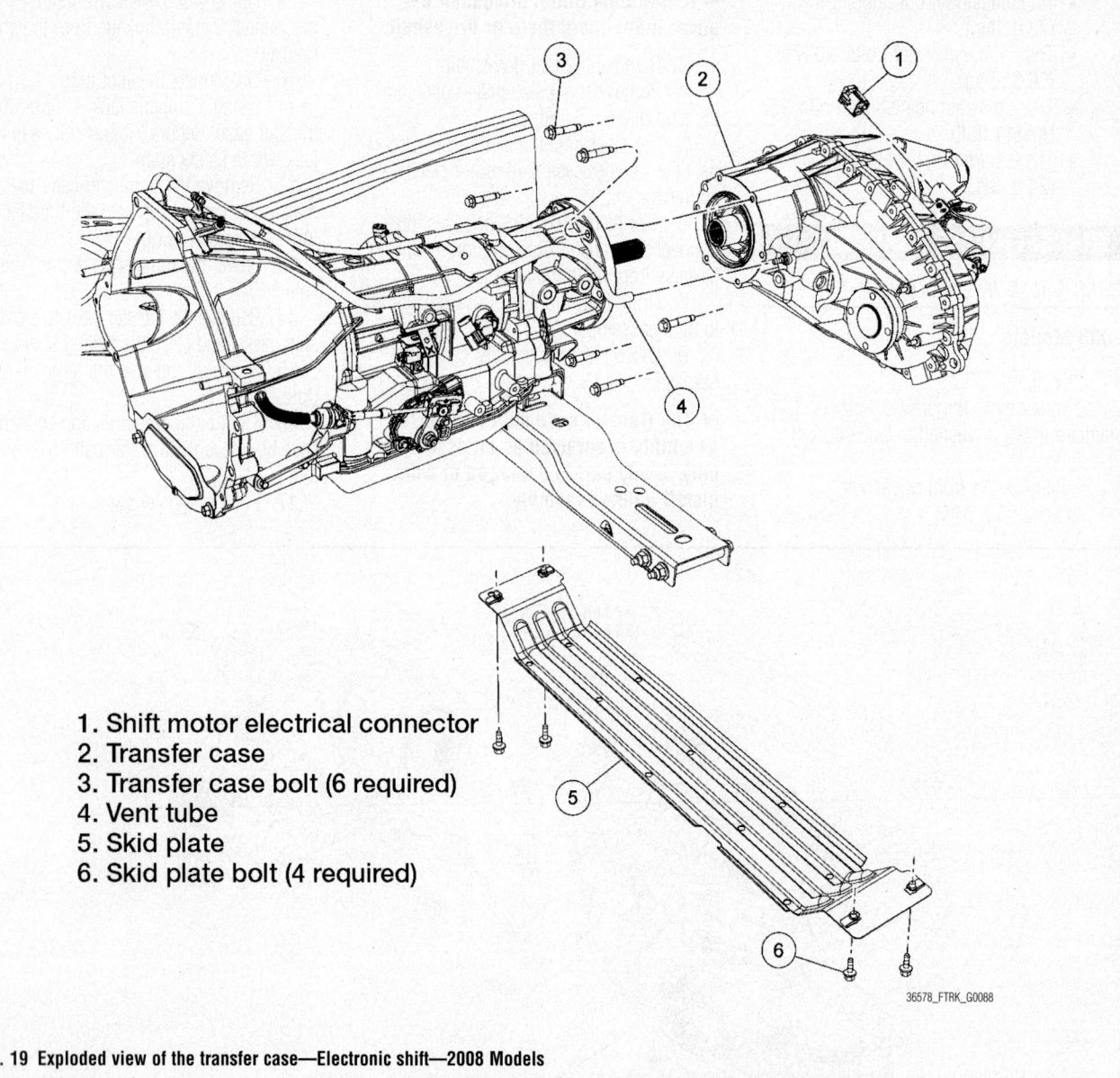

1. Shift motor electrical connector
2. Transfer case
3. Transfer case bolt (6 required)
4. Vent tube
5. Skid plate
6. Skid plate bolt (4 required)

36578_FTRK_G0088

Fig. 19 Exploded view of the transfer case—Electronic shift—2008 Models

2009 Models

See Figures 20 through 22.

1. With the vehicle in NEUTRAL, position it on a hoist.

2. Remove the 4 skid plate bolts and remove the skid plate, if equipped.

3. Drain the fluid if the transfer case is to be disassembled. Install the drain plug when finished draining.

➥**Index-mark the driveshaft to maintain initial driveshaft balance during installation.**

4. Remove the front driveshaft.

➥**Index-mark the driveshaft to maintain initial driveshaft balance during installation.**

5. Remove the rear driveshaft.

6. For vehicles with Electronic Shift-On-The-Fly (ESOF), disconnect the shift motor electrical connector and detach the 2 harness retainer clips from the transfer case.

7. For vehicles with Mechanical Shift-On-The-Fly (MSOF):

   a. Disconnect the cable end from the shift lever.

   b. Remove the 2 shift cable mounting bracket nuts and the bracket.

8. Disconnect the vent hose from the transfer case.

9. Remove the RH exhaust heat shield bolt from the crossmember.

10. Remove the LH exhaust heat shield bolt from the crossmember.

11. Support the front of the transmission.

12. Remove the 4 crossmember bolts and nuts.

13. Remove the 2 transmission mount nuts and the crossmember.

14. Remove the bolt from the LH exhaust support bracket.

15. Remove the 4 transmission mount bolts and the transmission mount.

16. Using a transmission jack, position it to the transfer case. Secure the transfer case to the jack with a safety strap.

17. Remove and discard the 9 transfer case-to-transmission bolts.

18. Separate the transfer case from the transmission and move the transfer case rearward. 25.4 mm (1 in). Move the transfer case rearward off the output shaft and lower it from the vehicle.

19. To install, reverse removal procedure. Refer to illustrations for torque specifications.

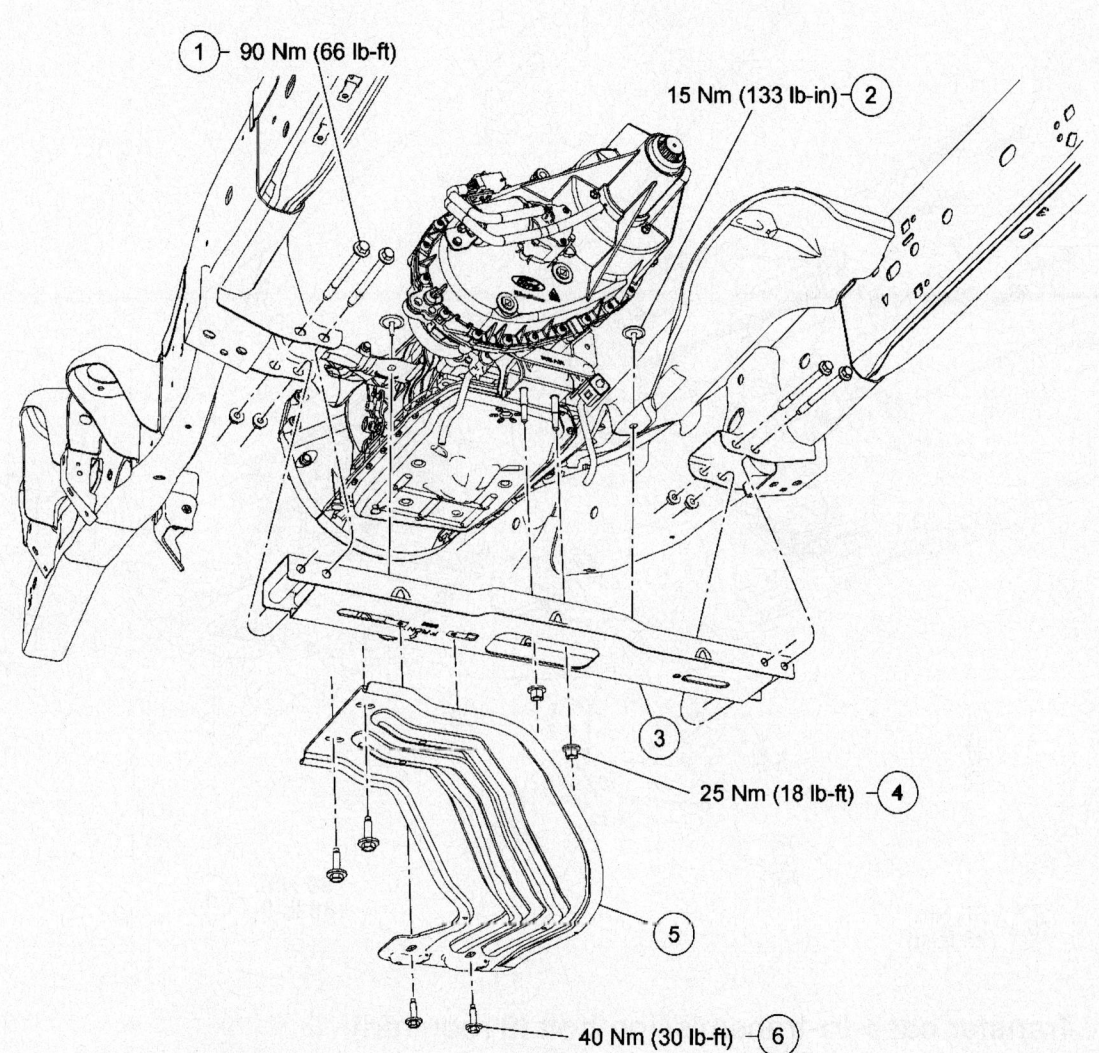

1. 90 Nm (66 lb-ft)
2. 15 Nm (133 lb-in)
4. 25 Nm (18 lb-ft)
6. 40 Nm (30 lb-ft)

1. Crossmember bolt (4 required)
2. Heat shield bolt (2 required)
3. Crossmember
4. Transmission mount nut (2 required)
5. Skid plate
6. Skid plate-to-frame bolt (4 required)

36578_FTRK_G0089

Fig. 20 Exploded view of the transfer case—Left Side —2009 Models

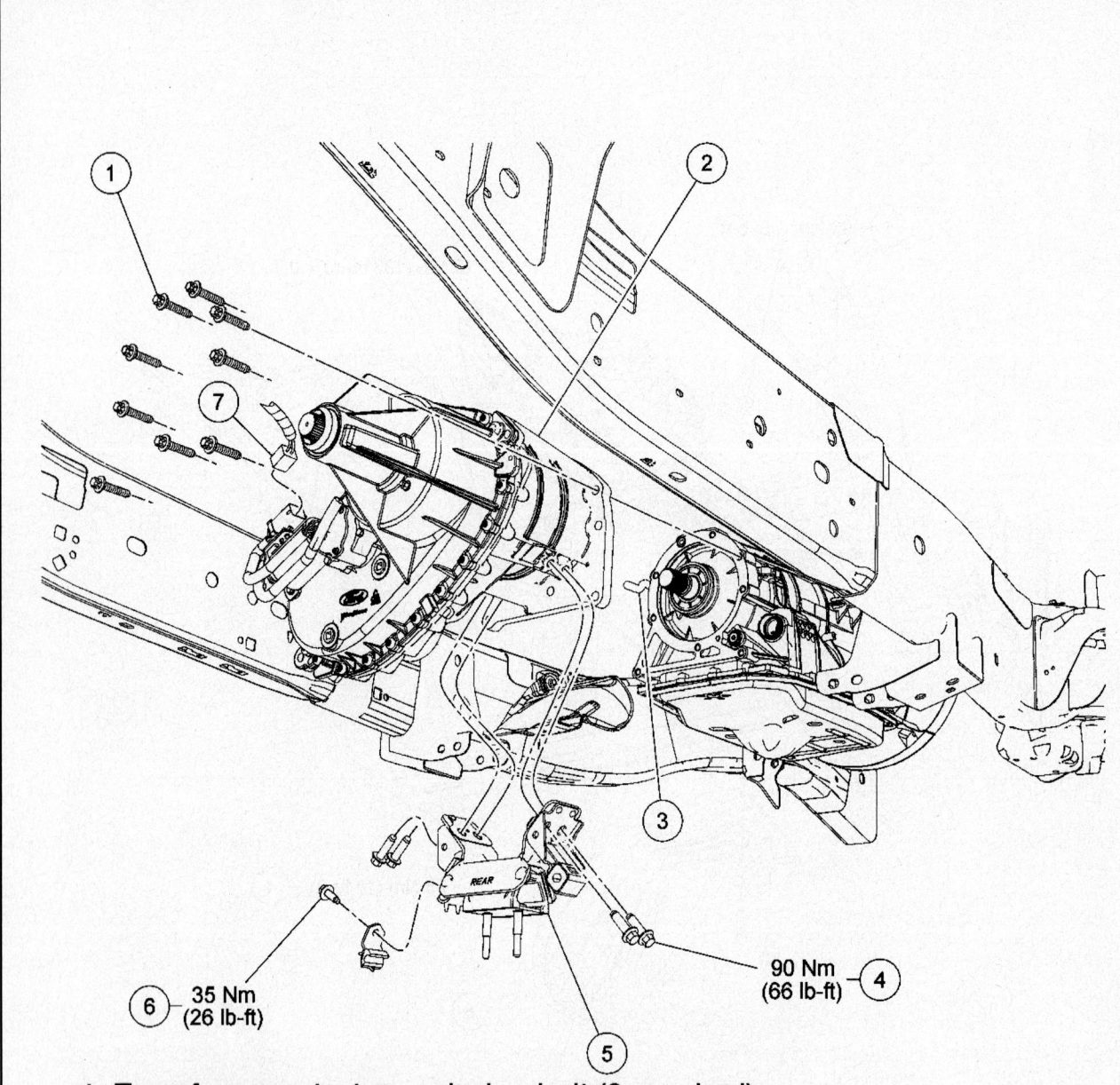

1. Transfer case-to-transmission bolt (9 required)
2. Transfer case
3. Vent tube
4. Transmission mount bolt (4 required)
5. Transmission mount
6. Exhaust support bracket bolt
7. Shift motor electrical connector — Electronic Shift-On-The-Fly (ESOF)

36578_FTRK_G0090

Fig. 21 Exploded view of the transfer case—Right Side—2009 Models

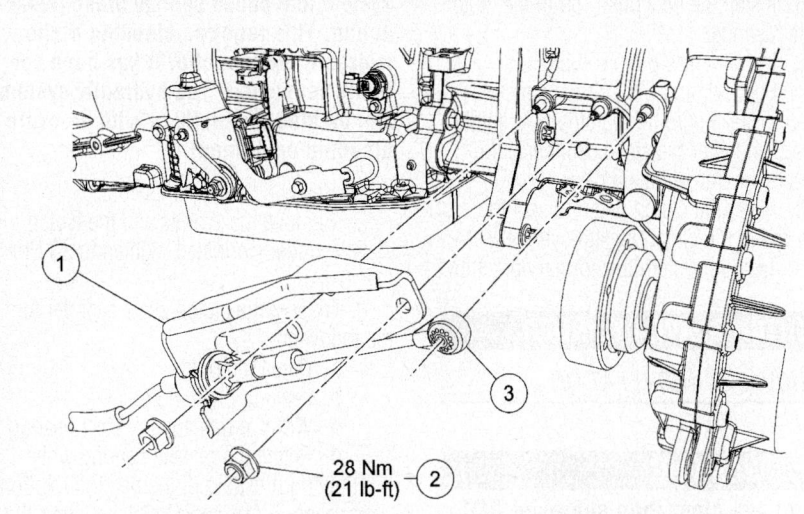

1. Transfer case shift cable mounting bracket
2. Transfer case shift cable mounting bracket nut
3. Transfer case shift cable

36578_FTRK_G0091

Fig. 22 Exploded view of the transfer case—Left Side—Mechanical shift—2009 Models

CLUTCH DRIVEN DISC & PRESSURE PLATE

REMOVAL & INSTALLATION

See Figures 23 and 24.

1. Remove the transmission.
2. If the original components are to be installed, index-mark the clutch pressure plate and Remove the clutch pressure plate bolts, clutch pressure plate and the clutch disc. the flywheel.
3. Remove the clutch pressure plate bolts, clutch pressure plate and the clutch disc.

To install:

4. Adjust the clutch pressure plate as follows:

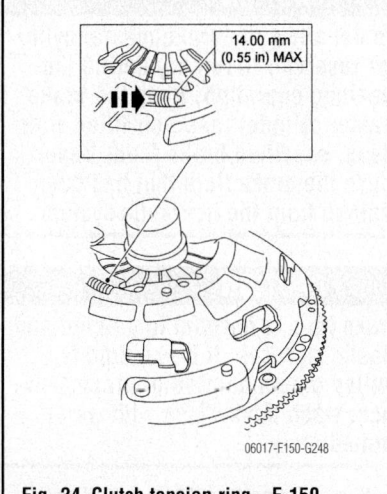

14.00 mm
(0.55 in) MAX

06017-F150-G248

Fig. 24 Clutch tension ring—F-150

5. Rotate the adjusting ring counter-clockwise until the tension springs are compressed.

6. Hold the adjusting ring, then release the pressure on the clutch pressure plate fingers. Using the special tool (308-090), position the clutch disc on the flywheel.

7. If installing the original clutch pressure plate, use the index marks made during removal.

8. Position the clutch pressure plate on the dowels, install the clutch pressure plate bolts and remove the special tool. Tighten to 41 ft. lbs. (55 Nm).

9. Install the transmission. Before securing the transmission to the engine, install the hydraulic line to the clutch slave cylinder.

10. Operate the vehicle to check clutch operation.

CLUTCH MASTER CYLINDER

REMOVAL & INSTALLATION

See Figure 25.

➡️Remove the entire clutch hydraulic system from the vehicle as an assembly when installing a new clutch master cylinder assembly. The clutch master cylinder is only serviced in the assembly.

1. Before servicing the vehicle, refer to the precautions in the beginning of this section.

2. Disconnect the clutch hydraulic tube from the dash clip.

3. With the vehicle in NEUTRAL, position it on a hoist.

4. The 5.4L and 6.8L clutch control system has a heat shield that covers most of the tube and clutch slave cylinder. To unlock the slave cylinder, slide the heat shield back and off of the slave cylinder. Slide the heat shield over the tube.

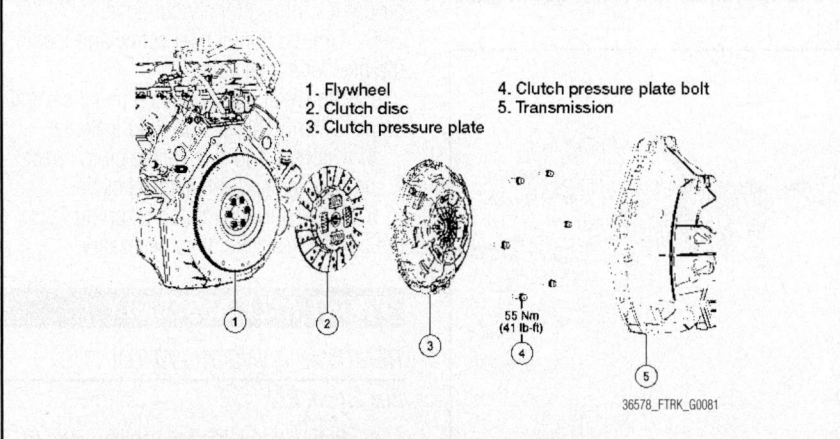

1. Flywheel
2. Clutch disc
3. Clutch pressure plate
4. Clutch pressure plate bolt
5. Transmission

55 Nm
(41 lb-ft)

36578_FTRK_G0081

Fig. 23 Exploded view of the clutch disc and pressure plate assembly

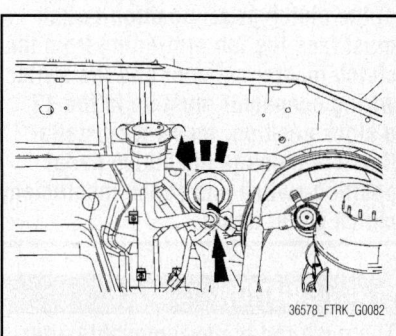

36578_FTRK_G0082

Fig. 25 Remove the clutch master cylinder from the clutch pedal and support bracket assembly

5. Compress and twist the clutch slave cylinder counterclockwise to unlock it from the transmission.

6. Disconnect the clutch hydraulic tube from the floor pan clip. Position the clutch slave cylinder and hydraulic tube forward below the left engine bank. This will make it easier to unlock the clutch master cylinder from the clutch pedal and support bracket by reducing tension on the hydraulic tube.

7. Lower the vehicle.

✳✳ WARNING

The clutch pedal is under spring tension.

8. Unlock the push rod retaining clips and separate the clutch master cylinder push rod from the clutch pedal.

9. Remove and discard the clutch master cylinder push rod bushing.

10. Remove the switch cover and the clutch pedal position switch from the clutch master cylinder push rod.

11. Separate the power distribution box from the bracket to gain access to the clutch master cylinder.

12. Compress and twist the clutch master cylinder clockwise 45 degrees to unlock it from the clutch pedal and support bracket. Remove the clutch master cylinder from the clutch pedal and support bracket.

13. Remove the clutch hydraulic system from the vehicle.

✳✳ CAUTION

Brake fluid is harmful to painted and plastic surfaces. If brake fluid is spilled onto a painted or plastic surface, wash the surface with water immediately.

14. To install, reverse the removal procedure.

✳✳ CAUTION

When installed correctly, the flat side of the clutch pedal position switch must face the tab protruding from the clutch master cylinder and the switch wiring connector must be in the 12 o'clock position. Incorrect installation will damage the clutch pedal position switch and cause insufficient clutch pedal travel.

✳✳ CAUTION

The push rod is not removable after installing it in the clutch master cylinder.

15. Install the new push rod in the clutch master cylinder.

16. Install a new push rod bushing.

17. For 5.4L and 6.8L clutch control systems, make sure to slide the heat shield forward and over the slave cylinder until it contacts the transmission case.

18. Press the clutch pedal to seat the push rod in the clutch master cylinder.

19. Test the system for normal operation.

CLUTCH SLAVE CYLINDER

REMOVAL & INSTALLATION

See Figure 26.

✳✳ WARNING

Use of any other than approved DOT 3 motor vehicle brake fluid will cause permanent damage to brake components and will render the brakes inoperative. Failure to follow these instructions may result in personal injury.

✳✳ CAUTION

Do not allow the brake master cylinder reservoir to run dry during the bleeding operation. Keep the brake master cylinder reservoir filled with clean, specified brake fluid. Never reuse the brake fluid that has been drained from the hydraulic system.

✳✳ CAUTION

Brake fluid is harmful to painted and plastic surfaces. If brake fluid is spilled onto a painted or plastic surface, wash the surface with water immediately.

➡When any part of the hydraulic system has been disconnected for repair or new installation, air may get into the

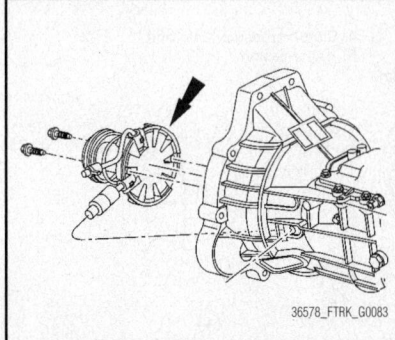

36578_FTRK_G0083

Fig. 26 Remove the clutch slave cylinder

system and cause spongy brake pedal action. This requires bleeding of the hydraulic system after it has been correctly connected. The hydraulic system can be bled manually or with pressure bleeding equipment.

1. Remove the transmission.

2. Remove the 2 bolts and the clutch slave cylinder. To install, tighten to 23 Nm (17 lb-ft).

3. Inspect the clutch slave cylinder for the following:

    a. Damaged boot.

    b. Leaking brake fluid.

    c. Worn or damaged release bearing.

    d. Rotate the release bearing while applying pressure. If the bearing rotation is rough, install a new clutch slave cylinder.

4. To install, reverse the removal procedure.

CLUTCH HYDRAULIC SYSTEM BLEEDING

1. Remove the clutch reservoir cap and diaphragm. Check the fluid level. Fill the reservoir to or above the step mark. Install the cap and diaphragm.

2. Depress and release the clutch pedal several times to stabilize the clutch hydraulic system.

3. With the vehicle in NEUTRAL, position it on a hoist.

4. Remove the bleeder screw cover and attach a vinyl hose to the bleeder hose. Place the other end of the vinyl hose into a clear container partially filled with brake fluid.

5. Have an assistant depress and release the clutch pedal 5 times, then hold the clutch pedal down. With the clutch pedal depressed, loosen the bleeder screw to let air escape the clutch system. Tighten the bleeder screw. Repeat this process until no air comes through the vinyl hose.

6. Tighten the bleeder screw and install the bleeder screw cover.

7. Slowly pump the clutch pedal several times to verify there is no fluid leakage.

8. Depress and release the clutch pedal 2 short cycles and 3 full-travel cycles.

9. Make sure the clutch reservoir is at the correct level. Refill as necessary.

FRONT AXLE ASSEMBLY

REMOVAL & INSTALLATION

See Figure 27.

1. Before servicing the vehicle, refer to the precautions section.

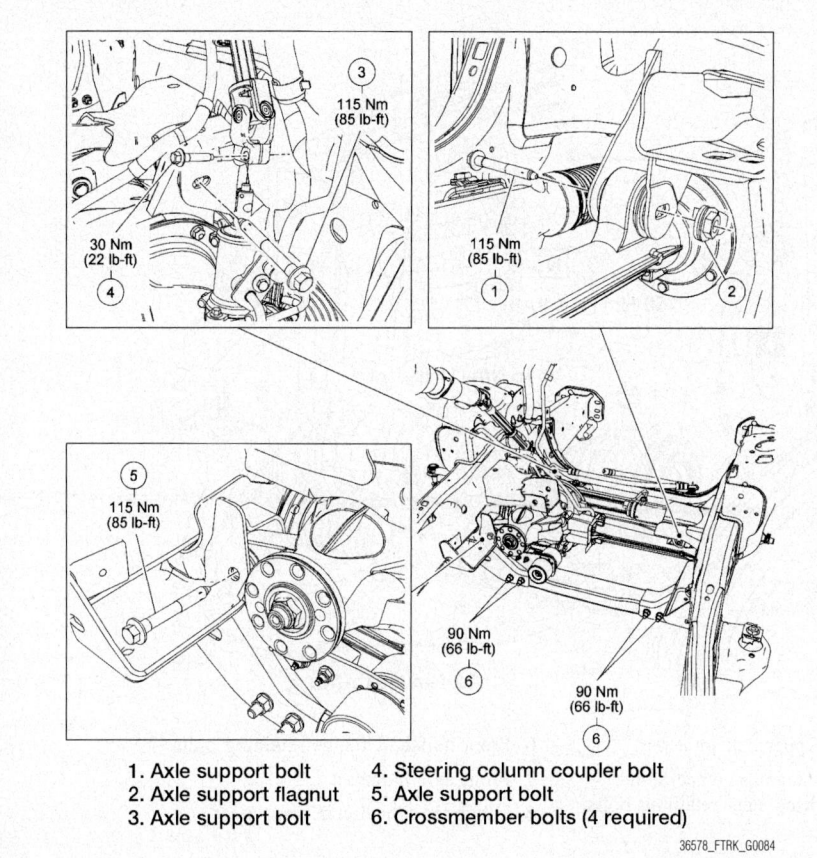

1. Axle support bolt
2. Axle support flagnut
3. Axle support bolt
4. Steering column coupler bolt
5. Axle support bolt
6. Crossmember bolts (4 required)

36578_FTRK_G0084

Fig. 27 Exploded view of the front axle assembly

2. With the transmission in NEUTRAL, raise and support the vehicle

3. Index-mark the front driveshaft to the universal joint drive pinion flange.

4. Disconnect and support the front driveshaft.

➡**Do not allow the driveshaft to hang unsupported.**

5. Remove the bolts, and disconnect both front drive halfshafts from the front axle shaft.

6. Remove the 4 crossmember bolts and the crossmember.

7. Use a high-lift jack to support the axle assembly.

8. Remove the axle housing isolator nut and bolts.

9. Remove the front mounting isolator bolt.

10. Remove the bolt from the lower steering shaft-to-steering gear and disconnect the coupler from the rack.

11. Remove the upper mounting isolator bolt.

12. Carefully lower the front drive axle assembly.

13. Disconnect the vent hose from the axle vent barbed fitting.

14. To Install, reverse the removal procedure and not the following:

FRONT HALFSHAFTS

REMOVAL & INSTALLATION

See Figure 28.

1. Before servicing the vehicle, refer to the Precautions Section.

2. Position the vehicle on a hoist.

3. Remove the front wheel and tire assembly.

4. Remove the dust cap and axle shaft nut.

5. Disconnect the tie rod end.

6. Disconnect the upper ball joint.

7. Remove the integrated wheel end disconnect retaining bolts.

8. Remove the halfshaft flange retaining bolts.

✳✳ WARNING

Do not damage the hub seal.

➡**Allow the steering knuckle to swing outboard while keeping the constant velocity shaft pushed inboard.**

9. Once clearance is available, remove the constant velocity shaft joint outboard end and integrated wheel end disconnect from the steering knuckle hub bearing.

10. Separate the halfshaft assembly from the axle assembly and remove the halfshaft assembly from the vehicle.

11. Carefully remove the integrated wheel end disconnect from the outboard constant velocity joint housing to avoid damage to the vacuum chamber.

12. To install, reverse the removal procedure. Take note of the following:

➡**Maintain a clean work surface.**

13. Compress the integrated wheel end disconnect on the bench to collapse the vacuum chamber.

14. While the integrated wheel end disconnect is collapsed, install a vacuum cap on the vacuum port.

✳✳ WARNING

Do not install the integrated wheel end disconnect in the knuckle. It must be installed on the outer constant velocity joint housing.

✳✳ WARNING

Do not dislodge the integrated wheel end disconnect seal spring when installing the integrated wheel end on the outer constant velocity joint housing.

15. Install the integrated wheel end disconnect on the outer constant velocity joint housing.

16. Install the front axle halfshaft in the vehicle. Install the halfshaft flange retaining bolts.

✳✳ WARNING

Verify the spline engagement by checking for spline lash before tightening the retainers of the integrated wheel end disconnect and the front axle halfshaft retaining nut.

17. Install and tighten the integrated wheel end disconnect retaining bolts.

18. Verify the front axle lubricant level is to specifications.

19. Observe the following torques:

- Tie rod stud nut: 111 ft. lbs. (150 Nm)
- Axle halfshaft (wheel end) nut: 20 ft. lbs. (27 Nm)
- Upper ball joint stud nut: 111 ft. lbs. (150 Nm)

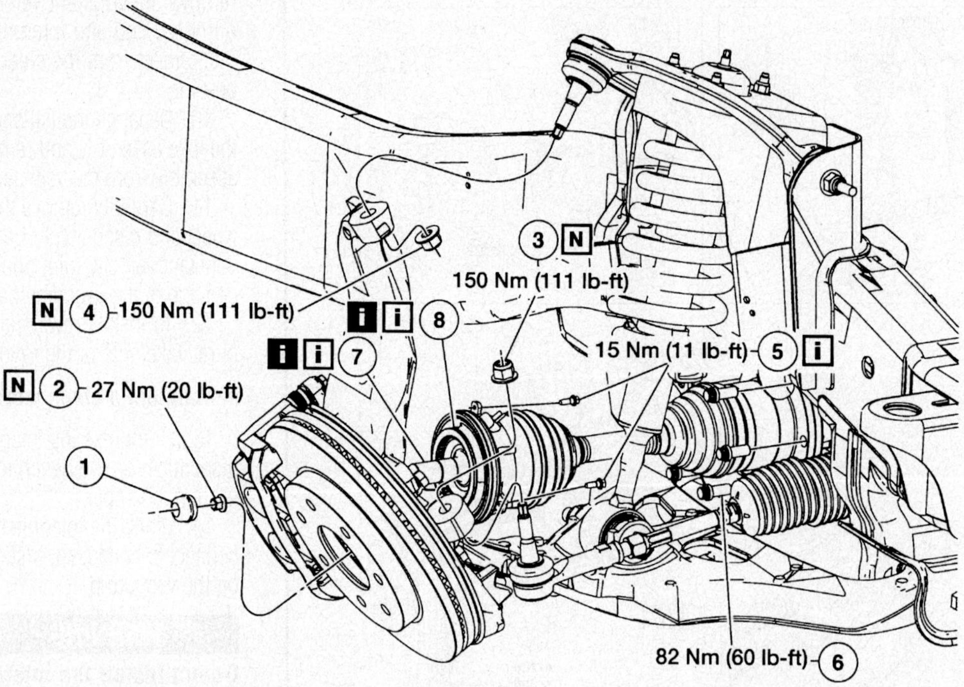

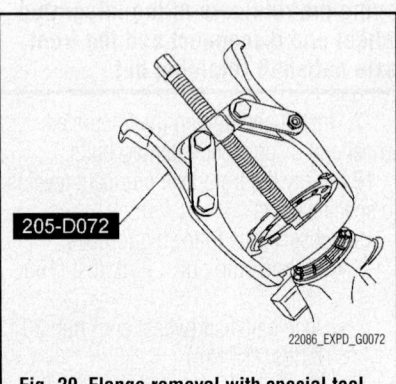

Fig. 28 Exploded view of the front axle halfshaft assembly

1	Dust cap	4	Upper ball joint nut	6	Front halfshaft flange retaining bolts
2	Axle halfshaft nut	5	Integrated wheel end disconnect retaining bolts	7	Front axle halfshaft
3	Tie-rod end nut			8	Integrated wheel end disconnect

- Integrated wheel end disconnect bolts: 108 inch lbs. (12 Nm)
- Halfshaft flange bolts: 60 ft. lbs. (82 Nm)

FRONT PINION SEAL

REMOVAL & INSTALLATION

See Figures 29 through 31.

1. Before servicing the vehicle, refer to the precautions section.
2. Position the vehicle on a hoist.

➡**Remove the front brake caliper to prevent drag during the drive pinion bearing preload adjustment.**

3. Remove the front brake calipers. Wire the caliper aside.
4. Index-mark the front driveshaft to the axle universal joint flange
5. Remove and discard the 6 bolts and 3 washers.

6. Carefully disconnect and support the front driveshaft

7. Using a Nm (inch/pound) torque wrench, measure the torque necessary to maintain pinion rotation. Record the measurement for reference during installation.

8. Install special tool 205-126 and remove the pinion nut

Fig. 29 Flange removal with special tool 205-D072

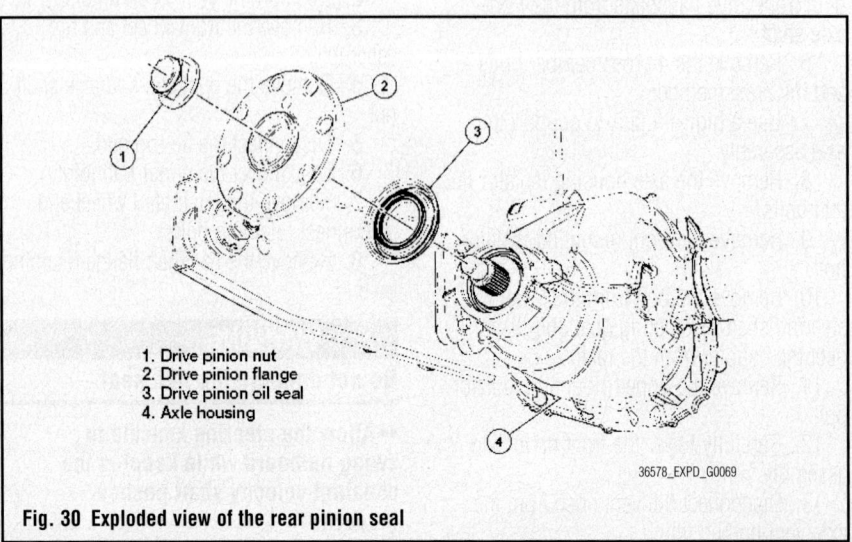

1. Drive pinion nut
2. Drive pinion flange
3. Drive pinion oil seal
4. Axle housing

Fig. 30 Exploded view of the rear pinion seal

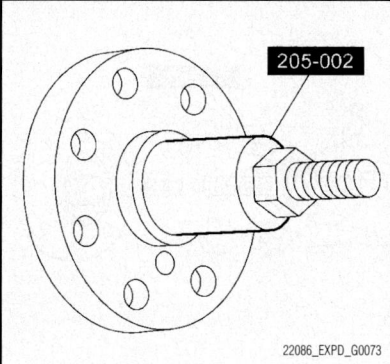

Fig. 31 Axle flange installation with special tool 205-002

9. Index-mark the axle universal joint flange to the pinion stem.

10. Using special tool 205-D072, separate the axle universal joint flange from the pinion gear.

11. Remove the flange.

12. Inspect the axle universal joint flange for burrs, the nut counterbore and the seal contact surface for nicks, and the bearing cone contact area for damage. Install a new flange if necessary.

13. Check the pinion stem splines for burrs. If burrs are evident, remove them with a fine crocus cloth.

To install:

14. Clean the pinion seal bore and use an oil seal installer to install the pinion seal.

15. Lubricate the axle universal joint flange splines and the pinion seal

➡**Disregard the scribe marks if installing a new flange.**

16. Align the index marks and position the axle universal joint flange on the pinion shaft.

➡**Rotate the pinion gear occasionally to make sure the pinion bearings seat correctly.**

17. Using special tool 205-002, install the axle universal joint flange.

18. Install the special tool, and tighten the pinion nut.

　a. Rotate the pinion gear occasionally to make sure the pinion bearings are seating correctly.

　b. Take frequent pinion bearing torque preload readings by rotating the pinion gear with a (Nm)inch/pound torque wrench.

　c. If the preload recorded prior to disassembly is lower than the specification for used bearings, then tighten the pinion nut to the specification 29 inch lbs. (1.8-3.3 Nm).

　d. If the preload recorded prior to disassembly is higher than the specification for used bearings, then tighten the pinion nut to the original reading as recorded.

19. Align the index-marks then attach the front driveshaft and tighten the 6 flange bolts to 41 ft. lbs. (55 Nm).

20. Inspect and, if necessary, fill the differential.

21. Lower the vehicle.

REAR AXLE SHAFT, BEARING & SEAL

REMOVAL & INSTALLATION

Ford 8.8 Inch Ring Gear, 9.75 Inch Ring Gear And 10.25 Inch Ring Gear Axles

See Figures 32 through 36.

1. Before servicing the vehicle, refer to the Precautions Section.

All Vehicles

2. Raise and support the vehicle.

3. Remove the wheel and tire assembly.

➡**Empty the lubricant into a clean container for reuse.**

4. Remove the 10 differential housing cover bolts and drain the lubricant from the rear axle housing.

5. Remove the differential housing cover.

Vehicles with drum brakes

6. Remove the rear brake drums.

Vehicles with disc brakes

7. Remove the rear disc brake caliper. Wire the rear disc brake caliper aside.

8. Remove the rear brake disc.

All vehicles

9. Remove and discard the differential pinion shaft lock bolt.

10. Remove the differential pinion shaft.

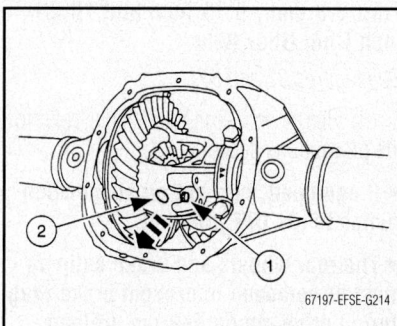

Fig. 32 Lock bolt (1); pinion shaft (2)— Ford 8.8 inch, 9.75 inch ring gear, and 10.25 inch ring gear axles

✳✳ WARNING

Do not damage the rubber O-rings in the axle shaft grooves.

11. Push in the axle shafts.

12. Remove the U-washers.

✳✳ WARNING

Do not damage the wheel bearing oil seal.

13. Remove the axle shaft.

➡**If the wheel bearing oil seal is leaking, the axle housing vent may be plugged with foreign material.**

➡**If only a new seal needs to be installed, use care to avoid damaging the seal bore.**

14. Using a suitable seal remover, remove the axle shaft oil seal. Discard the oil seal.

15. Inspect the rear wheel bearing and axle shaft for wear or damage.

16. If necessary, using the special tools, remove the rear wheel bearing.

To install:

17. Lubricate the new rear wheel bearing with rear axle lubricant.

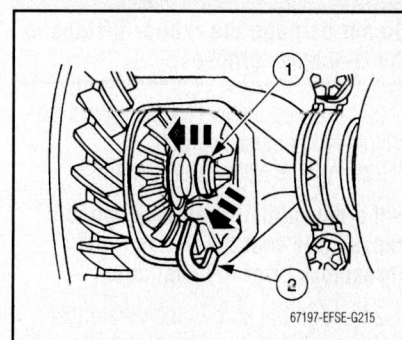

Fig. 33 Axle shaft (1); U-washer (2)—Ford 8.8 inch, 9.75 inch ring gear and 10.25 inch ring gear axles

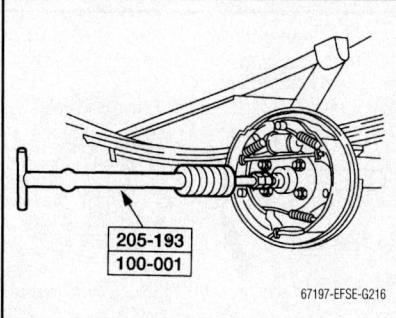

Fig. 34 Rear wheel bearing removal— Ford 8.8 inch, 9.75 inch ring gear and 10.25 inch ring gear axles

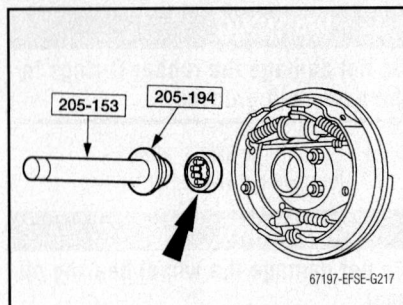

Fig. 35 Rear wheel bearing installation—Ford 8.8 inch, 9.75 inch ring gear and 10.25 inch ring gear axles

18. Using the special tools, install the rear wheel bearing.

19. Lubricate the lip of the new wheel bearing oil seal with grease.

20. Using the special tools, install the wheel bearing oil seal.

All vehicles

> ✳✳ **WARNING**
>
> **Do not damage the wheel bearing oil seal.**

21. Install the axle shaft.

> ✳✳ **WARNING**
>
> **Do not damage the rubber O-rings in the U-washer grooves.**

22. Position the two U-washers on the button end of the axle shafts.

23. Pull the axle shafts outward.

➡ **If a new pinion shaft lock bolt is unavailable coat the threads with Threadlock prior to installation.**

24. Align the hole in the differential pinion shaft with the case lock bolt hole.

25. Install a new differential pinion shaft lock bolt. Torque to 15–30 ft. lbs. (20–40 Nm).

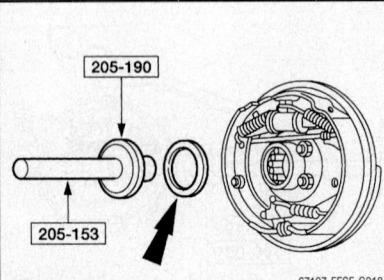

Fig. 36 Oil seal installation—Ford 8.8 inch, 9.75 inch ring gear and 10.25 inch ring gear axles

Vehicles with drum brakes

26. Install the rear brake drums.

Vehicles with disc brakes

27. Install the rear brake disc.

28. Install the rear disc brake caliper.

➡ **Clean the gasket mating surface of the rear axle and the differential housing cover.**

29. Apply a new continuous bead of sealant to the differential housing cover.

➡ **The differential housing cover must be installed within 15 minutes of application of the silicone, or new sealant must be applied. If possible, allow one hour before filling with lubricant to make sure the silicone sealant has correctly cured.**

30. Install the differential housing cover.

31. Install the 10 differential housing cover bolts. Torque to 33 ft. lbs. (45 Nm).

32. Fill the rear axle housing with 2.37 liters (5 pints) with the specified lubricant.

> ✳✳ **CAUTION**
>
> **Always remove any corrosion, dirt or foreign material present on the mounting surfaces of the wheel or the surface of the wheel hub or brake drum or disc that contacts the wheel. Installing wheels without correct metal-to-metal contact at the wheel mounting surfaces can cause the lug nut to loosen and the wheel to come off while the vehicle is in motion, causing loss of control.**

33. Clean the wheel hub and mounting surfaces.

34. Install the tire and wheel assembly.

REAR PINION SEAL

REMOVAL & INSTALLATION

Ford 8.8 inch, 9.75 inch and 10.25 inch Ring Gear Axle

See Figures 37 and 38.

1. Before servicing the vehicle, refer to the precautions section.

➡ **If equipped, turn the air suspension switch to the OFF position.**

➡ **The rear wheels and brake calipers must be removed to prevent brake drag during drive pinion bearing preload adjustment.**

2. With the vehicle in NEUTRAL, position the vehicle on a hoist.

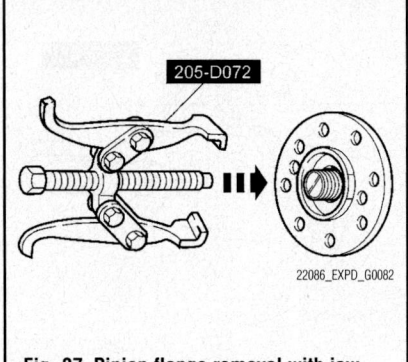

Fig. 37 Pinion flange removal with jaw puller

3. Remove the rear wheel and tire assemblies.

4. Remove the rear brake calipers and the brake discs.

5. Remove the rear driveshaft assembly.

6. Install a Nm (lb-in) torque wrench on the nut and record the torque necessary to maintain rotation of the drive pinion gear through several revolutions

> ✳✳ **WARNING**
>
> **After removing the pinion nut, discard it. Use a new nut for installation.**

7. Use the special tool to hold the pinion flange while removing the pinion nut.

8. Index-mark the drive pinion flange and the drive pinion gear stem to maintain initial balance during installation.

9. Using the special tool 205-D072, remove the drive pinion flange.

10. Force up on the metal flange of the drive pinion seal. Install gripping pliers and strike with a hammer until the pinion seal is removed.

To install:

11. Lubricate the lips of the new drive pinion seal with grease.

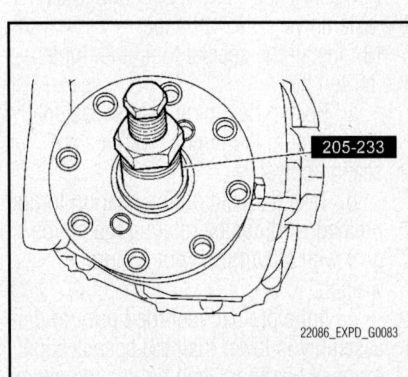

Fig. 38 Drive pinion flange installation with special tool

12. Using the special tool 205-208, install the drive pinion seal.

13. Lubricate the drive pinion flange splines with rear axle lubricant

14. Position the drive pinion flange.

15. Using the special tool 205-233, install the drive pinion flange.

16. Position the new drive pinion nut

❊❊ WARNING

Do not under any circumstance loosen the nut to reduce preload. If it is necessary to reduce preload, install a new drive pinion collapsible spacer and nut.

17. Use the special tool 205-126 to hold the pinion flange while tightening the nut.

- Rotate the pinion occasionally to make sure the pinion bearings seat correctly. Take frequent pinion bearing torque preload readings by rotating the drive pinion gear with a Nm (lb-in) torque wrench
- If the preload recorded prior to disassembly is lower than the specification for used bearings, tighten the nut to 16-29 inch lbs. (1.8-3.3 mm).
- If the preload recorded prior to disassembly is higher than the specification for used bearings, tighten the nut to the original reading as recorded.

➡**Install the driveshaft with new bolts. If new bolts are not available, apply sealer to the threads of the original bolts.**

18. Align the index marks.

➡**The driveshaft flange yoke fits tightly on the pinion flange pilot. To make sure that the yoke seats squarely on the flange, tighten the bolts evenly in a cross pattern as shown.**

19. Install the rear driveshaft.

20. Install the rear brake discs and the brake calipers.

21. Check fluid level and add if needed.

22. Install the rear wheel and tire assemblies.

23. Lower the vehicle.

24. If equipped with air suspension, reactivate the system.

ENGINE COOLING

ENGINE FAN

REMOVAL & INSTALLATION
See Figures 39 and 40.

Vehicles equipped with a 4.2L or 4.6L engine

1. Remove the air cleaner outlet pipe.

Vehicles equipped with a 5.4L engine

2. Remove the air cleaner intake pipe.

3. Remove the bolts and the air cleaner bracket.

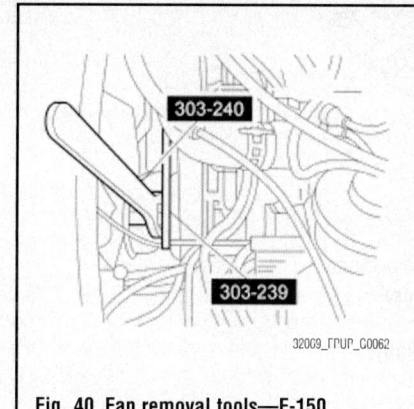

32009_FTUP_G0062

Fig. 40 Fan removal tools—F-150

Vehicles equipped with a 4.6L or 5.4L engine

4. Detach the battery cable harness from the radiator shroud.

All vehicles

5. sing the special tools, remove the cooling fan assembly and position it in the fan shroud.

6. Remove the bolts and the fan shroud and fan.

7. If necessary, remove the bolts and separate the fan and the fan clutch.

8. To install, reverse the removal procedure. Tighten the fan-to-clutch bolts to 17 Nm (13 ft. lbs.). Tighten the fan shroud bolts to 6 Nm (53 inch lbs.). Tighten the fan center bolt to 55 Nm (41 ft. lbs.).

RADIATOR

REMOVAL & INSTALLATION

2008 Models

See Figures 41 and 42.

1. Drain the engine cooling system.

2. Remove the cooling fan and shroud.

3. Release the clamp and disconnect the upper radiator hose.

4. Release the clamp and disconnect the upper degas bottle (coolant reservoir) hose.

5. Release the clamp and disconnect the lower radiator hose.

6. Using the special tool, disconnect the transmission cooler tubes.

7. Remove the bolts, the radiator support brackets and the upper radiator insulators

8. Remove the radiator.

9. Remove the lower radiator insulators.

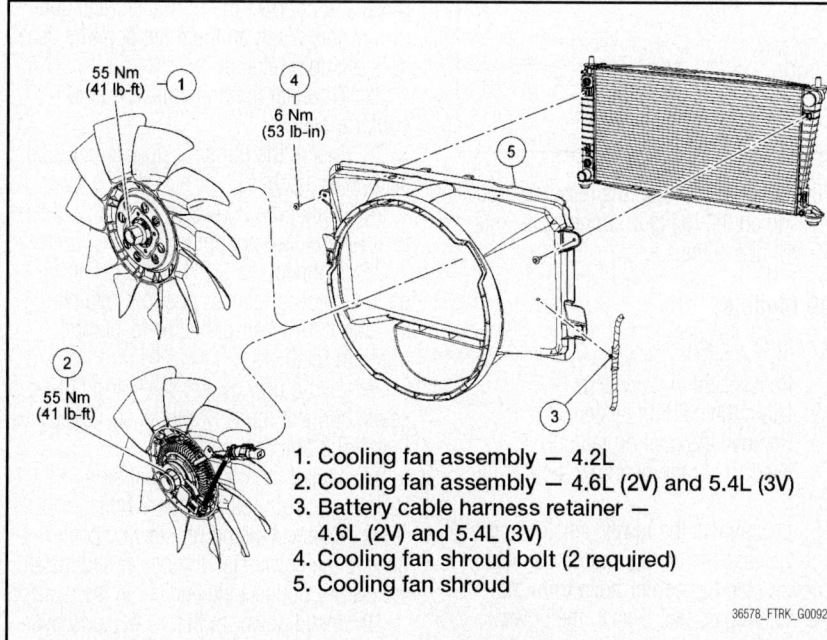

55 Nm (41 lb-ft) ① ④
6 Nm (53 lb-in)
⑤
② ③
55 Nm (41 lb-ft)

1. Cooling fan assembly — 4.2L
2. Cooling fan assembly — 4.6L (2V) and 5.4L (3V)
3. Battery cable harness retainer — 4.6L (2V) and 5.4L (3V)
4. Cooling fan shroud bolt (2 required)
5. Cooling fan shroud

36578_FTRK_G0092

Fig. 39 Exploded view of the fan blade, clutch and shroud

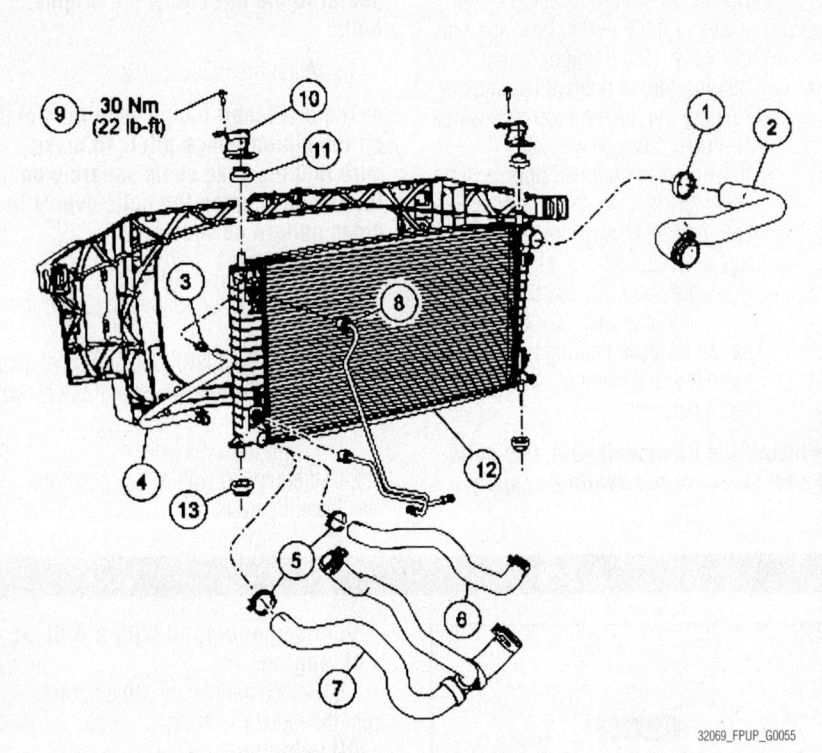

32069_FPUP_G0055

Fig. 41
1. Upper radiator hose clamp
2. Upper radiator hose
3. Upper degas bottle (coolant reservoir) hose clamp
4. Upper degas bottle (coolant reservoir) hose
5. Lower radiator hose clamp
6. Lower radiator hose 4.6L (2V) and 5.4L (3V)
7. Lower radiator hose 4.2L
8. Transmission cooler tubes
9. Radiator support bracket bolts
10. Radiator support bracket
11. Upper radiator insulators
12. Radiator
13. Lower radiator insulators
Radiator and related parts—2008 Models

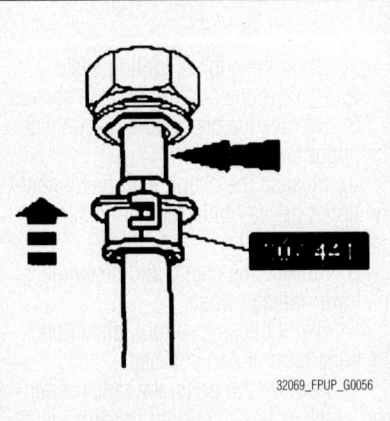

32069_FPUP_G0056

Fig. 42 Using the special tool, disconnect the transmission cooler tubes

10. To install, reverse the removal procedure. Tighten the radiator support brackets to 30 Nm (22 ft. lbs.).

2009 Models

See Figures 39 and 43.

1. Recover the A/C system.
2. Drain the cooling system.
3. Remove the cooling fan shroud.
4. Disconnect the overflow hose at the radiator.
5. Disconnect the lower radiator hose.
6. Release the clamp and disconnect the power steering cooler hose from the power steering cooler. Detach the power steering cooler hose retainer and position the hose aside.
7. Remove the 2 bolts and the coolant expansion tank/lower Air Cleaner (ACL) half.
8. Remove the bolt and nut and disconnect the A/C compressor-to-condenser tubes. Discard the gasket seals and the O-ring seals.
9. Disconnect the 3 RH and 2 LH air deflector-to-condenser pushpin retainers and the 3 lower air deflector-to-bumper pushpin retainers.
10. Disconnect the 2 RH and 2 LH air deflector-to-frame pushpin retainers
11. Remove the transmission cooler tube secondary latches.
12. Using the Transmission Cooler Line Disconnect Tool, disconnect the transmission fluid cooler tubes.
13. Disconnect the horn electrical connector and detach the wiring harness and ambient temperature sensor retainers. Position the wiring harness aside.
14. Remove the 2 bolts and the radiator/condenser core as an assembly.
15. Disconnect the 2 transmission fluid cooler hoses from the radiator.
16. Release the lock tabs and separate the radiator from the condenser core.

To install:

17. Position the condenser core into the radiator locking tabs.
18. Connect the transmission fluid cooler hoses to the radiator.
19. Position the radiator/condenser core assembly into the vehicle and onto the radiator insulators.
20. Install the 2 radiator bolts.
21. Position the wiring harness into place and connect the horn electrical connector and attach ambient temperature sensors pushpin retainer.
22. Connect the transmission fluid cooler tubes.
23. Install the transmission cooler tube secondary latches.
24. Install the 2 LH and 2 RH air deflector-to-frame rail pushpins
25. Connect the 3 RH and 2 LH air deflector-to-condenser pushpin retainers and the 3 lower air deflector-to-bumper pushpin retainers.
26. Using new gasket seals and O-ring seals, connect the A/C condenser tubes and install the bolt and nut.
27. Install the coolant expansion tank/lower ACL half and the 2 bolts.
28. Connect the power steering cooler hose to the power steering cooler and install the clamp. Connect the retainer to the radiator.
29. Install lower radiator hose and overflow hose.
30. Install the cooling fan shroud.

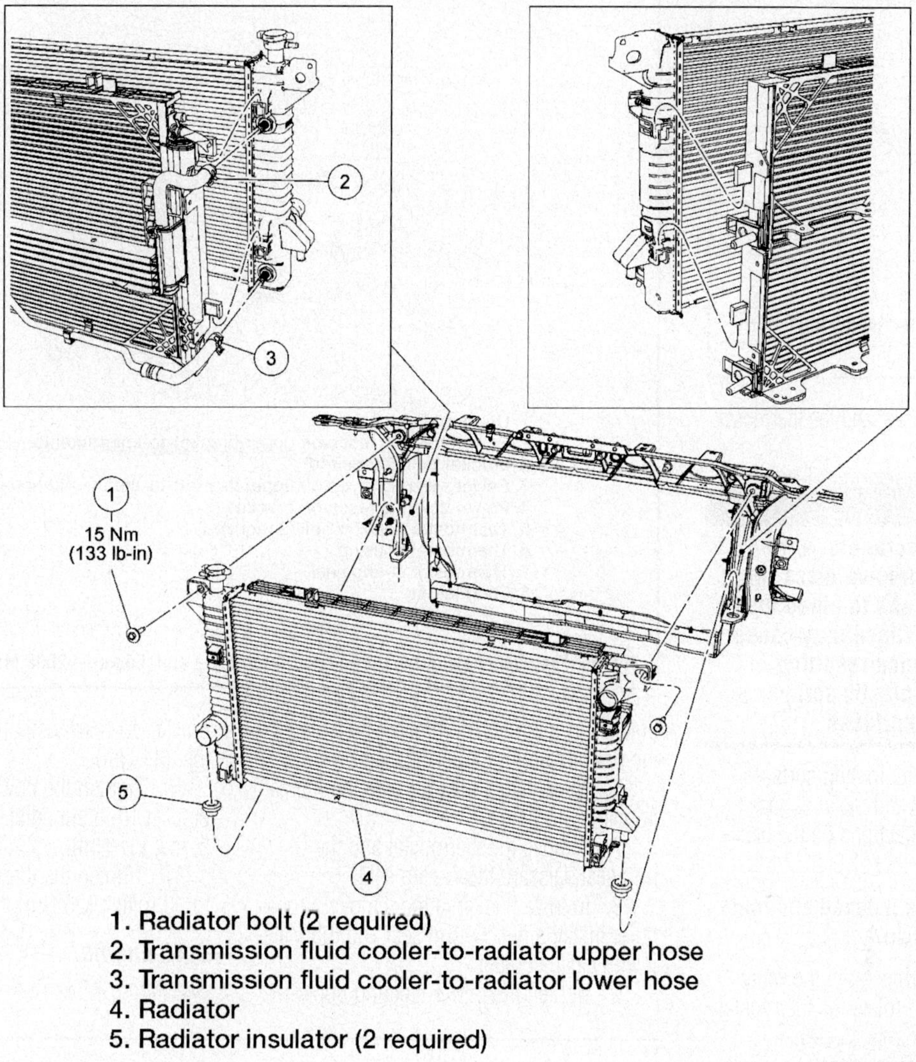

1. Radiator bolt (2 required)
2. Transmission fluid cooler-to-radiator upper hose
3. Transmission fluid cooler-to-radiator lower hose
4. Radiator
5. Radiator insulator (2 required)

36578_FTRK_G0093

Fig. 43 Exploded view of the radiator assembly—2009 Models

31. Filling the cooling system.
32. Fill the transmission with fluid and verify correct operation.
33. Evacuate and charge the A/C system.

THERMOSTAT

REMOVAL & INSTALLATION

2008 Models

4.2L Engine

See Figures 44 and 45.

1. Drain the cooling system.
2. Release the clamp and disconnect the upper radiator hose from the coolant outlet connection.
3. Remove the bolts and the thermostat housing.

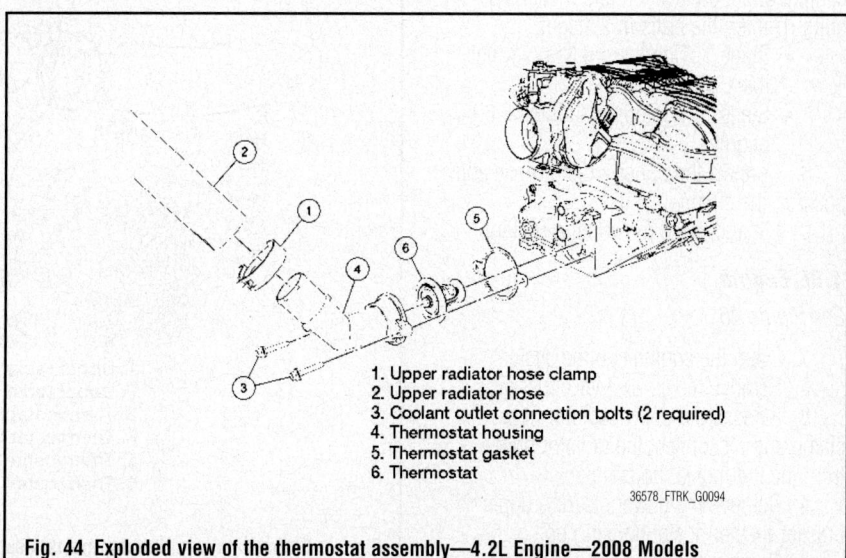

1. Upper radiator hose clamp
2. Upper radiator hose
3. Coolant outlet connection bolts (2 required)
4. Thermostat housing
5. Thermostat gasket
6. Thermostat

36578_FTRK_G0094

Fig. 44 Exploded view of the thermostat assembly—4.2L Engine—2008 Models

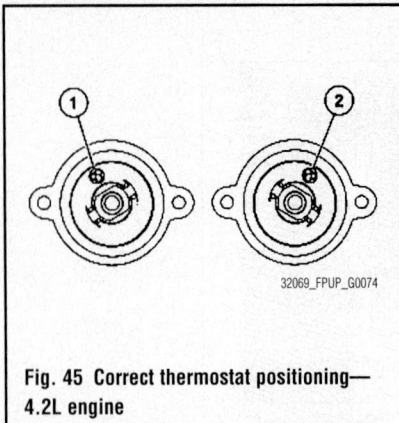

Fig. 45 Correct thermostat positioning—4.2L engine

4. Remove the gasket and the thermostat.

To install:

✳✳ WARNING

Do not use metal scrapers, wire brushes, power abrasive discs, or other abrasive means to clean the sealing surfaces. These may cause scratches and gouges resulting in leak paths. Use a plastic scraper to clean the sealing surfaces.

5. Clean the gasket mating surfaces with a plastic scraper and metal surface cleaner. Follow the directions on the packaging.

➡ **The thermostat is indexed and must be installed as shown.**

6. Install the thermostat in the water outlet connection and rotate the thermostat either clockwise or counterclockwise to engage the cam on the thermostat securely. The thermostat vent must be located either at the 11 o'clock or 1 o'clock position.

7. Position a new gasket and the coolant outlet connection and install the bolts. Tighten the bolts in 2 stages.
- Stage 1: Tighten to 8 Nm (71 inch lbs.).
- Stage 2: Tighten an additional 60 degrees.

8. Connect the upper radiator hose and position the clamp.

9. Fill and bleed the cooling system. .

4.6L Engine

See Figure 46.

1. Drain the engine cooling system.
2. Remove the air cleaner outlet pipe.
3. Release the upper radiator hose clamp and disconnect the radiator hose from the thermostat housing.
4. Remove the power steering upper bracket-to-thermostat housing bolt.
5. Remove the power steering upper

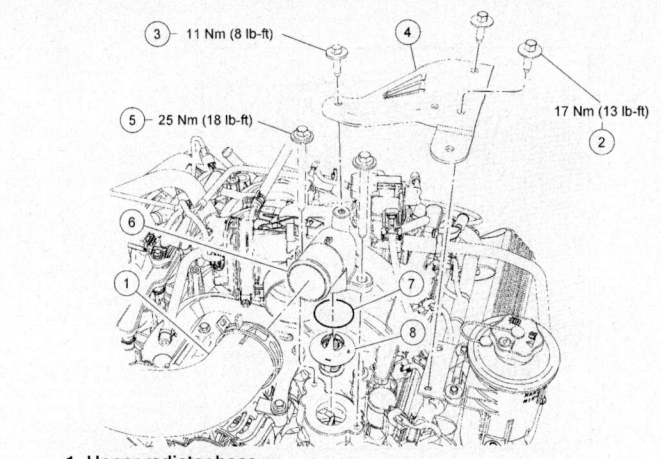

1. Upper radiator hose
2. Power steering reservoir upper bracket-to-intermediate bracket bolt (2 required)
3. Power steering reservoir upper bracket-to-thermostat housing bolt
4. Power steering reservoir bracket
5. Thermostat housing bolt (2 required)
6. Thermostat housing
7. Thermostat O-ring seal
8. Thermostat

36578_FTRK_G0095

Fig. 46 Exploded view of the thermostat assembly—4.6L Engine—2008 Models

bracket-to-intermediate bracket bolts and the power steering upper bracket.

6. Remove the bolts and the thermostat housing.

7. Remove the thermostat and the O-ring seal. Discard the O-ring seal.

8. To install, reverse the removal procedure. Install a new O-ring seal and lubricate it with clean coolant.

9. Tighten the power steering upper

bracket-to-thermostat housing bolt to 8 ft. lbs. (11 Nm).

10. Tighten the power steering upper bracket-to-intermediate bracket bolts to 13 ft. lbs. (17 Nm).

11. Tighten the thermostat housing bolts to 18 ft. lbs. (25 Nm).

5.4L Engine

See Figure 47.

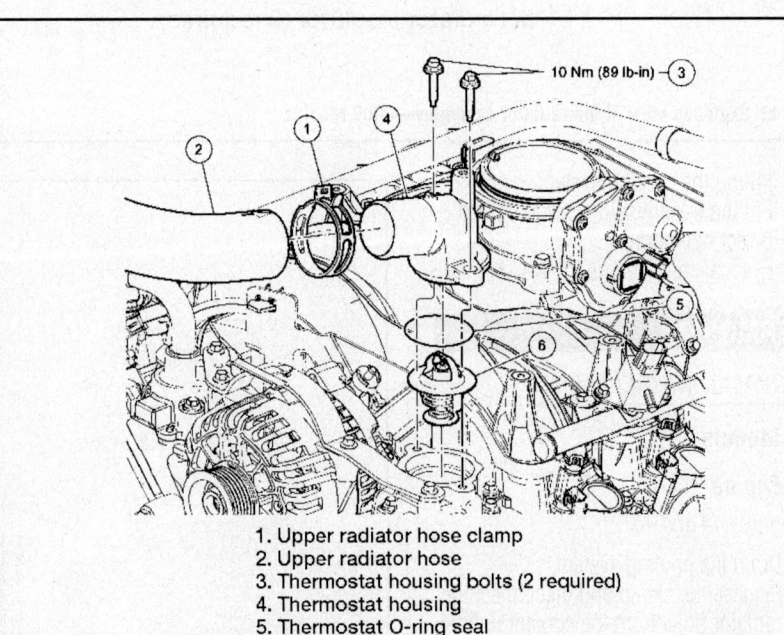

1. Upper radiator hose clamp
2. Upper radiator hose
3. Thermostat housing bolts (2 required)
4. Thermostat housing
5. Thermostat O-ring seal
6. Thermostat

36578_FTRK_G0096

Fig. 47 Exploded view of the thermostat assembly—5.4L Engine

1. Drain the engine cooling system.
2. Remove the air cleaner intake pipe.
3. Release the clamp and disconnect the upper radiator hose from the thermostat housing.
4. Remove the bolts and the thermostat housing.
5. Remove the thermostat and the O-ring seal. Discard the O-ring seal.
6. To install, reverse the removal procedure. Install a new O-ring seal and lubricate it with clean coolant. Torque the housing bolts to 89 inch lbs. (10 Nm).
7. Fill and bleed the cooling system.

2009 Models

4.6L Engine—2V

See Figure 48.

1. Drain the engine cooling system.
2. Remove the Air Cleaner (ACL) outlet pipe.
3. If servicing the thermostat housing, release the upper radiator hose clamp and disconnect the radiator hose from the thermostat housing.
4. Remove the 2 bolts, the thermostat housing and the thermostat. Discard the O-ring seal.
5. Inspect the mating surfaces. Clean the sealing surfaces with metal surface prep and silicone gasket remover. Follow the directions on the packaging.
6. If necessary, install a new thermostat with the spring facing down.
7. Install a new O-ring seal.

8. Make sure the thermostat housing is seated evenly by hand tightening the thermostat housing bolts prior to final tightening.
9. To install, tighten to 18 ft. lbs. (25 Nm).

10. To install, reverse the removal procedure.

4.6L Engine—3V

See Figure 49.

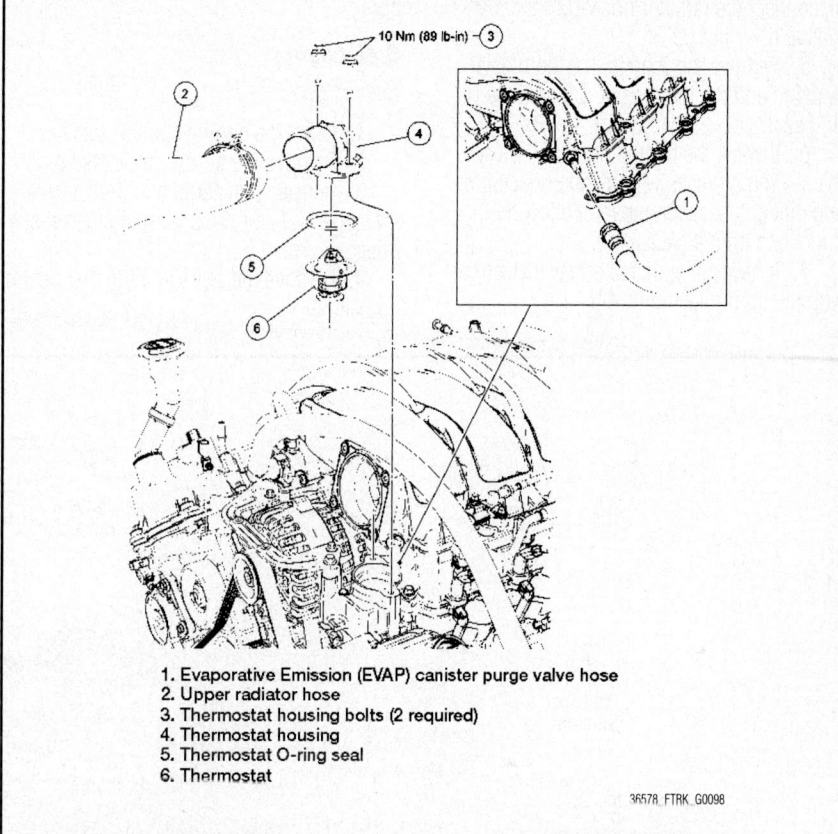

1. Evaporative Emission (EVAP) canister purge valve hose
2. Upper radiator hose
3. Thermostat housing bolts (2 required)
4. Thermostat housing
5. Thermostat O-ring seal
6. Thermostat

36578_FTRK_G0098

Fig. 49 Exploded view of the thermostat assembly—4.6L Engine—3V—2009 Models

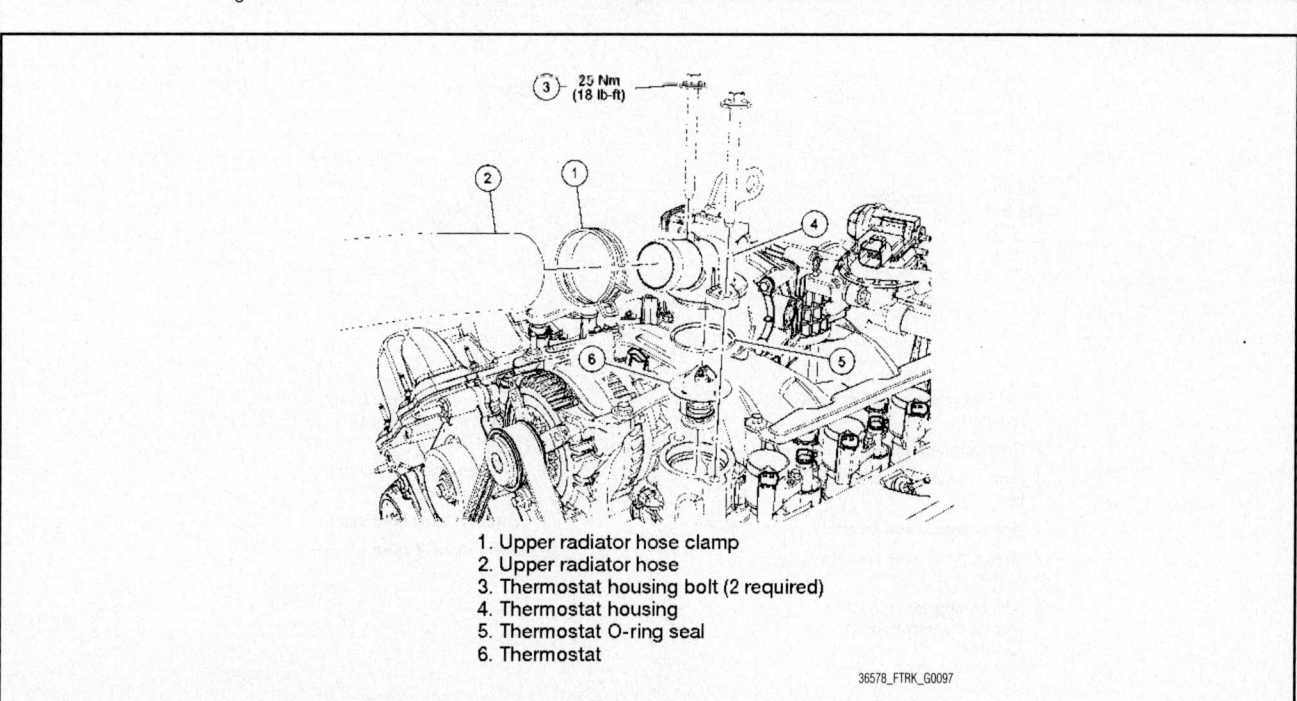

1. Upper radiator hose clamp
2. Upper radiator hose
3. Thermostat housing bolt (2 required)
4. Thermostat housing
5. Thermostat O-ring seal
6. Thermostat

36578_FTRK_G0097

Fig. 48 Exploded view of the thermostat assembly—4.6L Engine—2V—2009 Models

1. Drain the engine cooling system.
2. Remove the Throttle Body (TB).
3. Disconnect the Evaporative Emission (EVAP) canister purge valve hose.
4. If servicing the thermostat housing, release the upper radiator hose clamp and disconnect the radiator hose from the thermostat housing.
5. Remove the 2 bolts, the thermostat housing and the thermostat. Discard the O-ring seal.
6. Inspect the mating surfaces. Clean the sealing surfaces with metal surface prep and silicone gasket remover. Follow the directions on the packaging.
7. If necessary, install a new thermostat with the spring facing down.

8. Install a new O-ring seal.
9. Make sure the thermostat housing is seated evenly by hand tightening the thermostat housing bolts prior to final tightening.
10. To install, tighten to 18 ft. lbs. (25 Nm).
11. To install, reverse the removal procedure.

5.4L Engine
See Figure 47.

1. Drain the engine cooling system.
2. Remove the air cleaner intake pipe.
3. Release the clamp and disconnect the upper radiator hose from the thermostat housing.
4. Remove the bolts and the thermostat housing.

5. Remove the thermostat and the O-ring seal. Discard the O-ring seal.
6. To install, reverse the removal procedure. Install a new O-ring seal and lubricate it with clean coolant. Torque the housing bolts to 89 inch lbs. (10 Nm).
7. Fill and bleed the cooling system.

WATER PUMP

REMOVAL & INSTALLATION

4.2L Engine
See Figures 50 and 51.

1. Before servicing the vehicle, refer to the Precautions Section.
2. Drain the cooling system.

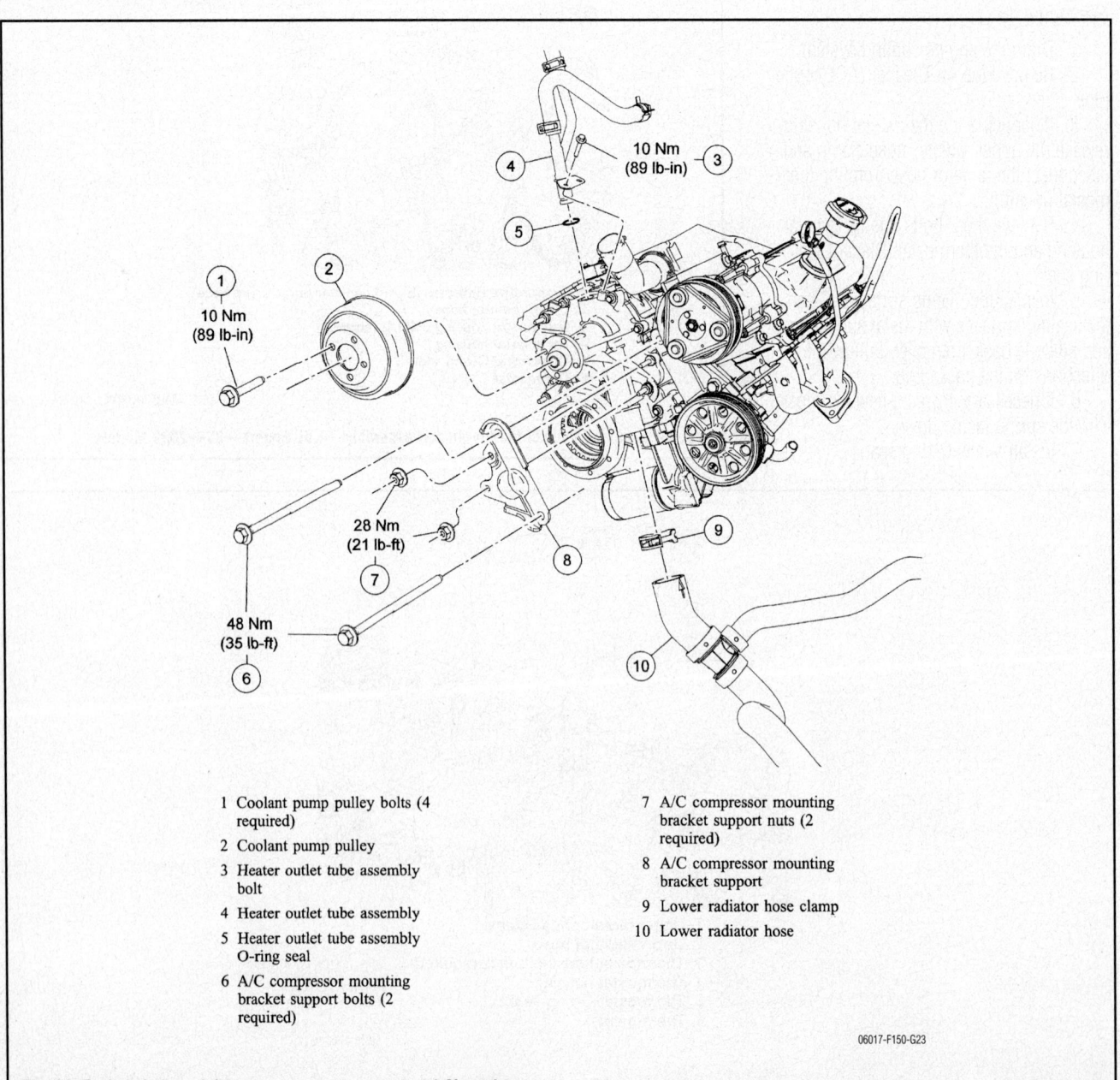

10 Nm
(89 lb-in)

10 Nm
(89 lb-in)

28 Nm
(21 lb-ft)

48 Nm
(35 lb-ft)

1 Coolant pump pulley bolts (4 required)
2 Coolant pump pulley
3 Heater outlet tube assembly bolt
4 Heater outlet tube assembly
5 Heater outlet tube assembly O-ring seal
6 A/C compressor mounting bracket support bolts (2 required)
7 A/C compressor mounting bracket support nuts (2 required)
8 A/C compressor mounting bracket support
9 Lower radiator hose clamp
10 Lower radiator hose

06017-F150-G23

Fig. 50 Exploded view of the water pump components—4.2L engine

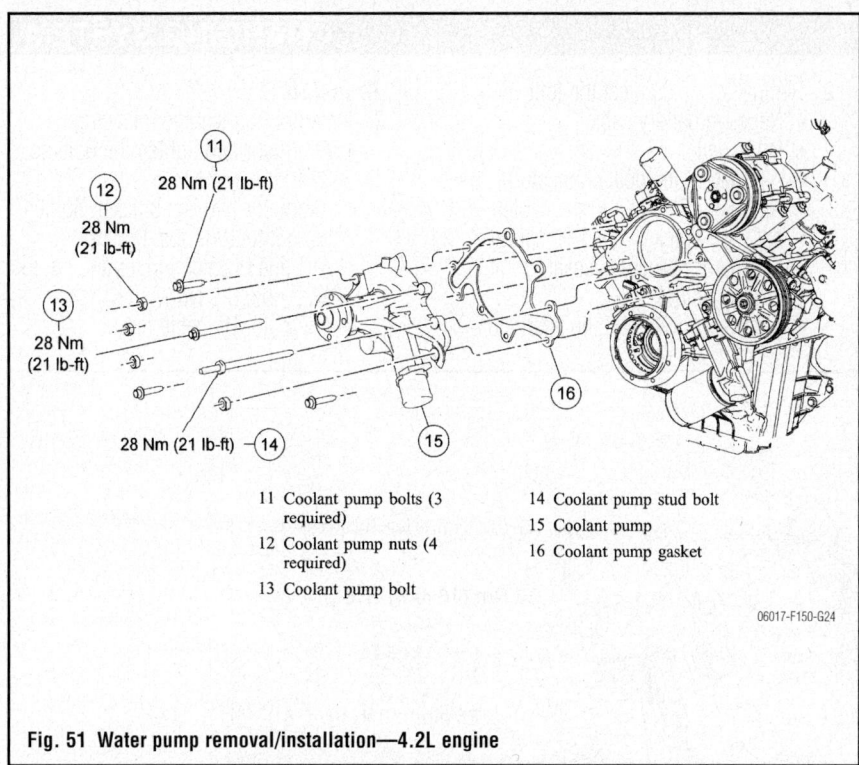

Fig. 51 Water pump removal/installation—4.2L engine

11 Coolant pump bolts (3 required)
12 Coolant pump nuts (4 required)
13 Coolant pump bolt
14 Coolant pump stud bolt
15 Coolant pump
16 Coolant pump gasket

06017-F150-G24

3. Remove the engine cooling fan and the fan shroud.

4. Remove the drive belt.

5. Remove the bolts and the coolant pump pulley.

6. Remove the bolt and disconnect the heater outlet tube assembly from the coolant pump.

7. Clean and inspect the O-ring seal. Install a new O-ring seal if necessary.

8. Remove the nuts for the A/C compressor mounting bracket support.

9. Remove the A/C compressor mounting bracket support upper bolt. Loosen the A/C compressor mounting bracket support lower bolt. Position the bracket and bolt forward until they contact the power steering pump pulley. Position the A/C compressor mounting bracket aside.

10. Release the clamp and disconnect the lower radiator hose.

11. Remove the fasteners and the coolant pump.

12. Remove and discard the coolant pump gasket.

☆☆ WARNING

Do not use metal scrapers, wire brushes, power abrasive discs, or other abrasive means to clean the sealing surfaces. These may cause scratches and gouges resulting in leak paths. Use a plastic scraper to clean the sealing surfaces.

13. Clean the coolant pump gasket mating surfaces with a plastic scraper and metal surface prep. Follow the directions on the packaging.

To install:

14. To install, reverse the removal procedure. Lubricate the O-ring seal with clean engine coolant. Observe the following torques:

- Water pump: 21 ft. lbs. (28 Nm)
- A/C compressor support bracket nuts: 21 ft. lbs. (28 Nm)
- A/C compressor support bracket bolts: 35 ft. lbs. (48 Nm)
- Heater outlet tube: 89 inch lbs. (10 Nm)

- Water pump pulley: 89 inch lbs. (10 Nm)
- Fan-to-fan clutch: 13 ft. lbs. (17 Nm)
- Fan shroud: 53 inch lbs. (6 Nm)
- Fan hub: 41 ft. lbs. (55 Nm)

4.6L & 5.4L Engines

See Figures 52 and 53.

1. Before servicing the vehicle, refer to the precautions section.

2. Drain the engine cooling system.

3. Remove the cooling fan.

4. Loosen the 4 coolant pump pulley bolts.

5. Rotate the belt tensioner clockwise and disconnect the accessory drive belt from the coolant pump pulley.

6. Remove the 4 bolts and the coolant pump pulley.

7. Remove the 4 bolts and the coolant pump. Discard the O-ring seal.

8. To install, reverse the removal procedure and note the following:

   a. Tighten water pump pulley bolts and water pump mounting bolts to 18 ft. lbs. (25 Nm).

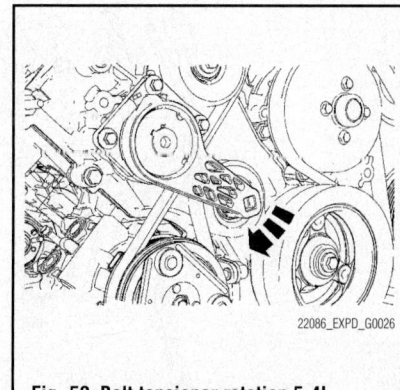

22086_EXPD_G0026

Fig. 52 Belt tensioner rotation 5.4L

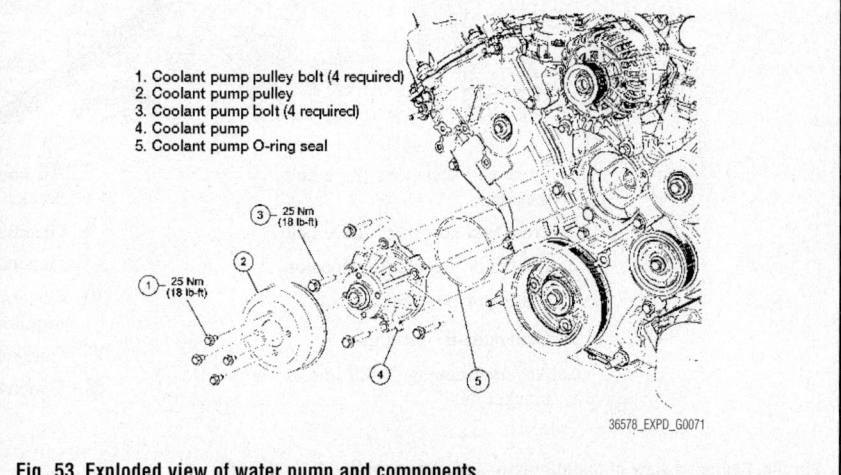

1. Coolant pump pulley bolt (4 required)
2. Coolant pump pulley
3. Coolant pump bolt (4 required)
4. Coolant pump
5. Coolant pump O-ring seal

36578_EXPD_G0071

Fig. 53 Exploded view of water pump and components

ALTERNATOR

REMOVAL & INSTALLATION

4.2L Engine

See Figure 54.

1. Before servicing the vehicle, refer to the Precautions Section.

2. Remove or disconnect the following:
   - Negative battery cable
   - Drive belt
   - Alternator electrical connectors
   - Alternator B+ nut and the cable
   - A/C line bracket (position aside)
   - Alternator harness bracket (position bracket aside)
   - Alternator bolts and the alternator

To install:

3. Install or connect the following:
   - Alternator and tighten the bolts to 35 ft. lbs. (47 Nm)
   - Alternator harness bracket; tighten the nut to 18 ft. lbs. (25 Nm)
   - A/C line bracket; tighten the nut to 18 ft. lbs. (25 Nm)
   - Alternator B+ cable nut

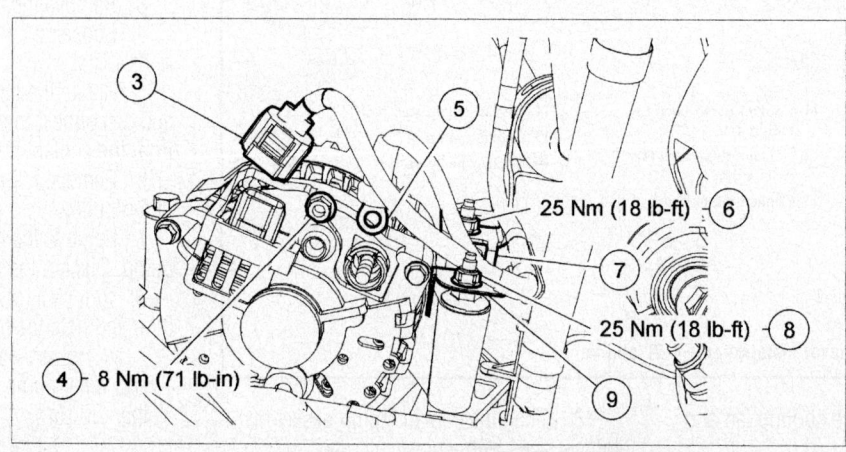

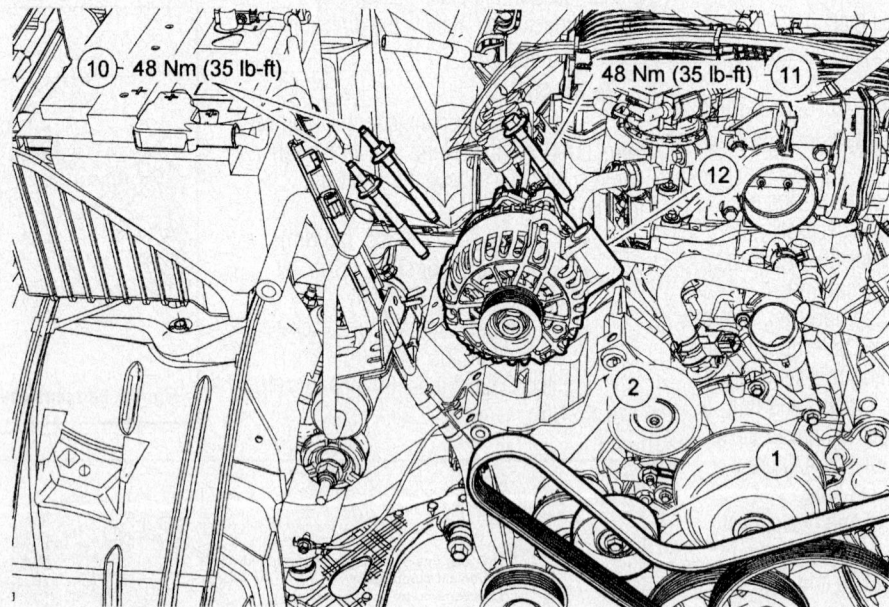

1 Front end accessory drive belt tensioner	7 Air conditioning (A/C) line bracket
2 Front end accessory drive belt	8 Generator harness bracket nut
3 Generator electrical connector	9 Generator harness bracket
4 Generator B+ terminal nut	10 Generator stud bolts (2 required)
5 Generator B+ terminal	11 Generator bolt
6 Air conditioning (A/C) line bracket nut	12 Generator

06017-F150-G13

Fig. 54 Exploded view of the alternator and components—4.2L engine

- Alternator stator and voltage regulator connectors
- Alternator electrical connectors
- Drive belt
- Negative battery cable

4.6L & 5.4L Engines

See Figure 55.

1. Before servicing the vehicle, refer to the Precautions Section.
2. Remove or disconnect the following:

- Negative battery cable
- Air cleaner outlet pipe
- Drive belt
- Alternator bracket bolts
- Ignition wire from the alternator
- Alternator bolts and the alternator

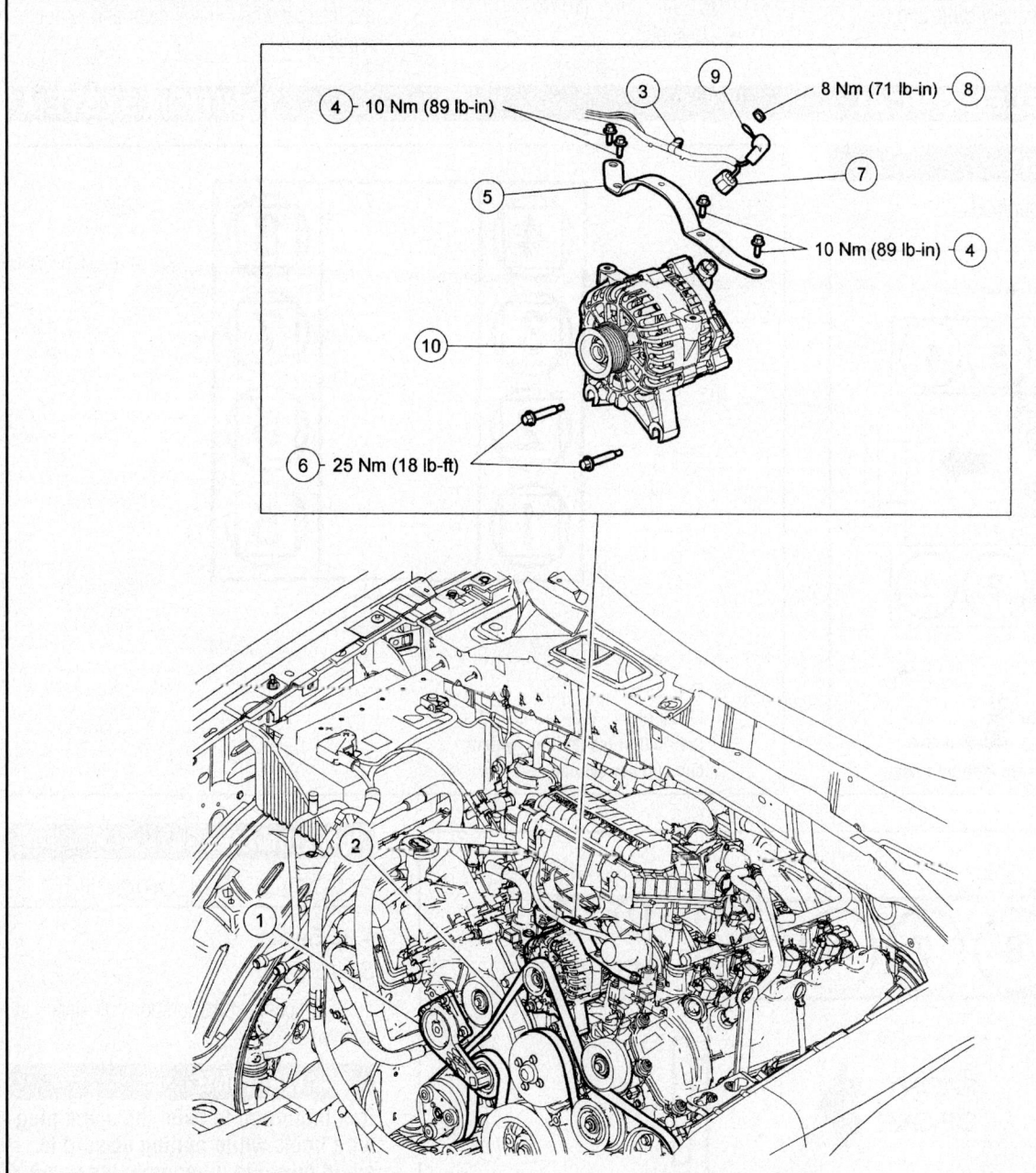

1   Front end accessory drive belt tensioner
2   Front end accessory drive belt
3   Generator harness locator
4   Generator bracket bolts (4 required)
5   Generator bracket
6   Generator bolts (2 required)
7   Generator electrical connector (part of 14305)
8   Generator B+ terminal nut
9   Generator B+ terminal
10 Generator

06017-F150-G14

Fig. 55 Exploded view of the alternator and components —5.4L engine; 4.6L similar

- Alternator electrical connectors
- Alternator stator and voltage regulator connectors
- Alternator battery cable nut and the cable

To install:

3. Install or connect the following:
  - Alternator battery cable and the nut

- Alternator stator and voltage regulator connectors
- Alternator electrical connectors
- Alternator and the bolts, tighten to 18 ft. lbs. (25 Nm)
- Ignition wire from the alternator
- Alternator bracket bolts and tighten to 89 inch lbs. (10 Nm)
- Drive belt

- Air cleaner outlet pipe
- Negative battery cable

VOLTAGE REGULATOR

REMOVAL & INSTALLATION

The voltage regulators on these vehicles are integral with the alternator and is not replaceable.

ENGINE ELECTRICAL

IGNITION SYSTEM

FIRING ORDERS

See Figures 56 through 58.

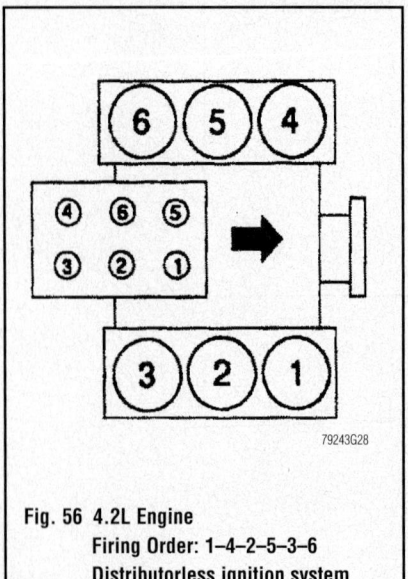

Fig. 56 4.2L Engine
Firing Order: 1–4–2–5–3–6
Distributorless ignition system

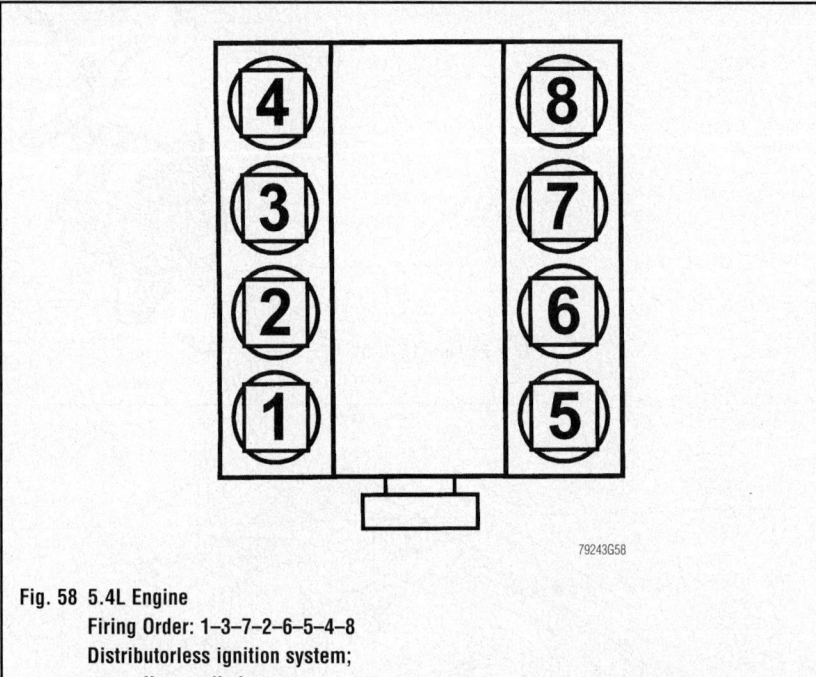

Fig. 58 5.4L Engine
Firing Order: 1–3–7–2–6–5–4–8
Distributorless ignition system;
one coil per cylinder

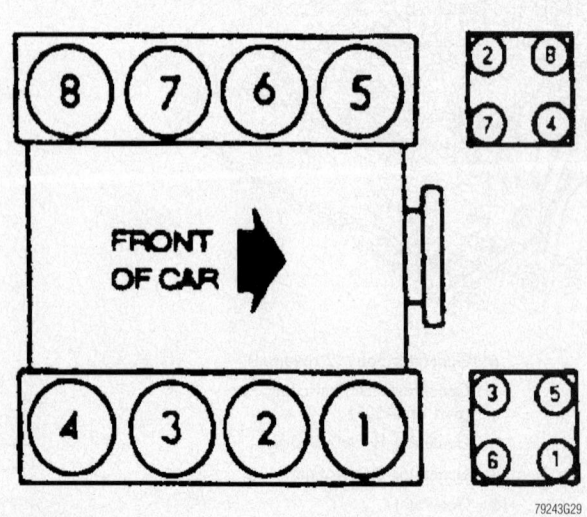

FRONT OF CAR

Fig. 57 4.6L Engine
Firing Order: 1–3–7–2–6–5–4–8
Distributorless ignition system

IGNITION COIL

REMOVAL & INSTALLATION

4.2L Engine

See Figure 59.

1. Disconnect the ignition coil electrical connector.

✸✸ WARNING

It is important to twist the spark plug wire boots while pulling upward to avoid possible damage to the spark plug wires. The spark plug wires must be connected in the correct firing order.

2. Disconnect the spark plug wires from the ignition coil by twisting while pulling upward.
3. Remove the bolts and the ignition coil.
4. Inspect the ignition coil for carbon tracks or damage.

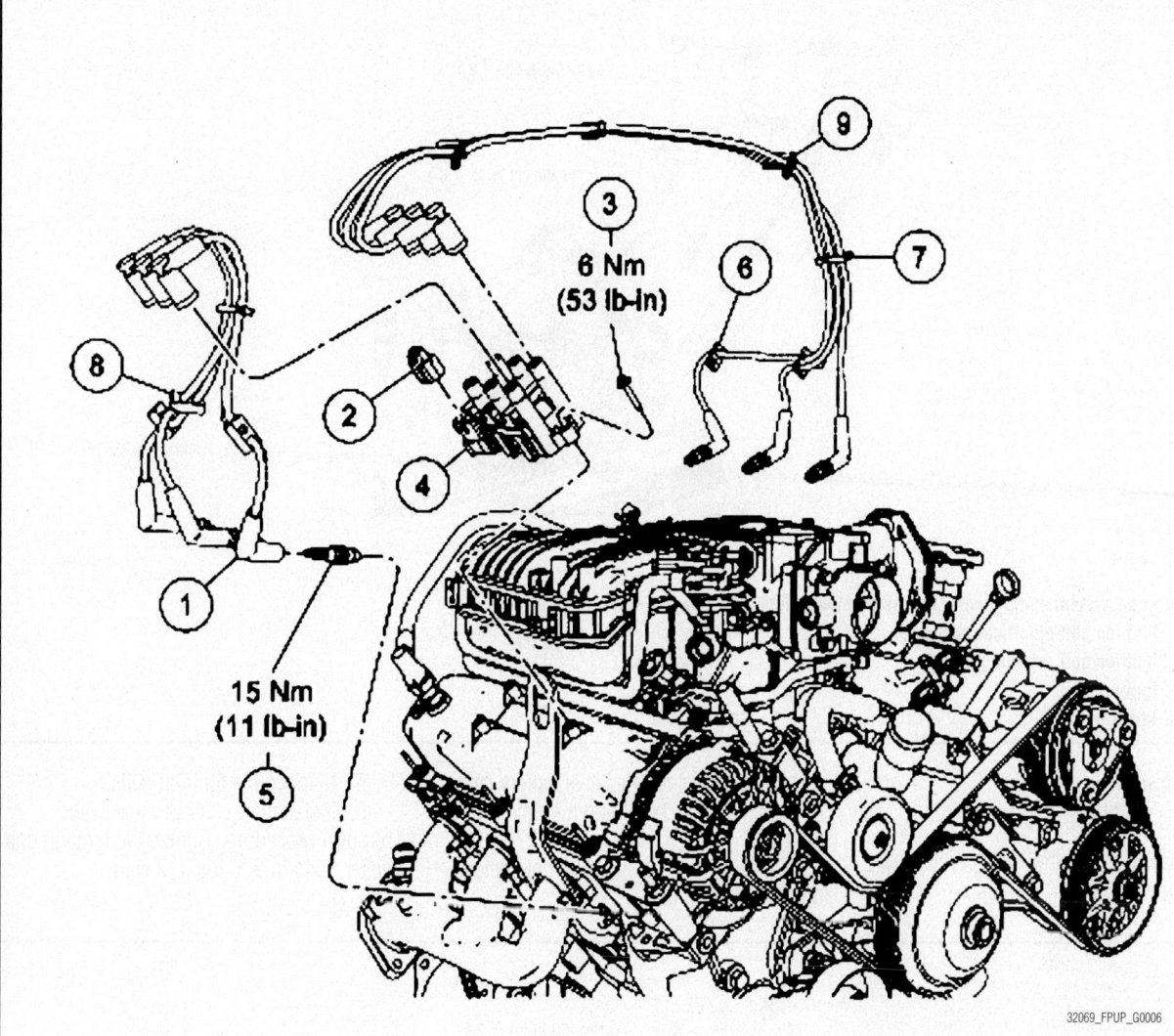

Fig. 59 Ignition system components—4.2L engine
1. Spark plug wire
2. Ignition coil electrical connector
3. Ignition coil bolts
4. Ignition coil
5. Spark plugs
6. Spark plug wire-to-valve cover retainers
7. Spark plug wire separators
8. Spark plug wire separator
9. Spark plug wire-to-intake manifold retainers

5. To install, reverse the removal procedure. Tighten to 6 Nm (53 inch lbs.). Apply silicone brake caliper grease and dielectric compound to the inside of the spark plug wire boots.

4.6L Engine

See Figure 60.

1. Disconnect the battery ground cable..

2. Disconnect the ignition coil electrical connector.

3. Remove the ignition coil retaining bolt.

4. Rotate the ignition coil clockwise 30–40 degrees to clear the fuel injection supply manifold. Use a twisting motion while pulling up on the ignition coil and remove.

➡Verify that the ignition coil spring is correctly located inside the ignition coil boot and that there is no damage to the tip of the boot.

5. To install, reverse the removal procedure. Apply dielectric compound to the inside of the coil boots before installing. Torque the ignition coil retaining bolt to 10 Nm (89 inch lbs.).

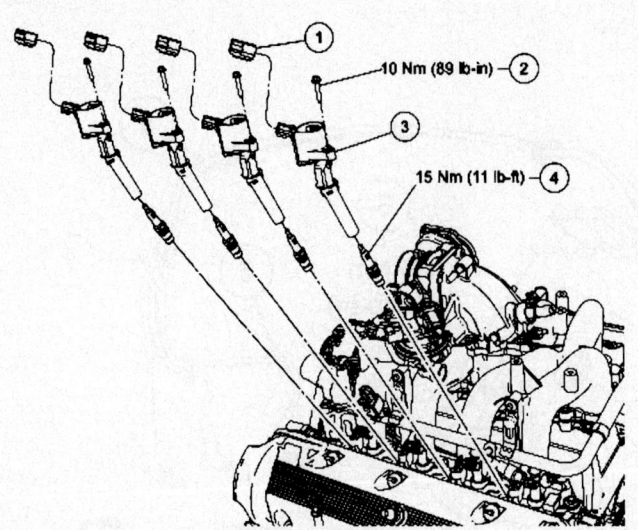

32069_FPUP_G0007

Fig. 60 Ignition system components. Left side shown; right side similar—4.6L engine
1. Ignition coil electrical connector
2. Ignition coil retaining bolt
3. Ignition coil
4. Spark plugs

5.4L Engine

See Figures 61 and 62.

1. Before servicing the vehicle, refer to the precautions section.

2. Disconnect the negative battery cable.

3. Remove the bolts and the ignition coil cover.

4. Disconnect the electrical connector from the ignition coil.

5. Remove the ignition coils.

6. Installation is the reverse of the removal procedure. Tighten the ignition coil cover bolts to 9 ft. lbs. (12 Nm).

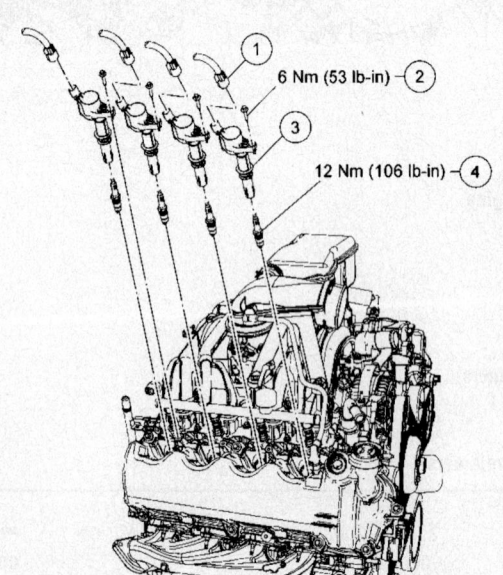

1. RH ignition coil electrical connector (4 required)
2. RH ignition coil retaining bolt (4 required)
3. RH ignition coil (4 required)
4. RH spark plug (4 required)

36578_EXPD_G0080

Fig. 61 Exploded view of the engine ignition components-RH

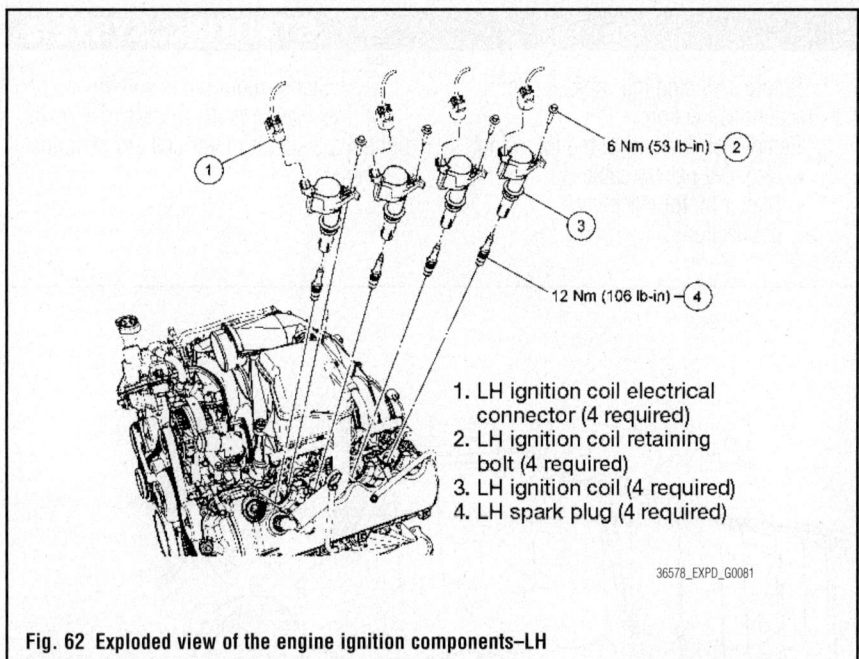

1. LH ignition coil electrical connector (4 required)
2. LH ignition coil retaining bolt (4 required)
3. LH ignition coil (4 required)
4. LH spark plug (4 required)

36578_EXPD_G0081

Fig. 62 Exploded view of the engine ignition components–LH

IGNITION TIMING

ADJUSTMENT

Base timing for distributorless ignition engines is set at the factory at 10 degrees Before Top Dead Center (BTDC) and is not adjustable.

SPARK PLUGS

REMOVAL & INSTALLATION

4.2L Engine

See Figure 63.

> **✳ WARNING**
> Spark plug wires must be connected in the correct firing order.

> **✳ WARNING**
> It is important to twist the spark plug wire boots while pulling upward to avoid possible damage to the spark plug wire.

1. Using the special tool shown, or equivalent, with a twisting motion pull the spark plug wire off the spark plug.

➡ **Use compressed air to remove any foreign material in the spark plug well before removing the spark plugs.**

➡ **If an original spark plug is reused, make sure it is installed in the same cylinder from which it was taken. New spark plugs can be used in any cylinder.**

2. Remove the spark plug.
3. Inspect the spark plug firing tip.
4. Adjust the spark plug gap as necessary.

➡ **Apply silicone brake caliper grease and dielectric compound to the inside of the spark plug wire boots.**

5. To install, reverse the removal procedure. See the torque Specifications Chart for spark plug tightening.

4.6L Engines

1. Disconnect the battery ground cable..
2. Disconnect the ignition coil electrical connector.
3. Remove the ignition coil retaining bolt.
4. Rotate the ignition coil clockwise 30–40 degrees to clear the fuel injection supply manifold. Use a twisting motion while pulling up on the ignition coil and remove.

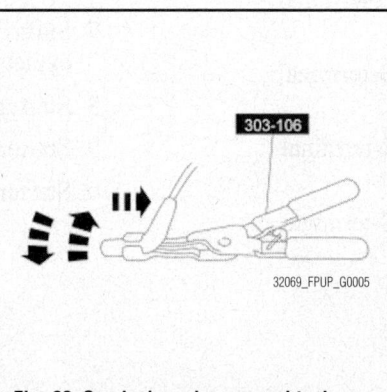

303-106

◀◀◀ ▶

32069_FPUP_G0005

Fig. 63 Spark plug wire removal tool

➡ **Verify that the ignition coil spring is correctly located inside the ignition coil boot and that there is no damage to the tip of the boot.**

➡ **Use compressed air to remove any foreign material from the spark plug well before removing the spark plugs.**

➡ **If an original spark plug is used, make sure it is installed in the same cylinder from which it was taken. New spark plugs can be used in any cylinder.**

5. Remove the spark plugs.
6. Inspect the spark plugs. Install new spark plugs as necessary.
7. To install, reverse the removal procedure. Apply dielectric compound to the inside of the coil boots before installing. See the torque Specifications Chart for spark plug tightening. Torque the ignition coil retaining bolt to 89 inch lbs. (10 Nm)

5.4L Engine

1. Disconnect the battery ground cable.
2. Disconnect the ignition coil electrical connector.
3. Remove the bolt and remove the ignition coil, using a twisting motion while pulling up on the ignition coil.

➡ **Verify that the ignition coil spring is correctly located inside the ignition coil boot and that there is no damage to the tip of the boot.**

➡ **Use compressed air to remove any foreign material from the spark plug well before removing the spark plugs.**

➡ **If an original spark plug is used, make sure it is installed in the same cylinder from which it was taken.**

4. New spark plugs can be used in any cylinder.
5. Remove the spark plugs.

> **✳ WARNING**
> The spark plug gap is NOT adjustable. Damage can occur to the ceramic if the gap is adjusted. Replace the spark plug if the gap is out of specification.

6. Inspect the spark plugs. Install new spark plugs as necessary.
7. To install, reverse the removal procedure. Apply a light coat of dielectric compound to the inside of the ignition coil boots. See the torque Specifications Chart for spark plug tightening. Tighten the coil bolt to 53 inch lbs. (6 Nm)

STARTER

REMOVAL & INSTALLATION

4.2L, 4.6L, 5.4L and 6.8L Engines

See Figures 64 and 65.

1. Before servicing the vehicle, refer to the Precautions Section.
2. Remove or disconnect the following:
   • Negative battery cable
   • Starter motor electrical connections
   • Starter motor bolts and the motor
3. Installation is the reverse of removal, tighten the starter motor bolts to 18 ft. lbs. (25 Nm).

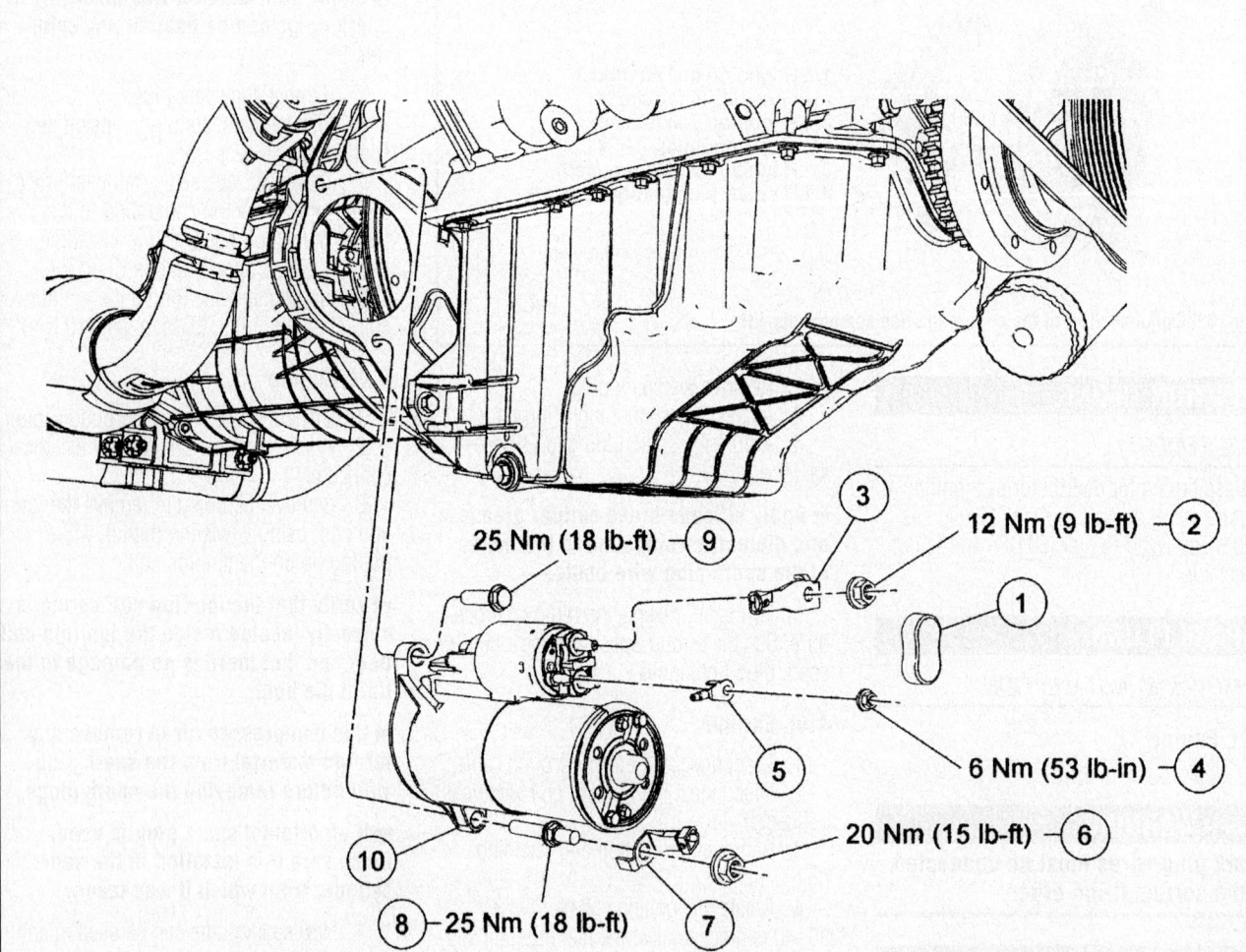

1	Terminal cover
2	Starter solenoid B-terminal nut
3	Starter solenoid B-terminal eyelet
4	Starter solenoid S-terminal nut
5	Starter solenoid S-terminal eyelet
6	Starter motor ground cable nut
7	Starter motor ground cable eyelet
8	Starter motor stud bolt
9	Starter motor bolt
10	Starter motor

06017-F150-G86

Fig. 64 Starter and related parts—4.2L engine

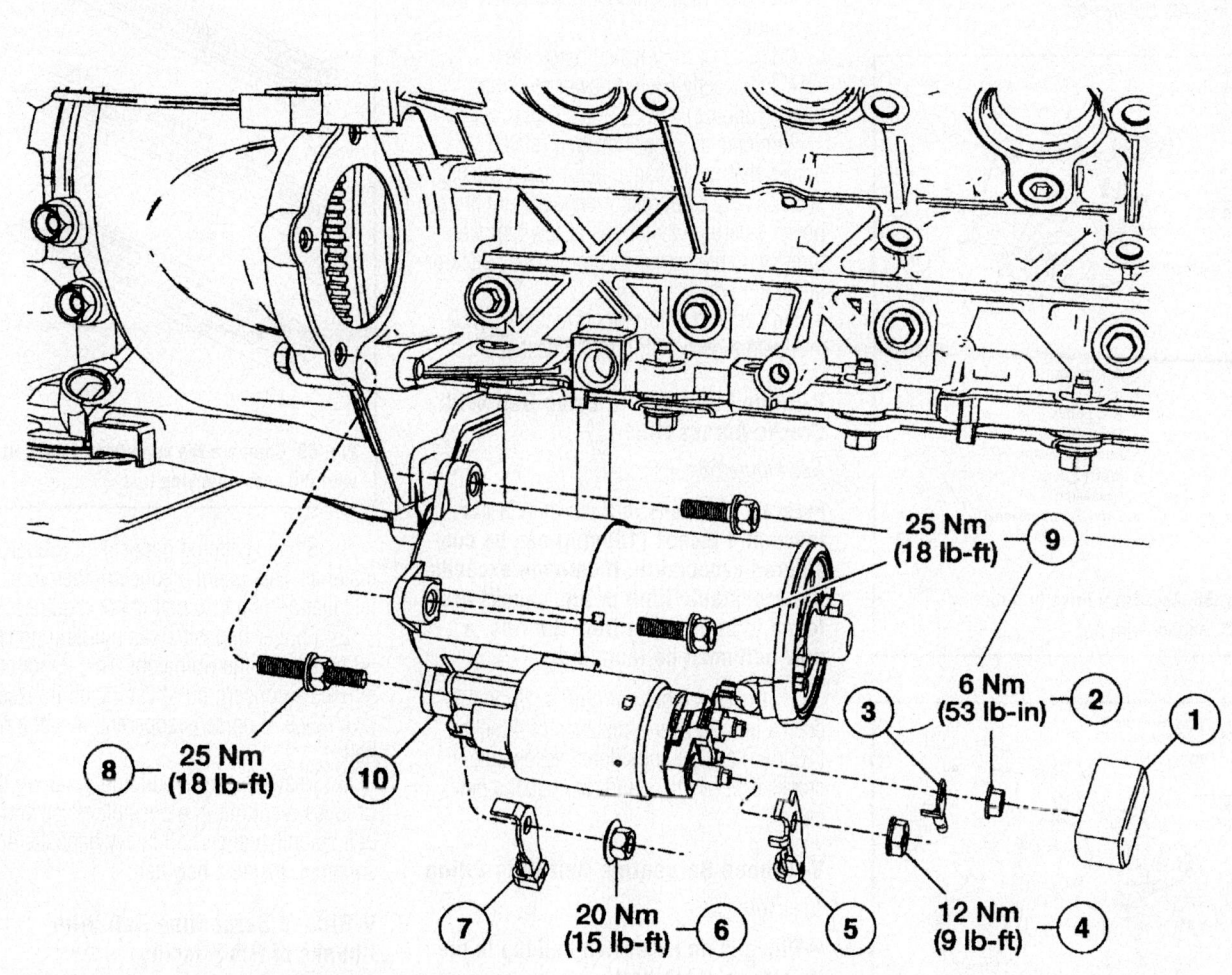

1 Terminal cover

2 Starter solenoid S-terminal nut

3 Starter solenoid S-terminal eyelet

4 Starter solenoid B-terminal nut

5 Starter solenoid B-terminal eyelet

6 Starter motor ground cable nut

7 Starter motor ground cable eyelet

8 Starter motor mounting stud bolt

9 Starter motor mounting bolt (2 required)

10 Starter motor

06017-F150-G87

Fig. 65 Starter and related parts—4.6L and 5.4L engines

ENGINE MECHANICAL

ACCESSORY DRIVE BELTS

ACCESSORY BELT ROUTING

See Figures 66 and 67.

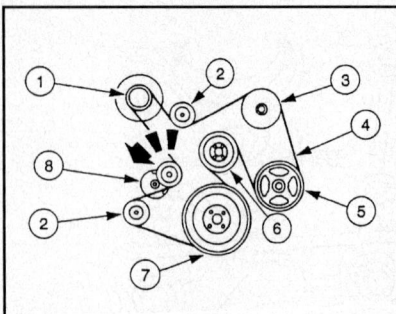

1. Alternator
2. Idler
3. A/C pulley
4. Drive Belt
5. Power Steering
6. Water Pump
7. Crankshaft
8. Drive Belt Tensioner

79244G88

Fig. 66 Accessory drive belt routing—4.2L engine with A/C

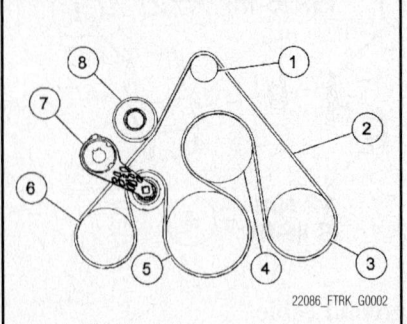

22086_FTRK_G0002

Fig. 67 Accessory drive belt routing—4.6L and 5.4L engines with A/C

INSPECTION

✳✳ WARNING

Under no circumstances should the accessory drive belt, tensioner or pulleys be lubricated as potential damage to the belt material and tensioner damping mechanism will occur. Do not apply any fluids or belt dressing to the accessory drive belt or pulleys.

Visual Inspection

Visually inspect the belt for obvious signs of mechanical damage:

- Drive belt cracking/chunking/wear
- Belt/pulley contamination
- Incorrectly routed belt
- Pulley misalignment or excessive pulley runout
- Loose or mislocated hardware
- Incorrectly routed power steering tubes (rubbing)

Eliminate all other non-belt related noises that could cause belt misdiagnosis, such as A/C compressor engagement chirp, power steering cavitations at low temperatures, variable camshaft timing (VCT) tick or generator whine.

If a concern is found, correct the condition before proceeding to the next section.

V-Ribbed Serpentine Drive Belt With Cracks Across Ribs

See Figure 68.

➡**Up to 15 cracks in a rib over a distance of 4 inches (100mm) can be considered acceptable. If damage exceeds the acceptable limit or any chunks are found to be missing from the ribs, a new belt must be installed.**

1. Check the belt for cracks. Up to 15 cracks in a rib over a distance of 4 inches (100mm) can be considered acceptable. If cracks exceed this standard, install a new belt.

V- Ribbed Serpentine Belt With Piling

See Figure 69.

➡**Piling is an excessive buildup in the V-grooves of the belt.**

The condition of the V-ribbed drive belt should be compared against the illustration and appropriate action taken.

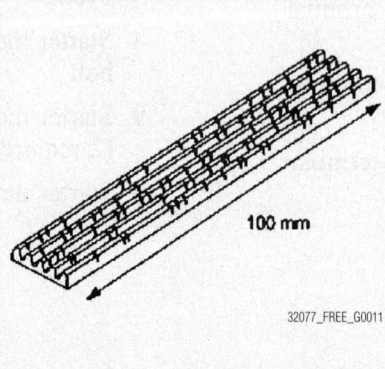

32077_FREE_G0011

Fig. 68 Up to 15 cracks in a rib over a distance of 4 inches (100mm) can be considered acceptable. If cracks exceed this standard, install a new belt

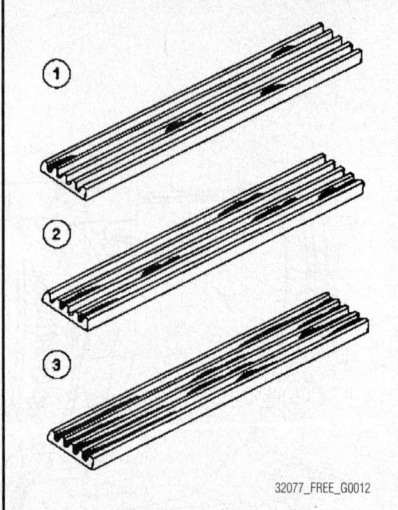

32077_FREE_G0012

Fig. 69 Compare the condition of the belt with the accompanying text

1. Small scattered deposits of rubber material. This is not a concern, therefore, installation of a new belt is not required.

2. Longer deposit areas building up to 50 percent of the rib height. This is not considered a concern but it can result in excessive noise. If noise is apparent, install a new belt.

3. Heavy deposits building up along the grooves resulting in a possible noise and belt stability concern. If heavy deposits are apparent, install a new belt.

V-Ribbed Serpentine Belt With Chunks of Rib Missing

See Figure 70.

There should be no chunks missing from the belt ribs. If the belt shows any evidence of this, install a new accessory drive belt.

Inspect the drive belt for signs of glazing or cracking. A glazed belt will be perfectly smooth from slippage, while a good belt

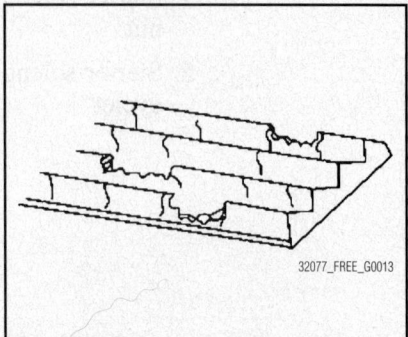

32077_FREE_G0013

Fig. 70 Replace the belt if missing chunks are found during inspection

will have a slight texture of fabric visible. Cracks will usually start at the inner edge of the belt and run outward. All worn or damaged drive belts should be replaced immediately.

ADJUSTMENT

The belts used on these vehicle are equipped with automatic (spring load) tensioners which maintain tension. No adjustment is necessary or possible.

REMOVAL & INSTALLATION

4.2L Engine

See Figure 71.

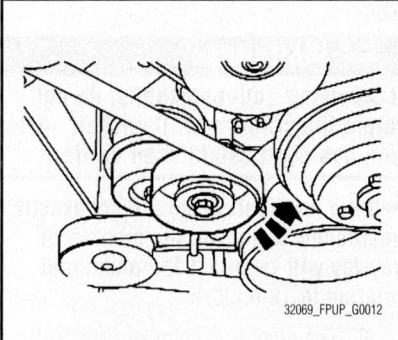

Fig. 71 Accessory drive belt removal—4.2L engine

1. Rotate the tensioner counterclockwise and remove the drive belt.
2. To install, reverse the removal procedure.

4.6L & 5.4L Engines

See Figure 72.

1. Remove the engine cooling fan and shroud.
2. Rotate the drive belt tensioner clockwise and remove the accessory drive belt.

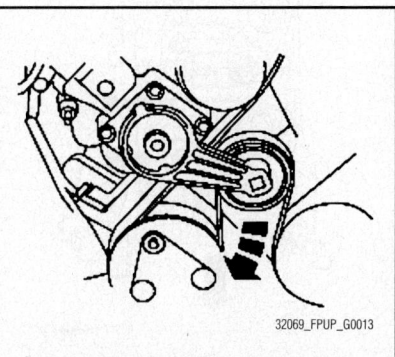

Fig. 72 Accessory drive belt removal—4.6L and 5.4L engines

3. To install, reverse the removal procedure.

CAMSHAFT AND VALVE LIFTERS

REMOVAL & INSTALLATION

4.2L Engine

See Figure 73.

➡It may be easier to remove the engine from the vehicle.

1. Before servicing the vehicle, refer to the Precautions Section.
2. Remove or disconnect the following:
   • Negative battery cable
   • Lower intake manifold
   • Rocker arm cover
   • Rocker arm hold-down bolt, then remove the rocker arm from the cylinder head.
   • Pushrods
   • Valve lifters by pulling them up out of their bores
   • Timing chain and sprockets; see procedure in this section
   • Camshaft key from the end of the camshaft, then slide the engine dynamic balance shaft drive gear off the camshaft.
   • The 2 camshaft thrust plate retaining bolts (1), then remove the thrust plate (2).
3. Remove the camshaft spacer (3), then slide the camshaft (4) out of the front of the engine block. Be cautious not to gouge or scratch the camshaft bearing journals.

To install:

4. Lubricate the camshaft with engine oil prior to installation.
5. Carefully slide the camshaft into the camshaft bore. Do not scratch the bearing surfaces.

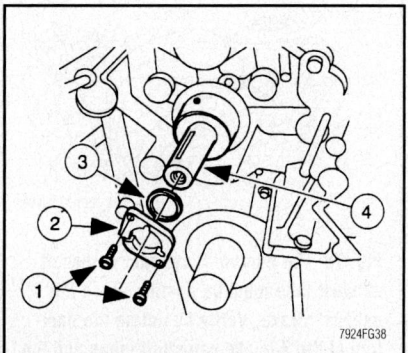

Fig. 73 Exploded view of the camshaft retaining hardware—4.2L engine

6. Install the camshaft thrust plate with the spacer. Tighten the thrust plate mounting bolts to 72–120 inch lbs. (8–14 Nm).
7. Slide the engine dynamic balance shaft drive gear onto the camshaft. Install the camshaft key to the camshaft groove.
8. Install the timing chain and sprockets.
9. Install the valve lifters, pushrods, intake manifolds and rocker arm covers.

4.6L Engines

See Figures 74 through 76.

1. Before servicing the vehicle, refer to the Precautions Section.
2. Remove the timing drive components. See "Timing Chain and Sprockets" in this section.
3. Install the special tool between the valve spring coils to protect the valve stem seal from damage.

➡The camshaft roller followers must be installed in their original locations. Record the camshaft roller follower locations.

➡The 3 rearmost camshaft roller followers on the RH side must use special tool 303-567 in the same manner as is shown in the illustration.

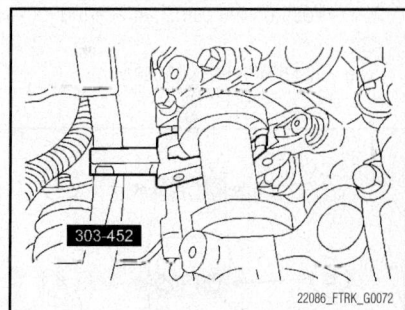

Fig. 74 The 3 rearmost camshaft roller followers on the RH side must use special tool 303-567 in the same manner as is shown

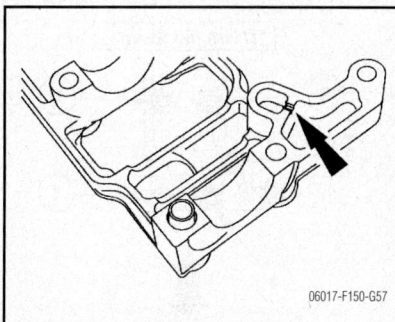

Fig. 75 One of the bearing caps contains an oil flow restriction groove—4.6L engine

4. Using the special tool, compress the valve spring and remove the camshaft roller follower.

5. Remove all of the camshaft roller followers from the camshaft being serviced.

6. Remove the bolt, camshaft sprocket and camshaft sprocket spacer from the camshaft being serviced.

7. Remove the special tools from the camshaft being serviced.

8. Remove the bolts, camshaft bearing caps and the camshaft.

9. Clean and inspect the camshaft bearing caps.

10. One of the bearing caps contains an oil flow restriction groove. Make sure the groove is free of foreign material.

11. Clean and inspect the camshaft bearing caps. One of the bearing caps contains an oil flow restriction groove. Make sure the groove is free of foreign material.

To install:

12. Install the camshaft and the camshaft bearing caps in their original locations, performing the following:

a. Lubricate the camshaft with clean engine oil.

b. Position the camshaft.

c. Lubricate the camshaft bearing caps with clean engine oil.

d. Position the camshaft bearing caps.

e. Install the bolts loosely.

13. Tighten the bolts in the sequence shown to 89 inch lbs. (10 Nm).

14. Install the camshaft sprocket. Install and tighten the bolt.

- Tighten in two stages.
- Stage 1: Tighten to 40 Nm (30 ft. lbs.).
- Stage 2: Tighten an additional 90 degrees.

15. Install the timing chains.

16. Install the camshaft roller followers.

5.4L Engines

Left Side

See Figures 77 through 82.

1. Before servicing the vehicle, refer to the Precautions Section.

> ❈❈ **WARNING**
>
> **The camshaft procedure must be followed exactly or damage to the valves and pistons will result.**

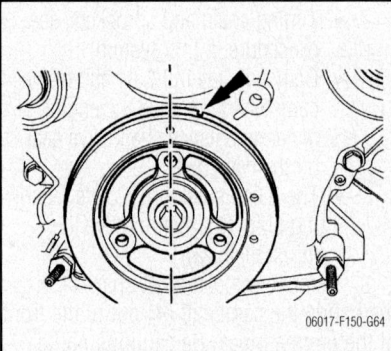

Fig. 77 Position the crankshaft damper spoke at the 12 o'clock position and the timing mark indentation at the 1 o'clock position—5.4L engine

Fig. 78 The number 5 cylinder camshaft exhaust lobe must be coming up on the exhaust stroke. Verify by noting the position of the 2 intake camshaft lobes and the exhaust lobe on the number 5 cylinder—5.4L engine

2. Remove the cooling fan shroud.

3. Position the crankshaft damper spoke at the 12 o'clock position and the timing mark indentation at the 1 o'clock position.

4. Remove the left valve cover.

> ❈❈ **WARNING**
>
> **Damage to the camshaft phaser sprocket assembly will occur if mishandled or used as a lifting or leveraging device.**

5. Loosen and back off the left camshaft phaser bolt 1 full turn.

6. Disconnect the left camshaft position (CMP) sensor electrical connector.

7. Remove the left CMP sensor and the bolt.

> ❈❈ **WARNING**
>
> **If servicing both camshafts, do not rotate the crankshaft. Camshaft position has been established earlier.**

➡ If the camshaft lobes are not exactly positioned as shown, the crankshaft keyway will require 1 full additional rotation to 12 o'clock.

8. The number 5 cylinder camshaft exhaust lobe must be coming up on the exhaust stroke. Verify by noting the position of the 2 intake camshaft lobes

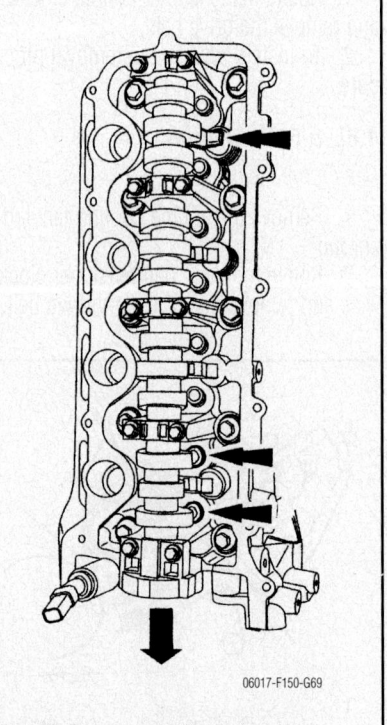

Fig. 79 Remove only these 3 roller followers at this time—5.4L engine

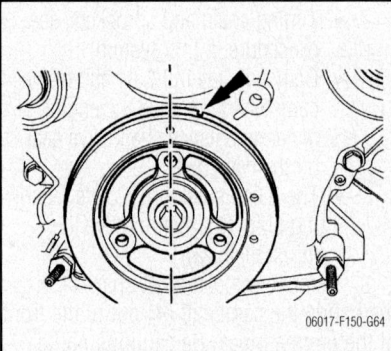

Fig. 76 Camshaft bearing cap torque sequence—4.6L engine

10 Nm (89 lb-in)

and the exhaust lobe on the number 5 cylinder.

9. Remove only the 3 roller followers shown in the illustration.

> ✳✳ **WARNING**
>
> **Do not allow the valve keepers to fall off the valve or the valve may drop into the cylinder.**

➡ The camshaft roller followers must be installed in their original locations. Record camshaft roller follower locations.

303-1039

06017-F150-G70

Fig. 80 Using special tool 303-1039— 5.4L engine

06017-F150-G71

Fig. 81 Rotate the crankshaft clockwise, as viewed from the front, positioning the crankshaft damper spoke at the 6 o'clock position and the timing mark indentation at the 7 o'clock position—5.4L engine

➡ It may be necessary to push the valve down while compressing the spring.

10. Using special tool 303-1039, remove only the 3 designated roller followers from the previous step.

> ✳✳ **WARNING**
>
> **The crankshaft cannot be moved past the 6 o'clock position once set.**

11. Rotate the crankshaft clockwise, as viewed from the front, positioning the crankshaft damper spoke at the 6 o'clock position and the timing mark indentation at the 7 o'clock position.

> ✳✳ **WARNING**
>
> **Engine is not freewheeling. Camshaft procedure must be followed exactly or damage to valves and pistons will result.**

> ✳✳ **WARNING**
>
> **The Timing Chain Wedge tool must be installed square to the timing chain and the engine block.**

➡ Front cover removed for clarity.

12. Install the special tools in the left timing chain as shown.

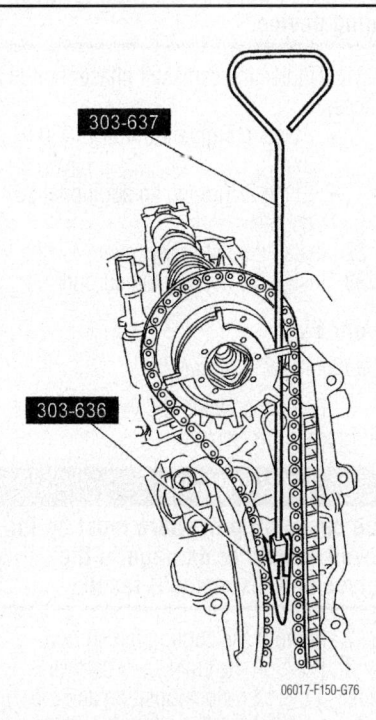

303-637

303-636

06017-F150-G76

Fig. 82 The Timing Chain Wedge tool must be installed square to the timing chain and the engine block—5.4L engine

> ✳✳ **WARNING**
>
> **Do not remove the timing chain wedge tool at any time during assembly. If the special tool is removed or out of placement, the engine front cover must be removed and the engine must be retimed.**

> ✳✳ **WARNING**
>
> **The timing chain must be installed in its original position onto the camshaft phaser sprocket using the scribed marks, or damage to valves and pistons will result.**

13. Scribe a location mark on the timing chain and the camshaft phaser sprocket assembly.

> ✳✳ **WARNING**
>
> **Remove the front thrust camshaft bearing cap straight upward from the bearing towers, or the bearing cap may be damaged from side loading.**

➡ The camshaft bearing caps must be installed in their original locations. Record camshaft bearing cap locations.

14. Remove the bolts in the sequence shown and remove the front camshaft bearing cap and then the remaining bearing caps.

15. Clean and inspect the left camshaft bearing caps. The camshaft front thrust bearing cap contains an oil metering groove. Make sure the groove is free of foreign material.

> ✳✳ **WARNING**
>
> **Damage to the camshaft phaser sprocket assembly will occur if mishandled or used as a lifting or leveraging device.**

> ✳✳ **WARNING**
>
> **Only use hand tools to remove the camshaft phaser sprocket bolt or damage may occur to the camshaft or camshaft phaser unit.**

> ✳✳ **WARNING**
>
> **Do not remove the timing chain wedge tool at any time during assembly. If the special tool is removed or out of placement, the engine front cover must be removed and the engine must be retimed.**

16. Remove the bolt and withdraw the camshaft from the phaser sprocket assembly leaving the sprocket assembly in place. Discard the bolt and washer.

To install:

17. Lubricate the camshaft and camshaft journals with clean engine oil.

✳ WARNING

Do not remove the timing chain wedge tool at any time during assembly. If the special tool is removed or out of placement, the engine front cover must be removed and the engine must be retimed.

✳ WARNING

Damage to the camshaft phaser sprocket assembly will occur if mishandled or used as a lifting or leveraging device.

✳ WARNING

Do not allow the roller followers to move out of position when installing the camshaft.

18. Install the camshaft into the camshaft phaser sprocket assembly and onto the head.

19. Install a new camshaft phaser bolt finger tight.

✳ WARNING

Do not remove the timing chain wedge tool at any time during assembly. If the special tool is removed or out of placement, the engine front cover must be removed and the engine must be retimed.

✳ WARNING

The timing chain must be installed in its original position onto the camshaft phaser sprocket using the scribed marks, or damage to valves and pistons will result. Verify the camshaft phaser sprocket and timing chain scribe marks are still in alignment.

✳ WARNING

Do not allow the roller followers to move out of position when installing the camshaft.

20. Lubricate the camshaft bearing caps with clean engine oil.

21. Position the front camshaft bearing cap.

22. Position the remaining camshaft bearing caps.

23. Install the bolts loosely.

24. Tighten the bolts in the sequence shown. Tighten to 10 Nm (89 inch lbs.).

25. Remove the special tools.

26. Rotate the crankshaft a half turn counterclockwise and position the crankshaft damper spoke at the 12 o'clock position and the timing mark indentation at the 1 o'clock position.

27. Verify correct cam position by noting the position of the number 5 cylinder intake and exhaust camshaft lobes.

28. Using the special tool, install the 3 originally removed roller followers.

29. Install the CMP sensor and the bolt.

30. Connect the CMP electrical connector.

✳ WARNING

Only use hand tools to install the camshaft phaser sprocket assembly or damage may occur to the camshaft or camshaft phaser unit.

✳ WARNING

Damage to the camshaft phaser sprocket assembly will occur if mishandled or used as a lifting or leveraging device.

31. Tighten the camshaft phaser bolt in 2 stages:
- Stage 1: Tighten to 40 Nm (30 ft. lbs.).
- Stage 2: Tighten an additional 90 degrees.

32. Install the left valve cover.

33. Install the cooling fan shroud.

Right Side

See Figures 83 through 89.

1. Before servicing the vehicle, refer to the Precautions Section.

✳ WARNING

The camshaft procedure must be followed exactly or damage to the valves and pistons will result.

2. Remove the cooling fan shroud.

3. Position the crankshaft damper spoke at the 12 o'clock position and the timing mark indentation at the 1 o'clock position.

4. Remove the right valve cover.

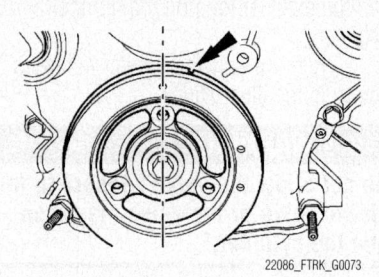

22086_FTRK_G0073

Fig. 83 The number 1 cylinder camshaft exhaust lobe must be coming up on the exhaust stroke. Verify by noting the position of the 2 intake camshaft lobes and the exhaust lobe on the number 1 cylinder—5.4L engine

✳ WARNING

Damage to the camshaft phaser sprocket assembly will occur if mishandled or used as a lifting or leveraging device.

5. Loosen and back off the right camshaft phaser bolt 1 full turn.

6. Disconnect the right camshaft position (CMP) sensor electrical connector.

7. Remove the bolt and the right CMP sensor.

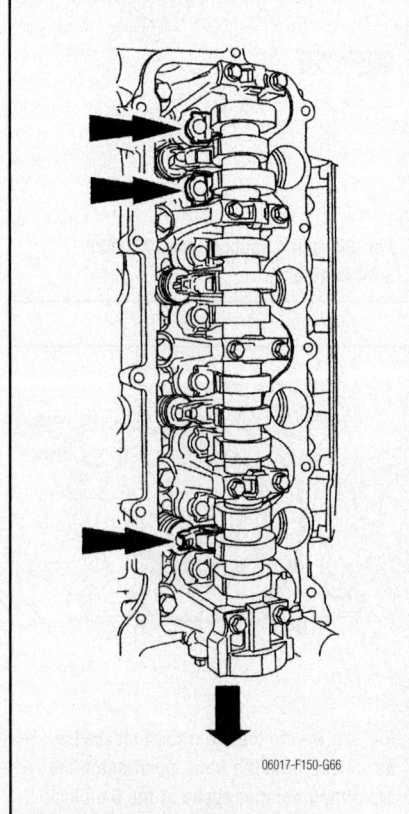

06017-F150-G66

Fig. 84 Remove only these 3 roller followers at this time—5.4L engine

➡If the camshaft lobes are not exactly positioned as shown, the crankshaft will require 1 full additional rotation to 12 o'clock.

8. The number 1 cylinder camshaft exhaust lobe must be coming up on the exhaust stroke. Verify by noting the position of the 2 intake camshaft lobes and the exhaust lobe on the number 1 cylinder.

9. Remove only the 3 roller followers shown in the illustration.

❊❊ WARNING

Do not allow the valve keepers to fall off the valve or the valve may drop into the cylinder.

➡The camshaft roller followers must be installed in their original locations. Record camshaft roller follower locations.

➡It may be necessary to push the valve down while compressing the spring.

10. Using special tool 303-1039, remove only the 3 designated roller followers from the previous step.

❊❊ WARNING

The crankshaft cannot be moved past the 6 o'clock position once set.

11. Rotate the crankshaft clockwise, as viewed from the front, positioning the crankshaft damper spoke at the 6 o'clock position and the timing mark indentation at the 7 o'clock position.

❊❊ WARNING

Engine is not freewheeling. Camshaft procedure must be followed exactly or damage to valves and pistons will result.

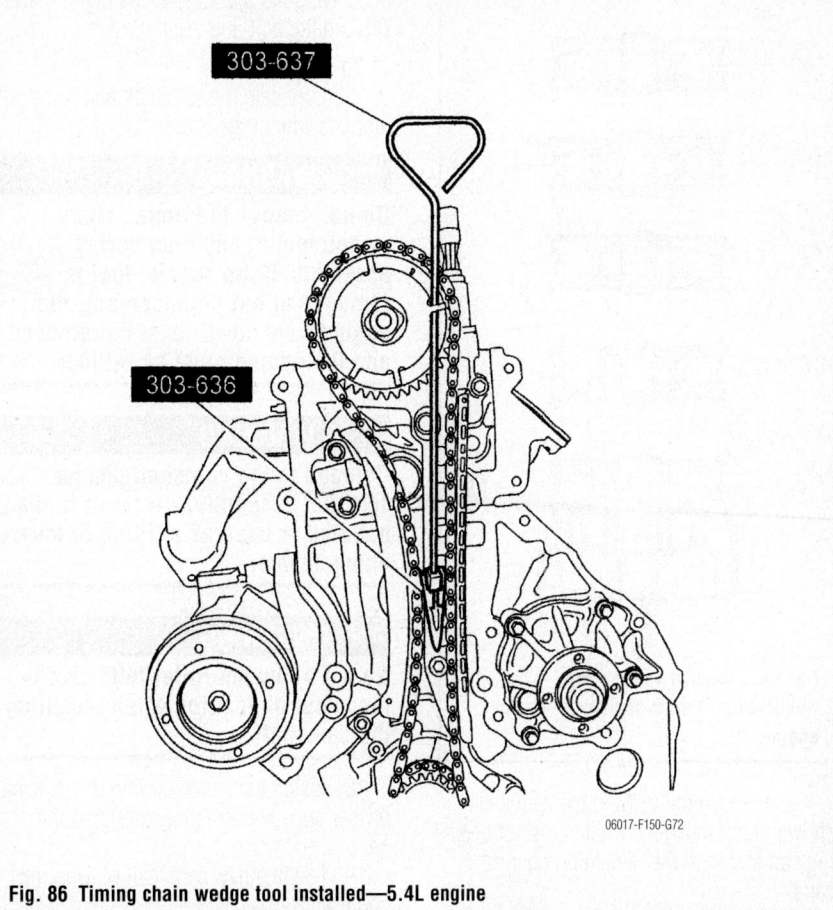

Fig. 86 Timing chain wedge tool installed—5.4L engine

❊❊ WARNING

The Timing Chain Wedge tool must be installed square to the timing chain and the engine block.

➡Front cover removed for clarity.

12. Install the special tools in the right timing chain as shown.

❊❊ WARNING

Do not remove the timing chain wedge tool at any time during assembly. If the special tool is removed or out of placement, the engine front cover must be removed and the engine must be retimed.

❊❊ WARNING

The timing chain must be installed in its original position onto the camshaft phaser sprocket using the scribed marks, or damage to valves and pistons will result.

13. Scribe a location mark on the timing chain and the camshaft phaser sprocket assembly.

❊❊ WARNING

Remove the front thrust camshaft bearing cap straight upward from the bearing towers, or the bearing cap may be damaged from side loading.

➡The camshaft bearing caps must be installed in their original locations. Record camshaft bearing cap locations.

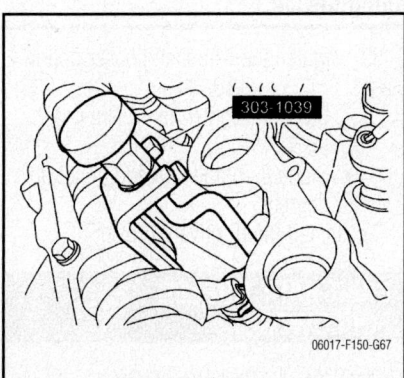

Fig. 85 Using special tool 303-1039— 5.4L engine

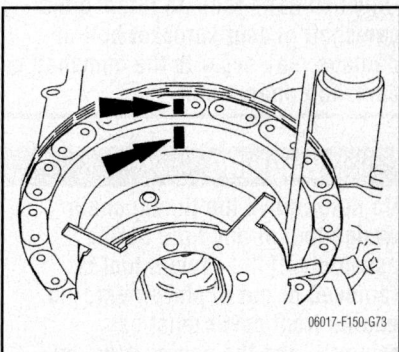

Fig. 87 Scribe a location mark on the timing chain and the camshaft phaser sprocket assembly—5.4L engine

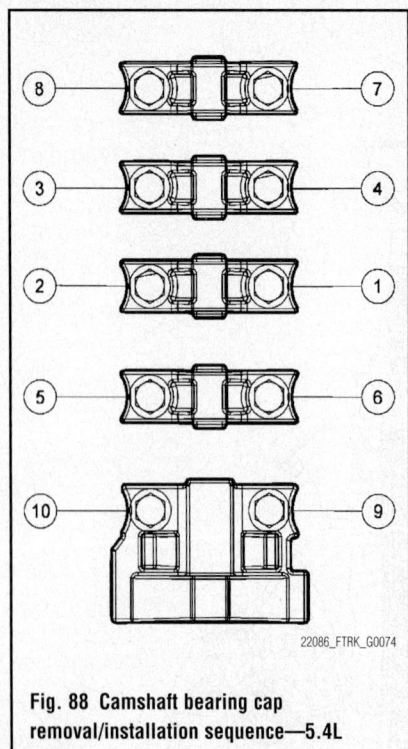

Fig. 88 Camshaft bearing cap removal/installation sequence—5.4L engine

14. Remove the bolts in the sequence shown and remove the front camshaft bearing cap and then the remaining bearing caps.

15. Clean and inspect the right camshaft bearing caps. The camshaft front thrust bearing cap contains an oil metering groove. Make sure the groove is free of foreign material.

✳✳ WARNING

Damage to the camshaft phaser sprocket assembly will occur if mishandled or used as a lifting or leveraging device.

✳✳ WARNING

Only use hand tools to remove the camshaft phaser sprocket bolt or damage may occur to the camshaft or camshaft phaser unit.

✳✳ WARNING

Do not remove the timing chain wedge tool at any time during assembly. If the special tool is removed or out of placement, the engine front cover must be removed and the engine must be retimed.

16. Remove the bolt and withdraw the camshaft from the phaser sprocket assem-

bly leaving the sprocket assembly in place. Discard the bolt and washer.

To install:

17. Lubricate the camshaft and camshaft journals with clean engine oil.

✳✳ WARNING

Do not remove the timing chain wedge tool at any time during assembly. If the special tool is removed or out of placement, the engine front cover must be removed and the engine must be retimed.

✳✳ WARNING

Damage to the camshaft phaser sprocket assembly will occur if mishandled or used as a lifting or leveraging device.

✳✳ WARNING

Do not allow the roller followers to move out of position when installing the camshaft.

18. Install the camshaft into the camshaft phaser sprocket assembly and onto the head.

19. Install a new camshaft phaser bolt finger tight.

✳✳ WARNING

Do not remove the timing chain wedge tool at any time during assembly. If the special tool is removed or out of placement, the engine front cover must be removed and the engine must be retimed.

✳✳ WARNING

The timing chain must be installed in its original position onto the camshaft phaser sprocket using the scribed marks, or damage to valves and pistons will result.

20. Verify the camshaft phaser sprocket and timing chain scribe marks are still in alignment.

✳✳ WARNING

Do not allow the roller followers to move out of position when installing the camshaft.

21. Lubricate the camshaft bearing caps with clean engine oil.

22. Position the front camshaft bearing cap.

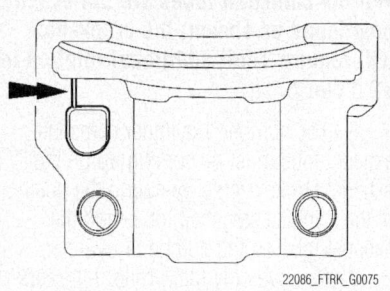

Fig. 89 The camshaft front thrust bearing cap contains an oil metering groove—5.4L engine

23. Position the remaining camshaft bearing caps.

24. Install the bolts loosely.

25. Tighten the bolts in the sequence shown. Tighten to 10 Nm (89 inch lbs.).

26. Remove the special tools.

27. Rotate the crankshaft a half turn counterclockwise and position the crankshaft damper spoke at the 12 o'clock position and the timing mark indentation at the 1 o'clock position.

28. Verify correct cam position by noting the position of the number 1 cylinder intake and exhaust camshaft lobes.

29. Using the special tool, install the 3 originally removed roller followers.

30. Install the CMP sensor and the bolt.

31. Connect the CMP electrical connector.

✳✳ WARNING

Only use hand tools to install the camshaft phaser sprocket assembly or damage may occur to the camshaft or camshaft phaser unit.

✳✳ WARNING

Damage to the camshaft phaser sprocket assembly will occur if mishandled or used as a lifting or leveraging device.

32. Tighten the camshaft phaser bolt in 2 stages:
   • Stage 1: Tighten to 40 Nm (30 ft. lbs.).
   • Stage 2: Tighten an additional 90 degrees.

33. Install the right valve cover.

CAMSHAFT ROLLER FOLLOWER

REMOVAL & INSTALLATION

4.6L Engines

See Figure 90.

Fig. 90 The 3 rearmost camshaft roller followers on the RH side must use special tool 303-567 in the same manner as is shown in the illustration

1. Before servicing the vehicle, refer to the Precautions Section.
2. Disconnect the negative battery cable.
3. Remove the valve covers. See "Valve (Rocker Arm) Covers" in this section.
4. Position the piston of the cylinder being serviced at the bottom of its travel.
5. Install the special tool (303-382) between the valve spring coils to protect the valve stem seal from damage.
6. Using a proper tool (303-452), compress the valve spring and remove the follower.

➡The camshaft roller followers must be installed in their original locations. Record the camshaft roller follower locations.

➡The 3 rearmost camshaft roller followers on the RH side must use special tool 303-567 in the same manner as is shown in the illustration.

7. Repeat the previous steps for each of the camshaft roller followers being serviced.

To install:
8. Position the piston of the cylinder being serviced at the bottom of its travel.
9. Install the special tool (303-382) between the valve spring coils to protect the valve stem seal from damage.
10. Apply clean engine oil to the rocker arm, valve stem tip and tappet bore.

➡Valve tappet should have no more than 1/16 inch (1.5mm) of travel before installing the rocker arm.

11. Compress the valve spring using the correct tool and install the follower.
12. Repeat the previous steps for each of the camshaft roller followers being serviced.

5.4L Engine
See Figure 91.

1. Before servicing the vehicle, refer to the Precautions Section.
2. Disconnect the negative battery cable.
3. Remove the valve covers. See "Valve (Rocker Arm) Covers" in this section.
4. Rotate the crankshaft until the piston for the valve being serviced is at the top of its stroke with the intake valve and the exhaust valves closed.

✳✳ CAUTION

If the components are to be reinstalled, they must be installed in the same positions. Mark the components for installation into their original locations.

5. Using the special tool, compress the valve spring and remove the camshaft roller follower.
6. Repeat the previous 2 steps for each camshaft roller follower being serviced.

➡On 6.8L engine, when removing roller follower on cylinder No. 7 or 10 intake cam, remove the 2 bolts and the camshaft roller follower

7. Inspect the camshaft roller follower; replace as necessary.

To install:

✳✳ CAUTION

If the components are to be reinstalled, they must be installed into their original locations.

➡Lubricate the camshaft roller follower with clean engine oil prior to installation.

8. Using the special tool, compress the valve spring and install the camshaft roller follower.
9. Lubricate the camshaft roller follower with clean engine oil prior to installation.

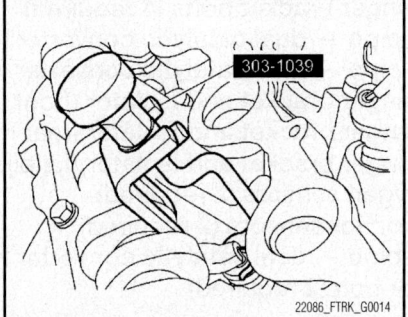

Fig. 91 Using the special tool, compress the valve spring and remove the camshaft roller follower

10. Repeat the previous steps for each camshaft roller follower being serviced.
11. Install the valve cover(s). See "Valve (Rocker Arm) Covers" in this section.

CATALYTIC CONVERTER

REMOVAL & INSTALLATION

2008 Models
See Figure 92.

✳✳ WARNING

Do not use oil or grease-based lubricants on isolators as they cause deterioration of rubber.

➡The exhaust Y-pipe dual catalytic converter is a 2-piece assembly. The RH and LH converters can be serviced separately as needed.

1. With the vehicle in NEUTRAL, position it on a hoist.
2. If equipped, remove the skid plate.
3. On 4.6L and 5.4L engines, disconnect the LH heated oxygen sensor (HO2S) electrical connector.
4. Disconnect the catalyst monitor sensors electrical connectors.

➡Whenever the exhaust Y-pipe dual catalytic converter-to-exhaust intermediate pipe coupling is loosened, a new exhaust Y-pipe dual catalytic converter-to-exhaust intermediate pipe coupling must be installed.

5. Loosen the exhaust Y-pipe dual catalytic converter-to-exhaust intermediate pipe coupling. Slide the coupling back onto the exhaust intermediate pipe.
6. Loosen the RH catalytic converter-to-LH catalytic converter clamp.
7. Remove the nuts on the LH catalytic converter-to-exhaust manifold joint.
8. Remove the nuts on the RH catalytic converter-to-exhaust manifold joint.
9. On 4.6L and 5.4L engines, let the RH catalytic convert drop down slightly and then disconnect the RH HO2S electrical connector.
10. Remove the heat shield bolts from the transmission crossmember.

➡ A special tool is available for use in removing the HO2S. An open-end wrench can be used for ease of removal.

➡ If necessary, lubricate the HO2S with penetrating and lock lubricant to assist in removal.

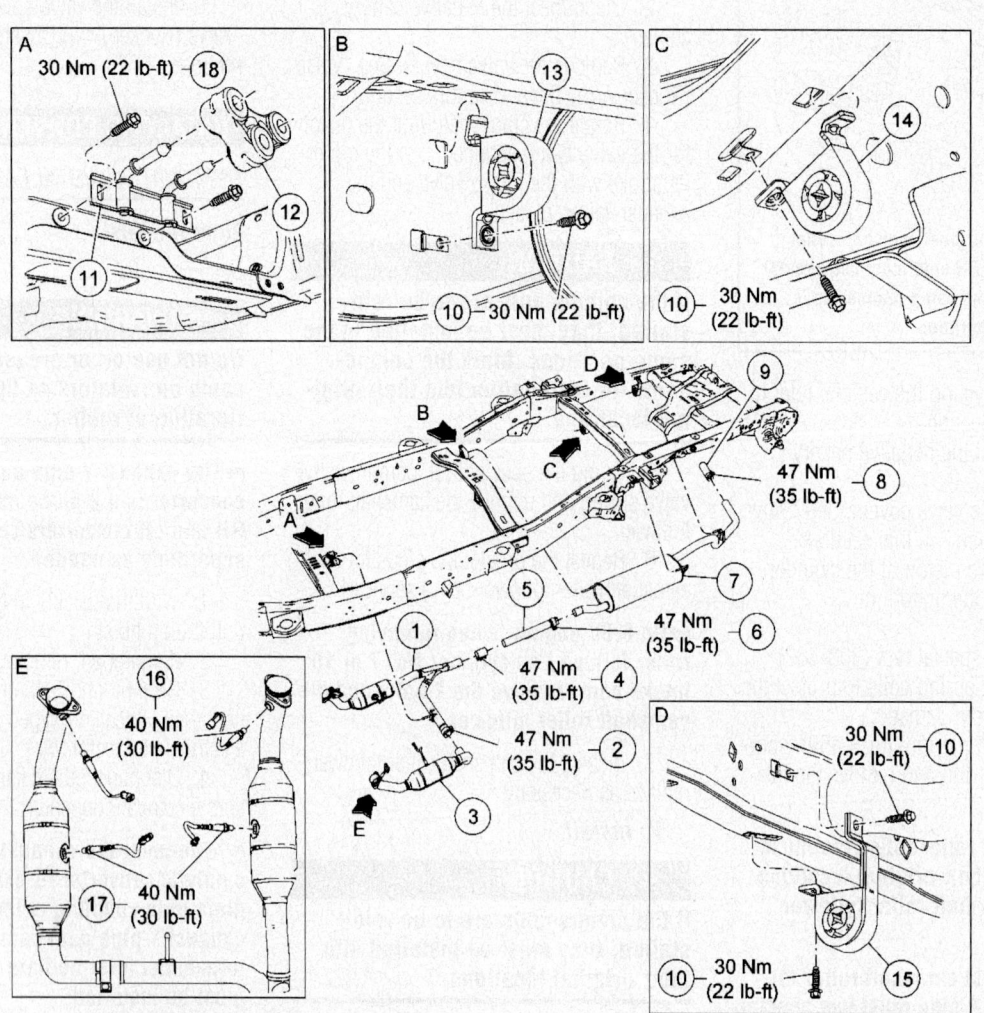

1. RH catalytic converter
2. Exhaust clamp
3. LH catalytic converter
4. Exhaust coupler
5. Exhaust intermediate pipe
6. Exhaust clamp
7. Muffler
8. Exhaust clamp
9. Exhaust tip (Mark LT only)
10. Exhaust hanger bracket bolts (4 required)
11. Exhaust Y-pipe — dual catalytic converter hanger bracket
12. Exhaust Y-pipe — dual catalytic converter isolator
13. Exhaust hanger bracket and isolator (front muffler)
14. Exhaust hanger bracket and isolator (rear muffler)
15. Exhaust hanger bracket and isolator (tailpipe)
16. Heated oxygen sensors (2 required)
17. Catalyst monitor sensors (2 required)
18. Exhaust Y-pipe — dual catalytic converter hanger bracket and isolator bolt (2 required)

36578_FTRK_G0101

Fig. 92 Exploded view of the catalytic converter(s) and components—5.4L shown, 4.6L and 4.2L similar

11. On 4.6L and 5.4L engines, remove the 2 HO2S.

➡ **A special tool is available for use in removing the catalyst monitor sensors. An open-end wrench can be used for ease of removal.**

➡ **If necessary, lubricate the HO2S with penetrating and lock lubricant to assist in removal.**

12. Remove the 2 catalyst monitor sensors.

13. Remove the exhaust Y-pipe dual catalytic converter hanger bracket and isolator bolts.

14. Remove the RH catalytic converter.

15. Remove the LH catalytic converter.

To install:

✳ CAUTION

Do not tighten the fasteners until all components are assembled and aligned, making sure to tighten all fasteners beginning at the front of the vehicle.

➡ **Clean the mating surfaces of the manifold outlet flare and the catalytic converter inlet flare. Make sure not to damage the manifold outlet flare, the converter inlet flare or the studs.**

➡ **Use caution installing the catalytic converter. Make sure not to damage the manifold outlet flare, the converter inlet flare or the studs.**

16. Position the RH catalytic converter.

➡ **Make sure to apply anti-seize lubricant to the threads of the sensors before installation. A special tool is available for use in installing the HO2S. An open-end wrench can be used for ease of installation.**

17. On 4.6L and 5.4L engines, install the RH HO2S sensors. Tighten to 30 ft. lbs. (40 Nm).

➡ **Make sure to apply anti-seize lubricant to the threads of the sensors before installation.**

➡ **A special tool is available for use in installing the catalyst monitor sensor. An open-end wrench can be used for ease of installation.**

18. Install the RH catalyst monitor. Tighten to 30 ft. lbs. (40 Nm).

19. Loosely install the exhaust Y-pipe-dual catalytic converter hanger bracket and isolator and RH exhaust Y-pipe dual catalytic converter hanger bracket and isolator

bolt. Let the LH side of the exhaust Y-pipe dual catalytic converter hanger bracket and isolator hang down.

20. On 4.6L and 5.4L engines, connect the RH HO2S sensor electrical connector.

➡ **Use caution installing the catalytic converter. Make sure not to damage the manifold outlet flare, the converter inlet flare or the studs.**

21. Using an abrasive pad, clean the exhaust clamp surface area of any surface rust.

22. Position the LH catalytic converter and loosely install the exhaust manifold nuts.

➡ **Make sure to apply anti-seize lubricant to the threads of the sensors before installation.**

➡ **A special tool is available for use in installing the catalyst monitor sensor. An open-end wrench can be used for ease of installation.**

23. Install the LH catalyst monitor sensor. Tighten to 30 ft. lbs. (40 Nm).

➡ **Make sure to apply anti-seize lubricant to the threads of the sensors before installation.**

➡ **A special tool is available for use in installing the HO2S. An open-end wrench can be used for ease of installation.**

24. On 4.6L and 5.4L engines, install the LH HO2S sensor. Tighten to 30 ft. lbs. (40 Nm).

25. Loosely install the bolt for the LH side of the exhaust Y-pipe dual catalytic converter hanger bracket and isolator.

➡ **Use caution installing the catalytic converter. Make sure not to damage the manifold outlet flare, the converter inlet flare or the studs.**

26. Push the RH catalytic converter into place and loosely install the exhaust manifold nuts.

➡ **Using an abrasive pad, clean the exhaust coupling surface area of any surface rust.**

➡ **Whenever the exhaust Y-pipe dual catalytic converter-to-exhaust intermediate pipe coupling is loosened, a new exhaust Y-pipe dual catalytic converter-to-exhaust intermediate pipe coupling must be installed.**

27. Loosely slide the exhaust Y-pipe-dual catalytic converter-to-exhaust intermediate pipe coupling into place.

28. Tighten the LH catalytic convert-to-exhaust manifold nuts in the following sequence:

   a. Tighten the lower nut to 15 ft. lbs. (20 Nm).

   b. Tighten the upper nut to 30 ft. lbs. (40 Nm).

   c. Tighten the lower nut to 30 ft. lbs. (40 Nm).

29. Tighten the RH catalytic convert-to-exhaust manifold nuts in the following sequence.

   a. Tighten the lower nut to 15 ft. lbs. (20 Nm).

   b. Tighten the upper nut to 30 ft. lbs. (40 Nm).

   c. Tighten the lower nut to 30 ft. lbs. (40 Nm).

30. Tighten the heat shield bolts to the transmission crossmember. Tighten to 11 ft. lbs. (15 Nm).

31. On 4.6L and 5.4L engines, connect the LH HO2S sensor electrical connectors.

32. Connect the 2 catalyst monitor sensor electrical connectors.

33. If equipped, install the skid plate.

34. Align the exhaust system and tighten the exhaust system clamps.

2009 Models

See Figure 93.

✳ CAUTION

Do not use oil or grease-based lubricants on the isolators. These lubricants may cause deterioration of the rubber. This can lead to separation of the isolator from the exhaust hanger bracket during vehicle operation.

➡ **The exhaust Y-pipe dual catalytic converter is a 2-piece assembly. The RH and LH converters can be serviced separately as needed.**

1. With the vehicle in NEUTRAL, position it on a hoist.

2. Disconnect the 2 Catalyst Monitor Sensor (CMS) electrical connectors.

3. Disconnect the 2 Heated Oxygen Sensor (HO2S) pushpins and electrical connectors.

4. Loosen the RH catalytic converter-to-LH catalytic converter Torca® clamp.

5. Remove the 2 nuts on the LH catalytic converter-to-exhaust manifold joint. Discard the nuts.

6. Remove the LH catalytic converter from the vehicle.

7. On Four-Wheel Drive (4WD) vehicles, remove the transfer case skid plate and 4 bolts, if equipped.

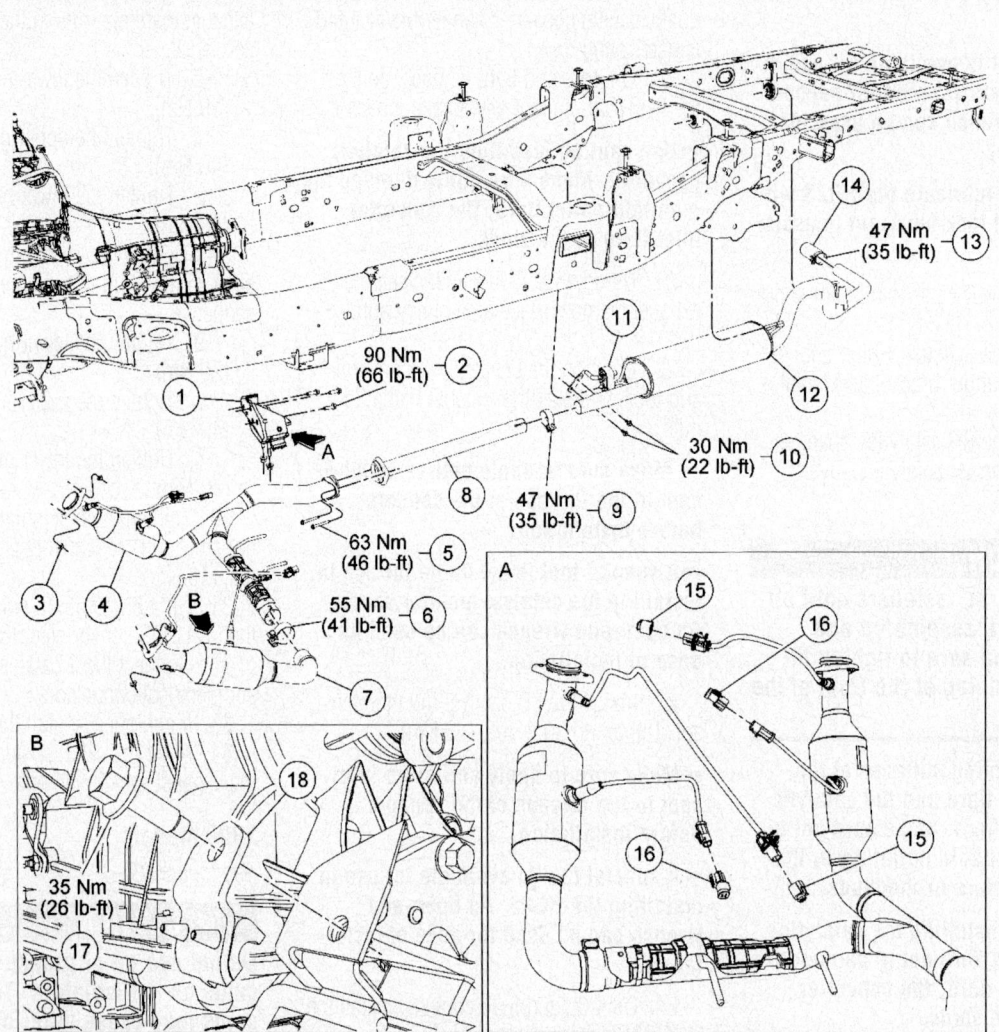

1. Exhaust and transmission mounting bracket
2. Exhaust and transmission mounting bracket bolt (3 required)
3. Exhaust Y-pipe dual catalytic converter-to-exhaust manifold nut (4 required)
4. RH catalytic converter
5. Exhaust Y-pipe dual catalytic converter-to-exhaust intermediate
   pipe bolt (2 required)
6. Torca® clamp
7. LH catalytic converter
8. Exhaust intermediate pipe
9. Exhaust clamp
10. Front muffler isolator and bracket assembly bolts
11. Front muffler isolator and bracket assembly
12. Muffler
13. Torca® clamp
14. Exhaust tip
15. Heated Oxygen Sensor (HO2S) electrical connectors (2 required)
16. Catalyst Monitor Sensor (CMS) electrical connectors (2 required)
17. LH isolator cap bolt
18. LH isolator cap

36578_FTRK_G0102

Fig. 93 Exploded view of the catalytic converter(s) and components—2WD shown, 4WD similar

8. Using an appropriate tool, support the transmission.

9. Remove the 2 heat shield bolts from the transmission crossmember.

10. Remove the 2 transmission mount nuts.

11. Remove the 4 transmission crossmember nuts and 4 bolts and remove the transmission crossmember from the vehicle.

12. Remove the LH isolator cap from the transmission mount.

13. On 4WD vehicles, remove the 4 transmission mount and isolator bolts and remove the transmission mount from the vehicle.

14. On 2-Wheel Drive (2WD) vehicles, remove the 3 transmission mount and isolator bolts and remove the transmission mount from the vehicle.

15. Remove the 2 RH catalytic converter-to-exhaust intermediate pipe bolts.

16. With help of an assistant, remove the 2 nuts on the RH catalytic converter-to-exhaust manifold joint and remove the RH catalytic converter from the vehicle. Discard the nuts.

To install:

➡ **Clean the mating surfaces of the manifold outlet flare and the catalytic converter inlet flare.**

17. With the help of an assistant, position the RH catalytic converter into the vehicle and loosely install 2 new RH catalytic converter-to-exhaust manifold nuts.

18. Loosely install the 2 RH catalytic converter-to-intermediate pipe bolts.

19. On 2WD vehicles, install the transmission mount and isolator and 3 bolts. Tighten to 66 ft. lbs. (90 Nm).

20. On 4WD vehicles, install the transmission mount and isolator and 4 bolts. Tighten to 66 ft. lbs. (90 Nm).

21. Loosely install the LH isolator cap and bolt onto the transmission mount.

22. Install the transmission crossmember, 4 bolts and 4 nuts. Tighten to 66 ft. lbs. (90 Nm).

23. Install the 2 transmission mount nuts. Tighten to 76 ft. lbs.(103 Nm).

24. Install the 2 heat shield bolts into the transmission crossmember.

25. On 4WD vehicles, install the transfer case skid plate and 4 bolts, if equipped. Tighten to 18 ft. lbs. (24 Nm).

26. Slide the LH catalytic converter into the RH catalytic converter up to the stop on the LH catalytic converter and position the LH catalytic converter into place.

27. Loosely install the 2 new LH catalytic converter-to-exhaust manifold nuts.

28. Tighten the 2 new RH catalytic converter-to-exhaust manifold nuts in the following sequence:

   a. Tighten the RH lower catalytic converter-to-exhaust manifold nut to 30 ft. lbs. (40 Nm).

   b. Tighten the RH upper catalytic converter-to-exhaust manifold nut to 30 ft. lbs. (40 Nm).

29. Tighten the LH isolator cap bolt. Tighten to 26 ft. lbs. (35 Nm).

30. Tighten the RH catalytic converter-to-LH catalytic converter Torca® clamp. Tighten to 41 ft. lbs. (55 Nm).

31. Tighten the 2 new LH catalytic converter-to-exhaust manifold nuts in the following sequence:

   a. Snug the LH inner catalytic converter-to-exhaust manifold nut.

   b. Tighten the LH outer catalytic converter-to-exhaust manifold nut to 30 ft. lbs. (40 Nm).

   c. Tighten the LH inner catalytic converter-to-exhaust manifold nut to 30 ft. lbs. (40 Nm).

32. Tighten the exhaust Y-pipe dual catalytic converter-to-exhaust intermediate pipe bolts in the following sequence:

   a. Snug the outer exhaust Y-pipe dual catalytic converter-to-exhaust intermediate pipe bolt.

   b. Tighten the inner exhaust Y-pipe dual catalytic converter-to-exhaust intermediate pipe bolt to 46 ft. lbs. (63 Nm).

   c. Tighten the outer exhaust Y-pipe dual catalytic converter-to-exhaust intermediate pipe bolt to 46 ft. lbs. (63 Nm).

33. Connect the 2 HO2S pushpins and electrical connectors.

34. Connect the 2 CMS electrical connectors.

CRANKSHAFT DAMPER

REMOVAL & INSTALLATION

4.2L Engine

See Figures 94 through 97.

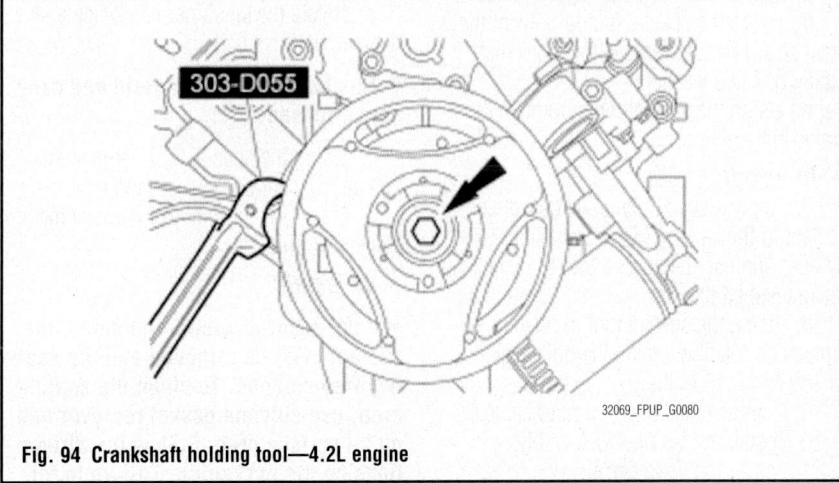

Fig. 94 Crankshaft holding tool—4.2L engine

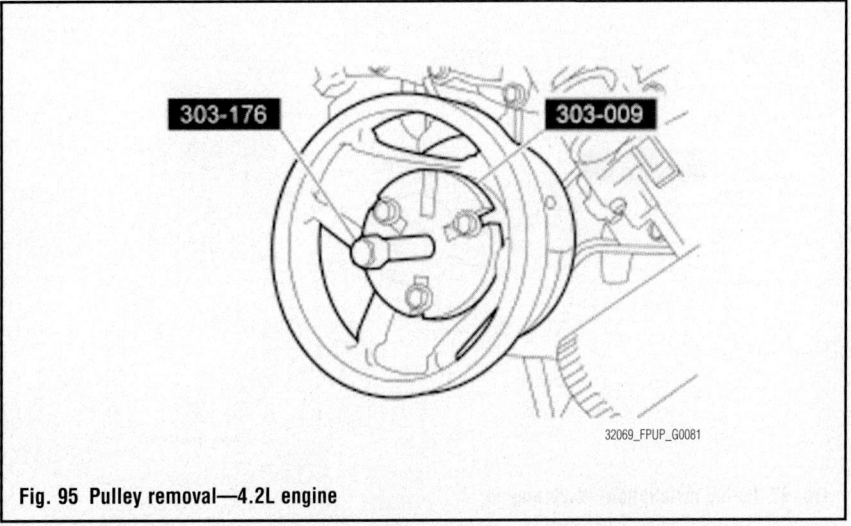

Fig. 95 Pulley removal—4.2L engine

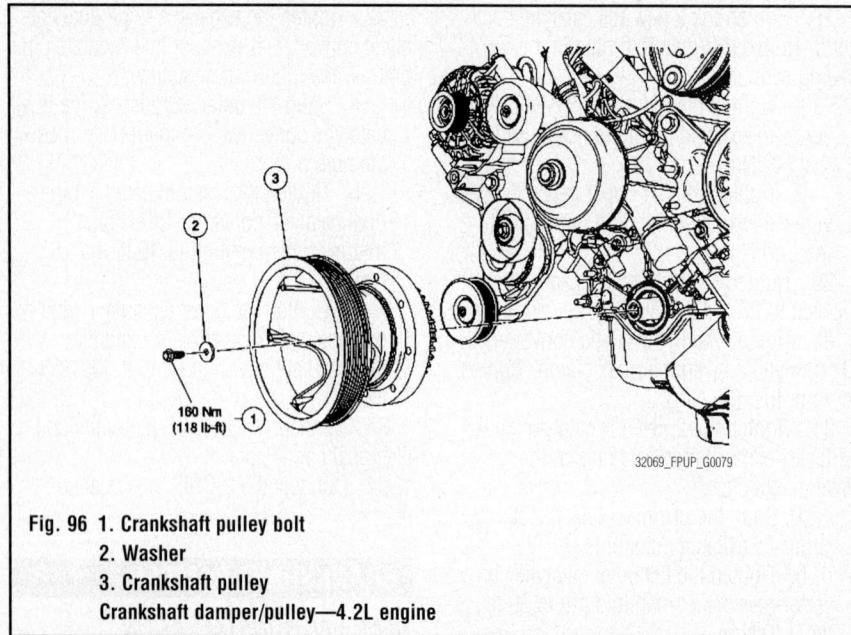

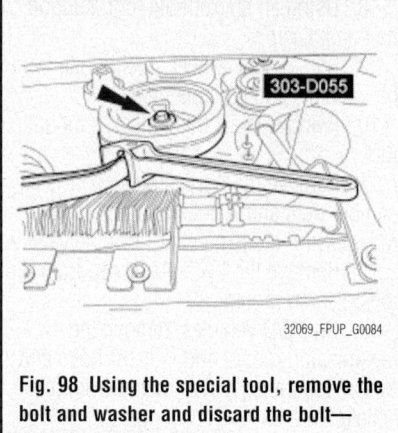

Fig. 98 Using the special tool, remove the bolt and washer and discard the bolt— 4.6L, 5.4L and 6.8L engine

Fig. 96 1. Crankshaft pulley bolt
2. Washer
3. Crankshaft pulley
Crankshaft damper/pulley—4.2L engine

1. Raise and safely support the vehicle.
2. Remove the accessory drive belt.
3. Remove the cooling fan assembly.
4. Disconnect the battery ground cable.
5. Using the special tool to prevent the crankshaft rotation, remove the crankshaft pulley bolt and washer.
6. Using the special tools, remove the crankshaft pulley.

To install:

7. Apply a bead of silicone gasket and sealant to the keyway in the crankshaft damper and use the special tool to install the crankshaft damper.
8. Using the special tool to prevent crankshaft rotation, install the bolt. Tighten to 160 Nm (118 ft. lbs.).
9. Connect the battery ground cable.
10. Install the fan blade assembly.
11. Install the drive belt.

4.6L & 5.4L Engines

See Figures 98 through 100.

1. Remove the cooling fan shroud.
2. Rotate the tensioner clockwise and remove the drive belt.

➡ **This bolt is torque-to-yield and cannot be reused.**

3. Using the special tool, remove the bolt and washer and discard the bolt.
4. Using the special tool, remove the crankshaft pulley.

To install:

➡ **If not secured within 4 minutes, the sealant must be removed and the sealing area cleaned. To clean the sealing area, use silicone gasket remover and metal surface prep. Follow the directions on the packaging. Failure to fol-**

low this procedure can cause future oil leakage.

5. Apply silicone gasket and sealant to the Woodruff key slot on the crankshaft pulley.
6. Using the special tool, install the crankshaft pulley.
7. Using a new crankshaft pulley bolt, install the crankshaft pulley bolt and washer. Using the special tool to hold the crankshaft pulley, tighten the bolt in 4 stages:
   - Stage 1: Tighten the bolt to 90 Nm (66 ft. lbs.).
   - Stage 2: Loosen the bolt one full turn.
   - Stage 3: Tighten the bolt to 50 Nm (37 ft. lbs.).
   - Stage 4: Tighten the bolt an additional 90 degrees without exceeding 200 Nm (148 ft. lbs.).
8. Rotate the tensioner clockwise and install the drive belt.
9. Install the cooling fan shroud.

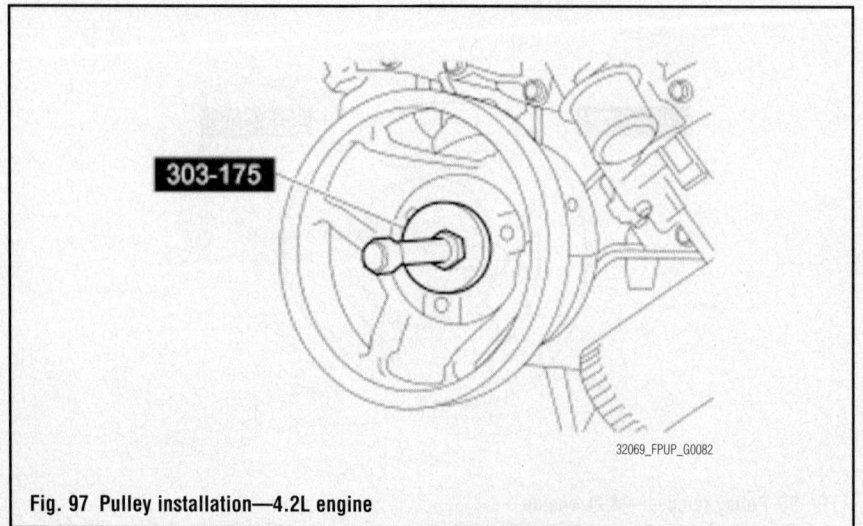

Fig. 97 Pulley installation—4.2L engine

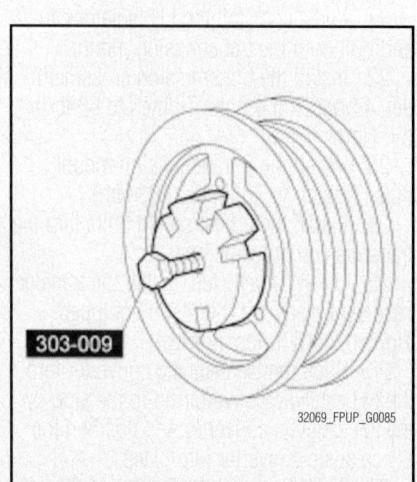

Fig. 99 Pulley removal tool—4.6L, 5.4L and 6.8L engine

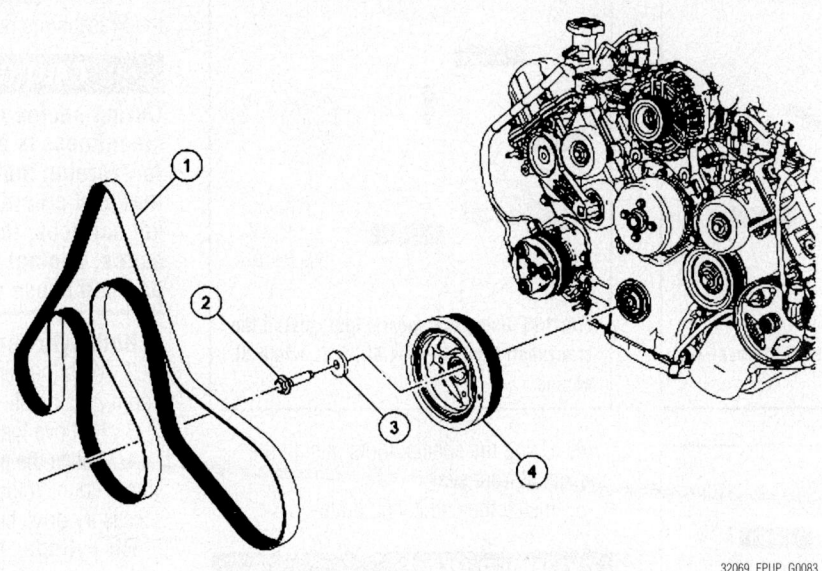

32069_FPUP_G0083

Fig. 100 1. Accessory drive belt
2. Crankshaft pulley bolt
3. Washer
4. Crankshaft pulley
Crankshaft pulley and related parts—4.6L, 5.4L and 6.8L engine

CRANKSHAFT FRONT SEAL

REMOVAL & INSTALLATION

4.2L Engine

See Figures 101 through 103.

1. Remove the crankshaft pulley.
2. Using the special tool, remove the crankshaft front seal. Discard the crankshaft front seal.

To install:

3. Inspect the crankshaft damper and the engine front cover for damage that may cause the crankshaft front seal to fail.

➡**Lubricate the crankshaft front seal with clean engine oil.**

4. Using the special tools, install the crankshaft front seal.

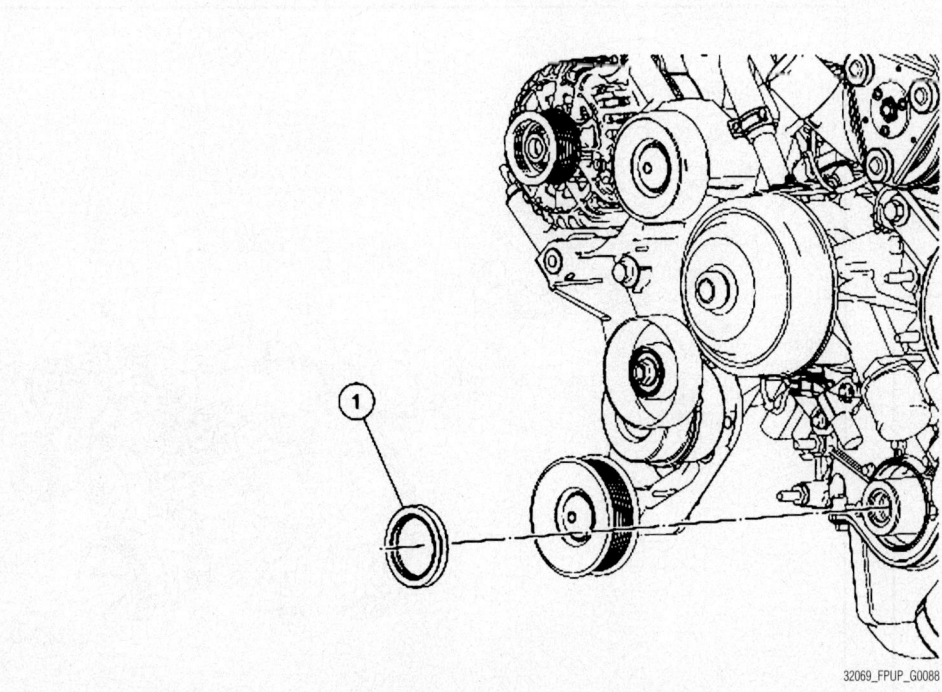

32069_FPUP_G0088

Fig. 101 Crankshaft front seal (1)—4.2L engine

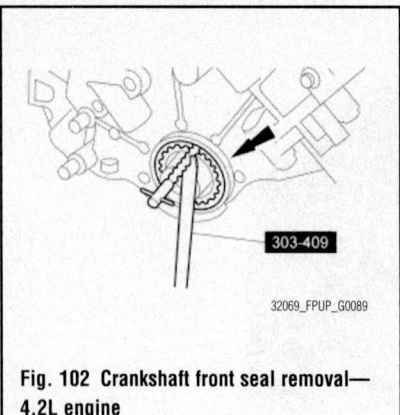

Fig. 102 Crankshaft front seal removal—4.2L engine

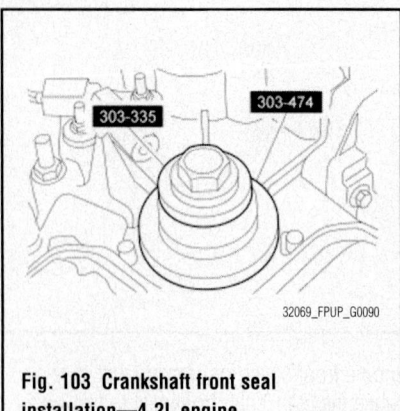

Fig. 103 Crankshaft front seal installation—4.2L engine

5. Install the crankshaft pulley. For additional information, refer to "Crankshaft Damper" in this section.

4.6L & 5.4L Engines

See Figures 104 and 105.

1. Remove the crankshaft pulley.
2. Using the special tool, remove the crankshaft front seal.

To install:

3. Lubricate the engine front cover and the crankshaft front seal inner lip with clean engine oil.

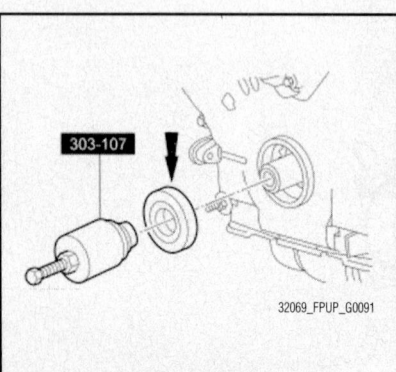

Fig. 104 Using the special tool, remove the crankshaft front seal—4.6L and 5.4L engines

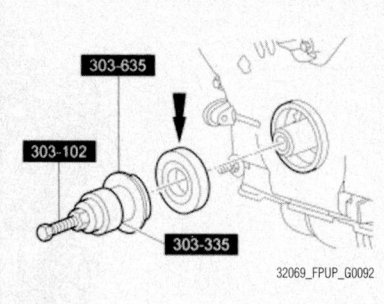

Fig. 105 Using the special tool, install the crankshaft front seal—4.6L, 5.4L and 6.8L engine

4. Using the special tools, install the crankshaft front seal.
5. Install the crankshaft pulley.

CYLINDER HEAD

REMOVAL & INSTALLATION

4.2L Engine

See Figures 106 through 109.

> ✺✺ CAUTION
>
> Fuel injection systems remain under pressure, even after the engine has been turned OFF. The fuel system pressure must be relieved before disconnecting any fuel lines. Failure to do so may result in fire and/or personal injury.

1. Before servicing the vehicle, refer to the Precautions Section.

> ✺✺ CAUTION
>
> During engine repair procedures, cleanliness is extremely important. Any foreign material, including any material created while cleaning gasket surfaces, that enters the oil passages, coolant passages or the oil pan can cause engine failure.

Both cylinder heads

2. With the vehicle in NEUTRAL, position it on a hoist.
3. Remove the lower intake manifold.
4. Rotate the accessory drive belt tensioner counterclockwise and remove the accessory drive belt.

RH cylinder head

5. Remove the bolt and the upper idler pulley.
6. Remove the 4 bolts and position the generator bracket, the generator, the accessory drive belt tensioner and the accessory drive belt idler pulley aside as an assembly.
7. Remove the bolt and position the radio interference capacitor aside.
8. Remove the RH exhaust manifold.
9. Detach the heated oxygen sensor (HO2S) electrical connector retainer from the rear of the RH cylinder head. Remove the bolt and detach the ground wire.

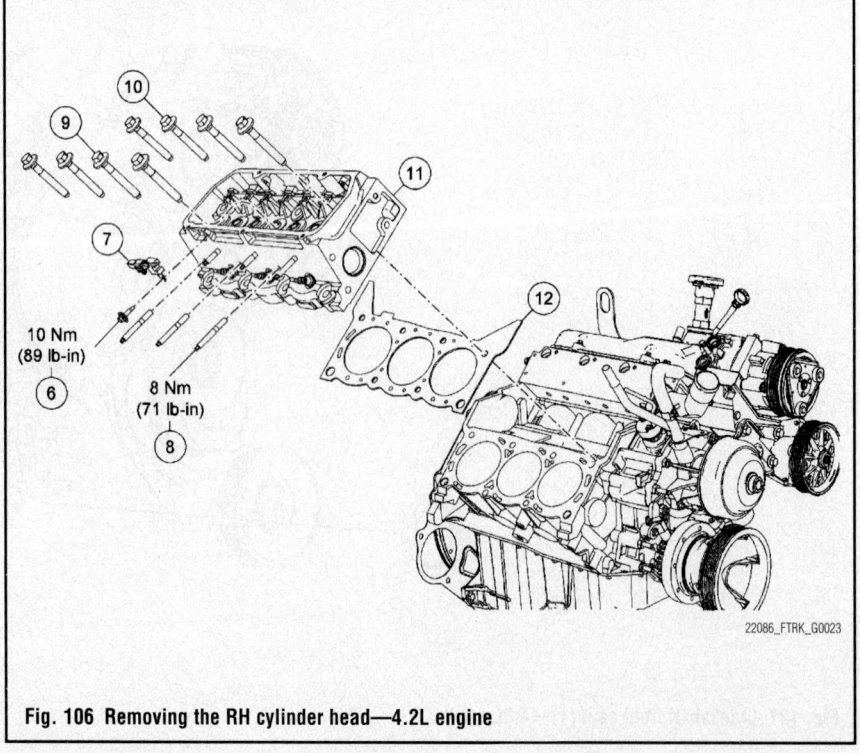

Fig. 106 Removing the RH cylinder head—4.2L engine

10. Remove the push rods from the RH cylinder head. For additional information, refer to Push Rod in this section.

LH cylinder head

11. If equipped, remove the A/C compressor.

12. Remove the nuts for the A/C compressor and power steering bracket brace.

13. Remove the A/C compressor mounting and power steering bracket brace upper bolt. Loosen the lower bolt and position it forward until it contacts the power steering pulley. Position the A/C compressor and power steering bracket brace aside.

14. Loosen the remaining bolt in the A/C compressor and power steering bracket. Position it forward until it contacts the power steering pulley and position the A/C compressor and power steering bracket aside.

15. Remove the LH exhaust manifold.

16. Disconnect the KS and CHT sensor electrical connectors. Detach the HO2S electrical connector retainer from the rear of the LH cylinder head.

17. Remove the push rods from the LH cylinder head.

Both cylinder heads

18. Remove the 2 cylinder block coolant drain plugs.

19. Remove and discard the 4 short and 4 long cylinder head bolts.

20. Remove the cylinder head and the gasket. Discard the gasket.

To install:

> **❋❋ CAUTION**
>
> **Do not use metal scrapers, wire brushes, power abrasive discs or other abrasive means to clean the sealing surfaces. These tools cause scratches and gouges that make leak paths. Use a plastic scraping tool to remove all traces of the head gasket.**

> **❋❋ CAUTION**
>
> **Observe all warnings or cautions and follow all application directions contained on the packaging of the silicone gasket remover and the metal surface prep.**

➡ If there is no residual gasket material present, metal surface prep can be used to clean and prepare the surfaces.

21. Clean the cylinder head-to-cylinder block mating surface of both the cylinder head and the cylinder block.

22. Remove any large deposits of silicone or gasket material with a plastic scraper.

23. Apply silicone gasket remover, following package directions and allow to set for several minutes.

24. Remove the silicone gasket remover with a plastic scraper. A second application of silicone gasket remover may be required

if residual traces of silicone or gasket material remain.

25. Apply metal surface prep, following package directions, to remove any traces of oil or coolant and to prepare the surfaces to bond with the new gasket. Do not attempt to make the metal shiny. Some staining of the metal surfaces is normal.

26. Inspect the cylinder head for distortion.

> **❋❋ CAUTION**
>
> **The use of sealing aids (aviation cement, copper spray and glue) is not permitted. The gasket must be installed dry.**

> **❋❋ CAUTION**
>
> **The cylinder head bolts must be discarded and new bolts installed. They are tighten-to-yield and cannot be reused.**

➡ Install the new cylinder head gaskets with the small hole to the front of the engine.

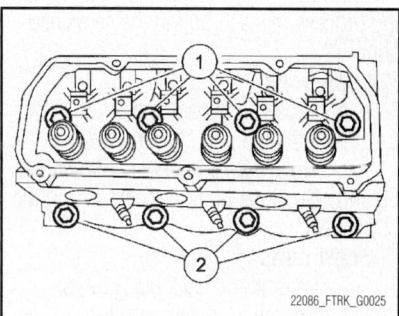

Fig. 108 Make sure the short bolts (1) and the long bolts (2) are installed in the correct locations

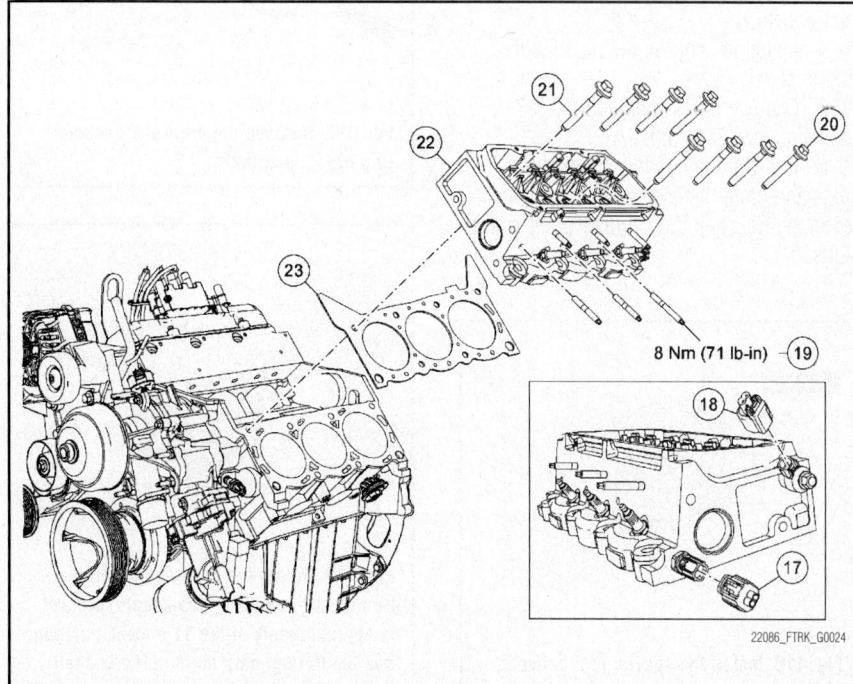

8 Nm (71 lb-in) —⑲

Fig. 107 Removing the LH cylinder head—4.2L engine

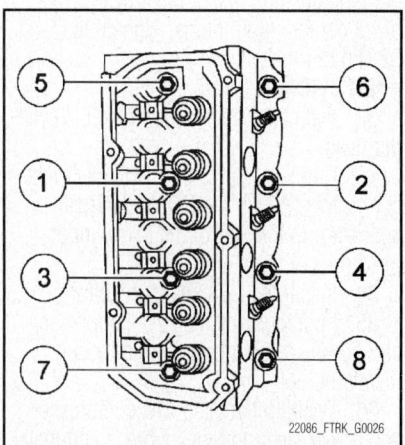

Fig. 109 Cylinder head bolt tightening sequence—4.2L engine

27. Position a new cylinder head gasket and the cylinder head.

⁂ CAUTION

Always use new bolts.

➡**Lubricate the bolts with clean engine oil prior to installation.**

28. Install the new bolts. Make sure the short and long bolts are installed in the correct locations.

29. Tighten the bolts in the sequence shown in 3 stages:

    a. Stage 1: Tighten to 20 Nm (15 lb-ft).

    b. Stage 2: Tighten to 40 Nm (30 lb-ft).

    c. Stage 3: Tighten to 50 Nm (37 lb-ft).

⁂ CAUTION

Each bolt must be loosened and the final tightening carried out prior to working on the next bolt in the sequence. Do not loosen all of the bolts at one time.

30. Carry out the following final tightening process on each bolt in the sequence shown:

Long bolts:

    a. Loosen and back out 3 turns.

    b. Tighten to 45 Nm (33 lb-ft).

    c. Tighten an additional 180 degrees.

    d. Continue on to the next bolt in the sequence.

Short bolts

    a. Loosen and back out 3 turns.

    b. Tighten to 25 Nm (18 lb-ft).

    c. Tighten an additional 180 degrees.

    d. Continue on to the next bolt in the sequence.

31. Apply thread sealant to the drain plug threads and install the 2 cylinder block coolant drain plugs. Tighten to 32 Nm (24 lb-ft).

LH cylinder head

32. Install the push rods in the LH cylinder head.

33. Connect the KS and CHT electrical connectors. Attach the HO2S electrical connector to the rear of the LH cylinder head.

34. Install the LH exhaust manifold.

35. Position back the A/C compressor and power steering bracket and loosely install the bolt.

36. Position back the A/C compressor and power steering bracket brace and install the 2 bolts. Tighten the 3 bolts. Tighten to 48 Nm (35 lb-ft).

37. Install the nuts for the A/C compressor and power steering bracket brace. Tighten to 25 Nm (18 lb-ft).

38. Install the A/C compressor.

RH cylinder head

39. Install the push rods in the RH cylinder head.

40. Attach the HO2S electrical connector retainer to the rear of the RH cylinder head. Position the ground wire and install the bolt. Tighten to 10 Nm (89 inch lbs.)

41. Install the RH exhaust manifold.

42. Position the radio interference capacitor and install the bolt. Tighten to 89 inch lbs. (10 Nm).

43. Position the generator bracket, the generator, the accessory drive belt tensioner and the accessory drive belt idler pulley as an assembly and install the 3 bolts. Tighten to 48 Nm (35 lb-ft).

44. Position the upper idler pulley and install the bolt. Tighten the bolt to 55 Nm (41 lb-ft).

Both cylinder heads

45. Rotate the accessory drive belt tensioner counterclockwise and install the accessory drive belt.

46. Install the lower intake manifold.

4.6L Engine

See Figures 110 through 131.

1. Before servicing the vehicle, refer to the Precautions Section.

2. Remove the engine. See "Engine Assembly" in this section.

3. Remove the bolts and the flexplate or the flywheel.

4. Install the engine onto a suitable engine stand.

5. Remove the 3 bolts and the RH engine support insulator.

6. Remove the cylinder block drain plugs and drain the coolant into a suitable container. Reinstall the cylinder block drain plugs.

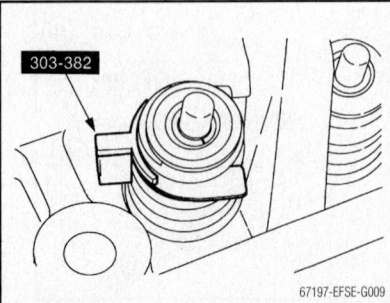

Fig. 110 Install the special tool between the valve spring coils to prevent valve stem seal damage

7. Remove or disconnect the following:

- Engine oil pressure (EOP) sensor electrical connector
- Knock sensor (KS) electrical connector and the wiring harness pin-type retainer
- Camshaft position (CMP) sensor electrical connector
- Crankshaft position (CKP) sensor electrical connector
- Upper radiator hose bracket.

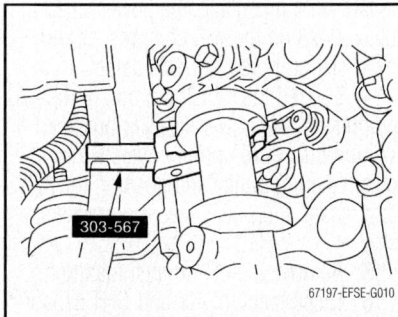

Fig. 111 Using the special tool, compress the valve springs and remove the camshaft roller followers

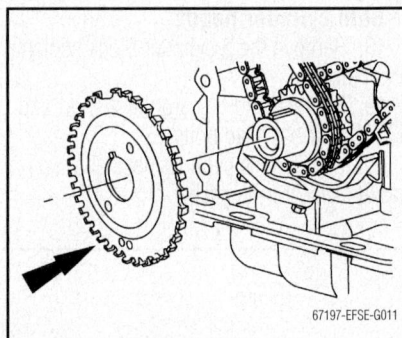

Fig. 112 Remove the crankshaft sensor ring from the crankshaft

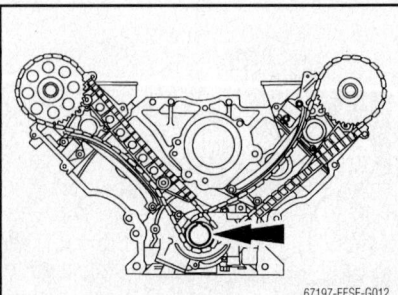

Fig. 113 Rotate the crankshaft until the timing mark on the RH camshaft sprocket is approximately at the 11 o'clock position and the timing mark on the LH camshaft sprocket is approximately at the 12 o'clock position

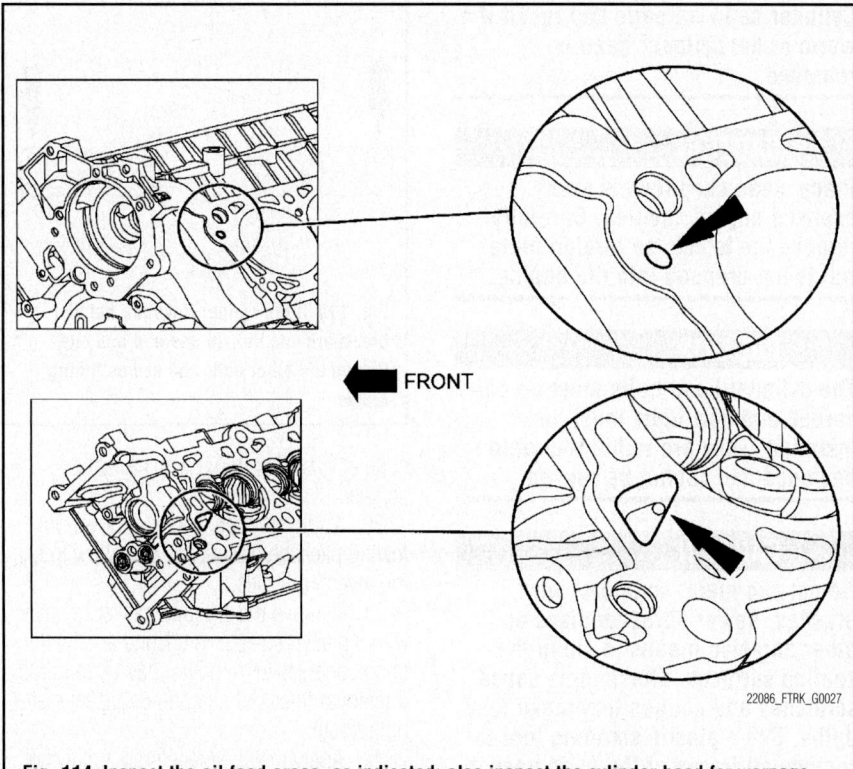

Fig. 114 Inspect the oil feed areas, as indicated; also inspect the cylinder head for warpage

- LH radio ignition interference capacitor and cylinder head temperature (CHT) sensor electrical connectors
- RH radio ignition interference capacitor electrical connector

- Engine wiring harness retainers from the valve cover studs and remove the electrical harness from the engine assembly
- 2 radio interference capacitors
- CMP sensor and the CKP sensor

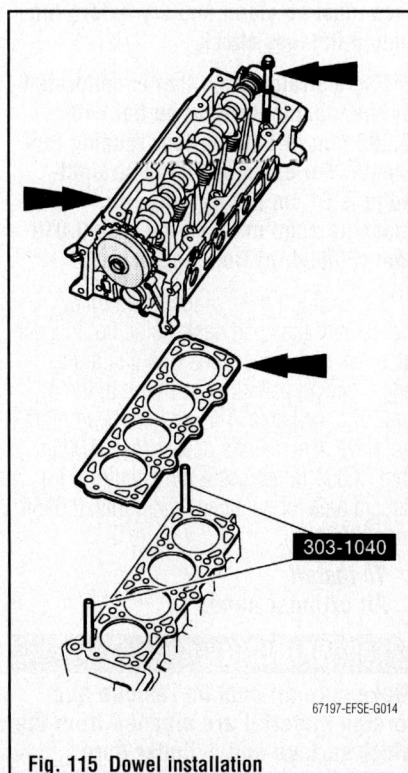

Fig. 115 Dowel installation

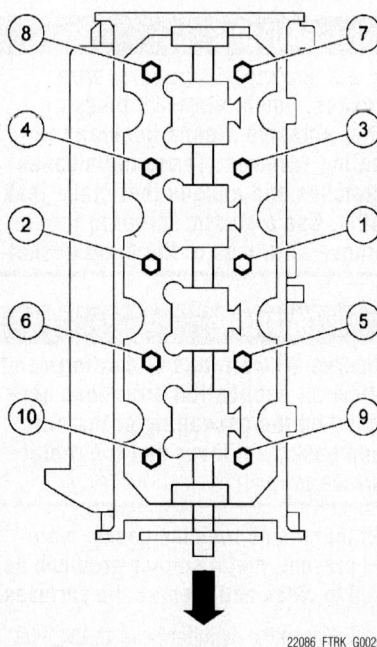

Fig. 116 Showing the LH cylinder head bolt tightening sequence

- Valve covers
- Accessory drive belt tensioner
- Crankshaft pulley bolt and washer (discard the bolt)
- Crankshaft pulley
- Crankshaft front seal
- 4 front oil pan bolts

8. Remove the engine front cover bolts engine and front cover from the front cover to cylinder.

9. Remove the 8 spark plugs.

10. Install the special tool between the valve spring coils to prevent valve stem seal damage.

11. The camshaft roller followers must be reinstalled in their original locations. Record the camshaft roller follower locations.

➡**Position the cam lobe away from the camshaft roller follower prior to removing each camshaft roller follower.**

12. Using the special tool, compress the valve springs and remove the camshaft roller followers.

13. Repeat the previous steps for each of the roller followers.

14. Remove the crankshaft sensor ring from the crankshaft.

15. Rotate the crankshaft until the timing mark on the RH camshaft sprocket is approximately at the 11 o'clock position and the timing mark on the LH camshaft sprocket is approximately at the 12 o'clock position.

✳✳ CAUTION

If one or both of the tensioner mounting bolts are loosened or removed, the tensioner-sealing head must be inspected for seal integrity. If cracks, tears, separation from the tensioner body or permanent compression of the seal bead is observed, install a new tensioner.

16. Remove the timing chain tensioning system from both timing chains.

17. Remove the bolts and the timing chain tensioners.

18. Remove the timing chain tensioner arms.

19. Remove the timing chains and crankshaft sprocket.

20. Remove the timing chain guides:
   a. Remove the bolts.
   b. Remove the LH timing chain guide.
   c. Remove the bolts.
   d. Remove the RH timing chain guide.

LH cylinder head

21. Remove the LH exhaust manifold.

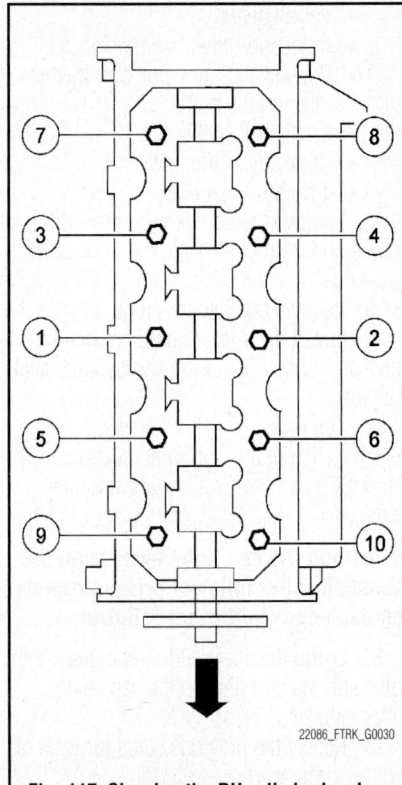

Fig. 117 Showing the RH cylinder head bolt tightening sequence

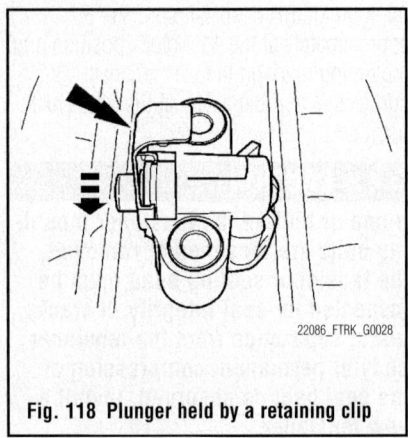

Fig. 118 Plunger held by a retaining clip

22. Remove the bolt and the oil level indicator tube.

RH cylinder head

23. Remove the RH exhaust manifold.
24. Disconnect the coolant hoses from the heater outlet tube and studs.
25. Remove the heater outlet tube and discard the O-ring seal.

All cylinder heads

26. Install the special lifting handles on both ends of the cylinder head being serviced.

✳✳ CAUTION

The cylinder head must be cool before removing it from the engine.

Cylinder head warpage can result if a warm or hot cylinder head is removed.

✳✳ CAUTION

Place clean shop towels over exposed engine cavities. Carefully remove the towels so foreign material is not dropped into the engine.

✳✳ CAUTION

The cylinder head bolts must be discarded and new bolts must be installed. They are tighten-to-yield designed and cannot be reused.

✳✳ CAUTION

Do not use metal scrapers, wire brushes, power abrasive discs or other abrasive means to clean the sealing surfaces. These tools cause scratches and gouges that make leak paths. Use a plastic scraping tool to remove all traces of the head gasket.

✳✳ CAUTION

Aluminum surfaces are soft and can be scratched easily. Never place the cylinder head gasket surface, unprotected, on a bench surface.

27. Remove the bolts and the cylinder head. Discard the gasket and bolts.

✳✳ CAUTION

Do not use metal scrapers, wire brushes, power abrasive discs or other abrasive means to clean the sealing surfaces. These tools cause scratches and gouges that make leak paths. Use a plastic scraping tool to remove all traces of the head gasket.

✳✳ CAUTION

Observe all warnings or cautions and follow all application directions contained on the packaging of the silicone gasket remover and the metal surface prep.

➡ If there is no residual gasket material present, metal surface prep can be used to clean and prepare the surfaces.

28. Clean the cylinder head-to-cylinder block mating surfaces of both the cylinder head and the cylinder block.
29. Remove any large deposits of sili-

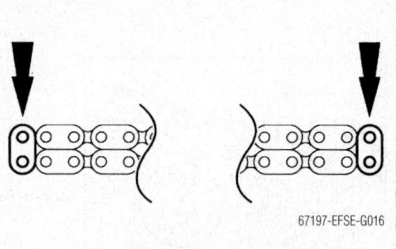

Fig. 119 If the copper links are not visible, mark one link on one end and one link on the other end, and use as timing marks

cone or gasket material with a plastic scraper.

30. Apply silicone gasket remover, following package directions, and allow to set for several minutes.
31. Remove the silicone gasket remover with a plastic scraper. A second application of silicone gasket remover may be required if residual traces of silicone or gasket material remain.
32. Apply metal surface prep, following package directions, to remove any remaining traces of oil or coolant and to prepare the surfaces to bond with the new gasket. Do not attempt to make the metal shiny. Some staining of the metal surfaces is normal.

➡ Make sure all cylinder head surfaces are clear of any gasket material, RTV, oil and coolant. The cylinder head surface must be clean and dry before running a flatness check.

➡ Use a straightedge that is calibrated by the manufacturer to be flat with 0.005 mm (0.0002 in) per running foot length. For example, if the straightedge is 61 cm (24 in) long, the machine edge must be flat with 0.010 mm (0.0004 in) from end to end.

33. Support the cylinder head on a bench with the head gasket side up. Inspect all areas of the deck face with a straightedge, paying particular attention to the oil pressure feed area. The cylinder head must not have depressions deeper than 0.0254 mm (0.001 in) across a 38.1 mm (1.5 in) square area, or scratches more than 0.0254 mm (0.001 in).

To install:
All cylinder heads

✳✳ WARNING

Make sure all coolant residue and foreign material are cleaned from the block surface and cylinder bore.

> ✳✳ **WARNING**
>
> The use of sealing aids. The gasket must be installed dry.

> ✳✳ **WARNING**
>
> The cylinder head bolts must be discarded and new bolts installed. They are tighten-to-yield designed and cannot be reused.

➥ Do not turn the crankshaft until instructed to do so.

34. Using the lifting tools, position the cylinder head gaskets and cylinder heads over the dowels and install the cylinder head bolts loosely.

35. Tighten the bolts in the sequence shown.

a. Stage 1: Tighten to 40 Nm (30 ft. lbs.).

b. Stage 2: Tighten an additional 90 degrees.

c. Stage 3: Tighten an additional 90 degrees.

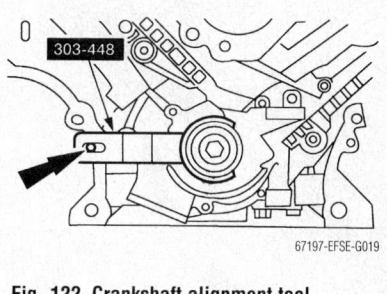

Fig. 122 Crankshaft alignment tool installed

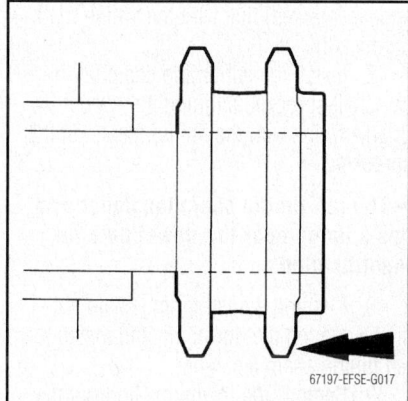

Fig. 120 Install the crankshaft sprocket, making sure the flange faces forward

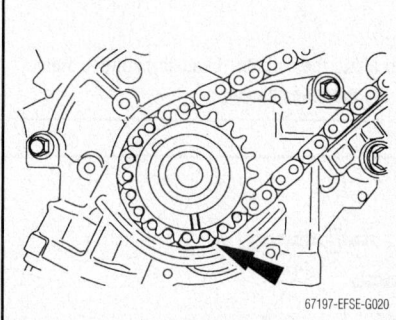

Fig. 123 Position the left (inner) timing chain on the crankshaft sprocket, aligning the copper (marked) link with the timing mark on the sprocket

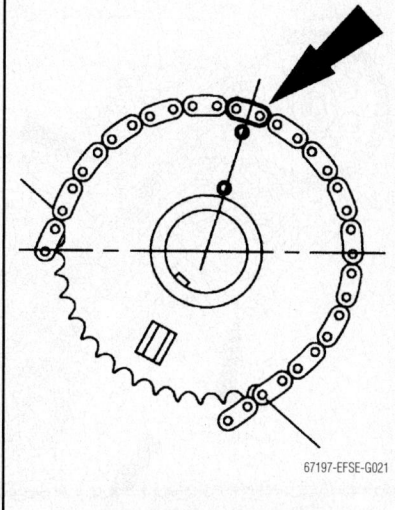

Fig. 124 Install the left timing chain on the camshaft sprocket, aligning the copper (marked) link with the timing marks on the sprocket

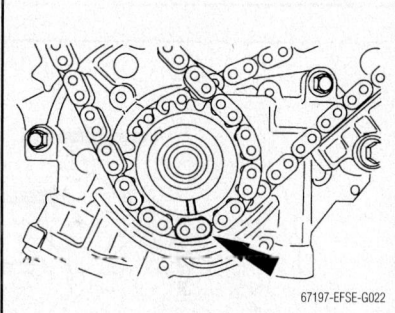

Fig. 125 Position the right (outer) timing chain on the crankshaft sprocket, aligning the copper (marked) link with the timing mark on the sprocket

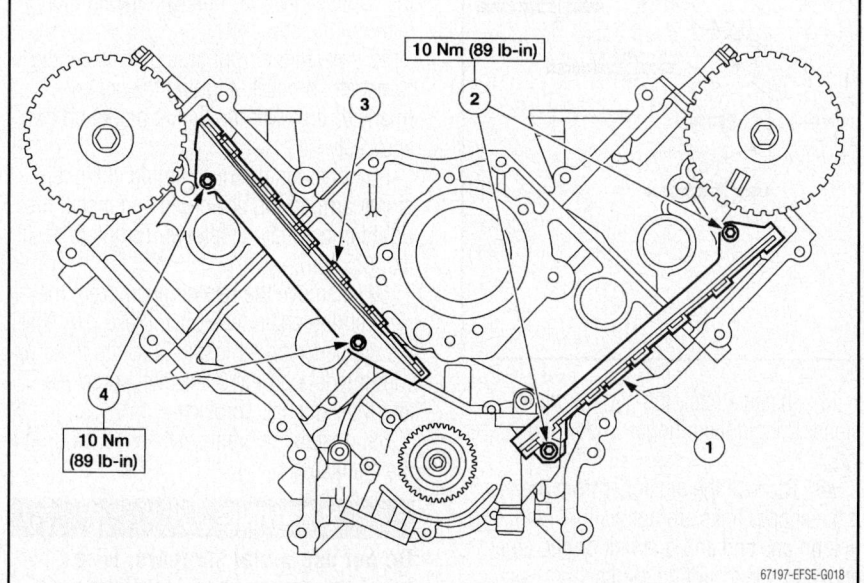

Fig. 121 Timing chain guide installation

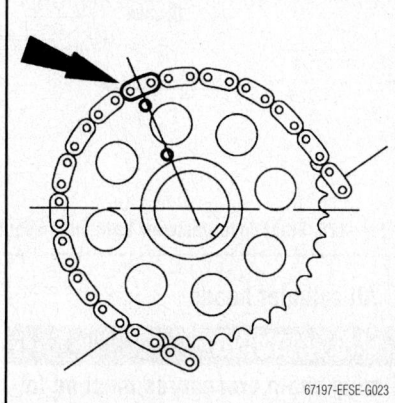

Fig. 126 Install the right timing chain on the camshaft sprocket, aligning the copper (marked) link with the timing marks on the sprocket

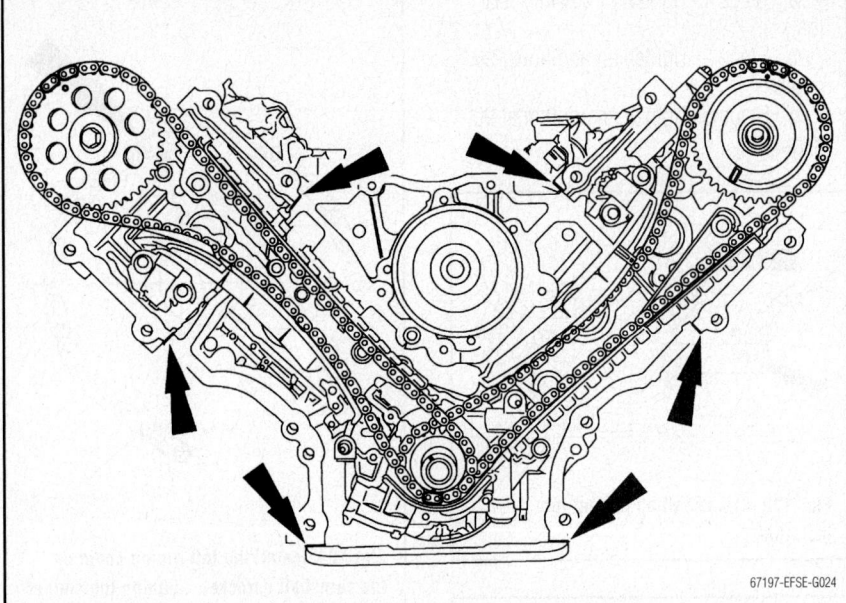

Fig. 127 Apply a bead of silicone gasket and sealant along the cylinder head-to-cylinder block surface and the oil pan-to-cylinder block surface, at the locations shown

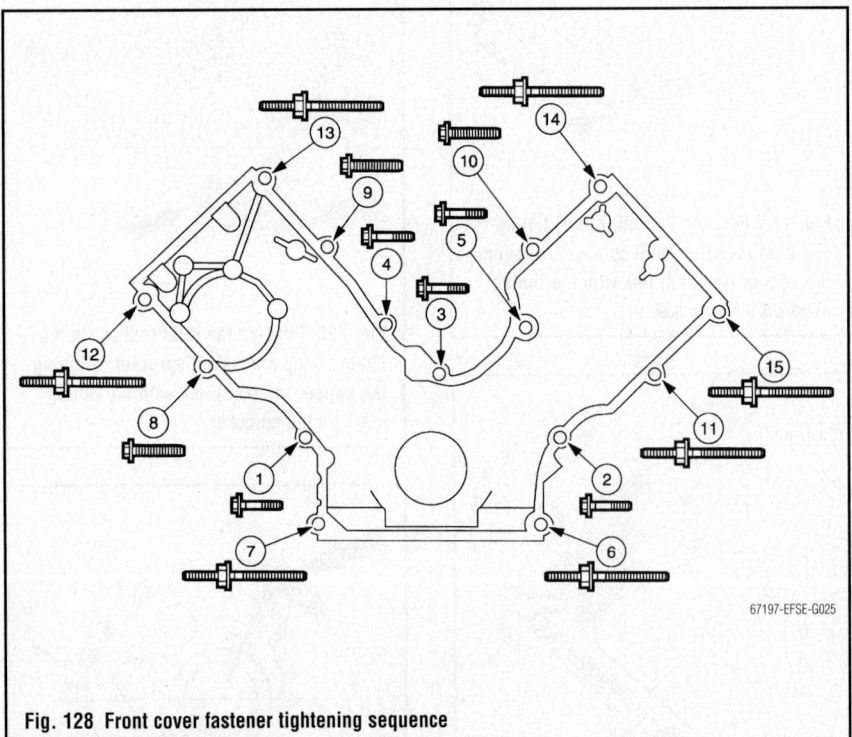

Fig. 128 Front cover fastener tightening sequence

All cylinder heads

❈❈ WARNING

Timing chain procedures must be followed exactly or damage to valves and pistons will result.

36. Compress the tensioner plunger, using a vise.

37. Install a retaining clip on the tensioner to hold the plunger in during installation.

38. Remove the tensioner from the vise. If the copper links are not visible, mark one link on one end and one link on the other end, and use as timing marks.

39. Install the crankshaft sprocket, making sure the flange faces forward.

40. Position the left timing chain guide.

41. Install and tighten the left bolts.

42. Position the right timing chain guide.

43. Install and tighten the right bolts.

44. Rotate the right camshaft sprocket until the timing mark is approximately at the 11 o'clock position. Rotate the left camshaft sprocket until the timing mark is approximately at the 12 o'clock position.

➡ **The number one cylinder is at top dead center (TDC) when the stud on the engine block fits into the slot in the handle of the special tool.**

45. Position the crankshaft so the number one cylinder is at TDC with the special tool.

46. Remove the Crankshaft Holding Tool.

47. Position the left (inner) timing chain on the crankshaft sprocket, aligning the copper (marked) link with the timing mark on the sprocket.

48. Install the left timing chain on the camshaft sprocket, aligning the copper (marked) link with the timing marks on the sprocket.

➡ **The left timing chain tensioner arm has a bump near the dowel hole for identification.**

49. Position the left timing chain tensioner arm on the dowel pin and install the left timing chain tensioner.

50. Remove the retaining clip from the left timing chain tensioner. Torque to 18 ft. lbs. (25 Nm).

51. Position the right (outer) timing chain on the crankshaft sprocket, aligning the copper (marked) link with the timing mark on the sprocket.

52. Install the right timing chain on the camshaft sprocket, aligning the copper (marked) link with the timing marks on the sprocket.

53. Position the right timing chain tensioner arm on the dowel pin and install the right timing chain tensioner. Torque to 18 ft. lbs. (25 Nm).

54. Remove the retaining clip from the right timing chain tensioner. Make sure that the copper (marked) chain links are lined up with the dots on the crankshaft sprockets and the camshaft sprocket.

55. Install the crankshaft sensor ring on the crankshaft.

❈❈ WARNING

Do not use metal scrapers, wire brushes, power abrasive discs or other abrasive means to clean the sealing surfaces. These tools cause

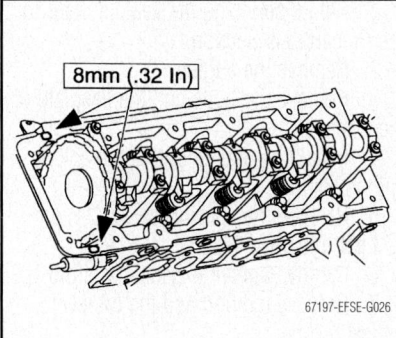

Fig. 129 Apply silicone gasket and sealant in two places where the engine front cover meets the cylinder head

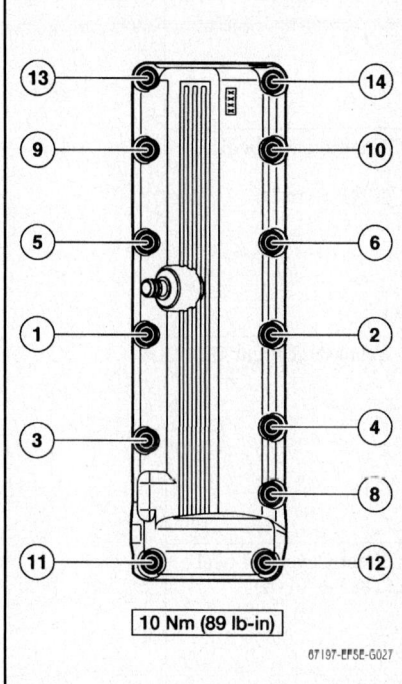

Fig. 130 Tighten the valve cover bolts in the sequence shown

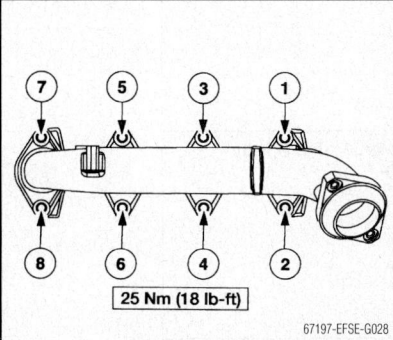

Fig. 131 Install the left exhaust manifold nuts in the sequence shown

scratches and gouges which make leak paths. Use a plastic scraping tool to remove all traces of old sealant.

➡ **If the engine front cover is not secured within four minutes, the sealant must be removed and the sealing area cleaned. To clean the sealing area, use silicone gasket remover and metal surface prep. Follow the directions on the packaging. Failure to follow this procedure can cause future oil leakage.**

➡ **Make sure that the engine front cover gasket is in place on the engine front cover before installation.**

56. Apply a bead of silicone gasket and sealant along the cylinder head-to-cylinder block surface and the oil pan-to-cylinder block surface, at the locations shown.

57. Install a new engine front cover gasket on the engine front cover. Position the engine front cover. Install the fasteners finger-tight.

58. Tighten the engine front cover fasteners in sequence in three stages.
   a. Stage 1: Tighten fasteners 1 through 5 to 25 Nm (18 ft. lbs.).
   b. Stage 2: Tighten fasteners 6 and 7 to 25 Nm (18 ft. lbs.).
   c. Stage 3: Tighten fasteners 8 through 15 to 25 Nm (18 ft. lbs.).

59. Install the left camshaft position (CMP) sensor and the bolt.

60. Lubricate the new O-ring seal with clean engine oil prior to installation.

61. Lubricate the engine front cover and the crankshaft seal inner lip with clean engine oil. Use a driver to install the crankshaft seal into the engine front cover.

➡ **If not secured within four minutes, the sealant must be removed and the sealing area cleaned. To clean the sealing area, use silicone gasket remover and metal surface prep. Follow the directions on the packaging. Failure to follow this procedure can cause future oil leakage.**

62. Apply silicone gasket and sealant to the Woodruff key slot on the crankshaft pulley. Use the special tool to install the crankshaft pulley.

63. Tighten the new crankshaft pulley bolt in four stages.
   a. Stage 1: Tighten to 90 Nm (66 ft. lbs.).
   b. Stage 2: Loosen 360 degrees.
   c. Stage 3: Tighten to 50 Nm (37 ft. lbs.).

   d. Stage 4: Tighten an additional 90 degrees.

64. Install the three accessory drive belt idler pulleys, the coolant pump pulley and the bolts.

65. Position the accessory drive belt tensioner and install the bolts.

66. Install a suitable tool between the valve spring coils to prevent valve stem seal damage.

➡ **The camshaft roller followers must be reinstalled in their original locations.**

➡ **Position the cam lobe away from the valve stem prior to installing each camshaft roller follower.**

67. Use a suitable tool to compress the valve springs, and install the camshaft roller follower. Remove the special tool.

➡ **The camshaft roller followers must be reinstalled in their original locations.**

68. Repeat the previous four steps for each of the camshaft roller followers.

69. Install the radio frequency interference capacitors.

Left cylinder head

⁕⁕ WARNING

Do not use metal scrapers, wire brushes, power abrasive discs or other abrasive means to clean sealing surfaces. These tools cause scratches and gouges which make leak paths.

70. Inspect and clean the valve cover sealing surfaces with metal surface cleaner.

71. Apply instant adhesive completely around the gasket groove in the left valve cover.

72. Install the new valve cover gasket.

➡ **If not secured within four minutes, the sealant must be removed and the sealing area cleaned. To clean the sealing area, use silicone gasket remover and metal surface prep.**

73. Follow the directions on the packaging. Failure to follow this procedure can cause future oil leakage.

74. Apply silicone gasket and sealant in two places where the engine front cover meets the cylinder head.

75. Position the left valve cover and gasket on the cylinder head and install the bolts loosely.

76. Tighten the valve cover bolts in sequence shown.

➡**Lubricate the O-ring seal with clean engine oil.**

77. Install the oil level indicator tube.

78. Install a new O-ring seal on the oil level indicator tube.

79. Install the oil level indicator tube.

80. Install the bolt.

81. Install the left exhaust manifold and the exhaust manifold gasket. Tighten the nuts in the sequence shown.

Right cylinder head

✳✳ WARNING

Do not use metal scrapers, wire brushes, power abrasive discs or other abrasive means to clean sealing surfaces. These tools cause scratches and gouges which make leak paths.

82. Inspect and clean the valve cover sealing surfaces with metal surface cleaner.

83. Apply instant adhesive completely around the gasket groove in the right valve cover. Install the new valve cover gasket.

➡**If not secured within four minutes, the sealant must be removed and the sealing area cleaned. To clean the sealing area, use silicone gasket remover and metal surface prep. Follow the directions on the packaging. Failure to follow this procedure can cause future oil leakage.**

84. Apply silicone gasket and sealant in two places where the engine front cover meets the cylinder head.

85. Position the right valve cover and gasket on the cylinder head and install the bolts loosely.

86. Tighten the valve cover bolts in the sequence shown.

87. Install the right exhaust manifold gaskets and the exhaust manifold. Tighten the nuts in the sequence shown.

88. Slide the heater outlet tube forward with a new O-ring seal into the cylinder block. Lubricate the O-ring seal with engine coolant.

89. Install the heater outlet tube studs.

90. Connect the coolant hoses to the heater outlet tube.

All cylinder heads

91. Connect the right radio ignition interference capacitor electrical connector.

92. Connect the left radio ignition interference capacitor and cylinder head temperature (CHT) sensor electrical connectors.

93. Connect the CMP sensor electrical connectors.

94. Connect the CKP sensor electrical connector.

95. Install a suitable tool.

96. Using a suitable floor crane, remove the engine from the engine stand.

97. Install the flexplate or the flywheel and bolts. Tighten the bolts in the sequence shown.

98. Install the engine.

5.4L Engine

See Figures 132 through 153.

1. Before servicing the vehicle, refer to the Precautions Section.

2. Remove the engine.

3. Remove the bolts and the flexplate or the flywheel.

4. Install the engine onto a suitable engine stand.

5. Remove the special tool.

Left cylinder head

6. Remove the left exhaust manifold.

7. Remove the bolt and the oil level indicator tube.

	Alignment Pins, Cylinder Head 303-1040 (SR-015486)
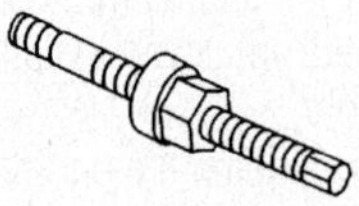	Installer, Crankshaft Vibration Damper 303-102 (T74P-6316-B)
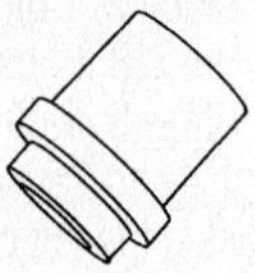	Installer, Crankshaft Front Oil Seal 303-635
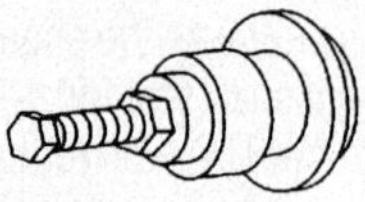	Installer, Front Cover Oil Seal 303-335 (T88T-6701-A)
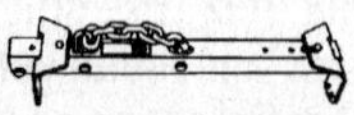	Modular Engine Lift Bracket 303-F047 (014-00073) or equivalent
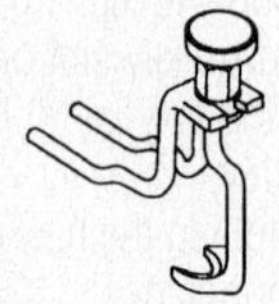	Compressor, Valve Spring 303-1039

67197-EFSE-G033

Fig. 132 Special tools needed for this procedure. These tools are referred to in the following procedure

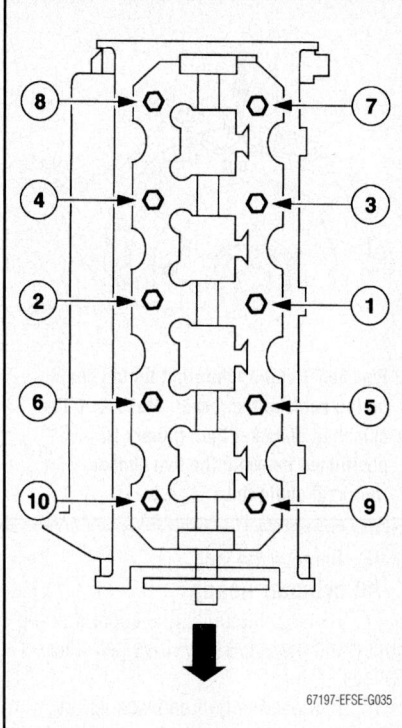

Fig. 133 Left cylinder head torque sequence—5.4L engine (RH cylinder head similar)

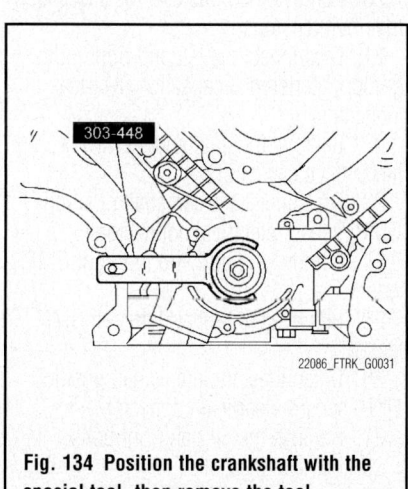

Fig. 134 Position the crankshaft with the special tool, then remove the tool

8. Remove the engine wiring harness retainers from the left valve cover studs.

✳✳ WARNING

When removing the valve cover, make sure to avoid damaging the variable camshaft timing (VCT) solenoid.

9. Remove the bolts and the left valve cover.

Right cylinder head

10. Remove the right exhaust manifold.
11. Remove the nuts.
12. Remove the right exhaust manifold.

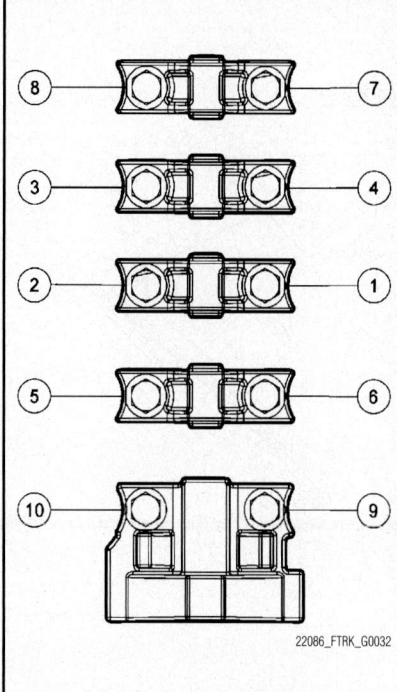

Fig. 135 Install the camshafts and tighten the bearing caps in the sequence shown

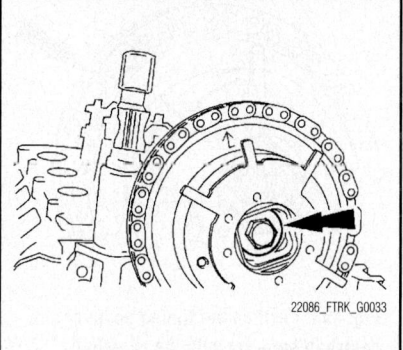

Fig. 136 Install the VCT phaser sprockets and new VCT phaser sprocket bolts finger tight

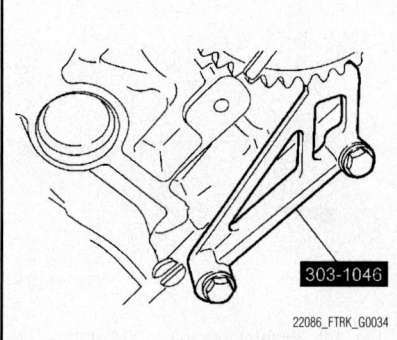

Fig. 137 Using the special tool, tighten the LH and RH VCT phaser sprocket bolts in 2 stages

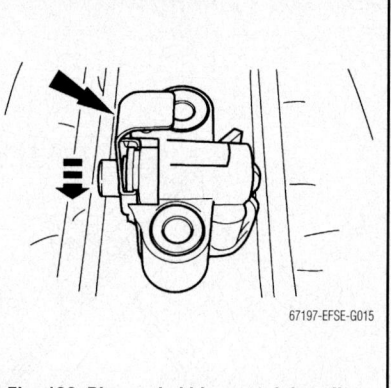

Fig. 138 Plunger held by a retaining clip

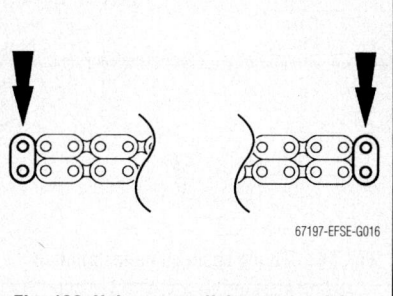

Fig. 139 If the copper links are not visible, mark one link on one end and one link on the other end, and use as timing marks

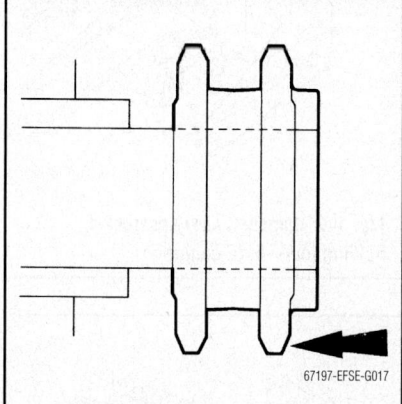

Fig. 140 Install the crankshaft sprocket, making sure the flange faces forward

13. Remove and discard the right exhaust manifold gasket.
14. Remove the engine wiring harness retainers from the right valve cover studs.

✳✳ WARNING

When removing the valve cover, make sure to avoid damaging the variable camshaft timing (VCT) solenoid.

15. Remove the bolts and the right valve cover.

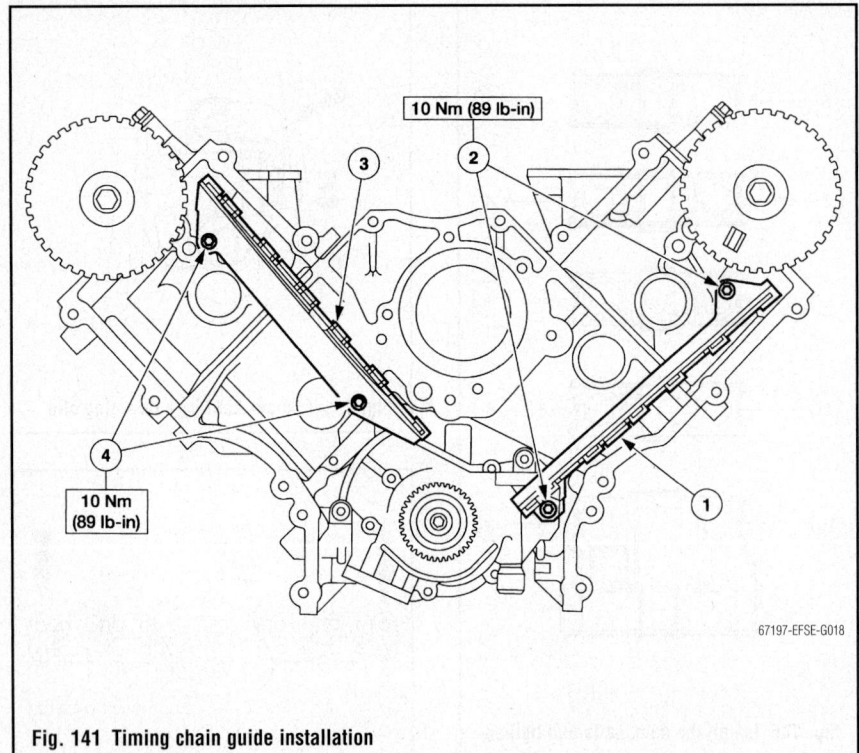

Fig. 141 Timing chain guide installation

10 Nm (89 lb-in)

10 Nm (89 lb-in)

67197-EFSE-G018

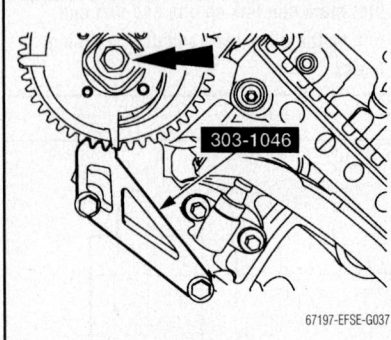

303-1046

67197-EFSE-G037

Fig. 142 Camshaft phaser sprocket holding tool—5.4L engine

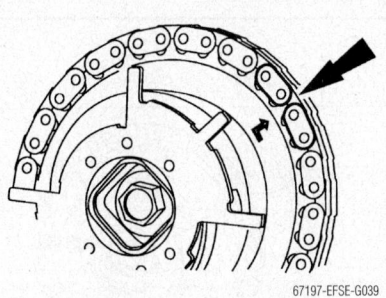

67197-EFSE-G039

Fig. 144 Position the timing chain on the camshaft sprocket with the camshaft sprocket timing mark positioned between the two copper (marked) chain links—5.4L engine

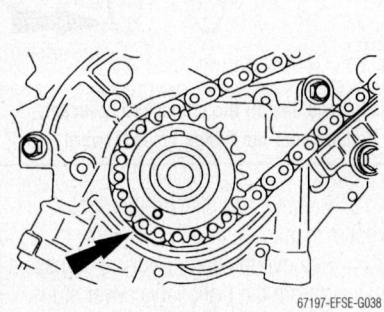

67197-EFSE-G038

Fig. 143 Position the lower end of the left (inner) timing chain on the crankshaft sprocket, aligning the timing mark on the outer flange of the crankshaft sprocket with the single copper (marked) link on the chain—5.4L engine

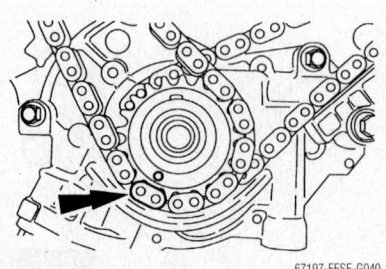

67197-EFSE-G040

Fig. 145 Position the lower end of the right (outer) timing chain on the crankshaft sprocket, aligning the timing mark on the sprocket with the single copper (marked) chain link

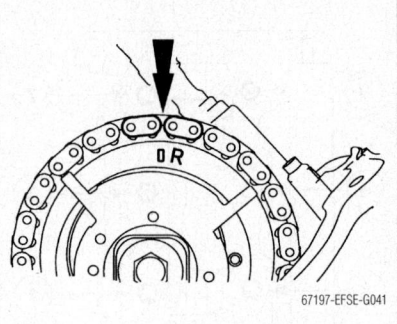

67197-EFSE-G041

Fig. 146 Position the right timing chain on the camshaft sprocket. Make sure the camshaft sprocket timing mark is positioned between the two copper (marked) chain links

16. Remove the stud.

All cylinder heads

17. Remove the bolts, the coolant pump pulley and the accessory drive belt idler pulleys.

18. Remove the bolt and washer and using a puller set, remove the crankshaft pulley. Discard the crankshaft bolt.

19. Using a suitable tool, remove the crankshaft seal.

20. Remove the bolts and the accessory drive belt tensioner.

21. Disconnect the left and right radio ignition interference capacitor electrical connectors.

22. Remove the nuts and the two radio interference capacitors.

23. Disconnect the camshaft position (CMP) sensor electrical connectors.

24. Remove the bolt and the right CMP sensor.

25. Remove the bolt and the left CMP sensor.

26. Disconnect the crankshaft position (CKP) sensor electrical connector.

27. Remove the oil pan front bolts.

28. Remove the bolts.

✷✷ WARNING

Do not use metal scrapers, wire brushes, power abrasive discs or other abrasive means to clean the sealing surfaces. These tools cause scratches and gouges which make leak paths. Use a plastic scraping tool to remove all traces of old sealant.

29. Remove the engine front cover from the front cover-to-cylinder block dowels.

30. Remove the engine front cover gaskets.

31. Clean the mating surfaces with sili-

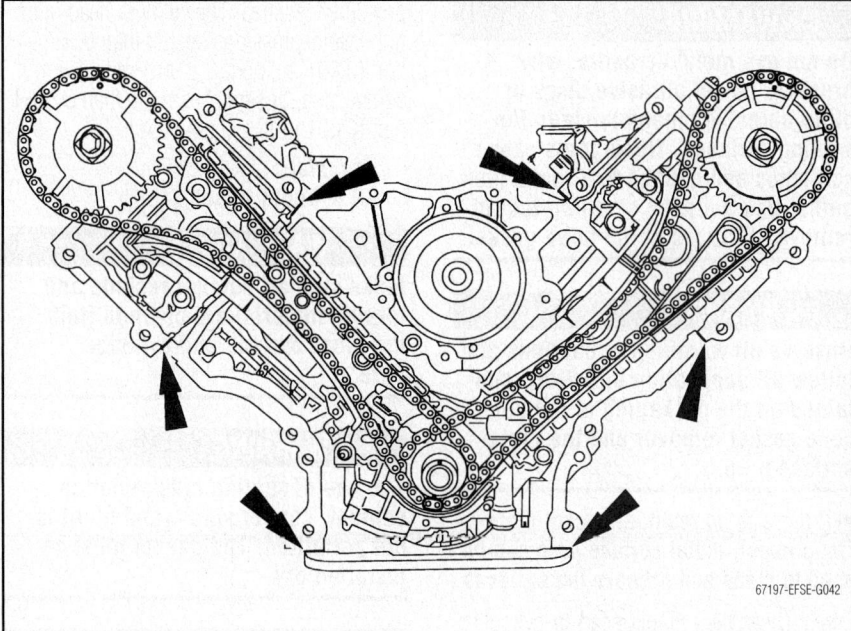

Fig. 147 Apply a bead of silicone gasket and sealant along the cylinder head-to-cylinder block surface and the oil pan-to-cylinder block surface, at the locations shown—5.4L engine

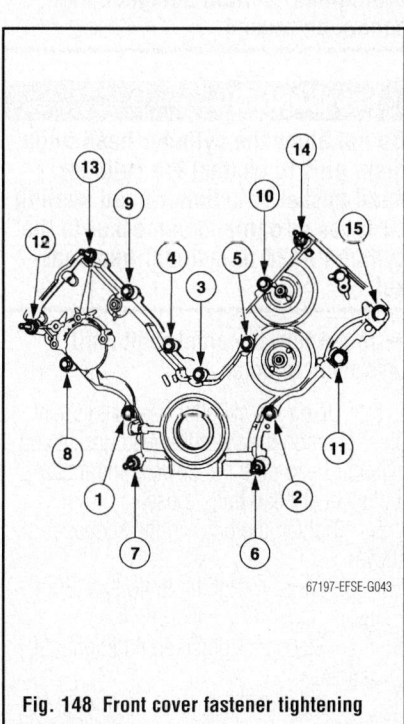

Fig. 148 Front cover fastener tightening sequence

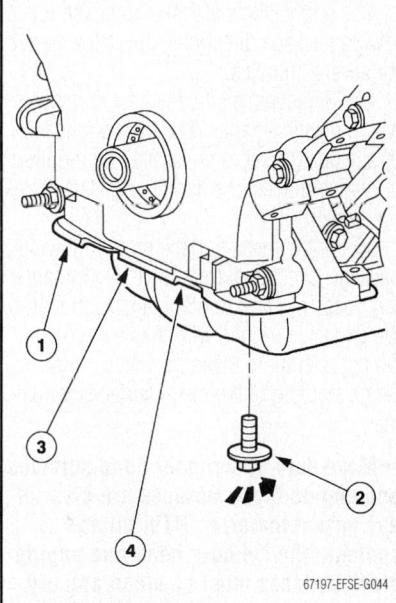

Fig. 149 Loosely install the pan-to-case bolts, then tighten the bolts in two stages, in the sequence shown

cone gasket remover and metal surface prep. Follow the directions on the packaging.

32. Inspect the mating surfaces.

> ✳✳ **WARNING**
>
> Do not allow the valve keepers to fall off of the valve or the valve can drop into the cylinder.

➡️ It may be necessary to push the valve down while compressing the valve spring.

➡️ The roller followers must be installed in their original positions.

33. Using a suitable tool, remove all of the roller followers. Record the roller follower positions.

34. Position the crankshaft keyway at the 12 o'clock position.

35. Remove the bolts, the left timing chain tensioner and tensioner arm.

36. Remove the bolts, the right timing chain tensioner and tensioner arm.

37. Remove the ignition pulse wheel from the crankshaft.

38. Remove the right timing chain from the camshaft sprocket.

39. Remove the right timing chain from the crankshaft sprocket.

40. Remove the left timing chain from the camshaft sprocket.

41. Remove the left timing chain and crankshaft sprocket.

42. Remove both timing chain guides.

> ✳✳ **WARNING**
>
> Use only hand tools to remove the camshaft phaser sprocket assembly or damage can occur to the camshaft or camshaft phaser sprocket.

43. If disassembly of the cylinder head is required, using a suitable tool, loosen the camshaft phaser sprocket bolt.

44. Install a suitable tool onto the left cylinder head. Install a suitable tool onto the right cylinder head.

> ✳✳ **WARNING**
>
> The cylinder head must be cool before removing it from the engine. Cylinder head warpage can result if a warm or hot cylinder head is removed.

> ✳✳ **WARNING**
>
> Do not use the variable camshaft timing (VCT) phaser sprocket as a lifting point or leveraging device when removing the cylinder head or damage to the VCT phaser sprocket can occur.

> ✳✳ **WARNING**
>
> Place clean shop towels over exposed engine cavities. Carefully remove the towels so foreign material is not dropped into the engine.

> ✳✳ **WARNING**
>
> The cylinder head bolts must be discarded and new bolts must be installed. They are tighten-to-yield designed and cannot be reused.

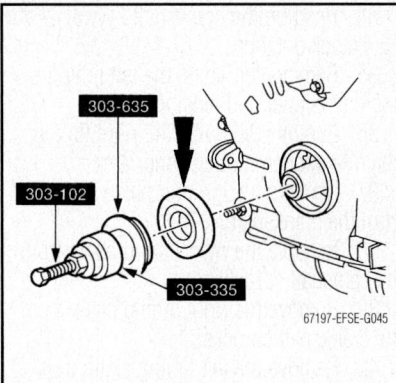

Fig. 150 Crankshaft seal installation tools

✳✳ WARNING

Do not use metal scrapers, wire brushes, power abrasive discs or other abrasive means to clean the sealing surfaces. These tools cause scratches and gouges that make leak paths. Use a plastic scraping tool to remove all traces of the head gasket.

✳✳ WARNING

Aluminum surfaces are soft and can be scratched easily. Never place the cylinder head gasket surface, unprotected, on a bench surface.

45. Remove the bolts and the cylinder head. Discard the cylinder head gasket. Discard the cylinder head bolts.

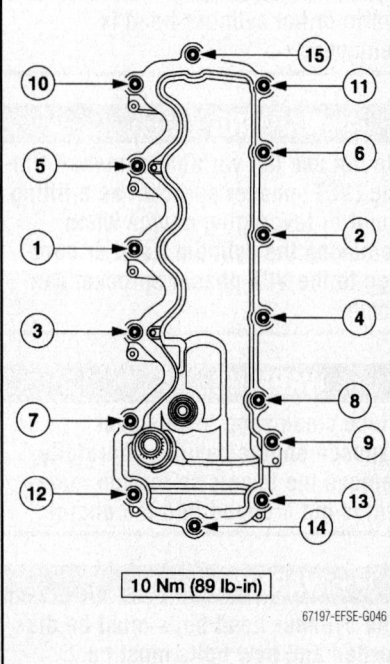

10 Nm (89 lb-in)

Fig. 151 Left valve cover torque sequence—5.4L engine

✳✳ WARNING

Do not use metal scrapers, wire brushes, power abrasive discs or other abrasive means to clean the sealing surfaces. These tools cause scratches and gouges that make leak paths. Use a plastic scraping tool to remove all traces of the head gasket.

✳✳ WARNING

Observe all warnings or cautions and follow all application directions contained on the packaging of the silicone gasket remover and the metal surface prep.

➡ If there is no residual gasket material present, metal surface prep can be used to clean and prepare the surfaces.

46. Clean the cylinder head-to-cylinder block mating surfaces of both the cylinder head and the cylinder block.

47. Remove any large deposits of silicone or gasket material with a plastic scraper.

48. Apply silicone gasket remover, following package directions, and allow to set for several minutes.

49. Remove the silicone gasket remover with a plastic scraper. A second application of silicone gasket remover may be required if residual traces of silicone or gasket material remain.

50. Apply metal surface prep, following package directions, to remove any remaining traces of oil or coolant, and to prepare the surfaces to bond with the new gasket. Do not attempt to make the metal shiny. Some staining of the metal surfaces is normal.

➡ Make sure all cylinder head surfaces and engine block surfaces are clear of any gasket material, RTV, oil and coolant. The cylinder head and engine block surfaces must be clean and dry before running a flatness check.

➡ Use a straightedge that is calibrated by the manufacturer to be flat within 0.005 mm (0.0002 in.) per running foot of length. For example, if the straightedge is 61 cm (24 in.) long, the machined edge must be flat with 0.010 mm (0.0004 in.) from end to end.

51. Support the cylinder head on a bench with the head gasket side up. Inspect all areas of the deck face with a straightedge, paying particular attention to the oil pressure feed area. The cylinder head must not have depressions deeper than 0.0254 mm (0.001 in.) across a 38.1 mm (1.5 in.) square area, or scratches more than 0.0254 mm (0.001 in.).

To install:
All cylinder heads

✳✳ WARNING

Make sure all coolant residue and foreign material are cleaned from the block surface and cylinder bore.

✳✳ WARNING

The use of sealing aids (aviation cement, copper spray, and glue) is not permitted. The gasket must be installed dry.

✳✳ WARNING

The cylinder head bolts must be discarded and new bolts installed. They are tighten-to-yield designed and cannot be reused.

✳✳ WARNING

Do not allow the cylinder head alignment pins to contact the cylinder head gasket or cylinder head sealing surfaces or damage can occur to the cylinder head or cylinder head gasket.

➡ Do not turn the crankshaft until instructed to do so.

52. Using the cylinder head alignment pins, position the cylinder head gasket and cylinder head onto the dowels and install the cylinder head bolts loosely.

53. Tighten the bolts in the sequence shown.

   a. Stage 1: Tighten to 40 Nm (30 ft. lbs.).

   b. Stage 2: Tighten an additional 90 degrees.

   c. Stage 3: Tighten an additional 90 degrees.

54. Remove the cylinder head lifting handle tools.

55. Remove the special tool from the cylinder head.

56. Install the hydraulic lash adjusters into the cylinder head. Lubricate the hydraulic lash adjusters with clean engine oil prior to installation.

57. Position a new gasket and the exhaust manifold and tighten the 8 nuts in

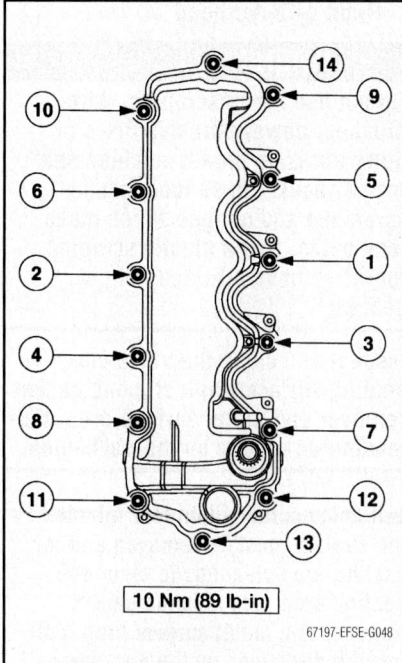

10 Nm (89 lb-in)

67197-EFSE-G048

Fig. 152 Right valve cover torque sequence—5.4L engine

the sequence shown. Tighten to 18 ft. lbs. (25 Nm).

58. Install the exhaust manifold shield and the 2 nuts. Tighten to 89 inch lbs. (10 Nm).

59. Position the crankshaft with the special tool, then remove the tool.

60. Install the LH and RH camshafts. Lubricate the camshaft and camshaft journals with clean engine oil prior to installation.

61. Install the LH and RH camshaft bearing caps in their original locations.

   a. Lubricate the camshaft bearing caps with clean engine oil.

   b. Position the front camshaft bearing cap.

   c. Position the remaining camshaft bearing caps.

   d. Install the bolts loosely.

   e. Tighten to 89 inch lbs. (10 Nm) in the sequence shown.

❊❊ CAUTION

Damage to the variable camshaft timing (VCT) phaser sprocket assembly will occur if mishandled or used as a lifting or leveraging device.

62. Install the VCT phaser sprockets and new VCT phaser sprocket bolts finger tight.

❊❊ CAUTION

Only use hand tools to remove the VCT phaser sprocket assembly or

damage may occur to the camshaft or VCT phaser sprocket.

63. Using the special tool, tighten the LH and RH VCT phaser sprocket bolts in 2 stages:

   a. Stage 1: Tighten to 30 ft. lbs. (40 Nm).

   b. Stage 2: Tighten an additional 90 degrees.

❊❊ WARNING

Timing chain procedures must be followed exactly or damage to valves and pistons will result.

64. Compress the tensioner plunger, using a vice.

65. Install a retaining clip on the tensioner to hold the plunger in during installation.

66. Remove the tensioner from the vise. If the copper links are not visible, mark two links on one end and one link on the other end, and use as timing marks.

❊❊ WARNING

Crankshaft keyway must be in the 12 o'clock position.

67. Install the timing chain guides.

68. Position the left timing chain guide.

69. Install the crankshaft sprocket, making sure the flange faces forward.

❊❊ WARNING

Only use hand tools to install the camshaft phaser sprocket assembly or damage may occur to the camshaft or camshaft phaser unit.

➡ **This step is only required if cylinder head was disassembled.**

70. Using a suitable tool, tighten the bolts in two stages:

   a. Stage 1: Tighten to 40 Nm (30 ft. lbs.).

   b. Stage 2: Tighten an additional 90 degrees.

71. Remove the special tool.

72. Position the lower end of the left (inner) timing chain on the crankshaft sprocket, aligning the timing mark on the outer flange of the crankshaft sprocket with the single copper (marked) link on the chain.

➡ **Make sure the upper half of the timing chain is below the tensioner arm dowel. Position the timing chain on the camshaft sprocket with the camshaft**

sprocket timing mark positioned between the two copper (marked) chain links.

➡ **The left timing chain tensioner arm has a bump near the dowel hole for identification.**

73. Position the left timing chain tensioner arm on the dowel pin and install the left timing chain tensioner.

74. Remove the retaining clip from the left timing chain tensioner.

75. Position the lower end of the right (outer) timing chain on the crankshaft sprocket, aligning the timing mark on the sprocket with the single copper (marked) chain link.

➡ **The lower half of the timing chain must be positioned above the tensioner arm dowel.**

76. Position the right timing chain on the camshaft sprocket. Make sure the camshaft sprocket timing mark is positioned between the two copper (marked) chain links.

77. Position the right timing chain tensioner arm on the dowel pin and install the right timing chain tensioner.

78. Remove the retaining clip from the right timing chain tensioner.

➡ **Both camshaft phaser sprockets are identical. Refer to the R timing mark to identify the right camshaft phaser sprocket and the L timing mark to identify the left camshaft phaser sprocket.**

79. As a post-check, verify correct alignment of all timing marks. Make sure the R and L timing marks on the sprockets correspond to the above note.

80. Install the crankshaft sensor ring on the crankshaft.

➡ **Lubricate the camshaft roller followers using clean engine oil.**

➡ **Using the mark on each camshaft roller follower, make sure it is returned to its original position.**

81. Using a suitable tool, install all of the camshaft roller followers.

❊❊ WARNING

Do not use metal scrapers, wire brushes, power abrasive discs or other abrasive means to clean the sealing surfaces. These tools cause scratches and gouges which make leak paths. Use a plastic scraping tool to remove all traces of old sealant.

➡️ If the engine front cover is not secured within four minutes, the sealant must be removed and the sealing area cleaned. To clean the sealing area, use silicone gasket remover and metal surface prep. Follow the directions on the packaging. Failure to follow this procedure can cause future oil leakage.

➡️ Make sure that the engine front cover gasket is in place on the engine front cover before installation.

82. Apply a bead of silicone gasket and sealant along the cylinder head-to-cylinder block surface and the oil pan-to-cylinder block surface, at the locations shown.

83. Install a new engine front cover gasket on the engine front cover. Position the engine front cover. Install the fasteners finger-tight.

84. Tighten the engine front cover fasteners in sequence in two stages.
   a. Stage 1: Tighten fasteners 1 through 15 to 25 Nm (18 ft. lbs.).
   b. Stage 2: Tighten fasteners 6 and 7 to 48 Nm (35 ft. lbs.).
   c. Loosely install the pan-to-case bolts, then tighten the bolts in two stages, in the sequence shown.
   d. Stage 1: Tighten to 20 Nm (15 ft. lbs.).
   e. Stage 2: Tighten an additional 60 degrees.

85. Install the left camshaft position (CMP) sensor and the bolt.

86. Lubricate the new O-ring seal with clean engine oil prior to installation.

87. Install the right CMP sensor and the bolt.

88. Lubricate the new O-ring seal with clean engine oil prior to installation.

89. Lubricate the engine front cover and the crankshaft seal inner lip with clean engine oil.

90. Use the special tools to install the crankshaft seal into the engine front cover.

91. If not secured within four minutes, the sealant must be removed and the sealing area cleaned. To clean the sealing area, use silicone gasket remover and metal surface prep. Follow the directions on the packaging. Failure to follow this procedure can cause future oil leakage.

92. Apply silicone gasket and sealant to the Woodruff key slot on the crankshaft pulley. Use a suitable tool to install the crankshaft pulley.

93. Tighten the new crankshaft pulley bolt in four stages.
   a. Stage 1: Tighten to 90 Nm (66 ft. lbs.).

b. Stage 2: Loosen 360 degrees.
   c. Stage 3: Tighten to 50 Nm (37 ft. lbs.).
   d. Stage 4: Tighten an additional 90 degrees.

94. Install the three accessory drive belt idler pulleys, the coolant pump pulley and the bolts. Torque all bolts to 25 Nm (18 ft. lbs.)

95. Position the accessory drive belt tensioner and install the bolts. Torque all bolts to 25 Nm (18 ft. lbs.)

96. Install the radio frequency interference capacitors.

Left cylinder head

⚠️ **WARNING**

Do not use metal scrapers, wire brushes, power abrasive discs or other abrasive means to clean sealing surfaces. These tools cause scratches and gouges which make leak paths. Use a plastic scraping tool to remove all traces of old sealant.

Inspect and clean the valve cover sealing surfaces with silicone gasket remover and metal surface prep. Follow the directions on the packaging.

➡️ If not secured within four minutes, the sealant must be removed and the sealing area cleaned. To clean the sealing area, use silicone gasket remover and metal surface prep. Follow the directions on the packaging. Failure to follow this procedure can cause future oil leakage.

97. Apply silicone gasket and sealant in two places where the engine front cover meets the cylinder head.

⚠️ **WARNING**

When installing the valve cover, make sure to avoid damaging the variable camshaft timing (VCT) solenoid.

98. Position the left valve cover and gasket on the cylinder head and install the bolts loosely. Tighten the bolts in the sequence shown.

➡️ Lubricate the O-ring seal with clean engine oil.

99. Install the oil level indicator tube.

100. Install a new O-ring seal on the oil level indicator tube.

101. Install the oil level indicator tube.

102. Install the bolt.

Right cylinder head

⚠️ **WARNING**

Do not use metal scrapers, wire brushes, power abrasive discs or other abrasive means to clean sealing surfaces. These tools cause scratches and gouges which make leak paths. Use a plastic scraping tool to remove all traces of old sealant.

Inspect and clean the valve cover sealing surfaces with silicone gasket remover and metal surface prep. Follow the directions on the packaging.

➡️ If not secured within four minutes, the sealant must be removed and the sealing area cleaned. To clean the sealing area, use silicone gasket remover and metal surface prep. Follow the directions on the packaging. Failure to follow this procedure can cause future oil leakage.

103. Apply silicone gasket and sealant in two places where the engine front cover meets the cylinder head.

⚠️ **WARNING**

When installing the valve cover, make sure to avoid damaging the variable camshaft timing (VCT) solenoid.

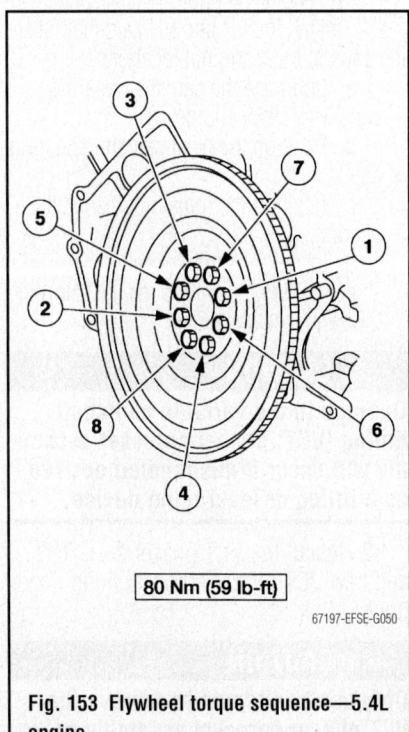

80 Nm (59 lb-ft)

67197-EFSE-G050

Fig. 153 Flywheel torque sequence—5.4L engine

104. Position the right valve cover and gasket on the cylinder head and install the bolts loosely. Tighten the bolts in the sequence shown.

105. Install the heater outlet tube stud.

All cylinder heads

106. Position the electrical harness on the valve cover and connect the engine wiring harness retainers to the valve cover studs.

107. Connect the right radio ignition interference capacitor electrical connector.

108. Connect the left radio ignition interference capacitor and cylinder head temperature (CHT) sensor electrical connectors.

109. Connect the CMP sensor electrical connectors.

110. Connect the CKP sensor electrical connector.

111. Install a suitable tool.

112. Using a suitable floor crane remove the engine from the engine stand.

113. Install the flexplate or the flywheel and bolts. Tighten the bolts in the sequence shown.

114. Install the engine.

ENGINE ASSEMBLY

REMOVAL & INSTALLATION

4.2L Engine

1. Before servicing the vehicle, refer to the Precautions Section.

All vehicles

2. Raise and safely support the vehicle.

3. Release the fuel system pressure.

4. Disconnect the battery ground cable.

5. Drain the cooling system.

6. Remove the hood.

7. Remove the cowl panel grille.

8. Remove the powertrain control module (PCM).

9. Detach the electrical connector, the wiring harness retainer and the washer hose from the cowl extension panel.

Vehicles equipped with a manual transmission

10. Remove the push pins and position the clutch master cylinder reservoir aside.

11. Disconnect the fuel vapor tubes from the purge valve.

All vehicles

12. Remove the 7 bolts and the cowl extension panel.

13. Remove the 9 push pins and the radiator sight shield.

14. Remove the upper intake manifold.

15. Remove the radiator, the cooling fan and the shroud.

16. Remove the air cleaner.

17. Release the clamp and disconnect the upper radiator hose from the thermostat housing. Remove the hose from the vehicle.

18. Release the clamps, disconnect the heater hoses and position the heater hoses aside.

19. Release the clamp and disconnect the lower radiator hose from the coolant pump.

20. Disconnect the intake manifold runner control (IMRC) actuator and the fuel charging wiring harness electrical connectors.

21. Disconnect the fuel supply spring lock coupling.

22. Remove the 4 bolts and the fuel rail, the fuel injectors, the fuel charging wiring harness and the vacuum harness as an assembly.

Vehicles equipped with an automatic transmission

23. Disconnect the fuel vapor tubes from the purge valve.

All vehicles

24. Using the special tool, with a twisting motion, pull the left spark plug wires off the spark plugs.

25. Detach the left spark plug wire retainers and remove the left spark plug wires.

26. Remove the bolts and position the power steering fluid reservoir aside.

27. If equipped, remove the compressor manifold and tube assembly.

28. Rotate the accessory drive belt tensioner counterclockwise and remove the accessory drive belt.

29. Remove the 2 power steering pump upper bolts.

30. Disconnect the alternator.

31. Detach the wiring harness retainer.

32. Using the special tool, with a twisting motion, pull the right spark plug wires off the spark plugs.

33. Detach the right spark plug wire retainers.

34. Disconnect the coil electrical connector.

35. Remove the bolts, the coil and the right spark plug wires as an assembly.

36. Disconnect the positive crankcase ventilation (PCV) valve hose from the PCV valve and remove the hose.

37. Disconnect the wiring harness in-line connector.

38. Remove the bolt and detach the ground wire.

39. Detach the wiring harness retainer from the rear of the right cylinder head.

40. Remove the power steering pressure hose bracket nut.

➡ **The front bolt cannot be removed from the power steering pump with the pressure hose in place. Remove the rear bolt first, then slide the power steering pump out while removing the second bolt.**

41. Remove the bolts and position the power steering pump aside.

42. Drain the engine oil. Install the drain plug when finished. Tighten to 23 Nm (17 ft. lbs.).

43. Remove the oil filter.

Vehicles equipped with an automatic transmission

44. Detach the transmission cooler tubes from the bracket.

All vehicles

45. Remove the nut and position the starter wiring harness aside.

46. If equipped, disconnect the engine block heater electrical connector.

47. Remove the 4 3-way catalytic converter-to-exhaust manifold nuts.

48. Remove the starter motor.

Vehicles equipped with an automatic transmission

49. Remove the cylinder block opening cover.

➡ **Rotate the crankshaft using the crankshaft pulley bolt to access all of the torque converter nuts.**

➡ **Mark the flexplate and one torque converter stud for installation reference.**

50. Remove the 4 torque converter nuts.

51. Remove the 3 oil pan-to-transmission bolts.

52. Remove the transmission-to-engine bolts.

53. Remove the left engine support insulator through bolt.

54. Remove the right engine support insulator nuts.

55. Remove the stud bolt, the bolts and the power steering fluid reservoir bracket.

56. Remove the nuts and the right engine lifting eye.

57. Install the lifting eye on the right side of the engine.

58. Remove the nuts and the left engine lifting eye.

59. Install the lifting eye on the left side of the engine.

➡ **Use 2 10mm (⅜ inch) spring links to connect the Engine Lifting Bracket 303-F047 to the Lifting Bracket, Engine 303-050.**

60. Install the lifting bracket.

61. Connect an engine crane to the special tool and lift the engine approximately 75 mm (3 in.).

62. Remove the bolts and the left engine support insulator.

63. Remove the bolts and the right engine support insulator.

64. Support the transmission with a floor jack and a wood block.

Vehicles equipped with an automatic transmission

65. Remove the engine from the vehicle.

Vehicles equipped with a manual transmission

66. Lift the engine while pulling the engine forward until the alternator pulley is above the radiator upper support.

67. Rotate the engine 90 degrees to the left and remove the engine from the vehicle.

To install:

Vehicles equipped with an automatic transmission

→Make sure the marks made on the torque converter stud and the flexplate are lined up.

68. Position the engine in the vehicle and mate it to the transmission.

Vehicles equipped with a manual transmission

69. Position the engine with the front of the engine facing the left side of the vehicle.

S0>Lower the engine until the alternator pulley is slightly higher than the radiator upper support.

70. Turn the engine 90 degrees to the right, lower the engine and mate it to the transmission.

All vehicles

71. Install the right engine support insulator and the bolts. Tighten to 63 Nm (46 ft. lbs.).

72. Install the left engine support insulator and the bolts. Tighten to 63 Nm (46 ft. lbs.).

73. Remove the floor jack and wood block from the transmission.

74. Lower the engine into position and remove the floor crane and the special tools.

75. Position the power steering fluid reservoir bracket and install the bolts and the stud bolt. Tighten to 20 Nm (15 ft. lbs.).

76. Install the right engine support insulator nuts. Tighten to 175 Nm (129 ft. lbs.).

77. Install the left engine support insulator through bolt. Tighten to 175 Nm (129 ft. lbs.).

78. Install the transmission-to-engine bolts. Tighten to 47 Nm (35 ft. lbs.).

79. Install the 3 oil pan-to-transmission bolts. Tighten to 34 Nm (24 ft. lbs.).

Vehicles equipped with an automatic transmission

→Rotate the crankshaft using the crankshaft pulley bolt to access all of the torque converter nuts.

80. Install the 4 torque converter nuts. Tighten to 36 Nm (27 ft. lbs.).

81. Install the cylinder block opening cover.

All vehicles

82. Install the starter motor.

83. Install the 4 3-way catalytic converter nuts. Tighten to 40 Nm (30 ft. lbs.).

84. If equipped, connect the engine block heater electrical connector.

85. Position the starter wiring harness bracket and install the nut. Tighten to 20 Nm (15 ft. lbs.).

Vehicles equipped with an automatic transmission

86. Attach the transmission cooler tubes to the bracket.

All vehicles

87. Install a new oil filter. Tighten to 12 Nm (9 ft. lbs.).

→Do not tighten the bolts until the 2 upper bolts are installed.

→Make sure the power steering pressure hose bracket is installed on the stud.

88. Position the power steering pump and install the bolts finger tight. Install the nut. Tighten to 10 Nm (89 inch lbs.).

89. Attach the wiring harness retainer to the rear of the right cylinder head.

90. Position the ground wire and install the bolt.

91. Connect the wiring harness in-line connector.

92. Connect the positive crankcase ventilation (PCV) valve hose to the PCV valve.

93. Position the coil and the right spark plug wires as an assembly and install the bolts. Tighten to 7 Nm (62 inch lbs.).

94. Connect the coil electrical connector.

95. Attach the right spark plug wire retainers.

96. Apply silicone dielectric compound to the inside of the spark plug wire boots.

97. Connect the spark plug wires to the spark plugs. Attach the wiring harness retainer.

98. Connect the alternator.

→Tighten the lower bolts at this time.

99. Install the power steering pump upper bolts. Tighten to 25 Nm (18 ft. lbs.).

100. Rotate the accessory drive belt tensioner counterclockwise and install the accessory drive belt.

101. If equipped, install the compressor manifold and tube assembly.

102. Position the power steering fluid reservoir and install the bolts. Tighten to 10 Nm (89 inch lbs.).

103. Position the left spark plug wires and attach the left spark plug wire retainers.

104. Apply silicone dielectric compound to the inside of the spark plug wire boots.

105. Connect the spark plug wires to the spark plugs.

Vehicles equipped with an automatic transmission

106. Connect the fuel vapor tubes to the purge valve.

All vehicles

107. Position the fuel rail, the fuel injectors, the fuel charging wiring harness and the vacuum harness as an assembly and install the bolts. Tighten to 10 Nm (89 inch lbs.).

108. Connect the fuel supply spring lock coupling.

109. Connect the intake manifold runner control (IMRC) actuator and the fuel charging wiring harness electrical connectors.

110. Connect the lower radiator hose to the coolant pump.

111. Connect the heater hoses.

112. Connect the upper radiator hose to the thermostat housing.

113. Install the air cleaner.

114. Install the radiator and the cooling fan and shroud.

115. Install the upper intake manifold.

116. Position the radiator sight shield and install the 9 push pins.

117. Position the cowl extension panel and install the 7 bolts.

Vehicles equipped with a manual transmission

118. Connect the fuel vapor tubes to the purge valve. Position the clutch master cylinder reservoir and install the push pins.

All vehicles

119. Attach the windshield washer hose, the wiring harness retainer and the electrical connector to the cowl extension panel.

120. Install the powertrain control module (PCM).

121. Install the cowl panel grille.

122. Position the hood and install the bolts. Tighten to 30 Nm (22 ft. lbs.).

123. Connect the battery ground cable.

124. Fill the engine with clean engine oil.

125. Fill and bleed the cooling system.

126. If equipped, evacuate and charge the A/C system.

4.6L Engine

1. Before servicing the vehicle, refer to the Precautions Section.

2. Raise and safely support the vehicle.

3. Remove the hood.

4. Remove the intake manifold. See "Intake Manifold" in this section.

5. Remove the radiator.

6. Remove the powertrain control module (PCM) and the support bracket.

7. Remove the cowl panel grille.

8. Detach the wiring harness and the windshield washer hose from the cowl panel extension.

9. Remove the bolts and the cowl panel extension.

10. Disconnect the electrical connector and remove the bolt and the ground strap.

11. Disconnect the heater hose.

12. Remove the nut and the A/C manifold and tube assembly support bracket.

13. Disconnect the A/C compressor electrical connector.

14. Disconnect the degas bottle (coolant reservoir) coolant hose.

15. Remove the bolts and position the power steering reservoir assembly aside.

16. Using the special tool, remove the power steering pump pulley.

17. Disconnect the power steering pressure tube. Drain the power steering fluid into a suitable container.

18. Remove the nut and position aside the power steering pressure tube.

19. Remove the power steering pump bolts and position the power steering pump assembly aside.

20. Remove the starter.

21. Disconnect the crankcase position (CKP) sensor electrical connector and harness retainer.

22. If equipped, remove the nut and the transmission cooler tube support bracket.

23. Remove the bolts and position the A/C compressor aside.

24. If equipped, disconnect the block heater electrical connector.

25. Detach the starter electrical harness support from the cylinder block.

26. Remove the drain plug and drain the engine oil.

27. Remove the oil filter.

28. Remove the bolts and the flexplate inspection cover.

29. Remove the cylinder block opening cover.

30. Remove the torque converter-to-flexplate nuts. Discard the nuts.

31. Disconnect the left heated exhaust gas oxygen sensor (HO2S) electrical connector and detach the electrical connector retainer.

32. Disconnect the shift cable and remove the shift cable bracket.

➡ **The left upper transmission-to-engine bolt will be removed later.**

33. Remove the 6 transmission-to-engine bolts.

34. Remove the bolt and position the transmission fluid filler tube aside.

35. Remove the 4 exhaust manifold flange nuts.

36. Remove the right motor mount nuts.

37. Remove the left motor mount bolt.

38. Support the transmission.

➡ **On 4x4 vehicles, it may be necessary to reposition the transfer case vent hose to access the bolt.**

39. Remove the left upper transmission-to-engine bolt.

40. Install the lifting bracket.

➡ **Raise the engine and position forward to disconnect the transmission wiring harness retainer at the rear of the right cylinder head and disconnect the right heated exhaust gas oxygen sensor (HO2S) electrical connector and detach the electrical connector retainer.**

41. Using a suitable floor crane, remove the engine assembly from the vehicle.

To install:

> ❊❊ **WARNING**
>
> **Clean the engine support insulator-to-frame mating surfaces of any dirt or foreign material prior to engine installation.**

➡ **Position the engine assembly forward to connect the right heated exhaust gas oxygen sensor (HO2S) electrical connector and the transmission harness retainers at the rear of the cylinder head.**

42. Using a suitable floor crane, position the engine assembly into the vehicle.

43. Apply High Strength Threadlocker to the bolt threads and install the left engine support insulator bolt.

   a. If the engine support insulator nut is missing or damaged, install a new nut using service part number W709375.

   b. If the engine support insulator nut cage is damaged or missing, install a new nut using service part number W520516-S301. Tighten to 175 Nm (129 ft. lbs.).

44. Apply High Strength Threadlocker to the bolt threads and install the right engine support insulator washer and nuts. Tighten to 175 Nm (129 ft. lbs.).

45. Install the 6 transmission-to-engine bolts. Tighten to 60 Nm (44 ft. lbs.).

46. Connect the shift cable and install the shift cable bracket and the bolts. Tighten to 25 Nm (18 ft. lbs.).

47. Connect the left heated exhaust gas oxygen sensor (HO2S) electrical connector and attach the electrical connector retainer.

➡ **Lubricate the O-ring seals with clean transmission fluid.**

48. Position the transmission fluid filler tube and install the bolt. Tighten to 12 Nm (9 ft. lbs.).

49. Install the 4 exhaust manifold-to-catalytic converter nuts. Tighten to 40 Nm (30 ft. lbs.).

50. Install the torque converter-to-flexplate nuts. Tighten to 35 Nm (26 ft. lbs.).

51. Install the cylinder block opening cover.

52. Install the flexplate inspection cover. Tighten to 34 Nm (25 ft. lbs.).

53. Install a new oil filter.

54. Install the drain plug. Tighten to 14 Nm (10 ft. lbs.).

55. Attach the starter electrical harness support to the cylinder block. Tighten to 10 Nm (89 inch lbs.).

56. If equipped, connect the block heater electrical connector.

57. Position the A/C compressor and install the bolts. Tighten to 25 Nm (18 ft. lbs.).

58. Install the starter.

59. Position the power steering reservoir and install the 2 lower bolts. Tighten to 23 Nm (17 ft. lbs.).

60. Position the power steering pump and install the bolts. Tighten to 25 Nm (18 ft. lbs.).

61. Using the special tool, install a new O-ring seal on the pressure line fitting.

62. Connect the power steering pressure tube. Tighten to 65 Nm (48 ft. lbs.).

63. Position the power steering pressure tube support bracket and install the nut. Tighten to 10 Nm (89 inch lbs.).

> ❊❊ **WARNING**
>
> **If the pulley has been removed and installed twice, install a new power steering pump pulley.**

64. Install the power steering pump pulley. Inspect the pulley for paint marks in the web area near the hub. If there are 2 paint marks, install a new pulley. If there is one

paint mark or none at all, use a pencil to mark the web area of the pulley near the hub.

65. If equipped, install the transmission cooler tube support bracket and nut. Tighten to 10 Nm (89 inch lbs.).

66. Connect the degas bottle (coolant reservoir) coolant hose.

67. Connect the A/C compressor electrical connector.

68. Connect the crankcase position (CKP) sensor electrical connector and the harness retainer.

69. Position the A/C manifold and tube assembly support bracket and install the nut. Tighten to 10 Nm (89 inch lbs.).

70. Remove the lifting bracket.

71. Install the upper transmission-to-engine bolts. Tighten to 60 Nm (44 ft. lbs.).

72. Connect the heater coolant hose.

73. Install the ground strap and the bolt and connect the electrical connector. Tighten to 10 Nm (89 inch lbs.).

74. Install the cowl panel extension.

75. Attach the wiring harness and the windshield washer hose to the cowl panel extension.

76. Install the cowl panel grill.

77. Install the powertrain control module (PCM) and the support bracket.

78. Install the intake manifold.

79. Install the radiator.

80. Install the hood and the 4 bolts. Tighten to 30 Nm (22 ft. lbs.).

81. Fill the engine with clean engine oil.

82. Fill and bleed the engine cooling system.

5.4L Engine

1. Before servicing the vehicle, refer to the Precautions Section.

All vehicles

2. Raise and safely support the vehicle.

3. Remove the hood.

4. Remove the intake manifold. See "Intake Manifold" in this section.

5. Remove the accessory drive belt.

6. Recover the A/C system.

7. Remove the radiator.

8. Remove the powertrain control module (PCM) and the support bracket.

9. Remove the cowl panel grille.

10. Detach the wiring harness and the windshield washer hose retainers from the cowl panel extension.

11. Remove the bolts and the cowl extension panel.

12. Disconnect the electrical connector and remove the bolt and the ground strap.

13. Disconnect the heater hose.

14. Remove the nut, disconnect the A/C manifold and tube assembly and position aside.

15. Remove the nut and the A/C manifold and tube assembly and support bracket.

16. Disconnect the coolant hose.

17. Remove the bolt and position the power steering reservoir assembly aside.

18. Disconnect the alternator wiring harness retainer from the right cylinder head.

19. Disconnect the A/C compressor and the A/C high pressure cut-off switch electrical connectors.

20. Disconnect the alternator wiring harness retainer from the right cylinder head and position the harness aside.

21. Disconnect the crankshaft position (CKP) sensor wiring harness retainer from the starter motor wiring harness.

22. Remove the nut and position aside the power steering pressure hose support bracket.

23. Using a puller, remove the power steering pump pulley.

24. Disconnect the power steering pressure tube. Drain the power steering fluid into a suitable container.

25. Remove the 3 bolts and position the power steering pump aside.

Manual transmission vehicles

26. Remove the clutch.

Automatic transmission vehicles

27. Remove the nut and position aside the transmission cooler tube support bracket.

28. Remove the starter.

29. Remove the 2 bolts and the flexplate inspection cover.

30. Remove the cylinder block opening cover.

31. Remove the 4 torque converter-to-flexplate nuts. Discard the nuts.

32. Disconnect the shift cable and remove the shift cable bracket.

➡**The upper 2 transmission-to-engine bolts will be removed later.**

33. Remove the lower 5 transmission-to-engine bolts.

34. Remove the bolt and position the transmission fluid filler tube aside.

All vehicles

35. Remove the drain plug and drain the engine oil.

36. Disconnect the right heated oxygen sensor (HO_2S) electrical connector and detach the wiring harness retainer.

37. Disconnect the left heated exhaust gas oxygen sensor electrical connector and detach the electrical connector retainer.

38. Remove the oil filter.

39. Disconnect the oil temperature sensor electrical connector.

40. Remove the bolts and position the A/C compressor aside.

41. If equipped, disconnect the block heater electrical connector.

42. Detach the starter electrical harness support from the cylinder block.

43. Remove the 4 exhaust manifold flange nuts.

44. Remove the right engine support insulator nuts and washer.

45. Remove the left engine support insulator bolt.

Automatic transmission vehicles

46. Support the transmission.

➡**On 4WD vehicles, it may be necessary to reposition the transfer case vent hose to access the bolts.**

47. Remove the upper 2 transmission-to-engine bolts.

All vehicles

48. Install the lifting bracket.

49. Using a suitable floor crane, remove the engine assembly from the vehicle.

To install:
All vehicles

50. Using a suitable floor crane, position the engine assembly into the vehicle.

✳✳ WARNING

Only use hand tools when installing the left engine mount bolt or damage to the engine mount can occur.

➡**Early build vehicles are equipped with an M14 through bolt. Late build vehicles are equipped with an M18 through bolt.**

51. Apply high strength threadlocker to the bolt threads and install the left engine support insulator bolt.

   a. If the M14 through bolt engine support insulator nut is missing or damaged, install a new nut using service part number W709375.

   b. If the M14 through bolt engine support insulator nut cage is damaged or missing, install a new nut using service part number W520516-S301.

   c. Early build vehicles, tighten to 220 Nm (162 ft. lbs.); Late build vehicles, tighten to 350 Nm (258 ft. lbs.).

✳✳ WARNING

Only use hand tools when installing the right engine mount nuts or damage to the engine mount can occur.

52. Apply high strength threadlocker to the stud threads and install the right engine support insulator washer and nuts. Tighten to 250 Nm (184 ft. lbs.).

53. Remove the lifting bracket.

Manual transmission vehicles

54. Install the clutch.

Automatic transmission vehicles

➡**The upper 2 transmission-to-engine bolts will be installed later.**

55. Install the lower 5 transmission-to-engine bolts. Tighten to 60 Nm (44 ft. lbs.).

56. Position the shift cable bracket and install the bolts and connect the shift cable. Tighten to 25 Nm (18 ft. lbs.).

57. Install 4 new torque converter-to-flexplate nuts. Tighten to 36 Nm (27 ft. lbs.).

58. Install the cylinder block opening cover.

59. Install the flexplate inspection cover and the 2 bolts. Tighten to 34 Nm (25 ft. lbs.).

60. Install the starter.

61. Position the transmission cooler tube support bracket and install the bolt. Tighten to 10 Nm (89 inch lbs.).

All vehicles

62. If equipped, connect the block heater electrical connector.

63. Connect the left and right heated exhaust gas oxygen sensor (HO2S) electrical connector and attach the electrical connector retainer.

64. Attach the starter electrical harness support bracket.

65. Connect the oil temperature sensor electrical connector.

66. Position the A/C compressor and install the 3 bolts. Tighten to 25 Nm (18 ft. lbs.).

67. Install the 4 exhaust manifold flange nuts. Tighten to 40 Nm (30 ft. lbs.).

Automatic transmission vehicles

68. Install the upper 2 transmission-to-engine bolts. Tighten to 60 Nm (44 ft. lbs.).

69. Position the transmission filler tube and install the bolt. Tighten to 20 Nm (15 ft. lbs.).

All vehicles

70. Connect the crankshaft position (CKP) sensor wiring harness retainer to the starter motor wiring harness.

71. Connect the alternator wiring harness retainer to the right cylinder head.

72. Connect the A/C compressor and the A/C high pressure cut-off switch electrical connectors.

73. Connect the alternator wiring harness retainer to the right cylinder head.

74. Position the power steering pump assembly and install the 3 bolts. Tighten to 25 Nm (18 ft. lbs.).

75. Install a new O-ring seal on the pressure line fitting.

76. Connect the power steering pressure tube. Tighten to 65 Nm (48 ft. lbs.).

77. Install the power steering pump pulley.

78. Position the power steering pressure hose support bracket and install the nut. Tighten to 10 Nm (89 inch lbs.).

79. Position the power steering reservoir assembly and install the bolt. Tighten to 23 Nm (17 ft. lbs.).

80. Using a new O-ring seal, connect the A/C manifold and tube assembly and install the nut. Tighten to 25 Nm (18 ft. lbs.).

81. Position the A/C manifold and tube assembly support bracket and install the nut. Tighten to 25 Nm (18 ft. lbs.).

82. Connect the heater hose.

83. Disconnect the coolant hose.

84. Connect the electrical connector and position the ground strap and install the bolt. Tighten to 10 Nm (89 inch lbs.).

85. Position the cowl extension panel and install the bolts.

86. Attach the wiring harness and the windshield washer hose retainers to the cowl panel extension.

87. Install the intake manifold.

88. Install the radiator.

89. Install the powertrain control module (PCM).

90. Install the cowl.

91. Install the hood.

92. Fill the crankcase with clean engine oil.

93. Evacuate and charge the A/C system.

94. Fill and bleed the power steering system.

EXHAUST MANIFOLD

REMOVAL & INSTALLATION

4.2L Engine

See Figures 154 and 155.

1. Before servicing the vehicle, refer to the Precautions Section.

2. Remove or disconnect the following:
   - Negative battery cable
   - For the right-hand manifold: the EGR valve-to-exhaust manifold tube
   - For the left-hand manifold: the oil level indicator tube bracket nut, then remove the oil level indicator tube. Remove and discard the oil level indicator tube O-ring.

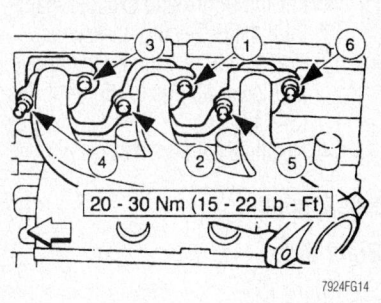

Fig. 154 Tighten the left-hand exhaust manifold bolts in the order shown—4.2L engine

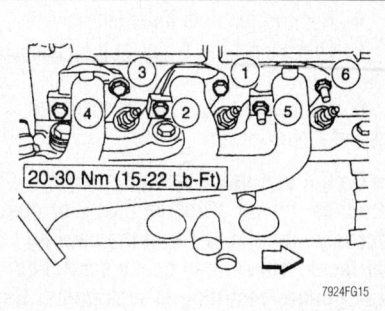

Fig. 155 Tighten the right-hand exhaust manifold bolts in the order shown—4.2L engine

- Oxygen Sensor (O2S) electrical connector
- The 2 catalytic converter-to-exhaust manifold nuts, then disconnect the Y-pipe from the left-hand exhaust manifold.
- Exhaust manifold stud bolts, then remove the manifold mounting bolts
- Exhaust manifold. Remove and discard the exhaust manifold gasket.

To install:

3. Install or connect the following:
   - New exhaust manifold gasket onto the engine, then install the exhaust manifold. Tighten the bolts and stud bolts in the sequence shown to 15–22 ft. lbs. (20–30 Nm).
   - Y-pipe to the exhaust manifold, then install and tighten the catalytic converter nuts to 25–34 ft. lbs. (34–46 Nm).
   - O2S connector, then lower the vehicle.
   - Left-hand exhaust manifold: a new oil level indicator tube O-ring onto the tube. Insert the tube into the engine block and tighten the bracket retaining nut to 15–22 ft. lbs. (20–30 Nm).

- For the right-hand exhaust manifold: the EGR valve-to-exhaust manifold tube. Tighten the upper and lower fittings to 25–34 ft. lbs. (34–47 Nm).
- Negative battery cable

4.6L Engine

Right Side

See Figure 156.

1. Before servicing the vehicle, refer to the Precautions Section.
2. With the vehicle in **Neutral**, position it on a hoist.
3. Remove the starter.
4. Remove the right inner fenderwell.
5. Disconnect the Y-pipe at the manifold.
6. Remove the manifold. Discard the gasket.

➡**Do not use metal scrapers, wire brushes, power abrasive discs, or other abrasive means to clean the sealing surfaces. These may cause scratches and gouges resulting in leak paths. Use a plastic scraper to clean the sealing surfaces.**

7. Clean the sealing surfaces with metal surface prep.

➡**Install a new exhaust manifold gasket.**

8. Position the right exhaust manifold and tighten the nuts in the sequence shown.
9. To install, reverse the removal procedure.

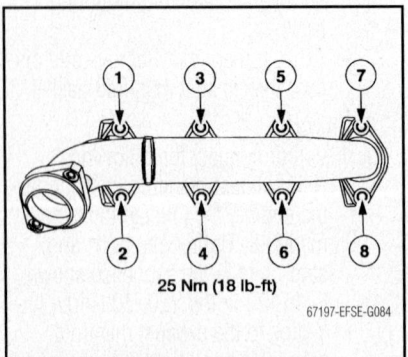

Fig. 156 Right exhaust manifold torque sequence—4.6L engine

Left Side

See Figure 157.

1. Before servicing the vehicle, refer to the Precautions Section.
2. With the vehicle in **Neutral**, position it on a hoist.

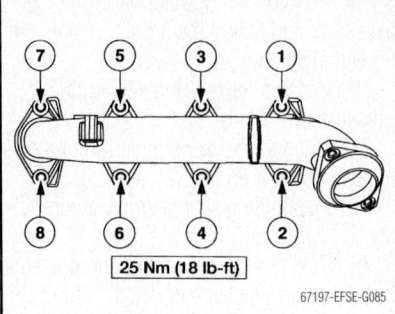

Fig. 157 Left exhaust manifold torque sequence—4.6L engines

3. Remove the left inner fenderwell.
4. Disconnect the Y-pipe at the manifold.
5. Disconnect the EGR tube.
6. Remove the manifold. Discard the gasket.

➡**Do not use metal scrapers, wire brushes, power abrasive discs, or other abrasive means to clean the sealing surfaces. These may cause scratches and gouges resulting in leak paths. Use**

a plastic scraper to clean the sealing surfaces.

7. Clean the sealing surfaces with metal surface prep.

➡**Install a new exhaust manifold gasket.**

8. Position the left exhaust manifold and tighten the exhaust manifold nuts in the sequence shown.
9. To install, reverse the removal procedure.

5.4L Engine

Right Side

See Figures 158 and 159.

1. Before servicing the vehicle, refer to the precautions section.
2. With the vehicle in NEUTRAL, position it on a hoist.
3. Remove the RH inner fender well.
4. Remove the RH engine support insulator.
5. Remove the 2 bolts and the exhaust manifold heat shield.

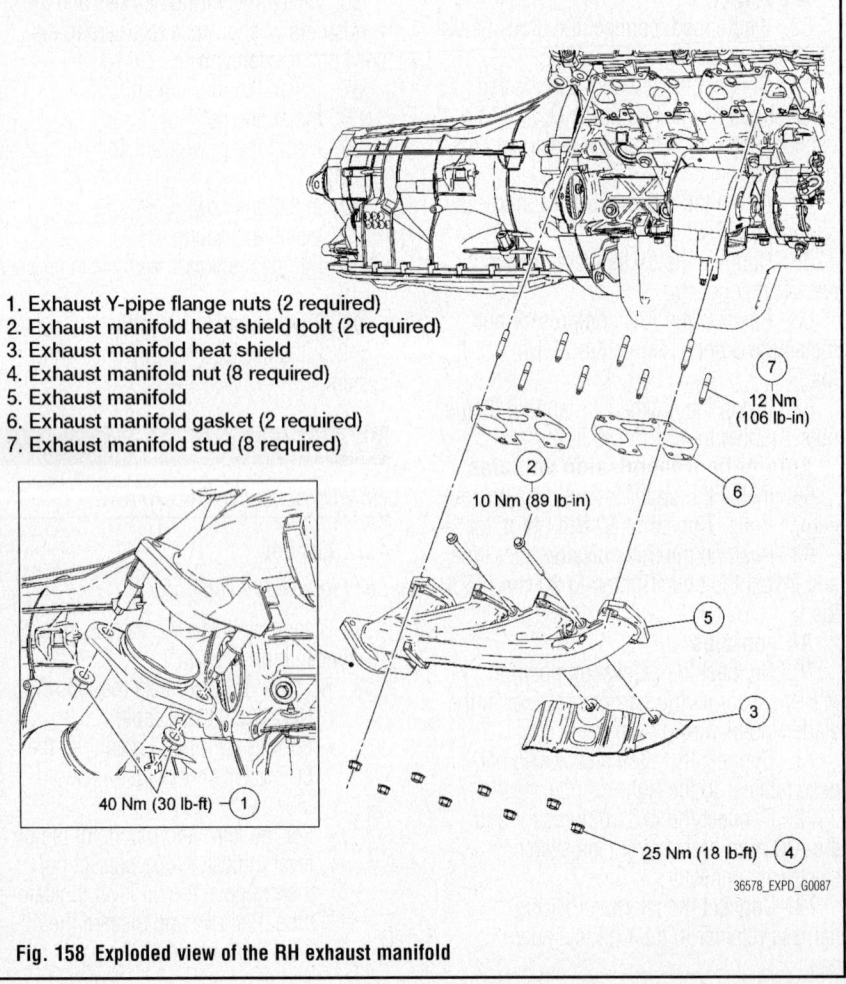

1. Exhaust Y-pipe flange nuts (2 required)
2. Exhaust manifold heat shield bolt (2 required)
3. Exhaust manifold heat shield
4. Exhaust manifold nut (8 required)
5. Exhaust manifold
6. Exhaust manifold gasket (2 required)
7. Exhaust manifold stud (8 required)

Fig. 158 Exploded view of the RH exhaust manifold

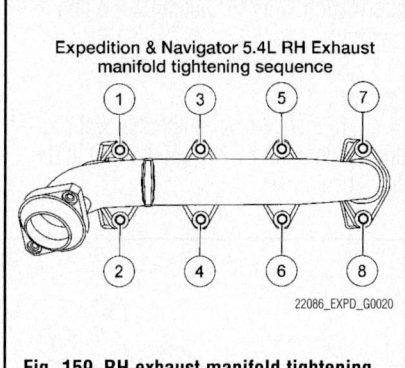

Fig. 159 RH exhaust manifold tightening sequence

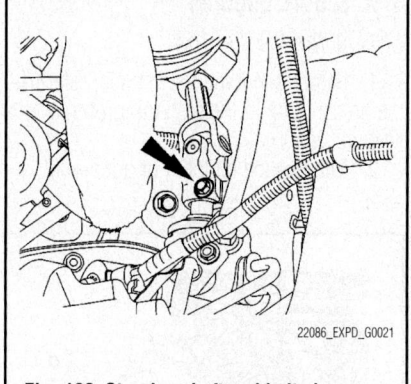

Fig. 160 Steering shaft and bolt view

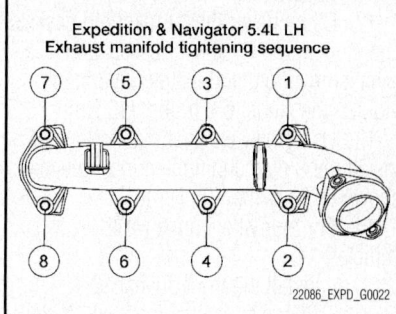

Fig. 162 LH exhaust manifold tightening sequence

6. Remove the 8 exhaust manifold nuts, studs and the exhaust manifold. Discard the exhaust manifold nuts and studs.

7. Remove and discard the exhaust manifold gaskets. Clean the sealing surfaces with metal surface prep.

8. Inspect the exhaust manifold.

To install:

9. Using new exhaust manifold gaskets and studs, position the 2 gaskets and exhaust manifold and install the 8 studs. Tighten the studs to 9 ft. lbs. (12 Nm).

10. Using new exhaust manifold nuts, install the 8 nuts and tighten in sequence shown to 18 ft. lbs. (25 Nm).

11. Position the exhaust manifold heat shield and install the 2 bolts. Tighten to 89 inch lbs. (10 Nm).

12. Install the RH engine support insulator and tighten the 2 stud bolts to 11 ft. lbs. (15 Nm).

13. Tighten the RH insulator bracket bolts to 46 ft. lbs. (63 Nm).

14. Install the RH inner fender well.

Left Side

See Figures 160 through 162.

1. Before servicing the vehicle, refer to the precautions section.

2. With the vehicle in NEUTRAL, position it on a hoist.

3. Remove the air cleaner outlet tube.

4. Remove the degas bottle.

❄❄ WARNING

Do not allow the steering column shaft to rotate while the intermediate shaft is disconnected or damage to the clock spring can result. If there is evidence that the shaft has rotated, the clockspring must be removed and recentered.

5. Remove the bolt and disconnect the steering shaft and position aside.

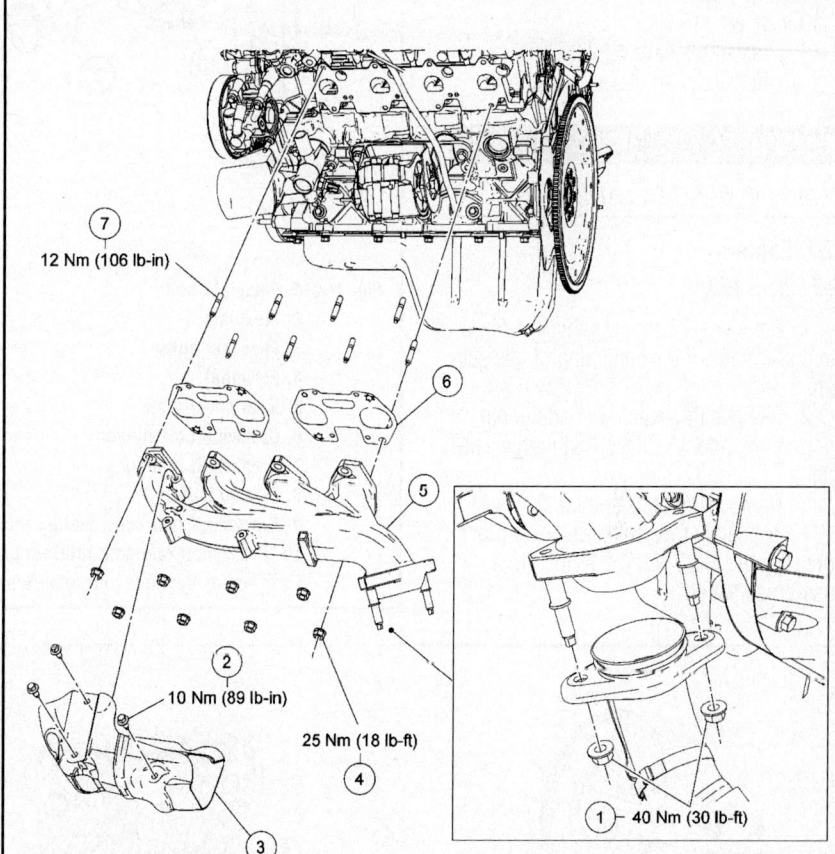

1. Exhaust Y-pipe flange nuts (2 required)
2. Exhaust manifold heat shield bolt (3 required)
3. Exhaust manifold heat shield
4. Exhaust manifold nut (8 required)
5. Exhaust manifold
6. Exhaust manifold gasket (2 required)
7. Exhaust manifold stud (8 required)

Fig. 161 Exploded view of the LH exhaust manifold

6. Remove the 4 (2 LH and 2 RH) exhaust manifold-to-catalytic converter nuts.

7. Remove the 3 bolts and the exhaust manifold heat shield.

8. Four wheel drive (4WD) vehicles:
   a. Remove the front driveshaft.

9. All vehicles: Remove the 8 exhaust manifold nuts, studs and the exhaust manifold.

10. Remove and discard the exhaust manifold gaskets. Clean the sealing surfaces with metal surface prep.

11. Inspect the exhaust manifold.

To install:

12. Using new exhaust manifold gaskets and studs, position the 2 gaskets and exhaust manifold and install the 8 studs. Tighten the studs to 9 ft. lbs. (12 Nm).

13. Using new exhaust manifold nuts, install the 8 nuts and tighten in sequence shown to 18 ft. lbs. (25 Nm).

14. For four wheel drive (4WD) vehicles:

   a. Install the front driveshaft.

   b. Connect the steering shaft, install and tighten bolt to 22 ft. lbs. (30 Nm).

   c. Install the 4 exhaust manifold-to-catalytic converter nuts.

   d. Position the exhaust manifold heat shield and install the 2 bolts. Tighten to 89 inch lbs. (10 Nm).

   e. Install the degas bottle.

   f. Install the air cleaner outlet tube.

FLYWHEEL

REMOVAL & INSTALLATION

4.2L Engine

See Figure 163.

1. Before servicing the vehicle, refer to the precautions in the beginning of this section.

2. Remove the clutch. For additional information, refer to Clutch R&I in this section.

3. Remove the bolts and the flywheel.

4. To install, reverse the removal procedure. Tighten to 80 Nm (59 ft. lbs.) in a criss-cross pattern.

4.6L & 5.4L Engines

See Figures 164 and 165.

1. Before servicing the vehicle, refer to the precautions in the beginning of this section.

2. Remove the clutch. For additional information, refer to Clutch R&I in this section.

3. Remove the 8 bolts and the flywheel.

4. To install, reverse the removal procedure. Tighten to 80 Nm (59 ft. lbs.) in the sequence shown.

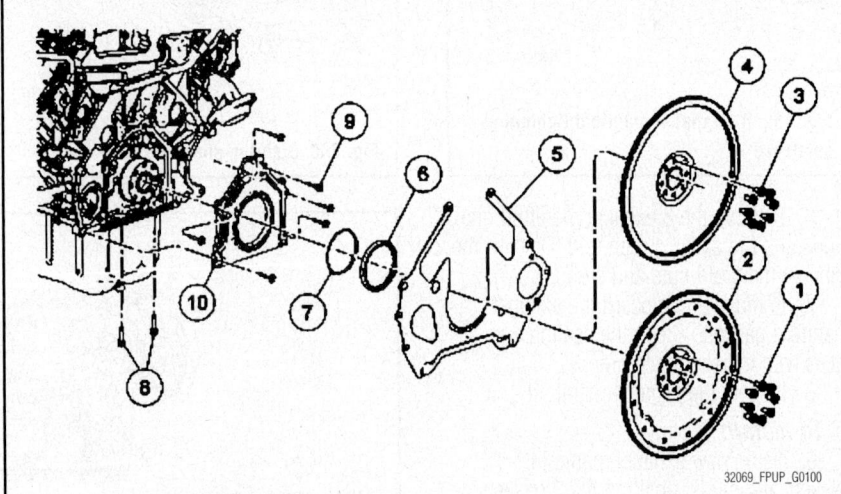

Fig. 164
1. Flexplate bolts
2. Flexplate
3. Flywheel bolts
4. Flywheel
5. Rear cover plate
6. Crankshaft oil slinger
7. Crankshaft rear seal
8. Oil pan bolts
9. Crankshaft rear seal retainer plate bolts
10. Crankshaft rear seal retainer plate
Flywheel or flexplate and related parts—4.6L, 5.4L and 6.8L engine

32069_FPUP_G0100

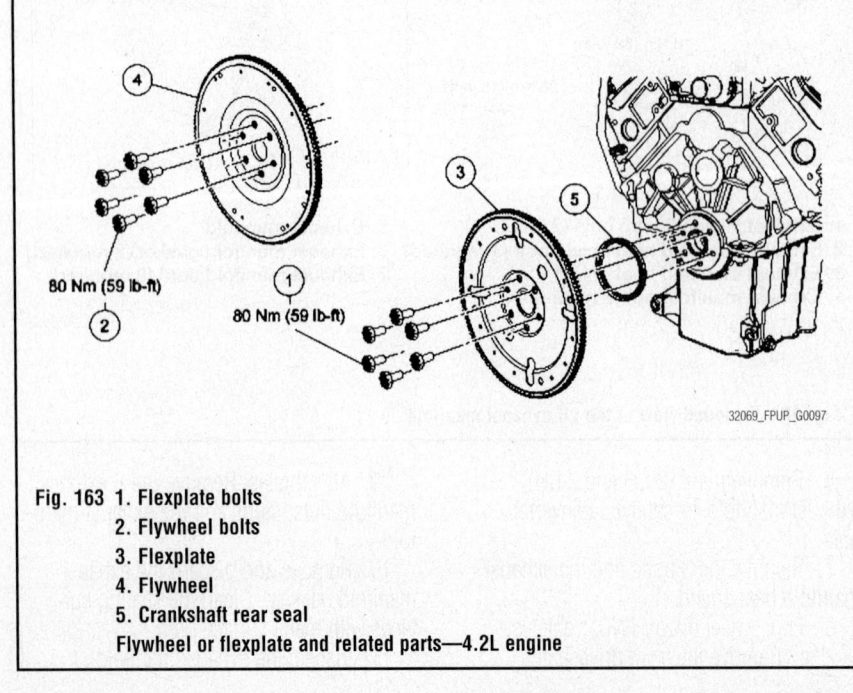

80 Nm (59 lb-ft)

80 Nm (59 lb-ft)

32069_FPUP_G0097

Fig. 163
1. Flexplate bolts
2. Flywheel bolts
3. Flexplate
4. Flywheel
5. Crankshaft rear seal
Flywheel or flexplate and related parts—4.2L engine

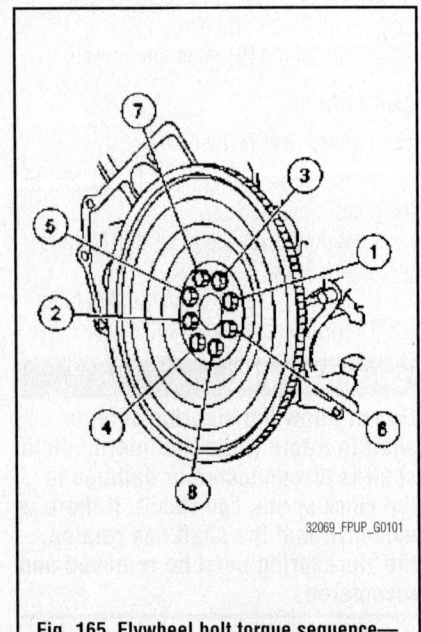

32069_FPUP_G0101

Fig. 165 Flywheel bolt torque sequence—4.6L, 5.4L and 6.8L engine

FLEXPLATE

REMOVAL & INSTALLATION

4.2L Engine

See Figure 163.

1. Before servicing the vehicle, refer to the precautions in the beginning of this section.
2. Remove the transmission. For additional information, refer to Automatic Transmission R&I in this section.
3. Remove the bolts and the flexplate.
4. To install, reverse the removal procedure. Tighten to 80 Nm (59 ft. lbs.) in a criss-cross pattern.

4.6L Engine

See Figures 166 and 167.

1. Before servicing the vehicle, refer to the precautions in the beginning of this section.
2. Raise and safely support the vehicle.
3. Remove the transmission. For additional information, refer to Automatic Transmission R&I in this section.

4. Remove the 6 flexplate bolts and the flexplate.

To install:

5. Install the flexplate and the 6 bolts. Tighten the bolts in 2 stages in the sequence shown.
   - Stage 1: Tighten to 20 Nm (15 inch lbs.).
   - Stage 2: Tighten to 80 Nm (59 ft. lbs.).
6. Install the transmission.

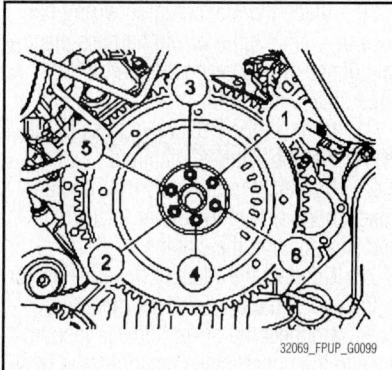

Fig. 167 Flexplate bolt torque sequence—4.6L engine

5.4L Engine

See Figure 168.

1. Before servicing the vehicle, refer to the precautions section.
2. Remove the transmission, as outlined in the Drive Train Section.
3. Remove the bolts and the flexplate.

To install:

4. Position the flexplate and install the bolts. Tighten the bolts in two stages:
   a. Stage 1: loosely install the bolts.
   b. Stage 2: tighten the bolts in sequence shown to 59 ft. lbs. (80 Nm).
5. Install the transmission.

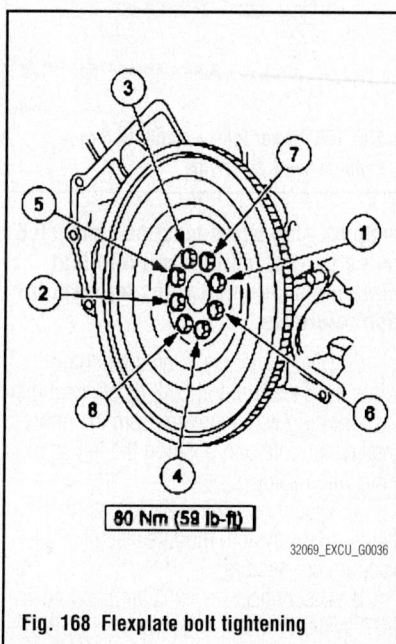

Fig. 168 Flexplate bolt tightening sequence

INTAKE MANIFOLD

REMOVAL & INSTALLATION

4.2L Engine

Upper

See Figure 169.

1. Before servicing the vehicle, refer to the Precautions Section.
2. Drain the engine cooling system.
3. Disconnect the battery ground cable.
4. Remove the air cleaner outlet pipe.
5. Remove the bolt and position the heater hoses aside.

❊❊ WARNING

It is important to twist the spark plug wire boots while pulling upward to avoid possible damage to the spark plug wire.

Fig. 166 1. Flexplate bolts
   2. Flexplate
   Flexplate and related parts—4.6L engine

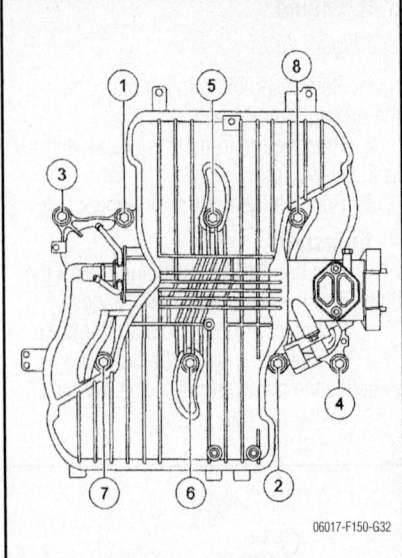

Fig. 169 Upper intake manifold torque sequence—4.2L engine

➡ **Spark plug wires must be connected to the correct ignition coil terminal. Mark the spark plug wires for installation reference.**

6. Disconnect the 3 left spark plug wires from the ignition coil, disconnect the 2 spark plug wire retainers from the upper intake manifold and position the left spark plug wires aside.

7. Disconnect the exhaust gas recirculation (EGR) system module electrical and vacuum connectors.

8. Disconnect the exhaust manifold-to-EGR system module tube from the EGR system module.

9. Disconnect the electronic throttle body electrical connector.

10. Release the clamp and disconnect the fuel vapor tube from the upper intake manifold.

11. Disconnect the 5 wiring harness retainers from the upper intake manifold.

12. Release the clamp and disconnect the brake booster vacuum hose from the upper intake manifold.

13. Disconnect the vacuum hose connector from the rear of the upper intake manifold.

14. Release the clamps and disconnect the 2 heated positive crankcase ventilation (PCV) coolant hoses from the rear of the upper intake manifold.

15. Disconnect the PCV valve hose from the rear of the upper intake manifold.

16. Detach the fuel charging wiring harness-to-main engine wiring harness electrical connector retainer from the rear of the upper intake manifold.

17. Remove the 8 bolts and the upper intake manifold.

To install:

18. Inspect the 6 upper intake manifold gaskets. Install new gaskets, if necessary.

19. Position the upper intake manifold and install the bolts. Tighten the bolts in the sequence shown in 2 stages.

- Stage 1: Tighten to 6 Nm (53 inch lbs.).
- Stage 2: Tighten to 10 Nm (89 inch lbs.).

20. Attach the fuel charging wiring harness-to-main engine wiring harness electrical connector retainer to the rear of the upper intake manifold.

21. Connect the PCV valve hose to the rear of the upper intake manifold.

22. Connect the 2 heated PCV coolant hoses to the rear of the upper intake manifold and position the clamps.

23. Connect the vacuum hose connector to the rear of the upper intake manifold.

24. Connect the brake booster vacuum hose to the upper intake manifold and position the clamp.

25. Connect the 5 wiring harness retainers to the upper intake manifold.

26. Connect the fuel vapor hose to the upper intake manifold and position the clamp.

27. Connect the electronic throttle body electrical connector.

28. Connect the exhaust manifold-to-EGR system module tube to the EGR system module. Tighten to 40 Nm (30 ft. lbs.).

29. Connect the EGR system module electrical and vacuum connectors.

➡ **Apply silicone brake caliper grease and dielectric compound to the inside of the spark plug wire boots.**

➡ **Spark plug wires must be connected to the correct ignition coil terminals.**

30. Position the spark plug wires, connect the 2 spark plug wire retainers to the upper intake manifold and connect the 3 spark plug wires to the ignition coil.

31. Position the heater hoses and install the bolt. Tighten to 5 Nm (44 inch lbs.).

32. Install the air cleaner outlet pipe.

33. Connect the battery ground cable.

34. Fill and bleed the engine cooling system.

Lower

See Figures 170 and 171.

1. Before servicing the vehicle, refer to the Precautions Section.

2. Relieve the fuel system pressure.

3. Disconnect the fuel supply spring lock coupling.

4. Remove the upper intake manifold. See the procedure above.

5. Disconnect the fuel charging wiring harness-to-main engine wiring harness and the intake manifold runner control (IMRC) actuator electrical connectors.

6. Remove the bolts and the fuel rail, the fuel charging wiring harness and the engine vacuum hose harness as an assembly.

7. Release the clamp and disconnect the heater outlet hose.

8. Release the clamp and disconnect the upper radiator hose.

9. Release the clamp and disconnect the bypass hose.

10. Release the clamp and disconnect the heater inlet hose.

11. Remove the 6 long and 8 short bolts, the lower intake manifold, the lower intake manifold gaskets and the front and rear seals.

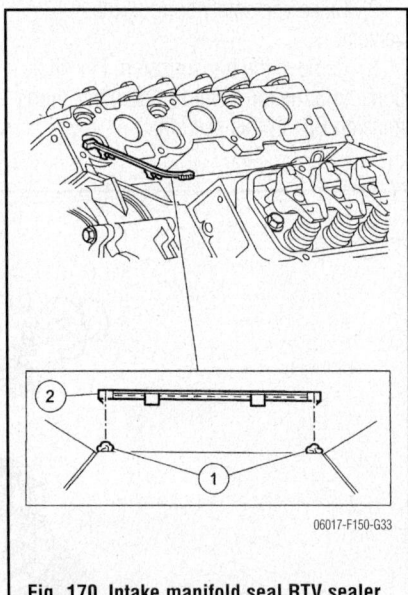

Fig. 170 Intake manifold seal RTV sealer application points—4.2L engine

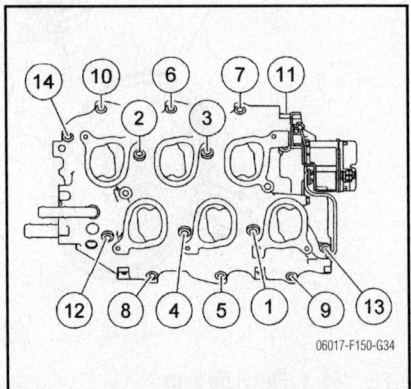

Fig. 171 Intake manifold bolt torque sequence—4.2L engine

To install:

✹✹ WARNING

Do not use metal scrapers, wire brushes, power abrasive discs or other abrasive means to clean the sealing surfaces. These tools cause scratches and gouges which make leak paths. Use a plastic scraping tool to remove all traces of old sealant.

12. Using a plastic scraping tool, silicone gasket remover and metal surface prep, clean the gasket mating surfaces. Follow the directions on the packaging.

➡ **If the lower intake manifold is not secured within 4 minutes, the sealant must be removed and the sealing area cleaned. To clean the sealing area, use silicone gasket remover and metal sur-** face prep. Follow the directions on the packaging. Failure to follow this procedure can cause future oil leakage.

13. Apply a bead of silicone gasket and sealant to the intake manifold front and rear seal mounting points as indicated.

14. Install the lower intake manifold front and rear seals.

4.6L Engine—2V

See Figures 172 and 173.

1. Before servicing the vehicle, refer to the Precautions Section.
2. Release the fuel system pressure.
3. Disconnect the battery ground cable.
4. Drain the cooling system.
5. Remove the 8 ignition coils.
6. Remove the generator.
7. Remove the EGR system module-to-exhaust manifold tube.

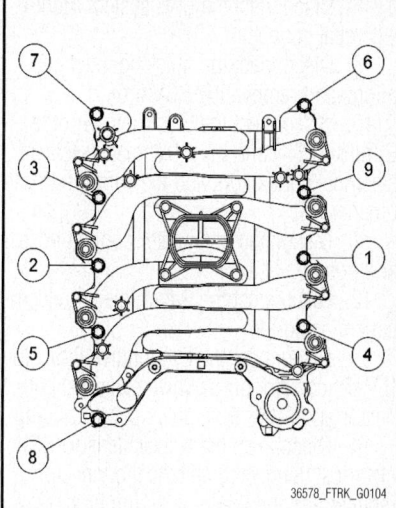

36578_FTRK_G0104

Fig. 173 Intake manifold tightening sequence

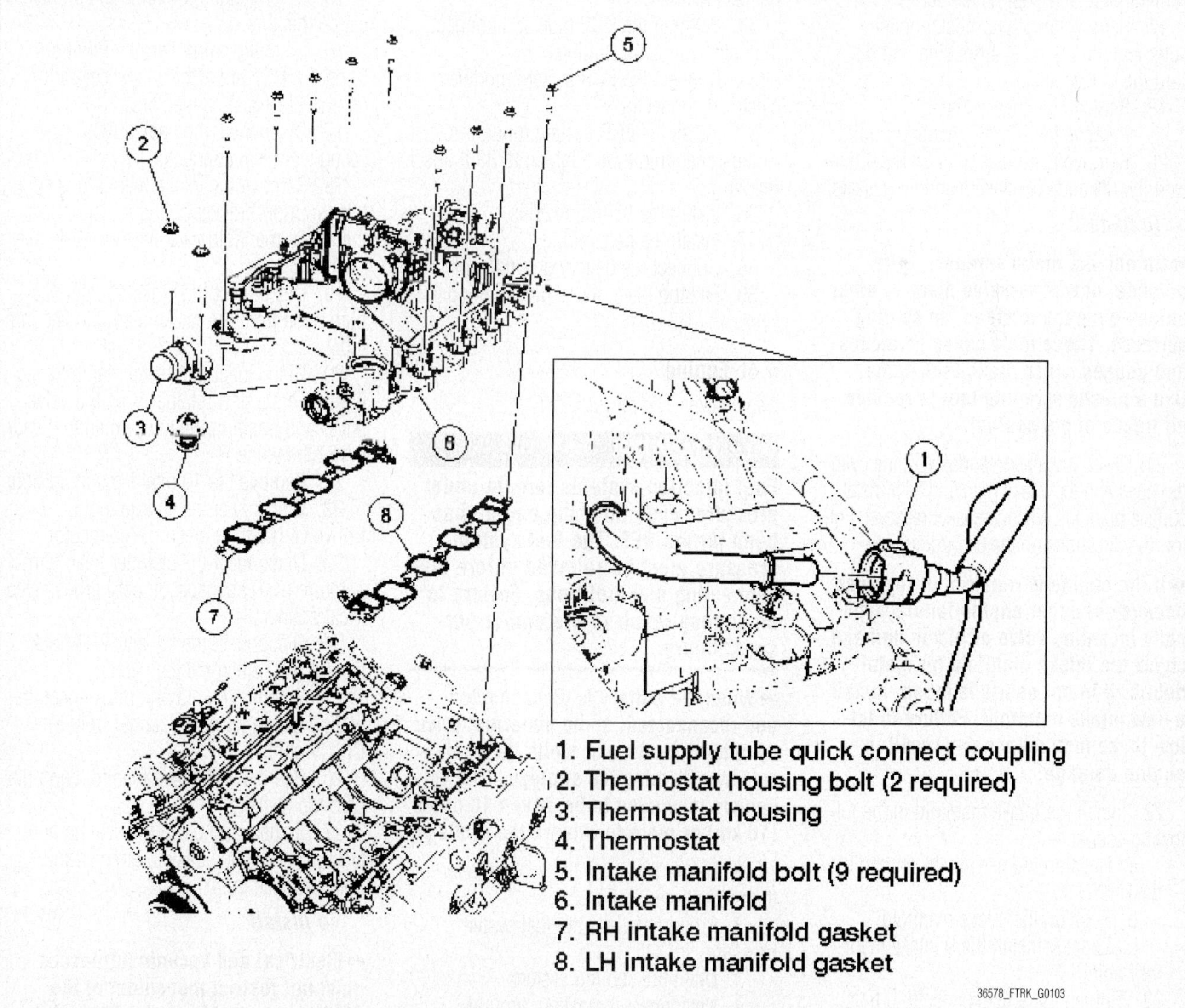

1. Fuel supply tube quick connect coupling
2. Thermostat housing bolt (2 required)
3. Thermostat housing
4. Thermostat
5. Intake manifold bolt (9 required)
6. Intake manifold
7. RH intake manifold gasket
8. LH intake manifold gasket

36578_FTRK_G0103

Fig. 172 Exploded view of the intake manifold, coolant crossover manifold and gasket assembly

8. Disconnect the EGR system module electrical connector.

9. Disconnect the quick connect couplings and remove the PCV tube.

10. Disconnect the Electronic Throttle Control (ETC) and the PCV heater element electrical connectors and the wiring harness retainer.

11. Disconnect the heater coolant hose and position aside.

12. Disconnect the 8 fuel injector electrical connectors.

13. Disconnect the Evaporative Emission (EVAP) canister purge valve electrical connector and EVAP tube quick connect fitting.

14. Disconnect the Knock Sensor (KS) electrical connector, electrical connector retainer and the 2 engine wiring harness retainers to the rear of the intake manifold.

15. Disconnect the brake booster vacuum hose.

16. Disconnect the upper radiator coolant hose and position aside.

17. Remove the 2 thermostat housing bolts and the thermostat housing and discard the O-ring seal.

18. Remove the thermostat.

19. Remove the 9 intake manifold bolts.

20. Remove the intake manifold and discard the RH and LH intake manifold gaskets.

To install:

➡ **Do not use metal scrapers, wire brushes, power abrasive discs or other abrasive means to clean the sealing surfaces. These tools cause scratches and gouges which make leak paths. Use a plastic scraping tool to remove all traces of old sealant.**

21. Clean the mating surfaces of the cylinder head and the intake manifold with metal surface prep and silicone gasket remover. Follow the directions on the packaging.

➡ **If the engine is repaired or replaced because of upper engine failure, typically including valve or piston damage, check the intake manifold for metal debris. If metal debris is found, install a new intake manifold. Failure to follow these instructions can result in engine damage.**

22. Install the intake manifold in the following sequence:

   a. Position the new intake manifold gaskets.

   b. Position the intake manifold.

   c. Loosely install the 9 intake manifold bolts.

23. Tighten the 9 intake manifold bolts in the sequence to 89 inch lbs. (10 Nm).

24. Install the thermostat, a new thermostat housing O-ring seal, the thermostat housing and the 2 bolts. Tighten to 18 ft. lbs. (25 Nm).

25. Connect the upper radiator coolant hose.

26. Connect the fuel supply tube quick connect coupling.

27. Connect the brake booster vacuum hose.

28. Connect the KS electrical connector, electrical connector retainer and the 2 engine wiring harness retainers to the rear of the intake manifold.

29. Connect the EVAP canister purge valve electrical connector and the EVAP tube quick connect fitting.

30. Connect the 8 fuel injector electrical connectors.

31. Connect the heater coolant hose.

32. Connect the ETC and the PCV heater element electrical connectors and the wiring harness retainer.

33. Position the PCV tube and connect the quick connect couplings.

34. Connect the EGR system module electrical connector.

35. Install the EGR system module-to-exhaust manifold tube. Tighten to 30 ft. lbs. (40 Nm).

36. Install the 8 ignition coils.

37. Install the generator.

38. Connect the battery ground cable.

39. Fill and bleed the engine cooling system.

5.4L Engine

See Figures 174 through 176.

✳✳ CAUTION

Fuel injection systems remain under pressure, even after the engine has been turned OFF. The fuel system pressure must be relieved before disconnecting any fuel lines. Failure to do so may result in fire and/or personal injury.

➡ **When the battery is disconnected and reconnected, some abnormal drive symptoms may occur while the vehicle relearns its adaptive strategy. The vehicle may need to be driven 10 miles (16 km) or more to relearn the strategy.**

1. Before servicing the vehicle, refer to the precautions section.

2. Properly relieve the fuel system pressure.

3. Drain the cooling system.

4. Disconnect the battery ground cable.

5. Disconnect the fuel supply hose spring lock coupling from the fuel rail.

6. Remove the generator.

7. Remove the air cleaner outlet pipe.

8. Disconnect the crankcase ventilation tube quick connect coupling from the intake manifold.

9. Disconnect the quick connect coupling and remove the evaporative emissions system (EVAP) hose from the intake manifold.

10. Disconnect the EVAP hose position retainer from the intake manifold.

11. Remove the 4 bolts and the air cleaner outlet pipe-to-TB adapter

12. Disconnect the heater coolant hose from the coolant bypass tube.

13. Disconnect the quick connect couplings and remove the positive crankcase ventilation (PCV) tube. For additional information

14. Disconnect the 8 fuel injector electrical connectors.

15. Disconnect the 8 ignition coil electrical connectors.

16. Disconnect the Throttle Position Sensor (TPS) and electronic acceleration control electrical connectors

17. Disconnect the heated PCV intake fitting electrical connector.

18. Remove the intake manifold vacuum tube support bracket bolt and disconnect the intake manifold vacuum tube-to-intake manifold hose.

19. Disconnect the brake booster vacuum hose from the intake manifold vacuum tube.

20. Disconnect the intake manifold vacuum tube support retainer from the valve cover and position the intake manifold vacuum tube aside

21. Remove the 10 intake manifold bolts.

22. Disconnect the charge motion control valve (CMCV) electrical connector.

23. Disconnect the cylinder head temperature (CHT) sensor jumper harness electrical connector.

24. Disconnect the LH and RH knock sensor (KS) electrical connectors.

25. Remove the nut and disconnect the engine wiring harness retainer from the CMCV stud.

26. Remove the intake manifold and discard the gaskets.

27. Inspect and clean the sealing surfaces with silicone gasket remover and metal surface prep.

To install:

➡ **Electrical and vacuum harnesses must not restrict movement of the CMCV control rods at rear of the intake manifold. Use extreme care on instal-**

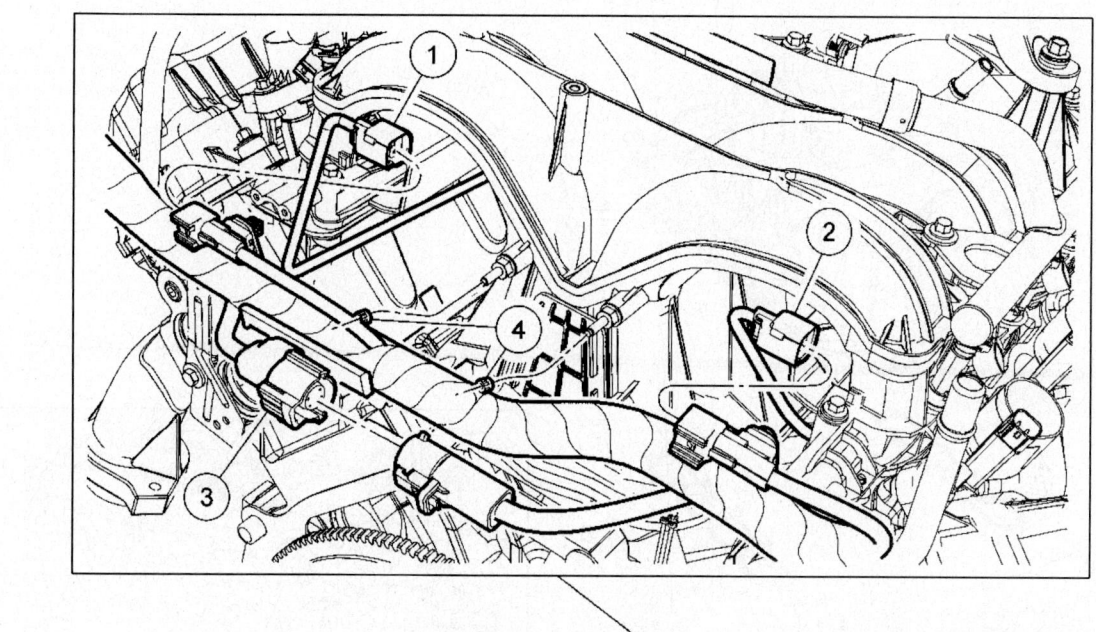

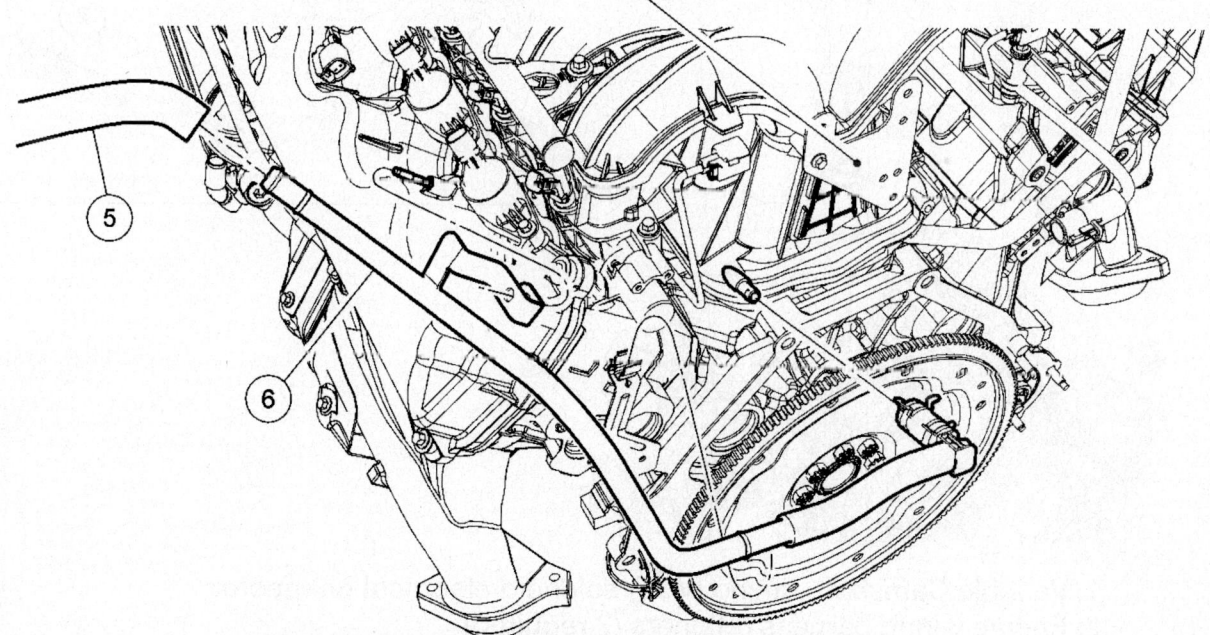

1. LH Knock Sensor (KS) electrical connector
2. RH KS electrical connector
3. Cylinder Head Temperature (CHT) electrical connector
4. Electrical wiring harness retainers
5. Brake booster vacuum hose
6. Intake manifold vacuum tube assembly

36578_EXPD_G0089

Fig. 174 View of the intake manifold vacuum tube assembly

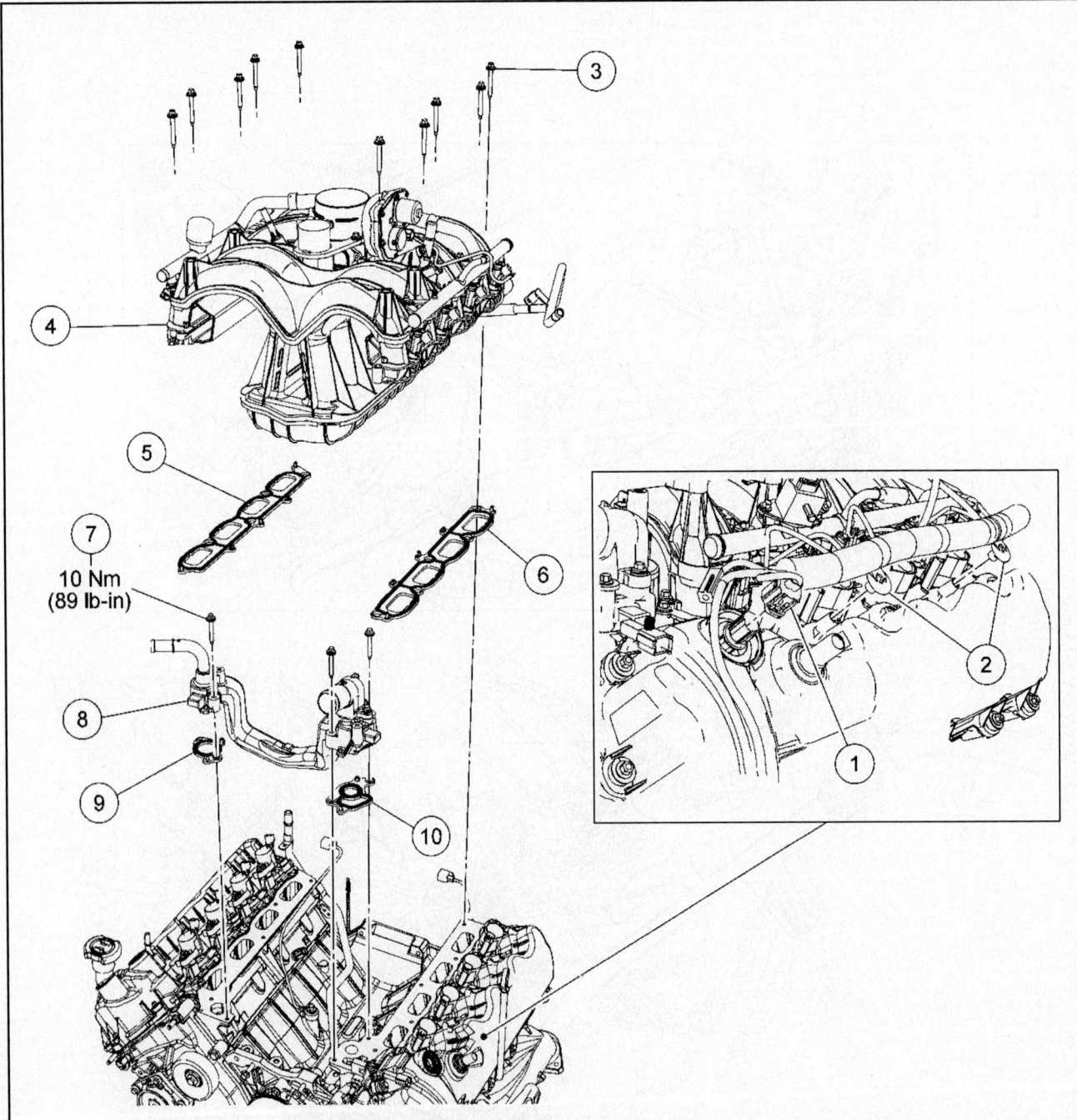

1. Variable Camshaft Timing (VCT) solenoid electrical connector
2. Engine wiring harness retainers (2 required)
3. Intake manifold bolt (10 required)
4. Intake manifold
5. RH intake manifold gasket
6. LH intake manifold gasket
7. Coolant crossover manifold assembly bolt (3 required)
8. Coolant crossover manifold assembly
9. RH coolant crossover manifold assembly gasket
10. LH coolant crossover manifold assembly gasket

36578_EXPD_G0090

Fig. 175 Exploded view of the intake manifold, coolant crossover manifold and gasket assembly

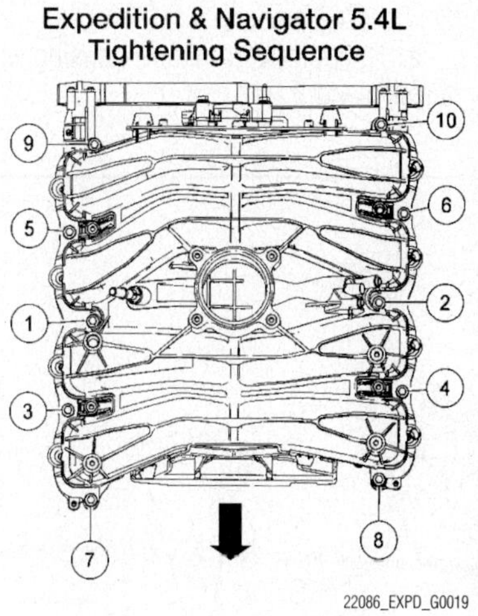

Expedition & Navigator 5.4L
Tightening Sequence

22086_EXPD_G0019

Fig. 176 Intake manifold tightening sequence

lation of the intake manifold to prevent any pinching of electrical and vacuum harnesses.

28. Using new intake manifold gaskets, position the intake manifold.

29. Connect the engine wiring harness retainer to the CMCV stud and install the nut. Tighten nut to 89 inch lbs. (10 Nm).

30. Connect the CMCV electrical connector.

31. Connect the CHT sensor jumper harness electrical connector.

32. Connect the LH and RH KS electrical connectors.

33. Install the intake manifold bolts and tighten in 2 stages, in the sequence shown.

   a. Stage 1: Tighten to 18 inch lbs. (2 Nm).

   b. Stage 2: Tighten to 89 inch lbs. (10 Nm).

34. Install the intake manifold vacuum tube support bracket bolt and connect the intake manifold vacuum tube-to-intake manifold hose. Tighten to 89 inch lbs. (10 Nm).

35. Connect the intake manifold vacuum tube support retainer to the valve cover and position the intake manifold vacuum tube aside

36. Connect the brake booster vacuum hose to the intake manifold vacuum tube.

37. Connect the heated PCV intake fitting electrical connector.

38. Connect the TPS and electronic acceleration control electrical connectors.

39. Connect the 8 fuel injector electrical connectors.

40. Connect the 8 ignition coil electrical connectors.

41. Position the air cleaner outlet pipe-to-TB adapter and install the 4 bolts. Tighten to 89 inch lbs. (10 Nm).

42. Connect the crankcase ventilation tube quick connect coupling to the intake manifold.

43. Position the EVAP hose and connect the quick connect coupling to the intake manifold.

44. Connect the EVAP hose position retainer to the intake manifold.

45. Position the PCV tube and connect the quick connect couplings.

46. Connect the heater coolant hose to the coolant bypass.

47. Connect the fuel supply spring lock coupling to the fuel rail.

48. Install the generator.

49. Install the air cleaner outlet pipe.

50. Connect the battery ground cable.

51. Fill and bleed the engine cooling system.

OIL PAN

REMOVAL & INSTALLATION

4.2L Engine

See Figure 177.

1. Before servicing the vehicle, refer to the Precautions Section.

✳✳ WARNING

During engine repair procedures, cleanliness is extremely important.

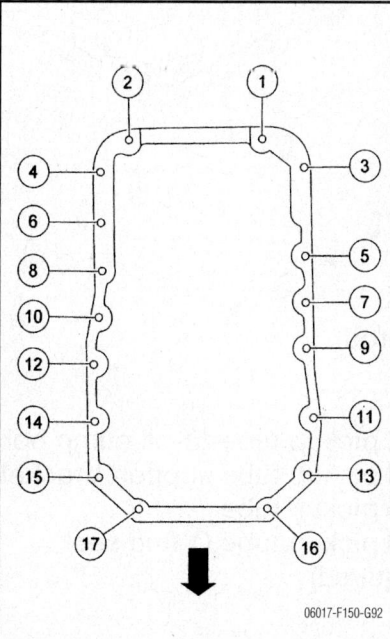

06017-F150-G92

Fig. 177 Oil pan torque sequence—4.2L engine

Any foreign material, including any material created while cleaning gasket surfaces, that enters the oil passages, coolant passages or the oil pan can cause engine failure.

2. Raise and safely support the vehicle.

3. Remove the starter.

4. Drain the engine oil. Install the drain plug when finished.

5. Remove the 4 bolts and the crossmember.

6. Remove the 3 oil pan-to-transmission bolts.

7. Remove the 17 bolts and the oil pan.

8. Remove and discard the oil pan rear seal.

To install:

✳✳ WARNING

Do not use metal scrapers, wire brushes, power abrasive discs or other abrasive means to clean the sealing surfaces. These tools cause scratches and gouges which make leak paths. Use silicone gasket remover and a plastic scraping tool to remove all traces of old sealant. Follow the directions on the packaging.

9. Clean the gasket mating surfaces using silicone gasket remover, a plastic scraping tool and metal surface prep. Follow the directions on the packaging.

➡ If the oil pan is not secured within 4 minutes, the sealant must be removed and the sealing areas cleaned. To clean the sealing area, use silicone gasket remover and metal surface prep. Follow the directions on the packaging. Failure to follow this procedure can cause future oil leakage.

10. Apply silicone gasket and sealant to the oil pan sealing areas shown and install the oil pan rear seal.

11. Apply silicone gasket and sealant to the rear main bearing cap.

12. Install the oil pan rear seal.

13. Apply a bead of silicone gasket and sealant to the oil pan mating surface.

14. Position the oil pan and install the bolts. Tighten the bolts in the sequence shown. Tighten to 10 Nm (89 inch lbs.).

15. Install the 3 oil pan-to-transmission bolts. Tighten to 34 Nm (25 ft. lbs)

16. Install the starter.

17. Position the crossmember and install the 4 bolts. Tighten to 90 Nm (66 ft. lbs.).

4.6L & 5.4L Engines

See Figures 178 and 179.

1. Before servicing the vehicle, refer to the precautions section.

2. Drain the engine oil.

3. Remove the bolts and the frame crossmember.

4. Remove the nut and remove the starter wiring harness and transmission fluid cooler tube support brackets from the stud bolt.

5. Remove the bolt and detach the wire harness bracket.

6. On 4WD models:

   a. Support the front axle housing with a jack stand.

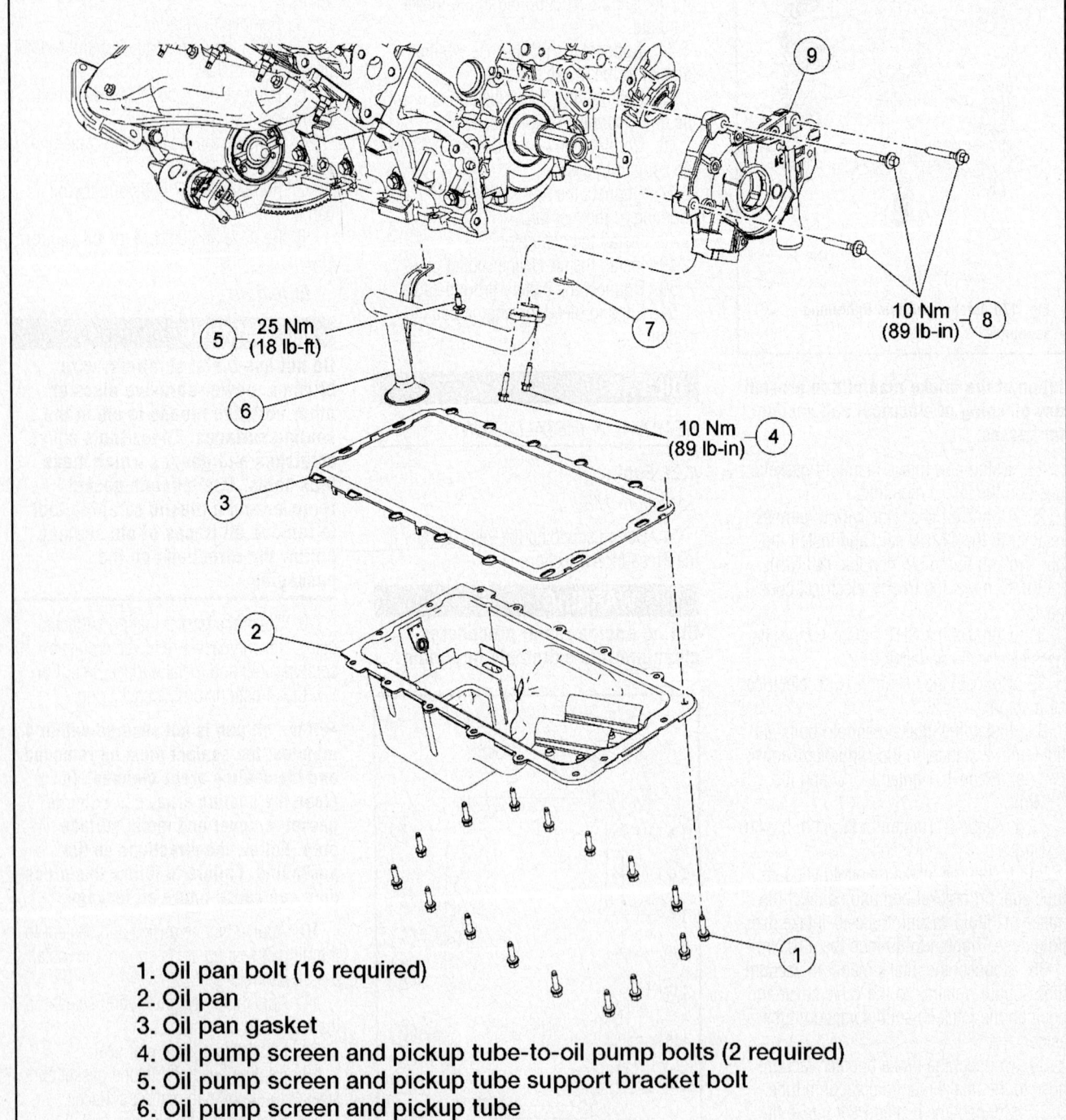

1. Oil pan bolt (16 required)
2. Oil pan
3. Oil pan gasket
4. Oil pump screen and pickup tube-to-oil pump bolts (2 required)
5. Oil pump screen and pickup tube support bracket bolt
6. Oil pump screen and pickup tube
7. Oil pump screen and pickup tube O-ring seal
8. Oil pump bolts (3 required)
9. Oil pump

36578_EXPD_G0091

Fig. 178 Exploded view of the engine lubrication system assembly

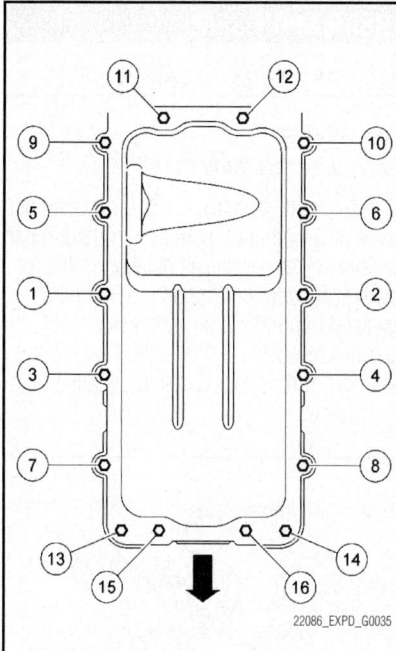

Fig. 179 Oil pan tightening sequence—5.4L engine

➡**Mark the bolt and bracket so that alignment can be maintained on installation.**

b. Remove the front axle housing right hand mounting bolt.

➡**Mark the bolt and brackct so that alignment can be maintained on installation.**

c. Remove the front axle housing left hand front mounting bolt.

➡**Mark the bolt and bracket so that alignment can be maintained on installation**

d. Remove the front axle housing left hand rear mounting bolt.

✷✷ CAUTION

Use care when lowering the front axle housing, or the vacuum lines to the axle solenoid may become disconnected or damaged.

e. Lower the axle to allow clearance for the oil pan to be removed.

➡**Be careful when removing the oil pan gasket. It is reusable.**

7. Remove the 16 bolts, the oil pan and the gaskets. Inspect the oil pan gasket for damage.

8. If damaged, discard the oil pan gasket and the oil pan-to-oil pump gaskets.

To install:

✷✷ CAUTION

Do not use metal scrapers, wire brushes, power abrasive discs or other abrasive means to clean the sealing surfaces. These tools cause scratches and gouges, which make leak paths. Use a plastic scraping tool to remove all traces of old sealant.

9. Inspect the oil pan. Clean the mating surface for the oil pan with silicone gasket remover and metal surface prep.

➡**If not secured within four minutes, the sealant must be removed and the sealing area cleaned. To clean the sealing area, use silicone gasket remover and metal surface prep. Follow the directions on the packaging. Failure to follow this procedure can cause future oil leakage.**

10. Apply silicone gasket and sealant at the crankshaft rear seal retainer plate-to-cylinder block sealing surface.

11. Apply silicone gasket and sealant at the engine front cover-to-cylinder block sealing surface.

12. Install the oil pan gasket and the oil pan and loosely install the 16 bolts.

13. Tighten the bolts in 3 steps, in the sequence illustrated.

a. Step 1: Tighten to 2 Nm (18 lb-in).

b. Step 2: Tighten to 15 ft. lbs. (20 Nm).

c. Step 3: Tighten an additional 60 degrees.

14. On 4WD models:

✷✷ CAUTION

Use care when positioning the front axle housing, or the vacuum lines to the axle solenoid may become disconnected or damaged.

a. Position the front axle housing and loosely install the three bolts, aligning the bolt location marks made during removal.

b. Install the front axle housing right hand mounting bolt. Tighten to 89 Nm (66 ft. lbs.).

c. Install the front axle housing left hand front mounting bolt. Tighten to 89 Nm (66 ft. lbs.).

d. Install the front axle housing left hand rear mounting bolt. Tighten to 89 Nm (66 ft. lbs.).

15. Position the frame crossmember and the 4 bolts. Tighten to 75 ft. lbs. (102 Nm).

16. Install the wire harness bracket and the bolt. Tighten to 89 inch lbs. (10 Nm).

17. Fill the crankcase with clean engine oil.

OIL PUMP

REMOVAL & INSTALLATION

4.2L Engine

See Figures 180.

1. Before servicing the vehicle, refer to the Precautions Section.

2. Raise and safely support the vehicle.

3. Drain the engine oil. Install the drain plug when finished.

4. Remove and discard the oil filter.

5. Remove the 6 bolts and the oil pump.

✷✷ WARNING

Do not reuse the oil pump seal. A new service seal must be installed.

6. Remove and discard the oil pump seal.

7. Remove and inspect the oil pump drive gear, the driven gear and the cover. Install new components if necessary.

8. Inspect the face of the oil pump for flatness.

To install:

9. Install a new service oil pump seal on the oil pump.

➡**Lubricate the parts with clean engine oil before assembly.**

10. Install the oil pump drive gear, the driven gear and the cover.

11. Position the oil pump and install the bolts. Tighten the bolts as shown.

- Bolts numbered 1: Tighten to 10 Nm (89 inch lbs.).
- Bolts numbered 2: Tighten to 25 Nm (18 ft. lbs.).

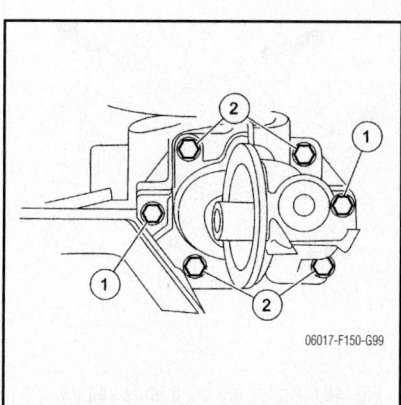

Fig. 180 Oil pump fasteners—4.2L engine

12. Install a new oil filter.
13. Fill the engine with clean engine oil.

4.6L & 5.4L Engines

See Figure 181.

1. Before servicing the vehicle, refer to the precautions section.
2. Disconnect the negative battery cable.
3. Remove the timing drive components.
4. Remove the oil pan.
5. Remove the 3 bolts and the oil pump screen and pickup tube.
6. Remove the 3 bolts and the oil pump.

To install:

➡ **Do not use metal scrapers, wire brushes, power abrasive discs or other abrasive means to clean the sealing surfaces. These tools cause scratches and gouges which make leak paths. Use a plastic scraping tool to remove all traces of old sealant.**

7. Clean the sealing surfaces with metal surface prep. Follow the directions on the packaging. Inspect the mating surfaces.
8. Position the oil pump and install the 3 bolts.

➡ **Make sure the O-ring is in place and not damaged. A missing or damaged O-ring can cause foam in the lubrication system, low oil pressure and severe engine damage.**

➡ **Clean and inspect the mating surfaces and install a new O-ring. Lubricate the O-ring with clean engine oil prior to installation.**

9. Position the oil pump screen and pickup tube and install the 3 bolts.
   a. Tighten the 2 oil pump screen and pickup tube-to-oil pump bolts to 10 Nm (89 lb-in).

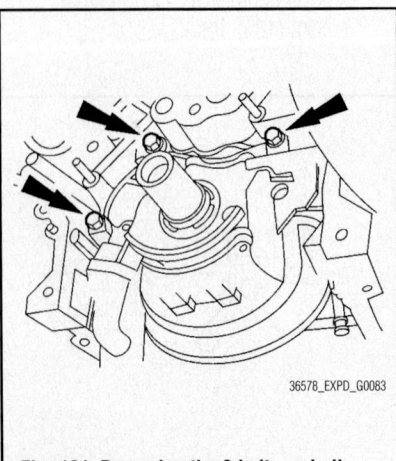

Fig. 181 Removing the 3 bolts and oil pump

b. Tighten the oil pump screen and pickup tube-to-spacer bolt to 25 Nm (18 lb-ft).
10. Install the oil pan.
11. Install the timing drive components.

PISTON AND RING

POSITIONING

See Figures 182 and 183.

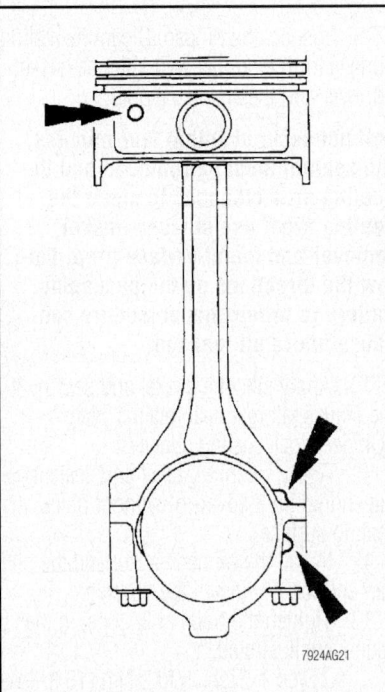

Fig. 182 Piston connecting rod to bearing cap orientation—all gasoline engines

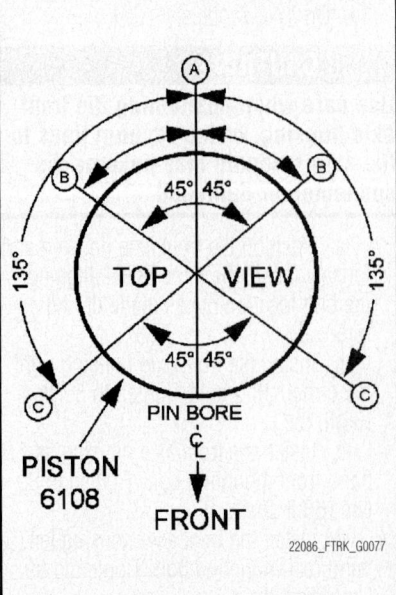

Fig. 183 Piston ring end gap positioning—all gasoline engines

REAR MAIN SEAL

REMOVAL & INSTALLATION

4.2L Engine

See Figures 184 through 187.

If the crankshaft rear oil seal replacement is the only operation being performed, it can be done in the vehicle as detailed in the following procedure. If the oil seal is being replaced in conjunction with a rear main bearing replacement, the engine must be removed from the vehicle and installed on a work stand.

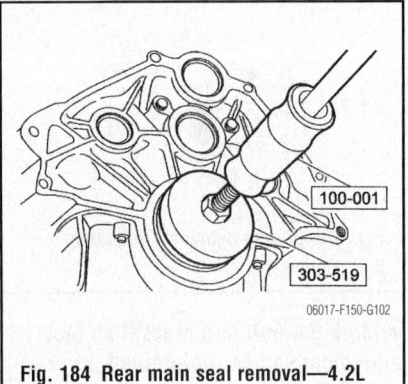

Fig. 184 Rear main seal removal—4.2L engine

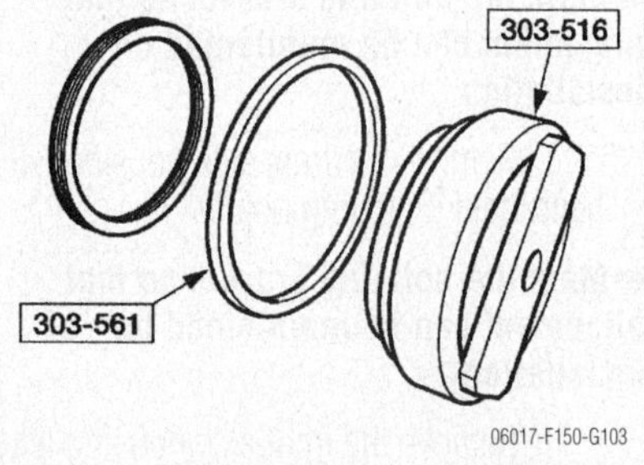

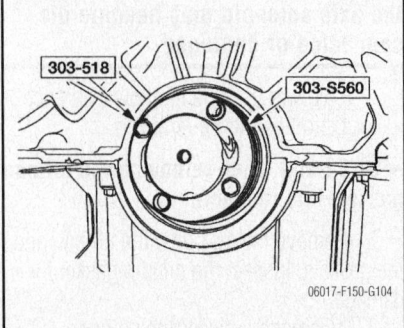

Fig. 185 Assembling the rear main seal and tools—4.2L engine

Fig. 186 Install tools 303-518 and 303-S560 on the crankshaft—4.2L engine

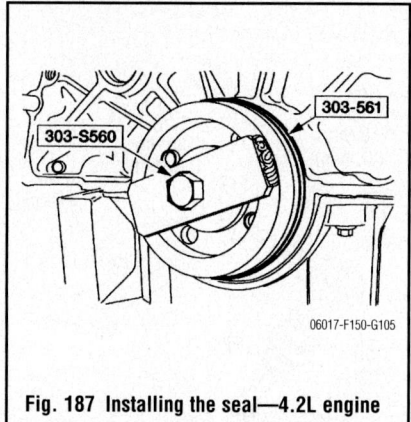

Fig. 187 Installing the seal—4.2L engine

1. Before servicing the vehicle, refer to the Precautions Section.
2. Disconnect the negative battery cable.
3. Remove the transmission from the vehicle.
4. Remove the flywheel/flexplate.
5. Use an appropriate seal removal tool to extract the rear crankshaft seal.
6. Clean the oil seal mating surface.

To install:

7. Coat the new oil seal and the crankshaft with a light film of engine oil.
8. Assemble the oil seal to the installer tool.
9. Install the oil seal until fully seated.
10. Install flywheel.
11. Install the transmission, following the recommended procedure.
12. Install the negative battery cable.

4.6L & 5.4L Engines

See Figures 188 through 192.

1. Before servicing the vehicle, refer to the precautions section.
2. Disconnect the negative battery cable.
3. Remove the transmission.
4. Remove the 8 bolts and the flexplate

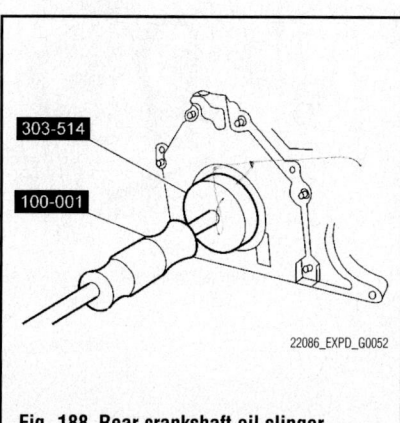

Fig. 188 Rear crankshaft oil slinger removal

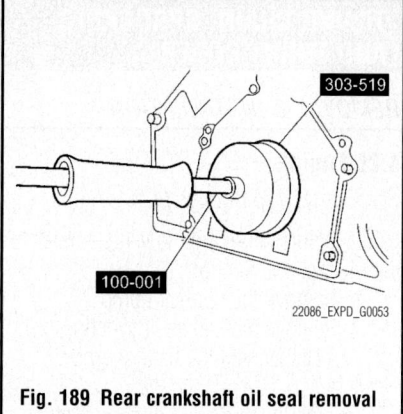

Fig. 189 Rear crankshaft oil seal removal

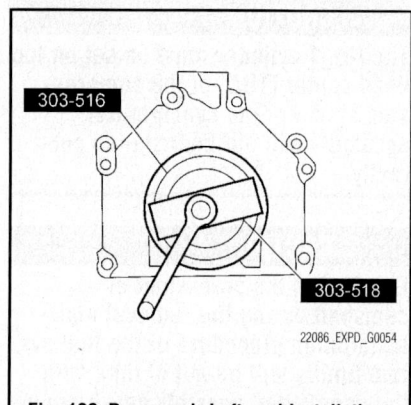

Fig. 190 Rear crankshaft seal installation

5. Using the special tools 303-514 and 108-001, remove the crankshaft oil slinger.
6. Using the special tools 303-519 and 100-001, remove the crankshaft rear seal.

To install:

7. Lubricate the inner lip of the crankshaft rear seal with clean engine oil.
8. Using the special tools 303-516 and 303-518, install a new crankshaft rear seal.
9. Using the special tools 303-516, 303-517 and 303-518, install a new crankshaft rear oil slinger.

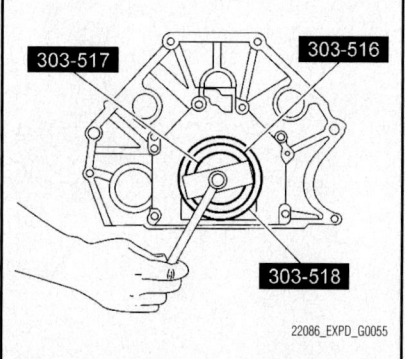

Fig. 191 Rear crankshaft oil slinger installation

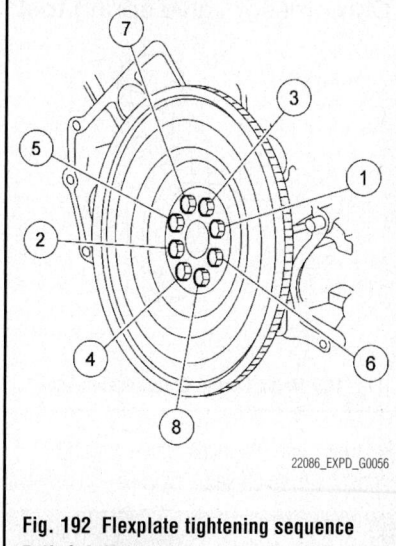

Fig. 192 Flexplate tightening sequence 5.4L & 6.8L engines

10. Install the flexplate and tighten the 8 bolts in the sequence shown to 59 ft. lbs. (80 Nm).
11. Install the transmission.

ROCKER ARMS/SHAFTS

REMOVAL & INSTALLATION

4.2L Engine

1. Before servicing the vehicle, refer to the Precautions Section.

➡**If removing more than 1 rocker arm, mark the components for proper location.**

2. Before servicing the vehicle, refer to the Precautions Section.
3. Disconnect the negative battery cable.
4. Remove the rocker arm cover.
5. Remove the rocker arm hold-down bolt, then remove the rocker arm from the cylinder head.

To install:

6. Position the rocker arms in place, then install the hold-down bolts. Tighten the bolts in 2 passes to:
   • Step 1: 44 inch lbs. (5 Nm)
   • Step 2: 24 ft. lbs. (32 Nm)
7. Install the rocker arm cover.
8. Connect the negative battery cable.

4.6L & 5.4L Engines

See Figures 193 and 194.

1. Depending on the camshaft roller follower being serviced, remove the LH or RH valve cover.
2. Rotate the crankshaft until the piston for the valve being serviced is at the top of

Compressor valve spring tool

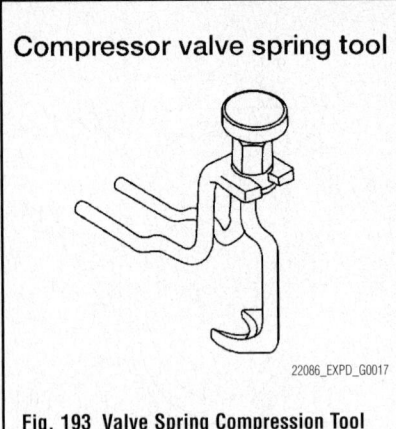

22086_EXPD_G0017

Fig. 193 Valve Spring Compression Tool

its stroke with the intake valve and the exhaust valves closed.

※※ WARNING

If the components are to be reinstalled, they must be installed in the same position. Mark the components for installation into the original location.

3. Using the special tool, compress the valve spring and remove the camshaft roller follower.

4. Repeat the previous 2 steps for each camshaft roller follower being serviced.

5. Inspect the camshaft roller follower.

To install:

➡Lubricate the camshaft roller followers with clean engine oil prior to installation.

6. Using the special tool, compress the valve spring and install the camshaft roller follower.

7. Repeat the previous step for each camshaft roller follower being serviced.

8. Depending on the camshaft roller follower being serviced, install the LH or RH valve cover.

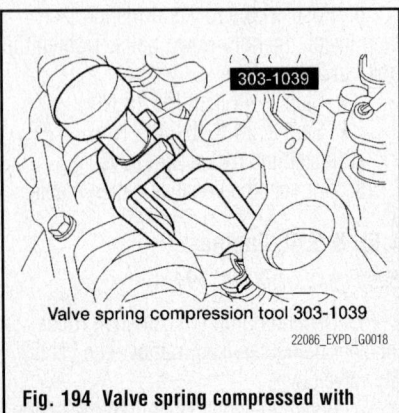

303-1039

Valve spring compression tool 303-1039

22086_EXPD_G0018

Fig. 194 Valve spring compressed with tool 303-1039 shown

TIMING CHAIN, SPROCKETS AND FRONT COVER

REMOVAL & INSTALLATION

4.2L Engine

See Figures 195 through 200.

1. Before servicing the vehicle, refer to the Precautions Section.

2. Remove the coolant pump.

3. Remove the camshaft synchronizer:

   a. Disconnect the battery ground cable.

   b. Drain the engine cooling system.

※※ CAUTION

The No. 1 cylinder must be set on top dead center (TDC) of the compression stroke or the synchronizer assembly will not be installed correctly.

※※ CAUTION

Do not turn the crankshaft or camshaft during the removal and installation procedure or the fuel system timing will be out of time with the engine and possibly cause engine damage.

   c. Rotate the crankshaft until the No. 1 cylinder is at TDC of the compression stroke.

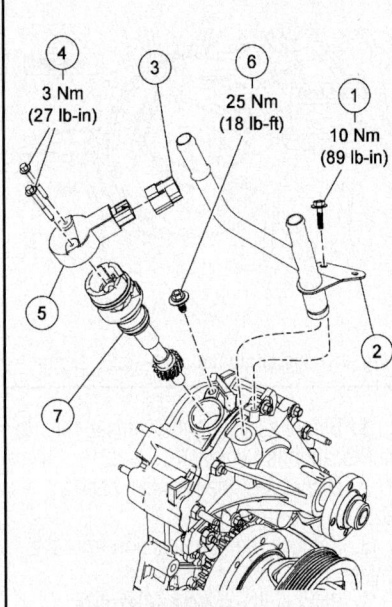

1. Heater outlet tube bolt
2. Heater outlet tube
3. Camshaft position (CMP) sensor electrical connector
4. CMP sensor bolts (2 required)
5. CMP sensor
6. Camshaft synchronizer bolt and washer assembly
7. Camshaft synchronizer

22086_FTRK_G0068

Fig. 196 Exploded view of the camshaft synchronizer and components

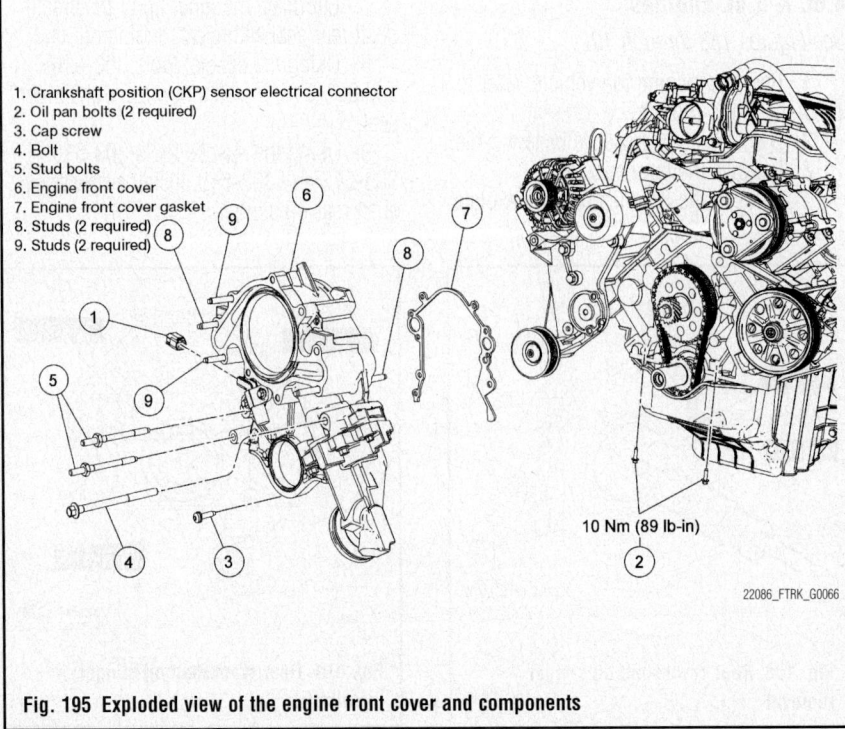

1. Crankshaft position (CKP) sensor electrical connector
2. Oil pan bolts (2 required)
3. Cap screw
4. Bolt
5. Stud bolts
6. Engine front cover
7. Engine front cover gasket
8. Studs (2 required)
9. Studs (2 required)

10 Nm (89 lb-in)

22086_FTRK_G0066

Fig. 195 Exploded view of the engine front cover and components

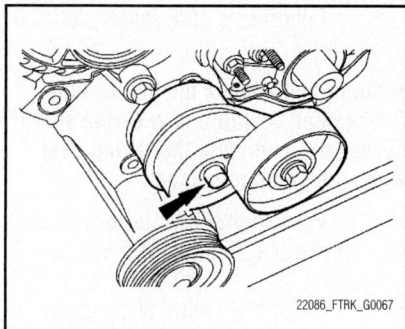

Fig. 197 Remove the bolt and the accessory drive belt tensioner

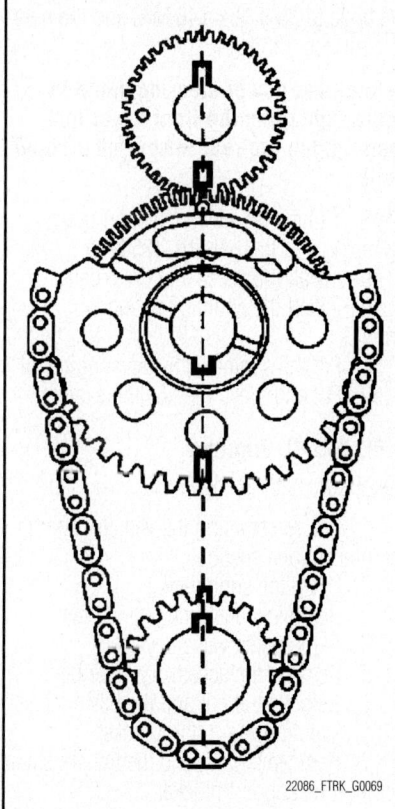

Fig. 198 Remove the bolt and the accessory drive belt tensioner

d. Remove the bolt and position the heater outlet tube aside.

e. Disconnect the camshaft position (CMP) sensor electrical connector.

f. Remove the bolts and the CMP sensor.

g. Remove the bolt and washer assembly and remove the camshaft synchronizer.

4. Remove the crankshaft front seal.

5. Disconnect the crankshaft position (CKP) sensor electrical connector.

6. Detach the wiring harness retainers from the engine front cover stud bolts.

7. Drain the engine oil. Install the drain plug when finished. Tighten to 17 ft. lbs. (23 Nm).

8. Remove the oil filter.

9. Remove the 2 oil pan-to-engine front cover bolts.

10. If equipped, remove the retaining nut and position the transmission coolant tube support bracket aside.

11. Remove the bolt and the accessory drive belt tensioner.

12. Loosen the 4 power steering pump bolts and slide the power steering pump out approximately 25 mm (1 in).

13. Remove the bolt and the A/C compressor and power steering pump bracket brace.

❋❋ CAUTION

The cap screw is concealed by the oil pump housing. Failure to remove this retainer will result in damage to the engine front cover.

14. Remove the bolt and the stud bolts. Slide the engine front cover from the studs. Remove and discard the gasket.

➡ **There are 2 different studs. Note the locations of the studs for installation reference.**

15. Remove the 4 studs.

16. Remove the camshaft synchronizer drive gear:

    a. Remove the bolt.

    b. Remove the camshaft synchronizer drive gear.

17. Rotate the crankshaft until the timing marks and keyways align.

18. Compress and install a retaining pin to hold the timing chain tensioner.

19. Remove the camshaft sprocket, the crankshaft sprocket and the timing chain as an assembly.

20. Remove the bolts and the timing chain tensioner.

To install:

21. Install the timing chain tensioner and the bolts. Tighten to 9 ft. lbs. (12 Nm).

22. If necessary, retract the tensioner pad retracting mechanism and insert a retaining pin.

23. Rotate the crankshaft so the No. 1 piston is at top dead center (TDC) and the key is at the 12 o'clock position.

24. Turn the camshaft sprocket so that the timing mark is at the 12 o'clock position and is lined up with the timing mark on the balance shaft at the 6 o'clock position.

25. Install the timing chain, the camshaft sprocket and the crankshaft sprocket.

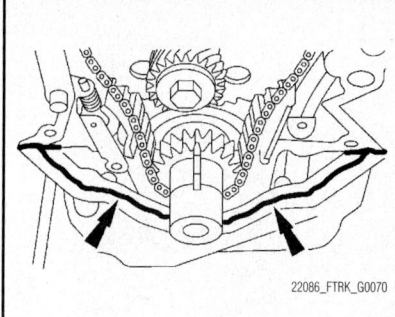

Fig. 199 Apply silicone gasket and sealant to the areas shown

26. Make sure that the timing marks and the keyways are aligned.

27. Remove the retaining pin.

28. Install the camshaft synchronizer drive gear and the bolt. Tighten to 33 ft. lbs. (45 Nm).

❋❋ CAUTION

In order to prevent foreign material from contaminating the engine block or the engine front cover, it is necessary to seal the coolant and oil passages of both components. Failure to follow these directions will result in engine damage.

❋❋ CAUTION

Do not use metal scrapers, wire brushes, power abrasive discs or other abrasive means to clean the sealing surfaces. These tools cause scratches and gouges which make leak paths. Use a plastic scraping tool to remove all traces of old sealant.

29. Clean and inspect the engine block and engine front cover as follows:

    a. Pack the exposed portion of the oil pan with clean shop towels.

    b. Plug the oil and coolant passages.

    c. Clean the gasket surfaces. Use silicone gasket remover and metal surface prep.

    d. Using compressed air, remove any remaining foreign material from the engine block and front cover.

    e. Remove the shop towels from the oil pan.

    f. Remove the plugs or seals from the oil and coolant passages.

30. Apply thread sealant to the threads on the studs and the cap screw.

31. Install the engine front cover studs. Tighten to 62 inch lbs. (7 Nm).

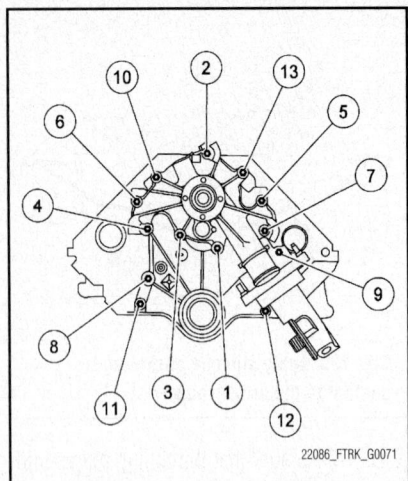

Fig. 200 Tighten the front cover screws in the sequence shown

22086_FTRK_G0071

➡If the engine front cover is not secured within 4 minutes, the sealant must be removed and the sealing areas cleaned. To clean the sealing area, use silicone gasket remover and metal surface prep. Failure to follow this procedure can cause future oil leakage.

32. Apply silicone gasket and sealant as shown.
33. Install the engine front cover gasket.

> ❋❋ **CAUTION**
>
> The coolant pump and gasket must be installed at this time to correctly tighten all of the engine front cover fasteners in sequence.

34. Install the engine front cover and coolant pump.
35. Position the engine front cover and install the bolt, the stud bolts and the cap screw finger tight.
36. Position a new coolant pump gasket and the coolant pump and install the fasteners finger tight.
37. Tighten the fasteners in the sequence shown
   a. Tighten capscrew No. 12 to 89 inch lbs. (10 Nm).
   b. Tighten all other fasteners to 21 ft. lbs. (28 Nm).
38. If equipped, position the transmission cooler tube bracket and install the nut. Tighten to 15 ft. lbs. (20 Nm).
39. Install the accessory drive belt tensioner and the bolt. Tighten to 41 ft. lbs. (55 Nm).
40. Install the 2 oil pan-to-engine front cover bolts. Tighten to 89 inch lbs. (10 Nm).
41. Install a new oil filter.

42. Connect the CKP sensor electrical connector.
43. Attach the wiring harness retainers to the engine front cover stud bolts.
44. Install the crankshaft front seal.
45. Install the camshaft synchronizer:

> ❋❋ **CAUTION**
>
> After installation, do not loosen the synchronizer bolt and rotate the synchronizer assembly. The synchronizer assembly is not adjustable. Do not loosen the synchronizer bolt after the alignment tool has been removed in order to align the CMP sensor electrical connector for any reason. If the electrical connector is not in the correct position, the synchronizer assembly must be removed, the alignment tool and the assembly reinstalled if the engine has not been rotated from TDC of the compression stroke on the No. 1 cylinder.

> ❋❋ **CAUTION**
>
> Do not turn the crankshaft or camshaft during the removal and installation procedure or the fuel system timing will be out of time with the engine and possibly cause engine damage.

> ❋❋ **CAUTION**
>
> A synchronizer alignment gauge must be used during the installation of the synchronizer assembly. Failure to follow these procedures will result in the fuel system being out of time with the engine and possibly cause engine damage.

   a. Install the special tool on the camshaft synchronizer by rotating the tool until it engages the notch on the camshaft synchronizer housing.

➡Coat the synchronizer drive gear with clean engine oil prior to installation.

➡During installation, the arrow in the synchronizer alignment tool will rotate clockwise as the gears engage.

   b. Install the camshaft synchronizer so the arrow on the synchronizer alignment gauge is 54 degrees from the centerline of the engine.
   c. Install the camshaft synchronizer bolt and washer assembly. Tighten to 18 ft. lbs. (25 Nm).
   d. Install the CMP sensor and the bolts.

   e. Connect the CMP sensor electrical connector.

➡Clean and inspect the heater tube O-ring seal. Install a new O-ring seal if necessary. Lubricate the O-ring seal with clean engine coolant.

   f. Position the heater outlet tube and install the bolt. Tighten to 89 inch lbs. (10 Nm).
46. Position the coolant pump pulley and install the bolts. Tighten to 89 inch lbs. (10 Nm).
47. Position the A/C compressor and power steering pump pulley bracket brace and install the 2 bolts and 2 nuts. Tighten the bolts to 35 ft. lbs. (48 Nm) and the nuts to 18 ft. lbs. (25 Nm).

➡Slide the power steering pump in while tightening the front lower bolt, then tighten the rear lower and 2 upper bolts.

48. Tighten the power steering pump bolts. Tighten to 18 ft. lbs. (25 Nm).
49. Install the accessory drive belt.
50. Install the cooling fan and fan shroud.
51. Fill the engine with clean engine oil.
52. Fill and bleed the cooling system.

4.6L & 5.4L Engines

See Figures 201 through 217.

1. Before servicing the vehicle, refer to the precautions section.
2. Drain the engine oil.
3. Remove the engine cooling fan.
4. Remove the valve covers.
5. Remove the accessory drive belt.
6. Remove the nut and the power steering pressure hose support bracket.
7. Remove the nut and the transmission cooler tube support bracket.
8. Remove the crankshaft pulley bolt and washer. Discard the crankshaft pulley bolt.
9. Using the tool 303-009, remove the crankshaft pulley.
10. Using the tool 303-107, remove the crankshaft front seal.
11. Remove the bolts and the accessory drive idler pulleys.
12. Remove the bolts and the coolant pump pulley.
13. Remove the bolts and the accessory drive belt tensioner.
14. Disconnect the right hand Camshaft Position (CMP) sensor. Discard the O-ring seal.
15. Disconnect the A/C compressor electrical connector.

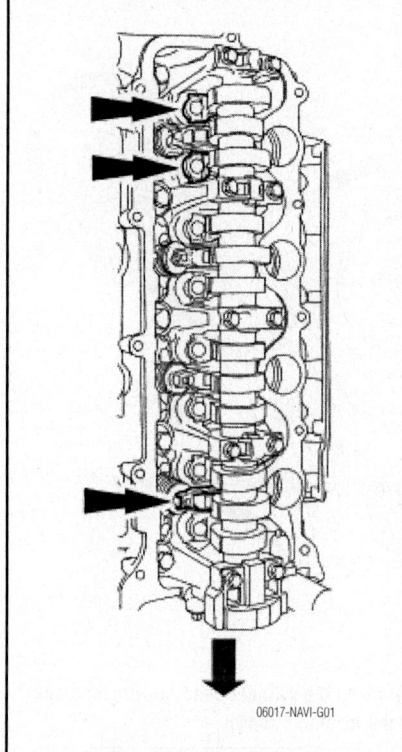

Fig. 201 Remove only the 3 roller followers shown from the right hand cylinder head

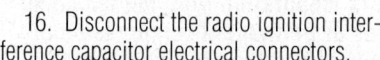

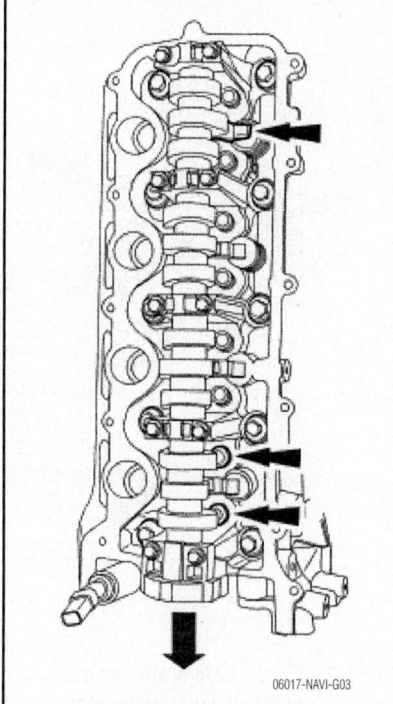

Fig. 203 Remove only the 3 roller followers shown from the left hand cylinder head

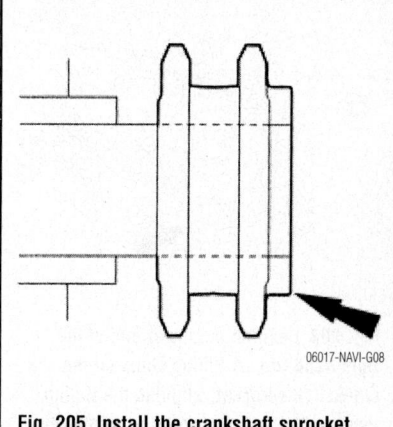

Fig. 205 Install the crankshaft sprocket, making sure the flange faces forward

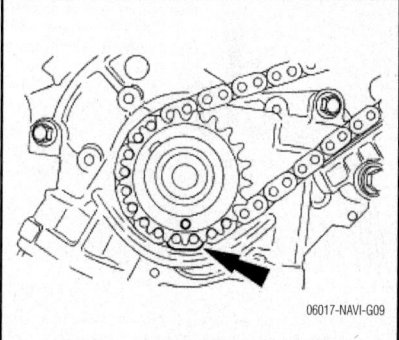

Fig. 206 Position the lower end of the left hand (inner) timing chain on the crankshaft sprocket, aligning the timing mark on the outer flange of the crankshaft sprocket with the single copper (marked) link on the chain

303-1039

Fig. 202 Remove the 3 designated roller followers from the right hand cylinder head

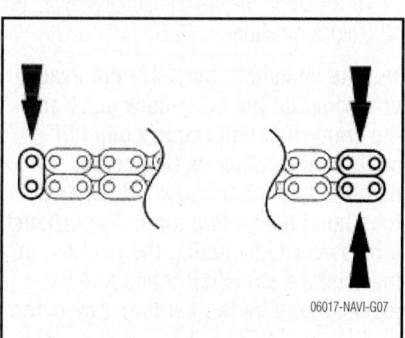

Fig. 204 If the copper links are not visible, mark two links on one end and one link on the other end, and use as timing marks

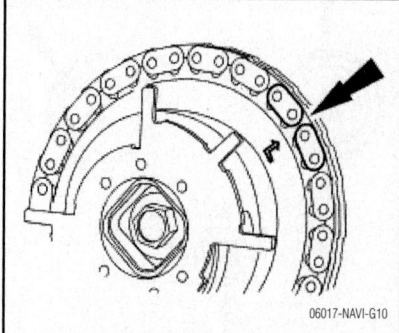

Fig. 207 Position the timing chain on the camshaft sprocket with the camshaft sprocket timing mark positioned between the two copper (marked) chain links

16. Disconnect the radio ignition interference capacitor electrical connectors.

17. Remove the nut and the right hand radio ignition interference capacitor.

18. Disconnect the left CMP sensor. Discard the O-ring seal.

19. Remove the nut and the left hand radio ignition interference capacitor.

20. Remove the bolts and position the power steering pump assembly aside.

21. Disconnect the wiring harness position retainer and the engine oil pressure (EOP) switch electrical connector and position the wiring harness aside.

22. Disconnect the Crankshaft Position (CKP) sensor connector.

23. Remove the 4 front oil pan bolts.

24. Remove the bolt and the CKP sensor. Discard the O-ring seal.

25. Remove the bolts and the studs from the front cover.

❊❊ CAUTION

Do not use metal scrapers, wire brushes, power abrasive discs or other abrasive means to clean the sealing surfaces. These tools cause scratches and gouges which make

leak paths. Use a plastic scraping tool to remove all traces of old sealant.

26. Remove the engine front cover from the front cover to cylinder block dowel.

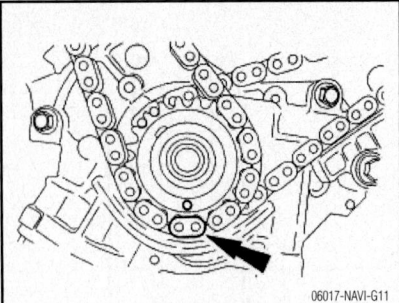

Fig. 208 Position the lower end of the right hand (outer) timing chain on the crankshaft sprocket, aligning the timing mark on the sprocket with the single copper (marked) chain link

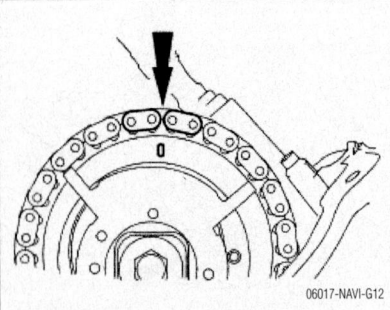

Fig. 209 Position the right hand timing chain on the camshaft sprocket. Make sure the camshaft sprocket timing mark is positioned between the two copper (marked) chain links

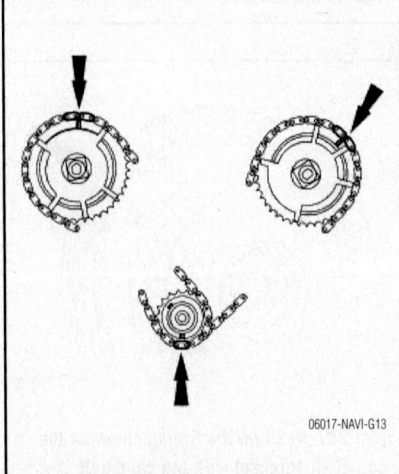

Fig. 210 Verify correct alignment of all timing marks

27. Remove the engine front cover gaskets.

28. Clean the mating surfaces with silicone gasket remover and metal surface prep. Follow the directions on the packaging.

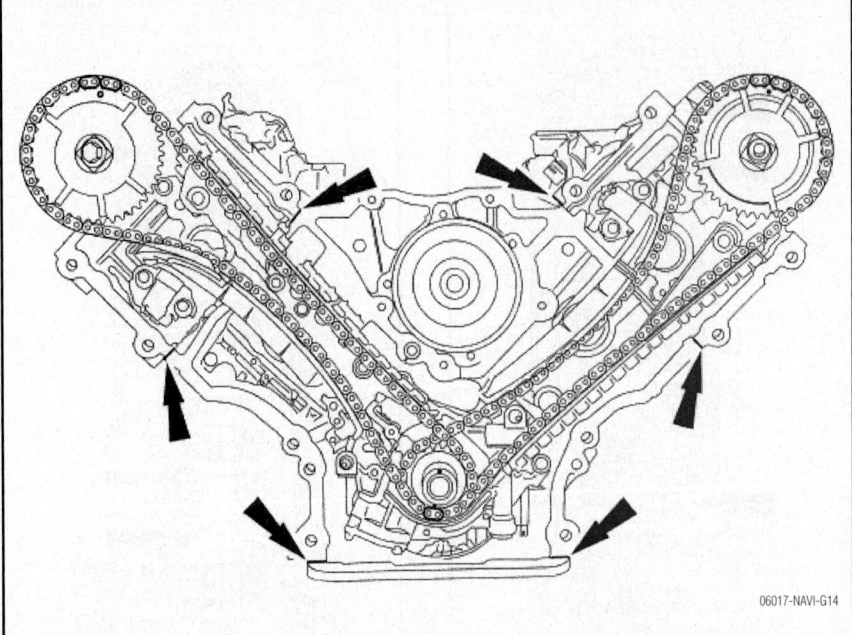

Fig. 211 Apply a bead of silicone gasket and sealant along the cylinder head-to-cylinder block surface and the oil pan-to-cylinder block surface, at the locations shown

29. Inspect the mating surfaces.

30. Remove the crankshaft sensor ring from the crankshaft.

31. Position the crankshaft keyway at the 12 o'clock position.

➡ If the camshaft lobes are not exactly positioned at the 12 o'clock position, the crankshaft will require one full additional rotation to 12 o'clock. The number 1 cylinder camshaft exhaust lobe must be coming up on the exhaust stroke. Verify by noting the position of the 2 intake camshaft lobes and the exhaust lobe on the number 1 cylinder.

➡ If the components are to be reinstalled, they must be installed in the same positions. Mark the components for installation into the original locations.

32. Remove only the 3 roller followers shown in the illustration from the right hand cylinder head.

✷✷ CAUTION

Do not allow the valve keepers to fall off the valve or the valve may drop into the cylinder.

➡ It may be necessary to push the valve down while compressing the spring.

33. Using the tool illustrated, remove the 3 designated roller followers in the previous step from the right hand cylinder head.

34. Remove only the 3 roller followers shown in the illustration from the left hand cylinder head.

35. Using the tool 303-1039, remove the 3 designated roller followers in the previous step from the left hand cylinder head.

✷✷ WARNING

The crankshaft cannot be moved past the 6 o'clock position once set.

36. Rotate the crankshaft clockwise and position the crankshaft keyway at the 6 o'clock position.

✷✷ CAUTION

If one or both of the tensioner mounting bolts are loosened or removed, the tensioner-sealing bead must be inspected for seal integrity. If cracks, tears, separation from the tensioner body or permanent compression of the seal bead is observed, install a new tensioner.

37. Remove the bolts, the left hand timing chain tensioner and tensioner arm.

38. Remove the bolts, the right hand timing chain tensioner and tensioner arm.

39. Remove the right hand and left hand timing chains and the crankshaft sprocket.

40. Remove the right hand timing chain from the camshaft sprocket.

41. Remove the right hand timing chain from the crankshaft sprocket.

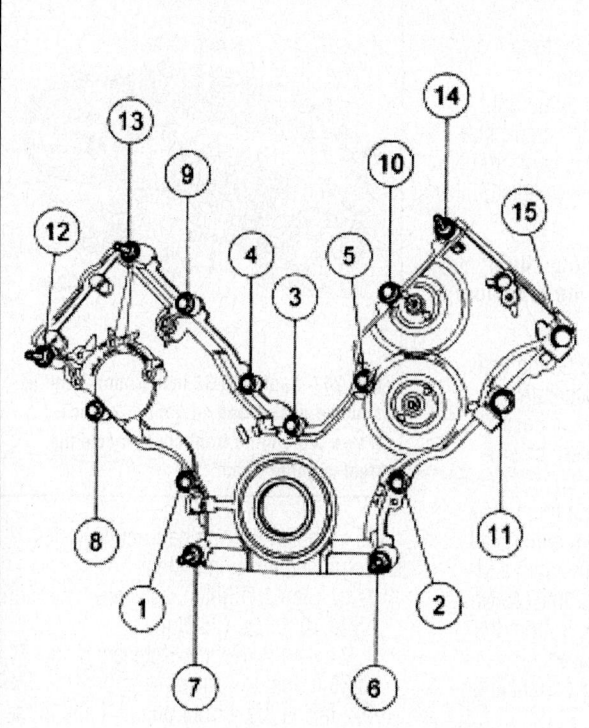

1 Bolt, Hex Flange Head Pilot, M8 x 1.25 x 50

2 Bolt, Hex Flange Head Pilot, M8 x 1.25 x 50

3 Bolt, Hex Flange Head Pilot, M8 x 1.25 x 50

4 Bolt, Hex Flange Head Pilot, M8 x 1.25 x 50

5 Bolts, Hex Flange Head Pilot, M8 x 1.25 x 50

6 Stud, Hex Head Pilot, M10 x 1.5 x 1.5 x 103

7 Stud, Hex Head Pilot, M10 x 1.5 x 1.5 x 103

8 Bolt, Hex Flange Head Pilot, M8 x 1.25 x 50

9 Bolt, Hex Flange Head Pilot, M8 x 1.25 x 50

10 Bolt, Hex Flange Head Pilot, M8 x 1.25 x 50

11 Bolt, Hex Flange Head Pilot, M8 x 1.25 x 50

12 Stud and Washer, Hex Head Pilot, M8 x 1.25 x 1.25 x 94

13 Stud and Washer, Hex Head Pilot, M8 x 1.25 x 1.25 x 94

14 Stud and Washer, Hex Head Pilot, M8 x 1.25 x 1.25 x 94

15 Bolt, Hex Head Pilot, M8 x 1.25 x 56

06017-NAVI-G15

Fig. 212 Engine front cover fastener location and torque sequence

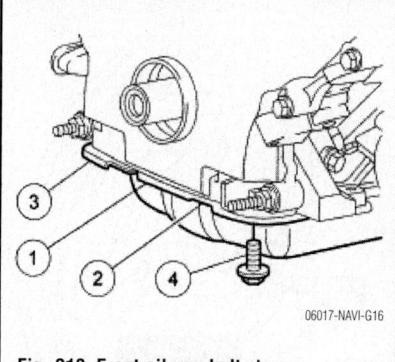

06017-NAVI-G16

Fig. 213 Front oil pan bolts torque sequence

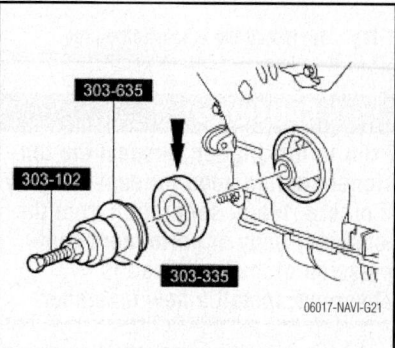

06017-NAVI-G21

Fig. 214 Install the crankshaft seal into the engine front cover

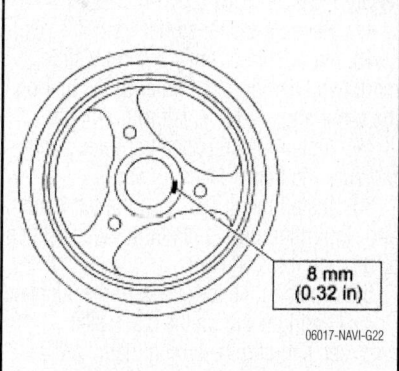

06017-NAVI-G22

Fig. 215 Apply a 0.32 inch (8mm) bead of silicone gasket and sealant to the Woodruff key slot on the crankshaft pulley

42. Remove the left hand timing chain from the camshaft sprocket.

43. Remove the left hand timing chain and crankshaft sprocket.

44. Remove the left hand and right hand timing chain guides.

To install:

❊❊ **CAUTION**

Timing chain procedures must be followed exactly or damage to valves and pistons will result.

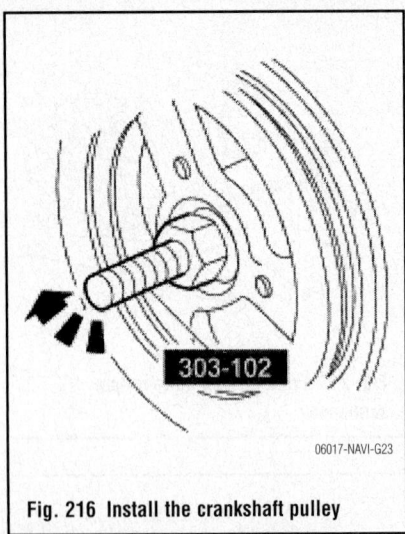

06017-NAVI-G23

Fig. 216 Install the crankshaft pulley

✳✳ CAUTION

Prior to installation, inspect the tensioner-sealing bead for seal integrity. If cracks, tears, separation from the tensioner body or permanent compression of the seal bead is observed, install a new tensioner.

45. Compress the tensioner plunger, using a vise.

46. Install a retaining clip on the tensioner to hold the plunger in during installation.

47. Remove the tensioner from the vise.

48. If the copper links are not visible, mark two links on one end and one link on the other end, and use as timing marks.

49. Install the crankshaft sprocket, making sure the flange faces forward.

50. Install the 4 bolts and the left hand and right hand timing chain guides. Tighten to 89 inch lbs. (10 Nm).

51. Position the lower end of the left hand (inner) timing chain on the crankshaft sprocket, aligning the timing mark on the outer flange of the crankshaft sprocket with the single copper (marked) link on the chain.

➡**Make sure the upper half of the timing chain is below the tensioner arm dowel.**

52. Position the timing chain on the camshaft sprocket with the camshaft sprocket timing mark positioned between the two copper (marked) chain links.

➡**The left hand timing chain tensioner arm has a bump near the dowel hole for identification.**

53. Position the left hand timing chain tensioner arm on the dowel pin and install the left hand timing chain tensioner and

bolts. Tighten the bolts to 18 ft. lbs. (25 Nm).

54. Remove the retaining clip from the left hand timing chain tensioner.

55. Position the lower end of the right hand (outer) timing chain on the crankshaft sprocket, aligning the timing mark on the sprocket with the single copper (marked) chain link.

➡**The lower half of the timing chain must be positioned above the tensioner arm dowel.**

56. Position the right hand timing chain on the camshaft sprocket. Make sure the camshaft sprocket timing mark is positioned between the two copper (marked) chain links.

57. Position the right hand timing chain tensioner arm on the dowel pin and install the right hand timing chain tensioner and bolts. Tighten the bolts to 18 ft. lbs. (25 Nm).

58. Remove the retaining clip from the right hand timing chain tensioner.

59. As a final-check, verify correct alignment of all timing marks.

60. Install the crankshaft sensor ring on the crankshaft.

61. Lubricate the roller followers with clean engine oil prior to installation.

62. Using tool 303-1039, install all of the camshaft roller followers.

✳✳ CAUTION

Do not use metal scrapers, wire brushes, power abrasive discs or other abrasive means to clean the sealing surfaces. These tools cause scratches and gouges which make leak paths. Use a plastic scraping tool to remove all traces of old sealant.

➡**If the engine front cover is not secured within 4 minutes, the sealant must be removed and the sealing area cleaned. To clean the sealing area, use silicone gasket remover and metal surface prep. Failure to follow this procedure can cause future oil leakage.**

➡**Make sure that the engine front cover gasket is in place on the engine front cover before installation.**

63. Apply a bead of silicone gasket and sealant along the cylinder head-to-cylinder block surface and the oil pan-to-cylinder block surface, at the locations illustrated.

64. Install a new engine front cover gasket on the engine front cover. Position the engine front cover onto the dowels. Install the fasteners finger-tight.

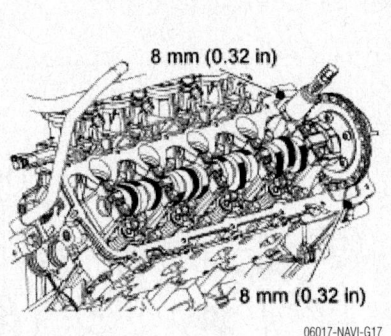

8 mm (0.32 in)

8 mm (0.32 in)

06017-NAVI-G17

Fig. 217 Apply a 0.32 inch (8mm) bead of silicone gasket and sealant in 2 places where the engine front cover meets the right cylinder head

65. Tighten the engine front cover fasteners in sequence in 2 steps:
   a. Step 1: Tighten fasteners 1 through 15 to 18 ft. lbs. (25 Nm).
   b. Step 2: Tighten fasteners 6 and 7 to 35 ft. lbs. (48 Nm).

66. Install the 4 front oil pan bolts in the sequence shown in 2 steps.
   a. Step 1: Tighten to 15 ft. lbs. (20 Nm).
   b. Step 2: Tighten an additional 60 degrees.

✳✳ CAUTION

Do not use metal scrapers, wire brushes, power abrasive discs or other abrasive means to clean sealing surfaces. These tools cause scratches and gouges which make leak paths. Use a plastic scraping tool to remove all traces of old sealant.

67. Connect the CKP sensor electrical connector.

68. Position the power steering pump assembly and install the bolts. Tighten to 18 ft. lbs. (25 Nm).

69. Position the power steering pressure hose support bracket and install the nut.

70. Position the transmission cooler tube support bracket and install the nut.

➡**Lubricate the O-ring seal with clean engine oil prior to installation.**

71. Using a new O-ring seal, install the right hand CMP sensor and the bolt.

72. Connect the right hand CMP sensor electrical connector.

73. Install the left hand radio ignition interference capacitor and the nut.

➡**Lubricate the O-ring seal with clean engine oil prior to installation.**

74. Using a new O-ring seal, install the left hand CMP sensor and the bolt.

75. Connect the left hand CMP sensor electrical connector.

76. Install the right hand radio ignition interference capacitor and the nut.

77. Connect the radio ignition interference capacitor electrical connectors.

78. Install the 3 accessory drive belt idler pulleys, the coolant pump pulley and the 7 bolts. Tighten the bolts to 18 ft. lbs. (25 Nm).

79. Lubricate the engine front cover and the crankshaft seal inner lip with clean engine oil.

80. Use the tools illustrated to install the crankshaft seal into the engine front cover.

➡**If not secured within 4 minutes, the sealant must be removed and the sealing area cleaned. To clean the sealing area, use silicone gasket remover and metal surface prep. Failure to follow this procedure can cause future oil leakage.**

81. Apply a 0.32 inch (8mm) bead of silicone gasket and sealant to the Woodruff key slot on the crankshaft pulley.

82. Use the tool illustrated to install the crankshaft pulley.

83. Tighten the new crankshaft pulley bolt in 4 steps:

  a. Step 1: Tighten to 66 ft. lbs. (90 Nm).

  b. Step 2: Loosen 360 degrees.

  c. Step 3: Tighten to 37 ft. lbs. (50 Nm).

  d. Step 4: Tighten an additional 90 degrees.

84. Install the accessory drive belt.

85. Clean the valve cover mating surface with silicone gasket remover and metal surface prep.

➡**If not secured within 4 minutes, the sealant must be removed and the sealing area cleaned. To clean the sealing area, use silicone gasket remover and metal surface prep. Failure to follow this procedure can cause future oil leakage.**

86. Apply a 0.32 inch (8mm) bead of silicone gasket and sealant in 2 places where the engine front cover meets the cylinder head.

⁂ **CAUTION**

When installing the valve cover, make sure to avoid damaging the Variable Camshaft Timing (VCT) solenoid.

87. Install the right hand valve cover and gasket on the cylinder head and tighten the bolts in sequence and tighten to 89 inch lbs. (10 Nm).

➡**If not secured within 4 minutes, the sealant must be removed and the sealing area cleaned. To clean the sealing area, use silicone gasket remover and metal surface prep. Failure to follow this procedure can cause future oil leakage.**

88. Apply a 0.32 inch (8mm) bead of silicone gasket and sealant in 2 places where the engine front cover meets the left cylinder head.

89. Install the left hand valve cover and gasket on the cylinder head and tighten the bolts in sequence shown and tighten to 89 inch lbs. (10 Nm).

90. Install the engine cooling fan.

91. Fill the crankcase with clean engine oil.

92. Check steering and transmission fluid, top off if needed.

93. Check all connections for leaks.

VALVE COVERS

REMOVAL & INSTALLATION

4.2L Engine

Left Side

See Figure 218.

1. Disconnect the crankcase breather hose.

2. Remove the bolt and position the oil level indicator and tube assembly aside.

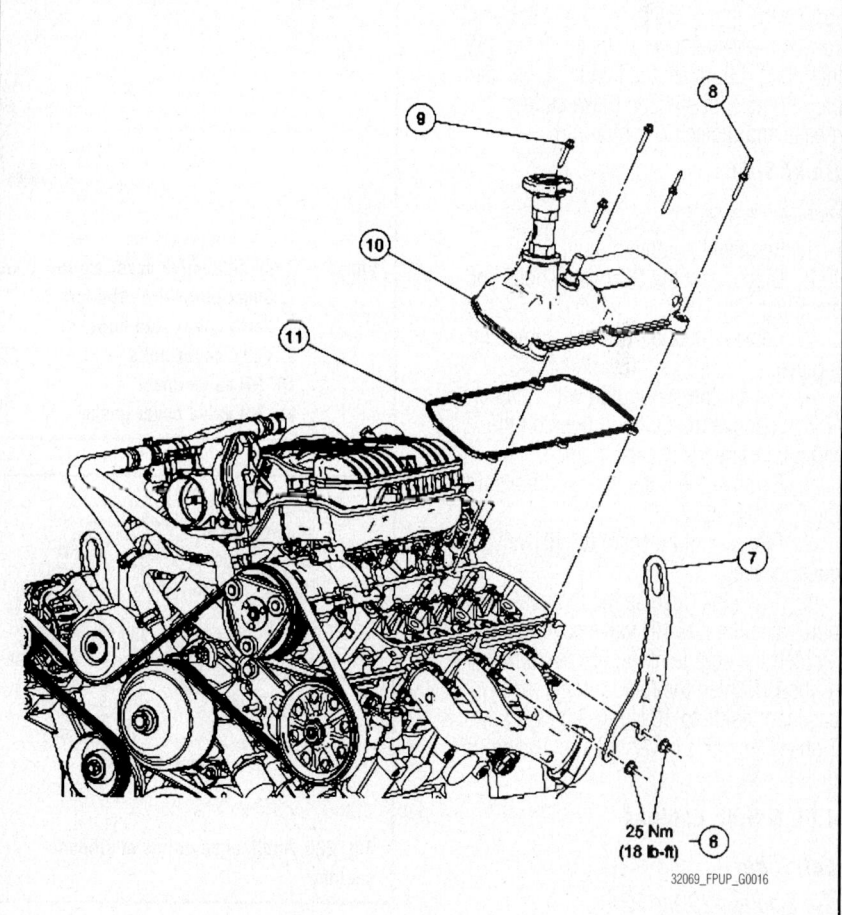

Fig. 218 Left side valve cover exploded view—4.2L engine

  6. Engine lifting eye nuts
  7. Engine lifting eye
  8. Valve cover stud bolts
  9. Valve cover bolts
  10. LH valve cover
  11. LH valve cover gasket

32069_FPUP_G0016

3. Remove the nuts and the engine lifting eye.

➡**Spark plug wires must be connected to the correct spark plug. Mark the spark plug wires for assembly reference. It is important to twist the spark plug boots while pulling upward to avoid possible damage to the spark plug wires.**

4. Using the special tool, with a twisting motion, disconnect the 3 spark plug wires from the spark plugs.

5. Disconnect the 2 spark plug wire retainers and position the spark plug wires aside.

6. Remove the 3 bolts, the 2 stud bolts and the LH valve cover.

7. Remove and discard the LH valve cover gasket.

8. To install, reverse the removal procedure. Install a new valve cover gasket. Torque the lifting eye to 25 Nm (18 ft. lbs.) Torque the valve cover bolts to 10 Nm (89 inch lbs.). Lubricate the inside of the spark plug boots with silicone brake caliper grease and dielectric compound.

Right Side

See Figure 219.

1. Remove the ignition coil.

2. Disconnect the PCV valve hose and electrical connector.

3. Remove the nuts and the engine lifting eye.

4. Detach the spark plug wire retainers.

5. Remove the bolt and position the radio interference capacitor aside.

6. Remove the bolts, the stud bolts and the RH valve cover.

7. Remove and discard the RH valve cover gasket.

8. To install, reverse the removal procedure. Install a new RH valve cover gasket. Tighten the engine lifting eye to 25 Nm (18 ft. lbs.). Tighten the radio interference capacitor aside to 10 Nm (89 inch lbs.). Tighten the valve cover bolts to 10 Nm (89 inch lbs.).

4.6L & 5.4L Engines

Left Side

See Figures 220 and 221.

1. Remove the air cleaner outlet pipe.

2. Remove the degas bottle.

3. Remove the LH ignition coils.

4. Disconnect the quick connect couplings and remove the positive crankcase ventilation (PCV) tube

5. Remove the bolt and position the oil level indicator tube aside.

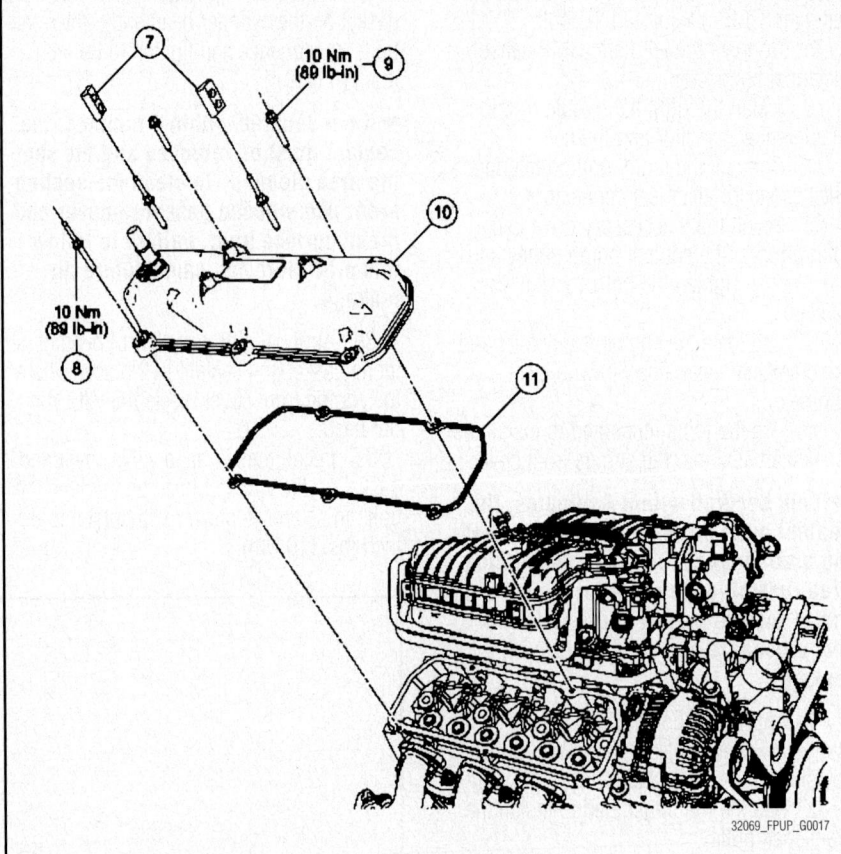

Fig. 219 Right side valve cover exploded view—4.2L engine

7. Spark plug wire retainers
8. Valve cover stud bolts
9. Valve cover bolts
10. RH valve cover
11. RH valve cover gasket

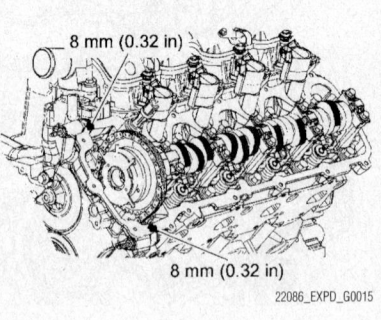

Fig. 220 Application points of silicone sealant

6. Disconnect the LH radio ignition interference capacitor electrical connector.

7. Disconnect the LH variable camshaft timing (VCT) solenoid electrical connector and the wiring harness retainers.

8. Disconnect the intake manifold vacuum tube hose from the brake booster.

9. Disconnect the intake manifold vacuum tube assembly from the support bracket and the valve cover stud and position aside.

※ **WARNING**

When removing the valve cover, make sure to avoid damaging the VCT solenoid.

10. Fully loosen the fasteners and remove the LH valve cover and gasket.

11. Clean the valve cover mating surface of the cylinder head with silicone gasket remover and metal surface prep.

➡**If the valve cover is not secured within 4 minutes, the sealant must be removed and the sealing area cleaned with metal surface prep and silicone gasket remover. Follow the directions on the packaging. Allow to dry until there is no sign of wetness, or 4 minutes, whichever is longer. Failure to follow this procedure can cause future oil leakage.**

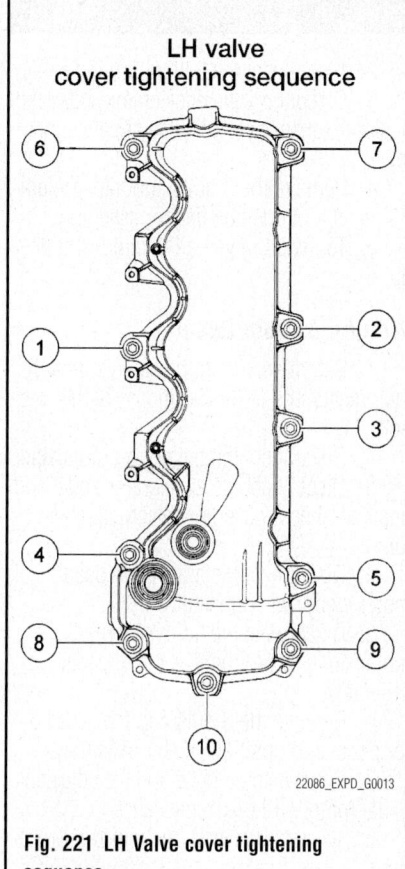

Fig. 221 LH Valve cover tightening sequence

To install:

12. Apply a bead of silicone gasket and sealant in 2 places where the engine front cover meets the cylinder head.

13. Position the LH valve cover and new gasket on the cylinder head and tighten the 10 fasteners in the sequence to 89 inch lbs. (10 Nm).

All vehicles

14. Position the intake manifold vacuum tube assembly onto the support bracket and the valve cover stud

15. Connect the intake manifold vacuum tube hose to the brake booster.

16. Connect the VCT solenoid electrical connector and the wiring harness retainers

17. Connect the radio ignition interference capacitor electrical connector.

18. Position the oil level indicator tube and install the bolt and tighten to 89 inch lbs. (10 Nm).

19. Position the PCV tube and connect the quick connect couplings.

20. Install the LH ignition coils and tighten mounting bolts to 53 inch lbs. (6 Nm).

21. Install the degas bottle and tighten mounting bolts to 11 ft. lbs. (15 Nm).

22. Fill the degas bottle with recommended coolant and mixture.

Right Side

See Figure 222.

1. Recover the A/C refrigerant.
2. Vehicles with auxiliary heat:
3. Drain the cooling system.
4. Disconnect the 2 auxiliary heat coolant hoses.
5. Disconnect the coolant hose from the intake manifold and position the coolant hose assembly aside.
6. All vehicles:
7. Disconnect the quick connect couplings and remove the crankcase vent tube.
8. Remove the nut and the ground cable and disconnect the wiring harness retainer.
9. Disconnect the powertrain control module (PCM) electrical connector.
10. Disconnect the 2 electrical connectors and the wiring harness retainer.
11. Disconnect the evaporator outlet and inlet fittings. Discard the O-ring seals
12. Disconnect the RH radio ignition interference capacitor and engine cooling fan clutch electrical connectors.
13. Remove the RH ignition coils.
14. Disconnect the RH variable camshaft timing (VCT) solenoid electrical connector
15. Disconnect the RH camshaft position (CMP) sensor electrical connector.
16. Disconnect the 2 engine wiring harness retainers from the RH valve cover studs.

➡**The fasteners are part of the valve cover and should not be removed.**

17. Fully loosen the fasteners and remove the RH valve cover and gasket.

18. Clean the valve cover mating surface of the cylinder head with silicone gasket remover and metal surface prep.

19. Discard the valve cover gasket. Clean the valve cover gasket groove with soap and water or a suitable solvent.

To install:

20. Apply a bead of silicone gasket and sealant in 2 places where the engine front cover meets the cylinder head.

21. Position the LH valve cover and new gasket on the cylinder head and tighten the 9 fasteners in the sequence to 89 inch lbs. (10 Nm).

22. Install the RH ignition coils and tighten mounting bolts to 53 inch lbs. (6 Nm).

23. Install new O-ring seals, and lubricate with fresh PAG oil, connect the evaporator outlet and inlet fittings.

24. Connect the 2 electrical connectors and the wiring harness retainer

25. Connect the PCM electrical connector.

26. Connect the wiring harness retainer and ground cable, install and tighten the nut to 89 inch lbs. (10 Nm).

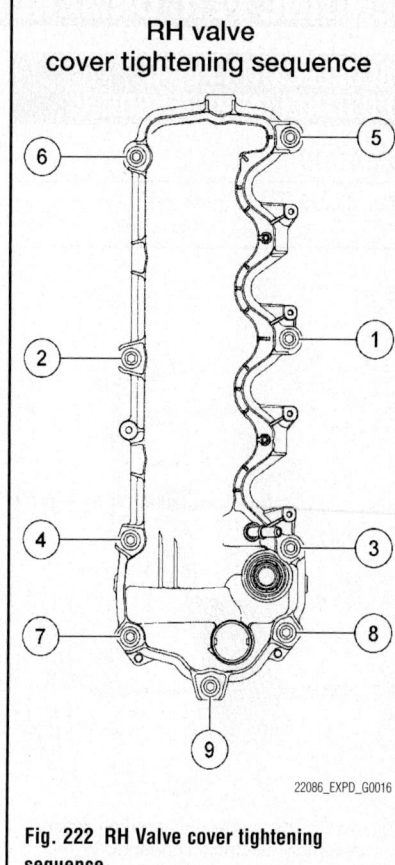

Fig. 222 RH Valve cover tightening sequence

27. Connect the RH radio ignition interference capacitor and engine cooling fan clutch electrical connectors.

28. Connect the RH VCT solenoid electrical connector.

29. Connect the RH CMP sensor electrical connector.

30. Connect the wiring harness retainers to the valve cover.

31. Position the crankcase vent tube and connect the quick connect couplings.

Vehicles with auxiliary heat

32. Position the coolant hose assembly and connect the coolant hose to the intake manifold.

33. Connect the 2 auxiliary heat coolant hoses.

34. Fill and bleed the coolant system.

All vehicles

35. Evacuate, leak test and charge the refrigerant system.

VALVE LASH

ADJUSTMENT

These engines do not require valve lash adjusting, because they utilize hydraulic lash components in their valve actuation systems.

ENGINE PERFORMANCE & EMISSION CONTROLS

ACCELERATOR PEDAL POSITION (APP) SENSOR

LOCATION

See Figures 223 through 226.

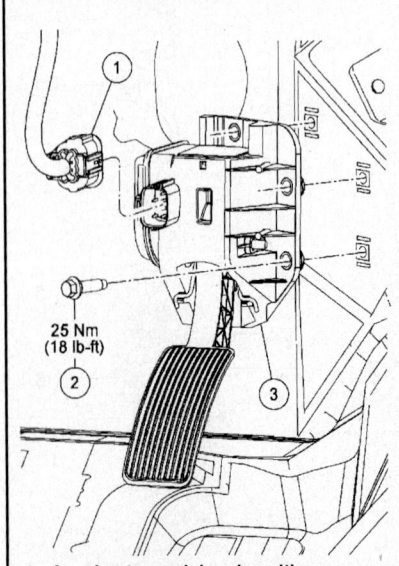

1. Accelerator pedal and position sensor assembly electrical connector
2. Accelerator pedal and position sensor assembly bolts (3 required)
3. Accelerator pedal and position sensor assembly

22086_FTRK_G0170

Fig. 223 Fixed Accelerator Pedal Assembly—2008 Models

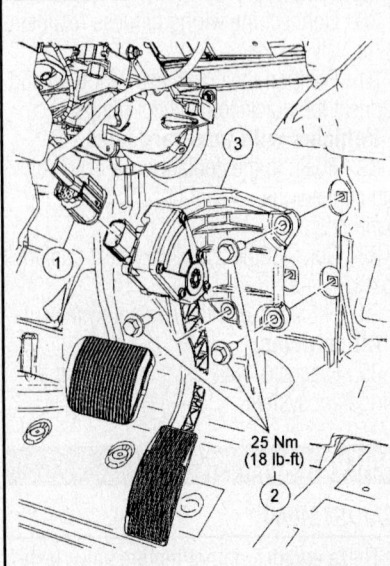

25 Nm (18 lb-ft)

22086_EXPD_G0189

Fig. 224 The Accelerator Pedal Position (APP) Sensor location view—2009 Models

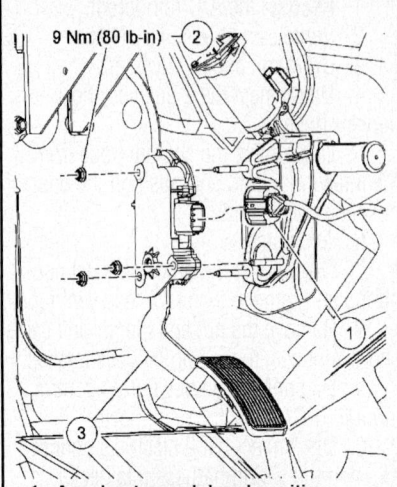

9 Nm (80 lb-in)

1. Accelerator pedal and position sensor assembly electrical connector
2. Accelerator pedal and position sensor assembly nuts (3 required)
3. Accelerator pedal and position sensor assembly

22086_FTRK_G0171

Fig. 225 Adjustable Accelerator Pedal Assembly—2008 Models

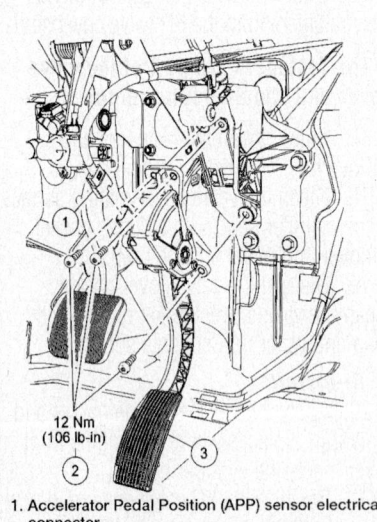

12 Nm (106 lb-in)

1. Accelerator Pedal Position (APP) sensor electrical connector
2. Accelerator pedal assembly bolts (3 required)
3. Accelerator pedal assembly

36578_FTRK_G0105

Fig. 226 Adjustable Accelerator Pedal Assembly—2009 Models

REMOVAL & INSTALLATION

With Fixed Pedal

1. Before servicing the vehicle, refer to the precautions in the beginning of this section.

2. Disconnect the battery ground cable.
3. Disconnect the accelerator pedal and position sensor assembly electrical connector.
4. Remove the 3 bolts and the accelerator pedal and position sensor assembly.
5. To install, reverse the removal procedure.

With Adjustable Pedal

1. Before servicing the vehicle, refer to the precautions in the beginning of this section.
2. Disconnect the battery ground cable.
3. Disconnect the accelerator pedal and position sensor assembly electrical connector.
4. Disconnect the adjustable pedal motor electrical connector.
5. Disconnect the adjustable pedal motor drive cable from the brake pedal assembly.
6. Remove the 3 nuts and the accelerator pedal and position sensor assembly.
7. Remove the 3 bolts and the adjustable pedal motor and bracket assembly.
8. To install, reverse the removal procedure.

✳✳ CAUTION

The adjustable pedal system must be indexed whenever the brake pedal assembly or accelerator pedal assembly is installed.

➡ **Make sure the electrical connector is connected to the adjustable pedal motor.**

9. Disconnect the adjustable pedal motor drive cable from the brake pedal drive.
10. Operate the accelerator pedal to the full rearward position.
11. Connect the adjustable pedal motor drive cable to the adjustable brake pedal drive.
12. Operate the adjustable pedals to the full forward position.
13. Disconnect the adjustable pedal motor drive cable from the adjustable brake pedal assembly.
14. Operate the adjustable accelerator pedal to the full forward position.
15. Connect the adjustable pedal motor drive cable to the adjustable brake pedal drive.
16. Check that the brake and accelerator pedals can be fully adjusted forward and rearward.

CAMSHAFT POSITION (CMP) SENSOR

LOCATION

4.2L Engine

Front of the engine, near the heater outlet tube.

4.6L Engine

At the front of the left cylinder head.

5.4L and 6.8L Engines

One at the front of each cylinder head.

REMOVAL & INSTALLATION

4.2L Engine

See Figure 227.

1. Before servicing the vehicle, refer to the precautions in the beginning of this section.
2. Disconnect the battery ground cable.
3. Drain the engine cooling system.

➡**Clean and inspect the heater outlet tube O-ring seal. Install a new O-ring seal if necessary. Lubricate the O-ring seal with clean engine coolant.**

4. Remove the bolt and position the heater outlet tube aside

5. Disconnect the camshaft position sensor (CMP) sensor electrical connector.
6. Remove the bolts and the CMP sensor.
7. To install, reverse the removal procedure.

4.6L Engine

See Figure 228.

1. Before servicing the vehicle, refer to the precautions in the beginning of this section.
2. Disconnect the battery ground cable.
3. Disconnect the camshaft position sensor (CMP) sensor electrical connector.
4. Remove the bolt and the CMP sensor.
5. To install, reverse the removal procedure.

5.4L Engine

See Figures 229 and 230.

1. Before servicing the vehicle, refer to the precautions in the beginning of this section.
2. Disconnect the battery ground cable.

3. For the left camshaft position (CMP) sensor, remove the air cleaner inlet pipe and resonator.
4. Disconnect the CMP sensor electrical connector.
5. Remove the bolt and the CMP sensor.
6. To install, reverse the removal procedure.

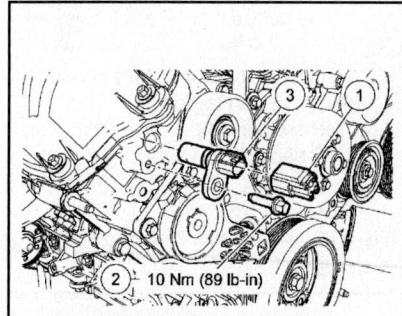

1. Camshaft position (CMP) sensor electrical connector
2. CMP sensor bolt
3. CMP sensor

22086_FTRK_G0139

Fig. 229 Right Camshaft Position Sensor—5.4L Engine

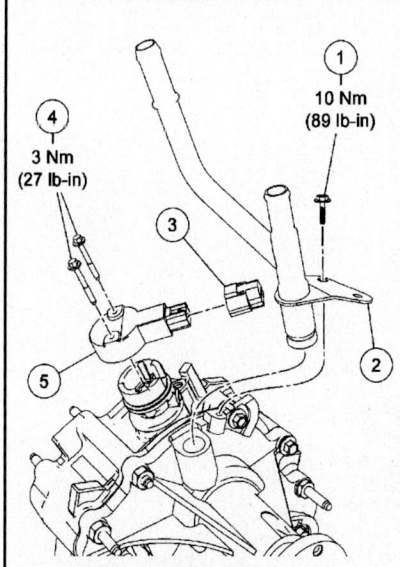

1. Heater outlet tube bolt
2. Heater outlet tube
3. Camshaft position (CMP) sensor electrical connector
4. CMP sensor bolts (2 required)
5. CMP sensor

22086_FTRK_G0137

Fig. 227 Camshaft Position Sensor—4.2L Engine

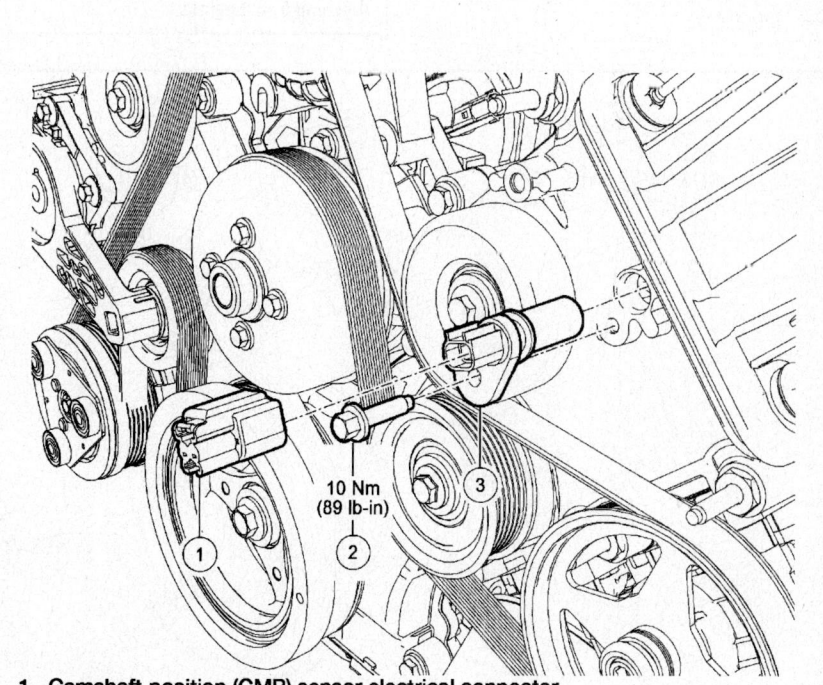

1. Camshaft position (CMP) sensor electrical connector
2. CMP sensor bolt
3. CMP sensor

22086_FTRK_G0138

Fig. 228 Camshaft Position Sensor—4.6L Engine

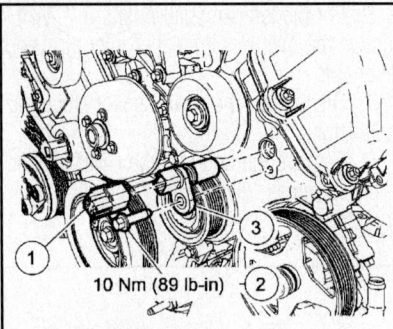

1. Camshaft position (CMP) sensor
   electrical connector
2. CMP sensor bolt
3. CMP sensor

22086_FTRK_G0140

**Fig. 230 Left Camshaft Position Sensor—
5.4L Engine**

CRANKSHAFT POSITION (CKP) SENSOR

LOCATION

Front of the engine, above the crankshaft damper.

REMOVAL & INSTALLATION

4.2L Engine

See Figure 231.

1. Before servicing the vehicle, refer to the precautions in the beginning of this section.
2. With the vehicle in NEUTRAL, position it on a hoist.
3. Disconnect the battery ground cable.
4. Disconnect the crankshaft position (CKP) sensor electrical connector.
5. Remove the bolts and the CKP sensor.
6. To install, reverse the removal procedure.

4.6L & 5.4L Engines

See Figure 232.

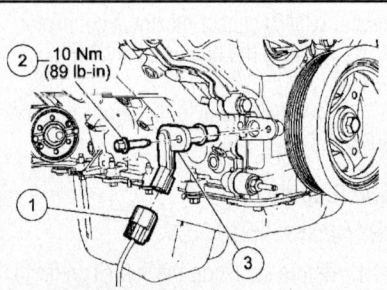

1. Crankshaft position (CKP) sensor
   electrical connector
2. CKP sensor bolt
3. CKP sensor

22086_FTRK_G0142

**Fig. 232 Crankshaft Position Sensor—
4.6L and 5.4L Engines**

1. Before servicing the vehicle, refer to the precautions in the beginning of this section.
2. With the vehicle in NEUTRAL, position it on a hoist.
3. Disconnect the battery ground cable.
4. Remove the accessory drive belt.
5. If equipped, remove the 2 bolts and position the power steering fluid cooler aside.
6. Loosen the A/C compressor bolts enough to slide the A/C compressor down 25 mm (1 in), to allow access to the crankshaft position (CKP) sensor.
7. Disconnect the CKP sensor electrical connector.
8. Remove the bolt and the CKP sensor.
9. To install, reverse the removal procedure.

CYLINDER HEAD TEMPERATURE (CHT) SENSOR

LOCATION

At the rear of the left cylinder head.

REMOVAL & INSTALLATION

4.2L Engine

See Figure 233.

1. Before servicing the vehicle, refer to the precautions in the beginning of this section.

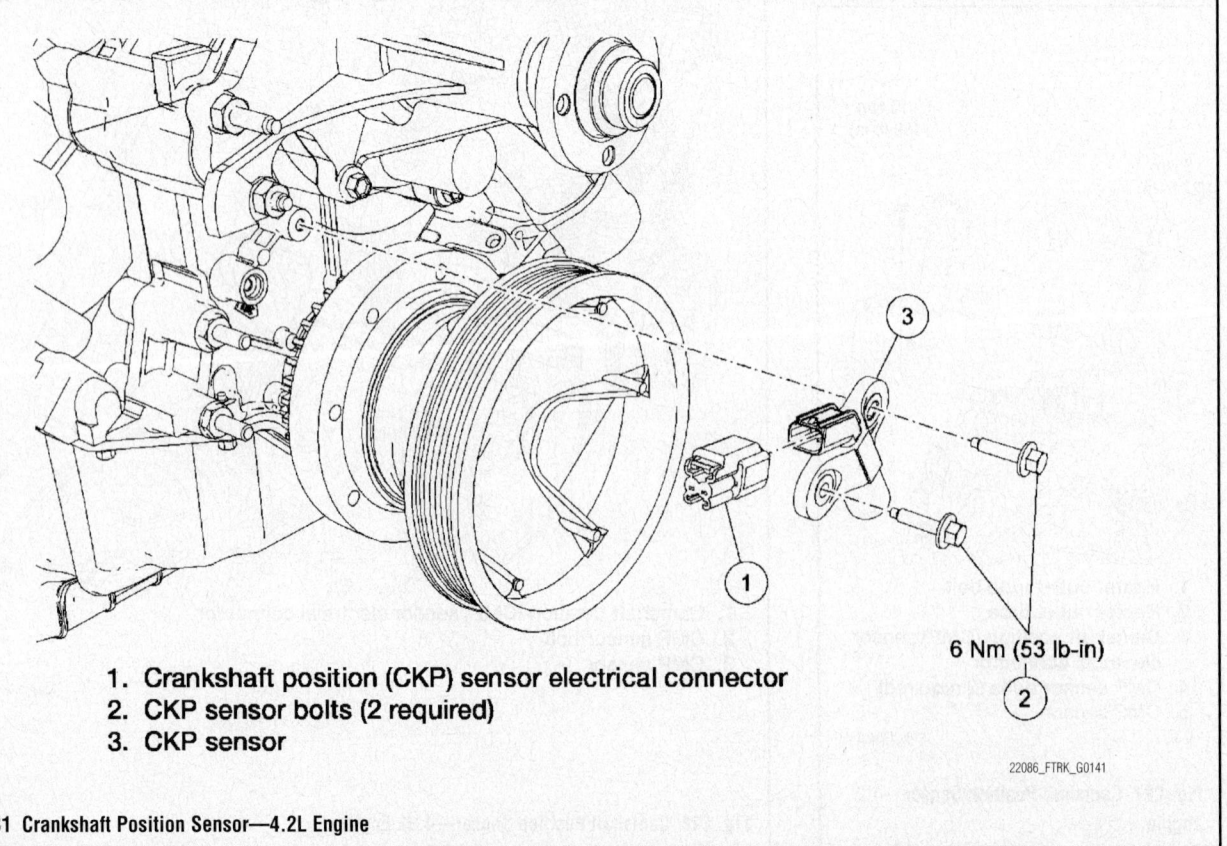

1. **Crankshaft position (CKP) sensor electrical connector**
2. **CKP sensor bolts (2 required)**
3. **CKP sensor**

22086_FTRK_G0141

Fig. 231 Crankshaft Position Sensor—4.2L Engine

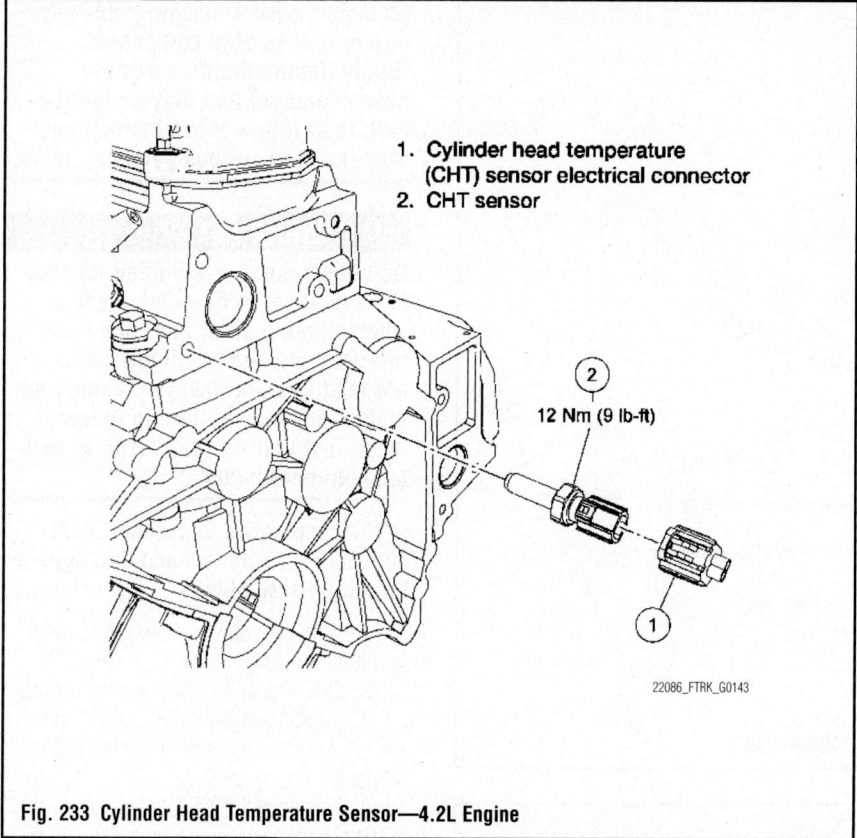

1. Cylinder head temperature
   (CHT) sensor electrical connector
2. CHT sensor

12 Nm (9 lb-ft)

22086_FTRK_G0143

Fig. 233 Cylinder Head Temperature Sensor—4.2L Engine

2. With the vehicle in NEUTRAL, position it on a hoist.
3. Disconnect the battery ground cable.
4. Disconnect the cylinder head temperature (CHT) sensor electrical connector.
5. Remove the CHT sensor.
6. To install, reverse the removal procedure.

4.6L Engine

See Figure 234.

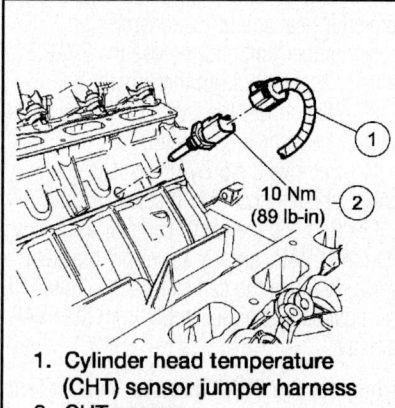

1. Cylinder head temperature
   (CHT) sensor jumper harness
2. CHT sensor

22086_FTRK_G0144

Fig. 234 Cylinder Head Temperature Sensor—4.6L Engine

1. Before servicing the vehicle, refer to the precautions in the beginning of this section.
2. Remove the generator.
3. Disconnect the cylinder head temperature (CHT) sensor electrical connector.
4. Remove the CHT sensor.
5. To install, reverse the removal procedure.

➡**Apply anti-seize to the threads of the CHT sensor.**

5.4L Engine

See Figure 235.

1. Before servicing the vehicle, refer to the precautions in the beginning of this section.
2. Remove the intake manifold.
3. Disconnect the cylinder head temperature (CHT) sensor electrical connector.
4. Remove the CHT.
5. To install, reverse the removal procedure.

➡**Apply anti-seize to the threads of the CHT sensor.**

EVAPORATIVE EMISSIONS (EVAP) CANISTER

LOCATION

See Figure 236.

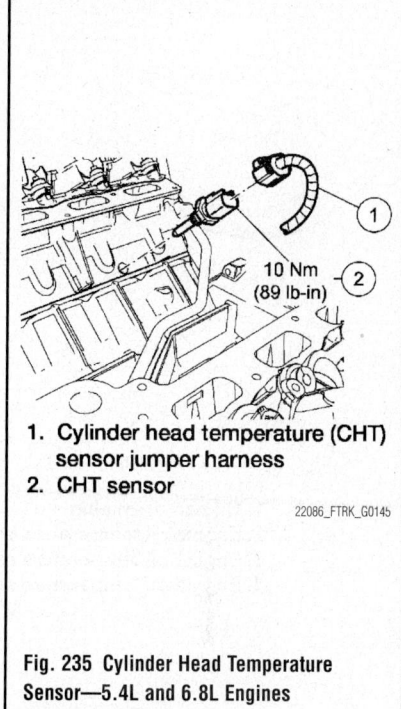

10 Nm
(89 lb-in)

1. Cylinder head temperature (CHT)
   sensor jumper harness
2. CHT sensor

22086_FTRK_G0145

Fig. 235 Cylinder Head Temperature Sensor—5.4L and 6.8L Engines

REMOVAL & INSTALLATION

2008 Models

See Figure 237.

1. With the vehicle in NEUTRAL, position it on a hoist.
2. Disconnect the battery ground cable.

➡**The evaporative emission (EVAP) canister assembly is located above the spare tire.**

3. Remove the spare tire.
4. Disconnect the fuel vapor tube quick connect coupling.
5. Disconnect the fuel vapor hose.
6. Remove the 2 front EVAP canister assembly bracket bolts. To install, tighten to 10 ft. lbs. (13 Nm).
7. Remove the 2 outer rear EVAP canister assembly bracket bolts. To install, tighten to 15 ft. lbs. (20 Nm).
8. Remove the 2 inner rear EVAP canister assembly bracket bolts. To install, tighten to 10 ft. lbs. (13 Nm).
9. Lower the EVAP canister assembly down slightly to disconnect the EVAP canister vent solenoid electrical connector and remove the EVAP canister vent solenoid harness pushpin retainer.
10. Remove the EVAP canister assembly.
11. Remove the EVAP canister heat shield.

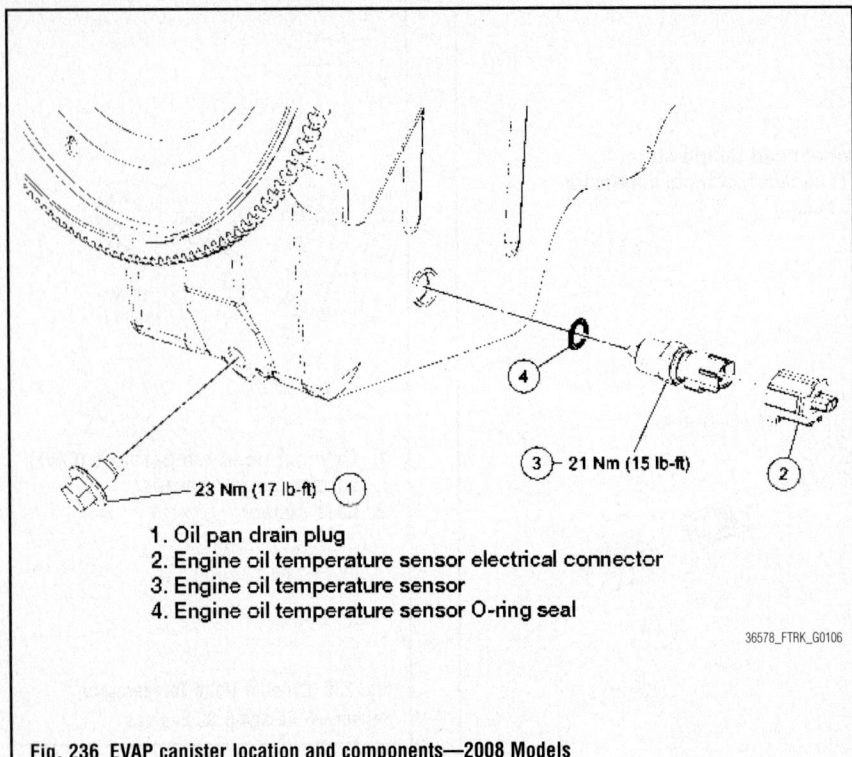

1. Oil pan drain plug
2. Engine oil temperature sensor electrical connector
3. Engine oil temperature sensor
4. Engine oil temperature sensor O-ring seal

36578_FTRK_G0106

Fig. 236 EVAP canister location and components—2008 Models

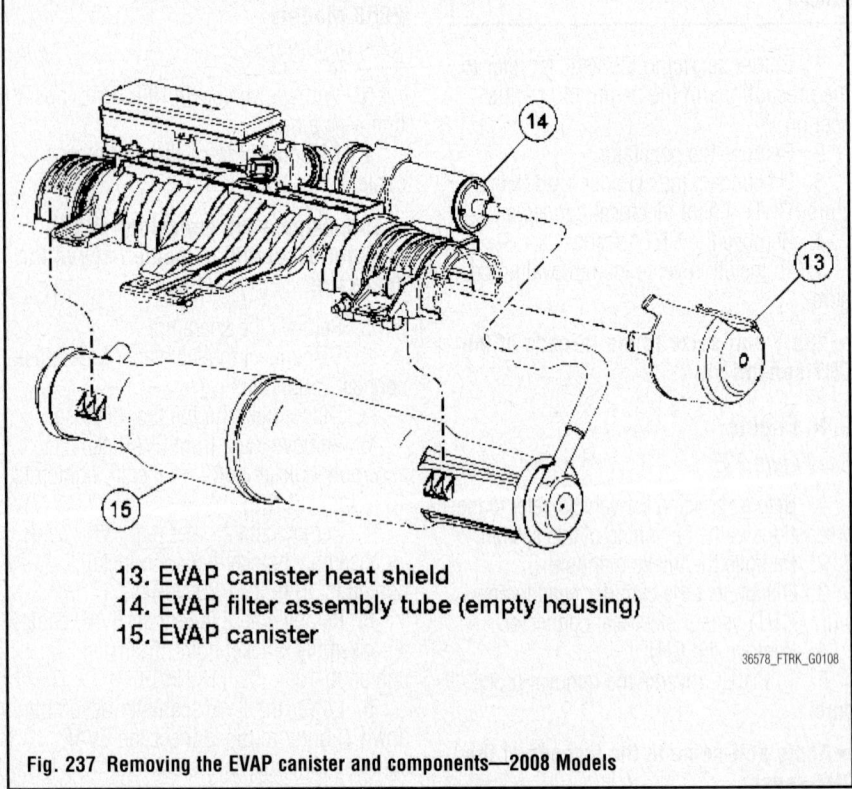

13. EVAP canister heat shield
14. EVAP filter assembly tube (empty housing)
15. EVAP canister

36578_FTRK_G0108

Fig. 237 Removing the EVAP canister and components—2008 Models

12. Disconnect the EVAP canister-to-EVAP filter assembly tube fuel vapor hose.
13. Remove the EVAP canister from the EVAP assembly.
14. To install, reverse the removal procedure.

2009 Models

See Figure 238.

⁂ **WARNING**

Always disconnect the battery ground cable at the battery when working on an evaporative emission (EVAP) system or fuel-related component. Highly flammable mixtures are always present and may be ignited. Failure to follow these instructions may result in serious personal injury.

⁂ **WARNING**

Do not smoke, carry lighted tobacco or have an open flame of any type when working on or near any fuel-related component. Highly flammable mixtures are always present and may be ignited. Failure to follow these instructions may result in serious personal injury.

➡The Evaporative Emission (EVAP) canister vent solenoid and dust separator are an assembly.

1. With the vehicle in NEUTRAL, position it on a hoist.
2. Disconnect the battery ground cable.
3. Disconnect the EVAP canister vent solenoid electrical jumper from the wiring harness.
4. Disconnect the Fuel Tank Pressure (FTP) sensor and vapor tube assembly-to-EVAP canister quick connect coupling.
5. Disconnect the EVAP canister purge valve vapor tube-to- EVAP canister quick connect coupling.
6. Disconnect the fresh air tube-to-canister vent solenoid and dust separator assembly quick connect coupling.
7. Remove the EVAP canister assembly bracket-to-frame rail bolt in the rear.
8. Remove the EVAP canister assembly bracket-to-frame rail bolt in the front.
9. Remove the EVAP canister assembly bracket and exhaust Y-pipe dual catalytic converter heat shield-to-transmission crossmember bolt and remove the EVAP canister assembly from the vehicle.
10. Disconnect the EVAP canister vent solenoid electrical connector.
11. Remove the 5 EVAP canister-to-EVAP canister assembly bracket bolts.
12. Remove the EVAP canister assembly from the EVAP canister assembly brackets.
13. Remove the canister vent solenoid and dust separator assembly from the EVAP canister.

➡Inspect the EVAP canister heat shield and if damaged, install a new EVAP canister heat shield.

14. To install, reverse the removal procedure.
15. Carry out the Evaporative Emission System Leak Test.

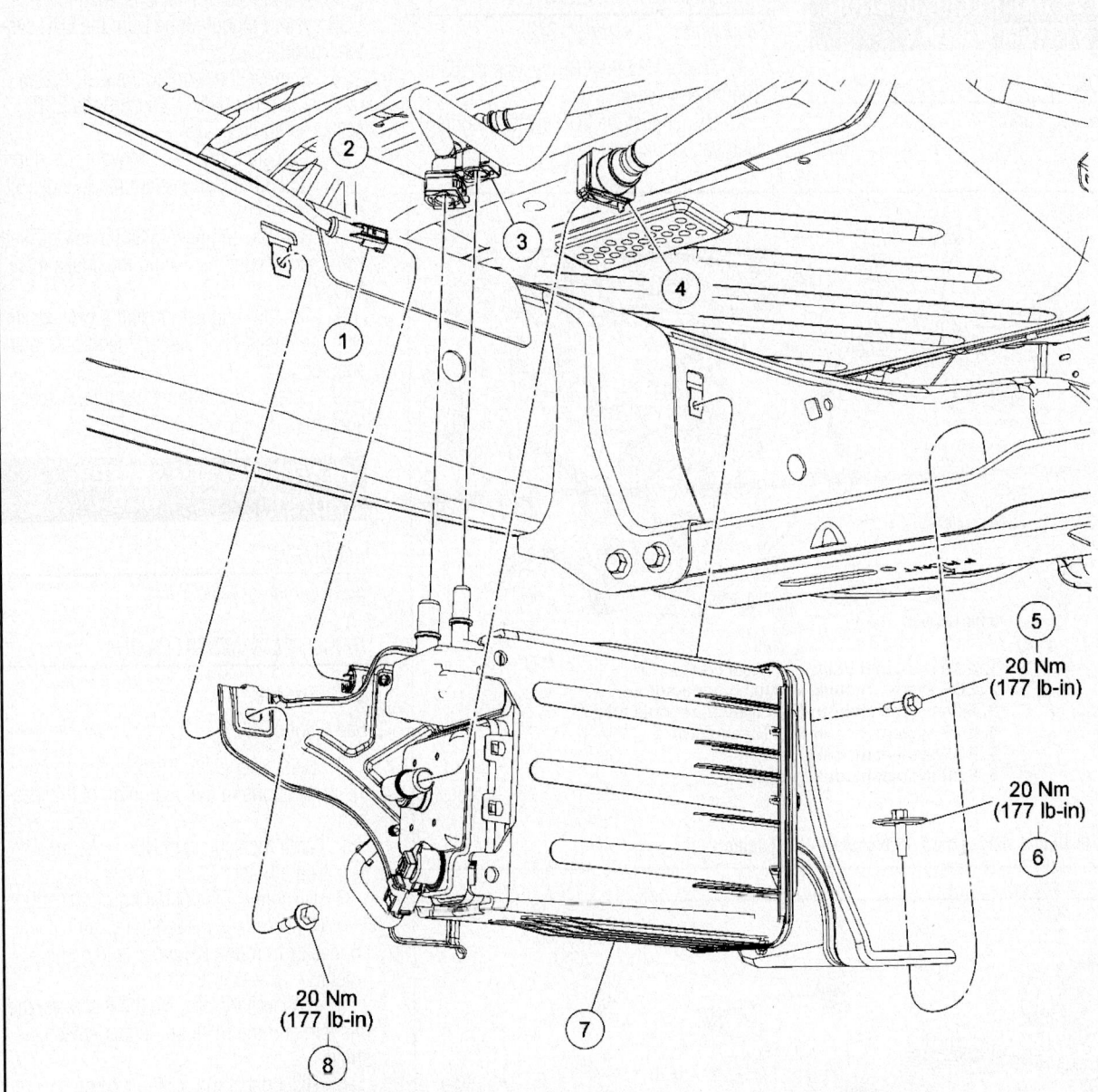

20 Nm
(177 lb-in)

20 Nm
(177 lb-in)

20 Nm
(177 lb-in)

1. Evaporative Emission (EVAP) canister vent solenoid electrical connector
2. Fuel Tank Pressure (FTP) sensor and vapor tube assembly-to- EVAP canister quick connect coupling
3. EVAP canister purge valve vapor tube-to- EVAP canister quick connect coupling
4. Fresh air tube-to-canister vent solenoid and dust separator assembly quick connect coupling
5. EVAP canister assembly bracket-to-frame rail bolt
6. EVAP canister assembly bracket and exhaust Y-pipe dual catalytic converter heat shield-to-transmission crossmember bolt
7. EVAP canister assembly
8. EVAP canister assembly bracket-to-frame rail bolt

36578_EXPD_G0092

Fig. 238 View of the EVAP canister assembly

EXHAUST GAS RECIRCULATION (EGR) SYSTEM MODULE

LOCATION

See Figures 239 and 240.

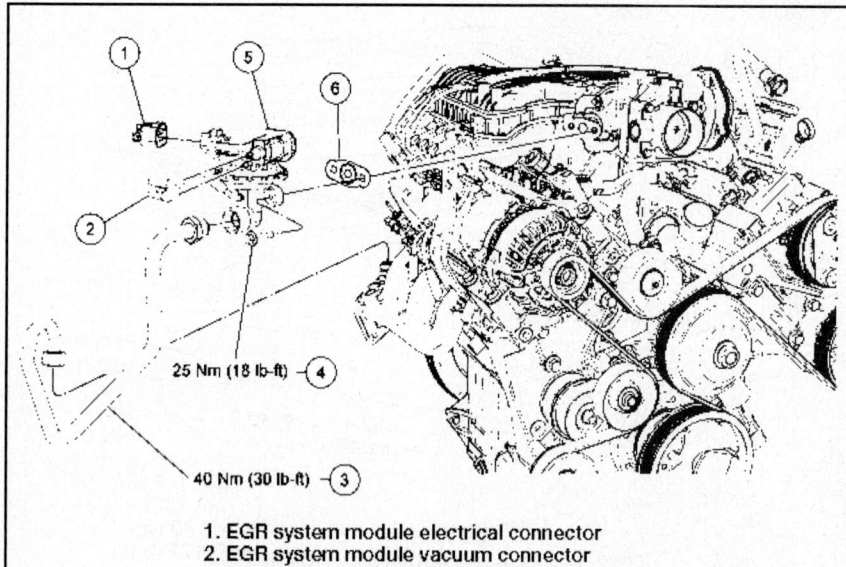

25 Nm (18 lb-ft) — 4

40 Nm (30 lb-ft) — 3

1. EGR system module electrical connector
2. EGR system module vacuum connector
3. Exhaust manifold-to-EGR system module tube
4. EGR system module bolt (2 required)
5. EGR system module
6. EGR system module gasket

36578_FTRK_G0111

Fig. 239 Exploded view of the EGR Module—4.2L Engine

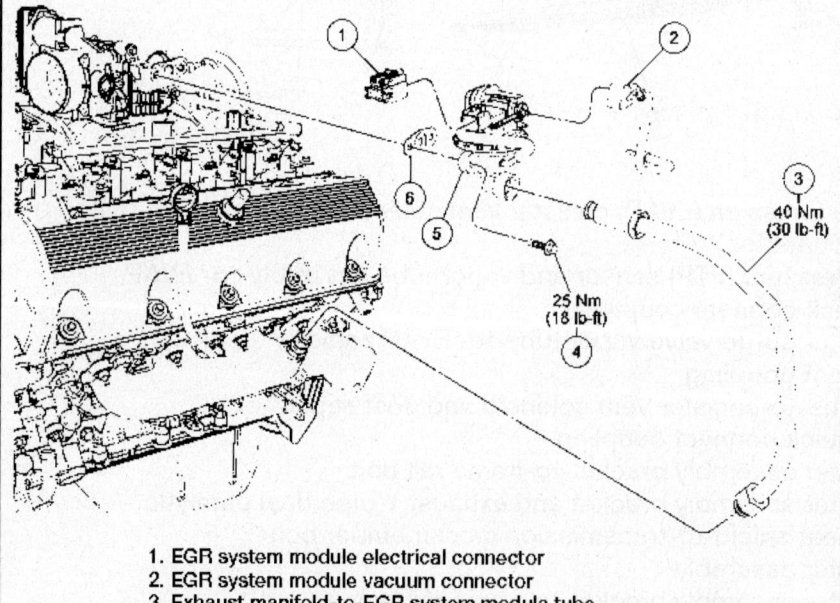

40 Nm (30 lb-ft)

25 Nm (18 lb-ft)

1. EGR system module electrical connector
2. EGR system module vacuum connector
3. Exhaust manifold-to-EGR system module tube
4. EGR system module bolt (2 required)
5. EGR system module
6. EGR system module gasket

36578_FTRK_G0112

Fig. 240 Exploded view of the EGR Module—4.2L Engine

REMOVAL & INSTALLATION

See Figures 241 through 242.

1. Disconnect the EGR system module vacuum connector.
2. Disconnect the EGR system module electrical connector.
3. Disconnect the exhaust manifold-to-EGR system module tube from the EGR system module.
4. Remove the 2 bolts, the EGR system module and the gasket. Discard the EGR system module gasket.
5. To install, reverse removal procedure.
6. Clean the EGR system module gasket mating surfaces.
7. On 4.2L engines, install a new gasket with the raised circle facing the intake manifold.
8. On 4.6L engines, install a new gasket with the raised circle facing the throttle body adapter.
9. Refer to illustrations for torque specifications.

HEATED OXYGEN SENSOR (HO2S)

LOCATION

See Figures 241 and 242.

REMOVAL & INSTALLATION

4.2L Engine

See Figure 241.

1. Before servicing the vehicle, refer to the precautions in the beginning of this section.
2. With the vehicle in NEUTRAL, position it on a hoist.
3. Disconnect the battery ground cable.
4. If necessary, detach the electrical connector from the RH inner fender splash shield.
5. If necessary, remove the 6 screws, the pushpin and the RH inner fender splash shield.
6. Disconnect the heated oxygen sensor (HO2S) electrical connector.

➡ **If necessary, lubricate the HO2S with lock lubricant to assist in removal.**

7. Remove the HO2S.
8. To install, reverse the removal procedure.

➡ **Apply anti-seize to the threads of the HO2S.**

4.6L and 5.4 Engines

See Figure 242.

1. Before servicing the vehicle, refer to the precautions in the beginning of this section.
2. With the vehicle in NEUTRAL, position it on a hoist.
3. Disconnect the battery ground cable.

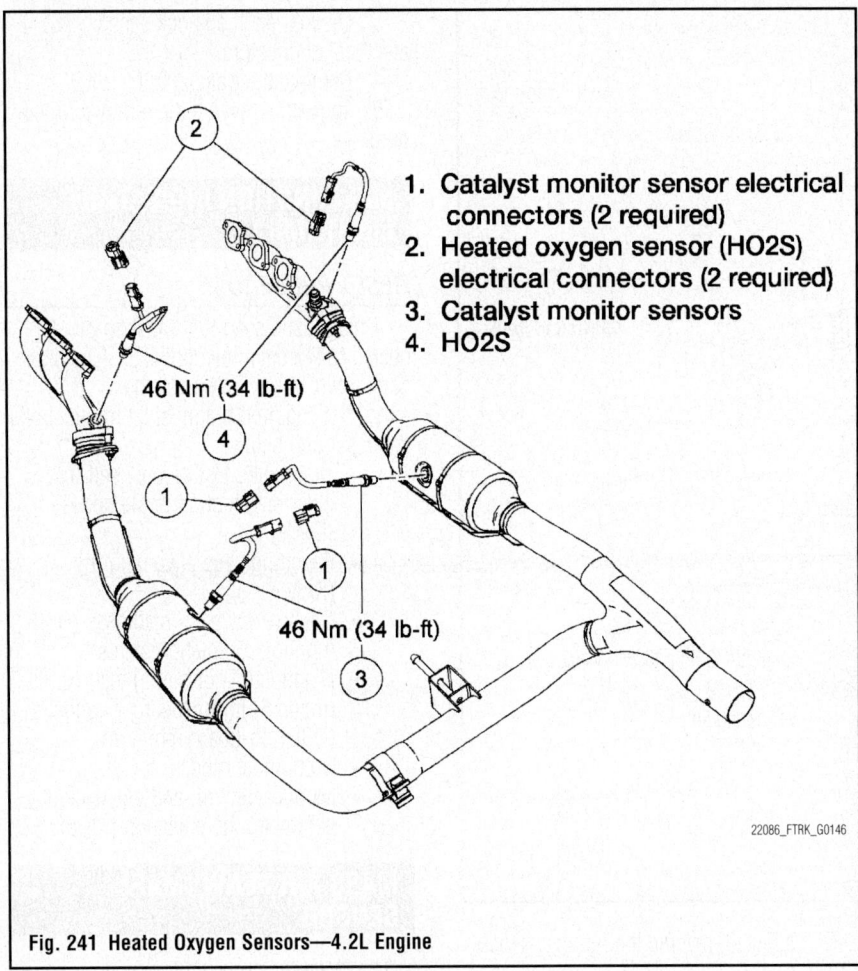

1. Catalyst monitor sensor electrical connectors (2 required)
2. Heated oxygen sensor (HO2S) electrical connectors (2 required)
3. Catalyst monitor sensors
4. HO2S

46 Nm (34 lb-ft)

46 Nm (34 lb-ft)

22086_FTRK_G0146

Fig. 241 Heated Oxygen Sensors—4.2L Engine

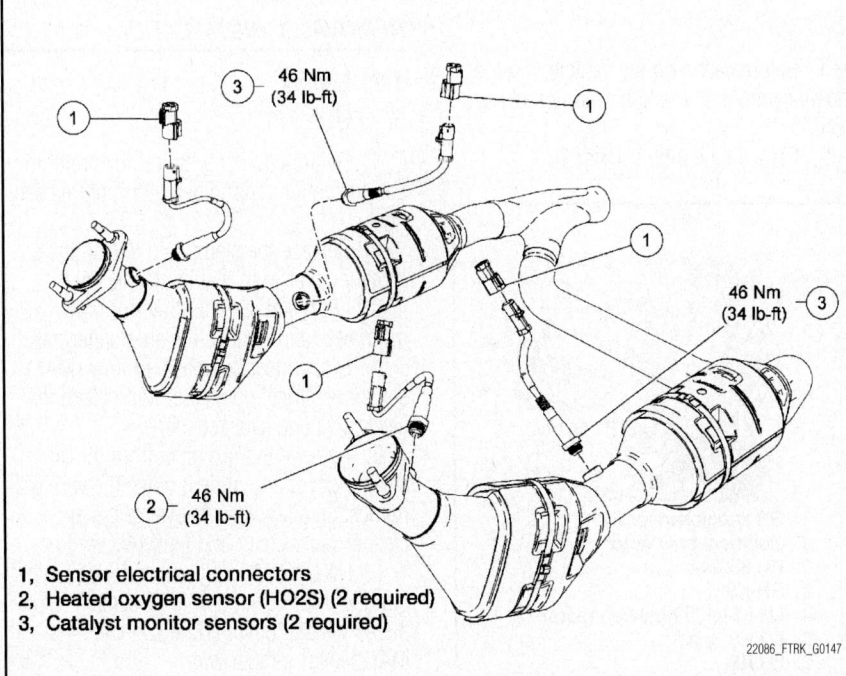

3 46 Nm (34 lb-ft)

46 Nm (34 lb-ft)

46 Nm (34 lb-ft)

1, Sensor electrical connectors
2, Heated oxygen sensor (HO2S) (2 required)
3, Catalyst monitor sensors (2 required)

22086_FTRK_G0147

Fig. 242 Heated Oxygen Sensors—5.4L Engine shown, 4.6L and 6.8L Engines similar

➡ **If necessary, lubricate the HO2S with penetrating and lock lubricant to assist in removal**

4. Remove the HO2S.
5. To install, reverse the removal procedure.

➡**Apply anti-seize to the threads of the HO2S.**

IDLE AIR CONTROL (IAC) VALVE

LOCATION

The Idle Air Control Valve is mounted on the intake manifold, just behind the throttle body.

REMOVAL & INSTALLATION

1. Disconnect the battery ground cable.
2. Disconnect the idle air control (IAC) valve electrical connector.
3. Disconnect the throttle bypass hose.
4. Remove the two bolts and the IAC valve.

To install:

5. Install the IAC valve and tighten the bolts in two stages:
   a. Stage 1: Tighten to 89 inch lbs. (10 Nm).
   b. Stage 2: Tighten an additional 90 degrees.
6. Connect the throttle bypass hose.
7. Connect the IAC electrical connector.
8. Connect the battery ground cable.

KNOCK SENSOR (KS)

LOCATION

4.2L Engine

Rear of the left cylinder head.

4.6L & 5.4L Engines

Under the intake manifold.

REMOVAL & INSTALLATION

4.2L Engine

See Figure 243.

1. Before servicing the vehicle, refer to the precautions in the beginning of this section.
2. With the vehicle in NEUTRAL, position it on a hoist.
3. Disconnect the battery ground cable.
4. Remove the bolt and position the fuel tube bracket aside.
5. Disconnect the knock sensor (KS) electrical connector.

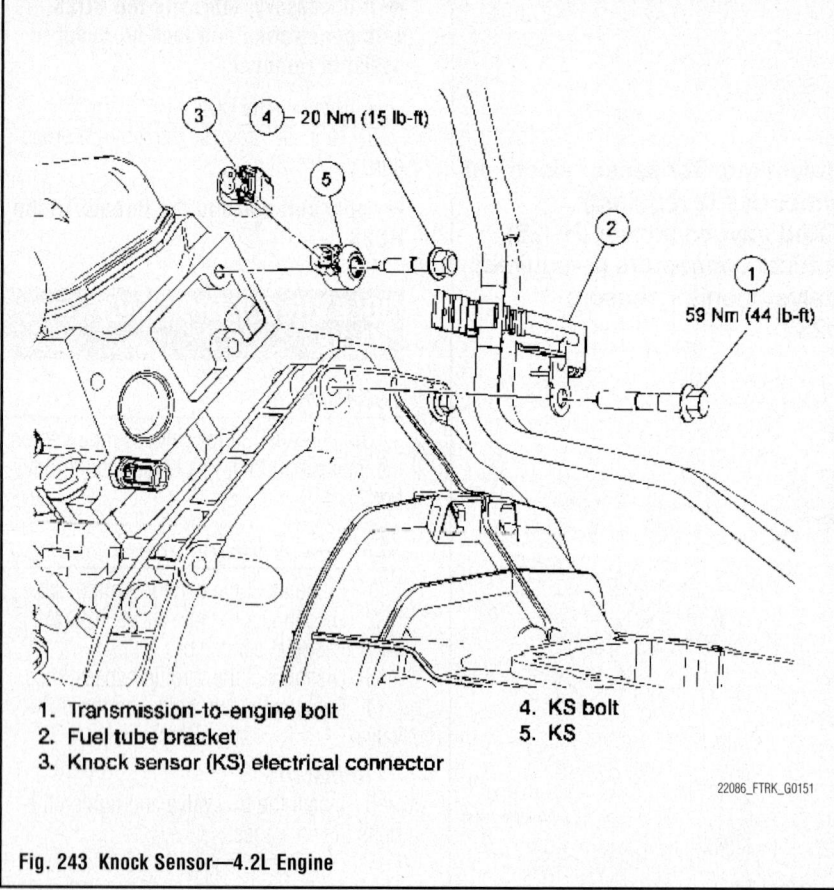

1. Transmission-to-engine bolt
2. Fuel tube bracket
3. Knock sensor (KS) electrical connector
4. KS bolt
5. KS

22086_FTRK_G0151

Fig. 243 Knock Sensor—4.2L Engine

6. Remove the bolt and the KS.
7. To install, reverse the removal procedure.

4.6L Engine

See Figure 244.

1. Before servicing the vehicle, refer to the precautions in the beginning of this section.
2. Remove the intake manifold.
3. Disconnect the knock sensor (KS) electrical connector.
4. Remove the bolt and the KS.

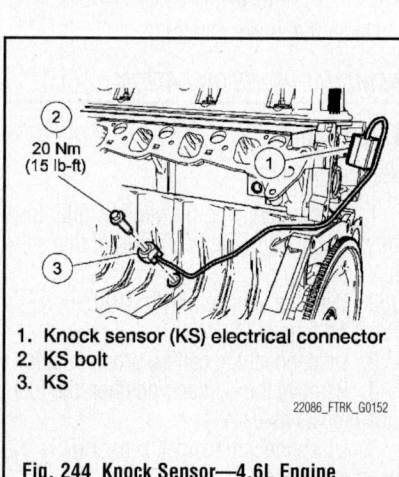

1. Knock sensor (KS) electrical connector
2. KS bolt
3. KS

22086_FTRK_G0152

Fig. 244 Knock Sensor—4.6L Engine

5. To install, reverse the removal procedure.

5.4L Engine

See Figure 245.

1. Before servicing the vehicle, refer to the precautions in the beginning of this section.
2. Remove the intake manifold.

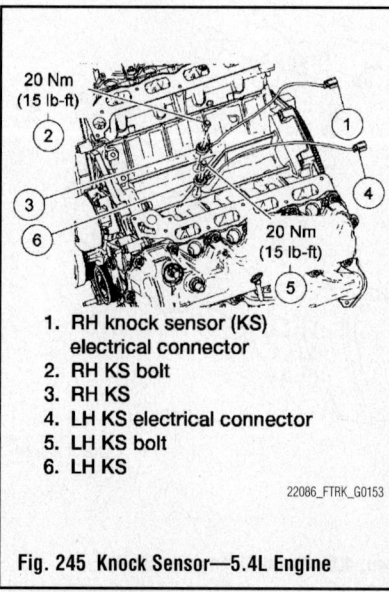

1. RH knock sensor (KS) electrical connector
2. RH KS bolt
3. RH KS
4. LH KS electrical connector
5. LH KS bolt
6. LH KS

22086_FTRK_G0153

Fig. 245 Knock Sensor—5.4L Engine

3. Disconnect the knock sensor (KS) electrical connectors.
4. Remove the bolts and the 2 KS.
5. To install, reverse the removal procedure.

MALFUNCTION INDICATOR LIGHT (MIL)

RESET PROCEDURE

A diagnostic scan tool must be connected to the data link connector (DLC) for communication with the vehicle.

1. The required diagnostic tool functions are described below:
   - Diagnostic test modes; self-test, clear diagnostic trouble codes (DTCs)
   - Resetting keep alive memory (KAM)
   - On-board system readiness (OBD monitor completion status)
   - Diagnostic monitoring test results (mode 6) for on-board diagnostic (OBD) on-board monitors
   - Output test mode
   - Monitor, record, and playback of parameter identification (PIDs)

MASS AIR FLOW (MAF) SENSOR

LOCATION

Attached to the air filter assembly.

REMOVAL & INSTALLATION

4.2L Engine

See Figure 246.

1. Before servicing the vehicle, refer to the precautions in the beginning of this section.
2. Release the clamp and detach the air cleaner cover from the air cleaner tray.
3. Lift the air cleaner tray from the grommets and remove the air cleaner tray.
4. Disconnect the mass air flow (MAF) sensor electrical connector and detach the electrical connector retainer.
5. Remove the grommet from the air cleaner cover and slide it down the wiring harness to allow the removal of the air cleaner inner cover and the MAF sensor.
6. Detach the air cleaner inner cover and pull the inner cover and MAF sensor out of the air cleaner cover and disconnect the MAF sensor jumper wire.
7. Remove the bolts and the MAF sensor.
8. To install, reverse the removal procedure.

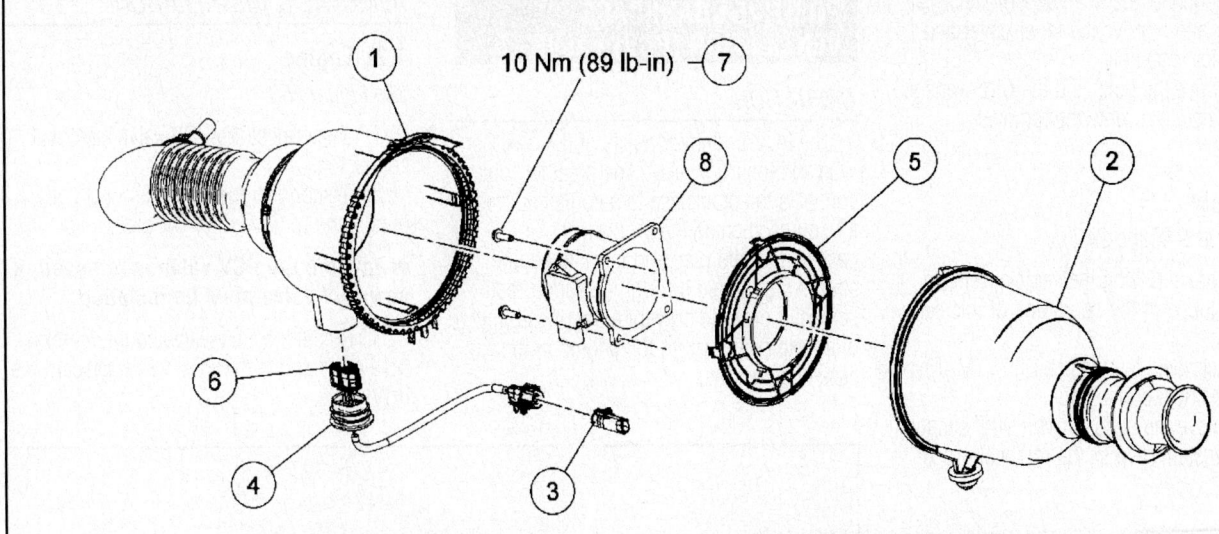

1. Air cleaner cover clamp
2. Air cleaner tray
3. Mass air flow (MAF) sensor electrical connector
4. Grommet
5. Air cleaner inner cover
6. MAF sensor jumper harness
7. MAF sensor bolt (2 required)
8. MAF sensor

22086_FTRK_G0154

Fig. 246 Mass Air Flow sensor—4.2L Engine

4.6L Engine

See Figure 247.

1. Before servicing the vehicle, refer to the precautions in the beginning of this section.

2. Open the clamp on the air cleaner and separate the tray from the cover.

3. Disconnect the mass air flow (MAF) sensor electrical connector and detach the connector retainer.

4. Remove the grommet from the air cleaner cover and slide it down the electrical harness.

5. Pull the air cleaner inner cover and MAF sensor out of the air cleaner cover.

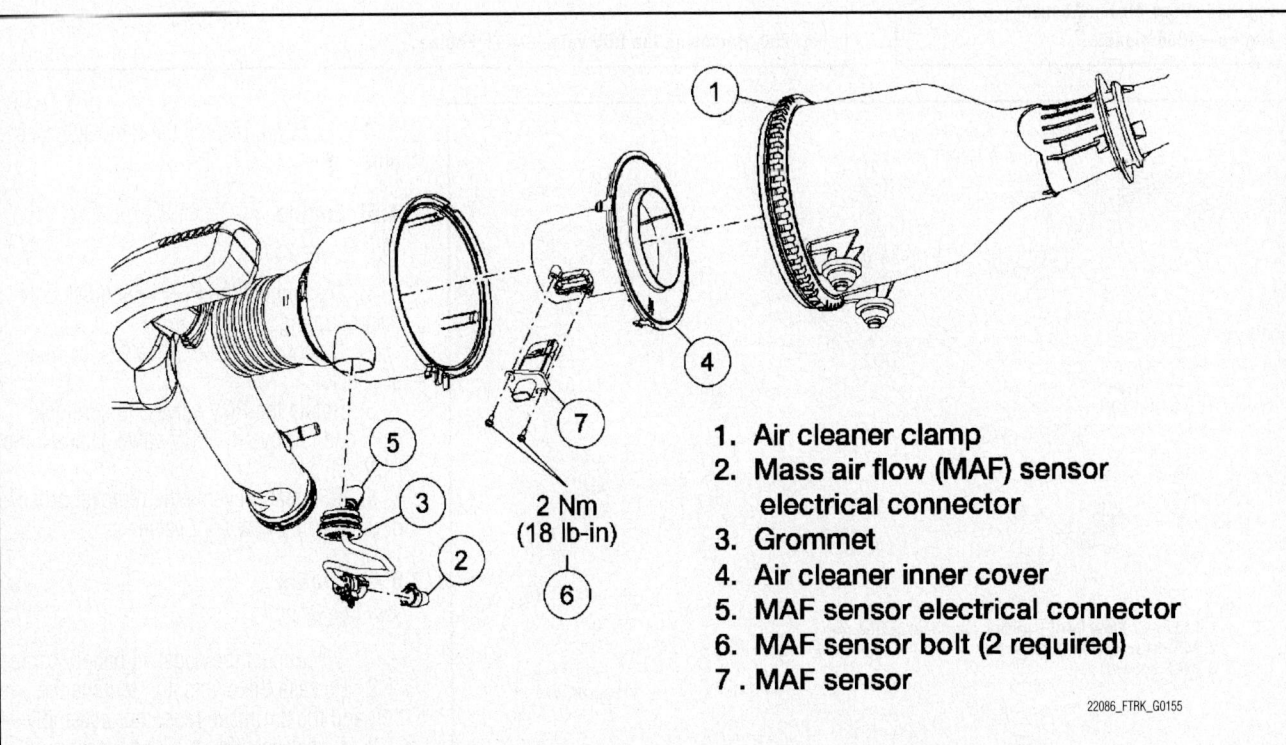

1. Air cleaner clamp
2. Mass air flow (MAF) sensor electrical connector
3. Grommet
4. Air cleaner inner cover
5. MAF sensor electrical connector
6. MAF sensor bolt (2 required)
7. MAF sensor

22086_FTRK_G0155

Fig. 247 Mass Air Flow sensor—4.6L Engine

6. Disconnect the MAF sensor electrical connector and remove the inner cover and MAF sensor assembly.

7. Remove the bolts and the MAF sensor.

8. To install, reverse the removal procedure.

5.4L Engine

See Figures 248 and 249.

1. Before servicing the vehicle, refer to the precautions in the beginning of this section.

2. Disconnect the mass air flow (MAF) sensor electrical connector.

3. Remove the bolts and the MAF sensor.

4. To install, reverse the removal procedure.

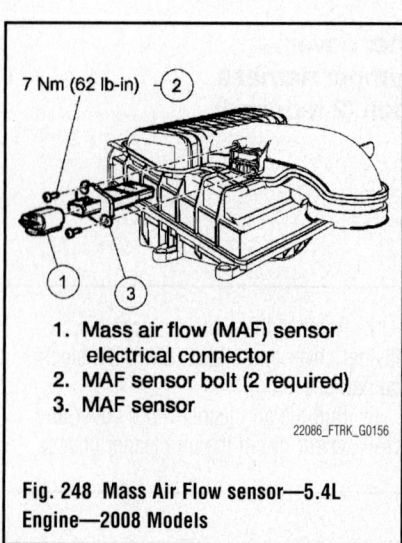

1. Mass air flow (MAF) sensor electrical connector
2. MAF sensor bolt (2 required)
3. MAF sensor

22086_FTRK_G0156

Fig. 248 Mass Air Flow sensor—5.4L Engine—2008 Models

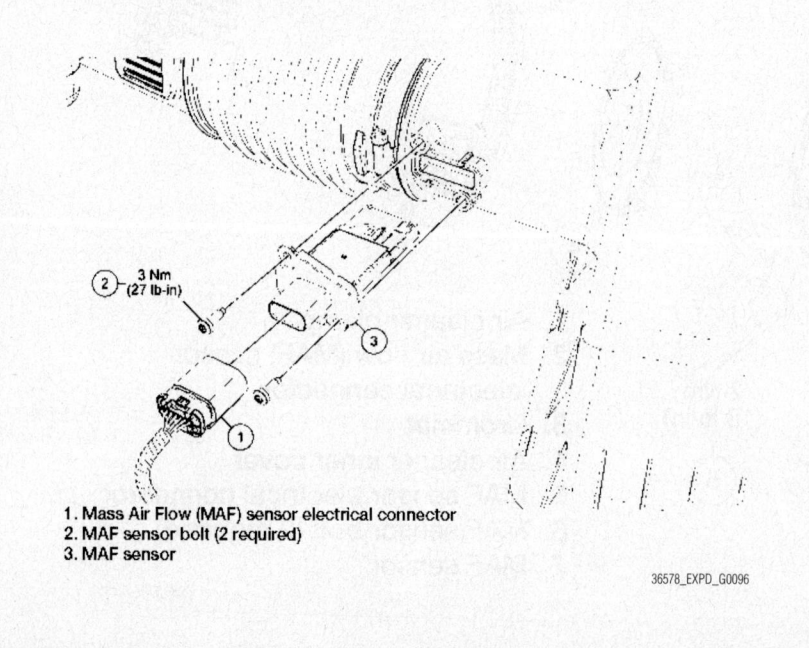

1. Mass Air Flow (MAF) sensor electrical connector
2. MAF sensor bolt (2 required)
3. MAF sensor

36578_EXPD_G0096

Fig. 249 Mass Air Flow sensor —5.4L Engine—2009 Models

POSITIVE CRANKCASE VENTILATION (PCV) VALVE

OPERATION

The PCV system consists of the breather tube and the PCV valve. The breather tube connects the crankcase to a contained fresh air source such as the air cleaner. Air passes into this tube and into the engine after being filtered through a spark arrestor screen in order to prevent a the possibility of an explosion within the engine in the case of a backfire.

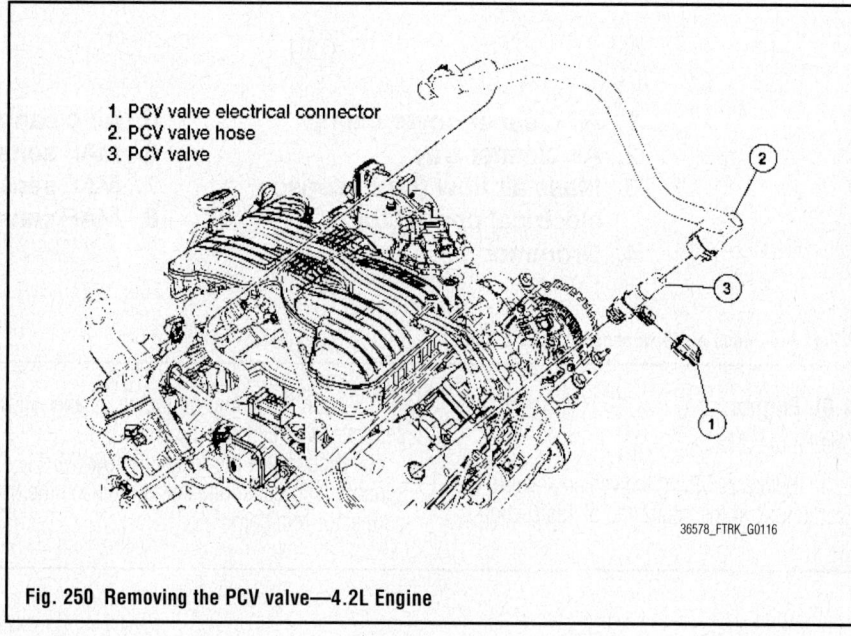

1. PCV valve electrical connector
2. PCV valve hose
3. PCV valve

36578_FTRK_G0116

Fig. 250 Removing the PCV valve—4.2L Engine

REMOVAL & INSTALLATION

4.2L Engine

See Figure 250.

1. Disconnect the PCV valve electrical connector.

2. Disconnect the quick connect couplings and remove the PCV tube.

➡**Anytime the PCV valve is removed, a new PCV valve must be installed.**

3. Rotate the PCV valve counterclockwise and remove the PCV valve. Discard the PCV valve.

4. To install, reverse the removal procedure.

4.6L Engine

See Figure 251.

1. Disconnect the PCV tube quick connect coupling.

2. Disconnect the PCV valve electrical connector.

3. Rotate the PCV valve counterclockwise and remove the PCV valve. Discard the PCV valve.

4. To install, reverse the removal procedure. Install a new PCV valve.

5.4L Engine

See Figure 252.

1. Disconnect the negative battery cable.

2. Release the clamp and remove the bolt and the air intake resonator assembly.

3. Disconnect the quick connect couplings and remove the PCV tube.

4. Disconnect the PCV heater element electrical connector.

5. Remove the 2 bolts and the PCV heater element.

6. Discard the O-ring seal.

7. To install, reverse removal procedure. Lubricate the o-ring with clean engine oil prior to installation.

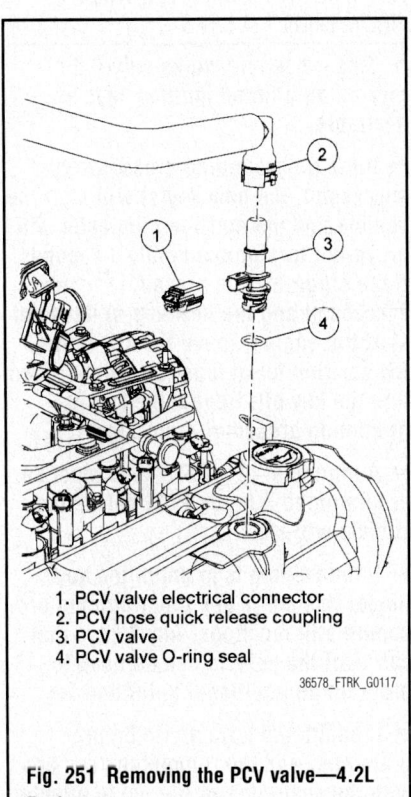

1. PCV valve electrical connector
2. PCV hose quick release coupling
3. PCV valve
4. PCV valve O-ring seal

36578_FTRK_G0117

Fig. 251 Removing the PCV valve—4.2L Engine

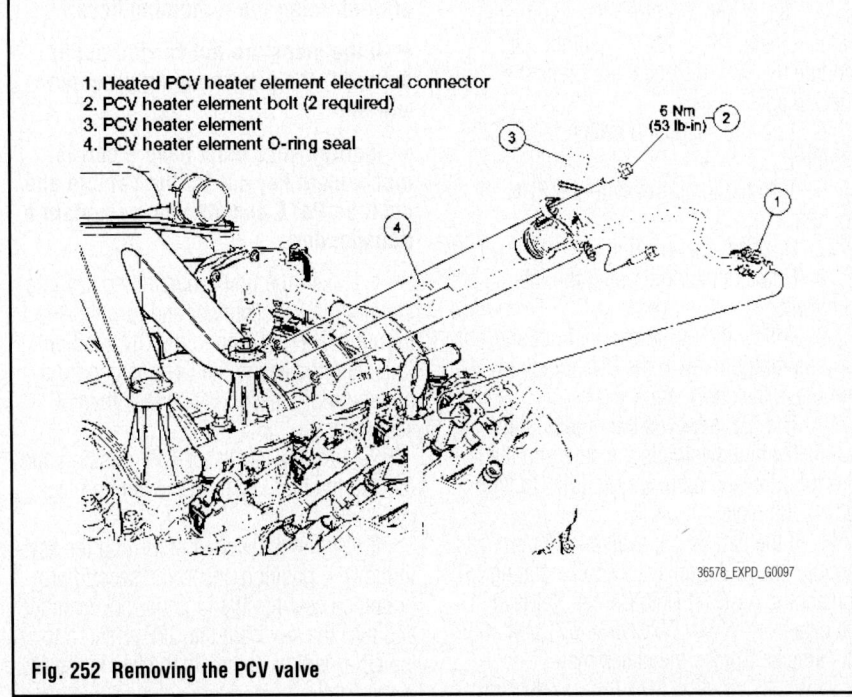

1. Heated PCV heater element electrical connector
2. PCV heater element bolt (2 required)
3. PCV heater element
4. PCV heater element O-ring seal

6 Nm (53 lb-in)

36578_EXPD_G0097

Fig. 252 Removing the PCV valve

POWERTRAIN CONTROL MODULE (PCM)

LOCATION

Passenger side of the engine compartment, mounted to the cowl.

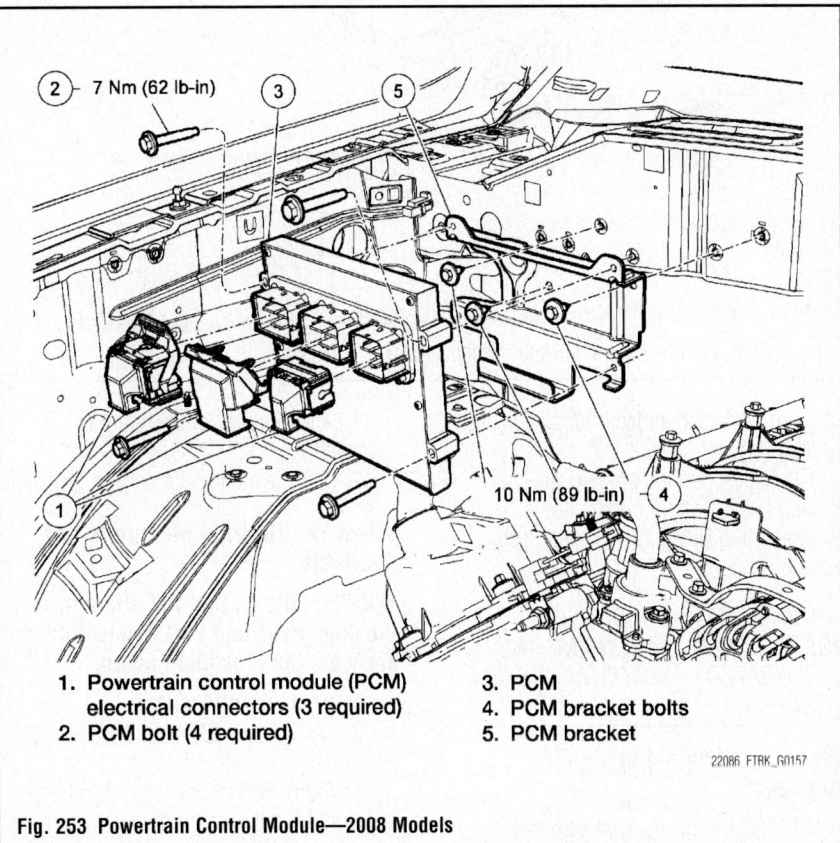

2 — 7 Nm (62 lb-in)

10 Nm (89 lb-in)

1. Powertrain control module (PCM) electrical connectors (3 required)
2. PCM bolt (4 required)
3. PCM
4. PCM bracket bolts
5. PCM bracket

22086_FTRK_G0157

Fig. 253 Powertrain Control Module—2008 Models

REMOVAL & INSTALLATION

See Figures 253 and 254.

➡ **Any powertrain control module (PCM) replacement will require that ALL customer keys are available to be reprogrammed** at the time of installation. **PCM replacement DOES NOT require new keys.**

1. Before servicing the vehicle, refer to the precautions in the beginning of this section.

2. Retrieve the module configuration. Carry out the module configuration retrieval steps of the Programmable Module Installation procedure.

3. Disconnect the PCM electrical connectors.

4. Remove the bolts and the PCM.

5. If necessary, remove the bolts and the PCM bracket.

To install:

6. If necessary, install the PCM bracket and the bolts.

7. Install the PCM and the bolts.

8. Connect the PCM electrical connectors.

9. Restore the module configuration. Carry out the module configuration restore

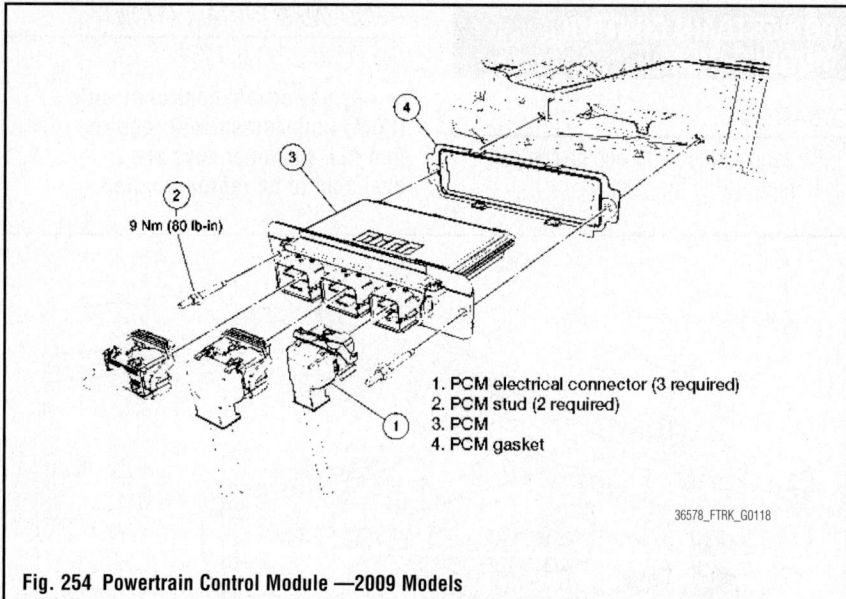

1. PCM electrical connector (3 required)
2. PCM stud (2 required)
3. PCM
4. PCM gasket

2 9 Nm (80 lb-in)

36578_FTRK_G0118

Fig. 254 Powertrain Control Module —2009 Models

steps of the Programmable Module Installation procedure.

10. Reprogram the passive anti-theft system (PATS). Carry out the Key Programming Using Two Programmed Keys procedure.

PROGRAMMABLE MODULE INSTALLATION (PMI) USING THE INTEGRATED DIAGNOSTIC SYSTEM (IDS)

When The Original Module Is Available

➡ **If PMI fails on the first attempt, exit the diagnostic tool PMI application and carry out the procedure again.**

1. Connect the IDS and ID the vehicle as normal.
2. From the Toolbox icon, select and highlight Module Programming and press the check mark.
3. Select and highlight Programmable Module Installation.
4. Follow the on-screen instructions, turn the ignition key to the OFF position, and press the check mark.
5. INSTALL the new module and press the check mark.
6. Turn the headlamp switch to the OFF position.
7. Turn the ignition key to the RUN position.
8. Open the driver's door.
9. Unlock the doors using the interior trim switch.
10. Follow the on-screen instructions, turn the ignition key to the ON position, and press the check mark.

11. The module configuration is complete.
12. Test the module for correct operation.

When The Original Module Is Not Available

➡ **If PMI fails on the first attempt, exit the diagnostic tool PMI application and carry out the procedure again.**

1. Install the new module.
2. Connect the IDS and ID the vehicle as normal.
3. From the Toolbox icon, select and highlight Module Programming. Then highlight the module that was installed and press the check mark.
4. Select and highlight Programmable Module Installation. Then highlight the module that was installed and press the check mark.
5. Turn the headlamp switch to the OFF position.
6. Turn the ignition key to the RUN position.
7. Open the driver's door.
8. Unlock the doors using the interior trim switch.
9. Follow the on-screen instructions, turn the ignition key to the RUN position and press the check mark.
10. The IDS retrieves the module data, automatically downloads the data into the new module, and displays Module Configuration Complete.
11. If the data is not available in the module, the IDS displays a screen stating to contact the As-Built Data Center. Retrieve the data from WWW.FMCDEALER.COM at this time and press the check mark.

12. Enter the module data (the module address and line are displayed to the left of the 3 entry boxes) and press the check mark.
13. The IDS downloads the data into the new module and displays Operation Successful - Programming Complete.
14. Test the module for correct operation.

KEY PROGRAMMING USING TWO PROGRAMMED KEYS

➡ **This procedure works only if 2 or more programmed ignition keys are available.**

➡ **If the programming procedure is successful, the new key(s) will start the vehicle and the anti-theft indicator will prove-out for approximately 3 seconds. If the programming procedure is not successful and the new key(s) does not start the engine, leave the key in the ON position for at least 3 seconds, then turn the key off. Repeat the key programming procedure from Step 1.**

➡ **A minimum of 2 PATS keys must be programmed into the PCM before the vehicle will start.**

➡ **If the vehicle is in unlimited key mode, this spare key programming procedure still functions. Any 2 keys that can start the vehicle can be used to program an additional unlimited key.**

➡ **If additional keys are to be programmed, and the remaining keys are with the customer, or are not available, instruct the customer to refer to the Owner's Literature for instructions on programming the remaining keys.**

➡ **If the steps are not carried out as outlined, the programming procedure will end.**

➡ **Ignition keys must have a correct mechanical key cut for the vehicle and must be PATS encoded keys (contain a transponder).**

1. Insert the first programmed key into the ignition lock cylinder and turn the key from the OFF position to the ON position (maintain the key in the ON position for a minimum of 3 seconds and less than 10 seconds).
2. Turn the key to the OFF position and remove the first key from the ignition lock cylinder.
3. Within 5 seconds of turning the key to the OFF position, insert the second programmed key into the ignition lock cylinder and turn the key from the OFF position to the ON position (maintain the key in the ON

position for a minimum of 3 seconds and less than 10 seconds).

4. Turn the key to the OFF position and remove the key from the ignition lock cylinder.

5. Within 10 seconds of turning the key to the OFF position, insert the unprogrammed key (the new key) into the ignition lock cylinder and turn the key from the OFF position to the ON position (maintain the key in the ON position for a minimum of 3 seconds and less than 10 seconds).

6. If it is desired to program additional key(s) (only up to 8 keys total can be programmed into the PCM), repeat Steps 1 - 5 for each additional key that needs to be programmed.

7. Start the vehicle with the new key(s).

THROTTLE POSITION SENSOR (TPS)

LOCATION

Mounted on the throttle body.

REMOVAL & INSTALLATION

5.4L Engine

See Figure 255.

1. Before servicing the vehicle, refer to the precautions in the beginning of this section.

2. Disconnect the throttle position (TP) sensor electrical connector.

❋❋ CAUTION

Failure to remove the TP sensor screws in the following manner will result in damage to the screws.

3. First loosen the screws 1-2 full turns using a hand tool and then use a suitable high speed driver to complete the removal.

4. Remove and discard the 2 screws and the TP sensor.

To install:

❋❋ CAUTION

Do not reuse the TP sensor and screws. A new TP sensor and screws must be installed.

❋❋ CAUTION

Do not use a high speed driver to install the new screws or damage to the TP sensor can occur.

➡ When installing the new TP sensor, make sure that the radial locator tab on the TP sensor is aligned with the radial locator hole on the throttle body (TB).

5. Position the new TP sensor and install the 2 new screws.

6. Tighten to 3 Nm (27 lb-in).
7. Connect the TP sensor electrical connector.

OUTPUT SHAFT SPEED (OSS) SENSOR

REMOVAL & INSTALLATION

See Figure 256.

1. Before servicing the vehicle, refer to the precautions in the beginning of this section.

2. With the vehicle in NEUTRAL, position it on a hoist.

3. Disconnect the output shaft speed (OSS) sensor electrical connector.

➡ Prior to removing the speed sensor, make sure that the area around the sensor is free of foreign material to prevent contamination of the transmission.

4. Remove the OSS sensor.

To install:

5. Lubricate the O-ring with clean automatic transmission fluid and install the OSS sensor.

6. Install the bolt and tighten to 9 Nm (80 lb-in).

7. Connect the OSS sensor electrical connector.

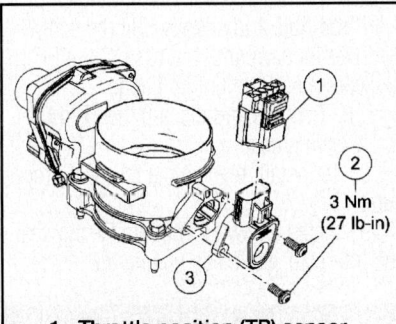

1. Throttle position (TP) sensor electrical connector
2. TP sensor screws (2 required)
3. TP sensor

22086_FTRK_G0158

Fig. 255 Throttle Position Sensor—5.4L Engine

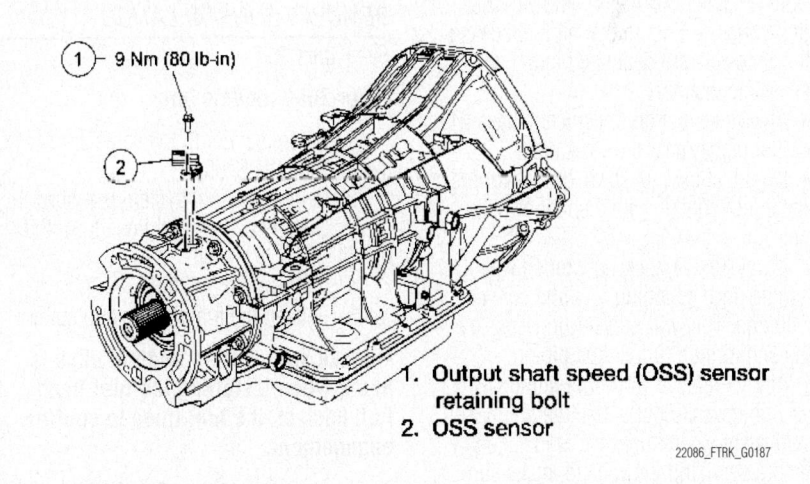

1. Output shaft speed (OSS) sensor retaining bolt
2. OSS sensor

22086_FTRK_G0187

Fig. 256 Output Shaft Speed sensor

FUEL SYSTEM SERVICE PRECAUTIONS

Safety is the most important factor when performing not only fuel system maintenance but any type of maintenance. Failure to conduct maintenance and repairs in a safe manner may result in serious personal injury or death. Maintenance and testing of the vehicle's fuel system components can be accomplished safely and effectively by adhering to the following rules and guidelines.

• To avoid the possibility of fire and personal injury, always disconnect the negative battery cable unless the repair or test procedure requires that battery voltage be applied.

• Always relieve the fuel system pressure prior to disconnecting any fuel system component (injector, fuel rail, pressure regulator, etc.), fitting or fuel line connection. Exercise extreme caution whenever relieving fuel system pressure to avoid exposing skin, face and eyes to fuel spray. Please be advised that fuel under pressure may penetrate the skin or any part of the body that it contacts.

• Always place a shop towel or cloth around the fitting or connection prior to loosening to absorb any excess fuel due to spillage. Ensure that all fuel spillage (should it occur) is quickly removed from engine surfaces. Ensure that all fuel soaked cloths or towels are deposited into a suitable waste container.

• Always keep a dry chemical (Class B) fire extinguisher near the work area.

• Do not allow fuel spray or fuel vapors to come into contact with a spark or open flame.

• Always use a back-up wrench when loosening and tightening fuel line connection fittings. This will prevent unnecessary stress and torsion to fuel line piping.

• Always replace worn fuel fitting O-rings with new. Do not substitute fuel hose or equivalent where fuel pipe is installed.

Before servicing the vehicle, make sure to also refer to the precautions in the beginning of this section as well.

RELIEVING FUEL SYSTEM PRESSURE

1. Before servicing the vehicle, refer to the Precautions Section.

➡The splash shield is located on the LH frame rail under the driver side door.

2. Disconnect the splash shield and position aside.

3. Disconnect the electrical connector.

4. Start the engine and allow it to idle until it stalls.

5. After the engine stalls, crank the engine for approximately 5 seconds to make sure the fuel rail pressure has been released.

6. Turn the ignition switch to the OFF position.

7. When fuel system service is complete, connect the electrical connector.

8. Reposition the splash shield and install a new push pin.

➡It may take more than one key cycle to pressurize the fuel system.

9. Cycle the ignition key and wait 3 seconds to pressurize the fuel system. Check for leaks before starting the engine.

10. Install the WDS diagnostic tool. Turn the key ON with the engine OFF. Cycle the key OFF, then ON. Select the appropriate vehicle and engine qualifier. Clear all diagnostic trouble codes (DTCs) and carry out a PCM reset.

11. Start the vehicle and check the fuel system for leaks.

FUEL FILTER

REMOVAL & INSTALLATION

See Figure 257.

➡For 2008 models only.

1. Before servicing the vehicle, refer to the Precautions Section.

2. Relieve the fuel system pressure.

3. Disconnect the fuel lines from the fuel filter.

4. Remove the fuel filter.

5. Loosen the fuel filter clamp screw.

➡Make sure that an audible click is heard when installing the fuel lines. Pull back on the fuel lines to confirm engagement.

6. To install, reverse the removal procedure.

FUEL PUMP MODULE

REMOVAL & INSTALLATION

See Figures 258 and 259.

1. With the vehicle in NEUTRAL, position it on a hoist.

2. Remove the fuel tank.

3. Using soapy water, clean a minimum of 76 mm (3 in) surface area around the fuel pump module.

4. Disconnect the fuel supply and fuel vapor tube assembly quick connect couplings at the fuel pump module and remove the fuel supply and fuel vapor tube assembly from the fuel tank.

5. Using the special tool, remove the fuel pump module locking ring.

6. For 2008 models, perform the following:

   a. Lift the fuel pump module out of the fuel tank enough to disconnect the internal fuel tank grade vent valves-to-fuel pump quick connect coupling.

⁂ CAUTION

The fuel pump module must be handled carefully to avoid damage to the float arm and the filter.

   b. Remove the fuel pump module.

   c. Remove and discard the fuel pump module O-ring seal.

7. For 2009 models, perform the following:

➡If the FP does not clear the FP mounting flange on the fuel tank, the use of a screwdriver may be necessary.

   a. Remove the FP module. If necessary, insert a screwdriver into the empty FP rod hole and slightly pull the screwdriver inboard until the base of the FP clears the FP mounting flange.

   b. Remove and discard the FP module O-ring seal.

8. To install, reverse the removal procedure.

9. Install a new FP module O-ring seal and lubricate with clean engine oil.

FUEL RAIL & INJECTORS

REMOVAL & INSTALLATION

4.2L Engine

See Figure 259.

1. Before servicing the vehicle, refer to the Precautions Section.

2. Release the fuel system pressure.

3. Disconnect the battery ground cable.

4. Disconnect the spring lock coupling at the fuel rail.

5. Remove the upper intake manifold.

6. Disconnect the fuel rail pressure sensor vacuum and electrical connectors.

7. Disconnect the 6 fuel injector electrical connectors.

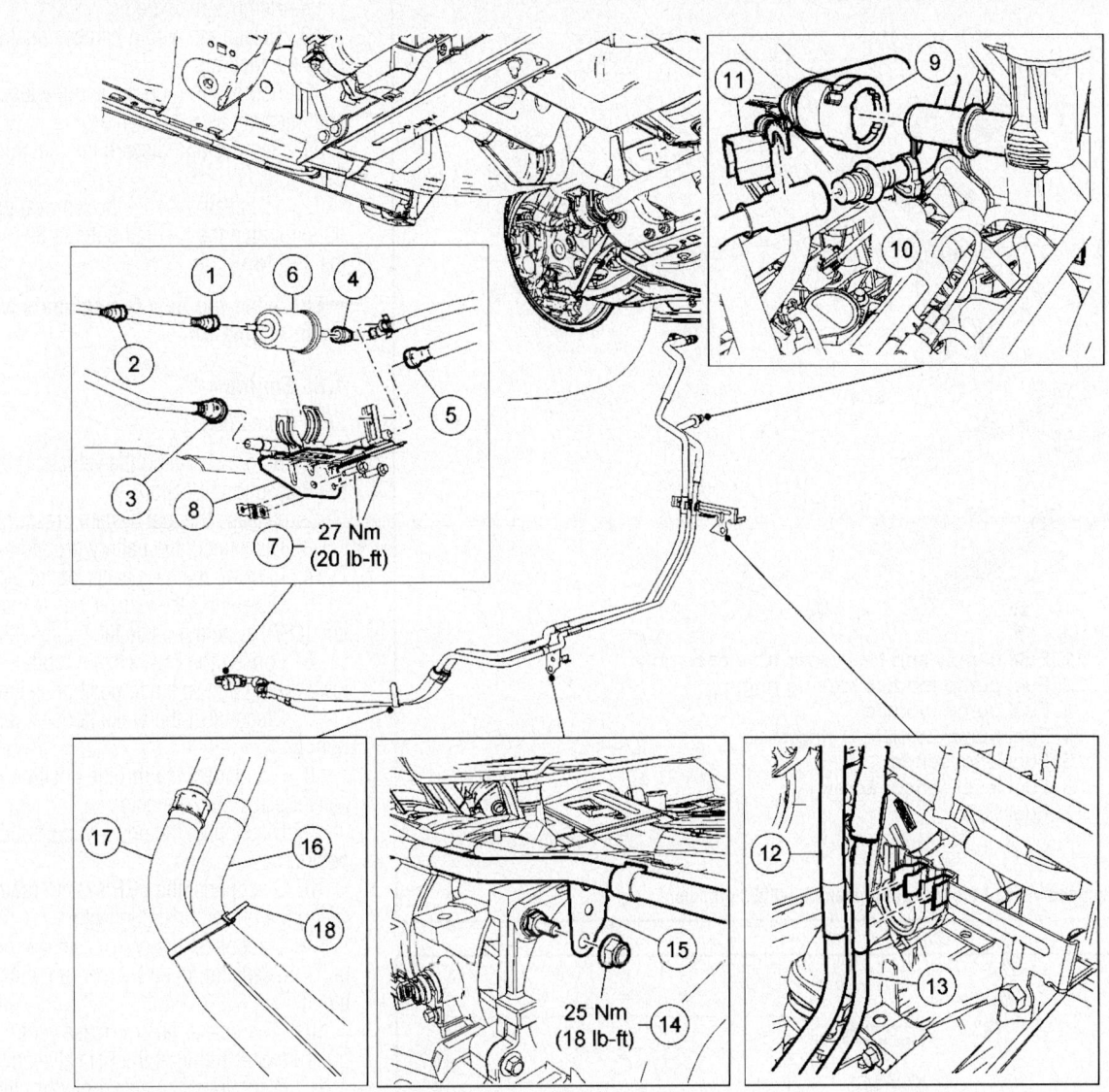

1. Fuel filter inlet fuel tube quick connect coupling
2. Fuel tube quick connect coupling
3. Fuel filter bracket inlet vapor tube quick connect coupling
4. Fuel filter outlet fuel tube spring lock coupling
5. Fuel filter bracket outlet vapor tube spring lock coupling
6. Fuel filter
7. Fuel filter bracket bolts (2 required)
8. Fuel filter bracket
9. Evaporative emission canister purge valve vapor tube quick connect coupling
10. Fuel rail spring lock coupling
11. Tether
12. Vapor tube
13. Fuel supply tube
14. Fuel tube assembly support bracket nut
15. Fuel tube assembly support bracket
16. Fuel supply tube
17. Vapor tube
18. Tie strap (if equipped)

36578_FTRK_G0119

Fig. 257 Exploded view of the fuel lines and fuel filter—2008 Models only

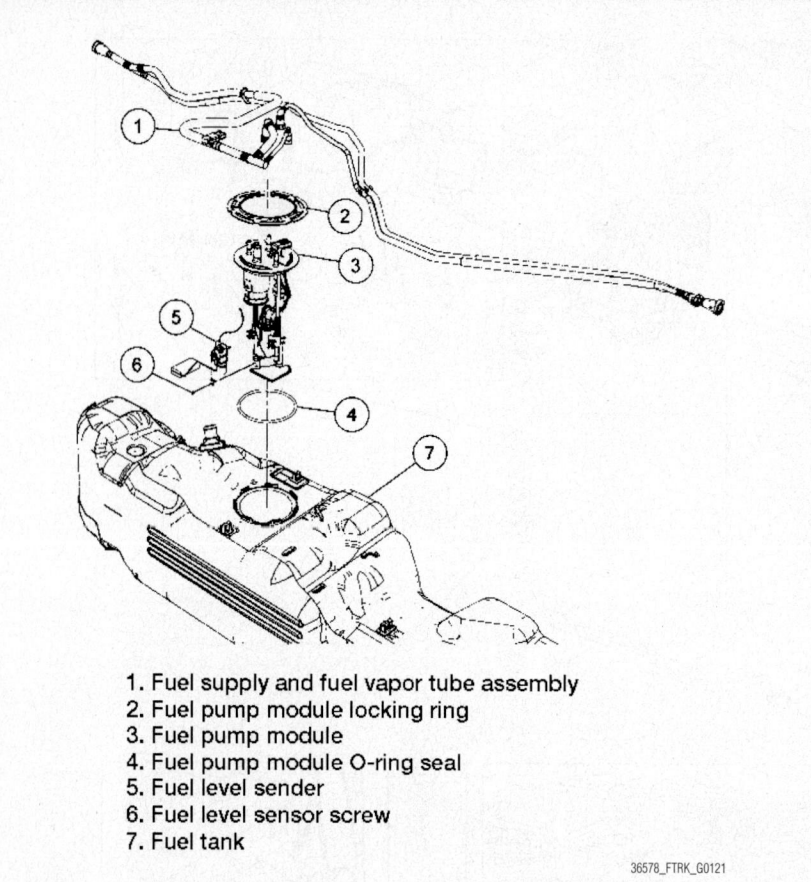

1. Fuel supply and fuel vapor tube assembly
2. Fuel pump module locking ring
3. Fuel pump module
4. Fuel pump module O-ring seal
5. Fuel level sender
6. Fuel level sensor screw
7. Fuel tank

36578_FTRK_G0121

Fig. 258 Exploded view of the fuel pump module—2008 Models

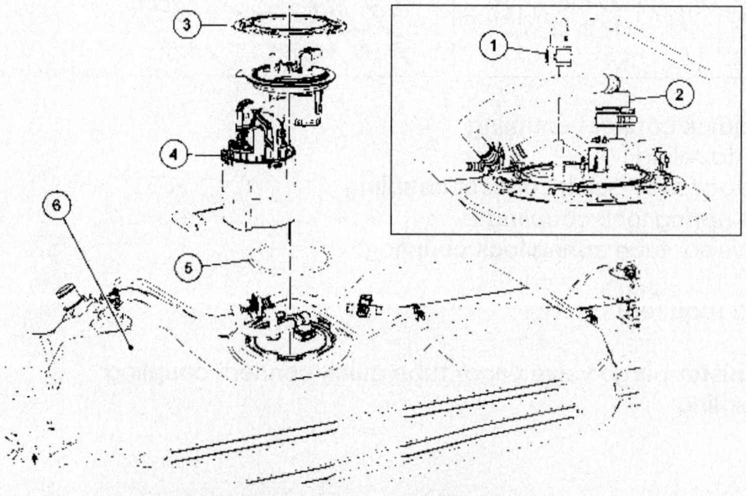

1. Fuel supply tube quick connect coupling
2. Fuel Tank Pressure (FTP) sensor and vapor tube assembly quick connect coupling
3. Fuel pump module locking ring
4. Fuel pump module
5. Fuel pump module O-ring seal
6. Fuel tank

36578_FTRK_G0122

Fig. 259 Exploded view of the fuel system components—2009 Models

8. Remove the wire tie.
9. Detach the wiring harness retainers from the fuel rail.
10. Remove the 4 bolts and the fuel rail and injectors as an assembly.
11. Remove and discard the fuel injector O-ring seals.
12. To install, reverse the removal procedure. Tighten the fuel rail bolts to 89 inch lbs. (10 Nm).

➡**Lubricate the new O-ring seals with clean engine oil.**

4.6L Engine

See Figure 260.

1. Before servicing the vehicle, refer to the Precautions Section.
2. Release the fuel system pressure.
3. Disconnect the battery ground cable.
4. Remove the air cleaner outlet pipe.
5. Disconnect the exhaust gas recirculation (EGR) system module tube upper fitting.
6. Loosen the EGR system module tube lower fitting and rotate to position aside.
7. Disconnect the brake booster vacuum hose.
8. Disconnect the throttle position (TP) sensor electrical connector.
9. Disconnect the upper vapor tube and position aside.
10. Disconnect the EGR system module vacuum and electrical connector.
11. Disconnect the crankcase vent hose quick-release fitting at the rear of the intake manifold.
12. Disconnect the crankcase vent hose quick-release fitting at the RH valve cover.
13. Disconnect the electronic throttle control electrical connector.
14. Disconnect the throttle body spacer vacuum hose.
15. Release the heated TB coolant hose clamp and remove and plug the coolant hose.
16. Release the heated TB coolant hose clamp and remove and plug the coolant hose.
17. Remove the 4 throttle body spacer bolts and the throttle body assembly and discard the gasket.
18. Disconnect the injection pressure sensor electrical connector.
19. Disconnect the 8 fuel injector electrical connectors.
20. Disconnect the injection pressure sensor vacuum connector.
21. Disconnect the fuel tube spring lock coupling.
22. Remove the 4 fuel rail bolts.
23. Remove the fuel rail.
24. Remove the 8 fuel injectors.

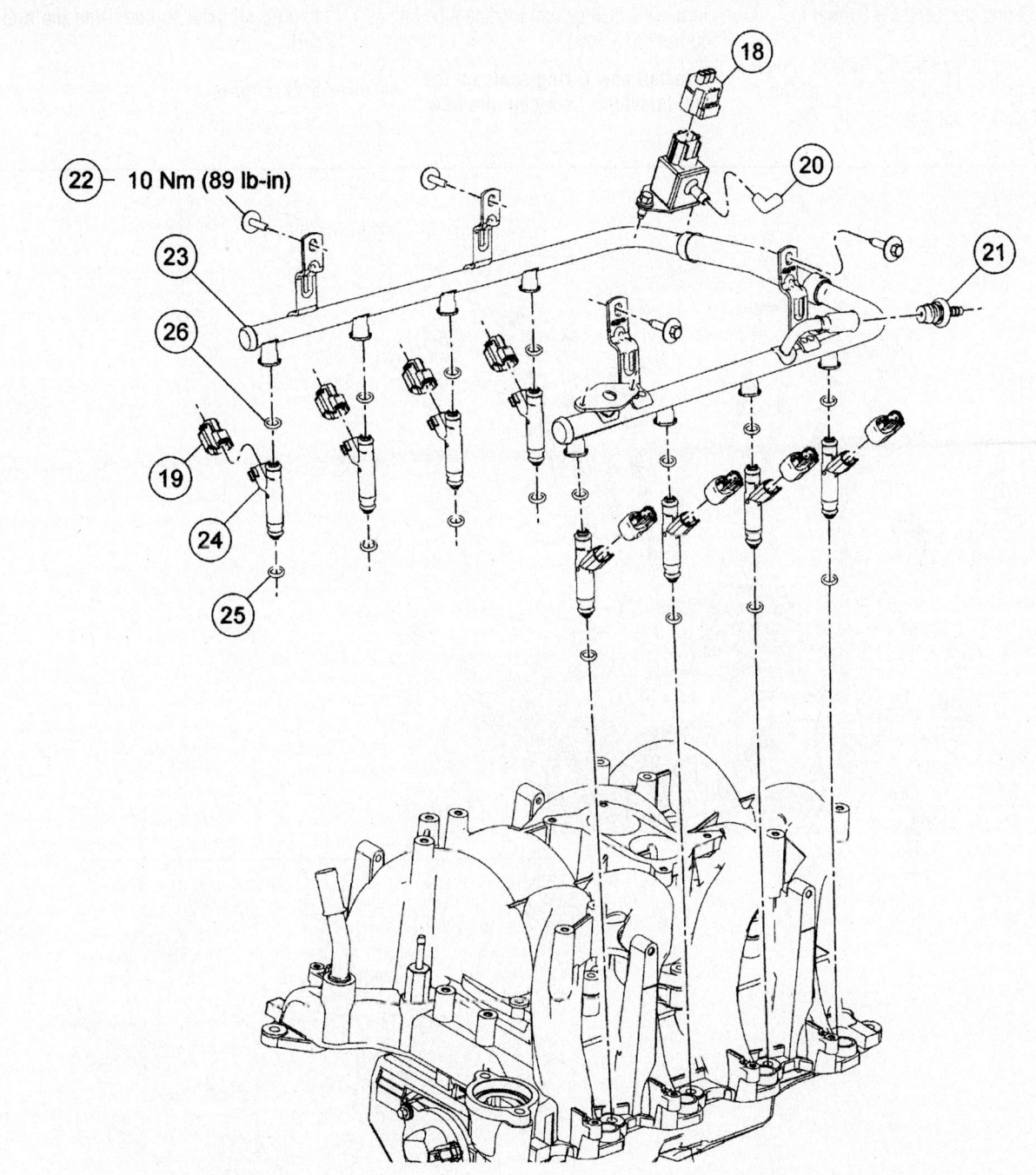

10 Nm (89 lb-in)

18 Injection pressure sensor electrical connector

19 Fuel injector electrical connector (8 required)

20 Injection pressure sensor vacuum connector

21 Fuel tube spring lock coupling

22 Fuel rail bolts (4 required)

23 Fuel rail

24 Fuel injector (8 required)

25 Fuel injector to intake manifold O-ring seal (8 required)

26 Fuel injector to fuel rail O-ring seal (8 required)

06017-F150-G235

Fig. 260 Fuel rail and injectors— 4.6L engine

25. Remove and discard the 8 upper fuel injector O-ring seals and the 8 lower fuel injector O-ring seals

26. To install, reverse the removal procedure. Torque the 4 fuel rail bolts to 10 Nm (89 inch lbs.).Torque the 4 throttle body spacer bolts to 10 Nm (89 inch lbs.). Torque the EGR system module tube fittings 40 Nm (30 ft. lbs.).

➡Install new O-ring seals on the fuel injectors. Lubricate the new fuel injector O-ring seals with clean engine oil prior to installing the fuel rail.

5.4L Engine

See Figure 261.

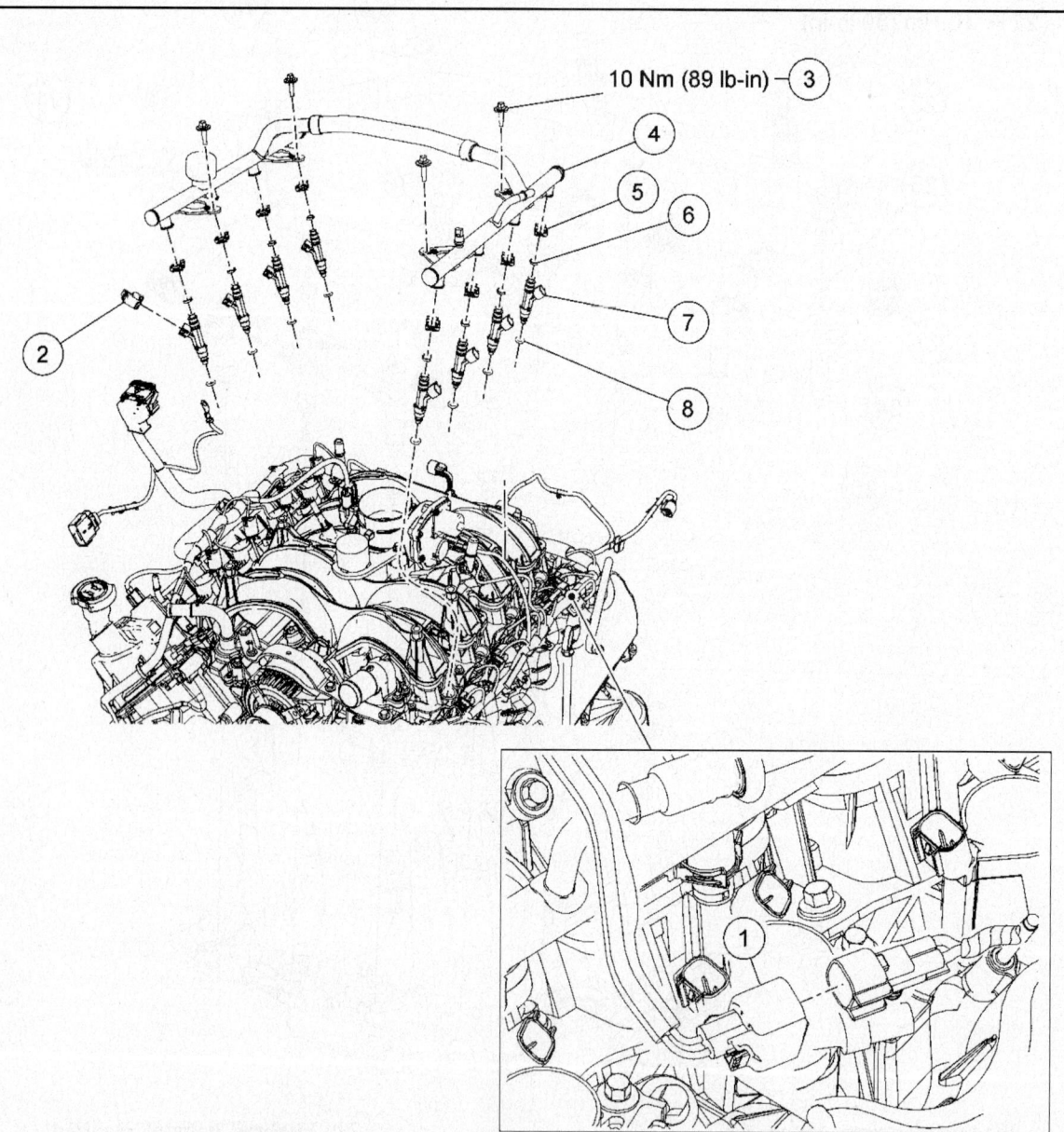

10 Nm (89 lb-in) — 3

1. Heated PCV intake fitting electrical connector
2. Fuel injector electrical connector (8 required)
3. Fuel rail bolt (4 required)
4. Fuel rail
5. Fuel injector-to-fuel rail locking clip (8 required)
6. Fuel injector-to-fuel rail O-ring (8 required)
7. Fuel injector (8 required)
8. Fuel injector-to-intake manifold O-ring (8 required)

36578_EXPD_G0107

Fig. 261 Exploded view of the fuel rail and fuel injectors

Fuel injection systems remain under pressure, even after the engine has been turned OFF. The fuel system pressure must be relieved before disconnecting any fuel lines. Failure to do so may result in fire and/or personal injury.

1. Before servicing the vehicle, refer to the precautions section.
2. Properly relieve the fuel system pressure.
3. Disconnect the negative battery cable.
4. Disconnect the fuel supply tube spring lock coupling.
5. Remove the air cleaner outlet pipe.
6. Disconnect the quick connect couplings and remove the crankcase vent tube.
7. Disconnect the generator wiring harness retainer from the air cleaner outlet pipe-to-throttle body (TB) adapter.
8. Remove the 4 bolts and the air cleaner outlet pipe-to-TB adapter.
9. Disconnect the quick connect couplings and remove the positive crankcase ventilation (PCV) tube.
10. Disconnect the electronic throttle control electrical connector
11. Disconnect the Throttle Position Sensor (TPS) electrical connector.
12. Disconnect the heated PCV intake fitting electrical connector.
13. Disconnect the 8 fuel injector electrical connectors.
14. Remove the 4 fuel rail bolts.

15. Remove the fuel rail and fuel injectors as an assembly.
16. Separate the fuel injectors from the fuel rail.

✳✳ **WARNING**

Use O-ring seals that are made of special fuel-resistant material. Use of ordinary O-rings can cause the fuel system to leak. Do not reuse the O-ring seals. Lubricate the O-ring seals with clean engine oil prior to installation.

17. To install, reverse the removal procedure and note the following:
   • Lubricate the air cleaner outlet pipe-to-TB adapter seal with clean engine coolant prior to installation
   • Tighten the fuel rail retainers to 89 inch lbs. (10 Nm).
   • Tighten the 4 bolts to the air cleaner outlet pipe-to-TB adapter, to 89 inch lbs. (10 Nm).

FUEL TANK

REMOVAL & INSTALLATION

✳✳ **CAUTION**

Fuel injection systems remain under pressure, even after the engine has been turned OFF. The fuel system pressure must be relieved before disconnecting any fuel lines. Failure to do so may result in fire and/or personal injury.

1. Before servicing the vehicle, refer to the Precautions Section.
2. Remove or disconnect the following:
   • Negative battery cable
   • Fuel pressure
   • Fuel tank skid plate bolts and lower the skid plate.
   • Fuel
   • Fuel tank filler pipe hose from the tank
   • Fuel tank filler pipe vent hose from the tank
   • Fuel lines from the fuel pump
   • Front fuel tank connections
   • Rear Evaporative Emissions (EVAP) hose clamp and the hose
   • Electrical connector from the fuel pump
3. Support the fuel tank with a jack.
   • Fuel tank support strap bolts and the fuel tank straps
   • Fuel tank

To install:
4. Installation is the reverse of removal. Note the following torques:
   a. Tighten the fuel tank strap bolts to: 35 ft. lbs. (47 Nm).

THROTTLE BODY

REMOVAL & INSTALLATION

4.2L Engine

See Figure 262.

➡ **The throttle body bore and plate area have a special coating and cannot be cleaned.**

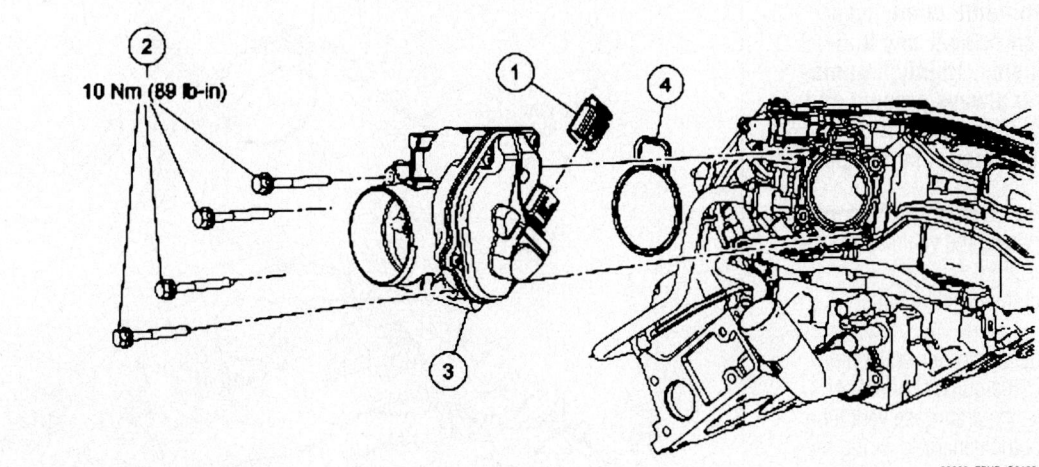

10 Nm (89 lb-in)

32069_FPUP_G0103

Fig. 262 1. Electronic throttle body electrical connector
2. Electronic throttle body bolts
3. Electronic throttle body
4. Electronic throttle body gasket
Throttle body and related parts—4.2L engine

1. Before servicing the vehicle, refer to the precautions in the beginning of this section.

2. Remove the air cleaner outlet tube.

3. Disconnect the electronic throttle body electrical connector.

4. Remove the bolts and the electronic throttle body.

5. Inspect the throttle body gasket. Install a new gasket, if necessary.

6. To install, reverse the removal procedure. Tighten to 10 Nm (89 inch lbs.).

4.6L Engine

See Figure 263.

➡ **The throttle body bore and plate area have a special coating and cannot be cleaned.**

1. Before servicing the vehicle, refer to the precautions in the beginning of this section.

2. Disconnect the battery ground.

3. Remove the air cleaner outlet pipe.

4. Disconnect the TP sensor electrical connector.

5. Disconnect the electronic throttle control electrical connector.

6. Remove the TB bolts and the TB and discard the gasket.

7. To install, reverse the removal procedure. Install a new TB gasket. To install, tighten to 9 Nm (80 inch lbs.). Tighten an additional 90 degrees.

5.4L Engine

See Figures 264 and 265.

✳✳ CAUTION

Do not smoke or carry lighted tobacco or open flame of any type when working on or near any fuel-related components. Highly flammable mixtures are always present and may be ignited. Failure to follow these instructions may result in personal injury.

1. Before servicing the vehicle, refer to the precautions section.

2. Disconnect the negative battery cable.

3. Remove the air cleaner outlet pipe.

4. Disconnect the quick connect couplings and remove the crankcase vent tube.

5. Disconnect the generator wiring harness retainer from the air cleaner outlet pipe-to-throttle body (TB) adapter.

6. Remove the 4 bolts and position aside the air cleaner outlet tube-to-TB adapter.

7. Disconnect the electronic throttle control electrical connector

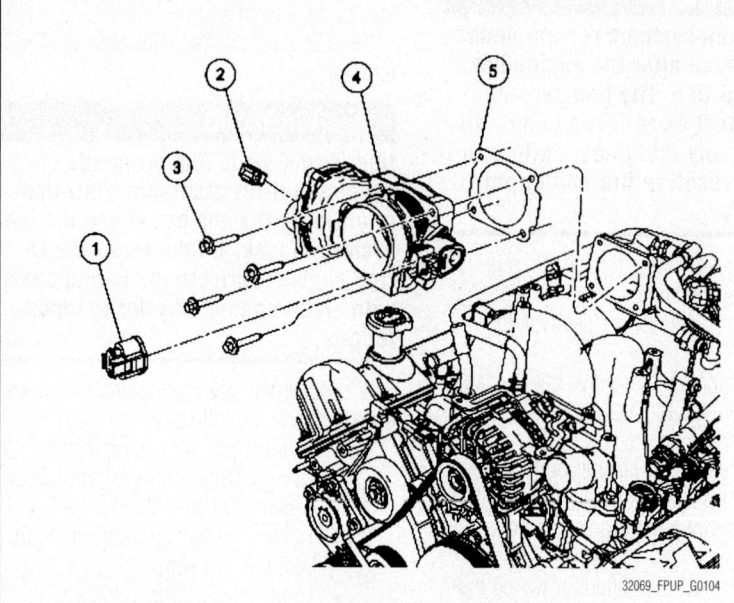

32069_FPUP_G0104

Fig. 263 1. Throttle position (TP) sensor electrical connector
2. Electronic throttle control electrical connector
3. Throttle body (TB) bolts
4. Throttle body
5. Throttle body gasket
Throttle body and related parts—4.6L engine

1. Crankcase ventilation tube
2. Air cleaner outlet pipe-to-throttle body adapter bolt (4 required)
3. Air cleaner outlet pipe-to-throttle body adapter

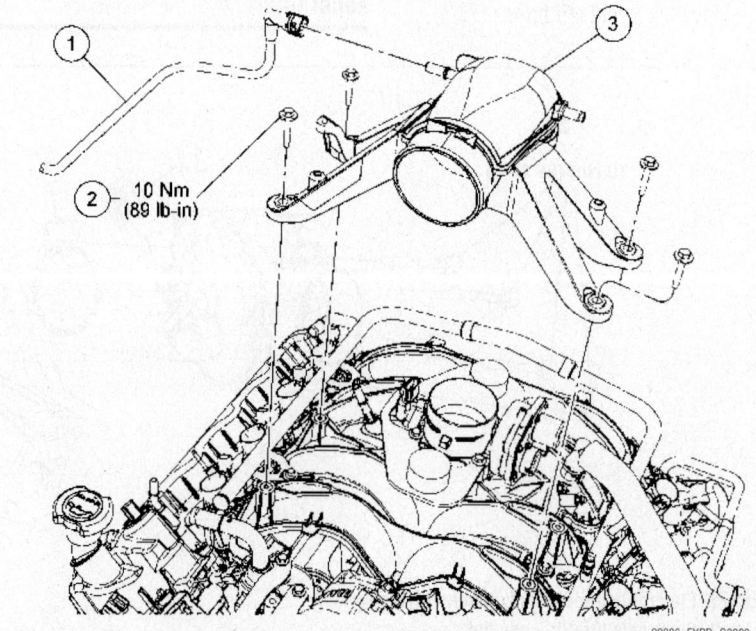

10 Nm
(89 lb-in)

22086_EXPD_G0060

Fig. 264 Air cleaner outlet pipe view

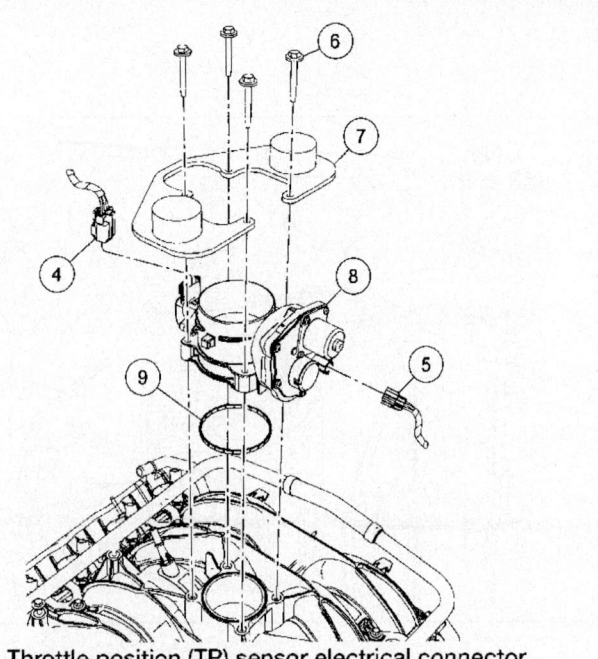

4. Throttle position (TP) sensor electrical connector
5. Electronic throttle control electrical connector
6. Throttle body bolt (4 required)
7. Vibration damper
8. Throttle body
9. Throttle body O-ring

22086_EXPD_G0059

Fig. 265 Throttle body

8. Disconnect the Throttle Position Sensor (TPS) electrical connector.

9. Remove the 4 bolts and the vibration damper

10. Remove the TB assembly.

To install:

11. Using a new O-ring seal, position the TB and vibration damper and tighten the 4 bolts in 2 stages.
   - Stage 1: Tighten to 80 inch lbs. (9 Nm).
   - Stage 2: Tighten an additional 90 degrees.

12. Connect the TPS electrical connector.

13. Connect the electronic throttle control electrical connector.

14. Lubricate the air cleaner outlet pipe-to-TB adapter seal with clean engine coolant prior to installation.

15. Position the air cleaner outlet pipe-to-TB adapter and install the 4 bolts.

16. Tighten bolts to 80 inch lbs. (9 Nm).

17. Connect the generator wiring harness retainer to the air cleaner outlet tube-to-TB adapter.

18. Position the crankcase vent tube and connect the quick connect couplings

19. Install the air cleaner outlet pipe.

20. Connect the negative battery cable.

HEATING & AIR CONDITIONING SYSTEM

BLOWER MOTOR

REMOVAL & INSTALLATION

See Figure 266.

1. Remove the RH lower A-pillar trim panel.

2. Position aside the carpet below the blower motor.

3. Disconnect the blower motor electrical connector.

4. Remove the 3 blower motor screws.

5. Remove the blower motor.

6. Remove the blower motor wheel clip.

7. Remove the blower motor wheel.

8. To install, reverse the removal procedure.

HEATER CORE

REMOVAL & INSTALLATION

2008 Models

See Figure 267 and 268.

1. Before servicing the vehicle, refer to the Precautions Section.

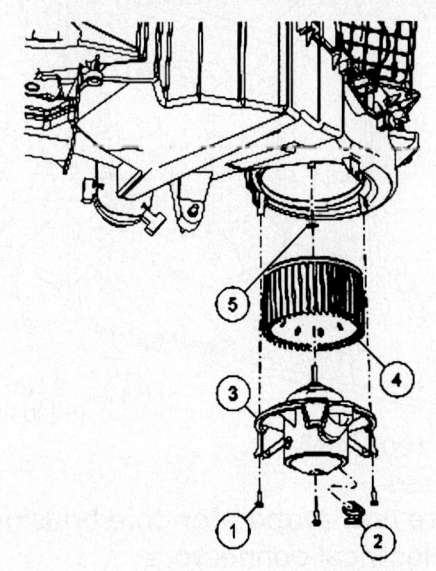

Fig. 266 1. Blower motor screw
2. Blower motor electrical connector
3. Blower motor
4. Blower motor wheel
5. Blower motor wheel clip
Blower motor—F-150 and Mark LT

32069_FPUP_G0205

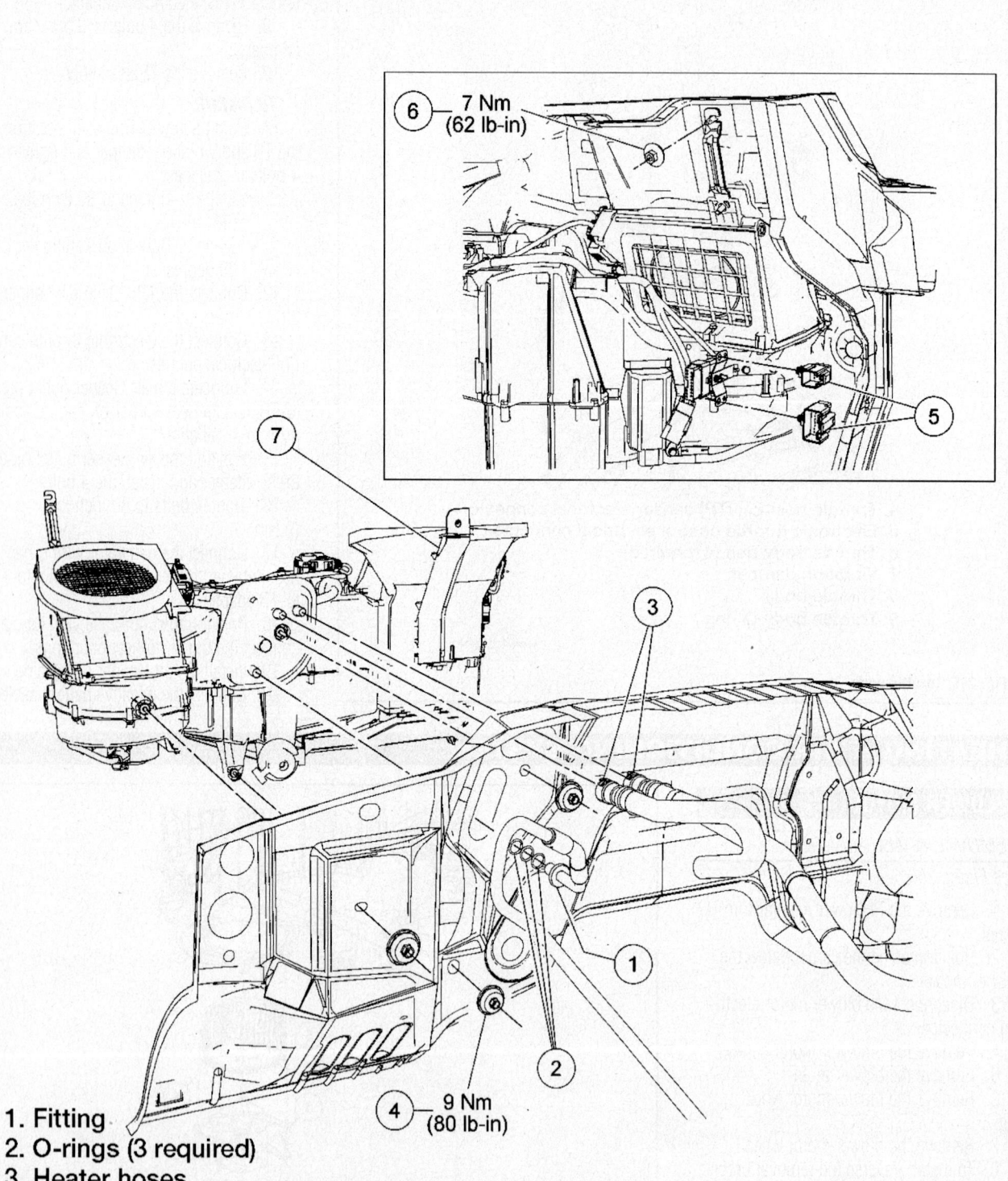

1. Fitting
2. O-rings (3 required)
3. Heater hoses
4. Heater core and evaporator core housing nut (3 required)
5. Harness electrical connectors
6. Air inlet duct bracket nut
7. Heater core and evaporator core housing

36578_FTRK_G0127

Fig. 267 Heater core and EVAP core housing removal—2008 Models

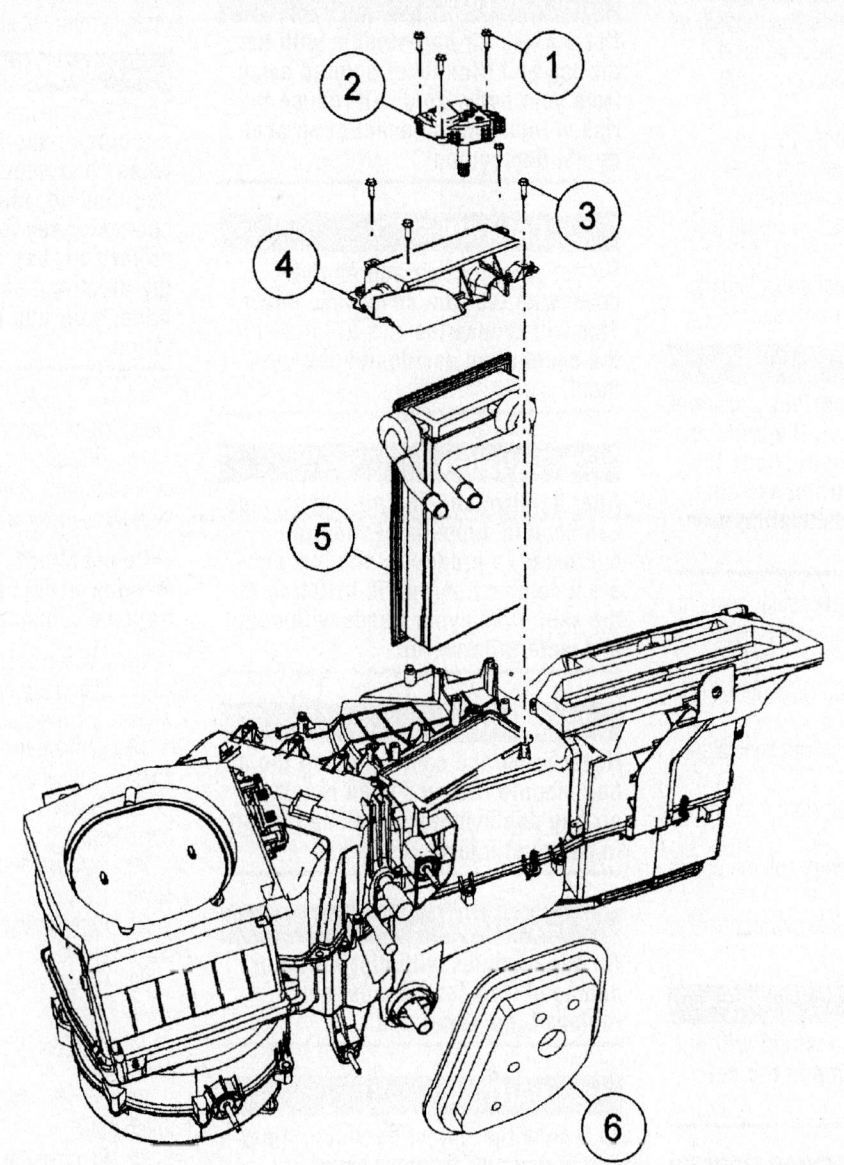

1 Temperature blend door
 actuator screw (3 required)

2 Temperature blend door
 actuator

3 Heater core cover screw (4
 required)

4 Heater core cover

5 Heater core

6 Dash panel seal

06017-F150-G30

Fig. 268 Heater core removal—2008 Models

2. If equipped with adjustable pedals, move the pedals to the full forward position.

3. If equipped with a floor console:

a. Remove the 3 floor trim panel push pins.

b. Remove the 2 floor trim panels.

c. Remove the shifter trim panel.

d. Disconnect the shifter cable.

e. Disconnect the floor console electrical connector.

f. Remove the 4 floor console bolts.

g. Remove the floor console.

✳ CAUTION

To reduce the risk of serious personal injury, read and follow all warnings, cautions, notes and instructions in the supplemental restraint system (SRS) deactivation/reactivation procedure.

4. De-power the supplemental restraint system (SRS). For additional information, refer to Steering.

5. Position the left and right door weatherstrip seals aside.

6. Remove the A-pillar trim panels and right cowl side trim panel.

7. Remove the left and right instrument panel side finish panels.

8. Remove the 2 steering column opening trim screws.

9. Remove the steering column opening trim.

✳ WARNING

Removing the steering wheel without using a puller can damage the column bearings.

✳ WARNING

Do not allow the steering column shaft to rotate while the intermediate shaft is disconnected or damage to the clockspring can result. If there is evidence that the shaft has rotated, the clockspring must be removed and re-centered.

10. Place the steering wheel in the straight-ahead position and turn the ignition switch to the OFF position.

✳ CAUTION

Always wear safety glasses when repairing an air bag supplemental restraint system (SRS) vehicle and when handling an air bag module. This will reduce the risk of injury in the event of an accidental deployment.

✳ CAUTION

Carry a live air bag module with the air bag and trim cover pointed away from your body. This will reduce the risk of injury in the event of an accidental deployment.

✳ CAUTION

Do not set a live air bag module down with the trim cover face down. This will reduce the risk of injury in the event of an accidental deployment.

✳ CAUTION

After deployment, the air bag surface can contain deposits of sodium hydroxide, a product of the gas generant combustion that is irritating to the skin. Wash your hands with soap and water afterwards.

✳ CAUTION

Never probe the connectors on the air bag module. Doing so can result in air bag deployment, which can result in personal injury.

✳ CAUTION

Air bag modules with discolored or damaged trim covers must be replaced, not repainted.

✳ CAUTION

To reduce the risk of personal injury, do not use any memory saver devices.

➡The air bag warning lamp illuminates when the RCM fuse is removed and the ignition switch is ON. This is normal operation and does not indicate a supplemental restraint system (SRS) fault.

➡The SRS must be fully operational and free of faults before releasing the vehicle to the customer.

➡Repair is made by installing a new part only. If the new part does not correct the condition, install the original part and perform the diagnostic procedure again.

11. Remove the 2 steering wheel back cover plugs.

12. Remove the 2 driver's air bag module bolts.

13. Partially remove the driver's air bag module from the steering wheel.

✳ WARNING

The clockspring electrical connectors are unique and cannot be reversed when connected to the driver's air bag module. Match the electrical connector key to the keyway in the driver's air bag module. Do not force the electrical connectors into the driver's air bag module during installation.

14. Disconnect the driver's air bag module electrical connectors.

15. Disconnect the horn switch electrical connector and remove the driver's air bag module.

➡Do not remove the bolt until the steering wheel has been separated from the column.

16. Loosen the steering wheel bolt.

17. Using a puller, separate the steering wheel from the steering column assembly.

18. Remove the steering wheel bolt and the steering wheel.

19. Remove the lower steering column cover screw.

20. Remove the lower steering column cover.

21. Remove the 2 upper steering column cover screws.

22. Remove the upper steering column cover.

23. Remove the instrument cluster finish panel.

24. Remove the instrument panel center finish panel.

25. Remove the instrument cluster center finish panel.

26. Remove the parking brake release handle bolt.

27. Position aside the parking brake release handle. Remove the parking brake release handle pin-type retainer.

28. Remove the hood release handle bolt.

29. Position aside the hood release handle.

30. Loosen the electrical connector screw and disconnect the bulkhead electrical connector.

31. Remove the ground bolt.

32. Disconnect the electrical connectors.

33. Position aside the front carpet.

34. Remove the 4 left center brace bolts.

35. Remove the left center brace.

36. If equipped, disconnect the transmission range indicator cable and position aside.

WARNING

To avoid damage to the clockspring, do not allow the steering column shaft to rotate while the intermediate shaft is disconnected.

37. Remove the steering column pinch bolt and disconnect the steering column intermediate shaft.
38. Disconnect the steering column electrical connector.
39. Remove the ground bolt.
40. Disconnect the radio antenna.
41. Disconnect the 4 PDB (B1, B2, L1 and L2) electrical connectors.
42. Disconnect the ETAC electrical connector.
43. Disconnect the instrument panel electrical connectors.
44. Position aside the front carpet.
45. Remove the 4 right center brace bolts.
46. Remove the right center brace.

➡ **If equipped with a floor console, remove the third center brace.**

47. If equipped, remove the 4 third center brace bolts.
48. If equipped, remove the third center brace.
49. Remove the 2 defrost grilles.
50. Disconnect the wiring harness pin-type retainer.

WARNING

To avoid damage to the instrument panel, an assistant is required to support the panel before carrying out this step.

51. Remove the 9 instrument panel bolts.

WARNING

Before removing the instrument panel, make sure all electrical connector wiring is free and not hindered.

52. Remove the instrument panel.

➡ **Installation of a new suction accumulator is not required when repairing the air conditioning system, except when there is physical evidence of contamination from a failed A/C compressor or damage to the suction accumulator.**

53. Recover the refrigerant.
54. Remove the powertrain control module (PCM).
55. Remove the battery and battery tray.
56. Remove the PCM bracket.

57. Remove the suction accumulator outlet fitting nut and disconnect the fitting.
58. Discard the O-ring seal.
59. Disconnect the suction accumulator inlet fitting. Discard the O-ring seals.
60. Remove the 2 suction accumulator bracket nuts.
61. Remove the suction accumulator.
62. Disconnect the evaporator core spring lock coupling. Discard the O-ring seals.
63. Clamp off and disconnect the 2 heater core quick disconnect fittings.
64. Remove the 3 heater core and evaporator core housing nuts.
65. Disconnect the 2 harness electrical connectors.
66. Remove the air inlet duct bracket nut.
67. Remove the bolt and position the junction box aside.
68. Loosen the nut and remove the heater core and evaporator core housing.
69. Remove the dash panel seal from the heater core tubes.
70. Position the temperature blend door actuator aside.
71. Remove the heater core cover.
72. Remove the heater core.

➡ **The heater core seal must be correctly installed to prevent airflow from bypassing the heater core.**

CAUTION

Incorrect centralization may result in premature component failure. If in doubt when centralizing the clockspring, repeat the centralizing procedure. Failure to follow this instruction may result in personal injury.

WARNING

Make sure the road wheels are in the straight-ahead position.

73. If the vehicle's clockspring has rotated out of center, follow these steps to center the clockspring.
    a. Hold the clockspring outer housing stationary.

WARNING

Overturning will destroy the clockspring. The internal ribbon wire acts as the stop and can be broken from its internal connection.

   b. While turning the rotor counterclockwise, carefully feel for the ribbon wire to run out of length and for a slight resistance. Stop turning at this point.

   c. Turn the clockspring clockwise approximately 3 turns. This is the center point of the clockspring. Do not allow the rotor to turn from this position. To prevent accidental rotation until the clockspring is installed, 2 pieces of tape may be applied to the clockspring.

➡ **Slight turning of the clockspring rotor is allowable for alignment purposes to the steering column.**

   d. With the flats of the clockspring aligned to the flats of the steering column, slide the clockspring onto the steering column. For vehicles receiving a new clockspring, remove the retaining pin. For vehicles reusing the clockspring that was removed, remove the tape.
74. To install, reverse the removal procedure. Evacuate, charge and leak test the system. Install new O-ring seals. Lubricate the refrigerant system with the correct amount of clean PAG oil.
75. Observe the following torques:
    - Heater core nut: 62 inch lbs. (7 Nm)
    - Air inlet duct bracket: 62 inch lbs. (7 Nm)
    - Heater core and evaporator core housing nuts: 80 inch lbs. (9 Nm)
    - Suction accumulator bracket nuts: 53 inch lbs. (6 Nm)
    - Suction accumulator outlet fitting nut: 71 inch lbs. (8 Nm)
    - PCM bracket: 89 inch lbs. (10 Nm)
    - Instrument panel bolts: 15 ft. lbs. (20 Nm)
    - Steering column pinch bolt: 30 ft. lbs. (40 Nm)
    - Steering wheel bolt and the steering wheel: 30 ft. lbs. (40 Nm)
    - Driver's air bag module bolts: 89 inch lbs. (10 Nm)
76. Fill the engine cooling system.

2009 Models

See Figures 269 and 270.

1. If a heater core leak is suspected, the heater core must be leak tested before it is removed from the vehicle.
2. Drain the engine coolant.
3. Recover the refrigerant.
4. Remove the instrument panel.
5. Disconnect the 2 heater core quick disconnect fittings at the heater core.
6. Remove the Thermostatic Expansion Valve (TXV) manifold and tube bracket bolt.
7. Remove the TXV fitting nut and disconnect the fitting. Discard the gasket seals.
8. Remove the 3 heater core and evaporator core housing nuts.

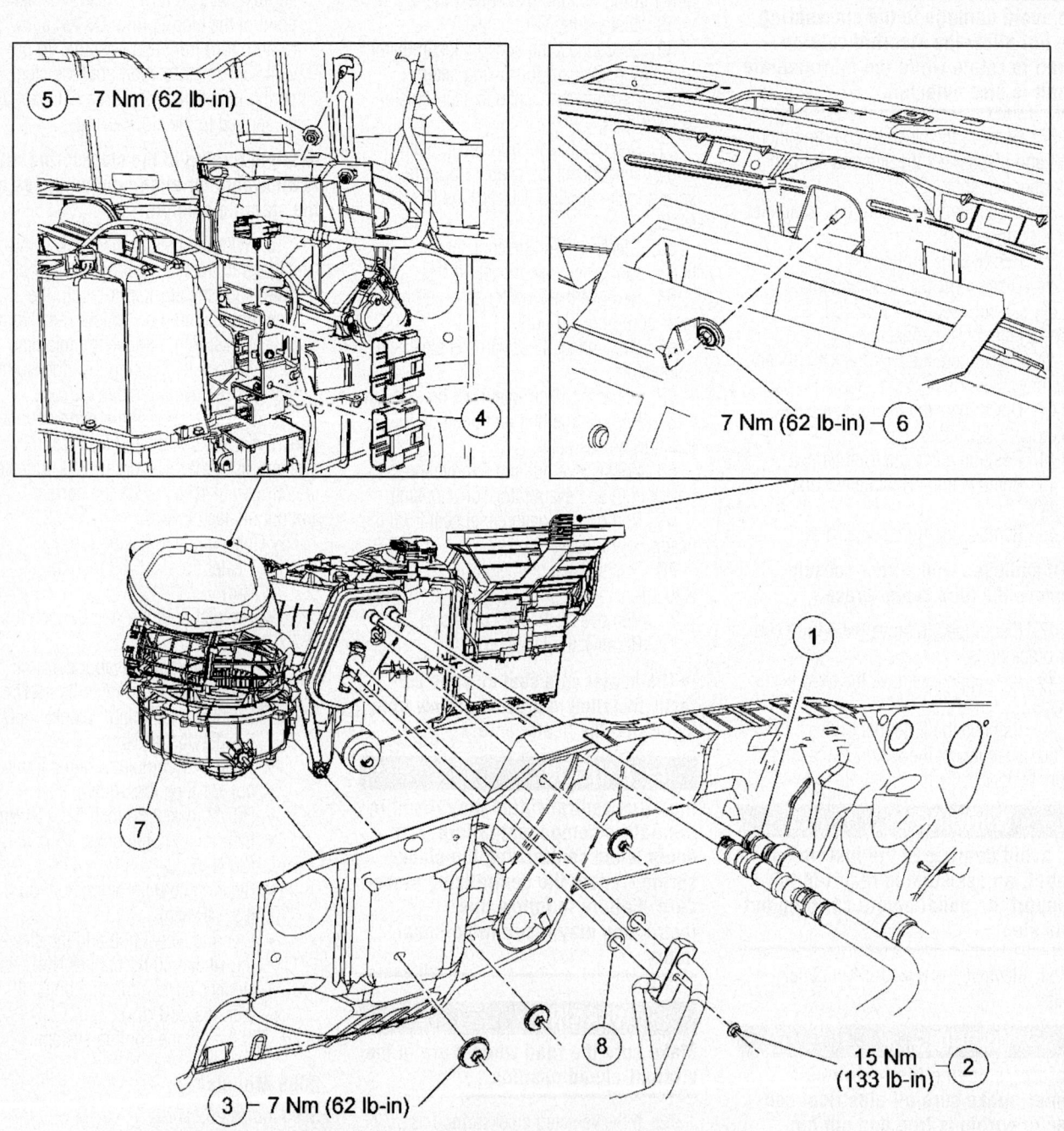

1. Heater hose quick disconnect fitting (2 required)
2. Thermostatic Expansion Valve (TXV) fitting nut
3. Heater core and evaporator core housing nut (3 required)
4. Body harness electrical connector (3 required)
5. Air inlet duct bracket nut
6. Plenum chamber nut
7. Heater core and evaporator core housing
8. Gasket seal (2 pieces from kit required)

36578_FTRK_G0128

Fig. 269 Heater core and EVAP core housing removal—2009 Models

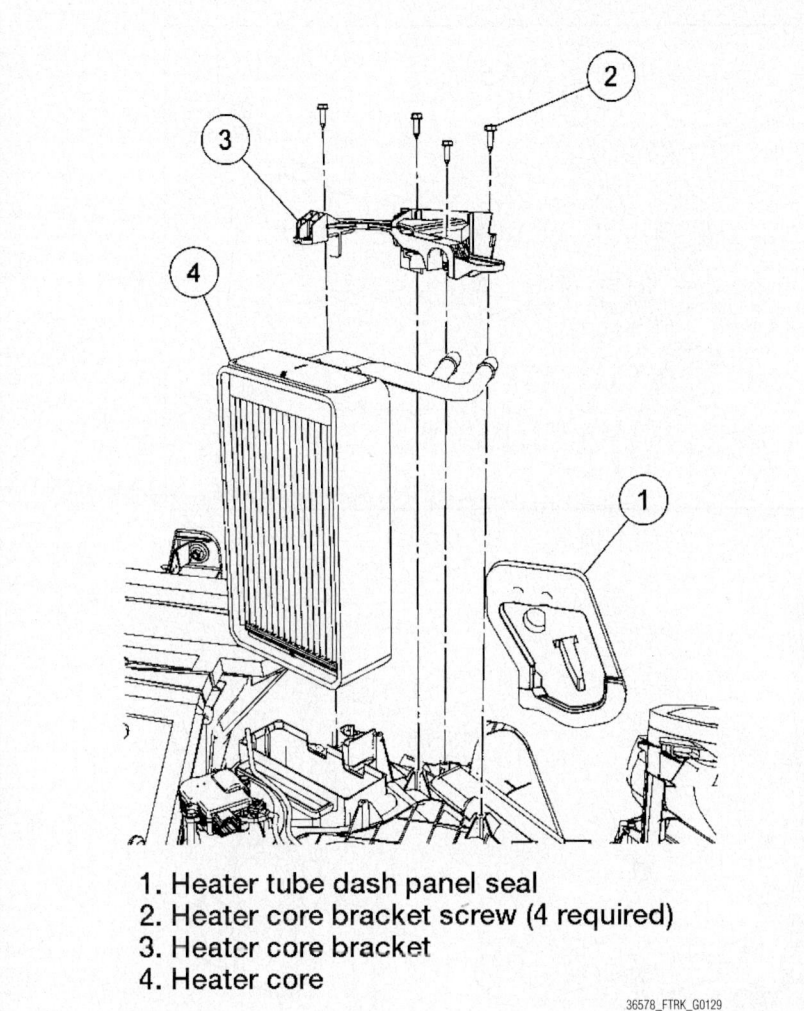

1. Heater tube dash panel seal
2. Heater core bracket screw (4 required)
3. Heater core bracket
4. Heater core

36578_FTRK_G0129

Fig. 270 Heater core removal—2009 Models

9. Detach the 3 harness electrical connectors from the heater core and evaporator core housing bracket.
10. Detach the 2 antenna cable retainers from the heater core and evaporator core housing (if equipped).
11. Remove the air inlet duct bracket nut.
12. Completely loosen the plenum chamber nut.
13. Detach the floor console duct from the heater core and evaporator core housing (if equipped).

➡**For vehicles equipped with a rear footwell duct, the heater core and evaporator core housing must be carefully detached from the dash panel and then tilted toward the rear of the vehicle to detach it from the rear footwell duct connection.**

14. Remove the heater core and evaporator core housing.
15. Remove the heater hose quick disconnect clips from the heater core.
16. Remove the heater tube dash panel seal.
17. Remove the 4 heater core bracket screws and the bracket.
18. Remove the heater core.

➡**The heater core seal must be correctly installed to prevent airflow from bypassing the heater core.**

19. To install, reverse the removal procedure.
20. Install new O-ring seals.
21. Add the correct amount of clean PAG oil to the refrigerant system.
22. Fill the engine cooling system.

STEERING

POWER RACK & PINION STEERING GEAR

REMOVAL & INSTALLATION

2008 Models
See Figure 271.

✳✳ CAUTION

While repairing the power steering system, care should be taken to prevent the entry of foreign material or failure of the power steering components may result.

➡**New O-ring seals must be installed any time the power steering lines are disconnected from the steering gear.**

1. With the vehicle in NEUTRAL, position it on a hoist.
2. If equipped, remove the 4 skid plate bolts and the skid plate.

✳✳ CAUTION

Do not allow the steering column to rotate while the steering column shaft is disconnected or damage to the clockspring may result. If there is evidence that the steering column has rotated, the clockspring must be removed and recentered.

3. Remove the lower steering column shaft-to-steering gear bolt and disconnect the lower steering column shaft.
4. Remove the 2 oil drip shield bolts and the drip shield.
5. New O-ring seals must be installed

any time the lines are disconnected from the steering gear.
6. Remove the steering line clamp plate bolt and disconnect the pressure line. Discard the O-ring seal.
7. Disconnect the return line. Discard the O-ring seal.
8. Loosen the 2 tie-rod jam nuts.
9. Remove the 2 outer tie-rod end nuts.

➡**Note the number of times the outer tie-rod ends turn for reference during assembly.**

10. Using the special tool, separate the outer tie-rod ends from the wheel knuckles and remove the outer tie-rod ends.
11. Remove the 2 steering gear bracket nuts.
12. Remove the 2 steering gear bracket bolts.

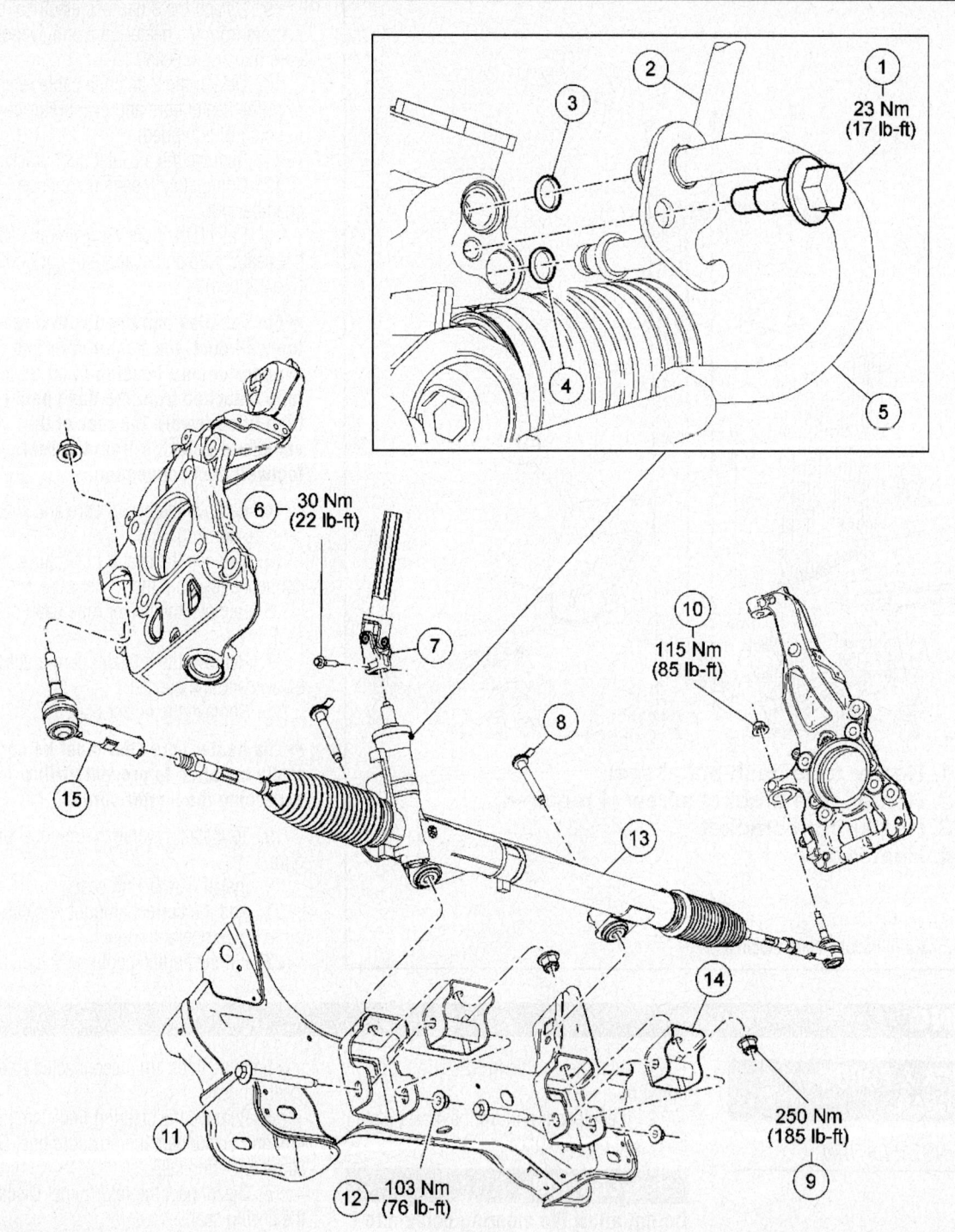

1. Steering line clamp plate bolt
2. Return line
3. O-ring seal
4. O-ring seal
5. Pressure line
6. Lower steering column shaft-to-steering gear bolt
7. Lower steering column shaft
8. Steering gear bolt (2 required)
9. Steering gear nut (2 required)
10. Outer tie-rod end nut (2 required)
11. Steering gear bracket bolt (2 required)
12. Steering gear bracket nut (2 required)
13. Steering gear
14. Steering gear mounting bracket (2 required)
15. Outer tie-rod end (2 required)

36578_FTRK_G0134

Fig. 271 Exploded view of the steering gear assembly—2008 Models

13. Remove the 2 steering gear nuts.

14. Remove the 2 steering gear bolts and the steering gear brackets.

15. Remove the steering gear.

16. Remove the steering gear through the LH wheel opening.

To install:

17. Install new O-ring seals on the pressure and return lines.

18. Position the steering gear. Install the steering gear through the LH wheel opening.

19. Install the 2 steering gear brackets and the steering gear bolts and nuts. Tighten to 185 ft. lbs. (250 Nm).

20. Install the 2 steering gear bracket bolts and nuts. Tighten to 76 ft. lbs. (103 Nm).

21. Connect the lower steering column shaft to the steering gear and install the lower steering column shaft-to-steering gear bolt. Tighten to 22 ft. lbs. (30 Nm).

22. Install the 2 outer tie-rod ends on the steering gear.

23. Position the 2 outer tie-rod ends on the wheel knuckles and install the nuts. Tighten to 85 ft. lbs. (115 Nm).

24. Tighten the 2 tie-rod jam nuts. Tighten to 76 ft. lbs. (103 Nm).

25. Connect the pressure line and install the steering line clamp plate bolt. Tighten to 17 ft. lbs. (23 Nm).

26. Position the oil drip shield and install the 2 bolts.

27. If equipped, install the skid plate and the 4 skid plate bolts. Tighten to 18 ft. lbs. (25 Nm).

28. Fill the power steering system. Check and, if necessary, adjust the front toe.

2009 Models

See Figure 272.

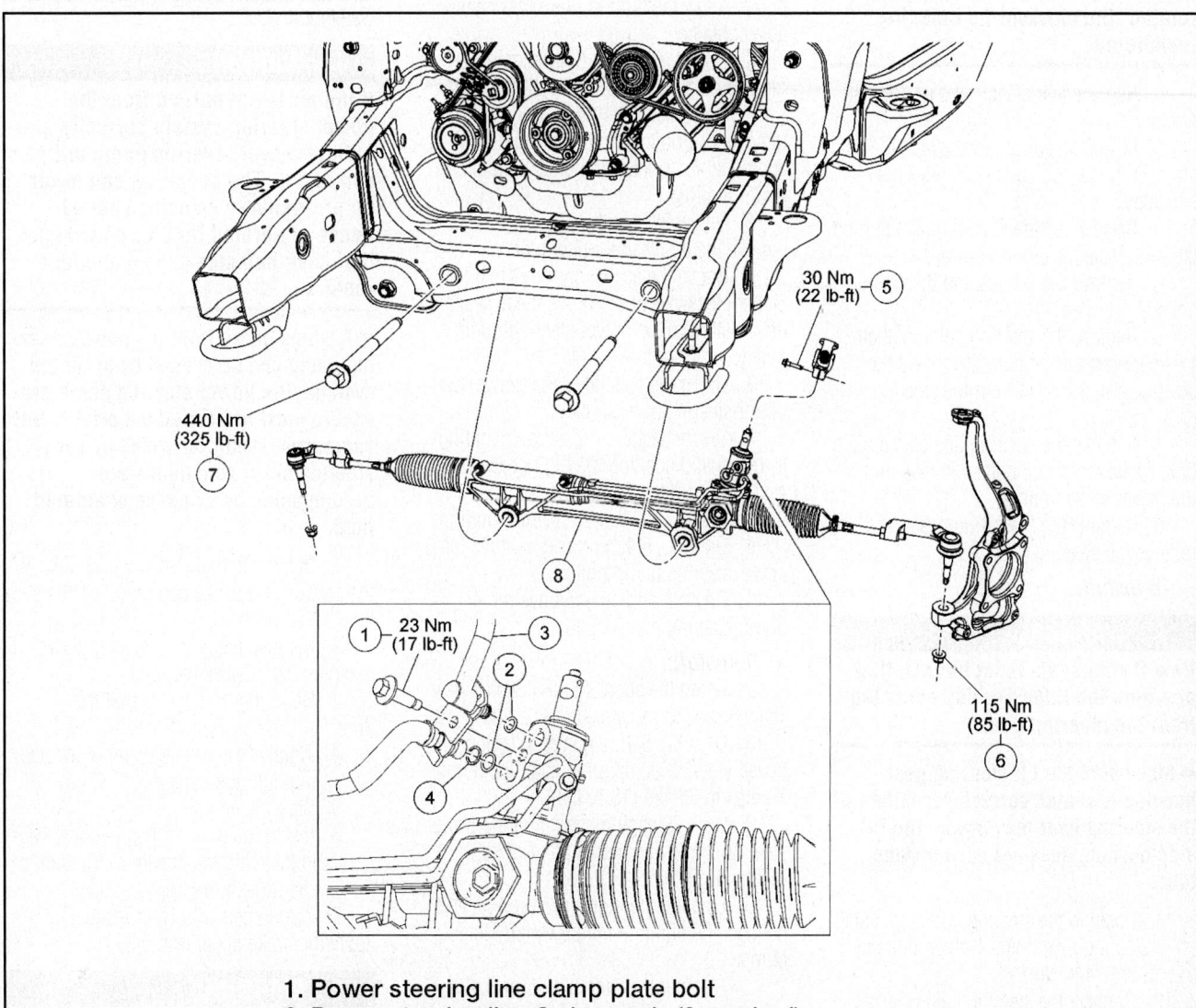

1. Power steering line clamp plate bolt
2. Power steering line O-ring seals (2 required)
3. Power steering return line
4. O-ring seal
5. Steering column shaft-to-steering gear bolt
6. Outer tie-rod end nut (2 required)
7. Steering gear-to-crossmember bolt (2 required)
8. Steering gear

36578_EXPD_G0117

Fig. 272 Exploded view of the power rack and pinion steering gear components

1. Before servicing the vehicle, refer to the precautions in the beginning of this section.

2. With the vehicle in NEUTRAL, position it on a hoist.

3. Hold the steering wheel in the straight ahead position using a suitable holding device.

❊❊ WARNING

Do not allow the steering column shaft to rotate while disconnected from the gear or damage to the clockspring can occur. if there is evidence that the steering column shaft has rotated, the clockspring must be recentered.

4. Remove and discard the tie-rod end nuts.

5. Using the special tool 204-592, disconnect the tie-rod ends from the wheel knuckles.

6. Release the lower cooling fan shroud tab and rotate the shroud upward.

7. Remove the 2 bolts and the oil drip shield.

8. Remove the steering column shaft-to-steering gear bolt and disconnect the steering column shaft from the steering gear.

9. Remove the steering line clamp plate bolt, rotate the clamp plate and disconnect the power steering lines

10. Remove the 2 steering gear bolts and remove the steering gear.

To install:

❊❊ WARNING

New O-ring seals must be installed any time the lines are disconnected from the steering gear.

➡**Make sure the LH steering gear bushing is seated correctly or failure of the steering gear may occur. The RH side bushing does not have locking tabs.**

11. Position the steering gear and install the 2 steering gear bolts. Tighten bolts to 325 ft. lbs. (440 Nm).

12. Connect the steering column shaft and install the bolt..

13. Connect the steering lines, rotate the clamp plate and install the clamp plate bolt. Tighten the bolt to 17 ft. lbs. (23 Nm).

14. Install the oil drip shield and tighten the 2 bolts to 8 ft. lbs. (11 Nm).

15. Release the lower cooling fan shroud tab and rotate the shroud downward.

16. Connect the tie-rod ends to the wheel knuckles, install and tighten the nuts to 85 ft. lbs. (115 Nm).

17. Fill the power steering system.

18. Check and, if necessary, align the front end.

POWER STEERING PUMP

REMOVAL & INSTALLATION

See Figures 273 and 274.

1. Raise and safely support the vehicle.

2. Release the clamp and disconnect the suction line from the power steering pump. Allow the fluid to drain into a suitable container.

3. On vehicles with 5.4L engine, remove the air cleaner intake pipe.

4. On vehicles with 4.6L engine, remove the cooling fan and shroud. For additional information, refer to Engine Fan & Shroud R&I.

5. On vehicles with 4.2L engine, remove the air cleaner outlet pipe.

6. Rotate the accessory drive belt tensioner clockwise and remove the accessory drive belt from the power steering pump pulley.

7. Using the special tool, remove the power steering pump pulley.

8. Disconnect the pressure line fitting-to-pump and position the high pressure line aside. Discard the Teflon® seal.

9. Remove the power steering pump.

10. On 4.6L, 5.4L engines, remove the 3 power steering pump bolts.

11. On 4.2L engines, remove the 4 power steering pump bolts.

To install:

12. Using the special tool, install a new Teflon® seal on the pressure line fitting.

13. On 4.6L, 5.4L engines, position the power steering pump and install the 3 bolts. Tighten to 25 Nm (18 ft. lbs.).

14. On 4.2L engines, position the power steering pump and install the 4 bolts. Tighten to 25 Nm (18 ft. lbs.).

15. Position the high pressure line and connect the fitting to the power steering pump.

   • If equipped with a 4.6L or 5.4L engine, tighten to 65 Nm (48 ft. lbs.).
   • If equipped with a 4.2L engine, tighten to 20 Nm (15 ft. lbs.).

16. Connect the suction line and install the clamp.

➡**Make sure the pulley is flush with the end of the power steering pump shaft.**

17. Using the special tool, install the power steering pump pulley.

18. Rotate the accessory drive belt tensioner and install the accessory drive belt on the power steering pump pulley.

19. On vehicles with 4.2L engine, install the air cleaner outlet pipe.

20. On vehicles with 4.6L engine, install the cooling fan and shroud.

21. On vehicles with 5.4L engine, Install the air cleaner intake pipe.

22. Install the power steering pump pulley. Fill the power steering system.

BLEEDING

See Figure 275.

❊❊ WARNING

If the air is not purged from the power steering system correctly, premature power steering pump failure can result. The condition can occur on pre-delivery vehicles with evidence of aerated fluid or on vehicles that have had steering component repairs.

➡**A whine heard from the power steering pump can be caused by air in the system. The power steering purge procedure must be carried out prior to any component repair for which power steering noise complaints are accompanied by evidence of aerated fluid.**

1. Before servicing the vehicle, refer to the precautions in the beginning of this section.

2. Remove the power steering pump reservoir cap. Check the fluid.

3. Raise the front wheels off the floor.

4. Tightly insert the stopper of the vacuum pump into the reservoir.

5. Start the engine.

6. Install the vacuum pump, apply vacuum and maintain the maximum vacuum of 68-85 kPa (20-25 in-Hg).

7. If equipped with Hydro-Boost®, apply the brake pedal twice.

❊❊ WARNING

Do not hold the steering wheel against the stops for more than 3 to 5 seconds at a time. Damage to the power steering pump can occur.

8. Cycle the steering wheel fully from stop-to-stop 10 times.

9. Stop the engine

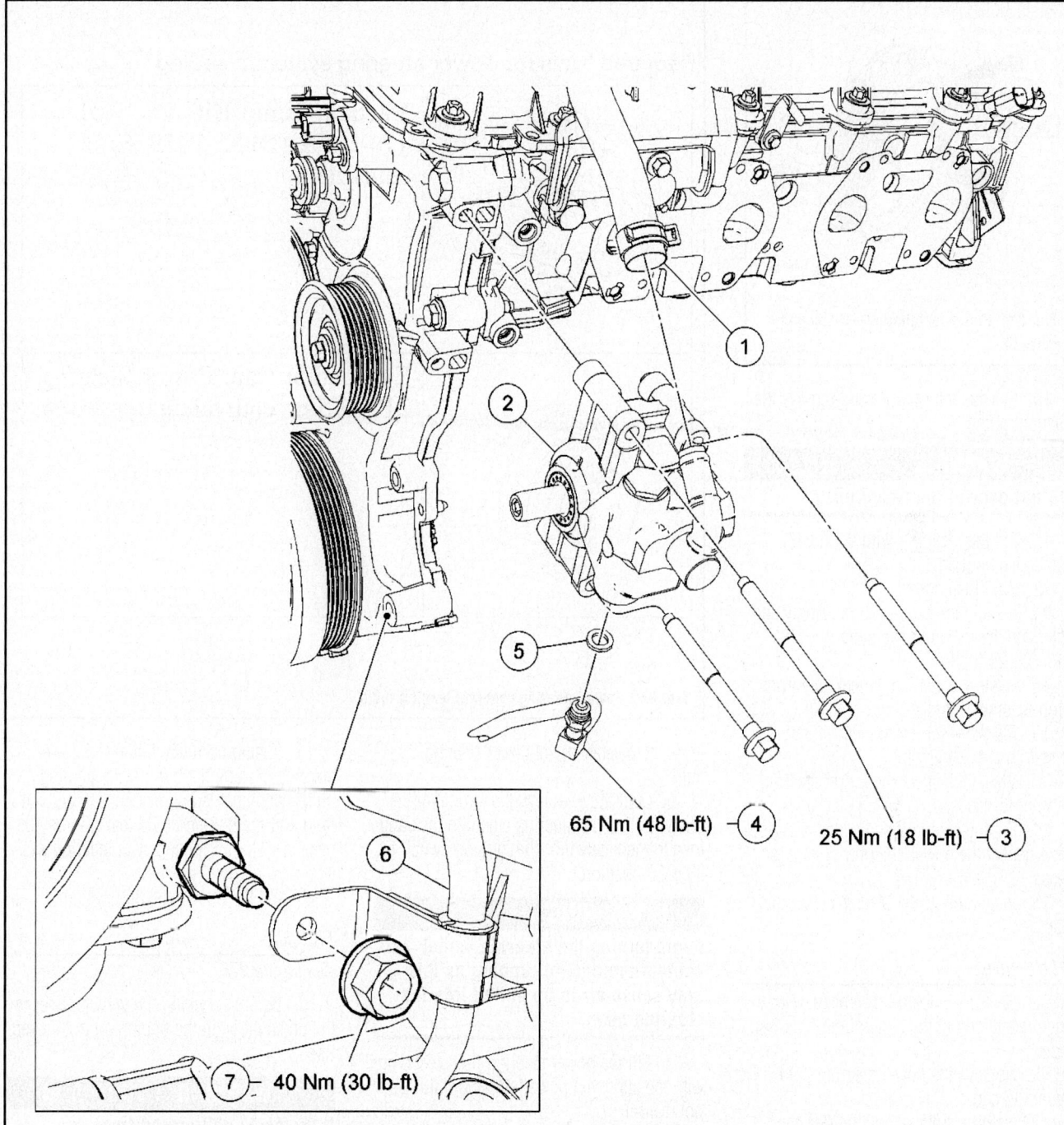

65 Nm (48 lb-ft) — 4

25 Nm (18 lb-ft) — 3

40 Nm (30 lb-ft)

1. Power steering fluid reservoir-to-pump supply hose
2. Power steering pump
3. Power steering pump bolt (3 required)
4. Power steering pressure line-to-power steering pump fitting
5. Power steering pressure line Teflon® seal
6. Power steering pressure line
7. Power steering pressure line bracket-to-engine nut

36578_EXPD_G0118

Fig. 273 View of the power steering pump and components—4.6L and 5.4L engine shown, 4.2L similar

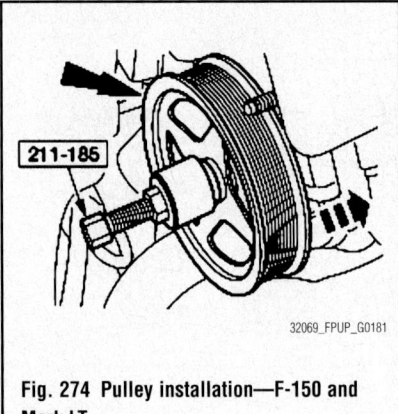

Fig. 274 Pulley installation—F-150 and Mark LT

10. Release the vacuum and remove the vacuum pump.

> ✳✳ **WARNING**
> **Do not overfill the reservoir.**

11. Fill the reservoir with approved transmission fluid.

12. Start the engine.

13. Install the vacuum pump. Apply and maintain the maximum vacuum of 68-85 kPa (20-25 in-Hg).

14. Cycle the steering wheel fully from stop-to-stop 10 times.

15. Fill the reservoir as needed and install the reservoir cap.

16. Visually inspect the power steering system for leaks.

17. Fill the reservoir as needed and visually inspect the power steering system for leaks.

18. Install the power steering reservoir cap.

FLUSHING

1. Before servicing the vehicle, refer to the precautions in the beginning of this section.

2. Remove the power steering fluid reservoir cap.

3. Using a suitable suction device, remove the power steering fluid from the reservoir.

4. Disconnect the power steering fluid return hose from the reservoir.

5. Plug the power steering fluid reservoir inlet port.

6. Attach an extension hose to the power steering return hose.

➡**Do not reuse the power steering fluid that has been flushed from the power steering system.**

7. Fill the power steering fluid reservoir with new fluid.

8. Do not allow the power steering pump

Required tools for power steering system bleeding

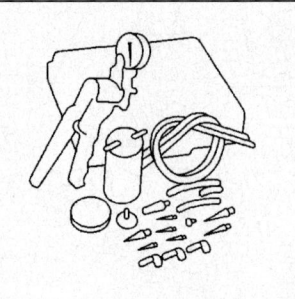	Vacuum Pump Kit 416-D002 (D95L-7559-A) or equivalent
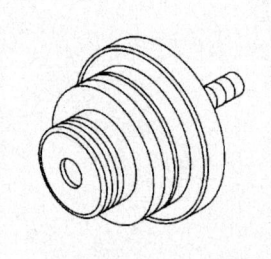	Evacuation Cap, Power Steering 211-265 or equivalent

Fig. 275 Power steering system bleeding tools

to run completely dry of power steering fluid.

9. Start the engine while simultaneously turning the steering wheel to lock and then immediately turn the ignition switch to the OFF position.

> ✳✳ **WARNING**
> **Avoid turning the steering wheel without the engine running as this may cause air to be pulled into the steering gear.**

10. Fill the power steering fluid reservoir with the approved power steering fluid. Do not overfill.

11. Repeat Steps 8 and 9, turning the steering wheel in the opposite direction each time, until the fluid exiting the power steering fluid return hose is clean and clear of foreign material.

12. Remove the extension hose from the power steering return hose.

13. Remove the plug from the power steering fluid reservoir inlet port.

14. Install the power steering return hose to the reservoir and the retaining clamp.

➡**It is necessary to correctly fill the power steering system to remove any trapped air and completely fill the power steering system components.**

15. If, after correctly filling the power steering system, there is power steering noise accompanied by evidence of aerated fluid and there are no fluid leaks, it may be necessary to purge the power steering system.

16. Fill the power steering system.

FILLING

See Figure 276.

1. Before servicing the vehicle, refer to the precautions in the beginning of this section.

> ✳✳ **WARNING**
> **If the air is not purged from the power steering system correctly, premature power steering pump failure can result. The condition can occur on pre-delivery vehicles with evidence of aerated fluid or on vehicles that have had steering component repairs.**

2. Remove the power steering pump reservoir cap.

3. Tightly install the evacuation cap to the power steering pump reservoir.

4. Install the hose from the fill adapter manifold tee to the evacuation cap on the power steering pump reservoir.

Tools required for power steering filling

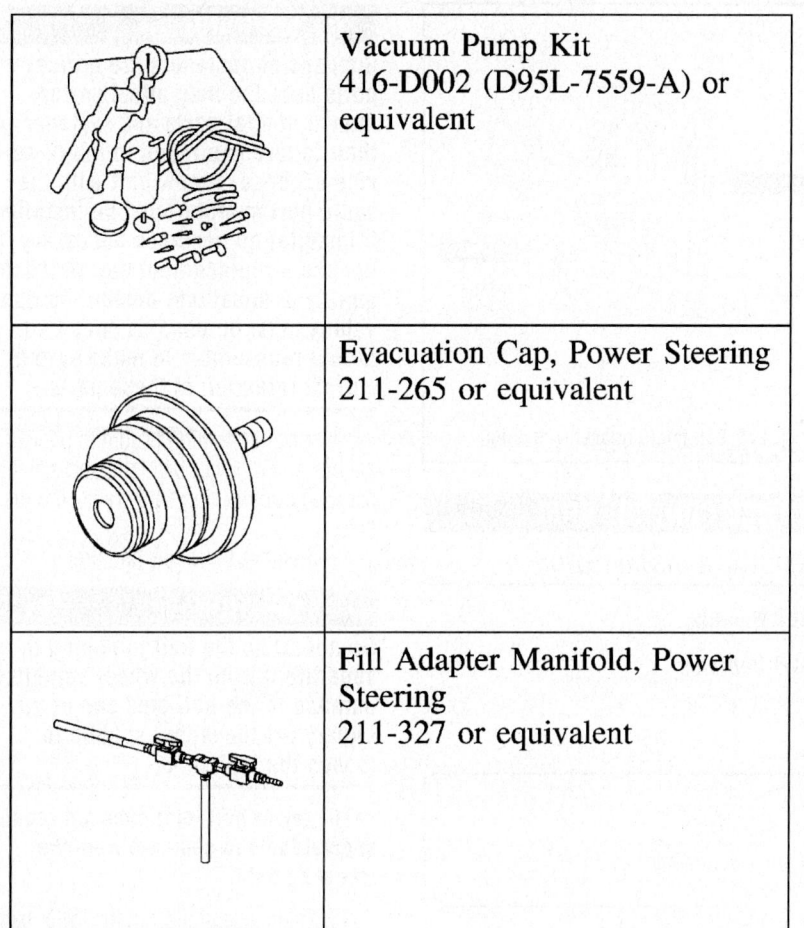

	Vacuum Pump Kit 416-D002 (D95L-7559-A) or equivalent
	Evacuation Cap, Power Steering 211-265 or equivalent
	Fill Adapter Manifold, Power Steering 211-327 or equivalent

22086_EXPD_G0118

Fig. 276 Power steering fluid filling tools

5. Install the vacuum pump to the fill adapter manifold control valve.

6. Install the hose to the opposite fill adapter manifold control valve and submerge the open end of the hose into a container of new power steering fluid.

➡**The fill adapter manifold control valves are in the open position when the point of the handles face the center of the fill adapter manifold.**

7. Close the fill adapter manifold control valve connected to the power steering fluid container.

8. Open the fill adapter manifold control valve connected to the vacuum pump

9. Using the vacuum pump, apply 68-85 kPa (20-25 in-Hg) of vacuum to the power steering system. Observe the vacuum gauge for 30 seconds.

10. If the vacuum gauge reading drops more than 3 kPa (0.88 in-Hg), correct any leaks in the power steering system or the filling tools before proceeding.

➡**The vacuum pump gauge reading will drop slightly during this step.**

11. Slowly open the fill adapter manifold control valve connected to the power steering fluid container until power steering fluid completely fills the hose.

12. Close the fill adapter manifold control valve connected to the power steering fluid container.

13. Using the vacuum pump, apply 68-85 kPa (20-25 in-Hg) of vacuum to the power steering system

14. Close the fill adapter manifold control valve connected to the vacuum pump.

15. Slowly open the fill adapter manifold control valve connected to the power steering fluid container

16. When the power steering fluid has drained from the hose connected to the power steering fluid container, close the fill adapter manifold control valve connected to the power steering fluid container.

17. Remove the tools from the vehicle.

18. Install the power steering reservoir cap.

✱✱ WARNING

Do not hold the steering wheel against the stops for more than 3 to 5 seconds at a time. Damage to the power steering pump can occur.

➡**There will be a slight drop in the power steering fluid level in the power steering fluid reservoir when the engine is started.**

19. Start the engine and turn the steering wheel from stop-to-stop.

20. If equipped with Hydro-Boost®, apply the brake pedal twice.

21. Turn the ignition switch to the OFF position.

✱✱ WARNING

Do not overfill the reservoir.

22. Remove the power steering reservoir cap and fill the reservoir.

23. Install the power steering reservoir cap.

LOWER BALL JOINT

REMOVAL & INSTALLATION

See Figures 277 and 278.

1. Remove the wheel knuckle.
2. Remove and discard the lower ball joint snap ring.
3. Using the special tools 205-086 and 204-358, remove the lower ball joint.
4. Clean and inspect the lower arm lower ball joint bore for damage before installing a new ball joint.
5. To install, reverse the removal procedure.

➡Make sure the lower ball joint is fully seated in the lower control arm, and new lower ball joint snap ring is fully seated.

❊❊ WARNING

Always install new nuts and cotter pins.

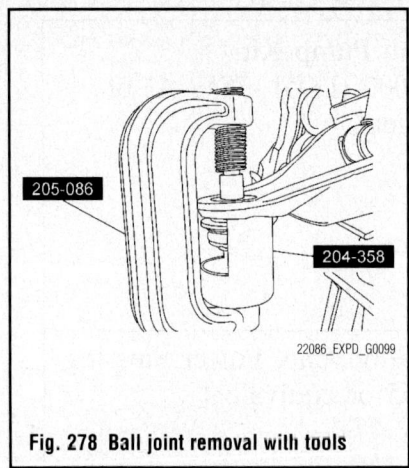

Fig. 278 Ball joint removal with tools

LOWER CONTROL ARM

REMOVAL & INSTALLATION

2008 Models

2WD Vehicles

See Figure 279.

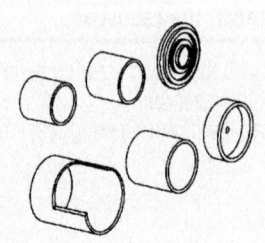

Installer/Remover, C-Frame and Screw 205-086	
Installer/Remover, Ball Joint 204-358	

Fig. 277 Ball joint removal tools

❊❊ WARNING

Suspension fasteners are critical parts because they affect performance of vital parts and systems and their failure can result in major service expense. A new part with the same part number must be installed if installation becomes necessary. Do not use a replacement part of lesser quality or substitute design. Torque values must be used as specified during reassembly to make sure of correct retention of these parts.

1. Use the holding feature to prevent the ball studs (lower ball joint and stabilizer bar link) from turning while removing the nuts.
2. Remove the wheel and tire.

❊❊ CAUTION

Do not strike the ball joint stud to separate it from the wheel spindle or damage to the ball stud can occur. Lightly tap the wheel spindle to loosen the ball stud.

➡The lower ball joint does not require special tools to separate from the wheel spindle.

3. Remove and discard the lower ball joint nut and separate the ball joint from the wheel spindle.
4. Remove and discard the stabilizer bar link lower nut.
5. Remove and discard the shock absorber lower nut and bolt.
6. Remove the lower arm nuts, bolts and the lower arm. Discard the nuts and bolts.

To install:

➡Use the holding feature to prevent the ball studs (lower ball joint and stabilizer bar link) from turning while installing the nuts.

➡Do not tighten the lower arm nuts at this time.

7. Install the lower arm and loosely install the lower arm bolts and nuts.
8. Position the lower ball joint into the wheel spindle and install the nut. Tighten to 150 Nm (111 lb-ft).
9. Install the shock absorber lower nut and bolt. Tighten the nut to 475 Nm (351 lb-ft).
10. Install the stabilizer bar link lower nut. Tighten to 90 Nm (66 lb-ft).

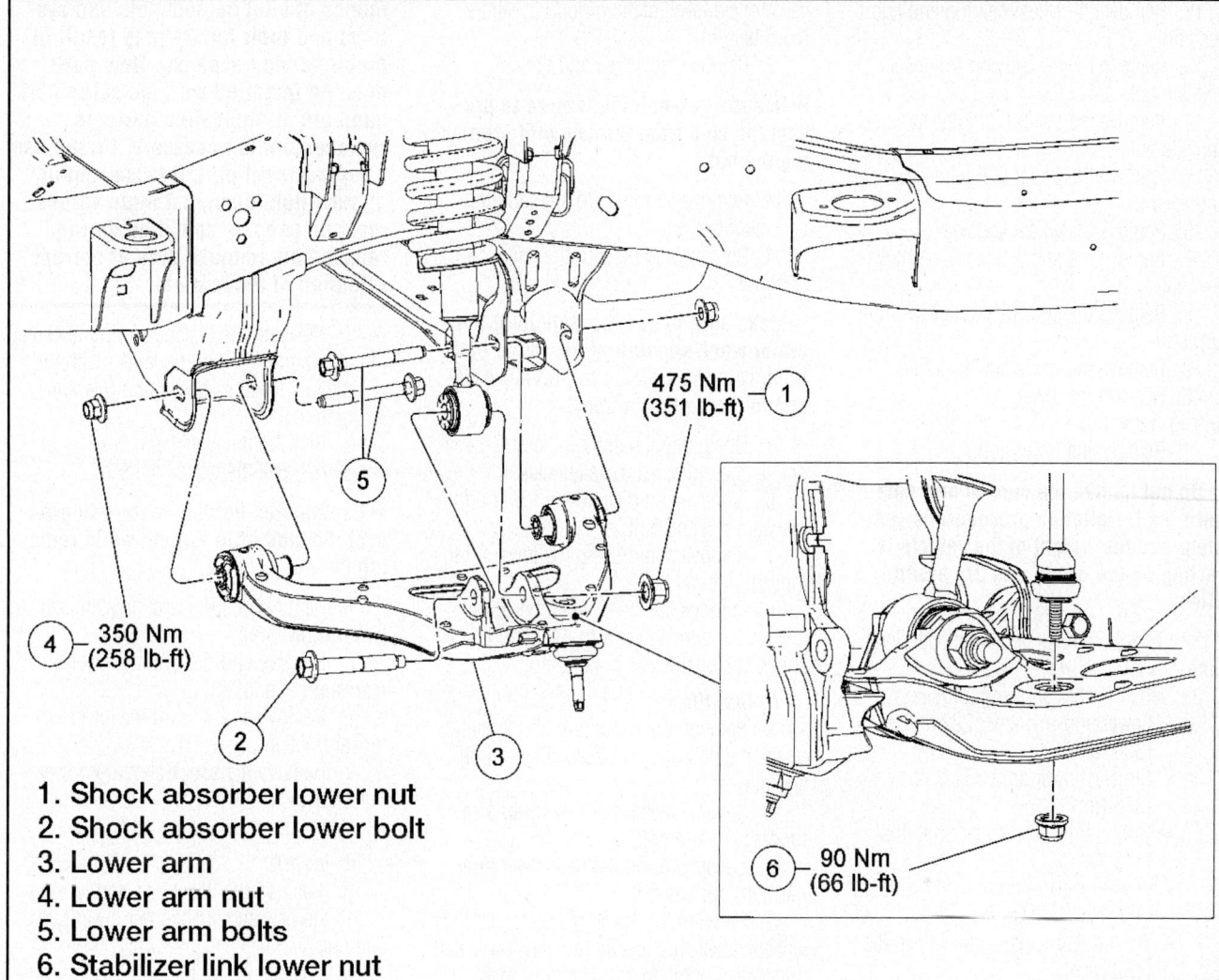

1. Shock absorber lower nut
2. Shock absorber lower bolt
3. Lower arm
4. Lower arm nut
5. Lower arm bolts
6. Stabilizer link lower nut

36578_FTRK_G0135

Fig. 279 Exploded view of the rear lower control arm and related parts—2008 2WD Models

11. Install the wheel and tire.

12. With the weight of the vehicle resting on the wheels and tires, tighten the lower arm nuts to 350 Nm (258 lb-ft).

13. Check and, if necessary, align the front end..

4WD Vehicles

1. Before servicing the vehicle, refer to the Precautions Section.

2. Loosen the axle retainer nut.

➡The wheel speed sensor electrical connectors are located in the engine compartment secured to the fender aprons.

3. Disconnect the wheel speed sensor.

4. Remove the wheel and tire assembly.

✳✳ WARNING

Use the hex holding feature to prevent the ball studs (upper control arm, lower control arm tie-rod end, and stabilizer bar links) from turning while removing and installing the nuts.

✳✳ WARNING

Do not hammer the ball studs to separate them from the wheel knuckle or stabilizer bar. Doing so can cause damage. Lightly tap the wheel knuckle or stabilizer bar to loosen the joints.

5. Remove the axle-to-wheel hub nut.

Remove the nut and separate the outboard CV-joint from the wheel hub.

6. Remove the wheel speed sensor harness connector.

7. Remove the anchor plate bolt.

8. Remove the brake caliper, pads and anchor plate .

✳✳ WARNING

Do not allow the brake caliper to hang from the hose or damage to the hose can occur.

9. Position the caliper, pads and anchor plate aside.

10. Remove the brake disc.

11. Remove the wheel hub-to-wheel knuckle bolts.

12. Remove the wheel bearing and hub assembly.

13. Remove the tie-rod end-to-wheel knuckle nut.

14. Remove the lower ball joint-to-wheel knuckle nut.

15. Remove the upper ball joint-to-wheel knuckle nut.

16. Remove the wheel knuckle.

17. Remove the shock absorber-to-lower arm nut.

18. Remove the shock absorber-to-lower arm bolt.

19. Remove the lower arm-to-frame nut.

20. Remove the lower arm-to-frame bolt.

21. Remove the lower arm.

➡ **Do not tighten the control arm nuts until the installation procedure is complete and the weight of the vehicle is resting on the wheel and tire assemblies.**

22. To install, reverse the removal procedure.

23. Observe the following torques:
- Lower arm-to-frame: 222 ft. lbs. (300 Nm)
- Strut-to-lower arm: 351 ft. lbs. (475 Nm)
- Upper arm-to-knuckle: 85 ft. lbs. (115 Nm)
- Lower arm-to-knuckle: 111 ft. lbs. (150 Nm)
- Tie rod end-to-knuckle: 111 ft. lbs. (150 Nm)
- Anchor plate: 148 ft. lbs. (200 Nm)

24. Check and, if necessary, align the front end.

2009 Models

2WD Vehicles

See Figure 280.

> ❈❈ **CAUTION**
>
> **Suspension fasteners are critical parts because they affect performance of vital components and systems and their failure may result in major service expense. New parts must be installed with the same part numbers or equivalent parts, if replacement is necessary. Do not use a replacement part of lesser quality or substitute design. Torque values must be used as specified during reassembly to make sure of correct retention of these parts.**

1. Measure the distance from the center of the hub to the lip of the fender with the vehicle in a level, static ground position (curb height).

2. Remove the wheel and tire.

➡ **Use the hex-holding feature to prevent the stud from turning while removing the nut.**

3. Remove and discard the stabilizer bar link lower nut.

4. Remove and discard the lower ball joint nut.

➡ **Make sure to use the Ball Joint Separator when separating the lower ball joint from the knuckle to prevent damage to the ball joint boot.**

5. Using the Ball Joint Separator, separate the ball joint from the knuckle.

6. Remove and discard the lower arm rearward nut and bolt.

7. Remove and discard the lower arm forward nut and bolt.

8. Remove the shock absorber lower nut, bolt and the lower arm. Discard the shock absorber lower nut and bolt.

To install:

9. Position the lower arm and loosely install the new shock absorber lower bolt and nut.

10. Loosely install the new lower arm forward nut and bolt.

11. Loosely install the new lower arm rearward nut and bolt.

12. Position the lower ball joint into the wheel knuckle and install the new lower ball joint nut. Tighten to 150 Nm (111 lb-ft).

13. Install the new stabilizer bar link lower nut. Tighten to 80 Nm (59 lb-ft).

14. Use a suitable jack to raise the suspension until the distance between the center of the hub and the lip of the fender is equal to the measurement taken in Step 1 (curb height).

➡ **Use a crowfoot wrench to tighten the lower arm rearward nut.**

15. Tighten the lower arm rearward nut to 258 ft. lbs. (350 Nm).

16. Tighten the lower arm forward nut to 258 ft. lbs. (350 Nm).

17. Tighten the shock absorber lower nut to 406 ft. lbs. (550 Nm).

18. Install the wheel and tire.

19. Check and, if necessary, align the front end.

4WD Vehicles

See Figure 281.

> ❈❈ **CAUTION**
>
> **Suspension fasteners are critical parts because they affect performance of vital components and systems and their failure may result in major service expense. New parts must be installed with the same part numbers or equivalent parts, if replacement is necessary. Do not use a replacement part of lesser quality or substitute design. Torque values must be used as specified during reassembly to make sure of correct retention of these parts.**

1. Measure the distance from the center of the hub to the lip of the fender with the vehicle in a level, static ground position (curb height).

2. Remove the wheel and tire.

3. Remove the wheel knuckle.

➡ **Use the hex-holding feature to prevent the stud from turning while removing the nut.**

4. Remove and discard the stabilizer bar link lower nut.

5. Remove and discard the lower arm rearward nut and bolt.

6. Remove and discard the lower arm forward nut and bolt.

7. Remove the shock absorber lower nut, bolt and the lower arm. Discard the shock absorber lower nut and bolt.

To install:

8. Position the lower arm and loosely install the new shock absorber lower bolt and nut.

9. Loosely install the new lower arm forward nut and bolt.

10. Loosely install the new lower arm rearward nut and bolt.

➡ **Use the hex-holding feature to prevent the stud from turning while installing the nut.**

11. Install the new stabilizer bar link lower nut. Tighten to 80 Nm (59 lb-ft).

12. Use a suitable jack to raise the suspension until the distance between the center of the hub and the lip of the fender is equal to the measurement taken in Step 1 (curb height).

➡ **Use a crowfoot wrench to tighten the lower arm rearward nut.**

13. Tighten the lower arm rearward nut to 258 ft. lbs. (350 Nm).

14. Tighten the lower arm forward nut to 258 ft. lbs. (350 Nm).

15. Tighten the shock absorber lower nut to 406 ft. lbs. (550 Nm).

16. Install the wheel and tire.

17. Check and, if necessary, align the front end.

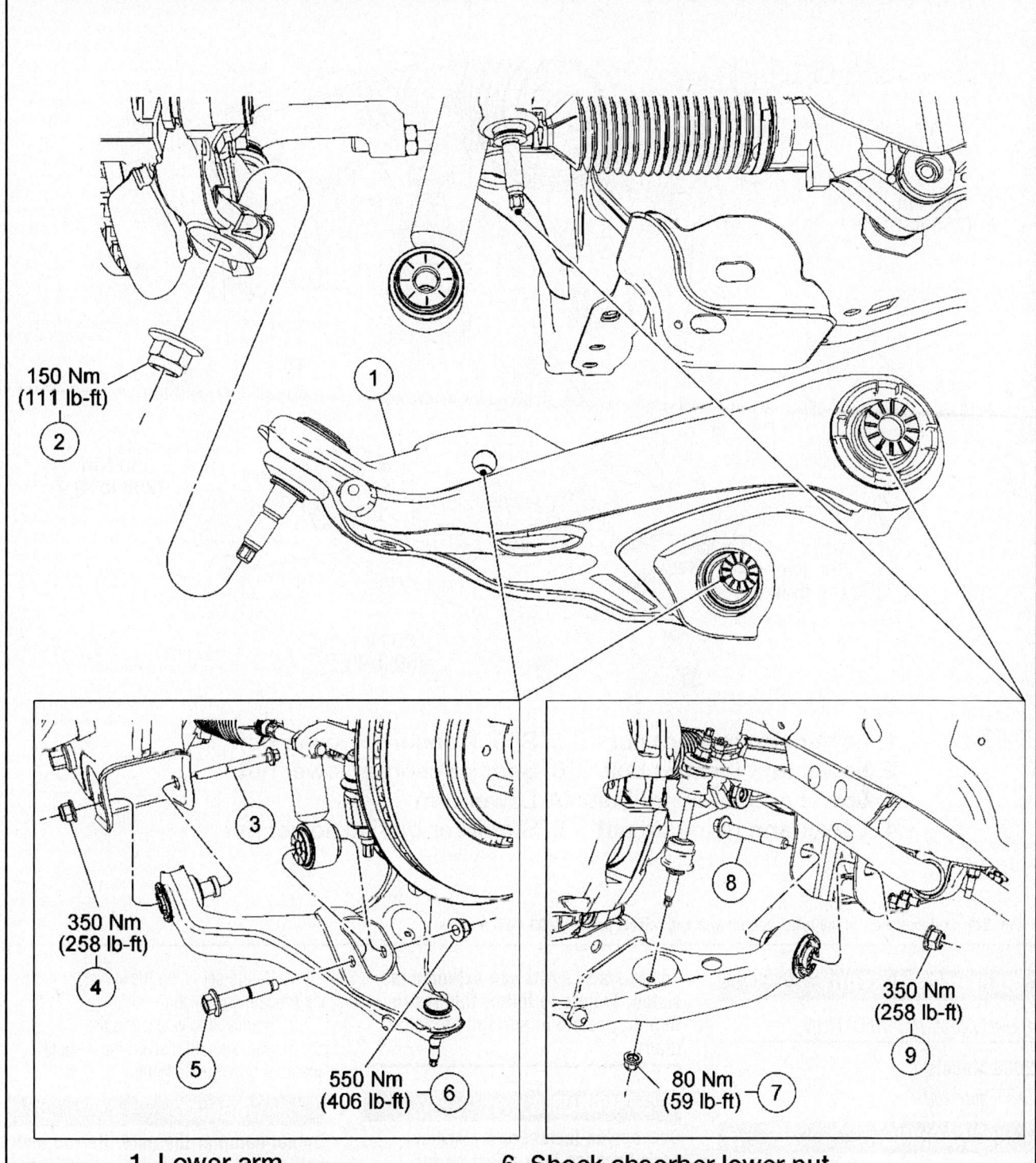

150 Nm
(111 lb-ft)
②

①

③

350 Nm
(258 lb-ft)
④

⑤

550 Nm
(406 lb-ft)   ⑥

⑧

80 Nm
(59 lb-ft)   ⑦

350 Nm
(258 lb-ft)
⑨

1. Lower arm
2. Lower ball joint nut
3. Lower arm forward bolt
4. Lower arm forward nut
5. Shock absorber lower bolt

6. Shock absorber lower nut
7. Stabilizer bar link lower nut
8. Lower arm rearward bolt
9. Lower arm rearward nut

36578_FTRK_G0136

Fig. 280 Exploded view of the lower control arm and related parts—2009 2WD Models

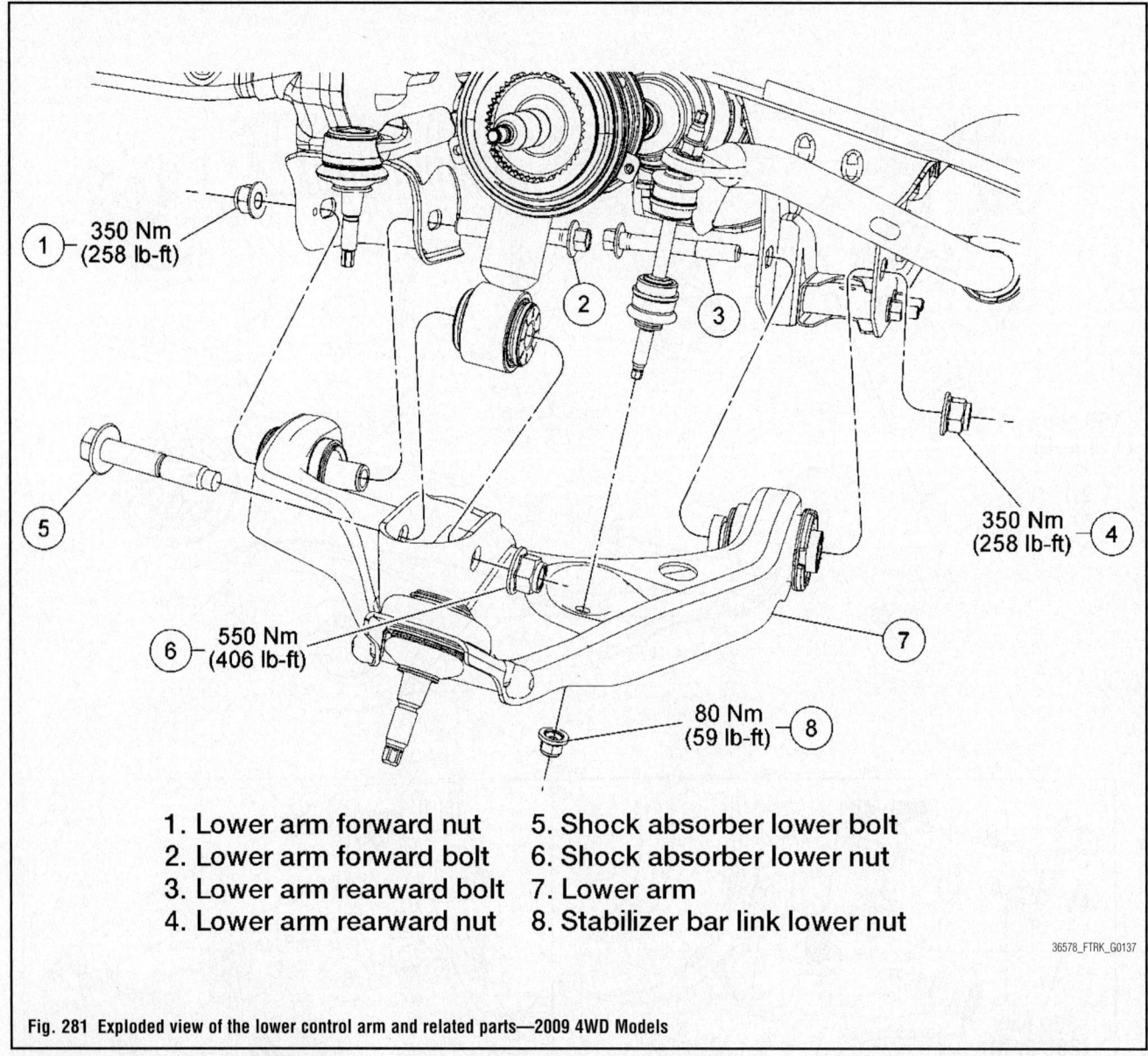

1. Lower arm forward nut
2. Lower arm forward bolt
3. Lower arm rearward bolt
4. Lower arm rearward nut
5. Shock absorber lower bolt
6. Shock absorber lower nut
7. Lower arm
8. Stabilizer bar link lower nut

36578_FTRK_G0137

Fig. 281 Exploded view of the lower control arm and related parts—2009 4WD Models

MACPHERSON STRUT

REMOVAL & INSTALLATION

2008 Models

See Figure 282.

✳✳ WARNING

Do not apply heat or flame to the shock absorber or strut tube. The shock absorber and strut tube are gas pressurized and could explode if heated. Failure to follow this instruction may result in serious personal injury.

✳✳ WARNING

Keep all body parts clear of shock absorbers or strut rods. Shock absorbers or struts can extend unassisted. Failure to follow this instruction may result in serious personal injury.

✳✳ WARNING

Suspension fasteners are critical parts because they affect performance of vital parts and systems and their failure can result in major service expense. A new part with the same part number must be installed if installation becomes necessary. Do not use a replacement part of lesser quality or substitute design. Torque values must be used as specified during reassembly to make sure of correct retention of these parts.

1. Before servicing the vehicle, refer to the Precautions Section.

2. Remove the wheel and tire.

3. Remove and discard the 3 shock absorber upper mount nuts.

✳✳ WARNING

Do not hammer the outer tie-rod end ball stud to separate the outer tie-rod end from the wheel spindle or damage to the ball stud can occur. Lightly tap the wheel spindle to loosen the ball stud.

➡Use the holding feature to prevent the outer tie-rod end ball stud from turning while removing the nut.

4. Remove and discard the outer tie-rod end nut and separate the tie-rod end from the wheel spindle.

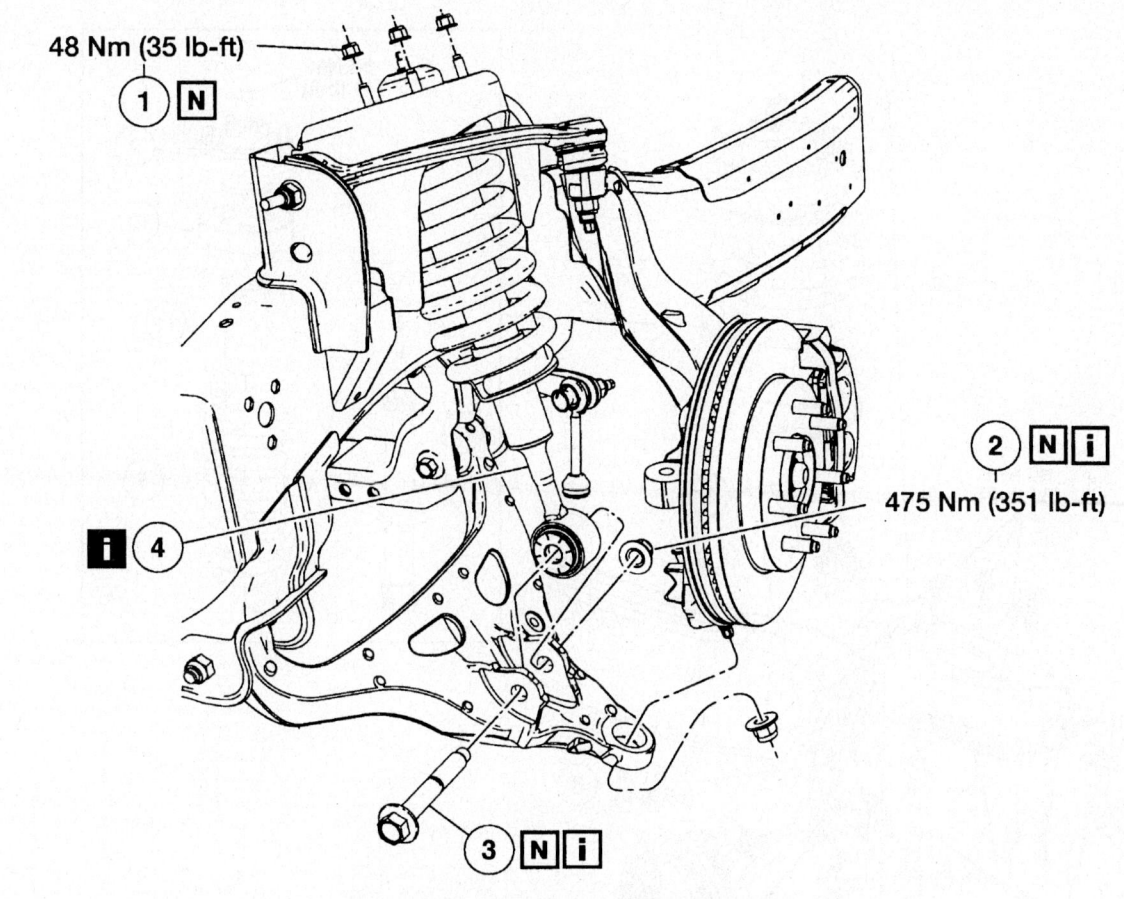

48 Nm (35 lb-ft)
① N

② N i
475 Nm (351 lb-ft)

i ④

③ N i

1 Shock absorber upper mount-to-frame nuts
2 Shock absorber-to-lower arm nut
3 Shock absorber-to-lower arm bolt
4 Shock absorber and spring assembly

67197-EFSE-G156

Fig. 282 Front strut mounting—F-150 and Mark LT

➡**Position the outer tie rod end as necessary to remove the shock absorber and spring assembly.**

5. Remove the shock absorber lower nut, bolt and the shock absorber and spring assembly. Discard the nut and bolt.

6. For additional information regarding disassembly and assembly of the shock absorber and spring assembly,

To install:

➡**Do not tighten the lower shock nut at this time.**

7. Install the shock absorber and spring assembly and loosely install the shock absorber lower bolt and nut.

➡**Use the holding feature to prevent the outer tie-rod end ball stud from turning while installing the nut.**

8. Position the outer tie-rod end and install the nut. Tighten to 85 ft. lbs. (115 Nm).

9. Install the 3 shock absorber upper mount nuts. Tighten to 35 ft. lbs. (48 Nm).

10. Install the wheel and tire..

11. With the weight of the vehicle resting on the wheels and tires, tighten the shock absorber lower nut to 351 ft. lbs. (475 Nm).

2009 Models
See Figure 283.

1. Before servicing the vehicle, refer to the precautions section.

✳✳ WARNING

Suspension fasteners are critical parts because they affect performance of vital parts and systems and their failure can result in major ser- vice expense. A new part with the same part number must be installed if installation becomes necessary. Do not use a replacement part of lesser quality or substitute design. Torque values must be used as specified during reassembly to make sure of correct retention of these parts.

✳✳ WARNING

Do not tighten the lower shock nut until the installation procedure is complete and the weight of the vehicle is resting on the wheel and tire assemblies.

2. Before servicing the vehicle, refer to the precautions section.

3. With the vehicle in NEUTRAL, position it on a hoist.

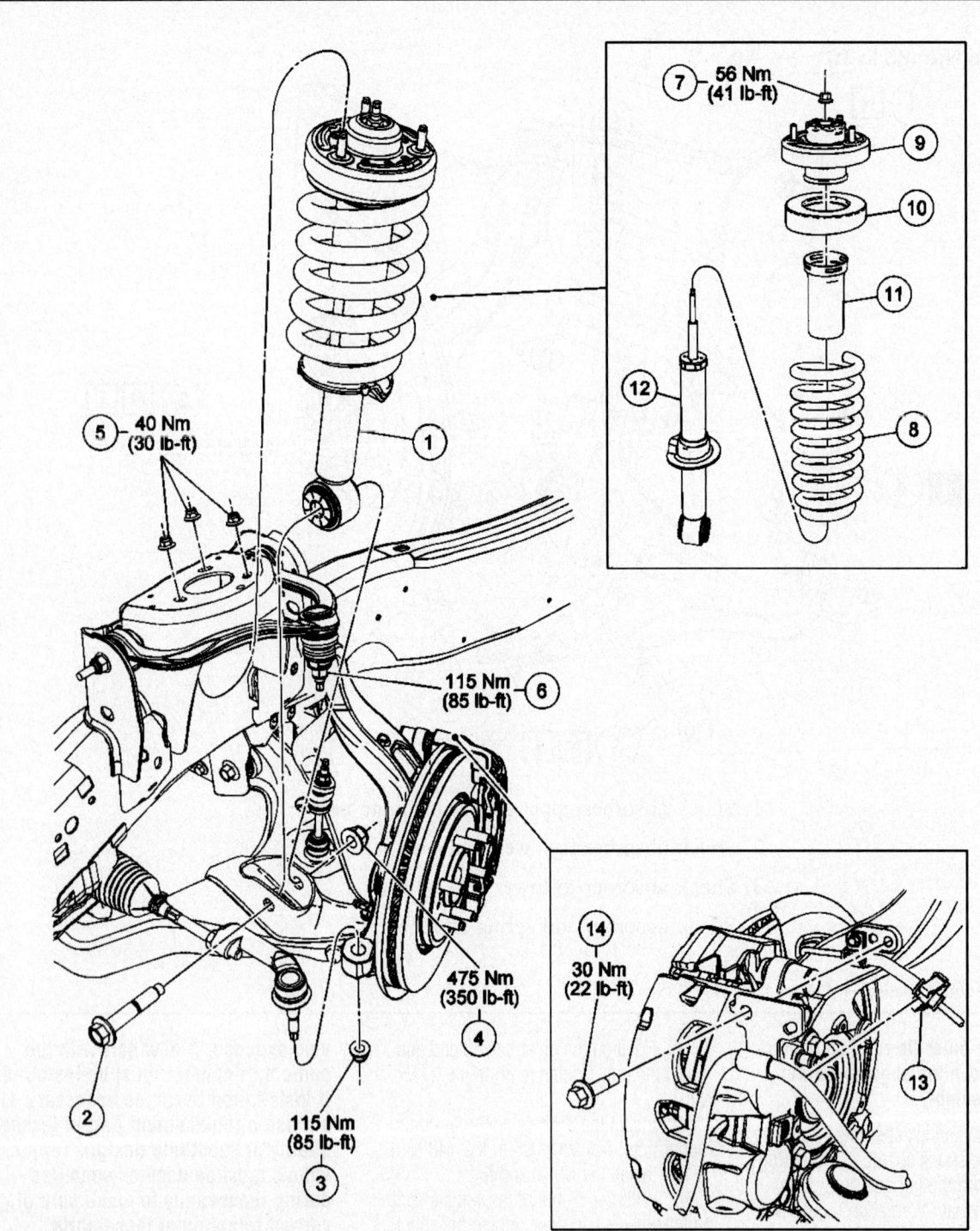

1. Shock absorber and spring assembly
2. Shock absorber lower bolt
3. Tie-rod end nut
4. Shock absorber lower nut
5. Shock absorber upper mount nuts (3 required)
6. Upper ball joint nut
7. Shock rod nut
8. Spring
9. Upper mount
10. Insulator
11. Dust boot
12. Shock absorber
13. Brake flexible hose retainer
14. Brake flexible hose bracket bolt

36578_EXPD_G0135

Fig. 283 Exploded view of the front shock absorber and components

4. Remove and discard the shock absorber and spring assembly upper nuts.

5. Remove and discard the tie-rod end nut.

6. Using the special tool 204-592, separate the upper ball joint from the wheel knuckle.

7. Remove and discard the upper ball joint nut.

8. Remove and discard the shock absorber and spring assembly lower nut and bolt

9. Using the special tool, disconnect the upper arm from the wheel knuckle and remove the shock absorber and spring assembly.

To install:

10. To install, reverse the removal procedure and note the following:

  a. Tighten lower shock absorber nut and bolt to 295 ft. lbs. (475 Nm).

  b. Tighten upper ball joint nut to 85 ft. lbs. (115 Nm).

  c. Tighten tie-rod end nut to 111 ft lbs. (150 Nm).

  d. Tighten the shock absorber and spring assembly upper nuts to 30 ft. lbs. (40 Nm).

OVERHAUL

See Figure 284.

1. Before servicing the vehicle, refer to the Precautions Section.

2. Remove the strut and spring assembly.

3. Using a suitable spring compressor, compress the spring until the tension is released from the shock absorber.

4. Remove the shock absorber-to-upper mount nut

5. Remove the upper shock mount

6. Remove the isolator

7. Remove the dust tube

8. Remove the coil spring

9. Remove the shock absorber

10. To assemble, reverse the disassembly procedure. Torque the nut to 22 ft. lbs. (30 Nm).

STEERING KNUCKLE

REMOVAL & INSTALLATION

2008 Models

See Figures 285 and 286.

❄❄ WARNING

Suspension fasteners are critical parts because they affect performance of vital parts and systems and their failure can result in major ser-

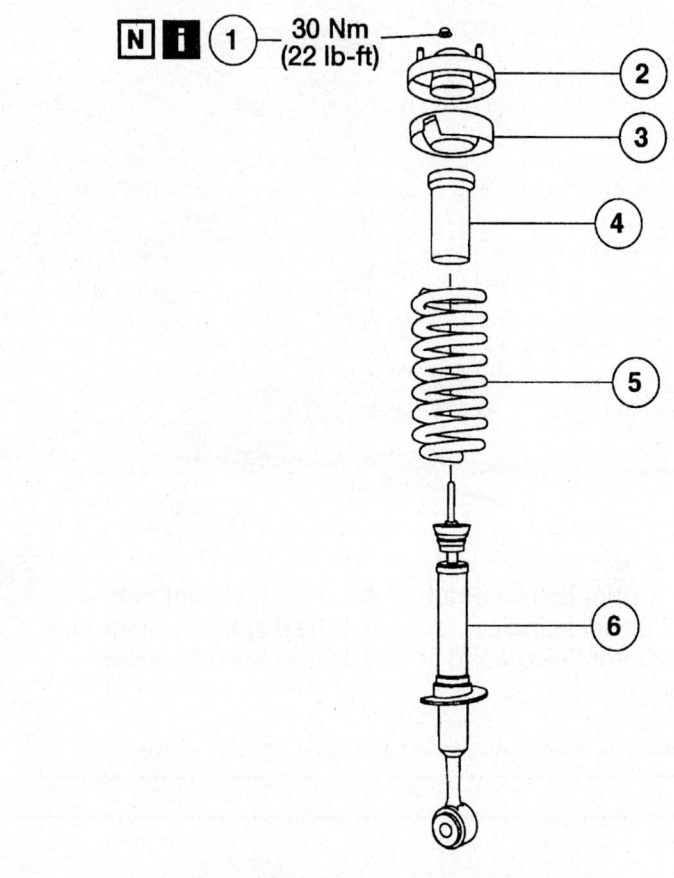

1 Shock absorber-to-upper mount nut
2 Upper shock mount (front/rear)
3 Isolator
4 Dust tube
5 Coil spring (front)
6 Shock absorber (front/rear)

67197-EFSE-G157

Fig. 284 Front strut disassembled

vice expense. A new part with the same part number must be installed if installation becomes necessary. Do not use a replacement part of lesser quality or substitute design. Torque values must be used as specified during reassembly to make sure of correct retention of these parts.

❄❄ CAUTION

Do not strike the ball studs to separate them from the wheel knuckle or damage to the ball studs can occur. Lightly tap the wheel spindle to loosen the ball studs.

➡Use the holding feature to prevent the stud (outer tie-rod end, lower ball joint and upper ball joint) from turning while removing or installing the nuts.

➡The upper ball joint, the lower ball joint and the outer tie-rod end ball studs do not require special tools to separate from the wheel spindle.

1. Remove the wheel bearing and wheel hub.

2. If equipped, remove the front wheel speed sensor bolt and position the wheel speed sensor aside.

3. Remove and discard the outer tie-rod end nut and detach the tie-rod end from the

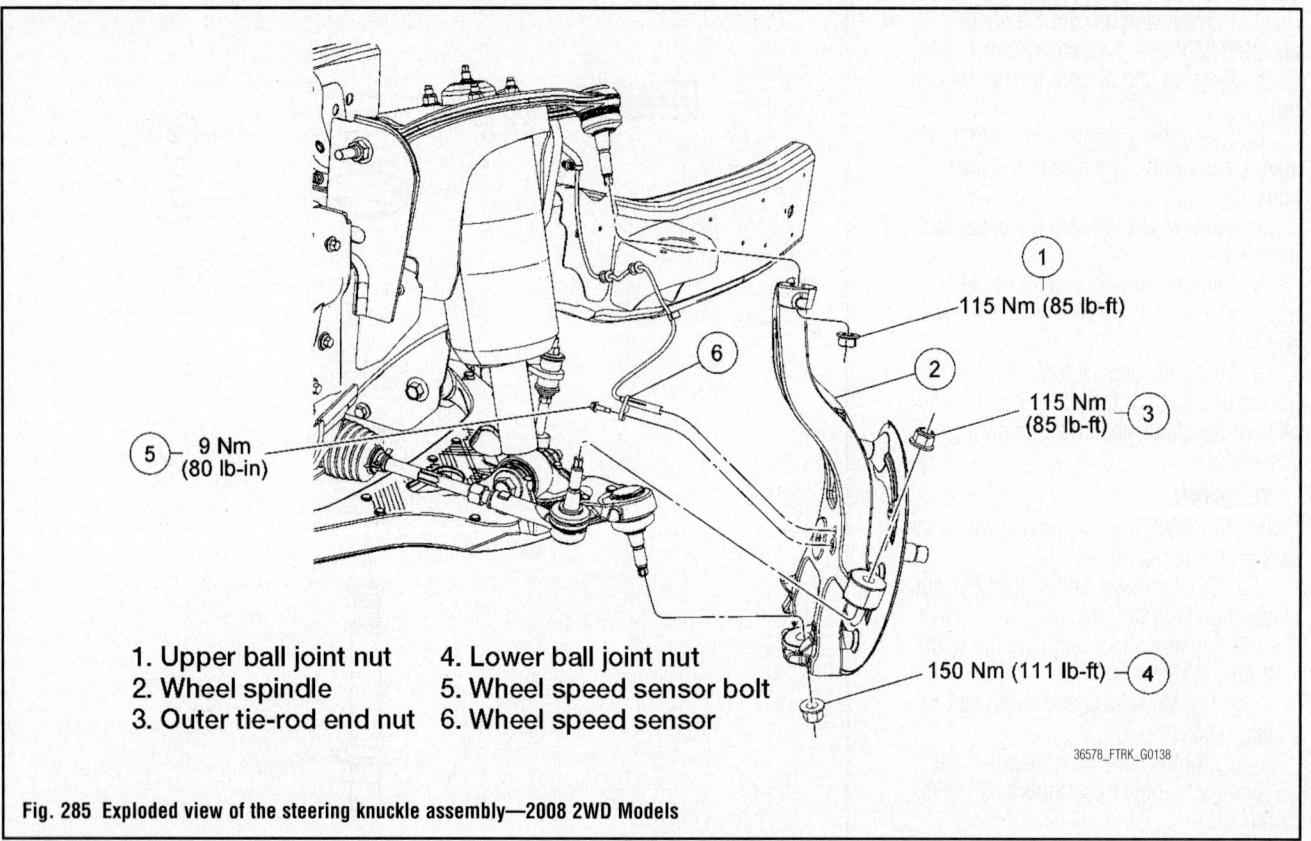

115 Nm (85 lb-ft) — ①

115 Nm (85 lb-ft) — ③

9 Nm (80 lb-in) — ⑤

150 Nm (111 lb-ft) — ④

1. Upper ball joint nut
2. Wheel spindle
3. Outer tie-rod end nut
4. Lower ball joint nut
5. Wheel speed sensor bolt
6. Wheel speed sensor

36578_FTRK_G0138

Fig. 285 Exploded view of the steering knuckle assembly—2008 2WD Models

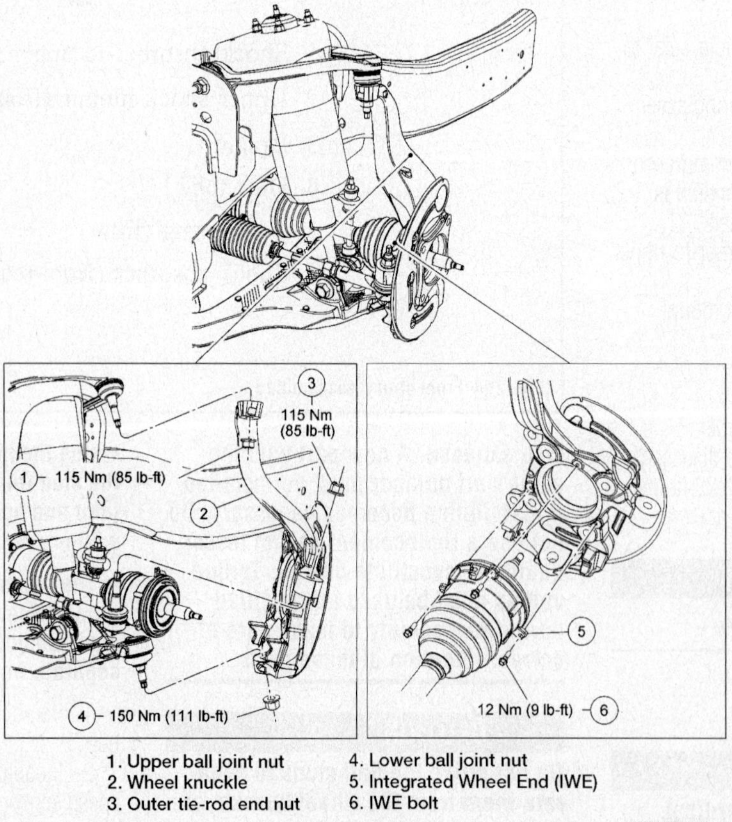

③ 115 Nm (85 lb-ft)

① 115 Nm (85 lb-ft)

④ 150 Nm (111 lb-ft)

⑤

12 Nm (9 lb-ft) — ⑥

1. Upper ball joint nut
2. Wheel knuckle
3. Outer tie-rod end nut
4. Lower ball joint nut
5. Integrated Wheel End (IWE)
6. IWE bolt

36578_FTRK_G0139

Fig. 286 Exploded view of the steering knuckle assembly—2008 4WD Models

wheel spindle. To install, tighten to 115 Nm (85 lb-ft).

4. Remove and discard the upper ball joint nut, then detach the upper ball joint from the wheel spindle and remove the wheel spindle.

5. For 4WD vehicles, remove the 3 integrated wheel end (IWE) bolts. To install, tighten to 9 ft. lbs. (12 Nm).

6. If necessary, remove the brake shield. To install, tighten to 115 Nm (85 lb-ft).

7. Remove and discard the lower ball joint nut and detach the lower ball joint from the wheel spindle. To install, tighten to 150 Nm (111 lb-ft).

8. To install, reverse the removal procedure.

9. Check and, if necessary, align the front end.

2009 Models

2WD Models

See Figure 287.

> ※ **CAUTION**
>
> **The electrical power to the air suspension system must be shut off prior to hoisting, jacking or towing an air suspension vehicle. This can be accomplished by turning off the air suspension switch located in the LH rear quarter trim panel. Failure to do so can result in unexpected inflation or deflation of the air springs, which can result in shifting of the vehicle during these operations.**

1. Before servicing the vehicle, refer to the precautions section.

2. If equipped, turn the air suspension to the OFF position.

3. Remove the wheel speed sensor harness bolt and detach the harness from the retainers.

4. Remove the wheel hub and bearing, as outlined in this section.

➡Use the hex holding feature to prevent the stud from turning while removing the nut.

5. Remove the nut and detach the tie-rod from the wheel knuckle. Discard the nut.

6. Remove the bolt and position the brake hose aside.

➡Use the hex holding feature to prevent the stud from turning while removing the nut.

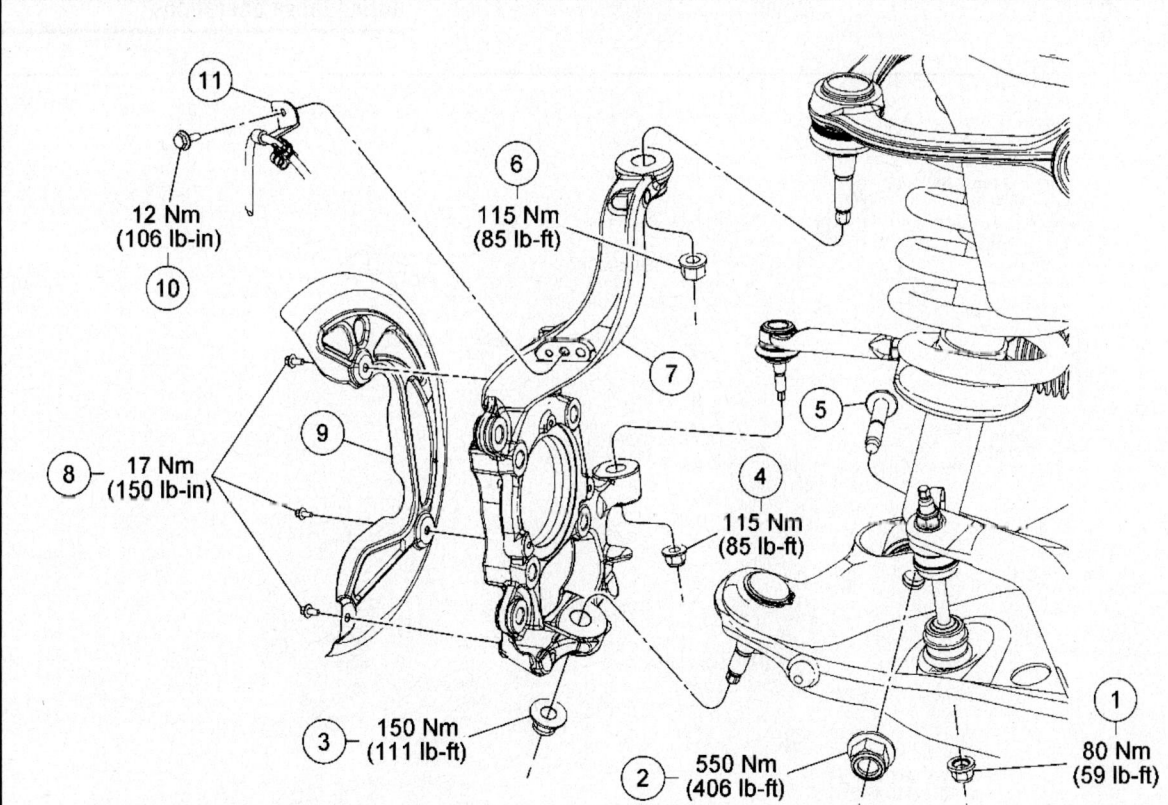

1. Stabilizer bar link lower nut
2. Shock absorber lower nut
3. Lower ball joint nut
4. Tie-rod end nut
5. Shock absorber lower bolt
6. Upper ball joint nut
7. Wheel knuckle
8. Brake disc shield bolts (3 required)
9. Brake disc shield
10. Wheel speed sensor harness bracket bolt
11. Wheel speed sensor harness bracket

36578_EXPD_G0124

Fig. 287 Exploded view of the front steering knuckle–2WD—2009 Models

7. Remove and discard the stabilizer bar link lower nut. Discard the nut.

8. Remove the shock absorber-to-lower arm nut and bolt. Discard the nut.

➡️ **Use the hex holding feature to prevent the stud from turning while removing the nut.**

➡️ **To separate the ball joints from the wheel knuckle, use tool 204-592.**

9. Remove the nut and separate the ball joint from the knuckle. Discard the nut.

➡️ **Use the hex holding feature to prevent the stud from turning while removing the nut.**

10. Remove the nut and the wheel knuckle. Discard the nut.

11. If necessary, remove the 3 brake disc shield bolts and remove the brake disc shield.

To install:

➡️ **Do not tighten the lower shock nut until the installation procedure is complete and the weight of the vehicle is resting on the wheel and tire assemblies.**

12. To install, reverse the removal procedure and note the following:
   a. Upper ball joint nut: 85 ft. lbs. (115 Nm).
   b. Lower ball joint nut: 111 ft. lbs. (150 Nm).
   c. Wheel bearing-to-knuckle bolts: 148 ft. lbs. (200 Nm)
   d. Shock absorber-to-lower control arm bolt and nut: 350 ft. lbs. (475 Nm)
   e. Stabilizer bar link-to-control arm nuts: 66 ft. lbs. (90 Nm)
   f. Brake hose bracket bolt: 9 ft. lbs. (12 Nm)

   g. Tie rod end nuts: 85 ft. lbs. (115 Nm).
   h. The brake disc shield bolts: 9 ft. lbs. (12 Nm).
13. Check and, if necessary, align the front end.

4WD Models
See Figure 288.

✴✴ CAUTION

The electrical power to the air suspension system must be shut off prior to hoisting, jacking or towing an air suspension vehicle. This can be accomplished by turning off the air suspension switch located in the LH rear quarter trim panel. Failure to do so can result in unexpected inflation or deflation of the air springs, which can result in shifting of the vehicle during these operations.

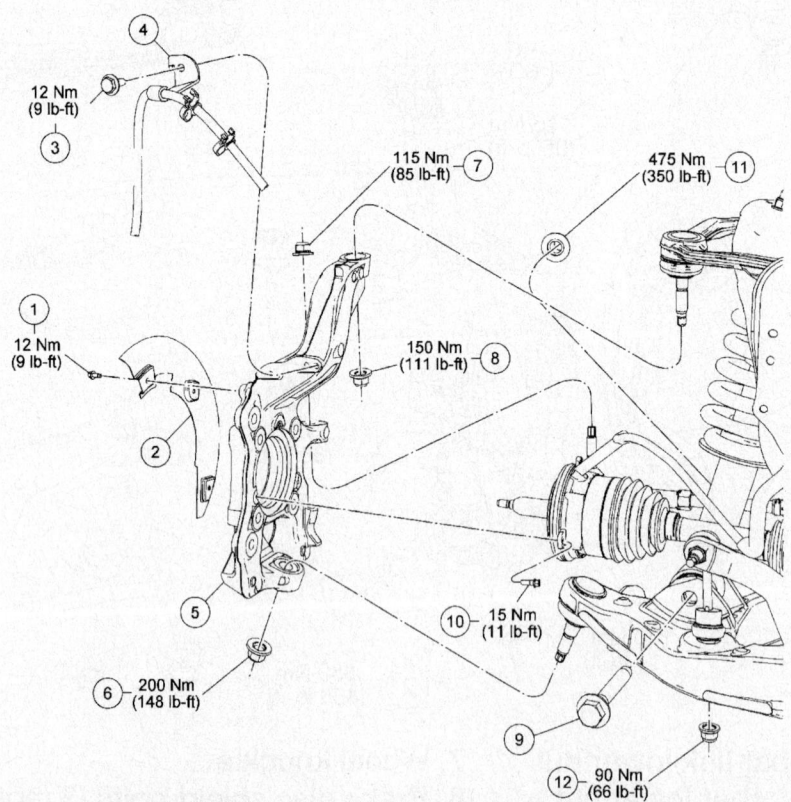

1. Brake disc shield bolt (3 required)
2. Brake disc shield
3. Brake hose bracket bolt
4. Brake hose bracket
5. Wheel knuckle
6. Lower ball joint nut
7. Tie-rod end nut
8. Upper ball joint nut
9. Shock absorber lower bolt
10. Integrated wheel end disconnect bolt (3 required)
11. Shock absorber lower nut
12. Stabilizer bar link lower nut

22086_EXPD_G0103

Fig. 288 Exploded view of the front steering knuckle–4WD–2009 Models

1. Before servicing the vehicle, refer to the precautions section.

2. If equipped, turn the air suspension to the OFF position.

3. Remove the wheel hub and bearing, as outlined in this section.

➡**Use the hex holding feature to prevent the stud from turning while removing the nut.**

4. Remove and discard the tie rod end nut.

5. Remove the bolt and position the brake hose aside.

➡**Use the hex holding feature to prevent the stud from turning while removing the nut.**

6. Remove and discard the stabilizer bar link-to-lower arm nut.

7. Remove the shock absorber-to-lower arm nut and bolt. Discard the nut.

8. Remove the three wheel end actuator-to-wheel knuckle bolts.

➡**Use the hex holding feature to prevent the stud from turning while removing the nut.**

9. Remove and discard the lower ball joint nut.

➡**Use the hex holding feature to prevent the stud from turning while removing the nut.**

➡**To separate the ball joints from the wheel knuckle, use tool 204-592.**

10. Remove the upper ball joint nut and the wheel knuckle. Discard the nut.

To install:

➡**Do not tighten the lower shock nut until the installation procedure is complete and the weight of the vehicle is resting on the wheel and tire assemblies.**

11. To install, reverse the removal procedure and note the following:

a. Upper ball joint nut: 111 ft. lbs. (150 Nm).

b. Lower ball joint nut: 148 ft. lbs. (200 Nm).

c. Wheel end actuator-to-wheel knuckle bolts and shield: 9 ft. lbs. (12 Nm)

d. Shock absorber-to-lower arm nut and bolt: 350 ft. lbs. (475 Nm)

e. Stabilizer bar link-to-lower arm nut: 66 ft. lbs. (90 Nm)

f. Brake hose bracket bolt: 9 ft. lbs. (12 Nm)

g. Tie rod end nut: 85 ft. lbs. (115 Nm)

12. Check and, if necessary, align the front end.

STABILIZER BAR

REMOVAL & INSTALLATION

2008 Models
See Figure 289.

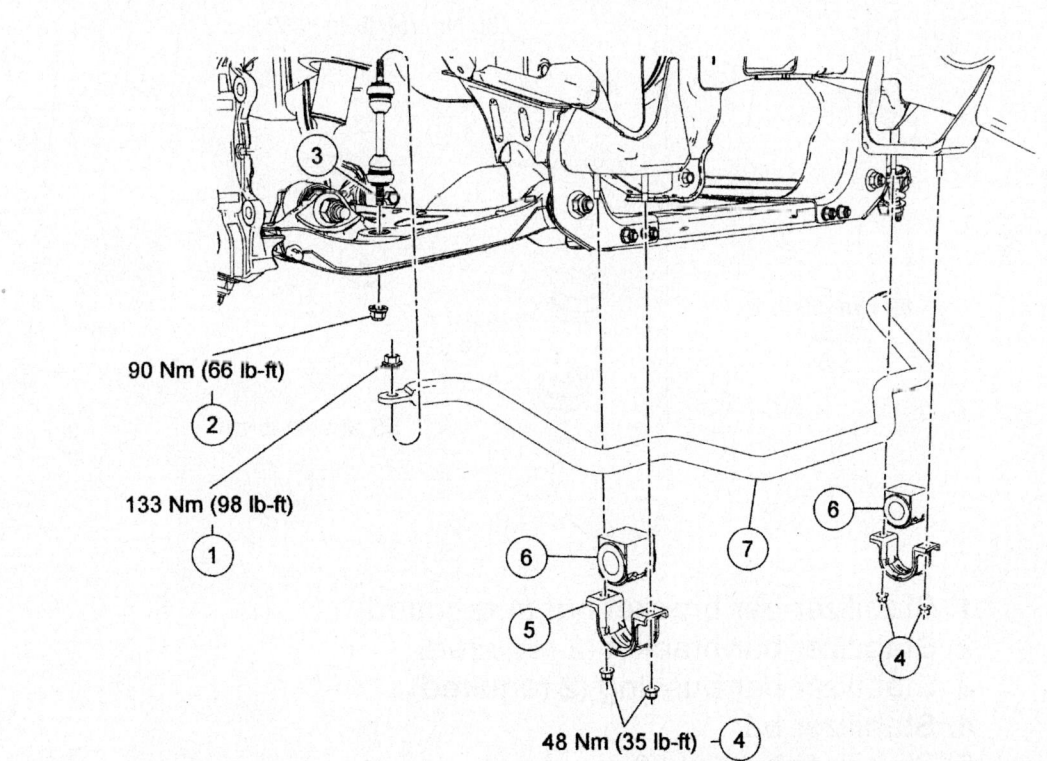

90 Nm (66 lb-ft)

133 Nm (98 lb-ft)

48 Nm (35 lb-ft)

1 Stabilizer bar link-to-stabilizer
   bar nut

2 Stabilizer bar link-to-lower
   control arm nut

3 Stabilizer bar link

4 Stabilizer bar-to-frame nuts

5 Bracket

6 Insulator (bushing)

7 Stabilizer bar

06017-F150-G270

Fig. 289 Stabilizer bar and link—2008 Models

1. Before servicing the vehicle, refer to the Precautions Section.

➡**Use the hex holding feature to prevent the ball studs (upper ball joint, lower ball joint, tie-rod end and stabilizer bar links) from turning while removing and installing the nuts.**

✳✳ WARNING

Do not hammer the ball studs to separate them from the wheel knuckle or stabilizer bar. Doing so can cause damage. Lightly tap the wheel knuckle or stabilizer bar to loosen the joints.

2. Remove the stabilizer bar link upper nuts.
3. Remove the stabilizer bar link lower nuts.
4. Remove the stabilizer bar links.
5. Remove the stabilizer bar bracket nuts, then, remove the stabilizer bar.

6. To install, reverse the removal procedure. Observe the following torques:
- Stabilizer bar bracket nuts: 48 Nm (35 ft. lbs.)
- Stabilizer bar link lower nuts: 90 Nm (66 ft. lbs.)
- Stabilizer bar link upper nuts: 133 Nm (98 ft. lbs.)

2009 Models

See Figure 290.

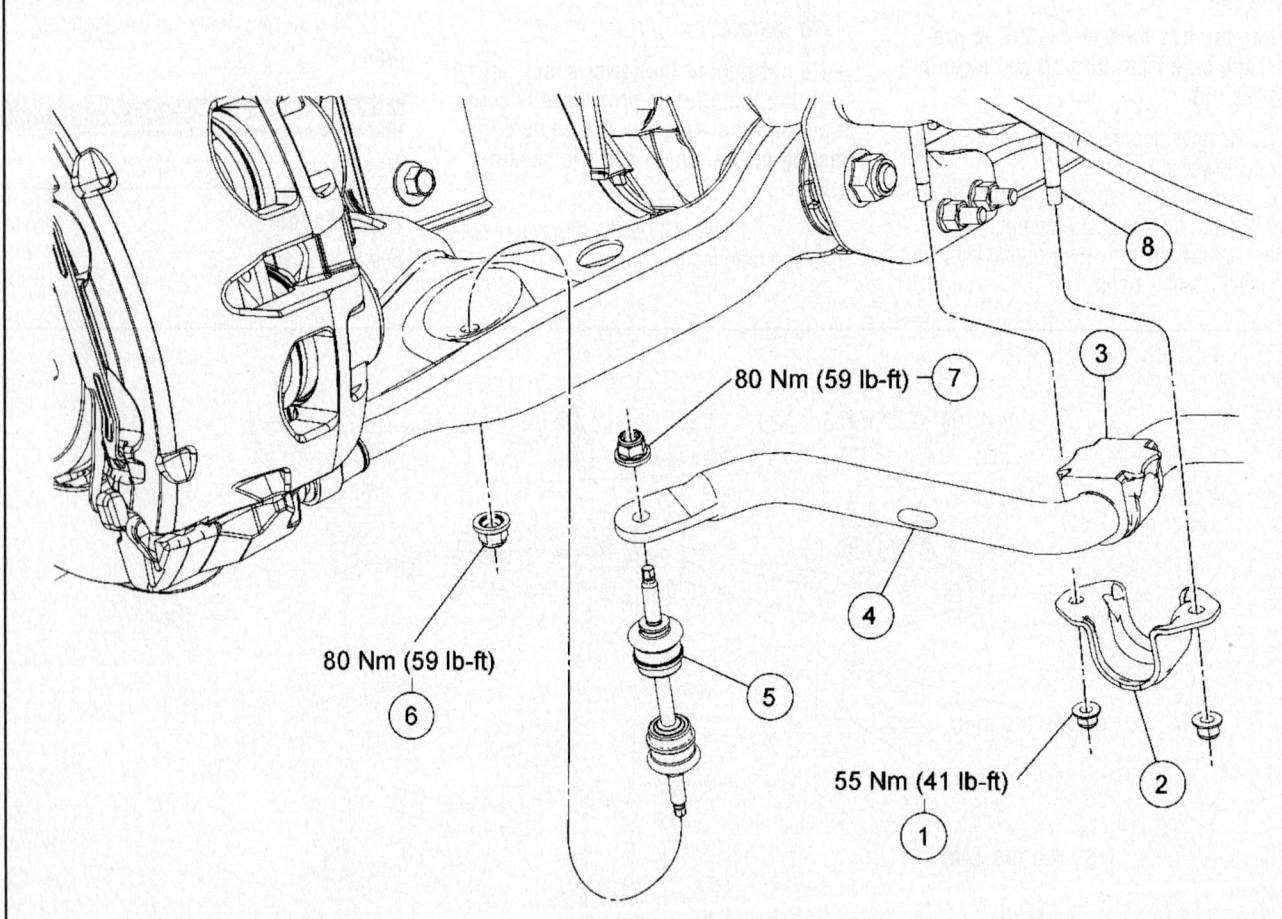

80 Nm (59 lb-ft) — 7

80 Nm (59 lb-ft)
6

55 Nm (41 lb-ft)
1

1. Stabilizer bar bracket nut (4 required)
2. Stabilizer bar bracket (2 required)
3. Stabilizer bar bushing (2 required)
4. Stabilizer bar
5. Stabilizer bar link (2 required)
6. Stabilizer bar link lower nut (2 required)
7. Stabilizer bar link upper nut (2 required)
8. Stabilizer bracket bolt plate

36578_EXPD_G0127

Fig. 290 Exploded view of the front stabilizer bar and control link

1. Before servicing the vehicle, refer to the precautions section.

2. With the vehicle in NEUTRAL, position it on a hoist.

➡**The hex holding feature can be used to prevent turning of the stud while removing the nut.**

3. Remove and discard the 2 stabilizer bar link upper nuts.

4. Remove and discard the 2 stabilizer bar link lower nuts and remove the 2 stabilizer bar links.

5. Remove the 4 stabilizer bar bracket nuts, brackets and the stabilizer bar. Discard the nuts.

6. Remove and discard the stabilizer bracket bolt plates.

➡**Make sure the stabilizer bar bushing upset is installed into the bracket groove**

7. Inspect and, if necessary, install new stabilizer bar bushings.

To install:

8. To install, reverse the removal procedure and note the following:

   a. Tighten upper and lower link nuts to 59 ft. lbs. (80 Nm).

   b. Tighten the stabilizer bar bracket nuts to 41 ft. lbs. (55 Nm).

UPPER BALL JOINT

REMOVAL & INSTALLATION

The upper ball joints on these models are an integral part of the control arm. If found to be defective the control arm must be replaced. Refer to control arm removal and installation.

UPPER CONTROL ARM

REMOVAL & INSTALLATION

2008 Models

See Figure 291.

❄❄ WARNING

Suspension fasteners are critical parts because they affect performance of vital parts and systems and their failure can result in major service expense. A new part with the same part number must be installed if installation becomes necessary. Do not use a replacement part of lesser quality or substitute design. Torque values must be used as specified during reassembly to make sure of correct retention of these parts.

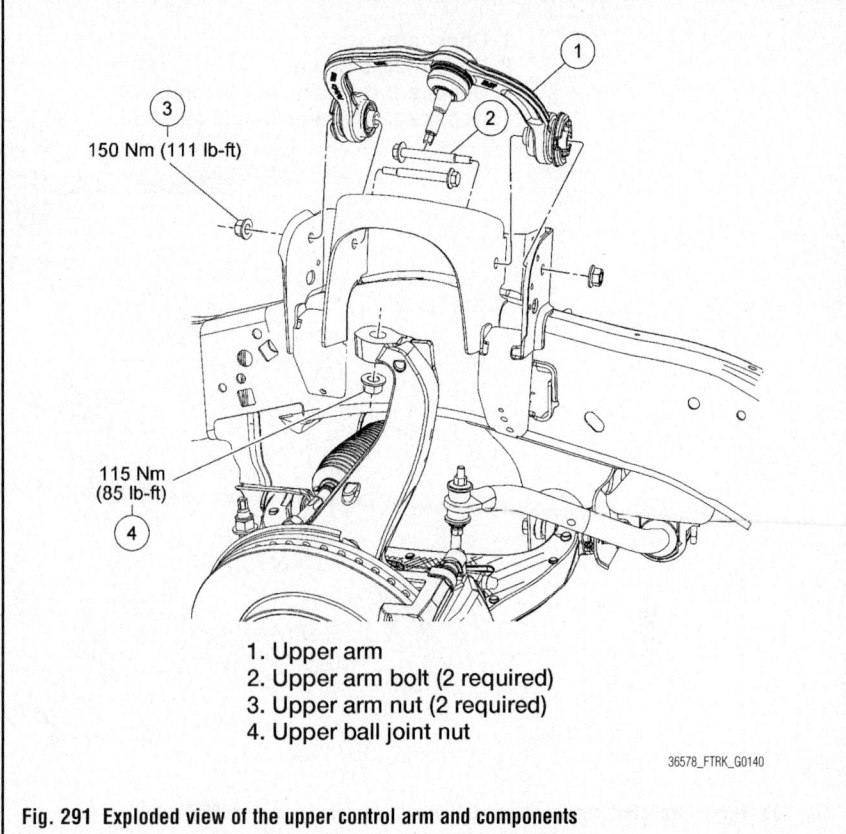

1. Upper arm
2. Upper arm bolt (2 required)
3. Upper arm nut (2 required)
4. Upper ball joint nut

36578_FTRK_G0140

Fig. 291 Exploded view of the upper control arm and components

1. Raise and safely support the vehicle.
2. Remove the wheel and tire assembly.
3. Remove the shock absorber and spring assembly.

❄❄ WARNING

Do not hammer the ball studs to separate them from the wheel knuckle or stabilizer bar. Doing so can cause damage. Lightly tap the wheel knuckle or stabilizer bar to loosen the joints.

➡**Use the hex holding feature to prevent the ball studs (upper control arm, lower control arm tie-rod end, and stabilizer bar links) from turning while removing and installing the nuts.**

➡**The upper ball joint does not require special tools to separate from the wheel spindle.**

4. Remove and discard the upper ball joint nut and separate the ball joint from the wheel spindle.

To install:

5. To install, reverse the removal procedure and note the following:

   a. Tighten the control arm nuts/bolts to 111 ft. lbs. (150 Nm).

   b. Tighten the upper control arm nut to 85 ft. lbs. (115 Nm).

2009 Models

See Figures 292 and 293.

➡**Before tightening any suspension bushing fasteners, use a suitable jack to raise the suspension until the distance between the center of the hub and the lip of the fender is equal to the measurement taken in Step 1 (curb height).**

1. Measure the distance from the center of the hub to the lip of the fender with the vehicle in a level, static ground position (curb height).

2. Before servicing the vehicle, refer to the precautions section.

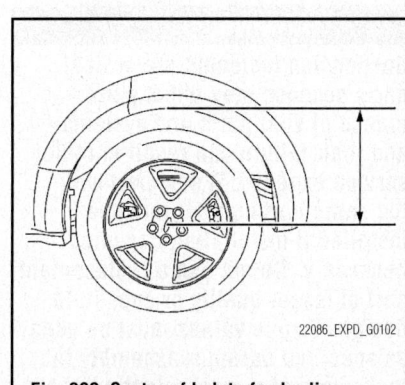

22086_EXPD_G0102

Fig. 292 Center of hub to fender lip measurement shown

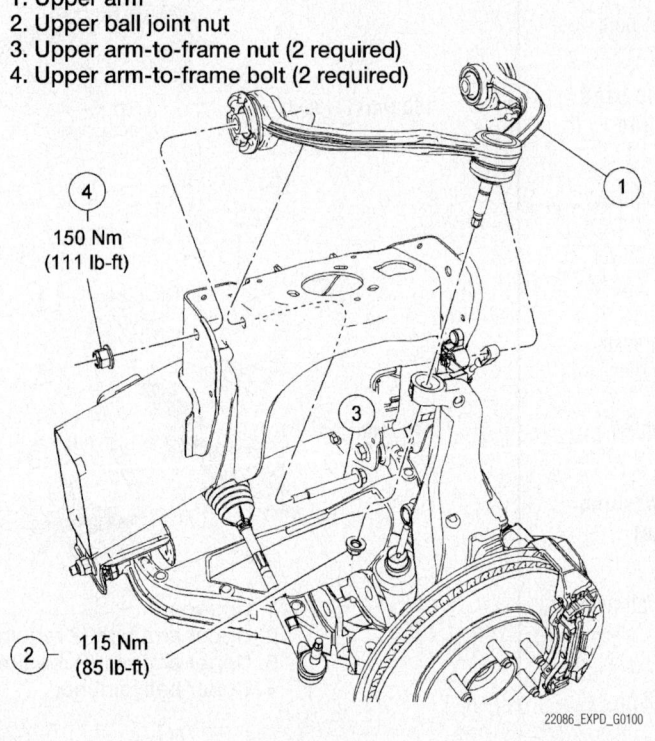

1. Upper arm
2. Upper ball joint nut
3. Upper arm-to-frame nut (2 required)
4. Upper arm-to-frame bolt (2 required)

150 Nm
(111 lb-ft)

115 Nm
(85 lb-ft)

22086_EXPD_G0100

Fig. 293 View of front left front upper control arm and related parts—2009 Models

❋❋ CAUTION

The electrical power to the air suspension system must be shut off prior to hoisting, jacking or towing an air suspension vehicle. This can be accomplished by turning off the air suspension switch located in the LH rear quarter trim panel. Failure to do so can result in unexpected inflation or deflation of the air springs, which can result in shifting of the vehicle during these operations. Failure to follow these instructions may result in personal injury.

❋❋ WARNING

Suspension fasteners are critical parts because they affect performance of vital parts and systems and their failure can result in major service expense. A new part with the same part number must be installed if installation becomes necessary. Do not use a replacement part of lesser quality or substitute design. Torque values must be used as specified during reassembly to make sure of correct retention of these parts.

3. Raise and safely support the vehicle.

4. Remove the wheel and tire assembly.

5. Remove the shock absorber and spring assembly.

6. On models with an air suspension, detach the height sensor from the upper arm.

➡Use the hex holding feature to prevent the stud from turning while removing the nut.

7. Remove and discard the upper ball joint nut.

8. Using the special tool 204-592, separate the upper ball joint from the wheel knuckle.

9. Remove the rearward upper arm-to-frame nut and bolt. Discard the nut.

10. Remove the forward upper arm-to-frame nut, bolt and the upper arm. Discard the nut.

To install:

11. To install, reverse the removal procedure and note the following:

a. Tighten the control arm nuts/bolts to 111 ft. lbs. (150 Nm).

b. Tighten the upper control arm nut to 85 ft. lbs. (115 Nm).

c. Check and, if necessary, align the front end

WHEEL HUB & BEARING

REMOVAL & INSTALLATION

2008 Models

2WD Vehicles

See Figure 294.

1. Before servicing the vehicle, refer to the Precautions Section.

2. Disconnect the wheel speed sensor.

3. Remove the wheel and tire assembly.

4. Remove the anchor plate bolts.

5. Remove the brake caliper, pads and anchor plate. Support the caliper to the vehicle.

6. Remove the axle-to-wheel hub nut, retainer and cotter pin.

7. Remove the brake disc/hub assembly.

8. To install, reverse the removal procedure.

❋❋ CAUTION

Do not apply lubricant to the threaded part of the axle.

9. To ease installation, lubricate the inner race of the bearing assembly using the specified lubricant.

10. Observe the following torques:
- Hub nut: 296 ft. lbs. (400 Nm)
- Anchor plate bolts: 148 ft. lbs. (200 Nm)

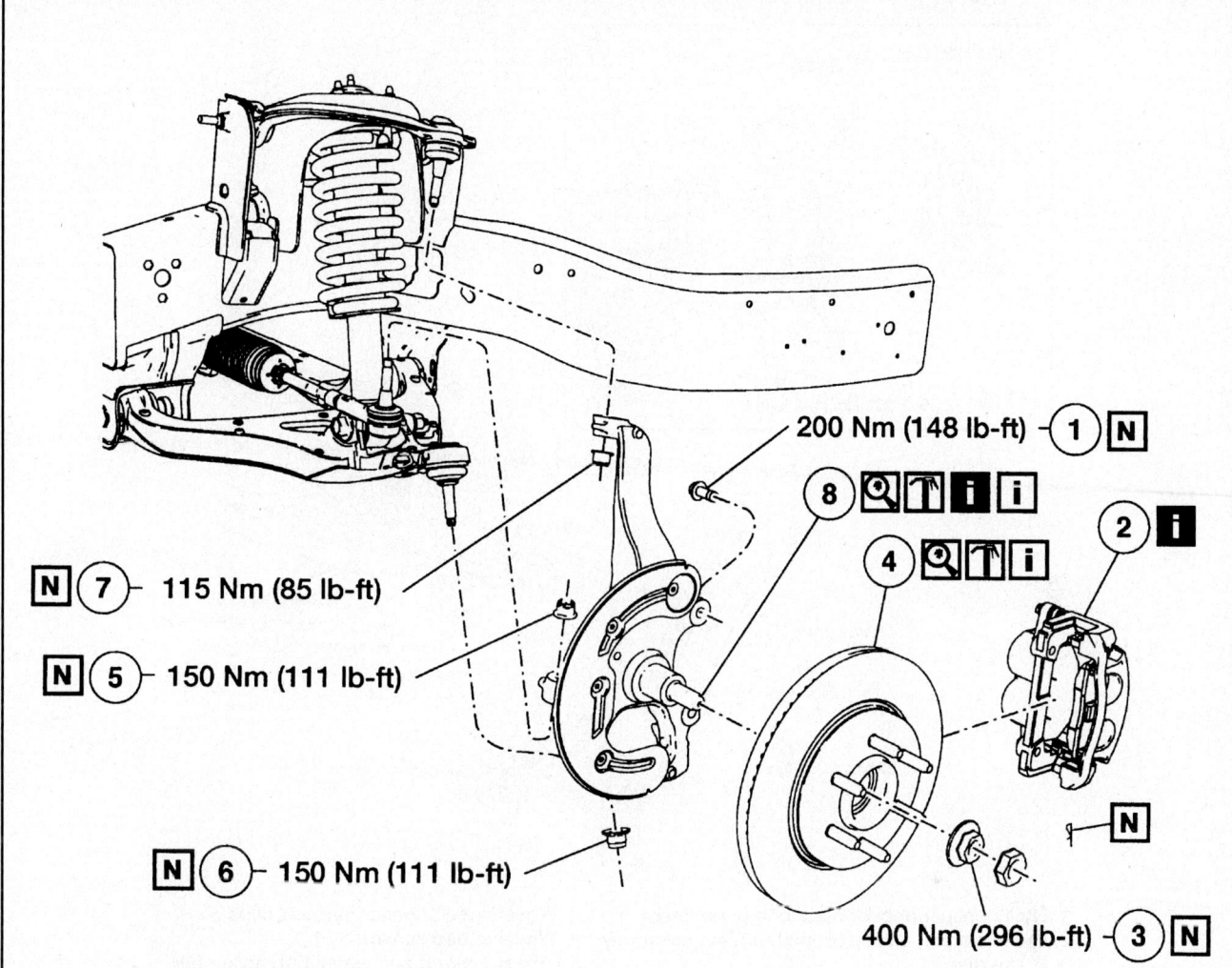

1 Anchor plate bolt

2 Brake caliper, pads and anchor plate

3 Axle-to-wheel hub nut (retainer/cotter pin)

4 Brake disc

5 Tie-rod end-to-wheel knuckle nut

6 Lower ball joint-to-wheel knuckle nut

7 Upper ball joint-to-wheel knuckle nut

8 Wheel knuckle

67197-EFSE-G193

Fig. 294 Front hub/bearing installation—2008 2WD models

4WD Vehicles

See Figure 295.

> ❊ **CAUTION**
>
> **Suspension fasteners are critical parts because they affect performance of vital components and systems and their failure may result in major service expense. New parts must be installed with the same part numbers or equivalent part, if replacement is necessary. Do not use a replacement part of lesser quality or substitute design. Torque values must be used as specified during reassembly to make sure of correct retention of these parts.**

1. Remove the wheel and tire.
2. Remove and discard the halfshaft nut. To install, tighten to 20 ft. lbs. (27 Nm).

> ❊ **CAUTION**
>
> **Do not allow the caliper and anchor plate assembly to hang from the brake hose or damage to the hose can occur.**

3. Remove the bolts and position the caliper and anchor plate assembly aside. Support the caliper and anchor plate assembly using mechanic's wire. To install, tighten to 148 ft. lbs. (200 Nm).
4. Remove the brake disc.
5. If equipped, detach the wheel speed sensor harness clips from the brake hose.
6. If equipped, remove the front wheel

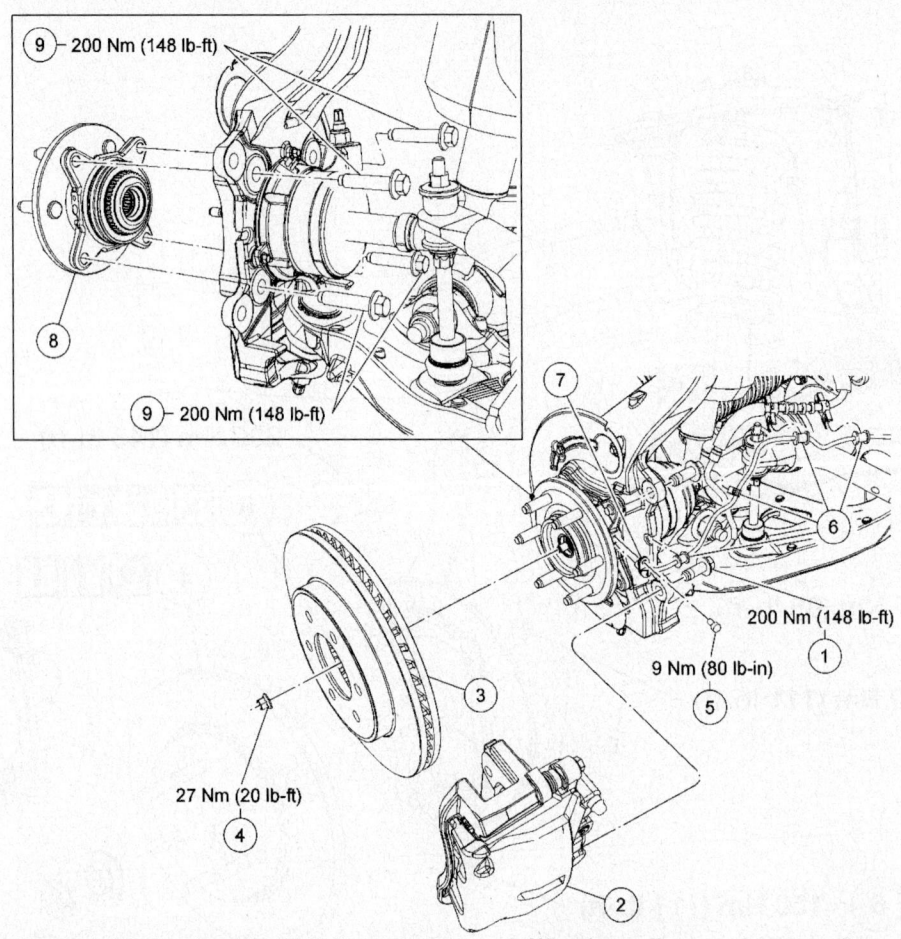

1. Brake caliper anchor plate bolt (2 required)
2. Brake caliper, pads and anchor plate assembly
3. Brake disc
4. Halfshaft nut
5. Wheel speed sensor bolt
6. Wheel speed sensor harness clips
7. Wheel speed sensor
8. Wheel bearing and wheel hub assembly
9. Wheel hub bolts (4 required)

36578_FTRK_G0141

Fig. 295 Exploded view of the wheel bearing and hub assembly—2008 4WD models

speed sensor bolt and position the sensor aside.

❋❋ CAUTION

Do not use a hammer to separate the halfshaft from the hub or damage to the halfshaft can occur.

7. Remove the 4 wheel hub bolts and the wheel bearing and wheel hub assembly. Discard the bolts. To install, tighten to 148 ft. lbs. (200 Nm).

❋❋ CAUTION

To prevent halfshaft or hub damage, verify the spline engagement by checking for spline lash before installing the halfshaft nut.

8. To install, reverse the removal procedure.

2009 Models

2WD Vehicles

See Figure 296.

❋❋ WARNING

The electrical power to the air suspension system must be shut off prior to hoisting, jacking or towing an air suspension vehicle. Failure to shut the system off may lead to an unexpected inflation or deflation of the air springs, which may result in a shift of the vehicle.

1. Before servicing the vehicle, refer to the precautions in the beginning of this section.

2. If equipped, turn the air suspension switch to the OFF position.

3. Disconnect the wheel speed sensor electrical connector.

4. With the vehicle in NEUTRAL, position it on a hoist.

5. Remove the wheel and tire assembly.

6. Remove the bolt and detach the brake line retainers.

❋❋ CAUTION

Do not allow the caliper to hang from the brake hose or damage to the hose can result.

7. Remove the caliper, pads and anchor plate and set aside.

8. Remove the brake rotor.

9. Remove the bolts and the wheel bearing and hub assembly.

10. If installing a new wheel bearing and wheel hub, remove the wheel speed sensor bolt and the wheel speed sensor.

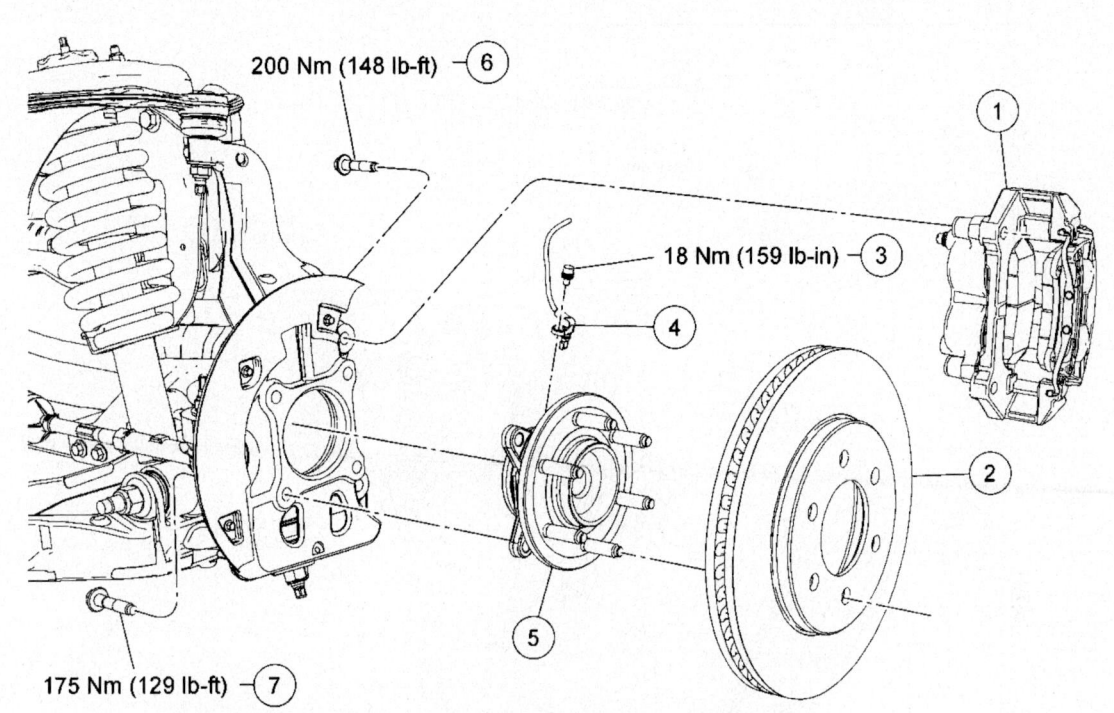

200 Nm (148 lb-ft) — 6

18 Nm (159 lb-in) — 3

175 Nm (129 lb-ft) — 7

1. Brake caliper and anchor plate assembly
2. Brake disc
3. Wheel speed sensor bolt
4. Wheel speed sensor
5. Wheel bearing and wheel hub
6. Brake caliper anchor plate bolt (2 required)
7. Wheel bearing and wheel hub bolt (4 required)

36578_EXPD_G0126

Fig. 296 Exploded view of the front wheel bearing and wheel hub—2009 2WD models

To install:

➡ If the original wheel bearing and hub is being reinstalled, make sure to install a new O-ring.

11. To install, reverse the removal procedure and note the following:

a. Wheel bearing/hub assembly bolts: 111 ft. lbs. (150 Nm).

b. Brake anchor plate: 148 ft. lbs. (200 Nm).

c. Speed sensor bolt: 13 ft. lbs. (18 Nm).

d. Retainer bracket bolts: 9 ft. lbs. (12 Nm).

4WD Vehicles

See Figure 297.

⁑ WARNING

The electrical power to the air suspension system must be shut off prior to hoisting, jacking or towing an air suspension vehicle. Failure to shut the system off may lead to an unexpected inflation or deflation of the air springs, which may result in a shift of the vehicle.

1. Before servicing the vehicle, refer to the precautions in the beginning of this section.

2. If equipped, turn the air suspension switch to the OFF position.

3. Disconnect the wheel speed sensor electrical connector.

4. Remove the wheel and tire assembly.

5. Remove the bolt and detach the brake line retainers.

⁑ CAUTION

Do not allow the caliper to hang from the brake hose or damage to the hose can result.

6. Remove the caliper, pads and anchor plate and set aside.

7. Remove the brake rotor.

8. Remove the dust cap.

9. Remove and discard the axle nut.

10. Remove the bolts and the wheel bearing and hub assembly.

To install:

⁑ CAUTION

If the original wheel bearing and hub is being reinstalled, make sure to install a new O-ring.

11. To install, reverse the removal procedure and note the following:

a. Wheel bearing/hub assembly bolts: 148 ft. lbs. (200 Nm).

b. Axle nut: 20 ft. lbs. (27 Nm).

c. Brake anchor plate: 148 ft. lbs. (200 Nm).

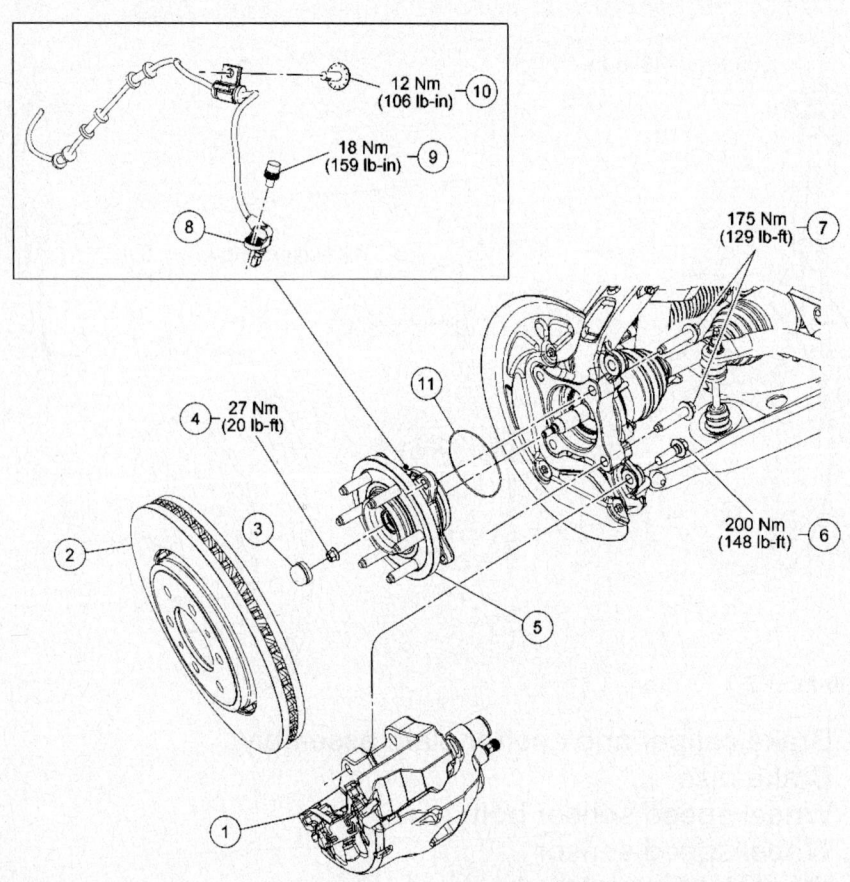

1. Brake caliper and anchor plate assembly
2. Brake disc
3. Dust cap
4. Halfshaft nut
5. Wheel bearing and wheel hub
6. Brake caliper anchor plate bolt (2 required)
7. Wheel bearing and wheel hub bolts (4 required)
8. Wheel speed sensor
9. Wheel speed sensor bolt
10. Wheel speed sensor harness bracket bolt
11. O-ring seal

36578_EXPD_G0125

Fig. 297 Exploded view of the front wheel bearing and wheel hub—2009 4WD models

SUSPENSION

LEAF SPRING

REMOVAL & INSTALLATION

2008 Models
See Figure 298.

1. Before servicing the vehicle, refer to the Precautions Section.
2. Remove the wheel and tire assembly.

✳✳ WARNING

Lower the rear axle only enough to gain access to the rear spring.

3. Use the jack to support and lower the rear axle housing assembly.
4. Remove the brake caliper and bolts

✳✳ WARNING

Do not allow the brake caliper to hang from the brake hose.

5. Position the brake caliper aside using mechanic's wire.
6. Disconnect the shock absorber at the lower end.
7. Remove the spring front eye bolt and nut.

➥**Lower the fuel tank to gain access to the spring shackle bolt.**

8. Remove the spring shackle bolt and nut (rear)
9. Remove the U-bolt nuts
10. Remove the U-bolt plate

REAR SUSPENSION

11. Remove the U-bolts
12. Remove the rear spring assembly
13. To install, reverse the removal procedure.

➥**Tighten the U-bolt nuts in a cross pattern in 3 even steps.**

14. Observe the following torques:
- U-bolt nuts. Light duty, in 3 equal steps: 85 ft. lbs. (115 Nm)
- U-bolt nuts. Heavy duty, in 3 equal steps: 184 ft. lbs. (250 Nm)
- Spring front eye bolt: 222 ft. lbs. (300 Nm)
- Spring rear shackle bolt: 98 ft. lbs. (133 Nm)
- Shock absorber nut: (66 ft. lbs. (90 Nm)

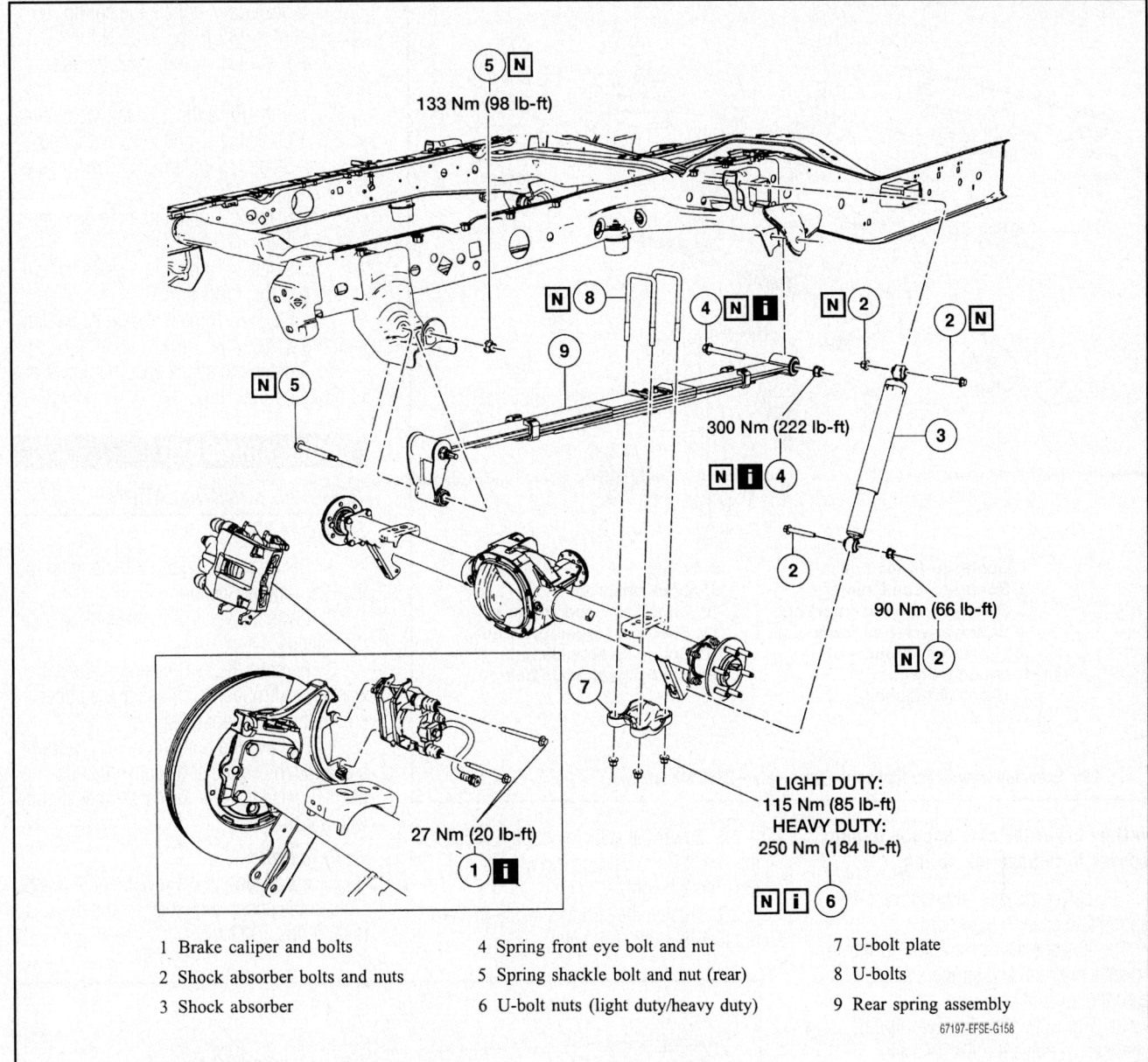

133 Nm (98 lb-ft)

300 Nm (222 lb-ft)

90 Nm (66 lb-ft)

LIGHT DUTY:
115 Nm (85 lb-ft)
HEAVY DUTY:
250 Nm (184 lb-ft)

27 Nm (20 lb-ft)

1 Brake caliper and bolts	4 Spring front eye bolt and nut	7 U-bolt plate
2 Shock absorber bolts and nuts	5 Spring shackle bolt and nut (rear)	8 U-bolts
3 Shock absorber	6 U-bolt nuts (light duty/heavy duty)	9 Rear spring assembly

67197-EFSE-G158

Fig. 298 Rear suspension components—2008 Models

2009 Models

See Figure 299.

※ WARNING

Do not apply heat or flame to the shock absorber or strut tube. The shock absorber and strut tube are gas pressurized and could explode if heated. Failure to follow this instruction may result in serious personal injury.

※ WARNING

Keep all body parts clear of shock absorbers or strut rods. Shock absorbers or struts can extend unassisted. Failure to follow this instruction may result in serious personal injury.

➡**Suspension fasteners are critical parts because they affect performance of vital components and systems and their failure may result in major service expense. New parts must be installed with the same part numbers or equivalent part, if replacement is necessary. Do not use a replacement part of lesser quality or substitute design. Torque values must be used as specified during reassembly to make sure correct retention of these parts.**

1. Remove the wheel and tire.
2. Using a suitable jack, support the axle.
3. Remove the shock absorber lower nut and bolt. Discard the nut and bolt.
4. Remove the 4 U-bolt nuts, the U-bolt plate and the 2 U-bolts. Discard the nuts and the U-bolts.
5. For the LH spring, lower the fuel tank to gain access to the spring shackle-to-frame bolt.
6. For the RH spring, remove the muffler to gain access to the spring-to-frame bolt.
7. Remove and discard the spring-to-frame nut and bolt.
8. Remove and discard the spring shackle-to-frame nut and bolt.

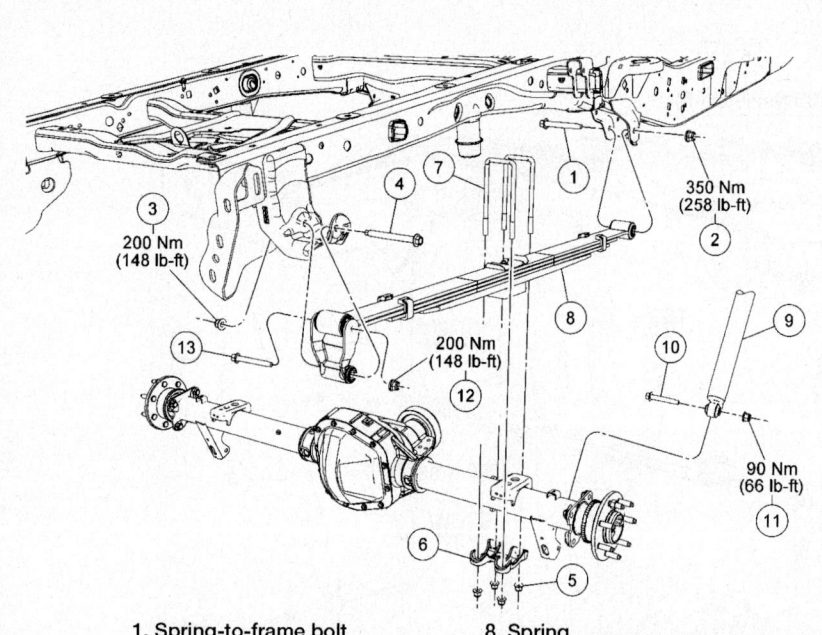

1. Spring-to-frame bolt
2. Spring-to-frame nut
3. Spring shackle-to-frame nut
4. Spring shackle-to-frame bolt
5. U-bolt nut (4 required)
6. U-bolt plate
7. U-bolt (2 required)
8. Spring
9. Shock absorber
10. Shock absorber lower bolt
11. Shock absorber lower nut
12. Spring-to-shackle nut
13. Spring-to-shackle bolt

36578_FTRK_G0142

Fig. 299 Exploded view of the leaf spring assembly—2009 Models

➡ **Only lower the axle enough to gain access to remove the spring.**

9. Lower the jack and remove the spring and shackle assembly.

10. If necessary, remove the spring-to-shackle nut, bolt and spring shackle. Discard the nut and bolt.

11. For Four-Wheel Drive (4WD) vehicles, remove the 4WD spring spacer.

To install:

12. For Four-Wheel 4WD vehicles, position the 4WD spring spacer and make sure that it is correctly seated between the axle and spring with the nose pointed to the front of the vehicle.

13. If necessary, install a new shackle-to-spring bolt and nut. Tighten until snug.

14. Position the spring and install a new spring shackle-to-frame bolt and nut. Tighten until snug.

15. Position the U-bolt plate and install the new U-bolts and nuts. Tighten until snug.

16. Install a new spring-to-frame bolt and nut. Tighten until snug.

17. Install a new shock absorber lower bolt and nut. Tighten until snug.

18. Install the wheel and tire.

19. Lower the vehicle until the weight of the vehicle is resting on the wheels and tires (curb height).

20. Tighten the spring shackle-to-frame nut to 148 ft. lbs. (200 Nm).

21. If necessary, tighten the spring-to-shackle nut to 148 ft. lbs. (200 Nm).

22. For the LH spring, raise the fuel tank.

23. For the RH spring, install the muffler.

24. Tighten the U-bolt nuts in 4 stages:
   a. Stage 1: Tighten in a cross pattern to 26 ft. lbs. (35 Nm).
   b. Stage 2: Tighten in a cross pattern to 52 ft. lbs. (70 Nm).
   c. Stage 3: Tighten in a cross pattern to 74 ft. lbs. (100 Nm).
   d. Stage 4: Tighten in a cross pattern to 98 ft. lbs. (133 Nm).

25. Tighten the shock absorber lower nut to 66 ft. lbs. (90 Nm).

SHOCK ABSORBER

REMOVAL & INSTALLATION

See Figure 300.

1. Before servicing the vehicle, refer to the Precautions Section.

2. Raise the vehicle and secure on support stands.

3. Remove the self-locking nut, steel washer, and rubber bushings at the upper end of the shock absorber.

4. Remove the bolt and nut at the lower end and remove the shock absorber. If needed, raise the rear axle assembly slightly with a jack.

To install:

5. Installation is the reverse of removal. Tighten the upper and lower mounting nuts to 66 ft. lbs. (90 Nm).

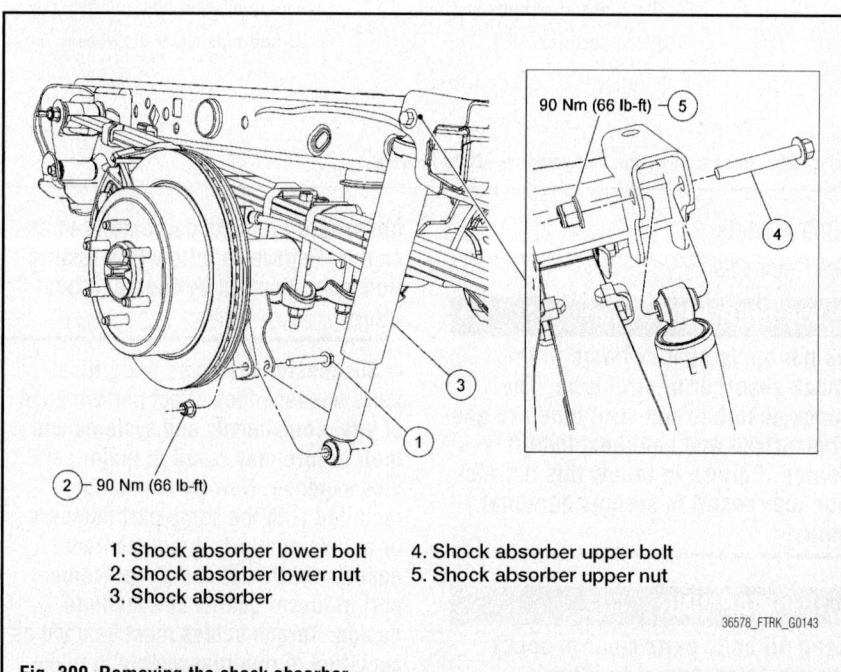

1. Shock absorber lower bolt
2. Shock absorber lower nut
3. Shock absorber
4. Shock absorber upper bolt
5. Shock absorber upper nut

36578_FTRK_G0143

Fig. 300 Removing the shock absorber

FORD

F-250 • F-350

SPECIFICATIONS AND MAINTENANCE CHARTS

ENGINE AND VEHICLE IDENTIFICATION

Engine							Model Year	
Code ①	Liters (cc)	Cu. In.	Cyl.	Fuel Sys.	Type	Eng. Mfg.	Code ②	Year
5 ③	5.4 (5409)	330	8	EFI	SOHV	Ford	8	2008
L	5.4 (5409)	330	8	EFI	SOHC	Ford	9	2009
R	6.4 (6400)	390	8	DDI	OHC	Ford		
S	6.8 (6800)	414	10	EFI	SOHC	Ford		
Y	6.8 (6800)	414	10	EFI	③	Ford		

EFI: Electronic Fuel Injection

DDI: Diesel Direct Injection

OHV: Overhead Valve

SOHC: Single Overhead Camshaft

① 8th digit of the Vehicle Identification Number (VIN)

② 10th digit of the Vehicle Identification Number (VIN)

③ 3 valves per cylinder

36578_F250_C0001

GENERAL ENGINE SPECIFICATIONS

Year	Model	Engine Displ. Liters	Engine VIN	Net Horsepower @ rpm	Net Torque @ rpm (ft. lbs.)	Bore x Stroke (in.)	Compression Ratio	Oil Pressure @ rpm
2008	F-250, F-350	5.4	5, L	300@5000	365@3750	3.55x4.17	9.8:1	40-75@2000
		6.4	R ①	NA	NA	3.87x 4.134	17.2:1	45@1800
		6.8	S, Y	362@4750	457@3250	3.55x4.16	9.2:1	40-75@2000
2009	F-250, F-350	5.4	5, L	300@5000	365@3750	3.55x4.17	9.8:1	40-75@2000
		6.4	R ①	NA	NA	3.87x 4.134	17.2:1	45@1800
		6.8	S, Y	362@4750	457@3250	3.55x4.16	9.2:1	40-75@2000

NA: Not Available

① Turbo diesel

36578_F250_C0002

GASOLINE ENGINE TUNE-UP SPECIFICATIONS

Year	Engine Displacement Liters	Engine VIN	Spark Plug Gap (in.)	Ignition Timing (deg.) ① MT	AT	Fuel Pump (psi) ②	Idle Speed (rpm) MT	AT	Valve Clearance In.	Ex.
2008	5.4	5, L	0.040-0.050	10B	10B	28-45	③	③	HYD	HYD
	6.8	S, Y	0.040-0.050	10B	10B	28-45	③	③	HYD	HYD
2009	5.4	5, L	0.040-0.050	10B	10B	28-45	③	③	HYD	HYD
	6.8	S, Y	0.040-0.050	10B	10B	28-45	③	③	HYD	HYD

NOTE: The Vehicle Emission Control Information label often reflects specification changes changes made during production. The label figures must be used if they differ from this chart.

B: Before top dead center

HYD: Hydraulic

NA: Information not Available

① Ignition timing is preset and cannot be adjusted

② With engine running

③ Idle speed is electronically controlled and cannot be adjusted

36578_F250_C0003

DIESEL ENGINE TUNE-UP SPECIFICATIONS

Year	Engine Displ. Liters	Engine VIN	Valve Clearance Intake (in.)	Exhaust (in.)	Injection Pump Setting (deg.)	Injection Nozzle Pressure (psi) New	Used	Idle Speed (rpm)	Cranking Compression Pressure (psi)
2008	6.4	R	HYD	HYD	①	NA	NA	②	NA
2009	6.4	R	HYD	HYD	①	NA	NA	②	NA

NOTE: The Vehicle Emission Control Information label often reflects specification changes made during production. The label figures must be used if they d from those in this chart

HYD: Hydraulic

NA: Not Available

① PCM controlled

② See underhood emission label

36578_F250_C0004

CAPACITIES

Year	Model	Engine Displ. Liters	Engine VIN	Engine Oil with Filter (qts.)	Transmission (pts.) MT	Transmission (pts.) Auto.*	Transfer Case (pts.)	Drive Axle Front (pts.)	Drive Axle Rear (pts.)	Fuel Tank (gal.)	Cooling System (qts.)
2008	F-250, F-350	5.4	5, L	7.0	11.6	19.0	4.0	6.38	①	②	20.6
		6.4	R A	15.0	11.6	19.0	4.0	6.38	①	②	27.5
		6.8	S, Y	7.0	11.6	19.0	4.0	6.38	①	②	27.5
2009	F-250, F-350	5.4	5, L	7.0	11.6	19.0	4.0	6.38	①	②	20.6
		6.4	R	15.0	11.6	19.0	4.0	6.38	①	②	27.5
		6.8	S, Y	7.0	11.6	19.0	4.0	6.38	①	②	27.5

NA: Information not available

NOTE: All capacities are approximate. Add fluid gradually and check to be sure a proper fluid level is obtained.

* Overhaul

① 10.5 inch: 6.9 pts.

Dana 80: 8.9 pts.

Dana S110 and S130: 14.0 pts.

② Aft-of-axle steel fuelt ank: 40 gal.

Auxiliary steel fuel tank (midship mounted): 19 gal.

Midship plastic fuel tank: 30 and 38 gal.

36578_F250_C0005

FLUID SPECIFICATIONS

Year	Model	Engine Displacement Liters	Engine ID/VIN	Engine Oil	Man. Trans.	Auto. Trans. ①	Drive Axle	Power Steering Fluid	Brake Master Cylinder
2008	F-250, F-350	5.4	5, L	5W-20	①	③	③	MERCON ATF	DOT 3
		6.4	R	15W-40	①	③	③	MERCON ATF	DOT 3
		6.8	S, Y	5W-20	①	③	③	MERCON ATF	DOT 3
2009	F-250, F-350	5.4	5, L	5W-20	①	③	③	MERCON ATF	DOT 3
		6.4	R	15W-40	①	③	③	MERCON ATF	DOT 3
		6.8	S, Y	5W-20	①	③	③	MERCON ATF	DOT 3

DOT: Department Of Transpotation

① Tremec 5-Speed: MERCON Type XT-5-QM

ZF 6-Speed: XT-M5-QS

② MERCON Type: XT-10-QLV

③ Fluid type varies per axle type usage:

With Ford 10.25 in.: SAE 75W-140 Synthetic Rear Axle Lubricant XY-75W140-QL

With DANA 80: SAE 75W-90 Premium Synthetic Transaxle Lubricant XT-75W90-QLS

With DANA S110 and S130: Motorcraft SAE 75W-140 Synthetic Rear Axle Lubricant XY-75W140-QL

With front driveshafts: Motorcraft 80W-90 Premium Rear Axle Lubricant XY-80W90-QL (US); CXY-80W90-1L (Canada) (Model 60/70 axles)

36578_F250_C0006

VALVE SPECIFICATIONS

Year	Engine Displ. Liters	Engine VIN	Seat Angle (deg.)	Face Angle (deg.)	Spring Test Pressure (lbs. @ in.)	Spring Installed Height (in.)	Stem-to-Guide Clearance (in.)		Stem Diameter (in.)	
							Intake	Exhaust	Intake	Exhaust
2008	5.4	5, L	44.5-45	45.5	79@1.66	1.660	0.0010-0.0020	0.0030-0.0040	0.2350-0.2360	0.2340-0.2350
	6.4	R	①	②	NA	NA	0.0040	0.0040	0.2735 0.2742	0.2735 0.2742
	6.8	S, Y	44.5-45	45.5	171@1.66	1.660	0.0010-0.0030	0.0020-0.0040	0.2350-0.2360	0.2340-0.2350
2009	5.4	5, L	44.5-45	45.5	79@1.66	1.660	0.0010-0.0020	0.0030-0.0040	0.2350-0.2360	0.2340-0.2350
	6.4	R	①	②	NA	NA	0.0040	0.0040	0.2735 0.2742	0.2735 0.2742
	6.8	S, Y	44.5-45	45.5	171@1.66	1.660	0.0010-0.0030	0.0020-0.0040	0.2350-0.2360	0.2340-0.2350

NA: Not Available

① Intake: 40
   Exhaust: 37.5

② Intake: 37
   Exhaust: 39.5

36578_F250_C0007

CAMSHAFT AND BEARING SPECIFICATIONS
All measurements are given in inches.

Year	Engine Displ. Liters	Engine VIN	Journal Diameter	Brg. Oil Clearance	Shaft End-play	Runout	Journal Bore	Lobe Lift	
								Intake	Exhaust
2008	5.4	5, L	1.1260-1.1270	0.0010-0.0030	0.001-0.0070	0.001	1.1280-1.1290	0.2173	0.2173
	6.4	R	2.4400-2.4410	0.0015-0.0060	0.0020-0.0080	0.002	2.4430-2.4460	0.2290	0.2326
	6.8	S, Y	2.4400-2.4410	0.0015-0.0060	0.0020-0.0080	0.002	2.4430-2.4460	0.2290	0.2326
2009	5.4	5, L	1.1260-1.1270	0.0010-0.0030	0.001-0.0070	0.001	1.1280-1.1290	0.2173	0.2173
	6.4	R	2.4400-2.4410	0.0015-0.0060	0.0020-0.0080	0.002	2.4430-2.4460	0.2290	0.2326
	6.8	S, Y	2.4400-2.4410	0.0015-0.0060	0.0020-0.0080	0.002	2.4430-2.4460	0.2290	0.2326

36578_F250_C0010

CRANKSHAFT AND CONNECTING ROD SPECIFICATIONS

All measurements are given in inches.

Year	Engine Displ. Liters	Engine VIN	Crankshaft				Connecting Rod		
			Main Brg. Journal Dia.	Main Brg. Oil Clearance	Shaft End-play	Thrust on No.	Journal Dia.	Oil Clearance	Side Clearance
2008	5.4	5, L	2.6568-2.6576	0.0009-0.0019	0.0030-0.0148	NA	2.0859-2.0867	0.0010-0.0025	0.0049-0.0187
	6.4	R	3.188-3.1890	0.0006-0.0035	0.0200	NA	2.9916-2.9926	0.0006-0.0035	0.0090-0.0420
	6.8	S, Y	3.188-3.1890	0.0006-0.0035	0.0200	NA	2.9916-2.9926	0.0006-0.0035	0.0090-0.0420
2009	5.4	5, L	2.6568-2.6576	0.0009-0.0019	0.0030-0.0148	NA	2.0859-2.0867	0.0010-0.0025	0.0049-0.0187
	6.4	R	3.188-3.1890	0.0006-0.0035	0.0200	NA	2.9916-2.9926	0.0006-0.0035	0.0090-0.0420
	6.8	S, Y	3.188-3.1890	0.0006-0.0035	0.0200	NA	2.9916-2.9926	0.0006-0.0035	0.0090-0.0420

NA: Information not available

36578_F250_C0009

PISTON AND RING SPECIFICATIONS

All measurements are given in inches.

Year	Engine Displ. Liters	Engine VIN	Piston Clearance	Ring Gap			Ring Side Clearance		
				Top Compression	Bottom Compression	Oil Control	Top Compression	Bottom Compression	Oil Control
2008	5.4	5, L	0.0010-0.0018	0.006-0.012	0.0098-0.0197	0.006-0.0256	0.0008-0.0031	0.0012-0.0028	0.1193-0.1201
	6.4	R	0.0018-0.0037	0.011-0.0310	0.056-0.0760	0.009-0.0290	NA	0.0020-0.0038	0.0015-0.0037
	6.8	S, Y	0.0010-0.0018	0.0059-0.0118	0.0098-0.0198	0.0059-0.0256	0.0012-0.0020	0.0012-0.0031	0.1193-0.1201
2009	5.4	5, L	0.0010-0.0018	0.006-0.012	0.0098-0.0197	0.006-0.0256	0.0008-0.0031	0.0012-0.0028	0.1193-0.1201
	6.4	R	0.0018-0.0037	0.011-0.0310	0.056-0.0760	0.009-0.0290	NA	0.0020-0.0038	0.0015-0.0037
	6.8	S, Y	0.0010-0.0018	0.0059-0.0118	0.0098-0.0198	0.0059-0.0256	0.0012-0.0020	0.0012-0.0031	0.1193-0.1201

NA: Information not available

36578_F250_C0008

TORQUE SPECIFICATIONS

All readings in ft. lbs.

	Engine Displ. Liters	Engine VIN	Cylinder Head Bolts	Main Bearing Bolts	Rod Bearing Bolts	Crankshaft Damper Bolts	Flywheel Bolts	Manifold		Spark Plugs	Oil Pan Drain Plug
								Intake *	Exhaust		
2008	5.4	5, L	①	②	③	④	59	⑤	18	25	10
	6.4	R	⑦	⑧	⑨	⑥	69	8	28 ⑩	NA	18
	6.8	Y	⑪	②	⑫	④	59	⑤	18	25	10
2009	5.4	5, L	①	②	③	④	59	⑤	18	25	10
	6.4	R	⑦	⑧	⑨	⑥	69	8	28 ⑩	NA	18
	6.8	Y	⑪	②	⑫	④	59	⑤	18	25	10

NA: Information not available

* NOTE: Applies to Lower Manifold only. For Upper Manifold, see the text.

① Step 1: 30 ft. lbs.

　　Step 2: Plus 85-95 degrees

　　Step 3: Plus 85-95 degrees

② Vertical bolts:

　　Step 1: 30 ft. lbs.

　　Step 2: plus 90 degrees

　　Side bolts:

　　Step 1: 22 ft. lbs.

　　Step 2: plus 90 degrees

③ Step 1: 18 ft. lbs.

　　Step 2: 33 ft. lbs.

　　Step 3: plus 90-120 degrees

④ Step 1: 66 ft. lbs.

　　Step 2: loosen 1 full turn

　　Step 3: 37 ft. lbs.

　　Step 4: + 90 deg. Without exceeding 148 ft. lbs.

⑤ Step 1: 18 inch lbs.

　　Step 2: 89 inch lbs.

⑥ Step 1: 50 ft. lbs.

　　Step 2: plus 90 degrees

　　See the text for torque sequence

⑦ See procedure in text.

⑧ Step 1: 90 ft. lbs.

　　Step 2: 120 ft. lbs.

　　Step 3: 170 ft. lbs.

　　Lower crankcase bolts: 23 ft. lbs.

⑨ Step 1: 33 ft. lbs.

　　Step 2: 50 ft. lbs.

⑩ Apply anti-seize compound

　　to bolt threads.

⑪ Step 1: 30 ft. lbs.

　　Step 2: plus 90 degrees

　　Step 3: plus 90 degrees

⑫ Step 1: 32 ft. lbs.

　　Step 2: 105 degrees

36578_F250_C0011

WHEEL ALIGNMENT

Year	Model	Style	Caster Range (+/-Deg.)	Caster Preferred Setting (Deg.)	Camber Range (+/-Deg.)	Camber Preferred Setting (Deg.)	Toe-in Front ① (Deg.)
2008	F-250, F-350	4x2	1.20	3.8	0.75	0.62	0.1+/-0.25
	F-250 Std. Susp.	4x4	1.20	3.3	0.75	0.15	0.1+/-0.25
	F-250 H.D. Susp.	4x4	1.30	2.6	0.75	0.15	0.1+/-0.25
	F-350 Std. Susp., Sgl. Rear Wheel	4x4	1.20	2.5	0.75	0.15	0.1+/-0.25
	F-350 H.D. Susp., Sgl. Rear Wheel	4x4	1.30	1.8	0.75	0.15	0.1+/-0.25
	F-350 Std. Susp., Dual Rear Wheel	4x4	1.20	3.0	0.75	0.15	0.1+/-0.25
	F-350 H.D. Susp., Dual Rear Wheel	4x4	1.30	2.4	0.75	0.15	0.1+/-0.25
	F-350 Chassis Cab, Std. Susp., Sgl. Rear Wheel	4x4	1.20	2.8	0.75	0.15	0.1+/-0.25
	F-350 Chassis Cab, H.D. Susp., Sgl. Rear Wheel	4x4	1.30	2.3	0.75	0.15	0.1+/-0.25
	F-350 Chassis Cab, Std. Susp., Dual Rear Wheel	4x4	1.20	2.5	0.75	0.15	0.1+/-0.25
	F-350 Chassis Cab, H.D. Susp., Dual Rear Wheel	4x4	1.30	1.9	0.75	0.15	0.1+/-0.25
2009	F-250, F-350	4x2	1.20	3.8	0.75	0.62	0.1+/-0.25
	F-250 Std. Susp.	4x4	1.20	3.3	0.75	0.15	0.1+/-0.25
	F-250 H.D. Susp.	4x4	1.30	2.6	0.75	0.15	0.1+/-0.25
	F-350 Std. Susp., Sgl. Rear Wheel	4x4	1.20	2.5	0.75	0.15	0.1+/-0.25
	F-350 H.D. Susp., Sgl. Rear Wheel	4x4	1.30	1.8	0.75	0.15	0.1+/-0.25
	F-350 Std. Susp., Dual Rear Wheel	4x4	1.20	3.0	0.75	0.15	0.1+/-0.25
	F-350 H.D. Susp., Dual Rear Wheel	4x4	1.30	2.4	0.75	0.15	0.1+/-0.25
	F-350 Chassis Cab, Std. Susp., Sgl. Rear Wheel	4x4	1.20	2.8	0.75	0.15	0.1+/-0.25
	F-350 Chassis Cab, H.D. Susp., Sgl. Rear Wheel	4x4	1.30	2.3	0.75	0.15	0.1+/-0.25
	F-350 Chassis Cab, Std. Susp., Dual Rear Wheel	4x4	1.20	2.5	0.75	0.15	0.1+/-0.25
	F-350 Chassis Cab, H.D. Susp., Dual Rear Wheel	4x4	1.30	1.9	0.75	0.15	0.1+/-0.25

36578_F250_C0012

TIRE, WHEEL AND BALL JOINT SPECIFICATIONS

| Year | Model | OEM Tires | | Tire Pressures (psi) | | Wheel Size | Ball Joint Inspection | Lug Nut Torque (ft. lbs.) |
		Standard	Optional	Front	Rear			
2008	F-250	NA	①	②	②	NA	③	165
	F-350	NA	①	②	②	NA	③	165
2009	F-250	NA	①	②	②	NA	③	165
	F-350	NA	①	②	②	NA	③	165

NA: Information not available

OEM: Original Equipment Manufacturer

PSI: Pounds Per Square Inch

① Multiple optional tires available; consult tire dealer.

② See placard on vehicle

③ Upper: 0.0.024 in.; Lower: 0.004 in.

36578_F250_C0013

BRAKE SPECIFICATIONS

All measurements in inches unless noted

| Year | Model | | Brake Disc | | | Brake Drum Diameter | | | Brake Caliper | |
			Original Thickness	Minimum Thickness	Maximum Runout	Original Inside Diameter	Max. Wear Limit	Maximum Machine Diameter	Bracket Bolts (ft. lbs.)	Mounting Bolts (ft. lbs.)
2008	F-250	F	NA	1.43	NA	NA	NA	NA	166	56
		R	NA	1.27	NA	NA	NA	NA	①	②
	F-350	F	NA	1.43	NA	NA	NA	NA	166	56
		R	NA	1.27	NA	NA	NA	NA	①	②
2009	F-250	F	NA	1.43	NA	NA	NA	NA	166	56
		R	NA	1.27	NA	NA	NA	NA	①	②
	F-350	F	NA	1.43	NA	NA	NA	NA	166	56
		R	NA	1.27	NA	NA	NA	NA	①	②

NOTE: Due to changes made during production, refer to manufacturer's specifications if they differ from those in this chart

NA: Information not available

① Caliper support bolts: 101 ft. lbs.
  Anchor plate bolts: 203 ft. lbs.

② F-250 and F-350 Single Rear Wheel: 26 ft. lbs.
  F-350 Dual Rear Wheels: 56 ft. lbs.

36578_F250_C0014

SCHEDULED MAINTENANCE INTERVALS
F-250 and F-350 Series with Gasoline Engines

TO BE SERVICED	TYPE OF SERVICE	VEHICLE MILEAGE INTERVAL (x1000)												
		5	10	15	20	25	30	35	40	45	50	55	60	65
Engine oil & filter	R	✓	✓	✓	✓	✓	✓	✓	✓	✓	✓	✓	✓	✓
Tires	Rotate	✓	✓	✓	✓	✓	✓	✓	✓	✓	✓	✓	✓	✓
Wheels	I ①			✓			✓			✓			✓	
Auto trans. fluid	I			✓			✓			✓			✓	
Brake pads/shoes	I			✓			✓			✓			✓	
Coolant hoses	S/I			✓			✓			✓			✓	
Steering linkage	I			✓			✓			✓			✓	
Suspension	I			✓			✓			✓			✓	
Driveshaft	I			✓			✓			✓			✓	
Cabin air filter	R			✓			✓			✓			✓	
Ball joints (2wd)	L			✓			✓			✓			✓	
Front drive axle U-joints	I/L			✓			✓			✓			✓	
NGV fuel filter	R					✓					✓			
Exhaust system	I						✓						✓	
Engine air filter	R						✓						✓	
Fuel filter	R						✓						✓	
Auto trans fluid (4R100 and	R						✓						✓	
Manual trans. fluid	R												✓	
Front wheel bearings (2wd)	L/Adj												✓	
Front wheel bearings grease	R												✓	
Accessory drive belts	I	every 100,000 miles												
Spark plugs	R	every 100,000 miles												
PCV valve ②	R	every 100,000 miles												
Premium Gold coolant	R	every 3 years or 100,000 miles												
Auto trans fluid (all exc. 4R100 and TorqShift)	R	every 120,000 miles												
PCV valve (5.4L 3v)	I	every 150,000 miles												
Front wheel bearings (2wd)	R	at 150,000 miles, if not previously done so												
Front drive axle needle bearings (F-Super Duty)	L	every 150,000 miles												
Fuel tank	I	every 150,000 miles												
Front drive axle fluid	R	every 150,000 miles												
Rear drive axle fluid	R	every 150,000 miles												
Transfer case fluid	R	every 150,000 miles												
Accessory drive belts	R	every 150,000 miles, if not previously done so												

NOTE: See next chart for footnotes.

36578_F250_C0015

SCHEDULED MAINTENANCE INTERVALS
F-250 and F-350 Series with Gasoline Engines
Footnotes

R: Replace   S: Service   I: Inspect   L: Lubricate

NGV: Natural gas vehicle

① Inspect for end play and noise

② Vehicles under 6,000 lbs. GVW, exc. 5.4L 3v engines

Special Operating Condition Requirements

When towing a trailer or using a camper or car-top carrier:

Change engine oil and install a new oil filter every 4,800 km (3,000 miles), 3 months or 200 hours of engine operation (whichever occurs first).

Change transfer case fluid every 96,000 km (60,000 miles).

Change manual transmission fluid as required.

Inspect and lubricate U-joints as required.

During extensive idling and/or low speed driving for long distances, as in heavy commercial use such as delivery, taxi, patrol car or livery:

Change engine oil and install a new oil filter every 4,800 km (3,000 miles), 3 months or 200 hours of engine operation (whichever occurs first).

Lube front lower control arm and steering linkage ball joints with zerk fittings (if equipped) every 4,800 km (3,000 miles) or 3 months.

Inspect brake system and check battery electrolyte level (Patrol cars) every 8,000 km (5,000 miles).

Install a new fuel filter every 24,000 km (15,000 miles).

Change automatic transmission fluid, lubricate 4x2 wheel bearings, install new grease seals and adjust bearings every

48,000 km (30,000 miles). If equipped, change the in-line service installed transmission fluid filter.

Install new spark plugs and change transfer case fluid every 96,000 km (60,000 miles).

Install a new cabin air filter as required.

When operating in dusty conditions such as unpaved or dusty roads:

Change engine oil and install a new oil filter every 4,800 km (3,000 miles) or 3 months.

Install a new fuel filter every 24,000 km (15,000 miles).

Change automatic transmission fluid every 48,000 km (30,000 miles). If equipped, change the in-line service installed transmission fluid filter.

Change transfer case fluid every 96,000 km (60,000 miles).

Install a new engine air filter as required.

Install a new cabin air filter as required.

When operating in off-road conditions:

Change automatic transmission fluid every 48,000 km (30,000 miles). If equipped, change the in-line service installed transmission fluid filter.

Change transfer case fluid every 96,000 km (60,000 miles).

Install a new cabin air filter as required.

Inspect and lubricate U-joints.

Inspect and lubricate steering linkage ball joints with zerk fittings.

Short trips in cold operating conditions:

Inspect and lubricate 4x2 ball joints and steering idler arms every 8,000 km (5,000 miles).

Change transfer case fluid every 96,000 km (60,000 miles).

36578_F250_C0016

SCHEDULED MAINTENANCE INTERVALS
All Vehicles with the 6.4L Diesel Engine

TO BE SERVICED	TYPE OF SERVICE	VEHICLE MILEAGE INTERVAL (x1000)												
		7.5	15	22.5	30	37.5	45	52.5	60	67.5	75	82.5	90	97.5
Engine oil & filter	R	✓	✓	✓	✓	✓	✓	✓	✓	✓	✓	✓	✓	✓
Tires	Rotate	✓	✓	✓	✓	✓	✓	✓	✓	✓	✓	✓	✓	✓
Air filter minder	I ①	✓	✓	✓	✓	✓	✓	✓	✓	✓	✓	✓	✓	✓
Wheels	I ②		✓		✓		✓		✓		✓		✓	
Brake pads, hoses, etc.	I		✓		✓		✓		✓		✓		✓	
Coolant hoses	I		✓		✓		✓		✓		✓		✓	
Steering linkage and suspension	I/L		✓		✓		✓		✓		✓		✓	
Cabin air filter	R					✓							✓	
Ball joints (2wd)	L		✓		✓		✓		✓		✓		✓	
Driveshaft	I/L		✓		✓		✓		✓		✓		✓	
4x4 front axle U-joints	L		✓		✓		✓		✓		✓		✓	
Exhaust system and heat shields	I		✓		✓		✓		✓		✓		✓	
Engine air filter	R		✓		✓		✓		✓		✓		✓	
Fuel filters ③	R		✓		✓		✓		✓		✓		✓	
Auto trans fluid ④	R				✓				✓				✓	
4x2 front wheel bearings	L								✓					
4x2 front wheel bearing grease seals	R								✓					
Accessory drive belts	I													✓
Manual trans. fluid	R								✓					
Rear differential fluid ⑤	R													✓
Coolant (Premium Gold)	R	every 105,000 miles												
Front drve axle fluid	R	every 150,000 miles												
Transfer case fluid	R	every 150,000 miles												
Accessory drive belts	R	every 150,000 miles, if not previously done so												

R: Replace   S: Service   I: Inspect   L: Lubricate   Adj: adjust

① Reset after new filter is installed
② Inspect for end play and noise
③ Frame-mounted and engine
④ Including external and in-line filters
⑤ Dana axles using non-synthetic fluid only

When towing a trailer or using a camper or car-top carrier:

Change engine oil and install a new oil filter every 4,800 km (3,000 miles), 3 months or 200 hours of engine operation (whichever occurs first).

Change transfer case fluid every 96,000 km (60,000 miles).

Change manual transmission fluid as required.

Inspect and lubricate U-joints as required.

During extensive idling and/or low speed driving for long distances, as in heavy commercial use such as delivery, taxi, patrol car or livery:

Change engine oil and install a new oil filter every 4,800 km (3,000 miles), 3 months or 200 hours of engine operation (whichever occurs first).

Lube front lower control arm and steering linkage ball joints with zerk fittings (if equipped) every 4,800 km (3,000 miles) or 3 months.

Inspect brake system and check battery electrolyte level (Patrol cars) every 8,000 km (5,000 miles).

Install a new fuel filter every 24,000 km (15,000 miles).

Change automatic transmission fluid, lubricate 4x2 wheel bearings, install new grease seals and adjust bearings every 48,000 km (30,000 miles). If equipped, change the in-line service installed transmission fluid filter.

Change transfer case fluid every 96,000 km (60,000 miles).

Install a new cabin air filter as required.

36578_F250_C0017

SCHEDULED MAINTENANCE INTERVALS

All Vehicles with the 6.4L Diesel Engine
Footnotes continued

When operating in dusty conditions such as unpaved or dusty roads:

Change engine oil and install a new oil filter every 4,800 km (3,000 miles) or 3 months.

Install a new fuel filter every 24,000 km (15,000 miles).

Change automatic transmission fluid every 48,000 km (30,000 miles). If equipped, change the in-line service installed transmission fluid filter.

Change transfer case fluid every 96,000 km (60,000 miles).

Install a new engine air filter or cabine air filter as required.

When operating in off-road conditions:

Change automatic transmission fluid every 48,000 km (30,000 miles). If equipped, change the in-line service installed transmission fluid filter.

Change transfer case fluid every 96,000 km (60,000 miles).

Install a new cabin air filter as required.

Inspect and lubricate U-joints.

Inspect and lubricate steering linkage ball joints with zerk fittings.

36578_F250_C0018

PRECAUTIONS

Before servicing any vehicle, please be sure to read all of the following precautions, which deal with personal safety, prevention of component damage, and important points to take into consideration when servicing a motor vehicle:

• Never open, service or drain the radiator or cooling system when the engine is hot; serious burns can occur from the steam and hot coolant.

• Observe all applicable safety precautions when working around fuel. Whenever servicing the fuel system, always work in a well-ventilated area. Do not allow fuel spray or vapors to come in contact with a spark, open flame, or excessive heat (a hot drop light, for example). Keep a dry chemical fire extinguisher near the work area. Always keep fuel in a container specifically designed for fuel storage; also, always properly seal fuel containers to avoid the possibility of fire or explosion. Refer to the additional fuel system precautions later in this section.

• Fuel injection systems often remain pressurized, even after the engine has been turned **OFF**. The fuel system pressure must be relieved before disconnecting any fuel lines. Failure to do so may result in fire and/or personal injury.

• Brake fluid often contains polyglycol ethers and polyglycols. Avoid contact with the eyes and wash your hands thoroughly after handling brake fluid. If you do get brake fluid in your eyes, flush your eyes with clean, running water for 15 minutes. If eye irritation persists, or if you have taken brake fluid internally, IMMEDIATELY seek medical assistance.

• The EPA warns that prolonged contact with used engine oil may cause a number of skin disorders, including cancer. You should make every effort to minimize your exposure to used engine oil. Protective gloves should be worn when changing oil. Wash your hands and any other exposed skin areas as soon as possible after exposure to used engine oil. Soap and water, or waterless hand cleaner should be used.

• All new vehicles are now equipped with an air bag system, often referred to as a Supplemental Restraint System (SRS) or Supplemental Inflatable Restraint (SIR) system. The system must be disabled before performing service on or around system components, steering column, instrument panel components, wiring and sensors. Failure to follow safety and disabling procedures could result in accidental air bag deployment, possible personal injury and unnecessary system repairs.

• Always wear safety goggles when working with, or around, the air bag system. When carrying a non-deployed air bag, be sure the bag and trim cover are pointed away from your body. When placing a non-deployed air bag on a work surface, always face the bag and trim cover upward, away from the surface. This will reduce the motion of the module if it is accidentally deployed. Refer to the additional air bag system precautions later in this section.

• Clean, high quality brake fluid from a sealed container is essential to the safe and proper operation of the brake system. You should always buy the correct type of brake fluid for your vehicle. If the brake fluid becomes contaminated, completely flush the system with new fluid. Never reuse any brake fluid. Any brake fluid that is removed from the system should be discarded. Also, do not allow any brake fluid to come in contact with a painted surface; it will damage the paint.

• Never operate the engine without the proper amount and type of engine oil; doing so WILL result in severe engine damage.

• Timing belt maintenance is extremely important. Many models utilize an interference-type, non-freewheeling engine. If the timing belt breaks, the valves in the cylinder head may strike the pistons, causing potentially serious (also time-consuming and expensive) engine damage. Refer to the maintenance interval charts for the recommended replacement interval for the timing belt, and to the timing belt section for belt replacement and inspection.

• Disconnecting the negative battery cable on some vehicles may interfere with the functions of the on-board computer system(s) and may require the computer to undergo a relearning process once the negative battery cable is reconnected.

• When servicing drum brakes, only disassemble and assemble one side at a time, leaving the remaining side intact for reference.

• Only an MVAC-trained, EPA-certified automotive technician should service the air conditioning system or its components.

BRAKES

ANTI-LOCK BRAKE SYSTEM (ABS)

GENERAL INFORMATION

PRECAUTIONS

• Certain components within the ABS system are not intended to be serviced or repaired individually.

• Do not use rubber hoses or other parts not specifically specified for and ABS system. When using repair kits, replace all parts included in the kit. Partial or incorrect repair may lead to functional problems and require the replacement of components.

• Lubricate rubber parts with clean, fresh brake fluid to ease assembly. Do not use shop air to clean parts; damage to rubber components may result.

• Use only DOT 3 brake fluid from an unopened container.

• If any hydraulic component or line is removed or replaced, it may be necessary to bleed the entire system.

• A clean repair area is essential. Always clean the reservoir and cap thoroughly before removing the cap. The slightest amount of dirt in the fluid may plug an orifice and impair the system function. Perform repairs after components have been thoroughly cleaned; use only denatured alcohol to clean components. Do not allow ABS components to come into contact with any substance containing mineral oil; this includes used shop rags.

• The Anti-Lock control unit is a microprocessor similar to other computer units in the vehicle. Ensure that the ignition switch is **OFF** before removing or installing controller harnesses. Avoid static electricity discharge at or near the controller.

• If any arc welding is to be done on the vehicle, the control unit should be unplugged before welding operations begin.

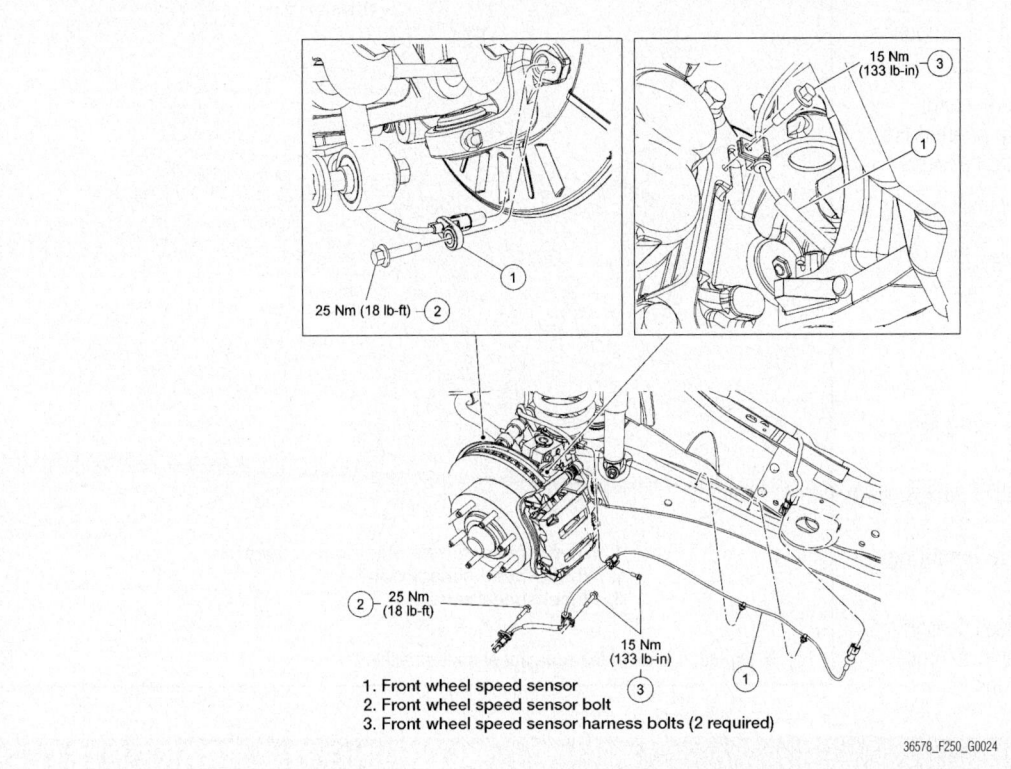

Fig. 1 Exploded view of the front wheel speed sensor—2WD models

1. Front wheel speed sensor
2. Front wheel speed sensor bolt
3. Front wheel speed sensor harness bolts (2 required)

36578_F250_G0024

WHEEL SPEED SENSORS

REMOVAL & INSTALLATION

Front

2WD Vehicles

See Figure 1.

1. Remove the wheel and tire.
2. Disconnect the wheel speed sensor electrical connector.
3. Remove the wheel speed sensor harness bolts and detach the harness from the radius arm.
4. Remove the wheel speed sensor bolt and the sensor. To install, tighten to 18 ft. lbs. (25 Nm).

➡**Make sure the wheel speed sensor harness is correctly routed to prevent the brake disc from damaging the harness. To install, reverse the removal procedure.**

4WD Vehicles

See Figure 2.

1. Remove the disc brake shield.
2. Disconnect the wheel speed sensor electrical connector.
3. Detach the wheel speed sensor harness from the radius arm.

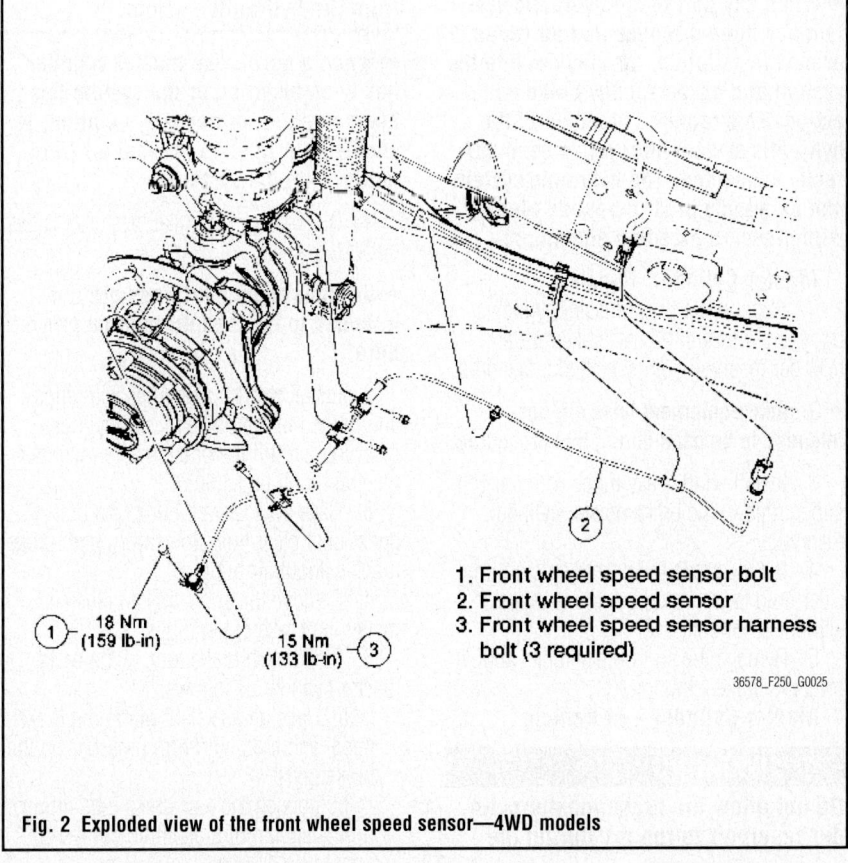

1. Front wheel speed sensor bolt
2. Front wheel speed sensor
3. Front wheel speed sensor harness bolt (3 required)

36578_F250_G0025

Fig. 2 Exploded view of the front wheel speed sensor—4WD models

4. Remove the 3 wheel speed sensor harness bolts.

5. Remove the wheel speed sensor bolt and the sensor.

➡**Make sure the wheel speed sensor harness is correctly routed to prevent the brake disc from damaging the harness.**

6. To install, reverse the removal procedure.

Rear

See Figure 3.

1. Raise and safely support the vehicle.

2. Disconnect the rear axle speed sensor electrical connector.

3. Remove the rear axle speed sensor bolt.

➡**Install a new O-ring before installing the rear axle speed sensor.**

4. Remove the rear axle speed sensor.

5. To install, reverse the removal procedure. Tighten to 15 Nm (11 ft. lbs.).

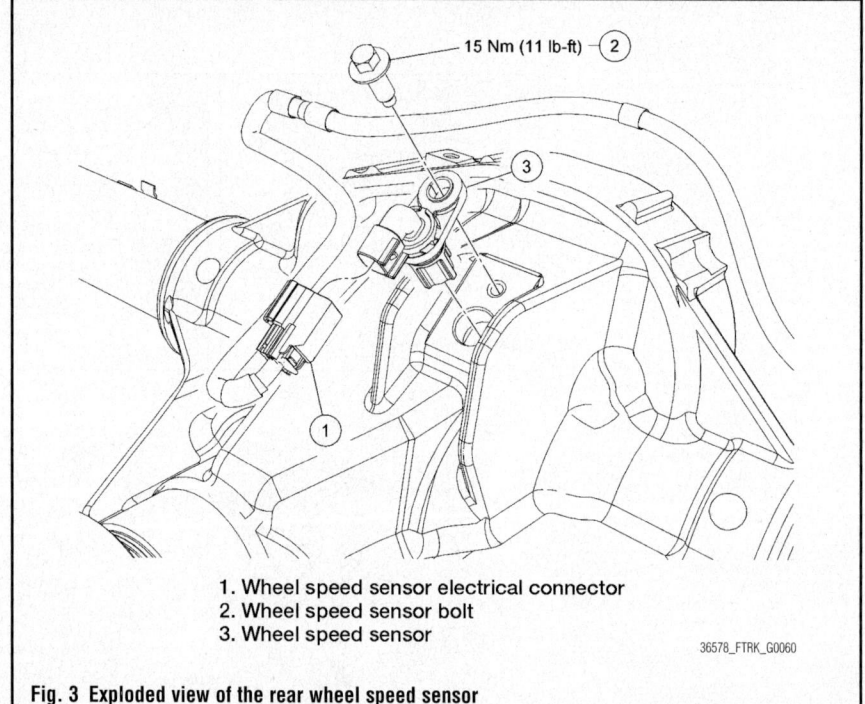

1. Wheel speed sensor electrical connector
2. Wheel speed sensor bolt
3. Wheel speed sensor

36578_FTRK_G0060

Fig. 3 Exploded view of the rear wheel speed sensor

BRAKES   BLEEDING THE BRAKE SYSTEM

BLEEDING PROCEDURE

1. Before servicing the vehicle, refer to the Precautions Section.

➡**When any part of the hydraulic system has been disconnected for repair or new installation, air may get into the system and cause spongy brake pedal action. This requires bleeding of the hydraulic system after it has been correctly connected. The hydraulic system can be gravity bled, manually bled or with pressure bleeding equipment.**

Master Cylinder, Bench

2. Support the brake master cylinder body in a vise and fill the brake master cylinder reservoir with specified brake fluid.

➡**Original equipment lines are not intended to be used during this procedure.**

3. Install short brake tubes with the ends submerged in the brake master cylinder reservoir.

4. Slowly press the primary piston until clear fluid flows from both brake tubes, without air bubbles.

5. Remove the short brake tubes and plug the brake tube ports.

Master Cylinder—In Vehicle

❋❋ WARNING

Do not allow the brake master cylinder reservoir to run dry during the bleeding operation. Keep the brake master cylinder reservoir filled with the specified brake fluid. Never reuse the brake fluid that has been drained from the hydraulic system.

➡**When a new brake master cylinder has been installed or the system has been emptied, or partially emptied, it should be primed to prevent air from getting into the system.**

1. Disconnect the brake master cylinder outlet tubes.

➡**Original equipment lines are not intended to be used during this procedure.**

2. Install short brake tubes with ends submerged in the brake master cylinder reservoir and fill the brake master cylinder reservoir with brake fluid.

3. Have an assistant pump the brake pedal until clear fluid flows from both brake tubes without air bubbles.

4. Remove the short brake tubes and install the brake outlet tubes.

5. Bleed each brake tube at the brake master cylinder as follows:

   a. Have an assistant pump the brake pedal and then hold firm pressure on the brake pedal.

   b. Loosen the rear brake tube fittings until a stream of brake fluid comes out.

Have an assistant maintain pressure on the brake pedal while tightening the brake tube fitting.

   c. Repeat this operation until clear, bubble-free fluid comes out.

   d. Refill the brake master cylinder reservoir as necessary. Repeat the bleeding operation at the front brake tube.

6. While the assistant maintains pressure on the brake pedal, tighten the brake tubes.

Gravity Bleeding

❋❋ WARNING

Do not allow the brake master cylinder reservoir to run dry during the bleeding operation. Keep the brake master cylinder reservoir filled with the specified brake fluid. Never reuse the brake fluid that has been drained from the hydraulic system.

➡**When a new brake master cylinder has been installed or the system has been emptied, or partially emptied, it should be primed to prevent air from getting into the system.**

1. Fill the brake master cylinder reservoir with brake fluid.

2. Connect a clear tube to the right rear disc brake caliper bleeder screw and the other end in a container partially filled with recommended brake fluid.

3. Open the bleeder screw and leave open until clear bubble-free brake fluid flows.

4. Refill the brake master cylinder reservoir as necessary.

5. Tighten the disc brake caliper bleeder screw.

6. Repeat Steps 1 through 4 for the three remaining brake calipers, going in order from the left rear disc brake caliper to the right front disc brake caliper ending with the left front disc brake caliper.

7. If the brake pedal feels spongy, repeat the bleed procedure.

Manual Bleeding

> ❊❊ **WARNING**
>
> **Do not allow the brake master cylinder reservoir to run dry during the bleeding operation. Keep the brake master cylinder reservoir filled with the specified brake fluid. Never reuse the brake fluid that has been drained from the hydraulic system.**

1. Fill the brake master cylinder reservoir with brake fluid.

2. Connect a clear tube to the right rear disc brake caliper bleeder screw and the other end in a container partially filled with recommended brake fluid.

3. Have an assistant pump the brake pedal and then hold firm pressure on the brake pedal.

4. Loosen the disc brake caliper bleeder screw until a stream of brake fluid comes out. Have an assistant maintain pressure on the brake pedal while tightening the disc brake caliper bleeder screw. Repeat until clear, bubble-free fluid comes out. Refill the brake master cylinder reservoir as necessary.

5. Tighten the disc brake caliper bleeder screw.

6. Repeat Steps 1 through 5 for the three remaining brake calipers, going in order from the left rear disc brake caliper to the right front disc brake caliper ending with the left front disc brake caliper.

7. If the brake pedal feels spongy, repeat the bleed procedure.

Anti-Lock Brake System Hydraulic Control Unit Bleeding

➡ **This procedure is only required when a new hydraulic control unit is installed.**

8. Connect diagnostic tool Worldwide Diagnostic System (WDS) 418-F224, New Generation STAR (NGS) Tester 418-F052, or equivalent diagnostic tool and follow the ABS system bleed instructions.

9. Use the gravity bleed or manual bleed procedure(s) to bleed the system. Begin at the right rear caliper.

BLEEDING THE ABS SYSTEM

Anti-Lock Brake System (ABS) Hydraulic Control Unit Bleeding

➡ **This procedure is required only when a new hydraulic control unit is installed. A diagnostic tool, or equivalent, is necessary.**

➡ **When any part of the hydraulic system has been disconnected for repair or new installation, air may get into the system and cause spongy brake pedal action. This requires bleeding of the hydraulic system after it has been correctly connected. See Bleeding the Brake System.**

1. Connect the diagnostic tool and follow the ABS system bleed instructions.

2. Use the manual bleed procedure(s) to bleed the system. Begin at the right rear caliper.

BRAKES

BRAKE CALIPER

REMOVAL & INSTALLATION
See Figure 4.

1. Before servicing the vehicle, refer to the Precautions Section.

2. Raise and safely support the vehicle.

3. Remove the brake flexible hose flow bolt and position the brake flexible hose aside. Discard the 2 copper washers.

> ❊❊ **WARNING**
>
> **Do not pry in the caliper sight hole to retract the pistons as this can damage the pistons and boots.**

4. Remove the 2 brake caliper bolts and the brake caliper. If leaks or damaged boots are found, install a new disc brake caliper.

To install:

> ❊❊ **WARNING**
>
> **Tighten the bottom caliper bolt before tightening the top caliper bolt.**

> ❊❊ **WARNING**
>
> **Make sure the caliper pin boots are correctly seated to prevent damage to the guide pins.**

5. Position the brake caliper and install the 2 bolts. Torque to 56 ft. lbs. (76 Nm).

FRONT DISC BRAKES

6. Using 2 new copper washers, position the brake flexible hose and install the brake caliper flow bolt. Torque to 35 ft. lbs. (48 Nm).

7. Bleed the brake caliper.

8. Test the brake system for normal operation.

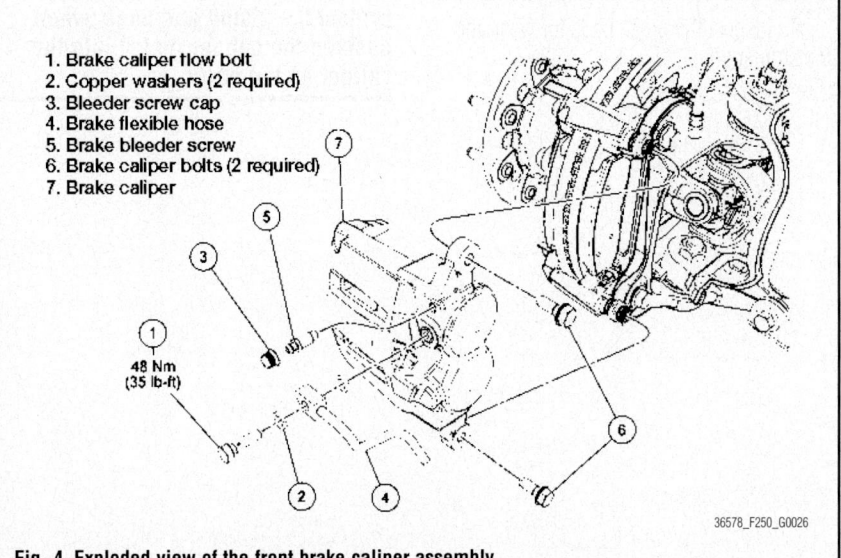

1. Brake caliper flow bolt
2. Copper washers (2 required)
3. Bleeder screw cap
4. Brake flexible hose
5. Brake bleeder screw
6. Brake caliper bolts (2 required)
7. Brake caliper

48 Nm
(35 lb-ft)

36578_F250_G0026

Fig. 4 Exploded view of the front brake caliper assembly

DISC BRAKE PADS

REMOVAL & INSTALLATION

See Figure 5.

1. Before servicing the vehicle, refer to the Precautions Section.

2. Check the brake fluid level in the brake master cylinder reservoir. If required, remove the fluid until the brake master cylinder reservoir is half full.

3. Raise and safely support the vehicle.

> **✳✳ WARNING**
>
> **Do not pry in the caliper sight hole to retract the pistons, as this can damage the pistons and boots.**

> **✳✳ WARNING**
>
> **Do not allow the brake caliper to hang from the brake caliper flexible hose. Use a suitable tool to support the brake caliper.**

4. Remove the 2 brake caliper bolts and position the caliper aside.

5. Remove the 2 brake pads and if equipped, remove the 4 retraction clips. Discard the retraction clips.

6. Measure the front brake disc thickness. Install a new front brake disc if it is not within specification.

> **✳✳ WARNING**
>
> **Install new brake pads if they are worn past the specified thickness above the metal backing plates. Install new brake pads in complete axle sets.**

7. Inspect the brake pads for wear and contamination.

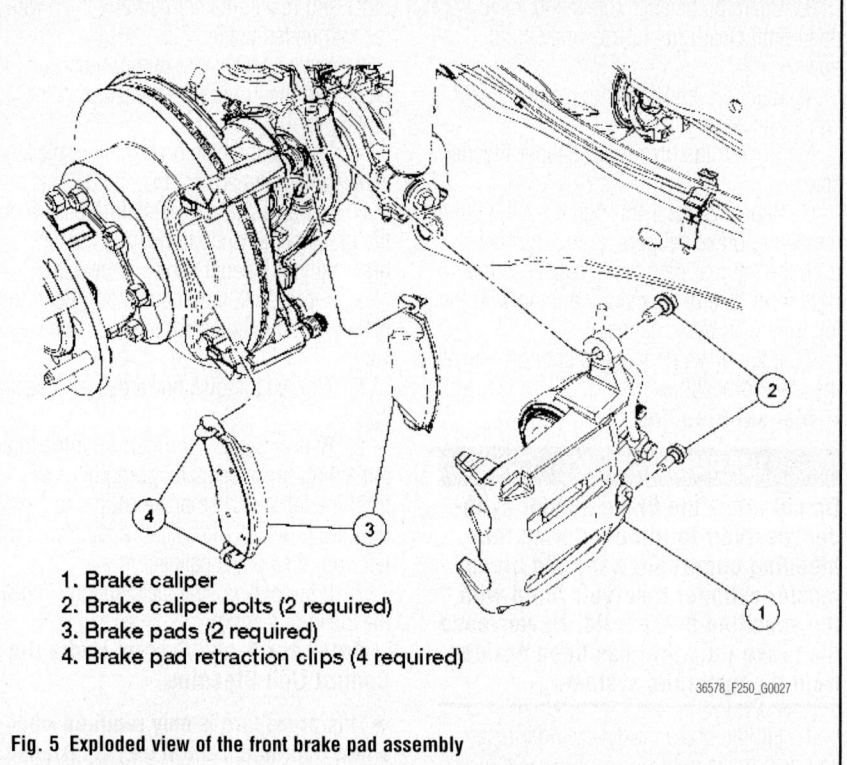

1. Brake caliper
2. Brake caliper bolts (2 required)
3. Brake pads (2 required)
4. Brake pad retraction clips (4 required)

36578_F250_G0027

Fig. 5 Exploded view of the front brake pad assembly

To install:

> **✳✳ WARNING**
>
> **Do not allow grease, oil, brake fluid or other contaminants to contact the pad lining material. Do not install contaminated pads.**

➡ Install all new hardware as supplied with the brake pad kit.

8. Install the 4 new retracting clips and the 2 brake pads.

> **✳✳ WARNING**
>
> **Protect the piston and boots when pushing the caliper piston into the caliper piston bores.**

9. Using a suitable tool, compress the disc brake caliper pistons into the caliper.

> **✳✳ WARNING**
>
> **Tighten the bottom caliper bolt before tightening the top caliper bolt**

> **✳✳ WARNING**
>
> **Make sure the caliper pin boots are correctly seated to prevent damage to the guide pins.**

10. Position the brake caliper and install the 2 bolts. Torque to 56 ft. lbs. (76 Nm).

11. Fill the brake master cylinder reservoir with clean brake fluid.

12. Test the brakes for normal operation.

BRAKES

BRAKE CALIPER

REMOVAL & INSTALLATION

See Figure 6.

1. Before servicing the vehicle, refer to the Precautions Section.
2. Raise and support the vehicle.
3. Remove the brake caliper flow bolt and discard the 2 copper washers.

> #### ✳✳ WARNING
> **Do not pry in the caliper sight hole to retract the pistons, as this can damage the pistons and boots.**

4. Remove the 2 brake caliper bolts and the caliper.

To install:

5. Position the brake caliper and install the 2 brake caliper bolts.
   - For F-250, F-350 single rear wheel caliper, tighten to 26 ft. lbs. (35 Nm).
   - For F-350 dual rear wheel caliper, tighten to 56 ft. lbs. (76 Nm).
6. Position the brake flexible hose, install the brake caliper flow bolt and 2 new copper washers. Torque to 26 ft. lbs. (35 Nm).
7. Bleed the brake system.

DISC BRAKE PADS

REMOVAL & INSTALLATION

See Figure 7.

1. Before servicing the vehicle, refer to the Precautions Section.
2. If necessary, remove the brake fluid until the brake master cylinder reservoir is half full.
3. Remove the wheel and tire assembly.

> #### ✳✳ WARNING
> **Do not pry in caliper sight hole to retract pistons as this can damage the pistons and boots.**

> #### ✳✳ WARNING
> **When removing the brake caliper, never allow it to hang from the brake flexible hose. Provide a suitable support.**

4. Remove the 2 brake caliper bolts and position the caliper aside.

➡**Install a new pads if they are worn past the specified thickness. Install new pads in complete axle sets.**

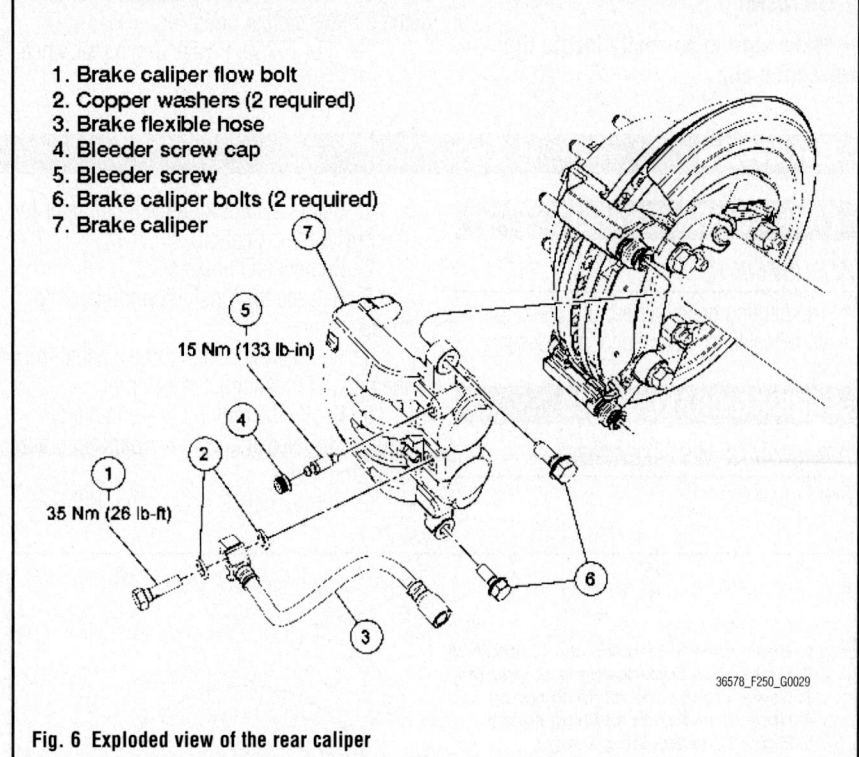

1. Brake caliper flow bolt
2. Copper washers (2 required)
3. Brake flexible hose
4. Bleeder screw cap
5. Bleeder screw
6. Brake caliper bolts (2 required)
7. Brake caliper

15 Nm (133 lb-in)

35 Nm (26 lb-ft)

36578_F250_G0029

Fig. 6 Exploded view of the rear caliper

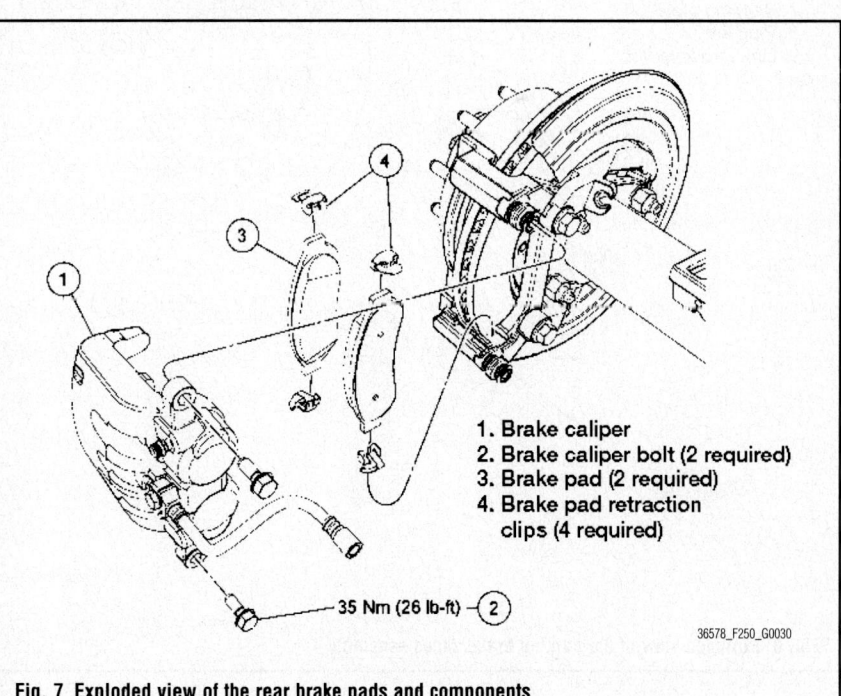

1. Brake caliper
2. Brake caliper bolt (2 required)
3. Brake pad (2 required)
4. Brake pad retraction clips (4 required)

35 Nm (26 lb-ft)

36578_F250_G0030

Fig. 7 Exploded view of the rear brake pads and components

5. Remove the brake pads and retraction clips.
6. Measure the brake disc thickness. Install a new brake disc if not within specification.
7. Inspect the disc brake caliper for leaks. If leaks are found a new caliper must be installed.

8. Inspect the disc brake anchor plate assembly.
   - Check the guide pin boots for damage.
   - Check the guide pins for binding and damage.
   - Replace worn or damaged pins.

Lube pins with Silicone Brake Caliper Compound.

To install:

➡ **Make sure to correctly locate the retraction clip.**

9. Install the brake pads and retraction clips.

10. Position the brake caliper and install the 2 brake caliper bolts.
- For F-250, F-350 single rear wheel

caliper, tighten to 26 ft. lbs. (35 Nm).
- For F-350 dual rear wheel caliper, tighten to 56 ft. lbs. (76 Nm).

BRAKES   PARKING BRAKE

PARKING BRAKE CABLES

ADJUSTMENT

The parking brake system utilizes an automatic adjuster. No adjustment is necessary.

PARKING BRAKE SHOES

REMOVAL & INSTALLATION
See Figure 8.

1. Before servicing the vehicle, refer to the Precautions Section.

2. Remove the brake disc.

3. Release the tension on the parking brake system.

4. Release the parking brake cable from the parking brake bracket assembly.

5. Rotate the parking brake cable 90 degrees to release it from the parking brake actuating lever.

6. Remove the 2 brake shoe hold-

down clips and the 2 brake shoe retaining pins.

7. Remove the brake shoe adjusting screw and the lower brake shoe retaining spring.

8. Remove the brake shoes and the upper brake shoe retaining spring.

9. To install, reverse the removal procedure.

10. Inspect the components for excessive wear or damage and install new as required.

11. Adjust the parking brake shoes.

ADJUSTMENT
See Figure 9.

1. Raise and support the vehicle.

2. Remove the wheel and tire assembly.

3. Remove the brake adjusting hole cover from the backing plate.

4. Turn the brake adjuster screw to expand the parking brake shoe and linings until they drag against the drum-in-hat rotor.

5. Back off the brake adjuster screw until no drag is evident.

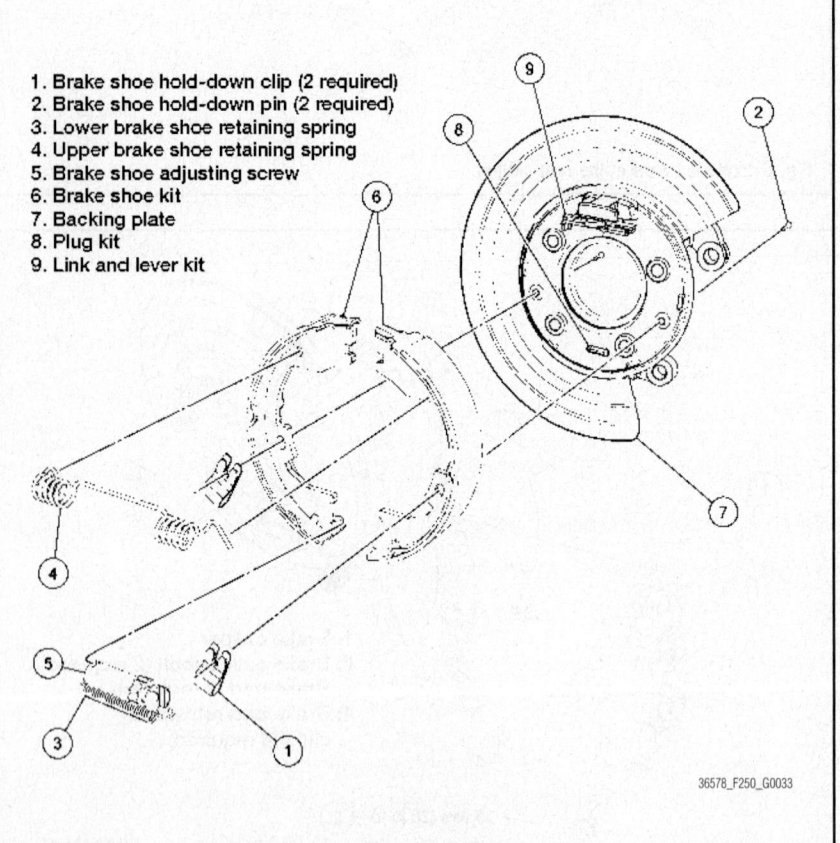

1. Brake shoe hold-down clip (2 required)
2. Brake shoe hold-down pin (2 required)
3. Lower brake shoe retaining spring
4. Upper brake shoe retaining spring
5. Brake shoe adjusting screw
6. Brake shoe kit
7. Backing plate
8. Plug kit
9. Link and lever kit

36578_F250_G0033

Fig. 8 Exploded view of the parking brake shoes assembly

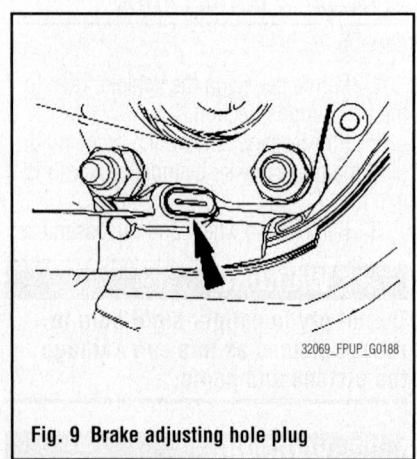

32069_FPUP_G0188

Fig. 9 Brake adjusting hole plug

GENERAL INFORMATION

✻✻ CAUTION

These vehicles are equipped with an air bag system. The system must be disarmed before performing service on, or around, system components, the steering column, instrument panel components, wiring and sensors. Failure to follow the safety precautions and the disarming procedure could result in accidental air bag deployment, possible injury and unnecessary system repairs.

SERVICE PRECAUTIONS

Disconnect and isolate the battery negative cable before beginning any airbag system component diagnosis, testing, removal, or installation procedures. Allow system capacitor to discharge for two minutes before beginning any component service. This will disable the airbag system. Failure to disable the airbag system may result in accidental airbag deployment, personal injury, or death.

Do not place an intact undeployed airbag face down on a solid surface. The airbag will propel into the air if accidentally deployed and may result in personal injury or death.

When carrying or handling an undeployed airbag, the trim side (face) of the airbag should be pointing towards the body to minimize possibility of injury if accidental deployment occurs. Failure to do this may result in personal injury or death.

Replace airbag system components with OEM replacement parts. Substitute parts may appear interchangeable, but internal differences may result in inferior occupant protection. Failure to do so may result in occupant personal injury or death.

Wear safety glasses, rubber gloves, and long sleeved clothing when cleaning powder residue from vehicle after an airbag deployment. Powder residue emitted from a deployed airbag can cause skin irritation. Flush affected area with cool water if irritation is experienced. If nasal or throat irritation is experienced, exit the vehicle for fresh air until the irritation ceases. If irritation continues, see a physician.

Do not use a replacement airbag that is not in the original packaging. This may result in improper deployment, personal injury, or death.

The factory installed fasteners, screws and bolts used to fasten airbag components have a special coating and are specifically designed for the airbag system. Do not use substitute fasteners. Use only original equipment fasteners listed in the parts catalog when fastener replacement is required.

During, and following, any child restraint anchor service, due to impact event or vehicle repair, carefully inspect all mounting hardware, tether straps, and anchors for proper installation, operation, or damage. If a child restraint anchor is found damaged in any way, the anchor must be replaced. Failure to do this may result in personal injury or death.

Deployed and non-deployed airbags may or may not have live pyrotechnic material within the airbag inflator.

Do not dispose of driver/passenger/curtain airbags or seat belt tensioners unless you are sure of complete deployment. Refer to the Hazardous Substance Control System for proper disposal.

Dispose of deployed airbags and tensioners consistent with state, provincial, local, and federal regulations.

After any airbag component testing or service, do not connect the battery negative cable. Personal injury or death may result if the system test is not performed first.

If the vehicle is equipped with the Occupant Classification System (OCS), do not connect the battery negative cable before performing the OCS Verification Test using the scan tool and the appropriate diagnostic information. Personal injury or death may result if the system test is not performed properly.

Never replace both the Occupant Restraint Controller (ORC) and the Occupant Classification Module (OCM) at the same time. If both require replacement, replace one, then perform the Airbag System test before replacing the other.

Both the ORC and the OCM store Occupant Classification System (OCS) calibration data, which they transfer to one another when one of them is replaced. If both are replaced at the same time, an irreversible fault will be set in both modules and the OCS may malfunction and cause personal injury or death.

If equipped with OCS, the Seat Weight Sensor is a sensitive, calibrated unit and must be handled carefully. Do not drop or handle roughly. If dropped or damaged, replace with another sensor. Failure to do so may result in occupant injury or death.

If equipped with OCS, the front passenger seat must be handled carefully as well. When removing the seat, be careful when setting on floor not to drop. If dropped, the sensor may be inoperative, could result in occupant injury, or possibly death.

If equipped with OCS, when the passenger front seat is on the floor, no one should sit in the front passenger seat. This uneven force may damage the sensing ability of the seat weight sensors. If sat on and damaged, the sensor may be inoperative, could result in occupant injury, or possibly death.

DISARMING THE SYSTEM

1. Before servicing the vehicle, refer to the Precautions Section.
2. Turn all vehicle accessories OFF.
3. Turn the ignition switch to OFF.
4. At the central junction box (CJB), located below the instrument panel, remove the trim panel, the cover, and the restraints control module (RCM) fuse from the CJB. See your Owner's Manual for fuse identification.
5. Turn the ignition ON and visually monitor the air bag indicator for at least 30 seconds. The air bag indicator will remain lit continuously (no flashing) if the correct RCM fuse has been removed. If the air bag indicator does not remain lit continuously, remove the correct RCM fuse before proceeding.
6. Turn the ignition OFF.

✻✻ CAUTION

To avoid accidental deployment and possible personal injury, the backup power supply must be depleted before repairing or replacing any front or side air bag supplemental restraint system (SRS) components and before servicing, replacing, adjusting or striking components near the front or side air bag sensors, such as doors, instrument panel, console, door latches, strikers, seats and hood latches.

7. To deplete the backup power supply energy, disconnect the battery ground cable and wait at least 1 minute. Be sure to disconnect auxiliary batteries and power supplies (if equipped).
8. Disconnect the battery ground cable and wait at least 1 minute.

ARMING THE SYSTEM

1. Before servicing the vehicle, refer to the Precautions Section.

2. Turn the ignition switch from OFF to ON.

3. Install the RCM fuse to the CJB and install the cover and trim panel.

❊❊ CAUTION

Be sure that nobody is in the vehicle and that there is nothing blocking or set in front of any air bag module when the battery ground cable is connected.

4. Connect the battery ground cable.

5. Prove out the supplemental restraint system (SRS) as follows:

6. Turn the ignition key from ON to OFF. Wait 10 seconds, then turn the key back to ON and visually monitor the air bag indicator with the air bag modules installed. The air bag indicator will light continuously for approximately 6 seconds and then turn off. If an air bag supplemental restraint system (SRS) fault is present, the air bag indicator will either:

- Fail to light
- Remain lit continuously
- Flash

7. The flashing might not occur until approximately 30 seconds after the ignition switch has been turned from the OFF to the ON position. This is the time required for the restraints control module (RCM) to complete the testing of the SRS. If the air bag indicator is inoperative and a SRS fault exists, a chime will sound in a pattern of 5 sets of 5 beeps. If this occurs, the air bag indicator and any SRS fault discovered must be diagnosed and repaired.

8. Clear all continuous DTCs from the restraints control module using a diagnostic tool.

CLOCKSPRING CENTERING

❊❊ WARNING

If the clockspring is not correctly centralized, it may fail prematurely. If in doubt, repeat the centralizing procedure. Failure to follow these instructions may increase the risk of serious personal injury or death in a crash.

➡ **Do not over-rotate the clockspring inner rotor. The internal ribbon wire is connected to the clockspring rotor. The internal ribbon wire acts as a stop and can be broken from its internal connection. Failure to follow this instruction may result in component damage and/or system failure.**

1. If a new clockspring was installed and the anti-rotation key has not been removed proceed to Step 5.

2. If a new clockspring was installed and the anti-rotation key has been removed before the steering wheel is installed or the same clockspring is being installed, rotate the clockspring inner rotor counterclockwise and carefully feel for the ribbon wire to run out of length with slight resistance. Stop rotating the clockspring inner rotor at this point

3. Starting with the clockspring rotated fully counterclockwise as indicated in Step 5, rotate the clockspring inner rotor, wiring and connector clockwise through 3 full revolutions to center the clockspring with the connector ending up in the 12 o'clock position. The clockspring is now centered.

4. Verify that the clockspring is correctly centralized by observing that the clockspring rotor, wiring and connector are in the 12 o'clock position.

5. Install the steering wheel. Refer to Steering Wheel in Steering.

6. If a new clockspring was installed, remove the anti-rotation key.

DRIVE TRAIN

AUTOMATIC TRANSMISSION ASSEMBLY

REMOVAL & INSTALLATION

Torq Shift®

See Figure 10.

1. Before servicing the vehicle, refer to the precautions in the beginning of this section.

2. With the vehicle in NEUTRAL, position it on a hoist.

3. For 4WD vehicles, remove the transfer case assembly.

4. For RWD vehicles, remove the driveshaft.

5. If transmission disassembly is required, drain the transmission fluid. Remove the transmission fluid pan drain plug and allow the transmission fluid to drain.

6. Install the transmission fluid pan drain plug.

7. Install a suitable high-lift transmission jack.

8. Remove the wire harness from the crossmember.

➡ **The transmission insulator studs may come out of the insulator while removing the nuts. Install new transmission insulator studs if the studs come out of the insulator.**

9. Remove the transmission insulator-to-crossmember nuts.

10. Remove the LH transmission support crossmember-to-frame bolts and nuts. Loosen, but do not remove.

11. Remove the RH crossmember bracket bolts and nuts.

a. Remove the transmission support crossmember-to-frame bracket bolts and nuts.

b. Remove the transmission support crossmember-to-frame bracket.

c. Remove the RH transmission support crossmember-to-frame bolts and nuts.

12. Remove the LH crossmember bolt, nut and the crossmember. Remove the transmission support crossmember-to-frame bolt and nut. Remove the crossmember.

13. Remove the transmission insulator-to-extension housing bolts from the extension housing and remove the transmission insulator.

➡ **To prevent selector lever cable damage, do not apply force to the selector lever cable assembly between the manual control lever and the selector lever cable bracket.**

14. Remove the selector lever cable.

a. Disconnect the selector lever cable from the manual control lever.

b. Remove the selector lever cable bracket bolts and position the selector lever cable and bracket aside.

15. Loosen the bolt and disconnect the transmission vehicle harness connector.

16. Disconnect the Output Shaft Speed (OSS) sensor.

17. Disconnect the Turbine Shaft Speed (TSS)/intermediate shaft speed sensor.

18. Disconnect the RH and LH wire harness from the side of the transmission.

19. While holding the case fitting, disconnect the rear transmission fluid cooler tube.

20. While holding the case fitting, disconnect the front transmission fluid cooler tube.

21. If equipped with dual generators, rotate the tensioner and remove the outer accessory drive belt from the crankshaft pulley.

22. Remove the cylinder block opening cover in order to gain access to the torque converter-to-flexplate nuts.

23. Remove the steering damper-to-frame bolt and nut, and position the steering damper aside.

24. Using a suitable tool, rotate the crankshaft pulley to gain access to the torque converter-to-flexplate nuts.

25. Remove and discard the 8 torque converter-to-flexplate nuts.

26. Remove the 9 transmission-to-engine mounting bolts.

27. Slide the transmission back enough to install the Torque Converter Retainer.

28. Carefully lower the transmission assembly.

29. Remove and discard the O-ring.

30. For vehicles equipped with a Power Take-Off (PTO) assembly, prior to installing the transmission, the PTO assembly must be flushed and cleaned to remove any foreign material. Failure to remove foreign material from the PTO assembly may result in subsequent transmission concerns

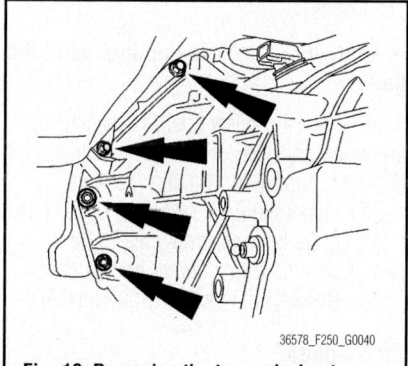

Fig. 10 Removing the transmission to engine bolts

To install:

➡Install a new Oil-To-Air (OTA) cooler as part of a transmission overhaul, or when installing a remanufactured transmission due to major metallic failure, multiple clutches or clutch plate failures or sufficient component wear, which results in metallic contamination.

➡Prior to installation of a new or overhauled transmission, the transmission fluid cooler tubes must be cleaned. Otherwise transmission failure can occur.

➡Prior to installation of the assembly, the torque converter pilot hub must be lubricated or damage to the torque converter or the engine crankshaft can occur.

31. Lubricate the torque converter pilot hub with multi-purpose grease.

32. Rotate the torque converter so the green or orange paint daub on the converter is in the 12 o'clock position.

33. If the Torque Converter Retainer has not been installed during the assembly of the transmission, install the Torque Converter Retainer to hold the torque converter in place while moving and positioning the transmission in place. Once the transmission is in place, prior to bolting it to the engine, remove the Torque Converter Retainer.

34. Install a new transmission fluid filler tube O-ring.

35. Position the transmission in place. While raising the transmission up into the engine compartment, align the transmission fluid filler tube with the stub tube on the transmission using the transmission fluid level indicator as a guide.

36. While installing the transmission to the engine, align the torque converter studs with the mounting holes in the flexplate.

37. Install the 9 transmission-to-engine bolts. Tighten to 35 ft. lbs. (47 Nm).

38. Using a suitable tool, rotate the crankshaft pulley to gain access to the torque converter-to-flexplate nuts.

39. Install the 8 new torque converter-to-flexplate nuts. Tighten to 35 ft. lbs. (47 Nm).

40. Install the cylinder block opening cover.

41. Position the steering damper and install the steering damper-to-frame bolt and nut. Tighten to 76 ft. lbs. (103 Nm).'

42. If equipped with dual generators, rotate the tensioner and Install the outer accessory drive belt onto the crankshaft pulley.

43. Install the front transmission fluid cooler tube. Tighten to 30 ft. lbs. (40 Nm).

44. Install the rear transmission fluid cooler tube. Tighten to 30 ft. lbs. (40 Nm).

45. Install the transmission insulator-to-extension housing bolts. Tighten to 76 ft. lbs. (103 Nm).

46. If required, install a new transmission insulator stud. Tighten to 55 ft. lbs. (75 Nm).

47. Position the crossmember to the transmission insulator and loosely install the transmission insulator-to-crossmember nut.

48. Install the LH crossmember-to-frame bolts. Tighten to 60 ft. lbs. (81 Nm).

49. Install the RH crossmember-to-frame bolts. Tighten to 60 ft. lbs. (81 Nm).

50. Install the bracket and loosely install the bracket bolts.

a. Install the transmission support crossmember-to-frame bracket.

b. Loosely install the transmission support crossmember-to-frame bracket bolts.

51. Tighten the RH crossmember-to-frame bolts. Tighten to 60 ft. lbs. (81 Nm).

52. Tighten the transmission insulator-to-crossmember nuts. Tighten to 85 ft. lbs. (115 Nm).

53. Reconnect the wire harness to the frame.

54. Connect the RH and LH wiring harness to the side of the transmission.

55. Connect the Output Shaft Speed (OSS) sensor.

56. Connect the Turbine Shaft Speed (TSS)/intermediate shaft speed sensor.

57. Connect the transmission vehicle harness connector.

➡**If the vehicle is equipped with a Power Take-Off (PTO) unit, all or part of the PTO unit will need to be installed.**

58. To prevent selector lever cable damage, do not apply force to the selector lever cable assembly between the manual control lever and the selector lever cable bracket.

59. Connect the selector lever cable.

60. Install the selector lever cable housing bracket and selector lever cable housing bracket bolts. Tighten to 35 ft. lbs. (47 Nm).

61. Install the selector lever cable to the manual control lever.

62. For 4WD vehicles, install the transfer case.

63. Install the rear driveshaft.

64. Use the following guidelines for the in-line transmission fluid filter:

a. If the transmission was overhauled and the vehicle was equipped with an in-line transmission fluid filter, install a new in-line transmission fluid filter.

b. If the transmission was overhauled and the vehicle was not equipped with the in-line transmission fluid filter, install a new in-line transmission fluid filter.

c. If the transmission is being installed for a non-internal repair, do not install an in-line transmission fluid filter or transmission fluid filter kit.

d. If installing a new or a Ford-authorized remanufactured transmission, install an in-line transmission fluid filter.

e. Prior to lowering the vehicle, install a new in-line transmission fluid filter or a transmission fluid filter kit.

65. With the installation of an overhauled or remanufactured transmission, the transmission fluid cooler tubes must be cleaned and back flushed, and then the

transmission fluid flow verified in order to prevent repeat repairs.

66. Adjust the selector lever cable. Verify that the vehicle starts in PARK and NEUTRAL and the reverse lamps illuminate in REVERSE.

67. With the engine running and the transmission at normal operating temperature 150-170°F (66-77°C), check and adjust the transmission fluid level, and check for any leaks.

68. If transmission fluid is needed, add transmission fluid in increments of 0.24L (0.5 pt) until the correct level is achieved (transmission fluid should be in the hot range cross-hatched area of the transmission fluid level indicator).

69. For vehicles equipped with a PTO assembly, prior to installing the transmission, the PTO assembly must be flushed and cleaned to remove any foreign material. Failure to remove foreign material from the PTO assembly may result in subsequent transmission concerns.

MANUAL TRANSMISSION ASSEMBLY

REMOVAL & INSTALLATION

Tremec 5 Speed

See Figure 11.

1. Before servicing the vehicle, refer to the Precautions Section.

2. With the vehicle in NEUTRAL, position it on a hoist.

3. Disconnect the battery ground cable.

4. Remove the 2 screws under the shift lever boot and slide the shift boot back, unseating it from the front tab.

5. Slide the upper shifter boot assembly up the shift lever to access the 2 shifter lever bolts.

6. Remove the 2 shift lever bolts and lever.

7. Remove the 4 bolts and the lower shift lever.

8. Disconnect the reverse lamp switch electrical connector.

9. If the transmission is being disassembled, remove the drain plug and drain the transmission fluid.

10. Remove the starter. For additional information, refer to Section 303-06A .

11. Remove the driveshaft. For additional information, refer to Section 205-01 .

12. Disconnect the wiring harness retainers from the transmission and crossmember and position the harness aside.

➡**Slide the heat shield back and rotate counterclockwise 45 degrees while pushing inward.**

13. Remove the clutch slave cylinder and position aside.

14. Disconnect the fuel tubes from the fuel tube clip on the transmission case and position aside.

15. Using the High Lift Transmission Jack, support the transmission. Securely strap the High Lift Transmission Jack to the transmission.

16. Remove the 2 transmission mount nuts from the crossmember.

17. Loosen the top 2 RH crossmember bracket nuts.

18. Remove the 4 lower RH crossmember nuts.

19. Remove the 3 LH crossmember bolts and remove the crossmember.

20. Remove 2 engine-to-transmission spacer plate bolts.

21. Remove the 7 transmission-to-engine bolts.

22. Remove the transmission by moving the transmission rearward until the input

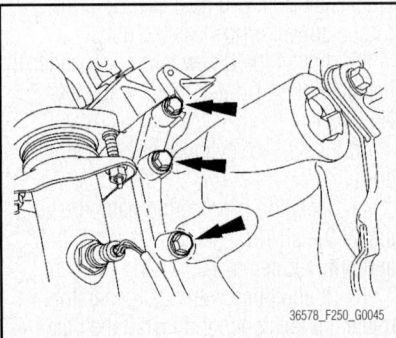

36578_F250_G0045

Fig. 11 Removing the transmission to engine bolts

shaft is clear of the clutch, then lower from the vehicle

To install:

23. Using the High Lift Transmission Jack, raise and position the transmission to the engine and clutch.

24. Install the 7 transmission-to-engine bolts. Tighten to 46 ft. lbs. (63 Nm).

25. Position the crossmember and install the 3 LH crossmember bolts. Tighten to 66 ft. lbs. (90 Nm).

26. Install the 4 RH crossmember nuts and tighten the upper 2 bracket nuts. Tighten to 52 ft. lbs. (70 Nm).

27. Install the 2 transmission mount nuts. Tighten to 60 ft. lbs. (81 Nm).

28. Install the 2 engine-to-transmission

spacer plate bolts. Tighten to 21 ft. lbs. (28 Nm).

29. Remove the transmission jack.

30. Position the clutch slave cylinder. Push in and rotate the clutch slave cylinder clockwise 45 degrees to the lock position.

31. Install the starter.

32. Install the rear driveshaft.

33. Connect the reverse lamp switch electrical connector then attach the wiring harness retainers to the transmission and crossmember.

34. Install the fuel tubes into the plastic clip on the transmission case.

➡**Refill the transmission with clean, specified lubricant. If drained, install the drain plug and refill the transmission. Tighten to 20 Nm (177 lb-in).**

➡**When installing, a slight wiggle may be necessary to seat the shifter lever between the detents.**

➡**Apply threadlock to the threads of the bolts.**

35. Install the lower gear shift lever and the 4 bolts.

➡**Apply threadlock to the threads of the bolts.**

36. Slide the shifter boot assembly up the lower gear shift lever and install the shift handle and bolts. Tighten to 21 ft. lbs. (28 Nm).

37. Install the front tab of the upper and lower shifter boot assembly under the floor pan. Install the 2 rear shifter boot screws.

38. Connect the battery ground cable.

ZF 6 Speed

See Figure 12.

1. Remove the four screws and the outer shift lever boot.

2. Remove the upper gearshift lever.

3. Remove the lower shift lever boot.

4. Remove the lower gearshift and shift housing.

Vehicles with a manual shift transfer case

5. Shift the transfer case into 4H.

6. Remove the screws that attach the bezel and boot assembly to the floor.

7. Remove the bolt that attaches the shift lever to the transfer case control lever assembly, and remove the shift lever, and the bezel and boot assembly.

All vehicles

8. Raise and support the vehicle.

9. If the transmission is being disassembled, drain the transmission fluid.

10. Remove the catalytic converter.

11. Remove the starter.

➡Index-mark the driveshaft to the transfer case flange. Remove and discard the driveshaft bolts.

12. Disconnect the rear driveshaft and position it aside.

13. Remove the transfer case, if equipped.

14. Disconnect the fuel lines from the transmission.

15. Remove any power take-off (PTO) equipment, if equipped.

16. Using a transmission jack, support the transmission.

✳✳ CAUTION

Securely strap the jack to the transmission.

17. Remove the four right crossmember nuts.

18. Remove the three left crossmember bolts.

19. Disconnect the wire harness from the crossmember.

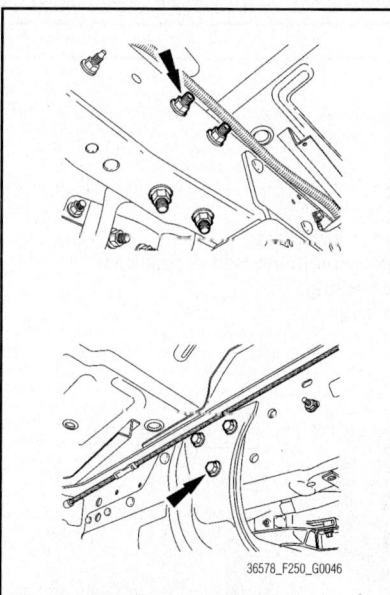

36578_F250_G0046

Fig. 12 Removing the LH and RH crossmember bolts

20. Remove the transmission mount nuts and the crossmember.

21. Disconnect the reverse lamp switch electrical connector.

22. Disconnect wiring harness from the transmission.

23. Push the clutch slave cylinder inward, then rotate counterclockwise 45 degrees to remove.

24. Disconnect the transmission cooling tubes.

25. Remove the dust cover bolts.

26. Remove the transmission-to-engine bolts.

27. Move the transmission rearward until the input shaft is clear of the clutch, then lower from the vehicle.

To install:
All vehicles

28. Using the transmission jack, raise and position the transmission to the engine and clutch.

29. Install the transmission-to-engine bolts. Torque to 46 ft. lbs. (63 Nm). Vehicles equipped with diesel engines have six bolts. Those equipped with gasoline engines, have seven bolts.

30. Position the crossmember in the vehicle. Install the transmission mount nuts. Torque to 60 ft. lbs. (81 Nm).

31. Install the left crossmember bolts. Torque to 52 ft. lbs. (70 Nm).

32. Install the right crossmember nuts. Torque to 52 ft. lbs. (70 Nm).

33. Attach the wire harness to the crossmember.

34. Install the dust cover bolts. Torque to 21 ft. lbs. (28 Nm).

➡6.0L equipped vehicles do not have a dust cover.

35. Remove the transmission jack.

36. Connect the transmission cooler tubes. Torque to 20 ft. lbs. (27 Nm).

37. Install the clutch slave cylinder. Rotate the clutch slave cylinder clockwise 45 degrees to lock in position.

38. Install the starter.

39. Install the catalytic converter.

40. Install the transfer case, if equipped. If the transfer case control lever assembly was removed from the transmission, it must be correctly aligned.

41. Connect the driveshaft.

42. Install any power take-off (PTO) equipment, if equipped.

43. Connect the fuel lines to the transmission.

44. Connect the reverse lamp switch electrical connector.

45. Connect the wiring harness to the transmission.

46. Refill the transmission to specification.

47. Lower the vehicle.

✳✳ WARNING

Do not use a silicone sealing compound.

➡Do not wait longer than ten minutes to tighten the six bolts due to the rapid cure time of the sealant.

48. Install the lower gearshift lever and shift housing assembly. Apply gasket maker

to the shift housing and the main case. Torque to 17 ft. lbs. (23 Nm).

49. Install the lower shift lever boot.

50. Apply threadlock and sealer to the gearshift lever bolts. Install the upper gearshift lever. Torque to 21 ft. lbs. (28 Nm).

51. Install the screws.

Vehicles with a manual shift transfer case

52. Position the shift lever with the bezel and boot assembly and install the bolt. Torque to 20 ft. lbs. (27 Nm).

53. Position the bezel and boot assembly and install the screws.

54. Verify the shift sequence from 2H to 4L to 2H.

CLUTCH DRIVEN DISC & PRESSURE PLATE

REMOVAL & INSTALLATION
See Figures 13 and 14.

1. Remove the transmission.

2. Index-mark the clutch pressure plate and the flywheel, if reinstalling these parts.

3. Remove the clutch pressure plate bolts, the clutch pressure plate and the clutch disc.

4. Inspect the transmission input shaft pilot bearing:

  a. For misalignment and looseness in the crankshaft (gasoline engine) or flywheel (diesel engine).

  b. Needle rollers for scoring, discoloration, wear and broken rollers.

  c. Seal for damage and lubricant leakage.

  d. Install a new transmission input shaft pilot bearing if any of these conditions are present.

➡Use emery cloth to remove minor imperfections in the clutch disc friction surface.

5. Inspect the clutch disc for:

  a. Oil and grease saturation.

  b. Worn and loose rivets at the hub.

  c. Broken springs.

  d. Wear and rust on the splines.

  e. Install a new clutch disc if any of these conditions are present.

➡If necessary, use a suitable cleaning solution to remove any oil film from the clutch pressure plate friction surface.

6. Inspect the clutch pressure plate levers for heavy wear associated with binding. Also, inspect for substantial difference in lever wear. Inspect the clutch pressure plate friction surface for scoring, burning, heat checking, distortion, warping and dishing.

7. Install a new clutch pressure plate if any of these conditions are present.

➡**If necessary, use a suitable cleaning solution to clean the flywheel clutch surface.**

8. Inspect the flywheel for:
   a. Surface cracks.
   b. Heat check.
   c. Glazing.
   d. Scoring.
   e. Scratches or grooves.
   f. For minor damage, finish the flywheel surface with coarse emery cloth or with a fine grade (400 grit) sandpaper. To polish the surface, stroke parallel to the machine lines.
9. Inspect the ring gear for worn, chopped or broken teeth.

To install:

➡**Sometimes, when removing the transmission, the input shaft will remove a considerable amount of lubricant from the transmission input shaft pilot bearing.**

10. Lubricate the transmission input shaft pilot bearing with grease, as necessary.

➡**When installing the original clutch pressure plate, reset the wear indicator before installing the clutch pressure plate on the flywheel.**

11. Reset the wear indicator.
   a. Using a suitable press and adapter, press downward on the fingers until the adjusting ring moves freely.
   b. Rotate the adjusting ring counterclockwise to compress the tension springs. Hold the adjusting ring in this position.
   c. Release the pressure on the fingers. The adjusting ring will now stay in the reset position.
12. Position the clutch disc on the flywheel and the clutch alignment tool in the pilot bearing to align the clutch disc.
   a. The 5.4L/6.8L engines accept a 1-1/4 in input shaft.
   b. The 6.4L engines accept a 1-3/8 in input shaft with 0.98 in pilot bearing inner diameter.

➡**Align the index marks if installing the original clutch pressure plate.**

13. Install the clutch pressure plate.
   a. Position the clutch pressure plate on the dowels.
   b. The diesel engine flywheel has 2 dowels. The gasoline engine flywheel has 3 dowels.

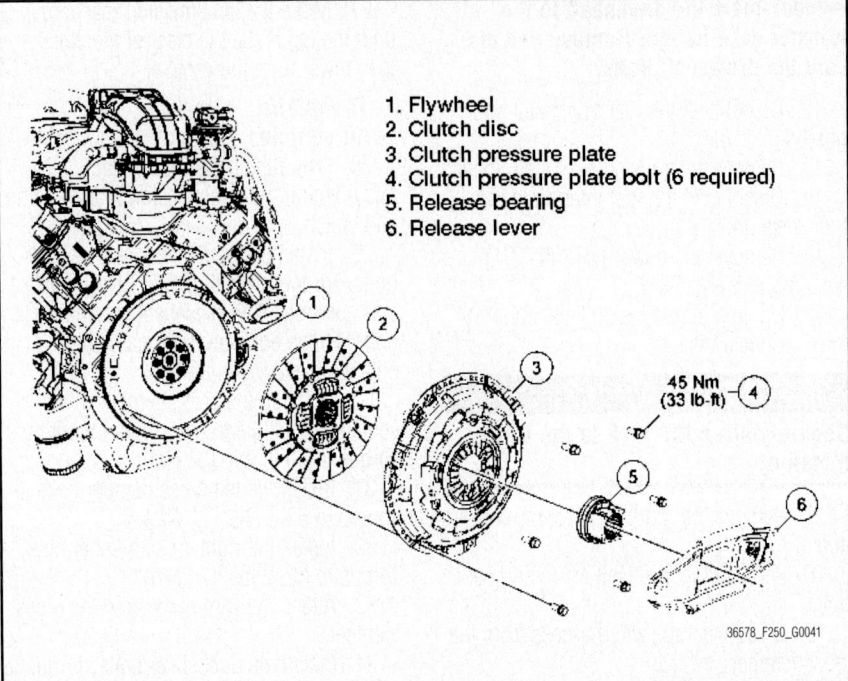

1. Flywheel
2. Clutch disc
3. Clutch pressure plate
4. Clutch pressure plate bolt (6 required)
5. Release bearing
6. Release lever

45 Nm (33 lb-ft)

36578_F250_G0041

Fig. 13 Exploded view of the driven disc and pressure plate assembly—5.4L and 6.8L Engines

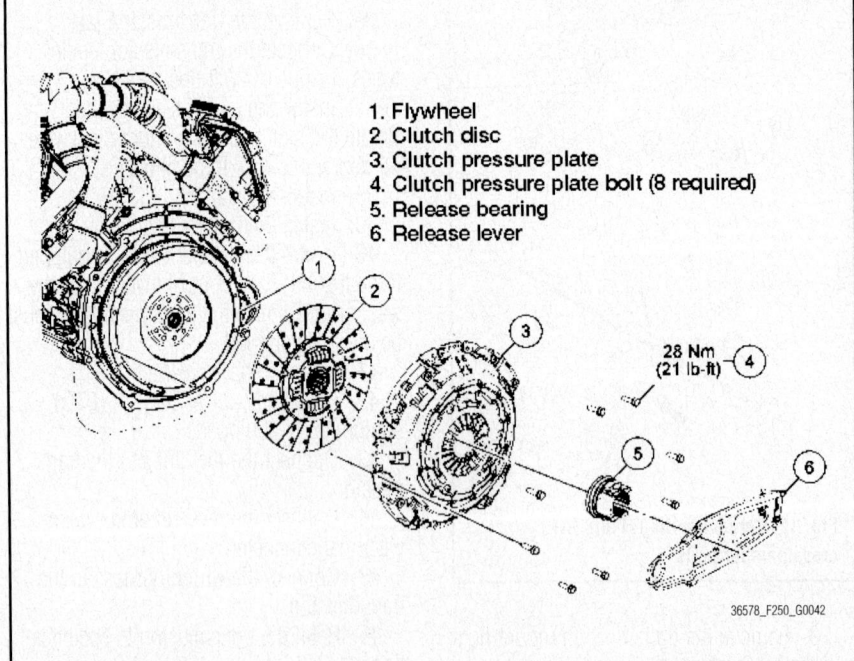

1. Flywheel
2. Clutch disc
3. Clutch pressure plate
4. Clutch pressure plate bolt (8 required)
5. Release bearing
6. Release lever

28 Nm (21 lb-ft)

36578_F250_G0042

Fig. 14 Exploded view of the driven disc and pressure plate assembly—5.4L and 6.8L Engines

c. Using a suitable clutch alignment tool, align the clutch disc and the pressure plate.
   d. Install the clutch pressure plate bolts and tighten in a star pattern sequence.
   e. For the 5.4L and 6.8L engines, tighten to 33 ft. lbs. (45 Nm).
   f. For the 6.4L engine, tighten to 21 ft. lbs. (28 Nm).
   g. Remove the clutch alignment tool.

14. Install the transmission.
15. Test the system for normal operation.

CLUTCH MASTER CYLINDER

REMOVAL & INSTALLATION

See Figure 15.

➡Remove the entire clutch hydraulic system from the vehicle as an assembly when installing a new clutch master cylinder assembly. The clutch master cylinder is only serviced in the assembly.

1. Before servicing the vehicle, refer to the precautions in the beginning of this section.

2. Disconnect the clutch hydraulic tube from the dash clip.

3. With the vehicle in NEUTRAL, position it on a hoist.

➡The clutch control system has a heat shield that covers most of the tube and clutch slave cylinder. To unlock the slave cylinder, slide the heat shield back and off of the slave cylinder. Slide the heat shield over the tube.

4. Compress and twist the clutch slave cylinder counterclockwise to unlock it from the transmission.

5. Disconnect the clutch hydraulic tube from the floor pan clip. Position the clutch slave cylinder and hydraulic tube forward below the left engine bank. This will make it easier to unlock the clutch master cylinder from the clutch pedal and support bracket by reducing tension on the hydraulic tube.

✴✴ WARNING

The clutch pedal is under spring tension.

6. Unlock the push rod retaining clips and separate the clutch master cylinder push rod from the clutch pedal.

7. Remove and discard the clutch master cylinder push rod bushing.

8. Remove the switch cover and the clutch pedal position switch from the clutch master cylinder push rod.

9. Separate the power distribution box from the bracket to gain access to the clutch master cylinder.

36578_FTRK_G0082

Fig. 15 Remove the clutch master cylinder from the clutch pedal and support bracket assembly

10. Compress and twist the clutch master cylinder clockwise 45 degrees to unlock it from the clutch pedal and support bracket. Remove the clutch master cylinder from the clutch pedal and support bracket.

11. Remove the clutch hydraulic system from the vehicle.

✴✴ CAUTION

Brake fluid is harmful to painted and plastic surfaces. If brake fluid is spilled onto a painted or plastic surface, wash the surface with water immediately.

12. To install, reverse the removal procedure.

✴✴ CAUTION

When installed correctly, the flat side of the clutch pedal position switch must face the tab protruding from the clutch master cylinder and the switch wiring connector must be in the 12 o'clock position. Incorrect installation will damage the clutch pedal position switch and cause insufficient clutch pedal travel.

✴✴ CAUTION

The push rod is not removable after installing it in the clutch master cylinder.

13. Install the new push rod in the clutch master cylinder.

14. Install a new push rod bushing.

15. Make sure to slide the heat shield forward and over the slave cylinder until it contacts the transmission case.

16. Press the clutch pedal to seat the push rod in the clutch master cylinder.

17. Test the system for normal operation.

CLUTCH SLAVE CYLINDER

REMOVAL & INSTALLATION

➡The clutch slave cylinder, the clutch master cylinder and the hydraulic lines make up the clutch hydraulic system. The clutch slave cylinder is only serviced in the assembly.

CLUTCH HYDRAULIC SYSTEM BLEEDING

1. Remove the clutch reservoir cap and diaphragm. Check the fluid level. Fill the reservoir to or above the step mark. Install the cap and diaphragm.

2. Depress and release the clutch pedal several times to stabilize the clutch hydraulic system.

3. With the vehicle in NEUTRAL, position it on a hoist.

4. Remove the bleeder screw cover and attach a vinyl hose to the bleeder hose. Place the other end of the vinyl hose into a clear container partially filled with brake fluid.

5. Have an assistant depress and release the clutch pedal 5 times, then hold the clutch pedal down. With the clutch pedal depressed, loosen the bleeder screw to let air escape the clutch system. Tighten the bleeder screw. Repeat this process until no air comes through the vinyl hose.

6. Tighten the bleeder screw and install the bleeder screw cover.

7. Slowly pump the clutch pedal several times to verify there is no fluid leakage.

8. Depress and release the clutch pedal 2 short cycles and 3 full-travel cycles.

9. Make sure the clutch reservoir is at the correct level. Refill as necessary.

FRONT AXLE ASSEMBLY

REMOVAL & INSTALLATION

➡Suspension fasteners are critical parts because they affect performance of vital components and systems and their failure can result in major service expense. They must be replaced with the same part number or an equivalent part if replacement is necessary. Do not use a replacement part of lesser quality or substitute design. Torque values must be used as specified during reassembly to make sure of correct retention of these parts.

1. Before servicing the vehicle, refer to the precautions in the beginning of this section.

2. With the vehicle in NEUTRAL, position it on a hoist.

3. Remove the wheel and tire.

4. Remove the wheel knuckles.

5. Remove and discard the stabilizer bar link bolt and disconnect the stabilizer bar from the frame. To install, tighten to 111 ft. lbs. (150 Nm).

6. Disconnect the ABS wire from the radius arms.

7. Remove the brake hose bracket bolts and brake hose brackets from the axle.

➡Index-mark the driveshaft to the pinion flange to maintain correct driveline balance.

8. Remove and discard the 4 driveshaft

flange bolts and 2 retainers, and disconnect the driveshaft at the front axle. Wrap electrical tape around the bearing cups and using mechanic's wire, position the front driveshaft aside. To install, tighten to 26 ft. lbs. (35 Nm).

➡It is necessary to load the suspension to remove the trackbar. Load the springs by allowing most of the front vehicle weight to rest on the axle.

9. Support the axle with a suitable jack, and lower the vehicle enough to relieve the tension on the trackbar.

10. Remove and discard the trackbar nut and disconnect the trackbar at the axle, then using mechanic's wire, position the trackbar aside.

   a. Relieve the load on the suspension after disconnecting the trackbar.

   b. Maintain the jack support of the axle assembly.

   c. To install, tighten to184 ft. lbs. (250 Nm).

11. Disconnect the vent tube and the routing clip.

12. Position aside the hublock vacuum hoses.

   a. On the LH side of the axle, remove the hublock vacuum hose bolt.

   b. Position aside the hublock vacuum hoses.

13. Remove and discard the 2 lower shock bolts. To install, tighten to 111 ft. lbs. (150 Nm).

14. Lower the axle.

15. Remove the front coil springs.

16. Remove and discard the 4 trailing arm bolts. To install, tighten to 221 ft. lbs. (300 Nm).

17. Lower the axle from the vehicle.

18. To install, reverse the removal procedure.

FRONT AXLE HOUSING

REMOVAL & INSTALLATION

See Figures 16 and 17.

1. Raise and safely support the vehicle.
2. Remove the wheel and tire assembly.
3. Remove the wheel knuckles. For additional information, refer to the procedure in this section.
4. Remove the stabilizer bar link nuts and disconnect the stabilizer bar links from the frame.
5. Disconnect the anti-lock brake system (ABS) wire from the radius arms.
6. Remove the brake hose bracket bolts and brake hose brackets from the axle.

➡Index-mark the driveshaft to the com-

panion flange to maintain proper driveline balance.

➡If new driveshaft flange bolts are not available, coat the threads of the driveshaft flange bolts with Threadlock and Sealer.

7. Remove and discard the driveshaft flange bolts and disconnect the driveshaft at the front axle. Wrap electrical tape around the bearing cups and using mechanic's wire, position the front driveshaft aside.

➡It is necessary to load the suspension to remove the track bar. Load the springs by allowing most of the front vehicle weight to rest on the axle.

8. Support the axle with a suitable jack, and lower the vehicle enough to relieve the tension on the track bar. Remove the track bar nut and disconnect the track bar at the axle, then using mechanic's wire, position the track bar aside.

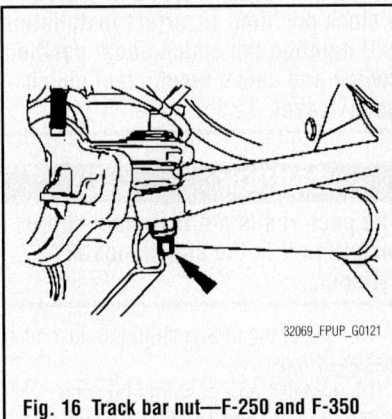

Fig. 16 Track bar nut—F-250 and F-350

9. Relieve the load on the suspension after disconnecting the track bar.

10. Leave the jack supporting the axle for removal from the vehicle.

11. Disconnect the vent tube and the routing clip.

12. Position aside the Hublock vacuum hoses. On the LH side of the axle, remove the Hublock vacuum hose bolt.

13. Remove the lower shock bolts.

14. Lower the axle.

15. Remove the front coil springs.

16. Remove the trailing arm bolts.

17. Lower the axle from the vehicle.

18. To install, reverse the removal procedure. Check and, if necessary, fill the axle with the specified lubricant. Observe the following torques:

- Trailing arm bolts: 300 Nm (221 ft. lbs.).
- Lower shock bolts: 150 Nm (111 ft. lbs.).

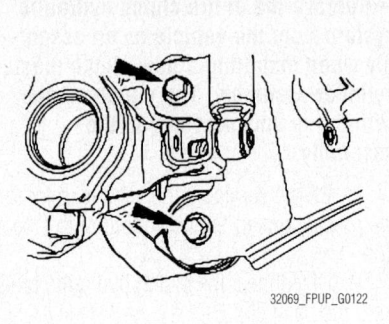

Fig. 17 Trailing arm bolts—F-250 and F-350

- Hublock vacuum hose bolt: 20 Nm (15 ft. lbs.).
- Track bar nut: 250 Nm (184 ft. lbs.).
- Driveshaft flange bolts: 35 Nm (26 ft. lbs.).
- Brake hose bracket bolts: 18 Nm (13 ft. lbs.).
- Stabilizer bar link nuts: 80 Nm (59 ft. lbs.).

FRONT PINION SEAL

REMOVAL & INSTALLATION

See Figures 18 through 20.

1. Before servicing the vehicle, refer to the Precautions Section.
2. With the vehicle in **Neutral**, raise and support the vehicle.
3. Match-mark the front driveshaft and the front axle flange to maintain driveline balance.
4. Disconnect the front driveshaft from the front axle flange, and position it aside.
5. Rotate the pinion with a Nm (inch lb.) torque wrench. Record the torque necessary to maintain rotation of the pinion through several revolutions.
6. Remove and discard the nut and

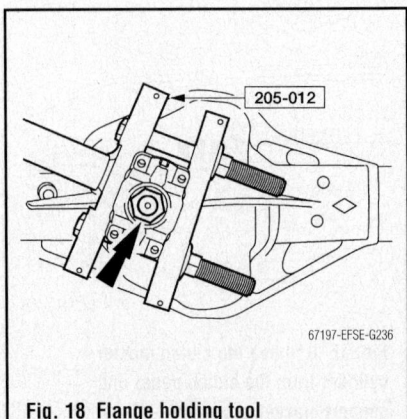

Fig. 18 Flange holding tool

washer. Use the special tool to prevent the flange from turning while removing the nut.

➡**Match-mark the flange and the pinion shaft.**

7. Using the special tool, remove the flange.

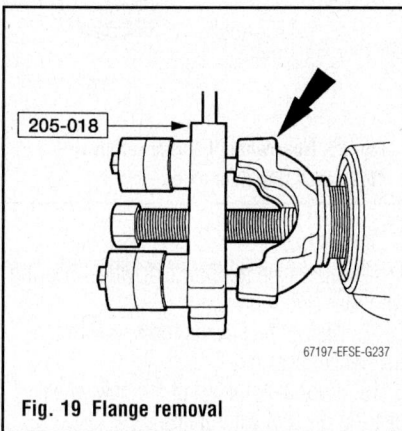

Fig. 19 Flange removal

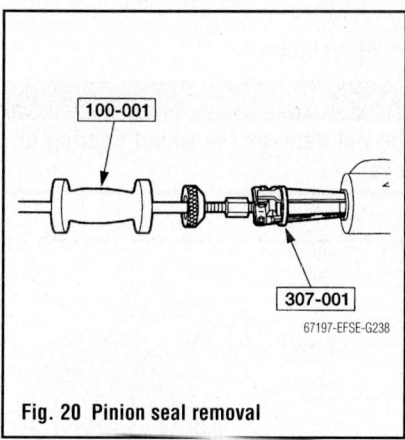

Fig. 20 Pinion seal removal

8. Using the special tools, remove the pinion seal. Discard the seal.
9. Clean and inspect the following:
   a. The seal mounting surface.
   b. The flange lugs and the flange end that contacts the bearing cone.
   c. Verify that the flange nut counterbore and the seal contact surfaces are smooth and free of nicks.

To install:
10. Using a suitable driver, install the pinion seal. Lightly coat the pinion seal lip with lubricant.

❋❋ WARNING

Never use a metal hammer on the pinion flange or install the flange with power tools. If necessary, use a plastic hammer to tap on a tight fitting flange.

➡**Align the index marks.**

11. Lightly coat the flange splines and seal mating area with lubricant, then install the flange with a new washer and nut.

❋❋ WARNING

Never back off the pinion nut to reduce preload. If preload reduction is necessary, install a new collapsible spacer and pinion nut.

12. Tighten the pinion nut as follows:
   a. Use the special tool to prevent the flange from turning while tightening the nut. Remove the special tool when taking pinion bearing torque preload readings.
   b. Take frequent pinion bearing torque preload readings.

➡**Never back off the pinion nut to reduce preload. If preload reduction is necessary, install a new collapsible spacer and pinion nut.**

   c. For new pinion bearing installation, tighten the pinion nut to a rotating torque of 1.7–3.4 Nm (15–30 inch lbs.) Pinion nut torque range is 217–678 Nm (160–500 ft. lbs.).
   d. For original pinion bearing installation, the reading must be 0.56 Nm (5 inch lbs.) more than the initial reading taken during the disassembly procedure.
13. Connect the front driveshaft to the front axle flange. Torque to 26 ft. lbs. (35 Nm).
14. Check and, if necessary, fill the axle with the specified lubricant.
15. Lower the vehicle.

REAR AXLE HOUSING

REMOVAL & INSTALLATION

Ford 10.5 Inch Axle And Dana 80 Axle
See Figures 21 and 22.

1. Remove the wheels and tires.
2. Disconnect the rear anti-lock brake sensor.
3. Remove the nuts and the stone shield.
4. Remove the caliper pin bolts.
5. Remove the rear disc brake caliper.

➡**Make sure the parking brake control is fully released.**

6. Release the tension on the parking brake system.
   a. Have an assistant pull the front parking brake cable and conduit to its full range.
   b. Insert a suitable retainer.

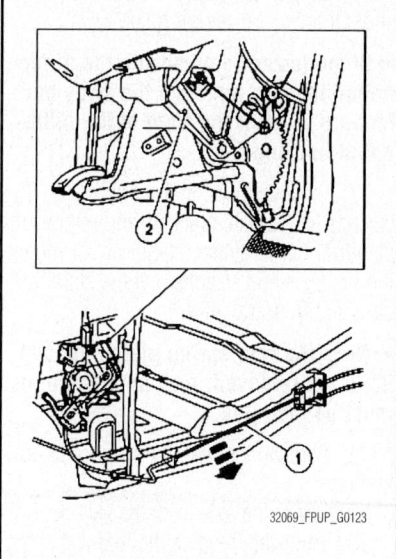

Fig. 21 Parking brake tension release— F-250 and F-350

7. Disconnect the parking brake cable at the parking brake lever.
8. Remove the cable clamp bolt.
9. Unclip the brake line and remove the retainer from the parking brake cable bracket and position the cable aside.
10. Remove the bolt from the brake hose bracket.
11. Remove the vent hose at the brake hose junction block.
12. Remove the brake junction block from the rear axle housing and let it hang.
13. Remove the brake lines from the rear axle housing tie strap (but not from the disc brake calipers) and let the tubing hang.

❋❋ CAUTION

Strap the axle securely to the jack.

14. Use a suitable transmission jack to support the axle.
15. Remove the lower shock absorber nuts and bolts.

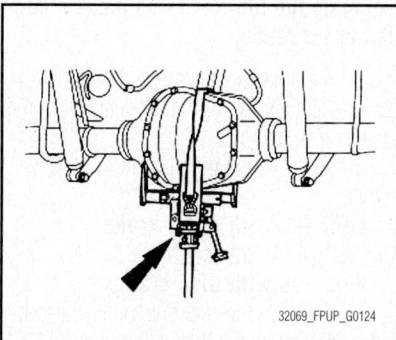

Fig. 22 Use a suitable transmission jack to support the axle—F-250 and F-350

16. Loosen the nuts from both lower ends of the stabilizer bar links.

➡ **When lowering or raising the differential housing, position the sway bar forward to clear the front of the differential housing.**

17. Remove the nuts from both stabilizer bar retainer-to-axle brackets and remove the stabilizer bar retainers, stabilizer bar mounting brackets and U-bolts. Let the stabilizer bar hang from the links.

➡ **Once the rear spring plate nuts and bolts are removed, new nuts and bolts must be installed.**

18. Remove the rear spring plate U-bolts and nuts.

19. Lower the axle from the vehicle.

20. To install, reverse the removal procedure. Observe the following torques:
- Spring plate U-bolt nuts: 186 ft. lbs. (251 Nm)
- Caliper pin bolts: 27 ft. lbs. (36 Nm)
- Stone shield nuts: 46 ft. lbs. (62 Nm)
- Shock absorber bolts: 47 ft. lbs. (63 Nm)
- Stabilizer bar bracket U-bolt nuts: 30 ft. lbs. (40 Nm)
- End links top and bottom: 52 ft. lbs. (70 Nm)

REAR AXLE SHAFT, BEARING & SEAL

REMOVAL & INSTALLATION

10.25 Inch Ring Gear Axles
See Figures 23 through 27.

1. Before servicing the vehicle, refer to the Precautions Section.

All Vehicles

2. Raise and support the vehicle.
3. Remove the wheel and tire assembly.

➡ **Empty the lubricant into a clean container for reuse.**

4. Remove the 10 differential housing cover bolts and drain the lubricant from the rear axle housing.
5. Remove the differential housing cover.

Vehicles with drum brakes

6. Remove the rear brake drums.

Vehicles with disc brakes

7. Remove the rear disc brake caliper. Wire the rear disc brake caliper aside.
8. Remove the rear brake disc.

All vehicles

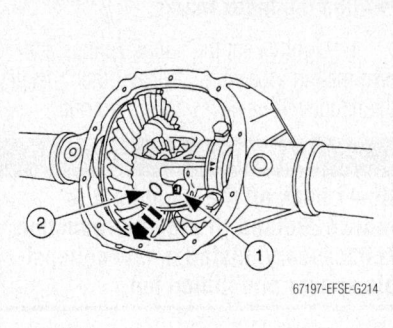

Fig. 23 Lock bolt (1); pinion shaft (2)—10.25 inch ring gear axles

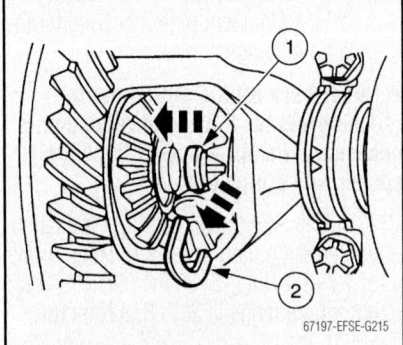

Fig. 24 Axle shaft (1); U-washer (2)—10.25 inch ring gear axles

9. Remove and discard the differential pinion shaft lock bolt.
10. Remove the differential pinion shaft.

❊❊ WARNING

Do not damage the rubber O-rings in the axle shaft grooves.

11. Push in the axle shafts.
12. Remove the U-washers.

❊❊ WARNING

Do not damage the wheel bearing oil seal.

13. Remove the axle shaft.

➡ **If the wheel bearing oil seal is leaking, the axle housing vent may be plugged with foreign material.**

➡ **If only a new seal needs to be installed, use care to avoid damaging the seal bore.**

14. Using a suitable seal remover, remove the axle shaft oil seal. Discard the oil seal.
15. Inspect the rear wheel bearing and axle shaft for wear or damage.
16. If necessary, using the special tools, remove the rear wheel bearing.

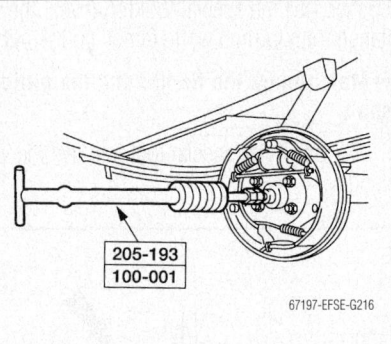

Fig. 25 Rear wheel bearing removal—10.25 inch ring gear axles

To install:
17. Lubricate the new rear wheel bearing with rear axle lubricant.
18. Using the special tools, install the rear wheel bearing.
19. Lubricate the lip of the new wheel bearing oil seal with grease.
20. Using the special tools, install the wheel bearing oil seal.

All vehicles

❊❊ WARNING

Do not damage the wheel bearing oil seal.

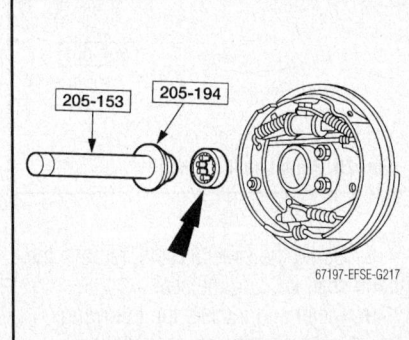

Fig. 26 Rear wheel bearing installation—10.25 inch ring gear axles

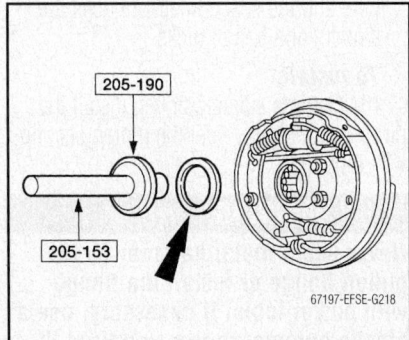

Fig. 27 Oil seal installation—10.25 inch ring gear axles

21. Install the axle shaft.

Do not damage the rubber O-rings in the U-washer grooves.

22. Position the two U-washers on the button end of the axle shafts.
23. Pull the axle shafts outward.

➡️**If a new pinion shaft lock bolt is unavailable coat the threads with Threadlock prior to installation.**

24. Align the hole in the differential pinion shaft with the case lock bolt hole.
25. Install a new differential pinion shaft lock bolt. Torque to 15–30 ft. lbs. (20–40 Nm).

Vehicles with drum brakes
26. Install the rear brake drums.

Vehicles with disc brakes
27. Install the rear brake disc.
28. Install the rear disc brake caliper.

➡️**Clean the gasket mating surface of the rear axle and the differential housing cover.**

29. Apply a new continuous bead of sealant to the differential housing cover.

➡️**The differential housing cover must be installed within 15 minutes of application of the silicone, or new sealant must be applied. If possible, allow one hour before filling with lubricant to make sure the silicone sealant has correctly cured.**

30. Install the differential housing cover.
31. Install the 10 differential housing cover bolts. Torque to 33 ft. lbs. (45 Nm).
32. Fill the rear axle housing with 2.37 liters (5 pints) with the specified lubricant.

Always remove any corrosion, dirt or foreign material present on the mounting surfaces of the wheel or the surface of the wheel hub or brake drum or disc that contacts the wheel. Installing wheels without correct metal-to-metal contact at the wheel mounting surfaces can cause the lug nut to loosen and the wheel to come off while the vehicle is in motion, causing loss of control.

33. Clean the wheel hub and mounting surfaces.
34. Install the tire and wheel assembly.

Ford Full-Floating Axle
See Figures 28 through 31.

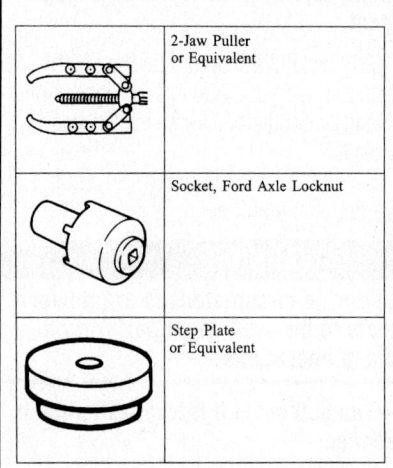

Fig. 28 Tools needed for the following hub removal on the Ford Full-Floating axle

1. Before servicing the vehicle, refer to the Precautions Section.
2. Set the parking brake.
3. Loosen the retaining bolts.
4. Raise the vehicle to the desired working height, keeping the axle parallel with the floor.
5. Release the parking brake.
6. Remove the wheel(s).
7. Remove the brake caliper and rotor on the single rear wheel axle.
8. Remove the retaining bolts and axle shaft.

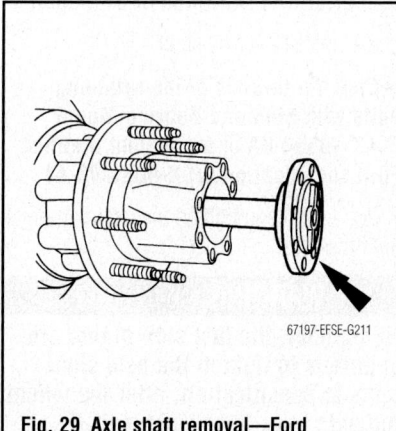

Fig. 29 Axle shaft removal—Ford full-floating axle

➡️**The hub nuts are right-hand thread (right hub) and left-hand thread (left hub). Each hub nut is stamped RH or LH.**

9. Install the Ford Axle Locknut Socket so that the drive tangs of the tool engage the four slots in the hub nut.

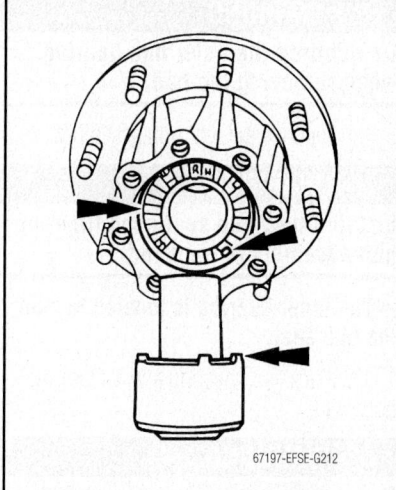

Fig. 30 Install the Ford Axle Locknut Socket so that the drive tangs of the tool engage the four slots in the hub nut

Discard the hub nut if the hub nut comes apart during removal.

Under no circumstances are power tools to be used when performing these operations.

➡️**The hub nut will ratchet during this operation.**

10. Remove the hub nut (counterclockwise for right-hand thread; clockwise for left-hand thread).
11. Install the Step Plate.
12. Install the 2-Jaw Puller and loosen the rear hub to the point of removal.

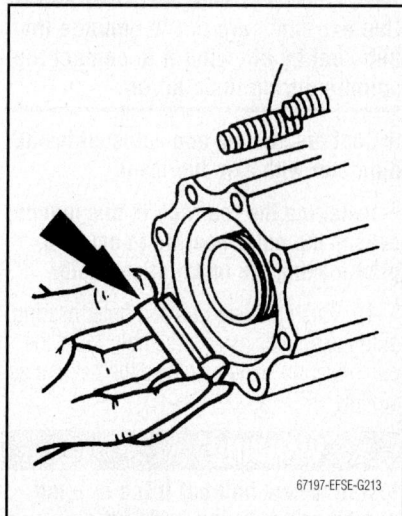

Fig. 31 Install the Step Plate—Ford full-floating axle

※※ WARNING

Do not drop the outer hub bearing when removing the hub.

13. Remove the rear hub assembly.

※※ WARNING

Install a new hub seal each time the hub assembly is removed.

➡ **The inner bearing is located behind the hub seal.**

14. Pack each bearing and replace the hub seals.

※※ WARNING

Use extreme care not to scratch or gouge the seal or bearing surfaces.

15. If after hub removal, the hub seal or seal inner sleeve remains on the spindle, remove using the Step Plate and the 2-Jaw Puller.

16. Inspect the seal surface and inner shoulder for scratches and damage. Remove all scratches, gouges or galling damage with No. 600 or finer crocus cloth.

To install:

➡ **Clean the spindle thoroughly after removing the rear hub.**

17. Coat the spindle with axle lubricant.

※※ WARNING

The hub bearings must be prelubed prior to installation.

18. Fill the hub cavity with 1 oz. of axle lubricant.

※※ WARNING

Use extreme care not to damage the hub seal by allowing it to contact the spindle during installation.

➡ **Coat the spindle and hub seal inside diameter with axle lubricant.**

➡ **Installing the rear hub in this manner causes the outer bearing to act as a pilot making the installation easier.**

19. Push the rear hub and outer bearing onto the spindle as an assembly. Hold the outer bearing seated and use the bearing as a pilot.

※※ WARNING

Install a new hub nut if the hub nut comes apart during installation.

➡ **Make sure the hub nut tab is located**

in the keyway prior to thread engagement.

20. Install the hub nut on the spindle. Turn the hub nut clockwise for right-hand thread or counterclockwise for left-hand thread.

21. Position the Ford Axle Locknut Socket on the hub nut.

※※ WARNING

Under no circumstances are power tools to be used when performing these operations.

➡ **The hub nut will ratchet as torque is applied.**

22. Tighten the hub nut, rotating the rear hub occasionally while tightening. Torque to 60 ft. lbs. (81 Nm).

23. Adjust hub nuts as follows:

a. For new bearings, ratchet back five teeth or notches (⅛ turn) on the hub nut. Five notches must be felt during this operation in order to have performed it correctly.

b. For used bearings, ratchet back seven teeth or notches (⅙ turn) on the hub nut. Seven notches must be felt during this operation to have performed it correctly.

24. Inspect the axle shaft O-ring seal for cracks, nicks or wear and replace it if required.

➡ **Lubricate the O-ring seal with lubricant prior to installation of axle shaft.**

25. Install the axle shaft.

➡ **Coat the threads of the retaining bolts with Stud and Bearing Mount E0AZ-19554-BA or equivalent meeting Ford specification WSK-M2G349-A1.**

26. Install and tighten the retaining bolts until they seat.

※※ WARNING

Remember, the last step of this procedure is to tighten the axle shaft bolts to specification, after the wheel lug nuts have been tightened.

27. Install the brake rotor and caliper on the single rear wheel axles.

28. Install the wheels and tires but do not tighten the lug nuts to specification at this time.

29. Check the axle lubricant level.

30. Lower the vehicle.

31. Tighten the wheel lug nuts.

32. Tighten the axle shaft retaining bolts. Torque to 80 ft. lbs. (109 Nm).

Dana Axle Full-Floating Axle

See Figures 32 and 33.

1. Before servicing the vehicle, refer to the Precautions Section.

All vehicles

2. Remove the tire and wheel assembly.
3. Remove the anchor plate.
4. Remove the axle shaft.

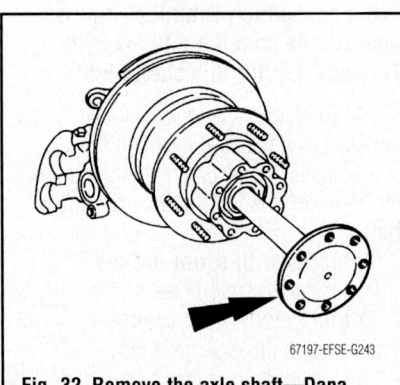

Fig. 32 Remove the axle shaft—Dana Axle Full-Floating Axle

Dana 70

➡ **Make sure that the drive tangs on the special tool engage the four slots of the hub nut.**

5. Using special tool 205-282, or equivalent, remove the hub nut.

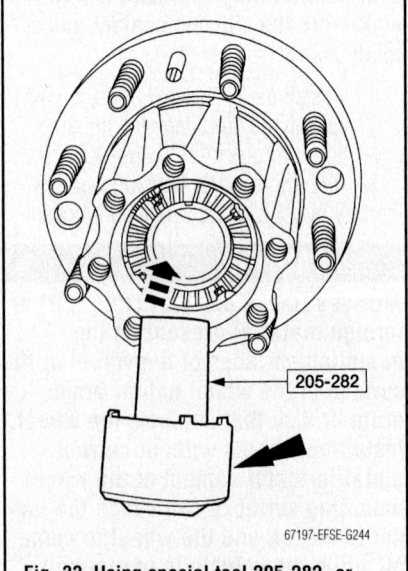

Fig. 33 Using special tool 205-282, or equivalent, remove the hub nut—Dana Axle Full-Floating Axle

All vehicles

6. Remove the outer rear wheel bearing.
7. Remove the rear hub and brake disc assembly.

8. Remove the bolts and separate the rear hub from the rear brake disc.

9. Inspect the rear hub for the following:

- Cracks and damage around the bolt holes.
- Oversized holes.

To install:

✳✳ WARNING

Install a new rear hub seal after removing the rear hub from the axle. A damaged or worn seal can permit bearing lubricant to reach the brake linings, resulting in ineffective brake operation. Failure to follow these instructions may result in personal injury.

✳✳ WARNING

Clean and remove any dirt or foreign material in the rear hub bolt holes.

10. Install a new rear hub seal.

11. Position the rear brake disc on the rear hub and install the bolts. Torque to 66–88 ft. lbs. (89–119 Nm).

✳✳ WARNING

Thoroughly clean the spindle. Wrap the spindle threads with electrician's tape to prevent damage while installing the rear hub and brake disc assembly.

✳✳ WARNING

Lightly coat the spindle and pack each rear wheel bearing with Premium Long-Life Grease XG-1-C or equivalent meeting Ford specification ESA-M1C75-B.

12. Prepare the spindle for rear hub installation.

13. Slide the rear hub and brake disc assembly over the axle housing spindle. Remove the electrician's tape.

14. Install the outer rear wheel bearing.

15. Start the hub nut making sure that the tab aligns correctly in the keyway prior to thread engagement.

➡**Apply inward pressure to the socket to separate the ratcheting components of the hub nut.**

16. To adjust the bearings, tighten the nut to 70 ft. lbs. (95 Nm).

17. Back off the nut 90 degrees.

18. Tighten the nut to 18 ft. lbs. (24 Nm). To verify that there is no side-to-side end

play, attach a magnetically mounted dial indicator to the spindle end and place the dial indicator tip on the outboard surface of the hub. Check for side-to-side end play. Final bearing adjustment has zero end play. The maximum torque to rotate the hub is 2.3 Nm (20 inch lbs.) when end play is zero.

19. Install the axle shaft.

20. Install the anchor plate.

21. Install the tire and wheel assembly.

Dana 80

1. Before servicing the vehicle, refer to the Precautions Section.

2. Remove the wheels and tires.

3. Remove the 2 nuts and the stone shield. To install, tighten to 46 ft. lbs. (62 Nm).

4. Remove the 2 caliper pin bolts. To install, tighten F-250/350 to 27 ft. lbs. (36 Nm).

➡**Do not allow the rear disc brake caliper to hang by the brake hose. Provide suitable support or damage to the component may occur.**

5. Position aside the rear disc brake caliper.

➡**Make sure the parking brake control is fully released.**

6. Release the tension on the parking brake system.

   a. Have an assistant pull the front parking brake cable and conduit to its full range.

   b. Insert a suitable retainer.

7. Disconnect the parking brake cable at the parking brake lever.

8. Disconnect the rear anti-lock brake sensor electrical connector. Release the harness clips and position the harness aside.

9. Remove the cable clamp bolt.

10. Unclip the brake line and remove the retainer from the parking brake cable bracket and position the cable aside.

11. Remove the bolt from the brake hose bracket.

12. Remove the brake tube from the brake tube retaining clip.

13. Remove the vent hose at the brake hose junction block.

14. Remove the brake junction block from the rear axle housing and position it aside.

15. Remove the brake tubes from the rear axle housing tie strap (but not from the disc brake calipers) and position it aside

✳✳ WARNING

Secure the assembly to the jack. Avoid any obstructions while lower-

ing and raising the jack. Contact with obstructions may cause the assembly to fall off the jack, which may result in serious personal injury.

16. Use a suitable transmission jack to support the axle.

17. Remove the 2 lower shock absorber nuts and bolts. To install, tighten to 66 ft. lbs. (90 Nm).

18. Loosen the 2 nuts from both lower ends of the stabilizer bar links. To install, tighten to 76 (103 Nm).

➡**When lowering or raising the differential housing, position the sway bar forward to clear the front of the differential housing.**

19. Remove the 4 nuts from both stabilizer bar retainer-to-axle brackets and remove the stabilizer bar retainers, stabilizer bar mounting brackets and U-bolts. Let the stabilizer bar hang from the links. To install, tighten to 30 ft. lbs. (40 Nm).

➡**Once the rear spring plate nuts and bolts are removed, new rear spring plate nuts and bolts must be installed.**

20. Remove the rear spring plate U-bolts and nuts. To install, tighten to 136 ft. lbs. (185 Nm).

21. Lower the axle from the vehicle.

22. To install, reverse the removal procedure.

23. Install the wheels and tires.

24. Make sure the axle is filled to specification.

Dana S110 and S130

See Figures 34 and 35.

1. Before servicing the vehicle, refer to the Precautions Section.

2. Remove the rear wheels and tires.

3. If equipped, remove the stabilizer bar.

4. Release the parking brake cable tension.

5. Disconnect the parking brake cables at the equalizer and the anchor plate.

6. Remove the frame anchors and position the parking brake cables aside.

7. Disconnect the rear wheel speed sensor electrical connector. Release the harness clips and position the harness aside.

8. For vehicles with split pin yoke, index-mark the driveshaft and pinion flange. Remove and discard the 4 driveshaft bolts and 2 retainers. To install, tighten the new yoke bolts to 46 ft. lbs. (62 Nm).

9. For vehicles with circular flange, index-mark the driveshaft and pinion flange.

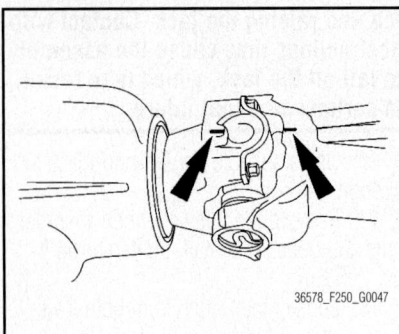

Fig. 34 Index-marking the driveshaft and pinion flange—Split pin yoke

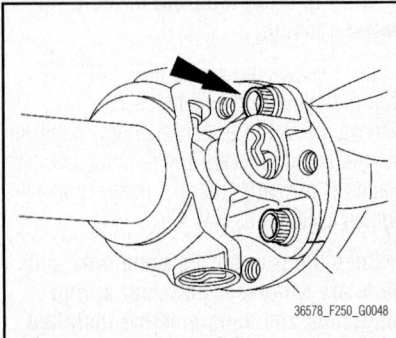

Fig. 35 Index-marking the driveshaft and pinion flange—Circular flange

Remove and discard the 4 bolts. To install, tighten the new flange bolts to 74 ft. lbs. (100 Nm).

✴✴ WARNING

Do not apply heat or flame to the shock absorber or strut tube. The shock absorber and strut tube are gas pressurized and could explode if heated. Failure to follow this instruction may result in serious personal injury.

10. Remove and discard the 2 lower shock absorber nuts and bolts. To install, tighten the new nuts and bolts to 66 ft. lbs. (90 Nm).

11. Disconnect the axle vent hose at the crossmember.

12. Disconnect the brake tube-to-flexible hose fitting at the crossmember. Remove the clip and position the flexible hose aside.

13. Plug the flexible hose and brake tube.

14. Support the axle with a suitable floor jack.

➡**Final tightening of the U-bolt nuts must be done with the suspension at curb height or incorrect clamp load may occur.**

15. Remove and discard the 8 U-bolt nuts and the 4 U-bolts.

✴✴ WARNING

Secure the assembly to the jack. Avoid any obstructions while lowering and raising the jack. Contact with obstructions may cause the assembly to fall off the jack, which may result in serious personal injury.

16. Carefully lower the axle and remove it from the vehicle.

17. To install, reverse the removal procedure.

18. To install the 8 U-bolt nuts and the 4 U-bolts, with the suspension at curb height, tighten the new nuts evenly in a cross-type pattern in 4 stages:

   a. Stage 1: Tighten to 74 ft. lbs. (100 Nm).
   b. Stage 2: Tighten to 148 ft. lbs. (200 Nm).
   c. Stage 3: Tighten to 222 ft. lbs. (300 Nm).
   d. Stage 4: Tighten to 295 ft. lbs. (400 Nm).

19. Bleed the brake system.

REAR PINION SEAL

REMOVAL & INSTALLATION

Ford 10.5 inch Ring Gear Axle
See Figures 36 through 38.

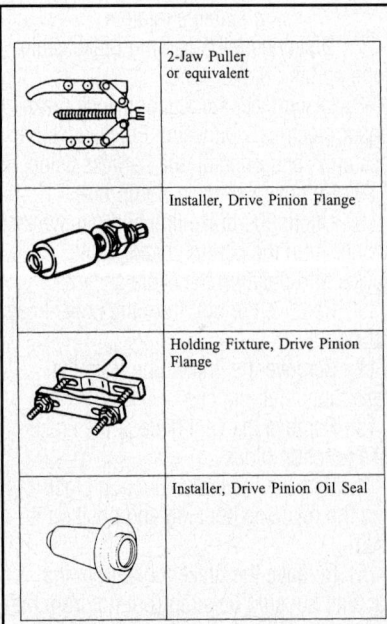

	2-Jaw Puller or equivalent
	Installer, Drive Pinion Flange
	Holding Fixture, Drive Pinion Flange
	Installer, Drive Pinion Oil Seal

Fig. 36 Tools necessary for this job—Ford 10.5 inch ring gear axle pinion seal replacement

1. Before servicing the vehicle, refer to the Precautions Section.

➡**The rear wheels and brake calipers must be removed to prevent brake drag during drive pinion bearing preload adjustment.**

2. Remove the rear brake calipers.

3. Remove the driveshaft.

4. Install an Nm (inch-pound) torque wrench on the pinion nut, and record the rotational torque required to maintain rotation of the pinion through several revolutions.

➡**After removal of the pinion nut, discard it. A new nut must be used for installation.**

5. Use a flange holder to hold the pinion flange while removing the pinion nut.

6. Mark the pinion flange in relation to the drive pinion stem to ensure proper alignment during installation.

7. Use a 2-jaw puller to remove the pinion flange.

8. Force up on the metal flange of the rear axle drive pinion seal. Install locking pliers to the seal flange and strike with a hammer until the rear axle drive pinion seal is removed.

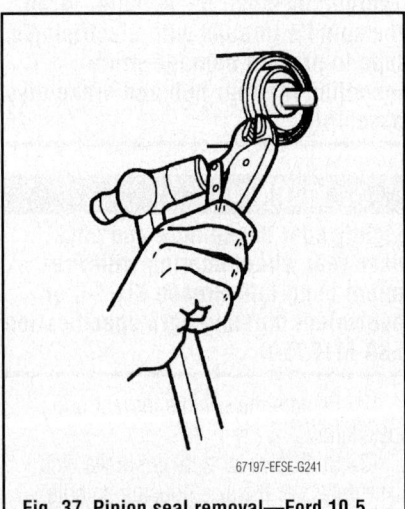

Fig. 37 Pinion seal removal—Ford 10.5 inch ring gear axle

To install:

9. Lubricate the new pinion seal. Use Premium Long-Life Grease XG-1-C or equivalent meeting Ford specification ESA-M1C75-B.

➡**If the rear axle drive pinion seal becomes misaligned during installation, remove the rear axle drive pinion seal and replace it with a new seal.**

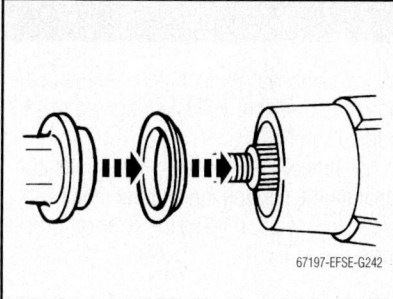

Fig. 38 Pinion seal installation—Ford 10.5 inch ring gear axle

10. Use the Pinion Seal Replacer to install the rear axle drive pinion seal.

11. Lubricate the pinion flange splines. Use SAE 75W-140 Synthetic Rear Axle Lubricant F1TZ-19580-B or equivalent meeting Ford specification WSL-M2C192-A.

➡**Disregard the scribe marks if a new pinion flange is being installed.**

12. Align the pinion flange with the drive pinion shaft.

13. With the pinion flange in place in the rear axle housing, install the pinion flange using the Companion Flange Replacer.

14. Position the new pinion nut.

➡**Under no circumstances is the pinion nut to be backed off to reduce preload. If reduced preload is required, a new collapsible spacer and pinion nut must be installed.**

15. Use the Flange Holder to hold the pinion flange while tightening the pinion nut.

   a. Tighten the pinion nut, rotating the pinion occasionally to make sure the cone and roller bearings are seating properly. Take frequent cone and roller bearing torque preload readings until the originally recorded preload reading is obtained by rotating the pinion with an Nm (inch-pound) torque wrench.

   b. If the original recorded preload is lower than specifications, tighten to the appropriate specification for used bearings. If the preload is higher than specification, tighten the nut to the original reading as recorded.

   c. Pinion bearing preload (used pinion bearing): 0.9–1.5Nm (8–14 inch lbs)

   d. Pinion bearing preload (new pinion bearing): 1.8–3.3Nm (16–29 inch lbs.)

   e. Initial minimum breakaway torque (Traction-Lok®): 27Nm (20 ft. lbs)

16. Install the driveshaft.

17. Install the brake calipers.

Dana 80 Rear Axle
See Figure 39.

1. Before servicing the vehicle, refer to the Precautions Section.

2. Raise the vehicle on a hoist or raise the rear end of the vehicle with a jack. Install safety stands under the frame rails and lower the jack or hoist far enough to allow the rear axle to drop into the rebound position for working clearance.

➡**To maintain driveline balance, mark the driveshaft components so they can be reinstalled in their original positions.**

3. Disconnect the driveshaft at the rear axle, and position it aside.

➡**Index-mark the flange to the pinion shaft.**

4. While using a flange holding tool to prevent the flange or yoke from turning, remove the pinion nut.

5. Using a 2-jaw puller, remove the flange or yoke.

6. Using a bushing remover and slide hammer, remove the pinion seal.

7. Clean the rear axle pinion seal seat.

To install:

➡**If the pinion seal becomes cocked during installation, remove the seal and install a new one. Make sure the garter spring remains in place during assembly. If the spring is dislodged, a new pinion seal must be installed.**

8. Install the seal using a suitable driver. Coat the pinion seal rubber lips with lubricant.

9. Using the special tool, 205-285, or equivalent, install the pinion flange.

✳✳ WARNING
Always install a new washer and locknut.

10. Install the new washer and locknut. Torque to 470 ft. lbs. (637 Nm).

11. Install the driveshaft at the rear axle. Observe the following torques:
- Split pin yoke: 26 ft. lbs. (35 Nm)
- Circular flange: 82 ft. lbs. (111 Nm)

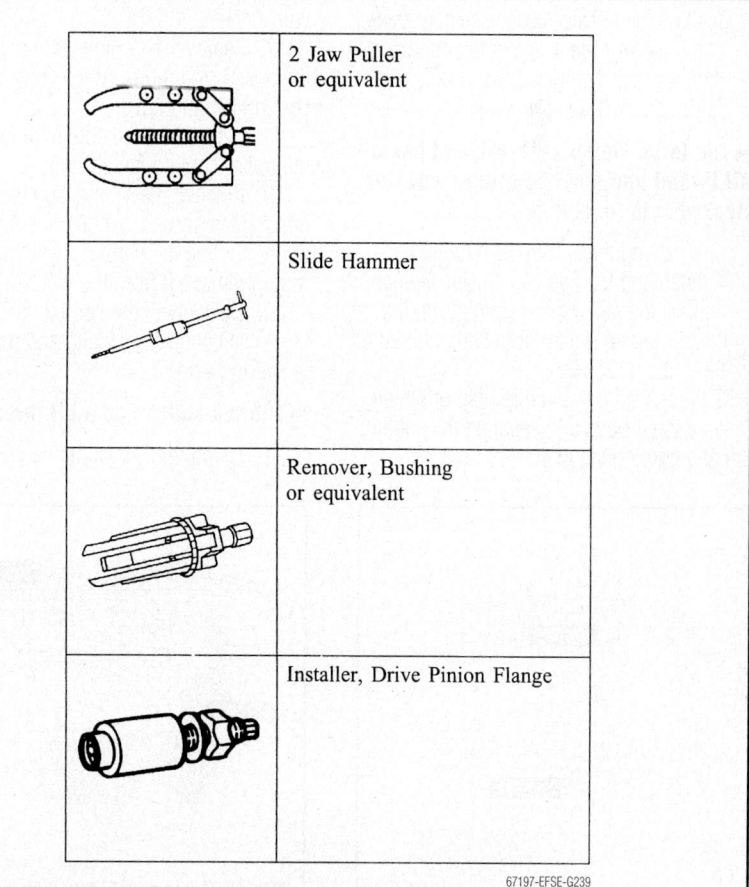

Fig. 39 Tools necessary for this job—Dana 80 axle

ENGINE COOLING

ENGINE FAN

REMOVAL & INSTALLATION

Gasoline Engines

See Figure 40.

1. For 5.4L engines:

   a. Remove the Air Cleaner (ACL) outlet pipe.

➡ **The large clutch assembly nut has a RH thread and must be rotated counterclockwise to remove it.**

   b. Using the Fan Pulley Holding Wrench and the Fan Clutch Nut Wrench, remove the fan and fan clutch from the coolant pump pulley. To install, tighten to 41 ft. lbs. (55 Nm).

2. For 6.8L engines:

   a. With the vehicle in NEUTRAL, position it on a hoist.

   b. Press the 5 position retaining tabs and rotate the lower cooling fan shroud upward until the position retainer tab locks into position.

   c. Disconnect the 2 lower radiator hose assembly position retainers and position the radiator hose assembly aside.

   d. Remove the 4 nuts and position the stabilizer bar downward. To install, tighten to 35 ft. lbs. (48 Nm).

➡ **The large clutch assembly nut has a RH thread and must be rotated counterclockwise to remove it.**

   e. Using the Fan Pulley Holding Wrench and the Fan Clutch Nut Wrench, remove the fan and fan clutch from the coolant pump pulley. To install, tighten to 98 ft. lbs. (133 Nm).

3. If servicing the cooling fan or clutch, remove the 4 bolts and separate the cooling fan and cooling fan clutch.

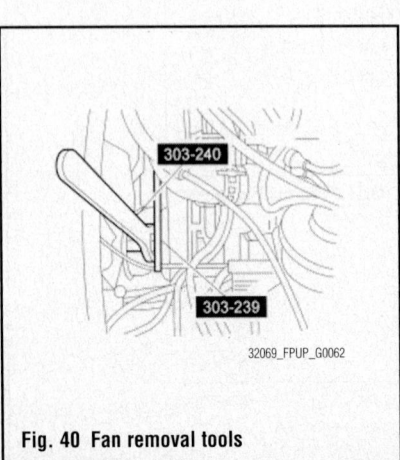

Fig. 40 Fan removal tools

4. To install, reverse the removal procedure.

Diesel Engines

See Figure 41.

1. Drain the cooling system.

2. Remove the RH Charge Air Cooler (CAC) tube.

3. Vehicles with vacuum pump (electric):

   a. Disconnect the vacuum solenoid electrical connector from the vacuum solenoid and disconnect the 2 pin-type retainers from the upper cooling fan shroud.

   b. Disconnect the vacuum hose at the RH battery box.

   c. Disconnect the vacuum hose at the degas bottle.

4. Loosen the clamp and disconnect the LH CAC tube from the turbocharger.

5. Remove the spring clip, disconnect the upper radiator hose from the radiator and position aside. To install, make sure the spring clip is seated correctly.

6. Disconnect the coolant pump-to-fuel cooler hose from the power steering reservoir.

7. Remove the 2 bolts and disconnect the power steering reservoir from the upper cooling fan shroud.

8. Disconnect the coolant hose from the upper cooling fan shroud.

9. Remove the 4 bolts and the upper cooling fan shroud. When removing the upper cooling fan shroud, raise the RH side first to remove it from the vehicle.

10. Disconnect the cooling fan clutch electrical connector. Unclip and position the fan wiring aside.

➡ **The fan clutch has a LH thread.**

11. Using the Fan Clutch Nut Wrench

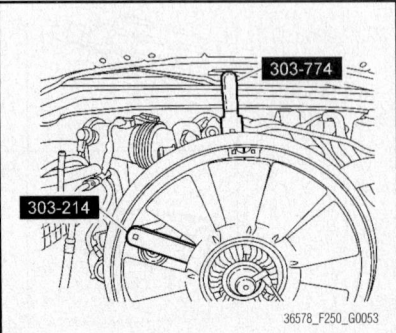

Fig. 41 Fan removal tools to remove the cooling fan and clutch

and Fan Hub Nut Wrench, remove the cooling fan and clutch. To install, tighten to 111 ft. lbs. (150 Nm).

12. If necessary, remove the 6 bolts and separate the cooling fan and the clutch.

13. To install, reverse the removal procedure

RADIATOR

REMOVAL & INSTALLATION

Gasoline Engines

See Figure 42.

1. Before servicing the vehicle, refer to the Precautions Section.

2. With the vehicle in NEUTRAL, position it on a hoist.

3. Drain the engine cooling system.

4. Remove the cooling fan.

5. Remove the cooling fan shroud.

6. Remove the 2 bolts and position the power steering fluid cooler aside.

7. Remove the 2 bolts and disconnect the A/C condenser from the radiator.

➡ **Failure to plug the openings for the transmission cooler hoses may result in siphoning of the transmission fluid. This may result in damage to the transmission, if the transmission fluid is not checked and topped-off after the repair is complete.**

8. Install plugs in the transmission cooler hoses.

9. Remove the 2 bolts and disconnect the 2 hoses and the transmission auxiliary fluid cooler from the radiator.

10. Disconnect the 2 radiator air deflector retainers.

11. Remove the clip and disconnect the lower radiator hose quick connect coupling.

12. If equipped, disconnect the hood switch electrical connector and pushpin retainer.

13. Remove the 4 radiator-to-radiator support bolts, the 2 radiator-to-radiator support clamps and the radiator.

14. If servicing the radiator, remove the radiator support insulators.

15. To install, reverse the removal procedure.

Diesel Engines

1. Remove the upper fan shroud.

2. Remove the 5 pushpins and the top air deflector.

3. Detach the battery cable from the radiator. Position the battery cable aside.

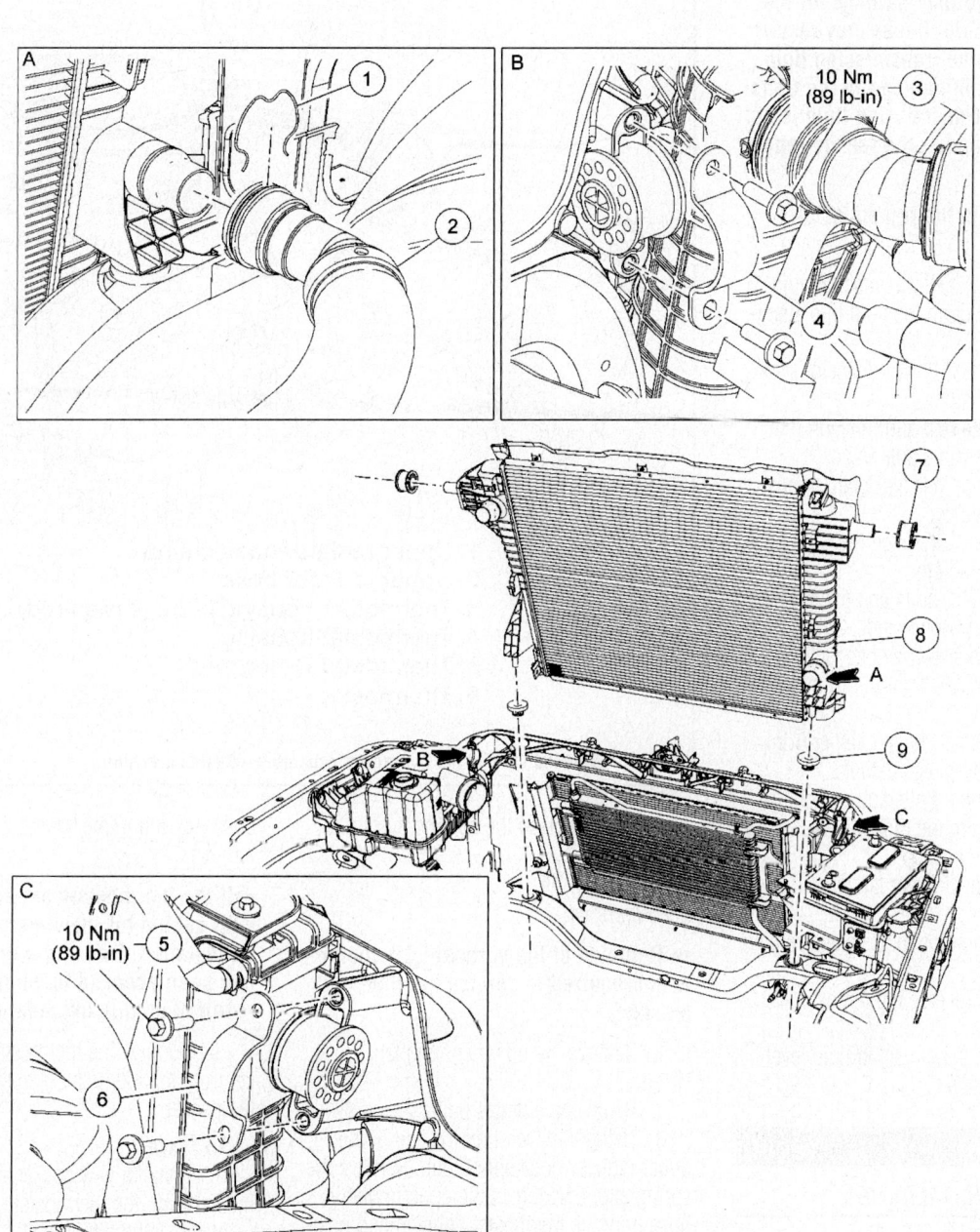

1. Lower radiator hose spring clip
2. Lower radiator hose
3. Radiator-to-radiator support LH bolt (2 required)
4. Radiator-to-radiator support LH bracket (without hood switch)
5. Radiator-to-radiator support RH bolt (2 required)
6. Radiator-to-radiator support RH bracket
7. Radiator upper insulator (2 required)
8. Radiator
9. Radiator lower insulator (2 required)

36578_F250_G0054

Fig. 42 Exploded view of the radiator assembly—Gasoline engines

4. Remove the spring clip and disconnect the lower radiator hose from the radiator.

➡**Failure to plug the openings for the transmission cooler hoses may result in siphoning of the transmission fluid. This may result in damage to the transmission, if the transmission fluid is not checked and topped-off after the repair is complete.**

➡**Install plugs in the transmission cooler hoses.**

5. Disconnect the transmission fluid cooler hoses and drain the fluid into a suitable container.

6. Remove the 2 RH air deflector push-pins from the radiator.

7. Remove the bolt and position the fuel cooling system radiator aside.

8. Remove the 2 LH air deflector push-pins from the radiator.

9. Detach the power steering fluid hose retainer from the radiator.

10. Remove the 2 bolts and position the transmission fluid cooler aside. Secure the transmission fluid cooler as needed.

11. Detach the A/C fitting from the RH battery tray.

12. Detach the A/C hose retainer from the RH inner fender splash shield.

13. Remove the 2 bolts and detach the A/C condenser from the radiator. Secure the A/C condenser as needed.

14. Remove the 2 lower fan shroud bolts.

15. With the help of an assistant, remove the radiator.

16. To install, reverse the removal procedure.

17. Check the transmission fluid level and fill as necessary.

THERMOSTAT

REMOVAL & INSTALLATION

Gasoline Engines

See Figure 43.

1. Drain the engine cooling system.
2. Remove the air cleaner intake pipe.
3. Release the clamp and disconnect the upper radiator hose from the thermostat housing.
4. Remove the bolts and the thermostat housing.
5. Remove the thermostat and the O-ring seal. Discard the O-ring seal.
6. To install, reverse the removal procedure. Install a new O-ring seal and lubricate it with clean coolant. Torque the housing bolts to 89 inch lbs. (10 Nm).

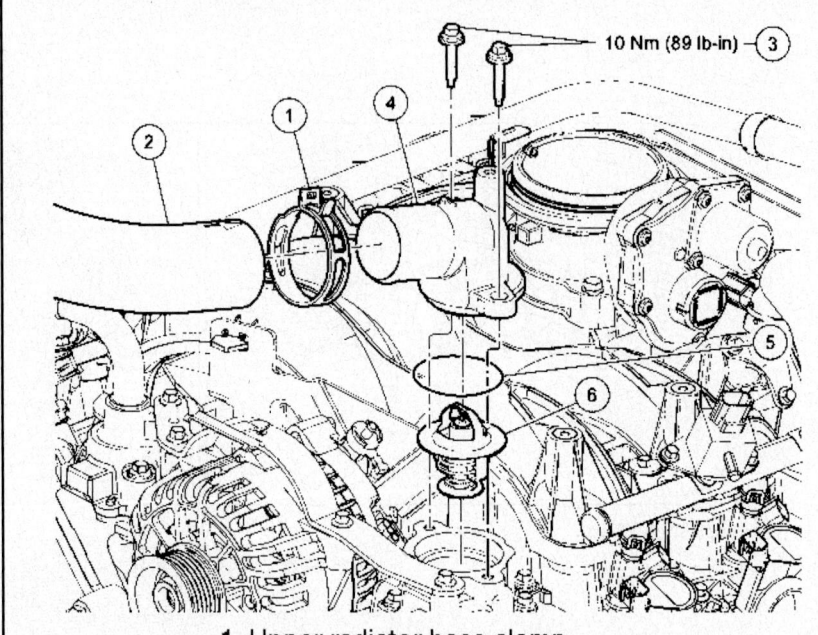

1. Upper radiator hose clamp
2. Upper radiator hose
3. Thermostat housing bolts (2 required)
4. Thermostat housing
5. Thermostat O-ring seal
6. Thermostat

36578_FTRK_G0096

Fig. 43 Exploded view of the thermostat assembly—Gasoline engine

7. Fill and bleed the cooling system.

Diesel Engines

See Figure 44.

➡ **Removal of the vertical EGR cooler is not required to service the thermostats.**

1. Remove the upper cooling fan shroud.
2. Remove the degas bottle.
3. Using a mirror, find the end of the upper radiator hose spring clip. Remove the spring clip, disconnect the upper radiator hose from the thermostat housing and position the upper radiator hose aside.
4. Remove and discard the nut and the vertical EGR cooler lower clamp.
5. Remove the bolt and the vertical EGR cooler lower bracket.
6. Disconnect the wiring from the heater return tube.
7. Remove the 2 bolts and position out the LH heater return tube. Remove and discard the O-ring seal.

➡**The 6.4L diesel engine uses 2 thermostats.**

8. Remove the 4 bolts, the collar and the thermostat housing. Lift the bottom of the

collar up and rotate toward the engine to remove.

➡**If the thermostats are contaminated with engine oil, new thermostats must be installed. Reusing a thermostat that has been exposed to engine oil may result in engine overheating.**

9. Remove the thermostats and the gasket from the thermostat housing. Discard the gasket.

To install:

10. Install a new gasket and the thermostats into the thermostat housing.
11. Install the thermostat housing, the collar and the 4 bolts.

➡**Install a new O-ring seal.**

12. Install the LH heater return tube and the 2 bolts.
13. Connect the wiring to the heater return tube.
14. Position the lower vertical EGR cooler bracket and loosely install the bolt.
15. Install a new vertical EGR cooler lower clamp. Tighten the clamp nut in 3 stages:

    a. Stage 1: Tighten the nut to 89 inch lbs. (10 Nm).

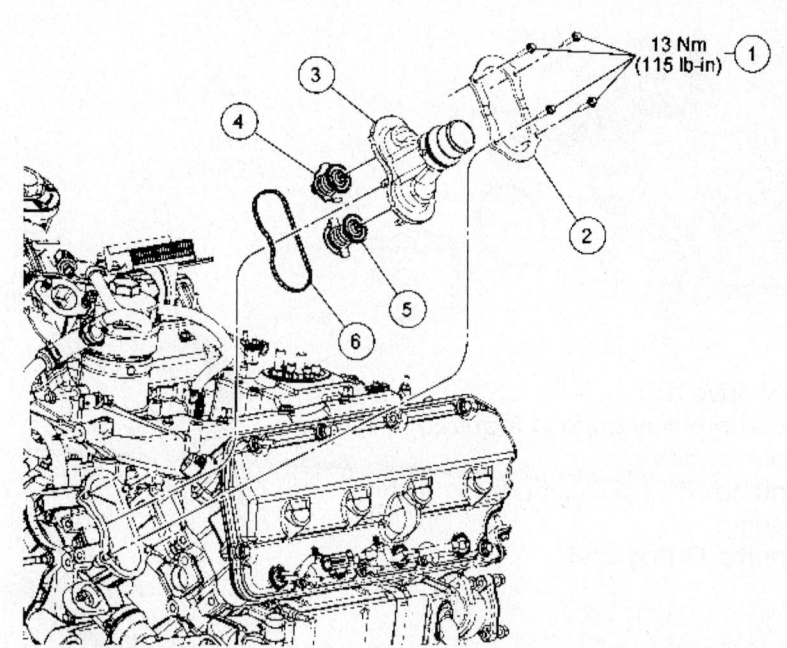

1. Thermostat housing bolts (4 required)
2. Thermostat housing collar
3. Thermostat housing
4. Thermostat without bypass
5. Thermostat with bypass
6. Thermostat housing gasket

36578_F250_G0055

Fig. 44 Exploded view of the thermostat assembly—Diesel engines

b. Stage 2: Loosen the nut 720 degrees (2 complete turns).

c. Stage 3: Tighten the nut to 71 inch lbs. (8 Nm).

16. Tighten the lower EGR cooler bracket bolt. Tighten to 46 ft. lbs. (62 Nm).

17. Connect the upper radiator hose to the thermostat housing. Install the spring clip. Verify the spring clip is correctly seated.

18. Install the degas bottle. For additional information, refer to Degas Bottle - 6.4L Diesel in this section.

19. Install the upper cooling fan shroud.

WATER PUMP

REMOVAL & INSTALLATION

See Figures 45 and 46.

1. Before servicing the vehicle, refer to the precautions section.
2. Drain the engine cooling system.
3. Remove the cooling fan.
4. Loosen the 4 coolant pump pulley bolts.
5. Rotate the belt tensioner clockwise and disconnect the accessory drive belt from the coolant pump pulley.
6. Remove the 4 bolts and the coolant pump pulley.

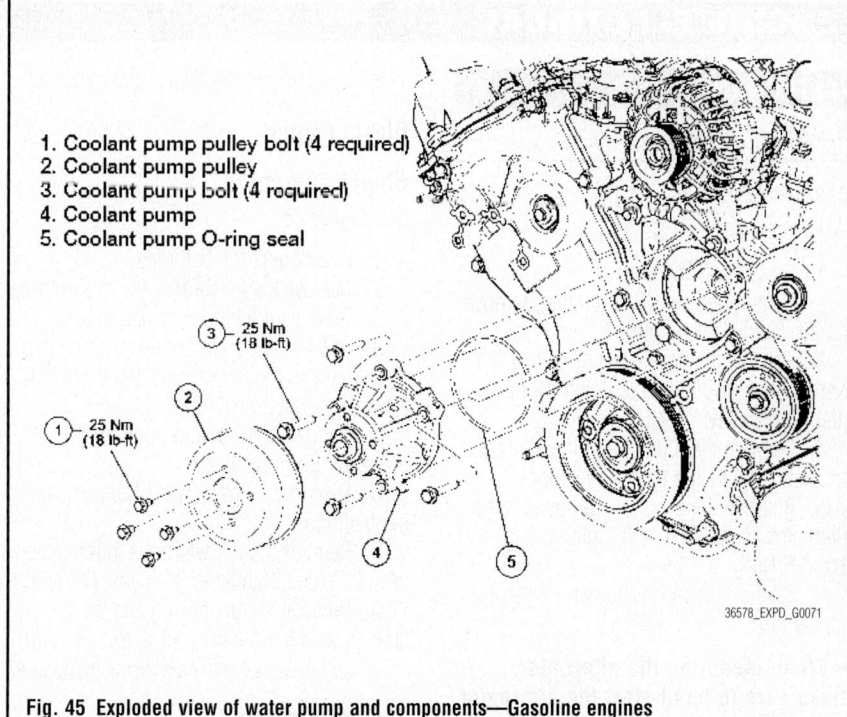

1. Coolant pump pulley bolt (4 required)
2. Coolant pump pulley
3. Coolant pump bolt (4 required)
4. Coolant pump
5. Coolant pump O-ring seal

36578_EXPD_G0071

Fig. 45 Exploded view of water pump and components—Gasoline engines

7. Remove the 4 bolts and the coolant pump. Discard the O-ring seal.

8. To install, reverse the removal procedure and note the following:

a. Tighten water pump pulley bolts and water pump mounting bolts to 18 ft. lbs. (25 Nm).

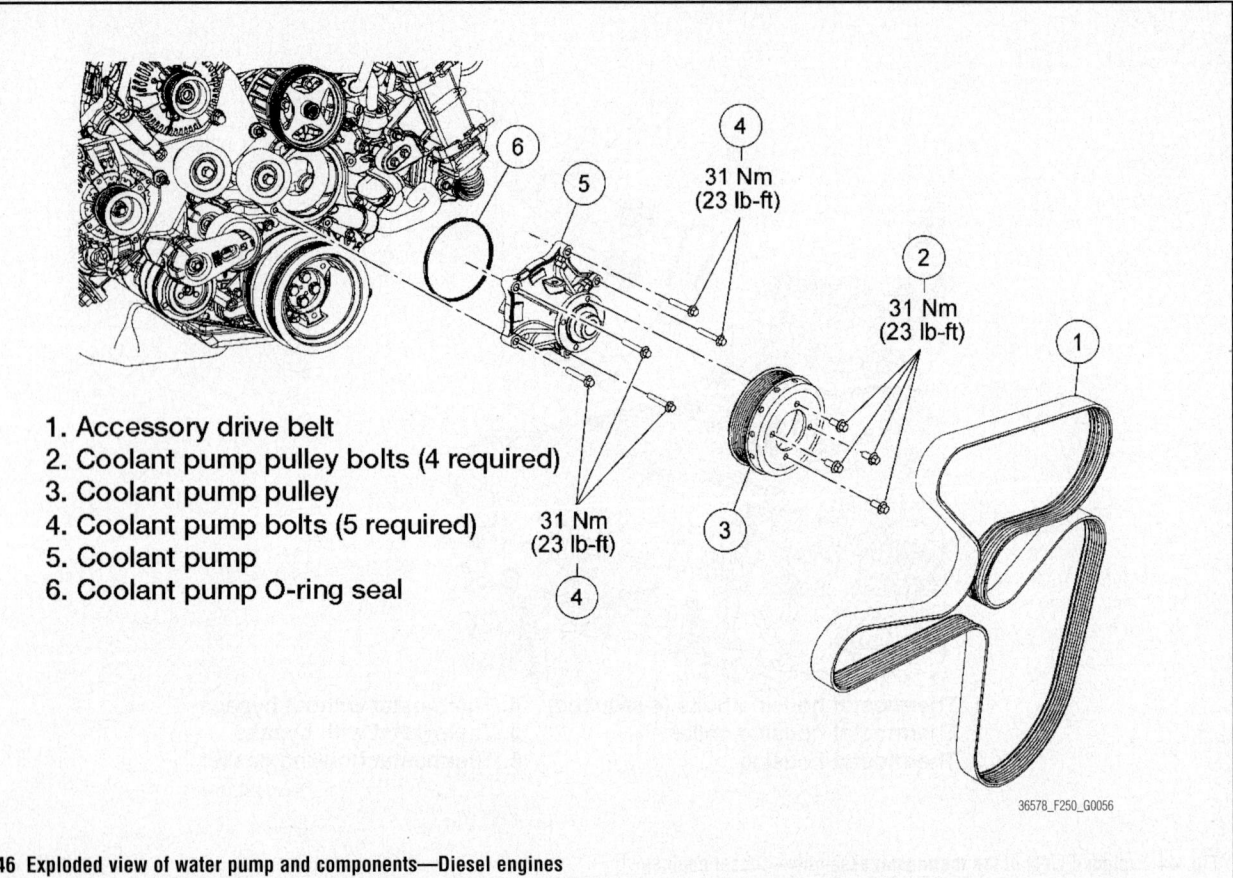

1. Accessory drive belt
2. Coolant pump pulley bolts (4 required)
3. Coolant pump pulley
4. Coolant pump bolts (5 required)
5. Coolant pump
6. Coolant pump O-ring seal

31 Nm (23 lb-ft)

36578_F250_G0056

Fig. 46 Exploded view of water pump and components—Diesel engines

ENGINE ELECTRICAL

ALTERNATOR

REMOVAL & INSTALLATION

Gasoline Engines

See Figure 47.

1. Disconnect the battery.
2. If equipped with 5.4L engine, remove the air cleaner intake pipe.
3. Release the accessory drive belt tension and remove the drive belt from the alternator pulley.
4. Remove the 4 bolts and the alternator bracket. Release the harness locator.
5. Remove the 2 bolts and position the alternator aside. To install, tighten to 18 ft. lbs. (25 Nm).
6. Disconnect the 2 alternator electrical connectors.

➡ **When installing the alternator, make sure to hand-start the alternator B+ terminal nut to prevent cross-threading.**

7. Remove the nut and position the alternator B+ terminal aside.
8. Remove the alternator.

9. To install, reverse the removal procedure.

Diesel Engines

Single Alternator

See Figure 48.

1. Disconnect the batteries.
2. Remove the Air Cleaner (ACL) assembly.
3. Remove the fender splash shield.
4. Rotate the accessory drive belt tensioner clockwise and remove the drive belt from the generator pulley.
5. Remove the nut and position the generator B+ terminal aside.
6. Disconnect the generator electrical connector.
7. Remove the 2 lower bolts to the generator. To install, tighten to 35 ft. lbs. (47 Nm).
8. Remove the upper bolt and the generator. To install, tighten to 35 ft. lbs. (47 Nm).
9. To install, reverse the removal procedure.

Dual Alternators

See Figure 49.

➡ **This procedure applies to the primary (lower) and/or secondary (upper) generator of the dual generator system.**

CHARGING SYSTEM

1. Disconnect the batteries.
2. Remove the air cleaner assembly.
3. For the primary generator. remove the fender splash shield.
4. For the secondary generator , loosen the RH Charge Air Cooler (CAC) tube clamp at the intake throttle adapter and position the CAC tube aside.
5. Rotate the accessory drive belt tensioner clockwise and remove the drive belt from the generator pulley.
6. Remove the nut(s) and position the generator B+ terminal(s) aside.
7. Disconnect the generator electrical connector.
8. Remove the 2 lower bolts to the generator. To install, tighten to 35 ft. lbs. (47 Nm).
9. Remove the upper bolt and the generator. To install, tighten to 35 ft. lbs. (47 Nm).
10. To install, reverse the removal procedure.

VOLTAGE REGULATOR

The voltage regulators on these vehicles are integral with the alternator and is not replaceable.

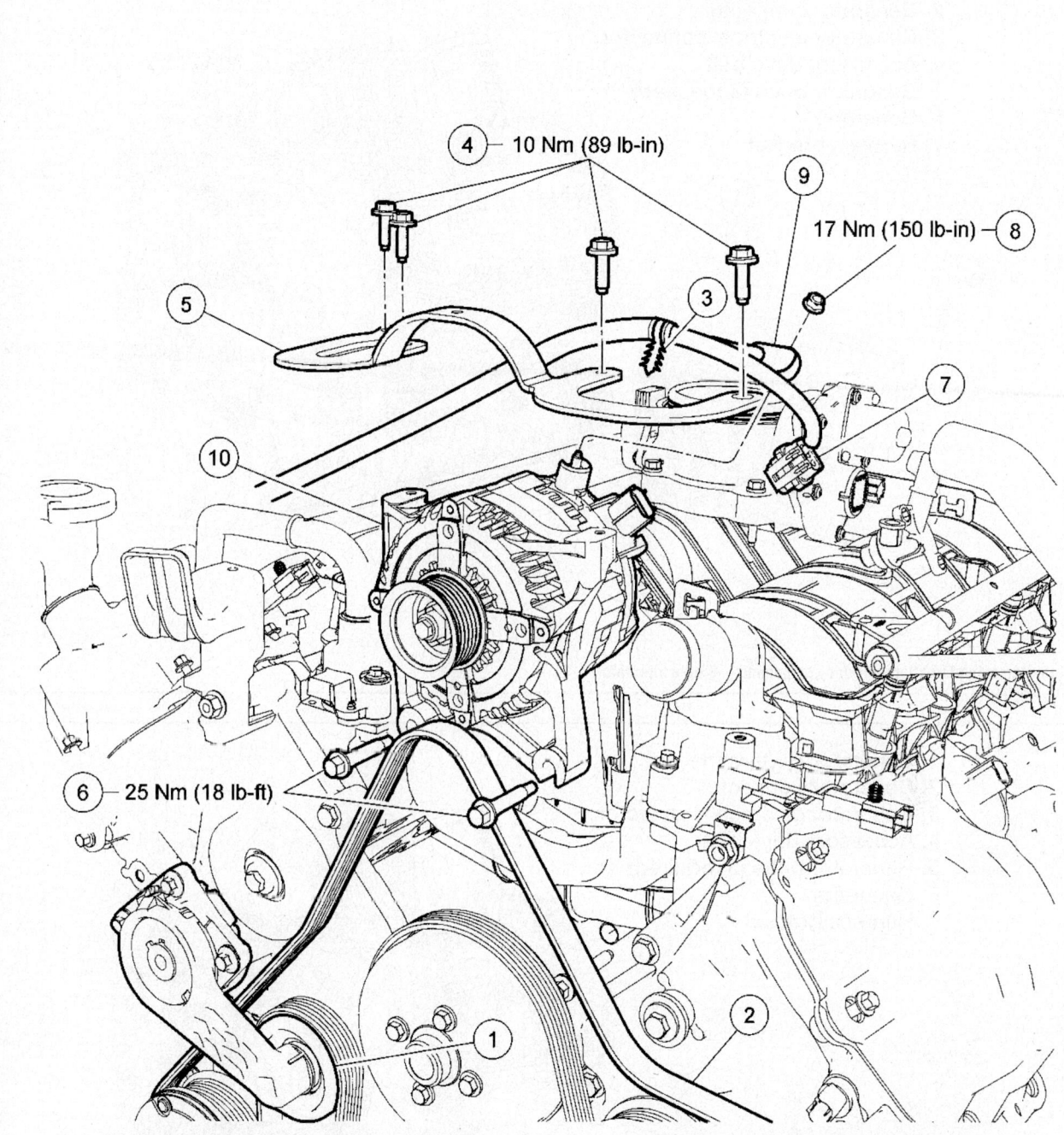

4 — 10 Nm (89 lb-in)

17 Nm (150 lb-in) — 8

6 — 25 Nm (18 lb-ft)

1. Accessory drive belt tensioner
2. Accessory drive belt
3. Generator harness locator
4. Generator bracket bolts (4 required)
5. Generator bracket
6. Generator bolts (2 required)
7. Generator electrical connectors
8. Generator B+ terminal nut
9. Generator B+ terminal
10. Generator

36578_F250_G0057

Fig. 47 Removing the alternator and components

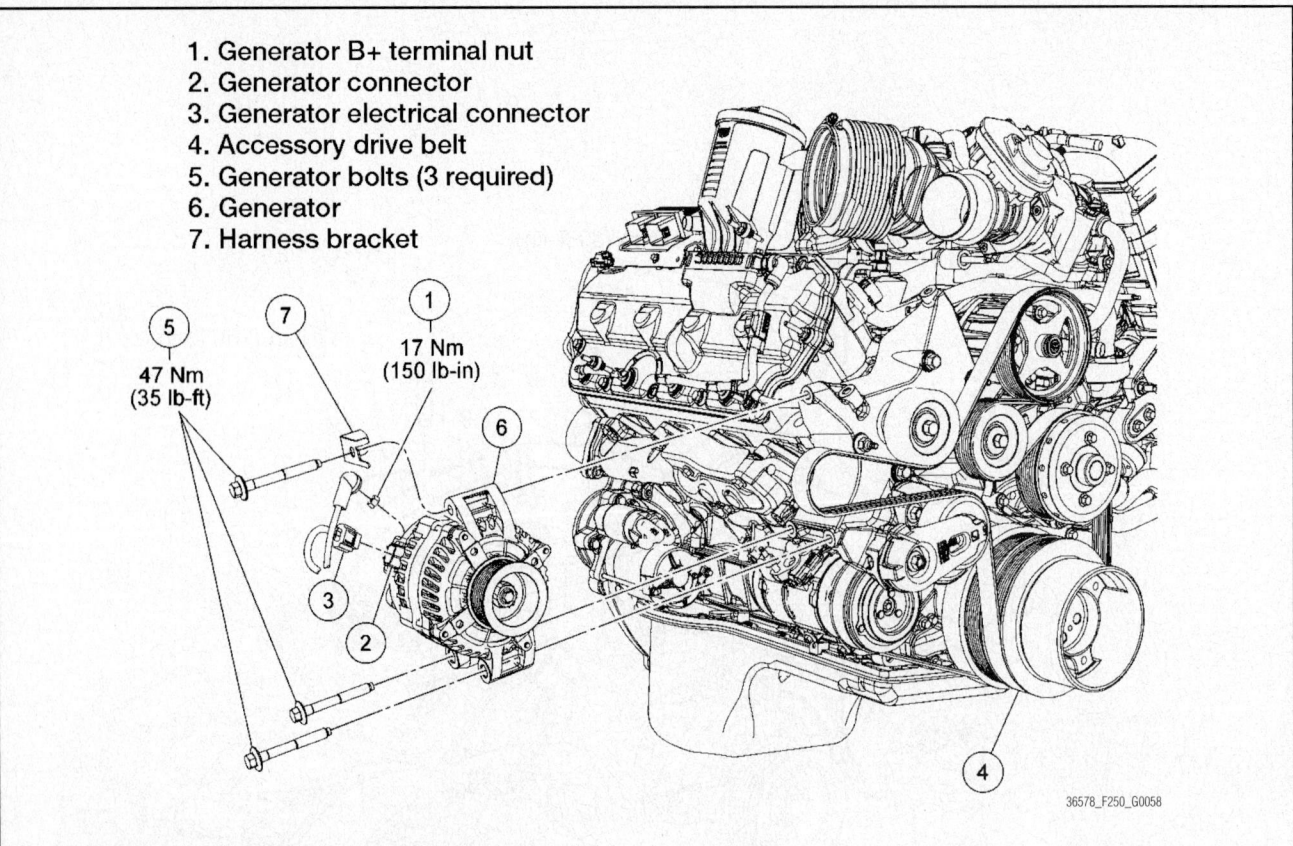

1. Generator B+ terminal nut
2. Generator connector
3. Generator electrical connector
4. Accessory drive belt
5. Generator bolts (3 required)
6. Generator
7. Harness bracket

5 — 47 Nm (35 lb-ft)
7
1 — 17 Nm (150 lb-in)
6
3
2
4

36578_F250_G0058

Fig. 48 Removing the alternator and components—Single alternator

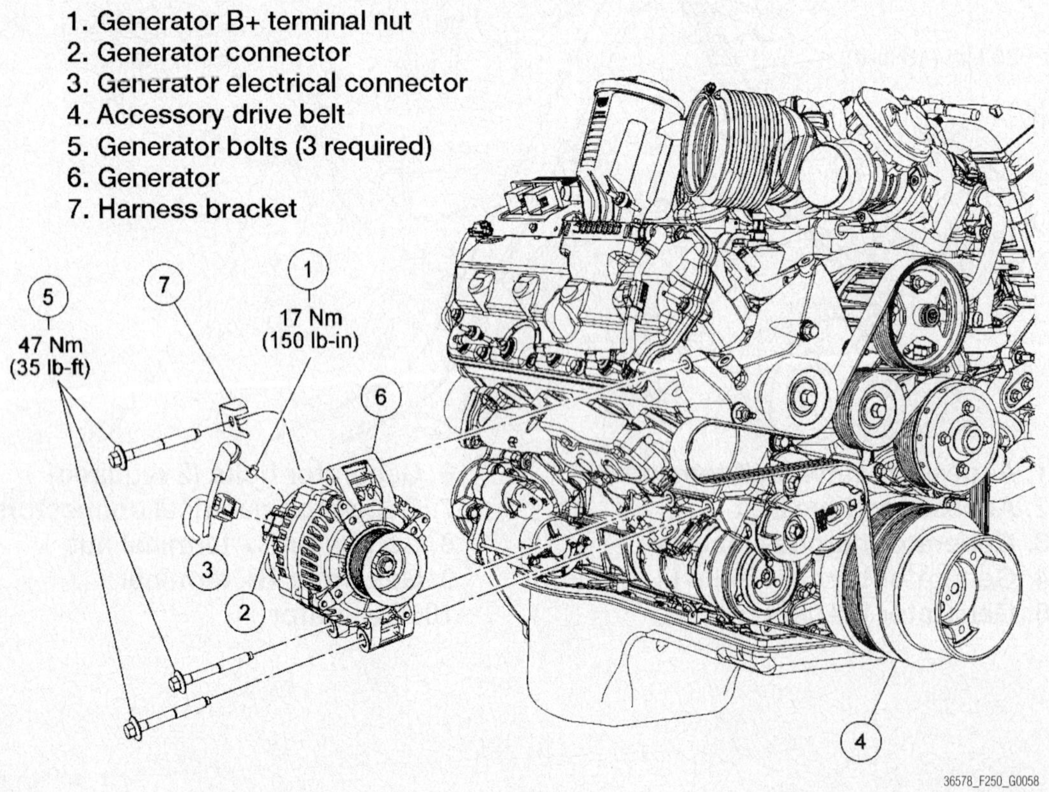

1. Generator B+ terminal nut
2. Generator connector
3. Generator electrical connector
4. Accessory drive belt
5. Generator bolts (3 required)
6. Generator
7. Harness bracket

5 — 47 Nm (35 lb-ft)
7
1 — 17 Nm (150 lb-in)
6
3
2
4

36578_F250_G0058

Fig. 49 Removing the dual alternator and components

ENGINE ELECTRICAL

IGNITION SYSTEM

FIRING ORDERS

See Figure 50.

79243G58

Fig. 50 5.4L Engine
Firing Order: 1–3–7–2–6–5–4–8
Distributorless ignition system;
one coil per cylinder

IGNITION COIL

REMOVAL & INSTALLATION

See Figures 51 and 52.

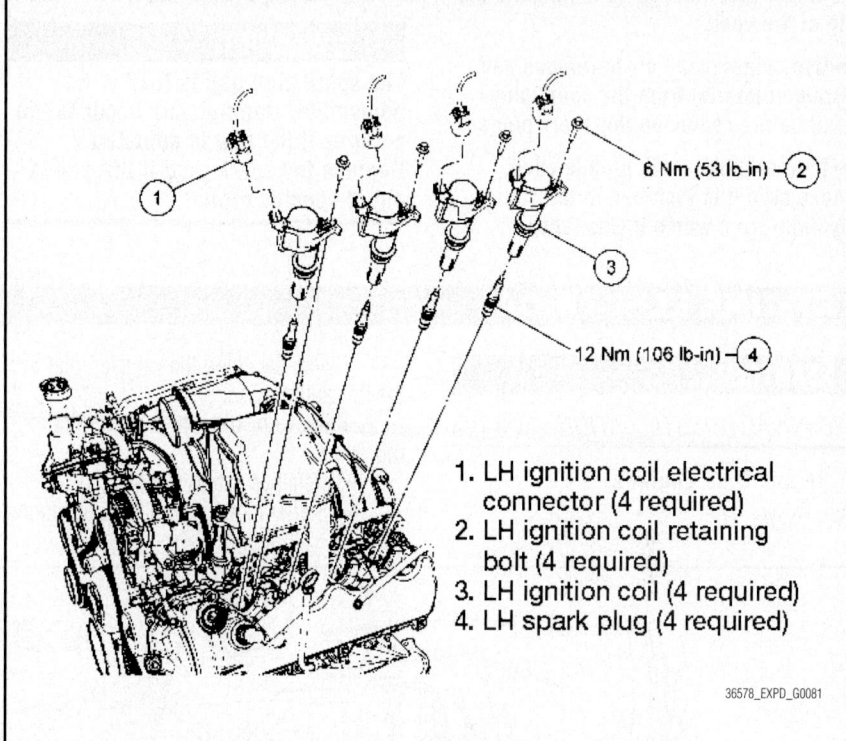

6 Nm (53 lb-in) – 2

12 Nm (106 lb-in) – 4

1. LH ignition coil electrical
   connector (4 required)
2. LH ignition coil retaining
   bolt (4 required)
3. LH ignition coil (4 required)
4. LH spark plug (4 required)

36578_EXPD_G0081

Fig. 52 Exploded view of the engine ignition components–LH

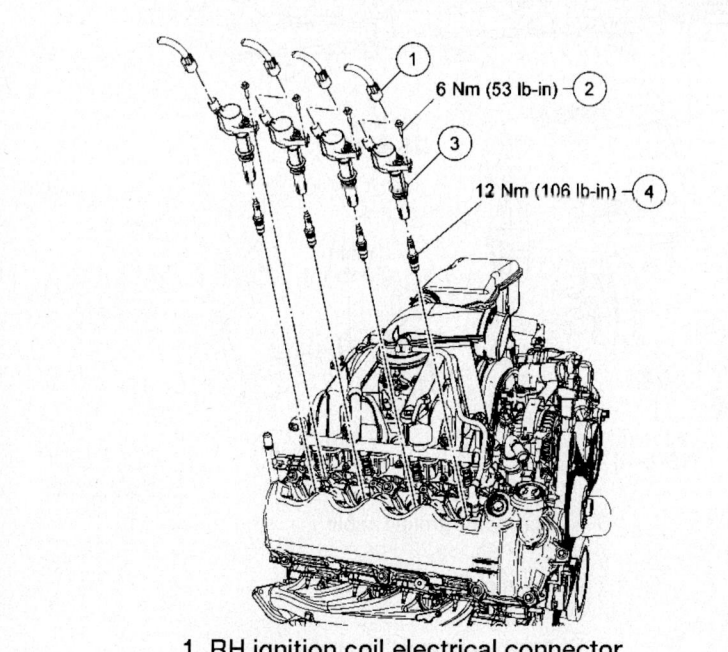

6 Nm (53 lb-in) – 2

12 Nm (106 lb-in) – 4

1. RH ignition coil electrical connector
   (4 required)
2. RH ignition coil retaining bolt (4 required)
3. RH ignition coil (4 required)
4. RH spark plug (4 required)

36578_EXPD_G0080

Fig. 51 Exploded view of the engine ignition components–RH

1. Before servicing the vehicle, refer to the precautions section.
2. Disconnect the negative battery cable.
3. Remove the bolts and the ignition coil cover.
4. Disconnect the electrical connector from the ignition coil.
5. Remove the ignition coils.
6. Installation is the reverse of the removal procedure. Tighten the ignition coil cover bolts to 9 ft. lbs. (12 Nm).

IGNITION TIMING

ADJUSTMENT

Base timing for distributorless ignition engines is set at the factory at 10 degrees Before Top Dead Center (BTDC) and is not adjustable.

SPARK PLUGS

REMOVAL & INSTALLATION

1. Disconnect the battery ground cable.
2. Disconnect the ignition coil electrical connector.
3. Remove the bolt and remove the ignition coil, using a twisting motion while pulling up on the ignition coil.

➡Verify that the ignition coil spring is correctly located inside the ignition coil boot and that there is no damage to the tip of the boot.

➡Use compressed air to remove any foreign material from the spark plug well before removing the spark plugs.

➡If an original spark plug is used, make sure it is installed in the same cylinder from which it was taken.

4. New spark plugs can be used in any cylinder.

5. Remove the spark plugs.

✳ WARNING

The spark plug gap is NOT adjustable. Damage can occur to the ceramic if the gap is adjusted. Replace the spark plug if the gap is out of specification.

6. Inspect the spark plugs. Install new spark plugs as necessary.

7. To install, reverse the removal procedure. Apply a light coat of dielectric compound to the inside of the ignition coil boots. See the torque Specifications Chart for spark plug tightening. Tighten the coil bolt to 53 inch lbs. (6 Nm).

ENGINE ELECTRICAL

STARTING SYSTEM

STARTER

REMOVAL & INSTALLATION

5.4L and 6.8L Engines

See Figure 53.

1. Before servicing the vehicle, refer to the Precautions Section.

2. Remove or disconnect the following:

   • Negative battery cable
   • Starter motor electrical connections

   • Starter motor bolts and the motor

3. Installation is the reverse of removal, tighten the starter motor bolts to 18 ft. lbs. (25 Nm).

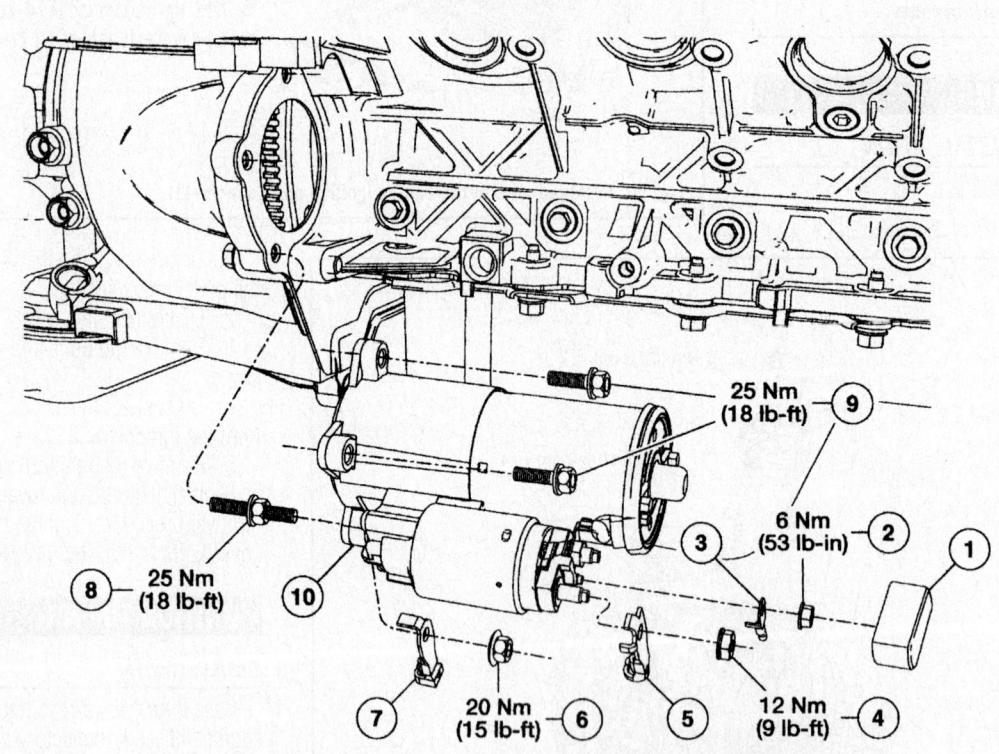

1	Terminal cover	6	Starter motor ground cable nut
2	Starter solenoid S-terminal nut	7	Starter motor ground cable eyelet
3	Starter solenoid S-terminal eyelet	8	Starter motor mounting stud bolt
4	Starter solenoid B-terminal nut	9	Starter motor mounting bolt (2 required)
5	Starter solenoid B-terminal eyelet	10	Starter motor

06017-F150-G87

Fig. 53 Starter and related parts—5.4L and 6.8L engines shown—6.4L engine similar

ENGINE MECHANICAL

ACCESSORY DRIVE BELTS

ACCESSORY BELT ROUTING

See Figures 54 through 57.

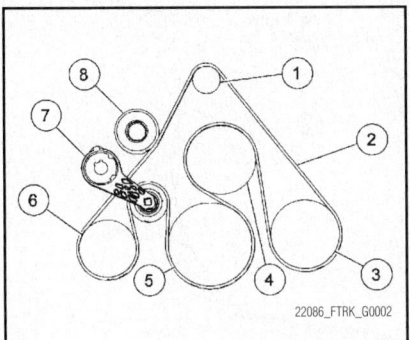

Fig. 54 Accessory drive belt routing— 5.4L and 6.8L engines

INSPECTION

Inspect the drive belt for signs of glazing or cracking. A glazed belt will be perfectly smooth from slippage, while a good belt will have a slight texture of fabric visible. Cracks will usually start at the inner edge of

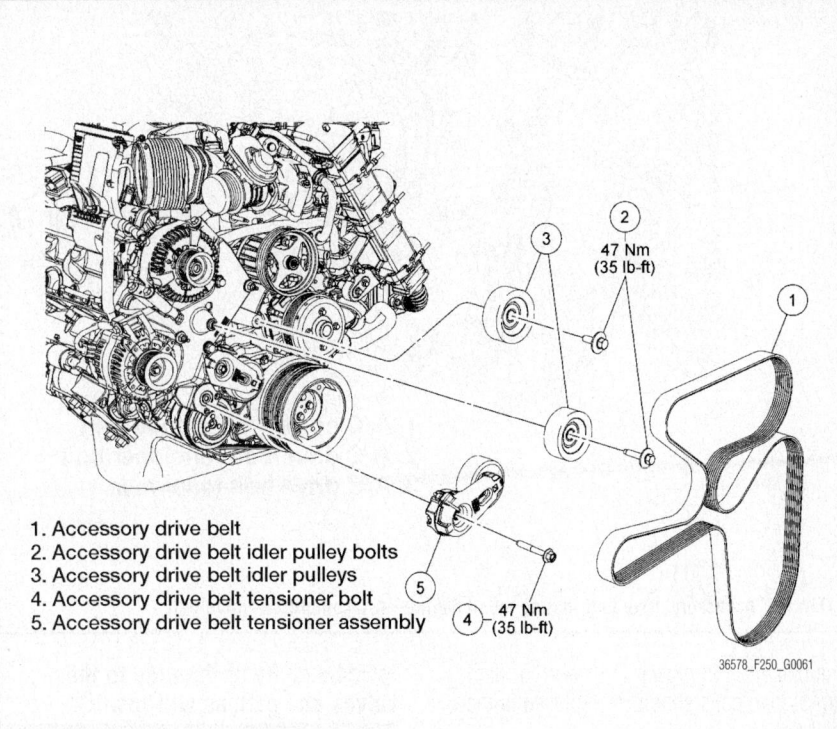

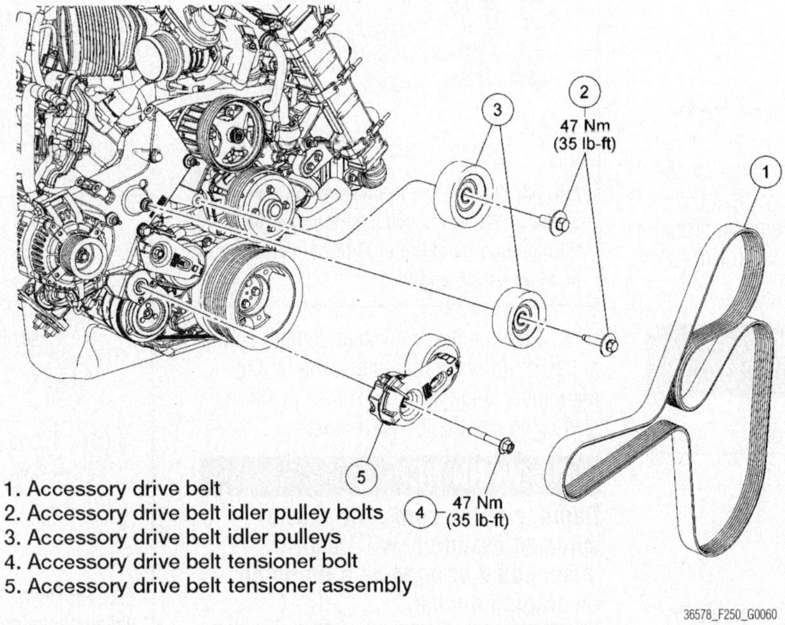

1. Accessory drive belt
2. Accessory drive belt idler pulley bolts
3. Accessory drive belt idler pulleys
4. Accessory drive belt tensioner bolt
5. Accessory drive belt tensioner assembly

47 Nm (35 lb-ft)

Fig. 56 Accessory drive belt routing—6.4L Engine—Dual alternators

1. Accessory drive belt
2. Accessory drive belt idler pulley bolts
3. Accessory drive belt idler pulleys
4. Accessory drive belt tensioner bolt
5. Accessory drive belt tensioner assembly

47 Nm (35 lb-ft)

Fig. 55 Accessory drive belt routing—6.4L Engine—Single alternator

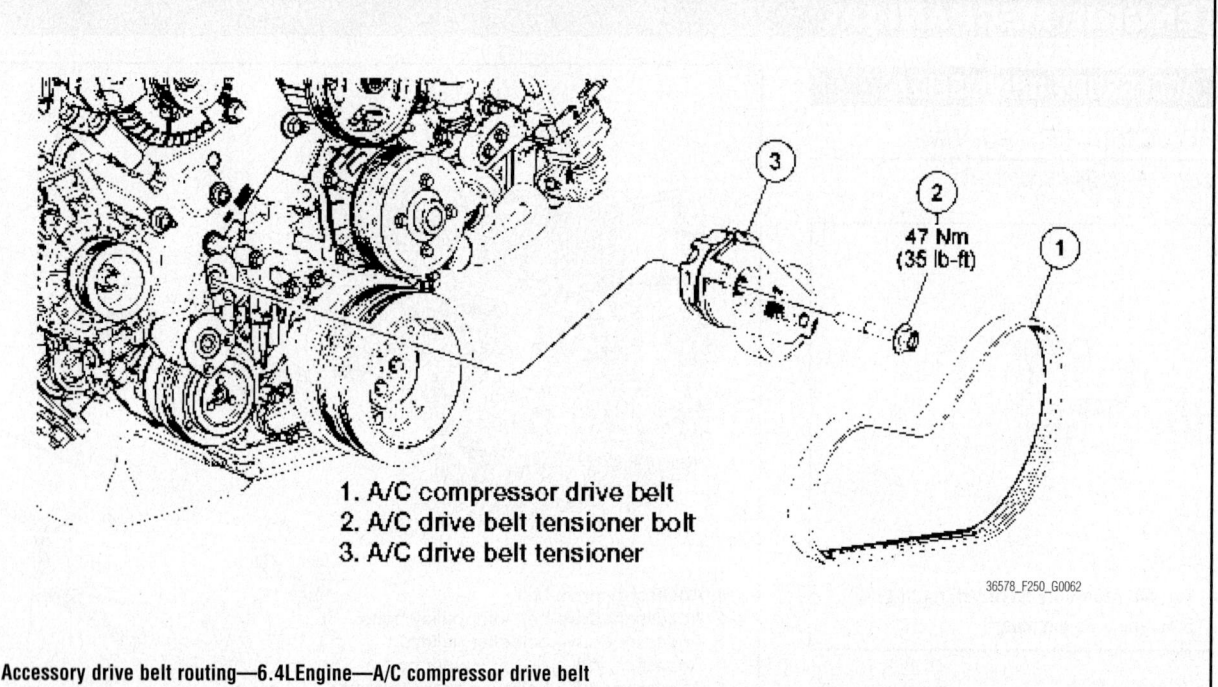

1. A/C compressor drive belt
2. A/C drive belt tensioner bolt
3. A/C drive belt tensioner

47 Nm
(35 lb-ft)

36578_F250_G0062

Fig. 57 Accessory drive belt routing—6.4LEngine—A/C compressor drive belt

the belt and run outward. All worn or damaged drive belts should be replaced immediately.

REMOVAL & INSTALLATION

5.4L and 6.8L Engines

1. Rotate the drive belt tensioner clockwise and remove the accessory drive belt.
2. To install, reverse the removal procedure.

6.4L Diesel Engine

1. Remove the cooling fan.
2. Remove the 4 bolts and cooling fan stator.
3. Rotate the drive belt tensioner clockwise and remove the accessory drive belt.
4. To install, reverse the removal procedure. Tighten the stator bolts to 40 Nm (30 ft. lbs.).

CAMSHAFT AND VALVE LIFTERS

REMOVAL & INSTALLATION

5.4L Engines

Left Side

See Figures 58 through 63.

1. Before servicing the vehicle, refer to the Precautions Section.

✳✳ WARNING

The camshaft procedure must be fol-

lowed exactly or damage to the valves and pistons will result.

2. Remove the cooling fan shroud.

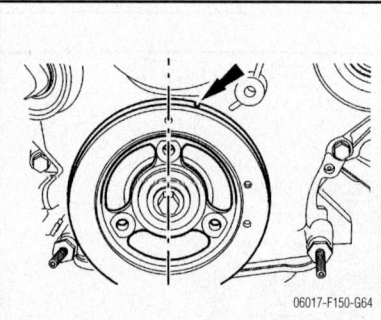

06017-F150-G64

Fig. 58 Position the crankshaft damper spoke at the 12 o'clock position and the timing mark indentation at the 1 o'clock position—5.4L engine

3. Position the crankshaft damper spoke at the 12 o'clock position and the timing mark indentation at the 1 o'clock position.
4. Remove the left valve cover.

✳✳ WARNING

Damage to the camshaft phaser sprocket assembly will occur if mishandled or used as a lifting or leveraging device.

5. Loosen and back off the left camshaft phaser bolt 1 full turn.
6. Disconnect the left camshaft position (CMP) sensor electrical connector.

7. Remove the left CMP sensor and the bolt.

✳✳ WARNING

If servicing both camshafts, do not rotate the crankshaft. Camshaft position has been established earlier.

➡**If the camshaft lobes are not exactly positioned as shown, the crankshaft keyway will require 1 full additional rotation to 12 o'clock.**

8. The number 5 cylinder camshaft exhaust lobe must be coming up on the exhaust stroke. Verify by noting the position

06017-F150-G68

Fig. 59 The number 5 cylinder camshaft exhaust lobe must be coming up on the exhaust stroke. Verify by noting the position of the 2 intake camshaft lobes and the exhaust lobe on the number 5 cylinder—5.4L engine

of the 2 intake camshaft lobes and the exhaust lobe on the number 5 cylinder.

9. Remove only the 3 roller followers shown in the illustration.

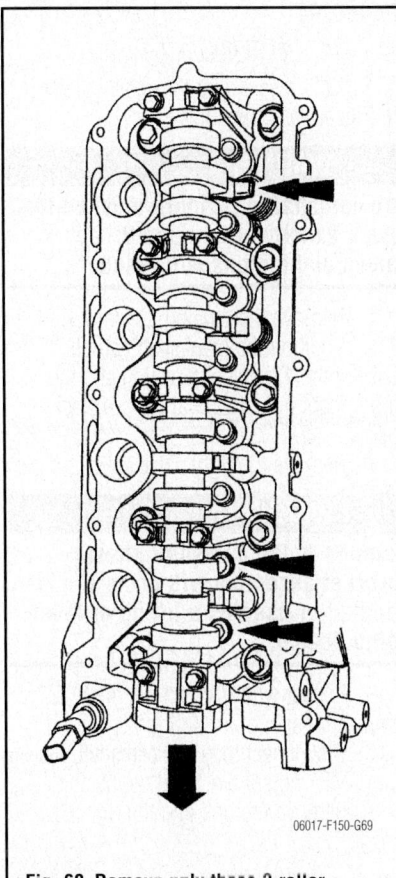

Fig. 60 Remove only these 3 roller followers at this time—5.4L engine

✳✳ WARNING

Do not allow the valve keepers to fall off the valve or the valve may drop into the cylinder.

➡The camshaft roller followers must be installed in their original locations. Record camshaft roller follower locations.

➡It may be necessary to push the valve down while compressing the spring.

10. Using special tool 303-1039, remove only the 3 designated roller followers from the previous step.

✳✳ WARNING

The crankshaft cannot be moved past the 6 o'clock position once set.

11. Rotate the crankshaft clockwise, as viewed from the front, positioning the

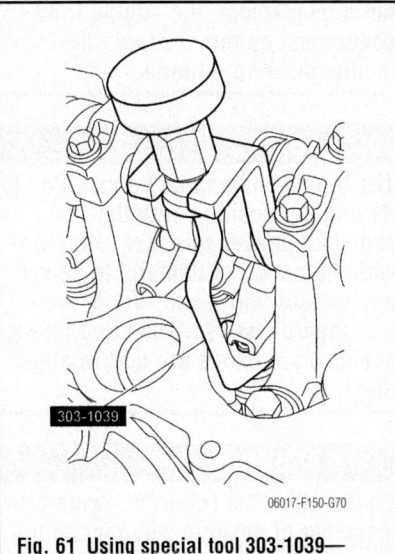

Fig. 61 Using special tool 303-1039—5.4L engine

Fig. 62 Rotate the crankshaft clockwise, as viewed from the front, positioning the crankshaft damper spoke at the 6 o'clock position and the timing mark indentation at the 7 o'clock position—5.4L engine

crankshaft damper spoke at the 6 o'clock position and the timing mark indentation at the 7 o'clock position.

✳✳ WARNING

Engine is not freewheeling. Camshaft procedure must be followed exactly or damage to valves and pistons will result.

✳✳ WARNING

The Timing Chain Wedge tool must be installed square to the timing chain and the engine block.

➡Front cover removed for clarity.

12. Install the special tools in the left timing chain as shown.

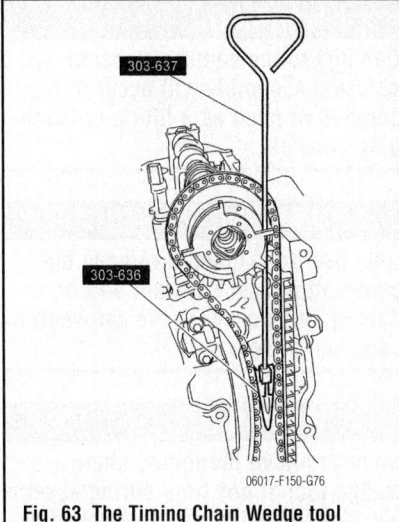

Fig. 63 The Timing Chain Wedge tool must be installed square to the timing chain and the engine block—5.4L engine

✳✳ WARNING

Do not remove the timing chain wedge tool at any time during assembly. If the special tool is removed or out of placement, the engine front cover must be removed and the engine must be retimed.

✳✳ WARNING

The timing chain must be installed in its original position onto the camshaft phaser sprocket using the scribed marks, or damage to valves and pistons will result.

13. Scribe a location mark on the timing chain and the camshaft phaser sprocket assembly.

✳✳ WARNING

Remove the front thrust camshaft bearing cap straight upward from the bearing towers, or the bearing cap may be damaged from side loading.

➡The camshaft bearing caps must be installed in their original locations. Record camshaft bearing cap locations.

14. Remove the bolts in the sequence shown and remove the front camshaft bearing cap and then the remaining bearing caps.

15. Clean and inspect the left camshaft bearing caps. The camshaft front thrust bearing cap contains an oil metering groove. Make sure the groove is free of foreign material.

✳✳ WARNING

Damage to the camshaft phaser sprocket assembly will occur if mishandled or used as a lifting or leveraging device.

✳✳ WARNING

Only use hand tools to remove the camshaft phaser sprocket bolt or damage may occur to the camshaft or camshaft phaser unit.

✳✳ WARNING

Do not remove the timing chain wedge tool at any time during assembly. If the special tool is removed or out of placement, the engine front cover must be removed and the engine must be retimed.

16. Remove the bolt and withdraw the camshaft from the phaser sprocket assembly leaving the sprocket assembly in place. Discard the bolt and washer.

To install:

17. Lubricate the camshaft and camshaft journals with clean engine oil.

✳✳ WARNING

Do not remove the timing chain wedge tool at any time during assembly. If the special tool is removed or out of placement, the engine front cover must be removed and the engine must be retimed.

✳✳ WARNING

Damage to the camshaft phaser sprocket assembly will occur if mishandled or used as a lifting or leveraging device.

✳✳ WARNING

Do not allow the roller followers to move out of position when installing the camshaft.

18. Install the camshaft into the camshaft phaser sprocket assembly and onto the head.

19. Install a new camshaft phaser bolt finger tight.

✳✳ WARNING

Do not remove the timing chain wedge tool at any time during assembly. If the special tool is removed or

out of placement, the engine front cover must be removed and the engine must be retimed.

✳✳ WARNING

The timing chain must be installed in its original position onto the camshaft phaser sprocket using the scribed marks, or damage to valves and pistons will result. Verify the camshaft phaser sprocket and timing chain scribe marks are still in alignment.

✳✳ WARNING

Do not allow the roller followers to move out of position when installing the camshaft.

20. Lubricate the camshaft bearing caps with clean engine oil.

21. Position the front camshaft bearing cap.

22. Position the remaining camshaft bearing caps.

23. Install the bolts loosely.

24. Tighten the bolts in the sequence shown. Tighten to 10 Nm (89 inch lbs.).

25. Remove the special tools.

26. Rotate the crankshaft a half turn counterclockwise and position the crankshaft damper spoke at the 12 o'clock position and the timing mark indentation at the 1 o'clock position.

27. Verify correct cam position by noting the position of the number 5 cylinder intake and exhaust camshaft lobes.

28. Using the special tool, install the 3 originally removed roller followers.

29. Install the CMP sensor and the bolt.

30. Connect the CMP electrical connector.

✳✳ WARNING

Only use hand tools to install the camshaft phaser sprocket assembly or damage may occur to the camshaft or camshaft phaser unit.

✳✳ WARNING

Damage to the camshaft phaser sprocket assembly will occur if mishandled or used as a lifting or leveraging device.

31. Tighten the camshaft phaser bolt in 2 stages:
- Stage 1: Tighten to 40 Nm (30 ft. lbs.).

- Stage 2: Tighten an additional 90 degrees.

32. Install the left valve cover.

33. Install the cooling fan shroud.

Right Side

See Figures 64 through 70.

1. Before servicing the vehicle, refer to the Precautions Section.

✳✳ WARNING

The camshaft procedure must be followed exactly or damage to the valves and pistons will result.

2. Remove the cooling fan shroud.

3. Position the crankshaft damper spoke at the 12 o'clock position and the timing mark indentation at the 1 o'clock position.

4. Remove the right valve cover.

✳✳ WARNING

Damage to the camshaft phaser sprocket assembly will occur if mishandled or used as a lifting or leveraging device.

5. Loosen and back off the right camshaft phaser bolt 1 full turn.

6. Disconnect the right camshaft position (CMP) sensor electrical connector.

7. Remove the bolt and the right CMP sensor.

➡If the camshaft lobes are not exactly positioned as shown, the crankshaft will require 1 full additional rotation to 12 o'clock.

8. The number 1 cylinder camshaft exhaust lobe must be coming up on the exhaust stroke. Verify by noting the position

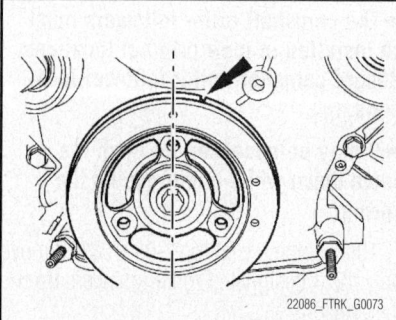

22086_FTRK_G0073

Fig. 64 The number 1 cylinder camshaft exhaust lobe must be coming up on the exhaust stroke. Verify by noting the position of the 2 intake camshaft lobes and the exhaust lobe on the number 1 cylinder—5.4L engine

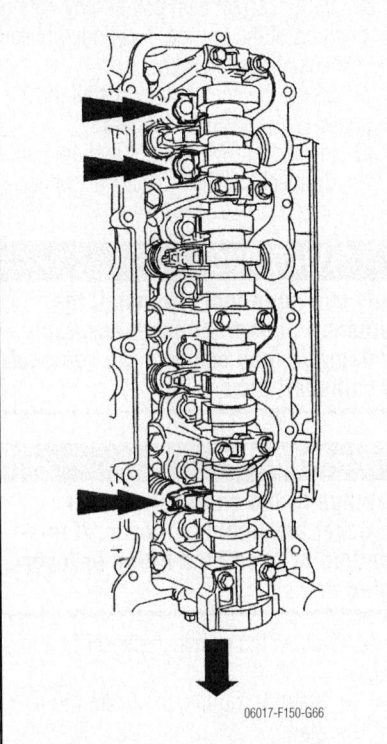

Fig. 65 Remove only these 3 roller followers at this time—5.4L engine

of the 2 intake camshaft lobes and the exhaust lobe on the number 1 cylinder.

9. Remove only the 3 roller followers shown in the illustration.

✳✳ WARNING

Do not allow the valve keepers to fall off the valve or the valve may drop into the cylinder.

➡The camshaft roller followers must be installed in their original locations. Record camshaft roller follower locations.

➡It may be necessary to push the valve down while compressing the spring.

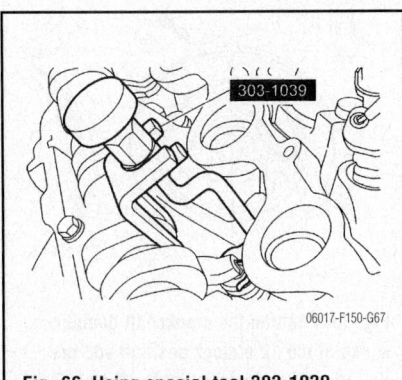

Fig. 66 Using special tool 303-1039—5.4L engine

10. Using special tool 303-1039, remove only the 3 designated roller followers from the previous step.

✳✳ WARNING

The crankshaft cannot be moved past the 6 o'clock position once set.

11. Rotate the crankshaft clockwise, as viewed from the front, positioning the crankshaft damper spoke at the 6 o'clock position and the timing mark indentation at the 7 o'clock position.

✳✳ WARNING

Engine is not freewheeling. Camshaft procedure must be followed exactly or damage to valves and pistons will result.

✳✳ WARNING

The Timing Chain Wedge tool must be installed square to the timing chain and the engine block.

➡Front cover removed for clarity.

12. Install the special tools in the right timing chain as shown.

✳✳ WARNING

Do not remove the timing chain wedge tool at any time during assembly. If the special tool is removed or out of placement, the engine front cover must be removed and the engine must be retimed.

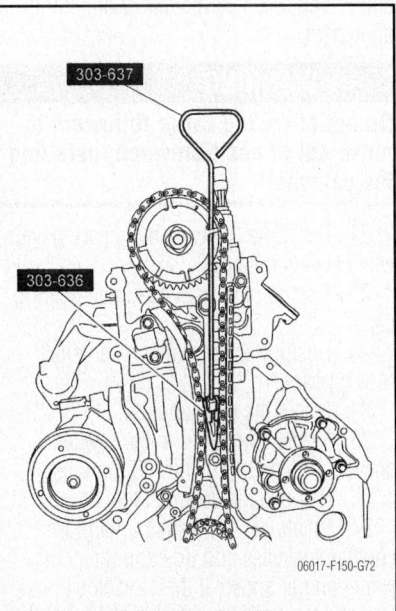

Fig. 67 Timing chain wedge tool installed—5.4L engine

✳✳ WARNING

The timing chain must be installed in its original position onto the camshaft phaser sprocket using the scribed marks, or damage to valves and pistons will result.

13. Scribe a location mark on the timing chain and the camshaft phaser sprocket assembly.

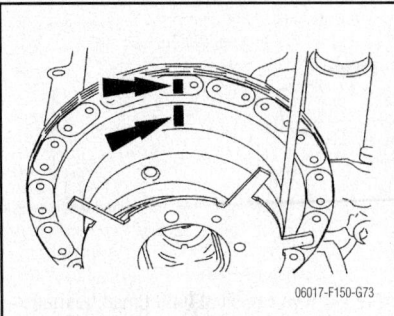

Fig. 68 Scribe a location mark on the timing chain and the camshaft phaser sprocket assembly—5.4L engine

✳✳ WARNING

Remove the front thrust camshaft bearing cap straight upward from the bearing towers, or the bearing cap may be damaged from side loading.

➡The camshaft bearing caps must be installed in their original locations. Record camshaft bearing cap locations.

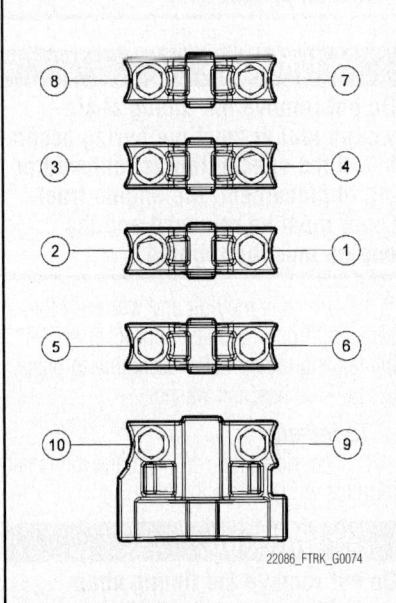

Fig. 69 Camshaft bearing cap removal/installation sequence—5.4L engine

14. Remove the bolts in the sequence shown and remove the front camshaft bearing cap and then the remaining bearing caps.

15. Clean and inspect the right camshaft bearing caps. The camshaft front thrust bearing cap contains an oil metering groove. Make sure the groove is free of foreign material.

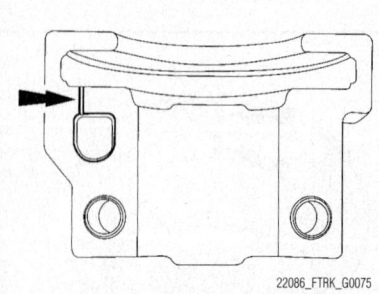

22086_FTRK_G0075

Fig. 70 The camshaft front thrust bearing cap contains an oil metering groove—5.4L engine

✳✳ WARNING
Damage to the camshaft phaser sprocket assembly will occur if mishandled or used as a lifting or leveraging device.

✳✳ WARNING
Only use hand tools to remove the camshaft phaser sprocket bolt or damage may occur to the camshaft or camshaft phaser unit.

✳✳ WARNING
Do not remove the timing chain wedge tool at any time during assembly. If the special tool is removed or out of placement, the engine front cover must be removed and the engine must be retimed.

16. Remove the bolt and withdraw the camshaft from the phaser sprocket assembly leaving the sprocket assembly in place. Discard the bolt and washer.

To install:

17. Lubricate the camshaft and camshaft journals with clean engine oil.

✳✳ WARNING
Do not remove the timing chain wedge tool at any time during assembly. If the special tool is removed or out of placement, the engine front

cover must be removed and the engine must be retimed.

✳✳ WARNING
Damage to the camshaft phaser sprocket assembly will occur if mishandled or used as a lifting or leveraging device.

✳✳ WARNING
Do not allow the roller followers to move out of position when installing the camshaft.

18. Install the camshaft into the camshaft phaser sprocket assembly and onto the head.

19. Install a new camshaft phaser bolt finger tight.

✳✳ WARNING
Do not remove the timing chain wedge tool at any time during assembly. If the special tool is removed or out of placement, the engine front cover must be removed and the engine must be retimed.

✳✳ WARNING
The timing chain must be installed in its original position onto the camshaft phaser sprocket using the scribed marks, or damage to valves and pistons will result.

20. Verify the camshaft phaser sprocket and timing chain scribe marks are still in alignment.

✳✳ WARNING
Do not allow the roller followers to move out of position when installing the camshaft.

21. Lubricate the camshaft bearing caps with clean engine oil.

22. Position the front camshaft bearing cap.

23. Position the remaining camshaft bearing caps.

24. Install the bolts loosely.

25. Tighten the bolts in the sequence shown. Tighten to 10 Nm (89 inch lbs.).

26. Remove the special tools.

27. Rotate the crankshaft a half turn counterclockwise and position the crankshaft damper spoke at the 12 o'clock position and the timing mark indentation at the 1 o'clock position.

28. Verify correct cam position by noting the position of the number 1 cylinder intake and exhaust camshaft lobes.

29. Using the special tool, install the 3 originally removed roller followers.

30. Install the CMP sensor and the bolt.

31. Connect the CMP electrical connector.

✳✳ WARNING
Only use hand tools to install the camshaft phaser sprocket assembly or damage may occur to the camshaft or camshaft phaser unit.

✳✳ WARNING
Damage to the camshaft phaser sprocket assembly will occur if mishandled or used as a lifting or leveraging device.

32. Tighten the camshaft phaser bolt in 2 stages:
   - Stage 1: Tighten to 40 Nm (30 ft. lbs.).
   - Stage 2: Tighten an additional 90 degrees.

33. Install the right valve cover.

6.8L Engine

Left Side

See Figures 71 through 78.

1. Before servicing the vehicle, refer to the Precautions Section.

✳✳ WARNING
The camshaft procedure must be followed exactly or damage to the valves and pistons will result.

2. Remove the cooling fan shroud.

3. Position the crankshaft damper

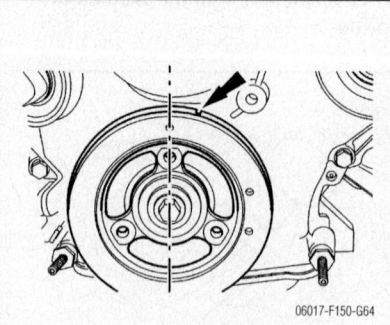

06017-F150-G64

Fig. 71 Position the crankshaft damper spoke at the 12 o'clock position and the timing mark indentation at the 1 o'clock position—6.8L engine

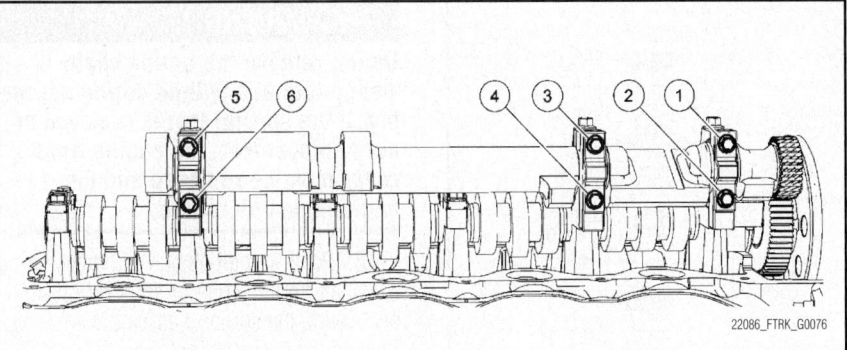

Fig. 72 Remove the 6 bolts in the sequence shown, the 3 bearing caps and the balance shaft

spoke at the 12 o'clock position and the timing mark indentation at the 1 o'clock position.

4. Remove the left valve cover.

5. Remove the 6 bolts in the sequence shown, the 3 bearing caps and the balance shaft.

➡Keep caps in exact order as removed for reinstallation.

✳✳ WARNING

Damage to the camshaft sprocket assembly will occur if mishandled or used as a lifting or leveraging device.

6. Loosen and back off the left camshaft bolt 1 full turn.

✳✳ CAUTION

If servicing both camshafts, do not rotate the crankshaft. Camshaft position has been established in the proper step in this procedure.

➡If the camshaft lobes are not exactly positioned as shown, the crankshaft keyway will require one full additional rotation to 12 o'clock. Do not rotate the crankshaft if servicing both camshafts.

7. The No. 6 cylinder camshaft exhaust lobe must be coming up on the exhaust stroke. Verify by noting the position of the 2 intake camshaft lobes and the exhaust lobe on the No. 6 cylinder.

8. Remove only the 3 roller followers shown in the illustration.

✳✳ WARNING

Do not allow the valve keepers to fall off the valve or the valve may drop into the cylinder.

➡The camshaft roller followers must be installed in their original locations.

Fig. 73 The number 6 cylinder camshaft exhaust lobe must be coming up on the exhaust stroke. Verify by noting the position of the 2 intake camshaft lobes and the exhaust lobe on the number 6 cylinder—6.8L engine

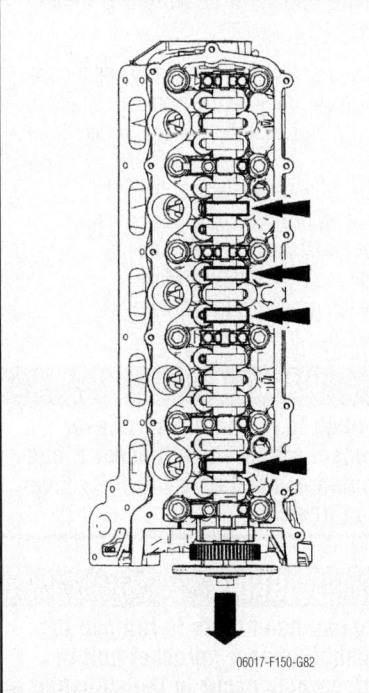

Fig. 74 Remove only these 3 roller followers at this time—6.8L engine

Record camshaft roller follower locations.

➡It may be necessary to push the valve down while compressing the spring.

9. Using special tool 303-1039, remove only the 3 designated roller followers from the previous step.

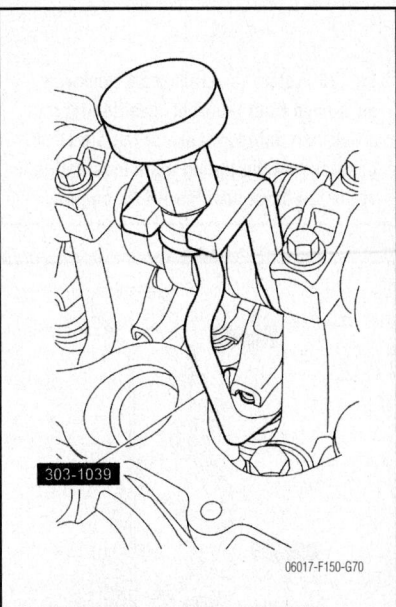

Fig. 75 Using special tool 303-1039—6.8L engine

✳✳ WARNING

The crankshaft cannot be moved past the 6 o'clock position once set.

10. Rotate the crankshaft clockwise, as viewed from the front, positioning the crankshaft damper spoke at the 6 o'clock position and the timing mark indentation at the 7 o'clock position.

✳✳ WARNING

Engine is not freewheeling. Camshaft procedure must be followed exactly or damage to valves and pistons will result.

✳✳ WARNING

The Timing Chain Wedge tool must be installed square to the timing chain and the engine block.

➡Front cover removed for clarity.

11. Install the special tools in the left timing chain as shown.

Fig. 76 Rotate the crankshaft clockwise, as viewed from the front, positioning the crankshaft damper spoke at the 6 o'clock position and the timing mark indentation at the 7 o'clock position—6.8L engine

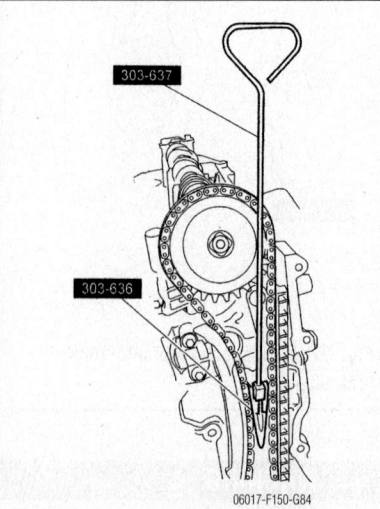

Fig. 77 The Timing Chain Wedge tool must be installed square to the timing chain and the engine block—6.8L engine

✳✳ WARNING

Do not remove the timing chain wedge tool at any time during assembly. If the special tool is removed or out of placement, the engine front cover must be removed and the engine must be retimed.

✳✳ WARNING

The timing chain must be installed in its original position onto the camshaft phaser sprocket using the scribed marks, or damage to valves and pistons will result.

12. Scribe a location mark on the timing chain and the camshaft phaser sprocket assembly.

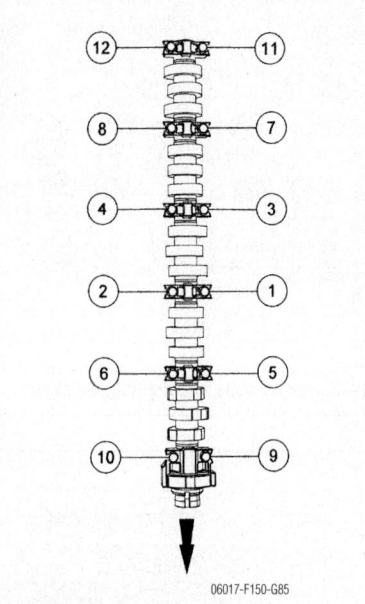

Fig. 78 Camshaft bearing cap removal/installation torque sequence— 6.8L engine

✳✳ WARNING

Remove the front thrust camshaft bearing cap straight upward from the bearing towers, or the bearing cap may be damaged from side loading.

➡ The camshaft bearing caps must be installed in their original locations. Record camshaft bearing cap locations.

13. Remove the bolts in the sequence shown and remove the front camshaft bearing cap and then the remaining bearing caps.

14. Clean and inspect the left camshaft bearing caps. The camshaft front thrust bearing cap contains an oil metering groove. Make sure the groove is free of foreign material.

✳✳ WARNING

Damage to the camshaft phaser sprocket assembly will occur if mishandled or used as a lifting or leveraging device.

✳✳ WARNING

Only use hand tools to remove the camshaft phaser sprocket bolt or damage may occur to the camshaft or camshaft phaser unit.

✳✳ WARNING

Do not remove the timing chain wedge tool at any time during assembly. If the special tool is removed or out of placement, the engine front cover must be removed and the engine must be retimed.

15. Remove the bolt and withdraw the camshaft from the phaser sprocket assembly leaving the sprocket assembly in place. Discard the bolt and washer.

To install:

16. Lubricate the camshaft and camshaft journals with clean engine oil.

✳✳ WARNING

Do not remove the timing chain wedge tool at any time during assembly. If the special tool is removed or out of placement, the engine front cover must be removed and the engine must be retimed.

✳✳ WARNING

Damage to the camshaft phaser sprocket assembly will occur if mishandled or used as a lifting or leveraging device.

✳✳ WARNING

Do not allow the roller followers to move out of position when installing the camshaft.

17. Install the camshaft into the camshaft phaser sprocket assembly and onto the head.

18. Install a new camshaft phaser bolt finger tight.

✳✳ WARNING

Do not remove the timing chain wedge tool at any time during assembly. If the special tool is removed or out of placement, the engine front cover must be removed and the engine must be retimed.

✳✳ WARNING

The timing chain must be installed in its original position onto the camshaft phaser sprocket using the scribed marks, or damage to valves and pistons will result. Verify the camshaft phaser sprocket and timing chain scribe marks are still in alignment.

Do not allow the roller followers to move out of position when installing the camshaft.

19. Lubricate the camshaft bearing caps with clean engine oil.
20. Position the front camshaft bearing cap.
21. Position the remaining camshaft bearing caps.
22. Install the bolts loosely.
23. Tighten the bolts in the sequence shown. Tighten to 10 Nm (89 inch lbs.).
24. Remove the special tools.
25. Rotate the crankshaft a half turn counterclockwise and position the crankshaft damper spoke at the 12 o'clock position and the timing mark indentation at the 1 o'clock position.
26. Verify correct cam position by noting the position of the number 5 cylinder intake and exhaust camshaft lobes.
27. Using the special tool, install the 3 originally removed roller followers.
28. Install the CMP sensor and the bolt.
29. Connect the CMP electrical connector.

Only use hand tools to install the camshaft phaser sprocket assembly or damage may occur to the camshaft or camshaft phaser unit.

Damage to the camshaft phaser sprocket assembly will occur if mishandled or used as a lifting or leveraging device.

30. Tighten the camshaft phaser bolt in 2 stages:
- Stage 1: Tighten to 40 Nm (30 ft. lbs.).
- Stage 2: Tighten an additional 90 degrees.
31. Install the left valve cover.
32. Install the cooling fan shroud.

Right Side

See Figures 79 through 85.

1. Before servicing the vehicle, refer to the Precautions Section.

The camshaft procedure must be followed exactly or damage to the valves and pistons will result.

2. Remove the cooling fan shroud.
3. Position the crankshaft damper spoke at the 12 o'clock position and the timing mark indentation at the 1 o'clock position.
4. Remove the right valve cover.

Damage to the camshaft phaser sprocket assembly will occur if mishandled or used as a lifting or leveraging device.

5. Loosen and back off the right camshaft phaser bolt 1 full turn.
6. Disconnect the right camshaft position (CMP) sensor electrical connector.
7. Remove the bolt and the right CMP sensor.

➡️ If the camshaft lobes are not exactly positioned as shown, the crankshaft will require 1 full additional rotation to 12 o'clock.

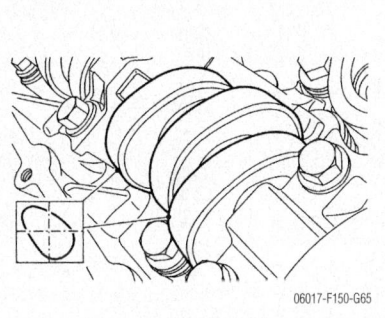

Fig. 79 The number 1 cylinder camshaft exhaust lobe must be coming up on the exhaust stroke. Verify by noting the position of the 2 intake camshaft lobes and the exhaust lobe on the number 1 cylinder—6.8L engine

8. The number 1 cylinder camshaft exhaust lobe must be coming up on the exhaust stroke. Verify by noting the position of the 2 intake camshaft lobes and the exhaust lobe on the number 1 cylinder.
9. Remove only the 3 roller followers shown in the illustration.

Do not allow the valve keepers to fall off the valve or the valve may drop into the cylinder.

➡️ The camshaft roller followers must be installed in their original locations. Record camshaft roller follower locations.

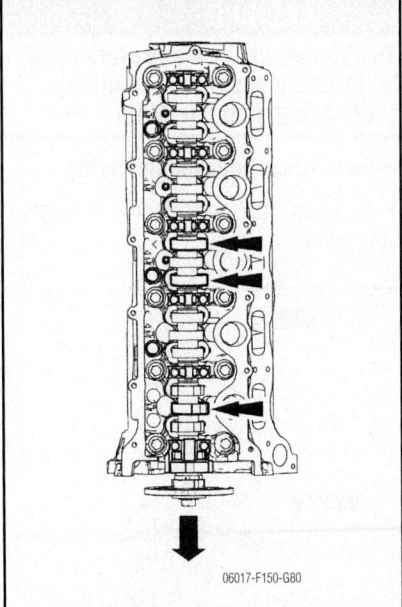

Fig. 80 Remove only these 3 roller followers at this time—6.8L engine

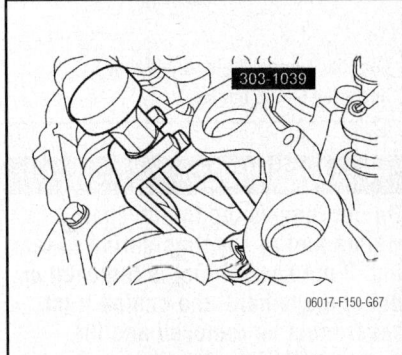

Fig. 81 Using special tool 303-1039—6.8L engine

➡️ It may be necessary to push the valve down while compressing the spring.

10. Using special tool 303-1039, remove only the 3 designated roller followers from the previous step.

The crankshaft cannot be moved past the 6 o'clock position once set.

11. Rotate the crankshaft clockwise, as viewed from the front, positioning the crankshaft damper spoke at the 6 o'clock position and the timing mark indentation at the 7 o'clock position.

Engine is not freewheeling. Camshaft procedure must be followed exactly or damage to valves and pistons will result.

✳✳ WARNING

The Timing Chain Wedge tool must be installed square to the timing chain and the engine block.

➡Front cover removed for clarity.

12. Install the special tools in the right timing chain as shown.

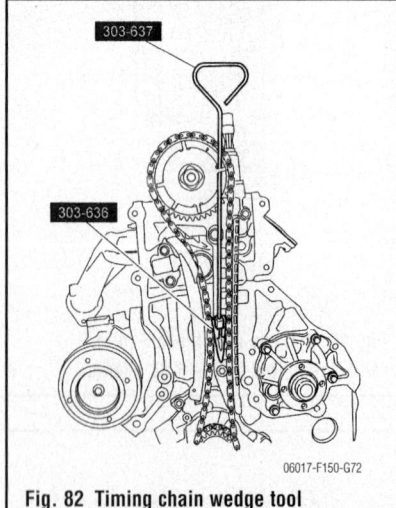

Fig. 82 Timing chain wedge tool installed—6.8L engine

✳✳ WARNING

Do not remove the timing chain wedge tool at any time during assembly. If the special tool is removed or out of placement, the engine front cover must be removed and the engine must be retimed.

✳✳ WARNING

The timing chain must be installed in its original position onto the camshaft phaser sprocket using the scribed marks, or damage to valves and pistons will result.

13. Scribe a location mark on the timing chain and the camshaft phaser sprocket assembly.

✳✳ WARNING

Remove the front thrust camshaft bearing cap straight upward from the bearing towers, or the bearing cap may be damaged from side loading.

➡The camshaft bearing caps must be installed in their original locations. Record camshaft bearing cap locations.

14. Remove the bolts in the sequence shown and remove the front camshaft bear-

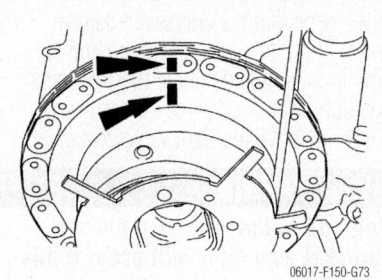

Fig. 83 Scribe a location mark on the timing chain and the camshaft phaser sprocket assembly—6.8L engine

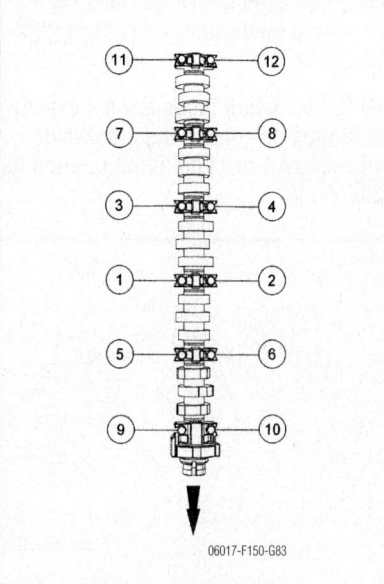

Fig. 84 Camshaft bearing cap removal/installation sequence—6.8L engine

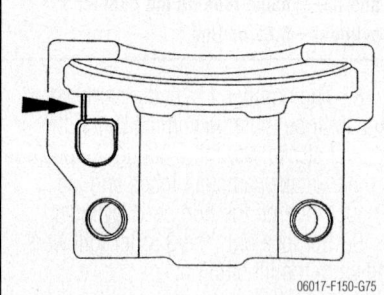

Fig. 85 The camshaft front thrust bearing cap contains an oil metering groove—6.8L engine

ing cap and then the remaining bearing caps.

15. Clean and inspect the right camshaft bearing caps. The camshaft front thrust bearing cap contains an oil metering

groove. Make sure the groove is free of foreign material.

✳✳ WARNING

Damage to the camshaft phaser sprocket assembly will occur if mishandled or used as a lifting or leveraging device.

✳✳ WARNING

Only use hand tools to remove the camshaft phaser sprocket bolt or damage may occur to the camshaft or camshaft phaser unit.

✳✳ WARNING

Do not remove the timing chain wedge tool at any time during assembly. If the special tool is removed or out of placement, the engine front cover must be removed and the engine must be retimed.

16. Remove the bolt and withdraw the camshaft from the phaser sprocket assembly leaving the sprocket assembly in place. Discard the bolt and washer.

To install:

17. Lubricate the camshaft and camshaft journals with clean engine oil.

✳✳ WARNING

Do not remove the timing chain wedge tool at any time during assembly. If the special tool is removed or out of placement, the engine front cover must be removed and the engine must be retimed.

✳✳ WARNING

Damage to the camshaft phaser sprocket assembly will occur if mishandled or used as a lifting or leveraging device.

✳✳ WARNING

Do not allow the roller followers to move out of position when installing the camshaft.

18. Install the camshaft into the camshaft phaser sprocket assembly and onto the head.

19. Install a new camshaft phaser bolt finger tight.

✳✳ WARNING

Do not remove the timing chain wedge tool at any time during assembly. If the special tool is removed or out of placement, the engine front cover must be removed and the engine must be retimed.

✳ WARNING

The timing chain must be installed in its original position onto the camshaft phaser sprocket using the scribed marks, or damage to valves and pistons will result.

20. Verify the camshaft phaser sprocket and timing chain scribe marks are still in alignment.

✳ WARNING

Do not allow the roller followers to move out of position when installing the camshaft.

21. Lubricate the camshaft bearing caps with clean engine oil.
22. Position the front camshaft bearing cap.
23. Position the remaining camshaft bearing caps.
24. Install the bolts loosely.
25. Tighten the bolts in the sequence shown. Tighten to 10 Nm (89 inch lbs.).
26. Remove the special tools.
27. Rotate the crankshaft a half turn counterclockwise and position the crankshaft damper spoke at the 12 o'clock position and the timing mark indentation at the 1 o'clock position.
28. Verify correct cam position by noting the position of the number 1 cylinder intake and exhaust camshaft lobes.
29. Using the special tool, install the 3 originally removed roller followers.
30. Install the CMP sensor and the bolt.
31. Connect the CMP electrical connector.

✳ WARNING

Only use hand tools to install the camshaft phaser sprocket assembly or damage may occur to the camshaft or camshaft phaser unit.

✳ WARNING

Damage to the camshaft phaser sprocket assembly will occur if mishandled or used as a lifting or leveraging device.

32. Tighten the camshaft phaser bolt in 2 stages:

- Stage 1: Tighten to 40 Nm (30 ft. lbs.).
- Stage 2: Tighten an additional 90 degrees.

33. Install the right valve cover.

CATALYTIC CONVERTER

REMOVAL & INSTALLATION

Gasoline Engines

See Figure 86.

➥Some applications are equipped with a catalytic converter delete pipe in place of the underbody catalytic converter. The catalytic converter delete pipe mounts in the exhaust system the same way as the underbody catalytic converter. The catalytic converter delete pipe does not have a Catalyst Monitor Sensor (CMS).

1. With the vehicle in NEUTRAL, position it on a hoist.
2. If equipped, remove the skid plate.
3. Remove the 2 exhaust Y-pipe flange bolts.
4. Loosen the catalytic converter-to-muffler Torca° clamp or, if equipped, the catalytic converter-to-exhaust intermediate pipe Torca° clamp.
5. If equipped, disconnect the exhaust intermediate pipe isolator and the front muffler isolator.
6. Disconnect the catalytic converter from the isolator.
7. Remove the catalytic converter.

To install:

8. Position the catalytic converter into the muffler or, if equipped, the exhaust intermediate pipe.
9. If equipped, connect the exhaust intermediate pipe isolator, the front muffler isolator and the catalytic converter isolator.
10. Install the 2 exhaust Y-pipe flange bolts. Tighten to 30 ft. lbs. (40 Nm).
11. Make sure the button on the catalytic converter is fully inserted into the button slot on the muffler or, if equipped, the exhaust intermediate pipe and tighten the catalytic converter-to-muffler Torca® clamp or, if equipped, the exhaust intermediate pipe Torca® clamp. Tighten to 41 ft. lbs. (55 Nm).

➥The exhaust system alignment procedure only needs to be carried out if the exhaust system isolators are not at zero load.

12. Check to see if the exhaust system isolators are at zero load. If the exhaust sys-

tem isolators are not at zero load, carry out the exhaust system alignment procedure.

13. If equipped, install the skid plate.

Diesel Engine

See Figures 87 through 89.

1. With the vehicle in NEUTRAL, position it on a hoist.
2. Vehicles equipped with a Diesel Particulate Filter (DPF):
   a. Remove the Diesel Particulate Filter (DPF) pressure sensor.
   b. Disconnect the Exhaust Gas Temperature (EGT) sensor electrical connectors.
3. Remove the resonator and tail pipe assembly.
4. Remove the 7 DPF or muffler-to-Oxidation Catalytic Converter (OC) nuts. Discard the nuts.
5. Disconnect the isolators and remove the DPF or muffler and, if equipped, the intermediate pipe as an assembly. Discard the DPF or muffler-to- OC gasket.
6. Support the OC .
7. Remove the OC -to-downpipe bolts.
8. Disconnect the OC isolators and remove the OC from the vehicle.

To install:

9. Position the OC in the vehicle and connect the isolators.
10. Install OC -to-downpipe bolts. Tighten to 30 ft. lbs. (40 Nm).

➥Make sure the DPF or muffler-to- OC gasket surface is clean.

11. Install a new DPF or muffler-to- OC gasket.
12. Position the DPF or muffler and, if equipped, the intermediate pipe as an assembly into the vehicle and connect the isolators.
13. Install the 7 new OC -to- DPF or muffler nuts. Tighten to 30 ft. lbs. (40 Nm).
14. Install the resonator and tail pipe assembly into the vehicle.

➥Make sure all 7 Oxidation Catalytic Converter (OC)-to-Diesel Particulate Filter (DPF) filter nuts have been installed before installing the DPF pressure sensor or damage to the DPF or DPF pressure sensor may occur.

15. Vehicles equipped with PDF, install the DPF pressure sensor. Connect the EGT sensor electrical connectors.

➥The exhaust system alignment procedure only needs to be carried out if the exhaust system isolators are not at zero load.

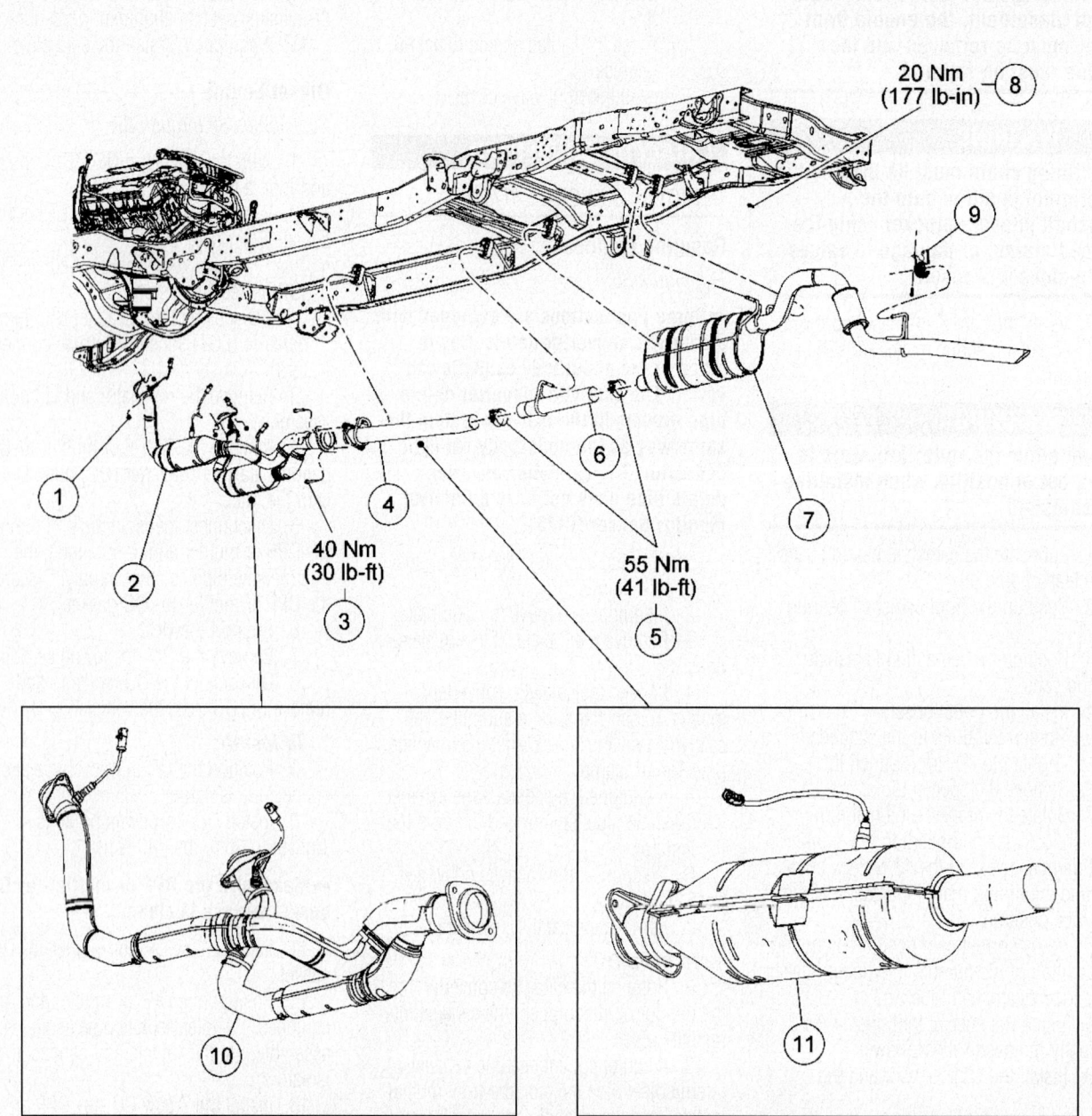

Fig. 86 Exploded view of the exhaust system

1. Exhaust Y-pipe-to-exhaust manifold nut (4 required)
2. Exhaust Y-pipe with dual catalytic converter
3. Exhaust Y-pipe-to-catalytic converter delete pipe bolt (2 required)
4. Catalytic converter delete pipe
5. Torca® clamps
6. Exhaust intermediate pipe
7. Muffler and tail pipe assembly
8. Tail pipe bracket and insulator bolt (2 required)
9. Tail pipe hanger
10. Exhaust Y-pipe without dual catalytic converters
11. Catalytic converter

36578_F250_G0063

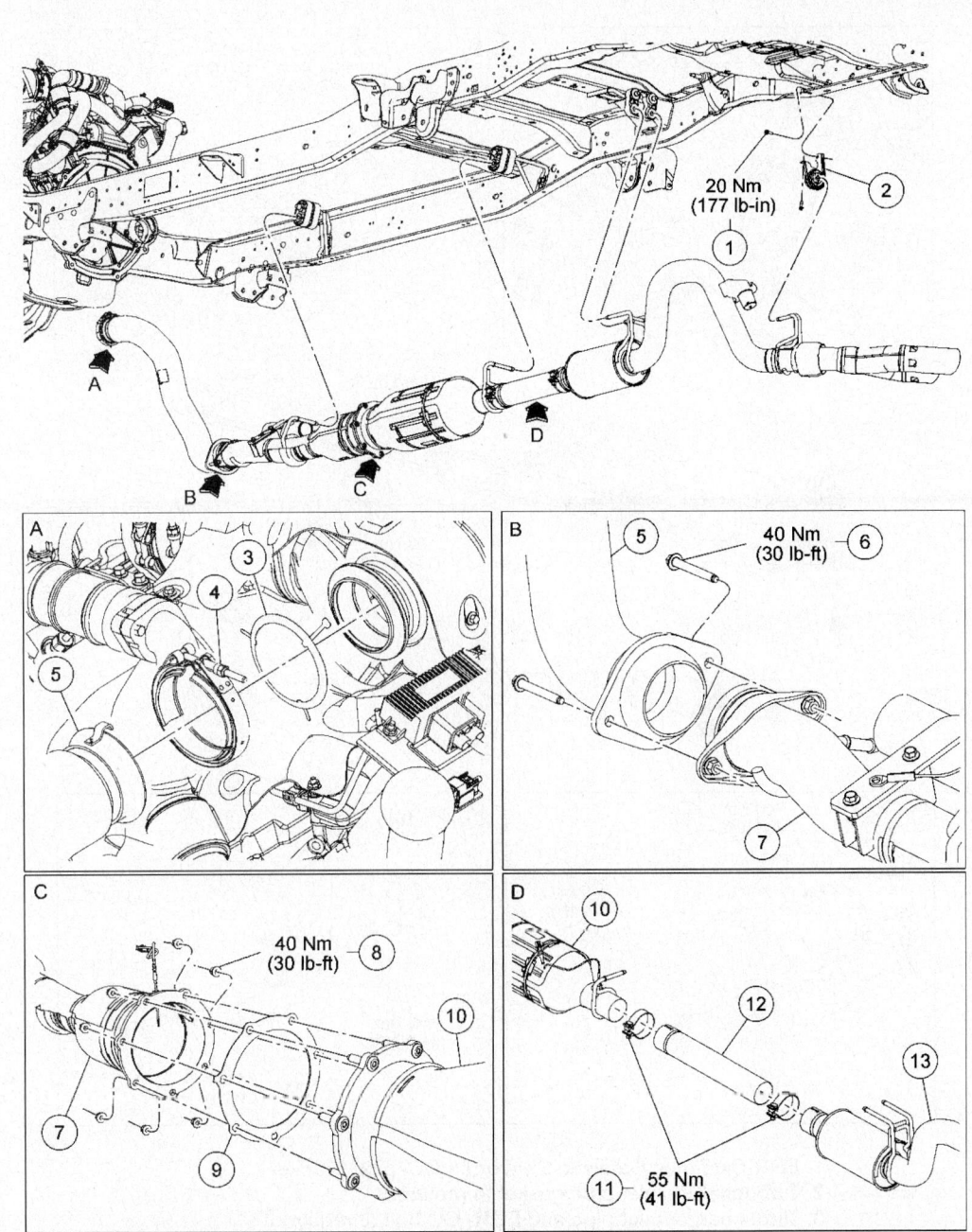

1. Tail pipe bracket and insulator bolt (2 required)
2. Tail pipe hanger
3. Exhaust downpipe-to-turbocharger gasket
4. Exhaust downpipe-to-turbocharger clamp
5. Exhaust downpipe
6. Exhaust downpipe-to-Oxidation Catalytic Converter (OC) bolt (2 required)
7. OC
8. OC -to-Diesel Particulate Filter (DPF) nut (7 required)
9. OC -to- DPF gasket
10. DPF
11. Torca® clamp
12. Exhaust intermediate pipe
13. Tail pipe

36578_F250_G0064

Fig. 87 Exploded view of the exhaust system—6.4L Diesel Engine with a Diesel Particulate Filter

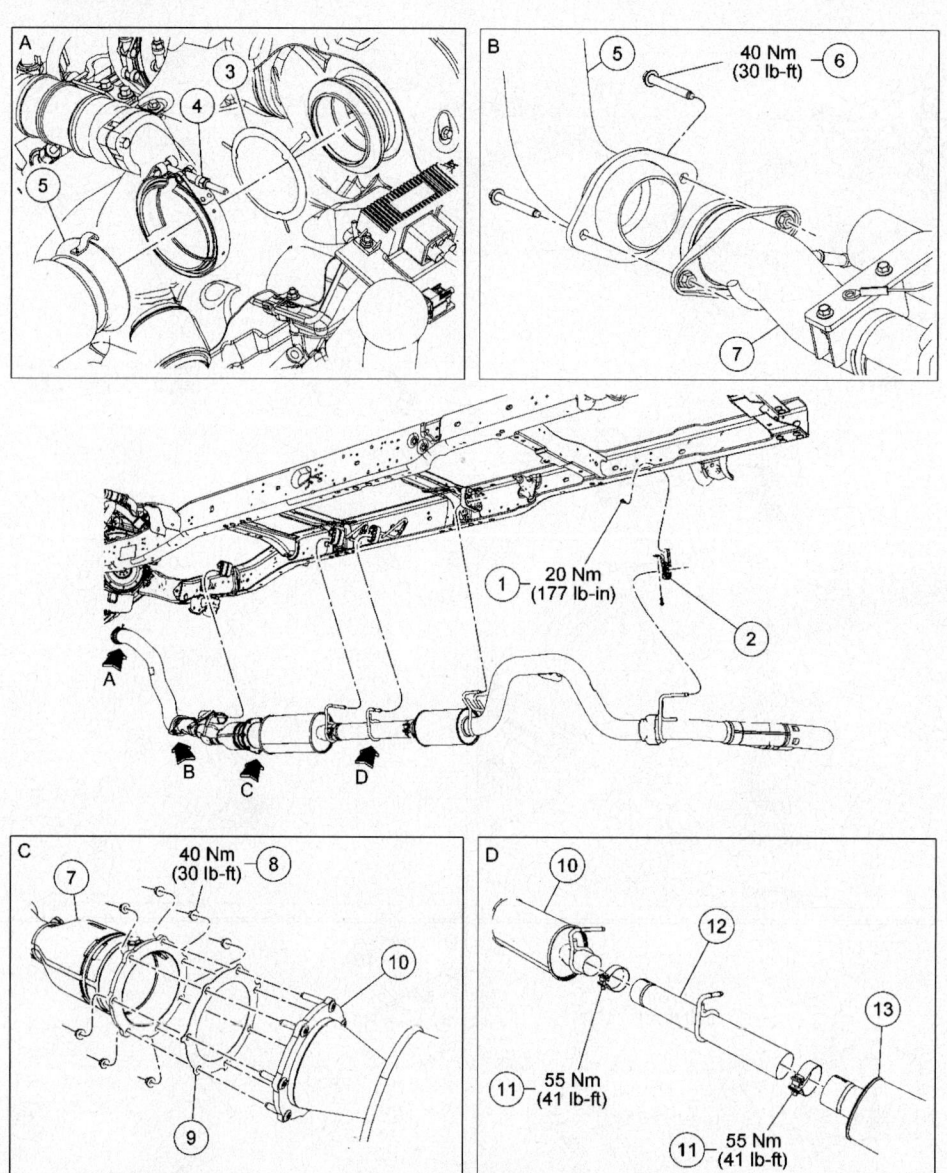

1. EGR-Oxidation Catalytic Converter (OC) pipe bracket
2. Turbocharger inlet pipe gasket (4 required)
3. Turbocharger inlet pipe and EGR- OC bolt (8 required)
4. LH turbocharger inlet pipe
5. EGR- OC pipe-to-EGR- OC pipe bracket bolt (2 required)
6. EGR- OC pipe gasket (2 required)
7. Exhaust Gas Temperature (EGT) sensor
8. RH turbocharger inlet pipe
9. EGR- OC pipe
10. EGR- OC pipe bracket-to-cylinder head bracket washer
11. Cylinder head bracket-to-cylinder head bolt
12. Cylinder head bracket-to-cylinder head washer (2 required)
13. EGR- OC pipe bracket-to-cylinder head bracket
14. EGR- OC pipe-to-EGR cooler bolt (2 required)
15. Turbocharger inlet pipe-to-exhaust manifold nut (6 required)
16. Turbocharger inlet pipe-to-exhaust manifold stud
17. LH turbocharger inlet pipe-to-exhaust manifold bolt (service only)
18. Exhaust Pressure (EP) sensor tube fitting

36578_F250_G0065

Fig. 88 Exploded view of the exhaust system—6.4L Diesel Engine with a muffler

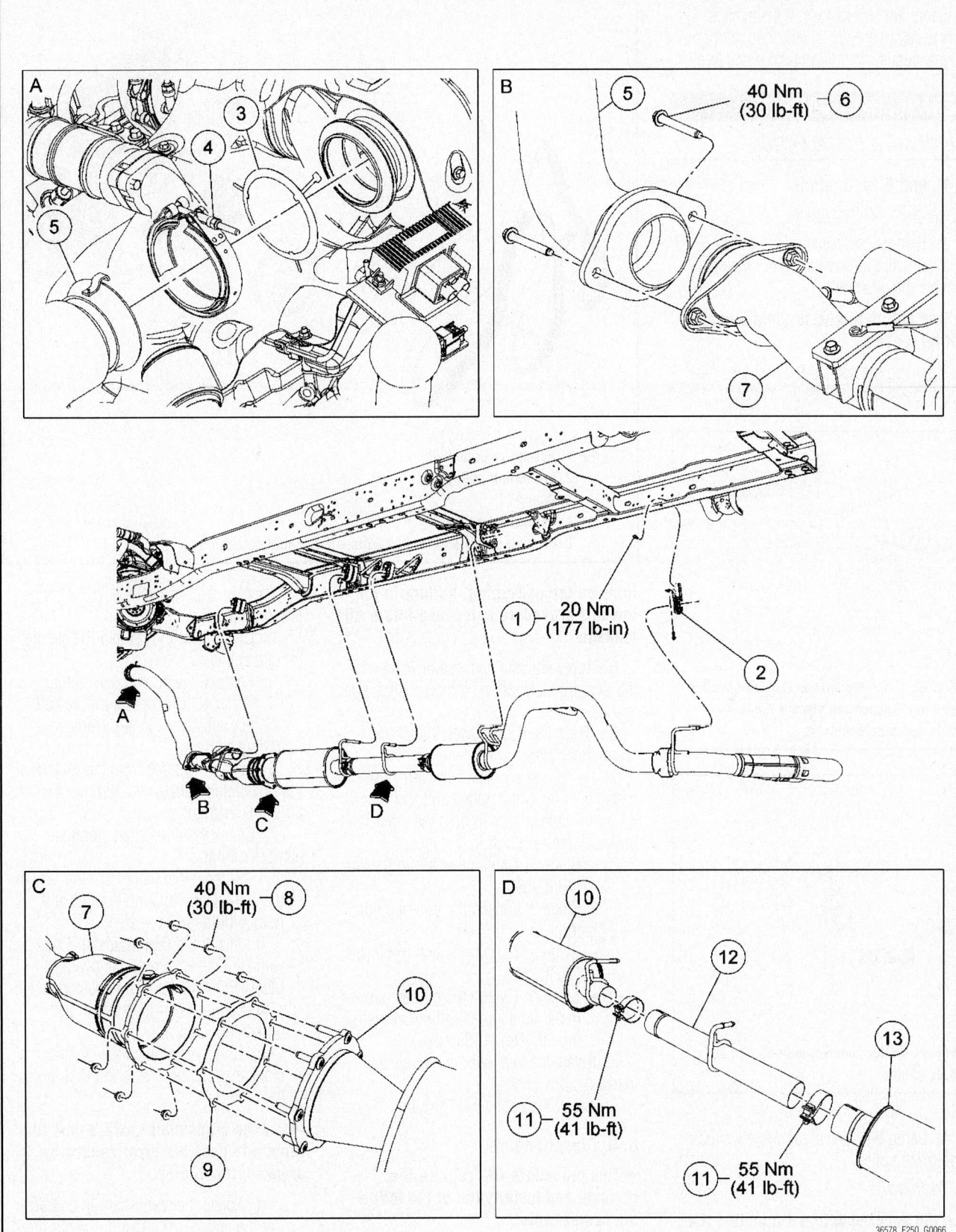

Fig. 89 Exploded view of the exhaust system—6.4L Diesel Engine with turbocharger inlet pipes and EGR OC pipe

36578_F250_G0066

16. Check to see if the exhaust system isolators are at zero load. If the exhaust system isolators are not at zero load, carry out the exhaust system alignment procedure.

CRANKSHAFT DAMPER

REMOVAL & INSTALLATION

5.4L and 6.8L Engines

See Figures 90 through 92.

1. Remove the cooling fan shroud.
2. Rotate the tensioner clockwise and remove the drive belt.

➡**This bolt is torque-to-yield and cannot be reused.**

3. Using the special tool, remove the bolt and washer and discard the bolt.

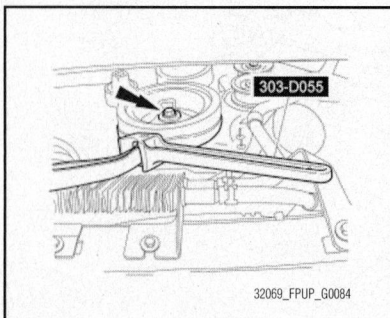

Fig. 90 Using the special tool, remove the bolt and washer and discard the bolt— 5.4L and 6.8L engine

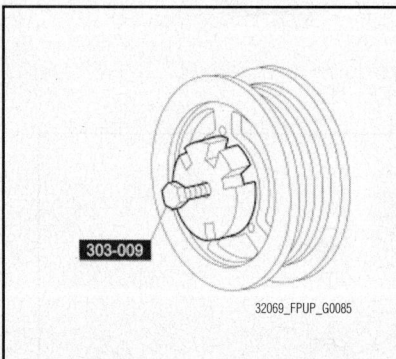

Fig. 91 Pulley removal tool—5.4L and 6.8L engine

4. Using the special tool, remove the crankshaft pulley.

To install:

➡**If not secured within 4 minutes, the sealant must be removed and the sealing area cleaned. To clean the sealing area, use silicone gasket remover and metal surface prep. Follow the direc-**

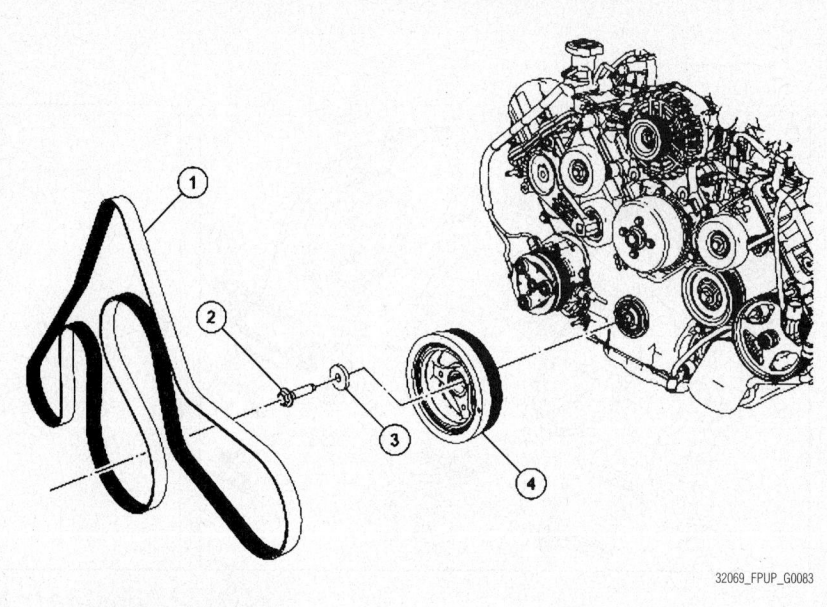

Fig. 92 1. Accessory drive belt
     2. Crankshaft pulley bolt
     3. Washer
     4. Crankshaft pulley
     Crankshaft pulley and related parts—5.4L and 6.8L engine

tions on the packaging. Failure to follow this procedure can cause future oil leakage.

5. Apply silicone gasket and sealant to the Woodruff key slot on the crankshaft pulley.
6. Using the special tool, install the crankshaft pulley.
7. Using a new crankshaft pulley bolt, install the crankshaft pulley bolt and washer. Using the special tool to hold the crankshaft pulley, tighten the bolt in 4 stages:
   - Stage 1: Tighten the bolt to 90 Nm (66 ft. lbs.).
   - Stage 2: Loosen the bolt one full turn.
   - Stage 3: Tighten the bolt to 50 Nm (37 ft. lbs.).
   - Stage 4: Tighten the bolt an additional 90 degrees without exceeding 200 Nm (148 ft. lbs.).
8. Rotate the tensioner clockwise and install the drive belt.
9. Install the cooling fan shroud.

6.4L Diesel Engine

➡**This procedure will require the removal and installation of the following components:**

  a. RH Charge Air Cooler (CAC) tube.
  b. Upper cooling fan shroud .
  c. Cooling fan.
  d. Cooling fan stator

1. With the vehicle in NEUTRAL, position it on a hoist.
2. Disconnect the LH and RH battery ground cable(s).
3. Remove the cooling fan stator.
4. Remove the accessory drive belt.
5. For vehicles with A/C, remove the A/C drive belt.
6. Remove the belt from the bottom of the A/C clutch pulley, then remove it from the crankshaft pulley.
7. Check the crankshaft vibration damper runout:
   a. Remove the paint from the face of the crankshaft vibration damper at 4 points, 90 degrees apart.
   b. Attach the Dial Indicator Gauge with Holding Fixture to the cylinder block. Position the Dial Indicator Gauge with Holding Fixture on one of the unpainted surfaces.
   c. Using a suitable tool, pry the crankshaft forward. Zero the Dial Indicator.

➡**Pry the crankshaft forward only to eliminate possible error caused by crankshaft end play.**

   d. Rotate the crankshaft 90 degrees. Pry the crankshaft forward. Record the measurement. Repeat at each unpainted surface.
   e. If the runout exceeds specification, install a new crankshaft vibration damper.

✳✳ **WARNING**

Support the vibration damper during mounting bolt removal. The damper can slide off the nose of the crankshaft. Failure to follow this instruction may result in serious personal injury.

8. Remove the 4 bolts and the crankshaft vibration damper. Discard the bolts.

To install:

➡ **To prevent engine damage, always install 4 new bolts when installing the vibration damper.**

➡ **Apply a light coat of engine oil to the bolts prior to installing the bolts.**

➡ **Use the Strap Wrench to prevent the engine from turning during the tightening of the bolts.**

9. Position the crankshaft pulley and install 4 new bolts in 2 stages, in sequence
   a. Stage 1: Tighten to 50 ft. lbs. (68 Nm).
   b. Stage 2: Tighten an additional 90 degrees.
10. Vehicles with A/C, install the A/C drive belt.
11. Install the accessory drive belt.
12. Install the cooling fan stator.
13. Connect the battery LH and RH ground cable(s).

CRANKSHAFT FRONT SEAL

REMOVAL & INSTALLATION

5.4L and 6.8L Engines
See Figures 93 and 94.

1. Remove the crankshaft pulley.
2. Using the special tool, remove the crankshaft front seal.

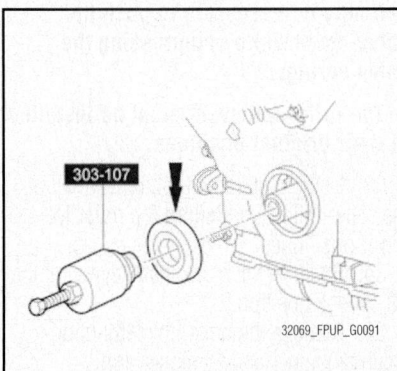

Fig. 93 Using the special tool, remove the crankshaft front seal—5.4L engines

To install:
3. Lubricate the engine front cover and the crankshaft front seal inner lip with clean engine oil.
4. Using the special tools, install the crankshaft front seal.

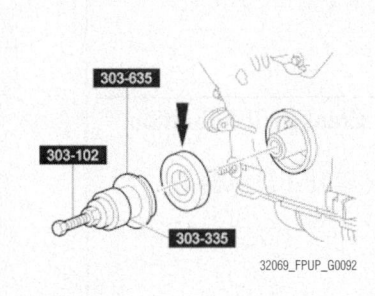

Fig. 94 Using the special tool, install the crankshaft front seal—5.4L and 6.8L engine

5. Install the crankshaft pulley.

6.4L Diesel Engine
See Figure 95.

1. Remove the crankshaft vibration damper. For additional information, refer to Crankshaft Damper in this section.
2. Punch two holes in the seal.
3. Using the special tool, remove the crankshaft seal.

➡ **Production engines will not have a wear sleeve.**

4. If equipped, remove the crankshaft seal wear sleeve.

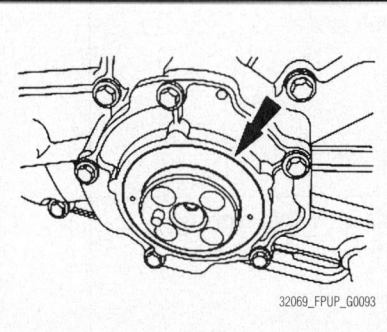

Fig. 95 Punch 2 holes in the seal—6.4L Diesel Engine

To install:
5. Thoroughly clean the crankshaft front seal mounting surface.
6. Apply High Strength Threadlocker to the outer circumference of the leading edge of the crankshaft.

➡ **New seal and wear sleeve must not be separated.**

7. Using the special tool, install the oil seal and wear sleeve assembly.
8. Install the crankshaft damper. For additional information, refer to Crankshaft Damper in this section.

CYLINDER HEAD

REMOVAL & INSTALLATION

5.4L Engine
See Figures 96 through 117.

1. Before servicing the vehicle, refer to the Precautions Section.
2. Remove the engine.
3. Remove the bolts and the flexplate or the flywheel.
4. Install the engine onto a suitable engine stand.
5. Remove the special tool.
Left cylinder head
6. Remove the left exhaust manifold.
7. Remove the bolt and the oil level indicator tube.
8. Remove the engine wiring harness retainers from the left valve cover studs.

✳✳ **WARNING**

When removing the valve cover, make sure to avoid damaging the variable camshaft timing (VCT) solenoid.

9. Remove the bolts and the left valve cover.
Right cylinder head
10. Remove the right exhaust manifold.
11. Remove the nuts.
12. Remove the right exhaust manifold.
13. Remove and discard the right exhaust manifold gasket.
14. Remove the engine wiring harness retainers from the right valve cover studs.

✳✳ **WARNING**

When removing the valve cover, make sure to avoid damaging the variable camshaft timing (VCT) solenoid.

15. Remove the bolts and the right valve cover.
16. Remove the stud.
All cylinder heads
17. Remove the bolts, the coolant pump pulley and the accessory drive belt idler pulleys.
18. Remove the bolt and washer and using a puller set, remove the crankshaft pulley. Discard the crankshaft bolt.

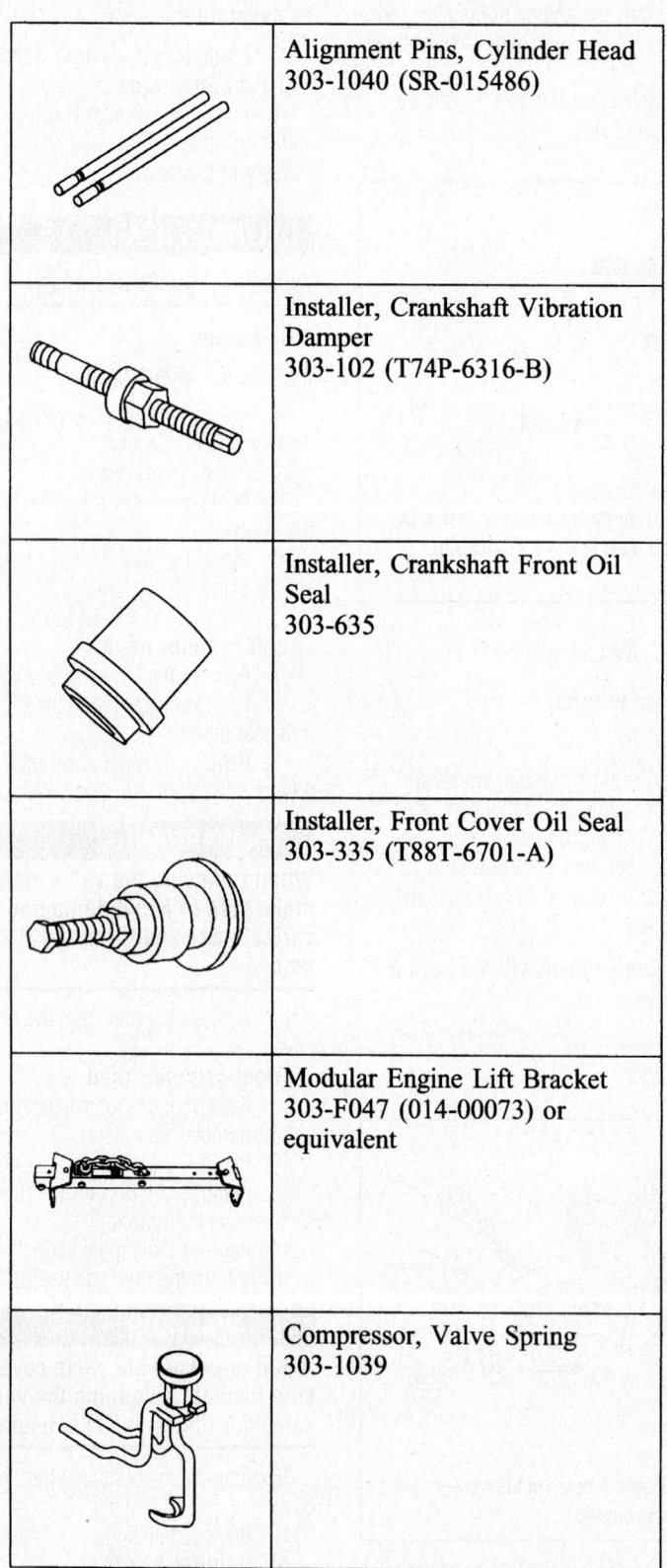

	Alignment Pins, Cylinder Head 303-1040 (SR-015486)
	Installer, Crankshaft Vibration Damper 303-102 (T74P-6316-B)
	Installer, Crankshaft Front Oil Seal 303-635
	Installer, Front Cover Oil Seal 303-335 (T88T-6701-A)
	Modular Engine Lift Bracket 303-F047 (014-00073) or equivalent
	Compressor, Valve Spring 303-1039

67197-EFSE-G033

Fig. 96 Special tools needed for this procedure. These tools are referred to in the following procedure

19. Using a suitable tool, remove the crankshaft seal.

20. Remove the bolts and the accessory drive belt tensioner.

21. Disconnect the left and right radio ignition interference capacitor electrical connectors.

22. Remove the nuts and the two radio interference capacitors.

23. Disconnect the camshaft position (CMP) sensor electrical connectors.

24. Remove the bolt and the right CMP sensor.

25. Remove the bolt and the left CMP sensor.

26. Disconnect the crankshaft position (CKP) sensor electrical connector.

27. Remove the oil pan front bolts.

28. Remove the bolts.

✳✳ WARNING

Do not use metal scrapers, wire brushes, power abrasive discs or other abrasive means to clean the sealing surfaces. These tools cause scratches and gouges which make leak paths. Use a plastic scraping tool to remove all traces of old sealant.

29. Remove the engine front cover from the front cover-to-cylinder block dowels.

30. Remove the engine front cover gaskets.

31. Clean the mating surfaces with silicone gasket remover and metal surface prep. Follow the directions on the packaging.

32. Inspect the mating surfaces.

✳✳ WARNING

Do not allow the valve keepers to fall off of the valve or the valve can drop into the cylinder.

➡ It may be necessary to push the valve down while compressing the valve spring.

➡ The roller followers must be installed in their original positions.

33. Using a suitable tool, remove all of the roller followers. Record the roller follower positions.

34. Position the crankshaft keyway at the 12 o'clock position.

35. Remove the bolts, the left timing chain tensioner and tensioner arm.

36. Remove the bolts, the right timing chain tensioner and tensioner arm.

37. Remove the ignition pulse wheel from the crankshaft.

38. Remove the right timing chain from the camshaft sprocket.

39. Remove the right timing chain from the crankshaft sprocket.

40. Remove the left timing chain from the camshaft sprocket.

41. Remove the left timing chain and crankshaft sprocket.

42. Remove both timing chain guides.

✳✳ WARNING

Use only hand tools to remove the camshaft phaser sprocket assembly or damage can occur to the camshaft or camshaft phaser sprocket.

43. If disassembly of the cylinder head is required, using a suitable tool, loosen the camshaft phaser sprocket bolt.

44. Install a suitable tool onto the left cylinder head. Install a suitable tool onto the right cylinder head.

✳✳ WARNING

The cylinder head must be cool before removing it from the engine. Cylinder head warpage can result if a warm or hot cylinder head is removed.

✳✳ WARNING

Do not use the variable camshaft timing (VCT) phaser sprocket as a lifting point or leveraging device when removing the cylinder head or damage to the VCT phaser sprocket can occur.

✳✳ WARNING

Place clean shop towels over exposed engine cavities. Carefully remove the towels so foreign material is not dropped into the engine.

✳✳ WARNING

The cylinder head bolts must be discarded and new bolts must be installed. They are tighten-to-yield designed and cannot be reused.

✳✳ WARNING

Do not use metal scrapers, wire brushes, power abrasive discs or other abrasive means to clean the sealing surfaces. These tools cause scratches and gouges that make leak paths. Use a plastic scraping tool to remove all traces of the head gasket.

✳✳ WARNING

Aluminum surfaces are soft and can be scratched easily. Never place the cylinder head gasket surface, unprotected, on a bench surface.

45. Remove the bolts and the cylinder head. Discard the cylinder head gasket. Discard the cylinder head bolts.

✳✳ WARNING

Do not use metal scrapers, wire brushes, power abrasive discs or other abrasive means to clean the sealing surfaces. These tools cause scratches and gouges that make leak paths. Use a plastic scraping tool to remove all traces of the head gasket.

✳✳ WARNING

Observe all warnings or cautions and follow all application directions contained on the packaging of the silicone gasket remover and the metal surface prep.

➡ If there is no residual gasket material present, metal surface prep can be used to clean and prepare the surfaces.

46. Clean the cylinder head-to-cylinder block mating surfaces of both the cylinder head and the cylinder block.

47. Remove any large deposits of silicone or gasket material with a plastic scraper.

48. Apply silicone gasket remover, following package directions, and allow to set for several minutes.

49. Remove the silicone gasket remover with a plastic scraper. A second application of silicone gasket remover may be required if residual traces of silicone or gasket material remain.

50. Apply metal surface prep, following package directions, to remove any remaining traces of oil or coolant, and to prepare the surfaces to bond with the new gasket. Do not attempt to make the metal shiny. Some staining of the metal surfaces is normal.

➡ Make sure all cylinder head surfaces and engine block surfaces are clear of any gasket material, RTV, oil and coolant. The cylinder head and engine block surfaces must be clean and dry before running a flatness check.

➡ Use a straightedge that is calibrated by the manufacturer to be flat within 0.005 mm (0.0002 in.) per running foot of length. For example, if the straight-

edge is 61 cm (24 in.) long, the machined edge must be flat with 0.010 mm (0.0004 in.) from end to end.

51. Support the cylinder head on a bench with the head gasket side up. Inspect all areas of the deck face with a straightedge, paying particular attention to the oil pressure feed area. The cylinder head must not have depressions deeper than 0.0254 mm (0.001 in.) across a 38.1 mm (1.5 in.) square area, or scratches more than 0.0254 mm (0.001 in.).

To install:
All cylinder heads

✳✳ WARNING

Make sure all coolant residue and foreign material are cleaned from the block surface and cylinder bore.

✳✳ WARNING

The use of sealing aids (aviation cement, copper spray, and glue) is not permitted. The gasket must be installed dry.

✳✳ WARNING

The cylinder head bolts must be discarded and new bolts installed. They are tighten-to-yield designed and cannot be reused.

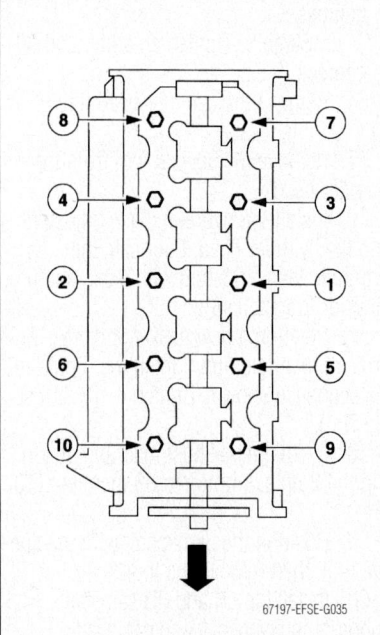

67197-EFSE-G035

Fig. 97 Left cylinder head torque sequence—5.4L engine (RH cylinder head similar)

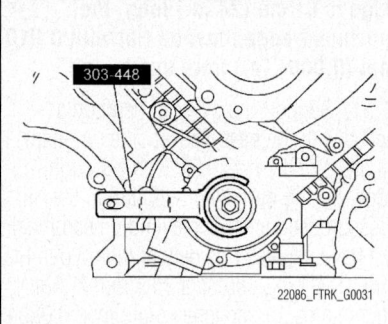

Fig. 98 Position the crankshaft with the special tool, then remove the tool

✳✳ WARNING

Do not allow the cylinder head alignment pins to contact the cylinder head gasket or cylinder head sealing surfaces or damage can occur to the cylinder head or cylinder head gasket.

➡**Do not turn the crankshaft until instructed to do so.**

52. Using the cylinder head alignment pins, position the cylinder head gasket and cylinder head onto the dowels and install the cylinder head bolts loosely.

53. Tighten the bolts in the sequence shown.

    a. Stage 1: Tighten to 40 Nm (30 ft. lbs.).

    b. Stage 2: Tighten an additional 90 degrees.

    c. Stage 3: Tighten an additional 90 degrees.

54. Remove the cylinder head lifting handle tools.

55. Remove the special tool from the cylinder head.

56. Install the hydraulic lash adjusters into the cylinder head. Lubricate the hydraulic lash adjusters with clean engine oil prior to installation.

57. Position a new gasket and the exhaust manifold and tighten the 8 nuts in the sequence shown. Tighten to 18 ft. lbs. (25 Nm).

58. Install the exhaust manifold shield and the 2 nuts. Tighten to 89 inch lbs. (10 Nm).

59. Position the crankshaft with the special tool, then remove the tool.

60. Install the LH and RH camshafts. Lubricate the camshaft and camshaft journals with clean engine oil prior to installation.

61. Install the LH and RH camshaft bearing caps in their original locations.

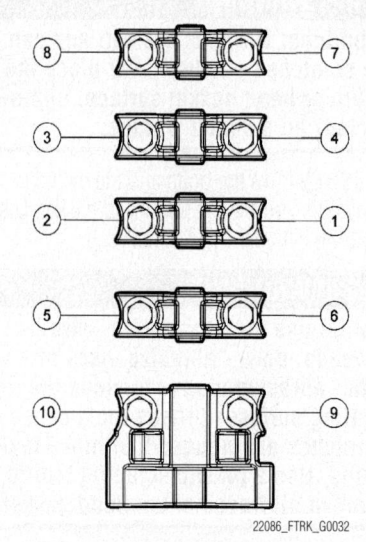

Fig. 99 Install the camshafts and tighten the bearing caps in the sequence shown

    a. Lubricate the camshaft bearing caps with clean engine oil.

    b. Position the front camshaft bearing cap.

    c. Position the remaining camshaft bearing caps.

    d. Install the bolts loosely.

    e. Tighten to 89 inch lbs. (10 Nm) in the sequence shown.

✳✳ CAUTION

Damage to the variable camshaft timing (VCT) phaser sprocket assembly will occur if mishandled or used as a lifting or leveraging device.

62. Install the VCT phaser sprockets and new VCT phaser sprocket bolts finger tight.

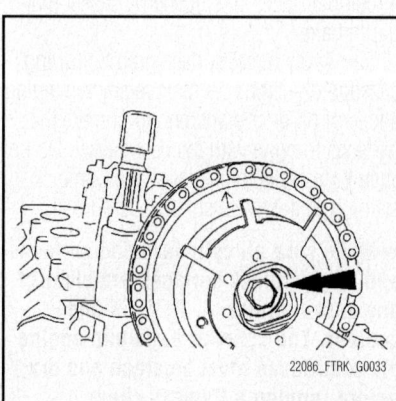

Fig. 100 Install the VCT phaser sprockets and new VCT phaser sprocket bolts finger tight

✳✳ CAUTION

Only use hand tools to remove the VCT phaser sprocket assembly or damage may occur to the camshaft or VCT phaser sprocket.

63. Using the special tool, tighten the LH and RH VCT phaser sprocket bolts in 2 stages:

    a. Stage 1: Tighten to 30 ft. lbs. (40 Nm).

    b. Stage 2: Tighten an additional 90 degrees.

✳✳ WARNING

Timing chain procedures must be followed exactly or damage to valves and pistons will result.

64. Compress the tensioner plunger, using a vice.

65. Install a retaining clip on the tensioner to hold the plunger in during installation.

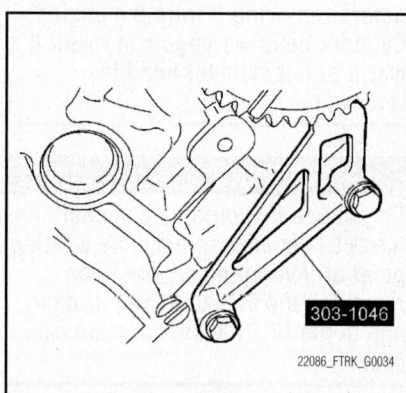

Fig. 101 Using the special tool, tighten the LH and RH VCT phaser sprocket bolts in 2 stages

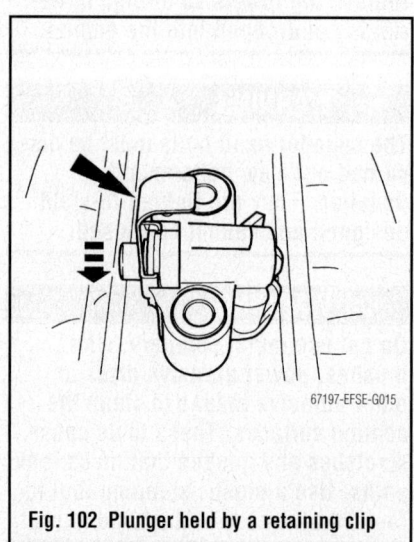

Fig. 102 Plunger held by a retaining clip

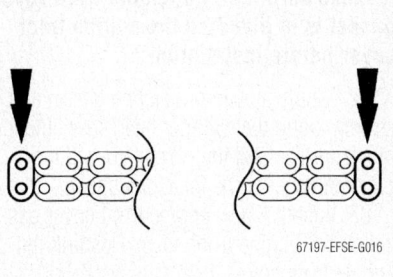

Fig. 103 If the copper links are not visible, mark one link on one end and one link on the other end, and use as timing marks

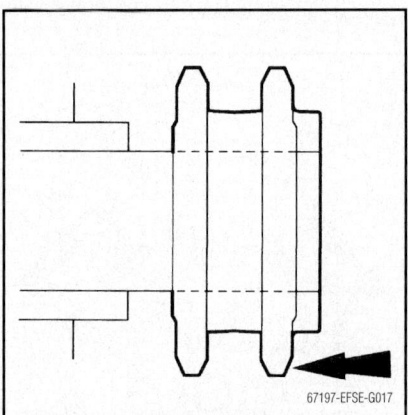

Fig. 104 Install the crankshaft sprocket, making sure the flange faces forward

66. Remove the tensioner from the vise. If the copper links are not visible, mark two links on one end and one link on the other end, and use as timing marks.

❊❊ WARNING
Crankshaft keyway must be in the 12 o'clock position.

67. Install the timing chain guides.
68. Position the left timing chain guide.
69. Install the crankshaft sprocket, making sure the flange faces forward.

❊❊ WARNING
Only use hand tools to install the camshaft phaser sprocket assembly or damage may occur to the camshaft or camshaft phaser unit.

➡This step is only required if cylinder head was disassembled.

70. Using a suitable tool, tighten the bolts in two stages:
   a. Stage 1: Tighten to 40 Nm (30 ft. lbs.).
   b. Stage 2: Tighten an additional 90 degrees.

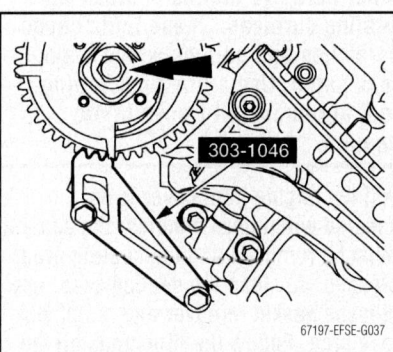

Fig. 106 Camshaft phaser sprocket holding tool—5.4L engine

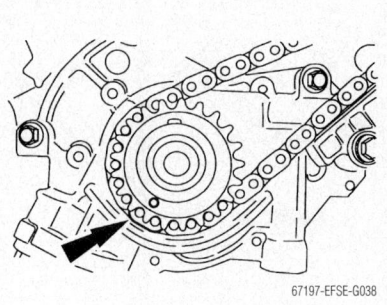

Fig. 107 Position the lower end of the left (inner) timing chain on the crankshaft sprocket, aligning the timing mark on the outer flange of the crankshaft sprocket with the single copper (marked) link on the chain—5.4L engine

71. Remove the special tool.
72. Position the lower end of the left (inner) timing chain on the crankshaft sprocket, aligning the timing mark on the outer flange of the crankshaft sprocket with the single copper (marked) link on the chain.

➡Make sure the upper half of the timing chain is below the tensioner arm dowel. Position the timing chain on the camshaft sprocket with the camshaft sprocket timing mark positioned between the two copper (marked) chain links.

➡The left timing chain tensioner arm has a bump near the dowel hole for identification.

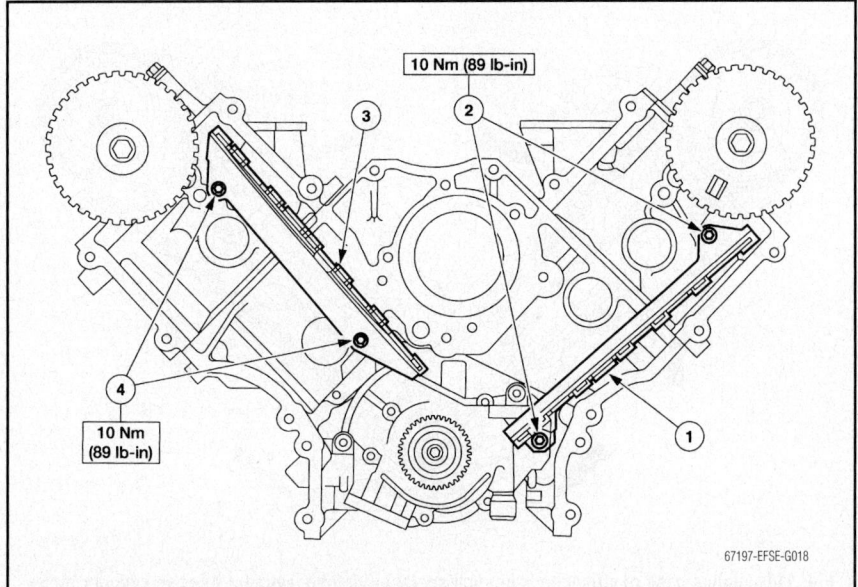

Fig. 105 Timing chain guide installation

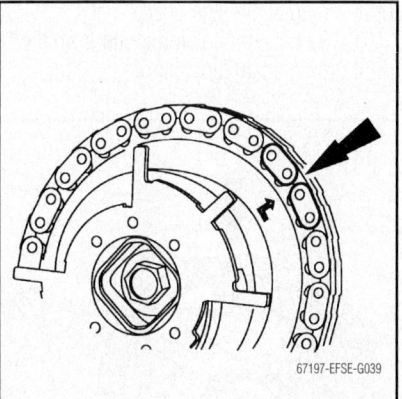

Fig. 108 Position the timing chain on the camshaft sprocket with the camshaft sprocket timing mark positioned between the two copper (marked) chain links—5.4L engine

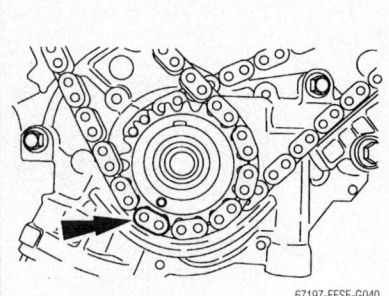

Fig. 109 Position the lower end of the right (outer) timing chain on the crankshaft sprocket, aligning the timing mark on the sprocket with the single copper (marked) chain link

73. Position the left timing chain tensioner arm on the dowel pin and install the left timing chain tensioner.

74. Remove the retaining clip from the left timing chain tensioner.

75. Position the lower end of the right (outer) timing chain on the crankshaft sprocket, aligning the timing mark on the sprocket with the single copper (marked) chain link.

➡**The lower half of the timing chain must be positioned above the tensioner arm dowel.**

76. Position the right timing chain on the camshaft sprocket. Make sure the camshaft sprocket timing mark is positioned between the two copper (marked) chain links.

77. Position the right timing chain tensioner arm on the dowel pin and install the right timing chain tensioner.

78. Remove the retaining clip from the right timing chain tensioner.

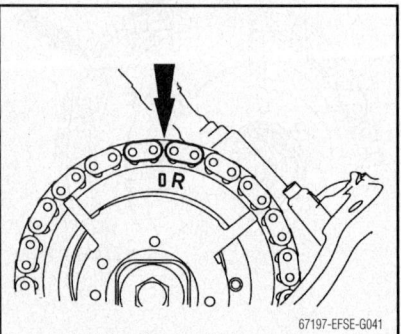

Fig. 110 Position the right timing chain on the camshaft sprocket. Make sure the camshaft sprocket timing mark is positioned between the two copper (marked) chain links

➡**Both camshaft phaser sprockets are identical. Refer to the R timing mark to identify the right camshaft phaser sprocket and the L timing mark to identify the left camshaft phaser sprocket.**

79. As a post-check, verify correct alignment of all timing marks. Make sure the R and L timing marks on the sprockets correspond to the above note.

80. Install the crankshaft sensor ring on the crankshaft.

➡**Lubricate the camshaft roller followers using clean engine oil.**

➡**Using the mark on each camshaft roller follower, make sure it is returned to its original position.**

81. Using a suitable tool, install all of the camshaft roller followers.

※※ WARNING

Do not use metal scrapers, wire brushes, power abrasive discs or other abrasive means to clean the sealing surfaces. These tools cause scratches and gouges which make leak paths. Use a plastic scraping tool to remove all traces of old sealant.

➡**If the engine front cover is not secured within four minutes, the sealant must be removed and the sealing area cleaned. To clean the sealing area, use silicone gasket remover and metal surface prep. Follow the directions on the packaging. Failure to follow this procedure can cause future oil leakage.**

➡**Make sure that the engine front cover gasket is in place on the engine front cover before installation.**

82. Apply a bead of silicone gasket and sealant along the cylinder head-to-cylinder block surface and the oil pan-to-cylinder block surface, at the locations shown.

83. Install a new engine front cover gasket on the engine front cover. Position the engine front cover. Install the fasteners finger-tight.

84. Tighten the engine front cover fasteners in sequence in two stages.
  a. Stage 1: Tighten fasteners 1 through 15 to 25 Nm (18 ft. lbs.).
  b. Stage 2: Tighten fasteners 6 and 7 to 48 Nm (35 ft. lbs.).

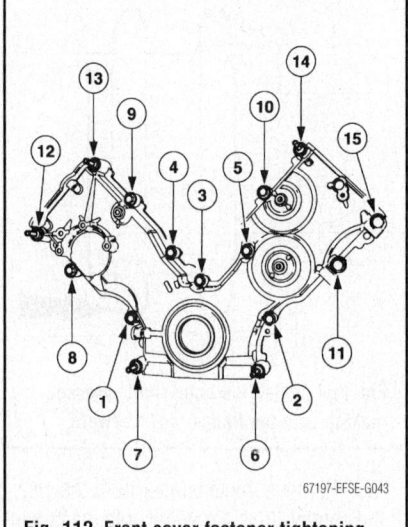

Fig. 112 Front cover fastener tightening sequence

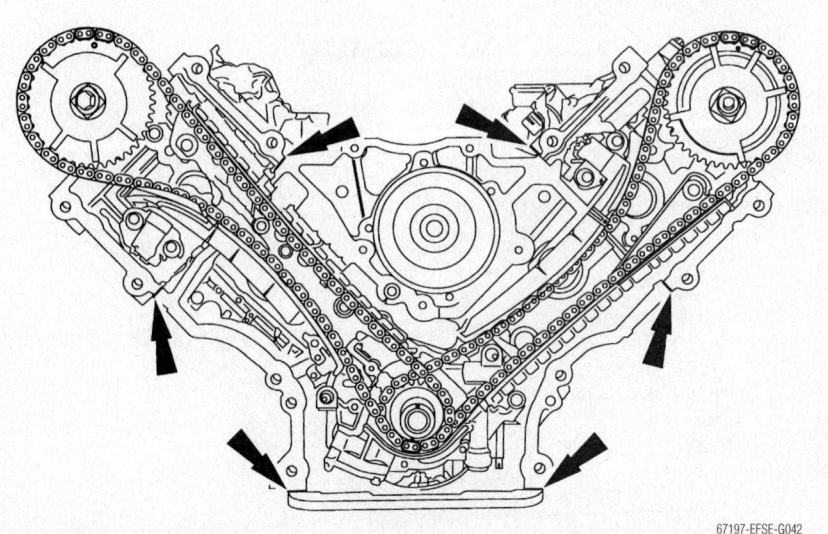

Fig. 111 Apply a bead of silicone gasket and sealant along the cylinder head-to-cylinder block surface and the oil pan-to-cylinder block surface, at the locations shown—5.4L engine

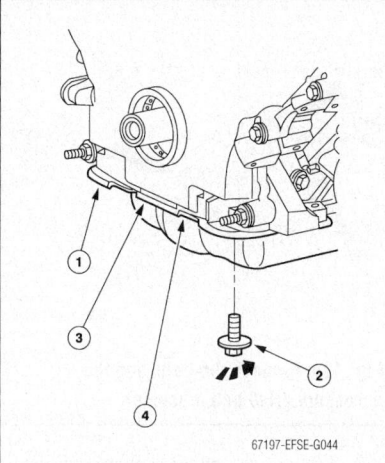

Fig. 113 Loosely install the pan-to-case bolts, then tighten the bolts in two stages, in the sequence shown

c. Loosely install the pan-to-case bolts, then tighten the bolts in two stages, in the sequence shown.

d. Stage 1: Tighten to 20 Nm (15 ft. lbs.).

e. Stage 2: Tighten an additional 60 degrees.

85. Install the left camshaft position (CMP) sensor and the bolt.

86. Lubricate the new O-ring seal with clean engine oil prior to installation.

87. Install the right CMP sensor and the bolt.

88. Lubricate the new O-ring seal with clean engine oil prior to installation.

89. Lubricate the engine front cover and the crankshaft seal inner lip with clean engine oil.

90. Use the special tools to install the crankshaft seal into the engine front cover.

91. If not secured within four minutes, the sealant must be removed and the seal-

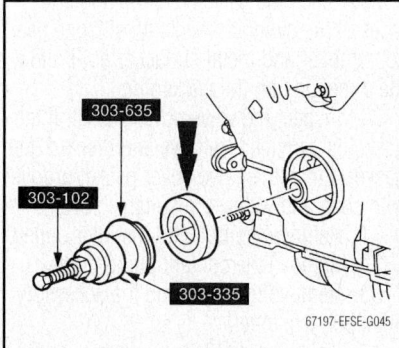

Fig. 114 Crankshaft seal installation tools

ing area cleaned. To clean the sealing area, use silicone gasket remover and metal surface prep. Follow the directions on the packaging. Failure to follow this procedure can cause future oil leakage.

92. Apply silicone gasket and sealant to the Woodruff key slot on the crankshaft pulley. Use a suitable tool to install the crankshaft pulley.

93. Tighten the new crankshaft pulley bolt in four stages.

a. Stage 1: Tighten to 90 Nm (66 ft. lbs.).

b. Stage 2: Loosen 360 degrees.

c. Stage 3: Tighten to 50 Nm (37 ft. lbs.).

d. Stage 4: Tighten an additional 90 degrees.

94. Install the three accessory drive belt idler pulleys, the coolant pump pulley and the bolts. Torque all bolts to 18 ft. lbs. (25 Nm).

95. Position the accessory drive belt tensioner and install the bolts. Torque all bolts to 18 ft. lbs. (25 Nm).

96. Install the radio frequency interference capacitors.

Left cylinder head

※※ WARNING

Do not use metal scrapers, wire brushes, power abrasive discs or other abrasive means to clean sealing surfaces. These tools cause scratches and gouges which make leak paths. Use a plastic scraping tool to remove all traces of old sealant. Inspect and clean the valve cover sealing surfaces with silicone gasket remover and metal surface prep. Follow the directions on the packaging.

➡If not secured within four minutes, the sealant must be removed and the sealing area cleaned. To clean the sealing area, use silicone gasket remover and metal surface prep. Follow the directions on the packaging. Failure to follow this procedure can cause future oil leakage.

97. Apply silicone gasket and sealant in two places where the engine front cover meets the cylinder head.

※※ WARNING

When installing the valve cover, make sure to avoid damaging the variable camshaft timing (VCT) solenoid.

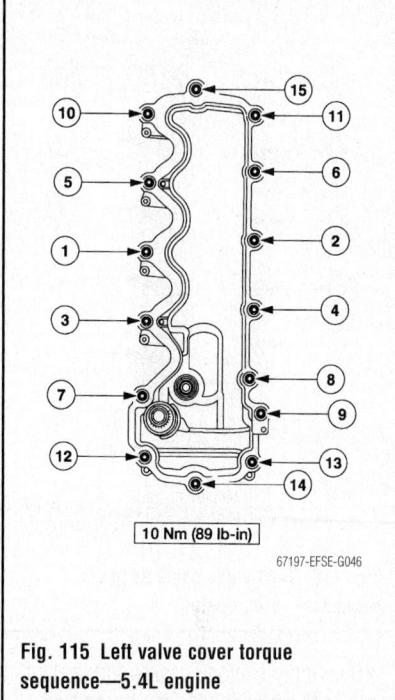

10 Nm (89 lb-in)

Fig. 115 Left valve cover torque sequence—5.4L engine

98. Position the left valve cover and gasket on the cylinder head and install the bolts loosely. Tighten the bolts in the sequence shown.

➡Lubricate the O-ring seal with clean engine oil.

99. Install the oil level indicator tube.

100. Install a new O-ring seal on the oil level indicator tube.

101. Install the oil level indicator tube.

102. Install the bolt.

Right cylinder head

※※ WARNING

Do not use metal scrapers, wire brushes, power abrasive discs or other abrasive means to clean sealing surfaces. These tools cause scratches and gouges which make leak paths. Use a plastic scraping tool to remove all traces of old sealant. Inspect and clean the valve cover sealing surfaces with silicone gasket remover and metal surface prep. Follow the directions on the packaging.

➡If not secured within four minutes, the sealant must be removed and the sealing area cleaned. To clean the sealing area, use silicone gasket remover and metal surface prep. Follow the directions on the packaging. Failure to follow this procedure can cause future oil leakage.

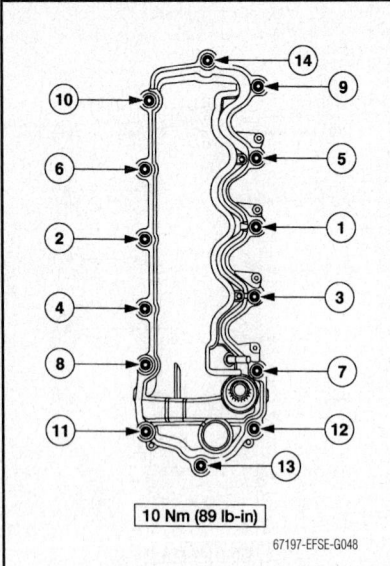

Fig. 116 Right valve cover torque sequence—5.4L engine

10 Nm (89 lb-in)

67197-EFSE-G048

103. Apply silicone gasket and sealant in two places where the engine front cover meets the cylinder head.

> ❊❊ **WARNING**
>
> **When installing the valve cover, make sure to avoid damaging the variable camshaft timing (VCT) solenoid.**

104. Position the right valve cover and gasket on the cylinder head and install the bolts loosely. Tighten the bolts in the sequence shown.

105. Install the heater outlet tube stud.

All cylinder heads

106. Position the electrical harness on the valve cover and connect the engine wiring harness retainers to the valve cover studs.

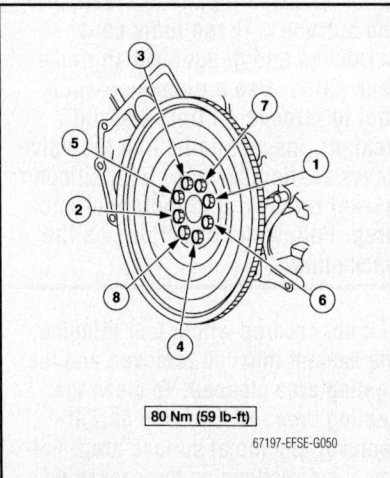

80 Nm (59 lb-ft)

67197-EFSE-G050

Fig. 117 Flywheel torque sequence—5.4L engine

107. Connect the right radio ignition interference capacitor electrical connector.

108. Connect the left radio ignition interference capacitor and cylinder head temperature (CHT) sensor electrical connectors.

109. Connect the CMP sensor electrical connectors.

110. Connect the CKP sensor electrical connector.

111. Install a suitable tool.

112. Using a suitable floor crane remove the engine from the engine stand.

113. Install the flexplate or the flywheel and bolts. Tighten the bolts in the sequence shown.

114. Install the engine.

6.8L Engine

See Figures 118 through 148.

1. Before servicing the vehicle, refer to the Precautions Section.

2. Remove the engine.

3. Remove the bolts and the flexplate or the flywheel.

> ❊❊ **CAUTION**
>
> **Do not use the oil pan to support the engine.**

4. Lower and support the engine assembly on wood blocks.

5. Using the special tools, remove and discard the crankshaft rear oil slinger.

6. Using the special tools, remove and discard the crankshaft rear seal.

7. Remove the bolts and the crankshaft rear seal retainer plate.

8. Mount the engine on a suitable work stand.

9. Remove the right engine mount.

10. Remove the cylinder block drain plugs and drain the coolant into a suitable container.

11. Disconnect the camshaft position (CMP) electrical connector.

12. Disconnect the right radio frequency interference capacitor electrical connector and the capacitor.

13. Disconnect the electrical connector retainer from the coolant tube support bracket.

14. Disconnect the 10 ignition coil electrical connectors.

15. Remove the 10 bolts and the 10 ignition coils.

16. Disconnect the cylinder head temperature (CHT) sensor electrical connector.

17. Disconnect the engine oil pressure (EOP) sensor electrical connector.

18. Remove the nut and the LH radio ignition interference capacitor.

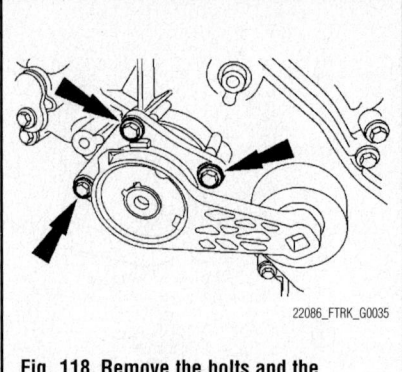

22086_FTRK_G0035

Fig. 118 Remove the bolts and the accessory drive belt tensioner

19. Disconnect the crankshaft position (CKP) sensor electrical connector.

20. Remove the nuts and position the wiring harness aside.

21. Remove the rear oil indicator tube and bracket.

22. Disconnect and remove the CMP sensor.

23. Remove the CKP sensor.

➡**The bolts are part of the valve cover and should not be removed.**

24. Loosen the 16 fasteners in an alternating sequence and remove the valve cover and gasket.

25. Clean the valve cover mating surface of the cylinder head with silicone gasket remover and metal surface prep. Follow the directions on the packaging.

26. Discard the valve cover gasket. Clean the valve cover gasket groove with soap and water or a suitable solvent.

27. Clean the valve cover mating surface of the cylinder head with silicone gasket remover and metal surface prep. Follow the directions on the packaging.

28. Inspect the valve cover gasket. If the gasket is damaged, remove and discard the gasket. Clean the valve cover gasket groove with soap and water or a suitable solvent.

29. Clean the valve cover mating surfaces of the cylinder head with silicone gasket remover and metal surface prep. Follow the directions on the packaging.

30. Inspect the valve cover gasket. If the gasket is damaged, remove and discard the gasket. Clean the valve cover gasket groove with soap and water or a suitable solvent.

31. Remove the bolt and the idler pulley.

32. Remove the coolant pump pulley.

33. Remove the bolts and the accessory drive belt tensioner.

34. Using a suitable tool, remove and discard the crankshaft pulley bolt. Remove the crankshaft pulley.

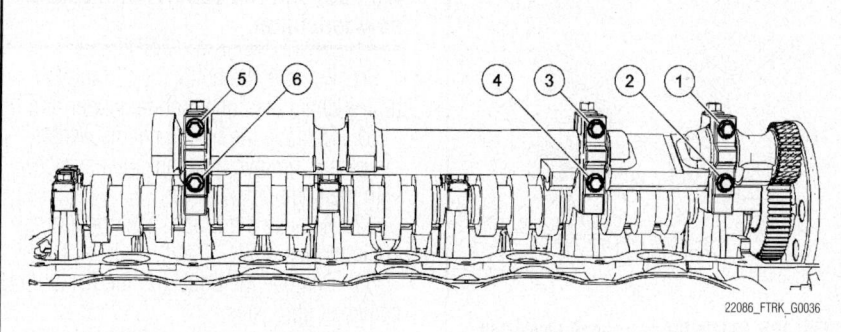

Fig. 119 Balance shaft cap bolt removal sequence—6.8L engine

35. Using a suitable tool, remove the crankshaft front seal.

36. Remove the front four oil pan bolts.

➡ Correct engine front cover fastener location is essential for assembly procedure. Record fastener location.

37. Remove the engine front cover fasteners.

38. Remove the engine front cover from the cylinder block.

✷✷ CAUTION
Only use hand tools to loosen the camshaft sprocket bolt or damage may occur to the camshaft or camshaft sprocket.

39. Loosen and back off the RH camshaft sprocket bolt 1 full turn.

40. Loosen the LH camshaft sprocket bolt.

➡ The balance shaft caps must be marked for installation in their original locations or damage to the engine may occur.

41. Remove the six bolts, in the sequence shown, and remove the balance shaft bearing caps.

42. Remove the balance shaft.

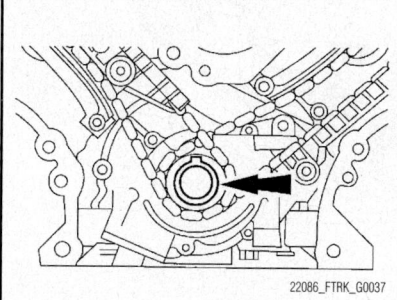

Fig. 120 Position the crankshaft with the keyway at the 12 o'clock position—6.8L engine

43. Remove the crankshaft sensor ring from the crankshaft.

44. Position the crankshaft with the keyway at the 12 o'clock position.

➡ If the camshaft lobes are not exactly positioned as shown, the crankshaft will require one full additional rotation to 12 o'clock.

➡ The No. 1 cylinder camshaft exhaust lobe must be coming up on the exhaust stroke. Verify by noting the position of the 2 intake camshaft lobes and the exhaust lobe on the No. 1 cylinder.

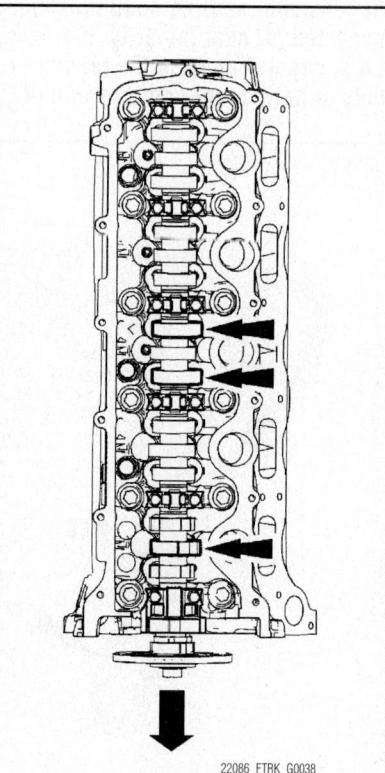

Fig. 121 Remove only the 3 camshaft roller followers shown in the illustration from the RH cylinder head—6.8L engine

✷✷ CAUTION
If the components are to be reinstalled, they must be installed in the same positions. Mark the components for installation into the original locations.

45. Remove only the 3 camshaft roller followers shown in the illustration from the RH cylinder head.

✷✷ CAUTION
Do not allow the valve keepers to fall off the valve or the valve may drop into the cylinder.

➡ It may be necessary to push the valve down while compressing the spring.

46. Using the special tool, remove the 3 designated camshaft roller followers in the previous step from the RH cylinder head.

✷✷ CAUTION
If the components are to be reinstalled, they must be installed in the same positions. Mark the components for installation into the original locations.

47. Remove only the 4 camshaft roller followers shown in the illustration from the LH cylinder head.

✷✷ CAUTION
Do not allow the valve keepers to fall off the valve or the valve may drop into the cylinder.

➡ It may be necessary to push the valve down while compressing the spring.

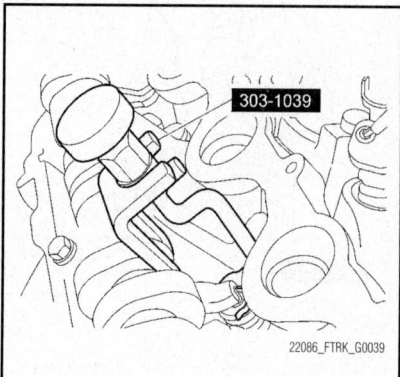

Fig. 122 Using the special tool, remove the 3 designated camshaft roller followers in the previous step from the RH cylinder head—6.8L engine

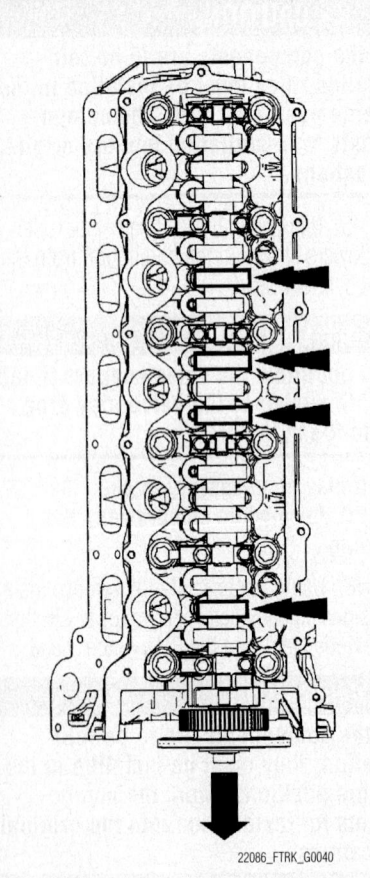

Fig. 123 Remove only the 4 camshaft roller followers shown in the illustration from the LH cylinder head—6.8L engine

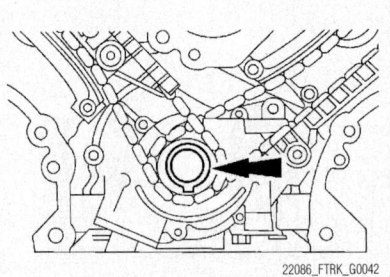

Fig. 125 Rotate the crankshaft clockwise and position the crankshaft keyway at the 6 o'clock position—6.8L engine

48. Using the special tool, remove the 4 designated camshaft roller followers in the previous step from the LH cylinder head.

✲✲ CAUTION

The crankshaft cannot be moved past the 6 o'clock position once set.

49. Rotate the crankshaft clockwise and position the crankshaft keyway at the 6 o'clock position.

✲✲ CAUTION

If one or both of the tensioner mounting bolts are loosened or removed, the tensioner-sealing bead must be inspected for seal integrity. If cracks, tears, separation from the tensioner body or permanent compression of

the seal bead is observed, install a new tensioner.

50. Remove the bolts, the LH and RH timing chain tensioner and tensioner arm.

51. Remove the timing chains. Where necessary, remove the crankshaft sprocket with the chain.

52. Remove the 4 bolts and the timing chain guides.

53. Remove the bolts and the RH and LH camshaft sprockets.

54. Remove the balance shaft drive gear from the LH camshaft.

✲✲ CAUTION

Remove the front thrust camshaft bearing cap straight upward from the bearing towers, or the bearing cap may be damaged from sideloading.

➡ **The camshaft bearing caps must be installed in their original locations. Record camshaft bearing cap locations.**

55. Remove the bolts in the sequence shown and remove the RH cylinder head front camshaft bearing cap and then the remaining bearing caps.

56. Clean and inspect the RH camshaft bearing caps.

57. The camshaft front thrust bearing cap contains an oil metering groove. Make sure the groove is free of foreign material.

Fig. 124 Using the special tool, remove the 4 designated camshaft roller followers in the previous step from the LH cylinder head—6.8L engine

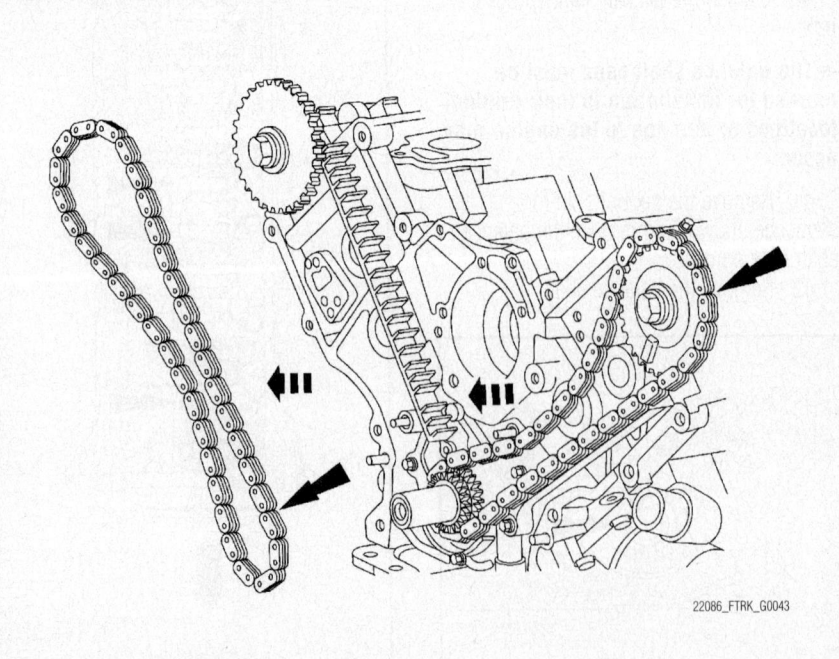

Fig. 126 Remove the timing chains; where necessary, remove the crankshaft sprocket with the chain—6.8L engine

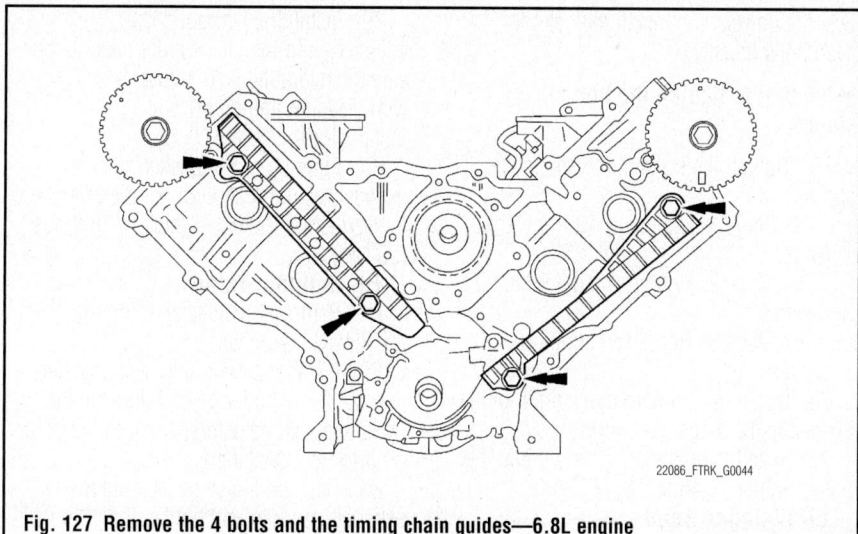

Fig. 127 Remove the 4 bolts and the timing chain guides—6.8L engine

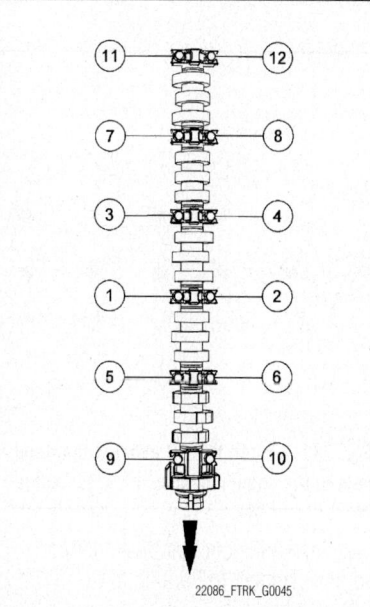

Fig. 128 Remove the bolts in the sequence shown and remove the RH cylinder head front camshaft bearing cap and then the remaining bearing caps—6.8L engine

58. Repeat the above steps for the LH camshaft.

59. Remove all of the remaining roller followers from the cylinder heads.

✳✳ CAUTION

If the components are to be reinstalled, they must be installed in the same positions. Mark the components for installation into their original locations.

60. Remove the hydraulic lash adjusters from the cylinder head.

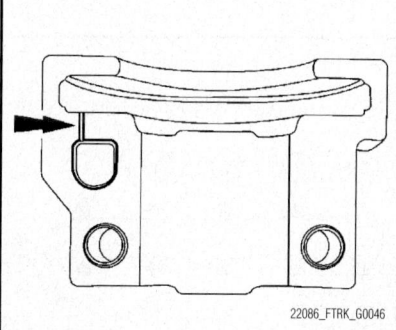

Fig. 129 The camshaft front thrust bearing cap contains an oil metering groove; make sure the groove is free of foreign material—6.8L engine

61. Install the special tool onto the cylinder head.

62. Remove the nuts and the exhaust manifold. Discard the gasket.

63. Remove the stud bolt and the coolant tube.

64. Discard the O-ring seals.

65. Remove the bolts and the cylinder head.

66. Discard the cylinder head gasket.

67. Discard the cylinder head bolts.

68. Clean the cylinder head-to-cylinder block mating surfaces of both the cylinder head and the cylinder block.

69. Remove any large deposits of silicone or gasket material with a plastic scraper.

70. Apply silicone gasket remover, following package directions, and allow to set for several minutes.

71. Remove the silicone gasket remover with a plastic scraper. A second application of silicone gasket remover may be required if residual traces of silicone or gasket material remain.

72. Apply metal surface prep, following package directions, to remove any remaining traces of oil or coolant, and to prepare the surfaces to bond with the new gasket. Do not attempt to make the metal shiny. Some staining of the metal surfaces is normal.

➡**Make sure all cylinder head surfaces are clear of any gasket material, RTV, oil and coolant. The cylinder head surface must be clean and dry before running a flatness check.**

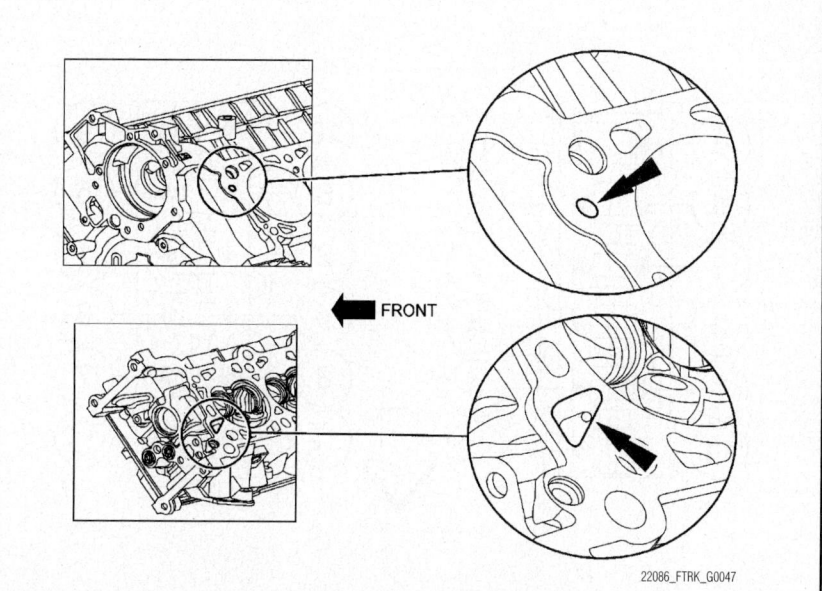

Fig. 130 Inspect all areas of the deck face with a straightedge, paying particular attention to the oil pressure feed area—6.8L engine

➡Use a straightedge that is calibrated by the manufacturer to be flat within 0.0002 inch (0.005 mm) per running foot length. For example, if the straightedge is 24 inch (61 cm) long, the machined edge must be flat within 0.0004 inch (0.010 mm) from end to end.

73. Support the cylinder head on a bench with the head gasket side up. Inspect all areas of the deck face with a straightedge, paying particular attention to the oil pressure feed area. The cylinder head must not have depressions deeper than 0.001 inch (0.0254 mm) across a 1.5 inch (38.1 mm) square area, or scratches longer than 0.001 inch (0.0254 mm).

To install:

✳✳ CAUTION

The use of sealing aids (aviation cement, copper spray and glue) is not permitted. The gasket must be installed dry.

✳✳ CAUTION

The cylinder head bolts must be discarded and new bolts installed. They are tighten-to-yield designed and cannot be reused.

➡**Do not turn the crankshaft until instructed to do so.**

74. Using the special tools, position the cylinder head gaskets and cylinder heads over the dowels and install the cylinder head bolts loosely.

➡**Be sure to tighten the bolts in 3 stages.**

75. Tighten the bolts in the sequence shown.
   a. Stage 1: Tighten to 40 Nm (30 lb-ft).
   b. Stage 2: Tighten an additional 90 degrees.
   c. Stage 3: Tighten an additional 90 degrees.
76. Install the cylinder block drain plugs. Tighten to 18 ft. lbs. (24 Nm).
77. Install the RH engine mount and the bolts. Tighten to 46 ft. lbs. (63 Nm).

LH Cylinder Head
78. Remove the special lifting tool from the LH cylinder head.

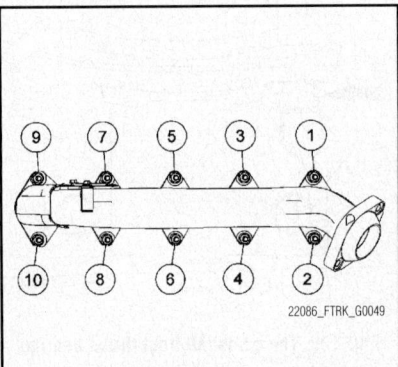

Fig. 132 Tighten the LH exhaust manifold nuts in the sequence shown—6.8L engine

79. Install the hydraulic lash adjusters into the LH cylinder head. Lubricate the hydraulic lash adjusters with clean engine oil prior to installation.
80. Position a new gasket, the LH exhaust manifold and tighten the 10 nuts in the sequence shown. Tighten to 18 ft. lbs. (25 Nm).

RH Cylinder Head
81. Remove the special lifting tool from the RH cylinder head.
82. Install the hydraulic lash adjusters into the RH cylinder head. Lubricate the hydraulic lash adjusters with clean engine oil prior to installation.
83. Position a new gasket, the RH exhaust manifold and tighten the 10 nuts in the sequence shown. Tighten to 18 ft. lbs. (25 Nm).

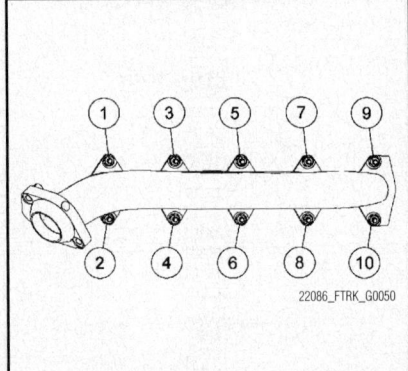

Fig. 133 Tighten the RH exhaust manifold nuts in the sequence shown—6.8L engine

84. Install the coolant tube and the stud bolt. Tighten to 89 inch lbs. (10 Nm).

All Cylinder Heads

✳✳ CAUTION

If the components are to be reinstalled, they must be installed into their original locations.

➡**Lubricate the camshaft roller followers with clean engine oil prior to installation.**

85. Install only the identified camshaft roller followers onto the RH cylinder head.

✳✳ CAUTION

If the components are to be reinstalled, they must be installed into their original locations.

➡**Lubricate the camshaft roller followers with clean engine oil prior to installation.**

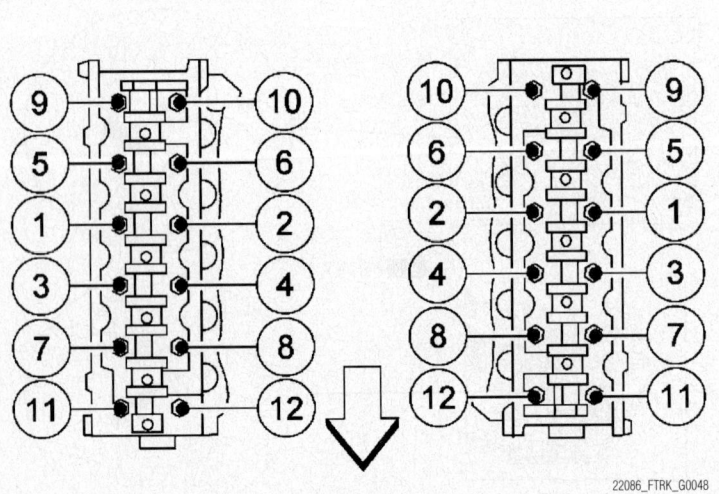

Fig. 131 Tighten the new cylinder head bolts in the sequence shown—6.8L engine

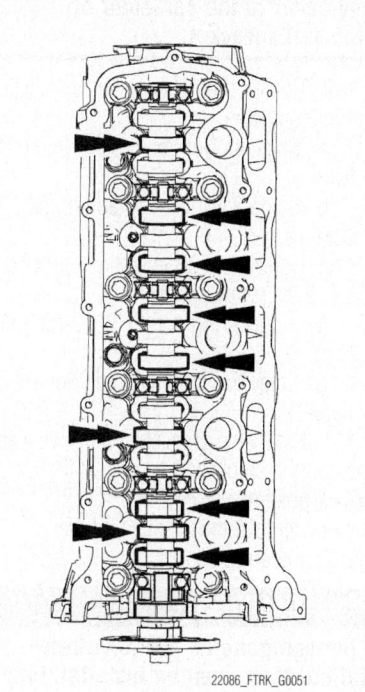

Fig. 134 Install only the identified camshaft roller followers onto the RH cylinder head (camshaft shown installed to clarify camshaft roller follower position)—6.8L engine

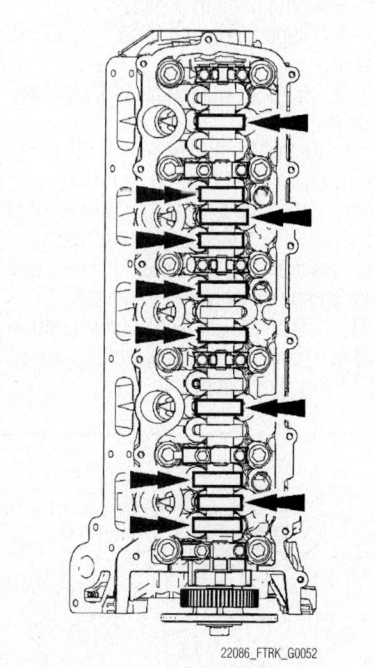

Fig. 135 Install only the identified camshaft roller followers onto the LH cylinder head (camshaft shown installed to clarify camshaft roller follower position)—6.8L engine

86. Install only the identified camshaft roller followers onto the LH cylinder head.

87. Install the LH and RH camshafts. Lubricate the camshaft and camshaft journals with clean engine oil prior to installation.

88. Install the LH and RH camshaft bearing caps in their original locations. Lubricate the camshaft bearing caps with clean engine oil.

89. Position the front camshaft bearing cap. Position the remaining camshaft bearing caps. Install the bolts loosely.

90. Tighten the LH camshaft bearing cap bolts in 2 stages:

    a. Stage 1: Tighten to 71 inch lbs. (8 Nm) in the sequence shown.

    b. Stage 2: Tighten an additional 45 degrees.

Tighten the RH camshaft bearing cap bolts in 2 stages:

Stage 1: Tighten to 8 Nm (71 lb-in) in the sequence shown.

Stage 2: Tighten an additional 45 degrees.

91. Install the balance shaft drive gear onto the LH camshaft.

92. Install both camshaft sprockets and camshaft sprocket bolts finger tight.

✳✳ CAUTION

Timing chain procedures must be followed exactly or damage to valves and pistons will result.

✳✳ CAUTION

Prior to installation, inspect the tensioner-sealing bead for seal integrity. If cracks, tears, separation from the tensioner body or permanent compression of the seal bead is observed, install a new tensioner.

93. Compress the tensioner plunger, using a vise.

94. Install a retaining clip on the tensioner to hold the plunger in during installation.

➡**There are 61 links in each timing chain.**

95. If copper links are not visible, mark 2 links on one end and 1 link on the other end, and use as timing marks.

96. Install the timing chain guides and the 4 bolts. Tighten to 89 inch lbs. (10 Nm).

97. Preposition the camshafts:

    a. Rotate the LH camshaft with the Camshaft Positioning Tool until the timing mark is approximately at 12 o'clock.

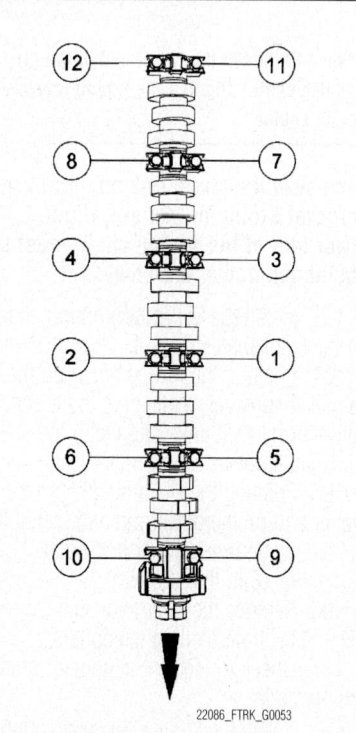

Fig. 136 Tighten the LH camshaft bearing cap bolts in 2 stages, in the sequence shown—6.8L engine

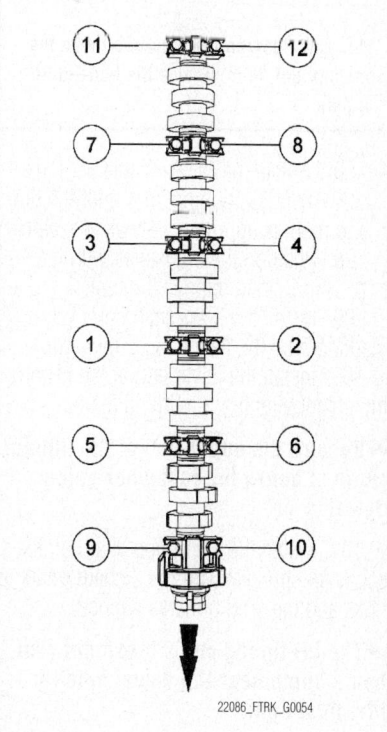

Fig. 137 Tighten the RH camshaft bearing cap bolts in 2 stages, in the sequence shown—6.8L engine

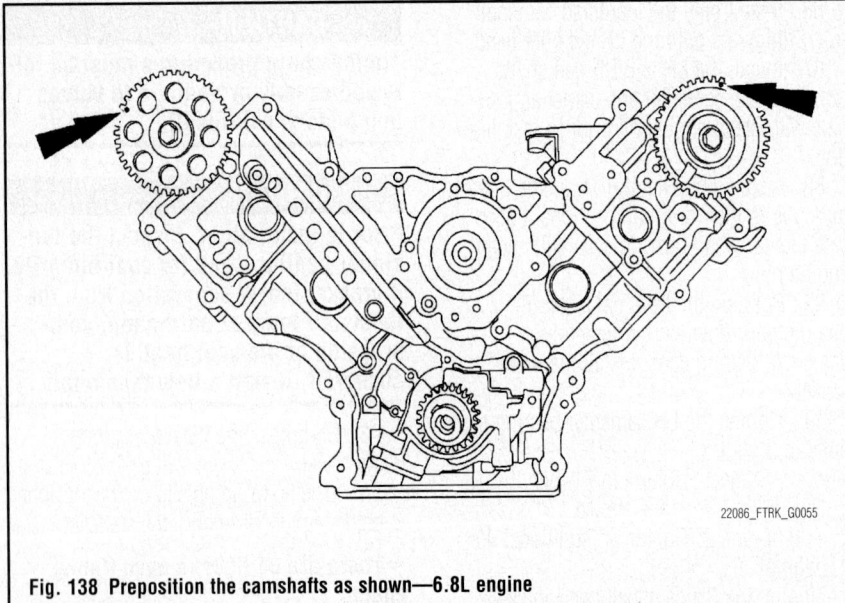

Fig. 138 Preposition the camshafts as shown—6.8L engine

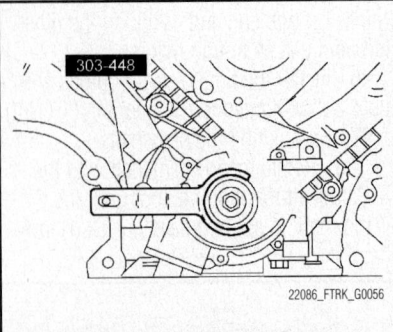

Fig. 139 Position the crankshaft with the special tool, then remove the tool—6.8L engine

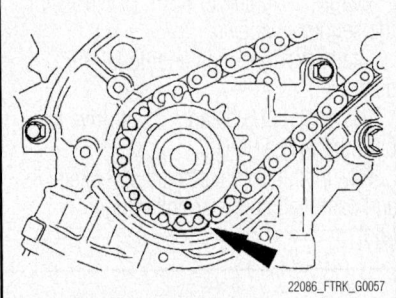

Fig. 140 Install the lower end of the LH timing chain, aligning the timing marks—6.8L engine

b. Rotate the RH camshaft with the Camshaft Positioning Tool until the timing mark is approximately at 11 o'clock.

98. Position the crankshaft with the special tool, then remove the tool.

99. Install the crankshaft sprocket, marking sure the flange faces forward.

100. Install the lower end of the LH timing chain, aligning the timing marks.

➡ **Be sure the upper half of the timing chain is below the tensioner guide dowel.**

101. Install the LH timing chain on the camshaft sprocket with the 2 chain (marked) links and the timing marks aligned.

➡ **The LH timing chain tensioner arm has a bump near the dowel hole for identification.**

102. Position the LH timing chain tensioner arm on the dowel pin and install the LH timing chain tensioner and bolts. Tighten to 18 ft. lbs. (25 Nm).

➡ **Be sure the chain link and crankshaft sprocket timing marks are aligned. The lower half of the timing chain must be positioned above the dowel.**

103. Install the RH (outer) timing chain on the crankshaft sprocket.

104. Position the timing chain on the camshaft sprocket. Make sure the 2 copper-colored (marked) links align with the camshaft sprocket timing mark.

105. Position the RH timing chain tensioner arm on the dowel pin and install the RH timing chain tensioner and bolts. Tighten to 18 ft. lbs. (25 Nm).

106. Remove the retaining clips from the RH and LH timing chain tensioners.

107. Check for correct alignment of all timing marks.

108. Install the crankshaft sensor ring on the crankshaft.

✳✳ **CAUTION**

Only use hand tools to tighten the camshaft sprocket bolt or damage

may occur to the camshaft or camshaft sprocket.

109. Tighten the RH camshaft sprocket bolt in 2 stages:
   a. Stage 1: Tighten to 30 ft. lbs. (40 Nm).
   b. Stage 2: Tighten an additional 90 degrees.

110. Tighten the LH camshaft sprocket bolt in 2 stages:
   a. Stage 1: Tighten to 30 ft. lbs. (40 Nm).
   b. Stage 2: Tighten an additional 90 degrees.

111. Rotate the crankshaft clockwise and position the crankshaft keyway at the 6 o'clock position.

112. Remove the 2 bolts and the camshaft bearing cap.

✳✳ **CAUTION**

If the components are to be reinstalled, they must be installed into their original locations or damage to the engine may occur.

113. Using the special tool, install the roller follower. Lubricate the camshaft roller follower with clean engine oil prior to installation.

114. Position the camshaft bearing cap and install the bolts in 2 stages:
   a. Stage 1: Tighten to 71 inch lbs. (8 Nm).
   b. Stage 2: Tighten an additional 45 degrees.

115. Repeat for the remaining roller followers with similar bearing cap.

116. Using the special tool, install all of the remaining camshaft roller followers. Lubricate the camshaft roller followers with clean engine oil prior to installation.

117. Rotate the crankshaft counterclockwise and position the crankshaft keyway at the 11 o'clock position.

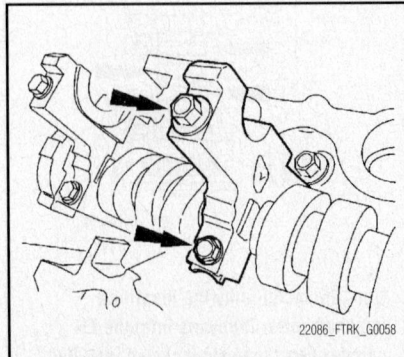

Fig. 141 Remove the 2 bolts and the camshaft bearing cap—6.8L engine

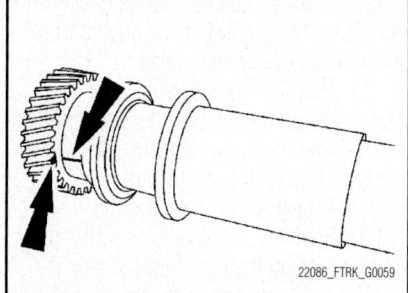

Fig. 142 Using the index mark on the balance shaft, mark the corresponding gear tooth with chalk—6.8L engine

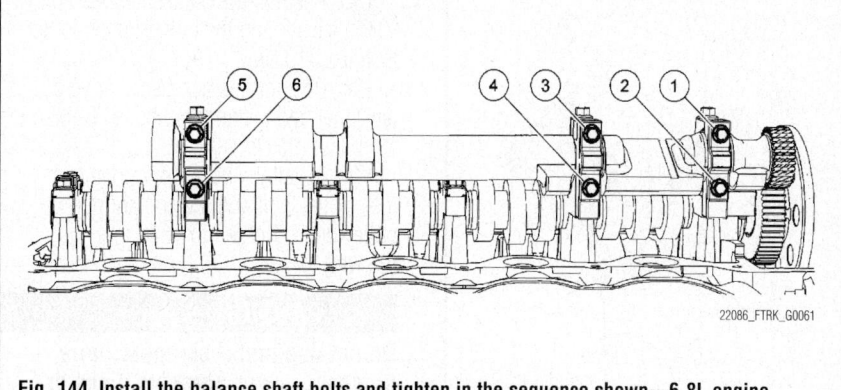

Fig. 144 Install the balance shaft bolts and tighten in the sequence shown—6.8L engine

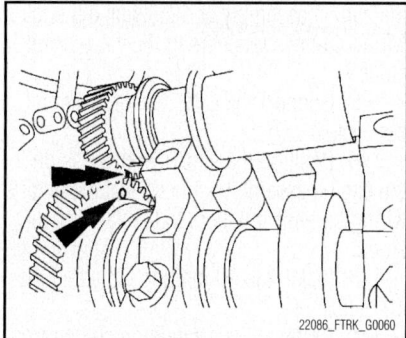

Fig. 143 Position the balance shaft on the journals and align the chalk mark on the balance shaft with the camshaft timing mark as shown—6.8L engine

118. Lubricate the balance shaft journals with clean engine oil.

119. Using the index mark on the balance shaft, mark the corresponding gear tooth with chalk.

120. Position the balance shaft on the journals.

➡**It may be necessary to use an inspection mirror to see the marks.**

121. Position the balance shaft on the journals and align the chalk mark on the balance shaft with the camshaft timing mark as shown.

➡**Install the balance shaft bearing caps in their original locations**

122. Install the bolts and tighten in the sequence shown. Tighten to 89 inch lbs. (10 Nm).

✳✳ CAUTION

Do not use metal scrapers, wire brushes, power abrasive discs or other abrasive means to clean the sealing surfaces. These tools cause scratches and gouges which make leak paths. Use a plastic scraping

tool to remove all traces of old sealant.

➡**If the engine front cover is not secured within 4 minutes, the sealant must be removed and the sealing area cleaned. To clean the sealing area, use silicone gasket remover and metal surface prep. Follow the directions on the packaging. Allow to dry until there is no sign of wetness, or 4 minutes, whichever is longer. Failure to follow this procedure can cause future oil leakage.**

➡**Make sure that the engine front cover gasket is in place on the engine front cover before installation.**

123. Apply a bead of silicone gasket and sealant along the cylinder head-to-cylinder block surface at the locations shown.

124. Install a new engine front cover gasket on the engine front cover. Position the engine front cover onto the dowels. Install the fasteners finger-tight.

125. Tighten the engine front cover fasteners, in sequence, in 2 stages.

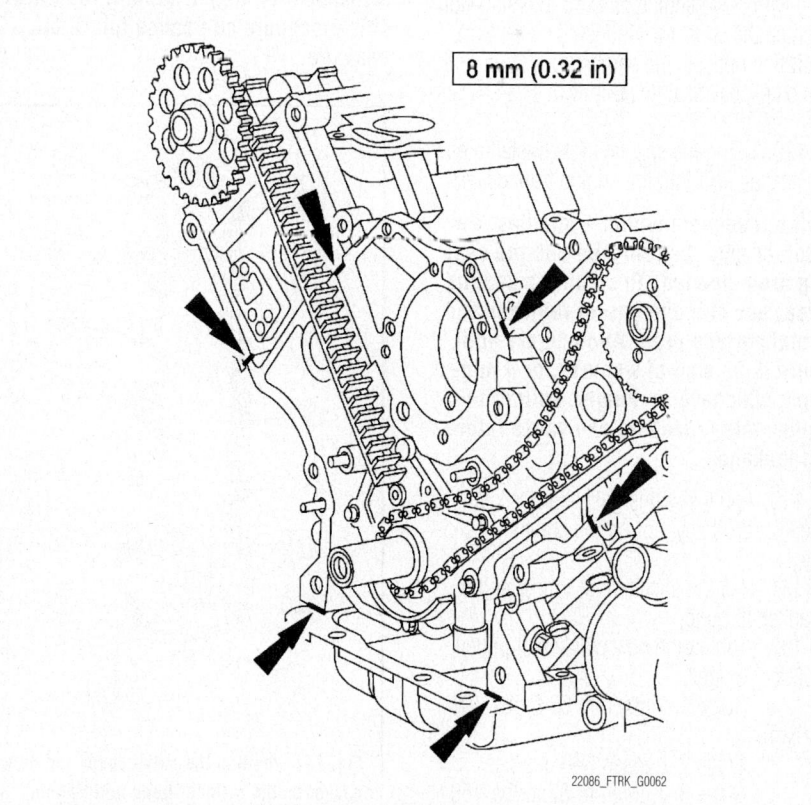

8 mm (0.32 in)

Fig. 145 Apply a bead of silicone gasket and sealant along the cylinder head-to-cylinder block surface at the locations shown—6.8L engine

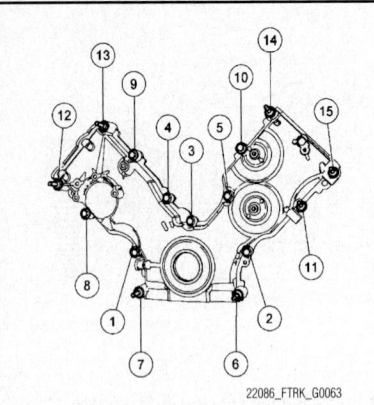

Fig. 146 Tighten the engine front cover fasteners, in sequence, in 2 stages—6.8L engine

a. Stage 1: Tighten fasteners 1 through 15 to 18 ft. lbs. (25 Nm).

b. Stage 2: Tighten fasteners 6 and 7 to 35 ft. lbs. (48 Nm).

126. Install the front 4 oil pan bolts in an alternating sequence, in 2 stages:

a. Stage 1: Tighten to 15 ft. lbs. (20 Nm).

b. Stage 2: Tighten an additional 60 degrees.

127. Install the camshaft position (CMP) sensor and the bolt. Lubricate the new O-ring seal with clean engine oil prior to installation. Tighten the sensor to 89 inch lbs. (10 Nm).

128. Lubricate the engine front cover and the crankshaft seal inner lip with clean engine oil.

129. Using the special tools, install a new crankshaft seal into the engine front cover.

➡️If not secured within 4 minutes, the sealant must be removed and the sealing area cleaned. To clean the sealing area, use silicone gasket remover and metal surface prep. Allow to dry until there is no sign of wetness, or 4 minutes, whichever is longer. Failure to follow this procedure can cause future oil leakage.

130. Apply silicone gasket and sealant to the Woodruff key slot on the crankshaft pulley.

131. Use the special tool to install the crankshaft pulley.

132. Tighten the new crankshaft pulley bolt in 4 stages.

a. Stage 1: Tighten to 66 ft. lbs. (90 Nm).

b. Stage 2: Loosen 360 degrees.

c. Stage 3: Tighten to 37 ft. lbs. (50 Nm).

d. Stage 4: Tighten an additional 90 degrees.

133. Position the crankshaft position (CKP) sensor and the bolt. Tighten to 89 inch lbs. (10 Nm).

134. Position the accessory drive belt tensioner and install the 3 bolts. Tighten to 18 ft. lbs. (25 Nm).

135. Install the accessory drive belt idler pulley bolt and the coolant pump pulley bolts. Tighten to 18 ft. lbs. (25 Nm).

✳✳ CAUTION

Do not use metal scrapers, wire brushes, power abrasive discs or other abrasive means to clean sealing surfaces. These tools cause scratches and gouges which make leak paths. Use a plastic scraping tool to remove all traces of old sealant.

136. Clean the valve cover mating surface with silicone gasket remover and metal surface prep.

➡️If the valve cover is not secured within 4 minutes, the sealant must be removed and the sealing area cleaned with silicone gasket remover and metal surface prep. Allow to dry until there is no sign of wetness, or 4 minutes, whichever is longer. Failure to follow this procedure can cause future oil leakage.

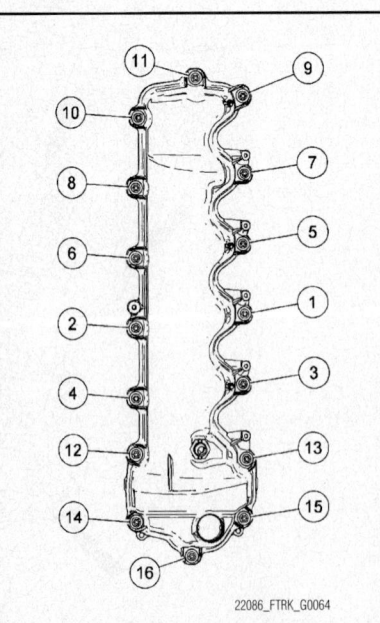

Fig. 147 Position the valve cover and new gasket on the cylinder head and tighten the 16 fasteners in the sequence shown— 6.8L engine (RH cover shown; LH cover sequence similar)

137. Apply a bead of silicone gasket and sealant in 2 places where the engine front cover meets the cylinder head.

138. Position the RH valve cover and new gasket on the cylinder head and tighten the 16 fasteners in the sequence shown. Tighten to 89 inch lbs. (10 Nm).

139. Repeat for the LH valve cover.

140. Position the oil level indicator and tube and install the bolt. Install a new O-ring seal and lubricate with clean engine oil prior to installation. Tighten to 89 inch lbs. (10 Nm).

141. Install the oil level indicator and tube front bolt. Tighten to 18 ft. lbs. (25 Nm).

142. Position the electrical harness on the engine assembly and connect the engine wiring harness retainers to the valve cover studs.

143. Connect the CKP sensor electrical connector.

144. Position the electrical harness on the engine assembly and connect the engine wiring harness retainers to the valve cover studs.

145. Install the 10 ignition coils and the 10 bolts.

146. Connect the 10 ignition coil electrical connectors.

147. Install the LH radio ignition interference capacitor and the stud bolt. Tighten to 18 ft. lbs. (25 Nm).

148. Connect the engine oil pressure (EOP) sensor electrical connector.

149. Connect the cylinder head temperature (CHT) sensor electrical connector.

150. Connect the electrical connector retainer to the coolant tube.

151. Install the RH radio ignition interference capacitor and the stud bolt. Tighten to 18 ft. lbs. (25 Nm).

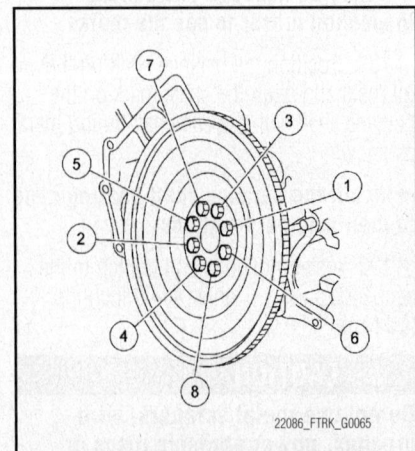

Fig. 148 Install the flexplate or flywheel and the 8 bolts in the sequence shown— 6.8L engine (RH cover shown; LH cover sequence similar)

152. Connect the CMP sensor electrical connector.

153. Using a suitable floor crane, remove the engine from the engine stand.

154. Lower and support the engine assembly on wood blocks.

155. Install the special engine lifting tool.

156. Using a suitable floor crane raise the engine.

157. Install the flexplate or flywheel and the 8 bolts in the sequence shown. Tighten to 59 ft. lbs. (80 Nm).

158. Install the engine.

6.4L Diesel Engine

See Figure 149.

➡ **It is recommend that this component be serviced with the vehicle body removed.**

1. Remove the engine.

2. Remove the 3 bolts and the starter.

3. Remove and discard the center bolt and the RH engine mount.

➡ **The engine mount bracket bolts must be discarded and new bolts installed or damage to the vehicle may occur. They are a torque-to-yield design and cannot be reused.**

4. Remove and discard the 4 bolts and the RH engine mount bracket.

➡ **Use a suitable engine stand with 6 mounting arms to support the engine. Failure to correctly support the engine may result in engine damage.**

5. Mount the engine on the Car/Truck Engine Stand.

6. Remove the 2 cylinder block coolant drain plugs on both cylinder heads.

7. Disconnect the glow plug electrical connector and pushpin retainers on the LH valve cover bracket.

8. Disconnect the Camshaft Position (CMP) sensor electrical connector and pushpin retainer.

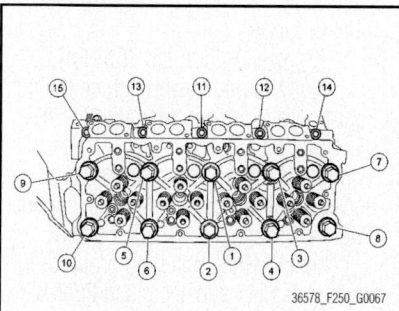

36578_F250_G0067

Fig. 149 Cylinder head tightening sequence—6.4L diesel engines

9. Disconnect the pushpin retainer and remove the harness from the retaining clip.

10. Disconnect the pushpin retainers from the oil drain back tube brackets.

11. Disconnect the Crankshaft Position (CKP) sensor electrical connector and pushpin retainer.

12. Disconnect the glow plug harness electrical connector and retainer from the RH valve cover. Remove the engine wiring harness from the engine.

13. LH cylinder head:

➡ **Do not disconnect the glow plug electrical connectors before dislodging the seals from the valve cover or the wiring harness may be damaged.**

➡ **Only one glow plug connector shown.**

a. Using an appropriate tool, dislodge the glow plug seals from the valve cover and disconnect the pin-type retainers.

b. Disconnect the glow plug electrical connectors by pulling on the glow plug wiring harness tee (above the seal at each glow plug) and remove the glow plug harness.

c. Remove the 2 bolts and the LH heater return tube. Remove and discard the O-ring seal.

d. Remove the bolt for the fuel supply and return tube retainer.

➡ **The coolant hose clamps used on this engine are constant tension worm gear clamps. Standard worm gear clamps cannot be used. Failure to use the correct coolant hose clamps can result in hose joint failure.**

e. Loosen the clamp for the EGR cooler hose.

f. Remove the 2 bolts and the EGR cooler tube. Remove and discard the O-ring seal and the clamp.

g. Remove the bolt and the fuel supply and return tubes.

h. Remove the retaining nut for the oil level indicator and tube.

i. Remove the bolt. Remove the oil level indicator and tube. Remove and discard the O-ring seal.

j. Remove the 3 retaining nuts and the LH valve cover bracket.

14. RH cylinder head:

➡ **Do not disconnect the glow plug electrical connectors before dislodging the seals from the valve cover or the wiring harness may be damaged.**

a. Using an appropriate tool, dislodge the glow plug seals from the valve cover and disconnect the retainers. Disconnect

the glow plug electrical connectors by pulling on the glow plug wiring harness tee (above the seal at each glow plug) and remove the glow plug harness.

b. Disconnect the crankcase vent oil separator tube at the crankcase.

c. Remove the nut, 2 bolts and the crankcase vent oil separator tube.

15. Both cylinder heads:

➡ **Mark the location of the stud bolts.**

16. Remove the 4 stud bolts, 6 bolts and valve covers. Remove and discard the press-in-place gaskets. Clean and inspect the sealing surfaces.

➡ **If engine coolant is found in the combustion chambers, it may be necessary to install a new glow plug sleeve.**

17. Remove the 8 glow plugs.

➡ **The Fuel Rail Pressure (FRP) sensor is located on the RH fuel rail. Disconnect the FRP sensor electrical connector.**

18. Using the Fuel Injector Connector Disconnect Tool, disconnect the fuel injector electrical connectors.

19. Disconnect the fuel charging harness from the high-pressure fuel rail.

➡ **The terminals in the fuel charging harness plug are not serviced, install a new fuel charging harness if damaged.**

20. Remove the 2 fuel charging harness electrical connectors from the valve cover base and remove the fuel charging harness.

➡ **Fuel injection equipment is manufactured to very precise tolerances and fine clearances. To prevent fuel system damage it is essential that absolute cleanliness is observed when working with these components. Always install Fuel System Caps to any open orifices or tubes.**

➡ **Use a back-up wrench on the fuel injector fittings.**

21. Remove and discard the 8 fuel injector supply tubes.

22. Remove the 4 bolts and the high-pressure fuel rails.

23. Prior to removing the injector assembly, insert clean shop towels in the oil drain holes adjacent to each glow plug.

➡ **Failure to account for all snap rings or pieces of snap rings prior to placing the vehicle back in service may cause engine damage. A missing snap ring can be ingested into the lube oil system causing severe engine damage.**

➡To prevent engine damage, do not use air tools to remove the fuel injectors. The snap ring that extracts the injector can dislodge and fall into the oil drain hole.

➡Failure to use the Injector Cups and the Fuel Injector Holding Rack may result in damage to the fuel injector.

➡There is no need to drain the fuel rail.

➡If engine coolant is found in the combustion chambers, it may be necessary to install a new injector sleeve.

24. Remove the bolt, the fuel injector hold down and the fuel injector.

25. Remove and discard the O-ring seal and soft steel washer.

26. Place the fuel injector in the fuel injector holding rack.

➡If a snap ring or piece of a snap ring is missing from the injector hold-down assembly, it must be located prior to removing the shop towels.

27. Remove the shop towels.

➡ Mark the location of the rocker arm assemblies prior to removing.

28. Remove the 16 bolts and the rocker arm assemblies.

29. Remove the 2 rocker arm spacer bars.

➡Mark the location of the valve bridges before removing.

30. Remove the 16 valve bridges.

➡To prevent engine damage, keep the push rods in the order in which they were removed. Install all push rods back in their original positions.

31. Mark the location and remove the 16 push rods.

32. Remove the 22 bolts and the valve cover bases.

33. Remove and discard the press-in-place gaskets.

34. Clean and inspect the sealing surfaces.

35. If necessary, remove and discard the high-pressure fuel rail seals.

36. Remove and discard the 10 head bolts from each cylinder head.

37. Remove the 5 outer bolts from each cylinder head.

38. Using the Heavy Duty Floor Crane and the Cylinder Head Lifting Bracket, remove the cylinder heads.

39. Check for cylinder head distortion.

40. Remove and discard the 2 cylinder head gaskets.

41. Remove and discard the 4 cylinder head dowel sleeves. Clean and inspect the sealing surfaces.

42. Check for cylinder block distortion.

To install:

43. Install the 4 new cylinder head dowels.

➡Install a new cylinder head gasket with the part number facing up. Verify the top 5 bolt holes and the head gasket push rod holes line up.

➡Use care to avoid scratching the blue compound on the cylinder head gaskets.

44. Place the 2 new cylinder head gaskets over the dowel sleeves and onto the crankcase.

45. Using the Heavy Duty Floor Crane and the Cylinder Head Lifting Bracket, install the cylinder heads.

46. Install the 10 outer bolts for the cylinder heads. Tighten finger-tight.

➡Using too much engine oil on the threads of the cylinder head bolts may cause damage to the threads and poor sealing. Using anti-seize compounds, grease or any other lubricants other than engine oil on the cylinder head bolt threads may affect the true torque value of the bolts.

➡Lightly lubricate the new cylinder head bolt threads and flanges with clean engine oil.

47. Install the 20 cylinder head retaining bolts for the cylinder heads. Tighten finger-tight.

➡If bolt chatter occurs during Stage 4 or 5, loosen the bolt and repeat Stage 3.

48. Tighten the cylinder head bolts in 7 stages in sequence shown:
   a. Stage 1: Tighten bolts 1 through 10 to 70 ft. lbs. (95 Nm).
   b. Stage 2: Loosen bolts 1 through 10.
   c. Stage 3: Tighten bolts 1 through 10 to 115 ft. lbs. (156 Nm).
   d. Stage 4: Tighten bolts in sequence, 1 through 10, an additional 90 degrees.
   e. Stage 5: Tighten bolts in sequence, 1 through 10, a second time, an additional 90 degrees.
   f. Stage 6: Tighten bolts 11 through 15 to 18 ft. lbs. (24 Nm).
   g. Stage 7: Tighten bolts 11 through 23 ft. lbs..

➡ Lubricate the seals with clean engine oil prior to installation.

49. If necessary, install a new seals for the high-pressure fuel rail.

50. Install the new press-in-place gaskets, the valve cover bases and the 22 bolts. Tighten to 115 inch lbs. (13 Nm).

➡To prevent engine damage, keep the push rods in the order in which they were removed. Install all push rods back in their original positions.

➡Install the copper ends of the push rods facing upward.

51. Apply clean engine oil to each end of the push rods and insert them into their respective positions.

➡Coat the end of each valve stem with clean engine oil.

52. Install the 16 valve bridges.

53. Position the 2 rocker arm spacer bars.

➡Apply clean engine oil to the top center of each valve bridge and rocker arm ball socket.

54. Install the rocker arm assemblies and the 16 bolts in the following sequence:
   a. Position the crankshaft with the No. 1 and the No. 4 cylinders at approximately Top Dead Center (TDC) by observing the damper dowel pin and clocking it to the 10:30 position (as viewed from the front of the engine).
   b. Determine which cylinder is actually in the firing position by observing the push rods for No. 3 intake and No. 8 intake valves.
   c. If the No. 3 intake push rod shows cam lift, this is the No. 1 firing position. Tighten only fulcrum plates No. 1, 2, 7 and 8 per Substeps d through f. If the No. 8 intake push rod shows cam lift, this is the No. 4 firing position. Tighten only fulcrum plates No. 3, 4, 5 and 6 per Substeps d through f.
   d. Partially run down both M10 bolts until they contact the fulcrum plate.
   e. Fully run down and tighten the inboard (upper) bolt.
   f. Tighten to 45 ft. lbs. (61 Nm).
   g. Fully run down and tighten the outboard (lower) bolt. Tighten to 45 ft. lbs. (61 Nm).
   h. Rotate the crankshaft one revolution to position it at the alternate cylinder TDC (dowel again at 10:30 position).
   i. Identify the remaining group of fulcrum plates per substep c and tighten per Substeps d through f.
   j. Verify that the pivot foot is centered on the valve bridge.

➡**The bead on the soft steel washer must be installed facing out.**

➡**Lubricate the fuel injector and O-ring seal with clean engine oil.**

55. Install a new O-ring seal and a soft steel washer on the fuel injector.

➡**Failure to tighten the fuel injector correctly can lead to engine failure.**

➡**To prevent engine damage, do not use air tools to install the fuel injectors. The snap ring that extracts the fuel injector can dislodge and fall into the oil drain hole.**

56. Install the fuel injector, the fuel injector hold down and bolt.

57. Install the high-pressure fuel rails and 4 bolts. Tighten hand-tight.

➡**Use a back-up wrench on the fuel injector fittings.**

58. Install the new fuel injector supply tubes in the following sequence:

   a. Remove the protective caps from the high-pressure fuel rails and fuel injectors one at a time prior to assembly of each tube.

   b. Position the 8 fuel injector supply tubes (one at a time) between the high-pressure fuel rail and fuel injectors, and fully hand start and seat the tube nuts onto the mating high-pressure fuel rail and fuel injector connectors. Snug the fuel injector supply tube nuts using the inside-out step sequence (2 inside tubes first, then 2 outside tubes).

   c. Calculate the correct torque wrench setting for the following torque. Tighten to 2 Nm (18 lb-in).

   d. Tighten the fuel injector hold-down clamp bolts. Tighten to 38 Nm (28 lb-ft).

   e. Tighten the high-pressure fuel rail bolts. Tighten to 31 Nm (23 lb-ft).

➡**Pre-tighten the 8 fuel injector tube nuts at the fuel injectors first, then the 8 nuts at the high-pressure fuel rails.**

   f. Pre-tighten the fuel injector tube nuts at the fuel injectors and at the high-pressure fuel rails. Tighten to 12 Nm (106 lb-in).

➡**Place a visible mark with a permanent marker on the high-pressure fuel rail and fuel injector threaded connection. Turning the tube nuts one flat of the nut is equal to 60 degrees.**

   g. Complete the tightening of the fuel injector tube nuts at the fuel injectors and at the high-pressure fuel rails. Tighten the tube nuts 60 degrees.

➡**The terminals in the fuel charging harness plug are not serviced, install a new the fuel charging harness if damaged.**

➡**Inspect the O-ring seals for damage or swelling prior to installing, install a new if necessary.**

59. Install the 2 fuel charging harness electrical connectors into the valve cover bases.

60. Position the fuel charging harness on the high-pressure fuel rail and connect the 8 fuel injector electrical connectors. Connect the Fuel Rail Pressure (FRP) sensor electrical connector.

61. Install the 8 glow plugs.

62. To complete installation, reverse remaining removal procedure.

ENGINE ASSEMBLY

REMOVAL & INSTALLATION

5.4L Engine

All vehicles

1. Raise and safely support the vehicle.
2. Remove the hood.
3. Remove the cowl vent grille.
4. Remove the radiator.
5. Remove the degas bottle (coolant reservoir).
6. Remove the intake manifold. See "Intake Manifold" in this section.
7. Remove the powertrain control module (PCM).
8. Remove the accessory drive belt.
9. Drain the engine oil.
10. Disconnect the degas bottle (coolant reservoir) coolant hose.
11. Disconnect the 2 electrical connectors on the left fender splash shield.
12. Remove the 3 bolts and position the power steering pump assembly aside.
13. Disconnect the alternator wiring harness retainer from the right cylinder head.
14. Disconnect the A/C compressor and the A/C high pressure cut-off switch electrical connectors.
15. Disconnect the alternator wiring harness retainer from the right cylinder head and position the harness aside.
16. Disconnect the crankshaft position (CKP) sensor wiring harness retainer from the starter motor wiring harness.
17. Disconnect the engine wiring harness retainer from the evaporative emissions (EVAP) canister purge valve bracket.
18. Disconnect the vacuum hose and engine wiring harness retainers.
19. Disconnect the EVAP tube quick connect couplings and the electrical connector from EVAP canister purge valve.

20. Remove the 3 nuts and remove the EVAP canister purge valve and bracket assembly.
21. Disconnect the body wiring harness retainer from the degas bottle (coolant reservoir) support bracket.
22. Remove the 3 nuts and the degas bottle (coolant reservoir) support bracket.
23. Remove the 2 nuts and the air cleaner outlet tube support bracket.
24. Disconnect the heater hose.

Manual transmission vehicles

25. Remove the clutch and pressure plate.

Automatic transmission vehicles

26. Remove the starter.
27. Remove the nut and position the transmission oil cooler lines and bracket aside.
28. Remove the 2 bolts and the flexplate inspection cover.
29. Remove the cylinder block opening cover.
30. Remove the 4 torque converter-to-flexplate nuts. Discard the nuts.

➡**The upper 2 transmission-to-engine bolts will be removed later.**

31. Remove the 5 transmission-to-engine bolts.
32. Remove the nut, the ground cable and position the transmission fluid filler tube aside.

All vehicles

33. If equipped, disconnect the block heater electrical connector.
34. Remove the stud bolt and position the ground strap aside.
35. Disconnect the oil temperature sensor electrical connector.
36. Remove the 3 bolts and position the A/C compressor aside.
37. Disconnect the 2 heated exhaust gas oxygen sensor (HO2S) electrical connectors.
38. Remove the 4 exhaust manifold flange nuts.
39. Remove the 6 right and left motor mount nuts.

Automatic transmission vehicles

40. Remove the upper 2 transmission-to-engine bolts.

All vehicles

41. Install the lifting bracket.
42. Using a suitable floor crane, remove the engine assembly from the vehicle.

To install:
All vehicles

43. Using a suitable floor crane, position the engine assembly into the vehicle.

> ✳✳ WARNING
>
> **Only use hand tools when installing the right engine mount nut or damage to the engine mount can occur.**

➡Align the engine-to-transmission dowels before installing the engine mount bolt.

44. Install the 6 engine mount nuts. Tighten to 175 Nm (129 ft. lbs.).
45. Remove the lifting bracket.

Manual transmission vehicles
46. Install the clutch.

Automatic transmission vehicles

➡The upper 2 transmission-to-engine bolts will be installed later.

47. Install the lower 5 transmission-to-engine bolts. Tighten to 35 Nm (26 ft. lbs.).
48. Install 4 new torque converter-to-flexplate nuts. Tighten to 35 Nm (26 ft. lbs.).
49. Install the cylinder block opening cover.
50. Install the flexplate inspection cover and the 2 bolts. Tighten to 34 Nm (25 ft. lbs.).
51. Install the transmission fluid filler tube, the ground strap and the nut. Tighten to 12 Nm (9 ft. lbs.).
52. Install the starter.

All vehicles
53. If equipped, connect the block heater electrical connector.
54. Position the starter electrical harness support bracket and install the bolt. Tighten to 10 Nm (89 inch lbs.).
55. Position the ground strap and install the stud bolt. Tighten to 10 Nm (89 inch lbs.).
56. Connect the oil temperature sensor electrical connector.
57. Position the A/C compressor and install the 3 bolts. Tighten to 25 Nm (18 ft. lbs.).
58. Install the 4 exhaust manifold flange nuts. Tighten to 40 Nm (30 ft. lbs.).
59. Connect the 2 heated exhaust gas oxygen sensor (HO2S) electrical connectors.

Automatic transmission vehicles
60. Install the transmission cooler tube support bracket and the nut. Tighten to 10 Nm (89 inch lbs.).
61. Install the upper 2 transmission-to-engine bolts. Tighten to 48 Nm (35 ft. lbs.).

All vehicles
62. Position the degas bottle (coolant reservoir) support bracket and install the 3 nuts. Tighten to 10 Nm (89 inch lbs.).
63. Connect the body wiring harness retainer to the degas bottle (coolant reservoir) support bracket.
64. Position the evaporative emissions (EVAP) canister purge valve and bracket assembly, and install the 3 nuts. Tighten to 10 Nm (89 inch lbs.).
65. Connect the electrical connector and the EVAP tube quick connect couplings to the EVAP canister purge valve.
66. Connect the engine wiring harness retainer to the EVAP canister purge valve bracket.
67. Connect the crankshaft position (CKP) sensor wiring harness retainer to the starter motor wiring harness.
68. Connect the alternator wiring harness retainer to the right cylinder head.
69. Connect the A/C compressor and the A/C high pressure cut-off switch electrical connectors.
70. Connect the alternator wiring harness retainer to the right cylinder head.
71. Position the power steering pump and install the 3 bolts. Tighten to 25 Nm (18 ft. lbs.).
72. Position the air cleaner outlet tube support bracket and install the 2 nuts. Tighten to 25 Nm (18 ft. lbs.).
73. Connect the 2 electrical connectors on the left fender splash shield.
74. Connect the degas bottle (coolant reservoir) coolant hose.
75. Install the intake manifold.
76. Install the radiator.
77. Install the degas bottle (coolant reservoir).
78. Install the powertrain control module (PCM).
79. Install the cowl vent grille.
80. Install the hood.
81. Fill the crankcase with clean engine oil.
82. Evacuate and charge the A/C system.
83. Fill and bleed the power steering system.

6.8L Engine

1. Before servicing the vehicle, refer to the Precautions Section.

All vehicles
2. Raise and safely support the vehicle.
3. Remove the hood.
4. Remove the radiator grille support.
5. Remove the A/C condenser core.
6. Remove the cowl vent grille.
7. Remove the radiator, fan shroud and engine cooling fan.
8. Remove the intake manifold.
9. Remove the degas bottle (coolant reservoir).
10. Remove the powertrain control module (PCM).
11. Disconnect the degas bottle (coolant reservoir) coolant hose.
12. Disconnect the 2 electrical connectors on the left fender splash shield.
13. If equipped, disconnect the block heater electrical connector.
14. Remove the 3 bolts and position the power steering pump aside.
15. Disconnect the alternator wiring harness retainer from the right cylinder head.
16. Disconnect the A/C compressor and the A/C high pressure cut-off switch electrical connectors.
17. Disconnect the alternator wiring harness retainer from the right cylinder head and position the harness aside.
18. Disconnect the crankshaft position (CKP) sensor wiring harness retainer from the starter motor wiring harness.
19. Disconnect the engine wiring harness retainer from the evaporative emissions (EVAP) canister purge valve bracket.
20. Disconnect EVAP tube quick connect couplings and the electrical connector from EVAP canister purge valve.
21. Remove the 3 nuts and remove EVAP canister purge valve and bracket assembly.
22. Disconnect the heater hose at the rear of the engine.
23. Disconnect the body wiring harness retainer from the degas bottle (coolant reservoir) support bracket.
24. Remove the 3 nuts and the degas bottle (coolant reservoir) support bracket.
25. Drain the engine oil.
26. Remove the 4 exhaust manifold-to-catalytic converter nuts.
27. Disconnect the 2 heated exhaust gas oxygen sensor (HO2S) electrical connectors.
28. Remove the nut and the ground cable.
29. Remove the 3 bolts and position the A/C compressor aside.

Manual transmission vehicles
30. Remove the clutch.

All vehicles
31. Remove and discard the oil filter.
32. Disconnect the coolant hoses from the oil cooler.
33. Loosen the threaded shaft and remove the oil cooler. Discard the oil cooler.

Automatic transmission vehicles
34. Remove the starter motor.
35. Remove the transmission filler tube.
36. Remove the bolts and position the transmission oil cooler lines and bracket aside.

All vehicles
37. Remove the stud bolt and position the ground strap aside.

38. Remove the nut and position the starter electrical harness support bracket aside.

Automatic transmission vehicles

39. Remove the 2 bolts and the flexplate inspection cover.

40. Remove the access plug.

41. Remove the 6 torque converter-to-flexplate nuts. Discard the nuts.

42. Remove the 5 lower transmission-to-engine bolts.

Automatic transmission vehicles

43. Remove the upper 2 transmission-to-engine bolts.

All vehicles

44. Install the lifting bracket and support the engine with a suitable floor crane.

✳✳ WARNING

Only use hand tools when removing the engine mount nut or damage to the engine mount can occur.

45. Remove the 4 engine mount nuts.

Automatic transmission vehicles

46. Support the transmission with a jack.

All vehicles

47. Using a suitable floor crane, remove the engine assembly from the vehicle.

To install:

All vehicles

48. Using a suitable floor crane, position the engine assembly into the vehicle.

✳✳ WARNING

Only use hand tools when installing the right engine mount nut or damage to the engine mount can occur.

➡**Align the engine-to-transmission dowels before installing the engine mount bolt.**

49. Install the 4 engine mount nuts. Tighten to 175 Nm (129 ft. lbs.).

50. Remove the lifting bracket.

Manual transmission vehicles

51. Install the clutch.

Automatic transmission vehicles

➡**The upper 2 transmission-to-engine bolts will be installed later.**

52. Install the lower 5 transmission-to-engine bolts. Tighten to 35 Nm (26 ft. lbs.).

53. Install 6 new torque converter-to-flexplate nuts. Tighten to 35 Nm (26 ft. lbs.).

54. Install the cylinder block opening cover.

55. Install the flexplate inspection cover and the 2 bolts. Tighten to 34 Nm (25 ft. lbs.).

56. Install the starter.

57. Install the transmission filler tube.

All vehicles

58. Install the ground strap and the nut. Tighten to 10 Nm (89 inch lbs.).

59. If equipped, connect the block heater electrical connector.

60. Position the starter electrical harness support bracket and install the bolt. Tighten to 10 Nm (89 inch lbs.).

61. Position the ground strap and install the stud bolt. Tighten to 10 Nm (89 inch lbs.).

62. Position the A/C compressor and install the 3 bolts. Tighten to 25 Nm (18 ft. lbs.).

63. Install the 4 exhaust manifold flange nuts. Tighten to 40 Nm (30 ft. lbs.).

64. Connect the 2 heated exhaust gas oxygen sensor (HO$_2$S) electrical connectors.

Automatic transmission vehicles

65. Install the transmission cooler tube support bracket and the nut. Tighten to 10 Nm (89 inch lbs.).

66. Install the upper 2 transmission-to-engine bolts. Tighten to 48 Nm (35 ft. lbs.).

All vehicles

67. Position the degas bottle (coolant reservoir) support bracket and install the 3 nuts. Tighten to 10 Nm (89 inch lbs.).

68. Connect the heater hose at the rear of the engine.

69. Connect the body wiring harness retainer to the degas bottle (coolant reservoir) support bracket.

70. Position the evaporative emissions (EVAP) canister purge valve and bracket assembly, and install the 3 nuts. Tighten to 10 Nm (89 inch lbs.)

71. Connect the electrical connector and the EVAP tube quick connect couplings to the EVAP canister purge valve.

72. Connect the engine wiring harness retainer to the EVAP canister purge valve bracket.

73. Connect the crankshaft position (CKP) sensor wiring harness retainer to the starter motor wiring harness.

74. Connect the alternator wiring harness retainer to the right cylinder head.

75. Connect the A/C compressor and the A/C high pressure cut-off switch electrical connectors.

76. Connect the alternator wiring harness retainer to the right cylinder head.

77. Position the power steering pump and install the 3 bolts. Tighten to 25 Nm (18 ft. lbs.).

78. Connect the 2 electrical connectors on the left fender splash shield.

79. Connect the degas bottle (coolant reservoir) coolant hose.

80. Install the intake manifold.

81. Install the radiator, fan shroud and engine cooling fan.

82. Install the degas bottle (coolant reservoir).

83. Install the powertrain control module (PCM).

84. Install the cowl vent grille.

85. Install the radiator grille support.

86. Install the A/C condenser core.

87. Install the hood.

88. Fill the crankcase with clean engine oil.

6.4L Diesel Engine

1. Before servicing the vehicle, refer to the Precautions Section.

2. With the vehicle in **Neutral**, position it on a hoist.

3. Disconnect the left and right battery ground cables.

Vehicles with manual transmission

➡**On vehicles equipped with manual transmissions, the transmission must be removed before the engine can be removed.**

4. Remove the transmission.

5. Remove the clutch.

All vehicles

6. Remove the air cleaner assembly.

7. Remove the radiator.

8. Remove the charge air cooler.

Vehicles with A/C

9. Remove the A/C condenser assembly.

All vehicles

10. Remove the parking lamp and the headlamp assemblies.

11. Remove the radiator grille, the radiator grille opening panel, and the upper radiator core supports.

12. Remove the front bumper.

13. Disconnect the transmission cooler hoses.

14. Remove the bolts and the transmission oil cooler.

15. Remove the bolts and position the power steering cooler out of the way.

16. Remove the intake manifold.

17. Remove the accessory drive idler pulley and bolt.

18. Disconnect the heater hose at the coolant pump.

19. Remove the battery cable cover.

20. Remove the nut and position the cable out of the way.

21. Disconnect the left glow plug electrical connector and wire retainer.

22. Disconnect the camshaft position (CMP) sensor electrical connector.

23. Remove the clips and disconnect the fuel lines.

24. Remove the lower radiator hose clamp and the hose.

25. Remove the power steering upper mounting bolts.

➡ **Bolts need to be removed evenly.**

26. Remove the bolts and position the power steering pump out of the way.

27. Remove the nut and the battery cable bracket.

28. Remove the ground stud and the ground cable.

29. If equipped, disconnect the injection control pressure (ICP) sensor electrical connector

30. Disconnect the glow plug electrical connectors.

31. Disconnect the right glow plug electrical connector and wire retainer.

Vehicles with A/C

32. Disconnect the A/C high pressure switch and the A/C clutch electrical connectors.

33. Disconnect the air conditioning manifold lines from the A/C compressor.

34. Remove the A/C compressor.

All vehicles

35. Disconnect the crankshaft position (CKP) sensor electrical connector and position the wiring aside.

Vehicles with automatic transmission

36. Remove the automatic transmission fluid indicator and tube.

All vehicles

37. Remove the ground strap at the back of the right head.

38. Remove the solenoid cap and disconnect the starter wiring.

39. Disconnect the block heater electrical connector.

40. Position the block heater and starter wiring harness out of the way.

Vehicles with automatic transmission

41. Remove the torque converter cover.

42. Remove the torque converter nuts.

All vehicles

43. Remove the bolts for the turbocharger adapter pipe.

44. Remove the motor mount nuts.

45. Loosen the nuts at the turbocharger adapter pipe flange.

Vehicles with automatic transmission

46. Remove the nine bell housing bolts.

All vehicles

47. Remove the turbocharger adapter pipe.

48. Remove the nuts and the fuel injector control module bracket.

49. Remove the left rear valve cover stud.

50. Remove the transmission cooler line bracket.

51. Secure the turbocharger outlet pipe.

52. Remove the manufacturer's lifting eye.

53. Install the engine lifting eye on the right cylinder head.

54. Install the front lifting brackets.

Vehicles with automatic transmission

55. Position a suitable jack under the transmission.

All vehicles

56. Install the Heavy Duty Floor Crane and Diesel Engine Lifting Bracket on the engine.

57. Raise the engine high enough to clear the No. 1 crossmember and pull the engine forward and clear of the vehicle.

To install:
All vehicles

58. With the vehicle in **Neutral**, position it on a hoist.

59. Raise the engine high enough to clear the No. 1 crossmember, then position the engine into the vehicle.

Vehicles with automatic transmission

60. Align the torque converter studs with the holes in the engine flywheel, then lower the engine onto the engine mount towers.

Vehicles with manual transmission

61. Lower the engine onto the engine mount towers.

All vehicles

62. Remove the Heavy Duty Floor Crane and the Diesel Engine Lifting Bracket.

Vehicles with automatic transmission

63. Remove the transmission jack.

64. Install the transmission-to-engine mounting bolts. Torque to 35 ft. lbs. (47 Nm).

65. Install the torque converter-to-flywheel retaining nuts. Torque to 26 ft. lbs. (35 Nm).

66. Install the flywheel housing cover.

All vehicles

67. Install the left and right side engine mount retaining nuts. Torque to 76 ft. lbs. (103 Nm).

68. Remove the engine lifting eye from the right side cylinder head.

69. Install the manufacturer's lifting bracket.

70. Remove the two engine lift adapters.

71. Position the turbocharger outlet pipe.

72. Install the transmission cooler tube bracket and nut.

73. Install the left rear valve cover stud.

74. Install the fuel injector control module bracket and nuts.

75. Position the turbocharger adapter pipe.

➡ **Do not tighten bolts at this time.**

➡ **Apply anti-seize lubricant to the threads prior to installing the bolts.**

76. Install the bolts for the turbocharger adapter pipe.

77. Position back the block heater and starter wiring.

78. Connect the block heater electrical connector.

79. Connect the starter wiring and install the solenoid cap.

80. Connect the ground strap on the right head and install the bolt.

Vehicles with automatic transmission

81. Install the automatic transmission fluid indicator and tube.

All vehicles

82. Position back the wiring and connect the crankshaft position (CKP) sensor electrical connector.

Vehicles with A/C

83. Install the A/C compressor. Torque to 18 ft. lbs. (25 Nm).

84. Position the A/C compressor manifold and install the bolt. Torque to 15 ft. lbs. (21 Nm).

85. Connect the A/C high pressure switch and the clutch electrical connectors.

All vehicles

86. Connect the right glow plug electrical connector and wire retainer.

87. Connect the glow plug module electrical connectors.

88. If equipped, connect the injection control pressure (ICP) sensor electrical connector.

89. Connect the ground cable and the ground stud.

90. Install the battery cable bracket and the nut.

➡ **The lower bolts need to be installed evenly.**

91. Position the power steering pump and install the lower bolts. Torque to 18 ft. lbs. (25 Nm).

92. Install the power steering pump upper bolts. Torque to 18 ft. lbs. (25 Nm).

93. Install the lower radiator hose and clamp.

94. Connect the fuel lines and install the clips.

95. Connect the camshaft position (CMP) sensor electrical connector.

96. Connect the left glow plug electrical connector and wire retainer.

97. Connect the battery crossover cable.

98. Install the battery cable cover.

99. Connect the heater hose at the coolant pump.

100. Install the accessory drive idler pulley and bolt. Torque to 35 ft. lbs. (47 Nm).

101. Install the intake manifold.

102. Tighten the turbocharger adapter pipe at the flanges. Torque to 20 ft. lbs. (27 Nm).

103. Tighten the nuts at the turbocharger adapter pipe flange. Torque to 35 ft. lbs. (47 Nm).

104. Position and install the power steering cooler and bolts.

105. Install the transmission oil cooler.

106. Connect the transmission cooler hoses.

107. Install the front bumper.

108. Install the upper radiator core support, radiator grill opening panel and the radiator grill.

109. Install the headlamp and the parking lamp assemblies.

Vehicles with A/C

110. Install the A/C condenser assembly.

All vehicles

111. Install the charge air cooler.

112. Install the radiator.

113. Install the air cleaner assembly.

Vehicles with manual transmission

114. Install the clutch assembly.

115. Install the transmission.

All vehicles

116. Fill the motor with clean engine oil.

117. Connect the left and right battery cables.

118. Fill the cooling system.

Vehicles with automatic transmission

119. Check and fill the automatic transmission.

EXHAUST MANIFOLD

REMOVAL & INSTALLATION

5.4L Engine

Left Side

See Figure 150.

1. Before servicing the vehicle, refer to the Precautions Section.

2. With the vehicle in **Neutral**, position it on a hoist.

3. Remove the front and rear oxygen sensors.

4. Disconnect the exhaust pipes from the catalytic converters and the crossmember brackets.

5. Remove the manifold. Discard the gasket.

➡ **Do not use metal scrapers, wire brushes, power abrasive discs, or other abrasive means to clean the sealing surfaces. These may cause scratches and gouges resulting in leak paths. Use a plastic scraper to clean the sealing surfaces.**

6. Clean the sealing surfaces with metal surface prep.

7. Install the manifold with a new gasket.

8. Tighten the exhaust manifold nuts in the sequence shown.

To install:

9. Installation is the reverse of the removal procedure. Note the following:

10. Tighten the manifold bolts, in the sequence shown, to 18 ft. lbs. (25 Nm).

11. Tighten the exhaust pipe bracket bolts to 18 ft. lbs. (25 Nm).

12. Tighten the exhaust pipe-to-converter nuts to 30 ft. lbs. (40 Nm).

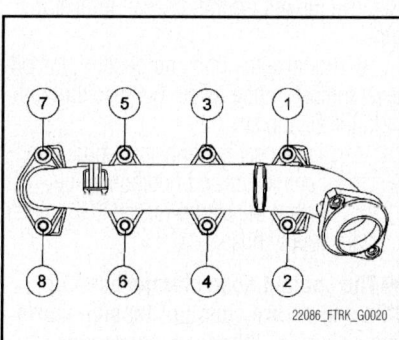

Fig. 150 Right side exhaust manifold nut tightening sequence—2005 4.6L engine

Right Side

See Figure 151.

1. Before servicing the vehicle, refer to the Precautions Section.

2. With the vehicle in **Neutral**, position it on a hoist.

3. Remove the starter.

4. Remove the right side inner fender well.

5. Disconnect the exhaust pipes at the manifolds and catalytic converters.

6. If equipped, remove the mounting bolts and position the sway bar aside.

7. Remove the manifold. Discard the gasket.

➡ **Do not use metal scrapers, wire brushes, power abrasive discs, or other abrasive means to clean the sealing surfaces. These may cause scratches**

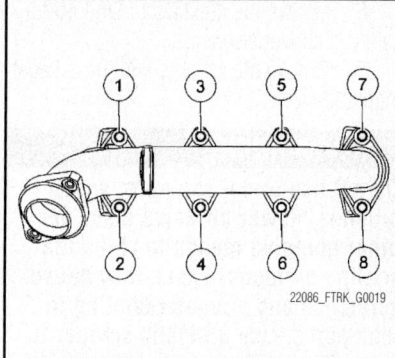

Fig. 151 Right side exhaust manifold nut tightening sequence—2005 4.6L engine

and gouges resulting in leak paths. Use a plastic scraper to clean the sealing surfaces.

8. Clean the sealing surfaces with metal surface prep.

9. Tighten the right exhaust manifold nuts in the sequence shown.

To install:

10. Installation is the reverse of the removal procedure. Note the following:

11. Tighten the manifold bolts, in the sequence shown, to 18 ft. lbs. (25 Nm).

12. If removed, install the sway bar nuts to 22 ft. lbs. (30 Nm).

13. Tighten the exhaust pipe flange and converter nuts to 30 ft. lbs. (40 Nm).

6.8L Engines

Left Side

See Figure 152.

1. Before servicing the vehicle, refer to the Precautions Section.

2. Raise and safely support the vehicle.

3. Remove the air cleaner housing.

4. Remove the 2 bolts and position the degas bottle (coolant reservoir) aside.

5. Disconnect and position the brake tube retainer aside.

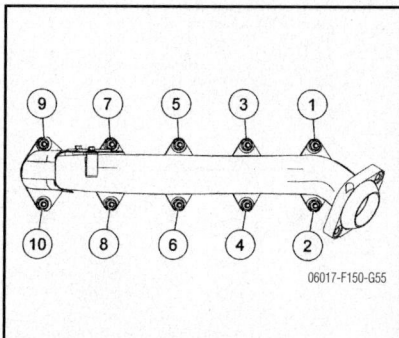

Fig. 152 Left side exhaust manifold torque sequence—6.8L engine

6. Remove the 4 exhaust manifold-to-catalytic converter nuts.

7. Remove the 10 nuts and the exhaust manifold.

❋❋ WARNING

Do not use metal scrapers, wire brushes, power abrasive discs or other abrasive means to clean the sealing surfaces. These may cause scratches and gouges resulting in leak paths. Use a plastic scraper to clean the sealing surfaces.

➡**Clean the sealing surfaces with metal surface prep. Follow the directions on the packaging.**

8. Remove and discard the exhaust manifold gaskets. Clean the sealing surfaces with metal surface prep.

9. To install, reverse the removal procedure.

10. Torque the manifold nuts to 18 ft. lbs. (25 Nm).

11. Torque the exhaust pipe-to-manifold nuts to 30 ft. lbs. (40 Nm).

Right Side

See Figure 153.

1. Before servicing the vehicle, refer to the Precautions Section.

2. Raise and safely support the vehicle.

3. If equipped, remove the transmission filler tube.

4. Remove the starter.

5. Remove the right inner fenderwell.

6. Remove the 4 exhaust manifold-to-catalytic converter nuts.

7. Remove the 10 nuts and the exhaust manifold.

❋❋ WARNING

Do not use metal scrapers, wire brushes, power abrasive discs or other abrasive means to clean the sealing surfaces. These may cause scratches and gouges resulting in leak paths. Use a plastic scraper to clean the sealing surfaces.

➡**Clean the sealing surfaces with metal surface prep. Follow the directions on the packaging.**

8. Remove and discard the exhaust manifold gaskets. Clean the sealing surfaces with metal surface prep.

9. To install, reverse the removal procedure. Torque the manifold nuts to 18 ft. lbs. (25 Nm). Torque the exhaust pipe-to-manifold nuts to 30 ft. lbs. (40 Nm).

6.4L Diesel Engine

Left Side

See Figure 154.

1. Remove the LH turbocharger inlet pipe.

2. Remove the degas bottle.

3. Remove the LH front tire and wheel.

4. Remove the LH fender splash shield.

5. Remove the oil level indicator. Remove the nut for the oil level indicator tube.

6. Remove the bolt and position the oil level indicator tube aside. Remove and discard the O-ring seal.

7. Disconnect the anti-lock module electrical connector and position aside.

8. Loosen the clamp for the EGR cooler coolant supply hose.

➡**The coolant hose clamps used on this engine are constant tension worm gear clamps. Standard worm gear clamps cannot be used. Failure to use the correct coolant hose clamps may result in hose joint failure.**

➡**Position a drain pan prior to removing the EGR cooler coolant supply tube.**

9. Remove the bolts and the EGR cooler coolant supply tube. Discard the clamp on the hose and the O-ring seal on the tube.

➡**The coolant hose clamps used on this engine are constant tension worm gear clamps. Standard worm gear clamps cannot be used. Failure to use the correct coolant hose clamps may result in hose joint failure.**

10. Loosen the clamp and disconnect the EGR cooler outlet coolant hose. Discard the clamp.

11. Remove the 2 nuts for the horizontal EGR cooler outlet.

12. Remove the 2 studs for the horizontal EGR cooler outlet. Remove and discard the gasket.

13. Remove the bolt and disconnect the steering shaft. Discard the bolt.

14. Remove the 2 nuts, separate the clamps and remove the horizontal EGR cooler.

15. Prior to removing the exhaust manifold, inspect the exhaust manifold for warpage with a feeler gauge between the manifold and the cylinder head. Record the measurement and compare to Specifications in this section.

16. Remove the 4 horizontal EGR cooler bracket bolts and the bracket. Discard the bolts.

17. Remove the 4 bolts, the exhaust manifold and the exhaust manifold gasket. Discard the bolts and gasket.

18. Remove the 2 pins from the back of the horizontal EGR cooler bracket. Remove and discard the EGR cooler clamps. Discard the nuts.

To install:

19. Position the new horizontal EGR cooler clamps and install 2 new pins.

20. Position the new gasket and the LH exhaust manifold. Loosely install the 4 new exhaust manifold bolts.

21. Position the horizontal EGR cooler bracket and loosely install the 4 new bolts.

22. Tighten the exhaust manifold bolts in 2 stages in the sequence shown:

    a. Stage 1: Tighten to 18 ft. lbs. (25 Nm).

    b. Stage 2: Tighten again to 18 ft. lbs. (25 Nm).

23. Insert the horizontal EGR cooler locating pin into the slot in the horizontal EGR cooler bracket and install the 2 new clamp nuts. Tighten the clamps for the horizontal EGR cooler in 3 stages:

    a. Stage 1: Tighten to 89 inch lbs. (10 Nm).

    b. Stage 2: Loosen the clamps 720 degrees.

    c. Stage 3: Tighten to 71 inch lbs. (8 Nm).

24. Position the steering shaft into the

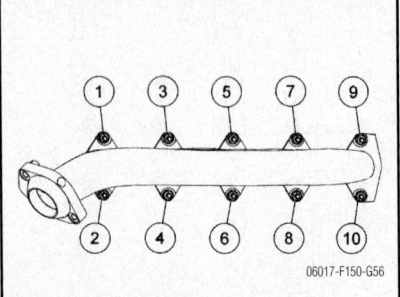

Fig. 153 Right side exhaust manifold torque sequence—6.8L engine

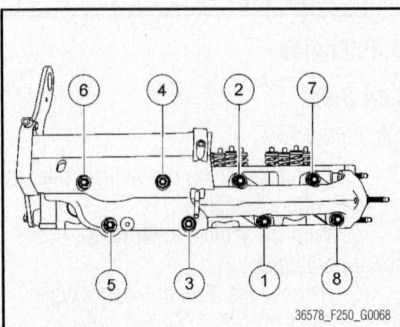

Fig. 154 Exhaust manifold tightening sequence—Left side

housing. Install the new steering shaft bolt. Tighten to 35 ft. lbs. (48 Nm).

25. Position a new horizontal EGR cooler outlet gasket and install the 2 studs.

➡**Do not bend or twist the Exhaust Gas Recirculation (EGR) cooler bellows or damage to the EGR cooler may occur.**

➡**Inspect the corrugation of the vertical EGR cooler inlet to make sure that the corrugation ribs are not touching and are not damaged.**

26. Install the 2 horizontal EGR cooler outlet nuts. Tighten to 23 ft. lbs. (31 Nm).

➡**The coolant hose clamps used on this engine are constant tension worm gear clamps. Standard worm gear clamps cannot be used. Failure to use the correct coolant hose clamps may result in hose joint failure.**

27. Using a new clamp, connect the EGR cooler coolant outlet hose to the horizontal EGR cooler.

➡**The coolant hose clamps used on this engine are constant tension worm gear clamps. Standard worm gear clamps cannot be used. Failure to use the correct coolant hose clamps may result in hose joint failure.**

➡**Install a new O-ring seal and clamp on the coolant supply tube.**

➡**Position the flexible section of hose on the EGR cooler prior to installing the tube.**

➡**Make sure the oil level indicator tube is positioned behind the EGR cooler coolant supply tube before installing the EGR cooler coolant supply tube.**

28. Position a new clamp and install the EGR cooler coolant supply tube and bolts. Tighten the clamp for the EGR cooler coolant supply hose.

29. Connect the anti-lock module electrical connector.

30. Install a new O-ring seal on the oil level tube prior to installing. Position the oil level indicator tube. Install the bolt.

31. Install the nut for the oil level indicator tube. Install the oil level indicator.

32. Install the LH fender splash shield.

33. Install the LH front tire and wheel.

34. Install the degas bottle.

35. Install the LH turbocharger inlet pipe.

Right Side
See Figure 155.

1. Remove the Air Cleaner (ACL) assembly.

2. Remove the auxiliary air intake tube.

3. Vehicles with A/C, recover the A/C system.

➡**Position a suitable material in front of the Charge Air Cooler (CAC) or damage to the CAC may occur.**

4. Disconnect the battery ground cables.

5. With the vehicle in NEUTRAL, position it on a hoist.

6. Remove the 2 exhaust downpipe-to-Oxidation Catalytic Converter (OC) pipe bolts.

7. Remove and discard the exhaust downpipe clamp. Position aside the exhaust downpipe. Remove and discard the exhaust downpipe gasket.

8. Disconnect the Exhaust Pressure (EP) sensor tube from the EGR- OC pipe.

9. Remove the EGR- OC pipe bracket-to-bracket bolt and washer. Remove the bracket-to-cylinder head bolt, washers and the bracket. Discard the bolts.

10. Remove the 2 EGR- OC -to-EGR cooler bolts. Discard the bolts and gasket.

11. Remove the 2 EGR- OC pipe bolts and the 2 EGR- OC -to-turbocharger bracket bolts. Position the EGR- OC pipe aside. Discard the bolts and gasket.

12. Remove the RH front tire and wheel.

13. Remove the RH fender splash shield.

14. Remove the Exhaust Gas Recirculation Temperature (EGRT) sensor from the RH turbocharger inlet pipe.

15. Remove and discard the 3 RH turbocharger inlet pipe-to-exhaust manifold nuts.

16. Remove the 3 RH turbocharger inlet pipe-to-exhaust manifold studs. Discard the studs.

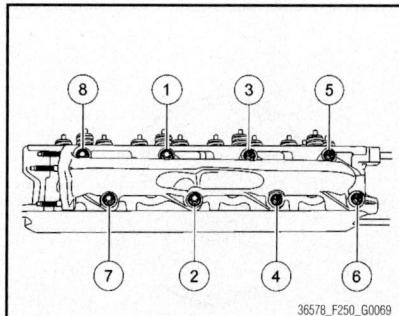

Fig. 155 Exhaust manifold tightening sequence—Right side

17. Remove the 3 RH turbocharger inlet pipe bolts.

18. Position the RH turbocharger inlet pipe aside. Discard the bolts and gasket.

19. Remove the nut and position the battery cable bracket aside.

20. Remove the cover for the starter terminals.

21. Remove the 2 retaining nuts for the starter solenoid wiring. Position the starter wiring aside.

22. Vehicles with A/C, disconnect the A/C compressor wire retainer. Position the wiring aside.

23. Remove the 2 nuts and position aside the A/C hoses. Discard the O-ring seal and gaskets. Plug or cap the openings.

24. Vehicles with automatic transmission, remove the retaining nut and position the transmission fluid indicator tube off the stud.

25. Prior to removing the exhaust manifold, inspect the exhaust manifold for warpage with a feeler gauge between the manifold and the cylinder head. Record the measurement and compare with the specifications.

26. Remove the 3 bolts and nut for the heat shield. Remove the heat shield.

27. Remove the 3 spacers from the exhaust manifold stud bolts.

➡**Mark the location of the fasteners prior to removing.**

28. Remove the 4 stud bolts and 4 bolts. Remove the exhaust manifold and exhaust manifold gasket. Discard the gasket, stud bolts and bolts.

To install:

29. Position a new exhaust manifold gasket and the exhaust manifold. Install the 4 new stud bolts and the 4 new bolts. Tighten in 2 stages in the sequence shown:

    a. Stage 1: Tighten to 18 ft. lbs. (25 Nm).

    b. Stage 2: Tighten again to 18 ft. lbs. (25 Nm).

30. To complete installation, reverse removal procedure.

FLYWHEEL

REMOVAL & INSTALLATION

5.4L and 6.8L Engines
See Figure 156.

1. Before servicing the vehicle, refer to the precautions in the beginning of this section.

2. Remove the clutch. For additional information, refer to Clutch R&I in this section.

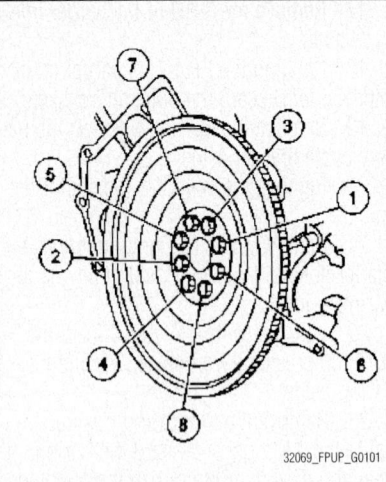

Fig. 156 Flywheel bolt torque sequence—5.4L and 6.8L engine

3. Remove the 8 bolts and the flywheel.

4. To install, reverse the removal procedure. Tighten to 59 ft. lbs. (80 Nm) in the sequence shown.

6.4L Diesel Engine

See Figure 157.

1. With the vehicle in NEUTRAL, position it on a hoist.

2. Remove the clutch disc and pressure plate.

3. Remove the 10 bolts, reinforcement ring and the flywheel. Discard the bolts.

4. To install, Install the flywheel, reinforcement ring and 10 new bolts. Tighten in 2 stages, in the sequence shown:

   a. Stage 1: Tighten to 44 inch lbs. (5 Nm).

   b. Stage 2: Tighten to 69 ft. lbs. (94 Nm).

5. Install the clutch disc and pressure plate.

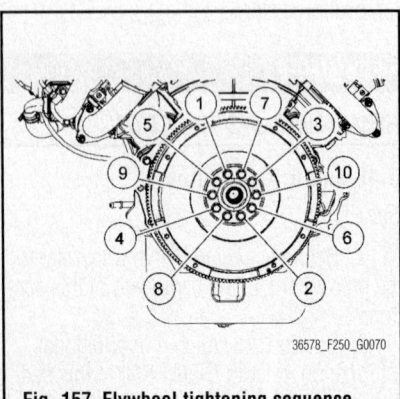

Fig. 157 Flywheel tightening sequence

FLEXPLATE

REMOVAL & INSTALLATION

5.4L and 6.8L Engines

See Figure 158.

1. Before servicing the vehicle, refer to the precautions in the beginning of this section.

2. Remove the transmission. For additional information, refer to Automatic Transmission R&I in this section.

3. Remove the 8 bolts and the flywheel.

4. To install, reverse the removal procedure. Tighten to 80 Nm (59 ft. lbs.) in the sequence shown.

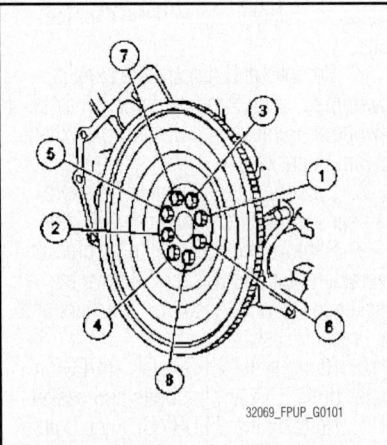

Fig. 158 Flexplate bolt torque sequence—5.4L and 6.8L engine

6.4L Diesel Engine

See Figure 159.

1. With the vehicle in NEUTRAL, position it on a hoist.

2. Remove the transmission.

3. Remove the 10 bolts, reinforcement ring and the flexplate. Discard the bolts.

4. To install, Install the flexplate, reinforcement ring and 10 new bolts. Tighten in 2 stages, in the sequence shown:

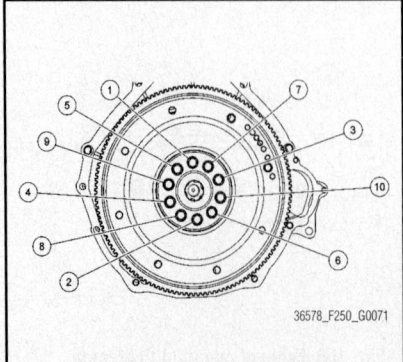

Fig. 159 Flexplate tightening sequence

   a. Stage 1: Tighten to 44 inch lbs. (5 Nm).

   b. Stage 2: Tighten to 69 ft. lbs. (94 Nm).

5. Install the transmission.

INTAKE MANIFOLD

REMOVAL & INSTALLATION

5.4L Engine

See Figure 160.

1. Before servicing the vehicle, refer to the Precautions Section.

2. Drain the cooling system.

3. Release the fuel system pressure.

4. Remove the alternator.

5. Remove the air cleaner.

6. Disconnect the upper radiator hose from the thermostat housing.

7. Disconnect the heater coolant hose from the coolant bypass tube.

8. Disconnect the quick connect coupling and remove the evaporative emissions (EVAP) tube from the intake manifold.

9. Disconnect the quick connect coupling and remove the positive crankcase ventilation (PCV) tube.

10. Disconnect the fuel supply spring lock coupling from the fuel rail.

11. Disconnect the fuel rail pressure and temperature sensor electrical connector and vacuum connector.

12. Disconnect the 8 fuel injector electrical connectors.

13. Disconnect the throttle position (TP) sensor and electronic throttle control electrical connectors.

14. Disconnect the heated PCV element electrical connector.

15. Disconnect the brake booster vacuum hose from the intake manifold vacuum tube.

16. Remove the 10 intake manifold bolts.

✴✴ WARNING

Do not use metal scrapers, wire brushes, power abrasive discs or other abrasive means to clean the sealing surfaces. These tools cause scratches and gouges which make leak paths. Use a plastic scraping tool to remove all traces of old sealant.

17. Remove the 3 bolts, the coolant bypass tube and discard the gaskets.

18. Clean and inspect the sealing surfaces with metal surface prep. Follow the directions on the packaging.

19. Disconnect the charge motion control valve (CMCV) electrical connector.

20. Disconnect the intake manifold vacuum tube from the valve cover stud and the support bracket.

21. Disconnect the cylinder head temperature (CHT) sensor jumper harness electrical connector.

22. Disconnect the LH and RH knock sensor (KS) electrical connectors.

23. Remove the nut and disconnect the engine wiring harness retainer from the CMCV stud.

✳✳ WARNING

Do not use metal scrapers, wire brushes, power abrasive discs or other abrasive means to clean the sealing surfaces. These tools cause scratches and gouges which make leak paths. Use a plastic scraping tool to remove all traces of old sealant.

24. Remove the intake manifold and discard the gaskets.

25. Clean and inspect the sealing surfaces with metal surface prep. Follow the directions on the packaging.

To install:

➡ **Electrical and vacuum harnesses must not restrict movement of the CMCV control rods at the rear of the intake manifold. Use extreme care on installation of the intake manifold to prevent any pinching of electrical and vacuum harnesses.**

26. Using new intake manifold gaskets, position the intake manifold.

27. Using new gaskets, position the coolant crossover and install the 3 bolts. Tighten to 10 Nm (89 inch lbs.).

28. Install the intake manifold bolts and tighten in 2 stages in the sequence shown.

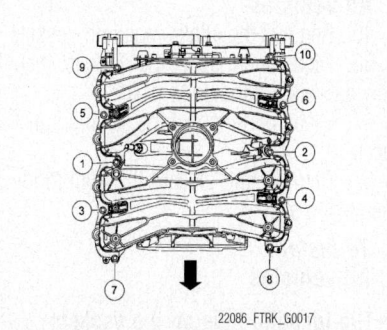

Fig. 160 Intake manifold bolt tightening sequence—5.4L engine

22086_FTRK_G0017

- Stage 1: Tighten to 18 inch. lbs. (2 Nm).
- Stage 2: Tighten to 89 inch lbs (10 Nm).

29. Connect the engine wiring harness retainer to the CMCV stud and install the nut.

30. Connect the CMCV electrical connector.

31. Connect the CHT sensor jumper harness electrical connector.

32. Connect the LH and RH KS electrical connectors.

33. Connect the intake manifold vacuum tube to the support bracket and the valve cover stud.

34. Connect the brake booster vacuum hose to the intake manifold vacuum tube.

35. Connect the heated PCV element electrical connector.

36. Connect the TP sensor and electronic throttle control electrical connectors.

37. Connect the 8 fuel injector electrical connectors.

38. Connect the fuel rail pressure and temperature sensor electrical connector and vacuum connector.

39. Connect the fuel supply spring lock coupling to the fuel rail.

40. Position the PCV tube and connect the quick connect coupling.

41. Position the EVAP tube and connect the quick connect coupling to the intake manifold.

42. Connect the heater coolant hose to the coolant bypass.

43. Connect the upper radiator hose to the thermostat housing.

44. Install the alternator.

45. Install the air cleaner.

46. Fill and bleed the engine cooling system.

6.8L Engine

See Figure 161.

✳✳ WARNING

Fuel in the fuel system remains under high pressure, even when the engine is not running.

1. Before servicing the vehicle, refer to the Precautions Section.

2. Relieve the fuel system pressure.

3. Disconnect the fuel supply spring lock coupling from the fuel rail.

4. Drain the cooling system.

5. Remove the alternator. See the "Alternator" section.

6. Remove the air cleaner outlet pipe.

7. Disconnect the upper radiator hose from the thermostat housing.

8. Disconnect the heater coolant hose from the coolant crossover assembly.

9. Disconnect the intake manifold runner control (IMRC) actuator electrical connector.

10. Disconnect the fuel rail pressure and temperature sensor electrical connector and vacuum connector.

11. Disconnect the 10 fuel injector electrical connectors.

12. Disconnect the positive crankcase ventilation (PCV) tube quick connect coupling from the intake manifold.

13. Disconnect the quick connect couplings and remove the evaporative emissions (EVAP) tube.

14. Disconnect the brake booster and engine vacuum hose connections from the rear of the intake manifold and position aside.

15. Disconnect the 2 heated PCV coolant hoses from the intake manifold.

16. Disconnect the throttle position (TP) sensor and electronic throttle control electrical connectors.

17. Disconnect the engine wiring harness position retainers from the intake manifold.

18. Remove the 12 intake manifold bolts.

✳✳ CAUTION

Do not use metal scrapers, wire brushes, power abrasive discs or other abrasive means to clean the sealing surfaces. These tools cause scratches and gouges which make leak paths. Use a plastic scraping tool to remove all traces of old sealant.

19. Remove the 2 bolts, the coolant crossover tube and discard the gaskets.

20. Clean and inspect the sealing surfaces with metal surface prep and silicone gasket remover. Follow the directions on the packaging.

21. Remove the intake manifold and discard the gaskets.

22. Clean and inspect the sealing surfaces with metal surface prep and silicone gasket remover.

To install:

23. Using new intake manifold gaskets, position the intake manifold.

24. Using new gaskets, position the coolant crossover tube and install the 2 bolts. Tighten to 89 inch lbs. (10 Nm).

25. Install the intake manifold bolts and tighten in 2 stages in the sequence shown, to the following:

- Stage 1: Tighten to 18 inch. lbs. (2 Nm).
- Stage 2: Tighten to 89 inch lbs (10 Nm).

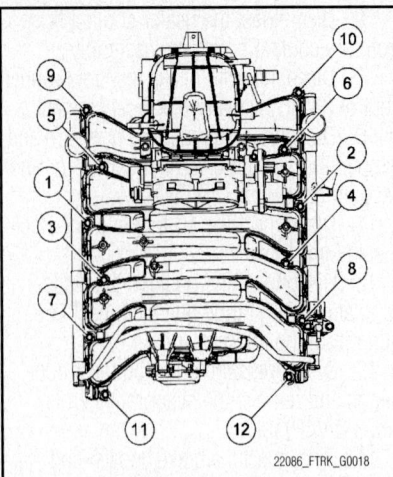

Fig. 161 Intake manifold bolt tightening sequence—6.8L engine

26. Connect the throttle position (TP) sensor and electronic throttle control electrical connectors.

27. Connect the engine wiring harness position retainers to the intake manifold.

28. Connect the brake booster and engine vacuum hose connections to the rear of the intake manifold.

29. Connect the positive crankcase ventilation (PCV) tube quick connect coupling to the intake manifold.

30. Position the evaporative emissions (EVAP) tube and connect the quick connect couplings.

31. Connect the 2 heated PCV coolant hoses to the intake manifold.

32. Connect the 10 fuel injector electrical connectors.

33. Connect the fuel rail pressure and temperature sensor electrical connector and vacuum connector.

34. Connect the intake manifold runner control (IMRC) actuator electrical connector.

35. Connect the fuel supply spring lock coupling to the fuel rail.

36. Connect the heater coolant hose to the coolant crossover assembly.

37. Connect the heated PCV coolant hose to the coolant crossover assembly.

38. Connect the upper radiator hose to the thermostat housing.

39. Install the alternator. See the "Alternator" section.

40. Install the air cleaner outlet pipe.

41. Fill and bleed the engine cooling system.

6.4L Diesel Engine

See Figure 162.

1. Before servicing the vehicle, refer to the Precautions Section.

2. Remove the auxiliary battery.

3. Remove the cooling fan stator.

4. Remove the degas bottle (coolant reservoir).

5. Remove the upper radiator hose.

6. Remove the turbocharger-to-charge air cooler duct.

Vehicles with dual alternators

7. Remove the accessory drive belt.

8. Remove the bolt and the accessory drive belt tensioner.

9. Remove the accessory drive belt.

10. Remove the bolts, bracket and accessory drive belt idler pulley.

11. Remove the bolts and the accessory drive belt tensioner.

12. Disconnect the wire retainer, alternator electrical connector and B+ wire.

13. Remove the bolts and the alternator with mounting bracket.

Vehicles with single alternator

14. Remove the accessory drive belt.

All vehicles

15. Position the boot back and disconnect the alternator B+ wire and electrical connector.

16. Remove the three bolts and the alternator.

17. Remove the turbocharger and the turbocharger pedestal.

Early build

18. Loosen the clamps and remove the charge air cooler duct.

Late build

19. Loosen the clamps and remove the charge air cooler duct.

20. Remove the bolts and position the heater hose tube aside.

21. Remove and discard the O-ring.

22. Disconnect the manifold absolute pressure (MAP) sensor hose.

23. Disconnect the engine coolant vent hose.

24. Remove the fuel injector control module.

25. Remove or position aside the heat insulating wrap.

26. Disconnect the wiring retainer, injector pressure regulator valve and injector control pressure (ICP) sensor (if equipped) electrical connectors.

27. Disconnect the exhaust gas recirculation (EGR) valve electrical connector.

28. Disconnect the engine oil pressure (EOP) sensor electrical connector.

29. Disconnect the engine oil temperature sensor electrical connector.

30. Disconnect the exhaust gas recirculation (EGR) throttle position control module electrical connector.

31. Disconnect the EGR throttle position sensor electrical connector.

32. Disconnect the pin-type retainer and engine coolant temperature (ECT) sensor.

33. Disconnect the intake air temperature (IAT2) sensor electrical connector and wiring connector.

34. Disconnect the exhaust backpressure sensor and retaining clip.

35. Disconnect the eight fuel injectors electrical connectors. Remove the nut and the fuel injector wiring harness.

➡**It is necessary to remove the fuel filter and drain the housing.**

36. Disconnect the fuel line fittings.

➡**It is necessary to remove the oil filter and drain the housing.**

37. Remove the four bolts and the oil filter housing.

38. Remove the bolt and the oil filter return tube.

39. Remove the fuel line.

40. Remove the bolt, and the banjo fitting from the fuel line.

41. Discard the sealing washers and remove the fuel line.

➡**Align the flat edge with the index feature located on the coolant supply port.**

42. Pull the EGR cooler clamp forward, twist and then slide the EGR cooler hose rearward to remove.

Early build

43. Remove the nuts and the turbocharger heat shield.

➡**Intake removed for clarity.**

44. Remove the EGR cooler V-clamp and gasket.

45. Remove the bolts and the intake manifold.

Late build

46. Remove the nuts and the turbocharger heat shield.

47. Remove the EGR cooler V-clamp and gasket.

48. Remove the bolts and the intake manifold.

All vehicles

49. Remove the intake manifold gaskets.

50. Clean and inspect the gaskets. Install new gaskets if necessary.

51. Clean and inspect the sealing surfaces.

52. Remove and discard the front module O-ring seal.

To install:
All vehicles

➡**The locating tabs on the gaskets must be up and toward the center of the engine, or a leak will occur.**

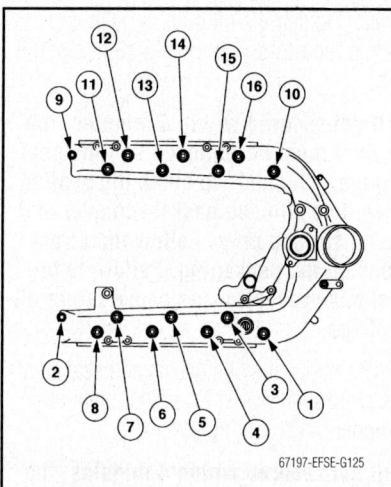

Fig. 162 Intake manifold torque sequence—6.4L Diesel Engine

53. Install the intake manifold gaskets and front module O-ring seal.

Late build

54. Install the intake manifold and bolts and tighten in the following sequence.

  a. Loosely install bolts 1–8.

  b. Tighten bolts 9– 8 ft. lbs. (11 Nm).

  c. Tighten all bolts to 8 ft. lbs. (11 Nm) in the sequence shown.

55. Install the gasket and the EGR cooler V-clamp.

56. Install the turbocharger heat shield and the nuts.

Early build

57. Install the intake manifold and bolts and tighten in the following sequence.

  a. Loosely install bolts 1–8.

  b. Tighten bolts 9–16 to 11 Nm (8 ft. lbs.).

  c. Tighten all bolts to 11 Nm (8 ft. lbs.) in the sequence shown.

58. Install the gasket and the EGR cooler V-clamp.

59. Install the turbocharger heat shield and the nuts.

All vehicles

60. Slide the EGR cooler hose forward and rotate flat to lock.

61. Install the fuel line.

62. Install new sealing washers.

63. Install the fuel line.

64. Install the banjo fitting and the bolt.

65. Install the oil filter return tube and bolt.

66. Install the oil filter housing and the four bolts.

67. Clean and inspect the housing O-rings. Install new O-rings if necessary.

68. Connect the fuel line fittings.

69. Position the fuel injector harness and install the retaining nut. Connect the

eight fuel injectors electrical connectors.

70. Connect the retaining clip and exhaust backpressure sensor electrical connector.

71. Connect the wiring retainer and the IAT2 sensor electrical connector.

72. Connect the engine coolant temperature (ECT) sensor and the pin-type retainer.

73. Connect the EGR throttle position sensor electrical connector.

74. Connect the EGR throttle position control module electrical connector.

75. Connect the engine oil temperature (EOT) sensor electrical connector.

76. Connect the engine oil pressure (EOP) sensor electrical connector.

77. Connect the EGR valve electrical connector.

78. Connect the wiring retainer, injector pressure regulator and ICP sensor (if equipped) electrical connectors.

79. Position back or install the heat insulating wrap.

80. Install the fuel injector control module.

81. Connect the engine coolant vent hose and clamp.

82. Connect the MAP sensor hose.

➡**Install a new O-ring on the heater hose tube.**

83. Install the heater hose tube and bolts.

Early build

84. Install the charge air cooler duct and tighten the clamps.

Late build

85. Install the charge air cooler duct and tighten the clamp.

86. Install the turbocharger pedestal and turbocharger.

87. Install the alternator and the three bolts.

88. Connect the alternator B+ wire land electrical connector and position the boot back.

Vehicles with single alternator

89. Install the accessory drive belt.

Vehicles with dual alternators

90. Install the alternator with mounting bracket and bolts.

91. Connect the B+ wire, alternator electrical connector and wire retainer.

92. Install the accessory drive belt tensioner and bolts.

93. Position the accessory drive belt idler pulley. Install the bracket and bolts.

94. Install the accessory drive belt.

95. Install the accessory drive belt tensioner and bolt.

96. Install the accessory drive belt.

All vehicles

97. Install the turbocharger-to-charge air cooler duct.

98. Install the upper radiator hose.

99. Install the degas bottle (coolant reservoir).

100. Install the auxiliary battery.

101. Install the cooling fan stator

OIL PAN

REMOVAL & INSTALLATION

5.4L Engine

1. Before servicing the vehicle, refer to the Precautions Section.

2. Remove the transmission.

3. Drain the engine oil.

4. Disconnect the engine oil temperature (EOT) sensor electrical connector.

5. Remove the nut and the starter wiring harness support bracket.

6. Remove the nut and position the transmission oil cooler lines and bracket aside.

7. Remove the 16 bolts and lower the oil pan onto the crossmember.

8. Remove the 3 bolts and position the oil pump screen and pickup tube into the oil pan.

➡**Be careful when removing the oil pan gasket. It is reusable.**

9. Remove the oil pan and the oil pump screen and pickup tube.

10. Inspect the oil pan gasket for damage. If damaged, discard the oil pan gasket and the oil pan-to-oil pump gaskets. Discard the oil pump screen and pickup tube O-ring seal.

To install:

✴✴ WARNING

Do not use metal scrapers, wire brushes, power abrasive discs or other abrasive means to clean the sealing surfaces. These tools cause scratches and gouges, which make leak paths. Use a plastic scraping tool to remove all traces of old sealant.

11. Inspect the oil pan. Clean the mating surface for the oil pan with silicone gasket remover and metal surface prep. Follow the directions on the packaging.

12. Position the oil pump screen and pickup tube in the oil pan and position the oil pan into the vehicle.

✳✳ WARNING

Make sure to install a new O-ring seal. A missing or damaged O-ring seal can cause foam in the lubrication system, low oil pressure and severe engine damage.

➡**Clean and inspect the mating surfaces and install a new O-ring seal. Lubricate the O-ring seal with clean engine oil prior to installation.**

13. Position the oil pump screen and pickup tube and install the bolts.

14. Tighten the oil pump screen and pickup tube-to-oil pump bolts to 10 Nm (89 inch lbs.).

15. Tighten the oil pump screen and pickup tube-to-spacer bolt to 25 Nm (18 ft. lbs.).

➡**If not secured within 4 minutes, the sealant must be removed and the sealing area cleaned. To clean the sealing area, use silicone gasket remover and metal surface prep. Follow the directions on the packaging. Failure to follow this procedure can cause future oil leakage.**

16. Apply silicone gasket and sealant at the crankshaft rear seal retainer plate-to-cylinder block sealing surface.

➡**If not secured within 4 minutes, the sealant must be removed and the sealing area cleaned. To clean the sealing area, use silicone gasket remover and metal surface prep. Follow the directions on the packaging. Failure to follow this procedure can cause future oil leakage.**

17. Apply silicone gasket and sealant at the engine front cover-to-cylinder block sealing surface.

18. Install the oil pan gasket and the oil pan and loosely install the 16 bolts.

19. Tighten the bolts in 3 stages, in the sequence shown.
- Stage 1: Tighten to 18 inch lbs. (2 Nm).
- Stage 2: Tighten to 15 ft. lbs. (20 Nm).
- Stage 3: Tighten an additional 60 degrees.

20. Install the wire harness bracket and the bolt. Tighten to 89 inch lbs. (10 Nm).

21. Position the starter wiring harness support bracket and install the nut. Tighten to 89 inch lbs. (10 Nm).

22. Connect the engine oil temperature (EOT) sensor electrical connector.

23. Install the transmission.

24. Fill the crankcase with clean engine oil.

6.8L ENGINE

Manual Transmission

1. Before servicing the vehicle, refer to the Precautions Section.

2. Remove the flywheel.

3. Remove the nut and the starter wiring harness support bracket.

4. Remove the 18 bolts and partially lower the oil pan.

5. Remove the 3 bolts and position the oil pump screen and pickup tube into the oil pan.

➡**Be careful when removing the oil pan gasket. It is reusable.**

6. Remove the oil pan and the oil pump screen and pickup tube.

7. Inspect the oil pan gasket for damage. If damaged, discard the oil pan gasket and the oil pan-to-oil pump gaskets. Discard the oil pump screen and pickup tube O-ring seal.

To install:

✳✳ WARNING

Do not use metal scrapers, wire brushes, power abrasive discs or other abrasive means to clean the sealing surfaces. These tools cause scratches and gouges, which make leak paths. Use a plastic scraping tool to remove all traces of old sealant.

8. Inspect the oil pan. Clean the mating surface for the oil pan with silicone gasket remover and metal surface prep. Follow the directions on the packaging.

9. Position the oil pump screen and pickup tube in the oil pan and position the oil pan into the vehicle.

✳✳ WARNING

Make sure to install a new O-ring seal. A missing or damaged O-ring seal can cause foam in the lubrication system, low oil pressure and severe engine damage.

➡**Clean and inspect the mating surfaces and install a new O-ring seal. Lubricate the O-ring seal with clean engine oil prior to installation.**

10. Position the oil pump screen and pickup tube and install the bolts.

11. Tighten the oil pump screen and pickup tube-to-oil pump bolts to 89 inch lbs. (10 Nm).

12. Tighten the oil pump screen and pickup tube-to-spacer bolt to 18 ft. lbs. (25 Nm).

➡**If not secured within 4 minutes, the sealant must be removed and the sealing area cleaned. To clean the sealing area, use silicone gasket remover and metal surface prep. Follow the directions on the packaging. Failure to follow this procedure can cause future oil leakage.**

13. Apply silicone gasket and sealant at the crankshaft rear seal retainer plate-to-cylinder block sealing surface.

➡**If not secured within 4 minutes, the sealant must be removed and the sealing area cleaned. To clean the sealing area, use silicone gasket remover and metal surface prep. Follow the directions on the packaging. Failure to follow this procedure can cause future oil leakage.**

14. Apply silicone gasket and sealant at the engine front cover-to-cylinder block sealing surface.

15. Install the oil pan gasket and the oil pan and loosely install the 18 bolts.

16. Tighten the bolts in 3 stages:.
- Stage 1: Tighten to 18 ft. lbs. (25 Nm).
- Stage 2: Tighten to 15 ft. lbs. (20 Nm).
- Stage 3: Tighten an additional 60 degrees.

17. Install the transmission cooler tube support bracket and the nut. Tighten to 89 inch lbs. (10 Nm).

18. Install the flywheel.

Automatic Transmission

1. Before servicing the vehicle, refer to the Precautions Section.

2. Raise and safely support the vehicle.

3. Remove the air cleaner outlet tube.

4. Remove the alternator.

5. Remove the cooling fan shroud.

6. Remove the starter.

7. Install the an engine crane and support the engine.

✳✳ WARNING

Only use hand tools when removing the transmission mount-to-crossmember nuts or damage to the transmission mount can occur.

8. Remove the transmission mount-to-crossmember nuts.

✳✳ WARNING

Only use hand tools when installing the right engine mount nut or damage to the engine mount can occur.

9. Remove the 6 engine mount nuts.

10. Remove the 4 exhaust manifold-to-catalytic converter nuts.

11. Remove the nut and the starter wiring harness support bracket.

12. Remove the nut and position the transmission oil cooler lines and bracket aside.

✳✳ WARNING

Damage to the TSS/OSS may occur and cause the transmission or torque converter operational concerns if the transmission is raised prior to removing TSS/OSS.

✳✳ WARNING

Sensor bosses must be cleaned prior to removal and then plugged to prevent contamination from damaging internal components.

13. If the vehicle is equipped with turbine shaft speed (TSS) and output shaft sensors (OSS), remove the sensors and install plugs in the transmission.

14. Using the crane, raise the engine.

✳✳ WARNING

Support the transmission on the oil pan rails only or internal transmission damage can occur.

15. Install a suitable transmission jack and raise the transmission.

16. Remove the 2 bolts and the flywheel inspection plate.

17. Remove the 18 bolts and partially lower the oil pan.

18. Remove the 3 bolts and position the oil pump screen and pickup tube into the oil pan.

➡**Be careful when removing the oil pan gasket. It is reusable.**

19. Remove the oil pan and the oil pump screen and pickup tube.

20. Inspect the oil pan gasket for damage. If damaged, discard the oil pan gasket and the oil pan-to-oil pump gaskets. Discard the oil pump screen and pickup tube O-ring seal.

To install:

✳✳ WARNING

Do not use metal scrapers, wire brushes, power abrasive discs or other abrasive means to clean the sealing surfaces. These tools cause scratches and gouges, which make leak paths. Use a plastic scraping tool to remove all traces of old sealant.

21. Inspect the oil pan. Clean the mating surface for the oil pan with silicone gasket remover and metal surface prep. Follow the directions on the packaging.

22. Position the oil pump screen and pickup tube in the oil pan and position the oil pan into the vehicle.

✳✳ WARNING

Make sure to install a new O-ring seal. A missing or damaged O-ring seal can cause foam in the lubrication system, low oil pressure and severe engine damage.

➡**Clean and inspect the mating surfaces and install a new O-ring seal. Lubricate the O-ring seal with clean engine oil prior to installation.**

23. Position the oil pump screen and pickup tube and install the bolts.

24. Tighten the oil pump screen and pickup tube-to-oil pump bolts to 89 inch lbs. (10 Nm).

25. Tighten the oil pump screen and pickup tube-to-spacer bolt to 18 ft. lbs. (25 Nm).

➡**If not secured within 4 minutes, the sealant must be removed and the sealing area cleaned. To clean the sealing area, use silicone gasket remover and metal surface prep. Follow the directions on the packaging. Failure to follow this procedure can cause future oil leakage.**

26. Apply silicone gasket and sealant at the crankshaft rear seal retainer plate-to-cylinder block sealing surface.

➡**If not secured within 4 minutes, the sealant must be removed and the sealing area cleaned. To clean the sealing area, use silicone gasket remover and metal surface prep. Follow the directions on the packaging. Failure to follow this procedure can cause future oil leakage.**

27. Apply silicone gasket and sealant at the engine front cover-to-cylinder block sealing surface.

28. Install the oil pan gasket and the oil pan and loosely install the 18 bolts.

29. Tighten the bolts in 3 stages, in the sequence shown.
- Stage 1: Tighten to 18 inch lbs. (2 Nm).
- Stage 2: Tighten to 15 ft. lbs. (20 Nm).
- Stage 3: Tighten an additional 60 degrees.

30. Install the flexplate inspection cover and the 2 bolts. Tighten to 25 ft. lbs. (34 Nm).

31. Lower the transmission.

32. Align the engine mount studs and lower the engine. Remove the special tool.

✳✳ WARNING

Only use hand tools when installing the right engine mount nut or damage to the engine mount can occur.

➡**Align the engine-to-transmission dowels before installing the engine mount bolt.**

33. Install the 6 engine mount nuts. Tighten to 129 ft. lbs. (175 Nm).

✳✳ WARNING

Only use hand tools when removing the transmission mount-to-crossmember nuts or damage to the transmission mount can occur.

34. Install the transmission mount-to-crossmember nuts. Tighten to 18 ft. lbs. (25 Nm).

35. Install the transmission cooler tube support bracket and the nut. Tighten to 89 inch lbs. (10 Nm).

36. Install the 4 exhaust manifold flange nuts. Tighten to 30 ft. lbs. (40 Nm).

37. If the vehicle is equipped with TSS and turbine/OSS, remove the plugs and install the sensors in the transmission.

38. Install the starter.

39. Install the alternator.

40. Install the cooling fan shroud.

41. Install the air cleaner outlet tube.

42. Fill the crankcase with clean engine oil.

6.4L Diesel Engine

Lower Oil Pan

See Figure 163.

1. Before servicing the vehicle, refer to the Precautions Section.

2. With the vehicle in **Neutral**, position it on a hoist.

3. Disconnect the negative battery cable.

⁜⁜ WARNING

Never remove the pressure relief cap while the engine is operating or when the cooling system is hot. Failure to follow these instructions can result in damage to the cooling system or engine or result in personal injury. To avoid having scalding hot coolant or steam blow out of the degas bottle (coolant reservoir) when removing the pressure relief cap, wait until the engine has cooled then wrap a thick cloth around the pressure relief cap and turn it slowly. Step back while the pressure is released from the cooling system. When certain all the pressure has been released, (still with a cloth) turn and remove the pressure relief cap. Failure to follow these instructions can result in personal injury.

⁜⁜ CAUTION

The coolant must be removed in a suitable, clean container for reuse. If the coolant is contaminated, it must be recycled or disposed of correctly and the system filled with new coolant.

➡Less than 80% of coolant capacity can be recovered with the engine in the vehicle. Dirty, rusty, or contaminated coolant requires replacement.

4. Place a suitable container below the radiator draincock. If equipped, disconnect the coolant return hose at the fluid cooler.

5. Remove the fill cap from the degas bottle (coolant reservoir).

6. Remove the oil pan drain plug and drain the engine oil.

7. Loosen the exhaust pipe retaining nuts.

8. Remove the motor mount retaining nuts.

9. Open the radiator draincock.

10. Disconnect the lower radiator hose.

11. Disconnect the transmission cooler tubes.

12. Remove the air cleaner assembly.

13. On vehicles with metal ducts, remove the charge air cooler duct.

14. On vehicles with blow molded ducts, loosen the clamps and remove the charge air cooler duct.

15. Remove the radiator support brackets.

16. Remove the 4 pin-type retainers and pull back the sight shield.

17. With the sight shield pulled back, remove the 3 pin-type retainers and the 2 wiring retainers and position the harness rearward out of the way.

18. Disconnect the upper radiator hose and the radiator overflow hose.

19. Remove the radiator and shroud as an assembly.

20. Disconnect the cooling fan electrical connector. Unclip and position the fan and wiring aside.

➡Use a hole in the fan hub to prevent the fan from turning.

21. Using the special tool 303-591, or equivalent, loosen the fan clutch. Remove the cooling fan.

22. Remove the bolts from the stator, remove the stator.

23. On vehicles with dual alternator perform the following:

   a. Remove the secondary accessory drive belt.

   b. Remove the bolt and the secondary accessory drive belt tensioner.

   c. Remove the primary accessory drive belt.

   d. Remove the bolts, bracket and secondary accessory drive belt idler pulley.

   e. Remove the bolts and the primary accessory drive belt tensioner.

   f. Disconnect the wire retainer, secondary alternator electrical connector and B+ wire.

   g. Remove the bolts and the secondary alternator with mounting bracket.

24. On vehicles with single alternator, remove the primary accessory drive belt.

25. Remove the bolts and position the alternator back.

26. Support the hood and disconnect the hood lift assemblies.

27. Install two lifting eyes 303-D030, or equivalent, on the right hand cylinder head.

28. Remove the retaining bolt for the fuel lines.

29. Disconnect the heater hose at the coolant pump.

30. Remove the fan shroud mounting stud.

31. Install one lifting eye 303-D030 on the left hand cylinder head.

⁜⁜ CAUTION

Do not use the special tool to raise the engine. Damage to the special tool or vehicle may occur.

➡The ball studs may have to be removed.

➡This procedure requires a second bolt hook assembly. The tools are available through Rotunda tools with the following numbers: bolt hook 303-F070-6, handle 303-F070-8, bracket 303-F070-7 and washer 303-F070-12004.

32. Install the special tool.

➡The engine must be raised evenly.

33. Using a lifting crane, raise the engine until the turbo charger is about to touch the cowl. Secure the engine with the special tool.

34. Remove the transmission cooler line bracket.

35. Remove the bolts and position back the oil pan until the oil pick-up tube bolts are accessible.

36. Remove the bolts and let the oil pick-up tube go into the oil pan. Remove the oil pan.

37. Remove the press-in-place gasket and discard.

38. Clean and inspect the sealing surfaces.

39. Remove and discard the oil pick-up tube O-ring.

To install:

40. Install a new O-ring on the oil pick-up tube and position the oil pick-up tube in the oil pan.

41. Install a new press-in-place gasket into the upper oil pan.

42. Position the oil pan in the vehicle.

43. Install the oil pick-up tube and bolts. Tighten to 10 ft. lbs. (13 Nm).

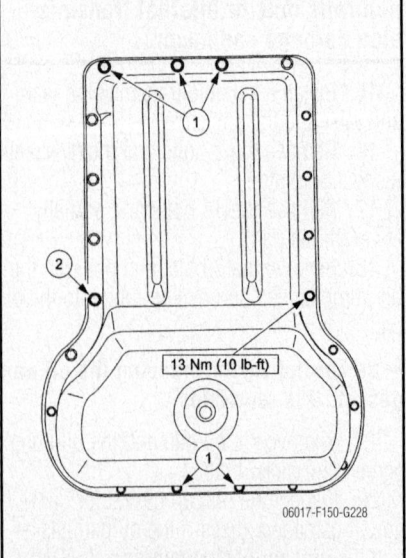

Fig. 163 Lower oil pan installation. (1) indicates the long bolts—6.4L Diesel Engine lower oil pan

44. Position the oil pan and install the bolts. Install the long bolts first. Tighten to 10 ft. lbs. (13 Nm).

45. Install the transmission cooler tube bracket and nut. Tighten to 18 inch lbs. (10 Nm).

46. Using the special tool 303-F070, lower the engine.

47. Remove the lifting eyes 303-D030 and the special tool.

48. Install the fan shroud mounting stud. Tighten to 30 ft. lbs. (40 Nm).

49. Connect the heater hose at the coolant pump.

50. Install the retaining bolt for the fuel lines. Tighten to 10 ft. lbs. (10 Nm).

51. If removed, install the ball studs.

52. Connect the hood lifts and remove the hood support.

53. Position the primary alternator and install the bolts.

54. On a vehicle with a single alternator, install the primary accessory drive belt.

55. On vehicles with dual alternators, perform the following:

    a. Install the secondary alternator with mounting bracket and bolts. Tighten to 35 ft. lbs. (47 Nm).

    b. Connect the B+ wire, secondary alternator electrical connector and wire retainer.

    c. Install the primary accessory drive belt tensioner and bolts. Tighten to 18 ft. lbs. (25 Nm).

    d. Position the secondary accessory drive belt idler pulley. Install the bracket and bolts. Tighten to 18 ft. lbs. (25 Nm).

    e. Install the primary accessory drive belt.

    f. Install the secondary accessory drive belt tensioner and bolt. Tighten to 18 ft. lbs. (25 Nm).

    g. Install the secondary accessory drive belt.

56. Install the stator and stator bolts. Tighten to 30 ft. lbs. (40 Nm).

57. Install the cooling fan clutch. Use the special tool 303-591 to tighten the cooling fan clutch. Tighten to 98 ft. lbs. (133 Nm).

58. Position and clip the cooling fan wiring. Connect the cooling fan electrical connector.

59. Install the radiator and shroud as an assembly.

60. Connect the upper radiator hose and the radiator overflow hose.

61. Position the harness wiring, install the 2 wiring retainers and 3 pin-type retainers.

62. Position the sight shield and install the 4 pin-type retainers.

63. Install the radiator support brackets. Tighten to 22 ft. lbs. (30 Nm).

64. On vehicles with metal ducts, install the charge air cooler duct and tighten the clamps.

65. On vehicles with blow molded ducts, install the charge air cooler duct and tighten the clamps.

66. Install the air cleaner assembly.

67. Connect the transmission cooler tubes. Tighten to the specifications illustrated.

68. Close the radiator draincock. Connect the lower radiator hose.

69. Install the motor mount retaining nuts. Tighten to 76 ft. lbs. (103 Nm).

70. Tighten the exhaust pipe retaining nuts to 35 ft. lbs. (47 Nm).

71. Clean and inspect the oil pan drain plug and gasket, install new if necessary.

72. Install the oil pan drain plug and tighten to 18 ft. lbs. (25 Nm).

73. Connect the negative battery cables.

74. Fill the engine with clean engine oil.

75. Fill the coolant system.

76. Run the engine and check for leaks

Upper Oil Pan

See Figure 164.

1. Before servicing the vehicle, refer to the Precautions Section.

2. Remove the oil pan.

3. Remove the bolts and the upper oil pan. Remove and discard the press-in-place gasket.

4. Clean and inspect the sealing surfaces.

➡ To install:

➡ Install a new press-in-place gasket.

5. Install the upper oil pan and bolts.

6. Install the lower oil pan.

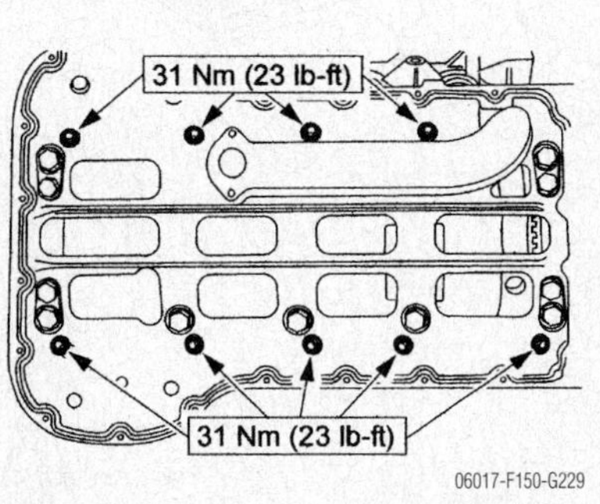

OIL PUMP

REMOVAL & INSTALLATION

5.4L and 6.8L Engine

See Figures 165 and 167.

1. Before servicing the vehicle, refer to the Precautions Section.

2. Raise and safely support the vehicle.

3. Remove the timing drive components.

4. Remove the oil pan.

5. Remove the 3 bolts, the oil pump screen and pickup tube and the spacer.

6. Remove the 3 bolts and the oil pump.

➡ To install:

➡ Lubricate the new O-ring seal with clean engine oil.

7. Clean and inspect the mating surfaces and install a new O-ring seal.

✳✳ WARNING

The oil pump must be primed prior to starting the engine.

8. Install the oil pump and loosely install the 3 bolts. Tighten the bolts in the sequence shown to 10 Nm (89 inch lbs.).

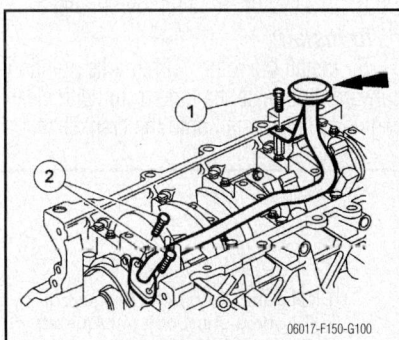

06017-F150-G100

Fig. 165 Pickup tube and spacer— 4.6L, 5.4L and 6.8L engines

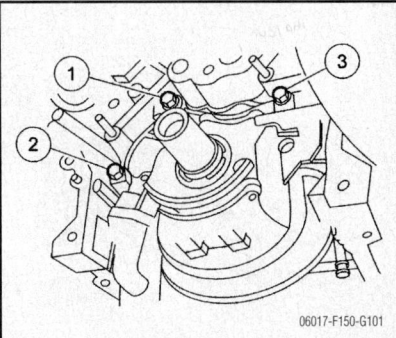

06017-F150-G101

Fig. 166 Oil pump fasteners—4.6L, 5.4L and 6.8L engines

31 Nm (23 lb-ft)

31 Nm (23 lb-ft)

06017-F150-G229

Fig. 164 Upper oil pan fasteners—6.4L Diesel Engine

❊❊ WARNING

Make sure the O-ring is in place and not damaged. A missing or damaged O-ring can cause foam in the lubrication system, low oil pressure and severe engine damage.

➡ **Install a new O-ring and lubricate with clean engine oil.**

9. Install the pickup tube spacer, oil pump screen and pickup tube and the 3 bolts. Tighten bolt 1 to 25 Nm (18 ft. lbs.). Tighten bolts 2 to 10 Nm (89 inch lbs.).

10. Install the oil pan.

11. Install the timing drive components.

6.4L Diesel Engine

1. Remove the crankshaft front seal.

➡ **Mark the location of the 4 short bolts to aid in installing the oil pump housing.**

2. Remove the bolts and the oil pump housing. Remove and discard the press-in-place gasket.

➡ **Mark the front of each drive rotor for correct reassembly orientation.**

3. Remove the inner and outer rotors.

4. Inspect the oil pump components.

To install:

5. Install the rotors with marks pointing outward. Lubricate the inner rotor with clean engine oil and install onto the crankshaft.

Lubricate the outer rotor with clean engine oil and mesh with the inner gear rotor.

➡ **Install a new press-in-place gasket.**

6. Install the oil pump housing and the bolts:

    a. Tighten the 7 long bolts to 23 ft. lbs. (31 Nm).

    b. Tighten the 4 short bolts to 16 ft. lbs. (22 Nm).

7. Install the crankshaft front seal.

PISTON AND RING

POSITIONING

See Figures 168 through 170.

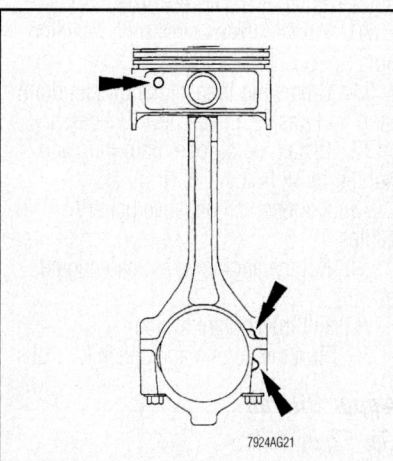

Fig. 168 Piston connecting rod to bearing cap orientation—all gasoline engines

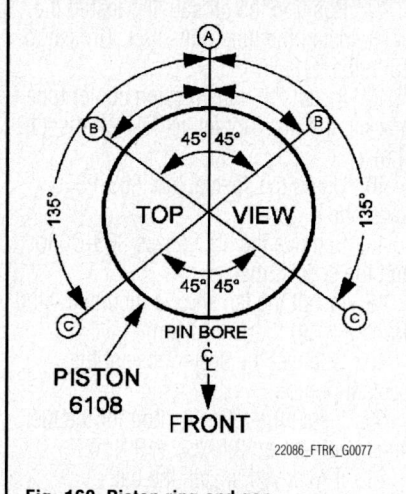

Fig. 169 Piston ring end gap positioning—all gasoline engines

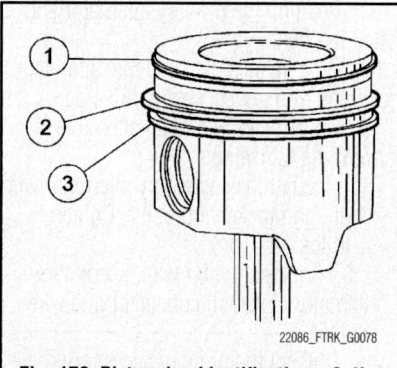

Fig. 170 Piston ring identification—6.4L diesel engine

REAR MAIN SEAL

REMOVAL & INSTALLATION

5.4L and 6.8L Engine

See Figures 171 through 175.

1. Before servicing the vehicle, refer to the precautions section.

2. Disconnect the negative battery cable.

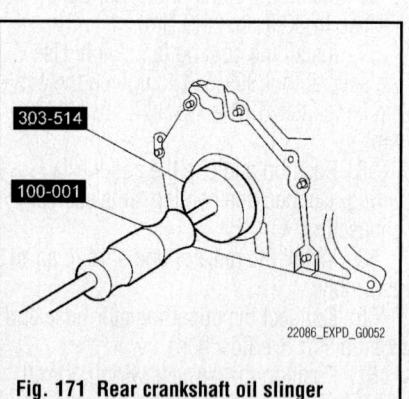

Fig. 171 Rear crankshaft oil slinger removal

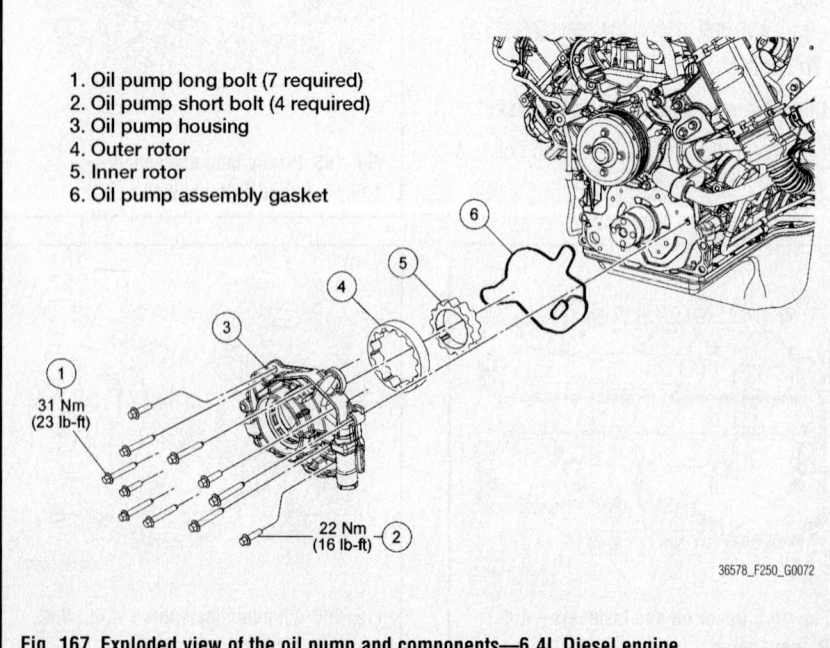

1. Oil pump long bolt (7 required)
2. Oil pump short bolt (4 required)
3. Oil pump housing
4. Outer rotor
5. Inner rotor
6. Oil pump assembly gasket

31 Nm (23 lb-ft)

22 Nm (16 lb-ft)

Fig. 167 Exploded view of the oil pump and components—6.4L Diesel engine

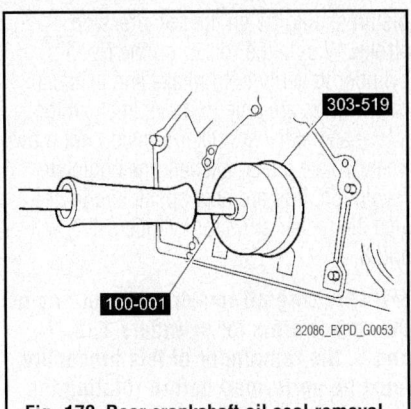

Fig. 172 Rear crankshaft oil seal removal

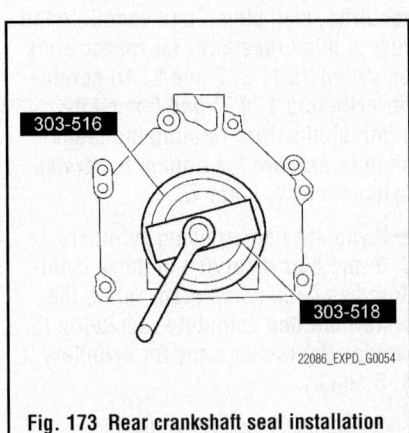

Fig. 173 Rear crankshaft seal installation

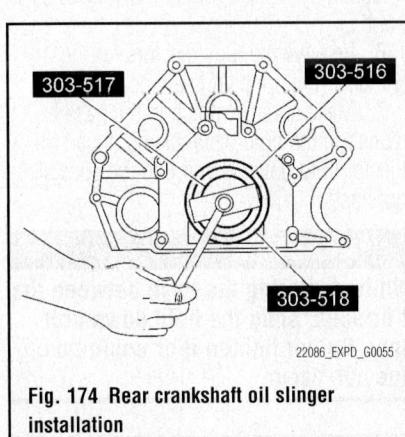

Fig. 174 Rear crankshaft oil slinger installation

3. Remove the transmission.

4. Remove the 8 bolts and the flexplate

5. Using the special tools 303-514 and 109-001, remove the crankshaft oil slinger.

6. Using the special tools 303-519 and 100-001, remove the crankshaft rear seal.

To install:

7. Lubricate the inner lip of the crankshaft rear seal with clean engine oil.

8. Using the special tools 303-516 and 303-518, install a new crankshaft rear seal.

9. Using the special tools 303-516, 303-517 and 303-518, install a new crankshaft rear oil slinger.

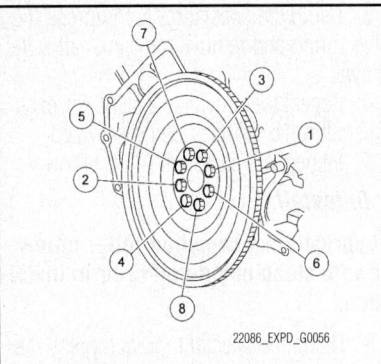

Fig. 175 Flexplate tightening sequence 5.4L & 6.8L engines

10. Install the flexplate and tighten the 8 bolts in the sequence shown to 59 ft. lbs. (80 Nm).

11. Install the transmission.

6.4L Diesel Engine

See Figures 176 and 177.

1. Remove the transmission.

2. Vehicles with manual transmission, remove the clutch disc and pressure plate.

3. Remove the 10 bolts and the flexplate or flywheel. Discard the bolts.

➡**Use extreme care when removing the flywheel front adapter to prevent damage to the alignment dowel pin.**

4. If equipped, remove the flywheel front adapter.

➡**To prevent engine damage, do not remove the rear primary crankshaft flange bolts under any circumstances. If the flange is removed and reinstalled, it may result in engine vibration and premature transmission component wear.**

➡**Drill only deep enough to penetrate the seal. Engine damage may occur if the seal is drilled too deep.**

➡**On early build vehicles, if equipped, the wear sleeve will be removed separately.**

5. Using a center punch, mark a location for 2 holes 180 degrees apart, 9.53 mm (0.37 in) from the outer diameter of the crankshaft flange. Using a drill bit of the appropriate size for the slide hammer dent puller attachment being used, drill a hole on each side of the crankshaft rear seal as shown. Drill the holes to a depth of 8.76 mm (0.34 in) to capture the metal case of the crankshaft seal.

6. Using the 2 drilled holes, the Slide Hammer and a commercially available body dent puller attachment, walk the seal out of

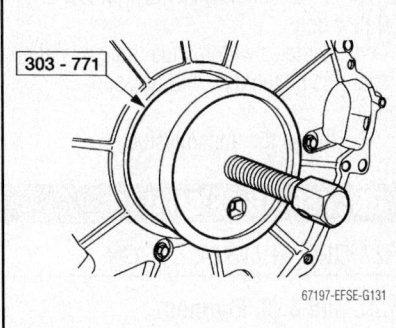

Fig. 176 Rear main seal wear sleeve removal—6.4L Diesel Engine

the rear cover by alternating from side to side to remove the seal. Discard the crankshaft rear seal.

7. Production seals will not have a wear sleeve. If a service part has been installed, it will have a wear sleeve.

8. If equipped with a crankshaft wear sleeve, use the Crankshaft Rear Seal and Wear Ring Remover to remove and discard the crankshaft rear wear sleeve

9. Clean and inspect the crankshaft sealing surface.

To install:

➡**The crankshaft rear oil seal and wear sleeve are installed as an assembly. Separating them may damage the seals.**

10. Lubricate the outer diameter of the rubber seal with a solution of dish soap and water (approximately 50/50 mix) prior to assembly. Do not use any other type of lubricant. Apply a bead of threadlock around the circumference of the outer rear edge of the secondary crankshaft flange.

11. Using the Crankshaft Rear Seal and Wear Ring Installer, install a new crankshaft rear seal.

12. If equipped, install the flywheel front adapter.

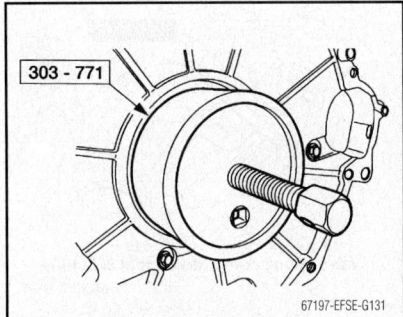

Fig. 177 Rear main seal wear sleeve removal—6.0L Diesel Engine

13. Install the flexplate or flywheel and 10 new bolts.

14. Vehicles with manual transmission, install the clutch disc and pressure plate.

15. Install the transmission.

ROCKER ARMS/SHAFTS

REMOVAL & INSTALLATION

5.4L and 6.8L Engines

See Figures 178 and 179.

1. Depending on the camshaft roller follower being serviced, remove the LH or RH valve cover.

2. Rotate the crankshaft until the piston for the valve being serviced is at the top of its stroke with the intake valve and the exhaust valves closed.

✳ WARNING

If the components are to be reinstalled, they must be installed in the same position. Mark the components for installation into the original location.

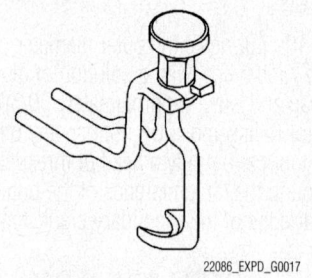

Compressor valve spring tool

22086_EXPD_G0017

Fig. 178 Valve Spring Compression Tool

Valve spring compression tool 303-1039

22086_EXPD_G0018

Fig. 179 Valve spring compressed with tool 303-1039 shown

3. Using the special tool, compress the valve spring and remove the camshaft roller follower.

4. Repeat the previous 2 steps for each camshaft roller follower being serviced.

5. Inspect the camshaft roller follower.

To install:

➡**Lubricate the camshaft roller followers with clean engine oil prior to installation.**

6. Using the special tool, compress the valve spring and install the camshaft roller follower.

7. Repeat the previous step for each camshaft roller follower being serviced.

8. Depending on the camshaft roller follower being serviced, install the LH or RH valve cover.

6.4L Diesel Engines

See Figures 180 through 185.

1. Before servicing the vehicle, refer to the Precautions Section.

➡**This procedure is performed with the engine in the vehicle.**

2. Remove the valve cover(s) for the cylinder bank being serviced. See "Valve (Rocker Arm) Covers" in this section.

3. Locate the dowel hole in the vibration damper. The dowel hole is located between 2 of the 4 bolts that attach the damper to the front of the crankshaft.

➡**For vehicles with a single generator, use a long arm box wrench to rotate the engine. Use an inspection mirror to verify that the dowel hole is in the 12 o'clock position.**

4. Rotate the crankshaft until the dowel hole is at the 12 o'clock position. The No. 1

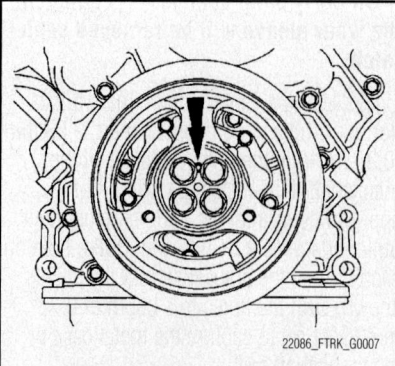

22086_FTRK_G0007

Fig. 180 The dowel hole is located between 2 of the 4 bolts that attach the damper to the front of the crankshaft

piston should be on the compression stroke. Wiggle the rocker on the No. 1 cylinder to verify both intake and exhaust rocker arms are able to move freely. If the intake and exhaust rocker arms do not move freely, rotate the crankshaft one complete revolution. You are now positioned to service the rocker arms for cylinders 1, 2, 7 and 8.

➡**If servicing all rocker arms, or any of the rocker arms for cylinders 1, 2, 7 and 8, the remainder of this procedure must be performed before rotating the crankshaft to prepare the engine to service cylinders 3, 4, 5 and 6. If required, skip step 5 and complete the rest of this procedure, for rocker arms on cylinders 1, 2, 7 and 8. All service for cylinders 1, 2, 7 and 8 must be completed before rotating the crankshaft to prepare the engine to service cylinders 3, 4, 5 and 6.**

➡**If you are not servicing cylinders 1, 2, 7 and 8 or if service to those cylinders has been completed, rotate the crankshaft one complete revolution to service the rocker arms for cylinders 3, 4, 5 and 6.**

5. Complete the rest of this procedure for rocker arms on cylinders 3, 4, 5 and 6.

6. Remove the fuel injectors for the cylinders that are being serviced.

7. Make sure the notch in the base is aligned in the hold down clamp. Insert the injector hold down clamp into the special tool base.

✳ CAUTION

While centering the base between the 2 bridges, snug the hold down bolt only. Do not tighten it or engine damage can occur.

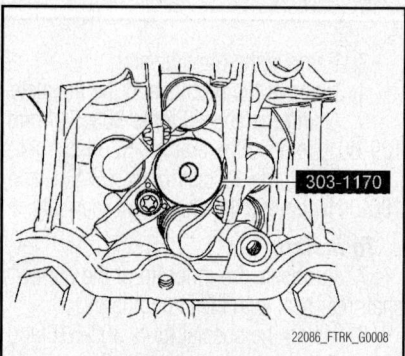

303-1170

22086_FTRK_G0008

Fig. 181 Install the assembly in between the bridges as if you are installing an injector

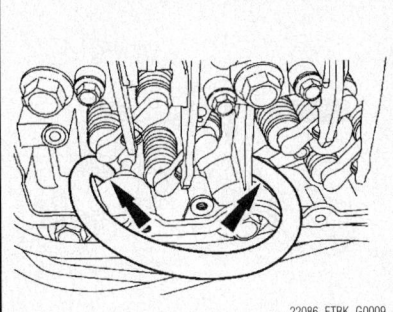

Fig. 182 Install the rubber hose in the oil drain holes for the cylinder on which the rocker arms are being serviced

8. Install the assembly in between the bridges as if you are installing an injector.

9. Use a piece of 457.2 mm (18 in) x 6.35 mm (0.25 in) vacuum hose to block the oil drain holes. Apply clean engine oil to the hose to aid in installing.

10. Install the rubber hose in the oil drain holes for the cylinder on which the rocker arms are being serviced. Verify that the oil drain holes are blocked.

✳✳ CAUTION

Only use hand tools to compress the valve springs. Do not use power tools or engine damage can occur.

➡ If the rocker arm is severely worn, insert a small pry bar between the exhaust rocker arm and bridge to gain clearance by compressing the valves slightly.

11. Install the special tool plate on top of the bridges with the small point of the plate in between the exhaust rocker and bridge. Install the special tool bolt and compress the valve springs until the plate contacts the top of the tool base.

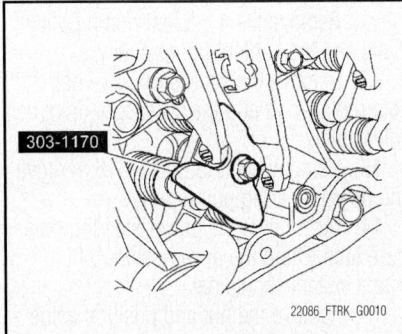

Fig. 183 Install the special tool bolt and compress the valve springs until the plate contacts the top of the tool base

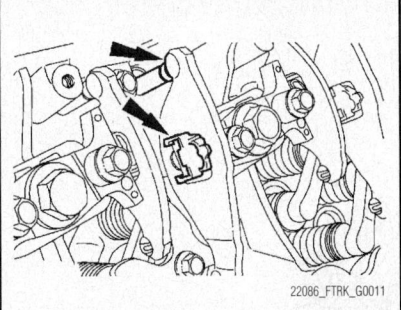

Fig. 184 Disengage the rocker arm from the push rod, then rotate the rocker arm out while compressing down on the rocker arm retaining clip

➡ When removing the rocker arm, be careful not to drop the ball from the fulcrum plate or rocker arm socket.

12. Disengage the rocker arm from the push rod. Then rotate the rocker arm out while compressing down on the rocker arm retaining clip.

13. Remove and discard the rocker arm retaining clip.

14. Repeat for the other rocker arm.

✳✳ CAUTION

To prevent engine damage, keep the push rods in the order in which they were removed. Install the push rods back in their original positions.

15. Remove the push rod.

16. Inspect each push rod for wear and deposits which may restrict the flow of oil into the rocker arm assembly, replace as necessary.

17. Check the push rod for flatness by rolling them on a flat surface if not within 0.01 in. (0.25 mm) of being straight, replace the push rod.

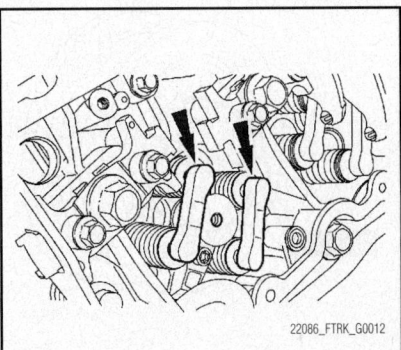

Fig. 185 Remove and discard the valve bridges

18. With the rocker arms removed, remove the special tool bolt and the special tool plate (303-1170) to gain access to the valve bridges.

19. Remove and discard the valve bridges.

To install:

➡ Apply clean engine oil on the valve stems prior to installing the valve bridges.

20. Install the new valve bridges. Install the special tool plate and bolt. Tighten the bolt until the plate contacts the top of the tool base.

✳✳ CAUTION

To prevent engine damage, keep the push rods in the order in which they were removed. Install all push rods back in their original positions.

21. Apply clean engine oil to each end of the push rods and insert them into their respective positions.

22. Place a dab of multi-purpose grease in the fulcrum socket to hold the ball in place while installing the rocker arms.

➡ Apply clean engine oil to the top center of the valve bridges prior to installing the rocker arms. Always replace the rocker arm retaining clip with the same color clip.

23. Insert the rocker arm under the fulcrum and ball, rotate the rocker arm into place and position onto the push rod. Install a new rocker arm retaining clip.

24. Repeat the step for the other rocker arm.

25. Remove the special tool bolt and plate.

26. Make sure the rocker arms remain in place and the fulcrum ball has not fallen out.

27. Remove the rubber hose from the oil drain holes.

28. Remove the injector hold down and special tool base.

29. Install the fuel injectors.

30. Install the valve covers.

TURBOCHARGER

REMOVAL & INSTALLATION

See Figure 186.

Refer to the accompanying illustration for turbocharger mounting.

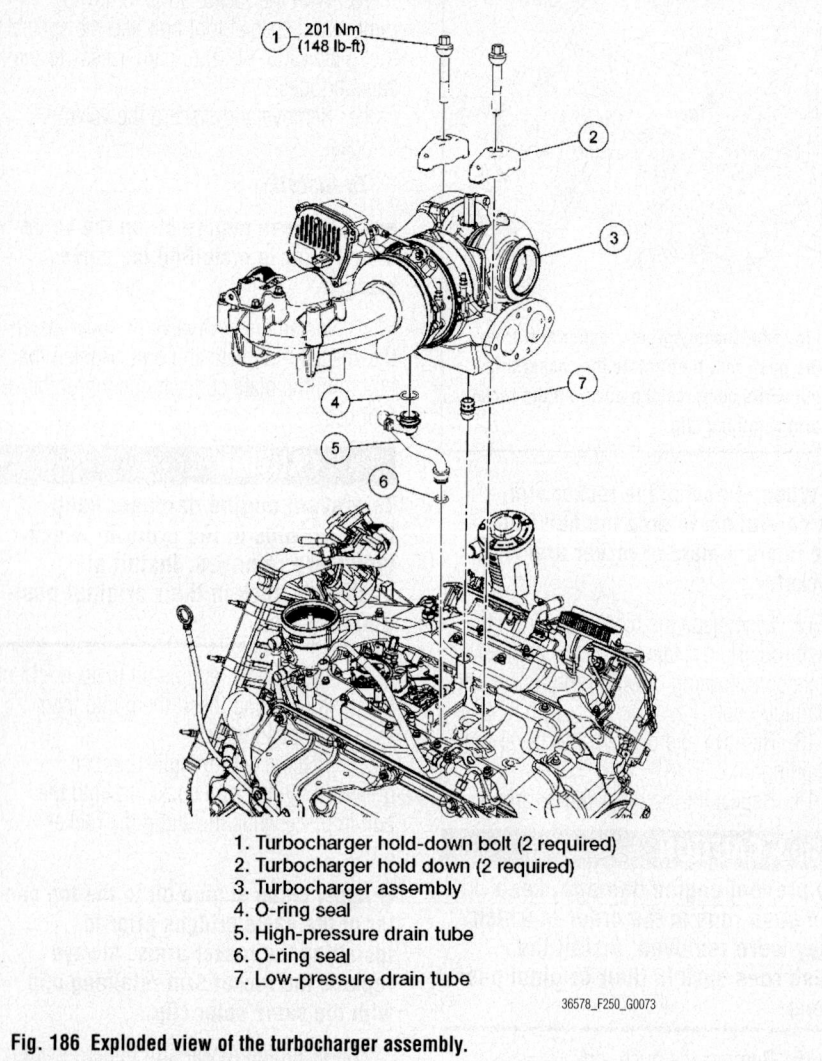

1. Turbocharger hold-down bolt (2 required)
2. Turbocharger hold down (2 required)
3. Turbocharger assembly
4. O-ring seal
5. High-pressure drain tube
6. O-ring seal
7. Low-pressure drain tube

36578_F250_G0073

Fig. 186 Exploded view of the turbocharger assembly.

TIMING CHAIN, SPROCKETS AND FRONT COVER

REMOVAL & INSTALLATION

5.4L Engine
See Figures 187 through 215.

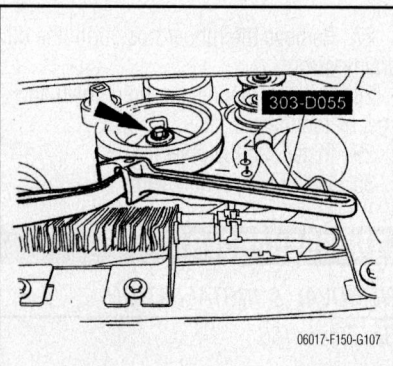

06017-F150-G107

Fig. 187 Using special tool 303-D055, remove the bolt and washer—5.4L engine

1. Before servicing the vehicle, refer to the Precautions Section.
2. Raise and safely support the vehicle.
3. Disconnect the battery ground cable.
4. Drain the engine oil.

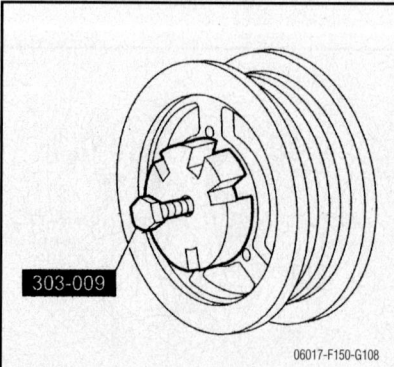

06017-F150-G108

Fig. 188 Using special tool 303-099, remove the crankshaft pulley—5.4L engine

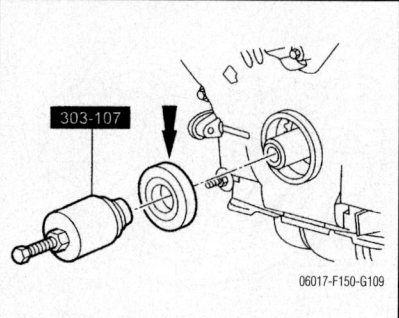

06017-F150-G109

Fig. 189 Using special tool 303-107, remove the crankshaft front seal—5.4L engine

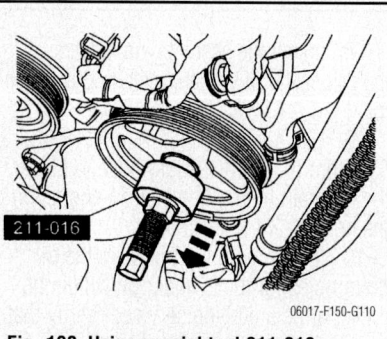

06017-F150-G110

Fig. 190 Using special tool 211-016, remove the power steering pump pulley—5.4L engine

5. Remove the cooling fan.
6. Remove the right valve cover.
7. Remove the left valve cover.
8. Rotate the tensioner clockwise and remove the drive belt. Using special tool 303-D055, remove the bolt and washer and discard the bolt.

✳✳ WARNING

This bolt is torque-to-yield and cannot be reused.

9. Using special tool 303-099, remove the crankshaft pulley.
10. Using special tool 303-107, remove the crankshaft front seal.
11. Remove the 4 coolant pump pulley bolts and the coolant pump pulley.
12. Remove the accessory drive belt idler pulley bolt and the accessory drive belt idler pulley.
13. Using special tool 211-016, remove the power steering pump pulley.
14. Disconnect the power steering pressure tube. Drain the power steering fluid into a suitable container.
15. Remove the nut and position aside the power steering pressure tube.
16. Remove the power steering pump bolts and position the power steering pump assembly aside.

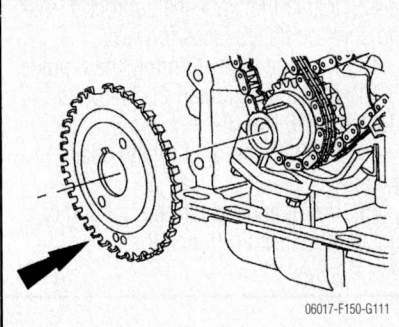

Fig. 191 Crankshaft sensor ring—5.4L engine

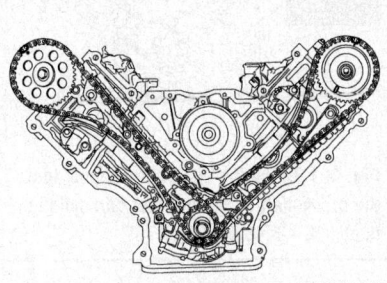

Fig. 192 Rotate the crankshaft until the timing mark on the right camshaft sprocket is approximately at the 11 o'clock position and the timing mark on the left camshaft sprocket is approximately at the 12 o'clock position—5.4L engine

17. Disconnect the camshaft position (CMP) sensor electrical connector.

18. Remove the CMP sensor bolt and the CMP sensor.

19. Remove the left radio interference capacitor nut and position the left radio interference capacitor aside.

20. Remove the nut and the upper radiator hose bracket.

21. Remove the right radio interference capacitor nut and position the right radio interference capacitor aside.

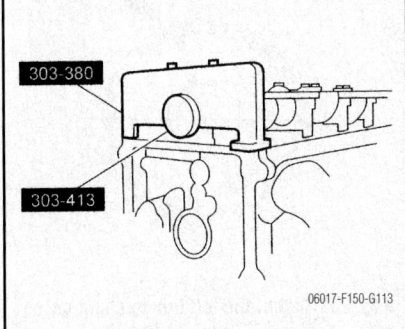

Fig. 193 Install the special tools on the camshaft—5.4L engine

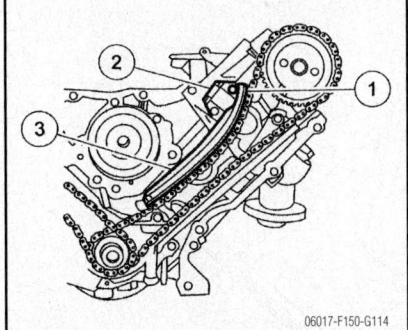

Fig. 194 Removing the tensioners and tensioner arms—5.4L engine

22. Disconnect the crankshaft position (CKP) sensor electrical connector.

23. Remove the 4 oil pan bolts.

24. Remove the nut and the A/C manifold and tube assembly support bracket.

25. If equipped, remove the nut and the transmission cooler tube support bracket.

26. Remove the bolts and the studs.

✳✳ WARNING

Do not use metal scrapers, wire brushes, power abrasive discs or other abrasive means to clean the sealing surfaces. These tools cause scratches and gouges which make leak paths. Use a plastic scraping tool to remove all traces of old sealant.

27. Remove the engine front cover from the front cover-to-cylinder block dowel.

28. Remove the engine front cover gaskets.

29. Clean the mating surfaces with silicone gasket remover and metal surface prep. Follow the directions on the packaging.

30. Inspect the mating surfaces.

31. Remove the CKP sensor bolt and the CKP sensor.

32. Remove the crankshaft sensor ring from the crankshaft.

33. Rotate the crankshaft until the timing mark on the right camshaft sprocket is approximately at the 11 o'clock position and the timing mark on the left camshaft sprocket is approximately at the 12 o'clock position.

34. Install the special tools on the camshaft as shown.

✳✳ WARNING

If one or both of the tensioner mounting bolts are loosened or removed, the tensioner-sealing bead must be inspected for seat integrity. If cracks, tears or separation from the tensioner body or permanent compression of the seal bead is observed, install a new tensioner.

35. Remove the bolts (1). Remove the timing chain tensioners (2). Remove the timing chain tensioner arms (3).

36. Remove the timing chains and crankshaft sprocket.

37. Remove the bolts (1). Remove the left timing chain guide (2).

38. Remove the bolts (3). Remove the right timing chain guide (4).

To install:

✳✳ WARNING

Timing chain procedures must be followed exactly or damage to valves and pistons will result.

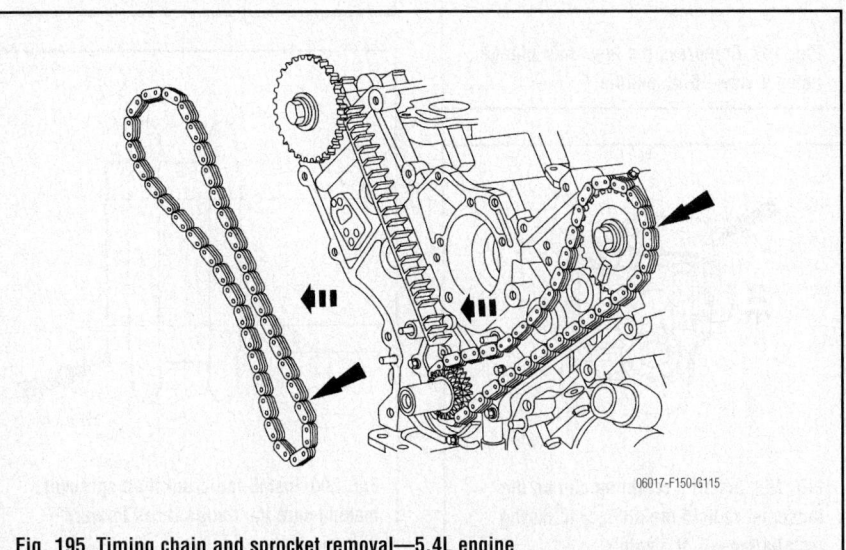

Fig. 195 Timing chain and sprocket removal—5.4L engine

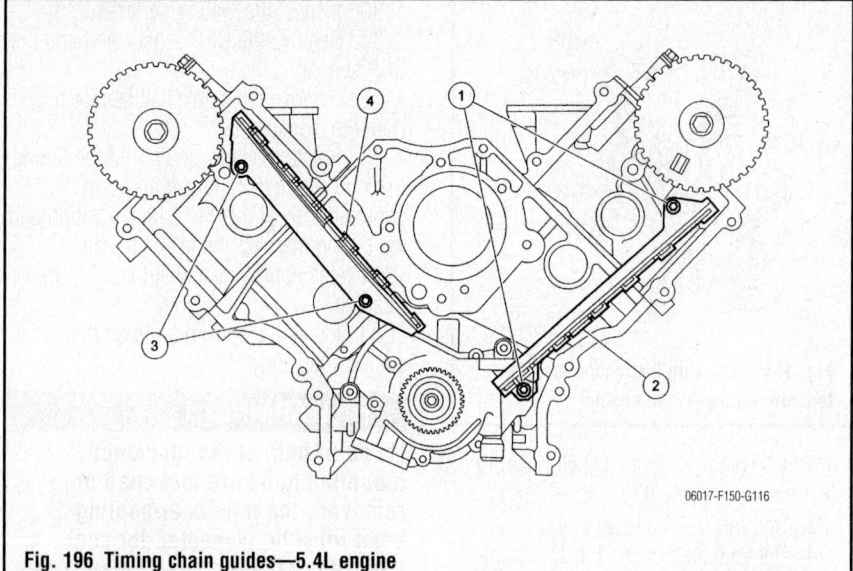

Fig. 196 Timing chain guides—5.4L engine

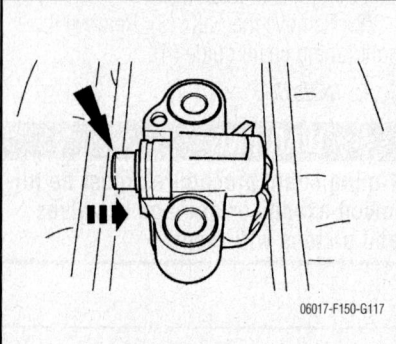

Fig. 197 Compress the tensioner plunger, using a vise—5.4L engine

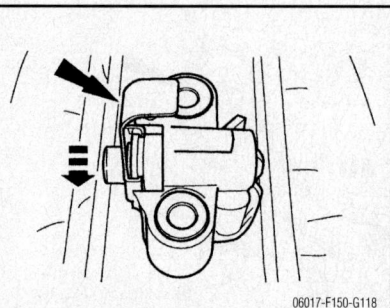

Fig. 198 Install a retaining clip on the tensioner to hold the plunger in during installation—5.4L engine

---

39. Compress the tensioner plunger, using a vise.

40. Install a retaining clip on the tensioner to hold the plunger in during installation.

41. If the copper links are not visible, mark one link on one end and one link on the other end, and use as timing marks.

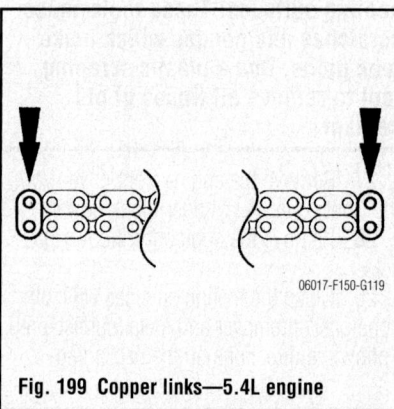

Fig. 199 Copper links—5.4L engine

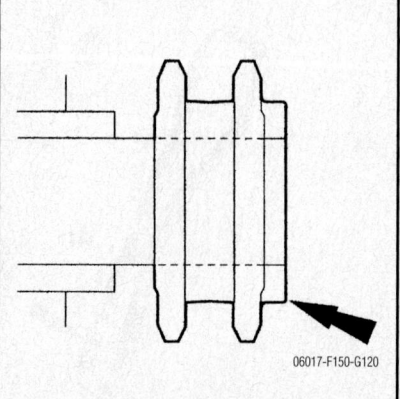

Fig. 200 Install the crankshaft sprocket, making sure the flange faces forward—5.4L engine

---

42. Install the crankshaft sprocket, making sure the flange faces forward.

43. Position the left timing chain guide.

44. Install and tighten the left bolts. Tighten to 10 Nm (89 inch lbs.).

45. Position the right timing chain guide.

46. Install and tighten the right bolts. Tighten to 10 Nm (89 inch lbs.).

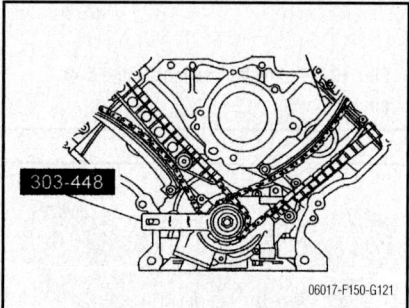

Fig. 201 Using the special tool, position the crankshaft so the number one cylinder is at TDC—5.4L engine

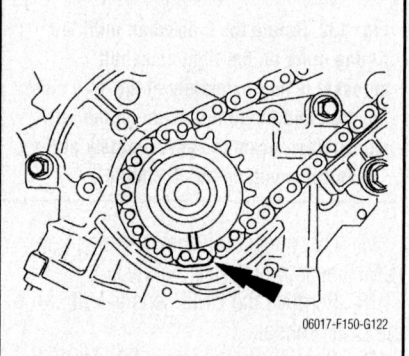

Fig. 202 Position the left (inner) timing chain on the crankshaft sprocket, aligning the copper (marked) link with the timing mark on the sprocket—5.4L engine

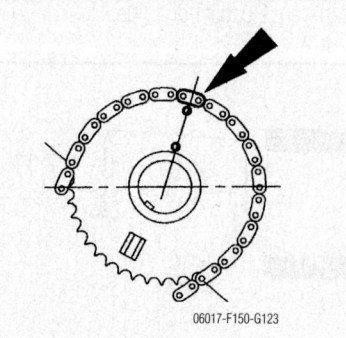

Fig. 203 Install the left timing chain on the camshaft sprocket, aligning the copper (marked) link with the timing marks on the sprocket—5.4L engine

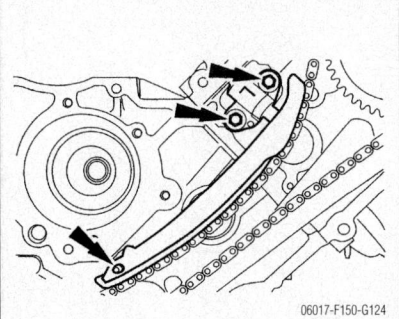

Fig. 204 Position the left timing chain tensioner arm on the dowel pin and install the left timing chain tensioner—5.4L engine

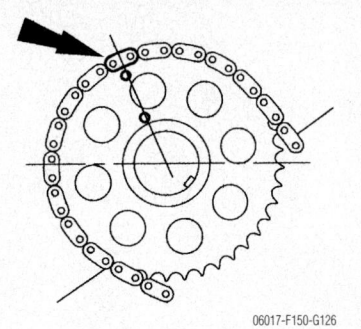

Fig. 206 Install the right timing chain on the camshaft sprocket, aligning the copper (marked) link with the timing marks on the sprocket—5.4L engine

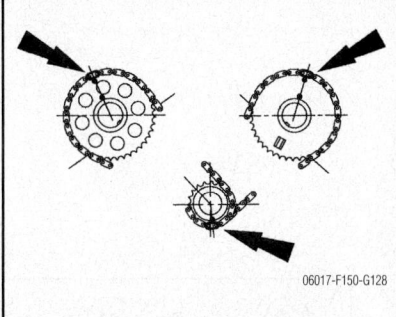

Fig. 208 Make sure that the copper (marked) chain links are lined up with the dots on the crankshaft sprockets and the camshaft sprocket—5.4L engine

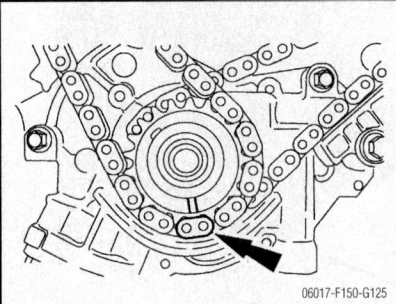

Fig. 205 Position the right (outer) timing chain on the crankshaft sprocket, aligning the copper (marked) link with the timing mark on the sprocket—5.4L engine

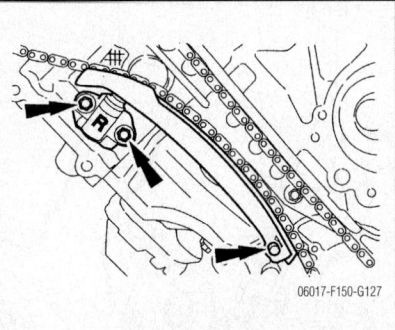

Fig. 207 Position the right timing chain tensioner arm on the dowel pin and install the right timing chain tensioner—5.4L engine

58. Install the crankshaft sensor ring on the crankshaft.

59. Install the CKP sensor and the CKP sensor bolt. Tighten to 10 Nm (89 inch lbs.).

✸✸ WARNING

Do not use metal scrapers, wire brushes, power abrasive discs or other abrasive means to clean the sealing surfaces. These tools cause scratches and gouges which make leak paths. Use a plastic scraping tool to remove all traces of old sealant.

➡If the engine front cover is not secured within 4 minutes, the sealant must be removed and the sealing area cleaned. To clean the sealing area, use silicone gasket remover and metal surface prep. Follow the directions on the packaging. Failure to follow this procedure can cause future oil leakage.

➡Make sure that the engine front cover gasket is in place on the engine front cover before installation.

60. Apply a bead of silicone gasket and sealant along the cylinder head-to-cylinder block surface and the oil pan-to-cylinder block surface, at the locations shown.

61. Install the engine front cover with the engine front cover gasket on the front cover-to-cylinder block dowel and loosely install the bolts.

62. Tighten the engine front cover fasteners in the sequence shown.

63. Loosely install the oil pan-to-front cover bolts, then tighten the bolts in 2 steps, in the sequence shown.
- Step 1: Tighten to 20 Nm (15 ft. lbs.).
- Step 2: Tighten an additional 60 degrees.

✸✸ WARNING

Unless otherwise instructed, do not rotate either the crankshaft or the camshafts, when the timing chains are removed and the cylinder heads are installed. Severe piston and valve damage will occur.

➡The number one cylinder is at top dead center (TDC) when the stud on the engine block fits into the slot in the handle of the special tool.

47. Remove the Crankshaft Holding Tool.

48. Position the left (inner) timing chain on the crankshaft sprocket, aligning the copper (marked) link with the timing mark on the sprocket.

49. Install the left timing chain on the camshaft sprocket, aligning the copper (marked) link with the timing marks on the sprocket.

➡The left timing chain tensioner arm has a bump near the dowel hole for identification.

50. Position the left timing chain tensioner arm on the dowel pin and install the left timing chain tensioner. Tighten to 25 Nm (18 ft. lbs.).

51. Remove the retaining clip from the left timing chain tensioner.

52. Position the right (outer) timing chain on the crankshaft sprocket, aligning the copper (marked) link with the timing mark on the sprocket.

53. Install the right timing chain on the camshaft sprocket, aligning the copper (marked) link with the timing marks on the sprocket.

54. Position the right timing chain tensioner arm on the dowel pin and install the right timing chain tensioner. Tighten to 25 Nm (18 ft. lbs.).

55. Remove the retaining clip from the right timing chain tensioner.

56. Make sure that the copper (marked) chain links are lined up with the dots on the crankshaft sprockets and the camshaft sprocket.

57. Remove the special tools from the camshaft.

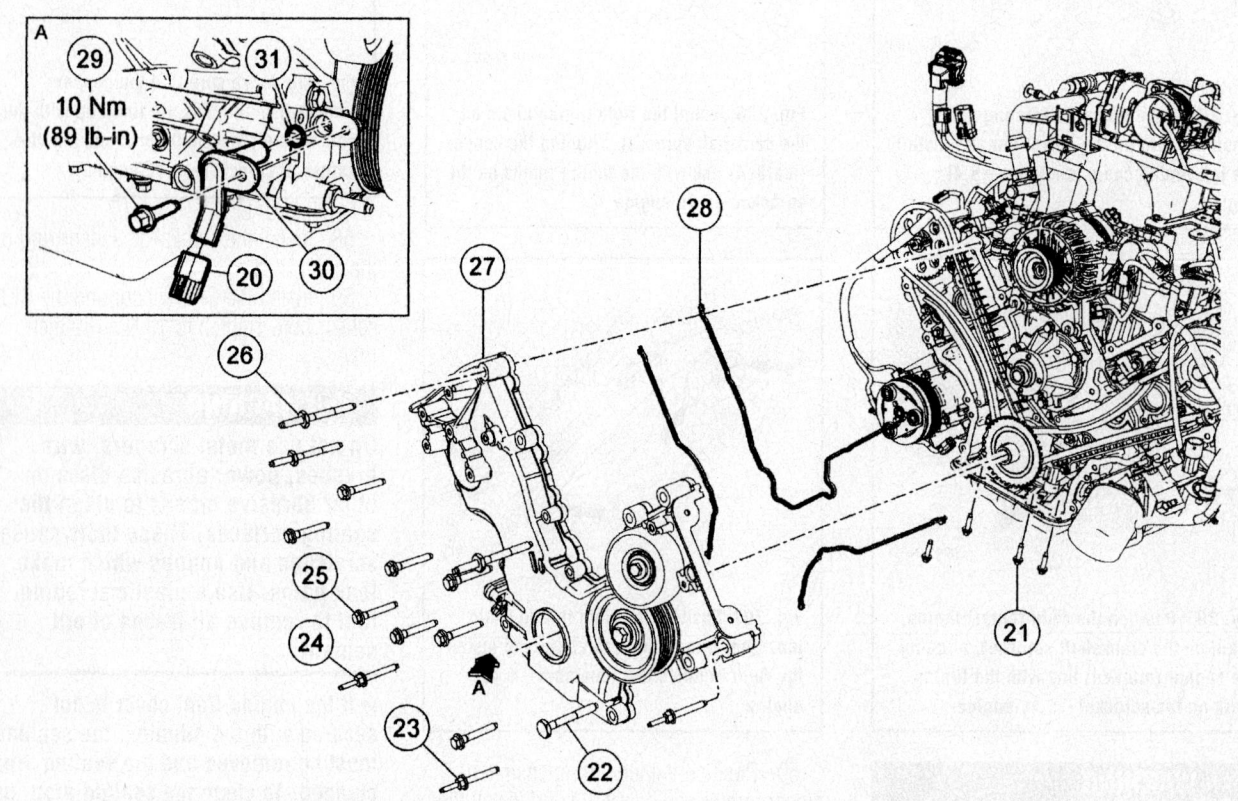

20   Crankshaft position (CKP) sensor electrical connector

21   Oil pan bolts (4 required)

22   Engine front cover bolt

23   Engine front cover lower stud bolt

24   Engine front cover lower stud bolt

25   Engine front cover bolts (8 required)

26   Engine front cover upper stud bolts (4 required)

27   Engine front cover

28   Engine front cover gaskets (3 required)

29   CKP sensor bolt

30   CKP sensor

31   CKP sensor O-ring seal

06017-F150-G129

Fig. 209 Front cover and related parts—5.4L engine

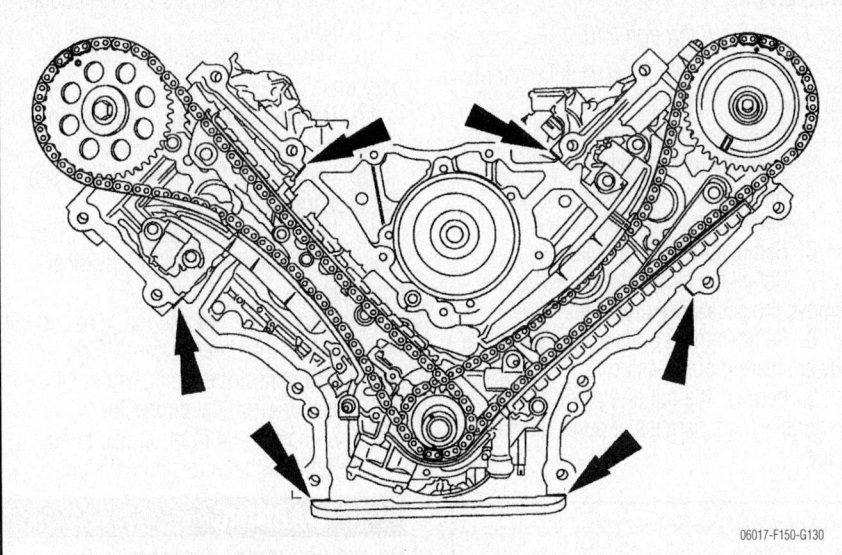

Fig. 210 Apply a bead of silicone gasket and sealant along the cylinder head-to-cylinder block surface and the oil pan-to-cylinder block surface, at the locations indicated—5.4L engine

64. If equipped, install the transmission cooler tube support bracket and nut. Tighten to 10 Nm (89 inch lbs.).

65. Install the A/C manifold and tube assembly support bracket and nut. Tighten to 10 Nm (89 inch lbs.).

66. Connect the CKP sensor electrical connector.

67. Position the right radio interference capacitor and install the nut. Tighten to 10 Nm (89 inch lbs.).

68. Position the upper radiator hose bracket and install the nut. Tighten to 10 Nm (89 inch lbs.).

69. Install the left radio interference capacitor and install the left radio interference capacitor nut. Tighten to 10 Nm (89 inch lbs.).

70. Install the CMP sensor and the bolt. Tighten to 10 Nm (89 inch lbs.).

71. Connect the CMP sensor electrical connector.

72. Position the power steering pump and install the bolts. Tighten to 25 Nm (18 ft. lbs.).

73. Using special tool 211-D207, install a new O-ring seal on the pressure line fitting.

74. Connect the power steering pressure tube. Tighten to 65 Nm (48 ft. lbs.).

75. Position the power steering pressure tube support bracket and install the nut. Tighten to 10 Nm (89 inch lbs.).

❋❋ WARNING

If the pulley has been removed and installed twice, install a new power steering pump pulley.

76. Using special tool 211-185, install the power steering pump pulley. Inspect the pulley for paint marks in the web area near the hub. If there are 2 paint marks, install a new pulley. If there is 1 paint mark or none at all, use a pencil to mark the web area of the pulley near the hub.

77. Install the accessory drive belt idler pulley and the 3 bolts. Tighten to 25 Nm (18 ft. lbs.).

78. Install the coolant pump pulley and the 4 bolts. Tighten to 25 Nm (18 ft. lbs.).

79. Lubricate the engine front cover and the crankshaft front seal inner lip with clean engine oil.

80. Using the special tools shown, install the crankshaft front seal.

➡**If not secured within 4 minutes, the sealant must be removed and the sealing area cleaned. To clean the sealing area, use silicone gasket remover and metal surface prep. Follow the directions on the packaging. Failure to follow this procedure can cause future oil leakage.**

81. Apply silicone gasket and sealant to the Woodruff key slot on the crankshaft pulley.

82. Using special tool 303-102, install the crankshaft pulley.

83. Using a new crankshaft pulley bolt, install the crankshaft pulley bolt and washer.

84. Using the special tool to hold the crankshaft pulley, tighten the bolt in 4 steps:
- Step 1: Tighten the bolt to 90 Nm (66 ft. lbs.).
- Step 2: Loosen the bolt one full turn.

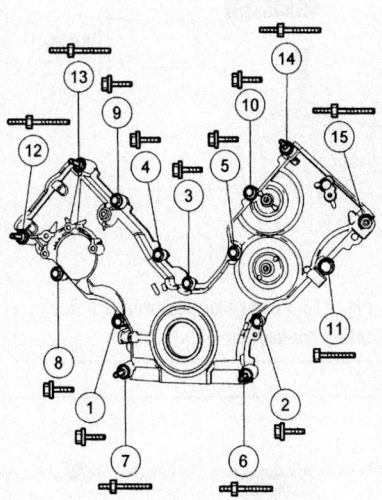

1 Bolt, Hex Flange Head Pilot, M8 x 1.25 x 53
2 Bolt, Hex Flange Head Pilot, M8 x 1.25 x 53
3 Bolt, Hex Flange Head Pilot, M8 x 1.25 x 53
4 Bolt, Hex Flange Head Pilot, M8 x 1.25 x 53
5 Bolts, Hex Flange Head Pilot, M8 x 1.25 x 53
6 Stud Hex Shoulder Pilot, M8 x 1.25 x 50— M6 x 1 x 10
7 Stud and Washer, Hex Head Pilot, M8 x 1.25 — M6 x 1 x 86.35
8 Bolt, Hex Flange Head Pilot, M8 x 1.25 x 53
9 Bolt, Hex Flange Head Pilot, M8 x 1.25 x 53
10 Bolt, Hex Flange Head Pilot, M8 x 1.25 x 53
11 Bolt, Hex Head Pilot, M8 x 1.25 x 53
12 Stud Hex Shoulder Pilot, M8 x 1.25 x 1.25 x 91.1
13 Stud Hex Shoulder Pilot, M8 x 1.25 x 1.25 x 91.1

Fig. 211 Front cover fastener identification—5.4L engine

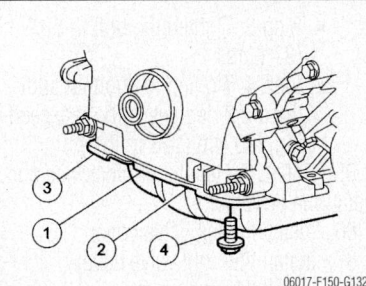

Fig. 212 Oil pan-to-front cover bolt torque sequence—5.4L engine

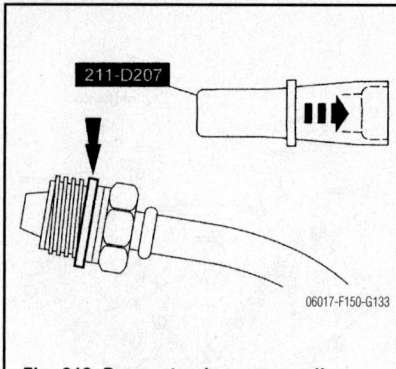

Fig. 213 Power steering pressure line fitting connection—5.4L engine

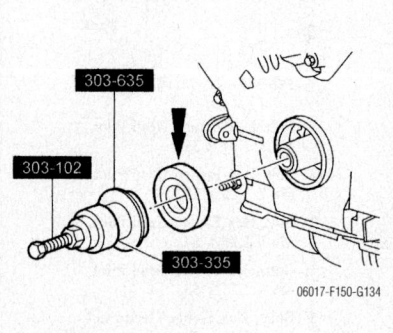

Fig. 214 Crankshaft front seal installation—5.4L engine

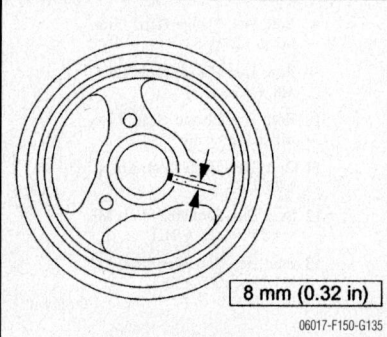

Fig. 215 Apply silicone gasket and sealant to the Woodruff key slot on the crankshaft pulley—5.4L engine

- Step 3: Tighten the bolt to 50 Nm (37 ft. lbs.).
- Step 4: Tighten the bolt an additional 90 degrees without exceeding 200 Nm (148 ft. lbs.).

85. Rotate the tensioner clockwise and install the drive belt.
86. Install the left valve cover.
87. Install the right valve cover.
88. Install the cooling fan.
89. Connect the battery ground cable.
90. Fill the engine with clean engine oil.

6.8L Engine

See Figures 216 through 240.

1. Before servicing the vehicle, refer to the Precautions Section.
2. Raise and safely support the vehicle.
3. Drain the engine oil.
4. Remove the engine cooling fan.
5. Remove the right valve cover.
6. Remove the left valve cover.
7. Rotate the tensioner clockwise and remove the accessory drive belt.
8. Remove the 3 bolts and position the power steering pump aside.
9. Remove the nut and position the starter electrical harness support bracket aside.

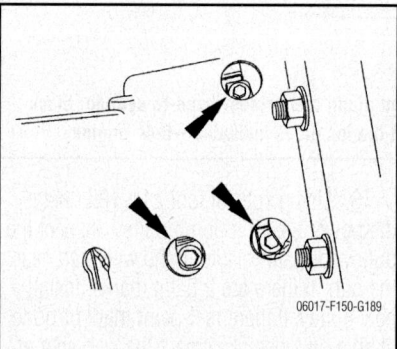

Fig. 216 Remove these 3 bolts from the A/C compressor—6.8L engine

10. Remove the 3 bolts and position the A/C compressor aside.
11. Remove the crankshaft pulley bolt and washer. Discard the crankshaft pulley bolt.
12. Using the special tool, remove the crankshaft pulley.

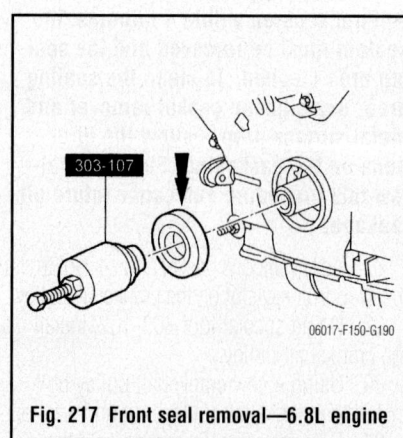

Fig. 217 Front seal removal—6.8L engine

13. Using the special tool, remove the crankshaft front seal.
14. Remove the bolt and the accessory drive idler pulley.

15. Remove the 4 bolts and the coolant pump pulley.
16. Remove the 3 bolts and the accessory drive belt tensioner.
17. Disconnect the camshaft position (CMP) sensor electrical connector.
18. Remove the bolt and the CMP sensor. Discard the O-ring seal.
19. Disconnect the right and left radio ignition interference capacitor electrical connectors.
20. Remove the nut and the right and left radio ignition interference capacitors.
21. Disconnect the crankshaft position (CKP) sensor electrical connector.
22. Remove the 4 front oil pan bolts.
23. Remove the bolts and the studs.

❋❋ WARNING

Do not use metal scrapers, wire brushes, power abrasive discs or other abrasive means to clean the sealing surfaces. These tools cause scratches and gouges which make leak paths. Use a plastic scraping tool to remove all traces of old sealant.

24. Remove the engine front cover from the front cover to cylinder block dowel.
25. Remove the engine front cover gaskets.
26. Clean the mating surfaces with silicone gasket remover and metal surface prep. Follow the directions on the packaging.
27. Inspect the mating surfaces.
28. Remove the bolt and the CKP sensor. Discard the O-ring seal.

❋❋ WARNING

Only use hand tools to loosen the camshaft sprocket bolt or damage may occur to the camshaft or camshaft sprocket.

29. Loosen and back off the right camshaft sprocket bolt 1 full turn.

❋❋ WARNING

Only use hand tools to loosen the sprocket bolt or damage may occur to the camshaft or camshaft sprocket.

30. Loosen the left camshaft sprocket bolt.

➡**The balance shaft bearing caps must be installed in their original locations. Record camshaft bearing cap locations.**

31. Remove the 6 bolts in the sequence shown, the 3 bearing caps and the balance shaft.

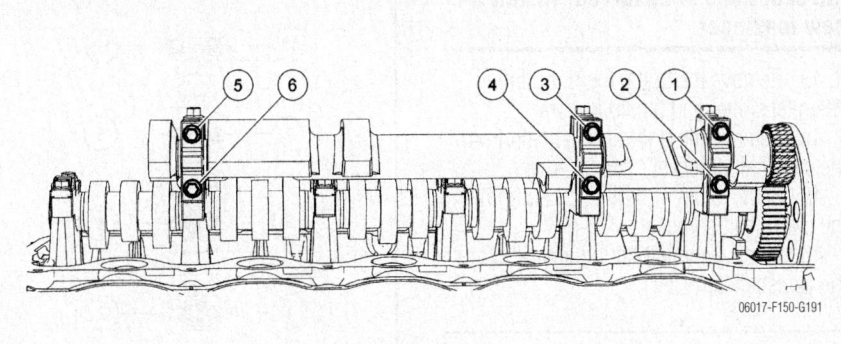

Fig. 218 Balance shaft bearing cap removal/installation sequence—6.8L engine

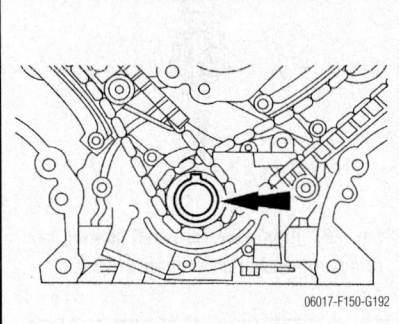

Fig. 219 Position the crankshaft keyway at the 12 o'clock position—6.8L engine

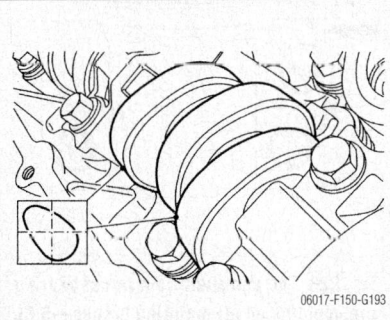

Fig. 220 The number 1 cylinder camshaft exhaust lobe must be coming up on the exhaust stroke. Verify by noting the position of the 2 intake camshaft lobes and the exhaust lobe on the number 1 cylinder—6.8L engine

32. Remove the crankshaft sensor ring from the crankshaft.

33. Position the crankshaft keyway at the 12 o'clock position.

➡If the camshaft lobes are not exactly positioned as shown, the crankshaft will require one full additional rotation to 12 o'clock.

34. The number 1 cylinder camshaft exhaust lobe must be coming up on the

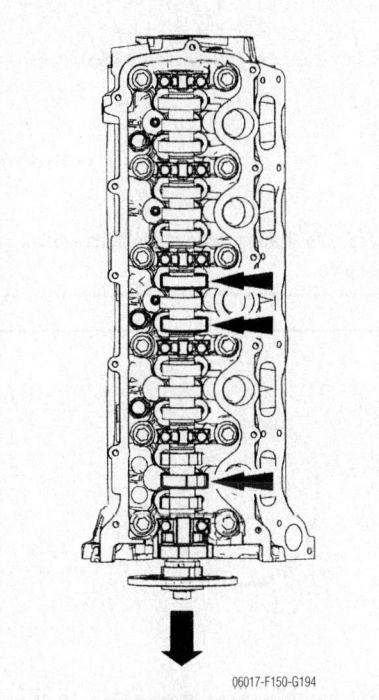

Fig. 221 Remove only these 3 roller followers from the right cylinder head—6.8L engine

exhaust stroke. Verify by noting the position of the 2 intake camshaft lobes and the exhaust lobe on the number 1 cylinder.

✳✳ WARNING

If the components are to be reinstalled, they must be installed in the same positions.

35. Mark the components for installation into the original locations.

36. Remove only the 3 roller followers shown in the illustration from the right cylinder head.

✳✳ WARNING

Do not allow the valve keepers to fall off the valve or the valve may drop into the cylinder.

➡It may be necessary to push the valve down while compressing the spring.

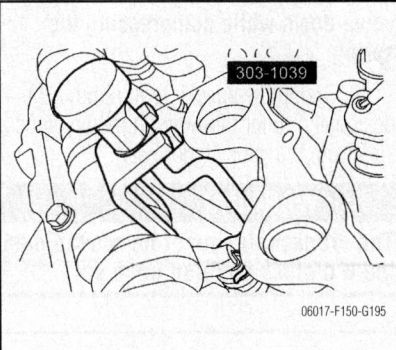

Fig. 222 Using special tool 303-1039—6.8L engine

37. Using special tool 303-1039, remove the 3 designated roller followers in the previous step from the right cylinder head.

✳✳ WARNING

If the components are to be reinstalled, they must be installed in the same positions.

38. Mark the components for installation into the original locations.

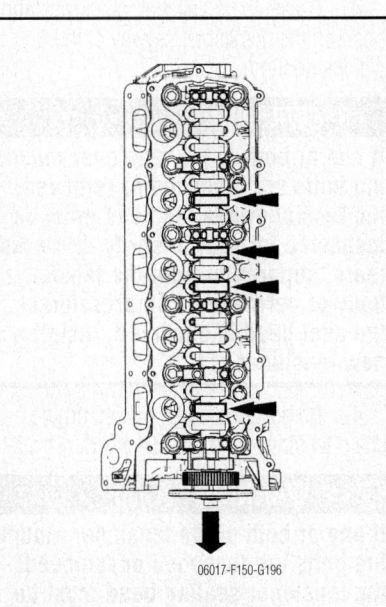

Fig. 223 Remove only these 4 roller followers from the left cylinder head—6.8L engine

39. Remove only the 4 roller followers shown in the illustration from the left cylinder head.

❊❊ WARNING

Do not allow the valve keepers to fall off the valve or the valve may drop into the cylinder.

➡️It may be necessary to push the valve down while compressing the spring.

40. Using the special tool, remove the 4 designated roller followers in the previous step from the left cylinder head.

❊❊ WARNING

The crankshaft cannot be moved past the 6 o'clock position once set.

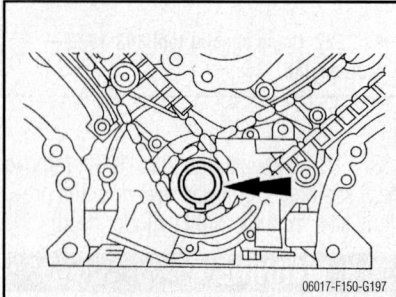

Fig. 224 Rotate the crankshaft clockwise and position the crankshaft keyway at the 6 o'clock position—6.8L engine

41. Rotate the crankshaft clockwise and position the crankshaft keyway at the 6 o'clock position.

❊❊ WARNING

If one or both of the tensioner mounting bolts are loosened or removed, the tensioner-sealing bead must be inspected for seal integrity. If cracks, tears, separation from the tensioner body or permanent compression of the seal bead is observed, install a new tensioner.

42. Remove the bolts, the left timing chain tensioner and tensioner arm.

❊❊ WARNING

If one or both of the tensioner mounting bolts are loosened or removed, the tensioner-sealing bead must be inspected for seal integrity. If cracks, tears, separation from the tensioner body or permanent compression of

the seal bead is observed, install a new tensioner.

43. Remove the bolts, the right timing chain tensioner and tensioner arm.
44. Remove the right timing chain from the camshaft sprocket.
45. Remove the right timing chain from the crankshaft sprocket.
46. Remove the left timing chain from the camshaft sprocket.

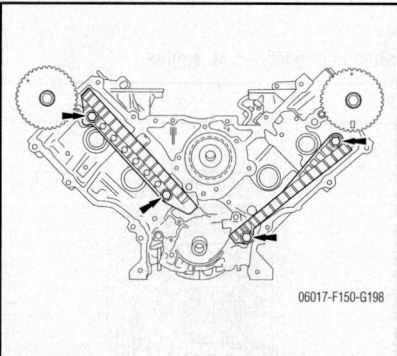

Fig. 225 Timing chain guide bolts—6.8L engine

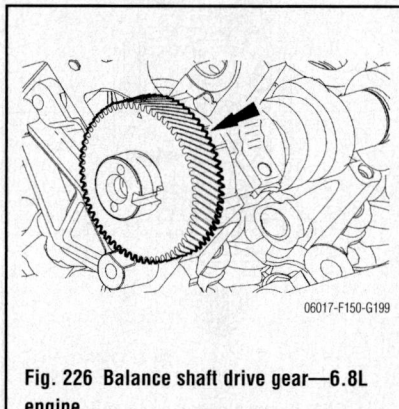

Fig. 226 Balance shaft drive gear—6.8L engine

47. Remove the left timing chain and the crankshaft sprocket.
48. Remove the bolts. Remove the timing chain guides.
49. Remove the bolts and the right and left camshaft sprockets.
50. Remove the balance shaft drive gear from the left camshaft.

❊❊ WARNING

Remove the front thrust camshaft bearing cap straight upward from the bearing towers, or the bearing cap may be damaged from side loading.

➡️The camshaft bearing caps must be installed in their original locations. Record camshaft bearing cap locations.

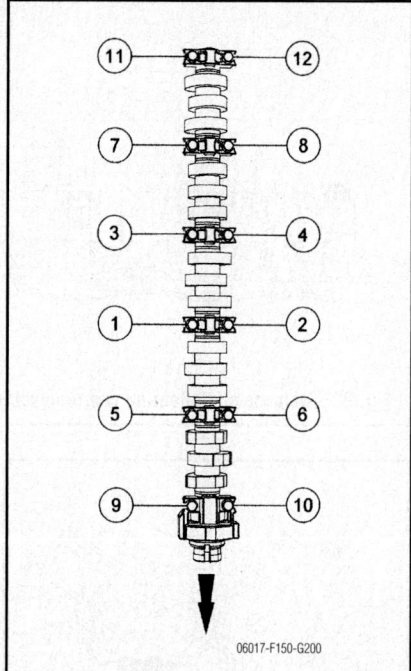

Fig. 227 Right side camshaft bearing cap removal/installation sequence—6.8L engine

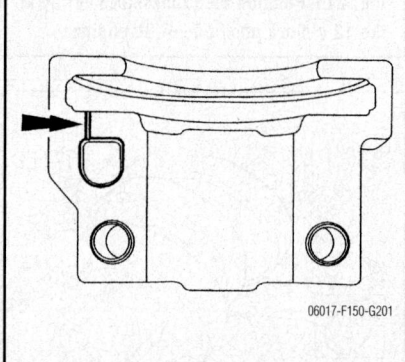

Fig. 228 The camshaft front thrust bearing cap contains an oil metering groove—6.8L engine

51. Remove the bolts in the sequence shown and remove the right cylinder head front camshaft bearing cap and then the remaining bearing caps.
52. Clean and inspect the right camshaft bearing caps. The camshaft front thrust bearing cap contains an oil metering groove. Make sure the groove is free of foreign material.
53. Remove the right camshaft.

❊❊ WARNING

Remove the front thrust camshaft bearing cap straight upward from the bearing towers, or the bearing cap may be damaged from side loading.

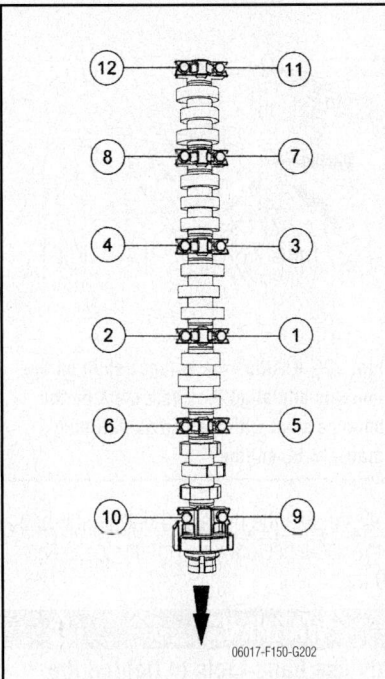

Fig. 229 Left side camshaft bearing cap removal/installation sequence—6.8L engine

➡**The camshaft bearing caps must be installed in their original locations. Record camshaft bearing cap locations.**

54. Remove the bolts in the sequence shown and remove the left cylinder head front camshaft bearing cap and then the remaining bearing caps.

55. Clean and inspect the left camshaft bearing caps. The camshaft front thrust bearing cap contains an oil metering groove. Make sure the groove is free of foreign material.

56. Remove the left camshaft.

❊❊ WARNING

If the components are to be reinstalled, they must be installed in the same positions.

57. Mark the components for installation into their original locations.
58. Remove all of the remaining roller followers from the cylinder heads.

To install:

❊❊ WARNING

Timing chain procedures must be followed exactly or damage to valves and pistons will result.

❊❊ WARNING

If the components are to be rein-

stalled, they must be installed into their original locations.

➡**Camshaft shown installed to clarify roller follower position.**

59. Install only the identified camshaft roller followers onto the right cylinder head.

❊❊ WARNING

If the components are to be reinstalled, they must be installed into their original locations.

➡**Camshaft shown installed to clarify camshaft roller follower position.**

60. Install only the identified camshaft roller followers onto the left cylinder head.
61. Install the left and right camshafts.
62. Lubricate the camshaft and camshaft journals with clean engine oil prior to installation.
63. Lubricate the camshaft bearing caps with clean engine oil.
64. Position the front camshaft bearing cap.
65. Position the remaining camshaft bearing caps.
66. Install the bolts loosely.
67. Tighten the left camshaft bearing cap bolts in 2 steps:
  • Step 1: Tighten to 8 Nm(71 inch lbs.) in the sequence shown.
  • Step 2: Tighten an additional 45 degrees.
68. Tighten the right camshaft bearing cap bolts in 2 steps:
  • Step 1: Tighten to 8 Nm (71 inch lbs.) in the sequence shown.
  • Step 2: Tighten an additional 45 degrees.
69. Install the balance shaft drive gear onto the left camshaft.
70. Install the camshaft sprockets and camshaft sprocket bolts finger tight.

❊❊ WARNING

Timing chain procedures must be followed exactly or damage to valves and pistons will result.

❊❊ WARNING

Prior to installation, inspect the tensioner-sealing bead for seal integrity. If cracks, tears, separation from the tensioner body or permanent compression of the seal bead is observed, install a new tensioner.

71. Compress the tensioner plunger, using a vise.

72. Install a retaining clip on the tensioner to hold the plunger in during installation.

➡**There are 61 links in each timing chain.**

73. If copper links are not visible, mark 2 links on one end and one link on the other end, and use as timing marks.
74. Install the timing chain guides and the 4 bolts. Tighten to 10 Nm (89 inch lbs.).

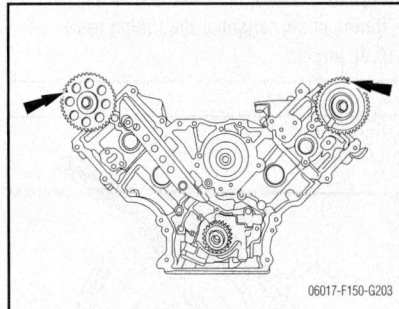

Fig. 230 Rotate the left camshaft until the timing mark is approximately at 12 o'clock. Rotate the right camshaft until the timing mark is approximately at 11 o'clock—6.8L engine

75. Rotate the left camshaft until the timing mark is approximately at 12 o'clock.
76. Rotate the right camshaft until the timing mark is approximately at 11 o'clock.

❊❊ WARNING

Rotate the crankshaft counterclockwise only. Do not rotate past the position shown or severe piston and/or valve damage can occur.

77. Position the crankshaft with special tool 303-448, then remove the tool.
78. Install the crankshaft sprocket, making sure the flange faces forward.

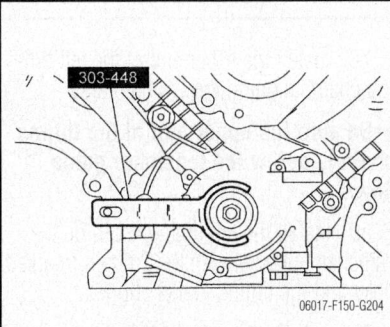

Fig. 231 Position the crankshaft with special tool 303-448—6.8L engine

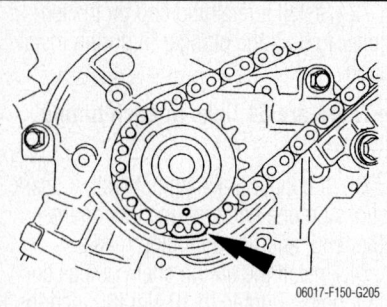

Fig. 232 Install the lower end of the left timing chain, aligning the timing marks—6.8L engine

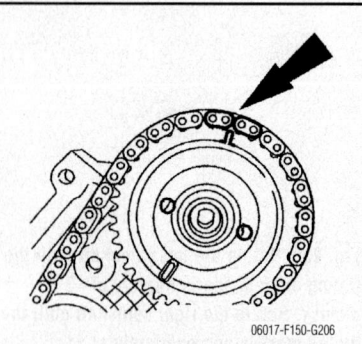

Fig. 233 Install the left timing chain on the camshaft sprocket with the 2 chain (marked) links and the timing marks aligned—6.8L engine

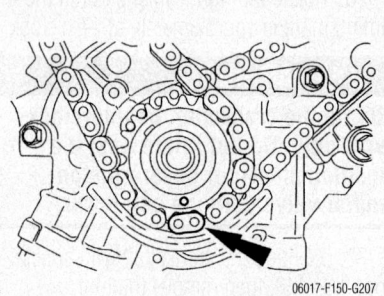

Fig. 234 Install the right (outer) timing chain on the crankshaft sprocket—6.8L engine

79. Install the lower end of the left timing chain, aligning the timing marks.

➡**Be sure the upper half of the timing chain is below the tensioner guide dowel.**

80. Install the left timing chain on the camshaft sprocket with the 2 chain (marked) links and the timing marks aligned.

➡**The left timing chain tensioner arm has a bump near the dowel hole for identification.**

81. Position the left timing chain tensioner arm on the dowel pin and install the left timing chain tensioner and bolts. Tighten to 25 Nm (18 ft. lbs.).

➡**Be sure the chain link and crankshaft sprocket timing marks are aligned.**

➡**The lower half of the timing chain must be positioned above the dowel.**

82. Install the right (outer) timing chain on the crankshaft sprocket.

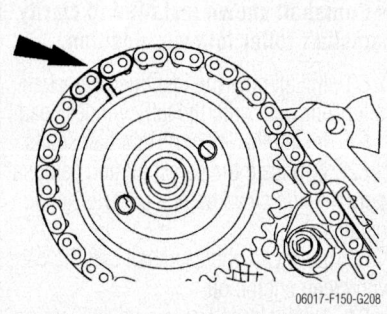

Fig. 235 Position the timing chain on the camshaft sprocket. Make sure the 2 copper-colored (marked) links align with the camshaft sprocket timing mark—6.8L engine

83. Position the timing chain on the camshaft sprocket. Make sure the 2 copper-colored (marked) links align with the camshaft sprocket timing mark.

84. Position the right timing chain tensioner arm on the dowel pin and install the right timing chain tensioner and bolts. Tighten to 25 Nm (18 ft. lbs.).

85. Remove the retaining clips from the right and left timing chain tensioners.

86. Check for correct alignment of all timing marks.

87. Install the crankshaft sensor ring on the crankshaft.

88. Lubricate the balance shaft journals with clean engine oil.

89. Using the index mark on the balance shaft, mark the corresponding gear tooth with chalk.

90. Position the balance shaft on the journals.

➡**It may be necessary to use an inspection mirror to see the marks.**

91. Position the balance shaft on the journals and align the chalk mark on the balance shaft with the camshaft timing mark as shown.

➡**Install the bearing caps in their original locations.**

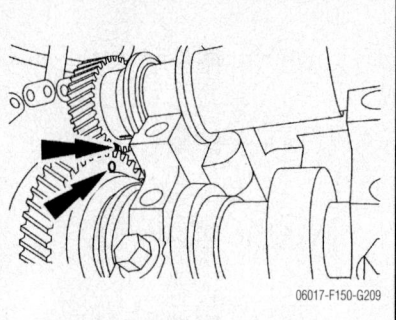

Fig. 236 Position the balance shaft on the journals and align the chalk mark on the balance shaft with the camshaft timing mark—6.8L engine

92. Install the bolts and tighten the bolts in the sequence shown. Tighten to 10 Nm (89 inch lbs.).

❊❊ WARNING

Only use hand tools to tighten the camshaft sprocket bolt or damage may occur to the camshaft or camshaft sprocket.

93. Tighten the right camshaft sprocket bolt in 2 steps:
- Step 1: Tighten to 40 Nm (30 ft. lbs.) in the sequence shown.
- Step 2: Tighten an additional 90 degrees.

❊❊ WARNING

Only use hand tools to tighten the camshaft sprocket bolt or damage may occur to the camshaft or camshaft sprocket.

94. Tighten the left camshaft sprocket bolt in 2 steps:
- Step 1: Tighten to 40 Nm (30 ft. lbs.) in the sequence shown.
- Step 2: Tighten an additional 90 degrees.

❊❊ WARNING

If the components are to be reinstalled, they must be installed into their original locations.

95. Using the special tool, install all of the remaining camshaft roller followers.

96. Lubricate the roller followers with clean engine oil prior to installation.

❊❊ WARNING

Do not use metal scrapers, wire brushes, power abrasive discs or other abrasive means to clean the sealing surfaces. These tools cause

scratches and gouges which make leak paths. Use a plastic scraping tool to remove all traces of old sealant.

➡If the engine front cover is not secured within 4 minutes, the sealant must be removed and the sealing area cleaned. To clean the sealing area, use silicone gasket remover and metal surface prep. Follow the directions on the packaging. Failure to follow this procedure can cause future oil leakage.

➡Make sure that the engine front cover gasket is in place on the engine front cover before installation.

97. Apply a bead of silicone gasket and sealant along the cylinder head-to-cylinder block surface and the oil pan-to-cylinder block surface, at the locations shown.

98. Install a new engine front cover gasket on the engine front cover. Position the engine front cover onto the dowels. Install the fasteners finger tight.

99. Tighten the engine front cover fasteners in sequence in 2 steps.
- Step 1: Tighten fasteners 1 through 15 to 25 Nm (18 ft. lbs.).
- Step 2: Tighten fasteners 6 and 7 to 48 Nm (35 ft. lbs.).

100. Loosely install the oil pan-to-front cover bolts, then tighten the bolts in 2 steps, in the sequence shown.

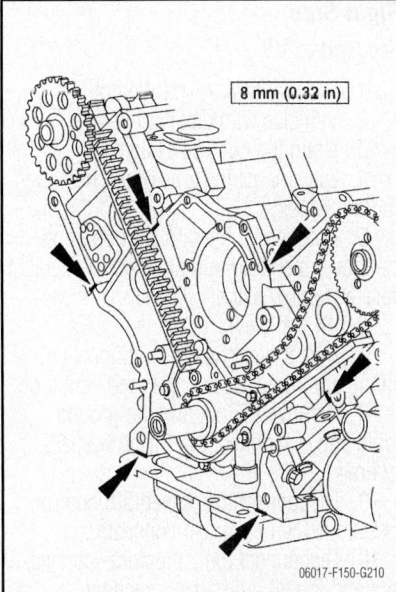

Fig. 237 Apply a bead of silicone gasket and sealant along the cylinder head-to-cylinder block surface and the oil pan-to-cylinder block surface—6.8L engine

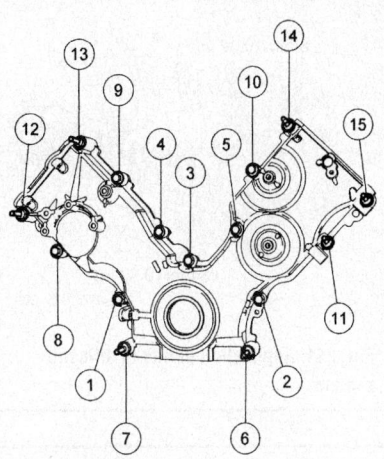

1	Bolt, Hex Flange Head Pilot, M8 x 1.25 x 50
2	Bolt, Hex Flange Head Pilot, M8 x 1.25 x 50
3	Bolt, Hex Flange Head Pilot, M8 x 1.25 x 50
4	Bolt, Hex Flange Head Pilot, M8 x 1.25 x 50
5	Bolts, Hex Flange Head Pilot, M8 x 1.25 x 50
6	Stud, Hex Head Pilot, M10 x 1.5 x 1.5 x 103
7	Stud, Hex Head Pilot, M10 x 1.5 x 1.5 x 103
8	Bolt, Hex Flange Head Pilot, M8 x 1.25 x 50
9	Bolt, Hex Flange Head Pilot, M8 x 1.25 x 50
10	Bolt, Hex Flange Head Pilot, M8 x 1.25 x 50
11	Stud and Washer, Hex Head Pilot, M8 x 1.25 x 1.25 x 94
12	Stud and Washer, Hex Head Pilot, M8 x 1.25 x 1.25 x 94
13	Stud and Washer, Hex Head Pilot, M8 x 1.25 x 1.25 x 94
14	Stud and Washer, Hex Head Pilot, M8 x 1.25 x 1.25 x 94
15	Stud and Washer, Hex Head Pilot, M8 x 1.25 x 56

06017-F150-G211

Fig. 238 Front cover torque sequence—6.8L engine

- Step 1: Tighten to 20 Nm (15 ft. lbs.).
- Step 2: Tighten an additional 60 degrees.

101. Using a new O-ring seal, install the crankshaft position (CKP) sensor and the bolt.

102. Lubricate the new O-ring seal with clean engine oil prior to installation. Tighten to 10 Nm (89 inch lbs.).

103. Connect the CKP sensor electrical connector.

104. Position the A/C compressor and install the 3 bolts. Tighten to 25 Nm (18 ft. lbs.).

105. Position the power steering pump and install the 3 bolts. Tighten to 25 Nm (18 ft. lbs.).

106. Position the starter electrical harness support bracket and install the bolt. Tighten to 10 Nm (89 inch lbs.).

➡Lubricate the O-ring seal with clean engine oil prior to installation.

107. Using a new O-ring seal, install the camshaft position (CMP) sensor and the bolt.

108. Tighten to 10 Nm (89 inch lbs.).

109. Connect the CMP sensor electrical connector.

110. Install the left radio ignition interference capacitor and the nut. Tighten to 10 Nm (89 inch lbs.).

111. Install the right radio ignition interference capacitor and the nut. Tighten to 10 Nm (89 inch lbs.).

112. Connect the radio ignition interference capacitor electrical connectors.

113. Install the accessory drive belt tensioner and the 3 bolts. Tighten to 25 Nm (18 ft. lbs.).

114. Install the coolant pump pulley and the 4 bolts. Tighten to 25 Nm (18 ft. lbs.).

115. Install the accessory drive idler pulley and the 3 bolts. Tighten to 25 Nm (18 ft. lbs.).

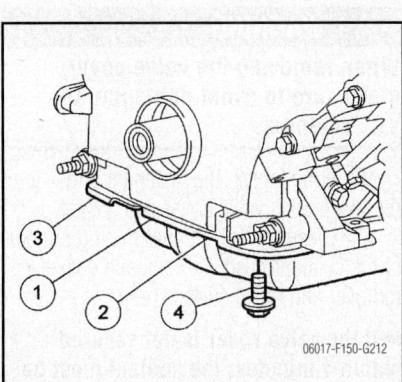

06017-F150-G212

Fig. 239 Oil pan-to-front cover bolt torque sequence—6.8L engine

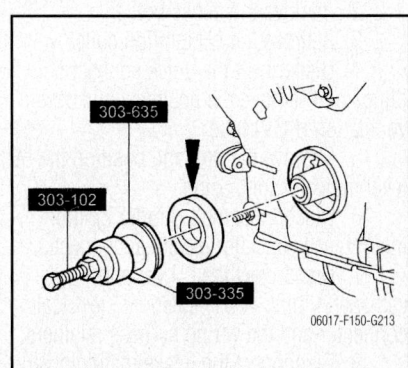

06017-F150-G213

Fig. 240 Front cover seal installation—6.8L engine

116. Lubricate the engine front cover and the crankshaft seal inner lip with clean engine oil.

117. Using the special tools, install the crankshaft seal into the engine front cover.

➡️ If not secured within 4 minutes, the sealant must be removed and the sealing area cleaned. To clean the sealing area, use silicone gasket remover and metal surface prep. Follow the directions on the packaging. Failure to follow this procedure can cause future oil leakage.

118. Apply silicone gasket and sealant to the Woodruff key slot on the crankshaft pulley.

119. Use the special tool to install the crankshaft pulley.

120. Tighten the new crankshaft pulley bolt in 4 steps.
- Step 1: Tighten to 90 Nm (66 ft. lbs.).
- Step 2: Loosen 360 degrees.
- Step 3: Tighten to 50 Nm (37 ft. lbs.).
- Step 4: Tighten an additional 90 degrees.

121. Rotate the tensioner clockwise and install the accessory drive belt.

122. Install the right valve cover.

123. Install the left valve cover. Install the engine cooling fan.

124. Fill the crankcase with clean engine oil.

VALVE COVERS

REMOVAL & INSTALLATION

5.4L Engine

Left Side

See Figures 241 and 242.

1. Remove the air cleaner outlet pipe.
2. Remove the degas bottle.
3. Remove the LH ignition coils.
4. Disconnect the quick connect couplings and remove the positive crankcase ventilation (PCV) tube
5. Remove the bolt and position the oil level indicator tube aside.
6. Disconnect the LH radio ignition interference capacitor electrical connector.
7. Disconnect the LH variable camshaft timing (VCT) solenoid electrical connector and the wiring harness retainers.
8. Disconnect the intake manifold vacuum tube hose from the brake booster.
9. Disconnect the intake manifold vacuum tube assembly from the support

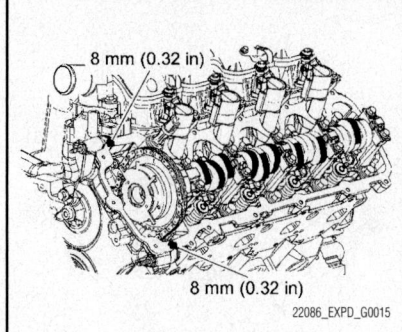

Fig. 241 Application points of silicone sealant

8 mm (0.32 in)

8 mm (0.32 in)

22086_EXPD_G0015

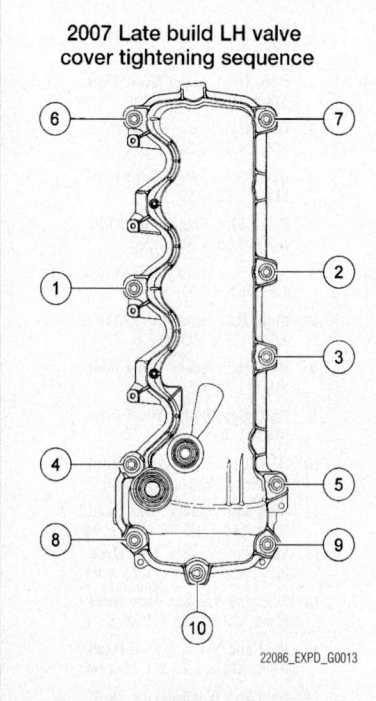

2007 Late build LH valve cover tightening sequence

22086_EXPD_G0013

Fig. 242 LH Valve cover tightening sequence

bracket and the valve cover stud and position aside.

❊❊ WARNING

When removing the valve cover, make sure to avoid damaging the VCT solenoid.

10. Fully loosen the fasteners and remove the LH valve cover and gasket.

11. Clean the valve cover mating surface of the cylinder head with silicone gasket remover and metal surface prep.

➡️ If the valve cover is not secured within 4 minutes, the sealant must be removed and the sealing area cleaned with metal surface prep and silicone gasket remover. Follow the directions

on the packaging. Allow to dry until there is no sign of wetness, or 4 minutes, whichever is longer. Failure to follow this procedure can cause future oil leakage.

To install:

12. Apply a bead of silicone gasket and sealant in 2 places where the engine front cover meets the cylinder head.

13. Position the LH valve cover and new gasket on the cylinder head and tighten the 10 fasteners in the sequence to 89 inch lbs. (10 Nm).

All vehicles

14. Position the intake manifold vacuum tube assembly onto the support bracket and the valve cover stud

15. Connect the intake manifold vacuum tube hose to the brake booster.

16. Connect the VCT solenoid electrical connector and the wiring harness retainers

17. Connect the radio ignition interference capacitor electrical connector.

18. Position the oil level indicator tube and install the bolt and tighten to 89 inch lbs. (10 Nm).

19. Position the PCV tube and connect the quick connect couplings.

20. Install the LH ignition coils and tighten mounting bolts to 53 inch lbs. (6 Nm).

21. Install the degas bottle and tighten mounting bolts to 11 ft. lbs. (15 Nm).

22. Fill the degas bottle with recommended coolant and mixture.

Right Side

See Figure 243.

1. Recover the A/C refrigerant.
2. Vehicles with auxiliary heat:
3. Drain the cooling system.
4. Disconnect the 2 auxiliary heat coolant hoses.
5. Disconnect the coolant hose from the intake manifold and position the coolant hose assembly aside.
6. All vehicles:
7. Disconnect the quick connect couplings and remove the crankcase vent tube.
8. Remove the nut and the ground cable and disconnect the wiring harness retainer.
9. Disconnect the powertrain control module (PCM) electrical connector.
10. Disconnect the 2 electrical connectors and the wiring harness retainer.
11. Disconnect the evaporator outlet and inlet fittings. Discard the O-ring seals
12. Disconnect the RH radio ignition interference capacitor and engine cooling fan clutch electrical connectors.

13. Remove the RH ignition coils.

14. Disconnect the RH variable camshaft timing (VCT) solenoid electrical connector

15. Disconnect the RH camshaft position (CMP) sensor electrical connector.

16. Disconnect the 2 engine wiring harness retainers from the RH valve cover studs.

➡ **The fasteners are part of the valve cover and should not be removed.**

17. Fully loosen the fasteners and remove the RH valve cover and gasket.

18. Clean the valve cover mating surface of the cylinder head with silicone gasket remover and metal surface prep.

19. Discard the valve cover gasket. Clean the valve cover gasket groove with soap and water or a suitable solvent.

To install:

20. Apply a bead of silicone gasket and sealant in 2 places where the engine front cover meets the cylinder head.

21. Position the LH valve cover and new gasket on the cylinder head and tighten the 9 fasteners in the sequence to 89 inch lbs. (10 Nm).

22. Install the RH ignition coils and tighten mounting bolts to 53 inch lbs. (6 Nm).

23. Install new O-ring seals, and lubricate with fresh PAG oil, connect the evaporator outlet and inlet fittings.

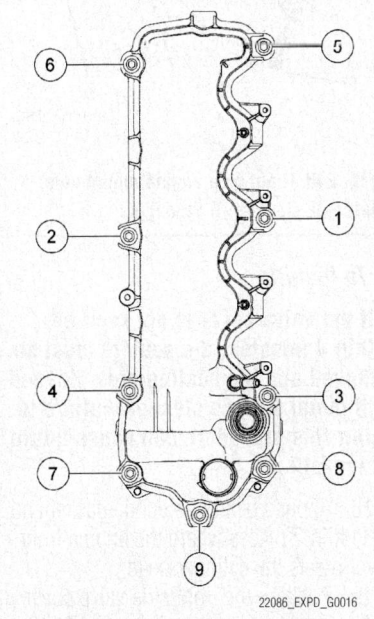

RH valve cover tightening sequence

22086_EXPD_G0016

Fig. 243 RH Valve cover tightening sequence

24. Connect the 2 electrical connectors and the wiring harness retainer

25. Connect the PCM electrical connector.

26. Connect the wiring harness retainer and ground cable, install and tighten the nut to 89 inch lbs. (10 Nm).

27. Connect the RH radio ignition interference capacitor and engine cooling fan clutch electrical connectors.

28. Connect the RH VCT solenoid electrical connector.

29. Connect the RH CMP sensor electrical connector.

30. Connect the wiring harness retainers to the valve cover.

31. Position the crankcase vent tube and connect the quick connect couplings.

Vehicles with auxiliary heat

32. Position the coolant hose assembly and connect the coolant hose to the intake manifold.

33. Connect the 2 auxiliary heat coolant hoses.

34. Fill and bleed the coolant system.

All vehicles

35. Evacuate, leak test and charge the refrigerant system.

6.8L Engine

Right Side

See Figures 244 through 250.

1. Remove the right side ignition coils.

2. If equipped, remove the automatic transmission filler tube.

✳✳ CAUTION

Do not smoke or carry lighted tobacco or open flame of any type when working on or near any fuel-related components. Highly flammable mixtures are always present and can be ignited. Failure to follow these instructions may result in personal injury.

3. Disconnect the battery ground cable.

4. Remove the throttle body (TB):

a. Disconnect the main vacuum harness from the TB spacer.

b. Disconnect the PCV tube from the TB spacer.

c. Disconnect the EVAP canister purge valve vacuum hose from the TB spacer.

d. Disconnect the brake booster vacuum hose.

e. Remove the 2 PCV heated element screws.

f. Remove the PCV heated element.

g. Remove the 2 upper TB spacer bolts.

h. Remove the 4 lower TB spacer bolts and the TB. Discard the TB spacer gasket.

5. Remove the alternator.

6. Remove the cooling fan shroud.

7. Install the special tools shown, or their equivalents.

✳✳ WARNING

Only use hand tools when removing the transmission mount-to-crossmember nuts or damage to the transmission mount can occur.

8. Loosen the transmission mount-to-crossmember nuts.

✳✳ WARNING

Only use hand tools when installing the right side engine mount nut or damage to the engine mount can occur.

9. Remove the 3 right side engine mount nuts and loosen the 3 left side engine mount nuts.

10. Remove the 4 exhaust manifold-to-catalytic converter nuts.

11. Disconnect the quick connect couplings and remove the evaporative emissions (EVAP) tube.

12. Disconnect the engine wiring harness retainers from the valve cover and position out of the way.

13. Disconnect the quick connect coupling and remove the positive crankcase ventilation (PCV) tube from the valve cover.

14. Using the special tools, raise the engine.

✳✳ WARNING

Do not use metal scrapers, wire brushes, power abrasive discs or other abrasive means to clean the sealing surfaces. These tools cause scratches and gouges which make leak paths. Use a plastic scraping tool to remove all traces of old sealant.

➡ **The bolts are part of the valve cover and should not be removed.**

15. Loosen the 16 fasteners in the sequence shown and remove the right side valve cover and gasket.

16. Clean the valve cover mating surface of the cylinder head with silicone gasket remover and metal surface prep. Follow the directions on the packaging.

17. Discard the valve cover gasket. Clean the valve cover gasket groove with soap and water or a suitable solvent.

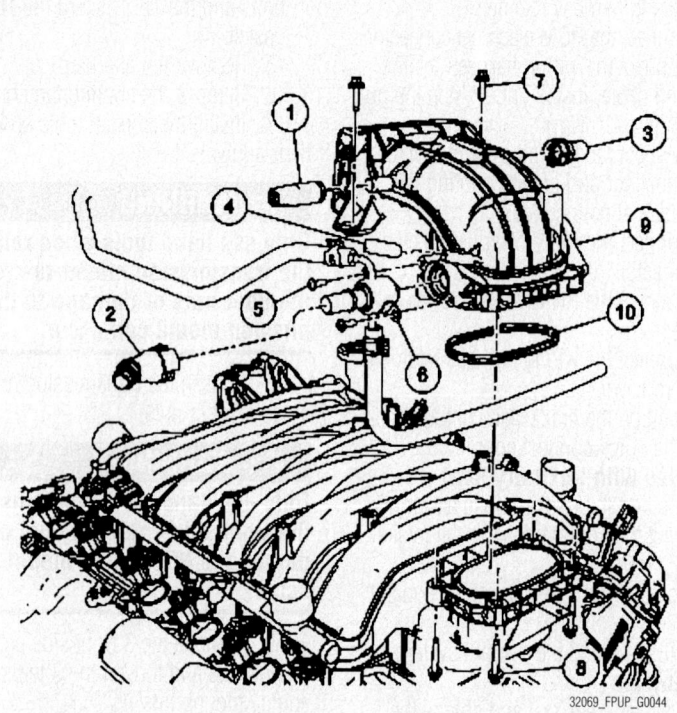

Fig. 244
1. Main vacuum harness
2. Positive crankcase ventilation (PCV) tube
3. Evaporative emission (EVAP) canister purge valve vacuum hose
4. Brake booster vacuum hose
5. PCV heater element screws
6. PCV heater element
7. Upper throttle body (TB) spacer bolts
8. Lower TB spacer bolts
9. TB spacer
10. TB spacer gasket
Throttle body spacer and related parts—6.8L engine

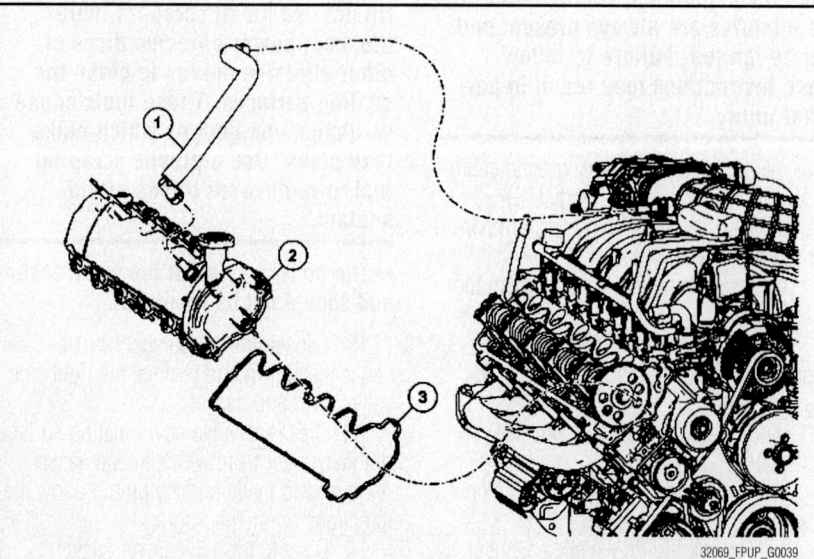

Fig. 245 Right side valve cover—6.8L engine–1. PCV tube, 2. valve cover, 3. gasket

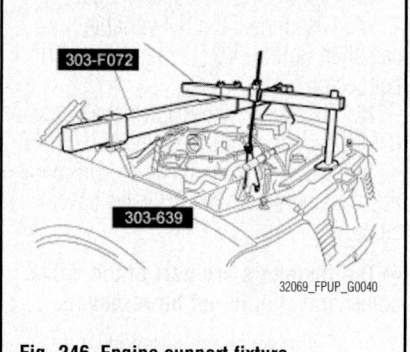

Fig. 246 Engine support fixture—6.8L engine

Fig. 247 Transmission mount-to-crossmember nuts—6.8L engine

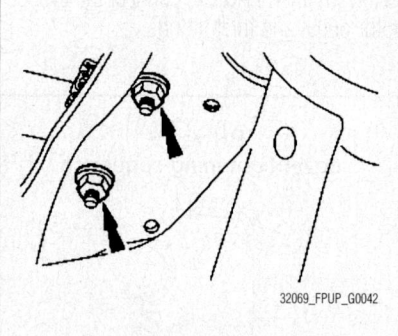

Fig. 248 Right side engine mount nuts; left side similar—6.8L engine

To install:

➡If the valve cover is not secured within 4 minutes, the sealant must be removed and the sealing area cleaned with metal surface cleaner. Failure to follow this procedure can cause future oil leakage.

18. Apply a bead of silicone gasket and sealant in 2 places where the engine front cover meets the cylinder head.

19. Position the right side valve cover and new gasket on the cylinder head and tighten the 16 fasteners in the sequence shown Tighten to 10 Nm (89 inch lbs.).

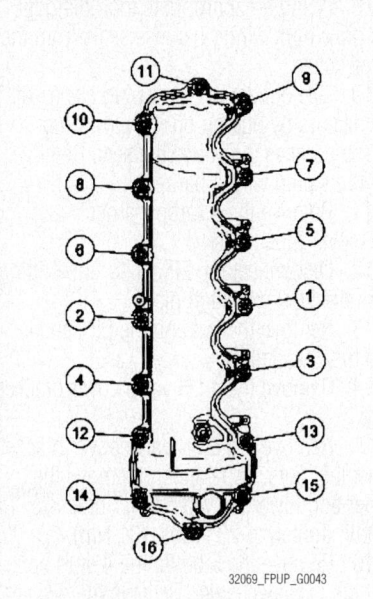

Fig. 249 Right side valve cover loosening/tightening sequence—6.8L engine

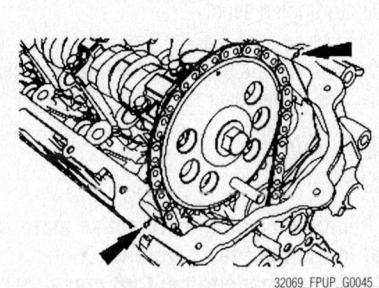

Fig. 250 Apply a bead of silicone gasket and sealant in 2 places where the engine front cover meets the cylinder head—6.8L engine

20. Lower the engine into position.

Only use hand tools when installing the right side engine mount nut or damage to the engine mount can occur.

21. Install the 6 engine mount nuts. Tighten to 175 Nm (129 ft. lbs.).
22. Position the Y-pipe and install the 4 nuts. Tighten to 40 Nm (30 ft. lbs.).

Only use hand tools when installing the transmission mount-to-crossmember nuts or damage to the transmission mount can occur.

23. Tighten the transmission mount-to-crossmember nuts. Tighten to 103 Nm (76 ft. lbs.).
24. Position the positive crankcase ventilation (PCV) tube and connect the quick connect coupling to the valve cover.
25. Position the engine wiring harness retainers onto the valve cover.
26. Position the evaporative emissions (EVAP) tube and connect the quick connect couplings.
27. Remove the special tools.
28. Install the generator.
29. Install the cooling fan shroud.
30. Install the throttle body adapter. Use new gaskets. Tighten the 2 upper TB spacer bolts to 9 Nm (80 inch lbs.). Tighten an additional 90 degrees. Tighten the 4 lower TB spacer bolts to 9 Nm (80 inch lbs.). Tighten an additional 90 degrees.
31. Install the right side ignition coils.
32. If equipped, install the automatic transmission filler tube.

Left Side

See Figures 251 through 253.

1. Remove the air cleaner outlet pipe.
2. Remove the left side ignition coils.
3. Remove the oil level indicator and tube.

4. Disconnect the quick connect couplings and remove the positive crankcase ventilation (PCV) tube.
5. Remove the 2 bolts and position the degas bottle (coolant reservoir) aside.
6. Disconnect the engine wiring harness retainers from the valve cover studs and position out of the way.

Do not use metal scrapers, wire brushes, power abrasive discs or other abrasive means to clean the sealing surfaces. These tools cause scratches and gouges which make leak paths. Use a plastic scraping tool to remove all traces of old sealant.

➡**The bolts are part of the valve cover and should not be removed.**

7. Loosen the 17 fasteners in the sequence shown and remove the left side valve cover and gasket. Clean the valve cover mating surface of the cylinder head with silicone gasket remover and metal surface prep. Follow the directions on the packaging. Discard the valve cover gasket. Clean the valve cover gasket groove with soap and water or a suitable solvent.

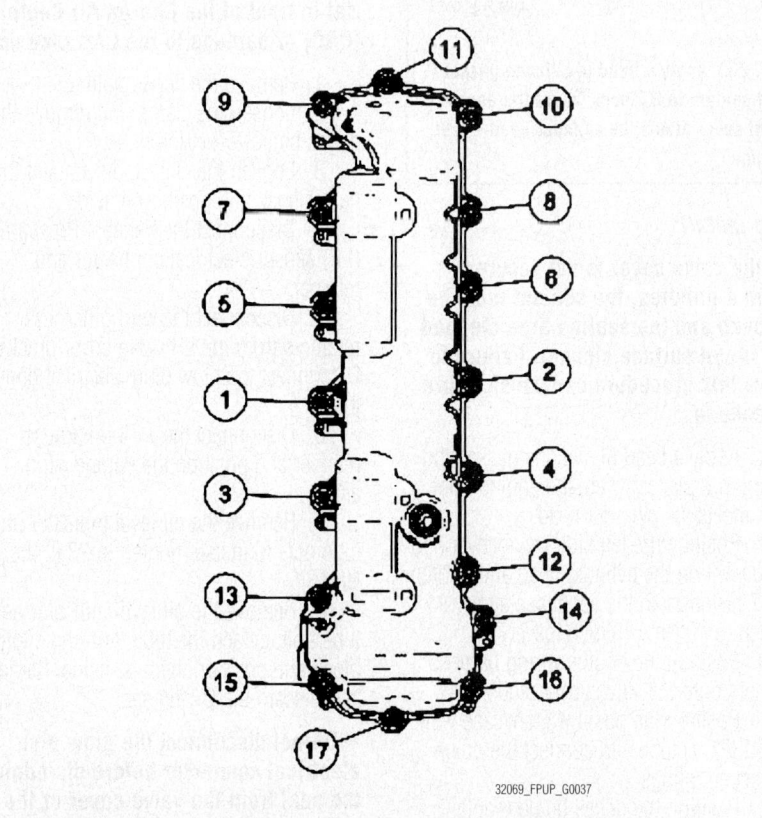

Fig. 251 Left side valve cover loosening and tightening sequence—6.8L engine

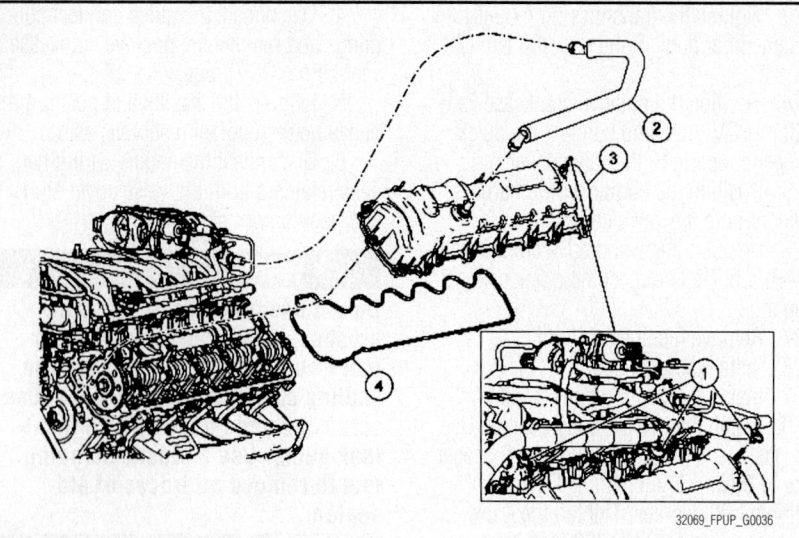

Fig. 252 Left side valve cover—6.8L engine–1. Wiring retainers, 2. PCV tube, 3. Valve cover, 4. Gasket

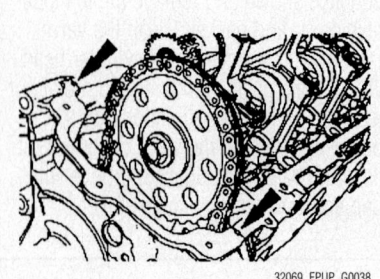

Fig. 253 Apply a bead of silicone gasket and sealant in 2 places where the engine front cover meets the cylinder head—6.8L engine

To install:

➡️**If the valve cover is not secured within 4 minutes, the sealant must be removed and the sealing area cleaned with metal surface cleaner. Failure to follow this procedure can cause future oil leakage.**

8. Apply a bead of silicone gasket and sealant in 2 places where the engine front cover meets the cylinder head.

9. Position the left side valve cover and new gasket on the cylinder head and tighten the 17 fasteners in the sequence shown. Tighten to 10 Nm (89 inch lbs.).

10. Position the engine wiring harness retainers onto the valve cover studs.

11. Position the positive crankcase ventilation (PCV) tube and connect the quick connect couplings.

12. Position the degas bottle (coolant reservoir) and install the 2 bolts. Tighten to 10 Nm (89 inch lbs.).

13. Install the left side ignition coils.

14. Install the oil level indicator and tube.

15. Install the air cleaner outlet tube.

6.4L Diesel Engine

Left Side

See Figure 254.

➡️**Position a suitable protective material in front of the Charge Air Cooler (CAC) or damage to the CAC may occur.**

1. Remove the degas bottle.

2. Loosen the clamp and remove the degas bottle-to-engine hose.

3. Loosen the clamp, disconnect the heater hose and position it aside.

4. Disconnect the Exhaust Pressure (EP) sensor electrical connector and retainer.

5. Disconnect the wiring harness retainers from the LH valve cover bracket. Disconnect the glow plug electrical connector.

6. Disconnect the wiring harness retainer and position the engine wiring aside.

7. Remove the oil level indicator and tube nut. To install, tighten to 23 ft. lbs. (31 Nm).

8. Remove the oil level indicator and tube bolt, detach the tube from the engine block and position the tube aside. Remove and discard the O-ring seal.

➡️**Do not disconnect the glow plug electrical connector before dislodging the seal from the valve cover or the wiring harness may be damaged.**

9. Using an appropriate tool, dislodge the glow plug wiring harness seals from the valve cover.

10. Disconnect the glow plug electrical connectors by pulling on the glow plug wiring harness tee above the seal. Remove the glow plug wiring harness.

11. Remove the 4 turbocharger crossover tube bolts.

12. Disconnect the EP sensor tube fitting from the EGR oxidation pipe.

13. Remove the nut and the EP sensor and tube assembly.

14. Remove the 4 LH valve cover bracket nuts.

15. Remove the 3 LH valve cover bracket assembly nuts. Separate and remove the upper and lower LH valve cover brackets. To install, tighten to 23 ft. lbs. (31 Nm).

16. Remove the 6 bolts, the 4 stud bolts and the LH valve cover. Remove the discard the valve cover gasket.

17. To install, reverse the removal procedure.

18. Install a new valve cover gasket.

19. Alternate tightening the valve cover bolts to tighten evenly.

20. Make sure that the turbocharger crossover tube is square to the turbocharger when the valve cover bracket is installed.

Right Side

See Figure 255.

➡️**Position a suitable protective material in front of the Charge Air Cooler (CAC) or damage to the CAC may occur.**

1. Position the vehicle on a hoist.

2. Disconnect the battery ground cable(s).

3. Remove the Air Cleaner (ACL) assembly.

4. Disconnect the crankcase vent oil separator tube from the crankcase vent oil separator.

5. Loosen the ACL outlet tube clamp and detach the ACL outlet tube from the turbocharger.

6. Remove the 4 bolts, the crankcase vent oil separator and the ACL outlet pipe as an assembly.

   a. Remove and discard the crankcase vent oil separator press-in-place gasket.

7. Disconnect the PCM electrical connector and retainer. Disconnect the in-line electrical connector and position the engine wiring harness on the engine.

8. Remove the 3 push nuts and the glow plug module heat shield. Discard the 3 push nuts.

9. Disconnect the high-pressure fuel injection pump electrical connector and

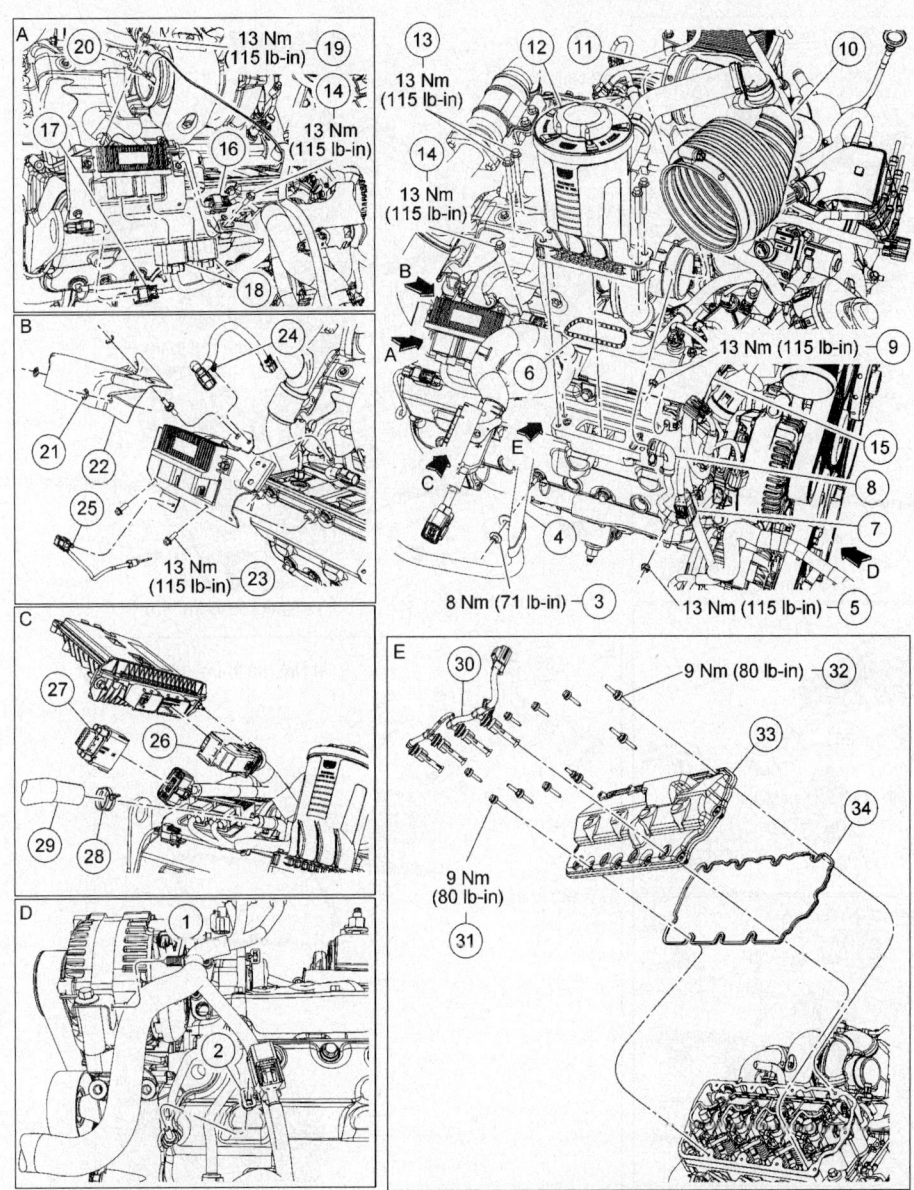

1. Wiring harness retainer
2. Wiring harness retainer
3. Transmission fluid tube and indicator nut (if equipped)
4. Transmission fluid tube and indicator (if equipped)
5. Crankcase vent oil separator tube nut
6. Crankcase vent oil separator gasket
7. Glow plug electrical connector and retainer
8. Crankcase vent oil separator drain tube
9. Heater supply tube nut
10. Air Cleaner (ACL) outlet pipe
11. ACL outlet pipe clamp
12. Crankcase vent oil separator
13. Crankcase vent oil separator bolts (4 required)
14. Engine wiring harness bolt
15. Engine wiring harness
16. High-pressure fuel injection pump electrical connector
17. Exhaust Gas Recirculation Temperature (EGRT) sensor electrical connector
18. Glow plug module electrical connectors
19. Ground wire nut
20. Ground wire
21. Glow plug module heat shield pushnut (3 required)
22. Glow plug module heat shield
23. Glow plug module bracket bolt (3 required)
24. High-pressure fuel injection pump electrical connector retainer
25. EGRT sensor electrical connector retainer
26. PCM electrical connector
27. In-line electrical connector
28. Heater inlet hose clamp
29. Heater inlet hose
30. RH glow plug wiring harness
31. RH valve cover bolt
32. RH valve cover stud bolt
33. RH valve cover
34. RH valve cover gasket

36578_F250_G0074

Fig. 254 Exploded view of the valve cover assembly and components—6.4L diesel engine—Left side

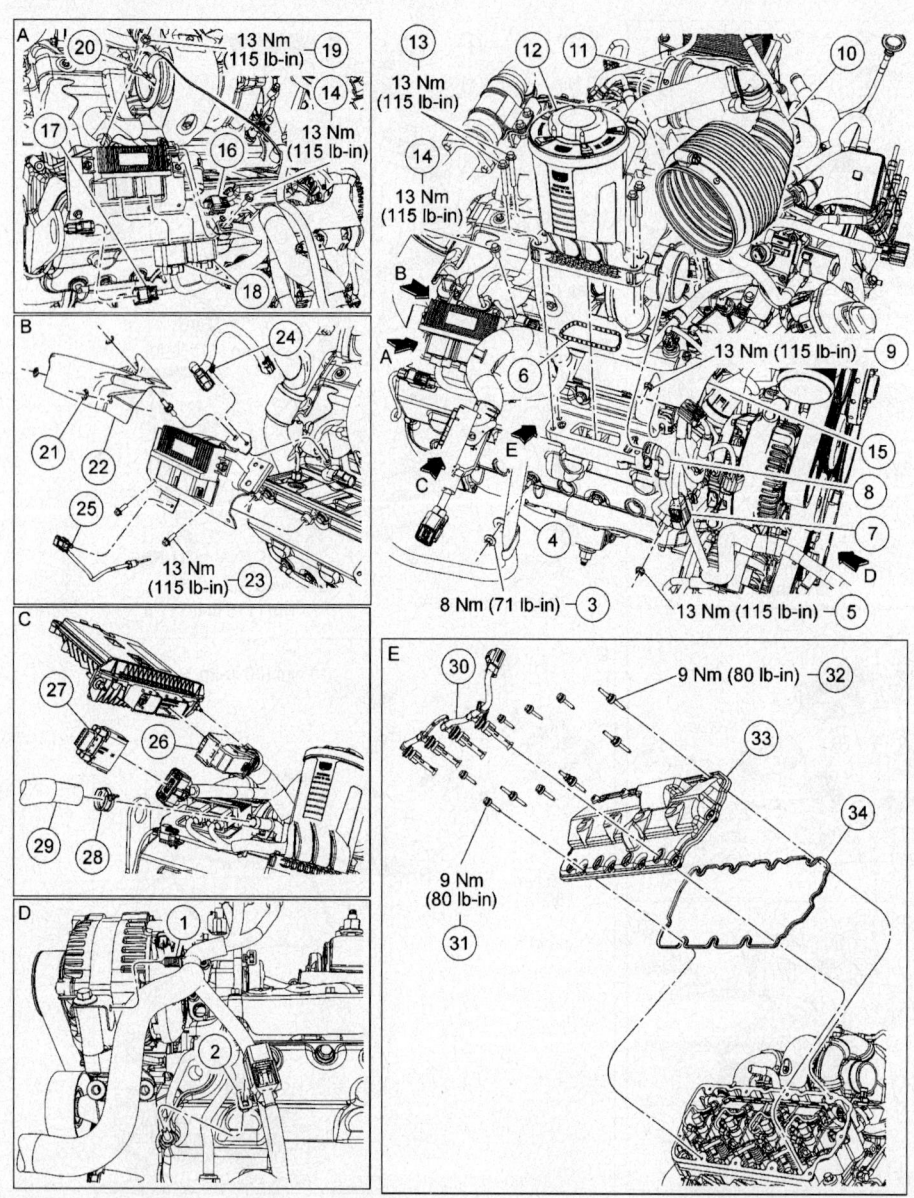

1. Wiring harness retainer
2. Wiring harness retainer
3. Transmission fluid tube and indicator nut (if equipped)
4. Transmission fluid tube and indicator (if equipped)
5. Crankcase vent oil separator tube nut
6. Crankcase vent oil separator gasket
7. Glow plug electrical connector and retainer
8. Crankcase vent oil separator drain tube
9. Heater supply tube nut
10. Air Cleaner (ACL) outlet pipe
11. ACL outlet pipe clamp
12. Crankcase vent oil separator
13. Crankcase vent oil separator bolts (4 required)
14. Engine wiring harness bolt
15. Engine wiring harness
16. High-pressure fuel injection pump electrical connector
17. Exhaust Gas Recirculation Temperature
   (EGRT) sensor electrical connector
18. Glow plug module electrical connectors
19. Ground wire nut
20. Ground wire
21. Glow plug module heat shield pushnut (3 required)
22. Glow plug module heat shield
23. Glow plug module bracket bolt (3 required)
24. High-pressure fuel injection pump electrical
   connector retainer
25. EGRT sensor electrical connector retainer
26. PCM electrical connector
27. In-line electrical connector
28. Heater inlet hose clamp
29. Heater inlet hose
30. RH glow plug wiring harness
31. RH valve cover bolt
32. RH valve cover stud bolt
33. RH valve cover
34. RH valve cover gasket

36578_F250_G0075

Fig. 255 Exploded view of the valve cover assembly and components—6.4L diesel engine—Right side

detach the retainer from the glow plug module bracket.

10. Disconnect the glow plug module and the EGRT sensor electrical connectors, detach the wiring retainer and position the wiring harnesses aside.

11. Remove the nut and position the ground strap aside.

12. Remove the engine wiring harness bolt.

13. Remove the heater supply tube nut.

14. Remove the 3 bolts and the glow plug module bracket.

15. Vehicles with automatic transmission, remove the nut and position the transmission fluid indicator tube aside.

➡**Do not disconnect the glow plug electrical connector before dislodging the seal from the valve cover or the wiring harness may be damaged.**

16. Using an appropriate tool, dislodge the glow plug wiring harness seals from the valve cover.

17. Disconnect the glow plug electrical connectors by pulling on the glow plug wiring harness tee above the seal. Remove the glow plug wiring harness.

18. Remove the nut and position the crankcase ventilation drain tube aside.

19. Disconnect the wiring harness retainer from the valve cover stud.

20. Disconnect the wiring harness retainer from the generator bracket.

21. Disconnect the A/C pressure switch electrical connector. Position the harness aside.

➡**Do not bend or flex the heater supply tube or damage to the tube may occur.**

22. Remove the 4 stud bolts, 6 bolts and the valve cover. Remove and discard the valve cover gasket.

23. To install, reverse the removal procedure.

24. Install a new valve cover gasket.

25. Alternate tightening the valve cover bolts to tighten evenly.

26. Install a new crankcase vent oil separator press-in-place gasket.

VALVE LASH

ADJUSTMENT

The 5.4L and 6.8L engines do not require valve lash adjusting, because they utilize hydraulic lash components in their valve actuation systems. 5.4L and 6.8L engines utilize hydraulic lash adjusters, all of which automatically adjust the valve lash. No valve lash adjustment is necessary.

Valve lash on the diesel engine is not adjustable.

ENGINE PERFORMANCE & EMISSION CONTROLS

ACCELERATOR PEDAL POSITION (APP) SENSOR

LOCATION

See Figures 256 and 257.

Part of the accelerator pedal assembly.

REMOVAL & INSTALLATION

With Fixed Pedal

See Figure 256.

1. Before servicing the vehicle, refer to the precautions in the beginning of this section.

2. Disconnect the battery ground cable.

3. Disconnect the accelerator pedal and position sensor assembly electrical connector.

4. Remove the 3 bolts and the accelerator pedal and position sensor assembly.

5. To install, reverse the removal procedure.

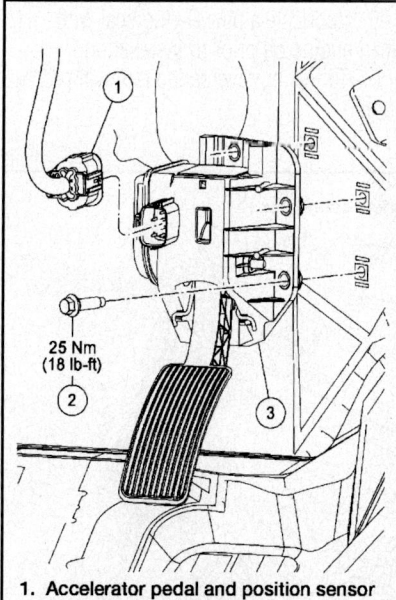

1. Accelerator pedal and position sensor assembly electrical connector
2. Accelerator pedal and position sensor assembly bolts (3 required)
3. Accelerator pedal and position sensor assembly

22086_FTRK_G0170

Fig. 256 Fixed Accelerator Pedal Assembly

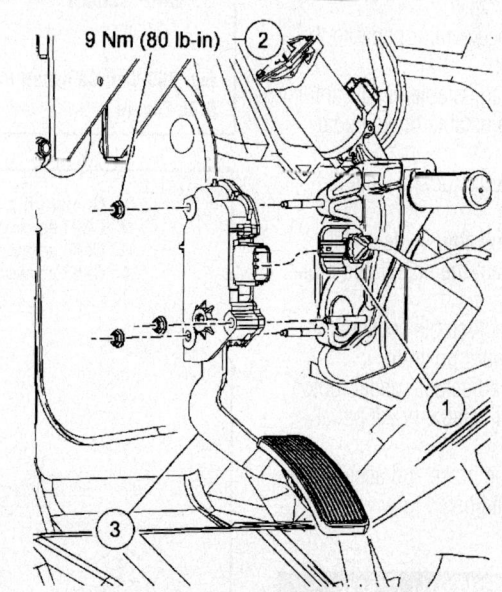

1. Accelerator pedal and position sensor assembly electrical connector
2. Accelerator pedal and position sensor assembly nuts (3 required)
3. Accelerator pedal and position sensor assembly

22086_FTRK_G0171

Fig. 257 Adjustable Accelerator Pedal Assembly

With Adjustable Pedal

See Figure 257.

1. Before servicing the vehicle, refer to the precautions in the beginning of this section.

2. Disconnect the battery ground cable.

3. Disconnect the accelerator pedal and position sensor assembly electrical connector.

4. Disconnect the adjustable pedal motor electrical connector.

5. Disconnect the adjustable pedal motor drive cable from the brake pedal assembly.

6. Remove the 3 nuts and the accelerator pedal and position sensor assembly.

7. Remove the 3 bolts and the adjustable pedal motor and bracket assembly.

8. To install, reverse the removal procedure.

✳✳ CAUTION

The adjustable pedal system must be indexed whenever the brake pedal assembly or accelerator pedal assembly is installed.

➡ **Make sure the electrical connector is connected to the adjustable pedal motor.**

9. Disconnect the adjustable pedal motor drive cable from the brake pedal drive.

10. Operate the accelerator pedal to the full rearward position.

11. Connect the adjustable pedal motor drive cable to the adjustable brake pedal drive.

12. Operate the adjustable pedals to the full forward position.

13. Disconnect the adjustable pedal motor drive cable from the adjustable brake pedal assembly.

14. Operate the adjustable accelerator pedal to the full forward position.

15. Connect the adjustable pedal motor drive cable to the adjustable brake pedal drive.

16. Check that the brake and accelerator pedals can be fully adjusted forward and rearward.

CAMSHAFT POSITION (CMP) SENSOR

LOCATION

5.4L and 6.8L Engines

See Figures 258 through 260.

One at the front of each cylinder head.

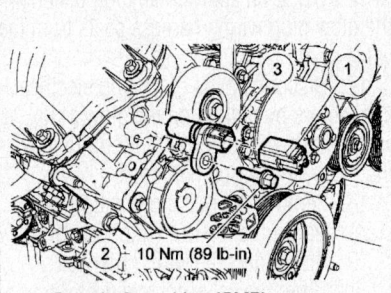

1. Camshaft position (CMP) sensor electrical connector
2. CMP sensor bolt
3. CMP sensor

10 Nm (89 lb-in)

22086_FTRK_G0139

Fig. 258 Right Camshaft Position Sensor—5.4L Engine

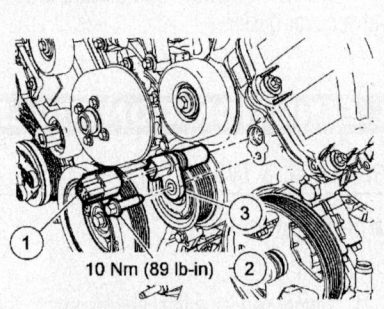

1. Camshaft position (CMP) sensor electrical connector
2. CMP sensor bolt
3. CMP sensor

10 Nm (89 lb-in)

22086_FTRK_G0140

Fig. 259 Left Camshaft Position Sensor—5.4L Engine

6.4L Diesel Engine

See Figure 261.

On the engine, under the power steering pump.

REMOVAL & INSTALLATION

5.4L Engine

See Figures 258 and 259.

1. Before servicing the vehicle, refer to the precautions in the beginning of this section.

2. Disconnect the battery ground cable.

3. For the left camshaft position (CMP) sensor, remove the air cleaner inlet pipe and resonator.

4. Disconnect the CMP sensor electrical connector.

5. Remove the bolt and the CMP sensor.

6. To install, reverse the removal procedure.

6.8L Engine

See Figure 260.

1. Before servicing the vehicle, refer to the precautions in the beginning of this section.

2. Disconnect the battery ground cable.

3. Disconnect the camshaft position (CMP) sensor electrical connector.

4. Remove the bolt and the CMP sensor. Discard the O-ring seal.

5. Lubricate a new O-ring seal with clean engine oil prior to installation.

6. To install, reverse the removal procedure.

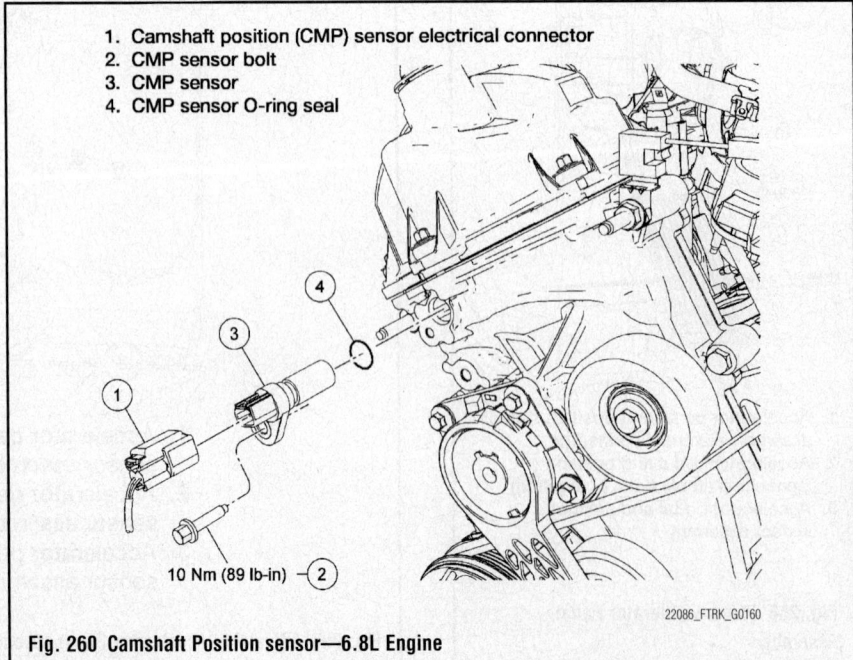

1. Camshaft position (CMP) sensor electrical connector
2. CMP sensor bolt
3. CMP sensor
4. CMP sensor O-ring seal

10 Nm (89 lb-in)

22086_FTRK_G0160

Fig. 260 Camshaft Position sensor—6.8L Engine

6.4L Diesel Engine

See Figure 261.

1. Before servicing the vehicle, refer to the precautions in the beginning of this section.

2. With the vehicle in NEUTRAL, position it on a hoist.

✱✱ CAUTION

Make sure the ignition switch is in the OFF position prior to working on the electronic engine controls.

3. Turn the ignition switch to the OFF position.

4. Rotate the accessory drive belt tensioner clockwise and remove the accessory drive belt from the power steering pump pulley.

5. Remove the 3 bolts and position the power steering pump aside.

➡ **The camshaft position (CMP) sensor is located behind the power steering pump.**

6. Disconnect the CMP sensor electrical connector.

7. Remove the bolt, the CMP sensor and discard the O-ring seal.

➡ **Apply clean engine oil to the new O-ring seal prior to installation.**

8. To install, reverse the removal procedure.

9. Verify that the accessory drive belt is correctly seated on the pulleys.

CRANKSHAFT POSITION (CKP) SENSOR

LOCATION

See Figures 262 and 263.

REMOVAL & INSTALLATION

5.4L and 6.8L Engines

See Figure 262.

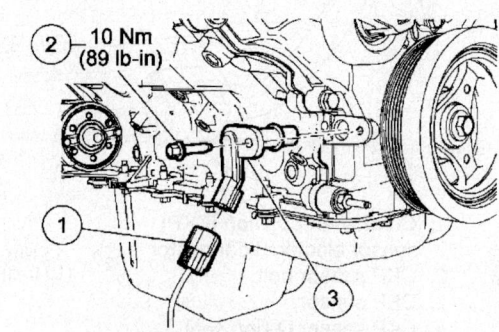

1. Crankshaft position (CKP) sensor electrical connector
2. CKP sensor bolt
3. CKP sensor

22086_FTRK_G0142

Fig. 262 Crankshaft Position Sensor—5.4L and 6.8L Engines

1. Before servicing the vehicle, refer to the precautions in the beginning of this section.

2. With the vehicle in NEUTRAL, position it on a hoist.

3. Disconnect the battery ground cable.

4. Remove the accessory drive belt.

5. If equipped, remove the 2 bolts and position the power steering fluid cooler aside.

6. Loosen the A/C compressor bolts enough to slide the A/C compressor down 25 mm (1 in), to allow access to the crankshaft position (CKP) sensor.

7. Disconnect the CKP sensor electrical connector.

8. Remove the bolt and the CKP sensor.

9. To install, reverse the removal procedure.

6.4L Diesel Engine

See Figure 263.

1. Before servicing the vehicle, refer to the precautions in the beginning of this section.

2. With the vehicle in NEUTRAL, position it on a hoist.

✱✱ CAUTION

Make sure the ignition switch is in the OFF position prior to working on the electronic engine controls.

3. Turn the ignition switch to the OFF position.

➡ **The crankshaft position (CKP) sensor is located underneath the air conditioning compressor.**

4. Remove the nut and position the positive battery cable and support bracket aside.

5. Remove the stud bolt and position the battery negative cable aside.

6. Disconnect the CKP sensor electrical connector.

7. Remove the bolt, the CKP sensor and discard the O-ring seal.

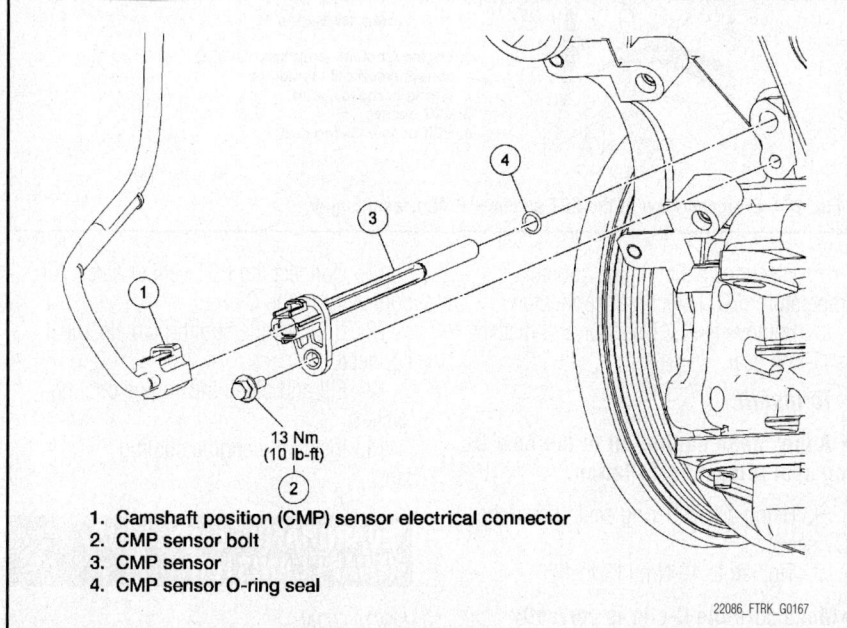

1. Camshaft position (CMP) sensor electrical connector
2. CMP sensor bolt
3. CMP sensor
4. CMP sensor O-ring seal

22086_FTRK_G0167

Fig. 261 Camshaft Position Sensor—6.4L Diesel Engine

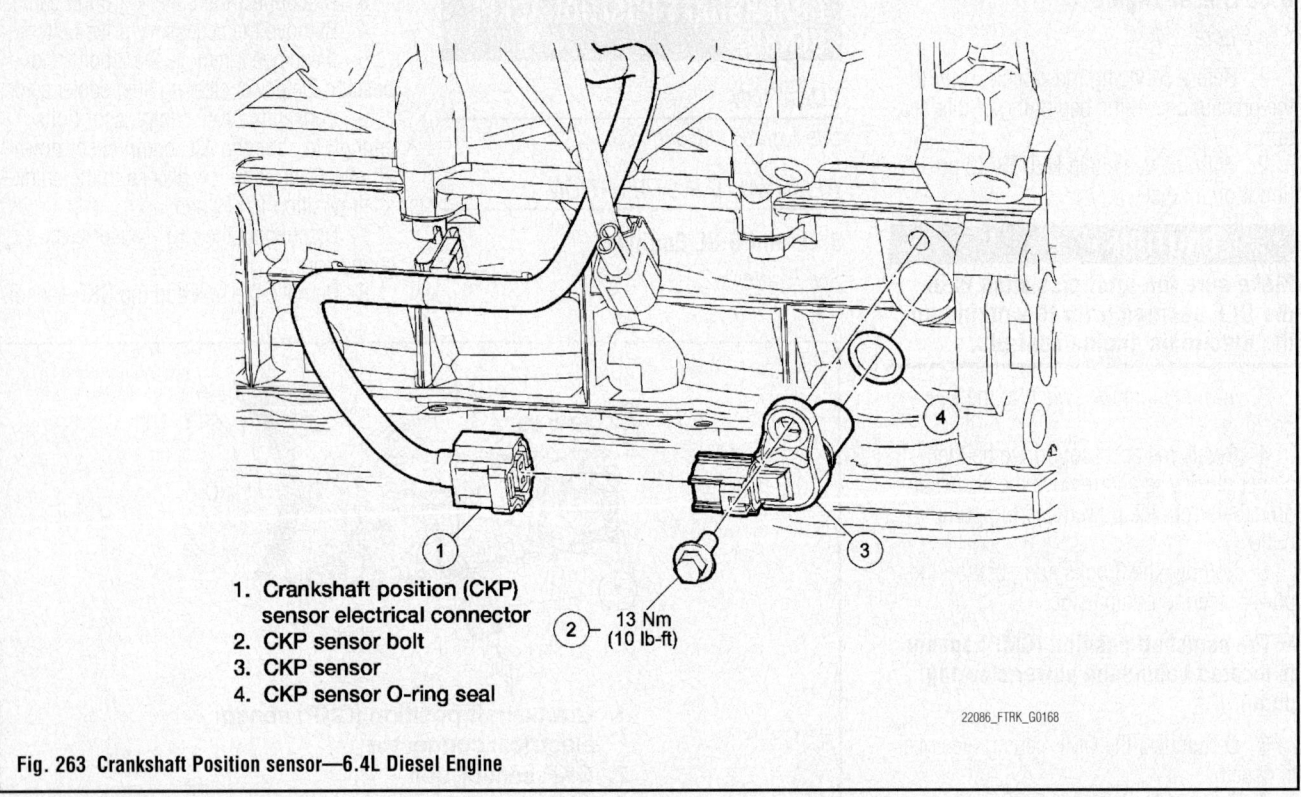

1. Crankshaft position (CKP)
   sensor electrical connector
2. CKP sensor bolt
3. CKP sensor
4. CKP sensor O-ring seal

13 Nm
(10 lb-ft)

22086_FTRK_G0168

Fig. 263 Crankshaft Position sensor—6.4L Diesel Engine

➡ **Apply clean engine oil to the O-ring seal prior to installation.**

8. To install, reverse the removal procedure.

ENGINE COOLANT TEMPERATURE (ECT) SENSOR

LOCATION

At the front and top of engine, near thermostat housing.

REMOVAL & INSTALLATION

See Figure 264.

✳✳ CAUTION

Make sure the ignition switch is in the OFF position prior to working on the electronic engine controls.

1. Before servicing the vehicle, refer to the precautions in the beginning of this section.
2. Turn the ignition switch to the OFF position.
3. Drain the engine cooling system.
4. Remove the engine cooling fan.
5. Detach the wiring harness C-clip from the Engine Coolant Temperature (ECT) sensor.
6. Disconnect the cooling fan electrical connector.

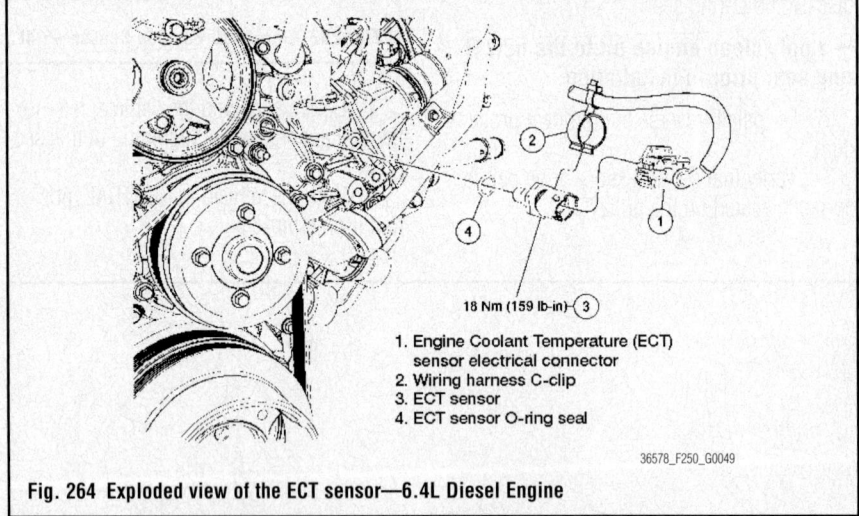

18 Nm (159 lb-in)—3

1. Engine Coolant Temperature (ECT)
   sensor electrical connector
2. Wiring harness C-clip
3. ECT sensor
4. ECT sensor O-ring seal

36578_F250_G0049

Fig. 264 Exploded view of the ECT sensor—6.4L Diesel Engine

7. Disconnect the engine coolant temperature (ECT) electrical connector.
8. Remove the ECT sensor and discard the O-ring seal.

To install:

➡ **Apply clean engine oil to the new O-ring seal prior to installation.**

9. Using a new O-ring seal, install the ECT sensor.
10. Tighten to 18 Nm (13 lb-ft).

➡**Make sure the C-clip is correctly installed or the wiring harness can be damaged by the accessory drive belt.**

11. Connect the ECT sensor electrical connector to the C clip.
12. Connect the cooling fan electrical connector.
13. Fill and bleed the engine cooling system.
14. Install the engine cooling fan.

EVAPORATIVE EMISSIONS (EVAP) CANISTER

LOCATION

See Figures 265 through 267.

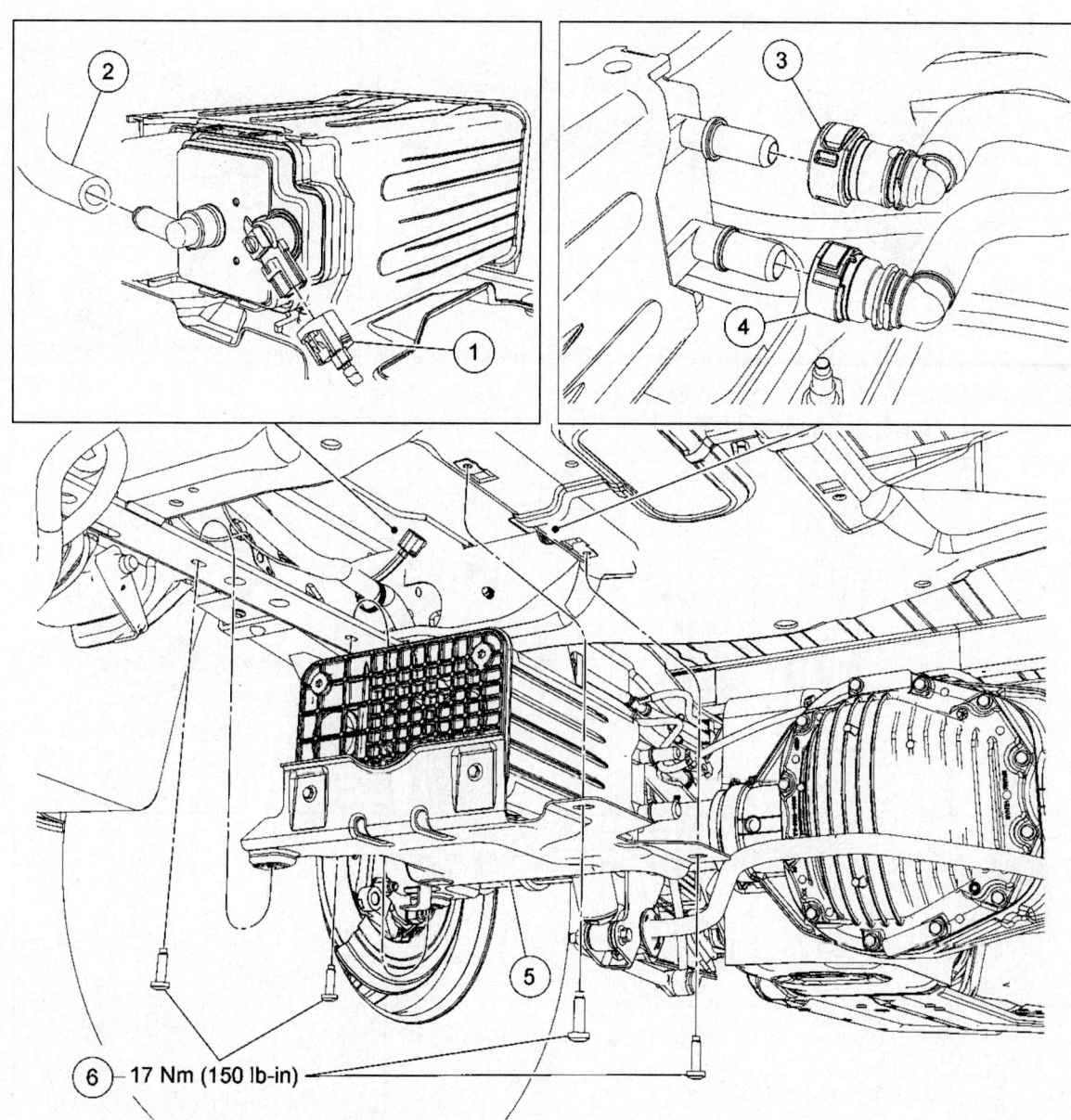

6 — 17 Nm (150 lb-in)

1. Evaporative Emission (EVAP) canister vent solenoid electrical connector
2. EVAP canister fresh air hose
3. EVAP canister purge valve vapor tube-to- EVAP canister assembly quick connect coupling
4. Fuel tank vapor tube-to- EVAP canister assembly quick connect coupling
5. EVAP canister and bracket assembly
6. EVAP canister assembly bracket bolts (4 required)

36578_F250_G0076

Fig. 265 View of EVAP canister and components—Midship fuel tank

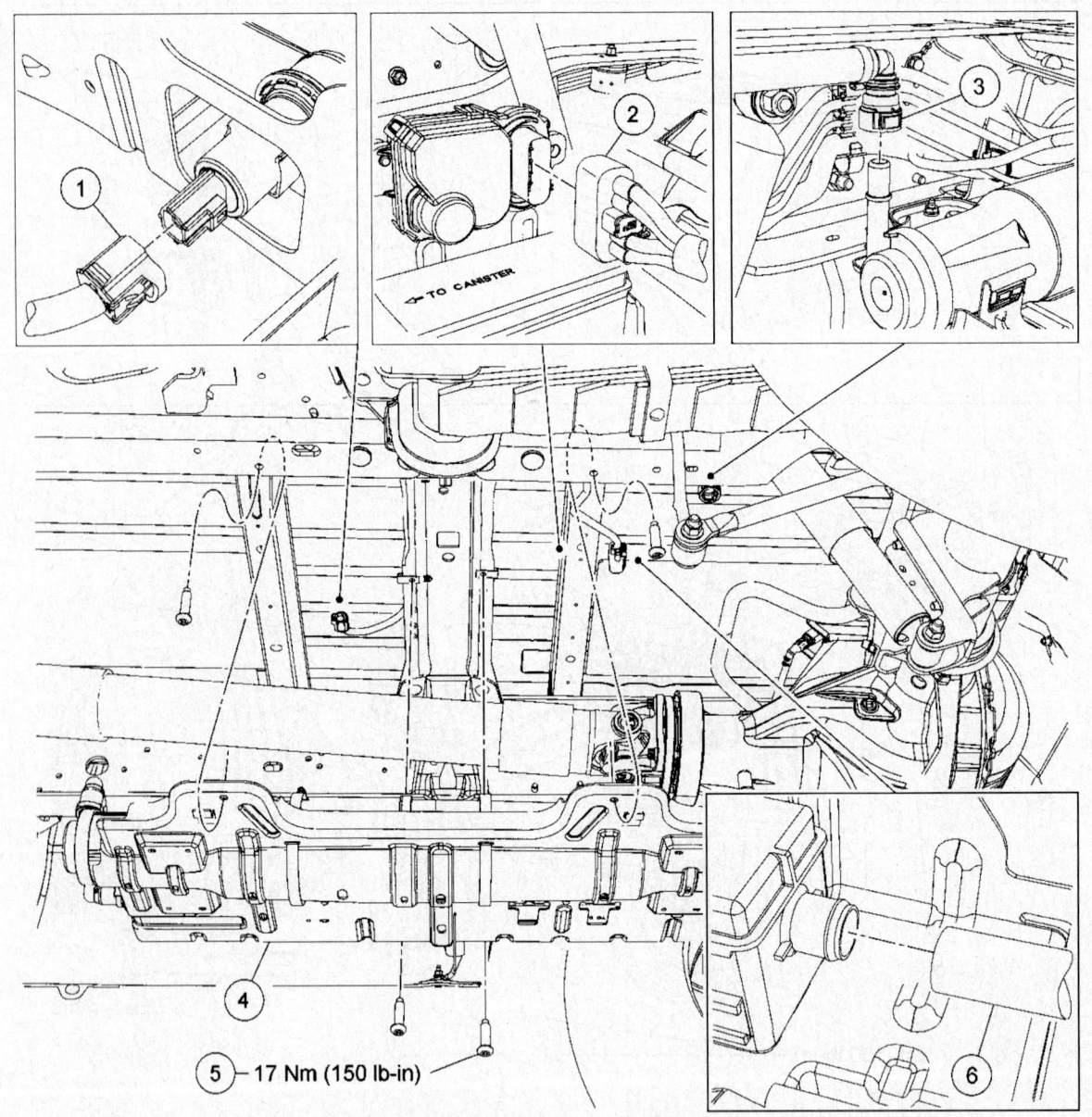

5 — 17 Nm (150 lb-in)

1. Evaporative Emission (EVAP) canister vent solenoid electrical connector
2. Fuel Pump Driver Module (FPDM) electrical connector
3. Fuel tank vapor tube-to- EVAP canister assembly quick connect coupling
4. EVAP canister and bracket assembly
5. EVAP canister assembly bracket bolt (4 required)
6. Fresh air kit

036578_F250_G0077

Fig. 266 View of EVAP canister and components—Aft axle fuel tank

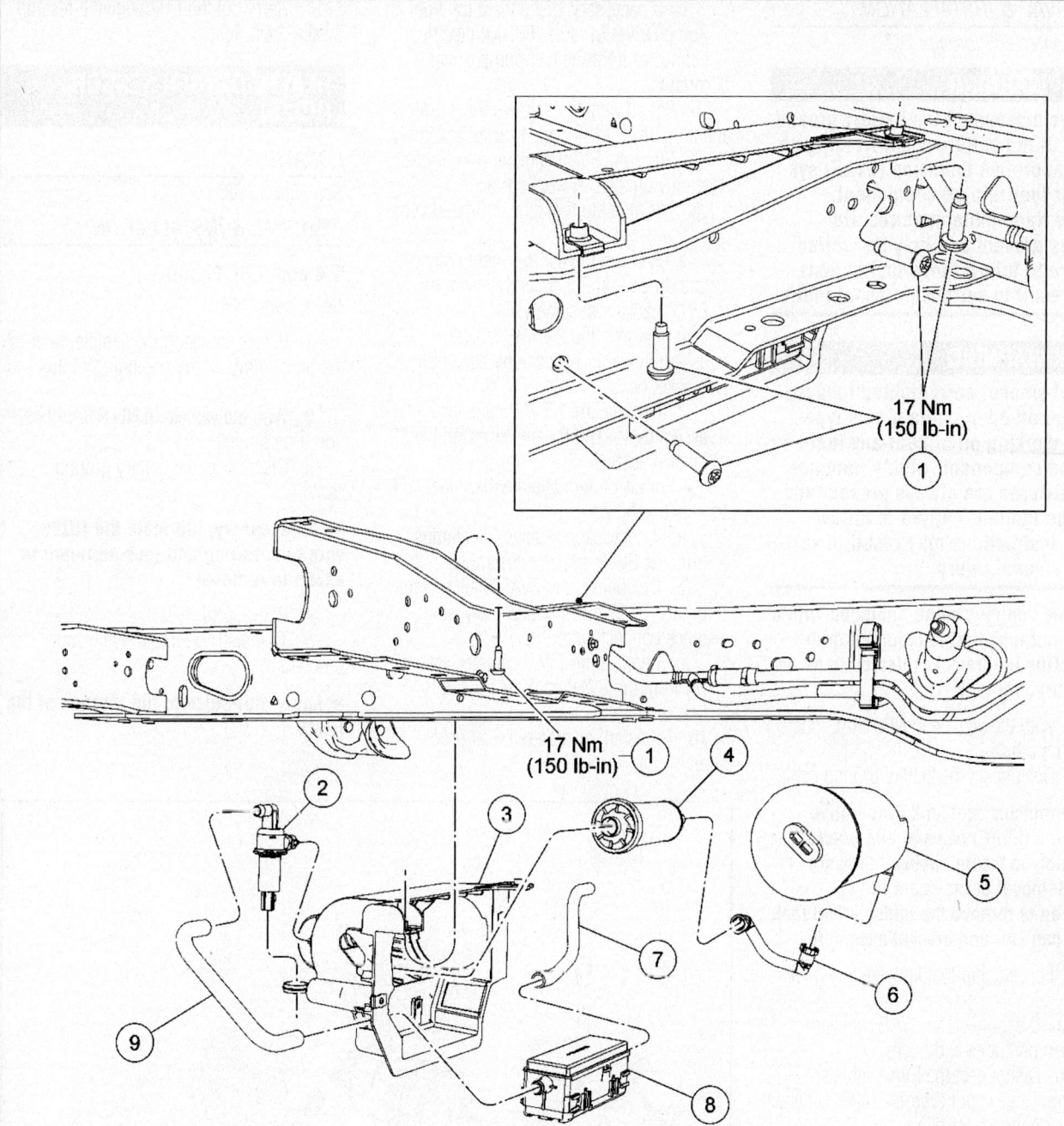

1. Evaporative Emission (EVAP) canister assembly bracket bolts (4 required)
2. EVAP canister vent solenoid
3. EVAP canister assembly bracket
4. EVAP filter assembly
5. EVAP canister assembly
6. EVAP filter assembly-to- EVAP canister tube
7. EVAP dust separator hose
8. EVAP dust separator
9. EVAP dust separator-to- EVAP canister vent solenoid hose

36578_F250_G0078

Fig. 267 View of EVAP canister and components—Auxiliary fuel tank

REMOVAL & INSTALLATION

See Figures 265 through 267.

※ WARNING

Always disconnect the battery ground cable at the battery when working on an Evaporative Emission (EVAP) system or fuel-related component. Highly flammable mixtures are always present and may be ignited. Failure to follow these instructions may result in serious personal injury.

※ WARNING

Do not smoke, carry lighted tobacco or have an open flame of any type when working on or near any fuel-related component. Highly flammable mixtures are always present and may be ignited. Failure to follow these instructions may result in serious personal injury.

➡ Some vehicles come equipped with a steel fuel tank that is mounted midship. This fuel tank is referred to as an auxiliary fuel tank.

1. With the vehicle in NEUTRAL, position it on a hoist.
2. Disconnect the battery ground cable.

➡ The midship fuel tank Evaporative Emission (EVAP) canister and bracket assembly is located above the spare tire. Removal of the spare tire is required to remove the midship fuel tank EVAP canister and bracket assembly.

3. For midship fuel tank equipped vehicles:
   a. Disconnect the EVAP canister assembly tubes and hoses.
   b. Disconnect the EVAP canister purge valve vapor tube-to- EVAP canister quick connect coupling.
   c. Disconnect fuel tank vapor tube-to- EVAP canister assembly quick connect coupling.
   d. Disconnect canister fresh air hose-to- EVAP canister vent solenoid and dust separator assembly tube.
4. On all vehicles, disconnect the EVAP canister vent solenoid electrical connector.
5. For aft-of-axle and auxiliary fuel tank equipped vehicles:
   a. Disconnect the fuel tank vapor tube-to- EVAP canister assembly quick connect coupling.
   b. Disconnect the EVAP dust separator hose or fresh air kit from the dust separator.

   c. If necessary, disconnect the Fuel Pump Driver Module (FPDM) electrical connector from the fuel pump driver module.
6. For all vehicles, remove the 4 bolts and the EVAP canister and bracket assembly.
7. Place the EVAP canister and bracket assembly on a clean work surface.
8. For midship fuel tank equipped vehicles:
   a. Remove the canister vent solenoid and dust separator assembly from the EVAP canister assembly.
   b. Remove the 2 EVAP canister assembly-to- EVAP canister assembly bracket bolts.
   c. Remove the 2 EVAP canister assembly-to- EVAP canister assembly bracket screws.
9. For aft-of-axle and auxiliary fuel tank equipped vehicles:
   a. If necessary, remove the clamps from the EVAP canister assembly.
   b. Disconnect the EVAP filter assembly-to- EVAP canister assembly tube quick connect coupling.
   c. Remove the EVAP canister assembly from the EVAP canister assembly bracket.
10. To install, reverse removal procedure.

11. Carry out the Evaporative Emission System Leak Test.

HEATED OXYGEN SENSOR (HO2S)

LOCATION

See Figure 268.

REMOVAL & INSTALLATION

5.4 and 6.8L Engines
See Figure 268.

1. Before servicing the vehicle, refer to the precautions in the beginning of this section.
2. With the vehicle in NEUTRAL, position it on a hoist.
3. Disconnect the battery ground cable.

➡ **If necessary, lubricate the HO2S with penetrating and lock lubricant to assist in removal**

4. Remove the HO2S.
5. To install, reverse the removal procedure.

➡ Apply anti-seize to the threads of the HO2S.

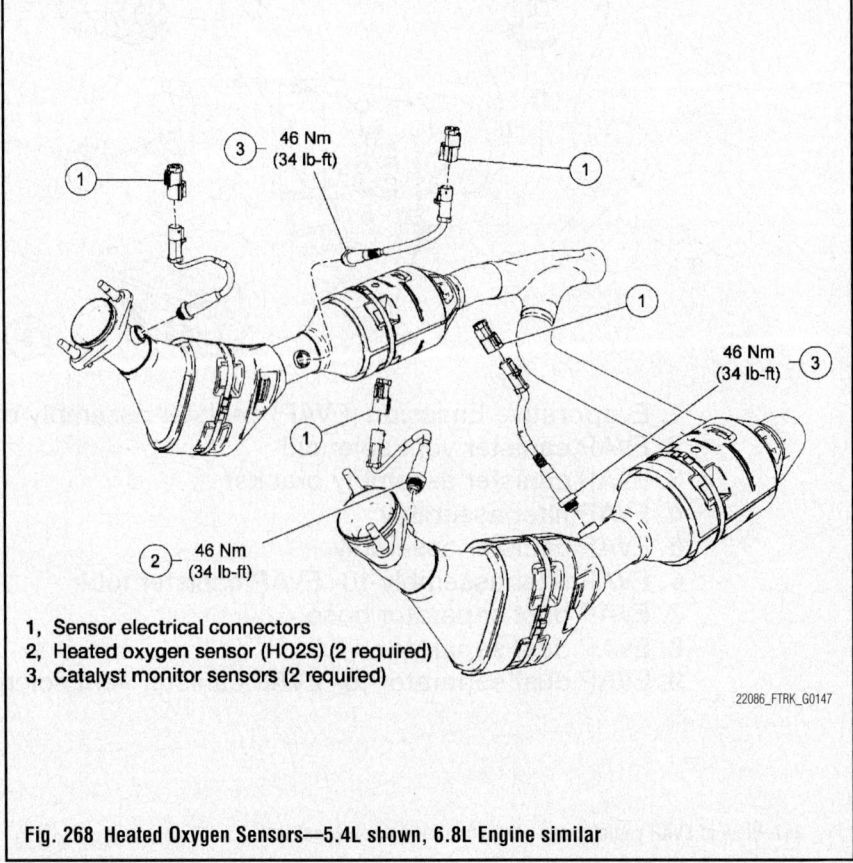

1, Sensor electrical connectors
2, Heated oxygen sensor (HO2S) (2 required)
3, Catalyst monitor sensors (2 required)

22086_FTRK_G0147

Fig. 268 Heated Oxygen Sensors—5.4L shown, 6.8L Engine similar

INTAKE AIR TEMPERATURE (IAT) SENSOR

LOCATION

See Figure 269.

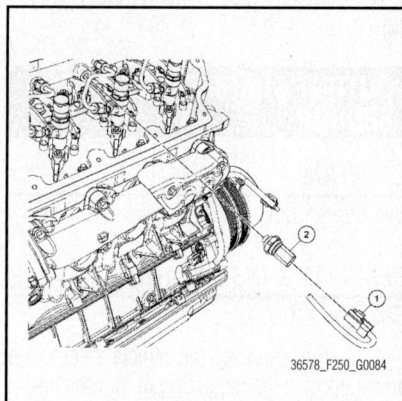

Fig. 269 Removing the IAT sensor—6.4L Diesel engines

REMOVAL & INSTALLATION

6.4L Diesel Engines

See Figure 269.

➡Make sure the ignition switch is in the OFF position prior to working on the electronic engine control or the vehicle may be damaged.

1. Turn the ignition switch to the OFF position.
2. Disconnect the Intake Air Temperature 2 (IAT2) electrical connector.
3. Remove the IAT2 sensor.
4. To install, reverse the removal procedure.

KNOCK SENSOR (KS)

TESTING

See Figures 270 and 271.

1. Before servicing the vehicle, refer to the precautions in the beginning of this section.

✳✳ WARNING

Use only a high-impedance multimeter, otherwise damage to the PCM and/or sensors can result.

2. With the key **ON** and the engine **OFF**, disconnect the knock sensor.
3. Measure resistance of the knock sensor. Standard value is 4.39M ohms— 5.35M ohms. If not, replace the knock sensor.

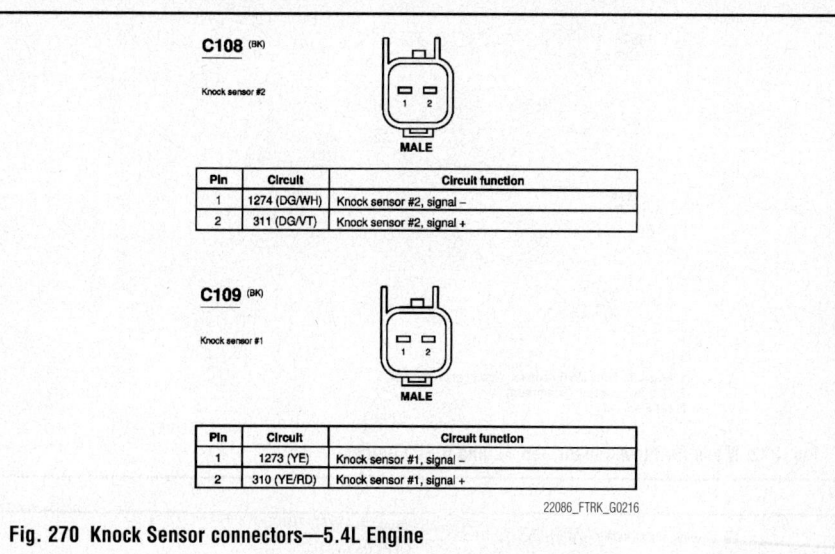

Pin	Circuit	Circuit function
1	1274 (DG/WH)	Knock sensor #2, signal –
2	311 (DG/VT)	Knock sensor #2, signal +

Pin	Circuit	Circuit function
1	1273 (YE)	Knock sensor #1, signal –
2	310 (YE/RD)	Knock sensor #1, signal +

Fig. 270 Knock Sensor connectors—5.4L Engine

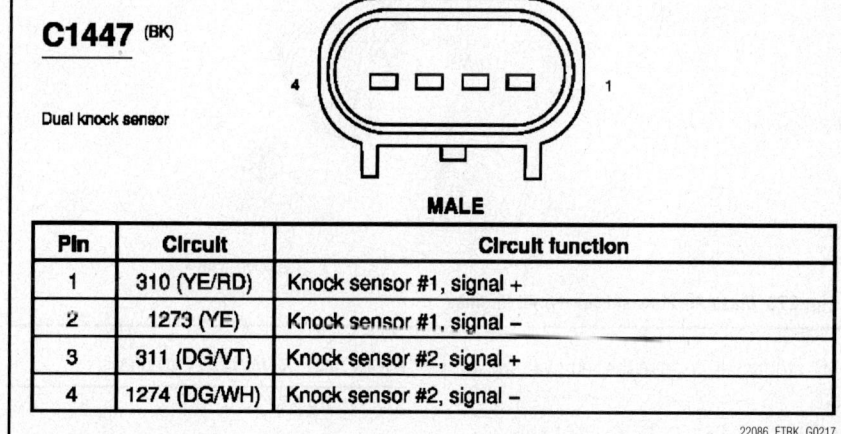

Pin	Circuit	Circuit function
1	310 (YE/RD)	Knock sensor #1, signal +
2	1273 (YE)	Knock sensor #1, signal –
3	311 (DG/VT)	Knock sensor #2, signal +
4	1274 (DG/WH)	Knock sensor #2, signal –

Fig. 271 Knock Sensor connector—6.8L Engine

MALFUNCTION INDICATOR LIGHT (MIL)

A diagnostic scan tool must be connected to the data link connector (DLC) for communication with the vehicle.

1. The required diagnostic tool functions are described below:
   - Diagnostic test modes; self-test, clear diagnostic trouble codes (DTCs)
   - Resetting keep alive memory (KAM)
   - On-board system readiness (OBD monitor completion status)
   - Diagnostic monitoring test results (mode 6) for on-board diagnostic (OBD) on-board monitors
   - Output test mode
   - Monitor, record, and playback of parameter identification (PIDs)

MASS AIR FLOW (MAF) SENSOR

LOCATION

See Figures 272 and 273.

REMOVAL & INSTALLATION

See Figures 272 and 273.

➡Make sure the ignition switch is in the OFF position prior to working on the electronic engine controls or the vehicle may be damaged.

1. Before servicing the vehicle, refer to the precautions in the beginning of this section.
2. Turn the ignition switch to the OFF position.
3. Disconnect the mass air flow (MAF) sensor electrical connector.
4. Remove the bolts and the MAF sensor.

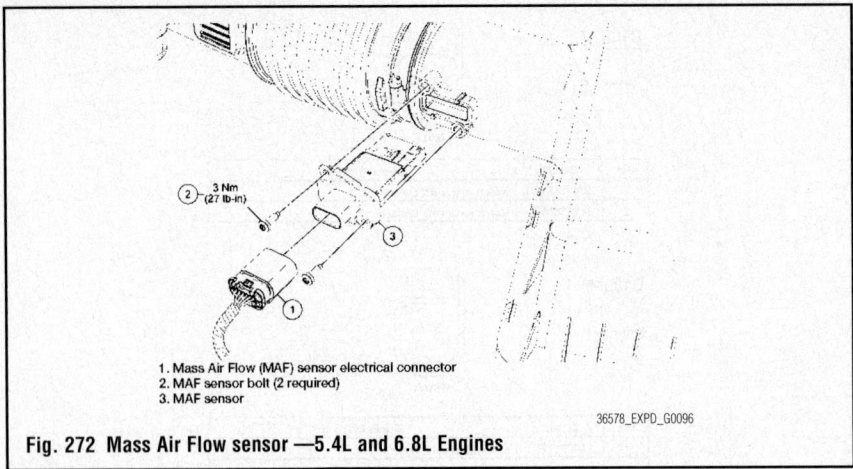

1. Mass Air Flow (MAF) sensor electrical connector
2. MAF sensor bolt (2 required)
3. MAF sensor

36578_EXPD_G0096

Fig. 272 Mass Air Flow sensor —5.4L and 6.8L Engines

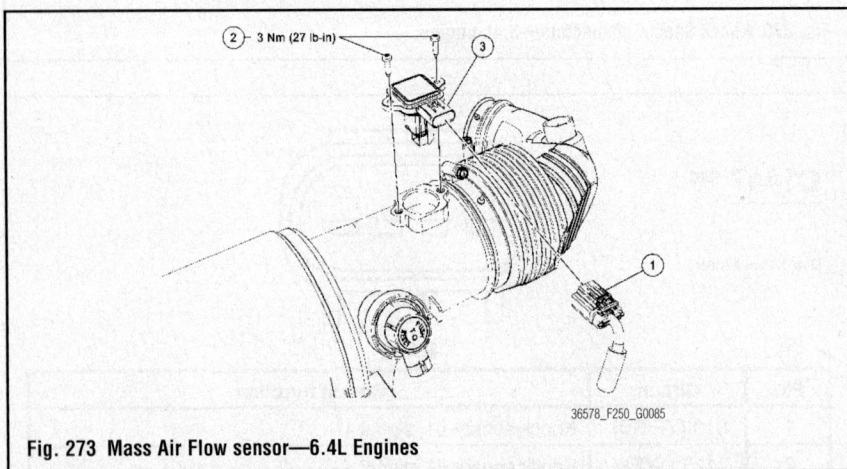

36578_F250_G0085

Fig. 273 Mass Air Flow sensor—6.4L Engines

5. To install, reverse the removal procedure.

MANIFOLD ABSOLUTE PRESSURE (MAP) SENSOR

LOCATION
See Figure 274.

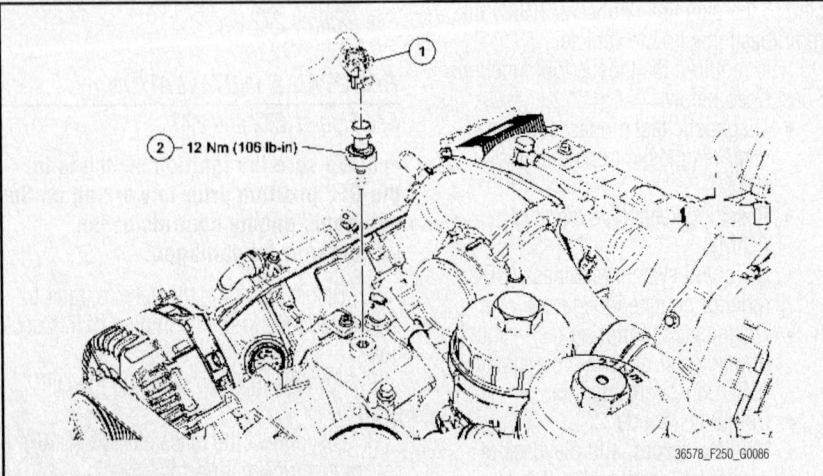

36578_F250_G0086

Fig. 274 MAP sensor—6.4L Diesel engine

REMOVAL & INSTALLATION
See Figure 274.

➡ **Make sure the ignition switch is in the OFF position prior to working on the electronic engine controls or the vehicle may be damaged.**

1. Before servicing the vehicle, refer to the precautions in the beginning of this section.

2. Turn the ignition switch to the OFF position.

3. Remove the air cleaner outlet tube.

4. Disconnect the Manifold Absolute Pressure (MAP) sensor electrical connector.

5. Remove the MAP sensor.

6. To install, reverse the removal procedure.

OUTPUT SHAFT SPEED (OSS) SENSOR

LOCATION
See Figure 275.

REMOVAL & INSTALLATION
See Figure 275.

1. Before servicing the vehicle, refer to the precautions in the beginning of this section.

2. With the vehicle in NEUTRAL, position it on a hoist.

3. Disconnect the output shaft speed (OSS) sensor electrical connector.

➡ **Prior to removing the speed sensor, make sure that the area around the sensor is free of foreign material to prevent contamination of the transmission.**

4. Remove the OSS sensor.

To install:
5. Lubricate the O-ring with clean automatic transmission fluid and install the OSS sensor.

6. Install the bolt and tighten to80 inch. lbs. (9 Nm).

7. Connect the OSS sensor electrical connector.

POSITIVE CRANKCASE VENTILATION (PCV) VALVE

LOCATION
See Figure 276.

5.4L Engine
See Figure 276.

1. Disconnect the negative battery cable.

2. Release the clamp and remove the bolt and the air intake resonator assembly.

3. Disconnect the quick connect couplings and remove the PCV tube.

4. Disconnect the PCV heater element electrical connector.

5. Remove the 2 bolts and the PCV heater element.

6. Discard the O-ring seal.

7. To install, reverse removal procedure. Lubricate the o-ring with clean engine oil prior to installation.

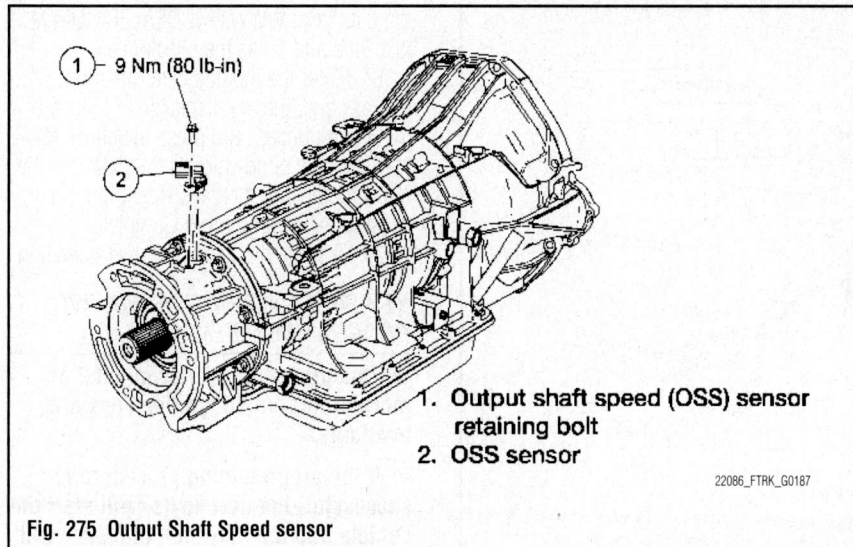

1. Output shaft speed (OSS) sensor
retaining bolt
2. OSS sensor

22086_FTRK_G0187

Fig. 275 Output Shaft Speed sensor

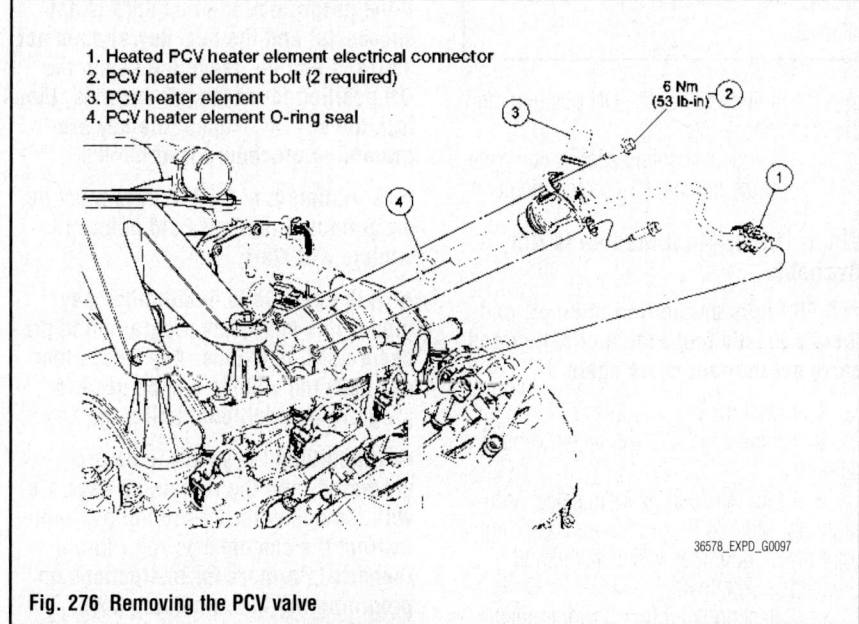

1. Heated PCV heater element electrical connector
2. PCV heater element bolt (2 required)
3. PCV heater element
4. PCV heater element O-ring seal

36578_EXPD_G0097

Fig. 276 Removing the PCV valve

POWERTRAIN CONTROL MODULE (PCM)

LOCATION
See Figures 277 and 278.

REMOVAL & INSTALLATION

Gasoline Engines
See Figure 277.

➡**Refer to the Powertrain Control/Emissions Diagnosis (PC/ED) manual for correct Vehicle Communication Module (VCM) hook-up procedure.**

1. If servicing the PCM, connect the scan tool to the vehicle. Allow the scan tool to identify the vehicle and obtain configuration data. All programmable module information will automatically be retrieved by the VCM.

2. Disconnect the 3 PCM electrical connectors.
3. Remove the 2 nuts and position the PCM wiring harness support bracket aside.
4. Remove the PCM.

➡**If the Instrument Cluster (IC) or the PCM is being replaced (or both), the parameters must be reset in both modules or the vehicle will experience a Passive Anti-Theft System (PATS) no-start. This will occur even if the vehicle is not equipped with PATS.**

5. To install, reverse the removal procedure.

Diesel Engines
See Figure 278.

➡**Make sure the ignition switch is in the OFF position prior to working on the electronic engine controls or the vehicle may be damaged.**

1. Turn the ignition switch to the OFF position.
2. Retrieve the module configuration. Carry out the module configuration retrieval steps of the Programmable Module Installation (PMI) procedure.
3. Remove the air cleaner element.
4. Remove the transmission fluid level indicator.
5. Disconnect the PCM electrical connectors.
6. Dctach the wiring harness retainer
7. Remove the 2 nuts and the PCM.

➡**If the Instrument Cluster (IC) or the PCM is being replaced (or both), the parameters must be reset in both modules or the vehicle will experience a Passive Anti-Theft System (PATS) no-start. This will occur even if the vehicle is not equipped with PATS.**

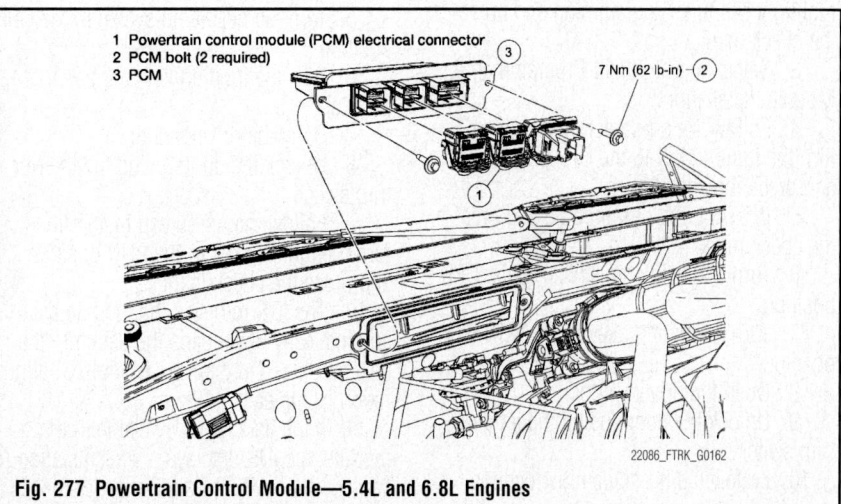

1 Powertrain control module (PCM) electrical connector
2 PCM bolt (2 required)
3 PCM

22086_FTRK_G0162

Fig. 277 Powertrain Control Module—5.4L and 6.8L Engines

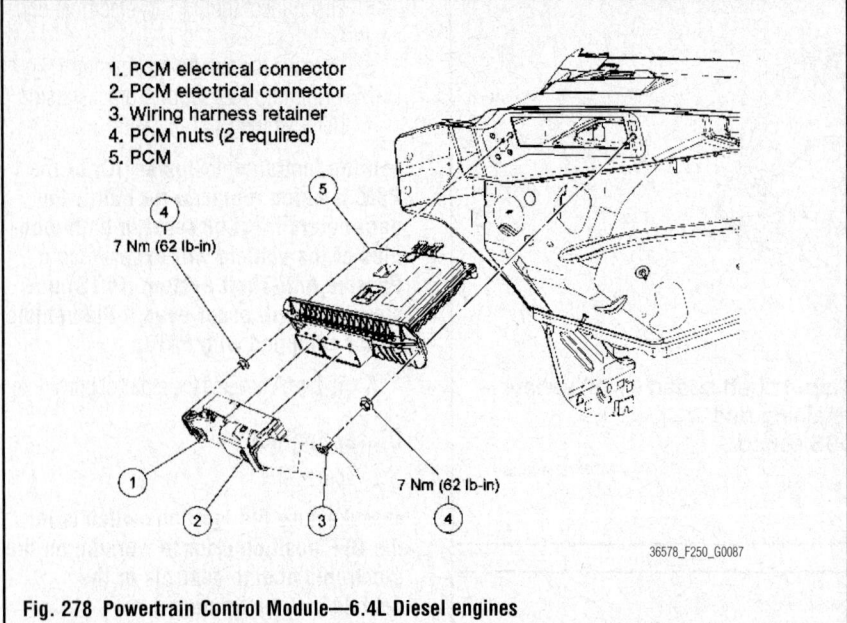

1. PCM electrical connector
2. PCM electrical connector
3. Wiring harness retainer
4. PCM nuts (2 required)
5. PCM

7 Nm (62 lb-in)

7 Nm (62 lb-in)

36578_F250_G0087

Fig. 278 Powertrain Control Module—6.4L Diesel engines

8. To install, reverse the removal procedure.

9. Restore the module configuration. Carry out the module configuration restore steps of the Programmable Module Installation (PMI) procedure.

10. Carry out the extended idle shut down initialization procedure.

PROGRAMMABLE MODULE INSTALLATION (PMI) USING THE INTEGRATED DIAGNOSTIC SYSTEM (IDS)

When The Original Module Is Available

➡ If PMI fails on the first attempt, exit the diagnostic tool PMI application and carry out the procedure again.

1. Connect the IDS and ID the vehicle as normal.

2. From the Toolbox icon, select and highlight Module Programming and press the check mark.

3. Select and highlight Programmable Module Installation.

4. Follow the on-screen instructions, turn the ignition key to the OFF position, and press the check mark.

5. INSTALL the new module and press the check mark.

6. Turn the headlamp switch to the OFF position.

7. Turn the ignition key to the RUN position.

8. Open the driver's door.

9. Unlock the doors using the interior trim switch.

10. Follow the on-screen instructions,

turn the ignition key to the ON position, and press the check mark.

11. The module configuration is complete.

12. Test the module for correct operation.

When The Original Module Is Not Available

➡ If PMI fails on the first attempt, exit the diagnostic tool PMI application and carry out the procedure again.

1. Install the new module.

2. Connect the IDS and ID the vehicle as normal.

3. From the Toolbox icon, select and highlight Module Programming. Then highlight the module that was installed and press the check mark.

4. Select and highlight Programmable Module Installation. Then highlight the module that was installed and press the check mark.

5. Turn the headlamp switch to the OFF position.

6. Turn the ignition key to the RUN position.

7. Open the driver's door.

8. Unlock the doors using the interior trim switch.

9. Follow the on-screen instructions, turn the ignition key to the RUN position and press the check mark.

10. The IDS retrieves the module data, automatically downloads the data into the new module, and displays Module Configuration Complete.

11. If the data is not available in the module, the IDS displays a screen stating to contact the As-Built Data Center. Retrieve

the data from WWW.FMCDEALER.COM at this time and press the check mark.

12. Enter the module data (the module address and line are displayed to the left of the 3 entry boxes) and press the check mark.

13. The IDS downloads the data into the new module and displays Operation Successful — Programming Complete.

14. Test the module for correct operation.

KEY PROGRAMMING USING TWO PROGRAMMED KEYS

➡ This procedure works only if 2 or more programmed ignition keys are available.

➡ If the programming procedure is successful, the new key(s) will start the vehicle and the anti-theft indicator will prove-out for approximately 3 seconds. If the programming procedure is not successful and the new key(s) does not start the engine, leave the key in the ON position for at least 3 seconds, then turn the key off. Repeat the key programming procedure from Step 1.

➡ A minimum of 2 PATS keys must be programmed into the PCM before the vehicle will start.

➡ If the vehicle is in unlimited key mode, this spare key programming procedure still functions. Any 2 keys that can start the vehicle can be used to program an additional unlimited key.

➡ If additional keys are to be programmed, and the remaining keys are with the customer, or are not available, instruct the customer to refer to the Owner's Literature for instructions on programming the remaining keys.

➡ If the steps are not carried out as outlined, the programming procedure will end.

➡ Ignition keys must have a correct mechanical key cut for the vehicle and must be PATS encoded keys (contain a transponder).

1. Insert the first programmed key into the ignition lock cylinder and turn the key from the OFF position to the ON position (maintain the key in the ON position for a minimum of 3 seconds and less than 10 seconds).

2. Turn the key to the OFF position and remove the first key from the ignition lock cylinder.

3. Within 5 seconds of turning the key to the OFF position, insert the second programmed key into the ignition lock cylinder

and turn the key from the OFF position to the ON position (maintain the key in the ON position for a minimum of 3 seconds and less than 10 seconds).

4. Turn the key to the OFF position and remove the key from the ignition lock cylinder.

5. Within 10 seconds of turning the key to the OFF position, insert the unprogrammed key (the new key) into the ignition lock cylinder and turn the key from the OFF position to the ON position (maintain the key in the ON position for a minimum of 3 seconds and less than 10 seconds).

6. If it is desired to program additional key(s) (only up to 8 keys total can be programmed into the PCM), repeat Steps 1 - 5 for each additional key that needs to be programmed.

7. Start the vehicle with the new key(s).

THROTTLE POSITION SENSOR (TPS)

LOCATION

See Figures 279 and 280.

REMOVAL & INSTALLATION

5.4L Engine

See Figure 279.

1. Before servicing the vehicle, refer to the precautions in the beginning of this section.

2. Disconnect the throttle position (TP) sensor electrical connector.

> ✳✳ **CAUTION**
>
> **Failure to remove the TP sensor screws in the following manner will result in damage to the screws.**

3. First loosen the screws 1-2 full turns using a hand tool and then use a suitable high speed driver to complete the removal.

4. Remove and discard the 2 screws and the TP sensor.

To install:

> ✳✳ **CAUTION**
>
> **Do not reuse the TP sensor and screws. A new TP sensor and screws must be installed.**

> ✳✳ **CAUTION**
>
> **Do not use a high speed driver to install the new screws or damage to the TP sensor can occur.**

➡ **When installing the new TP sensor, make sure that the radial locator tab on**

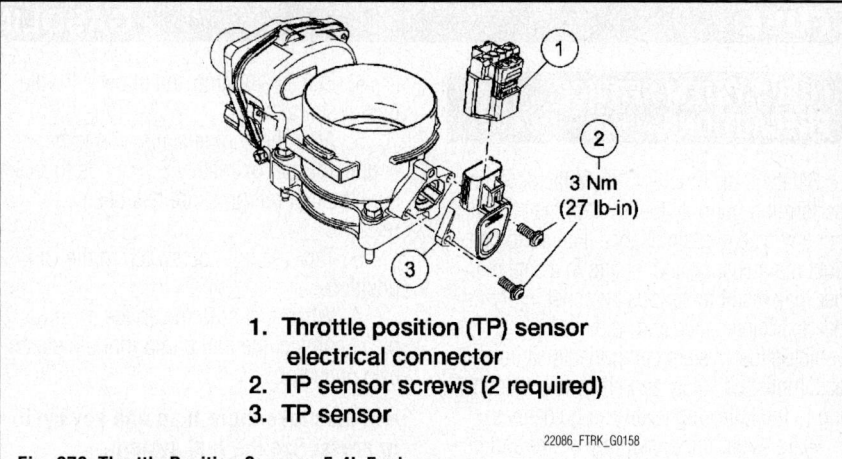

1. Throttle position (TP) sensor electrical connector
2. TP sensor screws (2 required)
3. TP sensor

22086_FTRK_G0158

Fig. 279 Throttle Position Sensor—5.4L Engine

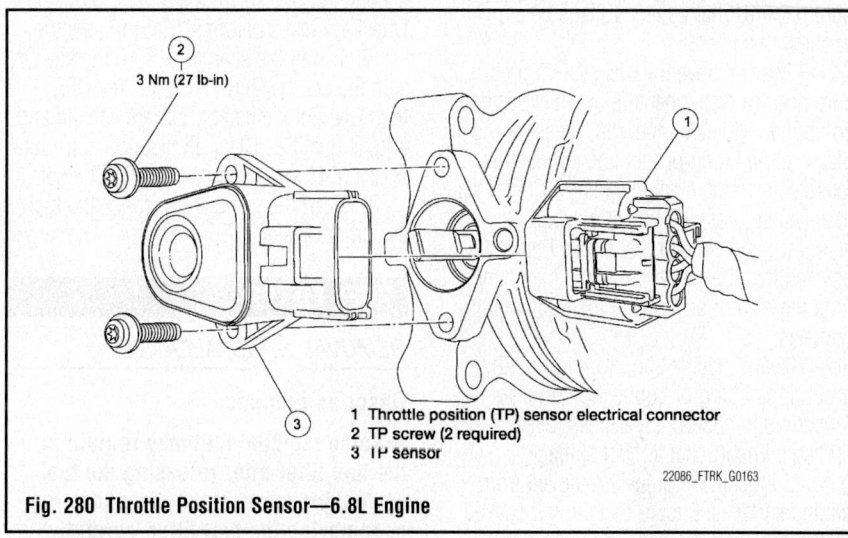

1 Throttle position (TP) sensor electrical connector
2 TP screw (2 required)
3 TP sensor

22086_FTRK_G0163

Fig. 280 Throttle Position Sensor—6.8L Engine

the TP sensor is aligned with the radial locator hole on the throttle body (TB).

5. Position the new TP sensor and install the 2 new screws.

6. Tighten to 3 Nm (27 lb-in).

7. Connect the TP sensor electrical connector.

6.8L Engine

See Figure 280.

1. Before servicing the vehicle, refer to the precautions in the beginning of this section.

2. Disconnect the throttle position (TP) sensor electrical connector.

> ✳✳ **CAUTION**
>
> **Failure to remove the TP sensor screws in the following manner will result in damage to the screws.**

3. First loosen the screws 1-2 full turns using a hand tool and then use a suitable high speed driver to complete the removal.

4. Remove and discard the 2 screws and the TP sensor.

To install:

> ✳✳ **CAUTION**
>
> **Do not reuse the TP sensor and screws. A new TP sensor and screws must be installed.**

> ✳✳ **CAUTION**
>
> **Do not use a high speed driver to install the new screws or damage to the TP sensor can occur.**

➡ **When installing the new TP sensor, make sure that the radial locator tab on the TP sensor is aligned with the radial locator hole on the throttle body (TB).**

5. Position the new TP sensor and install the 2 new screws.

6. Tighten to 3 Nm (27 lb-in).

7. Connect the TP sensor electrical connector.

FUEL SYSTEM SERVICE PRECAUTIONS

Safety is the most important factor when performing not only fuel system maintenance but any type of maintenance. Failure to conduct maintenance and repairs in a safe manner may result in serious personal injury or death. Maintenance and testing of the vehicle's fuel system components can be accomplished safely and effectively by adhering to the following rules and guidelines.

• To avoid the possibility of fire and personal injury, always disconnect the negative battery cable unless the repair or test procedure requires that battery voltage be applied.

• Always relieve the fuel system pressure prior to disconnecting any fuel system component (injector, fuel rail, pressure regulator, etc.), fitting or fuel line connection. Exercise extreme caution whenever relieving fuel system pressure to avoid exposing skin, face and eyes to fuel spray. Please be advised that fuel under pressure may penetrate the skin or any part of the body that it contacts.

• Always place a shop towel or cloth around the fitting or connection prior to loosening to absorb any excess fuel due to spillage. Ensure that all fuel spillage (should it occur) is quickly removed from engine surfaces. Ensure that all fuel soaked cloths or towels are deposited into a suitable waste container.

• Always keep a dry chemical (Class B) fire extinguisher near the work area.

• Do not allow fuel spray or fuel vapors to come into contact with a spark or open flame.

• Always use a back-up wrench when loosening and tightening fuel line connection fittings. This will prevent unnecessary stress and torsion to fuel line piping.

• Always replace worn fuel fitting O-rings with new. Do not substitute fuel hose or equivalent where fuel pipe is installed.

Before servicing the vehicle, make sure to also refer to the precautions in the beginning of this section as well.

RELIEVING FUEL SYSTEM PRESSURE

1. Before servicing the vehicle, refer to the Precautions Section.
2. Raise and safely support the vehicle.
3. Disconnect the fuel pump module electrical connector at the fuel tank.

4. Start the engine and allow it to idle until it stalls.
5. After the engine stalls, crank the engine for approximately 5 seconds to make sure the fuel rail pressure has been released.
6. Turn the ignition switch to the OFF position.
7. When fuel system service is complete, connect the fuel pump module electrical connector.

➡**It may take more than one key cycle to pressurize the fuel system.**

8. Cycle the ignition key and wait three seconds to pressurize the fuel system. Check for leaks before starting the engine.
9. Install the scan tool. Turn the key ON with the engine OFF. Cycle the key OFF, then ON. Select the appropriate vehicle and engine qualifier. Clear all diagnostic trouble codes (DTCs) and carry out a PCM reset.
10. Start the vehicle and check the fuel system for leaks.

FUEL FILTER

REMOVAL & INSTALLATION

Gasoline Engines

➡**Some residual fuel may remain in the fuel filter after releasing the fuel system pressure. Upon disconnecting or removing the fuel filter, carefully drain any residual fuel into a suitable container.**

1. With the vehicle in NEUTRAL, position it on a hoist.
2. Disconnect the fuel supply tube-to-fuel filter inlet quick connect coupling.
3. Disconnect the fuel supply tube-to-fuel filter outlet quick connect coupling.
4. Remove and discard the fuel filter.
5. To install, reverse the removal procedure.
6. Install a new fuel filter.

FUEL PUMP MODULE

REMOVAL & INSTALLATION
See Figures 281 and 282.

➡**This procedure is for gasoline applications only.**

➡**The fuel tank must be drained completely. Upon removal of the Fuel Pump (FP) module, the tank must be inspected for contamination.**

1. Remove the fuel tank. For additional information, refer to Fuel Tank —Aft of Axle or Fuel Tank— Auxiliary in this section.
2. Clean the fuel tank of any dirt or foreign material before servicing the Fuel Pump (FP) module. In extreme dirt or dusty conditions it may be necessary to wash the fuel tank using a water hose. Before removing the FP module, make sure that there is no residual dirt or foreign material around the FP module flange. If dirt or foreign material enter the fuel tank, damage to the FP module or other fuel system components may occur.
3. Clean the area around the FP mounting flange.

➡**Mark the orientation of the FP module on the fuel tank to aid in installation.**

4. For steel fuel tanks, remove the 6 bolts from the FP module.
5. For plastic fuel tanks, using the Lock Ring Wrench, remove the FP module lock ring.

➡**The Fuel Pump (FP) module must be handled carefully to avoid damage to the float arm.**

6. Completely remove the FP module from the fuel tank.

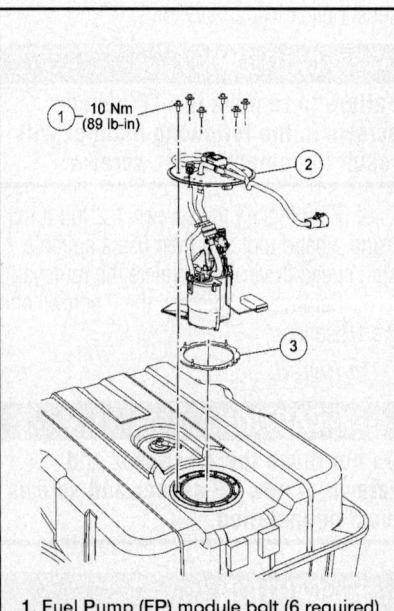

1. Fuel Pump (FP) module bolt (6 required)
2. FP module
3. FP module gasket

36578_F250_G0096

Fig. 281 Exploded view of the fuel level sensor—Steel fuel tank—Gasoline

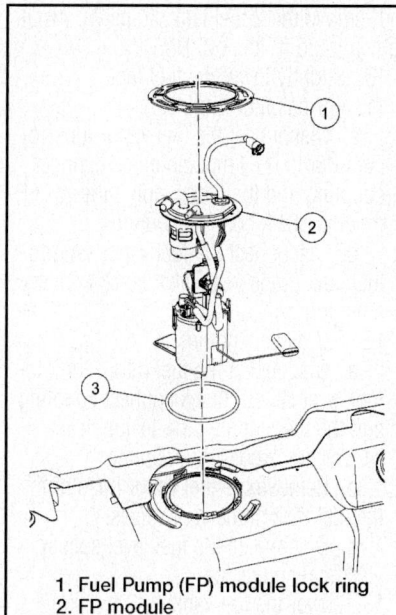

1. Fuel Pump (FP) module lock ring
2. FP module
3. FP module O-ring seal

36578_F250_G0097

Fig. 282 Exploded view of the fuel level sensor—Plastic fuel tank—Gasoline

➡️**Inspect the surfaces of the FP module flange and fuel tank gasket contact surfaces. Do not polish or adjust the gasket contact area of the fuel tank flange or the fuel tank. Install a new FP module or fuel tank if the gasket contact area is bent, scratched or corroded or fuel leakage could occur.**

➡️**Make sure to install a new FP module gasket or fuel leakage could occur.**

7. Remove and discard the FP module gasket.

To install:

8. Install a new FP module gasket.

➡️**The Fuel Pump (FP) module must be handled carefully to avoid damage to the float arm.**

➡️**Check the FP module orientation during installation so that the supply tube is positioned away from the float rod.**

9. Install the FP module into the fuel tank.
10. On steel fuel tanks, rotate the FP module clockwise until the alignment marks on the FP module and fuel tank meet and then install the 6 bolts.
11. On plastic fuel tanks, using the Lock Ring Wrench, install the new FP module lock ring. Make sure the alignment arrows on the FP module and the fuel tank meet before tightening the FP module lock ring
12. Install the fuel tank.

FUEL RAIL & INJECTORS

REMOVAL & INSTALLATION

5.4L Engine

See Figure 283.

1. Before servicing the vehicle, refer to the Precautions Section.
2. Release the fuel system pressure.
3. Disconnect the battery ground cable.
4. Remove the air cleaner and air cleaner intake pipe.
5. Disconnect the fuel vapor quick connect fitting from the evaporative emission (EVAP) canister purge valve and position aside.
6. Disconnect the heated positive crankcase ventilation (PCV) valve electrical connector.
7. Disconnect the PCV hose from the intake manifold and position aside.
8. Disconnect the electronic throttle control electrical connector.
9. Disconnect the throttle position (TP) sensor electrical connector.
10. Disconnect the vacuum hose near the rear of the right valve cover.

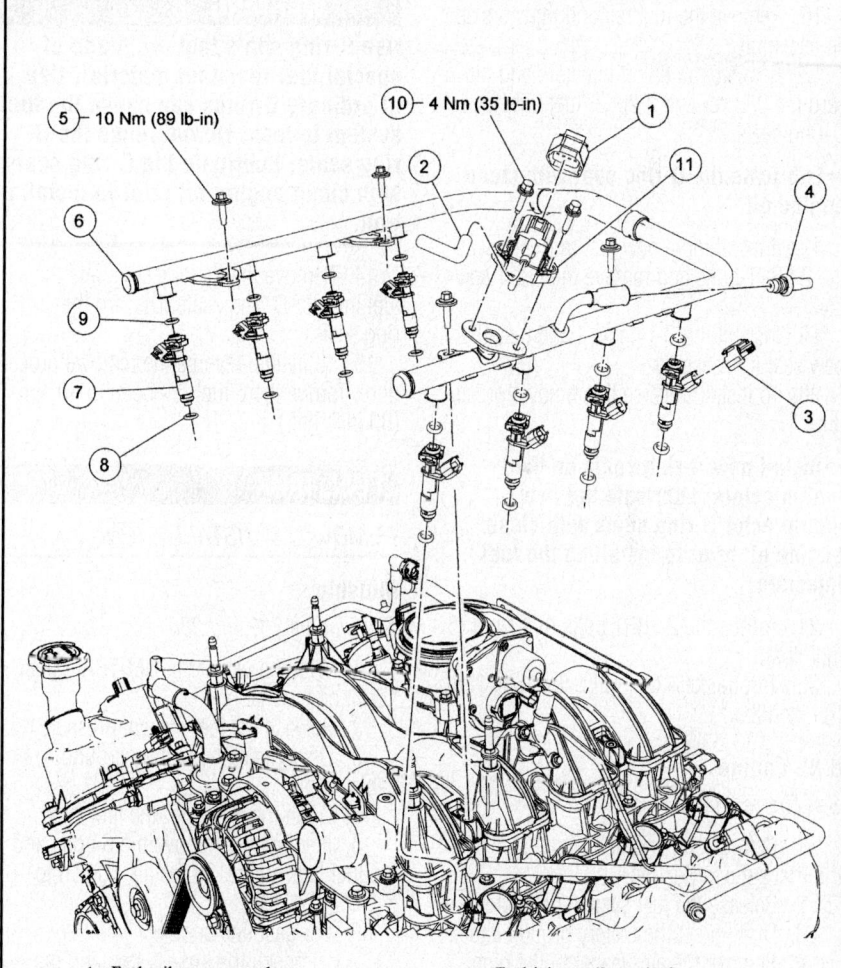

1 Fuel rail pressure and temperature (FRPT) sensor electrical connector
2 FRPT sensor vacuum connector
3 Fuel injector electrical connector (8 required)
4 Fuel tube spring lock couplings
5 Fuel rail bolts (4 required)
6 Fuel rail
7 Fuel injector (8 required)
8 Fuel injector to intake manifold O-ring seal (8 required)
9 Fuel injector to fuel rail O-ring seal (8 required)
10 FRPT sensor bolts (2 required)
11 FRPT sensor

06017-F150-G236

Fig. 283 F-Series 5.4L engine fuel rail and injectors

11. Disconnect the fuel rail pressure and temperature (FRPT) sensor electrical connector.

12. Disconnect the FRPT sensor vacuum hose.

13. Disconnect the 8 fuel injector electrical connectors.

14. Disconnect the spring lock couplings at the fuel rail.

15. Remove the 4 fuel rail bolts.

※※ WARNING

When installing the fuel injectors, make sure that the injectors are fully engaged in the fuel injector cups.

16. Remove the fuel rail and injectors as an assembly.

17. Remove the 8 fuel injectors and discard the 8 lower and 8 upper fuel injector O-ring seals.

➡**Lubricate the O-ring seal with clean engine oil.**

18. If installing a new fuel rail, remove the 2 FRPT bolts and remove the FRPT sensor.

19. Inspect the O-ring seal and install a new seal if necessary.

20. To install, reverse the removal procedure.

➡**Install new O-ring seals on the fuel injectors. Lubricate the new fuel injector O-ring seals with clean engine oil prior to installing the fuel injectors.**

21. Torque the 2 FRPT bolts to 4 Nm (35 inch lbs.).

22. Torque the 4 fuel rail bolts to 10 Nm (89 inch lbs.).

6.8L Engine

See Figure 284.

1. Before servicing the vehicle, refer to the Precautions Section.

2. Release the fuel system pressure.

3. Disconnect the battery ground cable.

4. Remove the air cleaner outlet pipe.

5. Disconnect the fuel supply tube spring lock coupling.

6. Disconnect the 2 electrical connectors from the throttle body (TB).

7. Disconnect the positive crankcase ventilation (PCV) tube from the TB spacer.

8. Disconnect the 2 vacuum lines from the TB spacer.

9. Disconnect the fuel rail pressure and temperature sensor electrical and vacuum connectors.

10. Disconnect the 10 fuel injector electrical connectors.

11. Detach the main engine wiring harness retainer from the RH valve cover.

12. Detach the 2 main engine wiring harness retainers from the intake manifold and position the harness for access to remove the fuel rail.

➡**When removing the fuel rail, leave the fuel injectors in the intake manifold. This will make removal of the fuel rail easier.**

13. Remove the 6 fuel rail bolts and the fuel rail.

※※ WARNING

Use O-ring seals that are made of special fuel-resistant material. Use of ordinary O-rings can cause the fuel system to leak. Do not reuse the O-ring seals. Lubricate the O-ring seals with clean engine oil prior to installation.

14. Remove the fuel injectors and the fuel injector O-ring seals. Discard the O-ring seals.

15. To install, reverse the removal procedure. Torque the 6 fuel rail bolts to 10 Nm (89 inch lbs.)

FUEL TANK

REMOVAL & INSTALLATION

Midship

See Figures 285 and 286.

1. With the vehicle in NEUTRAL, position it on a hoist.

2. Release the fuel system pressure.

3. Disconnect the battery ground cable.

4. Drain the fuel from the fuel tank.

5. If equipped, remove the 6 bolts and the fuel tank shield. To install, tighten to 16 ft. lbs. (22 Nm).

6. For gasoline engines:

a. Loosen the hose clamp and disconnect the fuel tank filler pipe from the fuel tank.

b. Disconnect the fuel tank filler pipe vent tube quick connect coupling.

7. For diesel engines, loosen the 2 hose clamps and disconnect the fuel tank filler pipe and fuel tank filler pipe vent tube from the fuel tank.

8. Place a suitable lifting device under the fuel tank.

9. Remove the 4 fuel tank strap bolts and remove the 2 fuel tank straps. To install, tighten to 30 ft. lbs. (40 Nm).

10. Slightly lower the fuel tank.

11. For gasoline engines:

a. Disconnect the fuel vapor tube-to-Fuel Pump (FP) module quick connect coupling and the fuel supply tube-to- FP module quick connect coupling.

b. Disconnect the fuel vapor tube-to-fuel tank grade vent valve quick connect couplings.

12. For diesel engines:

a. Disconnect the fuel return tube-to-fuel level sensor quick connect coupling and the fuel supply tube-to-fuel level sensor quick connect coupling.

b. Remove the fuel vapor hose from the fuel tank grade vent valves.

c. Disconnect the fuel level sensor electrical connector.

13. Lower the fuel tank.

14. To install, reverse the removal procedure.

Aft of Axle

See Figure 287.

1. With the vehicle in NEUTRAL, position it on a hoist.

2. Release the fuel system pressure.

3. Disconnect the battery ground cable.

4. Drain the fuel from the fuel tank.

5. Loosen the 2 hose clamps and disconnect the fuel tank filler pipe and fuel tank filler pipe vent hose from the fuel tank.

6. For gasoline engines:

a. Disconnect the fuel supply tube-to-Fuel Pump (FP) module quick connect coupling.

b. Disconnect the fuel vapor tube-to-fuel tank grade vent valve quick connect coupling.

7. For diesel engines:

a. Disconnect the fuel supply tube-to-fuel level sensor quick connect coupling.

b. Disconnect the fuel return tube-to-fuel level sensor quick connect coupling.

8. Place a suitable lifting device under the fuel tank shield.

9. Remove the 4 bolts from the fuel tank shield. To install, tighten to 66 ft. lbs. (90 Nm).

10. Lower the fuel tank.

11. Remove the 2 nuts from the fuel tank straps and remove the fuel tank straps. To install, tighten to 59 ft. lbs. (80 Nm).

12. Remove the fuel tank from the fuel tank shield.

13. To install, reverse the removal procedure.

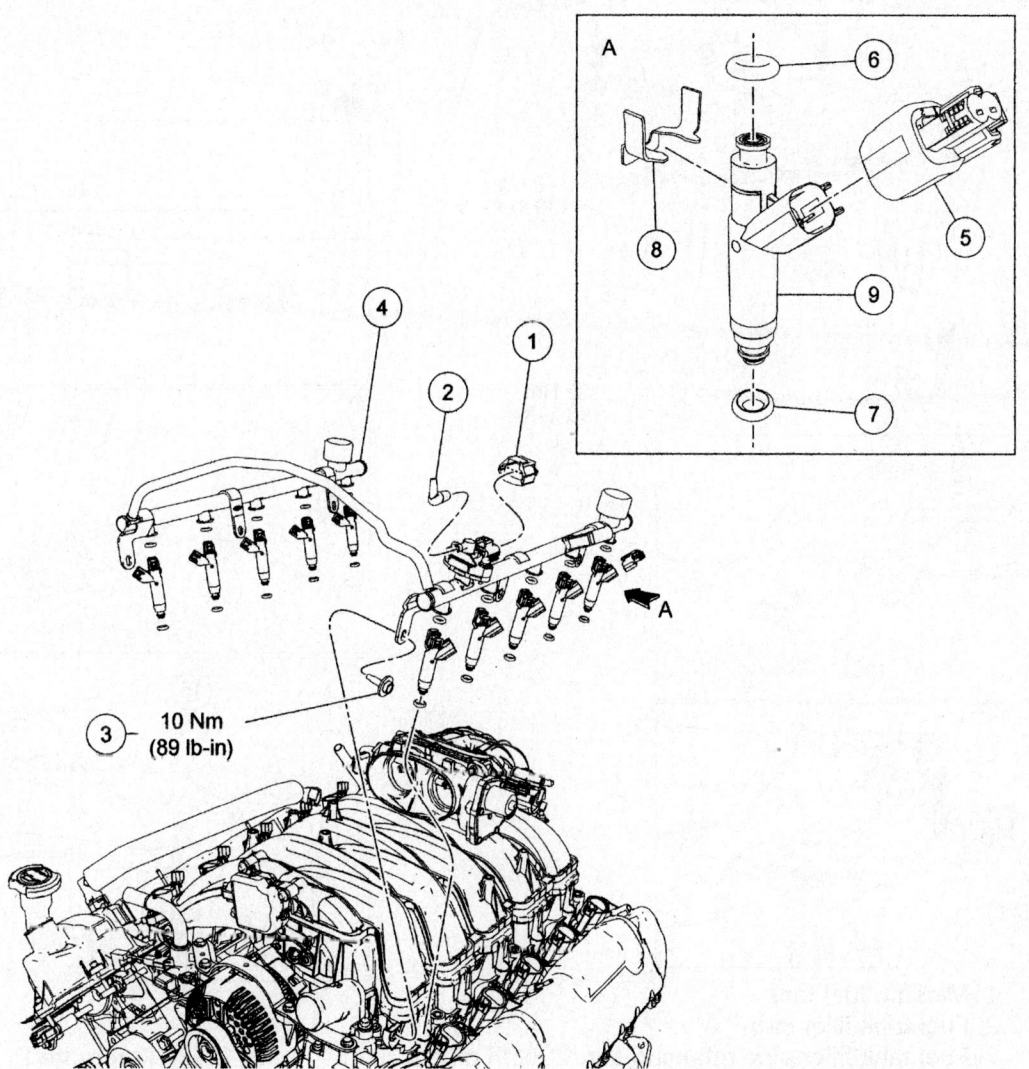

10 Nm
(89 lb-in)

1. Fuel rail pressure and temperature sensor electrical connector
2. Fuel rail pressure and temperature sensor vacuum hose
3. Fuel rail bolts (6 required)
4. Fuel rail
5. Fuel injector electrical connector (10 required)
6. Fuel injector-to-fuel rail O-ring (10 required)
7. Fuel injector-to-intake manifold O-ring (10 required)
8. Fuel injector-to-fuel rail locking clip (10 required)
9. Fuel injector (10 required)

06017-F150-G238

Fig. 284 Fuel rail and injectors—6.8L engine

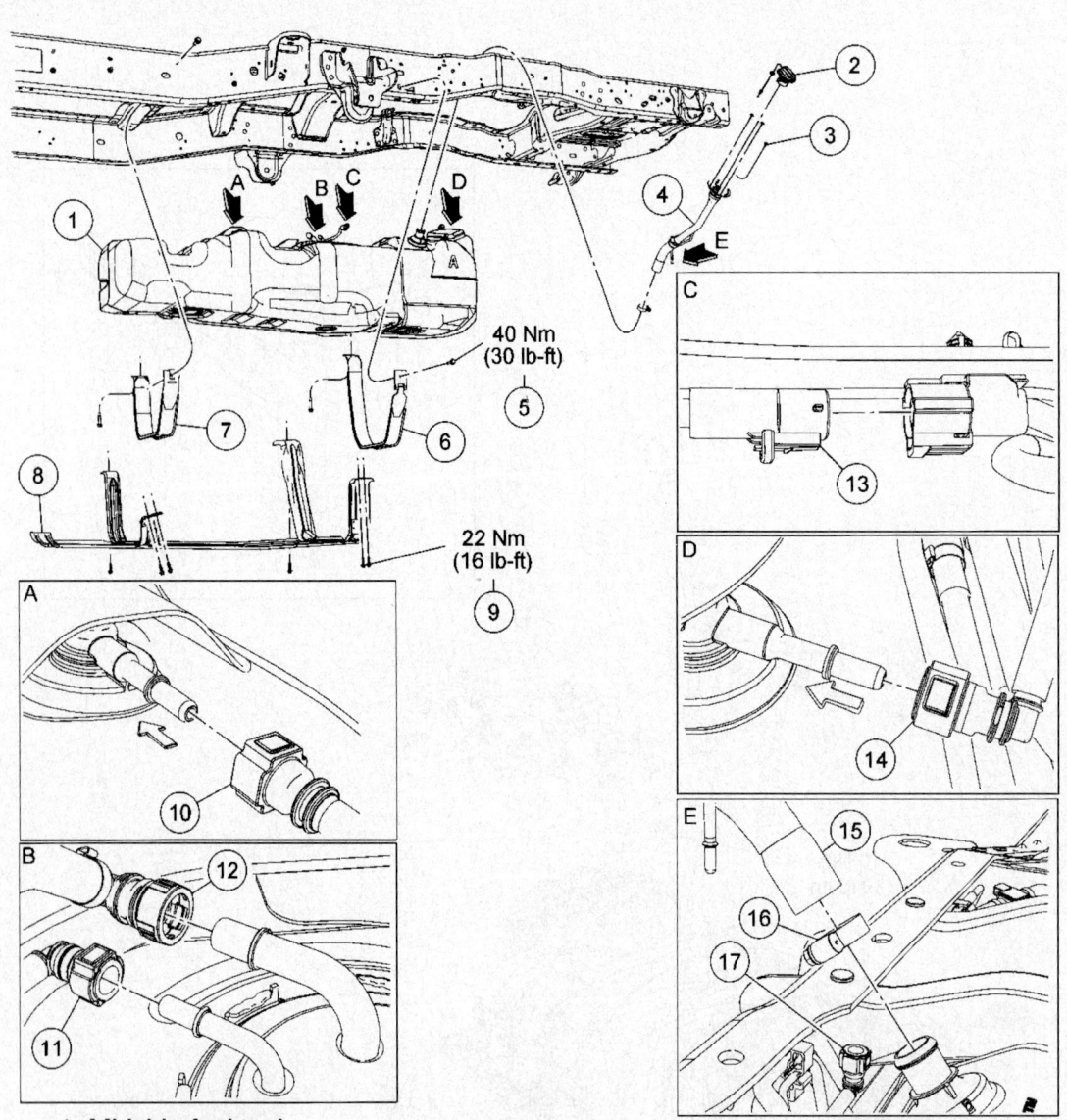

1. Midship fuel tank
2. Fuel tank filler cap
3. Fuel tank filler pipe retaining screw (with plastic inserts, early build) (3 required)
3. Fuel tank filler pipe retaining screw (without plastic inserts, late build) (3 required)
4. Fuel tank filler pipe assembly
5. Fuel tank strap bolt (4 required)
6. Rear fuel tank strap
7. Front fuel tank strap
8. Fuel tank shield
9. Fuel tank shield bolt (6 required)
10. Fuel vapor tube-to-fuel tank grade vent valve quick connect coupling
11. Fuel supply tube-to-Fuel Pump (FP) module quick connect coupling
12. Fuel vapor tube-to- FP module quick connect coupling
13. FP module electrical connector
14. Fuel vapor tube-to-fuel tank grade vent valve quick connect coupling
15. Fuel tank filler pipe
16. Fuel tank filler pipe-to-fuel tank hose clamp
17. Fuel vapor tube-to-fuel tank filler pipe vent tube quick connect coupling

36578_F250_G0098

Fig. 285 Exploded view of the fuel tank assembly—Midship—30 Gallon—Gasoline shown, diesel similar

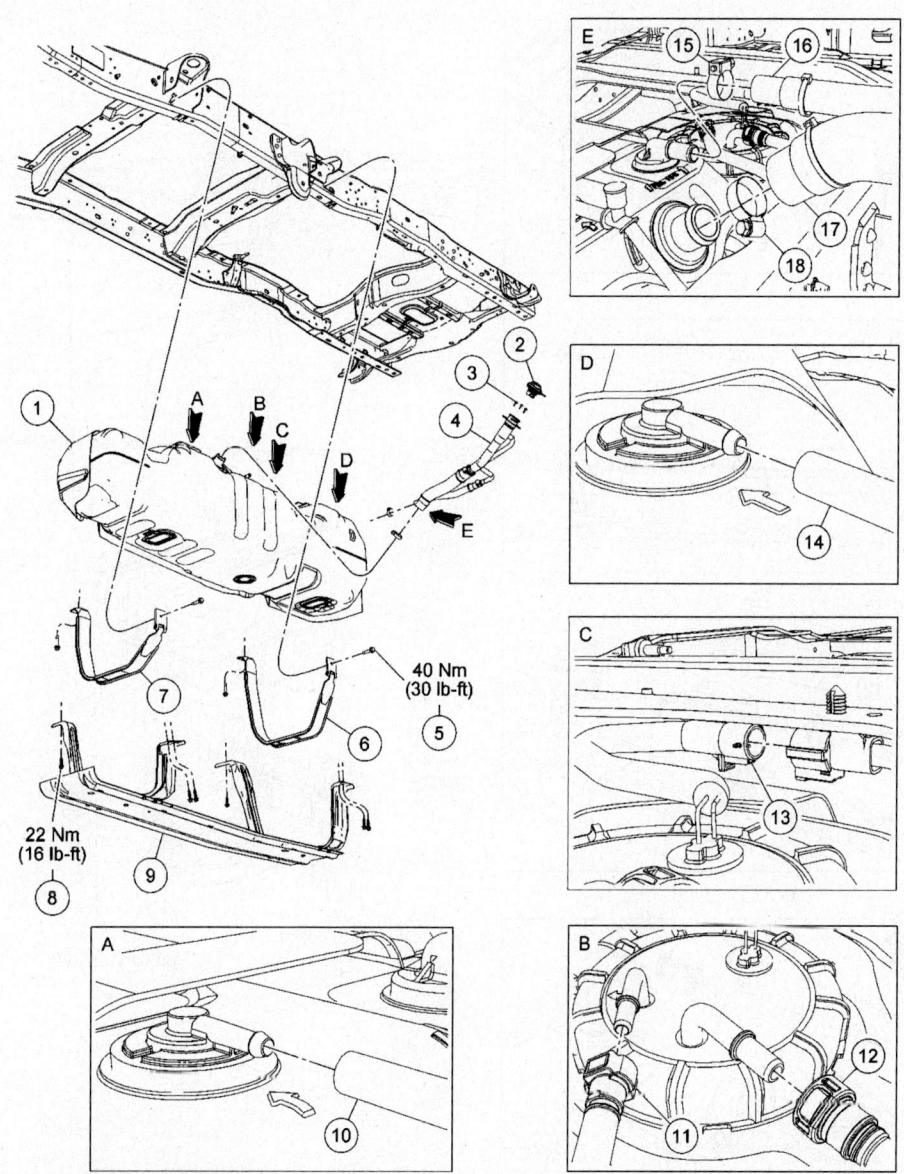

40 Nm
(30 lb-ft)

22 Nm
(16 lb-ft)

1. Midship fuel tank
2. Fuel tank filler cap
3. Fuel tank filler pipe retaining screw (with plastic inserts, early build) (3 required)
3. Fuel tank filler pipe retaining screw (without plastic inserts, late build) (3 required)
4. Fuel tank filler pipe assembly
5. Fuel tank strap bolt (4 required)
6. Rear fuel tank strap
7. Front fuel tank strap
8. Fuel tank shield bolt (6 required)
9. Fuel tank shield
10. Fuel vapor hose-to-fuel tank grade vent valve
11. Fuel return tube-to-fuel level sensor quick connect coupling
12. Fuel supply tube-to-fuel level sensor quick connect coupling
13. Fuel level sensor electrical connector
14. Fuel vapor hose-to-fuel tank grade vent valve
15. Fuel tank filler pipe vent hose-to-fuel tank hose clamp
16. Fuel tank filler pipe vent hose
17. Fuel tank filler pipe
18. Fuel tank filler pipe-to-fuel tank hose clamp

36578_F250_G0099

Fig. 286 Exploded view of the fuel tank assembly—Midship—38 Gallon—Diesel shown, gasoline similar

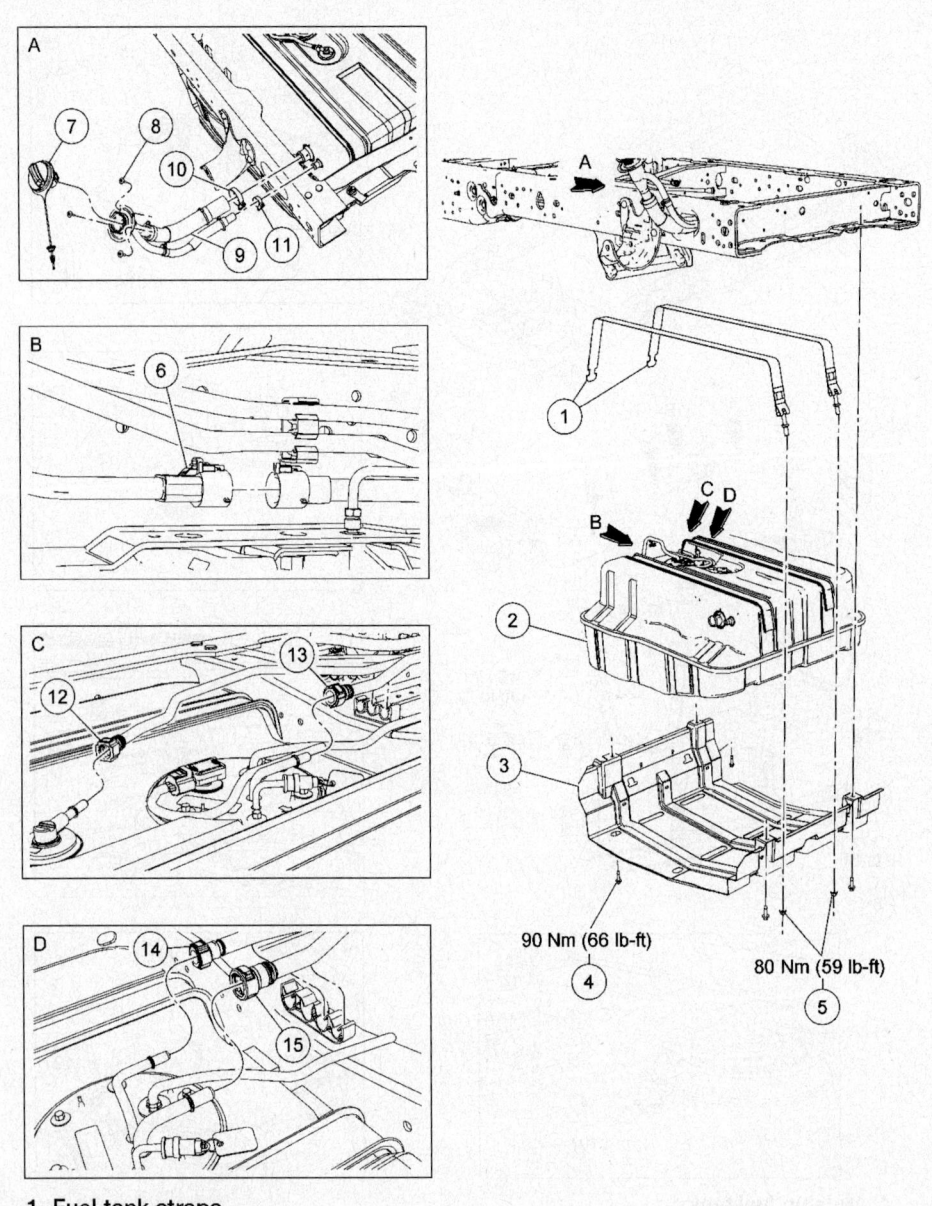

1. Fuel tank straps
2. Aft-of-axle fuel tank
3. Fuel tank shield
4. Fuel tank shield bolt (4 required)
5. Fuel tank strap nuts (2 required)
6. Fuel Pump (FP) module (gasoline engine)/fuel level sensor (diesel engine)
   electrical connector
7. Fuel tank filler cap
8. Fuel tank filler pipe retaining screw (with plastic inserts, early build) (3 required)
8. Fuel tank filler pipe retaining screw (without plastic inserts, late build) (3 required)
9. Fuel tank filler pipe assembly
10. Fuel tank filler pipe hose clamp
11. Fuel tank filler pipe vent hose clamp
12. Fuel vapor tube-to-fuel tank grade vent valve quick connect
    coupling (gasoline engine)
13. Fuel supply tube-to- FP module quick connect coupling (gasoline engine)
14. Fuel return tube-to-fuel level sensor quick connect coupling (diesel engine)
15. Fuel supply tube-to-fuel level sensor quick connect coupling (diesel engine)

36578_F250_G0100

Fig. 287 Exploded view of the fuel tank assembly—Aft of axle—40 Gallon

Auxiliary

See Figure 287.

➡**Some auxiliary tanks are stand alone applications and some are dual tank applications.**

1. With the vehicle in NEUTRAL, position it on a hoist.
2. Release the fuel system pressure.
3. Disconnect the battery ground cable.
4. Drain the fuel from the fuel tank.
5. Loosen the 2 hose clamps and disconnect the fuel tank filler pipe and the fuel tank filler pipe vent hose from the fuel tank.
6. For gasoline engines:
    a. Disconnect the fuel vapor tube-to-Fuel Pump (FP) module quick connect coupling and the fuel supply tube-to- FP module quick connect coupling.
    b. Disconnect the fuel vapor tube-to-fuel tank grade vent valve quick connect couplings.
    c. For diesel engine:
    d. Disconnect the fuel return tube-to-fuel level sensor quick connect coupling and fuel supply tube-to-fuel level sensor quick connect coupling.
7. Remove the 4 bolts and fuel tank heat shield. To install, tighten to 16 ft. lbs. (22 Nm).
8. Place a suitable lifting device under the fuel tank.
9. Remove 2 bolts and carefully position the 2 fuel tank straps aside. To install, tighten to 30 ft. lbs. (40 Nm).
10. Lower the fuel tank.
11. To install, reverse the removal procedure.

IDLE SPEED

Idle speed is maintained by the Powertrain Control Module (PCM). No adjustment is necessary or possible.

THROTTLE BODY

REMOVAL & INSTALLATION

5.4L Engine

See Figure 288.

➡**The throttle body bore and plate area have a special coating and cannot be cleaned.**

1. Before servicing the vehicle, refer to the precautions in the beginning of this section.
2. Disconnect the battery ground cable.
3. Remove the air cleaner and air cleaner intake pipe.
4. Disconnect the electronic throttle control electrical connector.

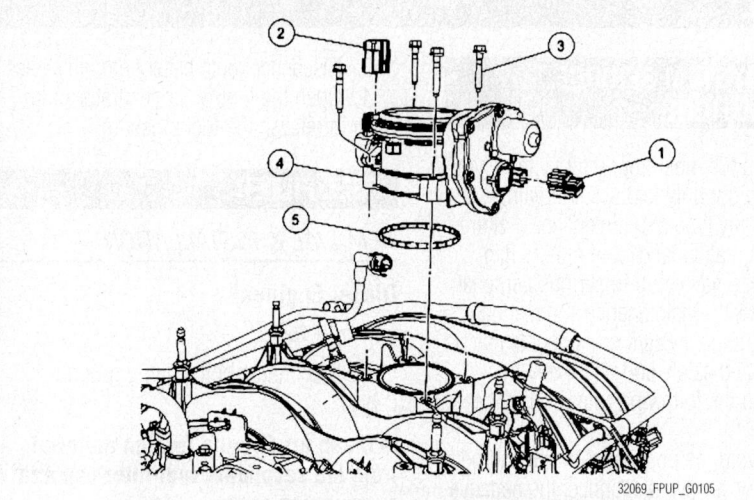

Fig. 288 1. Electronic throttle control electrical connector
2. Throttle position (TP) sensor electrical connector
3. Throttle body (TB) bolts
4. TB
5. TB O-ring seal Throttle body and related parts—5.4L engine

5. Disconnect the throttle position (TP) sensor electrical connector.
6. Remove the 4 throttle body (TB) bolts and the TB and discard the TB O-ring seal.
7. To install, reverse the removal procedure. To install, tighten to 9 Nm (80 inch lbs.). Tighten an additional 90 degrees.

6.8L Engine

See Figure 289.

1. Before servicing the vehicle, refer to the precautions in the beginning of this section.

2. Disconnect the battery ground cable.
3. Remove the air cleaner outlet tube.
4. Disconnect the electronic throttle control electrical connector.
5. Disconnect the TP sensor electrical connector.
6. Remove the 4 throttle body bolts and the throttle body and discard the throttle body gasket.
7. To install, reverse the removal procedure. To install, tighten to 9 Nm (80 inch lbs.). Tighten an additional 90 degrees.

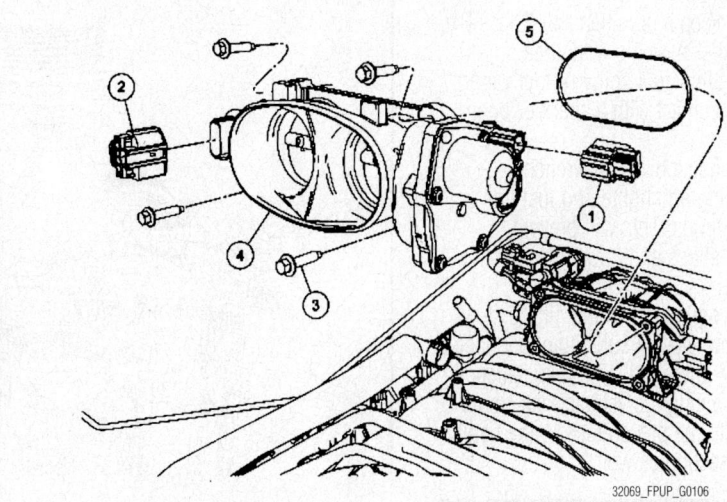

Fig. 289 1. Electronic throttle control electrical connector
2. Throttle position (TP) sensor electrical connector
3. Throttle body bolts
4. Throttle body
5. Throttle body gasket Throttle body and related parts—6.8L engine

FUEL SYSTEM SERVICE PRECAUTIONS

Safety is the most important factor when performing not only fuel system maintenance but any type of maintenance. Failure to conduct maintenance and repairs in a safe manner may result in serious personal injury or death. Maintenance and testing of the vehicle's fuel system components can be accomplished safely and effectively by adhering to the following rules and guidelines.

• To avoid the possibility of fire and personal injury, always disconnect the negative battery cable unless the repair or test procedure requires that battery voltage be applied.

• Always relieve the fuel system pressure prior to disconnecting any fuel system component (injector, fuel rail, pressure regulator, etc.), fitting or fuel line connection. Exercise extreme caution whenever relieving fuel system pressure to avoid exposing skin, face and eyes to fuel spray. Please be advised that fuel under pressure may penetrate the skin or any part of the body that it contacts.

• Always place a shop towel or cloth around the fitting or connection prior to loosening to absorb any excess fuel due to spillage. Ensure that all fuel spillage (should it occur) is quickly removed from engine surfaces. Ensure that all fuel soaked cloths or towels are deposited into a suitable waste container.

• Always keep a dry chemical (Class B) fire extinguisher near the work area.

• Do not allow fuel spray or fuel vapors to come into contact with a spark or open flame.

• Always use a back-up wrench when loosening and tightening fuel line connection fittings. This will prevent unnecessary stress and torsion to fuel line piping.

• Always replace worn fuel fitting O-rings with new. Do not substitute fuel hose or equivalent where fuel pipe is installed.

Before servicing the vehicle, make sure to also refer to the precautions in the beginning of this section as well.

RELIEVING FUEL SYSTEM PRESSURE

1. Before servicing the vehicle, refer to the Precautions Section.
2. Raise and safely support the vehicle.

3. Disconnect both battery ground cables.
4. Open the fuel/water separator drain valve to release the fuel pressure.

FUEL FILTER

REMOVAL & INSTALLATION

Diesel Engines
See Figure 290.

1. Disconnect both battery ground cables.

➡**Clean all dirt and foreign material from the secondary fuel filter cap and surrounding area.**

2. Remove the secondary fuel filter cap by turning the cap counterclockwise.
3. Remove the secondary fuel filter. Discard the secondary fuel filter.
4. Remove the O-ring seal from the secondary fuel filter cap. Discard the O-ring seal.

To install:
5. Carefully clean all mating surfaces.
6. Install a new O-ring seal onto the secondary fuel filter cap.

7. Install a new secondary fuel filter into the secondary fuel filter housing.

➡**Apply clean engine oil to the O-ring seal.**

8. Slowly install the secondary fuel filter cap allowing the fuel to soak into the secondary fuel filter until it contacts the secondary fuel filter housing.
9. Tighten the secondary fuel filter cap. Tighten to 20 ft. lbs. (27 Nm).
10. Bleed the low pressure fuel system.

DRAINING WATER FROM THE SYSTEM
See Figure 291.

1. Before servicing the vehicle, refer to the precautions in the beginning of this section.
2. With the vehicle in NEUTRAL, position it on a hoist.
3. Disconnect both battery ground cables.
4. Drain the fuel conditioning module by removing the drain plug.
5. Reinstall the drain plug once the fuel conditioning module is drained.

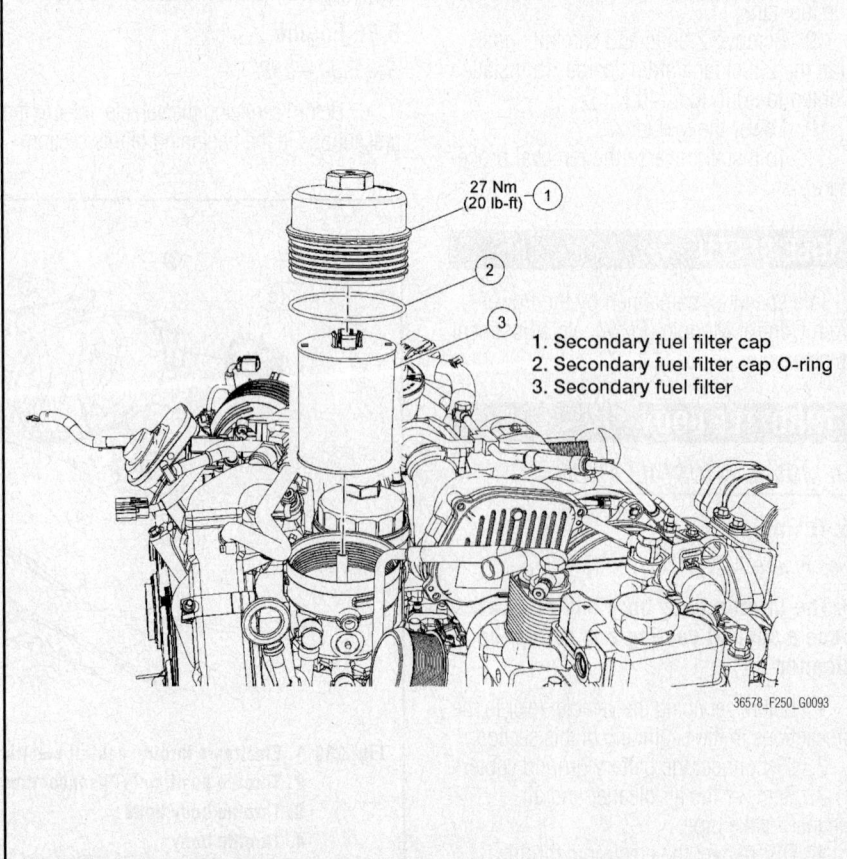

27 Nm
(20 lb-ft) — ①
②
③
1. Secondary fuel filter cap
2. Secondary fuel filter cap O-ring
3. Secondary fuel filter

36578_F250_G0093

Fig. 290 Exploded view of the Secondary fuel filter—6.4L Diesel engine

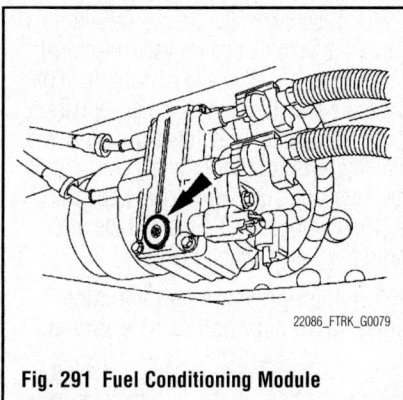

22086_FTRK_G0079

Fig. 291 Fuel Conditioning Module drain plug

FUEL LEVEL SENSOR

LOCATION

See Figures 292 and 293.

REMOVAL & INSTALLATION

See Figures 292 and 293.

➡**This procedure is for diesel applications only.**

➡**The fuel tank must be drained completely. Upon removal of the fuel level sensor, the tank must be inspected for contamination.**

1. Remove the fuel tank. For additional information, refer to Fuel Tank —Aft of Axle or Fuel Tank— Auxiliary in this section.

➡**Clean the fuel tank of any dirt or for-**

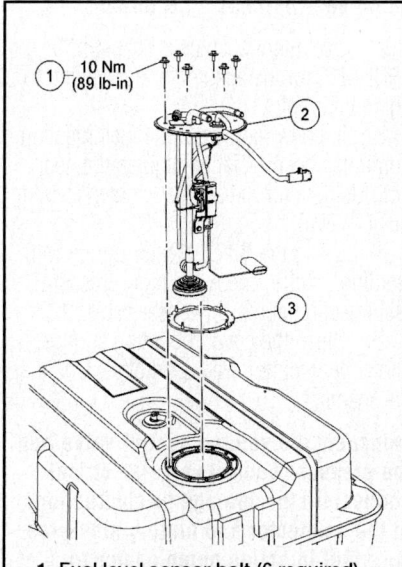

1. Fuel level sensor bolt (6 required)
2. Fuel level sensor
3. Fuel level sensor gasket

36578_F250_G0094

Fig. 292 Exploded view of the fuel level sensor—Steel fuel tank—Diesel

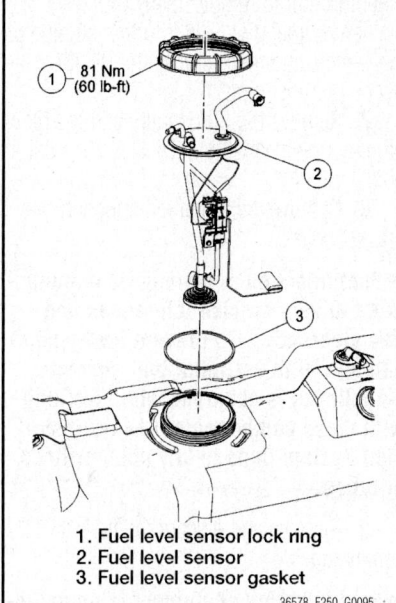

1. Fuel level sensor lock ring
2. Fuel level sensor
3. Fuel level sensor gasket

36578_F250_G0095

Fig. 293 Exploded view of the fuel level sensor—Plastic fuel tank—Diesel

eign material before servicing the fuel level sensor. In extreme dirt or dusty conditions it may be necessary to wash the fuel tank using a water hose. Before removing the fuel level sensor, make sure that there is no residual dirt or foreign material around the fuel level sensor flange. If dirt or foreign material enter the fuel tank, damage to the fuel level sensor or other fuel system components may occur.

2. Clean the area around the fuel level sensor mounting flange.

➡**Mark the orientation of the fuel level sensor on the fuel tank to aid in installation.**

3. On steel fuel tanks, remove the 6 bolts from the fuel level sensor.

4. On plastic fuel tanks, using the Fuel Tank Sender Unit Socket, remove the fuel level sensor lock ring. Tighten to 60 ft. lbs. (81 Nm) upon installation.

➡**The fuel level sensor must be handled carefully to avoid damage to the float arm.**

5. Completely remove the fuel level sensor from the fuel tank.

➡**Inspect the surfaces of the fuel level sensor flange and fuel tank gasket contact surfaces. Do not polish or adjust the gasket contact area of the fuel tank flange or the fuel tank. Install a new fuel level sensor or fuel tank if the gas-**

ket contact area is bent, scratched or corroded or fuel leakage could occur causing vehicle damage.

➡**Make sure to install a new fuel level sensor gasket or fuel leakage could occur causing vehicle damage.**

6. Remove and discard the fuel level sensor gasket.

7. To install, reverse the removal procedure.

8. Make sure the fuel level sensor is installed in the same orientation as the original

FUEL SUPPLY PUMP

REMOVAL & INSTALLATION

The fuel pump is located in the Fuel Conditioning Module.

FUEL SYSTEM PURGING

BLEEDING

Fuel pressure in the cylinder head fuel galleries is controlled by a fuel pressure regulator. The fixed orifice is an air bleed. It is the highest point in the fuel system. It allows the air behind the fuel pressure regulator to be vented to the fuel tank rather than ingested in the fuel galleries. The fuel pressure regulator contains a spring-loaded poppet valve, which opens to allow excess fuel to return to the fuel-conditioning module.

GLOW PLUGS

REMOVAL & INSTALLATION

See Figure 294.

1. Before servicing the vehicle, refer to the Precautions Section.

2. Disconnect the glow plug electrical connector.

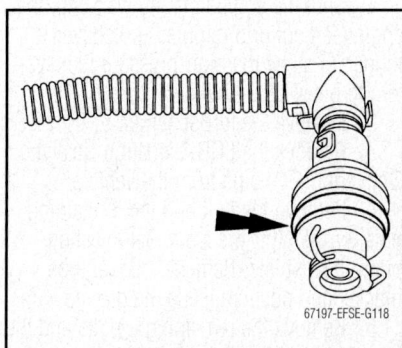

67197-EFSE-G118

Fig. 294 Apply clean engine oil to the O-rings—late build 6.0L Diesel Engines

❋❋ WARNING

Do not pull on the wiring to remove the glow plug connector or damage may occur.

3. Remove the glow plug harness.

➡**If coolant residue is found on the glow plug, a new glow plug sleeve may have to be installed.**

4. Remove the glow plug.

To install:

5. Install the glow plug. Torque to 14 ft. lbs. (19 Nm).
6. Clean and inspect the O-rings and install new if necessary.
7. Apply clean engine oil to the O-rings.
8. Install the glow plug harness.
9. Connect the glow plug electrical connector.

INJECTION LINES

REMOVAL & INSTALLATION

Refer to Injectors in this section.

INJECTION PUMP

REMOVAL & INSTALLATION

See Figure 295.

➡**It is recommended that this component be serviced with the vehicle body removed.**

❋❋ WARNING

Do not work on the fuel system until the pressure has been released and the engine has cooled. Fuel in the high-pressure fuel system is hot and under very high pressure. High-pressure fuel may cause cuts and contact with hot fuel may cause burns. Failure to follow these instructions may result in serious personal injury.

1. Shut the engine off and wait until the engine is cool or 5 minutes, whichever is longer, to allow the high-pressure fuel system to bleed off and the fuel to cool.
2. Remove the turbocharger.
3. Remove the EGR-Oxidation Catalytic Converter (OC) pipe from the vehicle.
4. Remove the bolt and the 5 retaining nuts for the high-pressure fuel injection pump heat shield. Remove the fuel tube bracket and position aside the ground wire.
5. Remove the remaining 2 bolts and the high-pressure fuel injection pump heat shield.
6. Remove the RH turbocharger inlet

pipe. In order to remove the RH turbocharger inlet pipe, roll it to the left side of the vehicle and then remove the RH turbocharger inlet pipe.

7. Remove the 3 pushnuts and the glow plug module heat shield. Discard the pushnuts.
8. Remove the 2 fuel rail supply tube bracket bolts.

➡**Fuel injection equipment is manufactured to very precise tolerances and fine clearances. To prevent fuel system damage, it is essential that absolute cleanliness is observed when working with these components. Always install Fuel System Caps to any open orifices or tubes.**

9. Remove and discard the fuel rail supply tubes.

➡**Fuel injection equipment is manufactured to very precise tolerances and fine clearances. To prevent fuel system damage, it is essential that absolute cleanliness is observed when working with these components. Always install Fuel System Caps to any open orifices or tubes.**

10. Disconnect the fuel injector return tube fitting from the check valve.
11. Remove the 2 high-pressure fuel injection pump supply tube bracket nuts.

➡**Fuel injection equipment is manufactured to very precise tolerances and fine clearances. To prevent fuel system damage, it is essential that absolute cleanliness is observed when working with these components. Always install Fuel System Caps to any open orifices or tubes.**

➡**Use a back-up wrench to prevent the fittings in the high-pressure fuel pump from turning.**

12. Remove the nuts and the copper sealing washers for the high-pressure fuel injection pump. Remove the high-pressure fuel injection pump supply tube and fuel injection pump-to-cooler return tube. Discard the copper sealing washers.
13. Disconnect the high-pressure fuel injection pump electrical connector.
14. Remove the 5 bolts and the high-pressure fuel injection pump cover.
15. Remove and discard the press-in-place gasket from the high-pressure pump cover.

➡**Use a thin gasket scraper to separate the gasket from the crankcase.**

16. Disconnect the pressure control valve and volume control valve electrical connectors. Remove and discard the high-pressure fuel injection pump cover gasket.
17. Using the Dial Indicator Gauge with Holding Fixture, check the high-pressure fuel injection pump drive gear backlash.
18. Remove the 3 bolts and the high-pressure fuel injection pump.

➡**The high-pressure fuel injection pump drive gear bolt is a LH thread.**

19. If a new pump is being installed, remove the bolt, washer and the high-pressure fuel injection pump gear.

To install:

➡ **The protruding hub of the high-pressure fuel injection pump drive gear must be facing the high-pressure fuel injection pump. Failure to install the gear correctly will result in engine damage.**

➡**The high-pressure fuel injection pump drive gear bolt is a LH thread.**

➡**The high-pressure fuel injection pump gear bolt will not be tightened at this time.**

➡**If a new pump is being installed, install the high-pressure fuel injection pump drive gear, washer and bolt.**

20. Install the high-pressure fuel injection pump and 3 bolts. Tighten to 45 ft. lbs. (61 Nm).

➡**The high-pressure fuel injection pump gear bolt has a LH thread.**

21. Use a tool such as a Snap-On® FRDHM15 torque adapter, or equivalent, to tighten the bolt.
22. If a new high-pressure fuel injection pump has been installed, tighten the gear bolt. Using a torque adapter, tighten to 57 ft. lbs. (77 Nm).
23. Using the Dial Indicator Gauge with Holding Fixture, check the high-pressure fuel injection pump drive gear backlash.
24. Clean the cover mounting surface and apply a dime-sized bead of sealant at the seams.

➡**Inspect the volume control valve and the pressure control valve electrical connectors for damage or obstructions at the connector and mating high-pressure fuel injection pump connector. Verify that the connectors are completely latched to the valve housings or engine damage may occur.**

25. Install a new high-pressure fuel injection pump cover gasket. Connect the

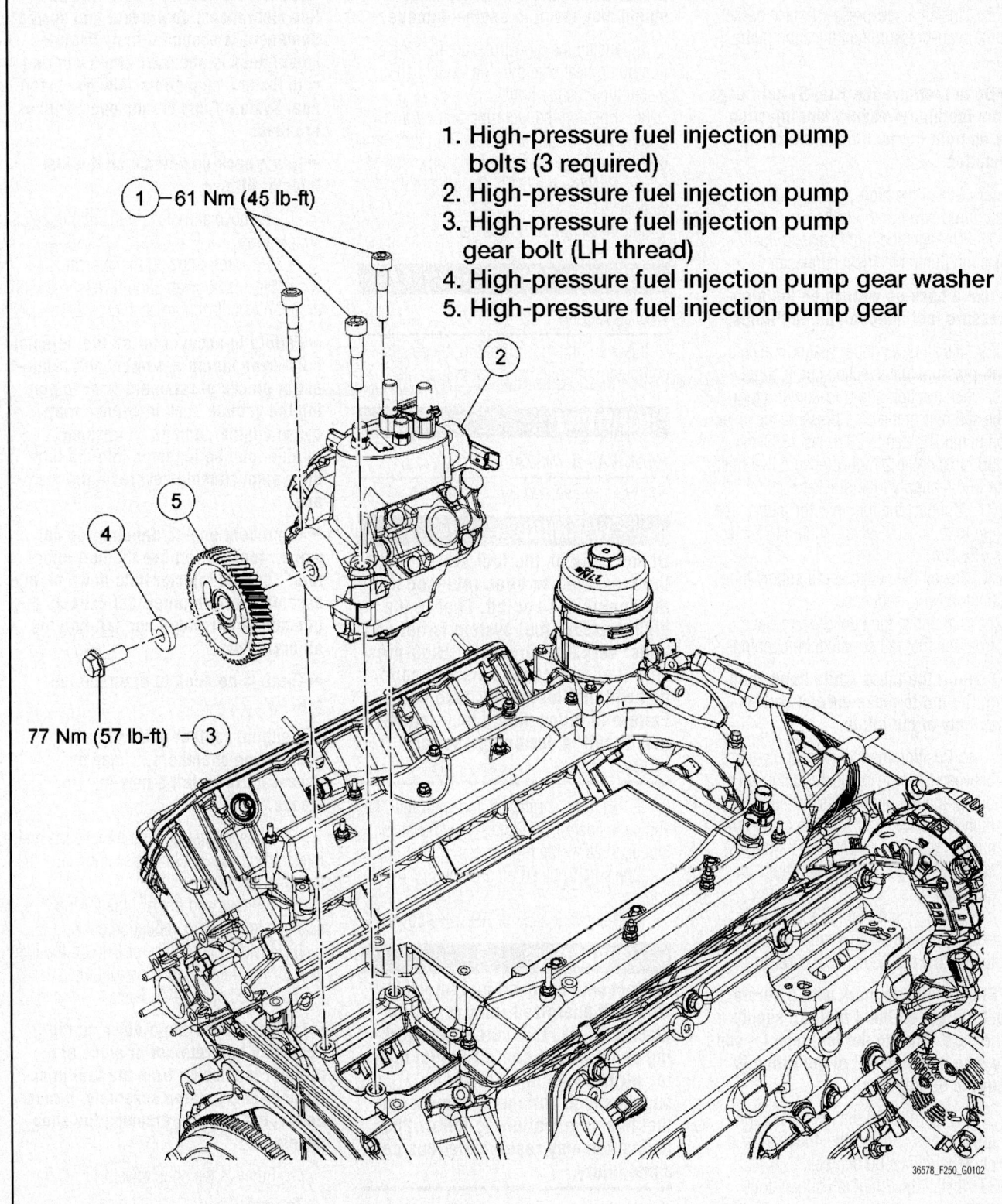

1. High-pressure fuel injection pump bolts (3 required)
2. High-pressure fuel injection pump
3. High-pressure fuel injection pump gear bolt (LH thread)
4. High-pressure fuel injection pump gear washer
5. High-pressure fuel injection pump gear

① — 61 Nm (45 lb-ft)

77 Nm (57 lb-ft) — ③

36578_F250_G0102

Fig. 295 Exploded view of the high pressure fuel injection pump

pressure control valve and volume control valve electrical connectors.

26. Install a new press-in-place gasket in the high-pressure fuel injection pump cover.

➡**Do not remove the Fuel System Caps from the high-pressure fuel injection pump until the fuel tubes are being installed.**

27. Install the high-pressure fuel injection pump cover and 5 bolts.

28. Connect the high-pressure fuel injection pump electrical connector.

➡**Use a back-up wrench on the high-pressure fuel injection pump fittings.**

29. Install new copper sealing washers, high-pressure fuel injection pump supply tube, fuel injection pump-to-cooler return tube and nuts at the high-pressure fuel injection pump. Tighten to 28 ft. lbs. (38 Nm).

30. Install the 2 high-pressure fuel injection pump supply tube bracket nuts.

31. Connect the fuel injector return tube fitting to the check valve. Tighten to 21 ft. lbs. (28 Nm).

32. Install the new fuel rail supply tubes in the following sequence:

a. Remove the Fuel System Caps from the fuel rail supply tube openings.

➡**Support the tubes while hand snugging the nut to make sure of correct assembly of the joints.**

b. Position the fuel rail supply tubes between the high-pressure fuel injection pump and the high-pressure fuel rail. Fully hand start and seat the 4 fuel rail supply tube fittings onto the high-pressure fuel injection pump and high-pressure fuel rails.

c. Snug the 4 fuel rail tube fittings.

d. Pre-tighten the 4 fuel rail supply tube fitting to 106 inch lbs. (12 Nm).

➡**Place a visible mark with a permanent marker on the 4 fuel rail supply tube nuts. Turning the fuel injector supply tube nuts one flat of the fitting is equal to 60 degrees.**

e. Final-tighten the fuel rail supply tube fittings. Tighten the 4 fuel rail supply tube fittings 60 degrees.

33. Install the 2 fuel rail supply tube bracket bolts.

➡**Use a socket to aid in installing the retainers. Install the glow plug module heat shield and 3 new pushnuts.**

34. Position the RH turbocharger inlet pipe in the vehicle.

➡**Failure to correctly install the high-pressure fuel injection pump heat shield may result in engine damage.**

35. Install the high-pressure fuel injection pump heat shield in the vehicle and install the 2 center bolts.

36. Position the fuel tube bracket and ground wire. Install the 5 retaining nuts and bolt for the high-pressure fuel pump shield.

37. Position the EGR- OC pipe in the vehicle.

38. Install the turbocharger.

INJECTION TIMING

ADJUSTMENT

Injection timing for the 6.4L diesels is computer controlled and not adjustable.

INJECTORS

REMOVAL & INSTALLATION
See Figures 296 and 297.

✳✳ WARNING

Do not work on the fuel system until the pressure has been released and the engine has cooled. Fuel in the high-pressure fuel system is hot and under very high pressure. High-pressure fuel may cause cuts and contact with hot fuel may cause burns. Failure to follow these instructions may result in serious personal injury.

1. Shut the engine off and wait until the engine is cool or 5 minutes, whichever is longer, to allow the high-pressure fuel system pressure to bleed off and the fuel to cool.

2. Remove the LH or RH valve cover.

✳✳ WARNING

Contact with exposed fuel injector wiring, if energized, may result in electric shock. Use care when working on or around energized fuel injector wiring. Fuel injector wiring supplies high voltage to operate the fuel injectors. Failure to follow this instruction may result in serious personal injury.

3. Make sure the ignition switch is in the OFF position.

4. Using the Fuel Injector Connector Disconnect Tool, disconnect the fuel injector electrical connector.

5. If necessary, disconnect the Fuel Rail Pressure (FRP) sensor electrical connector.

➡**Fuel injection equipment is manufactured to very precise tolerances and fine clearances. To prevent fuel system damage it is essential that absolute cleanliness is observed when working with these components. Always install Fuel System Caps on any open orifices or tubes.**

➡**Use a back-up wrench on the fuel injector fittings.**

6. Remove and discard the fuel injector supply tube.

7. Prior to removing the injector assembly, insert clean shop towels in the oil drain holes adjacent to each glow plug.

➡**Failure to account for all fuel injector hold-down clamp assembly bolt retainers or pieces of retainers prior to placing the vehicle back in service may cause engine damage. A missing retainer can be ingested into the lube oil system causing severe engine damage.**

➡**To prevent engine damage, do not use air tools to remove the fuel injectors. The fuel injector hold-down clamp assembly bolt retainer that extracts the injector can dislodge and fall into the oil drain hole.**

➡**There is no need to drain the fuel rail.**

➡**If engine coolant is found in the combustion chambers, it may be necessary to install a new injector sleeve.**

8. Loosen the bolt, and remove the fuel injector hold-down clamp assembly and the fuel injector.

9. Remove and discard the O-ring seal and soft steel combustion gasket.

10. Install a Fuel Injector Cup on the fuel injector nozzle and store the fuel injector in the Fuel Injector Holding Rack.

➡**f a fuel injector hold-down clamp assembly bolt retainer or piece of a retainer is missing from the fuel injector hold-down clamp assembly, it must be located prior to removing the shop towels.**

11. Remove the shop towels.

To install:

➡**Lubricate the fuel injector and O-ring seal with clean engine oil.**

12. Install a new O-ring seal and a soft steel combustion gasket on the fuel injector. Make sure the bead on the soft steel

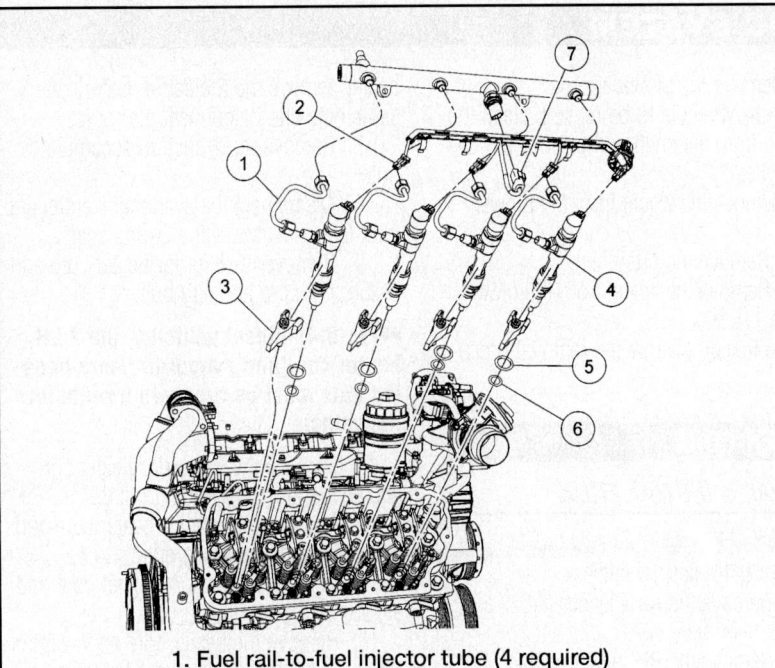

1. Fuel rail-to-fuel injector tube (4 required)
2. Fuel injector electrical connector
3. Fuel injector hold-down clamp assembly (4 required)
4. Fuel injector (4 required)
5. Fuel injector O-ring seal (4 required)
6. Combustion gasket (4 required)
7. Fuel Rail Pressure (FRP) sensor electrical connector

36578_F250_G0103

Fig. 296 Exploded view of the RH fuel injectors

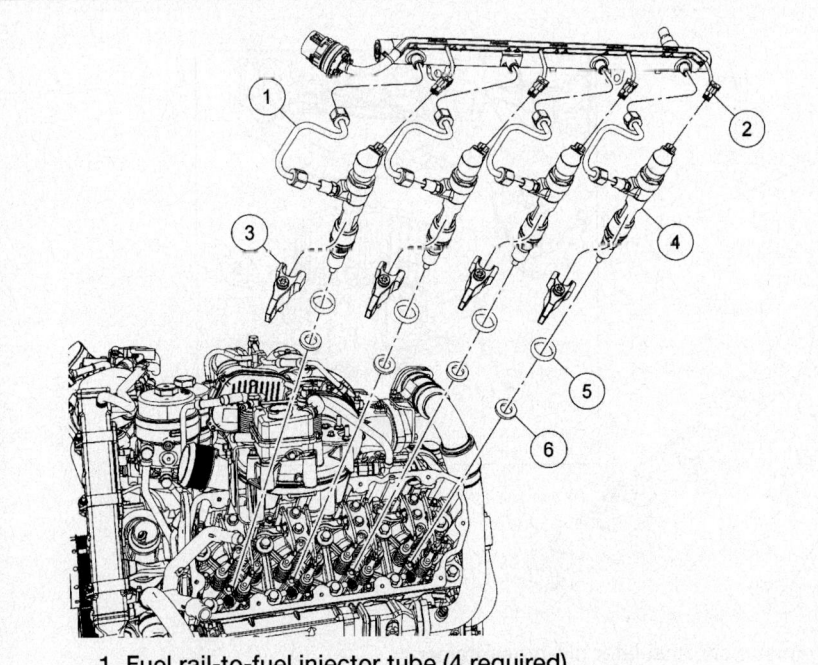

1. Fuel rail-to-fuel injector tube (4 required)
2. Fuel injector electrical connector
3. Fuel injector hold-down clamp assembly (4 required)
4. Fuel injector (4 required)
5. Fuel injector O-ring seal
6. Combustion gasket

36578_F250_G0104

Fig. 297 Exploded view of the LH fuel injectors

combustion gasket is facing the cylinder head.

➡ **Failure to tighten the injector correctly can lead to engine failure.**

➡ **To prevent engine damage, do not use air tools to install the fuel injectors. The fuel injector hold-down clamp bolt retainer that extracts the injector can dislodge and fall into the oil drain hole.**

➡ **If the fuel injector hold-down clamp assembly bolt retainer is damaged or missing, a new fuel injector hold-down clamp assembly must be installed, or the clamp assembly will not be able to remove the fuel injector.**

13. Install the fuel injector, the fuel injector hold-down clamp assembly and the bolt.

➡ **Use a back-up wrench on the fuel injector fittings.**

14. Install the new fuel injector supply tube in the following sequence:

a. Remove the Fuel System Caps from the high-pressure fuel rail and the fuel injector one at a time prior to assembly of each tube.

b. Position the new fuel injector supply tube between the high-pressure fuel rail and fuel injectors and fully hand-start and seat the tube fittings onto the mating high-pressure fuel rail and fuel injector high-pressure connectors. Snug the fuel injector supply tube fittings using the inside-out step sequence (the 2 inside tubes then the 2 outside tubes).

c. Tighten to 18 inch lbs. (2 Nm).

d. Tighten the fuel injector hold-down clamp bolt. Tighten to 38 Nm (28 lb-ft).

➡ **Pre-tighten the fuel injector fitting first, then the fuel rail fitting.**

e. Pre-tighten the fuel injector supply tube fittings. Using a torque adapter, tighten to 12 Nm (106 lb-in).

➡ **Place a visible mark with a permanent marker on the high-pressure fuel rail and fuel injector threaded connection. Turning the tube fittings one flat of the nut is equal to 60 degrees.**

f. Final tighten the fuel injector supply tube fittings. Tighten the fittings 60 degrees.

15. If necessary, connect the FRP sensor electrical connector.

16. Connect the fuel injector electrical connector.

17. Install the LH or RH valve cover.

18. Bleed the high-pressure fuel system.

HEATING & AIR CONDITIONING SYSTEM

BLOWER MOTOR

REMOVAL & INSTALLATION

See Figure 298.

➡**The blower motor vent tube must be completely removed from the blower motor before it can be rotated and disengaged from the heater core and evaporator core housing.**

1. Remove the RH lower instrument panel insulator.
2. Remove the RH lower A-pillar junction box trim cover.

➡**The carpet below the blower motor must be positioned aside to access the dash panel insulator.**

3. Position the dash panel insulator below the blower motor aside.
4. Detach the 2 blower motor vent tube clips and remove the vent tube.
5. Disconnect the blower motor electrical connector.
6. Rotate the blower motor counterclockwise to disengage it from the heater core and evaporator core housing.

7. Remove the blower motor.
8. If the wheel is to be reused, clean the corrosion from the shaft end prior to removing the wheel.
9. Remove the wheel from the blower motor:
   a. Remove the push clip.
   b. Remove the wheel from the blower motor.
10. To install, reverse the removal procedure

HEATER CORE

REMOVAL & INSTALLATION

See Figure 299.

1. For 6.4L diesel vehicles
   a. Remove the Air Cleaner (ACL) and ACL outlet tube.
   b. Remove the RH fender splash shield.
2. Recover the refrigerant.
3. Drain the engine coolant.
4. Remove the instrument panel.
5. Disconnect the heater hose quick disconnect fittings at the heater core.
6. Vehicles with electric auxiliary

heater, remove the 2 electric heater battery cable nuts and disconnect the cables.
7. Remove the 2 suction accumulator nuts.
8. Disconnect the evaporator outlet and inlet fittings. Discard the O-ring seals.
9. Remove the exterior heater core and evaporator core housing bolt.

➡**For 6.4L diesel vehicles, the 2 LH heater core and evaporator core housing nuts must be removed from below the vehicle.**

10. Remove the 3 exterior heater core and evaporator core housing nuts.
11. Remove the interior heater core and evaporator core housing nut.
12. Remove the interior heater core and evaporator core housing bolt.
13. Remove the heater core and evaporator core housing. Remove the heater tube dash panel seal. Remove the heater core bracket screw.
14. Vehicles with electric auxiliary heater:
   a. Disconnect the electric auxiliary heater battery cable connectors from the auxiliary heater.
   b. Detach the electric auxiliary heater

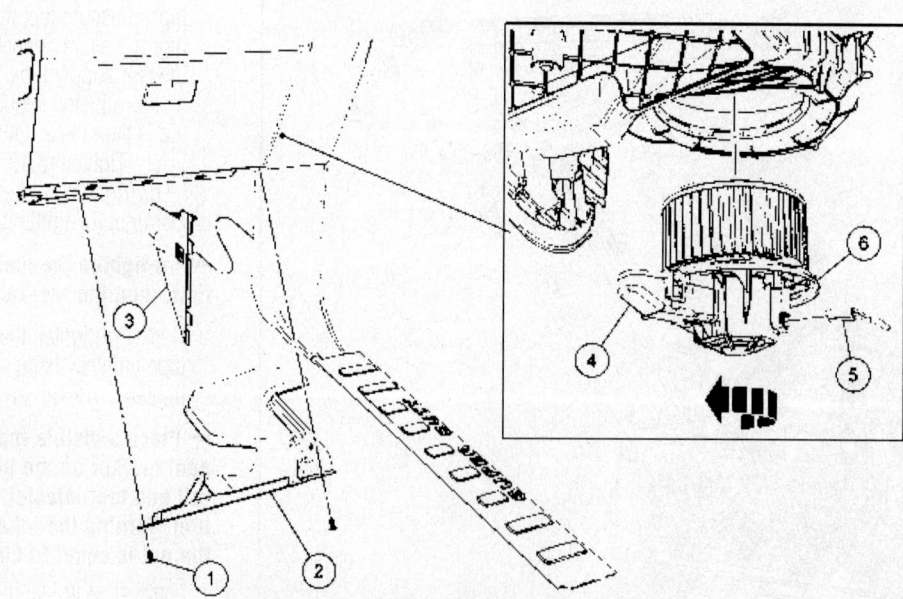

1. RH lower instrument panel insulator pin-type retainer
2. RH lower instrument panel insulator
3. RH lower A-pillar junction box trim cover
4. Blower motor vent tube (part on 19805)
5. Blower motor electrical connector
6. Blower motor

36578_F250_G0105

Fig. 298 Removing the blower motor

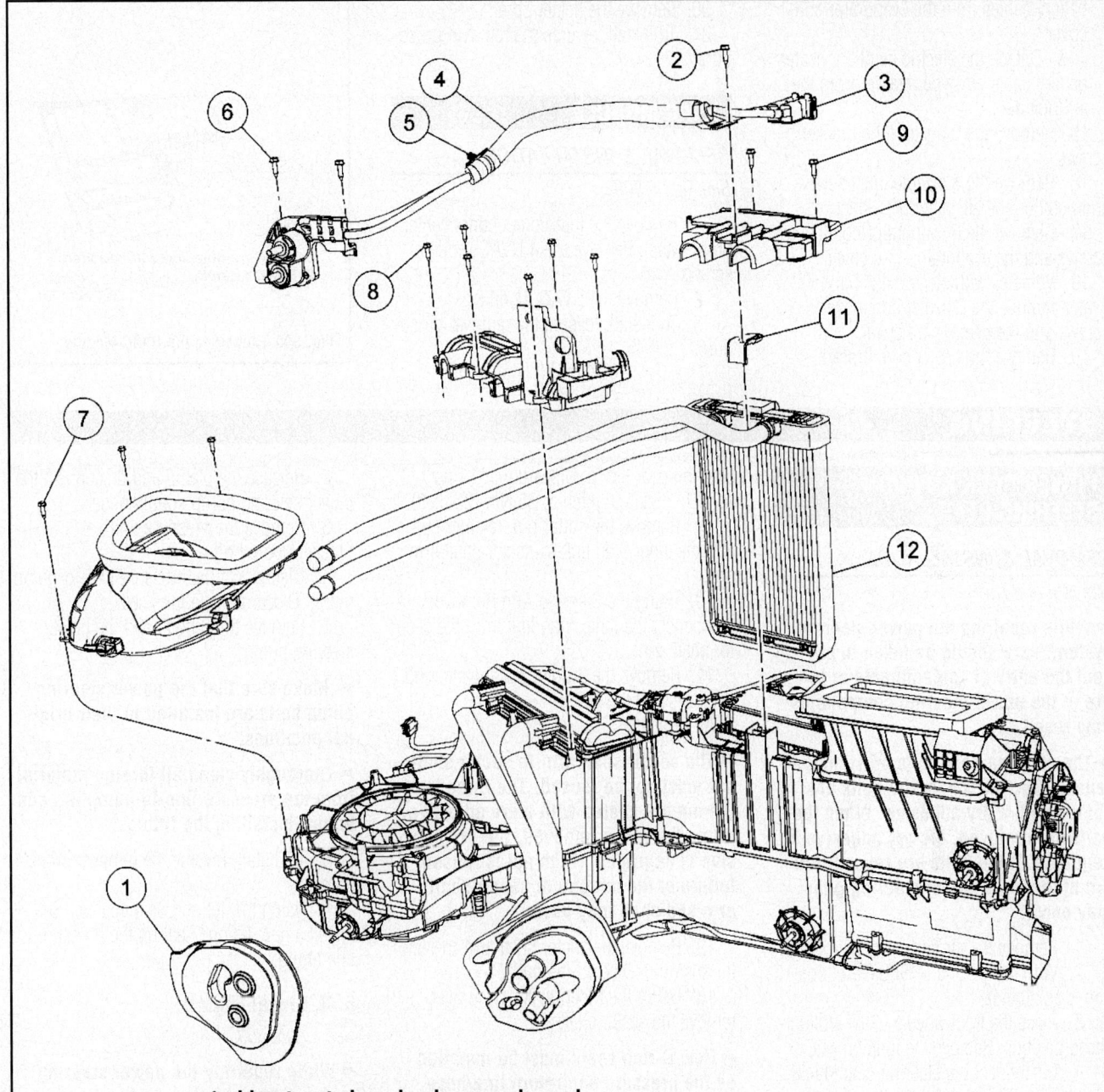

1. Heater tube dash panel seal
2. Heater core cover screw (3 required)
3. Electric auxiliary heater battery cable connector
4. Electric auxiliary heater battery cable
5. Electric auxiliary heater battery cable pin-type retainer
6. Heater tube bracket screw (2 required)
7. Air inlet duct screw (3 required)
8. Evaporator core cover screw (6 required)
9. Heater core cover screw (2 required)
10. Heater core cover
11. Heater core bracket
12. Heater core

36578_F250_G0110

Fig. 299 Exploded view of the heater core assembly

battery cables from the evaporator core cover.

   c. Detach the electric auxiliary heater battery cable pin-type retainer from the air inlet duct.

15. Remove the 2 heater tube bracket screws.

16. Remove the 3 air inlet duct screws and position the air inlet duct aside.

17. Remove the 6 evaporator core cover screws and the evaporator core cover.

18. Vehicles with electric auxiliary heater, remove the 2 heater core cover screws and the heater core cover.

19. Remove the heater core bracket.

20. Remove the heater core.

21. To install, reverse the removal procedure.

HVAC MODULE

REMOVAL & INSTALLATION

See Figure 300.

1. Remove the instrument panel center finish panel. Remove the 4 HVAC module screws.

2. Remove the HVAC module.

3. To install, reverse the removal procedure.

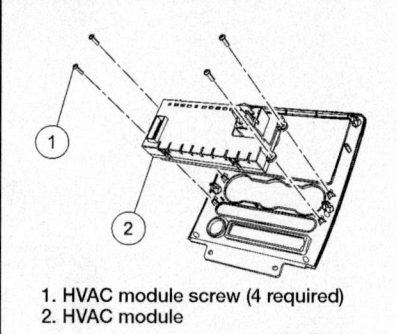

1. HVAC module screw (4 required)
2. HVAC module

36578_F250_G0111

Fig. 300 Removing the HVAC Module

STEERING

POWER RACK & PINION STEERING GEAR

REMOVAL & INSTALLATION

See Figure 301.

➡While repairing the power steering system, care should be taken to prevent the entry of contaminants or failure of the power steering components may result.

➡The steering gear bolts must not be reused. The threads of the bolts are coated with a dry adhesive. When the bolts are removed, the dry adhesive is degraded. If the bolts are reused, failure of the bolts and/or steering gear may occur.

1. Remove the air cleaner outlet pipe.

2. With the vehicle in NEUTRAL, position it on a hoist.

3. Place the front wheels in the straight-ahead position. Remove the ignition key.

4. Disconnect the steering gear shield from the line fitting and slide the shield upward on the lower steering column shaft.

➡Do not allow the steering column shaft to rotate while the intermediate shaft is disconnected or damage to the clockspring can result. If there is evidence that the shaft has rotated, the clockspring must be removed and recentered.

5. Remove the lower steering column shaft-to-steering gear bolt. Disconnect the lower steering column shaft from the steering gear.

6. Disconnect the return hose-to-steering gear fitting.

7. Discard the O-ring seal.

8. Disconnect the pressure line-to-

steering gear fitting. Discard the O-ring seal. To install, tighten to 35 Nm (26 lb-ft).

9. Remove the cotter pin, retainer cap and the inner drag link-to-sector shaft arm nut.

10. Using the Steering Arm Remover, disconnect the inner drag link from the sector shaft arm.

11. Remove the 3 bolts and the steering gear. Discard the bolts.

  All vehicles

➡The sector shaft arm-to-sector shaft nut must not be reused. The threads of the nut are coated with a dry adhesive. When the nut is removed, the dry adhesive is degraded. If the nut is reused, failure of the nut and/or sector shaft arm and shaft may occur.

12. Remove the sector shaft arm-to-sector shaft nut. Discard the nut.

13. Using the Steering Arm Remover, remove the sector shaft arm.

➡New O-ring seals must be installed on the pressure and return line/hose fittings or a fluid leak may occur.

14. To install, reverse the removal procedure.

15. Fill the power steering system..

POWER STEERING PUMP

REMOVAL & INSTALLATION

5.4L and 6.8L Engines

See Figure 302.

➡New Teflon® seals must be installed any time the power steering line fittings are disconnected.

1. Remove the power steering pump pulley.

2. Release the clamp and disconnect the power steering pump supply hose.

3. Remove the pressure line bracket/pump bolt.

4. Disconnect the pressure line-to-pump fitting. Discard the Teflon® seal.

5. Remove the 2 bolts and the power steering pump.

➡ Make sure that the power steering pump bolts are installed in their original positions.

➡Thoroughly clean all foreign material from the pressure line-to-pump threads before installing the fitting.

6. To install, reverse the removal procedure

7. Using the Teflon® Seal Installer Set, install a new Teflon® seal on the pressure line fitting.

6.4L Diesel Engines

See Figure 303.

➡While repairing the power steering system, care should be taken to prevent the entry of foreign material or failure of the power steering components may result.

➡New Teflon® seals must be installed any time the power steering line fittings are disconnected.

1. Remove the power steering pump pulley.

2. Remove the pressure line/supply hose bracket nut.

3. Release the clamp and disconnect the power steering pump supply hose.

4. Disconnect the pressure line-to-pump fitting. Remove and discard the Teflon® seal.

5. Remove the 3 bolts and the power steering pump.

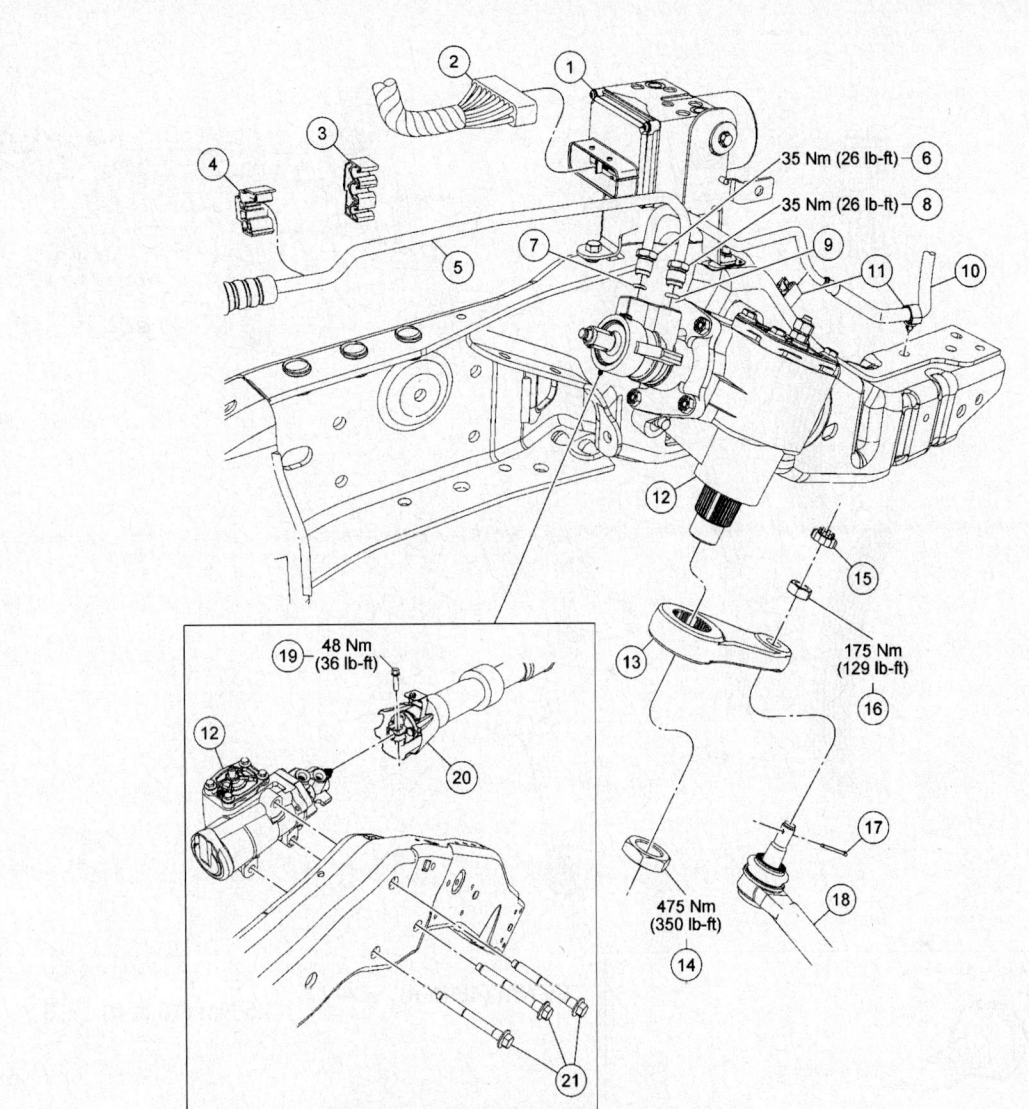

1. Hydraulic Control Unit (HCU)
2. ABS module electrical connector
3. Pressure line retainer
4. Pressure line retainer (5.4L, 6.8L engines only)
5. Pressure line
6. Return hose-to-steering gear fitting
7. O-ring seal
8. Pressure line-to-steering gear fitting
9. O-ring seal
10. Return hose
11. Pressure line retainers (2 required)
12. Steering gear
13. Sector shaft arm
14. Sector shaft arm-to-sector shaft nut
15. Nut retainer cap
16. Inner drag link-to-sector shaft arm nut
17. Cotter pin
18. Drag link
19. Lower steering column shaft-to-steering gear bolt
20. Steering gear shield
21. Steering gear bolts (3 required) (F-250/350)

36578_F250_G0115

Fig. 301 Removing the power steering gear

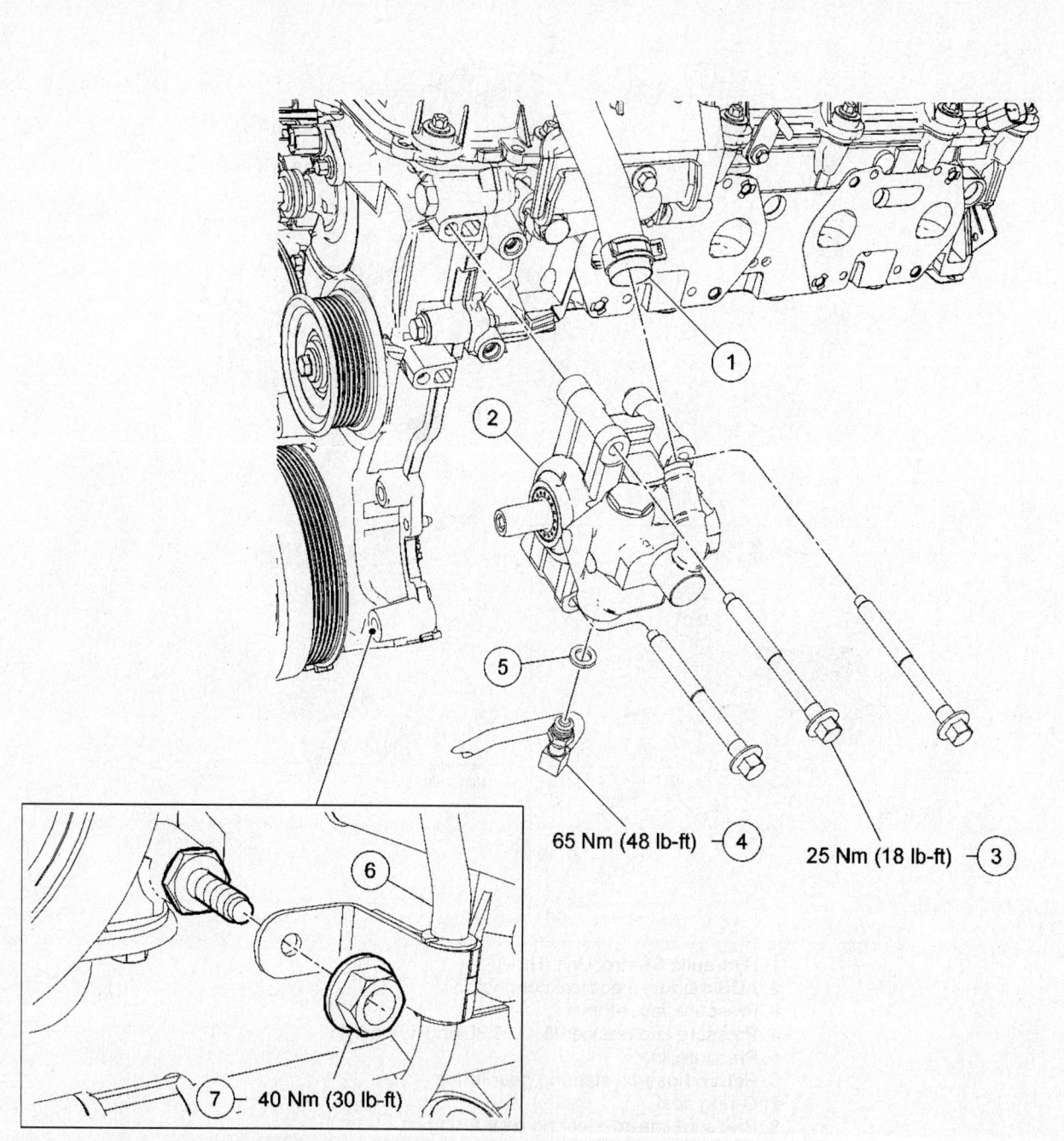

65 Nm (48 lb-ft) — 4   25 Nm (18 lb-ft) — 3

7 — 40 Nm (30 lb-ft)

1. Power steering fluid reservoir-to-pump supply hose
2. Power steering pump
3. Power steering pump bolt (3 required)
4. Power steering pressure line-to-power steering pump fitting
5. Power steering pressure line Teflon® seal
6. Power steering pressure line
7. Power steering pressure line bracket-to-engine nut

36578_EXPD_G0118

Fig. 302 View of the power steering pump and components—5.4L and 6.8L engines

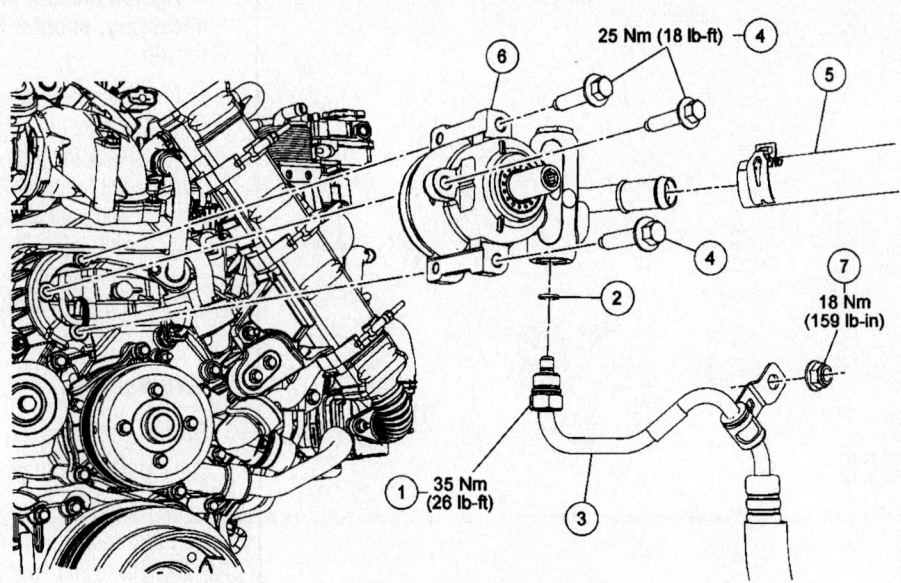

1. Pressure line-to-pump fitting
2. Teflon® seal
3. Hydraulic booster-to-power steering pump pressure line
4. Power steering pump bolts (3 required)
5. Power steering pump supply hose
6. Power steering pump
7. Pressure line/supply hose bracket nut

36578_F250_G0116

Fig. 303 Exploded view of the power steering pump components—6.4L Diesel engines

➡Make sure that the power steering pump bolts are installed in their original positions.

➡Thoroughly clean all foreign material from the pressure line-to-pump threads before installing the fitting.

6. To install, reverse the removal procedure.

7. Using the Teflon® Seal Installer Set, install a new Teflon® seal on the pressure line fitting.

SUSPENSION   FRONT SUSPENSION

COIL SPRING

REMOVAL & INSTALLATION
See Figure 304.

➡Suspension fasteners are critical parts because they affect performance of vital components and systems and their failure can result in major service expense. They must be replaced with the same part number or an equivalent part if replacement is necessary. Do not use a replacement part of lesser quality or substitute design. Torque values must be used as specified during reassembly to make sure of correct retention of these parts.

1. Remove the wheel and tire.
2. Using a suitable jack, support the front axle assembly
3. Remove the shock absorber lower

nut and washer, then detach the shock from the mounting stud. Discard the nut. To install, tighten the new nut to 59 ft. lbs. (80 Nm).
4. Remove the spring bracket bolt and bracket. Discard the bolt. To install, tighten the new bolt to 26 ft. lbs. (35 Nm).
5. Lower the front axle until the spring is free of the spring upper seat.
6. Using an extension through the top of the spring, remove and discard the spring lower nut. To install, tighten the new nut to 85 ft. lbs. (115 Nm).
7. Remove the spring lower retainer and the spring.

➡Inspect the spring upper and lower insulators, install new as necessary.

8. To install, reverse the removal procedure.

CONTROL LINKS

REMOVAL & INSTALLATION

Refer to Stabilizer Bar for Control Links removal and installation.

LOWER BALL JOINT

REMOVAL & INSTALLATION

2WD Vehicles

Upper & Lower

1. Before servicing the vehicle, refer to the Precautions Section.
2. Raise and support the vehicle.
3. Remove the wheel and tire assembly.
4. Remove the disc brake caliper and the front disc brake hub and rotor.
5. Remove the front disc brake rotor shield.
6. If equipped, remove the ABS sensor

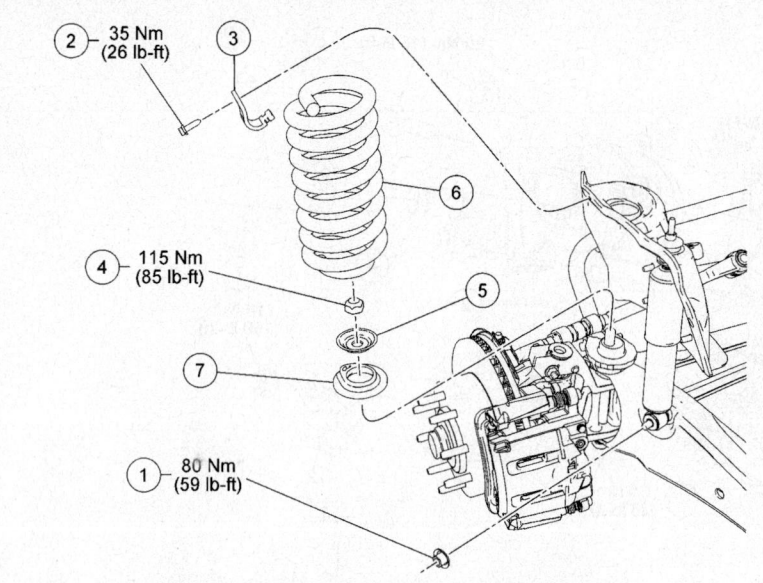

1. Shock absorber lower nut and washer
2. Spring bracket bolt
3. Spring bracket
4. Spring lower nut
5. Spring lower retainer
6. Spring
7. Spring lower insulator

36578_F250_G0122

Fig. 304 Exploded view of the front coil spring assembly

retaining bolt, ABS sensor harness retaining bolt and the ABS sensor. Position out of the way.

7. Disconnect the tie rod end.
   a. Remove and discard the cotter pin.
   b. Remove the castellated nut.
   c. Using the Pitman Arm Puller, remove the tie rod end.
8. Remove the pinch bolt.
9. Remove the camber adjuster.

✴✴ WARNING

To prevent damage to the ball joint seal and the ball joint socket, do not use a pickle fork-type remover to loosen the ball joints.

10. Remove the front wheel spindle.
   a. Remove and discard the cotter pin.
   b. Loosen, but do not remove, the castellated nut.
   c. Strike the lower end of the front axle to loosen the ball joint.
   d. Remove the castellated nut and the front wheel spindle.
11. Position the front wheel spindle in a vise, and remove the snapring from the lower ball joint.

✴✴ WARNING

To avoid damage to the components, do not use heat to aid ball joint removal.

12. Using the ball joint press tool and suitable receiver cup, remove the lower ball joint from the front wheel spindle.
13. Using the ball joint press tool and suitable receiver cup, remove the upper ball joint.

To install:

✴✴ WARNING

To avoid damage to components, do not use heat to aid installation.

➡ Clean the wheel knuckle ball joint bores.

➡ The lower ball joint must be installed first.

14. Using the ball joint press with suitable receiver cups, install the lower ball joint.
15. Using the ball joint press with suitable receiver cups, install the upper ball joint.
16. Install the snapring in the groove at the bottom of the ball joint.

➡ Tighten the ball joint nut further, if necessary, in order to insert a new cotter pin.

17. Using new fasteners, follow the removal procedure in reverse order.
18. Check the front end alignment. Observe the following torques:
- Ball joint stud nut: 99 ft. lbs. (133 Nm)
- Pinch bolt: 60 ft. lbs. (80 Nm)
- Tie rod end stud nut: 67 ft. lbs. (90 Nm)

4WD Vehicles

Upper

See Figures 305 through 308.

1. Before servicing the vehicle, refer to the Precautions Section.
2. Raise and support the vehicle.
3. Remove the wheel and tire assembly.
4. Remove the front brake disc.
5. Remove the wheel hub and bearing.
6. Using a drift, drive the axle shaft main seal out of the wheel knuckle.
7. Remove the axle shaft and main seal.
8. Remove the tie-rod end castellated nut.

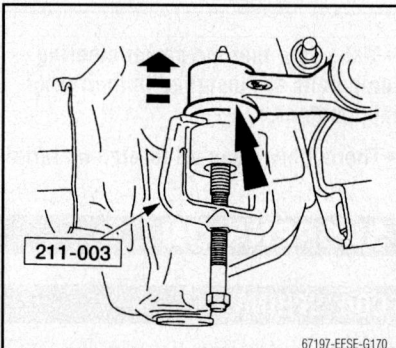

211-003

67197-EFSE-G170

Fig. 305 Disconnect the tie-rod end from the wheel knuckle—4WD models F-250 and F-350

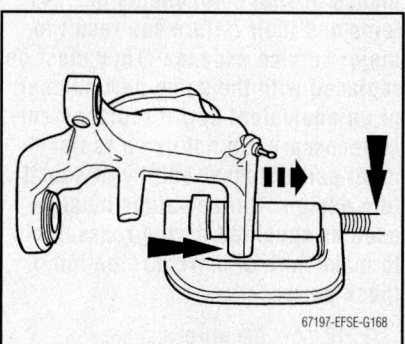

67197-EFSE-G168

Fig. 306 Removing the upper ball joint—4WD models F-250 and F-350

9. Disconnect the tie-rod end from the wheel knuckle.

10. Remove the upper ball joint castellated nut and the insert.

11. Remove the lower ball joint nut.

12. Remove the knuckle.

13. Clean and inspect the wheel knuckle ball joint bores.

14. Place the wheel knuckle into a suitable vise.

➡**Always remove the lower ball joint first.**

15. Remove the lower ball joint.

16. Using a suitable ball joint press, remove the upper ball joint.

To install:

17. Clean the wheel knuckle ball joint bores.

18. Using a suitable ball joint press, install the upper ball joint.

19. Install the lower ball joint.

20. Install the wheel knuckle.

21. Position the wheel knuckle onto the axle housing.

22. Install the nut onto the lower ball joint. Do not tighten the nut at this time.

23. Install the insert and the castellated nut onto the upper ball joint. Do not tighten the nut at this time.

24. Tighten the lower ball joint retaining nut. Pre-tighten the nut to 47 Nm (35 ft. lbs.).

➡**Do not loosen the castellated nut to install the cotter pin.**

25. Tighten the upper ball joint castellated nut. Torque to 69 ft. lbs. (94 Nm).

26. Install the cotter pin. If necessary, tighten the castellated nut until the cotter pin can be installed.

27. Tighten the lower ball joint nut to 204 Nm (150 ft. lbs.).

28. Position the tie-rod end into the wheel knuckle.

29. Install and tighten the castellated nut. Torque to 70 Nm (52 ft. lbs.).

30. Install the cotter pin.

31. Position the main seal onto the axle shaft.

32. Using the special tools and a hammer, seat the main seal onto the axle shaft.

33. Position the axle shaft into the axle housing.

34. Using the special tools and a hammer, install the main seal into the wheel knuckle.

35. Install the wheel hub and bearing.

36. Install the front brake disc.

37. Install the wheel and tire assembly.

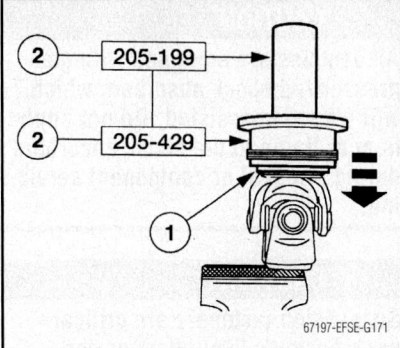

Fig. 307 Seat the main seal onto the axle shaft—4WD models F-250 and F-350

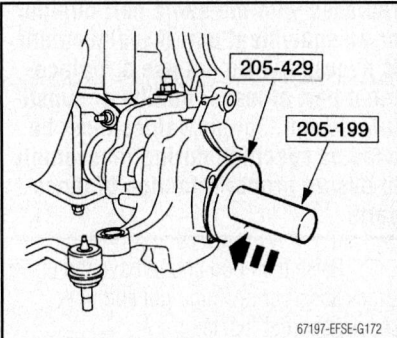

Fig. 308 Install the main seal into the wheel knuckle—4WD models F-250 and F-350

Lower

See Figures 309 through 311.

1. Raise and support the vehicle.

2. Remove the wheel and tire assembly.

3. Remove the front brake disc.

4. Remove the wheel hub and bearing.

5. Using a drift, drive the axle shaft main seal out of the wheel knuckle.

6. Remove the axle shaft and main seal.

7. Remove the tie-rod end castellated nut.

8. Disconnect the tie-rod end from the wheel knuckle.

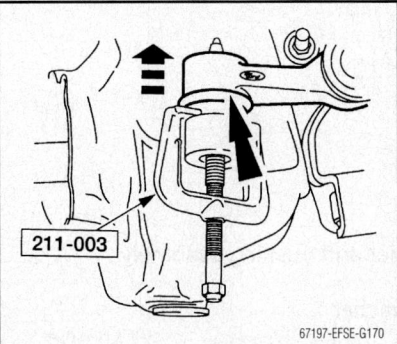

Fig. 309 Disconnect the tie-rod end from the wheel knuckle—F-250 and F-350

9. Remove the upper ball joint castellated nut and the insert.

10. Remove the lower ball joint nut.

11. Remove the knuckle.

12. Clean and inspect the wheel knuckle ball joint bores.

13. Place the wheel knuckle into a suitable vise.

14. Remove the lower ball joint.

To install:

15. Clean the wheel knuckle ball joint bores.

16. Install the lower ball joint.

17. Install the wheel knuckle.

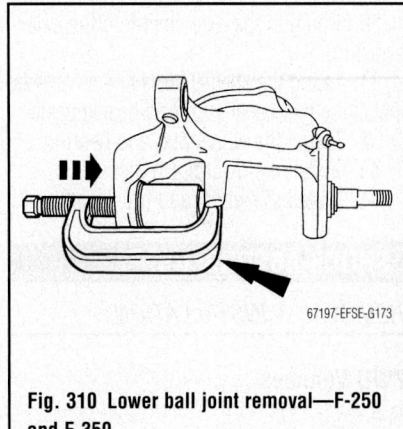

Fig. 310 Lower ball joint removal—F-250 and F-350

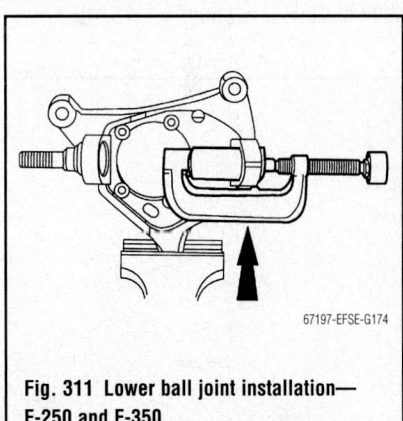

Fig. 311 Lower ball joint installation—F-250 and F-350

18. Position the wheel knuckle onto the axle housing.

19. Install the nut onto the lower ball joint. Do not tighten the nut at this time.

20. Install the insert and the castellated nut onto the upper ball joint. Do not tighten the nut at this time.

21. Tighten the lower ball joint retaining nut. Pre-tighten the nut to 47 Nm (35 ft. lbs.).

➡**Do not loosen the castellated nut to install the cotter pin.**

22. Tighten the upper ball joint castellated nut. Torque to 94 Nm (69 ft. lbs.).

23. Install the cotter pin. If necessary, tighten the castellated nut until the cotter pin can be installed.

24. Tighten the lower ball joint nut to 204 Nm (150 ft. lbs.).

25. Position the tie-rod end into the wheel knuckle.

26. Install and tighten the castellated nut. Torque to 52 ft. lbs. (70 Nm).

27. Install the cotter pin.

28. Position the main seal onto the axle shaft.

29. Using the special tools and a hammer, seat the main seal onto the axle shaft.

30. Position the axle shaft into the axle housing.

31. Using the special tools and a hammer, install the main seal into the wheel knuckle.

32. Install the wheel hub and bearing.

33. Install the front brake disc.

34. Install the wheel and tire assembly.

SHOCK ABSORBERS

REMOVAL & INSTALLATION

2WD Vehicles

See Figure 312.

1. Before servicing the vehicle, refer to the Precautions Section.

> **⁂ CAUTION**
>
> **All vehicles are equipped with gas-pressurized shock absorbers which will extend unassisted. Do not apply heat or flame to the shock absorbers during removal or component servicing.**

> **⁂ CAUTION**
>
> **Suspension fasteners are critical parts because they affect performance of vital components and systems and their failure can result in major service expense. They must be replaced with the same part number or an equivalent part if replacement is necessary. Do not use a replacement part of lesser quality or substitute design. Torque values must be used as specified during reassembly to ensure proper retention of these parts.**

---

2. Raise the hood and remove the upper shock absorber retaining nut and upper shock absorber insulator.

3. Raise and support the vehicle.

4. Remove the lower shock absorber retaining nut and remove the shock absorber.

5. Using new fasteners, follow the removal procedure in reverse order. Observe the following torques:
- Upper nut: 30 ft. lbs. (40 Nm)
- Lower nut: 60 ft. lbs. (80 Nm)

4WD Vehicles

See Figure 313.

1. Before servicing the vehicle, refer to the Precautions Section.

> **⁂ CAUTION**
>
> **All vehicles are equipped with gas-pressurized shock absorbers which will extend unassisted. Do not apply heat or flame to the shock absorbers during removal or component servicing.**

> **⁂ CAUTION**
>
> **Suspension fasteners are critical parts because they affect performance of vital components and systems and their failure can result in major service expense. They must be replaced with the same part number or an equivalent part if replacement is necessary. Do not use a replacement part of lesser quality or substitute design. Torque values must be used as specified during reassembly to ensure proper retention of these parts.**

---

2. With the vehicle in NEUTRAL, position it on a hoist.

3. Remove and discard the shock absorber upper nut, washer and bushing assembly (upper half). To install, tighten the new nut to 46 ft. lbs. (63 Nm).

4. Remove and discard the shock absorber lower bolt and flagnut. To install, tighten the new bolt to 111 ft. lbs. (150 Nm).

5. Remove the shock absorber.

6. To install, reverse the removal procedure

SPINDLE

REMOVAL & INSTALLATION

2WD Vehicles

1. Before servicing the vehicle, refer to the Precautions Section.

2. Raise and support the vehicle.

3. Remove the wheel and tire assembly.

4. Remove the disc brake caliper and the front disc brake hub and rotor.

5. Remove the front disc brake rotor shield.

6. If equipped, remove the ABS sensor

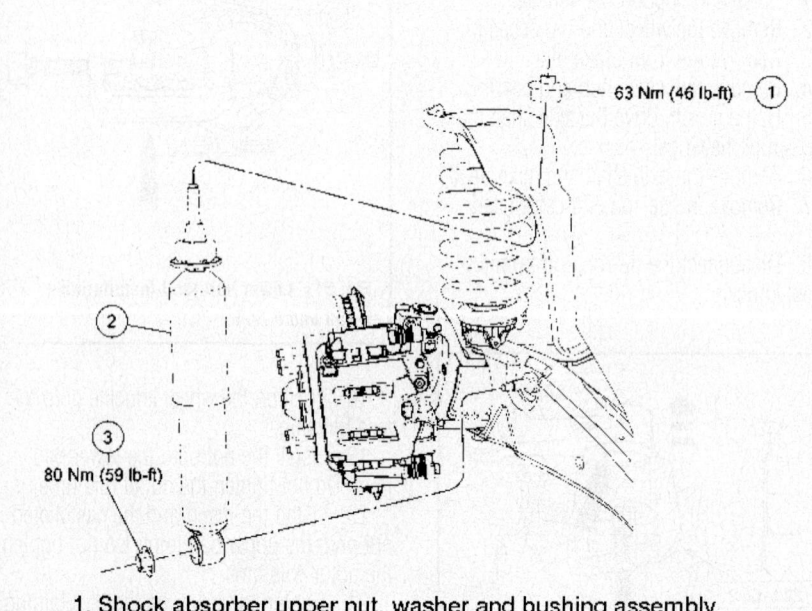

63 Nm (46 lb-ft) — ①

②

80 Nm (59 lb-ft)

1. Shock absorber upper nut, washer and bushing assembly
2. Shock absorber
3. Shock absorber lower nut and washer

36578_F250_G0123

Fig. 312 Removing the front shock absorber—2WD models

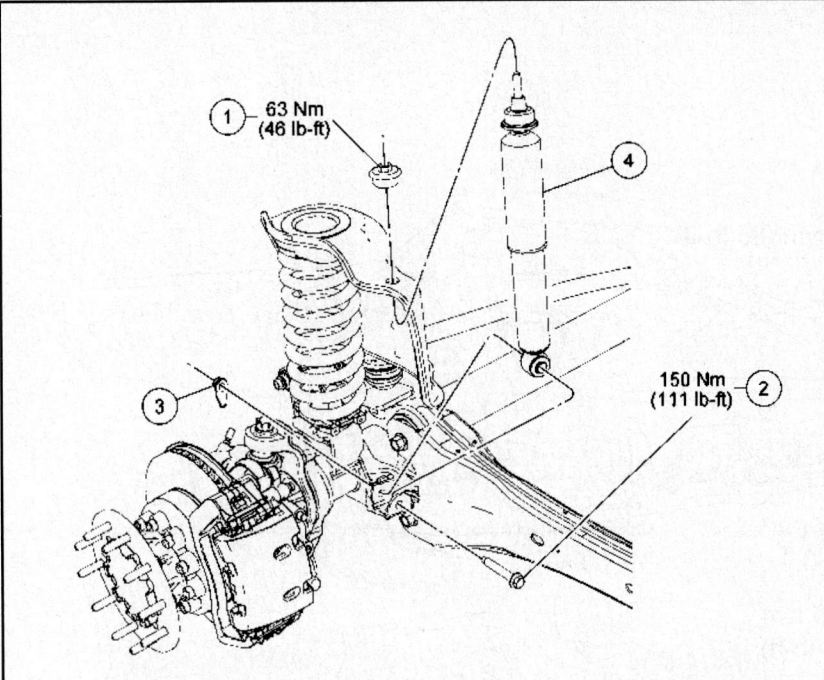

1. Upper nut, washer and bushing assembly (upper half)
2. Shock absorber lower bolt
3. Shock absorber lower flagnut
4. Shock absorber

36578_F250_G0124

Fig. 313 Removing the front shock absorber—4WD models

retaining bolt, ABS sensor harness retaining bolt and the ABS sensor. Position out of the way.

7. Remove and discard the cotter pin. Remove the castellated nut. Using a pitman arm puller, remove the tie rod end.

8. Remove the pinch bolt.

9. Remove the camber adjuster.

✳✳ WARNING

To prevent damage to the ball joint seal and the ball joint socket, do not use a pickle fork-type remover to loosen the ball joints.

10. Remove and discard the cotter pin. Loosen, but do not remove, the castellated nut. Strike the lower end of the front axle to loosen the ball joint.

11. Remove the castellated nut and the front wheel spindle.

➡**Tighten the ball joint nut further, if necessary, in order to insert a new cotter pin.**

12. Using new fasteners, follow the removal procedure in reverse order. Observe the following torques:

- Lower ball joint nut: 99 ft. lbs. (133 Nm)

- Pinch bolt: 60 ft. lbs. (80 Nm)
- Tie rod ball stud nut: 67 ft. lbs. (90 Nm)

13. Check the front end alignment.

STABILIZER BAR AND LINKS

REMOVAL & INSTALLATION

2WD Vehicles

See Figure 314.

1. With the vehicle in NEUTRAL, position it on a hoist.

2. Remove and discard the stabilizer bar link upper nuts, washers and bolts. To install, tighten the new nut to 85 ft. lbs. (115 Nm).

3. Remove the stabilizer bar link lower nuts, washers, bolts and the stabilizer bar links. Discard the nuts, bolts and washers. To install, tighten the new nuts, bolts and washers to 85 ft. lbs. (115 Nm).

4. Remove the stabilizer bar bracket nuts, brackets and the stabilizer bar. Discard the nuts. To install, tighten the new nuts to 33 ft. lbs. (48 Nm).

5. To install, reverse the removal procedure.

4WD Vehicles

See Figure 315.

1. With the vehicle in NEUTRAL, position it on a hoist.

2. Remove the stabilizer bar link lower bolt and washer. Discard the bolt. To install, tighten the new bolt to 111 ft. lbs. (150 Nm).

➡**If the clinch nut in the axle is stripped or damaged, remove the clinch nut and install a new flagnut (W711430) in place of the clinch nut.**

3. Remove and discard the stabilizer bar link upper nut, bolt and washer. To install, tighten the new nut to 111 ft. lbs. (150 Nm).

4. Remove the stabilizer bar link.

5. To install, reverse the removal procedure.

STEERING KNUCKLE

REMOVAL & INSTALLATION

4WD Vehicles

See Figures 316 and 317.

1. Before servicing the vehicle, refer to the Precautions Section.

2. Raise and support the vehicle.

3. Remove the wheel and tire assembly.

4. Remove the front brake disc.

5. Remove the wheel hub and bearing.

6. Using a drift, drive the axle shaft main seal out of the wheel knuckle.

7. Remove the axle shaft and main seal.

8. Remove the tie-rod end castellated nut.

9. Using the special tool, disconnect the tie-rod end from the wheel knuckle.

10. Remove the upper ball joint castellated nut and the insert.

11. Remove the lower ball joint nut.

12. Remove the knuckle.

13. Clean and inspect the wheel knuckle ball joint bores.

To install:

14. Position the wheel knuckle onto the axle housing.

15. Install the nut onto the lower ball joint. Do not tighten the nut at this time.

16. Install the insert and the castellated nut onto the upper ball joint. Do not tighten the nut at this time.

17. Tighten the lower ball joint retaining nut. Pre-tighten the nut to 47 Nm (35 ft. lbs.).

➡**Do not loosen the castellated nut to install the cotter pin.**

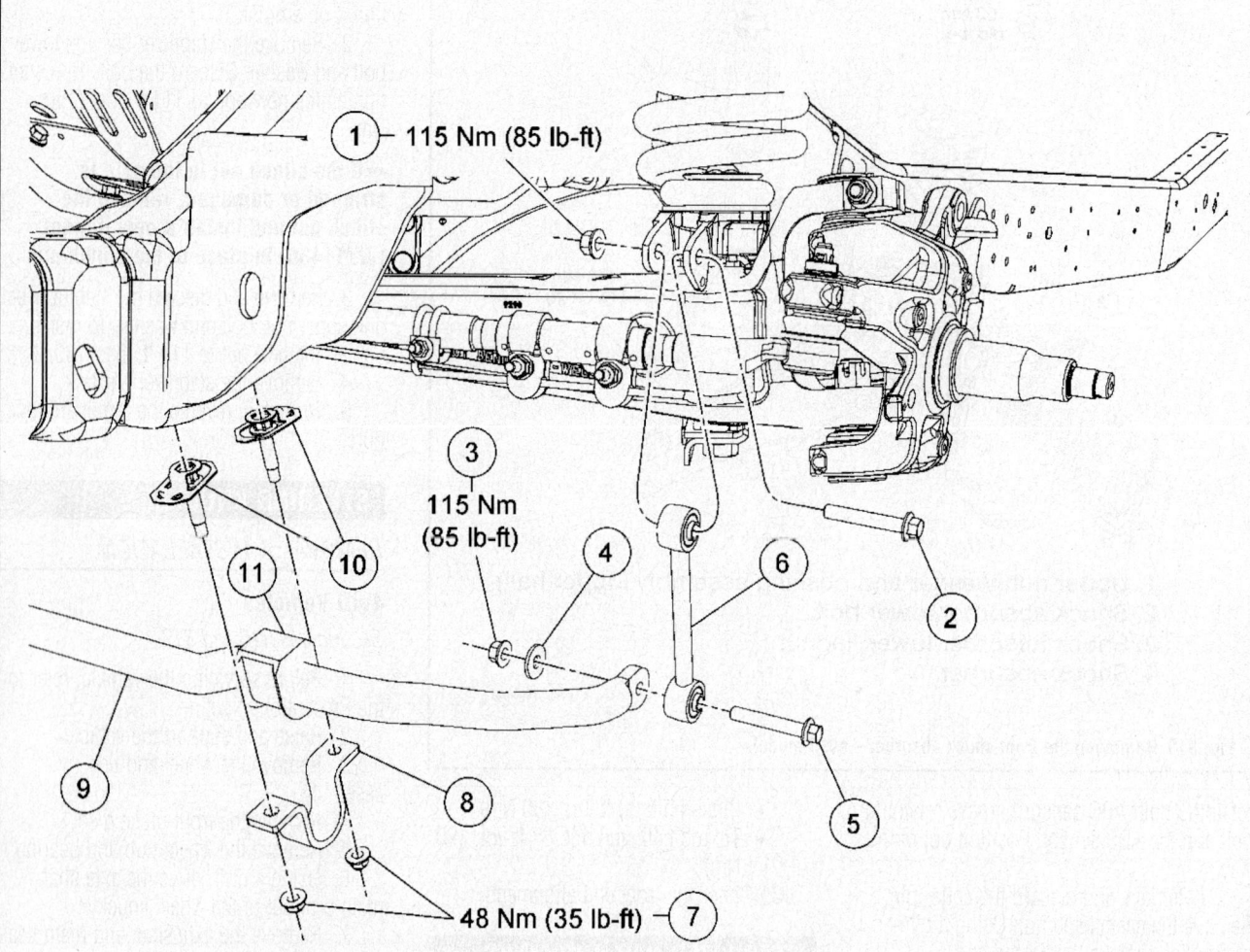

1. Stabilizer bar link upper nut (2 required)
2. Stabilizer bar link upper bolt (2 required)
3. Stabilizer bar link lower nut (2 required)
4. Washer (2 required)
5. Stabilizer bar link lower bolt (2 required)
6. Stabilizer bar link (2 required)
7. Stabilizer bar bracket nuts (4 required)
8. Stabilizer bar bracket
9. Stabilizer bar
10. Stabilizer bar bracket bolts and retainers (4 required)
11. Stabilizer bar bushing (2 required)

36578_F250_G0126

Fig. 314 Exploded view of the front stabilizer bar—2WD models

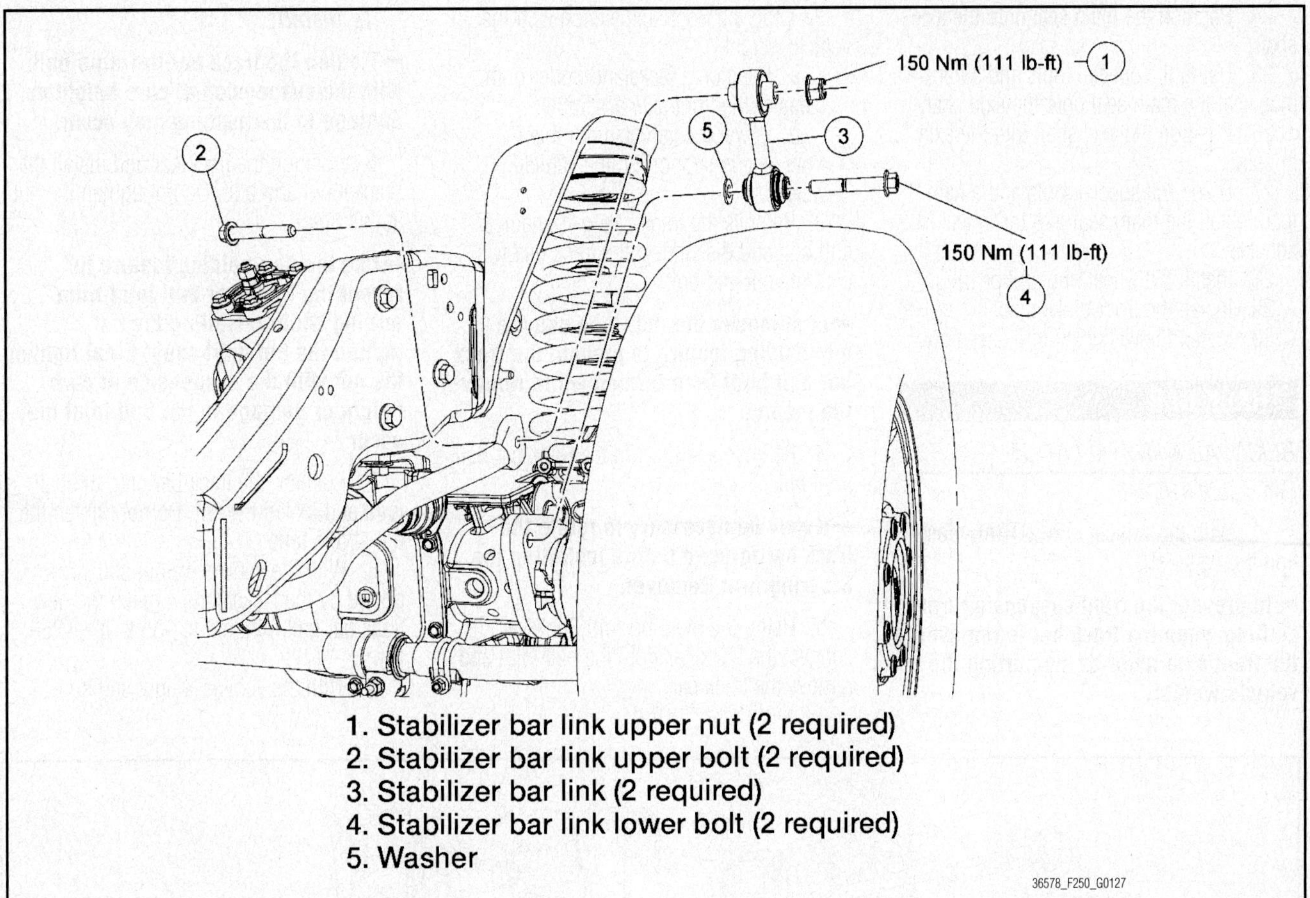

150 Nm (111 lb-ft)
1
2
3
5
150 Nm (111 lb-ft)
4
1. Stabilizer bar link upper nut (2 required)
2. Stabilizer bar link upper bolt (2 required)
3. Stabilizer bar link (2 required)
4. Stabilizer bar link lower bolt (2 required)
5. Washer
36578_F250_G0127

Fig. 315 Exploded view of the front stabilizer bar—4WD models

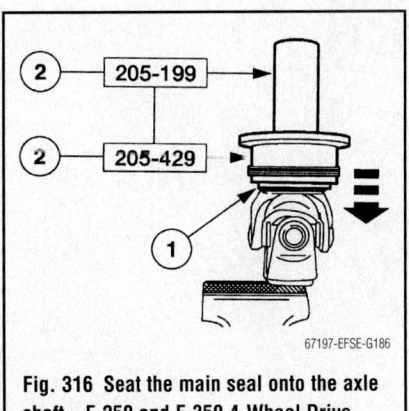

2
205-199
2
205-429
1
67197-EFSE-G186

Fig. 316 Seat the main seal onto the axle shaft—F-250 and F-350 4-Wheel Drive

18. Tighten the upper ball joint castellated nut. Torque to 69 ft. lbs. (94 Nm).
19. Install the cotter pin. If necessary, tighten the castellated nut until the cotter pin can be installed.
20. Tighten the lower ball joint nut to 204 Nm (150 ft. lbs.).
21. Position the tie-rod end into the wheel knuckle.
22. Install and tighten the castellated nut. Torque to 52 ft. lbs. (70 Nm).
23. Install the cotter pin.

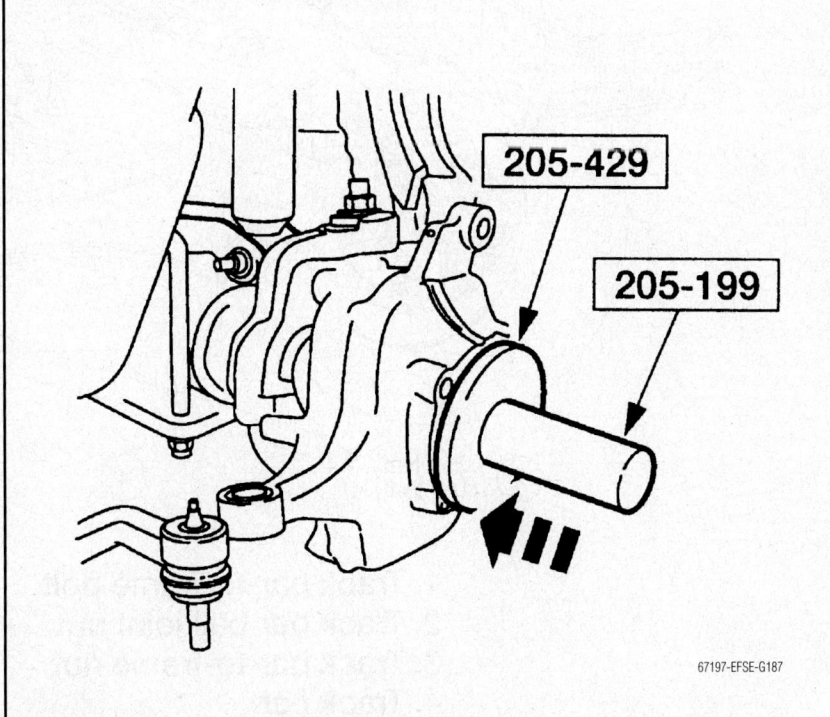

205-429
205-199
67197-EFSE-G187

Fig. 317 Install the main seal into the wheel knuckle—F-250 and F-350 4-Wheel Drive

24. Position the main seal onto the axle shaft.

25. Using the special tools and a hammer, seat the main seal onto the axle shaft.

26. Position the axle shaft into the axle housing.

27. Using the special tools and a hammer, install the main seal into the wheel knuckle.

28. Install the wheel hub and bearing.

29. Install the front brake disc.

30. Install the wheel and tire assembly.

TRACK BAR

REMOVAL & INSTALLATION

See Figure 318.

1. With the vehicle in NEUTRAL, position it on a hoist.

➡**To prevent the front suspension from shifting when the track bar is removed, the front axle must be supporting the vehicle weight.**

2. Load the front suspension with the vehicle weight.

   a. Position a jackstand under both sides of the front axle assembly.

   b. Lower the vehicle until the front axle is supporting the vehicle weight.

3. Remove the track bar-to-frame nut and bolt and disconnect the track bar. Discard the nut and bolt.

➡**First loosen the nut, then use the hex-holding feature to prevent the track bar ball joint from turning while removing the nut.**

4. Remove and discard the track bar ball joint nut.

➡**It may be necessary to rotate the track bar forward before installing the Steering Arm Remover.**

5. Using the Steering Arm Remover, disconnect the track bar from the ball joint and remove the track bar.

To install:

➡**Tighten the track bar-to-frame bolt with the suspension at curb height or damage to the bushing may occur.**

6. Position the track bar and install the bracket nut and bolt. Do not tighten the nut at this time.

➡**Use the hex-holding feature to revent the track bar ball joint from turning while installing the nut, tighten the nut until snug. Final tighten the nut with the suspension at curb height or damage to the ball joint may occur.**

7. Position the track bar onto the ball joint and install the nut. Do not tighten the nut at this time.

8. With the vehicle weight still supported by the jackstands, tighten the new track bar ball joint nut to 183 ft. lbs. (250 Nm).

9. With the vehicle weight still sup-

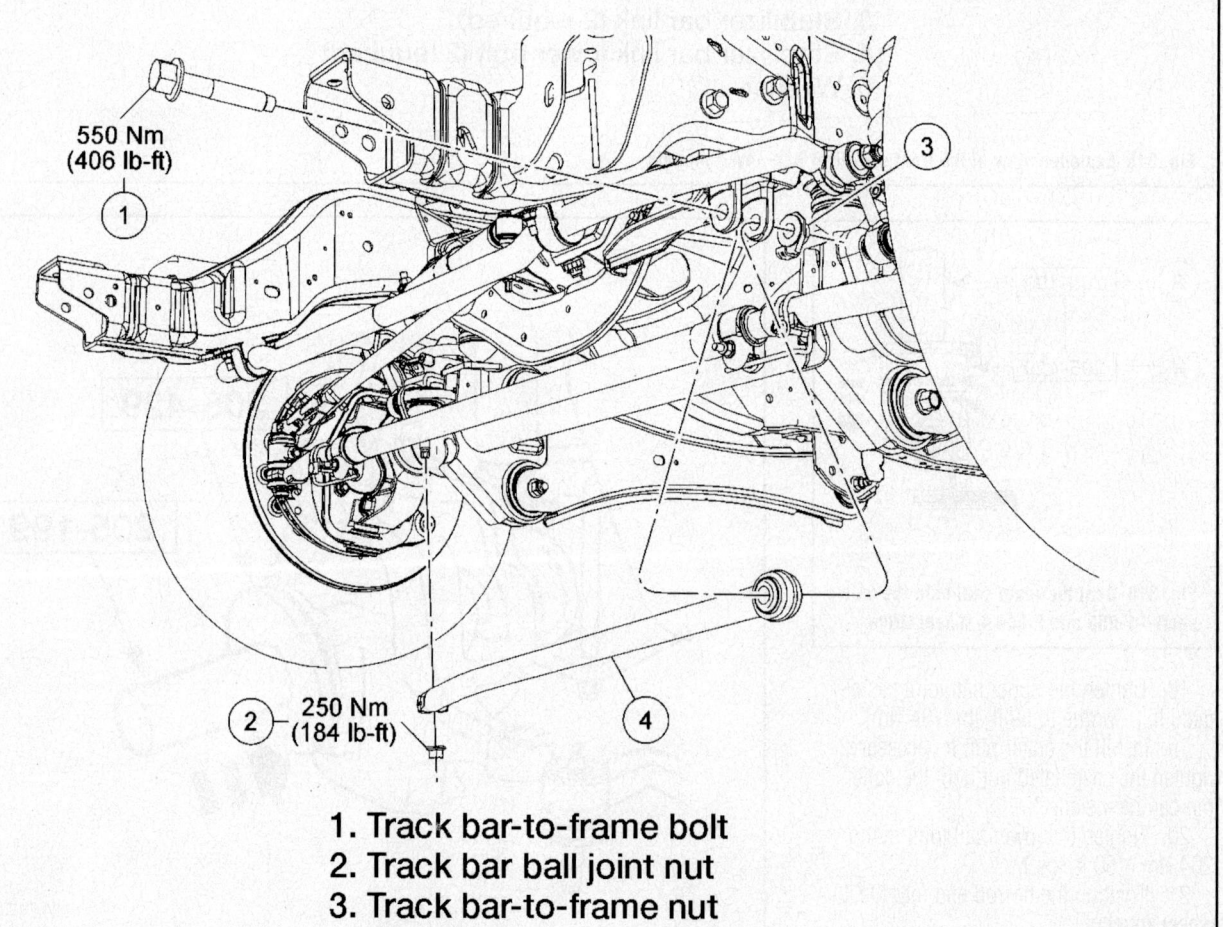

550 Nm
(406 lb-ft)
1

3

250 Nm
(184 lb-ft)
2

4

1. Track bar-to-frame bolt
2. Track bar ball joint nut
3. Track bar-to-frame nut
4. Track bar

36578_F250_G0128

Fig. 318 Exploded view of the front track bar

ported by the jackstands, tighten the new track bar-to-frame bolt to 406 ft. lbs. (550 Nm).

UPPER BALL JOINT

REMOVAL & INSTALLATION

Refer to Lower Ball Joint in this section.

RADIUS ARM

REMOVAL & INSTALLATION

See Figure 319.

1. Remove the spring.
2. Remove and discard the radius arm front nut and bolt. To install, tighten the new nut to 295 ft. lbs. (400 Nm).

➡**Tighten the radius arm rear nut with the suspension at curb height or damage to the bushing may occur.**

3. Remove and discard the radius arm rear nut and bolt. To install, tighten the new nut to 221 ft. lbs. (300 Nm).
4. Remove the radius arm.
5. To install, reverse the removal procedure.

WHEEL HUB &BEARING

REMOVAL & INSTALLATION

2WD Vehicles

See Figure 320.

1. Before servicing the vehicle, refer to the Precautions Section.
2. Raise and support the vehicle.
3. Remove the front wheel and tire assemblies.
4. Remove the front disc brake caliper and rotor, and position the caliper out of the way.
5. Remove the hub cap from the hub assembly.
6. Remove the cotter pin, adjusting nut and flat washer.

➡**Inspect the condition of the spindle and nut threads to ensure a free turning nut when reassembling.**

7. Remove the outer bearing cone and roller assembly, and pull the hub assembly from the spindle.
8. Using care not to damage the bearing cage, use a suitable slide hammer and bearing seal remover to remove the inner bearing cone and bearing seal.

To install:

➡Do not spin the bearing dry with compressed air.

➡Remove all traces of lubricant from the bearings, hub and axle spindle. Inspect bearings and bearing cups for pitting, spalling or unusual wear. If either bearings or bearing cups are worn or damaged, replace both bearings and bearing cups.

➡It is recommended that bearings and bearing cups be replaced in sets. If cups are worn or damaged, install the inner and outer bearing cups in the hub with an appropriate bearing cup driver tool. Check for proper seating of new bearing cups by trying to insert a 0.38-mm (0.0015 inch) feeler gauge between the bottom face of the cup and wheel hub seat. You should not be able to insert the feeler gauge.

9. Remove all burrs, nicks or scratches from the shoulder of the spindle and seal bore in the hub with emery cloth.

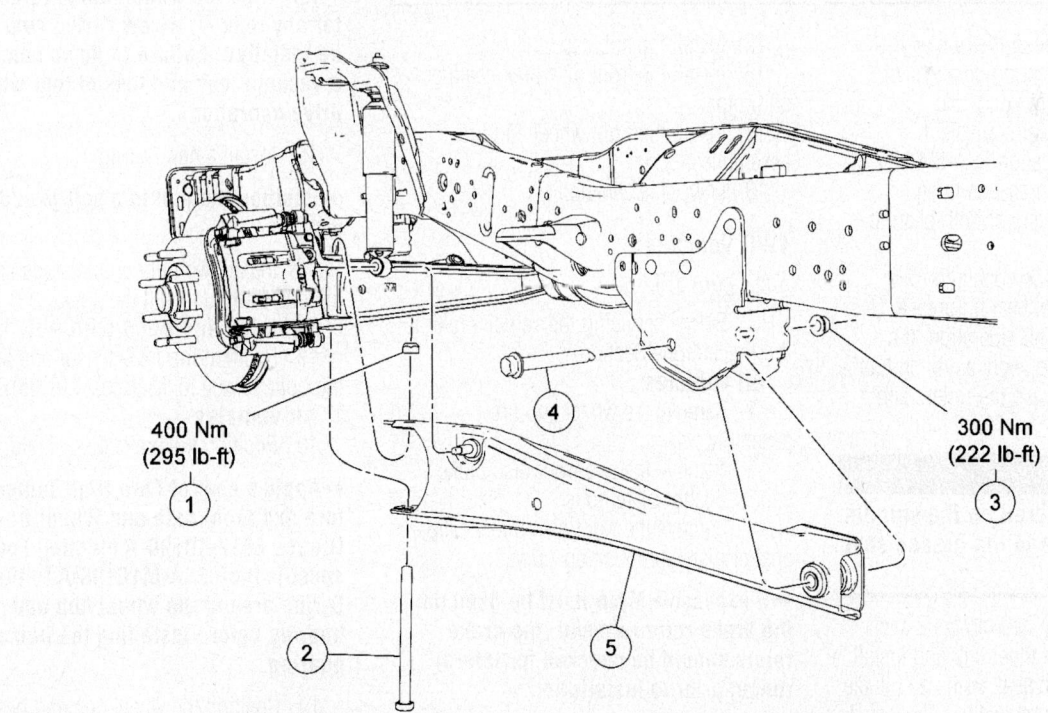

400 Nm
(295 lb-ft)
①

④

300 Nm
(222 lb-ft)
③

②

⑤

36578_F250_G0129

1. Radius arm front nut
2. Radius arm front bolt
3. Radius arm rear nut
4. Radius arm rear bolt
5. Radius arm

Fig. 319 View of the front radius arm

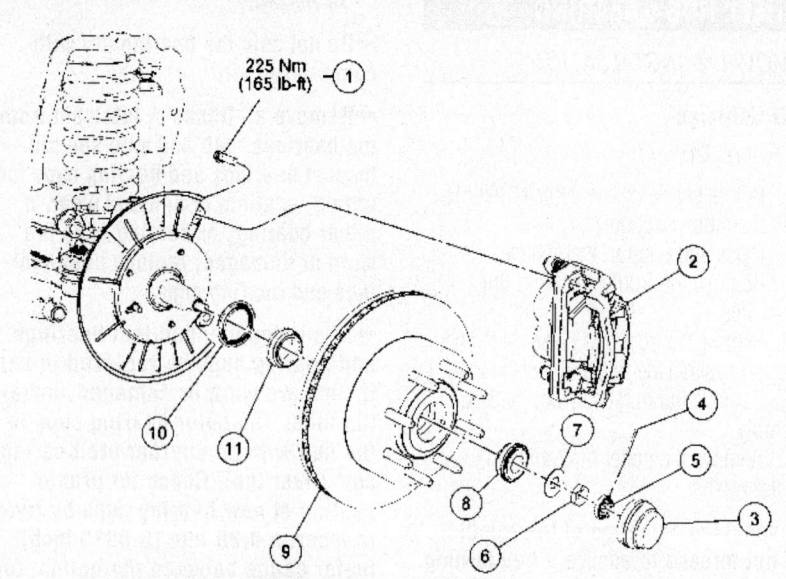

1. Brake caliper anchor plate bolt (2 required)
2. Brake caliper
3. Grease cap
4. Cotter pin
5. Wheel spindle nut retainer
6. Wheel spindle nut
7. Washer
8. Outer wheel bearing
9. Brake disc and hub assembly
10. Grease seal
11. Inner wheel bearing

36578_F250_G0130

Fig. 320 Exploded view of the wheel bearing and hub—2WD models

10. Pack the inside of the hub with lithium-base wheel bearing grease such as Motorcraft Premium Long-Life Grease XG-1-C or -K or equivalent meeting Ford specification ESA-M1C75-B. Fill the hub until the grease is flush with the inside diameters of both bearing cups.

11. Pack the bearing cone and roller assemblies with wheel bearing grease. Use a bearing packer for this operation. If a packer is not available, work as much lubricant as possible between the rollers and cages.

✳✳ WARNING

Keep the hub centered on the spindle to prevent damage to the grease seal or spindle threads.

12. Place the inner bearing cone and roller assembly in the inner cup and install the wheel bearing hub seal, using a suitable seal replacer. Make sure seal is fully seated and lubricated.

13. Install the hub assembly.

14. Install the outer bearing cone and roller assembly and the flat washer on the spindle and install the adjusting nut. Adjust the bearings. Install a new cotter pin.

15. Install the hub cap.

16. Install the front disc brake caliper and rotor.

17. Install the front wheel and tire assemblies.

18. Lower the vehicle.

4WD Vehicles

See Figure 321.

1. Before servicing the vehicle, refer to the Precautions Section.

All vehicles

2. Remove the wheel and tire assembly.

3. Remove the two front disc brake caliper anchor plate bolts.

4. Remove the front disc brake caliper anchor plate and position aside.

➡If excessive force must be used during brake rotor removal, the brake rotors should be checked for lateral runout prior to installation.

5. On F-250 and F-350 4x4 SRW vehicles, remove the rotor.

6. On DRW vehicles, remove the eight hub plate nuts. Remove the hub plate. Remove the rotor.

7. Remove the retainer ring. Pull outward and remove the hub lock.

8. Remove the snapring. Remove the three thrust washers.

Vehicles equipped with ABS

➡Do not remove the ABS sensor from the bearing.

9. Disconnect the ABS wheel sensor harness.

All vehicles

➡The wheel hub and bearing is a slip fit design and should not require a puller to remove it.

10. Remove the four lock nuts. Remove the wheel hub and bearing.

11. If necessary, remove the brake disc shield.

Vehicles with ABS

12. If necessary, remove the bolt and the ABS sensor.

All vehicles

➡If necessary, position the hub in a soft-jawed visc.

13. Install two nuts on the studs and use the inner nut to remove the studs.

14. Remove and discard the O-ring.

To install:
All vehicles

➡Any time the wheel hub is removed for any reason, a new O-ring seal must be installed. Failure to do so can cause a vacuum leak and loss of four wheel drive operations.

15. Install a new O-ring.

➡Position the hub in a soft-jawed vise.

16. Install two nuts on the studs and use the outer nut to install the studs.

Vehicles equipped with ABS

17. Position the ABS sensor and install the bolt. Torque to 13 ft. lbs. (18 Nm).

All vehicles

18. Position the brake disc shield.

➡Apply a coat of Ford High Temperature 4x4 Front Axle and Wheel Bearing Grease E8TZ-19590-A meeting Ford specification ESA-M1C198-A to the O-ring area of the wheel hub and bearing before installing the hub and bearing.

19. Position the wheel hub and bearing. Install the four lock nuts. Torque to 133 ft. lbs. (180 Nm).

Vehicle equipped with ABS

20. Connect the ABS sensor harness.

All vehicles

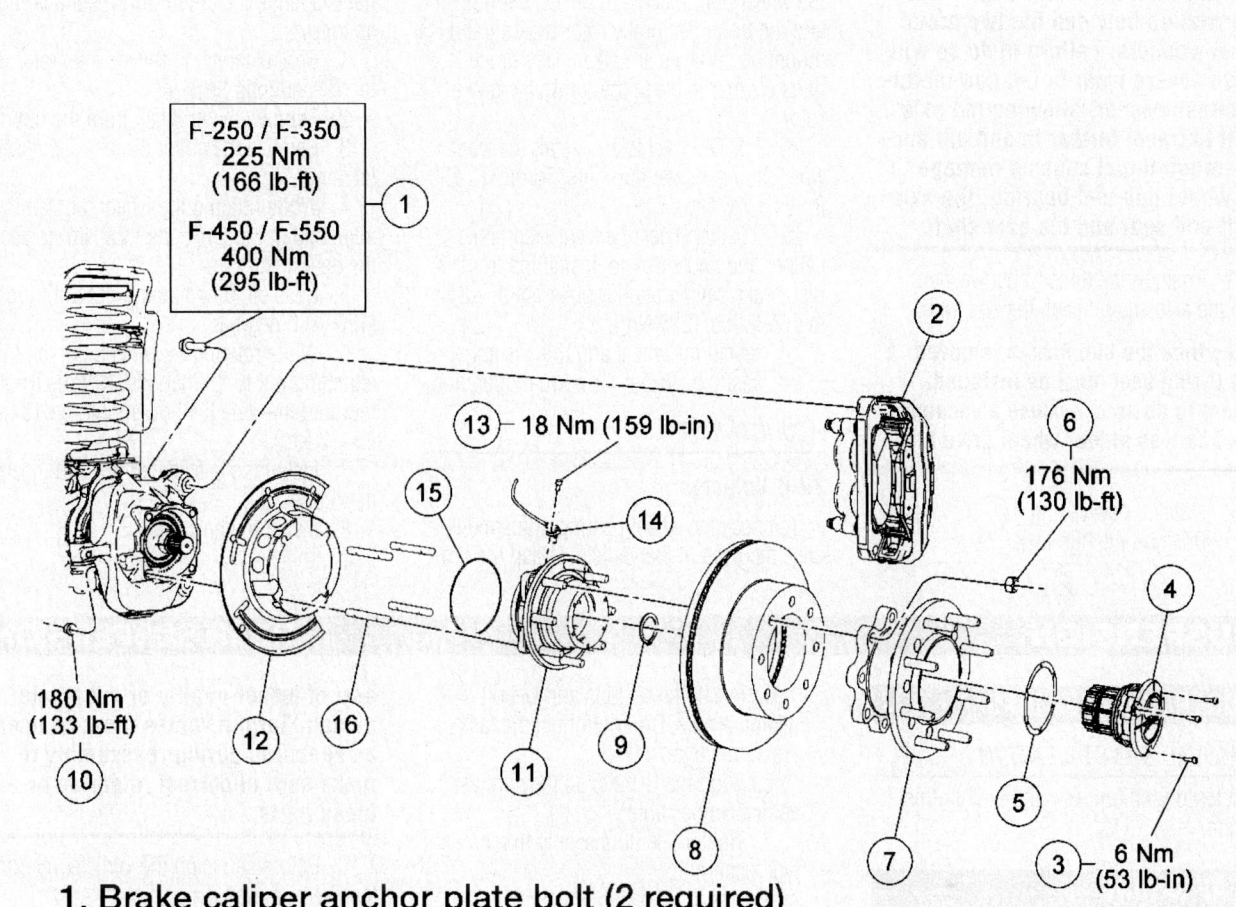

F-250 / F-350
225 Nm
(166 lb-ft)

F-450 / F-550
400 Nm
(295 lb-ft)

13 — 18 Nm (159 lb-in)

176 Nm
(130 lb-ft)

180 Nm
(133 lb-ft)

6 Nm
(53 lb-in)

1. Brake caliper anchor plate bolt (2 required)
2. Brake caliper
3. Hublock screw
4. Hublock
5. Hublock gasket
6. Wheel extension nut (8 required)
7. Wheel extension
8. Brake disc
9. Axle shaft snap ring
10. Wheel bearing and wheel hub nut (4 required)
11. Wheel bearing and wheel hub
12. Brake disc shield
13. Wheel speed sensor bolt
14. Wheel speed sensor
15. Wheel bearing and wheel hub O-ring
16. Wheel bearing and wheel hub stud

36578_F250_G0131

Fig. 321 Exploded view of the wheel bearing and hub—4WD models

❋❋ CAUTION

The non-metallic thrust washer must be installed between the two metal thrust washers. Failure to do so will cause severe wear to the non-metallic thrust washer, allowing the axle shaft to travel further in and out during torque thrust causing damage to the wheel hub and bearing, the axle shaft end seal and the axle shaft.

21. Position the three thrust washers onto the axle shaft. Install the snapring.

→**Any time the hub lock is removed, a new O-ring seal must be installed. Failure to do so can cause a vacuum leak and loss of four wheel drive functions.**

22. Install a new O-ring.
23. Position the hub lock.

24. Install the retainer ring.
25. Position the front disc brake rotor to the wheel hub. Make sure the wheel hub and the front disc brake rotor braking and mounting surfaces are clean. Use brake parts cleaner to clean the front disc brake rotor.
26. For DRW vehicles, install the front wheel hub extender and nuts. Torque to 130 ft. lbs. (176 Nm).
27. Position back the front disc brake caliper and anchor plate. Install the front disc brake caliper anchor plate bolts. Torque to 166 ft. lbs. (225 Nm).
28. Install the wheel and tire assembly.
29. Test the system for normal operation.

ADJUSTMENT

2WD Vehicles

To check the wheel bearing adjustment, raise the front of the vehicle. Grasp the tire at the sides, and alternately push inward and pull outward on the tire. If any looseness is felt, adjust the front wheel bearings as follows.

1. Before servicing the vehicle, refer to the Precautions Section.
2. Remove the hub cap from the hub.
3. Remove the cotter pin and the castellated nut.
4. While rotating the wheel, tighten the adjusting nut to 21 ft. lbs. (28 Nm) to seat the bearings.
5. Back off the adjusting nut until loose (120–180 degrees).
6. While rotating the wheel, tighten the adjusting nut to 18 inch lbs. (2Nm). Torque required to rotate the hub should be 18 inch lbs. (2 Nm).
7. Install the castellated nut and insert a new cotter pin.
8. Install the hub cap.

SUSPENSION

CONTROL ARMS/LINKS

REMOVAL & INSTALLATION

Refer to Stabilizer Bar and Link in this section.

LEAF SPRING

REMOVAL & INSTALLATION

See Figure 322.

1. Before servicing the vehicle, refer to the Precautions Section.
2. Raise and safely support the vehicle.
3. Remove the wheel and tire assembly.
4. Support the rear axle with a suitable jack.
5. Remove and discard the U-bolt retaining nuts and the U-bolts.
6. Remove the rear spring upper plate.
7. Remove the nut and bolt from the rear spring front hanger bracket.

→**If the rear spring has an auxiliary spring and spacer, it is serviced as part of the rear spring assembly.**

8. Remove the lower nut and bolt from the rear spring shackle bracket. Remove the rear spring assembly.
9. To install, follow the removal procedure in reverse order, using new fasteners.
10. Use the following procedure to correctly install the U-bolts.

a. Install the U-bolts and U-bolt retaining nuts. Do not tighten the fasteners at this time.
b. Align the U-bolts so they are as vertical as possible.
c. Tighten the nuts evenly in a cross-type pattern to:
- Step 1: 37 ft. lbs. (50 Nm)
- Step 2: 74 ft. lbs. (100 Nm)
- Step 3: 111 ft. lbs. (150 Nm)
- Step 4: 148 ft. lbs. (200 Nm).
11. Observe the following torques:
- Spring-to-front shackle, exc. waxed bracket: 277 ft. lbs. (375 Nm)
- Spring-to-front shackle, waxed bracket: 222 ft. lbs. (300 Nm)
- Spring-to-rear shackle: 185 ft. lbs. (250 Nm)
- Rear shackle-to-frame: 185 ft. lbs. (250 Nm)

SHOCK ABSORBER

REMOVAL & INSTALLATION

See Figure 323.

❋❋ WARNING

Suspension fasteners are critical parts because they affect performance of vital components and systems and their failure can result in major service expense. Install new parts with the same part number or an equivalent part if installation is necessary. Do not use an installation part of lesser quality or substitute design. Torque values must be used as specified during reassembly to make sure of correct retention of these parts.

1. Before servicing the vehicle, refer to the Precautions Section.

❋❋ WARNING

The low pressure gas shock absorbers are charged with nitrogen gas. Do not attempt to open, puncture or apply heat to shock absorbers.

2. Raise and support the vehicle.
3. Using a suitable jack, support the rear axle.
4. Remove the shock absorber lower retaining nut and bolt.
5. Remove the nut from the upper shock absorber mounting bracket and remove the shock.
6. To install, follow the removal procedure in reverse order, using new fasteners. Torque the upper bolt/nut to 46 ft. lbs. (62 Nm); the lower bolt/nut to 66 ft. lbs. (90 Nm).

STABILIZER BAR AND LINK

REMOVAL & INSTALLATION

See Figures 324 and 325.

1. Before servicing the vehicle, refer to the Precautions Section.

REAR SUSPENSION

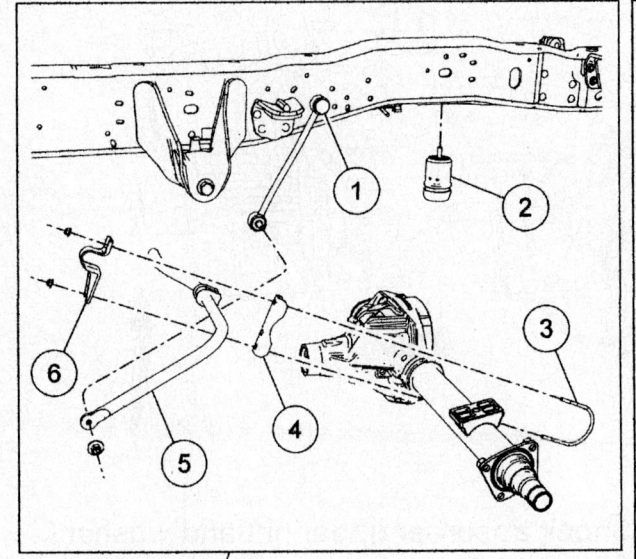

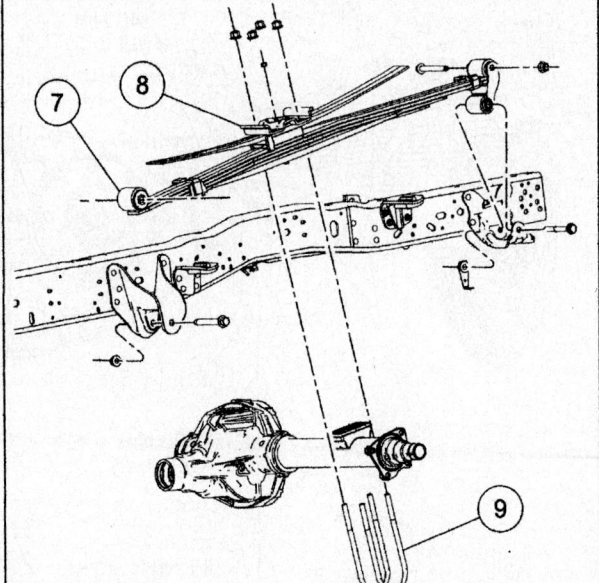

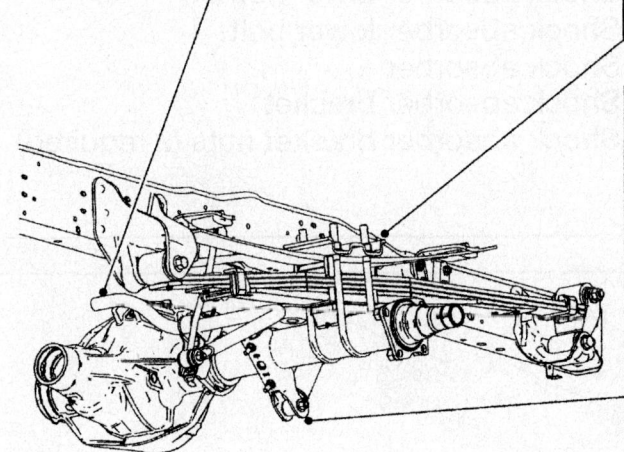

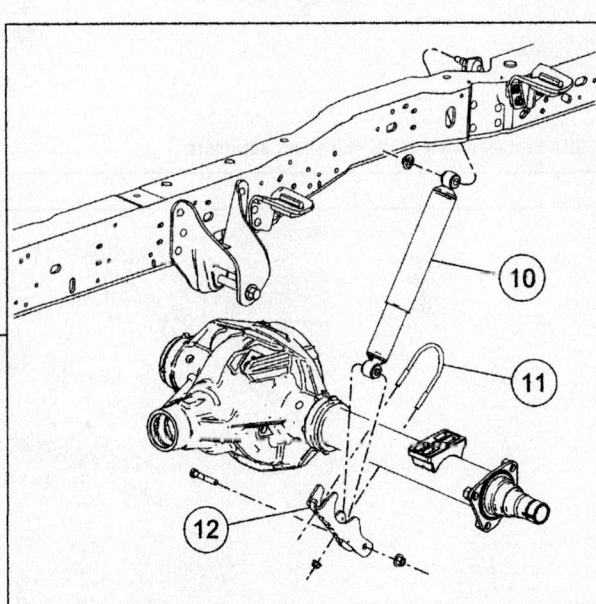

1 Link assembly

2 Rear axle bumper assembly

3 U-bolt, M10-1.75 x
137.5/161.5 (Ford axle only)

4 Rear stabilizer bar bracket
(Ford axle only)

5 Stabilizer bar assembly

6 Rear stabilizer bar retainer

7 Rear spring assembly

8 Rear spring plate

9 U-bolt, M16-2.0 x 108/225
(narrow frame 4 required,
wide frame 6 required)

10 Rear shock absorber

11 U-bolt, M10-1.50 x 101/136.7
(Ford axle only) (LH/RH)

12 Lower shock bracket (Ford
axle only)

06017-F150-G274

Fig. 322 F-250 and F-350 rear suspension

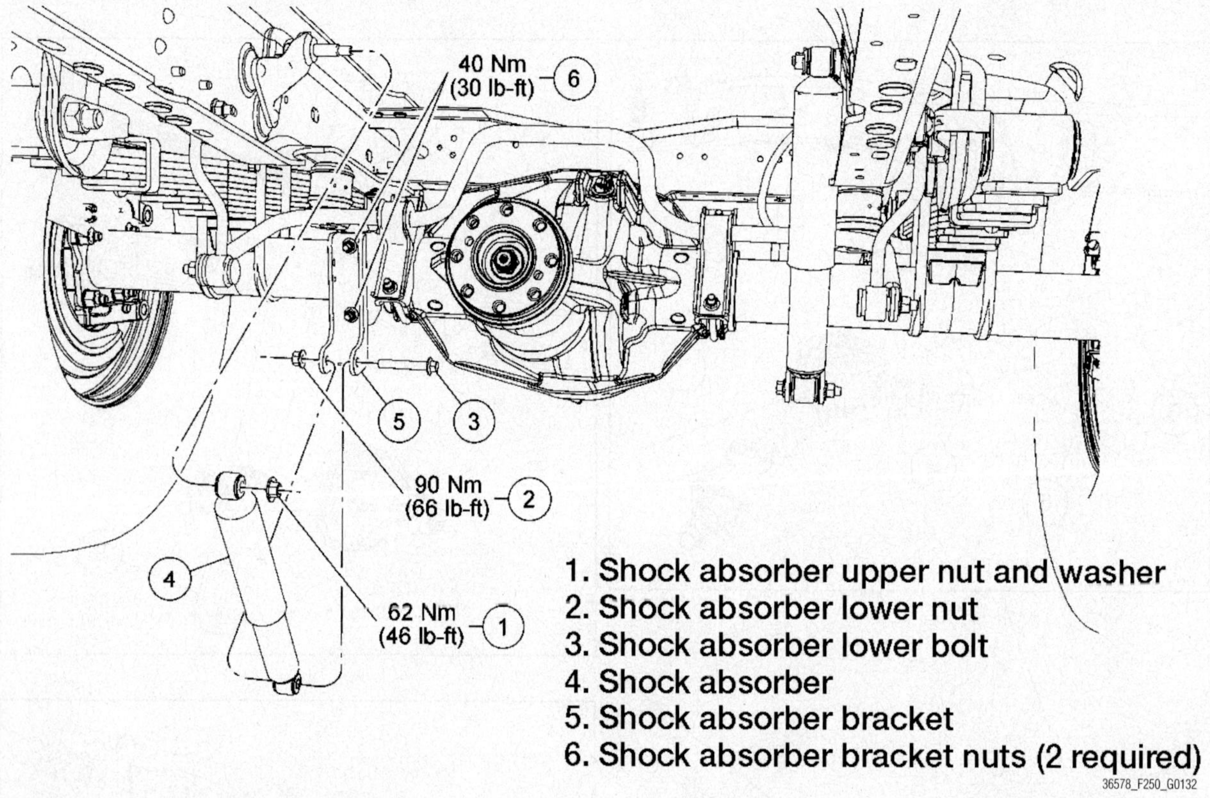

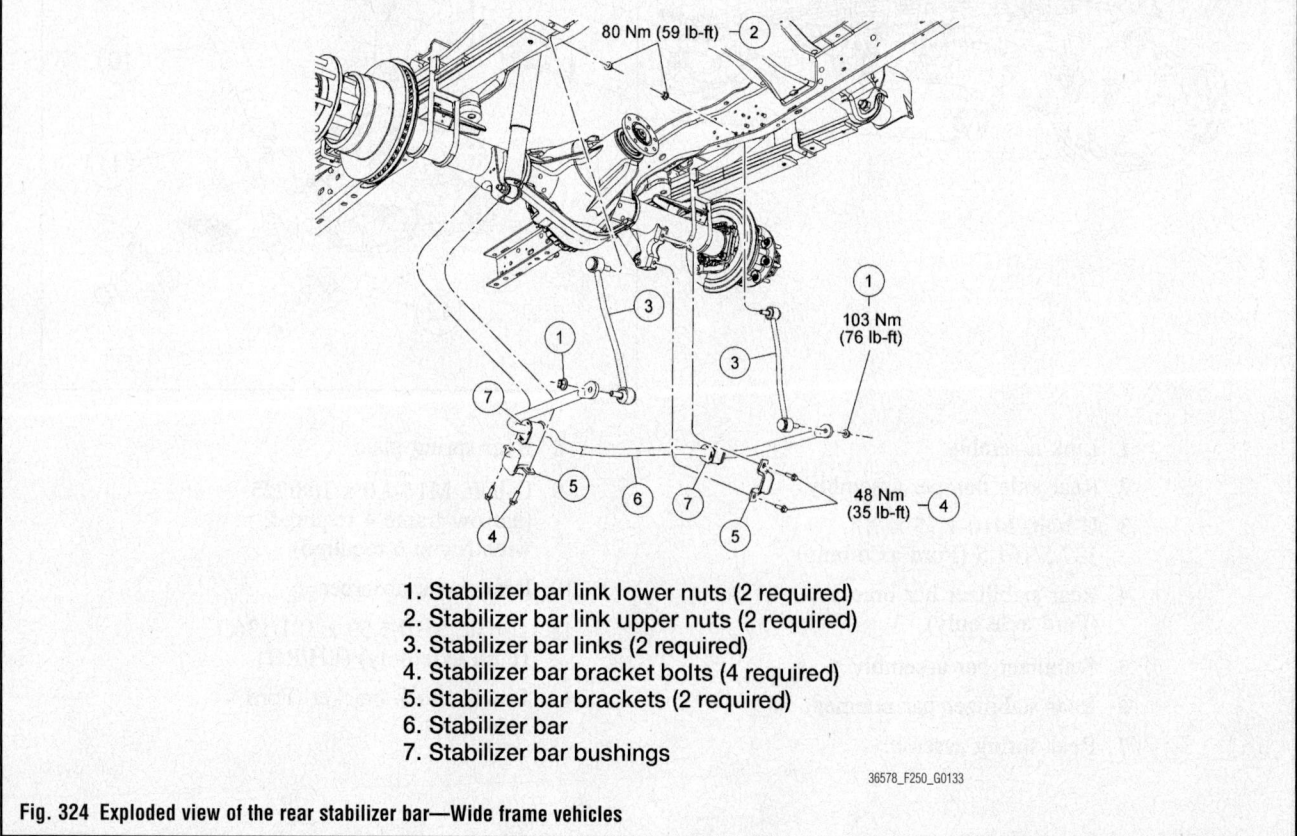

40 Nm
(30 lb-ft) 6
5
3
90 Nm
(66 lb-ft) 2
4
62 Nm
(46 lb-ft) 1
1. Shock absorber upper nut and washer
2. Shock absorber lower nut
3. Shock absorber lower bolt
4. Shock absorber
5. Shock absorber bracket
6. Shock absorber bracket nuts (2 required)
36578_F250_G0132

Fig. 323 Exploded view of the rear shock absorbers

80 Nm (59 lb-ft) 2
1
103 Nm
(76 lb-ft)
3
1
3
7
5
6
7
48 Nm
(35 lb-ft) 4
4
5
1. Stabilizer bar link lower nuts (2 required)
2. Stabilizer bar link upper nuts (2 required)
3. Stabilizer bar links (2 required)
4. Stabilizer bar bracket bolts (4 required)
5. Stabilizer bar brackets (2 required)
6. Stabilizer bar
7. Stabilizer bar bushings
36578_F250_G0133

Fig. 324 Exploded view of the rear stabilizer bar—Wide frame vehicles

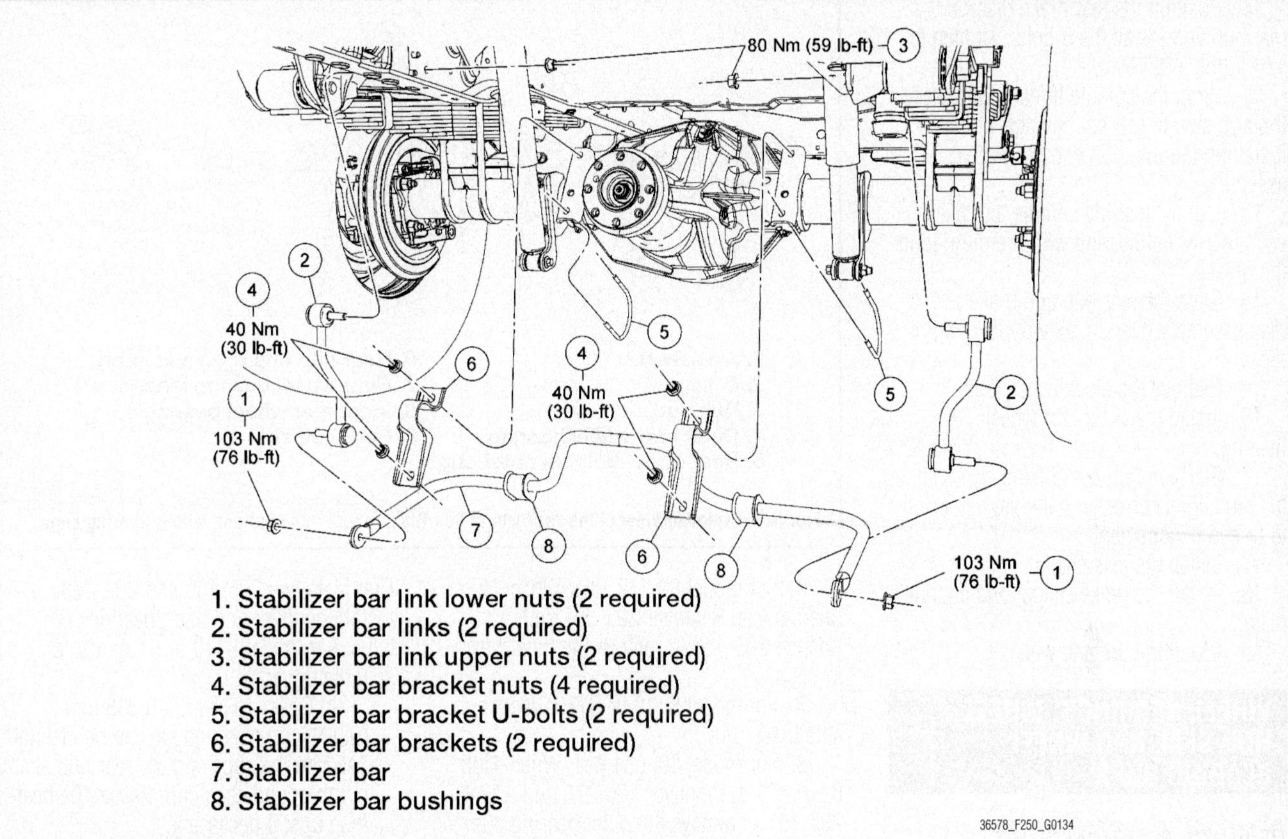

Fig. 325 Exploded view of the rear stabilizer bar—SRW and narrow frame vehicles

1. Stabilizer bar link lower nuts (2 required)
2. Stabilizer bar links (2 required)
3. Stabilizer bar link upper nuts (2 required)
4. Stabilizer bar bracket nuts (4 required)
5. Stabilizer bar bracket U-bolts (2 required)
6. Stabilizer bar brackets (2 required)
7. Stabilizer bar
8. Stabilizer bar bushings

36578_F250_G0134

2. With the vehicle in NEUTRAL, position it on a hoist.

3. Remove and discard the stabilizer bar link lower nuts. To install, tighten the new nuts to 76 ft. lbs. (103 Nm).

4. Remove and discard the stabilizer bar link upper nuts and remove the stabilizer bar links. To install, tighten the new nuts to 59 ft. lbs. (80 Nm).

5. For F-350 Single Rear Wheel (SRW), narrow frame vehicles:

   a. Remove the stabilizer bar bracket nuts, U-bolts, brackets and the stabilizer bar.

   b. Discard the nuts and U-bolts. To install, tighten the new nuts to 30 ft. lbs. (40 Nm).

6. For F-250/F-350 wide frame vehicles:

   a. Remove the stabilizer bar bracket bolts, brackets and the stabilizer bar.

   b. Discard the bolts. To install, tighten the new bolts to 35 ft. lbs. (48 Nm).

7. To install, reverse the removal procedure.

WHEEL HUB

REMOVAL & INSTALLATION

See Figure 326.

1. Remove the tire and wheel.
2. Remove the brake caliper anchor plate.
3. Remove the axle shaft.

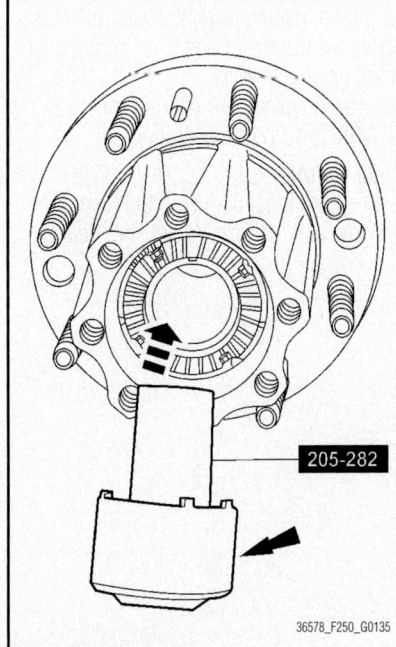

205-282

36578_F250_G0135

Fig. 326 Removing the hub with the Wheel Hub Nut Socket

➡ **Make sure that the drive tangs on the special tool engage the 4 slots of the hub nut.**

4. For the F-350, using the Wheel Hub Nut Socket, remove the hub nut.
5. Remove the outer rear wheel bearing.
6. Remove the rear hub and brake disc assembly.
7. Remove the 8 bolts and separate the rear hub from the rear brake disc.
8. Inspect the rear hub for the following:

   a. Cracks and damage around the bolt holes.

   b. Oversized holes.

To install:

➡ **Install a new rear hub seal after removing the rear hub from the axle. A damaged or worn seal can permit bearing lubricant to reach the brake linings, resulting in ineffective brake operation.**

➡ **Clean and remove any dirt or foreign material in the rear hub bolt holes or damage to components may occur.**

9. Install a new rear hub seal. For additional information, refer to Wheel Bearings, Wheel Hub Seal and Wheel Bearing Cups in this section.

10. Position the rear brake disc on the rear hub and install the 8 bolts. Tighten to 114 ft. lbs. (155 Nm).

11. Wrap the spindle threads with electrician's tape to prevent damage while installing the rear hub and brake disc assembly.

12. Lightly coat the spindle and pack each rear wheel bearing with premium long-life grease.

13. Slide the rear hub and brake disc assembly over the axle housing spindle.

14. Remove the electrician's tape.

15. Install the outer rear wheel bearing.

16. Start the hub nut making sure that the tab aligns correctly in the keyway prior to thread engagement.

17. Install the axle shaft.

18. Install the brake caliper and anchor plate.

19. Install the tire and wheel.

WHEEL BEARINGS, WHEEL HUB SEAL AND WHEEL BEARING CUPS

REMOVAL & INSTALLATION

F350 Models

Full Floating Axle—Dana

See Figure 327.

1. Remove the rear wheel hub.

2. Remove the rear hub seal and the inner rear wheel bearing. Discard the rear hub seal.

3. If not done previously, remove the 8 bolts and separate the rear hub from the brake disc.

4. Clean all the old grease and axle lubricant out of the rear hub.

5. Remove the inner and outer bearing cups.

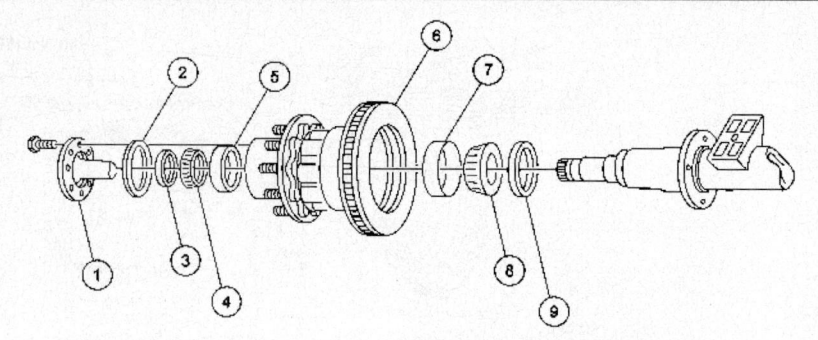

1. Axle shaft
2. O-ring
3. Hub nut
4. Outer rear wheel bearing
5. Rear wheel bearing outer cup
6. Rear hub and rotor assembly
7. Rear wheel bearing inner cup
8. Inner rear wheel bearing
9. Rear hub seal

36578_F250_G0136

Fig. 327 Exploded view of the rear wheel bearings, wheel hub seal and wheel bearing cups

6. For model 80, use Rear Wheel Hub Bearing Cup Remover 205-277 and Adapter 205-153 to remove the inner bearing cup.

7. For model S110 or S130, use a suitable brass drift.

8. For model 80, use Rear Wheel Hub Bearing Cup Remover 205-275 and Adapter 205-153 to remove the outer bearing cup. For model S110 or S130, use a suitable brass drift.

9. Clean the following components:
    a. The rear axle housing spindle.
    b. All the old grease and axle lubricant from the rear hub.
    c. The rear wheel bearings and cups.

10. Inspect the bearing races and rollers for pitting, galling or erratic wear patterns. Check the rollers for end wear. Discard the bearings, if necessary.
    a. A typical new bearing roller.
    b. A worn bearing roller.

To install:

11. For model 80, using the Rear Axle Drawbar and the Rear Wheel Hub Bearing

Cup Installers 205-100 and 205-278, install the inner and outer bearing cups. For model S110 or S130, use a suitable driver.
    a. Check to see if a 0.038 mm (0.0015 in) feeler gauge can be inserted between the cups and the rear hub at any point around each cup. Reseat the bearing cups, if necessary.

12. Install the inner rear wheel bearing in the rear hub.

13. Install a new rear hub seal.
    a. For model 80, use a suitable seal installer.
    b. For model S110 or S130, use the Wheel Hub Inner Wheel Installer and Adapter.

14. Position the rear brake disc on the rear hub and install the 8 bolts. Tighten to 114 ft. lbs. (155 Nm).

15. Install the rear wheel hub. For additional information, refer to Wheel Hub in this section.

FORD, LINCOLN AND MERCURY

Diagnostic Trouble Codes

DIAGNOSTIC TROUBLE CODES

OBD II VEHICLE APPLICATIONS

FORD

Crown Victoria
2008–2009
- 4.6L . . . . .VIN V
- 4.6L . . . . VIN W

Edge
2008–2009
- 3.5L . . . . .VIN C

Explorer, Explorer Sport Trac
2008–2009
- 4.0L . . . . .VIN E
- 4.6L . . . . .VIN 8

F-150, F-250, F-350
2008–2009
- 4.2L . . . . .VIN 2
- 4.6L . . . . VIN W
- 5.4L . . . . .VIN 5
- 5.4L . . . . .VIN L
- 5.4L . . . . .VIN V
- 6.8L . . . . .VIN S
- 6.8L . . . . .VIN Y

E-150, E-250, E-350
2008–2009
- 4.6L . . . . VIN W
- 5.4L . . . . .VIN L
- 6.0L . . . . .VIN P
- 6.8L . . . . .VIN S

Escape
2008–2009
- 2.3L . . . . .VIN Z
- 2.3L . . . . .VIN 7

- 3.0L . . . . .VIN 1
- 3.0L . . . . .VIN G

Escape Hybrid
2008–2009
- 2.3L . . . . .VIN H
- 2.3L . . . . .VIN 3

Expedition
2008–2009
- 5.4L . . . . .VIN 5

LINCOLN

Mark LT
2008
- 5.4L . . . . .VIN 5

MKX
2008–2009
- 3.5L . . . . .VIN C

Town Car
2008–2009
- 4.6L . . . . .VIN V
- 4.6L . . . . VIN W

MERCURY

Grand Marquis
2008–2009
- 4.6L . . . . .VIN V
- 4.6L . . . . VIN W

Navigator
2008–2009
- 5.4L . . . . .VIN 5

Mariner
2008–2009
- 2.3L . . . . .VIN Z
- 2.3L . . . . .VIN 7

- 3.0L . . . . .VIN 1
- 3.0L . . . . .VIN G

Mariner Hybrid
2008–2009
- 2.3L . . . . .VIN H
- 2.3L . . . . .VIN 3

Mountaineer
2008–2009
- 4.0L . . . . .VIN E
- 4.6L . . . . .VIN 8

INTRODUCTION

To use this information, first read and record all codes in memory along with any Freeze Frame data. *If the PCM reset function is done prior to recording any data, all codes and freeze frame data will be lost!* Look up the desired code by DTC number, Code Title and Conditions (enable criteria) that indicate why a code set, and how to drive the vehicle. **1T and 2T** indicate a 1-trip or 2-trip fault and the Monitor type.

Gas Engine OBD II Trouble Code List (P0xxx Codes)

DTC	Trouble Code Title, Conditions & Possible Causes
DTC: P0010 **2T CCM, MIL: Yes** **Years:** 2008, 2009, 2010 **Models:** All **Engines:** All **Transmissions:** All	**Intake Camshaft Position Actuator Circuit/Open (Bank 1)** Key on or engine running; and the PCM detected an unexpected high voltage or low voltage condition on the Variable Cam Timing (VCT) Solenoid 'A' control circuit during testing. **Note: This DTC is a circuit check. Testing should include the harness and solenoid coil.** **Possible Causes:** • Open VPWR circuit • Open or short in the VCT circuit • Open or short in the VCT solenoid valve
DTC: P0011 **2T CCM, MIL: Yes** **Years:** 2008, 2009, 2010 **Models:** All **Engines:** All **Transmissions:** All	**Intake Camshaft Position Timing - Over-Advanced (Bank 1)** Engine started; and the PCM detected the camshaft timing exceeded the maximum calibrated advance value, or the camshaft remained in an advanced position during the CCM test. **Note: This DTC may be accompanied by other DTCs. Diagnose all CMP sensor DTCs first. If no CMP sensor related DTCs are present, continue to follow diagnosis for this DTC.** **Possible Causes:** • Camshaft timing improperly set, or continuous oil flow to the VCT piston chamber • Camshaft advance mechanism (the VCT unit) is sticking or binding mechanically • VCT solenoid valve is stuck in open position • Radio Frequency Interference (RFI) interference • Open or short in the CMP sensor circuits • Damaged camshaft position (CMP) sensor • Open VPWR circuit
DTC: P0012 **2T CCM, MIL: Yes** **Years:** 2008, 2009, 2010 **Models:** All **Engines:** All **Transmissions:** All	**Intake Camshaft Position Timing - Over-Retarded (Bank 1)** The Powertrain Control Module (PCM) monitors the Variable Camshaft Timing (VCT) position for over-retarded camshaft timing. The test fails when the camshaft timing exceeds a maximum calibrated value or remains in a retarded position. **Note: This DTC may be accompanied by other DTCs. Diagnose all CMP sensor DTCs first. If no CMP sensor related DTCs are present, continue to follow diagnosis for this DTC.** **Possible Causes:** • Camshaft timing improperly set, or continuous oil flow to the VCT piston chamber • Camshaft advance mechanism (the VCT unit) is sticking or binding mechanically • VCT solenoid valve is stuck in open position • Radio Frequency Interference (RFI) interference • Open or short in the CMP sensor circuits • Damaged camshaft position (CMP) sensor • Open VPWR circuit
DTC: P0016 **2T CCM, MIL: Yes** **Years:** 2008, 2009, 2010 **Models:** All **Engines:** All **Transmissions:** All	**Crankshaft Position - Camshaft Position Correlation - Bank 1 Sensor A** The powertrain control module (PCM) monitors the variable camshaft timing (VCT) position for a misalignment between the camshaft and crankshaft. The test fails when the misalignment is 1 tooth or greater. This DTC can also be set due to VCT system concerns (oil contamination or VCT solenoid stuck). **Note: This DTC is a functional check of the VCT unit. Diagnose any base engine concerns related to the engine oil pressure or engine timing. Refer to the Workshop Manual Section 303-00 Engine System, Oil Pressure Test, to check the engine oil pressure. Refer to the Workshop Manual Section 303-01 Engine, Timing Drive Components, to check the engine timing.** **Possible Causes:** • Camshaft timing incorrectly set • VCT solenoid stuck in position • Camshaft advance mechanism binding (VCT unit)
DTC: P0018 **2T CCM, MIL: Yes** **Years:** 2008, 2009, 2010 **Models:** All **Engines:** All **Transmissions:** All	**Crankshaft Position - Camshaft Position Correlation - Bank 2 Sensor A** The powertrain control module (PCM) monitors the Variable Camshaft Timing (VCT) position for a misalignment between the camshaft and crankshaft. The test fails when the misalignment is 1 tooth or greater. This DTC can also be set due to VCT system concerns (oil contamination or VCT solenoid stuck). **Note: This DTC is a functional check of the VCT unit. Diagnose any base engine concerns related to the engine oil pressure or engine timing. Refer to the Workshop Manual Section 303-00 Engine System, Oil Pressure Test, to check the engine oil pressure. Refer to the Workshop Manual Section 303-01 Engine, Timing Drive Components, to check the engine timing.** **Possible Causes:** • Camshaft timing incorrectly set • VCT solenoid stuck in position • Camshaft advance mechanism binding (VCT unit)

DTC	Trouble Code Title, Conditions & Possible Causes

DTC: P0020
2T CCM, MIL: Yes
Years: 2008, 2009, 2010
Models: All
Engines: All
Transmissions: All
	Intake Camshaft Position Actuator Circuit/Open (Bank 2)
	Key on or engine running; and the PCM detected an unexpected high voltage or low voltage condition on the Variable Cam Timing (VCT) Solenoid 'A' control circuit during testing.
	Note: This DTC is a circuit check. Testing should include the harness and solenoid coil.
	Possible Causes:
	   • Open VPWR circuit
	   • Open or short in the VCT circuit
	   • Open or short in the VCT solenoid valve

DTC: P0021
2T CCM, MIL: Yes
Years: 2008, 2009, 2010
Models: All
Engines: All
Transmissions: All
	Intake Camshaft Position Timing - Over-Advanced (Bank 2)
	Engine started; and the PCM detected the camshaft timing exceeded the maximum calibrated advance value, or the camshaft remained in an advanced position during the CCM test.
	Note: This DTC may be accompanied by other DTCs. Diagnose all CMP sensor DTCs first. If no CMP sensor related DTCs are present, continue to follow diagnosis for this DTC.
	Possible Causes:
	   • Camshaft timing improperly set, or continuous oil flow to the VCT piston chamber
	   • Camshaft advance mechanism (the VCT unit) is sticking or binding mechanically
	   • VCT solenoid valve is stuck in open position
	   • Radio Frequency Interference (RFI) interference
	   • Open or short in the CMP sensor circuits
	   • Damaged camshaft position (CMP) sensor
	   • Open VPWR circuit

DTC: P0022
2T CCM, MIL: Yes
Years: 2008, 2009, 2010
Models: All
Engines: All
Transmissions: All
	Intake Camshaft Position Timing - Over-Retarded (Bank 2)
	The Powertrain Control Module (PCM) monitors the Variable Camshaft Timing (VCT) position for over-retarded camshaft timing. The test fails when the camshaft timing exceeds a maximum calibrated value or remains in a retarded position.
	Note: This DTC may be accompanied by other DTCs. Diagnose all CMP sensor DTCs first. If no CMP sensor related DTCs are present, continue to follow diagnosis for this DTC.
	Possible Causes:
	   • Camshaft timing improperly set, or continuous oil flow to the VCT piston chamber
	   • Camshaft advance mechanism (the VCT unit) is sticking or binding mechanically
	   • VCT solenoid valve is stuck in open position
	   • Radio Frequency Interference (RFI) interference
	   • Open or short in the CMP sensor circuits
	   • Damaged camshaft position (CMP) sensor
	   • Open VPWR circuit

DTC: P0030
2T CCM, MIL: Yes
Years: 2008, 2009, 2010
Models: All
Engines: All
Transmissions: All
	HO2S Heater Control Circuit (Bank 1, Sensor 1)
	The Powertrain Control Module (PCM) monitors the heater in the Heated Oxygen Sensor (HO2S) for correct operation. The PCM controls the heater on/off duty cycle to maintain a temperature of 780°C (1,436°F). The test fails when the sensor does not warm up to the required temperature in a calibrated amount of time. The test also fails when the PCM is not able to maintain the required temperature after the sensor is warm.
	Note: Inspect the connectors for signs of damage, water ingress, or corrosion.
	Possible Causes:
	   • Open UO2S circuit
	   • Open UO2SGREF circuit
	   • Open UO2SHTR circuit
	   • UO2SHTR circuit short to voltage
	   • Loose connection, and damaged or corroded terminals
	   • Exhaust temperature significantly higher than expected
	   • Damaged universal HO2S

DTC: P0040
2T CCM, MIL: Yes
Years: 2008, 2009, 2010
Models: E-Series, Expedition, F-150, Navigator
Engines: 4.6L VIN W, 5.4L L, 3.5L W
Transmissions: All
	Oxygen Sensor Signals Swapped Bank 1 Sensor 1/Bank 2 Sensor 1
	The heated oxygen sensor (HO2S) monitor determines if the HO2S signal response for a fuel shift corresponds to the correct engine bank. The test fails when there is no response from the HO2S being tested.
	Note: Connect the HO2S connector to the correct bank.
	Possible Causes:
	   • Crossed HO2S harness connectors
	   • Crossed HO2S wiring at the harness connectors
	   • Crossed HO2S wiring at the PCM connectors

DTC	Trouble Code Title, Conditions & Possible Causes
DTC: P0041 **2T CCM, MIL: Yes** **Years:** 2008, 2009, 2010 **Models:** All **Engines:** All **Transmissions:** All	**Oxygen Sensor Signals Swapped Bank 1 Sensor 2/Bank 2 Sensor 2** The Heated Oxygen Sensor (HO2S) monitor determines if the HO2S signal response for a fuel shift corresponds to the correct engine bank. The test fails when there is no response from the HO2S being tested. **Note: Connect the HO2S connector to the correct bank.** **Possible Causes:** • Crossed HO2S harness connectors • Crossed HO2S wiring at the harness connectors • Crossed HO2S wiring at the PCM connectors
DTC: P0050 **2T CCM, MIL: Yes** **Years:** 2008, 2009, 2010 **Models:** All **Engines:** All **Transmissions:** All	**HO2S Heater Control Circuit (Bank 2, Sensor 1)** The Powertrain Control Module (PCM) monitors the heater in the Heated Oxygen Sensor (HO2S) for correct operation. The PCM controls the heater on/off duty cycle to maintain a temperature of 780°C (1,436°F). The test fails when the sensor does not warm up to the required temperature in a calibrated amount of time. The test also fails when the PCM is not able to maintain the required temperature after the sensor is warm. **Note: Inspect the connectors for signs of damage, water ingress, or corrosion.** **Possible Causes:** • Open UO2S circuit • Open UO2SGREF circuit • Open UO2SHTR circuit • UO2SHTR circuit short to voltage • Loose connection, and damaged or corroded terminals • Exhaust temperature significantly higher than expected • Damaged universal HO2S
DTC: P0053 **2T CCM, MIL: Yes** **Years:** 2008, 2009, 2010 **Models:** All **Engines:** All **Transmissions:** All	**HO2S Heater Resistance (Bank 1, Sensor 1)** Heater current requirements too low or high in the Heated Oxygen Sensor (HO2S) heater control circuit **Note: Inspect the connectors for signs of damage, water ingress, or corrosion.** **Possible Causes:** • VPWR circuit open • HO2S heater circuit open • HO2S heater circuit short in the harness • Damaged HO2S heater
DTC: P0054 **2T CCM, MIL: Yes** **Years:** 2008, 2009, 2010 **Models:** All **Engines:** All **Transmissions:** All	**HO2S Heater Resistance (Bank 1, Sensor 2)** Heater current requirements too low or high in the Heated Oxygen Sensor (HO2S) heater control circuit **Note: Inspect the connectors for signs of damage, water ingress, or corrosion.** **Possible Causes:** • VPWR circuit open • HO2S heater circuit open • HO2S heater circuit short in the harness • Damaged HO2S heater
DTC: P0055 **2T CCM, MIL: Yes** **Years:** 2008, 2009, 2010 **Models:** All **Engines:** All **Transmissions:** All	**HO2S Heater Resistance (Bank 1, Sensor 3)** Heater current requirements too low or high in the Heated Oxygen Sensor (HO2S) heater control circuit **Note: Inspect the connectors for signs of damage, water ingress, or corrosion.** **Possible Causes:** • VPWR circuit open • HO2S heater circuit open • HO2S heater circuit short in the harness • Damaged HO2S heater
DTC: P0059 **2T CCM, MIL: Yes** **Years:** 2008, 2009, 2010 **Models:** All **Engines:** All **Transmissions:** All	**HO2S Heater Resistance (Bank 2, Sensor 1)** Heater current requirements too low or high in the Heated Oxygen Sensor (HO2S) heater control circuit **Note: Inspect the connectors for signs of damage, water ingress, or corrosion.** **Possible Causes:** • VPWR circuit open • HO2S heater circuit open • HO2S heater circuit short in the harness • Damaged HO2S heater

DTC	Trouble Code Title, Conditions & Possible Causes
DTC: P0060 **2T CCM, MIL: Yes** **Years:** 2008, 2009, 2010 **Models:** All **Engines:** All **Transmissions:** All	**HO2S Heater Resistance (Bank 2, Sensor 2)** Heater current requirements too low or high in the Heated Oxygen Sensor (HO2S) heater control circuit **Note: Inspect the connectors for signs of damage, water ingress, or corrosion.** **Possible Causes:** • VPWR circuit open • HO2S heater circuit open • HO2S heater circuit short in the harness • Damaged HO2S heater
DTC: P0068 **2T CCM, MIL: Yes** **Years:** 2008, 2009, 2010 **Models:** All **Engines:** All **Transmissions:** All	**Manifold Absolute Pressure (MAP)/Mass Air Flow (MAF) - Throttle Position Correlation** The Powertrain Control Module (PCM) monitors a vehicle operation rationality check by comparing sensed throttle position to mass air flow readings. If during a Key On Engine Running (KOER) self-test, the comparison of the Throttle Position (TP) sensor and MAF sensor readings are not consistent with the calibrated load values, the test fails and a DTC is stored in continuous memory. **Note: Diagnose any MAF or TP circuit DTCs first. Drive the vehicle and exercise the throttle and the TP sensor in all gears. A TP PID less than 4.82% (0.24 volt) with a LOAD PID greater than 55%, or a TP PID greater than 49.05% (2.44 volts) with a LOAD PID less than 30% indicates a concern is present.** **Possible Causes:** • Air leak between MAF sensor and throttle body • Damaged MAF sensor • TP sensor not seated correctly • Damaged TP sensor
DTC: P0097 **2T CCM, MIL: Yes** **Years:** 2008, 2009, 2010 **Models:** All **Engines:** All **Transmissions:** All	**Intake Air Temperature Sensor 2 Circuit Low** Indicates the sensor signal is less than the self-test minimum. The Intake Air Temperature 2 (IAT2) sensor minimum is 0.2 volt **Note: Monitor the IAT2 PID value. A typical IAT2 temperature should be greater than the IAT1 temperature.** **Possible Causes:** • Grounded circuit in the harness • Incorrect harness connection • Damaged sensor
DTC: P0098 **2T CCM, MIL: Yes** **Years:** 2008, 2009, 2010 **Models:** All **Engines:** All **Transmissions:** All	**Intake Air Temperature Sensor 2 Circuit High** Indicates the sensor signal is greater than the self-test maximum. The Intake Air Temperature 2 (IAT2) sensor maximum is 4.6 volts. **Note: Monitor the IAT2 PID value. A typical IAT2 temperature should be greater than the IAT1 temperature.** **Possible Causes:** • Open circuit in the harness • Sensor signal short to voltage • Incorrect harness connection • Damaged sensor
DTC: P0102 **2T CCM, MIL: Yes** **Years:** 2008, 2009, 2010 **Models:** All **Engines:** All **Transmissions:** All	**Mass or Volume Air Flow A Circuit Low** The mass air flow (MAF) sensor circuit is monitored by the powertrain control module (PCM) for low air flow (or voltage) input through the comprehensive component monitor (CCM). If during key on, engine running (KOER) the air flow (or voltage) changes below a minimum calibrated limit, the test fails. **Possible Causes** • MAF sensor disconnected • MAF circuit open to PCM • VPWR open to MAF sensor • PWR GND open to the MAF sensor • MAF RTN circuit open to PCM • MAF circuit shorted to GND • Intake air leak (near the MAF sensor) • A closed throttle indication (throttle position [TP] sensor system) • Damaged MAF sensor
DTC: P0103 **2T CCM, MIL: Yes** **Years:** 2008, 2009, 2010 **Models:** All **Engines:** All **Transmissions:** All	**Mass or Volume Air Flow A Circuit High** The Mass Air Flow (MAF) sensor circuit is monitored by the powertrain control module (PCM) for high air flow (or voltage) input through the Comprehensive Component Monitor (CCM). If during Key On, Engine Off (KOEO), or Key On, Engine Running (KOER), the air flow (or voltage) changes above a maximum calibrated limit, the test fails. **Possible Causes** • MAF sensor screen is blocked • MAF circuit shorted to voltage • Damaged MAF sensor

DTC	Trouble Code Title, Conditions & Possible Causes
DTC: P0104 **2T CCM, MIL: Yes** **Years:** 2008, 2009, 2010 **Models:** All **Engines:** All **Transmissions:** All	**Mass or Volume Air Flow A Circuit Intermittent/Erratic** A concern exists in the mass air flow (MAF) sensor A circuit, or the air tube containing the sensor, causing an incorrect air flow reading **Note: Verify the integrity of the MAF sensor circuit A for an intermittent concern. Check the MAF sensor tube for air leaks.** **Possible Causes:** • Intermittent circuit A open or short • Air leaks in the tube from the MAF to the throttle body
DTC: P0106 **2T CCM, MIL: Yes** **Years:** 2008, 2009, 2010 **Models:** All **Engines:** All **Transmissions:** All	**Manifold Absolute Pressure (MAP/BARO) Sensor Range/Performance** MAP sensor input to the powertrain control module (PCM) is monitored and is not within the calibrated value. **Note: The VREF voltage should be between 4.0 and 6.0 volts.** **Possible Causes:** • Slow responding MAP sensor • Electrical circuit failure • Damaged MAP sensor
DTC: P0107 **2T CCM, MIL: Yes** **Years:** 2008, 2009, 2010 **Models:** All **Engines:** All **Transmissions:** All	**Manifold Absolute Pressure (MAP)/Barometric Pressure (BARO) Sensor Low** MAP sensor operating voltage is below the minimum calibrated parameter of 0.024 volts **Note: The VREF voltage should be between 4.0 and 6.0 volts.** **Possible Causes:** • Open in the circuit, or short to ground • VREF circuit open, or short to ground • Damaged MAP sensor • PCM has failed
DTC: P0108 **2T CCM, MIL: Yes** **Years:** 2008, 2009, 2010 **Models:** All **Engines:** All **Transmissions:** All	**Manifold Absolute Pressure (MAP)/Barometric Pressure (BARO) Sensor High** Sensor operating voltage is greater than 4.96 volts. As a result it failed above the maximum allowable calibrated parameter **Note: The VREF voltage should be between 4.0 and 6.0 volts.** **Possible Causes:** • VREF shorted to VPWR • MAP signal shorted to VPWR • VREF should be less than 6.0 volts • Open circuit • PCM has failed
DTC: P0109 **2T CCM, MIL: Yes** **Years:** 2008, 2009, 2010 **Models:** All **Engines:** All **Transmissions:** All	**Manifold Absolute Pressure (MAP)/Barometric Pressure (BARO) Sensor Intermittent** The sensor signal to the Powertrain Control Module (PCM) is failing intermittently. **Note: Check the harness and connection.** **Possible Causes:** • Loose electrical connection • Damaged MAP sensor
DTC: P0111 **2T CCM, MIL: Yes** **Years:** 2008, 2009, 2010 **Models:** All **Engines:** All **Transmissions:** All	**Intake Air Temperature (IAT) Sensor 1 Circuit Range/Performance** Indicates the IAT rationality test has failed. This DTC indicates that the IAT value is higher than a calibrated value and could prevent one or more on-board diagnostic (OBD) monitors from completing. The powertrain control module (PCM) runs this logic after an engine off and a calibrated soak period (typically 6 hours). This soak period allows IAT and engine coolant temperature (ECT) or cylinder head temperature (CHT) to stabilize and not differ by more than a calibrated value. DTC P0111 sets when the IAT at engine start exceeds the ECT or CHT by more than a calibrated value, typically 17°C (30°F). **Note: Make sure the IAT and the CHT or ECT are similar when the engine is cold.** **Possible Causes:** • IAT Sensor
DTC: P0112 **2T CCM, MIL: Yes** **Years:** 2008, 2009, 2010 **Models:** All **Engines:** All **Transmissions:** All	**Intake Air Temperature (IAT) Sensor 1 Circuit Low** Indicates the sensor signal is less than the self-test minimum. The IAT sensor minimum is 0.2 volt or 121°C (250°F). **Note: An IAT V PID reading less than 0.2 volt with key ON engine OFF or during any engine operating mode indicates a concern is present** **Possible Causes:** • Grounded circuit in the harness • Damaged sensor • Incorrect harness connection

DTC	Trouble Code Title, Conditions & Possible Causes
DTC: P0113 **2T CCM, MIL: Yes** **Years:** 2008, 2009, 2010 **Models:** All **Engines:** All **Transmissions:** All	**Intake Air Temperature (IAT) Sensor 1 Circuit High** Indicates the sensor signal is greater than the self-test maximum. The IAT sensor maximum is 4.6 volts or −50°C (−58°F). **Note: An IAT PID reading greater than 4.6 volts with the key ON engine OFF or during any engine operating mode indicates a concern is present** **Possible Causes:** • Open circuit in the harness • Sensor signal short to voltage • Damaged sensor • Incorrect harness connection • PCM has failed
DTC: P0114 **2T CCM, MIL: Yes** **Years:** 2008, 2009, 2010 **Models:** All **Engines:** All **Transmissions:** All	**Intake Air Temperature (IAT) Sensor 1 Intermittent/Erratic** Indicates the sensor signal was intermittent during the Comprehensive Component Monitor (CCM). **Note: Monitor the IAT on a scan tool. Look for sudden changes in the reading when the harness is wiggled or the sensor is tapped** **Possible Causes:** • Damaged harness • Damaged sensor • Damaged harness connector • PCM has failed
DTC: P0116 **2T ECT, MIL: Yes** **Years:** 2008, 2009, 2010 **Models:** All **Engines:** All **Transmissions:** All	**Engine Coolant Temperature (ECT) Sensor 1 Circuit Range/Performance** Indicates the engine coolant temperature rationality test has failed. This DTC indicates that the ECT or Cylinder Head Temperature (CHT) value is higher than the calibrated value and could prevent one or more On-Doard Diagnostic (OBD) monitors from completing. The Powertrain Control Module (PCM) runs this logic after an engine off and a calibrated soak period (typically 6 hours). This soak period allows the Intake Air Temperature (IAT) and the CHT or ECT to stabilize and not differ by more than a calibrated value. DTC P0116 sets when all of the following conditions are met: The ECT at engine start exceeds the IAT at engine start by more than a calibrated value, typically 17°C (30°F).The ECT exceeds a calibrated value, typically 107°C (225°F). The fuel system, heated oxygen and misfire monitors have not completed. The calibrated time to set DTC P0116 has expired. **Note: Make sure the IAT and the ECT are similar when the engine is cold. Also make sure the ECT or CHT sensor and the actual engine operating temperatures are the same.** **Possible Causes:** • ECT or CHT sensor • Coolant system concern
DTC: P0117 **2T CCM, MIL: Yes** **Years:** 2008, 2009, 2010 **Models:** All **Engines:** All **Transmissions:** All	**Engine Coolant Temperature (ECT) Sensor 1 Circuit Low** Indicates the sensor signal is less than the self-test minimum. The ECT sensor minimum is 0.2 volt or 121°C (250°F). **Note: A concern is present if an ECT PID reading less than 0.2 volt with the key ON engine OFF or during any engine operating mode** **Possible Causes:** • Grounded circuit in the harness • Damaged sensor • Incorrect harness connection • PCM has failed
DTC: P0118 **2T CCM, MIL: Yes** **Years:** 2008, 2009, 2010 **Models:** All **Engines:** All **Transmissions:** All	**ECT Sensor Circuit High Input** Indicates the sensor signal is greater than the self-test maximum. The ECT sensor maximum is 4.6 volts or −50°C (−58°F). **Note: An ECT PID reading greater than 4.6 volts with the key ON engine OFF or during any engine operating mode indicates a concern is present** **Possible Causes:** • Open circuit in the harness • Sensor signal short to voltage • Incorrect harness connection • Damaged sensor • PCM has failed
DTC: P0119 **2T CCM, MIL: Yes** **Years:** 2008, 2009, 2010 **Models:** Explorer, Mountaineer **Engines:** 3.0L 1, 4.0L E, 4.0L N, **Transmissions:** All	**Engine Coolant Temperature (ECT) Sensor 1 Circuit Intermittent/Erratic** Indicates the ECT circuit became intermittently open or shorted while the engine was running. On vehicles that are not equipped with an ECT sensor, the Cylinder Head Temperature (CHT) sensor can be used and can set this DTC. **Note: Monitor the ECT or the CHT on a scan tool, look for sudden changes in the reading when the harness is wiggled or the sensor is tapped.** **Possible Causes:** • Damaged harness • Damaged sensor • Damaged harness connector • Low engine coolant

DTC	Trouble Code Title, Conditions & Possible Causes
DTC: P0121 **2T CCM, MIL: Yes** **Years:** 2008, 2009, 2010 **Models:** All **Engines:** All **Transmissions:** All	**Throttle/Pedal Position Sensor A Circuit Range/Performance** **(For Vehicles With an Idle Air Control (IAC) Valve)** The Throttle Position (TP) sensor circuit is monitored by the Powertrain Control Module (PCM) for a non-closed throttle position at idle. The test fails if the Key On Engine Running (KOER) self-test terminates upon placing the transmission gear selector in DRIVE or REVERSE or the TP closed throttle position is not achieved when closing the throttle (idle) after opening it (in PARK or NEUTRAL). **Note: Drive the vehicle, bring it to a stop, and turn the key to the OFF position. Start the engine, and run the KOER self-test at idle.** **Possible Causes:** • Binding throttle linkage • Damaged throttle body • TP circuit open to PCM • Damaged TP sensor • SIG RTN circuit open to the TP sensor
DTC: P0121 **2T CCM, MIL: Yes** **Years:** 2008, 2009, 2010 **Models:** All **Engines:** All **Transmissions:** All	**Throttle/Pedal Position Sensor A Circuit Range/Performance** **(For Vehicles Without an Idle Air Control (IAC) Valve)** The Electronic Throttle Control (ETC) Throttle Position (TP) sensor 1 circuit was flagged as a concern by the Powertrain Control Module (PCM) indicating an out of range in either the closed or Wide Open Throttle (WOT) modes. **Note: This concern exhibits a symptom of limited power.** **Possible Causes:** • Obstruction in the throttle plate movement • Damaged throttle body • TP circuit open to PCM • Damaged TP sensor • SIG RTN circuit open to the TP sensor • Self-test operator error (foot resting on the accelerator pedal during test)
DTC: P0122 **2T CCM, MIL: Yes** **Years:** 2008, 2009, 2010 **Models:** All **Engines:** All **Transmissions:** All	**Throttle/Pedal Position Sensor A Circuit Low** **(For Vehicles With an Idle Air Control (IAC) Valve)** The Throttle Position (TP) sensor circuit is monitored by the PCM for a high TP rotation angle (or voltage) input through the Comprehensive Component Monitor (CCM). The test fails if the TP rotation angle (or voltage) changes above the maximum calibrated limit. **Note: This concern exhibits a symptom of limited power. A TP PID reading less than 3.42% (0.17 volt) in key ON, engine OFF or key ON, engine running indicates a concern is present.** **Possible Causes:** • TP sensor not seated correctly • TP circuit open to PCM • VREF open to TP sensor • TP circuit short to GND • Damaged TP sensor • PCM has failed
DTC: P0122 **2T CCM, MIL: Yes** **Years:** 2008, 2009, 2010 **Models:** All **Engines:** All **Transmissions:** All	**Throttle/Pedal Position Sensor A Circuit Low** **(For Vehicles Without an Idle Air Control (IAC) Valve)** The Electronic Throttle Control (ETC) Throttle Position (TP) sensor 1 circuit was flagged as a concern by the Powertrain Control Module (PCM) indicating a low voltage or open circuit. **Note: This concern exhibits a symptom of limited power. A TP1 PID reading less than 0.25 volt in key ON, engine OFF or key ON, engine running indicates a concern is present.** **Possible Causes:** • Open ETC TP sensor harness • Short to ground in the ETC TP sensor harness • Damaged TP sensor • SIG RTN circuit open to the TP sensor • PCM has failed

DTC	Trouble Code Title, Conditions & Possible Causes
DTC: P0123 **2T CCM, MIL: Yes** **Years:** 2008, 2009, 2010 **Models:** All **Engines:** All **Transmissions:** All	**Throttle/Pedal Position Sensor A Circuit High** **(For Vehicles With an Idle Air Control (IAC) Valve)** The Throttle Position (TP) sensor circuit is monitored by the Powertrain Control Module (PCM) for a high TP rotation angle (or voltage) input through the Comprehensive Component Monitor (CCM). The test fails if the TP rotation angle (or voltage) changes above the maximum calibrated limit. **Note: A TP PID reading greater than 93% (4.65 volts) in key ON, engine OFF or key ON, engine running indicates a concern is present.** **Possible Causes:** • TP sensor not seated correctly • TP sensor harness is short to voltage • TP sensor harness short to VREF • SIG RTN circuit open to the TP sensor • Damaged TP sensor • PCM has failed
DTC: P0123 **2T CCM, MIL: Yes** **Years:** 2008, 2009, 2010 **Models:** All **Engines:** All **Transmissions:** All	**Throttle/Pedal Position Sensor A Circuit High** **(For Vehicles Without an Idle Air Control (IAC) Valve)** The Electronic Throttle Control (ETC) Throttle Position (TP) sensor 1 circuit was flagged as a concern by the Powertrain Control Module (PCM) indicating a high voltage. **Note: Drive the vehicle, bring it to a stop, and turn the key to the OFF position. Start the engine and carry out the Key On Engine Running (KOER) self-test at idle. Access the KOER DTCs on the scan tool. The TP1 signal is normally at a high voltage at closed throttle, and a lower voltage at Wide Open Throttle (WOT) (opposite of TP2). A TP1 PID reading greater than 4.75 volts in key ON, engine OFF or key ON, engine running indicates a concern is present.** **Possible Causes:** • TP sensor harness short to VREF • TP sensor harness is short to voltage • Damaged TP sensor • VREF circuit short to TP sensor • PCM has failed
DTC: P0125 **2T CCM, MIL: Yes** **Years:** 2008, 2009, 2010 **Models:** Explorer, Mountaineer **Engines:** 3.0L 1, 4.0L E, 4.0L N, **Transmissions:** All	**Insufficient Coolant Temperature For Closed Loop Fuel Control** Indicates the Engine Coolant Temperature (ECT) or the Cylinder Head Temperature (CHT) sensor has not achieved the required temperature level to enter closed loop operating conditions within a specified amount of time after starting the engine. **Note: Compare the thermostat specification to the actual ECT using the engine temperature PID (ECT or CHT). The temperature reading should be similar when the engine is at a normal operating temperature.** **Possible Causes:** • Insufficient warm up time • Low engine coolant level • Leaking or stuck open thermostat • Damaged ECT sensor • Damaged CHT sensor
DTC: P0127 **2T CCM, MIL: Yes** **Years:** 2008, 2009, 2010 **Models:** All **Engines:** All **Transmissions:** All	**Intake Air Temperature (IAT) Too High** Indicates that the IAT2 sensor has detected a concern in the Charge Air Cooler (CAC) system **Note: Monitor the IAT2 PID. A typical IAT2 temperature should be greater than the IAT1 temperature** **Possible Causes:** • Blockage of heat exchangers • Low fluid level • Fluid leakage • CAC pump or relay failure • Crossed CAC coolant lines
DTC: P0128 **2T CCM, MIL: Yes** **Years:** 2008, 2009, 2010 **Models:** All **Engines:** All **Transmissions:** All	**Coolant Thermostat (Coolant Temperature Below Thermostat Regulating Temperature)** Indicates that the thermostat monitor has not achieved the required engine operating temperature within a specified amount of time after starting the engine. **Possible Causes:** • Insufficient warm up time • Low engine coolant level • Leaking or stuck open thermostat • Damaged ECT sensor • Damaged CHT sensor

DTC	Trouble Code Title, Conditions & Possible Causes
DTC: P012B **2T CCM, MIL: Yes** **Years:** 2008, 2009, 2010 **Models:** All **Engines:** All with Turbocharger/Supercharger **Transmissions:** All	**Turbocharger/Supercharger Inlet Pressure Sensor Circuit High** Manifold Absolute Pressure (MAP) sensor input to the Powertrain Control Module (PCM) is monitored and is not within the calibrated value. **Note: The VREF voltage should be between 4.0 and 6.0 volts.** **Possible Causes:** • Slow responding MAP sensor • Electrical circuit failure • Damaged MAP sensor.
DTC: P012C **2T CCM, MIL: Yes** **Years:** 2008, 2009, 2010 **Models:** All **Engines:** All with Turbocharger/Supercharger **Transmissions:** All	**Turbocharger/Supercharger Inlet Pressure Sensor Circuit Low** MAP sensor operating voltage is below the minimum calibrated parameter of 0.25 volt. **Note: VREF voltage should be between 4.0 and 6.0 volts.** **Possible Causes:** • Open in the circuit, or short to ground • VREF circuit open, or short to ground • Damaged MAP sensor.
DTC: P012D **2T CCM, MIL: Yes** **Years:** 2008, 2009, 2010 **Models:** All **Engines:** All with Turbocharger/Supercharger **Transmissions:** All	**Turbocharger/Supercharger Inlet Pressure Sensor Circuit High** Manifold Absolute Pressure (MAP) sensor operating voltage is above the maximum calibrated parameter of 5 volts. **Note: VREF should be greater than 4.0 volts.** **Possible Causes:** • VREF shorted to VPWR • MAP signal shorted to VPWR • VREF circuit short to voltage • Open circuit
DTC: P012E **2T CCM, MIL: Yes** **Years:** 2008, 2009, 2010 **Models:** All **Engines:** All with Turbocharger/Supercharger **Transmissions:** All	**Turbocharger/Supercharger Inlet Pressure Sensor Circuit Intermittent/Erratic** The sensor signal to the Powertrain Control Module (PCM) is intermittent **Note: Check the harness and connection.** **Possible Causes:** • Loose electrical connection • Damaged Manifold Absolute Pressure (MAP) sensor
DTC: P0130 **2T O2HTR, MIL: Yes** **Years:** 2008, 2009, 2010 **Models:** All **Engines:** All **Transmissions:** All	**O2 Circuit (Bank 1, Sensor 1)** The Powertrain Control Module (PCM) monitors the Heated Oxygen Sensor (HO2S) for a circuit concern. The test fails when the PCM detects a concern with one of the circuits used to determine the oxygen content in the exhaust gas. **Possible Causes:** • Open UO2S circuit • Open UO2SGREF circuit • UO2S circuit short to voltage or ground • UO2SGREF circuit short to voltage or ground • UO2SPC circuit short to voltage or ground • UO2SPCT circuit short to voltage or ground • Damaged universal HO2S
DTC: P0132 **2T O2HTR, MIL: Yes** **Years:** 2008, 2009, 2010 **Models:** All **Engines:** All **Transmissions:** All	**O2 Circuit High Voltage (Bank 1, Sensor 1)** The Heated Oxygen Sensor (HO2S) signals are monitored for an over voltage condition. The code is set when the HO2S signal voltage is 1.5 volts or greater. **Note: An HO2S PID switching across 0.45 volt from 0.2 to 0.9 volt indicates a normal switching HO2S. An HO2S PID voltage of 1.5 volts or greater indicates a short to voltage.** **Possible Causes:** • Short to VPWR in the harness or HO2S • PCM has failed

DTC	Trouble Code Title, Conditions & Possible Causes

DTC: P0133
2T O2HTR, MIL: Yes
Years: 2008, 2009, 2010
Models: All
Engines: All
Transmissions: All
	O2 Circuit Slow Response (Bank 1, Sensor 1)
	The Powertrain Control Module (PCM) commands an air/fuel ratio that changes in the shape of a square wave. The PCM calculates the length of the resulting signal from the HO2S. The test fails when the length of the signal is less than a calibrated limit. For all others, the PCM checks the HO2S signal frequency and amplitude. The test fails when the frequency and amplitude less than a calibrated limit.
	Note: Access the HO2S test results from the generic OBD menu to verify the DTC.
	Possible Causes:
	    • Contaminated HO2S
	    • Exhaust leaks
	    • Short/open wiring
	    • Incorrect fueling
	    • MAF sensor
	    • Deteriorating HO2S
	    • Inlet air leaks
	    • PCM has failed

DTC: P0134
2T O2HTR, MIL: Yes
Years: 2008, 2009, 2010
Models: All
Engines: All
Transmissions: All
	O2 Circuit No Activity Detected (Bank 1, Sensor 1)
	The Powertrain Control Module (PCM) monitors the Heated Oxygen Sensor (HO2S) for a lack of movement concern. If the sensor signal value is not changing from the default value, the PCM commands an oscillating air/fuel ratio attempting to detect some movement in the signal value. The test fails when the PCM is unable to detect movement in the sensor signal while the air/fuel ratio is oscillating.
	Possible Causes:
	    • Open UO2SPC circuit
	    • Damaged universal HO2S
	    • PCM has failed

DTC: P0135
2T O2HTR, MIL: Yes
Years: 2008, 2009, 2010
Models: All
Engines: All
Transmissions: All
	O2 Heater Circuit (Bank 1, Sensor 1)
	During testing the Heated Oxygen Sensor (HO2S) heaters are checked for open and short circuits and excessive current draw. The test fails when the current draw exceeds a calibrated limit or an open or short circuit is detected.
	Note: Inspect the connectors for signs of damage, water ingress, or corrosion.
	Possible Causes:
	    • Vacuum hose disconnected on Exhaust Gas Recirculation (EGR) System Module (ESM) applications
	    • Short to VPWR in the harness or HO2S
	    • Water in the harness connector
	    • Open VPWR circuit
	    • Open UO2SHTR circuit
	    • Open GND circuit
	    • Low battery voltage
	    • Corrosion or poor mating terminals and wiring
	    • Damaged HO2S heater
	    • PCM has failed

DTC: P0138
2T O2HTR, MIL: Yes
Years: 2008, 2009, 2010
Models: All
Engines: All
Transmissions: All
	O2 Circuit High Voltage (Bank 1, Sensor 2)
	The Heated Oxygen Sensor (HO2S) signals are monitored for an over voltage condition. The code is set when the HO2S signal voltage is 1.5 volts or greater.
	Note: An HO2S PID switching across 0.45 volt from 0.2 to 0.9 volt indicates a normal switching HO2S. An HO2S PID voltage of 1.5 volts or greater indicates a short to voltage.
	Possible Causes:
	    • Short to VPWR in the harness or HO2S
	    • PCM has failed

DTC: P0139
2T O2HTR, MIL: Yes
Years: 2008, 2009, 2010
Models: All
Engines: All
Transmissions: All
	O2 Circuit Slow Response (Bank 1, Sensor 2)
	The Heated Oxygen Sensor (HO2S) monitor tracks the rate of voltage change during the rise and fall of the HO2S signal. When the rate of voltage change is less than a calibrated value, the Powertrain Control Module (PCM) begins to modify the fuel trim attempting to increase the HO2S voltage switch rate. The DTC sets when the PCM is at the allowable limit or has exceeded an allowable length of time for fuel trim modification, without detecting an acceptable rate of voltage change.
	Note: Access the HO2S test results from the generic OBD menu to verify the DTC.
	Possible Causes:
	    • Contaminated or damaged HO2S
	    • Deteriorating HO2S
	    • Exhaust leaks
	    • Aftermarket accessories
	    • Performance modifications

DTC	Trouble Code Title, Conditions & Possible Causes

DTC: P013A
2T O2HTR, MIL: Yes
Years: 2008, 2009, 2010
Models: All
Engines: All
Transmissions: All
	O2 Sensor Slow Response - Rich to Lean (Bank 1, Sensor 2)
	During a Deceleration Fuel Shut-Off (DFSO) event, the powertrain control module (PCM) monitors how quickly the rear Heated Oxygen Sensor (HO2S) switches from rich to lean. The measured rate of the rich to lean switch is compared to a calibrated fault threshold value. The threshold value takes into account the level of oxygen in the catalyst, which has an impact on how quickly the rich to lean switch occurs. The test fails when the measured value is slower than the threshold value.
	Note: Check for leaks in the exhaust system.
	Possible Causes:
	    • Exhaust leaks before or near the HO2S
	    • Damaged HO2S

DTC: P013C
2T O2HTR, MIL: Yes
Years: 2008, 2009, 2010
Models: All
Engines: All
Transmissions: All
	O2 Sensor Slow Response - Rich to Lean (Bank 2, Sensor 2)
	During a Deceleration Fuel Shut-Off (DFSO) event, the powertrain control module (PCM) monitors how quickly the rear Heated Oxygen Sensor (HO2S) switches from rich to lean. The measured rate of the rich to lean switch is compared to a calibrated fault threshold value. The threshold value takes into account the level of oxygen in the catalyst, which has an impact on how quickly the rich to lean switch occurs. The test fails when the measured value is slower than the threshold value.
	Note: Check for leaks in the exhaust system.
	Possible Causes:
	    • Exhaust leaks before or near the HO2S
	    • Damaged HO2S

DTC: P013E
2T O2HTR, MIL: Yes
Years: 2008, 2009, 2010
Models: All
Engines: All
Transmissions: All
	Sensor Delayed Response - Rich to Lean (Bank 1, Sensor 2)
	During a Deceleration Fuel Shut-Off (DFSO) event, the Powertrain Control Module (PCM) monitors the rear Heated Oxygen Sensor (HO2S) signal to determine if the signal is stuck in range. The PCM expects the signal to exceed a calibrated rich or lean value within a calibrated amount of time. If the signal voltage remains less than the rich value after a number of occurrences, the PCM intrusively controls the fuel system rich over increasing time periods in an attempt to force the signal to greater than the calibrated rich value. The test fails when after three consecutive intrusive attempts the signal cannot be forced greater than the calibrated rich value. Also, if the signal voltage remains greater than the lean value after a calibrated amount of time with the fuel injectors off, a counter is incremented. The test fails when after three consecutive occurrences the signal is not less than the calibrated lean value.
	Note: Check for leaks in the exhaust system. Check for an intermittent HO2S signal.
	Possible Causes:
	    • Exhaust leaks before or near the HO2S
	    • Aftermarket exhaust accessories or performance modifications
	    • Ethanol content in the fuel
	    • Circuit intermittent
	    • Damaged HO2S

DTC: P0141
2T O2HTR, MIL: Yes
Years: 2008, 2009, 2010
Models: All
Engines: All
Transmissions: All
	O2 Heater Circuit (Bank 1, Sensor 2)
	During testing the Heated Oxygen Sensor (HO2S) heaters are checked for open and short circuits and excessive current draw. The test fails when the current draw exceeds a calibrated limit or an open or short circuit is detected.
	Note: Inspect the connectors for signs of damage, water ingress, or corrosion.
	Possible Causes:
	    • Vacuum hose disconnected on Exhaust Gas Recirculation (EGR) system module (ESM) applications
	    • Short to VPWR in the harness or HO2S
	    • Water in the harness connector
	    • Open VPWR circuit
	    • Open UO2SHTR circuit
	    • Open GND circuit
	    • Low battery voltage
	    • Corrosion or poor mating terminals and wiring
	    • Damaged HO2S heater
	    • PCM has failed

DTC: P0144
2T O2HTR, MIL: Yes
Years: 2008, 2009, 2010
Models: All
Engines: All
Transmissions: All
	O2 Circuit High Voltage (Bank 1, Sensor 3)
	The Heated Oxygen Sensor (HO2S) signals are monitored for an over voltage condition. The code is set when the HO2S signal voltage is 1.5 volts or greater.
	Note: An HO2S PID switching across 0.45 volt from 0.2 to 0.9 volt indicates a normal switching HO2S. An HO2S PID voltage of 1.5 volts or greater indicates a short to voltage.
	Possible Causes:
	    • Short to VPWR in the harness or HO2S
	    • PCM has failed

DTC	Trouble Code Title, Conditions & Possible Causes
DTC: P0147 **2T O2HTR, MIL: Yes** **Years:** 2008, 2009, 2010 **Models:** All **Engines:** All **Transmissions:** All	**O2 Heater Circuit (Bank 1, Sensor 3)** During testing the Heated Oxygen Sensor (HO2S) heaters are checked for open and short circuits and excessive current draw. The test fails when the current draw exceeds a calibrated limit or an open or short circuit is detected. **Note: Inspect the connectors for signs of damage, water ingress, or corrosion.** **Possible Causes:** • Vacuum hose disconnected on Exhaust Gas Recirculation (EGR) system module (ESM) applications • Short to VPWR in the harness or HO2S • Water in the harness connector • Open VPWR circuit • Open UO2SHTR circuit • Open GND circuit • Low battery voltage • Corrosion or poor mating terminals and wiring • Damaged HO2S heater • PCM has failed
DTC: P0148 **2T FUEL, MIL: Yes** **Years:** 2008, 2009, 2010 **Models:** All **Engines:** All **Transmissions:** All	**Fuel Delivery Error** At least one bank is lean at Wide Open Throttle (WOT). **Possible Causes:** • Severely restricted fuel filter • Severely pinched or restricted fuel delivery line • Damaged or worn fuel pump • Damaged or contaminated mass air flow (MAF) sensor
DTC: P014A **2T O2HTR, MIL: Yes** **Years:** 2008, 2009, 2010 **Models:** All **Engines:** All **Transmissions:** All	**Sensor Delayed Response - Rich to Lean (Bank 2, Sensor 2)** During a Deceleration Fuel Shut-Off (DFSO) event, the Powertrain Control Module (PCM) monitors the rear Heated Oxygen Sensor (HO2S) signal to determine if the signal is stuck in range. The PCM expects the signal to exceed a calibrated rich or lean value within a calibrated amount of time. If the signal voltage remains less than the rich value after a number of occurrences, the PCM intrusively controls the fuel system rich over increasing time periods in an attempt to force the signal to greater than the calibrated rich value. The test fails when after three consecutive intrusive attempts the signal cannot be forced greater than the calibrated rich value. Also, if the signal voltage remains greater than the lean value after a calibrated amount of time with the fuel injectors off, a counter is incremented. The test fails when after three consecutive occurrences the signal is not less than the calibrated lean value. **Note: Check for leaks in the exhaust system. Check for an intermittent HO2S signal.** **Possible Causes:** • Exhaust leaks before or near the HO2S • Aftermarket exhaust accessories or performance modifications • Ethanol content in the fuel • Circuit intermittent • Damaged HO2S
DTC: P0150 **2T O2HTR, MIL: Yes** **Years:** 2008, 2009, 2010 **Models:** All **Engines:** All **Transmissions:** All	**O2 Circuit (Bank 2, Sensor 1)** The Powertrain Control Module (PCM) monitors the Heated Oxygen Sensor (HO2S) for a circuit concern. The test fails when the PCM detects a concern with one of the circuits used to determine the oxygen content in the exhaust gas. **Possible Causes:** • Open UO2S circuit • Open UO2SGREF circuit • UO2S circuit short to voltage or ground • UO2SGREF circuit short to voltage or ground • UO2SPC circuit short to voltage or ground • UO2SPCT circuit short to voltage or ground • Damaged universal HO2S
DTC: P0152 **2T O2HTR, MIL: Yes** **Years:** 2008, 2009, 2010 **Models:** All **Engines:** All **Transmissions:** All	**O2 Circuit High Voltage (Bank 2, Sensor 1)** The Heated Oxygen Sensor (HO2S) signals are monitored for an over voltage condition. The code is set when the HO2S signal voltage is 1.5 volts or greater. **Note: An HO2S PID switching across 0.45 volt from 0.2 to 0.9 volt indicates a normal switching HO2S. An HO2S PID voltage of 1.5 volts or greater indicates a short to voltage.** **Possible Causes:** • Short to VPWR in the harness or HO2S • PCM has failed

DTC	Trouble Code Title, Conditions & Possible Causes
DTC: P0153 **2T O2HTR, MIL: Yes** **Years:** 2008, 2009, 2010 **Models:** All **Engines:** All **Transmissions:** All	**O2 Circuit Slow Response (Bank 2, Sensor 1)** The Powertrain Control Module (PCM) commands an air/fuel ratio that changes in the shape of a square wave. The PCM calculates the length of the resulting signal from the HO2S. The test fails when the length of the signal is less than a calibrated limit. For all others, the PCM checks the HO2S signal frequency and amplitude. The test fails when the frequency and amplitude less than a calibrated limit. **Note: Access the HO2S test results from the generic OBD menu to verify the DTC.** **Possible Causes:** • Contaminated HO2S • Exhaust leaks • Short/open wiring • Incorrect fueling • MAF sensor • Deteriorating HO2S • Inlet air leaks • PCM has failed
DTC: P0154 **2T O2HTR, MIL: Yes** **Years:** 2008, 2009, 2010 **Models:** All **Engines:** All **Transmissions:** All	**O2 Circuit No Activity Detected (Bank 2, Sensor 1)** The Powertrain Control Module (PCM) monitors the Heated Oxygen Sensor (HO2S) for a lack of movement concern. If the sensor signal value is not changing from the default value, the PCM commands an oscillating air/fuel ratio attempting to detect some movement in the signal value. The test fails when the PCM is unable to detect movement in the sensor signal while the air/fuel ratio is oscillating. **Possible Causes:** • Open UO2SPC circuit • Damaged universal HO2S • PCM has failed
DTC: P0155 **2T O2HTR, MIL: Yes** **Years:** 2008, 2009, 2010 **Models:** All **Engines:** All **Transmissions:** All	**O2 Heater Circuit (Bank 2, Sensor 1)** During testing the Heated Oxygen Sensor (HO2S) heaters are checked for open and short circuits and excessive current draw. The test fails when the current draw exceeds a calibrated limit or an open or short circuit is detected. **Note: Inspect the connectors for signs of damage, water ingress, or corrosion.** **Possible Causes:** • Vacuum hose disconnected on Exhaust Gas Recirculation (EGR) system module (ESM) applications • Short to VPWR in the harness or HO2S • Water in the harness connector • Open VPWR circuit • Open UO2SHTR circuit • Open GND circuit • Low battery voltage • Corrosion or poor mating terminals and wiring • Damaged HO2S heater • PCM has failed
DTC: P0158 **2T O2HTR, MIL: Yes** **Years:** 2008, 2009, 2010 **Models:** All **Engines:** All **Transmissions:** All	**O2 Circuit High Voltage (Bank 2, Sensor 2)** The Heated Oxygen Sensor (HO2S) signals are monitored for an over voltage condition. The code is set when the HO2S signal voltage is 1.5 volts or greater. **Note: An HO2S PID switching across 0.45 volt from 0.2 to 0.9 volt indicates a normal switching HO2S. An HO2S PID voltage of 1.5 volts or greater indicates a short to voltage.** **Possible Causes:** • Short to VPWR in the harness or HO2S • PCM has failed
DTC: P0159 **2T O2HTR, MIL: Yes** **Years:** 2008, 2009, 2010 **Models:** All **Engines:** All **Transmissions:** All	**O2 Circuit Slow Response (Bank 2, Sensor 2)** The Heated Oxygen Sensor (HO2S) monitor tracks the rate of voltage change during the rise and fall of the HO2S signal. When the rate of voltage change is less than a calibrated value, the Powertrain Control Module (PCM) begins to modify the fuel trim attempting to increase the HO2S voltage switch rate. The DTC sets when the PCM is at the allowable limit or has exceeded an allowable length of time for fuel trim modification, without detecting an acceptable rate of voltage change. **Note: Access the HO2S test results from the generic OBD menu to verify the DTC.** **Possible Causes:** • Contaminated or damaged HO2S • Deteriorating HO2S • Exhaust leaks • Aftermarket accessories • Performance modifications

DTC	Trouble Code Title, Conditions & Possible Causes
DTC: P0161 **2T O2HTR, MIL: Yes** **Years:** 2008, 2009, 2010 **Models:** All **Engines:** All **Transmissions:** All	**O2 Heater Circuit (Bank 2, Sensor 2)** During testing the Heated Oxygen Sensor (HO2S) heaters are checked for open and short circuits and excessive current draw. The test fails when the current draw exceeds a calibrated limit or an open or short circuit is detected. **Note: Inspect the connectors for signs of damage, water ingress, or corrosion.** **Possible Causes:** • Vacuum hose disconnected on Exhaust Gas Recirculation (EGR) system module (ESM) applications • Short to VPWR in the harness or HO2S • Water in the harness connector • Open VPWR circuit • Open UO2SHTR circuit • Open GND circuit • Low battery voltage • Corrosion or poor mating terminals and wiring • Damaged HO2S heater • PCM has failed
DTC: P0171 **2T FUEL, MIL: Yes** **Years:** 2008, 2009, 2010 **Models:** All **Engines:** All **Transmissions:** All	**System Too Lean (Bank 1)** Engine started, engine running at cruise speed for 3 to 4 minutes, and the PCM detected the Bank 1 Adaptive Fuel Control System reached its rich correction limit (a lean A/F condition). **Possible Causes:** • Air leaks after the MAF sensor, or leaks in the PCV system • Exhaust leaks before or near where the HO2S is mounted • Fuel injector(s) restricted or not supplying enough fuel • Fuel pump not supplying enough fuel during high fuel demand conditions • Leaking EGR gasket, or leaking EGR valve diaphragm • MAF sensor dirty (causes PCM to underestimate airflow) • Vehicle running out of fuel or engine oil dip stick not seated
DTC: P0172 **2T FUEL, MIL: Yes** **Years:** 2008, 2009, 2010 **Models:** All **Engines:** All **Transmissions:** All	**System Too Rich (Bank 1)** Engine started, engine running at cruise speed for 3 to 4 minutes, and the PCM detected the Bank 1 Adaptive Fuel Control System reached its rich correction limit (a rich A/F condition). **Possible Causes:** • Fuel Rail Pressure (FRP) sensor bias • EVAP vapor recovery system failure • Leaking fuel injectors • MAF or MAP sensor values are incorrect or out-of-range • Engine oil contamination
DTC: P0174 **2T FUEL, MIL: Yes** **Years:** 2008, 2009, 2010 **Models:** All **Engines:** All **Transmissions:** All	**System Too Lean (Bank 2)** Engine started, engine running at cruise speed for 3 to 4 minutes, and the PCM detected the Bank 1 Adaptive Fuel Control System reached its rich correction limit (a lean A/F condition). **Possible Causes:** • Air leaks after the MAF sensor, or leaks in the PCV system • Exhaust leaks before or near where the HO2S is mounted • Fuel injector(s) restricted or not supplying enough fuel • Fuel pump not supplying enough fuel during high fuel demand conditions • Leaking EGR gasket, or leaking EGR valve diaphragm • MAF sensor dirty (causes PCM to underestimate airflow) • Vehicle running out of fuel or engine oil dip stick not seated
DTC: P0175 **2T FUEL, MIL: Yes** **Years:** 2008, 2009, 2010 **Models:** All **Engines:** All **Transmissions:** All	**System Too Rich (Bank 2)** Engine started, engine running at cruise speed for 3 to 4 minutes, and the PCM detected the Bank 1 Adaptive Fuel Control System reached its rich correction limit (a rich A/F condition). **Possible Causes:** • Fuel Rail Pressure (FRP) sensor bias • EVAP vapor recovery system failure • Leaking fuel injectors • MAF or MAP sensor values are incorrect or out-of-range • Engine oil contamination

DTC	Trouble Code Title, Conditions & Possible Causes
DTC: P0180 **2T CCM, MIL: Yes** **Years:** 2008, 2009, 2010 **Models:** All **Engines:** All **Transmissions:** All	**Fuel Temperature Sensor 'A' Circuit Malfunction** Engine runtime over 2 minutes, and the PCM detected the Engine Fuel Temperature (EFT) sensor 'A' signal was out-of-range (i.e., it was more than 4.54v [−46°F] or less than 0.21v [275°F]. **Note: Monitor the EFT PID value to identify an open or short circuit.** **Possible Causes:** • Open or short in the harness • Low ambient temperature operation • Incorrect harness connection • Damaged fuel temperature sensor • PCM has failed
DTC: P0181 **2T CCM, MIL: Yes** **Years:** 2008, 2009, 2010 **Models:** All **Engines:** All **Transmissions:** All	**Fuel Temperature Sensor A Circuit Range/Performance** The Comprehensive Component Monitor (CCM) monitors the fuel temperature sensor for acceptable operating temperature. The test fails if the voltage falls below or exceeds a calibrated limit, for a calibrated amount of time during testing. **Note: Verify the FRT PID value to determine an open or short.** **Possible Causes:** • Open or short in the harness • Low ambient temperature operation • Incorrect harness connection • Damaged fuel temperature sensor • PCM has failed
DTC: P0182 **2T CCM, MIL: Yes** **Years:** 2008, 2009, 2010 **Models:** All **Engines:** All **Transmissions:** All	**Fuel Temperature Sensor 'A' Circuit Low** The Comprehensive Component Monitor (CCM) monitors the fuel temperature sensor circuit to the Powertrain Control Module (PCM) for low voltage. The test fails if the voltage falls below a calibrated limit for a calibrated amount of time during testing **Note: Verify the FRT PID and VREF values to determine an open or short.** **Possible Causes:** • Short in the harness • VREF open or short • Low ambient temperature operation • Incorrect harness connection • Damaged fuel temperature sensor
DTC: P0183 **2T CCM, MIL: Yes** **Years:** 2008, 2009, 2010 **Models:** All **Engines:** All **Transmissions:** All	**Fuel Temperature Sensor 'A' Circuit High** The Comprehensive Component Monitor (CCM) monitors the fuel temperature sensor circuit to the Powertrain Control Module (PCM) for high voltage. The test fails if the voltage exceeds a calibrated limit for a calibrated amount of time during testing. **Note: Verify the FRT PID and VREF values to determine an open or short.** **Possible Causes:** • Open circuit • Open or short to voltage in the harness • Incorrect harness connection • Damaged fuel temperature sensor
DTC: P0190 **2T CCM, MIL: Yes** **Years:** 2008, 2009, 2010 **Models:** All **Engines:** All **Transmissions:** All	**Fuel Rail Pressure Sensor 'A' Circuit** The Comprehensive Component Monitor (CCM) monitors the Fuel Rail Pressure (FRP) sensor to the Powertrain Control Module (PCM) for VREF voltage. The test fails when the VREF voltage from the PCM drops to a voltage less than a minimum calibrated value. **Note: The sensor VREF should be between 4.0 to 6.0v at all times.** **Possible Causes:** • VREF open in harness • VREF open in sensor • Vacuum leaks
DTC: P0191 **2T CCM, MIL: Yes** **Years:** 2008, 2009, 2010 **Models:** All **Engines:** All **Transmissions:** All	**Fuel Rail Pressure Sensor 'A' Circuit Range/Performance** Engine started, and the PCM detected the FRP sensor signal was less than the minimum acceptable range or was more than the maximum acceptable range. With the engine running, the FRP PID should read between 20 psi (138 kPa) and 60 psi (413 kPa) for gasoline powered vehicles, or between 85 psi (586 kPa) and 105 psi (725 kPa) for Natural Gas (NG) powered vehicles. **Note: A FRP PID value during key ON, engine running of 138 kPa (20 psi) to 413 kPa (60 psi) is acceptable.** **Possible Causes:** • High fuel pressure • Low fuel pressure • Damaged FRP sensor • Excessive resistance in the circuit • Vacuum leaks • Low or no fuel

DTC	Trouble Code Title, Conditions & Possible Causes
DTC: P0192 **2T CCM, MIL: Yes** **Years:** 2008, 2009, 2010 **Models:** All **Engines:** All **Transmissions:** All	**Fuel Rail Pressure Sensor 'A' Circuit Low** Engine started, and the PCM detected the FRP sensor signal was less than 0.3v for gasoline vehicles or less than 0.5v for NG vehicles during the self-test. **Note: A FRP PID value during key ON, engine OFF or key ON, engine running less than 0.3 volt indicates a concern is present.** **Possible Causes:** • FRP signal short to SIG RTN or PWR GND • Damaged FRP sensor
DTC: P0193 **2T CCM, MIL: Yes** **Years:** 2008, 2009, 2010 **Models:** All **Engines:** All **Transmissions:** All	**Fuel Rail Pressure Sensor 'A' Circuit High** Engine started, and the PCM detected the FRP sensor was more than 4.5v for gasoline vehicles or more than 4.8v for NG vehicles. **Possible Causes:** • FRP sensor signal shorted to VREF or VPWR • FRP sensor signal circuit open (gasoline usage only) • Low fuel pressure (NG vehicle only) • FRP sensor is damaged or has failed
DTC: P0196 **2T CCM, MIL: Yes** **Years:** 2008, 2009, 2010 **Models:** All **Engines:** All **Transmissions:** All	**Engine Oil Temperature (EOT) Sensor Circuit Range/Performance** Engine started, KOER Self Test enabled, and the PCM detected the Engine Oil Temperature (EOT) sensor signal was not within a calibrated amount of the ECT sensor signal during the test. The EOT sensor value should be close to the engine oil temperature. **Possible Causes:** • Cooling system malfunction, or the thermostat is stuck • Engine not operating at normal operating temperature • EOT sensor is damaged or it has failed • EOT circuit failure
DTC: P0197 **2T CCM, MIL: Yes** **Years:** 2008, 2009, 2010 **Models:** All **Engines:** All **Transmissions:** All	**Engine Oil Temperature (EOT) Sensor Circuit Low** Key on or engine running; and the PCM detected that the Engine Oil Temperature (EOT) sensor was less than 0.20v during the test. The EOT sensor value should be close to the engine oil temperature. **Possible Causes:** • EOT sensor connector is damaged or shorted • EOT sensor signal circuit shorted to chassis or sensor ground • EOT sensor is damaged or it has failed
DTC: P0198 **2T CCM, MIL: Yes** **Years:** 2008, 2009, 2010 **Models:** All **Engines:** All **Transmissions:** All	**Engine Oil Temperature (EOT) Sensor Circuit High** Key on or engine running; and the PCM detected that the Engine Oil Temperature (EOT) sensor was less than 4.50v during the test. The EOT sensor value should be close to the engine oil temperature. **Possible Causes:** • EOT sensor connector is damaged or open • EOT sensor signal circuit is shorted to VPWR • EOT sensor is damaged or it has failed
DTC: P0201 **2T CCM, MIL: Yes** **Years:** 2008, 2009, 2010 **Models:** All **Engines:** All **Transmissions:** All	**Cylinder 1 Injector Circuit/Open** The Comprehensive Component Monitor (CCM) monitors the operation of the fuel injector drivers in the Powertrain Control Module (PCM). The test fails when the fuel injector circuitry is inoperative. **Note: Monitor the INJIF PID Fault "flags" with the Scan Tool. The appropriate INJF PID "flag" will read Yes when this code is set.** **Possible Causes:** • Injector 1 connector is damaged, open or shorted • Injector 1 control circuit is open, shorted to ground or to power • Damaged fuel injector 1 • PCM has failed
DTC: P0202 **2T CCM, MIL: Yes** **Years:** 2008, 2009, 2010 **Models:** All **Engines:** All **Transmissions:** All	**Cylinder 2 Injector Circuit/Open** The Comprehensive Component Monitor (CCM) monitors the operation of the fuel injector drivers in the Powertrain Control Module (PCM). The test fails when the fuel injector circuitry is inoperative. **Note: Monitor the INJIF PID Fault "flags" with the Scan Tool. The appropriate INJF PID "flag" will read Yes when this code is set.** **Possible Causes:** • Injector 2 connector is damaged, open or shorted • Injector 2 control circuit is open, shorted to ground or to power • Damaged fuel injector 2 • PCM has failed

DTC	Trouble Code Title, Conditions & Possible Causes
DTC: P0203 **2T CCM, MIL: Yes** **Years:** 2008, 2009, 2010 **Models:** All **Engines:** All **Transmissions:** All	**Cylinder 3 Injector Circuit/Open** The Comprehensive Component Monitor (CCM) monitors the operation of the fuel injector drivers in the Powertrain Control Module (PCM). The test fails when the fuel injector circuitry is inoperative. **Note: Monitor the INJIF PID Fault "flags" with the Scan Tool. The appropriate INJF PID "flag" will read Yes when this code is set.** **Possible Causes:** • Injector 3 connector is damaged, open or shorted • Injector 3 control circuit is open, shorted to ground or to power • Damaged fuel injector 3 • PCM has failed
DTC: P0204 **2T CCM, MIL: Yes** **Years:** 2008, 2009, 2010 **Models:** All **Engines:** All **Transmissions:** All	**Cylinder 4 Injector Circuit/Open** The Comprehensive Component Monitor (CCM) monitors the operation of the fuel injector drivers in the Powertrain Control Module (PCM). The test fails when the fuel injector circuitry is inoperative. **Note: Monitor the INJIF PID Fault "flags" with the Scan Tool. The appropriate INJF PID "flag" will read Yes when this code is set.** **Possible Causes:** • Injector 4 connector is damaged, open or shorted • Injector 4 control circuit is open, shorted to ground or to power • Damaged fuel injector 4 • PCM has failed
DTC: P0205 **2T CCM, MIL: Yes** **Years:** 2008, 2009, 2010 **Models:** All With V6, V8 or V10 Engine **Engines:** All V6, V8, V10 **Transmissions:** All	**Cylinder 5 Injector Circuit/Open** The Comprehensive Component Monitor (CCM) monitors the operation of the fuel injector drivers in the Powertrain Control Module (PCM). The test fails when the fuel injector circuitry is inoperative. **Note: Monitor the INJIF PID Fault "flags" with the Scan Tool. The appropriate INJF PID "flag" will read Yes when this code is set.** **Possible Causes:** • Injector 5 connector is damaged, open or shorted • Injector 5 control circuit is open, shorted to ground or to power • Damaged fuel injector 5 • PCM has failed
DTC: P0206 **2T CCM, MIL: Yes** **Years:** 2008, 2009, 2010 **Models:** All With V6, V8 or V10 Engine **Engines:** All V6, V8, V10 **Transmissions:** All	**Cylinder 6 Injector Circuit/Open** The Comprehensive Component Monitor (CCM) monitors the operation of the fuel injector drivers in the Powertrain Control Module (PCM). The test fails when the fuel injector circuitry is inoperative. **Note: Monitor the INJIF PID Fault "flags" with the Scan Tool. The appropriate INJF PID "flag" will read Yes when this code is set.** **Possible Causes:** • Injector 6 connector is damaged, open or shorted • Injector 6 control circuit is open, shorted to ground or to power • Damaged fuel injector 6 • PCM has failed
DTC: P0207 **2T CCM, MIL: Yes** **Years:** 2008, 2009, 2010 **Models:** All With V8 or V10 Engine **Engines:** All V8, V10 **Transmissions:** All	**Cylinder 7 Injector Circuit/Open** The Comprehensive Component Monitor (CCM) monitors the operation of the fuel injector drivers in the Powertrain Control Module (PCM). The test fails when the fuel injector circuitry is inoperative. **Note: Monitor the INJIF PID Fault "flags" with the Scan Tool. The appropriate INJF PID "flag" will read Yes when this code is set.** **Possible Causes:** • Injector 7 connector is damaged, open or shorted • Injector 7 control circuit is open, shorted to ground or to power • Damaged fuel injector 7 • PCM has failed
DTC: P0208 **2T CCM, MIL: Yes** **Years:** 2008, 2009, 2010 **Models:** All With V8 or V10 Engine **Engines:** All V8, V10 **Transmissions:** All	**Cylinder 8 Injector Circuit/Open** The Comprehensive Component Monitor (CCM) monitors the operation of the fuel injector drivers in the Powertrain Control Module (PCM). The test fails when the fuel injector circuitry is inoperative. **Note: Monitor the INJIF PID Fault "flags" with the Scan Tool. The appropriate INJF PID "flag" will read Yes when this code is set.** **Possible Causes:** • Injector 8 connector is damaged, open or shorted • Injector 8 control circuit is open, shorted to ground or to power • Damaged fuel injector 8 • PCM has failed

DTC	Trouble Code Title, Conditions & Possible Causes

DTC: P0209
2T CCM, MIL: Yes
Years: 2008, 2009, 2010
Models: All With V10 Engine
Engines: All V10
Transmissions: All
	Cylinder 9 Injector Circuit/Open
	The Comprehensive Component Monitor (CCM) monitors the operation of the fuel injector drivers in the Powertrain Control Module (PCM). The test fails when the fuel injector circuitry is inoperative.
	Note: Monitor the INJIF PID Fault "flags" with the Scan Tool. The appropriate INJF PID "flag" will read Yes when this code is set.
	Possible Causes:
	    • Injector 9 connector is damaged, open or shorted
	    • Injector 9 control circuit is open, shorted to ground or to power
	    • Damaged fuel injector 9
	    • PCM has failed

DTC: P0210
2T CCM, MIL: Yes
Years: 2008, 2009, 2010
Models: All With V10 Engine
Engines: All V10
Transmissions: All
	Cylinder 10 Injector Circuit/Open
	The Comprehensive Component Monitor (CCM) monitors the operation of the fuel injector drivers in the Powertrain Control Module (PCM). The test fails when the fuel injector circuitry is inoperative.
	Note: Monitor the INJIF PID Fault "flags" with the Scan Tool. The appropriate INJF PID "flag" will read Yes when this code is set.
	Possible Causes:
	    • Injector 10 connector is damaged, open or shorted
	    • Injector 10 control circuit is open, shorted to ground or to power
	    • Damaged fuel injector 10
	    • PCM has failed

DTC: P0217
2T CCM, MIL: Yes
Years: 2008, 2009, 2010
Models: All
Engines: All
Transmissions: All
	Engine Coolant Over-Temperature Condition
	Indicates an engine overheat condition was detected by the engine temperature sensor (CHT or ECT depending how the vehicle is equipped).
	Note: Monitor the engine temperature PID (CHT or ECT) for an overheat condition. Typical engine temperature should be close to cooling system thermostat specification.
	Possible Causes:
	    • Engine cooling system concerns
	    • Low engine coolant level.
	    • Base engine concerns

DTC: P0218
2T CCM, MIL: Yes
Years: 2008, 2009, 2010
Models: All
Engines: All
Transmissions: All
	Transmission Fluid Temperature Over-Temperature Condition
	Indicates a transmission overheat condition was sensed by the Transmission Fluid Temperature (TFT) sensor.
	Note: Monitor the transmission temperature PID TFT for an overheat condition.
	Possible Causes:
	    • Low transmission fluid level
	    • Transmission cooling system concerns

DTC: P0219
2T CCM, MIL: Yes
Years: 2008, 2009, 2010
Models: All
Engines: All
Transmissions: All
	Engine Over-Speed Condition
	Indicates the vehicle has been operated in a manner which caused the engine speed to exceed a calibrated limit. The engine RPM is continuously monitored and evaluated by the Powertrain Control Module (PCM). The DTC sets when the RPM exceeds the calibrated limit set within the PCM.
	Note: The DTC indicates the vehicle has been operated in a manner which caused the engine speed to exceed a calibrated limit.
	Possible Causes:
	    • Engine operated in the wrong transmission gear position
	    • Excessive engine speed with gear selector in Neutral position
	    • Wheel slippage due to wet, muddy or snowing conditions

DTC: P0221
2T CCM, MIL: Yes
Years: 2008, 2009, 2010
Models: All
Engines: All
Transmissions: All
	Throttle/Pedal Position Sensor/Switch B Circuit Range/Performance
	The Electronic Throttle Control (ETC) Throttle Position (TP) sensor 2 circuit was flagged as a concern by the Powertrain Control Module (PCM) indicating an out of range in either the closed or Wide Open Throttle (WOT) modes.
	Note: This concern exhibits a symptom of limited power.
	Possible Causes:
	    • Throttle body is damaged
	    • Throttle linkage is binding or sticking
	    • TP circuit open to PCM
	    • Damaged TP sensor
	    • SIG RTN circuit open to the TP sensor
	    • Self-test operator error (foot resting on the accelerator pedal during test)

DTC	Trouble Code Title, Conditions & Possible Causes
DTC: P0222 **2T CCM, MIL: Yes** **Years:** 2008, 2009, 2010 **Models:** Crown, Victoria, Grand Marquis, Town Car **Engines:** 4.6L VIN V, W **Transmissions:** All	**Throttle/Pedal Position Sensor/Switch B Circuit Low** The Electronic Throttle Control (ETC) Throttle Position (TP) sensor 2 circuit was flagged as a concern by the Powertrain Control Module (PCM) indicating a low voltage, or open circuit. **Note: This concern exhibits a symptom of limited power. A TP2 PID reading less than 0.25 volt in key ON, engine OFF or key ON, engine running indicates a concern is present.** **Possible Causes:** • Open ETC TP sensor harness • Short to ground in the ETC TP sensor harness • Damaged TP sensor • SIG RTN circuit open to the TP sensor • PCM has failed
DTC: P0223 **2T CCM, MIL: Yes** **Years:** 2008, 2009, 2010 **Models:** Crown, Victoria, Grand Marquis, Town Car **Engines:** 4.6L VIN V, W **Transmissions:** All	**Throttle/Pedal Position Sensor/Switch B Circuit High** The Electronic Throttle Control (ETC) Throttle Position (TP) sensor 2 circuit was flagged as a concern by the Powertrain Control Module (PCM) indicating a high voltage. **Note: This concern exhibits a symptom of limited power. A TP2 PID reading greater than 4.75 volts in key ON, engine OFF or key ON, engine running indicates a concern is present.** **Possible Causes:** • ETC TP sensor harness shorted to VREF • Damaged TP sensor • ETC TP2 circuit open • VREF circuit short to TP sensor
DTC: P0230 **2T CCM, MIL: Yes** **Years:** 2008, 2009, 2010 **Models:** All **Engines:** All **Transmissions:** All	**Fuel Pump Primary Circuit Malfunction** The Powertrain Control Module (PCM) monitors the Fuel Pump (FP) circuit output from the PCM. The test fails when the FP output is commanded ON (grounded) and excessive current draw is detected on the FP circuit. The test also fails when the FP output is commanded OFF and voltage is not detected on the FP circuit. The PCM expects to detect VPWR voltage coming through the fuel pump relay coil to the FP circuit. **Note: A concern is present when the FP_F PID reads YES. An open circuit or short to ground can only be detected with the fuel pump commanded OFF. A short to voltage can only be detected with the fuel pump commanded ON. During the Key On Engine Off (KOEO) and Key On Engine Running (KOER) self-test, the fuel pump output command is cycled on and off.** **Possible Causes:** • Open or shorted FP circuit • Open VPWR circuit to the fuel pump relay • Damaged fuel pump relay • PCM has failed
DTC: P0231 **2T CCM, MIL: Yes** **Years:** 2008, 2009, 2010 **Models:** All **Engines:** All **Transmissions:** All	**Fuel Pump Primary Circuit Low** The Powertrain Control Module (PCM) monitors the Fuel Pump Monitor (FPM) circuit. The test fails if the PCM commands the fuel pump ON and B+ voltage is not detected on the FPM circuit. **Note: During the Key On Engine Off (KOEO) self-test, the PCM commands the fuel pump ON so this test can be carried out.** **Possible Causes:** • Open B+ circuit to the fuel pump relay • Open FP PWR circuit between the fuel pump relay and its connection to the FPM circuit • Damaged fuel pump relay • PCM has failed
DTC: P0232 **2T CCM, MIL: Yes** **Years:** 2008, 2009, 2010 **Models:** All **Engines:** All **Transmissions:** All	**Fuel Pump Secondary Circuit High Input** The Powertrain Control Module (PCM) monitors the Fuel Pump Monitor (FPM) circuit. This test fails when the PCM detects voltage on the FPM circuit while the fuel pump is commanded OFF. The FPM circuit is wired to a pull-up voltage inside the PCM. The FPM circuit goes high if, with the key ON, engine OFF and the fuel pump commanded OFF, the FPM/FP PWR circuit loses its path to ground through the fuel pump. The FPM circuit also goes high if the FPM/FP PWR circuit is short to voltage. **Note: Continuous memory P0232 can be set if the IFS switch is tripped then reset, or if the fuel pump circuit is activated when the PCM expected the circuit to be off. This DTC may set during a fuel system test or prime procedure.** **Possible Causes:** • Inertia Fuel Shutoff (IFS) switch not reset or electrically open • Open circuit between the fuel pump and the FPM connection to the FP PWR circuit • Poor fuel pump ground • Fuel pump electrically open • Fuel pump secondary circuits short to voltage • Fuel pump relay contacts always closed • Open FPM circuit between the PCM and the connection to the FP PWR circuit

DTC	Trouble Code Title, Conditions & Possible Causes
DTC: P025A **2T CCM, MIL:** Yes **Years:** 2008, 2009, 2010 **Models:** All **Engines:** All **Transmissions:** All	**Fuel Pump Module Control Circuit/Open** The Powertrain Control Module (PCM) monitors the Fuel Pump Command (FPC) circuit for a concern. When the PCM commands the Fuel Pump (FP) ON, the PCM is able to detect a short to voltage on the FPC circuit. When the PCM commands the FP OFF, the PCM is able to detect an open circuit or a short to ground on the FPC circuit. The test fails if the voltage is less than or greater than a calibrated limit, for a calibrated amount of time. **Note: Check for any harness concerns.** **Possible Causes:** • FPC circuit open or short to ground • FPC circuit short to voltage • Damaged fuel pump control module
DTC: P025B **2T CCM, MIL:** Yes **Years:** 2008, 2009, 2010 **Models:** All **Engines:** All **Transmissions:** All	**Fuel Pump Module Control Circuit Range/Performance** The fuel pump control module monitors the duty cycle and frequency of the signal it receives from the Powertrain Control Module (PCM). The fuel pump control module determines if the signal from the PCM on the Fuel Pump Command (FPC) circuit is a valid duty cycle and frequency. If the duty cycle or frequency is invalid, the fuel pump control module sends a 20% duty cycle signal on the Fuel Pump Monitor (FPM) circuit to report the concern to the PCM. The test fails when the fuel pump control module is still reporting that it is receiving an invalid duty cycle or frequency from the PCM after a calibrated amount of time. **Note: Check the harness for routing, alterations, incorrect shielding, or electrical interference from other systems.** **Possible Causes:** • FPC circuit open or short to ground • FPC circuit short to voltage • Radio Frequency Interference/Electromagnetic Interference (RFI/EMI) • Damaged fuel pump control module • Damaged PCM
DTC: P0297 **2T CCM, MIL:** Yes **Years:** 2008, 2009, 2010 **Models:** All **Engines:** All **Transmissions:** All	**Vehicle Over-Speed Condition** Indicates the vehicle has been operated in a manner which caused the vehicle speed to exceed a calibration limit. The vehicle speed is continuously monitored and evaluated by the Powertrain Control Module (PCM). The DTC is set when the vehicle speed exceeds the calibrated limit set within the PCM. **Note: The DTC indicates the vehicle has been operated in a manner which caused the engine speed to exceed a calibrated limit.** **Possible Causes:** • Vehicle driven at a high rate of speed
DTC: P0298 **2T CCM, MIL:** Yes **Years:** 2008, 2009, 2010 **Models:** All **Engines:** All **Transmissions:** All	**Engine Oil Over Temperature Condition** Indicates the engine oil temperature protection strategy in the Powertrain Control Module (PCM) has been activated. This temporarily prohibits high engine speed operation by disabling injectors, to reduce the risk of engine damage from high engine oil temperature. On engines equipped with an oil temperature sensor, the PCM reads oil temperature to determine if it is excessive. When an oil temperature sensor is not present, the PCM uses an oil algorithm to determine actual temperature. Engine shutdown strategy function is the same on vehicles with and without oil temperature sensors. **Note: The engine is operating in high RPM range due to incorrect gear selection. This may cause a lack/loss of power or surge.** **Possible Causes:** • Very high engine RPM for an extended period of time • Overheating condition • Damaged Engine Oil Temperature (EOT) sensor or circuit (vehicles with an EOT sensor) • Base engine concerns
DTC: P0300 **1T MISFIRE** **MIL:** Yes **Years:** 2008, 2009, 2010 **Models:** All **Engines:** All **Transmissions:** All	**Random Misfire Detected** The random misfire DTC indicates multiple cylinders are misfiring or the Powertrain Control Module (PCM) cannot identify which cylinder is misfiring. **Note: One or more EGR passages may be blocked or partially blocked. If this is the case the misfire detection monitor indicates the EGR port to check for possible blockage.** **Possible Causes:** • Camshaft position (CMP) sensor • Low fuel (less than 1/8 tank) • Stuck open exhaust gas recirculation (EGR) valve • Blocked EGR passages

DTC	Trouble Code Title, Conditions & Possible Causes
DTC: P0301 **2T MISFIRE** **MIL: Yes** **Years:** 2008, 2009, 2010 **Models:** All **Engines:** All **Transmissions:** All	**Cylinder Number 1 Misfire Detected** The misfire detection monitor is designed to monitor engine misfire and identify the specific cylinder in which the misfire has occurred. Misfire is defined as lack of combustion in a cylinder due to absence of spark, poor fuel metering, poor compression, or any other cause. **Note: The Malfunction Indicator Lamp (MIL) blinks once per second when a misfire severe enough to cause catalyst damage is detected. If the MIL is on steady state due to a misfire, this indicates the threshold for emissions was exceeded and caused the vehicle to fail an inspection and maintenance tailpipe test.** **Possible Causes:** • Ignition system • Fuel injectors • Running out of fuel • Evaporative Emission (EVAP) canister purge valve • Fuel pressure • Evaporative emission system • Exhaust Gas Recirculation (EGR) system • Base engine
DTC: P0302 2T MISFIRE **MIL: Yes** **Years:** 2008, 2009, 2010 **Models:** All **Engines:** All **Transmissions:** All	**Cylinder Number 2 Misfire Detected** The misfire detection monitor is designed to monitor engine misfire and identify the specific cylinder in which the misfire has occurred. Misfire is defined as lack of combustion in a cylinder due to absence of spark, poor fuel metering, poor compression, or any other cause. **Note: The Malfunction Indicator Lamp (MIL) blinks once per second when a misfire severe enough to cause catalyst damage is detected. If the MIL is on steady state due to a misfire, this indicates the threshold for emissions was exceeded and caused the vehicle to fail an inspection and maintenance tailpipe test.** **Possible Causes:** • Ignition system • Fuel injectors • Running out of fuel • Evaporative Emission (EVAP) canister purge valve • Fuel pressure • Evaporative emission system • Exhaust Gas Recirculation (EGR) system • Base engine
DTC: P0303 2T MISFIRE **MIL: Yes** **Years:** 2008, 2009, 2010 **Models:** All **Engines:** All **Transmissions:** All	**Cylinder Number 3 Misfire Detected** The misfire detection monitor is designed to monitor engine misfire and identify the specific cylinder in which the misfire has occurred. Misfire is defined as lack of combustion in a cylinder due to absence of spark, poor fuel metering, poor compression, or any other cause. **Note: The Malfunction Indicator Lamp (MIL) blinks once per second when a misfire severe enough to cause catalyst damage is detected. If the MIL is on steady state due to a misfire, this indicates the threshold for emissions was exceeded and caused the vehicle to fail an inspection and maintenance tailpipe test.** **Possible Causes:** • Ignition system • Fuel injectors • Running out of fuel • Evaporative Emission (EVAP) canister purge valve • Fuel pressure • Evaporative emission system • Exhaust Gas Recirculation (EGR) system • Base engine

DTC	Trouble Code Title, Conditions & Possible Causes
DTC: P0304 **2T MISFIRE** **MIL: Yes** **Years:** 2008, 2009, 2010 **Models:** All **Engines:** All **Transmissions:** All	**Cylinder Number 4 Misfire Detected** The misfire detection monitor is designed to monitor engine misfire and identify the specific cylinder in which the misfire has occurred. Misfire is defined as lack of combustion in a cylinder due to absence of spark, poor fuel metering, poor compression, or any other cause. **Note: The Malfunction Indicator Lamp (MIL) blinks once per second when a misfire severe enough to cause catalyst damage is detected. If the MIL is on steady state due to a misfire, this indicates the threshold for emissions was exceeded and caused the vehicle to fail an inspection and maintenance tailpipe test.** **Possible Causes:** • Ignition system • Fuel injectors • Running out of fuel • Evaporative Emission (EVAP) canister purge valve • Fuel pressure • Evaporative emission system • Exhaust Gas Recirculation (EGR) system • Base engine
DTC: P0305 **2T MISFIRE** **MIL: Yes** **Years:** 2008, 2009, 2010 **Models:** All With V6, V8 or V10 Engine **Engines:** All V6, V8, V10 **Transmissions:** All	**Cylinder Number 5 Misfire Detected** The misfire detection monitor is designed to monitor engine misfire and identify the specific cylinder in which the misfire has occurred. Misfire is defined as lack of combustion in a cylinder due to absence of spark, poor fuel metering, poor compression, or any other cause. **Note: The Malfunction Indicator Lamp (MIL) blinks once per second when a misfire severe enough to cause catalyst damage is detected. If the MIL is on steady state due to a misfire, this indicates the threshold for emissions was exceeded and caused the vehicle to fail an inspection and maintenance tailpipe test.** **Possible Causes:** • Ignition system • Fuel injectors • Running out of fuel • Evaporative Emission (EVAP) canister purge valve • Fuel pressure • Evaporative emission system • Exhaust Gas Recirculation (EGR) system • Base engine
DTC: P0306 **2T MISFIRE** **MIL: Yes** **Years:** 2008, 2009, 2010 **Models:** All With V6, V8 or V10 Engine **Engines:** All V6, V8, V10 **Transmissions:** All	**Cylinder Number 6 Misfire Detected** The misfire detection monitor is designed to monitor engine misfire and identify the specific cylinder in which the misfire has occurred. Misfire is defined as lack of combustion in a cylinder due to absence of spark, poor fuel metering, poor compression, or any other cause. **Note: The Malfunction Indicator Lamp (MIL) blinks once per second when a misfire severe enough to cause catalyst damage is detected. If the MIL is on steady state due to a misfire, this indicates the threshold for emissions was exceeded and caused the vehicle to fail an inspection and maintenance tailpipe test.** **Possible Causes:** • Ignition system • Fuel injectors • Running out of fuel • Evaporative Emission (EVAP) canister purge valve • Fuel pressure • Evaporative emission system • Exhaust Gas Recirculation (EGR) system • Base engine

DTC	Trouble Code Title, Conditions & Possible Causes
DTC: P0307 **2T MISFIRE** **MIL: Yes** **Years:** 2008, 2009, 2010 **Models:** Models equipped with V8 or V10 engine **Engines:** All V8, V10 **Transmissions:** All	**Cylinder Number 7 Misfire Detected** The misfire detection monitor is designed to monitor engine misfire and identify the specific cylinder in which the misfire has occurred. Misfire is defined as lack of combustion in a cylinder due to absence of spark, poor fuel metering, poor compression, or any other cause. **Note: The Malfunction Indicator Lamp (MIL) blinks once per second when a misfire severe enough to cause catalyst damage is detected. If the MIL is on steady state due to a misfire, this indicates the threshold for emissions was exceeded and caused the vehicle to fail an inspection and maintenance tailpipe test.** **Possible Causes:** • Ignition system • Fuel injectors • Running out of fuel • Evaporative Emission (EVAP) canister purge valve • Fuel pressure • Evaporative emission system • Exhaust Gas Recirculation (EGR) system • Base engine
DTC: P0308 **2T MISFIRE** **MIL: Yes** **Years:** 2008, 2009, 2010 **Models:** Models equipped with V8 or V10 engine **Engines:** All V8, V10 **Transmissions:** All	**Cylinder Number 8 Misfire Detected** The misfire detection monitor is designed to monitor engine misfire and identify the specific cylinder in which the misfire has occurred. Misfire is defined as lack of combustion in a cylinder due to absence of spark, poor fuel metering, poor compression, or any other cause. **Note: The Malfunction Indicator Lamp (MIL) blinks once per second when a misfire severe enough to cause catalyst damage is detected. If the MIL is on steady state due to a misfire, this indicates the threshold for emissions was exceeded and caused the vehicle to fail an inspection and maintenance tailpipe test.** **Possible Causes:** • Ignition system • Fuel injectors • Running out of fuel • Evaporative Emission (EVAP) canister purge valve • Fuel pressure • Evaporative emission system • Exhaust Gas Recirculation (EGR) system • Base engine
DTC: P0309 **2T MISFIRE** **MIL: Yes** **Years:** 2008, 2009, 2010 **Models:** Models equipped with a V10 engine **Engines:** All V10 **Transmissions:** All	**Cylinder Number 9 Misfire Detected** The misfire detection monitor is designed to monitor engine misfire and identify the specific cylinder in which the misfire has occurred. Misfire is defined as lack of combustion in a cylinder due to absence of spark, poor fuel metering, poor compression, or any other cause. **Note: The Malfunction Indicator Lamp (MIL) blinks once per second when a misfire severe enough to cause catalyst damage is detected. If the MIL is on steady state due to a misfire, this indicates the threshold for emissions was exceeded and caused the vehicle to fail an inspection and maintenance tailpipe test.** **Possible Causes:** • Ignition system • Fuel injectors • Running out of fuel • Evaporative Emission (EVAP) canister purge valve • Fuel pressure • Evaporative emission system • Exhaust Gas Recirculation (EGR) system • Base engine

DTC	Trouble Code Title, Conditions & Possible Causes

DTC: P0310
2T MISFIRE
MIL: Yes
Years: 2008, 2009, 2010
Models: Models equipped with a V10 engine
Engines: All V10
Transmissions: All
	Cylinder Number 10 Misfire Detected
	The misfire detection monitor is designed to monitor engine misfire and identify the specific cylinder in which the misfire has occurred. Misfire is defined as lack of combustion in a cylinder due to absence of spark, poor fuel metering, poor compression, or any other cause.
	Note: The Malfunction Indicator Lamp (MIL) blinks once per second when a misfire severe enough to cause catalyst damage is detected. If the MIL is on steady state due to a misfire, this indicates the threshold for emissions was exceeded and caused the vehicle to fail an inspection and maintenance tailpipe test.
	Possible Causes:
	   • Ignition system
	   • Fuel injectors
	   • Running out of fuel
	   • Evaporative Emission (EVAP) canister purge valve
	   • Fuel pressure
	   • Evaporative emission system
	   • Exhaust Gas Recirculation (EGR) system
	   • Base engine

DTC: P0315
2T CCM, MIL: Yes
Years: 2008, 2009, 2010
Models: All
Engines: All
Transmissions: All
	Crankshaft Position System Variation Not Learned.
	The Powertrain Control Module (PCM) is unable to learn and correct for mechanical inaccuracies in crankshaft pulse wheel tooth spacing. This DTC disables the misfire monitor.
	Note: Requires visual inspection of the CKP sensor and the crankshaft pulse wheel teeth for damage.
	Possible Causes:
	     • Damaged crankshaft pulse wheel teeth
	     • Damaged crankshaft position (CKP) sensor

DTC: P0316
2T MISFIRE
MIL: Yes
Years: 2008, 2009, 2010
Models: All
Engines: All
Transmissions: All
	Misfire Detected On Startup (First 1000 Revolutions)
	DTC P0316 is set in addition to any type B misfire DTC which occurs in the first 1,000 revolution test interval following engine start.
	Note: Freeze frame data and the DTC P03xx are also stored, indicating which cylinder the misfire occurred.
	Possible Causes:
	     • Damaged Crankshaft Position (CKP) sensor
	     • Ignition system
	     • Fuel injectors
	     • Running out of fuel
	     • Fuel quality
	     • Base engine
	     • PCM has failed

DTC: P0320
2T CCM, MIL: Yes
Years: 2008, 2009, 2010
Models: All
Engines: All
Transmissions: All
	Ignition/Distributor Engine Speed Input Circuit
	The ignition engine speed sensor input signal to Powertrain Control Module (PCM) is continuously monitored. The test fails when the signal indicates two successive erratic Profile Ignition Pickup (PIP) pulses occurred.
	Note: The DTC indicates two successive erratic PIP pulses occurred.
	Possible Causes:
	     • Loose wires/connectors
	     • Arcing secondary ignition components (coil, wires and plugs)
	     • On-board transmitter (2-way radio)

DTC: P0325
2T CCM, MIL: Yes
Years: 2008, 2009, 2010
Models: All
Engines: All
Transmissions: All
	Knock Sensor 1 Circuit (Bank 1).
	The Knock Sensor (KS) detects vibrations upon increase and decrease in engine RPM. The knock sensor generates a voltage based on this vibration. A DTC is set if the voltage goes outside a calibrated level.
	Note: A knock sensor voltage greater than 0.5 volt with the key ON engine OFF indicates a concern is present.
	Possible Causes:
	     • KS circuit short to GND
	     • KS sensor circuit short to voltage
	     • KS circuit open
	     • Damaged KS

DTC: P0326
2T CCM, MIL: Yes
Years: 2008, 2009, 2010
Models: All
Engines: All
Transmissions: All
	Knock Sensor 1 Circuit Range/Performance (Bank 1)
	The Knock Sensor (KS) detects vibrations upon increase and decrease in engine RPM. The knock sensor generates a voltage based on this vibration. A DTC is set if the voltage goes outside a calibrated level.
	Note: A knock sensor voltage greater than 0.5 volt with the key ON engine OFF indicates a concern is present.
	Possible Causes:
	     • KS circuit short to GND
	     • KS sensor circuit short to voltage
	     • KS circuit open
	     • Damaged KS

DTC	Trouble Code Title, Conditions & Possible Causes
DTC: P0330 **2T CCM, MIL: Yes** **Years:** 2008, 2009, 2010 **Models:** All **Engines:** All **Transmissions:** All	**Knock Sensor 2 Circuit (Bank 2).** The Knock Sensor (KS) detects vibrations upon increase and decrease in engine RPM. The knock sensor generates a voltage based on this vibration. A DTC is set if the voltage goes outside a calibrated level. **Note: A knock sensor voltage greater than 0.5 volt with the key ON engine OFF indicates a concern is present.** **Possible Causes:** • KS circuit short to GND • KS sensor circuit short to voltage • KS circuit open • Damaged KS
DTC: P0331 **2T CCM, MIL: Yes** **Years:** 2008, 2009, 2010 **Models:** All **Engines:** All **Transmissions:** All	**Knock Sensor 2 Circuit Range/Performance (Bank 2)** The Knock Sensor (KS) detects vibrations upon increase and decrease in engine RPM. The knock sensor generates a voltage based on this vibration. A DTC is set if the voltage goes outside a calibrated level. **Note: A knock sensor voltage greater than 0.5 volt with the key ON engine OFF indicates a concern is present.** **Possible Causes:** • KS circuit short to GND • KS sensor circuit short to voltage • KS circuit open • Damaged KS
DTC: P0340 **2T CCM, MIL: Yes** **Years:** 2008, 2009, 2010 **Models:** All **Engines:** All **Transmissions:** All	**Camshaft Position Sensor A Circuit (Bank 1 or single sensor)** The test fails when the Powertrain Control Module (PCM) can no longer detect the signal from the Camshaft Position (CMP) sensor on bank 1. **Note: Harness routing, harness alterations, incorrect shielding, or electrical interference from other systems may have an intermittent impact on the CMP signal.** **Possible Causes:** • CMP circuit open • CMP circuit short to GND • CMP circuit short to voltage • SIG RTN open (VR sensor) • CMP GND open (Hall-effect sensor) • CMP circuit short to CMP2 circuit (if equipped) • CMP incorrectly installed (Hall-effect sensor) • Damaged CMP sensor shielding • Damaged CMP sensor • PCM has failed
DTC: P0341 **2T CCM, MIL: Yes** **Years:** 2008, 2009, 2010 **Models:** All **Engines:** All **Transmissions:** All	**Camshaft Position Sensor A Circuit Range/Performance (Bank 1 or single sensor)** The Powertrain Control Module (PCM) monitors the Camshaft Position (CMP) sensor for a noisy signal. **Note: Harness routing, harness alterations, incorrect shielding, or electrical interference from other systems may have an intermittent impact on the CMP signal.** **Possible Causes:** • Radio Frequency Interference/Electromagnetic Interference (RFI/EMI) • Damaged camshaft phaser and sprocket
DTC: P0344 **2T CCM, MIL: Yes** **Years:** 2008, 2009, 2010 **Models:** All **Engines:** All **Transmissions:** All	**Camshaft Position Sensor A Circuit Intermittent (Bank 1 or single sensor)** The test fails when the Powertrain Control Module (PCM) detects an intermittent signal from the Camshaft Position (CMP) sensor. **Note: Harness routing, harness alterations, incorrect shielding, or electrical interference from other systems may have an intermittent impact on the CMP signal.** **Possible Causes:** • Intermittent open circuit • Intermittent short circuit • Damaged sensor shielding • Damaged sensor

DTC	Trouble Code Title, Conditions & Possible Causes

DTC: P0345
2T CCM, MIL: Yes
Years: 2008, 2009, 2010
Models: All
Engines: All
Transmissions: All
	Camshaft Position Sensor A Circuit (Bank 2)
	The test fails when the Powertrain Control Module (PCM) can no longer detect the signal from the Camshaft Position (CMP) sensor on bank 2.
	Note: Harness routing, harness alterations, incorrect shielding, or electrical interference from other systems may have an intermittent impact on the CMP signal.
	Possible Causes:
	    • CMP circuit open
	    • CMP circuit short to GND
	    • CMP circuit short to voltage
	    • SIG RTN open (VR sensor)
	    • CMP GND open (Hall-effect sensor)
	    • CMP circuit short to CMP2 circuit (if equipped)
	    • CMP incorrectly installed (Hall-effect sensor)
	    • Damaged CMP sensor shielding
	    • Damaged CMP sensor
	    • PCM has failed

DTC: P0346
2T CCM, MIL: Yes
Years: 2008, 2009, 2010
Models: All
Engines: All
Transmissions: All
	Camshaft Position Sensor A Circuit Range/Performance (Bank 2)
	The Powertrain Control Module (PCM) monitors the Camshaft Position (CMP) sensor for a noisy signal.
	Note: Harness routing, harness alterations, incorrect shielding, or electrical interference from other systems may have an intermittent impact on the CMP signal.
	Possible Causes:
	    • Radio Frequency Interference/Electromagnetic Interference (RFI/EMI)
	    • Damaged camshaft phaser and sprocket

DTC: P0349
2T CCM, MIL: Yes
Years: 2008, 2009, 2010
Models: All
Engines: All
Transmissions: All
	Camshaft Position Sensor A Circuit Intermittent (Bank 2)
	The test fails when the Powertrain Control Module (PCM) detects an intermittent signal from the Camshaft Position (CMP) sensor.
	Note: Harness routing, harness alterations, incorrect shielding, or electrical interference from other systems may have an intermittent impact on the CMP signal.
	Possible Causes:
	    • Intermittent open circuit
	    • Intermittent short circuit
	    • Damaged sensor shielding
	    • Damaged sensor

DTC: P0350
2T CCM, MIL: Yes
Years: 2008, 2009, 2010
Models: All
Engines: All
Transmissions: All
	Ignition Coil Primary/Secondary Circuit Malfunction
	Each ignition primary circuit is continuously monitored. The test fails when the Powertrain Control Module (PCM) does not receive a valid Ignition Diagnostic Monitor (IDM) pulse signal from the ignition module (integrated in the PCM).
	Note: The PCM may disable the fuel injector for a cylinder that is misfiring to protect the exhaust system catalyst. Use the 12-volt non-powered test lamp to verify START/RUN voltage at the ignition coil harness connector. Check the coil driver circuit for open, short to VPWR, or short to ground.
	Possible Causes:
	    • Open or short in the ignition START/RUN circuit
	    • Open coil driver circuit
	    • Coil driver circuit short to ground
	    • Damaged coil or coil pack
	    • Coil driver circuit short to VPWR
	    • PCM has failed

DTC: P0351
2T CCM, MIL: Yes
Years: 2008, 2009, 2010
Models: All
Engines: All
Transmissions: All
	Ignition Coil 1 Primary/Secondary Circuit Malfunction
	Each ignition primary circuit is continuously monitored. The test fails when the Powertrain Control Module (PCM) does not receive a valid Ignition Diagnostic Monitor (IDM) pulse signal from the ignition module (integrated in the PCM).
	Note: The PCM may disable the fuel injector for a cylinder that is misfiring to protect the exhaust system catalyst. Use the 12-volt non-powered test lamp to verify START/RUN voltage at the ignition coil harness connector. Check the coil driver circuit for open, short to VPWR, or short to ground.
	Possible Causes:
	    • Open or short in the ignition START/RUN circuit
	    • Open coil driver circuit
	    • Coil driver circuit short to ground
	    • Damaged coil or coil pack
	    • Coil driver circuit short to VPWR
	    • PCM has failed

DTC	Trouble Code Title, Conditions & Possible Causes
DTC: P0352 **2T CCM, MIL: Yes** **Years:** 2008, 2009, 2010 **Models:** All **Engines:** All **Transmissions:** All	**Ignition Coil 2 Primary/Secondary Circuit Malfunction** Each ignition primary circuit is continuously monitored. The test fails when the Powertrain Control Module (PCM) does not receive a valid Ignition Diagnostic Monitor (IDM) pulse signal from the ignition module (integrated in the PCM). **Note: The PCM may disable the fuel injector for a cylinder that is misfiring to protect the exhaust system catalyst. Use the 12-volt non-powered test lamp to verify START/RUN voltage at the ignition coil harness connector. Check the coil driver circuit for open, short to VPWR, or short to ground.** **Possible Causes:** • Open or short in the ignition START/RUN circuit • Open coil driver circuit • Coil driver circuit short to ground • Damaged coil or coil pack • Coil driver circuit short to VPWR • PCM has failed
DTC: P0353 **2T CCM, MIL: Yes** **Years:** 2008, 2009, 2010 **Models:** All **Engines:** All **Transmissions:** All	**Ignition Coil 3 Primary/Secondary Circuit Malfunction** Each ignition primary circuit is continuously monitored. The test fails when the Powertrain Control Module (PCM) does not receive a valid Ignition Diagnostic Monitor (IDM) pulse signal from the ignition module (integrated in the PCM). **Note: The PCM may disable the fuel injector for a cylinder that is misfiring to protect the exhaust system catalyst. Use the 12-volt non-powered test lamp to verify START/RUN voltage at the ignition coil harness connector. Check the coil driver circuit for open, short to VPWR, or short to ground.** **Possible Causes:** • Open or short in the ignition START/RUN circuit • Open coil driver circuit • Coil driver circuit short to ground • Damaged coil or coil pack • Coil driver circuit short to VPWR • PCM has failed
DTC: P0354 **2T CCM, MIL: Yes** **Years:** 2008, 2009, 2010 **Models:** All **Engines:** All **Transmissions:** All	**Ignition Coil 4 Primary/Secondary Circuit Malfunction** Each ignition primary circuit is continuously monitored. The test fails when the Powertrain Control Module (PCM) does not receive a valid Ignition Diagnostic Monitor (IDM) pulse signal from the ignition module (integrated in the PCM). **Note: The PCM may disable the fuel injector for a cylinder that is misfiring to protect the exhaust system catalyst. Use the 12-volt non-powered test lamp to verify START/RUN voltage at the ignition coil harness connector. Check the coil driver circuit for open, short to VPWR, or short to ground.** **Possible Causes:** • Open or short in the ignition START/RUN circuit • Open coil driver circuit • Coil driver circuit short to ground • Damaged coil or coil pack • Coil driver circuit short to VPWR • PCM has failed
DTC: P0355 **2T CCM, MIL: Yes** **Years:** 2008, 2009, 2010 **Models:** All **Engines:** All V6, V8, V10 **Transmissions:** All	**Ignition Coil 5 Primary/Secondary Circuit Malfunction** Each ignition primary circuit is continuously monitored. The test fails when the Powertrain Control Module (PCM) does not receive a valid Ignition Diagnostic Monitor (IDM) pulse signal from the ignition module (integrated in the PCM). **Note: The PCM may disable the fuel injector for a cylinder that is misfiring to protect the exhaust system catalyst. Use the 12-volt non-powered test lamp to verify START/RUN voltage at the ignition coil harness connector. Check the coil driver circuit for open, short to VPWR, or short to ground.** **Possible Causes:** • Open or short in the ignition START/RUN circuit • Open coil driver circuit • Coil driver circuit short to ground • Damaged coil or coil pack • Coil driver circuit short to VPWR • PCM has failed

DTC	Trouble Code Title, Conditions & Possible Causes
DTC: P0356 **2T CCM, MIL: Yes** **Years:** 2008, 2009, 2010 **Models:** All **Engines:** All V6, V8, V10 **Transmissions:** All	**Ignition Coil 6 Primary/Secondary Circuit Malfunction** Each ignition primary circuit is continuously monitored. The test fails when the Powertrain Control Module (PCM) does not receive a valid Ignition Diagnostic Monitor (IDM) pulse signal from the ignition module (integrated in the PCM). **Note: The PCM may disable the fuel injector for a cylinder that is misfiring to protect the exhaust system catalyst. Use the 12-volt non-powered test lamp to verify START/RUN voltage at the ignition coil harness connector. Check the coil driver circuit for open, short to VPWR, or short to ground.** **Possible Causes:** • Open or short in the ignition START/RUN circuit • Open coil driver circuit • Coil driver circuit short to ground • Damaged coil or coil pack • Coil driver circuit short to VPWR • PCM has failed
DTC: P0357 **2T CCM, MIL: Yes** **Years:** 2008, 2009, 2010 **Models:** All **Engines:** All V8, V10 **Transmissions:** All	**Ignition Coil 7 Primary/Secondary Circuit Malfunction** Each ignition primary circuit is continuously monitored. The test fails when the Powertrain Control Module (PCM) does not receive a valid Ignition Diagnostic Monitor (IDM) pulse signal from the ignition module (integrated in the PCM). **Note: The PCM may disable the fuel injector for a cylinder that is misfiring to protect the exhaust system catalyst. Use the 12-volt non-powered test lamp to verify START/RUN voltage at the ignition coil harness connector. Check the coil driver circuit for open, short to VPWR, or short to ground.** **Possible Causes:** • Open or short in the ignition START/RUN circuit • Open coil driver circuit • Coil driver circuit short to ground • Damaged coil or coil pack • Coil driver circuit short to VPWR • PCM has failed
DTC: P0358 **2T CCM, MIL: Yes** **Years:** 2008, 2009, 2010 **Models:** All **Engines:** All V8, V10 **Transmissions:** All	**Ignition Coil 8 Primary/Secondary Circuit Malfunction** Each ignition primary circuit is continuously monitored. The test fails when the Powertrain Control Module (PCM) does not receive a valid Ignition Diagnostic Monitor (IDM) pulse signal from the ignition module (integrated in the PCM). **Note: The PCM may disable the fuel injector for a cylinder that is misfiring to protect the exhaust system catalyst. Use the 12-volt non-powered test lamp to verify START/RUN voltage at the ignition coil harness connector. Check the coil driver circuit for open, short to VPWR, or short to ground.** **Possible Causes:** • Open or short in the ignition START/RUN circuit • Open coil driver circuit • Coil driver circuit short to ground • Damaged coil or coil pack • Coil driver circuit short to VPWR • PCM has failed
DTC: P0359 **2T CCM, MIL: Yes** **Years:** 2008, 2009, 2010 **Models:** All **Engines:** All V10 **Transmissions:** All	**Ignition Coil 9 Primary/Secondary Circuit Malfunction** Each ignition primary circuit is continuously monitored. The test fails when the Powertrain Control Module (PCM) does not receive a valid Ignition Diagnostic Monitor (IDM) pulse signal from the ignition module (integrated in the PCM). **Note: The PCM may disable the fuel injector for a cylinder that is misfiring to protect the exhaust system catalyst. Use the 12-volt non-powered test lamp to verify START/RUN voltage at the ignition coil harness connector. Check the coil driver circuit for open, short to VPWR, or short to ground.** **Possible Causes:** • Open or short in the ignition START/RUN circuit • Open coil driver circuit • Coil driver circuit short to ground • Damaged coil or coil pack • Coil driver circuit short to VPWR • PCM has failed

DTC	Trouble Code Title, Conditions & Possible Causes
DTC: P0360 **2T CCM, MIL: Yes** **Years:** 2008, 2009, 2010 **Models:** All **Engines:** All V10 **Transmissions:** All	**Ignition Coil 10 Primary/Secondary Circuit Malfunction** Each ignition primary circuit is continuously monitored. The test fails when the Powertrain Control Module (PCM) does not receive a valid Ignition Diagnostic Monitor (IDM) pulse signal from the ignition module (integrated in the PCM). **Note: The PCM may disable the fuel injector for a cylinder that is misfiring to protect the exhaust system catalyst. Use the 12-volt non-powered test lamp to verify START/RUN voltage at the ignition coil harness connector. Check the coil driver circuit for open, short to VPWR, or short to ground.** **Possible Causes:** • Open or short in the ignition START/RUN circuit • Open coil driver circuit • Coil driver circuit short to ground • Damaged coil or coil pack • Coil driver circuit short to VPWR • PCM has failed
DTC: P0400 **2T EGR, MIL: Yes** **Years:** 2008, 2009, 2010 **Models:** All **Engines:** All with electric EGR valve **Transmissions:** All	**Exhaust Gas Recirculation (EGR) Flow (Vehicles with electric EGR valve)** The Electric EGR (EEGR) system is monitored once per drive cycle at high and low load conditions. The test fails when a concern is detected by Powertrain Control Module (PCM) calculations indicating the EGR flow is less or greater than expected. **Note: All of the following sensors input data to the PCM for correct operation of the EEGR system: Engine Coolant Temperature (ECT), Crankshaft Position (CKP), Intake Air Temperature (IAT), MAF, Throttle Position (TP), MAP. Any DTC relating to these sensors must be resolved prior to addressing DTC P0400.** **Possible Causes:** • EEGR valve stuck open or closed • Connector to EEGR not seated • EEGR motor winding circuits short or open • No voltage to the EEGR • Harness open or short to voltage or ground • Vacuum signal to Manifold Absolute Pressure (MAP) restricted or leaking • Mass Air Flow (MAF) sensor signal erroneous • Carbon build up in the EEGR valve seat area • One or more sensors is not responding or is out of range • PCM has failed
DTC: P0400 **2T EGR, MIL: Yes** **Years:** 2008, 2009, 2010 **Models:** All **Engines:** All with vacuum EGR valve **Transmissions:** All	**Exhaust Gas Recirculation (EGR) Flow (Vehicles with vacuum EGR valve)** Engine started, engine running under at cruise speed in closed loop, and the PCM detected a problem in the EGR system. Run the KOER self-test. If DTC P1406 is set, test the EGR valve operation. **Possible Causes:** • DPFE EGR valve hoses are damaged, leaking or restricted • DPFE EGR valve hoses may be reversed at the sensor • EGR valve connector is damaged, loose or shorted • EGR valve is damaged or it has failed • PCM has failed
DTC: P0401 **2T EGR, MIL: Yes** **Years:** 2008, 2009, 2010 **Models:** All **Engines:** All **Transmissions:** All	**Exhaust Gas Recirculation (EGR) Flow Insufficient Detected** The EGR system is monitored during steady state driving conditions while the EGR is commanded on. The test fails when the signal from the differential pressure feedback EGR sensor indicates that EGR flow is less than the desired minimum **Note: Carry out the Key On Engine Running (KOER) self-test and look for DTC P1408 as an indication of a hard fault. If DTC P1408 is not present, look for contamination, restrictions, leaks, and intermittent concerns.** **Possible Causes:** • Vacuum supply • EGR valve stuck closed • EGR valve leaks vacuum • EGR flow path restricted • EVR circuit short to voltage • VREF open to differential pressure feedback EGR sensor • Differential pressure feedback EGR sensor downstream hose is off or plugged • EVR circuit open • VPWR open to EGR vacuum regulator solenoid • Differential pressure feedback EGR sensor hoses are both off • Differential pressure feedback EGR sensor hoses are reversed • Damaged EGR orifice tube • Damaged EGR vacuum regulator solenoid

DTC	Trouble Code Title, Conditions & Possible Causes
DTC: P0402 **2T EGR, MIL: Yes** **Years:** 2008, 2009, 2010 **Models:** All **Engines:** All **Transmissions:** All	**Exhaust Gas Recirculation (EGR) Flow Excessive Detected** The EGR system is monitored for undesired EGR flow during idle. The EGR monitor looks at the Differential Pressure Feedback EGR (DPFE) signal at idle and compares it to the stored signal measured during Key On Engine Off (KOEO). The test fails when the signal at idle is greater than at KOEO by a calibrated amount. **Note: A DPFEGR PID reading that is greater at idle than during KOEO by 0.5 volt or a rough engine idle may indicate a hard fault.** **Possible Causes:** • EGR valve stuck open • Plugged EGR vacuum regulator solenoid vent • Plugged EGR tube • Slow responding differential pressure feedback EGR sensor • Damaged differential pressure feedback EGR sensor • Incorrect vacuum hose connection • Plugged vacuum hoses • EVR circuit short to ground • Damaged EGR vacuum regulator solenoid
DTC: P0403 **2T EGR, MIL: Yes** **Years:** 2008, 2009, 2010 **Models:** All **Engines:** All with electric EGR valve **Transmissions:** All	**Exhaust Gas Recirculation (EGR) Control Circuit (Vehicles with electric EGR valve)** The EEGR system is continuously monitored to check the four EEGR motor coils, circuits, and the powertrain control module (PCM) for opens, shorts to voltage and ground. If a concern is detected, the EEGR system is disabled and additional monitoring is suspended for the remainder of the drive until the next drive cycle. **Possible Causes:** • EEGR motor windings open • Connector to EEGR not seated • Open circuit in the harness from the PCM to the EEGR • Short circuit in the EEGR motor • Short circuit in the harness from the PCM to the EEGR • PCM has failed
DTC: P0403 **2T EGR, MIL: Yes** **Years:** 2008, 2009, 2010 **Models:** All **Engines:** All with vacuum EGR valve **Transmissions:** All	**Exhaust Gas Recirculation (EGR) Control Circuit (Vehicles with vacuum EGR valve)** This test checks the electrical function of the EGR vacuum regulator solenoid. The test fails when the EVR circuit voltage is either too high or too low when compared to the expected voltage range. The EGR system must be enabled for the test to be completed. **Note: The EGR vacuum regulator solenoid resistance is between 26 and 40 ohms.** **Possible Causes:** • EVR circuit open • EVR circuit short to voltage or ground • VPWR open to EGR vacuum regulator solenoid • EGR vacuum regulator solenoid • PCM has failed
DTC: P0405 **2T EGR, MIL: Yes** **Years:** 2008, 2009, 2010 **Models:** All **Engines:** All **Transmissions:** All	**Exhaust Gas Recirculation (EGR) Sensor A Circuit Low** The EGR monitor checks the differential pressure feedback EGR sensor signal to the Powertrain Control Module (PCM) for low voltage. The test fails when the average voltage to the PCM drops to a voltage less than the minimum calibrated value **Note: A DPFEGR PID reading less than 0.05 volt with the key ON, engine OFF or running indicates a hard fault.** **Possible Causes:** • Differential pressure feedback EGR circuit short to ground • Damaged differential pressure feedback EGR sensor. • VREF circuit short to ground • PCM has failed
DTC: P0406 **2T EGR, MIL: Yes** **Years:** 2008, 2009, 2010 **Models:** All **Engines:** All **Transmissions:** All	**Exhaust Gas Recirculation (EGR) Sensor A Circuit High** The EGR monitor checks the EGR sensor signal to the Powertrain Control Module (PCM) for high voltage. The test fails when the average voltage to the PCM exceeds the maximum calibrated value. **Note: A DPFEGR PID reading greater than 4.5 volts with the key ON, engine OFF or running indicates a hard fault.** **Possible Causes:** • Differential pressure feedback EGR circuit open • VREF circuit short to voltage • Damaged differential pressure feedback EGR sensor • Differential pressure feedback EGR circuit short to voltage • SIG RTN circuit open
DTC: P0410 **2T CCM, MIL: Yes** **Years:** 2008, 2009, 2010 **Models:** All **Engines:** All **Transmissions:** All	**Secondary Air Injection (AIR) System** The AIR system detected a lack of air flow with the secondary AIR pump ON. **Note: Measured air flow is less than expected. Visually inspect the secondary AIR inlet hose** **Possible Causes:** • AIR inlet hose leak. • AIR inlet hose disconnected.

DTC	Trouble Code Title, Conditions & Possible Causes
DTC: P0412 **2T CCM, MIL: Yes** **Years:** 2008, 2009, 2010 **Models:** All **Engines:** All **Transmissions:** All	**Secondary Air Injection (AIR) System - Switching Valve A Circuit** On the primary side of the AIR relay, open and short faults on the AIR command circuit are detected during normal operation by the Powertrain Control Module (PCM) output driver. **Note: For intermittent faults use the AIR PCM output driver fault PID (AIRF) during a harness wiggle test with the AIR PCM output driver in OFF and ON states. The AIR PCM output driver fault PID AIRF instantly detects open circuits and shorts to ground with the PCM output driver off. The AIR PCM output driver fault PID AIRF instantly detects open circuits and shorts to ground with the PCM output driver off. The AIR PCM output driver fault PID AIRF instantly detects a short to voltage or low resistance load with the PCM output driver on. Use the OTM to toggle the PCM output driver from OFF to ON.** **Possible Causes:** • Short to voltage or ground in the AIR command circuit • Open in the AIR command circuit • AIR bypass solenoid fault • AIR relay fault
DTC: P0420 **2T EGR, MIL: Yes** **Years:** 2008, 2009, 2010 **Models:** All **Engines:** All **Transmissions:** All	**Catalyst System Efficiency Below Threshold (Bank 1)** Indicates the bank 1 catalyst system efficiency is below the acceptable threshold. **Note: The signal line lengths of the downstream HO2Ss are compared against the signal line lengths of the upstream HO2Ss. Under normal closed loop fuel conditions, high efficiency catalysts have oxygen storage which reduces the frequency and amplitude of the downstream HO2S as compared with an upstream HO2S signal. As catalyst efficiency deteriorates, its ability to store oxygen declines and the downstream HO2S signal has an increased amplitude and frequency, approaching the amplitude and frequency of the upstream HO2S. Once beyond an acceptable limit the DTC is set. Vehicles with universal HO2Ss compare the signal line length of the downstream HO2Ss to an expected signal line length of the downstream HO2Ss with a deteriorated catalytic converter.** **Possible Causes:** • Use of leaded fuel • Damaged heated oxygen sensor (HO2S) • Out of range engine coolant temperature (ECT) sensor • High fuel pressure • Damaged exhaust manifold • Damaged catalytic converter • Oil contamination • Cylinder misfiring • Downstream HO2S wires incorrectly connected • Damaged exhaust system • Retarded spark timing • Leaking fuel injector
DTC: P0430 **2T CAT, MIL: Yes** **Years:** 2008, 2009, 2010 **Models:** All **Engines:** All **Transmissions:** All	**Catalyst System Efficiency Below Threshold (Bank 2)** Indicates the bank 1 catalyst system efficiency is below the acceptable threshold. **Note: The signal line lengths of the downstream HO2Ss are compared against the signal line lengths of the upstream HO2Ss. Under normal closed loop fuel conditions, high efficiency catalysts have oxygen storage which reduces the frequency and amplitude of the downstream HO2S as compared with an upstream HO2S signal. As catalyst efficiency deteriorates, its ability to store oxygen declines and the downstream HO2S signal has an increased amplitude and frequency, approaching the amplitude and frequency of the upstream HO2S. Once beyond an acceptable limit the DTC is set. Vehicles with universal HO2Ss compare the signal line length of the downstream HO2Ss to an expected signal line length of the downstream HO2Ss with a deteriorated catalytic converter.** **Possible Causes:** • Use of leaded fuel • Damaged Heated Oxygen Sensor (HO2S) • Out of range Engine Coolant Temperature (ECT) sensor • High fuel pressure • Damaged exhaust manifold • Damaged catalytic converter • Oil contamination • Cylinder misfiring • Downstream HO2S wires incorrectly connected • Damaged exhaust system • Retarded spark timing • Leaking fuel injector

DTC	Trouble Code Title, Conditions & Possible Causes
DTC: P0442 **2T EVAP, MIL: Yes** **Years:** 2008, 2009, 2010 **Models:** All **Engines:** All **Transmissions:** All	**Evaporative Emission System Leak Detected (Small Leak)** The Powertrain Control Module (PCM) monitors the complete Evaporative Emission (EVAP) control system for the presence of a small fuel vapor leak. System failure occurs when a fuel vapor leak from an opening as small as 1.016 mm (0.040 in) is detected by the EVAP running loss monitor test. **Note: Check for a missing fuel filler cap or the integrity of the cap. Verify the capless fuel tank filler pipe is sealed correctly (if equipped). Check for loose or damaged vapor hoses. Visually inspect the EVAP canister inlet port, CV solenoid filter, and canister vent hose assembly for contamination or debris.** **Possible Causes:** • Aftermarket EVAP hardware that does not conform to the required specifications • Small holes or cuts in the fuel vapor hoses/tubes • Canister vent solenoid stays partially open on closed command • Damaged, missing or loosely installed fuel filler cap • Capless fuel tank filler pipe damaged or not sealed correctly (if equipped) • Loose fuel vapor hose/tube connections to the EVAP system components • EVAP system component seals leaking at or near the EVAP canister purge valve, fuel tank pressure sensor, Canister Vent (CV) solenoid, fuel vapor control valve tube assembly or fuel vapor vent valve assembly
DTC: P0443 **2T EVAP, MIL: Yes** **Years:** 2008, 2009, 2010 **Models:** All **Engines:** All **Transmissions:** All	**Evaporative Emission System Purge Control Valve Circuit** The Powertrain Control Module (PCM) monitors the state of the Evaporative Emission (EVAP) canister purge valve circuit output driver. The test fails when the signal moves outside the minimum or maximum limit for the commanded state. **Note: To verify normal function, monitor the EVAP canister purge valve signal PID EVMV or EVAPCP and the signal voltage (PCM control side). With the valve closed, the EVMV indicates 0 mA (0% duty cycle for EVAPCP) and voltage approximately equal to battery voltage. When the valve is commanded fully open, EVMV indicates 1,000 mA (100% duty cycle for EVAPCP) and a voltage drop of 3 volts minimum is normal. Output test mode may be used to switch output on/off to verify function.** **Possible Causes:** • VPWR circuit open • EVAP canister purge valve circuit short to GND • Damaged EVAP canister purge valve • EVAP canister purge valve circuit open • EVAP canister purge valve circuit short to VPWR • PCM has failed
DTC: P0446 **2T EVAP, MIL: Yes** **Years:** 2008, 2009, 2010 **Models:** All **Engines:** All **Transmissions:** All	**Evaporative Emission System Vent Control Circuit** Monitors the Canister Vent (CV) solenoid circuit for an electrical failure. The test fails when the signal moves outside the minimum or maximum allowable calibrated parameters for a specified canister vent duty cycle by Powertrain Control Module (PCM) command. **Note: To verify normal functioning, monitor the EVAP canister vent solenoid signal PID EVAPCV and the signal voltage (PCM control side). With the valve open, EVAPCV indicates 0% duty cycle and a voltage approximately equal to battery voltage. When the valve is commanded fully closed, EVAPCV indicates 100% duty cycle, and a minimum voltage drop of 4 volts is normal. Output Test Mode (OTM) may be used to switch output on/off to verify function.** **Possible Causes:** • VPWR circuit open • KAPWR circuit open (vehicles equipped with Engine Off Natural Vacuum (EONV) EVAP leak check monitor) • CV solenoid circuit short to PWR GND or CHASSIS GND • Damaged CV solenoid • CV solenoid circuit open • CV solenoid circuit short to VPWR • CV solenoid circuit short to KAPWR (vehicles equipped with Engine Off Natural Vacuum (EONV) EVAP leak check monitor) • PCM has failed
DTC: P0451 **2T CCM, MIL: Yes** **Years:** 2008, 2009, 2010 **Models:** All **Engines:** All **Transmissions:** All	**Evaporative Emission System Pressure Sensor/Switch Range/Performance** This DTC sets for a Fuel Tank Pressure (FTP) sensor range (offset) concern. The FTP sensor output is offset by greater than 1.7 inches of water or less than −1.7 inches of water. **Note: With the FTP sensor at atmospheric pressure, the FTP PID normally indicates 0 inches of water.** **Possible Causes:** • Intermittent open or short in the FTP sensor or the FTP sensor signal • Contaminated or damaged sensor • Damaged FTP sensor • PCM has failed

DTC	Trouble Code Title, Conditions & Possible Causes
DTC: P0452 **2T CCM, MIL: Yes** **Years:** 2008, 2009, 2010 **Models:** All **Engines:** All **Transmissions:** All	**Evaporative Emission System Pressure Sensor/Switch Low** The Powertrain Control Module (PCM) monitors the Evaporative Emission (EVAP) control system Fuel Tank Pressure (FTP) sensor input signal to the PCM. The test fails when the signal average drops below a minimum allowable calibrated parameter. **Note: An FTP voltage PID reading less than 0.22 volt in key ON, engine OFF or key ON, engine running indicates a concern is present** **Possible Causes:** • Contamination internal to the FTP sensor connector • FTP circuit short to GND or SIG RTN • Damaged FTP sensor • PCM has failed
DTC: P0453 **2T CCM, MIL: Yes** **Years:** 2008, 2009, 2010 **Models:** All **Engines:** All **Transmissions:** All	**Evaporative Emission System Pressure Sensor/Switch High** The Powertrain Control Module (PCM) monitors the Evaporative Emission (EVAP) control system Fuel Tank Pressure (FTP) sensor input signal to the PCM. The test fails when the signal average jumps above a minimum allowable calibrated parameter. **Note: An FTP voltage PID reading greater than 4.85 volts in key ON, engine OFF or key ON, engine running indicates a concern is present.** **Possible Causes:** • FTP circuit open • VREF short to VPWR • FTP circuit short to VREF or VPWR • SIG RTN circuit open • Damaged FTP sensor
DTC: P0455 **2T EVAP, MIL: Yes** **Years:** 2008, 2009, 2010 **Models:** All **Engines:** All **Transmissions:** All	**Evaporative Emission System Pressure Sensor/Switch Intermittent** The fuel tank pressure changes greater than 14 inches of water in 0.10 seconds. **Note: Monitor the FTP PID and note if it changes from above 15 inches of water to below minus (−) 15 inches of water often in 1 minute.** **Possible Causes:** • Intermittent open or short in the Fuel Tank Pressure (FTP) sensor or the FTP sensor signal • Contaminated or damaged sensor
DTC: P0455 **2T EVAP, MIL: Yes** **Years:** 2008, 2009, 2010 **Models:** All **Engines:** All **Transmissions:** All	**Evaporative Emission System Leak Detected (Gross Leak/No Flow)** The Powertrain Control Module (PCM) monitors the complete Evaporative Emission (EVAP) control system for no purge flow, the presence of a large fuel vapor leak, or multiple small fuel vapor leaks. System failure occurs when no purge flow, which is attributed to fuel vapor blockages or restrictions, a large fuel vapor leak, or multiple fuel vapor leaks are detected by the EVAP running loss monitor test with the engine running, but not at idle **Note: Check for audible vacuum noise or significant fuel odor in the engine compartment or near the EVAP canister and fuel tank.** **Possible Causes:** • Aftermarket EVAP hardware that does not conform to the required specifications • Disconnected or cracked fuel EVAP canister tube, EVAP canister purge outlet tube, or EVAP return tube • EVAP canister purge valve stuck closed • Damaged EVAP canister • Damaged, missing or loosely installed fuel filler cap • Capless fuel tank filler pipe damaged or not sealed correctly (if equipped) • Loose fuel vapor hose/tube connections to the EVAP system components • Blockages or restrictions in the fuel vapor hoses/tubes • Fuel vapor control valve tube assembly or fuel vapor vent valve assembly blocked • Canister Vent (CV) solenoid stuck open • Mechanically inoperative Fuel Tank Pressure (FTP) sensor
DTC: P0456 **2T EVAP, MIL: Yes** **Years:** 2008, 2009, 2010 **Models:** All **Engines:** All **Transmissions:** All	**Evaporative Emission System Leak Detected (Very Small Leak)** The Powertrain Control Module (PCM) monitors the complete Evaporative Emission (EVAP) control system for the presence of a very small fuel vapor leak. The system failure occurs when a fuel vapor leak from an opening as small as 0.508 mm (0.020 inch) is detected by the EVAP running loss monitor test. **Note: Check for a missing fuel filler cap or the integrity of the cap. Verify the capless fuel tank filler pipe is sealed correctly (if equipped). Check for loose or damaged vapor hoses. Visually inspect the EVAP canister inlet port, CV solenoid filter, and canister vent hose assembly for contamination or debris.** **Possible Causes:** • Very small holes or cuts in the fuel vapor hoses/tubes • Loose fuel vapor hose/tube connections to the EVAP system components • EVAP system component seals leaking. (See the Possible Causes for DTC P0442)

DTC	Trouble Code Title, Conditions & Possible Causes

DTC: P0457
2T EVAP, MIL: Yes
Years: 2008, 2009, 2010
Models: All
Engines: All
Transmissions: All
	Evaporative Emission System Leak Detected (Fuel Cap Loose/Off)
	The Powertrain Control Module (PCM) continuously monitors the fuel level and retains the last updated value prior to the ignition switch being placed in the OFF position. After the ignition switch is placed in the ON position a new fuel level is taken and compared to the level recorded at key off. If the fuel level has increased, a flag is set in the PCM indicating the vehicle was refueled. If the Evaporative Emission (EVAP) monitor detects a gross leak while the refueling flag is set, a loose fuel filler cap or an incorrectly sealed fuel tank filler pipe (if equipped) is suspected and the DTC is set. On most vehicles when the DTC sets, either the check fuel cap indicator illuminates or a message on the instrument cluster displays to instruct the driver to check the fuel cap or capless fuel tank filler pipe (if equipped).
	Note: Check for a missing fuel filler cap or the integrity of the cap. Verify the capless fuel tank filler pipe is sealed correctly (if equipped). If OK, clear the continuous memory DTCs and test the system for correct operation.
	Possible Causes:
	    • Damaged, missing, or loosely installed fuel filler cap
	    • Capless fuel tank filler pipe damaged or not sealed correctly (if equipped)

DTC: P0460
2T CCM, MIL: Yes
Years: 2008, 2009, 2010
Models: All
Engines: All
Transmissions: All
	Fuel Level Sensor A Circuit
	The Powertrain Control Module (PCM) monitors the Fuel Level Input (FLI) communications network message for a concern. The test fails when the PCM determines that the value of the FLI signal is stuck. The PCM calculates the amount of fuel used during operation. If the FLI signal does not change or does not correspond with the calculated fuel usage, the DTC is set.
	Note: Check with the customer for driving and fueling habits that would keep the fuel level at approximately the same value. Monitor the FLI PIDs while attempting to move the fuel level float by adding or removing fuel as necessary.
	Possible Causes:
	    • Stuck float arm
	    • Fuel level is always greater than 95% due to refueling patterns
	    • Fuel level is always less than 5% due to refueling patterns
	    • Fuel level is always at the same level between 3% and 97% full due to refueling patterns
	    • Fuel Pump (FP) module concern
	    • Damaged Instrument Panel Cluster (IPC) (E-Series, MKS)
	    • Damaged Instrument Cluster (IC)

DTC: P0462
2T CCM, MIL: Yes
Years: 2008, 2009, 2010
Models: All
Engines: All
Transmissions: All
	Fuel Level Sensor A Circuit Low
	The Powertrain Control Module (PCM) monitors the Fuel Level Input (FLI) communications network message for a concern. The test fails when the FLI signal is less than the minimum allowable calibrated parameter for a specified fuel fill percentage in the fuel tank.
	Note: Monitor the FLI PIDs in key ON, engine running. A concern is present if the FLI percentage PID is at 25% fill and the FLI voltage PID is less than 0.90 volt with a non-matching fuel gauge or the FLI percentage PID is at 75% fill and the FLI voltage PID is greater than 2.45 volts with a non-matching fuel gauge.
	Possible Causes:
	    • Empty fuel tank
	    • Fuel Pump (FP) module concern
	    • Incorrectly installed fuel gauge
	    • Damaged Instrument Panel Cluster (IPC) (E-Series, MKS)
	    • Damaged Instrument Cluster (IC)
	    • Damaged fuel gauge
	    • FLI circuit short to ground

DTC: P0463
2T CCM, MIL: Yes
Years: 2008, 2009, 2010
Models: All
Engines: All
Transmissions: All
	Fuel Level Sensor A Circuit High
	The Powertrain Control Module (PCM) monitors the Fuel Level Input (FLI) communications network message for a concern. The test fails when the FLI signal is greater than the maximum allowable calibrated parameter for a specified fuel fill percentage in the fuel tank.
	Note: Monitor the FLI PIDs in key ON, engine running. A concern is present if the FLI percentage PID is at 25% fill and the FLI voltage PID is less than 0.90 volt with a non-matching fuel gauge or the FLI percentage PID is at 75% fill and the FLI voltage PID is greater than 2.45 volts with a non-matching fuel gauge.
	Possible Causes:
	    • Fuel pump (FP) module concern
	    • Incorrectly installed fuel gauge
	    • Damaged instrument panel cluster (IPC) (E-Series, MKS)
	    • Damaged Instrument Cluster (IC)
	    • FLI circuit open
	    • FLI short to VPWR
	    • Overfilled fuel tank
	    • Damaged fuel gauge

DTC	Trouble Code Title, Conditions & Possible Causes
DTC: P0480 **2T CCM, MIL: Yes** **Years:** 2008, 2009, 2010 **Models:** All with relay controlled cooling fan **Engines:** All **Transmissions:** All	**Fan 1 Control Circuit (Relay Controlled Electric Cooling Fan)** Monitors the Low Fan Control (LFC) primary circuit output from the Powertrain Control Module (PCM). The test fails when the PCM grounds the LFC circuit and excessive current draw is detected on the LFC circuit; or with the LFC circuit not grounded by the PCM the voltage is not detected on the LFC circuit (the PCM expects to detect VPWR voltage coming through the low speed fan control relay coil to the LFC circuit). **Note: When the LFC PID reads YES, a concern is currently present. During the Key On Engine Off (KOEO) self-test, the cooling fan is cycled on and off. A short to voltage can only be detected when the PCM is grounding the LFC circuit. During the KOEO and Key On Engine Running (KOER) self-test, the LFC circuit is cycled on and off.** **Possible Causes:** • Open or short LFC circuit • Open VPWR circuit to the low speed FC relay • FC relay power supply (VPWR) circuit is open • Damaged low speed FC relay • PCM has failed
DTC: P0480 **2T CCM, MIL: Yes** **Years:** 2008, 2009, 2010 **Models:** All with variable speed electric cooling fan **Engines:** All **Transmissions:** All	**Fan 1 Control Circuit (Variable Speed Electric Cooling Fan)** This test checks the Fan Control Variable (FCV) output circuit. The DTC sets if the Powertrain Control Module (PCM) detects that the voltage on the FCV circuit is not within the expected range. **Note: During the Key On Engine Off (KOEO) self-test, the cooling fan is cycled on and off.** **Possible Causes:** • FCV circuit open or short • B+ or ground circuit concern to cooling fan • VPWR open to cooling fan (if applicable) • Damaged cooling fan module
DTC: P0480 **2T CCM, MIL: Yes** **Years:** 2008, 2009, 2010 **Models:** All with cooling fan clutch **Engines:** All **Transmissions:** All	**Fan 1 Control Circuit (Cooling Fan Clutch)** This test checks the Fan Control Variable (FCV) output circuit for the cooling fan clutch. The DTC sets if the Powertrain Control Module (PCM) detects that the voltage on the FCV circuit is not within the expected range **Possible Causes:** • FCV circuit open in the harness • FCV circuit short to voltage or ground in the harness • Damaged cooling fan clutch solenoid
DTC: P0481 **2T CCM, MIL: Yes** **Years:** 2008, 2009, 2010 **Models:** All **Engines:** All **Transmissions:** All	**Fan 2 Control Circuit** Monitors the High Fan Control (HFC) primary circuit output from the Powertrain Control Module (PCM). The test fails, when the HFC output is commanded on (grounded) and excessive current draw is detected on the HFC circuit; or when the HFC circuit is commanded off and voltage is not detected on the HFC circuit (the PCM expects to detect VPWR voltage through the high speed FC relay coil to the HFC circuit). **Note: When the High Fan Control Fault (HFCF) PID reads YES, a concern is currently present. An open circuit or short to ground can only be detected when the PCM is not grounding the HFC circuit. A short to voltage can only be detected when the PCM is grounding the HFC circuit. During the Key On Engine Off (KOEO) and Key On Engine Running (KOER) self-test, the HFC circuit is cycled on and off.** **Possible Causes:** • Open or short HFC circuit • Open VPWR circuit to the high speed FC relay • Damaged high speed FC relay
DTC: P0482 **2T CCM, MIL: Yes** **Years:** 2008, 2009, 2010 **Models:** All **Engines:** All **Transmissions:** All	**Fan 3 Control Circuit** Monitors the Medium Fan Control (MFC) primary circuit output from the Powertrain Control Module (PCM). The test fails, when the MFC output is commanded on (grounded) and excessive current draw is detected on the MFC circuit; or when the MFC circuit is commanded off and voltage is not detected on the MFC circuit (the PCM expects to detect IGN START/RUN voltage through the medium speed FC relay coil to the MFC circuit). **Note: When the Medium Fan Control Fault (MFCF) PID reads YES, a concern is currently present. MFCF. An open circuit or short to ground can only be detected when the PCM is not grounding the MFC circuit. A short to voltage can only be detected when the PCM is grounding the MFC circuit. During the Key On Engine Off (KOEO) and Key On Engine Running (KOER) self-test, the MFC circuit is cycled on and off. Use output test mode to command the low speed/high speed fan on. The PCM also activates the medium speed fan output.** **Possible Causes:** • Open or short MFC circuit • Open IGN START/RUN circuit to the medium speed FC relay • Damaged medium speed FC relay

DTC	Trouble Code Title, Conditions & Possible Causes
DTC: P0483 **2T CCM, MIL: Yes** **Years:** 2008, 2009, 2010 **Models:** All with electric fan clutch **Engines:** All **Transmissions:** All	**Electronic Fan Clutch Performance** If the cooling fan clutch fan is binding, or the Powertrain Control Module (PCM) detects the fan speed is at or near 0 RPM, the DTC is set. **Note: Check for a mechanical concern with the cooling fan motor or for obstructions limiting the cooling fan motor operation.** **Possible Causes:** • Cooling fan motor mechanical concerns • Obstruction or binding conditions
DTC: P0483 **2T CCM, MIL: Yes** **Years:** 2008, 2009, 2010 **Models:** All with electrical fan **Engines:** All **Transmissions:** All	**Electrical Fan Performance** The PCM controls the fan speed and operation using a duty cycle output on the Fan Control Variable (FCV) circuit. **Note: Check for a mechanical concern with the cooling fan motor or for obstructions limiting the cooling fan motor operation.** **Possible Causes:** • Cooling fan motor mechanical concerns • Obstruction or binding conditions • Overheated controller
DTC: P0491 **2T CCM, MIL: Yes** **Years:** 2008, 2009, 2010 **Models:** All **Engines:** All **Transmissions:** All	**Secondary Air Injection (AIR) System Insufficient Flow (Bank 1)** The AIR system detected that there was insufficient mass air flow change during pump switching (ON/OFF). **Note: Measured air flow is less than expected. Visually inspect the secondary AIR inlet hose.** **Possible Causes:** • Secondary AIR pump with no or low air flow. • Secondary AIR by-pass solenoid leaking/blocked or stuck open/closed. • Secondary AIR diverter valve leaking/blocked or stuck open/closed. • Secondary AIR air hose restricted. • Secondary AIR vacuum hoes restricted or leaking.
DTC: P0500 **2T CCM, MIL: Yes** **Years:** 2008, 2009, 2010 **Models:** All **Engines:** All **Transmissions:** All	**Vehicle Speed Sensor (VSS) A** Indicates the Powertrain Control Module (PCM) detected an error in the vehicle speed information. Vehicle speed data is received from either the VSS, the Transfer Case Speed Sensor (TCSS) or the Anti-lock Brake System (ABS) control module. If the engine RPM is above the torque converter stall speed (automatic transmission) and the engine load is high, it can be inferred that the vehicle must be moving. If there is insufficient vehicle speed data input, a concern is indicated and a DTC is set. On most vehicle applications the Malfunction Indicator Lamp (MIL) is illuminated when this DTC is set. **Note: The PCM receives vehicle speed data from the Rear Wheel ABS (RABS) or 4-Wheel ABS (4WABS) on these applications.** **Note: Monitor the VSS PID while driving the vehicle. This DTC is set when the PCM detects a sudden loss of vehicle speed signal over a period of time. If vehicle speed data is lost, check the source of the vehicle speed input: VSS, TCSS or ABS. On some Manual Shift-On-the-Fly (MSOF) applications, VSS and TCSS PID can be monitored. However if no TCSS PID is available and VSS PID is zero, TCSS circuitry frequency must be checked for loss of sensor signal. If another vehicle electronic module has generated the P0500 and the vehicle does not receive its vehicle speed input from the VSS, TCSS or ABS, check the PCM for Output Shaft Speed (OSS) sensor DTCs. On OSS applications the PCM uses the OSS to calculate the vehicle speed. If no OSS DTCs are found check for correct PCM configuration, tire size and axle ratio.** **Possible Causes:** • VSC positive signal circuit is open or shorted to ground • VSC negative signal circuit is open • RABS or 4WABS control unit is damaged or has failed • One of the other modules (CTM or GEM) may be the cause of this trouble code. Diagnose other codes from these modules.
DTC: P0503 **2T CCM, MIL: Yes** **Years:** 2008, 2009, 2010 **Models:** All **Engines:** All **Transmissions:** A/T	**Vehicle Speed Sensor (VSS) A Intermittent/Erratic/High** Indicates poor or noisy VSS performance. Vehicle speed data is received from the VSS, the Transfer Case Speed Sensor (TCSS), or the Anti Lock Brake System (ABS) control module. **Note: Monitor the VSS PID while driving the vehicle, and check for intermittent vehicle speed indication. Verify the ignition and charging systems are functioning correctly.** **Possible Causes:** • Noisy VSS/TCSS input signal from the Radio Frequency Interference / Electromagnetic Interference (RFI/EMI) external sources, such as ignition components or the charging circuit • Damaged VSS or driven gears • Damaged TCSS • Damaged wiring harness or connectors • Concern in the module(s) or circuit connected to the VSS/TCSS circuit • Aftermarket add-on

DTC	Trouble Code Title, Conditions & Possible Causes
DTC: P0504 **2T CCM, MIL: Yes** **Years:** 2008, 2009, 2010 **Models:** All **Engines:** All **Transmissions:** A/T	**Brake Switch Correlation** The PCM does a comparison test between the Brake Pedal Switch (BPS) and the Brake Pedal Position (BPP) switch. **Note: Check the state of PID BPS and PID BPP. BPS is normally closed and BPP is normally open.** **Possible Causes:** • Damaged brake switch • Open or short in the BPS circuit • Open or short in the BPP circuit
DTC: P0505 **2T CCM, MIL: Yes** **Years:** 2008, 2009, 2010 **Models:** All with IAC valve **Engines:** All **Transmissions:** All	**Idle Air Control (IAC) System (Vehicles With IAC Valve)** The Powertrain Control Module (PCM) attempts to control engine speed during the Key On, Engine Running (KOER) self-test. The test fails when the desired RPM could not be reached or controlled during the self-test. **Possible Causes:** • IAC circuit open • VPWR to IAC solenoid open • B+ or VPWR to IAC solenoid open • Air inlet is plugged • IAC circuit shorted to PWR • Damaged IAC valve
DTC: P0505 **2T CCM, MIL: Yes** **Years:** 2008, 2009, 2010 **Models:** All without IAC valve **Engines:** All **Transmissions:** All	**Idle Air Control (IAC) System (Vehicles Without IAC Valve)** The Powertrain Control Module (PCM) attempts to control engine speed during the Key On, Engine Running (KOER) self-test. The test fails when the desired RPM could not be reached or controlled during the self-test. **Note: This DTC may be accompanied by other DTCs. Diagnose other DTCs first. If other DTCs are not present inspect the intake air system for air restrictions, vacuum leaks, and damage. If no concerns are present, clear the DTC and carry out the KOER self-test.** **Possible Causes:** • Failure Mode Effects Management (FMEM) condition is present • Intake air restriction • Exhaust restriction • Sludged throttle body • Vacuum leaks • Damaged Electronic Throttle Body (ETB) • PCM has failed
DTC: P0506 **2T CCM, MIL: Yes** **Years:** 2008, 2009, 2010 **Models:** All with IAC valve **Engines:** All **Transmissions:** All	**Idle Air Control (IAC) System RPM Lower Than Expected (Vehicles With IAC Valve)** This DTC is set when the Powertrain Control Module (PCM) detects an engine idle speed that is less than the desired RPM. **Note: Disconnect the IAC valve and look for little or no change in engine RPM as an indication of a stuck or damaged valve.** **Possible Causes:** • IAC circuit open • Air inlet is plugged • B+ or VPWR to IAC solenoid open • Damaged or incorrect IAC valve • IAC valve stuck closed • VPWR to IAC solenoid open • IAC circuit shorted to PWR
DTC: P0506 **2T CCM, MIL: Yes** **Years:** 2008, 2009, 2010 **Models:** All without IAC valve **Engines:** All **Transmissions:** All	**Idle Air Control (IAC) System RPM Lower Than Expected (Vehicles Without IAC Valve)** This DTC is set when the Powertrain Control Module (PCM) detects an engine idle speed that is less than the desired RPM. **Note: This DTC may be accompanied by other DTCs. Diagnose other DTCs first. If other DTCs are not present inspect the intake air system for air restrictions and damage. If no concerns are present, clear the DTC and carry out the KOER self-test.** **Possible Causes:** • Intake air restriction • Vacuum leaks • Exhaust restriction • Sludged throttle body • Vacuum leaks • Damaged Electronic Throttle Body (ETB) • PCM has failed

DTC	Trouble Code Title, Conditions & Possible Causes
DTC: P0507 **2T CCM, MIL: Yes** **Years:** 2008, 2009, 2010 **Models:** All with IAC valve **Engines:** All **Transmissions:** All	**Idle Air Control (IAC) System RPM Higher Than Expected (Vehicles With IAC Valve)** This DTC is set when the Powertrain Control Module (PCM) detects an engine idle speed that is greater than the desired RPM. **Note: Disconnect the IAC valve and look for little or no change in engine RPM as an indication of a stuck or damaged valve.** **Possible Causes:** • IAC circuit shorted to ground • Damaged or incorrect IAC valve • IAC valve stuck open • Intake air leak after throttle body • Vacuum leaks • Damaged EVAP system • PCM has failed
DTC: P0507 **2T CCM, MIL: Yes** **Years:** 2008, 2009, 2010 **Models:** All without IAC valve **Engines:** All **Transmissions:** All	**Idle Air Control (IAC) System RPM Higher Than Expected (Vehicles Without IAC Valve)** This DTC is set when the Powertrain Control Module (PCM) detects an engine idle speed that is greater than the desired RPM. **Note: This DTC is informational only and it may be accompanied by other DTCs. Diagnose other DTCs first. If other DTCs are not present inspect the intake air system for air or vacuum leaks and damage. If no concerns are present, clear the DTC and repeat the self-test.** **Possible Causes:** • Intake air leak after throttle body • Vacuum leaks • Damaged EVAP system • EGR valve leaks vacuum • Damaged Electronic Throttle Body (ETB) • Damaged EVAP system • PCM has failed
DTC: P050A **2T CCM, MIL: Yes** **Years:** 2008, 2009, 2010 **Models:** All **Engines:** All **Transmissions:** All	**Cold Start Idle Air Control Performance** The cold start emission reduction monitor has detected an airflow performance deficiency. The cold start emission reduction monitor validates the operation of the components of the system required to achieve the cold start emission reduction strategy, retarded spark timing (P050B) and elevated idle airflow (P050A). When the idle airflow test portion of the cold start emission reduction strategy is enabled, the idle air control system requests a higher idle RPM to increase the engine airflow. The cold start emission reduction monitor compares the actual airflow measured by the Mass Air Flow (MAF) sensor to the requested Powertrain Control Module (PCM) airflow. The DTC sets when the airflow is less than the calibrated limit. **Note: This DTC is an informational DTC and may be accompanied by other DTCs. Diagnose other DTCs first. If other DTCs are not present inspect the intake air system for air restrictions and damage. If no concerns are present, clear the DTCs and repeat the self-test. The cold start emission reduction monitor runs during a cold start. Before repeating the self-test, a 2 to 3 hour soak period is required for the cold start emission reduction monitor to run at start up.** **Possible Causes:** • Damaged intake air system tubes • Restricted air filter • Restricted or blocked idle air control or intake passages • Air or vacuum leaks • Base engine problem
DTC: P050B **2T CCM, MIL: Yes** **Years:** 2008, 2009, 2010 **Models:** All **Engines:** All **Transmissions:** All	**Cold Start Ignition Timing Performance** The cold start ignition timing performance has a functional response test of actual spark timing angle actual versus commanded spark timing in the Powertrain Control Module (PCM). **Note: Diagnose all other powertrain related DTCs first.** **Possible Causes:** • Spark timing • Spark capture circuit • Spark timing monitor • Spark capture circuit monitor

DTC	Trouble Code Title, Conditions & Possible Causes
DTC: P050E **2T CCM, MIL:** Yes **Years:** 2008, 2009, 2010 **Models:** All with IAC valve **Engines:** All **Transmissions:** All	**Cold Start Engine Exhaust Temperature Out of Range** The Powertrain Control Module (PCM) attempts to control engine speed during the Key On, Engine Running (KOER) self-test. The test fails when the desired RPM could not be reached or controlled during the self-test. **Note: The Powertrain Control Module (PCM) calculates the actual catalyst warm up temperature during a cold start. The PCM then compares the actual temperature to the expected catalyst temperature model. The difference between the actual and expected temperatures is a ratio. When this ratio exceeds the calibrated value this DTC is set and the Malfunction Indicator Lamp (MIL) illuminates.** **Possible Causes:** • IAC circuit open • VPWR to IAC solenoid open • B+ or VPWR to IAC solenoid open • IAC circuit shorted to PWR • Damaged IAC valve
DTC: P0511 **2T CCM, MIL:** Yes **Years:** 2008, 2009, 2010 **Models:** All with IAC valve **Engines:** All **Transmissions:** All	**Idle Air Control (IAC) Circuit** This DTC is set when the Powertrain Control Module (PCM) detects an electrical load failure on the IAC output circuit. **Possible Causes:** • IAC circuit open • VPWR to IAC solenoid open • B+ or VPWR to IAC solenoid open • IAC circuit shorted to PWR • Damaged IAC valve • IAC circuit short to GND
DTC: P0512 **2T CCM, MIL:** Yes **Years:** 2008, 2009, 2010 **Models:** All **Engines:** All **Transmissions:** All	**Starter Request Circuit** Indicates the one touch integrated starting system voltage circuit to the starter relay has a short to voltage. **Possible Causes:** • Short to voltage
DTC: P0528 **2T CCM, MIL:** Yes **Years:** 2008, 2009, 2010 **Models:** All **Engines:** All **Transmissions:** All	**Fan Speed Sensor Circuit No Signal** The Powertrain Control Module (PCM) uses the Fan Speed Sensor (FSS) input to monitor the cooling fan clutch speed. If the indicated fan speed is lower than the calibrated value during the Key On Engine Running (KOER) self-test, the DTC is set. **Note: Visually inspect the cooling fan clutch for damage or obstruction.** **Possible Causes:** • FSS VPWR circuit open in the harness • FSS PWRGND circuit open in the harness • FSS circuit open in the harness • FSS circuit short to voltage or ground in the harness • Damaged FSS sensor • PCM has failed
DTC: P052A **2T CCM, MIL:** Yes **Years:** 2008, 2009, 2010 **Models:** All **Engines:** All **Transmissions:** All	**Cold Start Camshaft Position Timing Over-Advanced (Bank 1)** The Powertrain Control Module (PCM) monitors the Variable Camshaft Timing (VCT) position for an over-advanced camshaft timing during cold start up. The test fails when the camshaft timing exceeds a maximum calibrated value or remains in an advanced position. **Note: This DTC is a functional check of the VCT unit. Diagnose any base engine concerns related to the engine oil pressure or engine timing** **Possible Causes:** • Camshaft timing incorrectly set • Continuous oil flow to the VCT piston chamber • VCT solenoid valve stuck open • Camshaft advance mechanism binding (VCT unit)

DTC	Trouble Code Title, Conditions & Possible Causes
DTC: P052B **2T CCM, MIL: Yes** **Years:** 2008, 2009, 2010 **Models:** All **Engines:** All **Transmissions:** All	**Cold Start Camshaft Position Timing Over-Retarded (Bank 1)** The Powertrain Control Module (PCM) monitors the Variable Camshaft Timing (VCT) position for over-retarded camshaft timing during cold start up. The test fails when the camshaft timing exceeds a maximum calibrated value or remains in a retarded position. **Note: This DTC is a functional check of the VCT unit. Diagnose any base engine concerns related to the engine oil pressure or engine timing.** **Possible Causes:** • Camshaft timing incorrectly set • Continuous oil flow to the VCT piston chamber • VCT solenoid valve stuck open • Camshaft advance mechanism binding (VCT unit)
DTC: P052C **2T CCM, MIL: Yes** **Years:** 2008, 2009, 2010 **Models:** All **Engines:** All **Transmissions:** All	**Cold Start Camshaft Position Timing Over-Advanced (Bank 2)** The Powertrain Control Module (PCM) monitors the Variable Camshaft Timing (VCT) position for over-advanced camshaft timing during cold start up. The test fails when the camshaft timing exceeds a maximum calibrated value or remains in an advanced position. **Note: This DTC is a functional check of the VCT unit. Diagnose any base engine concerns related to the engine oil pressure or engine timing** **Possible Causes:** • Camshaft timing incorrectly set • Continuous oil flow to the VCT piston chamber • VCT solenoid valve stuck open • Camshaft advance mechanism binding (VCT unit)
DTC: P052D **2T CCM, MIL: Yes** **Years:** 2008, 2009, 2010 **Models:** All **Engines:** All **Transmissions:** All	**Cold Start Camshaft Position Timing Over-Retarded (Bank 2)** The Powertrain Control Module (PCM) monitors the Variable Camshaft Timing (VCT) position for over-retarded camshaft timing during cold start up. The test fails when the camshaft timing exceeds a maximum calibrated value or remains in a retarded position. **Note: This DTC is a functional check of the VCT unit. Diagnose any base engine concerns related to the engine oil pressure or engine timing** **Possible Causes:** • Camshaft timing incorrectly set • Continuous oil flow to the VCT piston chamber • VCT solenoid valve stuck open • Camshaft advance mechanism binding (VCT unit)
DTC: P0532 **2T CCM, MIL: Yes** **Years:** 2008, 2009, 2010 **Models:** All **Engines:** All **Transmissions:** All	**A/C Pressure Refrigerant Sensor A Circuit Low** The Air Conditioning Pressure (ACP) transducer sensor inputs a voltage to the Powertrain Control Module (PCM). If the voltage is below the calibrated level the DTC sets. **Note: Verify the VREF voltage is between 4 and 6 volts.** **Possible Causes:** • ACP transducer sensor circuit short to GND or SIGRTN • VREF circuit open • Open ACP transducer sensor circuit • Damaged ACP transducer sensor
DTC: P0533 **2T CCM, MIL: Yes** **Years:** 2008, 2009, 2010 **Models:** All **Engines:** All **Transmissions:** All	**A/C Refrigerant Pressure Sensor A Circuit High** The Air Conditioning Pressure (ACP) transducer sensor inputs a voltage to the Powertrain Control Module (PCM). If the voltage is above a calibrated level the DTC sets **Note: Verify the VREF voltage is between 4 and 6 volts.** **Possible Causes:** • ACP transducer sensor circuit short to PWR • Open ACP transducer sensor circuit • ACP transducer sensor circuit short to VREF • Damaged ACP transducer sensor

DTC	Trouble Code Title, Conditions & Possible Causes

DTC: P0534
2T CCM, MIL: Yes
Years: 2008, 2009, 2010
Models: All
Engines: All
Transmissions: All
	A/C Refrigerant Charge Loss
	Indicates frequent A/C compressor clutch cycling.
	Note: This test is designed to protect the transmission. In some strategies, the PCM unlocks the torque converter during A/C clutch engagement. If a concern is present that results in frequent A/C clutch cycling, damage could occur if the torque converter is cycled at these intervals. This test detects this condition, sets the DTC and prevents the torque converter from excessive cycling.
	Possible Causes:
	    • Mechanical A/C system concern (such as low refrigerant charge, damaged A/C cycling switch)
	    • Intermittent open between the cycling pressure switch and the Powertrain Control Module (PCM)
	    • Intermittent open in the IGN RUN circuit to cycling pressure switch (if applicable)

DTC: P0537
2T CCM, MIL: Yes
Years: 2008, 2009, 2010
Models: All
Engines: All
Transmissions: All
	A/C Evaporator Temperature Sensor Circuit Low
	Indicates the air conditioning evaporator temperature (ACET) signal input was less than the self-test minimum. The self-test minimum is 0.13 volt.
	Note: The Powertrain Control Module (PCM) sources a low current 5 volts on the ACET circuit (this voltage can be measured with the sensor disconnected). As the A/C evaporator air temperature changes, the ACET circuit resistance to SIG RTN (ground) changes (which changes the voltage the PCM detects). When the ACET signal is detected below the self-test minimum, check for shorts to the SIG RTN or ground, which would pull the voltage low.
	Possible Causes:
	    • ACET circuit short to ground or SIG RTN
	    • Damaged ACET sensor

DTC: P0538
2T CCM, MIL: Yes
Years: 2008, 2009, 2010
Models: All
Engines: All
Transmissions: All
	A/C Evaporator Temperature Sensor Circuit High
	Indicates the Air Conditioning Evaporator Temperature (ACET) signal input was greater than the self-test maximum. The self-test maximum is 4.5 volts.
	Note: The Powertrain Control Module (PCM) sources a low current 5 volts on the ACET circuit (this voltage can be measured with the sensor disconnected). As the A/C evaporator air temperature changes, the ACET circuit resistance to SIG RTN (ground) changes (which changes the voltage the PCM detects). When the ACET signal is detected above the self-test maximum, check for open circuits (ACET or SIG RTN), which would cause the voltage to remain high. Although not as probable, also check for a short to voltage VREF.
	Possible Causes:
	    • ACET circuit open
	    • SIG RTN circuit open to the ACET sensor
	    • ACET circuit short to voltage (VREF)
	    • Damaged ACET sensor

DTC: P053A
2T CCM, MIL: Yes
Years: 2008, 2009, 2010
Models: All
Engines: All
Transmissions: All
	Positive Crankcase Ventilation (PCV) Heater Control Circuit / Open
	This DTC sets when the Powertrain Control Module (PCM) detects a Positive Crankcase Ventilation (PCV) heater circuit failure.
	Note: Make sure the PCV valve is correct for the engine application and the PCV heater connector is correctly connected.
	Possible Causes:
	    • Open or shorted PCV circuit
	    • Damaged PCV heater assembly

DTC: P0552
2T CCM, MIL: Yes
Years: 2008, 2009, 2010
Models: All
Engines: All
Transmissions: All
	Power Steering Pressure (PSP) Sensor/Switch Circuit Low
	Indicates the PSP sensor input signal was less than the self-test minimum
	Note: View the PSP PID to monitor the PSP input.
	Possible Causes:
	    • PSP sensor damaged
	    • SIG RTN circuit open
	    • VREF circuit open or shorted
	    • PSP sensor signal circuit open or shorted

DTC: P0553
2T CCM, MIL: Yes
Years: 2008, 2009, 2010
Models: All
Engines: All
Transmissions: All
	Power Steering Pressure (PSP) Sensor Circuit High Input
	Indicates the PSP sensor input signal was greater than the self-test maximum.
	Note: View the PSP PID to monitor the PSP input.
	Possible Causes:
	    • PSP sensor damaged
	    • VREF circuit shorted to voltage
	    • PSP sensor signal circuit open
	    • PSP sensor signal circuit shorted to voltage

DTC	Trouble Code Title, Conditions & Possible Causes
DTC: P0562 **2T CCM, MIL: Yes** **Years:** 2008, 2009, 2010 **Models:** All **Engines:** All **Transmissions:** All	**System Voltage Low** This DTC is set when the Powertrain Control Module (PCM) detects low system voltage. **Note: System voltage is monitored by the PCM. When the voltage is above or below a calibrated value, internal counter increments until a DTC is set.** **Possible Causes:** • Charging system concern
DTC: P0563 **2T CCM, MIL: Yes** **Years:** 2008, 2009, 2010 **Models:** All **Engines:** All **Transmissions:** All	**System Voltage High** This DTC is set when the Powertrain Control Module (PCM) detects high system voltage. **Note: System voltage is monitored by the PCM. When the voltage is above or below a calibrated value, internal counter increments until a DTC is set.** **Possible Causes:** • Charging system concern
DTC: P0571 **2T CCM, MIL: Yes** **Years:** 2008, 2009, 2010 **Models:** All **Engines:** All **Transmissions:** All	**Brake Switch A Circuit** The purpose of this DTC is to check whether the brake switch has toggled or not during the Key On Engine Running (KOER) test. **Note: Using the scan tool, check the BPP/BOO PID. The BPP/BOO PID should toggle on and off with brake pedal activation.** **Possible Causes:** • Open or short in the BPP circuit • Open or short in the stoplamp circuits • Concern in module(s) connected to the BPP circuit • Damaged brake switch • Misadjusted brake switch
DTC: P0572 **2T CCM, MIL: Yes** **Years:** 2008, 2009, 2010 **Models:** All **Engines:** All **Transmissions:** All	**Brake Switch A Circuit Low** This DTC indicates the brake switch is stuck in the ON position. **Note: Using the scan tool, check the BPP/BOO PID. The BPP/BOO PID should toggle on and off with brake pedal activation.** **Possible Causes:** • Open or short in the BPP circuit • Open or short in the stoplamp circuits • Damaged brake switch • Incorrectly adjusted brake switch
DTC: P0573 **2T CCM, MIL: Yes** **Years:** 2008, 2009, 2010 **Models:** All **Engines:** All **Transmissions:** All	**Brake Switch A Circuit High** This DTC indicates the brake switch is stuck in the OFF position. **Note: Using the scan tool, check the BPP/BOO PID. The BPP/BOO PID should toggle on and off with brake pedal activation.** **Possible Causes:** • Open or short in the BPP circuit • Open or short in the stoplamp circuits • Damaged brake switch • Misadjusted brake switch
DTC: P0579 **2T CCM, MIL: Yes** **Years:** 2008, 2009, 2010 **Models:** All **Engines:** All **Transmissions:** All	**Cruise Control Multifunction Input A Circuit Range / Performance** This DTC indicates the speed control is inoperative. **Possible Causes:** • Wiring, terminals or connectors • PCM not configured for speed control • Stoplamp switch • Speed control deactivator switch (integral to the stoplamp switch) • Speed control switches • Digital Transmission Range (TR) sensor • Vehicle speed signal • ABS module • Park brake • PCM has failed

DTC	Trouble Code Title, Conditions & Possible Causes
DTC: P0581 **2T CCM, MIL: Yes** **Years:** 2008, 2009, 2010 **Models:** All **Engines:** All **Transmissions:** All	**Cruise Control Multifunction Input A Circuit High** This DTC indicates the speed control is inoperative. **Possible Causes:** • Wiring, terminals or connectors • PCM not configured for speed control • Stoplamp switch • Speed control deactivator switch (integral to the stoplamp switch) • Speed control switches • Digital Transmission Range (TR) sensor • Vehicle speed signal • ABS module • Park brake • PCM has failed
DTC: P0600 **2T CCM, MIL: Yes** **Years:** 2008, 2009, 2010 **Models:** All **Engines:** All **Transmissions:** All	**Serial Communication Link** Indicates an error occurred in the Powertrain Control Module (PCM). This DTC may be set alone or in combination with P2105. **Possible Causes:** • Software incompatibility issue • PCM has failed
DTC: P0602 **1T PCM, MIL: Yes** **Years:** 2008, 2009, 2010 **Models:** All **Engines:** All **Transmissions:** All	**Powertrain Control Module (PCM) Programming Error** This DTC indicates a programming error within the Vehicle ID (VID) block. **Note: The VID block must be programmed.** **Possible Causes:** • VID data corrupted by the scan tool during VID reprogramming
DTC: P0603 **1T PCM, MIL: Yes** **Years:** 2008, 2009, 2010 **Models:** All **Engines:** All **Transmissions:** All	**Internal Control Module Keep Alive Memory (KAM) Error** Indicates the Powertrain Control Module (PCM) has experienced an internal memory concern. However, there are external items that can cause this DTC. **Note: If KAPWR is interrupted to the PCM because of a battery or PCM disconnect, this DTC can be generated on the first power-up.** **Possible Causes:** • Reprogramming • Battery terminal corrosion • KAPWR to PCM interrupt/open • Loose battery connection
DTC: P0604 **1T PCM, MIL: Yes** **Years:** 2008, 2009, 2010 **Models:** All **Engines:** All **Transmissions:** All	**Internal Control Module Random Access Memory (RAM) Error** Indicates the Powertrain Control Module (PCM) RAM has been corrupted. **Note: Reprogram or update the calibration. Check for other DTCs or drive symptoms for further action. Make sure to check for aftermarket performance products before installing a new PCM. If it is necessary to install a new PCM.** **Possible Causes:** • Module reprogramming • Aftermarket performance products. • PCM has failed
DTC: P0605 **1T PCM, MIL: Yes** **Years:** 2008, 2009, 2010 **Models:** All **Engines:** All **Transmissions:** All	**Internal Control Module Read Only Memory (ROM) Error** The Powertrain Control Module (PCM) ROM has been corrupted. **Note: Reprogram the vehicle identification VID block (use as built data). Check for other DTCs or drive symptoms for further action. Make sure to check for aftermarket performance products before installing a new Powertrain Control Module (PCM). If it is necessary to install a new PCM.** **Possible Causes:** • An attempt was made to change the calibration • Module programming error • Aftermarket performance products. • PCM has failed

DTC	Trouble Code Title, Conditions & Possible Causes
DTC: P0606 **1T PCM, MIL: Yes** **Years:** 2008, 2009, 2010 **Models:** All **Engines:** All **Transmissions:** All	**Control Module Processor** This DTC indicates an internal Powertrain Control Module (PCM) communication error. **Note: Reprogram or update the calibration. Check for other DTCs and diagnose those first. Make sure to check for aftermarket performance products before installing a new PCM. Clear the DTCs, repeat the self-test. If the DTC is retrieved again, install a new PCM.** **Possible Causes:** • Module programming error • Aftermarket performance products. • PCM has failed
DTC: P0607 **1T PCM, MIL: Yes** **Years:** 2008, 2009, 2010 **Models:** All **Engines:** All **Transmissions:** All	**Control Module Performance** Indicates that the Powertrain Control Module (PCM) internal Central Processing Unit (CPU) has encountered an error. The PCM monitors itself and carries out internal checks of its own CPU. If any of these checks returns an incorrect value, the DTC is set. **Note: Reprogram or update the calibration. Check for other DTCs and diagnose those first. Make sure to check for aftermarket performance products before installing a new PCM. Clear the DTCs, repeat the self-test. If the DTC is retrieved again, install a new PCM.** **Possible Causes:** • Module programming error • Aftermarket performance products. • PCM has failed
DTC: P060A **1T PCM, MIL: Yes** **Years:** 2008, 2009, 2010 **Models:** All **Engines:** All **Transmissions:** All	**Internal Control Module Monitoring Processor Performance** Indicates an error occurred in the Powertrain Control Module (PCM). This DTC may set in combination with P2105. **Note: Verify the PCM is at the latest calibration level.** **Possible Causes:** • Software incompatibility issue • PCM has failed
DTC: P060B **1T PCM, MIL: Yes** **Years:** 2008, 2009, 2010 **Models:** All **Engines:** All **Transmissions:** All	**Internal Control Module A/D Processing Performance** Indicates an error occurred in the Powertrain Control Module (PCM). This DTC may set in combination with P2104 or P2110. **Note: Inspect the harness for damage. Verify correct operation of the sensors using VREF and related circuits.** **Possible Causes:** • PCM has failed
DTC: P060C **1T PCM, MIL: Yes** **Years:** 2008, 2009, 2010 **Models:** All **Engines:** All **Transmissions:** All	**Internal Control Module Main Processor Performance** Indicates an error occurred in the Powertrain Control Module (PCM). **Note: Verify the PCM is at the latest calibration level.** **Possible Causes:** • Reprogramming • Software incompatibility issue • PCM has failed
DTC: P060D **1T PCM, MIL: Yes** **Years:** 2008, 2009, 2010 **Models:** All **Engines:** All **Transmissions:** All	**Internal Control Module Accelerator Pedal Position Performance** Indicates an error occurred in the Powertrain Control Module (PCM). If the PCM detects a concern identifying an issue with an Accelerator Pedal Position (APP) sensor signal or with processing the brake pedal sensor input, the DTC is set. **Note: Verify the PCM is at the latest calibration level.** **Possible Causes:** • Reprogramming • PCM has failed
DTC: P0610 **1T PCM, MIL: Yes** **Years:** 2008, 2009, 2010 **Models:** All **Engines:** All **Transmissions:** All	**Control Module Vehicle Options Error** Indicates a Powertrain Control Module (PCM) vehicle options error. **Note: Reprogram or update the calibration. Check for other DTCs or drive symptoms for further action. Make sure to check for aftermarket performance products before installing a new PCM. If it is necessary to install a new PCM.** **Possible Causes:** • Module programming error • Aftermarket performance products. • PCM has failed

DTC	Trouble Code Title, Conditions & Possible Causes
DTC: P0613 **1T PCM, MIL: Yes** **Years:** 2008, 2009, 2010 **Models:** All **Engines:** All **Transmissions:** A/T	**Transmission Control Module (TCM) Read-Only Memory (ROM) Error.** Indicates TCM has detected an internal software issue. Mechanical limp-home mode, default to 3rd or 5th gear. **Note: May turn on MIL, TCIL light on.** • Module programming error • Reprogramming • Software incompatibility issue • Aftermarket performance products. • TCM has failed
DTC: P061B **1T PCM, MIL: Yes** **Years:** 2008, 2009, 2010 **Models:** All **Engines:** All **Transmissions:** All	**Internal Control Module Torque Calculation Performance** Indicates a calculation error occurred in the Powertrain Control Module (PCM). **Note: Check for sensor and circuit related DTCs. Do not install a new Electronic Throttle Body (ETB) for this DTC.** **Possible Causes:** • PCM harness for damage • Correct operation of the sensors using ETCREF, VREF • Module programming error • Aftermarket performance products • PCM has failed
DTC: P061C **1T PCM, MIL: Yes** **Years:** 2008, 2009, 2010 **Models:** All **Engines:** All **Transmissions:** All	**Internal Control Module Engine RPM Performance** Indicates a calculation error occurred in the Powertrain Control Module (PCM). **Note: Verify correct operation of the CKP and CMP sensors and related circuits.** **Possible Causes:** • Crankshaft Position (CKP) sensor circuit is open or short • CKP sensor circuit intermittent • Damaged CKP sensor • Camshaft Position (CMP) sensor circuit is open or short • CMP sensor circuit intermittent • Damaged CMP sensor • PCM has failed
DTC: P061D **1T PCM, MIL: Yes** **Years:** 2008, 2009, 2010 **Models:** All **Engines:** All **Transmissions:** All	**Internal Control Module Engine Air Mass Performance** Indicates a calculation error occurred in the Powertrain Control Module (PCM). **Note: Verify the PCM is at the latest calibration level.** **Possible Causes:** • Reprogramming • Software incompatibility issue • PCM has failed
DTC: P061F **1T PCM, MIL: Yes** **Years:** 2008, 2009, 2010 **Models:** All **Engines:** All **Transmissions:** All	**Internal Control Module Throttle Actuator Controller Performance** Indicates a calculation error occurred in the Powertrain Control Module (PCM). **Note: Verify correct operation of the Electronic Throttle Control (ETC) components and related circuits** **Possible Causes:** • PCM harness for damage • Correct operation of the sensors using ETCREF, VREF • Module programming error • Aftermarket performance products. • PCM has failed
DTC: P0620 **1T PCM, MIL: Yes** **Years:** 2008, 2009, 2010 **Models:** All **Engines:** All **Transmissions:** All	**Generator Control Circuit** The Powertrain Control Module (PCM) reads the GENLI and sends a DTC through the network when the signal frequency of GENLI indicates a concern. **Possible Causes:** • Battery voltage high or low • Wiring, terminals or connectors • Radio Interference • Generator faulty • PCM has failed

DTC	Trouble Code Title, Conditions & Possible Causes

DTC: P0622
1T CCM, MIL: Yes
Years: 2008, 2009, 2010
Models: All
Engines: All
Transmissions: All
	Generator Field Terminal Circuit
	The Powertrain Control Module (PCM) monitors the generator load from the generator/regulator in the form of frequency. The frequency range is determined by the temperature of the voltage regulator, where 97% indicates a full load, and less than 6% indicates no load.
	Possible Causes:
	   • Battery voltage high or low
	   • Wiring, terminals or connectors
	   • Radio Interference
	   • Generator faulty
	   • PCM has failed

DTC: P0625
1T CCM, MIL: Yes
Years: 2008, 2009, 2010
Models: All
Engines: All
Transmissions: All
	Generator Field Terminal Circuit Low
	The Powertrain Control Module (PCM) monitors generator load from the generator/regulator in the form of frequency. The concern indicates the input is lower than the load should be in normal operation. The load input could be low when no generator output exists.
	Possible Causes:
	   • Battery voltage low
	   • Wiring, terminals or connectors
	   • Radio Interference
	   • Generator faulty
	   • PCM has failed

DTC: P0626
1T CCM, MIL: Yes
Years: 2008, 2009, 2010
Models: All
Engines: All
Transmissions: All
	Generator Field Terminal Circuit High
	The Powertrain Control Module (PCM) monitors generator load from the generator/regulator in the form of frequency. The concern indicates the input is lower than the load should be in normal operation. The load input could be low when no generator output exists.
	Possible Causes:
	   • Battery voltage high
	   • Wiring, terminals or connectors
	   • Radio Interference
	   • Generator faulty
	   • PCM has failed

DTC: P0627
1T CCM, MIL: Yes
Years: 2008, 2009, 2010
Models: All
Engines: All
Transmissions: All
	Fuel Pump A Control Circuit/Open
	The fuel pump control module monitors the fuel pump module and secondary circuits for a concern. If the fuel pump control module detects a concern with the fuel pump module or secondary circuits, the fuel pump control module sends an 80% duty cycle signal on the Fuel Pump Monitor (FPM) circuit to report the concern to the PCM. The test fails when the fuel pump control module is still reporting a concern with the fuel pump module or secondary circuits after a calibrated amount of time.
	Note: Check for any harness concerns. The fuel pump control module controls the speed of the fuel pump module by supplying a variable voltage to the fuel pump module on the FPPWR circuit.
	Possible Causes:
	   • FPPWR circuit open or short to ground
	   • FPRTN circuit open
	   • FPPWR circuit short to voltage
	   • FPRTN circuit short to voltage
	   • Damaged fuel pump module
	   • Damaged fuel pump control module

DTC: P062C
1T CCM, MIL: Yes
Years: 2008, 2009, 2010
Models: All
Engines: All
Transmissions: A/T
	Internal Control Module Vehicle Speed Performance
	Indicates an error occurred in the Powertrain Control Module (PCM).
	Note: Repair any ABS DTCs, ABS-related DTCs in other modules, or vehicle communication concerns.
	Possible Causes:
	   • Module communications network concerns
	   • Output Shaft Speed (OSS) sensor concern
	   • Turbine Shaft Speed (TSS) sensor concern
	   • Anti-lock Brake System (ABS) concern

DTC: P0634
1T CCM, MIL: Yes
Years: 2008, 2009, 2010
Models: All
Engines: All
Transmissions: A/T
	Transmissin Control Module (TCM) Temperature High
	Indicates TCM internal temperature is to high. Mechanical limp-home mode, default to 3rd or 5th gear.
	Note: May turn on MIL.
	   • Transmission cooler tubes for possible restrictions. (kinked or bent cooler)
	   • Operation/orientation of the thermal bypass valve
	   • TFT has failed
	   • TCM module sensor failed
	   • TCM has failed

DTC	Trouble Code Title, Conditions & Possible Causes
DTC: P0641 **1T CCM, MIL: Yes** **Years:** 2008, 2009, 2010 **Models:** All **Engines:** All **Transmissions:** All	**Transmissin Control Module (TCM) sensor Range/Performance** Indicates TCM internal temperature is to high. Mechanical limp-home mode, default to 3rd or 5th gear. **Note: May turn on MIL.** • Transmission cooler tubes for possible restrictions. (kinked or bent cooler) • Operation/orientation of the thermal bypass valve • Mechatronics unit failed • TFT has failed • TCM module sensor failed • TCM has failed
DTC: P0642 **1T CCM, MIL: Yes** **Years:** 2008, 2009, 2010 **Models:** All **Engines:** All **Transmissions:** All	**Sensor Reference Voltage A Circuit Low** Indicates the Reference Voltage (VREF) circuit is less than VREF minimum. **Note: This DTC is set due to an under voltage condition on the VREF circuit.** **Possible Causes:** • Accelerator Pedal Position (APP) sensor VREF circuit short to ground • Air Conditioning Pressure (ACP) sensor VREF circuit short to ground • Exhaust Gas Recirculation (EGR) sensor VREF circuit short to ground • EGR System Module (ESM) sensor VREF circuit short to ground • Fuel Rail Pressure Temperature (FRPT) sensor VREF circuit short to ground • Fuel Tank Pressure (FTP) sensor VREF circuit short to ground • Manifold Absolute Pressure (MAP) sensor VREF circuit short to ground • Power Steering Pressure (PSP) sensor VREF circuit short to ground • Throttle Position (TP) sensor VREF circuit short to ground • Powertrain Control Module (PCM) sensor VREF circuit short to ground • Damaged sensor • Incorrect harness connection
DTC: P0643 **1T CCM, MIL: Yes** **Years:** 2008, 2009, 2010 **Models:** All **Engines:** All **Transmissions:** All	**Sensor Reference Voltage A Circuit High** Indicates the Reference Voltage (VREF) circuit is less than VREF minimum. **Note: This DTC is set due to an over voltage condition on the VREF circuit.** **Possible Causes:** • Accelerator Pedal Position (APP) sensor VREF circuit short to voltage • Air Conditioning Pressure (ACP) sensor VREF circuit short to voltage • Exhaust Gas Recirculation (EGR) sensor VREF circuit short to voltage • EGR System Module (ESM) sensor VREF circuit short to voltage • Fuel Rail Pressure Temperature (FRPT) sensor VREF circuit short to voltage • Fuel Tank Pressure (FTP) sensor VREF circuit short to voltage • Manifold Absolute Pressure (MAP) sensor VREF circuit short to voltage • Power Steering Pressure (PSP) sensor VREF circuit short to voltage • Throttle Position (TP) sensor VREF circuit short to voltage • Powertrain Control Module (PCM) sensor VREF circuit short to voltage • Damaged sensor • Incorrect harness connection
DTC: P0645 **1T CCM, MIL: Yes** **Years:** 2008, 2009, 2010 **Models:** All **Engines:** All **Transmissions:** All	**Air Conditioning Clutch Relay (A/CCR) Control Circuit** Monitors the A/CCR circuit output from the Powertrain Control Module (PCM). The test fails when the PCM grounds the A/CCR circuit, excessive current draw is detected on the A/CCR circuit; or, with the A/CCR circuit not grounded by the PCM, and voltage is not detected on the A/CCR circuit (the PCM expects to detect VPWR voltage coming through the A/CCR relay coil to the A/CCR circuit). **Note: The A/CCR control circuit can be monitored using the WACF and WAC PID. When the WACF PID reads YES, a concern is present. An open circuit or short to ground can only be detected when the PCM is not grounding the circuit. A short to voltage can only be detected when the PCM is grounding the circuit. During the Key On Engine Off (KOEO) and Key On Engine Running (KOER) self-test, the WAC circuit is cycled on and off. Verify the A/C and the defrost were OFF during the KOEO and KOER self-tests. Check ACCS PID to verify. If the vehicle is not equipped with A/C, ignore DTC P0645.** **Possible Causes:** • Open or short A/CCR circuit • Damaged A/CCR relay • Open VPWR circuit to the A/CCR relay

DTC	Trouble Code Title, Conditions & Possible Causes
DTC: P064D **1T CCM, MIL: Yes** **Years:** 2008, 2009, 2010 **Models:** All **Engines:** All **Transmissions:** All	**Internal Control Module O2 Sensor Processor Performance (Bank 1)** The Powertrain Control Module (PCM) monitors the application-specific integrated circuit that controls and monitors the Heated Oxygen Sensor (HO2S). The test fails when the PCM detects an internal circuit or communication concern. **Note: Internal PCM concern.** **Possible Causes:** • PCM has failed
DTC: P064E **1T CCM, MIL: Yes** **Years:** 2008, 2009, 2010 **Models:** All **Engines:** All **Transmissions:** All	**Internal Control Module O2 Sensor Processor Performance (Bank 2)** The Powertrain Control Module (PCM) monitors the application-specific integrated circuit that controls and monitors the Heated Oxygen Sensor (HO2S). The test fails when the PCM detects an internal circuit or communication concern. **Note: Internal PCM concern.** **Possible Causes:** • PCM has failed

DTC: P0657
1T CCM, MIL: Yes
Years: 2008, 2009, 2010
Models: All
Engines: All
Transmissions: A/T
	Actuator Supply Voltage A Circuit/Low
	Voltage to all transmission solenoids has been interrupted. Mechanical limp-home mode, default to 3rd or 5th gear
	Possible Causes:
	   • Damaged sensor
	   • Power supply actuators short circuit to ground
	   • Incorrect harness connection
	   • Mechatronics unit failed
	   • Transmission Control Module (TCM)
	   • PCM has failed

DTC: P0658
1T CCM, MIL: Yes
Years: 2008, 2009, 2010
Models: All
Engines: All
Transmissions: A/T
	Actuator Supply Voltage A Circuit/Open
	Voltage to all transmission solenoids has been interrupted. Mechanical limp-home mode, default to 3rd or 5th gear
	Possible Causes:
	   • Damaged sensor
	   • Power supply actuators open
	   • Incorrect harness connection
	   • Mechatronics unit failed
	   • Transmission Control Module (TCM)
	   • PCM has failed

DTC: P0659
1T CCM, MIL: Yes
Years: 2008, 2009, 2010
Models: All
Engines: All
Transmissions: A/T
	Actuator Supply Voltage A Circuit/High
	Voltage to all transmission solenoids has been interrupted. Mechanical limp-home mode, default to 3rd or 5th gear
	Possible Causes:
	   • Damaged sensor
	   • Power supply actuators shorted to power
	   • Incorrect harness connection
	   • Mechatronics unit failed
	   • Transmission Control Module (TCM)
	   • PCM has failed

DTC: P065B
1T CCM, MIL: Yes
Years: 2008, 2009, 2010
Models: All
Engines: All
Transmissions: All
	Generator Control Circuit Range/Performance
	The Powertrain Control Module (PCM) reads the GENLI and sends a DTC through the network when the signal frequency of GENLI indicates a concern.
	Note: An IMTVM PID reading may indicate a fault.
	Possible Causes:
	   • Battery voltage high or low
	   • Wiring, terminals or connectors
	   • Radio Interference
	   • Generator faulty
	   • PCM has failed

DTC: P0660
1T CCM, MIL: Yes
Years: 2008, 2009, 2010
Models: All
Engines: All
Transmissions: All
	Intake Manifold Tuning Valve (IMTV) Control Circuit Open (Bank 1)
	The IMTV system is monitored for failure during continuous, Key On Engine Off (KOEO), or Key On Engine Running (KOER) self-tests. The test fails when the signal is more or less than an expected calibrated range.
	Possible Causes:
	   • IMTV signal circuit open, shorted to PWR GND or SIG RTN
	   • Damaged IMTV actuator

DTC	Trouble Code Title, Conditions & Possible Causes
DTC: P0663 **1T CCM, MIL: Yes** **Years:** 2008, 2009, 2010 **Models:** All **Engines:** All **Transmissions:** All	**Intake Manifold Tuning Valve (IMTV) Control Circuit Open (Bank 2)** The IMTV system is monitored for failure during continuous, Key On Engine Off (KOEO), or Key On Engine Running (KOER) self-tests. The test fails when the signal is more or less than an expected calibrated range. **Possible Causes:** • IMTV signal circuit open, shorted to PWR GND or SIG RTN • Damaged IMTV actuator
DTC: P0667 **1T CCM, MIL: Yes** **Years:** 2008, 2009, 2010 **Models:** All **Engines:** All **Transmissions:** All	**Powertrain Control Module (PCM) Transmission Control Module (TCM) Internal Temperature Sensor Range/Operation.** Substrate temperature sensor malfunction. **Possible Causes:** • Incorrect harness connection • Substrate temperature sensor Failed • Mechatronics unit failed • Transmission Control Module (TCM) • PCM has failed
DTC: P0685 **1T CCM, MIL: Yes** **Years:** 2008, 2009, 2010 **Models:** All **Engines:** All **Transmissions:** All	**Electronic Control Module (ECM)/Powertrain Control Module (PCM) Power Relay Control Circuit/Open** This DTC sets when the Ignition Switch Position Run (ISP-R) circuit indicates the key is in the OFF, ACC, or LOCK position, and the amount of time the PCM remains powered through the PCM power relay exceeds a predetermined amount of time. **Note: Ability to communicate with the PCM when the key is in the OFF, ACC, or LOCK position indicates a hard fault.** **Possible Causes:** • PCM Relay Control (PCMRC) circuit short to ground in the harness • Damaged PCM power relay • PCM has failed
DTC: P0689 **1T CCM, MIL: Yes** **Years:** 2008, 2009, 2010 **Models:** All **Engines:** All **Transmissions:** All	**Electronic Control Module (ECM)/Powertrain Control Module (PCM) Power Relay Sense Circuit Low** This DTC sets when the Passive Anti-Theft System (PATS) system indicates the key is in ON or START position and the ignition switch position run (ISP-R) circuit indicates OFF, ACC, or LOCK position. **Note: Diagnose and repair all PATS DTCs first.** **Possible Causes:** • Ignition circuit fuse • ISP-R circuit open in the harness • ISP-R circuit short to ground in the harness • Damaged ignition switch • Damaged PATS system
DTC: P0690 **1T CCM, MIL: Yes** **Years:** 2008, 2009, 2010 **Models:** All **Engines:** All **Transmissions:** All	**Electronic Control Module (ECM)/Powertrain Control Module (PCM) Power Relay Sense Circuit High** This DTC sets when the Passive Anti-Theft System (PATS) system indicates the key is in the OFF, ACC, or LOCK position and the Ignition Switch Position Run (ISP-R) circuit indicates ON or START position. **Note: Diagnose and repair all PATS DTCs first.** **Possible Causes:** • ISP-R circuit short to voltage in the harness • Damaged ignition switch • Damaged PATS system
DTC: P06B8 **1T CCM, MIL: Yes** **Years:** 2008, 2009, 2010 **Models:** All **Engines:** All **Transmissions:** All	**Internal Control Module Non-Volatile Random Access Memory (NVRAM) Error** This DTC indicates a concern with the ability of the Powertrain Control Module (PCM) to correctly store permanent DTCs. **Note: Check for other DTCs and diagnose those first. Make sure to check for aftermarket performance products. If an updated calibration is available, update the calibration to the latest level. Clear the DTCs and drive the vehicle. If an updated calibration is not available, install a new PCM.** **Possible Causes:** • Reprogramming • Aftermarket performance products • Software incompatibility issue • PCM has failed

DTC	Trouble Code Title, Conditions & Possible Causes
DTC: P0701 **2T CCM, MIL: Yes** **Years:** 2008, 2009, 2010 **Models:** All **Engines:** All **Transmissions:** A/T	**Transmission Control System. Range/Operation.** The TCM has detected a concern with the operational strategy. Dual DTC causing transmission default to a hydraulic limp-home mode. Mechanical limp-home mode, defaults to 3rd or 5th gear. **Note: Multiple DTC failure with conflicting failure mode actions. If other DTCs are present, REPAIR them first. MONITOR the appropriate PID. Turns on TCIL, may turn on MIL.** **Possible Causes:** • Incorrect harness connection • Transmission Range (TR) sensor failed • Mechatronics unit failed • Transmission Control Module (TCM) • PCM has failed
DTC: P0703 **1T CCM, MIL: Yes** **Years:** 2008, 2009, 2010 **Models:** All **Engines:** All **Transmissions:** All	**Brake Switch B Input Circuit** Indicates the Powertrain Control Module (PCM) did not receive a Brake Pedal Position (BPP) input. **Note: Verify the brake pedal was applied and released during the Key On Engine Running (KOER) self-test.** **Possible Causes:** • Open or short in the BPP circuit • Open or short in the stoplamp circuits • Damage in module(s) connected to the BPP circuit. • Damaged brake switch • Misadjusted brake switch
DTC: P0704 **1T CCM, MIL: Yes** **Years:** 2008, 2009, 2010 **Models:** All **Engines:** All **Transmissions:** M/T	**Clutch Switch Input Circuit** When the clutch pedal is applied the voltage goes to low. If the Powertrain Control Module (PCM) does not see this change from high to low the DTC is set. **Note: When the clutch pedal is applied and then released, the switch voltage should cycle.** **Possible Causes:** • Clutch Pedal Position (CPP) circuit short to voltage • Damaged CPP switch • CPP circuit open in the SIGRTN
DTC: P0705 **2T CCM, MIL: Yes** **Years:** 2008, 2009, 2010 **Models:** All **Engines:** All **Transmissions:** A/T	**Transmission Range (TR) Sensor A Circuit (PRNDL) Input** The TCM has detected aTR signal (P, R, N, D, 3, 2 or 1) is out of normal range. Mechanical limp-home mode, defaults to 3rd or 5th gear. **Note: Turns on TCIL, may turn on MIL.** **Possible Causes:** • DTR or TR sensor connector is damaged or open • DTR or TR sensor signal circuit is open • DTR or TR sensor is shorted to VREF (5v) • DTR or TR sensor is damaged • PCM has failed
DTC: P0706 **1T CCM, MIL: No** **Years:** 2008, 2009, 2010 **Models:** All **Engines:** All **Transmissions:** A/T	**Transmission Range (TR) Sensor A Circuit Range/Performance** TR sensor stuck in transition zone and possible no crank condition. Only PARK, REVERSE, NEUTRAL and 5th gear available. **Note: Will turn on wrench lamp.** **Possible Causes:** • DTR or TR sensor connector is damaged or open • DTR or TR sensor signal circuit is open • DTR or TR sensor is shorted to VREF (5v) • DTR or TR sensor is damaged • PCM has failed
DTC: P0707 **2T CCM, MIL: Yes** **Years:** 2008, 2009, 2010 **Models:** All **Engines:** All **Transmissions:** A/T	**Transmission Range (TR) Sensor A Circuit Low** Key on or engine running; and the PCM detected the Digital Transmission Range (DTR) or Transmission Range sensor (TR) input was more than the self-test maximum range in the test. **Possible Causes:** • DTR or TR sensor connector is damaged or open • DTR or TR sensor signal circuit is open • DTR or TR sensor is shorted to VREF (5v) • DTR or TR sensor is damaged • PCM has failed

DTC	Trouble Code Title, Conditions & Possible Causes
DTC: P0708 **2T CCM, MIL: Yes** **Years:** 2008, 2009, 2010 **Models:** All **Engines:** All **Transmissions:** A/T	**Transmission Range (TR) Sensor A Circuit High** Key on or engine running; and the PCM detected the Digital Transmission Range (DTR) or Transmission Range sensor (TR) input was more than the self-test maximum range in the test. **Possible Causes:** • DTR or TR sensor connector is damaged or open • DTR or TR sensor signal circuit is open • DTR or TR sensor is shorted to VREF (5v) • DTR or TR sensor is damaged • PCM has failed
DTC: P0709 **2T CCM, MIL: Yes** **Years:** 2008, 2009, 2010 **Models:** All **Engines:** All **Transmissions:** A/T	**Transmission Range (TR) Sensor A Circuit Range/Performance** TR sensor stuck in transition zone and possible no crank condition. Only PARK, REVERSE, NEUTRAL and 5th gear available. **Note: Will turn on wrench lamp.** **Possible Causes:** • DTR or TR sensor connector is damaged or open • DTR or TR sensor signal circuit is open • DTR or TR sensor is shorted to VREF (5v) • DTR or TR sensor is damaged • PCM has failed
DTC: P0711 **2T CCM, MIL: No** **Years:** 2008, 2009, 2010 **Models:** All **Engines:** All **Transmissions:** A/T	**TFT Sensor Circuit Range/Performance** Key on or engine running; and the PCM detected no change in the Transmission Fluid Temperature (TFT) sensor. **Possible Causes:** • TFT sensor signal circuit is open between the sensor and PCM • TFT sensor ground circuit is open between sensor and PCM • TFT sensor is damaged or has failed • PCM has failed
DTC: P0712 **2T CCM, MIL: No** **Years:** 2008, 2009, 2010 **Models:** All **Engines:** All **Transmissions:** A/T	**TFT Sensor Circuit Circuit Low** Key on or engine running; and the PCM detected low voltage in the Transmission Fluid Temperature (TFT) sensor. **Note: TCM has detected a voltage drop across TFT sensor exceeds scale set for temperature (grounded circuit).** **Possible Causes:** • TFT sensor signal circuit is shorted to ground • TFT sensor is damaged or has failed • PCM has failed
DTC: P0713 **2T CCM, MIL: No** **Years:** 2008, 2009, 2010 **Models:** All **Engines:** All **Transmissions:** A/T	**TFT Sensor Circuit High** Key on or engine running; and the PCM detected high voltage in the Transmission Fluid Temperature (TFT) sensor. **Possible Causes:** • TFT sensor signal circuit is shorted to power • TFT sensor is damaged or has failed • PCM has failed
DTC: P0714 **2T CCM, MIL: No** **Years:** 2008, 2009, 2010 **Models:** All **Engines:** All **Transmissions:** A/T	**TFT Sensor Circuit Intermittent/Erratic** Key on or engine running; and the PCM detected intermittent condition in the Transmission Fluid Temperature (TFT) sensor. **Possible Causes:** • TFT sensor signal circuit is open between the sensor and PCM • TFT sensor signal circuit is shorted to power • TFT sensor ground circuit is open between sensor and PCM • TFT sensor is damaged or has failed • PCM has failed
DTC: P0715 **2T CCM, MIL: No** **Years:** 2008, 2009, 2010 **Models:** All **Engines:** All **Transmissions:** A/T	**Turbine Shaft Speed (TSS) Sensor Error** Engine started, vehicle speed sensor signal over 1 mph, and the PCM detected a short circuit to power on the TSS signal circuit. **Note: Will turn onTCIL, holds in 3rd gear.** **Possible Causes:** • TSS signal wiring is damaged or contacting other signal wiring • TSS sensor is damaged or has failed • PCM has failed

DTC	Trouble Code Title, Conditions & Possible Causes ·

DTC: P0716
2T CCM, MIL: No
Years: 2008, 2009, 2010
Models: All
Engines: All
Transmissions: A/T
	Turbine Shaft Speed (TSS) Sensor Range/Performance
	Engine started, TSS signal more than 1 mph, and the PCM detected "noise" interference on the TSS sensor circuit.
	Note: Will turn onTCIL, holds in 3rd gear.
	Possible Causes:
	   • TSS sensor signal circuit is shorted to ground
	   • TSS sensor signal circuit is open
	   • TSS sensor circuit is shorted to power
	   • TSS sensor is damaged or it has failed
	   • PCM has failed

DTC: P0717
2T CCM, MIL: No
Years: 2008, 2009, 2010
Models: All
Engines: All
Transmissions: A/T
	Turbine Shaft Speed (TSS) Sensor No Signal
	Engine started, TCM has not detected a TSS signal. No TSS signal when Output Shaft Speed (OSS) signal is present.
	Note: Will turn onTCIL, holds in 3rd gear.
	Possible Causes:
	   • TSS sensor signal circuit is shorted to ground
	   • TSS sensor signal circuit is open
	   • TSS sensor circuit is shorted to power
	   • TSS sensor is damaged or it has failed
	   • PCM has failed

DTC: P0720
2T CCM, MIL: No
Years: 2008, 2009, 2010
Models: All
Engines: All
Transmissions: A/T
	Output Shaft Speed (OSS) Sensor Circuit
	The OSS sensor inputs a signal to the Powertrain Control Module (PCM) based on the speed of the output shaft of the transmission.
	Note: Verify the sensor signal output varies with the vehicle speed.
	Possible Causes:
	   • OSS sensor circuit shorted to GND
	   • OSS sensor circuit shorted to PWR
	   • OSS sensor circuit open
	   • Damaged OSS sensor

DTC: P0721
2T CCM, MIL: No
Years: 2008, 2009, 2010
Models: All
Engines: All
Transmissions: A/T
	Output Shaft Speed (OSS) Sensor Circuit Range/Performance
	The OSS sensor signal is very sensitive to noise. This noise distorts the input to the Powertrain Control Module (PCM).
	Note: Check the routing of the harness, and the wiring and the connector for damage.
	Possible Causes:
	   • Wiring misrouted
	   • Aftermarket add-on
	   • Wiring damaged
	   • Wiring insulation wear

DTC: P0722
2T CCM, MIL: No
Years: 2008, 2009, 2010
Models: All
Engines: All
Transmissions: A/T
	Output Shaft Speed (OSS) Sensor Circuit No Signal
	The OSS sensor failed to provide a signal to the Powertrain Control Module (PCM) upon initial movement of vehicle.
	Note: Check the wiring, connector, and sensor for damage.
	Possible Causes:
	   • Damaged OSS connector
	   • Damaged OSS sensor, or not installed correctly
	   • Harness intermittently shorted or open

DTC: P0723
2T CCM, MIL: No
Years: 2008, 2009, 2010
Models: All
Engines: All
Transmissions: A/T
	Output Shaft Speed (OSS) Sensor Circuit Intermittent
	The OSS sensor signal to the Powertrain Control Module (PCM) is irregular or interrupted.
	Note: Verify harness and connector integrity and correct installation of the OSS sensor. Will turn onTCIL.
	Possible Causes:
	   • Harness connector not correctly seated
	   • Harness intermittently shorted or open
	   • Harness connector damaged
	   • OSS sensor damaged, or not installed correctly

DTC	Trouble Code Title, Conditions & Possible Causes
DTC: P0729 **2T CCM, MIL: No** **Years:** 2008, 2009, 2010 **Models:** All **Engines:** All **Transmissions:** A/T	**Incorrect Sixth Gear Ratio** Engine started, vehicle operating with 6th Gear commanded "on", and the PCM detected an incorrect 6th gear ratio during the test. **Note: Verify harness and connector integrity and correct installation of the OSS sensor. Will turn onTCIL.** **Possible Causes:** • 6th Gear solenoid harness connector not properly seated • 6th Gear solenoid signal shorted to ground, or open • 6th Gear solenoid wring harness connector is damaged • 6th Gear solenoid is damaged or not properly installed
DTC: P0731 **2T CCM, MIL: No** **Years:** 2008, 2009, 2010 **Models:** All **Engines:** All **Transmissions:** A/T	**Incorrect First Gear Ratio** Engine started, vehicle operating with 1st Gear commanded "on", and the PCM detected an incorrect 1st gear ratio during the test. **Note: Verify harness and connector integrity and correct installation of the OSS sensor. Will turn onTCIL.** **Possible Causes:** • 1st Gear solenoid harness connector not properly seated • 1st Gear solenoid signal shorted to ground, or open • 1st Gear solenoid wring harness connector is damaged • 1st Gear solenoid is damaged or not properly installed
DTC: P0732 **2T CCM, MIL: No** **Years:** 2008, 2009, 2010 **Models:** All **Engines:** All **Transmissions:** A/T	**Incorrect Second Gear Ratio** Engine started, vehicle operating with 2nd Gear commanded "on", and the PCM detected an incorrect 2nd gear ratio during the test. **Note: Verify harness and connector integrity and correct installation of the OSS sensor. Will turn onTCIL.** **Possible Causes:** • 2nd Gear solenoid harness connector not properly seated • 2nd Gear solenoid signal shorted to ground, or open • 2nd Gear solenoid wiring harness connector is damaged • 2nd Gear solenoid is damaged or not properly installed
DTC: P0733 **2T CCM, MIL: No** **Years:** 2008, 2009, 2010 **Models:** All **Engines:** All **Transmissions:** A/T	**Incorrect Third Gear Ratio** Engine started, vehicle operating with 3rd Gear commanded "on", and the PCM detected an incorrect 3rd gear ratio during the test. **Note: Verify harness and connector integrity and correct installation of the OSS sensor. Will turn onTCIL.** **Possible Causes:** • 3rd Gear solenoid harness connector not properly seated • 3rd Gear solenoid signal shorted to ground, or open • 3rd Gear solenoid wiring harness connector is damaged • 3rd Gear solenoid is damaged or not properly installed
DTC: P0734 **2T CCM, MIL: No** **Years:** 2008, 2009, 2010 **Models:** All **Engines:** All **Transmissions:** A/T	**Incorrect Fourth Gear Ratio** Engine started, vehicle operating with 4th Gear commanded "on", and the PCM detected an incorrect 4th gear ratio during the test. **Note: Verify harness and connector integrity and correct installation of the OSS sensor. Will turn onTCIL.** **Possible Causes:** • 4th Gear solenoid harness connector not properly seated • 4th Gear solenoid signal shorted to ground, or open • 4th Gear solenoid wiring harness connector is damaged • 4th Gear solenoid is damaged or not properly installed
DTC: P0735 **2T CCM, MIL: No** **Years:** 2008, 2009, 2010 **Models:** All **Engines:** All **Transmissions:** A/T	**Incorrect Fifth Gear Ratio** Engine started, vehicle operating with 5th Gear commanded "on", and the PCM detected an incorrect 5th gear ratio during the test. **Possible Causes:** • 5th Gear solenoid harness connector not properly seated • 5th Gear solenoid signal shorted to ground, or open • 5th Gear solenoid wiring harness connector is damaged • 5th Gear solenoid is damaged or not properly installed
DTC: P0736 **2T CCM, MIL: No** **Years:** 2008, 2009, 2010 **Models:** All **Engines:** All **Transmissions:** A/T	**Incorrect Reverse Gear Ratio** Engine started, vehicle operating with Reverse Gear commanded "on", and the PCM detected an incorrect reverse gear ratio occurred. **Possible Causes:** • Reverse Gear solenoid harness connector not properly seated • Reverse Gear solenoid signal shorted to ground, or open • Reverse Gear solenoid wiring harness connector is damaged • Reverse Gear solenoid is damaged or not properly installed

DTC	Trouble Code Title, Conditions & Possible Causes
DTC: P0740 **2T CCM, MIL: No** **Years:** 2008, 2009, 2010 **Models:** All **Engines:** All **Transmissions:** A/T	**TCC Solenoid Circuit Malfunction** Key on, KOEO Self-Test enabled and the PCM did not detect any voltage drop across the TCC solenoid circuit during the test period. **Possible Causes:** • TCC solenoid control circuit is open • TCC solenoid control circuit is shorted to ground • TCC solenoid wiring harness connector is damaged • TCC solenoid is damaged or it has failed • PCM has failed
DTC: P0741 **2T CCM, MIL: No** **Years:** 2008, 2009, 2010 **Models:** All **Engines:** All **Transmissions:** A/T	**TCC Solenoid Circuit Open** Key on, KOEO Self-Test enabled and the PCM did not detect any voltage drop across the EPC solenoid circuit during the test period. **Possible Causes:** • TCC solenoid control circuit is open • TCC solenoid control circuit is shorted to ground • TCC solenoid wiring harness connector is damaged • TCC solenoid is damaged or it has failed • PCM has failed
DTC: P0750 **2T CCM, MIL: Yes** **Years:** 2008, 2009, 2010 **Models:** All **Engines:** All **Transmissions:** A/T	**A/T Shift Solenoid 1/A Circuit Malfunction** Engine started, vehicle driven with the solenoid applied, and the PCM detected an unexpected voltage condition on the SS1/A solenoid circuit was incorrect during the test. **Possible Causes:** • SS1/A solenoid control circuit is open • SS1/A solenoid control circuit is shorted to ground • SS1/A solenoid wiring harness connector is damaged • SS1/A solenoid is damaged or has failed • PCM has failed
DTC: P0751 **2T CCM, MIL: No** **Years:** 2008, 2009, 2010 **Models:** All **Engines:** All **Transmissions:** A/T	**A/T Shift Solenoid 2/B Circuit Malfunction** Engine started, vehicle driven with the solenoid applied, and the PCM detected an unexpected voltage condition on the SS2/B solenoid circuit was incorrect during the test. **Possible Causes:** • SS2/B solenoid control circuit is open • SS2/B solenoid control circuit is shorted to ground • SS2/B solenoid wiring harness connector is damaged • SS2/B solenoid is damaged or has failed • PCM has failed
DTC: P0752 **1T CCM, MIL: No** **Years:** 2008, 2009, 2010 **Models:** All **Engines:** All **Transmissions:** A/T	**A/T Shift Solenoid 2/B Function Range/Performance** Engine started, vehicle driven with the solenoid applied, and the PCM detected a mechanical failure while operating the Shift Solenoid 2/B during the CCM test period. **Possible Causes:** • SS2/B solenoid is stuck in the "on" position • SS2/B solenoid has a mechanical failure • SS2/B solenoid has a hydraulic failure • PCM has failed
DTC: P0753 **1T CCM, MIL: Yes** **Years:** 2008, 2009, 2010 **Models:** All **Engines:** All **Transmissions:** A/T	**A/T Shift Solenoid 2/B Function Range/Performance** Engine started, vehicle driven with the solenoid applied, and the PCM detected a mechanical failure while operating the Shift Solenoid 2/B during the CCM test period. **Possible Causes:** • SS2/B solenoid is stuck in the "on" position • SS2/B solenoid has a mechanical failure • SS2/B solenoid has a hydraulic failure • PCM has failed

DTC	Trouble Code Title, Conditions & Possible Causes
DTC: P0755 **1T CCM, MIL: Yes** **Years:** 2008, 2009, 2010 **Models:** All **Engines:** All **Transmissions:** A/T	**A/T Shift Solenoid 2/B Circuit Malfunction** Key on, KOEO Self-Test enabled, Shift Solenoid 2/B applied, and the PCM detected an unexpected voltage condition on the Shift Solenoid 2/B circuit during the CCM test period. **Possible Causes:** • Shift Solenoid 2/B connector is damaged, open or shorted • Shift Solenoid 2/B control circuit is open • Shift Solenoid 2/B control circuit is shorted to ground • Shift Solenoid 2/B is damaged or it has failed • PCM has failed
DTC: P0756 **1T CCM, MIL: Yes** **Years:** 2008, 2009, 2010 **Models:** All **Engines:** All **Transmissions:** A/T	**A/T Shift Solenoid 3/C Circuit Malfunction** Engine started, vehicle driven with Shift Solenoid 3/C applied, and the PCM detected an unexpected voltage condition on the Shift Solenoid 3/C circuit during the CCM test period. **Possible Causes:** • Shift Solenoid 3/C connector is damaged, open or shorted • Shift Solenoid 3/C control circuit is open • Shift Solenoid 3/C control circuit is shorted to ground • Shift Solenoid 3/C is damaged or it has failed • PCM has failed
DTC: P0757 **1T CCM, MIL: Yes** **Years:** 2008, 2009, 2010 **Models:** All **Engines:** All **Transmissions:** A/T	**A/T Shift Solenoid 3/C Function Range/Performance** Engine started, vehicle driven with Shift Solenoid 3/C applied, and the PCM detected a mechanical failure occurred (stuck "off") while operating Shift Solenoid 3/C during the test. **Possible Causes:** • SS3/C solenoid may be stuck "off" • SS3/C solenoid has a mechanical failure • SS3/C solenoid has a hydraulic failure • PCM has failed
DTC: P0758 **1T CCM, MIL: Yes** **Years:** 2008, 2009, 2010 **Models:** All **Engines:** All **Transmissions:** A/T	**A/T Shift Solenoid 3/C Function Range/Performance** Engine started, vehicle driven with Shift Solenoid 3/C applied, and the PCM detected a mechanical failure occurred (stuck "on") while operating Shift Solenoid 3/C during the test. **Possible Causes:** • SS3/C solenoid may be stuck "on" • SS3/C solenoid has a mechanical failure • SS3/C solenoid has a hydraulic failure • PCM has failed
DTC: P0760 **1T CCM, MIL: Yes** **Years:** 2008, 2009, 2010 **Models:** All **Engines:** All **Transmissions:** A/T	**A/T Shift Solenoid 4/D Circuit Malfunction** Engine started, vehicle driven with Shift Solenoid 4/D applied, and the PCM detected an unexpected voltage condition on Shift Solenoid 4/D circuit during the CCM continuous test. **Possible Causes:** • Shift Solenoid 4/D wiring harness or connector is damaged • Shift Solenoid 4/D control circuit is open or shorted to ground • Shift Solenoid 4/D is damaged or it has failed • PCM has failed
DTC: P0761 **1T CCM, MIL: No** **Years:** 2008, 2009, 2010 **Models:** All **Engines:** All **Transmissions:** A/T	**A/T 1 to 2 Shift Error** Engine started, vehicle driven in gear with VSS signals received, and the PCM detected the engine speed (rpm) did not decrease properly (i.e., an incorrect 1-2 gear ratio was detected during a shift event). **Possible Causes:** • SS1/A solenoid may be stuck • SS1/A solenoid has a hydraulic problem • SS2/B solenoid may be stuck • SS2/B has a hydraulic problem • Transmission may have damaged friction material • Transmission has internal damage and needs replacement

DTC	Trouble Code Title, Conditions & Possible Causes
DTC: P0762 **1T CCM, MIL: No** **Years:** 2008, 2009, 2010 **Models:** All **Engines:** All **Transmissions:** A/T	**A/T 2 to 3 Shift Error** Engine started, vehicle driven in gear with VSS signals received, and the PCM detected the engine speed (rpm) did not decrease properly (i.e., an incorrect 2-3 gear ratio was detected during a shift event). **Possible Causes:** • SS1/A solenoid may be stuck • SS1/A solenoid has a hydraulic problem • SS2/B solenoid may be stuck • SS2/B has a hydraulic problem • Transmission may have damaged friction material • Transmission has internal damage and needs replacement
DTC: P0765 **1T CCM, MIL: Yes** **Years:** 2008, 2009, 2010 **Models:** All **Engines:** All **Transmissions:** A/T	**A/T 3 to 4 Shift Error** Engine started, vehicle driven in gear with VSS signals received, and the PCM detected the engine speed (rpm) did not change properly (i.e., an incorrect 3-4 gear ratio was detected during the shift event). **Possible Causes:** • SS1/A solenoid may be stuck, or a hydraulic failure exists • SS2/B solenoid may be stuck, or a hydraulic failure exists • Transmission may have damaged friction material
DTC: P0767 **1T CCM, MIL: Yes** **Years:** 2008, 2009, 2010 **Models:** All **Engines:** All **Transmissions:** A/T	**A/T Shift Solenoid 4/D Functional Failure** Functional Failure (Stuck ON) or Main Control System Failure. (shift valves, orifices and sealing) **Possible Causes:** • SS4/D solenoid may be stuck, or a hydraulic failure exists • SS4/D solenoid may be stuck • SS4/D has a hydraulic problem • Transmission may have damaged friction material • Transmission has internal damage and needs replacement
DTC: P0768 **1T CCM, MIL: Yes** **Years:** 2008, 2009, 2010 **Models:** All **Engines:** All **Transmissions:** A/T	**A/T Shift Solenoid 4/D Circuit Failure** Functional Failure (Stuck ON) or Main Control System Failure. (shift valves, orifices and sealing) **Possible Causes:** • Transaxle harness connector • SS4/C solenoid may be open or shorted • PCM has failed
DTC: P0770 **1T CCM, MIL: Yes** **Years:** 2008, 2009, 2010 **Models:** All **Engines:** All **Transmissions:** A/T	**A/T Shift Solenoid 5/E Functional Failure** Functional Failure (Stuck ON) or Main Control System Failure. (shift valves, orifices and sealing) **Possible Causes:** • SS5/E solenoid may be stuck, or a hydraulic failure exists • SS5/E solenoid may be stuck • SS5/E has a hydraulic problem • Transmission may have damaged friction material • Transmission has internal damage and needs replacement
DTC: P0771 **1T CCM, MIL: Yes** **Years:** 2008, 2009, 2010 **Models:** All **Engines:** All **Transmissions:** A/T	**A/T Shift Solenoid 5/E Circuit Failure** Functional Failure (Stuck ON) or Main Control System Failure. (shift valves, orifices and sealing) **Possible Causes:** • Transaxle harness connector • SS5/E solenoid may be open or shorted • PCM has failed
DTC: P0775 **1T CCM, MIL: Yes** **Years:** 2008, 2009, 2010 **Models:** All **Engines:** All **Transmissions:** A/T	**Pressure Control Solenoid B (PCB)** Functional fault, Low pressure or circuit fault. Incorrect shift pattern indicating mechanical or hydraulic failure of the transmission **Possible Causes:** • Low transmission fluid level • Solenoid B has a hydraulic problem • Transmission may have damaged friction material • Transmission has internal damage and may need replacement
DTC: P0778 **1T CCM, MIL: Yes** **Years:** 2008, 2009, 2010 **Models:** All **Engines:** All **Transmissions:** A/T	**Pressure Control Solenoid B (PCB) Circuit Failure** Electrical failure of the solenoid detected, 2nd and 5th gear. **Possible Causes:** • Transmission internal harness open • Transmission internal harness shorted to ground • Solenoid B has failed

DTC	Trouble Code Title, Conditions & Possible Causes
DTC: P0780 **1T CCM, MIL: Yes** **Years:** 2008, 2009, 2010 **Models:** All **Engines:** All **Transmissions:** A/T	**Universal shifting Stuck Valve (Aisin AW21 Transmission)** Solenoid or valve internal to transaxle, valve stuck. Increase rpm during shifts. Slipping or erratic shifting. **Possible Causes:** • Main control valve body
DTC: P0781 **1T CCM, MIL: No** **Years:** 2008, 2009, 2010 **Models:** All **Engines:** All **Transmissions:** A/T	**A/T 4 to 5 Shift Error** Engine started, vehicle driven in gear with VSS signals received, and the PCM detected the engine speed (rpm) did not change properly (i.e., an incorrect 4-5 gear ratio was detected during a shift event). **Possible Causes:** • SS2/B solenoid may be stuck, or a hydraulic failure exists • SS3/C solenoid may be stuck, or a hydraulic failure exists • Transmission may have damaged friction material
DTC: P0782 **1T CCM, MIL: No** **Years:** 2008, 2009, 2010 **Models:** All **Engines:** All **Transmissions:** A/T	**A/T Reverse Switch Circuit Malfunction** Key on, engine off, KOEO Self Test enabled, and the PCM detected the reverse switch signal did not change as the selector was shifted in or out of reverse gear. **Note: The RS PID should change from ON to OFF while shifting.** **Possible Causes:** • Transmission shift not indicating neutral during the self-test • RS switch circuit shorted to VREF or VPWR • RS switch circuit is open or shorted to ground (signal return) • Reverse switch is damaged • PCM has failed
DTC: P0783 **1T CCM, MIL: No** **Years:** 2008, 2009, 2010 **Models:** All **Engines:** All **Transmissions:** A/T	**Transmission Control System Malfunction** Engine started, vehicle speed more than 1 in gear, and the PCM detected a problem in the Transmission Control System operation. **Possible Causes:** • Refer to the information in the Transmission Section of the appropriate Workshop Repair manual (i.e., the information for the particular vehicle that set this trouble code).
DTC: P0784 **1T CCM, MIL: No** **Years:** 2008, 2009, 2010 **Models:** All **Engines:** All **Transmissions:** A/T	**Transmission Control System Malfunction** Key on, engine off, KOEO Self Test enabled, and the PCM detected the reverse switch input did not change as the selector was shifted in or out of reverse (i.e., it was high when it should have been low). **Note: The RS PID should change from ON to OFF while shifting.** **Possible Causes:** • Refer to the information in the Transmission Section of the appropriate Workshop Repair manual (i.e., the information for the particular vehicle that set this trouble code).
DTC: P0791 **1T CCM, MIL: No** **Years:** 2008, 2009, 2010 **Models:** All **Engines:** All **Transmissions:** A/T	**Intermediate Shaft Speed Sensor No Signal** Insufficient input from the intermediate shaft speed sensor. PCM has detected a loss of the intermediate shaft speed sensor signal during operation. Harsh shifts. **Possible Causes:** • Wiring, terminals or connectors • Intermediate shaft speed sensor • Transmission has internal damage
DTC: P0794 **1T CCM, MIL: No** **Years:** 2008, 2009, 2010 **Models:** All **Engines:** All **Transmissions:** A/T	**Intermediate Shaft Speed Sensor Signal Noise** Intermediate shaft speed sensor signal noisy. PCM has detected a loss of the intermediate shaft speed sensor signal during operation. Harsh shifts. **Possible Causes:** • Wiring, terminals or connectors • Radio Interference • Intermediate shaft speed sensor • Transmission has internal damage
DTC: P0795 **1T CCM, MIL: No** **Years:** 2008, 2009, 2010 **Models:** All **Engines:** All **Transmissions:** A/T	**Pressure Control Solenoid C (PCC) Circuit Fault** Incorrect shift pattern indicating mechanical or hydraulic failure of the transmission. **Possible Causes:** • Incorrect transmission fluid level • Transmission fluid condition • Valves, springs damaged, misassembled, missing, stuck or bore damaged • Transmission has internal damage

DTC	Trouble Code Title, Conditions & Possible Causes
DTC: P0798 **1T CCM, MIL:** No **Years:** 2008, 2009, 2010 **Models:** All **Engines:** All **Transmissions:** A/T	**Pressure Control Solenoid C (PCC) Circuit Fault** Electrical failure of the solenoid detected. Incorrect gear ratio in 4th and 5th gear. **Possible Causes:** • Transmission harness circuit shorted to ground. • Transmission internal harness if an open • Transmission internal harness for a short to ground • Solenoid malfuntion
DTC: P0815 **1T CCM, MIL:** Yes **Years:** 2008, 2009, 2010 **Models:** All **Engines:** All **Transmissions:** A/T	**Upshift Switch Circuit** Key on or engine running; and the PCM detected an incorrect up shift. **Possible Causes:** • Incorrect transmission fluid level • Transmission fluid condition • Valves, springs damaged, misassembled, missing, stuck or bore damaged
DTC: P0830 **1T CCM, MIL:** Yes **Years:** 2008, 2009, 2010 **Models:** All **Engines:** All **Transmissions:** M/T	**Clutch Pedal Switch A Circuit** The Powertrain Control Module (PCM) monitors the clutch pedal position bottom of travel (CPP-BT) switch only during the calibrated engine speed range (cranking speed range). This DTC sets when the CPP-BT switch does not indicate that the clutch is disengaged (clutch pedal pressed) when the engine is cranked. **Note: Verify that the vehicle was not push-started with the clutch engaged. Check for aftermarket equipment such as remote starting devices which may bypass the clutch pedal position switch when cranking the engine.** **Possible Causes:** • Damaged CPP-BT switch • Damaged CPP-BT harness • Open PWRGND circuit to the CPP-BT switch • Vehicle push-started with the clutch engaged (clutch pedal released) • Aftermarket remote starting device
DTC: P0830 **1T CCM, MIL:** Yes **Years:** 2008, 2009, 2010 **Models:** All **Engines:** All **Transmissions:** M/T	**Clutch Pedal Switch B Circuit** The Powertrain Control Module (PCM) monitors the clutch pedal position top of travel (CPP-TT) switch only during the calibrated engine speed range (cranking speed range). This DTC sets when the CPP-TT does not indicate that the clutch is disengaged (clutch pedal pressed) when the engine is cranked. **Note: Verify that the vehicle was not push-started with the clutch engaged. Check for aftermarket equipment such as remote starting devices which may bypass the clutch pedal position switch when cranking the engine.** **Possible Causes:** • Damaged CPP-BT switch • Damaged CPP-BT harness • Open PWRGND circuit to the CPP-BT switch • Vehicle push-started with the clutch engaged (clutch pedal released) • Aftermarket remote starting device
DTC: P0840 **1T CCM, MIL:** Yes **Years:** 2008, 2009, 2010 **Models:** All **Engines:** All **Transmissions:** A/T	**Transmission Fluid Pressure Sensor/Switch A Circuit** The Transmission Control Module (TCM) monitors the transmission fliud pressure. This DTC sets when the TCC does not see the proper transmission fluid pressure. **Note: Check for the correct fluid level and condition.** **Possible Causes:** • Low or high transmission fluid level • Blockage in transmission cooler, lines or filter. • Transmission harness circuit shorted to ground or open • Transmission has internal damage • Sensor has failed
DTC: P0960 **1T CCM, MIL:** Yes **Years:** 2008, 2009, 2010 **Models:** All **Engines:** All **Transmissions:** A/T	**Pressure Control Solenoid A (PCA)** PCA circuit or Variable Force Solenoid (VFS 5) failed during operation. Max line pressure. **Note: Wil turn on the TCIL** **Possible Causes:** • Transmission internal harness circuit shorted to ground or open • PCA circuit or solenoid failure or open circuit • Mechatronic unit has failed

DTC	Trouble Code Title, Conditions & Possible Causes
DTC: P0962 **1T CCM, MIL: Yes** **Years:** 2008, 2009, 2010 **Models:** All **Engines:** All **Transmissions:** A/T	**Pressure Control Solenoid (PCA) Signal Fault** PCA solenoid signal or ground circuits either short or open solenoid circuit failure. Voltage through PCA solenoid (VFS-5) is checked. An error will be noted if tolerance is exceeded. **Note: Wil turn on the TCIL. Mechanical limp home mode, defaults to 3rd or 5th gear.** **Possible Causes:** • Transmission internal harness circuit shorted to ground or open • PCA circuit or solenoid failure or open circuit • Mechatronic unit has failed
DTC: P0963 **1T CCM, MIL: No** **Years:** 2008, 2009, 2010 **Models:** All **Engines:** All **Transmissions:** A/T	**Pressure Control Solenoid (PCA) Short To Voltage (VFS-5)** Voltage through PCA solenoid (VFS-5) is checked. An error will be noted if tolerance is exceeded. Max line pressure. Mechanical limp-home mode, default to 3rd or 5th gear. May turn on MIL. **Note: Wil turn on the TCIL.** **Possible Causes:** • Transmission internal harness circuit shorted to VPWR • PCA circuit or solenoid • Mechatronic unit has failed
DTC: P0972 **1T CCM, MIL: No** **Years:** 2008, 2009, 2010 **Models:** All **Engines:** All **Transmissions:** A/T	**Shift Solenoid A (SSA) Solenoid Failure (VFS-1)** SSA (VFS-1) circuit or solenoid failure. Mechanical limp-home mode, default to 3rd or 5th gear. May turn on MIL. **Note: Wil turn on the TCIL.** **Possible Causes:** • Transmission internal harness circuit shorted to , VPWP, ground or open • PCA circuit or solenoid failure • Mechatronic unit has failed
DTC: P0973 **1T CCM, MIL: No** **Years:** 2008, 2009, 2010 **Models:** All **Engines:** All **Transmissions:** A/T	**Shift Solenoid (SSA) Short To Ground (VFS-1)** SSA (VFS-1) circuit or solenoid failure. Mechanical limp-home mode, default to 3rd or 5th gear. May turn on MIL. **Note: Wil turn on the TCIL.** **Possible Causes:** • Transmission internal harness circuit short to GRND or open • PCA circuit or solenoid failure • Mechatronic unit has failed
DTC: P0974 **1T CCM, MIL: No** **Years:** 2008, 2009, 2010 **Models:** All **Engines:** All **Transmissions:** A/T	**Pressure Control Solenoid (PCA) Short To Voltage (VFS-1)** Voltage through PCA solenoid (VFS-1) is checked. An error will be noted if tolerance is exceeded. Max line pressure. Mechanical limp-home mode, default to 3rd or 5th gear. May turn on MIL. **Note: Wil turn on the TCIL.** **Possible Causes:** • Transmission internal harness circuit shorted to VPWR • PCA circuit or solenoid • Mechatronic unit has failed
DTC: P0975 **1T CCM, MIL: No** **Years:** 2008, 2009, 2010 **Models:** All **Engines:** All **Transmissions:** A/T	**Shift Solenoid (SSA) Short To Ground (VFS-2)** SSA (VFS-2) circuit or solenoid failure. Mechanical limp-home mode, default to 3rd or 5th gear. May turn on MIL. **Note: Wil turn on the TCIL.** **Possible Causes:** • Transmission internal harness circuit short to GRND or open • PCA circuit or solenoid failure • Mechatronic unit has failed
DTC: P0975 **1T CCM, MIL: No** **Years:** 2008, 2009, 2010 **Models:** All **Engines:** All **Transmissions:** A/T	**Shift Solenoid B (SSA) Solenoid Failure (VFS-2)** SSA (VFS-2) circuit or solenoid failure. Mechanical limp-home mode, default to 3rd or 5th gear. May turn on MIL. **Note: Wil turn on the TCIL.** **Possible Causes:** • Transmission internal harness circuit shorted to , VPWP, ground or open • PCA circuit or solenoid failure • Mechatronic unit has failed
DTC: P0976 **1T CCM, MIL: No** **Years:** 2008, 2009, 2010 **Models:** All **Engines:** All **Transmissions:** A/T	**Pressure Control Solenoid (PCA) Short To Voltage (VFS-2)** Voltage through PCA solenoid (VFS-2) is checked. An error will be noted if tolerance is exceeded. Max line pressure. **Note: Wil turn on the TCIL.** **Possible Causes:** • Transmission internal harness circuit shorted to VPWR • PCA circuit or solenoid • Mechatronic unit has failed

DTC	Trouble Code Title, Conditions & Possible Causes
DTC: P0978 **1T CCM, MIL: No** **Years:** 2008, 2009, 2010 **Models:** All **Engines:** All **Transmissions:** A/T	**Shift Solenoid C (SSA) Solenoid Failure (VFS-3)** SSA (VFS-3) circuit or solenoid failure. Mechanical limp-home mode, default to 3rd or 5th gear. May turn on MIL. **Note: Wil turn on the TCIL.** **Possible Causes:** • Transmission internal harness circuit shorted to , VPWP, ground or open • PCA circuit or solenoid failure • Mechatronic unit has failed
DTC: P0979 **1T CCM, MIL: No** **Years:** 2008, 2009, 2010 **Models:** All **Engines:** All **Transmissions:** A/T	**Shift Solenoid (SSA) Short To Ground (VFS-3)** SSA (VFS-3) circuit or solenoid failure. Mechanical limp-home mode, default to 3rd or 5th gear. May turn on MIL. **Note: Wil turn on the TCIL.** **Possible Causes:** • Transmission internal harness circuit short to GRND or open • PCA circuit or solenoid failure • Mechatronic unit has failed
DTC: P0980 **1T CCM, MIL: No** **Years:** 2008, 2009, 2010 **Models:** All **Engines:** All **Transmissions:** A/T	**Pressure Control Solenoid (PCA) Short To Voltage (VFS-3)** Voltage through PCA solenoid (VFS-3) is checked. An error will be noted if tolerance is exceeded. Max line pressure. Mechanical limp-home mode, default to 3rd or 5th gear. May turn on MIL. **Note: Wil turn on the TCIL.** **Possible Causes:** • Transmission internal harness circuit shorted to VPWR • PCA circuit or solenoid • Mechatronic unit has failed
DTC: P0981 **1T CCM, MIL: No** **Years:** 2008, 2009, 2010 **Models:** All **Engines:** All **Transmissions:** A/T	**Shift Solenoid D (SSA) Solenoid Failure (VFS-4)** SSA (VFS-4) circuit or solenoid failure. Mechanical limp-home mode, default to 3rd or 5th gear. May turn on MIL. **Note: Wil turn on the TCIL.** **Possible Causes:** • Transmission internal harness circuit shorted to , VPWP, ground or open • PCA circuit or solenoid failure • Mechatronic unit has failed
DTC: P0982 **1T CCM, MIL: No** **Years:** 2008, 2009, 2010 **Models:** All **Engines:** All **Transmissions:** A/T	**Shift Solenoid (SSA) Short To Ground (VFS-4)** SSA (VFS-4) circuit or solenoid failure. Mechanical limp-home mode, default to 3rd or 5th gear. May turn on MIL. **Note: Wil turn on the TCIL.** **Possible Causes:** • Transmission internal harness circuit short to GRND or open • PCA circuit or solenoid failure • Mechatronic unit has failed
DTC: P0983 **1T CCM, MIL: No** **Years:** 2008, 2009, 2010 **Models:** All **Engines:** All **Transmissions:** A/T	**Pressure Control Solenoid (PCA) Short To Voltage (VFS-4)** Voltage through PCA solenoid (VFS-4) is checked. An error will be noted if tolerance is exceeded. Max line pressure. Mechanical limp-home mode, default to 3rd or 5th gear. May turn on MIL. **Note: Wil turn on the TCIL.** **Possible Causes:** • Transmission internal harness circuit shorted to VPWR • PCA circuit or solenoid • Mechatronic unit has failed
DTC: P0984 **1T CCM, MIL: No** **Years:** 2008, 2009, 2010 **Models:** All **Engines:** All **Transmissions:** A/T	**Pressure Control Solenoid (PCA) Signal Circuit Short To Voltage (VFS-4)** Voltage through PCA solenoid (VFS-4) is checked. An error will be noted if tolerance is exceeded. Max line pressure. Mechanical limp-home mode, default to 3rd or 5th gear. May turn on MIL. **Note: Wil turn on the TCIL.** **Possible Causes:** • Transmission internal harness signal circuit shorted to VPWR • PCA signal circuit or solenoid • Mechatronic unit has failed

Gas Engine OBD II Trouble Code List (P1xxx Codes)

DTC	Trouble Code Title, Conditions & Possible Causes
DTC: P1000 **1T PCM, MIL: No** **Years:** 2008, 2009, 2010 **Models:** All **Engines:** All **Transmissions:** All	**On-Board Diagnostic (OBD) Systems Readiness Test Not Complete** Key on or engine running; the OBD monitors are carried out during the OBD drive cycle. This DTC is stored in continuous memory if any of the OBD monitors do not carry out their full diagnostic check. **Note: This DTC, Inspection/Maintenance (I/M) readiness function is part of the PCM strategy. A battery disconnection or clearing of the codes using a scan tool results in various I/M readiness bits being set to a not-ready condition. As each non-continuous OBD monitor completes a full diagnostic check, I/M readiness bit associated with that monitor is set to a ready condition. This may take one or two drive cycles based on whether concerns are detected or not. The readiness bits for Comprehensive Component Monitoring (CCM), misfire and fuel system monitoring are considered complete once all the non-continuous monitors have been evaluated. Because the EVAP system monitor requires certain ambient conditions to run, special logic can bypass the monitor for the purpose of clearing the EVAP and I/M readiness bit, due to continued presence of these extreme conditions. DTC P1000 does not need to be cleared from the PCM except to pass the I/M test. The Malfunction Indicator Lamp (MIL) flashes after a period of time with the key in the RUN position (engine not running) if DTC P1000 is set.** **Possible Causes:** • The vehicle is new from the factory • Battery or Powertrain Control Module (PCM) had recently been disconnected • An OBD monitor concern occurred before completion of an OBD drive cycle • PCM DTCs have recently been cleared with a scan tool • Power Take Off (PTO) circuit concern or PTO is on during testing.
DTC: P1001 **1T CCM, MIL: No** **Years:** 2008, 2009, 2010 **Models:** All **Engines:** All **Transmissions:** All	**KOER Self-Test Not Completed, KOER Test Aborted** This non-Malfunction Indicator Lamp (MIL) DTC is set when the KOER self-test does not complete in the time allowed. **Note: Carry out the KOEO self-test.** **Possible Causes:** • Incorrect self-test procedure • Unexpected response from the self-test monitors • Scan Tool has a communication problem • RPM out of specification
DTC: P1100 **2T CCM, MIL: Yes** **Years:** 2008, 2009, 2010 **Models:** All **Engines:** All **Transmissions:** All	**Mass Air Flow (MAF) Sensor Circuit Intermittent** Engine started, engine running at idle or cruise speed, and the PCM detected the MAF sensor signal above or below the calibrated limit. **Possible Causes:** • MAF sensor continuity problems at the connector • MAF sensor continuity through the wiring harness • MAF sensor circuit intermittent open inside the sensor • PCM has failed
DTC: P1101 **2T CCM, MIL: Yes** **Years:** 2008, 2009, 2010 **Models:** All **Engines:** All **Transmissions:** All	**Mass Air Flow (MAF) Sensor Out Of Self-Test Range** Key on and engine off, and the PCM detected the MAF sensor was more than 0.27v, or with the engine running, the MAF sensor voltage was not within a normal range of 0.46v to 2.44v. **Possible Causes:** • Low battery charge • MAF sensor partially connected, or the sensor is contaminated • MAF sensor power ground circuit or sensor signal (return) open • MAF sensor is damaged or it has failed • PCM has failed
DTC: P1112 **2T CCM, MIL: Yes** **Years:** 2008, 2009, 2010 **Models:** All **Engines:** All **Transmissions:** All	**Intake Air Temperature (IAT) Circuit Intermittent** Engine started, and the PCM detected an intermittent condition in the IAT sensor signal during the self-test. **Note: Select the IAT PID and monitor the signal for sudden changes when the harness is wiggled or the sensor is tapped.** **Possible Causes:** • IAT sensor wiring harness is damaged (wire may be open) • IAT sensor harness connector is damaged • IAT sensor is damaged or the PCM has failed
DTC: P1114 **2T CCM, MIL: Yes** **Years:** 2008, 2009, 2010 **Models:** All **Engines:** All **Transmissions:** All	**Intake Air Temperature 2 (IAT-2) Circuit Low** Engine started, and the PCM detected the IAT sensor signal was less than the self-test minimum of 0.20v (equivalent to 250°F). Monitor the IAT PID for very low signal. **Possible Causes:** • IAT sensor wiring harness is damaged (wire may be grounded) • IAT sensor harness connector is damaged (may be grounded) • IAT sensor is damaged or the PCM has failed

DTC	Trouble Code Title, Conditions & Possible Causes
DTC: P1115 **2T CCM, MIL: Yes** **Years:** 2008, 2009, 2010 **Models:** All **Engines:** All **Transmissions:** All	**Intake Air Temperature 2 (IAT-2) Circuit High** Engine started, and the PCM detected the IAT Sensor 2 signal was more than the self-test maximum of 4.60v (equivalent to 250°F). Monitor the IAT PID for very high signal. **Note: Monitor the IAT2 PID value. A typical IAT2 temperature should be greater than the IAT1 temperature** **Possible Causes:** • IAT sensor wiring harness or harness connector is damaged (wire may be open) • IAT sensor signal circuit is open, or the ground circuit is open • IAT sensor signal short to voltage • IAT sensor is damaged or has failed • PCM has failed
DTC: P1116 **1T CCM, MIL: Yes** **Years:** 2008, 2009, 2010 **Models:** All **Engines:** All **Transmissions:** All	**CHT or ECT Sensor Out of Self-Test Range** Indicates the ECT sensor is out of self-test range. The correct range is 0.3 to 3.7 **Note: The ECT must be greater than 10°C (50°F) to pass the Key On Engine Off (KOEO) self-test and greater than 82°C (180°F) to pass the Key On Engine Running (KOER) self-test.** **Possible Causes:** • Low engine coolant • Overheating condition • Damaged thermostat • ECT sensor is damaged • Damaged harness connector • KOER or KOER Self-Test performed with the engine "too cold"
DTC: P1117 **2T CCM, MIL: Yes** **Years:** 2008, 2009, 2010 **Models:** All **Engines:** All **Transmissions:** All	**CHT or ECT Sensor Signal Intermittent** Engine started, and the PCM detected an intermittent loss of the CHT or ECT sensor signal (it may have an open circuit condition). **Note: Monitor the CHT or ECT on a scan tool. Look for sudden changes in the reading when the harness is wiggled or the sensor is tapped.** **Possible Causes:** • Low engine coolant • ECT sensor harness connector is damaged, loose or shorted • ECT sensor is damaged or it has failed • Engine overheating condition present • Thermostat is faulty, or engine coolant level is low
DTC: P1120 **2T CCM, MIL: Yes** **Years:** 2008, 2009, 2010 **Models:** All **Engines:** All **Transmissions:** All	**Throttle Position (TP) Sensor A Out Of Range Low (Ratch Too Low)** Key on or engine running; the Throttle Position (TP) sensor circuit is monitored by the Powertrain Control Module (PCM) for a low TP rotation angle or voltage input below the closed throttle position through the Comprehensive Component Monitor (CCM). The test fails if the TP rotation angle or voltage remains within the calibrated self-test range, but falls between 3.42-9.85% (0.17-0.49 volt). **Note: A TP PID between 3.42-9.85% (0.17-0.49 volt) in key ON, engine OFF or key ON, engine running indicates a concern is present.** **Possible Causes:** • TP circuit with frayed wires • Corrosion or loose connection on the TP circuit connectors and pins • VREF open to TP sensor • VREF short to SIG RTN • PCM has failed
DTC: P1121 **2T CCM, MIL: Yes** **Years:** 2008, 2009, 2010 **Models:** All **Engines:** All **Transmissions:** All	**TP Sensor Inconsistent With MAF Sensor** Engine started; and the PCM detected the MAF and TP sensor signals were not consistent the calibrated values expected for these two sensors during the self-test. **Note: Drive the vehicle and monitor the TP PID in all gears. A TP PID of less than 0.24v (4.82%) with a LOAD PID over 55%, or a TP PID over 2.44v (49.05%) with a LOAD PID under 30% will set this code.** **Possible Causes:** • Air leak exists between MAF sensor and the throttle body • MAF sensor is damaged or it has failed • TP sensor is not seated properly • TP sensor is damaged • PCM has failed

DTC	Trouble Code Title, Conditions & Possible Causes
DTC: P1124 **1T CCM, MIL: Yes** **Years:** 2008, 2009, 2010 **Models:** All **Engines:** All with IAC valve **Transmissions:** All	**Throttle Position (TP) Sensor A Out Of Self-Test Range (Vehicles With an IAC Valve)** Key on, KOEO Self-Test enabled, and the PCM detected the TP sensor signal was less than 0.66v (13.27%), or with the engine running, KOER Self-Test enabled, the PCM detected the TP sensor signal was approximately 1.17v (23.52%). **Note: A TP V PID less than 4.82 % (0.24 volt) with a LOAD PID more than 55%; or the TP V PID more than 49.05% (2.44 volts) with a LOAD PID less than 30% indicates a hard fault is present.** **Possible Causes:** • Throttle linkage is binding, or TP sensor is not seated properly • Throttle plate below closed throttle position • Throttle plate screw is misadjusted • TP sensor is damaged or it has failed • PCM has failed
DTC: P1124 **1T CCM, MIL: Yes** **Years:** 2008, 2009, 2010 **Models:** All **Engines:** All without IAC valve **Transmissions:** All	**Throttle Position (TP) Sensor A Out Of Self-Test Range (Vehicles Without an IAC Valve)** During Key On Engine Off (KOEO) and Key On Engine Running (KOER) self-tests, the powertrain control module (PCM) monitors the Electronic Throttle Control (ETC) Throttle Position (TP) sensor inputs to determine if the TP1 and TP2 signals are less than an expected value. If either TP1 or TP2 is greater than the expected value, the DTC is set. **Note: Repeat the self-test without applying the accelerator pedal. Make sure the floor mat is not interfering with the accelerator pedal. Diagnose any TP circuit DTCs first.** **Possible Causes:** • Accelerator pedal applied during KOEO or KOER self-test • ETB damaged housing, harness connector, and harness • TP1-TP2 circuits open or shorted to ground, voltage • TP sensor is damaged or it has failed • PCM has failed
DTC: P1125 **2T CCM, MIL: Yes** **Years:** 2008, 2009, 2010 **Models:** All **Engines:** All with IAC **Transmissions:** All	**Throttle Position (TP) Sensor Circuit Malfunction (Vehicles With an IAC Valve)** Engine started, and the PCM detected the TP sensor rotational angle changed beyond the minimum or maximum calibrated limit. **Note: Monitor the TP V PID, and tap lightly on the TP sensor housing and wiggle the wiring harness. Watch for the value to suddenly go below 0.49v or over 4.65v.** **Possible Causes:** • TP sensor wiring harness or connector has an intermittent open • TP sensor has an intermittent open or shorted condition
DTC: P1127 **2T CCM, MIL: Yes** **Years:** 2008, 2009, 2010 **Models:** All **Engines:** All **Transmissions:** All	**Exhaust Temperature Out of Range, O2 Sensor Tests Not Completed** Engine started, KOER Self-Test enabled, and the PCM detected the inferred exhaust temperature was less than a minimum value. **Note: Monitor the HO2S heater PIDs to determine their ON/OFF state. DTC P1127 is present if the exhaust is not hot.** **Possible Causes:** • Engine not operating long enough prior to the KOER Self-Test • Exhaust system temperature too cold to run the self-test
DTC: P115E **2T CCM, MIL: Yes** **Years:** 2008, 2009, 2010 **Models:** All **Engines:** All **Transmissions:** All	**Throttle Actuator Control (TAC) Throttle Body Air Flow Trim at Max Limit** During idle, the Powertrain Control Module (PCM) monitors the throttle angle and air flow. If the air flow is determined to be less than expected, the PCM adjusts the throttle angle to compensate. The air flow reduction is typically the result of engine deposit buildup around the throttle plate. This DTC indicates the PCM has reached the maximum allowed compensation and is no longer able to compensate for the buildup. **Possible Causes:** • Engine deposits around the throttle plate • Throttle body is damaged
DTC: P117A **2T CCM, MIL: Yes** **Years:** 2008, 2009, 2010 **Models:** All **Engines:** All **Transmissions:** All	**Engine Oil Over Temperature (Forced Limited Power)** Indicates the engine oil protection strategy is enabled when the Engine Oil Temperature (EOT) reaches a predetermined level in the Powertrain Control Module (PCM). The PCM then limits the engine RPMs until the EOT returns to normal. **Note: This DTC is an informational DTC and may be set by an engine overheating concern. If the engine overheats, check the cooling system.** **Possible Causes:** • Engine overheating • Low engine coolant • Loaded weight is greater than the maximum vehicle weight rating.
DTC: P1184 **2T CCM, MIL: Yes** **Years:** 2008, 2009, 2010 **Models:** All **Engines:** All **Transmissions:** All	**Engine Oil Temperature (EOT) Sensor Out Of Self-Test Range** Engine started, and the PCM detected the EOT sensor circuit was open or shorted to ground (i.e., this fault can be caused by an intermittent loss of this signal). **Note: The engine should be at operating temperature before carrying out the self-test** **Possible Causes:** • EOT sensor circuit is open or shorted to ground (intermittent) • EOT sensor is corroded, damaged or it has failed • PCM has failed

DTC	Trouble Code Title, Conditions & Possible Causes
DTC: P1227 **1T CCM, MIL: Yes** **Years:** 2008, 2009, 2010 **Models:** All **Engines:** Supercharged **Transmissions:** All	**Wastegate Failed Closed (Over pressure)** Key on or engine running; Indicates that boost pressure is continuously higher than desired. **Note: This DTC is informational only and it may be accompanied by other DTCs. Diagnose other DTCs first.** **Possible Causes:** • EGR valve • MAF sensor • MAP sensor • Supercharger bypass actuator stuck closed • Supercharger
DTC: P1228 **1T CCM, MIL: Yes** **Years:** 2008, 2009, 2010 **Models:** All **Engines:** Supercharged **Transmissions:** All	**Wastegate Failed Open (Under pressure)** Key on or engine running; Indicates that boost pressure is continuously lower than desired. **Note: This DTC is informational only and it may be accompanied by other DTCs. Diagnose other DTCs first.** **Possible Causes:** • EGR valve • MAF sensor • MAP sensor • Supercharger bypass actuator stuck closed • Supercharger
DTC: P1229 **1T CCM, MIL: Yes** **Years:** 2008, 2009, 2010 **Models:** All **Engines:** Supercharged **Transmissions:** All	**Charge Air Cooler (CAC) Pump Driver** Key on or engine running; This DTC sets when the Powertrain Control Module (PCM) commands the supercharger CAC pump to operate but no current is detected. **Note: Check for voltage at the relay. Check the fuse in the voltage circuit. Check the ground connection of the CAC pump motor.** **Possible Causes:** • CAC pump motor open circuit • CAC pump relay coil open • Open circuit between the relay and pump • CAC pump motor shorted • Open circuit between the PCM and the relay • Poor CAC pump ground connection
DTC: P1231 **1T CCM, MIL: No** **Years:** 2008, 2009, 2010 **Models:** All **Engines:** All **Transmissions:** All	**Fuel Pump Secondary Low, High Speed Pump On** Key on, KOEO Self-Test enabled; High Speed Fuel Pump (HFP) relay energized, fuel pump driver in VLCM off (to VLCM Pin 7) off, the PCM detected voltage on the FPM circuit. **Possible Causes:** • HFP relay circuit to battery power (B+) is open • HFP relay is damaged or it has failed • Power-To-Pump circuit between HFP relay and splice is open
DTC: P1232 **2T CCM, MIL: Yes** **Years:** 2008, 2009, 2010 **Models:** All **Engines:** All **Transmissions:** All	**Low Speed Fuel Pump Primary Circuit Malfunction** Engine started, Low Speed Fuel Pump (LFP) relay energized, the PCM detected excessive current on the LFP circuit; or with LFP commanded off it detected power on the LFP circuit. **Possible Causes:** • Low fuel pump (LFP) circuit open or shorted • Low speed fuel pump relay VPWR circuit open • Low speed fuel pump relay is damaged • PCM has failed
DTC: P1233 **2T CCM, MIL: Yes** **Years:** 2008, 2009, 2010 **Models:** All **Engines:** All **Transmissions:** All	**Fuel Pump Driver Module Disabled or Off Line** The Powertrain Control Module (PCM) monitors the Fuel Pump Monitor (FPM) circuit from the Fuel Pump Driver Module (FPDM). With the key ON, engine OFF or key ON, engine running the FPDM continuously sends a duty cycle signal to the PCM through the FPM circuit. The test fails if the PCM stops receiving the duty cycle signal. **Note: The PCM expects to see one of the following duty cycle signals from the FPDM on the FPM circuit: 1) 50% (500 ms on, 500 ms off), all OK. 2) 25% (250 ms on, 750 ms off), FPDM did not receive a fuel pump (FP) duty cycle command from the PCM, or the duty cycle that was received was invalid. 3) 75% (750 ms on, 250 off), the FPDM detected a concern in the circuits between the FPDM and the fuel pump.** **Possible Causes:** • Inertia fuel shutoff (IFS) switch needs to be reset • Open FPDM ground circuit • Open circuit to FPDM2 PWR RLY • Open FPDM PWR circuit • Open or short FPM circuit (engine should start) • Damaged FPDM PWR RLY • Damaged FPDM

DTC	Trouble Code Title, Conditions & Possible Causes
DTC: P1234 **1T CCM, MIL: Yes** **Years:** 2008, 2009, 2010 **Models:** All **Engines:** All **Transmissions:** All	**Fuel System Disabled Or Offline** The Powertrain Control Module (PCM) monitors the Fuel Pump Monitor 2 (FPM2) circuit from the Fuel Pump Driver Module 2 (FPDM2). With the key ON, engine OFF or key ON, engine running the FPDM2 continuously sends a duty cycle signal to the PCM through the FPM2 circuit. The test fails if the PCM stops receiving the duty cycle signal. **Note: The PCM expects to see one of the following duty cycle signals from the FPDM2 on the FPM2 circuit: 1) 50% (500 ms on, 500 ms off), all OK. 2) 25% (250 ms on, 750 ms off), the FPDM2 did not receive a Fuel Pump (FP) duty cycle command from the PCM, or the duty cycle that was received was invalid. 3) 75% (750 ms on, 250 off), the FPDM2 detected a concern in the circuits between the FPDM2 and the fuel pump.** **Possible Causes:** • Inertia fuel shutoff (IFS) switch needs to be reset or has failed • Damaged IFS switch • Open FPDM2 ground circuit • Open circuit to FPDM2 PWR RLY • Open FPDM2 PWR circuit • Open or short FPM2 circuit (engine should start) • Damaged FPDM2 PWR RLY • Damaged FPDM2
DTC: P1235 **2T CCM, MIL: Yes** **Years:** 2008, 2009, 2010 **Models:** All **Engines:** All **Transmissions:** All	**Fuel Pump Control Out Of Range** Key on or engine running; and the PCM received a signal from the FPM over the SCP bus that the FPDM had received an invalid or missing fuel pump command from the PCM. **Note: The FPDM sends a 25% duty cycle (250 ms on, 750 ms off) through the FPM circuit to the PCM while the concern is being detected by the FPDM. If the concern is no longer detected, the FPDM returns to sending an all OK (50% duty cycle) message to the PCM. For ETC applications, check if ETC DTC P2105 is present. An ETC system concern could cause DTC P1235, and should be diagnosed first.** **Possible Causes:** • FP circuit is open or shorted • Electronic Throttle Control (ETC) system concern. Check for ETC DTCs • FPDM is damaged • PCM has failed
DTC: P1236 **2T CCM, MIL: No** **Years:** 2008, 2009, 2010 **Models:** All **Engines:** All **Transmissions:** All	**Fuel Pump Control Out Of Range** This DTC indicates the Fuel Pump Driver Module 2 (FPDM2) detected an invalid or missing Fuel Pump (FP) duty cycle signal on the Fuel Pump Control (FPC) circuit from the Powertrain Control Module (PCM). The FPDM2 sends a message to the PCM through the Fuel Pump Monitor 2 (FPM2) circuit, indicating this concern was detected. The PCM sets the DTC when the message is received. **Note: The FPDM2 sends a 25% duty cycle (250 ms on, 750 ms off) through the FPM2 circuit to the PCM while the concern is being detected by the FPDM2. If the concern is no longer detected, the FPDM2 returns to sending an all OK (50% duty cycle) message to the PCM.** **Possible Causes:** • FPC circuit is open or it is shorted • FPDM2 is damaged • PCM has failed
DTC: P1237 **2T CCM, MIL: Yes** **Years:** 2008, 2009, 2010 **Models:** All **Engines:** All **Transmissions:** All	**Fuel Pump Secondary Circuit Malfunction** Key on or engine running; and the PCM received a signal from the FPDM that it had detected a fault in the fuel pump secondary circuit. **Note: The FPDM sends a 75% duty cycle (750 ms on, 250 ms off) through the FPM circuit to the PCM while the concern is being detected by the FPDM. If the concern is no longer detected, the PCM returns to sending an all OK (50% duty cycle) message to the PCM. The FPDM controls pump speed by supplying a variable ground on the FP RTN circuit.** **Possible Causes:** • FP PWR circuit is open or shorted • FPDM fuel pump return circuit is open • Fuel pump windings are open or shorted, or the rotor is locked • FPDM is damaged
DTC: P1238 **2T CCM, MIL: Yes** **Years:** 2008, 2009, 2010 **Models:** All **Engines:** All **Transmissions:** All	**Fuel Pump Secondary Circuit Malfunction** Key on or engine running; and the PCM received a signal from the FPDM that it had detected a fault in the fuel pump secondary circuit. **Note: The FPDM2 sends a 75% duty cycle (750 ms on, 250 ms off) through the FPM2 circuit to the PCM while the concern is being detected by the FPDM2. If the concern is no longer detected, the PCM returns to sending an all OK (50% duty cycle) message to the PCM. The FPDM2 controls pump speed by supplying a variable ground on the FP2RTN circuit.** **Possible Causes:** • FP PWR circuit is open or shorted • FPDM fuel pump return circuit is open • Fuel pump windings are open or shorted • Fuel pump rotor is locked • FPDM is damaged

DTC	Trouble Code Title, Conditions & Possible Causes
DTC: P1244 **2T CCM, MIL: Yes** **Years:** 2008, 2009, 2010 **Models:** All **Engines:** All **Transmissions:** All	**Alternator Load High Input** The Powertrain Control Module (PCM) monitors generator load from the generator/regulator in the form of frequency. The concern indicates the input is higher than the load should be in normal operation. The load input could be high when a battery short to ground exists. **Possible Causes:** • Faulty battery • GENCMD circuit is shorted • Voltage regulator/ alternator is damaged • PCM has failed
DTC: P1245 **2T CCM, MIL: Yes** **Years:** 2008, 2009, 2010 **Models:** All **Engines:** All **Transmissions:** All	**Alternator Load High Low** The Powertrain Control Module (PCM) monitors generator load from the generator/regulator in the form of frequency. The concern indicates the input is lower than the load should be in normal operation. The load input could be low when no generator output exists. **Possible Causes:** • Faulty battery • Fauty drive belt tension • GENCMD circuit is open • Voltage regulator/ alternator is damaged • PCM has failed
DTC: P1246 **2T CCM, MIL: Yes** **Years:** 2008, 2009, 2010 **Models:** All **Engines:** All **Transmissions:** All	**Alternator Load Circuit Imput** The Powertrain Control Module (PCM) monitors the generator load from the generator/regulator in the form of frequency. The frequency range is determined by the temperature of the voltage regulator, where 97% indicates a full load, and less than 6% indicates no load. **Possible Causes:** • Faulty battery • Fauty drive belt tension • GENCMD circuit is open • Voltage regulator/ alternator is damaged • PCM has failed
DTC: P1260 **1T PCM, MIL: Yes** **Years:** 2008, 2009, 2010 **Models:** All **Engines:** All **Transmissions:** All	**Theft Detected, Vehicle Immobilized** Key on, and the PCM received a signal from the Anti-Theft System that a theft condition had occurred. The theft indicator on the dash will flash rapidly or remain on "solid" with the ignition switch in the "on" position. The engine may "start and stall", or may not crank if the vehicle is equipped with the PATS starter disable feature. **Possible Causes:** • Incorrectly programmed PCM • Incorrectly programmed IC • A Previous theft condition has occurred • Anti-Theft System is damaged or has failed
DTC: P1270 **1T CCM, MIL: Yes** **Years:** 2008, 2009, 2010 **Models:** All **Engines:** All **Transmissions:** All	**Engine RPM or Vehicle Speed Limiter Reached** Engine started, and after the PCM monitored the engine speed and VSS signals, it detected the vehicle was operated in a manner where the engine or vehicle speed exceeded its limit. **Possible Causes:** • Excessive wheel slippage due to water, ice, mud and snow • Excessive engine speed (rpm) with the gearshift in Neutral • Vehicle driven at a high rate of speed
DTC: P1285 **2T CCM, MIL: Yes** **Years:** 2008, 2009, 2010 **Models:** All **Engines:** All With CHT **Transmissions:** All	**Cylinder Head Over-Temperature Condition** Key on or engine running; and the PCM detected an engine overheat condition through inputs from the cylinder head temperature sensor. **Note: On some applications when this fault occurs, the engine temperature warning indicator illuminates or forces the temperature gauge to the full H (hot) zone. The warning indicator can be triggered by either grounding the engine temperature warning circuit when wired to the Powertrain Control Module (PCM), or by sending a PCM network message to the Instrument Cluster (IC).** **Possible Causes:** • Base engine problems or related concerns • CHT sensor has deteriorated or it has failed • Engine coolant level is too low • Engine cooling system has a problem

DTC	Trouble Code Title, Conditions & Possible Causes
DTC: P1288 **2T CCM, MIL: Yes** **Years:** 2008, 2009, 2010 **Models:** All **Engines:** All With CHT **Transmissions:** All	**Cylinder Head Temperature Sensor Out of Self-Test Range** Key on and KOEO Self-Test enabled, or engine running with the KOER Self-Test enabled, and the PCM detected the CHT sensor was out of its self-test range (i.e., the engine was too hot or it did not warm to its normal operating temperature) during the test period. **Possible Causes:** • CHT sensor harness connector is damaged • CHT sensor is damaged • Engine coolant level is too low • Engine is cold, or the engine is overheated
DTC: P1289 **2T CCM, MIL: Yes** **Years:** 2008, 2009, 2010 **Models:** All **Engines:** All With CHT **Transmissions:** All	**Cylinder Head Temperature Sensor Circuit High Input** Key on or engine running; and the PCM detected a Cylinder Head Temperature (CHT) sensor signal that was more than 4.60v. This code may be due to an intermittent fault. Wiggle the CHT sensor wiring and connector while monitoring the CHT PID for a sudden change in voltage. DTC P0118 may also be reported when this code is set, and either code will cause the PCM to activate the MIL. **Possible Causes:** • CHT sensor circuit is open in the wiring harness, or an open circuit exists in the CHT sensor circuit at the harness connector • CHT sensor is damaged or has failed • Engine coolant level is too low or the thermostat has failed • PCM has failed
DTC: P128A **2T CCM, MIL: Yes** **Years:** 2008, 2009, 2010 **Models:** All **Engines:** All With CHT **Transmissions:** All	**Cylinder Head Temperature (CHT) Sensor Circuit Intermittent/Erratic** Key on or engine running; Indicates the CHT circuit became intermittently open or shorted while the engine was running. **Note: Monitor the CHT on a scan tool. Look for sudden changes in the reading when the harness is wiggled or the sensor is tapped.** **Possible Causes:** • CHT sensor is damaged or has failed • CHT sensor harness or connector damaged
DTC: P1290 **2T CCM, MIL: Yes** **Years:** 2008, 2009, 2010 **Models:** All **Engines:** All With CHT **Transmissions:** All	**Cylinder Head Temperature (CHT) Sensor Circuit Low** Key on or engine running; and the PCM detected a Cylinder Head Temperature (CHT) sensor signal that was less than 0.2v. Note that this trouble code may be due to an intermittent type of fault. Wiggle the CHT sensor wiring and connector while monitoring the CHT V PID for signs of a sudden change in the voltage. DTC P0118 may also set along with this code (both codes will cause a MIL to be on). **Possible Causes:** • CHT sensor connector is damaged or a short circuit exists • CHT sensor signal circuit is shorted to sensor ground • CHT sensor is damaged • PCM has failed
DTC: P1299 **2T CCM, MIL: Yes** **Years:** 2008, 2009, 2010 **Models:** All **Engines:** All **Transmissions:** All	**Cylinder Head Over-Temperature Protection Active** Engine started, and after a period of time with the engine running, the PCM detected the engine was in an overheated condition. **Note: The PCM enables the Fail-Safe Cooling whenever this code is set to cool the engine (a Failure Mode Effects Strategy or FMEM).** **Possible Causes:** • Cooling system has a problem • Engine coolant level is too low • A Base Engine problem may be present
DTC: P1336 **2T CCM, MIL: Yes** **Years:** 2008, 2009, 2010 **Models:** All **Engines:** All **Transmissions:** All	**Crankshaft/Camshaft Sensor Range/Performance** Engine started, and the PCM detected an erratic signal from CKP sensor or the CMP sensor. It is possible for EMI/RFI interference to cause this code when they occur on these circuits. **Note: Check the harness for routing, alterations, incorrect shielding, or electrical interference from other systems.** **Possible Causes:** • Base Engine problem or concern exists • CKP sensor or CMP signal circuit is open or shorted to ground • CKP sensor or CMP sensor is damaged or failed • PCM has failed
DTC: P1397 **1T CCM, MIL: Yes** **Years:** 2008, 2009, 2010 **Models:** All **Engines:** All **Transmissions:** All	**System Voltage Out Of Self-Test Range** This DTC indicates that the 12-volt system voltage is too high or too low during the Key On Engine Off (KOEO) or Key On Engine Running (KOER) self-test. It sets if the system voltage falls below or exceeds the calibrated threshold at any time during the KOEO or KOER self-test. **Note: Make sure the battery voltage is between 11 and 18 volts before running a KOEO or KOER self-test.** **Possible Causes:** • Battery or charging system concern • PCM has failed

DTC	Trouble Code Title, Conditions & Possible Causes
DTC: P1405 **2T CCM, MIL: Yes** **Years:** 2008, 2009, 2010 **Models:** All **Engines:** All **Transmissions:** All	**Differential Pressure Feedback (DPFE) Sensor Upstream Hose Off or Plugged** While driving, the Exhaust Gas Recirculation (EGR) monitor commands the EGR valve closed and checks the differential pressure across the EGR orifice. The test fails when the signal from the differential pressure feedback EGR sensor indicates EGR flow is in the negative direction. **Note: Look for signs of water or icing in the hose. Verify the hose connection and routing (no excessive dips). Check the differential pressure feedback EGR sensor for correct mounting and function. View the DPFEGR PID while applying and releasing vacuum directly to the sensor with a hand pump.** **Possible Causes:** • DPFE sensor upstream hose is disconnected • DPFE sensor upstream hose is plugged (ice) • EGR tube is plugged or damaged
DTC: P1406 **2T CCM, MIL: Yes** **Years:** 2008, 2009, 2010 **Models:** All **Engines:** All **Transmissions:** All	**Differential Pressure Feedback (DPFE) Sensor Downstream Hose Off Or Plugged** Engine started; and the PCM detected the DPF EGR sensor signal indicated EGR flow existed with the EGR valve commanded closed. **Possible Causes:** • Check for signs of icing in the hose, or for a restricted tube • DPFE sensor downstream hose is disconnected • DPFE sensor downstream hose is plugged (ice) • EGR tube is plugged or damaged
DTC: P1408 **1T EGR, MIL: No** **Years:** 2008, 2009, 2010 **Models:** All **Engines:** All **Transmissions:** All	**Exhaust Gas Recirculation (EGR) Flow Out of Self-Test Range (Non-MIL)** This test is carried out during the Key On Engine Running (KOER) on demand self-test only. The EGR system is commanded on at a fixed engine speed. The test does not pass and the DTC is set when the measured EGR flow falls above or below the required calibration. **Note: For EEGR, use the output state control function of the scan tool and monitor the Manifold Absolute Pressure (MAP) PID and the EEGR PID (EGRMDSD) while commanding the EEGR on. If EGR is introduced into the engine at idle, the RPM drops or stalls out. For vacuum systems see diagnostic aids for DTC P0401.** **Possible Causes:** • For Electric EGR (EEGR) system, see possible causes for DTC P0400 • For vacuum activated systems, see the possible causes for DTC P0401
DTC: P1409 **2T CCM, MIL: Yes** **Years:** 2008, 2009, 2010 **Models:** All Except Crown Victoria, Grand Marquis & Town Car **Engines:** All **Transmissions:** All	**Exhaust Gas Recirculation (EGR) Vacuum Regulator Solenoid Circuit** Engine started, and the PCM detected a fault in the EGR VR solenoid circuit (i.e., the VR circuit was too high or low when compared to the expected range with the solenoid enabled). **Possible Causes:** • VPWR circuit is open to EGR Vacuum Regulator (VR)solenoid • EGR VR solenoid circuit is open, or shorted to ground • EGR vacuum regulator solenoid is damaged
DTC: P1409 **1T CCM, MIL: Yes** **Years:** 2008, 2009, 2010 **Models:** Crown Victoria, Grand Marquis, Town Car **Engines:** 4.6L VIN H, V, W **Transmissions:** All	**EGR Vacuum Regulator Solenoid Circuit Malfunction** Engine started, and the PCM detected a fault in the EGR VR solenoid circuit (i.e., the VR circuit was too high or low when compared to its expected range with the solenoid enabled). **Possible Causes:** • EGR VR solenoid circuit is open, or shorted to ground • EGR VR circuit is shorted to power or the VPWR circuit is open • EGR vacuum regulator solenoid is damaged or the PCM has failed • PCM has failed
DTC: P1436 **2T CCM, MIL: Yes** **Years:** 2008, 2009, 2010 **Models:** All **Engines:** All **Transmissions:** All	**A/C Evaporator Temperature (ACET) Circuit Low Input** Key on or engine running; and the PCM detected the ACET signal was less than the self-test minimum amount of 0.13v in the self-test. **Possible Causes:** • ACET circuit short to ground or SIG RTN • ACET sensor is damaged or has failed • PCM has failed
DTC: P1437 **2T CCM, MIL: Yes** **Years:** 2008, 2009, 2010 **Models:** All **Engines:** All **Transmissions:** All	**A/C Evaporator Temperature (ACET) Circuit High Input** Key on or engine running; Indicates the air conditioning evaporator temperature (ACET) signal input was less than the self-test minimum. The self-test minimum is 0.13 volt. **Possible Causes:** • ACET circuit open • SIGRTN circuit open to ACET sensor • ACET circuit short to voltage (VREF) • Damaged ACET sensor • PCM has failed

DTC	Trouble Code Title, Conditions & Possible Causes

DTC: P1443
2T EVAP, MIL: Yes
Years: 2008, 2009, 2010
Models: All
Engines: All
Transmissions: All
	Low Purge Flow Or No Purge Flow Condition Detected
	ECT sensor less than 90°Fat startup (cold engine), engine running at a steady cruise speed, and the PCM detected a fuel tank pressure change occurred of more than −7" H2O within 30 seconds with the purge flow less than 0.02 pounds per minute during testing.
	Possible Causes:
	  • EVAP canister purge valve stuck closed (mechanically)
	  • Fuel vapor hose blocked between EVAP purge valve and FTP sensor, or blocked between purge valve and intake manifold, or vacuum hose blocked between purge valve and intake manifold

DTC: P144A
1T CCM, MIL: Yes
Years: 2008, 2009, 2010
Models: All
Engines: All
Transmissions: All
	Evaporative Emission System Purge Vapor Line Restricted/Blocked
	The Powertrain Control Module (PCM) monitors the Evaporative Emission (EVAP) system for a blocked fuel vapor tube between the Fuel Tank Pressure (FTP) sensor and the fuel tank. During the initial phase of the EVAP monitor, the PCM closes the canister vent and a vacuum develops in the fuel vapor tubes and lines and in the fuel tank. The PCM monitors the FTP sensor to determine the amount of vacuum and how quickly the vacuum increases. The rate at which the vacuum increases is compared to an expected value. If the vacuum increases quicker than expected, a blocked fuel vapor tube is suspected and an intrusive test is carried out in the final phase of the EVAP monitor. If the intrusive test confirms a blockage a counter is incremented and once the counter reaches a calibrated number of completions, the DTC is.
	Note: Check the fuel vapor tube for blockage between the fuel tank pressure FTP sensor and the fuel tank.
	Possible Causes:
	  • Blocked fuel vapor tube between the FTP sensor and the fuel tank
	  • PCM has failed

DTC: P1450
2T EVAP, MIL: Yes
Years: 2008, 2009, 2010
Models: All
Engines: All
Transmissions: All
	Unable to Bleed Up Fuel Tank Vacuum
	ECT sensor less than 90°F at startup (cold engine), engine running at a steady cruise speed, and the PCM detected a high fuel tank vacuum condition was present during the EVAP test.
	Possible Causes:
	  • CV solenoid is stuck partially or fully open or filter is plugged
	  • EVAP canister tube or EVAP canister purge outlet tube blocked or kinked between fuel tank, purge valve and EVAP canister
	  • Fuel filler cap stuck closed (vacuum relief cannot occur)
	  • Contaminated fuel vapor elbow at the EVAP canister, or the EVAP canister is restricted or canister purge valve stuck open

DTC: P1450
2T EVAP, MIL: Yes
Years: 2008, 2009, 2010
Models: All
Engines: All
Transmissions: All
	Unable to Bleed Up Fuel Tank Vacuum
	Monitors the fuel vapor vacuum and pressure in the fuel tank. System failure occurs when the Evaporative Emission (EVAP) running loss monitor detects excessive fuel tank vacuum with the engine running, but not at idle.
	Note: Visually inspect the EVAP canister inlet port, CV solenoid filter, and canister vent hose assembly for contamination or debris. Check EVAP canister purge valve for vacuum leak.
	Possible Causes:
	  • CV solenoid is stuck partially or fully open or filter is plugged
	  • EVAP canister tube or EVAP canister purge outlet tube blocked or kinked between fuel tank, purge valve and EVAP canister
	  • Fuel filler cap stuck closed (vacuum relief cannot occur)
	  • Contaminated fuel vapor elbow at the EVAP canister, or the EVAP canister is restricted or canister purge valve stuck open
	  • FTP sensor is damaged

DTC: P1451
2T CCM, MIL: Yes
Years: 2008, 2009, 2010
Models: All
Engines: All
Transmissions: All
	Evaporative Emission System Vent Control Circuit
	Engine started, engine running at a steady cruise speed, canister vent solenoid enabled, and the PCM detected an unexpected voltage condition on the Canister Vent solenoid circuit.
	Note: To verify normal functioning, monitor the Evaporative Emission (EVAP) CV solenoid signal PID EVAPCV and the signal voltage on the PCM control side. With the valve open, the EVAPCV PID indicates 0% duty cycle and a voltage approximately equal to battery voltage. When the valve is commanded fully closed, the EVAPCV PID indicates 100% duty cycle, and a minimum voltage drop of 4 volts is normal. Output Test Mode (OTM) may be used to switch the output on and off to verify function.
	Possible Causes:
	  • VPWR circuit open
	  • CV solenoid circuit is open, shorted to ground or system power
	  • CV solenoid is damaged or has failed
	  • PCM has failed

DTC: P145E
1T CCM, MIL: Yes
Years: 2008, 2009, 2010
Models: All
Engines: All
Transmissions: All
	PCV Heater Control B Circuit
	This DTC sets when the Powertrain Control Module (PCM) detects a Positive Crankcase Ventilation (PCV) heater circuit failure.
	Note: Make sure the PCV valve is correct for the engine application and the PCV heater connector is correctly connected.
	Possible Causes:
	  • Open or shorted PCV circuit
	  • Damaged PCV heater assembly

DTC	Trouble Code Title, Conditions & Possible Causes
DTC: P1460 **1T CCM, MIL: Yes** **Years:** 2008, 2009, 2010 **Models:** All **Engines:** All **Transmissions:** All	**Wide Open Throttle A/C Cutout Relay Circuit Malfunction** Key on, and the PCM detected a malfunction in the A/C Wide-Open Throttle (WOT) circuit during the test. **Note: If this code sets on vehicles without an A/C system, ignore this code.** **Possible Causes:** • Open or short A/CCR circuit • Damaged A/CCR relay • Open VPWR circuit to the A/CCR relay • PCM has failed
DTC: P1461 **2T CCM, MIL: Yes** **Years:** 2008, 2009, 2010 **Models:** All **Engines:** All **Transmissions:** All	**A/C Pressure Sensor Circuit High Input** Engine started, and the PCM detected the A/C Pressure sensor signal was over the test limit. **Note: Verify a VREF voltage between 4 and 6 volts.** **Possible Causes:** • ACP sensor circuit shorted to VREF or to power (VPWR) • ACP sensor circuit is open, or the ground circuit is open • ACP sensor is damaged or has failed
DTC: P1462 **2T CCM, MIL: Yes** **Years:** 2008, 2009, 2010 **Models:** All **Engines:** All **Transmissions:** All	**Air Conditioning Pressure (A/CP) Sensor Low Voltage Detected** Engine started, and the PCM detected the A/C Pressure sensor signal was under the test limit. **Note: Verify a VREF voltage between 4 and 6 volts.** **Possible Causes:** • ACP circuit short to GND or SIGRTN • VREF circuit open • Open ACP circuit • Damaged ACP sensor
DTC: P1463 **2T CCM, MIL: Yes** **Years:** 2008, 2009, 2010 **Models:** All **Engines:** All **Transmissions:** All	**A/C Pressure Sensor Insufficient Pressure Change** Engine started, and with the A/C compressor operating, the PCM detected the A/C refrigerant pressure did not change as the compressor cycled during the self-test period. **Possible Causes:** • A/C system mechanical failure, or A/C clutch always engaged • ACP sensor signal open, or sensor ground circuit open • A/C sensor is damaged or the PCM has failed
DTC: P1464 **1T CCM, MIL: No** **Years:** 2008, 2009, 2010 **Models:** All **Engines:** All **Transmissions:** All	**A/C Demand Out of Self-Test Range** Key on, KOEO Self-Test enabled, or with the engine running, KOER Self-Test enabled, and the PCM detected the A/C demand switch signal was high during the self-test period. **Possible Causes:** • A/C switch was left "on" during the KOER self-test • A/C PWR circuit is shorted to power (N/C WAC relay contacts) • ACCS circuit is shorted to power • A/C Demand Switch, WAC relay or CCRM is damaged
DTC: P1469 **2T CCM, MIL: Yes** **Years:** 2008, 2009, 2010 **Models:** All **Engines:** All **Transmissions:** All	**Rapid A/C Cycling** Engine started, and with the A/C selected, PCM detected frequent cycling of the A/C compressor clutch. This test was designed to protect the transmission. In some strategies, the PCM will unlock the torque converter during A/C clutch engagement. If a concern is present that results in frequent A/C clutch cycling, damage could occur if the torque converter was cycled at these intervals. This test will detect this condition, set the code and prevent the torque converter from excessive cycling. **Possible Causes:** • Cycling pressure switch circuit open between pin 41 (ACCS) and the PCM, or the IGN RUN circuit is open to the cycling pressure switch circuit (if applicable) • Mechanical A/C system concern (i.e., low refrigerant charge, damaged A/C switch)
DTC: P1474 **2T CCM, MIL: Yes** **Years:** 2008, 2009, 2010 **Models:** All **Engines:** All **Transmissions:** All	**Fan Control Primary Circuit** Key on or engine running; Monitors the Low Fan Control (LFC) primary circuit output from the Powertrain Control Module (PCM). The test fails if the PCM grounds the LFC circuit. Excessive current draw is detected on the LFC circuit or with the LFC circuit not grounded by the PCM. Voltage is not detected on the LFC circuit (the PCM expects to detect VPWR voltage coming through the low speed FC relay coil to the LFC circuit). **Possible Causes:** • Open or short LFC circuit • Open VPWR circuit to the low speed FC relay • Damaged low speed FC relay

DTC	Trouble Code Title, Conditions & Possible Causes

DTC: P1477
2T CCM, MIL: Yes
Years: 2008, 2009, 2010
Models: All
Engines: All
Transmissions: All
	Additional Fan Relay Circuit
	Key on or engine running; Monitors the Medium Fan Control (MFC) primary circuit output from the Powertrain Control Module (PCM). The test fails if the MFC output commanded on (grounded), excessive current draw is detected on the MFC circuit or, with the MFC circuit commanded off, voltage is not detected on the MFC circuit (the PCM expects to detect IGN START/RUN voltage through the medium speed FC relay coil to the MFC circuit).
	Possible Causes:
	  • MFC circuit is open or shorted
	  • Open IGN START/RUN circuit to the medium speed FC relay
	  • Damaged medium speed FC relay

DTC: P1479
2T CCM, MIL: Yes
Years: 2008, 2009, 2010
Models: All
Engines: All
Transmissions: All
	High Fan Control Primary Circuit Malfunction
	Key on, High Cooling Fan (HFC) enabled, and the PCM detected excessive current draw in the circuit; or with the HFC commanded off, it detected voltage present on the HFC circuit.
	Possible Causes:
	  • HFC circuit is open
	  • HFC circuit is shorted to ground
	  • HFC relay power circuit (VPWR) is open
	  • High speed FC relay is damaged or it has failed

DTC: P1489
2T CCM, MIL: Yes
Years: 2008, 2009, 2010
Models: All
Engines: All
Transmissions: All
	PCV Heater Control Circuit
	Key on or engine running; This DTC sets when the Powertrain Control Module (PCM) detects a Positive Crankcase Ventilation (PCV) heater circuit failure.
	Note: Make sure the PCV valve is correct for the engine application and the PCV heater connector is correctly connected.
	Possible Causes:
	  • Open or shorted PCV circuit.
	  • Damaged PCV heater assembly

DTC: P1500
2T CCM, MIL: Yes
Years: 2008, 2009, 2010
Models: All
Engines: All
Transmissions: All
	Vehicle Speed Sensor (VSS) Signal Intermittent
	Engine running in gear with a VSS signal present, and the PCM detected that the VSS signal was intermitten.
	Note: Check the wiring, connector, and sensor for damage.
	Possible Causes:
	  • VSS pins damaged, loose or pushed in at the connector
	  • VSS circuit open or shorted in the wiring harness (insulation)
	  • VSS wiring harness routing incorrect or VSS mounting incorrect
	  • Damaged VSS

DTC: P1501 **1T CCM, MIL: No** **Years:** 2008, 2009, 2010 **Models:** All **Engines:** All **Transmissions:** All	**VSS Signal Out Of Self-Test Range** Engine started, KOER Self-Test enabled, and the PCM detected a VSS signal during the self-test (i.e., with the vehicle not moving). **Possible Causes:** • VSS signal is noisy due to Radio Frequency Interference/ Electro-Magnetic Interference (RFI/EMI) from outside devices (ignition wires, charging circuit or aftermarket devices)

DTC: P1502
1T CCM, MIL: Yes
Years: 2008, 2009, 2010
Models: All
Engines: All
Transmissions: All
	VSS Signal Intermittent
	Engine started, and the PCM detected an intermittent VSS signal. The TCIL will flash on the first trip that this code is set. The VSS signal is received from the VSS, transfer case speed sensor, ABS Control module, GEM or the Central Timer module (depends upon the vehicle).
	Possible Causes:
	  • VSS+ or VSS- harness circuit is open
	  • TCSS signal or TCSS signal return harness circuit is open
	  • VSS harness circuit, TCSS harness circuit is shorted to ground
	  • VSS harness circuit, CSS harness circuit is shorted to power
	  • VSS circuit open between the PCM and related control module
	  • VSS or TCSS, or wheel speed sensors circuits are damaged
	  • Modules connected to VSC/VSS harness circuits are damaged
	  • Mechanical drive mechanism for the VSS or TCSS is damaged

DTC: P1504
2T CCM, MIL: Yes
Years: 2008, 2009, 2010
Models: All
Engines: All
Transmissions: All
	Idle Air Control Circuit Malfunction
	Engine started, engine running for 1 minute, and the PCM detected an electrical load failure on the IAC motor circuit during the self-test.
	Possible Causes:
	  • IAC circuit is open, shorted to ground or to the VPWR circuit
	  • IAC solenoid VPWR circuit is open
	  • IAC valve is damaged or has failed
	  • PCM has failed

DTC	Trouble Code Title, Conditions & Possible Causes
DTC: P1506 **2T CCM, MIL: Yes** **Years:** 2008, 2009, 2010 **Models:** Crown Victoria, Grand Marquis Models **Engines:** 4.6L VIN V, W **Transmissions:** All	**Idle Air Control Overspeed Error** Engine started, engine running for 1 minute, and the PCM detected the idle speed was more than the desired engine Target Idle Speed. **Possible Causes:** • Base engine vacuum leaks present • EVAP system has a problem • IAC circuit shorted to ground • IAC valve is stuck open, or it is damaged • Throttle body or throttle plate is contaminated or very dirty
DTC: P1507 **2T CCM, MIL: Yes** **Years:** 2008, 2009, 2010 **Models:** All Except Crown Victoria, Grand Marquis & Town Car **Engines:** All **Transmissions:** All	**Idle Air Control Underspeed Error** Engine started, engine running for 1 minute, and the PCM detected the idle speed was less than the desired engine Target Idle Speed. **Possible Causes:** • Air inlet is plugged or the air filter element is severely clogged • IAC circuit is open, or shorted to the VPWR circuit • IAC circuit VPWR circuit is open • IAC solenoid is damaged or has failed • Throttle body or throttle plate is contaminated or very dirty
DTC: P1512 **2T CCM, MIL: Yes** **Years:** 2008, 2009, 2010 **Models:** All **Engines:** All **Transmissions:** All	**Intake Manifold Runner Control (IMRC) Stuck Closed (Bank 1)** Key on or engine running; this DTC is set when the vacuum actuated IMRC is commanded open, but the IMRC monitor indicates closed. **Note: Monitor the IMRC and IMRCM PIDs. The IMRCM state should change when the IMRC is commanded open or closed.** **Possible Causes:** • IMRC monitor circuit open • Suspect IMRC solenoid • Mechanical concern - bind, seize, damage, or obstruction of IMRC hardware • PCM has failed
DTC: P1513 **2T CCM, MIL: Yes** **Years:** 2008, 2009, 2010 **Models:** All **Engines:** All **Transmissions:** All	**Intake Manifold Runner Control (IMRC) Stuck Closed (Bank 2)** Key on or engine running; this DTC is set when the vacuum actuated IMRC is commanded open, but the IMRC monitor indicates closed. **Note: Monitor the IMRC and IMRCM PIDs. The IMRCM state should change when the IMRC is commanded open or closed.** **Possible Causes:** • IMRC monitor circuit open • Suspect IMRC solenoid • Mechanical concern - bind, seize, damage, or obstruction of IMRC hardware • PCM has failed
DTC: P1516 **2T CCM, MIL: Yes** **Years:** 2008, 2009, 2010 **Models:** All **Engines:** All **Transmissions:** All	**Intake Manifold Runner Control Input Error (Bank 1)** Key on or engine running; and the PCM detected the IMRC Monitor signal for Bank 1 was outside of its expected calibrated range during the Continuous self test. **Note: Monitor the IMRC and IMRCM PIDs. The IMRCM state should change when the IMRC is commanded open or closed.** **Possible Causes:** • Mechanical concern - bind, seize, damage, or obstruction of IMRC hardware
DTC: P1517 **2T CCM, MIL: Yes** **Years:** 2008, 2009, 2010 **Models:** All **Engines:** All **Transmissions:** All	**Intake Manifold Runner Control Input Error (Bank 2)** Key on or engine running; and the PCM detected the IMRC Monitor signal for Bank 2 was outside of its expected calibrated range during the Continuous self test. **Note: Monitor the IMRC and IMRCM PIDs. The IMRCM state should change when the IMRC is commanded open or closed.** **Possible Causes:** • Mechanical concern - bind, seize, damage, or obstruction of IMRC hardware
DTC: P1518 **2T CCM, MIL: Yes** **Years:** 2008, 2009, 2010 **Models:** All **Engines:** All **Transmissions:** All	**Intake Manifold Runner Control (IMRC) Stuck Open (Bank 1)** Key on, and this DTC is set when the electrically actuated IMRC is commanded closed, but the IMRC monitor indicates open. **Note: Monitor the IMRC and IMRCM PIDs. The IMRCM state should change when the IMRC is commanded open or closed.** **Possible Causes:** • IMRC monitor signal circuit shorted to PWR GND or SIG RTN • Damaged IMRC actuator • PCM has failed

DTC	Trouble Code Title, Conditions & Possible Causes
DTC: P1519 **2T CCM, MIL: Yes** **Years:** 2008, 2009, 2010 **Models:** All **Engines:** All **Transmissions:** All	**Intake Manifold Runner Control (IMRC) Stuck Closed (Bank 1)** Key on or engine running; and this DTC is set when the electrically actuated IMRC is commanded open, but the IMRC monitor indicates closed. **Note: Monitor the IMRC and IMRCM PIDs. The IMRCM state should change when the IMRC is commanded open or closed.** **Possible Causes:** • IMRC monitor circuit open • IMRC control circuit open • IMRC monitor circuit short to VREF • IMRC monitor return circuit open • Damaged IMRC actuator • IMRC VPWR circuit open
DTC: P151A **2T CCM, MIL: Yes** **Years:** 2008, 2009, 2010 **Models:** All **Engines:** All **Transmissions:** All	**Intake Manifold Runner Controller Performance** Key on or engine running; the Intake Manifold Runner Control (IMRC) system is monitored for failures. The test fails when the system detects a loss of bi-directional communication or signal(s) between the PCM and the IMRC solenoid. **Note: View the IMRCF PID to monitor for a fault.** **Possible Causes:** • IMRC control circuit open • Mechanical concern - bind, seize, damage, or obstruction of IMRC hardware • IMRC control circuit short to voltage • IMRC VPWR circuit open • IMRC GND circuit open • Damaged IMRC actuator
DTC: P1520 **2T CCM, MIL: Yes** **Years:** 2008, 2009, 2010 **Models:** All **Engines:** All **Transmissions:** All	**Intake Manifold Runner Control (IMRC) Circuit** Key on or engine running; this DTC indicates a failure in the IMRC primary control circuit. **Note: Monitor the IMRC and IMRCM PIDs. The IMRCM state should change when the IMRC is commanded open or closed.** **Possible Causes:** • IMRC control circuit open • PCM has failed
DTC: P1537 **2T CCM, MIL: Yes** **Years:** 2008, 2009, 2010 **Models:** All **Engines:** All **Transmissions:** All	**Intake Manifold Runner Control Stuck Open (Bank 1)** Key on or engine running; and the PCM detected the Bank 1 IMRC Monitor signal was more than its expected calibrated range at closed throttle (it may be stuck in open position). An IMRCM PID of VREF at 3000 rpm may indicate a fault is present. **Note: Monitor the IMRC and IMRCM PIDs. The IMRCM state should change when the IMRC is commanded open or closed.** **Possible Causes:** • IMRC monitor signal circuit shorted to PWR GND or SIG RTN • Damaged IMRC solenoid • Blocked vacuum hoses • PCM has failed
DTC: P1538 **2T CCM, MIL: Yes** **Years:** 2008, 2009, 2010 **Models:** All **Engines:** All **Transmissions:** All	**Intake Manifold Runner Control Stuck Open (Bank 2)** Key on or engine running; and the PCM detected the Bank 2 IMRC Monitor signal was more than its expected calibrated range at closed throttle (it may be stuck in open position). An IMRCM PID of VREF at 3000 rpm may indicate a fault is present. **Note: Monitor the IMRC and IMRCM PIDs. The IMRCM state should change when the IMRC is commanded open or closed.** **Possible Causes:** • IMRC monitor signal circuit shorted to PWR GND or SIG RTN • Damaged IMRC solenoid • Blocked vacuum hoses • PCM has failed
DTC: P1548 **1T CCM, MIL: Yes** **Years:** 2008, 2009, 2010 **Models:** All **Engines:** All **Transmissions:** All	**Engine Air Filter Restriction** Key on or engine running and the PCM monitors the Manifold Absolute Pressure (MAP) at various engine speeds during Wide Open Throttle (WOT) operation, and compares the information to a calibrated value. If the air flow is out of range, the DTC is set. **Note: If this DTC is set, inspect the intake air system and replace the air filter if no obstructions are found.** **Possible Causes:** • Intake air restriction • Clogged air filter

DTC	Trouble Code Title, Conditions & Possible Causes
DTC: P1549 **1T CCM, MIL: No** **Years:** 2008, 2009, 2010 **Models:** All **Engines:** All **Transmissions:** All	**Intake Manifold Communication Control (IMCC) Circuit (Bank 1)** KOER Self-Test enabled, and the IMCC or Intake Manifold Tuning Valve (IMTV) system is monitored for failure during continuous or Key On Engine Off (KOEO) self-test. The test fails when the Powertrain Control Module (PCM) detects a concern with the IMTV output circuit. **Note: An IMTV fault PID (IMTVF) displaying YES may indicate a fault.** **Possible Causes:** • Open IMTV circuit • Open VPWR circuit • Shorted IMTV circuit • Damaged IMTV • PCM has failed
DTC: P1572 **2T CCM, MIL: Yes** **Years:** 2008, 2009, 2010 **Models:** All **Engines:** All **Transmissions:** All	**Brake Pedal Switch Circuit Malfunction** KOER Self-Test enabled, the brake input rationality test for Brake Pedal Position (BPP) and Brake Pressure Switch (BPS) has detected a concern. One or both inputs to the Powertrain Control Module (PCM) did not change state when expected. On some vehicles with stability assist, the BPP switch is connected to the Anti lock Brake System (ABS) module and the ABS generates a driver brake application signal, which is then sent to the PCM. **Note: DTC P1572 sets when the PCM does not sense the correct sequence of the brake pedal input signal from both the BPP and BPS switches when the brake pedal is pressed and released.** **Possible Causes:** • Misadjusted brake switches, BPP or BPS • Blown fuse • Damaged BPP switch • Damaged BPS switch • Open or short in the BPP circuit • Open or short in the DBA circuit • Open or short in the BPS circuit • PCM has failed
DTC: P1575 **2T CCM, MIL: Yes** **Years:** 2008, 2009, 2010 **Models:** All **Engines:** All **Transmissions:** All	**Pedal Position Out Of Self Test Range** During Key On Engine Off (KOEO) self-test, the Powertrain Control Module (PCM) monitors the Accelerator Pedal Position (APP) sensor inputs to determine if the APP1 and APP2 signals are less than an expected value. If either APP1 or APP2 is greater than the expected value, the DTC is set. **Note: Repeat the self-test without applying the accelerator pedal. Make sure the floor mat is not interfering with the accelerator pedal. Diagnose any APP circuit DTCs first.** **Possible Causes:** • Accelerator pedal applied during KOEO self-test • Damaged APP switch • Open or short in the APP circuit • Open or short in the APP circuit • Open or short in the APP circuit • PCM has failed
DTC: P1633 **1T PCM, MIL: Yes** **Years:** 2008, 2009, 2010 **Models:** All **Engines:** All **Transmissions:** All	**Keep Alive Power (KAPWR) Voltage Too Low** Key on, and the PCM detected that the KAPWR circuit has experienced a voltage interrupt. **Note: Loss of KAPWR to the Powertrain Control Module (PCM) results in immediate Malfunction Indicator Lamp (MIL) illumination and DTC P1633.** **Possible Causes:** • KAPWR circuit has been interrupted (this problem may be an intermittent condition) • PCM has failed
DTC: P1635 **1T PCM, MIL: Yes** **Years:** 2008, 2009, 2010 **Models:** All **Engines:** All **Transmissions:** All	**Tire Axle/Ratio Out Of Acceptable Range** Key on, and the PCM detected the tire and axle information in the VID Block does not match the vehicle hardware. **Note: This code indicates that the PCM needs to be reprogrammed.** **Possible Causes:** • Incorrect tire size or Incorrect axle ratio • Incorrect VID configuration parameters • PCM need to be reprogrammed
DTC: P1636 **1T PCM, MIL: Yes** **Years:** 2008, 2009, 2010 **Models:** All **Engines:** All **Transmissions:** All	**Inductive Signature Chip Communication Error** Key on, and the PCM determined it had lost communication with the Inductive Signature Chip. The PCM has internal damage when this trouble code is present. **Possible Causes:** • PCM has failed and needs to be replaced

DTC	Trouble Code Title, Conditions & Possible Causes

DTC: P1639
1T PCM, MIL: Yes
Years: 2008, 2009, 2010
Models: All
Engines: All
Transmissions: All
	Vehicle ID Block Not Programmed Or Is Corrupt
	Key on, and the PCM determined the Vehicle ID Block information was incorrect.
	Note: Program the PCM to the most recent calibration available.
	Possible Causes:
	    • PCM may not be the correct application
	    • PCM may need to be reprogrammed
	    • VID configuration may not be correct

DTC: P1640 **1T PCM, MIL: Yes** **Years:** 2008, 2009, 2010 **Models:** All **Engines:** All **Transmissions:** All	**Powertrain DTCs Available in Another Module** Engine started, and the PCM received a request from another module to turn on the MIL due to a fault that could affect emissions. **Note: Vehicles using a secondary Engine Control Module can request that the PCM turn on the Check Engine Light when a failure occurs that could affect emissions. Request PID 0946 to determine which module made the request. Then select that module to read the related trouble code(s).** **Possible Causes:** • Trouble codes are stored in a secondary module, which in turn, requested that the PCM turn on the MIL when this code is set.
DTC: P1646 **1T PCM, MIL: Yes** **Years:** 2008, 2009, 2010 **Models:** All **Engines:** All **Transmissions:** All	**Linear O2 Sensor Control Chip (Bank 1)** The Powertrain Control Module (PCM) monitors the application-specific integrated circuit that controls and monitors the Heated Oxygen Sensor (HO2S). The test fails when the PCM detects an internal circuit or communication concern. **Note: Internal PCM concern.** **Possible Causes:** • PCM has failed
DTC: P1647 **1T PCM, MIL: Yes** **Years:** 2008, 2009, 2010 **Models:** All **Engines:** All **Transmissions:** All	**Linear O2 Sensor Control Chip (Bank 2)** The Powertrain Control Module (PCM) monitors the application-specific integrated circuit that controls and monitors the Heated Oxygen Sensor (HO2S). The test fails when the PCM detects an internal circuit or communication concern. **Note: Internal PCM concern.** **Possible Causes:** • PCM has failed

DTC: P1650
2T CCM, MIL: Yes
Years: 2008, 2009, 2010
Models: All
Engines: All
Transmissions: All
	Power Steering Pressure (PSP) Switch Out of Self-Test Range
	Engine started, and the PCM detected the PSP switch signal did not change after a certain number of vehicle speed transitions. The PCM counts the number of times that the vehicle speed transitions from 0 mph to a calibrated speed. The PCM expects the PSP switch input to change after a certain number of transitions.
	Possible Causes:
	    • Steering wheel must be turned during the KOER Self-Test
	    • PSP switch/shorting bar is damaged
	    • PSP signal circuit is open or shorted to ground
	    • PSP circuit open or shorted to signal return
	    • PCM has failed

DTC: P1651
2T CCM, MIL: Yes
Years: 2008, 2009, 2010
Models: All
Engines: All
Transmissions: All
	Power Steering Pressure (PSP) Switch Input
	Engine started, and the PCM detected the PSP switch signal did not change after a certain number of vehicle speed transitions.
	Note: The PCM counts the number of times that the vehicle speed transitions from 0 mph to a calibrated speed. The PCM expects the PSP switch input to change after a certain number of transitions. Observe the PSP PID while checking the wires for intermittent concerns.
	Possible Causes:
	    • Vehicle towed with the engine running
	    • The power steering hydraulic concern was repaired but the DTC was not erased
	    • Steering wheel must be turned during the KOER Self-Test
	    • PSP switch/shorting bar is damaged
	    • PSP signal circuit is open or shorted to ground
	    • PSP switch ground (return) circuit is open
	    • PCM has failed

DTC: P1674
2T CCM, MIL: Yes
Years: 2008, 2009, 2010
Models: All
Engines: All
Transmissions: All
	Control Module Software Corrupted
	Engine started, and the PCM detected an error occurred in the Powertrain Control Module (PCM). This DTC is set in combination with P2105.
	Note: Verify the PCM is at the latest calibration level.
	Possible Causes:
	    • Software incompatibility issue
	    • PCM has failed

DTC	Trouble Code Title, Conditions & Possible Causes

DTC: P1703
1T CCM, MIL: No
Years: 2008, 2009, 2010
Models: All
Engines: All
Transmissions: A/T
	Brake Switch Circuit Out of Self-Test Range
	Key on, KOEO Self-Test enabled; and the PCM detected the brake switch signal was high, or with the KOER Self-Test enabled, the PCM detected the switch signal did not cycle On / Off.
	Note: Check for correct function of the stoplamps. Using the scan tool, check the BPP PID. The stoplamps and PID should toggle on and off with brake pedal activation.
	Possible Causes:
	    • Open or short in the BPP circuit
	    • Open or short in the stoplamp circuits
	    • Concern in module(s) connected to the BPP circuit
	    • Damaged brake switch
	    • Incorrectly adjusted brake switch

DTC: P1705
1T CCM, MIL: No
Years: 2008, 2009, 2010
Models: All
Engines: All
Transmissions: A/T
	Transmission Range Sensor Out of Self-Test Range
	Key on, KOEO Self Test enabled, and the PCM detected it did not receive a Transmission Range (TR) sensor signal in Park or Neutral position.
	Possible Causes:
	    • Gear selector not in Park or Neutral during the self-test
	    • Digital TR sensor circuit is open or shorted to ground
	    • Digital TR sensor has failed
	    • PCM has failed

DTC: P1709
1T CCM, MIL: No
Years: 2008, 2009, 2010
Models: All
Engines: All
Transmissions: A/T
	Park/Neutral Position (PNP) Switch Out of Self-Test Range
	Key on, KOEO Self-Test enabled, and the PCM detected the PNP switch was high when is should have been low (wrong gearshift position).
	Note: When activating the PNP or CPP switch, the voltage should cycle from 5 volts to low.
	Possible Causes:
	    • Damaged PNP or Clutch Pedal Position (CPP) switch
	    • PNP/CPP circuit short to PWR
	    • PNP/CPP circuit open in the SIGRTN
	    • PCM has failed

DTC: P1710 **2T CCM, MIL: Yes** **Years:** 2008, 2009, 2010 **Models:** All **Engines:** All **Transmissions:** A/T	**TFT Sensor In-Range Circuit Malfunction** Engine started, vehicle driven to a speed over 1 mph, TFT sensor signal in-range, and the PCM did not detect any change in the TFT signal in the self-test. **Possible Causes:** • Refer to the appropriate Transmission Repair Manual or information in electronic media to perform a complete diagnosis of the automatic transmission when this code is set
DTC: P1711 **1T CCM, MIL: No** **Years:** 2008, 2009, 2010 **Models:** All **Engines:** All **Transmissions:** A/T	**TFT Sensor Out of Self-Test Range** Key on, KOER Self Test enabled; or engine running with the KOER Self Test enabled, and the PCM detected the Transmission Fluid Temperature (TFT) sensor was more than or less than the calibrated range (25°F to 240°F) during the self-test. **Possible Causes:** • Refer to the appropriate Transmission Repair Manual or information in electronic media to perform a complete diagnosis of the automatic transmission when this code is set
DTC: P1712 **1T CCM, MIL: No** **Years:** 2008, 2009, 2010 **Models:** All **Engines:** All **Transmissions:** A/T	**TFT Sensor Circuit Low Input** Engine started, and the PCM detected the TFT sensor signal was less than 0.2v (equivalent to a temperature of more than 357°F). **Possible Causes:** • Refer to the appropriate Transmission Repair Manual or information in electronic media to perform a complete diagnosis of the automatic transmission when this code is set
DTC: P1713 **1T CCM, MIL: No** **Years:** 2008, 2009, 2010 **Models:** All Models **Engines:** All **Transmissions:** A/T	**TFT Sensor No Activity or TFT Sensor Circuit Low Input** Engine started, VSS over 1 mph, and the PCM did not detect any change in the TFT low range circuit during the self-test. **Possible Causes:** • Refer to the appropriate Transmission Repair Manual or information in electronic media to perform a complete diagnosis of the automatic transmission when this code is set
DTC: P1714 **1T CCM, MIL: Yes** **Years:** 2008, 2009, 2010 **Models:** All **Engines:** All **Transmissions:** A/T	**Transmission Control System Malfunction** Engine started, VSS over 1 mph, and the PCM did not detect any change in the TFT low range circuit during the self-test. **Possible Causes:** • Refer to the appropriate Transmission Repair Manual or information in electronic media to perform a complete diagnosis of the automatic transmission when this code is set

DTC	Trouble Code Title, Conditions & Possible Causes
DTC: P1715 **1T CCM, MIL: Yes** **Years:** 2008, 2009, 2010 **Models:** All **Engines:** All **Transmissions:** A/T	**Transmission Control System Malfunction** Engine started, VSS over 1 mph, and the PCM detected a mechanical problem in the Shift Solenoid 'B' (SSB) during the test. **Possible Causes:** • Refer to the appropriate Transmission Repair Manual or information in electronic media to perform a complete diagnosis of the automatic transmission when this code is set
DTC: P1716 **2T CCM, MIL: No** **Years:** 2008, 2009, 2010 **Models:** All **Engines:** All **Transmissions:** A/T	**Transmission Control System Malfunction** Engine started, VSS over 1 mph, and the PCM detected a problem in the Transmission Control system during the self-test. **Possible Causes:** • Refer to the appropriate Transmission Repair Manual or information in electronic media to perform a complete diagnosis of the automatic transmission when this code is set
DTC: P1717 **1T CCM, MIL: No** **Years:** 2008, 2009, 2010 **Models:** All Models **Engines:** All **Transmissions:** A/T	**Transmission Control System Malfunction** Engine started, VSS over 1 mph, and the PCM detected a problem in the Transmission Control system during the self-test. **Possible Causes:** • Refer to the appropriate Transmission Repair Manual or information in electronic media to perform a complete diagnosis of the automatic transmission when this code is set
DTC: P1718 **1T CCM, MIL: No** **Years:** 2008, 2009, 2010 **Models:** All **Engines:** All **Transmissions:** A/T	**TFT Sensor No Activity Or TFT Sensor Circuit High Input** Engine started, VSS over 1 mph, and the PCM did not detect any change in the TFT high range circuit during the self-test. **Possible Causes:** • Refer to the appropriate Transmission Repair Manual or information in electronic media to perform a complete diagnosis of the automatic transmission when this code is set
DTC: P1719 **1T CCM, MIL: No** **Years:** 2008, 2009, 2010 **Models:** All **Engines:** All **Transmissions:** A/T	**Transmission Control System Malfunction** Engine started, VSS over 1 mph, and the PCM detected a problem in the Transmission Control system during the self-test. **Possible Causes:** • Refer to the appropriate Transmission Repair Manual or information in electronic media to perform a complete diagnosis of the automatic transmission when this code is set
DTC: P1727 **1T CCM, MIL: No** **Years:** 2008, 2009, 2010 **Models:** All **Engines:** All **Transmissions:** A/T	**Transmission Coast Clutch Solenoid Slip Malfunction** Engine started, VSS over 1 mph in gear, and the PCM detected a signal that indicated the coast clutch solenoid had a slippage fault. **Possible Causes:** • Refer to the appropriate Transmission Repair Manual or information in electronic media to perform a complete diagnosis of the automatic transmission when this code is set
DTC: P1728 **1T CCM, MIL: No** **Years:** 2008, 2009, 2010 **Models:** All **Engines:** All **Transmissions:** A/T	**Transmission Slip Malfunction** Engine started, VSS over 1 mph in gear, and the PCM detected a signal that indicated the transmission was slipping while in gear. **Possible Causes:** • Refer to the appropriate Transmission Repair Manual or information in electronic media to perform a complete diagnosis of the automatic transmission when this code is set
DTC: P1729 **1T CCM, MIL: No** **Years:** 2008, 2009, 2010 **Models:** All with 4WD **Engines:** All **Transmissions:** A/T	**4x4 Low Switch Circuit Malfunction** Engine running, the Powertrain Control Module (PCM) does not sense appropriate voltage when the switch is cycled on and off, a DTC sets for Mechanical Shift On The Fly (MSOF) systems. **Note: Verify the 4x4L switch cycles on/off.** **Possible Causes:** • The 4x4L harness between the PCM and the 4x4L switch is open or shorted • Damaged 4x4L switch • Electronic Shift Control Module is damaged or has failed, or the PCM has failed
DTC: P1740 **1T CCM, MIL: Yes** **Years:** 2008, 2009, 2010 **Models:** All Models **Engines:** All **Transmissions:** A/T	**Torque Conveter Clutch (TCC) Solenoid Mechanical Malfunction** Engine started, vehicle speed more than 20 mph, and the PCM detected that TCC lockup did not occur (the lockup event is inferred from other inputs). **Possible Causes:** • Refer to the appropriate Transmission Repair Manual or information in electronic media to perform a complete diagnosis of the automatic transmission when this code is set

DTC	Trouble Code Title, Conditions & Possible Causes
DTC: P1741 **1T CCM, MIL: No** **Years:** 2008, 2009, 2010 **Models:** All Models **Engines:** All **Transmissions:** A/T	**Torque Conveter Clutch (TCC) Engagement Error** Engine started, vehicle in gear at Cruise speed, and the PCM detected an error due to excessive TCC engagement. **Note: This problem can cause speed changes or vehicle surges.** **Possible Causes:** • Refer to the appropriate Transmission Repair Manual or information in electronic media to perform a complete diagnosis of the automatic transmission when this code is set
DTC: P1742 **1T CCM, MIL: Yes** **Years:** 2008, 2009, 2010 **Models:** All Models **Engines:** All **Transmissions:** A/T	**Torque Conveter Clutch (TCC) Solenoid Failed On (Electrical Or Mechanical Fault)** Engine started, vehicle in gear at Cruise speed, and the PCM detected that the Torque Converter Clutch system had failed "on". **Possible Causes:** • Refer to the appropriate Transmission Repair Manual or information in electronic media to perform a complete diagnosis of the automatic transmission when this code is set.
DTC: P1744 **1T CCM, MIL: Yes** **Years:** 2008, 2009, 2010 **Models:** All Models **Engines:** All **Transmissions:** A/T	**Torque Conveter Clutch (TCC) System Mechanically Stuck In Off Position** Engine started, vehicle in gear at Cruise speed, and the PCM detected the Torque Converter Clutch system had failed with the TCC in the mechanically "off" position. **Possible Causes:** • Refer to the appropriate Transmission Repair Manual or information in electronic media to perform a complete diagnosis of the automatic transmission when this code is set.

DTC: P1780
1T CCM, MIL: No
Years: 2008, 2009, 2010
Models: All
Engines: All
Transmissions: A/T
	Transmission Control Switch Out of Self-Test Range
	Engine started, KOER Self-Test enabled, and the PCM detected the Transmission Control Switch (TCS) was out of range during the test.
	Note: Verify the TCS switch cycles on/off.
	Possible Causes:
	   • TCS circuit open or shorted in the wiring harness
	   • TCS not cycled during the self-test
	   • TCS is damaged
	   • PCM has failed

DTC: P1781
1T CCM, MIL: No
Years: 2008, 2009, 2010
Models: All with 4WD
Engines: All
Transmissions: All
	4x4 Low Switch Out Of Self-Test Range
	Key on, KOEO Self-Test enabled, and the PCM detected the 4x4 switch input was not low with the switch engaged or "on".
	Note: Verify the 4x4L switch cycles on/off.
	Possible Causes:
	   • 4x4L switch circuit is open or shorted in the wiring harness
	   • Electronic Shift Module is damaged or has failed
	   • PCM has failed

DTC: P1783 **1T CCM, MIL: No** **Years:** 2008, 2009, 2010 **Models:** All **Engines:** All **Transmissions:** A/T	**Transmission Over-Temperature Malfunction** Engine started, engine runtime more than 5 minutes, vehicle in gear at Cruise speed, and the PCM detected the TFT sensor signal was more than 300°F during the CCM test period. **Possible Causes:** • Refer to the appropriate Transmission Repair Manual or information in electronic media to perform a complete diagnosis of the automatic transmission when this code is set.
DTC: P1784 **1T CCM, MIL: No** **Years:** 2008, 2009, 2010 **Models:** All **Engines:** All **Transmissions:** A/T	**Transmission System First Or Reverse Gear Malfunction** Engine started, vehicle speed over 1 mph in gear, shift command received for First or Reverse gear, and the PCM detected a problem in the Transmission Control system. **Possible Causes:** • Refer to the appropriate Transmission Repair Manual or information in electronic media to perform a complete diagnosis of the automatic transmission when this code is set.
DTC: P1785 **1T CCM, MIL: No** **Years:** 2008, 2009, 2010 **Models:** All **Engines:** All **Transmissions:** A/T	**Transmission System First Or Second Gear Malfunction** Engine started, vehicle speed over 1 mph in gear, shift command received for First or Second gear, and the PCM detected a problem in the Transmission Control system during the test. **Possible Causes:** • Refer to the appropriate Transmission Repair Manual or information in electronic media to perform a complete diagnosis of the automatic transmission when this code is set
DTC: P1786 **1T CCM, MIL: No** **Years:** 2008, 2009, 2010 **Models:** All **Engines:** All **Transmissions:** A/T	**Transmission System Second Or Third Gear Malfunction** Engine started, vehicle speed over 1 mph in gear, shift command received for Second or Third gear, and the PCM detected a problem in the Transmission Control system. **Possible Causes:** • Refer to the appropriate Transmission Repair Manual or information in electronic media to perform a complete diagnosis of the automatic transmission when this code is set.

DTC	Trouble Code Title, Conditions & Possible Causes
DTC: P1787 **1T CCM, MIL: No** **Years:** 2008, 2009, 2010 **Models:** All **Engines:** All **Transmissions:** A/T	**Transmission System Third Or Fourth Gear Malfunction** Engine started, vehicle speed over 1 mph in gear, shift command received for Third or Fourth gear, and the PCM detected a problem in the Transmission Control system during the test. **Possible Causes:** • Refer to the appropriate Transmission Repair Manual or information in electronic media to perform a complete diagnosis of the automatic transmission when this code is set.
DTC: P1788 **1T CCM, MIL: No** **Years:** 2008, 2009, 2010 **Models:** All **Engines:** All **Transmissions:** A/T	**3-2 Timing/Coast Clutch Solenoid Signal High Input** Engine started, vehicle in gear at Cruise speed, and the PCM detected the malfunction 3-2 Timing or Coast Clutch solenoid circuit. **Possible Causes:** • 3-2 Timing or Coast Clutch solenoid circuit open or grounded, or the solenoid has failed • Coast Clutch solenoid is damaged or has failed
DTC: P1789 **1T CCM, MIL: No** **Years:** 2008, 2009, 2010 **Models:** All **Engines:** All **Transmissions:** A/T	**3-2 Timing/Coast Clutch Solenoid Signal Low Input** Engine started, vehicle in gear at Cruise speed, and the PCM detected the malfunction 3-2 Timing or Coast Clutch solenoid circuit. **Possible Causes:** • 3-2 Timing or Coast Clutch solenoid circuit is shorted • 3-2 Timing solenoid is damaged or has failed • Coast Clutch solenoid is damaged or has failed
DTC: P1900 **1T CCM, MIL: No** **Years:** 2008, 2009, 2010 **Models:** All **Engines:** All **Transmissions:** A/T	**Output Shaft Speed (OSS) Sensor Circuit Intermittent** The OSS sensor signal to the Powertrain Control Module (PCM) is irregular or interrupted. **Note: Verify harness and connector integrity. Verify correct installation of the OSS sensor** **Possible Causes:** • Harness connector not correctly seated • Harness intermittently shorted or open • Harness connector damaged • OSS sensor damaged, or not installed correctly
DTC: P1901 **1T CCM, MIL: No** **Years:** 2008, 2009, 2010 **Models:** All **Engines:** All **Transmissions:** A/T	**Turbine Shaft Speed (TSS) Sensor Circuit Intermittent** The TSS sensor signal to the Powertrain Control Module (PCM) is irregular or interrupted. **Note: Verify harness and connector integrity. Verify correct installation of the OSS sensor.** **Possible Causes:** • Harness connector not correctly seated • Harness intermittently shorted or open • Harness connector damaged • TSS sensor damaged or not installed correctly
DTC: P1910 **1T CCM, MIL: No** **Years:** 2008, 2009, 2010 **Models:** All **Engines:** All **Transmissions:** All	**Reverse Lamp Control Circuit/Open** Engine started, vehicle in reverse, and the PCM detected no backup lamps. Backup lamp driver control circuit failed. **Possible Causes:** • Blown fuse • Wiring, terminals or connectors • Reversing lamps relay • Reversing lamp switch (manual transmission) • TCM has failed • PCM has failed

Gas Engine OBD II Trouble Code List (P2xxx Codes)

DTC	Trouble Code Title, Conditions & Possible Causes
DTC: P2004 **1T CCM, MIL: Yes** **Years:** 2008, 2009, 2010 **Models:** All **Engines:** All **Transmissions:** All	**Intake Manifold Runner Control (IMRC) Stuck Open (Bank 1)** This DTC is set when the IMRC is commanded closed, but the IMRC monitor indicates open. **Note: Monitor the IMRC and IMRCM PIDs. The IMRCM state should change when the IMRC is commanded open or closed** **Possible Causes:** • IMRC monitor signal circuit shorted to PWR GND or SIG RTN • Damaged IMRC actuator or solenoid • Blocked vacuum hoses

DTC	Trouble Code Title, Conditions & Possible Causes
DTC: P2005 **1T CCM, MIL: Yes** **Years:** 2008, 2009, 2010 **Models:** All **Engines:** All **Transmissions:** All	**Intake Manifold Runner Control (IMRC) Stuck Open (Bank 2)** This DTC is set when the IMRC is commanded closed, but the IMRC monitor indicates open. **Note: An IMRCM PID reading near approximately 1 volt at closed throttle may indicate a fault** **Possible Causes:** • IMRC monitor signal circuit shorted to PWR GND or SIG RTN • Damaged IMRC actuator or solenoid • Blocked vacuum hoses • PCM has failed
DTC: P2006 **1T CCM, MIL: Yes** **Years:** 2008, 2009, 2010 **Models:** All **Engines:** All **Transmissions:** All	**Intake Manifold Runner Control (IMRC) Stuck Closed (Bank 1)** This DTC is set when the IMRC is commanded open, but the IMRC monitor indicates closed. **Note: Monitor the IMRC and IMRCM PIDs. The IMRCM state should change when the IMRC is commanded open or closed.** **Possible Causes:** • IMRC monitor circuit open • IMRC control circuit open • IMRC monitor circuit short to VREF • Damaged IMRC actuator or solenoid
DTC: P2007 **1T CCM, MIL: Yes** **Years:** 2008, 2009, 2010 **Models:** All **Engines:** All **Transmissions:** All	**Intake Manifold Runner Control (IMRC) Stuck Closed (Bank 2)** Engine started, engine running the PCM detected the IMRC is commanded open, but the IMRC monitor indicates closed. **Possible Causes:** • IMRC monitor circuit open • IMRC control circuit open • IMRC monitor circuit short to VREF • Damaged IMRC actuator or solenoid
DTC: P2008 **1T CCM, MIL: Yes** **Years:** 2008, 2009, 2010 **Models:** All **Engines:** All **Transmissions:** All	**Intake Manifold Runner Control (IMRC) Circuit Open (Bank 1)** Engine started, engine running the PCM detected a failure in the IMRC primary control circuit. **Note: Monitor the IMRC and IMRCM PIDs. The IMRCM state should change when the IMRC is commanded open or closed.** **Possible Causes:** • IMRC monitor circuit open
DTC: P2014 **1T CCM, MIL: Yes** **Years:** 2008, 2009, 2010 **Models:** All **Engines:** All **Transmissions:** All	**Intake Manifold Runner Position Sensor/Switch Circuit (Bank 1)** The Intake Manifold Runner Control (IMRC) system is monitored for failure during continuous or Key On Engine Off (KOEO) self-test. Each DTC distinguishes the corresponding bank for IMRC actuator assemblies with dual monitor switches. The test fails when the signal on the monitor pin is outside an expected calibrated range. **Note: Monitor the IMRC and IMRCM PIDs. The IMRCM state should change when the IMRC is commanded open or closed.** **Possible Causes:** • IMRC monitor circuit open • Mechanical concern - bind, seize, damage or obstruction of IMRC hardware
DTC: P2015 **1T CCM, MIL: Yes** **Years:** 2008, 2009, 2010 **Models:** All **Engines:** All **Transmissions:** All	**Intake Manifold Runner Position Sensor/Switch Circuit Range/Performance (Bank 1)** The Intake Manifold Runner Control (IMRC) system is monitored for failures. Each DTC distinguishes the corresponding bank. The test fails when the system detects the presence of a broken or persistently out of range linkage. **Possible Causes:** • Mechanical concern - bind, seize, damage, or obstruction of IMRC hardware
DTC: P2019 **1T CCM, MIL: Yes** **Years:** 2008, 2009, 2010 **Models:** All **Engines:** All **Transmissions:** All	**Intake Manifold Runner Position Sensor/Switch Circuit (Bank 2)** The Intake Manifold Runner Control (IMRC) system is monitored for failure during continuous or Key On Engine Off (KOEO) self-test. Each DTC distinguishes the corresponding bank for IMRC actuator assemblies with dual monitor switches. The test fails when the signal on the monitor pin is outside an expected calibrated range. **Note: Monitor the IMRC and IMRCM PIDs. The IMRCM state should change when the IMRC is commanded open or closed.** **Possible Causes:** • IMRC monitor circuit open • Mechanical concern - bind, seize, damage, or obstruction of IMRC hardware
DTC: P2020 **1T CCM, MIL: Yes** **Years:** 2008, 2009, 2010 **Models:** All **Engines:** All **Transmissions:** All	**Intake Manifold Runner Position Sensor/Switch Circuit Range/Performance (Bank 2)** The Intake Manifold Runner Control (IMRC) system is monitored for failures. Each DTC distinguishes the corresponding bank. The test fails when the system detects the presence of a broken or persistently out of range linkage. **Possible Causes:** • Mechanical concern - bind, seize, damage, or obstruction of IMRC hardware

DTC	Trouble Code Title, Conditions & Possible Causes
DTC: P2065 **1T CCM, MIL: Yes** **Years:** 2008, 2009, 2010 **Models:** All **Engines:** All **Transmissions:** All	**Fuel Level Sensor B Circuit** Fuel level information is sent to the Powertrain Control Module (PCM) on the communication link. **Possible Causes:** • Communication link concern • Damaged Instrument Panel Cluster (IPC) (E-Series) • Damaged Instrument Cluster (IC) • Damaged PCM
DTC: P2066 **1T CCM, MIL: Yes** **Years:** 2008, 2009, 2010 **Models:** All **Engines:** All **Transmissions:** All	**Fuel Level Sensor B Circuit Range/Performance** Fuel level information is sent to the Powertrain Control Module (PCM) on the communication link. **Possible Causes:** • Communication link concern • Damaged Instrument Panel Cluster (IPC) (E-Series) • Damaged Instrument Cluster (IC) • Damaged PCM
DTC: P2067 **1T CCM, MIL: Yes** **Years:** 2008, 2009, 2010 **Models:** All **Engines:** All **Transmissions:** All	**Fuel Level Sensor B Circuit Low** Fuel level information is sent to the Powertrain Control Module (PCM) on the communication link. **Possible Causes:** • Communication link concern • Damaged Instrument Panel Cluster (IPC) (E-Series) • Damaged Instrument Cluster (IC) • Damaged PCM
DTC: P2068 **1T CCM, MIL:Yes** **Years:** 2008, 2009, 2010 **Models:** All **Engines:** All **Transmissions:** All	**Fuel Level Sensor B Circuit High** Fuel level information is sent to the Powertrain Control Module (PCM) on the communication link. **Possible Causes:** • Communication link concern • Damaged Instrument Panel Cluster (IPC) (E-Series) • Damaged Instrument Cluster (IC) • Damaged PCM
DTC: P2070 **2T CCM, MIL: Yes** **Years:** 2008, 2009, 2010 **Models:** All **Engines:** All **Transmissions:** All	**Intake Manifold Tuning Valve (IMTV) Stuck Open (Bank 1)** The IMTV system is monitored for failure during continuous, Key On Engine Off (KOEO), or Key On Engine Running (KOER) self-tests. The test fails when the signal is more or less than an expected calibrated range. **Note: An IMTVM PID reading may indicate a fault.** **Possible Causes:** • IMTV signal circuit shorted to PWR GND or SIG RTN • Damaged IMRC actuator • PCM has failed
DTC: P2071 **2T CCM, MIL: Yes** **Years:** 2008, 2009, 2010 **Models:** All **Engines:** All **Transmissions:** All	**Intake Manifold Tuning Valve (IMTV) Stuck Closed Bank 1** The IMTV system is monitored for failure during continuous, Key On Engine Off (KOEO), or Key On Engine Running (KOER) self-tests. The test fails when the signal is more or less than an expected calibrated range. **Note: An IMTVM PID reading may indicate a fault.** **Possible Causes:** • IMTV signal circuit shorted to PWR GND or SIG RTN • Damaged IMRC actuator • IMTV circuit open • PCM has failed
DTC: P2072 **2T CCM, MIL: Yes** **Years:** 2008, 2009, 2010 **Models:** All **Engines:** All **Transmissions:** All	**Throttle Actuator Control (TAC) System (Ice Breakage)** This DTC only identifies that the strategy has carried out several open and close cycles to remove potential ice build up. This DTC does not imply any system concerns, only that the mode has occurred, and that mode may be causing a long start time. **Note: Do not install a new Electronic Throttle Body (ETB) for this DTC. Check the PCV system for evidence of water or ice. Disconnect the intake air fresh air plenum from the throttle body. Check for water or oily residue at the PCV fresh air port. Disconnect the tube at the valve cover and check the tube for ice obstruction/ice. Start the engine and, to check the PCV system, place a piece of cardboard on the crankcase vent in the rocker cover. If the cardboard is held on the crankcase vent and fumes are not exiting, reconnect the tube to the valve cover and the intake air port. If the test passes, the PCV system is OK. If the cardboard is not held in place, turn off the engine and check the PCV valve side of the system for ice or obstruction and repair as necessary. If no obstruction is found there, isolate and repair any obstruction in the intake manifold connection. If no obstruction is found there, make sure the PCV coolant heater is functional and repair as necessary. If no concern is present, make sure the PCV valve is allowing the correct vacuum flow and repair as necessary.** **Possible Causes:** • Ice or oil in the intake air system could be the result of a Positive Crankcase Ventilation (PCV) system concern

DTC	Trouble Code Title, Conditions & Possible Causes
DTC: P2096 **2T CCM, MIL: Yes** Years: 2008, 2009, 2010 Models: All Models Engines: All Transmissions: All	**Post Catalyst Fuel Trim System Too Lean (Bank 1)** The Powertrain Control Module (PCM) monitors the correction value from downstream Heated Oxygen Sensor (HO2S) as part of the fore-aft oxygen sensor control routine. The test fails when the correction value is greater than a calibrated limit. **Possible Causes:** • Loose connection, and damaged or corroded terminals • Exhaust leaks • Contaminated HO2S
DTC: P2097 **2T CCM, MIL: Yes** Years: 2008, 2009, 2010 Models: All Engines: All Transmissions: All	**Post Catalyst Fuel Trim System Too Rich (Bank 1)** The Powertrain Control Module (PCM) monitors the correction value from downstream Heated Oxygen Sensor (HO2S) as part of the fore-aft oxygen sensor control routine. The test fails when the correction value is greater than a calibrated limit. **Possible Causes:** • Loose connection, and damaged or corroded terminals • Exhaust leaks • Contaminated HO2S
DTC: P2098 **2T CCM, MIL: Yes** Years: 2008, 2009, 2010 Models: All Engines: All Transmissions: All	**Post Catalyst Fuel Trim System Too Lean (Bank 2)** The Powertrain Control Module (PCM) monitors the correction value from downstream Heated Oxygen Sensor (HO2S) as part of the fore-aft oxygen sensor control routine. The test fails when the correction value is greater than a calibrated limit. **Possible Causes:** • Loose connection, and damaged or corroded terminals • Exhaust leaks • Contaminated HO2S
DTC: P2099 **2T CCM, MIL: Yes** Years: 2008, 2009, 2010 Models: All Engines: All Transmissions: All	**Post Catalyst Fuel Trim System Too Rich (Bank 2)** The Powertrain Control Module (PCM) monitors the correction value from downstream Heated Oxygen Sensor (HO2S) as part of the fore-aft oxygen sensor control routine. The test fails when the correction value is greater than a calibrated limit. **Possible Causes:** • Loose connection, and damaged or corroded terminals • Exhaust leaks • Contaminated HO2S
DTC: P2100 **2T CCM, MIL: Yes** Years: 2008, 2009, 2010 Models: All Engines: All Transmissions: All	**Throttle Actuator Control (TAC) Motor Circuit/Open** A Powertrain Control Module (PCM) fault flag is set indicating the motor circuit is open. May require cycling the key. **Note: A TAC motor circuit PID reading may indicate a concern, if available.** **Possible Causes:** • TAC motor has an open winding • TAC motor is damaged • TAC motor harness is open • TAC motor harness is short to PWR • TAC motor harness circuits are short together • TAC motor harness connector is unplugged
DTC: P2101 **2T CCM, MIL: Yes** Years: 2008, 2009, 2010 Models: All Engines: All Transmissions: All	**Throttle Actuator Control (TAC) Motor Range/Performance** A Powertrain Control Module (PCM) fault flag is set indicating the motor circuit is open, and may require cycling the key. **Note: A TAC motor circuit PID reading may indicate a concern, if available.** **Possible Causes:** • TAC motor circuits are cross-wired
DTC: P2104 **2T CCM, MIL: Yes** Years: 2008, 2009, 2010 Models: All Engines: All Transmissions: All	**Throttle Actuator Control (TAC) System (Forced Idle)** The TAC system is in the Failure Mode Effects Management (FMEM) mode of forced idle. **Note: This DTC is an informational DTC and may be set in combination with a number of other DTCs which are causing the FMEM. Diagnose other DTCs first.** **Possible Causes:** • Air cleaner and air inlet are not correctly seated • Check for self-test DTCs in all of the vehicle modules. • Accelerator Pedal Position (APP) sensor • Throttle Position (TP) sensor • Manifold Absolute Pressure (MAP) sensor • PCM has failed

DTC	Trouble Code Title, Conditions & Possible Causes
DTC: P2105 **2T CCM, MIL: Yes** **Years:** 2008, 2009, 2010 **Models:** All **Engines:** All **Transmissions:** All	**Throttle Actuator Control (TAC) System (Forced Engine Shutdown)** The TAC system is in the Failure Mode Effects Management (FMEM) mode of forced idle. **Note: This DTC is an informational DTC and may be set in combination with a number of other DTCs which are causing the FMEM. Diagnose other DTCs first.** **Possible Causes:** • Air cleaner and air inlet are not correctly seated • Check for self-test DTCs in all of the vehicle modules. • Accelerator Pedal Position (APP) sensor • Throttle Position (TP) sensor • Manifold Absolute Pressure (MAP) sensor • PCM has failed
DTC: P2107 **2T CCM, MIL: Yes** **Years:** 2008, 2009, 2010 **Models:** All **Engines:** All **Transmissions:** All	**Throttle Actuator Control (TAC) Module Processor** The Electronic Throttle Control (ETC) area of the Powertrain Control Module (PCM) failed the self-test. The concern could be the result of an incorrect Throttle Position (TP) command, or TAC motor wires shorted together. **Note: This DTC may be accompanied by other DTCs. If DTC P2110 is present along with other DTCs, disregard DTCs P2107 and P2110 at this time. Diagnose other DTCs first. A TAC motor circuit PID reading may indicate a concern, if available.** **Possible Causes:** • TAC motor harness circuit short to ground • TAC motor harness circuit short to voltage • Damaged Electronic Throttle Body (ETB) • PCM has failed
DTC: P2110 **2T CCM, MIL: Yes** **Years:** 2008, 2009, 2010 **Models:** All **Engines:** All **Transmissions:** All	**Throttle Actuator Control (TAC) System (Forced Limited RPM)** The TAC system is in the Failure Mode Effects Management (FMEM) mode of forced limited RPM. **Note: This DTC is an informational DTC and may be set in combination with a number of other DTCs which are causing the FMEM. Diagnose other DTCs first.** **Possible Causes:** • Air cleaner and air inlet are not correctly seated • Check for self-test DTCs in all of the vehicle modules. • Accelerator Pedal Position (APP) sensor • Throttle Position (TP) sensor • Manifold Absolute Pressure (MAP) sensor • PCM has failed
DTC: P2111 **2T CCM, MIL: Yes** **Years:** 2008, 2009, 2010 **Models:** All **Engines:** All **Transmissions:** All	**Throttle Actuator Control (TAC) System (Stuck Open)** This Powertrain Control Module (PCM) fault status indicates the throttle plate is at a greater angle than commanded. **Possible Causes:** • Binding throttle body, stuck open • TAC motor circuit open • TAC motor circuits are cross-wired • TAC motor harness circuits are shorted together • PCM has failed
DTC: P2112 **2T CCM, MIL: Yes** **Years:** 2008, 2009, 2010 **Models:** All **Engines:** All **Transmissions:** All	**Throttle Actuator Control (TAC) System - Stuck Closed** This Powertrain Control Module (PCM) fault status indicates the throttle plate is at a lower angle than commanded. **Possible Causes:** • Binding throttle body, stuck open • TAC motor circuit open • TAC motor circuits are cross-wired • TAC motor harness circuits are shorted together • PCM has failed
DTC: P2121 **2T CCM, MIL: Yes** **Years:** 2008, 2009, 2010 **Models:** All **Engines:** All **Transmissions:** All	**Throttle/Pedal Position Sensor/Switch D Circuit Range/Performance** The Accelerator Pedal Position (APP) sensor fault flag is set for sensor 1 by the Powertrain Control Module (PCM), indicating the signal is out of the normal self-test operating range. **Note: An APP1 sensor PID reading may indicate a concern.** **Possible Causes:** • APP sensor 1 is open, or short to ground or voltage • APP sensor signal circuits are short together • Damaged APP sensor • PCM has failed

DTC	Trouble Code Title, Conditions & Possible Causes
DTC: P2122 **2T CCM, MIL: Yes** **Years:** 2008, 2009, 2010 **Models:** All **Engines:** All **Transmissions:** All	**Throttle/Pedal Position Sensor/Switch D Circuit Low** The Accelerator Pedal Position (APP) sensor 1 is out of self-test range low. **Note: An APP1 sensor PID reading may indicate a concern.** **Possible Causes:** • APP sensor harness open (ETC system with a 2-track APP sensor) • APP sensor harness short to ground • Damaged APP sensor • PCM has failed
DTC: P2123 **2T CCM, MIL: Yes** **Years:** 2008, 2009, 2010 **Models:** All **Engines:** All **Transmissions:** All	**Throttle/Pedal Position Sensor/Switch D Circuit High** The accelerator pedal position (APP) sensor 1 is out of self-test range high. **Note: An APP1 sensor PID reading may indicate a concern.** **Possible Causes:** • APP sensor harness open (ETC system with a 3-track APP sensor) • APP sensor harness is short to VREF • Damaged APP sensor • PCM has failed
DTC: P2126 **2T CCM, MIL: Yes** **Years:** 2008, 2009, 2010 **Models:** All **Engines:** All **Transmissions:** All	**Throttle/Pedal Position Sensor/Switch E Circuit Range/Performance** The Accelerator Pedal Position (APP) sensor fault flag is set for sensor 2 by the Powertrain Control Module (PCM), indicating the signal is out of the normal self-test operating range. **Note: An APP2 sensor PID reading may indicate a concern.** **Possible Causes:** • APP sensor assembly is binding • Damaged APP sensor • PCM has failed
DTC: P2127 **2T CCM, MIL: Yes** **Years:** 2008, 2009, 2010 **Models:** All **Engines:** All **Transmissions:** All	**Throttle/Pedal Position Sensor/Switch E Circuit Low** The Accelerator Pedal Position (APP) sensor 2 is out of self-test range low. **Note: An APP2 sensor PID reading may indicate a concern.** **Possible Causes:** • APP sensor circuit is short to ground • APP sensor circuit is open • Damaged APP sensor • PCM has failed
DTC: P2128 **2T CCM, MIL: Yes** **Years:** 2008, 2009, 2010 **Models:** All **Engines:** All **Transmissions:** All	**Throttle/Pedal Position Sensor/Switch E Circuit High** The Accelerator Pedal Position (APP) sensor 2 is out of self-test range high. **Note: An APP2 sensor PID reading may indicate a concern.** **Possible Causes:** • APP sensor assembly is binding • APP sensor harness is short to voltage • Damaged APP sensor • PCM has failed
DTC: P2131 **2T CCM, MIL: Yes** **Years:** 2008, 2009, 2010 **Models:** All **Engines:** All **Transmissions:** All	**Throttle/Pedal Position Sensor/Switch F Circuit Range/Performance** The Accelerator Pedal Position (APP) sensor fault flag is set for sensor 3 by the Powertrain Control Module (PCM), indicating the signal is out of the normal self-test operating range. **Note: An APP3 sensor PID reading may indicate a concern.** **Possible Causes:** • APP sensor assembly is binding • Damaged APP sensor • PCM has failed
DTC: P2132 **2T CCM, MIL: Yes** **Years:** 2008, 2009, 2010 **Models:** All **Engines:** All **Transmissions:** All	**Throttle/Pedal Position Sensor/Switch F Circuit Low** The Accelerator Pedal Position (APP) sensor 3 is out of self-test range low. **Note: An APP3 sensor PID reading may indicate a concern.** **Possible Causes:** • APP sensor assembly is binding • APP sensor circuit is open • APP sensor harness short to ground • Damaged APP sensor • PCM has failed

DTC	Trouble Code Title, Conditions & Possible Causes
DTC: P2133 **2T CCM, MIL: Yes** **Years:** 2008, 2009, 2010 **Models:** All **Engines:** All **Transmissions:** All	**Throttle/Pedal Position Sensor/Switch F Circuit High** The Accelerator Pedal Position (APP) sensor 3 is out of self-test range high. **Note: An APP3 sensor PID reading may indicate a concern.** **Possible Causes:** • APP sensor assembly is binding • APP sensor harness is short to voltage • Damaged APP sensor • PCM has failed
DTC: P2135 **2T CCM, MIL: Yes** **Years:** 2008, 2009, 2010 **Models:** All **Engines:** All **Transmissions:** All	**Throttle/Pedal Position Sensor/Switch A/B Voltage Correlation** The Powertrain Control Module (PCM) flagged a concern indicating that Throttle Position (TP) 1 and TP2 disagree by more than a calibrated limit. **Note: Compare the TP1 and TP2 PID values for a full sweep and correlation. Check the wiring harness for an open or a short circuit. Check the TP sensor for an internal open or short circuit.** **Possible Causes:** • TP sensor shorted internally to VREF • TP sensor harness is short to voltage • TP sensor signal wires are short together • Damaged TP sensor
DTC: P2138 **2T CCM, MIL: Yes** **Years:** 2008, 2009, 2010 **Models:** All **Engines:** All **Transmissions:** All	**Throttle/Pedal Position Sensor/Switch D/E Voltage Correlation** The Powertrain Control Module (PCM) monitors the Accelerator Pedal Position (APP) sensor for a concern. The PCM compares the accelerator pedal position information from the APP sensor inputs, APP1 and APP2. If the APP sensor inputs APP1 and APP2 disagree on the position of the accelerator pedal by more than an expected value, the DTC is set. **Note: Monitor the APP_MAXDIFF PID while applying and releasing the accelerator pedal.** **Possible Causes:** • APP sensor circuit concerns • Damaged APP sensor. • Damaged TP sensor
DTC: P2195 **2T CCM, MIL: Yes** **Years:** 2008, 2009, 2010 **Models:** All **Engines:** All **Transmissions:** All	**O2 Sensor Signal Biased/Stuck Lean (Bank 1, Sensor 1)** A Heated Oxygen Sensor (HO2S) indicating lean at the end of a test is trying to correct for an over-rich condition. The test fails when the fuel control system no longer detects switching for a calibrated amount of time. **Possible Causes:** • Short to VPWR in the harness or HO2S • Water in the harness connector • Open/shorted HO2S circuit, • Open UO2SPC circuit • Corrosion or incorrect harness connections • Damaged HO2S • Fuel system problems • Intake air system leaks • Exhaust Gas Recirculation (EGR) System concerns • Base engine concerns • Exhaust leaks before or near the HO2S • PCM has failed
DTC: P2196 **2T CCM, MIL: Yes** **Years:** 2008, 2009, 2010 **Models:** All **Engines:** All **Transmissions:** All	**O2 Sensor Signal Biased/Stuck Rich - Bank 1, Sensor 1** A Heated Oxygen Sensor (HO2S) indicating lean at the end of a test is trying to correct for an over-lean condition. The test fails when the fuel control system no longer detects switching for a calibrated amount of time. **Possible Causes:** • Short to VPWR in the harness or HO2S • Water in the harness connector • Open/shorted HO2S circuit, • Open UO2SPC circuit • Corrosion or incorrect harness connections • Damaged HO2S • Fuel system problems • Intake air system leaks • Exhaust Gas Recirculation (EGR) System concerns • Base engine concerns • Exhaust leaks before or near the HO2S • PCM has failed

DTC	Trouble Code Title, Conditions & Possible Causes
DTC: P2197 **2T CCM, MIL: Yes** **Years:** 2008, 2009, 2010 **Models:** All **Engines:** All **Transmissions:** All	**O2 Sensor Signal Biased/Stuck Lean (Bank 2, Sensor 1)** A Heated Oxygen Sensor (HO2S) indicating lean at the end of a test is trying to correct for an over-rich condition. The test fails when the fuel control system no longer detects switching for a calibrated amount of time. **Possible Causes:** • Short to VPWR in the harness or HO2S • Water in the harness connector • Open/shorted HO2S circuit, • Open UO2SPC circuit • Corrosion or incorrect harness connections • Damaged HO2S • Fuel system problems • Intake air system leaks • Exhaust Gas Recirculation (EGR) System concerns • Base engine concerns • Exhaust leaks before or near the HO2S • PCM has failed
DTC: P2198 **2T CCM, MIL: Yes** **Years:** 2008, 2009, 2010 **Models:** All **Engines:** All **Transmissions:** All	**O2 Sensor Signal Biased/Stuck Rich - Bank 2, Sensor 1** A Heated Oxygen Sensor (HO2S) indicating lean at the end of a test is trying to correct for an over-lean condition. The test fails when the fuel control system no longer detects switching for a calibrated amount of time. **Possible Causes:** • Short to VPWR in the harness or HO2S • Water in the harness connector • Open/shorted HO2S circuit, • Open UO2SPC circuit • Corrosion or incorrect harness connections • Damaged HO2S • Fuel system problems • Intake air system leaks • Exhaust Gas Recirculation (EGR) System concerns • Base engine concerns • Exhaust leaks before or near the HO2S • PCM has failed
DTC: P2257 **1T CCM, MIL: Yes** **Years:** 2008, 2009, 2010 **Models:** All **Engines:** All **Transmissions:** All	**Secondary Air Injection (AIR) System Control A Circuit Low** The AIR system monitor circuit is low, indicating the secondary AIR pump is off although the secondary AIR pump was commanded on by the Powertrain Control Module (PCM). **Note: The AIR monitor circuit PCM input contains a pull up voltage through a resistance internal to the PCM. This voltage is normally held low by the resistance path through the secondary AIR pump when the secondary AIR pump is off. A single electrical open circuit component such as an AIR relay coil in this multi-component circuit is not detected by the PCM output driver, yet it sets DTC P2257.** **Possible Causes:** • Open B+ circuit • Open VPWR circuit • Open voltage circuit between the AIR relay and the secondary AIR pump • Damaged AIR relay
DTC: P2258 **1T CCM, MIL: Yes** **Years:** 2008, 2009, 2010 **Models:** All **Engines:** All **Transmissions:** All	**Secondary Air Injection (AIR) System Control A Circuit High** The AIR system monitor circuit is high, indicating the secondary AIR pump is on although the secondary AIR pump was commanded off by the Powertrain Control Module (PCM). **Note: The AIR monitor circuit PCM input contains a pull up voltage through a resistance internal to the PCM. This voltage is normally held low by the resistance path through the secondary AIR pump when the secondary AIR pump is off.** **Possible Causes:** • AIR relay fault (stuck closed) • Secondary AIR pump fault (circuit open in motor) • Open ground to secondary AIR pump • Open AIR monitor circuit between the secondary AIR pump and the PCM • Short to voltage in the AIR relay to secondary AIR pump voltage circuit

DTC	Trouble Code Title, Conditions & Possible Causes
DTC: P2270 **1T CCM, MIL: No** **Years:** 2008, 2009, 2010 **Models:** All **Engines:** All **Transmissions:** All	**O2 Sensor Signal Stuck Lean (Bank 1, Sensor 2)** The downstream Heated Oxygen Sensor (HO2S) is forced rich and lean and monitored by the Powertrain Control Module (PCM). The test fails if the PCM does not detect the output of the HO2S in a calibrated amount of time. **Possible Causes:** • Pinched, shorted, and corroded wiring and pins • Crossed HO2S wires • Exhaust leaks • Contaminated or damaged HO2S • PCM has failed
DTC: P2271 **1T CCM, MIL: No** **Years:** 2008, 2009, 2010 **Models:** All **Engines:** All **Transmissions:** All	**O2 Sensor Signal Stuck Rich (Bank 1, Sensor 2)** The downstream Heated Oxygen Sensor (HO2S) is forced rich and lean and monitored by the Powertrain Control Module (PCM). The test fails if the PCM does not detect the output of the HO2S in a calibrated amount of time. **Possible Causes:** • Pinched, shorted, and corroded wiring and pins • Crossed HO2S wires • Exhaust leaks • Contaminated or damaged HO2S • PCM has failed
DTC: P2272 **1T CCM, MIL: No** **Years:** 2008, 2009, 2010 **Models:** All **Engines:** All **Transmissions:** All	**O2 Sensor Signal Stuck Lean (Bank 2, Sensor 2)** The downstream Heated Oxygen Sensor (HO2S) is forced rich and lean and monitored by the Powertrain Control Module (PCM). The test fails if the PCM does not detect the output of the HO2S in a calibrated amount of time. **Possible Causes:** • Pinched, shorted, and corroded wiring and pins • Crossed HO2S wires • Exhaust leaks • Contaminated or damaged HO2S • PCM has failed
DTC: P2273 **1T CCM, MIL: No** **Years:** 2008, 2009, 2010 **Models:** All **Engines:** All **Transmissions:** All	**O2 Sensor Signal Stuck Rich (Bank 2, Sensor 2)** The downstream Heated Oxygen Sensor (HO2S) is forced rich and lean and monitored by the Powertrain Control Module (PCM). The test fails if the PCM does not detect the output of the HO2S in a calibrated amount of time. **Possible Causes:** • Pinched, shorted, and corroded wiring and pins • Crossed HO2S wires • Exhaust leaks • Contaminated or damaged HO2S • PCM has failed
DTC: P2274 **1T CCM, MIL: No** **Years:** 2008, 2009, 2010 **Models:** All **Engines:** All **Transmissions:** All	**O2 Sensor Signal Stuck Lean (Bank 1, Sensor 3)** The downstream Heated Oxygen Sensor (HO2S) is forced rich and lean and monitored by the Powertrain Control Module (PCM). The test fails if the PCM does not detect the output of the HO2S in a calibrated amount of time. **Possible Causes:** • Pinched, shorted, and corroded wiring and pins • Crossed HO2S wires • Exhaust leaks • Contaminated or damaged HO2S • PCM has failed
DTC: P2275 **1T CCM, MIL: No** **Years:** 2008, 2009, 2010 **Models:** All **Engines:** All **Transmissions:** All	**O2 Sensor Signal Stuck Rich (Bank 1, Sensor 3)** The downstream Heated Oxygen Sensor (HO2S) is forced rich and lean and monitored by the Powertrain Control Module (PCM). The test fails if the PCM does not detect the output of the HO2S in a calibrated amount of time. **Possible Causes:** • Pinched, shorted, and corroded wiring and pins • Crossed HO2S wires • Exhaust leaks • Contaminated or damaged HO2S • PCM has failed
DTC: P2448 **1T CCM, MIL: No** **Years:** 2008, 2009, 2010 **Models:** All **Engines:** All **Transmissions:** All	**Secondary Air Injection System High Airflow (Bank 1)** The AIR system detects excessive mass air flow change with the pump on and a rich exhaust system air fuel ratio. **Note: Measured air flow is less than expected. Visually inspect the secondary AIR inlet hose.** **Possible Causes:** • AIR outlet hose leak. • AIR outlet hose is disconnected.

DTC	Trouble Code Title, Conditions & Possible Causes
DTC: P260F **1T CCM, MIL: No** **Years:** 2008, 2009, 2010 **Models:** All **Engines:** All **Transmissions:** All	**Evaporative System Monitoring Processor Performance** This DTC sets when a concern is detected internal to the Powertrain Control Module (PCM). The microprocessor that controls the Engine Off Natural Vacuum (EONV) leak check monitor is separate from the main processor within the PCM. **Note: Verify the PCM is at the latest calibration level. Reprogram if necessary.** **Possible Causes:** • Module communications network concerns • PCM calibration level • PCM has failed
DTC: P2610 **1T CCM, MIL: No** **Years:** 2008, 2009, 2010 **Models:** All **Engines:** All **Transmissions:** All	**Electronic Control Module (ECM)/Powertrain Control Module (PCM) Internal Engine Off Timer Performance** Indicates an error in the internal PCM engine off timer processor. **Note: Verify the PCM is at the latest calibration level.** **Possible Causes:** • Battery cables loose or intermittent connections • Keep Alive Power (KAPWR) circuit to PCM concern • Engine Coolant Temperature (ECT) sensor • Engine cooling system concerns • Electrical interference around vehicle or PCM • PCM has failed

Gas Engine OBD II Trouble Code List (Uxxxx Codes)

DTC	Trouble Code Title, Conditions & Possible Causes
DTC: U0101 **1T PCM, MIL: No** **Years:** 2008, 2009, 2010 **Models:** All **Engines:** All **Transmissions:** All	**Lost Communication With Transaxle Control Module (TCM)** The Powertrain Control Module (PCM) continuously monitors the Controller Area Network (CAN) for messages from the TCM. This DTC sets when the PCM does not receive the TCM message within the defined amount of time. **Possible Causes:** • Damaged CAN communication bus circuit
DTC: U0109 **1T PCM, MIL: No** **Years:** 2008, 2009, 2010 **Models:** All **Engines:** All **Transmissions:** All	**Lost Communication With Fuel Pump Control Module** The Powertrain Control Module (PCM) monitors the Fuel Pump Monitor (FPM) circuit for the presence of a duty cycled signal. If the FPM circuit is fixed at a low or high voltage, the PCM begins to increment a counter. The test fails when the PCM is still not detecting a duty cycled signal on the FPM circuit after a calibrated amount of time. **Note: Check if the Inertia Fuel Shutoff (IFS) switch is tripped.** **Possible Causes:** • FPM circuit open or short to ground • FPM circuit short to voltage • VPWR fuel circuit open • PWRGND circuit open • Damaged Inertia Fuel Shutoff (IFS) switch (if equipped) • Damaged fuel pump control module relay
DTC: U0121 **1T PCM, MIL: No** **Years:** 2008, 2009, 2010 **Models:** All **Engines:** All **Transmissions:** All	**Lost Communication With Anti-lock Brake System (ABS) Control Module** The Powertrain Control Module (PCM) continuously monitors the Controller Area Network (CAN) for messages from the ABS. This DTC sets when the PCM fails to receive the ABS message within the defined amount of time. **Note: Network DTC concerns occur during module-to-module communication.** **Possible Causes:** • Damaged CAN communication bus circuit
DTC: U0155 **1T PCM, MIL: No** **Years:** 2008, 2009, 2010 **Models:** All **Engines:** All **Transmissions:** All	**Lost Communication With Instrument Panel Cluster Control Module** Missing message concerns are logged by a module upon failure to receive a message from another module within a defined retry period. **Note: Carry out the diagnostics for the associated network module.** **Possible Causes:** • Open VPWR circuit to the sending module • Open GND circuit to the sending module • Open network circuits to the sending module

DTC	Trouble Code Title, Conditions & Possible Causes
DTC: U0300 **1T PCM, MIL: No** **Years:** 2008, 2009, 2010 **Models:** All **Engines:** All **Transmissions:** All	**Internal Control Module Software Incompatibility** This DTC indicates there are incompatible software levels within the Powertrain Control Module (PCM) that control the Electronic Throttle Control (ETC) system. The ETC system uses multiple microprocessors within the PCM, each having its own software level and function. The microprocessors must have the correct level of software in order to communicate and function together. **Note: Verify the PCM is at the latest calibration level.** **Possible Causes:** • Program the PCM to the latest calibration. • Open VPWR circuit to the sending module • Open GND circuit to the sending module • PCM has failed
DTC: U1039 **1T PCM, MIL: No** **Years:** 2008, 2009, 2010 **Models:** All **Engines:** All **Transmissions:** All	**SCP (J1850) Invalid or Missing Data for Vehicle Speed** Key on, and the PCM detected that invalid or Missing Data from the Vehicle Speed Sensor was received on the SCP data bus. **Note: Network codes occur during module-to-module communication failures. Invalid and Missing data network faults are outlined below.** **Possible Causes:** • Invalid Data: Data transferred in normal inter-module messages with known invalid data. Transmitting module will set the code. • Missing Network Data: Missing message fault logged by a module upon failure to receive a message from another module within a defined retry period.
DTC: U210B **1T PCM, MIL: No** **Years:** 2008, 2009, 2010 **Models:** All **Engines:** All **Transmissions:** All	**Lost Communication Between Fuel Pump Control Module and Restraints Control** The fuel pump control module monitors the duty cycle and frequency of the signal it receives from the Restraints Control Module (RCM). The fuel pump control module determines if the signal on the Event Notification Signal (ENS) circuit from the RCM is a valid duty cycle and frequency. If the duty cycle or frequency is invalid, the fuel pump control module sends a 40% duty cycle signal on the Fuel Pump Monitor (FPM) circuit to report the concern to the PCM. The test fails when the fuel pump control module is still reporting that it is receiving an invalid duty cycle or frequency from the RCM after a calibrated amount of time. **Note: Check the harness for routing, alterations, incorrect shielding, or electrical interference from other systems. The ENS is used to notify the fuel pump control module of an event requiring the fuel pump to be disabled. This signal is used instead of an Inertia Fuel Shutoff (IFS) switch.** **Possible Causes:** • ENS circuit open or short to ground • ENS circuit short to voltage • Radio frequency interference/electromagnetic interference (RFI/EMI) • Damaged fuel pump control module • Damaged RCM

GLOSSARY

ABS: Anti-lock braking system. An electro-mechanical braking system which is designed to minimize or prevent wheel lock-up during braking.

ABSOLUTE PRESSURE: Atmospheric (barometric) pressure plus the pressure gauge reading.

ACCELERATOR PUMP: A small pump located in the carburetor that feeds fuel into the air/fuel mixture during acceleration.

ACCUMULATOR: A device that controls shift quality by cushioning the shock of hydraulic oil pressure being applied to a clutch or band.

ACTUATING MECHANISM: The mechanical output devices of a hydraulic system, for example, clutch pistons and band servos.

ACTUATOR: The output component of a hydraulic or electronic system.

ADVANCE: Setting the ignition timing so that spark occurs earlier before the piston reaches top dead center (TDC).

ADAPTIVE MEMORY (ADAPTIVE STRATEGY): The learning ability of the TCM or PCM to redefine its decision-making process to provide optimum shift quality.

AFTER TOP DEAD CENTER (ATDC): The point after the piston reaches the top of its travel on the compression stroke.

AIR BAG: Device on the inside of the car designed to inflate on impact of crash, protecting the occupants of the car.

AIR CHARGE TEMPERATURE (ACT) SENSOR: The temperature of the airflow into the engine is measured by an ACT sensor, usually located in the lower intake manifold or air cleaner.

AIR CLEANER: An assembly consisting of a housing, filter and any connecting ductwork. The filter element is made up of a porous paper, sometimes with a wire mesh screening, and is designed to prevent airborne particles from entering the engine through the carburetor or throttle body.

AIR INJECTION: One method of reducing harmful exhaust emissions by injecting air into each of the exhaust ports of an engine. The fresh air entering the hot exhaust manifold causes any remaining fuel to be burned before it can exit the tailpipe.

AIR PUMP: An emission control device that supplies fresh air to the exhaust manifold to aid in more completely burning exhaust gases.

AIR/FUEL RATIO: The ratio of air-to-gasoline by weight in the fuel mixture drawn into the engine.

ALDL (assembly line diagnostic link): Electrical connector for scanning ECM/PCM/TCM input and output devices.

ALIGNMENT RACK: A special drive-on vehicle lift apparatus/measuring device used to adjust a vehicle's toe, caster and camber angles.

ALL WHEEL DRIVE: Term used to describe a full time four wheel drive system or any other vehicle drive system that continuously delivers power to all four wheels. This system is found primarily on station wagon vehicles and SUVs not utilized for significant off road use.

ALTERNATING CURRENT (AC): Electric current that flows first in one direction, then in the opposite direction, continually reversing flow.

ALTERNATOR: A device which produces AC (alternating current) which is converted to DC (direct current) to charge the car battery.

AMMETER: An instrument, calibrated in amperes, used to measure the flow of an electrical current in a circuit. Ammeters are always connected in series with the circuit being tested.

AMPERAGE: The total amount of current (amperes) flowing in a circuit.

AMPLIFIER: A device used in an electrical circuit to increase the voltage of an output signal.

AMP/HR. RATING (BATTERY): Measurement of the ability of a battery to deliver a stated amount of current for a stated period of time. The higher the amp/hr. rating, the better the battery.

AMPERE: The rate of flow of electrical current present when one volt of electrical pressure is applied against one ohm of electrical resistance.

ANALOG COMPUTER: Any microprocessor that uses similar (analogous) electrical signals to make its calculations.

ANODIZED: A special coating applied to the surface of aluminum valves for extended service life.

ANTIFREEZE: A substance (ethylene or propylene glycol) added to the coolant to prevent freezing in cold weather.

ANTI-FOAM AGENTS: Minimize fluid foaming from the whipping action encountered in the converter and planetary action.

ANTI-WEAR AGENTS: Zinc agents that control wear on the gears, bushings, and thrust washers.

ANTI-LOCK BRAKING SYSTEM: A supplementary system to the base hydraulic system that prevents sustained lock-up of the wheels during braking as well as automatically controlling wheel slip.

ANTI-ROLL BAR: See stabilizer bar.

ARC: A flow of electricity through the air between two electrodes or contact points that produces a spark.

ARMATURE: A laminated, soft iron core wrapped by a wire that converts electrical energy to mechanical energy as in a motor or relay. When rotated in a magnetic field, it changes mechanical energy into electrical energy as in a generator.

ATDC: After Top Dead Center.

ATF: Automatic transmission fluid.

ATMOSPHERIC PRESSURE: The pressure on the Earth's surface caused by the weight of the air in the atmosphere. At sea level, this pressure is 14.7 psi at 32°F (101 kPa at 0°C).

ATOMIZATION: The breaking down of a liquid into a fine mist that can be suspended in air.

AUXILIARY ADD-ON COOLER: A supplemental transmission fluid cooling device that is installed in series with the heat exchanger (cooler), located inside the radiator, to provide additional support to cool the hot fluid leaving the torque converter.

AUXILIARY PRESSURE: An added fluid pressure that is introduced into a regulator or balanced valve system to control valve movement. The auxiliary pressure itself can be either a fixed or a variable value. (See balanced valve; regulator valve.)

AWD: All wheel drive.

AXIAL FORCE: A side or end thrust force acting in or along the same plane as the power flow.

AXIAL PLAY: Movement parallel to a shaft or bearing bore.

AXLE CAPACITY: The maximum load-carrying capacity of the axle itself, as specified by the manufacturer. This is usually a higher number than the GAWR.

AXLE RATIO: This is a number (3.07:1, 4.56:1, for example) expressing the ratio between driveshaft revolutions and wheel revolutions. A low numerical ratio allows the engine to work easier because it doesn't have to turn as fast. A high numerical ratio means that the engine has to turn more rpm's to move the wheels through the same number of turns.

BACKFIRE: The sudden combustion of gases in the intake or exhaust system that results in a loud explosion.

BACKLASH: The clearance or play between two parts, such as meshed gears.

BACKPRESSURE: Restrictions in the exhaust system that slow the exit of exhaust gases from the combustion chamber.

BAKELITE®: A heat resistant, plastic insulator material commonly used in printed circuit boards and transistorized components.

BALANCED VALVE: A valve that is positioned by opposing auxiliary hydraulic pressures and/or spring force. Examples include mainline regulator, throttle, and governor valves. (See regulator valve.)

BAND: A flexible ring of steel with an inner lining of friction material. When tightened around the outside of a drum, a planetary member is held stationary to the transmission/transaxle case.

BALL BEARING: A bearing made up of hardened inner and outer races between which hardened steel balls roll.

BALL JOINT: A ball and matching socket connecting suspension components (steering knuckle to lower control arms). It permits rotating movement in any direction between the components that are joined.

BARO (BAROMETRIC PRESSURE SENSOR): Measures the change in the intake manifold pressure caused by changes in altitude.

BAROMETRIC MANIFOLD ABSOLUTE PRESSURE (BMAP) SENSOR: Operates similarly to a conventional MAP sensor; reads intake manifold pressure and is also responsible for determining altitude and barometric pressure prior to engine operation.

BAROMETRIC PRESSURE: (See atmospheric pressure.)

BALLAST RESISTOR: A resistor in the primary ignition circuit that lowers voltage after the engine is started to reduce wear on ignition components.

BATTERY: A direct current electrical storage unit, consisting of the basic active materials of lead and sulfuric acid, which converts chemical energy into electrical energy. Used to provide current for the operation of the starter as well as other equipment, such as the radio, lighting, etc.

BEAD: The portion of a tire that holds it on the rim.

BEARING: A friction reducing, supportive device usually located between a stationary part and a moving part.

BEFORE TOP DEAD CENTER (BTDC): The point just before the piston reaches the top of its travel on the compression stroke.

BELTED TIRE: Tire construction similar to bias-ply tires, but using two or more layers of reinforced belts between body plies and the tread.

BEZEL: Piece of metal surrounding radio, headlights, gauges or similar components; sometimes used to hold the glass face of a gauge in the dash.

BIAS-PLY TIRE: Tire construction, using body ply reinforcing cords which run at alternating angles to the center line of the tread.

BI-METAL TEMPERATURE SENSOR: Any sensor or switch made of two dissimilar types of metal that bend when heated or cooled due to the different expansion rates of the alloys. These types of sensors usually function as an on/off switch.

BLOCK: See Engine Block.

BLOW-BY: Combustion gases, composed of water vapor and unburned fuel, that leak past the piston rings into the crankcase during normal engine operation. These gases are removed by the PCV system to prevent the buildup of harmful acids in the crankcase.

BOOK TIME: See Labor Time.

BOOK VALUE: The average value of a car, widely used to determine trade-in and resale value.

BOOST VALVE: Used at the base of the regulator valve to increase mainline pressure.

BORE: Diameter of a cylinder.

BRAKE CALIPER: The housing that fits over the brake disc. The caliper holds the brake pads, which are pressed against the discs by the caliper pistons when the brake pedal is depressed.

BRAKE HORSEPOWER (BHP): The actual horsepower available at the engine flywheel as measured by a dynamometer.

BRAKE FADE: Loss of braking power, usually caused by excessive heat after repeated brake applications.

BRAKE HORSEPOWER: Usable horsepower of an engine measured at the crankshaft.

BRAKE PAD: A brake shoe and lining assembly used with disc brakes.

BRAKE PROPORTIONING VALVE: A valve on the master cylinder which restricts hydraulic brake pressure to the wheels to a specified amount, preventing wheel lock-up.

BREAKAWAY: Often used by Chrysler to identify first-gear operation in D and 2 ranges. In these ranges, first-gear operation depends on a one-way roller clutch that holds on acceleration and releases (breaks away) on deceleration, resulting in a freewheeling coast-down condition.

BRAKE SHOE: The backing for the brake lining. The term is, however, usually applied to the assembly of the brake backing and lining.

BREAKER POINTS: A set of points inside the distributor, operated by a cam, which make and break the ignition circuit.

BRINNELLING: A wear pattern identified by a series of indentations at regular intervals. This condition is caused by a lack of lube, overload situations, and/or vibrations.

BTDC: Before Top Dead Center.

BUMP: Sudden and forceful apply of a clutch or band.

BUSHING: A liner, usually removable, for a bearing; an anti-friction liner used in place of a bearing.

CALIFORNIA ENGINE: An engine certified by the EPA for use in California only; conforms to more stringent emission regulations than Federal engine.

CALIPER: A hydraulically activated device in a disc brake system, which is mounted straddling the brake rotor (disc). The caliper contains at least one piston and two brake pads. Hydraulic pressure on the piston(s) forces the pads against the rotor.

CAPACITY: The quantity of electricity that can be delivered from a unit, as from a battery in ampere-hours, or output, as from a generator.

CAMBER: One of the factors of wheel alignment. Viewed from the front of the car, it is the inward or outward tilt of the wheel. The top of the tire will lean outward (positive camber) or inward (negative camber).

CAMSHAFT: A shaft in the engine on which are the lobes (cams) which operate the valves. The camshaft is driven by the crankshaft, via a belt, chain or gears, at one half the crankshaft speed.

CAPACITOR: A device which stores an electrical charge.

CARBON MONOXIDE (CO): A colorless, odorless gas given off as a normal byproduct of combustion. It is poisonous and extremely dangerous in confined areas, building up slowly to toxic levels without warning if adequate ventilation is not available.

CARBURETOR: A device, usually mounted on the intake manifold of an engine, which mixes the air and fuel in the proper proportion to allow even combustion.

CASTER: The forward or rearward tilt of an imaginary line drawn through the upper ball joint and the center of the wheel. Viewed from the sides, positive caster (forward tilt) lends directional stability, while negative caster (rearward tilt) produces instability.

CATALYTIC CONVERTER: A device installed in the exhaust system, like a muffler, that converts harmful byproducts of combustion into carbon dioxide and water vapor by means of a heat-producing chemical reaction.

CENTRIFUGAL ADVANCE: A mechanical method of advancing the spark timing by using flyweights in the distributor that react to centrifugal force generated by the distributor shaft rotation.

CENTRIFUGAL FORCE: The outward pull of a revolving object, away from the center of revolution. Centrifugal force increases with the speed of rotation.

CETANE RATING: A measure of the ignition value of diesel fuel. The higher the cetane rating, the better the fuel. Diesel fuel cetane rating is roughly comparable to gasoline octane rating.

CHECK VALVE: Any one-way valve installed to permit the flow of air, fuel or vacuum in one direction only.

CHOKE: The valve/plate that restricts the amount of air entering an engine on the induction stroke, thereby enriching the air/fuel ratio.

CHUGGLE: Bucking or jerking condition that may be engine related and may be most noticeable when converter clutch is engaged; similar to the feel of towing a trailer.

CIRCLIP: A split steel snapring that fits into a groove to hold various parts in place.

CIRCUIT BREAKER: A switch which protects an electrical circuit from overload by opening the circuit when the current flow exceeds a pre-determined level. Some circuit breakers must be reset manually, while most reset automatically.

CIRCUIT: Any unbroken path through which an electrical current can flow. Also used to describe fuel flow in some instances.

CIRCUIT, BYPASS: Another circuit in parallel with the major circuit through which power is diverted.

CIRCUIT, CLOSED: An electrical circuit in which there is no interruption of current flow.

CIRCUIT, GROUND: The non-insulated portion of a complete circuit used as a common potential point. In automotive circuits, the ground is composed of metal parts, such as the engine, body sheet metal, and frame and is usually a negative potential.

CIRCUIT, HOT: That portion of a circuit not at ground potential. The hot circuit is usually insulated and is connected to the positive side of the battery.

CIRCUIT, OPEN: A break or lack of contact in an electrical circuit, either intentional (switch) or unintentional (bad connection or broken wire).

CIRCUIT, PARALLEL: A circuit having two or more paths for current flow with common positive and negative tie points. The same voltage is applied to each load device or parallel branch.

CIRCUIT, SERIES: An electrical system in which separate parts are connected end to end, using one wire, to form a single path for current to flow.

CIRCUIT, SHORT: A circuit that is accidentally completed in an electrical path for which it was not intended.

CLAMPING (ISOLATION) DIODES: Diodes positioned in a circuit to prevent self-induction from damaging electronic components.

CLEARCOAT: A transparent layer which, when sprayed over a vehicle's paint job, adds gloss and depth as well as an additional protective coating to the finish.

CLUTCH: Part of the power train used to connect/disconnect power to the rear wheels.

CLUTCH, FLUID: The same as a fluid coupling. A fluid clutch or coupling performs the same function as a friction clutch by utilizing fluid friction and inertia as opposed to solid friction used by a friction clutch. (See fluid coupling.)

CLUTCH, FRICTION: A coupling device that provides a means of smooth and positive engagement and disengagement of engine torque to the vehicle powertrain. Transmission of power through the clutch is accomplished by bringing one or more rotating drive members into contact with complementing driven members.

COAST: Vehicle deceleration caused by engine braking conditions.

COEFFICIENT OF FRICTION: The amount of surface tension between two contacting surfaces; identified by a scientifically calculated number.

COIL: Part of the ignition system that boosts the relatively low voltage supplied by the car's electrical system to the high voltage required to fire the spark plugs.

COMBINATION MANIFOLD: An assembly which includes both the intake and exhaust manifolds in one casting.

COMBINATION VALVE: A device used in some fuel systems that routes fuel vapors to a charcoal storage canister instead of venting them into the atmosphere. The valve relieves fuel tank pressure and allows fresh air into the tank as the fuel level drops to prevent a vapor lock situation.

COMBUSTION CHAMBER: The part of the engine in the cylinder head where combustion takes place.

COMPOUND GEAR: A gear consisting of two or more simple gears with a common shaft.

COMPOUND PLANETARY: A gearset that has more than the three elements found in a simple gearset and is constructed by combining members of two planetary gearsets to create additional gear ratio possibilities.

COMPRESSION CHECK: A test involving removing each spark plug and inserting a gauge. When the engine is cranked, the gauge will record a pressure reading in the individual cylinder. General operating condition can be determined from a compression check.

COMPRESSION RATIO: The ratio of the volume between the piston and cylinder head when the piston is at the bottom of its stroke (bottom dead center) and when the piston is at the top of its stroke (top dead center).

COMPUTER: An electronic control module that correlates input data according to prearranged engineered instructions; used for the management of an actuator system or systems.

CONDENSER: An electrical device which acts to store an electrical charge, preventing voltage surges.

2. A radiator-like device in the air conditioning system in which refrigerant gas condenses into a liquid, giving off heat.

CONDUCTOR: Any material through which an electrical current can be transmitted easily.

CONNECTING ROD: The connecting link between the crankshaft and piston.

CONSTANT VELOCITY JOINT: Type of universal joint in a halfshaft assembly in which the output shaft turns at a constant angular velocity without variation, provided that the speed of the input shaft is constant.

CONTINUITY: Continuous or complete circuit. Can be checked with an ohmmeter.

CONTROL ARM: The upper or lower suspension components which are mounted on the frame and support the ball joints and steering knuckles.

CONVENTIONAL IGNITION: Ignition system which uses breaker points.

CONVERTER: (See torque converter.)

CONVERTER LOCKUP: The switching from hydrodynamic to direct mechanical drive, usually through the application of a friction element called the converter clutch.

COOLANT: Mixture of water and anti-freeze circulated through the engine to carry off heat produced by the engine.

CORROSION INHIBITOR: An inhibitor in ATF that prevents corrosion of bushings, thrust washers, and oil cooler brazed joints.

COUNTERSHAFT: An intermediate shaft which is rotated by a mainshaft and transmits, in turn, that rotation to a working part.

COUPLING PHASE: Occurs when the torque converter is operating at its greatest hydraulic efficiency. The speed differential between the impeller and the turbine is at its minimum. At this point, the stator freewheels, and there is no torque multiplication.

CRANKCASE: The lower part of an engine in which the crankshaft and related parts operate.

CRANKSHAFT: Engine component (connected to pistons by connecting rods) which converts the reciprocating (up and down) motion of pistons to rotary motion used to turn the driveshaft.

CURB WEIGHT: The weight of a vehicle without passengers or payload, but including all fluids (oil, gas, coolant, etc.) and other equipment specified as standard.

CURRENT: The flow (or rate) of electrons moving through a circuit. Current is measured in amperes (amp).

CURRENT FLOW CONVENTIONAL: Current flows through a circuit from the positive terminal of the source to the negative terminal (plus to minus).

CURRENT FLOW, ELECTRON: Current or electrons flow from the negative terminal of the source, through the circuit, to the positive terminal (minus to plus).

CV-JOINT: Constant velocity joint.

CYCLIC VIBRATIONS: The off-center movement of a rotating object that is affected by its initial balance, speed of rotation, and working angles.

CYLINDER BLOCK: See engine block.

CYLINDER HEAD: The detachable portion of the engine, usually fastened to the top of the cylinder block and containing all or most of the combustion chambers. On overhead valve engines, it contains the valves and their operating parts. On overhead cam engines, it contains the camshaft as well.

CYLINDER: In an engine, the round hole in the engine block in which the piston(s) ride.

DATA LINK CONNECTOR (DLC): Current acronym/term applied to the federally mandated, diagnostic junction connector that is used to monitor ECM/PC/TCM inputs, processing strategies, and outputs including diagnostic trouble codes (DTCs).

DEAD CENTER: The extreme top or bottom of the piston stroke.

DECELERATION BUMP: When referring to a torque converter clutch in the applied position, a sudden release of the accelerator pedal causes a forceful reversal of power through the drivetrain (engine braking), just prior to the apply plate actually being released.

DELAYED (LATE OR EXTENDED): Condition where shift is expected but does not occur for a period of time, for example, where clutch or band engagement does not occur as quickly as expected during part throttle or wide open throttle apply of accelerator or when manually downshifting to a lower range.

DETENT: A spring-loaded plunger, pin, ball, or pawl used as a holding device on a ratchet wheel or shaft. In automatic transmissions, a detent mechanism is used for locking the manual valve in place.

DETENT DOWNSHIFT: (See kickdown.)

DETERGENT: An additive in engine oil to improve its operating characteristics.

DETONATION: An unwanted explosion of the air/fuel mixture in the combustion chamber caused by excess heat and compression, advanced timing, or an overly lean mixture. Also referred to as "ping".

DEXRON®: A brand of automatic transmission fluid.

DIAGNOSTIC TROUBLE CODES (DTCs): A digital display from the control module memory that identifies the input, processor, or output device circuit that is related to the powertrain emission/driveability malfunction detected. Diagnostic trouble codes can be read by the MIL to flash any codes or by using a handheld scanner.

DIAPHRAGM: A thin, flexible wall separating two cavities, such as in a vacuum advance unit.

DIESELING: The engine continues to run after the car is shut off; caused by fuel continuing to be burned in the combustion chamber.

DIFFERENTIAL: A geared assembly which allows the transmission of motion between drive axles, giving one axle the ability to rotate faster than the other, as in cornering.

DIFFERENTIAL AREAS: When opposing faces of a spool valve are acted upon by the same pressure but their areas differ in size, the face with the larger area produces the differential force and valve movement. (See spool valve.)

DIFFERENTIAL FORCE: (See differential areas)

DIGITAL READOUT: A display of numbers or a combination of numbers and letters.

DIGITAL VOLT OHMMETER: An electronic diagnostic tool used to measure voltage, ohms and amps as well as several other functions, with the readings displayed on a digital screen in tenths, hundredths and thousandths.

DIODE: An electrical device that will allow current to flow in one direction only.

DIRECT CURRENT (DC): Electrical current that flows in one direction only.

DIRECT DRIVE: The gear ratio is 1:1, with no change occurring in the torque and speed input/output relationship.

DISC BRAKE: A hydraulic braking assembly consisting of a brake disc, or rotor, mounted on an axle shaft, and a caliper assembly containing, usually two brake pads which are activated by hydraulic pressure. The pads are forced against the sides of the disc, creating friction which slows the vehicle.

DISPERSANTS: Suspend dirt and prevent sludge buildup in a liquid, such as engine oil.

DOUBLE BUMP (DOUBLE FEEL): Two sudden and forceful applies of a clutch or band.

DISPLACEMENT: The total volume of air that is displaced by all pistons as the engine turns through one complete revolution.

DISTRIBUTOR: A mechanically driven device on an engine which is responsible for electrically firing the spark plug at a pre-determined point of the piston stroke.

DOHC: Double overhead camshaft.

DOUBLE OVERHEAD CAMSHAFT: The engine utilizes two camshafts mounted in one cylinder head. One camshaft operates the exhaust valves, while the other operates the intake valves.

DOWEL PIN: A pin, inserted in mating holes in two different parts allowing those parts to maintain a fixed relationship.

DRIVELINE: The drive connection between the transmission and the drive wheels.

DRIVE TRAIN: The components that transmit the flow of power from the engine to the wheels. The components include the clutch, transmission, driveshafts (or axle shafts in front wheel drive), U-joints and differential.

DRUM BRAKE: A braking system which consists of two brake shoes and one or two wheel cylinders, mounted on a fixed backing plate, and a brake drum, mounted on an axle, which revolves around the assembly.

DRY CHARGED BATTERY: Battery to which electrolyte is added when the battery is placed in service.

DVOM: Digital volt ohmmeter

DWELL: The rate, measured in degrees of shaft rotation, at which an electrical circuit cycles on and off.

DYNAMIC: An application in which there is rotating or reciprocating motion between the parts.

EARLY: Condition where shift occurs before vehicle has reached proper speed, which tends to labor engine after upshift.

EBCM: See Electronic Control Unit (ECU).

ECM: See Electronic Control Unit (ECU).

ECU: Electronic control unit.

ELECTRODE: Conductor (positive or negative) of electric current.

ELECTROLYSIS: A surface etching or bonding of current conducting transmission/transaxle components that may occur when grounding straps are missing or in poor condition.

ELECTROLYTE: A solution of water and sulfuric acid used to activate the battery. Electrolyte is extremely corrosive.

ELECTROMAGNET: A coil that produces a magnetic field when current flows through its windings.

ELECTROMAGNETIC INDUCTION: A method to create (generate) current flow through the use of magnetism.

ELECTROMAGNETISM: The effects surrounding the relationship between electricity and magnetism.

ELECTROMOTIVE FORCE (EMF): The force or pressure (voltage) that causes current movement in an electrical circuit.

ELECTRONIC CONTROL UNIT: A digital computer that controls engine (and sometimes transmission, brake or other vehicle system) functions based on data received from various sensors. Examples used by some manufacturers include Electronic Brake Control Module (EBCM), Engine Control Module (ECM), Powertrain Control Module (PCM) or Vehicle Control Module (VCM).

ELECTRONIC IGNITION: A system in which the timing and firing of the spark plugs is controlled by an electronic control unit, usually called a module. These systems have no points or condenser.

ELECTRONIC PRESSURE CONTROL (EPC) SOLENOID: A specially designed solenoid containing a spool valve and spring assembly to control fluid mainline pressure. A variable current flow, controlled by the ECM/PCM, varies the internal force of the solenoid on the spool valve and resulting mainline pressure. (See variable force solenoid.)

ELECTRONICS: Miniaturized electrical circuits utilizing semiconductors, solid-state devices, and printed circuits. Electronic circuits utilize small amounts of power.

ELECTRONIFICATION: The application of electronic circuitry to a mechanical device. Regarding automatic transmissions, electrification is incorporated into converter clutch lockup, shift scheduling, and line pressure control systems.

ELECTROSTATIC DISCHARGE (ESD): An unwanted, high-voltage electrical current released by an individual who has taken on a static charge of electricity. Electronic components can be easily damaged by ESD.

ELEMENT: A device within a hydrodynamic drive unit designed with a set of blades to direct fluid flow.

ENAMEL: Type of paint that dries to a smooth, glossy finish.

END BUMP (END FEEL OR SLIP BUMP): Firmer feel at end of shift when compared with feel at start of shift.

END-PLAY: The clearance/gap between two components that allows for expansion of the parts as they warm up, to prevent binding and to allow space for lubrication.

ENERGY: The ability or capacity to do work.

ENGINE: The primary motor or power apparatus of a vehicle, which converts liquid or gas fuel into mechanical energy.

ENGINE BLOCK: The basic engine casting containing the cylinders, the crankshaft main bearings, as well as machined surfaces for the mounting of other components such as the cylinder head, oil pan, transmission, etc.

ENGINE BRAKING: Use of engine to slow vehicle by manually downshifting during zero-throttle coast down.

ENGINE CONTROL MODULE (ECM): Manages the engine and incorporates output control over the torque converter clutch solenoid. (Note: Current designation for the ECM in late model vehicles is PCM.)

ENGINE COOLANT TEMPERATURE (ECT) SENSOR: Prevents converter clutch engagement with a cold engine; also used for shift timing and shift quality.

EP LUBRICANT: EP (extreme pressure) lubricants are specially formulated for use with gears involving heavy loads (transmissions, differentials, etc.).

ETHYL: A substance added to gasoline to improve its resistance to knock, by slowing down the rate of combustion.

ETHYLENE GLYCOL: The base substance of antifreeze.

EXHAUST MANIFOLD: A set of cast passages or pipes which conduct exhaust gases from the engine.

FAIL-SAFE (BACKUP) CONTROL: A substitute value used by the PCM/TCM to replace a faulty signal from an input sensor. The temporary value allows the vehicle to continue to be operated.

FAST IDLE: The speed of the engine when the choke is on. Fast idle speeds engine warm-up.

FEDERAL ENGINE: An engine certified by the EPA for use in any of the 49 states (except California).

FEEDBACK: A circuit malfunction whereby current can find another path to feed load devices.

FEELER GAUGE: A blade, usually metal, of precisely predetermined thickness, used to measure the clearance between two parts.

FILAMENT: The part of a bulb that glows; the filament creates high resistance to current flow and actually glows from the resulting heat.

FINAL DRIVE: An essential part of the axle drive assembly where final gear reduction takes place in the powertrain. In RWD applications and north-south FWD applications, it must also change the power flow direction to the axle shaft by ninety degrees. (Also see axle ratio).

FIRING ORDER: The order in which combustion occurs in the cylinders of an engine. Also the order in which spark is distributed to the plugs by the distributor.

FIRM: A noticeable quick apply of a clutch or band that is considered normal with medium to heavy throttle shift; should not be confused with harsh or rough.

FLAME FRONT: The term used to describe certain aspects of the fuel explosion in the cylinders. The flame front should move in a controlled pattern across the cylinder, rather than simply exploding immediately.

FLARE (SLIPPING): A quick increase in engine rpm accompanied by momentary loss of torque; generally occurs during shift.

FLAT ENGINE: Engine design in which the pistons are horizontally opposed. Porsche, Subaru and some old VW are common examples of flat engines.

FLAT RATE: A dealership term referring to the amount of money paid to a technician for a repair or diagnostic service based on that particular service versus dealership's labor time (NOT based on the actual time the technician spent on the job).

FLAT SPOT: A point during acceleration when the engine seems to lose power for an instant.

FLOODING: The presence of too much fuel in the intake manifold and combustion chamber which prevents the air/fuel mixture from firing, thereby causing a no-start situation.

FLUID: A fluid can be either liquid or gas. In hydraulics, a liquid is used for transmitting force or motion.

FLUID COUPLING: The simplest form of hydrodynamic drive, the fluid coupling consists of two look-alike members with straight radial varies referred to as the impeller (pump) and the turbine. Input torque is always equal to the output torque.

FLUID DRIVE: Either a fluid coupling or a fluid torque converter. (See hydrodynamic drive units.)

FLUID TORQUE CONVERTER: A hydrodynamic drive that has the ability to act both as a torque multiplier and fluid coupling. (See hydrodynamic drive units; torque converter.)

FLUID VISCOSITY: The resistance of a liquid to flow. A cold fluid (oil) has greater viscosity and flows more slowly than a hot fluid (oil).

FLYWHEEL: A heavy disc of metal attached to the rear of the crankshaft. It smoothes the firing impulses of the engine and keeps the crankshaft turning during periods when no firing takes place. The starter also engages the flywheel to start the engine.

FOOT POUND (ft. lbs., lbs. ft. or sometimes, ft. lb.): The amount of energy or work needed to raise an item weighing one pound, a distance of one foot.

FREEZE PLUG: A plug in the engine block which will be pushed out if the coolant freezes. Sometimes called expansion plugs, they protect the block from cracking should the coolant freeze.

FRICTION: The resistance that occurs between contacting surfaces. This relationship is expressed by a ratio called the coefficient of friction (CL).

FRICTION, COEFFICIENT OF: The amount of surface tension between two contacting surfaces; expressed by a scientifically calculated number.

FRONT END ALIGNMENT: A service to set caster, camber and toe-in to the correct specifications. This will ensure that the car steers and handles properly and that the tires wear properly.

FRICTION MODIFIER: Changes the coefficient of friction of the fluid between the mating steel and composition clutch/band surfaces during the engagement process and allows for a certain amount of intentional slipping for a good "shift-feel".

FRONTAL AREA: The total frontal area of a vehicle exposed to air flow.

FUEL FILTER: A component of the fuel system containing a porous paper element used to prevent any impurities from entering the engine through the fuel system. It usually takes the form of a canister-like housing, mounted in-line with the fuel hose, located anywhere on a vehicle between the fuel tank and engine.

FUEL INJECTION: A system replacing the carburetor that sprays fuel into the cylinder through nozzles. The amount of fuel can be more precisely controlled with fuel injection.

FULL FLOATING AXLE: An axle in which the axle housing extends through the wheel giving bearing support on the outside of the housing. The front axle of a four-wheel drive vehicle is usually a full floating axle, as are the rear axles of many larger (1 ton and over) pick-ups and vans.

FULL-TIME FOUR-WHEEL DRIVE: A four-wheel drive system that continuously delivers power to all four wheels. A differential between the front and rear driveshafts permits variations in axle speeds to control gear wind-up without damage.

FULL THROTTLE DETENT DOWNSHIFT: A quick apply of accelerator pedal to its full travel, forcing a downshift.

FUSE: A protective device in a circuit which prevents circuit overload by breaking the circuit when a specific amperage is present. The device is constructed around a strip or wire of a lower amperage rating than the circuit it is designed to protect. When an amperage higher than that stamped on the fuse is present in the circuit, the strip or wire melts, opening the circuit.

FUSIBLE LINK: A piece of wire in a wiring harness that performs the same job as a fuse. If overloaded, the fusible link will melt and interrupt the circuit.

FWD: Front wheel drive.

GAWR: (Gross axle weight rating) the total maximum weight an axle is designed to carry.

GCW: (Gross combined weight) total combined weight of a tow vehicle and trailer.

GARAGE SHIFT: initial engagement feel of transmission, neutral to reverse or neutral to a forward drive.

GARAGE SHIFT FEEL: A quick check of the engagement quality and responsiveness of reverse and forward gears. This test is done with the vehicle stationary.

GEAR: A toothed mechanical device that acts as a rotating lever to transmit power or turning effort from one shaft to another. (See gear ratio.)

GEAR RATIO. A ratio expressing the number of turns a smaller gear will make to turn a larger gear through one revolution. The ratio is found by dividing the number of teeth on the smaller gear into the number of teeth on the larger gear.

GEARBOX: Transmission

GEAR REDUCTION: Torque is multiplied and speed decreased by the factor of the gear ratio. For example, a 3:1 gear ratio changes an input torque of 180 ft. lbs. and an input speed of 2700 rpm to 540 Ft. lbs. and 900 rpm, respectively. (No account is taken of frictional losses, which are always present.)

GEARTRAIN: A succession of intermeshing gears that form an assembly and provide for one or more torque changes as the power input is transmitted to the power output.

GEL COAT: A thin coat of plastic resin covering fiberglass body panels.

GENERATOR: A device which produces direct current (DC) necessary to charge the battery.

GOVERNOR: A device that senses vehicle speed and generates a hydraulic oil pressure. As vehicle speed increases, governor oil pressure rises.

GROUND CIRCUIT: (See circuit, ground.)

GROUND SIDE SWITCHING: The electrical/electronic circuit control switch is located after the circuit load.

GVWR: (Gross vehicle weight rating) total maximum weight a vehicle is designed to carry including the weight of the vehicle, passengers, equipment, gas, oil, etc.

HALOGEN: A special type of lamp known for its quality of brilliant white light. Originally used for fog lights and driving lights.

HARD CODES: DTCs that are present at the time of testing; also called continuous or current codes.

HARSH(ROUGH): An apply of a clutch or band that is more noticeable than a firm one; considered undesirable at any throttle position.

HEADER TANK: An expansion tank for the radiator coolant. It can be located remotely or built into the radiator.

HEAT RANGE: A term used to describe the ability of a spark plug to carry away heat. Plugs with longer nosed insulators take longer to carry heat off effectively.

HEAT RISER: A flapper in the exhaust manifold that is closed when the engine is cold, causing hot exhaust gases to heat the intake manifold providing better cold engine operation. A thermostatic spring opens the flapper when the engine warms up.

HEAVY THROTTLE: Approximately three-fourths of accelerator pedal travel.

HEMI: A name given an engine using hemispherical combustion chambers.

HERTZ (HZ): The international unit of frequency equal to one cycle per second (10,000 Hertz equals 10,000 cycles per second).

HIGH-IMPEDANCE DVOM (DIGITAL VOLT-OHMMETER): This styled device provides a built-in resistance value and is capable of limiting circuit current flow to safe milliamp levels.

HIGH RESISTANCE: Often refers to a circuit where there is an excessive amount of opposition to normal current flow.

HORSEPOWER: A measurement of the amount of work; one horsepower is the amount of work necessary to lift 33,000 lbs. one foot in one minute. Brake horsepower (bhp) is the horsepower delivered by an engine on a dynamometer. Net horsepower is the power remaining (measured at the flywheel of the engine) that can be used to turn the wheels after power is consumed through friction and running the engine accessories (water pump, alternator, air pump, fan etc.)

HOT CIRCUIT: (See circuit, hot; hot lead.)

HOT LEAD: A wire or conductor in the power side of the circuit. (See circuit, hot.)

HOT SIDE SWITCHING: The electrical/electronic circuit control switch is located before the circuit load.

HUB: The center part of a wheel or gear.

HUNTING (BUSYNESS): Repeating quick series of up-shifts and downshifts that causes noticeable change in engine rpm, for example, as in a 4-3-4 shift pattern.

HYDRAULICS: The use of liquid under pressure to transfer force of motion.

HYDROCARBON (HC): Any chemical compound made up of hydrogen and carbon. A major pollutant formed by the engine as a by-product of combustion.

HYDRODYNAMIC DRIVE UNITS: Devices that transmit power solely by the action of a kinetic fluid flow in a closed recirculating path. An impeller energizes the fluid and discharges the high-speed jet stream into the turbine for power output.

HYDROMETER: An instrument used to measure the specific gravity of a solution.

HYDROPLANING: A phenomenon of driving when water builds up under the tire tread, causing it to lose contact with the road. Slowing down will usually restore normal tire contact with the road.

HYPOID GEARSET: The drive pinion gear may be placed below or above the centerline of the driven gear; often used as a final drive gearset.

IDLE MIXTURE: The mixture of air and fuel (usually about 14:1) being fed to the cylinders. The idle mixture screw(s) are sometimes adjusted as part of a tune-up.

IDLER ARM: Component of the steering linkage which is a geometric duplicate of the steering gear arm. It supports the right side of the center steering link.

IMPELLER: Often called a pump, the impeller is the power input (drive) member of a hydrodynamic drive. As part of the torque converter cover, it acts as a centrifugal pump and puts the fluid in motion.

INCH POUND (inch lbs.; sometimes in. lb. or in. lbs.): One twelfth of a foot pound.

INDUCTANCE: The force that produces voltage when a conductor is passed through a magnetic field.

INDUCTION: A means of transferring electrical energy in the form of a magnetic field. Principle used in the ignition coil to increase voltage.

INITIAL FEEL: A distinct firmer feel at start of shift when compared with feel at finish of shift.

INJECTOR: A device which receives metered fuel under relatively low pressure and is activated to inject the fuel into the engine under relatively high pressure at a predetermined time.

INPUT: In an automatic transmission, the source of power from the engine is absorbed by the torque converter, which provides the power input into the transmission. The turbine drives the input(turbine)shaft.

INPUT SHAFT: The shaft to which torque is applied, usually carrying the driving gear or gears.

INTAKE MANIFOLD: A casting of passages or pipes used to conduct air or a fuel/air mixture to the cylinders.

INTERNAL GEAR: The ring-like outer gear of a planetary gearset with the gear teeth cut on the inside of the ring to provide a mesh with the planet pinions.

ISOLATION (CLAMPING) DIODES: Diodes positioned in a circuit to prevent self-induction from damaging electronic components.

IX ROTARY GEAR PUMP: Contains two rotating members, one shaped with internal gear teeth and the other with external gear teeth. As the gears separate, the fluid fills the gaps between gear teeth, is pulled across a crescent-shaped divider, and then is forced to flow through the outlet as the gears mesh.

IX ROTARY LOBE PUMP: Sometimes referred to as a gerotor type pump. Two rotating members, one shaped with internal lobes and the other with external lobes, separate and then mesh to cause fluid to flow.

JOURNAL: The bearing surface within which a shaft operates.

JUMPER CABLES: Two heavy duty wires with large alligator clips used to provide power from a charged battery to a discharged battery mounted in a vehicle.

JUMPSTART: Utilizing the sufficiently charged battery of one vehicle to start the engine of another vehicle with a discharged battery by the use of jumper cables.

KEY: A small block usually fitted in a notch between a shaft and a hub to prevent slippage of the two parts.

KICKDOWN: Detent downshift system; either linkage, cable, or electrically controlled.

KILO: A prefix used in the metric system to indicate one thousand.

KNOCK: Noise which results from the spontaneous ignition of a portion of the air-fuel mixture in the engine cylinder caused by overly advanced ignition timing or use of incorrectly low octane fuel for that engine.

KNOCK SENSOR: An input device that responds to spark knock, caused by over advanced ignition timing.

LABOR TIME: A specific amount of time required to perform a certain repair or diagnostic service as defined by a vehicle or after-market manufacturer .

LACQUER: A quick-drying automotive paint.

LATE: Shift that occurs when engine is at higher than normal rpm for given amount of throttle.

LIGHT-EMITTING DIODE (LED): A semiconductor diode that emits light as electrical current flows through it; used in some electronic display devices to emit a red or other color light.

LIGHT THROTTLE: Approximately one-fourth of accelerator pedal travel.

LIMITED SLIP: A type of differential which transfers driving force to the wheel with the best traction.

LIMP-IN MODE: Electrical shutdown of the transmission/ transaxle output solenoids, allowing only forward and reverse gears that are hydraulically energized by the manual valve. This permits the vehicle to be driven to a service facility for repair.

LIP SEAL: Molded synthetic rubber seal designed with an outer sealing edge (lip) that points into the fluid containing area to be sealed. This type of seal is used where rotational and axial forces are present.

LITHIUM-BASE GREASE: Chassis and wheel bearing grease using lithium as a base. Not compatible with sodium-base grease.

LOAD DEVICE: A circuit's resistance that converts the electrical energy into light, sound, heat, or mechanical movement.

LOAD RANGE: Indicates the number of plies at which a tire is rated. Load range B equals four-ply rating; C equals six-ply rating; and, D equals an eight-ply rating.

LOAD TORQUE: The amount of output torque needed from the transmission/transaxle to overcome the vehicle load.

LOCKING HUBS: Accessories used on part-time four-wheel drive systems that allow the front wheels to be disengaged from the drive train when four-wheel drive is not being used. When four-wheel drive is desired, the hubs are engaged, locking the wheels to the drive train.

LOCKUP CONVERTER: A torque converter that operates hydraulically and mechanically. When an internal apply plate (lockup plate) clamps to the torque converter cover, hydraulic slippage is eliminated.

LOCK RING: See Circlip or Snapring

MAGNET: Any body with the property of attracting iron or steel.

MAGNETIC FIELD: The area surrounding the poles of a magnet that is affected by its attraction or repulsion forces.

MAIN LINE PRESSURE: Often called control pressure or line pressure, it refers to the pressure of the oil leaving the pump and is controlled by the pressure regulator valve.

MALFUNCTION INDICATOR LAMP (MIL): Previously known as a check engine light, the dash-mounted MIL illuminates and signals the driver that an emission or driveability problem with the powertrain has been detected by the ECM/PCM. When this occurs, at least one diagnostic trouble code (DTC) has been stored into the control module memory.

MANIFOLD ABSOLUTE PRESSURE (MAP) SENSOR: Reads the amount of air pressure (vacuum) in the engine's intake manifold system; its signal is used to analyze engine load conditions.

MANIFOLD VACUUM: Low pressure in an engine intake manifold formed just below the throttle plates. Manifold vacuum is highest at idle and drops under acceleration.

MANIFOLD: A casting of passages or set of pipes which connect the cylinders to an inlet or outlet source.

MANUAL LEVER POSITION SWITCH (MLPS): A mechanical switching unit that is typically mounted externally to the transmission/transaxle to inform the PCM/ECM which gear range the driver has selected.

MANUAL VALVE: Located inside the transmission/transaxle, it is directly connected to the driver's shift lever. The position of the manual valve determines which hydraulic circuits will be charged with oil pressure and the operating mode of the transmission.

MANUAL VALVE LEVER POSITION SENSOR (MVLPS): The input from this device tells the TCM what gear range was selected.

MASS AIR FLOW (MAF) SENSOR: Measures the airflow into the engine.

MASTER CYLINDER: The primary fluid pressurizing device in a hydraulic system. In automotive use, it is found in brake and hydraulic clutch systems and is pedal activated, either directly or, in a power brake system, through the power booster.

MacPherson STRUT: A suspension component combining a shock absorber and spring in one unit.

MEDIUM THROTTLE: Approximately one-half of accelerator pedal travel.

MEGA: A metric prefix indicating one million.

MEMBER: An independent component of a hydrodynamic unit such as an impeller, a stator, or a turbine. It may have one or more elements.

MERCON: A fluid developed by Ford Motor Company in 1988. It contains a friction modifier and closely resembles operating characteristics of Dexron.

METAL SEALING RINGS: Made from cast iron or aluminum, their primary application is with dynamic components involving pressure sealing circuits of rotating members. These rings are designed with either butt or hook lock end joints.

METER (ANALOG): A linear-style meter representing data as lengths; a needle-style instrument interfacing with logical numerical increments. This style of electrical meter uses relatively low impedance internal resistance and cannot be used for testing electronic circuitry.

METER (DIGITAL): Uses numbers as a direct readout to show values. Most meters of this style use high impedance internal resistance and must be used for testing low current electronic circuitry.

MICRO: A metric prefix indicating one-millionth (0.000001).

MILLI: A metric prefix indicating one-thousandth (0.001).

MINIMUM THROTTLE: The least amount of throttle opening required for upshift; normally close to zero throttle.

MISFIRE: Condition occurring when the fuel mixture in a cylinder fails to ignite, causing the engine to run roughly.

MODULE: Electronic control unit, amplifier or igniter of solid state or integrated design which controls the current flow in the ignition primary circuit based on input from the pick-up coil. When the module opens the primary circuit, high secondary voltage is induced in the coil.

MODULATED: In an electronic-hydraulic converter clutch system (or shift valve system), the term modulated refers to the pulsing of a solenoid, at a variable rate. This action controls the buildup of oil pressure in the hydraulic circuit to allow a controlled amount of clutch slippage.

MODULATED CONVERTER CLUTCH CONTROL (MCCC): A pulse width duty cycle valve that controls the converter lockup apply pressure and maximizes smoother transitions between lock and unlock conditions.

MODULATOR PRESSURE (THROTTLE PRESSURE): A hydraulic signal oil pressure relating to the amount of engine load, based on either the amount of throttle plate opening or engine vacuum.

MODULATOR VALVE: A regulator valve that is controlled by engine vacuum, providing a hydraulic pressure that varies in relation to engine torque. The hydraulic torque signal functions to delay the shift pattern and provide a line pressure boost. (See throttle valve.)

MOTOR: An electromagnetic device used to convert electrical energy into mechanical energy.

MULTIPLE-DISC CLUTCH: A grouping of steel and friction lined plates that, when compressed together by hydraulic pressure acting upon a piston, lock or unlock a planetary member.

MULTI-WEIGHT: Type of oil that provides adequate lubrication at both high and low temperatures.

needed to move one amp through a resistance of one ohm.

MUSHY: Same as soft; slow and drawn out clutch apply with very little shift feel.

MUTUAL INDUCTION: The generation of current from one wire circuit to another by movement of the magnetic field surrounding a current-carrying circuit as its ampere flow increases or decreases.

NEEDLE BEARING: A bearing which consists of a number (usually a large number) of long, thin rollers.

NITROGEN OXIDE (NOx): One of the three basic pollutants found in the exhaust emission of an internal combustion engine. The amount of NOx usually varies in an inverse proportion to the amount of HC and CO.

NONPOSITIVE SEALING: A sealing method that allows some minor leakage, which normally assists in lubrication.

O2 SENSOR: Located in the engine's exhaust system, it is an input device to the ECM/PCM for managing the fuel delivery and ignition system. A scanner can be used to observe the fluctuating voltage readings produced by an O2 sensor as the oxygen content of the exhaust is analyzed.

O-RING SEAL: Molded synthetic rubber seal designed with a circular cross-section. This type of seal is used primarily in static applications.

OBD II (ON-BOARD DIAGNOSTICS, SECOND GENERATION): Refers to the federal law mandating tighter control of 1996 and newer vehicle emissions, active monitoring of related devices, and standardization of terminology, data link connectors, and other technician concerns.

OCTANE RATING: A number, indicating the quality of gasoline based on its ability to resist knock. The higher the number, the better the quality. Higher compression engines require higher octane gas.

OEM: Original Equipment Manufactured. OEM equipment is that furnished standard by the manufacturer.

OFFSET: The distance between the vertical center of the wheel and the mounting surface at the lugs. Offset is positive if the center is outside the lug circle; negative offset puts the center line inside the lug circle.

OHM'S LAW: A law of electricity that states the relationship between voltage, current, and resistance. Volts = amperes x ohms

OHM: The unit used to measure the resistance of conductor-to-electrical flow. One ohm is the amount of resistance that limits current flow to one ampere in a circuit with one volt of pressure.

OHMMETER: An instrument used for measuring the resistance, in ohms, in an electrical circuit.

ONE-WAY CLUTCH: A mechanical clutch of roller or sprag design that resists torque or transmits power in one direction only. It is used to either hold or drive a planetary member.

ONE-WAY ROLLER CLUTCH: A mechanical device that transmits or holds torque in one direction only.

OPEN CIRCUIT: A break or lack of contact in an electrical circuit, either intentional (switch) or unintentional (bad connection or broken wire).

ORIFICE: Located in hydraulic oil circuits, it acts as a restriction. It slows down fluid flow to either create back pressure or delay pressure buildup downstream.

OSCILLOSCOPE: A piece of test equipment that shows electric impulses as a pattern on a screen. Engine performance can be analyzed by interpreting these patterns.

OUTPUT SHAFT: The shaft which transmits torque from a device, such as a transmission.

OUTPUT SPEED SENSOR (OSS): Identifies transmission/transaxle output shaft speed for shift timing and may be used to calculate TCC slip; often functions as the VSS (vehicle speed sensor).

OVERDRIVE: (1.) A device attached to or incorporated in a transmission/transaxle that allows the engine to turn less than one full revolution for every complete revolution of the wheels. The net effect is to reduce engine rpm, thereby using less fuel. A typical overdrive gear ratio would be .87:1, instead of the normal 1:1 in high gear. (2.) A gear assembly which produces more shaft revolutions than that transmitted to it.

OVERDRIVE PLANETARY GEARSET: A single planetary gearset designed to provide a direct drive and overdrive ratio. When coupled to a three-speed transmission/transaxle configuration, a four-speed/overdrive unit is present.

OVERHEAD CAMSHAFT (OHC): An engine configuration in which the camshaft is mounted on top of the cylinder head and operates the valve either directly or by means of rocker arms.

OVERHEAD VALVE (OHV): An engine configuration in which all of the valves are located in the cylinder head and the camshaft is located in the cylinder block. The camshaft operates the valves via lifters and pushrods.

OVERRUNCLUTCH: Another name for a one-way mechanical clutch. Applies to both roller and sprag designs.

OVERSTEER: The tendency of some vehicles, when steering into a turn, to over-respond or steer more than required, which could result in excessive slip of the rear wheels. Opposite of under-steer.

OXIDATION STABILIZERS: Absorb and dissipate heat. Automatic transmission fluid has high resistance to varnish and sludge buildup that occurs from excessive heat that is generated primarily in the torque converter. Local temperatures as high as 6000F (3150C) can occur at the clutch plates during engagement, and this heat must be absorbed and dissipated. If the fluid cannot withstand the heat, it burns or oxidizes, resulting in an almost immediate destruction of friction materials, clogged filter screen and hydraulic passages, and sticky valves.

OXIDES OF NITROGEN: See nitrogen oxide (NOx).

OXYGEN SENSOR: Used with a feedback system to sense the presence of oxygen in the exhaust gas and signal the computer which can use the voltage signal to determine engine operating efficiency and adjust the air/fuel ratio.

PARALLEL CIRCUIT: (See circuit, parallel.)

PARTS WASHER: A basin or tub, usually with a built-in pump mechanism and hose used for circulating chemical solvent for the purpose of cleaning greasy, oily and dirty components.

PART-TIME FOUR WHEEL DRIVE: A system that is normally in the two wheel drive mode and only runs in four-wheel drive when the system is manually engaged because more traction is desired. Two or four wheel drive is normally selected by a lever to engage the front axle, but if locking hubs are used, these must also be manually engaged in the Lock position. Otherwise, the front axle will not drive the front wheels.

PASSIVE RESTRAINT: Safety systems such as air bags or automatic seat belts which operate with no action required on the part of the driver or passenger. Mandated by Federal regulations on all vehicles sold in the U.S. after 1990.

PAYLOAD: The weight the vehicle is capable of carrying in addition to its own weight. Payload includes weight of the driver, passengers and cargo, but not coolant, fuel, lubricant, spare tire, etc.

PCM: Powertrain control module.

PCV VALVE: A valve usually located in the rocker cover that vents crankcase vapors back into the engine to be reburned.

PERCOLATION: A condition in which the fuel actually "boils," due to excessive heat. Percolation prevents proper atomization of the fuel causing rough running.

PICK-UP COIL: The coil in which voltage is induced in an electronic ignition.

PING: A metallic rattling sound produced by the engine during acceleration. It is usually due to incorrect ignition timing or a poor grade of gasoline.

PINION: The smaller of two gears. The rear axle pinion drives the ring gear which transmits motion to the axle shafts.

PINION GEAR: The smallest gear in a drive gear assembly.

PISTON: A disc or cup that fits in a cylinder bore and is free to move. In hydraulics, it provides the means of converting hydraulic pressure into a usable force. Examples of piston applications are found in servo, clutch, and accumulator units.

PISTON RING: An open-ended ring which fits into a groove on the outer diameter of the piston. Its chief function is to form a seal between the piston and cylinder wall. Most automotive pistons have three rings: two for compression sealing; one for oil sealing.

PITMAN ARM: A lever which transmits steering force from the steering gear to the steering linkage.

PLANET CARRIER: A basic member of a planetary gear assembly that carries the pinion gears.

PLANET PINIONS: Gears housed in a planet carrier that are in constant mesh with the sun gear and internal gear. Because they have their own independent rotating centers, the pinions are capable of rotating around the sun gear or the inside of the internal gear.

PLANETARY GEAR RATIO: The reduction or overdrive ratio developed by a planetary gearset.

PLANETARY GEARSET: In its simplest form, it is made up of a basic assembly group containing a sun gear, internal gear, and planet carrier. The gears are always in constant mesh and offer a wide range of gear ratio possibilities.

PLANETARY GEARSET (COMPOUND): Two planetary gearsets combined together.

PLANETARY GEARSET (SIMPLE): An assembly of gears in constant mesh consisting of a sun gear, several pinion gears mounted in a carrier, and a ring gear. It provides gear ratio and direction changes, in addition to a direct drive and a neutral.

PLY RATING: A. rating given a tire which indicates strength (but not necessarily actual plies). A two-ply/four-ply rating has only two plies, but the strength of a four-ply tire.

POLARITY: Indication (positive or negative) of the two poles of a battery.

PORT: An opening for fluid intake or exhaust.

POSITIVE SEALING: A sealing method that completely prevents leakage.

POTENTIAL: Electrical force measured in volts; sometimes used interchangeably with voltage.

POWER: The ability to do work per unit of time, as expressed in horsepower; one horsepower equals 33,000 ft. lbs. of work per minute, or 550 ft. lbs. of work per second.

POWER FLOW: The systematic flow or transmission of power through the gears, from the input shaft to the output shaft.

POWER-TO-WEIGHT RATIO: Ratio of horsepower to weight of car.

POWERTRAIN: See Drivetrain.

POWERTRAIN CONTROL MODULE (PCM): Current designation for the engine control module (ECM). In many cases, late model vehicle control units manage the engine as well as the transmission. In other settings, the PCM controls the engine and is interfaced with a TCM to control transmission functions.

Ppm: Parts per million; unit used to measure exhaust emissions.

PREIGNITION: Early ignition of fuel in the cylinder, sometimes due to glowing carbon deposits in the combustion chamber. Preignition can be damaging since combustion takes place prematurely.

PRELOAD: A predetermined load placed on a bearing during assembly or by adjustment.

PRESS FIT: The mating of two parts under pressure, due to the inner diameter of one being smaller than the outer diameter of the other, or vice versa; an interference fit.

PRESSURE: The amount of force exerted upon a surface area.

PRESSURE CONTROL SOLENOID (PCS): An output device that provides a boost oil pressure to the mainline regulator valve to control line pressure. Its operation is determined by the amount of current sent from the PCM.

PRESSURE GAUGE: An instrument used for measuring the fluid pressure in a hydraulic circuit.

PRESSURE REGULATOR VALVE: In automatic transmissions, its purpose is to regulate the pressure of the pump output and supply the basic fluid pressure necessary to operate the transmission. The regulated fluid pressure may be referred to as mainline pressure, line pressure, or control pressure.

PRESSURE SWITCH ASSEMBLY (PSA): Mounted inside the transmission, it is a grouping of oil pressure switches that inputs to the PCM when certain hydraulic passages are charged with oil pressure.

PRESSURE PLATE: A spring-loaded plate (part of the clutch) that transmits power to the driven (friction) plate when the clutch is engaged.

PRIMARY CIRCUIT: The low voltage side of the ignition system which consists of the ignition switch, ballast resistor or resistance wire, bypass, coil, electronic control unit and pick-up coil as well as the connecting wires and harnesses.

PROFILE: Term used for tire measurement (tire series), which is the ratio of tire height to tread width.

PROM (PROGRAMMABLE READ-ONLY MEMORY): The heart of the computer that compares input data and makes the engineered program or strategy decisions about when to trigger the appropriate output based on stored computer instructions.

PULSE GENERATOR: A two-wire pickup sensor used to produce a fluctuating electrical signal. This changing signal is read by the controller to determine the speed of the object and can be used to measure transmission/transaxle input speed, output speed, and vehicle speed.

PSI: Pounds per square inch; a measurement of pressure.

PULSE WIDTH DUTY CYCLE SOLENOID (PULSE WIDTH MODU-LATED SOLENOID): A computer-controlled solenoid that turns on and off at a variable rate producing a modulated oil pressure; often referred to as a pulse width modulated (PWM) solenoid. Employed in many electronic automatic transmissions and transaxles, these solenoids are used to manage shift control and converter clutch hydraulic circuits.

PUSHROD: A steel rod between the hydraulic valve lifter and the valve rocker arm in overhead valve (OHV) engines.

PUMP: A mechanical device designed to create fluid flow and pressure buildup in a hydraulic system.

QUARTER PANEL: General term used to refer to a rear fender. Quarter panel is the area from the rear door opening to the tail light area and from rear wheel well to the base of the trunk and roof-line.

RACE: The surface on the inner or outer ring of a bearing on which the balls, needles or rollers move.

RACK AND PINION: A type of automotive steering system using a pinion gear attached to the end of the steering shaft. The pinion meshes with a long rack attached to the steering linkage.

RADIAL TIRE: Tire design which uses body cords running at right angles to the center line of the tire. Two or more belts are used to give tread strength. Radials can be identified by their characteristic sidewall bulge.

RADIATOR: Part of the cooling system for a water-cooled engine, mounted in the front of the vehicle and connected to the engine with rubber hoses. Through the radiator, excess combustion heat is dissipated into the atmosphere through forced convection using a water and glycol based mixture that circulates through, and cools, the engine.

RANGE REFERENCE AND CLUTCH/BAND APPLY CHART: A guide that shows the application of clutches and bands for each gear, within the selector range positions. These charts are extremely useful for understanding how the unit operates and for diagnosing malfunctions.

RAVIGNEAUX GEARSET: A compound planetary gearset that features matched dual planetary pinions (sets of two) mounted in a single planet carrier. Two sun gears and one ring mesh with the carrier pinions.

REACTION MEMBER: The stationary planetary member, in a planetary gearset, that is grounded to the transmission/transaxle case through the use of friction and wedging devices known as bands, disc clutches, and one-way clutches.

REACTION PRESSURE: The fluid pressure that moves a spool valve against an opposing force or forces; the area on which the opposing force acts. The opposing force can be a spring or a combination of spring force and auxiliary hydraulic force.

REACTOR, TORQUE CONVERTER: The reaction member of a fluid torque converter, more commonly called a stator. (See stator.)

REAR MAIN OIL SEAL: A synthetic or rope-type seal that prevents oil from leaking out of the engine past the rear main crankshaft bearing.

RECIRCULATING BALL: Type of steering system in which recirculating steel balls occupy the area between the nut and worm wheel, causing a reduction in friction.

RECTIFIER: A device (used primarily in alternators) that permits electrical current to flow in one direction only.

REDUCTION: (See gear reduction.)

REGULATOR VALVE: A valve that changes the pressure of the oil in a hydraulic circuit as the oil passes through the valve by bleeding off (or exhausting) some of the volume of oil supplied to the valve.

REFRIGERANT 12 (R-12) or 134 (R-134): The generic name of the refrigerant used in automotive air conditioning systems.

REGULATOR: A device which maintains the amperage and/or voltage levels of a circuit at predetermined values.

RELAY: A switch which automatically opens and/or closes a circuit.

RELAY VALVE: A valve that directs flow and pressure. Relay valves simply connect or disconnect interrelated passages without restricting the fluid flow or changing the pressure.

RELIEF VALVE: A spring-loaded, pressure-operated valve that limits oil pressure buildup in a hydraulic circuit to a predetermined maximum value.

RELUCTOR: A wheel that rotates inside the distributor and triggers the release of voltage in an electronic ignition.

RESERVOIR: The storage area for fluid in a hydraulic system; often called a sump.

RESIN: A liquid plastic used in body work.

RESIDUAL MAGNETISM: The magnetic strength stored in a material after a magnetizing field has been removed.

RESISTANCE: The opposition to the flow of current through a circuit or electrical device, and is measured in ohms. Resistance is equal to the voltage divided by the amperage.

RESISTOR SPARK PLUG: A spark plug using a resistor to shorten the spark duration. This suppresses radio interference and lengthens plug life.

RESISTOR: A device, usually made of wire, which offers a preset amount of resistance in an electrical circuit.

RESULTANT FORCE: The single effective directional thrust of the fluid force on the turbine produced by the vortex and rotary forces acting in different planes.

RETARD: Set the ignition timing so that spark occurs later (fewer degrees before TDC).

RHEOSTAT: A device for regulating a current by means of a variable resistance.

RING GEAR: The name given to a ring-shaped gear attached to a differential case, or affixed to a flywheel or as part of a planetary gear set.

ROADLOAD: grade.

ROCKER ARM: A lever which rotates around a shaft pushing down (opening) the valve with an end when the other end is pushed up by the pushrod. Spring pressure will later close the valve.

ROCKER PANEL: The body panel below the doors between the wheel opening.

ROLLER BEARING: A bearing made up of hardened inner and outer races between which hardened steel rollers move.

ROLLER CLUTCH: A type of one-way clutch design using rollers and springs mounted within an inner and outer cam race assembly.

ROTARY FLOW: The path of the fluid trapped between the blades of the members as they revolve with the rotation of the torque converter cover (rotational inertia).

ROTOR: (1.) The disc-shaped part of a disc brake assembly, upon which the brake pads bear; also called, brake disc. (2.) The device mounted atop the distributor shaft, which passes current to the distributor cap tower contacts.

ROTARY ENGINE: See Wankel engine.

RPM: Revolutions per minute (usually indicates engine speed).

RTV: A gasket making compound that cures as it is exposed to the atmosphere. It is used between surfaces that are not perfectly machined to one another, leaving a slight gap that the RTV fills and in which it hardens. The letters RTV represent room temperature vulcanizing.

RUN-ON: Condition when the engine continues to run, even when the key is turned off. See dieseling.

SEALED BEAM: A automotive headlight. The lens, reflector and filament from a single unit.

SEATBELT INTERLOCK: A system whereby the car cannot be started unless the seatbelt is buckled.

SECONDARY CIRCUIT: The high voltage side of the ignition system, usually above 20,000 volts. The secondary includes the ignition coil, coil wire, distributor cap and rotor, spark plug wires and spark plugs.

SELF-INDUCTION: The generation of voltage in a current-carrying wire by changing the amount of current flowing within that wire.

SEMI-CONDUCTOR: A material (silicon or germanium) that is neither a good conductor nor an insulator; used in diodes and transistors.

SEMI-FLOATING AXLE: In this design, a wheel is attached to the axle shaft, which takes both drive and cornering loads. Almost all solid axle passenger cars and light trucks use this design.

SENDING UNIT: A mechanical, electrical, hydraulic or electromagnetic device which transmits information to a gauge.

SENSOR: Any device designed to measure engine operating conditions or ambient pressures and temperatures. Usually electronic in nature and designed to send a voltage signal to an on-board computer, some sensors may operate as a simple on/off switch or they may provide a variable voltage signal (like a potentiometer) as conditions or measured parameters change.

SERIES CIRCUIT: (See circuit, series.)

SERPENTINE BELT: An accessory drive belt, with small multiple v-ribs, routed around most or all of the engine-powered accessories such as the alternator and power steering pump. Usually both the front and the back side of the belt comes into contact with various pulleys.

SERVO: In an automatic transmission, it is a piston in a cylinder assembly that converts hydraulic pressure into mechanical force and movement; used for the application of the bands and clutches.

SHIFT BUSYNESS: When referring to a torque converter clutch, it is the frequent apply and release of the clutch plate due to uncommon driving conditions.

SHIFT VALVE: Classified as a relay valve, it triggers the automatic shift in response to a governor and a throttle signal by directing fluid to the appropriate band and clutch apply combination to cause the shift to occur.

SHIM: Spacers of precise, predetermined thickness used between parts to establish a proper working relationship.

SHIMMY: Vibration (sometimes violent) in the front end caused by misaligned front end, out of balance tires or worn suspension components.

SHORT CIRCUIT: An electrical malfunction where current takes the path of least resistance to ground (usually through damaged insulation). Current flow is excessive from low resistance resulting in a blown fuse.

SHUDDER: Repeated jerking or stick-slip sensation, similar to chuggle but more severe and rapid in nature, that may be most noticeable during certain ranges of vehicle speed; also used to define condition after converter clutch engagement.

SIMPSON GEARSET: A compound planetary gear train that integrates two simple planetary gearsets referred to as the front planetary and the rear planetary.

SINGLE OVERHEAD CAMSHAFT: See overhead camshaft.

SKIDPLATE: A metal plate attached to the underside of the body to protect the fuel tank, transfer case or other vulnerable parts from damage.

SLAVE CYLINDER: In automotive use, a device in the hydraulic clutch system which is activated by hydraulic force, disengaging the clutch.

SLIPPING: Noticeable increase in engine rpm without vehicle speed increase; usually occurs during or after initial clutch or band engagement.

SLUDGE: Thick, black deposits in engine formed from dirt, oil, water, etc. It is usually formed in engines when oil changes are neglected.

SNAP RING: A circular retaining clip used inside or outside a shaft or part to secure a shaft, such as a floating wrist pin.

SOFT: Slow, almost unnoticeable clutch apply with very little shift feel.

SOFTCODES: DTCs that have been set into the PCM memory but are not present at the time of testing; often referred to as history or intermittent codes.

SOHC: Single overhead camshaft.

SOLENOID: An electrically operated, magnetic switching device.

SPALLING: A wear pattern identified by metal chips flaking off the hardened surface. This condition is caused by foreign particles, overloading situations, and/or normal wear.

SPARK PLUG: A device screwed into the combustion chamber of a spark ignition engine. The basic construction is a conductive core inside of a ceramic insulator, mounted in an outer conductive base. An electrical charge from the spark plug wire travels along the conductive core and jumps a preset air gap to a grounding point or points at the end of the conductive base. The resultant spark ignites the fuel/air mixture in the combustion chamber.

SPECIFIC GRAVITY (BATTERY): The relative weight of liquid (battery electrolyte) as compared to the weight of an equal volume of water.

SPLINES: Ridges machined or cast onto the outer diameter of a shaft or inner diameter of a bore to enable parts to mate without rotation.

SPLIT TORQUE DRIVE: In a torque converter, it refers to parallel paths of torque transmission, one of which is mechanical and the other hydraulic.

SPONGY PEDAL: A soft or spongy feeling when the brake pedal is depressed. It is usually due to air in the brake lines.

SPOOLVALVE: A precision-machined, cylindrically shaped valve made up of lands and grooves. Depending on its position in the valve bore, various interconnecting hydraulic circuit passages are either opened or closed.

SPRAG CLUTCH: A type of one-way clutch design using cams or contoured-shaped sprags between inner and outer races. (See one-way clutch.)

SPRUNG WEIGHT: The weight of a car supported by the springs.

SQUARE-CUT SEAL: Molded synthetic rubber seal designed with a square- or rectangular-shaped cross-section. This type of seal is used for both dynamic and static applications.

SRS: Supplemental restraint system

STABILIZER (SWAY) BAR: A bar linking both sides of the suspension. It resists sway on turns by taking some of added load from one wheel and putting it on the other.

STAGE: The number of turbine sets separated by a stator. A turbine set may be made up of one or more turbine members. A three-element converter is classified as a single stage.

STALL: In fluid drive transmission/transaxle applications, stall refers to engine rpm with the transmission/transaxle engaged and the vehicle stationary; throttle valve can be in any position between closed and wide open.

STALL SPEED: In fluid drive transmission/transaxle applications, stall speed refers to the maximum engine rpm with the transmission/transaxle engaged and vehicle stationary, when the throttle valve is wide open. (See stall; stall test.)

STALL TEST: A procedure recommended by many manufacturers to help determine the integrity of an engine, the torque converter stator, and certain clutch and band combinations. With the shift lever in each of the forward and reverse positions and with the brakes firmly applied, the accelerator pedal is momentarily pressed to the wide open throttle (WOT) position. The engine rpm reading at full throttle can provide clues for diagnosing the condition of the items listed above.

STALL TORQUE: The maximum design or engineered torque ratio of a fluid torque converter, produced under stall speed conditions. (See stall speed.)

STARTER: A high-torque electric motor used for the purpose of starting the engine, typically through a high ratio geared drive connected to the flywheel ring gear.

STATIC: A sealing application in which the parts being sealed do not move in relation to each other.

STATOR (REACTOR): The reaction member of a fluid torque converter that changes the direction of the fluid as it leaves the turbine to enter the impeller vanes. During the torque multiplication phase, this action assists the impeller's rotary force and results in an increase in torque.

STEERING GEOMETRY: Combination of various angles of suspension components (caster, camber, toe-in); roughly equivalent to front end alignment.

STRAIGHT WEIGHT: Term designating motor oil as suitable for use within a narrow range of temperatures. Outside the narrow temperature range its flow characteristics will not adequately lubricate.

STROKE: The distance the piston travels from bottom dead center to top dead center.

SUBSTITUTION: Replacing one part suspected of a defect with a like part of known quality.

SUMP: The storage vessel or reservoir that provides a ready source of fluid to the pump. In an automatic transmission, the sump is the oil pan. All fluid eventually returns to the sump for recycling into the hydraulic system.

SUN GEAR: In a planetary gearset, it is the center gear that meshes with a cluster of planet pinions.

SUPERCHARGER: An air pump driven mechanically by the engine through belts, chains, shafts or gears from the crankshaft. Two general types of supercharger are the positive displacement and centrifugal type, which pump air in direct relationship to the speed of the engine.

SUPPLEMENTAL RESTRAINT SYSTEM: See air bag.

SURGE: Repeating engine-related feeling of acceleration and deceleration that is less intense than chuggle.

SWITCH: A device used to open, close, or redirect the current in an electrical circuit.

SYNCHROMESH: A manual transmission/transaxle that is equipped with devices (synchronizers) that match the gear speeds so that the transmission/transaxle can be downshifted without clashing gears.

SYNTHETIC OIL: Non-petroleum based oil.

TACHOMETER: A device used to measure the rotary speed of an engine, shaft, gear, etc., usually in rotations per minute.

TDC: Top dead center. The exact top of the piston's stroke.

TEFLON SEALING RINGS: Teflon is a soft, durable, plastic-like material that is resistant to heat and provides excellent sealing. These rings are designed with either scarf-cut joints or as one-piece rings. Teflon sealing rings have replaced many metal ring applications.

TERMINAL: A device attached to the end of a wire or cable to make an electrical connection.

TEST LIGHT, CIRCUIT-POWERED: Uses available circuit voltage to test circuit continuity.

TEST LIGHT, SELF-POWERED: Uses its own battery source to test circuit continuity.

THERMISTOR: A special resistor used to measure fluid temperature; it decreases its resistance with increases in temperature.

THERMOSTAT: A valve, located in the cooling system of an engine, which is closed when cold and opens gradually in response to engine heating, controlling the temperature of the coolant and rate of coolant flow.

THERMOSTATIC ELEMENT: A heat-sensitive, spring-type device that controls a drain port from the upper sump area to the lower sump. When the transaxle fluid reaches operating temperature, the port is closed and the upper sump fills, thus reducing the fluid level in the lower sump.

THROTTLE POSITION (TP) SENSOR: Reads the degree of throttle opening; its signal is used to analyze engine load conditions. The ECM/PCM decides to apply the TCC, or to disengage it for coast or load conditions that need a converter torque boost.

THROTTLE PRESSURE/MODULATOR PRESSURE: A hydraulic signal oil pressure relating to the amount of engine load, based on either the amount of throttle plate opening or engine vacuum.

THROTTLE VALVE: A regulating or balanced valve that is controlled mechanically by throttle linkage or engine vacuum. It sends a hydraulic signal to the shift valve body to control shift timing and shift quality. (See balanced valve; modulator valve.)

THROW-OUT BEARING: As the clutch pedal is depressed, the throwout bearing moves against the spring fingers of the pressure plate, forcing the pressure plate to disengage from the driven disc.

TIE ROD: A rod connecting the steering arms. Tie rods have threaded ends that are used to adjust toe-in.

TIE-UP: Condition where two opposing clutches are attempting to apply at same time, causing engine to labor with noticeable loss of engine rpm.

TIMING BELT: A square-toothed, reinforced rubber belt that is driven by the crankshaft and operates the camshaft.

TIMING CHAIN: A roller chain that is driven by the crankshaft and operates the camshaft.

TIRE ROTATION: Moving the tires from one position to another to make the tires wear evenly.

TOE-IN (OUT): A term comparing the extreme front and rear of the front tires. Closer together at the front is toe-in; farther apart at the front is toe-out.

TOP DEAD CENTER (TDC): The point at which the piston reaches the top of its travel on the compression stroke.

TORQUE: Measurement of turning or twisting force, expressed as foot-pounds or inch-pounds.

TORQUE CONVERTER: A turbine used to transmit power from a driving member to a driven member via hydraulic action, providing changes in drive ratio and torque. In automotive use, it links the driveplate at the rear of the engine to the automatic transmission.

TORQUE CONVERTER CLUTCH: The apply plate (lockup plate) assembly used for mechanical power flow through the converter.

TORQUE PHASE: Sometimes referred to as slip phase or stall phase, torque multiplication occurs when the turbine is turning at a slower speed than the impeller, and the stator is reactionary (stationary). This sequence generates a boost in output torque.

TORQUE RATING (STALL TORQUE): The maximum torque multiplication that occurs during stall conditions, with the engine at wide open throttle (WOT) and zero turbine speed.

TORQUE RATIO: An expression of the gear ratio factor on torque effect. A 3:1 gear ratio or 3:1 torque ratio increases the torque input by the ratio factor of 3. Input torque (100 ft. lbs.) x 3 = output torque (300 ft. lbs.)

TRACTION: The amount of usable tractive effort before the drive wheels slip on the road contact surface.

TORSION BAR SUSPENSION: Long rods of spring steel which take the place of springs. One end of the bar is anchored and the other arm (attached to the suspension) is free to twist. The bars' resistance to twisting causes springing action.

TRACK: Distance between the centers of the tires where they contact the ground.

TRACTION CONTROL: A control system that prevents the spinning of a vehicle's drive wheels when excess power is applied.

TRACTIVE EFFORT: The amount of force available to the drive wheels, to move the vehicle.

TRANSAXLE: A single housing containing the transmission and differential. Transaxles are usually found on front engine/front wheel drive or rear engine/rear wheel drive cars.

TRANSDUCER: A device that changes energy from one form to another. For example, a transducer in a microphone changes sound energy to electrical energy. In automotive air-conditioning controls used in automatic temperature systems, a transducer changes an electrical signal to a vacuum signal, which operates mechanical doors.

TRANSMISSION: A powertrain component designed to modify torque and speed developed by the engine; also provides direct drive, reverse, and neutral.

TRANSMISSION CONTROL MODULE (TCM): Manages transmission functions. These vary according to the manufacturer's product design but may include converter clutch operation, electronic shift scheduling, and mainline pressure.

TRANSMISSION FLUID TEMPERATURE (TFT) SENSOR: Originally called a transmission oil temperature (TOT) sensor, this input device to the ECM/PCM senses the fluid temperature and provides a resistance value. It operates on the thermistor principle.

TRANSMISSION INPUT SPEED (TIS) SENSOR: Measures turbine shaft (input shaft) rpm's and compares to engine rpm's to determine torque converter slip. When compared to the transmission output speed sensor or VSS, gear ratio and clutch engagement timing can be determined.

TRANSMISSION OIL TEMPERATURE (TOT) SENSOR: (See transmission fluid temperature (TFT) sensor.)

TRANSMISSION RANGE SELECTOR (TRS) SWITCH: Tells the module which gear shift position the driver has chosen.

TRANSFER CASE: A gearbox driven from the transmission that delivers power to both front and rear driveshafts in a four-wheel drive system. Transfer cases usually have a high and low range set of gears, used depending on how much pulling power is needed.

TRANSISTOR: A semi-conductor component which can be actuated by a small voltage to perform an electrical switching function.

TREAD WEAR INDICATOR: Bars molded into the tire at right angles to the tread that appear as horizontal bars when 1/16 in. of tread remains.

TREAD WEAR PATTERN: The pattern of wear on tires which can be "read" to diagnose problems in the front suspension.

TUNE-UP: A regular maintenance function, usually associated with the replacement and adjustment of parts and components in the electrical and fuel systems of a vehicle for the purpose of attaining optimum performance.

TURBINE: The output (driven) member of a fluid coupling or fluid torque converter. It is splined to the input (turbine) shaft of the transmission.

TURBOCHARGER: An exhaust driven pump which compresses intake air and forces it into the combustion chambers at higher than atmospheric pressures. The increased air pressure allows more fuel to be burned and results in increased horsepower being produced.

TURBULENCE: The interference of molecules of a fluid (or vapor) with each other in a fluid flow.

TYPE F: Transmission fluid developed and used by Ford Motor Company up to 1982. This fluid type provides a high coefficient of friction.

TYPE 7176: The preferred choice of transmission fluid for Chrysler automatic transmissions and transaxles. Developed in 1986, it closely resembles Dexron and Mercon. Type 7176 is the recommended service fill fluid for all Chrysler products utilizing a lockup torque converter dating back to 1978.

U-JOINT (UNIVERSAL JOINT): A flexible coupling in the drive train that allows the driveshafts or axle shafts to operate at different angles and still transmit rotary power.

UNDERSTEER: The tendency of a car to continue straight ahead while negotiating a turn.

UNIT BODY: Design in which the car body acts as the frame.

UNLEADED FUEL: Fuel which contains no lead (a common gasoline additive). The presence of lead in fuel will destroy the functioning elements of a catalytic converter, making it useless.

UNSPRUNG WEIGHT: The weight of car components not supported by the springs (wheels, tires, brakes, rear axle, control arms, etc.).

UPSHIFT: A shift that results in a decrease in torque ratio and an increase in speed.

VACUUM: A negative pressure; any pressure less than atmospheric pressure.

VACUUM ADVANCE: A device which advances the ignition timing in response to increased engine vacuum.

VACUUM GAUGE: An instrument used for measuring the existing vacuum in a vacuum circuit or chamber. The unit of measure is inches (of mercury in a barometer).

VACUUM MODULATOR: Generates a hydraulic oil pressure in response to the amount of engine vacuum.

VALVES: Devices that can open or close fluid passages in a hydraulic system and are used for directing fluid flow and controlling pressure.

VALVE BODY ASSEMBLY: The main hydraulic control assembly of the transmission/transaxle that contains numerous valves, check balls, and other components to control the distribution of pressurized oil throughout the transmission.

VALVE CLEARANCE: The measured gap between the end of the valve stem and the rocker arm, cam lobe or follower that activates the valve.

VALVE GUIDES: The guide through which the stem of the valve passes.

The guide is designed to keep the valve in proper alignment.

VALVE LASH (clearance): The operating clearance in the valve train.

VALVE TRAIN: The system that operates intake and exhaust valves, consisting of camshaft, valves and springs, lifters, pushrods and rocker arms.

VAPOR LOCK: Boiling of the fuel in the fuel lines due to excess heat. This will interfere with the flow of fuel in the lines and can completely stop the flow. Vapor lock normally only occurs in hot weather.

VARIABLE DISPLACEMENT (VARIABLE CAPACITY) VANE PUMP: Slipper-type vanes, mounted in a revolving rotor and contained within the bore of a movable slide, capture and then force fluid to flow. Movement of the slide to various positions changes the size of the vane chambers and the amount of fluid flow. **Note:** GM refers to this pump design as variable displacement, and Ford terms it variable capacity.

VARIABLE FORCE SOLENOID (VFS): Commonly referred to as the electronic pressure control (EPC) solenoid, it replaces the cable/linkage style of TV system control and is integrated with a spool valve and spring assembly to control pressure. A variable computer-controlled current flow varies the internal force of the solenoid on the spool valve and resulting control pressure.

VARIABLE ORIFICE THERMAL VALVE: Temperature-sensitive hydraulic oil control device that adjusts the size of a circuit path opening. By altering the size of the opening, the oil flow rate is adapted for cold to hot oil viscosity changes.

VARNISH: Term applied to the residue formed when gasoline gets old and stale.

VCM: See Electronic Control Unit (ECU).

VEHICLE SPEED SENSOR (VSS): Provides an electrical signal to the computer module, measuring vehicle speed, and affects the torque converter clutch engagement and release.

VESPEL SEALING RINGS: Hard plastic material that produces excellent sealing in dynamic settings. These rings are found in late versions of the 4T60 and in all 4T60-E and 4T80-E transaxles.

VISCOSITY: The ability of a fluid to flow. The lower the viscosity rating, the easier the fluid will flow. 10 weight motor oil will flow much easier than 40 weight motor oil.

VISCOSITY INDEX IMPROVERS: Keeps the viscosity nearly constant with changes in temperature. This is especially important at low temperatures, when the oil needs to be thin to aid in shifting and for cold-weather starting. Yet it must not be so thin that at high temperatures it will cause excessive hydraulic leakage so that pumps are unable to maintain the proper pressures.

VISCOUS CLUTCH: A specially designed torque converter clutch apply plate that, through the use of a silicon fluid, clamps smoothly and absorbs torsional vibrations.

VOLT: Unit used to measure the force or pressure of electricity. It is defined as the pressure needed to move one amp through the resistance of one ohm.

VOLTAGE: The electrical pressure that causes current to flow. Voltage is measured in volts (V).

VOLTAGE, APPLIED: The actual voltage read at a given point in a circuit. It equals the available voltage of the power supply minus the losses in the circuit up to that point.

VOLTAGE DROP: The voltage lost or used in a circuit by normal loads such as a motor or lamp or by abnormal loads such as a poor (high-resistance) lead or terminal connection.

VOLTAGE REGULATOR: A device that controls the current output of the alternator or generator.

VOLTMETER: An instrument used for measuring electrical force in units called volts. Voltmeters are always connected parallel with the circuit being tested.

VORTEX FLOW: The crosswise or circulatory flow of oil between the blades of the members caused by the centrifugal pumping action of the impeller.

WANKEL ENGINE: An engine which uses no pistons. In place of pistons, triangular-shaped rotors revolve in specially shaped housings.

WATER PUMP: A belt driven component of the cooling system that mounts on the engine, circulating the coolant under pressure.

WATT: The unit for measuring electrical power. One watt is the product of one ampere and one volt (watts equals amps times volts). Wattage is the horsepower of electricity (746 watts equal one horsepower).

WHEEL ALIGNMENT: Inclusive term to describe the front end geometry (caster, camber, toe-in/out).

WHEEL CYLINDER: Found in the automotive drum brake assembly, it is a device, actuated by hydraulic pressure, which, through internal pistons, pushes the brake shoes outward against the drums.

WHEEL WEIGHT: Small weights attached to the wheel to balance the wheel and tire assembly. Out-of-balance tires quickly wear out and also give erratic handling when installed on the front.

WHEELBASE: Distance between the center of front wheels and the center of rear wheels.

WIDE OPEN THROTTLE (WOT): Full travel of accelerator pedal.

WORK: The force exerted to move a mass or object. Work involves motion; if a force is exerted and no motion takes place, no work is done. Work per unit of time is called power. Work = force x distance = ft. lbs. 33,000 ft. lbs. in one minute = 1 horsepower

ZERO-THROTTLE COAST DOWN: A full release of accelerator pedal while vehicle is in motion and in drive range.

Commonly Used Abbreviations

2

2WD	Two Wheel Drive

4

4WD	Four Wheel Drive

A

A/C	Air Conditioning
ABDC	After Bottom Dead Center
ABS	Anti-lock Brakes
AC	Alternating Current
ACL	Air cleaner
ACT	Air Charge Temperature
AIR	Secondary Air Injection
ALCL	Assembly Line Communications Link
ALDL	Assembly Line Diagnostic Link
AT	Automatic Transaxle/Transmission
ATDC	After Top Dead Center
ATF	Automatic Transmission Fluid
ATS	Air Temperature Sensor
AWD	All Wheel Drive

B

BAP	Barometric Absolute Pressure
BARO	Barometric Pressure
BBDC	Before Bottom Dead Center
BCM	Body Control Module
BDC	Bottom Dead Center
BPT	Backpressure Transducer
BTDC	Before Top Dead Center
BVSV	Bimetallic Vacuum Switching Valve

C

CAC	Charge Air Cooler
CARB	California Air Resources Board
CAT	Catalytic Converter
CCC	Computer Command Control
CCCC	Computer Controlled Catalytic Converter
CCCI	Computer Controlled Coil Ignition
CCD	Computer Controlled Dwell
CDI	Capacitor Discharge Ignition
CEC	Computerized Engine Control
CFI	Continuous Fuel Injection
CIS	Continuous Injection System
CIS-E	Continuous Injection System - Electronic
CKP	Crankshaft Position
CL	Closed Loop
CMP	Camshaft Position
CPP	Clutch Pedal Position
CTOX	Continuous Trap Oxidizer System
CTP	Closed Throttle Position
CVC	Constant Vacuum Control
CYL	Cylinder

D

DBC	Dual Bed Catalyst
DC	Direct Current
DFI	Direct Fuel Injection
DIS	Distributorless Ignition System
DLC	Data Link Connector
DMM	Digital Multimeter
DOHC	Double Overhead Camshaft
DRB	Diagnostic Readout Box
DTC	Diagnostic Trouble Code
DTM	Diagnostic Test Mode
DVOM	Digital Volt/Ohmmeter

E

EBCM	Electronic Brake Control Module
ECM	Engine Control Module
ECT	Engine Coolant Temperature
ECU	Engine Control Unit or Electronic Control Unit
EDIS	Electronic Distributorless Ignition System
EEC	Electronic Engine Control
EEPROM	Electrically Erasable Programmable Read Only Memory
EFE	Early Fuel Evaporation
EGR	Exhaust Gas Recirculation
EGRT	Exhaust Gas Recirculation Temperature
EGRVC	EGR Valve Control
EPROM	Erasable Programmable Read Only Memory
EVAP	Evaporative Emissions
EVP	EGR Valve Position

F

FBC	Feedback Carburetor
FEEPROM	Flash Electrically Erasable Programmable Read Only Memory
FF	Flexible Fuel
FI	Fuel Injection
FT	Fuel Trim
FWD	Front Wheel Drive

G

GND	Ground

H

HAC	High Altitude Compensation
HEGO	Heated Exhaust Gas Oxygen sensor
HEI	High Energy Ignition
HO2 Sensor	Heated Oxygen Sensor

I

IAC	Idle Air Control
IAT	Intake Air Temperature
ICM	Ignition Control Module
IFI	Indirect Fuel Injection
IFS	Inertia Fuel Shutoff
ISC	Idle Speed Control
IVSV	Idle Vacuum Switching Valve

Commonly Used Abbreviations

K

KOEO	Key On, Engine Off
KOER	Key ON, Engine Running
KS	Knock Sensor

M

MAF	Mass Air Flow
MAP	Manifold Absolute Pressure
MAT	Manifold Air Temperature
MC	Mixture Control
MDP	Manifold Differential Pressure
MFI	Multiport Fuel Injection
MIL	Malfunction Indicator Lamp or Maintenance
MST	Manifold Surface Temperature
MVZ	Manifold Vacuum Zone

N

NVRAM	Nonvolatile Random Access Memory

O

O2 Sensor	Oxygen Sensor
OBD	On-Board Diagnostic
OC	Oxidation Catalyst
OHC	Overhead Camshaft
OL	Open Loop

P

P/S	Power Steering
PAIR	Pulsed Secondary Air Injection
PCM	Powertrain Control Module
PCS	Purge Control Solenoid
PCV	Positive Crankcase Ventilation
PIP	Profile Ignition Pick-up
PNP	Park/Neutral Position
PROM	Programmable Read Only Memory
PSP	Power Steering Pressure
PTO	Power Take-Off
PTOX	Periodic Trap Oxidizer System

R

RABS	Rear Anti-lock Brake System
RAM	Random Access Memory
ROM	Read Only Memory
RPM	Revolutions Per Minute
RWAL	Rear Wheel Anti-lock Brakes
RWD	Rear Wheel Drive

S

SBC	Single Bed Converter
SBEC	Single Board Engine Controller
SC	Supercharger
SCB	Supercharger Bypass
SFI	Sequential Multiport Fuel Injection
SIR	Supplemental Inflatable Restraint
SOHC	Single Overhead Camshaft
SPL	Smoke Puff Limiter
SPOUT	Spark Output
SRI	Service Reminder Indicator
SRS	Supplemental Restraint System
SRT	System Readiness Test
SSI	Solid State Ignition
ST	Scan Tool
STO	Self-Test Output

T

TAC	Thermostatic Air Cleaner
TBI	Throttle Body Fuel Injection
TC	Turbocharger
TCC	Torque Converter Clutch
TCM	Transmission Control Module
TDC	Top Dead Center
TFI	Thick Film Ignition
TP	Throttle Position
TR Sensor	Transaxle/Transmission Range Sensor
TVV	Thermal Vacuum Valve
TWC	Three-way Catalytic Converter

V

VAF	Volume Air Flow, or Vane Air Flow
VAPS	Variable Assist Power Steering
VRV	Vacuum Regulator Valve
VSS	Vehicle Speed Sensor
VSV	Vacuum Switching Valve

W

WOT	Wide Open Throttle
WU-TWC	Warm Up Three-way Catalytic Converter

ENGLISH TO METRIC CONVERSION: TORQUE

To convert foot-pounds (ft. lbs.) to Newton-meters (Nm), multiply the number of ft. lbs. by 1.36
To convert Newton-meters (Nm) to foot-pounds (ft. lbs.), multiply the number of Nm by 0.7376

ft. lbs.	Nm	ft. lbs.	Nm	ft. lbs.	Nm	ft. lbs.	Nm
0.1	0.1	34	46.2	76	103.4	118	160.5
0.2	0.3	35	47.6	77	104.7	119	161.8
0.3	0.4	36	49.0	78	106.1	120	163.2
0.4	0.5	37	50.3	79	107.4	121	164.6
0.5	0.7	38	51.7	80	108.8	122	165.9
0.6	0.8	39	53.0	81	110.2	123	167.3
0.7	1.0	40	54.4	82	111.5	124	168.6
0.8	1.1	41	55.8	83	112.9	125	170.0
0.9	1.2	42	57.1	84	114.2	126	171.4
1	1.4	43	58.5	85	115.6	127	172.7
2	2.7	44	59.8	86	117.0	128	174.1
3	4.1	45	61.2	87	118.3	129	175.4
4	5.4	46	62.6	88	119.7	130	176.8
5	6.8	47	63.9	89	121.0	131	178.2
6	8.2	48	65.3	90	122.4	132	179.5
7	9.5	49	66.6	91	123.8	133	180.9
8	10.9	50	68.0	92	125.1	134	182.2
9	12.2	51	69.4	93	126.5	135	183.6
10	13.6	52	70.7	94	127.8	136	185.0
11	15.0	53	72.1	95	129.2	137	186.3
12	16.3	54	73.4	96	130.6	138	187.7
13	17.7	55	74.8	97	131.9	139	189.0
14	19.0	56	76.2	98	133.3	140	190.4
15	20.4	57	77.5	99	134.6	141	191.8
16	21.8	58	78.9	100	136.0	142	193.1
17	23.1	59	80.2	101	137.4	143	194.5
18	24.5	60	81.6	102	138.7	144	195.8
19	25.8	61	83.0	103	140.1	145	197.2
20	27.2	62	84.3	104	141.4	146	198.6
21	28.6	63	85.7	105	142.8	147	199.9
22	29.9	64	87.0	106	144.2	148	201.3
23	31.3	65	88.4	107	145.5	149	202.6
24	32.6	66	89.8	108	146.9	150	204.0
25	34.0	67	91.1	109	148.2	151	205.4
26	35.4	68	92.5	110	149.6	152	206.7
27	36.7	69	93.8	111	151.0	153	208.1
28	38.1	70	95.2	112	152.3	154	209.4
29	39.4	71	96.6	113	153.7	155	210.8
30	40.8	72	97.9	114	155.0	156	212.2
31	42.2	73	99.3	115	156.4	157	213.5
32	43.5	74	100.6	116	157.8	158	214.9
33	44.9	75	102.0	117	159.1	159	216.2

METRIC TO ENGLISH CONVERSION: TORQUE

To convert foot-pounds (ft. lbs.) to Newton-meters (Nm), multiply the number of ft. lbs. by 1.36

To convert Newton-meters (Nm) to foot-pounds (ft. lbs.), multiply the number of Nm by 0.7376

Nm	ft. lbs.	Nm	ft. lbs.	Nm	ft. lbs.	Nm	ft. lbs.	Nm	ft. lbs.
0.1	0.1	34	25.0	76	55.9	118	86.8	160	117.6
0.2	0.1	35	25.7	77	56.6	119	87.5	161	118.4
0.3	0.2	36	26.5	78	57.4	120	88.2	162	119.1
0.4	0.3	37	27.2	79	58.1	121	89.0	163	119.9
0.5	0.4	38	27.9	80	58.8	122	89.7	164	120.6
0.6	0.4	39	28.7	81	59.6	123	90.4	165	121.3
0.7	0.5	40	29.4	82	60.3	124	91.2	166	122.1
0.8	0.6	41	30.1	83	61.0	125	91.9	167	122.8
0.9	0.7	42	30.9	84	61.8	126	92.6	168	123.5
1	0.7	43	31.6	85	62.5	127	93.4	169	124.3
2	1.5	44	32.4	86	63.2	128	94.1	170	125.0
3	2.2	45	33.1	87	64.0	129	94.9	171	125.7
4	2.9	46	33.8	88	64.7	130	95.6	172	126.5
5	3.7	47	34.6	89	65.4	131	96.3	173	127.2
6	4.4	48	35.3	90	66.2	132	97.1	174	127.9
7	5.1	49	36.0	91	66.9	133	97.8	175	128.7
8	5.9	50	36.8	92	67.6	134	98.5	176	129.4
9	6.6	51	37.5	93	68.4	135	99.3	177	130.1
10	7.4	52	38.2	94	69.1	136	100.0	178	130.9
11	8.1	53	39.0	95	69.9	137	100.7	179	131.6
12	8.8	54	39.7	96	70.6	138	101.5	180	132.4
13	9.6	55	40.4	97	71.3	139	102.2	181	133.1
14	10.3	56	41.2	98	72.1	140	102.9	182	133.8
15	11.0	57	41.9	99	72.8	141	103.7	183	134.6
16	11.8	58	42.6	100	73.5	142	104.4	184	135.3
17	12.5	59	43.4	101	74.3	143	105.1	185	136.0
18	13.2	60	44.1	102	75.0	144	105.9	186	136.8
19	14.0	61	44.9	103	75.7	145	106.6	187	137.5
20	14.7	62	45.6	104	76.5	146	107.4	188	138.2
21	15.4	63	46.3	105	77.2	147	108.1	189	139.0
22	16.2	64	47.1	106	77.9	148	108.8	190	139.7
23	16.9	65	47.8	107	78.7	149	109.6	191	140.4
24	17.6	66	48.5	108	79.4	150	110.3	192	141.2
25	18.4	67	49.3	109	80.1	151	111.0	193	141.9
26	19.1	68	50.0	110	80.9	152	111.8	194	142.6
27	19.9	69	50.7	111	81.6	153	112.5	195	143.4
28	20.6	70	51.5	112	82.4	154	113.2	196	144.1
29	21.3	71	52.2	113	83.1	155	114.0	197	144.9
30	22.1	72	52.9	114	83.8	156	114.7	198	145.6
31	22.8	73	53.7	115	84.6	157	115.4	199	146.3
32	23.5	74	54.4	116	85.3	158	116.2	200	147.1
33	24.3	75	55.1	117	86.0	159	116.9	201	147.8

ENGLISH/METRIC CONVERSION: TEMPERATURE

To convert Fahrenheit (F°) to Celsius (C°), take F° temperature and subtract 32, multiply the result by 5 and divide the result by 9
To convert Celsius (C°) to Fahrenheit (F°), take C° temperature and multiply it by 9, divide the result by 5 and add 32

F°	C°	F°	C°	C°	F°	C°	F°
-40	-40.0	150	65.6	-38	-36.4	46	114.8
-35	-37.2	155	68.3	-36	-32.8	48	118.4
-30	-34.4	160	71.1	-34	-29.2	50	122
-25	-31.7	165	73.9	-32	-25.6	52	125.6
-20	-28.9	170	76.7	-30	-22	54	129.2
-15	-26.1	175	79.4	-28	-18.4	56	132.8
-10	-23.3	180	82.2	-26	-14.8	58	136.4
-5	-20.6	185	85.0	-24	-11.2	60	140
0	-17.8	190	87.8	-22	-7.6	62	143.6
1	-17.2	195	90.6	-20	-4	64	147.2
2	-16.7	200	93.3	-18	-0.4	66	150.8
3	-16.1	205	96.1	-16	3.2	68	154.4
4	-15.6	210	98.9	-14	6.8	70	158
5	-15.0	212	100.0	-12	10.4	72	161.6
10	-12.2	215	101.7	-10	14	74	165.2
15	-9.4	220	104.4	-8	17.6	76	168.8
20	-6.7	225	107.2	-6	21.2	78	172.4
25	-3.9	230	110.0	-4	24.8	80	176
30	-1.1	235	112.8	-2	28.4	82	179.6
35	1.7	240	115.6	0	32	84	183.2
40	4.4	245	118.3	2	35.6	86	186.8
45	7.2	250	121.1	4	39.2	88	190.4
50	10.0	255	123.9	6	42.8	90	194
55	12.8	260	126.7	8	46.4	92	197.6
60	15.6	265	129.4	10	50	94	201.2
65	18.3	270	132.2	12	53.6	96	204.8
70	21.1	275	135.0	14	57.2	98	208.4
75	23.9	280	137.8	16	60.8	100	212
80	26.7	285	140.6	18	64.4	102	215.6
85	29.4	290	143.3	20	68	104	219.2
90	32.2	295	146.1	22	71.6	106	222.8
95	35.0	300	148.9	24	75.2	108	226.4
100	37.8	305	151.7	26	78.8	110	230
105	40.6	310	154.4	28	82.4	112	233.6
110	43.3	315	157.2	30	86	114	237.2
115	46.1	320	160.0	32	89.6	116	240.8
120	48.9	325	162.8	34	93.2	118	244.4
125	51.7	330	165.6	36	96.8	120	248
130	54.4	335	168.3	38	100.4	122	251.6
135	57.2	340	171.1	40	104	124	255.2
140	60.0	345	173.9	42	107.6	126	258.8
145	62.8	350	176.7	44	111.2	128	262.4

LENGTH CONVERSION

To convert inches (in.) to millimeters (mm), multiply the number of inches by 25.4
To convert millimeters (mm) to inches (in.), multiply the number of millimeters by 0.04

Inches	Millimeters	Inches	Millimeters	Inches	Millimeters	Inches	Millimeters
0.0001	0.00254	0.005	0.1270	0.09	2.286	4	101.6
0.0002	0.00508	0.006	0.1524	0.1	2.54	5	127.0
0.0003	0.00762	0.007	0.1778	0.2	5.08	6	152.4
0.0004	0.01016	0.008	0.2032	0.3	7.62	7	177.8
0.0005	0.01270	0.009	0.2286	0.4	10.16	8	203.2
0.0006	0.01524	0.01	0.254	0.5	12.70	9	228.6
0.0007	0.01778	0.02	0.508	0.6	15.24	10	254.0
0.0008	0.02032	0.03	0.762	0.7	17.78	11	279.4
0.0009	0.02286	0.04	1.016	0.8	20.32	12	304.8
0.001	0.0254	0.05	1.270	0.9	22.86	13	330.2
0.002	0.0508	0.06	1.524	1	25.4	14	355.6
0.003	0.0762	0.07	1.778	2	50.8	15	381.0
0.004	0.1016	0.08	2.032	3	76.2	16	406.4

ENGLISH/METRIC CONVERSION: LENGTH

To convert inches (in.) to millimeters (mm), multiply the number of inches by 25.4
To convert millimeters (mm) to inches (in.), multiply the number of millimeters by 0.04

| Inches | | Millimeters | Inches | | Millimeters | Inches | | Millimeters |
Fraction	Decimal	Decimal	Fraction	Decimal	Decimal	Fraction	Decimal	Decimal
1/64	0.016	0.397	11/32	0.344	8.731	11/16	0.688	17.463
1/32	0.031	0.794	23/64	0.359	9.128	45/64	0.703	17.859
3/64	0.047	1.191	3/8	0.375	9.525	23/32	0.719	18.256
1/16	0.063	1.588	25/64	0.391	9.922	47/64	0.734	18.653
5/64	0.078	1.984	13/32	0.406	10.319	3/4	0.750	19.050
3/32	0.094	2.381	27/64	0.422	10.716	49/64	0.766	19.447
7/64	0.109	2.778	7/16	0.438	11.113	25/32	0.781	19.844
1/8	0.125	3.175	29/64	0.453	11.509	51/64	0.797	20.241
9/64	0.141	3.572	15/32	0.469	11.906	13/16	0.813	20.638
5/32	0.156	3.969	31/64	0.484	12.303	53/64	0.828	21.034
11/64	0.172	4.366	1/2	0.500	12.700	27/32	0.844	21.431
3/16	0.188	4.763	33/64	0.516	13.097	55/64	0.859	21.828
13/64	0.203	5.159	17/32	0.531	13.494	7/8	0.875	22.225
7/32	0.219	5.556	35/64	0.547	13.891	57/64	0.891	22.622
15/64	0.234	5.953	9/16	0.563	14.288	29/32	0.906	23.019
1/4	0.250	6.350	37/64	0.578	14.684	59/64	0.922	23.416
17/64	0.266	6.747	19/32	0.594	15.081	15/16	0.938	23.813
9/32	0.281	7.144	39/64	0.609	15.478	61/64	0.953	24.209
19/64	0.297	7.541	5/8	0.625	15.875	31/32	0.969	24.606
5/16	0.313	7.938	41/64	0.641	16.272	63/64	0.984	25.003
21/64	0.328	8.334	21/32	0.656	16.669	1/1	1.000	25.400
			43/64	0.672	17.066			

CHILTON® LABOR GUIDE

Whether you are looking for labor times in print, or on CD-ROM, Chilton is your source! Chilton's editors have carefully crafted the latest edition of the famous Chilton Labor Guide to bring you the most accurate repair information available. Chilton's editors consider warranty times, component locations, component type, the environment in which technicians work, the training they receive, and the tools they use when calculating a labor time. To allow for vehicle age, operating conditions, and type of service, the Chilton Labor Guide provides standard and severe service times, plus OEM warranty times. Vehicle makes and models conform to current Automotive Aftermarket Industry Association (AAIA) standards.

978-1-1110-3608-9 Chilton 2010 Labor Guide Manual Set (Domestic & Import)
978-1-1110-3611-9 Chilton 2010 Labor Guide CD-ROM (Domestic & Import)

CD-ROM FEATURES

○ access labor times for 1981-2010 import and domestic vehicle models
○ save time with automatically calculated labor charges, taxes, & parts as total job is estimated
○ create professional estimates for your customer and worksheets for your technicians, printing them whenever needed
○ keep track of customers, prior estimates, and your own parts or package jobs with less paper
○ choose part names for estimates from an industry standard database to reduce typing
○ estimate and track your work status with improved forms
○ communicate easily with customers using re-designed printouts which show all labor and parts in an easy-to-read format.
○ simplify adding parts to your estimate or work order with a helpful parts list
○ locate information quick with a keyword search engine
○ quickly locate work requests by day, week and month using the calendar feature

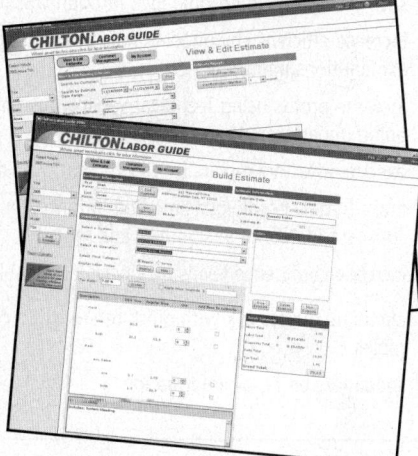

Manual FEATURES

○ more than 2,500 pages of updated Chilton labor times split into two volumes includes vehicle information from 1981 to 2010
○ trusted by more service professionals than any other labor guide
○ less flipping though pages with separate domestic and imported vehicle manuals
○ convenient tabs display contents by manufacturer and model
○ easy-to-find manufacturers are arranged alphabetically within each volume
○ search using two-indexes - labor operations and systems - in each model group
○ page numbers include manufacturer code so you know where you are in the book

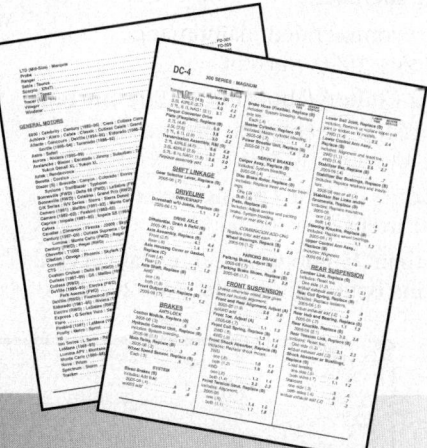

Chilton's labor times are so trusted, even a competing publisher uses them!

CHILTONPRO.COM
Where smart technicians click for service information.

ChiltonPRO is the alternative for professional technicians who want a cost-effective electronic automotive repair system. It combines Chilton's famous automotive repair information into one solution covering more than 20 years of domestic and imported vehicles. The information is delivered online and is updated regularly throughout the year.

Online Monthly Payment
ISBN: 978-14180-3002-5

Online Annual Payment
ISBN: 978-14180-2876-3

For a free demo visit ChiltonPRO.com

ChiltonPRO FEATURES

- make repairs even easier with videos & animations which explain system operations & contribute to technician knowledge
- create better estimates using labor times developed with real-world factors
- save money by accurately identifying and solving engine performance problems
- save time with expert guidance through OBDII diagnostics
- increase efficiency by understanding system operation through detailed explanations and theory
- increase profits using Technical Service Bulletins (TSBs) to ensure that work is not going unperformed
- execute effective repairs by viewing cutaway diagrams and actual photos
- make better use of your time with information that can be found quicker using AAIA standards for year, make, and model
- increase confidence levels by always being able to print what you need
- eliminate guesswork with quick reference to critical specifications in helpful tables
- spend less on repair information

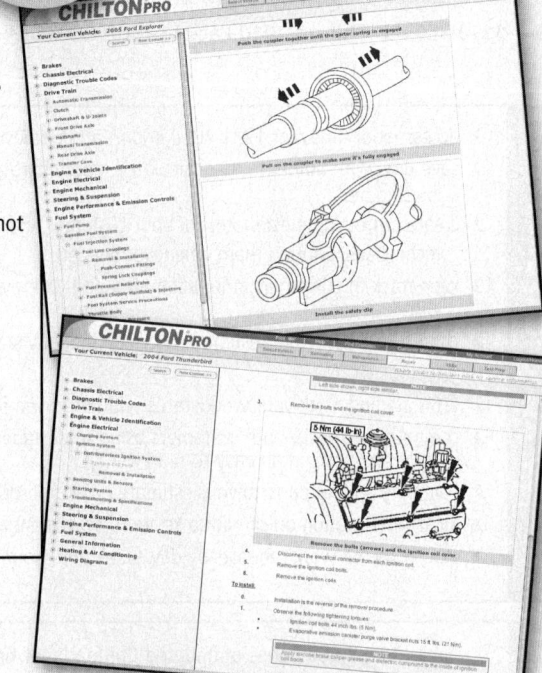

Coverage Includes:

- OEM recommended maintenance schedules, 1990–current
- trusted Chilton labor times, 1981–current
- step-by-step mechanical procedures, 1950s–current
- diagnostics designed by instructors, 1990–current
- More than 75,000 OEM Technical Service Bulletins issued during the past 20 years

System Requirements:
Web browser

- Internet Explorer 6.0 or above (recommended)
- Firefox 2 or 3, or Safari
- High-speed internet connection
- Adobe Flash Player
- Adobe Shockwave Player
- Windows XP or Vista

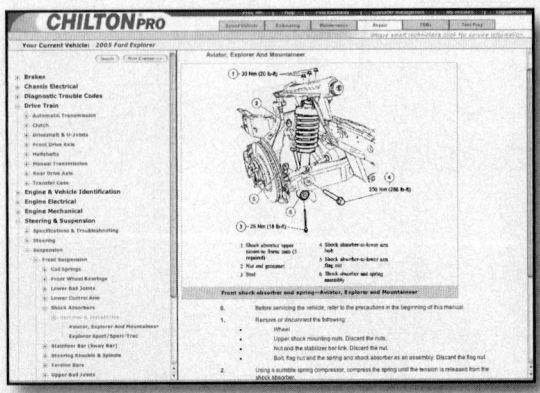

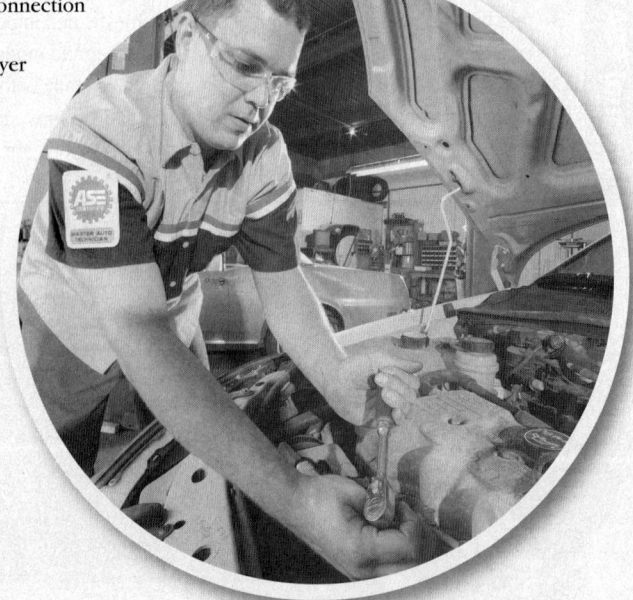

Chilton® 2010 Service Manuals

The Chilton 2010 Service Manuals now include even better graphics and expanded procedures! Chilton's editors have put together the most current automotive repair information available to assist users during daily repairs. These new manuals allow users to accurately and efficiently diagnose and repair late-model cars and trucks. Trust the step-by-step procedures and helpful illustrations that only Chilton can provide. The 2010 Service Manuals cover 2008 and 2009 models plus available 2010 models.

KEY FEATURES

- organized by vehicle manufacturer
- provides thousands of pages of expertly written content
- access new year, make, and model information without repeating previous edition's content
- comprehensive, technically detailed content, including exploded view illustrations, diagnostics and specification charts,   arranged alphabetically by model group for quick, easy access

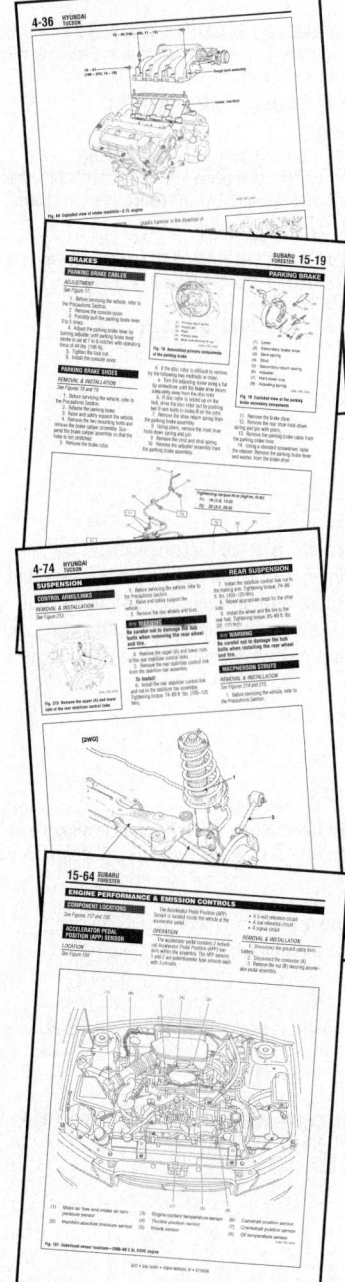

2010 EDITIONS

2010 Asian Service Manual Vol. 1*
ISBN 978-1-1110-3764-2
Part No. 163764

2010 Asian Service Manual Vol. 2*
ISBN 978-1-1110-3765-9
Part No. 163765

2010 Asian Service Manual Vol. 3*
ISBN 978-1-1110-3766-6
Part No. 163766

2010 Asian Service Manual Vol. 4*
ISBN 978-1-1110-3767-3
Part No. 163767

2010 Asian Service Manual Vol. 5*
ISBN 978-1-1110-3768-0
Part No. 163768

2010 European Service Manual*
ISBN 978-1-1110-3769-7
Part No. 163769

2010 Chrysler Service Manual,
Volumes 1 & 2
ISBN 978-1-1110-3654-6
Part No. 163654

2010 Ford Service Manual,
Vols. 1 & 2
ISBN 978-1-1110-3657-7
Part No. 163657

2010 General Motors Service
Manuals, Vols. 1, 2, & 3
ISBN 978-1-111-03661-4
Part No. 163661

2008 EDITIONS

2008 Chrysler Service Manual,
Vols. 1 & 2
ISBN 978-1-4283-2204-2
Part No. 142204

2008 Ford Service Manuals,
Vols. 1 & 2
ISBN 978-1-4283-2208-0
Part No. 142208

2008 Edition General Motors
Service Manuals, Vols. 1 & 2
ISBN 978-1-4283-2211-0
Part No. 142211

2008 Asian Service Manuals,
Vols. 1-4
ISBN 978-1-4283-2214-1
Part No. 142214

2008 Asian Service Manual, Vol. 1
ISBN 978-1-4283-2215-8
Part No. 142215

2008 Asian Service Manual, Vol. 2
ISBN 978-1-4283-2216-5
Part No. 142216

2008 Asian Service Manual, Vol. 3
ISBN 978-1-4283-2217-2
Part No. 142217

2008 Asian Service Manual, Vol. 4
ISBN 978-1-4283-2218-9
Part No. 142218

2008 European Service Manual
ISBN 978-1-4283-2220-2
Part No. 142220

2006 EDITIONS

2006 DaimlerChrysler Diagnostic
Service Manual
ISBN 978-1-4180-2118-4
Part No. 132118

2006 General Motors Diagnostic
Service Manual
ISBN 978-1-4180-2120-7
Part No. 132120

2006 Asian Diagnostic Service
Manual, Vol. 1
ISBN 978-1-4180-2913-5
Part No. 132913

2006 Asian Diagnostic Service
Manual, Vol. 2
ISBN 978-1-4180-2914-2
Part No. 132914

2006 Asian Diagnostic Service
Manual, Vol. 3
ISBN 978-1-4180-2915-9
Part No. 132915

2006 Asian Diagnostic Service
Manual, 3 Vol. Set
ISBN 978-1-4180-3212-8
Part No. 132986

2006 European Diagnostic Service
Manual
ISBN 978-1-4180-2924-1
Part No. 132924

2006 DaimlerChrysler Mechanical
Service Manual
ISBN 978-1-4180-0600-6
Part No. 130600

2006 Asian Mechanical Service
Manual, Vol. 1
ISBN 978-1-4180-0947-2
Part No. 130947

2006 Asian Mechanical Service
Manual, Vol. 2
ISBN 978-1-4180-0948-9
Part No. 130948

2006 Asian Mechanical Service
Manual, Vol. 3
ISBN 978-1-4180-0949-6
Part No. 130949

2006 Asian Mechanical Service
Manual, 3 Vol. Set
ISBN 978-1-4180-0603-7
Part No. 130603

2006 European Mechanical Service
Manual
ISBN 978-1-4180-0604-4
Part No. 130604

*Available December 2010

Order Today– Quantities are Limited

Chilton® Mechanical Service Manuals–Perennial Editions

These manuals contain repair and maintenance information for all major systems. Included are repair and overhaul procedures using thousands of illustrations.

CHILTON AUTO REPAIR MANUALS
1998-2002
ISBN 978-0-8019-9362-6/Part No. 9362
Covers all popular American and Canadian cars. An added feature includes scheduled maintenance interval charts.
1993-97
ISBN 978-0-8019-7919-4/Part No. 7919
Covers all popular American and Canadian cars.
1980-87
ISBN 978-0-8019-7670-4/Part No. 7670
Covers all popular American and Canadian cars.

CHILTON IMPORT AUTO REPAIR MANUALS
1998-2002
ISBN 978-0-8019-9363-3/Part No. 9363
Covers all popular Import cars. An added feature includes scheduled maintenance intervals charts.
1993-97
ISBN 978-0-8019-7920-0/Part No. 7920
Covers all popular Import cars.
1988-92
ISBN 978-0-8019-7907-1/Part No. 7907
Covers all popular Import cars.
1980-87
ISBN 978-0-8019-7672-8/Part No. 7672
Covers all popular Import cars.

CHILTON TRUCK AND VAN REPAIR MANUALS
1998-2002
ISBN 978-0-8019-9364-0/Part No. 9364
Covers popular U.S., Canadian, and Import Pick-Ups, Vans, and 4WDs. An added feature includes scheduled maintenance interval charts.

1993-97
ISBN 978-0-8019-7921-7/Part No. 7921
Covers popular U.S., Canadian, and Import Pick-Ups, Sport-Utilities, Vans, RVs and 4 wheel drives.
1991-95
ISBN 978-0-8019-7911-8/Part No. 7911
Covers popular U.S., Canadian, and Import Pick-Ups, Vans, RVs and 4 wheel drives.
1986-90
ISBN 978-08019-7902-6/Part No. 7902
Covers popular U.S., Canadian, and Import Pick-Us, Vans, RVs and 4 wheel drives.
1979-86
ISBN 978-08019-7655-1/Part No. 7655
Covers popular U.S., Canadian, and Import Pick-Ups, Vans, RVs and 4 wheel drives.

CHILTON SUV REPAIR MANUAL
1998-2002
ISBN 978-08019-9365-7/Part No. 9365
Covers popular U.S., Canadian, and import SUVs. An added feature includes scheduled maintenance intervals charts.

COLLECTOR'S SERIES
CHILTON AUTO REPAIR MANUAL 1964-1971
ISBN 978-08019-5974-5/Part No. 5974
1971-1978
ISBN 978-08019-7012-2/Part No. 7012

Chilton Timing Belts, 1985-2005

Timing belt procedures can represent increased profits for automotive repair shops and service stations, and this manual contains all the information automotive technicians need to properly service timing belts on domestic and imported cars, vans, and light trucks through 2005 models. Clear, straightforward procedures, illustrations, and specifications help to communicate 20 years of vehicle applications for fast, accurate inspection, replacement, and tensioning of timing belts. Users will learn how to perform key procedures quickly and safely, while learning the correct labor time to charge for the service.

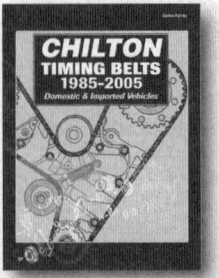

ISBN 978-1-4018-9880-9
Part No. 129880
544 pp, 8" x 11", SC, ©2006

ALSO AVAILABLE:
Quick-Reference Manuals
The Chilton Professional Series offers *Quick-Reference Manuals* for the automotive professional, providing complete coverage on repair and maintenance, adjustments, and diagnostic procedures for specific systems and components.

KEY FEATURES
- step-by-step procedures
- detailed illustrations and exploded views
- easy-to-use manufacturer and model indexing
- handy specifications or data charts

Heater Core Service 1990-2000,
ISBN 978-0-8019-9311-4
Part No. 9311
Brake Specifications and Service 1990-2000
ISBN 978-0-8019-9312-1
Part No. 9312

Electric Cooling Fans, Accessory Drive Belts & Water Pumps, 1995-1999,
ISBN 978-0-8019-9126-4
Part No. 9126
Powertrain Codes & Oxygen Sensors, 1990-1999,
ISBN 978-0-8019-9127-1
Part No. 9127

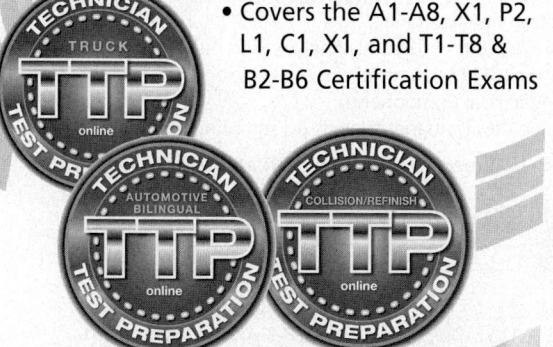
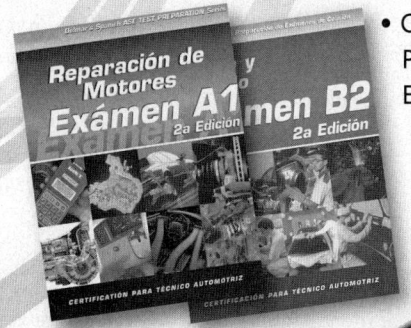

ASE CERTIFICATION TEST PREPARATION

You Deserve The Best When You Are Putting Your Skills To The Test!

ASE Test Preparation Manuals

133878	(A1) Engine Repair, 4E	978-1-4180-3878-6
133879	(A2) Transmissions and Transaxles, 4E	978-1-4180-3879-3
133880	(A3) Manual Drive Train and Axles, 4E	978-1-4180-3880-9
133881	(A4) Suspension and Steering, 4E	978-1-4180-3881-6
133882	(A5) Brakes, 4E	978-1-4180-3882-3
133883	(A6) Electrical/Electronic Systems, 4E	978-1-4180-3883-0
133884	(A7) Heating and Air Conditioning, 4E	978-1-4180-3884-7
133885	(A8) Engine Performance, 4E	978-1-4180-3885-4
133888	(L1) Advanced Engine Performance, 4E	978-1-4180-3888-5
133886	(X1) Exhaust Systems, 4E	978-1-4180-3886-1
133887	(P2) Parts Specialist, 4E	978-1-4180-3887-8
133889	(C1) Service Consultant, 2E	978-1-4180-3889-2
23664	(B2) Painting and Refinishing, 3E	978-1-4018-3664-1
23665	(B3) Non Structural Analysis and Damage Repair, 3E	978-1-4018-3665-8
23666	(B4) Structural Analysis and Damage Repair, 3E	978-1-4018-3666-5
23667	(B5) Mechanical and Electrical Components, 3E	978-1-4018-3667-2
23668	(B6) Damage Analysis and Estimation, 3E	978-1-4018-3668-9
16280	(M1) Cylinder Head Specialist	978-0-7668-6280-7
16281	(M2) Cylinder Block Specialist	978-0-7668-6281-4
16282	(M3) Assembly Specialist	978-0-7668-6282-1
134828	(T1) Gasoline Engines, 4E	978-1-4180-4828-0
134829	(T2) Diesel Engines, 4E	978-1-4180-4829-7
134830	(T3) Drive Train, 4E	978-1-4180-4830-3
134831	(T4) Brakes, 4E	978-1-4180-4831-0
134832	(T5) Suspension and Steering, 4E	978-1-4180-4832-7
134834	(T6) Electrical/Electronic Systems, 4E	978-1-4180-4834-1
134835	(T7) Heating, Ventilation, and Air Conditioning, 4E	978-1-4180-4835-8
134836	(T8) Preventive Maintenance, 4E	978-1-4180-4836-5
21822	(S2) Diesel Engines	978-1-4018-1822-7
21824	(S4) Brakes	978-1-4018-1824-1
21825	(S5) Suspension and Steering	978-1-4018-1825-8
153939	(H1) Compressed Natural Gas Engines	978-1-4354-3939-9
136570	(H2) Diesel Engines	978-1-4180-6570-6
155376	(H3) Drive Train	978-1-4354-5376-0
134998	(H4) Brakes	978-1-4180-4998-0
144011	(H5) Suspension & Steering	978-1-4283-4011-4
134999	(H6) Electrical/Electronic Systems	978-1-4180-4999-7
136571	(H7) Heating, Ventilation, & Air Conditioning	978-1-4180-6571-3
153938	(H8) Preventive Maintenance	978-1-4354-3938-2
153935	(E1) Truck Equipment Installation & Repair	978-1-4354-3935-1
153936	(E2) Electronic Systems Installation & Repair	978-1-4354-3936-8
153937	(E3) Auxilary Power Systems Installation & Repair	978-1-4354-3937-5

ASE Test Preparation in Spanish

131305	Spanish (A1) Engine Repair	978-1-4018-1014-6
131305	Spanish (A2) Transmissions and Transaxles	978-1-4018-1015-3
131305	Spanish (A3) Manual Drive Train and Axles	978-1-4018-1016-0
131305	Spanish (A4) Suspension and Steering	978-1-4018-1017-7
131305	Spanish (A5) Brakes	978-1-4018-1018-4
131305	Spanish (A6) Electrical/Electronic Systems	978-1-4018-1019-1
131305	Spanish (A7) Heating and Air Conditioning	978-1-4018-1020-7
131305	Spanish (A8) Engine Performance	978-1-4018-1021-4
131305	Spanish (L1) Advanced Engine Performance	978-1-4018-1022-1
131305	Spanish (X1) Exhaust Systems	978-1-4018-1024-5
131305	Spanish (P2) Parts Specialist	978-1-4018-1023-8
29255	Spanish (B2) Painting and Refinishin	978-1-4018-9255-5
22544	Spanish (B3) Non-Structural Analysis and Damage Repair	978-1-4018-2544-7
29131	Spanish (B4) Structural Analysis and Damage Repair	978-1-4018-9131-2
27759	Spanish (B5) Mechanical and Electrical Components	978-1-4018-7759-0
26573	Spanish (B6) Damage Analysis and Estimation	978-1-4018-6573-3

Online ASE Test Preparation
Place your order online at www.techniciantestprep.com

131305	*Online (A1) Engine Repair	978-1-4180-1305-9
131306	*Online (A2) Automatic Transmissions & Transaxles	978-1-4180-1306-6
131307	*Online (A3) Manual Drive Trains & Axles	978-1-4180-1307-3
131308	*Online (A4) Suspension & Steering	978-1-4180-1308-0
131309	*Online (A5) Brakes	978-1-4180-1309-7
131310	*Online (A6) Electrical/Electronic Systems	978-1-4180-1310-3
131311	*Online (A7) Heating & Air Conditioning	978-1-4180-1311-0
131312	*Online (A8) Engine Performance	978-1-4180-1312-7
131313	*Online (X1) Exhaust Systems	978-1-4180-1313-4
131314	*Online (P2) Automobile Parts Specialist	978-1-4180-1314-1
131315	*Online (L1) Advanced Engine Performance	978-1-4180-1315-8
131316	*Online (C1) Service Consultant	978-1-4180-1316-5
127897	Online (T1) Gasoline Engines	978-1-4018-7897-9
127898	Online (T2) Diesel Engines	978-1-4018-7898-6
127900	Online (T3) Drive Train	978-1-4018-7900-6
127901	Online (T4) Brakes	978-1-4018-7901-3
127903	Online (T5) Suspension & Steering	978-1-4018-7903-7
131879	Online (T6) Electrical/Electronic Systems	978-1-4180-1879-5
131880	Online (T7) Heating, Ventilation, & Air Conditioning	978-1-4180-1880-1
127906	Online (T8) Preventive Maintenance	978-1-4018-7906-8
154748	Online (B2) Painting & Refinishing	978-1-4354-4748-6
154749	Online (B3) Non-Structural Analysis & Damage Repair	978-1-4354-4749-3
154750	Online (B4) Structural Analysis and Repair	978-1-4354-4750-9
154751	Online (B5) Mechanical & Electrical Components	978-1-4354-4751-6
154752	Online (B6) Damage Analysis & Estimating	978-1-4354-4752-3

*Switch between English & Spanish at the click of a button!

Complete Series

CSAT-Automotive Series

The online *Comprehensive Skill Assessment Tool-Automotive Series* helps instructors and trainers implement the necessary training programs for individual areas needing improvement over various key automotive topics. As a true skill gap analysis tool, within each key topic, strategic learning areas are measured for knowledge of theory, hands-on application, and diagnostic skill. Areas of strength and areas needing improvement are identified. The combined phases of education and training, and post-assessment allow instructors to track skill level growth and target specific areas needing development.

Courses Available in the CSAT Automotive Series

Parts Specialist
ISBN 978-1-4180-3225-8

Service Consultant
ISBN 978-1-4180-3223-4

Advanced Engine Performance
ISBN 978-1-4180-0073-8

Brakes
ISBN 978-1-4180-0069-1

Electrical/Electronic Systems
ISBN 978-1-4180-0070-7

Engine Performance
ISBN 978-1-4180-0072-1

Engine Repair
ISBN 978-1-4180-0065-3

Exhaust Systems
ISBN 978-1-4180-0074-5

Heating and Air Conditioning
ISBN 978-1-4180-0071-4

Manual Drive Train & Axles
ISBN 978-1-4180-0067-7

Suspension & Steering
ISBN 978-1-4180-0068-4

Transmissions & Transaxles
ISBN 978-1-4180-0066-0

All-in-One (contains questions from all eight core automotive areas in one product)
ISBN 978-1-4354-2825-6

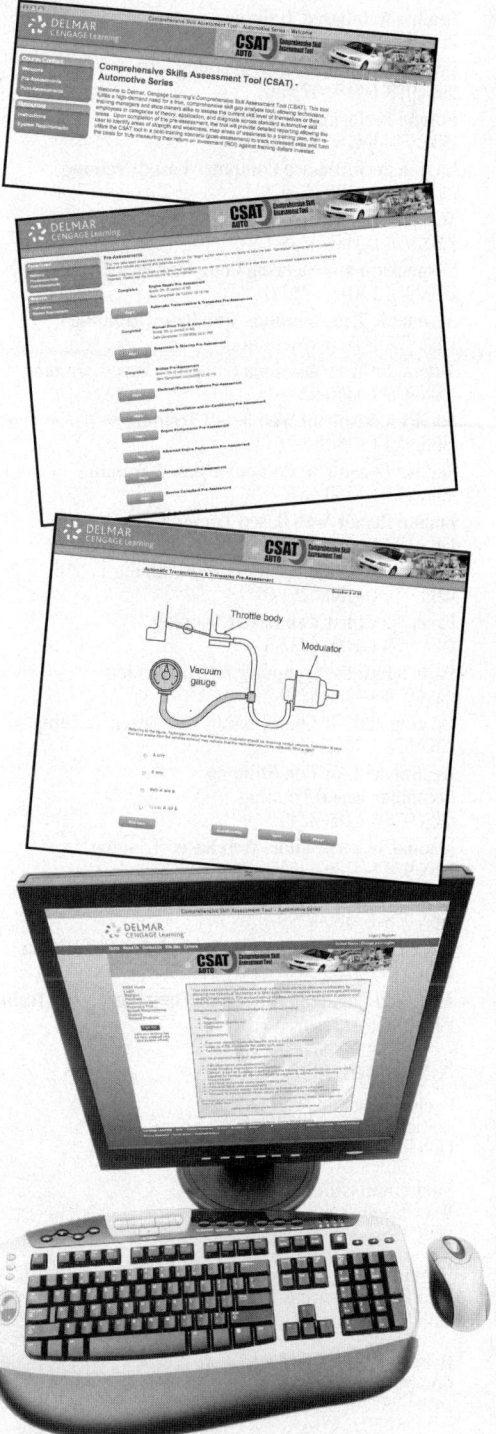

FEATURES

- available tests include Engine Repair, Transmissions and Transaxles, Manual Drive Train and Axles, Suspension and Steering, Brakes, Electrical/Electronic Systems, Heating and Air Conditioning, Engine Performance, Advanced Engine Performance, and Exhaust Systems
- can be utilized by companies to measure the technical skill level of individuals against an "ideal" to identify areas of strength and creates a skill gap analysis to help users address areas needing improvement
- questions are written and reviewed by experts in the industry and offer users the opportunity to receive instant feedback
- account set-up that enables instructors and trainers to assess and track the results of individual students
- acts as a true return on investment (ROI) tool for companies to ensure they invest their training dollars in the most appropriate areas

Visit **www.skillanalysis.com**
for a free demo!

Professional Automotive Technician Training Series: PATTS
Delmar

Delmar, the leader in providing first-rate educational materials for automotive technicians, now offers this exciting self-paced learning series. Choose the delivery method that best suits your needs-- CD-ROM or Web-based product -- and receive more than 8.5 hours worth of quality instruction. Combining theory, diagnosis, and repair information into one easy-to-use training tool, this highly interactive product helps technicians receive the most applicable delivery method for their needs, regardless of technical infrastructure.

KEY FEATURES

- attention-grabbing animations and learner interactions keep users interested and engaged throughout the course of the program
- bookmarking technology enables users to track their progress from beginning to end
- periodic progress checks and end-of-section reviews are integrated throughout to ensure the highest level of retention
- a certificate of completion can be printed by users achieving a score of 80% or higher on the final review of the course
- all material is completely AICC and SCORM compliant
- all material follows the latest ASE and NATEF standards

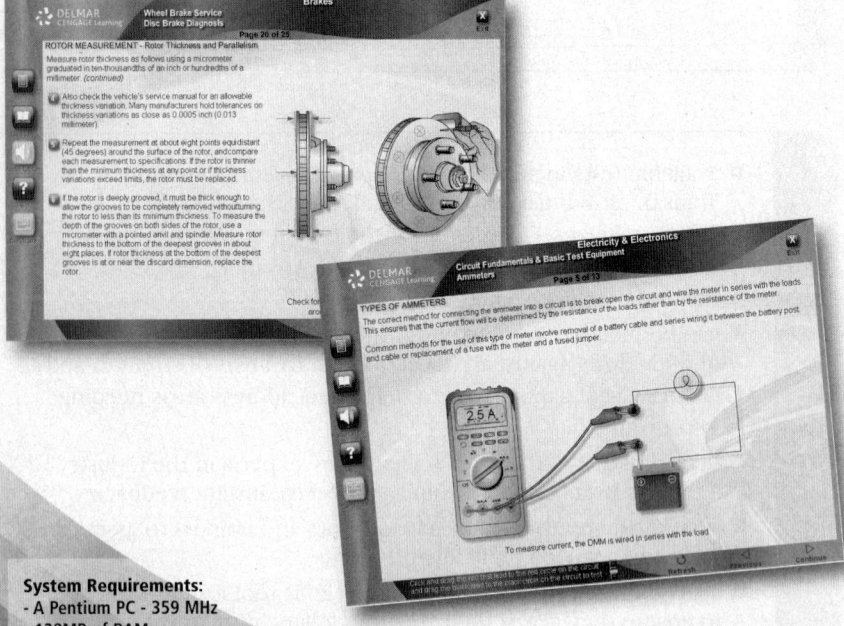

System Requirements:
- A Pentium PC - 359 MHz
- 128MB of RAM
- Windows 2000, Windows XP, Windows Vista
- Graphics adapter with Minimum 1024 x 768 display resolution, 32 bit depth
- Minimum Display Resolution 1024 x 768
- High Speed Internet Connection
- Internet Explorer 6, 7, or Firefox 2
- Not Mac Compatible

Basic Automotive Service and Maintenance Web Based Training
ISBN 978-1-4180-4101-4

Basic Automotive Service and Maintenance Computer Based Training
ISBN 978-1-4180-4100-7

Electricity and Electronics Web Based Training
ISBN 978-1-4180-4242-4

Electricity and Electronics Computer Based Training
ISBN 978-1-4180-4241-7

Brakes Web Based Training
ISBN 978-1-4180-4236-3

Brakes Computer Based Training
ISBN 978-1-4180-4235-6

Engine Performance Web Based Training
ISBN 978-1-4180-4240-0

Engine Performance Computer Based Training
ISBN 978-1-4180-4239-4

Suspension and Steering Web Based Training
ISBN 978-1-4180-4238-7

Suspension and Steering Computer Based Training
ISBN 978-1-4180-4237-0

Automatic Transmissions Web Based Training
ISBN 978-1-4180-4244-8

Automatic Transmissions Computer Based Training
ISBN 978-1-4180-4243-1

Service Consultant Web Based Training
ISBN 978-1-4180-4249-3

Service Consultant Computer Based Training
ISBN 978-1-4180-4247-9

Engine Repair Web Based Training
ISBN 978-1-4180-4254-7

Engine Repair Computer Based Training
ISBN 978-1-4180-4253-0

Parts Specialist Web Based Training
ISBN 978-1-4180-4252-3

Parts Specialist Computer Based Training
ISBN 978-1-4180-4250-9

Heating and Air Conditioning Web Based Training
ISBN 978-1-4180-4246-2

Heating and Air Conditioning Computer Based Training
ISBN 978-1-4180-4245-5

Manual Transmissions Web Based Training
ISBN 978-1-4180-4256-1

Manual Transmissions Computer Based Training
ISBN 978-1-4180-4255-4

Advanced Engine Performance Web Based Training
ISBN 978-1-4283-2098-7

Advanced Engine Performance Computer Based Training
ISBN 978-1-4283-2097-0

New Courses!

Fuels, Emissions, and Exhaust Computer Based Training
ISBN 978-1-4354-4148-4

Fuels, Emissions, and Exhaust Web Based Training
ISBN 978-1-4354-4147-7

Hybrid, Electric, and Fuel-Cell Vehicles Web Based Training
ISBN 978-1-4354-4144-6

Hybrid, Electric, and Fuel-Cell Vehicles Computer Based Training
ISBN 978-1-4354-4143-9

Visit **www.techniciantraining.com**
for a free demo!